3 Series

(E46)

Service Manual

M3, 323i, 323Ci, 325i, 325Ci, 325xi
328i, 328Ci, 330i, 330Ci, 330xi
Sedan, Coupe, Convertible and Sport Wagon
1999, 2000, 2001, 2002, 2003, 2004, 2005

[B] BentleyPublishers™
.com

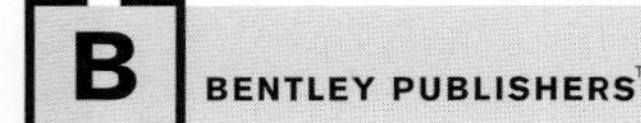

Bentley Publishers, a division of Robert Bentley, Inc.
1734 Massachusetts Avenue
Cambridge, MA 02138 USA
800-423-4595 / 617-547-4170

Information that makes the difference®

BentleyPublishers.com

Technical contact information

We welcome your feedback. Please submit corrections and additions to our BMW technical discussion forum at:

`http://www.BentleyPublishers.com`

Errata information

We will evaluate submissions and post appropriate editorial changes online as text errata or tech discussion. Appropriate errata will be incorporated with the book text in future printings. Read errata information for this book before beginning work on your vehicle. See the following web address for additional information:

`http://www.BentleyPublishers.com/errata/`

WARNING—important safety notice

Do not use this manual unless you are familiar with basic automotive repair procedures and safe workshop practices. This manual illustrates the workshop procedures required for most service work. It is not a substitute for full and up-to-date information from the vehicle manufacturer or for proper training as an automotive technician. Note that it is not possible for us to anticipate all of the ways or conditions under which vehicles may be serviced or to provide cautions as to all of the possible hazards that may result.

The vehicle manufacturer will continue to issue service information updates and parts retrofits after the editorial closing of this manual. Some of these updates and retrofits will apply to procedures and specifications in this manual. We regret that we cannot supply updates to purchasers of this manual.

We have endeavored to ensure the accuracy of the information in this manual. Please note, however, that considering the vast quantity and the complexity of the service information involved, we cannot warrant the accuracy or completeness of the information contained in this manual.

FOR THESE REASONS, NEITHER THE PUBLISHER NOR THE AUTHOR MAKES ANY WARRANTIES, EXPRESS OR IMPLIED, THAT THE INFORMATION IN THIS BOOK IS FREE OF ERRORS OR OMISSIONS, AND WE EXPRESSLY DISCLAIM THE IMPLIED WARRANTIES OF MERCHANTABILITY AND OF FITNESS FOR A PARTICULAR PURPOSE, EVEN IF THE PUBLISHER OR AUTHOR HAVE BEEN ADVISED OF A PARTICULAR PURPOSE, AND EVEN IF A PARTICULAR PURPOSE IS INDICATED IN THE MANUAL. THE PUBLISHER AND AUTHOR ALSO DISCLAIM ALL LIABILITY FOR DIRECT, INDIRECT, INCIDENTAL OR CONSEQUENTIAL DAMAGES THAT RESULT FROM ANY USE OF THE EXAMPLES, INSTRUCTIONS OR OTHER INFORMATION IN THIS BOOK. IN NO EVENT SHALL OUR LIABILITY WHETHER IN TORT, CONTRACT OR OTHERWISE EXCEED THE COST OF THIS MANUAL.

Your common sense and good judgment are crucial to safe and successful service work. Read procedures through before starting them. Think about whether the condition of your car, your level of mechanical skill, or your level of reading comprehension might result in or contribute in some way to an occurrence which might cause you injury, damage your car, or result in an unsafe repair. If you have doubts for these or other reasons about your ability to perform safe repair work on your car, have the work done at an authorized BMW dealer or other qualified shop.

Part numbers listed in this manual are for identification purposes only, not for ordering. Always check with your authorized BMW dealer to verify part numbers and availability before beginning service work that may require new parts.

Before attempting any work on your BMW, read the **WARNINGS** and **CAUTIONS** in **001 WARNINGS and CAUTIONS** and any **WARNING** or **CAUTION** that accompanies a procedure in the service manual. Review the **WARNINGS** and **CAUTIONS** each time you prepare to work on your BMW.

Special tools required to perform certain service operations are identified in the manual and are recommended for use. Use of tools other than those recommended in this manual may be detrimental to the car's safe operation as well as the safety of the person servicing the car.

Copies of this manual may be purchased from most automotive accessories and parts dealers specializing in BMW automobiles, from selected booksellers, or directly from the publisher.

This manual was published by Robert Bentley, Inc., Publishers. BMW has not reviewed and does not vouch for the accuracy of the technical specifications and procedures described in this manual.

Library of Congress Cataloging-in-Publication Data

BMW 3 series : service manual : M3, 323i, 323ci, 325i, 325ci, 325xi, 328i, 328ci, 330i,
330ci, 330xi : sedan, coupe, convertible, and sport wagon : 1999, 2000, 2001, 2002, 2003, 2004, 2005.
p. cm.
Includes bibliographical references and index.
ISBN 0-8376-1277-2 (pbk. : alk. paper)
1. BMW 3 series automobiles--Maintenance and repair--Handbooks, manuals, etc. I. Robert Bentley, inc.

TL215.B25B557 2005
629.28'72--dc22

2004030343

Bentley Stock No. B305

Editorial closing 01/05

11 10 09 08 07 10 9 8 7 6 5 4 3

The paper used in this publication is acid free and meets the requirements of the National Standard for Information Sciences-Permanence of Paper for Printed Library Materials. ∞

Manufactured in the United States of America

Foreword and Disclaimer

For the BMW owner with basic mechanical skills and for independent auto service professionals, this manual includes many of the specifications and procedures that were available in an authorized BMW dealer service department as this manual went to press. The BMW owner with no intention of working on his or her car will find that owning and referring to this manual will make it possible to be better informed and to more knowledgeably discuss repairs with a professional automotive technician.

The BMW owner intending to do maintenance and repair should have screwdrivers, a set of metric wrenches and sockets, and metric Allen and Torx wrenches, since these basic hand tools are needed for most of the work described in this manual. Many procedures will also require a torque wrench to ensure that fasteners are tightened properly and in accordance with specifications. Additional information on basic tools and other tips can be found in **010 General**. In some cases, the text refers to special tools that are recommended or required to accomplish adjustments or repairs. These tools are usually identified by their BMW special tool number and illustrated.

Disclaimer

We have endeavored to ensure the accuracy of the information in this manual. When the vast array of data presented in the manual is taken into account, however, no claim to infallibility can be made. We therefore cannot be responsible for the result of any errors that may have crept into the text. Please also read the **Important Safety Notice** on the copyright page at the beginning of this book.

A thorough pre-reading of each procedure, and **001 WARNINGS and CAUTIONS** at the front of the book and those that accompany the procedure is essential. Reading a procedure before beginning work will help you determine in advance the need for specific skills, identify hazards, prepare for appropriate capture and handling of hazardous materials, and the need for particular tools and replacement parts such as gaskets.

Bentley Publishers encourages comments from the readers of this manual with regard to errors, and/or suggestions for improvement of our product. These communications have been and will be carefully considered in the preparation of this and other manuals. If you identify inconsistencies in the manual, you may have found an error. Please contact the publisher and we will endeavor to post applicable corrections on our website. Posted corrections (errata) should be reviewed before beginning work. Please see the following web address:

`http://www.BentleyPublishers.com/errata/`

BMW offers extensive warranties, especially on components of the fuel delivery and emission control systems. Therefore, before deciding to repair a BMW that may be covered wholly or in part by any warranties issued by BMW of North America, LLC, consult your authorized BMW dealer. You may find that the dealer can make the repair either free or at minimum cost. Regardless of its age, or whether it is under warranty, your BMW is both an easy car to service and an easy car to get serviced. So if at any time a repair is needed that you feel is too difficult to do yourself, a trained BMW technician is ready to do the job for you.

Bentley Publishers

001 Warnings and Cautions

Please read these warnings and cautions before proceeding with maintenance and repair work.

WARNINGS—
See also ***CAUTIONS*** *on next page.*

- Read the important safety notice on the copyright page at the beginning of the book.
- Some repairs may be beyond your capability. If you lack the skills, tools and equipment, or a suitable workplace for any procedure described in this manual, we suggest you leave such repairs to an authorized BMW dealer service department or other qualified shop.
- A thorough pre-reading of each procedure, and the **WARNINGS** and **CAUTIONS** that accompany the procedure is essential. Posted corrections (errata) should also be reviewed before beginning work. Please see `www.BentleyPublishers.com/errata/`
- BMW is constantly improving its cars. Sometimes these changes, both in parts and specifications, are made applicable to earlier models. Therefore, before starting any major jobs or repairs to components on which passenger safety may depend, consult your authorized BMW dealer about Technical Bulletins that may have been issued.
- Do not re-use any fasteners that are worn or deformed in normal use. Many fasteners are designed to be used only once and become unreliable and may fail when used a second time. This includes, but is not limited to, nuts, bolts, washers, self-locking nuts or bolts, circlips and cotter pins. Always replace these fasteners with new parts.
- Never work under a lifted car unless it is solidly supported on stands designed for the purpose. Do not support a car on cinder blocks, hollow tiles or other props that may crumble under continuous load. Never work under a car that is supported solely by a jack. Never work under the car while the engine is running.
- If you are going to work under a car on the ground, make sure that the ground is level. Block the wheels to keep the car from rolling. Disconnect the battery negative (–) terminal (ground strap) to prevent others from starting the car while you are under it.
- Never run the engine unless the work area is well ventilated. Carbon monoxide kills.
- Finger rings, bracelets and other jewelry should be removed so that they cannot cause electrical shorts, get caught in running machinery, or be crushed by heavy parts.
- Tie long hair behind your head. Do not wear a necktie, a scarf, loose clothing, or a necklace when you work near machine tools or running engines. If your hair, clothing, or jewelry were to get caught in the machinery, severe injury could result.
- Do not attempt to work on your car if you do not feel well. You increase the danger of injury to yourself and others if you are tired, upset or have taken medication or any other substance that may keep you from being fully alert.
- Illuminate your work area adequately but safely. Use a portable safety light for working inside or under the car. Make sure the bulb is enclosed by a wire cage. The hot filament of an accidentally broken bulb can ignite spilled fuel, vapors or oil.
- Catch draining fuel, oil, or brake fluid in suitable containers. Do not use food or beverage containers that might mislead someone into drinking from them. Store flammable fluids away from fire hazards. Wipe up spills at once, but do not store the oily rags, which can ignite and burn spontaneously.
- Always observe good workshop practices. Wear goggles when you operate machine tools or work with battery acid. Gloves or other protective clothing should be worn whenever the job requires working with harmful substances.
- Greases, lubricants and other automotive chemicals contain toxic substances, many of which are absorbed directly through the skin. Read the manufacturer's instructions and warnings carefully. Use hand and eye protection. Avoid direct skin contact.
- Disconnect the battery negative (–) terminal (ground strap) whenever you work on the fuel system or the electrical system. Do not smoke or work near heaters or other fire hazards. Keep an approved fire extinguisher handy.
- Friction materials (such as brake pads or shoes or clutch discs) contain asbestos fibers or other friction materials. Do not create dust by grinding, sanding, or by cleaning with compressed air. Avoid breathing dust. Breathing any friction material dust can lead to serious diseases and may result in death.
- Batteries give off explosive hydrogen gas during charging. Keep sparks, lighted matches and open flame away from the top of the battery. If hydrogen gas escaping from the cap vents is ignited, it will ignite gas trapped in the cells and cause the battery to explode.
- Battery acid (electrolyte) can cause severe burns. Flush contact area with water, seek medical attention.
- Connect and disconnect battery cables, jumper cables or a battery charger only with the ignition switched off. Do not disconnect the battery while the engine is running.
- Do not quick-charge the battery (for boost starting) for longer than one minute. Wait at least one minute before boosting the battery a second time.
- Do not allow battery charging voltage to exceed 16.5 volts. If the battery begins producing gas or boiling violently, reduce the charging rate. Boosting a sulfated battery at a high rate can cause an explosion.
- The air conditioning system is filled with chemical refrigerant, which is hazardous. The A/C system should be serviced only by trained technicians using approved refrigerant recovery/recycling equipment, trained in related safety precautions, and familiar with regulations governing the discharging and disposal of automotive chemical refrigerants.

continued on next page

Please read these warnings and cautions before proceeding with maintenance and repair work.

WARNINGS— (continued)

- Do not expose any part of the A/C system to high temperatures such as open flame. Excessive heat will increase system pressure and may cause the system to burst.

- Some aerosol tire inflators are highly flammable. Be extremely cautious when repairing a tire that may have been inflated using an aerosol tire inflator. Keep sparks, open flame or other sources of ignition away from the tire repair area. Inflate and deflate the tire at least four times before breaking the bead from the rim. Completely remove the tire from the rim before attempting any repair.

- Cars covered by this manual are equipped with a supplemental restraint system (SRS), that automatically deploys airbags and pyrotechnic seat belt tensioners in the event of a frontal or side impact. These are explosive devices. Handled improperly or without adequate safeguards, they can be accidently activated and cause serious injury.

- Connect and disconnect a battery charger only with the battery charger switched off.

- Sealed or "maintenance free" batteries should be slow-charged only, at an amperage rate that is approximately 10% of the battery's ampere-hour (Ah) rating.

- Do not allow battery charging voltage to exceed 16.5 volts. If the battery begins producing gas or boiling violently, reduce the charging rate. Boosting a sulfated battery at a high charging rate can cause an explosion.

- The ignition system produces high voltages that can be fatal. Avoid contact with exposed terminals and use extreme care when working on a car with the engine running or the ignition switched on.

- Place jack stands only at locations specified by manufacturer. The vehicle lifting jack supplied with the vehicle is intended for tire changes only. A heavy duty floor jack should be used to lift vehicle before installing jack stands. See **03 Service and Maintenance**.

- Aerosol cleaners and solvents may contain hazardous or deadly vapors and are highly flammable. Use only in a well ventilated area. Do not use on hot surfaces (engines, brakes, etc.).

- Do not remove coolant reservoir or radiator cap with the engine hot. Danger of burns and engine damage.

CAUTIONS—
*See also **WARNINGS** on previous page.*

- If you lack the skills, tools and equipment, or a suitable workshop for any procedure described in this manual, we suggest you leave such repairs to an authorized BMW dealer or other qualified shop.

- BMW is constantly improving its cars and sometimes these changes, both in parts and specifications, are made applicable to earlier models. Therefore, part numbers listed in this manual are for reference only. Always check with your authorized BMW dealer parts department for the latest information.

- Before starting a job, make certain that you have all the necessary tools and parts on hand. Read all the instructions thoroughly, and do not attempt shortcuts. Use tools appropriate to the work and use only replacement parts meeting BMW specifications. Makeshift tools, parts and procedures will not make good repairs

- Use pneumatic and electric tools only to loosen threaded parts and fasteners. Never use these tools to tighten fasteners, especially on light alloy parts. Always use a torque wrench to tighten fasteners to the tightening torque specification listed.

- Be mindful of the environment and ecology. Before you drain the crankcase, find out the proper way to dispose of the oil. Do not pour oil onto the ground, down a drain, or into a stream, pond or lake. Dispose of in accordance with Federal, State and Local laws.

- The control module for the anti-lock brake system (ABS) cannot withstand temperatures from a paint-drying booth or a heat lamp in excess of 203° F (95° C) and should not be subjected to temperatures in excess of 185° F (85° C) for more than two hours.

- Before doing any electrical welding on cars equipped with ABS, disconnect the battery negative (–) terminal (ground strap) and the ABS control module connector.

- Always make sure ignition is off before disconnecting battery.

- Label battery cables before disconnecting. On some models, battery cables are not color coded.

- Disconnecting the battery may erase fault code(s) stored in control module memory. Using special BMW diagnostic equipment, check for fault codes prior to disconnecting the battery cables. If the Malfunction Indicator Light (MIL) is illuminated, see **OBD On-Board Diagnostics** at the back of this manual. This light is identified as the Check Engine light. If any other system faults have been detected (indicated by an illuminated warning light), see an authorized BMW dealer.

- If a normal or rapid charger is used to charge battery, the battery must be disconnected and removed from the vehicle in order to avoid damaging paint and upholstery.

- Do not quick-charge the battery (for boost starting) for longer than one minute. Wait at least one minute before boosting the battery a second time.

- Connect and disconnect a battery charger only with the battery charger switched off.

- Sealed or "maintenance free" batteries should be slow-charged only, at an amperage rate that is approximately 10% of the battery's ampere-hour (Ah) rating.

- Do not allow battery charging voltage to exceed 16.5 volts. If the battery begins producing gas or boiling violently, reduce the charging rate. Boosting a sulfated battery at a high charging rate can cause an explosion.

002 Vehicle Identification and VIN Decoder

Vehicle Identification Number (VIN), decoding

Some of the information in this manual applies only to cars of a particular model year or range of years. For example, 1999 refers to the 1999 model year but does not necessarily match the calendar year in which the car was manufactured or sold. To be sure of the model year of a particular car, check the Vehicle Identification Number (VIN) on the car.

The VIN is a unique sequence of 17 characters assigned by BMW to identify each individual car. When decoded, the VIN tells the country and year of manufacture; make, model and serial number; assembly plant and even some equipment specifications.

The BMW VIN is on a plate mounted on the top of the dashboard, on the driver's side where the number can be seen through the windshield. The 10th character is the model year code. The letters I, O, Q and U are not used for model year designation. Examples: X for 1999, Y for 2000, 1 for 2001, 2 for 2002, etc. The table below explains some of the codes in the VIN for 1999 through 2005 BMW E46 3 Series covered by this manual.

Sample VIN:	WBA	DC84	0	X	J	1	841989
position	1 2 3	4 5 6 7	8	9	10	11	12-17

VIN position	Description	Decoding information	
1 - 3	Country of manufacture	WBA WBS	BMW, AG. Munich, Germany BMW Motorsport, GmbH. Munich, Germany
4	Line	A B C E	323i, 328i (1999 - 2000) 325i, 330i (2001), 325i (2003) 323i, 328i (2000) 325Ci, 330Ci, M3 (2001 - 2005) 325i, 330i (2002 - 2003) 325i, 330i (2004 - 2005)
5	Series	L M N P R S T U V W X Z	M3 Coupe 323i, 328i Sedan (1999 - 2000), Coupe (2000) 325i, 325Ci, 330Ci (2001 - 2005) 325xi Sport Wagon (2002 - 2005) M3 Convertible 325Ci, 330Ci Convertible (2001 - 2005) 325i Sedan (2004 - 2005) 325xi Sedan (2002 - 2005) 325i, 330i, 330xi Sedan (2001 - 2005) 330xi (2002 - 2003), 325Ci, 330Ci Convertible (2004 - 2005) 325i Sport Wagon (2003 - 2005) 325i Sedan (2003 - 2005)
6	Engine type	3 5 9	2.5 liter, 6-cylinder (M52 TU, M54) 3.0 liter, 6-cylinder (M52 TU, M54) 3.2 liter, 6-cylinder (S54)
7	Vehicle type	3, 4, 7	Passenger vehicle
8	Restraint system	2 4	Manual belts with dual SRS airbags Manual belts with advanced SRS airbags
9	Check digit		0 - 9 or X, calculated by NHTSA
10	Model year	X Y 1 2 3 4 5	1999 2000 2001 2002 2003 2004 2005
11	Assembly plant	A, F, K B, C, D, G E, J, P	Munich, Germany Dingolfing, Germany Regensburg, Germany
12-17	Serial number		Sequential production number for specific vehicle

010 General

TABLES

GENERAL

This section is intended to help the do-it-yourselfer get started. Tips on workshop practices, basic tools, and a quick reference guide to emergencies can be found here.

> ***WARNING —***
> *Do not use this manual unless you are familiar with basic automotive repair procedures and safe workshop practices. This manual illustrates the workshop procedures required for most service work; it is not a substitute for full and up-to-date information from the vehicle manufacturer or for proper training as an automotive technician. Note that it is not possible for us to anticipate all of the ways or conditions under which vehicles may be serviced or to provide cautions as to all of the possible hazards that may result.*

HOW TO USE THIS MANUAL

> ***WARNING —***
> *Your common sense and good judgment are crucial to safe and successful service work. Read procedures through before starting them. Think about whether the condition of your car, your level of mechanical skill, or your level of reading comprehension might result in or contribute in some way to an occurrence that might cause you injury, damage your car, or result in an unsafe repair. If you have doubts for these or other reasons about your ability to perform safe repair work on your car, have the work done at an authorized BMW dealer or other qualified shop.*

The manual is divided into ten sections:

0 GENERAL DATA AND MAINTENANCE
1 ENGINE
2 TRANSMISSION
3 SUSPENSION, STEERING AND BRAKES
4 BODY
5 BODY EQUIPMENT
6 ELECTRICAL SYSTEM
7 EQUIPMENT AND ACCESSORIES
ELE ELECTRICAL WIRING DIAGRAMS
OBD ON-BOARD DIAGNOSTICS

0 GENERAL DATA AND MAINTENANCE covers general vehicle information (Repair Group 010) as well as the recommended maintenance schedules and service procedures to perform BMW scheduled maintenance work (Repair Group 020).

The next seven sections (Repair Groups 1 through 7) are repair based and organized by three digit repair groups. Most major sections begin with a **General** repair group, e.g. **100 Engine–General.** These "00" (double zero) groups are mostly descriptive in nature, covering topics such as theory of operation and troubleshooting. The remainder of the repair groups contain the service and repair information. The last two major sections contains detailed electrical wiring schematics and scan tool codes.

A master listing of the individual repair groups can be found on the inside front cover. A comprehensive index can be found at the back of the manual.

Warnings, cautions and notes

Throughout this manual are many passages with the headings **WARNING**, **CAUTION**, or **NOTE**. These very important headings have different meanings.

> ***WARNING —***
> *The text under this heading warns of unsafe practices that are very likely to cause injury, either by direct threat to the person(s) performing the work or by increased risk of accident or mechanical failure while driving.*

CAUTION —
A caution calls attention to important precautions to be observed during the repair work that will help prevent accidentally damaging the car or its parts.

NOTE —
A note contains helpful information, tips that will help in doing a better job and completing it more easily.

Please read every **WARNING**, **CAUTION**, and **NOTE** at the front of the manual and as they appear in repair procedures. They are very important. Read them before you begin any maintenance or repair job.

WARNING —
- *Never run the engine in the work area unless it is well-ventilated. The exhaust should be vented to the outside. Carbon monoxide (CO) in the exhaust kills.*
- *Remove all neckties, scarfs, loose clothing, or jewelry when working near running engines or power tools. Tuck in shirts. Tie long hair and secure it under a cap. Severe injury can result from these things being caught in rotating parts.*
- *Remove rings, watches, and bracelets. Aside from the dangers of moving parts, metallic jewelry conducts electricity and may cause shorts, sparks, burns, or damage to the electrical system when accidentally contacting the battery or other electrical terminals.*
- *Disconnect the battery negative (–) cable whenever working on or near the fuel system or anything that is electrically powered. Accidental electrical contact may damage the electrical system or cause a fire.*
- *Fuel is highly flammable. When working around fuel, do not smoke or work near heaters or other fire hazards. Keep an approved fire extinguisher handy.*
- *The fuel system is designed to retain pressure even when the ignition is off. When working with the fuel system, loosen the fuel lines slowly to allow the residual pressure to dissipate gradually. Take precautions to avoid spraying fuel.*
- *Illuminate the work area adequately and safely. Use a portable safety light for working inside or under the car. A fluorescent type light is best because it gives off less heat. If using a light with a normal incandescent bulb, use rough service bulbs to avoid breakage. The hot filament of an accidentally broken bulb can ignite spilled fuel or oil.*
- *Keep sparks, lighted matches, and any open flame away from the top of the battery. Hydrogen gas emitted by the battery is highly flammable. Any nearby source of ignition may cause the battery to explode.*
- *Never lay tools or parts in the engine compartment or on top of the battery. They may fall into confined spaces and be difficult to retrieve, become caught in belts or other rotating parts when the engine is started, or cause electrical shorts and damage to the electrical system.*

GETTING STARTED

Most of the necessary maintenance and minor repair that an automobile will need can be done with ordinary tools. Below is some important information on how to work safely, a discussion of what tools will be needed and how to use them.

Safety

Although an automobile presents many hazards, common sense and good equipment can help ensure safety. Many accidents happen because of carelessness. Pay attention and stick to safety rules in this manual.

Lifting the car

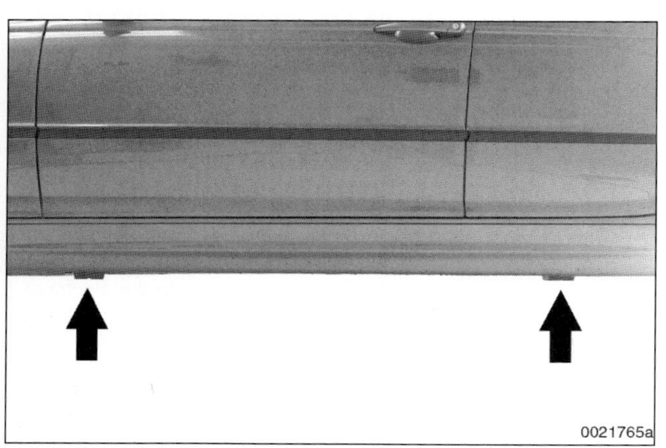

◀ The proper jacking points should be used to raise the car safely and avoid damage. The jack supplied with the car can only be used at the four side points (**arrows**)—just behind the front wheels or just in front of the rear wheels.

> ***WARNING —***
> - *Never work under a lifted car unless it is solidly supported on jack stands that are intended for that purpose.*
> - *When raising the car using a floor jack or a hydraulic lift, carefully position the jack pad to prevent damaging the car body. Plastic pads are provided for this purpose by the manufacturer at the jacking points.*
> - *Watch the jack closely. Make sure it stays stable and does not shift or tilt. As the car is raised, it may roll slightly and the jack may shift.*

Raising car safely

– Park car on flat, level surface.

– If changing a tire, loosen lug bolts before rasing car. See **Changing a tire**.

◀ Place jack into position. Make sure jack is resting on flat, solid ground. Use a board or other support to provide a firm surface for the jack, if necessary

– Raise car slowly while constantly checking position of jack and car.

– Once car is raised, block wheel that is opposite and farthest from jack to prevent car from unexpectedly rolling.

> ***WARNING —***
> - *Do not rely on the transmission or the emergency brake to keep the car from rolling. They are not a substitute for positively blocking the opposite wheel.*
> - *Never work under a car that is supported only by a jack. Use jack stands that are designed to support the car. See* **Tools**.

Working under car safely

- Disconnect negative (–) cable from battery so that no one can start car. Let others know what you will be doing.

> ***CAUTION —***
> *Prior to disconnecting the battery, read the battery disconnection cautions given at the front of this manual.*

- Raise car slowly as described above.

- Use at least two jack stands to support car. Use jack stands designed for the purpose of supporting a car. For more information on jack stands, see **Tools**.

> ***WARNING —***
> - *A jack is a temporary lifting device and should not be used alone to support the car while you are under it.*
> - *Do not use wood, concrete blocks, or bricks to support a car. Wood may split. Blocks or bricks, while strong, are not designed for that kind of load, and may break or collapse.*

- Place jack stands on firm, solid surface. If necessary, use a flat board or similar solid object to provide a firm footing.

- Lower car slowly until its weight is fully supported by jack stands. Watch to make sure that the jack stands do not tip or lean as the car settles on them.

- Observe all jacking precautions again when raising car to remove jack stands.

ADVICE FOR THE BEGINNER

The tips in the paragraphs that follow are general advice to help any do-it-yourself BMW owner perform repairs and maintenance tasks more easily and more professionally.

Planning ahead

To prevent getting in too deep, know what the whole job requires before starting. Read the procedure thoroughly, from beginning to end, in order to know just what to expect and what parts will have to be replaced.

Cleanliness

Keeping things organized, neat, and clean is essential to doing a good job. When working under the hood, fender covers will protect the finish from scratches and other damage. Make sure the car finish is clean so that dirt under the cover does not scratch the finish.

Any repair job will be less troublesome if the parts are clean. For cleaning old parts, there are many solvents and parts cleaners commercially available.

For cleaning parts prior to assembly, commercially available aerosol cans of parts cleaner or brake cleaner are handy to use, and the cleaner will evaporate completely.

> ***WARNING —***
> *Most solvents used for cleaning parts are highly flammable as well as toxic, especially in aerosol form. Use with extreme care. Do not smoke. Do not use these products indoors or near any source of heat, sparks or flame.*

Non-reusable fasteners

Many fasteners used on the cars covered by this manual must be replaced with new ones once they are removed. These include but are not limited to: bolts, nuts (self-locking, nylock, etc.), cotter pins, studs, brake fittings, roll pins, clips and washers. Genuine BMW parts should be the only replacement parts used for this purpose.

Some bolts are designed to stretch during assembly and are permanently altered rendering them unreliable once removed. These are known as torque-to-yield fasteners. Always replace fasteners where instructed to do so. Failure to replace these fasteners could cause vehicle damage and personal injury. See an authorized BMW dealer for applications and ordering information.

Tightening fasteners

When tightening the bolts or nuts that attach a component, it is always good practice to tighten the bolts gradually and evenly to avoid misalignment or over stressing any one portion of the component. For components sealed with gaskets, this method helps to ensure that the gasket will seal properly.

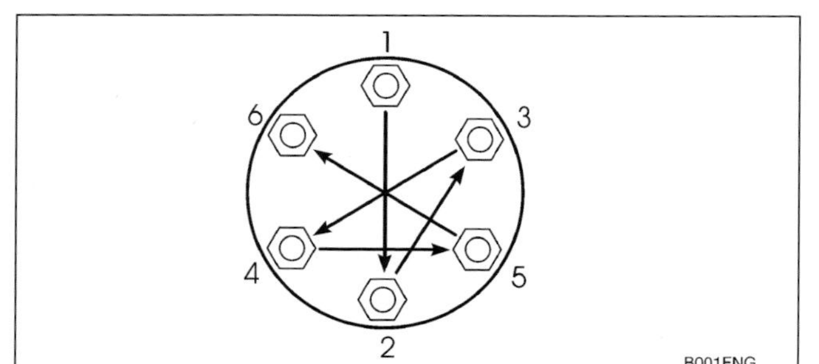

Where there are several fasteners, tighten them in a sequence alternating between opposite sides of the component. Repeat the sequence until all the bolts are evenly tightened to the proper specification.

For some repairs a specific tightening sequence is necessary, or a particular order of assembly is required. Such special conditions are noted in the text, and the necessary sequence is described or illustrated. Where no specific torque is listed, **Table a** can be used as a general guide for tightening fasteners.

WARNING —
Table a *is a general reference only. The values listed in the table are not intended to be used as a substitute for torques specifically called out in the text.*

NOTE —
- *Metric bolt classes or grades are marked on the bolt head.*
- *Do not confuse wrench size with bolt diameter. For a listing of the common wrenches used on various bolt diameters, see* **Basic tool requirements**.

Table a. General bolt tightening torques in Nm (max. permissible)

Bolt diameter	Bolt Class (according to DIN 267)					
	5.6	5.8	6.8	8.8	10.9	12.9
M5	2.5	3.5	4.5	6	8	10
M6	4.5	6	7.5	10	14	17
M8	11	15	18	24	34	40
M10	23	30	36	47	66	79
M12	39	52	62	82	115	140
M14	62	82	98	130	180	220
M16	94	126	150	200	280	340
M18	130	174	210	280	390	470

BUYING PARTS

Many of the maintenance and repair tasks in this manual call for the installation of new parts, or the use of new gaskets and other materials when reinstalling parts. Most often, the parts that will be needed should be on hand before beginning the job. Read the introductory text and the complete procedure to determine which parts will be needed.

NOTE —
For some bigger jobs, partial disassembly and inspection are required to determine a complete parts list. Read the procedure carefully and, if necessary, make other arrangements to get the necessary parts while your car is disassembled.

Genuine BMW parts

Genuine BMW replacement parts from an authorized BMW dealer are designed and manufactured to the same high standards as the original parts. They will be the correct material, manufactured to the same specifications, and guaranteed to fit and work as intended by the engineers who designed the car. Some genuine BMW parts have a limited warranty.

Many independent repair shops make a point of using genuine BMW parts, even though they may at times be more expensive. They know the value of doing the job right with the right parts. Parts from other sources can be as good, particularly if manufactured by one of BMWs original equipment suppliers, but it is often difficult to know.

BMW is constantly updating and improving their cars, often making improvements during a given model year. BMW may recommend a newer, improved part as a replacement, and your authorized dealer's parts department will know about it and provide it. The BMW parts organization is best equipped to deal with any BMW parts needs.

Non-returnable parts

Some parts cannot be returned. The best example is electrical parts. Buy electrical parts carefully, and be as sure as possible that a replacement is needed, especially for expensive parts such as electronic control units. It may be wise to let an authorized BMW dealer or other qualified shop confirm your diagnosis before replacing a non-returnable part.

Information you need to know

Model. When ordering parts it is important that you know the correct model designation for your car. Models covered in this E46 manual are 323i/Ci, 325i/Ci, 325Xi, 328i/Ci, 330i/Ci 330Xi, and M3 in Sedan, Coupe, Convertible and Sport Wagon body styles.

Model year. This is not necessarily the same as date of manufacture or date of sale. A 1999 model may have been manufactured in late 1998, and perhaps not sold until early 2000. It is still a 1999 model. Model years covered by this manual are 1999 to 2005.

Date of manufacture. This information is necessary when ordering replacement parts or determining if any of the warranty recalls are applicable to your car. The label on the driver's door below the door latch will specify the month and year that the car was built.

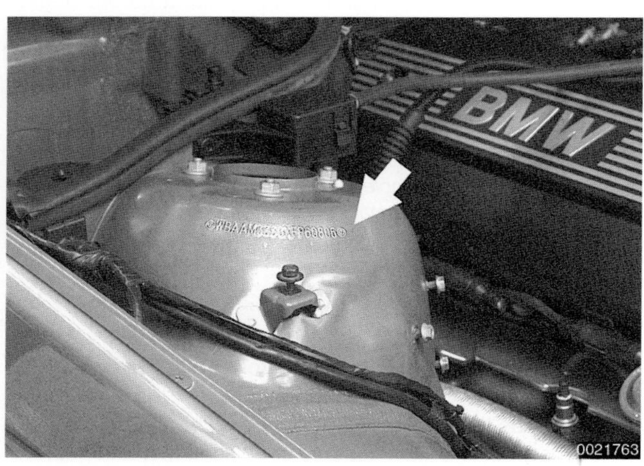

Vehicle Identification Number (VIN). This is a combination of letters and numbers that identify the particular car. The VIN appears on the state registration document, and on the car itself. One location is on the right front strut tower in the engine compartment (**arrow**), another in the lower left corner of the windshield.

Engine code. 3 Series cars covered in this manual are powered by 6-cylinder engines. For information on engine codes and engine applications, see **100 Engine–General**.

Transmission code. The transmission type with its identifying code may be important when buying clutch parts, seals, gaskets, and other transmission-related parts. For information on transmission codes and applications, see **200 Transmission–General**.

SERVICE

BMW dealers are uniquely qualified to provide service for BMW cars. Their authorized relationship with the large BMW service organization means that they are constantly receiving special tools and equipment, together with the latest and most accurate repair information.

The BMW dealer's service technicians are highly trained and very capable. Unlike many independent repair shops, authorized BMW dealers are committed to supporting the BMW product. On the other hand, there are many independent shops that specialize in BMW service and are capable of doing high quality repair work. Checking with other BMW owners for recommendations on service facilities is a good way to learn of reputable BMW shops in your area.

TOOLS

Most maintenance can be accomplished with a small selection of the right tools. Tools range in quality from inexpensive junk, which may break at first use, to very expensive and well-made tools for the professional. The best tools for most do-it-yourself BMW owners lie somewhere in between.

Many reputable tool manufacturers offer good quality, moderately priced tools with a lifetime guarantee. These are your best buy. They cost a little more, but they are good quality tools that will do what is expected of them. Sears' Craftsman® line is one such source of good quality tools.

Some of the repairs covered in this manual require the use of special tools, such as a custom puller or specialized electrical test equipment. These special tools are called out in the text and can be purchased through an authorized BMW dealer. As an alternative, some special tools mentioned may be purchased from the following tool manufacturers and/or distributors:

- Assenmacher Specialty Tools
  6440 Odell Place, Boulder, CO 80301
  303-530-2424
  http://www.asttool.com
- Baum Tools Unlimited, Inc.
  P.O. Box 5867, Sarasota, FL 34277-5867
  800-848-6657
  http://www.baumtools.com
- Diagnos.co.uk Ltd
  Cuxham Road, Watlington, Oxon, OX49 5NB, UK
  +44 (0)1491 614300
  http://www.autologic-diagnos.com
- Zelenda Machine and Tool Corp.
  65-60 Austin Street, Forest Hills, NY 11374-4695
  718-896-2288
  http://www.zelenda.com

Below is a list of typical bolt diameters and the corresponding wrench sizes.

Common bolt diameters and wrench sizes

- M5 . . . . 8 mm
- M6 . . . . 10 mm
- M8 . . . . 12 mm or 13 mm
- M10 . . . . 17 mm
- M12 . . . . 19 mm
- M14 . . . . 22 mm

Jack stands

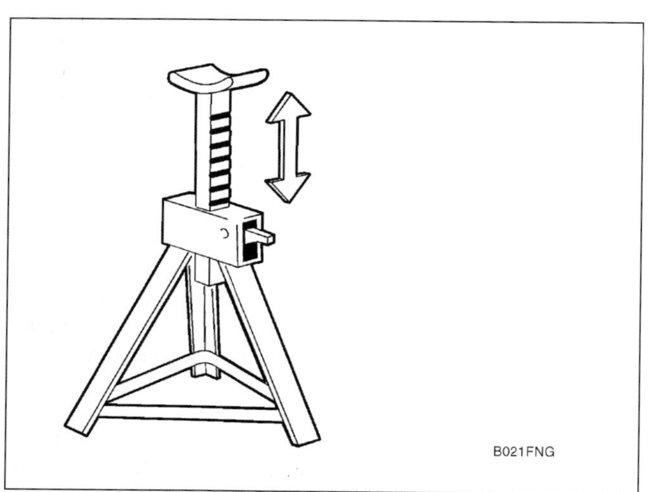
B021FNG

Strong jack stands are extremely important for any work that is done under the car. Use only jack stands that are designed for the purpose. Blocks of wood, concrete, bricks, etc. are not safe or suitable substitutes.

> ***WARNING —***
> *A jack should be used only to raise the vehicle and should not be used to support the car for a long period. Always use jack stands to support a raised vehicle.*

Jack stands are available in several styles. The best ones are made of heavy material for strength, have a wide base for stability, and are equipped to positively lock in their raised positions. Get the best ones available.

Oil change equipment

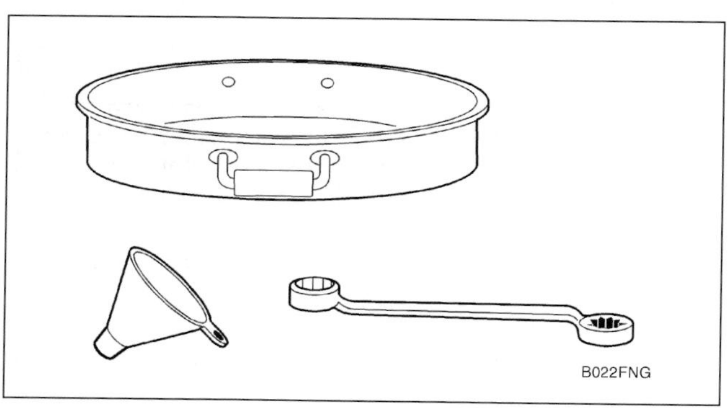
B022FNG

Changing engine oil requires a 17 mm socket or wrench to loosen and tighten the drain plug and a drain pan (at least 8 qt. capacity). A wide, low drain pan will fit more easily under the car. Use a funnel to pour the new oil into the engine.

The M52/M54 engines use an oil filter canister with a disposable filter cartridge insert. Therefore, an oil filter wrench is not required. See **020 Maintenance** for oil change instructions.

Torque wrench

A torque wrench is used to precisely tighten threaded fasteners to a predetermined value. Many of the repair procedures in this manual include BMW-specified torque values in Newton-meters (Nm) and the equivalent values in foot-pounds (ft-lb).

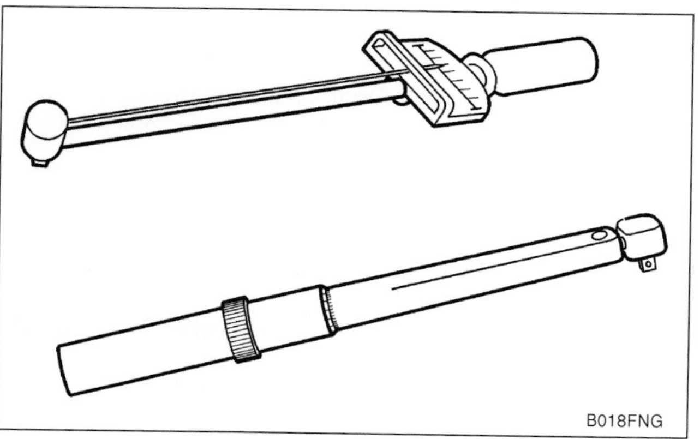
B018FNG

Several types of torque wrenches are available. An inexpensive beam-type (top) is adequate but must be read visually. A ratchet-type (bottom) can be preset to indicate (click) when the torque value has been reached. Follow the wrench manufacturer's directions for use to achieve the greatest accuracy.

Digital multimeter

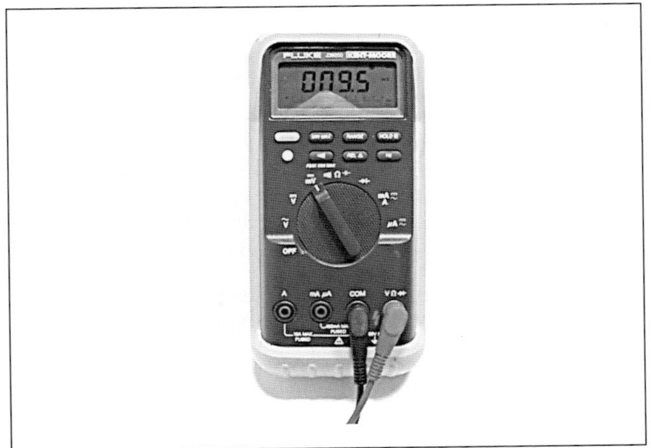

Many of the electrical tests in this manual call for the measurement of resistance (ohms) or voltage values. For safe and accurate tests of sensitive electronic components and systems, a multimeter or Digital Volt/Ohmmeter (DVOM) with high input impedance (at least 10,000 ohms) should be used. Some meters have automotive functions such as dwell and pulse width that are useful for troubleshooting ignition and fuel injection problems.

> ***CAUTION —***
> *Vehicle electronic systems may be damaged by the high current draw of a test light with a normal incandescent bulb. As a general rule, use a high impedance digital multimeter or an LED test light for all electrical testing.*

EMERGENCIES

Changing a tire

– Stop car on as flat a surface as possible, in a place where you can be easily seen by other drivers. Avoid stopping just over the crest of a hill.

– Turn on emergency flashers, and set out flares or emergency markers well behind car. Chock wheel (wheel chock located in trunk) diagonally opposite to the one being changed. Passengers should get out of car and stand well away from road.

> ***WARNING —***
> *If a tire goes flat while driving, pull well off the road. Changing a tire on a busy street or highway is very dangerous. If necessary, drive a short distance on the flat tire to get to a safe place. It is much better to ruin a tire or rim than to risk being hit.*

– Take jack and tools from tool area beneath trunk mat. Remove spare tire from tire storage tray.

– Loosen wheel bolts while car is on ground, but leave them a little snug.

0021505

Place jack in lifting point nearest wheel being changed. Use a board to provide a firm footing for jack if ground is soft. Raise car only far enough so that wheel is fully off ground and then remove wheel nuts and wheel.

– Install spare wheel. Install wheel nuts and tighten them hand tight using lug nut wrench.

– Lower car. With all wheels on ground, fully tighten nuts in a crisscross pattern. Torque wheel nuts when installing wheel. Check inflation pressure of spare tire.

Tightening torque

- Wheel to wheel hub . . . . 120 ± 10 Nm (90 ± 7 ft-lb)

Jump starting

Cars with discharged or dead batteries can be jump-started using the good battery from another car. When jump-starting the engine, always note the following warnings.

> ***WARNING —***
> - *Battery acid (electrolyte) can cause severe burns, and will damage the car and clothing. If electrolyte is spilled, wash the surface with large quantities of water. If it gets into eyes, flush them with water for several minutes and call a doctor.*
> - *Batteries produce explosive and noxious gasses. Keep sparks and flames away. Do not smoke near batteries.*
> - *Do not jump-start the engine if you suspect that the battery is frozen. Trapped gas may explode. Allow the battery to thaw first.*
> - *Do not quick-charge the battery (for boost starting) for longer than one minute, and do not exceed 16.5 volts at the battery with the boosting cables attached. Wait at least one minute before boosting the battery a second time.*

– Place cars close together, but do not allow them to touch each other.

- Turn off engine of car with good battery.
- Turn off ignition switch of car with discharged battery.

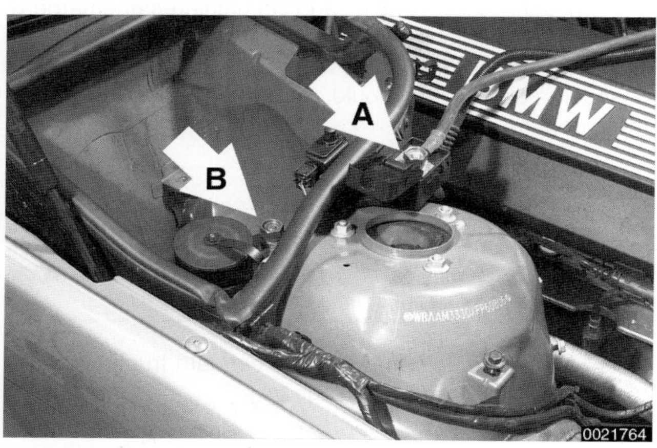

◀ Connect one end of positive (+) cable to positive (+) post of good battery. Remove cover from the positive (+) junction post (**A**) in engine compartment and connect other end of the positive (+) cable to the junction post.

– Connect one end of negative (–) cable to negative (–) battery post of good battery. Connect opposite end of negative cable (–) to ground lug (–) in engine compartment (**B**).

– Start car with good battery and run engine at about 2,000 rpm, then start car with dead battery.

– With engine at idle, switch on blower motor and rear window defogger to avoid a damaging voltage surge from alternator.

– Carefully disconnect jumper cables, starting with negative cable on ground lug. Turn all electrical consumers off.

NOTE —
The engine should be run for at least an hour to recharge the battery.

Indicator and warning lights

Many of the vehicle systems are self-monitored both statically and dynamically while driving. Generally, a red warning lamp that comes on during driving should be considered serious. If you cannot immediately determine the seriousness of the warning light, stop the vehicle in a safe place and turn the engine off as soon as possible. Consult the owner's manual in the glove box for additional information on the warning lamp and the recommended action.

If the Malfunction Indicator Lamp (MIL), "Check Engine" or "SERVICE ENGINE SOON" warning light, comes on or flashes, it indicates that an emissions-related fault has occurred. Faults such as a faulty oxygen sensor or a faulty fuel injector can cause the exhaust or evaporative emissions to exceed a specified limit. When these limits are exceeded, the MIL will be turned on. The car can be safely driven with the light on, although the emission systems should be checked as soon as possible. See **OBD On Board Diagnostics** for more information on the MIL and the On-board diagnostic system.

Towing

The cars covered by this manual should be towed with a tow truck using wheel lift or flat bed equipment. Do not tow the car on all four wheels except for very short distances to move it to a safe place.

> ***CAUTION —***
> *Do not tow with sling-type equipment. The front spoilers and bumper covers may sustain damage.*

To access threaded towing eye socket, pry open trim (**arrow**) on front or rear bumper.

NOTE —
A towing eye is provided in the luggage compartment tool kit. The towing eye can be screwed into the front or rear bumper.

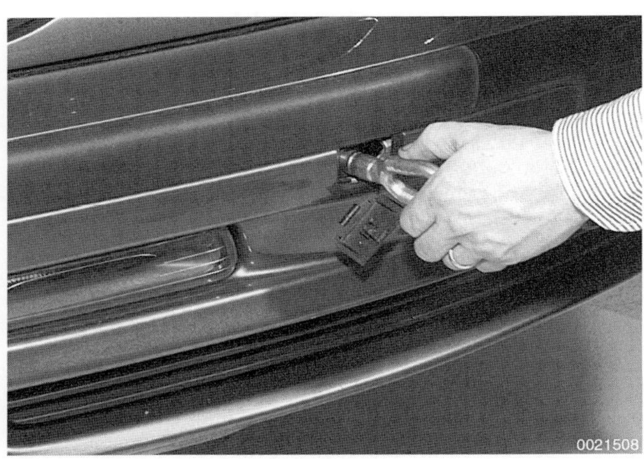

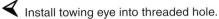

 Install towing eye into threaded hole.

– Standard transmission: A maximum towing distance of 20 miles is acceptable with the rear wheels on the ground and the transmission out of gear. If the car needs to be towed further, have the rear wheels placed on dollies.

– Automatic transmission: If absolutely necessary, car can be towed with rear wheels on ground, but the tow should not exceed 25 miles (40 km), at speeds at or below 30 mph (48 km/h).

- Be sure transmission fluid has been topped off before starting tow.
- Always tow car with transmission lever in "N" (neutral). If tow must exceed 25 miles (40 km), add one quart of ATF to transmission, or better yet, remove driveshaft.
- Be sure to drain or pump out added fluid once tow has been completed.

NOTE —
- *ATF draining and filling is covered in* **240 Automatic Transmission**. *Be sure to read the filling and draining procedure, as special service equipment is required to check the fluid level.*
- *Driveshaft removal is covered in* **260 Driveshaft**.

Spare parts kit

Carrying a basic set of spare parts can prevent a minor breakdown from turning into a major annoyance. Many of the following items won't allow you to do major repair work on the car, but they will help in the event of the failure of something that can disable the car or compromise its safety.

Spare parts kit – basic
- Poly-ribbed drive belt(s)
- Engine oil (one or two quarts)
- Engine coolant (1 gallon of premixed 50/50 BMW anti-freeze and water)
- Fuse assortment (7.5A, 10A, 15A, 20A, 30A, 50A)
- Radiator hoses (upper and lower)

Spare parts kit – additional contents
- Exterior lighting bulbs (headlight, brake light, turn signal, and taillight, except for models with Xenon headlights)
- Wiper blades
- Brake fluid (new unopened bottle, DOT 4 specification)
- Main relay for DME system

020 Maintenance

TABLES

GENERAL

The information given in this repair group includes the routine checks and maintenance steps that are both required by BMW under the terms of the vehicle warranty protection and recommended by BMW to ensure long and reliable vehicle operation.

NOTE —
Aside from keeping your car in the best possible condition, proper maintenance plays a role in maintaining full protection under BMW's new-car warranty coverage. If in doubt about the terms and conditions of your car's warranty, an authorized BMW dealer should be able to explain them.

Service Interval Indicator (SII)

For the E46 Series, BMW introduced an extended oil change interval of approximately 15,000 miles depending on engine operating conditions. The introduction of BMW High Performance Synthetic Oil has made this longer interval possible.

1999 to 6/2000 models. BMW uses a unique system to determine maintenance intervals. BMW's Service Interval Indicator (SII), calculates maintenance intervals based not only on elapsed mileage, but also on such inputs as engine speed, engine temperature, number of starts, length of trips, and the amount of fuel used. At the appropriate time, the system indicates, through lights in the instrument cluster, when the next routine maintenance is due.

6/2000 and later models. For the mid-2000 models BMW introduced new service interval software which calculates service based on the amount of fuel used. When SII detects total fuel consumption that equals the preset limits (in gallons), the instrument cluster indicates that service is required.

Using a 328i as an example:

- Standard transmission model: SII illuminates after consumption of 601 gallons of fuel.
- Automatic transmission model: SII illuminates after consumption of 667 gallons.

After the service is performed the SII can be reset to zero.

0021019c

The SII displays the mileage remaining before service is due. The type of service (OIL SERVICE or INSPECTION) is also illuminated in the display.

NOTE —
An OIL SERVICE interval will always be followed by an INSPECTION interval, which will then be followed by an OIL SERVICE interval, and so on.

When the ignition is turned on, the service recommendation and miles remaining are displayed for a few seconds. A flashing message and a negative (–) symbol in front of the number indicate that the service interval has been exceeded by the distance displayed.

The On-Board Computer uses the rate of fuel consumption in the period immediately preceding to calculate the mileage before the next service is due.

Service Interval Indicator (SII), resetting

The SII signals the need for basic routine maintenance including:

- Engine oil and oil filter change, after the engine has been warmed up.
- BMW-recommended additional maintenance as listed in **Table a**.

NOTE —

For reference, the BMW oil service requirements are approximately equivalent to the maintenance that other European manufacturers specify at intervals with a maximum of every 15,000 miles or 12 months.

When the specified maintenance has been carried out, the SII memory should be reset.

1999 to 6/2000 models

0021509

In vehicles equipped with the DLC in the right side engine compartment, the SII may be reset using the BMW diagnostic scan tool, or a specialty tool from another manufacturer. Plug the tool (**arrow**) into the DLC

CAUTION —

Follow the manufacturer's directions when resetting the SII. If the reset procedures are done incorrectly, the reset tool or the electronic Service Interval Indicator may be damaged.

Aftermarket reset tools that can reset all models with the DLC can be purchased from one of the following suppliers:

- Assenmacher Specialty Tools
  6440 Odell Place, Boulder, CO 80301
  303-530-2424
  http://www.asttool.com
- Baum Tools Unlimited, Inc.
  P.O. Box 5867, Sarasota, FL 34277-5867
  800-848-6657
  http://www.baumtools.com
- Peake Research, Automotive Products Division
  P.O. Box 28776
  San Jose, CA 95159
  408-369-0406
  http://www.peakeresearch.com

6/2000 and later models

On vehicles without the data link connector (DLC) in the engine compartment, the reset tool can no longer be used. Instead, the SII can be reset with the trip odometer reset button in the instrument cluster:

- The ignition key must be in OFF position.
- Press and hold trip odometer button in instrument cluster, and turn ignition key to ACCESSORY position.
- Keep button pressed for approx. 5 more seconds until any of the following appear in the display: “Oil Service” or “Inspection”, with “Reset” or “Re”.

- Press button again and hold for approx. 5 seconds until "Reset" or "Re" flash.
- While display is flashing, press button briefly to reset SII.
- After display has shown new interval, the following will appear in display for approx. 2 seconds: "End SIA".

The system can only be reset again after the vehicle has been driven approx. 50 to 75 miles (consumes at least 2.5 gal. fuel). If the display shows "Reset" or "Re" when resetting, the minimum driving distance has been fulfilled and the system can be reset again. It is possible to interrupt and end the reset procedure by changing the position of the ignition key.

Inspection I and Inspection II

The Service Interval Indicator signals the need for more comprehensive maintenance and inspection. There are two sets of inspection requirements. These inspections alternate throughout a car's maintenance history. If the last inspection interval was Inspection I, the next inspection interval (following an oil service) will be Inspection II, the next after that will be Inspection I, and so on.

Inspection I tasks are listed in **Table b**. Inspection II includes most of the tasks from Inspection I with additional Inspection II tasks. A complete listing of Inspection II tasks is in **Table c**.

NOTE —

For reference, the BMW Inspection I and Inspection II requirements are approximately equivalent to the maintenance requirements that other European manufacturers specify. Inspection I is normally due at intervals with a maximum of 30,000 miles or 24 months. Inspection II is normally due at intervals with a maximum of 60,000 miles or 48 months.

MAINTENANCE TABLES

The intervals for most tasks listed in the maintenance table below are determined by the SII.

Except where noted, the maintenance items listed apply to all models and model years covered by this manual. The columns on the right side of each table give quick-reference information about the job. The text in the "additional repair information" column refers to repair groups.

Table a. Oil service

Maintenance item	Tools required	New parts required	Warm engine required	Dealer service recommended	Additional repair information
Engine compartment maintenance					
Change oil and oil filter.	✻	✻	✻		**020**
Reset Service Interval Indicator (SII).	✻				**020**
Replace interior ventilation microfilter.		✻			**020**
Under car maintenance					
Check overall thickness of front and rear brake pads. If replacement is necessary: Examine brake disc surfaces. Clean brake pad contact points in calipers. Grease wheel centering hubs (alloy wheels only). Check thickness of parking brake linings only when replacing rear brake pads. Check operation of parking brake and adjust as necessary.	✻				**340**
Check and adjust tire pressures, including spare.	✻				**020**

Table b. Inspection I service

Maintenance item	Tools required	New parts required	Warm engine required	Dealer service recommended	Additional repair information
Under car maintenance					
Change engine oil and filter.	✻	✻	✻		**020**
Check transmission and differential(s) for external leaks. **325Xi/330Xi models**: Change oil in transfer case only if prompted by BMW diagnostic scan tool diagnostic test.					**230** **240**
Check CV joint boots for damage or leaks.					**311** **331**
Visually check fuel tank, fuel lines and connections for leaks.					**160**
Check condition, position, and mounting of exhaust system. Visually check for leaks.					**180**
Check power steering system for leaks. Check power steering fluid level and adjust if necessary.					**320**
Check steering rack and tie rods for tightness. Check condition of front axle joints, steering linkage and steering shaft joints.					**320**
Check overall thickness of front and rear brake pads using special BMW tool. If replacement is necessary: Examine brake disc surfaces. Clean brake pad contact points in calipers. Grease wheel centering hubs (alloy wheels only). Check thickness of parking brake linings only when replacing rear brake pads. Check operation of parking brake and adjust as necessary.	✻				**340**
Check front control arm bushings for damage or wear.					**310**

Table b. Inspection I service (continued)

Maintenance item	Tools required	New parts required	Warm engine required	Dealer service recommended	Additional repair information
Under car maintenance (continued)					
Check brake system connections and lines for leaks, damage and incorrect positioning.					340
Check parking brake actuator. Adjust if necessary.	*				340
Check all tire pressures (including spare) and correct if necessary. Check condition of tires (outer tread surfaces), tread wear pattern; in case of uneven tread wear, perform a wheel alignment if requested.	*				020
Inspect entire body according to terms of rust perforation limited warranty. (Must be performed at least every two years.)					
Engine compartment maintenance Read out on-board diagnostic (OBD II) system.	*				100 130
M3 models: check valve clearance (M3 only).	*	*	*	*	116
Check engine drive belt condition					
Check engine coolant system/heater hose connections for leaks. Check coolant level and antifreeze protection level. Add coolant as necessary.	*				170
Check windshield washer fluid level and antifreeze protection. Add washer fluid as necessary.					611
Replace ventilation microfilter. (Note: reduce replacement intervals in dusty operating conditions).		*			020
Reset service interval indicator.	*				020
Body/electrical Check operation of air conditioner.					640
Check operation of headlights, parking lights, back-up lights, license plate lights, interior lights, glove box light, engine compartment light, trunk light, turn signals, emergency flashers, stop lights, horns, headlight flasher and dimmer switch.					630
Check instrument panel and dashboard lights.					620
Check wipers and windshield washer system. Check aim of washer jets and adjust if necessary.					611
Check condition and function of seat belts.					720
Visually examine all airbag units for torn covers, obvious damage or attachment of decals, decorations or accessories.					721
Check central locking system and double lock.					515
Replace batteries for alarm remote controls in all master keys.	*	*			515
Check operation and condition of all door, hood and trunk latches.					410 515
Check heater, air conditioner blower, and rear window defogger operation.					640

Table b. Inspection I service (continued)

Maintenance item	Tools required	New parts required	Warm engine required	Dealer service recommended	Additional repair information
Body/electrical (continued) **Convertible models**: Check convertible top mechanism tension chords Activate automatic roll-over protection system via BMW diagnostic scan tool. Note: first remove hardtop or lower convertible top. Lubricate convertible top sliding hinge covers using a non-silicone spray.	*			*	541
Check all warning/indicator lights, check control.					620
Check operation of rear view mirrors.					
Road test Check braking performance, steering, heating, air conditioner operation. Check manual transmission and clutch operation or automatic transmission operation.					

Table c. Inspection II service

Maintenance item (incudes items from *Table b. Inspection I service*)	Tools required	New parts required	Warm engine required	Dealer service recommended	Additional repair information
Under car maintenance **M3 models**: change transmission fluid every inspection II. **All models except M3**: change automatic transmission fluid every 100,000 miles.	*	*	*		
M3 models: Change differential fluid.	*	*	*		
Engine compartment maintenance Replace air filter element. (Note: reduce replacement intervals in dusty operating conditions).	*	*			020
Brake system service Replace brake fluid every 2 years (time interval begins from vehicle production date).	*	*		*	340
Cooling system service **1999 -2003 models**: Replace coolant every 4 years. **2004-2005 models**: Engine coolant has lifetime rating, no change interval specified.	*	*			170
Oxygen sensor service Replace oxygen sensor: every 100,000 miles for 1999 - 2003 models and all M3 models. every 120,000 miles on 2004 -2005 models, ex. M56 engine. every 150,000 miles on M56 engine.	*	*			180
Spark plug service					

Table c. Inspection II service (continued)

Maintenance item (incudes items from *Table b. Inspection I service*)	Tools required	New parts required	Warm engine required	Dealer service recommended	Additional repair information
Replace spark plugs: every 100,000 miles on all models except M3 models. every 60,000 miles on M3.	*	*			020
General service					
Replace M-Mobility sealant cartridge every 4 years (M3 only).		*			

FLUID AND LUBRICANT SPECIFICATIONS

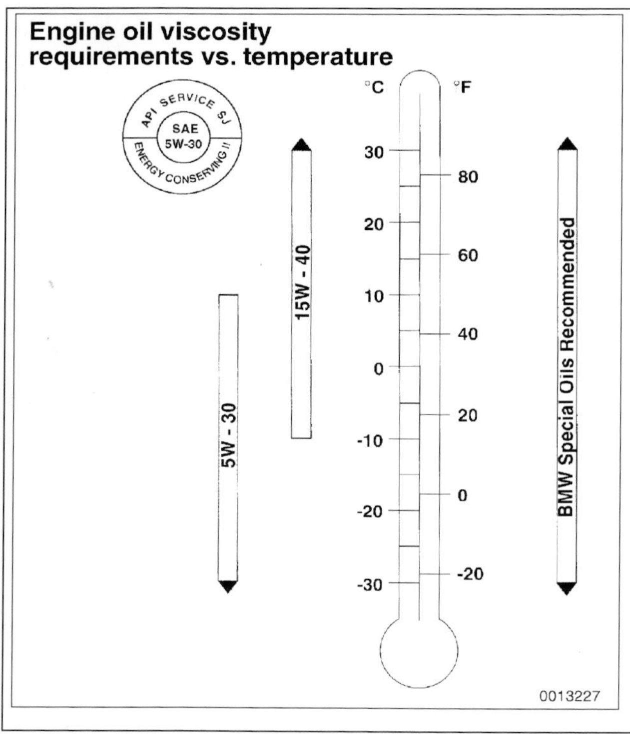

The illustration shows engine oil viscosity (SAE grade) vs. operating temperature range for BMW engines covered in this manual.

Fluid and lubricant capacities and specifications for E46 cars are listed in **Table d**.

> ***WARNING —***
> *The use of fluids that do not meet BMW's specifications may impair performance and reliability, and may void warranty coverage.*

Table d. Fluids and lubricants

Fluid	Approximate capacity	Specification
Engine oil with filter change		
Rear wheel drive All wheel drive	6.5 liters (6.9 US qt) 7.5 liters (8 US qt)	Synthetic 5W-30/40 API/SH or higher
M3 models	5.5 liters (5.8 US qt)	Synthetic 10W-60 API/SJ or higher
Manual transmission oil		
S5D 250G	1.1 liters (1.15 US q.)	BMW MTF-LT-1
S5D 320Z	1.3 liters (1.37 US qt)	BMW MTF-LT-1
S5D 280Z	1.3 liters (1.37 US qt)	BMW MTF-LT-1
S6S420G	1.9 liters (2.00 US qt)	BMW MTF-LT-2
S6X37BZ	1.6 liters (1.69 US qt)	BMW MTF-LT-2
Automatic transmission fluid (ATF) (drain and fill) (additional fluid required when installing a dry torque converter)		
A5S 325Z	4.0 liters (4.2 US qt)	Exxon LT 71141
A5S 360R/390R	6.2 liters (6.5 US qt)	ETL-7045 or Dexron III
Differential, front or rear (drain and fill) (Lifetime fluid; no fluid change required)		
Front differential:	0.7 liter (0.74 US qt)	
Rear differential: Rear wheel drive All wheel drive M3	 0.9 liter (0.95 US qt) 1.0 liter (1.06 US qt) 1.1 liter (1.20 US qt)	BMW SAF-XO synthetic oil

Table d. Fluids and lubricants (continued)

Fluid	Approximate capacity	Specification
Power steering fluid		
All models	Permanently sealed (no drain plug)	Dexron III® ATF
Brake fluid		
All models		SAE DOT4
Engine coolant		
i/Xi M3	8.4 liters (8.9 US qt) 10.0 liters (10.6 US qt)	50% BMW anti-freeze/ 50% distilled water

CAUTION —
Multi-viscosity engine oils should not be used in the manual transmission. Use of such an oil could shorten the service life of the transmission.

Brake fluid

Brake fluid absorbs moisture easily, and moisture in the fluid affects brake performance and reliability. This is why brake fluid should be flushed from the system every two years. When replacing or adding brake fluid, use only new fluid from previously unopened containers. Do not use brake fluid that has been bled from the system, even if it is brand new. Use only DOT 4 brake fluid.

NOTE —
See **340 Brakes** *for more brake fluid information.*

Engine coolant (anti-freeze)

BMW recommends coolant that is a 50/50 mixture of distilled water and phosphate/nitrate free anti-freeze containing ethylene glycol. Anti-freeze raises the boiling point and lowers the freezing point of the coolant. It also contains additives that help prevent cooling system corrosion.

Differential gear oil

BMW recommends using only a specially formulated synthetic gear oil (SAF-XO) that is available through an authorized BMW dealer parts department. For additional information on this lubricant and any other lubricants that may be compatible, contact an authorized BMW dealer service department.

Power steering fluid

The power steering fluid is Dexron III® ATF, or equivalent. The system is permanently filled and does not have a drain. Routinely adding ATF is not required unless the system is leaking.

Transmission fluid, automatic

The automatic transmissions installed in the E46 models are filled with special automatic transmission fluids, depending on transmission type and model year.

NOTE —

- *The transmission lubricant type can be found on the "type-plate" on the side of the transmission. See* **240 Automatic Transmission**.
- *Consult an authorized BMW dealer for alternate fluid use and the most-up-to-date information regarding transmission operating fluids.*
- *As of model year 2002, BMW has specified a 100,000 mile ATF change interval. It is recommended that this change interval be followed for earlier models.*

Transmission fluid, manual

The manual transmissions installed in the E46 models are normally filled with a special lifetime fluid (MTF-LT-1). Consult **230 Manual Transmission** for further information.

ENGINE OIL SERVICE

With the introduction of synthetic oil and extended oil change intervals, a new oil filter with improved filter paper design was introduced. The new filter paper resists deterioration caused by high oil temperatures over an extended time.

NOTE —

Early style oil filter numbers with BMW part numbers 11 42 1 427 908 or 11 42 1 745 390 should not be used in the 1999 and later BMW models.

Use any synthetic low viscosity oil to top off the engine oil level between oil changes, as long as it meets the API classification SH. Castrol is now the supplier of both the mineral based oil used in earlier models and the synthetic based oil used from model year 1999.

Oil recommendation

- i/Xi models . . . . 5W-30 or 5W-40
- M3 models 10W-60

NOTE —

- *The use of engine oil additives is not recommended when using BMW High Performance Synthetic engine oil.*
- *BMW is constantly upgrading recommended maintenance procedures and requirements. The information contained here is as accurate as possible at the time of publication. If there is any doubt about what procedures apply to a specific model or model year, or what intervals should be followed, remember that an authorized BMW dealer has the latest information on factory-recommended maintenance.*

Engine oil, checking level

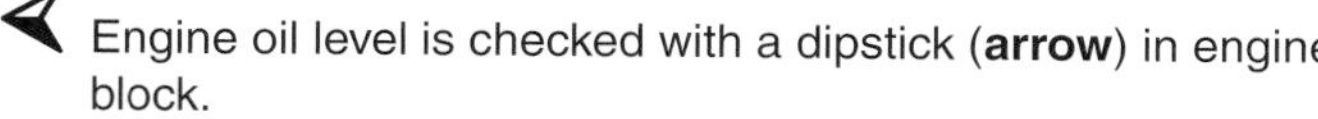

Engine oil level is checked with a dipstick (**arrow**) in engine block.

- Check oil level with car on a level surface, after engine has been stopped for at least a few minutes.
- Check level by pulling out dipstick and wiping it clean. Reinsert it all way and withdraw it again.
- Oil level is correct if it is between two marks near end of stick.

0021511

Add oil through filler cap (**arrow**) on top of cylinder head. Add only amount needed to bring oil level to **MAX** mark on dipstick, using an oil of correct viscosity and grade. Too much oil can be just as harmful as too little.

Engine oil and filter, changing

A complete oil change requires new oil, a new oil filter insert kit, and a new drain plug sealing washer. The tools needed, a 17 mm drain plug socket or box wrench and a drain pan (8 - 10 US qt. capacity), are described in **010 General**.

NOTE —

If using a "fast-lube" service facility for oil changes, make sure the technician hand-starts and torques the engine oil drain plug using hand-tools. Power tools can strip the threads of the plug and the oil pan.

– Run engine for a few minutes to warm engine oil. Shut engine off.

– With car on level ground, place drain pan under oil drain plug.

Using a 36 mm wrench, loosen and remove oil filter housing cover (**arrow**). Remove filter cartridge and discard any O-rings.

On Coupe or Convertible model: Remove oil drain plug access panel in center of front end reinforcement plate below engine.

Using a socket or box wrench, loosen drain plug at oil drain pan. Remove plug by hand and let oil drain into pan.

> **CAUTION —**
> *Pull the loose plug away from the hole quickly to avoid being scalded by hot oil. It will run out quickly when the plug is removed. If possible, use gloves to protect your hands.*

– When oil flow has diminished to an occasional drip, reinstall drain plug with a new metal sealing washer and torque plug.

Tightening torques
- Engine oil drain plug (M12 bolt) . . . . 25 Nm (18 ft-lb)

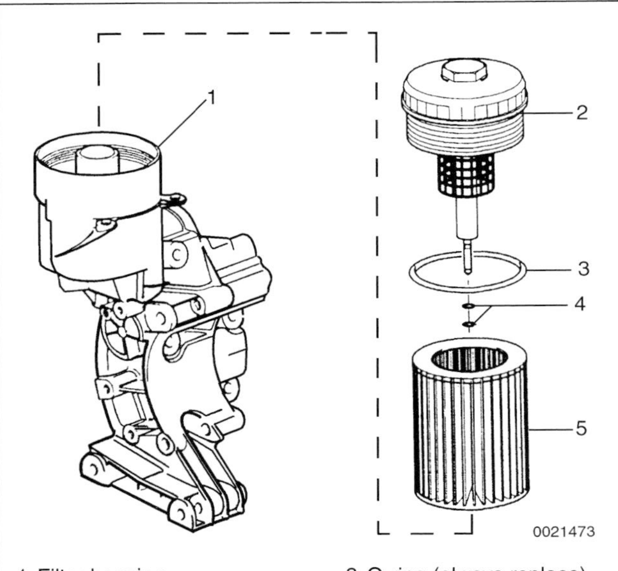

1. Filter housing
2. filter housing cover -tighten to 25 Nm (18 ft-lb)
3. O-ring (always replace)
4. O-rings (always replace)
5. Filter element

Working at oil filter housing:
- Lubricate and install new oil filter O-rings.
- Install a new filter cartridge and housing cover.
- Tighten cover.

Tightening torque
- Oil filter cover filter housing . . . . 25 Nm (18 ft-lb)

– Refill crankcase with oil. Approximate oil capacity is listed in **Table d**. Use dipstick to check correct oil level.

– Start engine and check that oil pressure warning light immediately goes out.

– Allow engine to run for a few minutes to circulate new oil, then check for leaks at drain plug and oil filter. Stop engine and recheck oil level.

ENGINE COMPARTMENT MAINTENANCE

The information under this heading describes routine maintenance other than oil change done in the engine compartment. It is not necessary for the car to be raised and supported off the ground. Information on oil change is given earlier in this group.

Accelerator linkage

The accelerator and throttle linkage should be lubricated periodically. Use a general purpose oil on the joints and bearings of the linkage. Use a multipurpose grease on the bearing points of the throttle plate.

Air filter, replacing

The specified replacement intervals for the air filter are based on normal use. If the car is operated primarily in dusty conditions, the air filter should be serviced more frequently.

NOTE —

M56 engines are fitted with an additional carbon filter element built into the top section of the air filter housing.

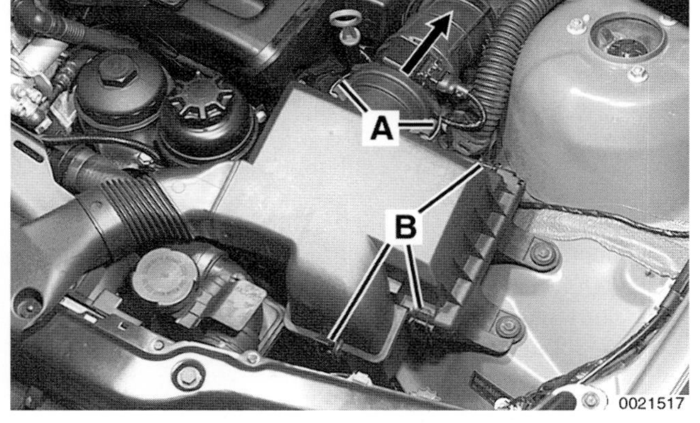

- Release mass air flow sensor clips (**A**) and pull sensor assembly out of air filter upper housing (**arrow**).
- Release upper air filter housing clips (**B**).

- Lift air filter upper housing, and then remove filter element insert from cartridge.
- On installation, install O-ring for mass air flow sensor (**arrow**) into retaining clips in air filter upper housing.

Cooling system service

Routine cooling system maintenance consists of maintaining the coolant level and inspecting hoses. Because the coolant's anti-corrosion and anti-freeze additives gradually lose their effectiveness, replacement of the coolant every four years is recommended.

> ***CAUTION —***
> *Use only BMW approved phosphate-free anti-freeze when filling the cooling system. Use of anti-freeze containing phosphates is considered to be harmful to the cooling system.*

The float in the radiator tank indicates coolant level, and should be inspected while the coolant is cold. When the upper mark on the float is level with the top of the filler neck, coolant is at the minimum allowable level. When the lower mark on the float is level with the top of the filler neck, the coolant is at the maximum level.

Hose connections should be tight and dry. Coolant seepage indicates either that the hose clamp is loose, that the hose is damaged, or that the connection is dirty or corroded. Dried coolant has a chalky appearance. Hoses should be firm and springy. Replace any hose that is cracked, that has become soft and limp, or has been contaminated by oil.

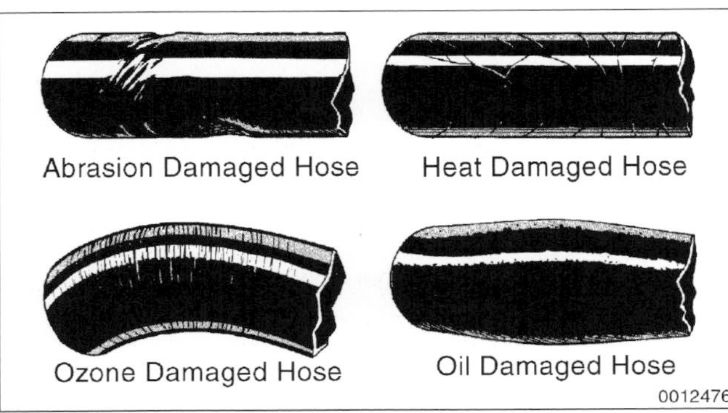

As a preventive measure, replacement of the cooling system hoses every four years is also recommended. The illustration shows examples of damage to coolant hoses. Any of conditions shown is cause for replacement. (Courtesy of Gates Rubber Company, Inc.)

Engine drive belt service

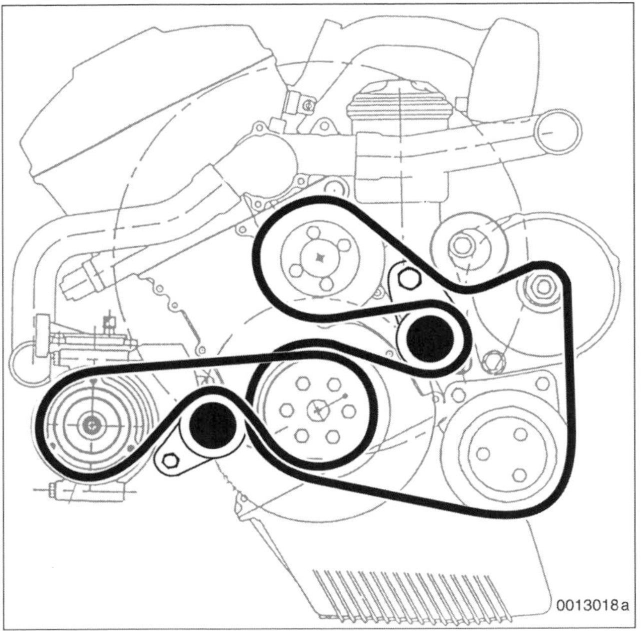

E46 models use two poly-ribbed (serpentine) belts:

- The outer belt only turns the A/C compressor.
- The inner, longer belt drives the alternator, coolant pump and power steering pump.

Inspect drive belts with the engine off. If the belt shows signs of wear, cracking, glazing, or missing sections, it should be replaced immediately. To reduce the chance of belt failure while driving, replacement of the belts every four years is recommended.

NOTE —
- *Note belt routing prior to removing belts.*
- *When belts are replaced with new ones, keep the old set for emergency use.*

To remove drive belts:

Prior to removing the inner belt, the outer (A/C compressor) belt must first be removed.

Two types of automatic belt tensioners are used to keep the belts tensioned properly; a hydraulic version and a mechanical version.The procedure for releasing the tension on the belt is similar for both types.

> ***CAUTION —***
> *Mark drive belt rotation direction if removing and reusing an old belt.*

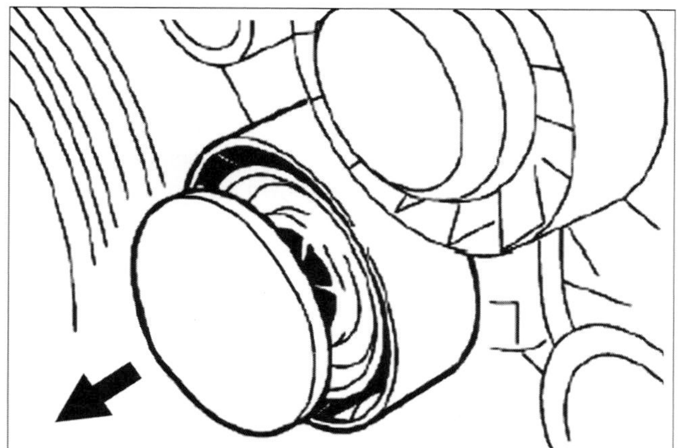

◄ Pry off dust cap from front of tensioner pulley.

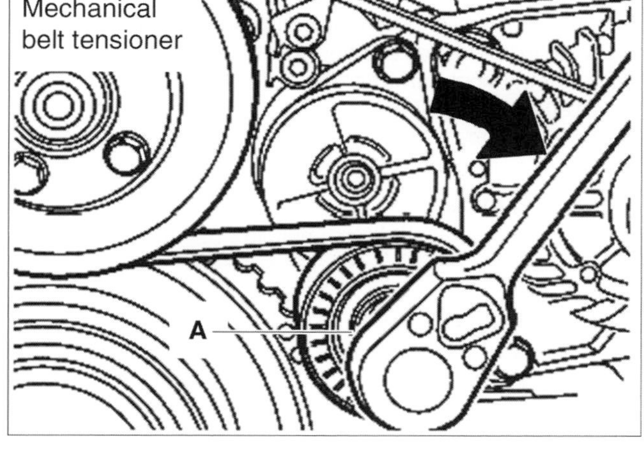

◄ Use long-handled wrench (8 mm hex bit), lever center bolt in tensioner pulley (**A**) clockwise, away from belt (**arrow**) to release belt tension (mechanical type tensioner shown in illustration).

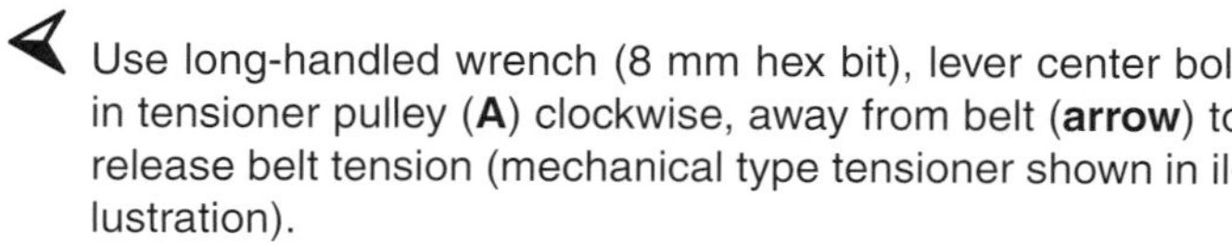

> ***WARNING —***
> *Observe care when replacing belts. Personal injury could result if a tensioner springs back into position uncontrollably.*

NOTE —
Mechanical belt tensioners have a cast hex boss on the body of the tensioner. Alternatively, use a 17 mm wrench on the hex boss to release belt tension.

– With tension released, slide belt off pulleys.

– When installing a new belt, gently pry it over the pulleys. Too much force may damage the belt or the accessory.

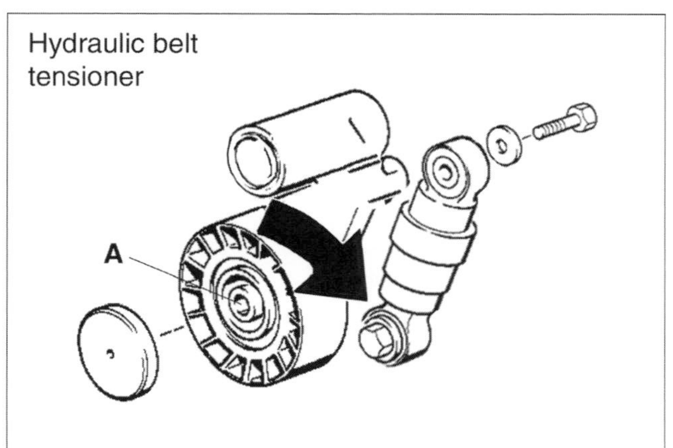

Idle speed

Engine idle speed can change due to a number of factors, including normal wear. The idle speed in E46 models is electronically adaptive and non-adjustable. See **130 Fuel Injection** for more information.

Oxygen sensors

The engine management system in E46 models is equipped with a regulating sensor mounted before each catalytic converter and a monitoring sensor down stream of each converter. This allows for tight control of the tail pipe emissions and also allows the ECM to diagnose converter problems. If the ECM detects that catalytic converter or oxygen sensor efficiency has degraded past a certain pre-programmed limit, it will turn on the Check Engine light, and store a diagnostic trouble code (DTC) in the ECM.

See **OBD On Board Diagnostics** in the rear of this manual for more information on OBD systems.

Replacement of oxygen sensors at the specified intervals ensures that the engine and emission control system will continue to operate as designed. Extending the replacement interval may void the emission control warranty coverage. See **180 Exhaust System** for information on replacing the oxygen sensors.

Tightening torque

- Oxygen sensor to exhaust manifold . . . . 50 Nm (37 ft-lb)

NOTE —
A special socket for replacing the oxygen sensor is available from most automotive parts stores. The socket has a groove cut down one side to allow the sensor to be installed without damaging the wire harness.

Power steering fluid, checking level

To check power steering fluid level in fluid reservoir:

- Park car on level ground with engine off.
- Level is correct if it is between **MIN** and **MAX** marks on dipstick.
- If level is below **MIN** mark, start engine and add fluid to reservoir to bring level up.
- Stop engine and recheck level.
- Hand-tighten reservoir cap.

Power steering fluid

- Recommended fluid . . . . Dexron III® ATF

Spark plugs, replacing

E46 engines use a "coil-over" configuration, with one ignition coil above each spark plug.

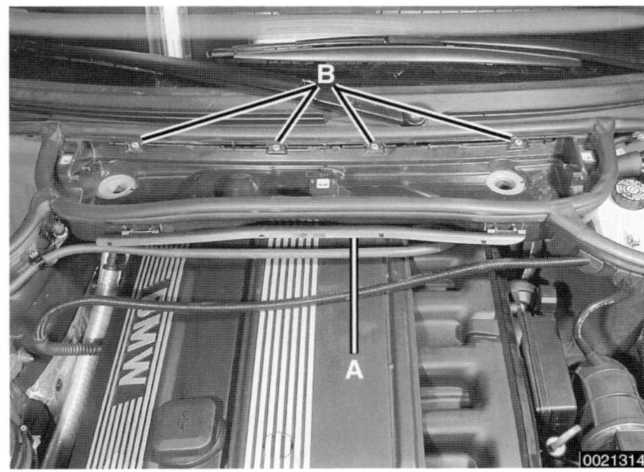

Remove microfilter housing:

- Remove microfilter for interior ventilation. See **Ventilation microfilter, replacing.**
- Open wiring harness loom (**A**), remove harness and lay aside.
- Unfasten screws (**B**) and take off lower microfilter housing.

Remove engine cover over ignition coils:

- Remove oil filler cap.
- Remove plastic trim covers (**arrows**).
- Remove cover hold down bolts.

Remove ignition coil grounding harnesses (**arrows**).

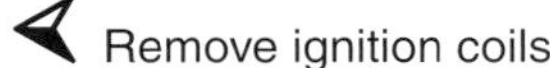

Remove ignition coils:

- Pull up on spring clips to disconnect ignition coil harness connectors.
- Remove coil mounting bolts. Remove coils.

– Remove spark plugs.

– Installation is reverse of removal, bearing in mind the following:

- Lightly lubricate new spark plug threads with copper-based anti-seize compound.
- Thread plugs into cylinder head by hand to prevent cross-threading.
- Be sure to reinstall coil grounding harness.

Spark plug recommendations

- i/Xi models . . . . NGK BKR6 EQUP
- M3 models . . . . NGK DCPR8 EKP

Tightening torque

- Spark plug to cylinder head . . . . 25 Nm (18 ft-lb)

Ventilation microfilter, replacing

Working at cowl housing inside engine compartment, twist microfilter cover retainers (**arrows**) 90° each and pull cover up.

Pull filter out and replace.

OTHER MECHANICAL MAINTENANCE

Battery, checking and cleaning

The battery is located in the right side of the luggage compartment. Simple maintenance of the battery and its terminal connections will ensure maximum starting performance, especially in winter when colder temperatures reduce battery power.

NOTE —
Design characteristics of the convertible body cause vibrations in the trunk area. Therefore, E46 Convertibles require a special battery designed for constant vibration. When replacing the battery, be sure the replacement is designed specifically for the Convertible.

Battery cables should be tight. The terminals, the cable clamps, and the battery case should be free of the white deposits that indicate corrosion and acid salts. Even a thin layer of dust containing conductive acid salts can cause battery discharge.

– To remove battery corrosion:
  - Disconnect battery cables. Disconnect negative (–) cable first.
  - Remove battery from trunk.
  - Clean terminal posts and cable clamps with a wire brush.
  - Clean main chassis ground terminal next to battery. Corrosion can be washed away with a baking soda and water solution that will neutralize acid. Apply solution carefully, though, since it will also neutralize acid inside battery.
  - Reconnect cable clamps, positive (+) cable first.
  - Lightly coat outside of terminals, hold down screws, and clamps with petroleum jelly, grease, or a commercial battery terminal corrosion inhibitor.

WARNING —
- *Prior to disconnecting the battery, read the battery disconnection cautions given at the front of this manual.*
- *Battery acid is extremely dangerous. Take care to keep it from contacting eyes, skin, or clothing. Wear eye protection. Extinguish all smoking materials and do not work near any open flames.*

Battery electrolyte should be maintained at the correct level just above the battery plates and their separators. The correct level is approximately 5 mm (¼ in.) above the top of battery plates or to the top of the indicator marks (if applicable). The battery plates and the indicator marks can be seen once the filler caps are removed. If the electrolyte level is low, replenish it by adding distilled water only.

NOTE —
The original equipment battery in E46 models is maintenance free. The original electrolyte will normally last the entire service life of the battery under moderate climate conditions.

Battery, replacing

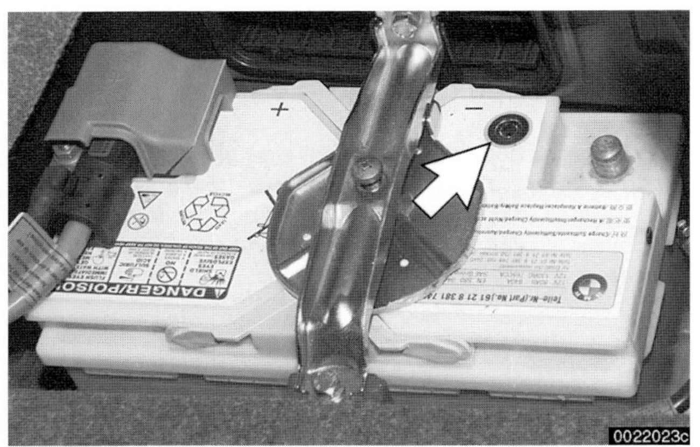

The original equipment BMW battery is equipped with a built-in hydrometer "magic eye" (**arrow**). Battery condition is determined by the color of the eye:

- Green: Adequate charge
- Black: Inadequate charge; recharge
- Yellow: Defective battery; replace

Batteries are rated by ampere hours (Ah), the number of hours a specific current drain can be sustained before complete discharge, or by cold cranking amps (CCA), the number of amps available to crank the engine in cold weather conditions. In general, replacement batteries should always be rated equal or higher than the original battery.

CAUTION —
Prior to disconnecting the battery, read the battery disconnection cautions given at the front of this manual.

The battery is held in place by a single hand screw and plate. A secure battery hold-down is important in order to prevent vibrations and road shock from damaging the battery.

NOTE —
- *Always disconnect the negative (–) cable first, and connect it last. While changing the battery, clean away any corrosion in or around the battery tray.*
- *Design characteristics of the convertible body cause vibrations to oscillate in the trunk area, requiring a special battery and battery retaining mechanism designed for vibration.*
- *More battery and charging system information is in* **121 Battery, Alternator, Starter**.

Brake fluid, replacing

BMW strictly recommends replacing the brake fluid every two years. This will help protect against corrosion and the effects of moisture in the fluid.

NOTE —
See **340 Brakes** *for brake fluid flushing procedures.*

Brake pad/rotor wear, checking

E46 cars are fitted with disc brakes at all four wheels. Although the brakes are equipped with a brake pad warning system, the system only monitors one wheel per axle. It is recommended that pad thickness should be checked whenever the wheels are off or brake work is being done.

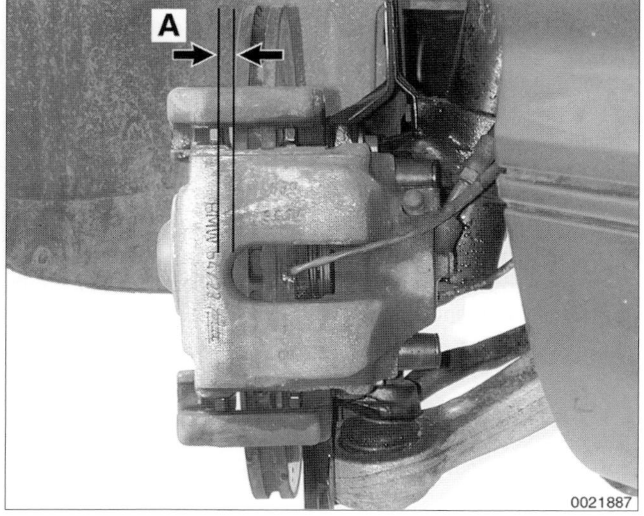

Disc brake pad wear can be checked through opening in caliper:

- Measure distance (**A**) of brake pad "ear" to brake rotor. See **340 Brakes**. Compare to specification below.

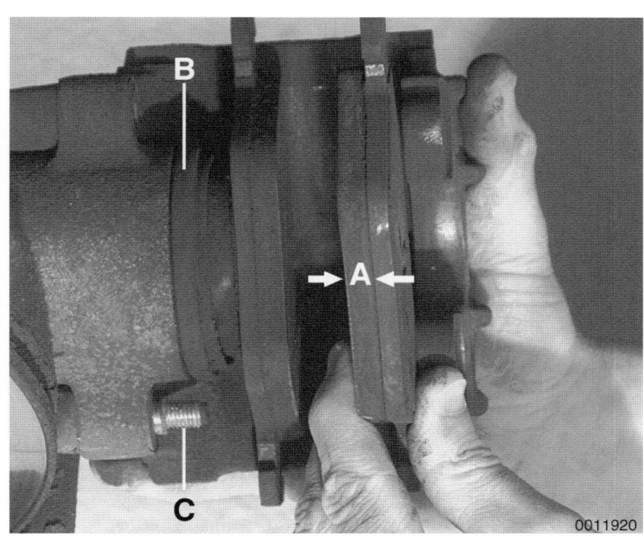

Unbolt caliper from steering arm to properly inspect:

- Brake pad thickness (**A**)
- Brake rotors
- Condition of caliper seal (**B**)
- Condition of caliper slider bolts (**C**)

NOTE —
Brake caliper removal and installation procedures are given in **340 Brakes**.

Brake pad lining minimum thickness

- Front or rear pad
  Dimension **A** . . . . 3.0 mm (0.12 in.)

Brake system, inspecting

Routine maintenance of the brake system includes maintaining the brake fluid in the reservoir, checking brake pads for wear, checking parking brake function, and inspecting the system for fluid leaks or other damage:

- Check that brake hoses are correctly routed to avoid chafing or kinking.
- Inspect unions and brake calipers for signs of fluid leaks.
- Inspect rigid lines for corrosion, dents, or other damage.
- Inspect flexible hoses for cracking.
- Replace faulty hoses or lines, see **340 Brakes**.

WARNING —
Incorrect installation or overtightening hoses, lines, and unions may cause chafing or leakage. This can lead to partial or complete brake system failure.

Parking brake, checking

The parking brake system is independent of the main braking system and may require periodic adjustment depending on use. Adjust the parking brake if the brake lever can be pulled up more than 8 clicks. Check that the cable moves freely. A description of the parking brake and parking brake adjustment can be found in **340 Brakes**.

NOTE —
The parking brake may lose some of its effectiveness if it is not used frequently. This is due to corrosion build-up on the parking brake drum. To remove corrosion, apply the parking brake just until it begins to grip, then pull the lever up one more stop (click). Drive the car approximately 400 meters (1,300 ft.) and release the brake. To recheck the adjustment of the parking brake see **340 Brakes**.

Clutch fluid, checking

The hydraulic clutch and the brake system share the same reservoir and the same brake fluid. Clutch fluid level and brake fluid level are checked at the same time.

NOTE —

- *See* **340 Brakes** *for more information.*
- *See* **210 Clutch** *for information on the clutch and the hydraulic clutch operating system.*

Drive axle joint (CV joint) boots, inspecting

CV joint protective boots must be closely inspected for cracks and any other damage that will allow contaminants to get into the joint. If the rubber boots fail, the water and dirt that enter the joint will quickly damage it.

NOTE —

Replacement of the CV joint boots and inspection of the joints are described in **311 Front Axle Final Drive** *and* **331 Rear Axle Final Drive**.

Exhaust system, inspecting

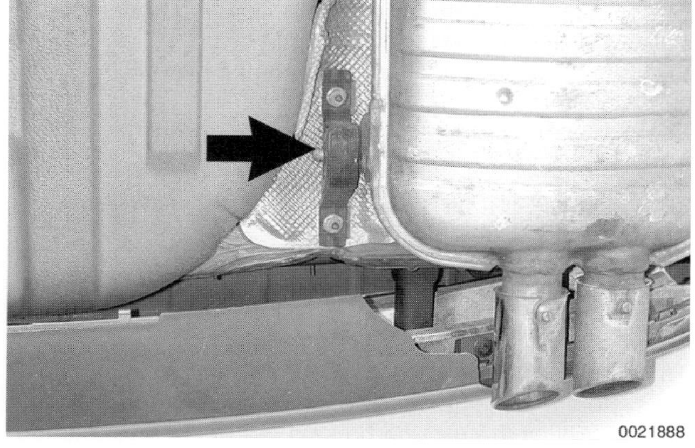

Scheduled maintenance of the exhaust system is limited to inspection:

- Check to see that all the hangers (**arrow**) are in place and properly supporting the system and that the system does not strike the body.
- Check for restrictions due to dents or kinks.
- Check for weakness or perforation due to rust.

NOTE —

Alignment of the system and the location of the hangers are described in **180 Exhaust System**.

Differential oil level, checking

The differential units in E46 models are filled with lifetime oil that ordinarily does not need to be changed.

 All wheel drive models: Check front differential fluid level at front differential filler plug (**arrow**).

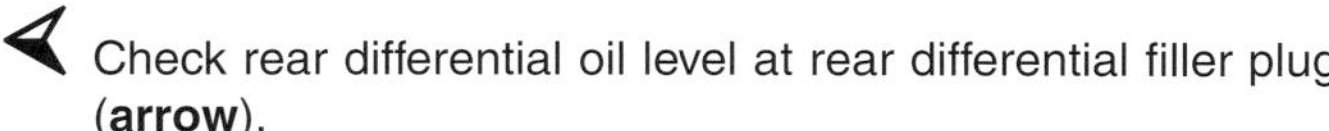
Check rear differential oil level at rear differential filler plug (**arrow**).

– Check lubricant level with car on a level surface:
- Remove oil filler plug.
- Level is correct when fluid just reaches edge of filler hole.
- If necessary, top up fluid.
- Install and tighten oil filler plug when oil level is correct.

The differential should be filled with a special BMW lubricant available through an authorized BMW dealer.

NOTE —
- *Use a 14 mm or 17 mm Allen socket to remove the drain plug.*
- *If the car is raised in the air, it should be level.*

Tightening torques
- Front differential filler plug to housing . . . 65 Nm (48 ft-lb)
- Rear differential filler plug
  - with sealing washer . . . . 65 Nm (48 ft-lb)
  - without sealing washer . . . . 60 Nm (44 ft-lb)

Fuel filter, replacing

The fuel filter is located beneath the center of the car, approximately under the driver's seat. A protective cover must be removed to access the filter.

NOTE —
325i models equipped with an automatic transmission and M56 engine use a lifetime fuel filter that is integral to the fuel tank assembly. Replacement of the fuel filter require replacement of the entire fuel tank assembly. For more information, see **160 Fuel Tank and Fuel Pump**.

0021522

Fuel filter for M52 TU engine is shown in illustration. Fuel filter for S54 engine applications is similar.

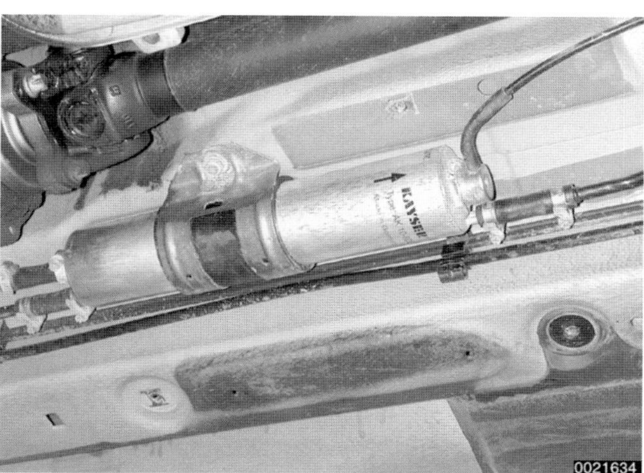
0021634

E46 cars with M54 engine are equipped with a fuel filter that has a built in fuel pressure regulator.

- Disconnect battery negative (–) cable.
- Drain fuel filter from inlet side into a container and inspect drained fuel. Check for rust, moisture and contamination.
- When replacing fuel filter:
  - Clamp filter inlet and outlet hoses to lessen fuel spillage.
  - Loosen center clamping bracket and hose clamps on either end of filter.
  - Note arrow or markings indicating direction of flow on new filter.
  - Install new filter using new hose clamps.

WARNING —
Fuel will be expelled when the filter is removed. Do not smoke or work near heaters or other fire hazards. Keep a fire extinguisher handy.

CAUTION —
Clean thoroughly around the filter connections before removing them.

NOTE —
When installing fuel filter cover, take care to reinstall foam rubber seal in front of cover correctly to prevent flooding of filter with rain splash water.

Fuel tank and fuel lines, inspecting

Inspect the fuel tank, fuel lines, and fuel system for damage or leaks. Check for fuel leaks in the engine compartment or fuel odors in the passenger compartment. Check for faulty flexible fuel lines by bending them. If any leaks are present, fuel should be expelled. Check for any evaporative emissions hoses that may have become disconnected, checking carefully at the charcoal canister and evaporative emissions purge system.

> ***WARNING —***
> *When checking for fuel leaks, the engine must be cold. A hot exhaust manifold or exhaust system could cause the fuel to ignite or explode causing serious personal injury. Ventilate the work area and clean up spilled fuel immediately.*

NOTE —
See **130 Fuel Injection** *and* **160 Fuel Tank and Fuel Pump** *for component locations and additional information.*

Suspension, front, inspecting

Inspection of the front suspension and steering includes a check of all moving parts for wear and excessive play. Inspect ball joint and tie-rod rubber seals and boots for cracks or tears that could allow the entry of dirt, water, and other contaminants.

On All wheel drive models check front differential fluid level and check CV joint boots for cracks.

NOTE —
See **310 Front Suspension** *and* **311 Front Axle Final Drive**.

Suspension, rear, inspecting

Differential and rear drive axle service consists of checking and changing the gear oil, inspecting for leaks, and checking the rear drive axle rubber boots for damage.

The areas where leaks are most likely to occur are around the drive shaft and drive axle mounting flanges.

NOTE —
For more information on identifying oil leaks and their causes, see **330 Rear Suspension** *and* **331 Rear Axle Final Drive**.

Tires, checking inflation pressure

Correct tire pressures are important to handling and stability, fuel economy, and tire wear. Tire pressures change with temperature. Pressures should be checked often during seasonal temperature changes. Correct inflation pressures can be found on the driver's door pillar and in the owner's manual. Note that tire pressures should be higher when the car is more heavily loaded.

> ***WARNING —***
> *Do not inflate any tire to a pressure higher than the tire's maximum inflation pressure listed on the sidewall. Use care when adding air to warm tires. Warm tire pressures can increase as much as 4 psi (0.3 bar) over their cold pressures.*

Tires, rotating

BMW does not recommend tire rotation. Due to the car's suspension design, the front tires begin to wear first at the outer shoulder and the rear tires begin to wear first at the middle of the tread or inner shoulder. Rotating the tires may adversely affect road handling and tire grip.

Transmission service, automatic

The automatic transmission is not equipped with a dipstick. Therefore, checking the ATF level is an involved procedure which includes measuring and maintaining a specified ATF temperature during the checking procedure.

NOTE —
For more complete ATF service information, including checking ATF level and ATF filter replacement procedures, see **240 Automatic Transmission**.

Transmission service, manual

Manual transmission service consists of inspecting for leaks and checking the fluid.

Evidence of transmission leaks is likely to be seen around the driveshaft mounting flange and at the bottom of the bell-housing.

NOTE —
For more information on identifying oil leaks and their causes, see **230 Manual Transmission** and **210 Clutch**.

Transmission fluid, checking and filling (manual transmission)

The manual transmission in E46 models is filled with lifetime oil that ordinarily does not need to be changed.

Check manual transmission oil level at transmission filler plug (**arrow**). Make sure car is on level surface.

NOTE —
Transmission fluid level checking and replacement procedures are covered in **230 Manual Transmission**.

Wheels, aligning

BMW recommends checking the front and rear alignment once a year and whenever new tires are installed.

NOTE —
See **320 Steering and Wheel Alignment** *for a more detailed discussion of alignment requirements and specifications.*

BODY AND INTERIOR MAINTENANCE

Body and hinges, lubricating

The door locks and lock cylinders can be lubricated with an oil that contains graphite.

The body and door hinges, the hood latch, and the door check rods should be lubricated with SAE 30 or SAE 40 engine oil. Lubricate the seat runners with multipurpose grease. Do not apply any oil to rubber parts. If door weather-strips are sticking, lubricate them with silicone spray or talcum powder. The hood release cable should be lubricated as well.

The use of winter lock de-icer sprays should be kept to an absolute minimum, as the alcohol in the de-icer will wash the grease out of the lock assemblies, and may cause the locks to corrode internally, or become difficult to operate.

Exterior washing

The longer dirt is left on the paint, the greater the risk of damaging the glossy finish, either by scratching or by the chemical effect dirt particles may have on the painted surface.

Do not wash the car in direct sunlight. If the engine hood is warm, allow it to cool. Beads of water not only leave spots when dried rapidly by the sun or heat from the engine, but also can act as small magnifying glasses and burn spots into the finish. Wash the car with a mixture of lukewarm water and a car wash product. Rinse using plenty of clear water. Wipe the body dry with a soft cloth towel or chamois to prevent water-spotting.

Interior care

Dirt spots can usually be removed with lukewarm soapy water or a dry foam cleaner. Use spot remover for grease and oil spots. Do not pour the liquid directly on the carpet or fabric, but dampen a clean cloth and rub carefully, starting at the edge of the spot and working inward. Do not use gasoline, naptha, or other flammable substances.

Leather upholstery and trim

Leather upholstery and trim should be periodically cleaned using a slightly damp cotton or wool cloth. The idea is to get rid of the dirt in the creases and pores that can cause brittleness and premature aging. On heavily soiled areas, use a mild detergent (such as Woolite®) or other specially formulated leather cleaners. Use two tablespoons to one quart of cold water. Dry the trim and upholstery completely using a soft cloth. Regular use of a good quality leather conditioner will reduce drying and cracking of the leather.

Polishing

Use paint polish only if the finish assumes a dull look after long service. Polish can be used to remove tar spots and tarnish, but afterwards a coat of wax should be applied to protect the clean finish. Do not use abrasive polish or cleaners on aluminum trim or accessories.

Seat belts

Dirt and other abrasive particles will damage seat belt webbing. If it is necessary to clean seat belts, use a mild soap solution. Bleach and other strong cleaning agents may weaken the belt webbing and should be avoided.

> ***WARNING —***
> *Do not clean the seat belt webbing using dry cleaning or other chemicals. Allow wet belts to dry before allowing them to retract.*

The condition of the belt webbing and the function of the retractor mechanisms should be inspected. See **720 Seat Belts** for seat belt inspection information.

Special cleaning

Tar spots can be removed with a bug and tar remover. Never use gasoline, kerosene, nail polish remover, or other unsuitable solvents. Insect spots also respond to tar remover. A bit of baking soda dissolved in the wash water will facilitate their removal. This method can also be used to remove spotting from tree sap.

Washing chassis

Periodic washing of the underside of the car, especially in winter, will help prevent accumulation of road salt and rust. The best time to wash the underside is just after the car has been driven in wet conditions. Spray the chassis with a powerful jet of water. Commercial or self-service car washes may not be best for this, as they may recycle the salt-contaminated water.

Waxing

For a long-lasting, protective, and glossy finish, apply a hard wax after the car has been washed and dried. Use carnauba or synthetic based products. Waxing is not needed after every washing. You can tell when waxing is required by looking at the finish when it is wet. If the water coats the paint in smooth sheets instead of forming beads that roll off, a new coat of wax is needed. Wax should not be applied to black trim pieces, rubber, or other plastic parts.

Windshield wiper blade maintenance

Common problems with the windshield wipers include streaking or sheeting, water drops after wiping, and blade chatter. Streaking is usually caused when wiper blades are coated with road film or car wash wax. Clean the blades using soapy water. If cleaning the blades does not cure the problem, they should be replaced. BMW recommends replacing the wiper blades twice a year, before and after the cold season.

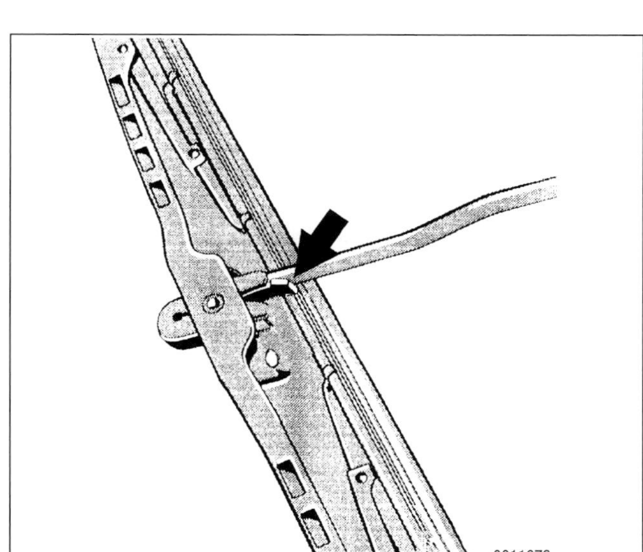

To replace wiper blade, depress retaining tab (**arrow**) and slide blade out of arm.

On older cars, check the tension spring that holds the wiper to the glass. Replace the wiper arm if the springs are weak.

Drops that remain behind after wiping are caused by oil, road film, or diesel exhaust coating the windshield. Use an alcohol or ammonia solution, or a non-abrasive cleanser to clean the windshield.

Wiper blade chatter may be caused by dirty or worn blades, by a dirty windshield, or by bent or twisted wiper arms. Clean the blades and windshield as described above. Adjust the wiper arm so that there is even pressure along the blade, and so that the blade is perpendicular to the windshield at rest. Lubricate the wiper linkage with a light oil. The linkage is located under the hood on the driver's side. If the problem persists, the blades are excessively aged or worn and should be replaced. See **611 Wipers and Washers** for more information.

100 Engine–General

TABLES

GENERAL

This section covers system descriptions and general information on engines and engine management systems. Also covered is basic engine troubleshooting.

For specific repair procedures, refer to the appropriate repair group:

- **110 Engine Removal and Installation**
- **113 Cylinder Head Removal and Installation**
- **116 Cylinder Head and Valvetrain**
- **117 Camshaft Timing Chains**
- **119 Lubrication System**
- **120 Ignition System**
- **130 Fuel Injection**
- **170 Radiator and Cooling System**

Engines

Three basic 6-cylinder engine 'families' are used in the 1999 through 2005 E46 cars covered by this manual. The M52 TU 2.5 and 2.8 liter double VANOS engines, the M54/M56 2.5 and 3.0 liter engines, and the S54 3.2 liter Motorsports engine.

The M52 TU engine was used in the 1999 and 2000 models. In model year 2001, the M54 (2.5 and 3.0 liter) engines were introduced. This engine featured fully electronic throttle control and enhanced emission controls. Beginning with MY 2003, the M56 engine was installed on a limited basis in the 325iA models. It was developed to meet stricter emission requirements in certain states.

Table a lists engine specifications for the vehicles covered by this manual.

Table a. Engine specifications

Model year	Engine code	Displacement cc (cu. in.)	Bore/ stroke	Compression ratio	Torque lb-ft/rpm	Horsepower Hp/rpm	Engine management
323i 1999 - 2000	M52 TU B25	2494 (152)	84 mm (3.307 in.) 75 mm (2.953 in.)	10.5: 1	181 / 3,500	170 / 5,500	Siemens MS 42.0
325i/Ci/xi 2001- 2005	M54 B25 M56 B25*	2494 (152)	84 mm (3.307 in.) 75 mm (2.953 in.)	10.5: 1	175 / 3,500	184 / 6,000	Siemens MS 43.0 MS 45.1
328i/Ci 1999 - 2000	M52 TU B28	2793 (170)	84 mm (3.307 in.) 84 mm (3.307 in.)	10.2: 1	206 / 3,500	193 / 5,500	Siemens MS 42.0
330i/Ci/xi 2001-2005	M54 B30	2979 (182)	84 mm (3.307 in.)/ 89.6 mm (3.528 in.)	10.2: 1	214 / 3,500	225 / 5,900	Siemens MS 43.0
330i Performance Package 2003 - 2005	M54 B30	2979 (182)	84 mm (3.307 in.)/ 89.6 mm (3.528 in.)	10.2: 1	222 / 3,500	235 / 5,900	Siemens MS 43.0
M3 2001 - 2005	S 54 B32	3246 (198)	87.0 mm (3.43 in.) 91.0 mm (3.58 in.)	11.5: 1	262 / 4,900	333 / 7,900	Siemens MS S54

*325iA (sedan, coupe and sport wagon) models sold in California, New York, and Massachusetts as of model year 2003 and in Vermont as of model year 2004 use an updated 2.5 liter engine designated **M56B25 SULEV** (Super Ultra Low Emission Vehicles). The M56 SULEV engine uses Siemens MS 45.1 engine management and includes many emission control system changes. The M56 B25 power output and performance is the same as the comparable models with the M54 B25 engine.

Cylinder block and crankshaft

On the 2.5, 2.8, and 3.0 liter engines, the cylinder block is cast aluminum alloy ($AlSi_9Cu_3$) with cast iron cylinder liners. The cylinders are exposed on all sides to circulating coolant.

On M3 models (3.2 liter engine), the cylinder block is cast iron to absorb the high forces produced by the crankshaft.

The 2.5 liter crankshaft is cast iron. The 2.8 and 3.0, and 3.2 liter engines use a forged steel crankshaft to accommodate the higher torque.

Connecting rods and pistons

The forged steel connecting rods use replaceable split-shell bearings at the crankshaft end and solid bushings at the piston pin end.

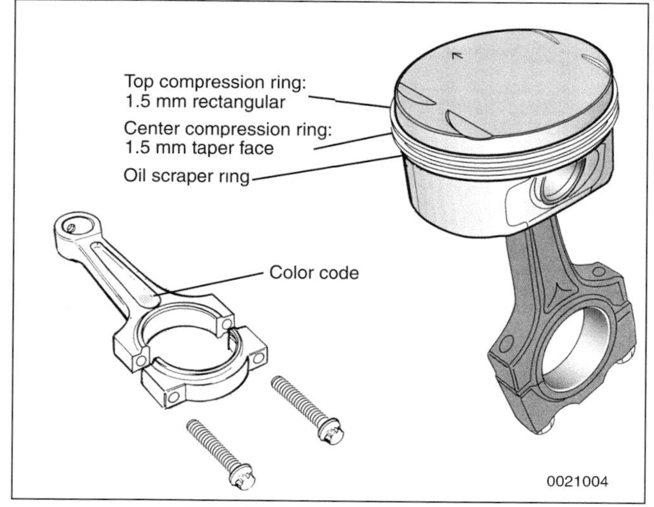

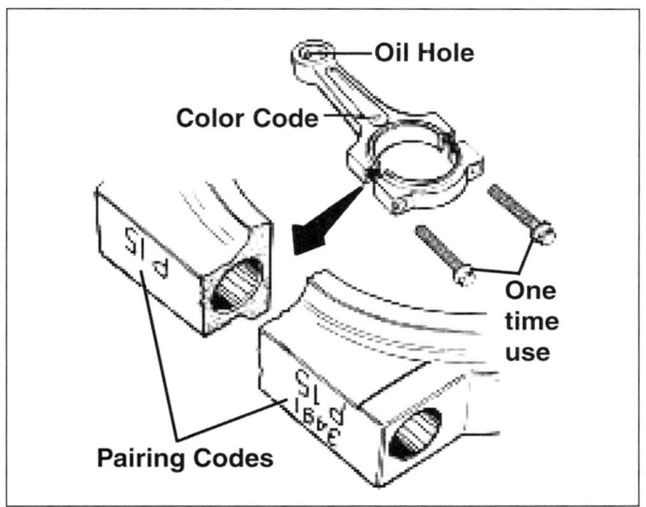

On S54 M3 engines, the connecting rod big end is fractured and split off leaving rough surfaces on both the cap and the rod. Centering of the cap on the rod is done through the structure of the split. Pairing codes are stamped into the rod to ensure proper assembly. Only a complete set of connecting rods (the same weight class) is available to maintain proper balance.

The pistons are of the three-ring type with two upper compression rings and a lower one-piece oil scraper ring. Full-floating piston pins are retained with circlips.

The 2.8 and 3.0, and 3.2 liter engines use a graphite coating on the piston skirts to reduce friction and noise.

On S54 engines, the pistons are cooled by oil spray nozzles that are bolted into the cylinder block. The nozzles deliver a constant oil spray to the underside of the pistons.

Cylinder head and valvetrain

The aluminum cylinder head uses chain-driven double overhead camshafts and four valves per cylinder. The cylinder head employs a crossflow design. Intake air enters the combustion chamber from one side while exhaust gasses exit from the other. The spark plugs are centrally located down the middle of the cylinder head.

Oilways in the head provide lubrication for the camshafts and valvetrain.

On 2.5, 2.8 and 3.0 liter engines, valve clearance is set by self-adjusting (zero-lash) hydraulic lifters for reduced valve noise and the elimination of routine valve adjustment.

On the 3.2 S54 engine, valve adjustment is not self-adjusting. Shims of varying thickness are used to adjust valve lash. See **116 Cylinder Head and Valvetrain**.

Exhaust manifolds

Each exhaust manifold assembly incorporates a catalytic converter. The converters are mounted close to the engine for faster heat up and light off. Pre- and post-catalyst oxygen sensors are a mounted in each exhaust manifold.

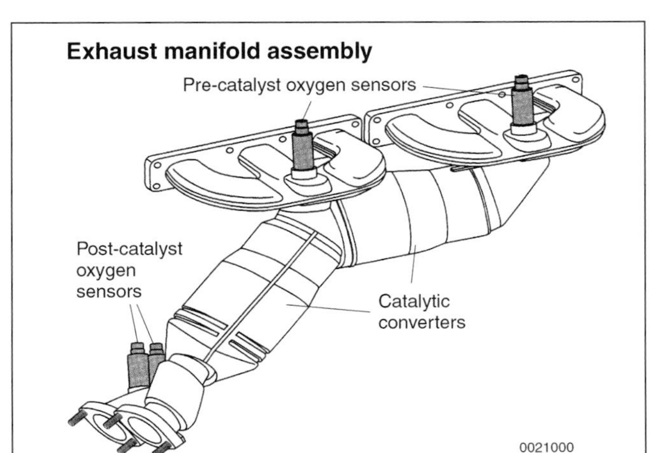

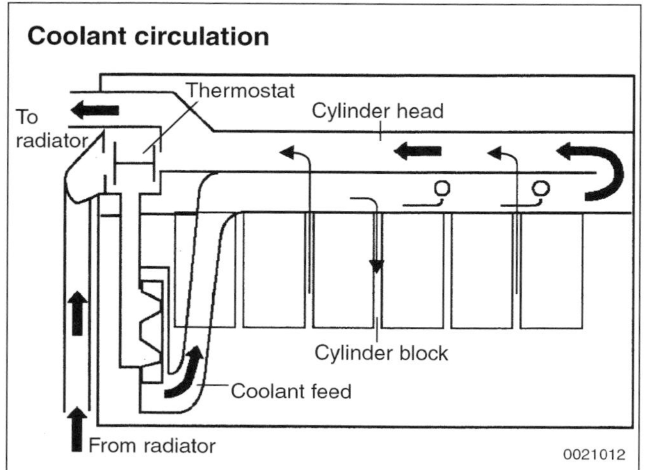

Cooling system

The cooling system circulation is designed so that coolant flows directly from the coolant pump to the cylinder head. The coolant is fed from the coolant pump through a cast coolant feed passage to the rear of the cylinder head. From there it flows forward to the thermostat housing, radiator and heater valve.

All models are equipped with a DME-controlled electric cooling fan. On some models, a supplemental cooling fan is used. See **170 Cooling System** for specific configuration and application information.

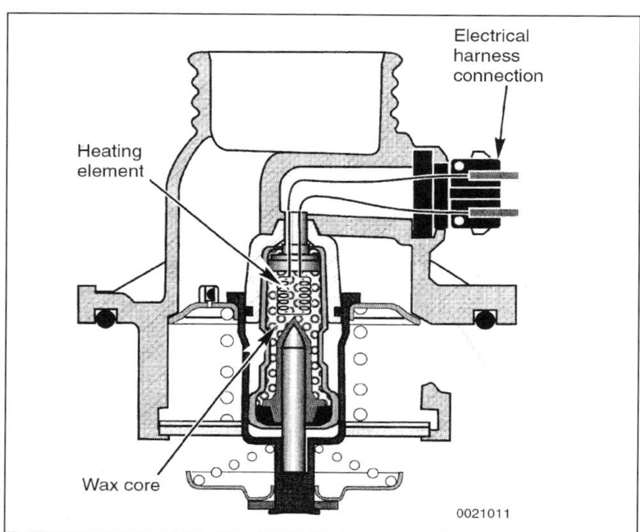

On all engines except the S54 (M3) engine, an electrically heated thermostat controls the flow of coolant through the radiator based on coolant and outside temperature, engine load, and driving speed, rather than just coolant temperature.

The DME-controlled heated thermostat allows the engine to be operated at higher controlled temperatures during low and part throttle. This optimizes operating temperatures in both cylinder head and block, reduces friction and thereby fuel consumption.

The DME-controlled heated thermostat functions to:

- Reduce operating temperatures of cylinder head. The result of lower temperatures is increased torque due to improved volumetric efficiency.
- Increase operating temperature of cylinder block.

The S54 engine uses a conventional type thermostat, mounted in the top of the coolant pump.

Lubrication system

The lubrication system is pressurized whenever the engine is running. The oil pump draws oil through a pickup in the bottom of the oil pan, then forces it through a replaceable oil filter and into the engine oil passages.

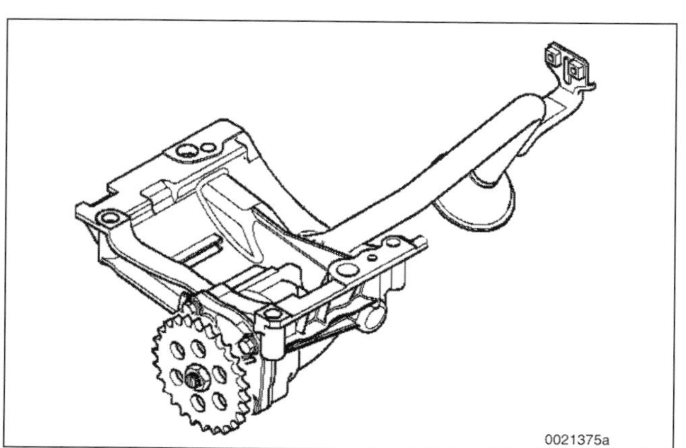

The chain-driven oil pump is bolted to the bottom of the cylinder block inside the oil pan. A pressure relief valve limits the maximum system pressure. A bypass valve prevents the oil filter from bursting and insures engine lubrication should the filter become plugged. See **119 Lubrication System** for additional information.

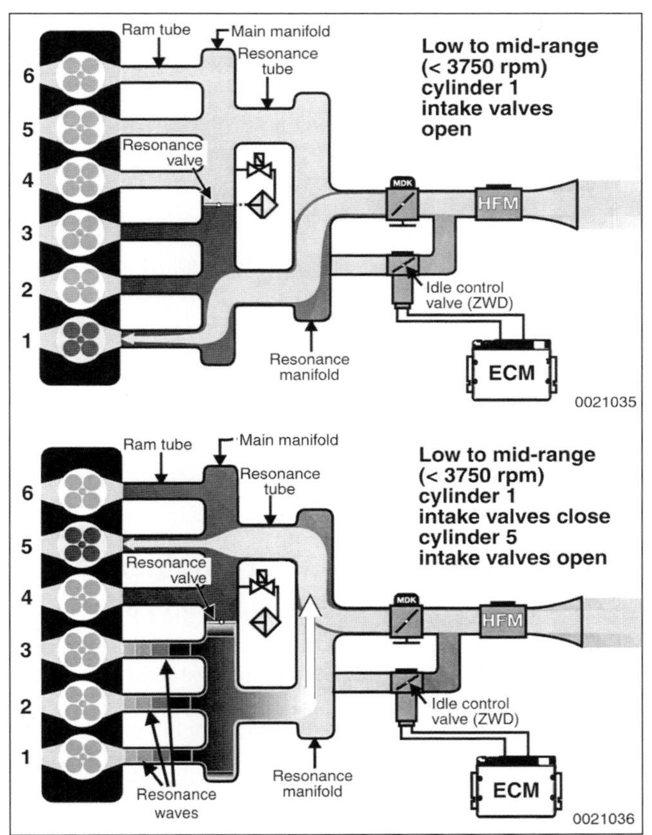

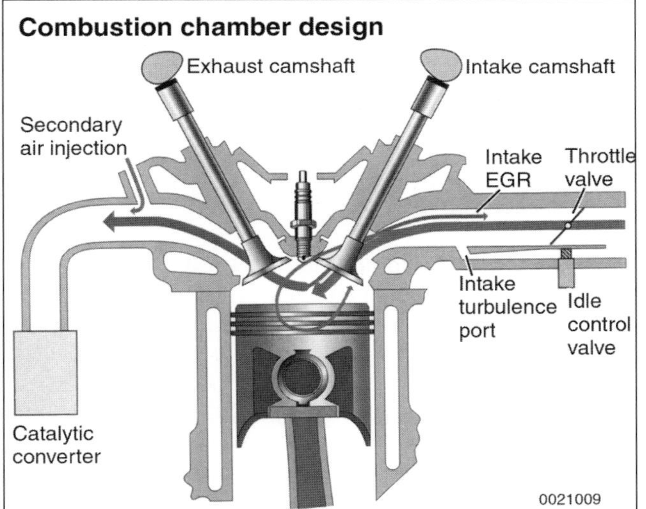

Intake system (M52 TU, M54, M56 engines)

The intake manifold, made of molded plastic, is configured as two sets of three runners. This design enhances low end torque by changing the intake air flow configuration for varying engine speeds. This helps achieve optimum torque throughout the entire RPM range.

During engine operation, a closed resonance valve gives the intake air charge the dynamic effect of long intake runners at low to mid-range RPM (up to 3750 rpm). This helps increase torque.

During mid-range to high rpm operation (above 4100 rpm), the solenoid is de-energized and the resonance valve is sprung open. This allows intake air to be drawn through both resonance tubes, providing the air volume necessary for additional power at the upper rpm range.

NOTE —

The rpm for resonance valve activation may vary slightly depending on temperature.

In addition, when the valve is closed, a dynamic effect is produced. For example, as intake air is flowing into cylinder 1, the intake valves will close. This blocks the onrushing air. The cylinder 1 air flow will stop and expand backward (resonance back pulse) to fill cylinder 5. The resonance wave along with the intake velocity enhances cylinder filling.

The intake manifold includes intake turbulence ports. The 5.5 mm (0.217 in.) turbulence ports channel idle and low speed air directly from the idle speed control valved to one intake valve of each cylinder.

Routing intake air to one intake valve per cylinder causes the air charge to swirl in the cylinder. Together with the high flow rate of intake air across the small (5.5 mm) port, intake fluctuations are reduced for more stable combustion.

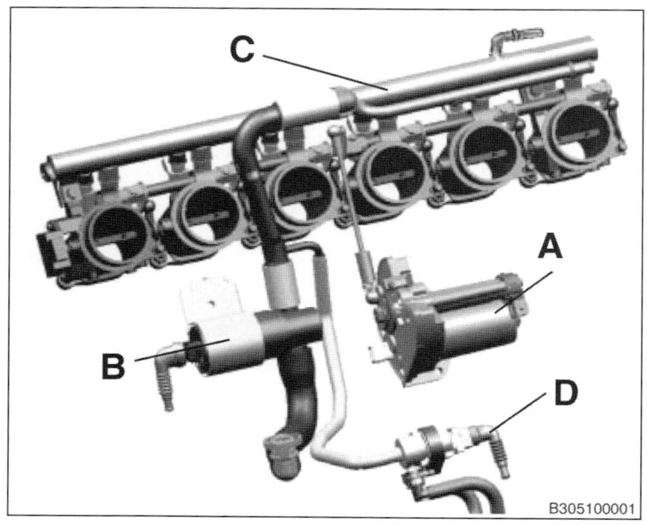

Intake system (S54 engine)

The S54 uses six individual throttle housings operated by an electronic throttle control actuator (**A**). For low engine speed and idling, intake air is provided by an idle air actuator (**B**). The idle air actuator regulates air flow through an external air distribution pipe (**C**) to the individual throttle housings. The Evaporative Emission Valve (**D**) regulates fuel tank vapor intake.

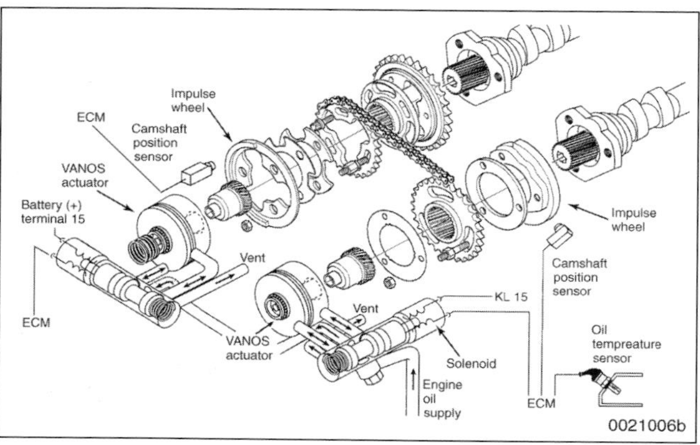

VANOS (M52 TU, M54, M56 engines)

A double VANOS system is used on both the M52 TU and the M54 and M56 engines. VANOS is fully variable and operates independently on both intake and exhaust sides.

When the VANOS solenoid is actuated, engine oil pressure is applied to the front side of the gear cup piston. This forces the gear cup into the camshaft helical gears to change camshaft timing.

In addition to offering increased power, the double VANOS system offers the following advantages:

- Increased torque at lower and medium RPM ranges
- More efficient combustion and improved idle quality
- Internal EGR in part-load range for lower NOx emissions.
- Quicker warm-up cycle for catalytic converter and faster reduction in emissions.
- Overall improved fuel economy.

See **117 Camshaft Timing Chain** for VANOS system testing and repair information.

VANOS (S54 engine)

The S54 M engine uses a high pressure (100 Bar) double VANOS system. VANOS is fully variable and operates independently on both intake and exhaust sides. The total adjustment range of the intake camshaft is 60°. The total adjustment range of the exhaust camshaft is 45°

See **117 Camshaft Timing Chain** for VANOS system testing and repair information.

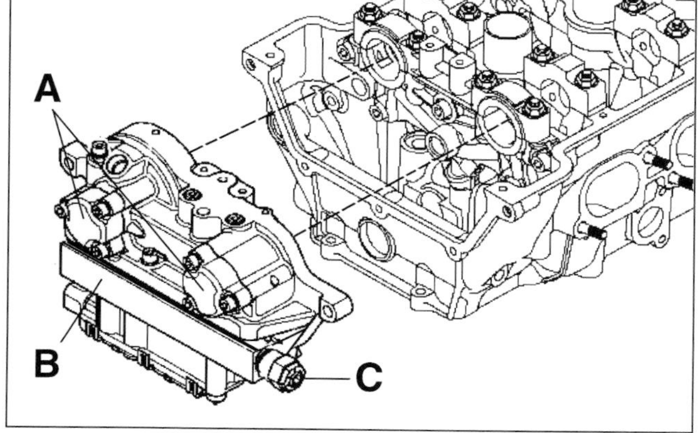

The S54 VANOS unit is mounted directly on the front of the cylinder head. The VANOS unit contains hydraulically actuated mechanical drives (**A**), electronically controlled oil pressure regulating solenoids (**B**) and a pressure regulating valve (**C**).

The VANOS solenoid electrical assembly (shown removed from the VANOS unit) contains four solenoids. Two solenoids are required for each adjusting piston circuit, one for advancing and one for retarding the camshaft timing. The solenoids are controlled by the Siemens MS S54 ECM.

VANOS mechanical operation is dependent on oil pressure applied to position the control pistons. The double VANOS camshafts are infinitely adjustable within the mechanical travel limits of the drive gears.

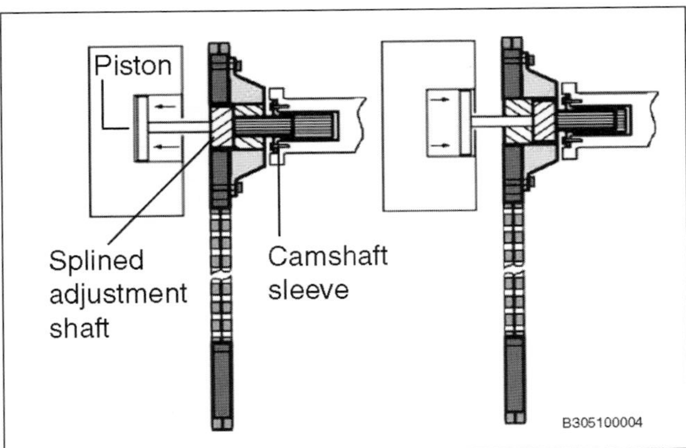

When oil pressure is applied to the control piston, the piston moves causing the splined adjustment shaft to move. The straight splines slide within the camshaft sleeve. The helical splines rotate the camshaft drive sprocket changing the position in relation to the camshaft position which advances or retards the camshaft timing.

Engine management systems

The Siemens engine management systems used in E46 cars combine fuel injection, ignition and other functions under the control of the engine control module (ECM). The Siemens systems are compliant with second generation on-board diagnostics (OBD II) standards. See **OBD (On-Board Diagnostics)** at the back of this manual for additional information.

Table b. Engine management systems

Year: Engine	**DME system**
1999 - 2000: M52 TU B25 M52 TU B28	Siemens MS 42.0
2001- 2005 M54 B25 / B30 M56 B25 (see **Table a**)	Siemens MS 43.0 Siemens MS 45.1
2001-2005 S54 B32	Siemens MS S54

0021391

Engine control module (ECM)

The engine control module (ECM) is mounted in the electronics box (E-box) next to the brake master cylinder.

– The ECM is flash-programmable and features 5 electrical harness connectors with a total of 134 pins.

- **Connector 1:** Voltages and grounds
- **Connector 2:** Ancillary signals (oxygen sensors, CAN, etc.)
- **Connector 3:** Engine signals
- **Connector 4:** Vehicle signals
- **Connector 5:** Ignition signals

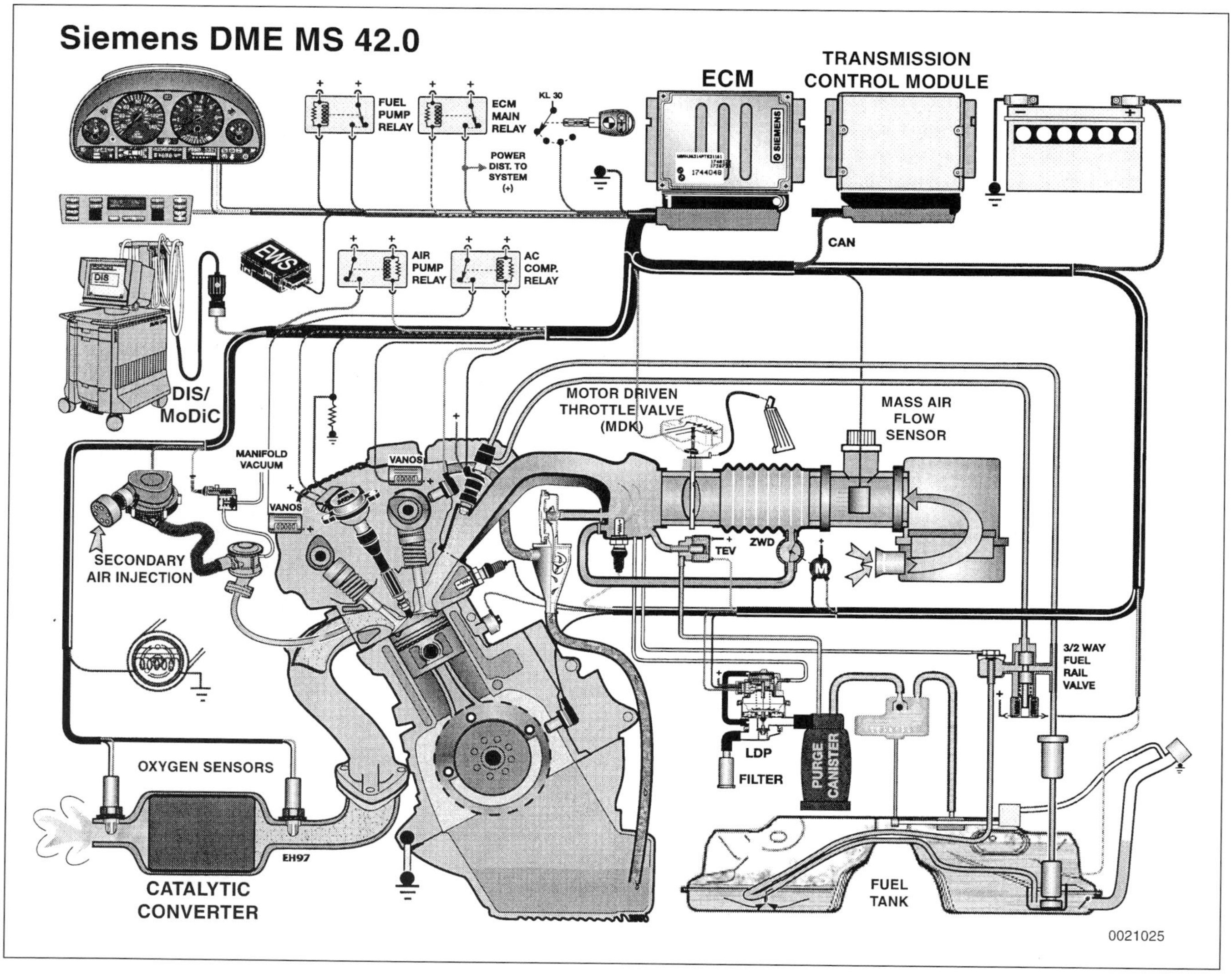

0021025

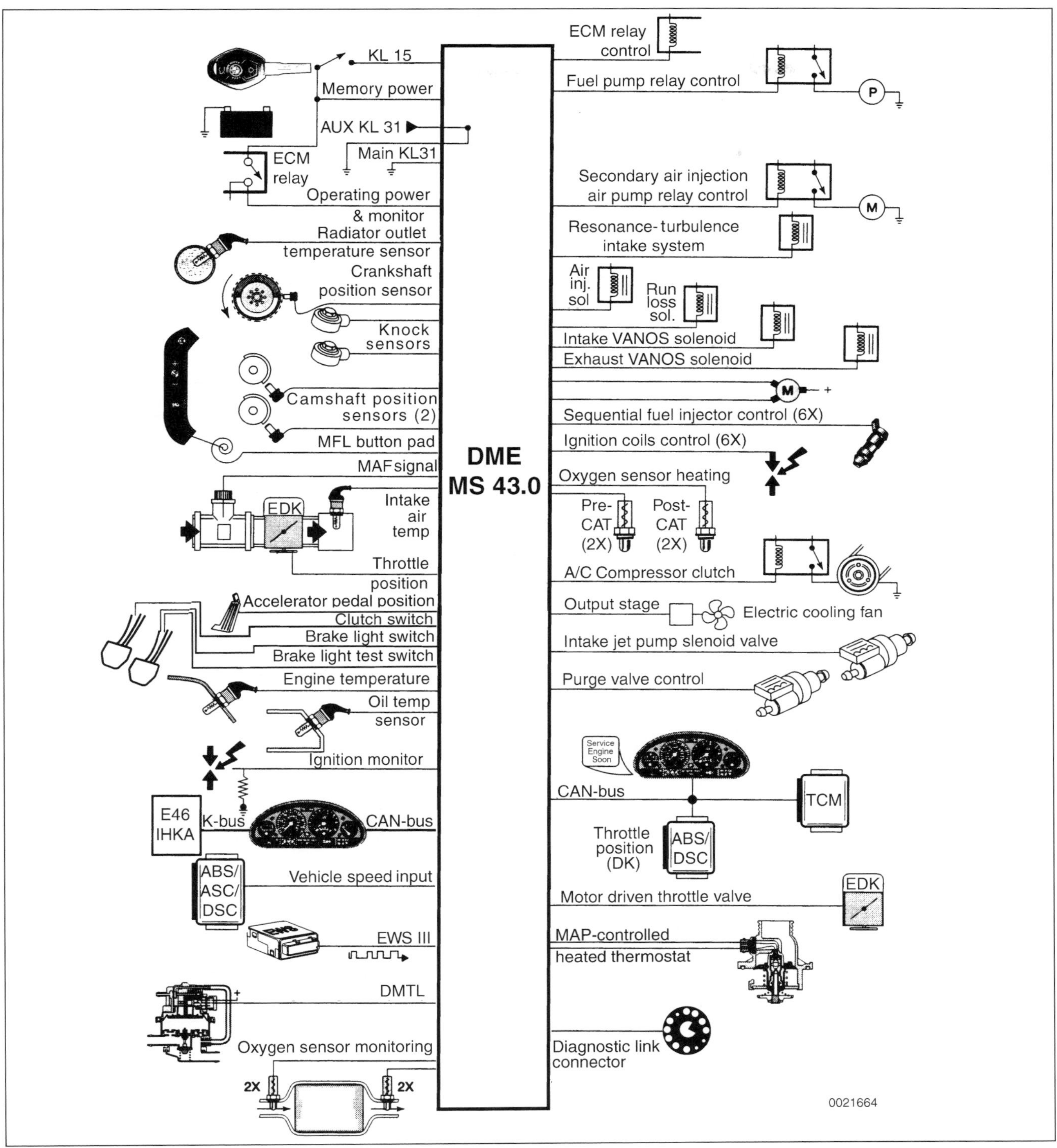
KL 15
Memory power
AUX KL 31
Main KL31
ECM relay
Operating power & monitor
Radiator outlet temperature sensor
Crankshaft position sensor
Knock sensors
Camshaft position sensors (2)
MFL button pad
MAFsignal
EDK
Intake air temp
Throttle position
Accelerator pedal position
Clutch switch
Brake light switch
Brake light test switch
Engine temperature
Oil temp sensor
Ignition monitor
E46 IHKA
K-bus
CAN-bus
ABS/ ASC/ DSC
Vehicle speed input
EWS III
DMTL
Oxygen sensor monitoring
2X
2X
DME MS 43.0
ECM relay control
Fuel pump relay control
P
Secondary air injection air pump relay control
M
Resonance-turbulence intake system
Air inj. sol
Run loss sol.
Intake VANOS solenoid
Exhaust VANOS solenoid
M
Sequential fuel injector control (6X)
Ignition coils control (6X)
Oxygen sensor heating
Pre-CAT (2X)
Post-CAT (2X)
A/C Compressor clutch
Output stage
Electric cooling fan
Intake jet pump slenoid valve
Purge valve control
Service Engine Soon
CAN-bus
TCM
Throttle position (DK)
ABS/ DSC
EDK
Motor driven throttle valve
MAP-controlled heated thermostat
Diagnostic link connector
0021664

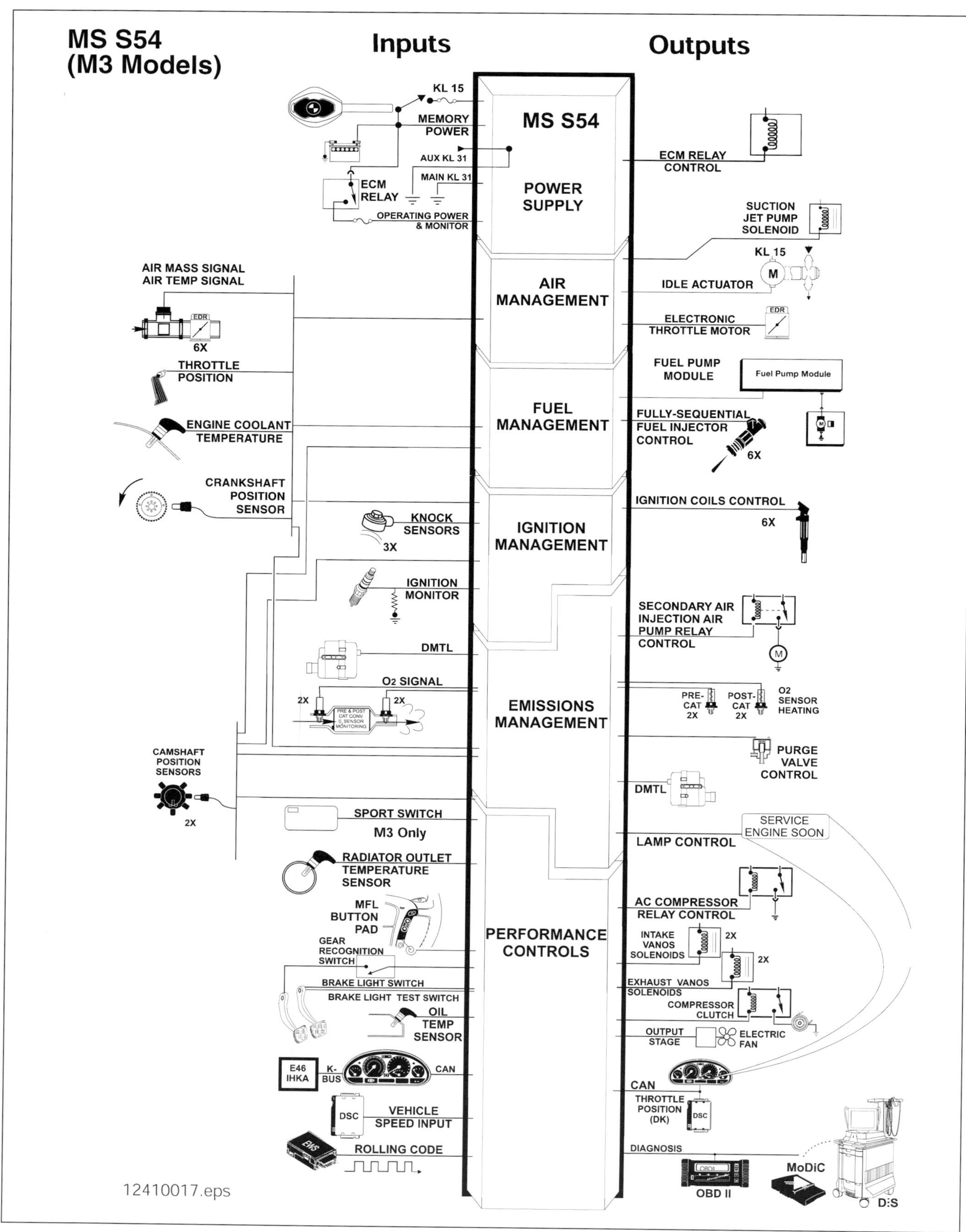

MS S54
(M3 Models)
Inputs
Outputs
KL 15
MEMORY POWER
AUX KL 31
MAIN KL 31
ECM RELAY
OPERATING POWER & MONITOR
MS S54
POWER SUPPLY
ECM RELAY CONTROL
SUCTION JET PUMP SOLENOID
KL 15
AIR MASS SIGNAL
AIR TEMP SIGNAL
EDR
6X
AIR MANAGEMENT
IDLE ACTUATOR
ELECTRONIC THROTTLE MOTOR
THROTTLE POSITION
FUEL PUMP MODULE
Fuel Pump Module
ENGINE COOLANT TEMPERATURE
FUEL MANAGEMENT
FULLY-SEQUENTIAL FUEL INJECTOR CONTROL
6X
CRANKSHAFT POSITION SENSOR
KNOCK SENSORS
3X
IGNITION MANAGEMENT
IGNITION COILS CONTROL
6X
IGNITION MONITOR
SECONDARY AIR INJECTION AIR PUMP RELAY CONTROL
M
DMTL
O2 SIGNAL
2X
2X
PRE & POST CAT CONV O2 SENSOR MONITORING
EMISSIONS MANAGEMENT
PRE-CAT 2X
POST-CAT 2X
O2 SENSOR HEATING
PURGE VALVE CONTROL
CAMSHAFT POSITION SENSORS
2X
DMTL
SPORT SWITCH
M3 Only
SERVICE ENGINE SOON
LAMP CONTROL
RADIATOR OUTLET TEMPERATURE SENSOR
MFL BUTTON PAD
GEAR RECOGNITION SWITCH
PERFORMANCE CONTROLS
AC COMPRESSOR RELAY CONTROL
INTAKE VANOS SOLENOIDS
2X
2X
EXHAUST VANOS SOLENOIDS
COMPRESSOR CLUTCH
BRAKE LIGHT SWITCH
BRAKE LIGHT TEST SWITCH
OIL TEMP SENSOR
OUTPUT STAGE
ELECTRIC FAN
E46 IHKA
K-BUS
CAN
CAN
THROTTLE POSITION (DK)
DSC
DSC
VEHICLE SPEED INPUT
ROLLING CODE
EWS
DIAGNOSIS
OBD II
MoDiC
D:S
12410017.eps

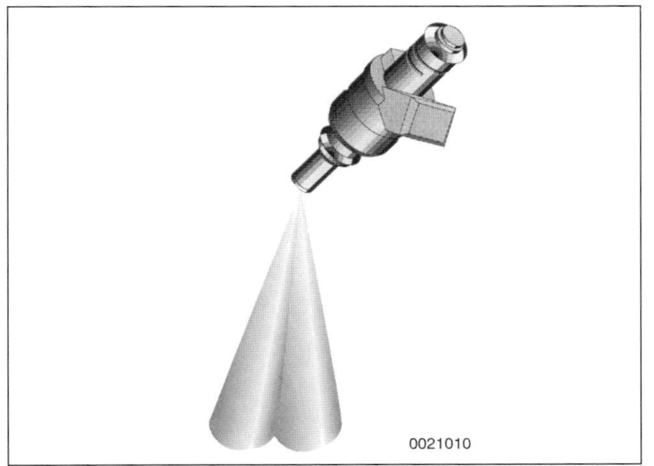

0021010

Fuel metering: The ECM meters fuel to the engine by changing the opening time (pulse width) of the electrically-operated fuel injectors. The exact amount of fuel injected is determined by the amount of time the injectors are open. To ensure that injector pulse width is the only factor that determines fuel metering, fuel pump pressure is maintained by a pressure regulator. The injectors are mounted to a common fuel rail.

The ECM monitors engine operating conditions to determine injector opening duration. Each injector can be individually controlled for cylinder selective fuel trim.

Air intake: Air entering the engine passes through a pleated paper air filter in the air cleaner. Intake air mass is then measured by a mass air flow (MAF) sensor. A reference current is used to heat a thin film in the sensor when the engine is running. The current needed to hold the temperature of the film constant is the basis of the electronically converted voltage measurement corresponding to the mass of the intake air.

Idle speed control: Idle speed is electronically controlled via the idle speed control valve by bypassing varying amounts of air around the closed throttle valve(s). Idle speed is not adjustable.

Throttle control: The throttle valve plate is electronically operated for precise throttle operation, OBD II compliant for fault monitoring, and ASC/DSC and cruise control. Adjusting electronic throttles is not permitted and the throttle assembly must be replaced as a unit if found to be faulty.

0021525

The throttle assembly for the MS 42.0 system is referred to as the MDK (Motor Driven Throttle Valve). The MDK is identified as follows:

- A throttle cable is used to actuate the accelerator pedal position potentiometers and also serves as a backup to open the throttle plate (full control) when the MDK system is in the failsafe mode.

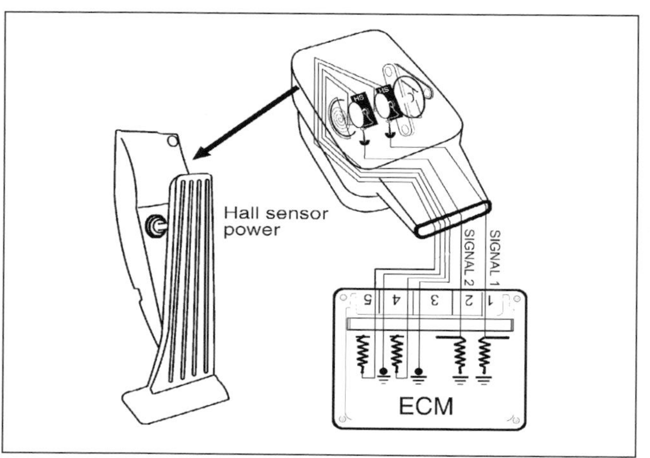

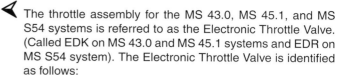

The throttle assembly for the MS 43.0, MS 45.1, and MS S54 systems is referred to as the Electronic Throttle Valve. (Called EDK on MS 43.0 and MS 45.1 systems and EDR on MS S54 system). The Electronic Throttle Valve is identified as follows:

- Accelerator position potentiometers (PWG) located in accelerator pedal assembly.
- The accelerator pedal is not mechanically linked to the EDK/EDR.

Ignition function: a distributorless ignition system with individual ignition coils for each cylinder is employed. The coils are mounted over the spark plugs and connect to the plugs via a short lead.

The Siemens systems use multiple spark ignition to reduce emissions and extend spark plug life.

Knock control. Knock (detonation) sensors monitor and control potentially damaging ignition knock through the ECM. The knock sensors function like microphones and are able to convert mechanical vibration (knock) into electrical signals. The ECM is programmed to react to frequencies that are characteristic of engine knock and adapt the ignition timing point accordingly. See **120 Ignition System** for further details.

NOTE —
The engines used in the E46 cars are designed to operate best with fuel octane of at least 91 anti-knock index (AKI). The adaptive engine management system, however, will allow use of fuel rated 87 AKI.

M56 SULEV 2.5 Liter engine

2003 and later 325iA (E46) sedan, coupe and sport wagon with automatic transmission are fitted with the M54 2.5 liter engine to meet stricter emission requirements. The M56B25 power output and performance is the same as the comparable models equipped with the M54B25 engine.

NOTE —
M56 equipped vehicles meet the SULEV tailpipe emission standard, which is approximately 1/5 of the previous ULEV standard. The vehicles also conforms to the Partial Zero Evaporative Emissions requirements (PZEV).

SULEV models are sold in California, New York and Massachusetts as of 2003 models and in Vermont starting in 2004 model year. The emission relevant components are warranted for 15 years or 150,000 miles.

The notable modifications to the M56 SULEV engine include:

- Additional carbon filter in the air filter housing and a closed throttle valve actuator for hydrocarbon blocking.
- Metal fuel system components are constructed of stainless steel and are fastened together using coupling type connectors. Stainless steel components include the fuel rail, injectors, tank ventilation valve, fuel tank, tank filler neck, and evaporative canister. The fuel pump is sealed inside the tank and is not serviceable.
- Crankcase ventilation valve in the aluminum cylinder head cover.
- Dual down stream catalytic converters (warm-up catalytic converters – high cell density technology).
- Wide band technology upstream oxygen sensors.
- Pistons with 3mm fire lands.
- VANOS – set to fixed position during start up.
- New style fuel injectors – 4 hole design
- External heat exchange surfaces of the radiator are coated with a catalyst to reduce ozone in the air drawn through the radiator.
- Secondary air system with secondary mass air flow sensor for improved monitoring of secondary air flow.

DRIVEABILITY TROUBLESHOOTING

The Siemens systems are sophisticated self-diagnosing OBD II systems. These systems continuously monitor components and record and store valuable diagnostic information.

If the ‘Check Engine’ or ‘Service Engine Soon’ light [also known as the malfunction indicator lamp (MIL)] is illuminated, the first diagnostic test should be to connect a BMW-compatible or OBD II scan tool and check the fault memory.

The diagnostic capabilities of these systems have the potential to save hours of diagnostic time, incorrect component replacement and possible damage to system components. See **On-Board Diagnostics** at the back of this manual.

Two of the most common causes of driveability problems are system voltage levels and poor grounds.

System voltage

The DME system requires that the system (battery) voltage be maintained within a narrow range. Voltage levels outside the operating range can cause havoc. When troubleshooting an illuminated MIL, make sure the battery is fully charged and capable of delivering all its power to the electrical system. If the battery is old (4 years or more), replacement is recommended.

To make a quick check of the battery charge, measure the voltage across the battery terminals with all cables attached and the ignition off. A fully charged battery will measure 12.6

volts or slightly more, compared to 12.15 volts for a battery with a 25% charge.

Even a fully charged battery cannot deliver power unless it is properly connected to the electrical system. Check the battery terminals for corrosion or loose cable connections. If the battery does not maintain the proper voltage, the charging system may be at fault. See **121 Battery, Starter, Alternator**.

If a battery cable connection has no visible faults, but is still suspect, measure the voltage drop across the connection. A large drop indicates excessive resistance, indicating that the connection is corroded, dirty, or damaged. Clean or repair the connection and retest.

NOTE —
For instructions on doing a voltage drop test and other general electrical troubleshooting information, see **600 Electrical System–General.**

The DME system operates at low voltage and current levels, making it sensitive to small increases in resistance. The electrical system is routinely subjected to corrosion, vibration and wear, so faults or corrosion in the wiring harness and connectors are not uncommon.

Visually inspect all wiring, connectors, switches and fuses in the system. Loose or damaged connectors can cause intermittent problems, especially the small terminals in the ECM connectors. Disconnect the wiring harness connectors to check for corrosion, and use electrical cleaning spray to remove contaminants.

Main grounds

Good grounds are critical to proper DME operation. If a ground connection has no visible faults but is still suspect, measure the voltage drop across the connection. A large voltage drop indicates high resistance, indicating that the connection is corroded, dirty or damaged. Clean or repair the connection and retest.

NOTE —
For instructions on conducting a voltage drop test and other general electrical troubleshooting information, see **600 Electrical System–General**.

Below is a listing of the main grounds for the fuel and ignition circuits of the DME system.

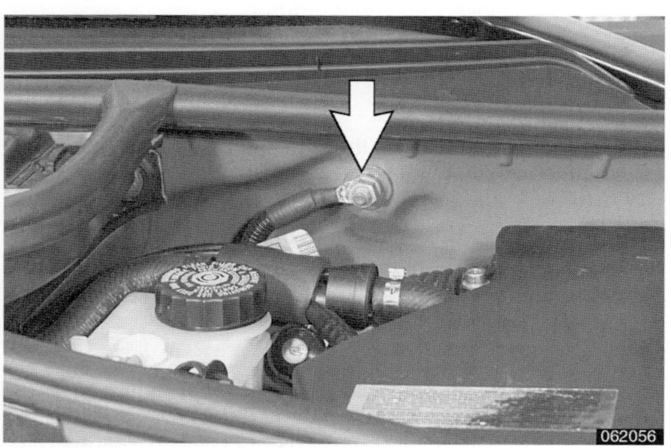

Main ground (**arrow**) for engine management system in left rear of engine compartment on bulkhead behind E-box (**M52 TU, M54 engines**).

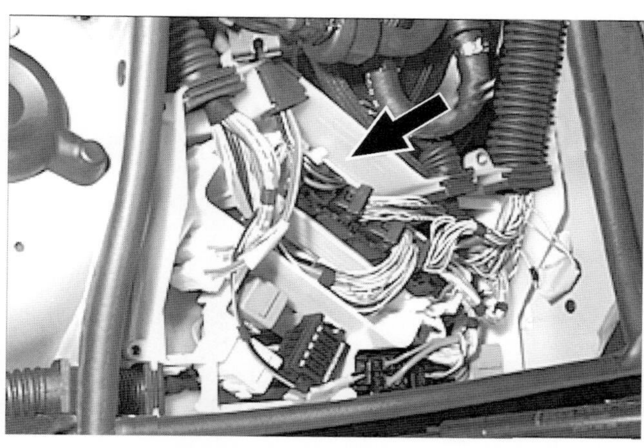

◀ Main ground (**arrow**) for engine management system in E-box in connector branch, left rear of engine compartment. (**M56, S54 engines**)

062007

◀ Main grounds for ignition coils (**arrows**).

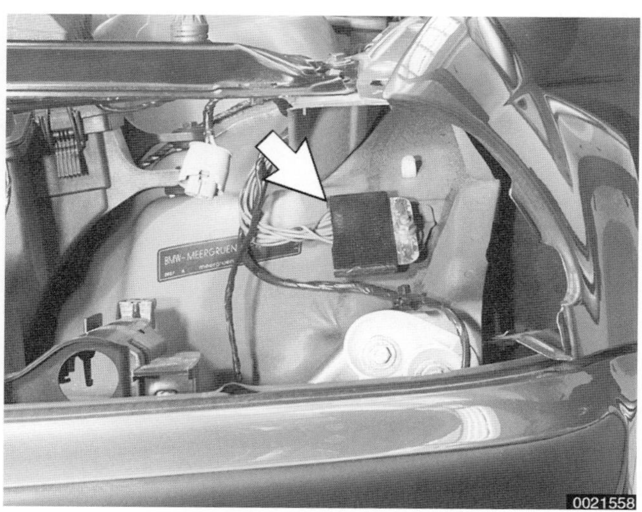

0021558

◀ Main chassis ground harness connection (**arrow**) in left front of engine compartment, behind left headlight assembly (headlight assembly shown removed).

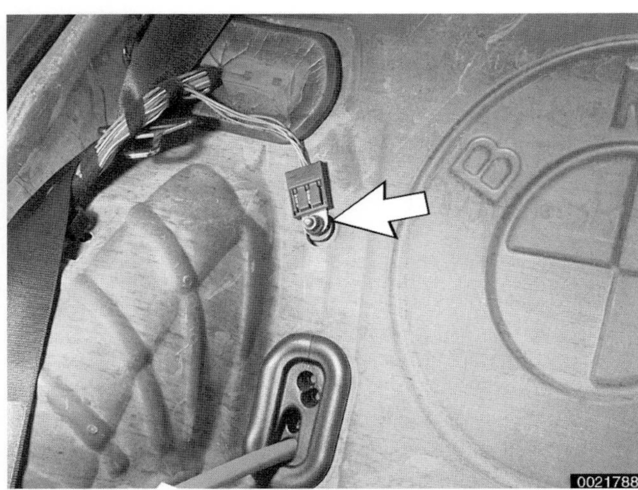

Main fuel pump ground (**arrow**) behind right rear seat back rest (**M52 TU, M54 engines**).

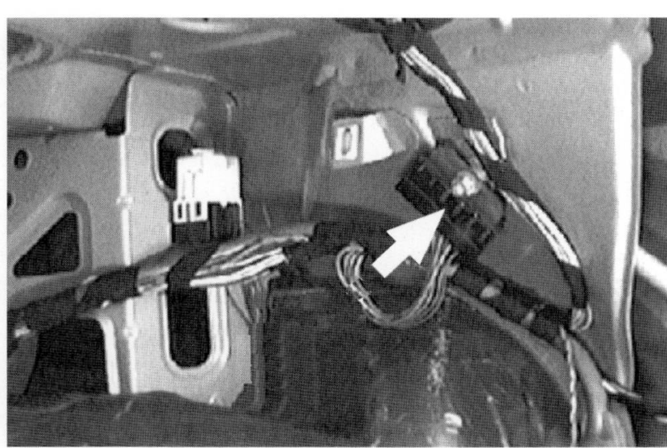

Main fuel pump ground (**arrow**) in right-hand side of luggage compartment (**S54, M56 engines**). Sedan shown, touring location similar.

110 Engine Removal and Installation

Special Tools

Special tools

A BMW 11 0 000 . . . . Engine lifting tool
B BMW 11 5 030 . . . . Cooling fan counterhold tool
C BMW 11 5 040 . . . . Cooling fan wrench
D BMW 13 5 281 / 13 5 282 . . . . Fuel line plugs
E BMW 16 1 050 . . . . Fuel line removal tool
F BMW 51 2 160 . . . . Service position hood props

GENERAL

Engine removal and installation are covered in this repair group. Procedures for this group are similar or the same for all models.

In order to remove the engine from the vehicle, the transmission must be removed first. This is best accomplished with the car raised on an automotive lift. For additional procedures required during engine removal, refer to the following repair groups:

- **020 Maintenance**
- **121 Battery, Alternator, Starter**
- **170 Radiator and Cooling System**
- **180 Exhaust System**
- **230 Manual Transmission**
- **231 Sequential Manual Gearbox (SMG)**
- **240 Automatic Transmission**
- **311 Front Axle Final Drive**
- **410 Fenders, Engine Hood**

Special tools

Some special tools are required for engine removal and installation. Be sure to have the necessary equipment on hand before starting the job.

> ***CAUTION —***
> *Disconnecting the battery may erase fault code(s) stored in memory. Check for fault codes prior to disconnecting the battery cables. If the MIL (Malfunction Indicator Light) is illuminated, see* **On-Board Diagnostics** *at the back of this manual for DME fault code information. If any other system faults have been detected (indicated by an illuminated warning light), see an authorized BMW dealer.*

ENGINE REMOVAL AND INSTALLATION

Be sure to cover all painted surfaces before beginning the removal procedure. As an aid to installation, label all components, wires and hoses before removing them. Do not reuse gaskets, O-rings or seals during reassembly.

> ***WARNING —***
> *Due to risk of personal injury, be sure the engine is cold before beginning the removal procedure.*

Engine assembly, removing and installing

– Remove engine hood or place hood in service position. See **410 Fenders, Engine Hood**.

NOTE —
It is not necessary to remove the engine hood, but it is helpful and will make engine removal and installation easier.

– Remove **intake manifold** as described later in this repair group.

NOTE —
The intake manifold must be removed as described earlier to facilitate engine assembly removal.

0021866

◀ **Except S54 engines**: remove cylinder head top cover:
- Remove plastic trim covers (**arrows**).
- Remove cover hold down bolts and lift off cover.

B305110029

◀ **S54 engines**: remove cylinder head top cover:
- Disconnect vent hose and remove oil filler cover.
- Remove cover bolts (**arrows**) and lift off cover.

– Remove engine splash guard and remove chassis reinforcement plate or reinforcement bar. See **310 Front Suspension**.

> ***WARNING —***
> - *The front chassis reinforcement plate or reinforcement bar mounting fasteners are stretch type bolts and must be replaced anytime they are removed.*
> - *The vehicle must not be driven with this component removed. See **310 Front Suspension** for additional information.*

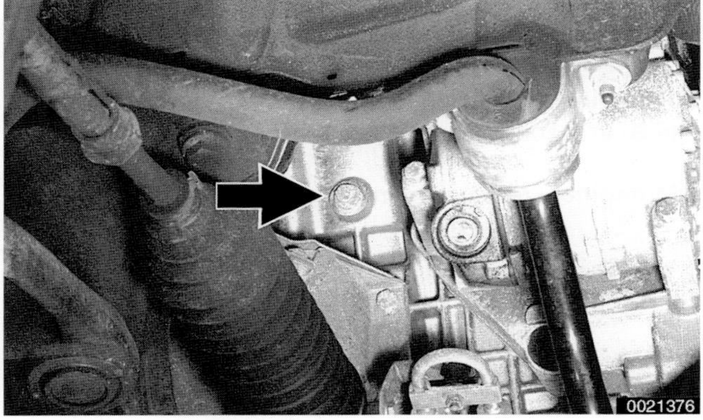

◄ Drain engine coolant and remove coolant hoses.

- Remove expansion tank cap on radiator.
- Place a 3-gallon pail beneath engine to capture coolant.
- Remove coolant drain plug located on exhaust side of cylinder 2 of engine block (**arrow**).

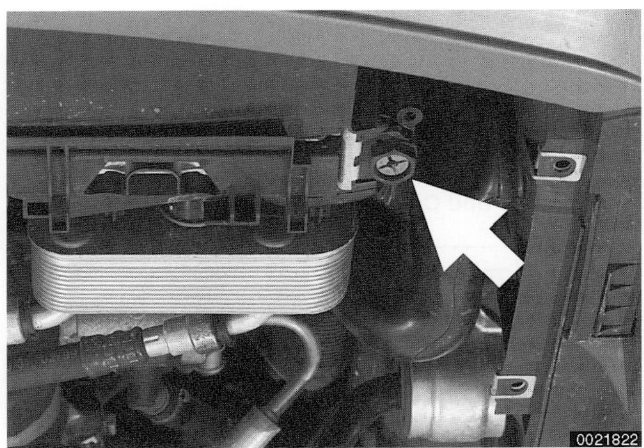

◄ Drain radiator into a 3-gallon pail by removing plastic drain plug completely (**arrow**).

> ***WARNING —***
> *Use caution when draining and disposing of engine coolant. Coolant is poisonous and lethal to humans and pets. Pets are attracted to coolant because of its sweet smell and taste. Consult a veterinarian immediately if coolant is ingested by an animal.*

NOTE —
Catch and dispose of drained coolant according to local, state, and federal laws.

◄ **Except S54 engines**: Remove hoses from thermostat housing by releasing locks (**arrows**).

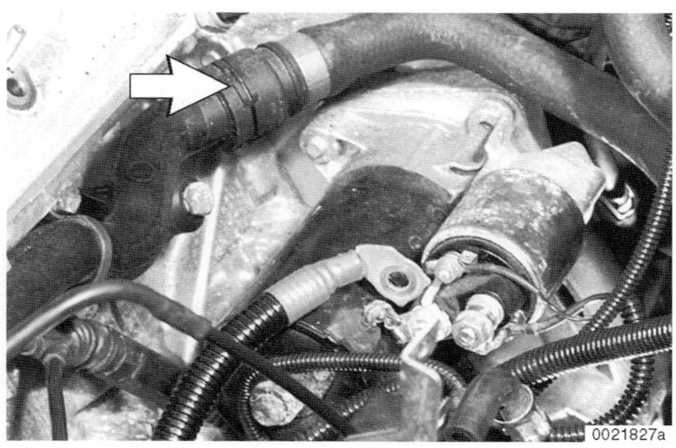

Except S54 engines: Disconnect coolant hose at rear left side of engine above starter by releasing lock (**arrow**).

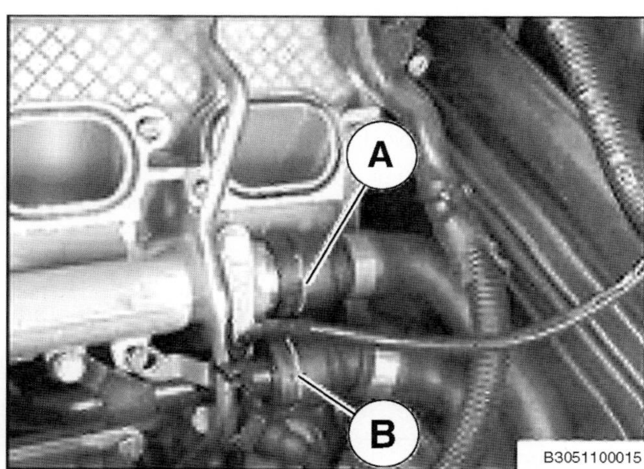

S54 engines: remove hose locks and disconnect hoses (**A** and **B**) at rear of cylinder head.

- **S54 engines**: remove engine oil cooler.

Remove radiator cooling fan and radiator as described in **170 Radiator and Cooling System**.

> ***CAUTION —***
> *32 mm radiator fan mounting nut has left hand threads.*

- **S54 engines**: remove engine oil cooler, located underneath radiator.

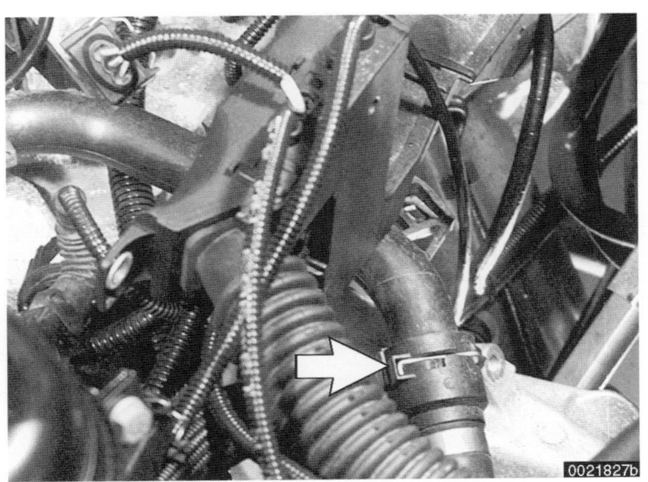

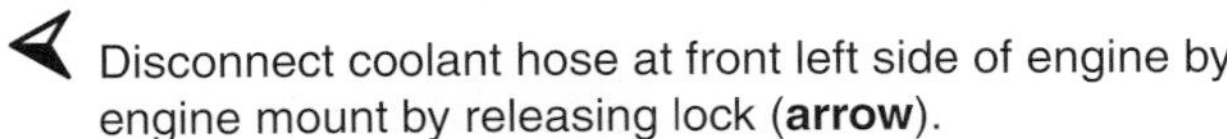

Disconnect coolant hose at front left side of engine by engine mount by releasing lock (**arrow**).

– **Except S54 engine**: Unbolt power steering fluid reservoir and pull aside without disconnecting hoses. Tie to fender with cord or stiff wire.

– **On S54 engine**: Drain power steering fluid reservoir and unbolt reservoir from mounting bracket. Tie reservoir to one side with cord or stiff wire.

NOTE —
Power steering fluid lines remain connected.

Working at E-box at left rear of engine compartment:
- Disconnect engine harness connectors (**arrows**).
- Lift off harness looms and lay over engine.

– Remove poly-ribbed drive belts. Mark belt direction of rotation if belts will be reused. See **020 Maintenance**.

– All wheel drive models: Remove front axle differential and output shaft bearing pedestal. See **311 Front Axle Final Drive**.

– Remove transmission from car. See **230 Manual Transmission**, **231 SMG Manual Transmission**, or **240 Automatic Transmission**.

NOTE —
Disconnect automatic transmission cooler lines from radiator, remove brackets holding lines to side of engine, and store lines in a clean environment.

– **On S54 Engines**: Disconnect steering spindle from steering rack. See **320 Steering and Wheel Alignment**.

– **On S54 Engines**: Remove starter motor. See **120 Battery, Alternator, Starter**.

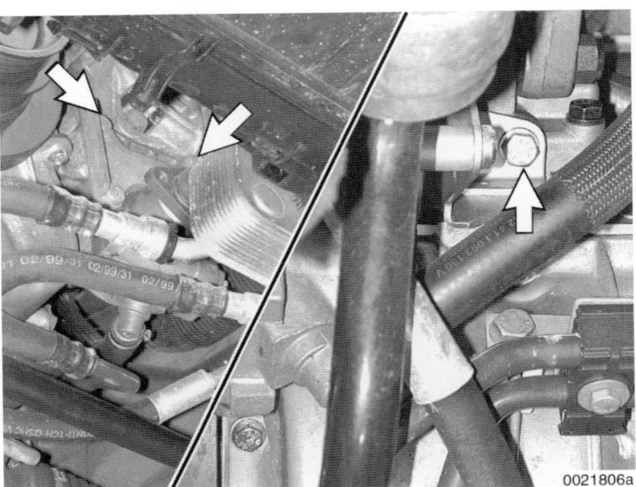

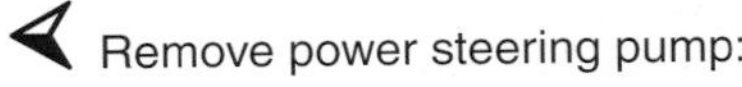

Remove power steering pump:
- Remove steering pump pulley.
- Remove front and rear pump mounting bolts (**arrows**).
- Hang pump from body using stiff wire.

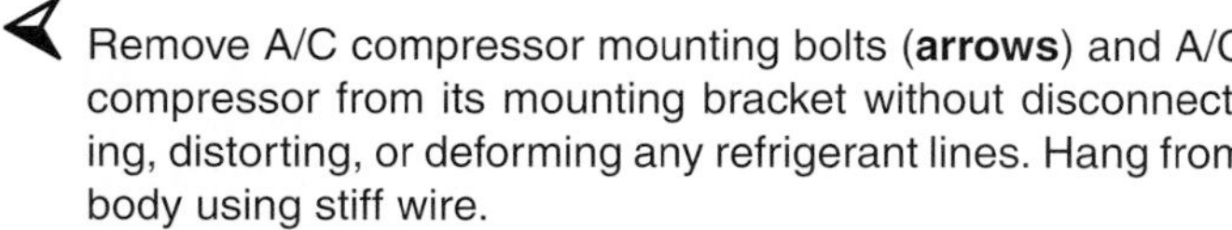

Remove A/C compressor mounting bolts (**arrows**) and A/C compressor from its mounting bracket without disconnecting, distorting, or deforming any refrigerant lines. Hang from body using stiff wire.

– Remove windshield and headlight washer reservoir:

- Remove bolt on top of reservoir.
- Lift tank and disconnect electrical connections to pump and to washer fluid level sensor.
- Disconnect hoses to windshield washer and headlight washer. Tilt reservoir to prevent fluid from leaking out.

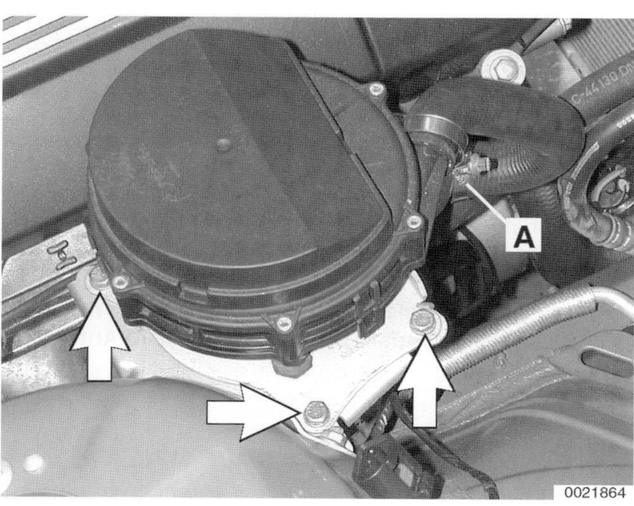

Remove secondary air pump:

- Remove hose at one-way valve (**A**).
- Remove bolts at support bracket on strut tower (**arrows**).
- Disconnect electrical harness from bottom of secondary air pump.
- Remove bracket from strut tower.
- **M56 engines**: disconnect and remove secondary air MAF sensor with air pump assembly.

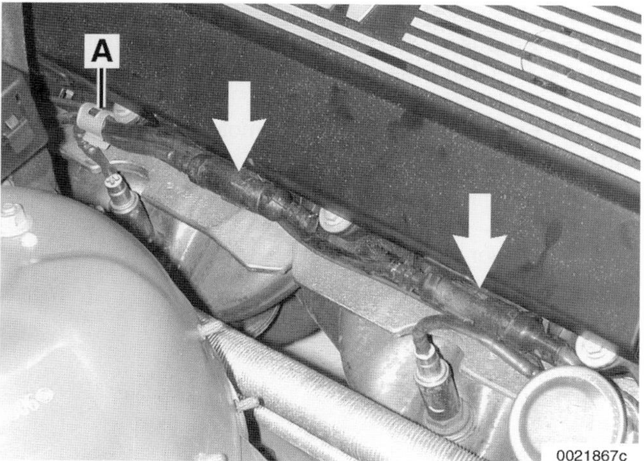

Separate oxygen sensor electrical harness connectors (**arrows**) and mounting clip (**A**) on right side of engine.

0021023

Remove chassis ground strap (**arrow**) at right engine mounting pedestal.

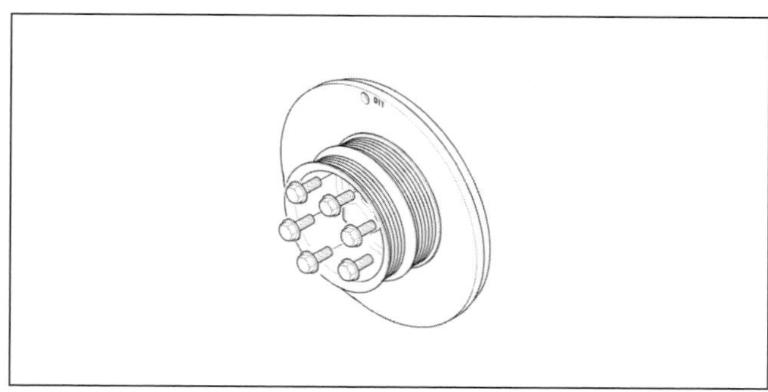

S54 engines: Remove 6 pulley mounting bolts. Remove center cover and pulley from vibration damper.

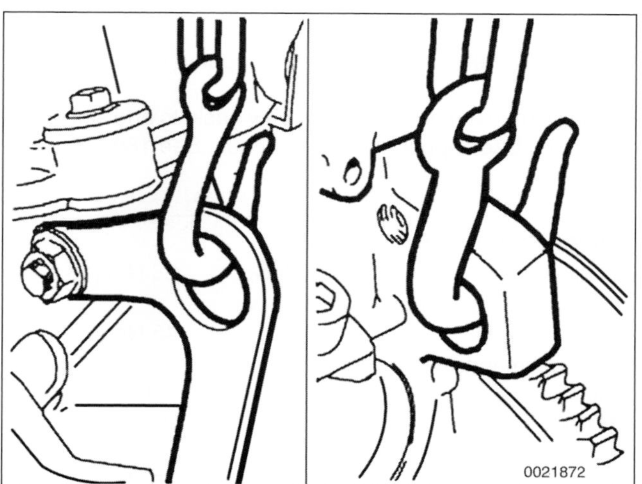
0021872

Install an engine lifting device (BMW 11 0 000 or equivalent) to the front and rear engine supports and raise engine until its weight is supported. Detach left and right engine mounts.

- Carefully raise engine out of car, checking for any wiring, fuel lines, or mechanical parts that might become snagged as engine is removed.

 When reinstalling, make sure locating pin on left engine mount (**arrow**) seats correctly in slot of subframe boss.

– Installation is reverse of removal, noting the following:

- Replace all gaskets, O-rings and seals.
- Use all new bolts when reinstalling chassis reinforcement plate or reinforcement bar. See **310 Front Suspension**.
- **On S54 Engines**, use a new bolt when installing steering spindle. See **320 Steering and Wheel Alignment**.
- Change engine oil and filter and check all other fluid levels. See **020 Maintenance**.
- Refill and bleed cooling system. See **170 Radiator and Cooling System**.
- Use new fuel injector seals.
- Carefully check intake manifold gaskets and replace if necessary.
- Inspect O-ring seal between mass air flow sensor and air filter housing. To facilitate reassembly, coat seal with acid-free grease.

> ***CAUTION —***
> *When reattaching throttle assembly harness connector, connector is fully tightened when arrows on connector and plug line up.*

> ***WARNING —***
> - *The front chassis reinforcement plate or reinforcement bar mounting fasteners are stretch type bolts and must be replaced anytime they are removed.*
> - *The vehicle must not be driven with this component removed. See **310 Front Suspension** for additional information.*

- Check that engine drive belts properly engage pulley grooves.
- Install exhaust manifolds using new gaskets and self-locking nuts. Use copper paste on threads. See **180 Exhaust System**.

Tightening torques

- Coolant drain plug to cylinder block .... 25 Nm (18 ft-lb)
- Engine mount to subframe
  M10 .... 45 Nm (33 ft-lb)
- Exhaust manifold to cylinder head
  M6 .... 10 Nm (8 ft-lb)
  M7 or M8 .... 20 Nm (15 ft-lb)
- Intake manifold to cylinder head
  M7 .... 15 Nm (11 ft-lb)
  M8 .... 22 Nm (16 ft-lb)
- Radiator cooling fan to coolant pump ... 40 Nm (30 ft-lb)
- Radiator drain screw to radiator ....2.5 Nm (22 in-lb)
- Pulley to vibration damper (S54 engine)
  grade 10.9 .... 34 Nm (25 ft-lb)
  grade 8.8 .... 22 Nm (16 ft-lb
- Reinforcement plate or reinforcement bar
  to chassis .... see **310 Front Suspension**

INTAKE MANIFOLD REMOVAL AND INSTALLATION

Intake manifold, removing and installing (M52 TU, M54, M56 engines)

– Disconnect negative (–) battery cable in luggage compartment.

> ***CAUTION —***
>
> *Prior to disconnecting the battery, read the battery disconnection cautions given at the front of this manual on page viii.*

◄ Remove housing for interior ventilation microfilter.

- Remove upper cover and microfilter.
- Open wiring harness loom cover (**A**) and remove wires.
- Unfasten screws (**B**) and remove lower microfilter housing.

◄ Remove intake manifold cover:

- Remove plastic trim covers (**arrows**).
- Remove cover hold down bolts and lift off cover.

◄ Working above engine, disconnect the following:

- **A** Positive engine lead at B+ terminal
- **B** Manifold vacuum line
- **C** Oxygen sensor connectors
- **D** Electrical harness connector for intake air temperature sensor
- **E** Positive lead hold-down bracket
- **F** Resonance valve electrical connector

> ***CAUTION —***
>
> *If oxygen sensor harness connectors are separated, be sure to mark them so that they can be reassembled as before.*

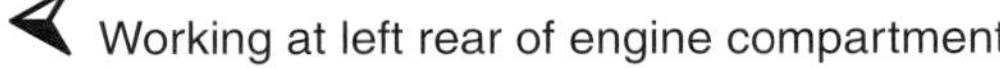

Working at left rear of engine compartment:

- Peel rubber edge seal off top of panel.
- Twist plastic panel retainers (**arrows**) 90° and pull out to remove.
- Disengage panel from hoses and wiring harnesses and remove from engine compartment.
- Separate brake booster vacuum hose at one way valve (**A**). Plug hose ends.

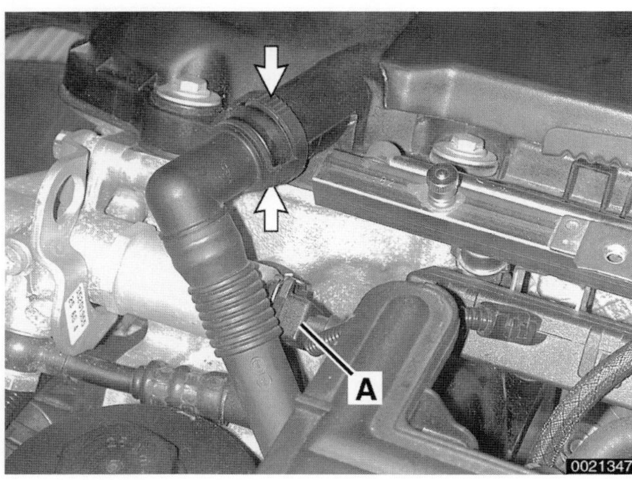

Disconnect engine vent hose from cylinder head cover by squeezing sides of spring clip (**arrows**). Disconnect VANOS solenoid electrical harness connector (**A**).

Disconnect fuel injector electrical connectors from injectors:

- Use small screwdriver to pry one corner of wire lock clip on fuel injector 1 connector.
- Repeat for all injectors.
- Lift off connector loom and lay aside.

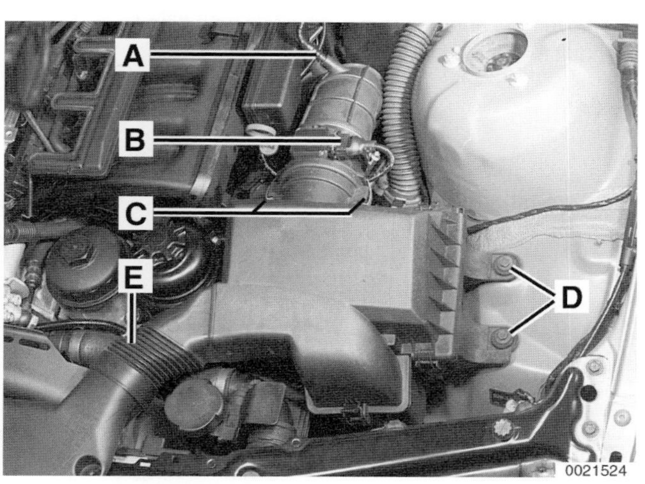

Remove complete air filter housing:

- Disconnect vacuum line at intake boot (**A**).
- Disconnect electrical harness connector on mass air flow sensor (**B**).
- Release mass air flow sensor clips (**C**).
- Remove filter housing mounting screws (**D**).
- Disconnect air duct connection (**E**) and lift complete air filter housing out of engine compartment, pulling it forward away from mass air flow sensor.

NOTE —

In this step, mass air flow sensor remains attached to rubber air duct.

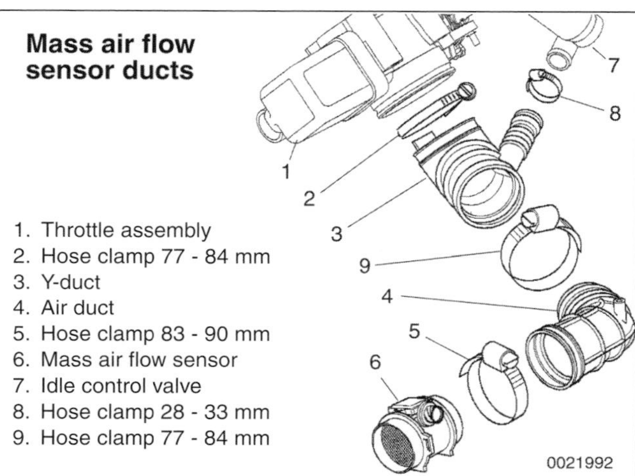

Loosen clamps **2** and **8** and remove mass air flow sensor and air ducts.

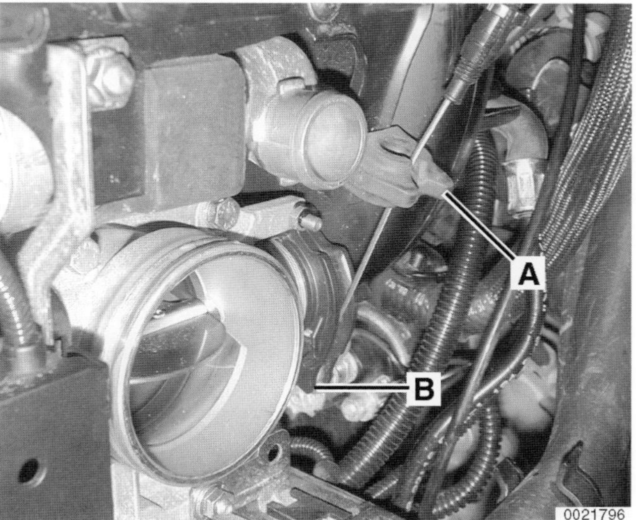

Where applicable: Pull throttle cable upwards out of rubber retainer (**A**) and unhook ball end of cable (**B**) from throttle actuator.

NOTE —

Models equipped with M54 and M56 engines do not use a throttle cable mounted to throttle housing.

Remove nuts and bolt (**arrows**) retaining wiring harness conduit to throttle body.

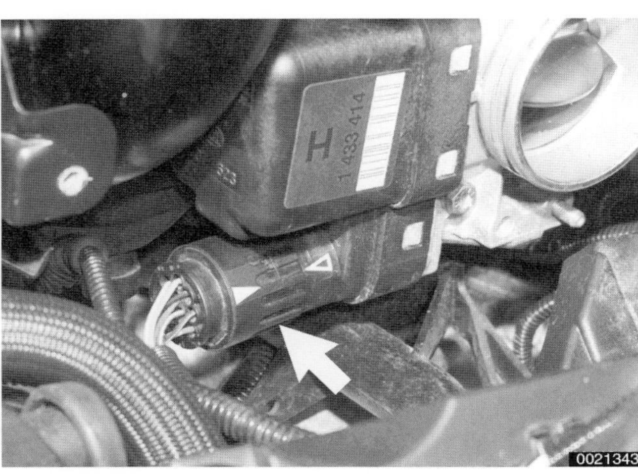

Working at throttle housing: Turn harness plug (**arrow**) counterclockwise and remove.

Disconnect electrical harness connector at idle speed control valve (**arrow**).

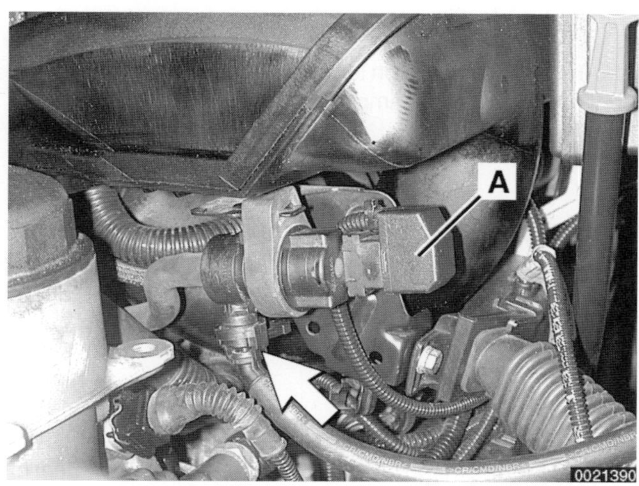

Disconnect electrical harness connector at fuel tank venting valve (**A**). Disconnect hose at quick disconnect fitting (**arrow**).

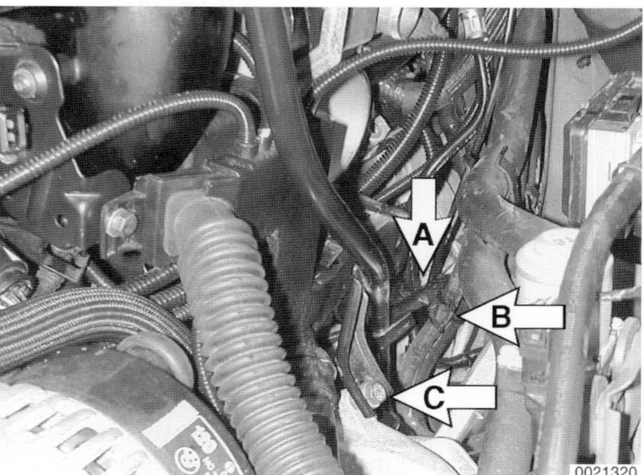

Remove dipstick guide tube:

- Disconnect wiring harness brackets from tube (**A**).
- Disconnect fuel lines from tube (**B**).
- Remove lower guide tube mounting bolt (**C**). Pull out dip stick guide tube.

Remove schræder valve cap (**arrow**) from air connection on fuel rail. Using a tire chuck, blow fuel back through feed line using a brief burst of compressed air (maximum of 3 bar or 43.5 psi).

WARNING —

- *Fuel in fuel line is under pressure (approx. 3 - 5 bar or 45 - 75 psi) and may be expelled under pressure. Do not smoke or work near heaters or other fire hazards. Keep a fire extinguisher handy. Before disconnecting fuel hoses, wrap a cloth around fuel hoses to absorb any leaking fuel. Catch and dispose of escaped fuel. Plug all open fuel lines.*
- *Always unscrew the fuel tank cap to release pressure in the tank before working on the tank or lines.*

– Raise car and support in a safe manner.

CAUTION —

Make sure the car is stable and well supported at all times. Use a professional automotive lift or jack stands designed for the purpose. A floor jack is not adequate support.

– Remove protective engine splash guard.

◀ Working beneath car (on left side under driver seat), remove fuel filter cover and clamp fuel hose(s).

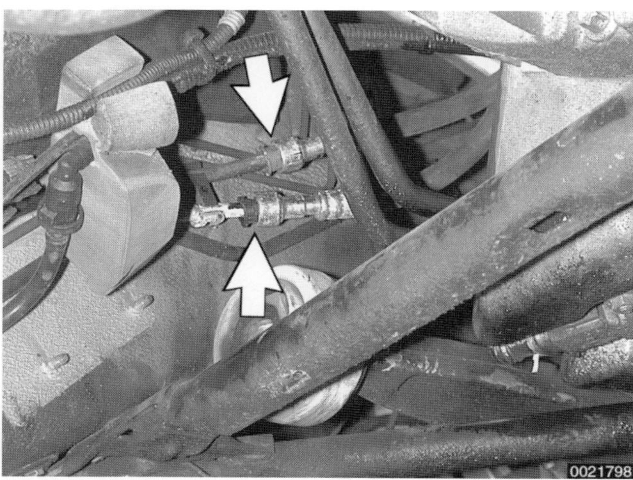

◀ Disconnect fuel hose(s) from fuel line(s) (**arrows**) using special fuel line removal tool 16 1 050 or equivalent. Seal off fuel line(s) with BMW special tools 13 5 281/13 5 282.

> ***CAUTION —***
> *Fuel may be expelled under pressure. Do not smoke or work near heaters or other fire hazards. Keep a fire extinguisher handy. Before disconnecting fuel hoses, wrap a cloth around fuel hoses to absorb any leaking fuel. Plug all open fuel lines.*

◀ Working underneath car, remove lower intake manifold support mounting bolt (**arrow**), located adjacent to left engine mount.

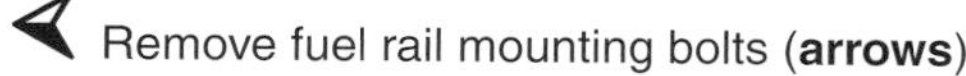

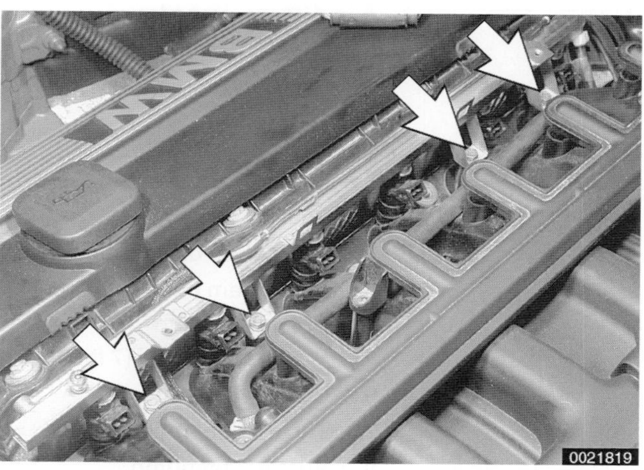

Remove fuel rail mounting bolts (**arrows**).

- Carefully pry fuel rail off manifold.
- Separate fuel line support bracket at rear of intake manifold.
- Thread fuel line(s) out of rear of engine compartment while lifting fuel rail out.

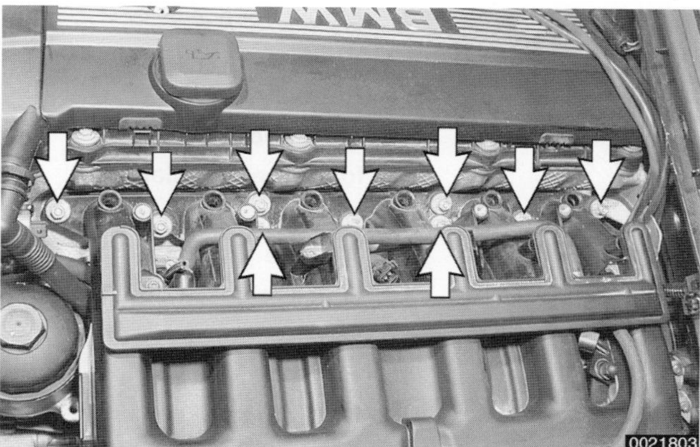

Remove manifold mounting nuts (**arrows**).

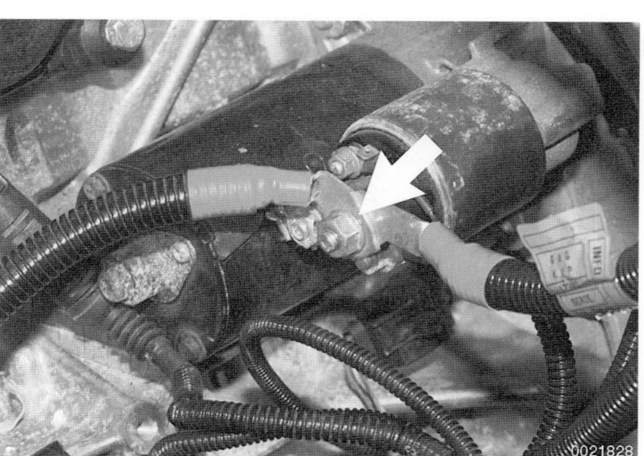

Lift up manifold just enough to disconnect positive cables from starter motor terminal 50 (**arrow**).

– Remove intake manifold from cylinder head while carefully checking for electrical connections or hoses.

> ***CAUTION —***
> *Stuff clean rags into open intake ports to prevent any parts from falling into the engine intake.*

– Intake manifold Installation is reverse of removal.

- Use new fuel injector seals.
- Carefully check intake manifold gasket and replace if necessary.
- Inspect O-ring seal between mass air flow sensor and air filter housing. To facilitate reassembly, coat seal with acid-free grease.

> ***CAUTION —***
> *When reattaching throttle assembly harness connector, connector is fully tightened when arrows on connector and plug line up.*

Tightening torques

- Intake manifold to cylinder head
  - M7 . . . . 15 Nm (11 ft-lb)
  - M8 . . . . 22 Nm (16 ft-lb)

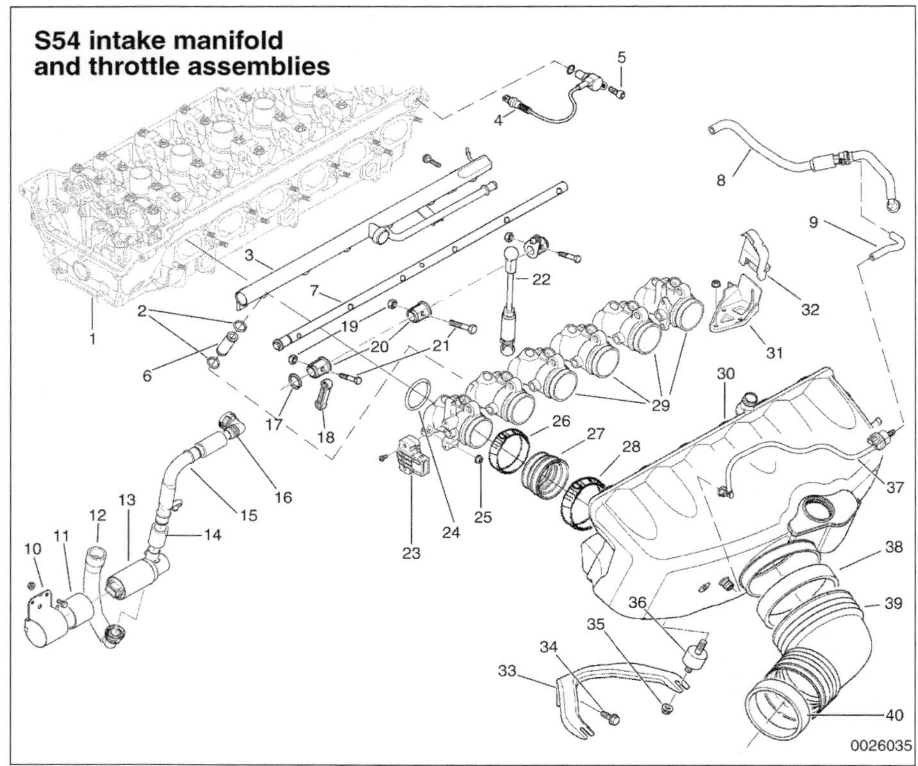

Air filter, intake manifold and throttle assemblies (S54 engine)

1. **Cylinder head**
2. **Sealing O-ring**
3. **Injector air distribution pipe**
4. **Intake cam position sensor**
5. **Bolt (M6)**
   - tighten to 10 Nm (7 ft-lb)
6. **Connection pipe**
7. **Throttle operating shaft**
8. **Sucking jet pump**
9. **Elbow hose**
10. **Bracket**
11. **Rubber damper**
12. **Elbow hose**
13. **Idle speed regulator**
14. **Hose**
15. **Air tube**
16. **Quick release coupling**
17. **Circlip**
18. **Pull rod**
19. **Nut (M5)**
20. **Operating lever**
21. **Bolt (M5)**
22. **Main throttle pull rod**
23. **Throttle position sensor**
24. **Intake manifold sealing O-ring (gasket)**
25. **Nut (M7)**
   - tighten to 15 Nm (11 ft-lb)
26. **Clamp 63 mm**
27. **Coupling hose**
28. **Clamp**
29. **Throttle housings**
30. **Intake manifold**
31. **Lower cover**
32. **Upper cover**
33. **Manifold support bracket**
34. **Bolt (M8)**
35. **Nut (M6)**
36. **Rubber mount**
37. **Duct hose with shut off valve**
38. **Gasket**
39. **Coupling hose**
40. **Gasket**

Intake manifold and throttle assemblies, removing and installing (S54 engine)

– With ignition key removed, disconnect negative (–) battery cable in luggage compartment.

> ***CAUTION —***
> *Prior to disconnecting the battery, read the battery disconnection cautions given at the front of this manual on page viii.*

◄ Pry out plastic expansion rivets (**arrows**) and remove intake hood with duct up and off.

– Remove strut cross brace mounting nuts and remove brace.

◄ Remove screw securing air filter housing to body (**arrows**).

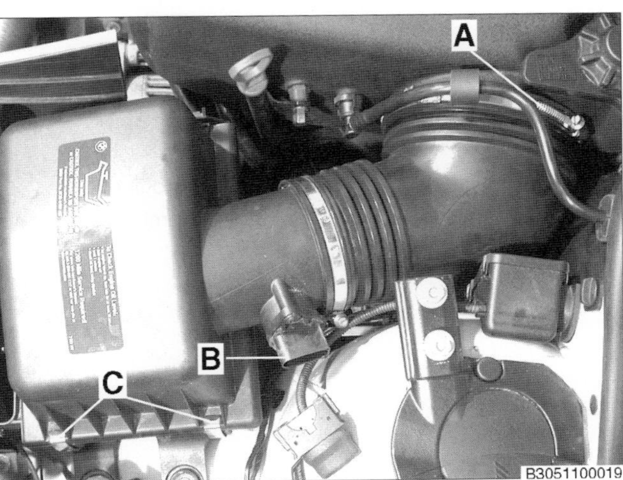

◄ Remove intake air filter housing

- Loosen hose clamp (**A**).
- Disconnect MAF sensor harness connector (**B**).
- Release air filter retainers (**C**).
- Lift top section of air filter housing up and rotate to disconnect intake hose from intake manifold and remove upper section of intake filter housing.
- Lift out air filter element.
- Remove lower section of intake filter housing towards top.

B305110021

On SMG equipped cars: Remove E-box cover at left rear of engine compartment and remove SMG hydraulic pump relay (**arrow**).

B305110022

On SMG equipped cars: Disconnect supply hose from SMG hydraulic fluid expansion tank at quick release coupling (**arrow**) at rear of intake manifold.

NOTE —

The SMG fluid expansion tank is mounted on the right rear of the intake manifold and connected to the hydraulic unit via a plastic supply hose with a quick release coupling. A valve in the expansion tank prevents oil loss when the supply hose is disconnected.

B305110023

Remove housing for interior ventilation microfilter.

- Unclip upper cover (**arrows**), lift up and remove cover and microfilter.

Open wiring harness loom cover (**A**) and lift out wiring. Unfasten screws (**arrows**) and lift out lower microfilter housing.

– Press quick release locks and disconnect crankcase vent hose from intake manifold.

– Working at side (rear) of intake manifold, unclip positive battery cable retaining clip by sliding upwards. Remove cable from retaining clip.

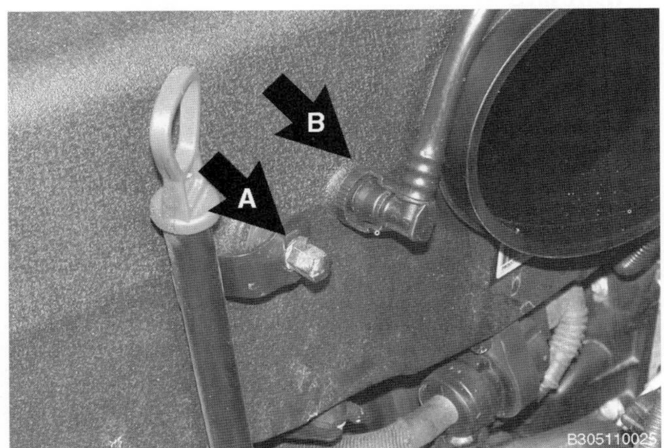

Remove nut and disconnect oil dipstick guide tube from intake manifold (**A**). Press quick release locks and disconnect vacuum hose from side of intake manifold (**B**).

– Working underneath intake manifold:
  - Disconnect EVAP vent valve from holder
  - Loosen retaining nuts at support bracket at front and rear support brackets at intake manifold.
  - Press quick release locks and disconnect vacuum hose from manifold.

Use BMW special tool 11 9 160 or equivalent hose clamp pliers to release clamps at throttle housings. Press clamp together until lock is opened.

– Press quick release locks and disconnect intake manifold condensate hose at top of oil pan.

– Raise intake manifold slightly and disconnect from throttle assembly.

– Feed out vacuum hose and wiring clipped to underside of manifold and remove intake manifold.

– Working at air distribution pipe, press quick release locks to diconnect idle speed regulator hose.

– Working underneath throttle housings, remove idle speed regulator mounting nuts. Remove regulator and bracket and place to one side.

– Detach vacuum lines and electrical harness connectors from throttle housings and fuel injectors.

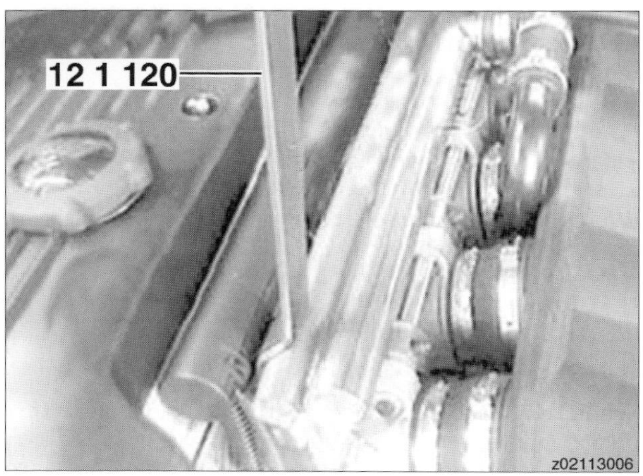

Working from outer ends and moving towards center, carefully pry off fuel injector electrical connector strip. Use BMW special tool 12 1 120 or equivalent.

> **CAUTION —**
> *Connector strip may break if it is removed without special tool 12 1 120.*

- Working underneath fuel rail, pry off fuel supply line locking clip. Wrap fuel line with shop rag and pull fuel line out of fuel rail.

> **WARNING —**
> - *Fuel in fuel line is under pressure (approx. 3 - 5 bar or 45 - 75 psi) and may be expelled under pressure. Do not smoke or work near heaters or other fire hazards. Keep a fire extinguisher handy. Before disconnecting fuel hoses, wrap a cloth around fuel hoses to absorb any leaking fuel. Catch and dispose of escaped fuel. Plug all open fuel lines.*
> - *Always unscrew the fuel tank cap to release pressure in the tank before working on the tank or lines.*

Remove retaining bolts (**arrow**) at front and rear of fuel rail.

- Pull fuel rail up and off fuel injectors, and store in safe place.
- Remove intake camshaft position sensor from left rear of cylinder head.

Pry off main throttle pull rod from center throttle operating lever (**arrow**).

- Unbolt and remove throttle housings (qty. 12 bolts) and remove, while carefully checking for electrical connections or hoses that might become snagged.

– On installation:

- Clean all sealing surfaces.
- Replace throttle housing sealing O-rings.
- Be sure throttle housing dowel sleeves fit into cylinder head correctly.
- Check fuel injector O-ring seals. Replace as necessary. Lubricate with SAE 90 oil before installing.
- Replace intake manifold to throttle housing clamps. Use BMW special tool 11 9 160 to install clamps.

> ***CAUTION —***
> *Use only original clamps. Use of non-original hose clamps may result in interference with the throttle linkage and cause the throttle to jam or stick in the open position.*

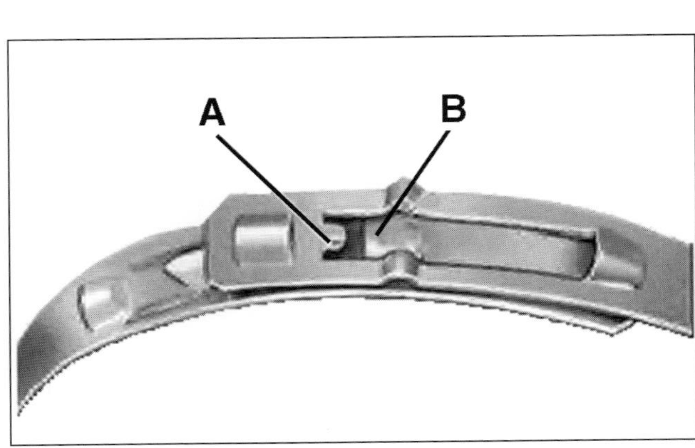

Use only new original style clamps. Press hose clamp together until lock (**A**) engages catch (**B**). Slide pre-assembled clamps onto the ducts prior to final installation.

- On cars with SMG, reinstall SMG hydraulic pump relay only after connecting line between expansion tank and hydraulic unit.

– After assembly:

- Check throttle position settings. See **130 Fuel Injection**.
- Test throttle system with factory scan tool or an equivalent scan tool.

Tightening torques	
Intake camshaft position sensor to cylinder head (M6)	10 Nm (7 ft-lb)
Throttle housing to cylinder head (M7)	15 ± 2 Nm (11 ± 1 ft-lb)

113 Cylinder Head Removal and Installation

113

GENERAL

This group covers cylinder head removal and installation as well as cylinder head/valve diagnosis procedures for the M52 TU, M54, and M65 engines.

NOTE —
Cylinder head removal for the S54 engine used in the M3 model is not included in the repair group. S54 cylinder head removal and installation is a highly complex job that requires a large and expensive assortment of BMW special tools and equipment and is therefore outside the scope of this manual.

The information given in this repair group assumes that the engine is installed in the engine bay. In order to remove the cylinder head from the engine block, the VANOS control unit and the camshafts must be removed from the cylinder head. For cylinder head and valvetrain reconditioning information, see **116 Cylinder Head and Valvetrain**.

NOTE —
If a head gasket problem is suspected, a compression test or leak-down test will usually detect the fault. See **Diagnostic Testing** *later in this group.*

Special tools

Special BMW service tools are required to properly remove and install the cylinder head on engines covered by this manual. The special tools are used to time the valvetrain to the crankshaft, to remove the VANOS control unit, the camshafts and the Torx (E12) head bolts. Read the entire procedure through before beginning the job.

Special Tools

A
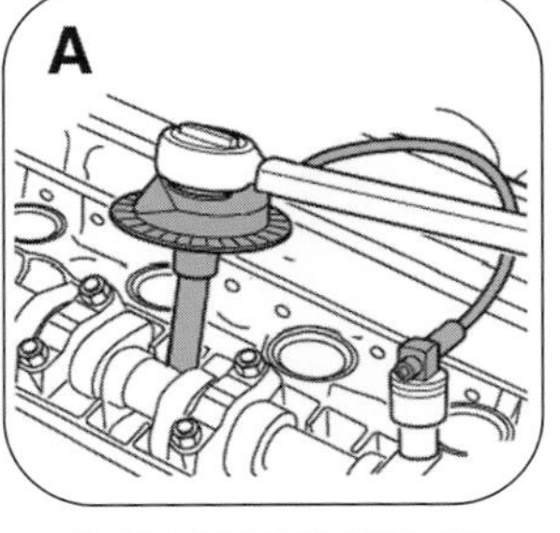

B
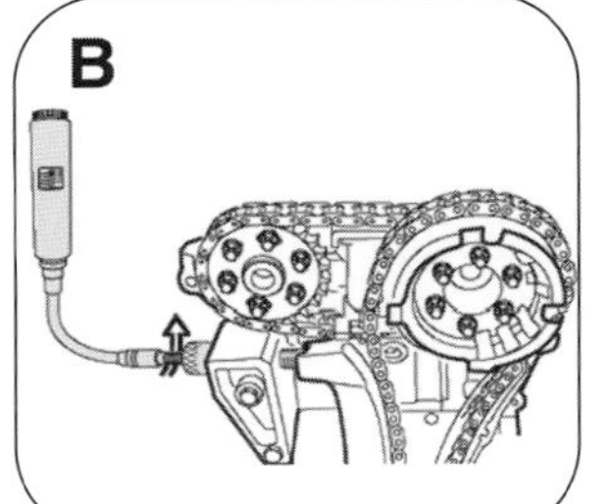

C
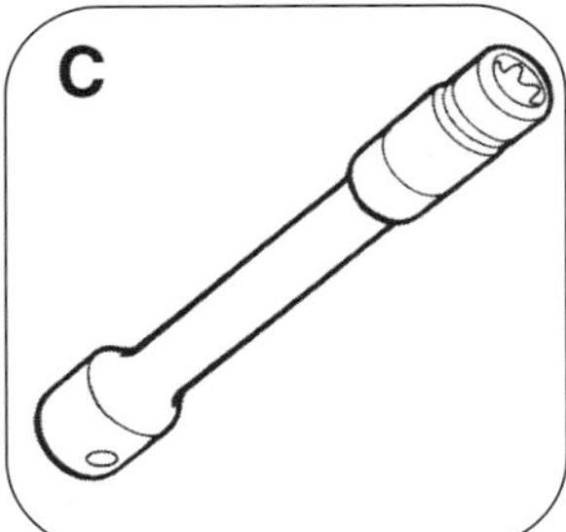

D
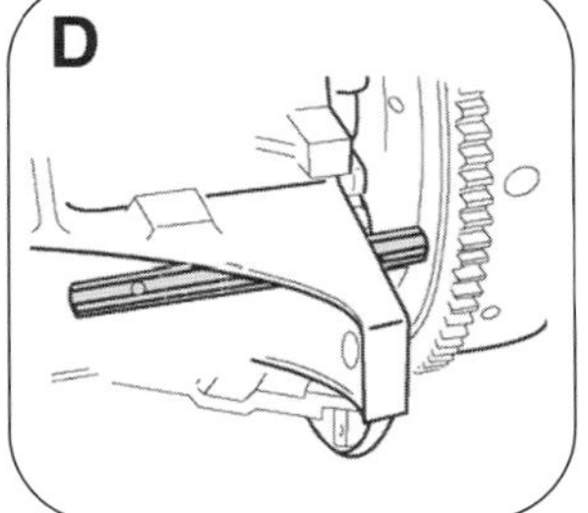

E

F
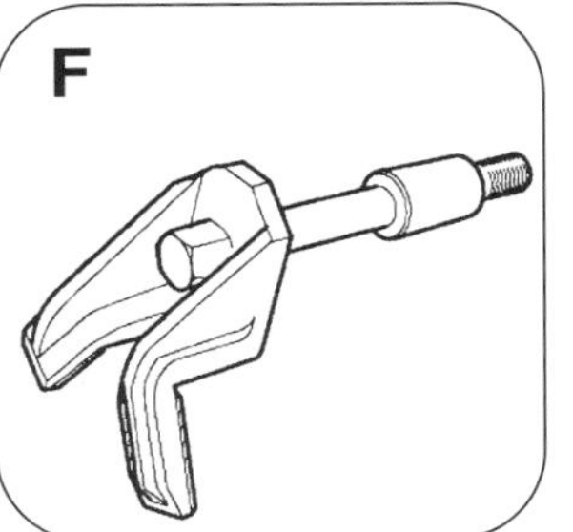

Special tools

A BMW special tool 00 9 120 . . . . Rotary angle dial gauge
B BMW special tool 00 9 250 . . Torque wrench w/ flex extension
C BMW special tool 11 2 250 . . . . E-12 Torx socket
D BMW special tool 11 2 300 . . . . Crankshaft locking tool
E BMW special tool 11 3 240 . . . . Camshaft locking tool
F BMW special tool 11 3 244 . . . . Camshaft locking tool bracket

Special Tools

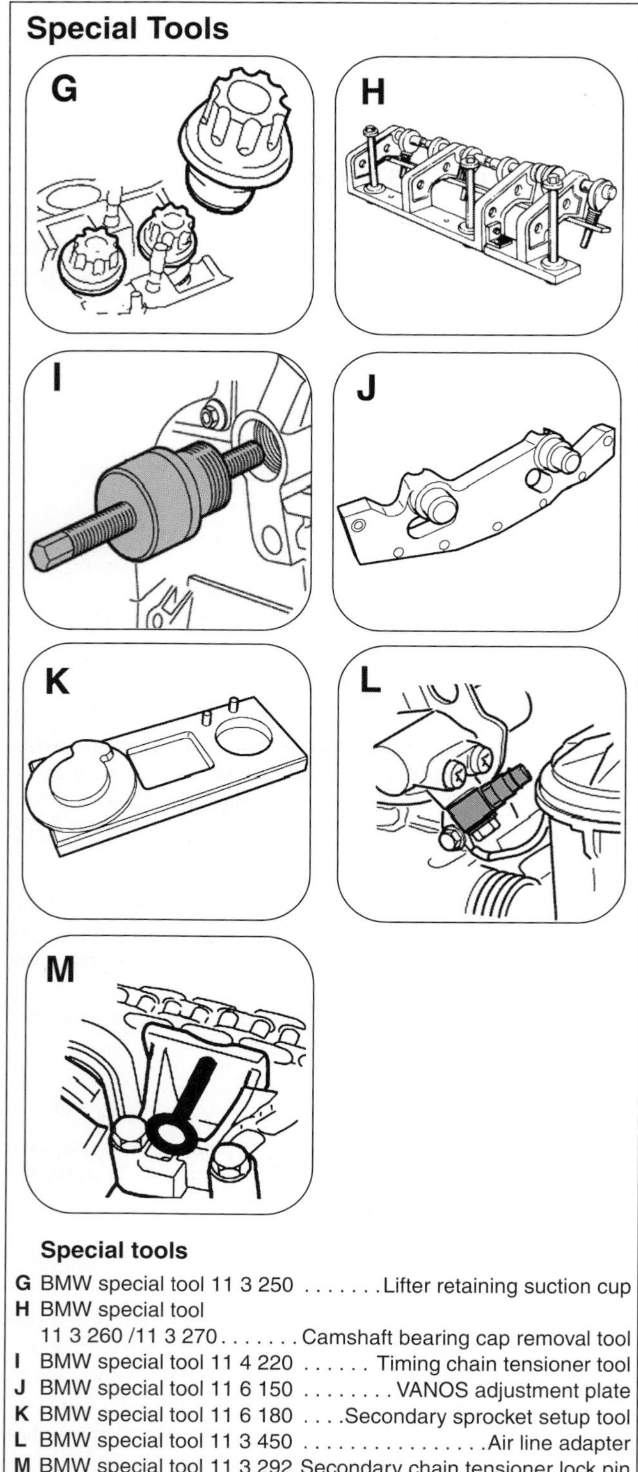

Special tools

G BMW special tool 11 3 250 .... Lifter retaining suction cup
H BMW special tool
11 3 260 /11 3 270....... Camshaft bearing cap removal tool
I BMW special tool 11 4 220 ...... Timing chain tensioner tool
J BMW special tool 11 6 150 .... VANOS adjustment plate
K BMW special tool 11 6 180 .... Secondary sprocket setup tool
L BMW special tool 11 3 450 .... Air line adapter
M BMW special tool 11 3 292 Secondary chain tensioner lock pin

CYLINDER HEAD REMOVAL (M52 TU, M54, M56)

> ***WARNING —***
> *Due to risk of personal injury, be sure the engine is cold before beginning the removal procedure.*

Cylinder head removal and installation is an involved repair procedure. VANOS control unit, timing chain, and camshaft removal and installation all require special tools. Read the entire procedure before beginning the repair.

> ***CAUTION —***
> *Cover all painted surfaces before beginning the removal procedure. As an aid to installation, label all components, wires, and hoses before removing them. Do not reuse gaskets, O-rings or seals during reassembly.*

To assist the technician in this repair, the procedure has been organized into discrete jobs. Please be advised that these individual jobs must be accomplished in the order in which they appear.

- **Intake manifold, removing**
  See **110 Engine Removal and Installation**
- **Cylinder head cover and spark plugs, removing**
- **VANOS adjustment unit, removing**
- **Camshafts and valvetrain, removing**
- **Cylinder head assembly, removing**

Intake manifold, removing

– Remove intake manifold as described in **110 Engine Removal and installation**.

> ***CAUTION —***
> - *Prior to disconnecting the battery, read the battery disconnection cautions given at the front of this manual on page viii.*
> - *Disconnecting the battery may erase fault code(s) stored in control module memory. Check for fault codes using special BMW diagnostic equipment.*

Cylinder head cover, removing

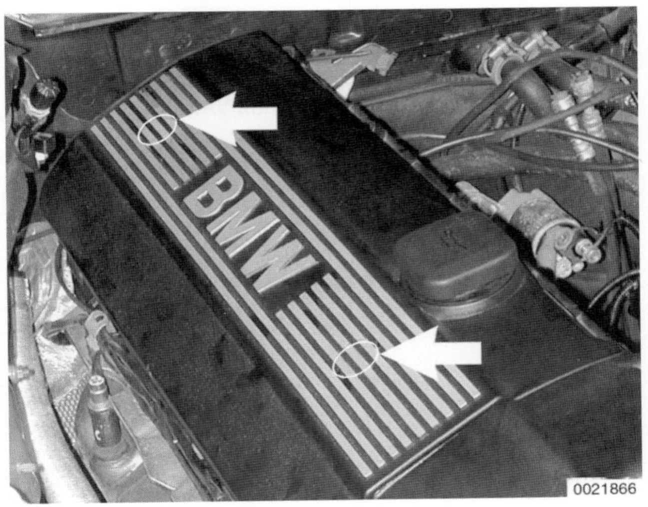

Remove cylinder head top cover:

- Remove plastic trim covers (**arrows**).
- Remove cover hold down nuts and lift off cover.

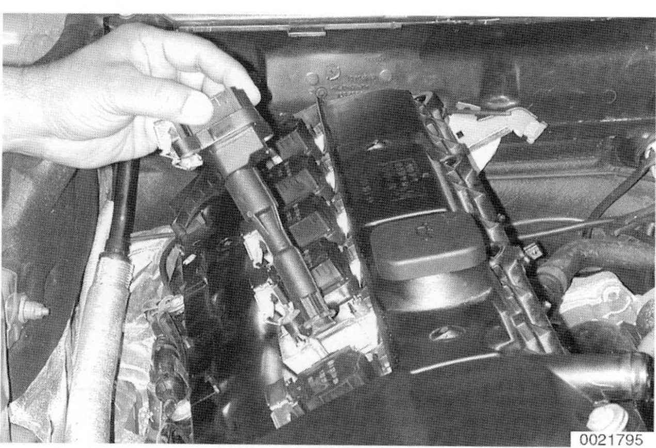

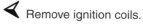

Remove ignition coils.

- Disconnect ignition coil harness connectors.
- Remove coil mounting fasteners.
- Remove coils.
- Remove ground straps.
- Set coil harness to left side of engine compartment.

NOTE —

On 2003 and later cars, a new style ignition coil (Bremi manufacture) was used. These thinner 'rod' type coils do not use hold down nuts. To remove the late style Bremi coil, swivel harness connector lock up, disconnect connector, and pull coil straight up.

– Remove cylinder head cover mounting fasteners and remove cylinder head cover.

NOTE —

The cylinder head cover mounting bolt insulators and gaskets should be reinstalled in their original locations. The three grounds mount to the first, second and fourth central studs. Make note of their arrangement during removal.

– Remove spark plugs.

> ***CAUTION —***
>
> *Stuff clean lint free rags into open intake ports to prevent any foreign matter from falling into the ports.*

Remove oil baffle cover from above intake camshaft.

VANOS control unit, removing

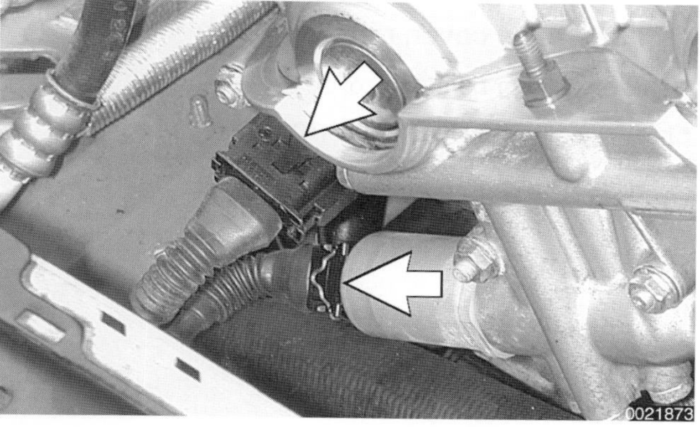

Disconnect electrical connections at exhaust camshaft position sensor and exhaust camshaft VANOS control valve (**arrows**).

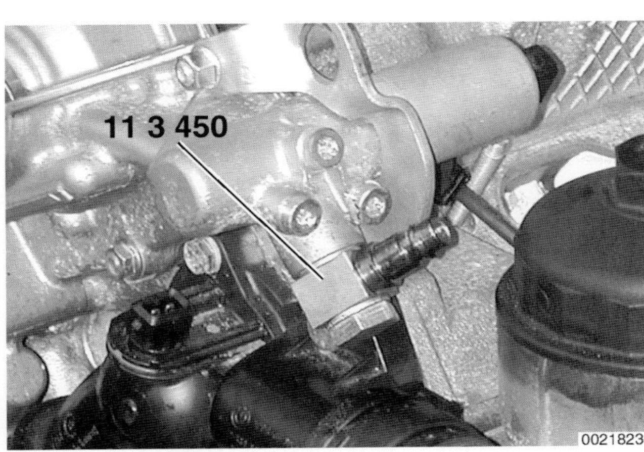

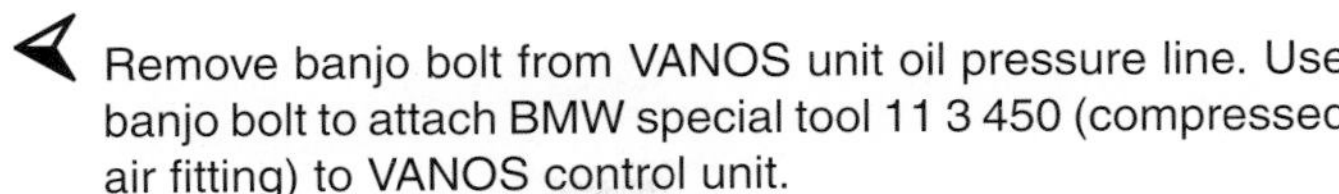

◄ Remove banjo bolt from VANOS unit oil pressure line. Use banjo bolt to attach BMW special tool 11 3 450 (compressed air fitting) to VANOS control unit.

◄ Cover oil hole (**arrow**) in VANOS unit with shop towel to capture oil which will spray when compressed air is applied.

– Connect compressed air line to air fitting. Apply air pressure set to 2 - 8 bar (30 - 110 psi).

◄ With compressed air line connected, rotate engine in direction of rotation (clockwise) at least two complete rotations, until cylinder 1 intake and exhaust camshaft lobes face each other (**arrows**) in the top dead center (TDC) position for cylinder 1.

> ***CAUTION —***
> *Do not rotate engine counterclockwise to reach the top dead center position. Instead, complete another two complete rotations.*

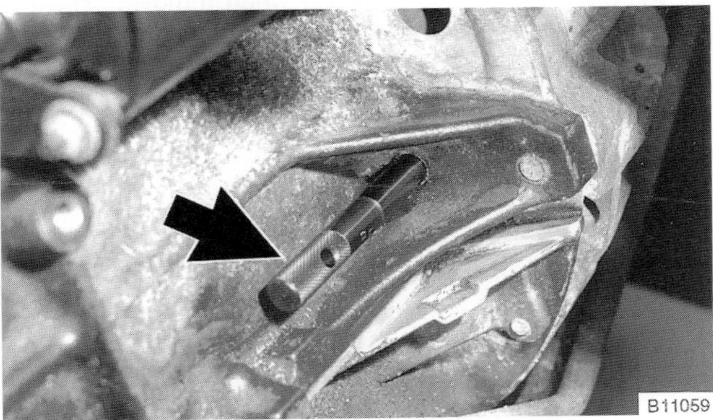

◄ Remove sealing plug from special tool bore on lower left side of engine block near flywheel. Secure crankshaft in TDC position with BMW special tool 11 2 300 (**arrow**).

Unscrew and remove two cylinder head cover studs (**arrows**) at rear of cylinder head.

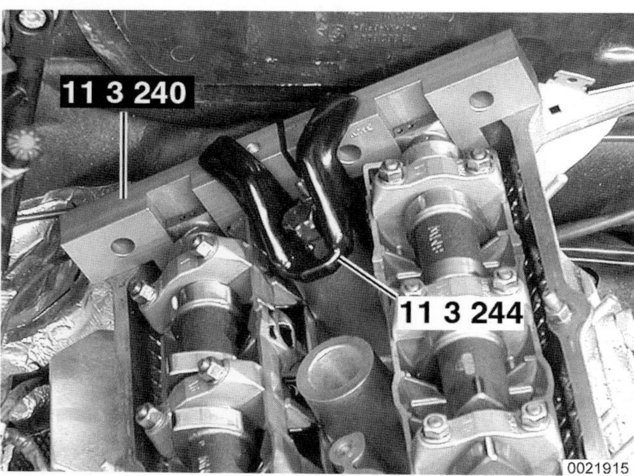

Secure camshafts in TDC position using BMW special tools 11 3 240 and 11 3 244.

– Disconnect compressed air line, leaving compressed air fitting attached to VANOS unit.

> ***CAUTION —***
> *Oil will drain from pressure line. Have a drain container and rags ready. Do not allow oil to run onto drive belts.*

Unscrew sealing plugs (**arrows**) from VANOS unit.

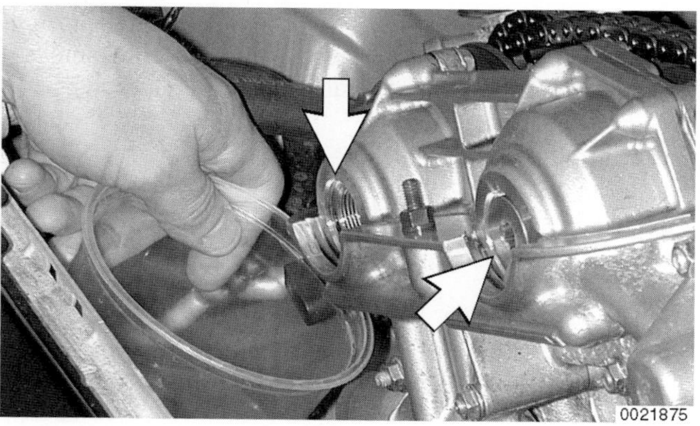

Oil will drain from plugs (**arrows**) when removed. Have a container and rags ready. Do not allow oil to run onto drive belts.

Pull sealing caps straight out of VANOS unit with BMW special tool 11 6 170, or with short nose pliers.

NOTE —

Additional oil may drain from VANOS unit.

Remove set screws (left-hand thread) on ends of intake and exhaust camshafts.

> ***CAUTION —***
>
> *Set screws have left hand threads. Remove in clockwise motion.*

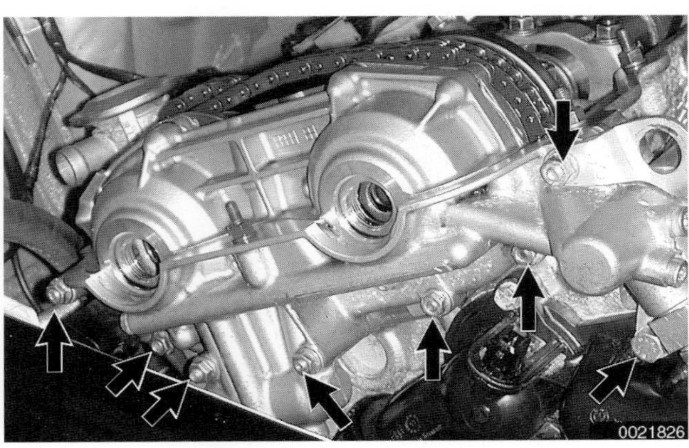

Remove VANOS unit:

- Remove engine support eye fasteners from side of VANOS unit.
- Remove VANOS mounting nuts (**arrows**) from cylinder head and pull VANOS unit and metal gasket off.

> ***CAUTION —***
>
> *Do not crank the engine with VANOS unit removed. The splined shaft on the intake camshaft might slip out of the VANOS spline teeth, causing the intake cam to no longer be positively connected to the timing chain, allowing for possible piston/valve interference.*

NOTE —

The VANOS unit will contain a small quantity of oil. Place shop towels to catch oil as unit is removed or tilted.

> ***CAUTION —***
>
> *If the VANOS adjustment unit is replaced, or if operations are completed that may change the timing of the camshafts, the camshaft timing must be checked as described later in this chapter.*

Camshafts and valvetrain, removing

Remove primary camshaft chain tensioner cylinder (**arrow**).

> ***CAUTION —***
> *Primary camshaft chain tensioning piston is under spring pressure.*

Press down on secondary chain tensioner and lock into place using BMW special tool 11 3 292 or a similar size pin.

Remove exhaust camshaft impulse wheel mounting nuts (**arrows**). Remove impulse wheel (**A**).

Remove spring plate (**A**).

Remove intake camshaft sprocket mounting nuts (**arrows**) and remove spring plate (labelled **FRONT**).

Remove torx screws from exhaust camshaft sprocket (**arrows**).

Lift off exhaust and intake sprockets together with secondary chain, thrust spacer (**A**) from exhaust camshaft, and splined shaft (**B**) from intake camshaft.

> ***CAUTION —***
> *Splined shafts share the same part number for both intake and exhaust camshafts. Remove and mark used splined shafts in order and reinstall in original locations.*

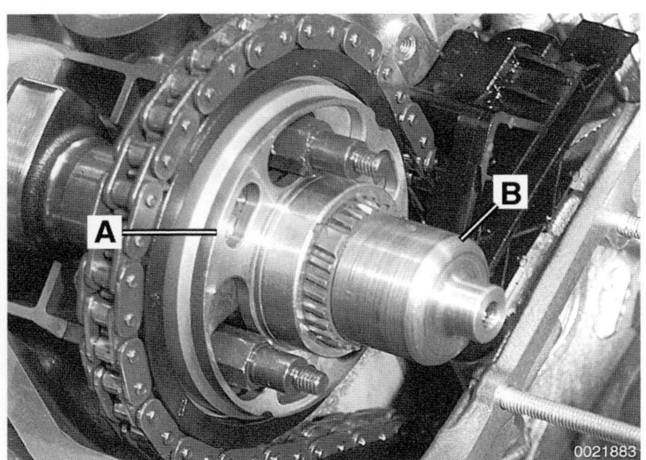

◀ Remove exhaust camshaft splined sleeve (**A**) and shaft (**B**).

◀ Remove primary chain sprocket mounting studs (**arrows**) on exhaust camshaft.

◀ Lift primary chain sprocket off exhaust camshaft. Remove sprocket from chain.

◀ Place timing chain on end of exhaust camshaft.

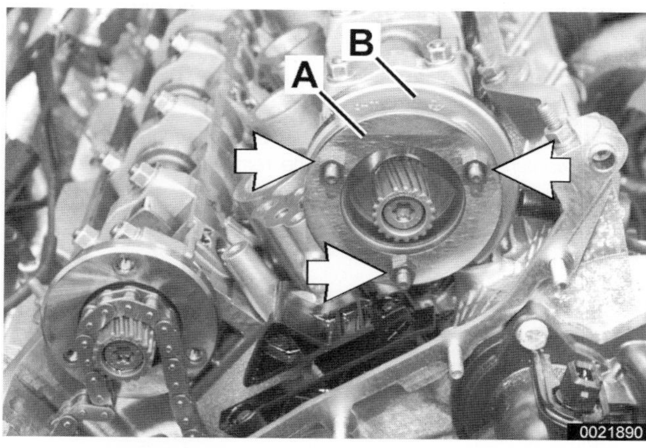

◀ Remove locating studs (**arrows**) from intake camshaft. Lift off intake camshaft thrust spacer (**A**) and impulse wheel (**B**).

◀ Do not remove end spline retaining screws from camshafts (**arrows**).

◀ Remove cylinder head cover mounting studs (**arrows**) from center of cylinder head.

– Remove flywheel locking tool from transmission bellhousing so that crankshaft is no longer secured.

◀ Lift primary chain and hold under tension, then rotate engine against direction of rotation (counterclockwise) approximately 30°.

> ***CAUTION —***
> *To prevent damaging valves while working on camshafts, no pistons should be in the TDC position.*

– Remove BMW special tools 11 3 240 and 11 3 244 from rear of cylinder head.

Remove retaining nuts (**arrows**) and bearing cap 1 of intake camshaft.

> ***CAUTION —***
> *Intake camshaft bearing cap 1 is centered with adapter sleeves. To avoid camshaft damage, it must be removed before any other caps.*

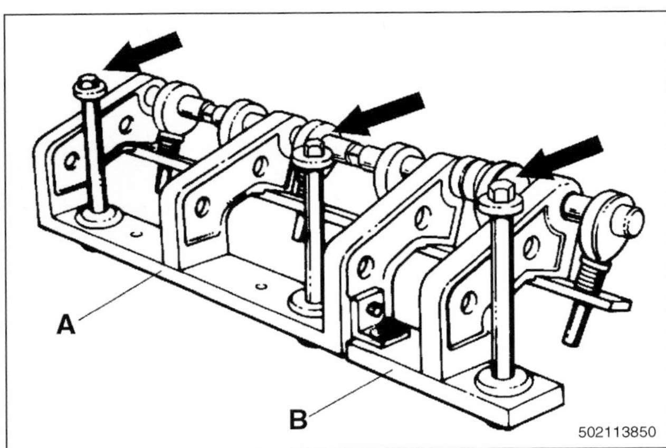

Fit BMW special tools 11 3 260 (**A**) and 11 3 270 (**B**) to cylinder head and screw long bolts (**arrows**) into spark plug threads. Tensioners will align with the bearing caps on the intake camshaft.

> ***CAUTION —***
> *Do not over torque bolts into spark plug holes.*

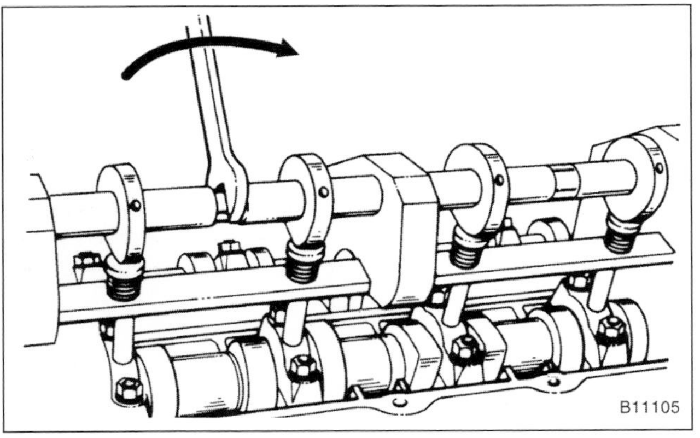

Turn eccentric shaft of special tool to pretension intake camshaft bearing caps. Remove nuts on remaining bearing caps.

- Release tension on eccentric shaft and remove BMW special tools 11 3 260 and 11 3 270. Remove bearing caps and set aside in order. Remove camshaft and store safely.
- Repeat procedure for exhaust camshaft.

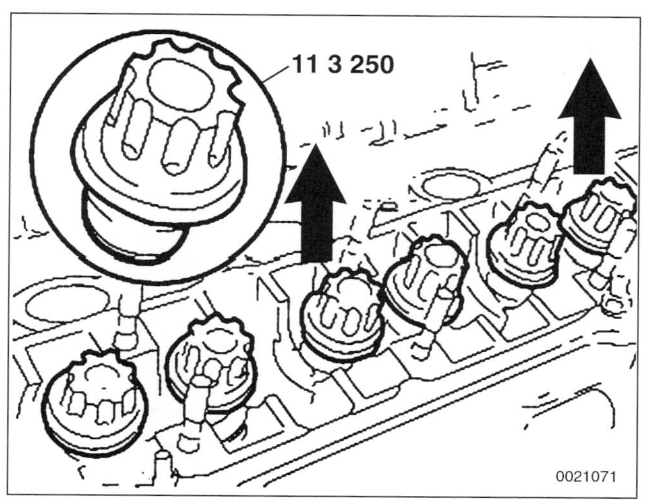

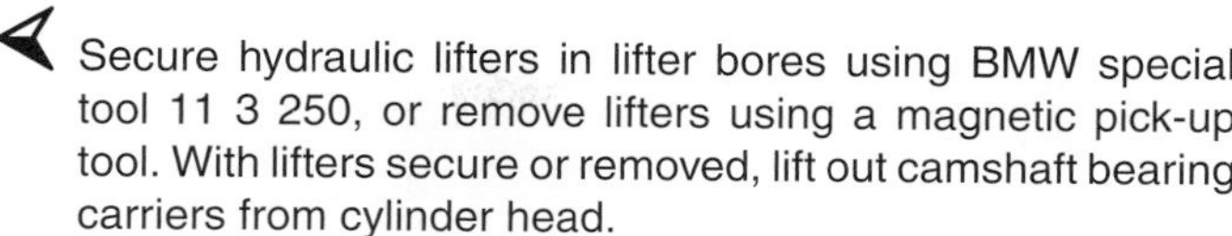

Secure hydraulic lifters in lifter bores using BMW special tool 11 3 250, or remove lifters using a magnetic pick-up tool. With lifters secure or removed, lift out camshaft bearing carriers from cylinder head.

> ***CAUTION—***
> - *Do not let the hydraulic lifters fall out as the camshaft carrier is removed.*
> - *Hydraulic lifters should be stored in an upright position.*
> - *Used hydraulic lifters must be replaced into original lifter bores.*

Cylinder head assembly, removing

– Remove exhaust manifolds. See **180 Exhaust System**.

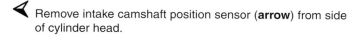

Remove intake camshaft position sensor (**arrow**) from side of cylinder head.

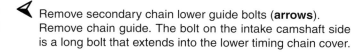

Remove secondary chain lower guide bolts (**arrows**). Remove chain guide. The bolt on the intake camshaft side is a long bolt that extends into the lower timing chain cover.

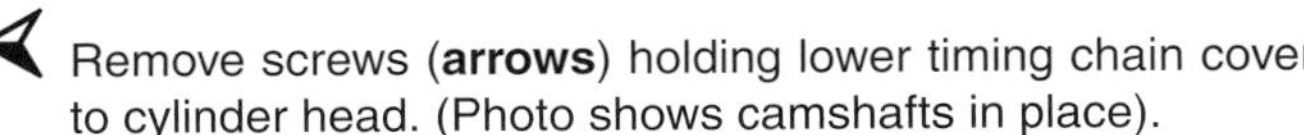

Remove screws (**arrows**) holding lower timing chain cover to cylinder head. (Photo shows camshafts in place).

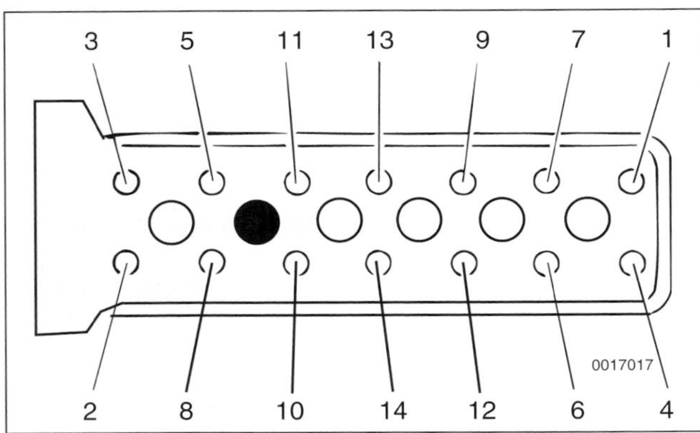

Using BMW special tool 11 2 250 or equivalent, loosen cylinder head bolts in several stages in sequence shown. Discard head bolts.

NOTE —
BMW special tool 11 2 250 is a thin-walled Torx E12 socket with an extended reach. The cylinder head bolts are recessed into the head below the camshaft towers with little working space.

– Lift off cylinder head. Refer to **116 Cylinder Head and Valvetrain** to evaluate the head.

CYLINDER HEAD INSTALLATION (M52 TU, M54, M56)

Clean cylinder head and gasket surfaces of cylinder block and all timing chain covers.

Remove foreign matter and liquid from bolt holes.

CAUTION —
Do not use a metal scraper or wire brush to clean the aluminum cylinder head or pistons. If necessary, use a hard wooden or plastic scraper. Also available are abrasive discs to be used in conjunction with an electric drill. Be sure to use the correct disc for the type of metal being cleaned.

Evaluate cylinder head as shown in **116 Cylinder Head and Valvetrain**.

NOTE —
If the cylinder head has been machined, a special 0.3 mm (0.011 in.) thicker gasket should be installed. The thicker gasket is available from an authorized BMW dealer. Cylinder head and valve specifications are covered in **116 Cylinder Head and Valvetrain**.

Lubricate camshafts, camshaft carriers, bearing caps, hydraulic lifters, friction washers, splined shafts and spline hubs with assembly lubricant before installation.

The procedure has been organized as separate operations. Please be advised that these individual jobs must be accomplished in the order in which they appear.

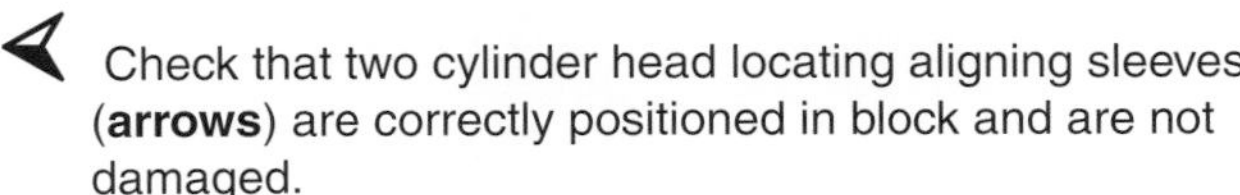

- **Cylinder head assembly, installing**
- **Camshafts and valvetrain, installing**
- **VANOS adjustment unit, installing**
- **Cylinder head cover, manifolds, cooling system, installing**

Cylinder head assembly, installing

Check that two cylinder head locating aligning sleeves (**arrows**) are correctly positioned in block and are not damaged.

– Apply permanently elastic sealing compound 3 Bond® 1209 to joints with timing belt cover.

– Place new cylinder head gasket on cylinder block.

NOTE —
The word OBEN, printed on the gasket, should face up. The cylinder head gasket will fit correctly in only one orientation.

– Set cylinder head in position, guiding primary chain through cylinder head opening.

> ***CAUTION —***
> *Make sure the crankshaft, which had been rotated approximately 30° opposite the direction of engine rotation from TDC, is still in that position before lowering the cylinder head into position. All pistons must be out of TDC position to prevent valve/piston interference when the camshafts are installed.*

– Lightly lubricate new cylinder head bolts. Install bolts and washers finger tight. Install cylinder head-to-lower timing chain cover bolts finger tight.

NOTE —
- *Cylinder head bolts should not be reused. They are stretch-type bolts and must always be replaced whenever loosened.*
- *Check that all washers for the head bolts are in place before installing the bolts. Some of the washers may be staked to the cylinder head.*

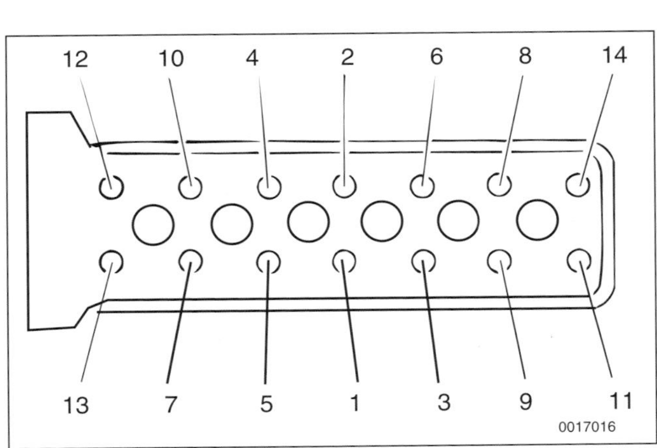

Tighten cylinder head bolts in correct sequence (1-14).

> ***CAUTION —***
> *The bolts should be tightened in three stages as listed below. The final stages require the use of a BMW special tool 11 2 110 or a suitable protractor to tighten the bolts to a specified torque angle.*

– Secure cylinder head bolts by torquing an additional 90° each for Stage 2 and 3.

Tightening torques
- Cylinder head to engine block (Torx E12 M10 bolts)
  - Stage 1 . . . . 40 Nm (30 ft-lb)
  - Stage 2 . . . . +90°
  - Stage 3 . . . . +90°

◀ Install intake camshaft position sensor (**arrow**).

◀ Install lower secondary chain guide. Tighten Torx bolts (**arrows**) to specifications. The bolt on the intake camshaft side is long and extends into the engine block.

Tightening torque

- Secondary chain guide to cylinder head . . . . 10 Nm (89 in-lb)

◀ Install and tighten cylinder head-to-lower timing chain cover bolts (**arrows**). (Photo shows camshafts in place)

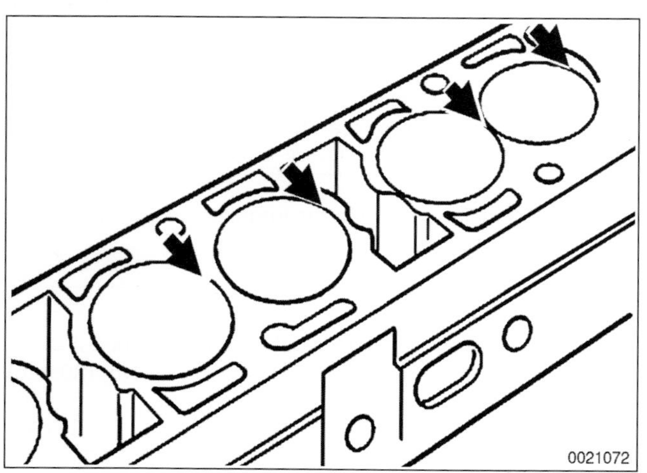

Camshafts and valvetrain, installing

CAUTION —

A minimum waiting time is required for the hydraulic lifters to "bleed down" after installing the camshafts into the cylinder head, but before synchronizing the crankshaft and valve train timing. When the camshafts are removed, the hydraulic lifters can expand. This expansion can cause increased valve lift when the camshafts are bolted down, possibly resulting in piston interference.

◀ Before installing camshaft carriers, examine bearing points (**arrows**) on hydraulic lifter bores for signs of wear.

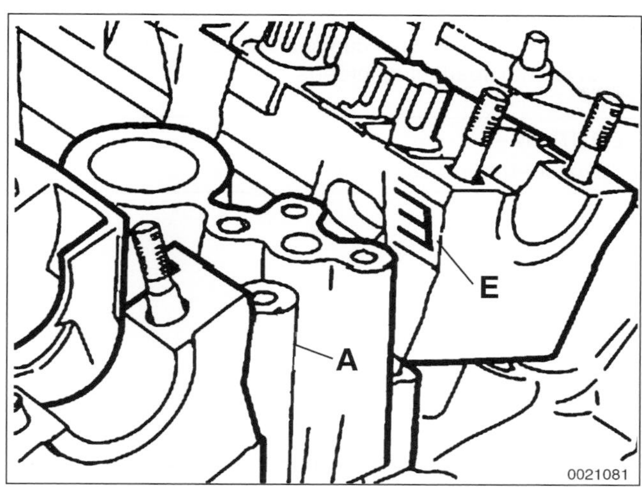

◀ Install camshaft carriers with hydraulic lifters into cylinder head. Note marks on carriers: (**E)** for intake side and (**A**) for exhaust side.

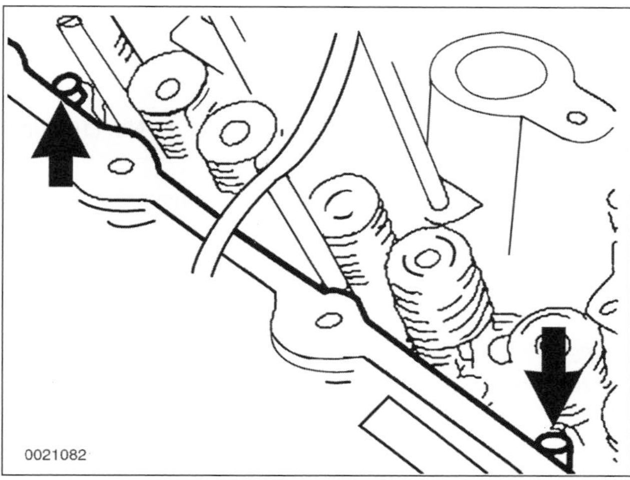

◀ Center camshaft carrier on pins (**arrows**) at bearing positions 2 and 7.

- Lift timing chain and place exhaust camshaft onto exhaust camshaft carrier. Place intake camshaft on intake camshaft carrier.

◀ Rotate camshafts so that intake and exhaust lobes for cylinder 1 face each other (**arrows**).

> ***CAUTION —***
> *Be sure that crankshaft is still positioned at least 30° back from TDC.*

- Place bearing caps on cams, but do not install retaining nuts.

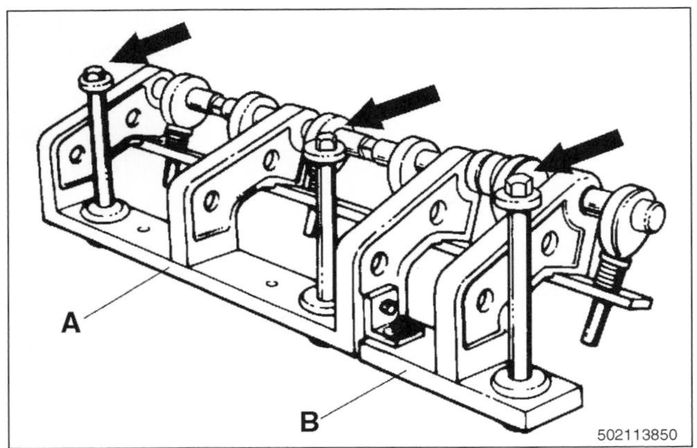

Fit BMW special tools 11 3 260 (**A**) and 11 3 270 (**B**) to cylinder head over intake camshaft and screw long bolts (**arrows**) into spark plug threads.

> ***CAUTION —***
> *Do not overtighten bolts into spark plug holes.*

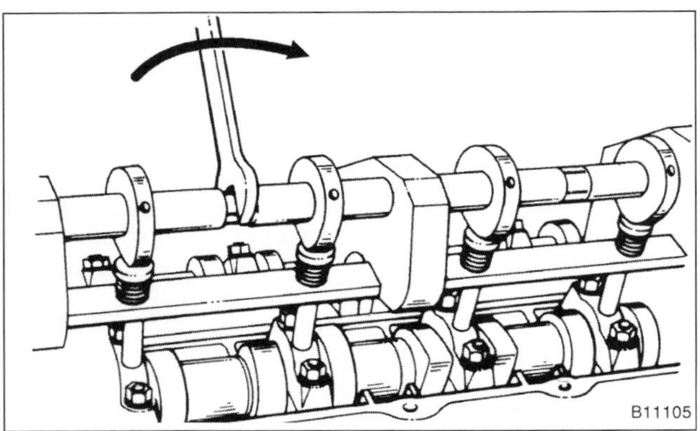

Turn eccentric shaft of special tool to pretension bearing caps. Install and torque nuts on intake camshaft bearing caps.

Tightening torque

- Camshaft bearing cap to cylinder head (M7) . . . . 14 Nm (10 ft-lb)

- Release tension on eccentric shaft and remove BMW special tool 11 3 260/270.

- Repeat procedure for exhaust camshaft.

NOTE —
Before the next step, observe waiting time for lifter bleed down before continuing with camshaft installation.

Crankshaft / valve timing waiting times

- 68°F (20°C) and higher. . . . . 5 minutes
- 50 - 68°F (10 - 20°C) . . . . 14 minutes
- 32 - 50°F (0 - 10°C) . . . . 30 minutes

Secure camshafts in TDC position using BMW special tools 11 3 240 and 11 3 244.

11 3 240
11 3 244
0021915

◀ If necessary, turn camshaft so that special tools are squarely seated on cylinder head.

◀ Lift timing chain and hold under tension.

◀ While maintaining tension on timing chain, rotate crankshaft from 30° before TDC in direction of rotation up to cylinder 1 TDC position (**0|T** on front pulley lined up with pointer on lower timing chain cover).

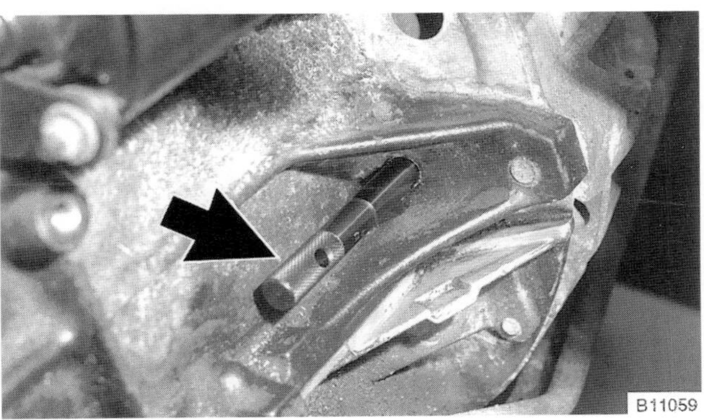

◀ Secure crankshaft in TDC position with BMW special tool 11 2 300 (**arrow**).

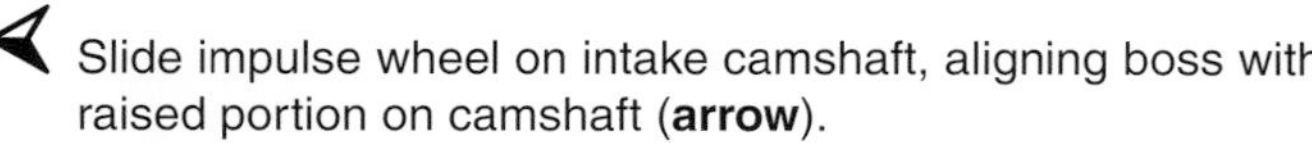

Slide impulse wheel on intake camshaft, aligning boss with raised portion on camshaft (**arrow**).

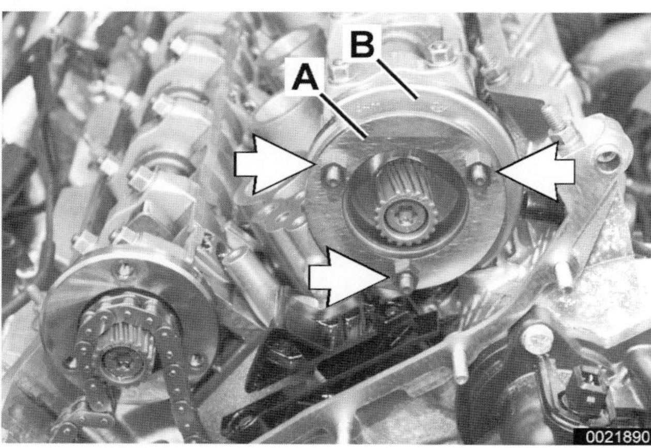

Fit thrust spacer to intake camshaft and tighten down with threaded locating studs (place longer threaded portion of studs into camshaft).

Tightening torque
- Impulse wheel studs to intake camshaft (M7) . . . . 20 Nm (15 ft-lb)

Fit top sprocket to primary timing chain and install on exhaust camshaft so that pointer on sprocket (**arrow**) lines up with cylinder head sealing surface.

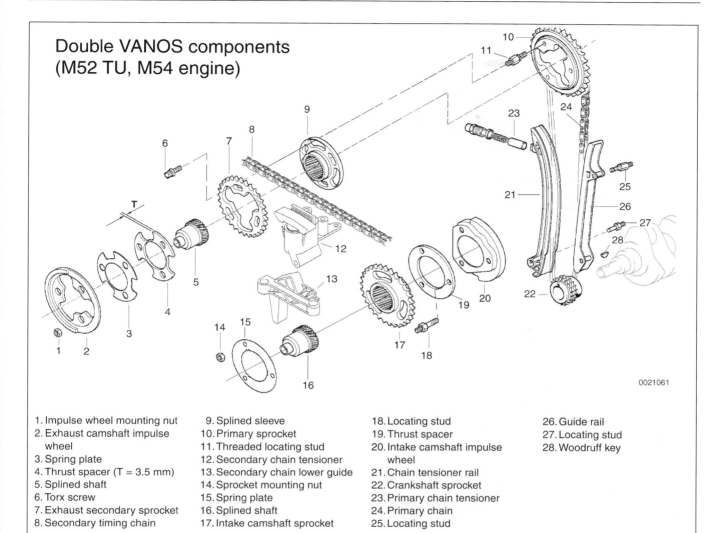

Double VANOS components (M52 TU, M54 engine)

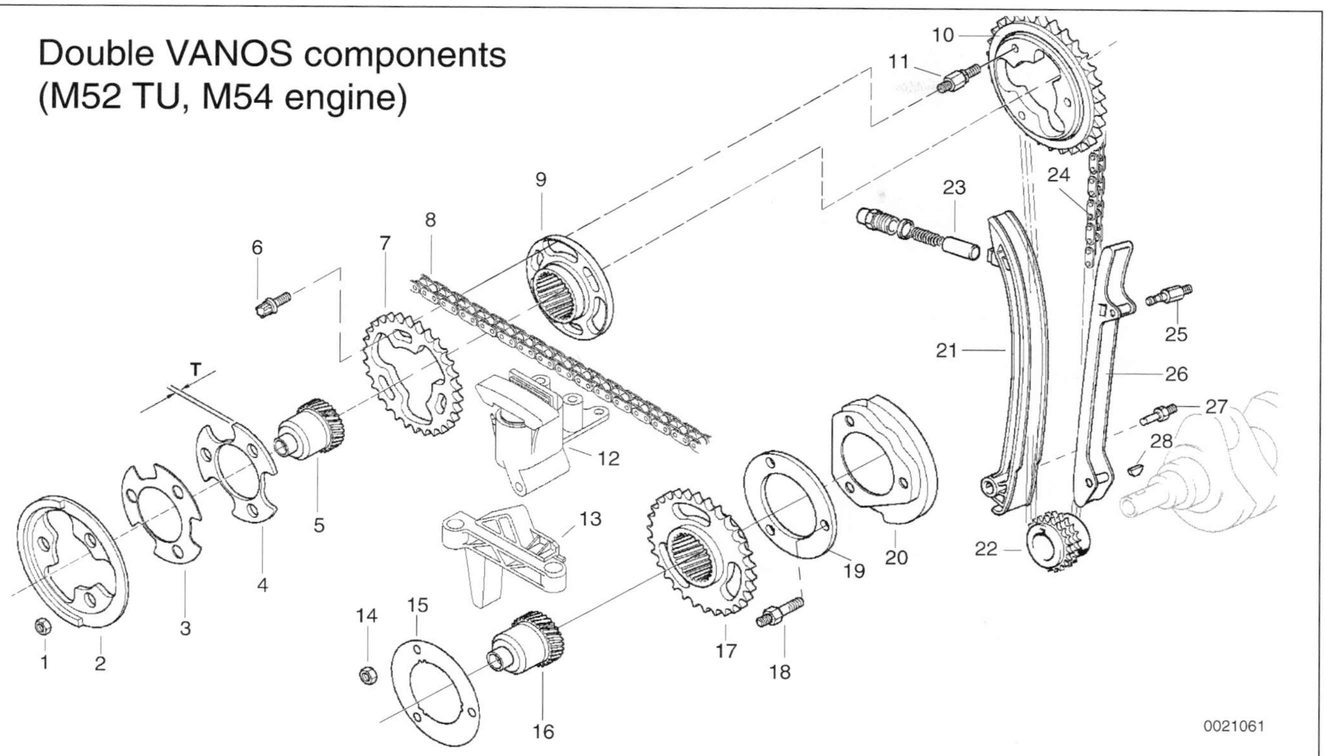

0021061

1. Impulse wheel mounting nut
2. Exhaust camshaft impulse wheel
3. Spring plate
4. Thrust spacer (T = 3.5 mm)
5. Splined shaft
6. Torx screw
7. Exhaust secondary sprocket
8. Secondary timing chain
9. Splined sleeve
10. Primary sprocket
11. Threaded locating stud
12. Secondary chain tensioner
13. Secondary chain lower guide
14. Sprocket mounting nut
15. Spring plate
16. Splined shaft
17. Intake camshaft sprocket
18. Locating stud
19. Thrust spacer
20. Intake camshaft impulse wheel
21. Chain tensioner rail
22. Crankshaft sprocket
23. Primary chain tensioner
24. Primary chain
25. Locating stud
26. Guide rail
27. Locating stud
28. Woodruff key

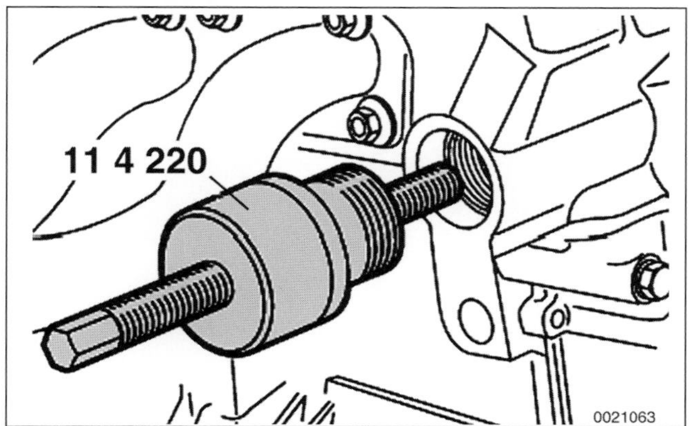

Insert BMW special tool 11 4 220 into timing chain tensioning piston bore and bring adjustment screw into contact with tensioning rail, but do not pretension timing chain.

NOTE —

BMW special tool 11 4 220 is a dummy primary chain tensioner and simulates the function of the tensioner.

– Recheck that arrow on top primary sprocket is aligned with upper edge of cylinder head. Reposition sprocket if necessary.

0021885

Insert and tighten down threaded locating studs (**arrows**) in end of exhaust camshaft.

Tightening torques

- Exhaust camshaft locating stud . . . . 20 Nm (15 ft-lb)

0021884

Install secondary chain tensioner on cylinder head (**arrows**). Keep tensioner compressed using BMW special tool 11 3 292 or suitable pin.

0021918

Fit exhaust camshaft splined sleeve. Confirm that gap in sleeve splines aligns with corresponding gap in camshaft splines (**arrows**).

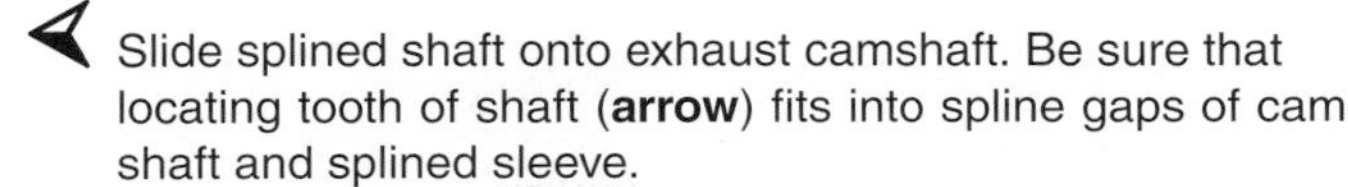

Slide splined shaft onto exhaust camshaft. Be sure that locating tooth of shaft (**arrow**) fits into spline gaps of camshaft and splined sleeve.

- Slide splined shaft in further until three small slots on splined sleeve are centered on three threaded holes in primary chain sprocket.

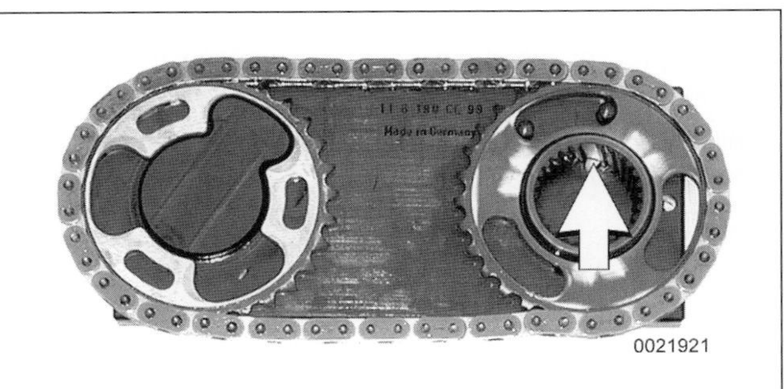

Place intake and exhaust sprockets in BMW special tool 11 6 180. Position spline gap on intake sprocket (**arrow**) as shown and place secondary chain on sprockets.

Remove chain and sprockets from tool and slide sprockets on camshafts. Confirm that gap in intake sprocket splines lines up with corresponding gap in camshaft splines (**arrow**).

> ***CAUTION —***
> *Do not alter position of sprockets with respect to chain when removing from special tool 11 6 180.*

Slide splined shaft onto intake camshaft until approx. 1 mm (0.04 in.) of splines (**arrows**) are visible. Confirm that locating tooth of shaft fits into spline gaps on camshaft and sprocket.

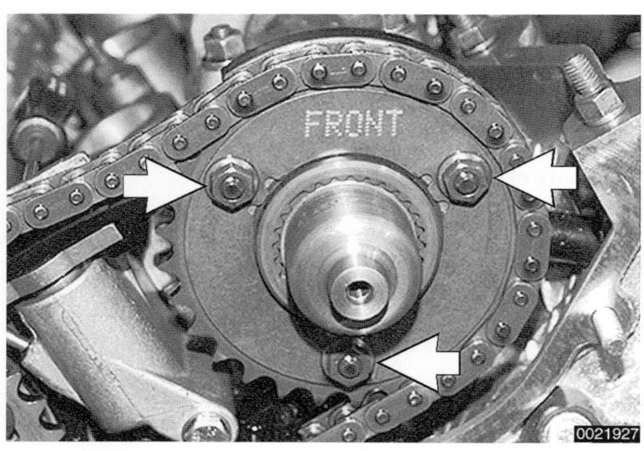

Install intake camshaft spring plate so that **FRONT** mark is visible. Install mounting nuts (**arrows**) finger tight.

Insert sprocket mounting bolts (**arrows**) on exhaust side camshaft assembly.

- Initially tighten to approx. 5 Nm (44 in-lb) and then back off by half a turn.

Fit thrust spacer (**A**) on exhaust camshaft.

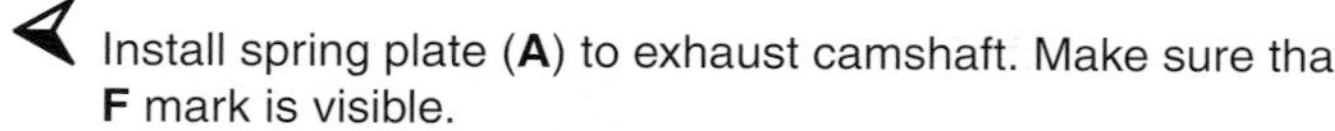

Install spring plate (**A**) to exhaust camshaft. Make sure that **F** mark is visible.

NOTE —

*If **F** mark is no longer visible, install spring plate so that convex side points forward (toward front of car).*

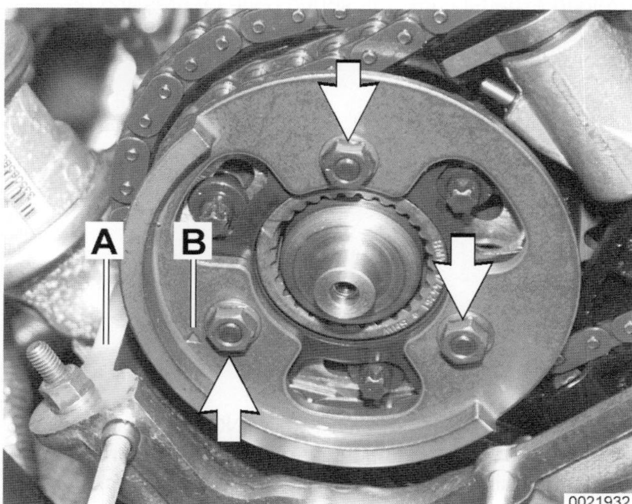

Install exhaust camshaft impulse wheel, aligning pointer (**B**) with top edge of cylinder head (**A**). Install mounting nuts (**arrows**) finger tight.

Pull out exhaust camshaft splined shaft to stop.

– Press down on secondary chain tensioner and remove tensioner lock-down tool.

Preload primary chain:

- Tighten adjusting screw on BMW special tool 11 4 220 to specified torque.

Tightening torque

- Primary chain tensioner preload. . . . . . . .0.7 Nm (6 in-lb)

Preload exhaust camshaft spring plate by pressing on impulse wheel while tightening mounting nuts (**arrows**) finger tight.

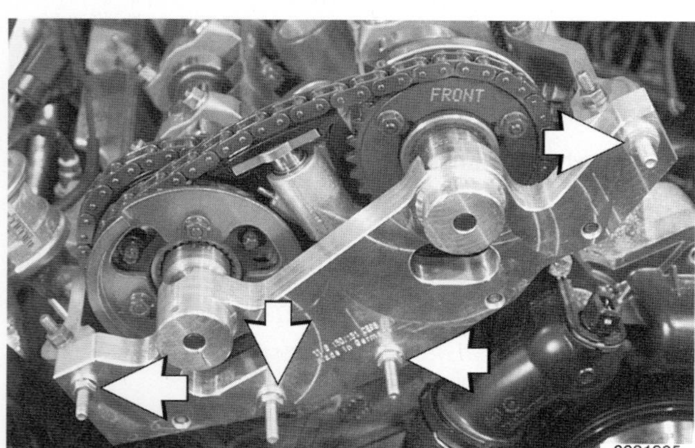

Install BMW special tool 11 6 150 (VANOS setup bracket) to front of cylinder head timing case. Install nuts (**arrows**) finger tight, then tighten down uniformly until special tool is in full contact with cylinder head.

> ***CAUTION —***
> *Make sure all gasket material is removed from face of cylinder head. Clean sealing face and keep free of oil. If any foreign material is present on the sealing surface, the camshaft timing will be incorrect.*

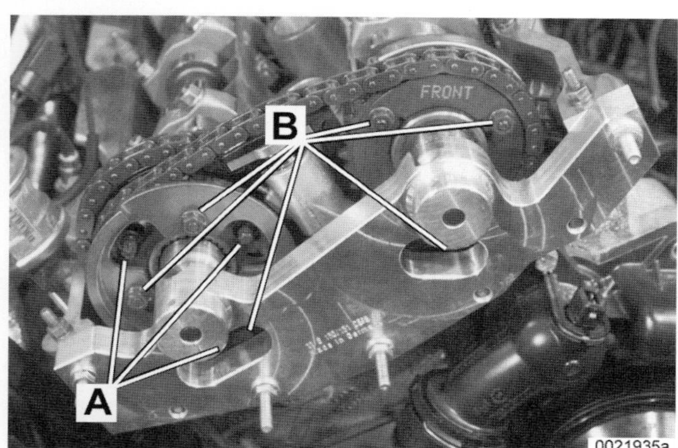

Secure camshaft sprockets and impulse wheels:

- Tighten mounting screws (**A**) on exhaust camshaft impulse wheel to approx. 5 Nm (44 in-lb).
- Tighten mounting nuts (**B**) on exhaust and intake sprocket assemblies to approx. 5 Nm (44 in-lb).
- Torque down mounting screws (**A**) and nuts (**B**) to final specifications.

Tightening torques
- Sprocket assembly to camshaft initial torque . . . . 5 Nm (44 in-lb)
- Sprocket assembly wheel to camshaft
  M7 Torx screws (**A**). . . . . 20 Nm (15 ft-lb)
  M6 mounting nut (**B**). . . . . 10 Nm (8 ft-lb)

– Remove flywheel locking tool from transmission bellhousing so that crankshaft is no longer secured.

– Remove camshaft locking tools from cylinder head.

Turn engine over twice in direction of rotation until cylinder 1 intake and exhaust camshaft lobes (**arrows**) face each other.

– Secure crankshaft in TDC position with BMW special tool 11 2 300.

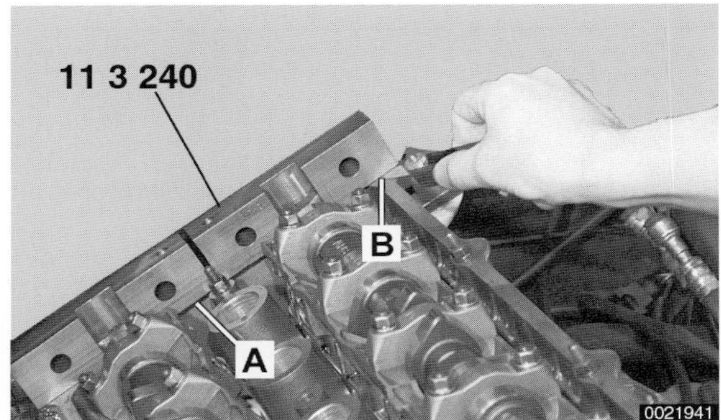

Place BMW special tool 11 3 240 over camshafts and measure clearances.

NOTE —
- *If the exhaust side of the tool (**A**) is not flush with the head, camshaft timing is incorrect. Reset camshaft timing as described in* **117 Camshaft Timing Chain**.
- *Due to flexible sprocket design, VANOS unit tolerances and play in the VANOS splines, when the camshaft timing is set correctly, the intake side of special tool 11 3 240 (**B**) may be up to 1 mm (0.04 in) above the surface of the cylinder head. This is normal. Reassemble engine. Otherwise, reset camshaft timing as described in* **117 Camshaft Timing Chain.**

– Remove BMW special tool 11 6 150 from front of cylinder head.

VANOS control unit, installing

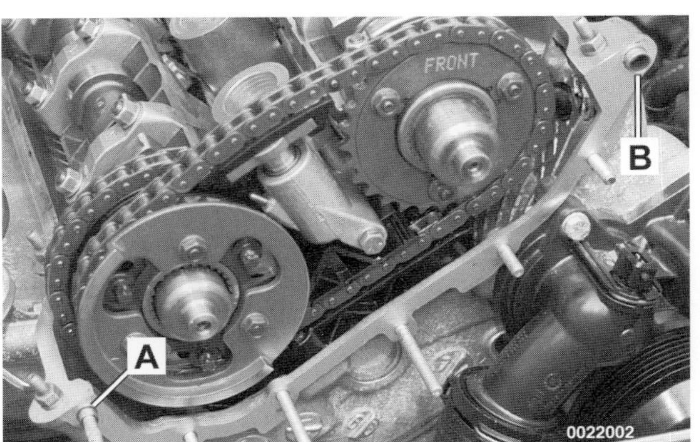

Clean contact edges of cylinder head face and VANOS unit and apply a thin coat of sealing compound 3-Bond®1209 or equivalent to surfaces.

CAUTION —
- *Make sure all gasket material is removed from face of cylinder head. Clean sealing face and keep free of oil. If any foreign material is present on the sealing surface, the camshaft timing will be incorrect.*
- *Check locating dowel (**A**) and dowel sleeve (**B**) at top of cylinder head for damage or incorrect installation.*

– Replace steel gasket.

– Install VANOS unit to front of cylinder head.

NOTE —
If Double VANOS control unit is being replaced, be sure to check and adjust camshaft timing as described in **117 Camshaft Timing Chain**.

– Reinstall engine support hook.

Tightening torque

- VANOS unit to cylinder head
  M6 nut. . . . . 10 Nm (89 in-lb)
  M7 nut. . . . . 14 Nm (10 in-lb)

– Reconnect electrical harness connectors to camshaft position sensors and VANOS solenoid valves.

◀ Insert and tighten down VANOS hydraulic piston set screws (**arrows**) in splined shafts on intake and exhaust camshafts.

> ***CAUTION —***
> *Set screws have left hand thread. Tighten counterclockwise.*

Tightening torque

- Hydraulic piston to splined shaft
  M6 set screw. . . . . 10 Nm (89 in-lb)

◀ Replace sealing caps inside VANOS unit with BMW special tool 11 6 170, or short flat nosed pliers.

◀ Insert and secure VANOS sealing plugs (**arrows**) with new sealing O-rings.

Tightening torque

- Sealing plug to VANOS unit . . . . 50 Nm (37 ft-lb)

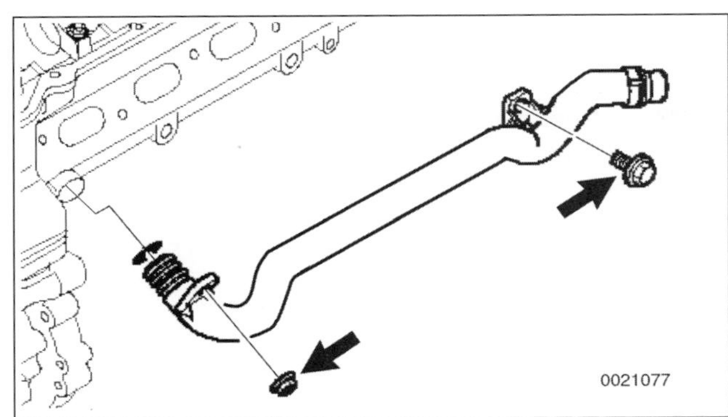

◄ Install coolant pipe fasteners at base of cylinder head and tighten fasteners (**arrows**).

NOTE —
Use new sealing O-ring on coolant pipe.

– Install VANOS oil line banjo bolt with new seals. Attach oil line to VANOS unit.

Tightening torque
- Oil line to VANOS unit (banjo bolt) . . . . . 32 Nm (24 ft-lb)

– Remove BMW special tool 11 4 220 and reinstall chain tensioner cylinder.

Tightening torque
- Primary chain tensioner cylinder to cylinder head . . . . 70 Nm (52 ft-lb)

– Remove flywheel locking tool from transmission bellhousing. Replace special tool bore sealing plug.

– Remove camshaft locking tools from cylinder head.

Cylinder head cover, manifolds, cooling system, installing

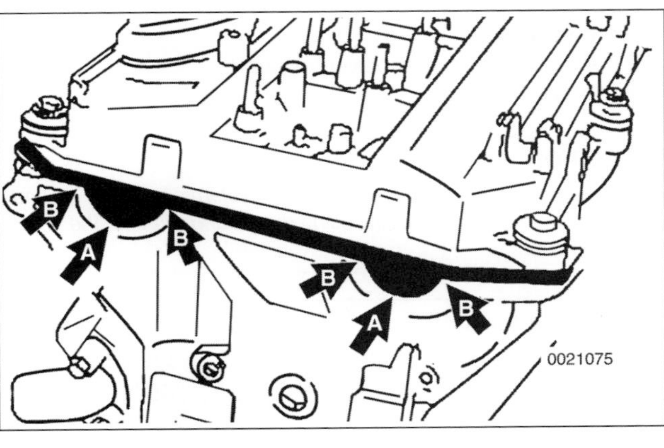

◄ Install intake camshaft cover and cylinder head cover.

- Check for correct seating of half-moon seals (**A**) in back of cylinder head cover.
- Use a small amount of 3-Bond®1209 or equivalent sealant at corners (**B**) of half-moon cutouts.
- Seat gasket and seal corners in front of cylinder head at VANOS unit.

Tightening torque
- Cylinder head cover to cylinder head (M6) . . . . 10 Nm (89 in-lb)

– Install exhaust manifolds using new gaskets and nuts. Coat manifold studs with copper paste prior to installing nuts.

Tightening torque
- Exhaust manifold to cylinder head (M7) . . . . 20 Nm (15 ft-lb)

– Install electrical harness connectors for oil pressure sender and coolant temperature sensor before installing intake manifold.

Intake manifold brackets and mounts

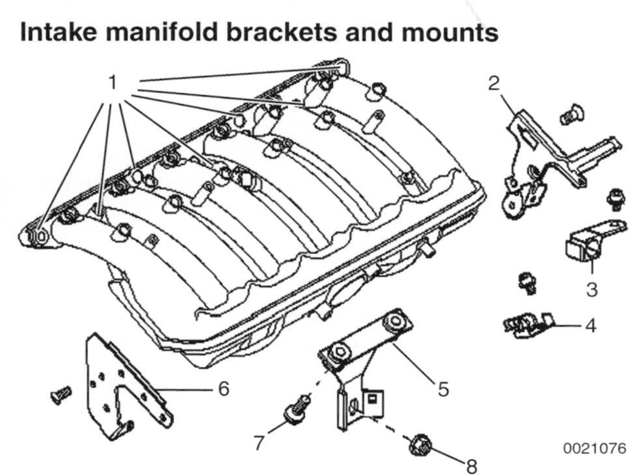

1. Manifold mounting nuts -tighten to 15 Nm (11 ft-lb)
2. Fuel pipe bracket
3. Fuel pipe bracket
4. Vacuum pump bracket
5. Manifold mounting bracket
6. Tank venting valve bracket
7. Mounting bracket to manifold bolt (M6) -tighten to 10 Nm (7 ft-lb)
8. Mounting bracket to cylinder block nut (M10) -tighten to 47 Nm (33 ft-lb)

Intake manifold Installation is reverse of removal. See **110 Engine Removal and Installation**.

- Use new fuel injector seals.
- Carefully check intake manifold gasket and replace if necessary.
- Inspect O-ring seal between mass air flow sensor and air filter housing. To facilitate reassembly, coat seal with acid-free grease.

CAUTION —

When reattaching throttle assembly harness connector, connector is fully tightened when arrows on connector and plug line up.

Tightening torques

- Intake manifold to cylinder head
  M7 . . . . 15 Nm (11 ft-lb)
  M8 . . . . 22 Nm (16 ft-lb)
- Mounting bracket to cylinder block (M10) . . . . 47 Nm (33 ft-lb)
- Mounting bracket to intake manifold (M6) . . . . 10 Nm (7 ft-lb)

– Installation of remaining parts is reverse of removal, noting the following:

- Refill cooling system as described in **170 Radiator and Cooling System**.
- Change engine oil and filter as described in **020 Maintenance**.
- If necessary, adjust accelerator cable.
- Reconnect battery.

CAUTION —

To prevent damaging engine electronic systems, install all ground wires previously removed, including the ground wires for the ignition coils.

Tightening torques

- Coolant drain plug to cylinder block . . . . 25 Nm (18 ft-lb)
- Radiator cooling fan to coolant pump . . . 40 Nm (30 ft-lb)
- Radiator drain screw to radiator . . . . . . .2.5 Nm (22 in-lb)
- Spark plug to cylinder head . . . . 25 Nm (18 ft-lb)

DIAGNOSTIC TESTING

Cylinder compression, checking

A compression gauge is needed to make a compression test. For accurate test, the battery and starter must be capable of cranking the engine at least 300 rpm, and the engine should be at normal operating temperature.

NOTE —
Performing a compression test may cause a fault to set in the ECM and may illuminate the engine service light. The light can only be turned out using either BMW special service scan tools or an equivalent aftermarket scan tool. Disconnecting the battery will not erase the fault memory nor turn out the light.

◄ Disable ignition system by removing DME main relay (**arrow**) from the electronics box (E-box) in left rear of engine compartment

> ***WARNING —***
> - *The ignition system produces high voltages that can be fatal. Avoid contact with exposed terminals and use extreme caution when working on a car with the ignition switched on or the engine running.*
> - *Do not touch or disconnect ignition components while the engine is running or being cranked by the starter.*

> ***CAUTION —***
> *Failure to remove the DME main relay or attempting to disable the ignition system by other methods may result in damage to the engine control module (ECM).*

◄ Remove housing for interior ventilation microfilter.

- Remove upper cover and microfilter.
- Open wiring harness loom cover (**A**) and remove wires.
- Unfasten screws (**B**) and remove lower microfilter housing.

– Remove oil filler cap.

– Remove engine cover over ignition coils. Replace oil filler cap.

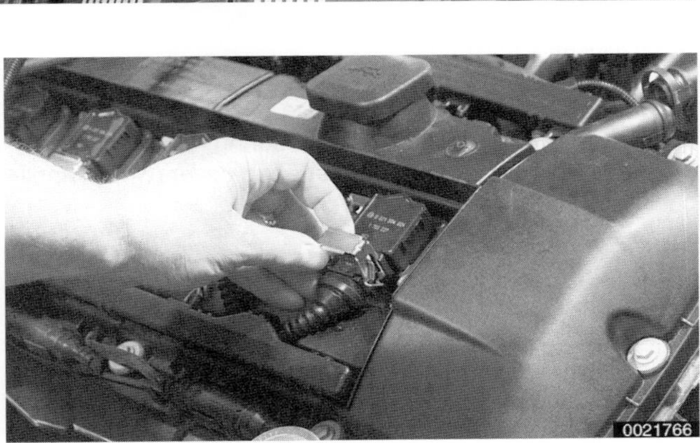

◄ Remove ignition coils.

- Pull up on spring clips to disconnect ignition coil harness connectors.
- Remove coil mounting nuts and grounding straps.
- Remove coils.
- Remove spark plugs.

NOTE —

On 2003 and later cars, a new style ignition coil (Bremi manufacture) was used. These thinner 'rod' type coils do not use hold down nuts. To remove rod-type Bremi coil, swivel harness connector lock up, disconnect connector, and pull coil out.

0021022

- Install compression gauge in first cylinder's spark plug hole, tight enough to form a good seal.

- With parking brake set, transmission in PARK or NEUTRAL, and accelerator pedal pressed to floor, crank engine with starter. Record highest value indicated by gauge.

NOTE —

- *The compression gauge reading should increase with each compression stroke and reach near its maximum reading in about 4-6 strokes.*
- *All cylinders should reach maximum compression in the same number of strokes. If a cylinder needs significantly more strokes to reach maximum compression, there is a problem.*

- Release pressure at compression gauge valve, then remove gauge from spark plug hole. Repeat test for each cylinder and compare results with values given below.

Compression pressures

- Minimum
  M52 TU, M54, M56 . . . . 10 - 11 bar (142 - 156 psi)
  S54 . . . . 11 - 12 bar (160 - 174 psi)
- Maximum difference
  between cylinders . . . . 0.5 bar (7 psi)

- Compression readings may be interpreted as follows:
  - Low compression indicates a poorly sealed combustion chamber.
  - Relatively even pressures that are below specification normally indicate worn piston rings and/or cylinder walls.
  - Erratic values tend to indicate valve leakage.
  - Dramatic differences between cylinders are often the sign of a failed head gasket, burned valve, or broken piston ring.

- Reinstall spark plugs and ignition coils.

NOTE —

Used spark plugs should be reinstalled in the same cylinder from which they were removed.

- Remainder of installation is reverse of removal. Be sure to reinstall all wires disconnected during test, especially ground wires at coils and cylinder head cover (where applicable).

Tightening torque

- Spark plug to cylinder head . . . . 25 Nm (18 ft-lb)

Wet compression test

To further help analyze the source of poor compression, a wet compression test is the next step:

- Repeat compression test, this time with about a teaspoon of oil squirted into each cylinder. (The oil will temporarily help seal between piston rings and cylinder wall, practically eliminating leakage past rings for a short time.)

- If this test yields higher compression reading than "dry" compression test, there is probably leakage between piston rings and cylinder walls, due either to wear or to broken piston rings.

- Little or no change in compression reading indicates other leakage, probably from valves.

Cylinder leak-down test

The most conclusive diagnosis of low compression symptoms requires a cylinder leak-down test. Using a special tester and compressed air, each cylinder, in turn, is pressurized. The rate at which the air leaks out of the cylinder, as well as where the air leaks out, can accurately pinpoint the magnitude and location of the leakage.

Before attempting any repair that requires major engine disassembly, use a leak-down test to confirm low compression.

116 Cylinder Head and Valvetrain

Special Tools

Special tools

A BMW 00 1 490 . . . . Cylinder head jig
B BMW 00 3 580 . . . . Valve seat grinder set
C BMW 00 4 210 . . . . Valve guide reamer set (6, 7, 8 mm)
D BMW 11 1 200 . . . . Valve stem seal driver
E BMW special tool 11 1 480 . . . . Valve stem seal puller
F BMW special tool 11 1 960 . . . . Valve stem seal guide

GENERAL

This repair group covers cylinder head and valvetrain service and repair. Procedures described here require that the cylinder head first be removed as described in **113 Cylinder Head Removal and Installation**.

NOTE —

- *For timing chain and VANOS repair information, see* **117 Camshaft Timing Chain**.
- *If it is determined that the cylinder head will require significant reconditioning work, a remanufactured cylinder head may be a good alternative. Remanufactured cylinder heads are available from an authorized BMW dealer.*

The information given in this repair group is organized according to engine code. For engine application information, see **100 Engine–General**.

Special tools

BMW special tools are required for most cylinder head service described. Many of the tools are expensive and only available through an authorized BMW dealer. Be sure to read each procedure thoroughly before starting a job to determine which special tools and equipment will be necessary.

Most of the repairs to a cylinder head require precision machine work to specific tolerances. This type of work should be performed by an authorized BMW repair facility or an ASE certified machinist.

CYLINDER HEAD

The disassembled cylinder head should be inspected for warpage and cracks. Check the valve guides and valve seats for wear before machining a warped head. Always decarbonize and clean the head before inspecting it. A high-quality straight edge can be used to check for warpage.

Visually inspect the cylinder head for cracks. If a cracked cylinder head is suspected and no cracks are detected through the visual inspection, have the head further tested for cracks by an authorized BMW dealer or an ASE certified machinist. A cracked cylinder head must be replaced.

NOTE—
When disassembling and inspecting the cylinder head on an engine, be sure to check the camshaft carrier bearing surfaces for warpage.

A warped cylinder head can be machined provided no more than 0.3 mm (0.012 in.) of material is removed. If further machining is required, the head should be replaced. Removing more than this amount will reduce the size of the combustion chamber and adversely affect engine performance. A 0.3 mm thicker gasket is available from an authorized BMW parts department for machined heads.

Before machining the head to correct for warpage, measure the total height (**A**) (thickness of the cylinder head). Minimum height specifications are given in **Table a**.

NOTE—
S54 engine (M3) cylinder head resurfacing is not recommend by BMW.

Table a. Cylinder head height

New	Minimum height (dimension A)
M52 TU, M54, M56 engines 140.0 mm (5.512 in)	139.7 mm (5.500 in)
S54 engine 146.0 ± 0.05 mm (5.748 ± 0.002 in.)	Cylinder head must not be machined

Valves, leak test

To test the valves for leakage, the cylinder head must be disassembled with camshafts and camshaft carriers removed. Install the valve assemblies and the spark plugs in each cylinder. Place the cylinder head on a workbench with the combustion chamber facing upward. Fill each combustion chamber with a thin non-flammable liquid, such as a parts cleaning fluid. After fifteen minutes, check the level of the fluid. If the fluid level in any cylinder drops, that cylinder is not sealing properly.

Camshaft

Camshaft wear is usually caused by insufficient lubrication. Visually inspect camshaft lobes and journals for wear. Camshaft wear specifications are given in **Table b**.

Table b. Camshaft wear limits

M52 TU, M54, M56 engines	
Axial play	0.150-0.330 mm (0.0060-0.0130 in.)
Radial play (Plastigage)	0.020-0.054 mm (0.0008-0.0021 in.)
S54 engine	
Axial play	0.100-0.183 mm (0.0040-0.0072 in.)
Radial play (bearing 1)	0.034-0.066 mm (0.0013-0.026 in.)
Radial play (bearing 2-7)	0.027-0.053 mm (0.0011-0.0021 in.)

CAUTION —

If the camshaft is being replaced due to cam lobe wear, it is recommended that the corresponding lifters should also be replaced to avoid damaging the replacement camshaft.

Hydraulic lifters, checking and replacing

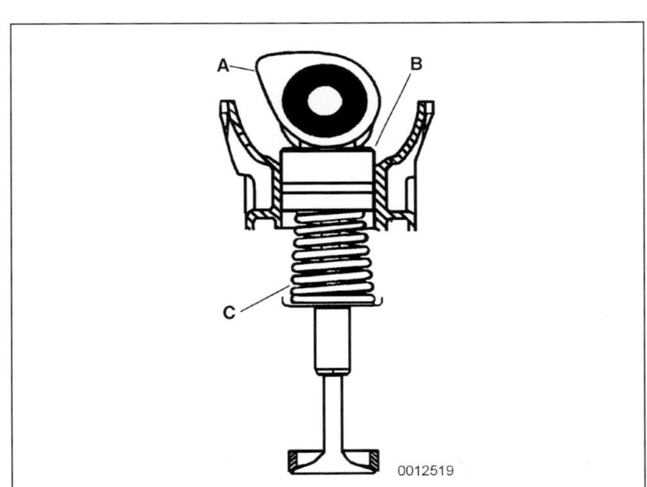

Except for S54 engines, all engines use self-adjusting hydraulic lifters to keep the valve clearances within a limited working range. (**A)** Section view of camshaft, (**B**) the hydraulic lifters are sealed units and require no maintenance, (**C**) valve with conical valve spring.

NOTE —

The S54 engines requires periodic valve adjustment, as described later in this repair group.

Under some circumstances, such as a cold start, the cam followers may become noisy. Hydraulic lifter noise is usually a high-pitched tapping or chattering noise. In most instances, this is considered normal as long as the noise goes away in a few minutes (maximum 20 minutes). If the noise does not go away, either the lifter is faulty or the oil pressure to the lifter is low. Hydraulic lifter replacement requires that the camshaft first be removed.

NOTE —

Before checking hydraulic lifters, make sure engine oil is fresh and at the proper level.

– Run engine until it reaches normal operating temperature.

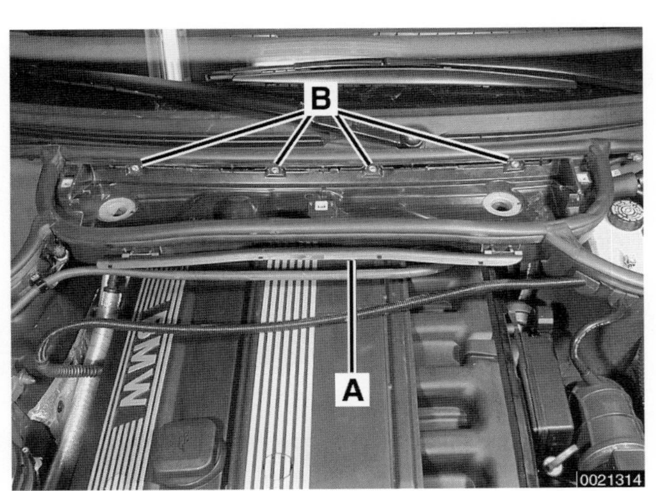

– Remove microfilter housing:

- Remove microfilter for interior ventilation.
- Open wiring harness loom (**A**), remove harness and lay aside.
- Unfasten screws (**B**) and take off lower microfilter housing.

– Remove engine cover.

0021795a

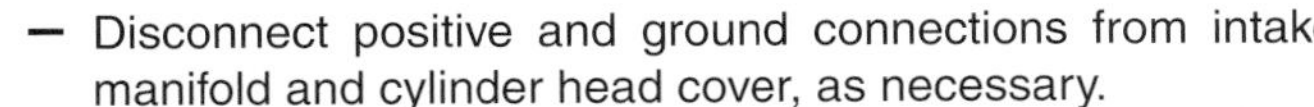

– Disconnect positive and ground connections from intake manifold and cylinder head cover, as necessary.

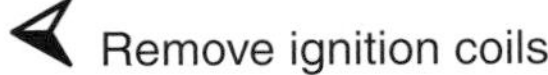

Remove ignition coils.

- Disconnect ignition coil harness connectors and lay harness aside.
- Remove coil grounding straps.
- Remove coils.
- Remove spark plugs.

NOTE —

On 2003 and later cars, a new style ignition coil (Bremi manufacture) was used. These thinner 'rod' type coils do not use hold down nuts. To remove the late style Bremi coil, swivel harness connector lock up, disconnect connector, and twist and pull coil straight up.

– Remove cylinder head cover mounting fasteners and remove cylinder head cover.

NOTE —

The cylinder head cover mounting bolt insulators and gaskets should be reinstalled in their original locations. Make note of their arrangement during removal.

B11119

Remove oil baffle cover from above intake camshaft.

0021730

Use a plastic or wooden stick to press down on top of lifter. If there is any noticeable clearance, the lifter is faulty and should be replaced.

NOTE —

When checking a hydraulic lifter, make sure the corresponding camshaft lobe is facing up so that there is no valve spring pressure on the follower.

– To replace a hydraulic lifter, remove appropriate camshaft. Refer to camshaft removal procedures given in **113 Cylinder Head Removal and Installation**.

– Once camshaft is removed, withdraw faulty lifter and replace with new one. Inspect lifter bores for wear and scoring.

– Camshaft, timing chain and cylinder head cover reassembly is reverse of disassembly.

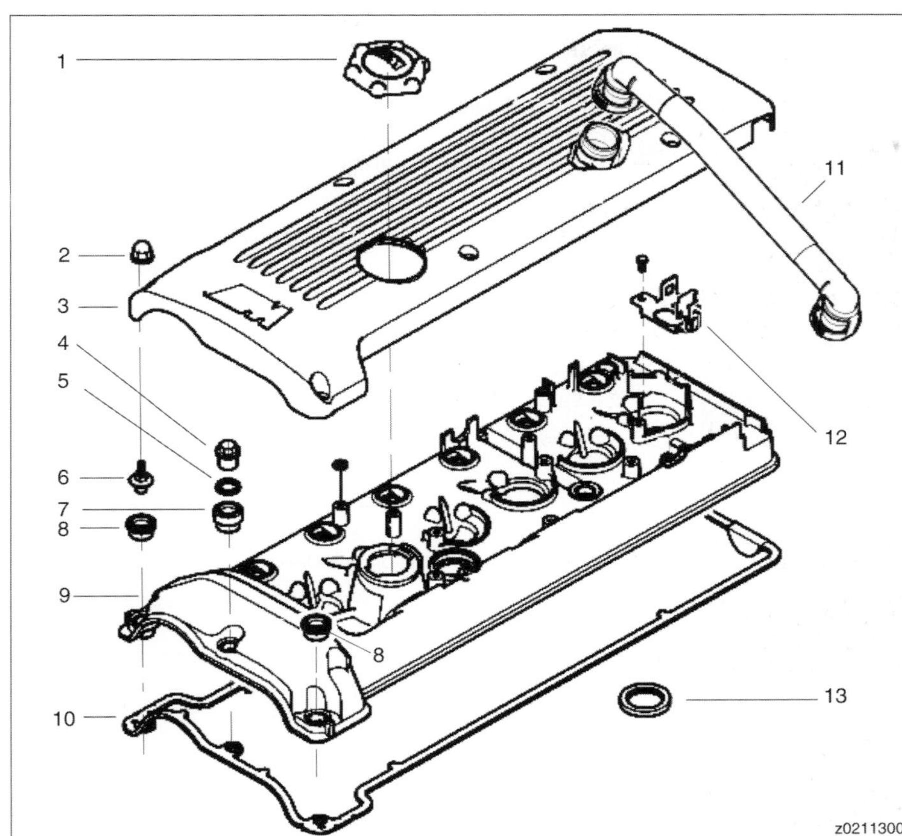

Cylinder head cover components (S54 engine)

1. **Oil filler cap**
2. **Cap nut (M6)**
3. **Cap nut (M6)**
4. **Top engine plastic cover**
5. **Washer**
6. **Shoulder stud**
7. **Rubber insulator**
   (note different size insulators)
8. **Rubber insulator**
   (note different size insulators)
9. **Cylinder head cover**
10. **Cylinder head cover gasket**
11. **Engine vent hose**
12. **Oxygen sensor connector bracket**
13. **Spark plug well seal**

Cylinder head cover, removing and installing (S54 engine)

> ***WARNING —***
> *To avoid personal injury, be sure the engine is cold before starting the procedure.*

– Disconnect negative (–) battery cable.

> ***CAUTION —***
> *Prior to disconnecting the battery, read the battery disconnection cautions given in* **001 General Warnings and Cautions**.

Remove housing for interior ventilation microfilter.

- Unclip upper cover (**arrows**), lift up and remove cover and microfilter.

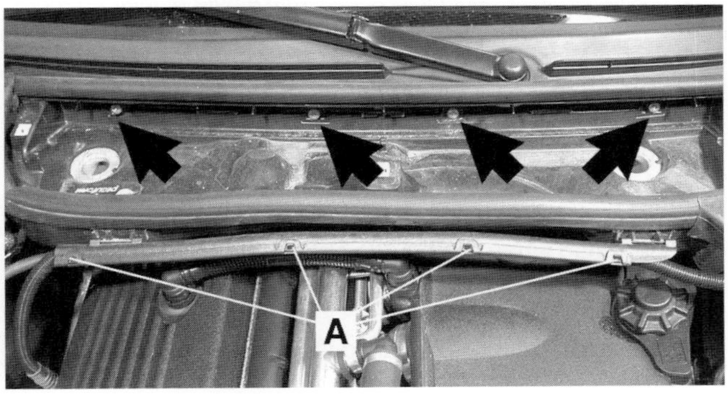

Open wiring harness loom cover (**A**) and lift out wiring. Unfasten screws (**arrows**) and lift out lower microfilter housing.

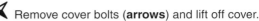

- Press quick release locks and disconnect crankcase vent hose from intake manifold and cylinder head cover.
- Remove oil filler cap.

Remove cover bolts (**arrows**) and lift off cover.

NOTE —

Remove oil filler cap to allow removal of plastic cover. Be sure to replace it on the oil filler immediately to prevent debris from entering the engine.

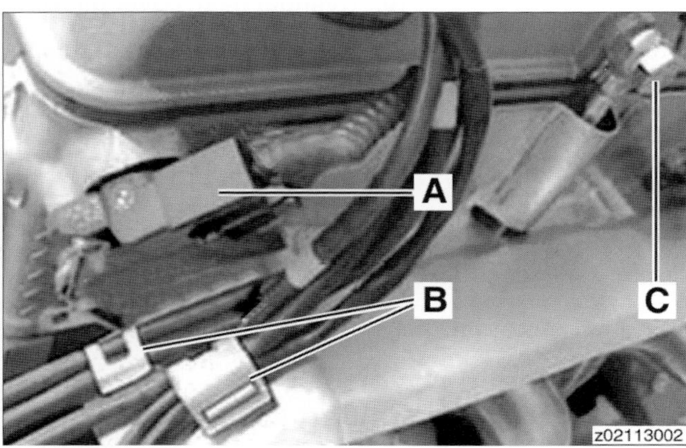

Working at right rear of cylinder head:

- Disconnect exhaust camshaft position sensor electrical harness connector (**A**).
- Release oxygen sensor wiring harnesses from exhaust heat shield brackets (**B**).
- Remove vent line banjo bolt (**C**).

CAUTION —

Make sure that sealing ring between banjo bolt and cylinder head does not drop down side of engine.

- Disconnect ignition coils grounding strap at right side of cylinder head.

Unclip and separate oxygen sensor harness connectors (**arrows**) at top of cylinder head cover.

- Disconnect and remove ignition coils. See **120 Ignition System**.
- Lay ignition and oxygen sensor harnesses to one side.
- Remove cylinder head cover mounting fasteners and remove cylinder head cover.

NOTE —

In order to reinstall cylinder head cover mounting bolt insulators and gaskets in their original locations, make note of their arrangement during removal.

- Remove old gasket material from sealing faces.
- Use a small amount of 3-Bond®1209 adhesive or equivalent on left and right sides at transition between cylinder head and VANOS adjustment unit. Apply same sealer are rear of cylinder head where half moon shapes transition to cylinder head gasket surface.
- Replace spark plug well sealing O-rings.

– Lay new cylinder head cover gasket on cylinder head. Note that gasket is secured with molded rubber guide pins on cylinder head and on VANOS adjustment unit.

> ***CAUTION —***
> - *The rubber guide pins may buckle very slightly during installation. Make sure that guide pins mate exactly with the bore holes.*
> - *Make sure gasket is seated correctly on front and rear of cylinder head.*

– Install cover and sealing insulators. Install nuts hand tight. Align cover and then tighten nuts diagonally, working from inside to outside.

– Install vent line using new sealing washers. Tighten banjo bolt.

Tightening torque
- Cylinder head cover vent line to cylinder head cover (banjo bolt) . . . . 25 Nm (18 ft-lb)

Cylinder head cover, removing and installing (M52 TU, M54, M56 engines)

> ***WARNING —***
> *To avoid personal injury, be sure the engine is cold before starting the procedure.*

NOTE —
The illustrations in this procedure depict an M52 TU (6-cylinder) engine. Models with M54 and M56 engines are similar.

– Disconnect negative (–) battery cable.

> ***CAUTION —***
> *Prior to disconnecting the battery, read the battery disconnection cautions given in* **001 General Warnings and Cautions**.

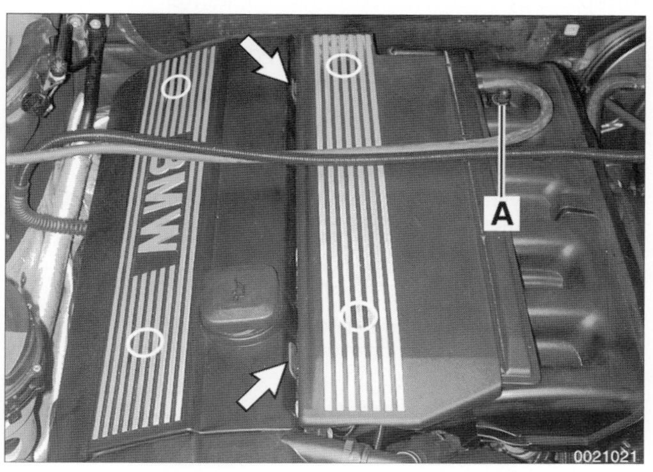

 Working at top of engine:
- Remove protective cover from positive (+) jumper post. Loosen and remove battery lead mounting nut (**A**). Remove lead and push down through intake manifold.
- Remove trim covers (**white circles**) from engine plastic covers. Remove cover hold down fasteners and lift off covers.
- Make sure rubber insulators (**arrows**) on either side of large cover do not fall off during cover removal.

NOTE —
Remove oil filler cap to allow removal of large plastic cover. Be sure to replace it on the oil filler immediately to prevent debris from entering the engine.

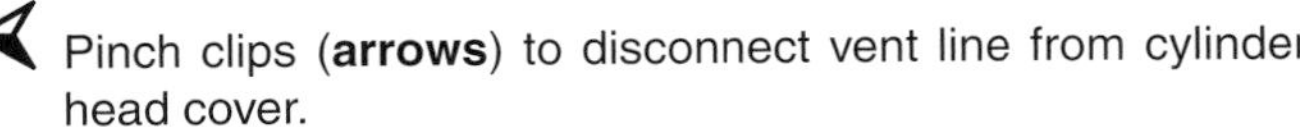

Pinch clips (**arrows**) to disconnect vent line from cylinder head cover.

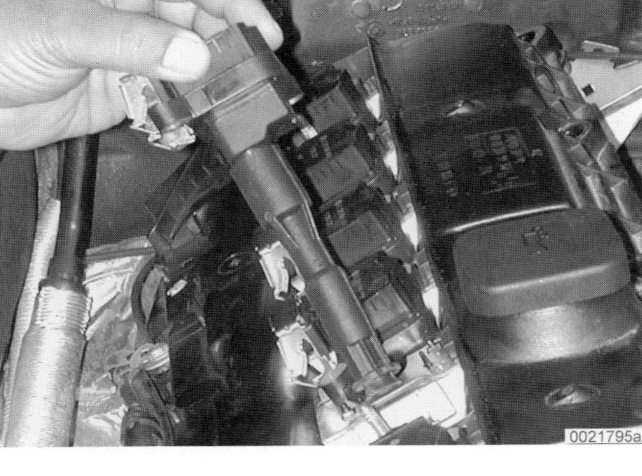

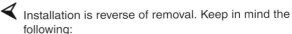

Remove ignition coils:

- Disconnect ignition coil harness connectors.
- Remove coil mounting fasteners.
- Remove coils.
- Remove ground straps.
- Set coil harness to side of engine compartment.

> ***CAUTION—***
> *Note location of all ground wires. Failure to reinstall grounds can result in permanent damage to engine control module or ignition system components.*

– Remove cylinder head cover mounting fasteners and remove cylinder head cover.

NOTE—
In order to reinstall cylinder head cover mounting bolt insulators and gaskets in their original locations, make note of their arrangement during removal.

Installation is reverse of removal. Keep in mind the following:

- Make sure sealing surfaces are clean and free of old gasket material.
- Replace cylinder head cover gasket, as well as rubber insulators and seals as necessary.
- Use a small amount of 3-Bond®1209 adhesive or equivalent at corners (**arrows**) of half-moon cut-outs at back of cylinder head.
- Seat gasket and seal corners in front of cylinder head at VANOS unit.
- Inspect cylinder head cover mounting screw assembly rubber seals. Replace if rubber is cracked or brittle.

Tightening torque
- Cylinder head cover to cylinder head . . . 10 Nm (89 in-lb)

VALVES

Valve clearance, checking and adjusting (S54 engine)

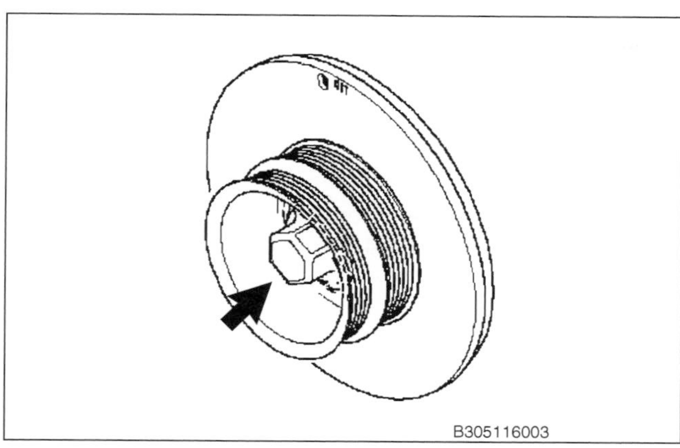

- Remove cylinder head cover. See **Cylinder head cover, removing (S54 engine)** given in this repair group.

- Remove fan clutch with fan impeller and fan cowl. See **170 Radiator and Cooling System**.

- Remove spark plugs. See **120 Ignition System**.

- Using socket wrench on vibration damper center cover (**arrow**), turn engine over (in normal direction of rotation) until camshaft lobes at cylinder no. 1 are pointing up.

NOTE —

Early M3 models (before 01/01 production) are not fitted with the vibration damper center cover. On these early cars, use BMW special tool 11 5 100 to aid in turning engine over.

- With cams pointing upwards, measure valve clearance with feeler gauge (BMW special tool 11 3 160 or equivalent).

- Record measured values. Valve clearance specifications are listed in **Table c**. If clearance is not within specified range, adjust as described below.

CAUTION —

It is very easy for the adjustment plates to fall down.

Table c. Valve clearance (S54 engine)

Valve clearance (measure at max. temp. of 95° F)	S54 engine
intake exhaust	0.18 - 0.23 mm (0.0070 - 0.0090 in.) 0.28 - 0.33 mm (0.0110 - 0.0130 in.)

- Place clean cloth around valve to be adjusted.

- Seal off all openings using lint free rags or tape, including oil return and vent holes, opening to timing case cover at first cylinder no. 1, and all spark plug holes.

Remove retaining clip from rocker arm shaft by pulling straight up (**arrow**).

– Carefully slide rocker arm to one side.

> ***CAUTION —***
> *Adjustment plates can easily fall off valve when sliding rocker arm.*

– Remove adjustment plate from top of valve using magnetic tool (BMW special tool 11 4 400 or equivalent).

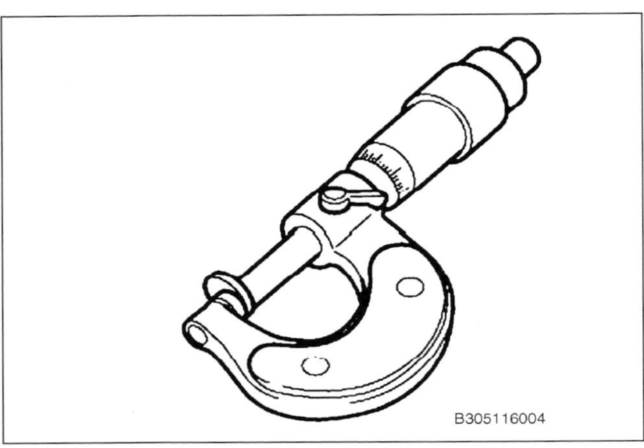

Using a micrometer, measure removed adjustment plate. Calculate new plate required to obtain correct valve clearance.

- Using difference between specified clearance and clearance recorded using feeler gauge, add difference to measured plate to obtain thickness of replacement plate.

NOTE —

- *Generally, the measured clearance is excessive and a thicker replacement adjustment plate is required. If clearance is too tight, a thinner plate must be selected.*
- *Valve adjustment plates are available in thicknesses ranging from 1.72 mm to 2.60 mm, in 0.04 mm increments.*

– Carefully install new adjustment plate to valve stem with magnetic tool (BMW special tool 11 4 400 or equivalent).

– Carefully push rocker arm back and check correct position of adjustment plates.

> ***CAUTION —***
> *Adjustment plates can easily fall off valve when sliding rocker arm.*

– Install rocker arm retaining clip. Retaining clip must snap into place on rocker arm shaft.

– Check valve clearance using feeler gauge.

– Repeat checking adjustment sequence for remainder of valves.

– Reassemble engine:

- Install cylinder head cover. See **Cylinder head cover, removing (S54 engine)** given in this repair group.
- Install fan clutch with fan impeller and fan cowl. See **170 Radiator and Cooling System**.
- Install spark plugs. See **120 Ignition System**.

Valves, removing and installing

– Remove cylinder head as described in **113 Cylinder Head Removal and Installation**.

> ***CAUTION —***
> - *Do not let the hydraulic lifters fall out as the camshaft carrier is removed. Special suction cups are available from BMW to hold the hydraulic lifters in place during carrier removal.*
> - *Hydraulic cam lifters should be stored in an upright position. If necessary, use a magnetic tool to aid in removal of the lifters.*

NOTE —
Cylinder head removal for the S54 engine used in the M3 model is not included in this repair manual. S54 cylinder head removal and installation is a highly complex job that requires a large and expensive assortment of BMW special tools and equipment and is therefore outside the scope of this manual.

– Remove valves using a valve spring compressor.

> ***CAUTION —***
> *Label each valve assembly as it is removed so it can be installed in its original position.*

– Remove and discard valve stem oil seals from valve guides. See **Valve stem oil seals** later in this section.

– Valve installation is reverse of removal.

Valve specifications are listed in **Table d** and **Table e**. Remove carbon deposits from the valves using a wire brush or wire wheel.

Table d. Valve specifications (M52 TU, M54, M56 engines)

Specification	M 52TU, M 54, M56 engines
Valve head dia. Intake Exhaust	 33.0 mm (1.299 in.) 30.5 mm (1.201 in.)
Valve stem dia. Standard Intake Exhaust	 $6.0^{-0.025 \text{ to } -0.040}$ mm ($0.2362^{-0.00098 \text{ to } -0.00157}$ in.) $6.0^{-0.040 \text{ to } -0.055}$ mm ($0.2362^{-0.00157 \text{ to } -0.00216}$ in.)
Oversize 1 Intake Exhaust	 $6.1^{-0.025 \text{ to } -0.040}$ mm ($0.2401^{-0.00098 \text{ to } -0.00157}$ in.) $6.1^{-0.040 \text{ to } -0.055}$ mm ($0.2401^{-0.00157 \text{ to } -0.00216}$ in.)
Oversize 2 Intake Exhaust	 $6.2^{-0.025 \text{ to } -0.040}$ mm ($0.2441^{-0.00098 \text{ to } -0.00157}$ in.) $6.2^{-0.040 \text{ to } -0.055}$ mm ($0.2441^{-0.00157 \text{ to } -0.00216}$ in.)

Table e. Valve specifications (S54 engine)

Specification	S54 engine
Valve head dia. Intake Exhaust	 35.0 mm (1.378 in.) 30.5 mm (1.201 in.)
Valve stem dia. Standard Intake Exhaust	 $6.0^{-0.025 \text{ to } -0.040}$ mm ($0.2362^{-0.00098 \text{ to } -0.00157}$ in.) $6.0^{-0.040 \text{ to } -0.055}$ mm ($0.2362^{-0.00157 \text{ to } -0.00216}$ in.)

Valve guides

BMW does not supply valve guides as replacement parts. If a valve guide is excessively worn, it should be reamed to accept oversized valve stems. Valve guide specifications are listed in **Table f**.

Valve guides should be checked for wear using a new valve. Be sure to thoroughly inspect the cylinder head to ensure that it can be reused before reworking the guides.

NOTE —

- *International Organization for Standardization (ISO) allowances are based on nominal sizes and should be used to determine proper fit. Most machine shops should have this information available.*
- *Replacement valve guides may be available through aftermarket suppliers. Valve guide replacement requires special tools and a press. It is also necessary to heat the cylinder head and chill the valve guides when replacing the guides*
- *At the time of this printing, oversized valve stems were not available from BMW for the S54 engine.*

Table f. Valve guide specifications

Specifications	M52TU / M54 engine (1999 - 2001)
Valve guide wear, maximum (valve tilt clearance measured with new valve)	0.5 mm (0.020 in.)
Valve guide inside diameter, installed (tolerance per ISO allowance H7) Standard Oversize 1 Oversize 2	 6.0 mm (0.236 in.) 6.1 mm (0.240 in.) 6.2 mm (0.244 in.)

Valve stem oil seals

The purpose of the valve stem oil seal is to prevent excess oil from entering the combustion chamber. The sign of faulty valve stem oil seals is excessive oil consumption and smoke from the exhaust immediately after starting and during deceleration.

NOTE —

Valve stem oil seals should not be reused. If valves are removed, new valve stem oil seals should be installed.

Valve stem oil seal replacement requires that the cylinder head be disassembled and the valves removed as described above under **Valves, removing and installing**.

NOTE —

BMW special tools are available to remove the valve stem oil seals. As an alternative, standard valve seal removal tools are available from most automotive parts stores.

Lubricate new seal and install using hand pressure only. Be sure to install valve spring seat(s) before installing seal.

Valve seats

The valve seats should be resurfaced whenever new valves or valve guides are installed. Cutters are required to resurface the seats. Always check the valves for leaks after reconditioning a valve seat as described above. **Table e** lists valve seat dimensions.

NOTE —

Standard size replacement valve seats are not available from BMW. Replacement valve seats are only available from BMW in 0.4 mm oversize (oversized in both height and diameter). The manufacturer does not provide specifications for valve seat replacement for the engines covered by this manual.

Table g. Valve seat specifications

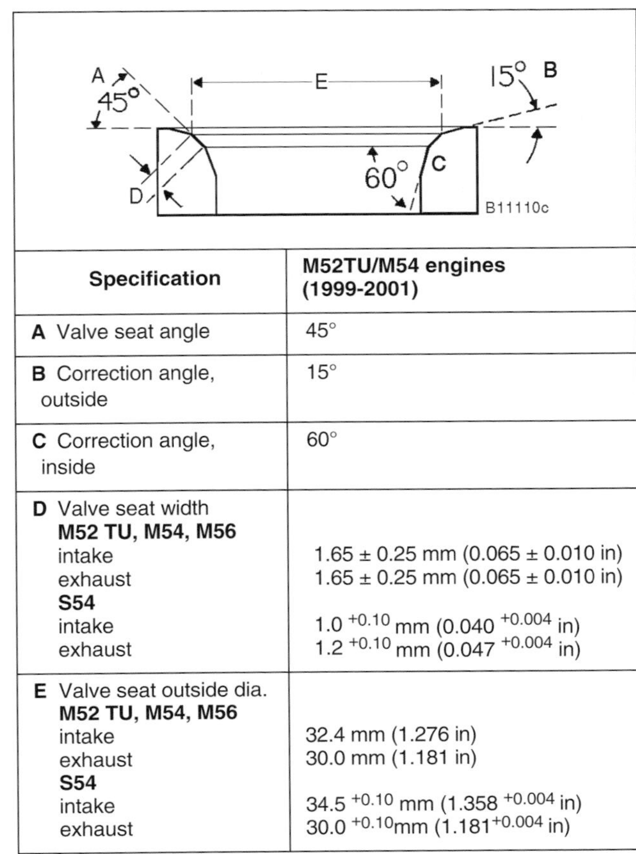

Specification	M52TU/M54 engines (1999-2001)
A Valve seat angle	45°
B Correction angle, outside	15°
C Correction angle, inside	60°
D Valve seat width **M52 TU, M54, M56** intake exhaust **S54** intake exhaust	 1.65 ± 0.25 mm (0.065 ± 0.010 in) 1.65 ± 0.25 mm (0.065 ± 0.010 in) $1.0^{+0.10}$ mm ($0.040^{+0.004}$ in) $1.2^{+0.10}$ mm ($0.047^{+0.004}$ in)
E Valve seat outside dia. **M52 TU, M54, M56** intake exhaust **S54** intake exhaust	 32.4 mm (1.276 in) 30.0 mm (1.181 in) $34.5^{+0.10}$ mm ($1.358^{+0.004}$ in) $30.0^{+0.10}$mm ($1.181^{+0.004}$ in)

Valve springs

The valve springs should be checked for fatigue. To quickly check the springs, line them up in a row. Place a straight edge across the top of the springs. Any spring that is significantly shorter than the others is worn and should be replaced.

NOTE —
Valve spring specifications and wear limits are not available from BMW.

117 Camshaft Timing Chains

Special Tools

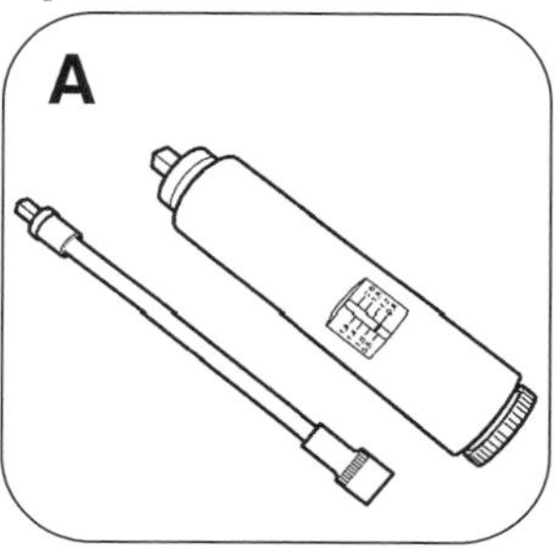

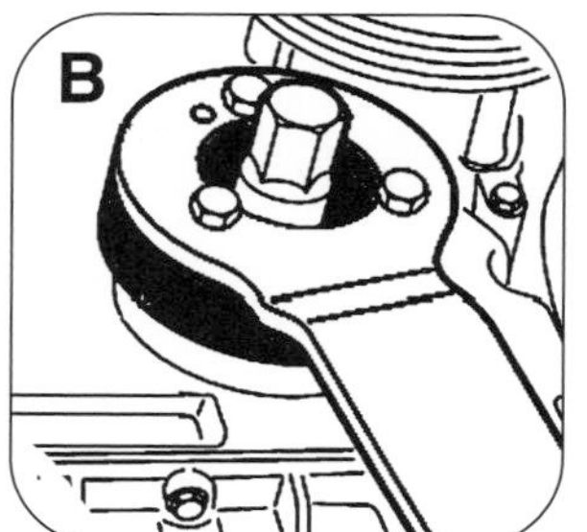

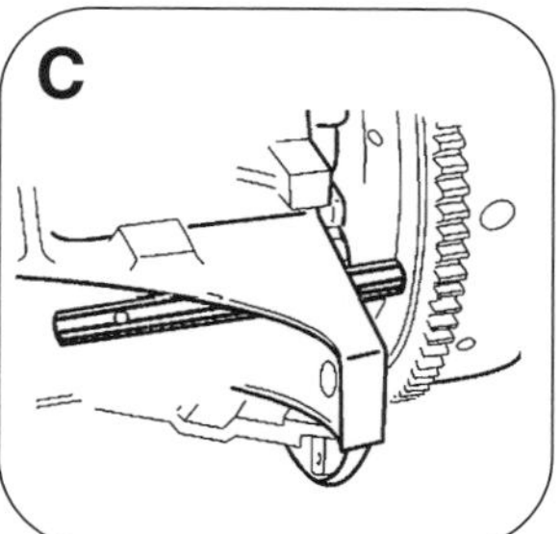

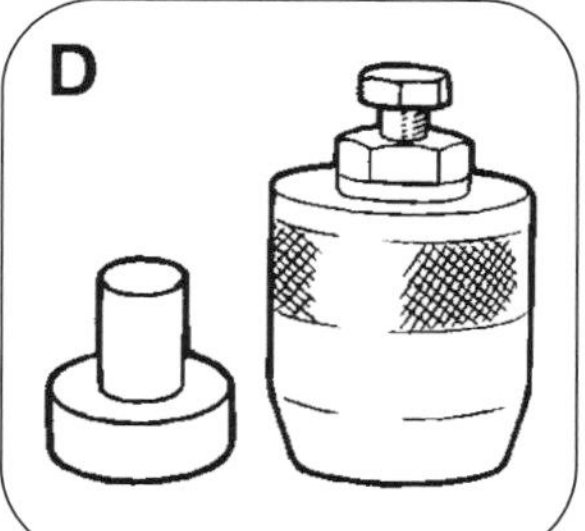

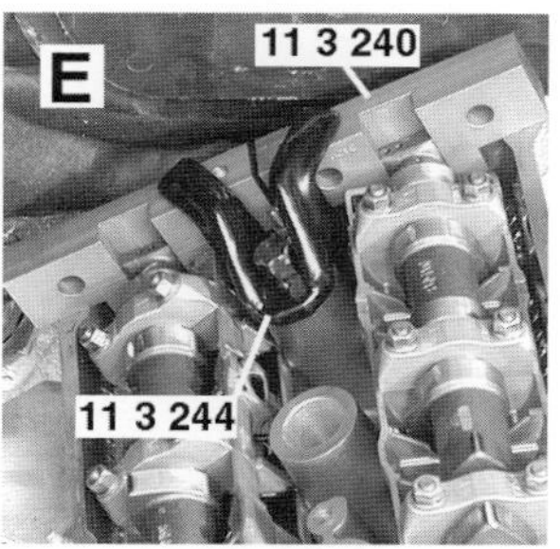

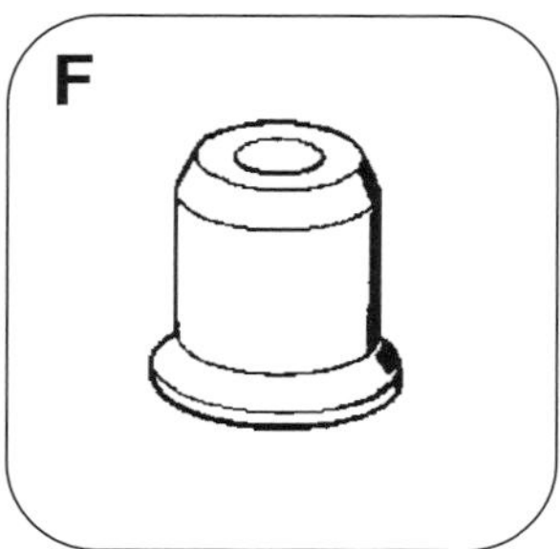

Special tools

A BMW 00 9 250 . . . . Torque wrench w/ flex extension
B BMW 11 2 150 /11 2 410/11 0 280 . Crankshaft hub locking tools
C BMW 11 2 300 . . . . Crankshaft locking tool
D BMW 11 2 380 (includes 11 2 384/385) . . . . Seal extractor tool
E BMW 11 3 240/11 3 244. . . . . Camshaft locking tools
F BMW 11 3 280 (Ex. S54 engine. . . . . .seal installer bush
BMW 11 1 220 (S54 engine)

GENERAL

This repair group covers timing chain and Variable Camshaft Timing (VANOS) repair information.

The timing chains are lubricated by engine oil and do not require maintenance. Worn timing chains and sprockets can lead to noisy operation and erratic valve timing. A faulty tensioner can also cause timing chain noises.

NOTE —

- *Timing chain service for the S54 engine used in the M3 model is not included in the repair group. The S54 high-pressure VANOS and timing chain service requires an extensive assortment of BMW special tools and equipment and is therefore outside the scope of this manual.*
- *See* **100 Engine–General** *for engine code and application information.*

Special tools

Special BMW service tools are needed to remove and disassemble the timing chain, the VANOS control unit, the camshafts and the valvetrain. Many of these tools are expensive and only available through an authorized BMW dealer. Be sure to read each procedure thoroughly before starting a job to determine which special tools will be necessary.

In addition, VANOS system diagnosis can only be carried out by using BMW specific electronic scan tools, such as BMW DIS or MoDiC or equivalent.

CAUTION —
The VANOS system must be removed and installed exactly as described later in this repair group.

Special Tools

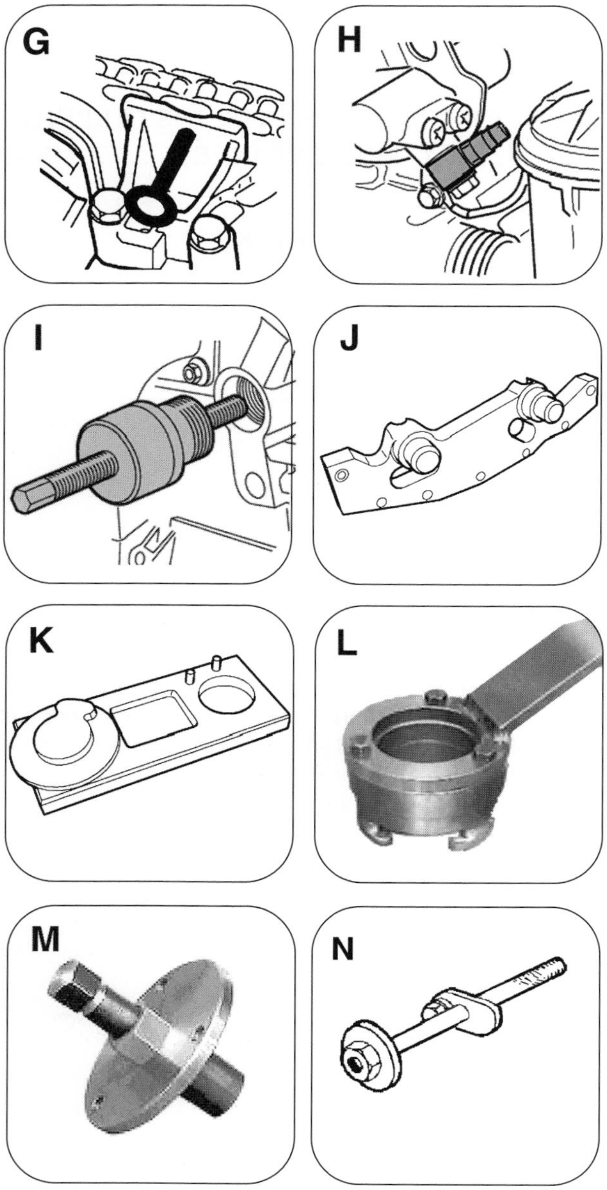

G

H

I

J

K

L

M

N

Special tools

G	BMW 11 3 292	Secondary chain tensioner locking pin
H	BMW 11 3 450	Air line fitting
I	BMW 11 4 220	Primary chain tensioner tool
J	BMW 11 6 150	VANOS setup bracket
K	BMW 11 6 180	Secondary sprocket tool
L	BMW 11 8 190 /11 8 200	Crankshaft hub locking tool
M	BMW 11 8 210	Puller for crankshaft hub
N	BMW 11 1 220	Crankshaft oil seal installation fixture (S54)

CRANKSHAFT FRONT OIL SEAL

The crankshaft front seal is located in the lower timing cover on the front of the engine, behind the vibration damper.

Front oil seal, removing and installing (M52 TU, M54, M56 engines)

NOTE —

Non-M3 cars built up to January 2000 are fitted with a 2-piece vibration damper and hub assembly. Non-M3 cars built from January 2000 use an integral vibration damper and hub assembly. If the early vibration damper needs to be replaced, only the single piece with integral hub is available from BMW.

– Disconnect negative (–) cable from battery.

CAUTION —

- *Disconnecting the battery may erase fault code(s) stored in control module memory. Check for fault codes using special BMW diagnostic equipment.*
- *Prior to disconnecting the battery, read the battery disconnection cautions given at the front of this manual.*

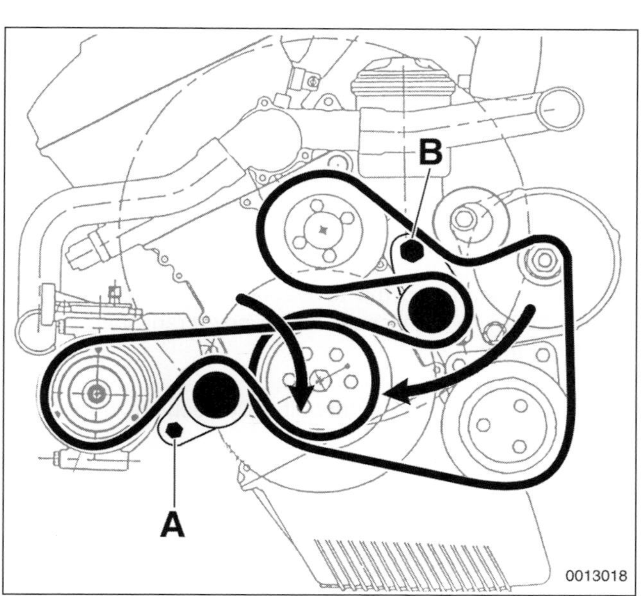

 Remove drive belts:

- Use long-handled wrench to turn A/C belt tensioner hex (**A**) clockwise (against spring tension). Remove A/C belt.
- Similarly, turn main engine drive belt tensioner hex (**B**) clockwise and remove belt.

– Secure crankshaft hub using special holding tools:

- Up to 1/2000 production: 11 2 150 and 11 2 410.
- From 01/2000 production: 11 8 190 and 11 8 200.

CAUTION —

Do not use BMW special tool 11 2 300 to hold crankshaft stationary to loosen or tighten crankshaft hub center bolt. Use only the special tools specified, or equivalent hub holding tool.

NOTE —

The crankshaft hub center bolt is tightened to a torque of 410 Nm (300 ft-lb).

– On cars built up to 1/2000 (2-piece vibration damper assembly), remove vibration damper mounting bolts and remove vibration damper and pulley from hub.

– Remove crankshaft hub (up to 1/2000 production) or vibration damper (1/2000 and later production).

NOTE —

If necessary, use BMW special tool 11 8 219 or equivalent puller to remove hub from crankshaft.

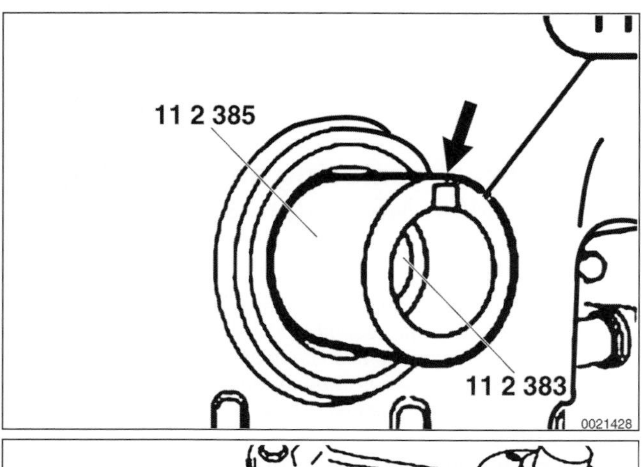

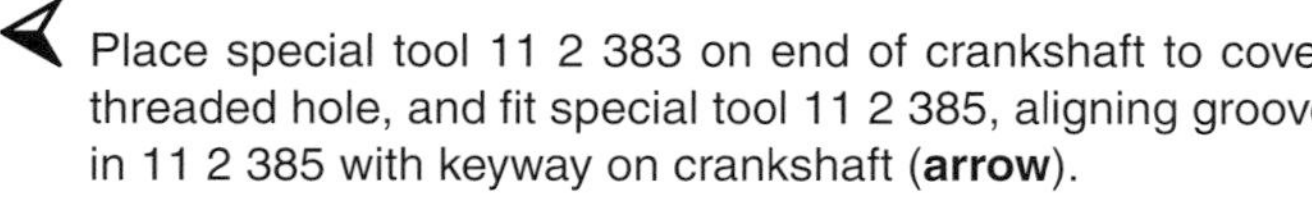

Place special tool 11 2 383 on end of crankshaft to cover threaded hole, and fit special tool 11 2 385, aligning groove in 11 2 385 with keyway on crankshaft (**arrow**).

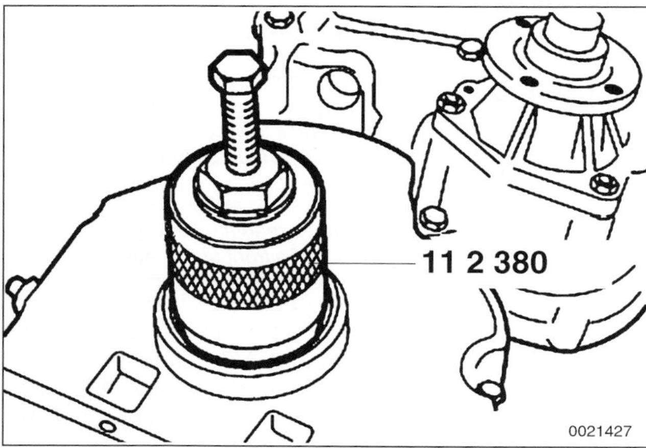

Put special tool 11 2 380 over tools installed on crankshaft, and screw in until it makes firm contact with the seal. Tighten screw in end of 11 2 380 to draw out seal.

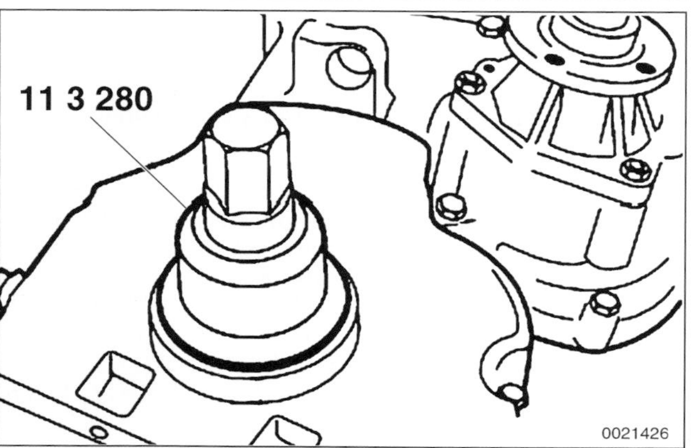

To install new seal, coat with oil, and use special tool 11 3 280 and crankshaft center bolt to draw seal in flush with timing case cover.

- Install crankshaft hub (up to 1/2000) or vibration damper (from 1/2000) to crankshaft. Install new crankshaft center bolt finger tight.

- Torque crankshaft hub center bolt while securing crankshaft with special tool.

Tightening torque

Vibration damper hub to crankshaft
- M52 TU, M54, M56 engines . . . . 410 Nm (302 ft-lb)

> ***CAUTION —***
> *Do not use BMW special tool 11 2 300 to hold crankshaft stationary to loosen or tighten crankshaft hub center bolt. Use only the special tools specified, or equivalent hub holding tool.*

Install vibration damper mounting bolts, where applicable. Note hub locating dowel (**arrow**).

Tightening torque

- Vibration damper to crankshaft hub (M8) . . . . 22 Nm (16 ft-lb)

Front oil seal, removing and installing (S54 engine)

– Disconnect negative (–) cable from battery.

> ***CAUTION —***
> - *Disconnecting the battery may erase fault code(s) stored in control module memory. Check for fault codes using special BMW diagnostic equipment.*
> - *Prior to disconnecting the battery, read the battery disconnection cautions given at the front of this manual.*

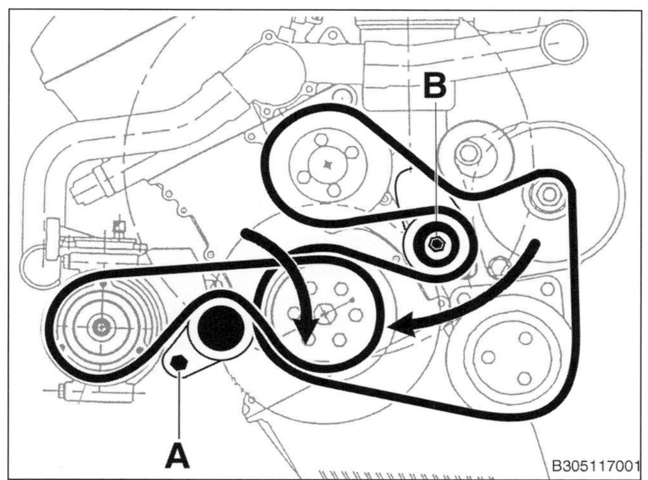

– Remove radiator fan and fan shroud. See **170 Radiator and Cooling System**.

◄ Remove drive belts:

- Use long-handled wrench to turn A/C belt tensioner hex (**A**) clockwise (against spring tension). Remove A/C belt.
- Similarly, turn main engine drive belt tensioner hex (**B**) clockwise and remove belt.

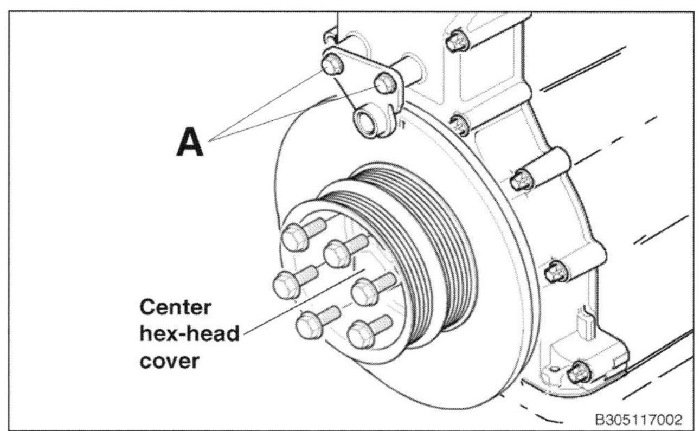

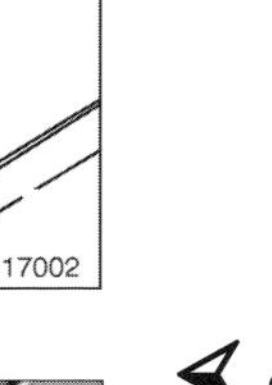

◄ Remove TDC bracket mounting bolts (**A**) and bracket. Remove pulley mounting bolts and remove pulley with center hex-head cover.

NOTE —
Early M3 models (before 01/01 production) are not fitted with the vibration damper center (hex-head) cover.

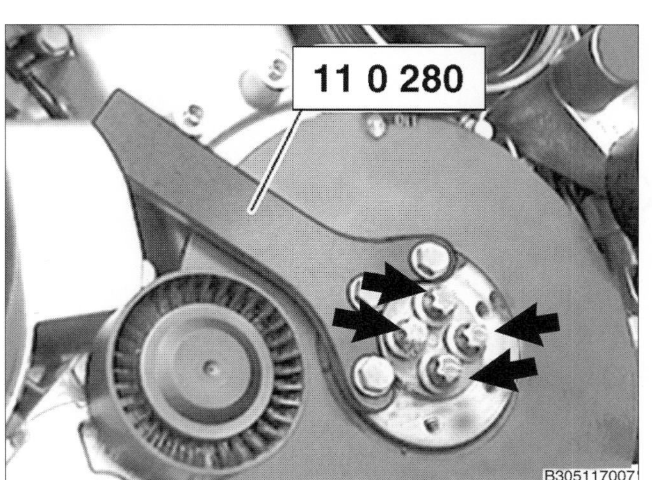

◄ Secure crankshaft hub using BMW special tool 11 0 280. Loosen vibration damper mounting bolts (**arrows**). Remove vibration damper by lifting out from below first (to clear coolant pump pulley).

NOTE —
Special tool 11 0 280 rests on A/C compressor bracket when loosening center bolts.

> ***CAUTION —***
> *Use only the special tools specified, or equivalent hub holding tool to loosen bolts.*

Place special tool 11 2 384 into crankshaft center.

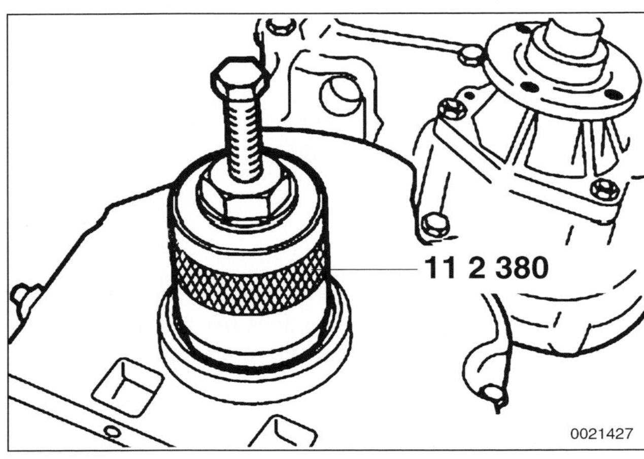

Install special tool 11 2 380 over crankshaft, and screw in until it makes firm contact with the seal. Tighten screw in end of 11 2 380 to draw out seal.

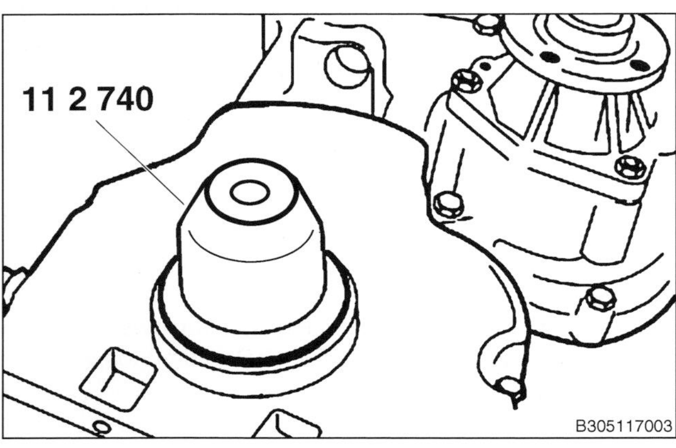

To install new seal, coat with oil. Place special tool 11 2 740 onto crankshaft. Install new seal until it is seated on timing chain cover. Remove special tool 11 2 740.

> ***CAUTION —***
> *Do not touch sealing lips on new seal with your fingers.*

Fasten special tool 11 5 090 to crankshaft.

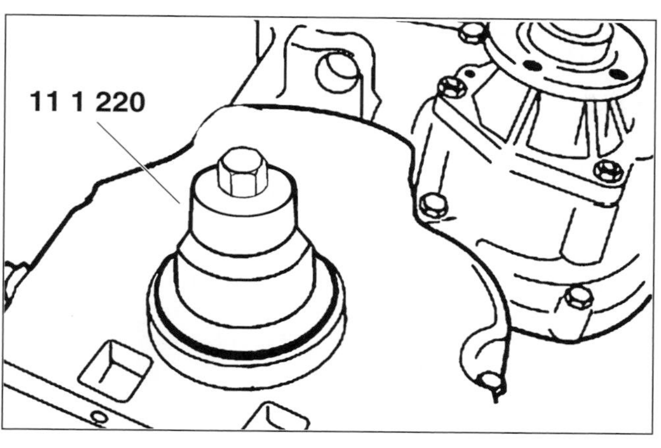

◀ Install special tool 11 1 220 and draw seal in flush with timing case cover.

– Install vibration damper to crankshaft, making sure to align locating hole in damper to dowel in crankshaft hub. Install new bolts finger tight.

> **CAUTION—**
> *Always use new stretch bolts when installing vibration damper.*

– Torque crankshaft center bolts while securing crankshaft with special tool.

Tightening torque

Vibration damper hub to crankshaft
- S54 engine (*use new bolts!*)
  - stage 1 . . . . 60 Nm (44 ft-lb)
  - stage 2 (angle torque) . . . . 50 °
  - stage 3 (angle torque) . . . . 50 °

– Install pulley and TDC bracket. Make sure dowels for TDC bracket are correctly located in timing chain cover.

Tightening torque

- Pulley to vibration damper (S54 engine)
  - grade 10.9. . . . . 34 Nm (25 ft-lb)
  - grade 8.8. . . . . 22 Nm (16 ft-lb)

CAMSHAFT TIMING CHAINS, REMOVING (M52 TU, M54, M56 ENGINES)

Camshaft timing chain removal requires that the oil pan be removed. This requires raising the engine and/or lowering the front suspension subframe. See **119 Lubrication System**. Also required is removal of the VANOS unit and disassembly of the intake and exhaust camshaft sprocket assemblies as described later in this repair group.

Special BMW service tools are needed for timing chain removal and installation procedures. The special tools assure proper timing of the valvetrain. Precise marks to set the timing on the camshafts are not provided for reassembly. Read the procedures through before beginning the job.

> **CAUTION—**
> *If the camshafts are not properly timed, the pistons can contact the valves.*

– Disconnect negative (–) cable from battery.

> **CAUTION—**
> - *Disconnecting the battery may erase fault code(s) stored in control module memory. Check for fault codes using special BMW diagnostic equipment.*
> - *Prior to disconnecting the battery, read the battery disconnection cautions given at the front of this manual.*

Double Vanos Components (M52 TU, M54, M56 engines)

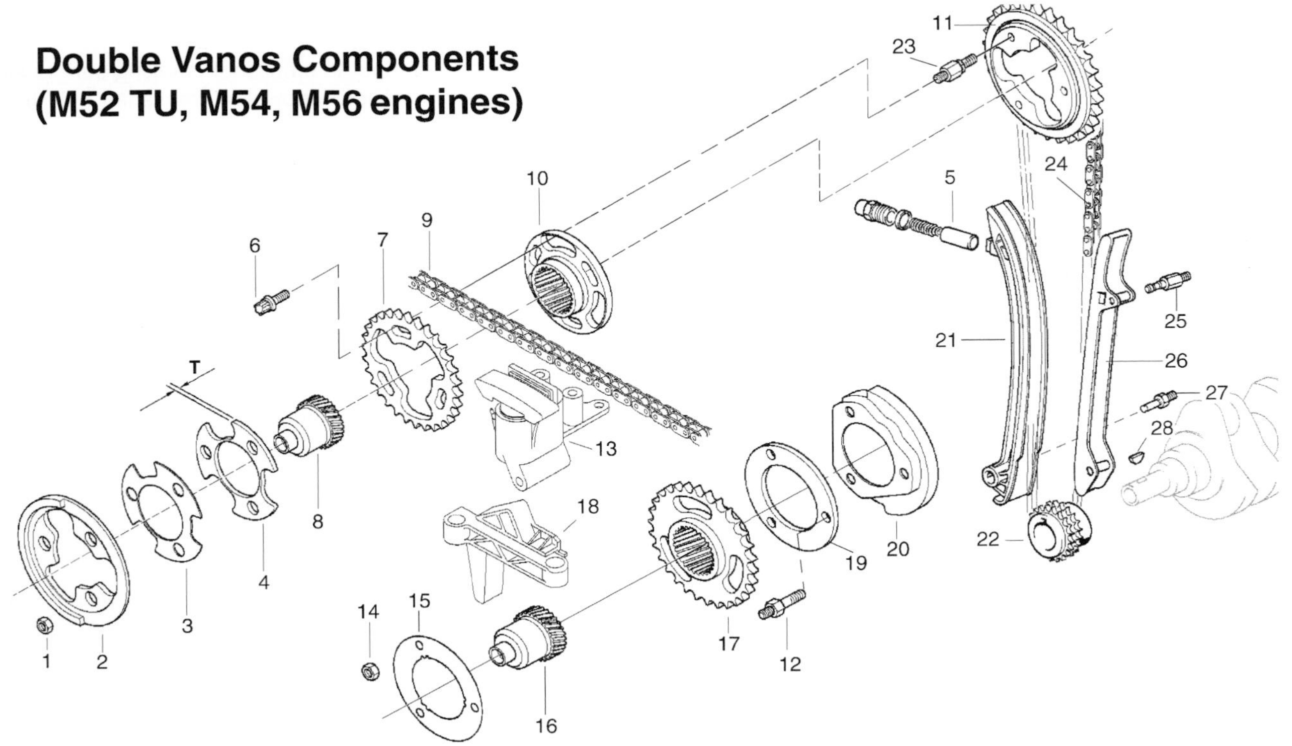

1. Impulse wheel mounting nut
2. Camshaft impulse wheel (exh.)
3. Spring plate
4. Thrust spacer (T = 3.5 mm)
5. Primary chain tensioner
6. Torx screw
7. Exhaust secondary sprocket
8. Splined shaft
9. Secondary timing chain
10. Splined sleeve
11. Primary sprocket
12. Threaded stud
13. Secondary chain tensioner
14. Sprocket mounting nut
15. Spring plate
16. Splined shaft
17. Intake camshaft sprocket
18. Secondary chain lower guide
19. Thrust spacer
20. Camshaft impulse wheel (intake)
21. Chain tensioner rail
22. Crankshaft sprocket
23. Threaded stud
24. Primary chain
25. Threaded stud
26. Guide rail
27. Threaded stud
28. Woodruff key

 Remove microfilter for interior ventilation.

Remove microfilter housing:

- Open wiring harness loom (**A**), remove harness and lay aside.
- Unfasten screws (**B**) and take off lower microfilter housing.

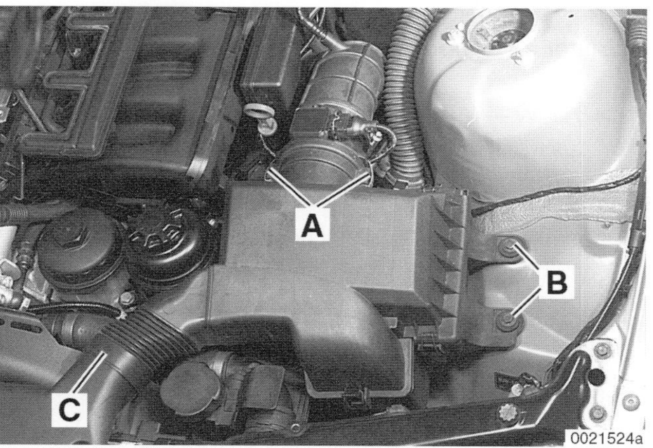

Remove complete air filter housing:

- Release mass air flow sensor clips (**A**).
- Remove filter housing mounting screws (**B**).
- Disconnect air duct connections (**C**) and lift complete air filter housing out of engine compartment, pulling it forward away from mass air flow sensor.

NOTE —
Mass air flow sensor remains attached to air duct in above step.

Remove engine covers:

- Remove plastic trim covers (**arrows**).
- Remove cover hold down bolts.

Drain engine coolant and remove coolant hoses.

- Remove expansion tank cap on radiator.
- Place a 3-gallon pail beneath engine to capture coolant.
- Remove engine block drain plug on exhaust side near cylinder 2 (**arrow**).

> ***WARNING —***
> - *Allow engine to cool before opening or draining cooling system.*
> - *Use caution when draining and disposing of engine coolant. Coolant is poisonous and lethal to humans and pets. Pets are attracted to coolant because of its sweet smell and taste. Consult a veterinarian immediately if ingested by an animal.*

– Drain radiator into 3-gallon pail by removing plastic drain plug at lower left corner of radiator.

– Remove radiator cooling fan shroud and viscous clutch cooling fan (cars with automatic transmission) or electric cooling fan (cars with manual transmission). See **170 Radiator and Cooling System**

> ***CAUTION —***
> *On cars with viscous clutch, 32 mm cooling fan mounting nut has left hand threads.*

Release locking clips and pull hoses from thermostat housing (**arrows**). Unbolt and remove thermostat houses.

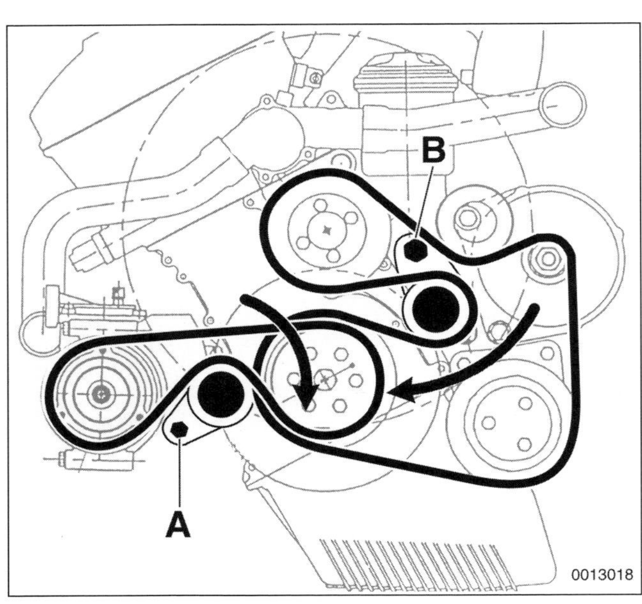

Remove drive belts:

- Use long-handled wrench to turn A/C belt tensioner hex (**A**) clockwise (against spring tension). Remove A/C belt.
- Similarly, turn main engine drive belt tensioner hex (**B**) clockwise and remove belt.

– Remove coolant pump pulley.

– Remove alternator cooling duct at radiator support.

– Drain engine oil and remove oil pan as described in **119 Lubrication System**.

– On cars produced up to 1/2000 with 2-piece vibration damper: Remove vibration damper mounting bolts and separate vibration damper and pulley from crankshaft hub.

> ***NOTE —***
> *Cars built up to January 2000 are fitted with a 2-piece vibration damper and hub assembly. Cars built from January 2000 use an integral vibration damper and hub assembly.*

– Using BMW special holding tool, secure crankshaft hub to prevent crankshaft from turning. Loosen but do not remove crankshaft hub center bolt.

> ***CAUTION —***
> *Do not use BMW special tool 11 2 300 (flywheel locking tool) to hold crankshaft stationary to loosen or tighten crankshaft hub center bolt. Use only the special tools specified, or equivalent hub holding tool.*

NOTE —
The crankshaft hub center bolt is tightened to a torque of 410 Nm (300 ft-lb). BMW special tools 11 2 150 and 11 2 410 (up to 1/2000 models) or 11 8 190 and 11 8 200 (1/2000 and later models) should be used to hold the crankshaft stationary while the bolt is loosened.

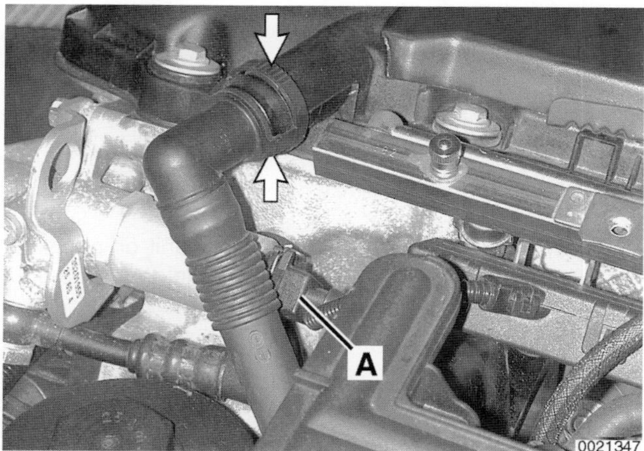

◄ Working at top center of engine, disconnect vent hose by squeezing at fitting (**arrows**).

– Disconnect electrical connection at VANOS soleniod (**A**).

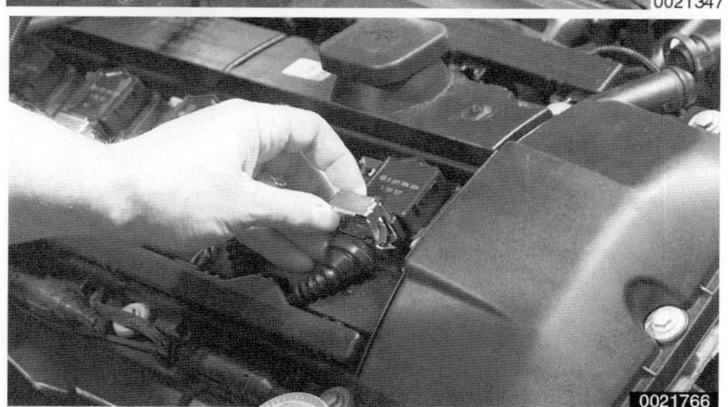

◄ Remove ignition coils and spark plugs:

- Pull up on retaining clips to disconnect ignition coil harness connectors.
- Remove grounding straps at coil mounting studs.
- Remove all ignition coils.
- Remove spark plugs.

– Remove cylinder head cover mounting fasteners and remove cylinder head cover.

NOTE —
The cylinder head cover mounting bolt insulators, gaskets and coil grounds should be reinstalled in their original locations.

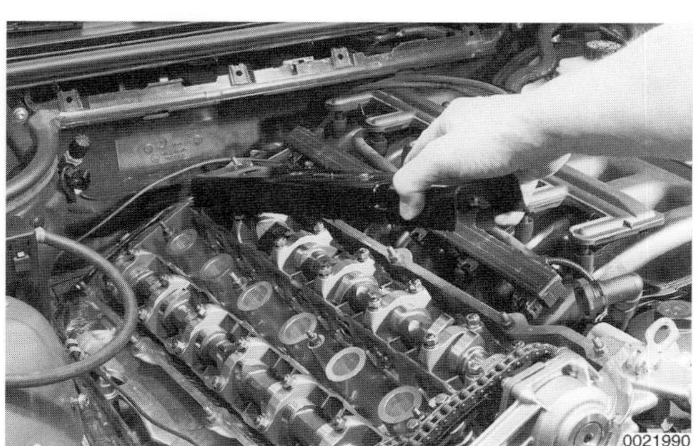

◄ Remove oil baffle cover from intake camshaft.

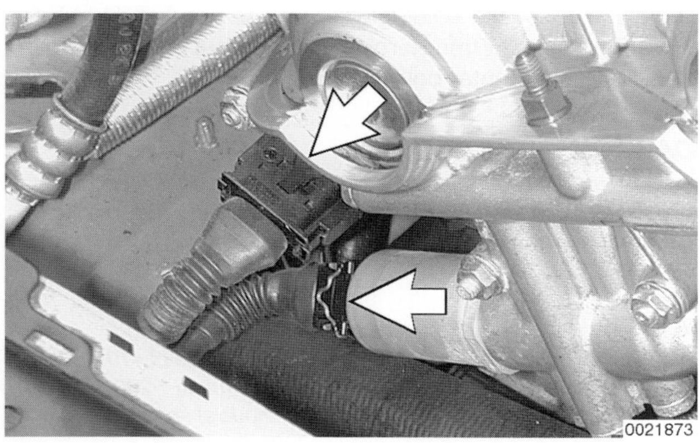

Working at left front of cylinder head, disconnect electrical connections at exhaust camshaft position sensor and exhaust camshaft VANOS control valve (**arrows**).

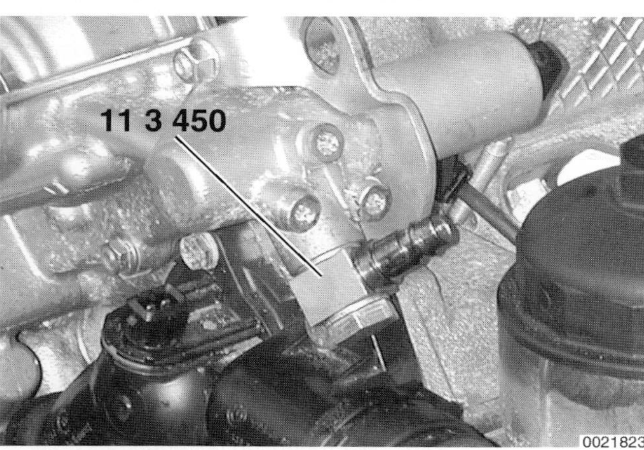

Remove banjo bolt from VANOS control unit oil pressure line. Use banjo bolt to attach BMW special tool 11 3 450 (compressed air fitting) (**arrow**) to VANOS unit.

Cover oil hole in VANOS unit (**arrow**) with shop towel to capture oil which will spray when compressed air line is connected.

- Connect compressed air line to air fitting. Apply air pressure set to 2 - 8 bar (30 - 110 psi).

With compressed air line connected, rotate engine in direction of rotation (clockwise) at least two full rotations, leaving cylinder 1 intake and exhaust camshaft lobes facing each other, as shown (**arrows**).

> ***CAUTION —***
> *Do not rotate engine counterclockwise to reach the top dead center position. Instead, complete another two complete rotations.*

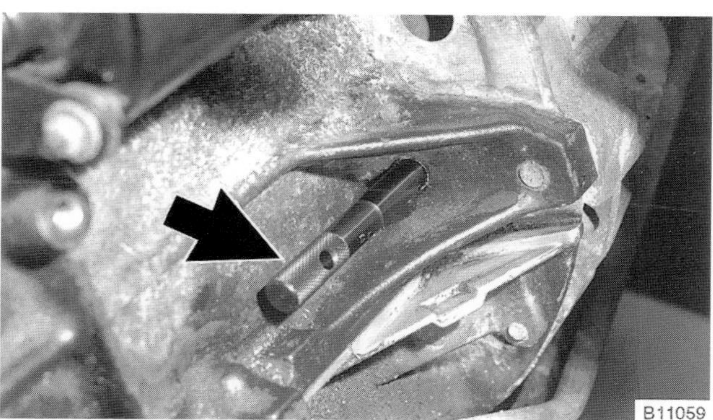
B11059

Remove sealing plug from bore on lower left side of engine block below starter. Secure crankshaft in TDC position with BMW special tool 11 2 300 (**arrow**).

0021871

Unscrew and remove threaded studs (**arrows**) at rear of cylinder head.

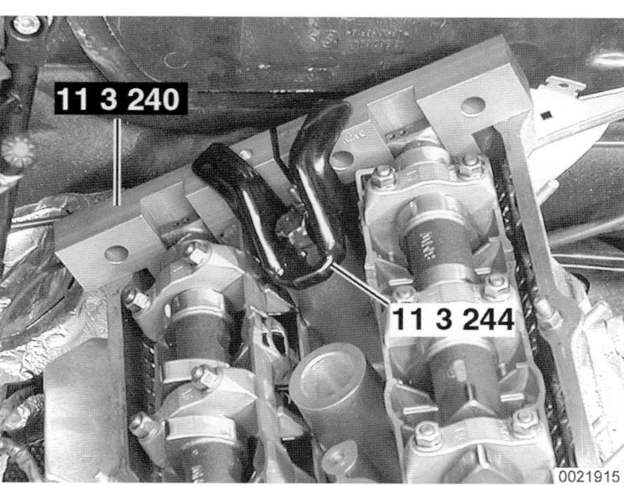

0021915

Secure camshafts in TDC position using BMW special tools 11 3 240 and 11 3 244.

- Detach compressed air line, leaving compressed air fitting attached to VANOS unit.

NOTE —
Oil will drain from pressure line. Have a container and rags ready.

0021769

Unscrew sealing plugs from VANOS unit (**arrows**).

NOTE —
Oil will drain from sealing plug bores. Have a container and rags ready.

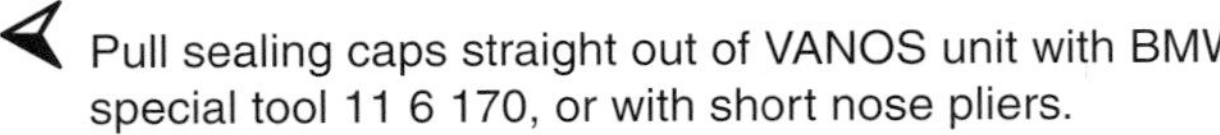

Pull sealing caps straight out of VANOS unit with BMW special tool 11 6 170, or with short nose pliers.

NOTE —
Additional oil may drain from VANOS unit.

Remove set screws (left hand thread) on ends of intake and exhaust camshafts.

> ***CAUTION —***
> *Set screws have left hand threads. Remove with a clockwise motion.*

Remove VANOS unit:

- Remove fasteners from engine support eye.
- Remove VANOS mounting nuts (**arrows**) from cylinder head. Slide VANOS unit and metal gasket off.

> ***CAUTION —***
> *Do not crank or turn over engine with VANOS unit removed. Piston/valve interference is possible.*

NOTE —
- *The VANOS unit will contain residual oil. Place shop towels beneath adjustment unit when removing.*
- *If the VANOS control unit is replaced, or if repair operations are completed that may change camshaft timing, the camshaft timing must be checked as described later in this chapter.*

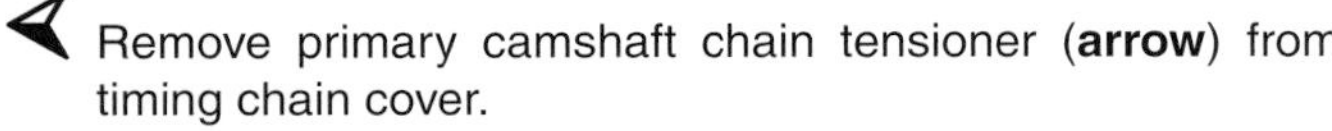

Remove primary camshaft chain tensioner (**arrow**) from timing chain cover.

> ***CAUTION —***
> *Primary camshaft chain tensioning piston is under spring pressure.*

◄ Press down on secondary chain tensioner and lock into place using BMW special tool 11 3 292 or a similar size rod.

◄ Remove exhaust camshaft impulse wheel mounting nuts (**arrows**). Remove impulse wheel (**A**).

◄ Remove spring plate (**A**).

◄ Remove intake camshaft sprocket mounting nuts (**arrows**) and remove spring plate (labelled FRONT).

0021881

Remove torx screws from exhaust camshaft sprocket (**arrows**).

0021882

Lift off exhaust and intake sprockets together with secondary chain, thrust spacer (**A**) and splined shaft (**B**).

> ***CAUTION —***
> *Splined shafts for both intake and exhaust camshafts share the same part number. Remove and mark used splined shafts in order to reinstall in original locations.*

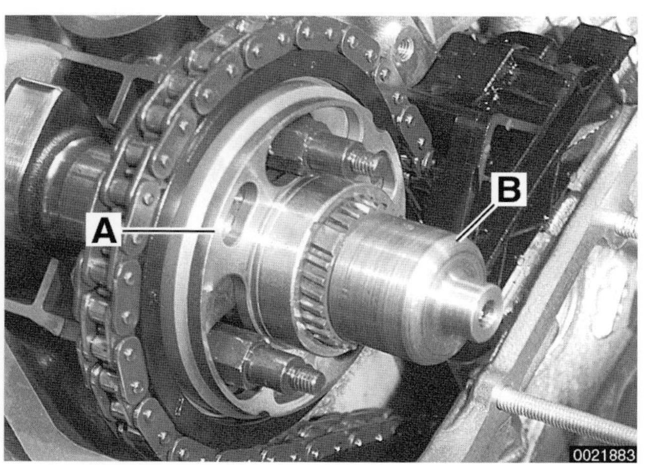

0021883

Remove exhaust camshaft splined sleeve (**A**) and shaft (**B**).

0021884

Remove secondary chain tensioner mounting bolts (**arrows**). Remove tensioner while keeping locking pin in place.

0021885

Remove primary chain sprocket mounting studs (**arrows**) on exhaust camshaft.

0021886

Lift primary chain sprocket off exhaust camshaft. Remove sprocket from chain.

0021889

< Set timing chain on exhaust camshaft end.

0021898

< Working in cylinder head cavity, remove timing chain cover bolts (**arrows**).

0021897

< Remove secondary chain lower guide bolts (**arrows**). Remove chain guide.

NOTE —

Bolt on intake camshaft side is long and extends into timing chain cover.

– Remove crankshaft hub center bolt and remove crankshaft hub (to 1/2000 models) or vibration damper (models from 1/2000).

CAUTION —

The crankshaft must not be allowed to rotate when the timing chains are loosened or removed. The pistons can contact the valves.

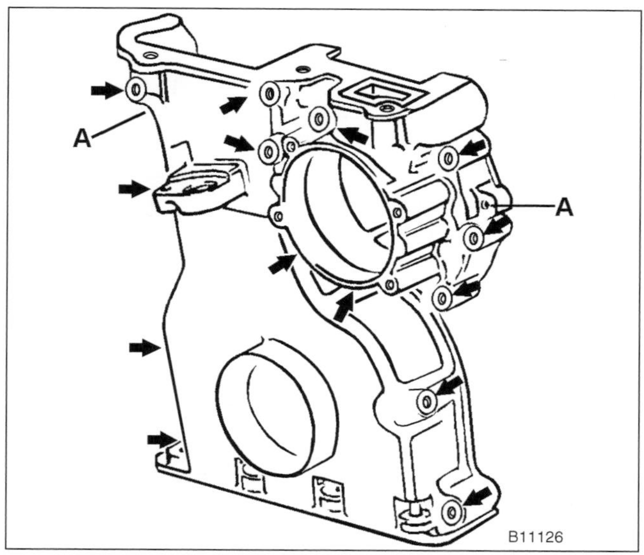

Using a drift of less than 5 mm diameter, drive two locating dowels (**A**) in left and right sides of lower timing chain cover toward rear of car. Remove cover mounting bolts (**arrows**) and carefully lift cover off.

> ***CAUTION —***
> *Use care when removing the cover from the cylinder head gasket. If the cover is stuck, use a sharp knife to separate it from the head gasket.*

NOTE —

- *The chain cover can be removed with the coolant pump installed.*
- *Use care when removing the cover from the coolant pipe at rear.*

– Push primary chain tensioner guide rail aside and remove chain.

CAMSHAFT TIMING CHAINS, INSTALLING (M52 TU, M54, M56 ENGINES)

> ***CAUTION —***
> *The procedure outlined below assumes that the camshafts and the crankshaft are locked in the TDC installation position with special locking tools as shown earlier.*

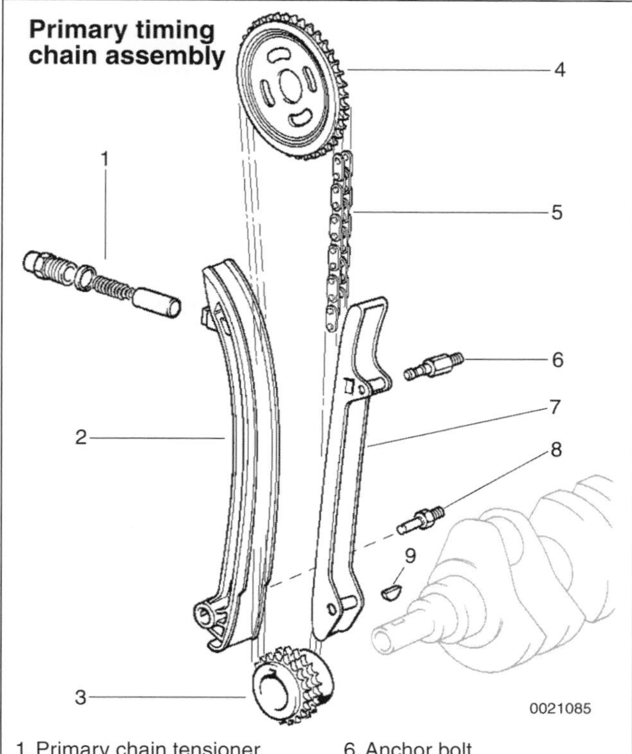

1. Primary chain tensioner
2. Chain tensioner rail
3. Crankshaft sprocket
4. Exhaust camshaft sprocket
5. Primary chain
6. Anchor bolt
7. Guide rail
8. Anchor bolt
9. Woodruff key

Inspect timing chain sprockets. Inspect guide rail and tensioner rail for deep grooves caused by chain contact. Replace any part that is worn or damaged.

NOTE —

If sprockets are being replaced for wear, the chain should also be replaced. If the crankshaft sprocket requires replacement, the oil pump drive sprocket and chain must be removed. See **119 Lubrication System** *for oil pump removal information.*

– Install primary timing chain to crankshaft sprocket and hang upper end from exhaust camshaft.

– If necessary, replace crankshaft seal as described earlier.

– To install lower timing case cover:
  - Clean cover and cylinder block sealing surfaces.
  - Use new gaskets and coolant pipe O-ring.
  - Drive timing cover dowels in until they just protrude slightly from sealing surface.
  - Apply a small bead of silicon sealer (3-Bond 1209® or equivalent) to corners of cylinder head where timing cover meets cylinder head and engine block.
  - Tap cover into position to engage dowels.
  - Install all bolts hand tight, including two Torx bolts from above.
  - Install secondary chain lower guide.
  - Drive dowels in flush to front of cover.
  - Tighten cover mounting bolts alternately and in stages.

– Install oil pan with new gasket. See **119 Lubrication System**.

Tightening torques

- Lower timing cover to cylinder block (M6) . . . . 10 Nm (89 in-lb)

Tightening torque

- Oil pan to engine block (M6)
  8.8 grade. . . . . 10 Nm (89 in-lb)
  10.9 grade. . . . . 12 Nm (9 ft-lb)

Install crankshaft hub or vibration damper to crankshaft. Install crankshaft center bolt finger tight. Make sure hub is fully seated, noting alignment dowel (**arrow**), where applicable.

NOTE —

Cars built up to January 2000 are fitted with a 2-piece vibration damper and hub assembly. Cars built from January 2000 use an integral vibration damper and hub assembly. If the early vibration damper needs to be replaced, only the single piece with integral hub is available from BMW.

Tightening torque

- Vibration damper to crankshaft hub (M8) . . . . 22 Nm (16 ft-lb)

Fit top sprocket to primary timing chain and install on exhaust camshaft so that pointer (**arrow**) on sprocket lines up with cylinder head sealing surface.

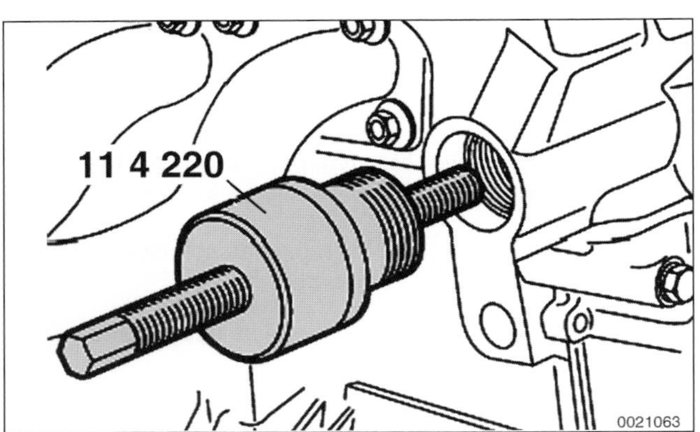

Insert BMW special tool 11 4 220 in cylinder head and screw in adjustment screw by hand just until it contacts tensioning rail.

NOTE —

BMW special tool 11 4 220 is a dummy primary chain tensioner and simulates the function of the tensioner.

– Make sure arrow on top primary sprocket is still lined up with upper edge of cylinder head. Reposition sprocket if necessary.

Install and tighten down threaded locating studs (**arrows**) in end of exhaust camshaft.

Tightening torques

- Exhaust camshaft locating stud . . . . 20 Nm (15 ft-lb)

Install secondary chain tensioner on cylinder head.

- Make sure tensioner is locked in compressed position as described earlier.

Fit exhaust camshaft splined sleeve, aligning gap in sleeve splines with corresponding gap on camshaft splines (**arrows**).

Slide splined shaft onto exhaust camshaft, aligning larger tooth with corresponding gap of splined sleeve.

- Slide splined shaft in further until 3 small slots in splined sleeve are centered on 3 threaded holes in sprocket.

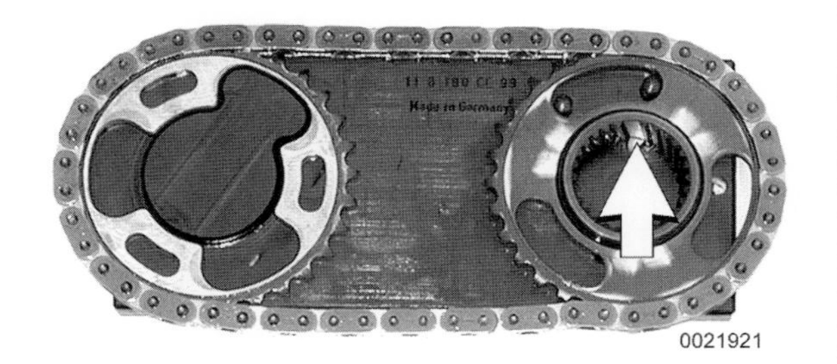

Place intake and exhaust sprockets in BMW special tool 11 6 180. Position spline gap on intake sprocket (**arrow**) as shown and place secondary chain on sprockets.

0021922

Carefully remove chain and sprockets from tool and slide onto camshafts. Align gap in intake sprocket splines with corresponding gap in camshaft splines (**arrow**).

> ***CAUTION —***
> *Do not alter position of sprockets with respect to chain when removing from special tool 11 6 180.*

0021926

Slide splined shaft onto intake camshaft until approx. 1 mm (0.04 in.) of splines can still be seen.

0021927

Install intake camshaft spring plate so that **FRONT** mark is visible. Install mounting nuts (**arrows**) finger tight.

Working at exhaust side, insert sprocket mounting Torx screws into threaded holes (**arrows**).

- Initially tighten screws to approx. 5 Nm (44 in-lb). Back off half a turn.

Fit thrust spacer (**A**) on exhaust camshaft.

Install spring plate (**A**) to exhaust camshaft. Make sure that **F** marking is visible.

NOTE —

*If **F** marking is no longer visible, install spring plate so that convex side points forward (toward front of car).*

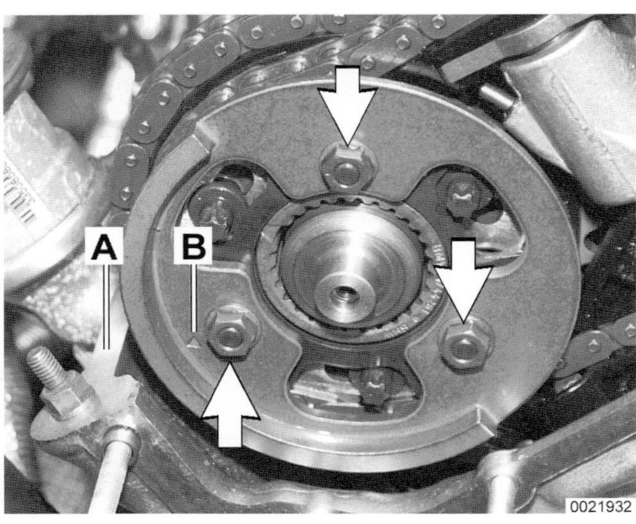

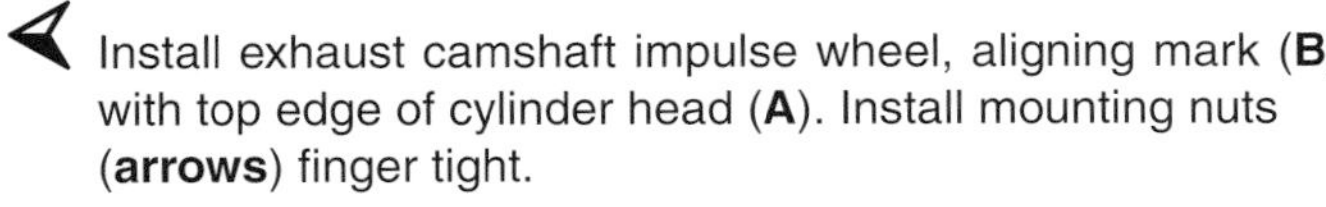

Install exhaust camshaft impulse wheel, aligning mark (**B**) with top edge of cylinder head (**A**). Install mounting nuts (**arrows**) finger tight.

Pull out exhaust splined shaft until it stops.

– Press down on secondary chain tensioner and remove tensioner lock-down tool.

Preload primary chain:

- Tighten adjusting screw on BMW special tool 11 4 220 to specified torque.

Tightening torque

- Primary chain tensioner preload. . . . . . . .0.7 Nm (6 in-lb)

Preload exhaust camshaft spring plate by pressing on impulse wheel while tightening mounting nuts (**arrows**) finger tight.

Install BMW special tool 11 6 150 (VANOS setup bracket) to front of cylinder head timing case.

– Tighten tool mounting nuts (**arrows**) by hand, and then tighten down uniformly until special tool is firmly contacting cylinder head.

> ***CAUTION —***
> *Make sure all gasket material is removed from face of cylinder head. Clean sealing face and keep free of oil. If any foreign material is present on the sealing surface, the camshaft timing will be incorrect.*

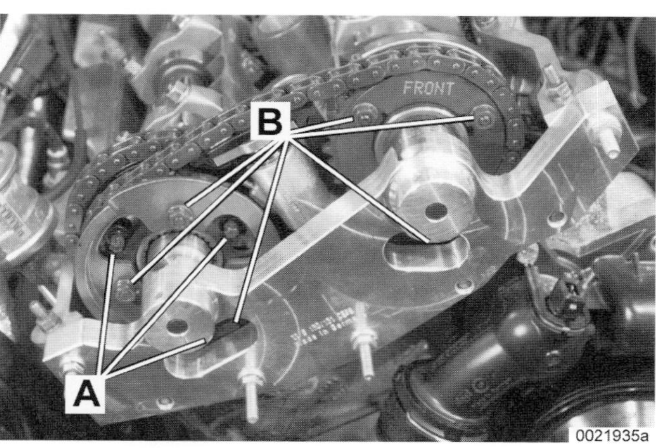

Secure camshaft sprockets and impulse wheels:

- Tighten mounting screws (**A**) on exhaust camshaft impulse wheel to approx. 5 Nm (44 in-lb).
- Tighten mounting nuts (**B**) on exhaust and intake sprocket assemblies to approx. 5 Nm (44 in-lb).
- Torque down mounting screws (**A**) and nuts (**B**) to final specifications.

Tightening torques

- Sprocket assembly to camshaft initial torque . . . . 5 Nm (44 in-lb)
- Sprocket assembly to camshaft
  M7 Torx screw (**A**). . . . . 20 Nm (15 ft-lb)
  M6 mounting nut (**B**) . . . . 10 Nm (89 in-lb)

– Remove flywheel locking tool from transmission bellhousing so that crankshaft is no longer secured.

– Remove camshaft locking tools from rear of camshafts.

Crank engine over by hand twice in direction of rotation until cylinder 1 intake and exhaust camshaft lobes (**arrows**) face each other.

– Secure crankshaft in TDC position with BMW special tool 11 2 300.

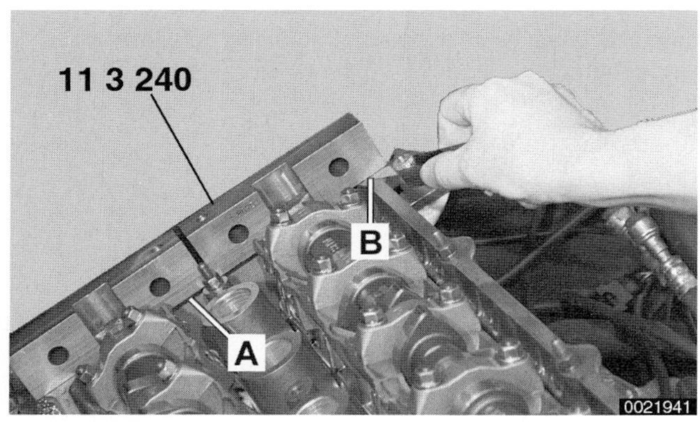

 Place BMW special tool 11 3 240 over camshaft ends and measure clearance of tool to cylinder head surface.

NOTE —

- *If the exhaust side of the tool is not flush with the head (gap **A**), retime the camshafts as described later in this repair group.*
- *Due to flexible sprocket design, VANOS unit tolerances, and play in the VANOS splines, when the camshaft timing is set correctly, the intake side of special tool 11 3 240 may be up to 1 mm (0.04 in) above the surface of the cylinder head (gap **B**). This is normal. Otherwise, retime the camshafts as described later in this repair group.*

– Remove VANOS setup bracket from front of cylinder head.

– Install VANOS unit. See **VANOS control unit, installing**, given later.

– Install intake camshaft oil baffle

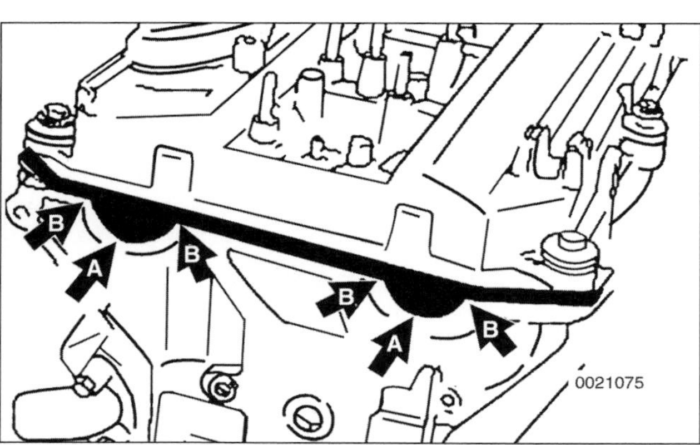

 Install cylinder head cover.

- Check for correct seating of half-moon seals (**A**) in back of cylinder head cover.
- Use a small amount of 3-Bond® 1209 or equivalent sealant at corners (**B**) of half-moon cutouts. Seal corners in front of cylinder head at VANOS unit.

Tightening torque

- Cylinder head cover to cylinder head . . . 10 Nm (89 in-lb)

– Reassemble remainder of engine:

- Torque crankshaft hub center bolt, using special tools 11 2 150/11 2 410 (to 1/2000) or 11 8 190/11 8 200 (from 1/2000).

CAUTION —

Do not use BMW special tool 11 2 300 (flywheel locking tool) to hold crankshaft stationary to loosen or tighten crankshaft hub center bolt. Use only the special tools specified, or equivalent hub holding tool.

- Reinstall air filter housing, engine covers, interior ventilation microfilter housing.
- Secure all coolant hoses, thermostat housing, engine coolant drains.
- Reinstall engine oil drain plug.
- Refill engine oil and coolant before running engine. Check for leaks.

Tightening torques

- Coolant drain plug to cylinder block . . . . 25 Nm (18 ft-lb)
- Radiator cooling fan (viscous clutch) to coolant pump . . . . 40 Nm (30 ft-lb)
- Radiator drain screw to radiator . . . . . . 2.5 Nm (22 in-lb)
- Vibration damper hub to crankshaft . . 410 Nm (302 ft-lb)

– Use scan tool to check VANOS operation with engine idling.

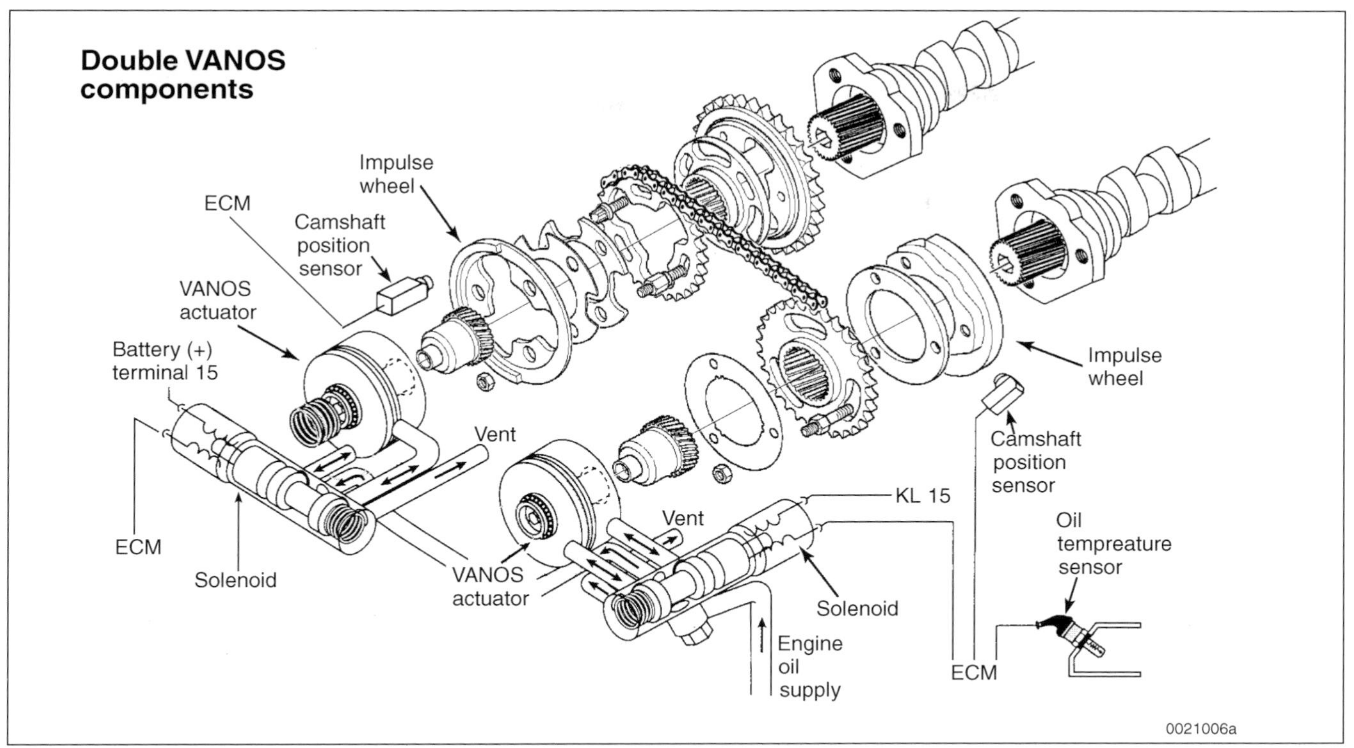

VANOS (M52 TU, M54, M56 ENGINES)

The main components of the double VANOS system are:

- Intake and exhaust camshafts with helical spline inserts
- Camshaft sprockets with adjustable gears
- VANOS actuators (two position piston housing with internal/external helical spline cup)
- Three-way solenoid switching valves
- Camshaft position impulse wheels
- Hall effect camshaft position sensors

Camshaft position is varied based on engine rpm, throttle position signal, intake air and coolant temperature.

When engine is started, camshafts are in deactivated position:

- Intake camshaft is held in RETARDED position by oil pressure.
- Exhaust camshaft is held in ADVANCED position by preload spring and oil pressure.

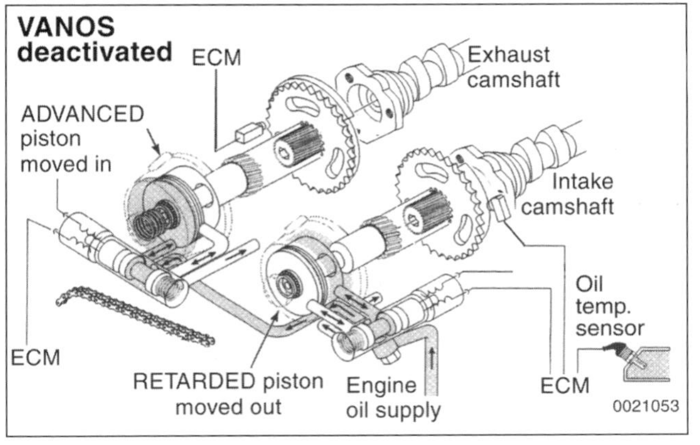

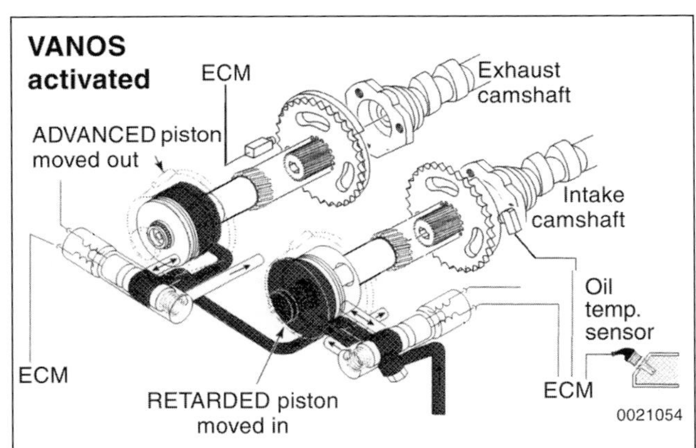

Within 2 - 5 seconds (50 engine revolutions), the ECM begins monitoring and controlling camshaft positions.

The Double VANOS system allows full variability of camshaft timing up to the limits of the system. When the ECM detects that the camshafts are in optimum position, the solenoids are modulated at approximately 100 - 220 Hz to maintain oil pressure on both sides of the actuator pistons to maintain timing.

In models with DME MS 43.0 and MS 45.1, the engine control module (ECM) detects camshaft position before the engine starts, thereby adjusting camshaft timing immediately upon start-up.

NOTE —

- *BMW does not provide diagnostic information or specifications for the Double VANOS system. VANOS system troubleshooting and diagnostics is best accomplished using a scan tool.*
- *Diagnostic Trouble Codes (DTCs) pertaining to the VANOS system are listed in* **Table a**. *See also* **On-Board Diagnostics** *at the back of this manual.*
- *Elevated oil temperatures can cause VANOS to deactivate. Oil that is too thick (high viscosity) may cause a DTC to be set in the ECM. If VANOS is deactivated (limp-home mode), there will be a noticeable loss of power.*

Table a. VANOS fault codes

BMW code	P-code	Fault description
19	P1529	VANOS solenoid valve activation, exhaust
21	P1525	VANOS solenoid valve activation, intake
103	P1519	VANOS faulty reference value intake
104	P1520	VANOS faulty reference value exhaust
105	P1522	VANOS stuck (Bank 1) intake
106	P1523	VANOS stuck (Bank 2) exhaust

VANOS control unit, removing

NOTE —

If the Double VANOS control unit is being replaced, camshaft timing must be checked as described later in this group. This procedure requires multiple special tools. Be sure to read the procedures through before beginning the repair.

– Working inside trunk, disconnect negative (–) battery cable.

CAUTION —

- *Prior to disconnecting the battery, read the battery disconnection cautions given at the front of this manual.*
- *Disconnecting the battery may erase fault code(s) stored in control module memory. Check for fault codes using special BMW diagnostic equipment.*

VANOS control unit

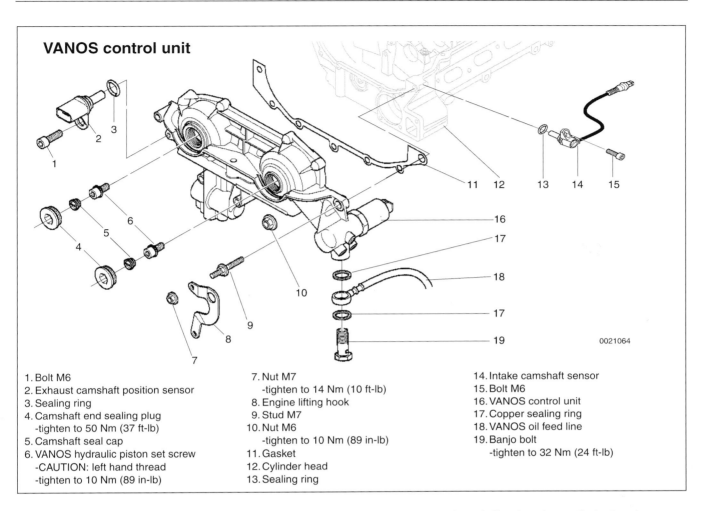

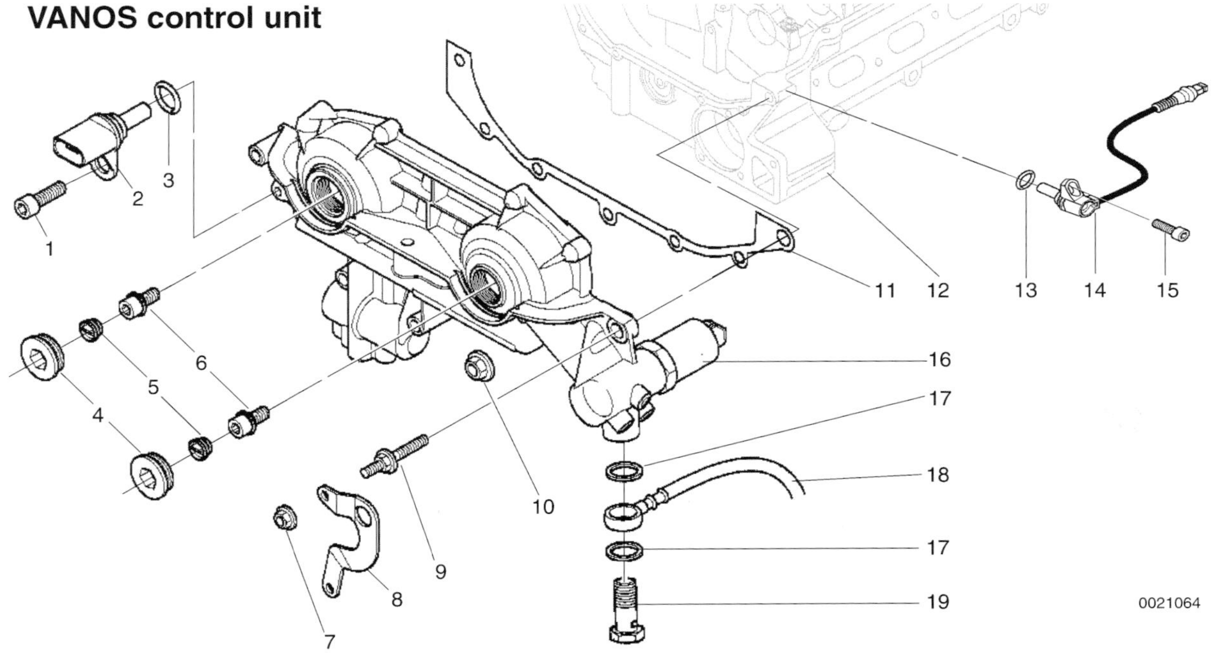

1. Bolt M6
2. Exhaust camshaft position sensor
3. Sealing ring
4. Camshaft end sealing plug
   -tighten to 50 Nm (37 ft-lb)
5. Camshaft seal cap
6. VANOS hydraulic piston set screw
   -CAUTION: left hand thread
   -tighten to 10 Nm (89 in-lb)
7. Nut M7
   -tighten to 14 Nm (10 ft-lb)
8. Engine lifting hook
9. Stud M7
10. Nut M6
    -tighten to 10 Nm (89 in-lb)
11. Gasket
12. Cylinder head
13. Sealing ring
14. Intake camshaft sensor
15. Bolt M6
16. VANOS control unit
17. Copper sealing ring
18. VANOS oil feed line
19. Banjo bolt
    -tighten to 32 Nm (24 ft-lb)

– Remove complete air filter housing, cylinder head cover, intake camshaft plastic cover and spark plugs, as described earlier in **Camshaft timing chains, removing**.

◀ Remove banjo bolt from VANOS unit oil pressure line. Use banjo bolt to attach BMW special tool 11 3 450 (compressed air fitting) to VANOS unit.

> ***CAUTION —***
>
> - *Oil will drain from pressure line. Have a container and rags ready. Do not allow oil to run onto drive belts.*
> - *Cover top of VANOS unit with lint-free shop cloth. Compressed air will force oil to spray out of oil bore on top of unit.*

– Connect compressed air line (with line pressure set to 2 - 8 bar or 30 - 110 psi) to air fitting.

With compressed air line connected, turn engine at least twice in direction of rotation until cylinder 1 intake and exhaust camshaft lobes (**arrows**) face each other.

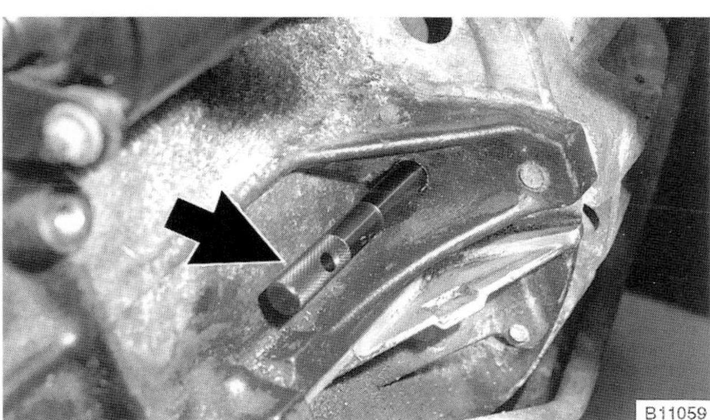

Remove sealing plug from bore on lower left side of engine block (flywheel end). Secure crankshaft in TDC position with BMW special tool 11 2 300 (**arrow**).

– Unscrew and remove cylinder head cover studs at rear of cylinder head.

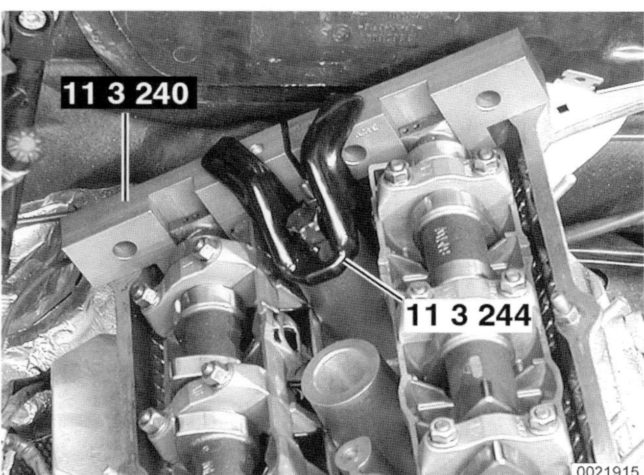

Secure camshafts in TDC position using BMW special tools 11 3 240 ans 11 3 244.

– Detach compressed air line, leaving compressed air fitting attached to VANOS unit.

NOTE —
Oil will drain from fittings when air line is removed. Have a container and rags ready. Do not allow oil to run onto drive belts.

Unscrew sealing plugs (**arrows**) from VANOS unit.

NOTE —
Oil will drain from plugs when removed. Have a container and rags ready. Do not allow oil to run onto drive belts.

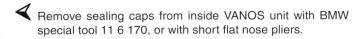

0021824

Remove sealing caps from inside VANOS unit with BMW special tool 11 6 170, or with short flat nose pliers.

NOTE —
Additional oil may drain from VANOS unit.

0021825

Remove set screws (left hand thread) on ends of intake and exhaust camshaft hydraulic pistons.

CAUTION —
Set screws have left-hand threads. Remove with a clockwise motion.

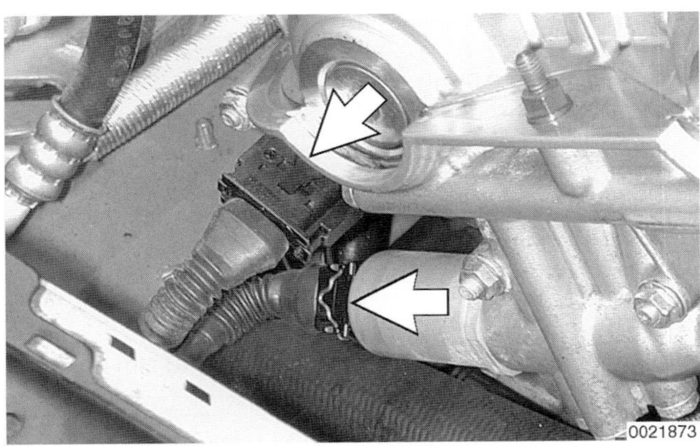
0021873

Disconnect electrical harness connectors from camshaft position sensors and solenoid valves on both exhaust and intake sides of VANOS unit.

0021826

Remove VANOS unit:

- Remove fasteners from engine support eye.
- Remove VANOS mounting nuts (**arrows**) from cylinder head. Slide VANOS unit and metal gasket off.

CAUTION —
Do not crank or turn over engine with VANOS unit removed. Piston/valve interference is possible.

VANOS control unit, installing

 Clean contact edges of cylinder head face and VANOS unit and apply a thin coat of sealing compound (3-Bond® 1209 or equivalent) to surfaces.

> ***CAUTION —***
> - *Make sure all gasket material is removed from face of cylinder head. Clean sealing face and keep free of oil. If any foreign material is present on the sealing surface, the camshaft timing will be incorrect.*
> - *Check locating dowel (**A**) and dowel sleeve (**B**) at top of cylinder head for damage or incorrect installation.*

NOTE —
- *If the Double VANOS control unit is being replaced, be sure to check and adjust camshaft timing as described later in this group.*
- *If work being carried out has no effect on camshaft timing, it is not necessary to recheck the timing. It is recommended however that the VANOS operation be checked using a compatible scan tool.*

– Using new gasket, install VANOS unit to cylinder head.
- Reinstall engine support eye.

Tightening torque
- VANOS unit to cylinder head
  M6 nut . . . . 10 Nm (89 in-lb)
  M7 nut . . . . 14 Nm (10 ft-lb)

 Insert and tighten down VANOS hydraulic piston set screws on intake and exhaust camshafts.

> ***CAUTION —***
> *Set screws have left hand thread. Tighten counterclockwise.*

Tightening torque
- Hydraulic piston to splined shaft
  M6 set screw . . . . 10 Nm (89 in-lb)

 Replace sealing caps inside VANOS unit with BMW special tool 11 6 170, or short flat nosed pliers.

Insert and secure VANOS sealing plugs (**arrows**), using new sealing O-rings.

Tightening torque
- Sealing plug to VANOS unit . . . . 50 Nm (37 ft-lb)

– Remove compressed air fitting from VANOS unit.

– Fit VANOS oil line banjo bolt with new seals. Attach oil line to VANOS unit.

Tightening torque
- Oil line to VANOS unit (banjo bolt) . . . . . 32 Nm (24 ft-lb)

– Attach electrical harness connectors to camshaft position sensors and VANOS solenoid valves.

– Remove BMW special locking tools from rear of cylinder head.

– Remove BMW special locking tool from flywheel and replace dust guard.

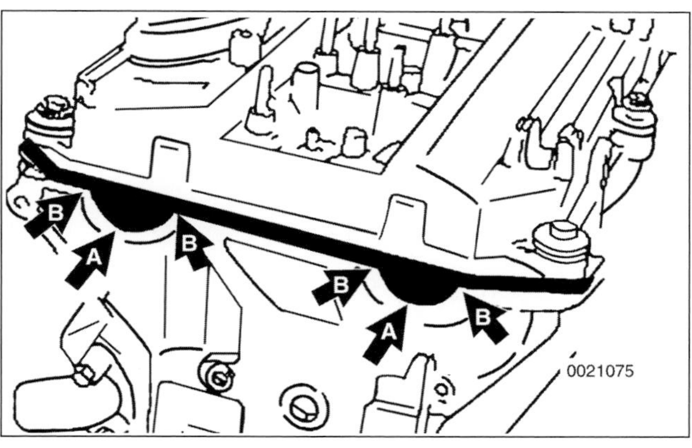

Install intake camshaft plastic baffle and then install cylinder head cover.

- Check for correct seating of half-moon seals (**A**) in back of cylinder head cover.
- Use a small amount of 3-Bond®1209 or equivalent sealant at corners (**B**) of half-moon cutouts.
- Similarly, seat gasket and seal corners in front of cylinder head, at VANOS unit.

Tightening torque
- Cylinder head cover to cylinder head (M6) . . . . 10 Nm (89 in-lb)

– Remainder of installation is reverse of removal.

Tightening torques
- Radiator fan (viscous clutch) to coolant pump . . . . 40 Nm (30 ft-lb)
- Spark plug to cylinder head . . . . 25 Nm (18 ft-lb)

Camshaft timing, adjusting

Use this procedure to check and, if necessary, adjust camshaft timing. This procedure assumes that the cylinder head cover and intake camshaft plastic baffle have been removed as described under **Camshaft timing chain, removing**. Also, be sure the cooling fan behind the radiator and the spark plugs have been removed.

Remove primary camshaft chain tensioner cylinder (**arrow**).

> ***CAUTION —***
> *Primary camshaft chain tensioning piston is under spring pressure.*

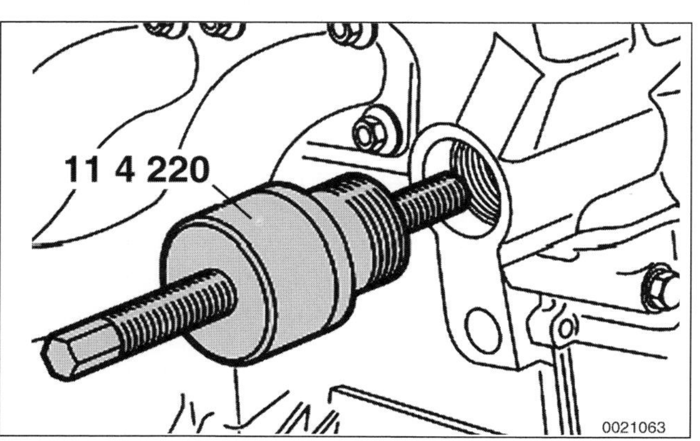

Insert BMW special tool 11 4 220 in cylinder head and bring adjustment screw into contact with tensioning rail.

NOTE —
BMW special tool 11 4 220 is a dummy primary chain tensioner and simulates the function of the tensioner.

Preload primary chain tensioner rail:

- Tighten adjusting screw on BMW special tool 11 4 220.

Tightening torque
- Primary chain tensioner preload. . . . . . . .0.7 Nm (6 in-lb)

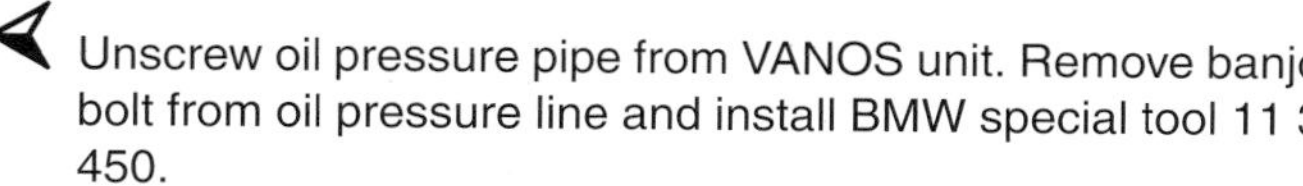

Unscrew oil pressure pipe from VANOS unit. Remove banjo bolt from oil pressure line and install BMW special tool 11 3 450.

> ***CAUTION —***
> *Cover top of VANOS unit with lint-free shop cloth. Attachment of compressed air line will force oil to spray out of bore.*

– Connect compressed air line to air fitting. Apply air pressure set to 2 - 8 bar (30 - 110 psi).

With compressed air line connected, turn engine at least twice in direction of rotation until cylinder 1 intake and exhaust camshaft lobes (**arrows**) face each other.

> ***CAUTION —***
> *Do not rotate engine counterclockwise to reach the top dead center position. Instead, complete another two complete rotations.*

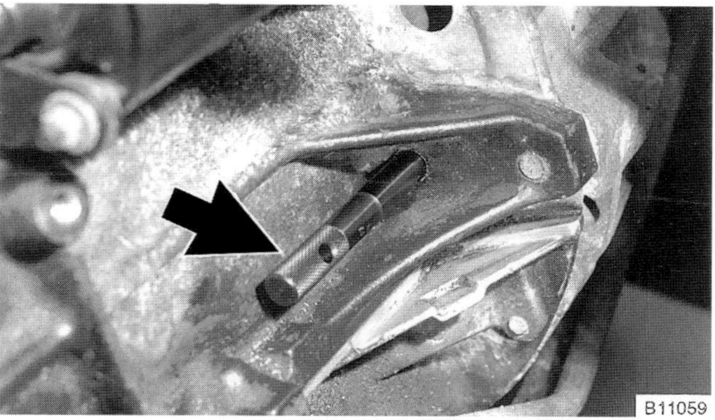

Remove sealing plug from bore on lower left side of engine block near flywheel. Secure crankshaft in TDC position with BMW special tool 11 2 300 (**arrow**).

– Unscrew and remove cylinder head cover studs at rear of cylinder head.

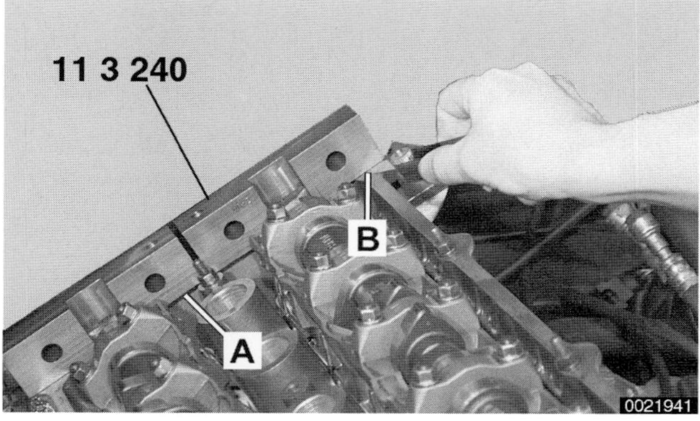

Place BMW special tool 11 3 240 over camshafts ends and measure clearance of tool to cylinder head surface.

NOTE —

- *If the exhaust side of the tool (**A**) is not flush with the head, retime the camshafts as described below.*
- *Due to flexible sprocket design, VANOS unit tolerances and play in the VANOS splines, when the camshaft timing is set correctly, the intake side of special tool 11 3 240 (**B**) may be up to 1 mm (0.04 in) above the surface of the cylinder head. This is normal. Reassemble engine. Otherwise, retime the engine as described below.*

– Remove Double VANOS unit as described earlier.

◄ Press down on secondary chain tensioner and lock into place using BMW special tool 11 3 292 or equivalent.

– Make sure primary chain tensioner dummy tool (special tool 11 4 220) is installed in side of cylinder head and just touching tensioning rail. Do not preload chain yet.

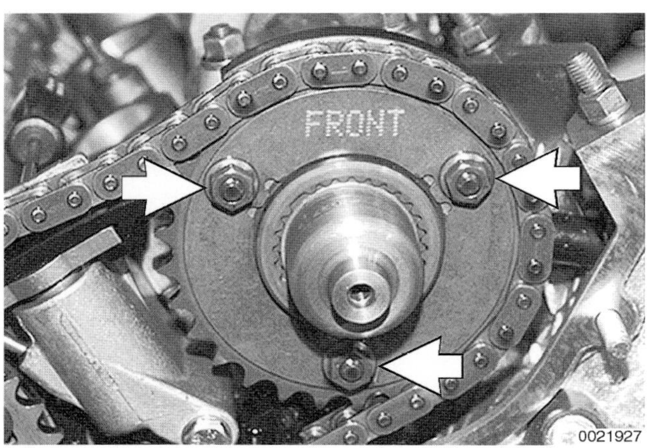

◄ Loosen intake camshaft sprocket mounting nuts (**arrows**) by 1 turn.

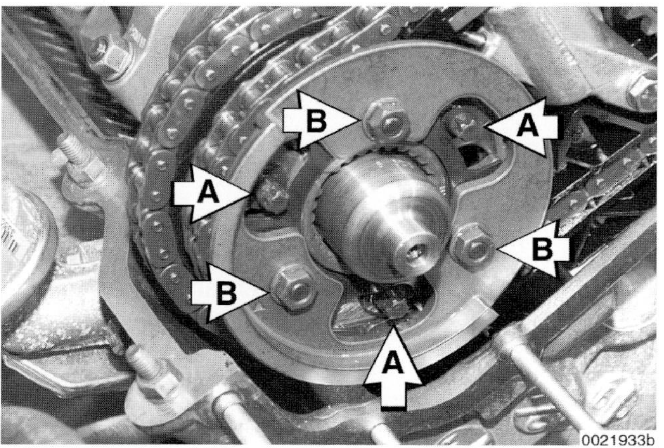

◄ Loosen exhaust camshaft sprocket mounting bolts (**A**) ½ turn.

- Loosen exhaust camshaft impulse wheel mounting nuts (**B**) 2 turns.

◄ Slide out intake camshaft splined shaft until approx. 1 mm (0.04 in) of splines (**arrows**) can be seen.

◄ Pull out exhaust camshaft splined shaft to stop.

– Make sure camshafts are secured in TDC position using BMW special tools 11 3 240 and 11 3 244.

◄ Preload primary chain tensioning rail:

- Tighten adjusting screw on BMW special tool 11 4 220.

Tightening torque

- Primary chain tensioner preload . . . . .0.7 Nm (6 in-lb)

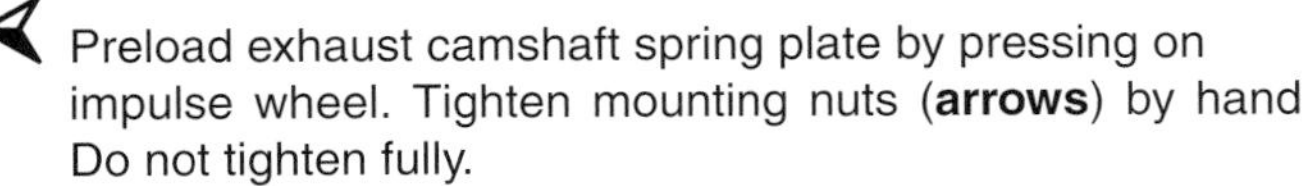

Preload exhaust camshaft spring plate by pressing on impulse wheel. Tighten mounting nuts (**arrows**) by hand. Do not tighten fully.

Install BMW special tool 11 6 150 (VANOS setup bracket) to front of cylinder head timing case. Tighten nuts (**arrows**) by hand, and then tighten down uniformly until special tool is in full contact with cylinder head.

> ***CAUTION —***
> *Make sure all gasket material is removed from face of cylinder head. Clean sealing face and keep free of oil. If any foreign material is present on the sealing surface, the camshaft timing will be incorrect.*

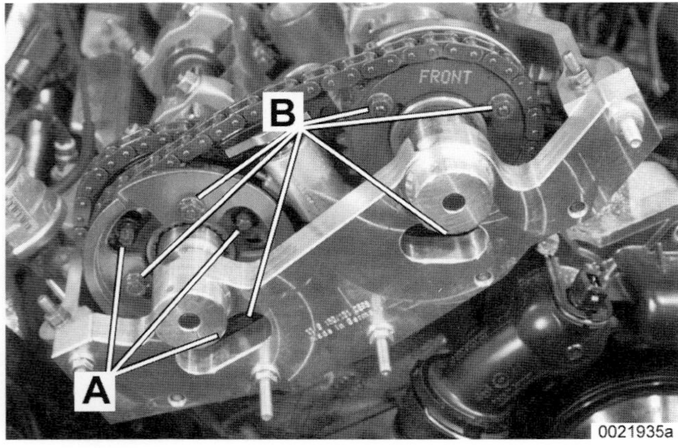

Secure camshaft impulse sprockets and wheels:

- Pretighten Torx screws (**A**) on exhaust camshaft impulse wheel to approx. 5 Nm (44 in-lb).
- Pretighten mounting nuts (**B**) on exhaust and intake sprocket assemblies to approx. 5 Nm (44 in-lb).
- Torque down Torx screws (**A**) and nuts (**B**) to final specifications.

Tightening torques

- Sprocket assembly to camshaft
  initial torque . . . . 5 Nm (44 in-lb)
- Sprocket assembly to camshaft
  M7 Torx screw (**A**). . . . . 20 Nm (15 ft-lb)
  M6 mounting nut (**B**) . . . . 10 Nm (89 in-lb)

– Remove flywheel locking tool from transmission bellhousing so that crankshaft is no longer locked.

– Remove camshaft locking tools from rear of cylinder head.

– Crank engine over twice by hand in direction of rotation until cylinder 1 intake and exhaust camshaft lobes face each other again.

– Secure crankshaft with BMW special tool 11 2 300.

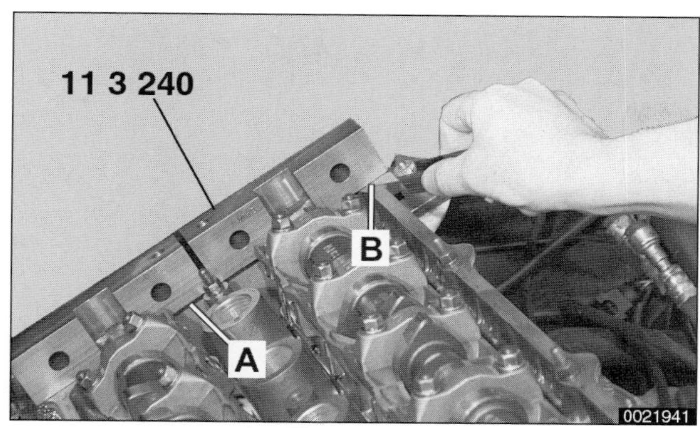

Place BMW special tool 11 3 240 over camshaft ends and measure clearance of tool to cylinder head surface.

NOTE —

- *If the exhaust side of the tool (**A**) is not flush with the head, camshaft timing is incorrect. Repeat camshaft timing procedure.*
- *Due to flexible sprocket design, VANOS unit tolerances and play in the VANOS splines, when the camshaft timing is set correctly, the intake side of special tool 11 3 240 (**B**) may be up to 1 mm (0.04 in) above the surface of the cylinder head. This is normal. Otherwise, repeat camshaft timing procedure.*

– Remove camshaft locking tools from rear of camshafts.

– Remove BMW special tool 11 4 220 (dummy primary chain tensioner). Reinstall primary chain tensioner.

Tightening torque

- Primary chain tensioner cylinder to cylinder head . . . . 70 Nm (52 ft-lb)

– Remove flywheel locking tool from transmission bellhousing Reinstall sealing plug.

– Remove VANOS setup bracket from front of cylinder head.

– Install VANOS control unit as described earlier in this group.

– Remove compressed air fitting (special tool 11 3 450) from VANOS unit.

– Fit VANOS oil line banjo bolt with new seals. Attach oil line to VANOS unit.

Tightening torque

- Oil line to VANOS unit (banjo bolt) . . . . . 32 Nm (24 ft-lb)

– Remainder of engine assembly is reverse of disassembly.

Tightening torques

- Radiator cooling fan (viscous clutch) to coolant pump . . . . 40 Nm (30 ft-lb)
- Cylinder head cover to cylinder head . . . 10 Nm (89 in-lb)
- Spark plug to cylinder head . . . . 25 Nm (18 ft-lb)

119 Lubrication System

119

GENERAL

This repair group covers lubrication system troubleshooting as well as oil pan removal and oil pump replacement.

Special tools

The engine needs to be properly supported while the front suspension subframe is removed to access the lubrication system. If BMW special tools 00 0 200 / 00 0 208 are not available, a device to support the weight of the engine from above would be suitable.

Special Tools

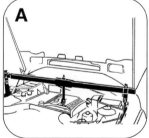

A

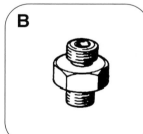

B

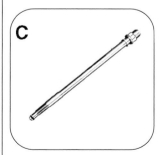

C

Special tools

A BMW 00 0 200/00 0 208 . . . . Engine support bracket
B BMW 11 4 050 . . . . .Adapter for BMW oil pressure gauge
C BMW 11 4 390 . . . Adapter screw for BMW oil pressure gauge

NOTE —
Oil change procedure and oil filter replacement are covered in **020 Maintenance**.

Engine lubrication

Oil pressure is generated by a gear-type pump bolted to the bottom of the engine block. The oil pump is chain driven off the front of the crankshaft.

Oil passages in the cylinder block and cylinder head connect the oil pump to components such as camshafts, crankshaft and valve lifters.

Engine oil change capacity

- Rear wheel drive. . . . .
  M52 TU, M54, M56 engines . . . . 6.5 liters (6.9 qt.)
  S54 engine 5.5 liters (5.8 qt.)
- All wheel drive. 7.5 liters (7.9 qt.)

Oil pressure, checking (M52 TU, M54, M56 engines)

In some engines access to the oil pressure warning switch port may be extremely restricted.

– Unscrew oil filter cap in order to allow engine oil to drain back down into oil pan.

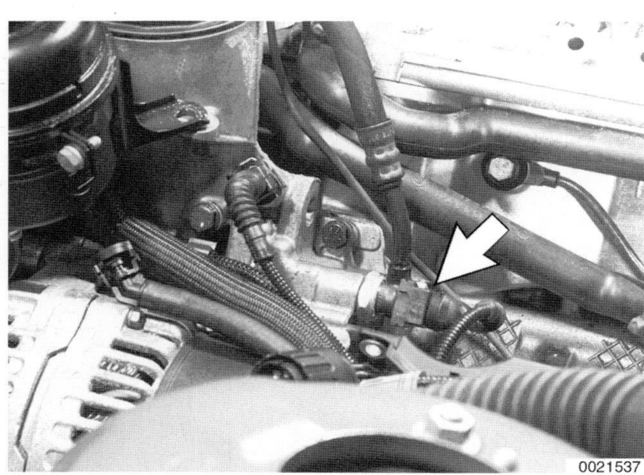

◀ Disconnect harness connector from oil pressure switch (**arrow**) and remove switch.

> ***CAUTION —***
> *Running the engine with the oil pressure switch disconnected may set a fault code (DTC).*

NOTE —
- *Thoroughly clean around the oil pressure switch before removing.*
- *Be prepared to catch leaking oil with a shop towel.*

Component location
- Oil pressure switch . . . . base of oil filter housing

---

– Install pressure gauge in place of switch.

– With gauge installed, start engine and allow to reach operating temperature. Check oil pressure both cold and hot.

NOTE —
For the most accurate test results, the engine oil and filter should be new. The oil should be the correct grade.

Oil pressure
- Idle (minimum)
  M52 TU, M54, M56 engines . . . . 0.5 bar (7 psi)
- Regulated pressure
  (elevated engine speed) . . . . 4.0 bar (59 psi)

– Remove pressure gauge and reinstall pressure switch.

Tightening torque
- Oil pressure switch to oil filter housing . . 27 Nm (20 ft-lb)

If testing shows low oil pressure, one or more of the following conditions may be indicated:

- Worn or faulty oil pump
- Worn or faulty engine bearings
- Severe engine wear

All of these conditions indicate the need for major repairs.

Oil pressure, checking (S54 engine)

BMW special tool 11 4 390 and an appropriate pressure gauge (0-25 bar range) is required to check engine oil pressure. The special tool is substituted in place of the long center oil filter cover bolt as an adapter to connect the oil pressure gauge.

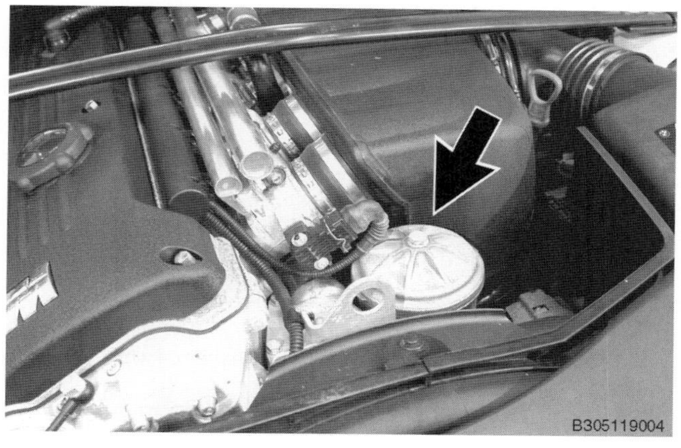
B305119004

◄ Unscrew center bolt (**arrow**) from oil filter cover. Allow engine oil to drain back down into oil pan and then remove long screw from filter cover.

NOTE —

- *Thoroughly clean around oil filter cover bolt before removing it.*
- *Be prepared to catch any leaking oil with a shop towel.*

– Install BMW special tool 11 4 390 (screw adapter) in oil filter cover. Install cover and tighten screw adapter.

– Connect pressure gauge to adapter (BMW special tool 11 4 390), start engine and allow to reach operating temperature. Check oil pressure both cold and hot.

NOTE —

For the most accurate test results, the engine oil and filter should be new. The oil should be the correct grade.

Oil pressure

- Idle (minimum)
  S54 engine . . . . 0.7 bar (9 psi)
- Regulated pressure
  (elevated engine speed) . . . . 4.0 bar (59 psi)

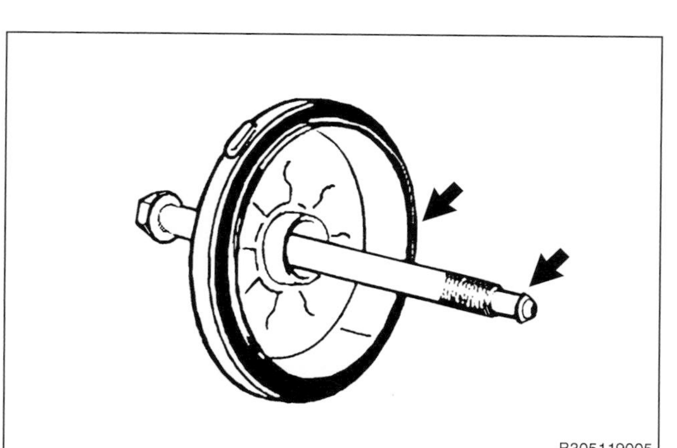
B305119005

 Remove pressure gauge and reinstall oil filter cover bolt. Replace O-ring in cover and at base of center bolt if necessary (**arrows**).

Tightening torque

- Oil cover bolt to oil filter housing. . . . . . . 33 Nm (24 ft-lb)

If testing shows low oil pressure, one or more of the following conditions may be indicated:

- Worn or faulty oil pump
- Worn or faulty engine bearings
- Severe engine wear

All of these conditions indicate the need for major repairs.

Oil pressure warning system, testing

The oil pressure warning system consists of an oil pressure switch mounted in the oil circuit and an instrument panel warning light. Other safety features include:

- Dynamic oil level warning
- Engine oil temperature monitoring (S54 engine)
- A filter bypass to provide lubrication should the oil filter become clogged
- An oil pump pressure relief valve to prevent excessive system pressure.

NOTE —
The MS S54 engine management system on M3 models monitors engine oil temperature and signals the instrument cluster over the CAN line for operation of the oil temperature gauge and illumination of the instrument cluster LEDs.

CAUTION —
If the red oil pressure warning comes on or flashes on while driving, always assume that the oil pressure is low.

When the ignition is turned on, the oil pressure warning light comes on. When the engine is started and the oil pressure rises slightly, the oil pressure switch opens and the warning light goes out. Make sure the oil level is correct before making tests.

— Turn ignition switch on.

- Warning light on instrument panel must light up.

— Remove connector from oil pressure switch.

- Warning light on instrument panel must go out.

CAUTION —
Running the engine with the oil pressure switch disconnected may set a fault code (DTC).

NOTE —
If the light does not go out, the wiring to the switch is most likely grounded somewhere between the switch terminal and the warning light. See **Electrical Wiring Diagrams** *at rear of manual for electrical schematics.*

The oil pressure warning switch circuit varies depending on engine application.

Oil pressure switch circuit

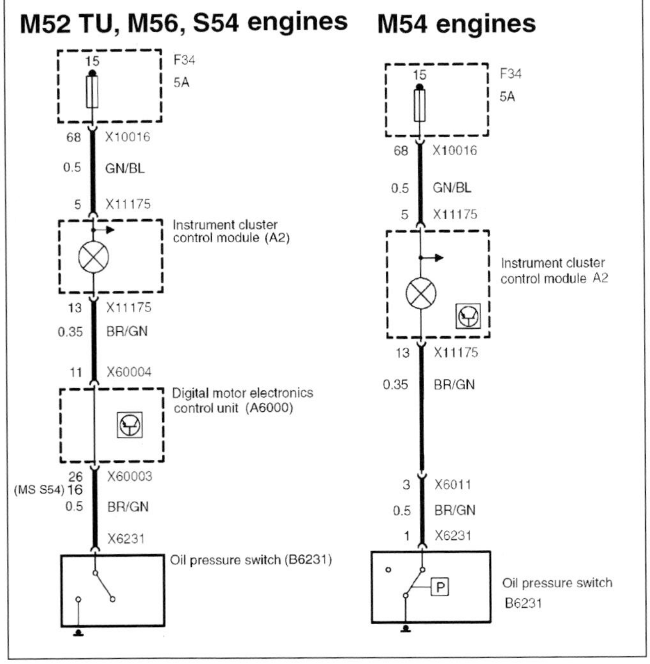

M52 TU, M56, S54 engines

15
F34
5A
68 X10016
0.5 GN/BL
5 X11175
Instrument cluster control module (A2)
13 X11175
0.35 BR/GN
11 X60004
Digital motor electronics control unit (A6000)
26 X60003
(MS S54) 16
0.5 BR/GN
X6231
Oil pressure switch (B6231)

M54 engines

15
F34
5A
68 X10016
0.5 GN/BL
5 X11175
Instrument cluster control module A2
13 X11175
0.35 BR/GN
3 X6011
0.5 BR/GN
1 X6231
P
Oil pressure switch B6231

— If warning light does not light when ignition is on, remove connector from oil pressure switch and use a jumper wire to ground connector terminal to a clean metal surface.

- To test switch, connect an ohmmeter between terminal in switch body and ground. With engine off, there should be continuity. With engine running, oil pressure should open switch and there should be no continuity. Replace a faulty switch.

> ***CAUTION —***
> *Keep in mind that low oil pressure may be preventing the switch from turning the light out. If the light remains on while the engine is running, check the oil pressure as described earlier. Do not drive the car until the problem is corrected. The engine may be severely damaged.*

OIL PAN

The oil pan removal procedure requires that the engine be supported from above and the front suspension subframe be unbolted and lowered from the chassis.

Oil pan, removing and installing (rear wheel drive models)

- Raise car and place securely on jack stands.

> ***WARNING —***
> *Make sure the car is stable and well supported at all times. Use a professional automotive lift or jack stands designed for the purpose. A floor jack is not adequate support.*

◀ Working underneath car, remove engine splash guard and remove chassis reinforcement plate or reinforcement bar. See **310 Front Suspension**.

NOTE —
Chassis reinforcement consists of a triangulated bar for Sedan (shown) or Wagon or a reinforced plate for Convertible or Coupe and M3 models.

> ***WARNING —***
> - *The front chassis reinforcement plate or reinforcement bar mounting fasteners are stretch type bolts and must be replaced anytime they are removed.*
> - *The vehicle must not be driven with this component removed. See* **310 Front Suspension** *for additional information.*

- Drain engine oil as described in **020 Maintenance**.

- Remove air filter housing complete with mass air flow sensor.

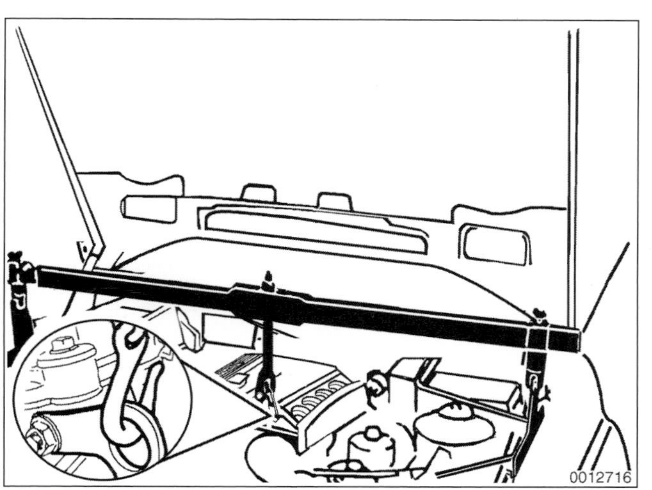

◀ Install engine lifting equipment at front engine lifting point and raise approximately 10 mm (1/2 inch) until engine weight is supported.

> **CAUTION —**
> *Check that the radiator cooling fan does not damage fan shroud when raising engine. If necessary, remove fan shroud. See* **170 Radiator and Cooling System**.

– On cars with automatic transmission, remove ATF cooler line brackets from oil pan.

S54 engines: Remove nut and disconnect oil dipstick guide tube from intake manifold (**A**).

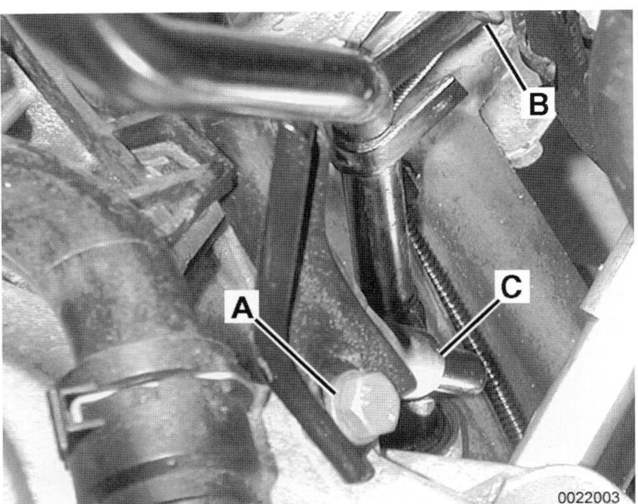

Remove oil dipstick guide tube:

- **M52 TU, M54, M56 engines**:
  - Remove bolt (**A**) from left engine mounting bracket.
  - Disconnect fuel lines and wiring harness brackets (**B**).
  - Disconnect oil separator hose (**C**) from base of guide tube and remove tube from oil pan.
- **S54 engine**:
  - Remove dipstick guide tube bracket at top of oil pan. Separate guide tube from oil pan.
  - Disconnect oil separator hose at top of oil pan (quick-disconnect fitting).
  - Unclip wiring harness secured to top of oil pan.

NOTE —
The dipstick guide tube is sealed in the block using an O-ring. Check that the O-ring comes out with the tube.

Center steering wheel, then working from below separate steering column shaft from steering rack at universal joint.

> **CAUTION —**
> *Prior to separating the steering column shaft, center the front wheels and remove the ignition key to lock steering wheel. Once the column is separated, the steering wheel rotation is no longer limited and if allowed to spin freely can result in damage to airbag system electrical components.*

Remove power steering pump belt. Remove pump bracket mounting bolts from the front (**arrows**).

NOTE —

- *Do not detach power steering fluid lines from pump.*
- *Power steering pump mounting may vary slightly depending on model.*

Remove third power steering pump mounting bolt (**arrow**) and remove pump from its mounting bracket. Use stiff wire to suspend pump from chassis.

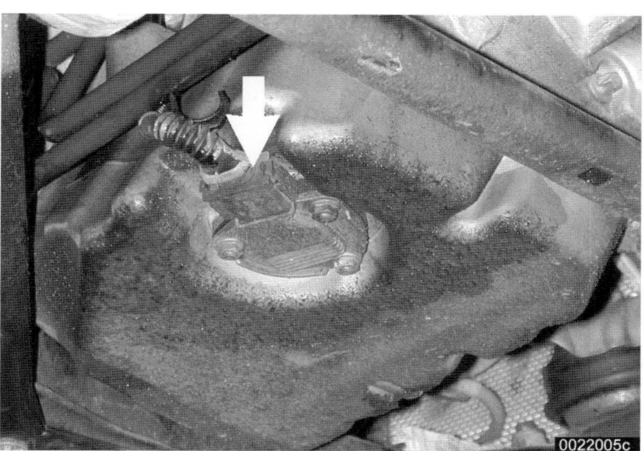

Disconnect electrical harness connector (**arrow**) at oil level sensor.

0022007

◀ Loosen top engine mount fasteners (**arrow**) at left and right sides.

NOTE —
Right side is shown in photo. Left is similar.

0022017

◀ Remove lower engine mount fasteners (**arrows**).

NOTE —
Right side is shown in photo. Left is similar.

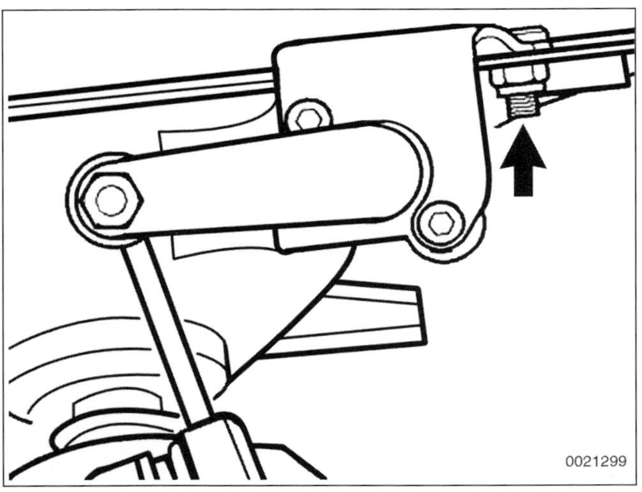
0021299

◀ If applicable, remove front ride level sensor mounting bolt (**arrow**) and lay sensor aside.

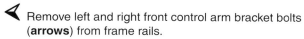

0022008

Remove left and right front control arm bracket bolts (**arrows**) from frame rails.

NOTE —
Right side is shown in photo. Left is similar.

– Detach left and right stabilizer bar anchors from frame rails.

0022010

Remove left control arm ball joint mounting nut (**arrow**) at front suspension subframe.

• Drive ball joint out from subframe using soft hammer.
• Push control arm aside.
• Repeat for left side.

0022013

Support suspension subframe from below using appropriate jacking equipment. Remove subframe mounting bolts (**arrows**) and lower subframe as far as possible.

NOTE —
Right side is shown in photo. Left is similar.

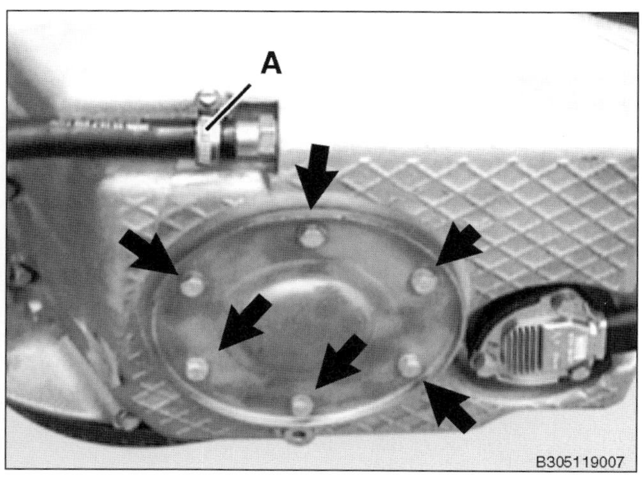

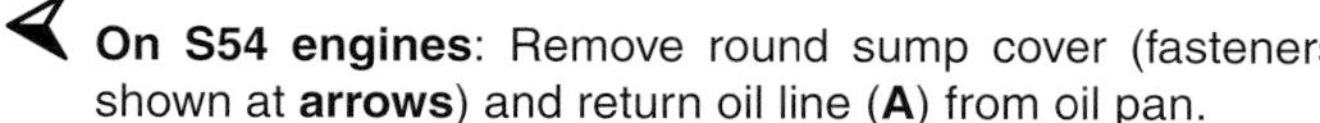
On S54 engines: Remove round sump cover (fasteners shown at **arrows**) and return oil line (**A**) from oil pan.

NOTE —

Some residual oil will drip from sump cover once removed. Have shop rags ready.

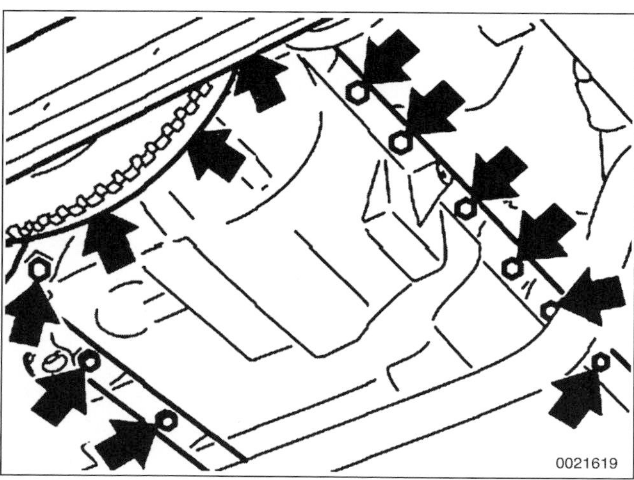

Remove oil pan screws (**arrows**) at cylinder block. Lower oil pan forward to remove.

CAUTION —

If the oil pan does not separate easily from the engine cylinder block, a few taps with a rubber mallet should break it free. Do not pry the oil pan loose.

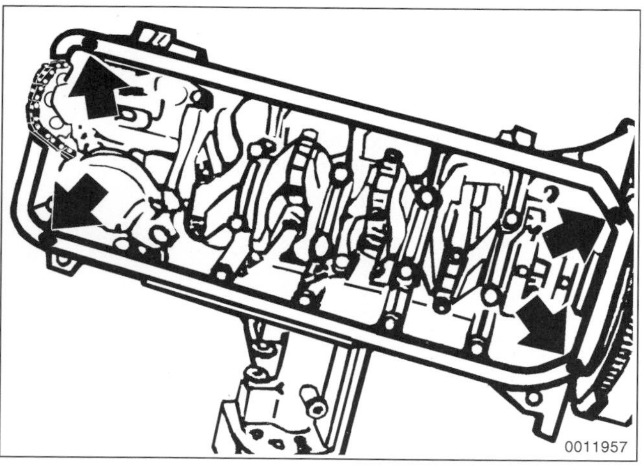

When installing oil pan:

- Thoroughly clean all old gasket material from mating surfaces and use a new gasket.
- Apply a small amount of non-hardening sealer (3-Bond 1209® or equivalent) to oil pan gasket directly below joints (**arrows**) for end cover and front timing case cover. Apply a bead 3 mm wide by 2 mm high.
- Tighten oil pan bolts to cylinder block evenly all around.
- Tighten transmission bellhousing bolts last.

Tightening torque

- Oil drain plug to oil pan (M12). . . . . 25 Nm (18 ft-lb)
- Oil pan to engine block
  M6, 8.8 grade . . . . 10 Nm (89 in-lb)
  M6, 10.9 grade . . . . 12 Nm (106 in-lb)

– Remainder of installation is reverse of removal.
  - Replace self-locking nuts when reinstalling front suspension components.
  - Match up key ways while installing steering column shaft. See **320 Steering and Wheel Alignment** for more specific procedures. Use a new bolt.
  - Use new oil dipstick tube sealing O-ring.
  - S54 engine: use new gasket at round sump cover.
  - Fill engine with oil and then check oil level as described in **020 Maintenance**.
  - After adding engine oil, start and run engine. Raise engine speed to 2,500 rpm until oil pressure warning lamp goes out (about 5 seconds).

NOTE —

- *See chart in the beginning of this repair group for engine oil capacities and specifications.*
- *S54 engine: A small quantity of oil, which otherwise would stay inside the oil pan during regular oil and filter service, is drained when the pan is removed. When refilling the engine, add an extra 1.0 liter / 1.1 US qt. of oil (for a total of 6.5 liters / 6.9 US qt). Be sure to check oil level as the final step.*
- *BMW does not specify a front end alignment following this procedure.*

Tightening torques

- Control arm ball joint to suspension subframe . . . . 90 Nm (66 ft-lb)
- Front subframe to frame rails (M12, use new bolts)
  8.8 grade. . . . . 77 Nm (57 ft-lb)
  10.9 grade. . . . . 110 Nm (81 ft-lb)
  12.9 grade. . . . . 105 Nm (77 ft-lb)
- Front end reinforcement to frame rails or suspension subframe (use new bolts) . . .See **310 Front Suspension**
- Stabilizer bar to frame rail (M8 nut). . . . . 22 Nm (16 ft-lb)
- Steering column universal joint clamping screw (M8 bolt, use new bolt) . . . . 22 Nm (16 ft-lb)

Oil pan, removing and installing (all wheel drive models)

– Raise car and place securely on jack stands.

WARNING —
Make sure the car is stable and well supported at all times. Use a professional automotive lift or jack stands designed for the purpose. A floor jack is not adequate support.

– Remove splash shield from under engine.

– Drain engine oil as described in **020 Maintenance**.

– Remove air filter housing complete with mass air flow sensor.

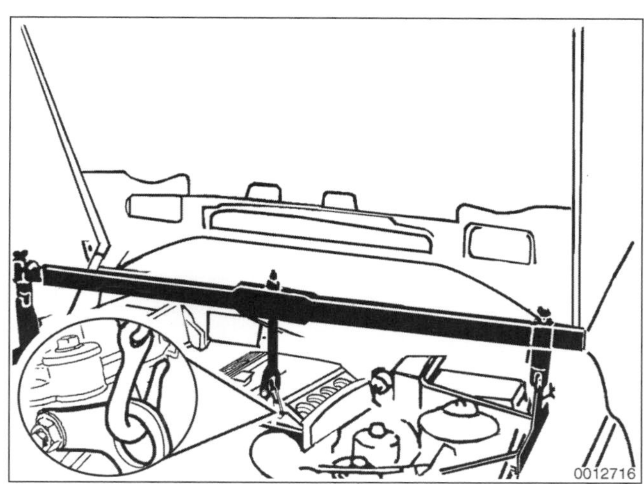

◄ Install engine lifting equipment at front engine lifting point and raise approximately 5 mm (¼ inch) until engine weight is supported.

– Remove fuel line clamping brackets from oil pan.

– On cars with automatic transmission, remove ATF cooler line brackets from oil pan and from transmission.

NOTE —
Place drain pan under lines to catch ATF drips.

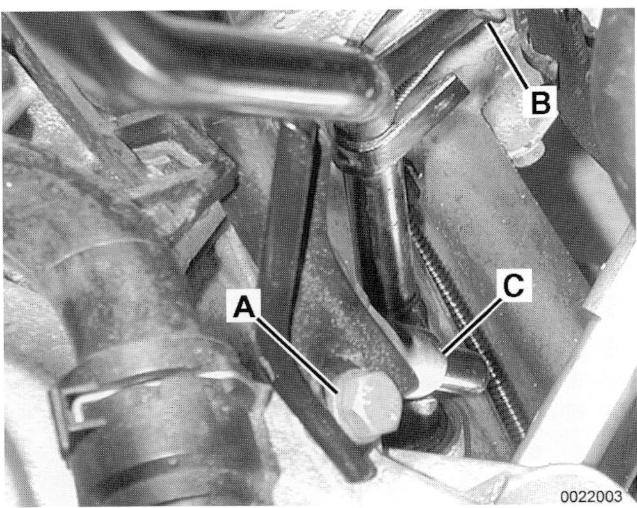

◀ Remove oil dipstick guide tube:

- Detach mounting bolt (**A**) from left engine mounting bracket.
- Detach fuel lines and wiring harness brackets (**B**).
- Disconnect oil separator hose (**C**) from base of guide tube and remove tube from oil pan.

NOTE —
The guide tube is sealed in the block using an O-ring. Check that the O-ring comes out with the tube.

◀ Separate steering column shaft from steering rack at universal joint. Point wheels straight ahead before disconnecting shaft from rack. See **320 Steering and Wheel Alignment**.

◀ Remove power steering pump pulley. Remove two mounting bolts from the front (**arrows**).

NOTE —
Do not detach power steering fluid lines from pump.

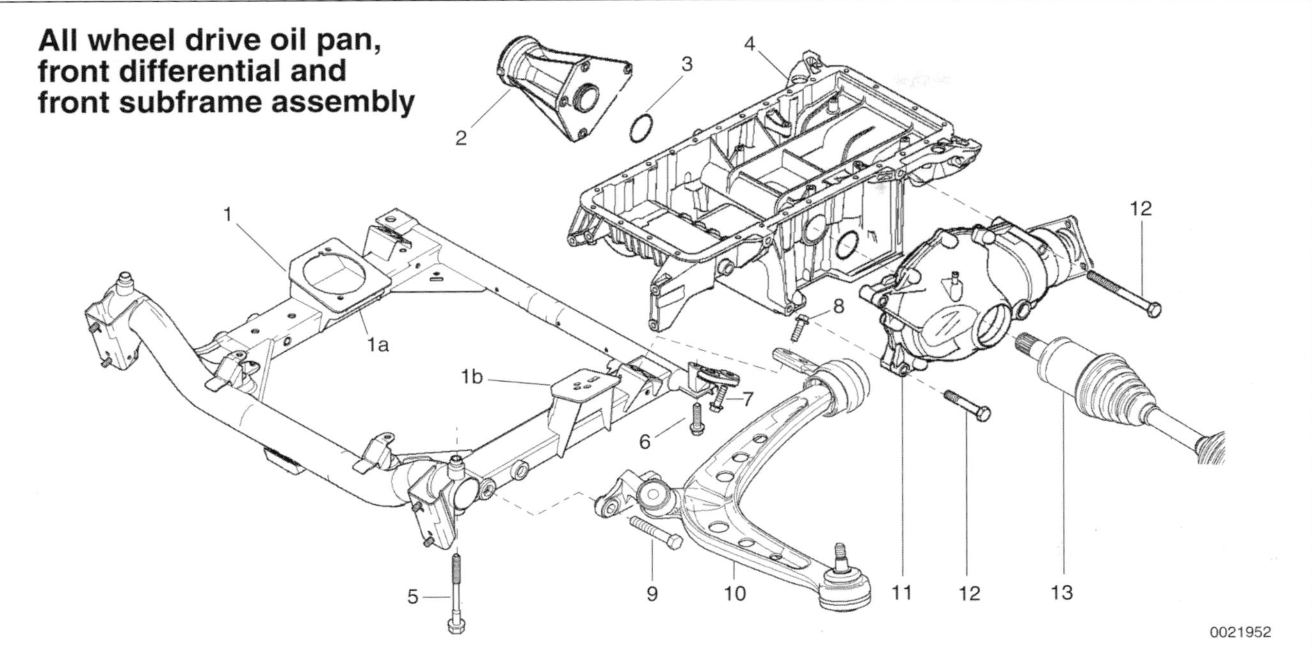

1. Front subframe
1a. Right engine mounting point
1b. Left engine mounting point
2. Right axle inner bearing pedestal
3. Sealing O-ring
4. Oil pan
5. Bolt M12 (always replace)
   - -8.8 grade tighten to 77 Nm (57 ft-lb)
   - -10.9 grade tighten to 110 Nm (81 ft-lb)
   - -12.9 grade tighten to 105 Nm (77 ft-lb)
6. Bolt M12 (always replace)
   - -tighten to 110 Nm (81 ft-lb)
7. Bolt M10 (always replace)
   - -tighten to 59 Nm (44 ft-lb)
8. Bolt M10 (always replace)
   - -tighten to 59 Nm (44 ft-lb)
9. Bolt M12
   - -tighten to 77 Nm (57 ft-lb)
10. Front control arm with ball joint and rear mounting bracket
11. Front differential
12. Bolt M10
    - -tighten to 45 Nm (33 ft-lb)
13. Left front axle

Remove third power steering mounting bolt (**arrow**) and remove pump from its mounting bracket. Use stiff wire to suspend pump from chassis.

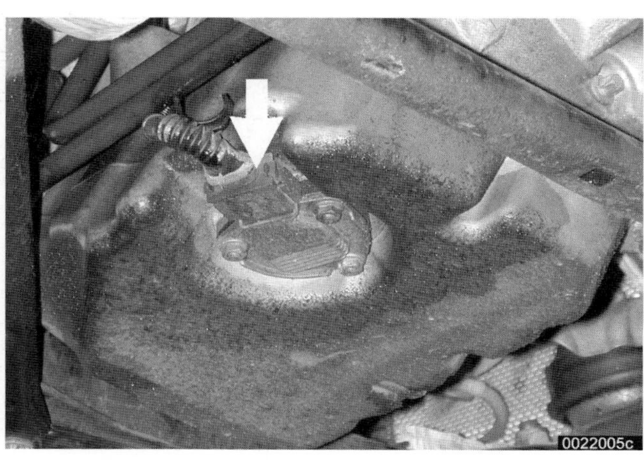
0022005c

◀ Detach electrical harness connector at oil level sensor.

– Remove lower engine mount fasteners.

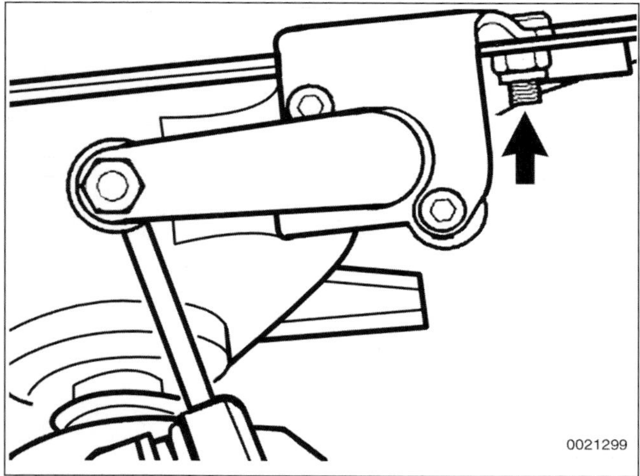
0021299

◀ If applicable, remove front ride level sensor mounting bolt (**arrow**) and lay sensor aside.

0021625

◀ Working at rear right corner of front subframe, unhook heatshield from subframe (**arrow**).

– Detach stabilizer bar anchors from frame rails.

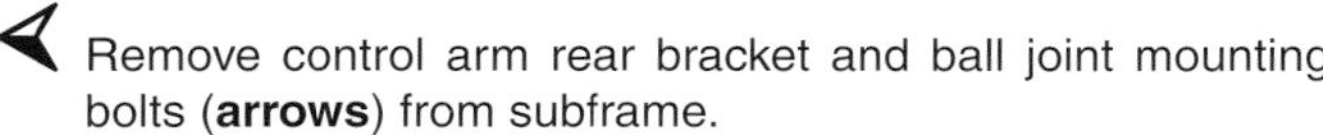

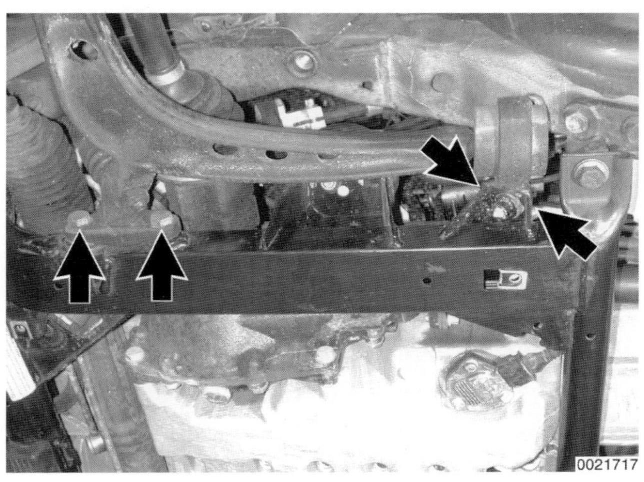

Remove control arm rear bracket and ball joint mounting bolts (**arrows**) from subframe.

- Remove control arms and front drive axles as described in **310 Front Suspension**.
- Remove front differential and right axle inner bearing pedestal as described in **311 Front Axle Final Drive**.

Support subframe while removing four mounting bolts (**arrows**).

> ***CAUTION —***
> *Lower subframe as far as possible without damaging power steering lines. Make sure it is adequately supported throughout the remainder of this procedure.*

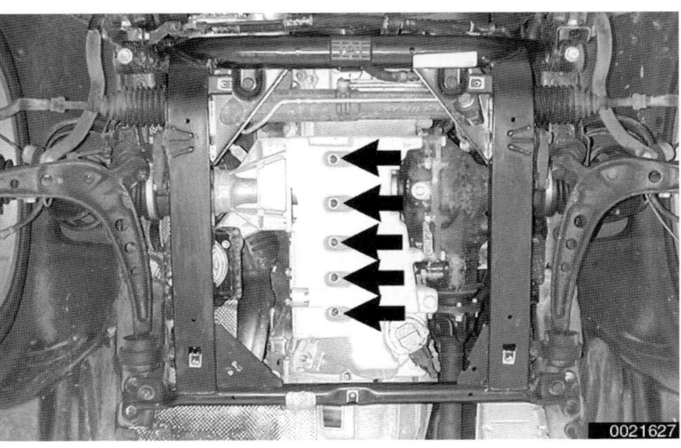

Remove oil pan:

- Remove bellhousing bolts from oil pan.
- Remove all oil pan periphery bolts.
- Remove center oil pan bolts (**arrows**).
- Lower oil pan to remove.

> ***CAUTION —***
> *If the oil pan does not separate easily from the engine cylinder block, a few taps with a rubber mallet should break it free. Do not pry the oil pan loose.*

- When reinstalling oil pan:
  - Thoroughly clean all old gasket material from mating surfaces and use a new gasket.
  - Apply a small amount of non-hardening sealer (3-Bond 1209® or equivalent) to oil pan gasket directly below joints for end cover and front timing case cover. Apply a bead 3 mm wide by 2 mm high.
  - Tighten oil pan bolts to cylinder block evenly all around.
  - Tighten transmission bellhousing bolts last.

Tightening torque

- Oil drain plug to oil pan (M12). . . . . 25 Nm (18 ft-lb)
- Oil pan to engine block
  M6, 8.8 grade . . . . 10 Nm (89 in-lb)
  M6, 10.9 grade . . . . 12 Nm (106 in-lb)
  M8, 8.8 grade . . . . 22 Nm (16 ft-lb)
- Transmission bellhousing to oil pan
  M8 Allen . . . . 24 Nm (17 ft-lb)
  M8 Torx. . . . . 21 Nm (15 ft-lb)

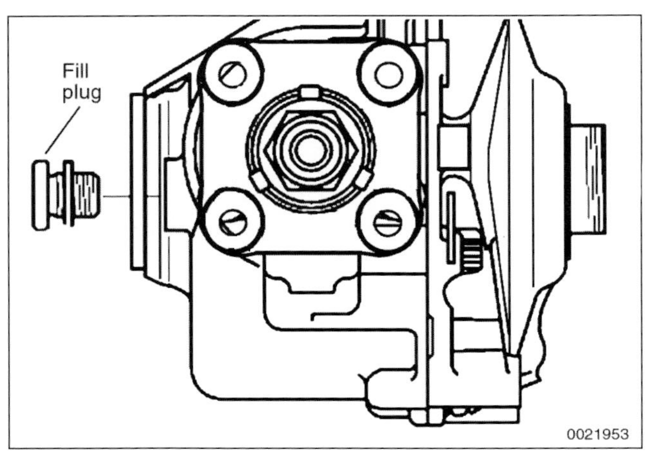

Reinstall front differential and right axle inner bearing pedestal. See **311 Front Axle Final Drive**.

- Fill differential to lower edge of fill plug.

Tightening torques

- Fill or drain plug to front differential. . . . . 65 Nm (48 ft-lb)
- Front differential to oil pan (M10) . . . . . . 45 Nm (33 ft-lb)

– Reinstall front axles, control arms and front steering arms as described in **310 Front Suspension**.

NOTE —

- *Be sure to replace seals on differential output flanges.*
- *Replace self-locking fasteners when reinstalling front suspension components.*

Tightening torques

- Control arm ball joint bracket to subframe
  M12 bolt . . . . 77 Nm (57 ft-lb)
- Control arm mounting bracket to subframe
  M10 bolt (always replace). . . . . 59 Nm (44 ft-lb)

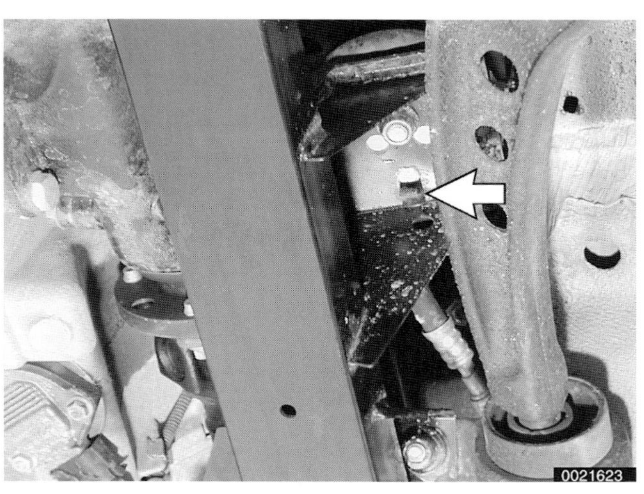

When reattaching engine to subframe, be sure that left engine mount locating tab (**arrow**) is seated correctly in subframe slot.

Tightening torques

- Engine mount to subframe
  M10 self-locking nut . . . . 45 Nm (33 ft-lb)
- Front of subframe to frame rail (M12 bolt, always replace)
  8.8 grade. . . . . 77 Nm (57 ft-lb)
  10.9 grade. . . . . 110 Nm (81 ft-lb)
  12.9 grade. . . . . 105 Nm (77 ft-lb)
- Rear of subframe to mounting adapter
  M12 bolt (always replace). . . . . 110 Nm (81 ft-lb)

– Remainder of installation is reverse of removal.

- Match up key ways while installing steering column shaft. See **320 Steering and Wheel Alignment** for more specific procedures.
- Use new oil dipstick tube sealing O-ring.
- Fill engine with oil as described in **020 Maintenance**.
- After adding engine oil, start and run engine. Raise engine speed to 2,500 rpm until oil pressure warning lamp goes out (about 5 seconds).

NOTE —
Be sure to align the front end after completing this procedure.

Tightening torques
- Stabilizer bar to frame rail (M8 nut). . . . . 22 Nm (16 ft-lb)
- Steering column universal joint clamping screw (M8 bolt, use new bolt)-. 22 Nm (16 ft-lb)

COMPONENT REPLACEMENT

Engine oil cooler, removing and installing (S54 engine)

The engine oil cooler is mounted directly below the radiator.

– Raise car and support. Remove splash guard from below engine.

◄ Remove engine oil drain plug **(arrow)** and drain engine oil. See **020 Maintenance.**

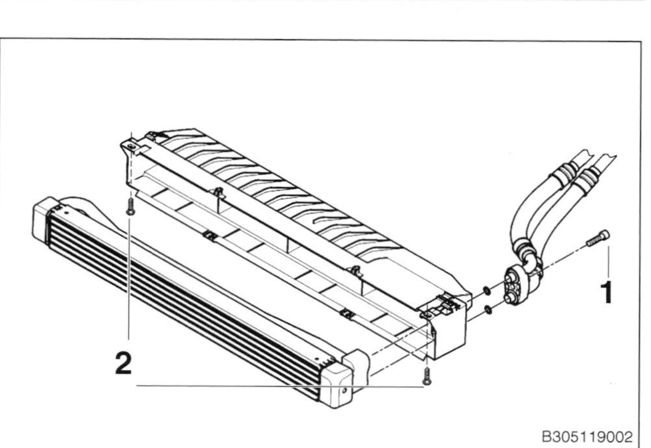

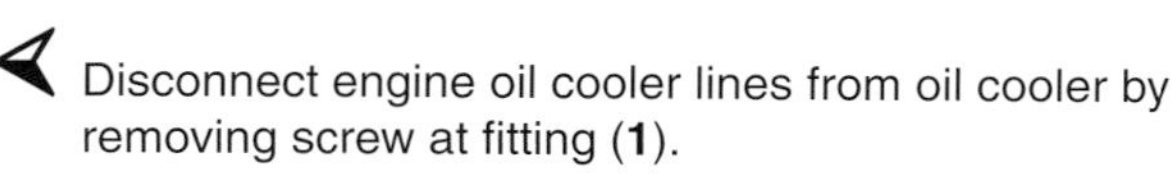

◄ Disconnect engine oil cooler lines from oil cooler by removing screw at fitting (**1**).

– Remove engine oil cooler carrier mounting screws (**2**). Pull oil cooler with carrier straight off.

– Installation is reverse of removal. Replace O-rings at oil line fitting if necessary. Install and torque drain plug. Fill engine with oil.

Tightening torque

- Engine oil drain plug to oil pan . . . . 25 Nm (18 ft-lb)

Oil pressure warning switch

The pressure warning switch is located in the rear of the oil filter housing.

NOTE —
Switch replacement may require intake manifold removal on some models.

Tightening torque

- Oil pressure switch to oil filter housing . . 27 Nm (20 ft-lb)

Oil level warning switch

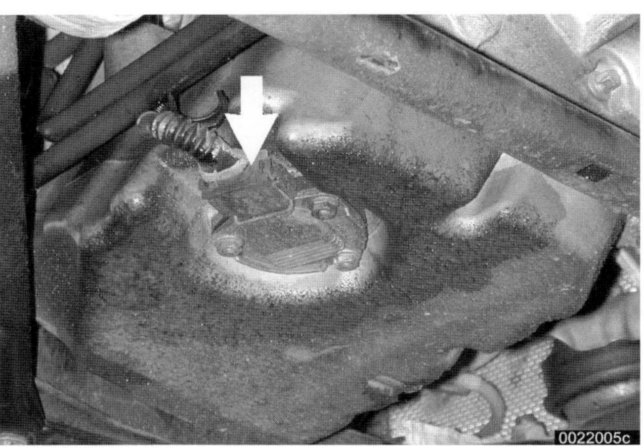

The oil level warning switch is located at the bottom of the engine oil pan. Drain engine oil before removing level switch.

NOTE —
Anytime the oil level warning switch is removed, be sure to replace the sealing O-ring between switch and oil pan.

Oil pump, removing and installing

NOTE —
Oil pump removal requires lowering the front suspension subframe to remove the oil pan.

- Drain oil as described in **020 Maintenance**.
- Remove oil pan as described earlier.

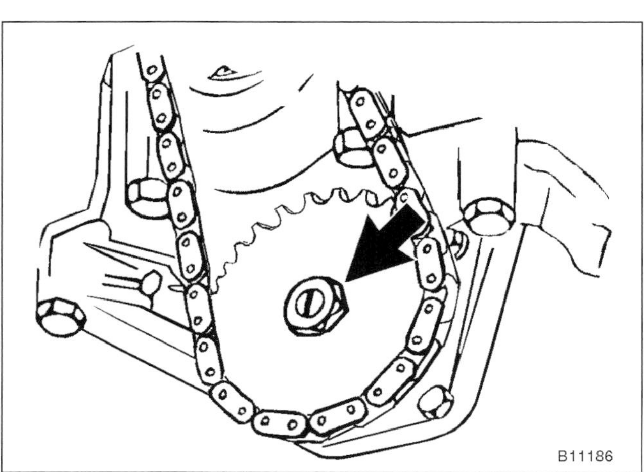

Remove oil pump sprocket mounting nut (left-hand thread) (**arrow**).

> *CAUTION —*
> ***On S54 engines**: The chain tensioner can be easily damaged by the chain when loosening the sprocket nut. Hold the sprocket stationary when loosening left-hand thread nut.*

- Lift sprocket off together with drive chain.

NOTE —
On S54 engines, press out on chain tensioner when lifting sprocket off pump to relieve chain tension.

Oil pump assembly
M52 TU, M54, M56 (to 1/2000)

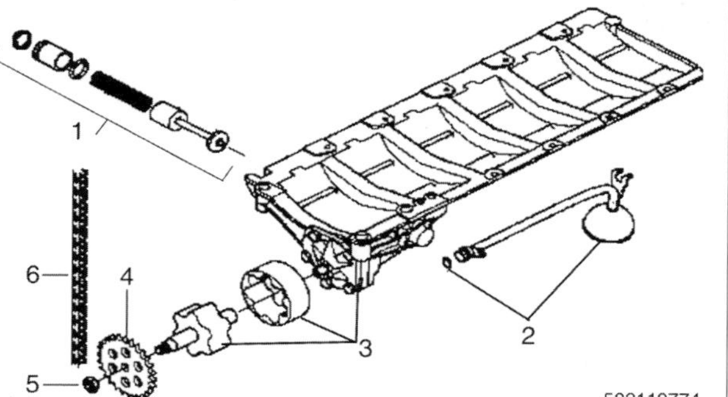

1. Oil pressure relief valve assembly
2. Oil pump suction pickup and seal
3. Oil pump
4. Oil pump sprocket
5. Oil pump shaft locking nut (left-hand thread)
6. Oil pump drive chain

Oil pump assembly
M52 TU, M54, M56 (from 1/2000)

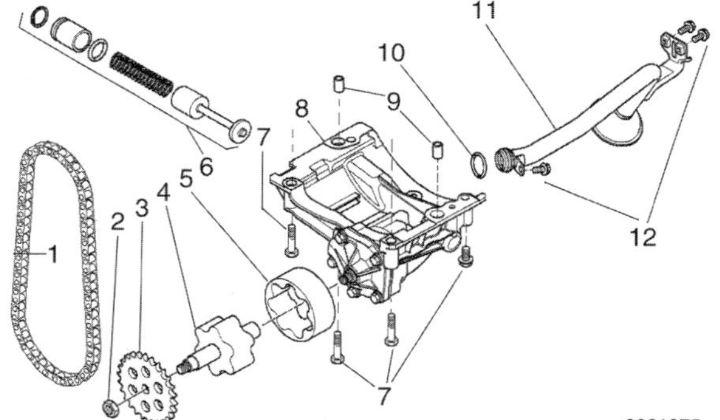

1. Drive chain
2. Nut M10x1left-hand thread -tighten to 25 Nm (18 ft-lb)
3. Oil pump sprocket
4. Inner rotor
5. Outer rotor
6. Oil pressure relief valve assembly
7. Bolt M8 -tighten to 22 Nm (16 ft-lb)
8. Oil pump housing
9. Locating dowels
10. Sealing O-ring
11. Oil pick-up pipe
12. Bolt M6 -tighten to 10 Nm (89 in-lb)

– Remove mounting bolts from oil pump pickup tube(s). Withdraw tube.

NOTE —

- *Note any spacers between pump and engine block.*
- *Note positions of locating dowels.*

◄ **Version 1** (engine with integrated oil pump and oil deflector): Unbolt oil pump with deflector.

◄ **Version 2** (engine with separate oil pump and oil deflector): Remove oil pump mounting bolts. Remove oil pump assembly.

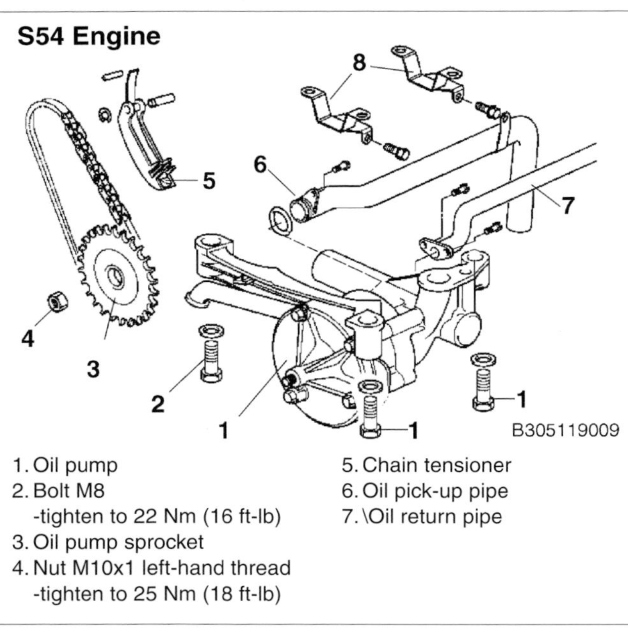

1. Oil pump
2. Bolt M8
   -tighten to 22 Nm (16 ft-lb)
3. Oil pump sprocket
4. Nut M10x1 left-hand thread
   -tighten to 25 Nm (18 ft-lb)
5. Chain tensioner
6. Oil pick-up pipe
7. \Oil return pipe

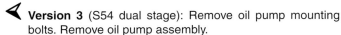

Version 3 (S54 dual stage): Remove oil pump mounting bolts. Remove oil pump assembly.

– Remove cover from oil pump and check for wear or scoring. Spin oil pump shaft and check that gears turn smoothly. Replace pump if gears spin with difficulty or any wear is present.

– Installation is reverse of removal, noting the following:
  - Align sprocket splines to oil pump shaft splines before tightening sprocket nut.

Tightening torques
- Oil drain plug to oil pan (M12). . . . . 25 Nm (18 ft-lb)
- Oil pan to engine block
  M6, 8.8 grade . . . . 10 Nm (89 in-lb)
  M6, 10.9 grade . . . . 12 Nm (106 in-lb)
- Oil pump to engine block (M8) . . . . 22 Nm (16 ft-lb)
- Oil pump sprocket to oil pump shaft
  M10x1 left-hand thread. . . . . 25 Nm (18 ft-lb)

Oil pump pressure relief valve

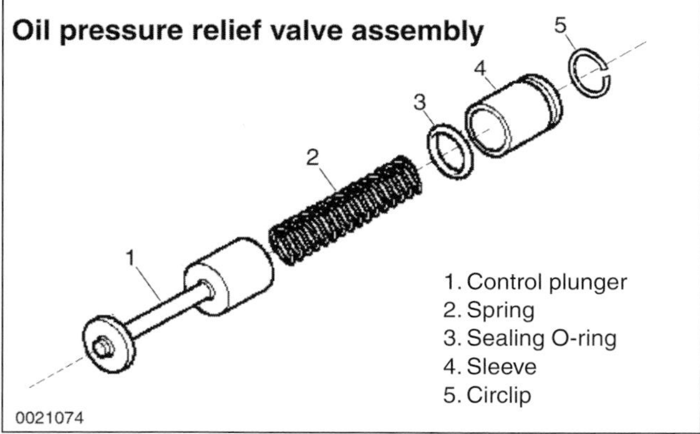

1. Control plunger
2. Spring
3. Sealing O-ring
4. Sleeve
5. Circlip

The oil pump pressure relief valve is held in the side of the oil pump with a circlip.

120 Ignition System

TABLES

GENERAL

This repair group covers component replacement information for the ignition system.

When diagnosing engine management problems, including on-board diagnostics (OBD II) fault code analysis, also refer to these repair groups:

- **100 Engine–General**
- **130 Fuel Injection**
- **Electrical Wiring Diagrams** at the rear of this manual
- **On Board Diagnostics** at the rear of this manual

Special tools

Owing to the coil-per-cylinder configuration, system diagnosis and testing requires special test equipment.

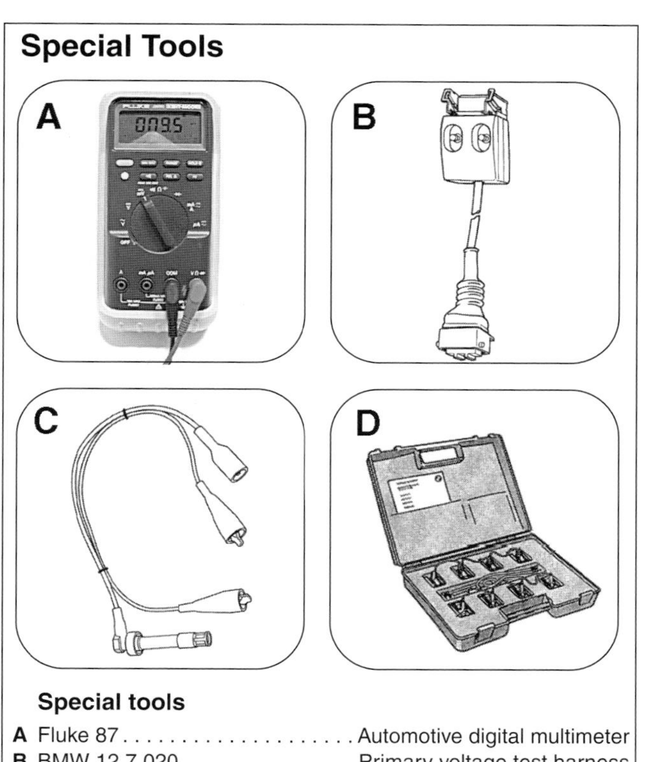

Special tools

A Fluke 87 . . . . Automotive digital multimeter
B BMW 12 7 020 . . . . Primary voltage test harness
C BMW 12 7 030 . . . . Secondary voltage test harness
D BMW 12 7 040 . . . . Ignition coil test adapters

Engine management

BMW E46 engines use an advanced engine management system known as Digital Motor Electronics (DME). DME incorporates on-board diagnostics, fuel injection, ignition and other engine control functions. DME variants are listed in **Table a**.

Second generation On-Board Diagnostics (OBD II) is incorporated into the engine management systems used on the cars covered by this manual. Using a BMW-specific or OBD II electronic scan tool, it is possible to access Diagnostic Trouble Codes (DTCs) that pinpoint ignition and other engine management problems.

Additional information about DTCs and engine management system electronic system diagnosis is provided in **On Board Diagnostics** at the rear of this manual.

Table a. Engine management systems

Year: Engine	DME system
1999 – 2000: M52 TU B25 M52 TU B28	Siemens MS 42.0
2001-2005 M54 B25 M54 B30	Siemens MS 43.0
2003- 2005 M56 B25	Siemens MS 45.1
2002 - 2005 S54	Siemens MS S54

Ignition system

All engines are fitted with individual ignition coils for each cylinder. There is no distributor cap or ignition rotor.

Ignition coil wiring

ECM
Fuse 5 30A
Fuse panel
1
10
0.5 GRN
2.5 RED
8
6
86
30
85
87
Unloader relay
4
2
1
to Ignition coils
0.5 BRN
1.0 GRN
3
Ignition coil
1
2
1.0 BLK/WHT
1.0 BRN
ECM

Wiring color code	
BLK	= black
BRN	= brown
GRN	= green
GRY	= grey
RED	= red
VIO	= violet
WHT	= white
YEL	= yellow

0021043

Each coil can be controlled by the Engine Control Module (ECM) on a cylinder-by-cylinder basis.

NOTE —

Schematic diagram of ignition coil circuit shown is for MS 42.0 engine management system. For ignition wiring for other systems, see **Electrical Wiring Diagrams**.

WARNING —

- *Do not touch or disconnect any cables from the coils while the engine is running or being cranked by the starter.*
- *The ignition system produces high voltages that can be fatal. Avoid contact with exposed terminals. Use extreme caution when working on a car with the ignition switched on or the engine running.*
- *Connect and disconnect the DME system wiring and test equipment leads only when the ignition is OFF.*
- *Before operating the starter without starting the engine (for example when making a compression test) always disable the ignition.*

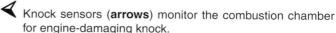

Knock sensors (**arrows**) monitor the combustion chamber for engine-damaging knock.

- **M52 TU, M54, M56 engines**: Two sensors monitor three cylinders each. If engine knock is detected, the ignition point is retarded by the ECM.
- **S54 engines**: Three knock sensors are bolted to the engine block between cylinders 1 and 2, 3 and 4 and 5 and 6. If ignition knock is detected, the ECM retards the ignition timing for that cylinder.

NOTE —

When knock is detected, ignition timing will be retarded at the selective cylinder(s) by 3° increments. If knock is no longer detected, the timing will be advanced in 1° increments.

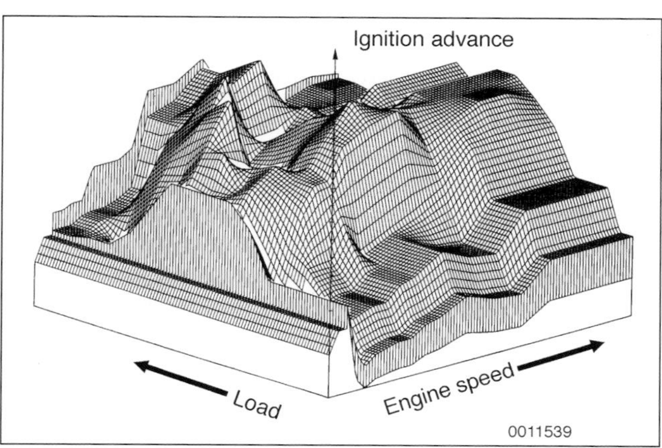

Ignition timing is electronically mapped and not adjustable. The ECM uses engine load, engine speed, coolant temperature, knock detection and intake air temperature as the basic inputs for timing control. A three dimensional map similar to the one shown is digitally stored in the ECM.

The initial ignition point is determined by the crankshaft speed sensor during cranking. Once the engine is running, timing is continually adjusted based on operating conditions.

Basic troubleshooting principles

Poor driveability may have a variety of causes. The fault may lie with the ignition system, the fuel system, parts of the emission control system, or a combination of the three. Because of these interrelated functions and their effects on each other, it is often difficult to know where to begin looking for problems.

For this reason, effective troubleshooting should always begin with an interrogation of the On-Board Diagnostics (OBD II) system. The OBD II system detects engine management malfunctions, including cylinder-specific ignition coil faults.

When faults are detected, the OBD II system stores a Diagnostic Trouble Code (DTC) in the Engine Control Module (ECM) along with other pertinent fault information. In addition, the Malfunction Indicator Light (MIL) may also be illuminated. Additional OBD II information, including a DTC lookup table can be found in the back of this manual under **On Board Diagnostics**.

NOTE —

On model year 1999 and 2000 cars, the MIL is labeled Check Engine. On model year 2001 and later cars, the MIL is labeled Service Engine Soon.

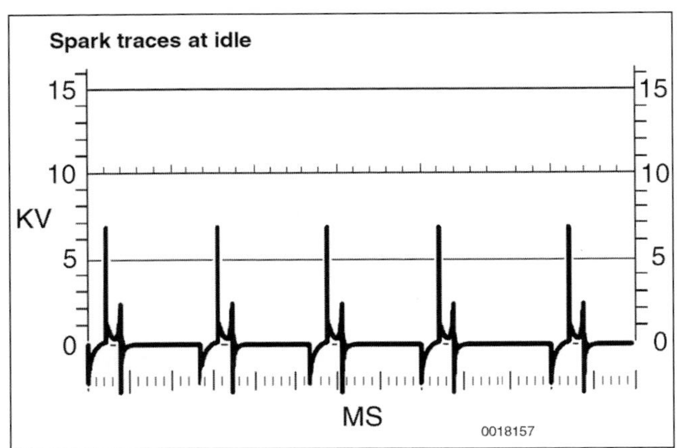

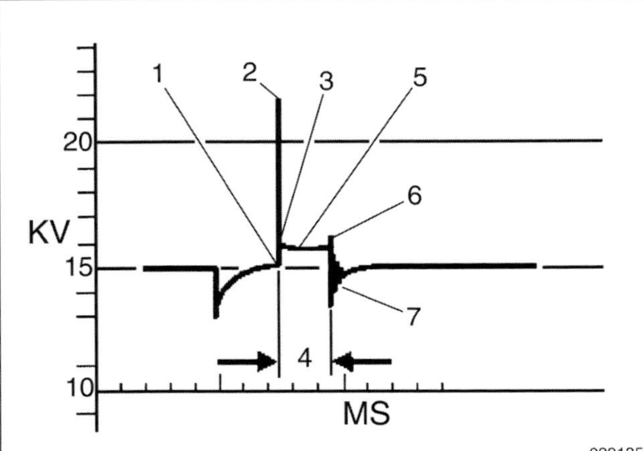

1. Start of ignition voltage peak
2. Level of ignition voltage
3. Level of combustion voltage
4. Period of combustion
5. Combustion curve characteristics
6. Start of decay process
7. Termination oscillations

> ***WARNING —***
> *Inefficient combustion (rich air/fuel mixture) can cause elevated hydrocarbon exhaust emissions and catalytic converter damage. For this reason, if a severe misfire is detected, the fuel injector will be turned off to the specific cylinder and the MIL be illuminated. a misfire due to An overheated catalytic converter can also be a fire hazard.*

One way to diagnose a faulty coil on a car that is running is to use an oscilloscope to analyze spark quality. The illustrations show normal scope trace of spark at idle.

Table b lists common ignition coil voltage faults and related causes.

NOTE —
Note the length of sparking period and the up-down voltage attenuations. A short sparking period and/or an irregular/low voltage attenuation usually indicates a faulty coil.

A normal oscilloscope pattern for a six cylinder engine.

Table b. Ignition trace diagnostics

Parameter	Ignition voltage low	Ignition voltage high
Spark plug electrode gap	too small	too big
Spark plug electrode condition	—	worn/burnt
Spark plug electrode temperature	too high	too low
Engine compression	too low	too high
Spark plug wire(s)	—	faulty
Fuel air mixture	—	too lean

Engine misfire, the result of inefficient combustion in one or more cylinders, may be caused by a variety of malfunctions in various subsystems.

The OBD II system incorporated within the engine management system is designed to detect and warn of misfire faults during engine operation. For a detailed list of fault codes see **On Board Diagnostics**.

Warnings and cautions

The engine management system contains sensitive electronic components. To protect the system and for general safety, the following warnings and cautions should be observed during ignition system troubleshooting, maintenance or repair work.

WARNING —
- *Do not touch or disconnect any cables from the coils while the engine is running or being cranked by the starter.*
- *The ignition system produces high voltages that can be fatal. Avoid contact with exposed terminals. Use extreme caution when working on a car with the ignition switched on or the engine running.*
- *Connect and disconnect the DME system wiring and test equipment leads only when the ignition is OFF.*
- *Before operating the starter without starting the engine (for example when making a compression test) always disable the ignition.*

CAUTION —
- *Prior to disconnecting the battery, read the battery disconnection cautions given at the front of this manual.*
- *Do not attempt to disable the ignition by removing the coils from the spark plugs.*
- *Connect or disconnect ignition system wires, multiple wire connectors, and ignition test equipment leads only while the ignition is off. Switch multimeter functions or measurement ranges only with the test probes disconnected.*
- *Do not disconnect the battery while the engine is running.*
- *A high impedance digital multimeter should be used for all voltage and resistance tests. An LED test light should be used in place of an incandescent-type test lamp.*
- *In general, make test connections only as specified by BMW, as described in this manual, or as described by the instrument manufacturer.*

IGNITION SYSTEM SERVICE

Ignition firing order

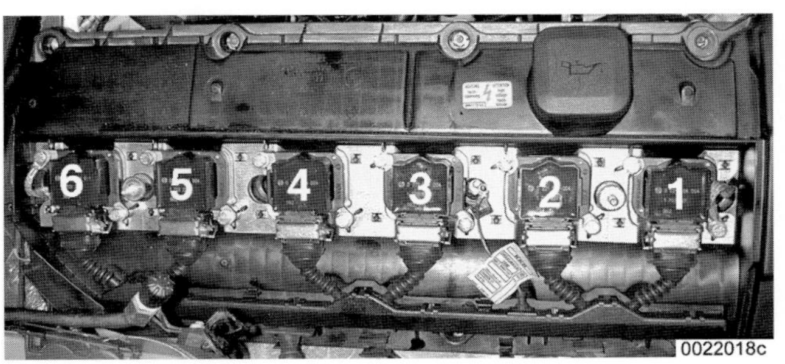

 Each ignition coil is mounted above the corresponding spark plug. Cylinder 1 is at the front of the engine.

Ignition firing order
- M52 TU, M54, M56, S54. . . . . 1 - 5 - 3 - 6 - 2 - 4

Disabling ignition system

The ignition system operates in a lethal voltage range and should therefore be disabled any time engine service or repair work is being done that requires the ignition to be switched on.

0021391c

The engine management system can be disabled by removing the DME main relay (**arrow**). The relay is located in the electronics box (E-box) in the left rear of the engine compartment.

> ***CAUTION —***
> *Relay locations may vary. Use care when identifying relays. The main relay has a large (4 mm²) red wire at terminal 30 and a large (4 mm²) red/white wire at terminal 87. See* **610 Electrical Component Locations**.

Checking for spark

> ***CAUTION —***
> *If a spark test is done incorrectly, damage to the Engine Control Module (ECM) or the ignition coils may result.*

NOTE —
Spark plug replacement is covered in **020 Maintenance**.

Checking for spark is difficult to do on the DME system without special test harnesses and test equipment.

Inspect the ignition coils carefully. A bad coil will often show signs of damage, such as cracking in the casting or oozing or melted casting material. Try removing the spark plugs and inspecting for differences between them. A poor-firing plug may be wet with fuel and/or black and sooty, but not always. If a coil is not operating, the engine management system will electrically disable the fuel injector to that cylinder. The key is to look for differences between cylinders.

Ignition coil, testing and replacing

> ***CAUTION —***
> *Use a digital multimeter for the following tests.*

0021792

Remove interior ventilation microfilter.

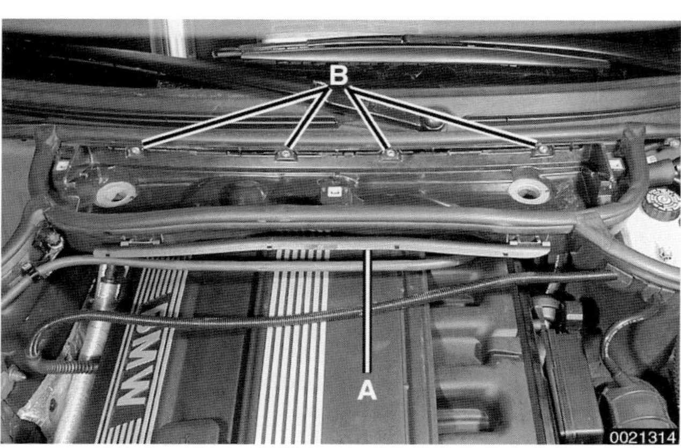

Remove housing for microfilter for interior ventilation.

- Open wiring harness loom (**A**) and remove wires.
- Unfasten screws (**B**) and remove lower microfilter housing.

– Remove plastic engine cover from top of valve cover by prying off bolt covers and removing cover mounting bolts.

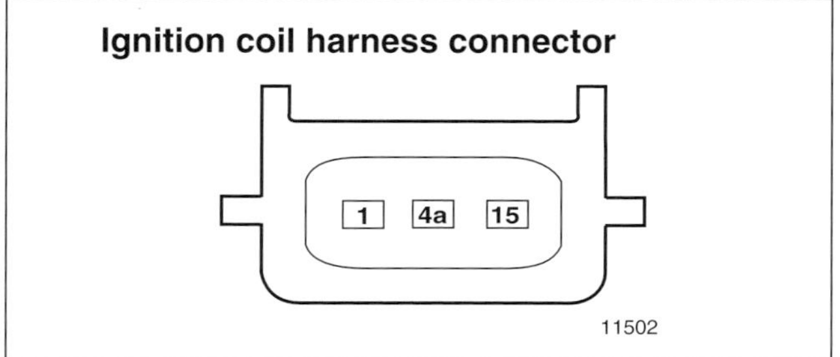

Disconnect harness connector from coil. Connect multimeter between terminal **15** (+) in connector and ground.

– Turn ignition on and check for battery voltage.

- If battery voltage is not present, check wiring, fuses and applicable relay. See **Electrical Wiring Diagrams** for specific circuit information.
- On MS 42 cars, check fuse no. 5 (30 amp) and unloader relay (K6326) circuit.
- On MS 43, MS 45, and MS S54 cars, check fuse no. 1 (30 amp) and DME main relay (K6300) circuit.

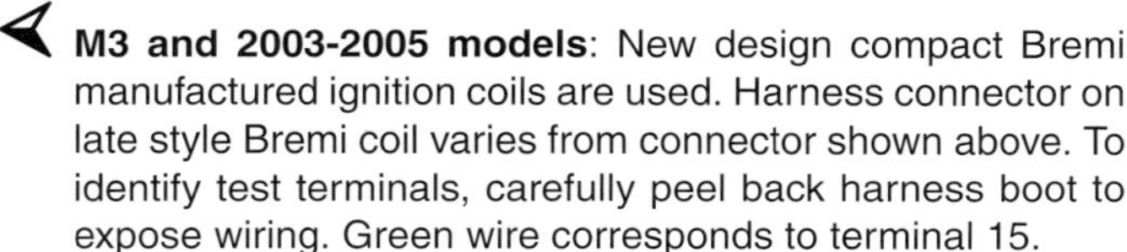

M3 and 2003-2005 models: New design compact Bremi manufactured ignition coils are used. Harness connector on late style Bremi coil varies from connector shown above. To identify test terminals, carefully peel back harness boot to expose wiring. Green wire corresponds to terminal 15.

– Turn ignition off.

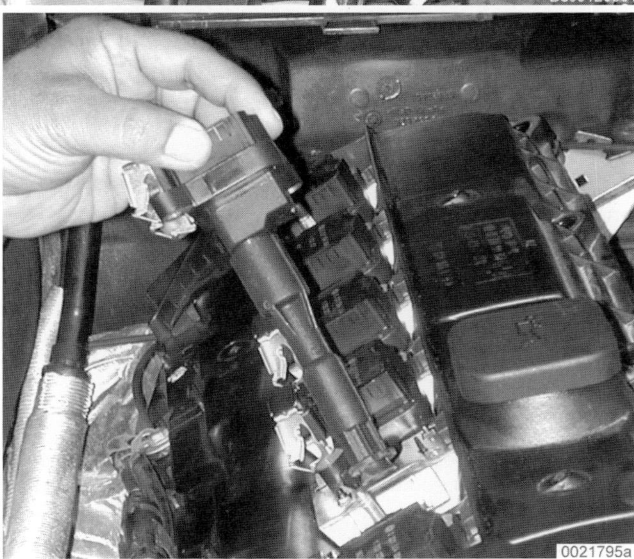

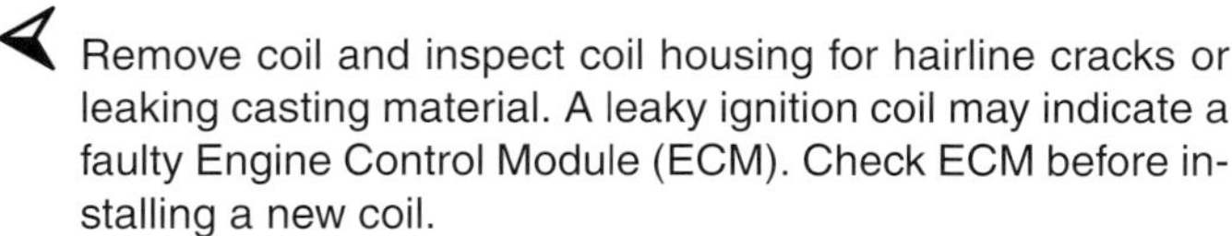

Remove coil and inspect coil housing for hairline cracks or leaking casting material. A leaky ignition coil may indicate a faulty Engine Control Module (ECM). Check ECM before installing a new coil.

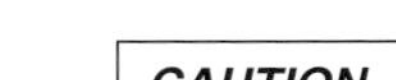

CAUTION—

Note location of coil ground straps before coil removal; reinstall in the same location.

NOTE—

The compact 'rod' type Bremi coils do not use hold down nuts. To remove the late style Bremi coil, swivel harness connector lock up, disconnect connector, and twist and pull coil straight up.

– Use a multimeter to test:

- Coil primary resistance at coil terminals
- Spark plug connector resistance
- Compare results to specification in **Table c**.

NOTE —
The information in the **Table c** *below applies to the M52 TU engine. Coil specifications for other engines is not available from BMW. Use this information as a guide when testing coils on engines other than the M52 TU.*

Table c. Ignition coil resistance (M52 TU engine)

Component	Terminals	Resistance
Coil primary	**1** (–) and **15** (+)	approx. 0.8 Ω
Coil secondary		N.A.
Spark plug connector: Bosch Beru		 1 kΩ ± 20% 1.8 kΩ ± 20%

– Replace ignition coil or spark plug connector if resistance readings do not meet specifications.

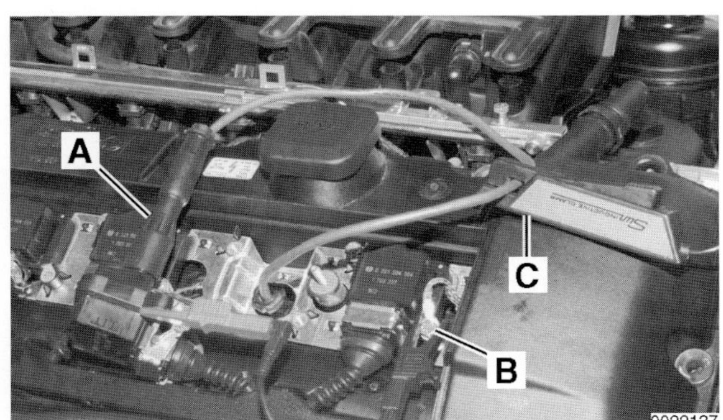

◄ Remove ignition coil to be tested.

- **A**: Install BMW special tool 12 7 030 on coil to be tested.
- **B:** Connect ground jumper between coil mounting point and engine ground point.
- **C**: Clip scope pick-up lead around ignition lead.
- Start engine.
- Compare scope pattern with diagrams in **Basic troubleshooting principles**.

NOTE —
When replacing ignition coils, ensure that the replacements are from the same manufacturer with the same part/code numbers. If individual coils with the correct specifications are not available, all coils should be replaced.

Crankshaft speed sensor, replacing

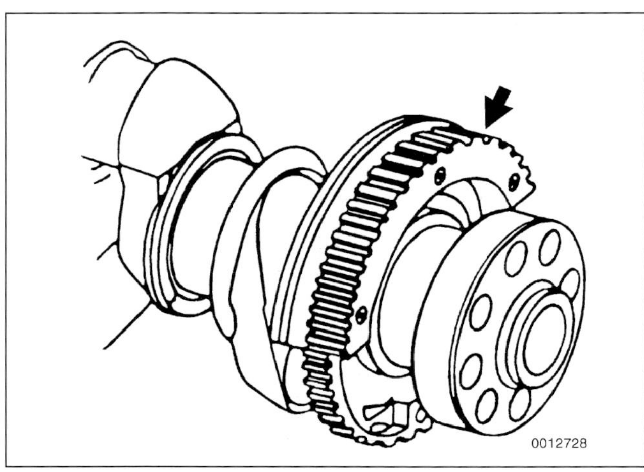

◄ The crankshaft speed sensor is mounted in the left rear side of the cylinder block below the starter. The sensor reads a toothed pulse wheel (**arrow**) mounted to the end of the crankshaft.

If the Engine Control Module (ECM) does not receive a signal from the crankshaft speed sensor during cranking, the engine will not start.

If the OBD II system misfire detection protocol detects a catalyst damaging fault due to a malfunction in crankshaft speed sensor components, the Check Engine light (Malfunction Indicator Light or MIL) will be illuminated.

NOTE —
If the crankshaft speed sensor pulse wheel is damaged, the engine will have to be disassembled down to the crankshaft to replace the wheel.

0022131

– Make certain ignition has been turned off.

– Raise car and support in a safe manner.

> ***WARNING —***
> *Make sure the car is stable and well supported at all times. Use a professional automotive lift or jack stands designed for the purpose. A floor jack is not adequate support.*

– Remove under-engine splash guards.

< Working just underneath starter:

- Cut wire tie securing crankshaft speed sensor harness connector (**arrow**) to sensor.
- Disconnect harness connector.

0022500c

< Remove sensor mounting screw (**arrow**) and remove sensor from cylinder block.

– Installation is reverse of removal, noting the following:

- Use a new O-ring when installing sensor.
- Be sure wiring is rerouted in same orientation.
- Secure sensor using new wire ties.
- Use scan tool to read out and clear ECM fault memory.

Camshaft position sensors

The camshaft position sensors are used by the engine management system for VANOS control, sequential fuel injection and knock control. A faulty cam position sensor should store a DTC (diagnostic trouble code) in fault memory and turn on the MIL (malfunction indicator light).

Intake camshaft position sensor, replacing (M52 TU, M54, M56 engines)

– Make certain ignition has been turned off.

– Remove housing for the microfilter for interior ventilation as shown earlier.

– Remove plastic cover from above fuel injectors by prying off bolt covers and removing cover mounting bolts.

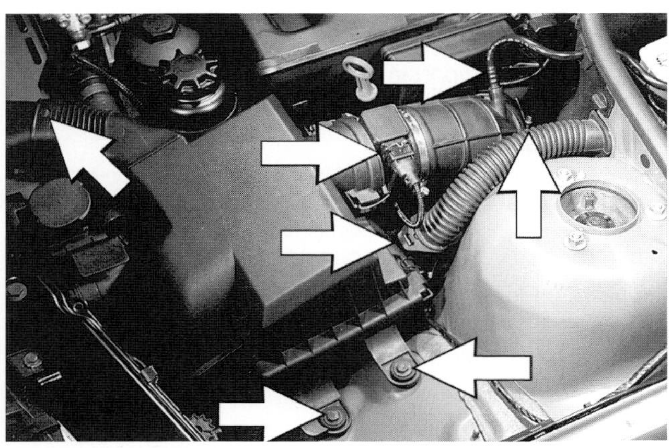

Remove complete air filter housing:

- Disconnect electrical harness connector on mass air flow sensor (**B**).
- Detach vacuum line at intake boot (**A**).
- Remove filter housing mounting screws (**D**).
- Loosen hose clamp at intake boot and detach air duct connections (**C**).
- Disconnect cold air duct tube (**E**).

– Disconnect harness connector from VANOS solenoid and unscrew solenoid from VANOS control unit. Be prepared with shop rags to catch oil released from VANOS unit.

Remove camshaft sensor (**arrow**) from left front of cylinder head, next to top of oil filter housing.

– Disconnect camshaft sensor harness from under intake manifold. Prior to removal, attach a stiff piece of wire to the harness connector end to preserve proper routing of harness for reinstallation.

– Installation is reverse of removal.

- Use new self-locking bolt and new O-ring when installing sensor.
- Be sure wiring is rerouted in same orientation.
- Use scan tool to read out and clear ECM fault memory.

Tightening torques

- Intake camshaft sensor to cylinder head .... 10 Nm (7 ft-lb)
- VANOS solenoid to VANOS control unit .... 30 Nm (22 ft-lb)

Intake camshaft position sensor, replacing (S54 engine)

The intake camshaft position sensor is located on the rear left-hand side of the cylinder head. Replacement requires that the intake manifold first be removed.

– Make certain ignition has been turned off.

– Remove intake manifold. See **110 Engine Removal and Installation**.

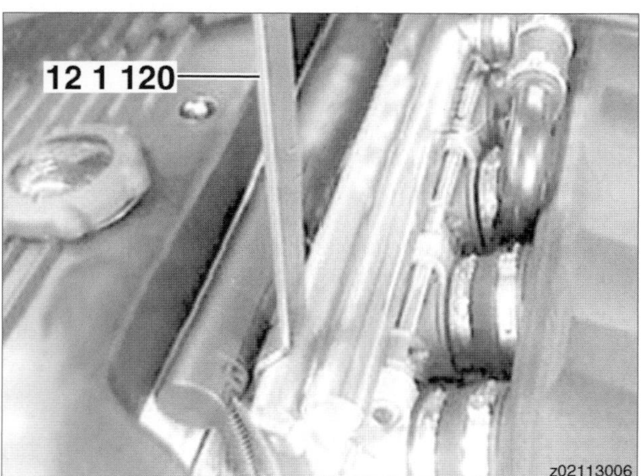

Working from outer ends and moving towards center, carefully pry off fuel injector electrical connector strip. Use BMW special tool 12 1 120 or equivalent.

> ***CAUTION —***
> *Connector strip may break if it is removed without special tool 12 1 120.*

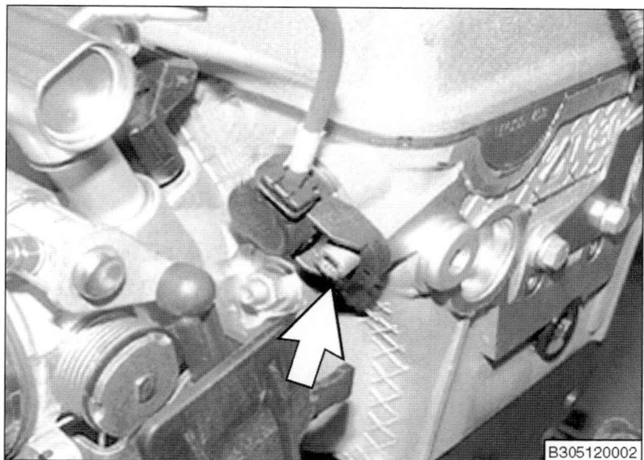

◄ Remove camshaft sensor (**arrow**) from left rear of cylinder head.

– Disconnect camshaft sensor harness.

– Installation is reverse of removal.

- Use new self-locking bolt and new O-ring when installing sensor.
- Be sure wiring is rerouted in same orientation.
- Use scan tool to read out and clear ECM fault memory.

Tightening torques

- Intake camshaft sensor to cylinder head . . . . 10 Nm (7 ft-lb)

Exhaust camshaft position sensor, replacing (M52 TU, M54, M56 engines)

– Make certain ignition has been turned off.

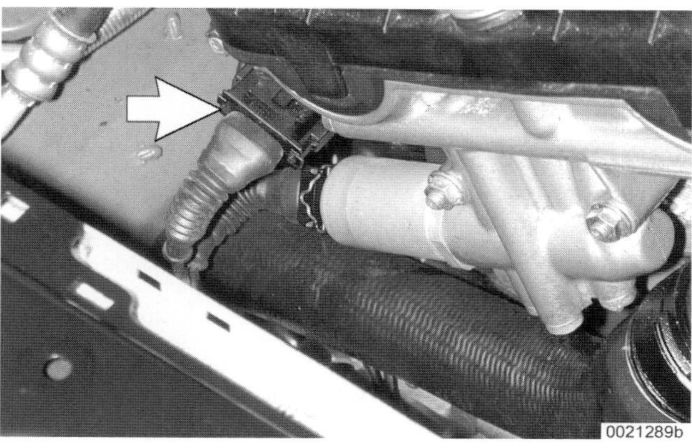

◄ Working at front of engine on exhaust (right) side, detach exhaust camshaft position sensor electrical harness connector (**arrow**).

– Remove camshaft sensor from right front of cylinder head.

– Installation is reverse of removal.

- Use a new self-locking bolt and new O-ring when installing sensor.
- Be sure wiring is rerouted in same orientation.
- Use scan tool to read out and clear ECM fault memory.

Tightening torque

- Exhaust camshaft sensor to cylinder head . . . . 10 Nm (7 ft-lb)

Exhaust camshaft position sensor, replacing (S54 engine)

– Make certain ignition has been turned off.

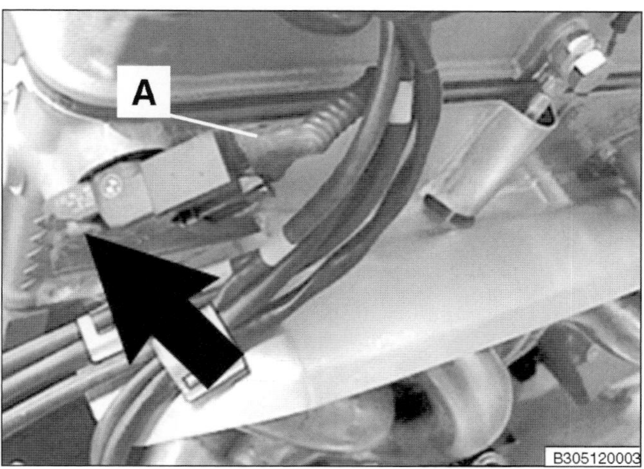

◄ Working at rear of engine on exhaust (right) side, detach exhaust camshaft position sensor electrical harness connector (**A**).

– Remove camshaft sensor mounting bolt and remove sensor from cylinder head.

– Installation is reverse of removal.

- Use a new self-locking bolt and new O-ring when installing sensor.
- Use scan tool to read out and clear ECM fault memory.

Tightening torque

- Exhaust camshaft sensor to cylinder head . . . . 10 Nm (7 ft-lb)

Knock sensors, replacing

The knock sensors are bolted to the left side of the cylinder block under the intake manifold.

NOTE —
M52 TU, S54, and S56 engines are fitted with two knock sensors. The S54 engine uses three knock sensors.

– Remove intake manifold as described in **110 Engine Removal and Installation**.

◀ **On S54 engines**: Remove idle speed control valve mounting nuts (arrows) and set valve aside.

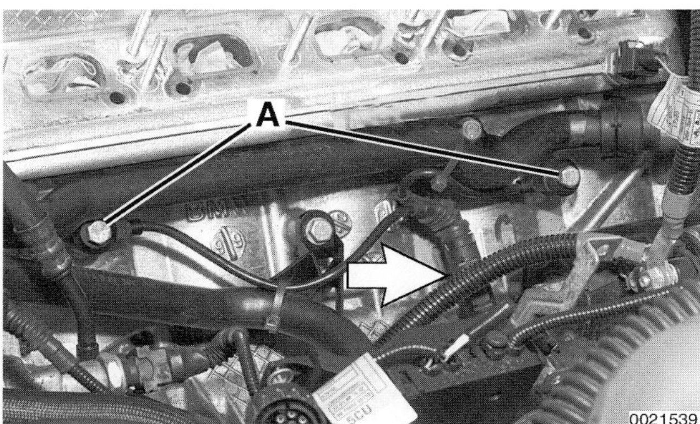

◀ Disconnect knock sensor electrical harness connector (**arrow**) on left side of engine cylinder block.

- Remove knock sensor mounting bolts (**A**) on side of cylinder block. Remove sensors.

CAUTION —
Note the installed angle of the knock sensor on the block before removing it. Reinstall the sensor in the same position. Be sure to use a torque wrench when tightening the sensor mounting bolt.

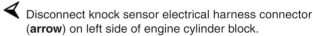

◀ Clean contact surface on engine block and sensor (**arrows**) before installing knock sensor.

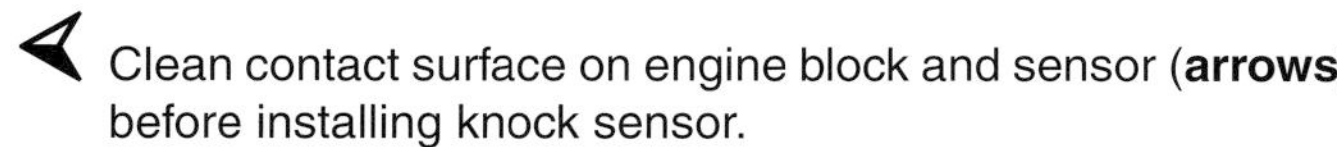

Tightening torque
- Knock sensor to cylinder block . . . . . . .20 Nm (15 ft. lbs.)

– Use scan tool to read out and clear ECM fault memory.

121 Battery, Alternator, Starter

TABLES

Special Tools

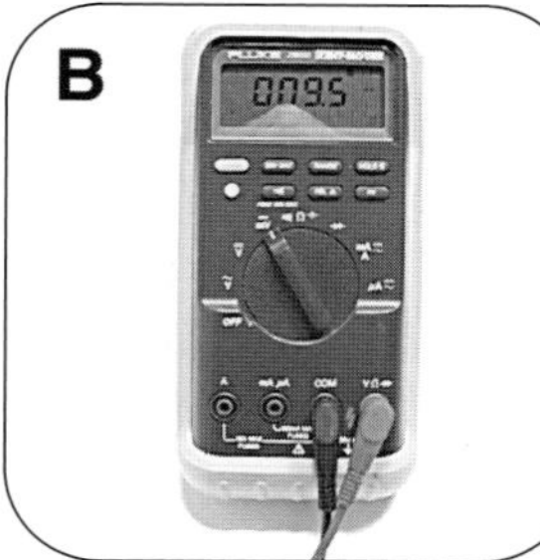

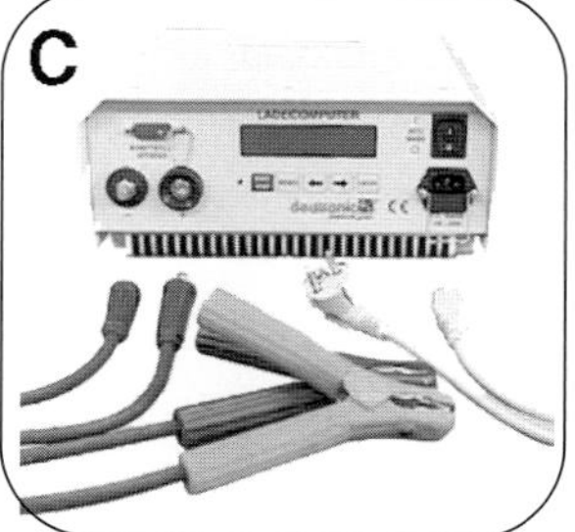

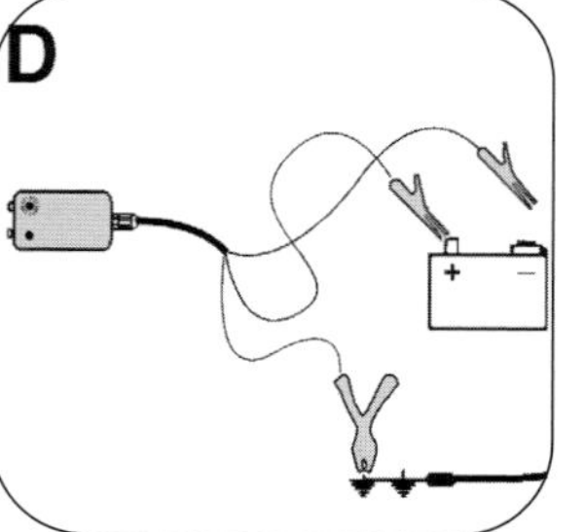

Special tools

A BMW 12 7 110 . . . . .Alternator pulley nut removal tool
B Fluke 87 . . . . Automotive digital multimeter
C BMW 61 2 300 . . .Closed-circuit current measurement adapter
D Deutronic DBL 1000-14 . . . . Electronic battery charger

GENERAL

This section covers the battery, alternator and starter components of the electrical system. For additional electrical troubleshooting information that may apply to these components, see **600 Electrical System–General**.

Special tools

Only use a digital multimeter when testing automotive electrical malfunctions.

Engine electrical system

The alternator and starter are wired directly to the battery. To prevent accidental shorts that might blow a fuse or damage wires and electrical components, the negative (–) battery cable should always be disconnected before working on the electrical system.

Various versions of alternators, voltage regulators, starters, and batteries are used in the E46 cars. It is important to replace components according to the original equipment specification. Check with an authorized BMW dealer for specific application and parts information.

Warnings and cautions

WARNING —

- *Wear goggles, rubber gloves and a rubber apron when working around the battery or battery acid (electrolyte).*
- *Battery acid contains sulfuric acid and can cause skin irritation and burning. If acid is spilled on your skin or clothing, flush the area at once with large quantities of water. If electrolyte gets into your eyes, flush them with large quantities of clean water for several minutes and see a physician.*
- *Batteries that are being charged or are fully charged give off explosive hydrogen gas. Keep sparks and open flames away. Do not smoke.*

CAUTION —

- *Only use a digital multimeter when testing automotive electrical components.*
- *Prior to disconnecting the battery, read the battery disconnection cautions in* **001 General Warnings and Cautions**.
- *Before disconnecting the battery, switch the ignition OFF. Otherwise, diagnostic troubles codes (DTCs) may be set in some electronic control modules.*
- *Disconnecting the battery cables may erase DTCs stored in ECM memory.*
- *Disconnecting the battery erases the radio presets. Therefore, note stored stations and restore them after connecting the battery.*
- *Stored settings of the on-board computer and clock are also lost when the battery is disconnected.*
- *Always disconnect the negative (–) battery cable first and reconnect it last. Cover the battery post with an insulating material whenever the cable is removed.*
- *Do not disconnect battery, alternator or starter wires while the engine is running.*
- *Never reverse the battery cables. Even a momentary wrong connection can damage the alternator and other electrical components.*
- *Do not depend on the color of insulation to tell battery positive and negative cables apart. Label cables before removing.*

BATTERY

The E46 uses a six-cell, 12-volt lead acid battery mounted in the right hand side of the luggage compartment.

BMW batteries are rated by ampere/hours (Ah) and cold cranking amps (CCA) rating. The Ah rating is determined by the average amount of current the battery can deliver over time without dropping below a specified voltage. The CCA is determined by the battery's ability to deliver starting current at 0°F (-18°C) without dropping below a specified voltage.

Battery testing

Battery testing determines the state of battery charge. On conventional or low-maintenance batteries the most common method of testing the battery is that of checking the specific gravity of the electrolyte using a hydrometer. Before testing the battery, check that the cables are tight and free of corrosion.

Hydrometer testing

The hydrometer is a glass cylinder with a freely moving float inside. When electrolyte is drawn into the cylinder, the level to which the float sinks indicates the specific gravity of the electrolyte. The more dense the concentration of sulfuric acid in the electrolyte, the less the float will sink, resulting in a higher reading and indicating a higher state of charge.

NOTE —

Electrolyte temperature affects hydrometer reading. Check the electrolyte temperature with a thermometer. Add 0.004 to the hydrometer reading for every 6°C (10°F) that the electrolyte is above 27°C (80°F). Subtract 0.004 from the reading for every 6°C (10°F) that the electrolyte is below 27°C (80°F).

Before checking the specific gravity of a battery, load the battery with 15 amperes for one minute. If the battery is installed in the vehicle, this can be done by turning on the headlights without the engine running. **Table b** lists the percentage of charge based on specific gravity values.

Table a. Specific gravity of battery electrolyte at 80°F (27°C)

Specific gravity	State of charge
1.265	Fully charged
1.225	75% charged
1.190	50% charged
1.155	25% charged
1.120	Fully discharged

The battery is in satisfactory condition if the average specific gravity of the six cells is at least 1.225. If the specific gravity is above this level, but the battery lacks power for starting, determine the battery's service condition with a load voltage test, as described below. If the average specific gravity of the six cells is below 1.225, remove the battery from the luggage compartment and recharge. If, after recharging, the specific gravity varies by more than 0.005 between any two cells, replace the battery.

Battery, charging

Discharged batteries can be recharged using a battery charger. Always remove battery from vehicle during charging.

Prolonged charging causes electrolyte evaporation to a level that can damage the battery. It is best to use a low-current charger (6 amperes or less) to prevent battery damage caused by overheating.

> ***WARNING —***
> *Hydrogen gas given off by the battery during charging is explosive. Do not smoke. Keep open flames away from the top of the battery, and prevent electrical sparks by turning off the battery charger before connecting or disconnecting it.*

> ***CAUTION —***
> - *Battery electrolyte (sulfuric acid) can damage the car. If electrolyte is spilled, clean the area with a solution of baking soda and water.*
> - *Always allow a frozen battery to thaw before attempting to recharge it.*
> - *Always disconnect both battery cables and remove battery from vehicle during battery charging. Do not exceed 16.5 charging voltage at the battery.*

Battery open-circuit voltage test

Before making the test, load the battery with 15 amperes for one minute with a battery load-tester or turn on the headlights for about one minute without the engine running.Then disconnect the battery negative (–) cable and connect a digital voltmeter across the battery terminals. Open-circuit voltage levels are given in **Table b**.

If the open-circuit voltage is OK but the battery still lacks power for starting, make a load voltage test. If the open-circuit voltage is below 12.4 volts, recharge the battery and retest.

Table b. Open-circuit voltage and battery charge

Open-circuit voltage	State of charge
12.6 V or more	Fully charged
12.4 V	75% charged
12.2 V	50% charged
12.0 V	25% charged
11.7 V or less	Fully discharged

Battery load voltage test

A battery load tester is required for a load voltage test. The test is made by applying a high resistive load to the battery terminals and then measuring battery voltage. The battery should be fully charged for the most accurate results. The battery cables must be disconnected before making the test. If the voltage is below that listed in **Table d**, the battery should be replaced.

> ***WARNING —***
> *Always wear protective goggles and clothing when performing a load test.*

Table c. Battery load test–minimum voltage (apply 200 amp load for 15 seconds)

Ambient temperature	Voltage
27°C (80°F)	9.6 V
16°C (60°F)	9.5 V
4°C (40°F)	9.3 V
-7°C (20°F)	8.9 V
-18°C (0°F)	8.5 V

Battery safety terminal (BST), replacing

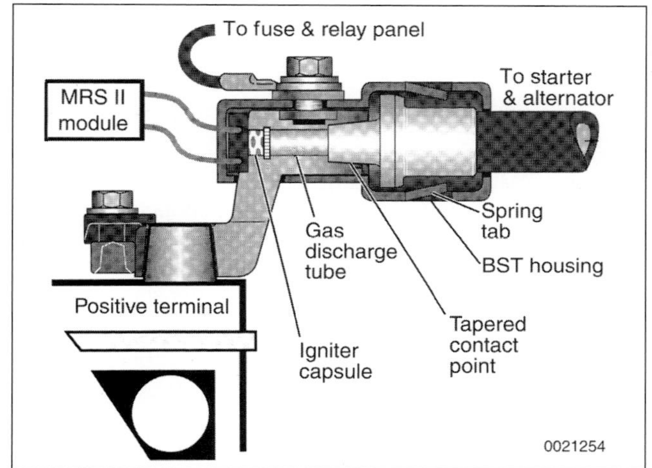

The E46 features a Battery Safety Terminal (BST) controlled by the Multiple Restraint System (MRS). This system is designed to disconnect electrical power to the engine compartment in the event of an impact or collision. Depending on the severity of an impact, the MRS system fires an encapsulated pyrotechnic device in the battery terminal that disconnects power to the engine compartment, but maintains power to the exterior lights and interior of the vehicle.

If the BST (also referred to as SBK) has been triggered, investigate and correct the cause prior to replacement.

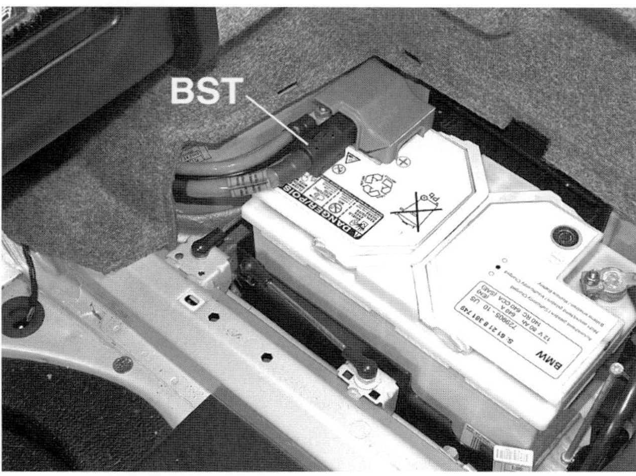

Working in right side of trunk, remove battery trim panel to access battery.

- Disconnect negative (–) battery terminal and cover with insulator.
- Disconnect positive (+) cable from battery.
- Release positive (+) cable from cable brackets on trunk side wall. Lay new repair cable parallel to positive cable.
- Mark off length of new cable on old cable. Allow 10 cm (2.5 in) of slack.

- Saw through old cable.

> ***CAUTION —***
> *Do not use bolt cutters or similar tools to cut through cable. A cable end that has been squashed flat may not fit into the clamping sleeve of the new cable.*

- Strip approximately 15 mm (0.6 in) of insulation from cable end.

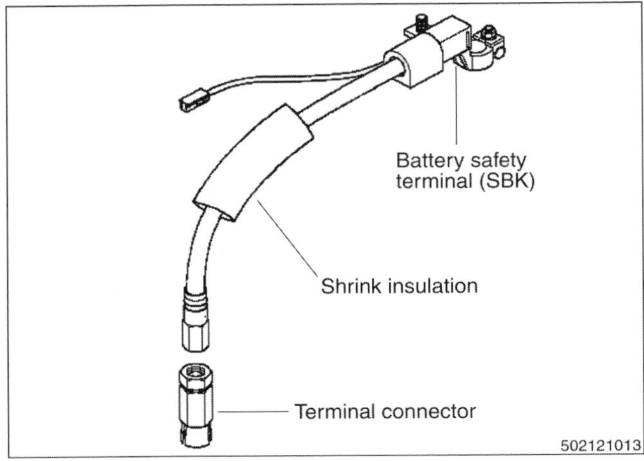

- ◄ Push terminal connector of new cable over stripped end of old cable. Tighten clamp.
- Slip shrink-fit insulation over positive cable. Attach new safety harness to end of positive cable. Shrink insulation with hot air blower.
- Reinstall cable in cable bracket and attach to battery.
- Reattach negative battery cable. Reinstall trunk trim.
- Use BMW scan tool to read out airbag control module (SRS) fault memory. Correct faults, then clear fault memory.

Closed-circuit current measurement

If the vehicle battery is discharged for an unknown reason, perform a closed-circuit current measurement as the first test.

This test requires a special closed circuit current adapter harness (BMW special tool 61 2 300). The test adapter allows current measurement without disconnecting the battery. For diagnostic purposes, it is important to not disconnect the battery. Disconnecting the battery may reset a faulty control unit, preventing proper diagnosis.

The following test should be carried out overnight using a multimeter with a recording function.

- Check that battery voltage is 12 VDC or higher. If lower, recharge battery.
- Switch off all electrical consumers.
- Open trunk and remove battery trim panel. Use screwdriver to lock latch on trunk lid or hatch, simulating closed trunk. Close other doors. **Leave trunk open**.
- Open driver's door, then close it, simulating driver entering vehicle.
- Switch ignition to RUN position for at least five seconds, then turn ignition OFF. This simulates driving vehicle.
- Open and close driver's door, simulating driver leaving vehicle. Lock car and arm alarm.

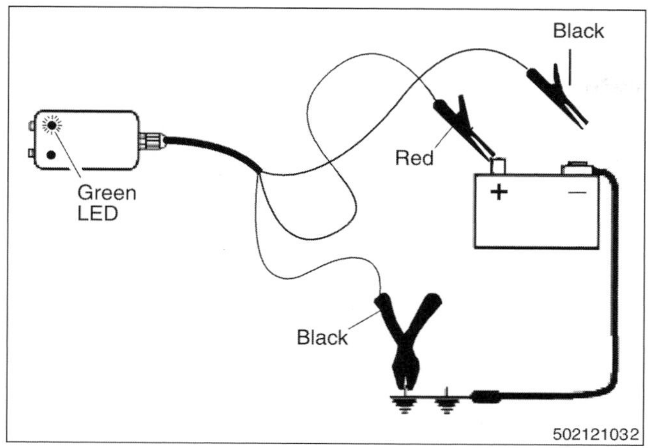

– Wait at least 16 minutes for electrical consumer sleep mode to set in.

NOTE —
The consumer sleep mode function interrupts battery voltage to vehicle circuits, preventing inadvertent battery drain if one of the consumers remains activated.Automatic transmission cars: amber shifter LED goes out when consumer sleep mode sets in.

◄ Attach closed-circuit current measurement adapter (BMW special tool 61 2 300):

- Connect red clamp to positive battery terminal.
- Connect large black clamp to chassis ground point.

NOTE —
Green LED lights up to indicate correct adapter installation.

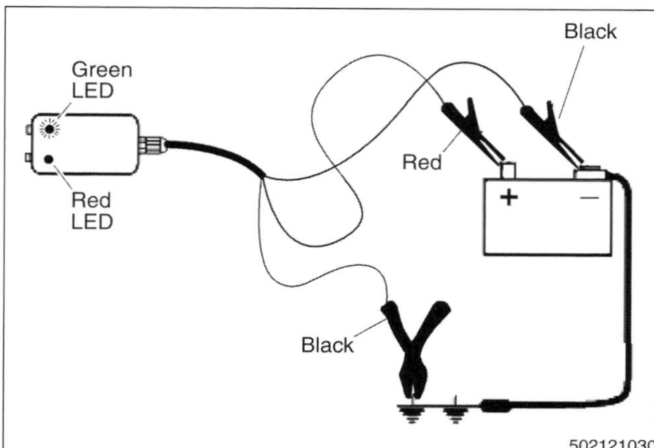

◄ Connect small black clamp to negative battery terminal. Green LED light goes out.

NOTE —
Electrical overloading is indicated by the illuminated red LED. If the red LED lights up, recheck adapter connections.

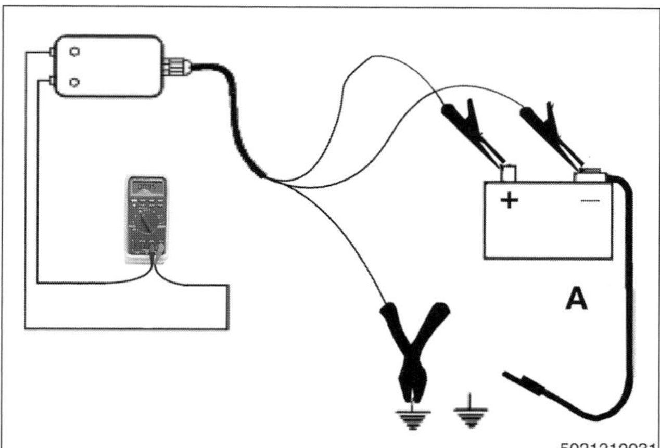

◄ Set multimeter to 2 - 5 A measuring range and connect to adapter.

NOTE —
- *Set multimeter to record average readings.*
- *If possible, turn off powersaving features of multimeter which prevent a long term (overnight) test by automatically powering down meter.*

– Disconnect battery ground strap (**A**) at chassis mounting point.

– Record closed-circuit current using multimeter.

– After measuring current, reconnect battery ground before removing large tester clamp. Switch on ignition for at least 5 seconds and then off again to prevent setting faults in control modules.

– Investigate readings over 30 mA.

NOTE —
Momentary spikes may be recorded intermittently due to use of remote-control keys in other vehicles nearby or other radio transmitters. These spikes can be ignored as a cause of battery discharge.

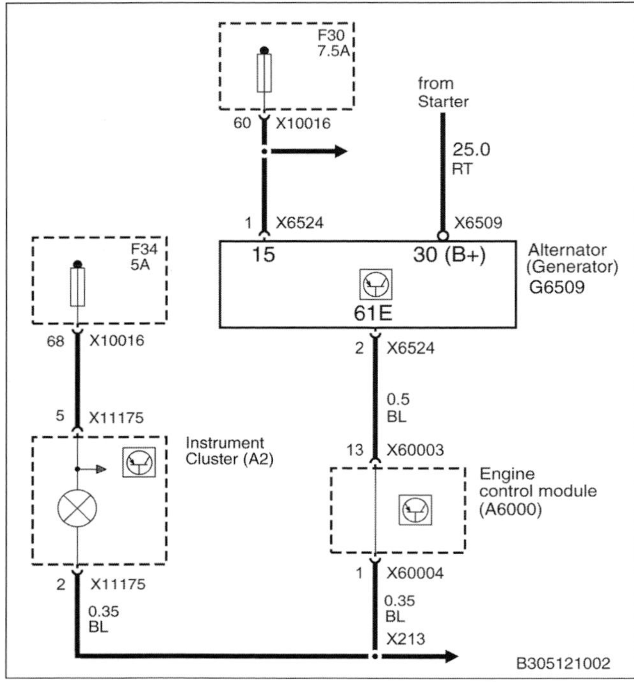

ALTERNATOR

Before checking the alternator and regulator, make sure the battery is fully charged and capable of holding a charge. Check that the battery terminals are clean and tight and the alternator drive belt is properly tensioned and not severely worn.

Several versions of alternators have been used in E46 models. Be sure that replacement alternators are correct for the application.

Alternator with multifunction controller (MFR)

The multifunction controller (MFR) alternator charge warning light is activated by means of an electronic switch integrated in the MFR. This switch receives its voltage supply from terminal 15 on the 3–pin connector at the rear of the alternator. The MFR measures internally the voltage difference between terminal 30 and terminal 15 to turn the charge warning light ON and OFF.

NOTE —
The schematic diagram is for the charging circuit for cars with MS 42.0 engine management (M52 TU engines). For model specific diagrams, consult **Electrical Wiring Diagrams**.

The controller features integrated fault detection. The battery charge warning light illuminates in case of:

- Drive belt failure
- No charging current due to an electrical or electronic fault
- Interruption in excitation circuit
- Over-voltage due to a defective MFR output stage
- Fault or break in charging line
- Alternator fault

Charging system troubleshooting

Charging system diagnostics requires special test equipment. If the test equipment is not available, charging system fault diagnosis can be performed by an authorized BMW dealer or other qualified repair shop. See **Table a** for general electrical component troubleshooting.

Before checking the alternator, make sure the battery is fully charged and capable of holding a charge. Check that the battery terminals are clean and tight and the alternator drive belt is properly tensioned and not severely worn.

NOTE —
The alternator requires up to 15 second to reach full output.

Table d. Battery, alternator and starter troubleshooting

Symptom	Probable cause	Corrective action
Starter motor does not operate	a. Battery cables loose, dirty or corroded b. Battery fully discharged c. Poor connection at starter motor terminal 30 d. Starter motor or solenoid faulty e. EWS (drive away protection) system fault	a. Clean or replace battery cables. b. Charge battery and test, replace if necessary. c. Inspect ground strap. Clean, tighten or replace if necessary. d. Check connections, test for voltage at starter. Test for voltage at neutral safety or clutch interlock switch. e. Connect BMW scan tool and interrogate EWS system for faults. Re-align EWS control module to DME control module using scan tool.
Engine cranks slowly or solenoid clicks when starter is operated.	a. Battery cables loose, dirty or corroded b. Battery discharged c. Body ground strap loose, dirty or corroded d. Poor connection at starter motor terminal 30 e. Starter motor or solenoid faulty	a. Clean or replace cables. b. Charge battery and test, replace if necessary. c. Inspect ground strap. Clean, tighten or replace if necessary. d. Check connections, test for voltage at starter. Test for voltage at neutral safety or clutch interlock switch. e. Test starter.
Battery will not stay charged more than a few days.	a. Short circuit draining battery b. Short driving trips and high electrical drain on charging system does not allow battery to recharge. c. Drive belt(s) worn or damaged d. Battery faulty e. Battery cables loose, dirty or corroded f. Alternator or voltage regulator faulty	a. Test for excessive current drain with everything electrical off. b. Evaluate driving style. Where possible, reduce electrical consumption when making short trips. c. Inspect or replace multi-ribbed belt(s). See **020 Maintenance**. d. Test battery and replace if necessary. e. Clean or replace cables. f. Test alternator and voltage regulator.
Battery loses water.	a. Battery overcharging or damaged	a. Test voltage regulator for proper operation.
Lights dim, light intensity varies with engine speed.	a. Drive belt worn or damaged b. Alternator or voltage regulator faulty c. Body ground straps loose, dirty or corroded	a. Inspect or replace multi-ribbed belt(s). See **020 Maintenance**. b. Test alternator and voltage regulator. c. Inspect ground straps. Clean, tighten or replace as necessary.

Charging system quick-check

Use a digital multimeter to measure voltage across the battery terminals with key off and then again with engine running.

Battery voltage	
Engine at rest, battery fully charged	12.6 vdc
Engine running, regulated voltage	13.2 - 14.5 vdc
Faulty regulator or MFR	>14.8 vdc

Check for clean and tight battery cables. Check ground cable running from negative (–) battery terminal to chassis and ground cable running from engine to chassis. Check alternator drive belt condition and tension. Check wiring connections at alternator.

NOTE —
Drive belt service is covered in **020 Maintenance**.

Charging system, checking

> ***CAUTION —***
> - *Do not disconnect battery while engine is running. Damage to alternator and/or engine electronic systems may result.*
> - *Only use a digital multimeter when testing charging system components.*

Charge indicator lamp

502620805

- Turn ignition key on. Check that charge warning light comes on.

NOTE —
If the warning light does not come on, repair bulb or wiring faults before continuing to check the charging system.

- Using BMW diagnostic scan tool, Read out engine control module (ECM) fault memory.
- Test alternator output using a load tester.
- If a load tester is not available, a quick output test can be done by running engine at about 2000 rpm and turning on electrical loads (fans, lights and rear window defroster, wipers). With all accessories on, battery voltage should be above 12.6 VDC.
- Connect BMW diagnostic scan tool or oscilloscope to check alternator function.

NOTE —
An alternator output pattern other than "normal" indicates that the alternator needs rebuilding or replacement.

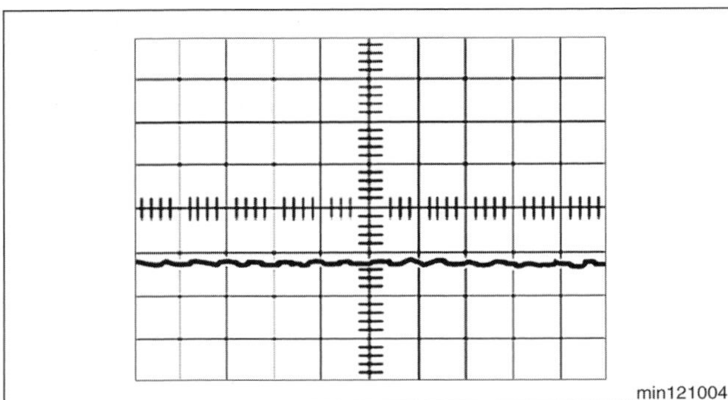

min121004

- Normal alternator pattern

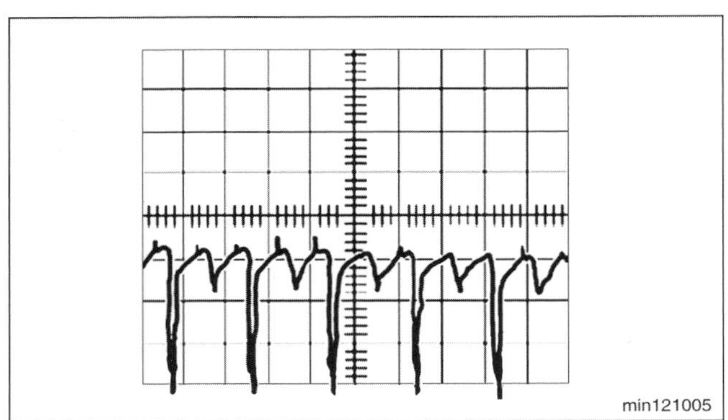

min121005

- One phase interrupted

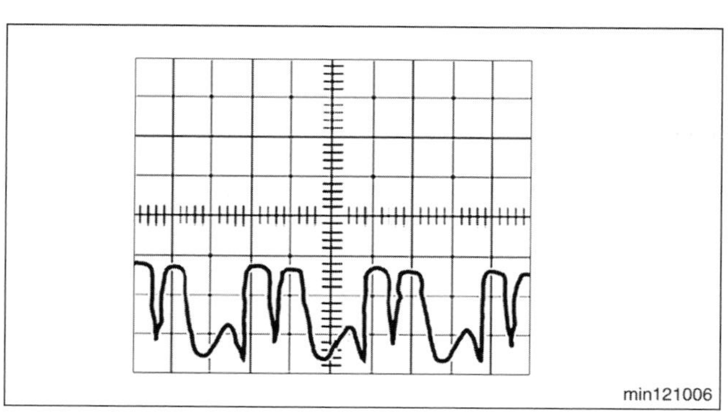
min121006

Interturn (short circuit in rotor windings) fault

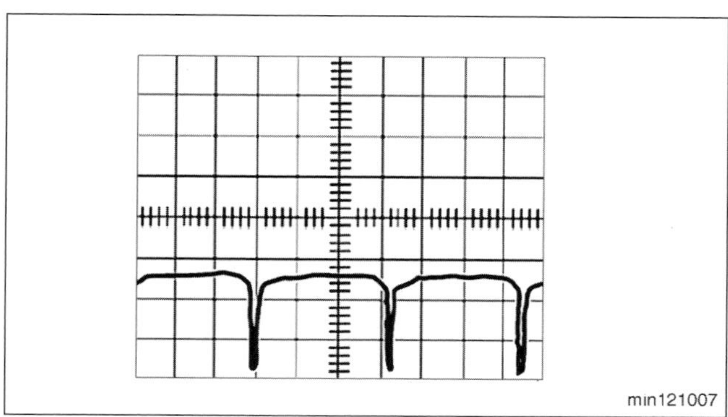
min121007

Open circuit in negative diode

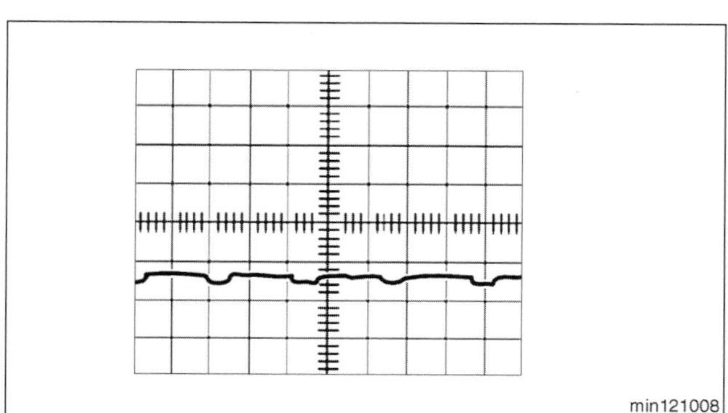
min121008

Short circuit in positive diode

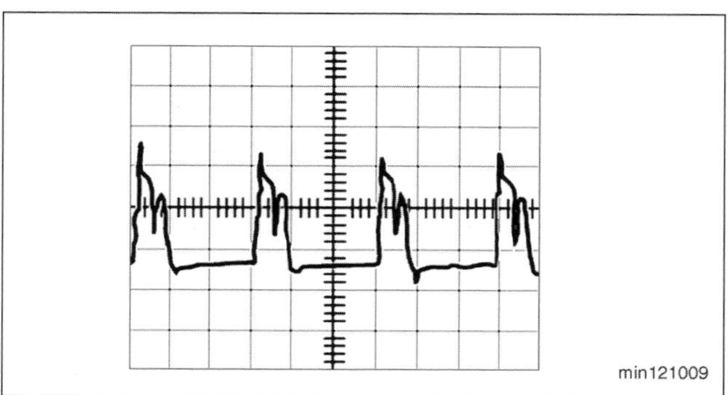
min121009

Open circuit in positive diode

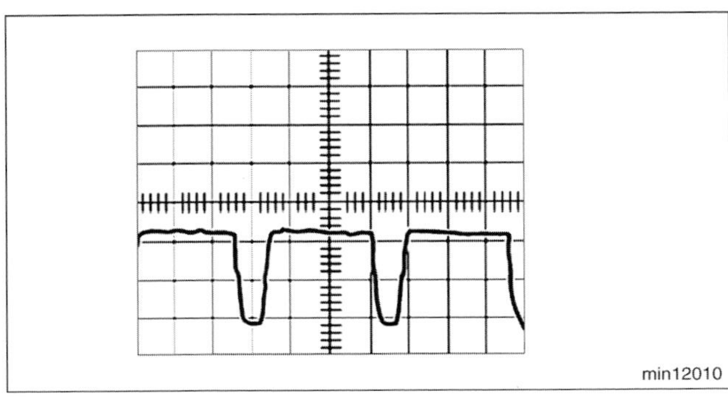

Open circuit in exciter diode

Alternator, removing and installing

A replacement alternator should have the same rating as the original. Alternator manufacturer and ampere rating are normally marked on the alternator housing.

– Disconnect negative (–) battery cable.

> ***CAUTION —***
> *Prior to disconnecting the battery, read the battery disconnection cautions given at the front of this manual on page viii.*

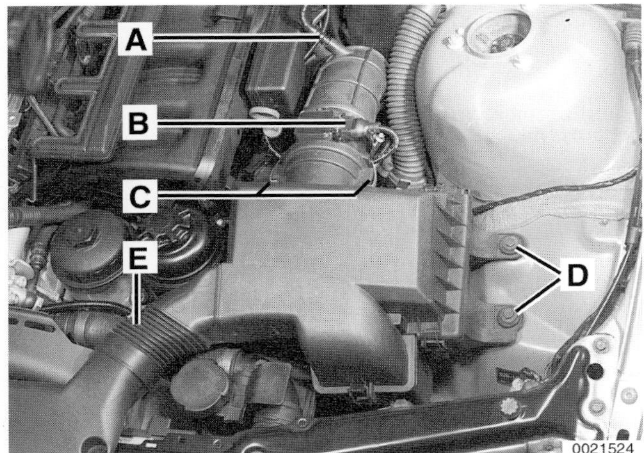

Remove complete air filter housing:

- Disconnect electrical harness connector on mass air flow sensor (**B**).
- Detach vacuum line at intake boot (**A**).
- Remove filter housing mounting screws (**D**).
- Loosen hose clamp at intake boot and detach air duct connections (**C**).
- Disconnect cold air duct tube (**E**).

Remove alternator cooling duct fasteners (**arrows**). Pull back ducts and disconnect wiring from rear of alternator.

– Remove radiator cooling fan and fan shroud. See **170 Radiator and Cooling System**.

> ***NOTE —***
> *On automatic transmission equipped vehicles the radiator cooling fan nut (32 mm wrench) has left-hand threads.*

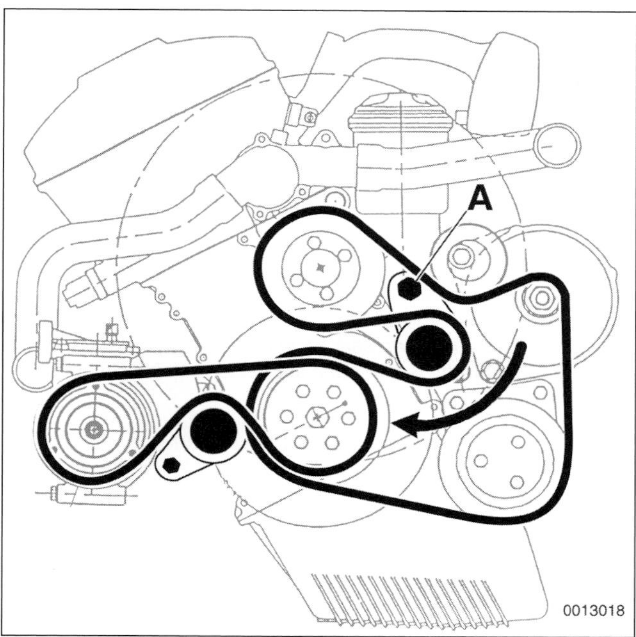

Remove alternator drive belt using a long-handled wrench to turn alternator belt tensioner release lug (**A**) clockwise (against spring tension). Remove belt.

NOTE —
If reusing drive belt, mark direction of rotation on belt before removing.

– Remove upper and lower mounting bolts and lift out alternator.

– Counterhold alternator shaft with Allen wrench and use BMW special tool 12 7 110 or equivalent thin-walled 24 mm socket wrench to remove alternator pulley bolt.

– Installation is reverse of removal.

Tightening torques
- B+ wire to alternator (M8 nut) . . . . 13 Nm (10 ft-lb)
- Pulley to alternator (M16 nut) . . . . 70 Nm (44 ft-lb)

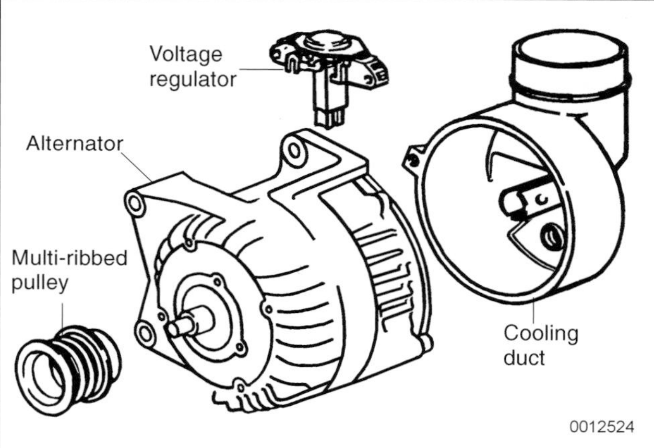

Voltage regulator, removing and installing

– Disconnect negative (–) cable from battery.

– Remove alternator as described earlier.

Remove voltage regulator mounting screws and remove regulator from alternator.

– Installation is reverse of removal. Clean brush contact surfaces in alternator and check brush length as described later.

STARTER

Starter troubleshooting

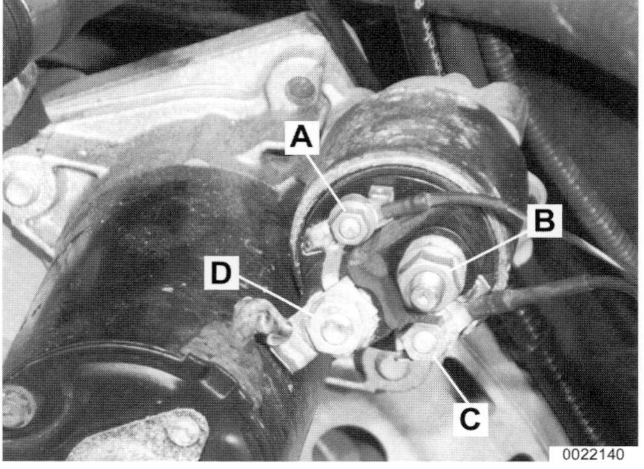

Typical starter wiring terminal identification. Large wire at terminal **30** is direct battery voltage. Smaller wire at terminal **50** operates starter solenoid via ignition switch.

- A - Terminal 30h
- B - Terminal 30 to battery
- C - Terminal 50 to ignition switch
- D - Starter field terminal

If the starter turns the engine slowly or fails to operate when the ignition is in the start position, check the battery first. Inspect the starter wires, terminals, and ground connections for good contact. In particular, make sure the ground connections between the battery, the body and the engine are completely clean and tight. Check clutch pedal operated starter lock-out switch or gear position switch (automatic). If no faults can be found, the starter may be faulty and should be replaced.

NOTE —
- *A factory-installed drive-away protection system, also referred to as EWS, is used on all E46 cars. This system prevents operation of the starter if an incorrectly coded ignition key is used. See* **515 Central Locking and Anti-theft**.
- *On cars with automatic transmission, the transmission gear position switch signals EWS III to prevent the engine from starting in gear positions other than park or neutral. If voltage is not present at terminal* ***50*** *with the key in the start position, check these components.*
- *On cars with manual transmissions, a starter immobilization switch at the clutch pedal is used to prevent the starter from operating unless the clutch pedal is pushed fully to the floor.*

To make the most accurate check of the battery cables and starter wiring, make a voltage drop test on the cables and wiring as described in **600 Electrical System–General**.

Check for battery voltage at terminal **50** of starter motor with key in start position. If voltage is not present, check wiring between ignition switch and starter terminal. If voltage is present and no other visible wiring faults can be found, problem is most likely in starter motor.

If solenoid audibly clicks but motor does not turn, switch on rights and turn key to start position. If lights go out while attempting to start, battery cable may be loose or starter may have a short circuit. If lights stay on, solenoid is most likely at fault.

Starter, removing and installing

The starter on a car with manual transmission is removed from below.

NOTE —
- *Starter removal on some vehicles may be easier with air filter housing removed and throttle cable disconnected. See* **110 Engine Removal and Installation.**
- *Starter removal on all wheel drive equipped vehicles may be easier with the transmission lowered 5 cm.*

– Disconnect negative (–) battery cable.

– Raise vehicle and support safely.

– Remove engine underbody shield.

– Remove reinforcing cross brace from under transmission.

– Remove cover from fuel filter and fuel lines on left side underneath car. Detach fuel lines and harness connectors from retaining brackets, as necessary.

– Disconnect wiring from starter.

– Using a long extension and universal joint from output end of transmission, remove bolts fastening starter to transmission bell housing and engine block.

– Remove starter from below.

– Check starter pinion gear and flywheel teeth for damage.

– Installation is reverse of removal.

Tightening torques
- Starter to engine block . . . . 47 Nm (35 ft-lb)
- Support bracket to starter (M5 nut). . . . . . 5 Nm (44 in-lb)
- Support bracket
  to engine block (M10 bolt) . . . . 47 Nm (35 ft-lb)
- Wire to terminal 50 (M6 nut) . . . . 6 Nm (53 in-lb)
- Wire to terminal 30 (M8 nut) . . . . 12 Nm (9 ft-lb)

Solenoid switch, removing and installing

– Remove starter as described above.

– Disconnect field winding strap between starter motor and solenoid switch.

NOTE —
The condition of the field winding strap is critical. If it is damaged, burned or partially melted through, a new or rebuilt starter motor is needed.

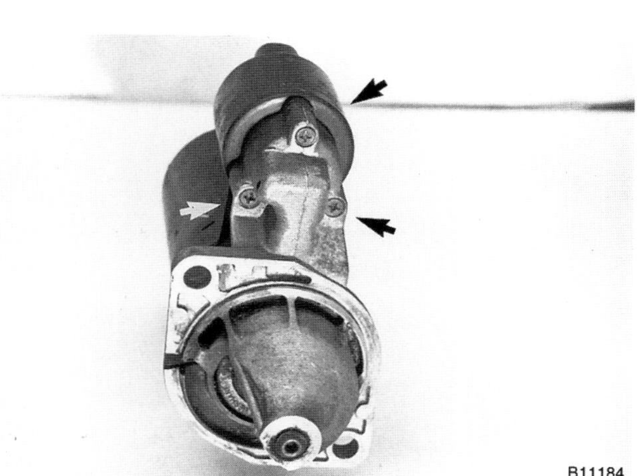
B11184

 Remove solenoid switch mounting screws, and separate solenoid from starter.

CAUTION —
When installing field winding strap to starter, position it so that it does not contact the starter body.

– Installation is reverse of removal. Lubricate solenoid piston with light grease.

Tightening torque
- Field winding strap to starter (M8) . . . . . . 12 Nm (9 ft-lb)

130 Fuel Injection

TABLES

GENERAL

This repair group covers service and repair for the Siemens MS 42.0, MS 43.0, and MS 45.1 engine management systems used on the E46 models. For additional engine management information see the following repair groups:

- **120 Ignition System**
- **131 Fuel Injection (M3 models)**
- **160 Fuel Tank and Fuel Pump**
- **Electrical Wiring Diagrams**

NOTE —
Fuel pressure testing and fuel pump repair information is covered in **160 Fuel Tank and Fuel Pump**.

Table a. Engine management systems

Model year: Engine code	DME system
1999 - 2000: M52 TU B25 M52 TU B28	Siemens MS 42.0
2001 - 2005 M54 B25 M54 B30	Siemens MS 43.0
2003 - 2005 M56 B25	Siemens MS 45.1
2001 - 2005 S54 B34	Siemens MS S54 *see* **131 Fuel Injection (M3 models)**

The Siemens systems are sophisticated self-diagnostic OBD II systems. These systems continuously monitor components and record and store valuable diagnostic information about operating conditions.

When faults arise, or if the MIL (malfunction indicator lamp) in the instrument cluster is illuminated, begin troubleshooting by connecting a BMW-compatible scan tool. The diagnostic capabilities of these systems have the potential to save hours of diagnostic time, and prevent incorrect component replacement and possible damage to system components. See **On-Board Diagnostics** at the back of this manual.

NOTE —

- *Beginning in the 2003 model year, 325i models equipped with an automatic transmission destined for sale in California, New York, Massachusetts, and Vermont are fitted with the M56 B25 engine, and achieve SULEV (Super Low Emissions Vehicle) classification. Through the addition of upgrades to the fuel delivery and emissions systems, and a 15 year / 150,000 mile warranty on emissions equipment, these vehicles are considered PZEV (Partial Zero Emissions Vehicles). Repair procedures for these models have been included where information is available.*
- *As of 3/2003 production, M54 B25 and M54 B30 engines installed in E46 models (except xi) receive the emissions classification ULEV2 (Ultra Low Emissions Vehicle II) in all 50 states. These vehicles are equipped with revised catalytic converters and wideband pre-catalyst oxygen sensors.*

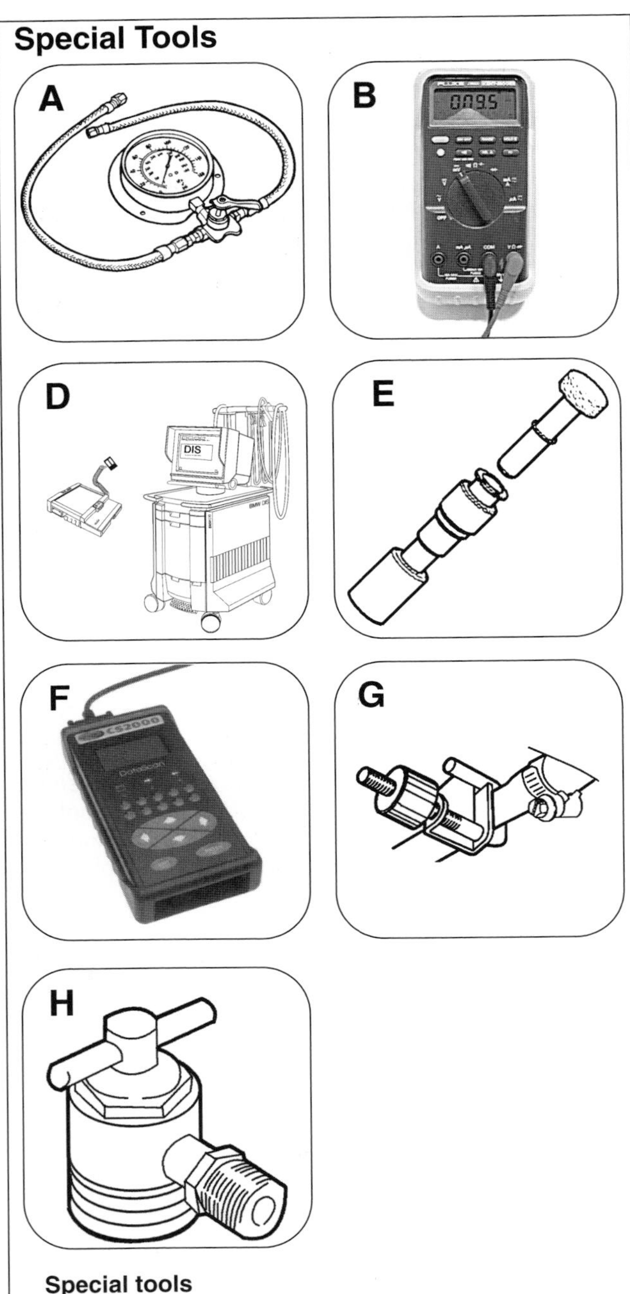

Special tools

A Baum 1318 . . . . Fuel pressure gauge (Source: Baum Tools Unlimited)
B Automotive digital multimeter
C BMW GT1 . . . . Factory scan tool
D BMW 13 5 281 / 13 5 282 . . . . Fuel line plugs
E Aftermarket DTC scan tool
F BMW 13 3 010 . . . . Fuel line clamp
G BMW 13 5 220 . . . . Fuel rail to pressure gauge fitting

Tools and test equipment

Special tools may be required to properly service the DME system and to replace system components. If the special equipment is unavailable, it is recommended that these repairs be left to an authorized BMW dealer or other qualified BMW repair facility. Read the procedure through before beginning a repair.

NOTE —

- *In addition to the BMW professional line of scan tools, there are many inexpensive 'generic' OBD II scan tool software programs and handheld units available. Although these tools have limited capabilities as compared to the dedicated tools, they are powerful diagnostic tools. These tools read live data streams, freeze frame information for DTCs (diagnostic trouble codes) and impending DTCs, as well as a host of other valuable diagnostic data.*
- *For the DIY owner, simple aftermarket DTC readers are also available. These inexpensive BMW-only tools are capable of checking for DTCs as well as turning off the illuminated MIL, and resetting the service indicator lights.*
- *See* **020 Maintenance** *for specialty tool manufacturer contact information.*

Principle of operation

The DME fuel injection system is completely electronic in operation. Intake air, engine coolant temperature, crankshaft and camshaft positions, engine speed and many other engine operating parameters are measured electronically and the information is supplied to the engine control module (ECM).

Based on input information, the ECM controls the ignition coils, fuel injectors, motor driven throttle valve, double VANOS system, radiator cooling fan, electrically heated thermostat, as well as other outputs.

The illustration on the following page shows the MS 42.0 ECM inputs and outputs. The MS 43.0 system is similar in operation, with the main difference being the fully electronic 'drive-by-wire' throttle valve. MS 45.1 is also similar to MS 42.0 and 43.0, but uses revised emission control and fuel delivery systems to achieve Partial Zero Emissions Vehicle (PZEV) certification. Additional information can be also found in **100 Engine–General**.

Warnings and cautions

For personal safety, as well as the protection of sensitive electronic components, adhere to the warnings and cautions on the following pages.

WARNING —

- *Gasoline is highly flammable and its vapors are explosive. Do not smoke or work on a car near heaters or other fire hazards when diagnosing and repairing fuel system problems. Have a fire extinguisher available in case of an emergency.*
- *When working on an open fuel system, wear suitable hand protection, as prolonged contact with fuel can cause illnesses and skin disorders.*
- *The ignition system produces high voltages that can be fatal. Avoid contact with exposed terminals. Use extreme caution when working on a car with the ignition switched on or the engine running.*
- *Do not touch or disconnect any cables from the coils while the engine is running or being cranked by the starter.*
- *Connect and disconnect the DME system wiring and test equipment leads only when the ignition is switched off.*
- *Renew fuel system hoses, clamps and O-rings any time they are removed.*
- *Before making any electrical tests that require the engine to be cranked using the starter, disable the ignition system as described in* **120 Ignition System**.

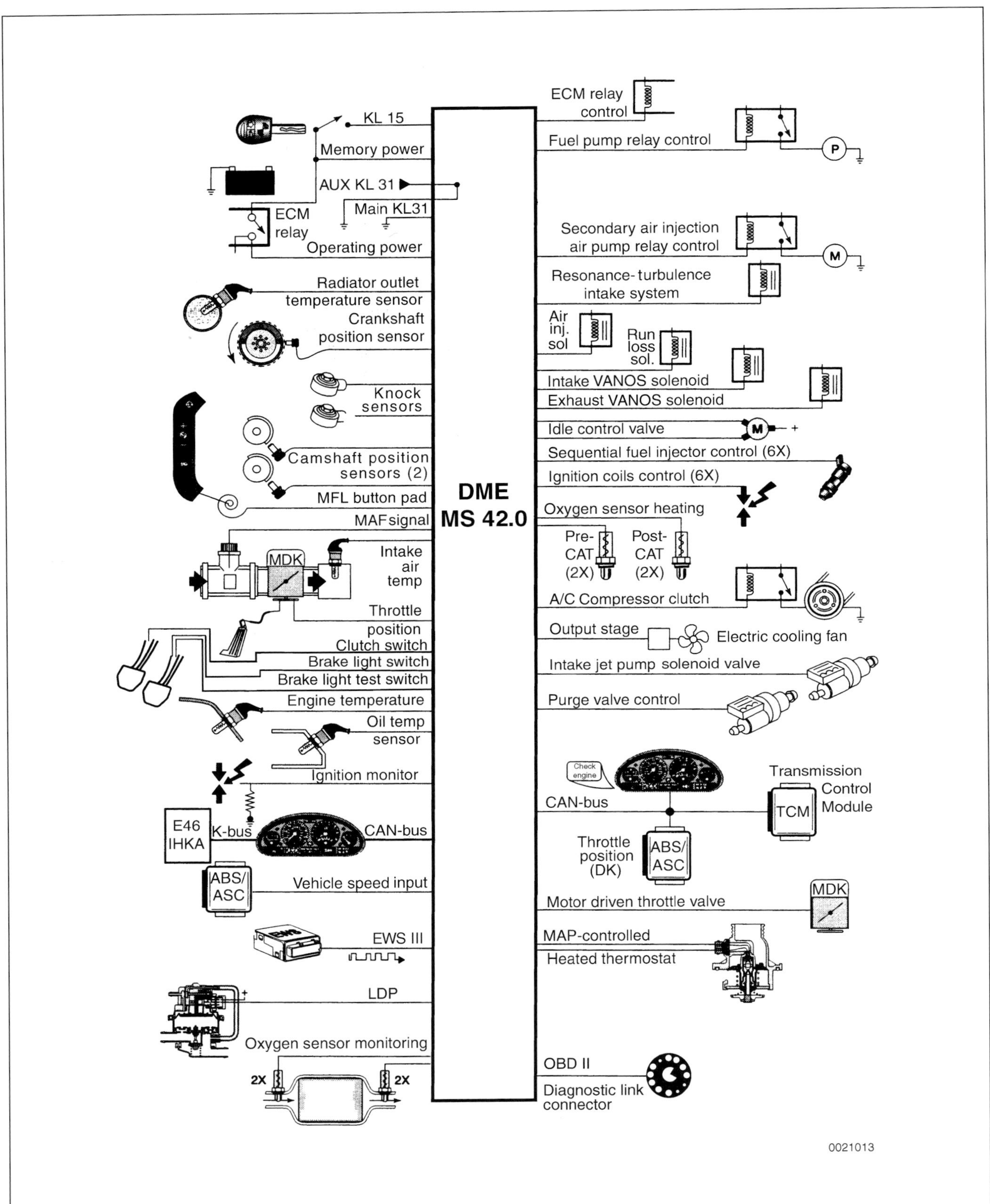
KL 15
Memory power
AUX KL 31
Main KL31
ECM relay
Operating power
Radiator outlet temperature sensor
Crankshaft position sensor
Knock sensors
Camshaft position sensors (2)
MFL button pad
MAFsignal
MDK
Intake air temp
Throttle position
Clutch switch
Brake light switch
Brake light test switch
Engine temperature
Oil temp sensor
Ignition monitor
E46 IHKA
K-bus
CAN-bus
ABS/ ASC
Vehicle speed input
EWS III
LDP
Oxygen sensor monitoring
2X
2X
DME MS 42.0
ECM relay control
Fuel pump relay control
P
Secondary air injection air pump relay control
M
Resonance-turbulence intake system
Air inj. sol
Run loss sol.
Intake VANOS solenoid
Exhaust VANOS solenoid
Idle control valve
M
Sequential fuel injector control (6X)
Ignition coils control (6X)
Oxygen sensor heating
Pre-CAT (2X)
Post-CAT (2X)
A/C Compressor clutch
Output stage
Electric cooling fan
Intake jet pump solenoid valve
Purge valve control
Check engine
CAN-bus
Transmission Control Module
TCM
Throttle position (DK)
ABS/ ASC
MDK
Motor driven throttle valve
MAP-controlled
Heated thermostat
OBD II
Diagnostic link connector
0021013

CAUTION —
- *Prior to disconnecting the battery, read the battery disconnection cautions in* **001 Warnings and Cautions**.
- *Do not connect any test equipment that delivers a 12-volt power supply to terminal 15 (+) of the ignition coil. The current flow may damage the ECM. In general, connect test equipment only as specified by BMW or the equipment maker.*
- *Only use a digital multimeter for electrical tests.*
- *Only use an LED test light for quick tests.*
- *Disconnecting the battery may erase fault code(s) stored in memory. Check for fault codes prior to disconnecting the battery cables.*
- *Wait at least 40 seconds after turning off the ignition before removing the engine control module (ECM) connector. If the connector is removed before this time, residual power in the system relay may damage the control module.*
- *Cleanliness is essential when working on an open fuel system. Thoroughly clean fuel line connections and surrounding areas before loosening. Avoid moving the car. Only install clean parts.*
- *Fuel system cleaners and other chemical additives other than those specifically recommended by BMW may damage the catalytic converter, the oxygen sensor or other fuel supply components.*

ELECTRICAL CHECKS AND COMPONENT TESTING

Troubleshooting and fault diagnosis on OBD II cars is best performed using an electronic scan tool.

CAUTION —
- *Some of the tests in this section may set fault codes (DTCs) in the ECM and illuminate the MIL. After all testing tests is completed, access and clear DTC fault memory using a BMW compatible scan tool. See* **On-Board Diagnostics** *at the back of this manual.*
- *Only use a digital multimeter for electrical tests.*
- *Relay positions can vary. Be sure to confirm relay position by identifying the wiring in the socket using the wiring diagrams found at the rear of this manual.*

DME main relay, testing

The DME main relay is energized via the engine control module (ECM) and supplies battery positive (B+) power to many of the engine management components and subsystems. If this relay is faulty, the engine will not start.

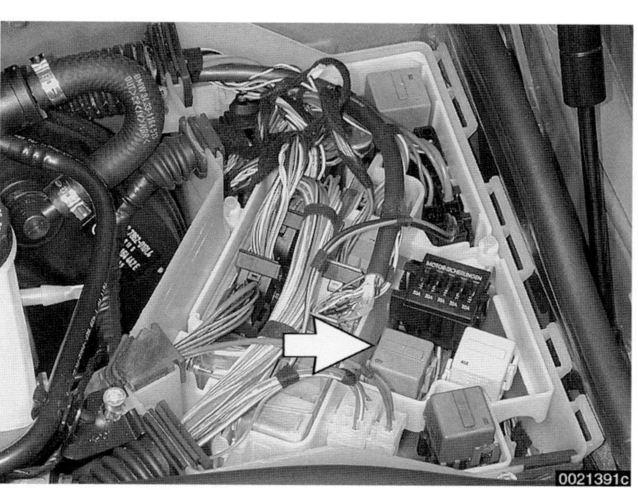

With ignition off, remove main relay (**arrow**) in electronics box (E-box) at left rear of engine compartment.

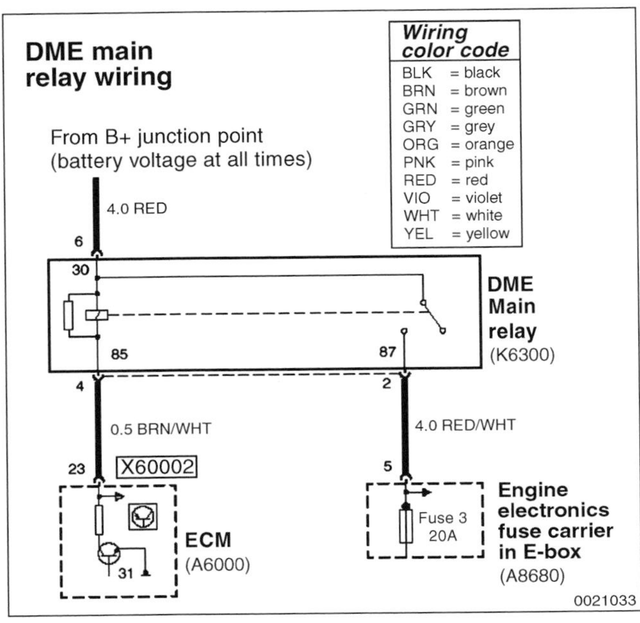

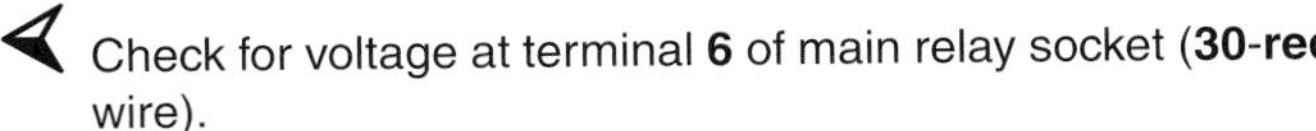

Check for voltage at terminal **6** of main relay socket (**30-red** wire).

- If battery voltage is present continue testing.
- If battery voltage is not present, check large red wire in relay socket. See **Electrical Wiring Diagrams.**

– Reinstall relay and turn ignition on. Gain access to underside of relay socket and check for ground at terminal **4** (**85-brown/white** wire).

- If ground is present continue testing.
- If ground is not present, signal from ECM (connector X60002, pin **23**) is missing. Check wire between ECM and relay.

– With ignition on and relay installed, check for battery voltage at terminal **2** (**87-red/white** wire).

- If battery voltage is present, relay has energized and is functioning correctly.
- If battery voltage is not present and all earlier tests are OK, relay is faulty and should be replaced.

Fuel pump relay, testing (MS 42.0 and MS 43.0)

NOTE —
Models equipped with Siemens DME MS 45.1 and MS S54 operate the fuel pump through an electronically controlled relay (fuel pump control module). For more information, see **160 Fuel Tank and Fuel Pump**. *The fuel pump relay/fuel pump control module on these cars is mounted in the right-hand side of the luggage compartment, behind the trim panel.*

On DME MS 42.0 and MS 43.0, the ECM energizes the fuel pump relay by providing the coil side of the relay with ground. During engine cranking, the fuel pump runs as long as the ignition switch is in the start position and continues to run once the engine starts. If the relay is faulty the fuel pump will not run.

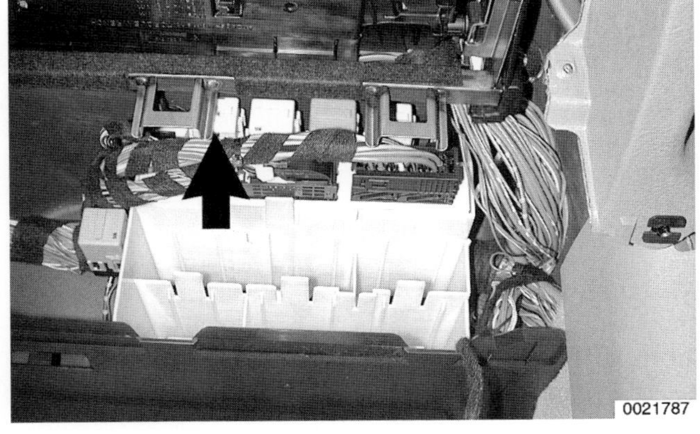

Fuel pump relay (**arrow**) is located behind glove compartment. Remove glove compartment. See **513 Interior Trim**.

– Remove fuel pump relay from socket.

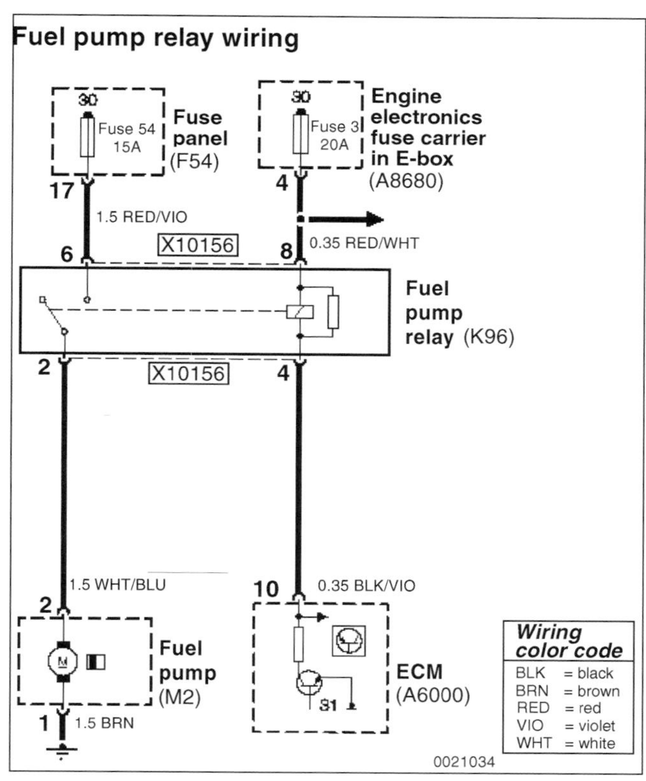

With ignition in START position, check for battery voltage at relay connector (X10156) terminals **6** and **8** (**red/violet** and **red/white** wires).

> ***CAUTION —***
> *Ensure that manual transmission vehicles are not in gear, and automatic transmission vehicles are in Park or Neutral prior to operating ignition in START position.*

– With ignition in START position, use digital multimeter to check for ground at terminal **4** (**black/violet** wire).

NOTE —
The ground at terminal 4 is switched by the ECM. The ECM harness must be connected to check the switched ground connection.

– If no faults are found up to this point, turn ignition key off. Using a fused (14 gauge) jumper wire, connect relay connector terminal **6** to terminal **2**. The fuel pump should run.

- If pump runs and all other tests are as specified, fuel pump relay is probably faulty.
- If pump does not run, test fuel pump operation as described in **160 Fuel Tank and Fuel Pump**.

> ***CAUTION —***
> *The jumper wire should be 1.5 mm² (14 ga.) and include an in-line fuse holder with a 15 amp fuse. To avoid fuse/relay panel damage from repeated connecting and disconnecting, also include a toggle switch.*

Fuel delivery and fuel pressure

Checking fuel delivery volume and fuel pressure is a fundamental part of troubleshooting and diagnosing the engine management system. Fuel pressure directly influences fuel delivery. Procedures for measuring the fuel pressure and fuel volume are given in **160 Fuel Tank and Fuel Pump**.

Relieving fuel pressure

The fuel system retains fuel pressure in the system when the engine is turned off. To prevent fuel from spraying on a hot engine, system fuel pressure should be relieved before disconnecting fuel lines. One method is to tightly wrap a shop towel around a fuel line fitting and loosen or disconnect the fitting.

Cleanliness is essential when working with fuel circuit components. Thoroughly clean the unions before disconnecting fuel lines.

> ***WARNING —***
> - *Gasoline is highly flammable and its vapors are explosive. Do not smoke or work on a car near heaters or other fire hazards when diagnosing and repairing fuel system problems. Have a fire extinguisher available in case of an emergency.*
> - *When working on an open fuel system, wear suitable hand protection. Prolonged contact with fuel can cause illnesses and skin disorders.*

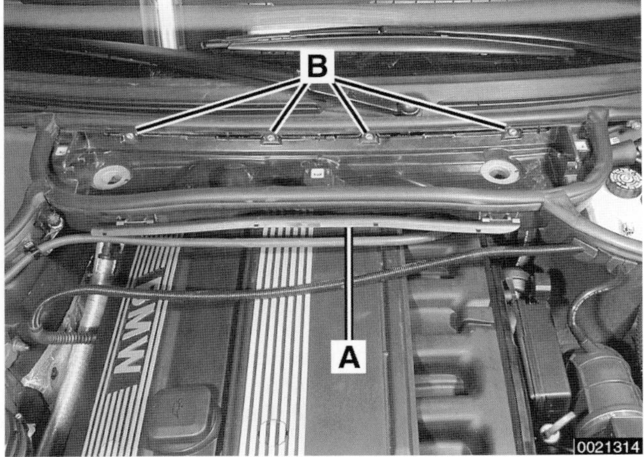

 Remove housing for interior ventilation microfilter.

- Remove upper cover and microfilter.
- Open wiring harness loom (**A**) and move wiring out of way.
- Unfasten screws (**B**) and remove lower microfilter housing.

Remove fuel rail cover by prying off nut covers (**arrows**) and removing nuts.

– Following the fuel rail to the rear of engine compartment, disconnect fuel line at fitting.

> ***WARNING —***
> - *Be sure to wrap fuel line disconnect fittings with a shop rag before disconnecting line.*
> - *Fuel in fuel line is under pressure (approx. 3 - 5 bar or 45 - 75 psi) and may be expelled under pressure. Do not smoke or work near heaters or other fire hazards. Keep a fire extinguisher handy. Before disconnecting fuel hoses, wrap a cloth around fuel hoses to absorb any leaking fuel. Catch and dispose of escaped fuel. Plug all open fuel lines.*
> - *Always unscrew fuel tank cap to release pressure in the tank before working on the tank or lines.*

COMPONENT REPLACEMENT

After diagnosing and replacing a faulty engine management component, be sure to use a BMW-compatible scan tool to check and clear the fault memory in the ECM. Diagnostic trouble codes are given in **On-Board Diagnostics** at the back of this book.

Fuel rail and injectors, removing and installing (MS 42.0 and MS 43.0)

NOTE —

- *On DME MS 45.1 equipped vehicles the fuel injectors are mounted to a stainless steel fuel rail via specialized compression fittings. Removal and installation of the fuel rail and injectors requires specialized equipment and tools. See an authorized BMW repair facility for service.*
- *DME MS 45.1 equipped vehicles are classified as PZEV (Partial Zero Emissions Vehicles) and are covered by a 15 year/150,000 mile warranty on fuel delivery and emissions control equipment.*

– Disconnect negative (–) battery cable.

> ***CAUTION —***
> *Prior to disconnecting the battery, read the battery disconnection cautions in* **001 Warnings and Cautions**.

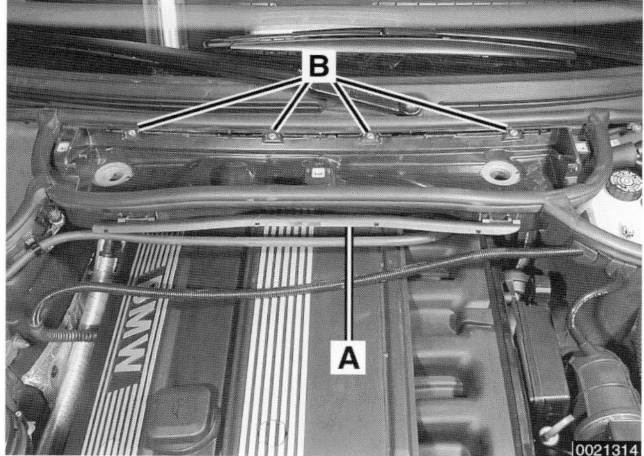

Remove housing for interior ventilation microfilter.

- Remove upper cover and microfilter.
- Open wiring harness loom (**A**) and remove wires.
- Unfasten screws (**B**) and remove lower microfilter housing.

Remove fuel rail cover by prying off nut covers (**arrows**) and removing nuts.

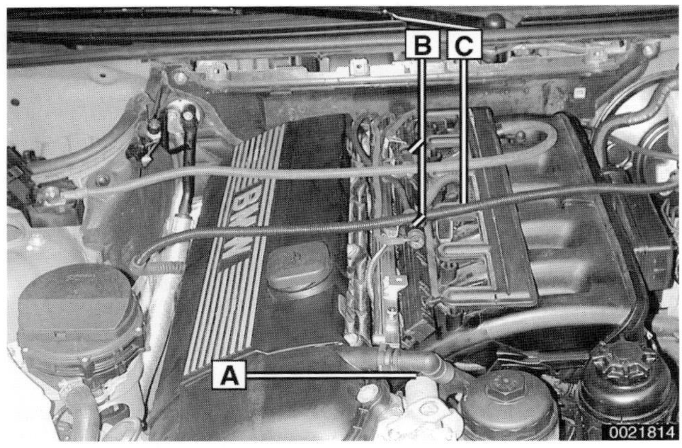

Working above engine, disconnect electrical harness connectors:

- VANOS control unit harness connector (**A**)
- Connectors for oxygen sensors (**B**)
- Connector for intake air temperature sensor (**C**)

> ***CAUTION —***
> *Mark oxygen sensor harness connectors in order to avoid reversing them during installation. Incorrect reconnection can cause serious engine damage.*

Disconnect fuel injector electrical connectors from injectors:

- Use small screwdriver to pry one corner of wire lock clip on fuel injector 1 connector.
- Repeat for all injectors.
- Lift off connector loom and set aside.

Unscrew Schræder valve cap (**arrow**) from fuel rail. Unscrew fuel tank cap to release pressure to vent tank.

– Using a brief burst of compressed air (maximum of 3 bar or 43.5 psi) blow fuel back through return line into fuel tank.

> ***WARNING —***
> - *Do not smoke or work near heaters or other fire hazards. Keep a fire extinguisher handy. Before disconnecting fuel hoses, wrap a cloth around fuel hoses to absorb any leaking fuel. Catch and dispose of escaped fuel. Plug all open fuel lines.*
> - *Always unscrew the fuel tank cap to release pressure in the tank before working on the tank or lines.*

– Raise car and support in a safe manner.

> ***CAUTION —***
> *Make sure the car is stable and well supported at all times. Use a professional automotive lift or jack stands designed for the purpose. A floor jack is not adequate support.*

– Remove protective engine splash guard.

Working beneath car (on left side under driver seat), remove fuel filter cover and clamp off fuel hose(s).

NOTE —

MS 42.0 vehicle shown. Fuel line arrangement on MS 43.0 vehicles varies from that shown. The MS 43.0 system uses a non-return fuel rail. Only a single fuel line leads to the engine compartment.

Disconnect fuel hose(s) from fuel line(s) (**arrows**) using special fuel line removal tool 16 1 050 or equivalent. Seal off fuel line(s) with BMW special tools 13 5 281/13 5 282.

> ***CAUTION —***
>
> *Fuel may be expelled under pressure. Do not smoke or work near heaters or other fire hazards. Keep a fire extinguisher handy. Before disconnecting fuel hoses, wrap a cloth around fuel hoses to absorb any leaking fuel. Plug all open fuel lines.*

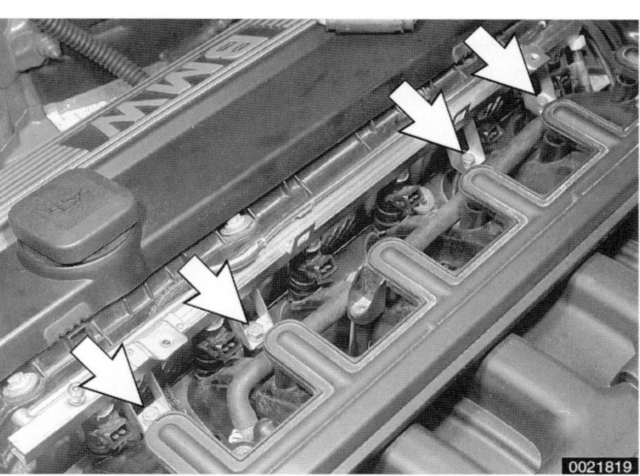

Remove fuel rail mounting bolts (**arrows**).

- Carefully pry fuel rail off manifold.
- Separate fuel line support bracket at rear of intake manifold.
- Guide fuel line(s) out of rear of engine compartment while lifting fuel rail out.

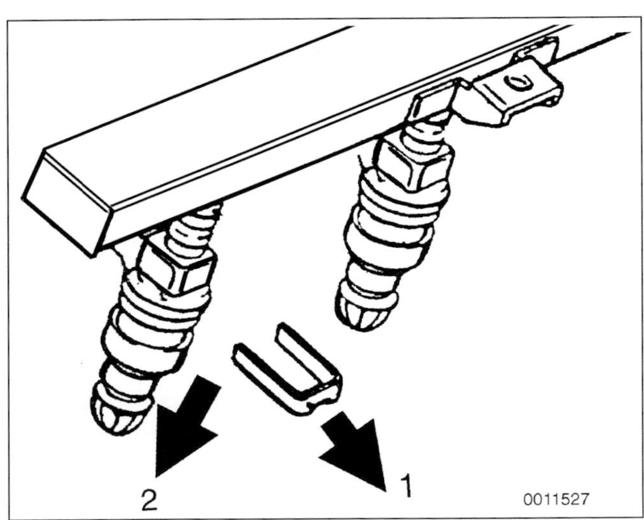

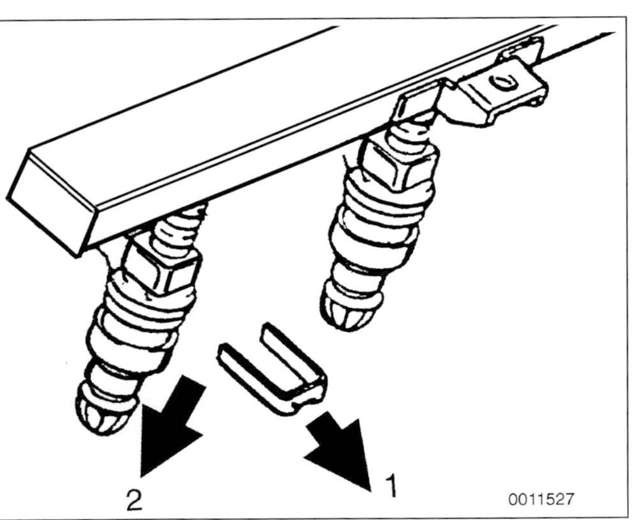

Remove individual injectors:

- Pry retaining clip from injector (**1**).
- Pull injector from rail (**2**).

– Installation is reverse of removal.

- Fit new O-rings when installing injectors. For ease of installation, lightly lubricate all fuel system O-rings with assembly lubricant.
- Check that injector electrical connections are correctly fitted and that injectors are fully seated prior to installing fuel rail mounting bolts.
- Replace any wire ties removed during removal procedure.

> ***CAUTION —***
> *Replace any flexible fuel lines which were pinched shut during testing.*

Fuel pressure regulator, replacing (MS 42.0 and MS 43.0)

E46 fuel pressure regulator location

- DME MS 42.0 . . . . under left side of car, in 3/2-way valve
- DME MS 43.0 . . . . under left side of car, in fuel filter
- MS 45.1 . . . . inside fuel tank (sealed).

NOTE —

- *On models with DME MS 43.0, the fuel pressure regulator (**arrow**) is an integral part of the fuel filter. Fuel filter replacement procedure is covered in* **020 Maintenance**.
- *On models equipped with DME 45.1, the fuel tank is permanently sealed. No internal replacement parts, including the fuel pump, are available from BMW. See **160 Fuel Tank and Fuel Pump** for more details.*

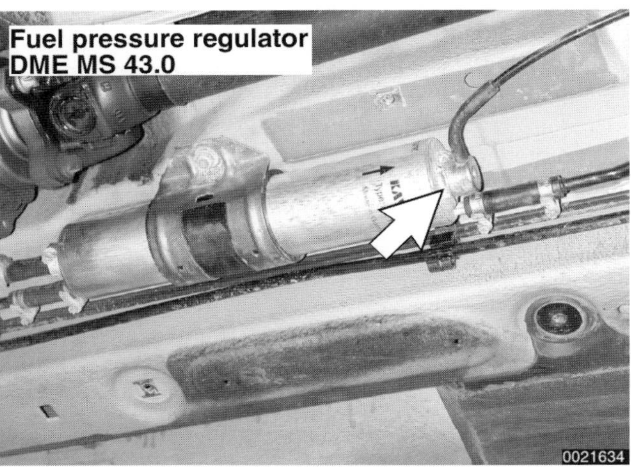

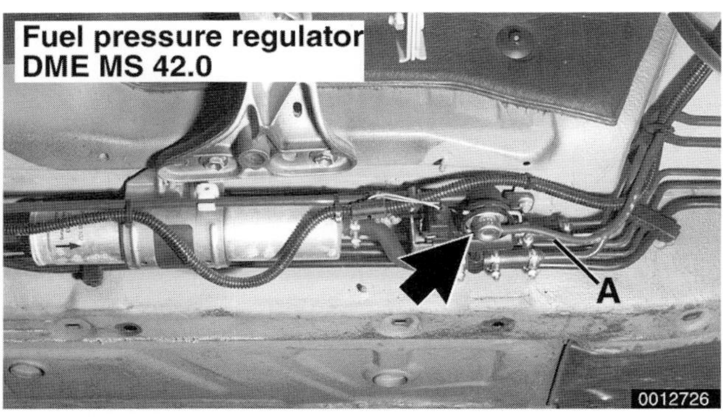

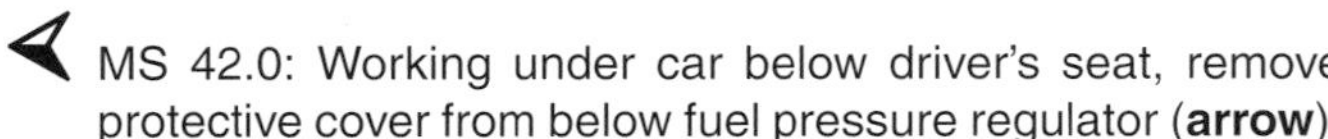

MS 42.0: Working under car below driver's seat, remove protective cover from below fuel pressure regulator (**arrow**).

– Disconnect vacuum hose (**A**) from fuel pressure regulator.

– Remove locking spring clip retaining fuel pressure regulator.

– Wrap a shop rag around regulator, then remove regulator from 3/2-way valve by pulling straight down.

– Installation is reverse of removal. Replace sealing O-rings.

Mass air flow (MAF) sensor, removing and installing (MS 42.0 and MS 43.0)

> ***CAUTION—***
> *Be sure the ignition is OFF before replacing DME system components.*

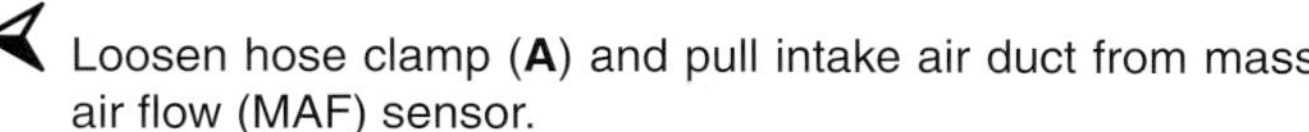

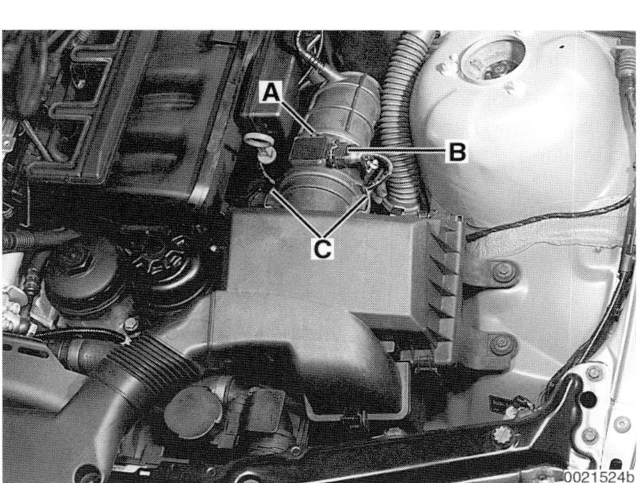

- Loosen hose clamp (**A**) and pull intake air duct from mass air flow (MAF) sensor.
- Disconnect electrical harness connector (**B**) and unclip fasteners (**C**).
- Remove sensor. Inspect protective screen in sensor housing. Replace sensor if screen is damaged.
- Inspect air intake ducting for damage and cracks. Replace rubber parts as necessary.
- Installation is reverse of removal.
  - Replace O-ring between sensor and air filter housing.

NOTE—
No adjustment to air flow sensor is possible.

Engine coolant temperature (ECT) sensor, replacing (MS 42.0 and MS 43.0)

The engine coolant temperature (ECT) sensor is located toward the rear of the cylinder head below intake runner 6. Intake manifold removal is required to access the ECT sensor.

> ***CAUTION—***
> *Be sure ignition is OFF before replacing DME system components.*

- Remove intake manifold, see **110 Engine Removal and Installation**.

> ***WARNING—***
> *Due to risk of personal injury, be sure engine is cold before beginning the removal procedure.*

- Working at rear of cylinder head, disconnect harness connector (**arrow**) from ECT sensor.
- Remove sensor. Catch leaking coolant using shop rags.
- Installation is reverse of removal.
  - Use a new copper sealing washer when installing sensor.
  - Replace lost coolant.

Tightening torque
- ECT sensor to cylinder head . . . . 13 Nm (10 ft-lb)

Intake air temperature (IAT) sensor, replacing (MS 42.0 and MS 43.0)

The intake air temperature (IAT) sensor is located at the top center of the intake manifold. The intake air temperature sensor functions to adapt or fine tune the fuel mixture and engine timing based on varying intake air temperatures.

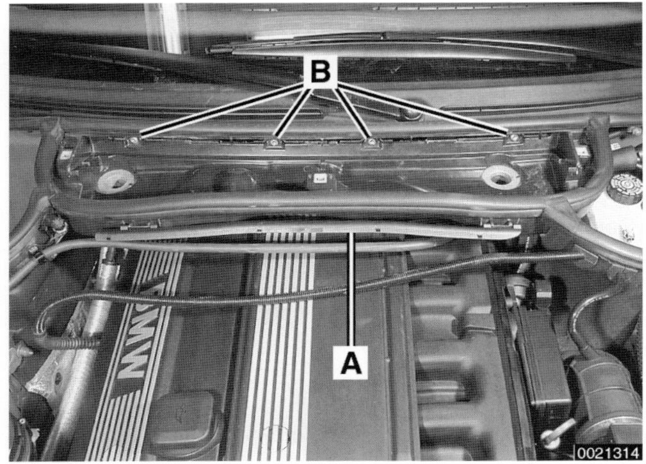

Remove housing for interior ventilation microfilter.

- Remove upper cover and microfilter.
- Open wiring harness loom (**A**) and remove wires.
- Unfasten screws (**B**) and remove lower microfilter housing.

Remove fuel rail cover by prying off plastic covers (**arrows**) and removing nuts.

Remove electrical harness connector (**arrow**) from IAT sensor.

> ***CAUTION —***
> *Be sure the ignition is OFF.*

– Depress locking clip on side of temperature sensor and pull straight out of intake manifold.

– Installation is reverse of removal.

- Use a new sealing O-ring at base of sensor and lubricate with assembly lubricant for ease of installation.

Throttle assembly, removing and installing (MS 42.0 and MS 43.0)

Throttle assembly faults may reset the engine control module (ECM) adaption values. After repairs to the throttle assembly, be sure to use BMW diagnostic tools to reset adaption values.

If the electronic throttle assembly is replaced, ECM throttle setting and adaption values must be reconfigured as described at the end of this procedure.

> **CAUTION —**
> *If the adaptation process is not completed correctly, the engine will not start.*

– Disconnect battery negative (–) cable in luggage compartment.

> **CAUTION —**
> *Prior to disconnecting the battery, read the battery disconnection cautions in* **001 Warnings and Cautions**.

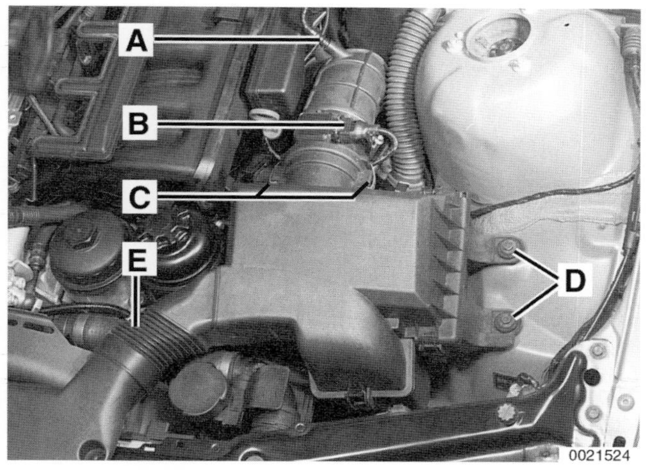

Remove complete air filter housing:

- Disconnect vacuum line at intake boot (**A**).
- Disconnect electrical harness connector on mass air flow sensor (**B**).
- Release mass air flow sensor clips (**C**).
- Remove filter housing mounting screws (**D**).
- Disconnect air duct connections (**E**) and lift complete air filter housing out of engine compartment, pulling it forward away from mass air flow sensor.

NOTE —
In this step, mass air flow sensor remains attached to rubber air duct.

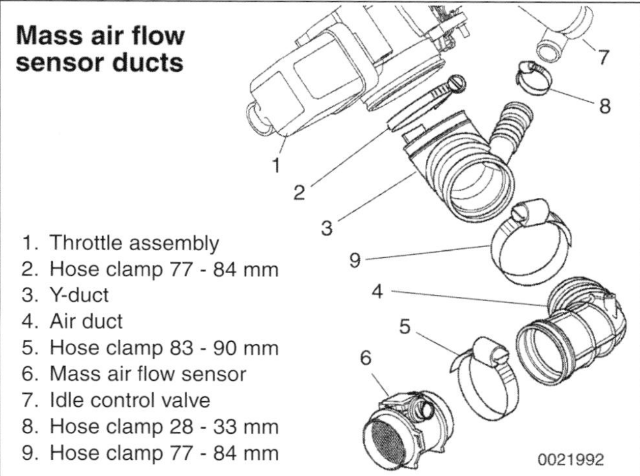

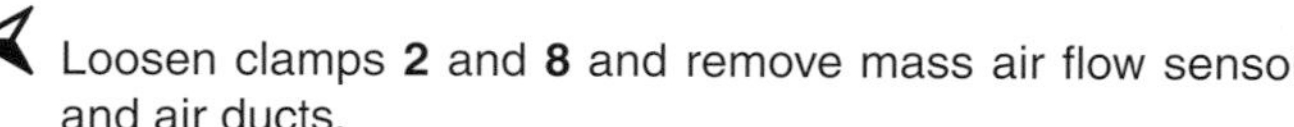

Loosen clamps **2** and **8** and remove mass air flow sensor and air ducts.

On MS 42.0 vehicles: Pull throttle cable upwards out of rubber retainer (**A**) and unhook ball end of cable (**B**) from throttle actuator.

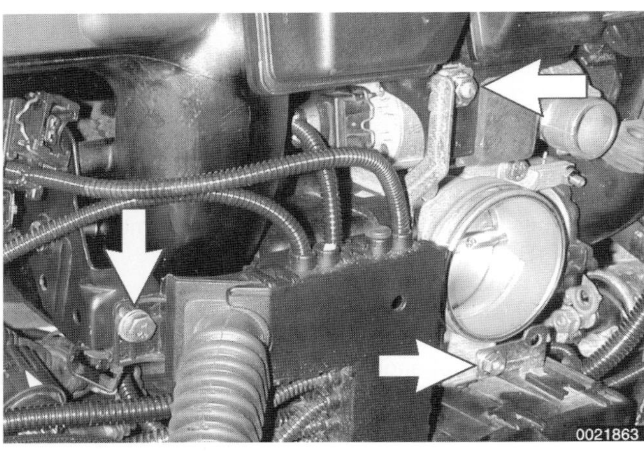

Remove nuts and bolt (**arrows**) retaining wiring harness conduit to throttle body.

Working at throttle housing: Turn harness plug (**arrow**) counterclockwise and remove.

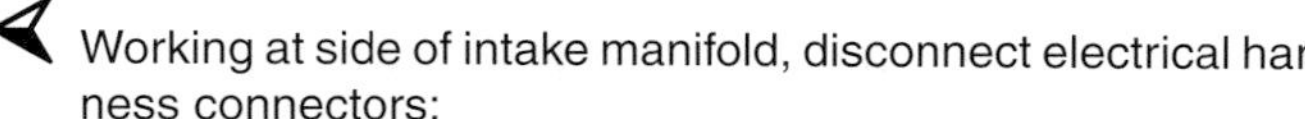

Working at side of intake manifold, disconnect electrical harness connectors:

- Idle control valve (**A**)
- Intake manifold resonance valve (**B**)

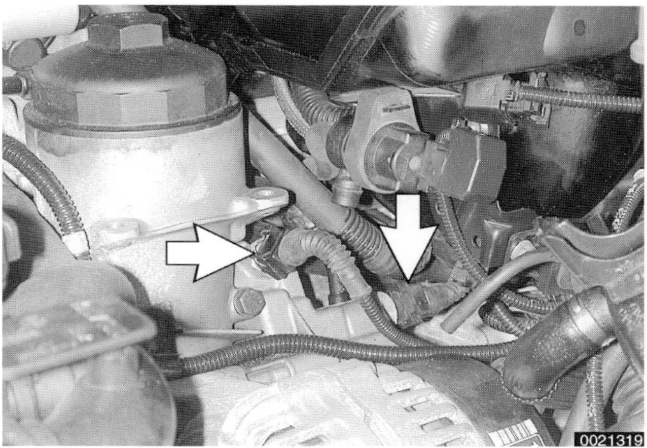

Disconnect electrical harness connectors (**arrows**) at oil pressure sender and oil temperature sender at base of oil filter housing.

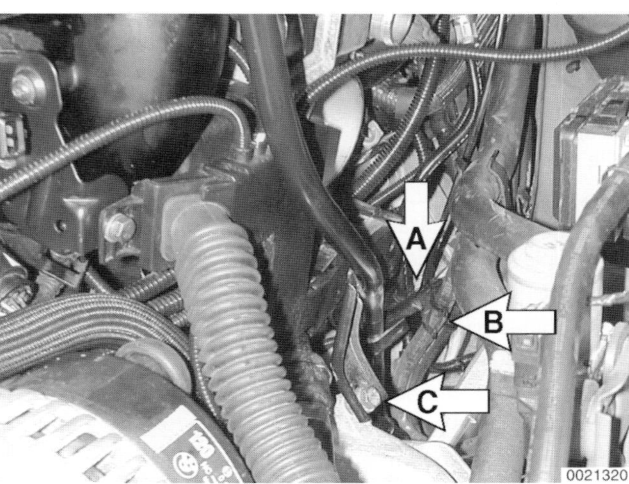

Remove dipstick guide tube:

- Disconnect wiring harness brackets from tube (**A**).
- Unclip fuel lines from tube (**B**).
- Remove lower guide tube mounting bolt (**C**). Pull out dipstick guide tube.

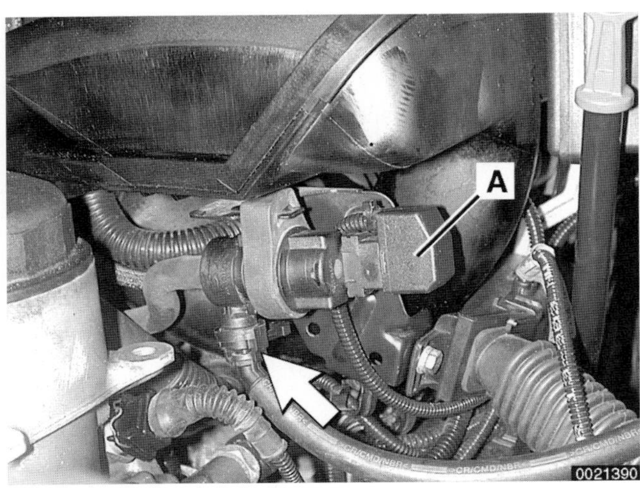

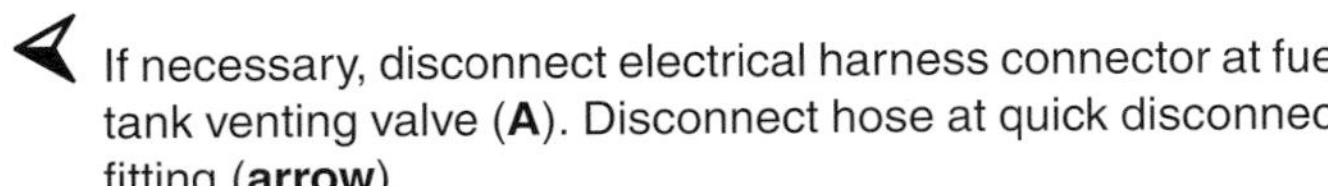

If necessary, disconnect electrical harness connector at fuel tank venting valve (**A**). Disconnect hose at quick disconnect fitting (**arrow**).

– Remove throttle assembly mounting screws at all corners and pull assembly off manifold.

– Installation is reverse of removal.

- Replace sealing ring between throttle assembly and intake manifold.
- Reattach throttle assembly harness connector with care. Arrow on fully tightened connector must line up with corresponding arrow on throttle assembly housing.
- On DME MS 42.0: Reattach throttle cable and adjust as described later.

– If EDK throttle assembly (DME MS 43.0) is replaced, reconfigure throttle settings and ECM adaption as follows:

- Turn ignition ON (KL 15) for 10 seconds (do not try to start engine).
- Turn ignition off for 10 seconds.
- Start engine.

Throttle cable, adjusting (MS 42.0)

Models with DME MS 42.0 are equipped with a throttle cable. Cable should be adjusted any time it is disconnected or replaced. This procedure requires the factory scan tool or an equivalent to read and adjust throttle angle. It is recommended that this procedure be done by an authorized BMW dealer service department.

Basic adjustment:

- Ensure that at idle (accelerator pedal in rest position) throttle cable has detectable play at throttle lever attaching point. Play must not exceed maximum allowable.
- Adjust by turning knurled adjustor (**arrow**) on end of throttle cable sheath at throttle housing.

Throttle cable clearance

- Max. play at throttle plate lever . . . . 3 mm (0.125 in.)

– Full throttle adjustment (manual transmission):

- With ignition key on press pedal fully to stop. Check throttle angle using scan tool. Adjust pedal stop if necessary.

Throttle angle specifications

- Manual transmisssion:
  Full throttle . . . . 80° - 84°

– Full throttle adjustment (automatic transmission):

- With ignition key on, press accelerator until pedal touches kickdown stop. Check throttle angle. Press accelerator pedal down beyond kickdown stop pressure point. Check throttle angle. Adjust kickdown stop if necessary, recheck.
- Press accelerator down fully against stop. Check throttle angle.
- Use scan tool diagnostic program or road test vehicle to confirm transmission downshifts when kickdown is actuated.

Throttle angle specifications

- Automatic transmission:

Kickdown stop contacted	76° - 80°
Kickdown pressure point range	84° - 88°
Full-load downshift	100%

Idle speed control valve, replacing (MS 42.0 and MS 43.0)

The idle speed control valve is mounted under the intake manifold adjacent to the dipstick tube bracket. The valve can be removed with the manifold in place, although the job is easier if the manifold is first removed. Intake manifold removal is described in **113 Cylinder Head Removal and Installation**.

– Disconnect battery negative (–) cable in trunk.

> ***CAUTION —***
> *Prior to disconnecting the battery, read the battery disconnection cautions given at the front of this manual on page viii.*

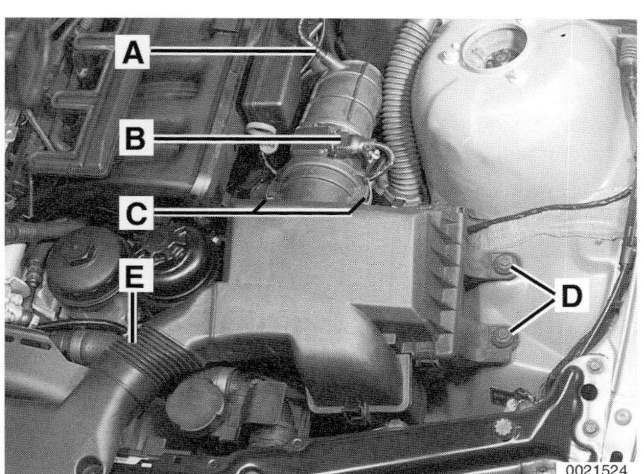

Remove complete air filter housing:

- Disconnect vacuum line at intake boot (**A**).
- Disconnect electrical harness connector on mass air flow sensor (**B**).
- Release mass air flow sensor clips (**C**).
- Remove filter housing mounting screws (**D**).
- Disconnect air duct connections (**E**) and lift complete air filter housing out of engine compartment, pulling it forward away from mass air flow sensor.

NOTE —
In this step, mass air flow sensor remains attached to intake duct.

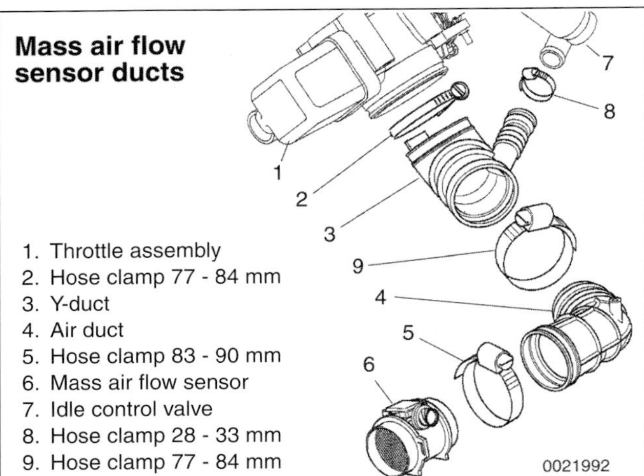

◀ Loosen clamps **2** and **8** and remove mass air flow sensor and air ducts.

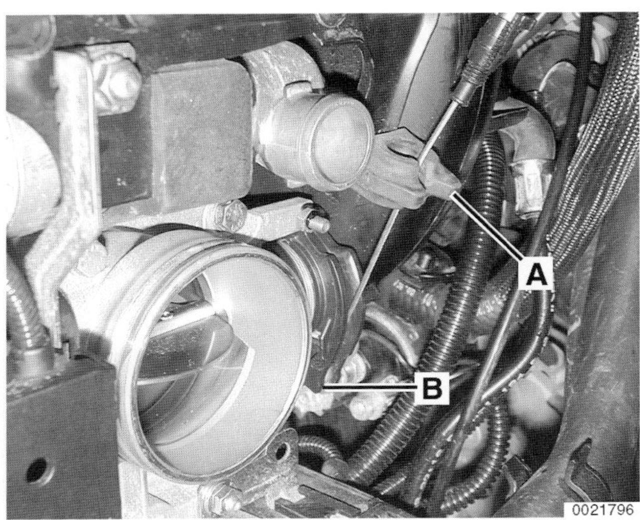

◀ DME MS 42.0: Pull throttle cable upwards out of rubber retainer (**A**) but leave attached to throttle actuator (**B**).

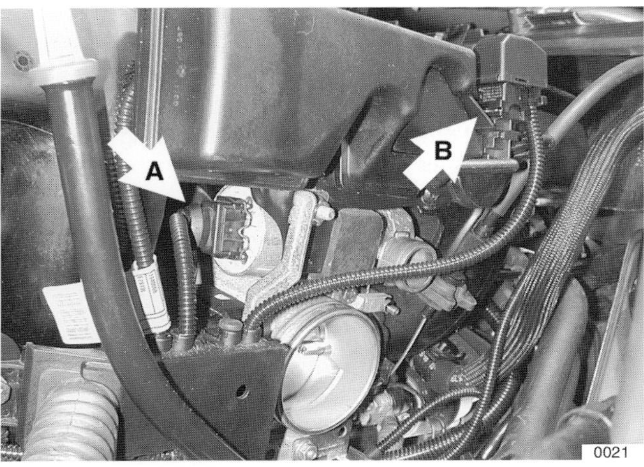

◀ Working at side of intake manifold, disconnect electrical harness connectors:

- Idle control valve (**A**)
- Intake manifold resonance valve (**B**)

– Disconnect bypass hose from idle control valve.

– Remove idle control valve:

- Remove idle control valve bracket mounting fasteners.
- Slide control valve with bracket out from between intake manifold and throttle assembly.
- Pull control valve from rubber retainer.

– Installation is reverse of removal.

- Use new gaskets and O-ring seals when installing. Use assembly lubricant to facilitate reassembly.
- Install idle control valve rubber seal in intake manifold first, then insert control valve.
- Similarly, install mass air flow sensor into intake duct, then install to throttle assembly.

Engine control module (ECM), removing and installing

NOTE —

Replacement ECMs must be coded with application information (i.e. engine code, transmission type, etc.) prior to installation. Consult an authorized BMW dealer before replacing the ECM. Alternatively, coded ECMs may be available at an additional cost.

– Disconnect negative (–) battery cable. Wait at least three minutes.

> ***CAUTION —***
>
> *Prior to disconnecting the battery, read the battery disconnection cautions in* **001 Warnings and Cautions**.

– Remove E-box cover at left rear of engine compartment. Cover is retained with four captive screws.

0021391

◀ ECM (**arrow**) is located in right rear of E-box, as identified with five electrical harness connectors.

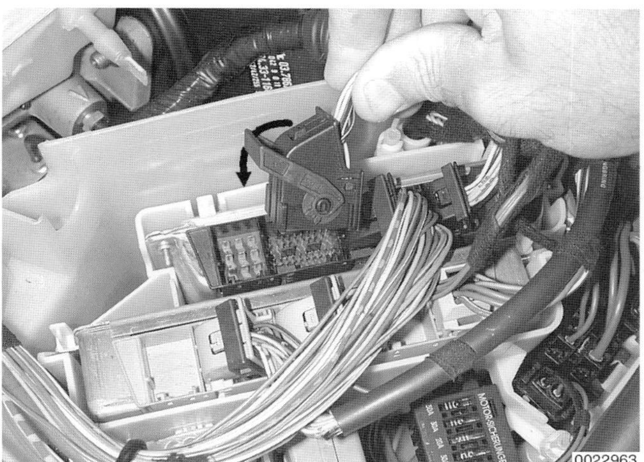

0022963

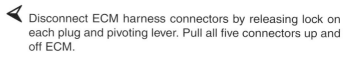

◀ Disconnect ECM harness connectors by releasing lock on each plug and pivoting lever. Pull all five connectors up and off ECM.

– Remove ECM from retaining brackets and pull from its holder.

– Installation is reverse of removal.

ECM PIN ASSIGNMENTS

ECM pin assignments are given in **Table b**. This information may be helpful when diagnosing faults to or from the ECM. If all inputs and wiring are OK but operational problems still exist, the ECM itself may be faulty.

Generally, absence of voltage or continuity means there is a wiring or connector problem. Test results with incorrect values do not necessarily mean that a component is faulty. Check for loose, broken or corroded connections and wiring before replacing components. If the results are still incorrect, check the component itself.

For engine management system electrical schematics, see **Electrical Wiring Diagrams**.

> ***CAUTION —***
> - *Always wait at least three minutes after turning off the ignition before removing the connector from the engine control module (ECM). If the connector is removed before this time, residual power in the system relay may damage the ECM.*
> - *Always connect or disconnect the control module connector and meter probes with the ignition off.*

When making checks at the ECM itself, a breakout box should be used to allow tests to be made with the connector attached to the ECM. This also prevents damage to the small terminals in the connector. As an alternative, the harness connector housing can be separated so that electrical checks can be made from the back of the connector.

Table b. ECM pin assignment—DME MS 42.0 and MS 43.0

Pin	Signal	Component/function	Notes
Connector X60001 9-pin black			
1	Output	Terminal 15	Unloader relay terminal 15
2		not used	
3		not used	
4	Ground	Ground	Ground point
5	Ground	Ground	Ground connector
6	Ground	Ground	Ground connector
7	Input	Terminal 30 (Fuse 80 amp)	B+ Terminal
8	Input	Voltage supply (Fuse 2)	Fuse carrier, engine electronics
9	Input	Voltage supply	Fuse carrier, engine electronics
Connector X60002 24-pin black			
1	Input	Heater, precatalyst oxygen sensor 1	Heated oxygen sensor 1 in front of catalytic converter
2		not used	
3	Input/output	CAN bus signal, low	Transmission control module
4	Input/output	CAN bus signal, high	Transmission control module
5		not used	
6	Input/output	Transmit diagnosis line (TXD) data link signal	Transmission control module
7	Input	Heater, post-catalyst oxygen sensor 1	Heated oxygen sensor 1 behind catalytic converter
8		not used	
9		not used	
10		not used	
11		not used	
12	Input	Signal, 3/2-way valve, running losses (MS 42.0)	3/2 way valve, running losses (MS 42.0)
13	Input	Heater, precatalyst oxygen sensor 2	Heated oxygen sensor 2 in front of catalytic converter
14	Input	Signal, precatalyst oxygen sensor 1	Heated oxygen sensor 1 in front of catalytic converter
15	Input	Signal, precatalyst oxygen sensor 2	Heated oxygen sensor 2 in front of catalytic converter
16	Input	Signal, post-catalyst oxygen sensor 1	Heated oxygen sensor 1 behind catalytic converter
17		not used	
18	Input	Signal, post-catalyst oxygen sensor 2	Heated oxygen sensor 2 behind catalytic converter
19	Input	Heater, post catalyst oxygen sensor 2	Heated oxygen sensor 2 behind catalytic converter
20	Ground	Ground, precatalyst oxygen sensor 1	Heated oxygen sensor 1 in front of catalytic converter
21	Ground	Ground, precatalyst oxygen sensor 2	Heated oxygen sensor 2 in front of catalytic converter
22	Ground	Ground, post-catalyst oxygen sensor 1	Heated oxygen sensor 1 behind catalytic converter
23	Input	DME main relay signal activation	DME main relay
24	Ground	Ground, post-catalyst oxygen sensor 2	Heated oxygen sensor 2 behind catalytic converter
Connector X60003 52-pin black			
1	Input	Signal, mass air flow sensor	Hot film mass air flow sensor
2	Input	Signal, exhaust camshaft sensor 1	Camshaft position sensor II
3	Input	Signal, suction jet pump valve (2.8 L, 3.0 L)	Suction jet pump valve
4	Output	Throttle valve supply (MS 42.0)	Throttle valve (MS 42.0)
5	Input	Signal, intake camshaft position sensor	Camshaft position sensor I
6		not used	
7	Output	Throttle valve supply	Throttle valve
8	Input	Signal, crankshaft position sensor	Crankshaft position sensor
9	Input	Signal, pedal position sensor 2 (MS 42.0)	Throttle valve (MS 42.0)

Table b. ECM pin assignment—DME MS 42.0 and MS 43.0

Pin	Signal	Component/function	Notes
Connector X60003 52-pin black (cont.)			
10	Input	Signal, throttle position potentiometer 2	Throttle valve
11		not used	
12	Input	Feedback signal, engine start	Starter
13	Input	Signal, battery charge indicator lamp	Generator (Alternator)
14	Ground	Ground, throttle position sensor (MS 42.0)	Throttle valve (MS 42.0)
15	Ground	Ground, exhaust camshaft sensor 1	Camshaft position sensor II
16	Input	Signal, pedal position sensor 1 (MS 42.0)	Throttle valve (MS 42.0)
17	Ground	Ground, mass air flow sensor	Hot film mass air flow sensor
18	Ground	Ground, intake camshaft sensor 1	Camshaft position sensor I
19	Input	Signal, throttle potentiometer 1	Throttle valve
20	Ground	Ground, throttle position sensor	Throttle valve
21	Ground	Ground, crankshaft position sensor	Crankshaft position sensor
22	Output	Signal, intake air temperature	Intake air temperature sensor
23	Ground	Ground, intake air temperature sensor	Intake air temperature sensor
24	Output	Signal, coolant temperature sensor	Coolant temperature sensor
25	Ground	Ground, coolant temperature sensor	Coolant temperature sensor
26	Input	Signal, oil pressure (MS 42.0)	Oil pressure switch
27	Output	Signal, engine oil temperature	Oil temperature sensor
28	Ground	Ground, engine oil temperature sensor	Oil temperature sensor
29	Output	Signal, knock sensor	Knock sensor
30	Output	Signal, knock sensor	Knock sensor
31	Output	Signal, knock sensor	Knock sensor
32	Output	Signal, knock sensor	Knock sensor
33	Input	Signal, cylinder 1 fuel injector	Cylinder 1 fuel injector
34	Input	Signal, cylinder 2 fuel injector	Cylinder 2 fuel injector
35	Input	Signal, cylinder 3 fuel injector	Cylinder 3 fuel injector
36	Input	Signal, cylinder 4 fuel injector	Cylinder 4 fuel injector
37	Input	Signal, cylinder 5 fuel injector	Cylinder 5 fuel injector
38	Input	Signal, cylinder 6 fuel injector	Cylinder 6 fuel injector
39	Input	Signal, oil level sensor	Oil level sensor
40	Input	Signal, VANOS inlet valve	VANOS inlet valve
41	Input	Signal, VANOS outlet valve	VANOS outlet valve
42	Input	Signal, evaporative emissions valve	Evaporative emissions valve
43	Input	Signal, throttle valve drive	Throttle valve
44	Input	Signal, throttle valve drive	Throttle valve
45	Input	Signal, engine coolant thermostat	Engine coolant thermostat (map controlled)
46	Input	Signal, close idle speed control valve	Idle speed control valve
47	Input	Signal, open idle speed control valve	Idle speed control valve
48	Ground	Signal shield, knock sensor	Shield, knock sensor
49	Input	Signal, resonance valve intake system	Resonance valve intake system
50		not used	
51		not used	
52	Input	Signal, secondary air injection pump valve	Secondary air injection valve

Table b. ECM pin assignment—DME MS 42.0 and MS 43.0

Pin	Signal	Component/function	Notes
Connector X60004 40-pin black			
1	Input	Signal, battery charge indicator lamp	Instrument cluster control unit
2	Input	Feedback signal, engine start	Instrument cluster control module
3	Input	Signal, secondary air injection pump	Secondary air injection pump relay
4	Input	Signal, electric fan	Auxiliary fan motor
5		not used	
6		not used	
7		Pedal position sensor (PWG) (MS 43.0)	Pedal position sensor (PWG) (MS 43.0)
8		Signal, pedal position sensor (PWG) (MS 43.0)	Pedal position sensor (PWG) (MS 43.0)
9		Pedal position sensor (PWG) (MS 43.0)	Pedal position sensor (PWG) (MS 43.0)
10	Input	Signal, fuel pump relay 1	Fuel pump relay 1
11	Input	Signal, oil pressure switch	Instrument cluster control module
12		Pedal position sensor (PWG) (MS 43.0)	Pedal position sensor (PWG) (MS 43.0)
13		Signal, pedal position sensor (PWG) (MS 43.0)	Pedal position sensor (PWG) (MS 43.0)
14		Pedal position sensor (PWG) (MS 43.0)	Pedal position sensor (PWG) (MS 43.0)
15		not used	
16		not used	
17	Input	Speed signal (MS 42.0 up to 6-00) (MS 42.0 from 6-00 and MS 43.0)	 Data link connector OBDII 16 pin connector)
18		not used	
19		not used	
20	Output	Diagnostic module tank leak (DMTL) detection (MS 43.0)	Leak detection (DMTL) (MS 43.0)
21	Input	Signal, oil level sensor	Instrument cluster control module
22	Input	Signal, processed wheel speed, right rear	ABS/ASC module, ABS/DSC module
23	Output	Signal, clutch pedal position switch	Clutch pedal position switch
24	Input	Signal, brake light switch	Light switching center control unit
25		not used	
26	Input	Terminal 15	Fuse F29
27	Output	Voltage supply, multifunction steering wheel	Volute spring
28	Input	Signal, brake light switch	Brake light switch
29	Input	Signal, relay, A/C compressor	A/C compressor relay
30		Signal, leakage diagnosis pump (MS 42.0) Signal diagnostic module (MS43.0)	Leakage diagnosis pump Leak detection (MS 43.0)
31		not used	
32	Input/output	Transmit diagnosis line (TXD) data link signal	Data link connector (MS 42.0) OBD II connector (MS 43.0)
33	Input	Electronic vehicle immobilization	Electronic immobilizer control module
34		Signal, leakage diagnosis pump (LDP) (MS 42.0)	Leakage diagnosis pump (LDP) (MS 42.0)
35		not used	
36	Input/output	CAN bus signal, high	Connector, CAN bus
37	Input/output	CAN bus signal, low	Connector, CAN bus
38	Ground	Ground, coolant outlet temperature sensor	Temperature sensor
39	Output	Signal, coolant outlet temperature	Temperature sensor
40		not used	

Table b. ECM pin assignment—DME MS 42.0 and MS 43.0

Pin	Signal	Component/function	Notes
Connector X60005 9-pin black			
1	Input	Signal, ignition coil 3	Ignition coil 3
2	Input	Signal, ignition coil 2	Ignition coil 2
3	Input	Signal, ignition coil 1	Ignition coil 1
4		not used	
5	Ground	Ground	Ground connector
6	Ground	Ground	Ground connector
7	Input	Signal, ignition coil 6	Ignition coil 6
8	Input	Signal, ignition coil 5	Ignition coil 5
9	Input	Signal, ignition coil 4	Ignition coil 4

Table c. ECM pin assignment—DME MS 45.1

Pin	Signal	Component/function	Notes
Connector X60001 9-pin black			
1	Output	Terminal 15	Relay, fuel injectors
2		not used	
3		Diagnosis signal, TDX	SMG II Transmission control module
4	Ground	Ground	Ground point
5	Ground	Ground	Ground connector
6	Ground	Ground	Ground connector
7	Input	Terminal 30	B+ Terminal (Fuse 102)
8	Input	Voltage supply, Terminal 87	Fuse carrier, engine electronics
9		not used	
Connector X60002 24-pin black			
1	Output	Heater ground, precatalyst oxygen sensor 1	Heated oxygen sensor 1 in front of catalytic converter
2	Output	Heater ground, precatalyst oxygen sensor 2	Heated oxygen sensor 2 in front of catalytic converter
3	Input/ Output	Signal, CAN bus low	Transmission control unit
4	Input/ Output	Signal, CAN bus high	Transmission control unit
5		not used	
6	Output	Heater ground, post-catalyst oxygen sensor 1	Heated oxygen sensor 1 behind catalytic converter
7	Ground	Ground, precatalyst oxygen sensor 1	Heated oxygen sensor 1 behind catalytic converter
8	Ground	Ground, post-catalyst oxygen sensor 2	Heated oxygen sensor 2 behind catalytic converter
9	Ground	Ground, precatalyst oxygen sensor 2	Heated oxygen sensor 2 in front of catalytic converter
10	Ground	Ground, post-catalyst oxygen sensor 1	Heated oxygen sensor 1 in front of catalytic converter
11		not used	
12	Output	Heater ground, post-catalyst oxygen sensor 2	Heated oxygen sensor 2 behind catalytic converter
13	Output	Heater, precatalyst oxygen sensor 1	Heated oxygen sensor 1 in front of catalytic converter
14	Input	Signal, post-catalyst oxygen sensor 2	Heated oxygen sensor 2 behind catalytic converter
15	Output	Signal, precatalyst oxygen sensor 2	Heated oxygen sensor 2 in front of catalytic converter
16	Input	Signal, post-catalyst oxygen sensor 1	Heated oxygen sensor 1 behind catalytic converter
17		not used	
18		not used	

Table c. ECM pin assignment—DME MS 45.1

Pin	Signal	Component/function	Notes
Connector X60002 24-pin black (cont.)			
19	Input	Signal, precatalyst oxygen sensor 1	Heated oxygen sensor 1 in front of catalytic converter
20	Input	Signal, precatalyst oxygen sensor 1	Heated oxygen sensor 1 in front of catalytic converter
21	Input	Signal, precatalyst oxygen sensor 2	Heated oxygen sensor 2 in front of catalytic converter
22	Input	Signal, precatalyst oxygen sensor 2	Heated oxygen sensor 2 in front of catalytic converter
23	Output	DME main relay signal activation	DME main relay
24		not used	
Connector X60003 52-pin black			
1	Input	Signal, mass air flow sensor	Hot film mass air flow sensor
2		not used	
3	Input	Signal, crankshaft position sensor	Crankshaft position sensor
4	Output	Voltage supply, mass air flow sensor	Hot film mass air flow sensor
5	Output	Voltage supply, throttle potentiometer	
6	Output	Signal, cylinder 2 fuel injector	Cylinder 2 fuel injector
7	Output	Signal, cylinder 4 fuel injector	Cylinder 4 fuel injector
8	Output	Signal, cylinder 6 fuel injector	Cylinder 6 fuel injector
9	Output	Signal, VANOS outlet valve	
10	Output	Signal, VANOS inlet valve	
11	Output	Signal, cylinder 5 fuel injector	Cylinder 5 fuel injector
12	Output	Signal, thermostat, map cooling	
13	Output	Signal, cylinder 1 fuel injector	Cylinder 1 fuel injector
14	Ground	Suction jet pump shut-off valve, Mass air-flow sensor	
15	Ground	Ground, throttle potentiometer	Electric throttle actuator
16	Input	Signal, oil pressure	Oil pressure switch
17		not used	
18		not used	
19		Bi-directional data interface	Alternator (generator)
20		not used	
21	Output	Signal, evaporative emissions valve	
22	Output	Signal, close idle speed control valve	Idle speed control valve
23	Output	Signal, open idle speed control valve	Idle speed control valve
24		not used	
25		not used	
26	Output	Signal, cylinder 3 fuel injector	Cylinder 3 fuel injector
27	Input	Signal, intake air temperature	
28	Input	Signal, engine coolant temperature sensor	
29	Input	Signal, camshaft position 1	Camshaft position sensor 1
30	Input	Signal, camshaft position 2	Camshaft position sensor 2
31	Input	Signal, electric throttle actuator	EDK
32	Input	Signal, electric throttle actuator	EDK
33	Input	Signal, double knock sensor	Double knock sensor
34	Input	Signal, double knock sensor	Double knock sensor
35	Ground	Ground, engine coolant temperature sensor	
36	Ground	Ground, camshaft position sensor 1	Camshaft position sensor 1

Table c. ECM pin assignment—DME MS 45.1

Pin	Signal	Component/function	Notes
Connector X60003 52-pin black (cont.)			
37	Ground	Ground, crankshaft position sensor	Crankshaft position sensor
38	Input/ Output	Local CAN bus high	
39	Output	Signal, secondary air injection pump valve	
40	Output	Signal, valve, individual control intake system	
41		not used	
42	Output	Signal, electric throttle actuator	EDK
43	Output	Signal, electric throttle actuator	EDK
44	Input	Signal, engine oil temperature	Engine oil temperature sensor
45	Ground	Ground, engine oil temperature	Engine oil temperature sensor
46	Input	Signal, double knock sensor	Double knock sensor
47	Input	Signal, double knock sensor	Double knock sensor
48		not used	
49	Ground	Ground, camshaft position sensor 2	Camshaft position sensor 2
50	Input	Signal, oil level sensor	Oil level sensor
51	Input/ Output	Local CAN bus low	
52		not used	
Connector X60004 40-pin black			
1		not used	
2	Output	Signal, heater for fuel tank diagnosis	Diagnostic module, fuel tank leakage
3	Output	Signal, secondary air injection pump	Secondary air injection pump relay
4	Output	Signal, electric fan	Auxiliary fan motor
5	Ground	Ground, secondary air injection, mass-air flow meter	Ground point
6		not used	
7	Ground	Ground, pedal position sensor	Pedal position sensor
8	Input	Signal, pedal position sensor	Pedal position sensor
9	Output	Voltage supply, pedal position sensor	Pedal position sensor
10		not used	
11		not used	
12	Ground	Ground, pedal position sensor	Pedal position sensor
13	Input	Signal, pedal position sensor	Pedal position sensor
14	Output	Voltage supply, pedal position sensor	Pedal position sensor
15	Input	Signal, secondary air injection, mass-air flow meter	
16		not used	
17	Output	Speed signal	Data link connector
18		not used	
19	Output	Signal, E-box fan	E-box fan
20	Output	Activation, pump, fuel tank leak detection	Diagnostic module, fuel tank leakage (USA only)
21		not used	
22	Input	Signal, processed wheel speed, right rear	ABS/ASC module, ABS/DSC module
23		not used	
24	Input	Signal, brake light switch	Light switching center control unit

Table c. ECM pin assignment—DME MS 45.1

Pin	Signal	Component/function	Notes
Connector X60004 40-pin black (cont.)			
25		not used	
26	Input	Terminal 15	Fuse F29
27	Input	Data link, MFL	Volute spring
28	Input	Signal, brake light test signal	Brake light switch
29	Output	Signal, relay, A/C compressor	A/C compressor relay
30	Output	Signal, leakage diagnosis pump	Diagnostic module, fuel tank leakage
31	Input/output	Local CAN bus, low	Connector, CAN bus
32	Input/output	Transmit diagnosis line (TXD) data link signal	Data link connector
33	Input	Electronic vehicle immobilization	Electronic immobilizer control module
34		not used	
35	Input/output	Local CAN bus, high	Connector, CAN bus
36	Input/output	Signal, CAN bus, high	Connector, CAN bus
37	Input/output	Signal, CAN bus, low	Connector, CAN bus
38	Ground	Ground, coolant outlet temperature sensor	Temperature sensor
39	Input	Signal, coolant outlet temperature	Temperature sensor
40		not used	
Connector X60005 9-pin black			
1	Output	Signal, ignition coil 5	Ignition coil 5
2		not used	
3		not used	
4	Output	Signal, ignition coil 3	Ignition coil 3
5	Ground	Ground	Ground connector
6	Output	Signal, ignition coil 1	Ignition coil 1
7	Output	Signal, ignition coil 2	Ignition coil 2
8	Output	Signal, ignition coil 4	Ignition coil 4
9	Output	Signal, ignition coil 6	Ignition coil 6

131 Fuel Injection (M3 Models)

GENERAL

This repair group covers service and repair for the Siemens MS S54 engine management systems used in E46 M3 models. For additional engine management information see the following repair groups:

- **120 Ignition System**
- **160 Fuel Tank and Fuel Pump**
- **Electrical Wiring Diagrams**

NOTE —
Fuel pressure testing and fuel pump repair information is covered in **160 Fuel Tank and Fuel Pump**.

The Siemens DME MS S54 is a sophisticated self-diagnostic OBD II system. When faults arise, or if the MIL (malfunction indicator lamp) in the instrument cluster is illuminated, begin troubleshooting by connecting a BMW-compatible scan tool.

The self diagnostic capabilities of these systems have the potential to save hours of diagnostic time, and prevent incorrect component replacement and possible damage to system components. See **On-Board Diagnostics** at the back of this manual.

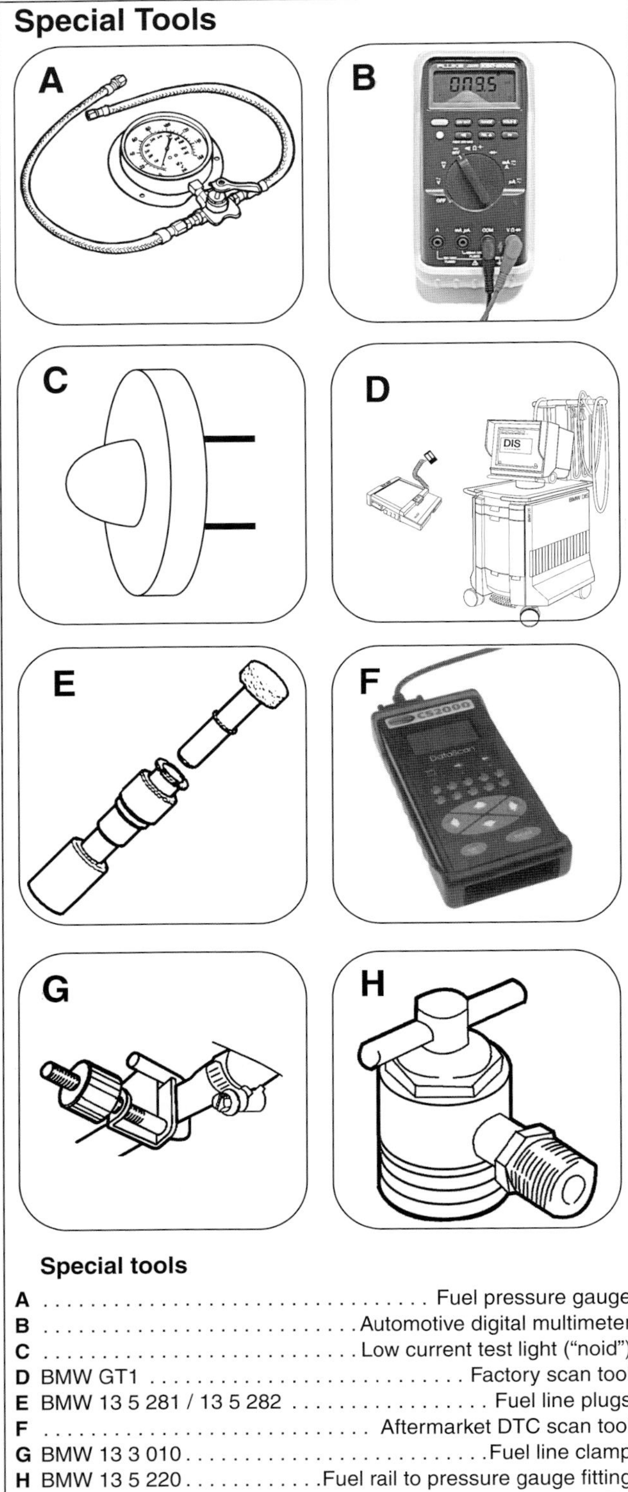

Special tools

A .... Fuel pressure gauge
B .... Automotive digital multimeter
C .... Low current test light ("noid")
D BMW GT1 .... Factory scan tool
E BMW 13 5 281 / 13 5 282 .... Fuel line plugs
F .... Aftermarket DTC scan tool
G BMW 13 3 010........................... Fuel line clamp
H BMW 13 5 220............ Fuel rail to pressure gauge fitting

Tools and test equipment

Special tools may be required to properly service the DME system and to replace system components. If the special equipment is unavailable, it is recommended that these repairs be left to an authorized BMW dealer or other qualified BMW repair facility. Read the procedure through before beginning a repair.

NOTE —

- *In addition to the BMW professional line of scan tools, there are many inexpensive 'generic' OBD II scan tool software programs and handheld units available. Although these tools have limited capabilities as compared to the dedicated tools, they are powerful diagnostic tools. These tools read live data streams, freeze frame information for DTCs (diagnostic trouble codes) and impending DTCs, as well as a host of other valuable diagnostic data.*
- *For the DIY owner, simple aftermarket DTC readers are also available. These inexpensive BMW-only tools are capable of checking for DTCs as well as turning off the illuminated MIL, and resetting the service indicator lights.*
- *See* **020 Maintenance** *for specialty tool manufacturer contact information.*

Principle of operation

The DME fuel injection system is completely electronic in operation. Intake air, engine coolant temperature, crankshaft and camshaft positions, engine speed and many other engine operating parameters are measured electronically and the information is supplied to the engine control module (ECM).

Based on input information, the ECM controls the ignition coils, fuel injectors, motor driven throttle valve (EDR), double VANOS system, radiator cooling fan, as well as other outputs.

The illustration on the following page shows the MS S54 ECM inputs and outputs. Additional system operational information can be found in **100 Engine–General**.

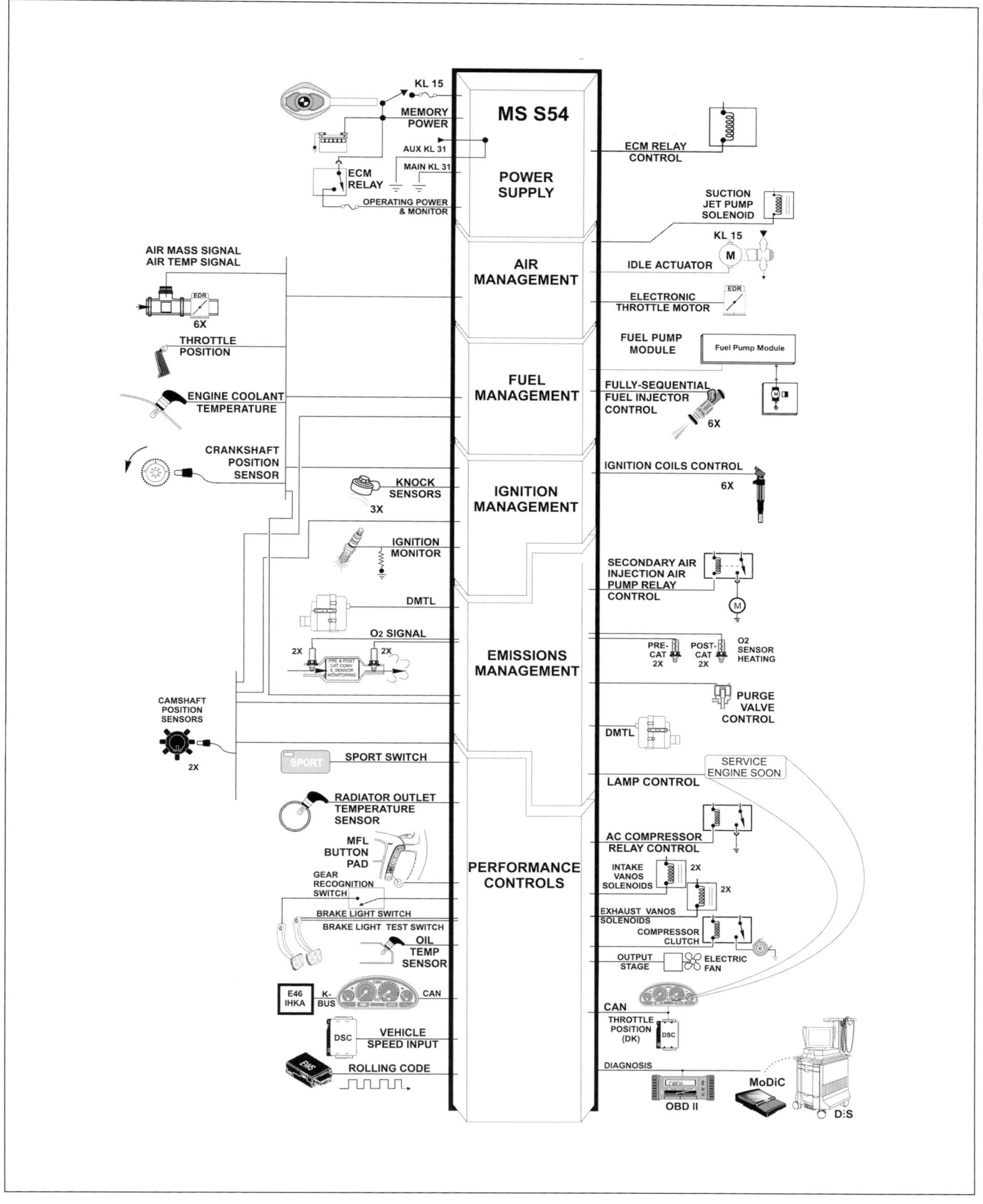
KL 15
MEMORY POWER
AUX KL 31
MAIN KL 31
ECM RELAY
OPERATING POWER & MONITOR
MS S54
POWER SUPPLY
AIR MANAGEMENT
FUEL MANAGEMENT
IGNITION MANAGEMENT
EMISSIONS MANAGEMENT
PERFORMANCE CONTROLS
ECM RELAY CONTROL
SUCTION JET PUMP SOLENOID
IDLE ACTUATOR
ELECTRONIC THROTTLE MOTOR
EDR
FUEL PUMP MODULE
Fuel Pump Module
FULLY-SEQUENTIAL FUEL INJECTOR CONTROL
6X
IGNITION COILS CONTROL
SECONDARY AIR INJECTION AIR PUMP RELAY CONTROL
PRE-CAT 2X
POST-CAT 2X
O2 SENSOR HEATING
PURGE VALVE CONTROL
DMTL
SERVICE ENGINE SOON
LAMP CONTROL
AC COMPRESSOR RELAY CONTROL
INTAKE VANOS SOLENOIDS
2X
EXHAUST VANOS SOLENOIDS
COMPRESSOR CLUTCH
OUTPUT STAGE
ELECTRIC FAN
CAN
THROTTLE POSITION (DK)
DSC
DIAGNOSIS
OBD II
MoDiC
D:S
AIR MASS SIGNAL
AIR TEMP SIGNAL
THROTTLE POSITION
ENGINE COOLANT TEMPERATURE
CRANKSHAFT POSITION SENSOR
KNOCK SENSORS
3X
IGNITION MONITOR
O2 SIGNAL
PRE & POST CAT CONV O2 SENSOR MONITORING
CAMSHAFT POSITION SENSORS
SPORT
SPORT SWITCH
RADIATOR OUTLET TEMPERATURE SENSOR
MFL BUTTON PAD
GEAR RECOGNITION SWITCH
BRAKE LIGHT SWITCH
BRAKE LIGHT TEST SWITCH
OIL TEMP SENSOR
E46 IHKA
K-BUS
VEHICLE SPEED INPUT
EWS
ROLLING CODE

Warnings and cautions

For personal safety, as well as the protection of sensitive electronic components, adhere to the following warnings and cautions.

WARNING —

- *Gasoline is highly flammable and its vapors are explosive. Do not smoke or work on a car near heaters or other fire hazards when diagnosing and repairing fuel system problems. Have a fire extinguisher available in case of an emergency.*
- *When working on an open fuel system, wear suitable hand protection, as prolonged contact with fuel can cause illnesses and skin disorders.*
- *The ignition system produces high voltages that can be fatal. Avoid contact with exposed terminals. Use extreme caution when working on a car with the ignition switched on or the engine running.*
- *Do not touch or disconnect any cables from the ignition coils while the engine is running or being cranked by the starter.*
- *Connect and disconnect the DME system wiring and test equipment leads only when the ignition is switched off.*
- *Renew fuel system hoses, clamps and O-rings any time they are removed.*
- *Before making any electrical tests that require the engine to be cranked using the starter, disable the ignition system as described in* **120 Ignition System**.

CAUTION —

- *Prior to disconnecting the battery, read the battery disconnection cautions in* **001 Warnings and Cautions**.
- *Do not connect any test equipment that delivers a 12-volt power supply to terminal 15 (+) of the ignition coil. The current flow may damage the ECM. In general, connect test equipment only as specified by BMW or the equipment maker.*
- *Only use a digital multimeter for electrical tests.*
- *Only use an LED test light for quick tests.*
- *Disconnecting the battery may erase fault code(s) stored in memory. Check for fault codes prior to disconnecting the battery cables.*
- *Wait at least 1 minute after turning off the ignition before removing the engine control module (ECM) connector. If the connector is removed before this time, residual power in the system relay may damage the control module.*
- *Cleanliness is essential when working on an open fuel system. Thoroughly clean fuel line connections and surrounding areas before loosening. Avoid moving the car. Only install clean parts.*
- *Fuel system cleaners and other chemical additives other than those specifically recommended by BMW may damage catalytic converters, oxygen sensors or other fuel supply components.*

ELECTRICAL CHECKS AND COMPONENT TESTING

Troubleshooting and fault diagnosis on OBD II cars is best performed using an electronic scan tool. However, it may be necessary to perform basic tests of the engine management main components, fuel system or wiring.

> ***CAUTION —***
>
> - *Tests in this section may set fault codes (DTCs) in the ECM and illuminate the MIL. After all testing is completed, access and clear DTC fault memory using a BMW compatible scan tool. See* **On-Board Diagnostics** *at the back of this manual.*
> - *Only use a digital multimeter for electrical tests.*
> - *Relay positions can vary. Be sure to confirm relay position by identifying the wiring in the socket using the wiring diagrams found at the rear of this manual.*

DME main relay, testing

The DME main relay is energized via the engine control module (ECM) and supplies battery positive (B+) power to many of the engine management components and subsystems. If this relay is faulty, the engine will not start.

- With ignition off, remove main relay (**arrow**) in electronics box (E-box) at left rear of engine compartment.

DME main relay wiring

From B+ junction point (battery voltage at all times)

4.0 RED

6

30

DME Main relay (K6300)

85

87

4

2

0.5 BRN/WHT

4.0 RED/WHT

23 X60002

5

ECM (A6000)

31

Fuse 3 20A

Engine electronics fuse carrier in E-box (A8680)

Wiring color code	
BLK	= black
BRN	= brown
GRN	= green
GRY	= grey
ORG	= orange
PNK	= pink
RED	= red
VIO	= violet
WHT	= white
YEL	= yellow

0021033

- Check for voltage at terminal **6** of main relay socket (**30-red** wire).
  - If battery voltage is present continue testing.
  - If battery voltage is not present, check large red wire in relay socket. See **Electrical Wiring Diagrams.**
- Reinstall relay and turn ignition on. Gain access to underside of relay socket and check for ground at terminal **4** (**85-brown/white** wire).
  - If ground is present continue testing.
  - If ground is not present, signal from ECM (connector X60002, pin **23**) is missing. Check wire between ECM and relay.
- With ignition on and relay installed, check for battery voltage at terminal **2** (**87-red/white** wire).
  - If battery voltage is present, relay has energized and is functioning correctly.
  - If battery voltage is not present and all earlier tests are OK, relay is faulty and should be replaced.

Fuel pump control module

The ECM controls activation of the MS S54 fuel pump through the solid-state fuel pump control module. The fuel pump module varies the voltage to the pump based on engine load conditions. For more information, see **160 Fuel Tank and Fuel Pump**.

NOTE —
The fuel pump control module is identified as the Fuel Pump Relay (K96) in the electrical schematic for the MS S54 DME system. The fuel pump control module/relay used on the MS S54 system is electronically controlled and specific to the MS S54 system.

Fuel delivery and fuel pressure

Checking fuel delivery volume and fuel pressure is a fundamental part of troubleshooting and diagnosing the engine management system. Fuel pressure directly influences fuel delivery. Procedures for measuring the fuel pressure and fuel volume are given in **160 Fuel Tank and Fuel Pump**.

Relieving fuel pressure

The fuel system retains fuel pressure when the engine is turned off. To prevent fuel from spraying on a hot engine, fuel pressure should be relieved before disconnecting fuel lines. See **160 Fuel Tank and Fuel Pump** for more information.

COMPONENT REPLACEMENT

After diagnosing and replacing a faulty engine management component, be sure to use a BMW-compatible scan tool to check and clear the fault memory in the ECM. Diagnostic trouble codes are given in **On-Board Diagnostics** at the back of this book.

Fuel rail and injectors, removing and installing

– Disconnect negative (–) battery cable.

> ***CAUTION —***
> *Prior to disconnecting the battery, read the battery disconnection cautions in* **001 Warnings and Cautions**.

 Remove housing for interior ventilation microfilter.

- Unclip upper cover (**arrows**). Lift up and remove cover and microfilter.

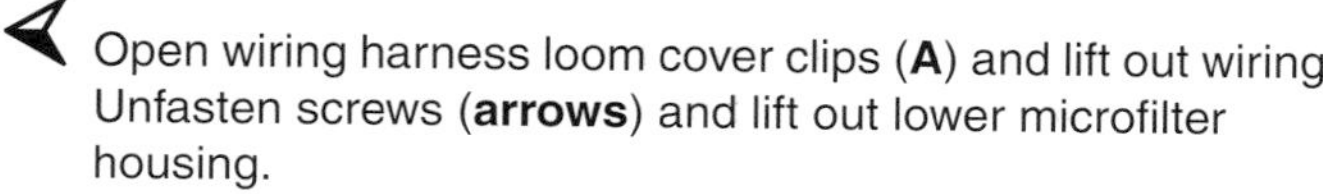

◄ Open wiring harness loom cover clips (**A**) and lift out wiring. Unfasten screws (**arrows**) and lift out lower microfilter housing.

◄ Release harness (**arrow**) from retaining clip.

– Working at back of fuel rail, remove fuel injector electrical harness from retainer.

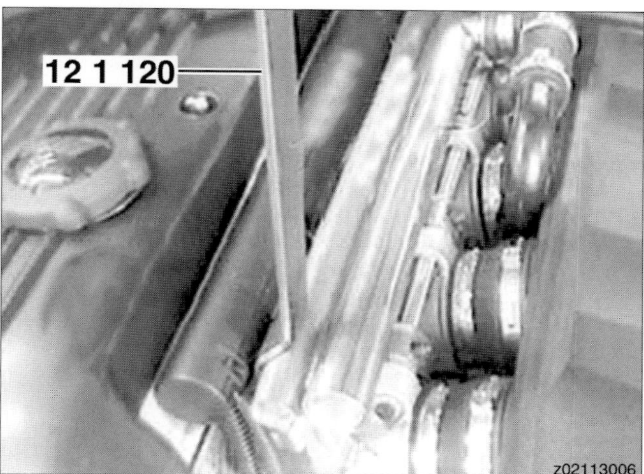

◄ Unlock fuel injector electrical connector strip using BMW special tool 12 1 120. Lay connector strip to the side of the engine.

> ***WARNING —***
> *Fuel injector connector strip may break if not removed using BMW special tool 12 1 120.*

– Remove retaining clip, and pull fuel line from fuel injector rail.

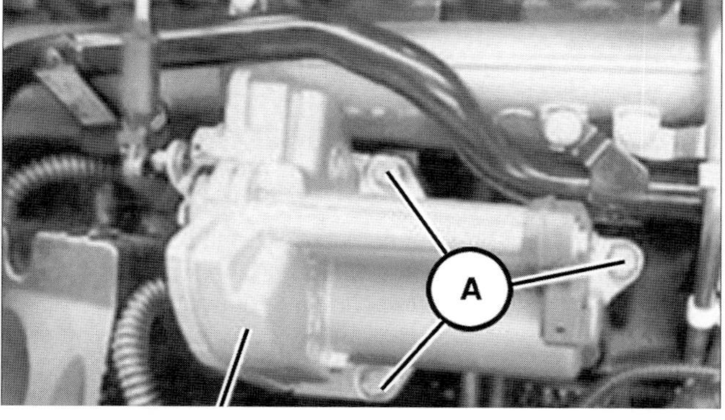

◄ Remove fuel rail retaining screws (**arrows**). Lift fuel injector rail up and away from engine.

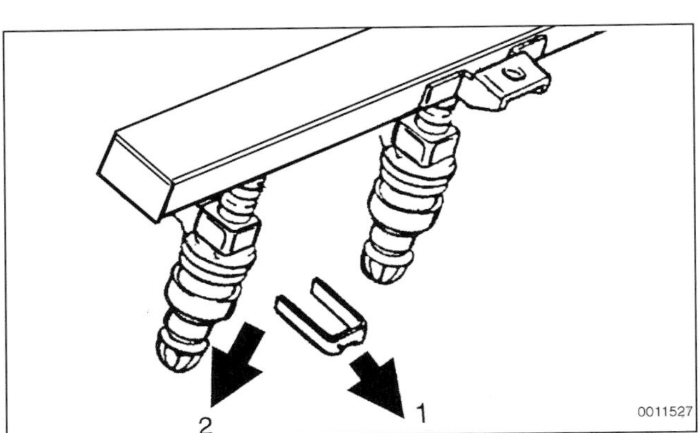

Lever out locking retainers (**1**) and remove injectors (**2**) from injector rail.

– Installation is reverse of removal, noting the following:
  - Check fuel injector O-rings for cracks of damage. Replace as necessary.
  - When installing, lubricate O-rings with SAE 90 weight oil.

Fuel pressure regulator, replacing

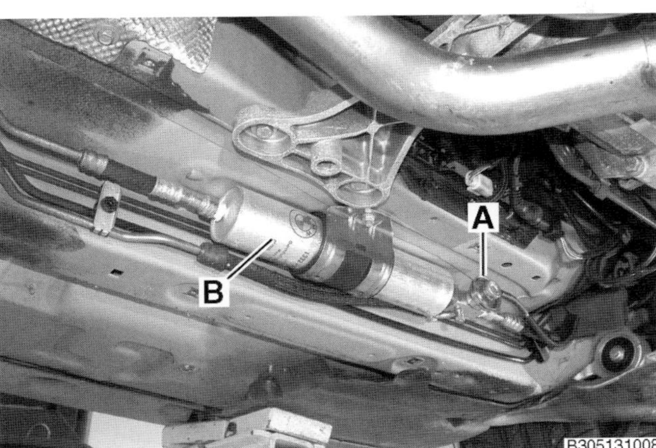

Fuel pressure regulator (**A**) is located under left side of car, along with fuel filter assembly (**B**) and fuel return line.

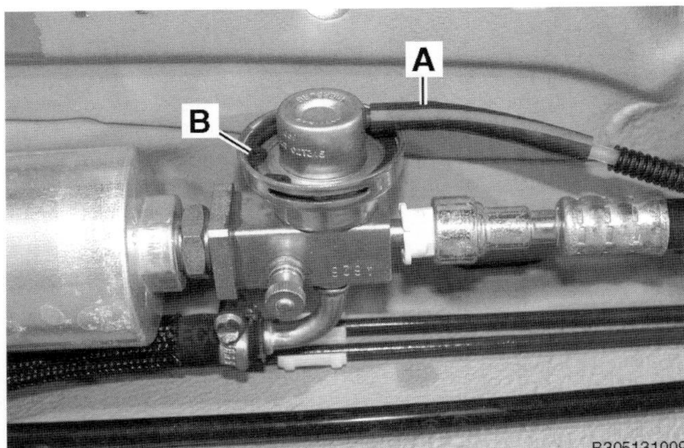

Disconnect vacuum hose (**A**) from fuel pressure regulator.
  - Remove locking spring clip (**B**) retaining fuel pressure regulator.
  - Wrap a shop rag around regulator, then remove by pulling regulator valve from regulator body.

– Installation is reverse of removal. Replace sealing O-rings as necessary.

Mass air flow (MAF) sensor, removing and installing

The mass air flow (MAF) sensor used on the MS S54 system also contains an intake air temperature sensor. Data provided by these sensors allow the engine control module (ECM) to calculate air volume and density for proper engine performance and efficiency. The MAF is non-adjustable.

> ***CAUTION —***
> *Be sure the ignition is OFF before replacing DME system components.*

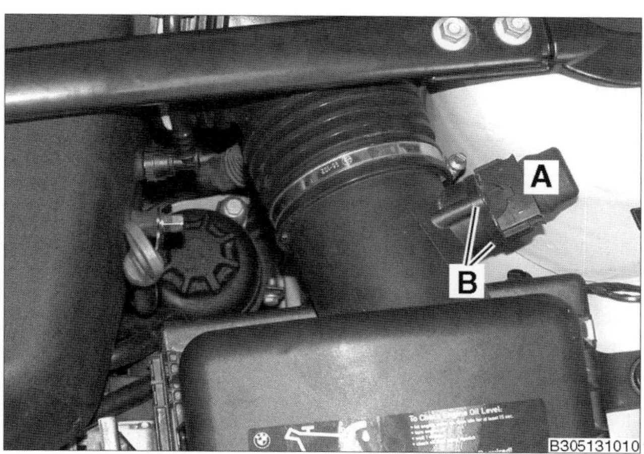

◀ Working under the hood at driver's side front corner, remove electrical harness connector (**A**) from MAF sensor. Remove screws **(B)** and pull MAF sensor from intake air duct.

– Installation is reverse of removal.

- Replace sealing O-ring between sensor and intake air ducts as necessary.

Engine coolant temperature (ECT) sensor, removing and installing

The engine coolant temperature (ECT) sensor is located below intake runner 1 in the coolant return pipe. Intake manifold removal is required to access the ECT sensor.

> ***CAUTION —***
> *Be sure the ignition is OFF before replacing DME system components.*

– Remove intake manifold as described in **110 Engine Removal and Installation**.

> ***WARNING —***
> *Due to risk of personal injury, be sure engine is cold before beginning the removal procedure.*

– Working under cylinder 1 throttle body, disconnect harness connector from idle speed control valve.

- Unplug harness connector at engine coolant temperature sensor, and unscrew sensor.
- Remove sensor. Catch leaking coolant using shop rags.

– Installation is reverse of removal, noting the following:

- Use a new copper sealing washer when installing new sensor. Replace lost coolant.

Tightening torque
- ECT sensor. . . . . 13 Nm (10 ft-lb)

Throttle assemblies, removing and installing

M3 models are equipped with a unique intake manifold assembly that mounts to six individual throttle assemblies attached directly to the cylinder head. For information on removing and installing the intake manifold and throttle assemblies, see **110 Engine Removal and Installation**.

After repairs to the throttle assembly, be sure to use to reset adaption values using the BMW specific diagnostic scan tool (diagnostic computer).

NOTE —
If the throttle assembly is removed, throttle setting and adaption values must be reconfigured within the ECM as described in the following procedure.

> ***CAUTION —***
> *If the adaptation process is not completed correctly, the engine will not start.*

Throttle actuator (EDR motor), removing and installing

The throttle actuator, or EDR motor, is located below the intake manifold.

> ***WARNING —***
> *After working on the throttle system (throttle assembly, throttle actuator, or throttle position sensor), a throttle function test must be carried out using a BMW specific diagnostic scan tool (diagnostic computer). Do not drive the vechicle until proper throttle operation has been confirmed using the factory test procedure. Using the BMW diagnostic scan tool, interrogate the system for any faults and correct as necessary before driving vehicle.*

– Turn off ignition. Remove ignition key.

– Remove intake manifold. See **110 Engine Removal and Installation**.

◄ Disconnect hose (**B**) from air pipe (**A**).

◄ Pry off pull rod (**A**) from ball head on throttle actuator lever. Disconnect harness connector from actuator (**B**).

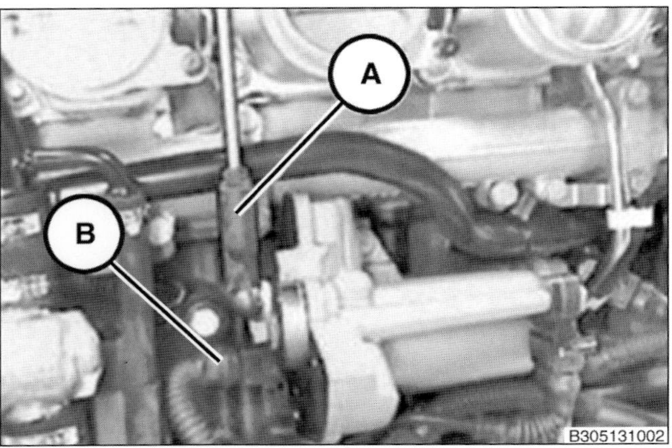

– Remove idle speed control valve mounting nuts and lay valve to side.

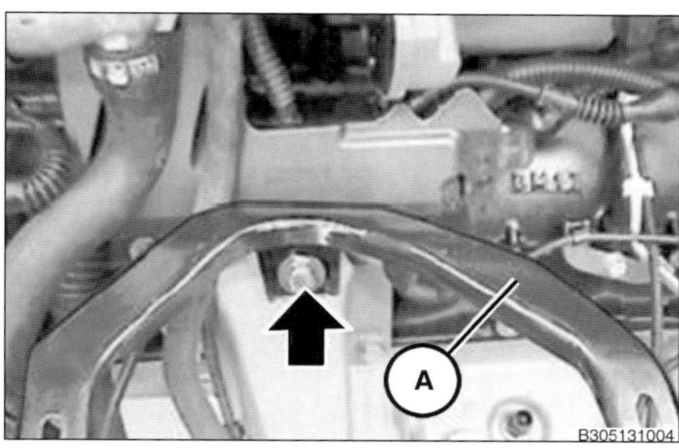

Remove mounting nut (**arrow**) and remove manifold support bracket (**A**).

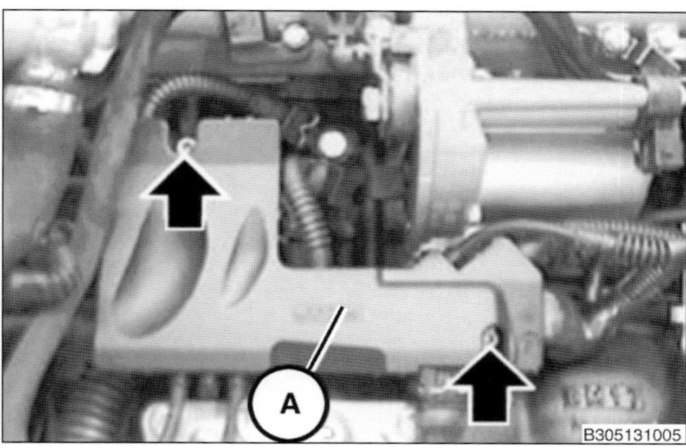

Remove wiring harness cover screws (**arrows**) and lay cover (**A**) to one side.

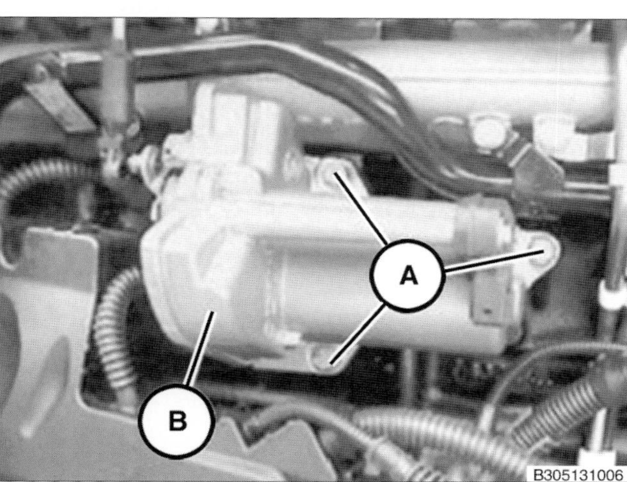

Remove throttle actuator mounting bolts (**A**) and remove throttle actuator (**B**).

– Check throttle actuator threaded sleeves in engine block for damage. If no damage is found, install actuator and tighten bolts.

– Check and adjust full-load stop as described in this repair group. See **Basic throttle setting, checking and adjusting**.

Tightening torque

- Throttle actuator to engine block. . . . . . . 13 Nm (10 ft-lb)

– Install intake manifold as described in **110 Engine Removal and Installation**.

NOTE —

Tighten manifold support bracket to engine block only after installing intake manifold to throttle assembly.

– Carry out throttle function test using a BMW specific scan tool (diagnostic computer). After throttle function test has been satisfactorily performed, check for stored faults and correct faults as necessary. Clear fault memory. Road test vehicle to check for proper throttle operation.

> ***WARNING —***
> *Do not drive the vechicle until proper throttle operation has been confirmed using the factory test procedure. Interrogate the system for any faults and correct as necessary before driving vehicle.*

Basic throttle setting, checking and adjusting

Check throttle setting whenever any work on the throttle system (throttle assembly, throttle actuator, throttle position sensor) has been carried out.

> ***WARNING —***
> - *If throttle setting adjustment is required, a BMW specific scan tool (diagnostic computer) must be used to initialize throttle settings. It is recommended that procedure be done by an authorized BMW dealer service department.*
> - *Idle stop screws for the throttle assemblies are set at the factory and secured with locking paint and plastic caps. Do not remove caps or screws.*

– Remove intake manifold assembly. See **110 Engine Removal and Installation**.

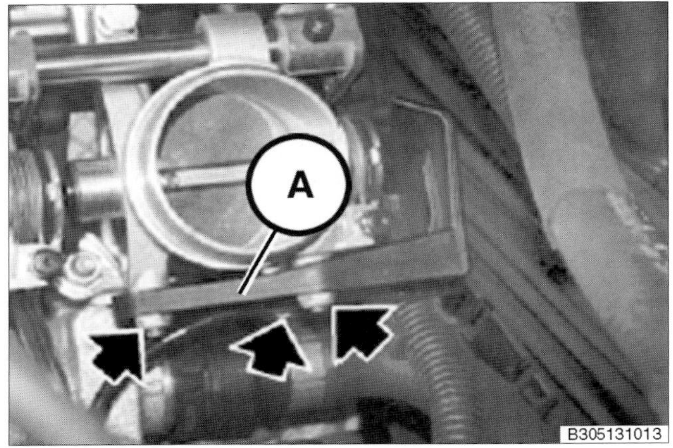

◄ Remove retaining nuts (**arrows**) and remove bracket (**A**) from throttle 6 at rear of engine.

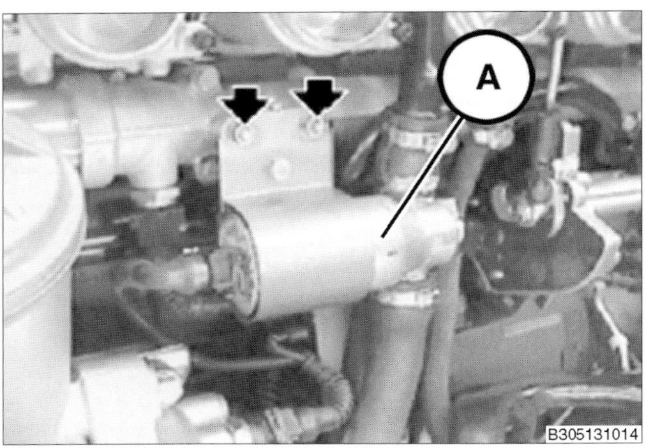

◄ Remove retaining nuts (**arrows**) and remove idle speed control valve (**A**) under throttle assemblies at cylinders 1 and 2.

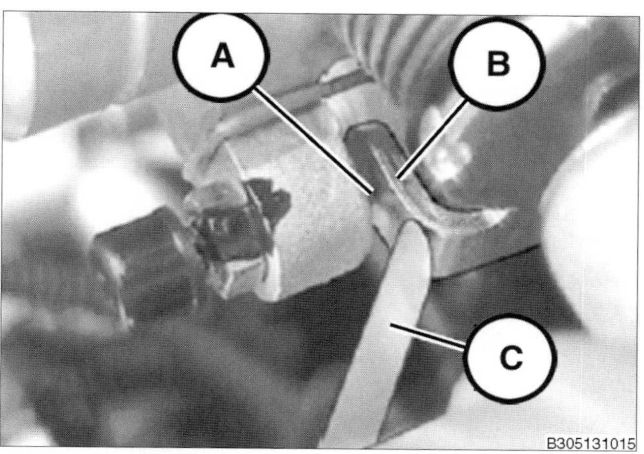

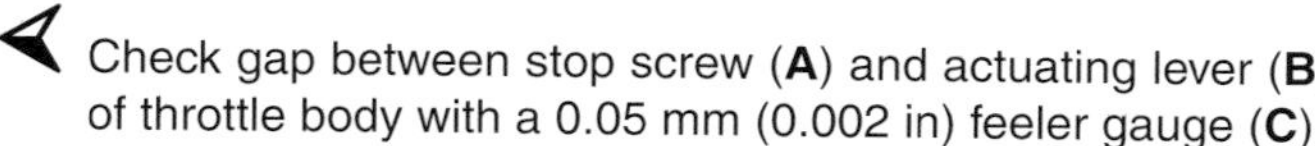

Check gap between stop screw (**A**) and actuating lever (**B**) of throttle body with a 0.05 mm (0.002 in) feeler gauge (**C**).

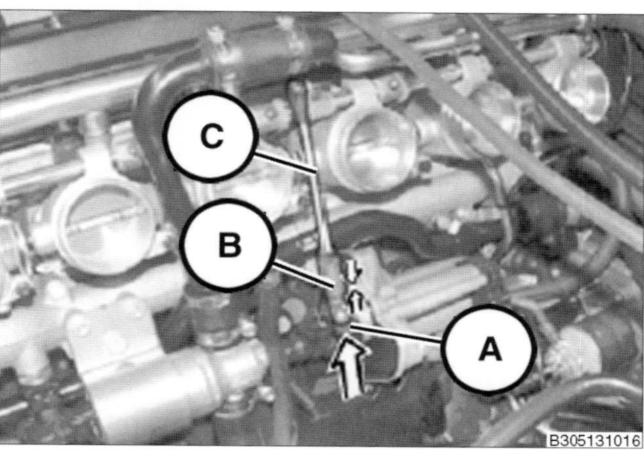

To check gap:

- Slide feeler gauge between stop screw and actuating lever.
- Press throttle rod (**A**) towards closed position to compress overload spring (**B**) in pull rod (**C**).
- Release throttle rod.

NOTE —

When correctly adjusted, feeler gauge will fit between screw and lever without falling out. Perform check on each individual throttle.

– If gap is larger than 0.05 mm (0.002 in), readjust at throttle 2 through 6.

CAUTION —

When loosening or tightening throttle hardware at actuating rod, hold wrenches perpendicular to actuating rod to prevent torque from being exerted on actuating rod assembly

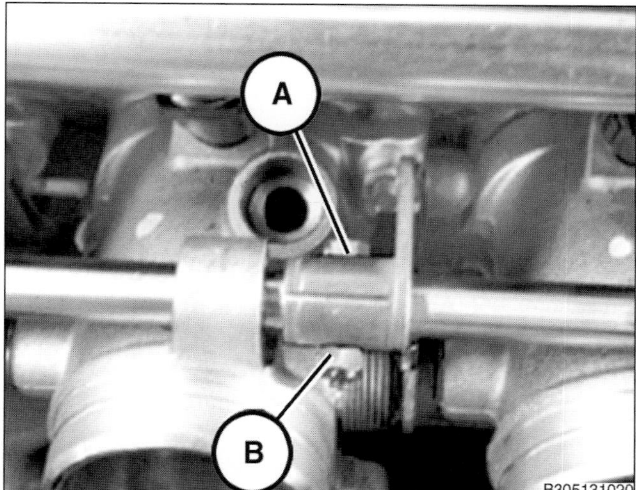

To begin throttle adjustment, loosen actuating arm hardware beginning at throttle 2.

- Using two open ended wrenches, counterhold bolt (**A**) and release nut (**B**).
- Continue for throttles 3 though 6.

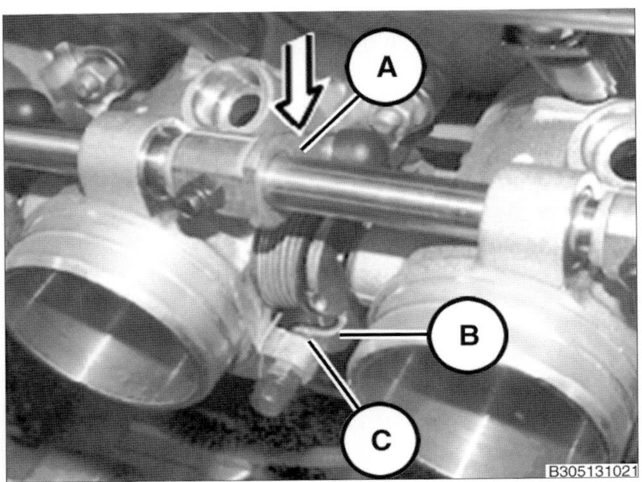

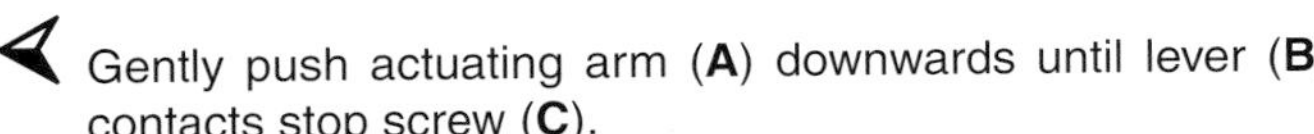

Gently push actuating arm (**A**) downwards until lever (**B**) contacts stop screw (**C**).

> ***CAUTION —***
> *Do not force linkage or throttle assembly to stop position.*

– Tighten actuating arm hardware to specification, noting the following:

- Replace fasteners.
- Keep wrenches perpendicular to actuating rod to prevent stressing actuating rod.
- Counterhold bolt and tighten retaining nut.
- Continue for throttle 3-6, checking basic adjustment upon completion.
- With basic throttle settings completed, continue by adjusting full-throttle stop.

Tightening torque

- Throttle actuating arm hardware. . . . . 7 Nm (5 ft-lb)

Full-throttle stop (adaptation), checking and adjusting

Adjusting full-throttle stop requires activating the electronic throttle actuator using a BMW diagnostic computer and following the instructions provided.

Activate EDR throttle actuator to full throttle position using a BMW specific scan tool (diagnostic computer) until throttles are fully open and stop screw (**A**) rests on detent lug.

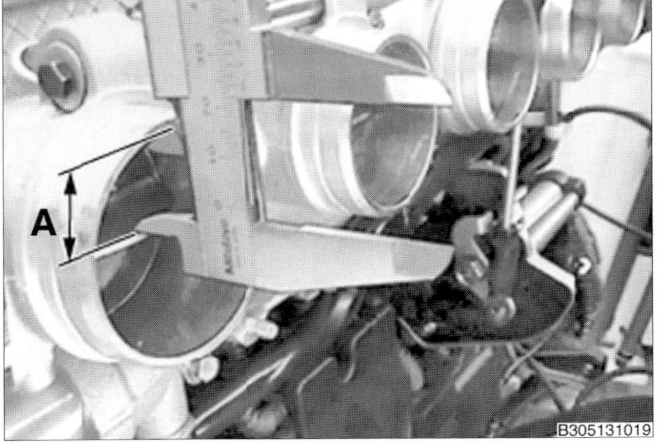

Measure full throttle opening at throttle 1.

- Adjust full throttle measurement to specification by turning stop screw on throttle motor housing.
- Activate throttle motor several times and check whether measurement (**A**) is within range.

Full throttle opening specification

- (**A**). . . . . 24.6 mm± 0.2mm(0.97 in ± 0.008 in)

Idle speed control valve, replacing

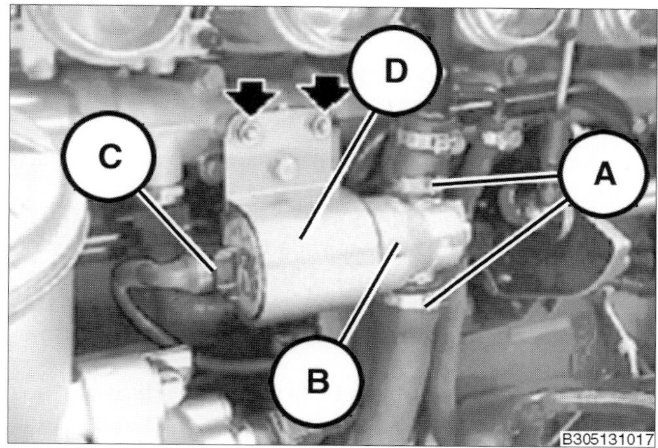

The idle speed control valve is mounted under the intake manifold. In order to remove the valve, the intake manifold must be removed. Intake manifold removal is described in **110 Engine Removal and Installation**.

◄ With intake manifold removed:

- Release hose clamps (**A**) from idle speed control valve (**B**).
- Disconnect electrical harness connector (**C**).
- Remove retaining nuts (**arrows**) and remove bracket (**D**) with idle speed control valve in place.

– Installation is reverse of removal. Clear stored fault codes from engine control module after installation.

Engine control module (ECM), removing and installing

NOTE —

Recode replacement ECM with application information (i.e. engine code, transmission type, etc.) prior to installation. Replacement ECMS need to be coded to the vehicle prior to installation. Consult an authorized BMW dealer before replacing the ECM.

– Disconnect negative (–) battery cable. Wait at least 1 minute.

> *CAUTION —*
>
> *Prior to disconnecting the battery, read the battery disconnection cautions given at the front of this manual.*

– Remove E-box cover at left rear of engine compartment. Cover is retained with four captive screws.

◄ ECM (**arrow**) is located in right rear of E-box, as identified with five electrical harness connectors.

◄ Disconnect ECM harness connectors by releasing lock on each plug and pivoting lever. Pull all five connector up and off ECM.

– Remove ECM from retaining brackets and pull from holder.

– Installation is reverse of removal.

ECM PIN ASSIGNMENTS

ECM pin assignments are given in **Table a**. This information may be helpful when diagnosing faults to or from the ECM. If all inputs and wiring are OK but operational problems still exist, the ECM itself may be faulty.

Generally, absence of voltage or continuity means there is a wiring or connector problem. Test results with incorrect values do not necessarily mean that a component is faulty. Check for loose, broken or corroded connections and wiring before replacing components. If the results are still incorrect, check the component itself. For engine management system electrical schematics, see **Electrical Wiring Diagrams**.

When making checks at the ECM itself, use a breakout box to allow tests to be made with the connector attached to the ECM. This also prevents damage to the small terminals in the connector. As an alternative, the harness connector housing can be separated so that electrical checks can be made from the back of the connector.

CAUTION—
- *Always wait at least one minute after turning off the ignition before removing the connector from the engine control module (ECM). If the connector is removed before this time, residual power in the system relay may damage the ECM.*
- *Always connect or disconnect the control module connector and meter probes with the ignition off.*

Table a. ECM pin assignment—DME MS S54

Pin	Signal	Component/function	Notes
Connector X60001 9-pin black			
1	Output	Fuel injector relay, terminal 15	Relay, fuel injectors
2	Output	Voltage supply, EDR throttle actuator	
3	Input/output	Diagnosis signal, TDX	SMG II transmission control module
4	Ground	Ground	Ground point
5	Ground	Ground	
6	Ground	Ground	
7	Input	Terminal 30	B+ Terminal (Fuse 102)
8	Input	Voltage supply (Fuse 2)	Fuse carrier, engine electronics
9	Ground	Ground, EDR throttle actuator	
Connector X60002 24-pin black			
1	Input	Heater, precatalyst oxygen sensor 1	Heated oxygen sensor 1 in front of catalytic converter
2		not used	
3		not used	
4		not used	
5	Ground	Ground	Ground connector
6		not used	
7	Input	Heater, post-catalyst oxygen sensor 1	Heated oxygen sensor 1 behind catalytic converter
8		not used	
9		not used	

Table a. ECM pin assignment—DME MS S54

Pin	Signal	Component/function	Notes
Connector X60002 24-pin black (cont.)			
10	Input	Signal, exhaust temperature	Exhaust temperature sensor (B5351)
11	Output	Signal, fuel pump relay 1	USA only
12	Output	Signal, E-box fan	
13	Input	Heater, precatalyst oxygen sensor 2	Heated oxygen sensor 2 in front of catalytic converter
14	Input	Signal, precatalyst oxygen sensor 1	Heated oxygen sensor 1 in front of catalytic converter
15	Input	Signal, precatalyst oxygen sensor 2	Heated oxygen sensor 2 in front of catalytic converter
16	Input	Signal, post-catalyst oxygen sensor 1	Heated oxygen sensor 1 behind catalytic converter
17		not used	
18	Input	Signal, post-catalyst oxygen sensor 2	Heated oxygen sensor 2 behind catalytic converter
19	Input	Heater, post catalyst oxygen sensor 2	Heated oxygen sensor 2 behind catalytic converter
20	Input	Signal, gear recognition switch	
21	Input/output	CAN bus signal, low	SMG II transmission control module
22	Input/output	CAN bus signal, high	SMG II transmission control module
23	Input	DME main relay signal activation	DME main relay
24		not used	
Connector X60003 52-pin black			
1	Input	Signal, mass air flow sensor	Hot film mass air flow sensor
2	Input	Signal, exhaust camshaft sensor 1	Camshaft position sensor II
3		not used	
4	Output	Signal, VANOS inlet valve, advance	
5	Input	Signal, intake camshaft position sensor	Camshaft position sensor I
6	Input	Signal, exhaust camshaft position sensor	Camshaft position sensor II
7	Output	Voltage supply, mass air flow sensor and EDR throttle actuator (throttle potentiometer)	Hot film mass air flow sensor and EDK throttle actuator
8	Input	Signal, crankshaft position sensor	
9		not used	
10	Input	Signal, EDR throttle actuator (throttle potentiometer)	
11		not used	
12		not used	
13	Input	Signal, battery charge indicator lamp	Generator (alternator, terminal 61)
14	Output	Voltage supply, throttle position sensor	
15		not used	
16		not used	
17	Ground	Ground, mass air flow sensor	Hot film mass air flow sensor
18		not used	
19		not used	
20	Ground	Ground, EDK throttle actuator (throttle potentiometer)	
21	Input	Ground, crankshaft position sensor	
22	Input	Signal, intake air temperature	
23	Input	Signal, throttle position sensor	
24	Output	Signal, coolant temperature sensor	
25	Ground	Ground, coolant temperature sensor, shield, knock sensor	
26	Input	Signal, oil pressure	Oil pressure switch

Table a. ECM pin assignment—DME MS S54

Pin	Signal	Component/function	Notes
Connector X60003 52-pin black (cont.)			
27		not used	
28		not used	
29	Input	Signal, knock sensor 1	
30	Input	Signal, knock sensor 3	
31	Input	Signal, knock sensor 2	
32		not used	
33	Input	Signal, cylinder 1 fuel injector	
34	Input	Signal, cylinder 2 fuel injector	
35	Input	Signal, cylinder 3 fuel injector	
36	Input	Signal, cylinder 4 fuel injector	
37	Input	Signal, cylinder 5 fuel injector	
38	Input	Signal, cylinder 6 fuel injector	
39	Input	Signal, oil level sensor	
40		not used	
41		not used	
42	Input	Signal, evaporative emissions valve	
43	Output	Signal, VANOS exhaust valve, retard	
44	Output	Signal, VANOS exhaust valve, advance	
45		not used	
46	Input	Signal, idle speed control valve	Idle speed control valve, close signal
47	Input	Signal, idle speed control valve	Idle speed control valve, open signal
48		not used	
49		not used	
50	Output	Signal, VANOS inlet valve, retard	
51	Output	Signal, valve, sucking jet pump	
52		not used	
Connector X60004 40-pin black			
1	Output	Signal, battery charge lamp (terminal 61)	Instrument cluster control unit
2	Input	Feedback signal, engine start (terminal 30h)	Instrument cluster control module
3	Input	Signal, secondary air injection pump	Secondary air injection pump relay
4	Input	Signal, electric fan	Auxiliary fan motor
5	Ground	Ground	
6	Output	Signal, terminal 50, ignition lock	Instrument cluster control unit
7	Ground	Ground, pedal position sensor	
8	Input	Signal, pedal position sensor	
9	Output	Voltage supply, pedal position sensor	
10	Output	Signal, fuel pump relay 1	Fuel pump relay 1, USA only
11	Output	Signal, oil pressure switch	Instrument cluster control module
12	Ground	Ground, pedal position sensor	
13	Input	Signal, pedal position sensor	
14	Output	Voltage supply, pedal position sensor	
15	Input	Signal, driving dynamics	Switching center
16	Input	Driving dynamics active LED	Switching center
17	Output	Speed signal	Data link connector

Table a. ECM pin assignment—DME MS S54

Pin	Signal	Component/function	Notes
Connector X60004 40-pin black (cont.)			
18	Output	Activation, heater, leak detection (From 09/2001 only)	Diagnostic module, fuel tank leakage (USA only)
19		not used	
20	Output	Activation, heater, leak detection (From 09 / 2001 only)	Diagnostic module, fuel tank leakage (USA only)
21	Output	Signal, oil level sensor	Instrument cluster control module
22	Input	Signal, processed wheel speed, right rear	ABS / ASC module, ABS / DSC module
23		not used	
24	Input	Signal, brake light switch	Light switching center control unit
25		not used	
26	Input	Terminal 15	Fuse F29
27	Input	Voltage supply, multifunction steering wheel	Data link, airbag contact (volute) spring
28	Output	Signal, leakage diagnosis pump (not used after 09 / 2001)	Diagnostic module, fuel tank leakage
29	Input	Signal, relay, A/C compressor	A/C compressor relay
30	Output	Signal, leakage diagnosis pump (not used after 09 / 2001)	Diagnostic module, fuel tank leakage
31		not used	
32	Input/output	Transmit diagnosis line (TXD) data link signal	Data link connector
33	Input	Electronic vehicle immobilization	Electronic immobilizer control module
34	Input	Signal, brake light switch	Brake light switch
35		not used	
36	Input/output	CAN bus signal, high	Connector, CAN bus
37	Input/output	CAN bus signal, low	Connector, CAN bus
38	Ground	Ground, coolant outlet temperature sensor	Temperature sensor
39	Output	Signal, coolant outlet temperature sensor	Temperature sensor
40		not used	
Connector X60005 9-pin black			
1	Output	Signal, ignition coil 1	
2	Output	Signal, ignition coil 2	
3	Output	Signal, ignition coil 3	
4		not used	
5	Ground	Ground	
6	Output	Signal, ignition coil 5	
7	Output	Signal, ignition coil 6	
8		not used	
9	Output	Signal, ignition coil 4	

160 Fuel Tank and Fuel Pump

TABLES

GENERAL

This repair group covers service information specifically for the fuel supply system. Information on the fuel injection system is covered in **130 Fuel Injection**.

In the descriptions and procedures given below, engine and engine management (DME) systems are referred to by manufacturer code. If necessary, see **100 Engine–General** for model year, engine code, and DME applications.

Fuel filter replacement is covered in **020 Maintenance**.

Special tools

Some of the procedures in this group require the use of special tools.

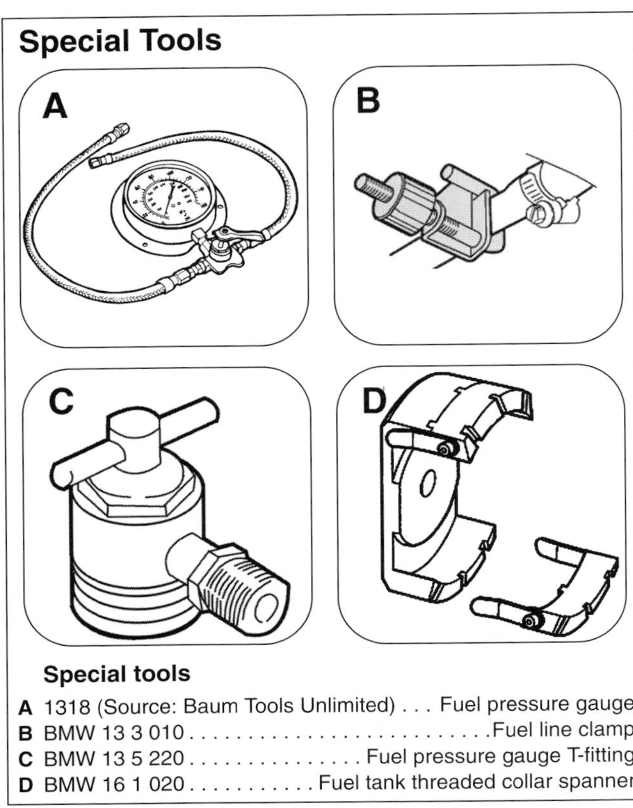

Special tools

A 1318 (Source: Baum Tools Unlimited) . . . Fuel pressure gauge
B BMW 13 3 010 . . . . .Fuel line clamp
C BMW 13 5 220 . . . . Fuel pressure gauge T-fitting
D BMW 16 1 020 . . . . Fuel tank threaded collar spanner

Fuel pump

On models equipped with DME MS 42.0, MS 43.0, and MS S54, the electric fuel pump is mounted in the fuel tank in tandem with the right side fuel level sender. The fuel pump delivers fuel at high pressure to the fuel injection system. A pressure regulator maintains system pressure. The quantity of fuel supplied exceeds demand, so excess fuel returns to the fuel tank via a return line. See **130 Fuel Injection** for more information on system pressure and the fuel pressure regulator.

NOTE —
Fuel pump removal procedures are given under **Fuel level sender (right side) and fuel pump, removing and installing**.

Fuel pump control module (MS S54 and MS 45.1)

On DME MS S54 (S54 engines) and MS 45.1 (M56 engines), the fuel pump is operated via the fuel pump control module. The fuel pump control module is controlled by the DME control module based on engine operating conditions. The fuel pump module varies the voltage to the pump based on engine load conditions.

NOTE —
On MS S54 engines, the fuel pump control module is identified as the Fuel Pump Relay (K96) in the electrical schematics at the rear of this book.

Fuel tank evaporative control system

Evaporative control is designed to prevent fuel system evaporative losses from venting into the atmosphere. The components of this system allow control and monitoring of evaporative losses by the on-board diagnostic (OBD II) software incorporated into the engine control module (ECM).

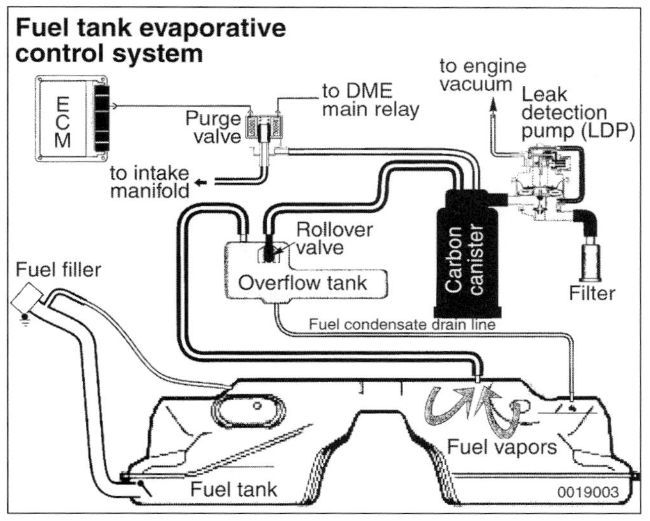

For DME MS 42.0, the main components of the evaporative control system are:

- **Fuel overflow tank** acts as a liquid/vapor separator.
- **Carbon canister** stores evaporated fuel.
- **Plumbing** ducts vapors from the fuel tank to the canister and from the canister to the intake manifold.
- **Carbon canister purge valve** is controlled by the engine control module (ECM).
- **Running losses (3/2-way) valve** shunts excess fuel volume directly back to the fuel tank before it circulates through the injector fuel rail.
- **Leak detection unit** pressurizes the fuel tank and the evaporative system to monitor system leaks.

For DME MS 43.0 and MS S54 the only significant change is that the running losses (3/2-way) valve and the fuel injector loop are no longer used. The fuel pressure regulator is located in or near the fuel filter and shunts excess fuel directly back to the tank.

NOTE —

3/2-way valve, running losses valve and fuel changeover valve are used interchangeably in BMW technical literature.

Partial Zero Emissions Vehicle (PZEV) (MS 45.1)

Beginning in the 2003 model year, 325i models equipped with an automatic transmission for sale in California, Massachusetts, New York and Vermont are fitted with an updated engine, identified as the M56 B25. The PZEV M56 B25 is a further development of the M54 2.5 liter engine with the addition of the following:

- Dual down-stream catalytic converters featuring high cell density technology.
- Wide-band Oxygen sensors mounted upstream of the catalysts
- High-pressure, four outlet fuel injectors.
- Revised VANOS system with a fixed position for reduced emissions at start-up.
- Secondary Air Injection system with mass air flow sensor.
- Carbon filter added to the air intake to reduce hydrocarbon emissions.
- Stainless steel fuel injectors and fuel rail, tank vent valve, and evaporative canister.
- Sealed stainless steel fuel tank with integrated fuel pump, fuel pressure regulator, and fuel filter.
- Aluminum cylinder head cover with integrated ventilation valve.
- 15 year / 150,000 mile warranty on emissions equipment.

NOTE —

Due to the nature of the sealed stainless steel fuel tank with integrated fuel pump, filter, and fuel pressure regulator, a component failure requires replacement of the fuel tank unit as a complete unit. Service and repair information for this model has been included where available.

Evaporative system troubleshooting

Troubleshooting and testing of the evaporative system should start by accessing DTCs using a BMW or BMW compatible aftermarket scan tool.

For purposes of OBD II emissions compliance, the DME system sets a diagnostic trouble code (DTC) when it detects a leak that is equal or larger than the minimum leak sensed by the system.

The Malfunction Indicator Light (MIL) is illuminated upon a second recurrence of the fault. See **On-Board Diagnostics** at the back of this manual. BMW recommends that an independent pressure test of the fuel system should be conducted with a chemical leak detector present to confirm the presence of the fuel system leak.

NOTE —

In 1999 cars, the MIL illuminates a "Check Engine" light. In cars manufactured in mid-2000 and later, the MIL illuminates a "Service Engine Soon" light.

When leak testing, observe the following conditions to obtain plausible results:

- Fuel tank must be ¼ to ¾ full.
- Park vehicle in shop for at least 2 hours before test to allow fuel to reach room temperature. Ideal fuel temperature is 10° - 20°C (50° - 68°F).
- Do not refuel immediately before leak test.

If a leak is detected, check the following areas:

- Fuel filter cap (leaky or off)
- Fuel tank ventilation lines leaky at fuel tank or activated carbon canister
- Tank ventilation valve leaky (in engine compartment)
- Fuel level sensor/fuel pump cap leaky

Evaporative system component replacement is covered later in this group in **Fuel Tank and Fuel Lines**.

Warnings and cautions

The following warnings and cautions should be observed when servicing the fuel system.

> ***WARNING —***
> - *The fuel system is designed to retain pressure even when the ignition is off. When working with the fuel system, loosen the fuel lines slowly to allow residual fuel pressure to dissipate. Avoid spraying fuel. Use shop rags to capture leaking fuel.*
> - *Before beginning any work on the fuel system, place a fire extinguisher in the vicinity of the work area.*
> - *Fuel is highly flammable. When working around fuel, do not disconnect any wires that could cause electrical sparks. Do not smoke or work near heaters or other fire hazards.*
> - *Always unscrew the fuel tank cap to release pressure in the tank before working on the tank or lines.*
> - *Do not use a work light with an incandescent bulb near any fuel. Fuel may spray on the hot bulb causing a fire.*
> - *Make sure the work area is properly ventilated.*

> ***CAUTION —***
> - *Prior to disconnecting the battery, read the battery disconnection cautions in* **001 Warnings and Cautions**.
> - *Before making any electrical tests with the ignition turned on, disable the ignition system as described in* **120 Ignition System**. *Be sure the battery is disconnected when replacing components.*
> - *To prevent damage to the ignition system or other DME components, including the ECM, always connect and disconnect wires and test equipment with the ignition off.*
> - *Cleanliness is essential when working with the fuel system. Thoroughly clean the fuel line unions before disconnecting any of the lines.*
> - *Use only clean tools. Keep removed parts clean and sealed or covered with a clean, lint-free cloth, especially if completion of the repair is delayed.*
> - *Do not move the car while the fuel system is open.*
> - *Avoid using high pressure compressed air to blow out lines and components. High pressure can rupture internal seals and gaskets.*
> - *Always replace seals, O-rings and hose clamps.*

FUEL SYSTEM TROUBLESHOOTING

Fuel pump fuse and relay (MS 42.0 and MS 43.0)

Troubleshooting of any fuel pump fault should begin with checking the fuel pump fuse and the fuel pump relay. The DME main relay should also be checked. The fuel pump relay is located in the relay panel behind the glove compartment.

NOTE —

- *Special tools are required for some of the tests described here.*
- *DME MS S54 and MS 45.1 fuel pumps use a fuel pump control module instead of fuel pump relay. Control modules are signaled through the CAN bus, and require special diagnostic tools for troubleshooting.*

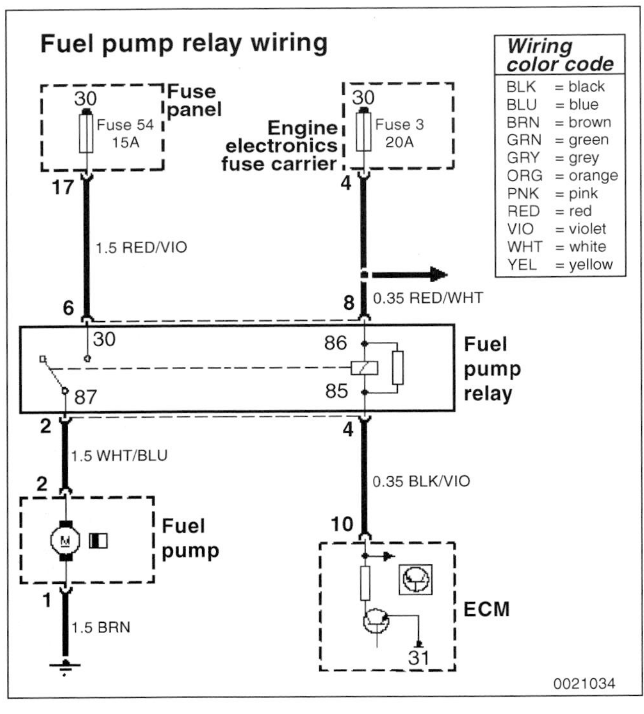

The fuel pump circuit is protected by fuse 54 located in the fuse panel above the glove compartment.

Fuse 3 in the engine electronics fuse carrier in the E-box supplies power to the coil side of the fuel pump relay. The engine control module (ECM) supplies switched ground to the relay. During starting, the fuel pump runs as long as the ignition switch is in the start position and continues to run once the engine starts. If an electrical system fault interrupts power to the fuel pump, the engine will not run.

Operating fuel pump for tests (MS 42.0 and MS 43.0)

To operate the fuel pump for testing purposes without having to run the engine, the fuel pump relay can be bypassed to power the pump directly.

NOTE —

DME MS S54 and MS 45.1 fuel pumps use a fuel pump control module instead of fuel pump relay. Control modules are signaled through the CAN bus, and require special diagnostic tools for troubleshooting.

– To run fuel pump, remove glove box and right footwell trim panel as described in **513 Interior trim**.

Remove relay panel support bolt (**arrow**).

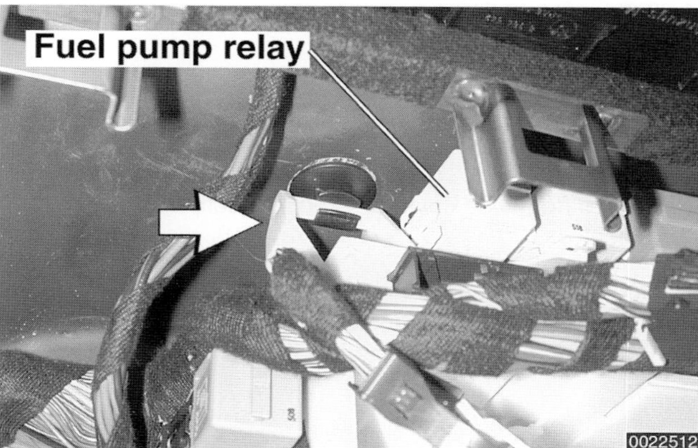

0022512

Pull relay panel at top to release mounting clips (**arrow**) at left and right sides. Pull relay panel down and remove fuel pump relay.

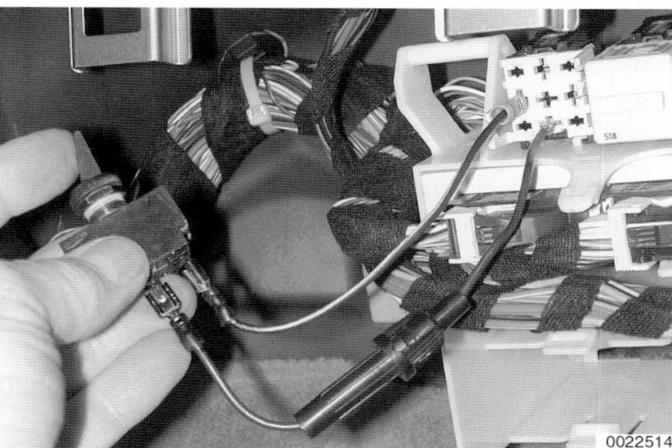
0022514

Connect socket for relay terminal **6** (30–red/violet wire) to socket for relay terminal **2** (87–white/blue wire) with a fused jumper wire. After completing tests, remove jumper wire.

> ***CAUTION —***
> - *Relay locations may vary. Use care when identifying relays and making electrical checks at the fuse/relay panel. See* **610 Electrical Component Locations** *for additional information.*
> - *The fuel pump relay has a 1.5 mm² red/violet wire at terminal 6 in the relay socket. Terminal 2 has a 1.5 mm² white/blue wire. See* **Electrical Wiring Diagrams** *for additional wiring information.*

NOTE —
Jumper wire should be 1.5 mm² (14 ga.) and include an in-line fuse holder with a 15 amp fuse. To avoid f damage from repeated connecting and disconnecting, also include a toggle switch.

– If pump does not run with jumper installed, fault could be in fuel pump, fuses 3 or 54, or wiring to pump. Check pump, fuses and its wiring as described below.

Fuel pump electrical circuit, testing (MS 42.0 and MS 43.0)

The test given below assumes that the fuel pump relay circuit is functioning correctly as described earlier. Access to the pump is from below the rear seat bottom cushion.

NOTE —
DME MS S54 and MS 45.1 fuel pumps use a fuel pump control module instead of fuel pump relay. Control modules are signaled through the CAN bus, and require special diagnostic tools for troubleshooting.

– Remove fuel pump relay and operate fuel pump as described earlier under **Operating fuel pump for tests**.

> ***CAUTION —***
> *Fuse and relay locations may vary. Use care when troubleshooting the electrical system at the fuse/relay panel. To resolve problems in identifying a relay, see an authorized BMW dealer.*

- Remove rear seat lower cushion by lifting front edge off left and right catches.
- Peel forward lip of carpet from beneath seat cushion and carefully peel back insulation to expose fuel tank access cover.
  - Remove right side cover to expose electrical harness connector.

◀ Disconnect harness connector from tank sender unit by sliding lock back, then lifting connector.

◀ With jumper wire connected in place of fuel pump relay as described above, check for positive (+) battery voltage at harness connector terminals.

- If voltage and ground are present, fuel pump is probably faulty. If there is no voltage, check wiring between from fuel pump and relay.

Fuel pump power consumption, testing (MS 42.0 and MS 43.0)

To achieve accurate test results, the battery voltage at the fuel pump connector should be approx. 12.6 volts. Charge the battery as necessary.

A higher than normal power consumption may indicate a worn fuel pump, which may cause intermittent fuel starvation due to pump overheating and seizure. The only remedy is pump replacement. A lower than normal power consumption may indicate a blockage. Be sure to check that the return line and the pump pickup are not obstructed before replacing the pump.

- To access top of fuel tank:
  - Remove rear seat lower cushion by lifting front edge off catches.
  - Peel forward lip of carpet and carefully peel back insulation to expose fuel tank access cover.
  - Remove cover.

◀ Disconnect harness connector from tank sender unit by sliding lock back, then lifting connector.

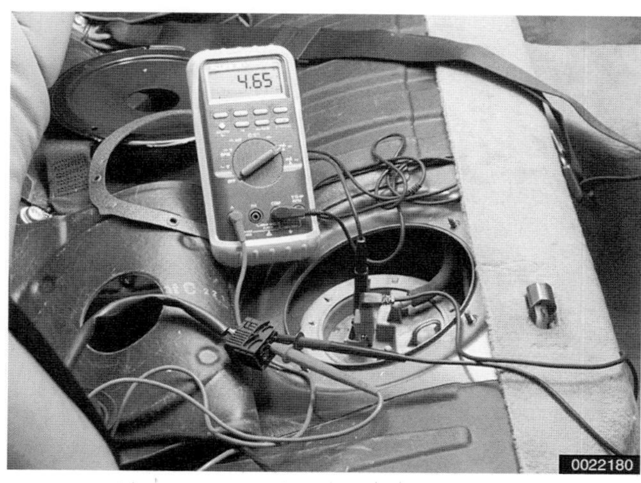

0022180

Test fuel pump for current draw by attaching ammeter between pump and harness (terminal 2, white/blue wire) and connect a jumper wire between the pump and harness (terminal 1, brown wire) as shown

- Run pump, see **Operating fuel pump for tests**.
- Compare ammeter reading with specification listed in **Table a**.

> ***CAUTION —***
> *Do not allow the test leads to short to ground.*

NOTE —
See **600 Electrical System–General** *for information on electrical tests using a digital multimeter.*

Table a. Fuel pump current

Maximum current consumption	5.0 amps

Fuel delivery tests

Checking fuel delivery is a fundamental part of troubleshooting and diagnosing the DME system. Fuel pressure directly influences fuel delivery. An accurate fuel pressure gauge will be needed to make the tests.

There are three significant fuel delivery values to be measured:

- **System pressure**—created by the fuel pump and maintained by the pressure regulator.
- **Fuel delivery volume**—created by the fuel pump and affected by restrictions, such as clogged fuel filter.
- **Residual pressure**—the pressure maintained in the closed system after the engine and fuel pump are shut off.

Residual fuel pressure is checked using the procedure detailed in **130 Fuel Injection**.

NOTE —
Vehicles equipped with DME MS 45.1 use a sealed fuel system with specialized connectors. The fuel pump and fuel pressure regulator that integral to the fuel tank and non-replaceable. Testing these components is beyond the scope of this manual.

MS 42.0 and MS 43.0

– Remove interior microfilter and housing. See **110 Engine removal and Installation**.

0021021

Remove fuel rail cover by prying off nut covers (**arrows**) and removing nuts.

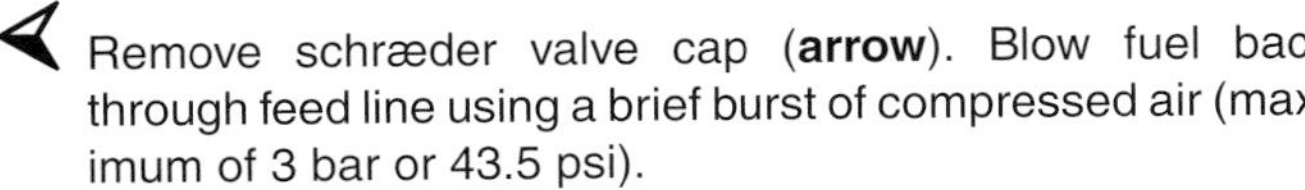
Remove schræder valve cap (**arrow**). Blow fuel back through feed line using a brief burst of compressed air (maximum of 3 bar or 43.5 psi).

> ***WARNING —***
> - *Fuel in fuel line is under pressure (approx. 3 - 5 bar or 45 - 75 psi) and may be expelled under pressure. Do not smoke or work near heaters or other fire hazards. Keep a fire extinguisher handy. Before disconnecting fuel hoses, wrap a cloth around fuel hoses to absorb any leaking fuel. Catch and dispose of escaped fuel. Plug all open fuel lines.*
> - *Always unscrew the fuel tank cap to release pressure in the tank before working on the tank or lines.*

NOTE —

The schræder valve must be opened to the fuel pressure gauge connection. Either remove the valve using a standard tire valve removal tool or use the BMW special tool 15 5 220.

MS S54

Fuel delivery tests may be performed using the schræder valve located at the fuel pressure regulator, under the left side of the car.

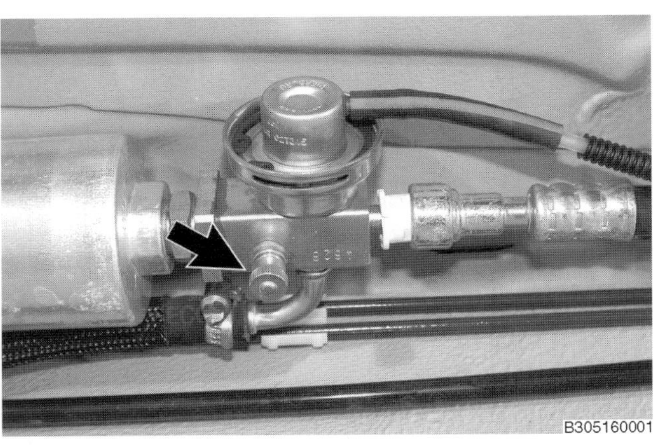

Remove schræder valve cap (**arrow**). Blow fuel back through feed line using a brief burst of compressed air (maximum of 5 bar or 72.5 psi).

> ***WARNING —***
> - *Fuel in fuel line is under pressure (approx. 3 - 5 bar or 45 - 75 psi) and may be expelled under pressure. Do not smoke or work near heaters or other fire hazards. Keep a fire extinguisher handy. Before disconnecting fuel hoses, wrap a cloth around fuel hoses to absorb any leaking fuel. Catch and dispose of escaped fuel. Plug all open fuel lines.*
> - *Always unscrew the fuel tank cap to release pressure in the tank before working on the tank or lines.*

0022146

All models

 Attach fuel pressure gauge to special tool 13 5 220 (T-fitting) or equivalent. Attach T-fitting to schræder valve.

> **WARNING —**
> *The fuel pressure gauge must be securely connected to prevent it from coming loose under pressure.*

> **CAUTION —**
> *When using the BMW special tool, use care when turning the T-handle in to open the schræder valve. Screw the handle in just until the schræder valve opens. Turning the handle in too far will damage the schræder valve.*

NOTE —
The fuel pressure gauge should have a minimum range of 0 to 5 bar (0 to 75 psi).

System pressure, testing

System pressure is the pressure created by the fuel pump and maintained by the pressure regulator. System pressure is not adjustable.

> **CAUTION —**
> *The fuel pump is capable of developing a higher pressure than that regulated by the pressure regulator. In the event the fuel pump check valve is faulty (stuck closed), make sure the fuel pressure does not rise above 6.0 bar (87 psi). Damage to the fuel lines or fuel system components could result.*

Fuel pressure regulator (DME MS 42.0)

Fuel return to tank
Fuel in from fuel rail
Diaphragm
Spring
Connection to crankcase breather
B588

NOTE —
- *DME MS 42.0 fuel pressure regulator is shown in illustration. Fuel pressure deflects diaphragm to return fuel to tank when pressure reaches desired limit.*
- *DME MS 43.0 fuel pressure regulator is integrated with fuel filter.*
- *DME MS S54 pressure regulator is located just ahead of fuel filter.*
- *DME MS 45.1 fuel pressure regulator is located in the permanently sealed fuel tank.*

– Remove fuel tank filler cap.

– Relieve fuel pressure and connect a pressure gauge to fuel rail as described earlier.

> **WARNING —**
> *Fuel will be discharged. Wrap a shop towel around the fuel line fitting when disconnecting the fuel line. Do not smoke or work near heaters or other fire hazards. Keep an approved fire extinguisher handy.*

> ***CAUTION —***
> *When using the BMW special tool 11 5 220, use care when turning the T-handle in to open the schræder valve. Screw the handle in just until pressure shows on the gauge.*

– Operate fuel pump as described earlier under **Operating fuel pump for tests**. Check that fuel pressure corresponds to specifications listed in **Table b**.

- If pressure is low, repeat test while gradually pinching off return hose to fuel tank. Pressure should rise rapidly. If not, fuel pump is most likely faulty. If pressure rises, the fuel pressure regulator is most likely faulty.
- If pressure is too high, check return line from pressure regulator to tank. Check for kinks in hose. If no faults can be found, pressure regulator is most likely faulty. **See 130 Fuel Injection** for testing and replacement procedures.

> ***WARNING —***
> *Fuel under pressure is present during the test. Use hose clamps at all connections.*

Table b. Fuel pressure specifications

Engine	Fuel pressure
MS 42.0 and MS 43.0	3.5 ± 0.2 bar (50.76 ± 2.9 psi)
MS S54	5.0 ± 0.2 bar (72.5 ± 2.9 psi)

– When finished, disconnect pressure gauge and fitting. Replace schræder valve if removed during testing. Replace fuel filler cap.

Fuel delivery volume, testing

0022146

◀ Working in engine compartment, connect BMW special tool 13 5 220 and a length of hose to schræder valve fitting on front end of fuel rail. Place open end of hose in a suitable container for catching fuel (2-quart capacity).

> ***WARNING —***
> *Fuel will be discharged during this test. Do not smoke or work near heaters or other fire hazards. Keep an approved fire extinguisher handy.*

– Run fuel pump for exactly 30 seconds as described earlier under **Operating fuel pump for tests** and measure fuel collected. Refer to **Table c**.

Table c. Fuel pump delivery specifications

Engine	Delivery rate (30 seconds @ 12V)
All	1.12 liter (1.16 qt)

– When finished testing, remove fuel rail connection.

– Using BMW diagnostic scan tool or equivalent, access and clear ECM fault memory.

Residual fuel pressure, testing

For quick restarts and to avoid vapor lock when the engine is hot, the fuel injection system is designed to retain fuel pressure after the engine has been turned off. This residual pressure is primarily maintained by the fuel pressure regulator and a check valve at the fuel pump outlet.

NOTE —
On MS 42.0 and MS S54 cars, the fuel pressure regulator is under the car, below the driver's seat near the fuel filter. On MS 43.0 cars, the fuel pressure regulator is integrated into the fuel filter. In MS 45.1 cars, the fuel pressure regulator is integral to the fuel tank.

– Relieve fuel pressure and connect a pressure gauge to fuel rail as described earlier.

> ***WARNING —***
> *Fuel will be discharged. Wrap a shop towel around the fuel line fitting when disconnecting the fuel line. Do not smoke or work near heaters or other fire hazards. Keep an approved fire extinguisher handy.*

> ***CAUTION —***
> *When using the BMW special tool 11 5 220 use care when turning the T-handle in to open the schræder valve. Screw the handle in just until pressure shows on the gauge.*

– Operate fuel pump for approximately one minute by running engine and observe fuel pressure. Shut off engine.

– Observe fuel pressure gauge after 20 minutes. The pressure should not drop off more than 0.5 bar from system pressure listed in **Table d**.

– When finished, disconnect pressure gauge and fitting. Replace schræder valve if removed during testing.

– If fuel system does not maintain pressure:

- Check visually for leaks in fuel lines or at unions.
- Check for leaking injector.
- Check for faulty fuel pump check valve.

– To test fuel pump check valve:

- Repeat residual pressure test.
- Immediately after turning engine off, pinch off fuel delivery line using special fuel hose pinch clamp 13 3 010.
- If pressure is now maintained, fault is most likely at fuel pump check valve.
- If pressure again drops below specifications, fault is most likely in fuel pressure regulator.

Table d. Fuel pressure specifications

Parameter	Fuel pressure
MS 42.0/MS 43.0 System pressure Residual pressure	 3.5 ± 0.2 bar (50.76 ± 2.9 psi) > 3.0 bar (> 43.51 psi)

Table d. Fuel pressure specifications

Parameter	Fuel pressure
MS S54 System pressure Residual pressure	 5.0 ± 0.2 bar (72.5 ± 2.9 psi) > 4.5 bar (> 65.2 psi)

NOTE —
The fuel pressure check valve is not available as a replacement part. If the check valve is faulty, the pump assembly should be replaced.

FUEL PUMPS AND FUEL LEVEL SENDERS

E46 models use a two-lobed fuel tank and each lobe of the tank has its own fuel level sending unit.

The right side fuel level sender is integrated with the fuel pump. Each sender has a float connected to a variable resistance wiper contact for fuel level. When replacing the sender/pump assembly always replace hose clamps, gaskets and O-rings.

To equalize fuel level between the two tank lobes, a siphon pump is installed in the left lobe.

WARNING —
When removing the fuel level sender or the fuel pump, the fuel tank should be drained to 1/4 tank or below as described later in this repair group.

NOTE —
- *Models equipped with DME MS 45.1 use a sealed, stainless steel fuel tank with intergrated fuel pump and fuel pressure regulator. These fuel tanks and components must be replace as a complete unit. Diagnostic and service information has been included where available.*
- *The compensating siphon pump maintains the fuel level between the right and left tank lobes. If the resistances do not match those given in* **Table e**, *remove the senders and visually inspect the level in each lobe. If the levels are different, check the siphon pump.*

Table e. Fuel level sender resistances

Float position	Test result (ohms)
Right side empty	70.0 ± 1.2 Ω
Right side full	394.5 ± 4.5 Ω
Left side empty	70.0 ± 1.2 Ω
Left side full	310.2 ± 3.6 Ω

Fuel level sender (right side) and fuel pump, removing and installing (MS 42.0, MS 43.0 and MS S54)

– Drain fuel from tank as described later.

– Disconnect negative (–) cable from battery.

> ***CAUTION —***
> *Prior to disconnecting the battery, read the battery disconnection cautions given at the front of this manual on page viii.*

– To access top of fuel tank, remove rear seat lower cushion by lifting front edge off catches.

0022141

Peel forward lip of carpet from beneath seat cushion and carefully peel back insulation to expose fuel tank access cover.

- Remove right side cover to expose electrical harness connector.

– Disconnect hose.

– Disconnect harness connector from tank sender unit by sliding lock back, then lifting connector.

– Unscrew threaded collar from fuel pump/fuel level sender.

NOTE —
BMW special spanner 16 1 022 should be used to remove and install the threaded collar. Damage to the collar may result if the special tool is not used.

0022158

Slowly withdraw assembly from tank, allowing fuel to drain.

- If necessary, push level sender arm toward fuel pump assembly to facilitate removal.

> ***WARNING —***
> *Fuel may be spilled. Do not smoke or work near heaters or other fire hazards.*

– To reinstall:

- Use new sealing ring at tank collar.
- Be sure that fuel line connections point in same direction as they came out.
- Reconnect harness connector and hose.
- Fill tank and check for leaks by running engine.
- Install access cover and its mounting nuts.

– After finishing repairs but before starting engine, fill fuel tank with at least 5 liters (1.5 gallons) of fuel.

> ***CAUTION —***
> *The fuel pump will be damaged if you run it without fuel.*

NOTE —
It is common practice to replace the fuel filter any time the fuel pump unit is replaced.

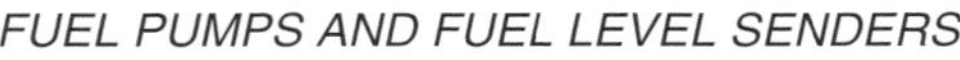

Fuel level sender (left side), removing and installing (MS 42.0, MS 43.0 and MS S54)

The procedure for removing and replacing the left side fuel level sender is similar to that used for the right side. There is no fuel pump on the left side.

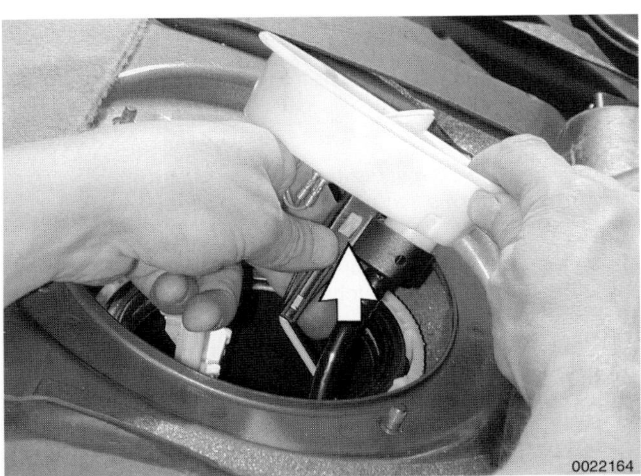
0022164

◀ Once level sensor unit has been lifted partially out of tank, disconnect tank siphon hose by pressing in detent (**arrow**).

0022163

◀ Inspect siphon pump to make sure one-way valve (**arrow**) is in siphon hose.

NOTE —
Tank siphon pump removal is covered later.

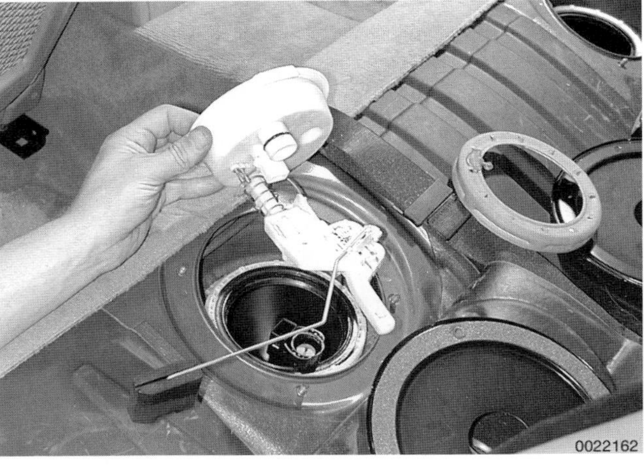
0022162

◀ Remove fuel level sender and set aside.

0022157

◄ Inspect bottom of tank to make sure lower siphon hose (**arrow**) is firmly engaged in tank baffle.

– Installation is reverse of removal.
  - Attach tank siphon hose to sender unit firmly.
  - Use new sealing ring at tank collar.
  - Be sure that fuel sender float points in same direction as during removal.
  - Reconnect harness connector.
  - Fill tank and check for leaks by running engine.

– After finishing repairs but before starting engine, fill fuel tank with at least 5 liters (1.5 gallons) of fuel.

> ***CAUTION —***
> *The fuel pump will be damaged if you run it without fuel.*

Siphon pump, removing and installing (MS 42.0, MS 43.0 and MS S54)

The fuel compensating siphon pump equalizes fuel level between the two fuel tank lobes.

– Drain fuel tank as described later.

> ***WARNING —***
> *Fuel may be spilled. Do not smoke or work near heaters or other fire hazards.*

– Remove left and right fuel level sensors as described earlier.

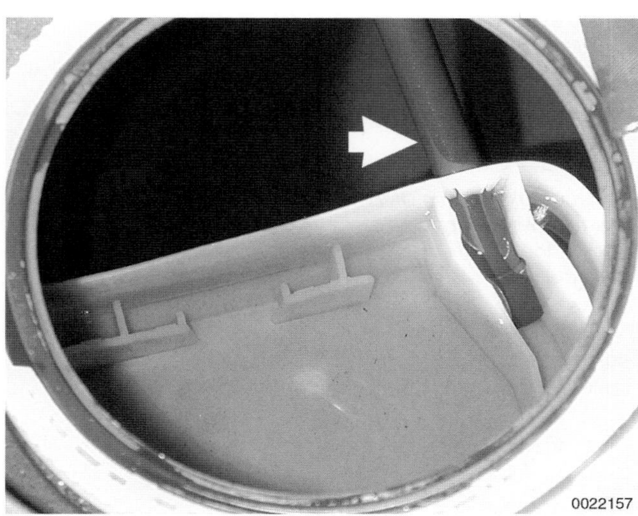
0022157

◄ Working in left tank opening, detach lower siphon hose (**arrow**) from tank baffle and carefully remove siphon pump and hose assembly.

> ***CAUTION —***
> *Use care not to kink hose when removing.*

0022163

◄ Inspect siphon assembly to make sure one-way valve (**arrow**) is in siphon hose.

– Reinstallation is reverse of removal.
  - Inspect left bottom of tank (on inside) to make sure lower siphon hose is firmly engaged in tank baffle.
  - Attach tank siphon hose to left sender unit firmly.
  - Use new sealing ring at tank collars.
  - Be sure that fuel sender floats point in same direction as during removal.
  - Reconnect harness connectors.
  - Before starting engine, fill fuel tank with at least 5 liters (1.5 gallons) of fuel.
  - Check for leaks by running engine.

> ***CAUTION —***
> *The fuel pump will be damaged if you run it without fuel.*

FUEL TANK AND FUEL LINES

The plastic fuel tank is mounted beneath the center of the car (beneath the rear seat). Mounted in the fuel tank are the fuel pump and fuel level sending units. Connecting lines for the evaporative emission control system and expansion tank are also attached to the tank.

Fuel tank capacity for E46 models

- Tank capacity .63 liters (16.6 gal)
- Reserve capacity . . . . .5 liters (1.3 gal)

Fuel tank, draining (MS 42.0, MS 43.0 and MS S54)

The fuel tank should be drained into a safe storage unit using an approved fuel pumping device.

WARNING —

- *Before draining tank, be sure that all hot components, such as the exhaust system, are completely cooled down.*
- *Fuel may be spilled. Do not smoke or work near heaters or other fire hazards.*

NOTE —

Models equipped with DME MS 45.1 use a sealed, stainless steel fuel tank with intergrated fuel pump and fuel pressure regulator. Due to the nature of their construction, these tanks cannot be drained.

– Start engine and allow to run 10 - 15 seconds to fill fuel compensating siphon assembly. This will allow both lobes of fuel tank to be drawn off through fuel filler pipe.

– Disconnect negative (–) cable from battery.

CAUTION —

Prior to disconnecting the battery, read the battery disconnection cautions given at the front of this manual on page viii.

– Remove fuel tank filler cap.

– Slide suction hose into filler neck about 130 cm (55 in.), twisting as necessary. Withdraw fuel into storage unit.

– Monitor fuel level reduction in both lobes:

- Remove rear seat cushion and access both fuel tank sender harness connectors.
- Use multimeter to measure resistance at both senders. Resistance should drop as fuel level drops.

– If siphoning mechanism is faulty, drain left tank lobe separately by removing sender cover and pumping fuel directly out of left lobe.

– Remove suction hose from tank filler neck carefully to avoid damaging filler neck baffle plate.

– After finishing repairs but before starting engine, fill fuel tank with at least 5 liters (1.5 gallons) of fuel.

> ***CAUTION —***
> *The fuel pump will be damaged if you run it without fuel.*

Fuel tank, removing and installing (MS 42.0, MS 43.0 and MS S54)

– Remove fuel tank filler cap and drain tank as described under **Fuel tank, removing and installing (MS 451.)**.

– Disconnect negative (–) cable from battery.

> ***CAUTION —***
> *Prior to disconnecting the battery, read the battery disconnection cautions in* **001 Warnings and Cautions**.

– Remove rear seat bottom cushion. Peel forward lip of carpet from beneath seat cushion and carefully peel back insulation to expose fuel tank access cover on left and right sides.

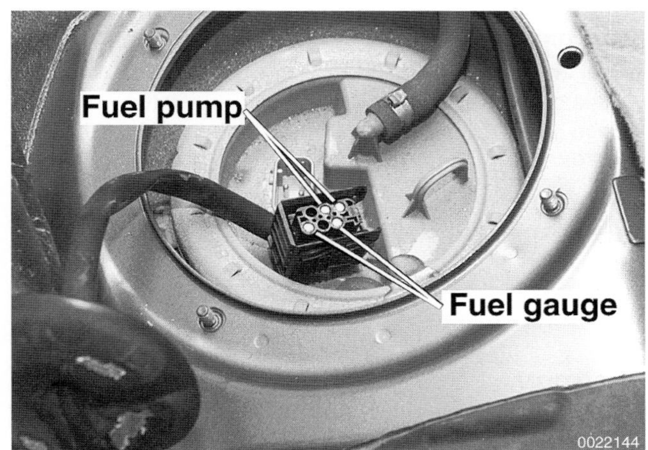

◄ Disconnect right side supply hose.

– Disconnect harness connector from tank sender unit by sliding lock back, then lifting connector.

– Detach left side return hose and electrical harness connector.

– Working inside car, disconnect parking brake cable ends from parking brake lever. See **340 Brakes**.

– Lift car and support safely.

> ***CAUTION —***
> *Make sure the car is stable and well supported at all times. Use a professional automotive lift or jack stands designed for the purpose. A floor jack is not adequate support.*

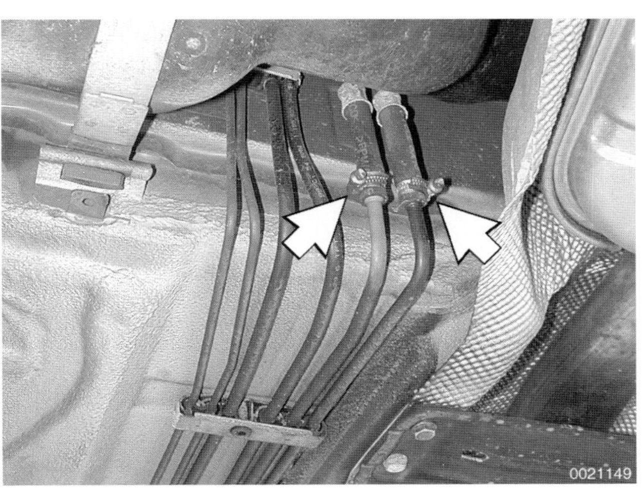

– Remove complete exhaust system and heat shield. See **180 Exhaust System**.

– Remove drive shaft. See **260 Driveshaft**.

◄ Working underneath car, pinch off supply and return fuel hoses (**arrows**) before disconnecting from rigid metal lines.

– Remove plastic trim pieces from under fuel tank and rocker panels.

– Pull parking brake cables backward away from bottom of fuel tank, disengaging them from guide tubes as needed.

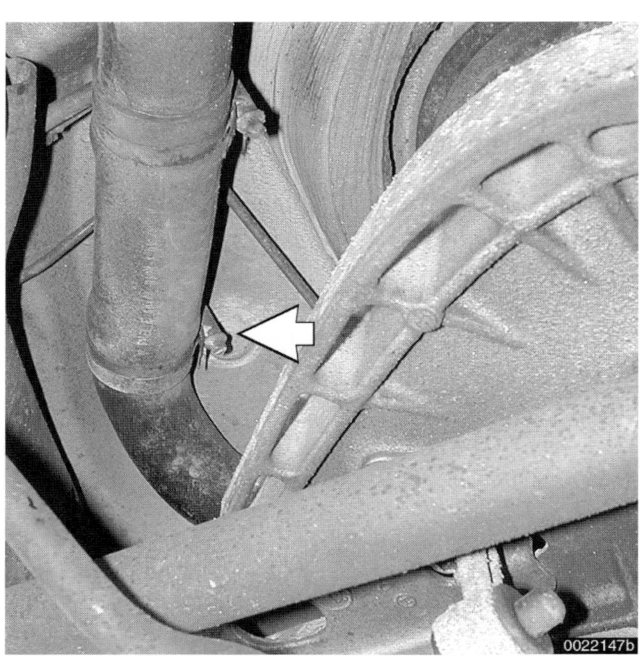

◀ Working underneath car, loosen hose clamp and disconnect filler pipe from tank.

– Support tank from below. Remove tank strap mounting bolts. Lower and remove tank, disconnecting right side vent and other hoses/electrical connectors as necessary.

– Installation is reverse of removal.

- Always use new seals, gaskets, O-rings, and hose clamps.
- Inspect hoses and replace any that are chafed, dried out or cracked.
- Inspect heat shield and replace if corroded.
- Inspect rubber buffers and liners on fuel tank, support straps and on underside of body. Replace rubber parts that are hardened or damaged.

– After finishing repairs but before starting engine, fill fuel tank with at least 5 liters (1.5 gallons) of fuel.

> ***CAUTION—***
> - *The fuel pump will be damaged if you run it without fuel.*
> - *If the filler neck has been removed from the body, be sure to reattach the neck grounding screw (where applicable). Check electrical resistance between the ground tab and wheel hub. The resistance should be no higher than 0.6 ohms.*

Tightening torques

- Fuel tank to body (M8 bolt) . . . . 23 Nm (17 ft-lb)
- Hose clamp 8 - 13 mm dia . . . . 2 Nm (18 in-lb)
- Hose clamp 13 - 16 mm dia. . . . . 3 Nm (27 in-lb)
- Hose clamp 42 - 48 mm dia. . . . . 4 Nm (36 in-lb)

Fuel tank, removing and installing (MS 45.1)

– Disconnect negative (–) cable from battery.

> ***CAUTION—***
> *Prior to disconnecting the battery, read the battery disconnection cautions given at the front of this manual on page viii.*

– Remove rear seats, see **520 Seats**. Peel forward lip of carpet from beneath seat cushion and carefully peel back insulation to expose fuel tank access cover.

– Remove exhaust system from catalyst back, see **180 Exhaust System**.

– Remove driveshaft, see **260 Driveshafts**.

– Remove rear differential, see **331 Rear Axle Final Drive**.

– Remove right rear fender liner.

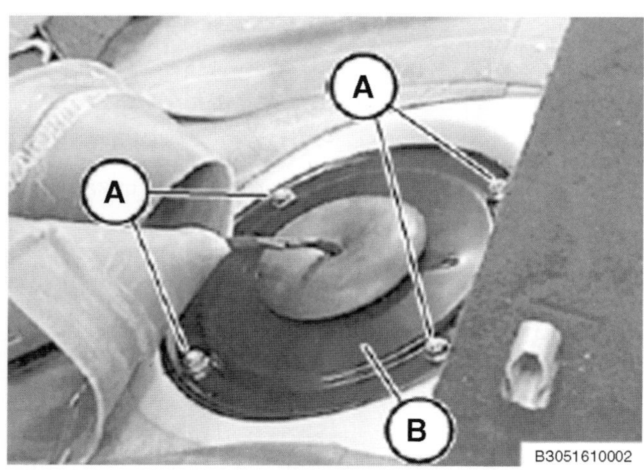

◀ Release nuts (**A**) and remove cover (**B**).

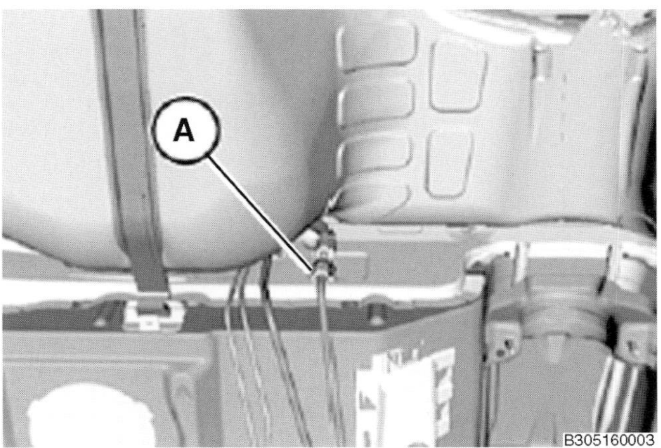

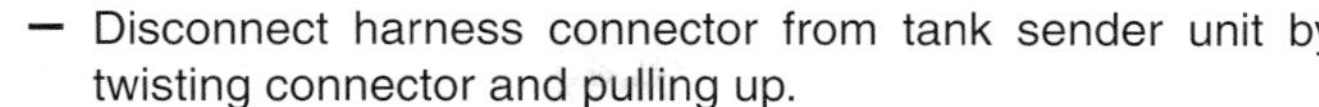

– Disconnect harness connector from tank sender unit by twisting connector and pulling up.

◄ Working underneath vehicle, disconnect fuel line (**A**).

> ***WARNING —***
> *Fuel will be discharged. Wrap a shop towel around the fuel line fitting when disconnecting the fuel line. Do not smoke or work near heaters or other fire hazards. Keep an approved fire extinguisher handy.*

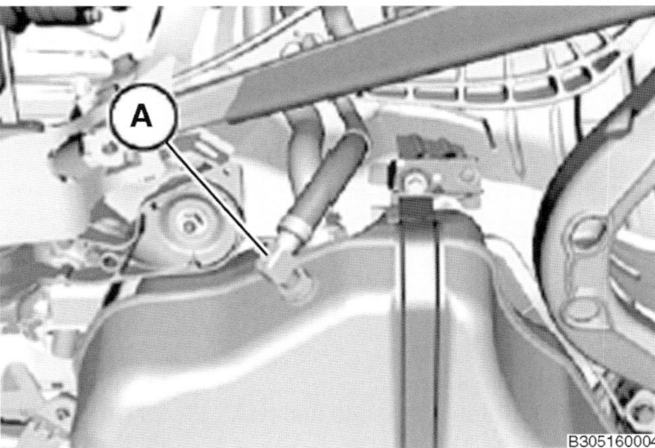

◄ Disconnect vent line (**A**) from fuel tank.

◄ Remove fuel filler pipe (**arrows**).

– Support fuel tank with transmission jack or other suitable lift.

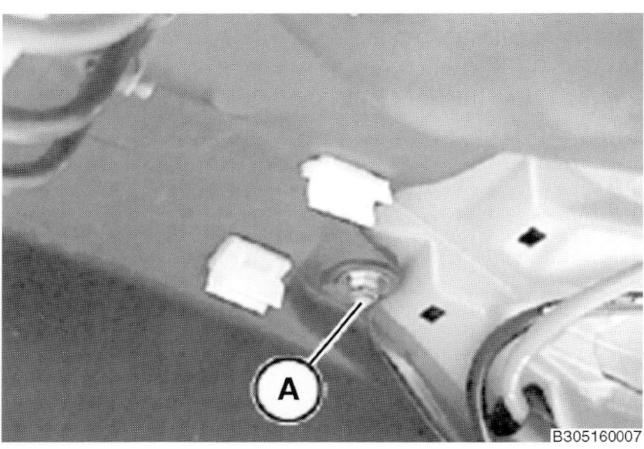

Remove fuel tank retaining bolt (**A**).

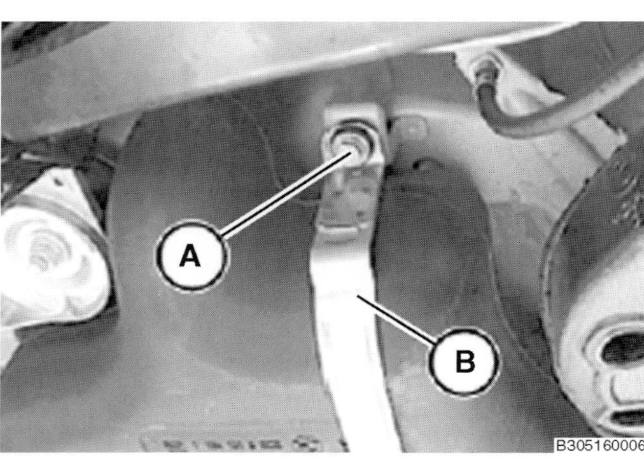

Remove retaining bolts (**A**) at left and right fuel tank straps (**B**).

– Lower fuel tank.

– Installation is reverse of removal.

Tightening torques

- Fuel tank to body .... 19 Nm(14 ft-lb)
- Tension strap to body .... 19 Nm(14 ft-lb)
- Fuel filler pipe to body................. 4 Nm (3 ft-lb)
- Feed line to fuel tank.................. 26 Nm(19 ft-lb)
- Carbon canister vent line to fuel tank .... 26 Nm(19 ft-lb)
- Tank vent line to filler pipe............. 26 Nm(19 ft-lb)

Fuel expansion tank, removing and installing (MS 42.0, MS 43.0 and MS S54)

– Raise rear end of car and support safely.

> ***CAUTION —***
> *Make sure the car is stable and well supported at all times. Use a professional automotive lift or jack stands designed for the purpose. A floor jack is not adequate support.*

– Remove right rear wheel and wheel housing inner shield.

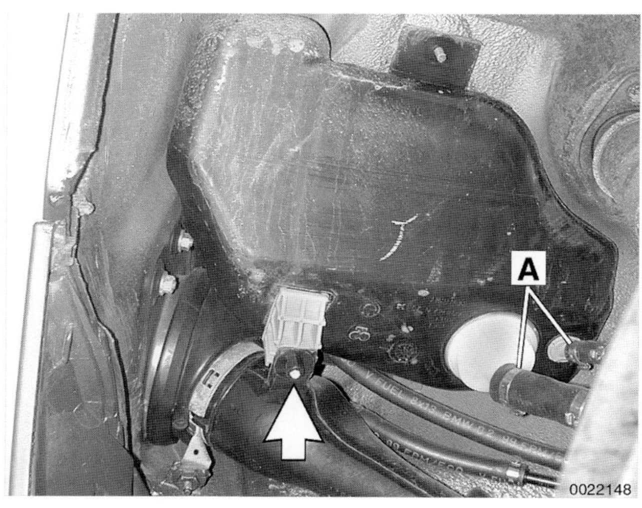

Remove plastic nut (**arrow**) and detach hoses (**A**).

Pull expansion tank slightly forward and tilt down. Working at top of tank, detach hose (**arrow**) and remove tank.

– Installation is reverse of removal. Use new hose clamps.

Tightening torques
- Hose clamp 8 - 13 mm dia . . . . 2 Nm (18 in-lb)
- Hose clamp 13 - 16 mm dia. . . . . 3 Nm (27 in-lb)
- Hose clamp 42 - 48 mm dia. . . . . 4 Nm (36 in-lb)

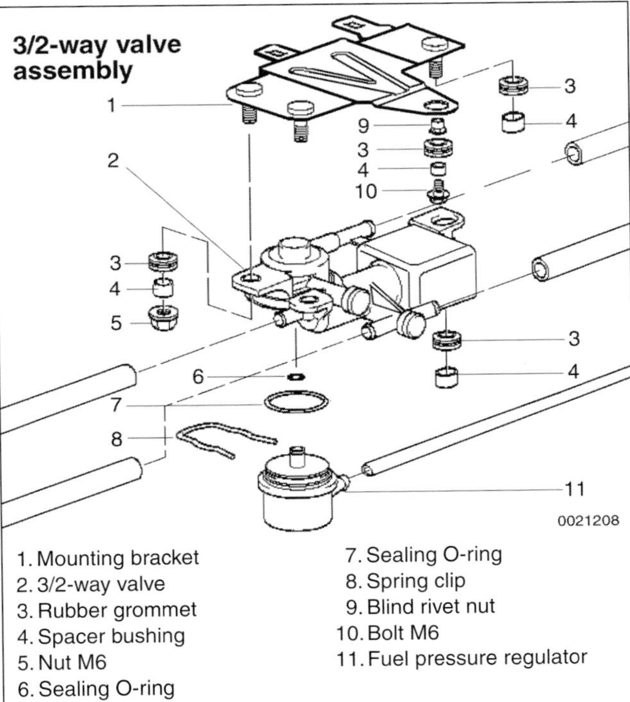

1. Mounting bracket
2. 3/2-way valve
3. Rubber grommet
4. Spacer bushing
5. Nut M6
6. Sealing O-ring
7. Sealing O-ring
8. Spring clip
9. Blind rivet nut
10. Bolt M6
11. Fuel pressure regulator

Running losses (3/2-way) valve, removing and installing (DME MS 42.0)

The running losses (3/2-way) valve in DME MS 42.0 systems is located below the driver's seat underneath the car, just ahead of the fuel filter. A protective cover shields fuel system components in this location from road hazards.

The ECM controls the operation of the 3/2 way valve (pulse-width modulated). The valve's solenoid is energized for 20 seconds on engine start up to supply full fuel volume to the fuel rail. After 20 seconds, the solenoid is deactivated and sprung closed (the by-pass is opened). This reduces the amount of fuel circulating through the fuel rail and diverts the excess to return through the fuel pressure regulator.

The fuel injectors are supplied with regulated fuel, but the returned fuel by-passes the fuel rail. This lowers the temperature and amount of vaporization that takes place in the fuel tank. The valve is also activated briefly if an engine misfire is detected. This provides full fuel flow through the fuel rail to determine if the misfire was caused by a lean fuel condition. The valve is monitored by the ECM for faults.

To remove and install:

– Using BMW scan tool DIS or MoDiC or equivalent, access ECM fault memory.

– Turn off ignition.

– Raise car and support safely.

– Working under car, below driver's seat, remove protective tray covering 3/2- way valve assembly.

– Clamp off all fuel lines at 3/2-way valve using appropriate fuel line clamping tools.

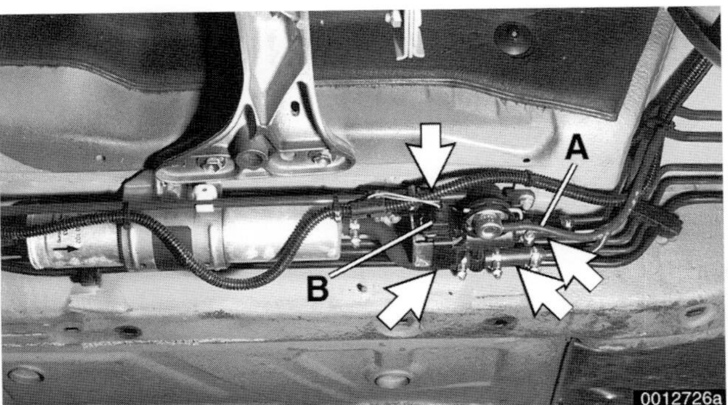

To remove 3/2-way valve:
- Remove vacuum hose (**A**) from fuel pressure regulator.
- Disconnect electrical harness connector (**B**) from valve.
- Remove hose clamps and disconnect fuel lines (**arrows**).
- Remove M6 mounting nuts and lower 3/2-way valve.

> ***WARNING —***
> *Fuel will be spilled. Do not smoke or work near heaters or other fire hazards.*

– Installation is reverse of removal. Use new hose clamps.

NOTE —
Be sure to install protective cover and seals correctly to keep moisture and road dirt out of underbody fuel system components.

Tightening torques
- Hose clamp 10 - 16 mm dia . . . . 2 Nm (18 in-lb)
- Hose clamp 18 mm dia. . . . . 3 Nm (27 in-lb)

Leak detection pump (with activated carbon canister), removing and installing (MS 42.0, MS 43.0 and MS S54)

– Raise rear end of car and support safely.

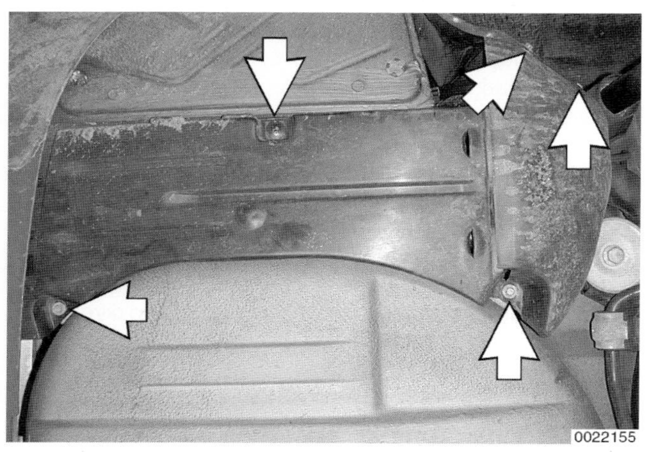

Working underneath rear of car, remove carbon canister protective panels by removing retaining nuts and screws (**arrows**).

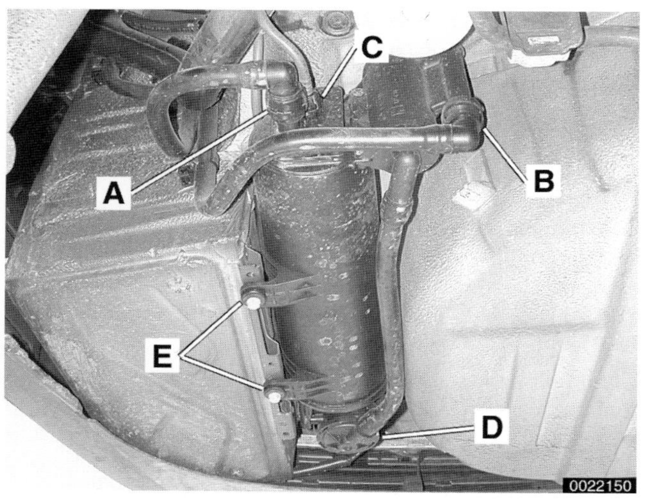

Remove fuel tank leak detection unit/carbon canister:

- Pinch and remove quick-disconnect fittings at hose to expansion tank (**A**), intake line to air filter housing (**B**), and scavenging air line (**C**).
- Detach electrical harness connector (**D**) from fuel tank leak detection unit.
- Remove mounting screws (**E**) and lower canister with fuel tank leak detection unit.

– Installation is reverse of removal.

Tightening torques
- Hose clamp 8 - 13 mm dia . . . . 2 Nm (18 in-lb)
- Hose clamp 13 - 16 mm dia. . . . . 3 Nm (27 in-lb)

Fuel tank leakage diagnosis module, removing and installing (MS 45.1)

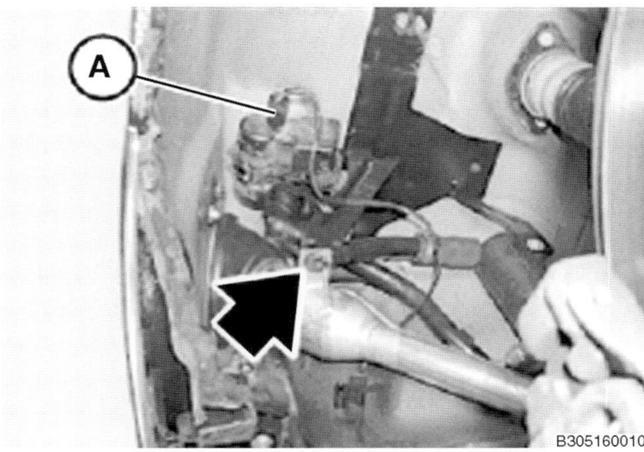

– Raise rear end of car and support safely.

– Remove right rear wheel and fender liner.

Remove connector (**A**) and remove retaining nut (**arrow**).

– Remove module with bracket and dust filter.

– Disconnect vent lines, and remove retaining screws from module mounting bracket.

– Installation is reverse of removal.

Tightening torques
- Filler pipe to body . . . . 4 Nm (35 in-lb)
- Bracket to diagnosis module. . . . . 2 Nm (18 in-lb)

Activated carbon canister/, removing and installing (MS 45.1)

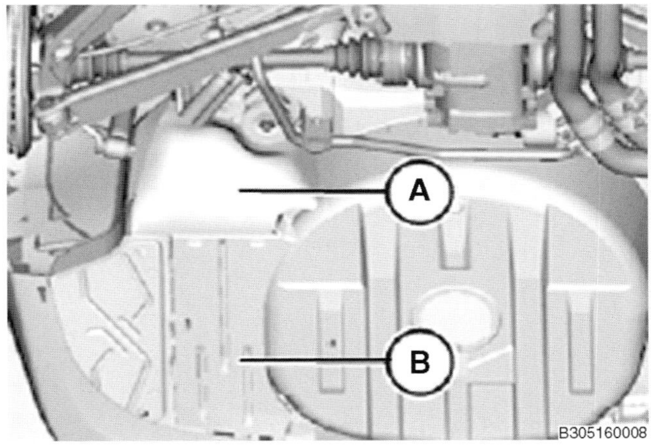

– Raise rear end of car and support safely.

Working underneath rear of car, remove carbon canister protective panels (**A**) and (**B**) by removing retaining nuts and screws.

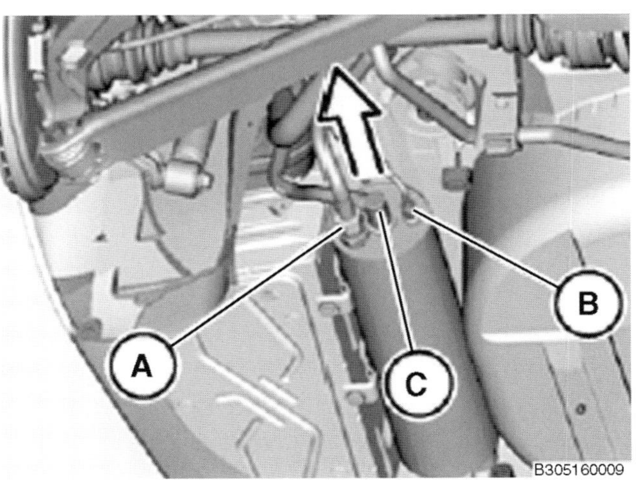

Remove carbon canister/fuel tank leak detection unit:

- Release line to fuel filler pipe (**A**), vent line to fuel tank (**B**), and vent line to leak detection pump (**C**).
- Remove mounting screws and lower canister.

– Installation is reverse of removal.

Tightening torques
- Carbon canister to body . . . . 9 Nm (7 ft-lb)

170 Radiator and Cooling System

TABLES

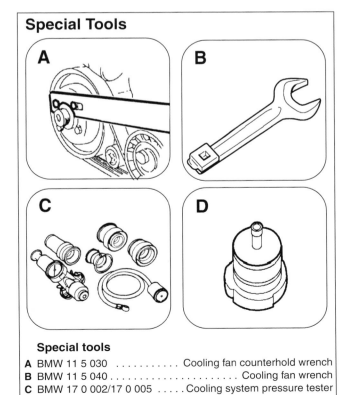

Special Tools

A

B

C

D

Special tools

A BMW 11 5 030 . . . . Cooling fan counterhold wrench
B BMW 11 5 040 . . . . Cooling fan wrench
C BMW 17 0 002/17 0 005 . . . . . Cooling system pressure tester
D BMW 17 0 007 . . . . Expansion tank cap test adapter

GENERAL

This section covers component repair information for the engine cooling system.

The E46 cooling system uses a centrifugal-type belt-driven coolant pump, an electric primary cooling fan, and an electrically heated thermostat (except M3 models). The cooling fan and the thermostat (except M3 models) are controlled and monitored by the DME engine management system. Therefore, cooling system faults can be diagnosed using an appropriate diagnostic scan tool.

NOTE —
E46 M3 models use a conventional non-heated thermostat.

Heater valve replacement is covered in **640 Heating and Air Conditioning**.

Special tools

Special tools are necessary for fan clutch removal and pressure testing the cooling system.

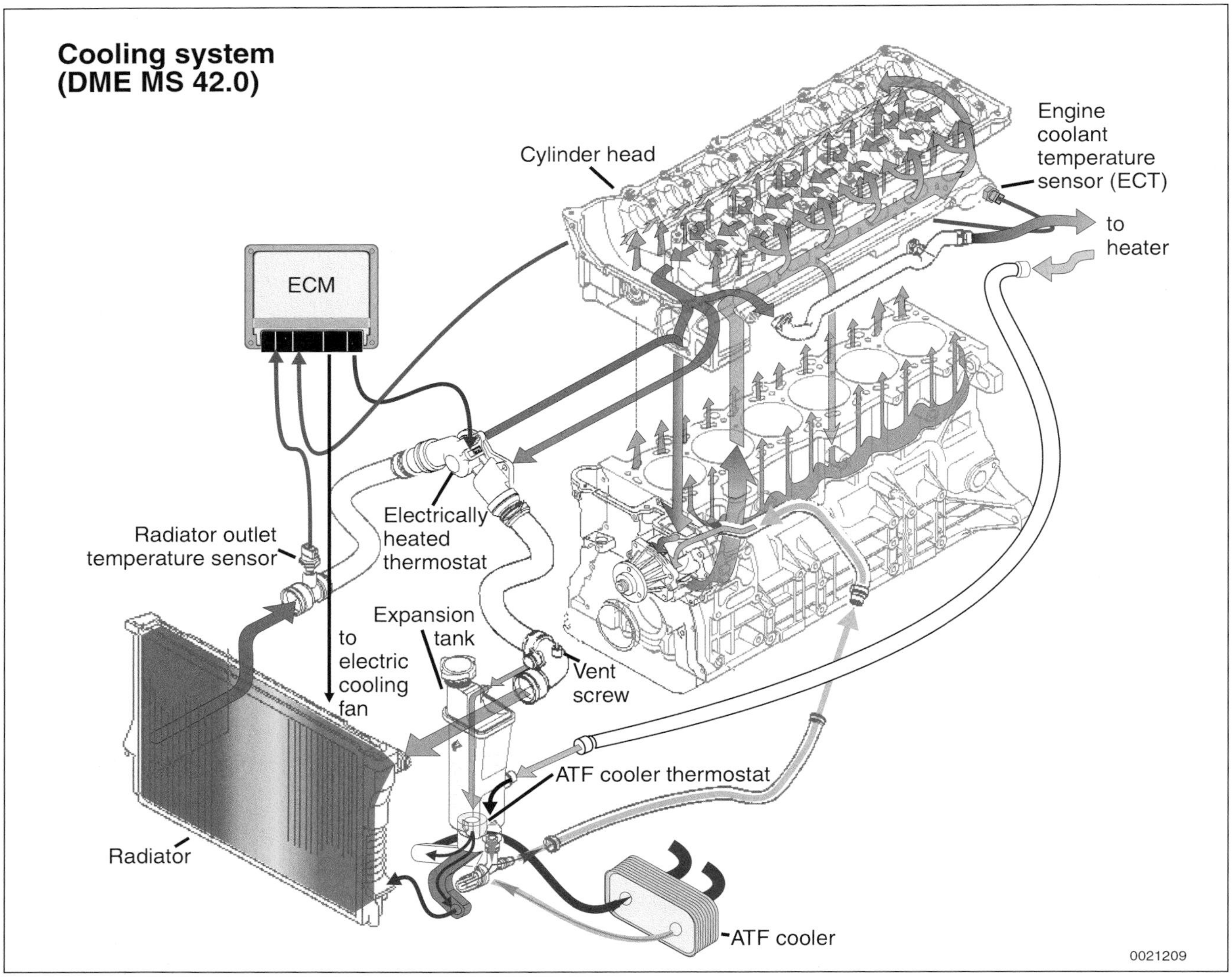

Cooling system (DME MS 42.0)

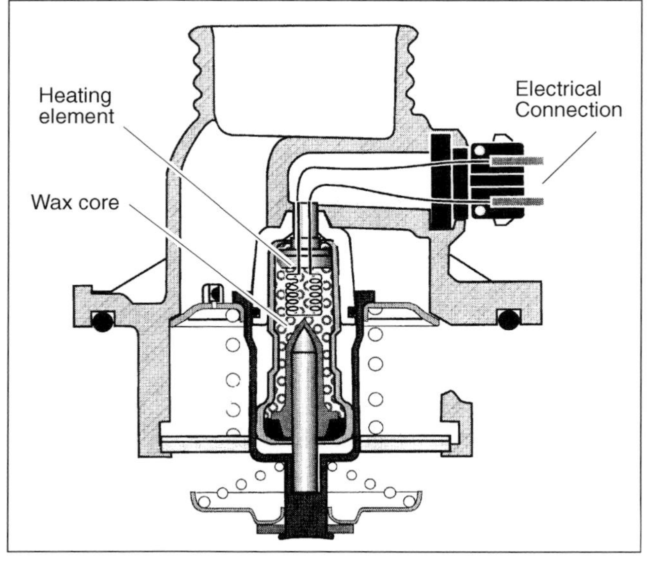

Coolant pump

A centrifugal-type coolant pump is mounted to the front of the engine. The belt-driven pump circulates coolant through the system whenever the engine is running.

Electrically heated thermostat

On all models except M3 models, an electrically heated thermostat regulates the engine coolant temperature and is controlled by the DME control module. The heated thermostat allows the engine to be operated at higher temperatures at idle and at part throttle. Having the ability to control the engine coolant temperature electronically results in improved emissions and performance. Problems with the heated thermostat can be diagnosed using a BMW diagnostic scan tool.

Radiator and expansion tank

The radiator is a crossflow design. An expansion tank provides for coolant expansion at higher temperatures and easy monitoring of the coolant level.

On cars with automatic transmission, ATF is circulated through an additional heat exchanger (ATF cooler).

Cooling fan (primary)

The are two cooling fan configurations used on the cars covered by this manual, depending on transmission application.

On cars with **automatic transmissions**, the main fan is electric and mounted on the bumper side of the radiator. The fan is controlled by the DME control module via the output final stage. Additionally a belt-driven fan via a viscous fluid coupling (clutch) is attached to the front of the coolant pump. The fan clutch controls the speed of the fan based on engine compartment temperature.

On cars with **manual transmissions**, a single multi-speed electric cooling fan is used. The fan is mounted on the engine side of the radiator and controlled by the DME control module via the output final stage.

On both configurations, the output final stage is mounted on the fan housing, next to the fan motor. The fan is operated using a pulse width modulated (PWM) signal and is protected by a 50-amp fuse. Electric fan activation is based on the following inputs to the ECM:

- Radiator outlet temperature
- Catalyst temperature (calculated temperature)
- Vehicle speed
- Battery voltage
- A/C pressure (calculated pressure)

When the vehicle is first started, The ECM activates the electric fan briefly at 20% of its maximum speed, then switches off. This is for diagnostic monitoring. The voltage generated by the fan when it slows down (acting as a generator) must match the stored 'rpm' values in the fan power output stage to confirm that the fan is operating correctly.

NOTE —

- *If the ECM stored a cooling fan fault, check that the fan is not seized and that is spins freely.*
- *When A/C is switched ON, the electric fan is not immediately turned on.*
- *After the engine is switched OFF, the fan may continue to run at varying speeds for up to 10 minutes, based on calculated catalyst temperature.*

Warnings and cautions

The following warnings and cautions should be observed when working on the cooling system.

> ***WARNING —***
>
> - *At normal operating temperature the cooling system is pressurized. Allow the system to cool as long as possible before opening—a minimum of an hour—then release the cap slowly to allow safe release of pressure.*
> - *Releasing the cooling system pressure lowers the coolant boiling point and the coolant may boil suddenly. Use heavy gloves and wear eye and face protection to guard against scalding.*
> - *Use extreme care when draining and disposing of engine coolant. Coolant is poisonous and lethal to humans and pets. Pets are attracted to coolant because of its sweet smell and taste. Consult a veterinarian immediately if coolant is ingested by an animal.*

> ***CAUTION —***
>
> - *Avoid adding cold water to the coolant while the engine is hot or overheated. If it is necessary to add coolant to a hot system, do so only with the engine running and coolant pump turning.*
> - *To avoid excess silicate gel precipitation in the cooling system and loss of cooling capacity, use BMW coolant or equivalent low silicate antifreeze.*
> - *If oil enters the cooling system, the radiator, expansion tank and heating circuit must be flushed with cleaning agent. BMW recommends removal of the radiator and expansion tank to flush.*
> - *When working on the cooling system, cover the alternator to protect it against coolant drips.*
> - *Prior to disconnecting the battery, read the battery disconnection cautions given at the front of this manual on page viii.*

TROUBLESHOOTING

Begin the diagnosis of cooling system problems with a thorough visual inspection. If no visual faults are found, it is recommend that the DME system be checked for stored diagnostic fault codes (DTCs) using BMW scan tools DIS (Diagnostic Information System) or MoDiC (Mobile Diagnostic Computer) or an aftermarket equivalent.

Common cooling system faults can be grouped into one of four categories:

- Cooling system leaks
- Poor coolant circulation
- Radiator cooling fan faults
- Electrical/electronic faults

Be sure to check the condition and tension of the coolant pump drive belt. Check hoses for cracks or softness. Check clamps for looseness. Check the coolant level and check for evidence of coolant leaks from the engine.

Check that the radiator fins are not blocked with dirt or debris. Clean the radiator using low-pressure water or compressed air. Blow outward, from the engine side out.

To check coolant pump:

- Lever tensioner clockwise using wrench on hex (**large arrow**) and slip belt off pulley.
- Firmly grasp opposite sides of pulley and check for play in all directions.
- Spin pulley and check that shaft runs smoothly without play.

NOTE —

The coolant provides lubrication for the pump shaft, so an occasional drop of coolant leaking from the pump is acceptable. If coolant drips steadily from the vent hole, the pump should be replaced.

The cooling system becomes pressurized at normal operating temperature, which raises the boiling point of the coolant. Leaks may prevent the system from becoming pressurized, allowing the coolant to boil at a lower temperature. If visual evidence is inconclusive, a cooling system pressure test can help to pinpoint hard-to-find leaks.

If the cooling system is full of coolant and holds pressure, the next most probable causes of overheating are:

- Faulty radiator fan or DME control circuit. Use an appropriate scan tool to interrogate the DME control module for faults.
- Loose or worn drive belt.
- Failed thermostat or coolant pump impeller. Some pumps may be fitted with plastic impellers.
- Clogged/plugged radiator or coolant passages.

Cooling system pressure test

A cooling system pressure test is used to check for internal leaks. Some of the common sources of internal leaks are a faulty cylinder head gasket, a cracked cylinder head, or a cracked cylinder block.

To do a cooling system pressure test, a special pressure tester is needed.

WARNING —

At normal operating temperature the cooling system is pressurized. Allow the system to cool before opening. Release the cap slowly to allow safe release of pressure.

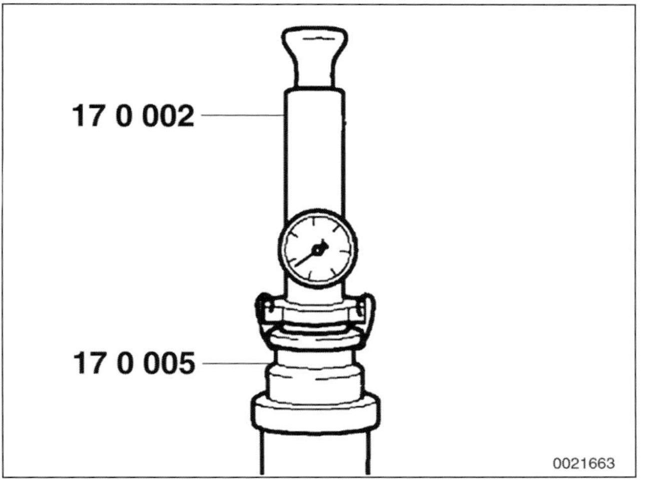

With engine cold, install pressure tester (BMW special tools 17 0 002/17 0 005 or equivalent) to expansion tank. Pressurize system to specification listed in **Table A**.

- Pressure should not drop more than 0.1 bar (1.45 psi) for at least two minutes.
- If pressure drops rapidly and there is no sign of external leakage, cylinder head gasket may be faulty. Perform com-

pression and leak-down tests as described in **100 Engine—General**.

- Also test expansion tank cap using pressure tester and correct adapter (BMW special tool 17 0 007 or equivalent). Replace faulty cap or cap gasket.

Table a. Cooling system test pressures

Component	Test pressure
Radiator	1.5 bar (21.75 psi)
Radiator cap	2 bar (29 psi)

> ***CAUTION —***
> *Exceeding the specified test pressure could damage the radiator or other system components.*

Combustion chamber leak test

— If you suspect that combustion chamber pressure is leaking into the cooling system past the cylinder head gasket, use an exhaust gas analyzer to test the vapors rising from the coolant at the expansion tank.

> ***CAUTION —***
> - *Use an extension tube above the reservoir neck to maintain distance between the top of the coolant and the gas analyzer nozzle. The gas analyzer is easily damaged if it is allowed to inhale liquid coolant.*
> - *While running engine to check for causes of overheating, observe coolant temperature carefully in order to avoid engine damage.*

Thermostat, checking

If the engine overheats or runs too cool and no other cooling system tests indicate trouble, the thermostat may be faulty.

On cars with an electrically heated thermostat, check for DME diagnostic fault codes (DTCs) using BMW scan tools DIS or MoDiC or equivalent. DTCs pertaining to cooling system malfunctions are listed in **Table b**. See also **On-Board Diagnostics** at the back of this manual.

Table b. Cooling system fault codes

BMW fault code	Explanation	Possible cause(s)
10	Engine coolant temperature out of predefined range	Faulty thermostat or cooling fan. Faulty wiring to cooling fan or thermostat.
222	Insufficient coolant temperature signal to permit closed loop operation	Faulty thermostat. Faulty thermostat electrical circuit

COOLING SYSTEM SERVICE

Coolant, draining and filling

> ***WARNING —***
> *Allow the cooling system to cool before opening or draining the cooling system.*

– Raise front of car and support safely.

> ***CAUTION —***
> *Make sure the car is stable and well supported at all times. Use a professional automotive lift or jack stands designed for the purpose. A floor jack is not adequate support.*

– Remove splash shield from under engine.

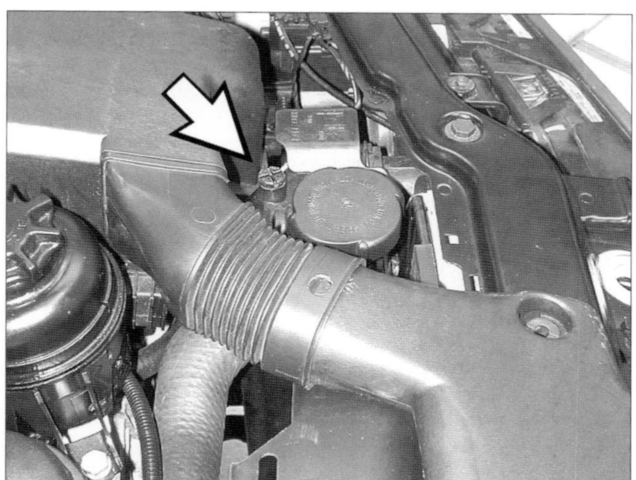

0022349

◄ Loosen radiator bleed screw at top radiator fitting (**arrow**).

– Remove cap from radiator expansion tank. Set temperature controls to full warm.

– Place 3-gallon pail underneath radiator.

0021822

◄ Remove drain plug (**arrow**) on bottom of radiator.

> ***WARNING —***
> *Coolant is poisonous. It is especially lethal to pets. Clean up spills immediately and rinse the area with water.*

◀ Place empty 3-gallon pail underneath exhaust side of engine block. Loosen and remove engine block coolant drain plug (**arrow**).

NOTE —
The block drain plug is located on the exhaust side of the engine block at cylinder 2.

– Reinstall radiator and engine block drain plugs using new sealing washers.

– Before refilling radiator:
  - Switch ignition to ON.
  - Set temperature controls to full warm.
  - Set blower control to low.

– Using a coolant mixture of 50% antifreeze and 50% distilled water, fill expansion tank *slowly*. Continue until coolant emerges from bleed screw. Cooling system capacity is listed in **Table c**.

NOTE —
- *Be sure radiator bleed screw is loose when filling cooling system.*
- *Tap water may cause corrosion of radiator, engine and coolant hoses.*
- *Coolant can often be reused provided it is clean and less than two years old. Do not reuse coolant when replacing damaged engine parts. Contaminated coolant may damage the engine or cooling system.*

Table c. Cooling system capacity

Engine	Capacity
M52 TU/M54	8.4 liters (8.8 qt.)
S54	10.0 liters (10.6 qt.)

Tightening torques
- Engine block drain plug to block . . . . 25 Nm (18 ft-lb)
- Radiator drain plug to radiator . . . 2 - 3 Nm (18 - 27 in-lb)

Cooling system, bleeding

Air may become trapped in the system during cooling system service. Trapped air can prevent proper coolant circulation. Whenever the coolant is drained and filled, the system should be bled of trapped air.

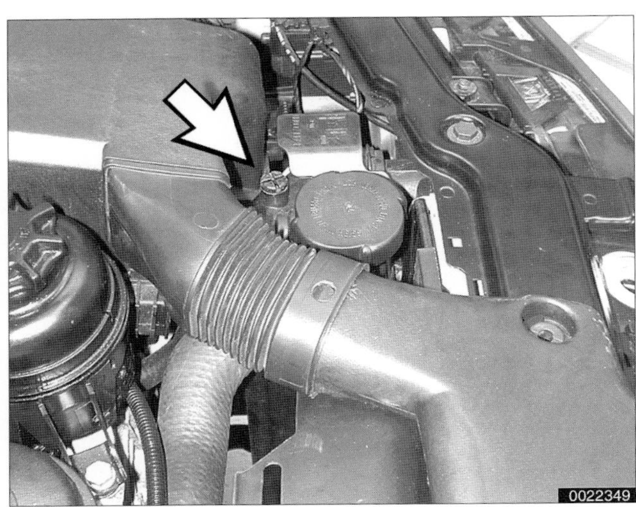

◀ Loosen bleed screw (**arrow**) on radiator expansion tank.

– Set temperature controls in passenger compartment to full warm, set blower to low setting and turn ignition to ON position (do *not* start engine).

– *Slowly* add coolant until it spills from bleed screw. When coolant spilling from bleed screws is free of air bubbles, tighten screw.

Run engine until it reaches operating temperature.

- After engine has cooled, recheck coolant level.
- Top up so that coolant level indicator is at MAX.

> ***CAUTION —***
> *Always use genuine BMW coolant or its equivalent to avoid the formation of harmful, clogging deposits in the cooling system. Use of other antifreeze solutions may be harmful to the cooling system.*

Tightening torque

- Radiator bleed screw . . . . 2.5 Nm (22 in-lb)

Cooling fan cowl, removing (models with automatic transmission)

To gain access to viscous clutch fan or electric fan at front of the engine:

- Remove expansion rivets (**arrows**) and remove intake duct.

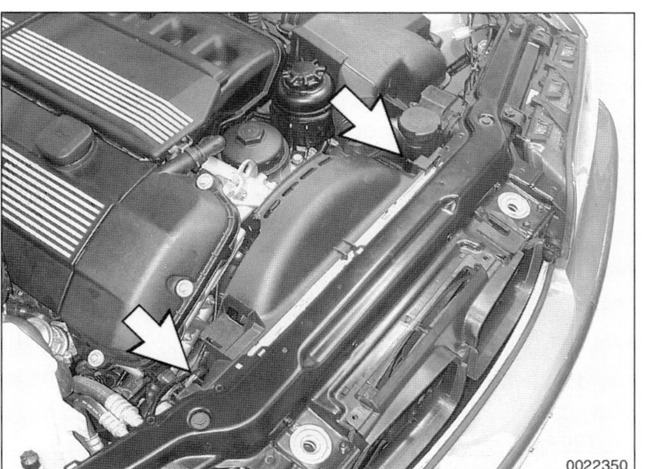

Working at top of fan shroud, remove screw and expansion rivet (**arrows**) holding fan shroud to radiator. Unclip or disconnect electrical connector(s) from right side of shroud.

> ***NOTE —***
> *Shroud is detached from radiator at this point but can only be removed later when fan and clutch assembly is removed.*

– Remove viscous clutch cooling fan, see following procedure.

Cooling fan cowl, removing (M3 models)

– Remove underbody splash shield.

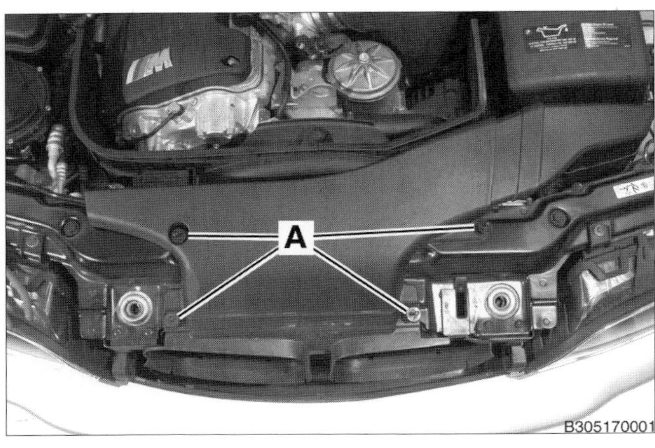

◀ Remove expansion rivets (**A**) and remove intake duct.

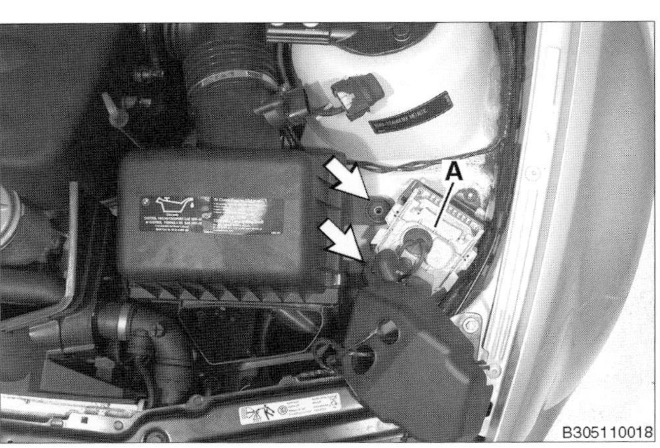

◀ Remove control unit for left xenon light (**A**) and remove screw securing air filter housing to body (**arrows**).

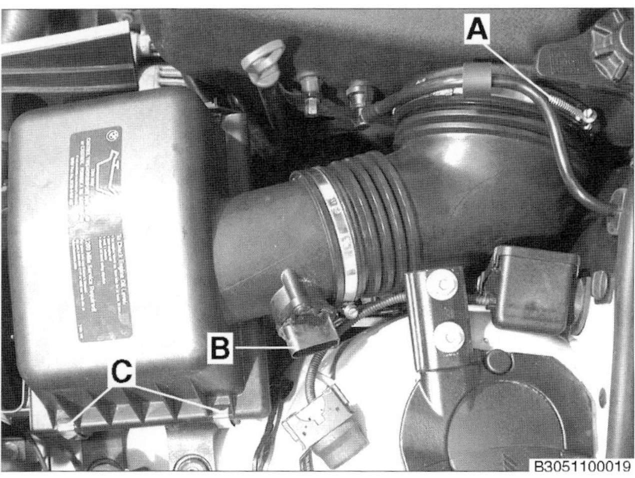

◀ Remove intake air filter housing

- Loosen hose clamp (**A**).
- Disconnect MAF sensor harness connector (**B**).
- Release air filter retainers (**C**).
- Lift top section of air filter housing up and rotate to disconnect intake hose from intake manifold and remove upper section of intake filter housing.
- Lift out air filter element.
- Remove lower section of intake filter housing towards top.

– Pry expansion rivets out of left and right air ducts. Lay left air duct (with coolant hose) aside.

– Remove radiator mounting screw at upper left corner of radiator, underneath cooling outlet neck.

– Remove viscous clutch cooling fan, see following procedure.

Viscous clutch cooling fan, replacing

B11183A

◄ Using 32 mm wrench (BMW special tool 11 5 040) on fan clutch nut (**arrow**), turn wrench quickly in a clockwise direction (working from front of car) to loosen. Spin fan off coolant pump.

NOTE —

- *The radiator cooling fan nut (32 mm wrench) has left-hand threads.*
- *If fan nut is difficult to loosen, use BMW special tool 11 5 030 to counterhold coolant pump pulley.*

— Lift fan and shroud together out of engine compartment.

— To replace fan clutch, remove fan mounting bolts and separate viscous clutch from fan.

— Installation is reverse of removal.

Tightening torques

- Clutch nut to coolant pump (left-hand threads)
  without BMW tool 11 5 040 . . . . 40 Nm (29 ft-lb)
  with BMW tool 11 5 040 . . . . 30 Nm (22 ft-lb)
- Fan to viscous clutch . . . . 10 Nm (89 in-lb)

Electric cooling fan, replacing (models with manual transmission)

On models with manual transmission, the primary cooling fan is electrically operated and is mounted on the engine side of the radiator.

— Remove air intake duct as described above.

0022350

◄ Working at top of fan shroud, remove screw and expansion rivet (**arrows**) holding fan shroud to radiator. Unclip or disconnect electrical connector(s) from right side of shroud.

— Lift fan assembly straight up and off radiator. If necessary, push center top area of fan shroud toward engine to unhook shroud from radiator crossmember.

— Fan can be separated from shroud on bench.

> ***CAUTION —***
> *Do not carry fan by the blades; it may disturb the balance.*

— Installation is reverse of removal.

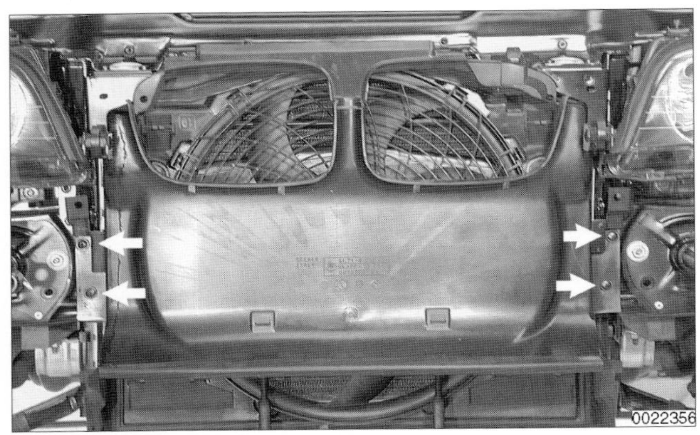

Electric cooling fan, replacing (models with automatic transmission)

The electric cooling fan on cars with automatic transmission is mounted behind the front bumper, in front of the A/C condenser.

- Remove air intake duct as described above.
- Remove front bumper. See **510 Exterior Trim, Bumpers**.
- Disconnect fan electrical connector (**arrow**) on right side of radiator shroud
- Pull out plastic expansion rivets (**arrows**) and remove cover from front of fan.
- Remove fan mounting nuts (**arrows**) and lift out fan.
- Installation is reverse of removal. Install front bumper. See **510 Exterior Trim, Bumpers**.

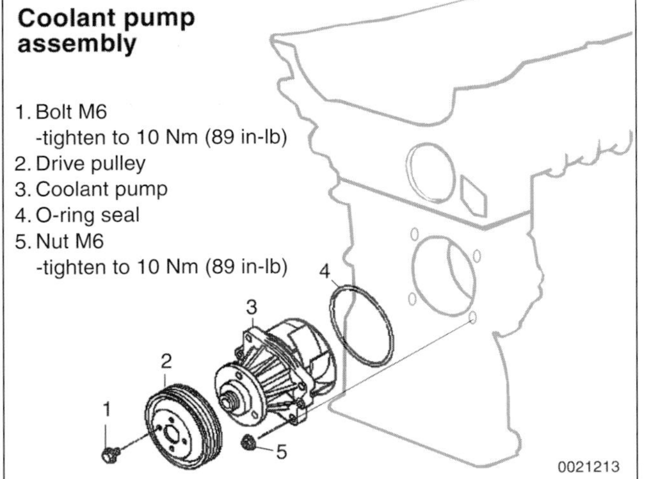

Coolant pump, replacing (except M3 models)

The engine coolant pump is mounted in the front of the engine in the timing chain cover.

- Drain cooling system as described earlier.

> ***WARNING —***
> *Allow cooling system to cool before opening or draining system.*

- Remove air intake duct, cooling fan and fan shroud as described earlier.

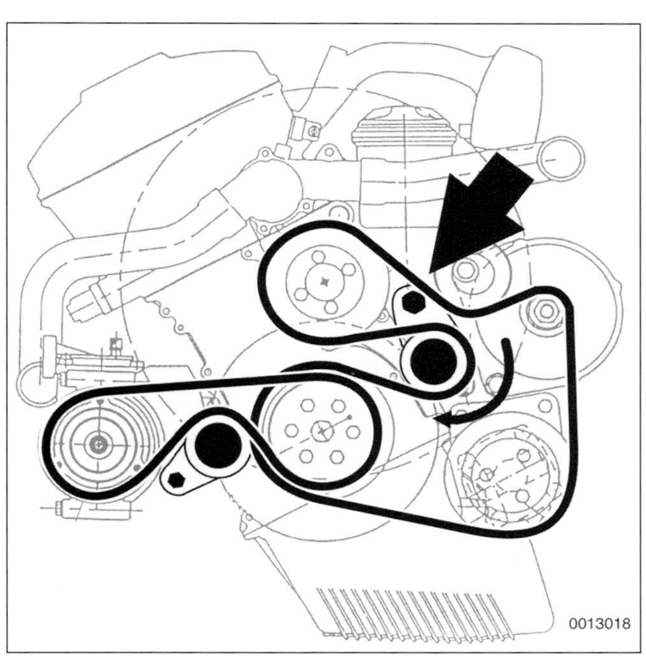

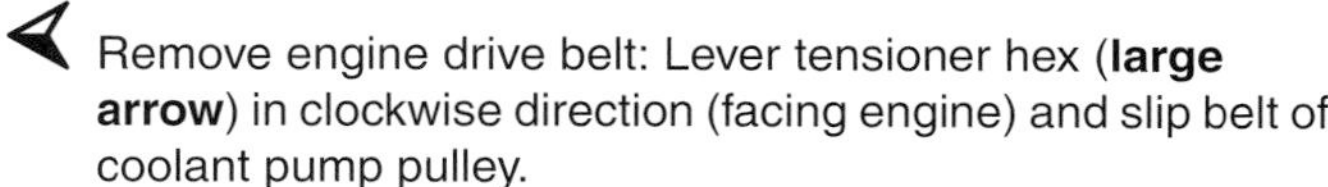

Remove engine drive belt: Lever tensioner hex (**large arrow**) in clockwise direction (facing engine) and slip belt off coolant pump pulley.

NOTE —
Mark direction of drive belt rotation if reusing belt.

- Remove coolant pump pulley bolts and remove pulley from pump.
- Remove pump mounting nuts (qty. 4).

NOTE —
The coolant pump is mounted on studs and retained by nuts.

Insert two M6 screws (**arrows**) in tapped bores and tighten uniformly until pump is free from timing chain cover. (Thermostat and hoses have been removed for visual access.)

- Installation is reverse of removal, noting the following:
  - Be sure to replace sealing O-ring and gaskets.
  - Coat O-ring with lubricant during installation.

Tightening torques
- Coolant pump to timing chain cover . . . . 10 Nm (89 in-lb)
- Coolant pump pulley to coolant pump. . . 10 Nm (89 in-lb)
- Engine block drain plug to block . . . . 25 Nm (18 ft-lb)
- Radiator drain plug to radiator . . . . . 2-3 Nm (18-27 in-lb)

Thermostat, replacing (except M3 models)

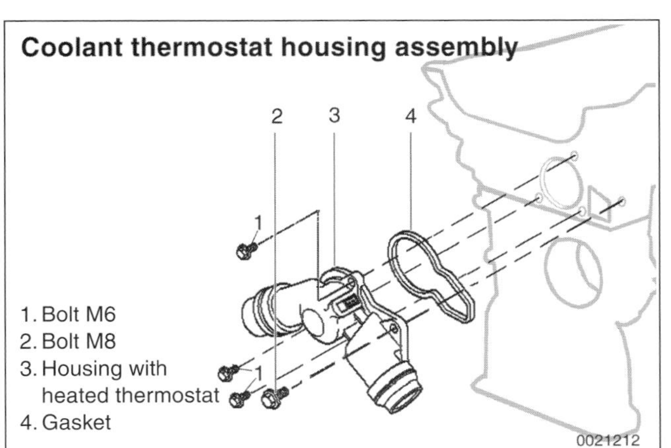

The electrically-heated thermostat is an integral part of the thermostat housing. The operation of the thermostat is monitored by the DME control module. If a faulty thermostat is suspected, the DME control module should be interrogated for stored fault codes using an appropriate scan tool.

- Drain radiator and engine block as described above under **Coolant, draining and filling**.

WARNING —
Allow cooling system to cool before opening or draining the system.

- Remove air intake duct, cooling fan and fan shroud as described earlier.

– Disconnect electrical harness connector from thermostat housing.

◄ Lever out retaining clips (**arrows**) and pull hose fittings off housing.

– Unbolt and remove thermostat housing from front of engine. Loosen nut at top of engine lifting eye to facilitate removal.

– Installation is reverse of removal, noting the following:

- Keep sealing faces free of oil.
- Use new sealing gasket.
- Fill system with coolant as described under **Coolant, draining and filling.**

Tightening torques
- Engine block drain plug to block . . . . 25 Nm (18 ft-lb)
- Radiator drain plug to radiator . . . 2 - 3 Nm (18 - 27 in-lb)

Coolant pump, replacing (M3 models)

– With engine cold, drain cooling system. See **Coolant, draining and filling** in this repair group.

> ***WARNING —***
> *At normal operating temperature the cooling system is pressurized. Allow the system to cool thoroughly (a minimum of one hour), then release the cooling system pressure cap slowly to allow safe release of pressure.*

> ***CAUTION —***
> *When working on the cooling system, cover the alternator to protect it against coolant drips.*

– Remove cooling cowl and cooling fan. See **Cooling fan cowl, removing (M3 models)** in this repair group.

> ***CAUTION —***
> *The viscous fan clutch nut has left-hand threads.*

– Remove coolant pump drive belt. See **020 Maintenance**.

NOTE —
If reusing belt, mark direction of rotation on belt.

– Remove coolant pump pulley bolts and remove pulley from pump.

– Remove thermostat. See **Thermostat, replacing (M3 models)** in this repair group.

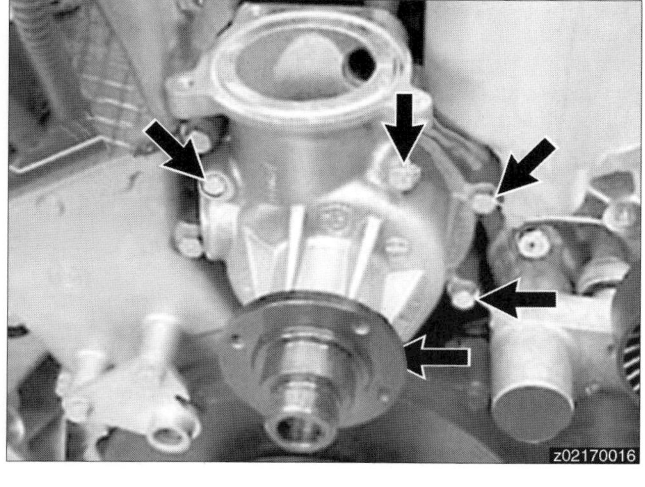

◄ Remove coolant pump mounting bolts (**arrows**).

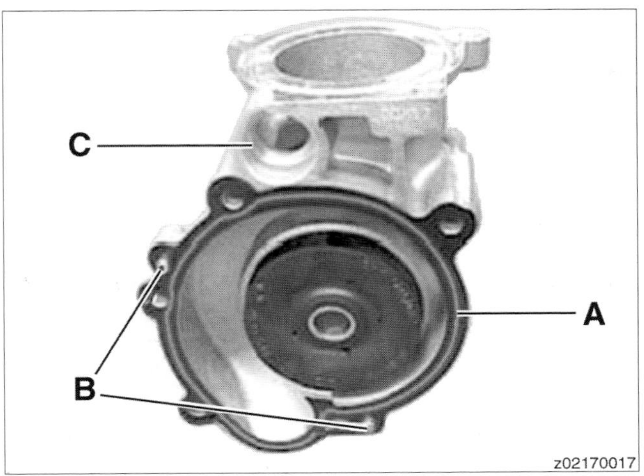

– Remove pump from engine block. Pry gently to disengage from coolant Y-pipe.

When installing, make sure:

- New coolant pump gasket (**A**) is installed.
- Locating dowels (**B**) are undamaged and positioned correctly.
- Bore for Y-pipe connection (**C**) is clean. Install new sealing O-ring on end of Y-pipe and lubricate with water-based lubricant. Slide pump on pipe carefully.

> ***CAUTION —***
> *O-ring seal is easily damaged when installing pump.*

Tightening torque

- Coolant pump to timing chain cover . . . . . 10 Nm (7 ft-lb)

– Remainder of installation is reverse of removal. Fill and bleed cooling system. See **Cooling system, bleeding** in this repair group.

Tightening torque

- Thermostat cover to coolant pump . . . . . . 10 Nm (7 ft-lb)

Thermostat, replacing (M3 models)

The coolant thermostat is installed in a housing at the top of the coolant pump, at the front of the engine.

– With engine cold, partially drain cooling system. See **Coolant, draining and filling** in this repair group.

> ***WARNING —***
> *At normal operating temperature the cooling system is pressurized. Allow the system to cool thoroughly (a minimum of one hour), then release the cooling system pressure cap slowly to allow safe release of pressure.*

> ***CAUTION —***
> *When working on the cooling system, cover the alternator to protect it against coolant drips.*

– Remove engine cooling fan and fan shroud. See **Cooling fan cowl, removing (M3 models)** in this repair group.

> ***CAUTION —***
> *The viscous fan clutch nut has left-hand threads.*

– Remove air filter housing with mass air flow sensor. See **130 Fuel Injection**.

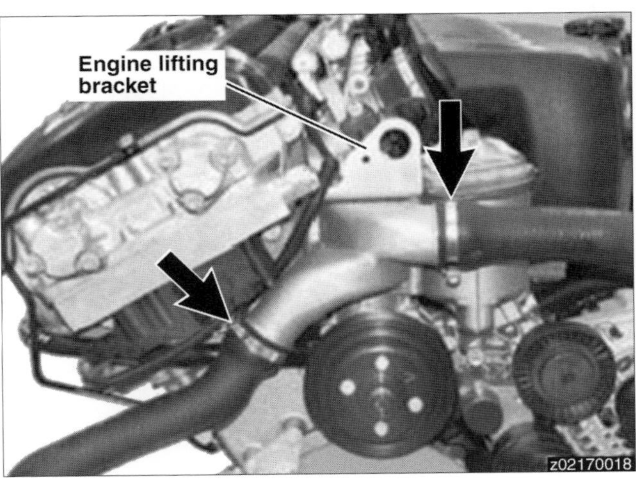

Working at thermostat cover:

- Loosen or cut coolant hose clamps (**arrows**).
- Pull hoses off housing.
- Detach electrical harness loom from engine lifting bracket. Unbolt and remove bracket.

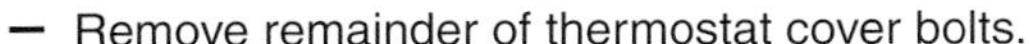

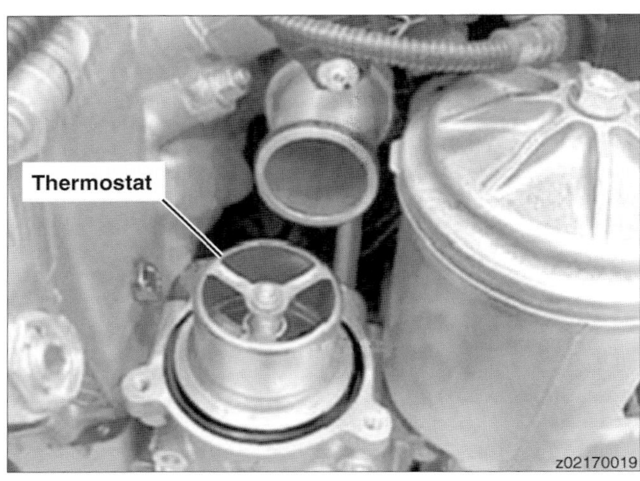

– Remove remainder of thermostat cover bolts.

- Remove thermostat cover, disengaging from coolant return pipe.
- Remove thermostat.

– Replace sealing O-rings on coolant pump and return pipe. Lubricate with water-based lubricant.

◄ Place new thermostat on coolant pump.

– Remainder of installation is reverse of removal. Fill and bleed cooling system. See **Cooling system, bleeding** in this repair group.

Tightening torque

- Coolant hose clamp (32 - 48 mm) . . . . .2.5 Nm (22 in-lb)
- Thermostat housing to cylinder head . . . . 10 Nm (7 ft-lb)

Radiator, removing and installing

– Raise front of car and support safely.

CAUTION —
Make sure the car is stable and well supported at all times. Use a professional automotive lift or jack stands designed for the purpose. A floor jack is not adequate support.

– Remove splash shield from under engine.

– Drain radiator and engine block as described earlier.

WARNING —
Allow cooling system to cool before opening or draining system.

– Remove complete air filter housing.

– Remove air intake duct, cooling fan and fan shroud as described earlier.

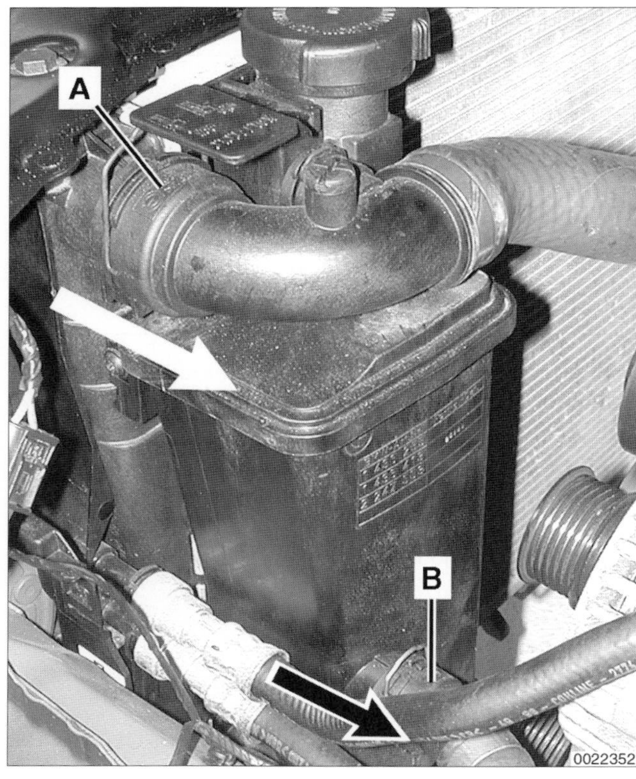

◄ Working on left side of radiator, lever out hose retaining clips and disconnect coolant hose fittings from radiator (**A**) and radiator expansion tank (**B**).

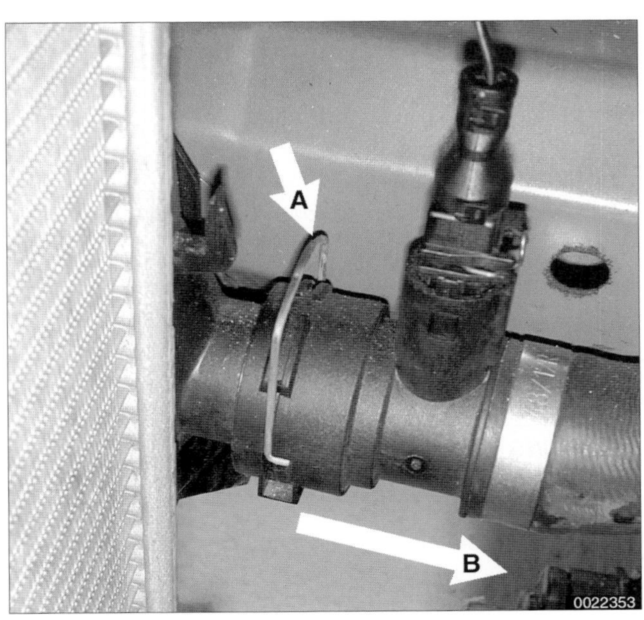

◄ Working on ride side of radiator, release hose retaining clips (**A**) and disconnect lower coolant hose fitting from radiator (**B**).

– Working underneath radiator, disconnect harness connector from coolant level sensor.

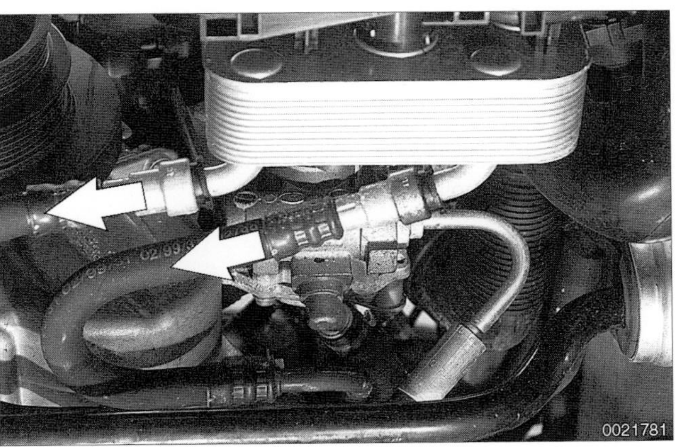

◄ Where applicable, disconnect automatic transmission fluid (ATF) cooler lines from ATF cooler at quick disconnect unions (**arrows**) as follows:

- Push hose toward oil cooler.
- Press black locking ring into hose fitting while pulling hose off cooler.

> ***CAUTION —***
> *Be sure to have a drain pan ready to catch spilled ATF.*

NOTE —
Alternatively, detach ATF cooler from radiator by pulling up on quick release clips and pulling cooler from radiator tank.

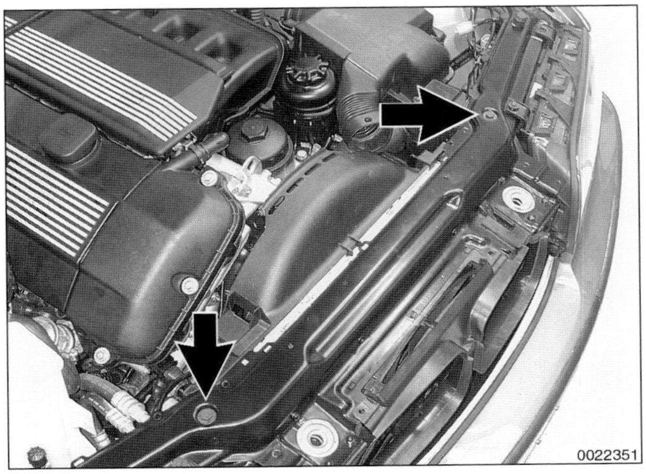

◄ Remove plastic bolts at top of radiator (**arrows**). Pull radiator up and out of car.

– Installation is reverse of removal, noting the following:

- Do not coat sealing O-rings with anti-seize paste.
- Fill radiator and cooling system as described under **Coolant, draining and filling.**
- Check ATF level and, if necessary, top up. See **240 Automatic Transmission**.

Tightening torques
- Engine block drain plug to block . . . . 25 Nm (18 ft-lb)
- Radiator drain plug to radiator . . . 2 - 3 Nm (18 - 27 in-lb)

Coolant expansion tank, removing and installing

– Raise front of car and support safely.

> **CAUTION —**
> *Make sure the car is stable and well supported at all times. Use a professional automotive lift or jack stands designed for the purpose. A floor jack is not adequate support.*

– Remove splash shield from under engine.

– Drain radiator and engine block as described earlier.

> **WARNING —**
> *Allow cooling system to cool before opening or draining system.*

– Remove complete air intake filter housing.

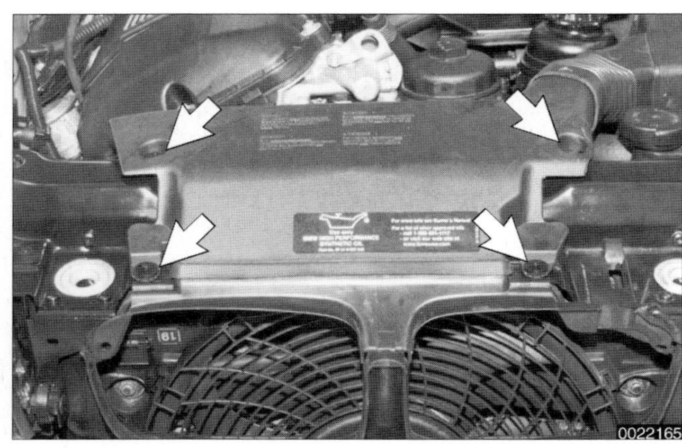

◀ Working at front of engine compartment, remove expansion rivets (**arrows**) retaining air intake duct to radiator support and remove intake duct.

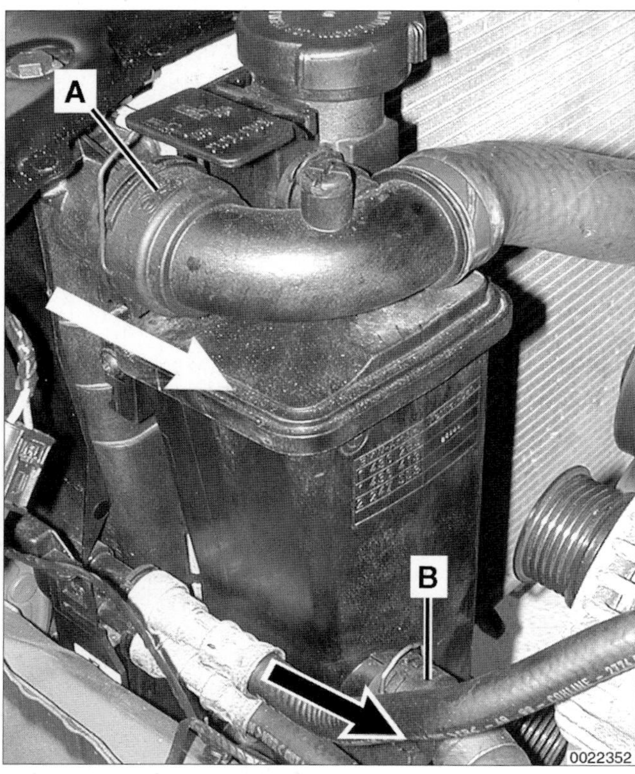

◀ Release hose retaining clips and disconnect coolant hose fittings (**A** and **B**) from expansion tank.

– Working underneath radiator, disconnect harness connector from coolant level sensor.

Coolant expansion tank assembly

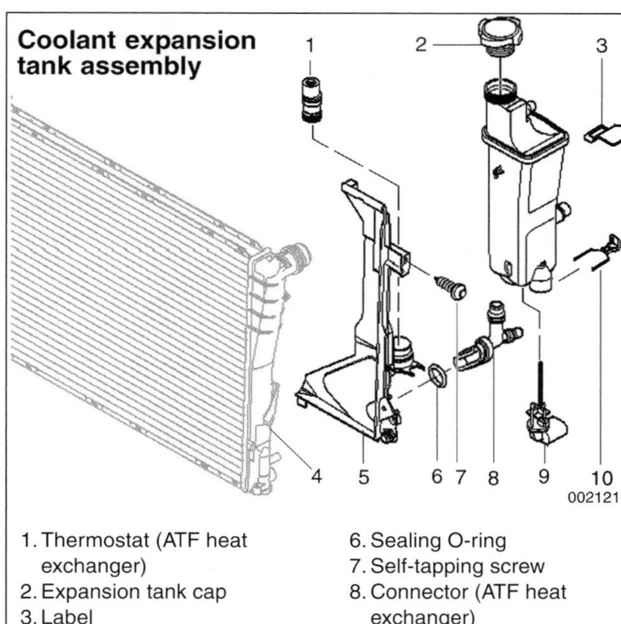

1. Thermostat (ATF heat exchanger)
2. Expansion tank cap
3. Label
4. Radiator
5. Mounting bracket
6. Sealing O-ring
7. Self-tapping screw
8. Connector (ATF heat exchanger)
9. Coolant level sensor
10. Locking clip

< Remove coolant level sensor (**9**) by twisting counterclockwise and pulling out of bottom of tank.

– Pull out expansion tank by detaching from radiator at top. Then pull up from mounting bracket at bottom.

– Installation is reverse of removal.

- Do not coat O-rings with anti-seize paste.
- Fill radiator and cooling system as described under **Coolant, draining and filling.**

Tightening torques

- Engine block drain plug to block .... 25 Nm (18 ft-lb)
- Radiator drain plug to radiator ... 2 - 3 Nm (18 - 27 in-lb)

180 Exhaust System

GENERAL

The exhaust system is designed to be maintenance free, although inspection should be performed during routine services.

New fasteners, clamps, rubber mounts and gaskets should be used when replacing exhaust system components. A liberal application of penetrating oil to the exhaust system nuts and bolts in advance may make removal easier. Heating fasteners is also often used for freeing up components. Illustrations of exhaust systems for rear wheel drive and all-wheel-drive (xi) models are given on the following pages.

NOTE —
See **130 Fuel Injection** *for information on oxygen sensor checking.*

Special tools

Some procedures require the use of special tools.

Special Tools

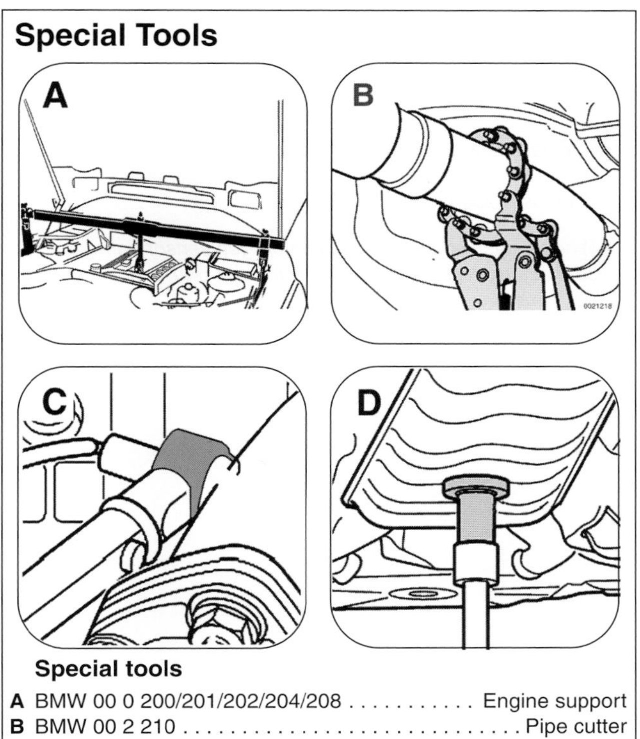

Special tools

A BMW 00 0 200/201/202/204/208 .... Engine support
B BMW 00 2 210 .... Pipe cutter
C BMW 11 7 030 .... Oxygen sensor socket (postcat)
D BMW 31 2 220 .... Exhaust system support

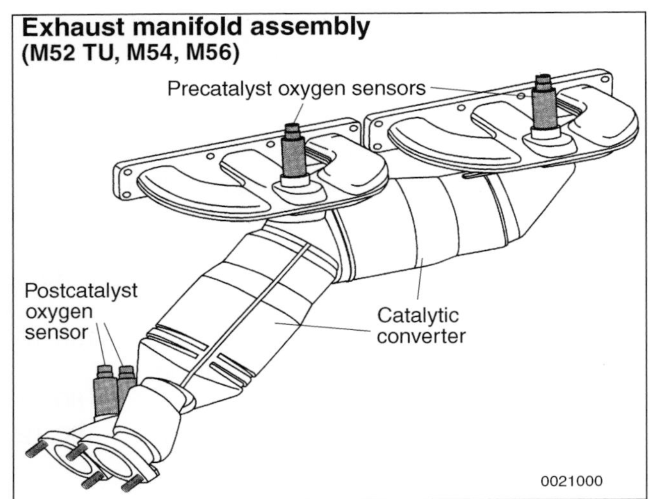

Exhaust manifolds and catalytic converters

The exhaust manifolds incorporate the catalytic converters. Mounting the catalytic converters close to the engine allows them to come up to operating temperature quicker. Two pre-catalyst and two post-catalyst oxygen sensors are mounted in the exhaust manifold assembly.

Under normal conditions the catalytic converters do not require replacement unless damaged.

Warnings and cautions

Observe the following warnings and cautions when servicing the exhaust system.

WARNING —

- *Exhaust gases are colorless, odorless, and very toxic. Run the engine only in a well-ventilated area. Immediately repair any leaks in the exhaust system or structural damage to the car body that might allow exhaust gases to enter the passenger compartment.*
- *The exhaust system and catalytic converter operate at high temperatures. Allow components to cool before servicing. Wear protective clothing to prevent burns. Do not use flammable chemicals near a hot catalytic converter.*
- *Old, corroded exhaust system components crumble easily and often have exposed sharp edges. To avoid injury, wear eye protection and heavy gloves when working with old exhaust parts.*

CAUTION —

- *When removing the exhaust manifolds, take care that the oxygen sensors are not damaged.*
- *A "catalyst damaging" fault code stored in the ECM does NOT automatically indicate a defective catalytic converter. Use a diagnostic scan tool to pinpoint the problem.*
- *When detaching and reattaching oxygen sensor harness connectors, take care that the front and rear connectors are not mixed up.*

Exhaust system, rear wheel drive models

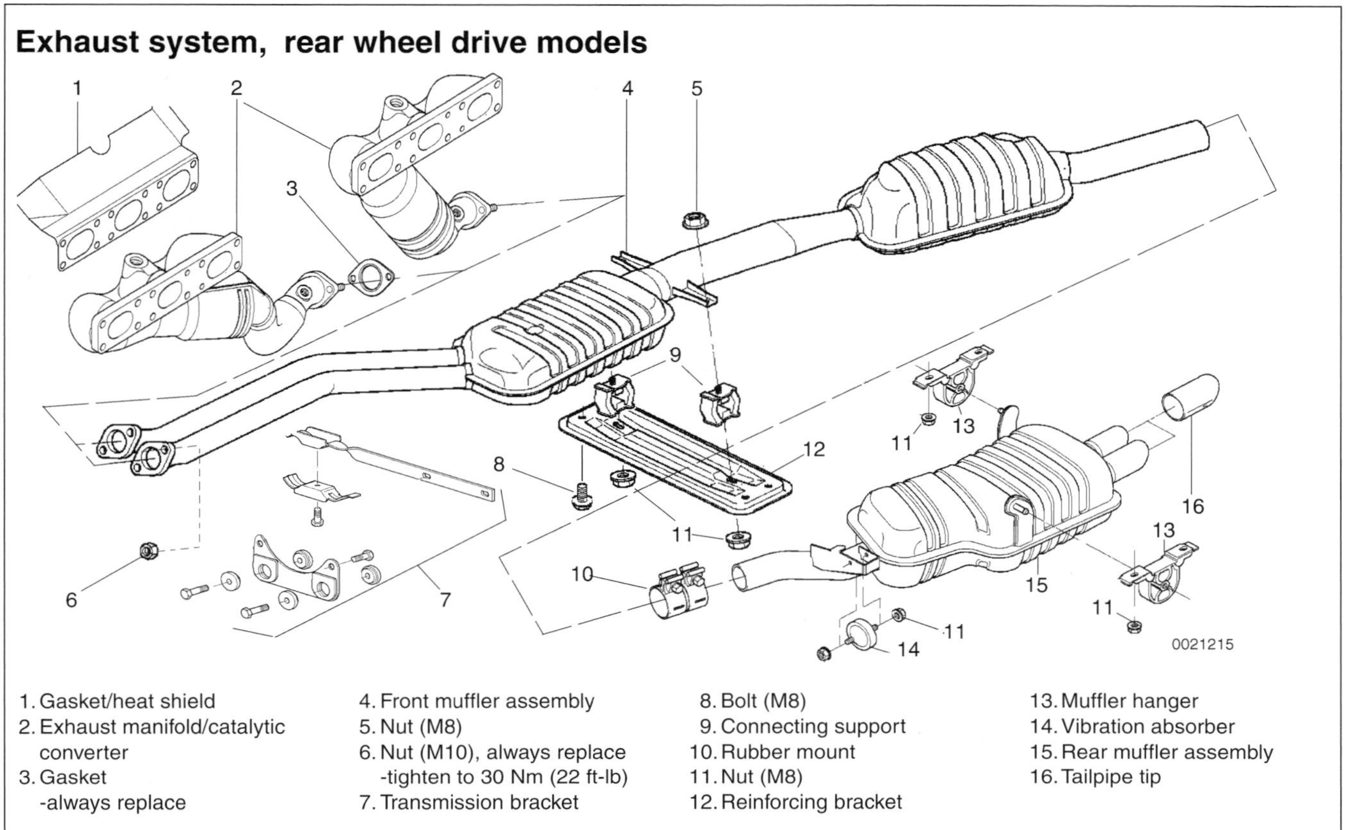

1. Gasket/heat shield
2. Exhaust manifold/catalytic converter
3. Gasket -always replace
4. Front muffler assembly
5. Nut (M8)
6. Nut (M10), always replace -tighten to 30 Nm (22 ft-lb)
7. Transmission bracket
8. Bolt (M8)
9. Connecting support
10. Rubber mount
11. Nut (M8)
12. Reinforcing bracket
13. Muffler hanger
14. Vibration absorber
15. Rear muffler assembly
16. Tailpipe tip

EXHAUST REPLACEMENT

New fasteners, clamps, rubber mounts and gaskets should be used when replacing exhaust system components.

Exhaust system, removing and installing

Non-M3 models: Exhaust system should be removed as a complete unit. Once the system is removed from the car, individual pipes and mufflers can be replaced more easily.

M3 models: Exhaust system should be removed in three sections; the rear muffler, the intermediate pipes, and the front system.

– Raise and support car for access to exhaust system.

> ***WARNING —***
> - *Do not work under a lifted car unless it is solidly supported on jack stands designed for that purpose. Never work under a car that is supported solely by a jack.*
> - *The exhaust system operates at high temperatures. Allow components to cool before servicing. Wear protective clothing to prevent burns.*

– **M3 models:** remove rear muffler from intermediate pipes.

Exhaust system, all wheel drive (xi) models

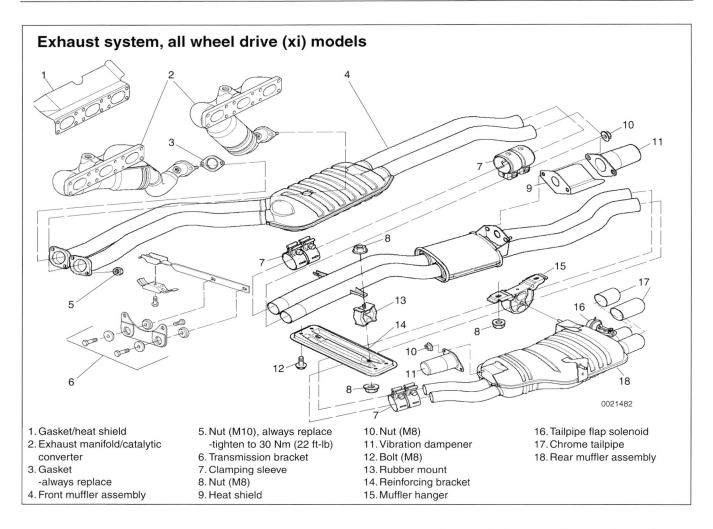

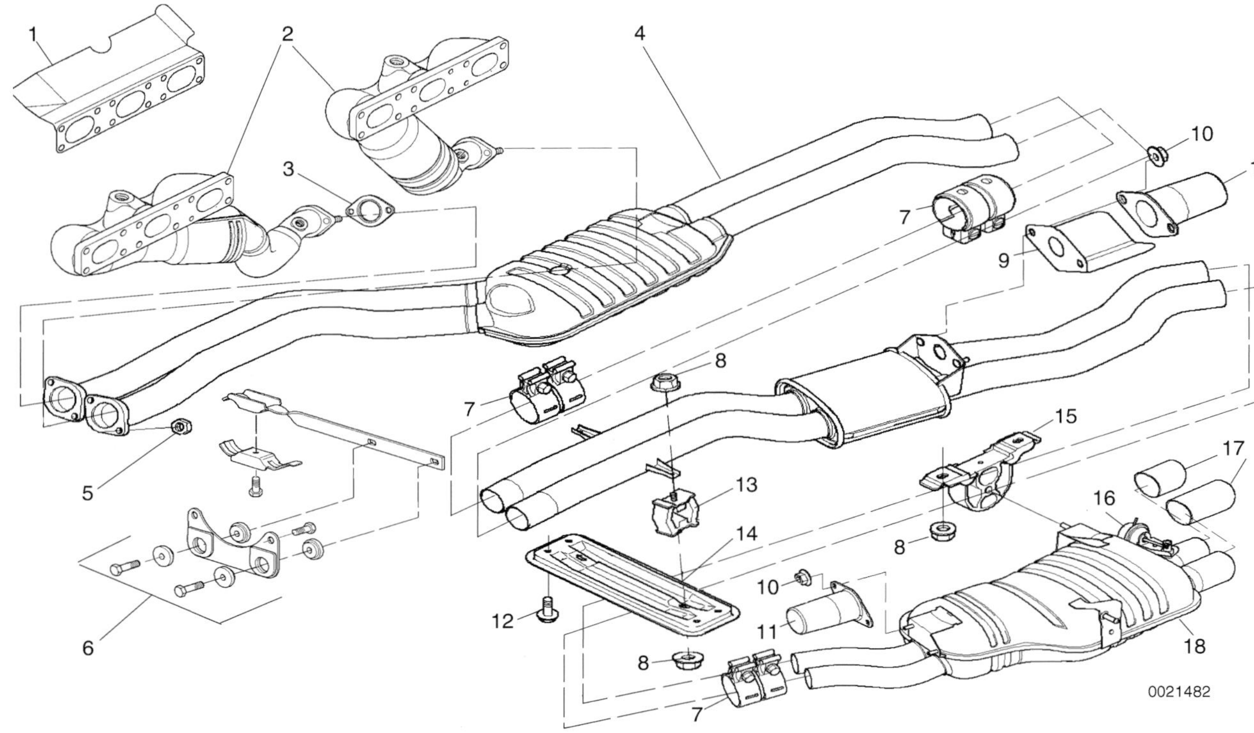

0021482

1. Gasket/heat shield
2. Exhaust manifold/catalytic converter
3. Gasket -always replace
4. Front muffler assembly
5. Nut (M10), always replace -tighten to 30 Nm (22 ft-lb)
6. Transmission bracket
7. Clamping sleeve
8. Nut (M8)
9. Heat shield
10. Nut (M8)
11. Vibration dampener
12. Bolt (M8)
13. Rubber mount
14. Reinforcing bracket
15. Muffler hanger
16. Tailpipe flap solenoid
17. Chrome tailpipe
18. Rear muffler assembly

– Loosen and remove fasteners holding mid pipes to front exhaust pipes, and front exhaust pipes to exhaust manifolds (where applicable).

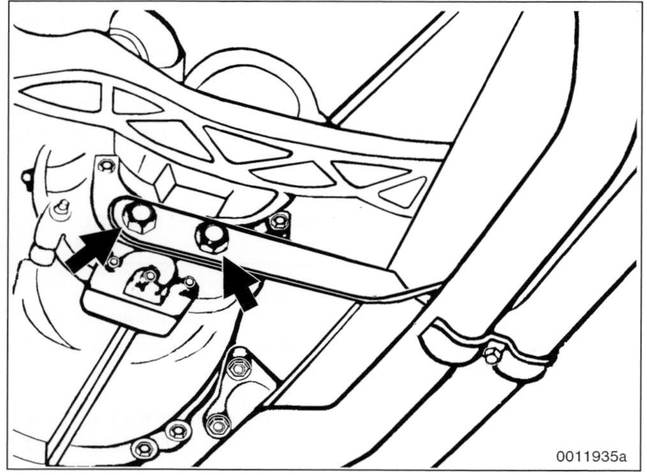

◄ Remove bolts (**arrows**) and detach exhaust support bracket assembly from transmission.

– While supporting exhaust system from below (use BMW special tool 31 2 220 or equivalent), remove mounting bolts from reinforcing bracket(s).

NOTE —

Rubber hangers attach reinforcing bracket(s) to exhaust pipes.

– **M3 and convertible models:** Remove rear body reinforcing crossbrace.

Exhaust system, M3 models

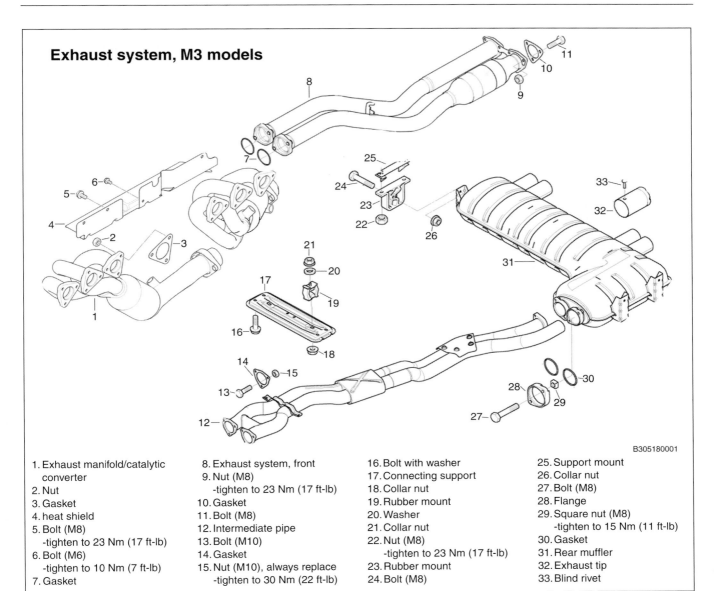

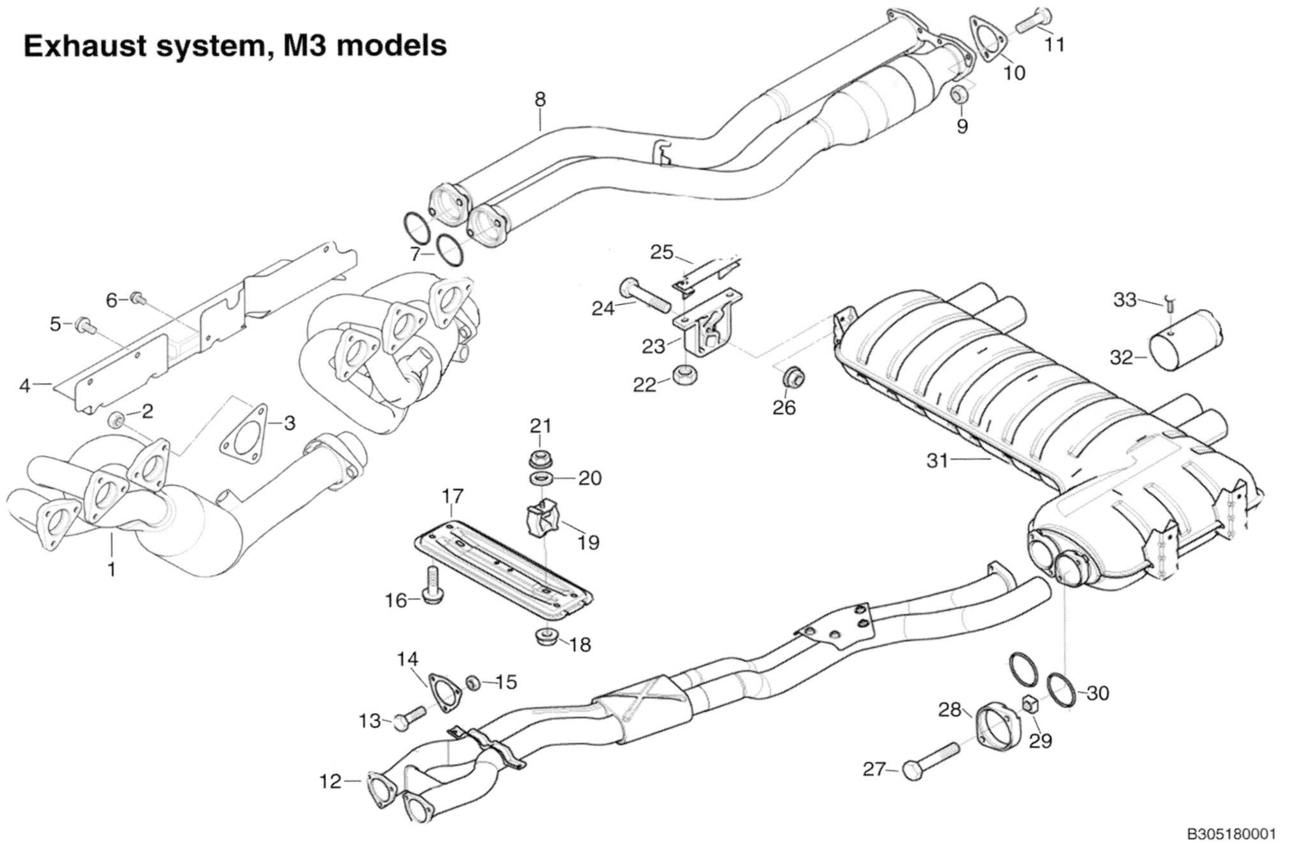

B305180001

1. Exhaust manifold/catalytic converter
2. Nut
3. Gasket
4. heat shield
5. Bolt (M8)
   -tighten to 23 Nm (17 ft-lb)
6. Bolt (M6)
   -tighten to 10 Nm (7 ft-lb)
7. Gasket
8. Exhaust system, front
9. Nut (M8)
   -tighten to 23 Nm (17 ft-lb)
10. Gasket
11. Bolt (M8)
12. Intermediate pipe
13. Bolt (M10)
14. Gasket
15. Nut (M10), always replace
    -tighten to 30 Nm (22 ft-lb)
16. Bolt with washer
17. Connecting support
18. Collar nut
19. Rubber mount
20. Washer
21. Collar nut
22. Nut (M8)
    -tighten to 23 Nm (17 ft-lb)
23. Rubber mount
24. Bolt (M8)
25. Support mount
26. Collar nut
27. Bolt (M8)
28. Flange
29. Square nut (M8)
    -tighten to 15 Nm (11 ft-lb)
30. Gasket
31. Rear muffler
32. Exhaust tip
33. Blind rivet

If applicable, remove vacuum hose (**arrow**) from tailpipe flap solenoid.

◄ Unscrew mounting nuts (**arrows**) and remove rear exhaust hanger rubber(s) from left and right sides of rear muffler.

– Separate exhaust system sections (where applicable), and carefully lower exhaust system and remove.

– Installation is reverse of removal.

- Where necessary, transfer parts from old system to replacement system. Replace any deformed or damaged rubber hangers or support members.
- Coat exhaust system mounting studs with copper paste before installing nuts. Use new gaskets and self-locking nuts at front pipe connection.
- Be sure to reinstall exhaust system vibration damper(s) where applicable.
- Loosely install all exhaust system mounting hardware and hangers before tightening fasteners to their final torque.

NOTE —
To prevent exhaust system rattles and vibration, align support bracket at transmission so that there is no tension on exhaust system.

Tightening torques

- Exhaust support bracket to transmission . . . . 21 Nm (15 ft-lb)
- Front exhaust pipe to exhaust manifold (self-locking nut (M10); always replace) . 30 Nm (22 ft-lb)

Muffler, replacing

BMW offers individual mufflers as replacement parts for the original one-piece assembly. Replacement of a rear muffler may be possible with the system installed on the car. Replacement of the front or middle muffler should only be done with the exhaust removed from the car as described earlier.

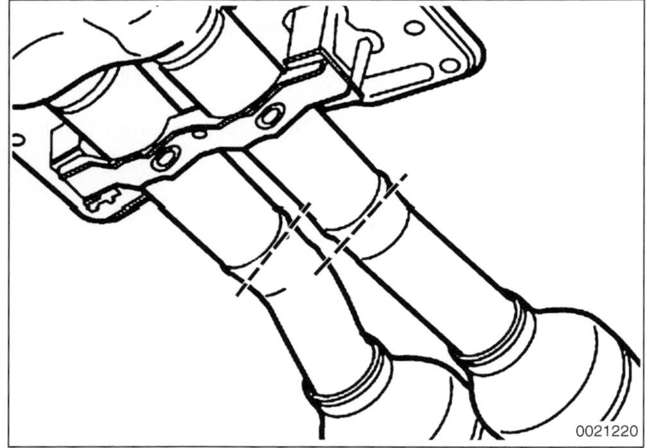

◄ Mark length of new muffler pipe(s) on old system.

– Use exhaust pipe cutter to cut pipe(s). Deburr cut pipe end(s).

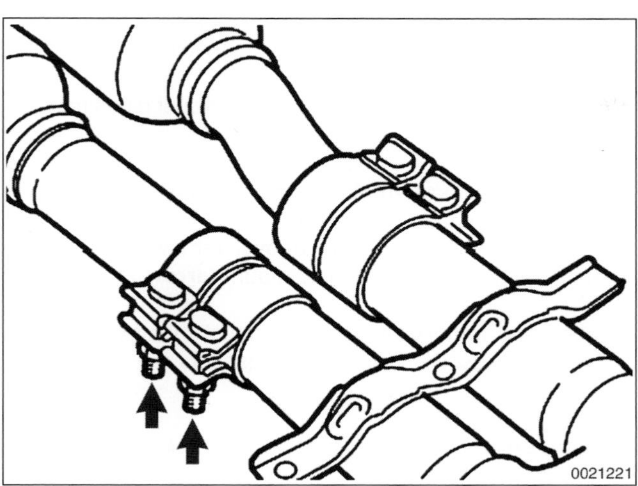

 Use clamping sleeves to join new pipe(s) to old.

- Make sure pipe ends are centered inside sleeve.
- Point clamping sleeve bolt threads (**arrows**) down.

– Reinstall exhaust system.

Tailpipe flap vacuum tank

In E46 vehicles with a tailpipe flap, vacuum to operate the flap is supplied from a tank mounted underneath the motor on the driver's side. Access to the tank requires removal of the splash shield and front body crossbrace underneath engine compartment.

The tailpipe flap functions to reduce noise at low engine speeds (idle). During idle the flap is closed. Once the engine reaches a specified speed, the DME control module signals the solenoid to open the flap.

Exhaust manifolds, removing and installing (except M3 models)

Always use new retaining nuts and gaskets when removing and installing the exhaust manifolds.

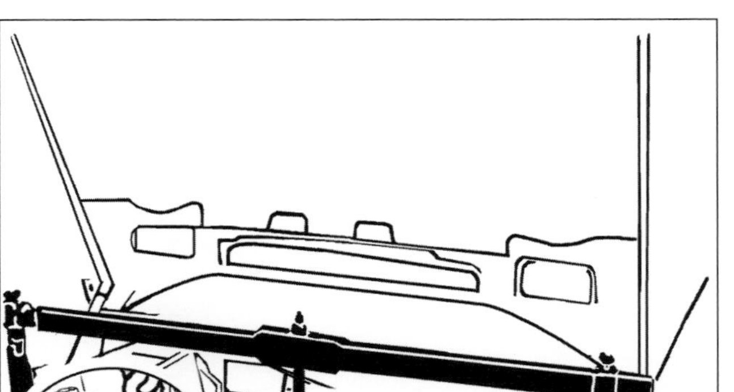

 Using engine support equipment (BMW special tools 00 0 200/201/202/204/208 or equivalent), connect to lifting eye on front of engine. Raise engine approx. 5 mm (¼ in).

– With exhaust system cold, raise and support car for access to exhaust system.

> ***WARNING —***
> *Do not work under a lifted car unless it is solidly supported on jack stands designed for that purpose. Never work under a car that is supported solely by a jack.*

– In order to avoid damaging oxygen sensors:

- Detach oxygen sensor harness connectors.
- Remove oxygen sensors from exhaust manifolds as described later in this group.

> ***CAUTION —***
> *Take care that the front and rear oxygen sensor connectors are not mixed up.*

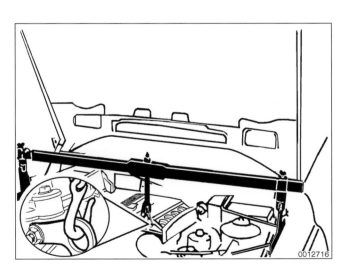

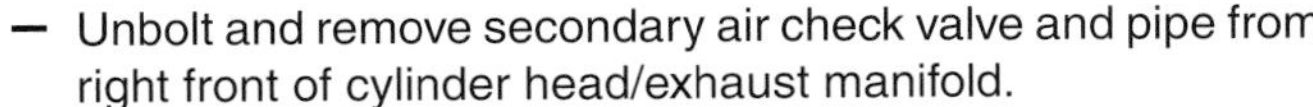

– Unbolt and remove secondary air check valve and pipe from right front of cylinder head/exhaust manifold.

– Working underneath car, unbolt front exhaust pipes from exhaust manifolds.

– If necessary, remove front body crossbrace.

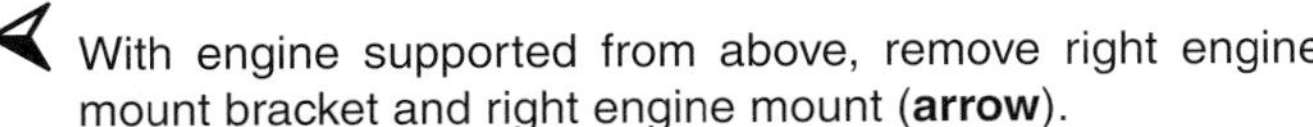

With engine supported from above, remove right engine mount bracket and right engine mount (**arrow**).

– Loosen and remove nuts from exhaust manifolds and remove manifolds. Discard nuts and gaskets.

NOTE —
The front exhaust manifold must be removed before the rear manifold.

– Installation is reverse of removal.

- Coat exhaust mounting studs with CRC or equivalent copper paste.
- Use new gaskets and self-locking nuts.

Tightening torque

- Exhaust manifold to cylinder head (self-locking (M7) nut; always replace) . . 20 Nm (15 ft-lb)
- Front exhaust pipe to exhaust manifold (self-locking (M10) nut; always replace) . 30 Nm (22 ft-lb)
- Oxygen sensor to manifold . . . . 50 Nm (37 ft-lb)

Exhaust manifolds, removing and installing (M3 models)

Always use new retaining nuts and gaskets when removing and installing the exhaust manifolds.

Remove housing for interior ventilation microfilter.

- Unclip upper cover (**arrows**), lift up and remove cover and microfilter.

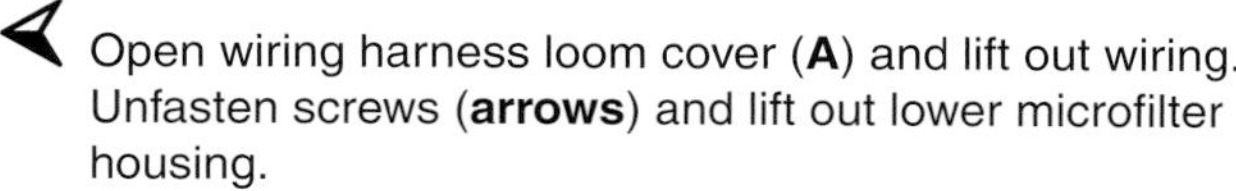

Open wiring harness loom cover (**A**) and lift out wiring. Unfasten screws (**arrows**) and lift out lower microfilter housing.

– Remove expansion rivets and remove air duct from right side of engine.

Remove cylinder head top cover:

- Disconnect vent hose and remove oil filler cover.
- Remove cover bolts (**arrows**) and lift off cover.

– Remove engine splash guard and remove chassis reinforcement plate or reinforcement bar. See **310 Front Suspension**.

WARNING —

- *The front chassis reinforcement plate mounting fasteners are stretch type bolts and must be replaced anytime they are removed.*
- *The vehicle must not be driven with this component removed. See **310 Front Suspension** for additional information.*

Working at the rear of the cylinder head, disconnect oxygen sensor electrical harness connectors (**arrows**) and lift out lower microfilter housing.

– Drain coolant, see **170 Radiator and Cooling System**.

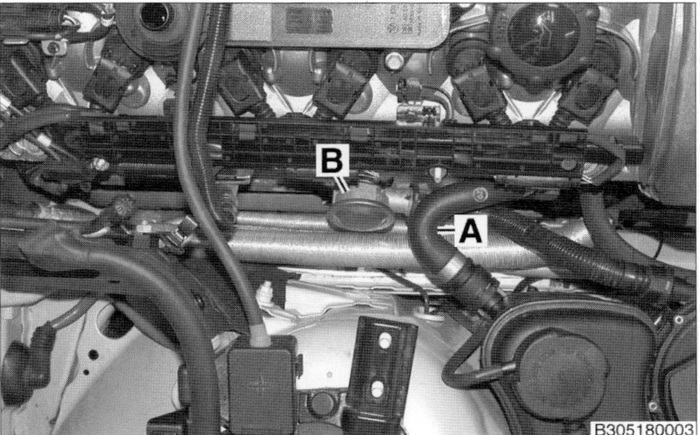

Disconnect coolant hose (**A**) from cooling system reservoir. Remove air injection valve (**B**) from cylinder head.

– Unclip oxygen sensor harnesses from heatshield.

– Remove exhaust manifold heat shield.

– Remove front pipes of exhaust system.

– Remove exhaust manifolds mounting nuts and remove manifolds:
  - Remove front manifold from cylinder head and rest on engine mount.
  - Remove rear manifold from cylinder head and feed front and rear manifolds out together.

NOTE —
Oxygen sensors can be damaged during manifold removal. To avoid costly replacement, remove from manifolds before removing manifolds from cylinder head.

– Installation is reverse of removal, noting the following:
  - Clean all gasket mounting surfaces.
  - Coat exhaust mounting studs with CRC or equivalent copper paste.
  - Use new gaskets and self-locking nuts.

Tightening torque
- Mounting nuts to cylinder head. . . . . 23 Nm (37 ft-lb)

Oxygen sensor (precatalyst), replacing (except M3 models)

The precatalyst oxygen sensors are installed at the top of the exhaust manifolds.

WARNING —
Allow components to cool before servicing.

– Using BMW specific diagnostic scan tool, or equivalent, read out and clear ECM fault codes.

◄ Working at right side of engine above exhaust manifolds, remove front or rear oxygen sensor harness connector (**arrows**) from bracket, then separate plug.

NOTE —
In photo, secondary air pump has been removed for clarity.

– Remove oxygen sensor using special oxygen sensor removal socket.

– Installation is reverse of removal.
  - New sensor threads come coated with anti-seize paste.
  - If reusing a sensor, apply thin coat of anti-seize paste to threads only. Do not contaminate tip of sensor with paste or lubricants of any sort.
  - Install harness and connector in original location.

Tightening torque
- Oxygen sensor to manifold . . . . 50 Nm (37 ft-lb)

Oxygen sensor (post-catalyst), replacing (except M3 models)

The post-catalyst oxygen sensors are installed at the rear of the catalytic converters.

> ***WARNING —***
> *Allow components to cool before servicing.*

– Using BMW diagnostic scan tool or equivalent, read out and clear ECM fault codes.

< Remove interior ventilation microfilter housing.

- Remove upper cover and microfilter.
- Open wiring harness loom (**A**) and remove wires.
- Unfasten screws (**B**) and remove lower microfilter housing.

– Remove large cover from above fuel rail/intake manifold.

< Label and disconnect sensor harness connectors (**arrows**).

> ***CAUTION —***
> *Label connectors so that front and rear connectors are not mixed up.*

– Detach harness from guides and brackets

– Remove oxygen sensor from exhaust manifold using special tool 11 7 030 or equivalent.

– Installation is reverse of removal.

- New sensor threads come coated with anti-seize paste.
- If reusing a sensor, apply thin coat of anti-seize paste to threads only. Do not contaminate tip of sensor with paste or lubricants of any sort.
- Install harness and connector in original location.

Tightening torque

- Oxygen sensor to manifold . . . . 50 Nm (37 ft-lb)

> ***CAUTION —***
> *Do not allow undercoating to get on oxygen sensor.*

Oxygen sensors, replacing (M3 models)

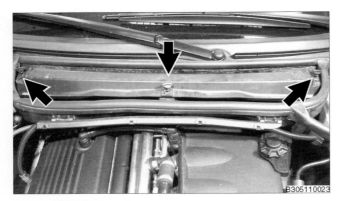

Remove housing for interior ventilation microfilter.

- Unclip upper cover (**arrows**), lift up and remove cover and microfilter.

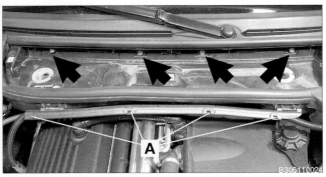

Open wiring harness loom cover (**A**) and lift out wiring. Unfasten screws (**arrows**) and lift out lower microfilter housing.

– Remove expansion rivets and remove air duct from right side of engine.

Remove cylinder head top cover:

- Disconnect vent hose and remove oil filler cover.
- Remove cover bolts (**arrows**) and lift off cover.

Working at the rear of the cylinder head, disconnect oxygen sensor electrical harness connectors (**arrows**) and lift out lower microfilter housing. Label harnesses for correct reassembly.

– Unclip oxygen sensor harnesses from heatshield.

– Remove engine splash guard and remove chassis reinforcement plate. See **310 Front Suspension**.

> ***WARNING —***
> - *The front chassis reinforcement plate mounting fasteners are stretch type bolts and must be replaced anytime they are removed.*
> - *The vehicle must not be driven with this component removed. See **310 Front Suspension** for additional information.*

– Use BMW special tools 11 7 030 and 11 9 150, or equivalent oxygen sensor wrench to remove oxygen sensors from exhaust manifolds.

– Installation is reverse of removal, noting the following:

- New oxygen sensor threads are coated with antiseize compound from the factory.
- If a sensor is reused, apply a thin coat of copper paste to the threads only.
- Reroute electrical harnesses as before.
- Check fault codes and clear/reset ECM memory.

> ***CAUTION —***
> *Do not clean sensor tip, and make sure tip does not contact any lubricants or antiseize compounds.*

Tightening torque

- Oxygen sensor to manifold . . . . 50 Nm (37 ft-lb)

200 Transmission–General

GENERAL

This section covers the repairs related to the clutch, manual and automatic transmissions, shift linkages, driveshafts, and transfer case (all wheel drive vehicles only). For repairs related to drive axles and front and rear final drive differentials, see **311 Front Axle Final Drive** and **331 Rear Axle Final Drive**.

Drivetrain

E46 models are equipped with a longitudinal drivetrain. The transmission is bolted directly to the rear of the engine. In rear wheel drive models, a driveshaft connects the output shaft of the transmission to the rear final drive. On all wheel drive models, a transfer case is mounted to the rear of the transmission, with drive shafts leading to front and rear final drive assemblies. Individual drive axles with integrated constant velocity joints transfer rotational power from the final drive units to the drive wheels.

Manual transmission

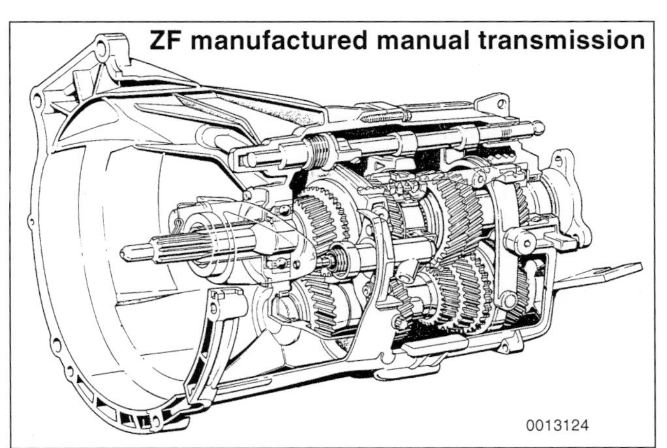

ZF manufactured manual transmission

Due to different power characteristics and performance requirements, manual transmisison application varies depending on engine application, model and model year. See **Table a**.

> ***NOTE —***
> *For transmission gear ratio information and repair information, see* **230 Manual Transmission**.

The manual transmissions use a single clutch disc with dual-mass flywheel. For further information, see **210 Clutch**.

Manual transmissions have a metal ID plate mounted on the side of the transmission. Do not rely on numbers cast on the transmission case for identification.

Table a. Manual transmission applications

Model	Year	Transmission
323i/Ci	1999 - 2000	S5D250G
325i/Ci	2001 - 2005 2004- 2005 (opt)	S5D250G S6S37BZ SMG
325xi	2001 -2005	S5D320Z
328i/Ci	1999 - 2000	S5D 320Z
330i/Ci	2001 - 2003 2003 - 2005 2004- 2005 (opt)	S5D320Z (up to 03/03) GS637BZ (from 03/03) GS637BZ SMG
330xi	2000 - 2003 2004 - 2005	S5D 280Z (up to 03/03) S6X37BZ (from 03/03)
M3	2001 - 2004 2003 - 2005 (opt)	S6S420G S6S420G SMG

Available as an option, the Sequential Manual Gearbox (SMG) functions like a clutchless manual transmission. Clutch operation is handled via a computer controlled hydraulic unit that engages and disengages the clutch automatically, as well as physically shifting the transmission into gear.

Two different SMG transmission systems are used, one on M3 models (Getrag manufactured), the second (ZF manufactured), available on rear wheel drive models equipped with M54 engines.

For more information on the SMG transmission, see **231 Sequential Manual Gearbox (SMG)**.

Automatic transmission

Automatic transmission applications vary, depending on model and model year and/or production date. All of the automatic transmissions are electrohydraulically controlled with five forward speeds. Automatic transmission applications are given in **Table b**.

For automatic transmission repair information, see **240 Automatic Transmission**.

Transmission Identification codes for automatic transmissions are located on metal ID tags mounted to the body of the transmission.

Table b. Automatic transmission applications

Model	Year	Transmission
323i/Ci	1999 - 2000	A5S360R (up to 03/00) A5S325 Z (from 03/00)
325i (M54)	2001 - 2005	A5S325 Z (up to 03/02) A5S390R (from 03/02)
325i (M56)	2003 - 2005	A5S325 Z
325Ci	2001 - 2005	A5S325 Z (up to 03/03) A5S390R (from 03/03)
328i/Ci	1999 - 2000	A5S360R
330i/Ci	2001 - 2005	A5S325 Z (up to 03/03) A5S390R (from 03/03)
325xi **330xi**	2001 - 2005	A5S390R

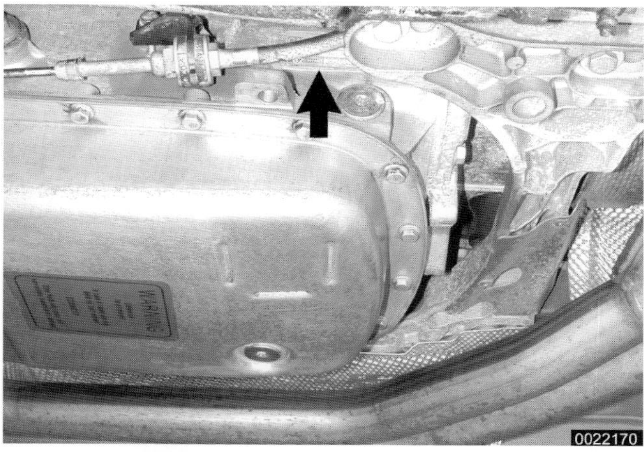

GM manufactured transmissions have the ID tag located on the left hand side of the transmission housing, behind the transmission selector cable, just above the transmission pan (**arrow**).

ZF manufactured transmissions have the ID tags mounted on the left side of the rear of the transmissions, just above the automatic transmission pan (**arrow**).

Transmission lubricants

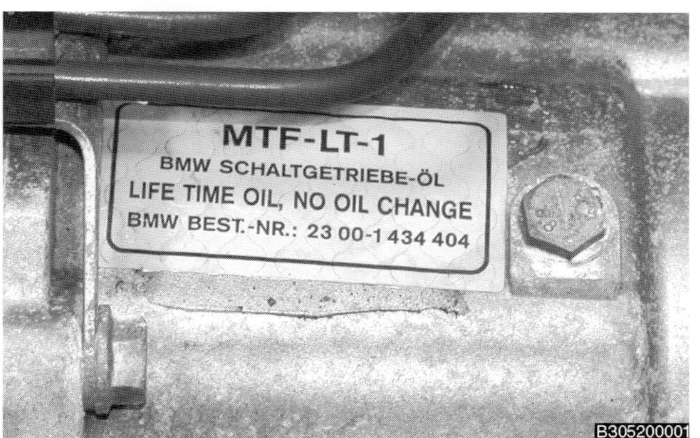

The lubricant used varies between transmissions and model years. Fluid application information is clearly marked on a label on the transmission.

On manual transmissions, either ATF (orange label reads ATF-Oil) or special BMW lubricants (yellow label reads MTF-LT 1 or MTF-LT2) is used. See **230 Manual Transmission**.

Automatic transmissions are filled with either Dexron III ATF (black transmission ID plate reads ATF-Oil), a special lifetime oil (green transmission ID plate reading Life-Time Oil). See **240 Automatic Transmission**.

CAUTION —
If in doubt as to the type of fluid installed in a particular transmission, consult authorized BMW dealer service department for the latest in operating fluids.

210 Clutch

GENERAL

This repair group covers replacement of the clutch mechanical and hydraulic components. Read the procedure through before beginning a job.

NOTE —
See **200 Transmission–General** *for transmission application information.*

Special tools

Special Tools

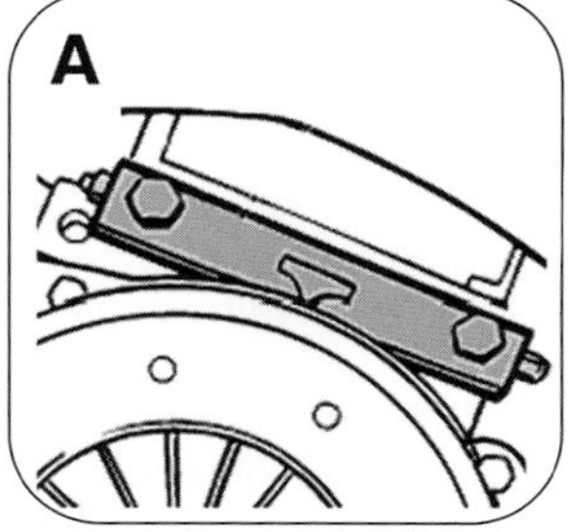

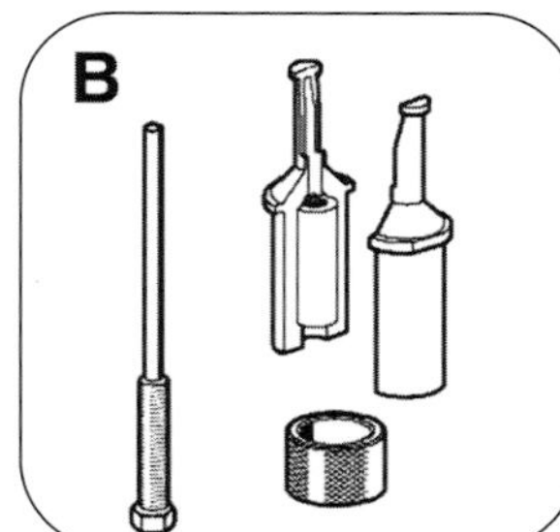

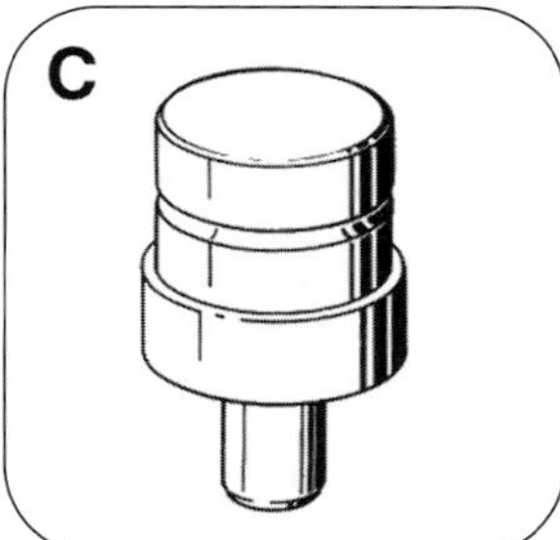

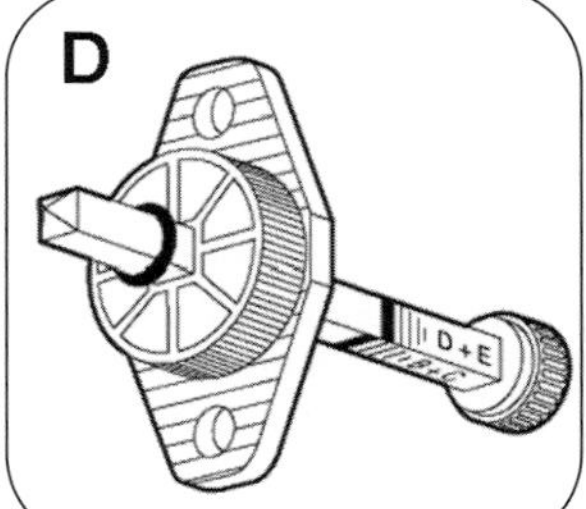

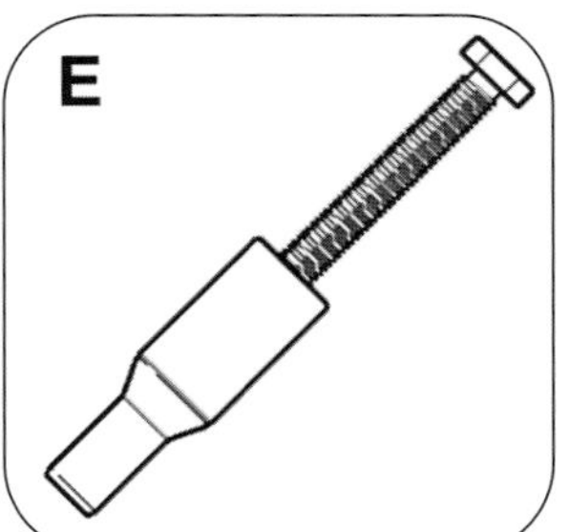

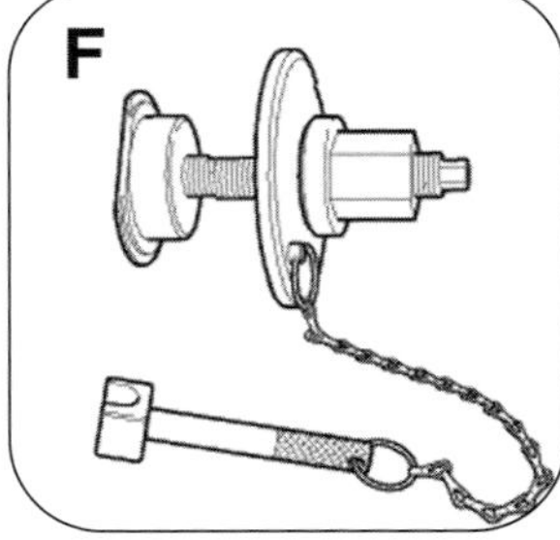

Special tools
- **A** BMW 11 2 170 . . . . Flywheel locking tool
- **B** BMW 11 2 340 . . . . Pilot bearing removal tool
- **C** BMW 11 2 350 . . . . Pilot bearing installation tool
- **D** BMW 21 2 080 . . . . Clutch lining gauge
- **E** BMW 21 2 142 . . . . .Clutch centering mandrel
- **F** BMW 21 2 150 . . . . .SAC clutch lock tool

The 3 Series BMW employs a traditional style clutch layout with a self adjusting clutch for manual transmission cars. BMW suggests some specific tools for fitting and removing the self adjusting clutch (SAC) assembly. These tools are required for aligning and assembling the clutch disk, as well as locking the flywheel in place and aligning the SAC assembly to the dual mass flywheel.

CLUTCH HYDRAULICS

The clutch is hydraulically actuated by the master and slave cylinders. Clutch disc wear is automatically taken up through the self adjusting pressure plate springs, making periodic adjustments unnecessary.

A soft or spongy feel to the clutch pedal, long pedal freeplay, or grinding noises from the gears while shifting can all indicate problems with the clutch hydraulics. In these circumstances it is best to start with a clutch fluid flush, followed, if necessary, by replacement of the hydraulic parts.

Clutch hydraulic information for models equipped with the Sequential Manual Gearbox (SMG) is covered in **231 Sequential Manual Gearbox (SMG)**.

Special Tools

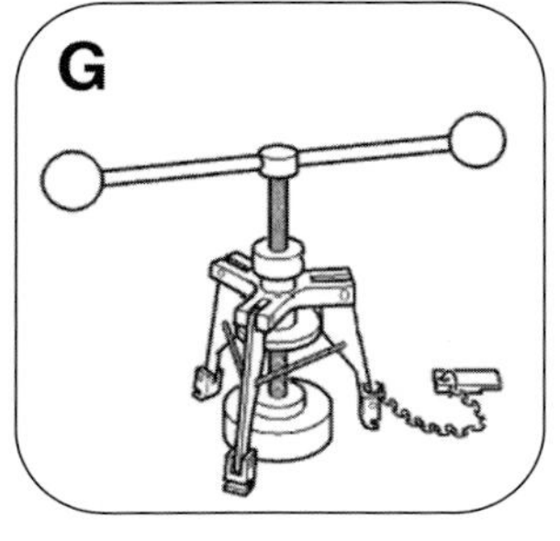

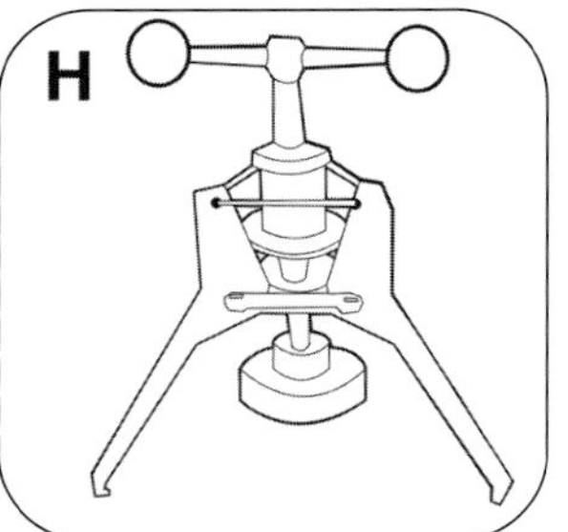

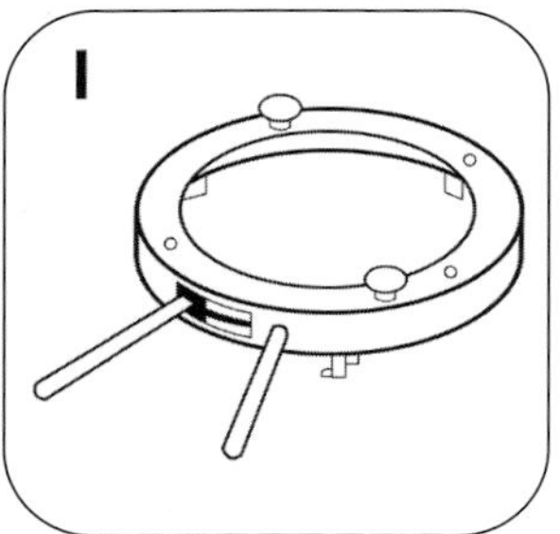

Special tools

G BMW 21 2 160 ....Clutch diaphragm tensioning too
H BMW 21 2 170 ....SAC tensioning tool
I BMW 21 2 180 ....SAC locating ring

NOTE —
The clutch hydraulic system shares the fluid reservoir and fluid with the brake hydraulic system.

Clutch hydraulic system, bleeding and flushing

If the clutch/brake fluid is murky or muddy, or has not been changed within the last two years, the system should be flushed. Flushing the old fluid from the clutch lines is done using a brake system pressure bleeder.

– Raise and safely support vehicle.

– Remove under transmission splash guard if applicable.

– Remove brake fluid reservoir cap. Using a clean syringe, remove brake fluid from reservoir. Refill reservoir with clean DOT 4 brake fluid.

◀ Attach pressure brake bleeder to fluid reservoir and pump bleeder a few times to pressurize hydraulic fluid system.

CAUTION —
- *Do not exceed 2 bar (29 psi) pressure at the fluid reservoir when bleeding or flushing the hydraulic system.*
- *Brake fluid is poisonous, highly corrosive and dangerous to the environment. Wear safety glasses and rubber gloves when working with brake fluid. Do not siphon brake fluid with your mouth. Immediately clean away any fluid spilled on painted surfaces and wash with water, as brake fluid will remove paint.*
- *Always use new brake fluid from a fresh, unopened container. Brake fluid will absorb moisture from the air. This can lead to corrosion problems in the hydraulic systems, and will also lower the brake fluid's boiling point. Dispose of brake fluid properly.*

◀ Connect a length of hose from clutch slave cylinder bleeder valve (**arrow**) to a container.

– Open bleeder valve and allow brake fluid to expel until clean fluid comes out free of air bubbles.

– Close bleeder valve and disconnect pressure bleeding equipment from fluid reservoir. Hose on bleeder valve remains connected.

– Slowly operate clutch pedal about 10 times. Fill reservoir with clean fluid as necessary.

– Unbolt slave cylinder from transmission. Fit BMW special tool 21 5 030. Press slave cylinder pushrod completely into slave cylinder.

– Hold slave cylinder so that bleeder valve is at the highest point.

– Open bleeder valve.

- Once brake fluid appears with out air bubbles, withdraw pushrod completely.
- Press slave cylinder pushrod all the way in.
- If brake fluid appears without air bubbles close bleeder valve and slowly release pushrod. Repeat procedure until fluid runs out clear and without bubbles.

– Disconnect bleeder hose. Install slave cylinder to transmission. Add clean brake fluid to reservoir as necessary. Check clutch operation.

Tightening torque

- Clutch slave cylinder to transmission . . . . 22 Nm (16 ft-lb)

Clutch master cylinder, replacing

The clutch master cylinder is mounted to the pedal assembly directly above the clutch pedal.

– Disconnect negative (–) cable from battery.

CAUTION —
Prior to disconnecting the battery, read the battery disconnection cautions given at the front of this manual.

– Raise and safely support vehicle.

– Remove under transmission splash guard if applicable.

– Remove brake fluid reservoir cap. Using a clean syringe, remove brake fluid from reservoir.

– Disconnect fluid supply hose from brake master cylinder. Place a pan under hose to catch any excess fluid.

– Working in engine compartment, disconnect fluid line fitting from master cylinder.

◄ Working at left rear of engine compartment:

- Peel rubber edge seal off top of panel.
- Twist plastic panel retainers (**arrows**) 90° and pull out to remove.
- Disengage panel from hoses and wiring harnesses and remove from engine compartment.
- Separate brake booster vacuum hose at one way valve (**A**). Plug hose ends.

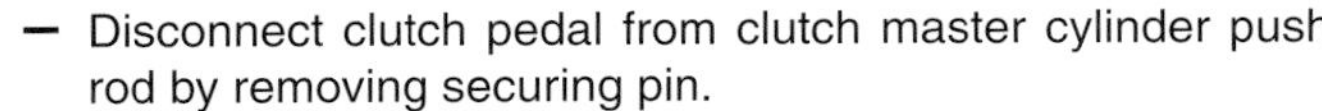

– Disconnect clutch pedal from clutch master cylinder push rod by removing securing pin.

◄ Remove master cylinder mounting bolts (**arrows**).

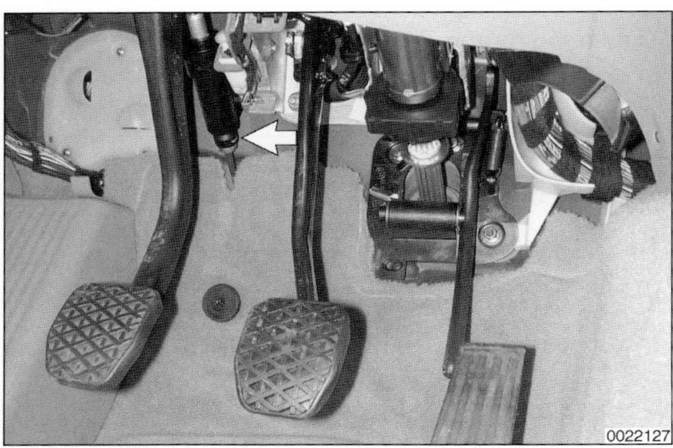

◄ Remove clip (**arrow**) retaining hydraulic line to master cylinder. Be prepared to catch any excess brake fluid remaining in hydraulic line.

NOTE —

Wrap clutch master cylinder with shop rags when removing hydraulic fluid lines from master cylinder to prevent brake fluid spill.

– Pull hydraulic line from master cylinder. Remove master cylinder with supply hose.

– Installation is reverse of removal. Fill fluid reservoir with clean fluid. Bleed clutch hydraulics as described earlier. Connect negative cable to battery last.

Tightening torques

- Clutch master cylinder to pedal cluster. . 22 Nm (16 ft-lb)
- Fluid line to master cylinder or slave cylinder . . . . 20 + 5 Nm (15 + 4 ft-lb)

Clutch slave cylinder, replacing

– Pinch off brake fluid supply hose to clutch master cylinder using BMW special tool 13 3 010 or equivalent fuel line clamp tool.

– Remove transmission splash guard if applicable.

– Disconnect fluid hose from slave cylinder. Place a pan under hose to catch any excess fluid.

◄ Remove mounting nuts (**arrows**) from slave cylinder on left side of transmission.

– Installation is reverse of removal, noting the following:
  - Check for wear on slave cylinder. Any other wear except on tip is caused by misalignment of clutch components.
  - Lightly coat pushrod tip with molybdenum disulfide grease (Molykote® Longterm 2 or equivalent).
  - During installation be sure pushrod tip engages recess in clutch release lever.
  - Fill fluid reservoir with clean fluid.
  - Bleed clutch hydraulics as described earlier.

Tightening torques
- Clutch slave cylinder to transmission . . . . 22 Nm (16 ft-lb)
- Fluid line to slave cylinder. . . . . . 20 + 5 Nm (15 + 4 ft-lb)

CLUTCH MECHANICAL

The transmission must be removed from the engine to access the clutch mechanical components. It is recommended that the clutch disc, pressure plate and release bearing be replaced during a clutch overhaul. Be sure to check the bottom of the bellhousing for oil. If engine oil is found, check for a faulty rear crankshaft oil seal.

Due to the construction of the self adjusting clutch (SAC) disc special tools must be used when removing the SAC style clutch. The pressure plate of the SAC clutch uses a wedge ring which rotates against the diaphragm springs to accommodate for clutch disc wear. The wedge ring adjusts by means of spring tension, so special tools must be used to apply and relieve spring tension as the clutch pressure plate is removed and installed. For special tools needed for clutch replacement procedures refer to the **Special tools.**

Table a. Clutch disc diameter

Model	Diameter
323i/Ci 325i/Ci/xi	228 mm (8.98 in.)
328i/Ci 330i/Ci/xi M3	240 mm (9.45 in.)

Clutch, removing

– On all wheel drive vehicles: Remove transfer case. See **270 Transfer Case**.

– Remove transmission from engine. See **230 Manual Transmission** or **231 Sequential Manual Gearbox (SMG)**.

– Remove release bearing from transmission input shaft.

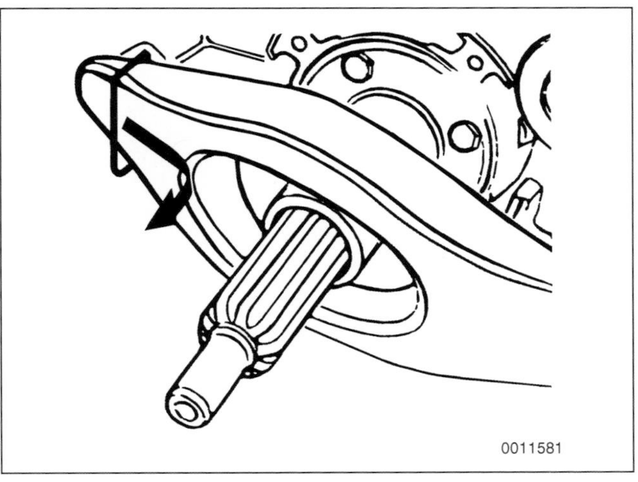

◄ Remove clutch release lever by pulling away from spring clip in direction of **arrow**.

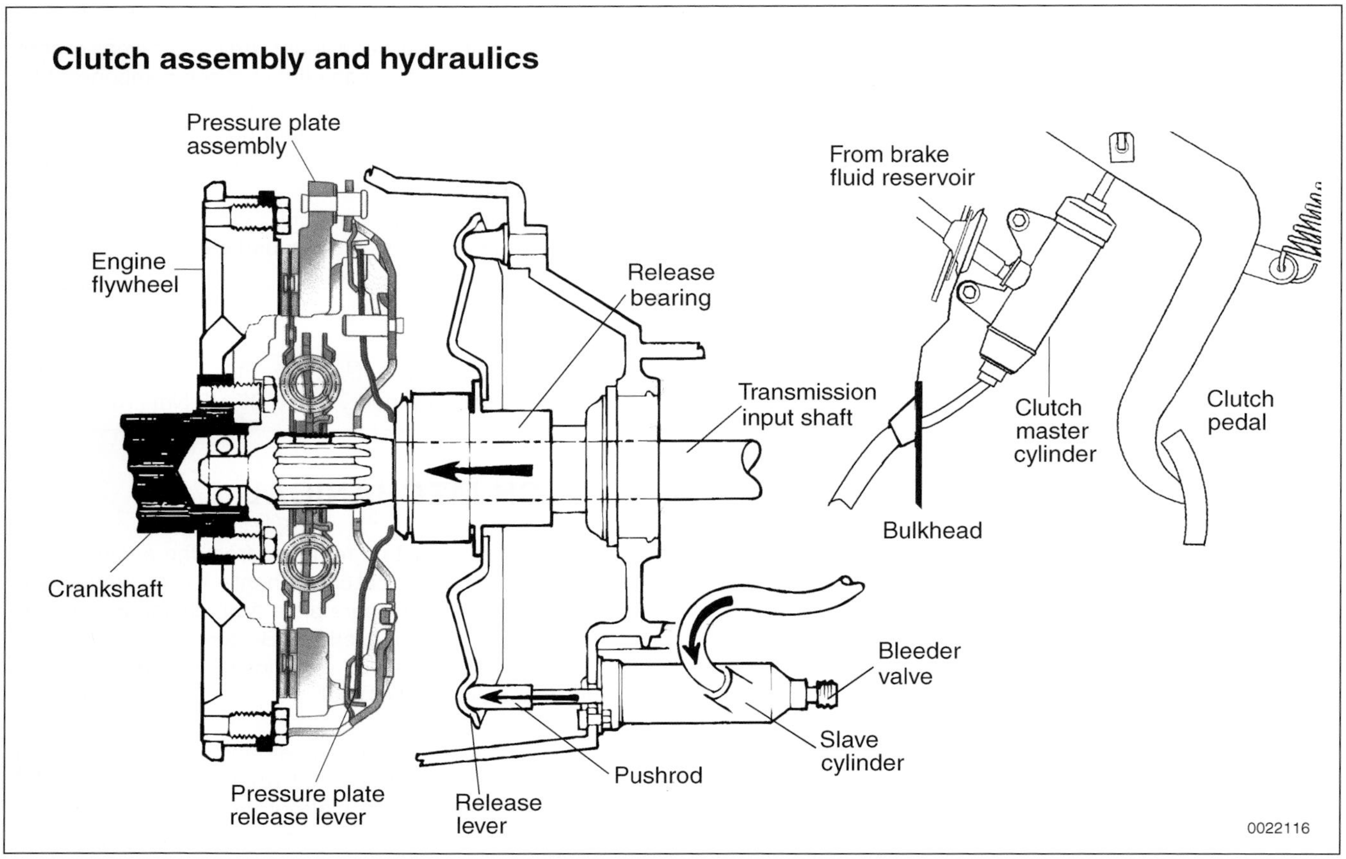

Clutch assembly and hydraulics

Pressure plate assembly
Engine flywheel
Crankshaft
Pressure plate release lever
Release lever
Pushrod
Release bearing
Transmission input shaft
From brake fluid reservoir
Bulkhead
Clutch master cylinder
Clutch pedal
Bleeder valve
Slave cylinder
0022116

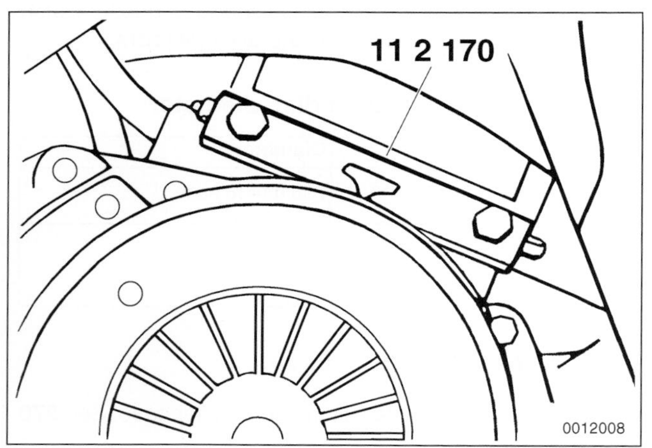

Lock flywheel in position using BMW special tool 11 2 170 or equivalent.

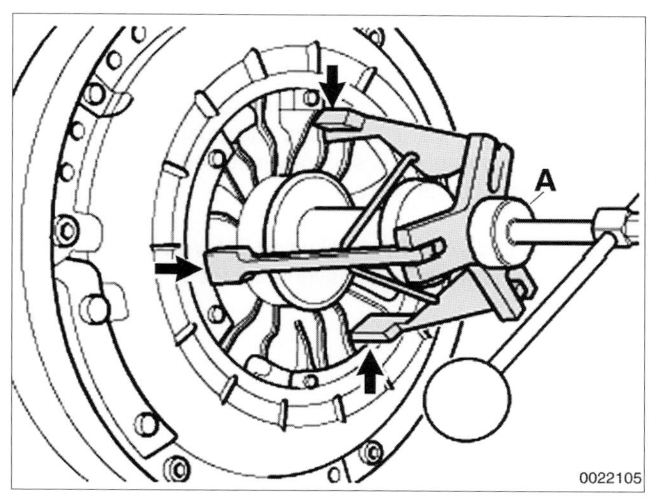

Install BMW special tool 21 2 160 or 21 2 170 with feet (**arrows**) clamping on to pressure plate at openings for self-adjusting springs. Tighten down head nut (**A**) to lock feet into position.

> ***CAUTION —***
> *Self adjusting clutch tool feet must engage in the openings for adjusting springs to safely remove the SAC pressure plate.*

- Turn tool handle in until clutch diaphragm spring is fully tensioned.
- Remove six bolts from perimeter of pressure plate. Remove self adjusting clutch unit and clutch disk.

Clutch, inspecting

- Inspect clutch disc for wear, cracks, loose rivets, contamination or excessive runout (warping). Replace if necessary.

NOTE —
Measure the depth of clutch lining at lining rivets. If shallowest rivet depth is less than 1 mm (0.04 in.), replace clutch disk.

- Inspect flywheel for scoring, hot spots, cracks or loose or worn guide pins. Replace flywheel if any faults are found.

> ***WARNING —***
> *If flywheel is removed from vehicle, use new bolts during installation. The old stretch-type bolts should not be reused.*

- Inspect transmission pilot bearing in end of crankshaft. The bearing should rotate smoothly without play. If necessary, replace as described later.

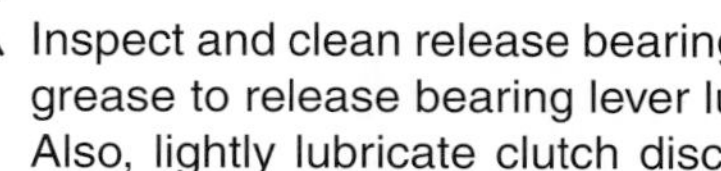

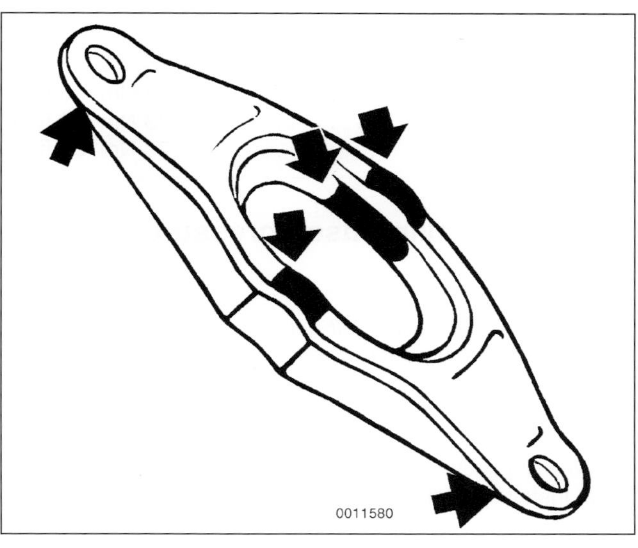

Inspect and clean release bearing lever. Apply a thin coat of grease to release bearing lever lubrication points (**arrows**). Also, lightly lubricate clutch disc splines and transmission input shaft splines.

Clutch, installing new pressure plate

New self adjusting clutch (SAC) pressure plates come with a locking plate installed that maintains spring tension on the self adjusting springs. This locking ring must not be removed until the pressure plate is securely installed on the flywheel with the clutch disk in place.

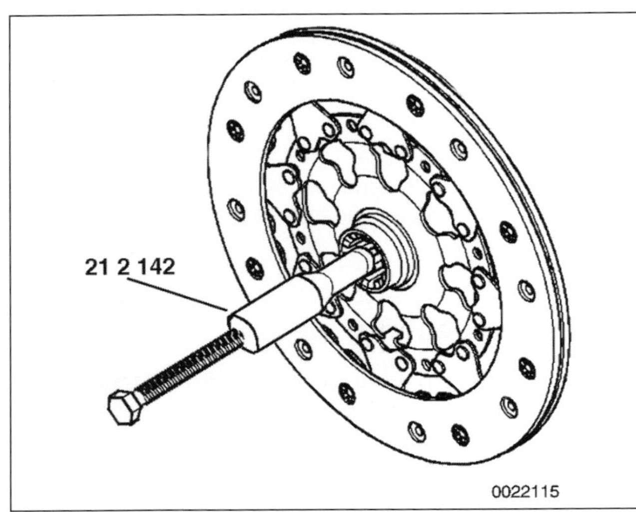

< Center clutch disk on flywheel using BMW special tool 21 2 142, or an equivalent clutch alignment tool.

NOTE —
The sides of a replacement clutch disk are labelled engine side and transmission side. Be sure to install clutch disk orientated in the proper direction.

— Install self adjusting clutch pressure plate onto dowel pins at flywheel. Tighten each bolt one turn at a time until pressure plate is fully seated, and then torque to specification

Tightening torque
- Clutch to flywheel
  M8 (8.8 grade) . . . . 24 Nm (18 ft-lb)
  M8 (10.9 grade) . . . . 34 Nm (25 ft-lb)

— Using a 14 mm allen wrench, carefully screw out locking plate in a clockwise direction.

— Remove BMW special tool 21 2 142 with bolt or screw enclosed with replacement clutch disk.

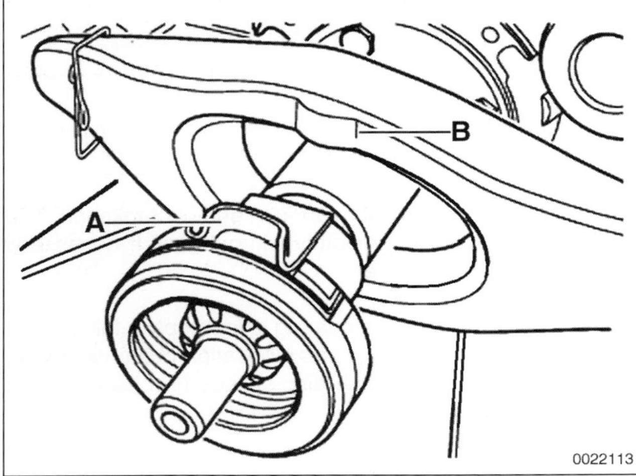

< Clean and inspect release bearing guide sleeve on transmission. Install release lever and release bearing. Bearing tabs (**A**) align with contact points (**B**) on release lever.

— Install transmission. See **230 Manual Transmission**.

Tightening torques
- Transmission to engine (Torx bolts)
  M8. . . . . 22 Nm (16 ft-lb)
  M10. . . . . 43 Nm (32 ft-lb)
  M12. . . . . 72 Nm (53 ft-lb)

Clutch, installing used pressure plate

NOTE —
- *Before installing a used Self Adjusting Clutch (SAC) pressure plate, be sure to reset self adjusting ring to the new position*
- *Locating hooks of BMW special tool 21 2 180 must engage in openings of SAC pressure plate*

— Place self adjusting clutch pressure plate on clean work surface. Install special tool 21 2 180 onto pressure plate.

- Squeeze handles of 21 2 180 together. Tighten down knurled knobs of 21 2 180. SAC adjustment ring is now in installation position.

- Install special tool 21 2 170 over 2 12 180 on SAC pressure plate. Screw in handle of 21 2 170 until diaphragm spring of SAC pressure plate is pretensioned.

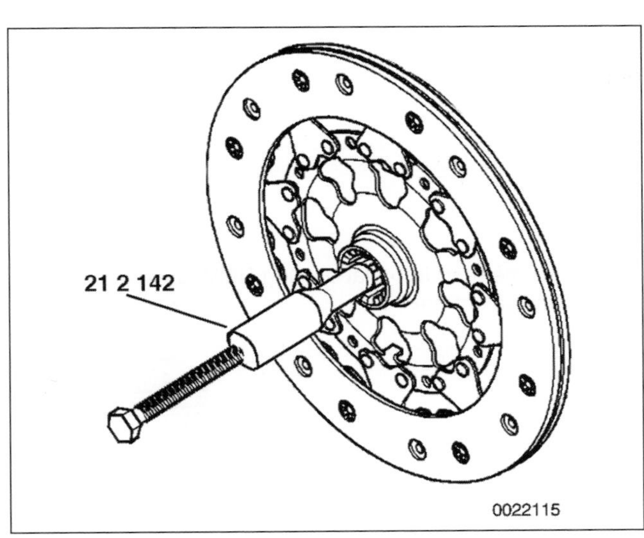

◄ Center clutch disk with BMW special tool 21 2 142. A comparable clutch alignment tool may be used. Remove threaded handle of clutch alignment tool

> ***WARNING —***
> *Be sure clutch disc is facing the correct way. The disc should be marked* ***engine side*** *or* ***transmission side****.*

- Mount self adjusting clutch assembly on flywheel, noting location of alignment pins.

- Tighten each bolt one turn at a time until pressure plate is fully seated, and then torque to specification.

Tightening torque

- Clutch to flywheel

M8 (8.8 grade)	24 Nm (17-ft-lb)
M8 (10.9 grade)	34 Nm (25 ft-lb)

- Unscrew handle of special tool until load is removed from diaphragm. Remove BMW special tool 21 2 180 from pressure plate.

- Remove clutch alignment tool from disk.

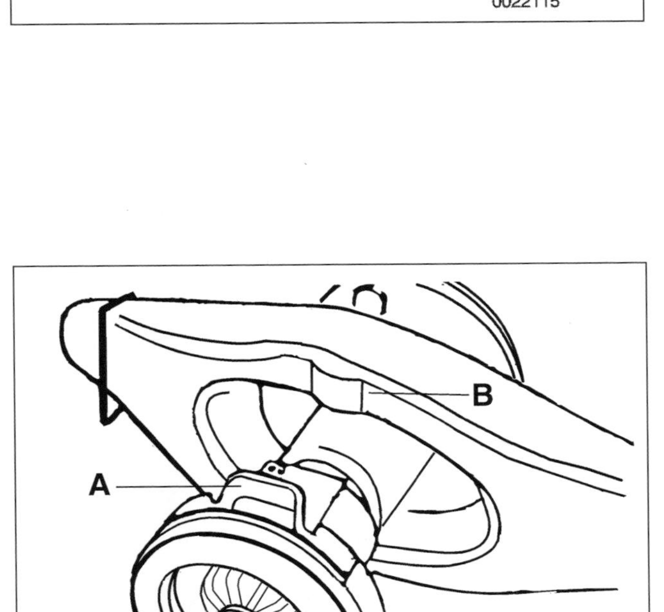

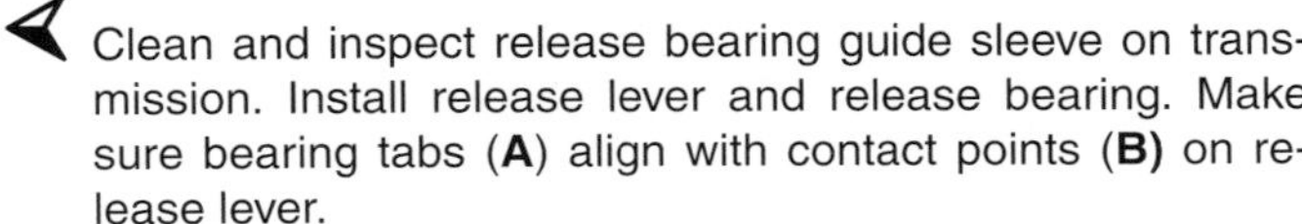

◄ Clean and inspect release bearing guide sleeve on transmission. Install release lever and release bearing. Make sure bearing tabs (**A**) align with contact points (**B**) on release lever.

- Install transmission. See **230 Manual Transmission**.

Tightening torques

- Transmission to engine (Torx bolts)

M8	22 Nm (16 ft-lb)
M10	43 Nm (32 ft-lb)
M12	72 Nm (53 ft-lb)

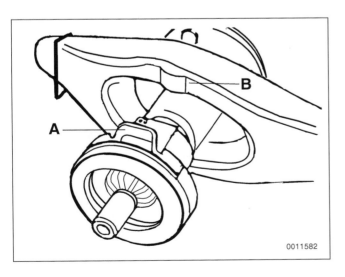

Transmission pilot bearing, replacing

- Remove clutch as described earlier.

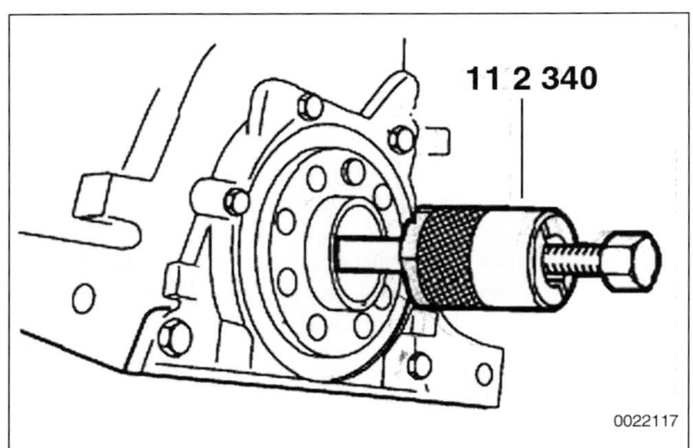

Remove transmission pilot bearing from end of crankshaft using BMW special tool 11 2 340 or equivalent puller.

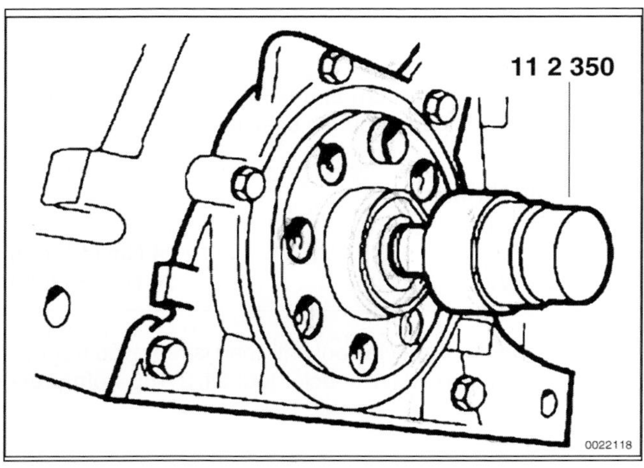

Press new bearing into place using BMW special tool 11 2 350 or equivalent driver.

230 Manual Transmission

230

GENERAL

This repair group covers external transmission service, including removal and installation of the transmission unit. Internal transmission repair is not covered. Special press tools and procedures are required to disassemble and service the internal geartrain.

For information on Sequential Manual Gearbox (SMG) transmissions, see **231 Sequential Manual Gearbox (SMG)**.

Special tools

BMW specified tools are recommended for removal and installation of the manual transmission, as well as the removal and installation of seals at the transmission input, output, and selector shafts. If these tools are unavailable, equivalent tools may be substituted.

Manual transmissions used are based on engine application. Consult **200 Transmission–General** for transmission application information. **Table a** lists gear ratio specifications.

NOTE —
Do not rely on forged casting numbers for transmission code identification.

Special Tools

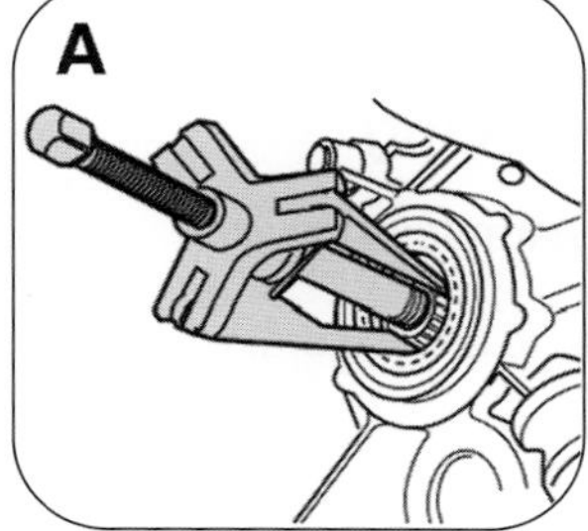

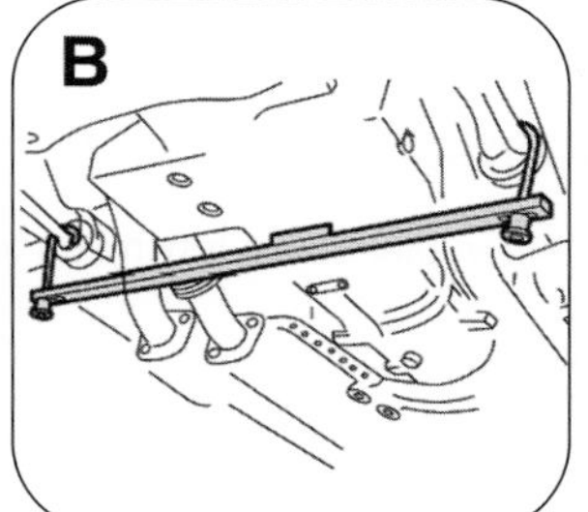

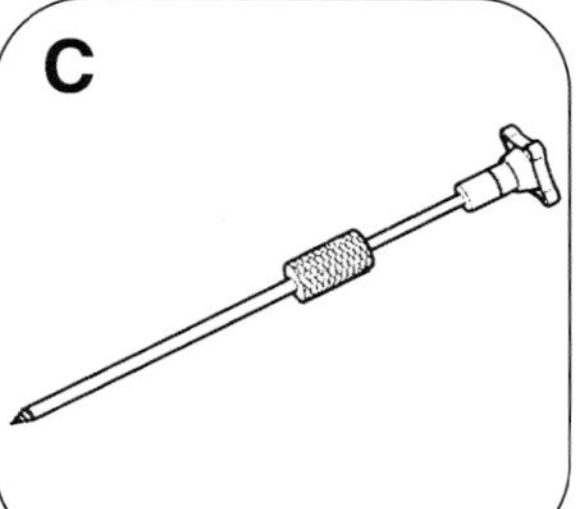

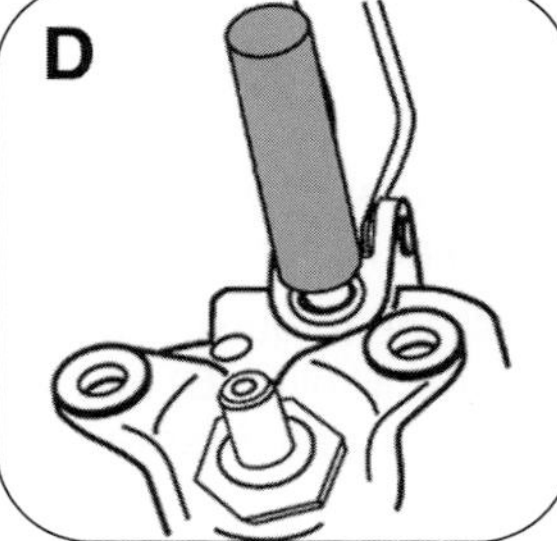

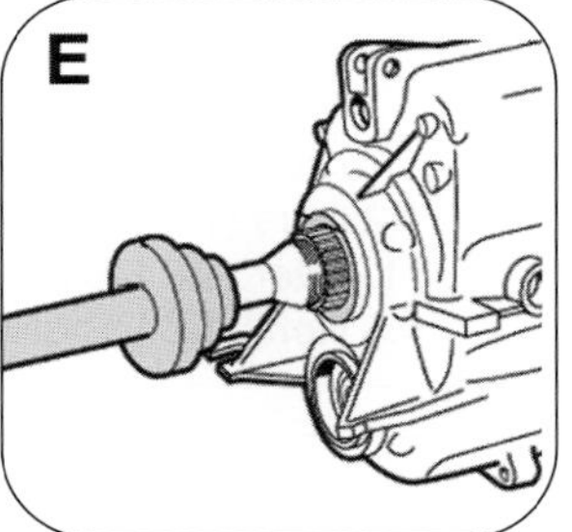

Special tools

A BMW 00 5 010 . . . . Seal puller
B BMW 11 8 022 . . . . Engine support bracket (lower)
C BMW 23 0 490 . . . . Input shaft seal puller (slide hammer)
D BMW 23 0 220 . . . . .Selector seal drift
E BMW 23 2 300 . . . . Output seal drift

TRANSMISSION FLUID SERVICE

Manual transmissions installed in the 3 Series are normally filled with a "Lifetime" manual transmission fluid (either BMW MTF LT-1 or MTF LT-2) and do not require periodic fluid changes. Transmissions filled with MTF LT-1 or MTF LT-2 lifetime oil are identified with a yellow label near the transmission fill plug labeled "Lifetime Oil MTF-LT-1" or "Lifetime Oil MTF-LT-2".

NOTE —
BMW MTF LT-2 supersedes MTF LT-1, as an approved replacement fluid for MTF LT-1.

Transmission fluid level, checking

Checking the transmission fluid level involves simply removing the side fill plug and inserting a finger into the hole to check the fluid level. If the fluid level is up to the bottom of the fill hole (finger is wetted by transmission fluid), the level is correct.

Transmission fluid, replacing

– Drive vehicle for a few miles to warm transmission.

– Raise and safely support vehicle to access drain plug.

CAUTION —
Make sure the car is stable and well supported at all times. Use a professional automotive lift or jack stands designed for the purpose. A floor jack is not adequate support.

Place a drain pan under transmission and remove drain plug (**A**) at bottom of transmission.

- Install and torque drain plug.
- Remove fill plug (**B**) from side of transmission.
- Slowly fill transmission with fluid until fluid overflows fill hole.
- Install and torque fluid fill plug.

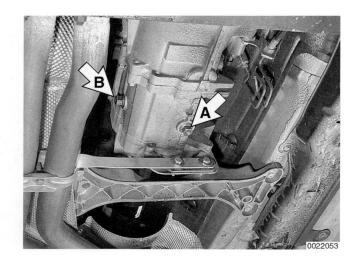

Fluid capacity

- Getrag transmission . . . . 1.0 liter (1.1 US qts)
- ZF transmission . . . . 1.2 liters (1.3 US qts)
- S6S420G transmission . . . . 1.7 liter (1.8 US qts)
- GS6-37BZ transmission . . . . 1.5 liters (1.6 US qts)

Tightening torque

- Transmission drain or fill plug . . . . 50 Nm (37 ft-lb)
- S6S420G drain or fill plug. . . . . 52 Nm (38 ft-lb)
- GS6-37BZ drain or fill plug . . . . 35 Nm (26 ft-lb)

TRANSMISSION SERVICE

Back-up light switch, replacing

< Raise and safely support vehicle to access back-up light switch (**arrow**). Unscrew switch from transmission.

NOTE —
- *Getrag transmission is illustrated. The back-up light switch is in the left side of the transmission.*
- *The back-up light switch on ZF transmission is in the right front of the transmission.*

— Install new switch.

Tightening torque
- Back-up light switch to transmission . . . . 18 Nm (13 ft-lb)

— Check transmission fluid level before lowering vehicle.

Selector shaft seal, replacing (transmission installed)

— Raise and safely support vehicle.

— Support transmission with transmission jack.

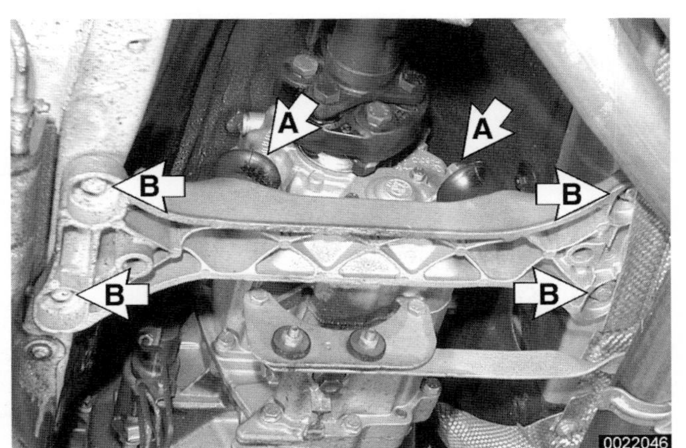

< On rear wheel drive cars:
- Remove driveshaft. See **260 Driveshafts**.
- Remove transmission mount bolts (**A**).
- Remove transmission crossmember bolts (**B**) and tilt down rear of transmission.

On all wheel drive cars:

- Remove front and rear driveshafts. See **260 Driveshafts.**
- Remove transfer case crossmember bolts (**arrows**) and remove transfer case. See **270 Transfer Case**.

> ***CAUTION —***
> *Tilting the engine to lower the transmission can lead to damage to various components due to lack of clearance.*

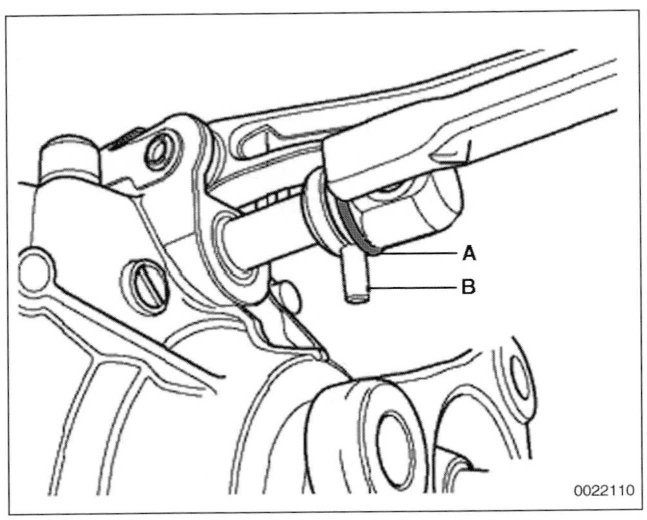

Working at rear of selector shaft, pry snap ring (**A**) out of groove with a small screwdriver. Push snap ring towards gear selector rod joint and drive out pin (**B**).

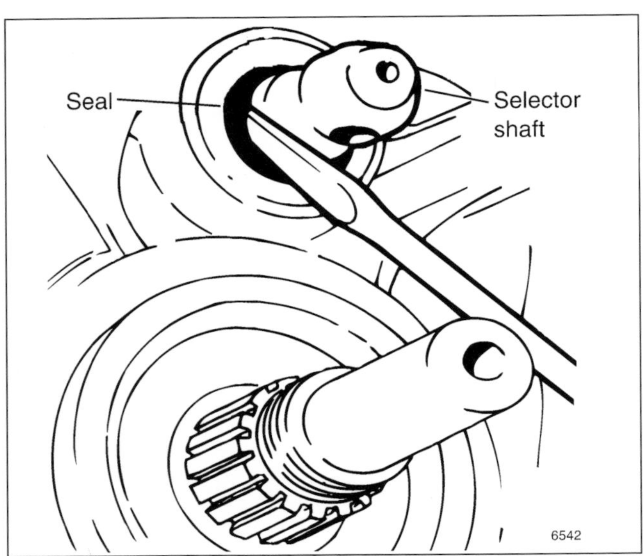

Carefully pry out selector shaft oil seal with a narrow seal remover or small screwdriver.

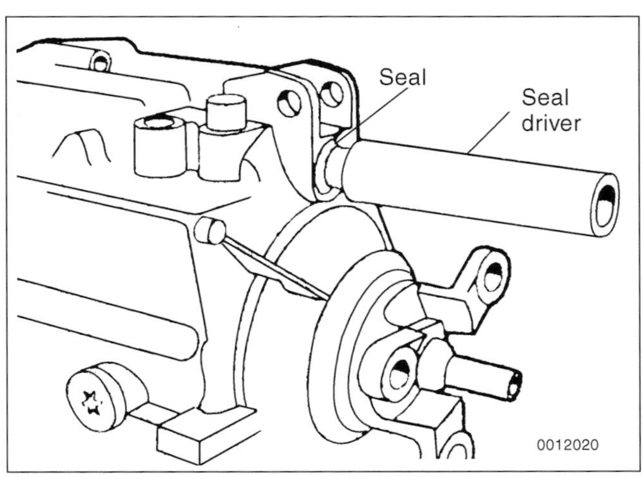

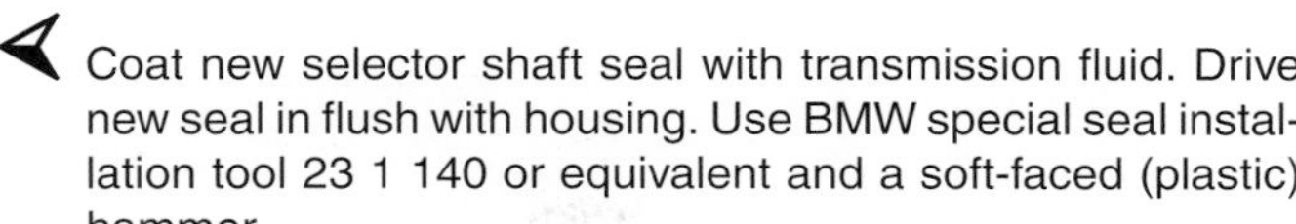

Coat new selector shaft seal with transmission fluid. Drive new seal in flush with housing. Use BMW special seal installation tool 23 1 140 or equivalent and a soft-faced (plastic) hammer.

– Installation is reverse of removal, noting the following;

- Install driveshaft using new lock nuts.
- Check transmission oil level, topping up as necessary.

Tightening torques

- Center bearing (driveshaft) to body .... 21 Nm (15 ft-lb)
- Clamping sleeve (driveshaft) .... 10 Nm (89 in-lb)
- Driveshaft to final drive flange
  With U-joint (M10 ribbed nut) .... 80 Nm (59 ft-lb)
  With U-joint (M10 compressed nut) .... 64 Nm (47 ft-lb)
- Flex-disc to driveshaft or transmission flange
  M10 (8.8 grade) .... 48 Nm (35 ft-lb)
  M10 (10.9 grade) .... 60 Nm (44 ft-lb)
  M12 (10.9 grade) .... 100 Nm (74 ft-lb)
- Transmission / transfer case crossmember
  to chassis (M8) .... 21 Nm (15 ft-lb)
- Transfer case to transmission (M10) ... 41 Nm (30 ft-lb)

Output shaft seal, replacing (transmission installed)

– Raise and safely support vehicle.

– Support transmission with transmission jack.

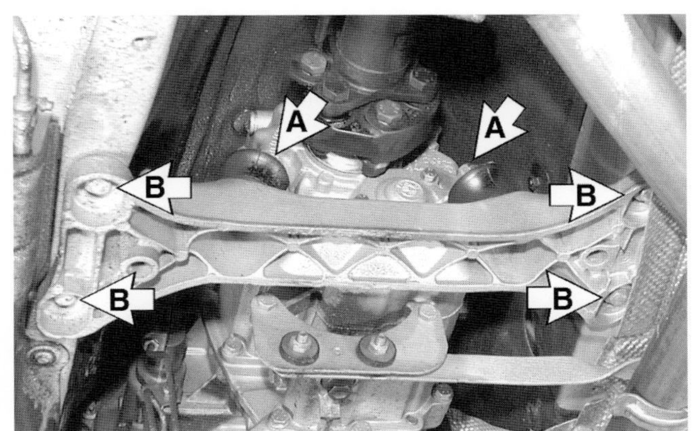

On rear wheel drive cars:

- Remove driveshaft. See **260 Driveshafts**.
- Remove transmission mount bolts (**A**).
- Remove transmission crossmember bolts (**B**) and tilt down rear of transmission.

On all wheel drive cars:

- Remove front and rear driveshafts. See **260 Driveshafts.**
- Remove transfer case crossmember bolts (**arrows**) and remove transfer case. See **270 Transfer Case**.

> ***CAUTION —***
> *Tilting the engine to lower the transmission can lead to damage to various components due to lack of clearance.*

– Bend back and remove transmission output collar nut lock-plate.

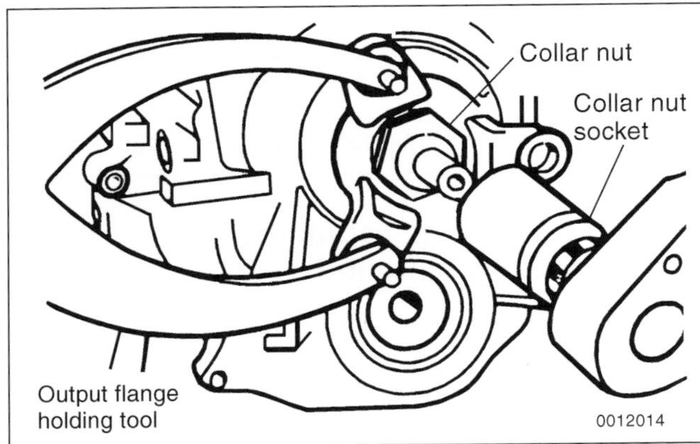

Remove collar nut with 30 mm thin-walled deep socket. Counterhold output flange to prevent it from turning.

– Remove output flange. If necessary, use a puller.

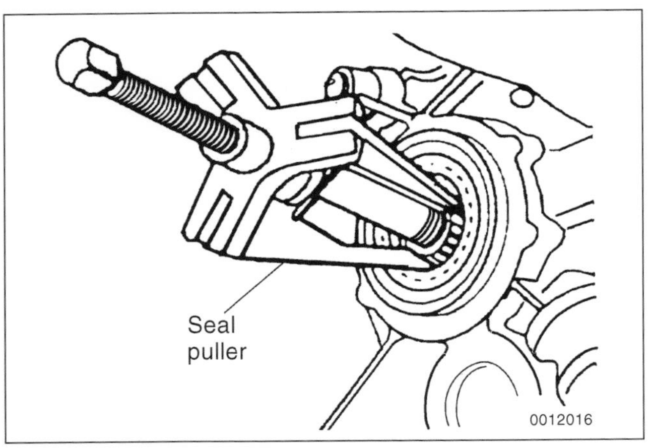

Use a seal puller to remove seal from transmission housing

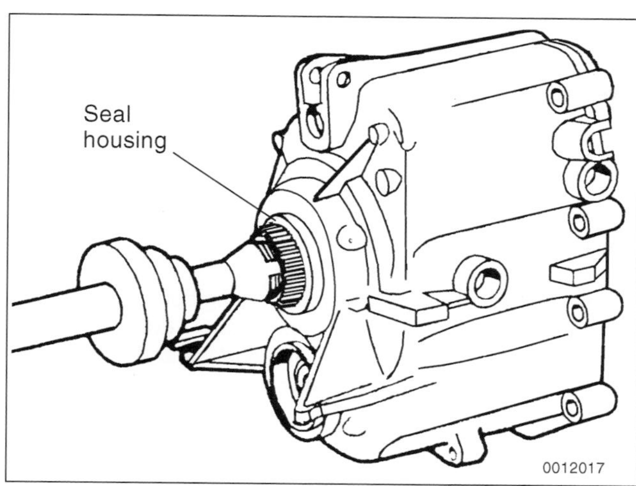

Coat new seal with transmission fluid and drive into position until it is flush with housing. Use seal driver (BMW special tool 23 2 300) or equivalent.

– Reinstall output flange (and shims, if applicable) to output shaft.

NOTE —
On Getrag S5D 250G transmissions BMW recommends heating the output flange to about 176°F (80°C) to aid installation. This can be done by placing the flange in hot water.

– Coat bearing surface of collar nut with sealer and install nut. Tighten collar nut in two stages. Install new lockplate. Bend tabs into flange grooves.

NOTE —
BMW recommends the use of a sealer such as Loctite® 242 when installing the flange collar nut to prevent oil from leaking past the threads.

– Installation is reverse of removal, noting the following:
- Install driveshaft using new nuts. See **260 Driveshafts**.
- Check transmission and transfer case fluid level, if applicable, topping up as necessary.

Tightening torque
- Transmission crossmember to chassis
  M8 . . . . 21 Nm (15 ft-lb)
- Transmission output flange to output shaft
  Stage I . . . . 190 Nm (140 ft-lb)
  Stage II (after loosening) . . . . 120 Nm (89 ft-lb)

Input shaft seal, replacing (transmission removed)

Replacement of the input shaft seal requires the removal of the transmission from the vehicle as described later in this repair group.

– Remove clutch release bearing and release lever from inside bellhousing.

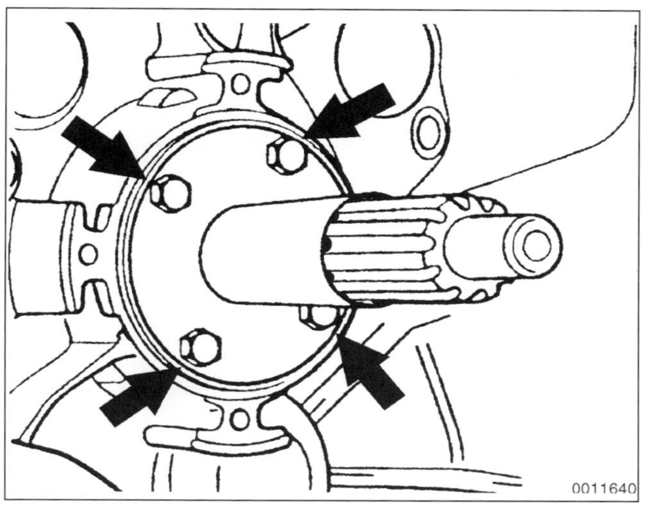

Remove bolts (**arrows**) for clutch release-bearing guide sleeve, noting bolt lengths (Getrag transmission shown). Remove sleeve and any spacers (shims) under it.

– With transmission on a workbench, remove input shaft seal cover from inside bell-housing.

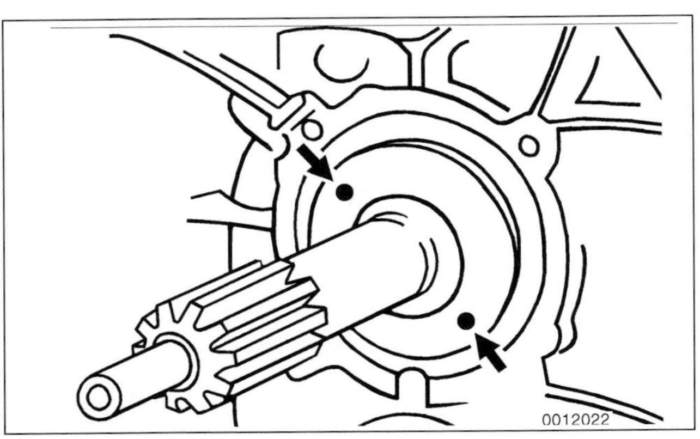

Locate two indents (**arrows**) in seal. Thread a slide hammer seal puller at indents and remove seal.

- Use care not to scratch or damage input shaft. Use a protective sleeve or tape the shaft when removing and installing the seal.

- Lubricate new seal with transmission oil and drive into place using an appropriate drift.

- Thoroughly clean guide sleeve mounting bolts, sealing surfaces, and threads in case. Apply sealer (Loctite® 242 or equivalent) to guide sleeve sealing surface and bolts. Reinstall guide sleeve and any spacer(s).

Tightening torque

- Guide sleeve to transmission M6x12 bolt . . . . 10 Nm (89 in-lb)

TRANSMISSION REMOVAL AND INSTALLATION

Removal and installation of the transmission is best accomplished on a lift using a transmission jack. The engine must be supported from above using appropriate support equipment. This allows the engine to pivot on its mounts to access the upper Torx-head bolts at the bellhousing.

> ***WARNING —***
> - *Make sure the car is stable and well supported at all times. Use a professional automotive lift or jack stands designed for the purpose. A floor jack is not adequate support.*
> - *The removal of the transmission may upset the balance of the vehicle on a lift.*

Transmission, removing and installing

- Disconnect negative (–) cable from battery.

> ***CAUTION —***
> *Prior to disconnecting the battery, read the battery disconnection cautions given at the front of this manual.*

Remove engine cooling intake hood fasteners (**arrows**) at front of engine compartment.

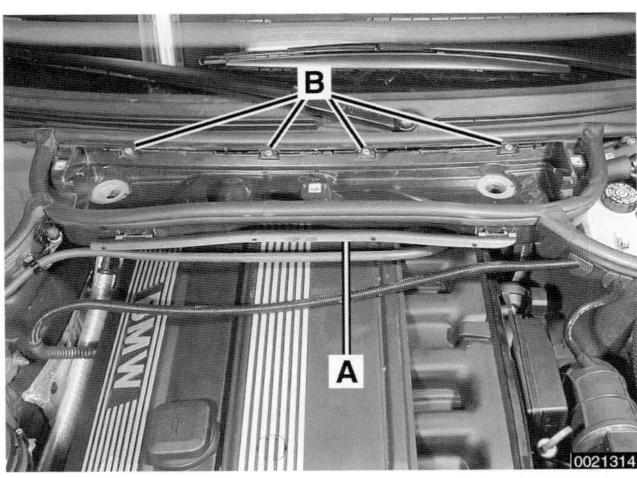

Remove housing for interior ventilation microfilter.

- Remove upper cover and microfilter.
- Open wiring harness loom cover (**A**) and remove wires.
- Unfasten screws (**B**) and remove lower microfilter housing.

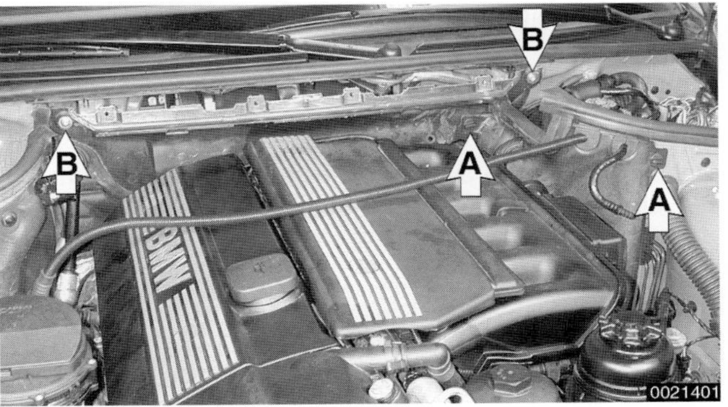

Remove heater bulkhead cover.

- Remove engine compartment side trim panel. Turn locking knobs (**A**) and slide trim panel from mounting lip.
- Remove heater bulkhead cover mounting screws (**B**) and lift cover up and out from firewall.

– On M3 models, remove intake manifold, see **110 Engine Removal and Installation**.

– Raise and safely support vehicle.

– Remove engine splashguard from underside of vehicle.

– On M3 models, remove engine driven cooling fan and fan clutch, see **170 Radiator and Cooling System**.

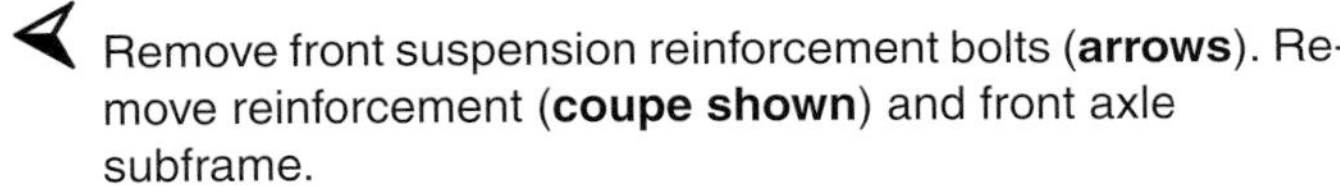

Remove front suspension reinforcement bolts (**arrows**). Remove reinforcement (**coupe shown**) and front axle subframe.

NOTE —

- *Tubular style front end reinforcements are used in rear wheel drive 3 Series sedans and wagons built up to 11/00 and coupes built up to 10/99.*
- *Pan style front end reinforcements are used on rear wheel drive sedans and wagons built after 12/00, coupes built after 11/99 and all convertibles.*
- *All wheel drive models require no reinforcement due to the construction of the front subframe.*

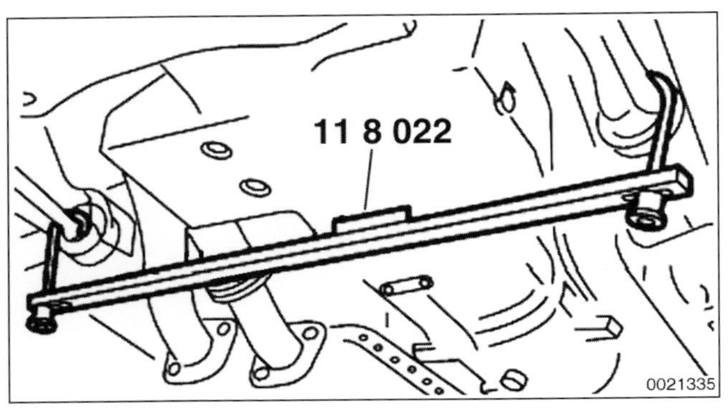

- Attach BMW special tool 11 8 022 to left and right lower control arms. Tighten knurled screws until tool makes contact with engine oil pan.

- Support transmission with transmission jack. Remove reinforcing cross brace from below engine/transmission.

- Disconnect harness connector from back-up light switch on transmission. On M3 models, disconnect harness connector for gear detection switch.

- Remove exhaust system and heat shield. See **180 Exhaust System**.

- Remove driveshaft. See **260 Driveshafts**.

- On all wheel drive vehicles: Remove transfer case. See **270 Transfer Case**.

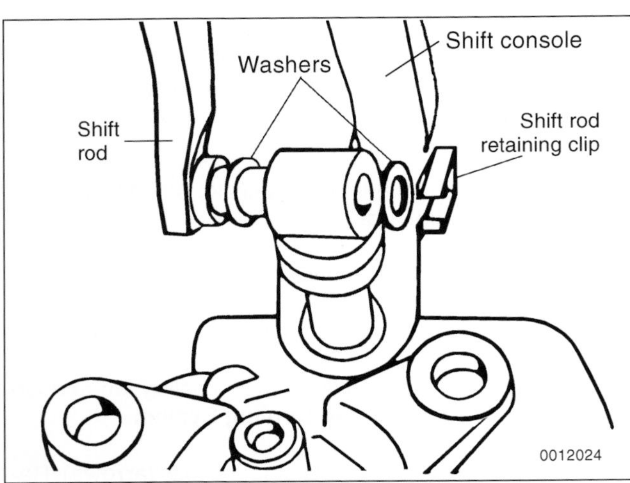

- Disconnect shift rod from selector shaft coupling.

- Disconnect shift console from top of transmission. See **250 Gearshift Linkage**.

- Unbolt clutch slave cylinder from side of transmission. Do not disconnect fluid hose. Suspend slave cylinder from chassis using stiff wire.

> **CAUTION —**
> *Do not operate clutch pedal with slave cylinder removed from transmission.*

- Loosen knurled screws of BMW special tool 11 8 022 until transmission/engine assembly is just above, but not in contact with fire wall and heater connections.

> **CAUTION —**
> *Tilting the engine to lower the transmission can lead to damage to various components due to lack of clearance at rear of engine -Remove brake fluid reservoir if necessary.*

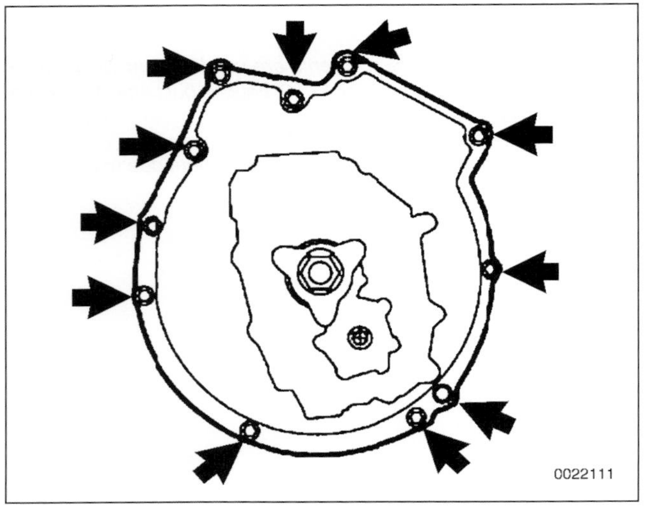

- Remove transmission mounting Torx-head bolts (**arrows**). Note length and location of bolts.

- Remove transmission by pulling backward until the transmission input shaft clears the clutch disc splines, then pull downwards. Lower jack and remove transmission.

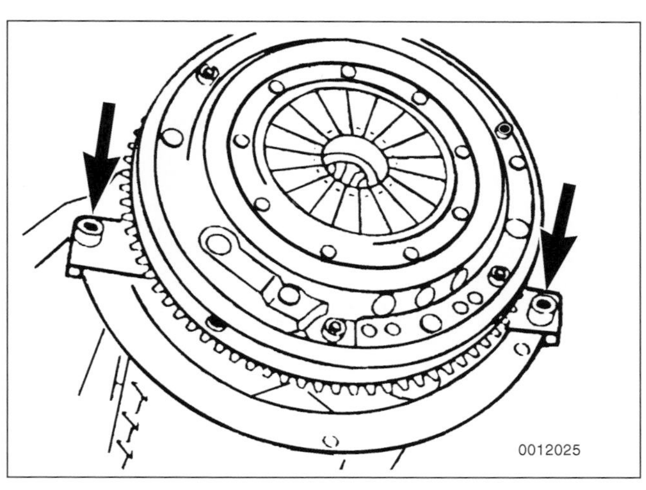

Installation is reverse of removal, keeping in mind the following:

- When installing a new transmission, be sure to transfer parts from old transmission if applicable.
- Thoroughly clean input shaft and clutch disc splines. Lightly lubricate transmission input shaft before installing.
- Be sure bellhousing dowels (**arrows**) are correctly located.
- Center rear of transmission in driveshaft tunnel before tightening transmission support bracket.
- Always replace front end reinforcement mounting fasteners on vehicles equipped with the plate style reinforcement.

NOTE —

Torx-head mounting bolts should always be used with washers to prevent difficult removal in the future.

– Install driveshaft and preload center bearing bracket. Use new nuts when mounting driveshaft to transmission/flex disc and final drive. See **260 Driveshafts**.

– Refill transmission with appropriate lubricant before starting or towing the car. See **Transmission Fluid Service** earlier in this repair group.

Tightening torques

- Front end reinforcement to chassis and subframe (M10)
  (tubular style) . . . . 42 Nm (31 ft-lb)
  (pan style) . . . . 59 Nm (44 ft-lb) + 90°
- Rubber mount to transmission or bracket nut (M8) . . . . 21 Nm (15 ft-lb)
- Slave cylinder to transmission . . . . 22 Nm (16 ft-lb)
- Transmission crossmember to chassis
  M8 . . . . 21 Nm (15 ft-lb)
- Transmission to engine (Torx-head)
  M8 . . . . 22 Nm (16 ft-lb)
  M10 . . . . 43 Nm (32 ft-lb)
  M12 . . . . 72 Nm (53 ft-lb)
- Transmission drain/fill plug . . . . 50 Nm (37 ft-lb)

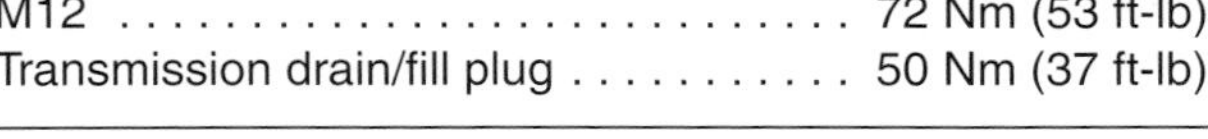

231 Sequential Manual Gearbox (SMG)

231

GENERAL

This repair group covers basic transmission service for the Sequential Manual Gearbox (SMG) transmissions, including SMG Clutch/Hydraulic system service and transmission removal and installation. Internal transmission repair is not covered.

Special Tools

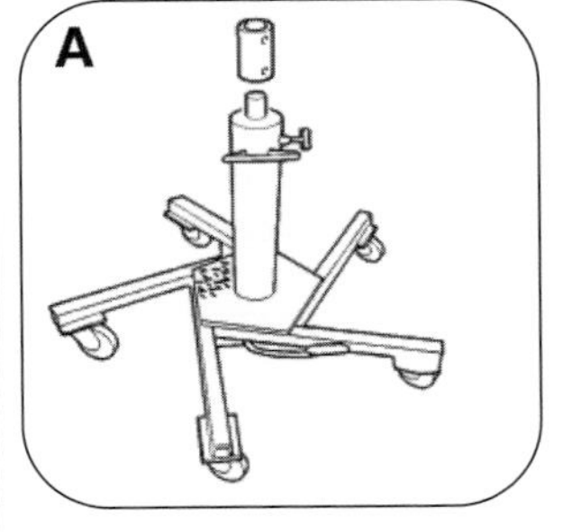

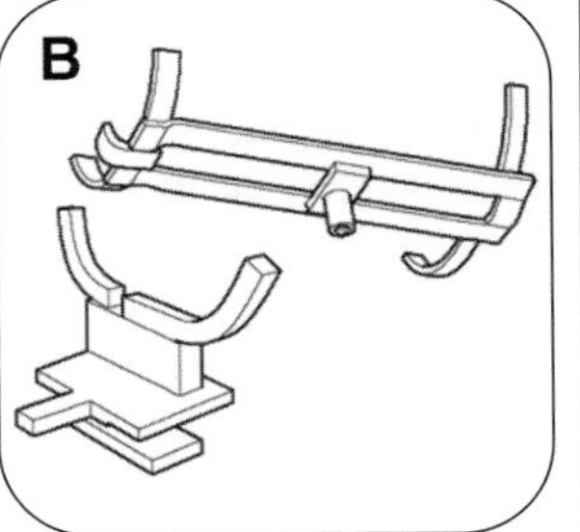

Special tools
A BMW 00 2 030 .... Transmission jack
B BMW 23 0 030 / 23 0 140 .... Transmission fixture sets

Special tools

BMW specified tools are recommended for removal and installation of the SMG manual transmission.

For transmission seal replacement, see **230 Manual Transmission**.

For clutch replacement information, see **210 Clutch**.

SMG transmissions used are based on engine code. **Table a** lists model and gear ratio specifications.

NOTE —
Do not rely on forged casting numbers for transmission code identification.

Table a. SMG transmission gear ratios

Transmission	S6S420G SMG (S54 engine)	GS6S37BZ SMG (M54 engine)
Gear Ratios:		
1st	4.23	4.35
2nd	2.53	2.49
3rd	1.67	1.66
4th	1.24	1.24
5th	1.00	1.00
6th	0.83	0.85
reverse	3.75	3.93

TRANSMISSION FLUID SERVICE

SMG transmissions installed in the 3 Series use "Lifetime" manual transmission fluid (BMW MTF LT-1 or LT-2) and do not require periodic fluid changes. Transmissions filled with MTF LT-1 lifetime oil are identified with a yellow label near the transmission fill plug labeled "Lifetime Oil MTF-LT-1".

Transmission fluid level, checking

Checking the transmission fluid level involves removing the side fill plug and inserting a finger into the hole to check the fluid level. If the fluid level is up to the bottom of the fill hole (finger is wetted by transmission fluid), the level is correct.

Transmission fluid, replacing

– Drive vehicle for a few miles to warm transmission.

– Raise and safely support vehicle to access drain plug.

> ***CAUTION —***
> *Make sure the car is stable and well supported at all times. Use a professional automotive lift or jack stands designed for the purpose. A floor jack is not adequate support.*

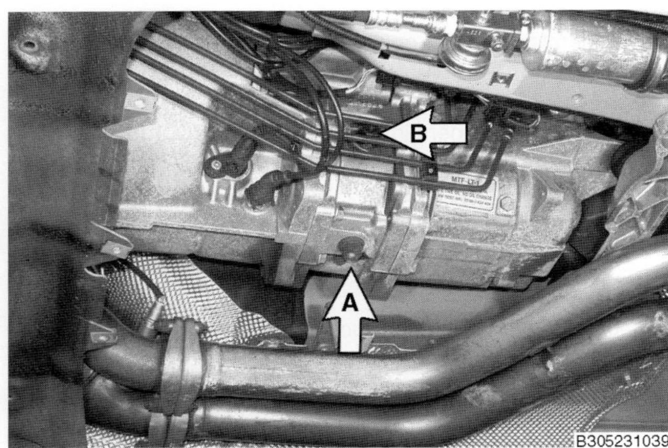

Place a drain pan under transmission and remove drain plug (**A**) at bottom of transmission.

- Install and torque drain plug.
- Remove fill plug (**B**) from side of transmission.
- Slowly fill with fluid until fluid overflows fill hole.
- Install and torque fluid fill plug.

Fluid capacity

- S6S 420G transmission . . . . 1.7 liters (1.8 US qts)
- GS6S37BZ transmission . . . . 1.5 liters (1.6 US qts)

Tightening torque

- S6S 420G drain or fill plug . . . . 52 Nm (38 ft-lb)
- GS6S37BZ drain or fill plug . . . . 35 Nm (26 ft-lb)

SMG CLUTCH / HYDRAULIC SYSTEM SERVICE

While the clutch components of an SMG transmission are very similar to a traditional manual transmission, clutch release and engagement is governed by a computer controlled hydraulic module and slave cylinder. The computer controlled hydraulic module also activates hydraulic cylinders that control gear selection.

For clutch replacement information, see **210 Clutch**.

Some SMG hydraulic system service procedures require the use of factory diagnostic equipment. These procedures are identified where noted.

Hydraulic fluid level, checking (M3 models)

- Turn ignition switch to “On” position without starting the car.
- Depress brake pedal.
- Move gear selector back and forth from “0” to “R”, or “0” to “E” until transmission stops performing gearshifts. Wait until hydraulic pump stops.

◀ Open hydraulic fluid expansion tank and fill to “MAX” level with **Pentosin CHF 11S** hydraulic fluid.

Hydraulic fluid level, checking (except M3 models)

- Turn ignition switch to “On” position without starting the car.
- Depressurize clutch hydraulic system using BMW DIS diagnostic computer.

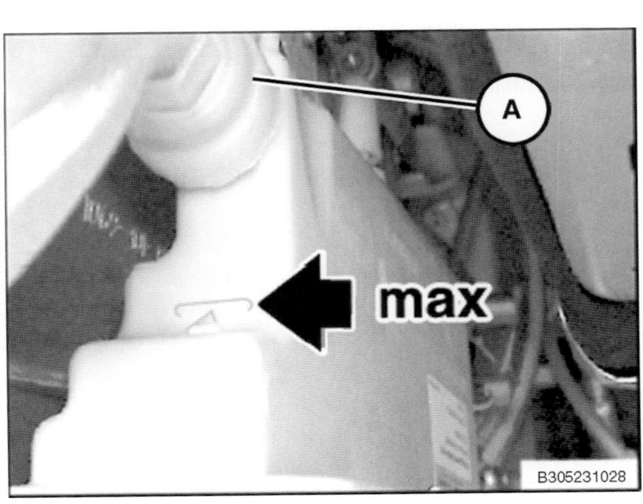

◀ Working at side of transmission, open hydraulic fluid expansion tank (**A**) and fill to “MAX” level with **Pentosin CHF 11S** hydraulic fluid.

Hydraulic system depressurization (M3 models)

– Remove e-box cover.

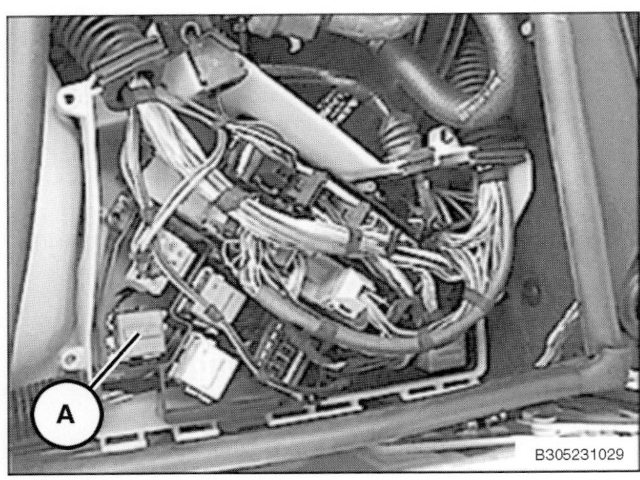

◄ Remove hydraulic pump relay (**A**).

– Turn ignition switch to "On" position without starting the car.

– Move gear selector back and forth from "0" to "R", or "0" to "E" until transmission stops performing gearshifts. Wait until hydraulic pump stops.

– Check accumulator pressure using BMW DIS diagnostic computer.

NOTE —
Residual pressure drops after a brief period.

– Before re-inserting hydraulic pump relay, begin the following service functions using BMW DIS diagnostic computer:

- Transmission actuator
- Clutch slave cylinder

Hydraulic system depressurization (except M3 models)

SMG clutch hydraulic system depressurization is performed using BMW DIS diagnostic computer.

Hydraulic unit, removing and installing (M3 models)

– Depressurize hydraulic system.

– Disconnect battery. Disconnect battery positive (+) lead from connection point.

– Remove intake manifold, see **110 Engine Removal and Installation**.

◄ Working from below, at driver's side front control arm, disconnect electrical harness connector (**arrow**) on hydraulic unit.

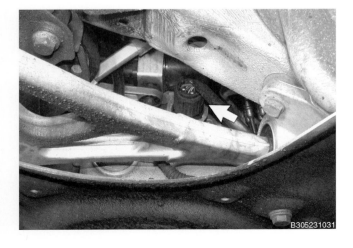

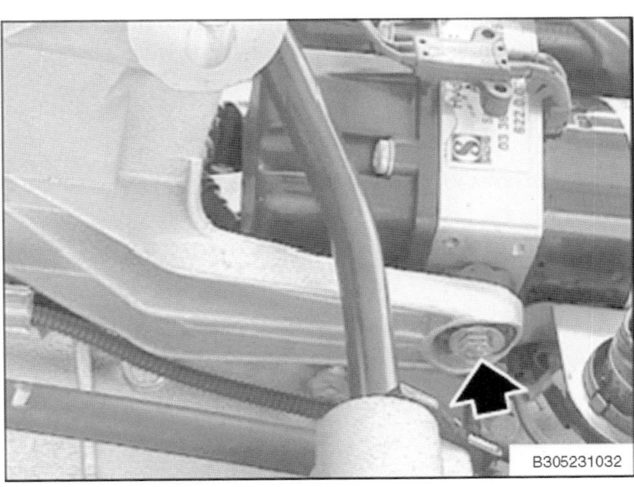
B305231032

< Remove bolt (**arrow**).

B305231033

< Remove bolt (**arrow**).

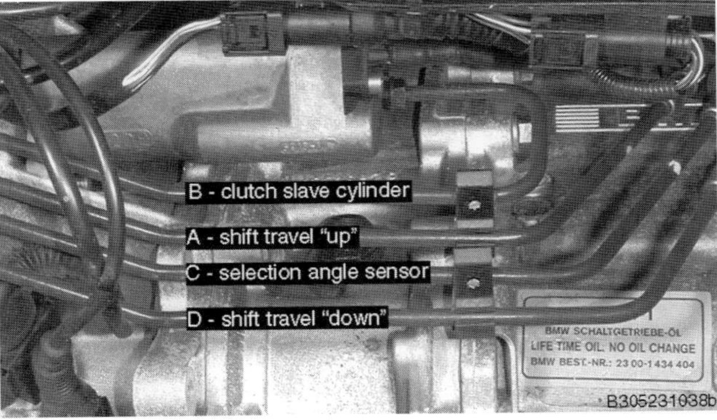

B305231038b

< Mark position and function of hydraulic lines as they correspond to locations at hydraulic unit.

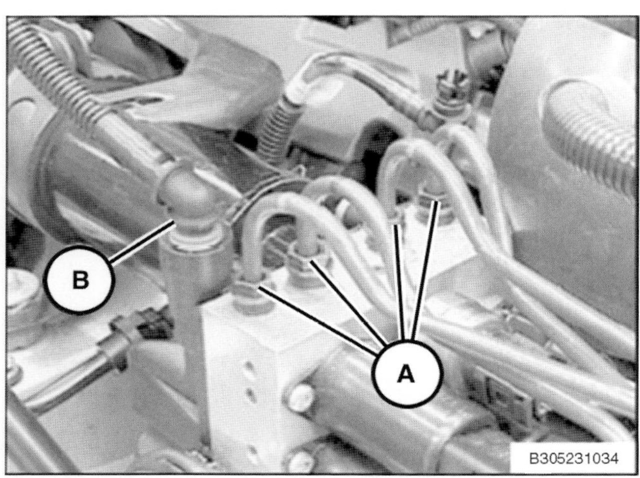

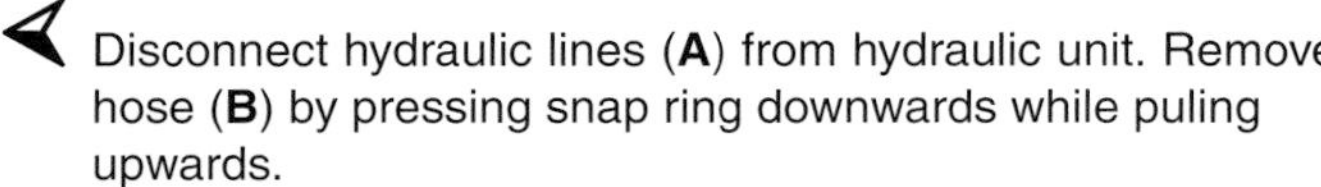

◄ Disconnect hydraulic lines (**A**) from hydraulic unit. Remove hose (**B**) by pressing snap ring downwards while puling upwards.

NOTE —
Plug or cap holes with suitable plastic caps.

◄ Disconnect electrical harness connector (**A**) at carbon canister.

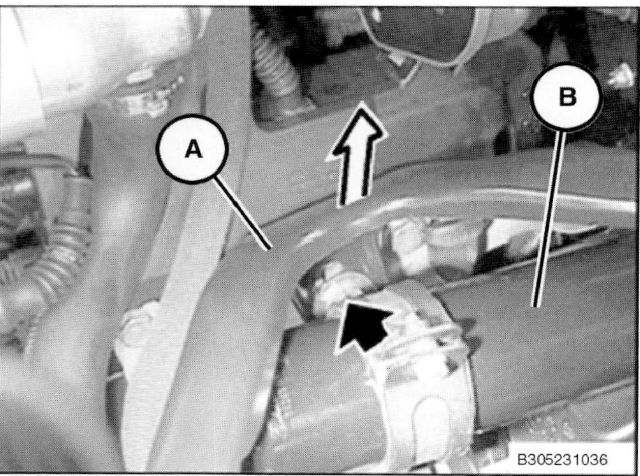

◄ Remove screw on manifold support (**A**).

- Pull manifold support upwards slightly.
- Lift out hydraulic unit (**B**).

– Installation is reverse of removal, noting the following:

- Guide pin of hydraulic unit must engage in lower retaining fixture.
- Align manifold support before tightening screw.

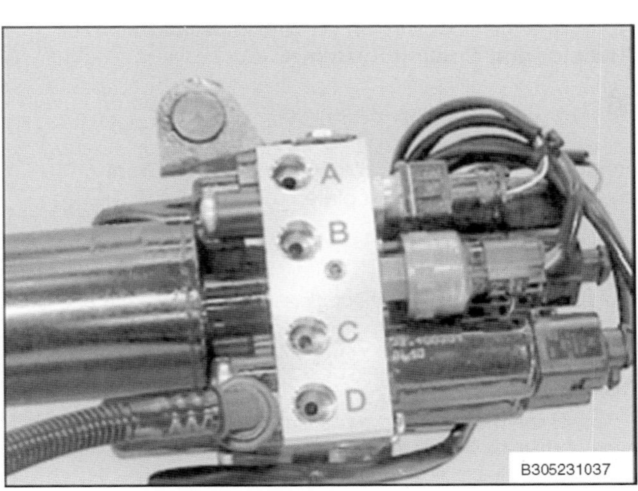

Observe correct installation positions of hydraulic lines.

- A - shift travel "up"
- B - clutch slave cylinder
- C - selection angle sensor
- D - shift travel "down"

Hydraulic unit, removing and installing (except M3 models)

Removal and installation of the hydraulic unit on non-M3 models equipped with the SMG transmission requires transmission removal, the use of specialized BMW transmission tools, and the use of a BMW diagnostic computer. This procedure is beyond the scope of this manual, and should be performed by a BMW trained service technician.

TRANSMISSION REMOVAL AND INSTALLATION

Removal and installation of the transmission is best accomplished on a lift using a transmission jack. The engine must be supported from above using appropriate support equipment. This allows the engine to pivot on its mounts to access the upper Torx-head bolts at the bellhousing.

> ***WARNING —***
> - *Make sure the car is stable and well supported at all times. Use a professional automotive lift or jack stands designed for the purpose. A floor jack is not adequate support.*
> - *The removal of the transmission may upset the balance of the vehicle on a lift.*

Transmission, removing and installing (M3 models)

– Disconnect negative (–) cable from battery.

> ***CAUTION —***
> *Prior to disconnecting the battery, read the battery disconnection cautions given at the front of this manual.*

– Remove engine intake manifold. See **110 Engine Removal and Installation**.

- Remove engine cooling fan with fan impeller. See **170 Radiator and Cooling System**.

- Remove underbody splash shields.

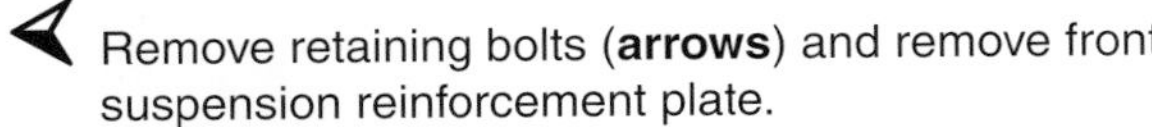

◄ Remove retaining bolts (**arrows**) and remove front suspension reinforcement plate.

NOTE —
Front suspension reinforcement plate retaining bolts are one time use only.

> ***CAUTION —***
> *Front suspension reinforcement plate is a critical structural member for the front suspension. Do not drive vehicle without plate installed.*

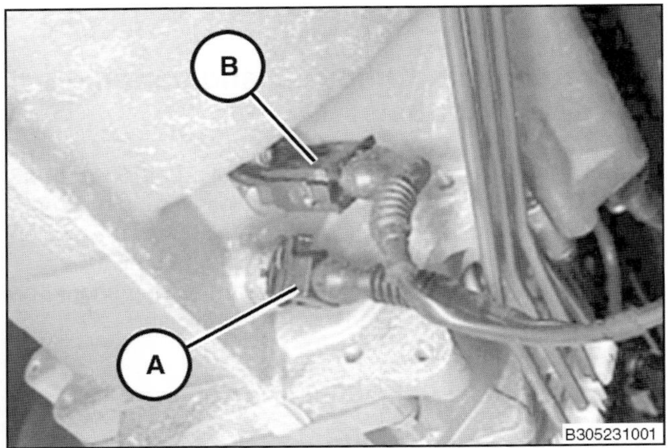

- Remove exhaust system including exhaust manifolds and heatshields. See **180 Exhaust System**. Remove rear bracket for underbody splashshield.

◄ Disconnect electrical harness connectors for transmission oil temperature sensor (**A**) and transmission speed sensor (**B**).

◄ Disconnect electrical harness connector for back-up light switch (**A**).

Unclip hydraulic lines at bellhousing (**arrow**).

Unclip hydraulic lines from side of transmission (**arrow**). Remove nuts (**A**) and remove clutch slave cylinder from transmission.

NOTE —

Hydraulic line remains connected. Slowly relieve tension on clutch slave cylinder when removing to prevent air from being drawn in though sealing sleeve.

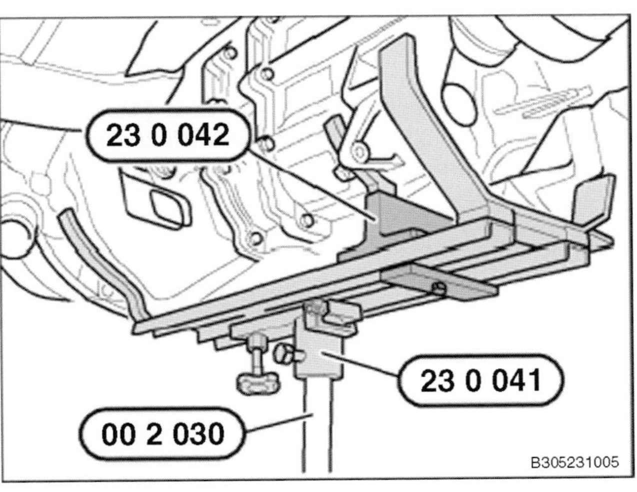

Support transmission using BMW special tools 00 2 030, 23 0 041, and 23 0 042.

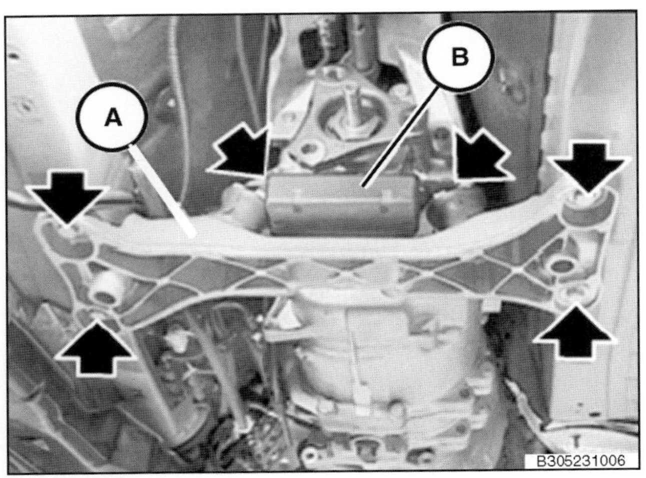

Remove bolts (**arrows**) and remove crossmember (**A**). Lower transmission until cylinder head touches rear bulkhead. Support engine at oil pan.

NOTE —
*Note position of vibration damper (**B**).*

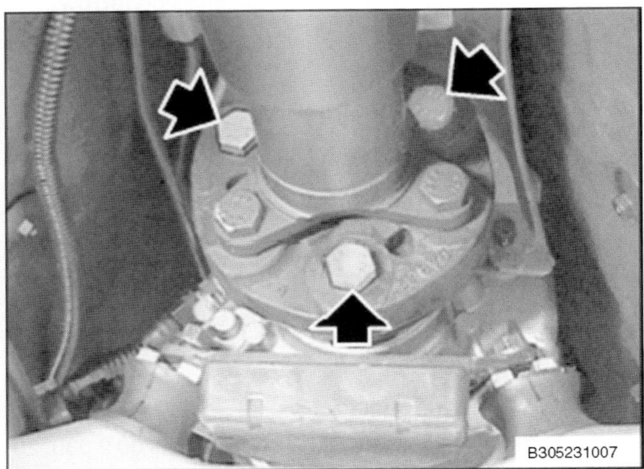

Holding the driveshaft stationary, loosen bolts holding driveshaft guibo to transmission output flange.

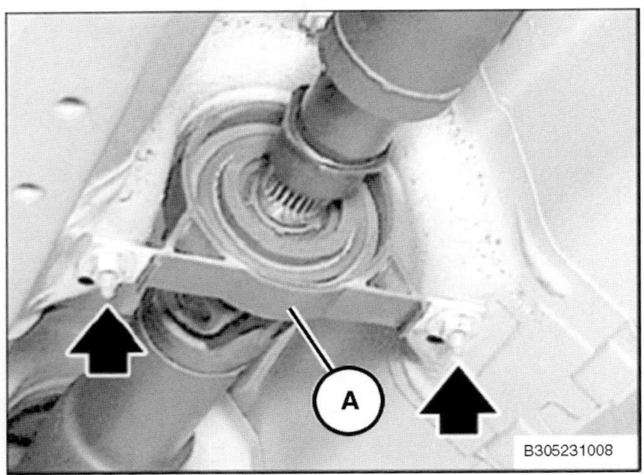

Remove retaining bolts at center bearing (**A**) and from transmission output flange. Bend driveshaft to remove and secure t to underside of body using mechanic's wire.

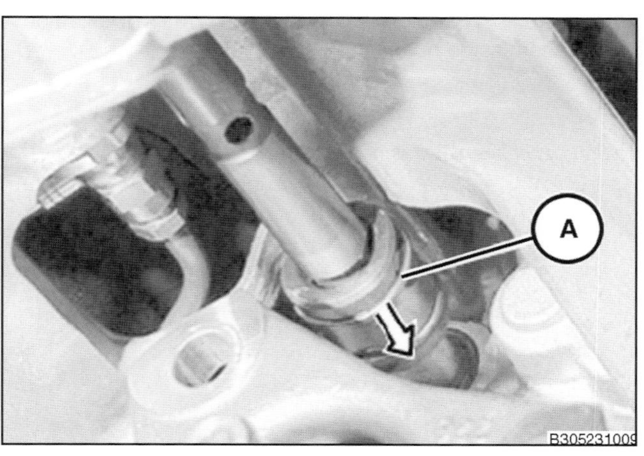

Working at top of transmission, lever retaining ring (**A**) out of groove. Push ring slightly forward.

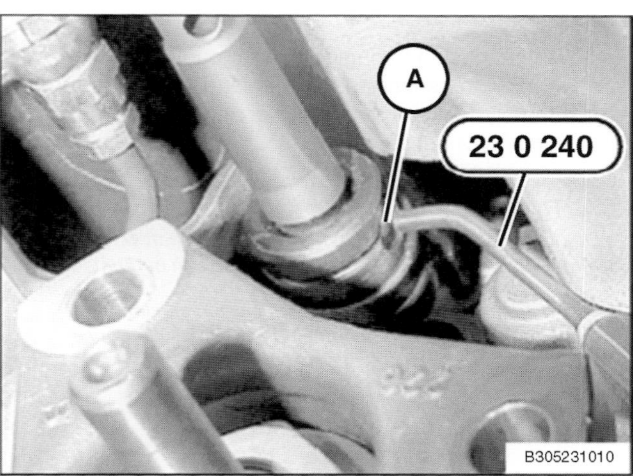

Drive retaining pin (**A**) out of selector rod with BMW special tool 23 0 240.

Unbolt (**arrows**) actuator from transmission housing.

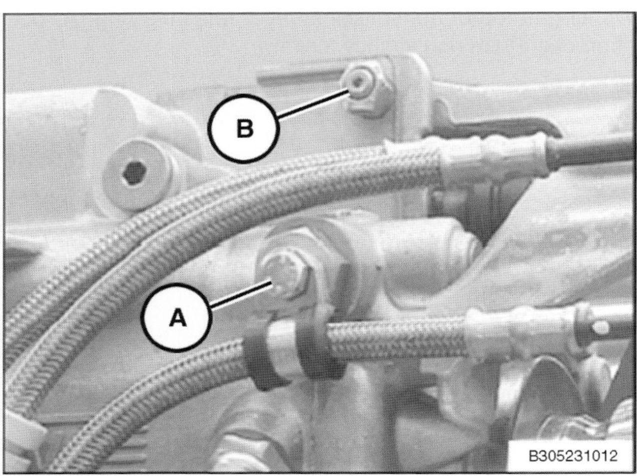

Remove bolt (**A**) and nut (**B**), and remove hydraulic lines from transmission housing.

NOTE —

Hydraulic lines remain connected.

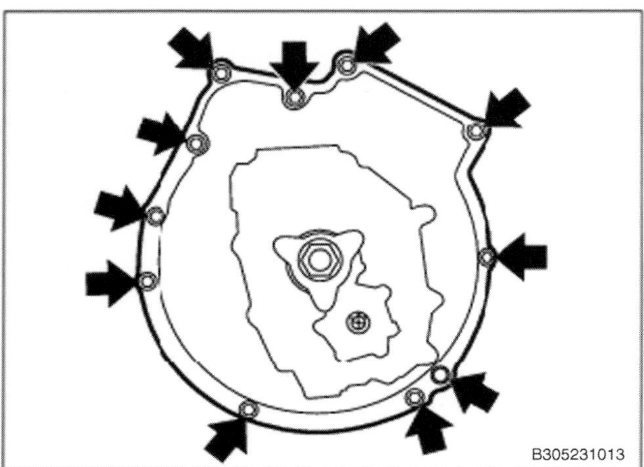

Remove bellhousing to engine block mounting bolts (**arrows**). Pull transmission back as far as possible, turn approximately 10° counterclockwise, and slide transmission off of clutch/flywheel assembly.

CAUTION —

- *Do not allow transmission to hang on input shaft while removing and installing as the clutch disc can be damaged.*
- *Tilting the engine to lower the transmission can lead to damage to various components due to lack of clearance.*

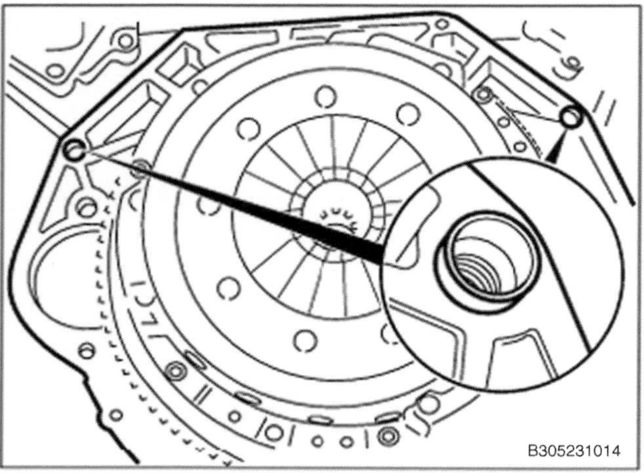

Before installing transmission, note the correct position of dowel sleeves and bellhousing cover plate, replace if damaged.

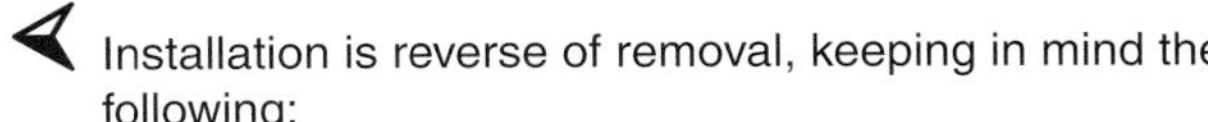

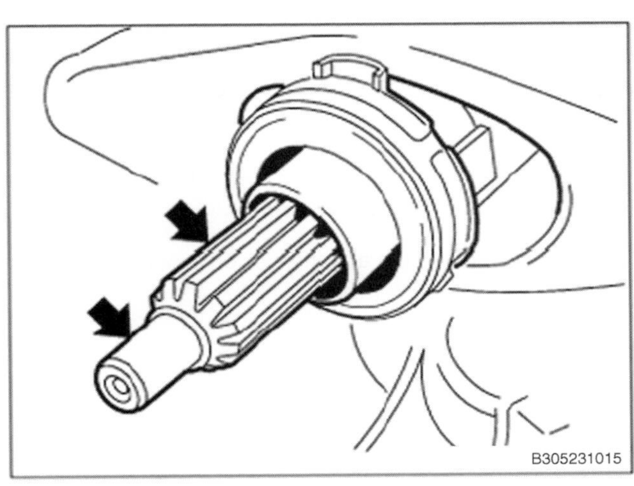

Installation is reverse of removal, keeping in mind the following:

- When installing a new transmission, be sure to transfer parts from old transmission if applicable.
- Check lubrication of transmission input shaft for sticky consistency. If grease is sticky, replace clutch disc.
- Thoroughly clean input shaft and clutch disc splines.
- Lightly lubricate transmission input shaft (**arrows**) before installing.
- Center rear of transmission in driveshaft tunnel before tightening transmission support bracket.

NOTE —
Torx-head mounting bolts should always be used with washers to prevent difficult removal in the future.

– Install driveshaft and preload center bearing bracket. Use new nuts when mounting driveshaft to transmission/flex disc and final drive. See **260 Driveshafts**.

– Refill transmission with appropriate lubricant before starting or towing the car. See **Transmission Fluid Service** earlier in this repair group.

Tightening torques

- Front end reinforcement to front subframe or body frame rails: M10 bolt (always replace)
  - Stage 1 . . . . 59 Nm (43 ft-lb)
  - Stage 2 . . . . torque angle 90°
- Rubber mount to transmission or bracket nut (M8) . . . . 21 Nm (15 ft-lb)
- Slave cylinder to transmission . . . . 22 Nm (16 ft-lb)
- Transmission crossmember to chassis M8. . . . . 21 Nm (15 ft-lb)
- Transmission to engine (Torx-head)
  - M8. . . . . 22 Nm (16 ft-lb)
  - M10 . . . . 43 Nm (32 ft-lb)
  - M12 . . . . 72 Nm (53 ft-lb)
- Transmission drain/fill plug . . . . 50 Nm (37 ft-lb)

Transmission, removing and installing (except M3 models)

– Disconnect negative (–) cable from battery.

CAUTION —
Prior to disconnecting the battery, read the battery disconnection cautions given at the front of this manual.

– Remove underbody splash shield.

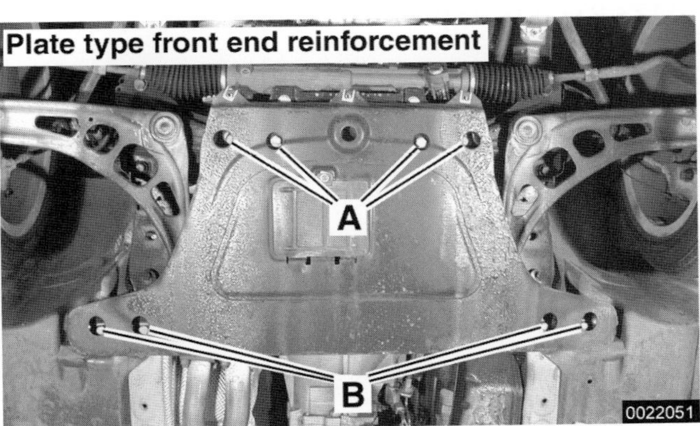

Remove front suspension reinforcement plate retaining bolts (**A** and **B**) and remove reinforcement plate.

NOTE —
Front suspension reinforcement bolts are one time use only.

> ***CAUTION —***
> *Front suspension reinforcement plate is a critical structural member for the front suspension. Do not drive vehicle without plate installed.*

– Remove complete exhaust system and exhaust heat shields. See **180 Exhaust System**.

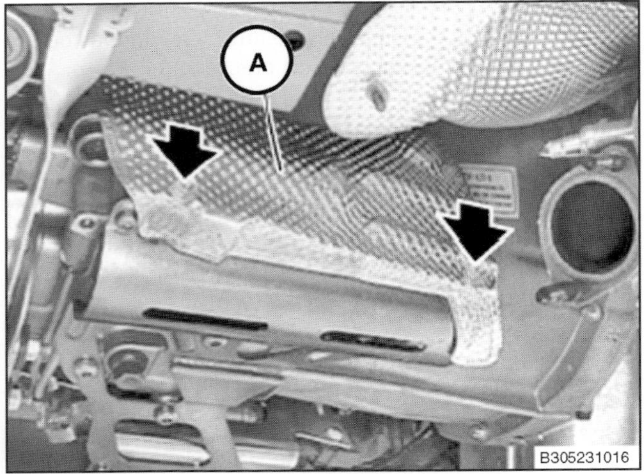

◀ Remove heat shield (**A**) at transmission expansion tank.

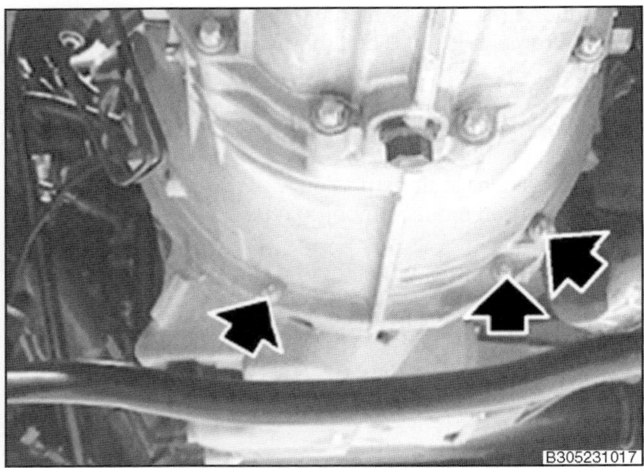

◀ Remove screws (**arrows**) to support transmission.

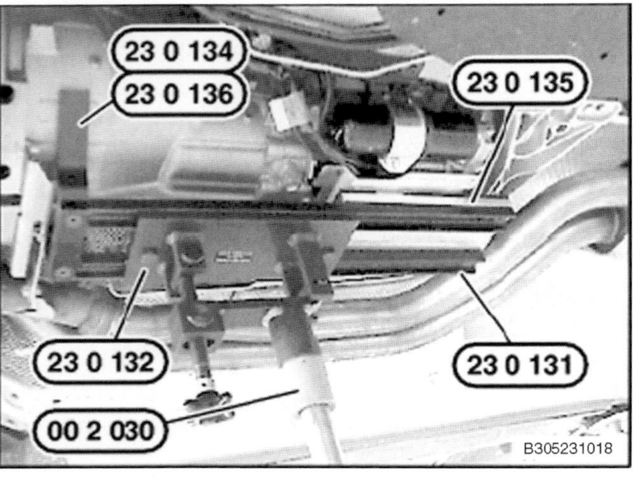

◀ Support transmission with BMW special tools 00 2 030, 23 0 123, 23 0 131, 23 0 134, and 21 0 135.

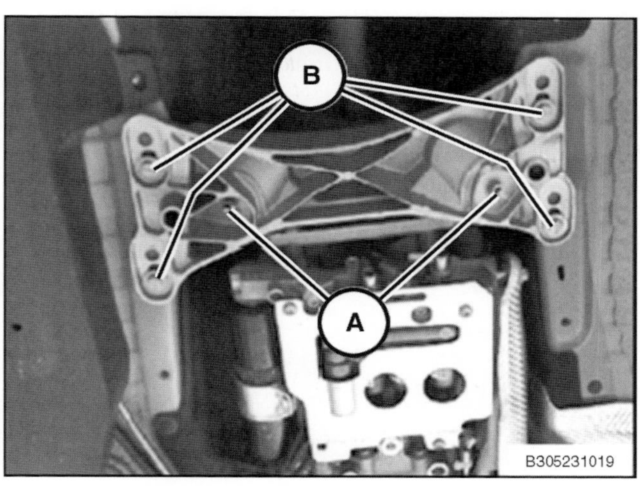

< Remove transmission hardware (**A**).Remove crossmember hardware (**B**) and crossmember.

– Remove driveshaft from transmission. See **260 Driveshafts**.

- Release center bearing.
- Secure driveshaft to body using mechanic's wire.

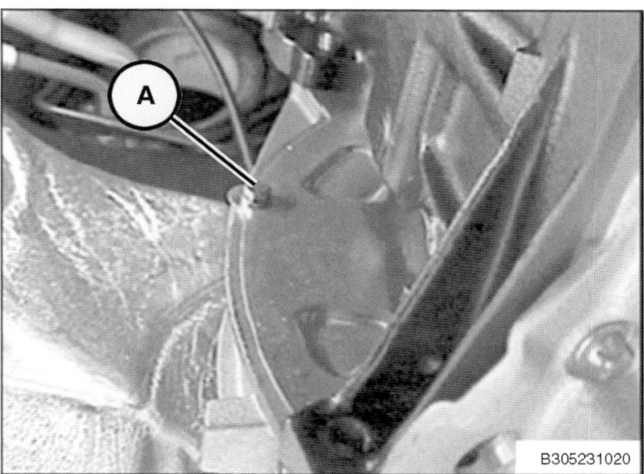

< Remove screw (**A**).

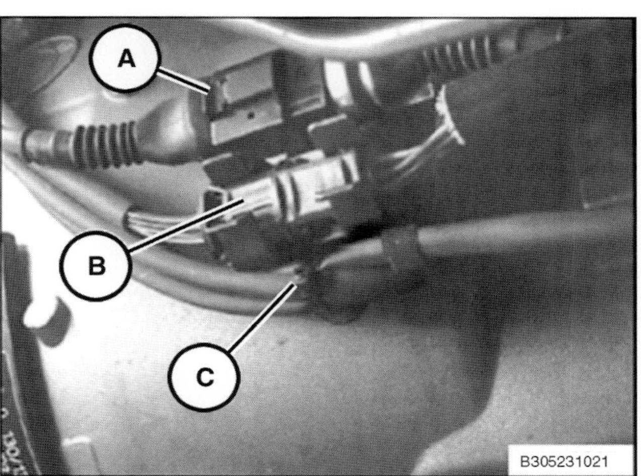

< Disconnect electrical harness connectors (**A**) and (**B**). Release cable strap (**C**).

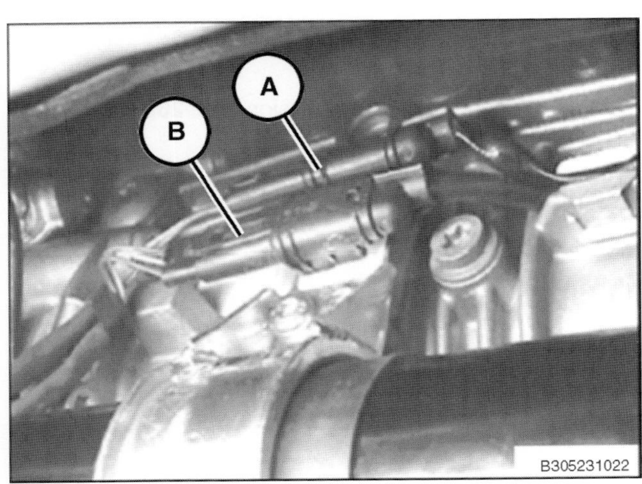

Disconnect electrical harness connectors (**A**) and (**B**), uncliping cable from holder.

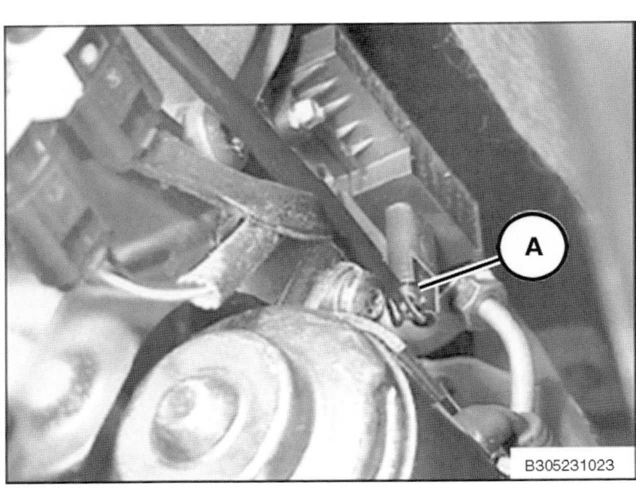

Disconnect electrical harness connector (**A**) from clutch travel sensor.

Disconnect electrical harness connector (**A**) from sensor.

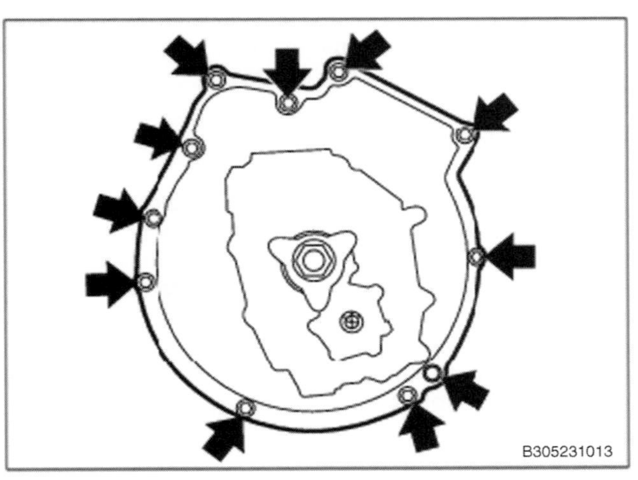

Remove bellhousing to engine block mounting bolts (**arrows**), and slide transmission off of clutch/flywheel assembly.

CAUTION —
- *Do not allow transmission to hang on input shaft while removing and installing as the clutch disc can be damaged.*
- *Tilting the engine to lower the transmission can lead to damage to various components due to lack of clearance.*

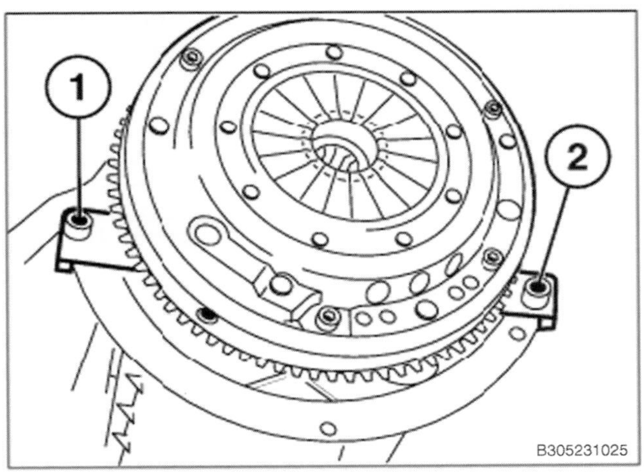

Before installing transmission, note the correct position of dowel sleeves (**1** and **2**) and bellhousing cover plate, replace if damaged.

Remove and clean release bearing and release lever.

- Push grease scraper, BMW special tool 21 2 221 onto input shaft (**A**) as far as it will go.
- Grease splines of input shaft, using Unirex S2 grease.
- Slide grease scraper off of input shaft.

– Installation is reverse of removal, keeping in mind the following:

- When installing a new transmission, be sure to transfer parts from old transmission if applicable.

NOTE —
Torx-head mounting bolts should always be used with washers to prevent difficult removal in the future.

– Install driveshaft and preload center bearing bracket. Use new nuts when mounting driveshaft to transmission/flex disc and final drive. See **260 Driveshafts**.

– Refill transmission with appropriate lubricant before starting or towing the car. See **Transmission Fluid Service** earlier in this repair group.

Tightening torques

- Transmission to engine
- Front end reinforcement to front subframe or body frame rails: M10 bolt (always replace)
  Stage 1 . . . . 59 Nm (43 ft-lb)
  Stage 2 . . . . torque angle 90°
- Rubber mount to transmission or bracket nut (M8) . . . . 21 Nm (15 ft-lb)
- Slave cylinder to transmission . . . . 22 Nm (16 ft-lb)
- Transmission crossmember to chassis
  M8. . . . . 21 Nm (15 ft-lb)
- Transmission to engine (Torx-head)
  M8. . . . . 22 Nm (16 ft-lb)
  M10 . . . . 43 Nm (32 ft-lb)
  M12 . . . . 72 Nm (53 ft-lb)
- Transmission drain/fill plug . . . . 50 Nm (37 ft-lb)

240 Automatic Transmission

GENERAL

This section covers maintenance and replacement of the E46 automatic transmission. Internal repairs to the automatic transmission are not covered. Special tools and procedures are required to disassemble and service internal automatic transmission components.

Automatic transmissions are identified by code letters found on a data plate located on the side or rear of the transmission case. See **200 Transmission–General** for application information. For gear ratio specifications, see **Table a**.

> ***CAUTION —***
> *ATF does not circulate unless the engine is running. When towing an automatic transmission vehicle, use a flat-bed truck or raise the rear wheels off the ground. All wheel drive vehicles equipped with automatic transmissions must be towed using a flat-bed truck only.*

The electronic transmission control module (TCM) monitors transmission operation for faults and alerts the driver by illuminating the transmission fault indicator on the instrument panel. On-board diagnostic codes stored in the TCM must be downloaded and interpreted by trained technicians using special BMW diagnostic equipment.

Special tools

Special Tools

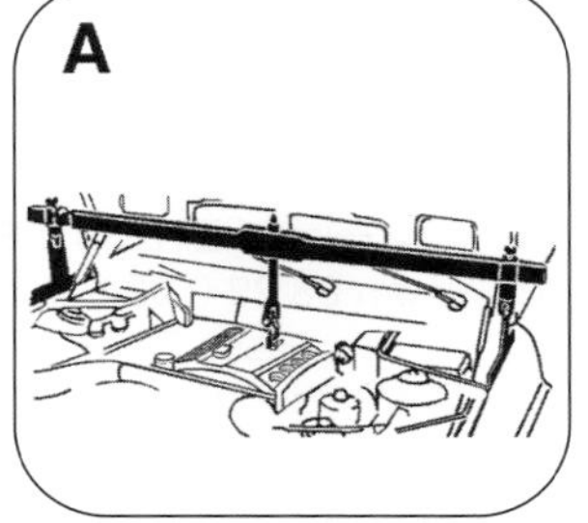

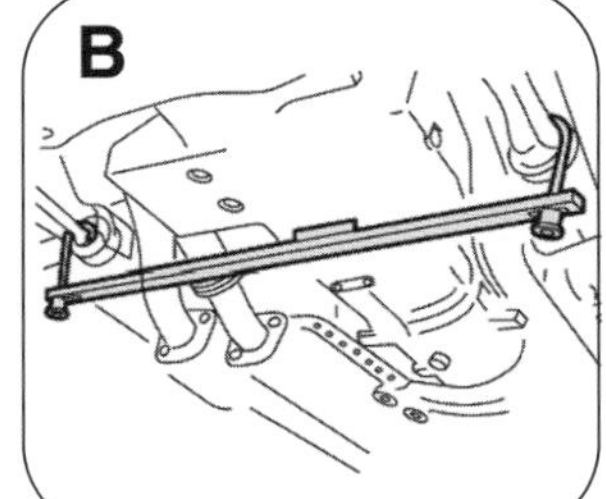

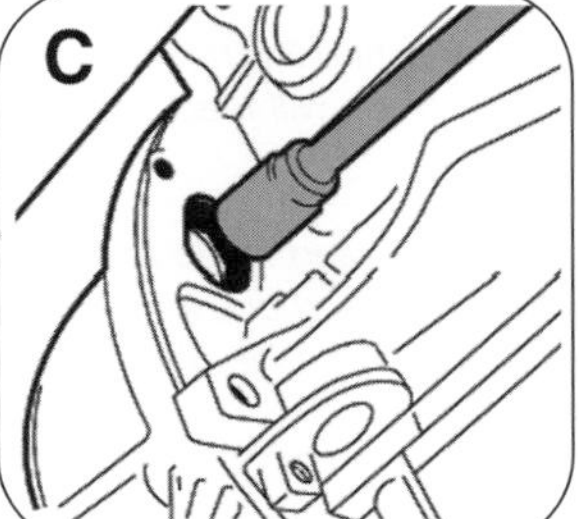

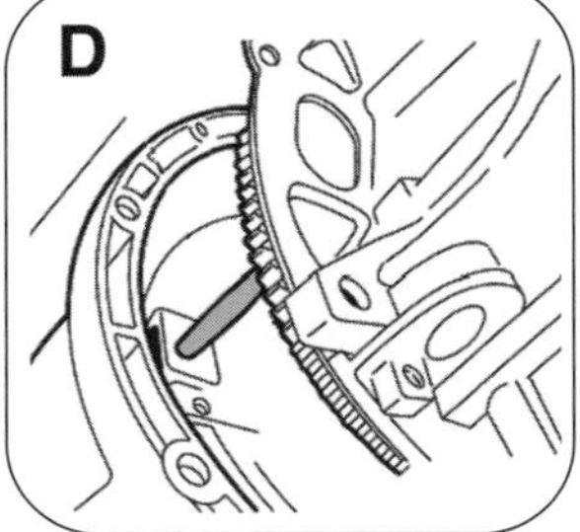

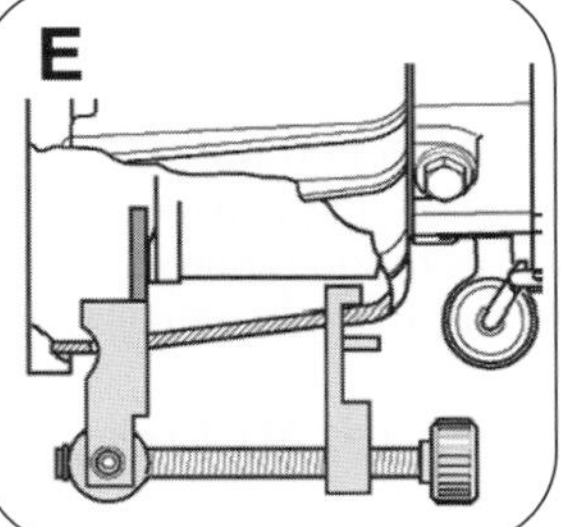

Special tools

- **A** BMW 00 0 200 / 208 . . . . Engine support bracket
- **B** BMW 11 8 022 . . . . Oil pan support bracket
- **C** BMW 24 1 100 . . . . Torque converter socket
- **D** BMW 24 2 300 . . . . Spline bore alignment tool
- **E** BMW 24 4 131 / 135 . . . . Torque converter clamp

Some special tools are recommended for the removal and installation of an automatic transmission on the E46 BMW models. While these tools are not absolutely necessary, they are especially helpful when dealing with the removal and replacement of the torque converter.

Internal repairs to the automatic transmission require special service equipment and knowledge. If it is determined that internal service is required, consult an authorized BMW dealer about a factory reconditioned unit or a transmission rebuild.

Table a. Automatic transmission applications

Model	Year	Transmission
323i/Ci	1999 - 2000	A5S360R (up to 03/00) A5S325Z (from 03/00)
325i (M54)	2001 - 2005	A5S325Z (up to 03/02) A5S390R (from 03/02)
325i (M56)	2003 - 2005	A5S325Z
325Ci	2001 - 2005	A5S325Z (up to 03/03) A5S390R (from 03/03)
328i/Ci	1999 - 2000	A5S360R
330i/Ci	2001 - 2005	A5S325Z (up to 03/03) A5S390R (from 03/03)
325xi **330xi**	2001 - 2005	A5S390R

TRANSMISSION SERVICE

0021333

The automatic transmissions installed in the 3 Series are filled with a number of different transmission fluids. Each transmission should have a colored label on the ATF sump identifying the fluid type installed..

ATF fluid type labels

- Orange . . . . Dexron III
- Yellow . . . . Texaco ETL 7045E (BMW p/n 83 22 0 026 922)
- Green . . . . Texaco ETL 8072B (BMW p/n 83 22 0 024 359)
- Blue . . . . Esso 71141 LT (BMW p/n 83 2 29 407 807)

> ***CAUTION—***
> - *Only re-fill or top off using ATF fluid specified for the transmission. Mixing or adding incorrect ATF fluids will lead to transmission damage.*
> - *ATF specifications are subject to change and fluids are constantly being improved and updated. Always check with an authorized BMW dealer parts department for the latest transmission operating fluids information.*

Automatic transmission fluid (ATF) level, checking

The automatic transmission is not equipped with a dipstick. Checking the ATF level requires measuring and maintaining the ATF temperature within a narrow range (approx. 100° F) with the engine running and the vehicle raised safely in air.

– Raise and safely support vehicle to access ATF fill plug. The vehicle must be level and unloaded.

> ***CAUTION—***
> *Make sure the car is stable and well supported at all times. Use a professional automotive lift or jack stands designed for the purpose. A floor jack is not adequate support.*

– Warm up drivetrain by running engine until ATF reaches specified temperature. Switch on air conditioning to increase idle speed and to ensure all fluid passages in transmission are filled.

ATF level checking
- Fluid temperature . . . . 30° - 50°C (85° - 120°F)

– Apply parking brake firmly and step on brake pedal. Shift through all gears several times, pausing briefly between gear changes.

0022168

◄ With engine running and selector lever in Park, remove ATF filler plug (**arrow**).

- If a small stream of fluid runs out, fluid level is correct.
- If no oil fluid out, fluid level is too low. Add oil until it fluid starts to overflow.

> ***WARNING —***
> *Hot ATF can scald. Wear eye protection and protective clothing and gloves during the check. If the transmission was overfilled, hot ATF will spill from the filler hole when the fill plug is removed.*

– Reinstall fill plug using new sealing ring.

Tightening torques
- ATF drain plug to ATF sump
  A5S 360R / A5S 390R(M14). . . . . 20 Nm (15 ft-lb)
  A5S 325Z . . . . 35 Nm (26 ft-lb)
- ATF fill plug to transmission
  A5S 360R / A5S 390R(M14). . . . . 20 Nm (15 ft-lb)
  A5S 325Z . . . . 30 Nm (22 ft-lb)

ATF, draining and filling

The procedure given here includes removal and installation of the ATF fluid strainer (filter).

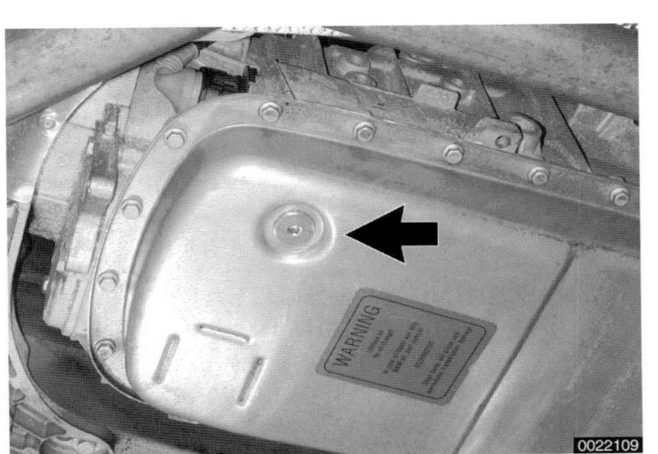

0022109

◄ Remove ATF drain plug **(arrow)** and drain fluid into clean measuring container. Record quantity of fluid drained.

> ***WARNING —***
> *The ATF must not be hot when draining. Do not drain the ATF if the engine and/or transmission is hot. Hot ATF can scald. Wear eye protection, protective clothing and gloves.*

– Remove transmission pan mounting bolts and remove pan.

– Remove pan gasket and clean gasket sealing surface.

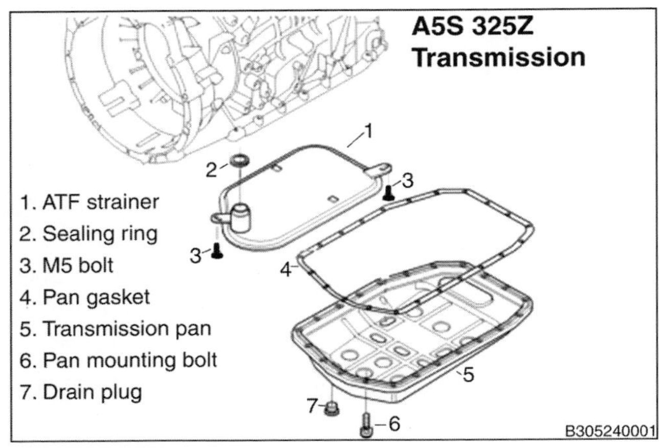

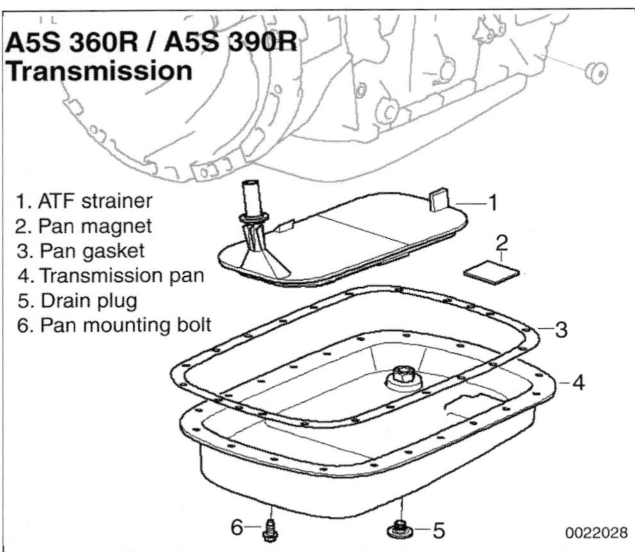

- **ZF transmission (A5S 325Z)**: Remove ATF fluid strainer mounting bolts and remove strainer from transmission valve body.
- **GM transmissions (A5S 360R / A5S 390R)**: Pull ATF fluid strainer from transmission pump housing. If strainer sealing ring remains in pump housing remove using a seal puller.
- Installation is reverse of removal.
  - Always replace seal for drain plug and all gasket(s) and O-rings.
  - Clean sump and sump magnet(s) using a lint-free cloth.
  - Tighten transmission pan bolts in sequential order.
  - Fill transmission with approved fluid. Add quantity of fluid drained and then check fluid level as described under **ATF level, checking**

CAUTION —
Only re-fill or top off using ATF fluid specified for the transmission. Mixing or swapping ATF fluids will lead to transmission damage.

NOTE —
Use new sump bolts purchased from BMW. Alternatively, clean old bolts and coat with Loctite® thread locking compound or equivalent.

Automatic transmission fluid capacity
- A5S 360R / A5S 390R
  with torque converter . . . . 9 liters (9.5 qt)
  without torque converter . . . . 4 liters (4.2 qt)
- A5S 325Z (2.5 liter)
  with torque converter . . . . 8.9 liters (9.4 qt)
  without torque converter . . . . 6.2 liters (6.5 qt)
- A5S 325Z (3.0 liter)
  with torque converter . . . . 8.7 liter (9.2 qt)
  without torque converter . . . . 6.1 liter (6.4 qt)

Tightening torques
- ATF drain plug to ATF sump
  A5S 360R / A5S 390R(M14) . . . . 18 Nm (14 ft-lb)
  A5S 325Z . . . . 35 Nm (26 ft-lb)
- ATF fill plug to ATF sump
  A5S 360R / A5S 390R (M14) . . . . 18 Nm (14 ft-lb)
  A5S 325Z . . . . 30 Nm (23 ft-lb))
- ATF sump to transmission
  A5S 360R / A5S 390R (M14) . . . . 10 Nm (7 ft-lb)
  A5S 325Z . . . . 6 Nm (4 ft-lb)

TRANSMISSION REMOVAL AND INSTALLATION

Removal and installation of the transmission is best accomplished on a lift using a transmission jack. Use caution and safe workshop practices when working beneath car and lowering transmission.

> ***CAUTION —***
> - *Be sure the vehicle is properly supported. The removal of the transmission may upset the balance of the vehicle on a lift.*
> - *Tilting the engine to remove the transmission can lead to damage to various components due to lack of clearance.*
>   *-On cars with AST remove throttle body.*
>   *-Remove brake fluid reservoir if necessary.*

Torx-head bolts are used to mount the transmission to the bellhousing. Be sure to have appropriate tools on hand before starting the job.

Transmission, removing and installing

– Disconnect negative (–) cable from battery.

> ***CAUTION —***
> *Prior to disconnecting the battery, read the battery disconnection cautions given at the front of this manual.*

◄ Remove engine cooling intake hood fasteners (**arrows**) at front of engine compartment.

– Remove engine driven cooling fan, unfasten cooling fan cowl and pull slightly upwards. See **170 Radiator and Cooling System**.

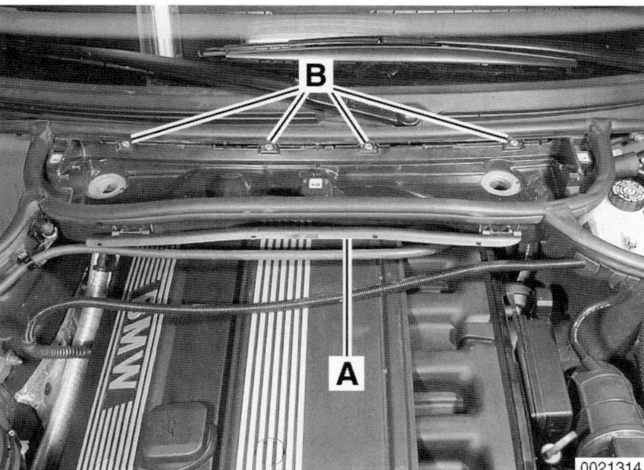

◄ Remove housing for interior ventilation microfilter.

- Remove upper cover and microfilter.
- Open wiring harness loom cover (**A**) and remove wires.
- Unfasten screws (**B**) and remove lower microfilter housing.

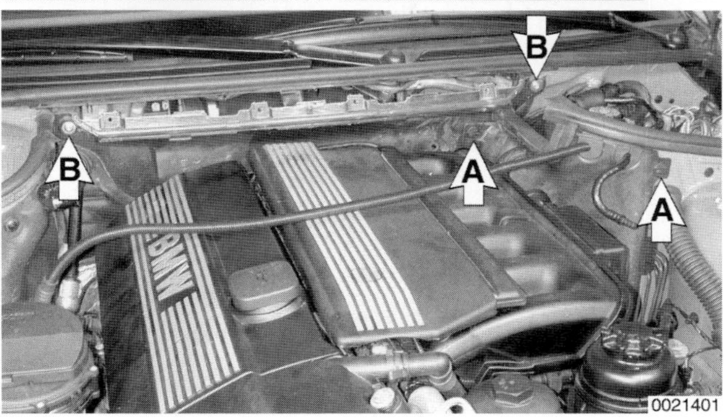

◄ Remove heater bulkhead cover.

- Remove engine compartment side trim panel. Turn locking knobs (**A**) and slide trim panel from mounting lip.
- Remove heater bulkhead cover mounting screws (**B**) and lift cover up and out from firewall.

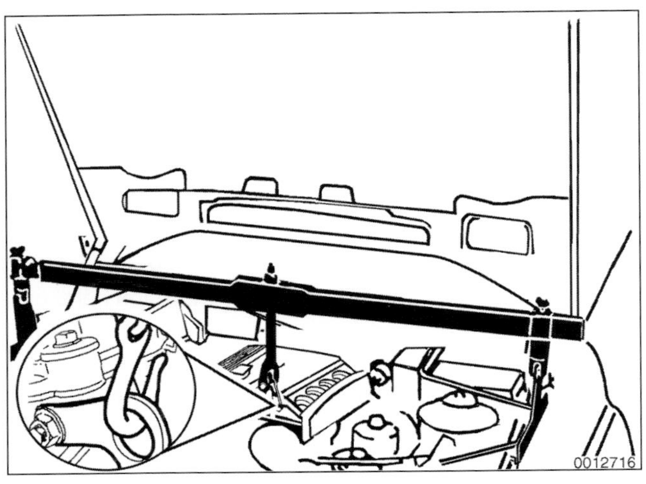

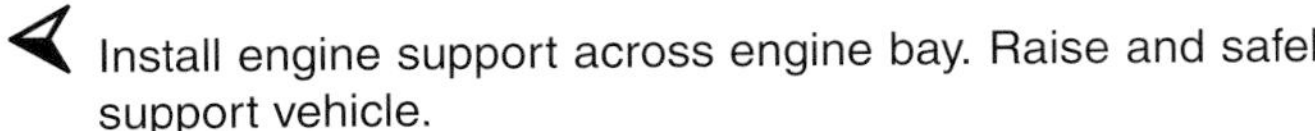

Install engine support across engine bay. Raise and safely support vehicle.

> ***CAUTION —***
> - *Make sure the car is stable and well supported at all times. Use a professional automotive lift or jack stands designed for the purpose. A floor jack is not adequate support.*
> - *Removal of transmission will cause engine to tip unless engine support is used.*

– Remove engine splash guard from underside of vehicle.

– Remove front suspension reinforcement at lower control arms and front subframe.

– Drain ATF from transmission as described earlier.

– Remove exhaust system and exhaust heat shield. See **180 Exhaust System**.

– Remove driveshaft(s). See **260 Driveshafts**.

– On all wheel drive equipped vehicles: Remove transfer case. See **270 Transfer Case**.

With selector lever in **Park**, disconnect shift selector lever cable from lever and remove cable bracket.

- Counterhold clamping bushing (**A**) when loosening nut.
- Loosen cable clamping nut (**B**) and remove cable from bracket. (A5S 325Z transmission shown.)

A5S 325Z ZF Transmission

A5S 360R / A5S 390R GM Transmission

Disconnect electrical harness connector(s) from transmission by turning bayonet lock ring(s) (**arrows**) counterclockwise.

- On A5S 325Z disconnect two connectors on the left side of the transmission.
- On A5S 360R / A5S 390R disconnect the harness connector at the right rear of the transmission.
- Remove wiring harness(s) from transmission housing.

– Disconnect transmission cooler line clamps from engine. Disconnect cooler lines from transmission.

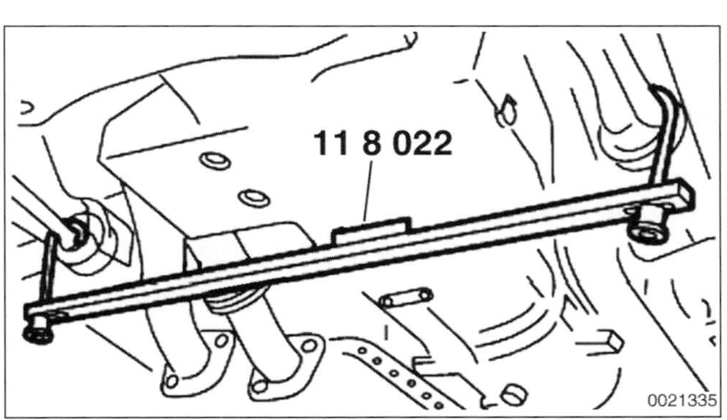

◀ Attach BMW special tool 11 8 022 to lower control arms.

– Support transmission with transmission jack. Remove transmission support crossmember.

– Lower transmission until engine cylinder head touches firewall. Tighten knurled screws of BMW special tool 11 8 022 until tool supports engine oil pan securely.

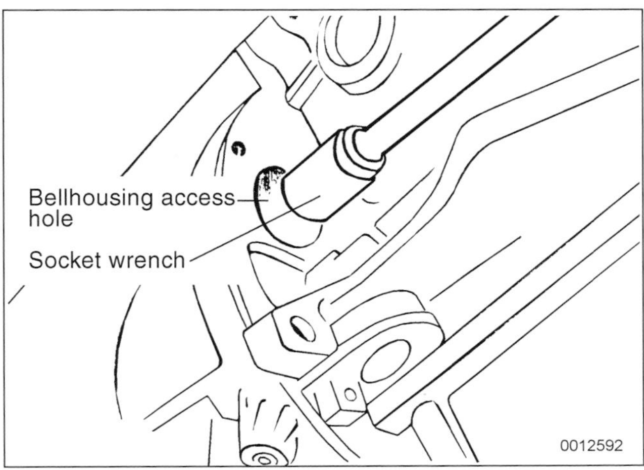

◀ Remove access plug in cover plate on right side of engine block and remove torque converter bolts. Turn crankshaft to access bolts.

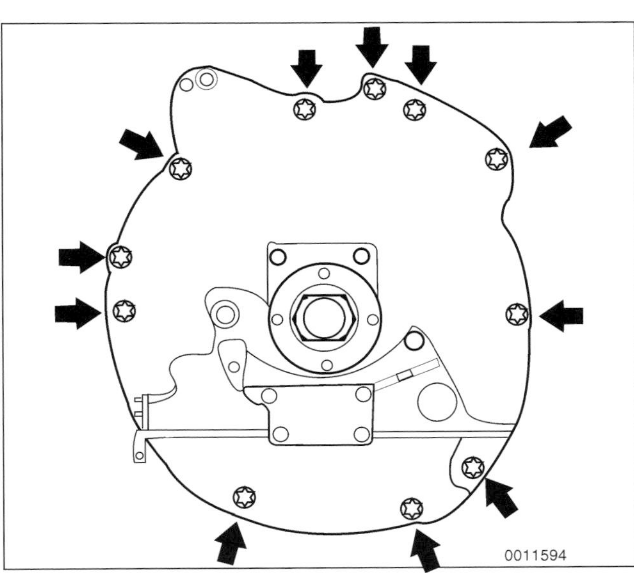

◀ Remove bellhousing-to-engine mounting bolts (**arrows**).

– Install BMW special tools 24 4 131 and 24 4 135 to secure torque converter in place during transmission removal.

> ***CAUTION —***
> *Do not allow the torque converter to fall off the transmission input shaft.*

– Remove transmission by pulling back and down. Lower jack to allow transmission to clear vehicle.

– Installation is reverse of removal, noting the following:
  - Blow out oil cooler lines with low-pressure compressed air and flush cooler with clean ATF twice before reattaching lines to transmission.

> ***CAUTION —***
> - *Wear safety glasses when working with compressed air.*
> - *Do not reuse ATF after flushing.*

  - Install new sealing washers on hollow bolts.
  - Install new O-rings on transmission cooler lines, where applicable.
  - Inspect engine drive plate for cracks or elongated holes. Replace if necessary.
  - Check to be sure torque converter is seated correctly in transmission during final installation.
  - When mounting transmission to engine, the three mounting tabs on torque converter must be aligned with indentations on drive plate. Use an alignment dowel to line up bolt holes, if necessary.
  - Fill transmission with clean ATF until oil level is even with fill hole. Then check fluid level. See **Automatic transmission fluid (ATF) level, checking** in this repair group.
  - Adjust gearshift mechanism. See **250 Gearshift Linkage**.

NOTE —
Torx-head mounting bolts should always be used with washers to prevent difficult removal in the future.

Tightening torques

- ATF drain plug to ATF sump
  - A5S 325Z . . . . 35 Nm (26 ft-lb)
  - A5S 360R . . . . 20 Nm (15 ft-lb)
- ATF fill plug to ATF sump
  - A5S 325Z . . . . 30 Nm (22 ft-lb)
  - A5S 360R . . . . 20 Nm (15 ft-lb)
- Front suspension reinforcement to chassis (M10) . . . . 42 Nm (30 ft-lb)
- Torque converter to drive plate (M10) . . . . 45 Nm (33 ft-lb)
- Transmission support crossmember to chassis . . . . 23 Nm (17 ft-lb)
- Transmission to engine (Torx-head with washer)
  - M8 . . . . 21 Nm (15 ft-lb)
  - M10 . . . . 42 Nm (31 ft-lb)
  - M12 . . . . 72 Nm (53 ft-lb)

250 Gearshift Linkage

GENERAL

This repair group covers transmission gearshift and linkage service for both manual and automatic transmission equipped vehicles.

Special tools

BMW suggests the use of one special tool in the removal of the gear shift lever for manual transmission equipped vehicles.

To gain access to the complete gearshift mechanism it is necessary to remove the exhaust system and the driveshaft as described in **180 Exhaust System** and **260 Driveshafts**.

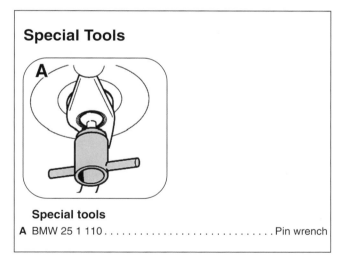

Special Tools

Special tools

A BMW 25 1 110 . . . . Pin wrench

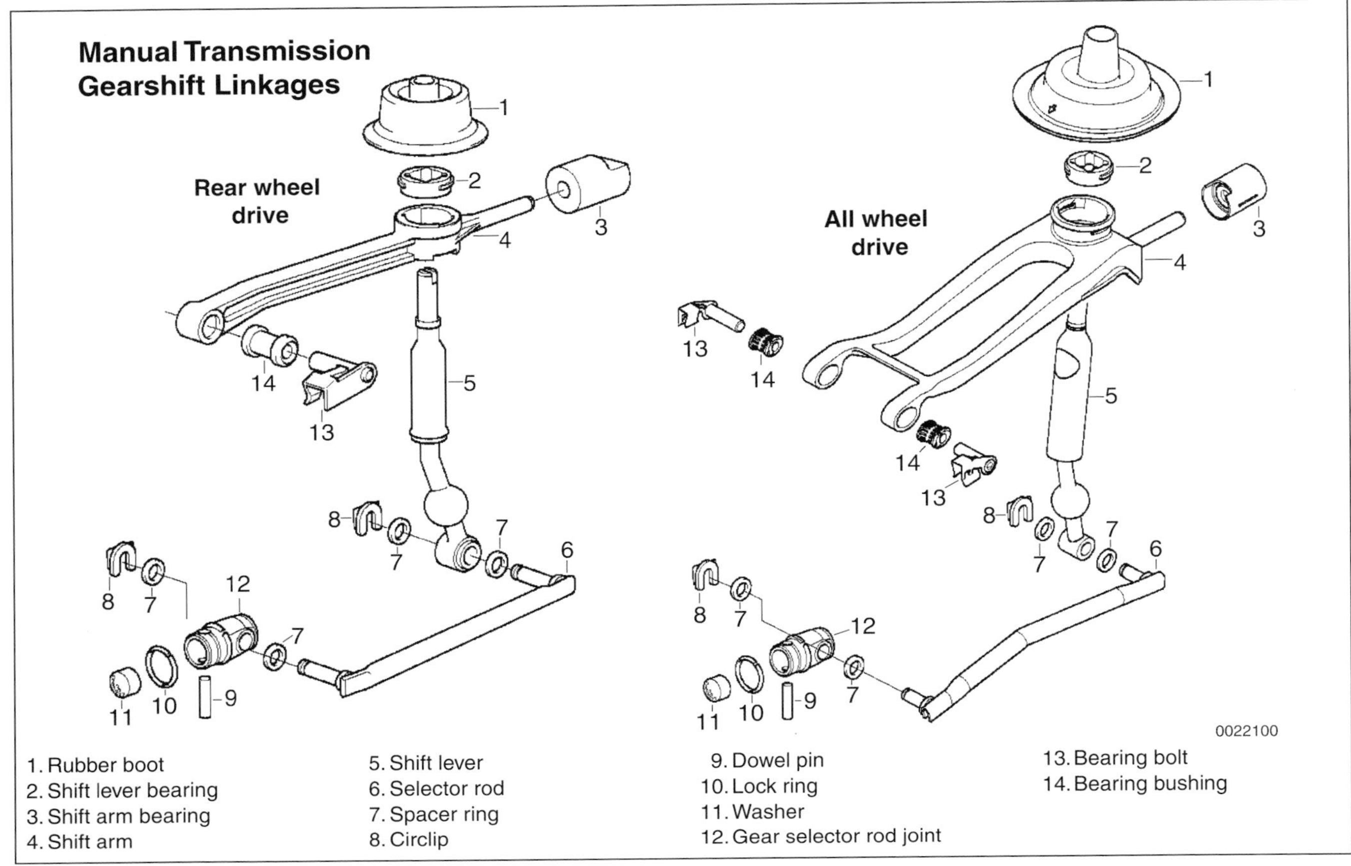

MANUAL TRANSMISSION GEARSHIFT

Gearshift lever, removing (manual transmission)

Use the above illustration as a guide when removing and installing the linkage.

– Remove shift knob by pulling knob straight off the manual gearshift.

NOTE —

Removal of the shift knob will require about 90 lbs. of force. Do not twist knob or locating key can be damaged.

– Pry up on rear of shift boot to unclip, then remove boot from front retainers.

– Raise vehicle to gain access to underside of vehicle.

– Remove complete exhaust system. See **180 Exhaust System**.

> ***WARNING —***
> *Make sure the car is stable and well supported at all times. Use a professional automotive lift or jack stands designed for the purpose. A floor jack is not adequate support.*

– Remove driveshaft(s). See **260 Driveshafts**.

◀ Support transmission with transmission jack. Remove crossmember (**arrow**) from rear of transmission.

– Lower rear of transmission to access gearshift linkage.

> ***CAUTION —***
> *Tilting the engine to lower the transmission can lead to damage to various components due to lack of clearance.*

0022046

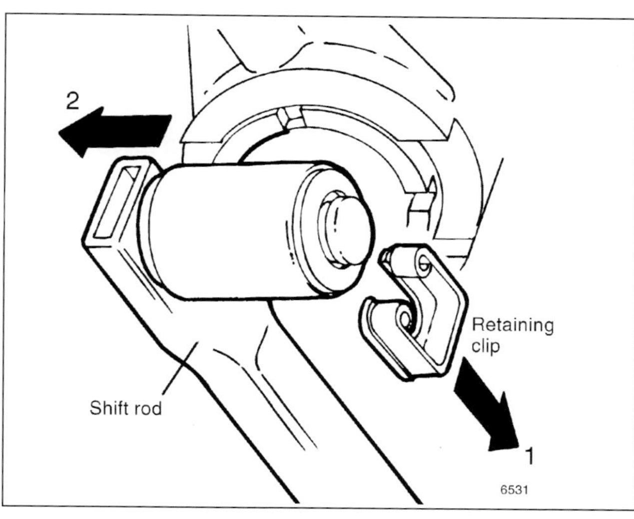

◀ Working above transmission, disconnect shift rod from gearshift lever by pulling off shift rod retaining clip in direction of arrow (**1**). Disengage shift rod from gearshift lever (**2**). Note washers on either side of shift rod end.

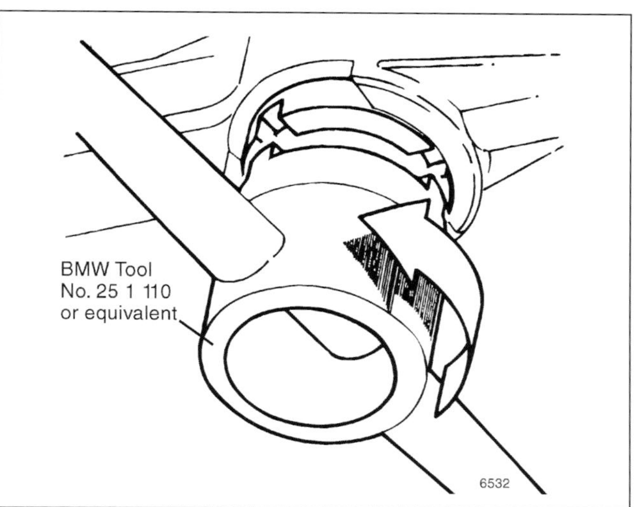

◀ Release gearshift lever retaining ring from below using BMW special tool 25 1 110. Turn tool 90° (¼ turn) counterclockwise.

– Raise transmission and temporarily install transmission crossmember.

– Lower vehicle. Working from inside passenger compartment, pull up on gearshift lever to remove it together with retaining ring and rubber grommet.

Gearshift lever, installing (manual transmission)

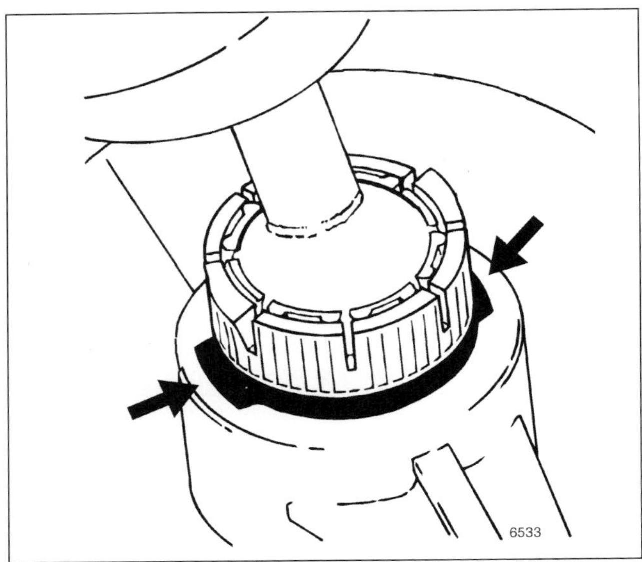

◀ Install shift lever, aligning locking tabs with openings in shift console (**arrows**). Press down on retaining ring until it clicks into place.

– Install rubber grommet with arrow pointing forward. Install shift rod and shift boot.

NOTE —
Install rubber grommet correctly so that it seals out water.

– Connect shift rod to shift lever. Install transmission crossmember. Lift transmission and tighten crossmember bolts.

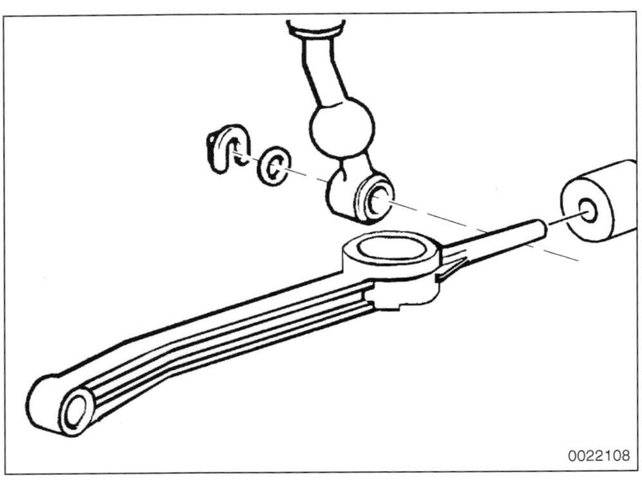

◀ Before connecting the shift rod to the lever, be sure the gearshift lever is facing the correct way as illustrated.

– Install driveshaft(s) and heat shield. See **260 Driveshafts**.

– Reinstall exhaust system. See **180 Exhaust System.**

– Lower vehicle. Install shift boot cover. Push shift knob onto lever.

Tightening torques

- Rear driveshaft to final drive flange
  With U-joint (M10 ribbed nut) . . . . 80 Nm (59 ft-lb)
  With U-joint (M10 compressed nut) . . . . 64 Nm (47 ft-lb)
- Flex-disc to driveshaft or transmission flange
  M10 (8.8 grade) . . . . 48 Nm (35 ft-lb)
  M10 (10.9 grade . . . . 60 Nm (44 ft-lb)
  M12 (10.9 grade) . . . . 100 Nm (74 ft-lb)
- Front driveshaft to final drive
  flange (with U-joint)(M10) . . . . 70 Nm (52 ft-lb)
- Transmission crossmember
  to body (M8) . . . . 21 Nm (15 ft-lb)

AUTOMATIC TRANSMISSION GEARSHIFT

In E46 models, the electronic immobilizer (EWS) prevents starter operation unless the gear position is **Park** or **Neutral**.

Gearshift mechanism, adjusting (automatic transmission)

- Position gearshift lever in **Park**.
- Raise vehicle to gain access to shift linkage.

> ***WARNING —***
> *Make sure the car is stable and well supported at all times. Use a professional automotive lift or jack stands designed for the purpose.*

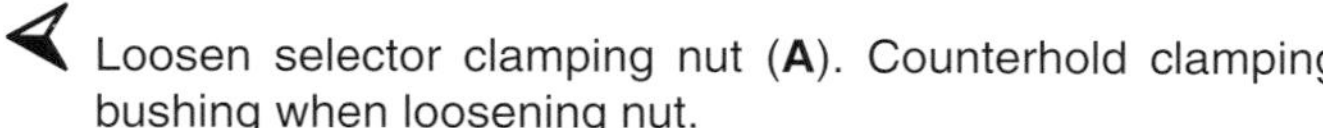

Loosen selector clamping nut (**A**). Counterhold clamping bushing when loosening nut.

- Push shift lever of transmission forward toward engine (**Park** position) while applying light pressure on cable end. Tighten cable clamping nut.

NOTE —
Do not overtighten the nut so that it twists the cable.

Tightening torque
- Shift cable clamping nut . . . . 10 - 12 Nm (7.5 - 9 ft-lb)

Automatic shiftlock, checking function (automatic transmission)

The automatic shiftlock uses an electric solenoid to lock the selector lever in **Park** or **Neutral**. Depressing the foot brake with the ignition on energizes the solenoid, allowing the lever to be moved into a drive gear. The solenoid is energized only when the engine speed is below 2,500 rpm and the vehicle speed is below 3 mph. The solenoid is mounted in the right-hand side of the selector lever housing.

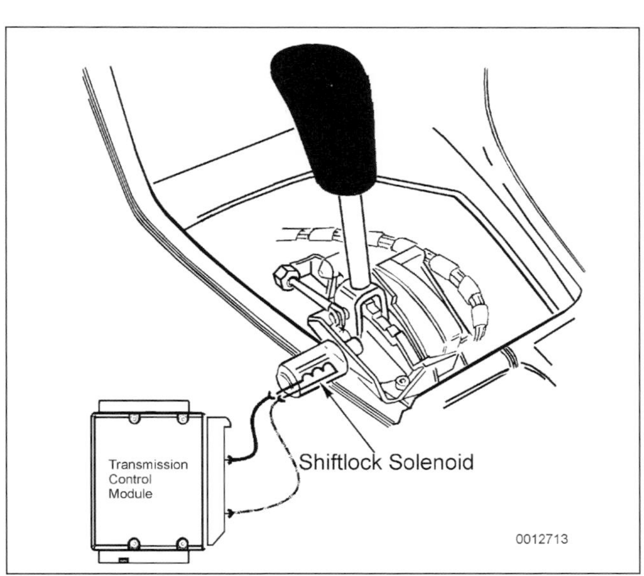

Automatic shiftlock prevents drive gear selection until the brake pedal is depressed.

- With engine running and car stopped, place selector lever in **Park** or **Neutral**.
- Without depressing brake pedal, check that selector lever is locked in position **Park** or **Neutral**.

- Depress brake pedal firmly. Solenoid should be heard to energize.
- Check that selector lever can now be moved out of **Park** or **Neutral**.

NOTE —
The next test should be performed in an open area with the parking brake on and with extreme caution.

- With selector lever in **Park** or **Neutral** and brake pedal depressed, raise engine above 2,500 rpm. Check that selector lever cannot be moved out of **Park** or **Neutral**.

If any faults are found check the electrical operation of the shiftlock solenoid and check for wiring faults to or from the transmission control module (TCM). See **610 Electrical Component Locations** and **Electrical Wiring Diagrams**.

NOTE —
The solenoid is controlled via the TCM, using brake pedal position, engine speed, and road speed as controlling inputs.

Automatic transmission gearshift mechanism

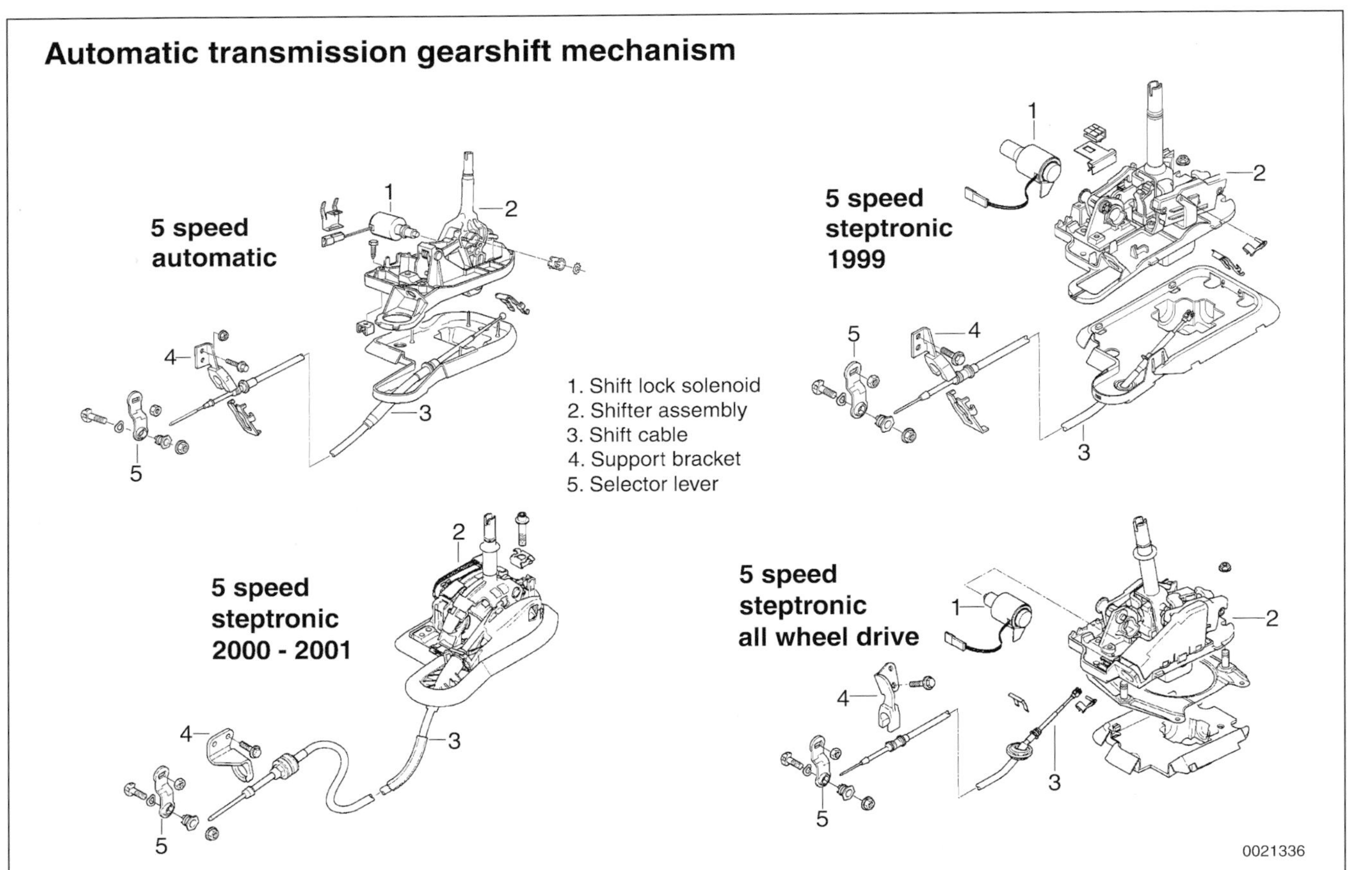

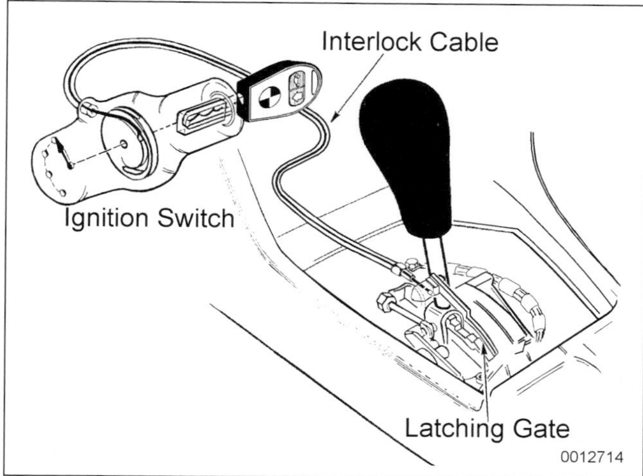

Shift interlock, checking function (automatic transmission)

The shift interlock uses a cable between the ignition switch and the shift lever to lock the shift lever in the park position when the key is in the off position or removed. This feature also prevents the key from being removed from the ignition lock until the selector lever is in **Park**.

– Shift selector lever to **Park** position and turn ignition key to the off position.

– Remove ignition key. Check that selector lever cannot be shifted out of **Park** position.

- Turn ignition key on and depress brake pedal. Check that selector lever moves freely from gear to gear.
- With selector lever in a gear position other than **Park**, attempt to turn key to off position and remove. Key should not go into off position.
- If any faults are found check cable for kinks and check cable attachment points for damage or faults.

NOTE—

- *It must only be possible to remove ignition key with selector lever in **Park** position.*
- *Shift interlock cable must not be kinked.*

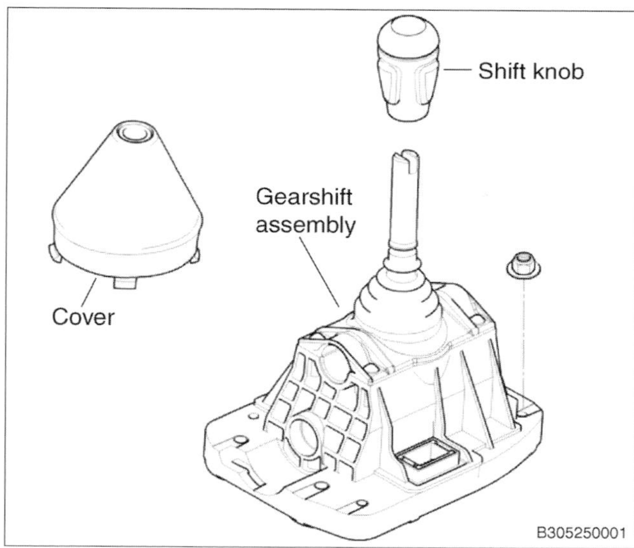

SEQUENTIAL MANUAL GEARBOX (SMG) GEARSHIFT

E46 models equipped with the Sequential Manual Gearbox (SMG) transmissions use a shift lever with no mechanical connection to the transmission.

The gear shift lever sits in a spring loaded assembly containing eight hall effect sensors that determine the desired gear / mode selection. When the lever is moved, sensors signal the SMG control unit to shift the transmission to the selected gear or mode. Manaul shifting of the SMG gearbox is made by either pulling the gearshift lever backward to upshift, or pushing the lever forward to downshift.

To start the engine, the brake pedal must be depressed, and the gearshift moved to the neutral position. With the engine running, and the brake pedal depressed, the driver can select from either reverse or forward (with manual shifting or automatic mode). A shift lock is built into the assembly to prevent the transmission from slipping out of gear.

Shifts can also be made using the paddles located on either side of the steering wheel.

260 Driveshafts

GENERAL

This repair group covers the repair and replacement of drive-shafts and driveshaft components. Drive axles are covered in **311 Front Axle Final Drive** and **331 Rear Axle Final Drive**.

Special tools

BMW suggests the use of a special tool in the release of the clamping sleeve which acts as a grease seal for the splined shaft to the rear of the driveshaft center bearing.

Special Tools

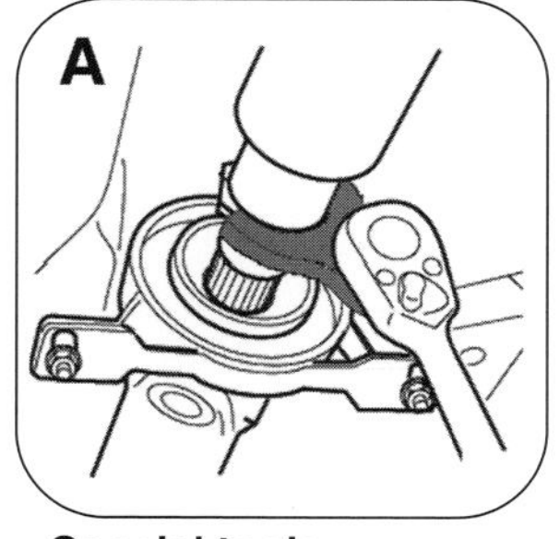

Special tools

A BMW 26 1 040 . . . . Clamping sleeve adjustment tool

Front and rear driveshafts

The rear driveshaft is a two-piece unit joined in the center by a sliding splined coupling. This coupling compensates for fore and aft movement of the drive line. The driveshaft is connected to the transmission by a rubber flex-disc and to the rear final drive by a universal joint. It is supported in the middle by a center support bearing. The bearing is mounted in rubber to isolate vibration.

All wheel drive models incorporate two driveshafts. The rear driveshaft is a two-piece unit with splined center coupling much like that of a rear wheel drive model, but it is shorter and connects the transfer case to the rear differential. A short, one-piece driveshaft runs from the transfer case to the front differential. The front driveshaft bolts to the transfer case and differential directly, using no flexible rubber disk.

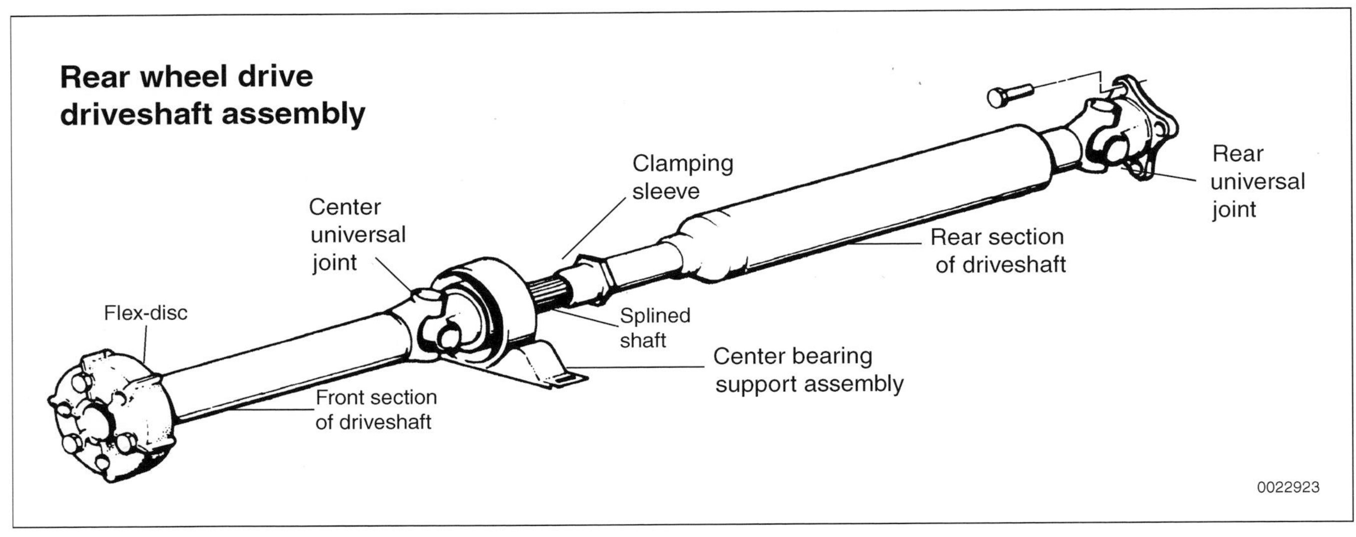

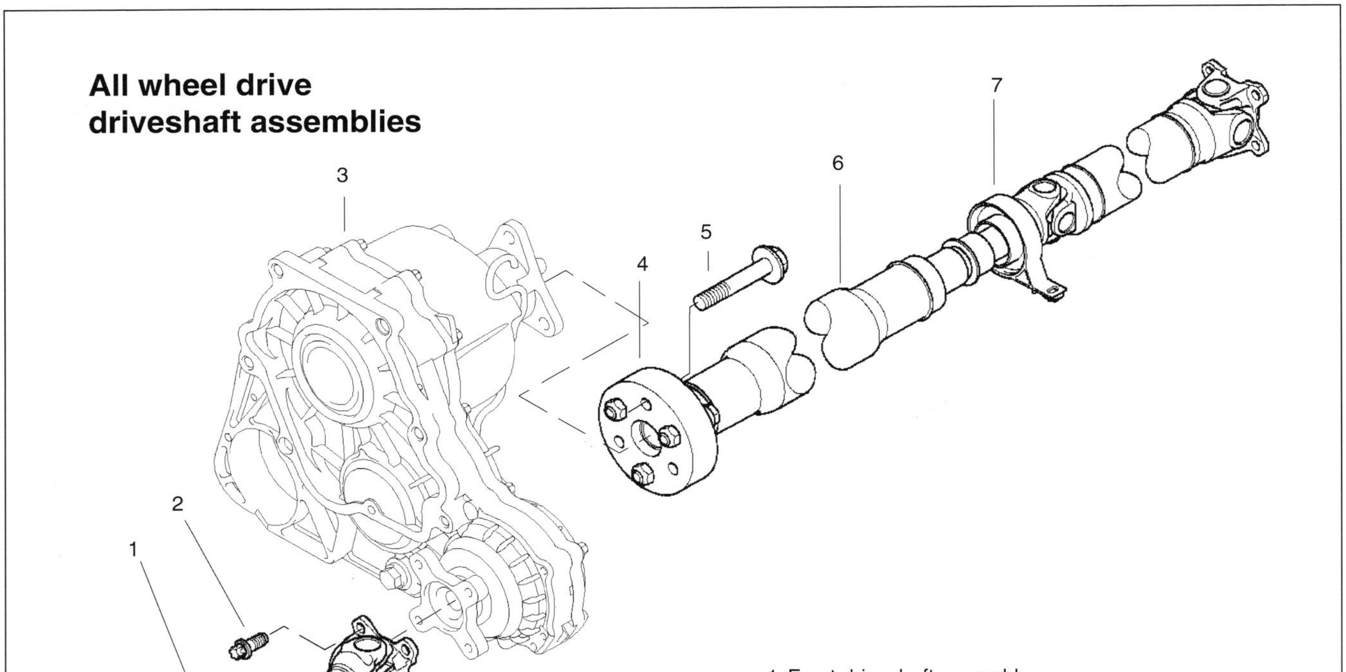

All wheel drive driveshaft assemblies

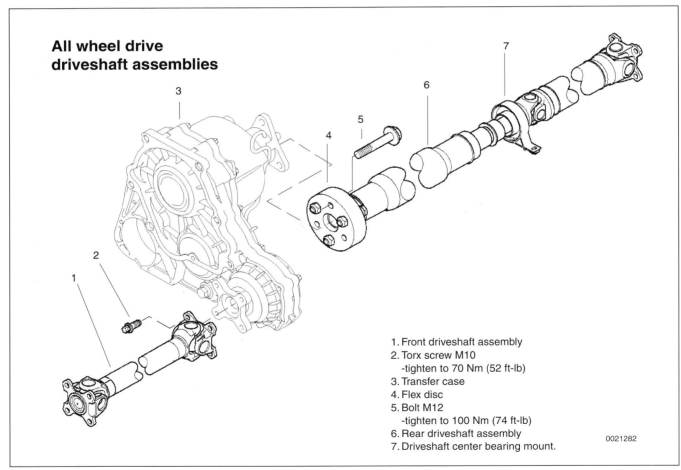

1. Front driveshaft assembly
2. Torx screw M10
   -tighten to 70 Nm (52 ft-lb)
3. Transfer case
4. Flex disc
5. Bolt M12
   -tighten to 100 Nm (74 ft-lb)
6. Rear driveshaft assembly
7. Driveshaft center bearing mount.

0021282

Troubleshooting

The source of driveline vibrations and noise can be difficult to pinpoint. Engine, transmission, front and rear axle, or wheel vibrations can be transmitted through the driveshaft to the car body. Noises from the car may be caused by final drive problems, or by faulty wheel bearings, drive axles, or even worn or improperly inflated tires.

NOTE —
For drive axle repair information, see **311 Front Axle Final Drive** *or* **331 Rear Axle Final Drive**.

Driveshaft noise or vibration may be caused by worn or damaged components. Check the universal joints for play. With the driveshaft installed, pull and twist the driveshaft while watching the joint. The BMW specification for play is very small, so almost any noticeable play could indicate a problem.

Check the torque of the fasteners at the flange connections. At the rear driveshaft check the rubber of the flex-disc and center bearing for deterioration or tearing and check for preload at the center bearing with a visual inspection. Check the driveshafts for broken or missing balance weights. The weights are welded tabs on the driveshaft tubes. In addition to inspecting for faulty driveshaft parts, the installed angles of the driveshaft should also be considered.

Further inspection requires removal of the driveshafts. Check the front centering guide on the transmission output flange for damage or misalignment. Also check runout at the transmission or transfer case output flange and output shaft, and at the final drive input flange. Check the bolt hole bores in the flange for wear and elongation.

Driveshaft flange runout (max. allowable)

- Transmission / transfer case output flange
  axial play . . . . 0.10 mm (0.004 in.)
  radial play . . . . 0.07 mm (0.003 in.)
- Final drive input flange radial play (measured at driveshaft centering lip). . . . . 0.07 mm (0.003 in.)

Spin the rear driveshaft center bearing and check for smooth operation without play. Check that the splines of the sliding coupling move freely. Clean and lubricate the splines with molybdenum disulfide grease (Molykote® Longterm 2 or equivalent).

Check the universal joints for wear or binding. If any joint is difficult to move or binds, the driveshaft section should be replaced.

Universal joint play

- Maximum allowable . . . . 0.15 mm (0.006 in.)

Table a lists symptoms of driveshaft problems and their probable causes. Most of the repair information is contained within this repair group.

Table a. Driveshaft troubleshooting

Symptom	Probable cause	Corrective action
Vibration when starting off (forward or reverse).	Incorrect preload of center bearing.	Check preload of center bearing. Readjust preload.
	Center bearing rubber deteriorated.	Inspect center bearing and rubber. Replace if necessary.
	Flex-disc damaged or worn.	Inspect flex-disc. Replace if necessary.
	Engine or transmission mounts faulty.	Inspect engine and transmission mounts. Align or replace, if necessary.
	Front centering guide worn, or driveshaft mounting flanges out of round.	Check front centering guide and replace if necessary. Check runout of driveshaft flanges.
	Universal joints worn or seized.	Check universal joint play and movement. Replace driveshaft if necessary.
	Sliding coupling seized.	Remove driveshaft and check movement of sliding coupling. Clean coupling splines and replace parts as necessary.
	Driveshaft misaligned.	Check driveshaft alignment.
Noise during on/off throttle or when engaging clutch.	Final drive components worn or damaged (excessive pinion-to-ring-gear clearance).	Remove final drive and repair.
	Drive axle or CV joint faulty.	Inspect drive axles and CV joints. Repair or replace as necessary.
	Sliding coupling seized.	Remove driveshaft and check movement of sliding coupling. Clean coupling splines and replace parts as necessary.
Vibration at 25 to 30 mph (40 to 50 km/h).	Front centering guide worn, or driveshaft mounting flanges out of round or damaged.	Check front centering guide and replace if necessary. Check runout of driveshaft mounting flanges.
	Universal joints worn or seized.	Check universal joint play and movement. Replace driveshaft if necessary.
	Flex-disc damaged or worn.	Inspect flex-disc. Replace if necessary.
	Center bearing rubber deteriorated.	Inspect center bearing. Replace if necessary.
	Sliding coupling seized.	Remove driveshaft and check movement of sliding coupling. Clean coupling splines and replace parts as necessary.
	Misaligned installed position.	Check driveshaft alignment.
Vibration, audible rumble over 35 mph (60 km/h).	Front centering guide worn, or driveshaft mounting flanges out of round or damaged.	Check front centering guide and replace if necessary. Check runout of driveshaft mounting flanges.
	Mounting flange bolts loose or holes worn.	Remove driveshaft and check transmission output flange and final drive input flange. Replace if necessary.
	Driveshaft unbalanced.	Check driveshaft for loose or missing balance weights. Have driveshaft rebalanced or replace if necessary.
	Universal joints worn or seized.	Check universal joint play and movement. Replace driveshaft if necessary.
	Sliding coupling seized.	Remove driveshaft and check movement of sliding coupling. Clean coupling splines or replace parts as necessary.
	Incorrect preload of center bearing.	Check preload of center bearing. Readjust if necessary.
	Center bearing faulty.	Replace center bearing.
	Final drive rubber mount faulty.	Inspect final drive rubber mount and replace if necessary.
	Driveshaft misaligned.	Check driveshaft alignment.

NOTE —
With the driveshaft installed, the actual amount that the universal joints pivot is limited. For the most accurate test, check universal joints in their normal range of movement.

If inspection reveals nothing wrong with the driveshaft, it may need to be rebalanced. This can be done by a speciality driveshaft repair shop. Also, check the alignment of the driveshaft. See **Rear driveshaft, aligning**.

NOTE —
Minor driveshaft vibrations can often be corrected simply by disconnecting the driveshaft at the final drive and repositioning it 90°, 180° or 270° in relation to the final drive input flange.

REAR DRIVESHAFT SERVICE

Rear drive shaft assembly

0022104

1. Hex bolt, M12
2. Centering sleeve
3. Flexible disk
4. Front section of driveshaft
5. Clamping sleeve
6. Clamping ring
7. Torx screw
8. Rear section of drive shaft
9. Center bearing
10. Nut
11. Center bearing support
12. Lock ring

Repair kits for the universal joints are not available for BMW driveshafts. Worn or damaged universal joints usually require replacement of the driveshaft.

The driveshaft is balanced to close tolerances. Whenever it is removed or disassembled, the mounting flanges and driveshaft sections should be marked with paint or a punch before proceeding with work. This will ensure that the driveshaft can be installed in the original orientation.

Rear driveshaft, aligning

The alignment of the driveshaft does not normally need to be checked unless the engine/transmission or the final drive have been removed and installed. If all other parts of the driveshaft have been inspected and found to be okay, but there is still noise or vibration, driveshaft alignment should be checked.

There are two important driveshaft alignment checks. The first is to make sure that the driveshaft runs straight from the transmission to the final drive, without any variation from side-to-side caused by misalignment of the engine/transmission in its mounts. Make a basic check by sighting along the driveshaft from back to front. Any misalignment should be apparent from the center bearing forward.

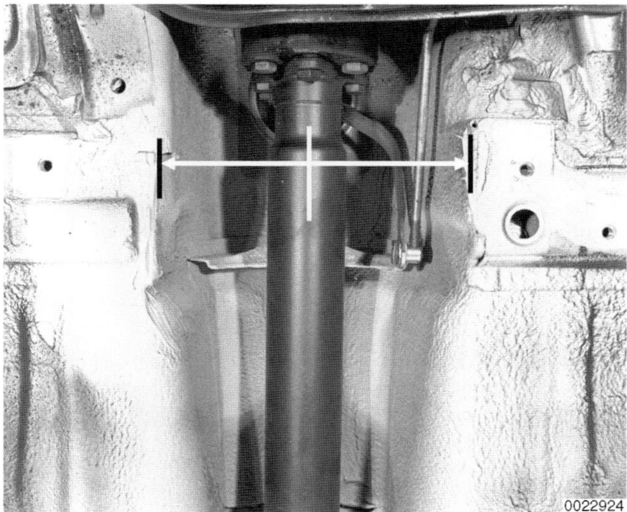

To adjust the side-to-side alignment, loosen transmission or engine mounts to reposition them, then retighten mounts. The driveshaft should be exactly centered in driveshaft tunnel.

The second important driveshaft alignment check is more complicated. It checks the amount the driveshaft is angled vertically at the joints. This angle is known as driveshaft deflection.

In general, there should be little deflection in the driveshaft between the engine, the center bearing, and the final drive. Precise checks require the use of a large protractor or some other means of measuring the angle of the engine and the final drive and comparing these angles to the angle of the driveshaft sections.

To change the deflection angle, shims can be placed between the center bearing and the body or between the transmission and its rear support. When using shims to change a deflection angle, keep in mind that the angle of adjacent joints will also change. Deflection angles should be as small as possible.

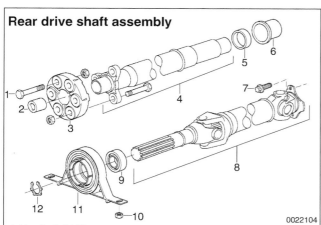

Rear driveshaft, removing

> ***WARNING —***
> - *Be sure the wheels are off the ground before removing the driveshaft. Set the parking brake before removing the driveshaft.*
> - *Once the driveshaft has been removed, the vehicle can roll regardless of whether the transmission is in gear or not.*
> - *The driveshaft is mounted to the transmission and final drive with self-locking nuts. These nuts are designed to be used only once and should be replaced during reassembly.*

– Remove complete exhaust system. See **180 Exhaust System**.

– Remove exhaust heat shields.

– Matchmark front and rear driveshaft connections at transmission and final drive.

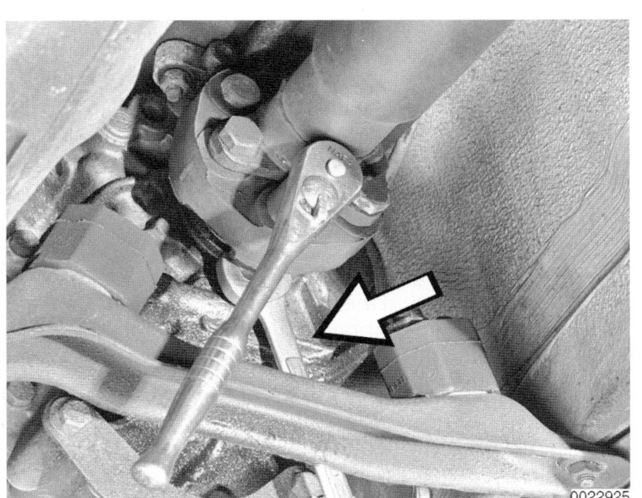

◄ Remove driveshaft mounting bolts. Discard old nuts. Note open-end wrench (**arrow**) being used to counterhold bolt at transmission flex-disc.

– Support driveshaft sections from body using stiff wire.

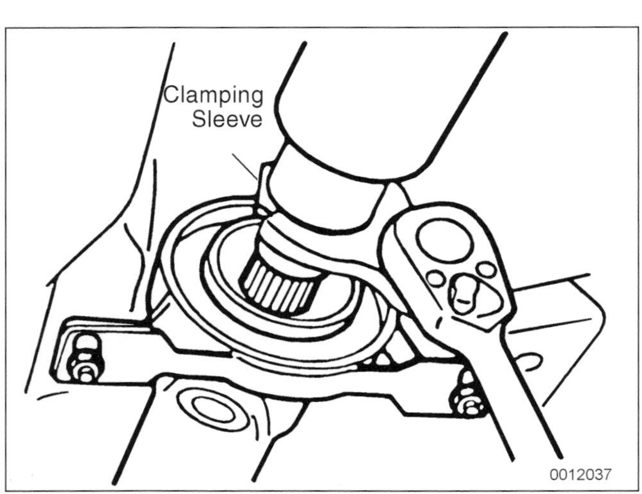

◄ Using BMW special tool 26 1 040, loosen threaded clamping sleeve on driveshaft a few turns.

– Remove center support bearing mounting bolts.

– Remove driveshaft but do not separate two halves. Pull down on center of driveshaft to facilitate removal.

NOTE —
If driveshaft halves were separate and not matchmarked, see **Rear driveshaft, installing**. *If a vibration occurs, disassemble driveshaft and rotate one section 180°.*

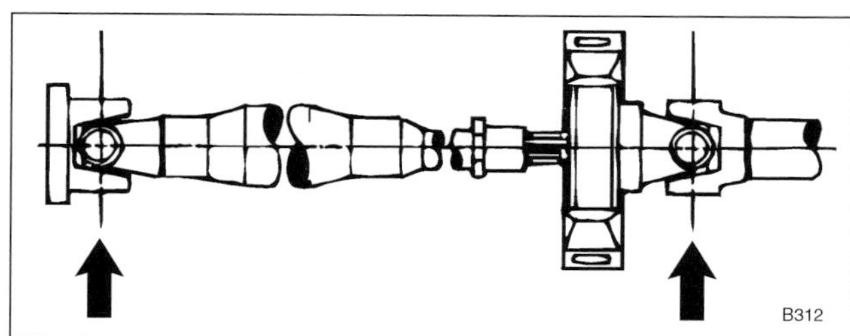

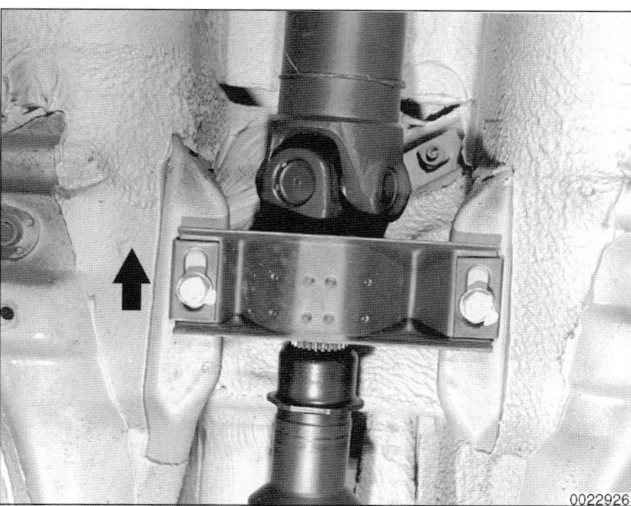

Rear driveshaft, installing

◄ Align driveshaft matchmarks at final drive and transmission flange. Centerlines of universal joints (**arrows**) must be parallel or at 90° to each other. Position center support bearing and start attaching nuts. Use new self-locking nuts.

– Tighten flange nuts while preventing bolts from twisting in coupling. Tighten final drive flange first, then tighten coupling at transmission.

◄ Preload center support bearing by pushing bearing forward (**arrow**) 4-6 mm (0.16-0.24 in.) from center. Tighten attaching bolts.

> ***CAUTION —***
> *The maximum allowable change in height of the center bearing or transmission support using shims is 3 mm (0.12 in.).*

– Tighten threaded sleeve on driveshaft to proper torque.

– Install heat shields.

– Install exhaust system. See **180 Exhaust System**. Connect wiring harness to oxygen sensors.

– Road test vehicle to check for noise or vibration.

> ***WARNING —***
> - *Do not reuse self-locking nuts. These nuts are designed to be used only once.*
> - *Avoid stressing the flex-disc when torquing the bolts. Hold the bolts steady and turn the nuts on the flange side.*

Tightening torques

- Center bearing to body . . . . 21 Nm (15 ft-lb)
- Clamping sleeve . . . . 10 Nm (89 in-lb)
- Drive axle to differential flange
  - M10 Torx bolt . . . . 83 Nm (61 ft-lb)
  - M10 with locking teeth (replace bolts). . . 96 Nm (71 ft-lb)
  - M10 with ribbed teeth (black) . . . . 100 Nm (74 ft-lb)
  - M10 with ribbed teeth (silver) ZNS (replace bolts). . . . . 80 Nm (59 ft-lb)
- Flex-disc to driveshaft or transmission flange
  - M10 (8.8 grade) . . . . 48 Nm (35 ft-lb)
  - M10 (10.9 grade) . . . . 60 Nm (44 ft-lb)
  - M12 (10.9 grade) . . . . 100 Nm (74 ft-lb)
  - M12 (10.9 grade) M3 models . . . . 114 Nm (84 ft-lb)
  - M14. . . . . 140 Nm (103 ft-lb)
  - Rolled on shim . . . . 50 Nm (74 ft-lb) + 90°
- Transmission crossmember to body (M8) . . . . 21 Nm (15 ft-lb)

NOTE —
Bolt grade is marked on the bolt head. When replacing bolts, only use bolts of the same strength and hardness as the originals installed.

Flex-disc, replacing

The flex-disc between the front section of the rear driveshaft and the output flange of the transmission or transfer case should be checked for cracks, tears, missing pieces, or distortion. Check for worn bolt hole bores in the flange.

— Remove driveshaft as described earlier.

NOTE —

It is possible to only partially remove the driveshaft, leaving it connected to the final drive. The driveshaft can be tilted down in the center and slid off the transmission flange once the clamping sleeve is loosened and the center bearing bracket is unbolted. Suspend the driveshaft using stiff wire in as close to the installed position as possible. If the driveshaft hangs unsupported, the rear universal joint may be damaged.

— Unbolt flex-disc from driveshaft.

NOTE —

Removal and installation of the bolts may be made easier by placing a large hose clamp around the flex-disc, and tightening the clamp slightly to compress the coupling.

 Install new flex-disc using new self-locking nuts. Molded arrows on coupling should face flange arms.

— Install driveshaft as described earlier.

NOTE —

Torque only the nuts while holding the bolt heads. This will prevent damaging or fatiguing the rubber.

Tightening torques

- Center bearing to body . . . . 21 Nm (15 ft-lb)
- Clamping sleeve . . . . 10 Nm (89 in-lb)
- Drive axle to differential flange
  - M10 Torx bolt . . . . 83 Nm (61 ft-lb)
  - M10 with locking teeth (replace bolts). . . 96 Nm (71 ft-lb)
  - M10 with ribbed teeth (black) . . . . 100 Nm (74 ft-lb)
  - M10 with ribbed teeth (silver) ZNS (replace bolts). . . . . 80 Nm (59 ft-lb)
- Flex-disc to driveshaft or transmission flange
  - M10 (8.8 grade) . . . . 48 Nm (35 ft-lb)
  - M10 (10.9 grade) . . . . 60 Nm (44 ft-lb)
  - M12 (10.9 grade) . . . . 100 Nm (74 ft-lb)
  - M12 (10.9 grade) M3 models . . . . 114 Nm (84 ft-lb)
  - M14. . . . . 140 Nm (103 ft-lb)
  - Rolled on shim . . . . 50 Nm (74 ft-lb) + 90°
- Transmission crossmember to body (M8) . . . . 21 Nm (15 ft-lb)

Center bearing assembly, replacing

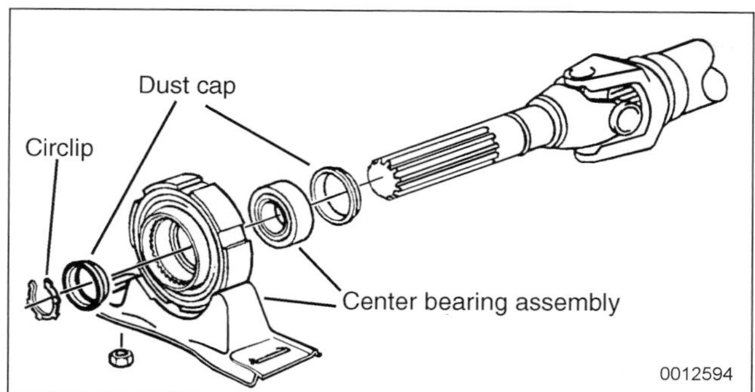

◀ To replace the center bearing assembly, the driveshaft must be removed from the car. The center bearing assembly consists of a grooved ball bearing in a rubber mount. The bearing assembly is pressed onto the front section of the driveshaft and secured by a circlip.

– Remove rear driveshaft. See **Rear driveshaft, removing**.

– Match mark front and rear driveshaft sections before separating.

– Loosen clamping sleeve fully and pull driveshaft sections apart. Remove rubber bushing, washer, and clamping sleeve from front section.

– Inspect condition of rubber bushing for splined coupling. Replace worn or damaged parts.

◀ Remove center bearing circlip (**arrow**) and dust guard.

– Install puller so that it pulls on inner hub of bearing. Pulling on outer ring of mount may tear rubber, and entire bearing assembly will need to be replaced.

– Before installation, make sure dust guard is on driveshaft, and then press center mount onto driveshaft flush with dust guard.

– Place clamping sleeve, washer, and rubber bushing on front driveshaft section. Lubricate splines with molybdenum disulfide grease (Molykote® Longterm 2 or equivalent) and then reassemble driveshaft.

NOTE —
Do not retighten clamping sleeve until driveshaft is installed.

– Install driveshaft. See **Rear driveshaft, installing**.

– Tighten clamping sleeve.

Tightening torque
• Clamping sleeve . . . . 10 Nm (7.5 ft-lb)

Front centering guide, replacing

The front centering guide centers the driveshaft in relation to the transmission or transfer case. The guide is press-fit into a cavity in the front of the driveshaft and slides onto the transmission output shaft.

No specifications are given for wear of the guide, but generally the guide should fit snugly on the transmission output shaft.

NOTE —
Some driveshafts have a dust cap installed on the end of the driveshaft, over the centering guide. The dust cap may become bent or distorted when the driveshaft is removed or installed. Damage to the dust cap should not affect the centering guide and should not be mistaken for guide wear.

– Remove driveshaft. See **Rear driveshaft, removing**.

– Pack cavity behind centering guide with heavy grease until grease is flush with bottom edge of guide.

– Insert 14 mm (approximately ½ in.) diameter mandrel or metal rod into guide. Strike guide with hammer to force centering guide out.

NOTE —
The mandrel should fit snugly in the centering guide so that the grease cannot escape around the sides of the mandrel.

– Remove old grease from driveshaft, lubricate new centering guide with molybdenum disulfide grease (Molykote® Longterm 2 or equivalent) and drive it into driveshaft.

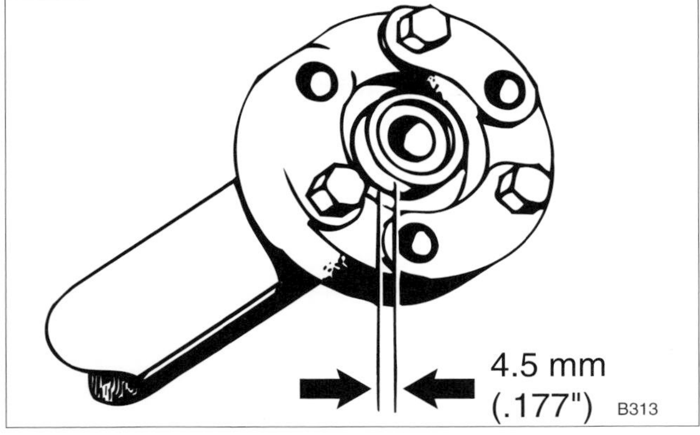

When installing new driveshaft centering guide, the sealing lip of the guide should face outward and it should be driven into the driveshaft to a protrusion depth of 4.5 mm (.177 in.).

– Install driveshaft as described earlier.

FRONT DRIVESHAFT SERVICE

Repair kits for the universal joints are not available for BMW driveshafts. Worn or damaged universal joints usually require replacement of the driveshaft.

Front driveshaft, removing and installing

> ***CAUTION —***
> *Do not move vechicle using engine power once front driveshaft has been removed.*

– Raise vehicle and safely support to access front driveshaft.

> ***WARNING —***
> - *When raising the car using a floor jack or a hydraulic lift, carefully position the jack pad to prevent damaging the car body. A suitable liner (wood, rubber, etc.) should be placed between the jack and the car to prevent body damage.*
> - *Watch the jack closely. Make sure it stays stable and does not shift or tilt. As the car is raised, the car may roll slightly and the jack may shift.*

– Remove underbody splash guard.

0021626

◄ Remove bolts holding driveshaft to transfer case output flange and front differential input flange (**arrows**).

– Installation is reverse of removal.

Tightening torques
- Driveshaft to drive flange (M10) . . . . 70 Nm (52 ft-lb)

270 Transfer Case

GENERAL

This repair group covers removal and installation of the all wheel drive transfer case. Internal transfer case repair is not covered. Special press tools and procedures are required to disassemble and service the internal geartrain.

Some procedures covered in this repair group will require you to refer to the following repair groups:

- **180 Exhaust System**
- **260 Driveshafts**

The transfer case is used in all wheel drive models to direct power from the transmission to both the front and rear differentials via driveshafts. This transfer case is unique in that it delivers 38% of the transmission's torque output to the front differential, and 62% of the torque to the rear. Unlike the transfer cases used in many four wheel drive trucks, the transfer case used is a single range unit, permanently engaged to drive all four wheels all of the time.

TRANSFER CASE

Transfer case, removing and installing

– Raise vehicle and safely support to access transfer case.

> ***WARNING —***
> - *When raising the car using a floor jack or a hydraulic lift, carefully position the jack pad to prevent damaging the car body. A suitable liner (wood, rubber, etc.) should be placed between the jack and the car to prevent body damage.*
> - *Watch the jack closely. Make sure it stays stable and does not shift or tilt. As the car is raised, the car may roll slightly and the jack may shift.*

– Remove engine splash guard from underside of vehicle.

– Remove exhaust system. See **180 Exhaust System**.

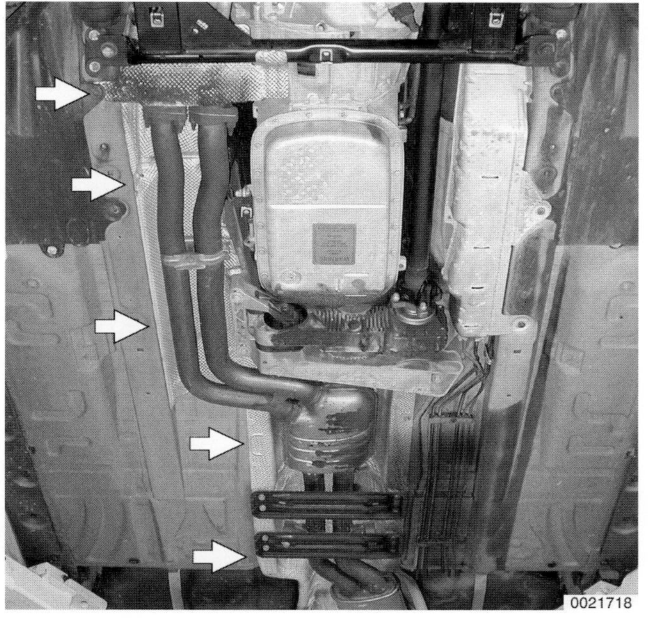
0021718

< Remove exhaust system heat shields (**arrows**).

– Remove front drive shaft. See **260 Driveshafts**.

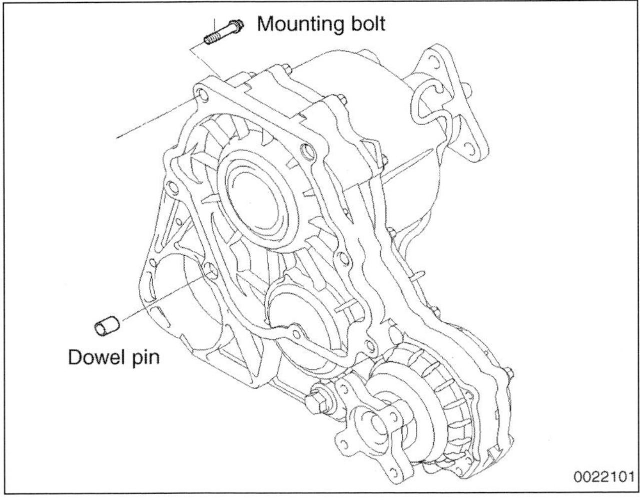

- Support transmission with transmission jack or suitable shop hoist.

◄ Remove transmission crossmember (**arrows**).

- Detach transfer case vent tube.

- Keeping the driveshaft in place, remove nuts retaining rear driveshaft to transfer case at flexible disc.

> ***CAUTION —***
> *Do not allow the driveshaft to hang down. This may damage universal joints at drive shaft ends.*

- Support rear driveshaft center bearing and release mounting nuts.

- Lower rear driveshaft at center bearing and remove from transmission output flange at flexible disk. Support from vehicle body using stiff wire.

◄ Remove bolts retaining transfer case to transmission and remove transfer case.

- Installation is reverse of removal, noting the following:
  - Replace dowel pins in transfer case mounting surface if damaged.
  - Coat dowel pins with anti-seize before installing.
  - On manual transmission cars: Replace sealing O-ring between transmission and transfer case.

NOTE —
When refilling transfer case, recheck oil level again after driving car approximately 200 meters (600 ft).

Tightening torques
- Transmission crossmember to body (M8) . . . . 21 Nm (15 ft-lb)
- Transfer case to transmission (M10) . . . 41 Nm (30 ft-lb)
- Transfer case filler plug (M18) . . . . 33 Nm (24 ft-lb)

Fluid capacities
- Transfer case oil change. . . . . 0.16 liter (0.16 qt.)
- New transfer case fill. . . . . 0.24 liter (0.25 qt.)

300 Suspension, Steering and Brakes–General

TABLES

GENERAL

This section covers general information for front and rear suspension, steering system, and the electronic braking and stability control systems.

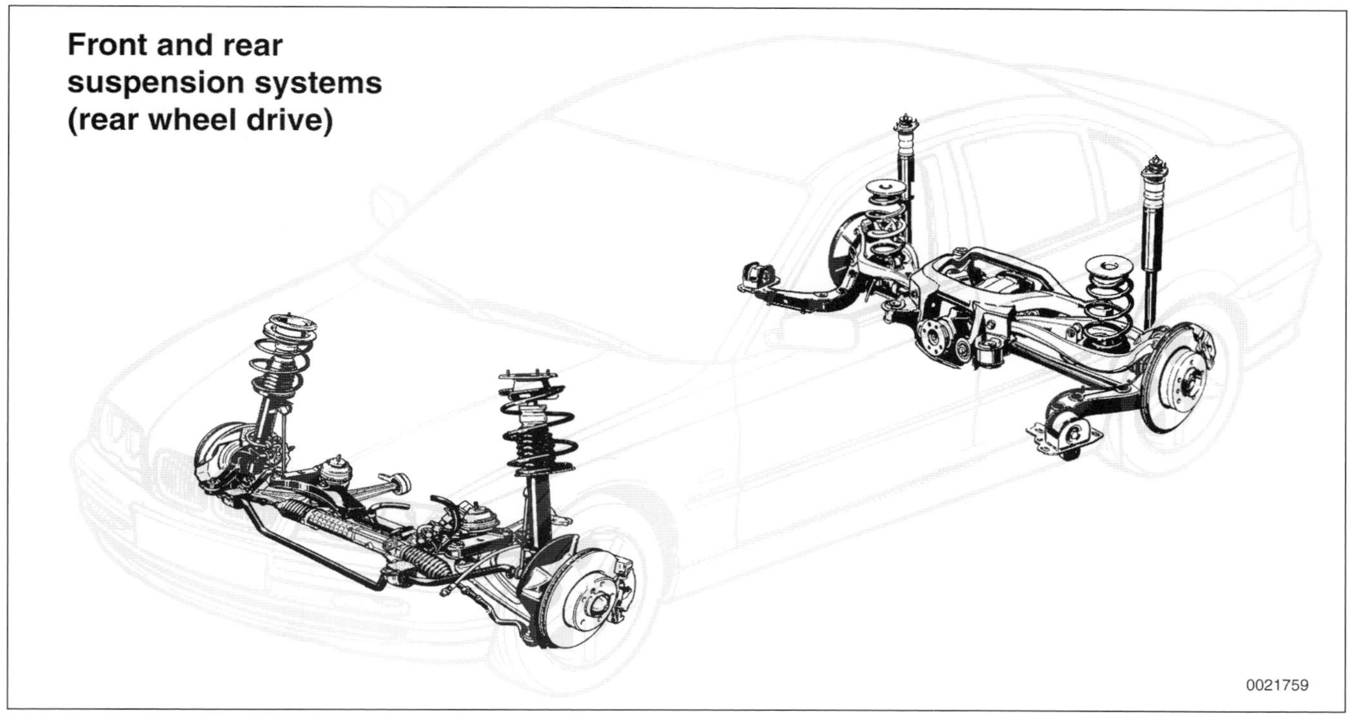

Front and rear suspension systems (rear wheel drive)

Front suspension

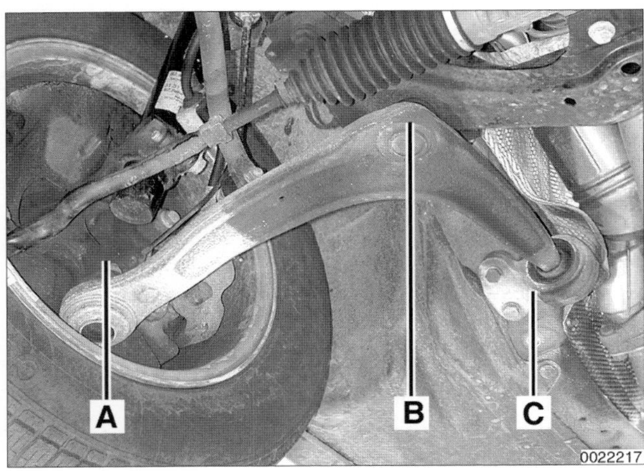

In rear wheel drive cars, the control arm on each side connects the steering arm (**A**) to mounting points on the subframe (**B**) and the body frame rail (**C**). On all wheel drive cars the rear mounting of the control arm is to the subframe.

Each front strut assembly includes a tubular strut housing with an integrated shock absorber and a large coil spring. The upper strut mount includes a coil spring seat and strut bearing. A rubber bump stop limits suspension travel. The steering arm clamps the lower end of the strut assembly. The strut assembly pivots between the upper strut mount bearing and a ball joint on the control arm.

The front suspension is designed with minimum positive steering offset. This geometry contributes to stability when traction is unequal from side to side.

Front suspension, rear wheel drive cars

The control arms are constructed of forged aluminum. This design lowers the overall weight of the car and reduces the amount of unsprung mass. By reducing unsprung mass, softer, more comfortable springs can be used and accurate handling is maintained.

The three point mounting of each L-shaped control arm precisely controls the front-to-rear and side-to-side position of the strut, while the flexibility of the joints and mounts also allows the movement necessary for suspension travel. The control arm mounting points are designed with anti-dive geometry. This design reduces the normal tendency for the front of the vehicle to dive under hard braking.

Control arm position is fixed, with no adjustment provisions for altering front wheel alignment.

A stabilizer bar mounted to both strut housings helps to reduce body roll when cornering.

For the 2001 model year, the E46 coupe and convertible were available as an M3 model. Numerous changes were made to the E46 coupe body to accommodate the increased horsepower and torque of the M3 model:

- Track width increased by 37 mm (1.46 in)
- Aluminum thrust plate installed to strengthen front suspension mounting points
- Revised aluminum control arms
- Unique steering arms, wheel bearings, bushings, mounts and reinforcement braces

Front suspension, all wheel drive cars

For model year 2001, the E46 Sedan and Sport Wagon were offered with optional all wheel drive. The all wheel drive models are known as 325xi or 330xi.

NOTE —
The internal BMW designation of these models is E46/16.

The all wheel drive system adds approx. 100 kg (220 lbs.) to the weight of the car. Weight distribution is largely unaffected at 52.7% front, 47.3% rear.

The front suspension for all wheel drive vehicles was redesigned to provide clearance for the front axle differential and drive shafts. All suspension components are constructed of steel.

The front subframe consists of two square frame sections welded to two tubes to form a box structure. Four bolts (**arrows**) attach it to the undercarriage of the vehicle.

The steel control arms, smaller than the aluminum arms used on rear wheel drive models, attach at the rear to the subframe. The control arm inner ball joints are bolted to the subframe. The hydraulic engine mounts are different from the rear wheel drive version and are also relocated to provide front axle clearance.

The front stabilizer bar was increased in diameter to accommodate the additional weight. See **Table a**.

The front struts are shorter than the rear wheel drive version. Reinforcement plates were added between the strut upper mounting and the strut towers to prevent sheet metal deformation when traveling on poor road surfaces. The spring travel of the E46 all wheel drive is approximately 20 mm (¾ in) less than the rear wheel drive version. The shorter front axle spring travel is due to the limited angle of deflection of the front axle shafts.

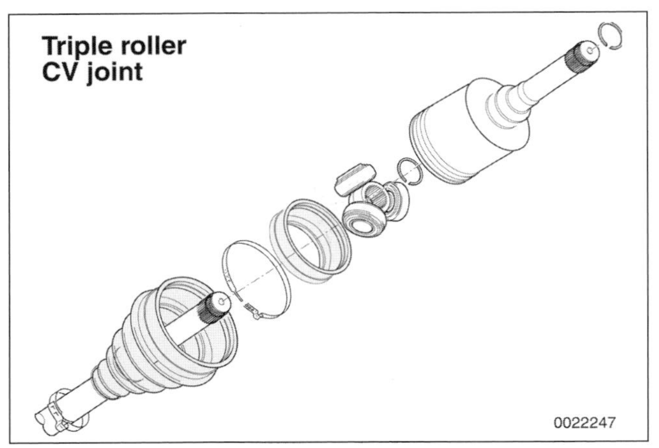

Each front drive axle shaft has a conventional constant velocity (CV) joint at the outboard end and a triple roller bearing CV joint at the inboard end. The right inner joint shaft is supported by a bearing pedestal bolted to the oil pan. The shaft extends through the engine oil pan into the front differential.

The front axle differential, bolted to the left side of the engine oil pan, is driven by a 40 mm (1.57 in) single piece driveshaft. Universal joints are located at both ends of the driveshaft.

Steering

The variable-assist power steering system consists of an engine-driven hydraulic pump, rack-and-pinion type steering, and connecting linkage to the road wheels. Steering effort in E46 models is engine-speed dependent. At low speeds, maximum power assist is provided to ease parking and city driving. At high speeds, assist is reduced to ensure stability.

The steering linkage connects the rack-and-pinion unit through tie rods to the steering arms. The tie rod ends allow the wheels to pivot and react to suspension travel.

On all wheel drive models, the rack and pinion steering is constructed with a larger diameter piston than the rear wheel drive version. This is necessary to counter the additional drag of the all wheel drive system and the wider standard wheels and tires.

The lower steering column in all wheel drive models connects to the steering rack via a universal joint, whereas there is flexible ("guibo") joint on the rear wheel drive models. The turning radius of the all wheel drive vehicle is 35.8 feet, 1.4 feet greater than the rear wheel drive vehicle.

Rear suspension

The rear suspension subframe (final drive carrier) is the main mounting point for the differential housing and rear suspension components. It is bolted to the vehicle undercarriage using four large bolts through rubber bushings (**arrows**).

Trailing arms locate the rear wheels and anchor the springs, shock absorbers and stabilizer bar. Drive axles with constant-velocity (CV) joints at both ends transfer power from the differential to the road wheels. The differential is mounted to the subframe through rubber mounts and bushings to help isolate drivetrain noise and vibration.

In all wheel drive models, the rear suspension and the rear differential have the same layout as the rear wheel drive version.

Convertible and M3 models are fitted with a V-brace with tension struts (**arrows**) which tie the rear differential to the rear suspension pick-up points. These struts work to limit rear body twist and increase structural rigidity.

The rear suspension travel of the E46 all wheel drive is approx. 17 mm (0.67 in) less than the rear wheel drive version. The reason for the reduced travel in the rear is to prevent excessive body roll as a result of the higher body profile.

The rear stabilizer bar diameter was increased to accommodate the additional vehicle weight. See **Table a**.

Table a. E46 stabilizer bars

Model	Front diameter	Rear diameter
Rear wheel drive	23.0 mm (0.906 in)	18 mm (0.709 in)
All wheel drive	23.5 mm (0.925 in)	20 mm (0.787 in)
Sport suspension (n/a on awd)	24.0 mm (0.945 in)	19 mm (0.748 in)
M3	26.0 mm (1.024 in)	21.5 mm (0.846 in)

For M3 models, the rear suspension was modified to accommodate the increased horsepower and torque of the M3 driveline.

- Track width increased by 47mm (1.85 in)
- Control arms revised to use ball joints at outer ends
- V-strut brace added to stiffen rear subframe

Brakes

E46 cars are equipped with power disc brakes with integral antilock brakes (ABS). The parking brake is a dual-drum system integrated with the rear brake rotors.

Power assist is provided by a vacuum booster when the engine is running. The brake pedal pushrod is connected directly to the master cylinder, so failure of the vacuum booster does not normally result in total brake failure.

Each disc brake uses a caliper with a single hydraulic cylinder. Brake pads in the left front and right rear contain wear sensors. When the pads need replacement, the sensors illuminate a light on the dashboard.

Tires and wheels

Tire size is critical to the proper operation of the anti-lock brake system and traction control system. Several different styles of wheels in 15, 16, 17, 18, and 19 inch diameters are available from an authorized BMW dealer.

On all wheel drive cars, standard wheel size is 17x 7.0 to ensure there is enough room for the front axles and brakes. Tire size is 205/50 R17.

Tire and rim size applications are listed in **Table b**.

Table b. Rim and tire sizes

Model	Standard		Option	
	Rim size	Tire size	Rim size	Tire size
323i	15 x 6.5	195 / 65R 15	16 x 7	205 / 55R 16
323Ci 325i / Ci 328i	16 x 7	205 / 55R 16	17 x 8	225 / 45R 17
328Ci	16 x 7	205 / 55R 16	17 x 7.5 / 8.5	225 / 45R 17 245 / 45R 17
330i / Ci	17 x 7	205 / 50R 17	17 x 7.5 / 8.5 18 x 8 / 8.5	225 / 45R 17 245 / 40R 17 225 / 40ZR 18 255 / 35ZR 18
325xi	16 x 7	205 / 55R 16	17 x 7	205 / 50R 17
330xi	17 x 7	205 / 50R 17		
M3	18 x 8 / 9	225 / 45ZR 18 255 / 40ZR 18	19 x 8 / 9	225 / 40ZR 19 255 / 35ZR 19

NOTE —
Select aftermarket wheels with care. Improperly fitted wheels can contact and damage suspension, brake or body components and may adversely affect vehicle stability.

ELECTRONIC BRAKE AND STABILITY CONTROL SYSTEMS

E46 vehicles are equipped with antilock braking (ABS). Early production models featured ABS with Automatic Stability Control (ABS / ASC). Later models came equipped with ABS and Dynamic Stability Control (ABS / DSC). DSC builds upon the existing ABS / ASC system to provide electronic control of drive and braking systems to insure vehicle stability.

This manual refers to these systems as ABS. ASC or DSC is specified when necessary. See the accompanying illustrations for individual system identification.

ABS system description

The electronically controlled ABS maintains vehicle stability and control during emergency braking by preventing wheel lock-up. ABS provides optimum deceleration and stability during adverse conditions. It automatically adjusts brake system hydraulic pressure at each wheel to prevent wheel lock-up.

The system's main components are the wheel speed (pulse) sensors, the ABS / ASC or ABS / DSC control module, and the hydraulic control unit.

E46 Electronic braking and stability control systems

1999 - 2000
Automatic Stability Control
Teves MK 20 ASC

1. Brake master cylinder and fluid reservoir, left rear of engine compartment
2. ASC control module and hydraulic unit, left rear of engine compartment under master cylinder
3. Rear wheel speed sensor, at each rear wheel hub
4. Front wheel speed sensor, at each front steering arm

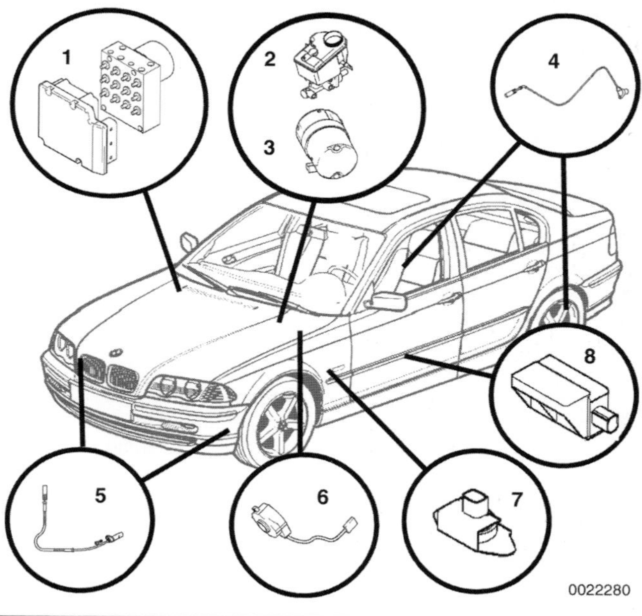

1999 - 2000,
2001 - 2005 M3
Dynamic Stability Control
Teves MK 20 EI DSC III

1. DSC control module and hydraulic unit, right rear of engine compartment
2. Brake fluid reservoir, master cylinder and DSC brake pressure sensors, left rear of engine compartment
3. DSC precharge pump, left rear of engine compartment, under brake master cylinder
4. Rear wheel speed sensor, at each rear wheel hub
5. Front wheel speed sensor, at each front steering arm
6. Steering angle sensor, at base of upper steering column
7. Lateral acceleration sensor, behind driver kick panel
8. Rotational acceleration (yaw) sensor, under driver seat, underneath rug

E46 Electronic braking and stability control systems

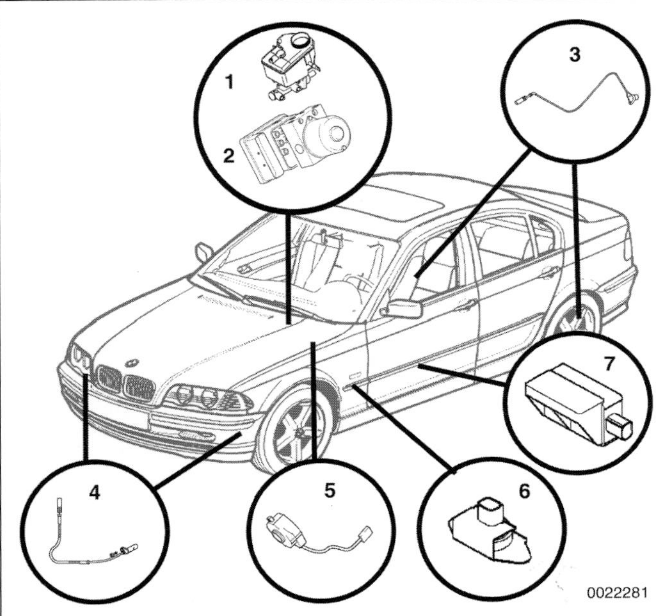

0022281

2001 - 2005 rear wheel drive
Dynamic Stability Control
Teves MK 60 DSC III

1. Brake fluid reservoir and master cylinder, left rear of engine compartment
2. DSC control module and hydraulic unit, left rear of engine compartment, under brake master cylinder
3. Rear wheel speed sensor, at each rear wheel hub
4. Front wheel speed sensor, at each front steering arm
5. Steering angle sensor, at base of upper steering column
6. Lateral acceleration sensor, behind driver kick panel
7. Rotational acceleration (yaw) sensor, under driver seat, underneath rug

Note: There is no precharge pump in this system.

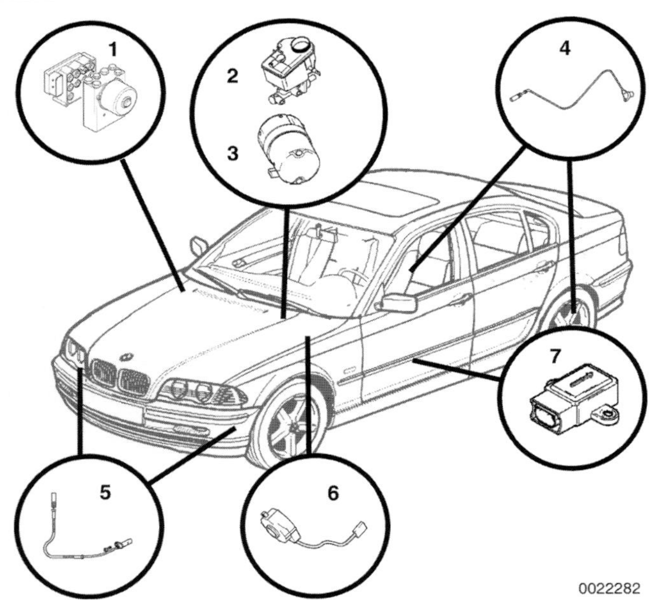

0022282

2001 - 2005 all wheel drive
Dynamic Stability Control
Bosch DSC III 5.7

1. DSC control module, hydraulic unit and DSC brake pressure sensor, right rear of engine compartment
2. Brake fluid reservoir and master cylinder, left rear of engine compartment
3. DSC precharge pump, left rear of engine compartment, under brake master cylinder
4. Rear wheel speed sensor, at each rear wheel hub
5. Front wheel speed sensor, at each front steering arm
6. Steering angle sensor, at base of upper steering column
7. Lateral acceleration sensor and rotational acceleration (yaw) sensor, under driver seat, underneath rug

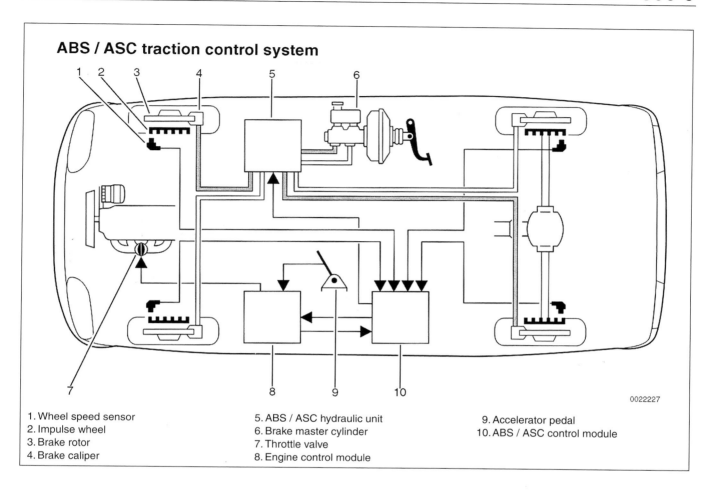

ABS / ASC traction control system

0022227

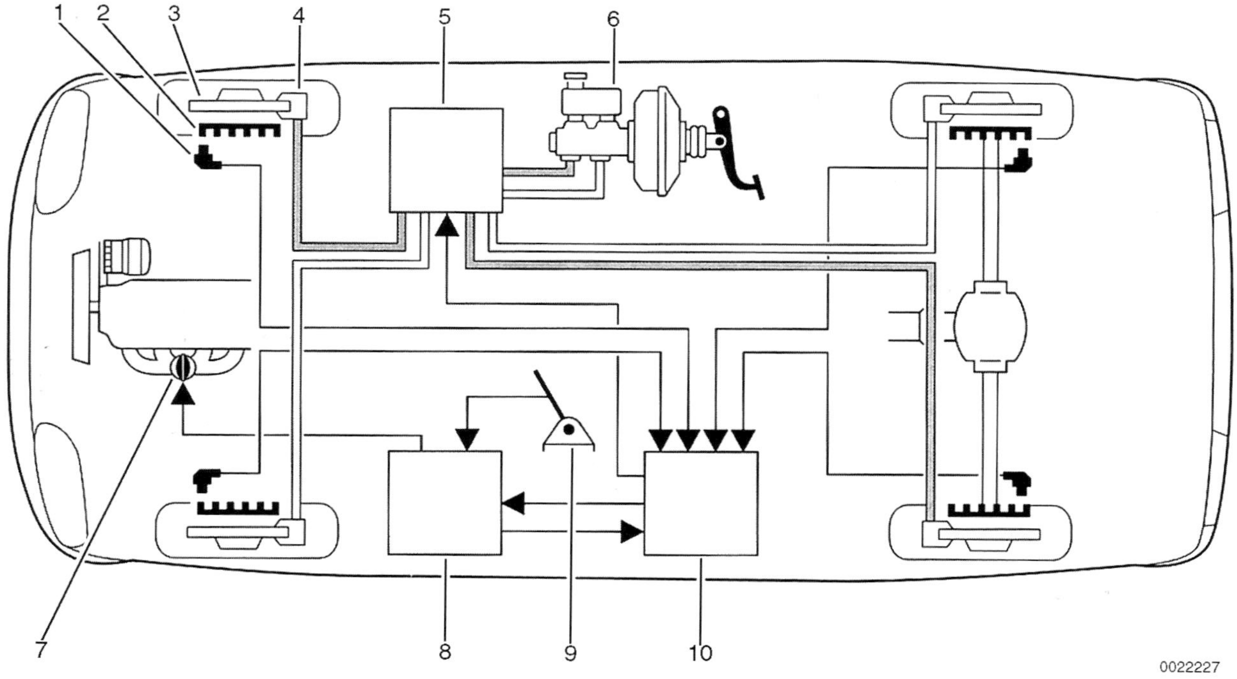

1. Wheel speed sensor
2. Impulse wheel
3. Brake rotor
4. Brake caliper
5. ABS / ASC hydraulic unit
6. Brake master cylinder
7. Throttle valve
8. Engine control module
9. Accelerator pedal
10. ABS / ASC control module

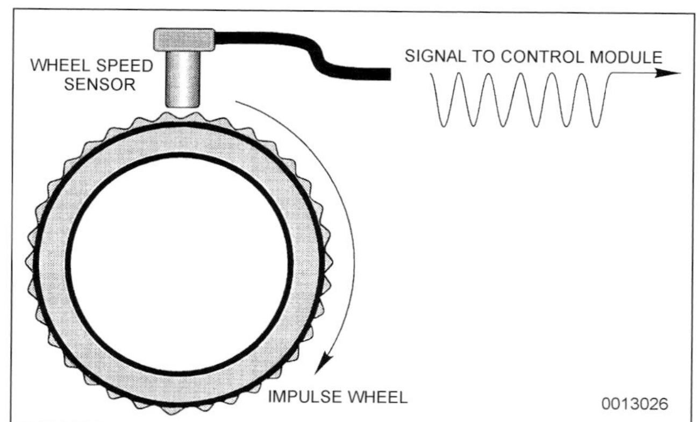

◄ The wheel speed sensors continuously send wheel speed signals to the control module. The control module compares these signals to determine, in fractions of a second, if one wheel is slowing down faster than others during braking. If a wheel is nearing lock-up, the module signals the ABS hydraulic unit to maintain or reduce brake fluid pressure at that wheel. Pressure is modulated by electrically-operated solenoid valves in the hydraulic unit.

Automatic Stability Control (ASC)

The Automatic Stability Control (ASC) system works in conjunction with the Antilock Brake System (ABS) and the engine management system to enhance vehicle control. The main function of the ASC system is to maintain the rolling contact between the tires and the road surface under all driving conditions. This is achieved through exact application and management of braking and drivetrain forces.

NOTE —

The traction control system referred to as ASC (Automatic Stability Control) may also be referred to as ASC+T (Automatic Stability Control+Traction).

The ASC system improves traction by electronically applying the rear brakes when the rear drive wheels are spinning at a faster rate than the front wheels. The combined ABS / ASC control module, operating through the ABS hydraulic control unit, modulates braking force at the rear wheels.

In addition, ASC deactivates individual fuel injectors and overrides the motor driven throttle to reduce engine torque and maintain vehicle traction. Because the throttle is controlled electronically the driver cannot increase the engine power output during ASC intervention regardless of how far the accelerator pedal is pushed.

The components that comprise the ASC system also function to replace the limited slip differential available in previous models. Even with the ASC system turned off, if the ASC control module senses a difference in wheel speed (one wheel spinning) the control module applies modulated braking force to the slipping wheel until traction is regained, but does not override fuel injection function.

Traction control also comes into operation during closed throttle deceleration. Decelerating on snowy or icy road surfaces can lead to rear wheel slip. If a rear wheel starts to drag or lock up, the ASC system can limit the problem by adjusting throttle, fuel injection and ignition timing.

A switch on the center console is used to toggle the ASC on or off.

The ASC system is designed to be maintenance free. There are no adjustments that can be made. Repair and troubleshooting of the ASC system requires special test equipment and knowledge and should be performed only by an authorized BMW dealer. **Table c** lists the conditions indicated by the ASC indicator light in the instrument cluster.

ASC

0022266

Table c. ASC indicator light function

Indicator light	Condition	Action / use
Light ON	Normal ASC start-up	Automatic ASC self-test
Light OFF	ASC monitoring mode	Automatic ASC operation
Press ASC button, light ON	ASC OFF (disabled)	Rocking the car to get out of snow or other loose surface Driving with snow chains
Press ASC button, light OFF	ASC monitoring mode	Automatic ASC operation
Light flashes	ASC active mode	Normal ASC operation as it controls wheel speed
Light ON after start up or while driving	Defect in ASC	Consult BMW dealer for diagnosis / repair (vehicle operation remains normal)

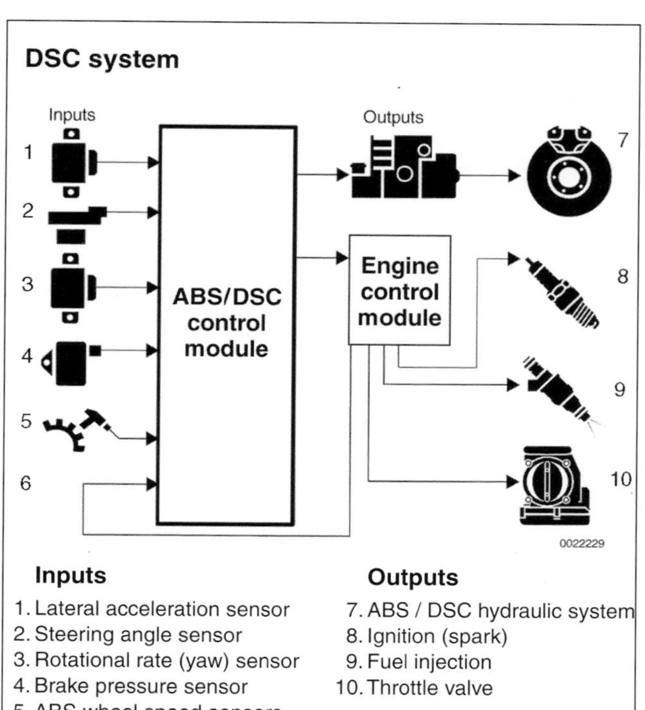

Inputs

1. Lateral acceleration sensor
2. Steering angle sensor
3. Rotational rate (yaw) sensor
4. Brake pressure sensor
5. ABS wheel speed sensors
6. Engine control module

Outputs

7. ABS / DSC hydraulic system
8. Ignition (spark)
9. Fuel injection
10. Throttle valve

Dynamic Stability Control (DSC)

Dynamic Stability Control (DSC), standard in 2000 and later E46 models, utilizes many principles and components of the ASC traction control system. DSC is active throughout the driving experience, unlike ASC which is only active during acceleration and braking. DSC helps stabilize the vehicle in cornering and avoidance maneuvers by adjusting engine controls such as throttle, ignition, fuel injection and the application of brake pressure to the wheels individually.

The DSC control module uses various inputs to determine vehicle instability during braking, cornering, or reduced traction situations. Based upon these inputs the ABS / DSC control module sends outputs to the engine control module and the ABS / DSC hydraulic unit to activate torque reduction protocols and braking intervention.

The DSC system can be toggled on and off by a switch mounted on the center console. Turning off the DSC system does not disable ABS or ASC functions.

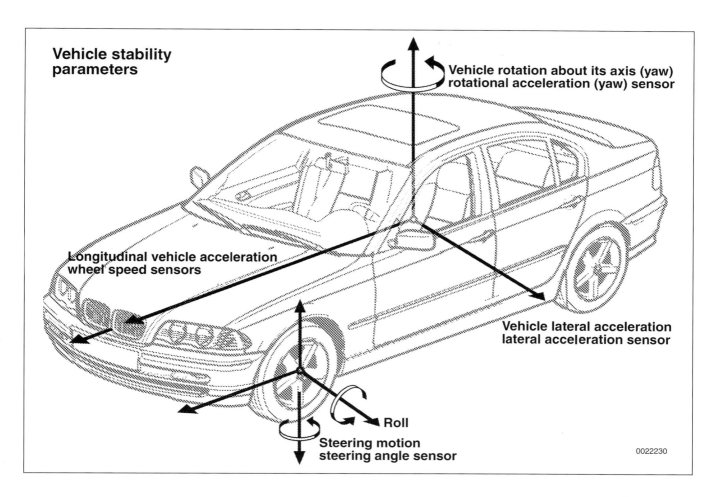

Vehicle stability parameters

Vehicle rotation about its axis (yaw)
rotational acceleration (yaw) sensor

Longitudinal vehicle acceleration
wheel speed sensors

Vehicle lateral acceleration
lateral acceleration sensor

Roll

Steering motion
steering angle sensor

0022230

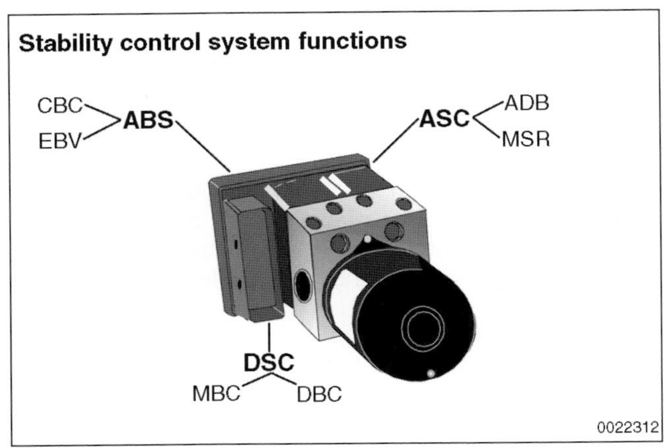

System functions

Each of the electronic braking and stability control systems include sub-systems which use the hydraulic unit / control module and sensors to carry out additional system functions. The foundation of the stability control systems is ABS with the following basic functions:

- Cornering brake control (CBC)
- Electronic brake proportioning (EBV)

The Teves MK 20 ASC system functions as a basic ABS system, but adds additional system functions:

- Brake intervention (ADB)
- Drag torque reduction (MSR)

All of the dynamic stability control systems are based on the ABS / ASC system, but add DSC system functions

- Dynamic brake control (DBC)
- Maximum brake control (MBC)

Cornering brake control (CBC)

Cornering brake control reduces brake pressure build up on the inside rear wheel brake circuit during cornering if activation threshold values are exceeded.

Electronic brake proportioning (EBV)

Electronic brake proportioning adjusts braking force to the rear wheels based upon vehicle load, front to rear, to maximize vehicle braking power.

Using wheel speed sensors, the control module compares individual wheel deceleration rates as the brakes are applied. If the difference in wheel speeds exceeds the programmed threshold values, EBV is activated. EBV activation modulates inlet valves to the rear wheels to regulate braking force.

Brake intervention (ADB)

Brake intervention is applied to the individual drive wheel which is losing traction by activating the rear brake calipers in three phases:

- Pressure build
- Pressure hold
- Pressure release

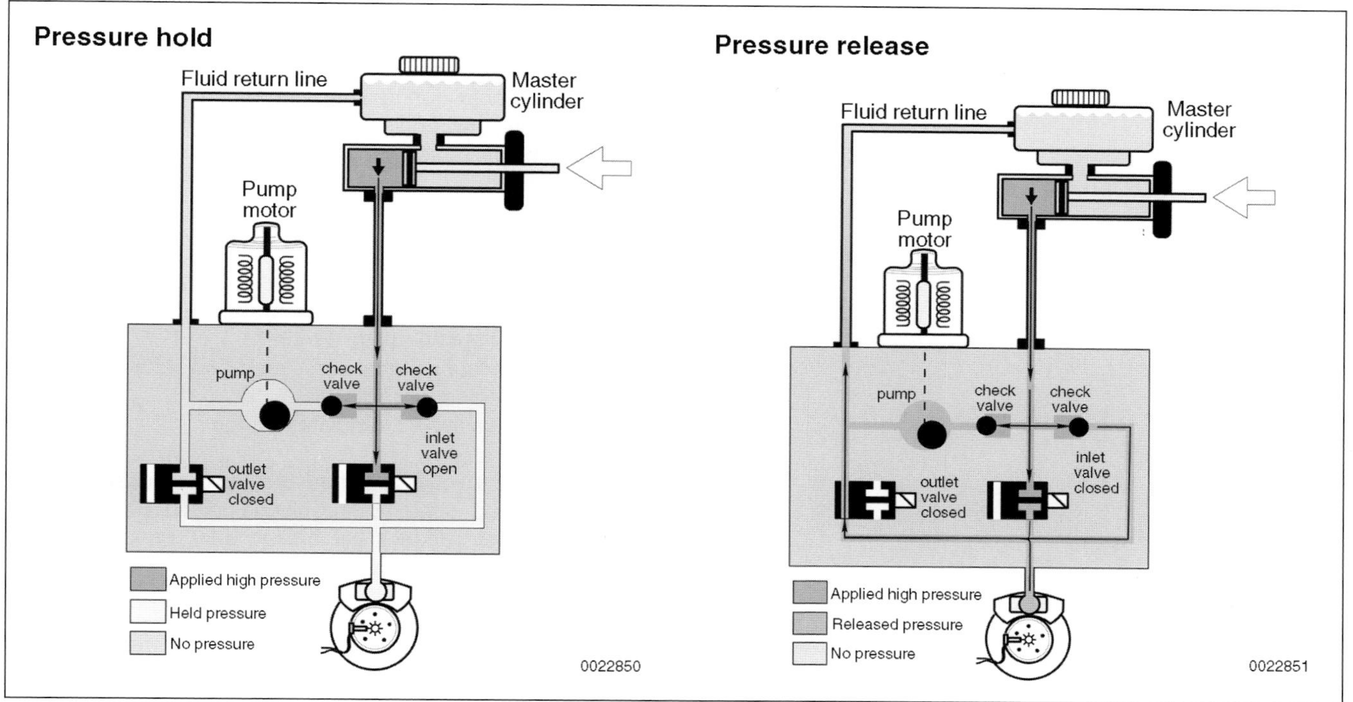

When intervention is necessary:

- The changeover valve in the hydraulic unit energizes and closes inlet valves for the two front wheels and the rear wheel with traction.
- The rear brake circuit intake valve is energized and opened to rear wheel without traction.
- Return / pressure pump is activated and draws in brake fluid from the master cylinder and delivers pressurized brake fluid to wheel without traction.
- Pressure hold and pressure release cycles are run by cycling inlet and outlet valve to rear brake caliper without traction.

Drive torque reduction

In low traction conditions, the ABS control module request is sent to the engine control module (ECM) via the CAN-bus. The ECM accomplishes torque reduction by implementing the following measures:

- Reduced throttle opening angle
- Retarded ignition
- Individual cylinder fuel injector cut-off

Drag torque reduction (MSR)

During closed-throttle deceleration, engine braking can cause the rear wheels of a vehicle to lock on low traction surfaces, especially in high speed, low gear driving. This can lead to loss of traction in the rear. When drive wheel speed is slower than front wheel speed the ECM suspends vehicle coasting by increasing throttle opening angle and engine torque.

Dynamic brake control (DBC)

The DBC function provides increased braking pressure, up to ABS threshold, during emergency braking situations. The DSC control unit implements DBC function when brake pressure builds rapidly with application of the brake pedal.

DBC triggering conditions:

- Brake light switch on
- Brake pressure in master cylinder above ABS threshold
- Brake pressure build up speed above threshold
- Vehicle road speed above 3 mph
- Pressure sensor self-test completed and sensors OK
- Vehicle travelling forward
- Not all wheels in ABS regulation range

When DBC function is activated, braking pressure increases at all wheels up to the ABS regulation point. DBC continues until the driver releases the brake pedal, brake pressure drops, or the vehicle slows to under 3 mph.

Maximum brake control (MBC)

Maximum brake control is designed to assist in stability control by increasing rear brake pressure when the front wheels are under ABS regulation. MBC intervention is triggered when the brakes are applied too slowly to reach DBC threshold.

MBC triggering conditions:

- Both front wheels in ABS regulation
- Vehicle speed above 3 mph
- DBC and pressure sensor self test completed and OK
- Vehicle travelling forward
- Rear wheels not under ABS regulation

MBC activates the return pump to increase rear wheel pressure build up. The function is terminated under the following conditions:

- Front wheels drop out of ABS regulation
- Driver releases brake pedal
- Brake pressure falls below threshold
- Vehicle road speed drops below 3 mph

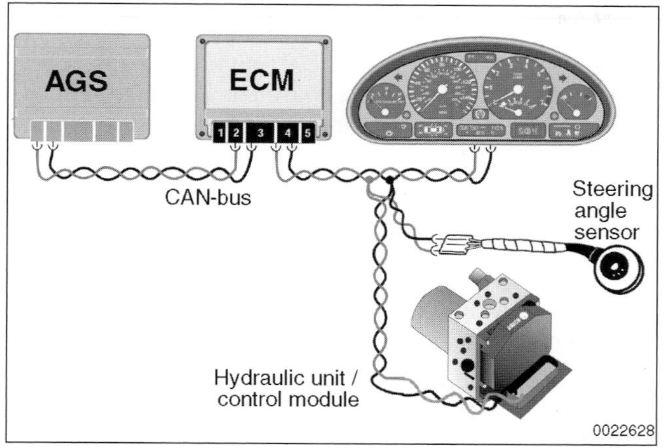

Vehicle network

The hydraulic unit / control module communicates with some sensors and many other control modules over the CAN-bus. The CAN-bus is a system of wiring that functions like a computer network, allowing different components to communicate over the same data line, at the same time, by varying electronic signals.

Component communication dialogs take place between multiple control units and sensors over the CAN-bus:

- Engine control module (ECM) provides current engine torque to ABS control module.
- ABS control module provides wheel speed sensor signals (vehicle speed) to other modules.
- ABS control module signals ECM to increase / reduce torque, ECM adjusts motor driven throttle (MDK / EDK).
- ABS control module commands transmission control module (AGS) to suppress shifts during ASC/DSC regulation.
- DSC receives yaw, lateral acceleration & steering angle sensor information.
- ABS control module receives signal from ASC / DSC switch on dash.
- ABS control module signals cause instrument cluster warning lights to turn ON during ASC / DSC regulation.

Hydraulic unit / control module

The hydraulic unit is mounted in conjunction with the control module. While the hydraulic unit and control module function as one unit, they are replaceable individually. All ABS / ASC or ABS / DSC processing functions are performed by the control module. The control module is linked to the engine control module (ECM) and transmission control module (AGS) (if applicable) by the CAN-bus network.

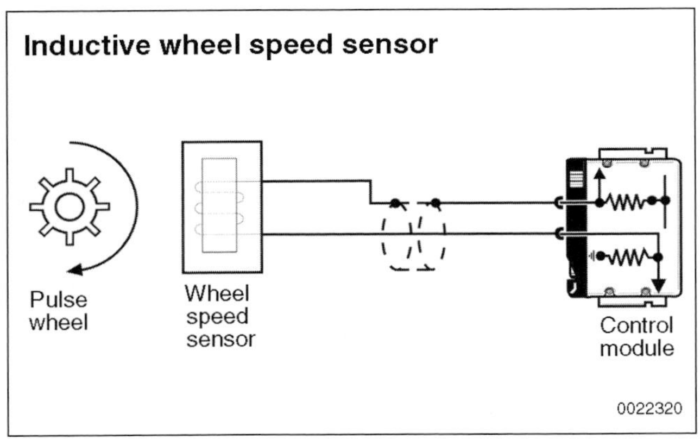

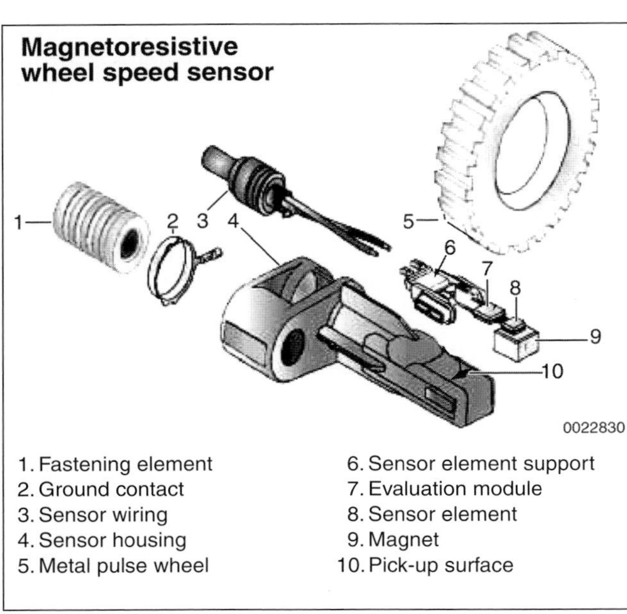

1. Fastening element
2. Ground contact
3. Sensor wiring
4. Sensor housing
5. Metal pulse wheel
6. Sensor element support
7. Evaluation module
8. Sensor element
9. Magnet
10. Pick-up surface

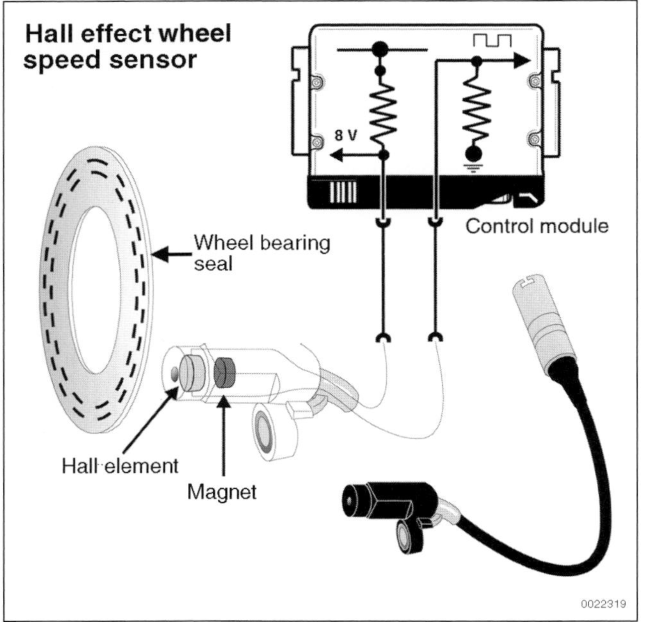

Wheel speed sensors

Wheel speed sensors are a crucial component in every ABS system. Control modules use these sensor inputs to determine overall vehicle speed and individual wheel speed for both ABS braking and stability control functions.

Three different types of wheel speed sensor are used in the E46 electronic braking and stability control systems:

- Teves MK 20 ASC / DSC: Inductive
- Teves MK 60 DSC: Magnetoresistive
- Bosch DSC III 5.7: Hall effect

CAUTION—

The magnetoresistive and the Hall effect sensor for the rear wheel are physically interchangeable. However, the electronic properties are not the same and they must not be interchanged.

DSC lateral acceleration sensor

The lateral acceleration sensor provides the DSC control module with an input signal based on the degree of lateral acceleration (g forces) that the vehicle experiences. Based on a 5 volt reference voltage, the sensor returns an output voltage that ranges between 0.5 and 4.5 volts to the DSC control module, with 1.8 volts as a standing voltage. This input, along with other DSC inputs, determines the amount of DSC regulation needed to maintain vehicle stability.

DSC rotational rate (yaw) sensor

Combined rotational rate / lateral acceleration sensor

reference voltage
signal voltage
acceleration sensor input
12 V
2.5v
yaw
-50
+50
0.5 - 4.5 v
Rotational rate / lateral acceleration sensor
DSC control module
0022629

The rotational rate sensor provides a analog voltage signal to the DSC control module to indicate the rotational speed (yaw) of the vehicle on its vertical axis. The control module supplies a 5 volt reference voltage to the sensor. The sensor returns a voltage between 0.25 and 4.65 volts based on the amount of yaw. If the vehicle's yaw exceeds preset parameters, the DSC control module activates a DSC regulation cycle to increase vehicle stability while cornering.

A defective sensor sends a constant voltage to the DSC control unit.

DSC steering angle sensor

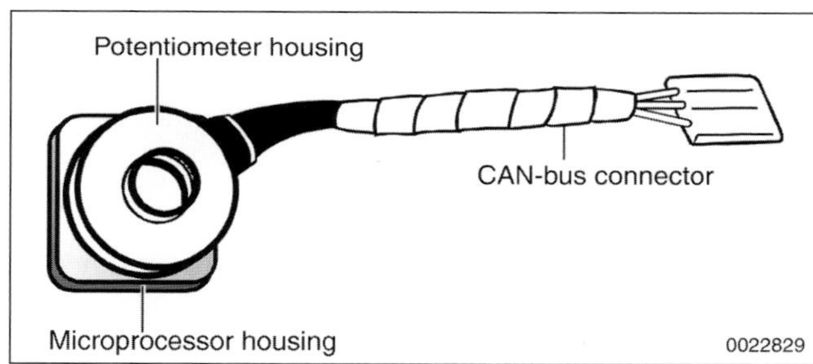

Using two potentiometers, the steering angle sensor determines the steering angle and the rate of steering change. The sensor processes the two potentiometer outputs and provides a digital signal to the DSC control unit via CAN-bus.

After sensor replacement or repairs to the steering column, recalibrate sensor using BMW scan tool (DISplus, GT1, MoDiC) or equivalent.

DSC pressure sensor

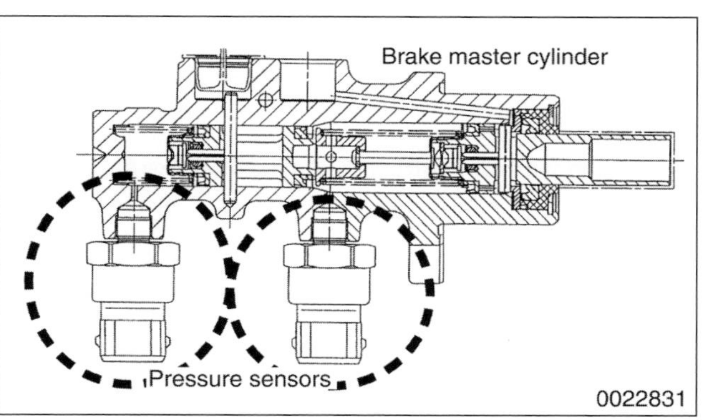

The DSC pressure sensor(s) provides the ABS/DSC control module an analog voltage signal in proportion to brake pressure in the master cylinder.

The DSC MK 20 and MK 60 systems use two switches installed at the brake master cylinder.

The Bosch DSC III 5.7 system uses one switch installed at the DSC hydraulic unit.

DSC precharge pump

The DSC precharge pump, used in the Teves MK 20 DSC and Bosch DSC III 5.7 systems, provides the hydraulic unit with the necessary supply of hydraulic brake fluid. When the DSC system is activated, the precharge pump delivers brake fluid from the reservoir to the hydraulic unit at 10 bar (150 psi).

Switches and indicators

ASC/DSC control button

The control button is used to deactivate the stability control functions of either the ASC system or the DSC system.

Brake light switch

The brake light switch input signal is used by the control module to determine which stability control routine is necessary. The control module interrupts Automatic Stability Control (ASC) functions if the brake pedal is depressed during ASC operation. On vehicles equipped with DSC, DSC operation is not cancelled during braking situations.

Parking brake switch

The switch for the parking brake warning light is used to signal the control module if the parking brake is engaged. This signal is used in stability control system logic to cancel system functions.

Brake fluid level switch

The reed-type brake fluid level switch monitors the level of brake fluid available in the brake fluid reservoir. When an adequate amount of fluid is present, the switch completes a ground circuit for the control module. When fluid level is too low, the circuit is broken and the ASC/DSC functions are turned off. Normal braking and ABS remains unaffected.

Warning lights

ASC/DSC warning light. Illuminates solidly when traction control is OFF. Blinks when traction control is in intervention mode.

Brake warning light. Indicates when parking brake is engaged, or when brake system hydraulic fluid level is low.

ABS warning light. Indicates that ABS system is deactivated, or when there is an ABS system malfunction.

Brake pad warning light. Indicates worn brake pads.

Braking and stability control warning lights

1 2 3 4

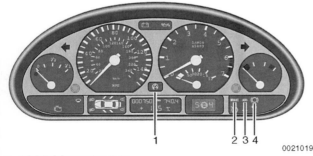

0021019

1. ASC/DSC warning light
2. Brake warning light
3. Antilock brake system (ABS) warning light

> ***WARNING —***
> *If the brake warning light, ABS warning light, and ASC / DSC warning light are all illuminated at the same time, there is an ABS and stability control system failure. Do not drive vehicle without diagnosing and repairing the problem.*

TROUBLESHOOTING

Stable handling and ride comfort both depend on the integrity of the suspension and steering components. Any symptom of instability or imprecise road feel may be caused by worn or damaged suspension components.

When troubleshooting suspension and steering problems, also consider the condition of tires, wheels and their alignment. Tire wear and incorrect inflation pressures can dramatically affect handling. Subtle irregularities in wheel alignment angles also affect stability. Mixing different types or sizes of tires, particularly on the same axle, can affect alignment and may unbalance handling.

Table d lists the symptoms of common suspension and steering problems and their probable causes, and suggests corrective actions. **Bold type** indicates the repair groups in this manual where applicable test or repair procedures can be found.

Table d. Suspension and steering troubleshooting

Symptom	Probable cause	Repairs (Repair Group shown in bold)
Breaking away while braking	Worn struts or shock absorbers	Replace struts or shock absorbers. **310**, **330**
Car pulls to one side, wanders	Incorrect tire pressure	Check and correct tire pressures. **020**
	Incorrect wheel alignment	Check and adjust wheel alignment. **320**
	Faulty brakes (pulls only when braking)	Check for sticking/damaged front caliper. **340**
Front end or rear end vibration or shimmy	Worn struts or shock absorbers	Replace struts or shock absorbers. **310**, **330**
	Worn suspension bushings (control arm or trailing arm)	Replace worn bushings. **310**, **330**
	Worn front suspension ball joints (control arm, steering arm or steering tie-rod end)	Replace worn ball joints. **310**
	Unbalanced or bent wheels/tires	Balance tires. Check tires for uneven wear patterns. Check wheels for damage.
	Loose wheel lug bolts	Tighten lug bolts to proper torque.
Poor handling, poor directional stability	Rear control arm or rear subframe bushings worn or damaged	Replace rear suspension bushings as necessary. **330**
	Rear alignment incorrect	Check and adjust wheel alignment. **320**
Poor stability, repeated bouncing after bumps, suspension bottoms out easily	Worn struts or shock absorbers	Replace struts or shock absorbers. **310**, **330**
Rear end hop with hard braking	Rear trailing arm busing worn or damaged	Replace trailing arm bushing. **330**
Steering heavy, poor return-to-center	Worn upper strut mounts	Replace strut mounts. **310**
	Incorrect tire pressure	Check and correct tire pressures. **020**
	Power steering system faulty	Check power steering fluid level. **320**
Steering loose, imprecise	Incorrect tire pressure	Check and correct tire pressures. **020**
	Loose steering rack mounting bolt(s)	Inspect and tighten bolts. **320**
	Worn tie rod end(s)	Replace tie rod(s) and align wheels. **320**
	Faulty front wheel bearing	Replace wheel bearing. **310**
	Worn or damaged steering rack	Adjust or replace steering rack. **320**
	Worn tires	Replace tires.
Suspension noise, especially over bumps (drumming, rattling)	Worn front upper strut mounts	Replace upper strut mounts. **310**
	Worn suspension bushings (control arm or trailing arm)	Replace worn bushings. **310**, **330**
	Worn stabilizer bar rubber mounts	Replace stabilizer bar rubber mounts. **310**, **330**
	Loose suspension subframe	Check subframe for damage. Tighten mounting bolts.
Tail skid when braking	Rear trailing arm front bushing worn or damaged	Replace trailing arm bushing. **330**
Tire flat spots	Worn struts or shock absorbers	Replace struts or shock absorbers. **310**, **330**
Uneven ride height	Incorrect coil springs	Measure ride height. **300**
	Bent or damaged suspension components	Inspect, repair/replace as necessary. **310**, **330**
	Sagging coil springs	Replace springs as necessary. **310**, **330**

Table d. Suspension and steering troubleshooting (continued)

Symptom	Probable cause	Repairs (Repair Group shown in bold)
Unsteady in curves, self-steering, poor rear end stability	Rear subframe bushings worn or damaged	Replace rear suspension bushings as necessary. **330**
	Differential bushings worn or damaged	Replace rear suspension bushings as necessary. **330**
	Rear shock absorbers worn	Replace rear shock absorbers. **330**
Wheel noise, continuous growling, may be more noticeable when turning	Worn wheel bearing	Replace wheel bearing. **310, 330**
Wheel-hop on normal road surface	Worn struts or shock absorbers	Replace struts or shock absorbers. **310, 330**

ABS troubleshooting

ABS is designed to be maintenance free. There are no adjustments that can be made to the system. Repair and troubleshooting of major ABS components requires special test equipment and knowledge and should be performed by an authorized BMW dealer.

ABS is self-tested by the control module each time the car is started. Once the test is complete, the ABS dashboard warning light turns OFF. If the light remains lit or comes ON at any time while driving, a system fault has occurred and ABS is electronically disabled. The conventional braking system remains fully functioning.

When a system or component failure occurs in the electronic braking and stability control systems, either the brake warning light, ABS warning light, or the ASC / DSC warning light illuminates.

Troubleshoot electronic braking and stability control systems using BMW scan tool (DISplus, GT1, MoDiC) or equivalent.

Perform brake bleeding functions and component coding and initialization using BMW scan tool or equivalent.

ABS system inspection

A visual inspection of the ABS system components may help to locate system faults. If no visual faults can be found and the ABS light remains ON, have the system diagnosed by an authorized BMW dealer.

Carefully inspect the entire ABS wiring harness, particularly the wheel speed sensor harnesses and connectors near each wheel. Look for chafing or damage due to incorrectly routed wires.

Carefully remove the wheel speed sensors. Clean the sensor tips. Inspect toothed wheel on wheel hub, if applicable. Check for missing, clogged or corroded teeth, or other damage that could alter the clearance between the sensor tip and toothed wheel.

Ride height

Ride height measurement (**A**) at either axle is taken from center of wheel arch to bottom of wheel rim.

If the ride height is outside the specification listed, install new springs. Be sure to have the old spring code number on hand when ordering new spring.

Table e and **Table f** list suspension ride height specifications.When checking ride height or installing suspension components that require the car to be "normally loaded," load the car as follows:

Normal loaded position

- Each front seat . . . . .68 Kg (150 lbs)
- Rear seat (center). . . . . .68 Kg (150 lbs)
- Trunk. . . . . .21 Kg (46 lbs)
- Fuel tank. . . . . .full

Table e. Front ride height specifications (measurement A)

Wheel size	Standard suspension	Sport suspension	Rough road suspension	All wheel drive suspension
15 inch	576 mm (22.67 in)	561 mm (22.08 in)	593 mm (23.35 in)	
16 inch	589 mm (23.19 in)	574 mm (22.59 in)	606 mm (23.86 in)	606 mm (23.85 in)
17 inch	604 mm (23.77 in)	589 mm (23.19 in)	621 mm (24.44 in)	621 mm (24.44 in)
18 inch (M3)	617 mm (24.29 in) 605 mm (23.82 in)	602 mm (23.71 in)	634 mm (24.96 in)	634 mm (24.96 in)
19 inch (M3)	619mm (24.37 in)			
Maximum variation between sides: 10 mm (0.4 in) Maximum deviation from specifications: 10 mm (0.4 in)				

Table f. Rear ride height specifications (measurement A)

Wheel size	Standard suspension	Sport suspension	Rough road suspension	All wheel drive suspension
15 inch	542 mm (21.33 in)	526 mm (20.70 in)	562 mm (22.12 in)	
16 inch	555 mm (21.85 in)	539 mm (21.22 in).	575 mm (22.64 in)	572 mm (22.52 in)
17 inch	570 mm (22.44 in)	554 mm (21.81 in)	590 mm (23.22 in).	587 mm (23.11 in)
18 inch (M3)	583 mm (22.95 in) 587 mm (23.11 in)	567 mm (22.32 in)	603 mm (23.74 in)	600 mm (23.62 in)
19 inch (M3)	600mm (23.62 in)			
Maximum variation between sides: 10 mm (0.4 in) Maximum deviation from specifications: 10 mm (0.4 in)				

310 Front Suspension

TABLES

GENERAL

This repair group covers the repair and replacement of components that make up the front suspension of E46 cars.

See **300 Suspension, Steering and Brakes–General** for a description of the front suspension and components, as well as ride height specifications.

Special tools

Special service tools are required for most of the work described in this repair group. In addition to the tools depicted in the illustrations, a variety of press tools are necessary for control arm bushing replacement.

Read the procedures through before beginning any job.

Special tools

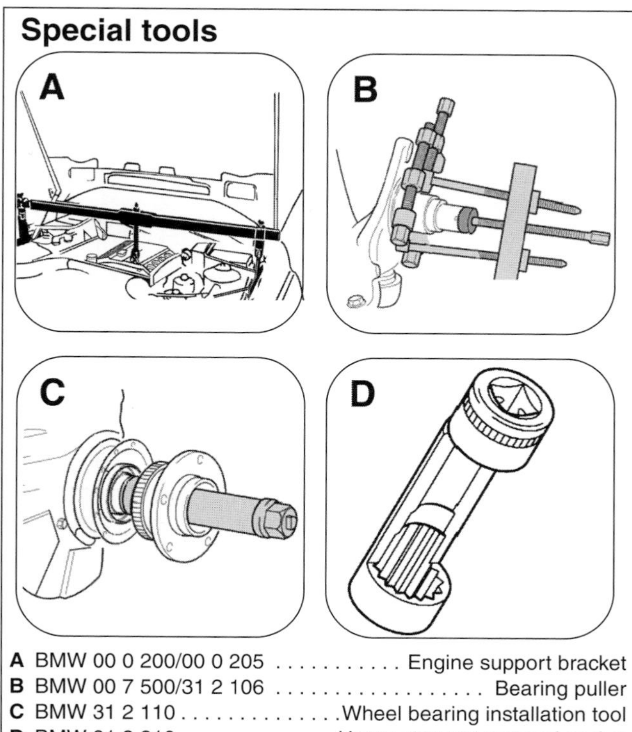

A BMW 00 0 200/00 0 205 . . . . . Engine support bracket
B BMW 00 7 500/31 2 106 . . . . . Bearing puller
C BMW 31 2 110 . . . . . Wheel bearing installation tool
D BMW 31 2 210 . . . . . Upper strut nut removal socket

Special Tools

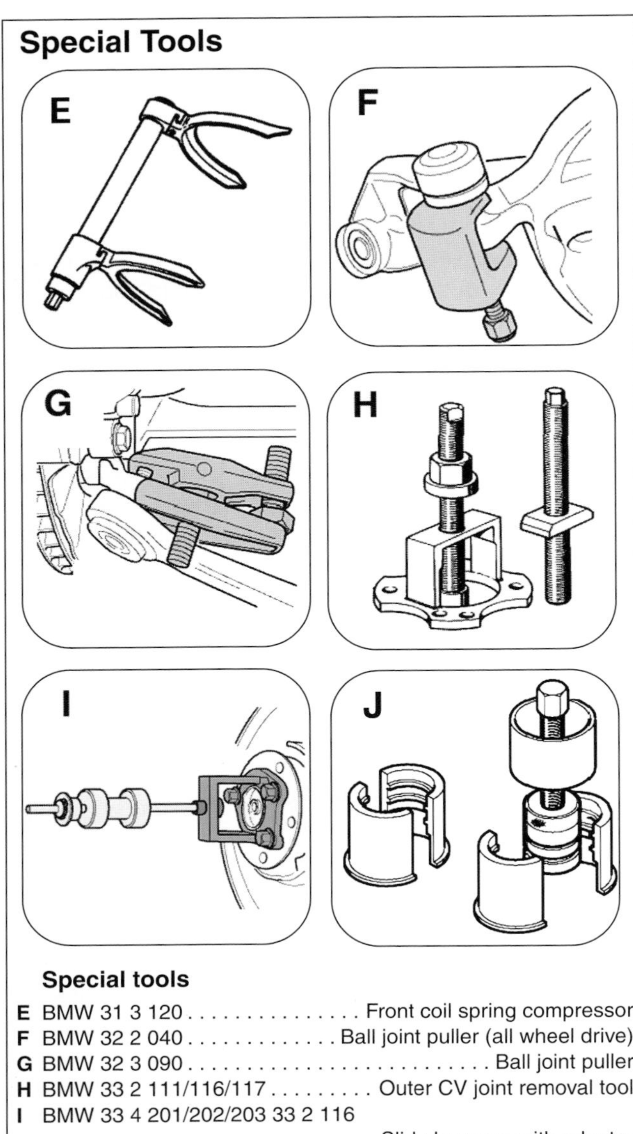

Special tools

E BMW 31 3 120 . . . . Front coil spring compressor
F BMW 32 2 040 . . . . Ball joint puller (all wheel drive)
G BMW 32 3 090 . . . . Ball joint puller
H BMW 33 2 111/116/117 . . . . Outer CV joint removal tool
I BMW 33 4 201/202/203 33 2 116
. . . . Slide hammer with adapter
J BMW 33 4 400 . . . . Inner bearing race puller

Front suspension construction

Some front suspension components are constructed of weight saving materials. For example, front control arms in rear wheel drive models are forged aluminum. This allows for weight reduction in the car, as well as a lower unsprung mass for better handling. However, the aluminum construction prevents removal or replacement of the pressed-in ball joints.

WARNING —

- *Physical safety could be impaired if procedures described here are undertaken without the proper service tools and equipment. Be sure to have the right tools on hand before beginning any job.*
- *Do not reuse self-locking nuts or bolts. They are designed to be used only once and may fail if reused. Always replace self-locking fasteners any time they are loosened or removed.*
- *Do not install bolts and nuts coated with undercoating wax, as the correct tightening torque cannot be assured. Always clean the threads with solvent before installation, or install new parts.*
- *Do not attempt to weld or straighten any suspension components. Replace damaged parts.*

CAUTION —

Due to the aluminum construction of the control arms, observe the following precautions when working on and around the front suspension:

- *When replacing any damaged front end components, always check the condition of the control arms.*
- *Do not clean control arm with wire brush made of brass or iron. Only use stainless steel brush.*
- *Do not expose control arms to temperatures exceeding 80°C (176°F); sparks created by grinding; battery acid or other highly corrosive materials; or steel welding splashes.*

SHOCK ABSORBERS AND SPRINGS

NOTE —

Setting the ride height is covered in **300 Suspension, Steering and Brakes–General***.*

The front suspension shock absorbers in E46 cars are MacPherson struts. The strut is a major component of the suspension and supports the spring. Most strut assembly components are available as replacement parts. Replace struts and springs in pairs.

Front strut, upper strut mount or spring replacement is a two-step procedure:

- Removal of strut assembly from vehicle
- Disassembly and replacement of components on workbench

Front suspension assembly (rear wheel drive)

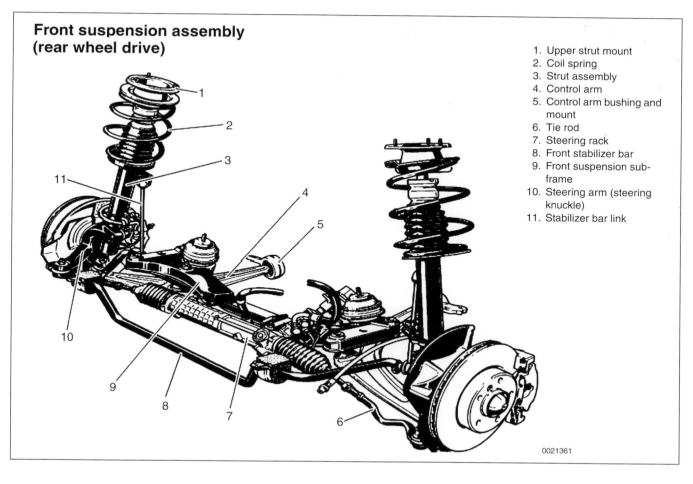

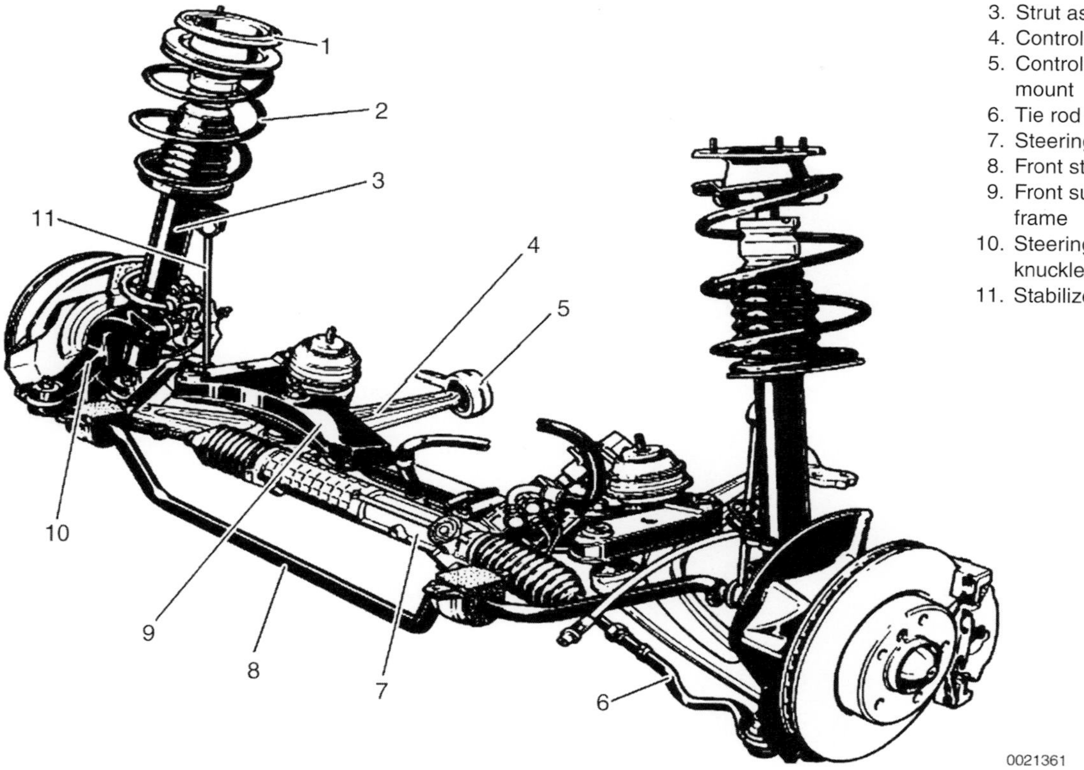

1. Upper strut mount
2. Coil spring
3. Strut assembly
4. Control arm
5. Control arm bushing and mount
6. Tie rod
7. Steering rack
8. Front stabilizer bar
9. Front suspension sub-frame
10. Steering arm (steering knuckle)
11. Stabilizer bar link

0021361

Strut assembly, removing and installing

– Raise car and remove front wheel.

> ***WARNING —***
> *Make sure the car is firmly supported on jack stands designed for the purpose. Place jack stands underneath structural chassis points, not under suspension parts.*

< Pull brake fluid hose and ABS sensor wire harness off bracket at steering arm pinch bolt.

> ***NOTE —***
> *Right side shown. Left side bracket also holds brake pad wear sensor wire.*

– Unbolt brake caliper assembly, keeping brake hose connected. Suspend brake caliper from chassis using stiff wire. See **340 Brakes**.

◀ Remove ABS wheel speed sensor mounting bolt (**arrow**). Slide sensor out of steering arm and lay aside.

NOTE —
Rear wheel drive vehicle shown.

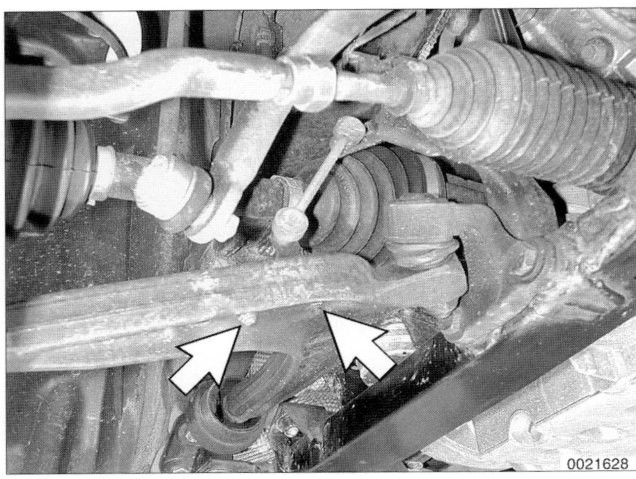

◀ Vehicle with xenon headlights: Remove headlight vertical aim sensor link bracket mounting nuts (**arrows**) from right control arm.

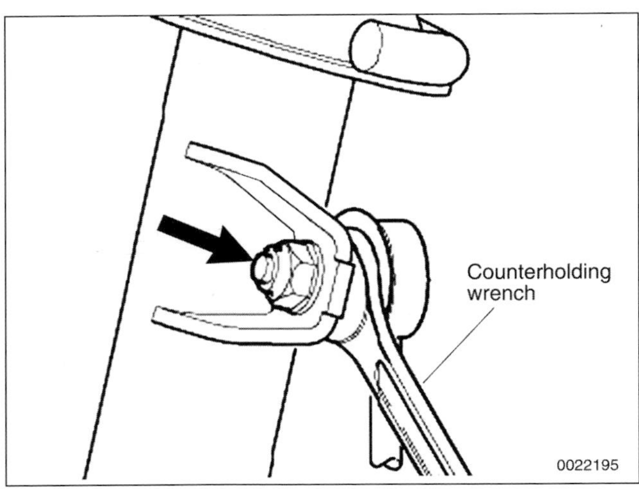

◀ Loosen and remove stabilizer bar link mounting nut (**arrow**) from strut. Detach link from strut housing.

NOTE —
Use a thin wrench to counterhold shaft of stabilizer bar link ball joint while removing mounting nut.

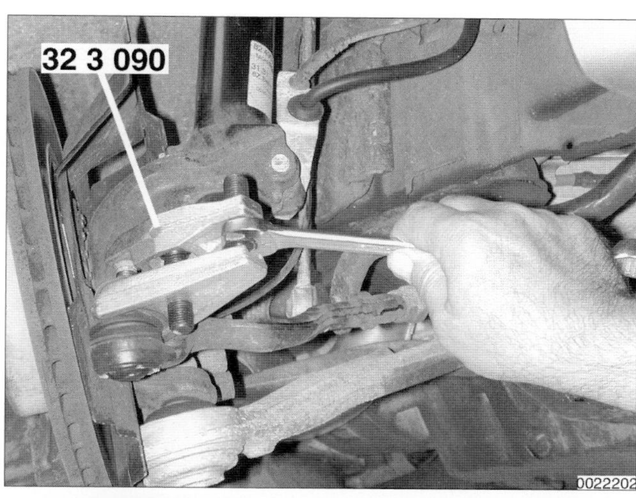

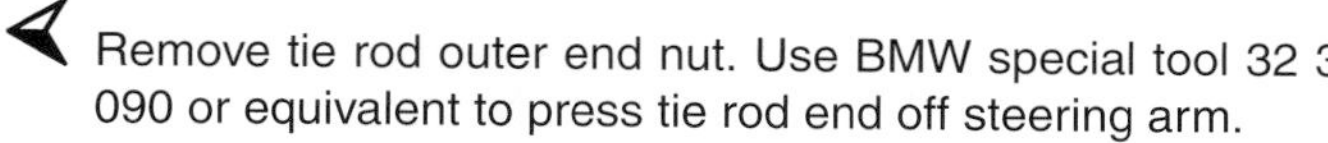

◄ Remove tie rod outer end nut. Use BMW special tool 32 3 090 or equivalent to press tie rod end off steering arm.

– Remove lower ball joint nut. Use BMW special tool 32 3 090 or equivalent to separate steering arm from control arm.

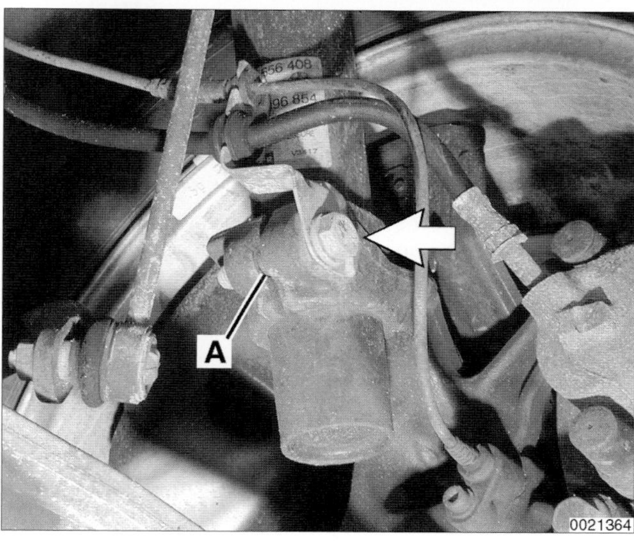

◄ Support steering arm from below. Loosen pinch bolt (**arrow**) at top of steering arm. Spread clamping collar at slot **A**, if necessary, to slide steering arm off strut assembly.

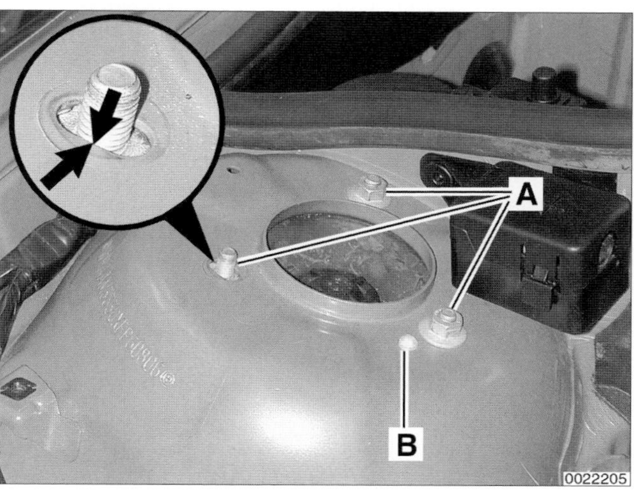

◄ Support strut assembly from below.

- Working in engine compartment at strut tower, remove three strut mounting nuts (**A**) on strut tower.
- If factory alignment locating pin (**B**) is missing, be sure to mark location of strut mounting studs in strut tower slots (**arrows**).

> ***CAUTION —***
> *Do not remove center strut retaining nut.*

– Lower strut assembly from car.

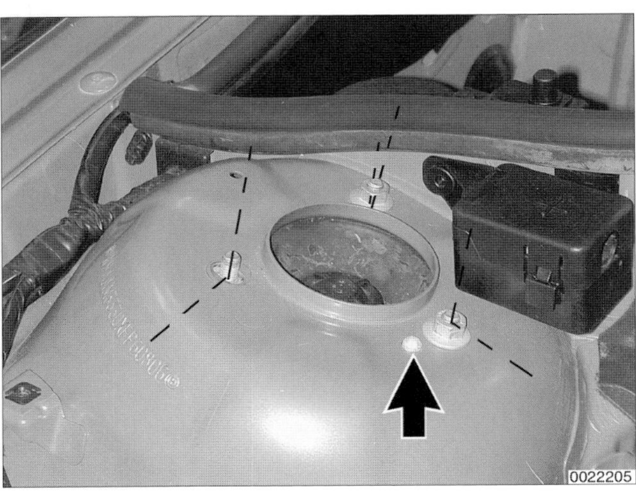

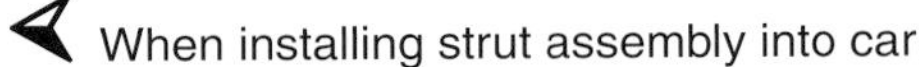

When installing strut assembly into car:

- Make sure locating pin (**arrow**) of strut bearing is positioned correctly in strut tower.
- If factory alignment locating pin is missing, make sure three upper mounting studs are positioned correctly in slotted holes according to marks made previously.

When installing steering arm to strut assembly, insert positioning pin (**arrow**) of strut into slot of steering arm clamping collar. To ensure proper alignment specifications, slide steering arm up on strut until stop is reached.

– Remainder of installation is reverse of removal.

- Be sure to use new self-locking nuts and bolts.
- Use new steering arm mounting bolts, or clean bolts and use Loctite® 270 or equivalent thread-locking compound.
- When attaching stabilizer link to strut, use a thin wrench to counterhold link ball joint while tightening nut.
- Have car professionally aligned when job is complete.

Tightening torques

- Brake caliper to steering arm . . . . 110 Nm (81 ft-lb)
- Road wheel to hub . . . . 120 ± 10 Nm (90 ± 7 ft-lb)
- Stabilizer bar link to strut . . . . 59 Nm (44 ft-lb)
- Steering tie rod to steering arm . . . . 65 Nm (48 ft-lb)
- Steering arm to control arm . . . . 65 Nm (48 ft-lb)
- Steering arm pinch bolt
  at strut housing . . . . 81 Nm (60 ft-lb)
- Strut assembly to strut tower
  (self-locking nuts) . . . . 24 Nm (18 ft-lb)
- Upper strut mount to strut tower,
  self-locking M8 flanged nut:
  18 mm flange . . . . 24 Nm (18 ft-lb)
  21 mm flange . . . . 34 Nm (25 ft-lb)

Front spring and upper strut mount assembly (not M3)

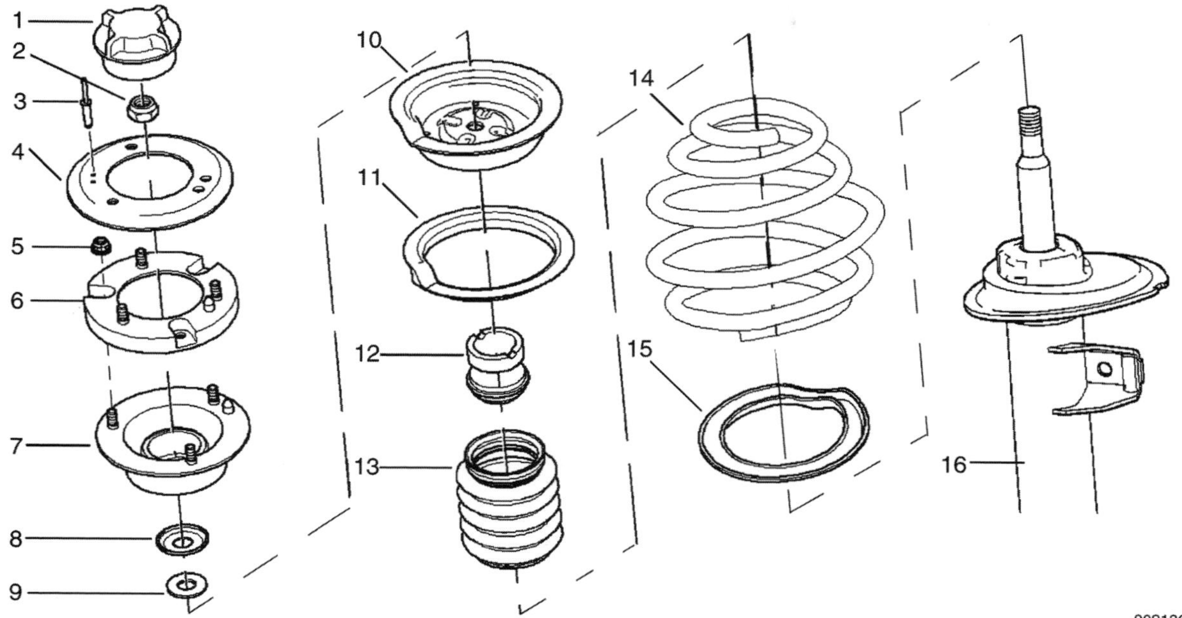

1. Cap
2. Upper strut self-locking nut M14 -tighten to 64 Nm (47 ft-lb)
3. Rivet (all wheel drive or rough road package only)
4. Strut bearing reinforcement (all wheel drive or rough road package only)
5. Self-locking flanged nut M8 -tighten to:
   24 Nm (18 ft-lb) (18 mm flange)
   34 Nm (25 ft-lb) (21 mm flange)
6. Spacer plate (all wheel drive or rough road package only)
7. Upper strut bearing
8. Sealing ring
9. Flat washer
10. Upper spring seat
11. Upper spring pad
12. Rubber bump stop
13. Dust boot
14. Spring
15. Lower spring pad
16. Strut

Strut assembly, disassembling and assembling

Replacing the strut, upper strut mount or spring requires that the strut assembly first be removed from the car and disassembled. For a guide to parts used during component replacement, see the accompanying diagram.

– Remove strut assembly. See **Strut assembly, removing and installing** in this repair group. Place in shop vice, or support securely.

– Using spring compressor, compress spring until spring force on upper mount is relieved.

> ***WARNING —***
> - *Do not attempt to disassemble the struts without a spring compressor designed specifically for this job.*
> - *Make sure the spring compressor grabs the spring fully and securely before compressing it.*

M3 front spring and upper strut mount assembly

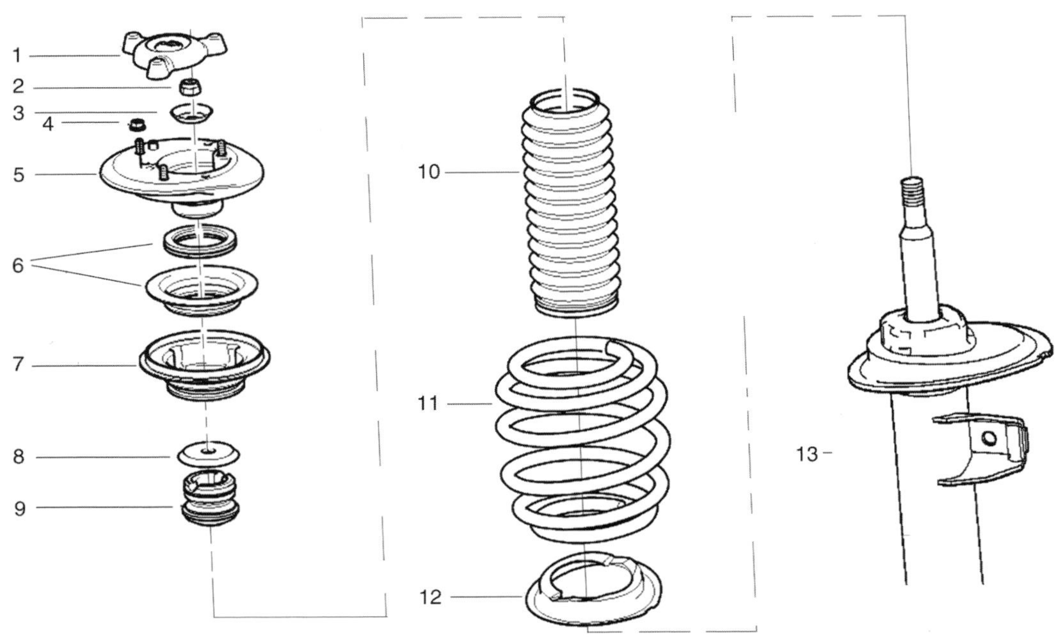

1. Cap
2. Upper strut self locking nut M14 -tighten to 64 Nm (47 ft-lb)
3. Sealing plate
4. Self-locking flanged nut M8 -tighten to: 34 Nm (25 ft-lb)
5. Upper strut bearing
6. Upper spring pocket with axial cage bearing
7. Upper spring pad
8. Support
9. Rubber bumper stop
10. Dust boot
11. Coil spring
12. Lower spring pad
13. Strut

– Pry protective cover off top of strut assembly. Use BMW special tool 31 2 210 or equivalent socket to remove strut top (center) nut. Counterhold strut shaft using 6 mm Allen wrench.

– Remove upper strut bearing and related components.

– Replace strut, upper strut mount or spring, as needed.

NOTE —
- *Replace springs and struts in pairs only.*
- *The part number is stamped near the large end of the spring.*

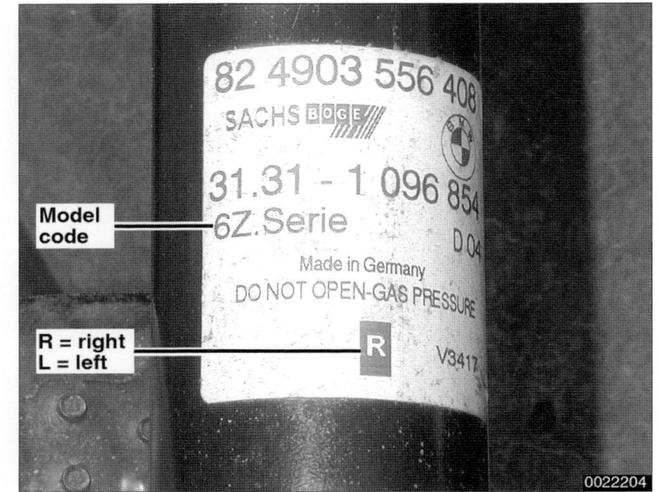

Be sure that replacement struts are marked with the same code as the ones being removed.

NOTE —
Aftermarket struts are not marked.

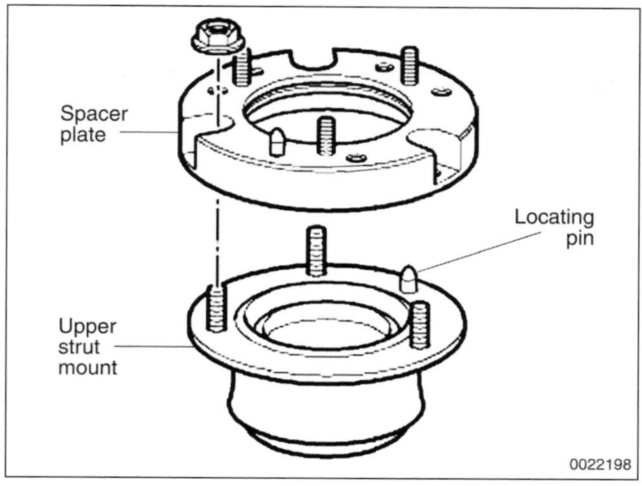

Vehicles with "rough road" package are equipped with a spacer plate above the upper strut mount. Make sure the strut mount locating pin fits in the corresponding bore of the spacer plate.

NOTE —

If there is no locating bore in the strut tower for the pin in the replacement upper strut mount to fit, drive out the pin before installing the new mount.

Front strut top mount assembly (not M3)

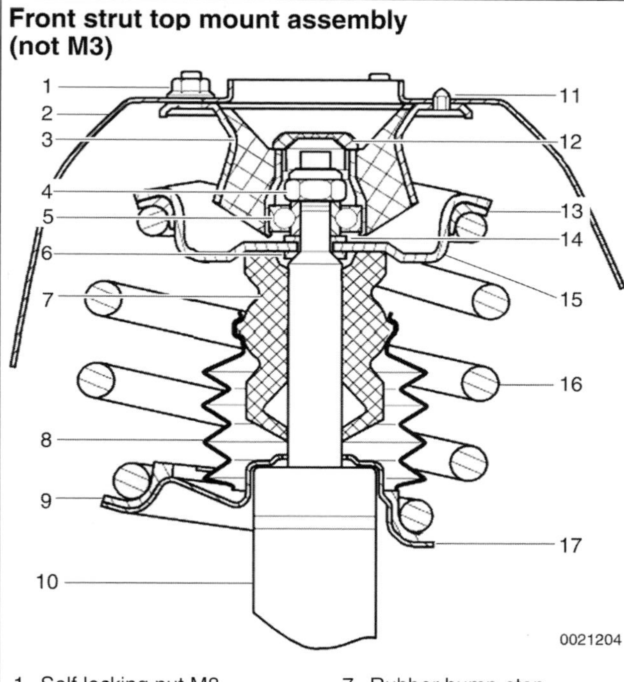

1. Self locking nut M8
   -tighten to:
   24 Nm (18 ft-lb) (18 mm flange)
   34 Nm (25 ft-lb) (21 mm flange)
2. Strut tower
3. Upper strut mount
4. Upper strut self locking nut M14
   -tighten to 64 Nm (47 ft-lb)
5. Upper strut bearing
6. Sealing ring
7. Rubber bump-stop
8. Dust shield
9. Lower spring pad
10. Strut housing
11. Locating pin
12. Protective cap
13. Upper spring pad
14. Washer
15. Upper spring seat
16. Spring
17. Lower spring seat

Assembly is reverse of disassembly, noting the following:

- Line up slot in spring pad with corresponding slot in lower spring seat.
- Use a new upper strut self locking nut. Tighten nut fully before releasing spring compressor.
- Be sure upper spring pad is correctly installed to upper spring seat and spring end is correctly seated in upper and lower spring seats.
- Release spring compressor carefully and evenly, allowing spring to expand slowly.
- Have car professionally aligned when job is complete.

Tightening torque

- Upper strut mount to strut shaft
  M14 self-locking nut . . . . 64 Nm (47 ft-lb)

FRONT END REINFORCEMENT

Rear wheel drive: Front end reinforcement is bolted to the rear of the subframe and attached to the frame rails.

> ***CAUTION —***
> *Do not drive vehicle without the front end reinforcement in place. Damage to chassis or front suspension may result.*

Tubular front end reinforcement

The tubular front end reinforcement is installed with 4 bolts (**arrows**) in the following cars:

- Rear wheel drive Sedan or Sport Wagon manufactured until production date 12 / 2000.
- Coupe manufactured until production date 11 / 1999.

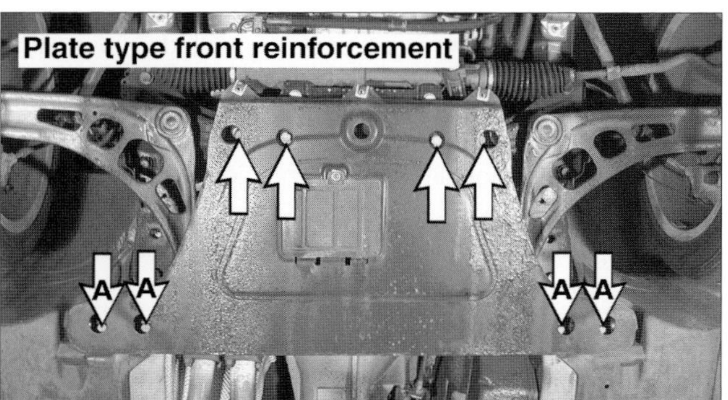

The aluminum plate type front end reinforcement is installed in the following cars:

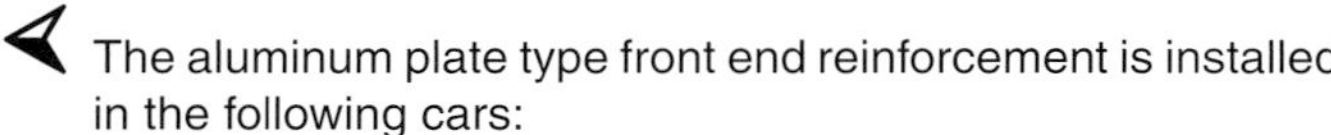

- Convertibles
- Coupe manufactured from production date 11 / 1999.
- Rear wheel drive Sedan or Sport Wagon manufactured from production date 12 / 2000.

NOTE —

- *After 02 / 2001, the front reinforcement plate was produced with larger cast depressions to accommodate the larger (66 mm) front control arm bushings. The difference in the early production and later plates can only be discerned by removing the plate.*
- *In order to safely use an early production plate in a car with larger bushings, insert appropriate sized washers between frame rails and reinforcement plate at bolts* **A**.

M3 Coupe or Convertible uses a 3 mm thick aluminum plate front end reinforcement.

– When reinstalling front end reinforcement:
  - Replace mounting bolts (**arrows**).
  - Torque bolts in 2 stages, as shown below. Use BMW special tool 00 9 120 or equivalent torque angle protractor.

Tightening torque

- Front end reinforcement to front subframe or body frame rails: M10 bolt (always replace)
  Stage 1 . . . . 59 Nm (43 ft-lb)
  Stage 2 . . . . torque angle 90° + 30°

FRONT SUBFRAME

The front subframe provides rigid mounting points for the engine, suspensions and steering components. The subframe is not normally subject to wear and should only be replaced if structurally damaged.

Rear wheel drive and all wheel drive models differ significantly in the design of the front subframe.

Removing the front subframe requires engine lifting equipment to support the weight of the engine from above so that the subframe can be removed from below.

> ***CAUTION —***
> *Removal or replacement of the subframe may affect suspension and steering geometry, including front wheel alignment. Make appropriate matching marks during removal and have the front end aligned once repairs are complete.*

Front subframe, removing and installing (rear wheel drive)

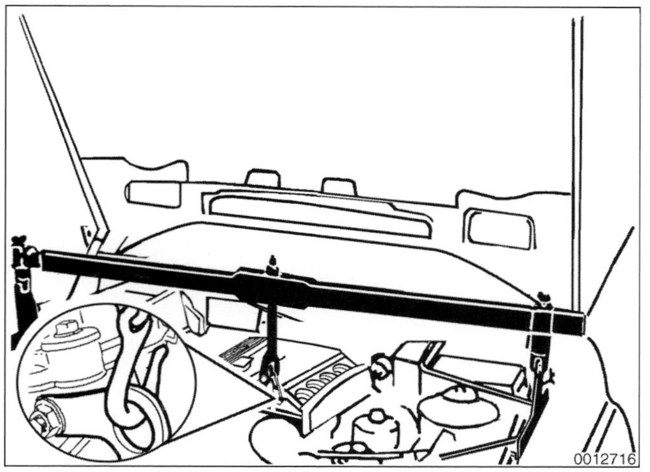

- Using engine support equipment, raise engine until weight of engine is supported.

- Raise car and remove front wheels.

> ***WARNING —***
> *Make sure the car is firmly supported on jack stands designed for the purpose. Place jack stands underneath structural chassis points, not under suspension parts.*

- Remove splash shield under engine compartment.

- Remove front end reinforcement. See **Front End Reinforcement** earlier in this group.

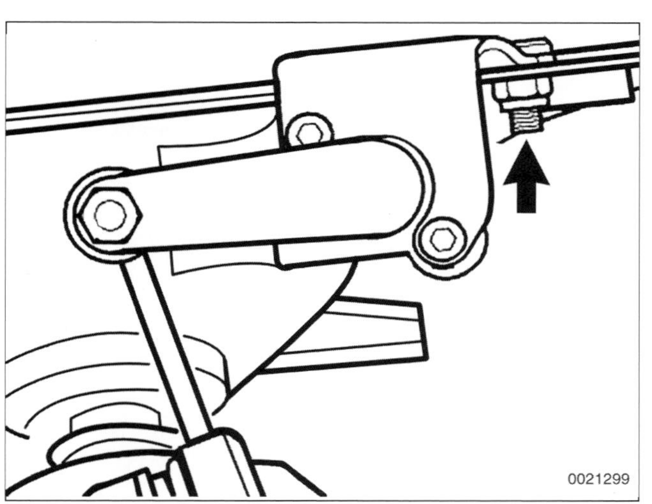

- On cars equipped with xenon headlights: Remove front ride level sensor mounting fastener (**arrow**) and lay sensor aside.

◀ Remove right front control arm bracket bolts (**arrows**) from frame rail.

– Repeat for left side.

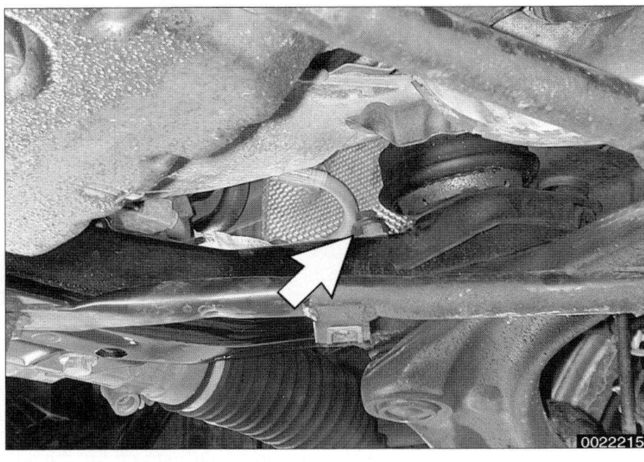

◀ Remove right inner control arm ball joint mounting nut (**arrow**) at subframe.

- Drive ball joint shaft out of subframe using soft hammer.
- Push control arm aside.
- Repeat for left side.

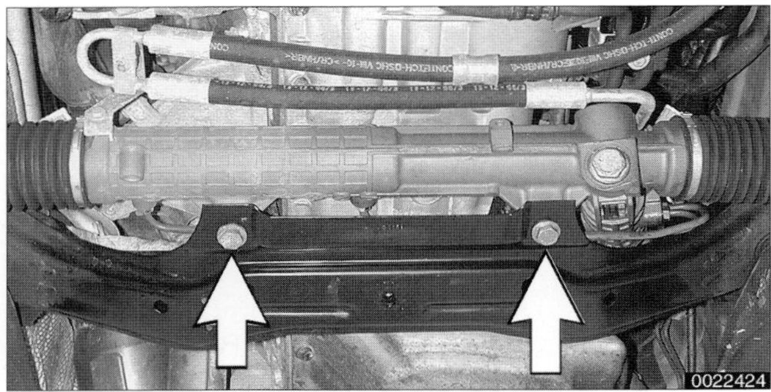

◀ Remove steering rack mounting bolts (**arrows**) at front of subframe. Suspend rack out of the way with stiff wire.

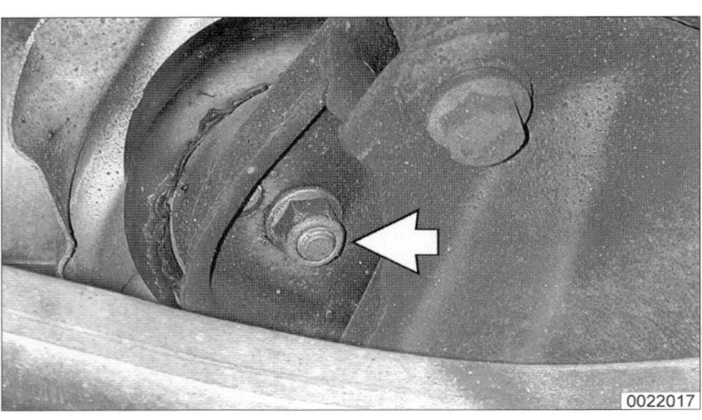

◀ Remove right lower engine mount fastener (**arrow**).

– Repeat on left side

Support suspension subframe from below using appropriate jacking equipment. Remove subframe mounting bolts (**arrows**). Remove subframe.

NOTE —

Right side is shown in photo. Left is similar.

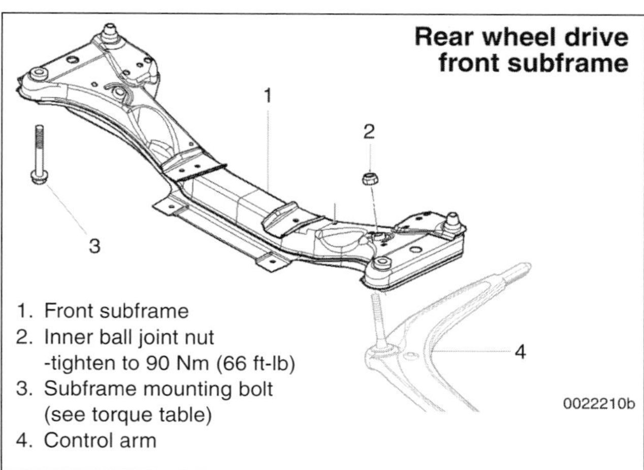

1. Front subframe
2. Inner ball joint nut -tighten to 90 Nm (66 ft-lb)
3. Subframe mounting bolt (see torque table)
4. Control arm

Installation is reverse of removal, noting the following:

- Make sure all bolts, bolt holes, and mating surfaces are clean to ensure proper tightening and alignment. Use new self-locking nuts or bolts, where applicable.
- Lower engine on engine mounts and allow it to settle fully before tightening engine mount fasteners.
- When the job is completed, have front end professionally aligned.

Tightening torques

- Control arm ball joint to subframe
  M14 self-locking nut (always replace) . . 90 Nm (66 ft-lb)
- Control arm bushing carrier to body
  M10 bolt (always replace). . . . . 59 Nm (43 ft-lb)
- Front end reinforcement to front subframe or body frame rails: M10 bolt (always replace)
  Stage 1 . . . . 59 Nm (43 ft-lb)
  Stage 2 . . . . torque angle 90° + 30°
- Steering rack to subframe (M10 bolt) . . . 42 Nm (31 ft-lb)
- Subframe to body
  M12 (8.8 grade bolt) . . . . 77 Nm (57 ft-lb)
  M12 (10.9 grade bolt) . . . . 110 Nm (81 ft-lb)
  M12 (12.9 grade bolt) . . . . 105 Nm (77 ft-lb)

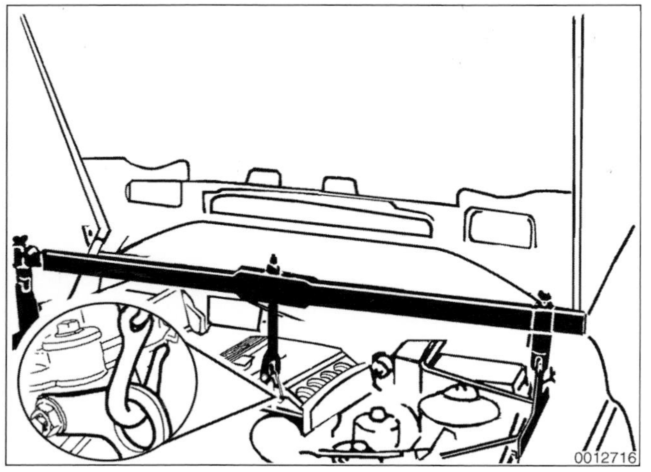

Front subframe, removing and installing (all wheel drive)

- Using engine support equipment, raise engine until weight of engine is supported.

- Raise car and remove front wheels.

> ***WARNING —***
> *Make sure the car is firmly supported on jack stands designed for the purpose. Place jack stands underneath structural chassis points, not under suspension parts.*

- Remove splash shield under engine compartment.

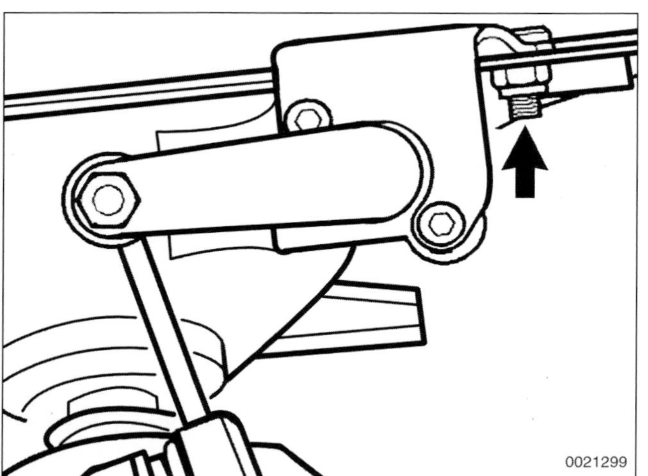

- On cars equipped with xenon headlights: Remove front ride level sensor mounting fastener (**arrow**) and lay sensor aside.

- Working at rear right corner of front subframe, unhook heat-shield from subframe (**arrow**).

0021623

◀ Remove left engine mount fastener (**arrow**).

– Repeat for right side.

– Working at right front of subframe, detach power steering lines.

0021627

◀ Remove stabilizer bar anchor fasteners (**arrows**) from front corners of subframe. Suspend stabilizer bar from chassis using stiff wire.

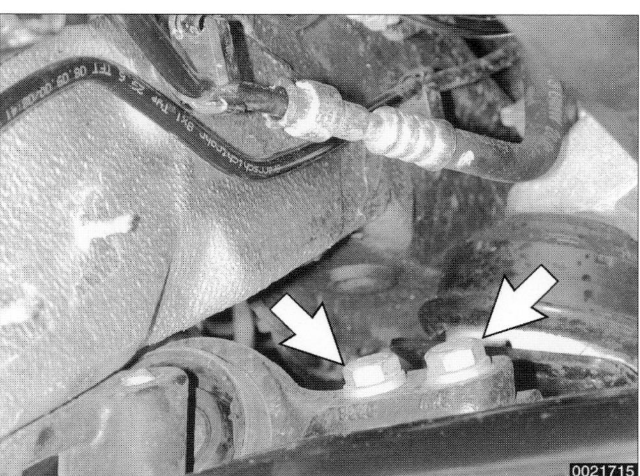
0021715

◀ Working at left rear corner of subframe, remove control arm rear bracket mounting bolts (**arrows**).

– Repeat for right side.

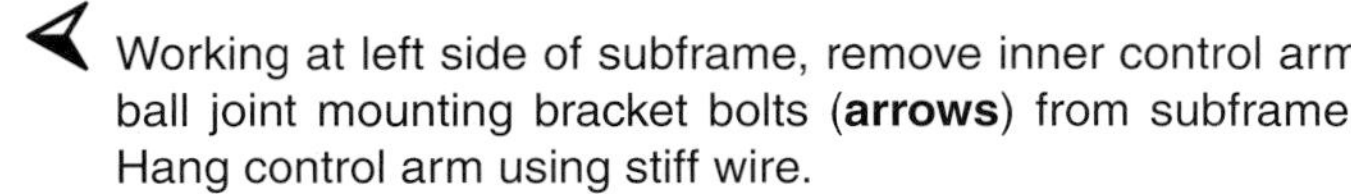
Working at left side of subframe, remove inner control arm ball joint mounting bracket bolts (**arrows**) from subframe. Hang control arm using stiff wire.

> **WARNING —**
> *Do not allow the control arm to hang from the outer (steering arm) ball joint. This can damage the ball joint.*

Working underneath subframe, remove steering rack mounting bolts (**arrows**). Suspend rack with stiff wire.

Support subframe from below. Remove subframe mounting bolts (**arrows**).

- Slowly lower subframe, making sure heat shields, wiring harnesses and other underbody components are clear during removal.

All wheel drive front subframe

1. Front subframe
2. Blind rivet nut
3. Engine mounting flange
4. Steering rack mounting flange
5. Stabilizer bar mounting
6. Subframe to body adapter
7. Bolt M10 (always replace) -tighten to 59 Nm (44-ft-lb)
8. Bolt M10 (always replace) -tighten to 59 Nm (44 ft-lb)
9. Control arm rear bracket
10. Bolt M12 (always replace) -tighten to 110 Nm (81 ft-lb)
11. Jack point
12. Subframe mounting bolt M12 (see torque table)
13. Control arm inner ball joint
14. Bolt M12 -tighten to 77 Nm (57 ft-lb)
15. Self locking nut M14 (always replace) -tighten to 80 Nm (59 ft-lb)

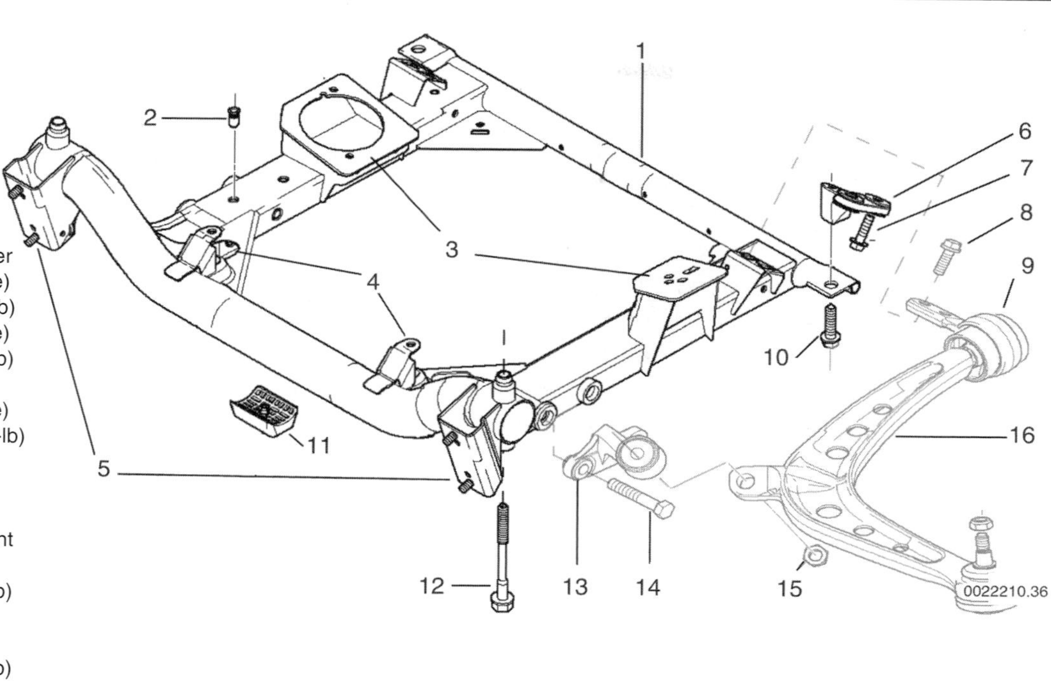

Installation is reverse of removal, noting the following:

- Make sure all bolts, bolt holes, and mating surfaces are clean to ensure proper alignment and torque. Use new self-locking nuts or bolts where applicable.
- Lower engine onto engine mounts, making sure locating pin on left mount (**arrow**) seats correctly in slot of subframe boss.
- Allowing engine to settle fully on mounts before tightening engine mount fasteners.
- When the job is completed have front end professionally aligned.

Tightening torques

- Control arm rear bracket to subframe
  M10 bolt (always replace) . . . . 59 Nm (44 ft-lb)
- Engine mount to subframe
  M10 self locking nut . . . . 45 Nm (33 ft-lb)
- Inner ball joint to control arm
  M14 self-locking nut (always replace) . . . 80 Nm (59 ft-lb)
- Inner ball joint mount to subframe
  M12 bolt . . . . 77 Nm (57 ft-lb)
- Stabilizer anchor to subframe (M8) . . . . . 22 Nm (16 ft-lb)
- Steering rack to subframe (M10 bolt) . . . 42 Nm (31 ft-lb)
- Subframe adapter to body
  M10 bolt (always replace) . . . . 59 Nm (44 ft-lb)
- Subframe to body
  M12 (8.8 grade bolt) . . . . 77 Nm (57 ft-lb)
  M12 (10.9 grade bolt) . . . . 110 Nm (81 ft-lb)
  M12 (12.9 grade bolt) . . . . 105 Nm (77 ft-lb)
- Subframe rear to adapter
  M12 bolt (always replace) . . . . 110 Nm (81 ft-lb)

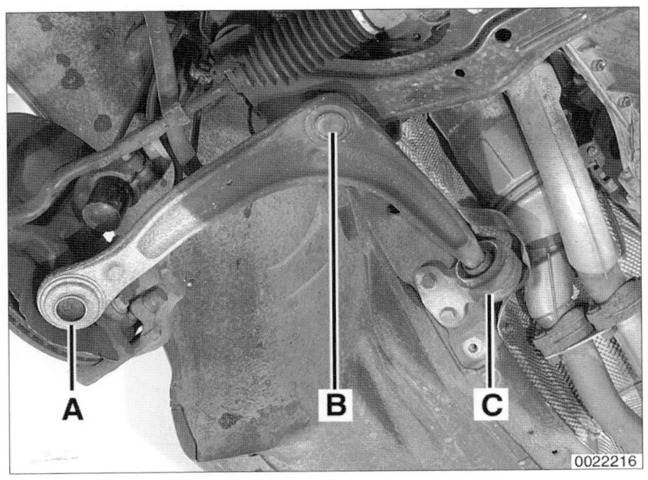

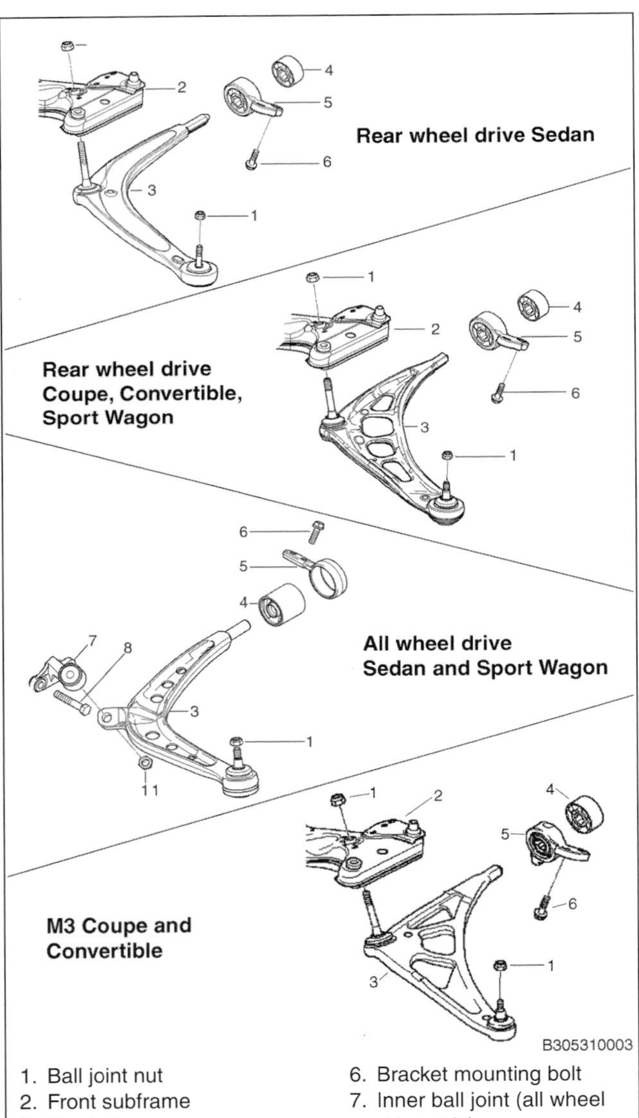

1. Ball joint nut
2. Front subframe
3. Control arm
4. Rear bushing
5. Bushing bracket
6. Bracket mounting bolt
7. Inner ball joint (all wheel drive only)
8. Ball joint mounting bolt

CONTROL ARMS

 Each front control arm has three attachment points:

- **A** Outer ball joint attached to steering arm
- **B** Inner ball joint attached to front subframe
- **C** Bushing and bracket attached to frame rail (rear wheel drive) or front subframe (all wheel drive)

NOTE —
Rear wheel drive Sedan front control arm is shown in illustration. Other models are similar.

The control arm rear bushing is available as a replacement part.

Ball joint replacement:

- Rear wheel drive: Both ball joints are pressed into control arm at factory.
- All wheel drive: Outer (steering arm) ball joint is pressed into control arm.

Because of the aluminum construction of the control arm, pressed-in ball joints are not separately replaceable. If worn or damaged, replace the complete control arm with ball joint(s), available from BMW.

 There are four different styles of control arm in E46 vehicles. Make sure a replacement control arm is identical to the original.

Control arm, removing and installing (rear wheel drive)

– Raise car and remove wheel.

WARNING —
Make sure the car is firmly supported on jack stands designed for the purpose. Place jack stands underneath structural chassis points, not under suspension parts.

– Remove splash shield under engine compartment.

– Remove front end reinforcement.

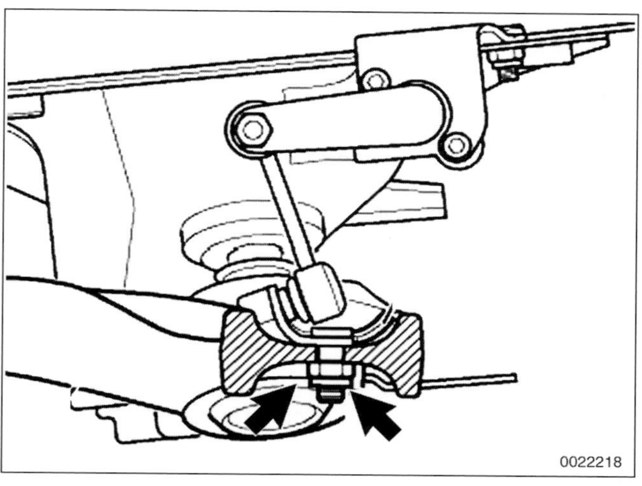

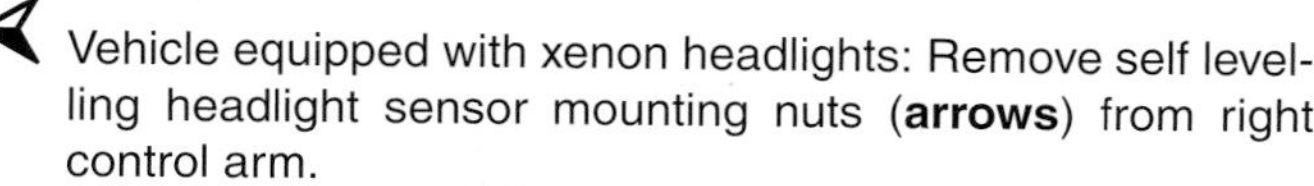

Vehicle equipped with xenon headlights: Remove self leveling headlight sensor mounting nuts (**arrows**) from right control arm.

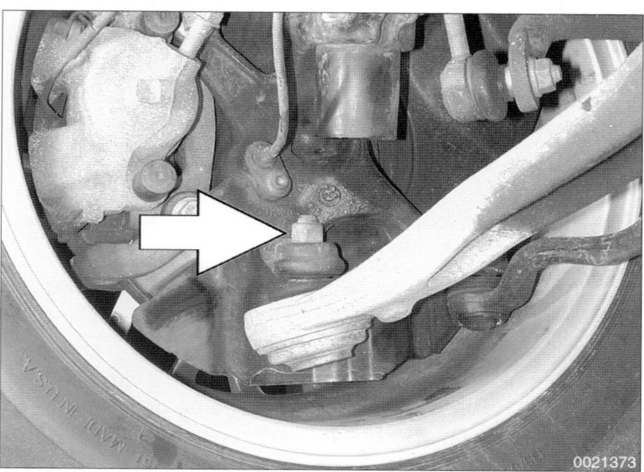

Working at steering arm, remove outer ball joint nut (**arrow**). Use BMW special tool 32 3 090 or equivalent to separate steering arm from control arm.

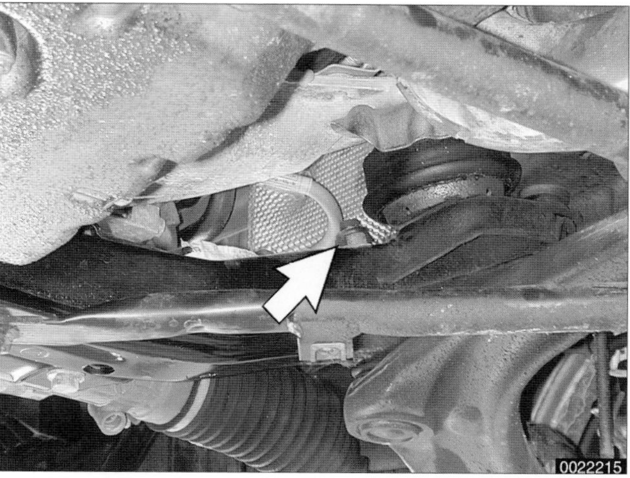

Remove control arm inner ball joint mounting nut (**arrow**) at subframe.

- Drive ball joint shaft out of subframe using soft-faced hammer.

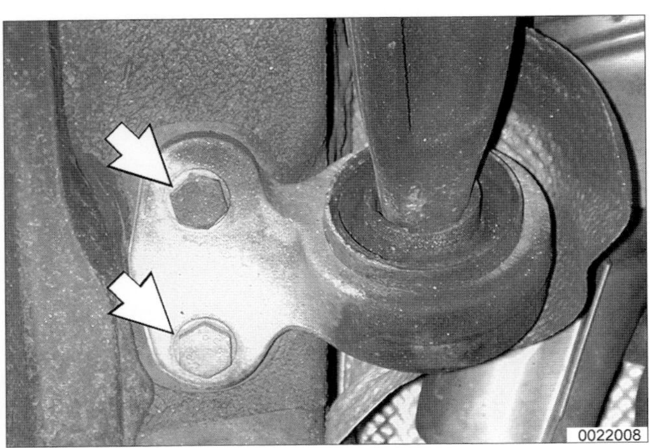

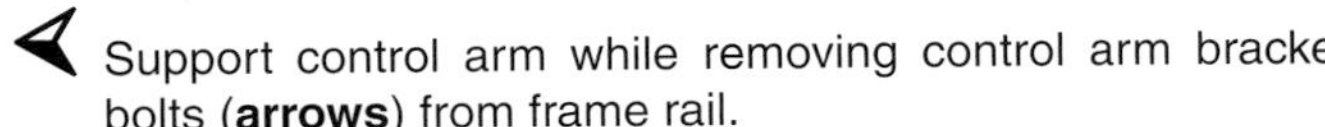

Support control arm while removing control arm bracket bolts (**arrows**) from frame rail.

– Remove control arm and inspect for wear and damage.
  - Check rear bracket rubber bushing for wear.
  - Check ball joints for damage, looseness, or torn boots.
  - Replace control arm if ball joints are damaged.

> ***CAUTION —***
> - *If a control arm is deformed due to an accident, inspect the inner ball joint mounting bore in the subframe for damage or eccentricity.*
> - *If one control arm rear rubber bushing is damaged, replace bushings on both sides. See* **Control arm bushing, removing and installing (rear wheel drive)** *in this repair group.*

– Installation is reverse of removal, noting the following:
  - Make sure all thread bores, bolts, nuts and mating surfaces are clean.
  - Use new self-locking nuts or bolts, where applicable.
  - Have vehicle alignment checked after assembly.

> ***WARNING —***
> *Do not reuse self-locking nuts or bolts. They are designed to be used only once and may fail if reused.*

Tightening torques
- Control arm rear bracket to frame rails
  M10 bolt (always replace) . . . . 59 Nm (44 ft-lb)
- Front end reinforcement to front subframe or body frame rails: M10 bolt (always replace)
  Stage 1 . . . . 59 Nm (44 ft-lb)
  Stage 2 . . . . torque angle 90° + 30°
- Inner ball joint to subframe
  M14 self-locking nut (always replace) . . . 90 Nm (66 ft-lb)
- Outer ball joint to steering arm
  M12 self-locking nut (always replace) . . . 65 Nm (48 ft-lb)
- Road wheel to hub . . . . 120 ± 10 Nm (90 ± 7 ft-lb)

Control arm, removing and installing (all wheel drive)

– Raise car and remove wheel.

> ***WARNING —***
> *Make sure the car is firmly supported on jack stands designed for the purpose. Place jack stands underneath structural chassis points, not under suspension parts.*

– Remove splash shield under engine compartment.

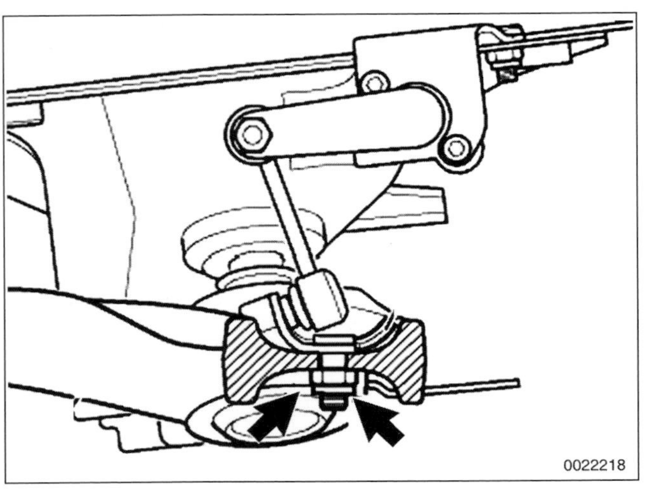

Vehicle equipped with xenon headlights: Remove headlight vertical aim sensor mounting nuts (**arrows**) from right control arm.

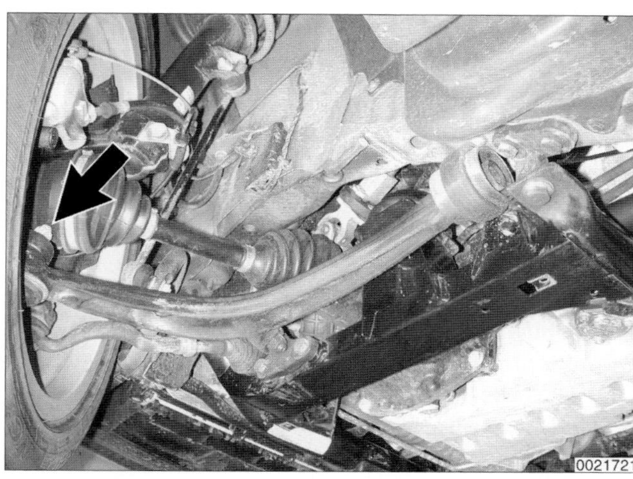

0021721

Working at steering arm, remove outer ball joint nut (**arrow**). Use BMW special tool 32 3 090 or equivalent to separate steering arm from control arm.

0021719

Remove inner ball joint mounting bracket bolts (**arrows**) from subframe.

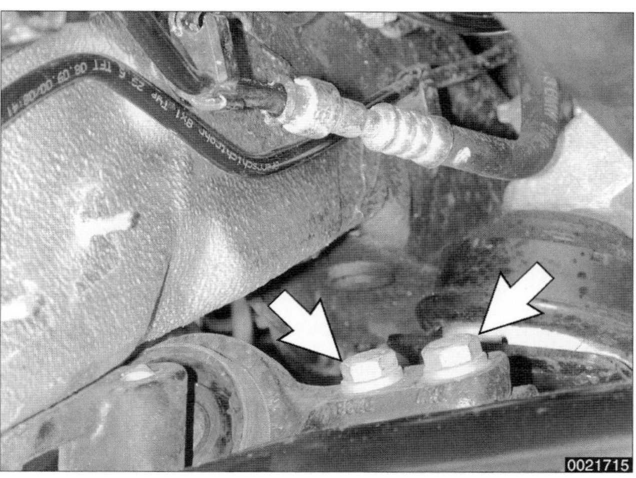

0021715

Support control arm. Working at rear of subframe, remove control arm rear bracket mounting bolts (**arrows**).

– Remove control arm and inspect for wear and damage.
  - Check rear bracket rubber bushing for wear.
  - Check ball joints for damage, looseness, or torn boots.
  - Replace inner ball joint, if damaged. See **Inner ball joint, replacing (all wheel drive)** in this repair group.
  - Replace control arm if outer (steering arm) ball joint is damaged.

> ***CAUTION—***
> - *If a control arm is deformed due to an accident, inspect the inner ball joint mounting bore in the subframe for damage or eccentricity.*
> - *If one control arm rear rubber bushing is damaged, replace bushings on both sides. See* **Control arm bushing, removing and installing (all wheel drive)** *in this repair group.*

– Installation is reverse of removal, noting the following:
  - Make sure all thread bores, bolts, nuts and mating surfaces are clean.
  - Use new self-locking nuts or bolts, where applicable.
  - Have vehicle alignment checked after assembly.

> ***WARNING —***
> *Do not reuse self-locking nuts or bolts. They are designed to be used only once and may fail if reused.*

Tightening torques
- Control arm rear bracket to subframe
  M10 bolt (always replace) . . . . 59 Nm (44 ft-lb)
- Inner ball joint mount to subframe
  M12 bolt . . . . 77 Nm (57 ft-lb)
- Outer ball joint to steering arm
  M12 self-locking nut (always replace) . . . 65 Nm (48 ft-lb)
- Road wheel to hub . . . . 120 ± 10 Nm (90 ± 7 ft-lb)

Inner ball joint, replacing (all wheel drive)

– Raise car and support safely

> ***WARNING —***
> *Make sure the car is firmly supported on jack stands designed for the purpose. Place jack stands underneath structural chassis points, not under suspension parts.*

– Remove splash shield under engine compartment.

◄ Remove inner ball joint fasteners from control arm and subframe.
  - Remove nut (**A**) from ball joint shaft.
  - Remove bolts (**B**) from subframe.

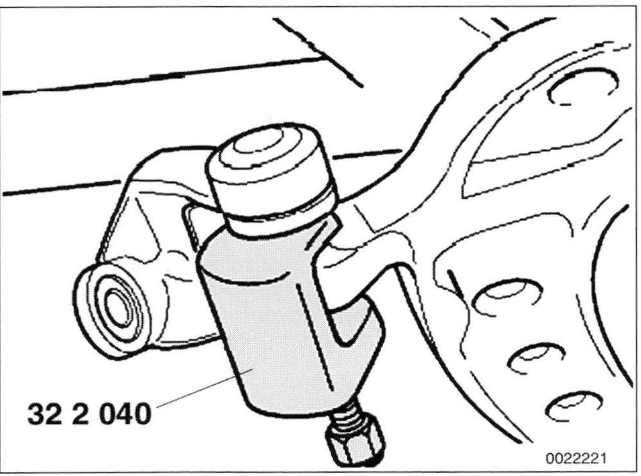

◄ Use BMW special tool 32 2 040 or equivalent to separate ball joint from control arm.

– Installation is reverse of removal, noting the following:
  - Make sure thread bores, bolts, nuts and mating surfaces are clean.
  - Use new self-locking nuts or bolts.

Tightening torques
- Inner ball joint mount to subframe
  M12 bolt . . . . 77 Nm (57 ft-lb)
- Inner ball joint to control arm
  M14 self-locking nut (always replace) . . . 80 Nm (59 ft-lb)

Control arm bushing, removing and installing (rear wheel drive)

> ***CAUTION—***
> - *Do not reuse a rubber bushing that has been pulled off the control arm. The rubber coated inner sleeve is destroyed when it is pulled off dry.*
> - *Check with an authorized BMW parts dealer for the latest information about control arm bushing applications.*

Replace control arm bushings in pairs. Make sure both bushings and bushing carriers have the same markings, indicating same manufacturer.

– Remove control arm. See **Control arm, removing and installing (rear wheel drive)** in this repair group.

– Use puller to remove rear bracket and bushing from control arm.

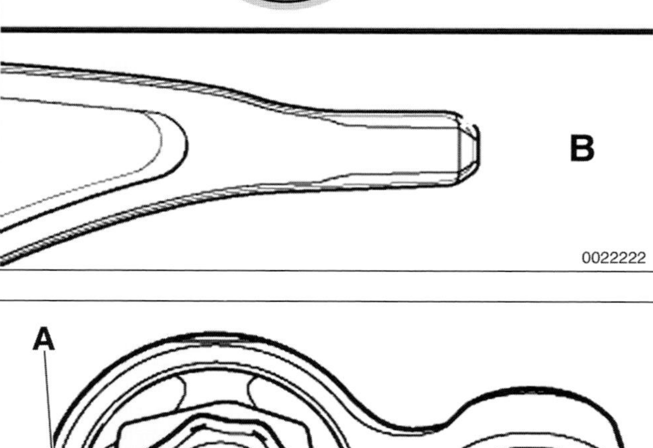

◄ Inspect pin (rubber bushing) end of control arm. Replace control arm with end **A**.

NOTE—
*Control arms with pin shape **A** are superseded by parts with pin shape **B**.*

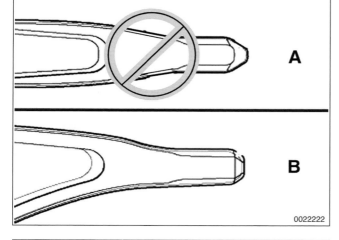

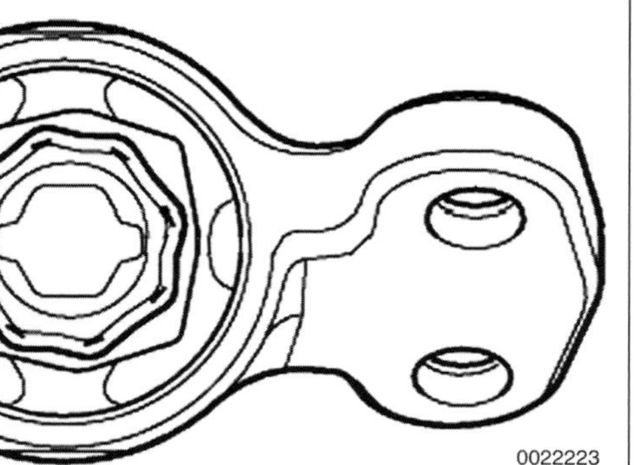

◄ Inspect bushing bracket. Replace bracket if there is a center punch mark at boss **A**.

> ***WARNING—***
> *If a bushing bracket with the center punch mark is reused with a new bushing, the bushing may fall out.*

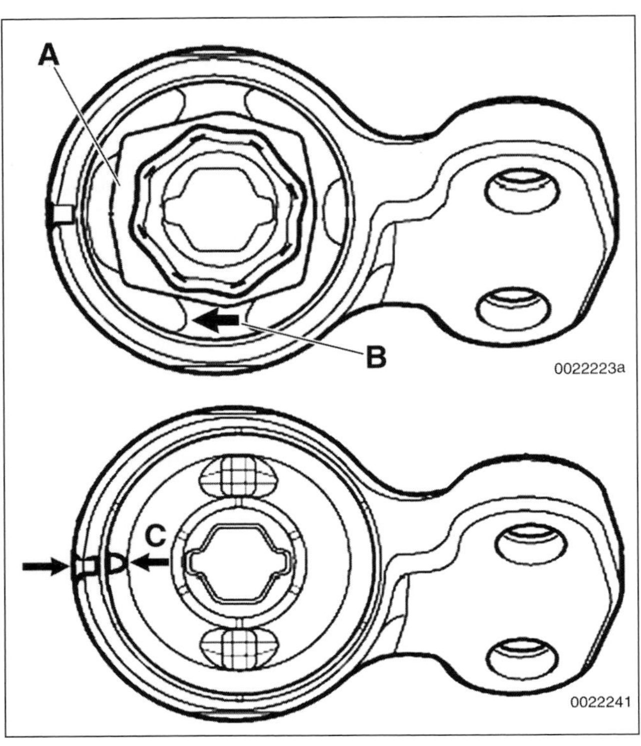

Use press tools to remove old bushing and press in new. Be sure to line up marks on new bushing with boss on bracket. Depending on manufacturer, mark on bushing may consist of:

- Extra buffer on inner part of bushing (**A**)
- Arrow on rubber webbing of bushing (**B**)
- Indent on outer casing of bushing (**C**)

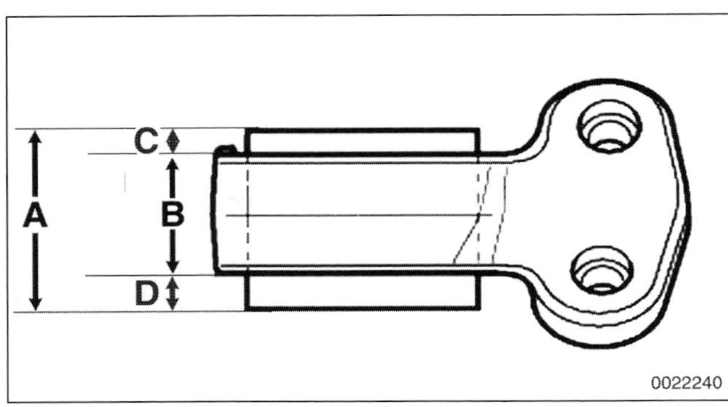

Press in new bushing so that it protrudes correct distance from edges of bracket. See **Table a**.

Table a. Control arm bushing protrusion (rear wheel drive)

Dimension	60 mm bushing	66 mm bushing
A = Total bushing length (nominal)	50.5 mm (1.99 in.)	53.5 mm (2.11 in.)
B = Bracket width (nominal)	34.0 mm (1.36 in.)	
C = Fixed measurement	8.5 mm (0.33 in.)	12.0 mm (0.47 in.)
D = Protrusion	8.0 mm (0.31 in)	7.5 mm (0.29 in.)

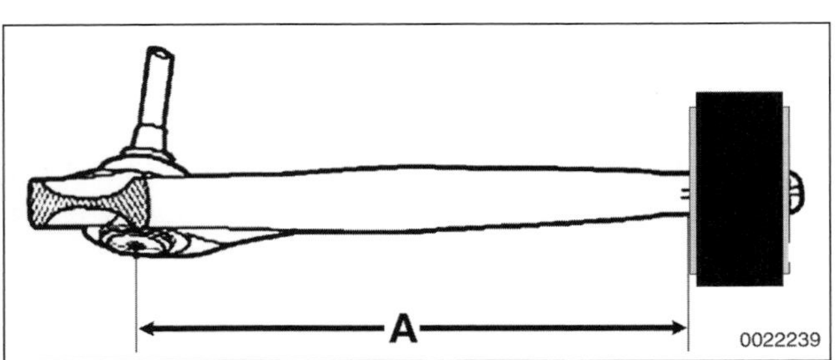

When installing bushing on control arm:

- Use soapy water on control pin and rubber bushing to facilitate assembly.
- Make sure dimension **A** (distance from inner ball joint to edge of control arm bushing) is correct after assembly. See **Table b**.

Table b. Control arm bracket installation distances (rear wheel drive)

Bushing diameter	Bushing distance A
60 mm	289 ± 1 mm (11.38 ± 0.04 in.)
66 mm	290.9 ± 1 mm (11.45 ± 0.04 in.)

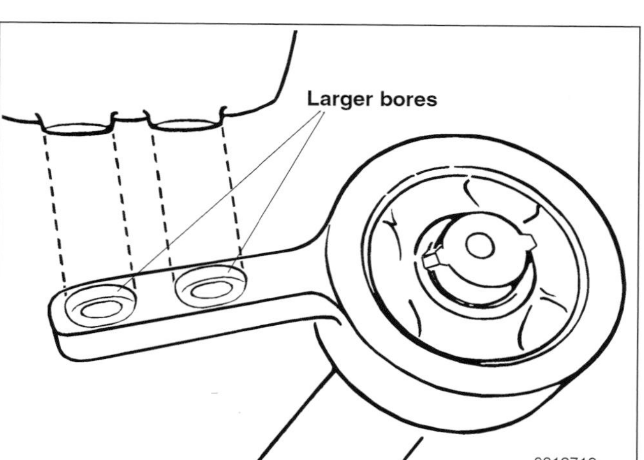

Be sure to reinstall bushing bracket to frame rail correctly, with larger centering bores facing up toward body.

Tightening torque

- Control arm rear bracket to frame rail M10 bolt (always replace) . . . . 59 Nm (44 ft-lb)

Control arm bushing, removing and installing (all wheel drive)

CAUTION —

- *Do not reuse a rubber bushing that has been pulled off the control arm. The rubber coated inner sleeve is destroyed when it is pulled off dry.*
- *Check with an authorized BMW parts dealer for the latest information about control arm bushing applications.*

Replace control arm bushings in pairs. Make sure both bushings and bushing carriers have the same markings, indicating same manufacturer.

– Remove control arm. See **Control arm, removing and installing (all wheel drive)** in this repair group.

– Use puller to remove rear bracket and bushing from control arm.

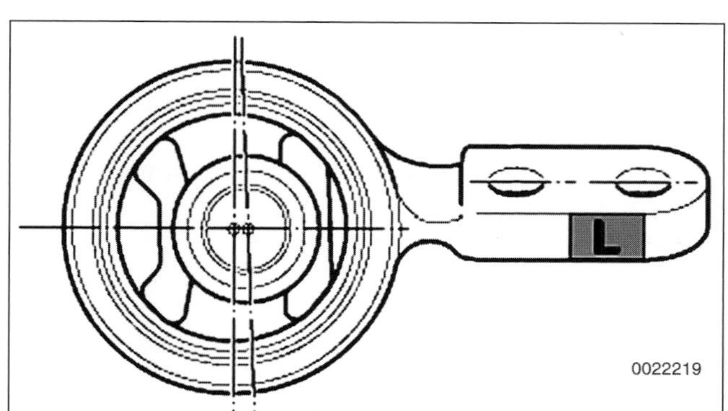

Use press tools to remove old bushing and press in new.

- Align bushing with bracket as shown in accompanying illustration.

CAUTION —

Never reuse a rubber bushing that has been pulled off the control arm. The rubber coated inner sleeve is destroyed when it is pulled off dry.

NOTE —

Brackets are marked L or R for left or right.

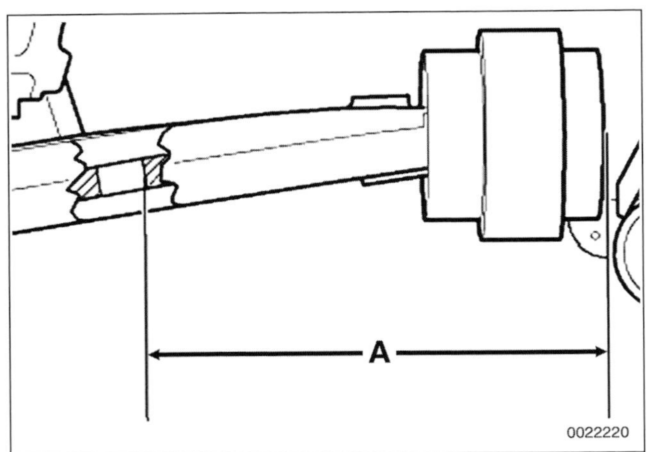

When installing bushing on control arm:

- Coat control arm pin and rubber mount with appropriate lubricant to facilitate installation.
- Make sure dimension **A** (distance from first bore in control arm to outer edge of control arm bushing) is correct after assembly. See **Table c**.

NOTE —

Slacken pressing tool when measuring installation distance. For measurement to be accurate, allow rubber bushing to relax.

Table c. Control arm bracket installation distance (all wheel drive)

Measurement **A**	170 ± 1 mm (6.69 ± 0.04 in.)

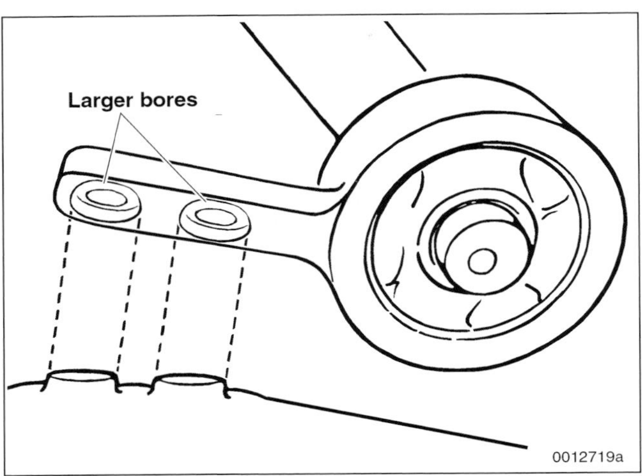

Bolt bracket and control arm to front subframe and steering arm immediately after pressing on bushing. Be sure to reinstall bushing bracket to subframe correctly, with larger centering bores facing subframe surface.

Tightening torque

- Control arm rear bracket to subframe M10 bolt (always replace) . . . . 59 Nm (44 ft-lb)

WARNING —

- *After installation, leave car undisturbed for a minimum of 30 minutes. Leave car on the ground but avoid major movement.*
- *After approx. 30 minutes, the lubricant used to slide on the bushing will have evaporated and the control arm will be correctly seated in the rubber.*
- *Serious handling problems could result if these instructions are not carried out.*

STABILIZER BAR

Stabilizer bar, removing and installing

Front stabilizer bar links attach to the strut assemblies.

– Raise car and support safely.

WARNING —

Make sure the car is firmly supported on jack stands designed for the purpose. Place jack stands underneath structural chassis points, not under suspension parts.

– Remove front underbody shields, if installed.

Remove stabilizer bar connecting link mounting nut (**arrow**) from stabilizer bar on right side. Counterhold ball joint with flat wrench. (Rear wheel drive model shown.)

– Repeat on left side.

Remove stabilizer bar bushing anchor nuts (**arrows**) on right side.

- Repeat on left side.
- Remove bar.

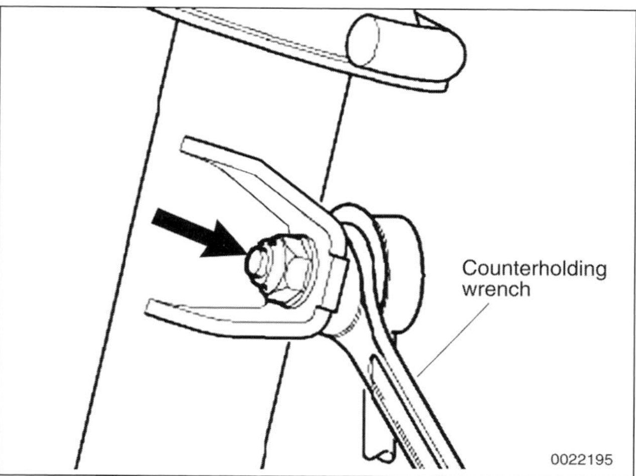

If necessary, loosen and remove stabilizer bar link mounting nut (**arrow**) from strut. Detach link from strut housing.

NOTE —
Use a thin wrench to counterhold shaft of stabilizer bar link ball joint while removing mounting nut.

- Installation is reverse of removal, noting the following
  - Use new self-locking nuts on connecting links.
  - When attaching stabilizer link to strut or bar, use a thin wrench to counterhold ball joints on link while tightening nut.
  - Installation of stabilizer bar is easiest with car level (front wheels at the same height) and as near to normal ride height as possible.

Tightening torques

- Stabilizer bar bushing brackets to subframe. . . . . 22 Nm (16 ft-lb)
- Stabilizer bar link to stabilizer bar M10 self locking nut (always replace) . . . 65 Nm (48 ft-lb)
- Stabilizer bar link to strut M10 self locking nut (always replace) . . . 65 Nm (48 ft-lb)

Front wheel bearing and stub axle (rear wheel drive models)

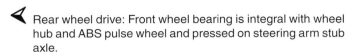

1. Steering arm and stub axle
2. Dust guard
3. Wheel hub, bearing and ABS pulse wheel
4. Stub axle collar nut -tighten to 290 Nm (214 ft-lb)
5. Dust cap

FRONT WHEEL BEARINGS

The front wheel bearings are permanently sealed and require no maintenance.

Rear wheel drive: Front wheel bearing is integral with wheel hub and ABS pulse wheel and pressed on steering arm stub axle.

All wheel drive: Front wheel bearing is pressed into steering arm. Wheel hub is pressed into bearing and outer CV joint stub axle is pressed into hub. ABS front pulse wheel is inner (ridged) seal of front wheel bearing.

Special press tools are required to replace front wheel bearings. Read procedures through before beginning.

Front wheel bearing, replacing (rear wheel drive)

– Raise car and remove front wheel.

> ***WARNING —***
> *Make sure the car is firmly supported on jack stands designed for the purpose. Place jack stands underneath structural chassis points, not under suspension parts.*

Pry off dust cap from center of wheel hub. Bend back staked part (**arrow**) of wheel hub (axle) collar nut.

– Remount wheel and lug bolts.

– Lower car to ground. With an assistant applying brakes, loosen collar nut. Do not remove completely.

> ***CAUTION —***
> *The wheel hub collar nut is tightened to a torque of 290 Nm (214 ft-lb). Make sure the car is firmly on the ground.*

– Raise car and remove wheel.

Remove ABS wheel speed sensor (**arrow**).

– Remove brake caliper assembly and brake rotor. See **340 Brakes**. Leave brake hose connected to caliper. Suspend caliper assembly from chassis using stiff wire.

– Remove wheel hub collar nut.

0011200

Remove wheel hub with integral wheel bearing from steering arm using a slide hammer puller (BMW special tools 33 4 201, 33 4 202, 33 4 203 and 33 2 116) or conventional puller as illustrated.

– If outermost bearing inner race stays on steering arm stub axle, use BMW special tool set 33 4 400 or two-jaw puller to remove race.

> ***CAUTION —***
> *Do not reuse a wheel bearing assembly once it has been removed. The removal process destroys the bearing.*

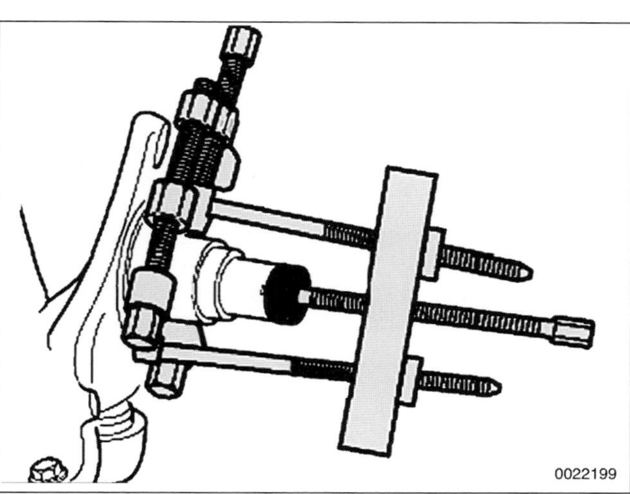
0022199

To remove innermost inner race:

- Unbolt brake rotor dust shield.
- Bend back wheel bearing dust guard.
- Use BMW special tools 00 7 500 and 31 2 106 to pull race off stub axle.

– Install splash guard and new dust shield behind bearing. Press new wheel hub/bearing assembly on stub axle using BMW special tool 31 2 110 or equivalent.

> ***CAUTION —***
> *The BMW special tool insures that only the inner bearing race is used to press on the hub and bearing assembly. The bearing is damaged if it is not pressed on using the inner race.*

– Install new collar nut. Do not tighten nut to its final torque at this time.

- Install brake rotor and brake caliper. See **340 Brakes**.
- Mount wheel and lug bolts. Lower car to ground to gain leverage.

Tightening torques
- Brake caliper to steering arm . . . . 110 Nm (81 ft-lb)
- Brake rotor to wheel hub. . . . . 16 Nm (12 ft-lb)
- Road wheel to hub . . . . 120 ± 10 Nm (90 ± 7 ft-lb)

– With an assistant applying brakes, tighten collar nut.

Tightening torque
- Collar nut to stub axle. . . . . 290 Nm (214 ft-lb)

– Raise car and remove wheel.

– Stake axle nut and caulk threads of stub axle.

– Install a new grease cap, using Loctite® 638 sealant or equivalent. Install wheel and lower car.

– Install ABS pulse sensor.

Tightening torques

• ABS pulse sensor to steering arm . . . . . . 8 Nm (71 in-lb)

Front wheel bearing, replacing (all wheel drive)

Removal and installation of the all wheel drive front wheel bearing is best accomplished by removing the steering arm and wheel hub from the car and separating the components on the bench.

– Raise car and remove front wheel.

> ***WARNING —***
> *Make sure the car is firmly supported on jack stands designed for the purpose. Place jack stands underneath structural chassis points, not under suspension parts.*

◀ Bend back staked part of wheel hub (axle) collar nut (**arrow**).

– Remount wheel and lug bolts.

– Lower car to ground. With an assistant applying brakes, loosen collar nut. Do not remove completely.

> ***CAUTION —***
> *The wheel hub collar nut is tightened to a torque of 420 Nm (310 ft-lb). Make sure the car is firmly on the ground.*

– Raise car and remove front wheel.

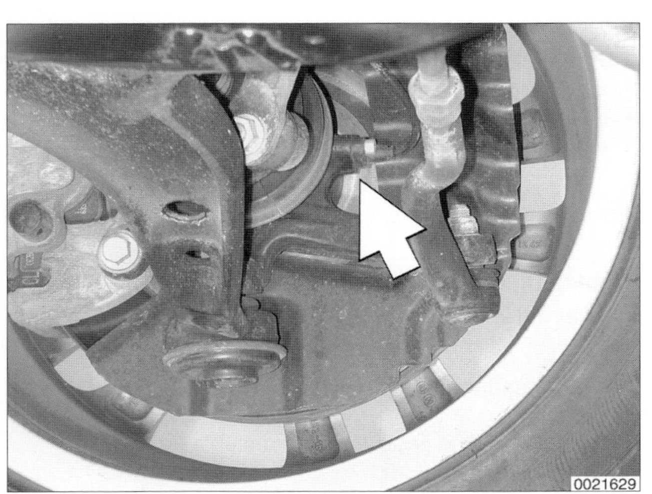

◀ Remove ABS wheel speed sensor (**arrow**).

– Remove brake caliper assembly and brake rotor. See **340 Brakes**. Leave brake hose connected to caliper. Suspend caliper assembly from chassis using stiff wire.

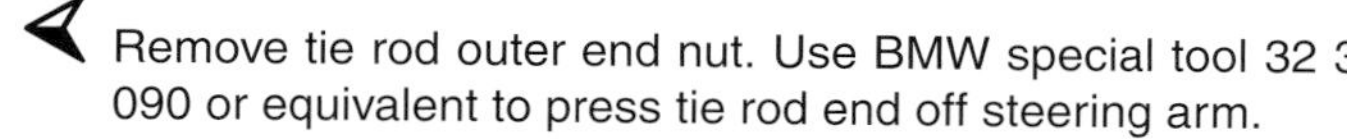

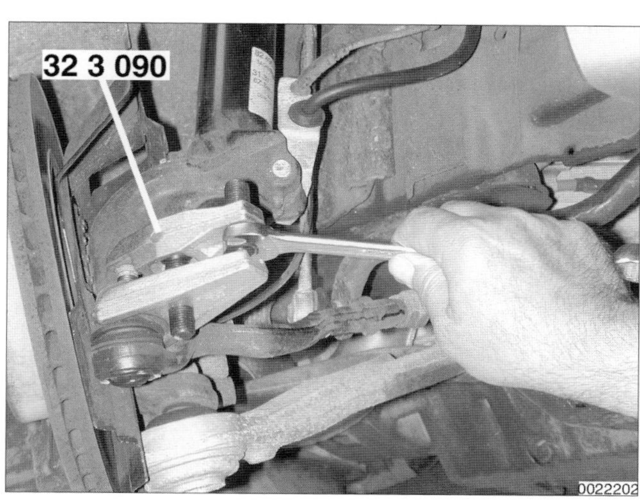

◀ Remove tie rod outer end nut. Use BMW special tool 32 3 090 or equivalent to press tie rod end off steering arm.

– Detach control arm from front axle subframe. See **Control arm, removing and installing (all wheel drive)** in this repair group.

– Remove outer ball joint nut. Use BMW special tool 32 3 090 or equivalent to separate steering arm and strut assembly from control arm.

– Attach BMW special tool 33 2 111 /116 /117, or equivalent puller, to steering arm using five lug bolts and press outer CV joint stub axle inward, out of steering arm.

◀ Support steering arm from below. Loosen pinch bolt (**arrow**) at top of steering arm. Spread clamping collar at slot **A**, if necessary, to slide steering arm off strut assembly.

– Working at bench, clamp steering arm in a vise.

> ***CAUTION —***
> *Use a vise with aluminum jaws to protect steering arm from damage when clamping in vise.*

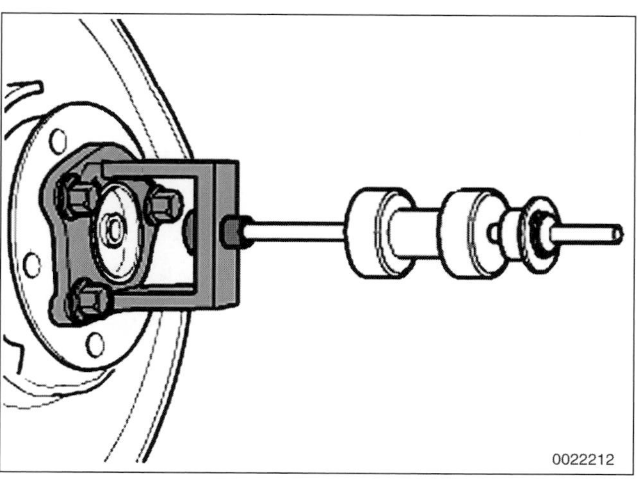

◀ Remove wheel hub with integral wheel bearing from steering arm using a slide hammer puller (BMW special tools 33 4 201, 33 4 202, 33 4 203 and 33 2 116).

– If bearing inner race stays on wheel hub, use BMW special tool set 33 4 400 or two-jaw puller to remove race.

Front wheel bearing and steering arm (all wheel drive models)

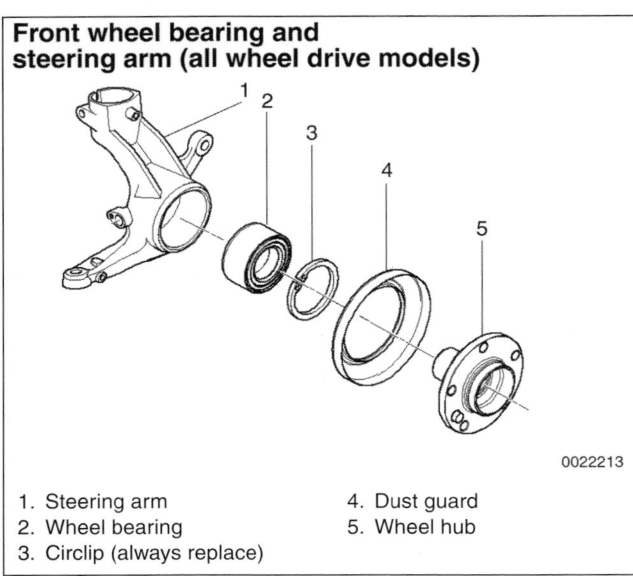

1. Steering arm
2. Wheel bearing
3. Circlip (always replace)
4. Dust guard
5. Wheel hub

◀ Remove circlip (**3**) from steering arm.

– Drive wheel bearing out of steering arm using a press with appropriate adapters.

> ***CAUTION —***
> *Do not reuse a wheel bearing assembly once it has been removed. The removal process destroys the bearing.*

– Press in bearing using a press with appropriate adapters.

- Coat bearing seat in steering arm over 50% of its length with Loctite® 648.
- Make sure press fit surfaces are clean and free of grease.

> ***CAUTION —***
> *When installing the front wheel bearing into the steering arm, be sure that the ridged bearing seal (ABS impulse wheel) is facing inboard. Start the bevelled edge of the bearing into the bore first.*

– Replace circlip and make sure it is seated correctly.

– Place dust guard over steering arm hub.

– Drive wheel hub into bearing using shop press.

> ***CAUTION —***
> *Press only on the inner race. The bearing is damaged if it is not pressed on using the inner race.*

– Installation of steering arm to car is reverse of removal, noting the following:

- Replace control arm bracket bolts.
- Torque stub axle collar nut with vehicle on ground. Stake nut and caulk stub axle threads.
- Have vehicle professionally aligned.

Tightening torques

- Ball joint to steering arm . . . . 65 Nm (48 ft-lb)
- Brake caliper to steering arm . . . . 110 Nm (81 ft-lb)
- Brake rotor to wheel hub. . . . . 16 Nm (12 ft-lb)
- Collar nut to wheel hub . . . . 420 Nm (310 ft-lb)
- Control arm bracket to subframe . . . . . . 59 Nm (44 ft-lb)
- Steering arm pinch bolt at strut housing . . . . 81 Nm (60 ft-lb)
- Road wheel to hub . . . . 120 ± 10 Nm (90 ± 7 ft-lb)
- Tie rod to steering arm . . . . 65 Nm (48 ft-lb)

311 Front Axle Final Drive

Special tools

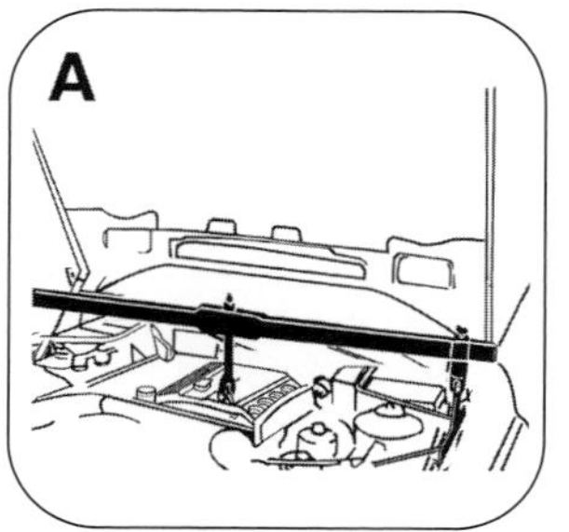

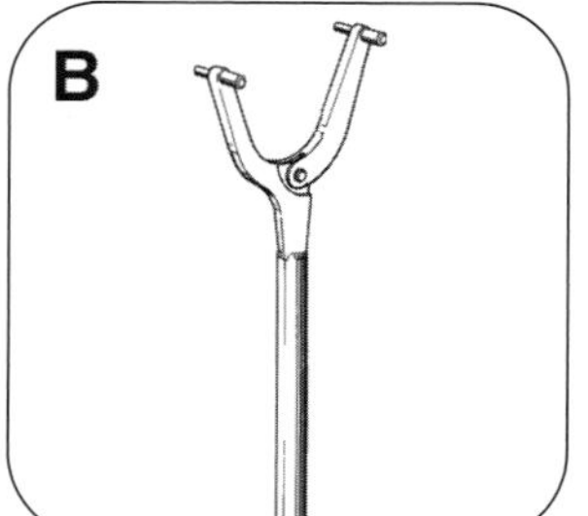

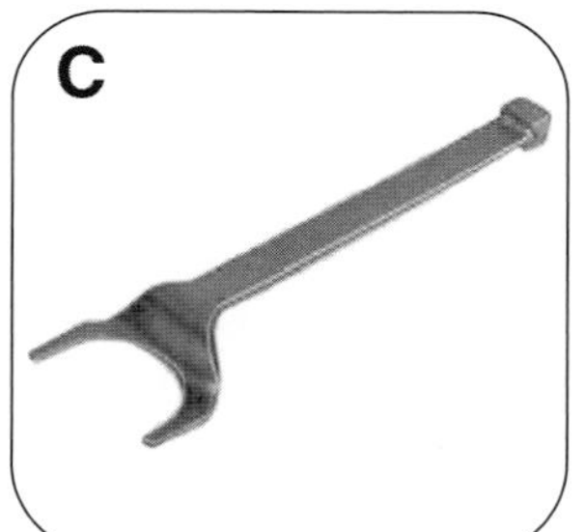

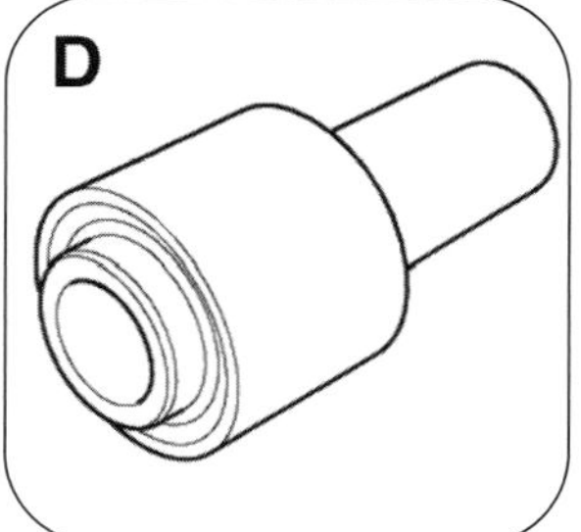

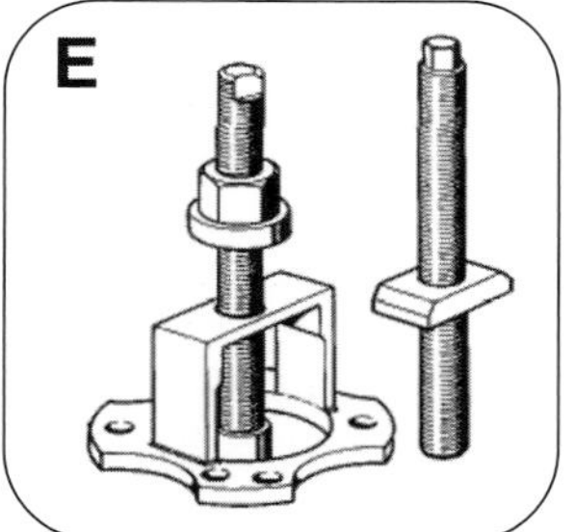

A BMW 00 0 200 . . . . Engine support bracket
B BMW 23 0 020 . . . . Transmission flange holder
C BMW 31 1 170 . . . . Inner CV joint puller
D BMW 31 5 130 . . . . Impact drift
E BMW 33 2 111/116/117 . . . . Outer CV joint removal tool

GENERAL

This repair group covers service and replacement of front drive axles and front differential for all wheel drive models.

See **300 Suspension, Steering and Brakes–General** for a general description of the front suspension.

For additional information, see also the following repair groups:

- **260 Driveshafts**
- **270 Transfer Case**
- **310 Front Suspension**
- **340 Brakes**

Procedures involving the internal repairs of the front differential are not included in this manual.

Special tools

BMW recommends special tools for the removal of the drive axles as well as the installation of the front differential input drive flange seal. Commonly available pullers and drifts can often be substituted for the specified tools. Read the procedures through before beginning any job.

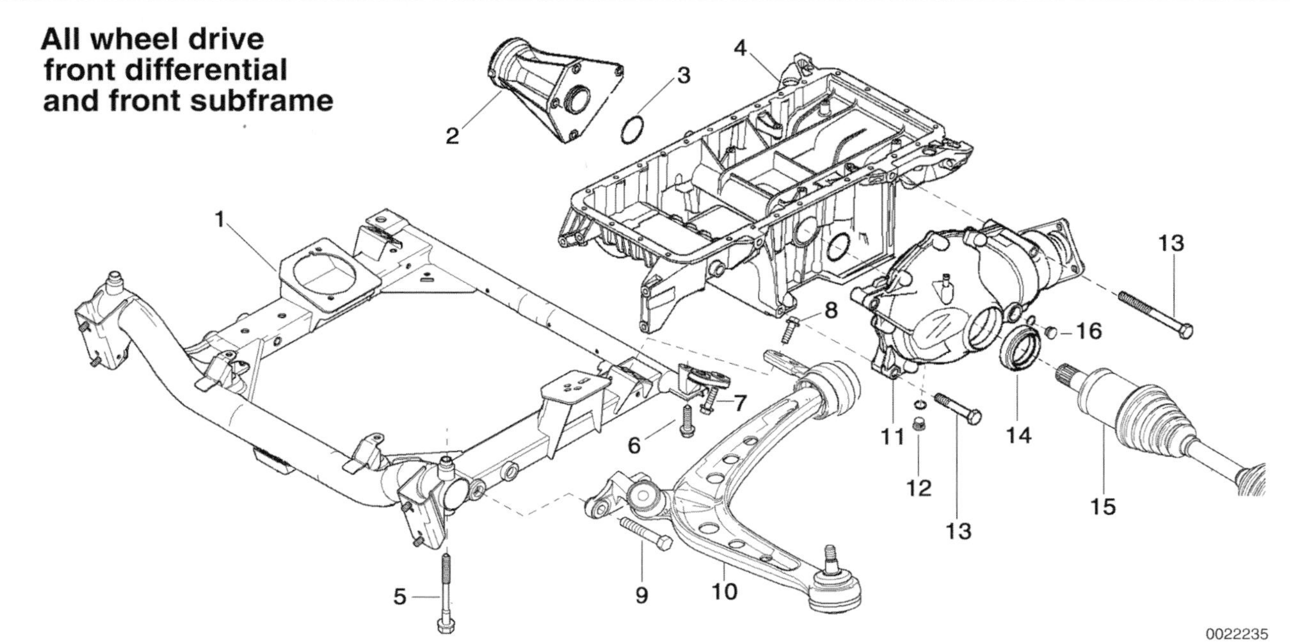

1. Front subframe
2. Right axle bearing pedestal
3. Sealing O-ring
4. Oil pan
5. Bolt M12 (always replace)
   -8.8 grade tighten to 77 Nm (57 ft-lb)
   -10.9 grade tighten to 110 Nm (81 ft-lb)
   -12.9 grade tighten to 105 Nm (77 ft-lb)
6. Bolt M12 (always replace)
   -tighten to 110 Nm (81 ft-lb)
7. Bolt M10 (always replace)
   -tighten to 59 Nm (44 ft-lb)
8. Bolt M10 (always replace)
   -tighten to 59 Nm (44 ft-lb)
9. Bolt M12
   -tighten to 77 Nm (57 ft-lb)
10. Front control arm with ball joint and rear mounting bracket
11. Front differential
12. Front differential drain plug
    -tighten to 65 Nm (48 ft-lb)
13. Bolt M10
    -tighten to 45 Nm (33 ft-lb)
14. Drive axle radial seal
15. Drive axle
16. Front differential fill plug
    -tighten to 65 Nm (48 ft-lb)

System description

The front axle final drive unit is integrated into the engine oil pan. The front differential and the right side bearing pedestal bolt to each side of a modified oil pan. Power is transmitted to the front differential from the transfer case via a driveshaft, and out to front drive hubs through two drive axles.

DRIVE AXLES

The front drive axles use two different types of constant-velocity (CV) joint.

The outer CV joint is a traditional design that allows power to be delivered from the axle to the joint continuously through rotation.

The inner is a triple roller bearing joint which minimizes the amount of vibration and noise transmitted back through the vehicle drivetrain, while also allowing the axle to move in and out to compensate for suspension travel.

To replace a CV joint or dust boot, remove the drive axle from the car.

Drive axle, removing and installing

NOTE —
If removing the drive axle for service, it is a good idea to replace the drive axle radial seal while the axle is removed from the vehicle.

– Carefully remove center cap from wheel.

< Break free staked collar nut (**arrow**) at steering arm.

– Lift vehicle and support safely.

> ***WARNING —***
> *Make sure the car is stable and well supported at all times. Use a professional automotive lift or jack stands designed for the purpose. A floor jack is not adequate support.*

– Remove front wheel.

– Remove splash shield from below engine compartment.

– If working on right side, remove right side heat shield from front axle support.

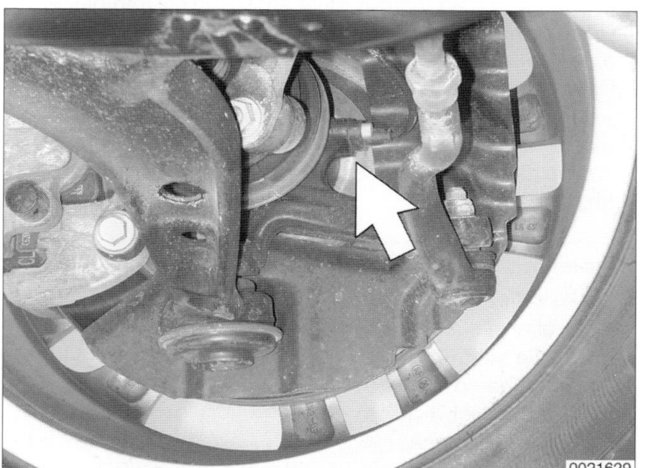

< Remove ABS sensor (**arrow)** from steering arm.

– Unclip brake hose from mounting bracket.

– Unbolt brake caliper and suspend from body using stiff wire.

– Vehicles with Xenon lighting: Detach headlight vertical aim sensor from control arm.

– Unfasten stabilizer link from stabilizer bar.

– Remove collar nut from drive axle at steering arm.

– Using BMW special tool 33 2 111 / 116 / 117, or similar tool, press outboard end of axle out from drive flange at steering arm.

< Remove inner ball joint mounting bracket bolts (**arrows**) from subframe.

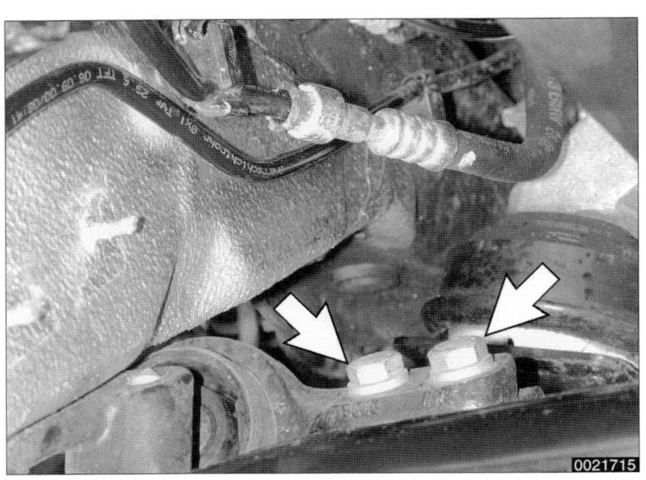

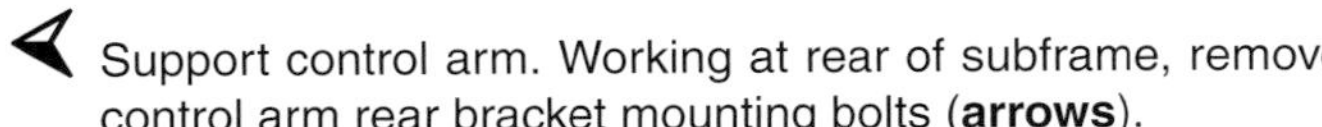

Support control arm. Working at rear of subframe, remove control arm rear bracket mounting bolts (**arrows**).

– Tilt steering arm to one side, out of the way.

– Using BMW special tool 31 1 170 or equivalent pry bar, pry inboard CV joint out of front differential or bearing pedestal.

NOTE —

Be prepared to catch oil drips from differential or right side bearing pedestal.

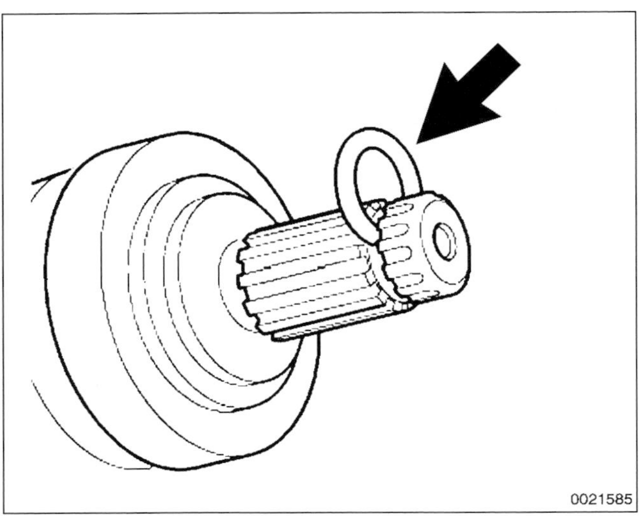

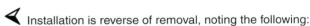

Installation is reverse of removal, noting the following:

- Replace drive axle radial seal before replacing drive axle.
- Before installing drive axle, replace inboard CV joint spring clip (**arrow**).
- When pressing drive axle into front axle differential or bearing pedestal, be sure to press axle beyond resistance of spring clip. Spring clip must snap audibly into place.
- Replace bolts holding control arm bushing bracket to front axle subframe.
- Be sure to restake new collar nut at outboard end of drive axle after tightening to correct torque specifications. Caulk axle threads.
- Top up differential fluid. See **Front differential oil, checking and filling.**

Tightening torques

- Brake caliper to steering arm . . . . 110 Nm (81 ft-lb)
- Control arm bushing bracket to front axle subframe (replace bolts) . . . . . 59 Nm (44 ft-lb)
- Drive flange collar nut to front hub . . . 420 Nm (310 ft-lb)
- Inner ball joint bracket to front axle subframe . . . . 77 Nm (57 ft-lb)
- Road wheel to hub . . . . 120 ± 10 Nm (90 ± 7 ft-lb)
- Stabilizer link to stabilizer bar . . . . 65 Nm (48 ft-lb)

Drive axle radial seal, replacing

NOTE —

If only replacing drive axle radial seal, the axle does not need to be completely removed from the vehicle. Only the inboard CV joint needs to be removed from either the front axle differential or the right axle bearing pedestal. The front suspension may be partially disassembled for radial seal replacement.

– Lift vehicle and support safely.

> ***WARNING —***
> *Make sure car is stable and well supported at all times. Use a professional automotive lift or jack stands designed for the purpose. A floor jack is not adequate support.*

– Remove splash shield from below engine compartment.

Remove inner ball joint mounting bracket bolts (**arrows**) from subframe.

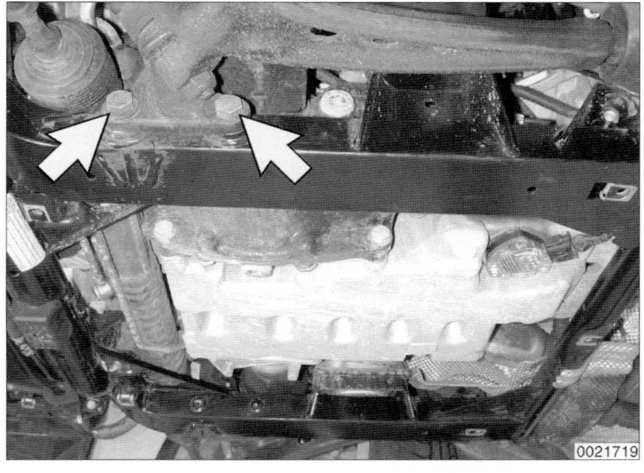

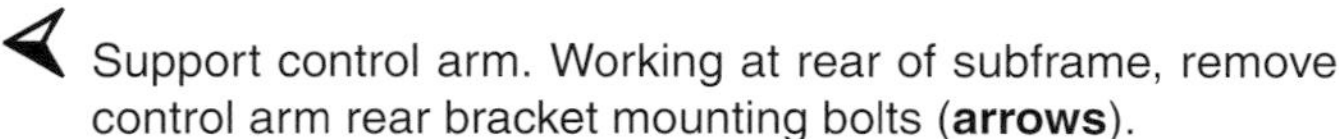

Support control arm. Working at rear of subframe, remove control arm rear bracket mounting bolts (**arrows**).

– Tilt steering arm to one side, out of the way.

– Using BMW special tool 31 1 170 or equivalent pry bar, pry inboard CV joint out of front differential or bearing pedestal.

NOTE —

Be prepared to catch oil drips from differential or right side bearing pedestal.

Front axle differential and housing

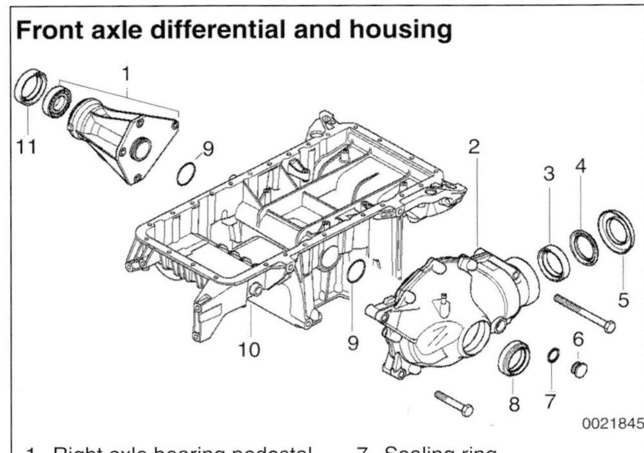

1. Right axle bearing pedestal
2. Front differential
3. Input shaft seal
4. Small dustcover
5. Large dustcover
6. Differential fill plug
7. Sealing ring
8. Drive axle radial seal with lock ring, left
9. O-ring
10. Engine oil pan
11. Drive axle radial seal with lock ring, right

◄ Pry radial seal out of differential housing or bearing pedestal using a flat screwdriver.

NOTE —
Remove protective sleeve from new drive axle radial seal before installing seal and save for use during drive axle installation. Drive axle radial seal is equipped with protective covering to prevent sealing lip from damage during installation.

– Using BMW special tool 31 5 130 or equivalent drift, drive radial seal into differential housing or bearing pedestal.
- Coat sealing lip of radial seal with transmission fluid.
- Drive radial seal into differential or bearing pedestal.
- Insert protective sleeve into radial seal.
- Insert inboard end of drive axle partially into differential housing or bearing pedestal.
- Withdraw protective sleeve from sealing lip, cut protective sleeve and remove sleeve.
- Continue pressing drive axle in until spring clip snaps audibly into place.

NOTE —
Always replace spring clip on inboard end of drive axle before reinstalling into differential housing or bearing pedestal.

– Remainder of installation is reverse of removal, noting the following:
- Make sure end of drive axle audibly snaps into place.
- Replace control arm bracket bolts.
- Top up differential fluid. See **Front differential oil, checking and filling.**

Tightening torques
- Inner ball joint bracket to front axle subframe . . . . 77 Nm (57 ft-lb)
- Brake caliper to steering arm . . . . 110 Nm (81 ft-lb)
- Control arm bracket to front axle subframe (replace bolts) . . . . . 59 Nm (44 ft-lb)

Outer CV joint boot, replacing

NOTE —
When replacing CV boot, use a complete boot repair kit available from an authorized BMW dealer parts department. The kit includes new boot, clamping bands, special lubricant and a new outer CV joint axle circlip.

– Remove drive axle. See **Drive axle, removing and installing** in this repair group.

– Release retaining clamps from both ends of outer CV boot.

– Using a hammer, pound outer CV joint off drive axle.

– Using a flat blade screw driver, pry spring clip off drive axle splines.

– Clean old lubricant off axle splines.

– Inspect CV joint carefully.
  - Look for galling, pitting and other signs of wear or physical damage.
  - Polished surfaces or visible ball tracks alone are not necessarily cause for replacement.
  - Discoloration (overheating) indicates lack of lubrication.

– Place new clamping bands and CV boot over drive axle.

– Replace spring clip on splined end of drive axle.

– Apply Loctite® 270 or an equivalent heavy-duty locking compound to drive axle splines.

> ***WARNING —***
> *Do not let locking compound contact balls in joint. Apply only a thin coat to cover splines.*

– Pack outer CV joint with fresh grease. Tap CV joint onto splined end of drive axle until spring clip snaps audibly into place.

CV joint lubricant capacity
- Outer CV joint . . . . 80 gram (2.8 oz.)

– Using clamp pliers, secure retaining clamp into position tightly sealing large end of boot against CV joint.

NOTE —
Before installing each small boot clamp be sure to "burp" boot by flexing CV joint as far over as it will go. A small screw-driver inserted between boot and axle-shaft will help the process.

– With outer CV boot full of grease, and any air eliminated from boot, secure small end of CV boot on CV joint by pinching clamp with pliers.

– Installation is reverse of removal, noting the following:
  - Make sure inboard end of drive axle audibly snaps into place.
  - Replace control arm bracket bolts.
  - Be sure to restake new collar nut at outboard end of drive axle after tightening to correct torque specifications. Caulk axle threads.
  - Top up differential fluid. See **Front differential oil, checking and filling.**

Tightening torques
- Ball joint bracket to front axle subframe . . . . 77 Nm (57 ft-lb)
- Brake caliper to steering arm . . . . 110 Nm (81 ft-lb)
- Control arm bushing bracket to front axle subframe . . . . 59 Nm (44 ft-lb)
- Drive flange collar nut to front hub . . . 420 Nm (310 ft-lb)

Inner CV joint boot, replacing

NOTE —
When replacing CV boot, use a complete boot repair kit available from an authorized BMW dealer parts department. The kit includes new boot, clamping bands, special lubricant and a new outer CV joint axle circlip.

– Remove drive axle. See **Drive axle, removing and installing** in this repair group.

– Release retaining clamp on both ends of inner CV boot. Pull back inner boot and detach inner CV joint housing.

– Remove circlip retaining triple roller bearing to drive axle and remove triple roller bearing.

– Slide boot off drive axle. Separate inner CV joint boot adapter from boot.

– Clean old lubricant off axle splines and triple roller bearing splines.

– Install new inner CV joint boot:
  - Attach boot to boot adapter.
  - Slide retaining clamps and boot over drive axle.
  - Secure retaining clamp using clamp pliers, tightly sealing small end of boot against drive axle.

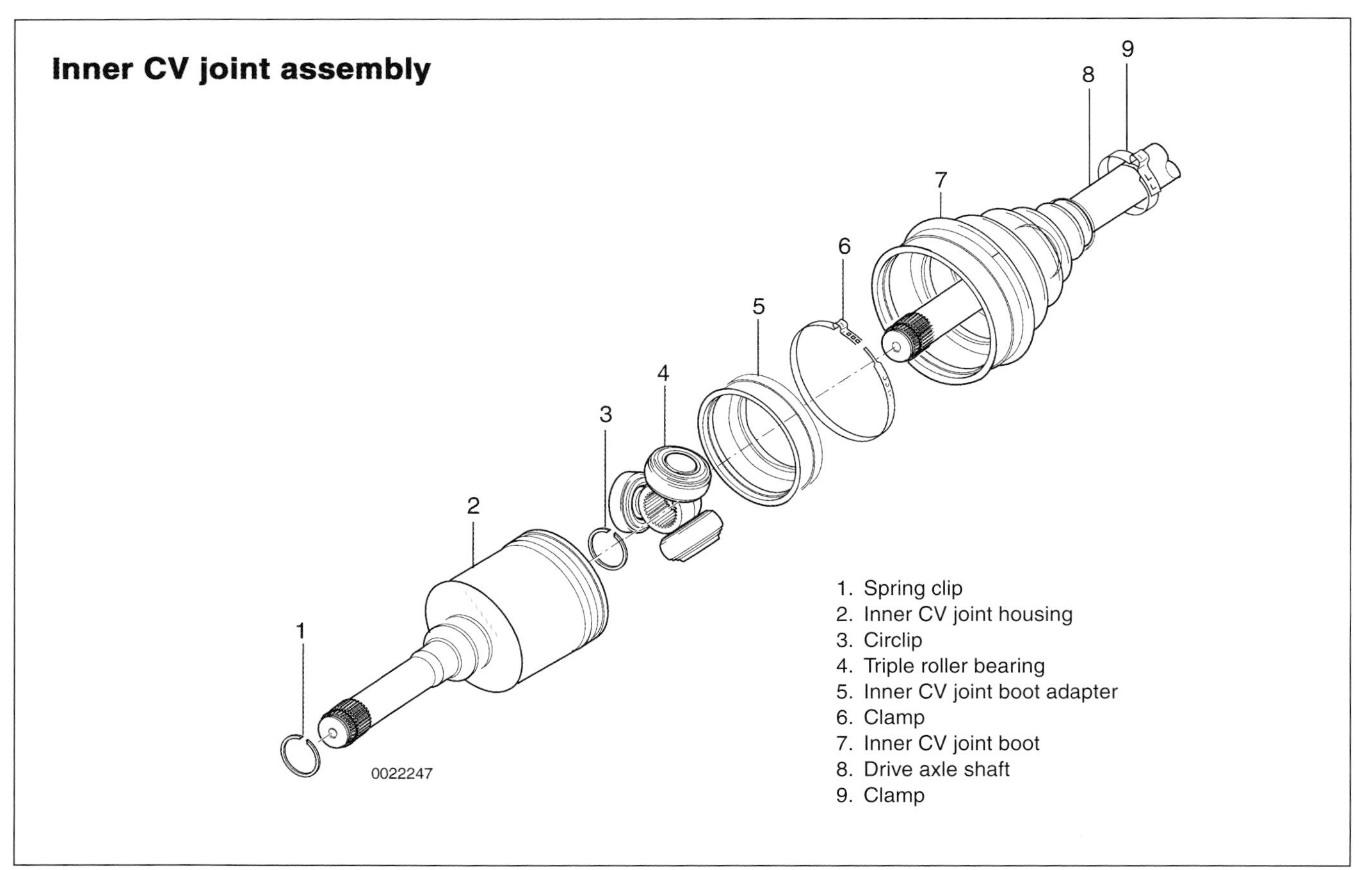

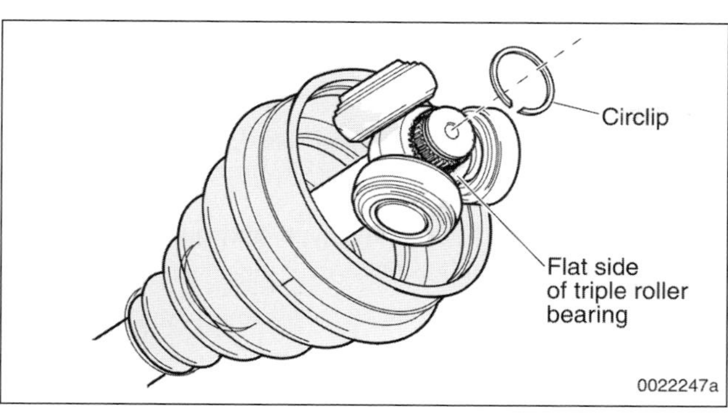

◄ Install triple roller bearing with flat edge of joint facing retaining circlip.

– Replace inner CV joint housing shaft circlip.

– Pack triple roller bearing and inner CV joint boot with fresh grease.

CV joint lubricant capacity
- Inner CV joint . . . . 85 gram (3.0 oz.)

– Insert triple roller bearing into inner CV joint housing.

– Secure boot connection to boot adapter using clamp supplied with boot kit.

– Installation is reverse of removal, noting the following:
- Make sure inboard end of drive axle snaps audibly into place.
- Replace control arm bracket bolts.
- Be sure to restake new collar nut at outboard end of drive axle after tightening to correct torque specifications. Caulk axle threads.
- Top up differential fluid. See **Front differential oil, checking and filling.**

Tightening torques
- Ball joint bracket to front axle subframe . . . . 77 Nm (57 ft-lb)
- Brake caliper to steering arm . . . . 110 Nm (81 ft-lb)
- Control arm bracket to front axle subframe (replace bolts) . . . . . 59 Nm (44 ft-lb)
- Drive flange collar nut to front hub . . . 420 Nm (310 ft-lb)

FRONT DIFFERENTIAL

Procedures for replacement of O-ring seal between the engine oil pan and the front differential or right side bearing pedestal are covered in **Front differential, removing and installing** and **Right axle bearing pedestal, removing and installing**.

Front differential oil, checking and filling

NOTE —
The E46 all wheel drive front differential is filled with lifetime lubricant.

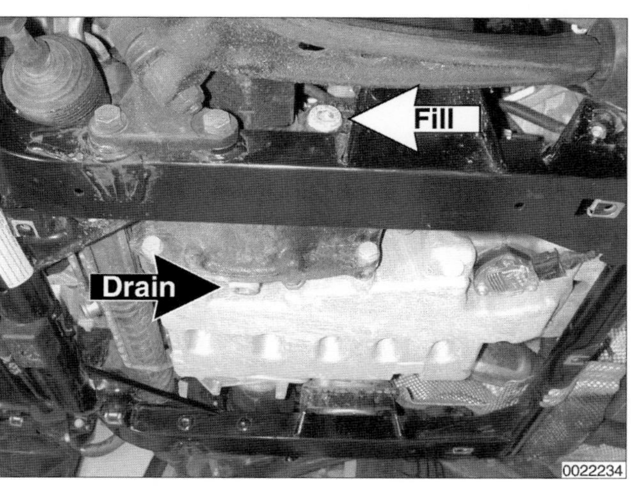

◄ Front differential drain plug and fill plug (**arrows**).

NOTE —
Use an Allen bit socket to remove drain plug. Alternatively, cut approximately 30 mm (1.2 in) from an Allen key and use a box end wrench on key stub.

– Remove oil filler plug.

NOTE —
Differential fluid level is correct when fluid begins to spill from fill plug.

– Fill differential with appropriate type and quantity of lubricant to bottom of fill plug bore.

– Install and tighten fill plug.

Final drive drain and fill
- Oil specifications . . . . BMW SAF-XO synthetic oil
- Front axle differential oil capacity . . . . 0.7 liters (0.74 US qts)

Tightening torque
- Front axle differential drain / fill plug . . . . 65 Nm (48 ft-lb)

Front differential, removing and installing

– Disconnect battery negative (–) ground at battery.

CAUTION —
Prior to disconnecting battery, read battery disconnection cautions given at front of this manual.

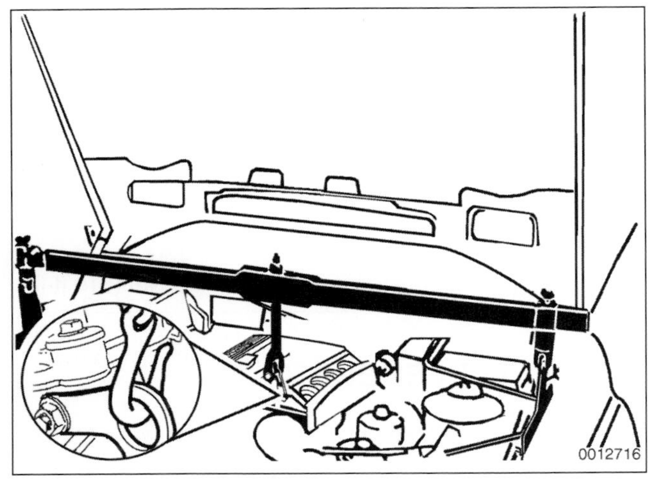

◄ Support engine using appropriate lifting device.

– Lift vehicle and support safely.

WARNING —
Make sure car is stable and well supported at all times. Use a professional automotive lift or jack stands designed for purpose. A floor jack is not adequate support.

– Remove engine splash shield.

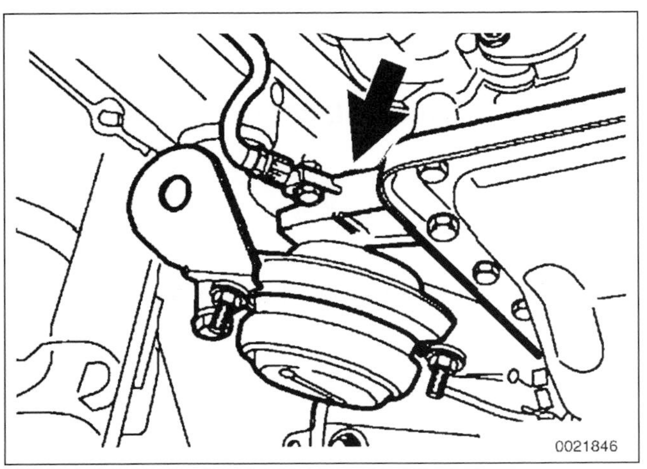

◄ Release nut at top on right engine mount (**arrow**).

0021582

◄ Remove nut (**arrow)** at bottom on left engine mount.

– Raise engine approximately 10 mm (0.4 in).

– Remove front wheels. Unbolt brake calipers and suspend from body using stiff wire. See **340 Brakes**.

– Remove front driveshaft. See **260 Driveshafts**.

0021719

◄ Remove left inner ball joint mounting bracket bolts (**arrows**) from subframe.

– Repeat for right side.

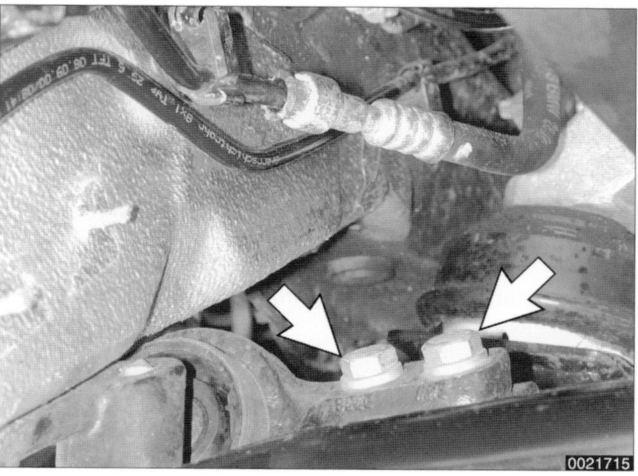
0021715

◄ Support left control arm. Working at rear of subframe, remove control arm rear bracket mounting bolts (**arrows**).

– Repeat for right side.

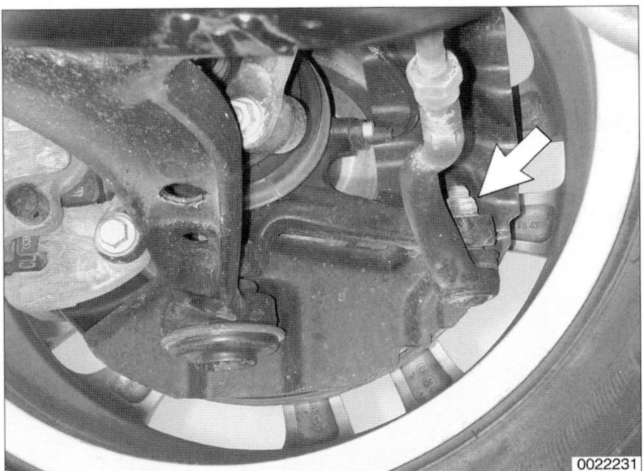

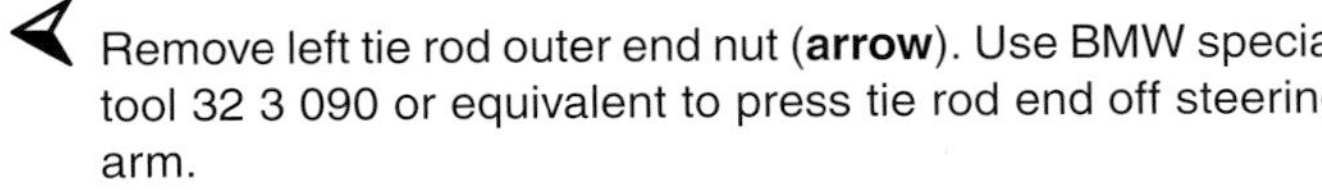

- Remove left tie rod outer end nut (**arrow**). Use BMW special tool 32 3 090 or equivalent to press tie rod end off steering arm.

- Repeat for right side.

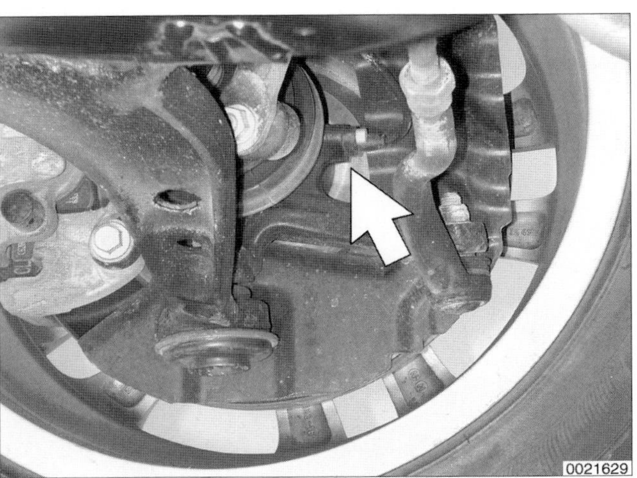

- Remove left ABS sensor (**arrow)** from steering arm.

- Repeat for right side.

- Unclip brake hoses and electrical harness wires from mounting brackets.

- Swing control arms and steering arms out of the way. Using BMW special tool 31 1 170 or equivalent pry bar, pry inner CV joints out of front differential and bearing pedestal.

NOTE —

Be prepared to catch oil drips from differential or right side bearing pedestal.

- Working on left side of car:
  - Release pinch bolt (**arrow**) at top of steering arm.
  - Pull steering arm down from strut assembly.
  - Remove steering arm, drive axle, and control arm assembly as one unit.
  - Repeat for right side.

- Remove lower steering column. See **320 Steering and Wheel Alignment**.

- Remove stabilizer bar anchors from front subframe.

Working underneath car, remove fluid line banjo bolts (**arrows**) from steering rack.

> ***CAUTION —***
> *Plug off power steering lines and connections to keep out contamination.*

– Remove front axle subframe and steering rack from frame rails. **See 310 Front Suspension**.

NOTE —
Make sure heat shields, wiring harnesses and other under body components are clear during removal.

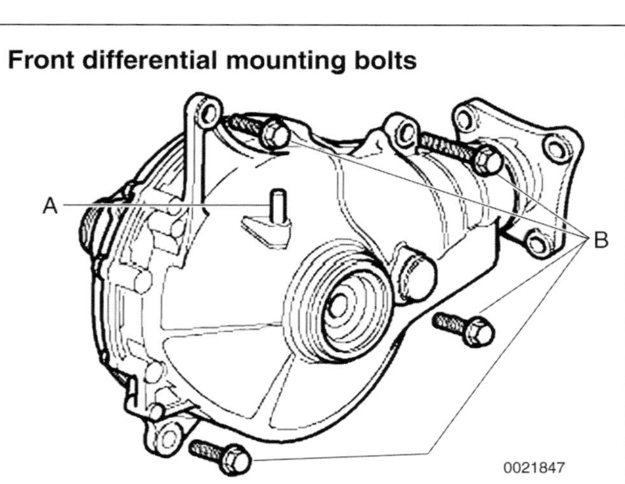

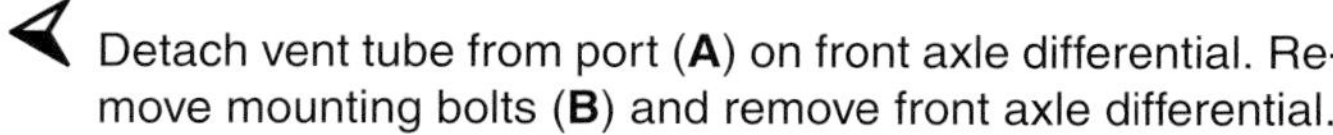
Detach vent tube from port (**A**) on front axle differential. Remove mounting bolts (**B**) and remove front axle differential.

– Install new sealing ring, coating inside edge with assembly lubricant. Push assembly ring up to sealing ring.

NOTE —
- *Replace sealing and assembly rings between oil pan and differential before reinstalling differential.*
- *Assembly ring prevents damage when front axle differential is installed.*
- *When front axle differential is installed on oil pan, the assembly ring is forced over sealing ring and remains in place.*

– Installation is reverse of removal, noting the following:
- Replace drive axle radial seal of differential before installing drive axles.
- Top up differential fluid. See **Front differential oil, checking and filling.**
- Replace sealing rings when reinstalling banjo bolts to steering rack.

Tightening torques
- Brake caliper to steering arm . . . . 110 Nm (81 ft-lb)
- Control arm bracket to front suspension subframe
  (replace bolts) . . . . 59 Nm (44 ft-lb)
- Engine mount to subframe
  M10 self locking nut . . . . 45 Nm (33 ft-lb)
- Front axle differential to oil pan . . . . 45 Nm (33 ft-lb)
- Front axle differential fill plug . . . . 65 Nm (48 ft-lb)
- Hydraulic hoses to power steering pump
  M14 banjo bolt . . . . 35 Nm (26 ft-lb)
  M16 banjo bolt . . . . 40 Nm (30 ft-lb)
- Inner ball joint to
  front suspension subframe . . . . 77 Nm (57 ft-lb)
- Stabilizer bar bushing brackets
  to subframe . . . . 22 Nm (16 ft-lb)
- Steering arm to lower ball joint . . . . 65 Nm (48 ft-lb)
- Steering arm clamping bolt
  at strut housing . . . . 81 Nm (60 ft-lb)

Tightening torques (cont.)

- Steering column to steering rack . . . . . . 22 Nm (16 ft-lb)
- Steering tie rod to steering arm . . . . 65 Nm (48 ft-lb)
- Subframe to body
  M12 (8.8 grade bolt) . . . . 77 Nm (57 ft-lb)
  M12 (10.9 grade bolt) . . . . 110 Nm (81 ft-lb)
  M12 (12.9 grade bolt) . . . . 105 Nm (77 ft-lb)
- Subframe rear to adapter
  M12 bolt (always replace) . . . . 110 Nm (81 ft-lb)

Right axle bearing pedestal, removing and installing

– Lift vehicle and support safely.

> ***WARNING —***
> *Make sure car is stable and well supported at all times. Use a professional automotive lift or jack stands designed for purpose. A floor jack is not adequate support.*

– Remove right front wheel.

– Release nut and remove tie rod end from right steering arm assembly.

– Remove ABS sensor from steering arm.

– Unclip brake hose from mounting bracket.

– Unbolt brake caliper and suspend from body using stiff wire.

◀ Remove inner ball joint mounting bracket bolts (**arrows**) from subframe.

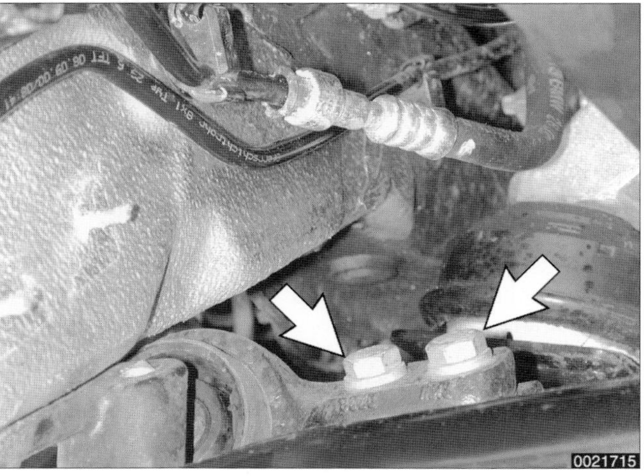

◀ Support control arm. Working at rear of subframe, remove control arm rear bracket mounting bolts (**arrows**).

– Using BMW special tool 31 1 170 or equivalent pry bar, pry inner CV joint out of bearing pedestal.

– Release pinch bolt at top of steering arm. Pull steering arm down from strut assembly and remove steering arm, drive axle, and control arm assembly.

– Remove grounding strap on bearing pedestal. Remove four bolts retaining bearing pedestal to oil pan, and remove pedestal.

– Install new sealing ring, coating inside edge with assembly lubricant. Push assembly ring up to sealing ring.

NOTE —

- *Replace sealing and assembly rings between oil pan and differential before reinstalling differential.*
- *Assembly ring prevents damage when bearing pedestal is installed.*
- *When bearing pedestal is installed on oil pan, the assembly ring is forced over sealing ring and remains in place.*

– Installation is reverse of removal, noting the following:

- Replace drive axle radial seal before installing drive axle.
- Top up differential fluid. See **Front differential oil, checking and filling**.

Tightening torques

- Bearing pedestal to oil pan . . . . 45 Nm (33 ft-lb)
- Brake caliper to steering arm . . . . 110 Nm (81 ft-lb)
- Control arm bracket to front suspension subframe (replace bolts) . . . . 59 Nm (44 ft-lb)
- Inner ball joint to front suspension subframe . . . . 77 Nm (57 ft-lb)
- Steering arm to lower ball joint . . . . 65 Nm (48 ft-lb)
- Steering arm clamping bolt at strut housing . . . . 81 Nm (60 ft-lb)
- Steering tie rod to steering arm . . . . 65 Nm (48 ft-lb)

Input flange radial seal, replacing

– Lift vehicle and support safely.

WARNING —
Make sure car is stable and well supported at all times. Use a professional automotive lift or jack stands designed for purpose. A floor jack is not adequate support.

– Remove front driveshaft. See **260 Driveshafts**.

– Pry out input flange retaining nut lock plate.

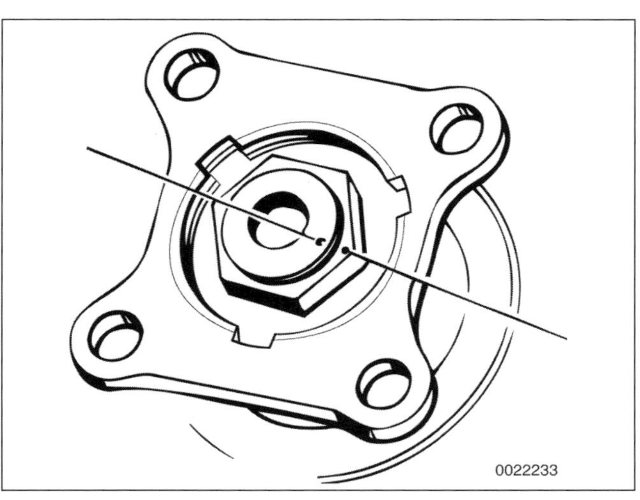

◄ Using a centerpunch, mark relation of input flange retaining nut to output shaft.

0022232

◄ Counterhold input flange using BMW special tool 23 0 020 and remove nut.

– Pull input flange out from differential using hub puller.

– Remove input seal dust shields.

– Using a seal puller or flat screwdriver, pry radial seal out of differential housing.

– Coat sealing edges of radial seal with transmission fluid and drive into differential housing using BMW special tool 31 5 130 or equivalent drift.

– Replace dust shields.

– Clean input flange and install into differential housing.
  - Tighten down nut until punch marks align.
  - Install new input flange retaining nut locking plate.

> ***CAUTION —***
> - *Do not torque input flange retaining nut beyond matchmarks. Over-torquing can damage differential internals.*
> - *Do not replace input flange or input flange locking nut.*

– Installation is reverse of removal.

Tightening torque
- Input flange collar nut to differential . . . . until matchmarks align

320 Steering and Wheel Alignment

TABLES

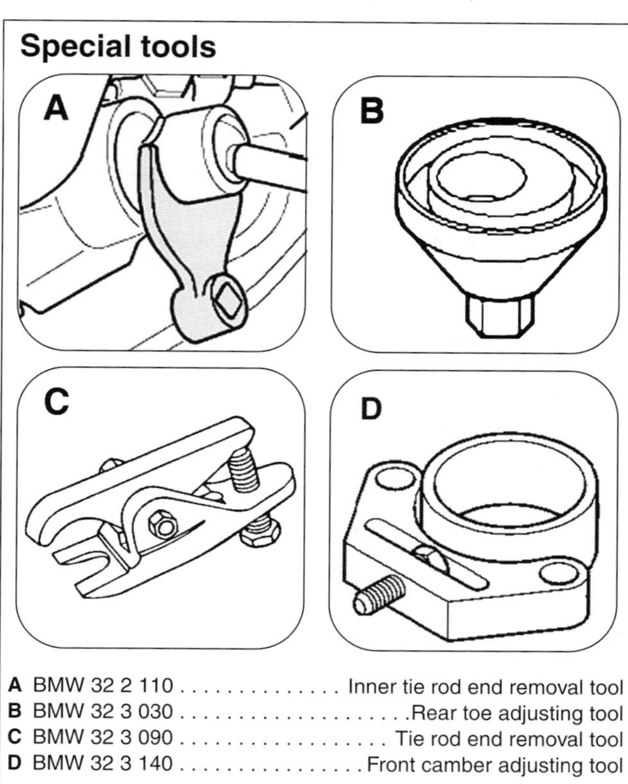

A BMW 32 2 110 . . . . Inner tie rod end removal tool
B BMW 32 3 030 . . . . Rear toe adjusting tool
C BMW 32 3 090 . . . . Tie rod end removal tool
D BMW 32 3 140 . . . . Front camber adjusting tool

GENERAL

This repair group covers steering wheel and column removal and steering system service, including wheel alignment information.

NOTE —
- *Ignition cylinder replacement is covered in this repair group.*
- *For information on steering column mounted switches including the ignition switch, see* **612 Switches.**

Special tools

Some special tools are necessary to carry out the repairs and adjustments required for steering service and wheel alignment. Be sure to read the procedures through before starting work on the vehicle.

Steering system

The variable-assist power steering system consists of an engine-driven hydraulic pump, rack-and-pinion steering rack with integral hydraulic control valve and connecting linkage to road wheels.

At low speeds, maximum power assist is provided to ease parking and city driving. At high speeds, assist is reduced to ensure stability. The power steering system varies assist based on engine speed.

Power assist is provided by a belt-driven pump on the lower left front of the engine, just below the alternator.

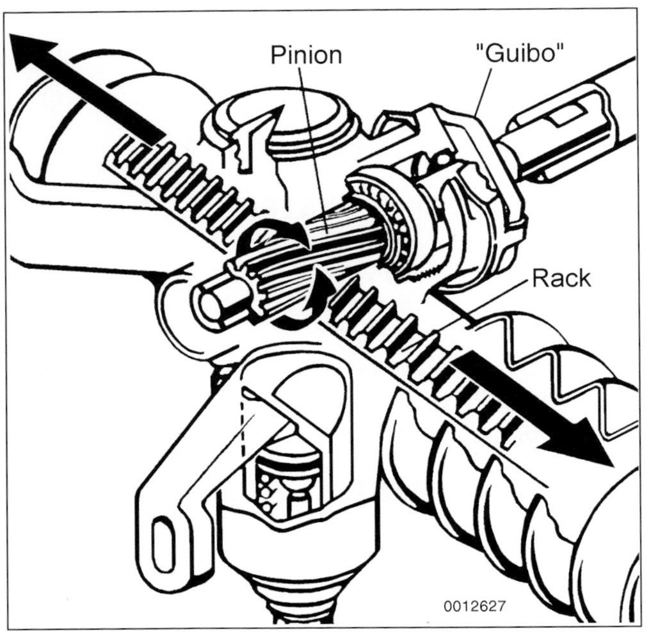

The steering rack is bolted to the front subframe underneath the engine. The steering wheel connects to the rack via a telescoping column which incorporates a rubber coupling ("guibo") to dampen vibration and noise.

The power steering fluid is fed from the fluid reservoir to the pump and to the rack via rubber / metal hoses. The return line from the steering rack to the reservoir loops into the airstream in front of the vehicle and is used as a steering fluid cooler.

The steering rack and linkage require no maintenance other than alignment and periodic inspection for worn components. Inspect rubber rack boots and tie-rod end boots for tears or damage and replace if necessary.

WARNING —

- *The BMW airbag system (MRS) is complex. Special precautions must be observed when servicing the system. Serious injury may result if system service is attempted by persons unfamiliar with the BMW airbag system and its approved service procedures. BMW specifies that all inspection and service should be performed by an authorized BMW dealer.*
- *The BMW E46 is equipped with an airbag mounted in the steering wheel. The airbag is an explosive device and should be treated with extreme caution. Follow the airbag removal procedure as outlined in* **721 Airbag System (SRS)**.
- *BMW airbags are equipped with a back-up power supply inside the airbag control module. After disconnecting the battery, observe a 1 minute waiting period before beginning work on airbag components. This allows the reserve power supply to discharge.*
- *Do not reuse self-locking nuts. They are designed to be used only once and may fail if reused. Replace with new locking nuts.*
- *Do not install bolts and nuts coated with undercoating wax, as correct tightening torque cannot be assured. Clean threads with solvent before installation, or install new parts.*
- *Do not attempt to weld or straighten any steering components. Replace damaged parts.*

NOTE —

The airbag system is traditionally referred to as Supplemental Restraint System (SRS). The BMW version of SRS used in E46 models is known as the Multiple Restraint System (MRS).

STEERING WHEEL

Steering wheel, removing and installing

- Center steering wheel. Make sure front wheels are pointed straight ahead.

- Disconnect negative (–) cable from battery.

> ***CAUTION —***
> *Prior to disconnecting the battery, read the battery disconnection cautions given at the front of this manual.*

- Carefully remove airbag from front of steering wheel. See **721 Airbag System (SRS)**. Store airbag unit in a safe place.

> ***WARNING —***
> *Store the airbag with the horn pad facing up. If stored facing down, accidental deployment could propel it violently into the air, causing injury.*

> ***CAUTION —***
> *Avoid damaging the convenience switches such as radio and cruise controls installed in the steering wheel of some models.*

- Remove steering wheel center bolt.

◄ Confirm steering column and steering wheel factory match marks (**arrow**). Remove steering wheel.

- When reinstalling steering wheel:
  - Align steering wheel and column match marks.
  - Align steering wheel to alignment pins located on steering column switch block.
  - Install steering column center bolt. Do not over-torque.

Tightening torque
- Steering wheel to steering shaft . . . . 63 Nm (46 ft-lb)

- Carefully install airbag.

Tightening torque
- Airbag to steering wheel . . . . 8 Nm (71 in-lb)

NOTE —
The airbag in some models is attached to the steering wheel using spring clips instead of mounting screws. See **721 Airbag System (SRS)**.

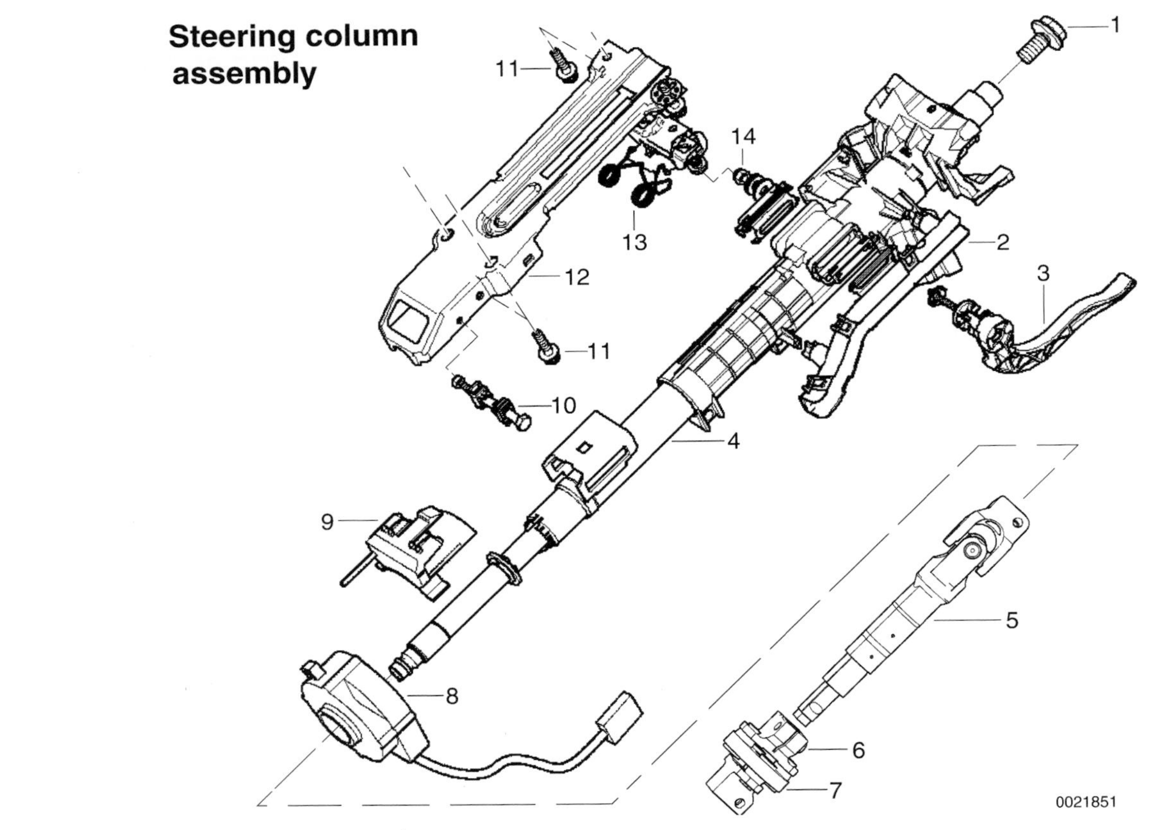

1. Bolt (M14 x 1.5)
   -tighten to 63 Nm (46 ft-lb)
2. Cable duct
3. Steering column adjustment lever
4. Upper steering column
5. Lower steering column with universal joint
6. Torx bolt (M8 x 33)
   -tighten to 22 Nm (16 ft-lb)
7. Flexible joint (guibo)
8. Steering angle sensor
9. Steering angle sensor bracket
10. Column pivot bushing
11. Bolt (M8 x 36)
    -tighten to 22 Nm (16 ft-lb)
12. Steering column mounting bracket
13. Column return spring
14. Nut (M8)
    -tighten to 4.8 Nm (3.5 ft-lb)
    -recheck as necessary

STEERING COLUMN

Ignition lock cylinder, removing and installing

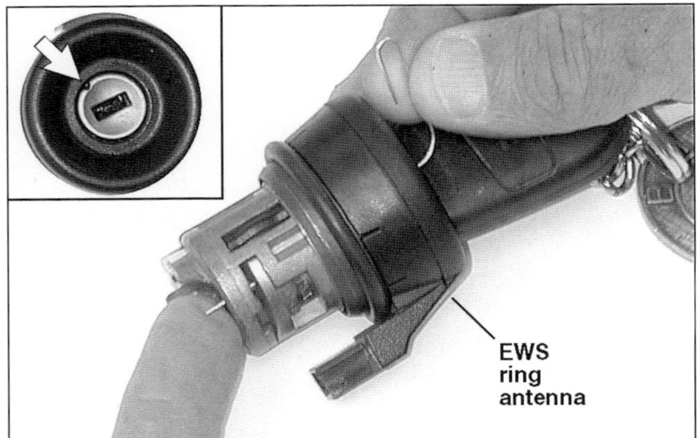

To remove EWS ring antenna prior to removing ignition lock cylinder, remove upper and lower steering column trim. Use BMW special tool 61 3 300 to lever ring antenna off lock cylinder. Alternatively, remove lock cylinder first.

With ignition key in ON position (60° from LOCKED):

- Insert a thin piece of stiff wire into opening (**arrow**) in lock cylinder and pull cylinder out.
- Detach ring antenna harness connector.
- Gently work ring antenna off lock cylinder.
- Reinstallation is reverse of removal.

Lower steering column, removing and installing

– Lift vehicle and support safely.

> ***WARNING —***
> *Make sure the car is firmly supported on jack stands designed for the purpose. Place jack stands underneath structural chassis points, not under suspension parts.*

– Remove engine splash guard.

◄ Remove lower steering column flexible joint pinch bolt (**arrow**). Slide lower column up and pull flexible joint off steering rack shaft.

> ***CAUTION —***
> *When the lower steering column is removed there is no longer an end stop for the steering wheel. To prevent damage to the airbag contact ring in steering column:*
> *-Unlock steering wheel.*
> *-Move steering wheel to straight ahead position.*
> *-Lock steering wheel and remove ignition key.*

NOTE —

Do not remove alignment flange from steering rack.

◄ Working near bulkhead, remove pinch bolt at universal joint and remove lower steering column.

NOTE —
Upper steering column is keyed to lower steering column universal joint. It can only be installed in one position.

◄ Installation is reverse of removal, noting the following:

- Replace flexible and universal joint pinch bolts.
- Align lower steering column to keyed upper steering column.
- Align tab (**arrow**) on steering rack flange with lower steering column flexible joint.

Tightening torque

- Pinch bolt at steering column joint . . . . 22 Nm (16 ft-lb)

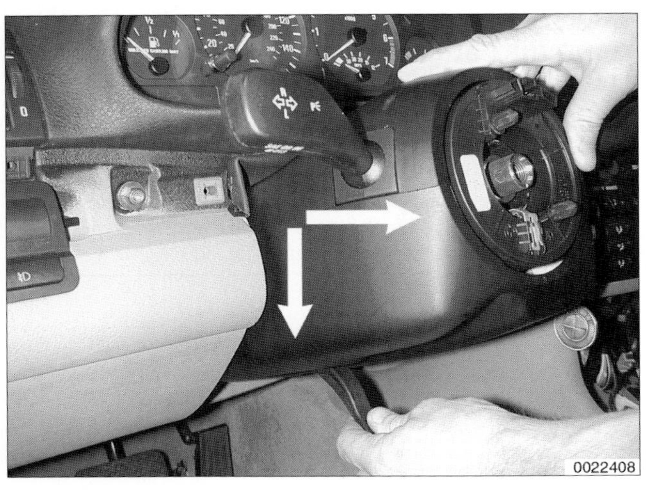

Upper steering column, removing and installing

– Remove steering wheel. See **Steering wheel, removing and installing** in this repair group.

◄ Fully lower and extend (**arrows**) adjustable steering column.

– Remove retaining screw from top of steering column upper trim cover.

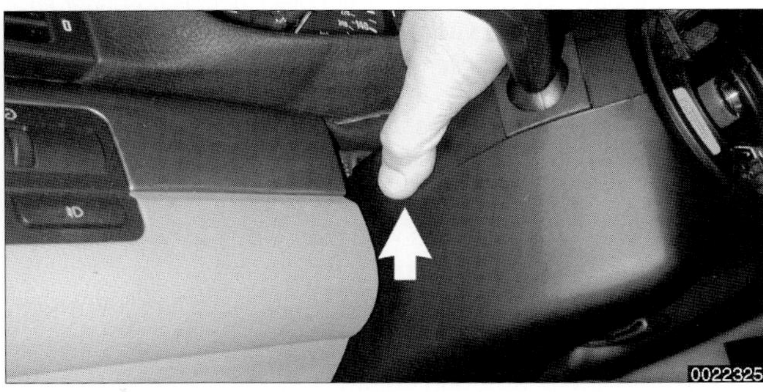

◄ Push in sides of upper trim cover (**arrows**) to release from lower trim. Pull back and up on upper trim.

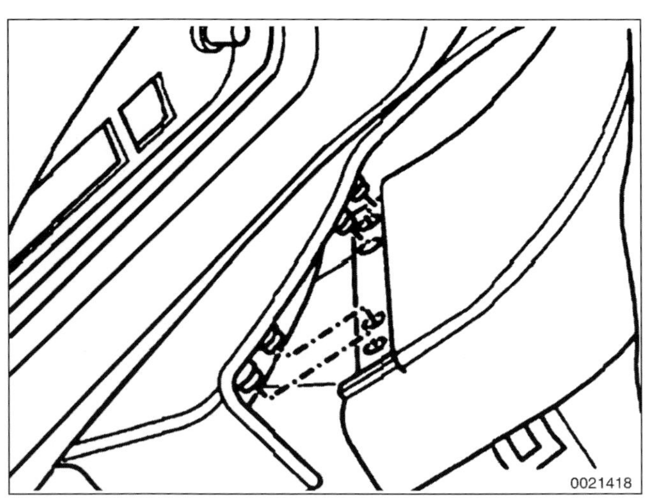

◄ Pry gently to detach flexible cover from upper trim. Lift off trim.

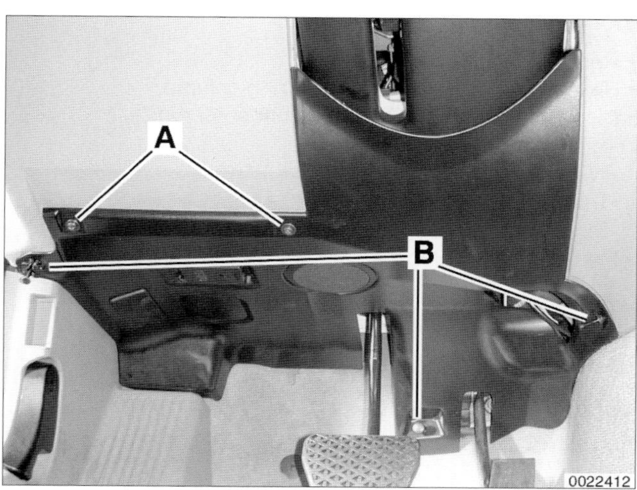

Remove left footwell (pedal cluster) trim panel.

- Remove screws (**A**).
- Remove fasteners (**B**).

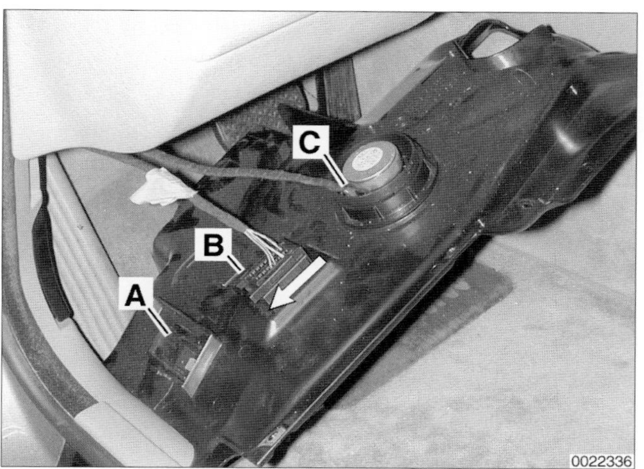

Disconnect electrical harness connectors at left footwell trim panel and remove panel:

- Unplug connector at footwell interior light (**A**), if equipped.
- Slide lock at OBD II connector (**B**) in direction of **arrow**.
- Unplug connector at cellular phone speaker (**C**), if equipped.

– Remove lower steering column. See **Lower steering column, removing and installing** in this repair group.

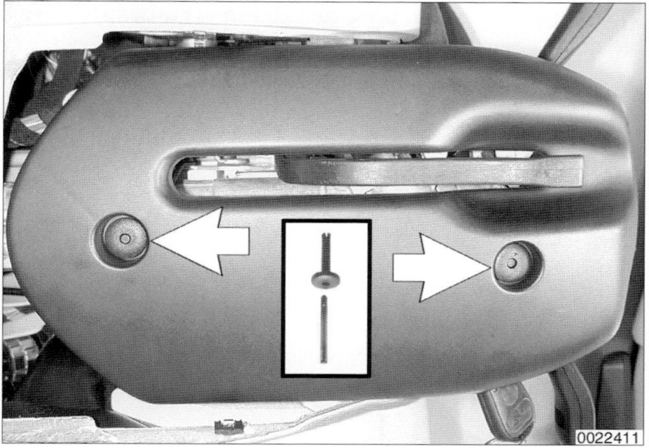

To remove steering column lower trim, drive pins into expansion rivets (**arrows**) to release. Pull down on trim.

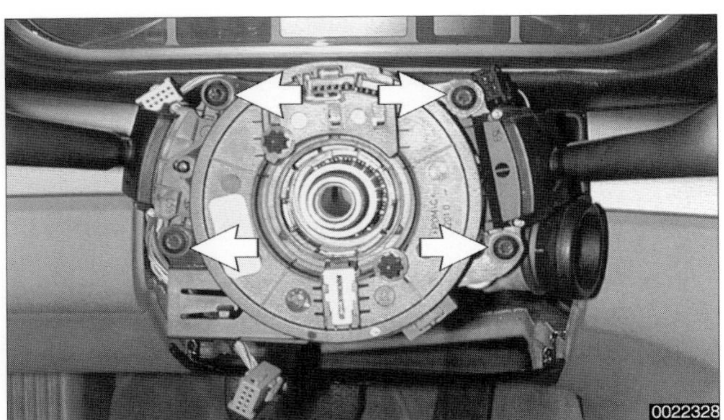

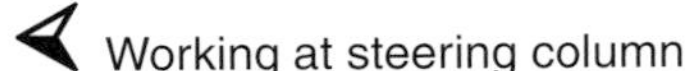
Working at steering column:

- Remove screws (**arrows**).
- Slide switch block out from steering column.
- Disconnect electrical harness connectors at:
  - -Ignition switch
  - -Wiper switch
  - -Turn signal / high beam switch
  - -Steering wheel functions / airbag connector
- Remove switch block.

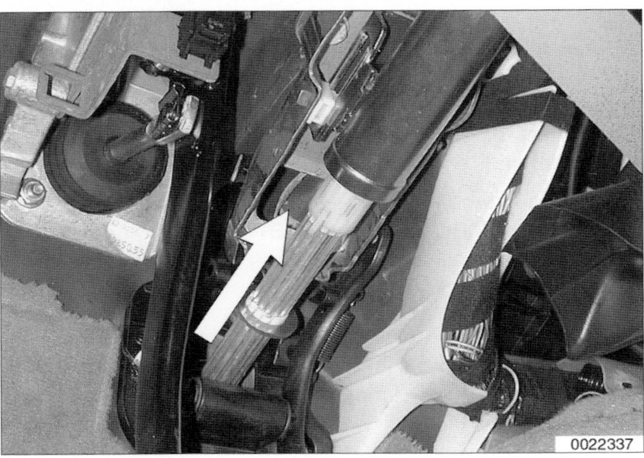

Slide lower section of upper steering column into upper section (**arrow**).

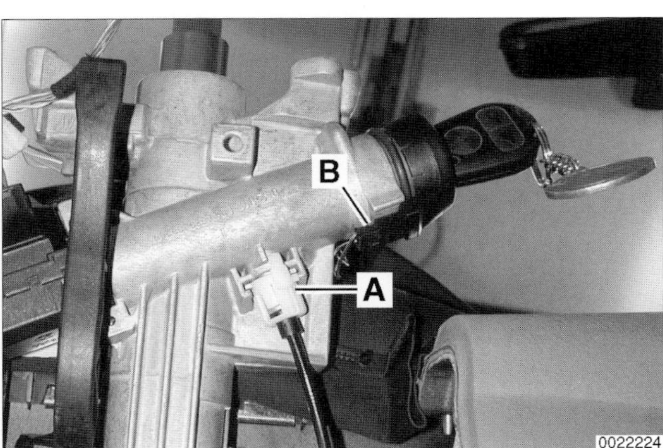

Remove shift interlock cable (**A**) if necessary.

– Disconnect electrical harness connector at EWS ring antenna (**B**).

– Working at steering column, detach wiring harness from cable duct.

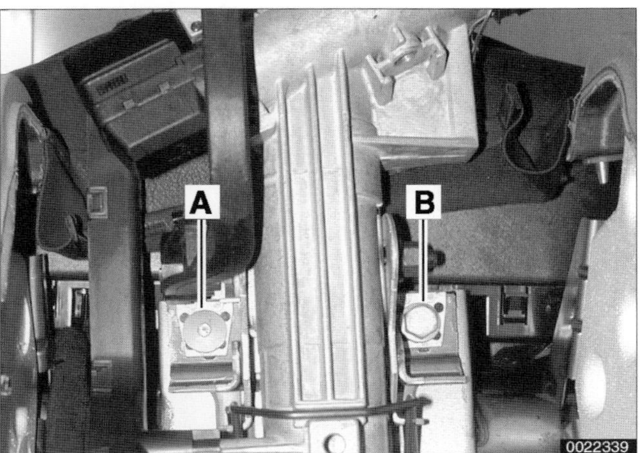

Drill out steering column mounting shear bolt (**A**), and remove mounting bolt (**B**).

< Remove lower steering column mounting bolts (**arrows**). Remove upper steering column.

– Installation is reverse of removal, noting the following:

- Replace shear bolt at steering column mounting bracket. Tighten until bolt head shears off.
- Make sure interlock cable snaps into place.
- When installing column top trim panel, replace expansion nut for trim retaining screw.
- When installing lower trim panel, push expansion rivet pin into rivet until pin head is flush with rivet head.

Tightening torques

- Universal joint pinch bolt at steering column . . . . 22 Nm (16 ft-lb)
- Steering column to dashboard carrier . . . . 22 Nm (16 ft-lb)

POWER STEERING SYSTEM

The power steering fluid reservoir is located on the lower left front of the engine.

CAUTION —

- *Maintain clean conditions when working with open power steering fluid lines.*
- *Plug off opened steering fluid lines and connections to keep out contamination.*

Power steering fluid

- Recommended fluid . . ATF (automatic transmission fluid)

Power steering system, bleeding and filling

– With engine off, fill power steering fluid reservoir with clean fluid. Fill level to **MAX** mark on dip stick.

– Start engine. Slowly turn steering wheel from lock to lock a minimum of two times.

– Turn engine off and check fluid level, adding more if necessary.

Power steering pump, removing and installing

– Empty power steering fluid reservoir using clean syringe. Do not reuse fluid.

– Remove drive belt from power steering pump. See **020 Maintenance**. Mark direction of rotation for reinstallation.

Power steering system

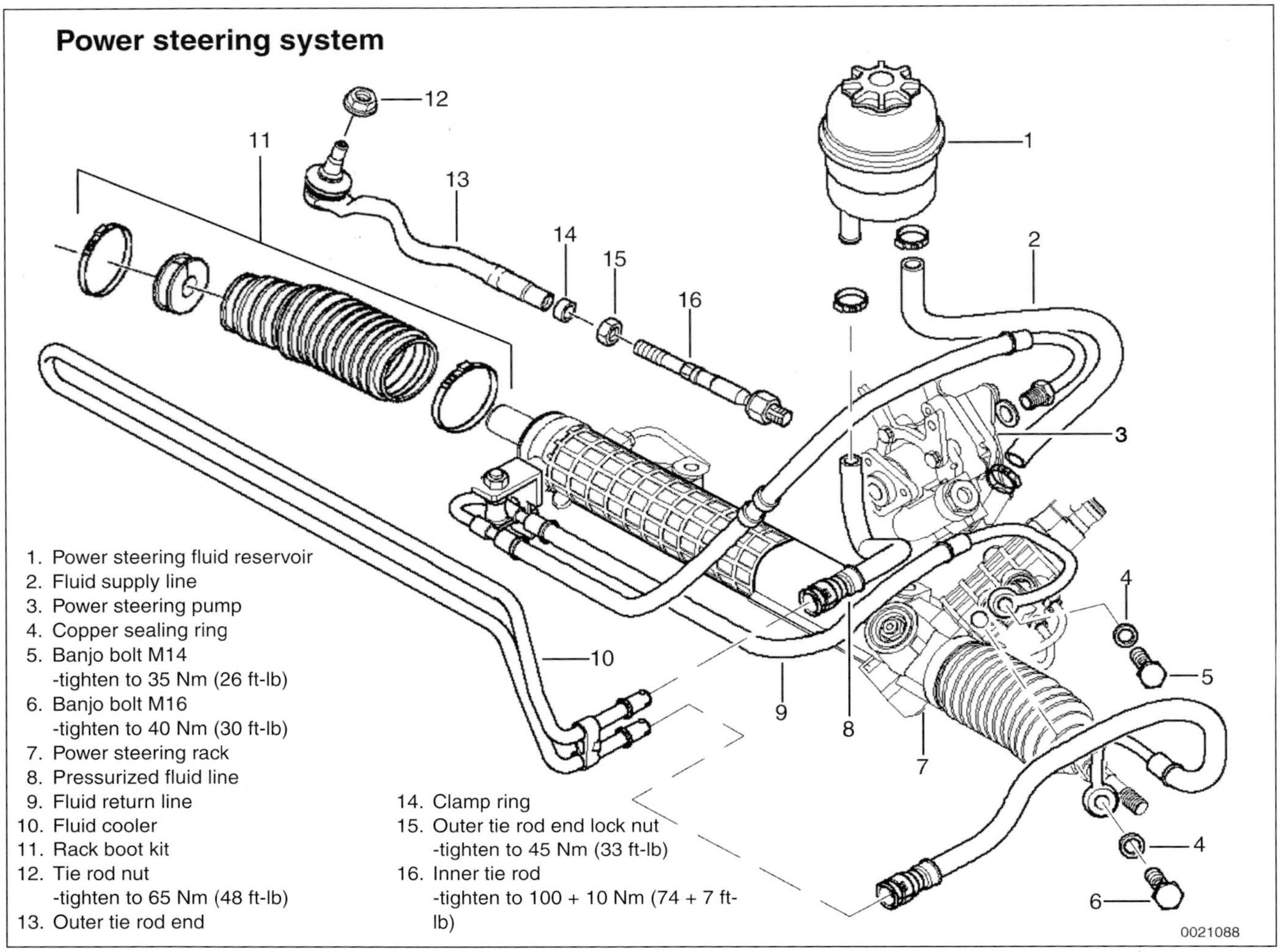

1. Power steering fluid reservoir
2. Fluid supply line
3. Power steering pump
4. Copper sealing ring
5. Banjo bolt M14
   -tighten to 35 Nm (26 ft-lb)
6. Banjo bolt M16
   -tighten to 40 Nm (30 ft-lb)
7. Power steering rack
8. Pressurized fluid line
9. Fluid return line
10. Fluid cooler
11. Rack boot kit
12. Tie rod nut
    -tighten to 65 Nm (48 ft-lb)
13. Outer tie rod end
14. Clamp ring
15. Outer tie rod end lock nut
    -tighten to 45 Nm (33 ft-lb)
16. Inner tie rod
    -tighten to 100 + 10 Nm (74 + 7 ft-lb)

0021088

– Raise front of car. Remove splash shield from under engine.

> ***WARNING —***
> *Make sure the car is firmly supported on jack stands designed for the purpose. Place jack stands underneath structural chassis points, not under suspension parts.*

– Remove power steering pump drive pulley.

– Remove fluid hoses from pump. Plug openings in pump and hose ends.

– Remove brake rotor cooling duct on left side.

– Remove front stabilizer bar anchors and swing stabilizer bar down out of the way. See **310 Front Suspension**.

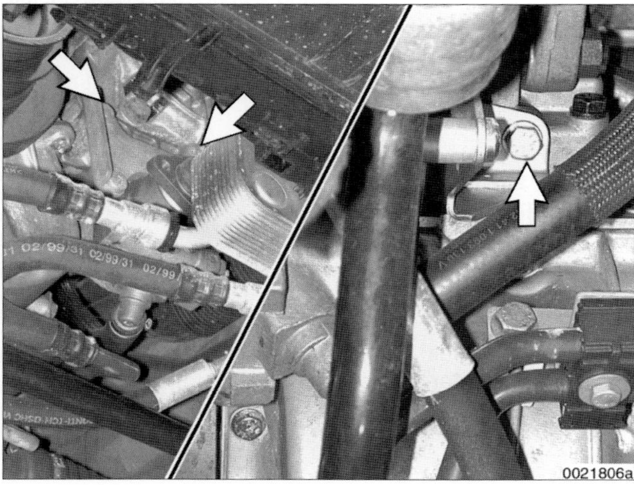

◄ Remove pump mounting bolts (**arrows**) and remove pump. Rear wheel drive model shown.

– Installation is reverse of removal, noting the following:
  - Make sure thread bores, bolts, nuts, fluid couplings and mating surfaces are clean, and inside surface of drive belt is free of grease and dirt.
  - Use new sealing washers when reattaching power steering pressure lines.
  - Make sure hoses have adequate clearance from chassis. Do not over-torque banjo bolts.
  - Fill and bleed power steering system. See **Power steering system, bleeding and filling** in this repair group.

Tightening torques

- Hydraulic hoses to power steering pump
  M14 banjo bolt .... 35 Nm (26 ft-lb)
  M16 banjo bolt .... 40 Nm (30 ft-lb)
- Power steering pump to bracket
  M8 self-locking nuts 22 Nm (16 ft-lb)
- Power steering pump bracket to engine block
  M8 self-locking nuts .... 22 Nm (16 ft-lb)

Steering rack, removing and installing

– Empty power steering fluid reservoir using clean syringe. Do not reuse fluid.

– Raise front of car, and remove wheels. Remove splash shield from under engine.

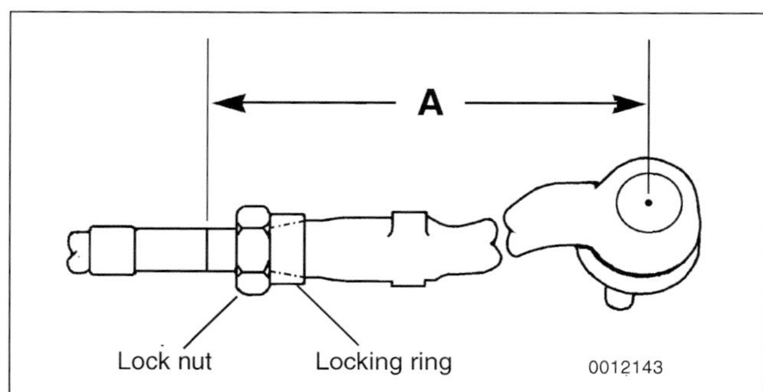

◄ Make reference measurement (**A**) of left outer tie rod end to tie rod. Record measurement.

NOTE —

- *Accurate measurement of the tie rod end with reference to the tie rod will help approximate correct wheel alignment when new parts are installed.*
- *Note correct placement of inner taper on locking ring*

– Repeat for right side.

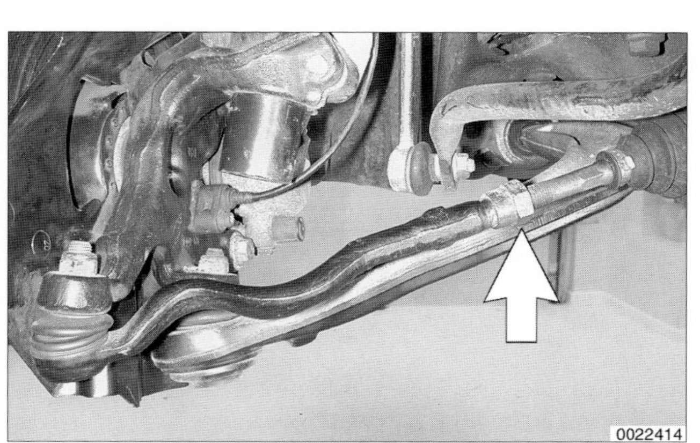

◄ Loosen left outer tie rod end lock nut (**arrow**).

– Unscrew left tie rod end from steering rack by turning inner tie rod shaft.

> ***CAUTION —***
> *Grip end of rack boot to keep it from twisting as the tie rod shaft is unscrewed.*

– Repeat for right tie rod.

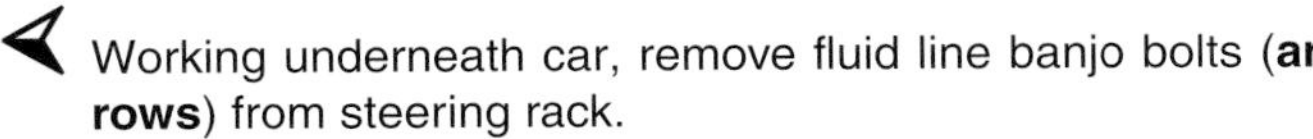

Working underneath car, remove fluid line banjo bolts (**arrows**) from steering rack.

> ***CAUTION —***
> *Plug off power steering lines and connections to keep out contamination.*

NOTE —
It may be necessary to remove other components to gain access to steering rack.

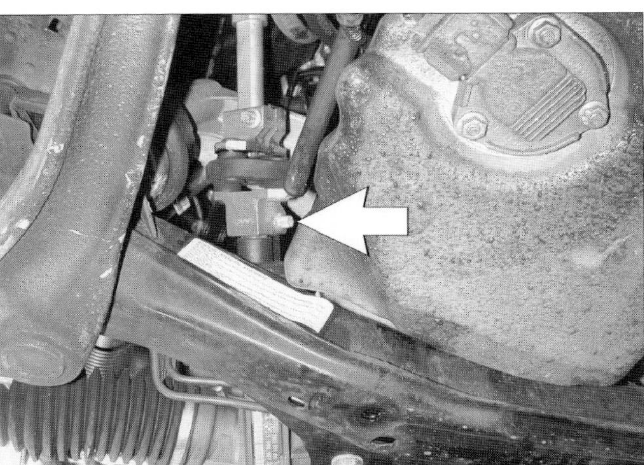

Remove lower steering column flexible joint pinch bolt (**arrow**). Pull flexible joint off steering rack shaft.

> ***CAUTION —***
> *When the lower steering column is detached from the steering rack, there is no longer an end stop for the steering wheel. To prevent damage to the airbag contact ring in steering column:*
> *-Unlock steering wheel.*
> *-Move steering wheel to straight ahead position.*
> *-Lock steering wheel and remove ignition key.*

– All wheel drive:
  - Support front subframe with a shop hoist or appropriate jack.
  - Detach subframe from engine and lower approx. 20 mm (¾ in). See **310 Front Suspension.**

0022424

Remove steering rack mounting bolts (**arrows**). Remove steering rack from subframe by sliding it forward.

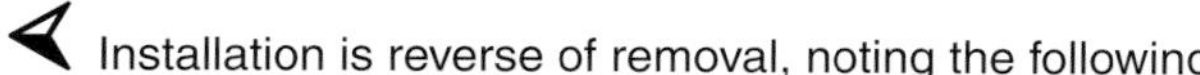

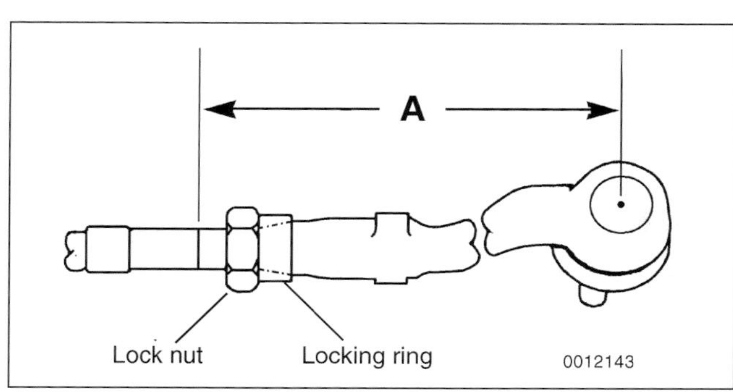

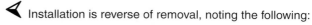

Installation is reverse of removal, noting the following:

- Make sure thread bores, bolts, nuts, splines and mating surfaces are clean. Use anti-seize paste on inner tie rod threads.
- Use new self-locking nuts wherever applicable.
- Use keyed components to reassemble steering column flexible joint to steering rack shaft. Make sure wheels are straight ahead.
- Use new sealing rings on banjo fittings. Do not over-torque banjo bolts.
- Use tie rod measurement previously made (measurement **A**) to temporarily set toe.
- Fill and bleed power steering system as described earlier.
- Have car professionally aligned.

Tightening torques

- Outer tie rod end to steering arm replace self-locking nut . . . . 65 Nm (48 ft-lb)
- Outer tie rod end lock nut . . . . 45 Nm (33 ft-lb)
- Steering column flexible joint to steering rack shaft . . . . 22 Nm (16 ft-lb)
- Steering rack to subframe M10 bolt . . . . 42 Nm (32 ft-lb)
- Steering fluid lines
  M14 banjo bolt . . . . 35 Nm (26 ft-lb)
  M16 banjo bolt . . . . 40 Nm (30 ft-lb)

Outer tie rod end, replacing

– Raise front of car. Remove road wheel.

> ***WARNING —***
> *Make sure the car is firmly supported on jack stands designed for the purpose. Place jack stands underneath structural chassis points, not under suspension parts.*

Remove outer tie rod ball joint nut. Separate outer tie rod end from steering arm using BMW special tool 32 3 090 or equivalent.

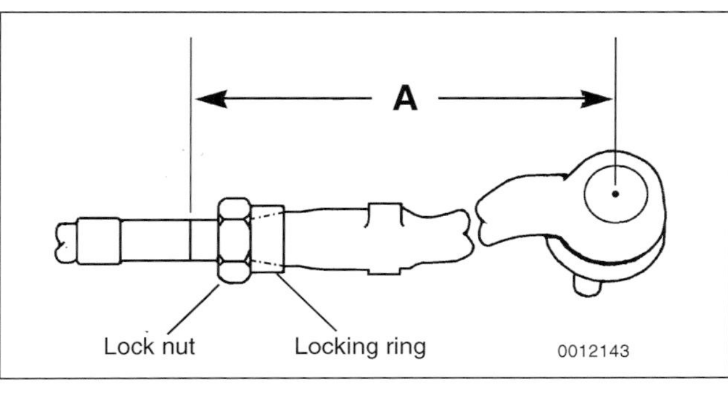

Make reference measurement (**A**) of outer tie rod end to tie rod. Record measurement.

NOTE —

- *Accurate measurement of the tie rod end with reference to the tie rod will help approximate correct wheel alignment when new parts are installed.*
- *Note correct placement of inner taper on locking ring*

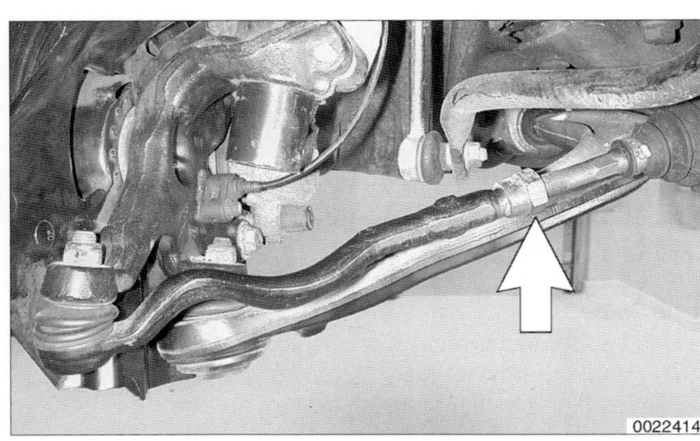

◀ Loosen outer tie rod end lock nut (**arrow**).

– Unscrew tie rod end from tie rod shaft.

– Installation is reverse of removal.
  - Make sure threaded parts are clean. Use antiseize paste on inner tie rod threads.
  - Use new self-locking nuts where applicable.
  - Use tie rod measurement (**A**) to set toe.
  - Have car professionally aligned.

Tightening torques

- Outer tie rod end to steering arm (replace self locking nut) . . . . 65 Nm (48 ft-lb)
- Outer tie rod end lock nut . . . . 45 Nm (33 ft-lb)

Tie rod or rack boot, replacing

– Raise front of car. Remove splash shield from under engine.

> ***WARNING —***
> *Make sure the car is firmly supported on jack stands designed for the purpose. Place jack stands underneath structural chassis points, not under suspension parts.*

– Remove outer tie rod end self-locking nut, and separate outer tie rod end ball joint. See **Outer tie rod end, replacing** in this repair group.

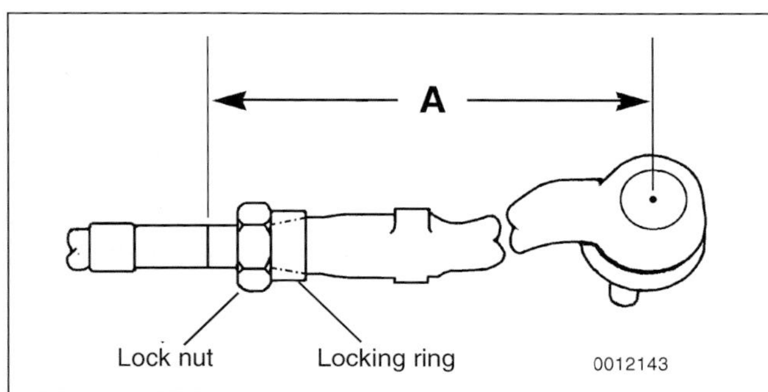

◀ Make a reference measurement of outer tie rod end to tie rod. Record measurement.

NOTE —

- *Accurate measurement of the tie rod end with reference to the tie rod will help approximate correct wheel alignment when new parts are installed.*
- *Note correct placement of inner taper on locking ring*

– Cut rack boot band clamp and slide bellows back. Inspect boot for damage. Replace if necessary.

NOTE —
New rack boot kit comes with new band clamp.

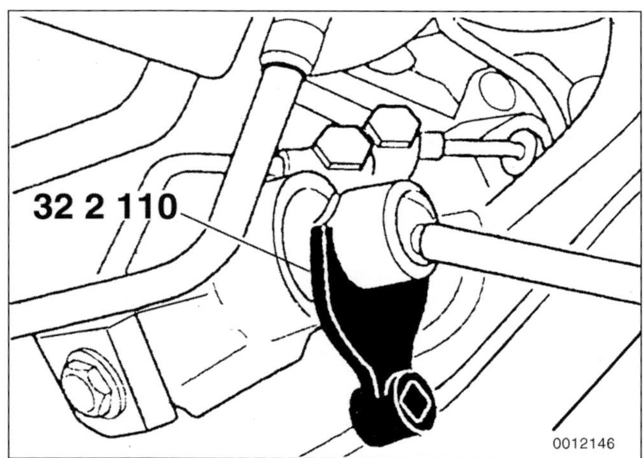

◀ Using BMW special tool 32 2 110 remove inner tie rod shaft from steering rack.

> ***CAUTION —***
> *To avoid damage to steering rack while removing tie rod, turn steering until end of rack is as far as possible in housing*

◄ When reassembling, grease tie rod taper so that rack boot support buffer or small end of rack boot (**inset**) slides on tie rod when tie rod is tightened, preventing rack boot from twisting.

– Installation is reverse of removal, noting the following:

- Make sure threaded parts are clean. Replace self-locking nuts.
- Install outer tie rod end to new tie rod using reference measurement (**A**) recorded earlier.
- Have car professionally aligned.

Tightening torques

- Outer tie rod end to steering arm . . . . . . 65 Nm (48 ft-lb)
- Outer tie rod end lock nut . . . . 45 Nm (33 ft-lb)
- Inner tie rod to steering rack . . 100 + 10 Nm (74 + 7 ft-lb)

WHEEL ALIGNMENT

Proper handling, stability, tire wear and driving ease depend upon the correct alignment of all four wheels. The front axle is aligned in relation to the rear axle, then the front wheels are aligned in relation to one another. This is known as a four-wheel or thrust-axis alignment.

The BMW E46 uses a sophisticated multi-link suspension at the front and rear of the car. Proper alignment requires computerized alignment equipment.

Make sure the following apply prior to alignment:

- Correct wheels and tires in good condition and at correct inflation pressures
- Steering and suspension parts and bushings undamaged with no signs of abnormal wear
- Wheel bearings in good condition
- Ride height in accordance with specifications. See **300 Suspension, Steering and Brakes-General**.
- Car in normal loaded position

See **Table a** for front wheel alignment specifications, **Table b** for rear wheel alignment specifications.

> ***WARNING —***
> *While performing alignment procedures, make sure the car is stable and well supported at all times. Use a professional automotive lift or jack stands designed for the purpose. A floor jack is not adequate support.*

Normal loaded position

- Each front seat . . . . .68 Kg (150 lb)
- Rear seat (center). . . . . .68 Kg (150 lb)
- Trunk . . . . .21 Kg (46 lb)
- Fuel tank. . . . . .full

Table a. Front wheel alignment specifications

Parameter	Standard suspension	All wheel drive suspension	Sport suspension	Rough road suspension	M3 suspension
Toe angle (total)	0° 14' ± 8'				0° 16' ± 7'
Camber (difference between left/right max. 30') track differential angle with 20° lock on inside wheel	–20' ± 20' –1° 34' ± 30'	20' ± 20' –53' ± 30'	43' ± 20' –1° 34' ± 30'	+8' ± 20' –1° 34' ± 30'	–1° ± 20' –1° 32' ± 30'
Caster (difference between left/right max. 30') with ± 10° wheel lock with ± 20° wheel lock	 5° 26' ± 30' 5° 37' ± 30'	 5° 27' ± 30' 5° 37' ± 30'	 5° 36' ± 30' 5° 47' ± 30'	 5° 17' ± 30' 5° 27' ± 30'	 7° 25' ± 30' 7° 40' ± 30'
Front wheel displacement	0° ± 15'				0° ± 10'

Table b. Rear wheel alignment specifications

Parameter	Standard suspension	All wheel drive suspension	Sport suspension	Rough road suspension	M3 suspension
Toe angle (total)	0° 16' ± 6'				0° 22' ± 6'
Camber (difference between left/right max. 15') maximum allowable deviation between sides	–1° 30' ± 15'	–1° 15' ±15'	–2° 04' ±15'	–46' ±15'	–1° 45' ±15'
Geometrical axis deviation	0° ± 6'				0° ± 4'

Front wheel camber

Any change to the camber will also change the toe setting. Always adjust camber prior to adjusting toe.

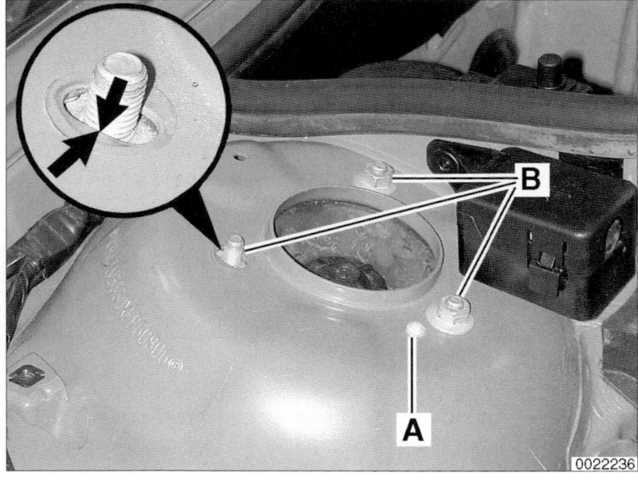

Front wheel camber adjustment can be made by driving out factory strut alignment pin (**A**) in upper strut housing.

– Loosen upper strut mount nuts (**B**).

– Use BMW special tool 32 3 140 to adjust position of upper strut mount studs in slotted holes (**arrows**).

Tightening torque
- Upper strut mount to body . . . . 24 Nm (17 ft-lb)

Front wheel toe

Front wheel toe is adjusted at tie rod ends:

- Loosen tie rod lock nut (**A**).
- Adjust tie rod by turning inner tie rod (**B**) to change length.

NOTE —

- *Steering rack can be centered by aligning centering mark on steering shaft with lug on steering rack.*
- *To keep steering wheel centered, adjust both tie rods equal amounts.*
- *Make sure the rubber boot on the rack moves freely on the tie rod and does not twist.*

Tightening torque

- Tie rod lock nut . . . . 45 Nm (33 ft-lb)

Rear wheel camber

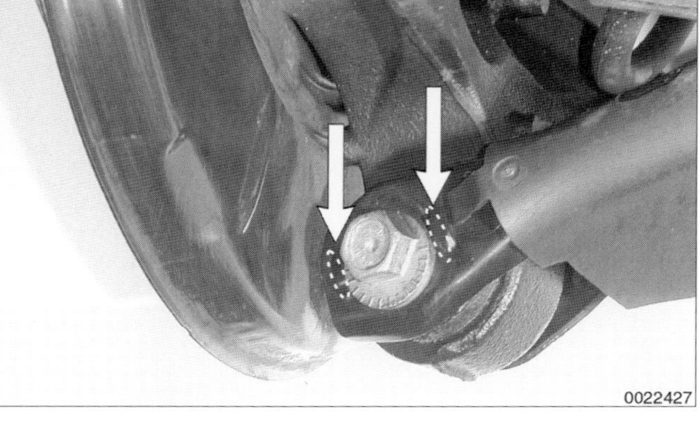

Rear wheel camber is adjusted at outer end of rear lower control arm using camber adjusting bolt.

- Make sure bolt remains between two alignment lugs (**arrows**) on end of control arm.
- Check toe setting. See **Rear wheel toe** in this repair group.

Tightening torque

- Rear lower control arm to rear trailing arm. . . . . 77 Nm (57 ft-lb)

Rear wheel toe

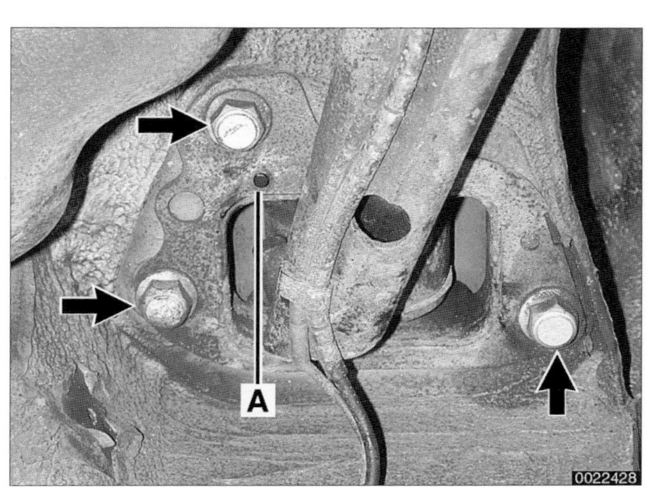

Loosen trailing arm bracket mounting bolts (**arrows**).

– Install BMW special tool 32 3 030 over alignment lug (**A**) and adjacent bolt.

- Use tool to adjust position of bracket.
- Remove tool and tighten trailing arm bracket mounting bolts.

Tightening torque

- Rear trailing arm bracket to body . . . . . . 77 Nm (57 ft-lb)

330 Rear Suspension

Special tools

A BMW I 00 7 500 . . . . Wheel bearing splitter
B BMW set 33 2 115/116/119 . . . . .Drive axle press
C BMW set 33 2 116/4 201/4 202/4 203 . . . . Flange puller
D BMW set 33 4 400 . . . . Inner wheel bearing race puller
E B90 . . . . Wheel bearing extractor
(Source: Baum Tools Unlimited)

GENERAL

This repair group covers removal and replacement of E46 rear suspension components.

A general description of the rear suspension, ride height specifications and a troubleshooting guide is in **300 Suspension, Steering and Brakes–General**.

For additional information, see:

- **310 Front Suspension**
- **311 Front Axle Final Drive**
- **320 Steering and Wheel Alignment**
- **331 Rear Axle Final Drive**

Special tools

Special service tools are recommended for some of the work described in this repair group. Most of these tools are specialized presses and pullers. It may be possible to substitute standard presses and pullers of various sizes.

Read the procedures through before beginning any job.

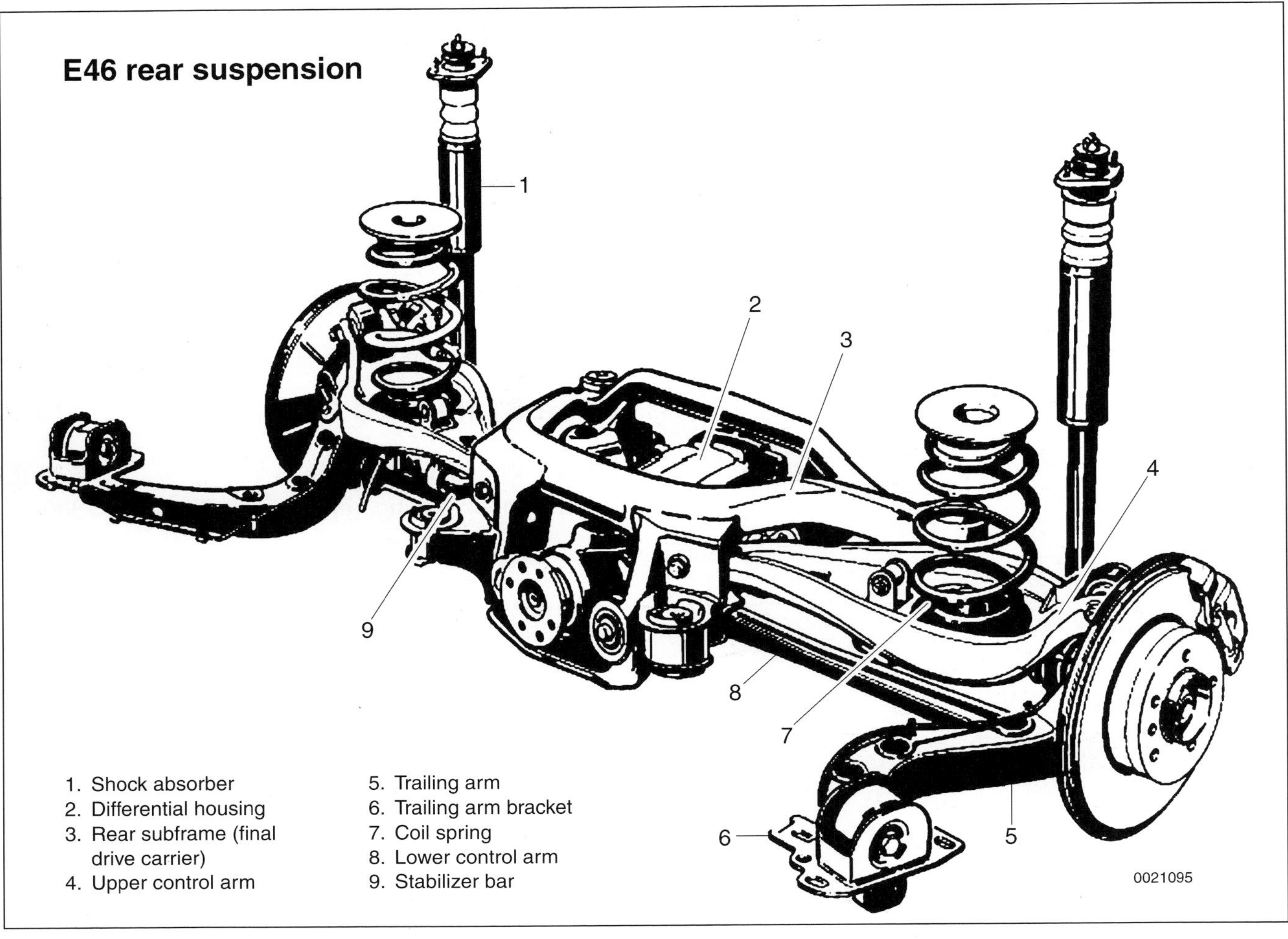

Rear suspension description

BMW uses an independent rear suspension consisting of an upper and a lower control arm and a trailing arm on each side. The weight of the car is supported by coil springs. There is a rear stabilizer bar attached to the upper control arms. Gas-pressure shock absorbers round out the rear suspension.

The rear subframe (final drive carrier) supports the rear differential and provides mounting points for the upper and lower control arms. The upper control arm on each side provides the lower spring perch for the coil spring. The upper and lower control arm on each side are attached to the trailing arm. The trailing arms contain the wheel bearings for the rear drive hubs. Rear brake calipers are bolted to the trailing arms.

REAR SHOCK ABSORBERS AND SPRINGS

Replace shock absorbers and springs in pairs only.

Rear shock absorber, removing and installing

– Raise car and remove rear wheels.

> ***WARNING —***
> *Make sure the car is firmly supported on jack stands designed for the purpose. Place jack stands underneath structural chassis points, not under suspension parts.*

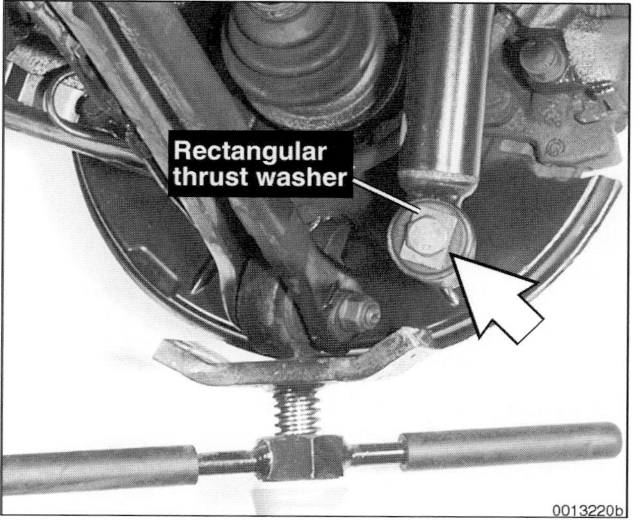

◀ Support trailing arm from below using an adjustable jackstand. Remove shock absorber lower mounting bolt (**arrow**).

> ***CAUTION —***
> *The shock absorber prevents the drive axle from dropping too far. Support the trailing arm before removing the lower shock absorber bolt to avoid damage to drive axle CV joints.*

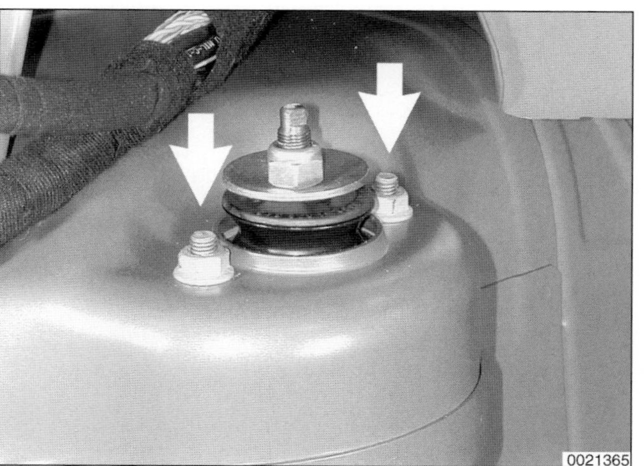

◀ Sedan or Coupe: Working in trunk, pry out trim liner retaining clips. Peel back liner to gain access to upper shock absorber mounting nuts (**arrows**).

– Convertible: Open convertible top storage compartment to access upper shock absorber mount.

– Sport Wagon: Working in cargo compartment, remove side trim next to rear seat backrests.

– Support shock absorber from below while removing upper mounting nuts. Lower shock absorber out of wheel housing.

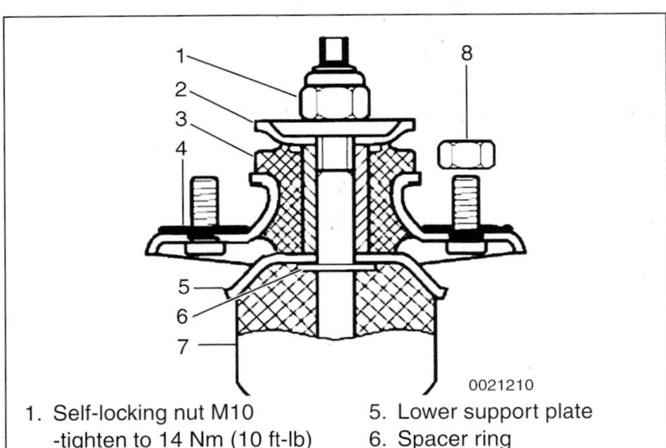

1. Self-locking nut M10 -tighten to 14 Nm (10 ft-lb)
2. Upper support plate
3. Top mounting plate
4. Body seal
5. Lower support plate
6. Spacer ring
7. Rubber bump stop
8. Self-locking nut M8 -tighten to 24 Nm (17 ft-lb)

Transfer shock absorber top mounting plate, dust cover (if applicable) and related components to new shock absorber.

– Installation is reverse of removal, noting the following:
  - Make sure all threaded bolts, nuts and mating surfaces are clean.
  - Install shock absorber into shock tower using a new upper mounting seal and new self-locking nuts.
  - Make sure rectangular thrust washer on lower mounting bolt is between bolt head and shock absorber rubber.
  - Tighten lower shock absorber bolt to its final torque once car is on ground.

Tighting torques

- Road wheel to hub . . . . 120 ± 10 Nm (90 ± 7 ft-lb)
- Shock absorber to trailing arm (car in normal loaded position) . . . . 100 Nm (74 ft-lb)
- Shock absorber to upper mount . . . . 14 Nm (10 ft-lb)
- Shock absorber upper mount to body M8 self-locking nuts . . . . 28 Nm (21 ft-lb)

Coil spring, removing and installing

– Raise car and remove rear wheel.

Remove drive axle to differential mounting bolts (**arrows**).
  - Detach drive axle from differential.
  - Suspend drive axle from chassis using stiff wire.

– M3: Remove rear reinforcing V-brace.

– Remove rear underbody splash shields as applicable.

– Detach stabilizer bar from rear subframe.

Remove rear brake line bracket mounting bolt (**arrow**). Detach bracket from trailing arm.

> ***CAUTION —***
> *Avoid damaging the brake hose by stretching when the trailing arm is lowered.*

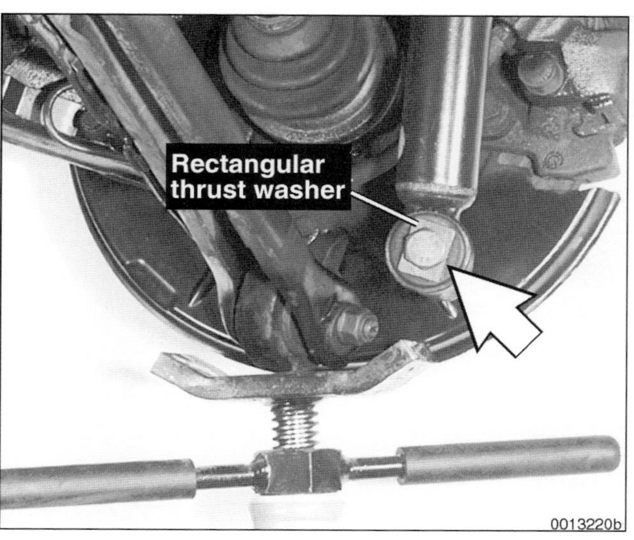

◀ Support trailing arm from below using an adjustable jack-stand. Remove shock absorber lower mounting bolt (**arrow**).

– Lower trailing arm slowly and carefully until the compressed coil spring is fully unloaded. Remove spring.

– If spring is to be reused:

- Inspect spring for any surface damage or corrosion.
- Inspect top and bottom spring seat rubber pads for signs of damage.
- Replace parts showing evidence of wear or damage.

NOTE —

In the "rough road package", the top spring seat pad is 14.5 mm (0.57 in) thick.

– To install spring:

- Coat top spring pad with anti-friction paste (*e.g.*, tire mounting paste).
- Slowly lift suspension back into position, making sure coil spring is correctly seated in upper and lower spring seats.
- When suspension is lifted sufficiently, reattach shock absorber to trailing arm. Make sure rectangular thrust washer on lower shock absorber mounting bolt is between bolt head and shock absorber rubber.
- Tighten lower shock absorber bolt to its final torque once car is on ground.

– Remainder of installation is reverse of removal.

Tightening torques

- Drive axle to differential flange
  M10 x 20 mm Torx bolt . . . . 83 Nm (61 ft-lb)
  M10 x 46 mm bolt (black) . . . . 100 Nm (74 ft-lb)
  M10 x 46 mm bolt (silver)
  (always replace) . . . . 80 Nm (59 ft-lb)
- Road wheel to hub . . . . 120 ± 10 Nm (90 ± 7 ft-lb)
- Shock absorber to trailing arm
  (car in normal loaded position) . . . . 100 Nm (74 ft-lb)
- V-brace to differential or body
  (M10, use new bolts). . . . . .59 Nm (44 ft-lb) + 90°

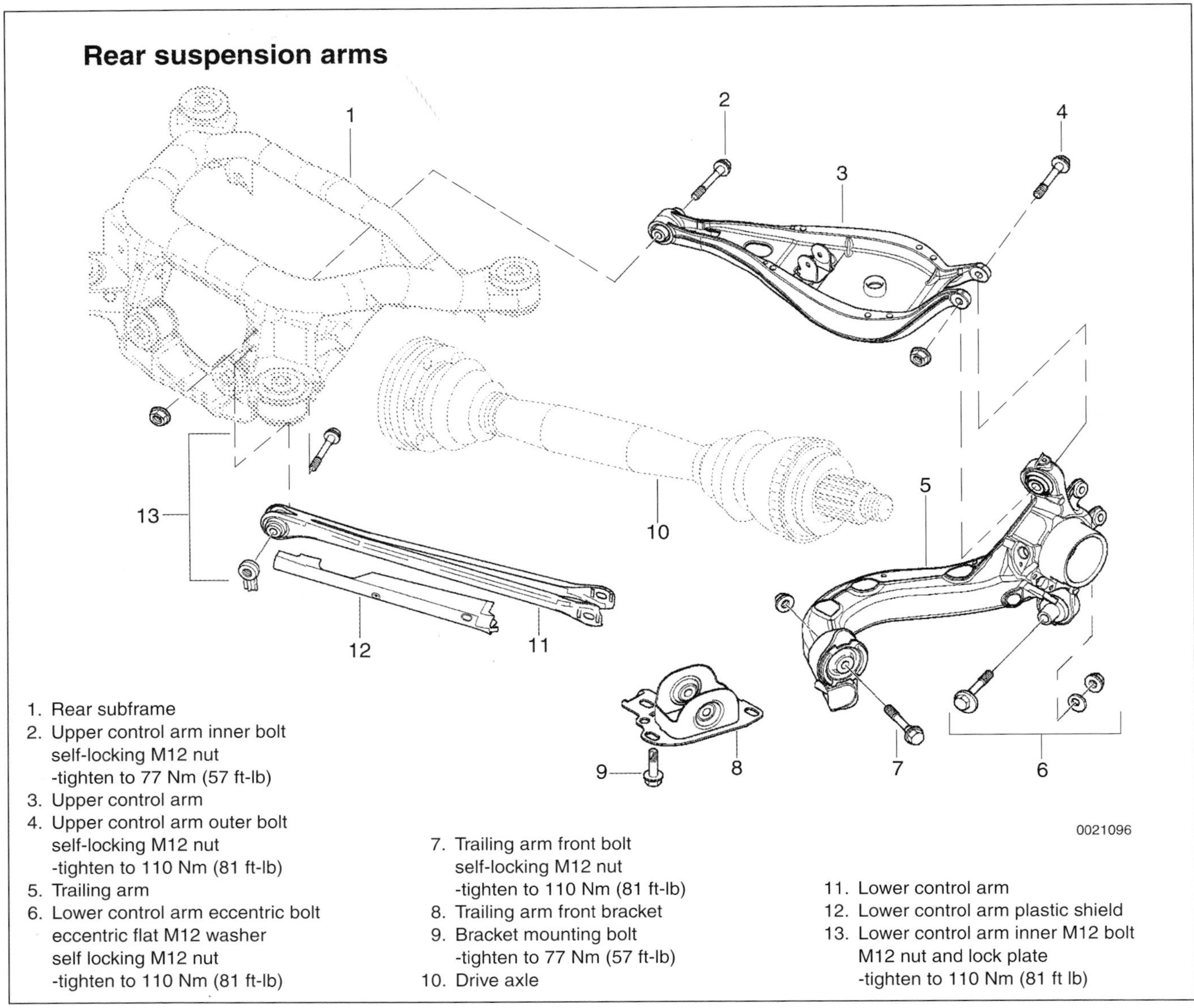

1. Rear subframe
2. Upper control arm inner bolt
   self-locking M12 nut
   -tighten to 77 Nm (57 ft-lb)
3. Upper control arm
4. Upper control arm outer bolt
   self-locking M12 nut
   -tighten to 110 Nm (81 ft-lb)
5. Trailing arm
6. Lower control arm eccentric bolt
   eccentric flat M12 washer
   self locking M12 nut
   -tighten to 110 Nm (81 ft-lb)
7. Trailing arm front bolt
   self-locking M12 nut
   -tighten to 110 Nm (81 ft-lb)
8. Trailing arm front bracket
9. Bracket mounting bolt
   -tighten to 77 Nm (57 ft-lb)
10. Drive axle
11. Lower control arm
12. Lower control arm plastic shield
13. Lower control arm inner M12 bolt
    M12 nut and lock plate
    -tighten to 110 Nm (81 ft lb)

REAR SUSPENSION ARMS, SUBFRAME AND BUSHINGS

The trailing arms, control arms and rear suspension bushings control the position of the rear wheels. A damaged suspension arm or worn bushings changes rear wheel alignment and may adversely affect handling and stability.

> ***WARNING —***
> *Do not attempt to straighten a damaged suspension arm. Bending or heating may weaken the original part. If the suspension arm shows any signs of damage or excessive corrosion, replaced it.*

Trailing arm, removing and installing

– Raise rear end of car and remove wheel.

> ***WARNING —***
> *Make sure the car is firmly supported on jack stands designed for the purpose. Place jack stands underneath structural chassis points, not under suspension parts.*

– M3: Remove rear reinforcing V-brace.

– Remove rear underbody splash shields as applicable.

– Remove drive axle. See **331 Rear Axle Final Drive**.

– Right side: Detach brake pad sensor connector at brake caliper.

– Remove brake rotor and caliper. See **340 Brakes**. Do not remove brake line from caliper. Suspend caliper from body using stiff wire.

– Remove parking brake cable from brake shoe expander. See **340 Brakes**.

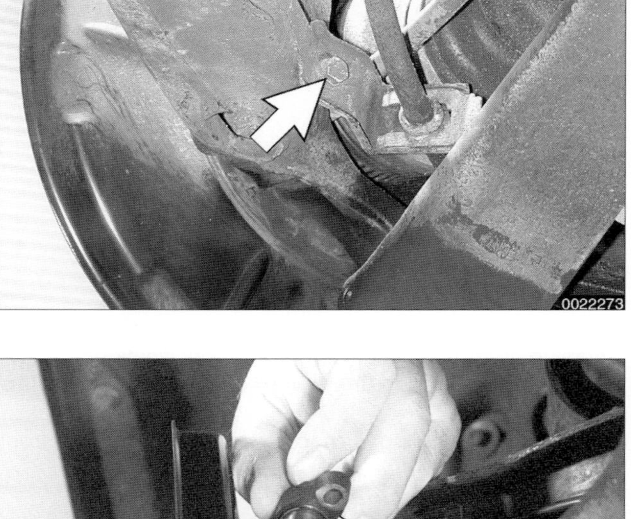

◄ Remove rear brake line bracket mounting bolt (**arrow**). Detach bracket from trailing arm.

> ***CAUTION —***
> *Avoid damaging the brake hose by stretching when the trailing arm is lowered.*

◄ Remove ABS pulse sensor from trailing arm.

– Unclip pulse sensor and pad sensor (if applicable) harnesses from control arm and lay aside.

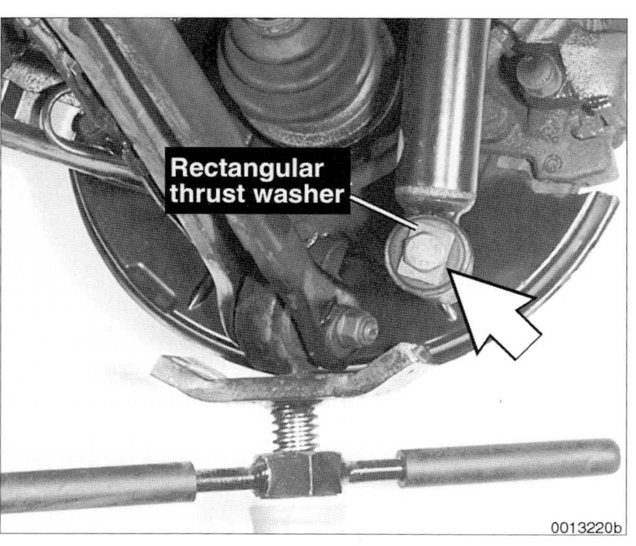

Support trailing arm from below using an adjustable jack-stand. Remove shock absorber lower mounting bolt (**arrow**).

- Slowly lower suspension until coil spring can be safely removed.

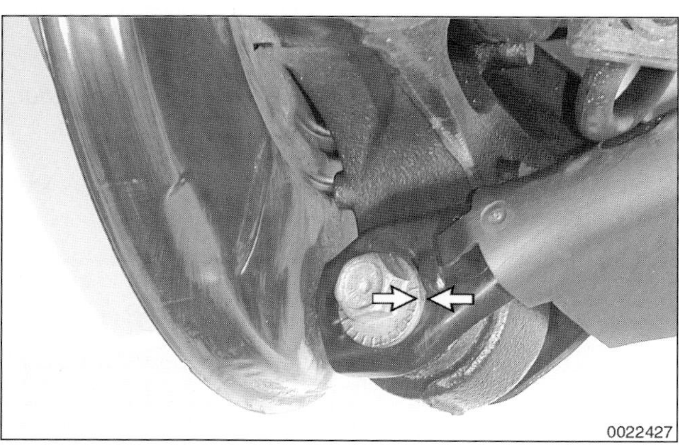

Mark position (**arrows**) of lower control arm eccentric mounting bolt.

- Unbolt upper and lower control arms from trailing arm. Note direction of bolt insertion in both arms.

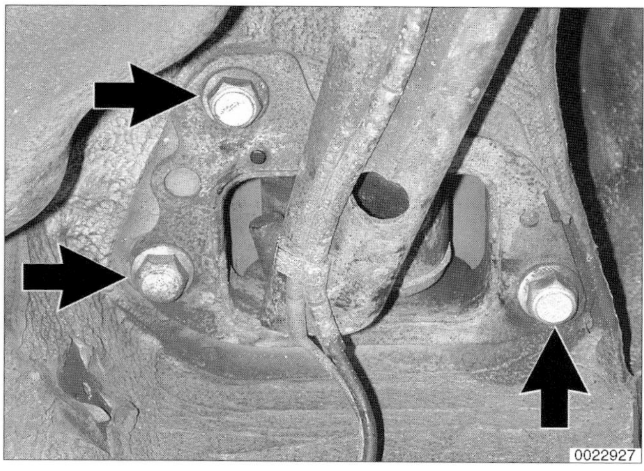

To remove trailing arm:

- Make reference marks to locate trailing arm bracket to body in order to maintain alignment specifications.
- Remove trailing arm front bracket mounting bolts (**arrows**).
- Working with trailing arm on workbench, detach front bracket from arm.

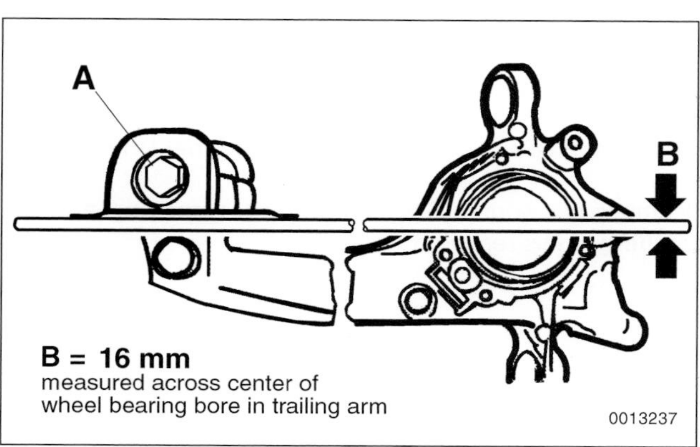

When reinstalling, preload trailing arm front bracket bushing:

- Install bolt (**A**) through bracket and arm and install nut finger tight.
- Using 16 mm bar stock as shown in illustration, align base of bracket so that it is parallel with center of wheel bearing bore on trailing arm.
- Torque bracket bolt (**A**).

Tightening torque
- Trailing arm to front bracket . . . . 110 Nm (81 ft-lb)

– Remainder of installation is reverse of removal, noting the following:

- Install new rear wheel bearings.
- Insert control arm mounting bolts as marked.
- Use new self-locking nuts.
- Transfer brake system components to new arm.
- Have car professionally aligned when job is complete.

NOTE —
BMW-supplied replacement trailing arms come with control arm bushings installed. Install a new wheel bearing.

Tightening torques
- Drive axle collar nut to drive flange
  M24. . . . . 250 Nm (184 ft-lb)
  M27. . . . . 300 Nm (221 ft-lb)
- Drive axle to differential flange
  M10 x 20 mm Torx bolt . . . . 83 Nm (61 ft-lb)
  M10 x 46 mm bolt (black) . . . . 100 Nm (74 ft-lb)
  M10 x 46 mm bolt (silver)
  (always replace) . . . . 80 Nm (59 ft-lb)
- Road wheel to hub . . . . 120 ± 10 Nm (90 ± 7 ft-lb)
- Shock absorber to trailing arm
  (car in normal loaded position) . . . . 100 Nm (74 ft-lb)
- Trailing arm bracket to body (M12 bolt). . 77 Nm (57 ft-lb)
- Trailing arm to upper
  or lower control arm (M12 bolt). . . . . . . 110 Nm (81 ft-lb)
- V-brace to differential or body
  (M10, use new bolts). . . . . .59 Nm (44 ft-lb) + 90°

WARNING —
If a rear brake line was disconnected to remove the trailing arm, bleed the complete braking system. See **340 Brakes**.

Upper control arm, removing and installing

– Raise rear end of car.

WARNING —
Make sure the car is firmly supported on jack stands designed for the purpose. Place jack stands underneath structural chassis points, not under suspension parts.

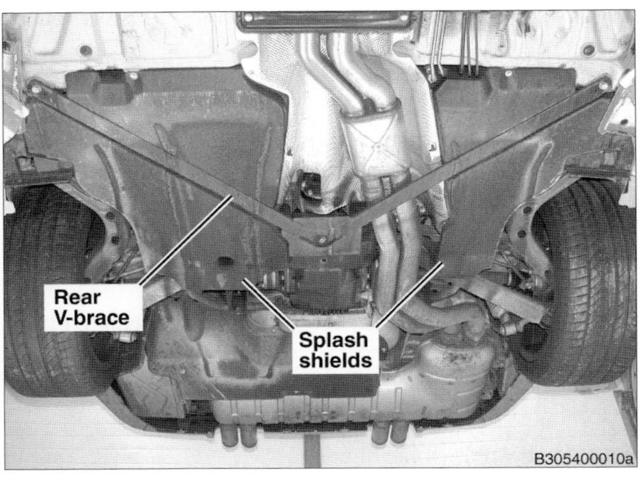

M3: Remove rear reinforcing V-brace.

- Remove rear underbody splash shields as applicable.
- Remove drive axle. See **331 Rear Axle Final Drive**.
- Remove coil spring. See **Coil spring, removing and installing** in this repair group.

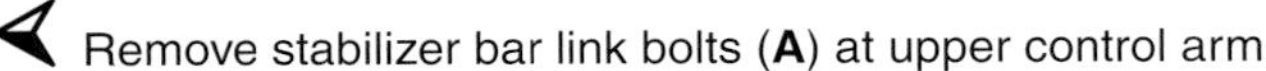

Remove stabilizer bar link bolts (**A**) at upper control arm.

- Remove stabilizer bar anchor bolts (**B**).
- Carefully push stabilizer bar aside.

NOTE —

Do not twist stabilizer bar link bushing on end of bar. See **Rear Stabilizer Bar** *in this repair group.*

- If necessary, remove ride level sensor from upper control arm.
- Unbolt upper control arm from both trailing arm and rear subframe. Note direction of bolt insertion.

NOTE —

If necessary for clearance, unbolt the differential from the subframe and push it toward the rear of the car in order to remove the control arm mounting bolt from the subframe.

- Installation is reverse of removal, noting the following;
  - Insert mounting bolts in direction previously marked
  - Use new self-locking nuts.
  - Have car professionally aligned when job is complete.

Tightening torques

- Drive axle collar nut to drive flange
  M24 . . . . 250 Nm (184 ft-lb)
  M27 . . . . 300 Nm (221 ft-lb)
- Drive axle to differential flange
  M10 x 20 mm Torx bolt . . . . 83 Nm (61 ft-lb)
  M10 x 46 mm bolt (black) . . . . 100 Nm (74 ft-lb)
  M10 x 46 mm bolt (silver)
  (always replace) . . . . 80 Nm (59 ft-lb)
- Road wheel to hub . . . . 120 ± 10 Nm (90 ± 7 ft-lb)
- Shock absorber to trailing arm
  car in normal loaded position . . . . 100 Nm (74 ft-lb)
- Upper control arm to rear subframe
  M12 bolt . . . . 77 Nm (57 ft-lb)

Tightening torques (cont.)

- Upper control arm to trailing arm
  M12 bolt . . . . 110 Nm (81 ft-lb)
- V-brace to differential or body
  (M10, use new bolts). . . . . 59 Nm (44 ft-lb) + 90°

Lower control arm, removing and installing

– Raise rear end of car.

> ***WARNING —***
> *Make sure the car is firmly supported on jack stands designed for the purpose. Place jack stands underneath structural chassis points, not under suspension parts.*

– M3: Remove rear reinforcing V-brace.

– Remove rear underbody splash shields as applicable.

– Support trailing arm from below using an adjustable jackstand.

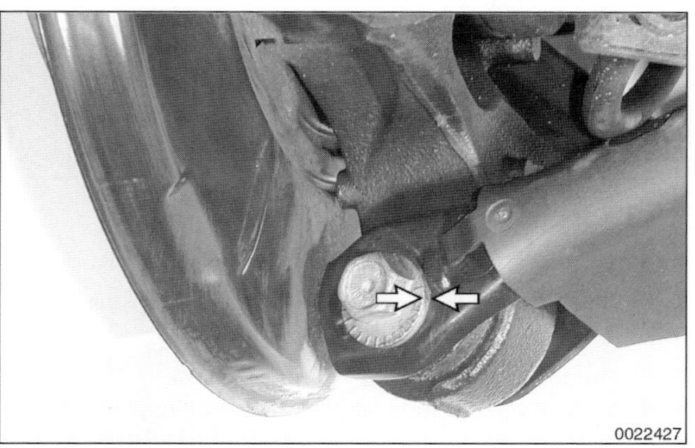

< Mark position (**arrows**) of lower control arm eccentric mounting bolt.

– Remove lower control arm plastic shield.

– Remove both lower control arm mounting bolts. Note direction of bolt insertion.

NOTE —
If necessary for clearance, unbolt the differential from the subframe and push it toward the rear of the car in order to remove the control arm mounting bolt from the subframe.

– Use soft hammer to tap control arm out of its mounting points.

– Installation is reverse of removal.

- Welded seam of control arm faces upward.
- To install mounting hardware at subframe, insert lock plate into opening in subframe from below.
- Line up eccentric bolt head with marks made previously.
- Have car professionally aligned when job is complete.

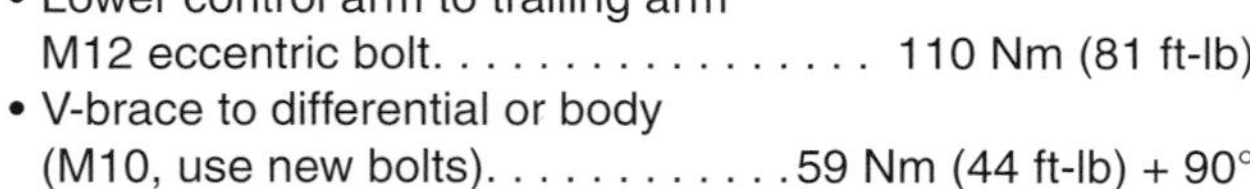

Tightening torque

- Lower control arm to rear subframe
  M12 bolt . . . . 110 Nm (81 ft-lb)
- Lower control arm to trailing arm
  M12 eccentric bolt. . . . . 110 Nm (81 ft-lb)
- V-brace to differential or body
  (M10, use new bolts). . . . . 59 Nm (44 ft-lb) + 90°

Rear subframe assembly

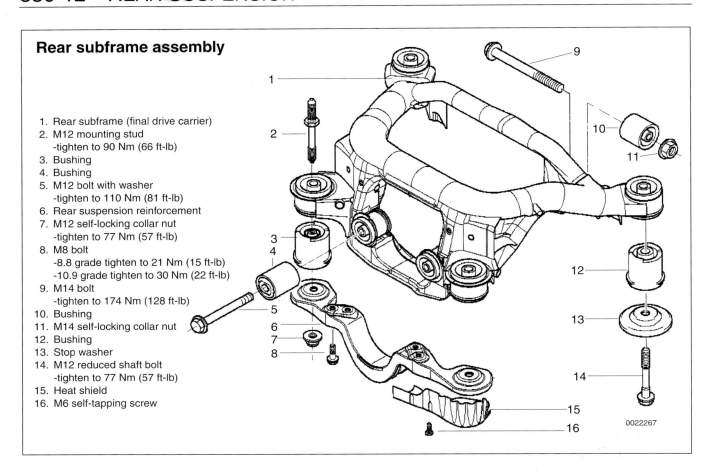

1. Rear subframe (final drive carrier)
2. M12 mounting stud
   -tighten to 90 Nm (66 ft-lb)
3. Bushing
4. Bushing
5. M12 bolt with washer
   -tighten to 110 Nm (81 ft-lb)
6. Rear suspension reinforcement
7. M12 self-locking collar nut
   -tighten to 77 Nm (57 ft-lb)
8. M8 bolt
   -8.8 grade tighten to 21 Nm (15 ft-lb)
   -10.9 grade tighten to 30 Nm (22 ft-lb)
9. M14 bolt
   -tighten to 174 Nm (128 ft-lb)
10. Bushing
11. M14 self-locking collar nut
12. Bushing
13. Stop washer
14. M12 reduced shaft bolt
    -tighten to 77 Nm (57 ft-lb)
15. Heat shield
16. M6 self-tapping screw

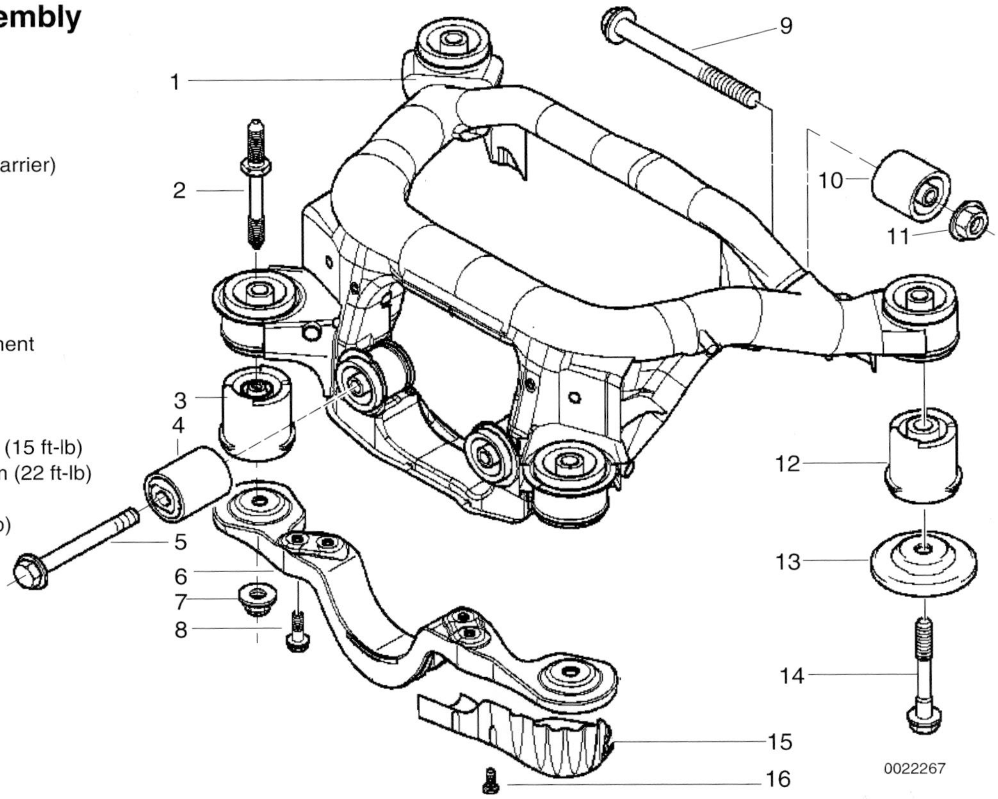

0022267

Rear subframe

– In case of damage to the subframe, or if a pressed-in bushing is worn, remove subframe.

- M3: Remove rear reinforcing V-brace.
- Remove rear underbody splash shields as applicable.
- Remove exhaust system. See **180 Exhaust System**.
- Detach rear driveshaft from rear differential. See **260 Driveshafts**.
- Detach rear drive axles from rear differential. Remove rear differential. See **331 Rear Axle Final Drive**.
- Detach rear control arms. See **Upper control arm, removing and installing** and **Lower control arm, removing and installing** in this repair group.

◄ Remove rear subframe mounting fasteners (**arrows**) while supporting subframe securely.

– In case of damage to subframe mounting stud threads, replace stud.

– In case of damage to subframe mounting stud threads in body, repair using Helicoil thread insert M12 x 1.5 x 18.

Tightening torques

- Differential to subframe front bolt (M12) . . . . 110 Nm (81 ft-lb)
- Differential to subframe rear bolt (M14) . . . 174 Nm (128 ft-lb)
- Drive axle to differential flange
  M10 x 20 mm Torx bolt . . . . 83 Nm (61 ft-lb)
  M10 x 46 mm bolt (black) . . . . 100 Nm (74 ft-lb)
  M10 x 46 mm bolt (silver)
  (always replace) . . . . 80 Nm (59 ft-lb)
- Driveshaft to differential flange
  M10 compression nut . . . . 64 Nm (47 ft-lb)
  M10 Torx bolt . . . . 85 Nm (63 ft-lb)
- Lower control arm to subframe (M12). . 110 Nm (81 ft-lb)
- Subframe to body (M12) . . . . 77 Nm (57 ft-lb)
- Upper control arm to subframe (M12). . . 77 Nm (57 ft-lb)
- V-brace to differential or body
  (M10, use new bolts). . . . . .59 Nm (44 ft-lb) + 90°

Rear suspension bushings

When replacing a rear suspension bushing, be sure to measure and record orientation and protrusion of old bushing.

– Lift rear of car and support securely.

> ***WARNING —***
> *Make sure the car is firmly supported on jack stands designed for the purpose. Place jack stands underneath structural chassis points, not under suspension parts.*

Trailing arm front bushing

– Remove trailing arm. Be sure to mark position of trailing arm front bracket on body to facilitate resetting of rear toe. See **Trailing arm, removing and installing** in this repair group.

 Using appropriate press tools:

- Press bushing out of trailing arm.
- Clean trailing arm bore.
- Press new bushing into trailing arm.
- Line up slot in bushing with mark (**A**) on trailing arm bore.
- Fully pressed in, Make sure cylindrical bushing protrudes from trailing arm bore by measurement **B** = 2.5 mm (0.1 in)

– Have car professionally aligned when job is complete.

Tightening torques

- Trailing arm to front bracket . . . . 110 Nm (81 ft-lb)
- Trailing arm bracket to body . . . . 77 Nm (57 ft-lb)

A
Slot
B
0021200a

Upper or lower control arm outer bushing (in trailing arm)

– Upper control arm bushing:

- Remove trailing arm.
- Be sure to mark position of trailing arm front bracket on body to facilitate resetting of rear toe.
- See **Trailing arm, removing and installing** in this repair group.

– Lower control arm bushing:

- Detach lower control arm from trailing arm. There is no need to remove trailing arm.
- Be sure to mark position of eccentric mounting bolt to facilitate resetting of rear camber.
- Note direction of bolt insertion.

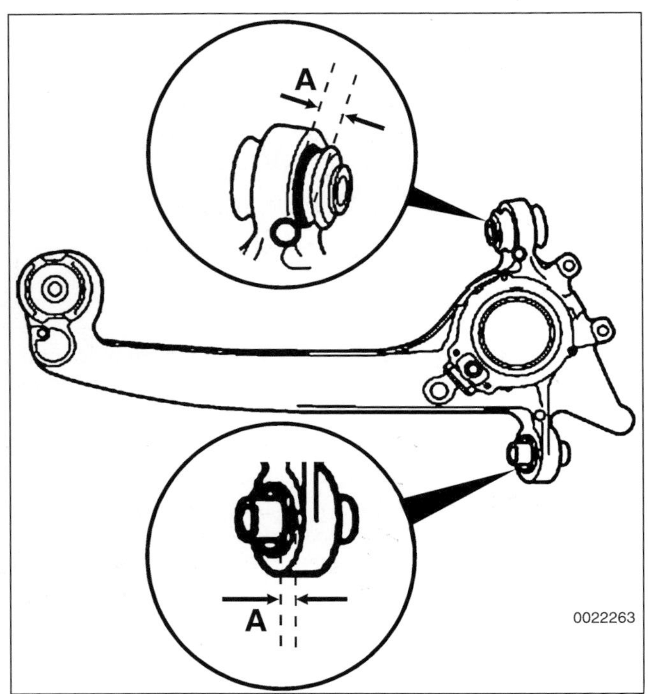

To replace bushing:

- Measure and record protrusion (**A**) of old bushing from trailing arm boss.
- Press old bushing out and install new bushing, using protrusion measurement **A** as a reference.

– Have car professionally aligned when job is complete.

Tightening torques

- Lower control arm to trailing arm M12 eccentric bolt. . . . . 110 Nm (81 ft-lb)
- Upper control arm to rear subframe M12 bolt . . . . 77 Nm (57 ft-lb)
- Upper control arm to trailing arm M12 bolt . . . . 110 Nm (81 ft-lb)

Upper control arm inner bushing

– Remove upper control arm. See **Upper control arm, removing and installing** in this repair group.

– Press old bushing out using appropriate press tools.

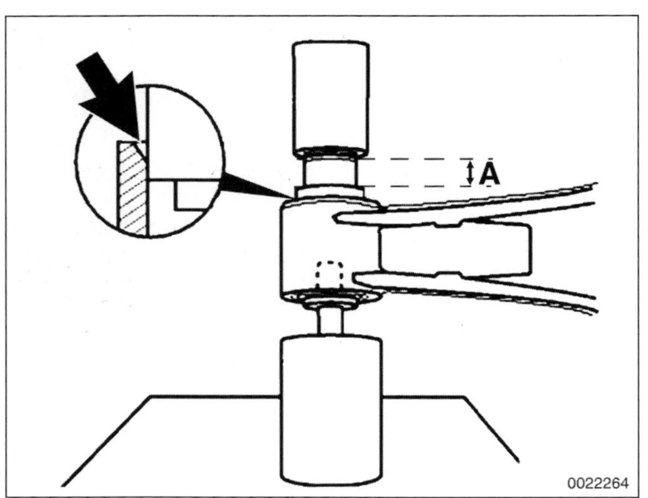

Press new bushing starting at inner bevelled end (**arrow**) of control arm bore.

- Make sure that longer collar of bushing (**A**) is on same side as bevel in control arm.
- Make sure that outer bushing housing is flush with control arm bore when fully pressed in.
- Have car professionally aligned when job is complete.

Tightening torque

- Upper control arm to rear subframe M12 bolt . . . . 77 Nm (57 ft-lb)
- Upper control arm to trailing arm M12 bolt . . . . 110 Nm (81 ft-lb)

Rear subframe bushings

All others

Right front

0022265

Rear subframe bushing

– Remove rear subframe. See **Rear subframe** in this repair group.

– Press old bushing out and install new bushing using appropriate press tools. Coat new bushing with Circolight® or equivalent rubber bonding agent.

< Bushing position and orientation:

- Right front bushing has elongated hole (**arrow**).
- Orient all bushings with triangular arrow heads pointing front/aft on car.
- Have car professionally aligned when job is complete.

Tightening torque

- Lower control arm to subframe (M12). . 110 Nm (81 ft-lb)
- Subframe to body (M12) . . . . 77 Nm (57 ft-lb)
- Upper control arm to rear subframe M12 bolt . . . . 77 Nm (57 ft-lb)

REAR STABILIZER BAR

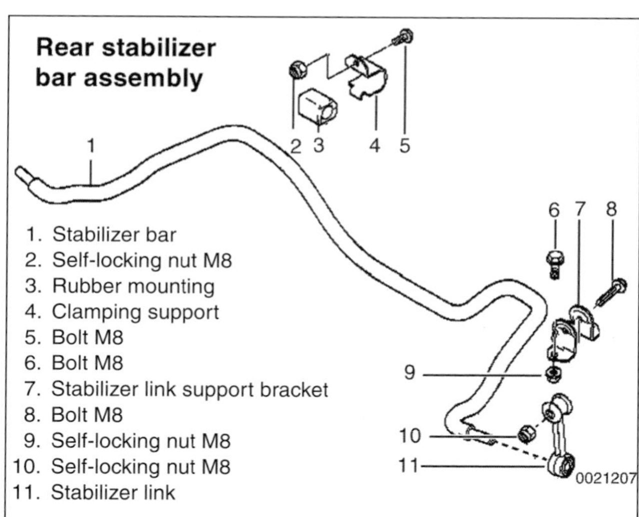

< The rear stabilizer bar is mounted to the rear subframe and attached via stabilizer bar links to the rear upper control arms.

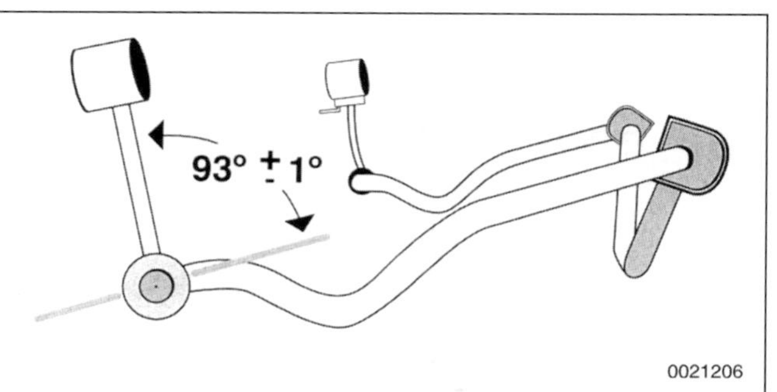

< When installing new stabilizer link:

- Clean rubber seating surface at end of stabilizer bar.
- Moisten end of bar and inside rubber mount (in link end). with Circolight® or equivalent rubber bonding agent.
- Push bar into rubber mount and position as shown in illustration. Once rubber bond has set, do not twist stabilizer link.

REAR WHEEL BEARINGS

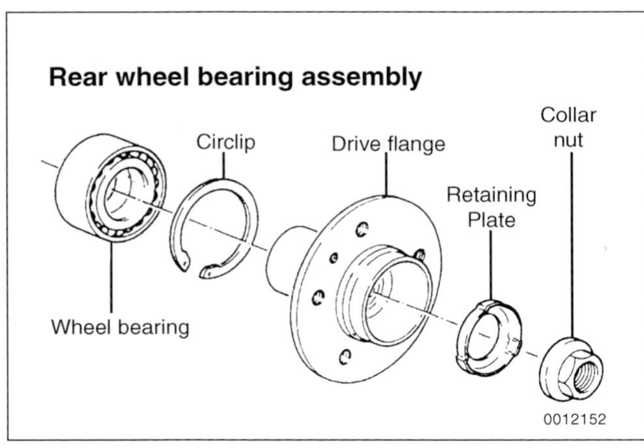

◀ The rear wheel bearing is a unitized assembly and is not repairable separately.

Special press tools, to be used with the trailing arm attached to the car, are required to replace a wheel bearing. Read the procedure through before beginning the job.

Rear wheel bearing, replacing

– Raise rear of car and support securely.

> ***WARNING —***
> *Make sure the car is firmly supported on jack stands designed for the purpose. Place jack stands underneath structural chassis points, not under suspension parts.*

– Remove drive axle. See **331 Rear Axle Final Drive.**

– Right side: Detach brake pad sensor connector at brake caliper.

– Remove brake caliper assembly and rotor. See **340 Brakes**. Leave brake hose connected to caliper. Suspend caliper assembly from chassis using stiff wire.

◀ Remove ABS pulse sensor at trailing arm.

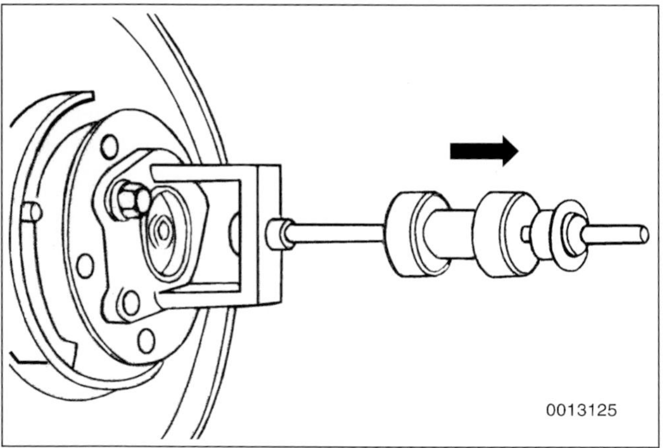

◀ Remove drive flange from bearing assembly using BMW impact puller 33 2 116, 33 4 201 / 202 / 203 or equivalent.

> ***CAUTION —***
> *The wheel bearing is destroyed when the drive flange is removed. Do not attempt to reuse bearing.*

NOTE —
Use BMW special tool set 33 4 400 or equivalent to separate inner bearing race from drive flange.

– Remove bearing retaining circlip from bearing housing in trailing arm.

– Using BMW bearing extraction tools 33 3 261 / 262 / 263 or equivalent, pull bearing assembly out of trailing arm bearing housing.

– Inspect bearing housing for damage or contamination.

  • Clean housing bore thoroughly before installing bearing.
  • Make sure mating surfaces are clean

– Install new bearing assembly using BMW press tools 33 3 261 / 264 / 265 or equivalent.

– Install new circlip.

> ***CAUTION —***
> - *Apply force only to outer race when installing bearing.*
> - *Make sure that the bearing is pressed in far enough to contact the shoulder at the back side of the housing and that the circlip is fully seated in its groove.*
> - *Always use a new retaining circlip.*

– Press drive flange into bearing using BMW press tools 33 3 261 / 262 / 263 or equivalent.

> ***CAUTION —***
> *BMW specifies special tools to pull the drive flange through the wheel bearing into position. If using alternative tools, be sure to support the bearing inner race when pressing or pulling the drive flange into place.*

– Install brake caliper assembly and rotor. See **340 Brakes**.

– Reinstall drive axle.

Tightening torques

- Brake rotor to drive flange (M8) .... 16 Nm (12 ft-lb)
- Brake caliper to trailing arm (M12) ..... 67 Nm (50 ft-lb)
- Drive axle collar nut to drive flange
  M24 .... 250 Nm (184 ft-lb)
  M27 .... 300 Nm (221 ft-lb)
- Drive axle to differential flange
  M10 x 20 mm Torx bolt .... 83 Nm (61 ft-lb)
  M10 x 46 mm bolt (black) .... 100 Nm (74 ft-lb)
  M10 x 46 mm bolt (silver)
  (always replace) .... 80 Nm (59 ft-lb)
- Road wheel to hub .... 120 ± 10 Nm (90 ± 7 ft-lb)

331 Rear Axle Final Drive

GENERAL

This repair group covers removal and repair information for the rear drive axle shafts, CV joints and CV joint boots. Also covered is rear differential (final drive) removal and seal replacement.

Internal repairs of the differential assembly are not covered in this manual.

Special tools

BMW recommends some special tools for the removal of the drive axles as well as the installation of rear differential input and output drive flange seals. Common pullers and drifts can often be substituted for these tools.

Special tools

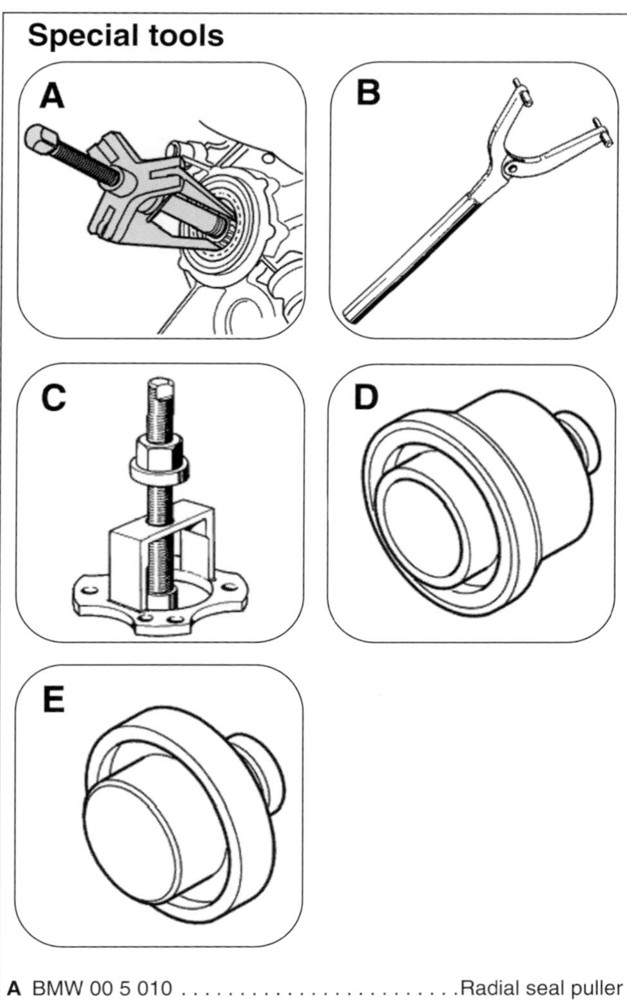

A BMW 00 5 010 . . . . .Radial seal puller
B BMW 23 0 020 . . . . .Flange counterhold tool
C BMW 33 2 110 . . . . Drive axle puller
D BMW 33 3 400 . . . . Output flange seal drift
E BMW 33 3 430 . . . . .Input flange seal drift

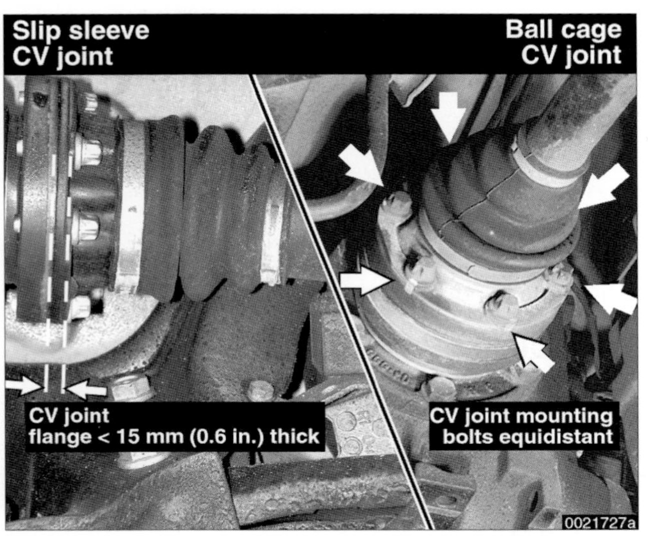

DRIVE AXLES

The drive axles use constant-velocity (CV) joints on both ends. Two different styles of rear inner CV joints are in E46 vehicles. Refer to the accompanying illustration:

- **Ball cage CV joint**. Traditional design CV joint with thick metal housing (approx. 40 mm / 1.6 in. thick). Balls slide in non-parallel grooves.
- **Slip sleeve CV joint**. Thin bolt-on flange (approx. 15 mm / 0.6 in. thick). CV joint has splined shaft that slides into end of drive axle.

For replacement parts, only CV joints boots or complete axles are offered by BMW. To replace a CV joint boot, remove the drive axle from the car.

Rear drive axle, removing and installing

With an assistant applying brakes, break free staked collar nut (**arrow**) at center of rear wheel hub. Do not remove completely.

NOTE —

The drive flange collar nut is tightened to a torque of over 250 Nm (184 ft-lb). Make sure the car is firmly on the ground.

– Raise rear of car. Remove rear wheel.

WARNING —

Make sure that the car is firmly supported on jack stands designed for the purpose. Place the jack stands beneath a structural chassis point. Do not place jack stands under suspension parts.

– Detach rear stabilizer bar anchor bolts from rear subframe and tilt stabilizer down.

– Left axle: Detach rear of exhaust system and tilt down. Support rear muffler securely.

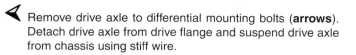

◀ Remove drive axle to differential mounting bolts (**arrows**). Detach drive axle from drive flange and suspend drive axle from chassis using stiff wire.

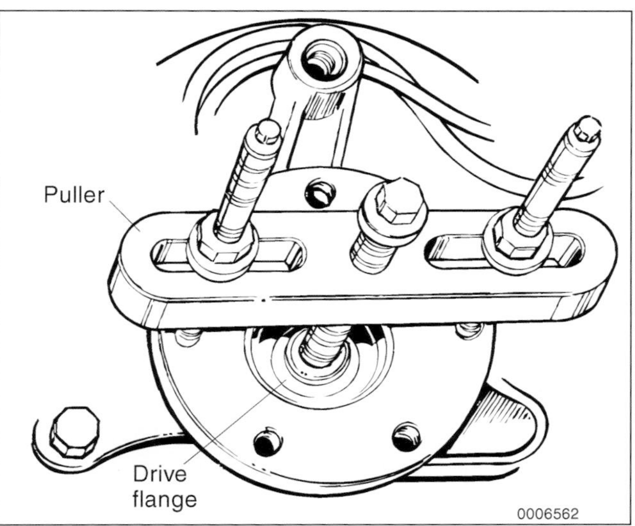

◀ Press drive axle from wheel bearing housing using an appropriate puller.

– Installation is reverse of removal.

- Apply light coating of oil to contact face of collar nut and install loosely.
- Install road wheel and lower car to ground.
- With an assistant applying brakes, tighten drive axle collar nut to its final torque.
- Stake and caulk collar nut.

Tightening torques

- Drive axle collar nut to drive flange
  M24 . . . . 250 Nm (184 ft-lb)
  M27 . . . . 300 Nm (221 ft-lb)
- Drive axle to differential flange
  M10 x 20 mm Torx bolt . . . . 83 Nm (61 ft-lb)
  M10 x 46 mm bolt (black) . . . . 100 Nm (74 ft-lb)
  M10 x 46 mm bolt (silver)
  (always replace) . . . . 80 Nm (59 ft-lb)
- Road wheel to hub . . . . 120 ± 10 Nm (90 ± 7 ft-lb)

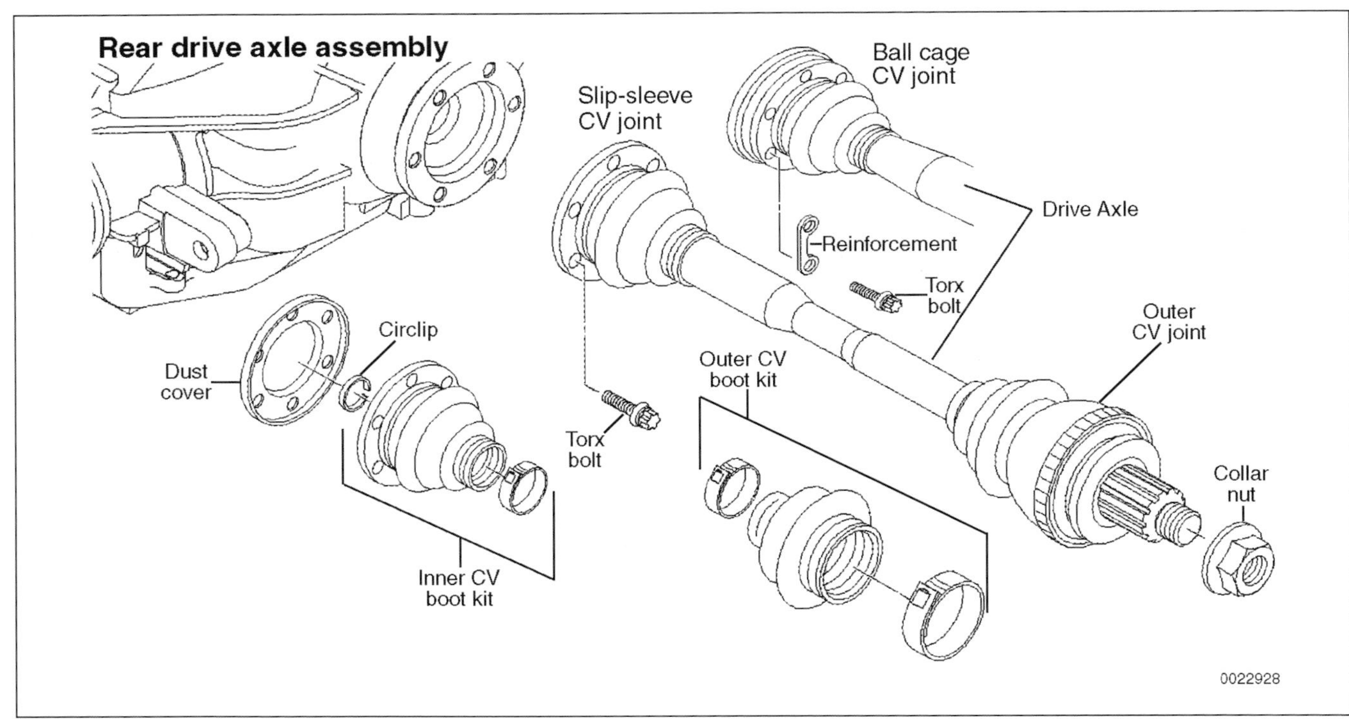

CV joint boots

NOTE —

When replacing CV joint boot, use a complete boot repair kit available from an authorized BMW dealer parts department. The kit includes new boot, clamping bands, special lubricant and a new outer CV joint axle circlip.

The outer CV joint cannot be removed from the axle shaft. In order to replace the outer CV boot, remove the inner joint and boot first. If the CV joints are worn or defective, a complete rebuilt axle shaft is available from an authorized BMW dealer parts department.

– Remove rear drive axle. See **Rear drive axle, removing and installing** in this repair group. Place axle shaft on workbench.

– Cut off old boot clamps and remove boots. Clean old grease off joints and shafts.

Ball cage CV joint boot

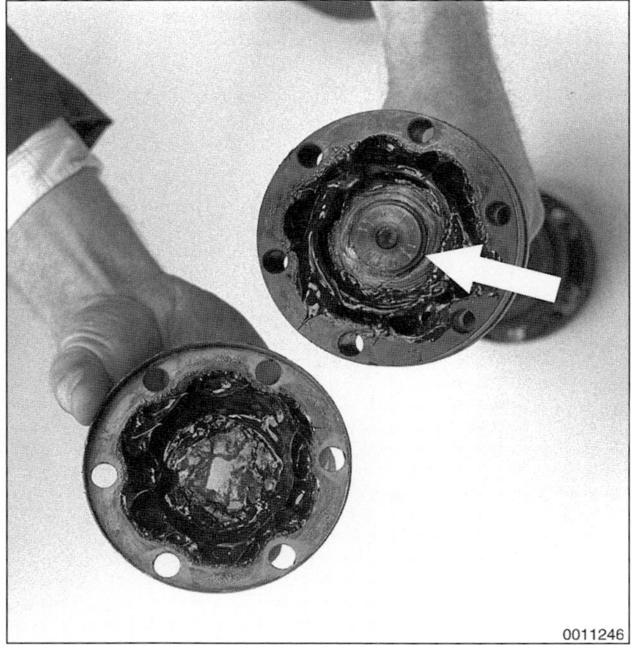

◄ Lift off dust cover from inner CV joint and remove circlip (**arrow**) retaining joint inner hub to axle shaft.

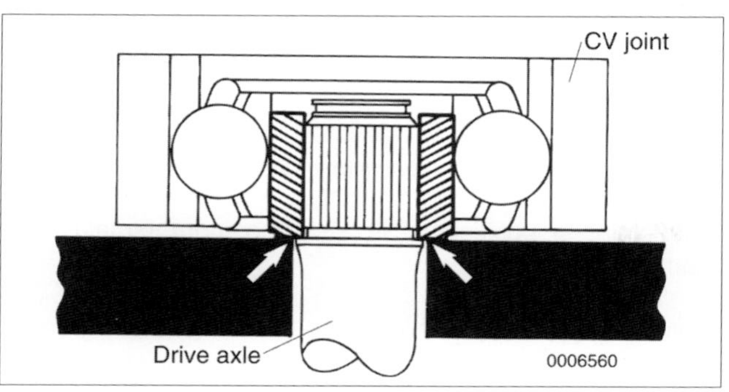

◄ Support inner hub at **arrows** when pressing axle shaft out of joint.

– Clean all old lubricant off shaft splines and inner joint splines.

> ***CAUTION —***
> *If disassembling CV joint for cleaning and inspection, be sure to matchmark inner and outer race and intermediate ball cage. This allows reassembly of parts in their original positions.*

NOTE —

To inspect a CV joint, clean away the grease and look for galling, pitting and other signs of wear or physical damage. Polished surfaces or visible ball tracks alone are not necessarily cause for replacement. Discoloration due to overheating indicates lack of lubrication.

– Apply Loctite® 270 or equivalent heavy-duty thread locking compound to drive axle splines. Position new CV joint on shaft so that raised or taller side of hub is facing shaft.

> ***WARNING —***
> *Do not let the locking compound contact the balls in the joint. Apply only a thin coat to cover the splines.*

– While supporting axle shaft, press inner hub of CV joint onto shaft. Install new circlip.

NOTE —

- *Do not let the ball hub pivot more than 20° in the outer ring of the joint. The balls will fall out if the hub is pivoted too far.*
- *Before installing each small boot clamp be sure to "burp" the boot by flexing the CV joint as far over as it will go. A small screwdriver inserted between the boot and the axle shaft will help the process.*
- *BMW recommends Bostik® 1513 or Epple® 4851 adhesive, and Epple® 39 or Curil® T sealer.*

CV joint lubricant capacity

- Wheel hub end . . . . 80 gram (2.8 oz.)
  (M3) . . . . 85 gram (3.0 oz.)
- Differential end . . . . 85 gram (3.0 oz.)
  M3. . . . . 100 gram (3.5 oz.)

– Use sealing gel to seal dust cover to CV joint prior to reinstallation.

Slip sleeve CV joint boot

– Pull CV joint partially out of axle shaft. Matchmark relative position of joint to shaft.

> ***CAUTION —***
> *If the joint and shaft are not reassembled in their original position the assembly may be out of balance and vibrate during operation.*

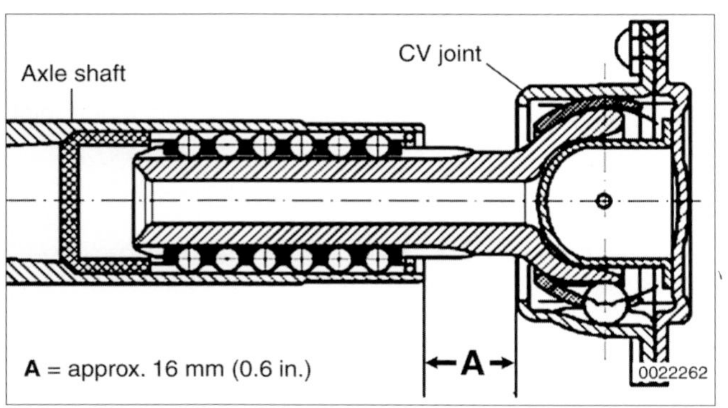

When reinstalling joint, push joint into shaft as far as it will go, then pull it out to measurement **A** (16 mm / 0.6 in).

NOTE —
This step insures uniform lubrication of the CV joint.

– Keep joint in position while installing inner (small) boot clamp.

– Make sure sealing lip of joint and boot are free of grease. The boot could otherwise slide off when boot clamp is tightened.

Slip sleeve joint boot lengths

- Inner boot . . . . 65 mm (2.6 in)
- Outer boot. . . . . 55 mm (2.2 in)

NOTE —
- *On the differential end CV joint, position large boot clamp so that crimp in clamp faces rivet on CV joint flange.*
- *Install large clamps of inner and outer CV joints so that the crimps are offset by 180°.*

REAR DIFFERENTIAL

NOTE —
Rear subframe (differential carrier) removal is covered in **330 Rear Suspension**.

Rear differential oil, checking and filling

NOTE —
E46 rear differential is filled with lifetime lubricant.

– Lift vehicle and support safely.

> ***WARNING —***
> *Make sure the car is stable and well supported at all times. Use a professional automotive lift or jack stands designed for the purpose. A floor jack is not adequate support.*

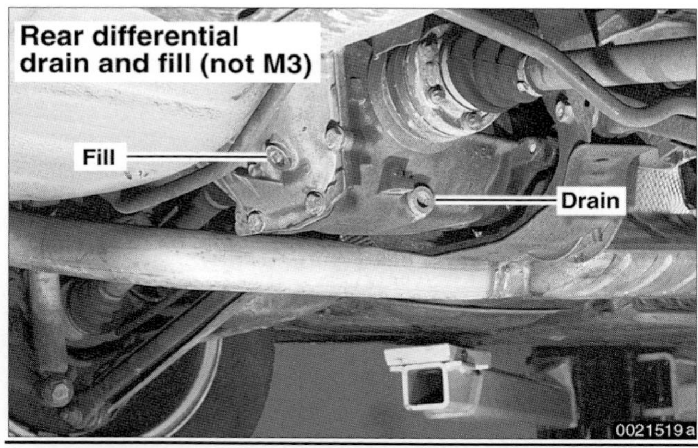

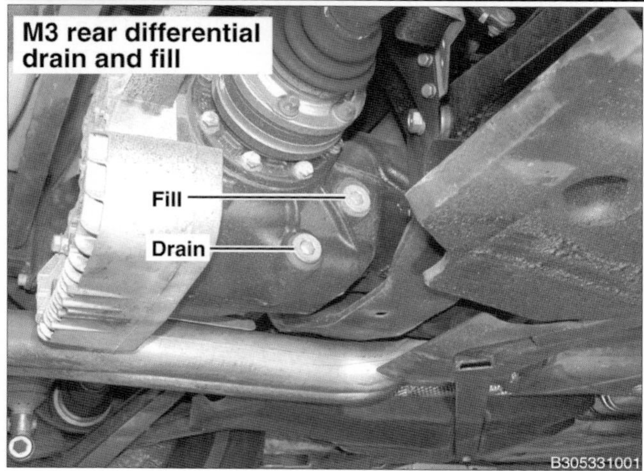

Remove rear differential oil filler plug. Use a 14 mm Allen socket to remove the fill plug. Alternatively, cut approximately 30 mm (1.2 in) from an Allen key and use a box end wrench on stub.

– Insert finger into fill hole. If finger is wetted from oil, level is correct.

– If necessary, fill differential with appropriate type and quantity of lubricant.

NOTE —
The differential fluid level is correct when the fluid begins to spill from the fill plug.

– Install and tighten fill plug.

Differential oil

- Differential oil capacity
  Automatic transmission. . . . . 0.9 liter (0.95 US qt.)
  Manual transmission. . . . . 1.0 liter (1.06 US qt.)
  M3. . . . . 1.3 liter (1.37 US qt.)
- Oil specification. . . . . BMW SAF-XO synthetic oil

Tightening torques

- Differential drain or fill plug
  With O-ring . . . . 60 Nm (44 ft-lb)
  With sealing washer . . . . 65 Nm (48 ft-lb)

Rear differential, removing and installing

– Raise rear end of car and support it securely on jack stands.

> ***WARNING —***
> *Make sure the car is stable and well supported at all times. Use a professional automotive lift or jack stands designed for the purpose. A floor jack is not adequate support.*

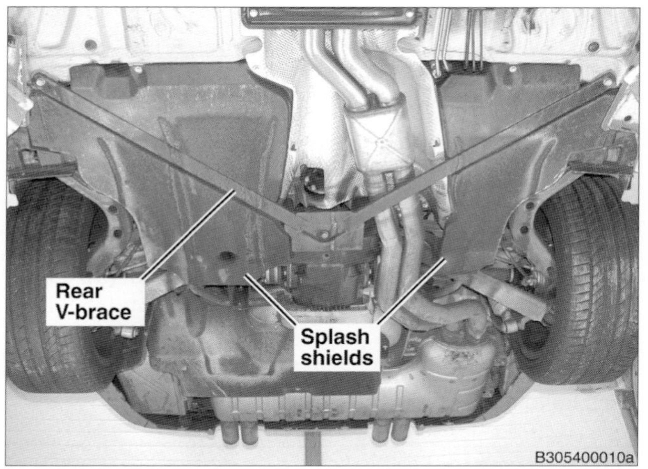

– Remove rear drive axles. See **Rear drive axle, removing and installing** in this repair group.

– If necessary, drain differential oil.

◄ M3: Remove rear reinforcing V-brace.

– Remove rear underbody splash shields as applicable.

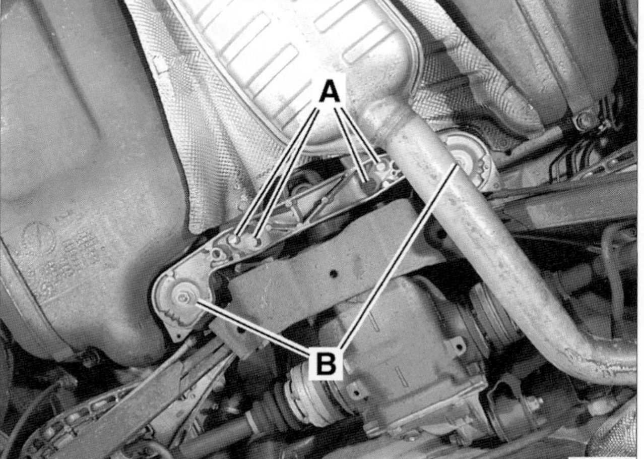

◄ Remove rear suspension reinforcement brace:

- Remove heat shield between reinforcement brace and exhaust pipe.
- Remove bolts (**A**) mounting brace to undercarriage.
- Remove nuts (**B**) mounting brace and front of rear subframe to undercarriage.
- Lower and remove reinforcement.

NOTE —
If necessary, tilt rear half of exhaust system down. Support exhaust system securely.

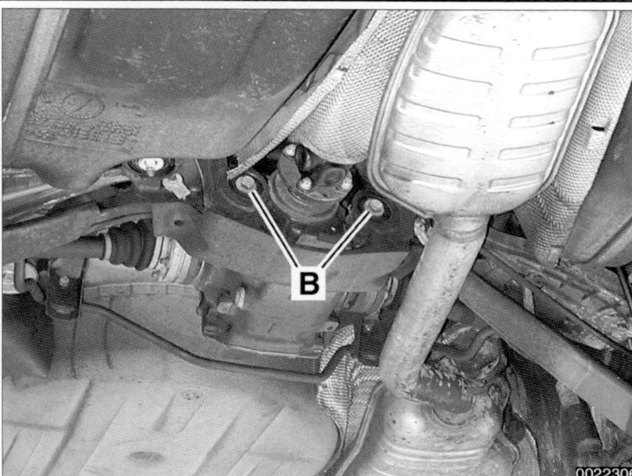

– Detach driveshaft from differential input shaft flange and suspend. See **260 Driveshaft**.

> ***CAUTION —***
> *Suspend the detached drive axle from the car body with a stiff wire hook to prevent damage to the outer CV joint.*

– Remove rear stabilizer bar.

Support differential with transmission jack. Remove rear (**A**) and front (**B**) mounting bolts at subframe.

– Slowly lower differential unit and remove toward rear.

– Installation is reverse of removal. In order to prevent excess vibration and noise, follow sequence for tightening differential mounting bolts:

- Install bolts finger tight.
- Tighten front bolts (**B**).
- Tighten rear bolt (**A**).

Tightening torques

- Differential drain or fill plug . . . . 70 Nm (52 ft-lb)
- Differential to rear subframe
  Front mount (M12 bolts) . . . . 95 Nm (70 ft-lb)
  Rear mount (M14 bolt) . . . . 174 Nm (128 ft-lb)
- Drive axle to differential flange
  M10 x 20 mm Torx bolt . . . . 83 Nm (61 ft-lb)
  M10 x 46 mm bolt (black) . . . . 100 Nm (74 ft-lb)
  M10 x 46 mm bolt (silver)
  (always replace) . . . . 80 Nm (59 ft-lb)
- Driveshaft to differential flange
  M10 compression nut . . . . 64 Nm (47 ft-lb)
  M10 Torx bolt . . . . 85 Nm (63 ft-lb)
- Rear suspension reinforcement to undercarriage
  M12 self-locking nut . . . . 77 Nm (57 ft-lb)
  M8 bolt 8.8 grade . . . . 21 Nm (15 ft-lb)
  M8 bolt 10.9 grade . . . . 30 Nm (22 ft-lb)

– Be sure to refill differential.

Differential oil

- Differential oil capacity
  Rear wheel drive, auto trans. . . . . 0.9 liter (0.95 US qt.)
  Rear wheel drive, manual trans
  and All wheel drive . . . . 1.0 liter (1.06 US qt.)
  M3. . . . . 1.3 liter (1.37 US qt.)
- Oil specification. . . . . BMW SAF-XO synthetic oil

Differential mounting bushings

– If rear differential mounting bushing are worn, damaged or oil soaked:

  - Remove differential from rear subframe. See **Rear differential, removing and installing** in this repair group.
  - Working at subframe, use bushing press tools to remove old bushings and install new ones.
  - Carefully note installation marks (arrows) on new bushings.

NOTE —
BMW uses bushings from different manufacturers in the course of production. Always check with an authorized BMW dealer for the latest information on suspension bushings.

REAR DIFFERENTIAL OIL SEALS

Low oil level caused by faulty oil seals may be the cause of noisy differential operation. The drive flange (side) and input shaft (front) oil seals can be replaced while the differential is installed.

NOTE —
Do not mistake leaking CV joint grease for flange seal leaks. Degrease the differential to pinpoint the source of the leak prior to replacing seals.

Output drive flange oil seal, replacing

– Raise car and support safely.

> ***WARNING —***
> *Make sure the car is stable and well supported at all times. Use a professional automotive lift or jack stands designed for the purpose. A floor jack is not adequate support.*

– Left side: Detach rear of exhaust system and tilt down. Support rear muffler securely.

– Detach stabilizer bar from rear subframe.

– Detach drive axle from differential. See **Rear drive axle, removing and installing** in this repair group.

> ***CAUTION —***
> *Suspend the detached drive axle from the car body with a stiff wire hook to prevent damage to the outer CV joint.*

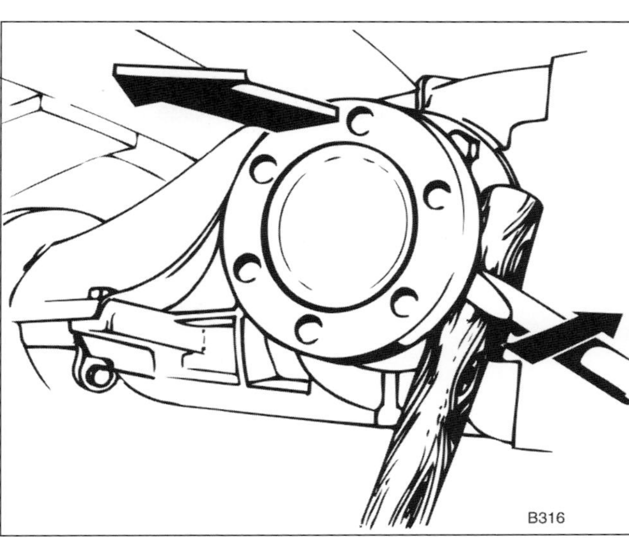

 Pry output flange from differential. For leverage, use a wooden dowel as shown.

NOTE —
- *Be prepared to catch dripping oil in a pan.*
- *Inspect flange at the point where the oil seal rides on the shaft. Replace the flange if there is a groove worn in the shaft.*

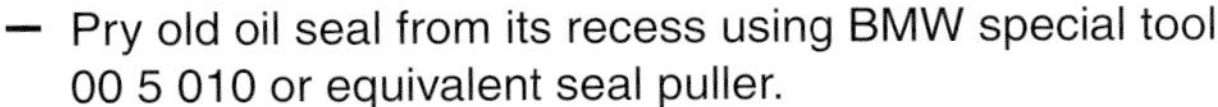

– Pry old oil seal from its recess using BMW special tool 00 5 010 or equivalent seal puller.

> **_CAUTION —_**
> *Be careful not to mar the differential housing when removing the seal.*

– Dip new seal in differential lubricant and drive into place until fully seated.

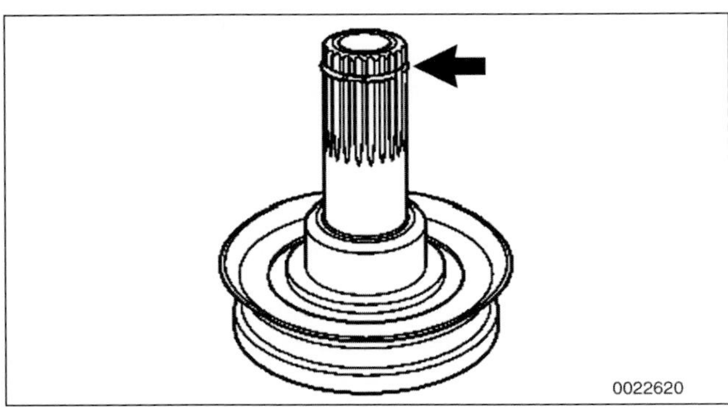

◄ Replace locking circlip (**arrow**) on output flange.

– Install flange by pressing it in by hand until snap ring engages. If necessary, turn flange slightly while pushing.

– Attach drive axle and tighten bolts.

– Top off differential with oil.

Tightening torque
- Drive axle to differential flange
  M10 x 20 mm Torx bolt . . . . 83 Nm (61 ft-lb)
  M10 x 46 mm bolt (black) . . . . 100 Nm (74 ft-lb)
  M10 x 46 mm bolt (silver)
  (always replace) . . . . 80 Nm (59 ft-lb)

Input drive flange oil seal, replacing

– Raise car and support safely.

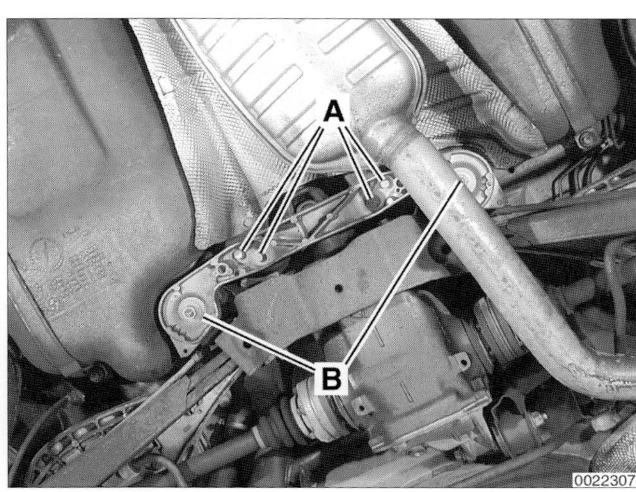

◄ Remove rear suspension reinforcement brace:
- Remove heat shield between reinforcement brace and exhaust pipe.
- Remove bolts (**A**) mounting brace to undercarriage.
- Remove nuts (**B**) mounting brace and front of rear subframe to undercarriage.
- Lower and remove reinforcement.

NOTE —
If necessary, tilt rear half of exhaust system down. Support exhaust system securely.

– Remove driveshaft from differential input shaft flange. See **260 Driveshaft**. Tie end of driveshaft to side.

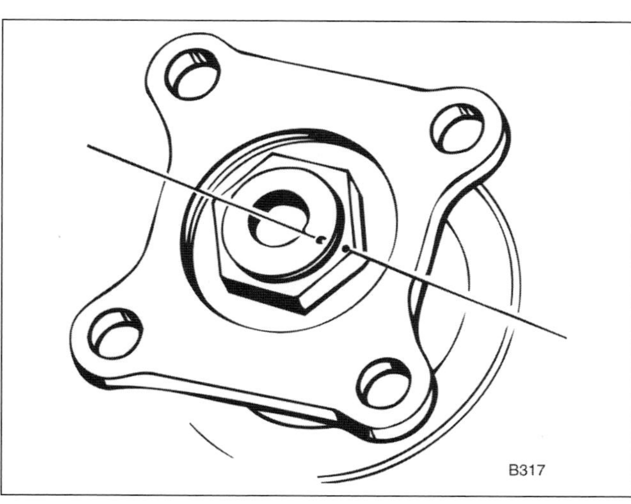

Make matching marks on differential input shaft, collar nut and driveshaft flange.

– Pry lock plate from nut. Counterhold input flange with BMW special tool 23 0 020 or equivalent and remove collar nut.

– If necessary, use puller to remove input flange.

NOTE —
Be prepared to catch dripping oil in a pan.

– Pry old oil seal from its recess using BMW special tool 00 5 010 or equivalent seal puller.

CAUTION —
Be careful not to mar the differential housing when removing the seal.

– Dip new seal in differential lubricant and drive it into position.

– Lightly lubricate input shaft and press input flange back on. Install collar nut and slowly tighten until matching marks line up.

CAUTION —
If the flange collar nut is tightened past the marks, interior components of the differential will be damaged.

– Install a new lock plate and refill differential with lubricant.

Differential oil

- Differential oil capacity
  Rear wheel drive, auto trans. . . . . 0.9 liter (0.95 US qt.)
  Rear wheel drive, manual trans
  and All wheel drive . . . . 1.0 liter (1.06 US qt.)
  M3. . . . . 1.3 liter (1.37 US qt.)
- Oil specification. . . . . BMW SAF-XO synthetic oil

– Remainder of assembly is reverse of disassembly.

Tightening torques

- Driveshaft to differential flange
  M10 compression nut . . . . 64 Nm (47 ft-lb)
  M10 Torx bolt . . . . 85 Nm (63 ft-lb)
- Differential drain or fill plug
  With O-ring . . . . 60 Nm (44 ft-lb)
  With sealing washer . . . . 65 Nm (48 ft-lb)

340 Brakes

TABLES

GENERAL

This repair group covers brake service:

- Brake pads, calipers, and rotors
- Master cylinder, brake booster, and parking brake
- ABS / ASC and ABS / DSC component replacement

ABS / ASC and ABS / DSC system descriptions are in **300 Suspension, Steering and Brakes–General**.

Special tools

BMW requires the use of the dedicated diagnostic scan tool (DISplus, GT1) to safely and completely bleed the braking and traction control systems if system hydraulic components are replaced or if air is trapped in the hydraulic system. Read procedures through before beginning a job.

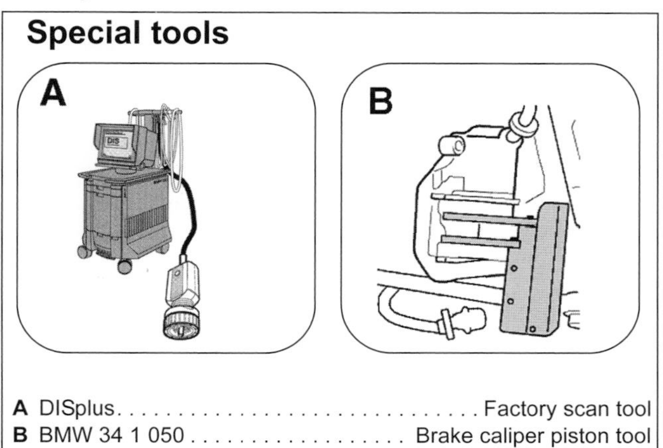

A DISplus. . . . . Factory scan tool
B BMW 34 1 050 . . . . . Brake caliper piston tool

Special tools

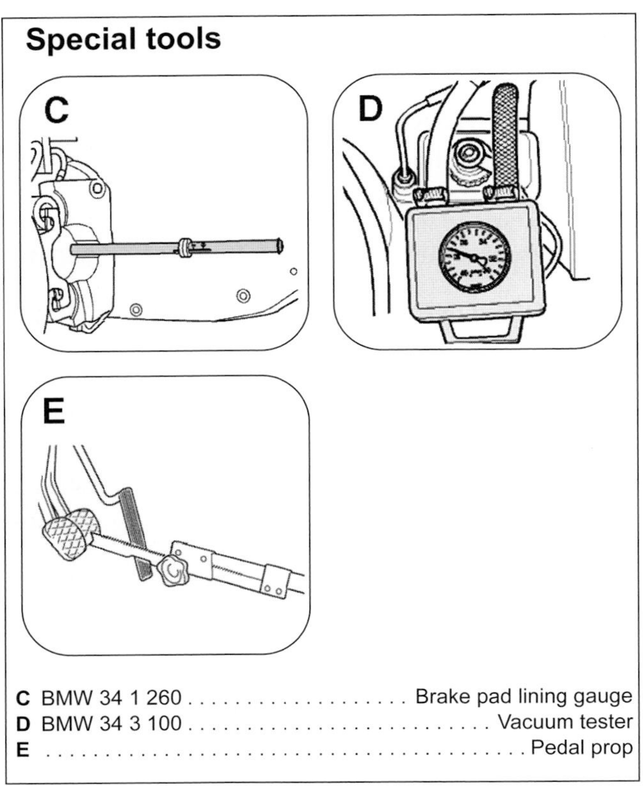

C BMW 34 1 260 . . . . Brake pad lining gauge
D BMW 34 3 100 . . . . Vacuum tester
E . . . . Pedal prop

E46 brake system

BMW E46 models are equipped with vacuum power-assisted four-wheel disc brakes with integral antilock braking (ABS). Single-piston calipers act on vented front and rear rotors. A brake pad wear sensor for each axle indicates when brake pads need replacement. The dual drum-type parking brake system is integrated with the rear brake rotors.

Electronic braking and stability control

E46 models were introduced with Automatic Stability Control (ASC). ASC is a computer controlled traction control system that uses the ABS system in conjunction with engine management to control wheel spin and maintain vehicle stability while braking.

Added midway through the 1999 model year was Dynamic Stability Control (DSC). This system uses ASC technology, but implements wheel speed modulation throughout all stages of driving. DSC is able to reduce understeer by applying differing amounts of braking force to each wheel, as well as overriding the engine management system during hard cornering.

A summary of distinguishing characteristics of the various systems is shown in **Table a**.

For ABS system and component descriptions, see **300 Suspension, Steering and Brakes–General**.

> ***WARNING —***
> *A car with electronic stability control is still subject to normal physical laws. Avoid excessive speeds for the road conditions encountered.*

Table a. E46 electronic braking and stability control systems

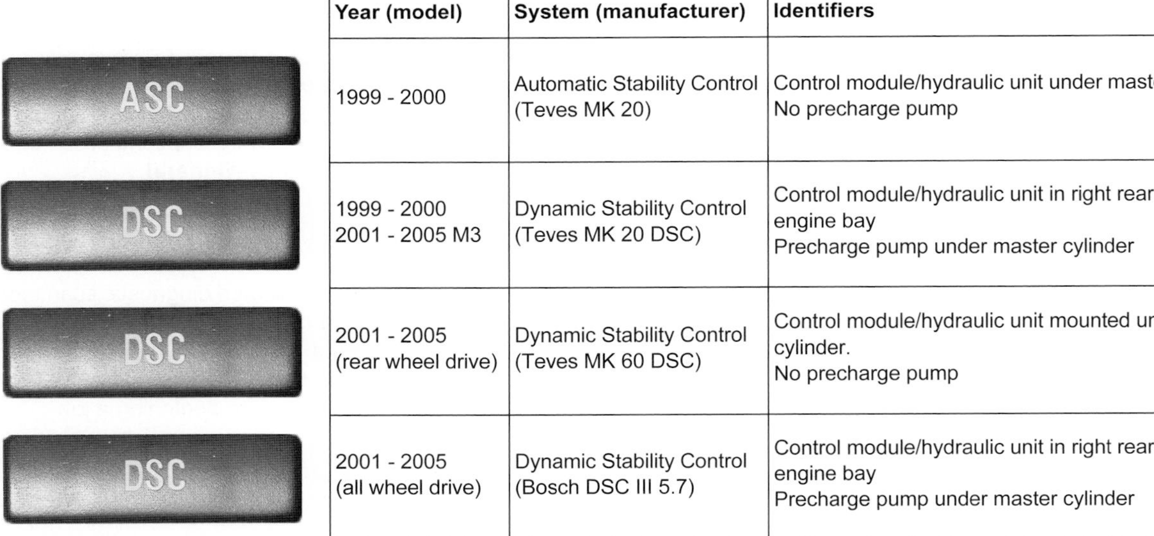

Year (model)	System (manufacturer)	Identifiers
1999 - 2000	Automatic Stability Control (Teves MK 20)	Control module/hydraulic unit under master cylinder No precharge pump
1999 - 2000 2001 - 2005 M3	Dynamic Stability Control (Teves MK 20 DSC)	Control module/hydraulic unit in right rear compartment of engine bay Precharge pump under master cylinder
2001 - 2005 (rear wheel drive)	Dynamic Stability Control (Teves MK 60 DSC)	Control module/hydraulic unit mounted under master cylinder. No precharge pump
2001 - 2005 (all wheel drive)	Dynamic Stability Control (Bosch DSC III 5.7)	Control module/hydraulic unit in right rear compartment of engine bay Precharge pump under master cylinder

Troubleshooting

Brake performance is mainly affected by three things:

- Level and condition of brake fluid
- The system's ability to create and maintain hydraulic pressure
- Condition of friction components

Air in the brake fluid makes the brake pedal feel spongy during braking or increases the brake pedal force required to stop. Fluid contaminated by moisture or dirt corrodes the system. Inspect the brake fluid inside the reservoir. If it is dirty or murky, or is more then two years old, flush the fluid.

Visually check the hydraulic system starting at the master cylinder. To check the function of the master cylinder hold the brake pedal down hard with the engine running. The pedal should feel solid and stay solid. If the pedal slowly falls to the floor, either the master cylinder is leaking internally, or fluid is leaking externally. Check brake fluid lines and couplings for leaks, kinks, chafing and corrosion. If no leaks can be found, the master cylinder is faulty and should be replaced.

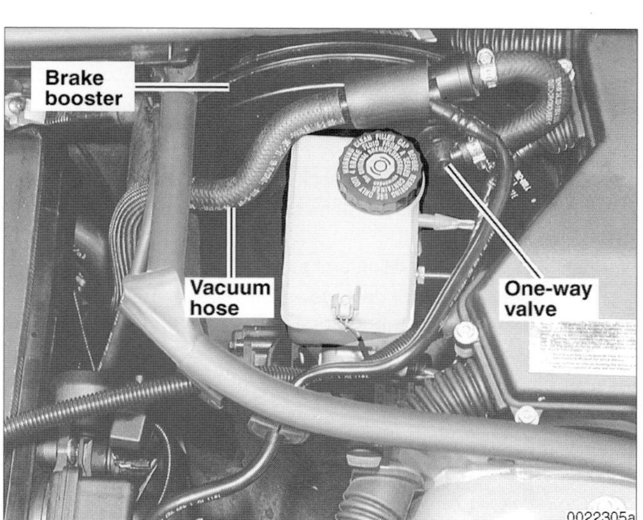

 Check brake booster:

- Remove vacuum hose from brake booster and install BMW special tool 34 3 100 between connection and hose on one-way check-valve.
- Start engine and check build-up of partial vacuum. Switch engine off.
- Press brake pedal to set partial vacuum of no more than 0.8 bar (11.6 psi). Wait for vacuum value to stabilize.
- When pedal is released, partial vacuum should not drop by more then 0.06 bar (0.8 psi) over 1 hour.

— If vacuum values are not reached:

- Check connections of vacuum hoses.
- Replace vacuum non-return valve (**B**).
- Check seal between brake booster and master cylinder.
- If values still cannot be reached, replace brake booster.

Worn or contaminated brake pads cause poor braking performance. Oil-contaminated or glazed pads cause stopping distances to increase. Inspect rotors for glazing, discoloration and scoring.

Steering wheel vibration while braking at speed is often caused by warped rotors, but can also be caused by worn suspension components.

When troubleshooting, keep in mind that tire inflation, wear and temperature all have an affect on braking. See **300 Suspension, Steering and Brakes–General** for additional suspension and brake system troubleshooting.

Table b lists symptoms of brake problems, probable causes, and suggested corrective actions. Unless it is noted otherwise, repairs are described later in this repair group

Table b. Brake system troubleshooting

Symptom	Probable cause	Repairs
Brake squeal	Incorrectly installed brake pads or parking brake shoes	Check component installation.
	Brake pad carriers dirty or corroded	Remove brake pads and clean calipers.
	Brake pad anti-rattle springs faulty or missing	Install / replace anti-rattle springs.
	Brake pads heat-glazed or oil-soaked	Replace brake pads. Clean rotors. Replace leaking calipers as required.
	Wheel bearings worn (noise most pronounced when turning)	Replace worn bearings. See **310 Front Suspension** or **330 Rear Suspension**.
Pedal goes to floor when braking	Brake fluid level low due to system leaks	Check fluid level and inspect hydraulic system for signs of leakage. Fill and bleed system.
	Master cylinder faulty	Replace master cylinder.
Low pedal after system bleeding	Master cylinder faulty	Replace master cylinder.
Pedal spongy or brakes work only when pedal is pumped	Air in brake fluid	Bleed system.
	Master cylinder faulty (internal return spring weak)	Replace master cylinder.
	Leaking line or hose unions	Repair or replace lines and hoses. Bleed system.
Excessive braking effort	Brake pads wet	Use light pedal pressure to dry pads while driving.
	Brake pads heat-glazed or oil-soaked	Replace brake pads. Clean rotors. Replace leaking calipers.
	Vacuum booster or vacuum hose connections to booster faulty	Inspect vacuum lines. Test vacuum booster and replace as required. Test vacuum check valve for one-way air flow.
Brakes pulsate, chatter or grab	Warped brake rotors	Resurface or replace rotors.
	Brake pads worn	Replace brake pads.
	Brake pads heat-glazed or oil-soaked	Replace brake pads. Clean rotors. Replace leaking calipers.
Uneven braking, car pulls to one side, rear brakes lock	Incorrect tire pressures or worn tires	Inspect tire condition. Check and correct tire pressures.
	Brake pads on one side of car heat-glazed or oil-soaked	Replace brake pads. Clean rotors. Replace leaking calipers.
	Caliper or brake pads binding	Clean and recondition brakes.
	Worn suspension components	Inspect for worn or damaged suspension components. See **310 Front Suspension** or **330 Rear Suspension**.

Warnings and cautions

WARNING —

- *Semi-metallic and metallic brake friction materials in brake pads or shoes produce dangerous dust. Avoid breathing in brake dust.*
- *Treat brake dust as a hazardous material. Do not create dust by grinding, sanding, or cleaning brake friction surfaces with compressed air.*
- *Brake fluid is poisonous, corrosive and dangerous to the environment. Wear safety glasses and rubber gloves when working with brake fluid. Do not siphon brake fluid with your mouth. Dispose of brake fluid properly.*
- *Do not reuse self-locking nuts, bolts or fasteners. They are designed to be used only once and may fail if reused. Replace with new self-locking fasteners.*

> ***CAUTION—***
> - *Models covered by this manual require special BMW service equipment to properly bleed the brake hydraulic system. See* **Bleeding Brakes** *for more information.*
> - *Immediately clean brake fluid spilled on painted surfaces and wash with water, as brake fluid removes paint.*
> - *Use new brake fluid from an unopened container. Brake fluid absorbs moisture from the air. This can lead to corrosion problems in the braking system, and also lowers the fluid boiling point.*
> - *Plug open lines and brake fluid ports to prevent contamination.*
> - *Only tighten brake hoses on front wheels with wheels in straight ahead position.*
> - *If carrying out electric welding work, be sure to disconnect electrical harness connector from electronic control module.*
> - *Do not expose electronic control modules to high sustained heat, such as in a paint drying booth. Maximum heat exposure: 95°C (203°F) for short periods of time, 85°C (185°F) for long periods (approx. 2 hours).*

BLEEDING BRAKES

Brake bleeding is usually done for one of two reasons: either to replace old brake fluid as part of routine maintenance or to expel trapped air in the system that resulted from opening the brake hydraulic system during repairs.

When adding or replacing brake fluid, add new brake fluid from an unopened container. It is important to bleed the entire system when any part of the hydraulic system has been opened.

If you are certain no air was introduced into the master cylinder or traction control hydraulic unit, bleed brakes at the calipers using a pressure bleeder. See **Brake calipers, bleeding** in this repair group.

If air was introduced into the master cylinder or traction control hydraulic unit, or you are unsure, bleed brakes using a BMW scan tool (DISplus / GT1) or bring the car to an authorized BMW dealer. See **Brake system, bleeding** in this repair group.

> ***WARNING—***
> - *The ASC and DSC systems use electronic controls and a sophisticated hydraulic unit. Once air enters the hydraulic unit, it is difficult to remove using traditional methods. For this reason, pressure bleed the brakes using the BMW service tester (DISplus / GT1).*
> - *When flushing brake fluid from the system, use extreme care to not let the brake fluid reservoir run dry. If air enters the hydraulic unit, the BMW service tester MUST be used to bleed the brake system before the vehicle is driven.*

When bleeding the brakes, start at the wheel farthest from the master cylinder and progress in the following order:

- right rear brake
- left rear brake
- right front brake
- left front brake

Brake calipers, bleeding

– To begin work, jack up car and support securely. Remove wheels.

> ***WARNING —***
> *Make sure the car is stable and well supported at all times. Use a professional automotive lift or jack stands designed for the purpose. A floor jack is not adequate support.*

– Top off brake fluid in reservoir and connect pressure bleeder to reservoir. Connect bleeder hose and bottle to right rear caliper bleeder screw. Pressurize system to approximately 2 bar (29 psi).

> ***CAUTION —***
> *Do not exceed a pressure of 2 bar (29 psi) when pressure bleeding the brake system. Excessive pressure damages the brake fluid reservoir.*

– Have a helper hold brake pedal down.

0022301

 Open bleeder screw (**arrow**). Have helper slowly pump brakes about 10 times with bleeder screw open, holding pedal down on the last pump. When escaping fluid is free of air bubbles, close bleeder screw.

> ***CAUTION —***
> *Make sure bleeder hose remains submersed in clean brake fluid whenever the bleeder valve is open.*

– Close bleeder screw and release brake pedal. Refill brake fluid reservoir and proceed to left rear wheel.

– Continue bleeding remaining wheels in the following order:

- left rear
- right front
- left front

Tightening torques

- Bleeder screws (wrench size):
  - 7 mm screw . . . . 3.5 - 5 Nm (2 - 4 ft-lb)
  - 9 mm screw . . . . 7 - 11 Nm (5 - 8 ft-lb)
  - 11 mm screw. . . . . 12 - 16 Nm (9 - 12 ft-lb)

Brake system, bleeding

The procedure below requires a BMW service tester (DIS-plus / GT1).

– Determine type of traction control (ASC, DSC). Be sure to use correct specification brake fluid, according to application table below.

Brake fluid applications
- ABS / ASC . . . . DOT 4 brake fluid
- ABS / DSC . . . . DOT 4 low viscosity brake fluid

NOTE —
Brake fluid specifications are subject to change. Consult your authorized BMW parts department for the latest operating fluids information.

– Top off brake fluid in reservoir and connect BMW service tester to 20-pin DLC in engine compartment (1999 models) or 16-pin OBD II connector (2000 - 2005 models) under dashboard.

– Call up service function Bleeding ABS / ASC or service function Bleeding ABS / DSC, depending on installed system.

– Fill pressure bleeding device with correct brake fluid and connect to brake fluid reservoir. Pressurize system.

CAUTION —
Do not exceed a pressure of 2 bar (29 psi) when pressure bleeding the brake system. Excessive pressure damages the brake fluid reservoir.

– Jack up car and support securely. Remove wheels.

WARNING —
Make sure the car is stable and well supported at all times. Use a professional automotive lift or jack stands designed for the purpose. A floor jack is not adequate support.

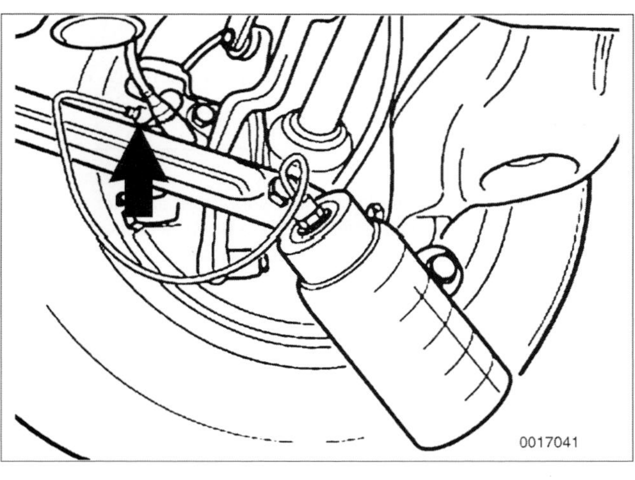

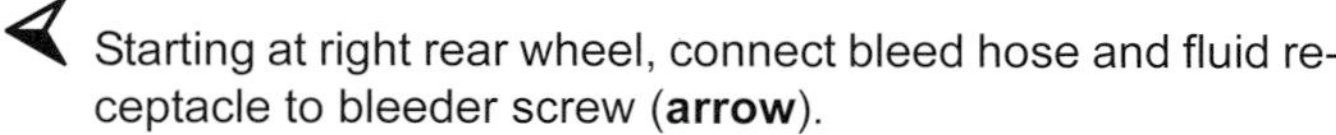
Starting at right rear wheel, connect bleed hose and fluid receptacle to bleeder screw (**arrow**).

– Following on-screen instructions, open bleeder screw and flush fluid until it runs clear and bubble-free. Close bleeder.

CAUTION —
Make sure bleeder hose remains submersed in clean brake fluid whenever the bleeder valve is open.

– Follow same bleeding procedure in the following order:
- left rear
- right front
- left front

– Reattach bleeder assembly to **right rear** brake caliper. Open bleeder screw. Carry out bleeding procedure with BMW service tester until clear, bubble-free fluid flows.

- Models with ASC: Close **right rear** bleeder.
- Models with DSC: After BMW service tester bleeding routine has finished, press brake pedal to floor 5 times until clear, bubble-free fluid flows. Close **right rear** bleeder.

– Repeat procedure at **left rear** brake.

– Repeat BMW service tester bleeding at **right front** brake.

- Models with ASC: After BMW service tester bleeding routine has finished, press brake pedal to floor 12 times until clear, bubble-free fluid flows. Close **right front** bleeder.
- Models with DSC: After BMW service tester bleeding routine has finished, press brake pedal to floor 5 times until clear, bubble-free fluid flows. Close **right front** bleeder.

– Repeat procedure at **left front** brake.

– Remove brake bleeding apparatus and disconnect BMW service tester. Top up brake fluid. Check to make sure brake fluid reservoir cap seal is intact.

Tightening torques

- Bleeder screws (wrench size):
  7 mm screw . . . . 3.5 - 5 Nm (2 - 4 ft-lb)
  9 mm screw . . . . 7 - 11 Nm (5 - 8 ft-lb)
  11 mm screw. . . . . 12 - 16 Nm (9 - 12 ft-lb)

BRAKE PADS, CALIPERS AND ROTORS

Brake pads can be replaced without disconnecting the brake fluid hose from the caliper or having to bleed the brakes. The rotors can be replaced without disassembling wheel hub and bearing. Machine or replace rotors in axle pairs. Replace pads in axle sets.

Refer to the accompanying illustration (next page) and the detail notes (indicated in **bold**) during replacement procedures.

– To begin work, jack up car and support securely. Remove wheels.

> ***WARNING —***
> *Make sure the car is stable and well supported at all times. Use a professional automotive lift or jack stands designed for the purpose. A floor jack is not adequate support.*

Caliper removal

B305340002

◄ Insert pedal prop and depress brake pedal slightly. This prevents brake fluid from escaping when brake lines are detached.

Brake pads, calipers and rotors

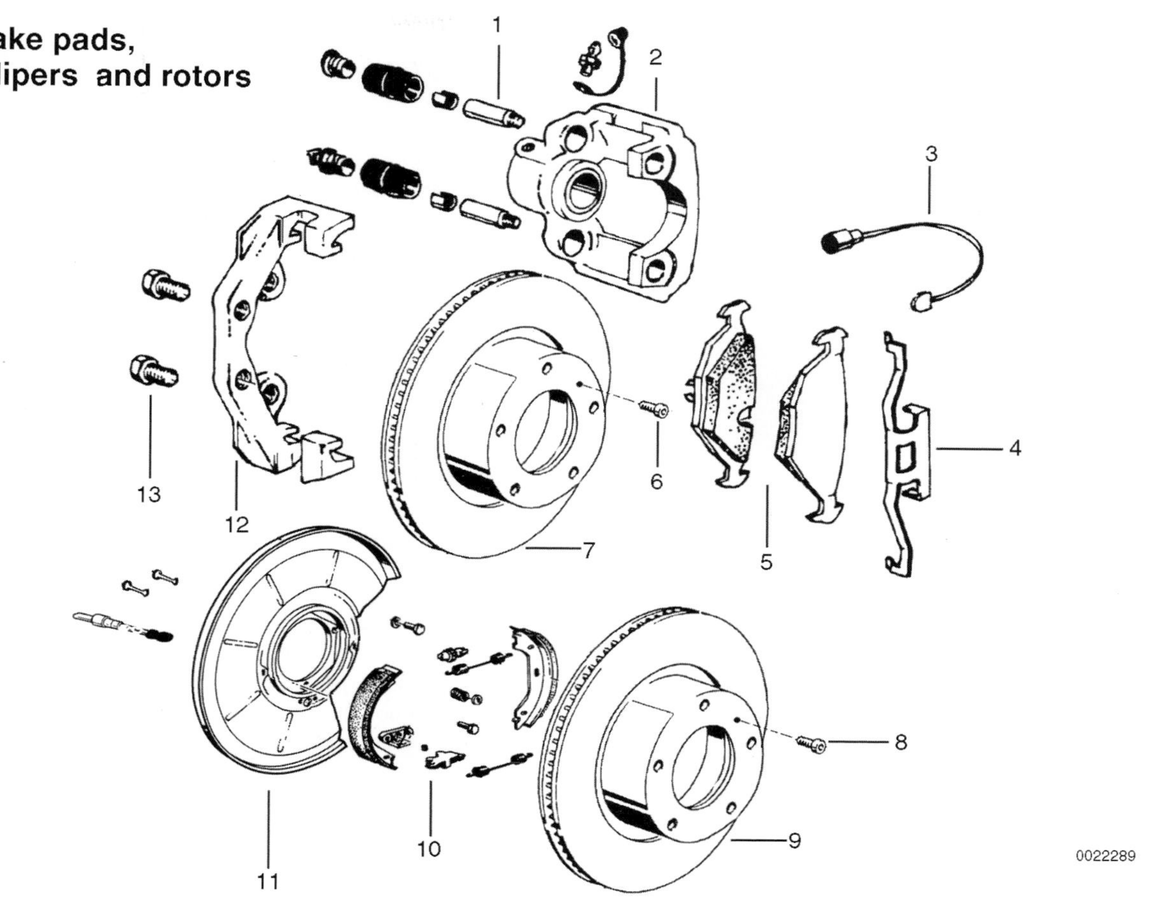

1. Brake caliper guide bolts
   7 mm Allen head,
   -torque to 30 Nm (22 ft-lb).
2. Brake caliper
   -torque brake line to 18 Nm (13 ft-lb)
   See **Caliper removal**.
3. Brake pad wear sensor
   See **Brake pad wear sensor**.
4. Brake pad anti-rattle clip
   See **Brake pad anti-rattle clip**.
5. Brake pads
   replacement warning at 3.0 mm (0.11 in.)
6. Front brake rotor retaining screw
   -torque to 16 Nm (12 ft-lb)
7. Front brake rotor
   Make sure contact surfaces are clean and free from grease.
   See **Brake rotor removal**.
8. Rear brake rotor retaining screw
   Torque to 16 Nm (12 ft-lb)
9. Rear brake rotor
   Make sure contact surfaces are clean and grease-free.
   Parking brake drum dia. 160 mm (6.3 in.)
   See **Brake rotor removal**.
   For brake rotor specifications see **Table c** and **Table d**.
10. Parking brake shoes with hardware:
    Min. lining thickness 1.5 mm (0.06 in.)
11. Rear brake dust shield
12. Brake pad carrier
    Make sure contact surfaces are clean and grease-free.
    See **Brake pad carrier removal**.
13. Brake pad carrier retaining bolts:
    Front: torque to 110 Nm (81 ft-lb).
    Rear: torque to 65 Nm (48 ft-lb).
    Oil bolts lightly. Make sure contact surfaces are clean and grease-free.

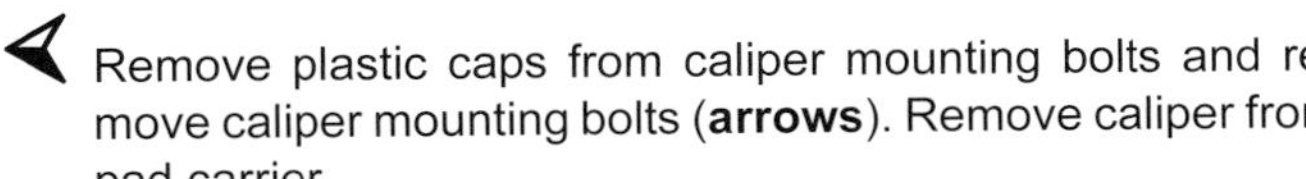

Remove plastic caps from caliper mounting bolts and remove caliper mounting bolts (**arrows**). Remove caliper from pad carrier.

> ***CAUTION —***
> *Do not let brake caliper hang from brake hose. Suspend it from chassis using stiff wire.*

- Inspect brake caliper for signs of leakage. Check that caliper piston slides smoothly into caliper. Replace caliper if faults are found.

- Detach brake caliper hydraulic line only when replacing brake caliper with a new unit. If removing brake caliper to service brake pads or rotors, leave hydraulic line connected.

- If there is a ridge on rotor edge, press caliper piston back into caliper before removing caliper.

> ***CAUTION —***
> *Pressing caliper piston in may cause brake fluid reservoir to overflow. To prevent this, use a clean syringe to first remove some fluid from reservoir.*

- Open caliper bleeder screw only when applying force to piston. Do not allow air to be drawn in through bleeder screw. Catch expelled fluid in appropriate container.

- Thoroughly clean all contact points on caliper and brake pad carrier. Clean guide bolts and make sure they slide freely. Do not lubricate guide bolts.

- After installation, bleed brake system if hydraulic line to caliper was detached. See **Brake calipers, bleeding** in this repair group.

Tightening torque
- Caliper to brake pad carrier . . . . 30 Nm (22 ft-lb)

Brake pad wear sensor

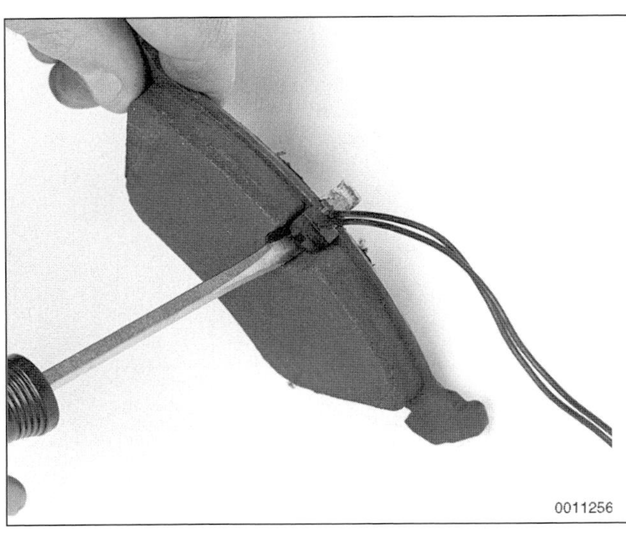

Carefully pry pad wear sensor from brake pad.

- Insert brake pad wear sensor into cutout in new pad where applicable.

- If brake pad wear warning light illuminated prior to brake pad replacement, replace wear sensor.

- Route pad wear sensor wiring through caliper opening and bleeder dust cap.

> ***NOTE —***
> *After replacing pads and sensors, turn the ignition key on and leave on for approx. 2 minutes. This resets the brake pad wear warning light.*

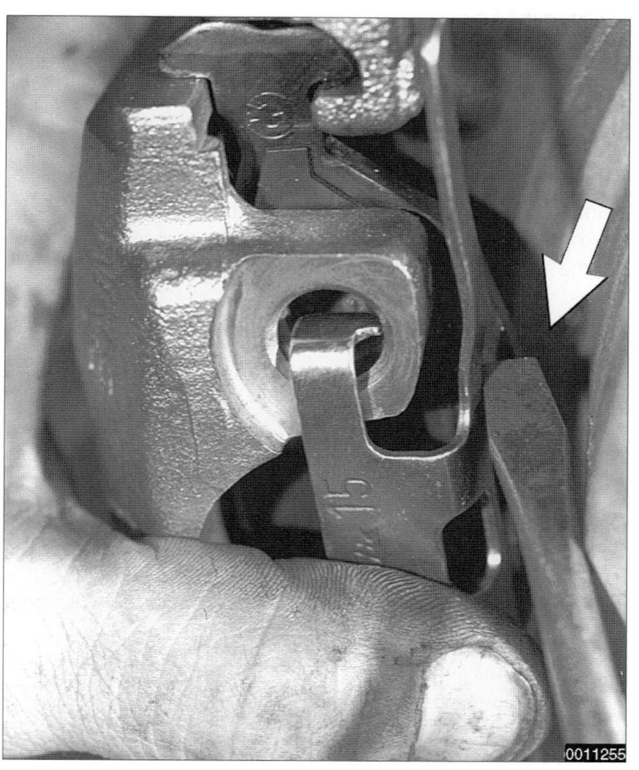

Brake pad anti-rattle clip

◄ Remove anti-rattle clip by unhooking at top and bottom. Use screwdriver as an aid (**arrow**).

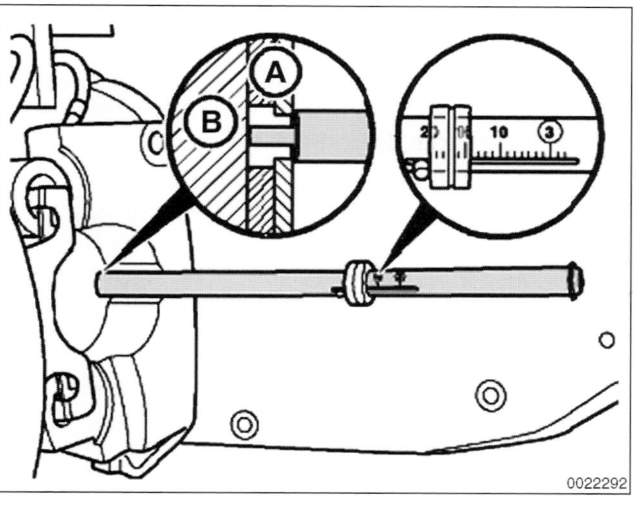

Brake pad lining thickness

◄ Insert BMW special tool 34 1 260 at either front right wheel or left rear wheel.

– Move wheel until notch for brake wear indicator can be seen through wheel opening.

– Insert tip of tool into notch so that the body of tool rests on brake pad backing plate (**A**), and tip touches brake disc (**B**).

– Replace pads if thickness is 3.0 mm (0.12 in.) or less.

Brake rotor removal

Remove brake rotor mounting screw (**arrow**).

- Inspect rotor for cracks, signs of overheating and scoring.
- Original equipment rotor: Minimum allowable thickness is stamped on rotor hub. Measure rotor braking surface with a micrometer at eight to ten different points and use the smallest measurement recorded. See **Table c**.
- If rotor does not pass minimum thickness requirements or is damaged, replace.
- Replace brake rotors in pairs.
- Clean rotor with brake cleaner before installing.
- After installing new rear brake rotors, adjust parking brake. See **Parking brake shoes, adjusting** in this repair group.

Table c. Brake rotor reconditioning specifications

	Front	Rear
Vented rotor wear limit (min. thickness) M3	20.4 mm (0.80 in) 26.4 mm (1.04 in)	17.4 mm (0.68 in) 18.4 mm (0.73 in)
Max. machine limit per friction ring side	0.8 mm (0.03 in)	0.8 mm (0.03 in)

> ***WARNING —***
> *Confirm rotor wear limit specifications given in* **Table c** *with specifications stamped on rotor shell and identified with "MIN TH".*

Table d. Brake rotor sizes

Model	Front	Rear
323 i / Ci	286 x 22 mm (11.3 x 0.9 in)	276 x 19 mm (10.8 x 0.7 in)
325 i / Ci / xi 328 i / Ci	300 x 22 mm (11.8 x 0.9 in)	294 x 19 mm (11.6 x 0.7 in)
330 i / Ci / xi	325 x 25 mm (12.8 x 1.0 in)	320 x 22 mm (12.6 x 0.9 in)
M3	325 x 28 mm (12.8 x 1.1 in)	328 x 20 mm (12.6 x 0.8 in)
M3 CSL	345 x28 mm (13.6 x 1.1 in)	328 x 20 mm (12.9 x 0.8 in)

Tightening torque

- Brake rotor to hub mounting screw. . . . . 16 Nm (12 ft-lb)

Brake pad carrier removal

Remove brake pad carrier mounting bolts (**arrows**) and remove pad carrier from steering arm or trailing arm.

Tightening torques

- Pad carrier to front steering arm . . . . . . .110 Nm (81 ft-lb)
- Pad carrier to rear trailing arm . . . . 65 Nm (48 ft-lb)

BRAKE MASTER CYLINDER

The brake master cylinder is mounted to the front of the vacuum booster on the driver side bulkhead.

Master cylinder, removing and installing

– Using a clean syringe, empty brake fluid reservoir.

> ***WARNING —***
> *Brake fluid is highly corrosive and dangerous to the environment. Dispose of it properly.*

Remove interior ventilation microfilter housing:

- Remove upper cover and microfilter.
- Open wiring harness loom (**A**) and remove wires.
- Unfasten screws (**B**) and remove lower microfilter housing.

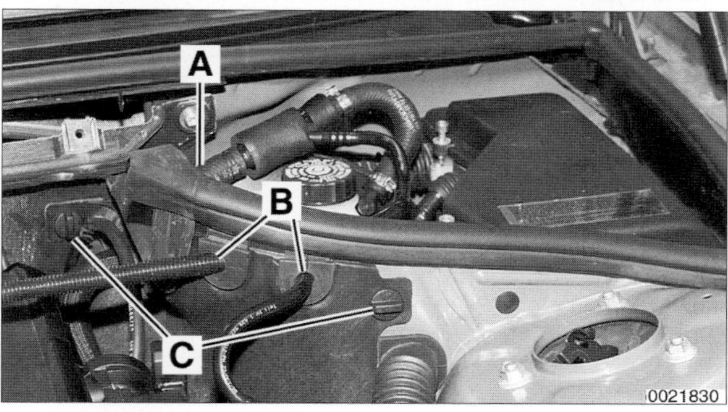

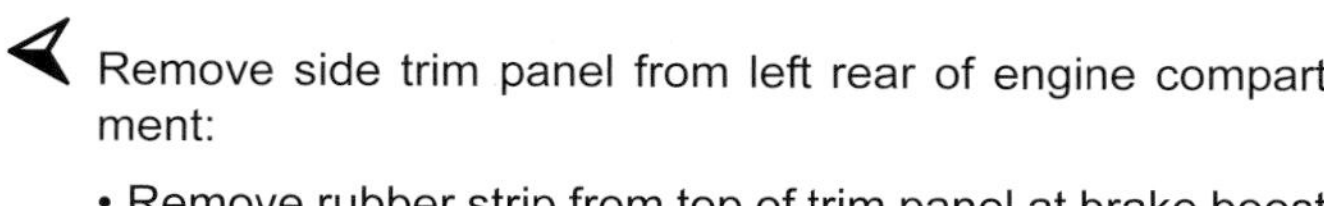

Remove side trim panel from left rear of engine compartment:

- Remove rubber strip from top of trim panel at brake booster.
- Detach vacuum line (**A**) from brake booster Y-connector, unhook from trim panel and push to side.
- Unhook plastic vacuum line and positive starter cable (**B**) from trim panel and pull forward.
- Release locking clips (**C**) on edges of trim panel and remove panel by pulling upward.

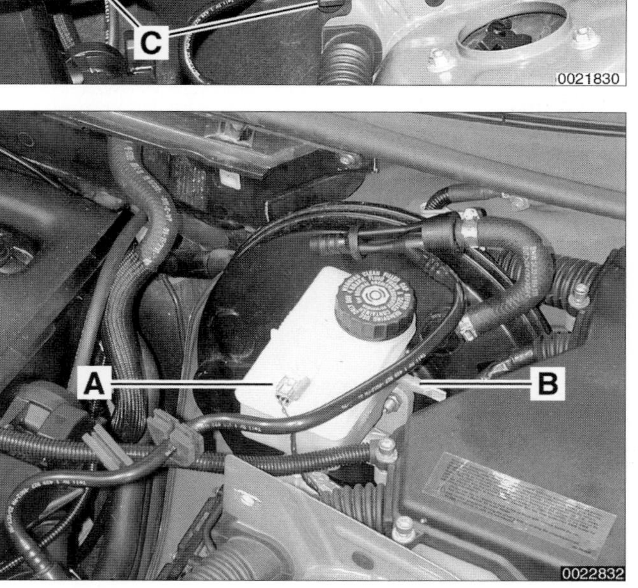
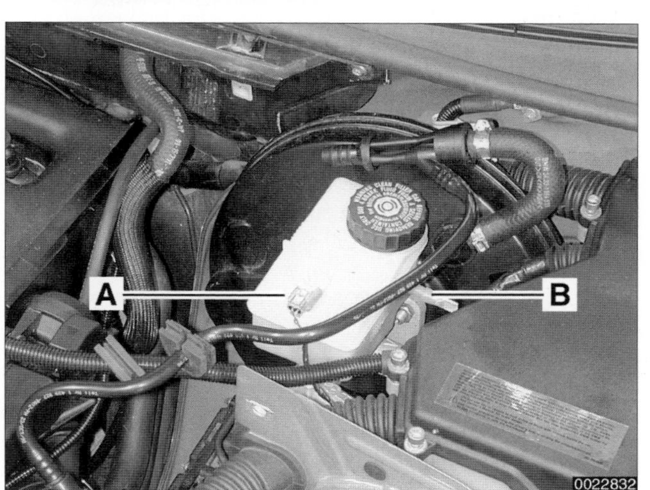

Working at brake master cylinder:

- Disconnect brake fluid level sensor connector (**A**) from fluid reservoir.
- Disconnect hydraulic clutch system supply line (**B**) if applicable. Plug open brake fluid ducts to prevent fluid leakage or contamination.

> ***CAUTION —***
> *Keep clutch supply line supported and above clutch master cylinder to prevent any air bubbles from reaching the clutch hydraulic system.*

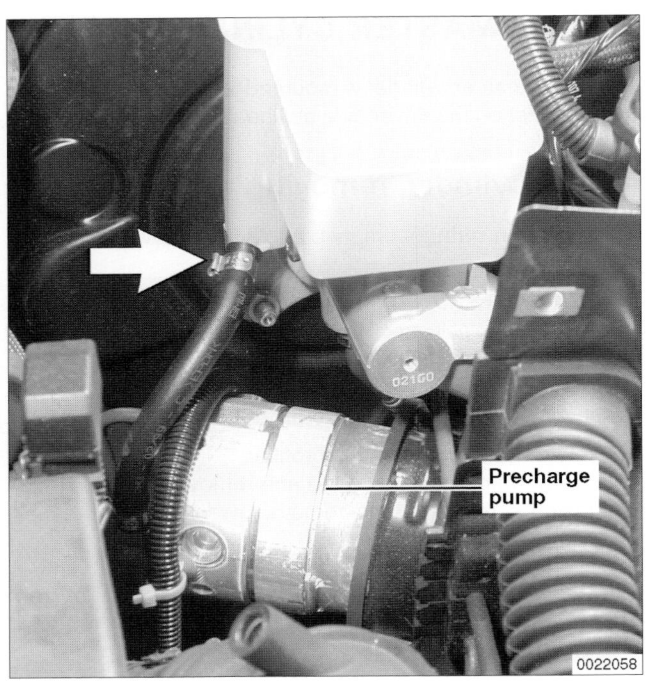

If DSC precharge pump is installed below brake master cylinder:

- Release hose clamp (**arrow**) at brake fluid reservoir and remove precharge pump supply hose.
- Plug hose and reservoir to prevent fluid leakage or contamination.

— Remove brake fluid reservoir.

— Working at master cylinder:

- Disconnect brake fluid lines and electrical harness connectors from master cylinder as needed.
- If equipped with Teves DSC: Remove brake system pressure sensors if replacing master cylinder.
- Unscrew mounting nuts and remove master cylinder from brake booster.
- Plug open brake lines to prevent contamination.

— Make sure fasteners, fluid couplings, thread bores, and mating surfaces are clean.

— Mount master cylinder to brake booster using a new O-ring and new self-locking nuts.

> ***CAUTION —***
> - *Be sure to align master cylinder pushrod and booster pushrod.*
> - *Do not over-torque master cylinder mounting nuts. This could damage brake booster and prevent proper vacuum build-up.*

Tightening torque
- Brake master cylinder to brake booster . . . . 26 Nm (19 ft-lb)

— Connect brake fluid lines to master cylinder.

Tightening torque
- Brake fluid lines to master cylinder . . . . 18 Nm (13 ft-lb)

NOTE —
If equipped with Teves MK 20 ASC: Leave flex in flexible brake lines between master cylinder and hydraulic unit.

— Carefully reinstall fluid reservoir using new sealing grommets.

— Reconnect precharge pump supply hose to brake fluid reservoir, if applicable.

— Connect hydraulic clutch hose to brake fluid reservoir, if applicable.

— Remainder of installation is reverse of removal. Bleed entire brake system. See **Brake system, bleeding** in this repair group.

BRAKE BOOSTER

The brake booster is mounted to the bulkhead on driver's side of engine compartment, directly behind brake master cylinder.

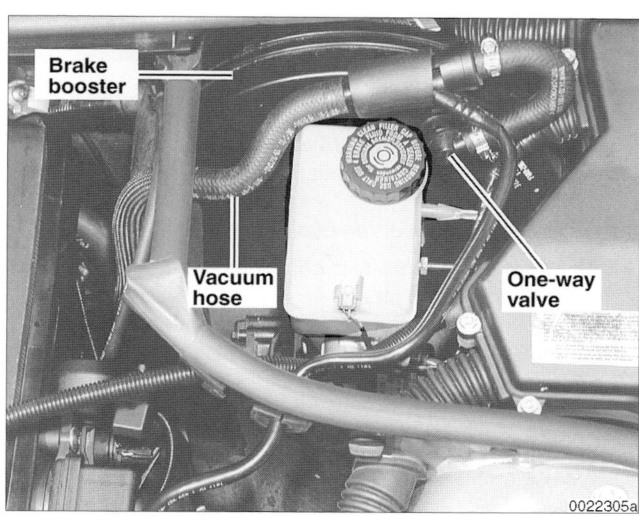

Intake manifold vacuum acts on a large diaphragm in brake booster to reduce brake pedal effort.

Brake booster, removing and installing

– Disconnect negative (–) cable from battery.

> ***CAUTION —***
> *Prior to disconnecting the battery, read the battery disconnection cautions given at front of this manual.*

– Using a clean syringe, empty brake fluid reservoir.

> ***WARNING —***
> *Brake fluid is highly corrosive and dangerous to the environment. Dispose of it properly.*

– Remove brake master cylinder. See **Master cylinder, removing and installing** in this repair group. Make sure to plug openings at brake fluid lines.

– Detach engine vacuum hose from brake booster.

– Remove hydraulic unit or precharge pump below master cylinder. See **Hydraulic unit / control module, removing and installing** or **DSC precharge pump, removing and installing** in this repair group.

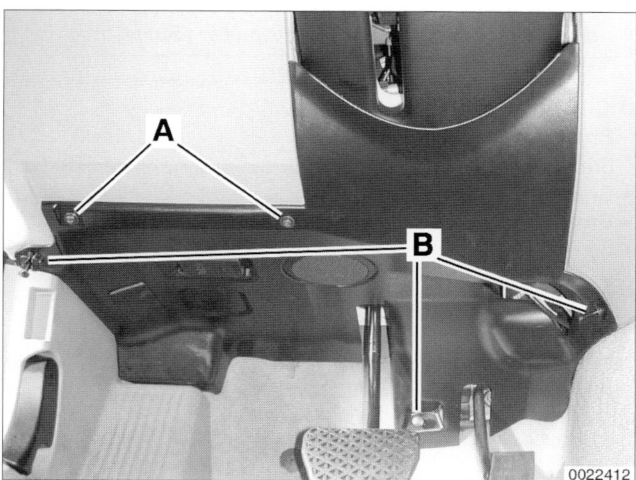

Working in vehicle interior, remove left footwell (pedal cluster) trim panel.

- Remove screws (**A**).
- Remove fasteners (**B**).

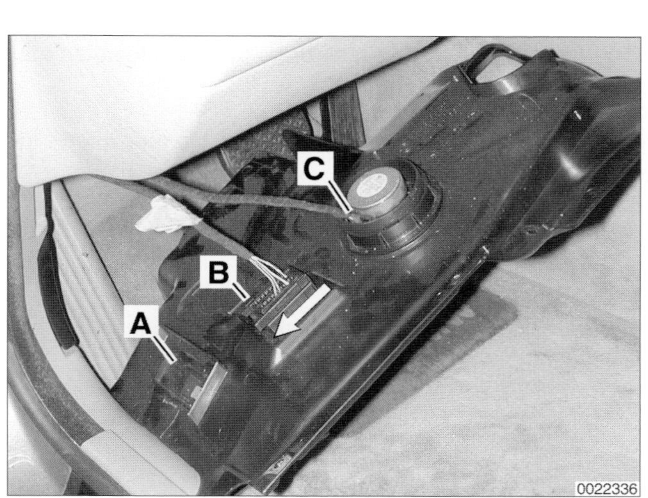

Disconnect electrical harness connectors at left footwell trim panel and remove panel:

- Unplug connector at footwell interior light (**A**), if equipped.
- Slide lock at OBD II connector (**B**) in direction of **arrow**.
- Unplug connector at speaker (**C**).

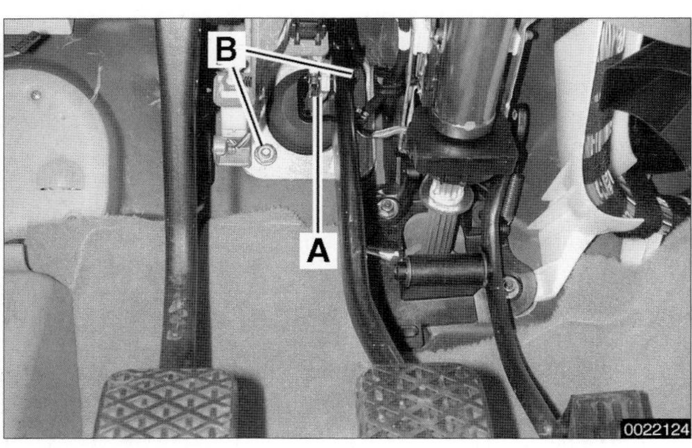

Remove clip (**A**) and slide brake booster pushrod off brake pedal pin. Remove brake booster mounting nuts (**B**).

– Working in engine compartment, carefully separate brake booster from engine compartment bulkhead.

> ***CAUTION —***
> *Do not use force on booster when separating from bulkhead. This can damage booster and pushrod.*

– Remove booster by tilting brake booster out in direction of engine. Lift booster up and out from engine compartment.

– Installation is reverse of removal, noting the following:

- Make sure fasteners, fluid couplings, thread bores, and mating surfaces are clean.
- Replace brake booster self-locking mounting nuts.
- Replace sealing O-ring between master cylinder and brake booster.
- Bleed brake system as described earlier.

> ***CAUTION —***
> - *Be sure to align master cylinder pushrod and booster pushrod.*
> - *Do not over-torque master cylinder mounting nuts. This could damage brake booster and prevent proper vacuum build-up.*

Tightening torques

- Brake master cylinder to brake booster . . . . 26 Nm (19 ft-lb)
- Brake booster to bulkhead . . . . 22 Nm (16 ft-lb)
- Brake fluid line to master cylinder or hydraulic unit. . . . . 18 Nm (13 ft-lb)

NOTE —
When replacing the brake booster one-way check-valve or vacuum hose, install the valve so that the molded arrow is pointing toward the intake manifold. Use new hose clamps.

PARKING BRAKE

The parking brake is a brake drum system integrated into the rear brake rotors.

The parking brake can be adjusted with the rear wheels installed but off the ground.

Adjust the parking brake under the following circumstances:

- Replacing parking brake shoes
- Replacing rear brake rotors
- Excessive stroke of parking brake handle required for actuation (more then 10 notches)
- Replacement of adjustment unit or parking brake cables

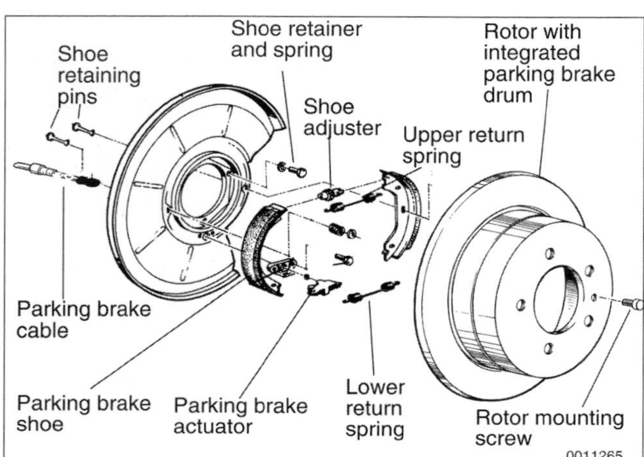

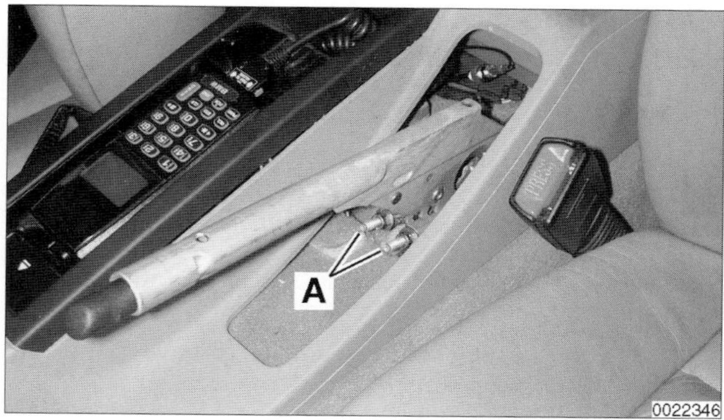

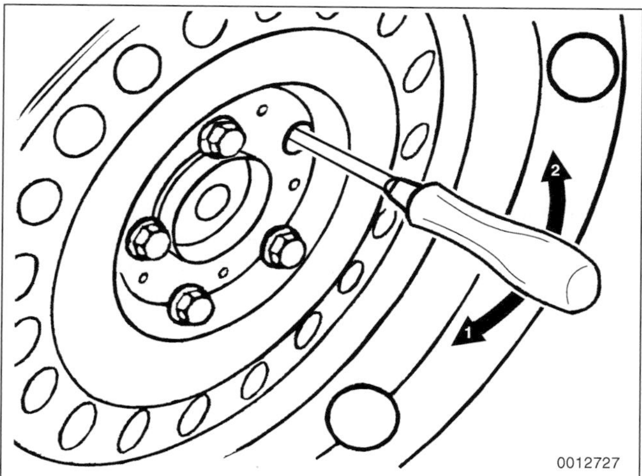

Parking brake shoes, adjusting

 Lift parking brake lever boot out of console. While holding cables stationary, loosen parking brake cable nuts (**A**) until cables are completely slack.

– Raise rear of car.

> ***WARNING —***
> *Make sure the car is stable and well supported at all times. Use a professional automotive lift or jack stands designed for the purpose. A floor jack is not adequate support.*

– Remove one lug bolt from each rear wheel. Turn road wheel until lug bolt hole lines up with parking brake adjuster (approximately 65° to rear of wheel centerline).

< Use flat-bladed screwdriver to turn adjuster.

- Left wheel: Turn adjuster in direction **1** to expand shoes.
- Right wheel: Turn adjuster in direction **2** to expand shoes.

– Using a screwdriver, turn adjuster to expand brake shoes until road wheel can no longer turn, then back adjuster off. Repeat procedure on other rear wheel.

Parking brake adjusting (initial)
- Tighten adjuster . . . . until wheel lock-up
- Back off adjuster . . . . 10 notches

– Working inside car, set parking brake several times to seat cable. Then pull parking brake lever up two notches. Tighten cable adjusting nuts until it is just possible to turn rear wheels with slight resistance.

– Release lever and make sure rear wheels turn freely.

– Turn on ignition. Pull up parking brake lever 1 notch and make sure that parking brake warning light comes on.

– Pull parking brake lever up one more notch and check that rear wheels do not move and parking brake warning light stays lit. If parking brake light goes out, adjust contact switch.

– Install parking brake lever boot. Install road wheel lug bolts.

Tightening torque
- Road wheel to hub . . . . .120 ± 10 Nm (90 ± 7 ft-lb)

Parking brake shoes, removing and installing

- Raise rear of car and remove road wheels.

> ***WARNING —***
> *Make sure the car is stable and well supported at all times. Use a professional automotive lift or jack stands designed for the purpose. A floor jack is not adequate support.*

- Without disconnecting brake fluid hose, remove rear brake calipers from trailing arms. Remove rear brake rotors. See **Brake Pads, Calipers and Rotors**.

> ***CAUTION —***
> *Do not let the brake caliper assembly hang from the brake hose. Support caliper from chassis with strong wire.*

- Unhook upper return spring from brake shoes. Remove shoe retainers by pushing them in and rotating ¼ turn. If needed, use BMW special tool 34 4 000 to remove retainers.
- Spread shoes apart and lift out.
- Inspect shoe expander to make sure it functions properly. Apply a thin coat of grease to sliding parts and pins.
- Installation is reverse of removal. Be sure to adjust parking brake cables. See **Parking brake shoes, adjusting** in this repair group.

Parking brake cable, replacing

The parking brake is actuated by two separate Bowden cables between the parking brake handle and the parking brake shoe actuators at the rear brake backing plates. Each cable can be replaced separately.

To replace a cable it is not necessary to disassemble the rear brakes. Remove the complete exhaust system and lower the exhaust system heat shield to access the front end of the parking brake cable housing.

- Working inside car, gain access to base of parking brake handle by removing center console storage tray and center armrest, as necessary.

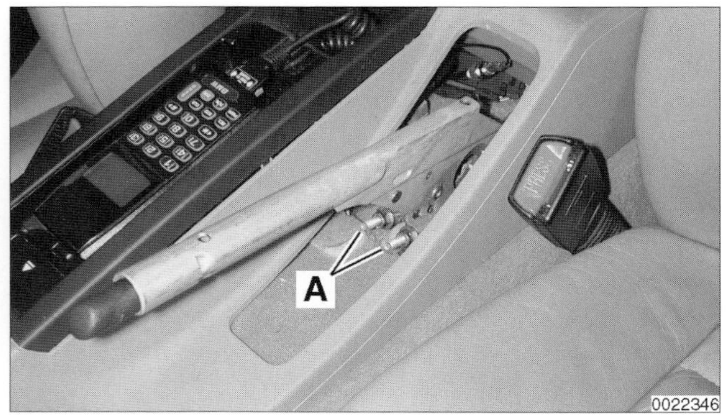

◄ Use BMW special tool 34 1 030 or equivalent deep 10 mm socket to remove parking brake cable lock nuts (**A**) at base of parking brake handle.

- Raise rear of car.

> ***WARNING —***
> *Make sure the car is stable and well supported at all times. Use a professional automotive lift or jack stands designed for the purpose. A floor jack is not adequate support.*

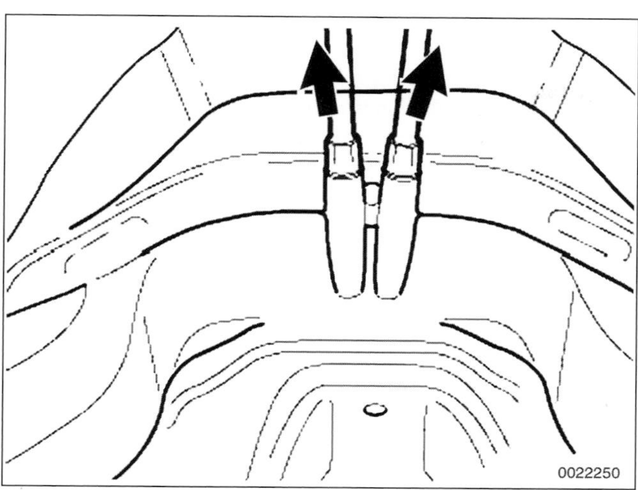

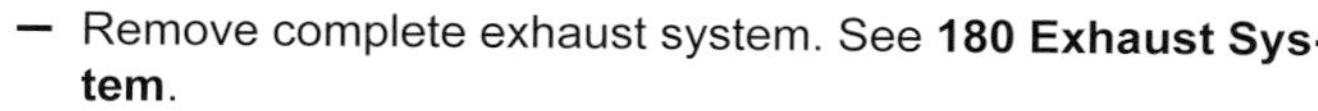
- Remove complete exhaust system. See **180 Exhaust System**.

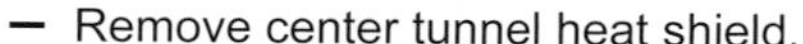
- Remove center tunnel heat shield.

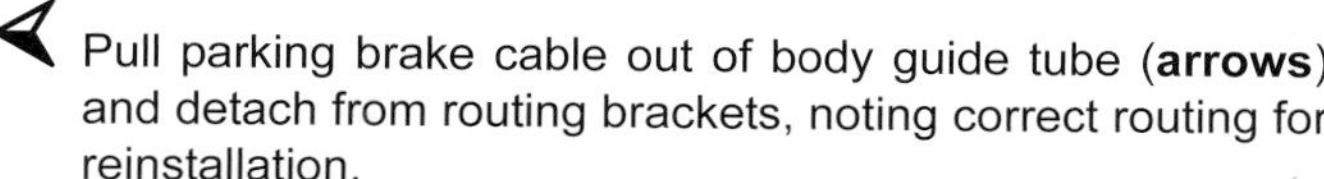
- Pull parking brake cable out of body guide tube (**arrows**) and detach from routing brackets, noting correct routing for reinstallation.

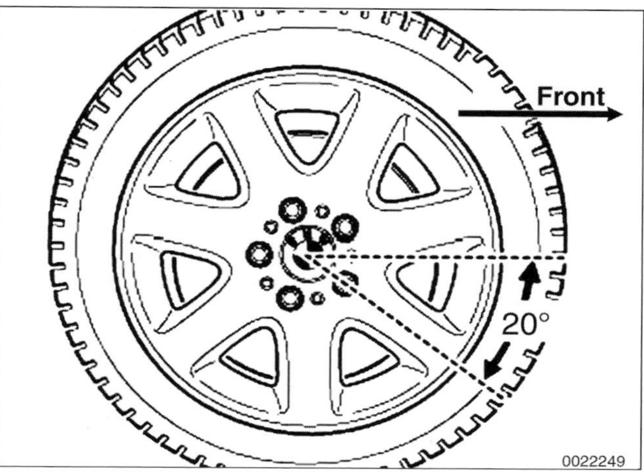

- Remove one lug bolt from rear wheel. To access end of parking brake cable, turn wheel until lug bolt hole is approx. 20° below horizontal.

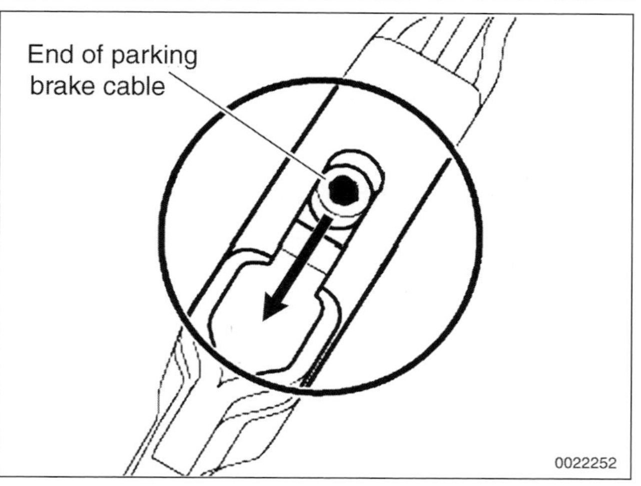

- Disconnect cable from parking brake actuator:
  - Push free (parking brake handle) end of cable into housing to create slack inside brake drum.
  - Poke thin screwdriver through lug bolt hole and pry end of parking brake cable downward (**arrow**).
  - Pull cable out of back of backing plate.
- To reinstall:
  - Push new cable housing into hole in back of backing plate.
  - Push free (parking brake handle) end of cable into housing until end of cable snaps audibly into holder inside brake drum.

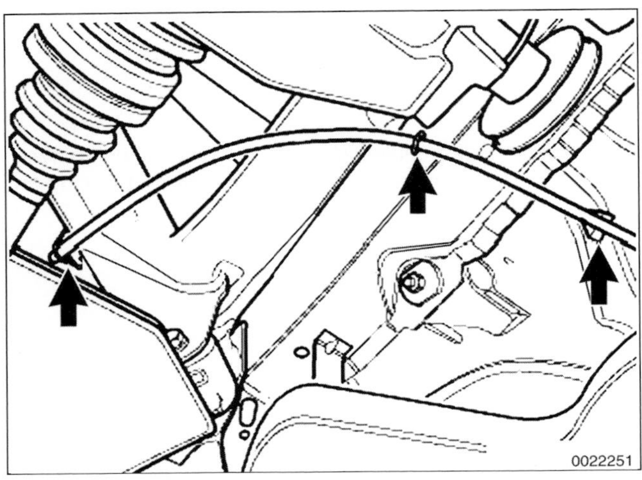

Reroute new cable under car, attaching to brackets (**arrows**).

– Remainder of installation is reverse of removal. Adjust parking brake. See **Parking brake shoes, adjusting** in this repair group.

ABS COMPONENT REPLACEMENT

> ***CAUTION—***
> - *If the tires on the car are of different makes, the ASC system may over-react. Only fit tires of the same make and tread pattern.*
> - *In adverse conditions, such as trying to rock the car out of deep snow or another soft surface, or when snow chains are fitted, switch off ASC and allow the car's driveline to operate conventionally.*

E46 vehicles are equipped with antilock braking (ABS). Early production models featured ABS with Automatic Stability Control (ABS / ASC). Later models came equipped with ABS and Dynamic Stability Control (ABS / DSC). This manual will refer to these systems as ABS (ASC or DSC will be specified when necessary).

For ABS system and component descriptions, see **300 Suspension, Steering and Brakes–General**.

Wheel speed sensor, replacing

> ***CAUTION—***
> *Magnetoresistive & Hall effect wheel speed sensors can be interchanged physically in the rear wheels, but function is not similar.*

– Raise applicable end of car.

> ***WARNING—***
> *Make sure the car is stable and well supported at all times. Use a professional automotive lift or jack stands designed for the purpose. A floor jack is not adequate support.*

Front sensor: Unscrew mounting bolt at steering arm (**arrow**).

◀ Rear sensor: Remove sensor from its bore (**arrow**) in the rear trailing arm.

NOTE —
ABS wheel speed sensor application may vary depending on traction control system installed.

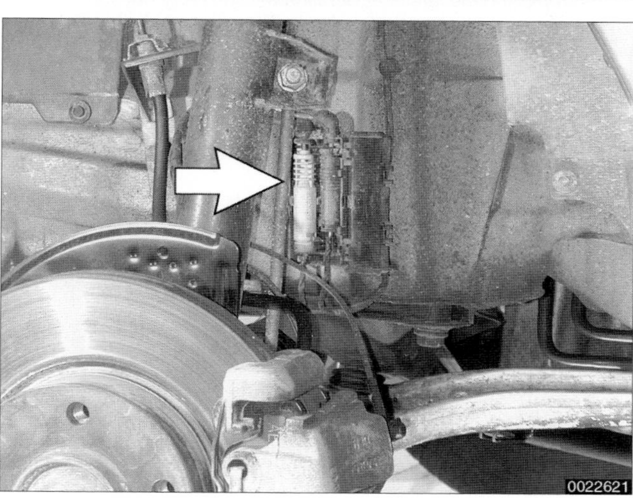

◀ Disconnect and remove impulse sensor electrical harness (**arrow**) from retaining mounts. (Left front wheel shown).

– During installation, apply thin coat of Molykote® Longterm 2 or an equivalent grease to impulse sensor and housing.

– Installation is reverse of removal.

Tightening torque
- ABS wheel speed sensor to steering arm / trailing arm . . . . 8 Nm (6 ft-lb)

ABS impulse wheel

ABS impulse wheel replacement may be needed in case of damage or impulse teeth corrosion.

Front impulse wheel

– Rear wheel drive: Impulse wheel is integral with front wheel bearing hub.

– All wheel drive: Impulse wheel is integral with inner seal of front wheel bearing.

See **310 Front Suspension** for front wheel bearing replacement procedure.

NOTE —
When installing the front wheel bearing on an all wheel drive car, be sure that the ridged bearing seal (ABS impulse wheel) is facing inboard.

Rear impulse wheel

- Impulse wheel is pressed on outer CV joint, but it is not replaceable separately.

See **331 Rear Axle Final Drive** for CV joint and drive axle replacement.

DSC lateral acceleration sensor, replacing

Rear wheel drive: Lateral accleration sensor is located in left side driver footwell, behind trim.

All wheel drive: Lateral acceleration sensor is combined into one unit with rotational rate (yaw) sensor and mounted under driver seat, in front of left seat rail. See **DSC rotational rate (yaw) sensor, replacing** in this repair group.

> ***CAUTION —***
> *After replacing the lateral accleration sensor, carry out sensor adjustment using the BMW diagnostic scan tool (DISplus or GT1) under menu "Service Functions".*

- Remove footwell trim on left side A-pillar. Fold foot trim panel and insulating mat to one side.
- Disconnect sensor electrical harness connector. Remove mounting screw and nut. Remove sensor.
- Installation is reverse of removal.

DSC rotational rate (yaw) sensor, replacing

Rear wheel drive: DSC rotational rate sensor is located on left side of car, under driver seat.

All wheel drive: Rotational rate sensor is combined into one unit with lateral acceleration sensor. It is mounted under driver seat, in front of left seat rail.

- Remove driver seat. See **520 Seats**.
- Remove plastic trim as necessary. Lift carpet for driver footwell and fold toward center console. Move insulation forward to gain access to sensor.
- Remove sensor bracket mounting screws.
- Disconnect electrical harness connector at sensor.
- Remove sensor to bracket mounting screws. Lift sensor away from bracket.

– Installation is reverse of removal.

> ***CAUTION —***
> *Be sure to tighten rotational rate sensor and mounting bracket to specified torques. The sensor is vibration sensitive and subject to cause DSC malfunctions if installed improperly.*

Tightening torques
- Rotational rate sensor to bracket . . . . 8 Nm (6 ft-lb)
- Sensor bracket to body. . . . . 8 Nm (6 ft-lb)

DSC steering angle sensor

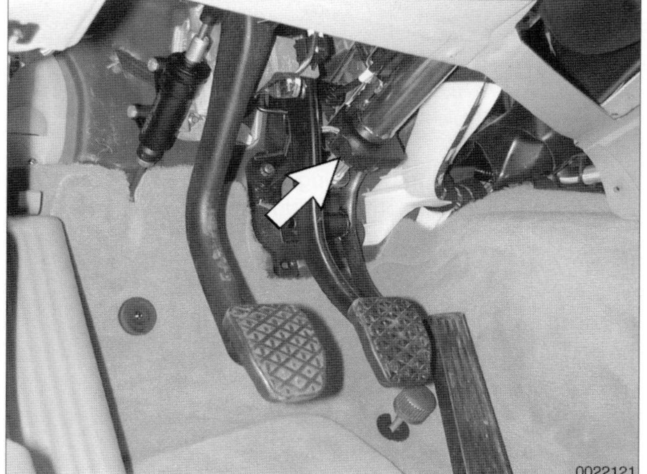
0022121

The DSC steering angle sensor (**arrow**) is mounted to the steering column right above the pedal cluster.

After removal or replacement calibrate steering angle sensor using BMW diagnostic scan tool (DISplus, GT1) or equivalent. Once calibrated, the sensor sends a confirmation ID code to the DSC control module to indicate proper calibration.

For steering column removal see **320 Steering and Wheel Alignment**.

DSC pressure sensor

Rear wheel drive: Two DSC pressure sensors are used, mounted in brake master cylinder.

All wheel drive: One DSC pressure sensor is used, mounted on DSC hydraulic unit.

Tightening torques
- Pressure sensor to hydraulic unit. . . . . 19 Nm (14 ft-lb)
- Pressure sensor to master cylinder . . . . .15 + 4 Nm (11 + 3 ft-lb)

Hydraulic unit / control module, removing and installing

The procedure for removing the ABS / ASC or ABS / DSC hydraulic unit / control module is similar for all models. The location of the units varies.

– Read fault codes from control module memory and print out diagnostic record.

– Hydraulic unit mounted beneath master cylinder: Remove master cylinder. See **Master cylinder, removing and installing** in this repair group.

– Disconnect electrical harness connector at hydraulic unit / control module.

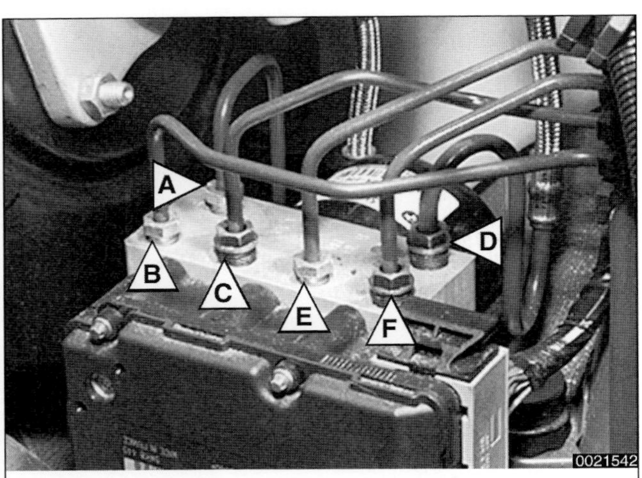

A. Front from master cylinder
B. Left front
C. Right front
D. Rear from master cylinder
E. Right rear
F. Left rear

◄ Mark brake lines placement on hydraulic unit. (Teves MK 20 ASC hydraulic unit shown.)

- Detach brake fluid lines.
- Seal open brake fluid lines and bores with suitable plugs to prevent contamination.

– Detach brake lines from retainers or grommets and pull away from hydraulic unit / control module

> ***CAUTION—***
> *Make sure not to bend or kink brake lines while separating rubber grommet from retainer.*

– Remove hydraulic unit housing mounting screws and remove hydraulic unit / control module from engine bay.

– If necessary, separate hydraulic unit from control module.

– Installation is reverse of removal, noting the following:

- Check rubber mount for hydraulic unit/control module. Replace if damaged.
- Make sure fasteners, fluid couplings, thread bores, and mating surfaces are clean.
- Make sure brake lines are securely seated in grommets before installing brake lines in hydraulic unit bores.
- Bleed brakes. See **Brake system, bleeding** in this repair group.

Tightening torques

- Brake lines to hydraulic unit . . . . 18 Nm (13 ft-lb)
- Brake master cylinder to brake booster . . . . 26 Nm (19 ft-lb)
- Hydraulic unit to body . . . . 8 Nm (6 ft-lb)
- Mounting bracket to hydraulic unit . . . . 8 Nm (6 ft-lb)

– After completing work, perform function test on control module using BMW diagnostic scan tool (DISplus, GT1) or equivalent.

DSC precharge pump, removing and installing

The precharge pump is mounted below the brake master cylinder in the left side of the engine compartment.

– Read fault codes from control module memory and print out diagnostic record.

– Using a clean syringe, empty brake fluid reservoir.

> ***WARNING —***
> *Brake fluid is highly corrosive and dangerous to the environment. Dispose of it properly.*

 Remove interior ventilation microfilter housing.

- Remove upper cover and microfilter.
- Open wiring harness loom (**A**) and remove wires.
- Unfasten screws (**B**) and remove lower microfilter housing.

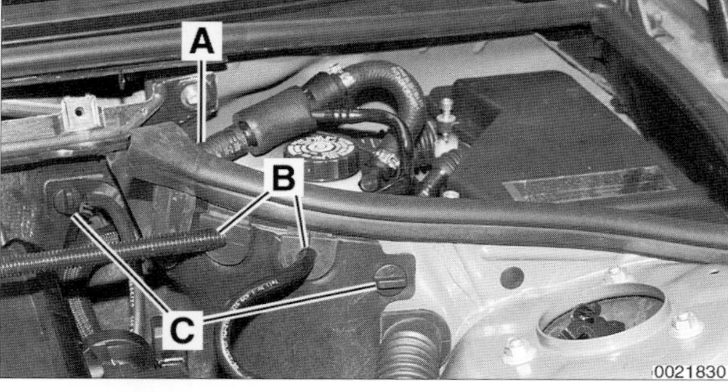

 Remove side trim panel from left rear of engine compartment:

- Remove rubber strip (**A**) from top of trim panel at brake booster.
- Remove vacuum line and positive battery cable with grommets (**B**) from trim panel.
- Release locking clips (**C**) on edges of trim panel and remove panel by pulling upwards.

 Working at precharge pump beneath brake master cylinder:

- Remove brake fluid supply line (**arrow**) from brake fluid reservoir.
- Remove brake fluid intake and output lines from pump.
- Remove electrical harness connector.
- Lift pump to release from lower mounting pad.
- Slide pump out of retaining ring.

– Installation is reverse of removal, noting the following:

- Be sure to replace rubber pump mounts if damaged or worn.
- When installing vacuum hose and battery cable at trim panel, make sure isolating grommets are securely seated.
- Bleed brakes. See **Brake system, bleeding** in this repair group.

400 Body–General

GENERAL

This section covers system descriptions and general information for the repair groups found in **4 Body** and **5 Body Equipment**.

400

BODY ASSEMBLY

The body styles of E46 cars covered by this manual are the 4-door Sedan, 4-door Sport Wagon, 2-door Coupe and M3, and 2-door Convertible and M3 Convertible. Body dimensions vary slightly among models. Dimensions are given in inches.

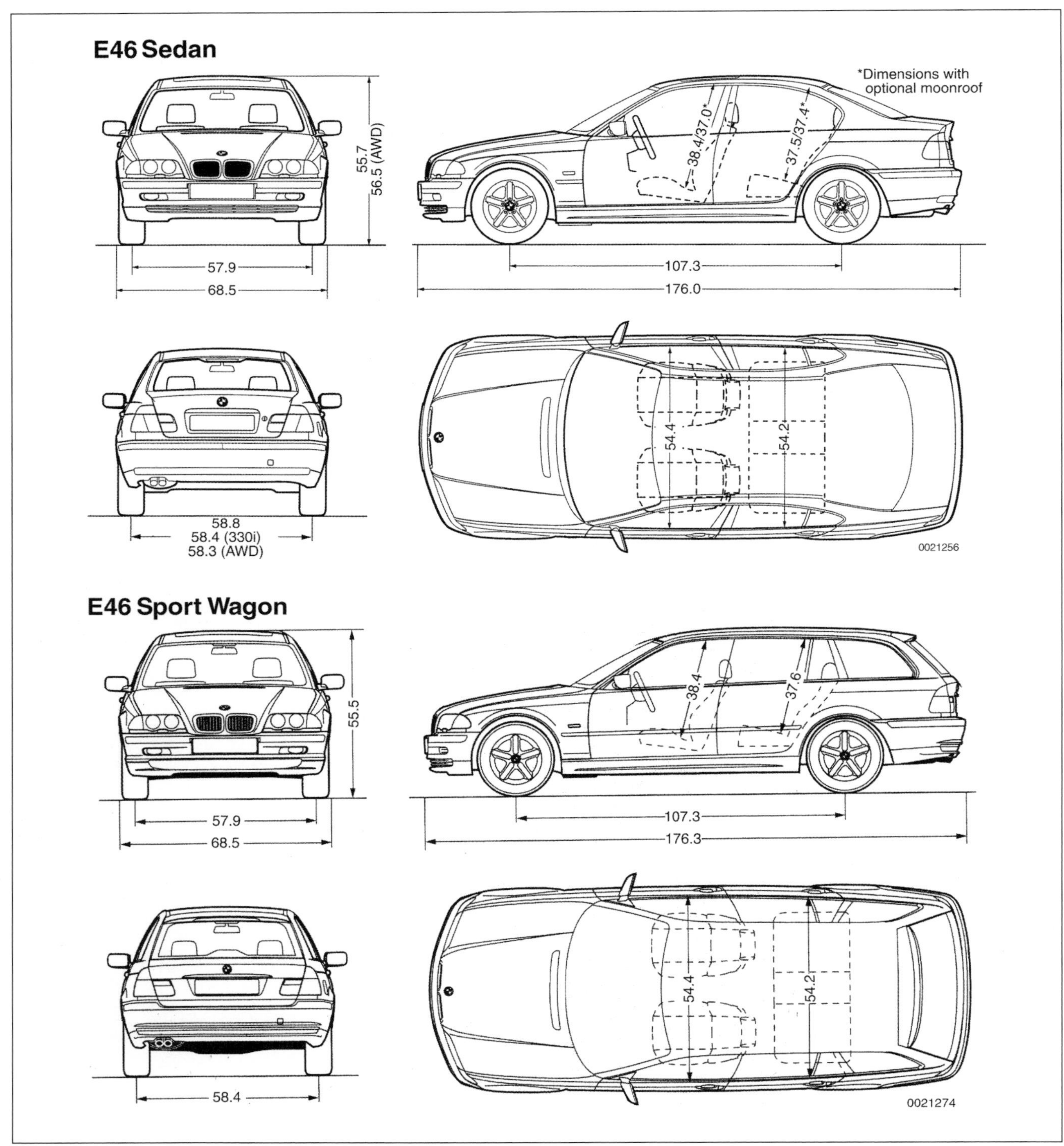

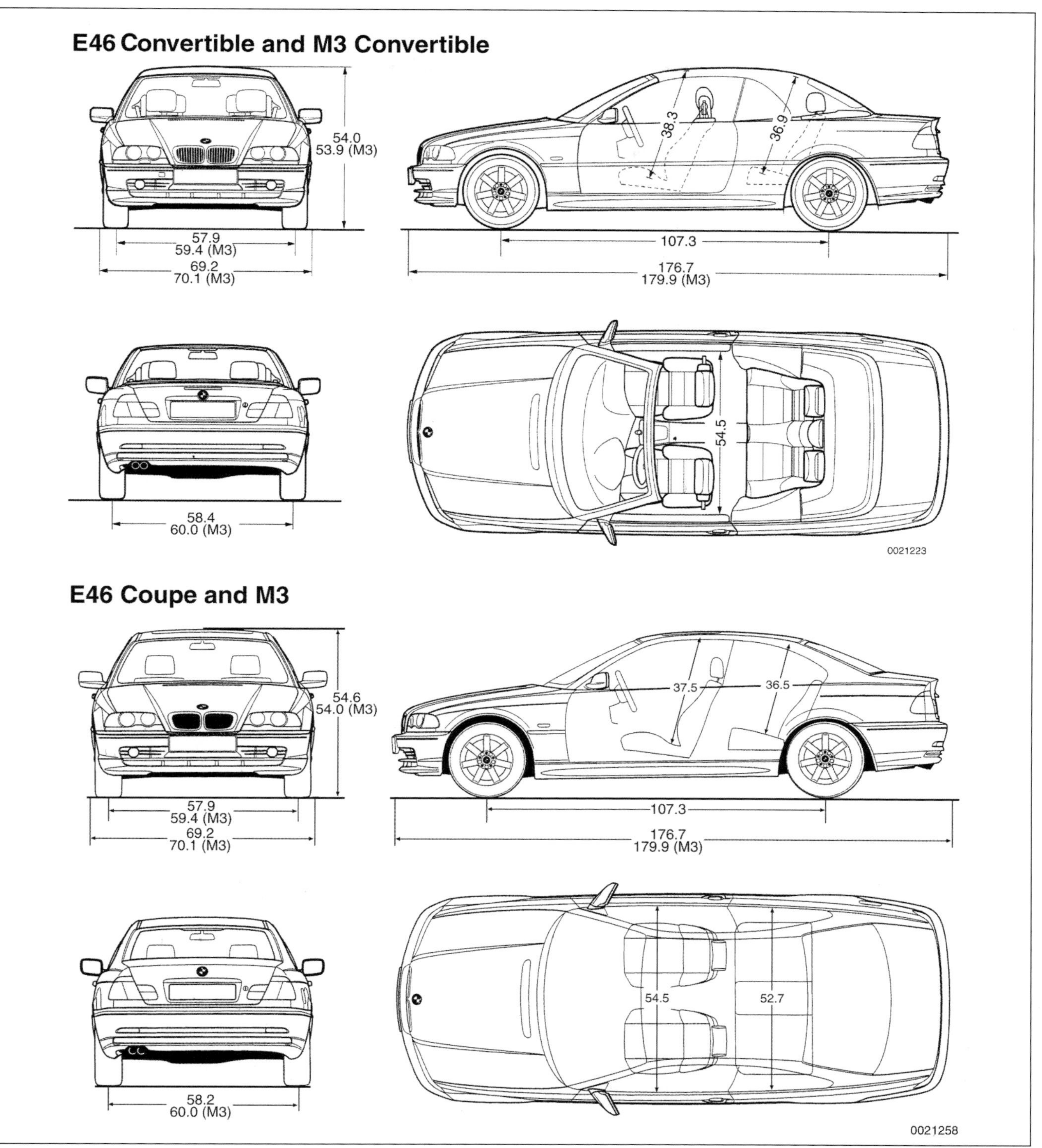
E46 Convertible and M3 Convertible
54.0
53.9 (M3)
38.3
36.9
57.9
59.4 (M3)
69.2
70.1 (M3)
107.3
176.7
179.9 (M3)
54.5
58.4
60.0 (M3)
0021223
E46 Coupe and M3
54.6
54.0 (M3)
37.5
36.5
57.9
59.4 (M3)
69.2
70.1 (M3)
107.3
176.7
179.9 (M3)
54.5
52.7
58.2
60.0 (M3)
0021258

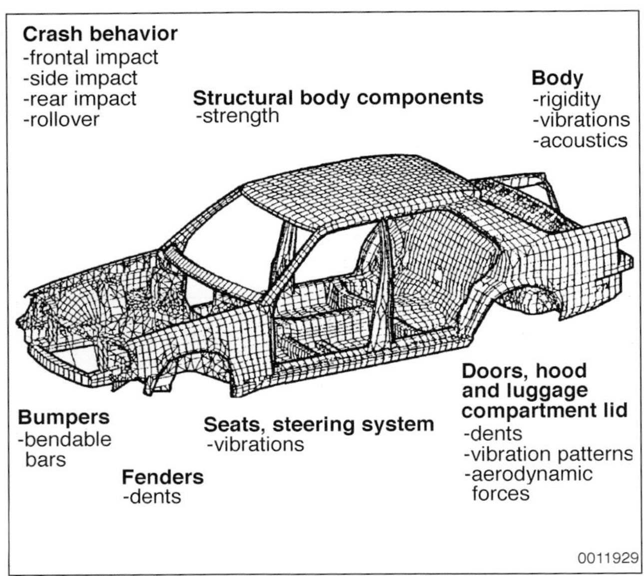

Body shell

The BMW 3 Series chassis is a unibody design constructed of high strength steel. Attaching parts, such as the front fenders, rear quarter panels, doors, trunk lid and hood are also constructed of steel.

Computer aided design (CAD) techniques have been used in refining E46 body models to reduce vehicle weight while retaining strength and increasing torsional rigidity. For good handling purposes, the more rigid the structure the more precisely the suspension can operate. High strength steels now account for 50% of the body shell weight. The body shell's resistance to twisting forces has been almost doubled over the previous 3 Series platform. To help insure long-lasting strength, 85% of the body (in surface area) is made of galvanized steel. This resists corrosion and maintains body strength over time.

The E46 body shell was designed so that the vibrations of torsional twisting and bending are separated into discrete components and in the inaudible range. The current Sedan design ensures that the body twists at 29 hertz and bends at 26 hertz.

Exterior and aerodynamics

With its traditional styling features, such as the kidney grille, circular headlights behind a glass cover (for reasons of streamlining), and the "kick" in the rearmost roof pillar (C-pillar), the E46 can be immediately recognized as a BMW.

Wind resistance. Windows bonded flush to the body and the guided flow of cooling air into the engine compartment provide a good coefficient of drag (C_d).

E46 cars are designed for balanced aerodynamics but not necessarily an extremely low C_d.

- A low coefficient of lift (C_l) promotes stability at high speeds. The current design has a front C_l of 0.08 and a rear C_l of 0.10.
- Windshield wipers are designed for effectiveness at speeds up to and beyond 200 kph (124 mph).
- Body, window and exterior mirror shapes are refined for lower wind noise and reduced soiling of mirrors and windows. Coupe side mirrors are specially shaped and include five ribs (**arrows**) on the top edge for further wind noise reduction.

All this has resulted in a C_d of approximately 0.31 for the Sedan and 0.32 for Coupe models.

Fenders. The exterior panels are corrosion-resistant zinc coated (galvanized) steel. The front fenders are bolted on. For front fender replacement information, see **410 Fenders, Engine Hood**.

Bumpers. Front and rear bumpers are clad in high quality deformable plastic and provide protection with virtually no damage to the bumper or the vehicle at solid barrier impact speeds of 4 kph (2.5 mph). In addition to hydraulic dampeners, which absorb the initial impact energy, these bumpers are backed by compressible tubes. These deform in a controlled manner at higher impact speeds. This helps avoid expensive damage to the body at impact speeds up to 14 kph (9 mph).

Coupe

The E46 Coupe is similar to the 4-door Sedan, but has a more stretched and sleeker appearance. Thus, with the same wheelbase and identical length, it looks different but still familiar.

The 2-door Coupe differs from the 4-door (2-wheel drive) Sedan by a longer front end, a flatter hood line with air slits, and a roof 2.7 cm (1.1 in.) lower. Additional differences include wider doors with frameless windows, glass-covered door-posts (B-pillars) and a shorter and lower trunk lid in the Coupe.

Convertible

The E46 Convertible is an all-season vehicle with a high level of functionality, excellent interior comfort and acoustic refinement. Interior materials and colors, the soft top and the light-alloy wheels are carefully matched.

Although the automatic Convertible roof is standard, a hardtop in body color with heated rear window is available as an option for the cold season.

The Convertible body structure includes many passive safety refinements over its fixed-top counterpart.

- To achieve a more rigid underbody, an aluminum reinforcement plate (**arrow**) is bolted to the front undercarriage and reinforcing struts are bolted to the rear undercarriage.

NOTE —
The aluminum reinforcement plate is used in all rear wheel drive E46 models produced from December 2000.

- Transverse seat support reinforcements in the floor pan accommodate the seat-integrated seat belts (SGS).
- The windshield frame is reinforced with stepped reinforcing tubes which allow it to act as roll-over protection.
- The windshield is bonded into its frame.
- There are tubular door reinforcements.
- The rollover protection system is tripped into position in a fraction of second. With this feature, two bars fully independent of each other come up behind each rear-seat backrest when the vehicle is in danger of turning over.

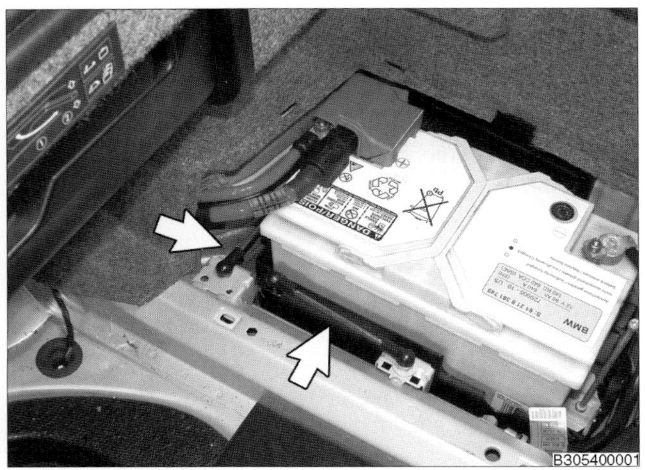
B305400001

A Convertible body normally flexes and vibrates, transferring oscillations to the passenger compartment. In the E46 Convertible, BMW utilizes a unique battery tray with link rods (**arrows**) in the trunk as a vibration dampening system to counteract this oscillation.

> ***CAUTION —***
> *The E46 Convertible requires a special battery which is designed for constant vibration.*

Information for the Convertible top and its related mechanisms can be found **541 Convertible Top**.

Sport Wagon

Introduced in 2000, the E46 Sport Wagon is identical to the E46 Sedan from the front bumper to the B pillar (middle door-post). From the B pillar back the Sport Wagon features:

- Remodelled rear doors
- Tailgate and hinge mechanism
- Rear (tailgate) window that flips up to open, independent from the tailgate, held open by compact torsional coil springs
- New rear bumper
- Roof rails (optional equipment)

Structural, safety and comfort features in the Sport Wagon are comparable to the E46 Sedan and Coupe.

Sport Wagon capacities

- Cargo capacity:
  Rear seat backrest up. . . . . .435 liters (15.4 cu. ft.)
  Rear seat backrest folded down . .1345 liters (47.5 cu. ft.)
- Load capacity:
  In cargo compartment. . . . . 540 Kg (1191 lb.)
  On roof . . . . 75 Kg (165 lb.)

B305400007

M3 Coupe, M3 Convertible

Available beginning in the 2001 model year, the M3 Coupe and Convertible are based on regular E46 platforms, but each have several modifications to strengthen their chassis for the increased engine output, dynamic driving characteristics, and sporting design of the M models.

Body structure. Increased body rigidity through the use of gusset plates welded to the side frame, wheel arches, and C-pillar.

Exterior:

- Wider front and rear fenders
- Aluminum engine hood
- Special front bumper and spoiler ensemble
- Widened wheel-opening flares
- Clear front and rear turn-signal lenses
- Aerodynamic outside mirrors with power fold-up feature
- Side gills incorporating M3 logos
- Special rear bumper and air diffuser
- Special M colors

Interior:

- 10-way manual sport seats with Nappa leather / M cloth or Nappa leather upholstery
- Optional 8-way power and 2-way manual sport seats
- Memory system for driver seat & outside mirrors
- Automatic tilt-down feature for right exterior mirror
- Optional power-adjustable front-seat backrest width and 4-way power lumbar support

Suspension:

- Firmer springs, struts and shock absorbers
- Unique lower front control arms
- Specially developed suspension bushings and low-friction ball joints

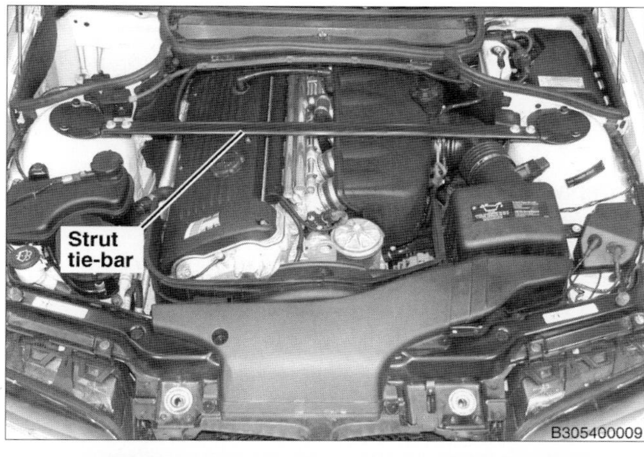

Front strut tie-bar reinforces front-suspension strut towers.

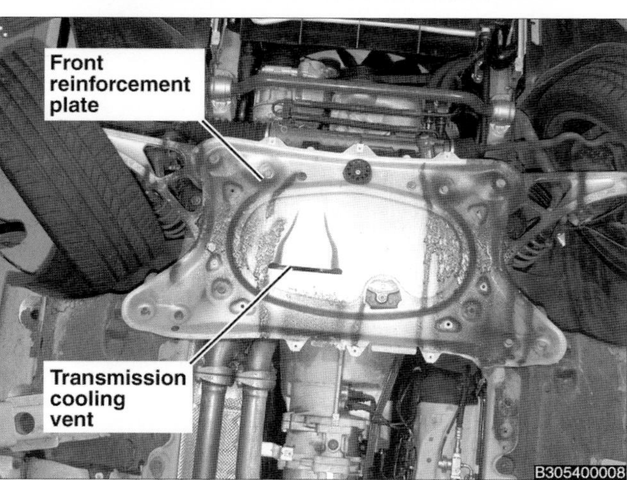

Front reinforcement plate, made of 3 mm thick aluminum and complete with transmission cooling vent, adds front chassis rigidity to handle M3 cornering thrust.

V-brace at rear suspension adds rigidity at chassis rear.

Dynamic Stability Control (DSC) with special M logic to accommodate ultra-high performance.

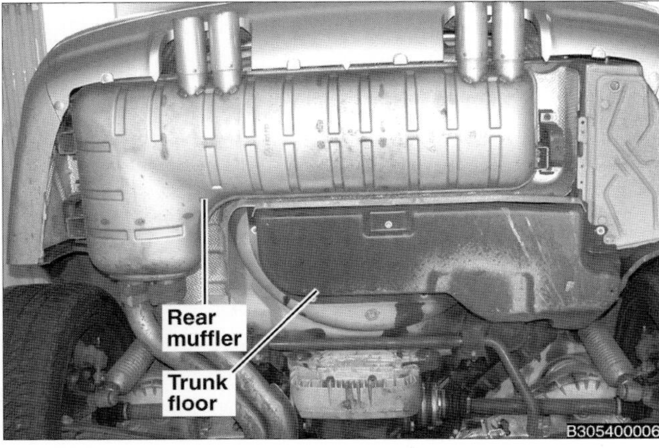

Trunk floor modified to fit larger rear muffler assembly.

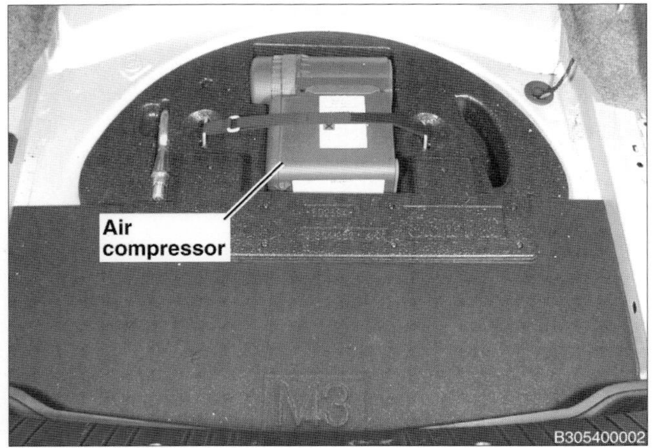

No spare tire. Vehicle trunk fitted with a specialized air compressor with tire sealant in lieu of spare tire.

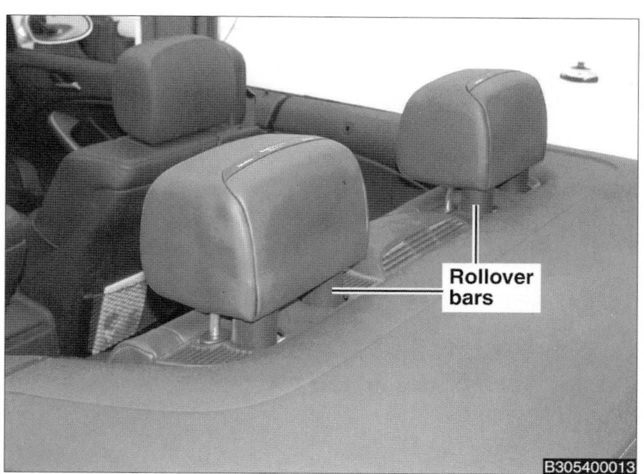

M3 Convertible features:

- Fully automatic, fully lined power convertible top. Variable convertible top storage compartment in trunk; provides greater trunk space when top is raised
- Nappa leather upholstery
- 10-way power and 2-way manual sport seats including power head-restraint and safety-belt height
- Optional 4-way power lumbar support
- Front safety belts fully integrated with seats for optimum belt fit and ease of rear-seat entry and exit
- Power easy-entry feature: front seats can be moved forward for easier rear-seat entry and exit
- Optional rear side-impact airbags
- Rollover Protection System: structural bars behind rear seats deploy automatically in case of impending rollover accident

SAFETY AND SECURITY

A large number of new or improved safety and security features are incorporated in E46 cars.

Safety cage

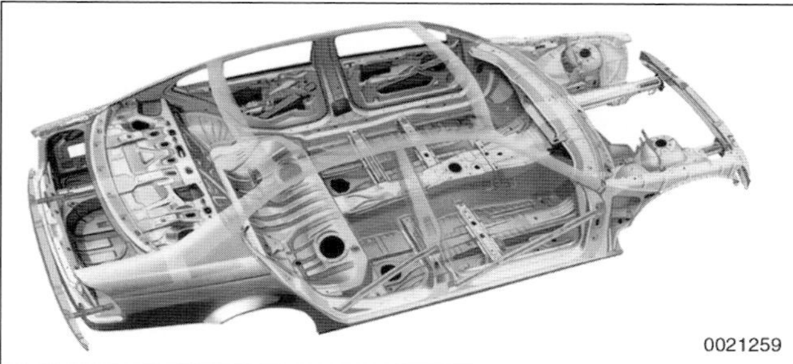

The body safety cage is a continuation of an established BMW concept for passenger protection. Tubular impact structures built into the body provide protection against passenger injury during front or rear impacts.

Door anchoring system

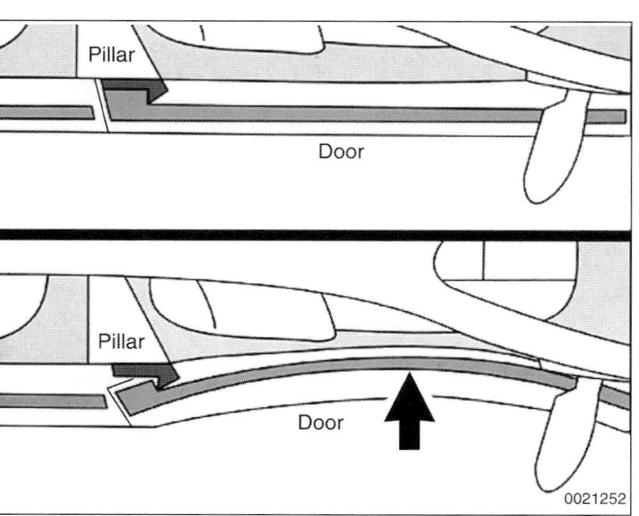

Each door is reinforced with a diagonal aluminum bar with a metal hook at the rear edge.

Upon severe side impact, the hook locks into a recessed notch in the B or C pillar, thus providing unitized protection against buckling of the door. The body side holds together as a unit, offering significantly greater strength.

After most impacts, the door springs back and unhooks from the notch. It can then be opened again.

Door locks and door handles

The bow type door handles allow easy door opening, but are secure in accidents.

Electrical components in the locks are fully encapsulated and cannot be picked easily. The new door handles, latches and lock assemblies offer improved reliability and security against theft.

Door position and lock condition are detected by Hall sensors.

See **515 Central Locking and Anti-theft** for door lock repair procedures.

Roof padding

In addition to the side and head protection airbags, there is supplementary padding at the roof pillars and along the roof above the doors. This is positioned to present energy absorbing surfaces to passengers thrown around by side impact forces.

Seat belts

In Sedan, Coupe and Sport Wagon, each front seat belt assembly has a height-adjustable anchor at the B-pillar.

An automatic pyrotechnic (explosive charge) tensioner tightens the front belt at the buckle upon impact, snugging up lap and shoulder segments of the belt. The tensioners are designed to automatically tension the belts by about 2 inches (55 mm) in the event of a collision.

A force limiter puts an upper limit on the amount of force each belt can exert on the passenger.

Convertible seat belts are integrated into the seat, but otherwise have features similar to the other models.

See **720 Seat Belts** for repair procedures.

Airbags

As many as 8 airbags are installed in E46 cars, depending on model.

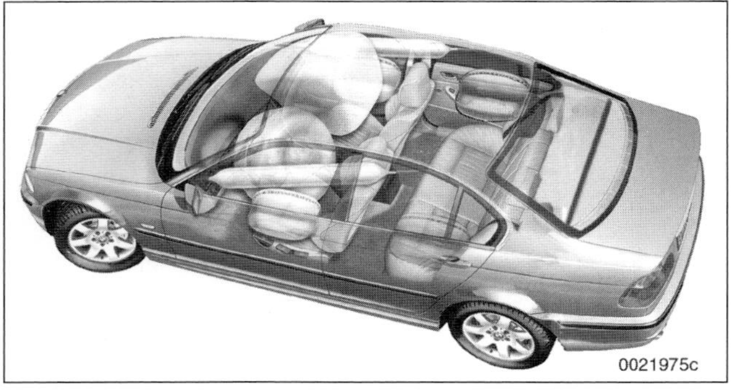

The front airbags operate without sodium azide propellant, widely considered an irritant when an airbag is deployed.

Starting with 2000 models, "smart" front passenger and driver airbags were installed. These are of the dual-threshold, dual stage design, including a sensor to help prevent the unnecessary deployment of the passenger side airbag if the seat is unoccupied.

Depending on options chosen, one airbag may be installed in each door of Sedan and Sport Wagon models, protecting passengers against side impacts. Coupe and Convertible models are equipped with door-installed airbags as well. An option on M3 Convertible is rear side-impact airbags.

Head Protection System (HPS) airbags stretch diagonally across the tops of the front doors in solid-top models.

Airbag deployment automatically triggers fuel shut-off, turns on the hazard and interior lights, and unlocks the doors.

See **721 Airbag System (SRS)** for repair procedures.

> ***WARNING —***
> - *Airbags are inflated by an explosive device. Handled improperly or without adequate safeguards, airbag units can be very dangerous. Special precautions must be observed prior to any work at or near any of the airbags. See* **721 Airbag System (SRS)**.
> - *Always disconnect the battery and cover the negative (–) battery terminal with an insulator before starting diagnostic, troubleshooting or service work on cars fitted with SRS, and before doing any welding on the car.*

Battery safety terminal (BST)

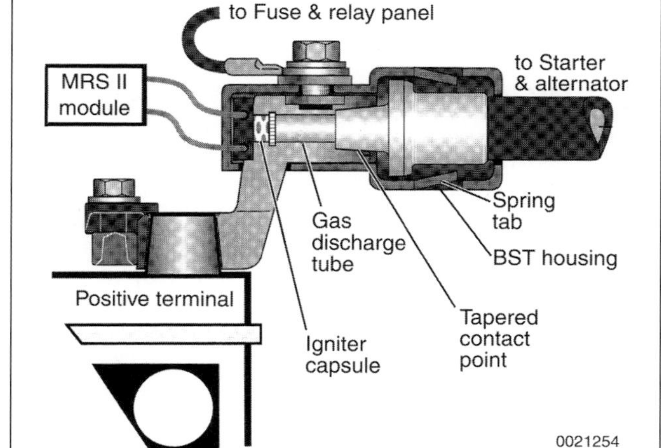

A pyrotechnic (explosive charge) device automatically disconnects the battery positive terminal during impacts or collisions.

See **121 Battery, Starter, Alternator** for further details.

The seatbelt system, airbag system and battery safety terminal are controlled by the Multiple Restraint System (MRS) control module.

Security

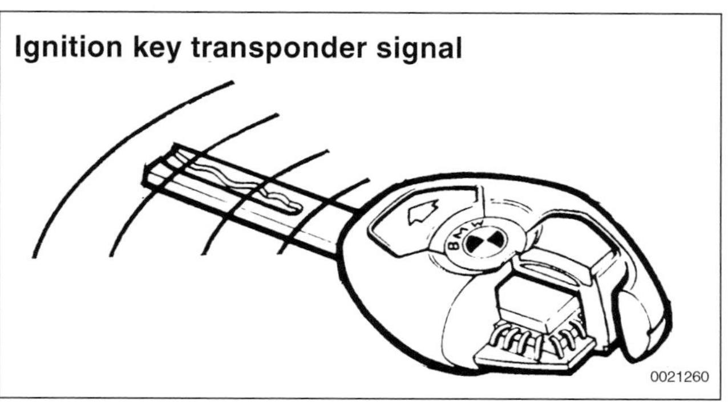

Electronic immobilization (EWS). E46 vehicles are equipped with electronic immobilization (EWS). This system uses a wireless communication link between a transponder chip in the ignition key and the ring antenna surrounding the ignition switch. The EWS control module blocks the starting of the vehicle unless the correct coded ignition key is used.

NOTE —
Electronic immobilization is sometimes referred to as the driveaway protection system.

Anti-theft alarm (DWA). This is a dealer-installed option for which the E46 vehicles are factory-wired. When armed, the system monitors door lock contacts and trunk and engine hood locks and sounds a siren if it detects tampering.

Tilt sensor. Located in the right side of the trunk above the battery, the tilt sensor monitors the vehicle parked angle when DWA is armed. The siren is activated if the vehicle angle is changed. This helps prevent theft of the car using a ramp truck.

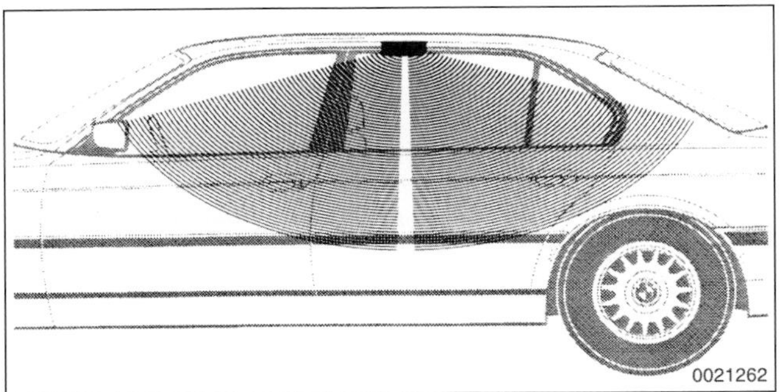

Ultrasonic interior protection (UIS). An interior ultrasonic emitter/detector is installed in the center of the headliner of Sedan, Coupe and Sport Wagon models. The DWA alarm is triggered if motion is detected inside the car.

Short distance radar (SDR) is the interior motion detector system used in Convertible models. The SDR emitter is located on the driveshaft tunnel under the center console next to the parking brake.

See **515 Central Locking and Anti-theft** for additional information and repair procedures.

Emergency location

If emergency assistance is needed, the on-board navigation system (if equipped) uses GPS technology to pinpoint the location of the vehicle.

INTERIOR FEATURES

E46 interiors have a unique character, with a combination of sporty features and innovative design. All body versions offer a wide choice of interior and exterior colors. New colors with matching leather or leatherette upholstery were introduced for each model year, including light-alloy wheels in new designs.

Driving comfort is enhanced by power steering, tilt steering wheel, height-adjustable front seats, and electrically adjustable and heated rear-view mirrors. Inside the car there are reading lights at four seating positions.

Noise reduction

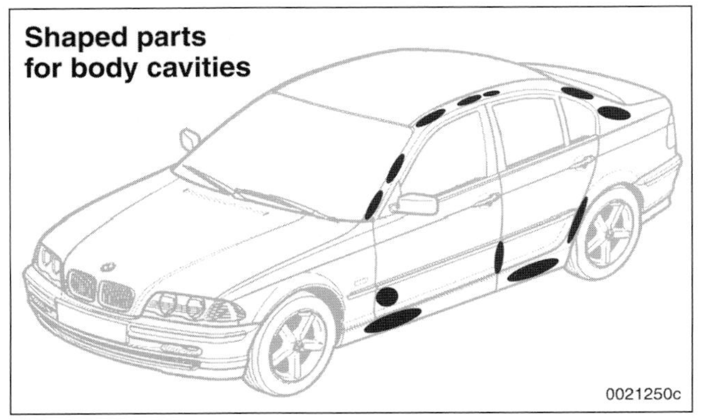

To reduce interior noise, certain body cavities are sealed with shaped parts installed during the manufacturing process. The body is heated to approx 180°C (356°F) and kept at that temperature for approx. 20 minutes, during which interval the shaped parts expand to fit the shapes of the cavities.

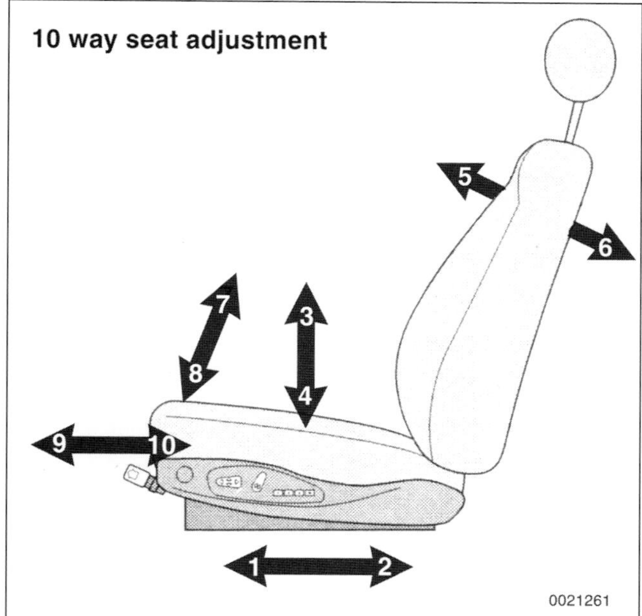

Seats

Anatomically correct seats are constructed from polyurethane foam containing areas or "zones" of different firmness. They offer good lateral support without constricting the occupant.

Driving comfort is enhanced by power steering, tilt steering wheel, height-adjustable front seats, and electrically adjustable and heated rear-view mirrors.

The seats have a passive internal ventilation system: Cylindrical cavities within the cushions and backrests generate a pumping effect as ride motions cause occupant motion. This helps remove moisture and feeds fresh air into the seats.

Other features of the seating system:

- Seat bases with steel springs for added support and strength.
- Seat control switches along outside edge of seat.
- Optional heated seats.
- Seat position memory: Three different seat configurations memorized by seat control module(s).
- Seat memory coordinated with outside mirror memory.
- Convertible: Pressing seat back switch forward causes comfort entry aid system to move seat forward and lowers headrest to prevent it from contacting sun visor. Seat and headrest then returned to memorized positions. These functions controlled by seat memory module.
- For security reasons, rear seat backrest release lever installed in trunk.
- Sport Wagon: Rear seat backs split 60/40. Center arm rest on left seat back incorporates non adjustable headrest, opens out with cup-holders and storage compartment when folded down.

See **520 Seats** for more details.

Instruments and controls

Everything in the interior passenger compartment essential to the driver is logically grouped and easy to reach. All instruments and controls have been arranged ergonomically and are fully integrated into the overall design of the vehicle. The following features are optional in some models.

Tilt-telescopic steering wheel has 30 mm (1.2 in.) of vertical and longitudinal adjustment.

Multi-function steering wheel contains two key pads containing controls for the sound system, telephone and cruise control.

Padded dashboard houses the instrument cluster and the ventilation and heating system.

Instrument cluster uses large easy-to-read analog instruments and is removable as a unit without removing the dashboard. On-board computer and Check Control functions are integrated into the instrument cluster displays.

Service Interval Display calculates vehicle service needs, based on current driving patterns, and indicates to the driver when the car requires service.

Integrated on-board navigation system, based on Global Positioning System (GPS) technology, is optionally available on E46 cars. When installed, a multi-function monitor is included in the center of the dash above the radio. In addition to displaying navigation system information, this monitor accesses to On-Board Computer functions, audio system controls, mobile phone dialling and memory, and automatic ventilation.

Park Distance Control (PDC) is an optional system which uses ultra-sonic sensors (**arrows**) in the rear bumper trim to warn the driver of approaching too close to obstacles when parking.

Central Body Electronics (ZKE V)

E46 cars are equipped with a sophisticated centralized body electric/electronics plan. Central Body Electronics (ZKE V) is self-diagnostic and incorporates many functions into a single control module. The consolidation of several systems into a single control module minimizes power requirements and the incorporation of the diagnostic link results in more efficient and accurate troubleshooting.

ZKE V directly controls the following functions:

- Windshield wiper / washer system. See **611 Wipers and Washers**.
- Central locking with power trunk or tailgate release. See **515 Central Locking and Anti-theft**.
- Keyless entry (FZV).
- Power window control. See **512 Door Windows**.
- Car Memory / Key Memory. See **515 Central Locking and Anti-theft**.
- Interior lighting. See **630 Lights**.
- Alarm system (DWA). See **515 Central Locking and Anti-theft**.
- Electronic consumer sleep mode. See **600 Electrical System–General**.

Other functions not directly controlled by ZKE V but interconnected:

- Rain sensor (AIC). See **611 Wiper and Washers**.
- Sunroof operation. See **540 Sunroof**.
- Seat memory. See **520 Seats**.
- Outside rear-view mirror control and heating.
- Windshield washer jet heating.

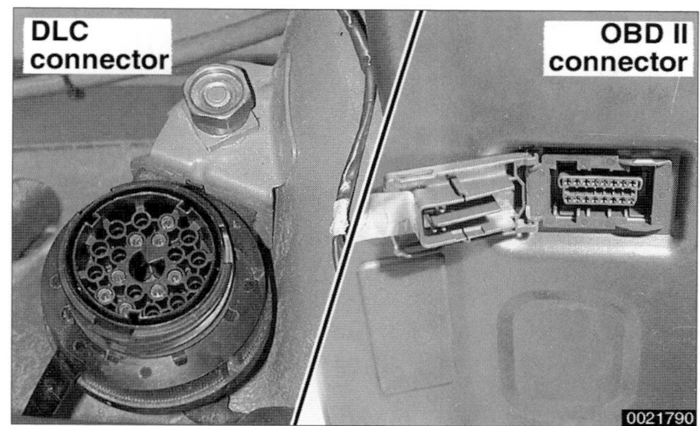

ZKE V diagnostic trouble codes (DTCs) are accessible electronically through the data-link connector (DLC). See **610 Electrical Component Locations**.

NOTE —

- *1999 models and cars produced through June 2000 are equipped with the DLC socket in the rear right corner of the engine compartment.*
- *In cars produced after June 2000, the DLC socket in the engine compartment was discontinued. All scan tool codes can be accessed through the OBD II interface socket on the driver side of the dashboard, left and below the instrument cluster, under a cover.*

Heating and air conditioning (IHKA)

The integrated heating and air conditioning (IHKA) system uses an extra large, infinitely variable radial blower motor for good distribution of air. Fresh air enters through the grille below the engine hood and into the passenger compartment via the dashboard and footwell vents.

Repair information for the heating and air conditioning system is covered in **640 Heating and Air Conditioning**.

0022032

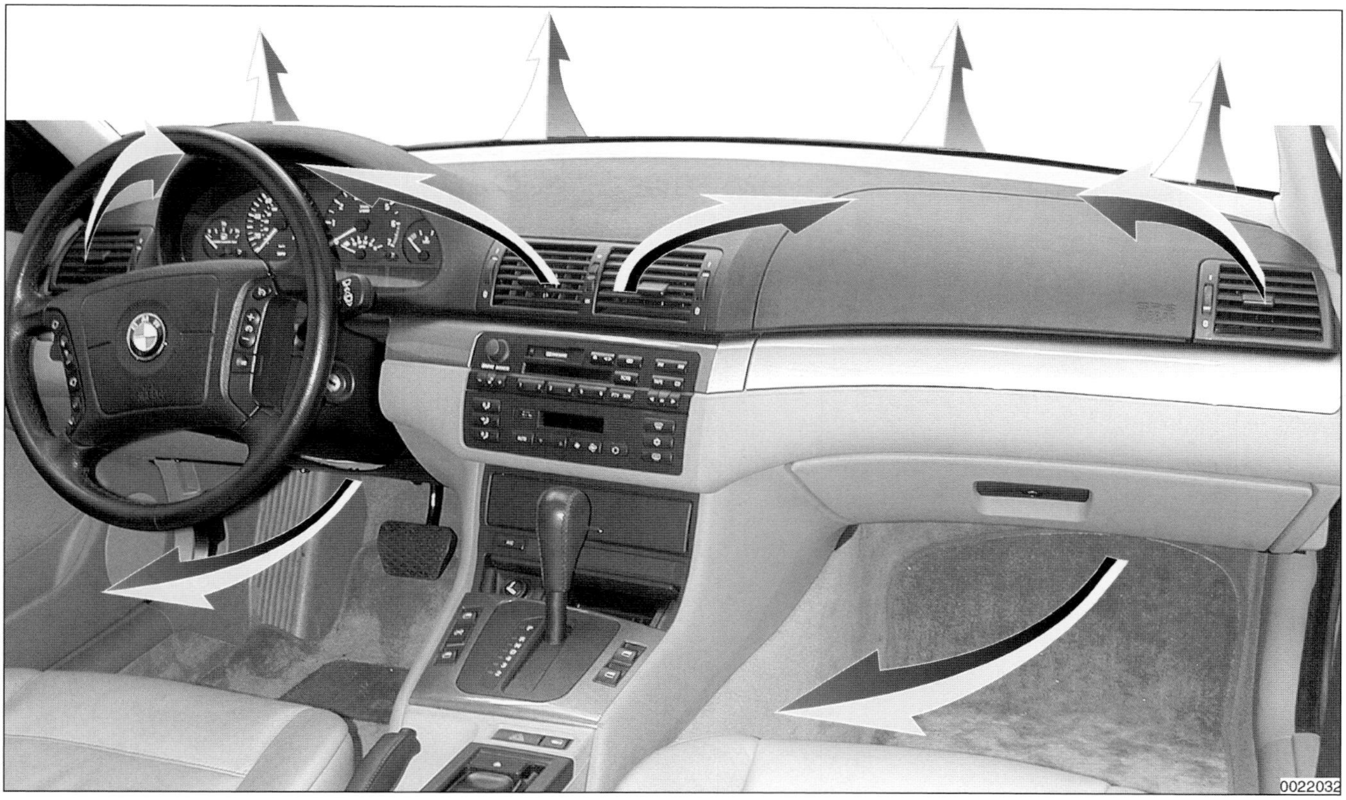

Sport Wagon interior features

Child seats. There are three child seat hold down anchors behind the rear seat back rest. Plastic trim covers are used to hide the anchors.

Cargo area. There is a spring-loaded blind and a cargo safety net installed behind the rear seat.

Storage. There are extra storage compartments on the left and right sides in the rear. These house the rear window washer fluid reservoir and sound system components.

Power socket. A 12 volt power socket is in the left side of the cargo area behind the rear seat backrest.

410 Fenders, Engine Hood

GENERAL

This repair group covers replacement of the front fenders and removal and installation of the engine hood.

Special tools

Most body repairs can be performed using regular automotive service tools. BMW special tools are required to set engine hood into service position.

Special tools

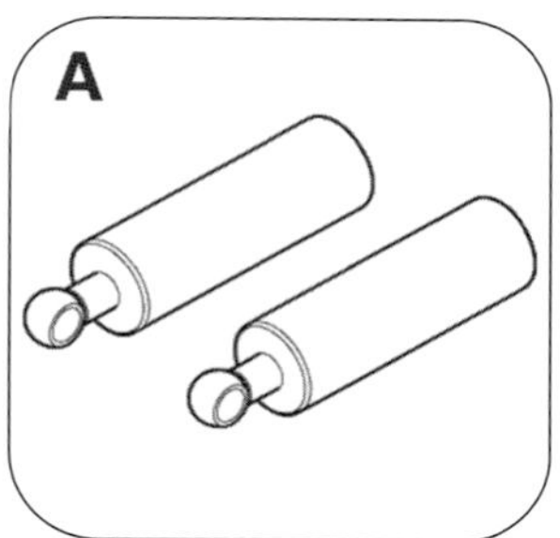

A BMW 51 2 160 . . . . Service position hood props

> ***CAUTION —***
> *The body is painted at the factory after assembly. Realignment of body panels may expose unpainted metal. Paint all exposed metal once the work is complete.*

FRONT FENDERS

Front fender, removing and installing

- Raise hood. Raise and safely support front of vehicle.

> ***WARNING —***
> *Make sure the car is firmly supported on jack stands designed for the purpose. Place jack stands underneath structural chassis points, not under suspension parts.*

- Remove front wheel. Remove inner plastic liner from wheel housing.
- Remove front turn signal/lens assembly from fender corner. Carefully pry out side directional from fender and disconnect. See **630 Lights**.
- Remove body colored trim panel underneath headlight assembly.

Working at cowl, peel corner of side trim panel cover away from side of fender. Gently lift panel cover upwards and remove retaining screw (**arrow**).

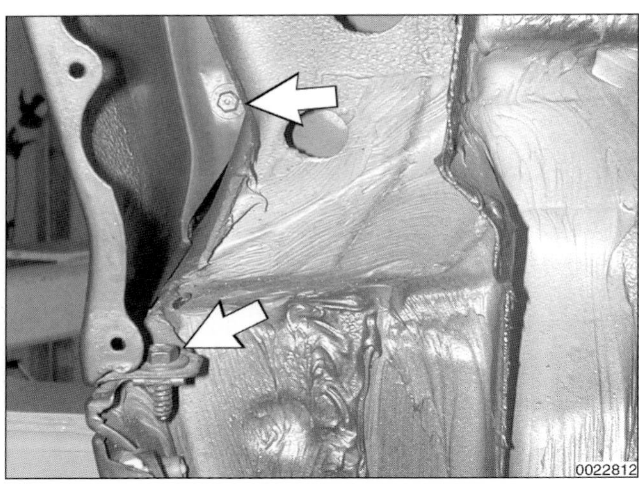

Remove lower fender attaching bolts (**arrows**) at rear of wheel housing.

With door open, remove upper fender mounting bolt (**arrow**).

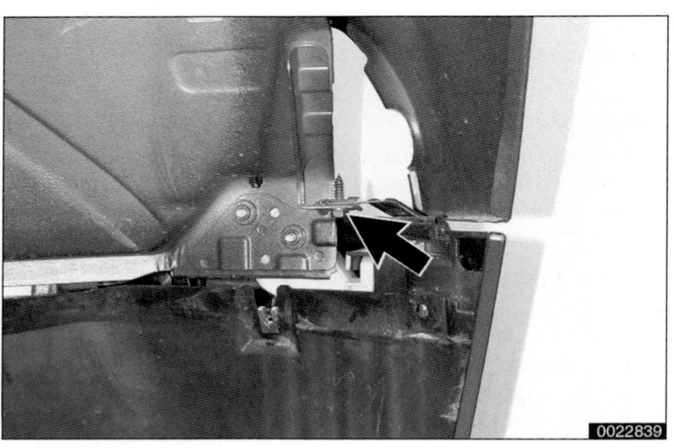

Remove screw (**arrow**) at front of fender.

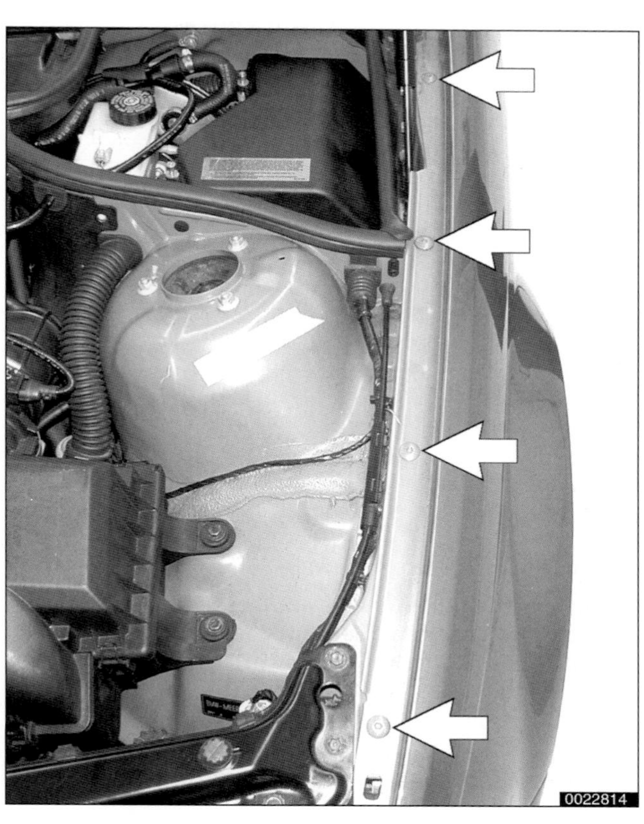

Remove bolts (**arrows**) along top edge of fender.

– Carefully remove fender from body.

– Installation is reverse of removal, noting the following:
  - Before installing new fender, clean old sealant and protective coating from mounting surfaces.
  - Position new fender and loosely install all mounting bolts. Align fender with door pillar and inner fender, then tighten bolts.
  - Repair paint damage and paint exposed metal.
  - Reseal and apply protective coating to mounting surfaces.

Clearance specification

- Fender to front hood or to door . . 4.25 ± 0.75 mm (0.167 ± 0.03 in)

ENGINE HOOD

Hood, raising to service position

CAUTION —

- *Do not switch on the windshield wipers with the engine hood raised. As a precaution, remove the wiper motor fuse. See* **610 Electrical Component Locations**.
- *The hood is heavy. Before removing the hood supports, be sure to have an assistant help support the hood.*

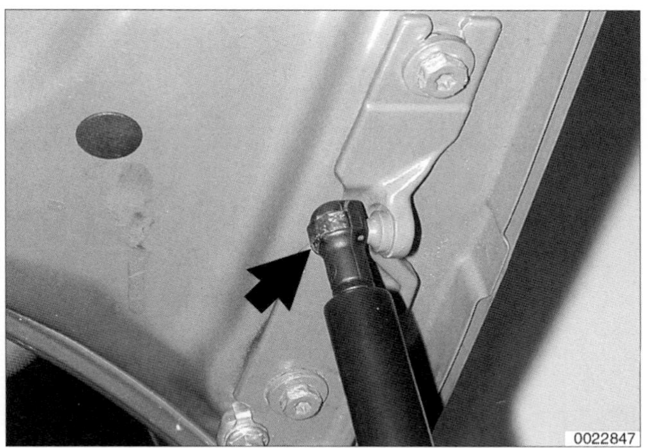

Open hood fully. With help of assistant, support hood and remove retaining clips (**arrow**) on upper end of pressurized lifting struts. Pull struts off hood.

– Raise hood higher and install BMW special tools 51 2 160 in between hood lift struts and hood brackets to hold hood in service position.

Hood, removing and installing

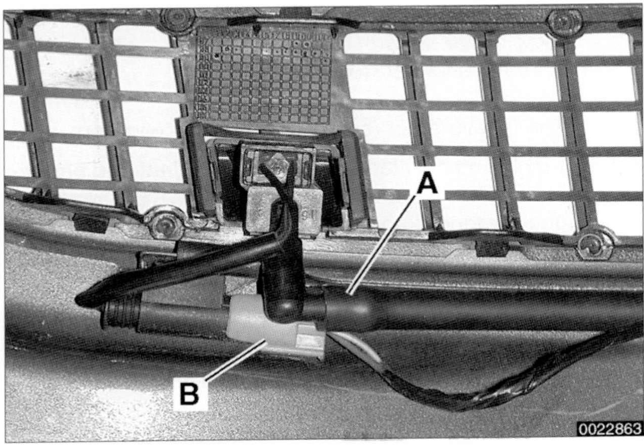

Raise hood:

- Disconnect washer fluid hose (**A**) from washer nozzles.
- Where applicable, disconnect electrical harness connector (**B**) from heated nozzles.

— Detach gas-charged hood supports from hood.

> ***CAUTION —***
> *The hood is heavy. Before removing the hood supports or hood retaining bolts, be sure to have an assistant help support the hood.*

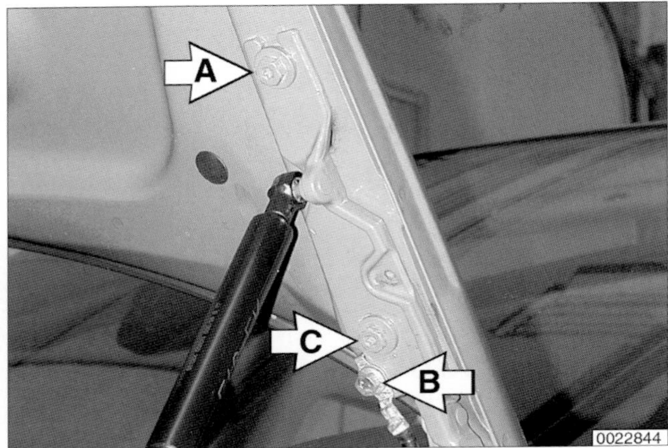

Loosen upper hood hinge bolts (**A**). Remove ground strap (**B**) and remove lower hinge bolts (**C**). Lift hood off carefully.

— Installation is reverse of removal.

- Repair paint damage and paint exposed metal.
- Check hood alignment. See **Hood, aligning** in this repair group.

NOTE —
The hood was fitted and attached to an unfinished body at the factory. Touch up unfinished surfaces exposed by this procedure.

Hood, aligning

When installing the hood, align the hinges as close to the original paint marks as possible. Movement of the hood on its attaching hardware may require touch-up paint.

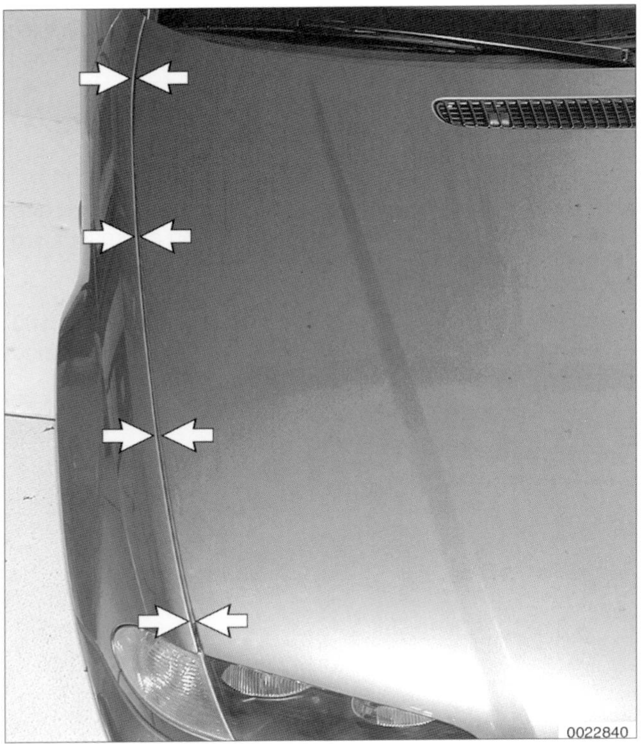

Align hood so that gap to fender (**arrows**) is as even as possible.

Clearance specification

- Hood edges to adjoining body panel (gap) . . . . 5.5 mm (0.216 in)

0022841

⊲ If height adjustment at rear of hood cannot be completed using upper hinge, loosen lower hinge bolts (**arrows**) and reposition as necessary.

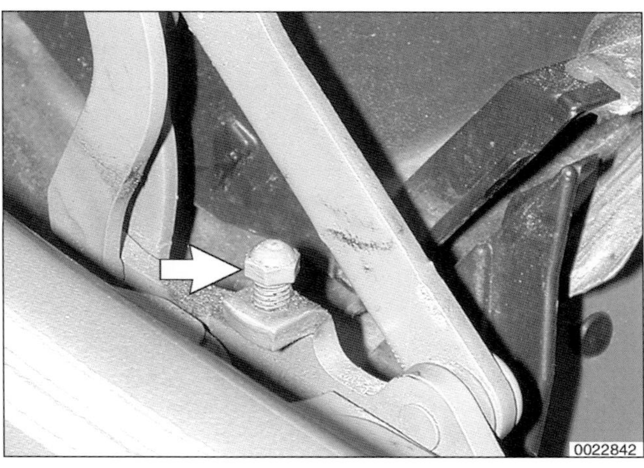
0022842

⊲ Plastic coating on top of hinge stop screw must not be damaged or missing.

0022843

⊲ Stop disk for front of hood (**arrow**) is eccentric, and is marked 0-10. Initial setting is with the 0 setting forward, for minimal clearance. Turn stop disk to move hood front stop further out.

– Height at front of hood is set using spring pins and rubber stop buffers.

Hood latch components

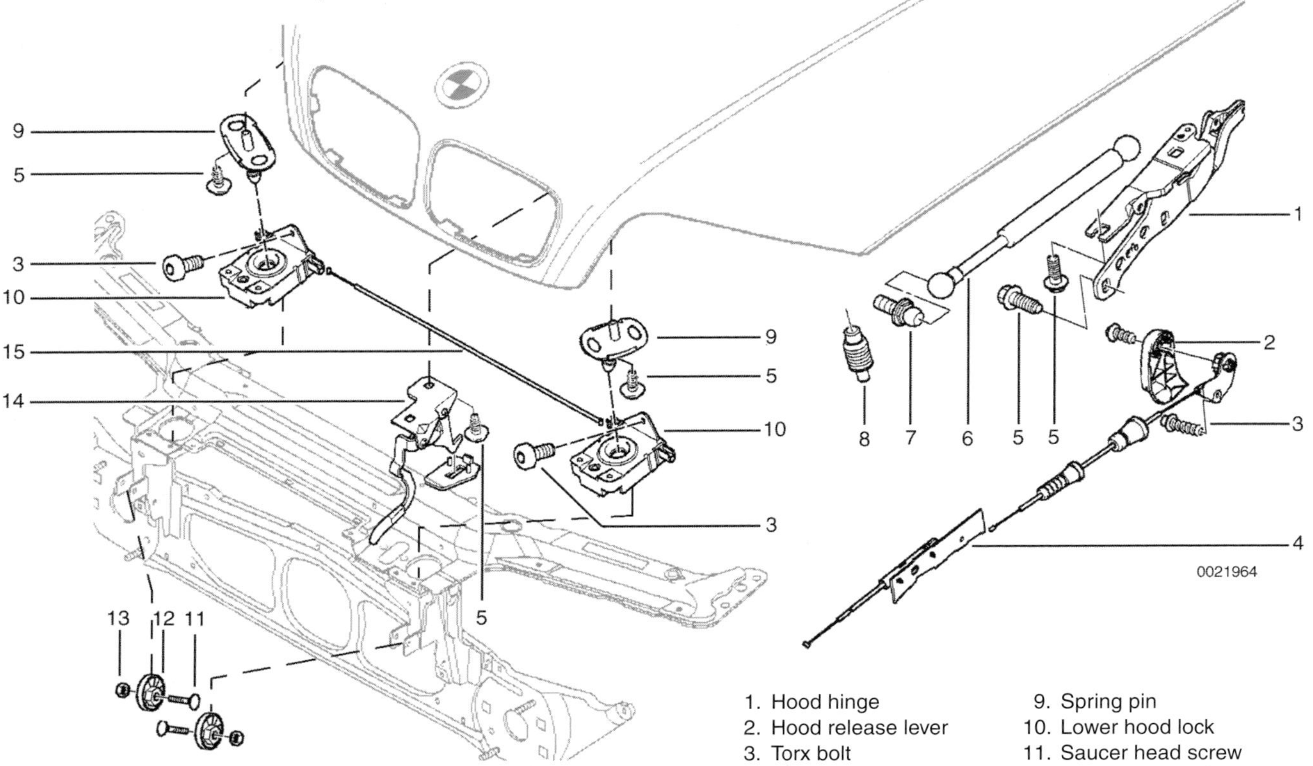

0021964

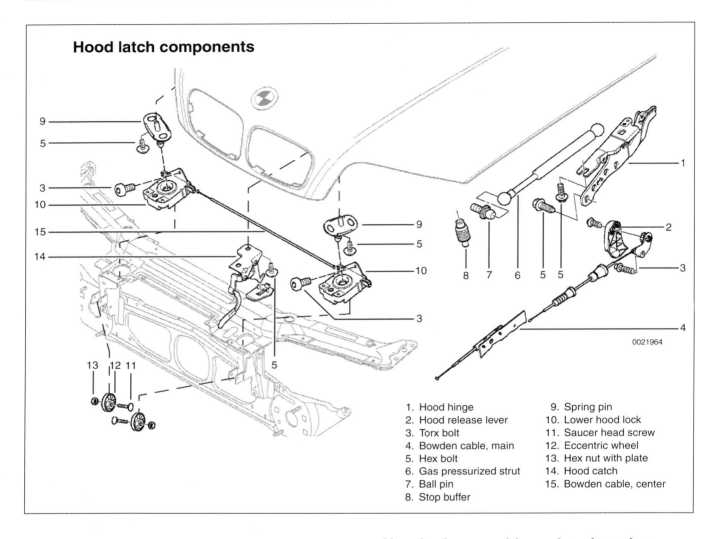

1. Hood hinge
2. Hood release lever
3. Torx bolt
4. Bowden cable, main
5. Hex bolt
6. Gas pressurized strut
7. Ball pin
8. Stop buffer
9. Spring pin
10. Lower hood lock
11. Saucer head screw
12. Eccentric wheel
13. Hex nut with plate
14. Hood catch
15. Bowden cable, center

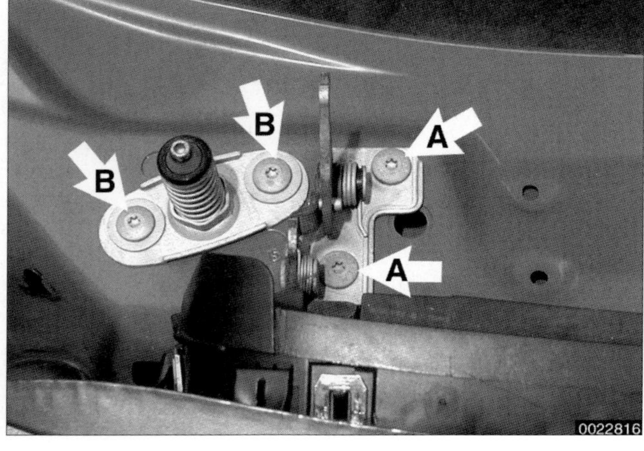

Hood release cable and spring pins, adjusting

Before adjusting hood pins, be sure the hood is aligned evenly to fenders and front panel.

– Make sure bowden cable, which connects both hood locks together, is seated in lock guide on both left and right locks.

◄ Loosen hood spring pin bolts (**A**) and retaining hook bolts (**B**) at hood on left and right sides just enough to allow movement.

– Turn rubber stop buffers over headlights inwards to provide clearance.

– Lower (but do not fully latch) hood several times so pins on hood center themselves in lower locks.

> ***CAUTION —***
> *Do not let hood lock with latch bolts loose.*

– Tighten hood spring pin bolts and latch bolts when alignment is correct.

– Remove one bolt at a time from each side, clean and coat with Loctite®270 or equivalent, and reinstall. Repeat with other bolt.

– Unscrew rubber stop buffers above headlight assemblies until they support hood when closed without movement.

– Test hood for correct closure and opening. If hood does not spring open, lengthen spring pins.

◄ To lengthen spring pin, loosen locknut (**arrow**) with wrench inserted through spring, then turn pin counterclockwise.

411 Doors

GENERAL

This repair group covers front and rear door repair information. It includes removal and installation of interior front door trim panel, rear door trim panel for Sedan or Sport Wagon and rear trim panel for Coupe or Convertible.

See the following repair groups for related repair information:

- **512 Door Windows** for power door windows and door glass replacement
- **515 Central Locking and Anti-theft** for power door locking system

> ***WARNING —***
> *E46 cars are fitted with side-impact airbags in the front doors. Some are equipped with airbags in the rear doors as well. M3 Convertible may be equipped with rear side-impact airbags. When servicing windows or interior panels on a vehicle with side-impact airbags, see* **721 Airbag System (SRS)** *for warnings and cautions and procedures relating to the airbag system.*

DOORS

Front or rear door, removing and installing

– If working on a door with side-impact airbag, disconnect negative (–) battery cable.

> ***CAUTION —***
> *Prior to disconnecting the battery, read the battery disconnection cautions given at the front of this manual on page viii.*

0022822

Remove harness connector mounting bolt (**arrow**) at door pillar.

0022820

Pull up on locking clip and separate connector.

0022823

With door fully open, remove pin bolts (**arrow**) from top and bottom door hinges.

0022825

Remove door check mounting bolt (**arrow**).

– Remove door by lifting up off lower hinge halves.

> ***CAUTION —***
> *Be careful not to damage door or other painted body surfaces. Make sure no load is placed on wiring harness.*

– Installation is reverse of removal. Keep in mind the following:
  - 4-door: Mount and align rear door first, followed by front door.
  - Align door so that panel gaps are equal on either side. See **Door hinge adjustment** in this repair group.
  - Adjust door striker so that trailing edge of front door is slightly higher (1 mm / 0.04 in) than leading edge of rear door. See **515 Central Locking and Anti-theft**.
  - Repair paint damage and paint exposed metal.

> ***CAUTION —***
> *2-door: Removing and installing the door may upset the adjustment and alignment of the window. Be sure to carry out window adjustment to avoid damaging the glass. See* **512 Door Windows**.

Door adjustment

- Front fender to front door gap . . . approx. 4.25 mm ± 0.25 mm (0.17 ± 0.01 in)
- Front door to rear door gap approx. . . . . 4.5 mm ± 0.25 mm (0.18 ± 0.01 in)
- Rear door to rear fender approx. . . . . 4.0 mm ± 0.25 mm (0.16 ± 0.01 in)
- Max. deviation from parallel . . . . .1.0 mm (0.04 in)

Tightening torque

- Door hinge to door . . . . 20 Nm (15 ft-lb)

Door check, replacing

– Close door window completely.

– Disconnect negative (–) battery cable.

> ***CAUTION —***
>
> *Prior to disconnecting the battery, read the battery disconnection cautions given at the front of this manual on page viii.*

– Remove interior door panel. See **Door trim panel, removing and installing** in this repair group.

– Where applicable, remove side-impact airbag from door. See **721 Airbag System (SRS)**. Remove door vapor barrier.

< Remove door check mounting bolt (**arrow**).

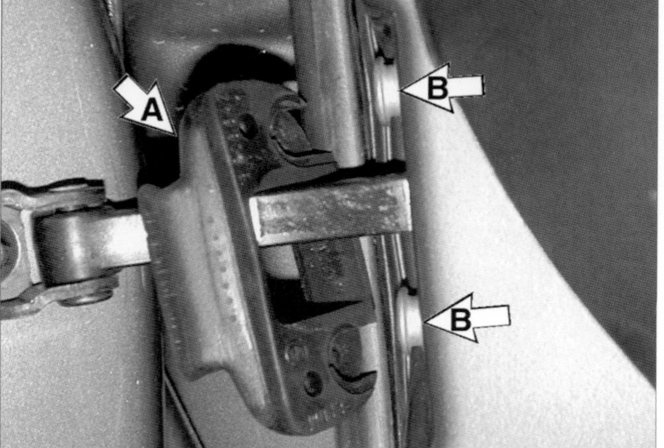

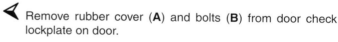

< Remove rubber cover (**A**) and bolts (**B**) from door check lockplate on door.

– Remove door check from inside door.

– Installation is reverse of removal.

- Lubricate door check before installing.
- Use new mounting bolts when reinstalling side-impact airbag to door (where applicable).

Tightening torque

- Door check to door . . . . 24 Nm (16 ft-lb)

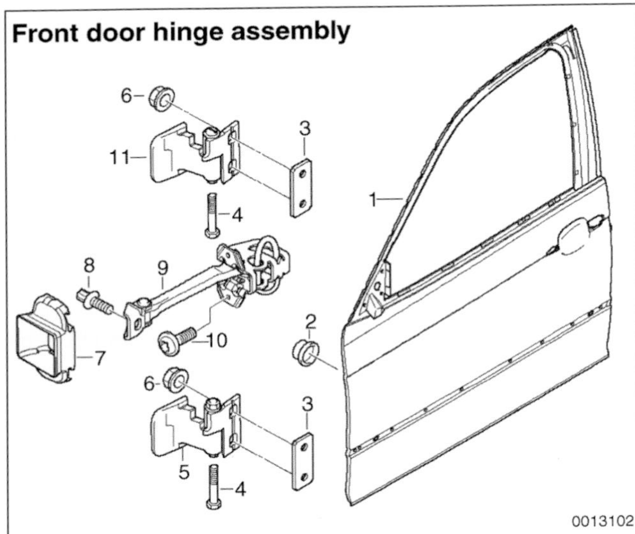

1. Door
2. Protective cap
3. Spacer plate
4. Hex bolt
5. Lower door hinge
6. Hex nut with plate
7. Door check gasket
8. Torx bolt with washer
9. Door check
10. Torx bolt
11. Upper door hinge

Door hinge adjustment

If installed door is uneven or out of parallel, place shims behind hinge plate to correct its position. Shim are available in two different thicknesses (0.5 mm and 1.0 mm).

Front and rear doors are similar.

Tightening torques

- Door hinge to door . . . . 20 Nm (15 ft-lb)

DOOR PANELS

WARNING —

E46 cars are fitted with side-impact airbags in the front doors. Some are equipped with airbags in the rear doors as well. M3 Convertible may be equipped with rear side-impact airbags. When servicing windows or interior panels on a vehicle with side-impact airbags, see **721 Airbag System (SRS)** *for warnings and cautions and procedures relating to the airbag system.*

Door trim panel, removing and installing

– Disconnect negative (–) battery cable.

CAUTION —

Prior to disconnecting the battery, read the battery disconnection cautions given at the front of this manual on page viii.

Gently pry off door panel trim strip.

◄ Carefully pry out mirror adjustment switch and disconnect harness connector from switch.

– For rear trim panel: Pry out window switch at top of armrest.

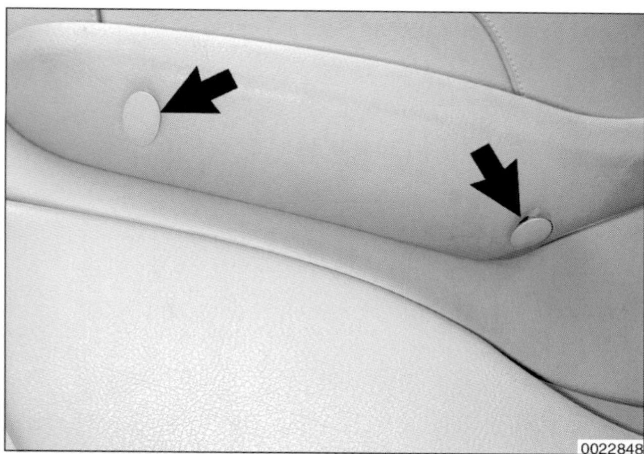

◄ Pry off concealing plugs (**arrows**) from under armrest.

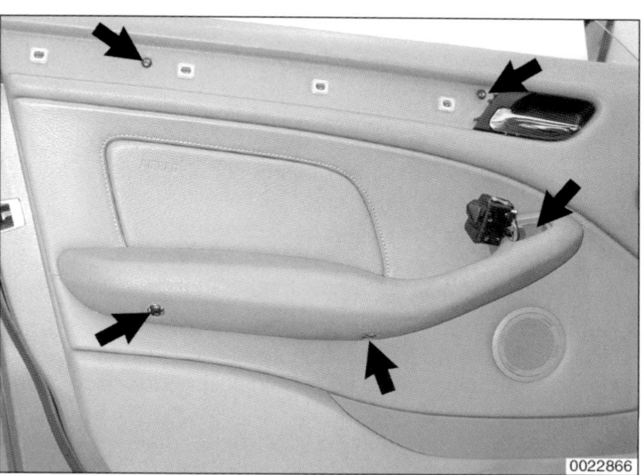

◄ Remove door panel retaining screws (**arrows**).

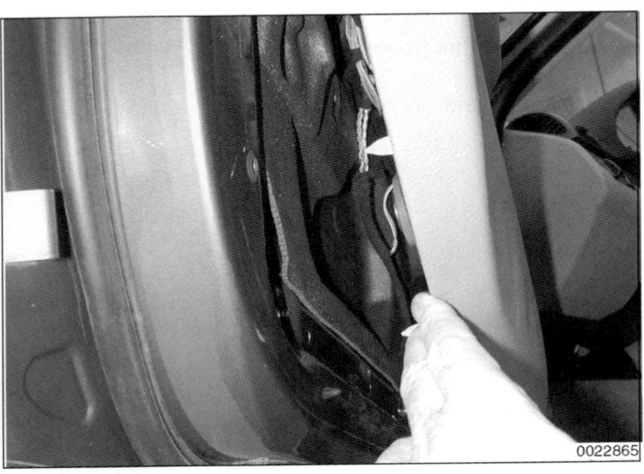

Unclip door panel from door perimeter using a trim panel tool. Pull panel retaining clips off one at a time.

Pry off inside door release Bowden cable at end of clip (**arrow**).

Pull off panel: Detach cable from interior door release lever.

– Disconnect radio speaker harness connector.

– Installation is reverse of removal, noting the following:
  - Replace damaged plastic parts or clips.
  - Renew vapor barrier if it is damaged.
  - Use new mounting bolts when reinstalling side-impact airbag to door.
  - When installing door panel, align metal retainers on window sill with openings on top of door panel.
  - Check door-lock mechanism and window for ease of movement.

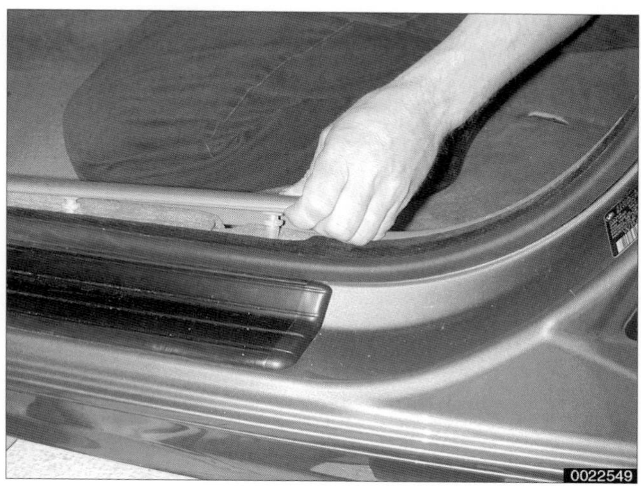

Rear side trim panel, removing and installing (Coupe)

– Remove rear seat cushion. Remove rear backrest side section. See **520 Seats**.

< Using a trim tool, gently pry up door threshold trim. Starting at A-pillar, press radius of trim downwards while sliding trim forward off trim clips. Remove clips from body using pliers.

– Remove trim plugs on armrest. Remove panel mounting screws. Gently pry off panel using trim tool.

– Disconnect electrical harness connectors as necessary. Remove side panel by lifting up and toward interior.

– Installation is reverse of removal. Replace damaged plastic parts or clips.

Rear side trim panel, removing and installing (Convertible)

> ***WARNING —***
> *M3 Convertible, as an option, may have side-impact airbags for rear seat passengers. See* **721 Airbag System (SRS)** *for warnings and cautions and procedures relating to the airbag system.*

– Remove rear seat cushion. Remove rear backrest side section. See **520 Seats**.

– Lower side windows; open convertible roof.

– Remove side panel insert:

- Remove trim plugs on side panel armrest.
- Remove insert panel retaining screws.
- Gently pry side panel insert from upper and lower side panels.
- Disconnect electrical harness connectors as necessary.

– Remove upper side trim panel:

- Remove trim retaining rivet from upper corner at door. Pull trim cap upwards from weather-stripping.
- Unhook spring from linkage at convertible top.
- Remove retaining screws from lower edge of upper panel.
- Gently pull weather-stripping from rear edge of upper panel as necessary.
- Pry up on upper panel and remove.

– Remove lower side trim panel:

- Gently pry lower side trim panel from body.
- Make sure to feed lower front corner of side trim panel out from door threshold trim.

– Installation is reverse of removal. Replace broken trim clips.

412 Trunk Lid, Tailgate

GENERAL

This repair group covers trunk lid and tailgate removal and installation. Also included here are replacement procedures for the gas-charged support struts that hold the trunk lid or tailgate in the open position.

> ***CAUTION —***
> *The body is painted at the factory after assembly. Realignment of body panels may expose unpainted metal. Paint all exposed metal once the work is complete.*

TRUNK LID

Trunk lid, removing and installing

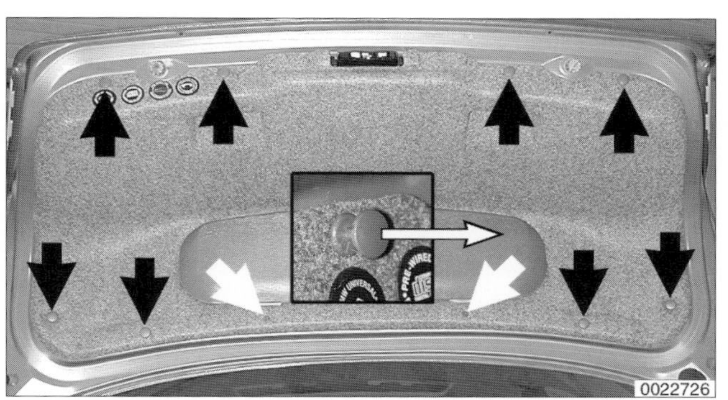

 Raise trunk lid.

- Open tool kit and remove tool kit mounting screws (**white arrows**).
- Unclip retaining strap at trunk lid and remove tool kit.
- Remove insulating liner expansion rivets (**black arrows**), by prying out outer pin (**inset**).
- Lift off trunk liner.

– Detach electrical connectors from trunk lock assembly, trunk lock cylinder, third brake light assembly and license plate lights assembly. Remove wiring harness from trunk lid.

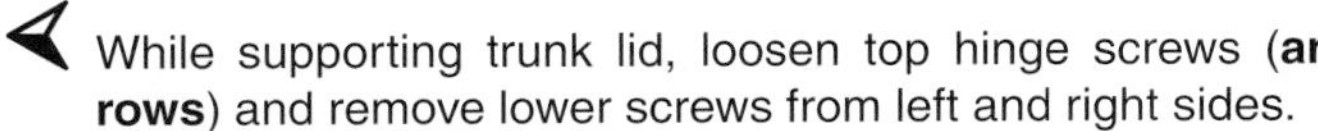

While supporting trunk lid, loosen top hinge screws (**arrows**) and remove lower screws from left and right sides.

NOTE —

Before loosening hinge bolts, mark hinge and hinge bolt locations for reinstallation.

– Installation is reverse of removal. If necessary, align trunk lid to body. See **Trunk lid, aligning** in this repair group.

Trunk lid, aligning

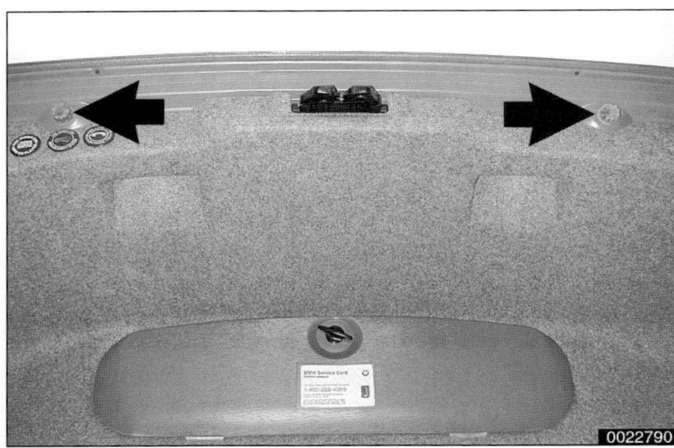

Raise trunk lid. Working at lower corners of trunk lid, unscrew rubber buffers (**arrows**) on left and right sides.

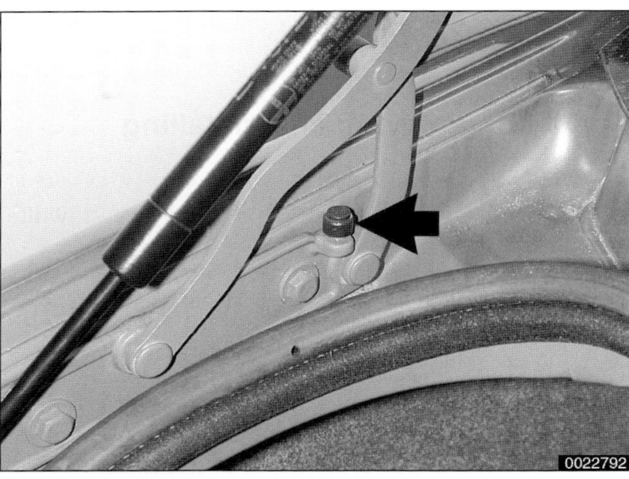

Check stop screw at trunk lid hinge:

- If stop screw has a round plastic head, cut or grind off bolt head. If head is removed, replace round headed stop screw with flat head screw and protective cap.
- If stop screw has removable protective cap (**arrow**) remove protective cap from stop screw.

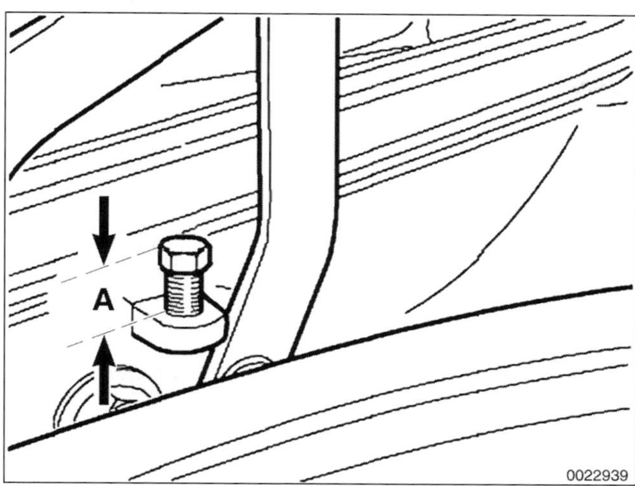

Adjust stop screw so that head is set to (**A**).
A = 10 mm (0.40 in) above bore height

Adjust trunk lid gap at rear fender:

- Loosen bolts retaining trunk hinge to trunk lid (**arrows**) until trunk lid is just able to move.
- If range of adjustment is insufficient, loosen lower bolts on trunk hinge
- Once trunk lid gap is within specification, tighten trunk hinge to lid bolts.

Trunk lid gap specification

- Trunk lid
  to rear fender . . . . 4.25 ± 0.75 mm (0.17 ± 0.03 in)

> ***CAUTION —***
> *Before closing truck lid, be sure that trunk lid and body do not scrape.*

Adjust trunk lock:

- Remove protective caps from trunk rear trim panel. Loosen lock striker screws until striker can just be moved.
- Inspect pads (**arrows**) on each side of striker assembly for damage or wear. Replace if necessary.
- Insert key in trunk lock and hold in unlock position to prevent lock from latching. Close trunk lid to center striker.
- Open trunk lid and tighten striker screws.
- Check adjustment of trunk lock and striker. Repeat adjustment process if necessary. Replace protective caps on trim panel.

– Screw in trunk lid detent buffers until left and right sides of lid rest on buffers with trunk lid closed.

> ***CAUTION —***
> *Make sure top surface of trunk lid is even with top surfaces of fenders.*

– Adjust stop screw at trunk lid hinge:
  - Working at trunk lid hinge, set stop screw to a height of 10 mm (0.40 in). Place a strip of paper on top of stop screw, and gently close trunk lid.
  - Adjust height of stop screw until paper strip can be removed with slight resistance. Once stop screw height has been adjusted, lower adjusted height of stop screw 2.5 mm (0.1 in) to allow room for stop screw protective cap.
  - Fit protective cap on stop screw. Check that trunk lid is in correct position. Adjust if necessary.

> ***CAUTION —***
> *Check that excessive force is not needed to close trunk lid.*

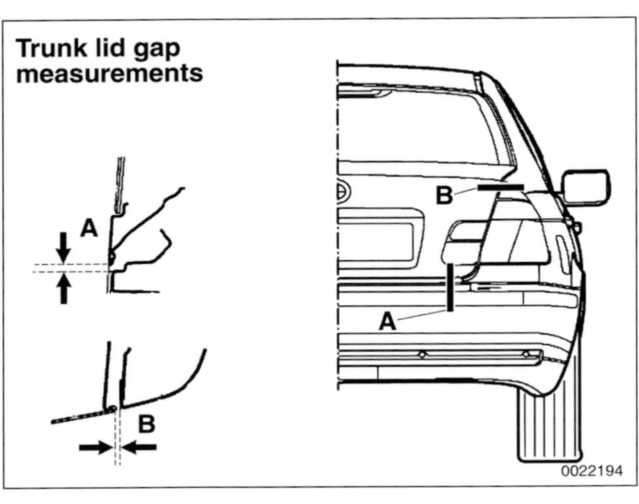

Set gap measurements as listed below.

Trunk position gap adjustment
- Trunk lid to trunk panel (**A**) . . . . 5 ± 1.5 mm (0.2 ± 0.06 in)
- Trunk lid to rear fender (**B**) . . . . . . 4.25 ± 0.75 mm (0.17 ± 0.03 in)

Trunk lid support strut, removing and installing

> ***WARNING —***
> *Make sure to support trunk lid before removing strut.*

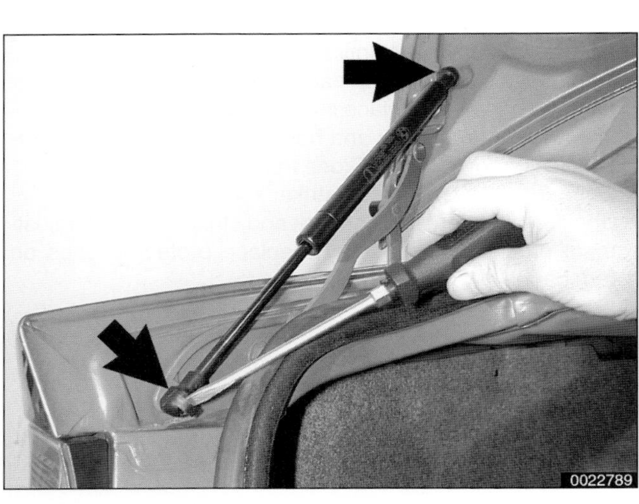

Open trunk lid and support in open position. Remove spring clips (**arrows**) from support strut ends.

– Remove strut from trunk lid.

– Installation is reverse of removal. Replace retaining clips damaged during removal.

TAILGATE (SPORT WAGON)

Tailgate emergency lock release is shown in **515 Central Locking and Anti-theft**.

Tailgate, removing and installing

– Raise tailgate. Remove tailgate inside trim.

– Detach electrical connectors from tailgate lock, rear wiper, rear window defogger, third brake light and license plate light assembly. Remove wiring harness from tailgate.

– Disconnect left and right support struts. See **Tailgate support strut, removing and installing** in this repair group.

– While supporting tailgate, remove hinge bolts for tailgate on left and right sides.

> ***CAUTION—***
> *The tailgate is very heavy. Use assistance to support both sides prior to removal of hinge bolts.*

– Installation is reverse of removal. To align, see **Rear spoiler, rear window and tailgate alignment**.

Tightening torque
- Tailgate to tailgate hinge (M8). . . . . 20 Nm (15 ft-lb)

Tailgate support strut, removing and installing

0021496

 Open tailgate fully. Support tailgate and remove retaining clip (**arrow**) on upper end of pressurized support strut.

> ***CAUTION—***
> *The tailgate is very heavy and will close without both pressurized struts installed. Properly support tailgate prior to removal of a strut.*

– Pull strut off tailgate.

– Remove retaining clip from lower end of support strut. Remove strut.

– Installation is reverse of removal. Replace retaining clips if damaged during removal.

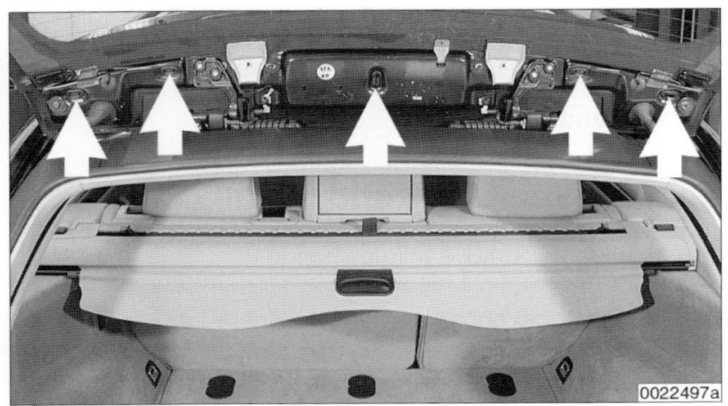

Rear spoiler, removing and installing

Raise rear window. Remove inner trim from glass panel by releasing clips on trim from retainers (**arrows**). For clarity, trim is shown removed in photo.

NOTE —

Use two plastic prying wedge tools to release each pin retaining trim.

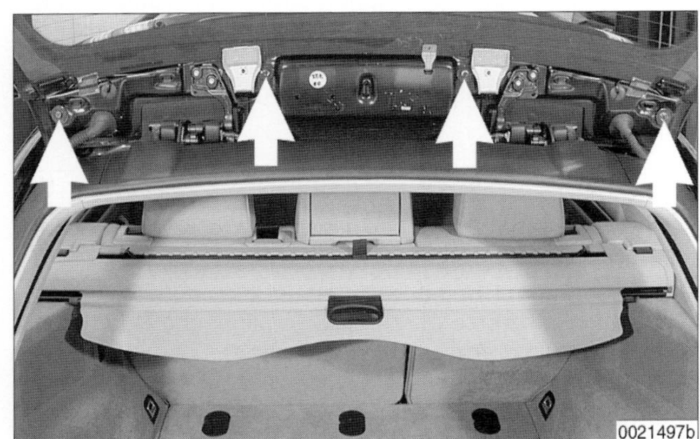

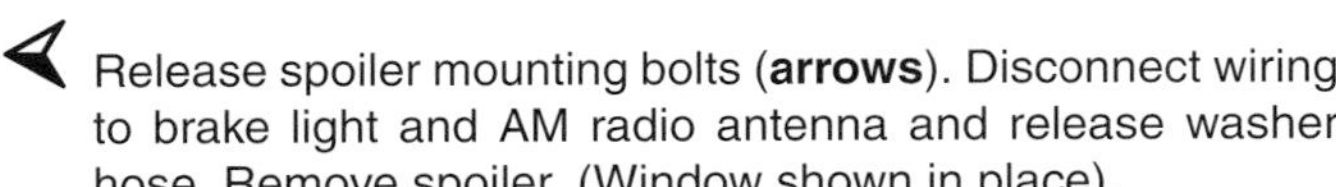
Release spoiler mounting bolts (**arrows**). Disconnect wiring to brake light and AM radio antenna and release washer hose. Remove spoiler. (Window shown in place).

– Installation is reverse of removal. Replace waterproofing sheeting where disturbed. Adjust spoiler. See **Rear spoiler, rear window and tailgate alignment** in this repair group.

Rear window, removing and installing

– Remove rear spoiler. See **Rear spoiler, removing and installing** in this repair group.

– Working at top outside of window, remove waterproofing sheeting over antenna amplifier and disconnect wiring connections. Release tape retaining wiring harnesses.

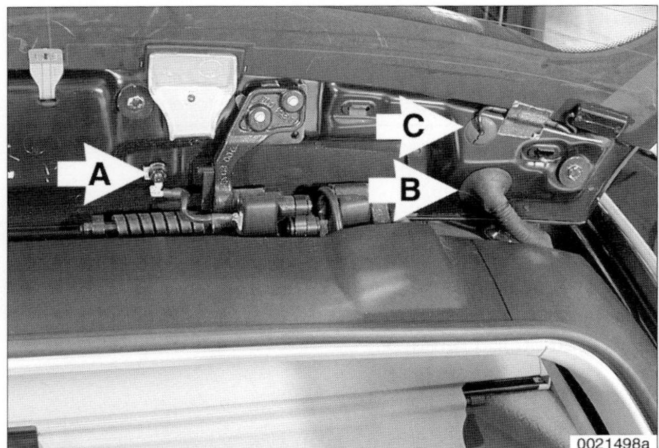

Release grounds (**A**) and rubber grommets (**B, C**) at both hinges.

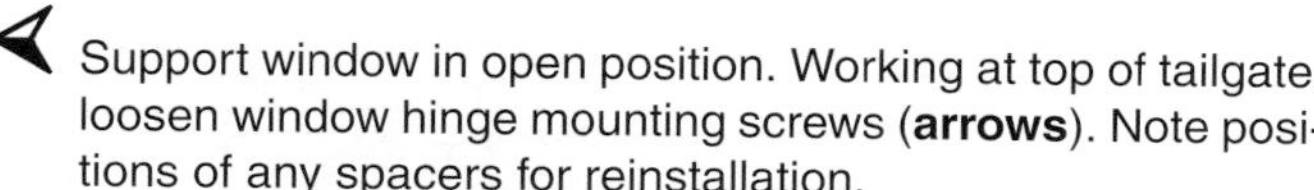

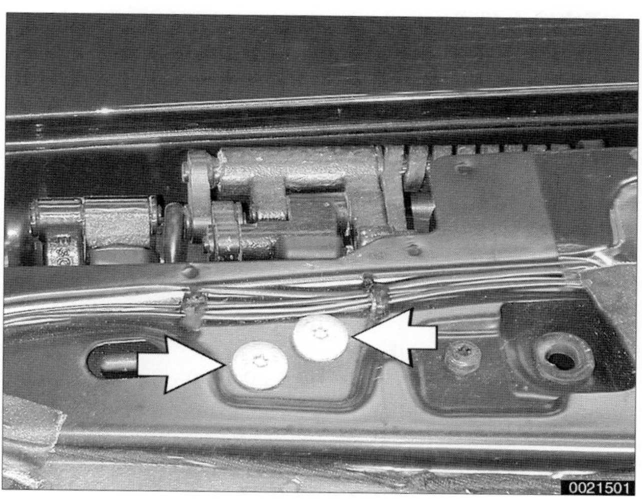

Support window in open position. Working at top of tailgate, loosen window hinge mounting screws (**arrows**). Note positions of any spacers for reinstallation.

> ***CAUTION —***
> *Rear window is heavy. Use a second person to support window prior to releasing from hinges.*

- Detach rear window defogger and antenna harness connectors.
- Remove hinge mounting screws and lift off window.
- Installation is reverse of removal. Replace waterproofing sheeting where disturbed. Align window. See **Rear spoiler, rear window and tailgate alignment** in this repair group.

Tightening torque
- Tailgate window to hinge (M8) . . . . 16 Nm (12 ft-lb)

Rear spoiler, rear window and tailgate alignment

Alignment procedures involve adjusting tailgate, window, and spoiler to have equal space between left and right sides and to be flush with body. Measurement locations and specific dimensions are shown in **Table a**.

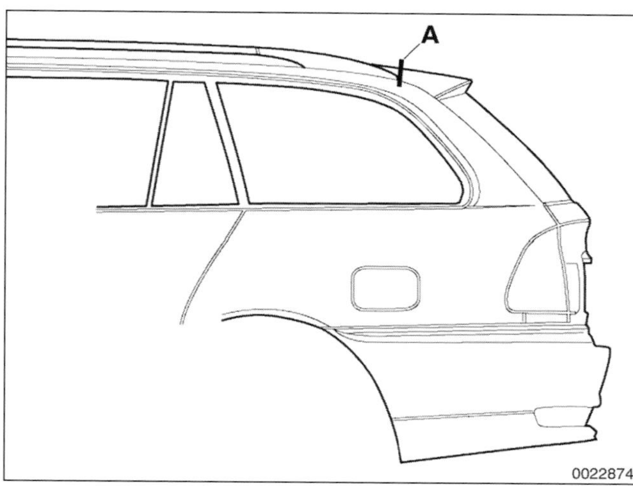

If alignment is disturbed during repair, adjust fit of tailgate to body. Then adjust fit of rear window to hatch.

- Adjust rear window clearance by adding or removing shims between hinge bracket and rear window (maximum of three shims).
- Adjust spoiler gap to body last. Height of spoiler is set by rear hatch alignment. Adjust spoiler gap by adjusting spoiler attachment bolts.

Seam clearance specification
- Rear spoiler to roof (**A**) . . . 4.25 - 5 mm (0.167 - 0.197 in)
- Max. deviation from parallel . . . . 0.5 mm (0.019 in)

- Adjust lateral and vertical alignment using window and tailgate hinge bolts. Use rubber stop buffers and latch assembly for fine adjustments. See **Table a**.

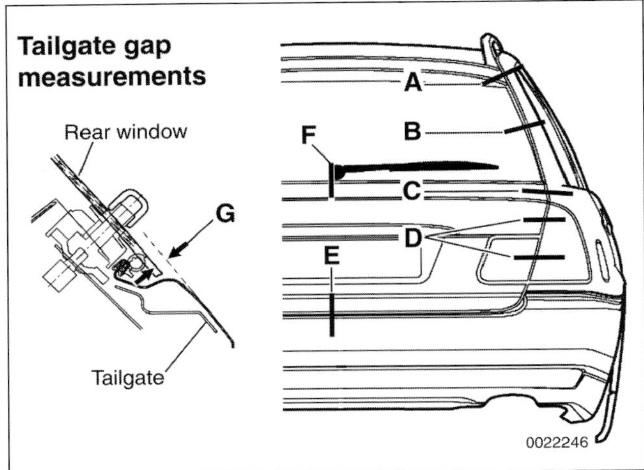

Table a. Tailgate to body gap measurements

Parameter (from sketch)	Gap measurement
Rear spoiler to side panel (**A**)	3.75 ± 1.3 mm (0.15 ± 0.05 in)
Rear window to side panel (**B**)	3.5 ± 1.4 mm (0.14 ± 0.06 in)
Tailgate to side panel (**C**)	3.6 mm ± 0.75 mm (0.14 ± 0.03 in)
Tailgate to side panel (height)	Flush to 2 mm (0.08 in) lower
Tailgate light to corner light (**D**)	4.25 ± 0.75 mm (0.17 ± 0.03 in)
Tailgate to rear bumper (**E**)	5 ± 1 mm (0.2 ± 0.04 in)
Rear window to tailgate (**F**)	4 ± 1 mm (0.16 ± 0.04 in)
Rear window to tailgate (**G**)	5.4 ± 1 mm (0.21 ± 0.04 in)

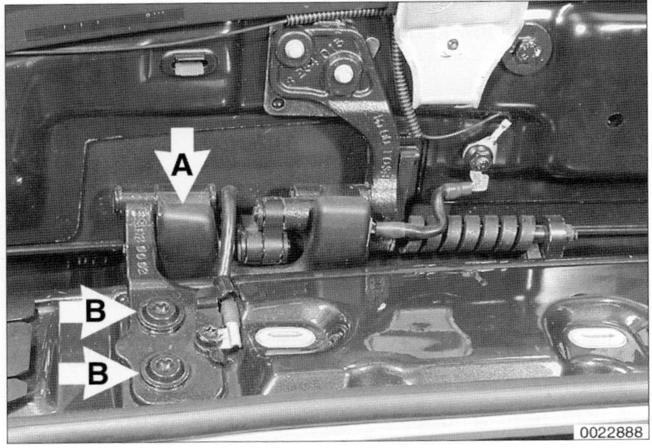

Adjust fit of tailgate to body:

- Close tailgate and open rear window.
- Center tailgate hinge bolts (**A**, behind trim) both vertically and horizontally within their adjustment range. When centered, tighten bolts.
- Loosen screws (**B**) on left and right to adjust horizontal location (gap on left and right). When gap is correct, tighten screws.
- To prevent damage or poor operation, adjust rear window if tailgate vertical adjustment is changed.
- Window hinge must be parallel to the tailgate hinge.

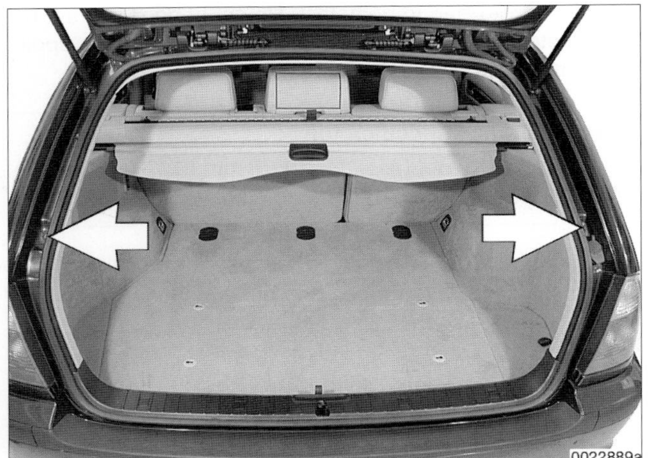

Stop buffers (**arrows**) are adjustable and set height between tailgate and body at sides.

- To adjust buffers, remove inner trim panel and loosen lock nut.
- Initially adjust buffers to just contact tailgate when closed, then tighten buffers one turn. Tighten lock nut.

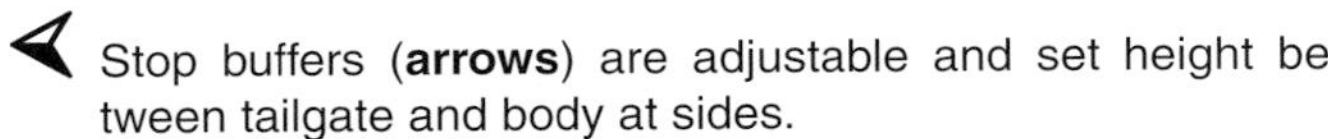

Tightening torque

- Lock nut for stop buffer (M8) . . . . 15 Nm (11 ft-lb)

– Adjustment of tailgate window lock and tailgate lock is covered in **515 Central Locking and Anti-theft**.

510 Exterior Trim, Bumpers

GENERAL

This repair group includes repair information for the outside rear view mirror, front and rear bumpers, and the easily removable exterior trim parts.

OUTSIDE REAR VIEW MIRRORS

Mirror components separately available from an authorized BMW dealer include mirror glass and outside plastic housing.

Outside mirror glass, replacing

> ***CAUTION —***
> *Mirror should be at or above room temperature before removal. Otherwise, small plastic parts or glass may break.*

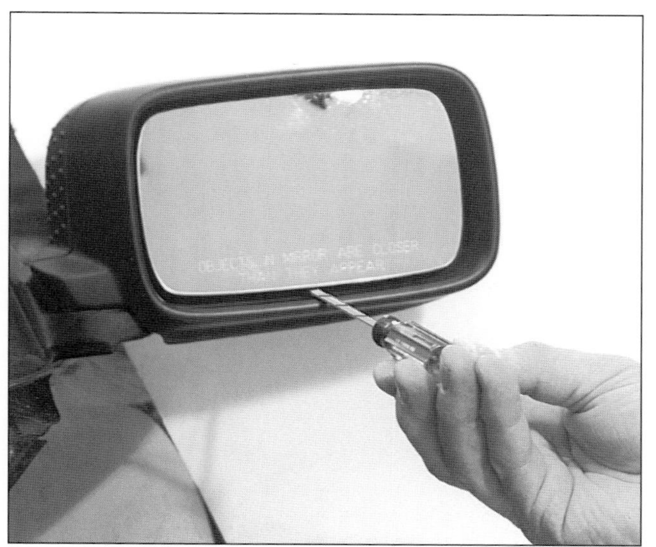

 Insert thin pry tool (wooden or tape-wrapped screwdriver) between bottom mirror edge and mirror housing and carefully pry out mirror glass from housing.

– Heated mirror: Remove heating element harness connectors from back of mirror glass.

– Install new glass into position by pressing firmly until it snaps into place.

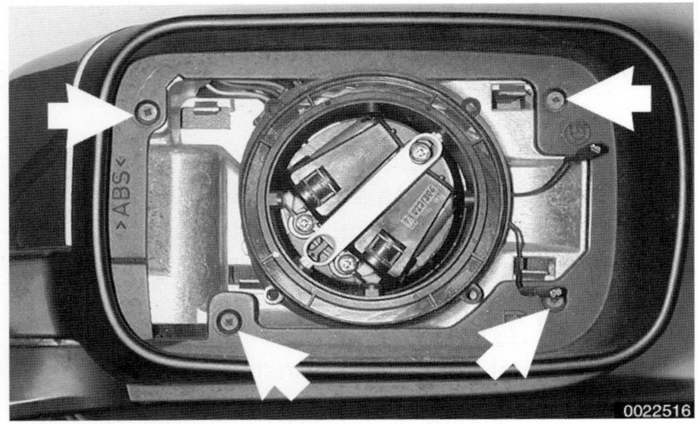

Outside mirror housing, removing and installing

– Remove mirror glass. See **Outside mirror glass, replacing** in this repair group.

◄ Remove housing retaining screws (**arrows**) and lift off rear housing.

0022518

◄ Tilt mirror housing forward. Gently squeeze plastic tabs (**arrows**) and lift off front housing.

NOTE —

The front mirror housing is retained by either three or four tabs, depending on model.

– Installation is reverse of removal. Check mirror function before installing covering parts.

Outside mirror, removing and installing

– Remove front door panel trim. **See 411 Doors.**

◄ Working at door hinge, remove door inner edge trim retaining pins (**arrows**).

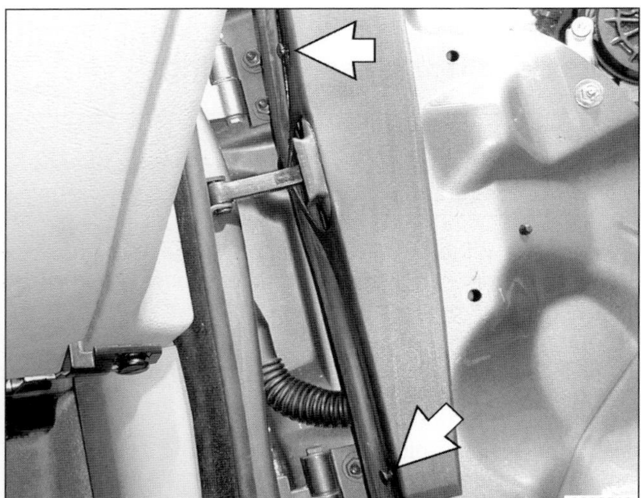

Gently pry off door edge trim from retaining clips (**arrows**).

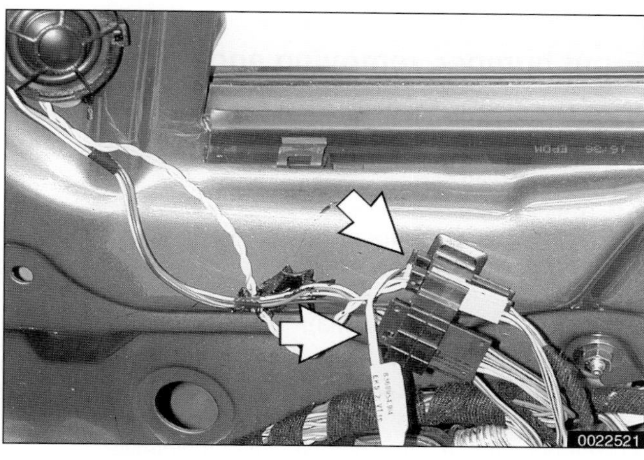

Disconnect electrical harness connectors for window pinch-protection strip and speaker (**arrows**).

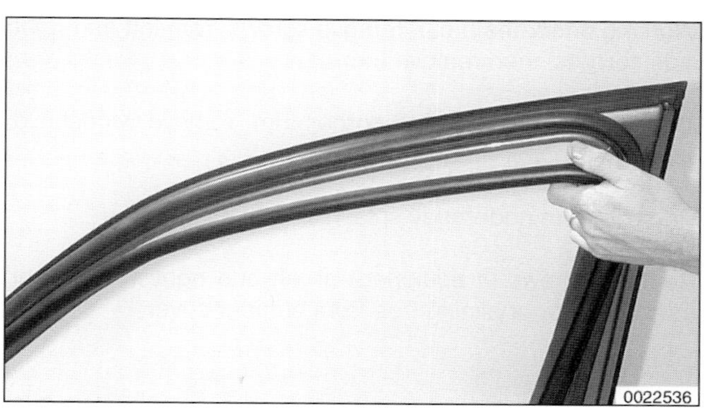

Remove inner door panel trim. On sedan model, trim strip extends around window to door latch area.

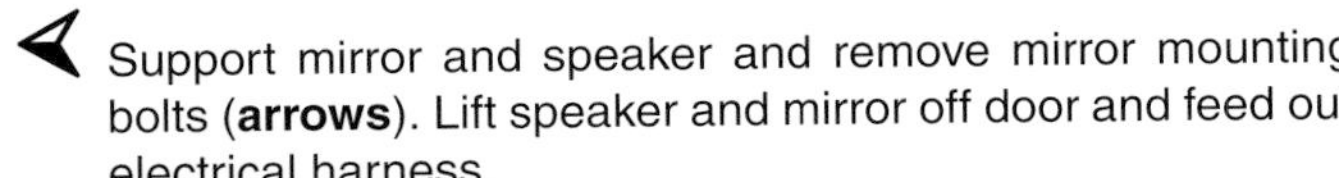

Support mirror and speaker and remove mirror mounting bolts (**arrows**). Lift speaker and mirror off door and feed out electrical harness.

– Installation is reverse of removal. Check mirror function before installing covering parts.

Tightening torque
- Outside mirror to door (M6) . . . . 6 Nm (4.5 ft-lb)

BUMPERS

Front bumper, removing and installing

– Raise and safely support vehicle.

> ***WARNING —***
> *Make sure the car is firmly supported on jack stands designed for the purpose. Place jack stands underneath structural chassis points, not under suspension parts.*

Coupe or Convertible (non-M3):

- Remove fog lamp trim:
- Snap out catches (**A**) on grill assembly (**B**), and gently pull from bumper.
- Lever out catch (**C**) and detach trim completely.

– Working underneath car, remove screws from left and right side corners, then remove trim.

– M3: working at right side corner trim, remove windshield washer reservoir mounting screw.

– Remove front underbody splash shield.

– Remove screws (if equipped) at left and right front wheel arch lining, or pry lining free from bumper cover.

Remove bumper cover mounting screws (**arrows**).

Front bumper assembly

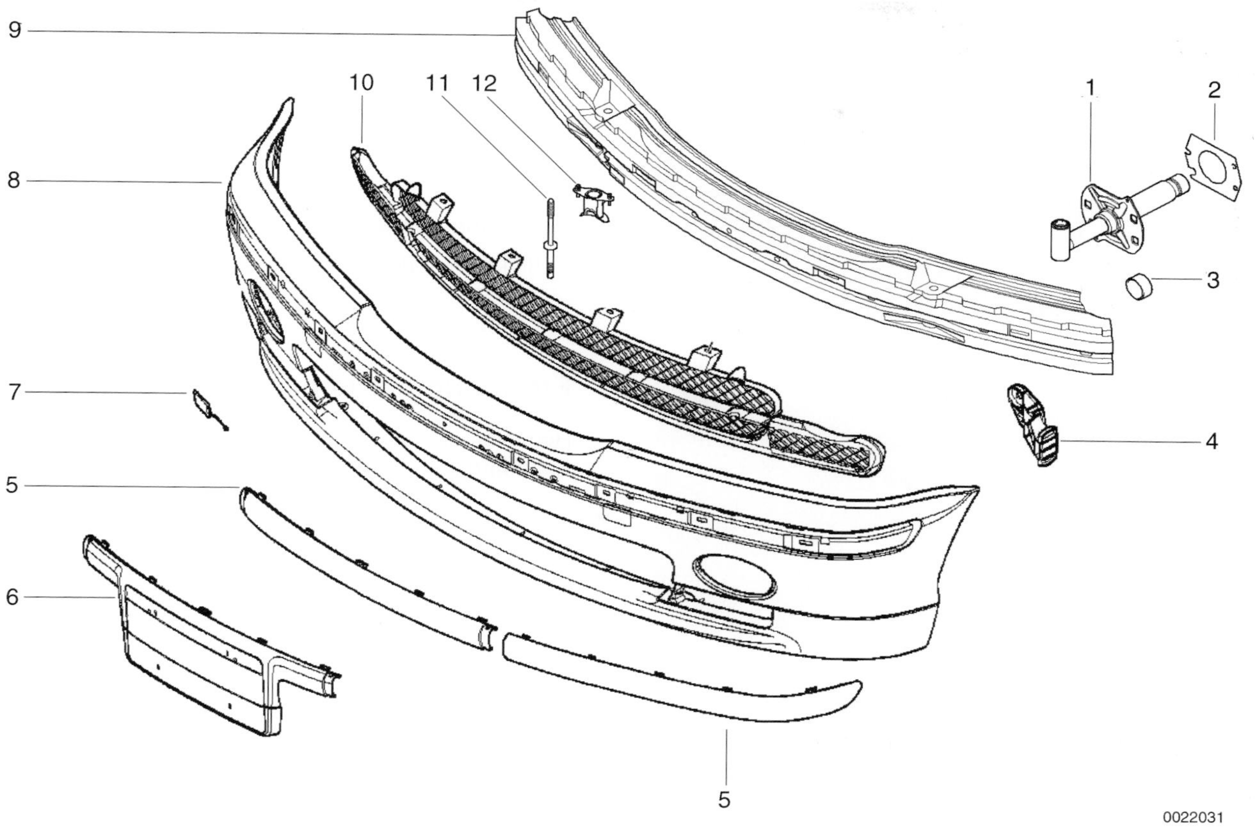

0022031

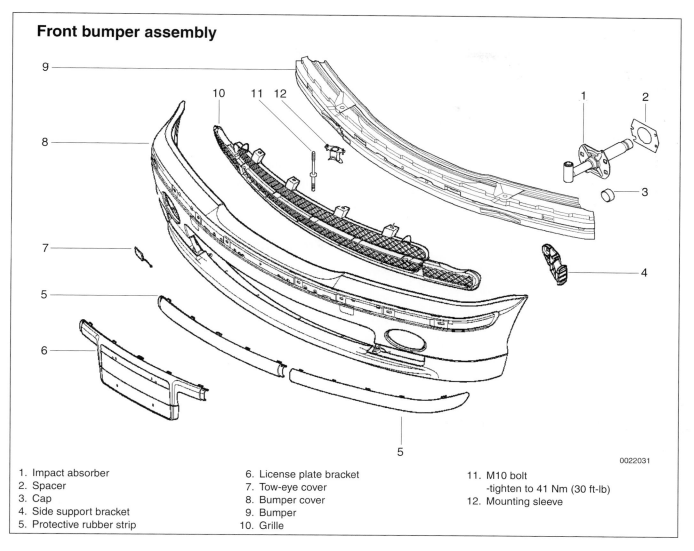

1. Impact absorber
2. Spacer
3. Cap
4. Side support bracket
5. Protective rubber strip
6. License plate bracket
7. Tow-eye cover
8. Bumper cover
9. Bumper
10. Grille
11. M10 bolt
    -tighten to 41 Nm (30 ft-lb)
12. Mounting sleeve

◄ Remove bumper mounting bolts (**arrows**).

– Slide bumper assembly out a few inches and disconnect the following:
  - Headlight washer hoses (if applicable)
  - Horn (if applicable)
  - Foglight assemblies
  - Outside temperature sensor

– Slide bumper straight off side support brackets, watching carefully for fasteners or wiring harnesses that might become snagged.

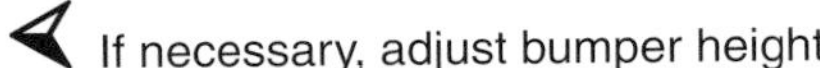

If necessary, adjust bumper height:

- Use 14 mm Allen socket to turn height adjuster collar at bumper impact absorber.
- See **Bumper height, adjusting** in this repair group.

— Installation is reverse of removal, noting the following:

- Carefully slide bumper on side brackets.
- Set gap between body and bumper to approximately 5 ± 1 mm (¼ in). Make sure gap is even.

Tightening torque

- Bumper to impact absorber (M10) ..... 41 Nm (30 ft-lb)

Front bumper impact absorber, replacing

— Remove front bumper. See **Front bumper, removing and installing** in this repair group.

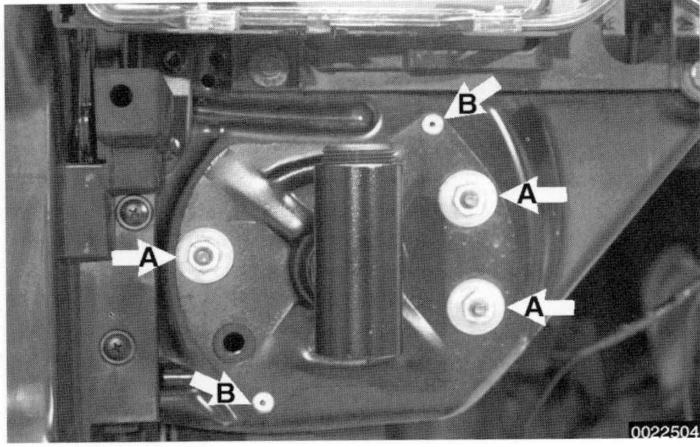

Remove bumper impact absorber mounting nuts (**A**) and drill out pop rivets (**B**).

— Installation is reverse of removal.

Tightening torques

- Bumper to impact absorber (M10) ..... 41 Nm (30 ft-lb)
- Impact absorber to body (M8 nut)...... 18 Nm (13 ft-lb)

Rear bumper, removing and installing

— Raise and safely support vehicle.

> ***WARNING —***
> *Make sure the car is firmly supported on jack stands designed for the purpose. Place jack stands underneath structural chassis points, not under suspension parts.*

— Pull off lower bumper trim. If necessary, disconnect electrical harness connectors for park distance control sensors.

Remove bumper support bolts (**arrows**) using BMW special tool 00 2 150 (short T50 Torx driver).

> ***CAUTION —***
> *Place protective cloth or fabric tape on body parts to prevent paint damage from tool.*

Rear bumper assembly

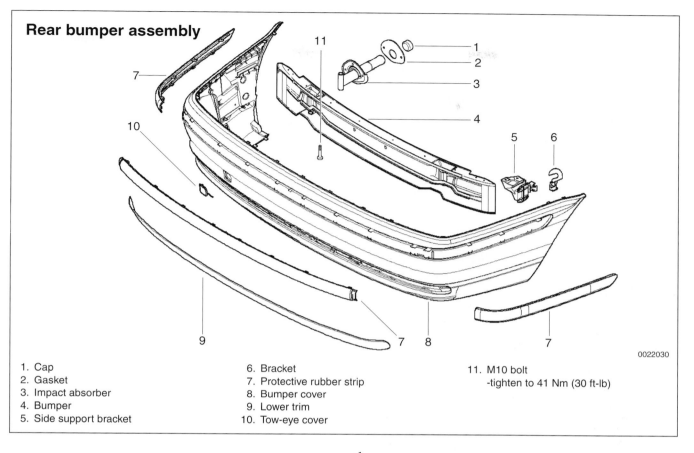

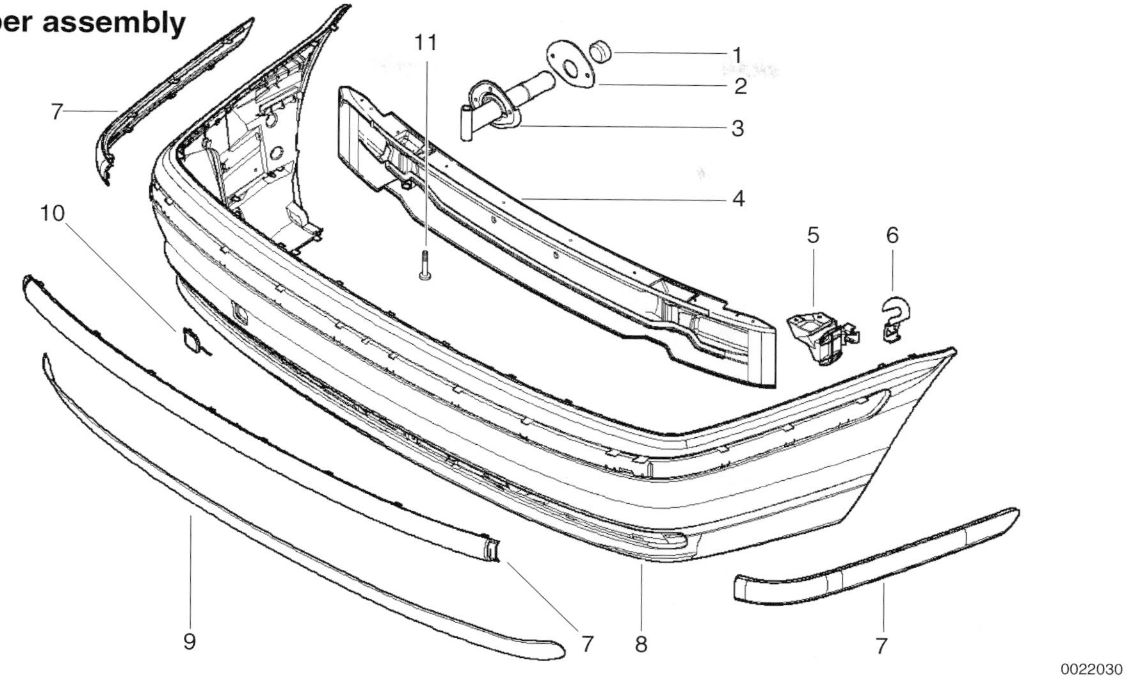

0022030

1. Cap
2. Gasket
3. Impact absorber
4. Bumper
5. Side support bracket
6. Bracket
7. Protective rubber strip
8. Bumper cover
9. Lower trim
10. Tow-eye cover
11. M10 bolt
    -tighten to 41 Nm (30 ft-lb)

◀ Models to 9 / 2001:

- Remove nut (**arrow**) from bumper cover mounting bracket at rear of left and right rear wheel wells. Remove bracket.
- Remove expansion pins from lower wheel wells.

– Models from 10 / 2001: Disengage bumper cover from mounting lugs by pressing detent lug downward.

– Remove wheel well liner from left and right sides.

– Pull bumper rearward to remove, watching carefully for fasteners or wiring harnesses that might become snagged. If necessary, detach wiring harnesses inside trunk and pull out of body with insulating grommet.

– Installation is reverse of removal, noting the following:

- Carefully slide bumper on side brackets.
- Set gap between body and bumper to approximately 2 ± 1 mm (1/8 in). Make sure gap is even. See **Bumper height, adjusting** in this repair group.

Tightening torque

- Bumper cover mounting bracket to wheel well . . . . 3 Nm (27 in-lb)
- Bumper to impact absorber (M10) . . . . . 41 Nm (30 ft-lb)

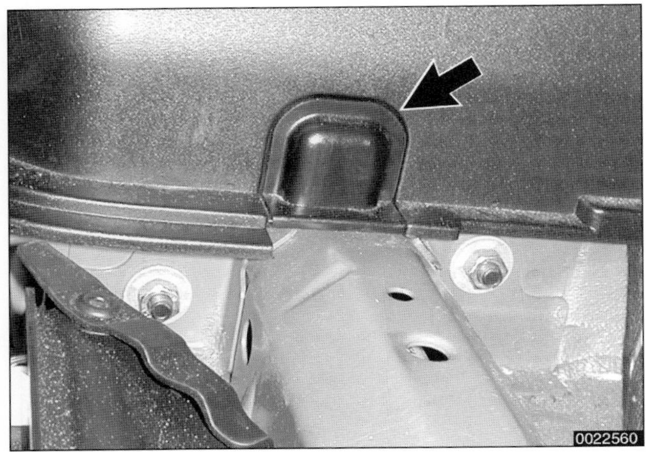

Rear bumper impact absorber, replacing

– Remove rear bumper. See **Rear bumper, removing and installing** in this repair group.

– Remove trunk floor covering.

– Remove battery and battery tray on right side and trunk trim panel on left side.

◄ Remove trim caps (**arrow**) at rear of frame rails.

◄ Remove bumper impact absorber mounting nuts (**arrows**) on inside of vehicle trunk. Remove absorber.

– Installation is reverse of removal. Replace body seal and protective cap if necessary.

Tightening torques
- Bumper to impact absorber (M10) . . . . . 41 Nm (30 ft-lb)
- Impact absorber to body (M8 nut). . . . . . 22 Nm (16 ft-lb)

Bumper height, adjusting

The adjustment procedure applies to either front or rear bumper. Use a 14 mm Allen socket to make adjustments.

– Raise and properly support vehicle.

> ***WARNING —***
> *Make sure the car is firmly supported on jack stands designed for the purpose. Place jack stands underneath structural chassis points, not under suspension parts.*

– Rear bumper: Remove lower bumper trim.

– Front or rear bumper: Remove bumper bracket mounting bolt at impact absorber.

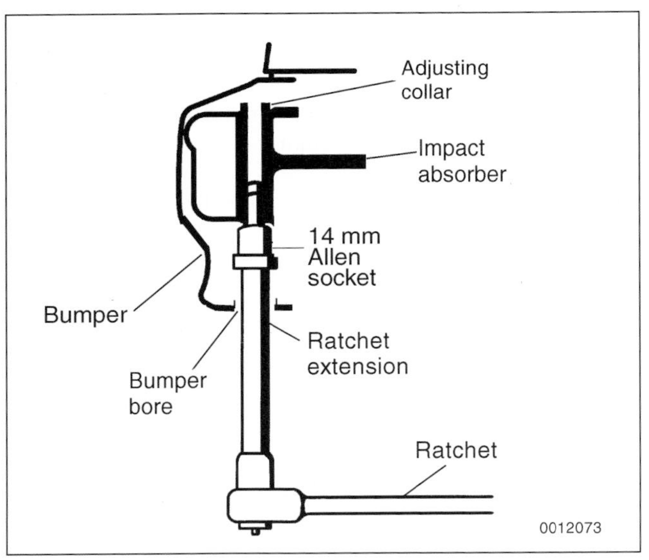

◄ Use 12-inch extension and 14 mm Allen socket to turn adjusting collar clockwise or counterclockwise as needed to change height of bumper.

– Reinstall mounting bolts and check bumper height. Refit trim.

Tightening torque
- Bumper to impact absorber (M10) . . . . . 41 Nm (30 ft-lb)

EXTERIOR TRIM

Exterior trim is retained to the body by plastic clips and fasteners that may be damaged during removal. Be sure to have necessary fasteners on hand when reinstalling exterior trim pieces.

BMW emblem, removing and installing

The procedure given below applies to both front and rear emblems.

– Wrap end of a screwdriver with tape.

> **CAUTION —**
> *Protect hood by covering area around emblem with tape.*

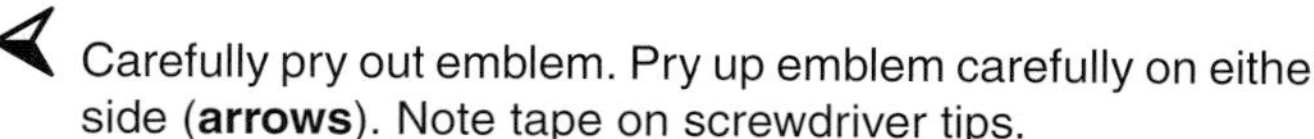

◄ Carefully pry out emblem. Pry up emblem carefully on either side (**arrows**). Note tape on screwdriver tips.

– Installation is reverse of removal.
  - Replace plastic inserts in body if damaged.
  - If emblem fits loosely, use a small amount of body molding tape or adhesive on rear of emblem before installing.

Body side molding, replacing

To remove body side moldings, carefully pry moldings straight off.

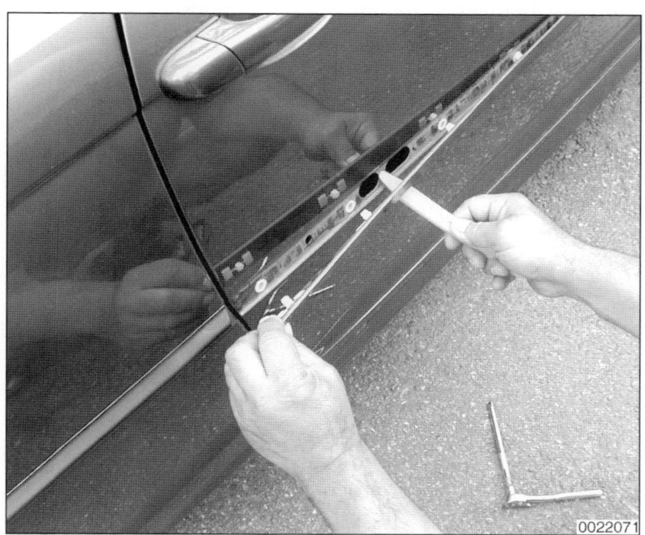

◄ Installation is reverse of removal. Replace clips or clip covers damaged during removal.

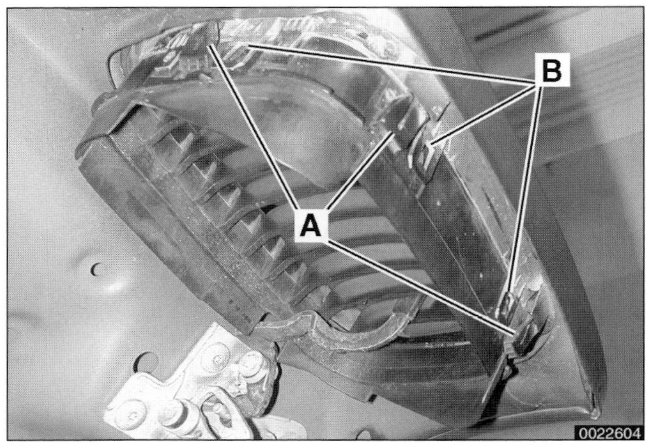

Radiator grill, removing and installing

- Open hood.

- Gently pry out tab on left or right side of grill trim ring (**A**), as well as tabs on bottom.

- Feed grill out through opening. Be careful of hood lever on driver's side grill.

- Once grill is removed, pry remaining tabs (**B**) to separate inner grill from chrome trim ring.

- Before installation, assemble chrome trim ring and grill insert securely. Replace components if tabs or catches are broken or missing.

- To install, align grill and trim ring in hood opening. Press on trim ring until grill snaps into place.

Headlight housing trim, removing and installing

- Open hood.

- Remove headlight washer nozzle, if applicable. **See 611 Wipers and Washers.**

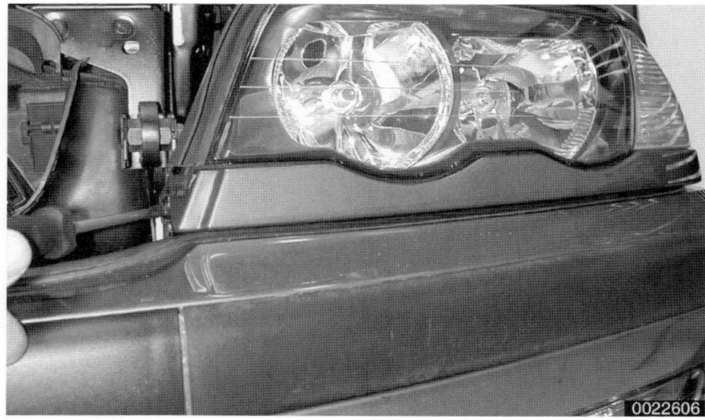

- Unclip inner tab at radiator support.

- Press panel downward, out of retaining brackets. Feed out retaining hook at fender.

- Installation is reverse of removal.

512 Door Windows

GENERAL

This repair group covers door glass, window regulator and power window motor repair information.

Electric window switch replacement is covered in **612 Switches**.

The windshield, rear window, fixed rear door glass, and cargo compartment glass (Sport Wagon) are bonded using special adhesives and tools. It is recommended that bonded glass replacement be done by an authorized BMW service facility or an automotive glass installer.

Special tools

Some window repair operations require the use of special tools.

Special tools

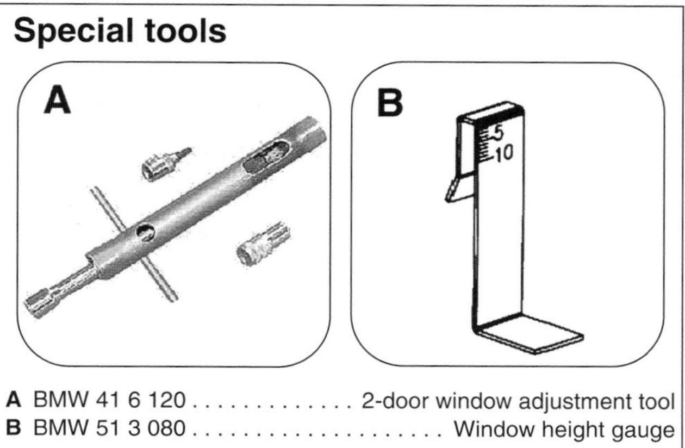

A BMW 41 6 120 . . . . 2-door window adjustment tool
B BMW 51 3 080 . . . . Window height gauge

512

Power windows

Power window features in E46 models include:

- Door window motor controlled directly by General Module (GM V).
- One-touch operation in both directions on all four windows, where applicable.
- Cable type window regulator used for all door windows.
- Window switch pulled up to raise the window, pushed down to lower.
- 4-door: Each rear door with window switch in door pull-handle.
- Rear window switches deactivated by child lock-out switch in center console.
- Convenience closing / opening of windows from driver's lock cylinder. Convenience opening only from FZV remote key. FZV operation can be owner customized with Car Memory function. See **515 Central Locking and Anti-theft**.
- After ignition is switched off, electric windows operable until a door is opened or until 16 minutes has elapsed.
- GM V bases window motor end position on current draw (load). Maximum window motor run time is 8 seconds. Window motor then switched off even if end position load sensor fails.

Window switches

The push-pull type window switch provides the GM V with a coded ground signal. Holding a switch at the first detent provides a single ground signal on one wire requesting the GM V to open the window. When released, the ground signal is removed and the window motor stops.

Momentarily pushing the switch to the second detent and releasing provides an additional ground signal on the second wire requesting "one touch mode". The GM V lowers the window automatically until it reaches the end position.

The switch functions in the same manner for window closing but the ground signal sequence is reversed.

NOTE —

- *Coupe: Rear window switches are used for operating the rear swing-out vent windows.*
- *M3 Convertible from 03 / 2003 and Convertible from 09 / 2003: To activate pinch protection, standardize power window motor. See* **Window motor standardization (Convertibles)** *in this repair group.*
- *Window switch replacement is covered in* **612 Switches**.

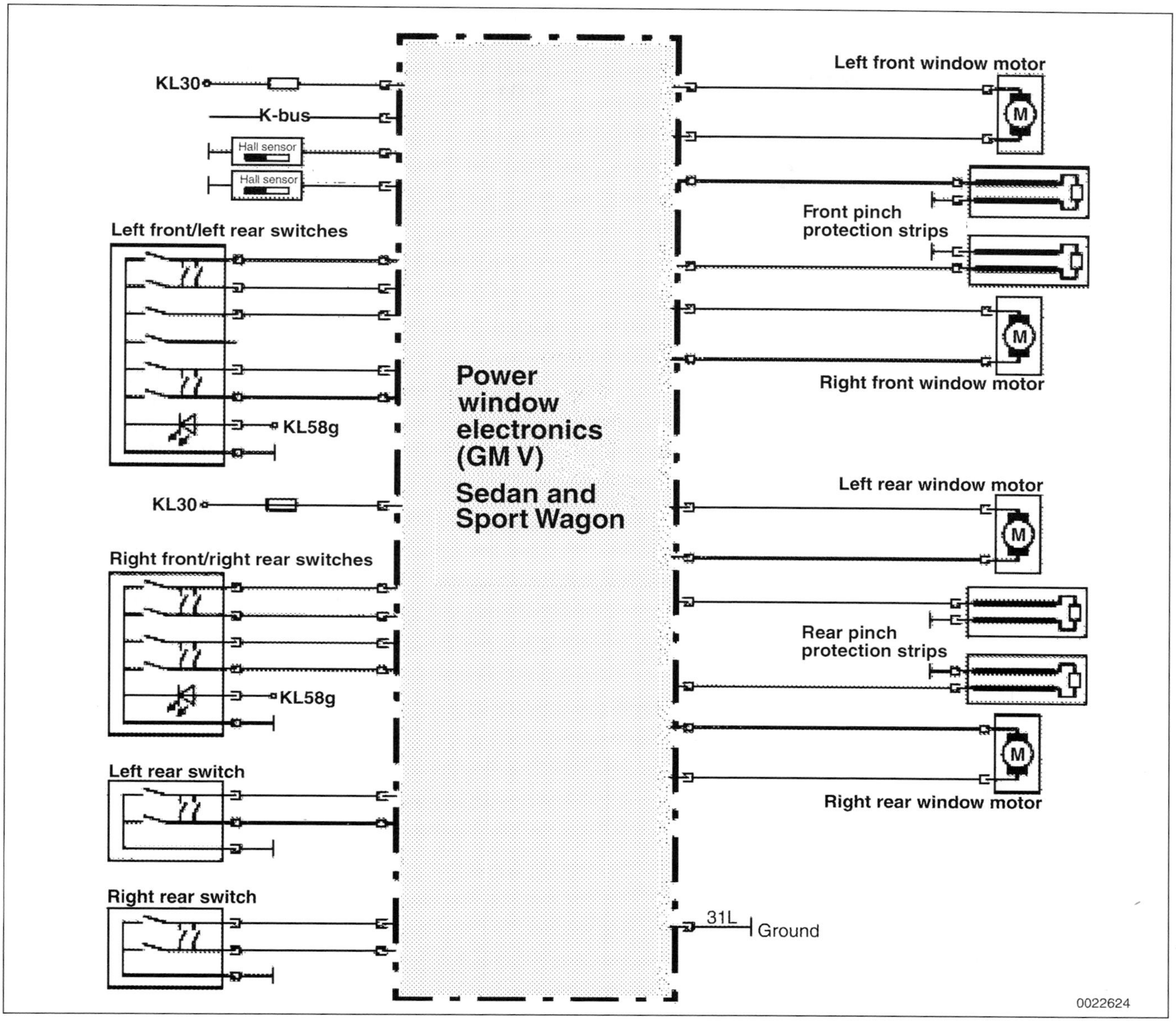

KL30
K-bus
Hall sensor
Hall sensor
Left front/left rear switches
KL58g
KL30
Right front/right rear switches
KL58g
Left rear switch
Right rear switch
Power window electronics (GM V)
Sedan and Sport Wagon
Left front window motor
M
Front pinch protection strips
M
Right front window motor
Left rear window motor
M
Rear pinch protection strips
M
Right rear window motor
31L
Ground
0022624

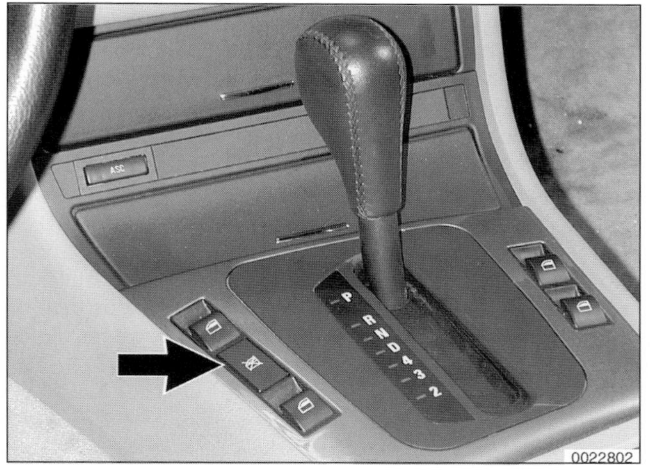

0022802

Rear window child lockout switch

4-door: Rear window child lockout switch (**arrow**) is incorporated in the driver's window switch block to the left of the shifter. When activated, it provides a constant ground signal to the GM V, preventing the windows from being operated from the rear door switches.

The lockout switch ground signal is overridden by the GM V if a Multiple Restraint System (MRS) crash signal is received.

NOTE —

Convertible: The four-window control switch is in the position occupied by the rear window lockout switch in 4-door model.

Power window motors

The window motors are mounted on cable regulators. The window motor control circuit consists of two wires for operating the motor in both directions.

Relays in the GM V provide either power or ground to the window motors, depending on the direction of window travel. The GM V controls the polarity based on a request to run the window from a window switch or a convenience opening / closing signal.

Convenience opening / closing

The GM V provides the convenience open / close feature, providing control of the power windows (and sunroof) from outside the vehicle with the key in the driver's door lock. The FZV (remote key) provides the same function for window opening only.

Pinch protection is active during convenience closing from the driver's door lock.

If the GM receives a request to operate convenience closing or opening for more than 110 seconds, the function is deactivated and a fault code is stored.

Window pinch protection

In 4-door models, a rubber pressure guard located at the top edge of each door frame consists of two contact strips that close when subjected to pressure. When the contact strip closes (for example, a hand is trapped between the top of the window and the door frame), a pinch signal is sent to the GM V. The window immediately (within 10 milliseconds) reverses direction. This feature does not require initialization.

The E46 pressure sensitive pinch protection strip has a resistance of 3 KΩ and it is monitored for open circuit. When pressed, the monitored resistance changes to < 1 KΩ. If pinch protection becomes faulty, one-touch window closing is disabled.

Window pinch protection is only active in the one-touch and convenience close modes of operation. If the window switch is pulled and held, pinch protection does not function.

Window pinch protection was added to the front windows of Convertible models beginning with M3 models in 03 / 2003 and all Convertibles in 09 / 2003.

The Convertible pinch protection system differs from 4-door models. Electrical system load on the electric lift motor is monitored to determine if the window lift path is obstructed. When an obstruction is detected, the window reverses direction.

Window motor limit stop function

If repeated window activation (up / down cycles) exceeds one minute, the GM V deactivates the internal relays and disregards any further up / down requests. The GM V provides motor activation after a short duration but not for the full one minute monitoring cycle.

The GM V monitors the number of times a window motor is activated. It counts each cycle and stores the number in memory. After the stop function limit is reached and the window motor is deactivated, the GM V slowly reverses the count until the stored number equals 0, thus allowing the window motor to cool down.

Convertible windows

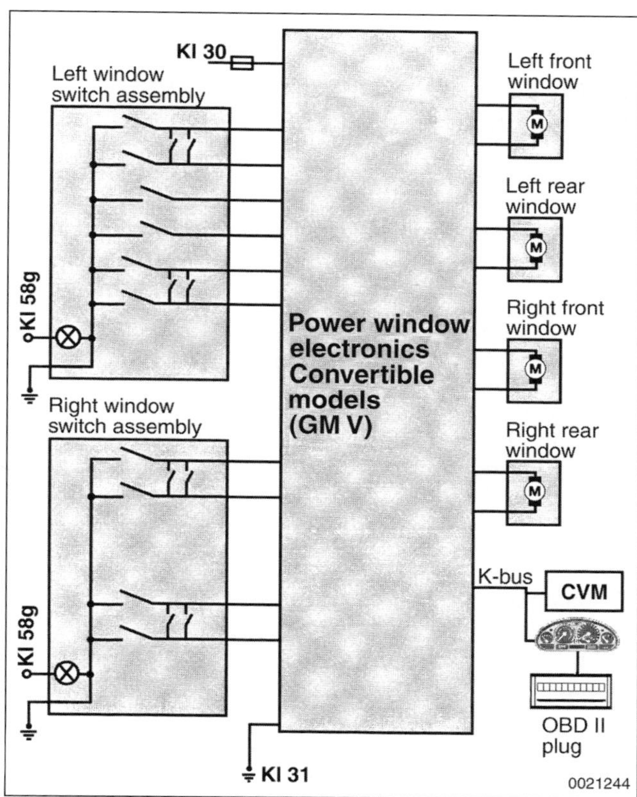

A central power window switch is located in the Convertible console between the left side window switches. This switch allows all four windows to be opened with one-touch operation and closed if the switch is held.

When the convertible top is opened the power windows are lowered slightly for approx. 1.5 seconds to ensure clearance for the top. Once the top is stored in the storage compartment, the windows close again if the top switch is held in the open position.

WARNING —

- *E46 cars are fitted with side-impact airbags in the front doors. Some are equipped with airbags in the rear doors as well. When servicing the door window on a vehicle with side-impact airbags, see* **721 Airbag System (SRS)** *for warnings and cautions and procedures relating to the airbag system.*

- *When connecting or disconnecting side-impact airbag harness connector, make sure the battery is disconnected.*

- *The airbags system contains a back-up power supply within the SRS control module. Allow a 60 second discharge period after disconnecting the battery cable.*

- *If the airbag warning light on the dashboard illuminates after completion of window repairs, the airbags will not deploy in case of an accident. Be sure to have the SRS system diagnosed and repaired immediately.*

- *When working on door window, disconnect the harness connector to the window regulator to prevent pinching fingers in the moving window mechanism.*

- *Wear hand and eye protection when working with broken glass.*

- *If a window is broken, vacuum all of the glass bits out of the door cavity. Use a blunt screwdriver to clean out any remaining glass pieces from the window guide rails.*

WINDOW SERVICE, 4-DOOR

Sedan and Sport Wagon doors are similar. Use the following procedures for window service on these models.

Window pinch protection strip, testing

Pinch protection strip is integrated into the molding strip of the door window frame.

– To test function of pinch protection strip on any window:
  - With key ON and window down, pull up window switch to second detent, thus activating one-touch close operation.
  - Insert wooden block or other soft object between glass and upper door frame.
  - When window contacts block, it immediately reverses direction and lowers by approx. 25 mm (1 in).

Front window pinch protection strip, removing

– Remove front door panel and vapor barrier. See **411 Doors**.

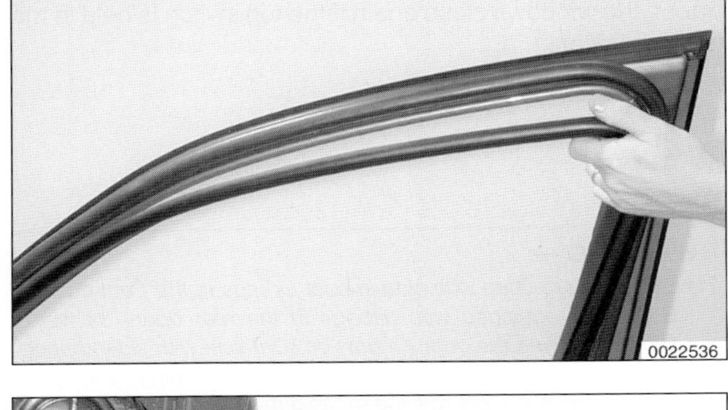
0022536

◄ Detach window frame molding strip and peel toward inside of vehicle.

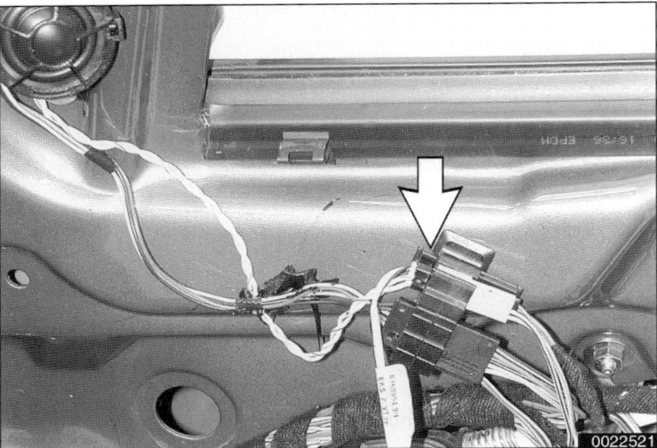
0022521

◄ Separate pinch protection electrical harness connector (**arrow**) at top front of door.

NOTE —
Wire colors for pinch protection strip are black-white.

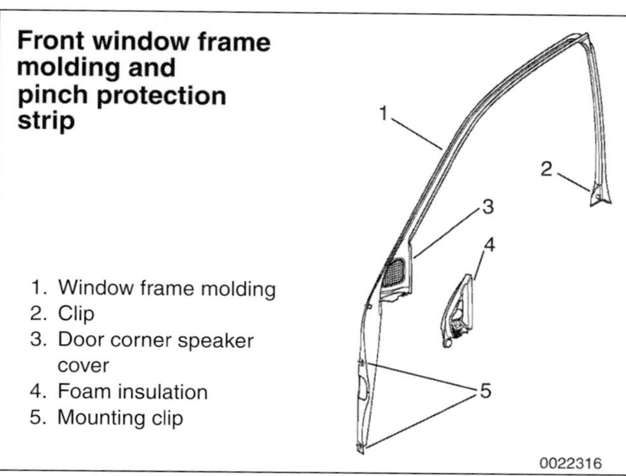

Front window frame molding and pinch protection strip

1. Window frame molding
2. Clip
3. Door corner speaker cover
4. Foam insulation
5. Mounting clip

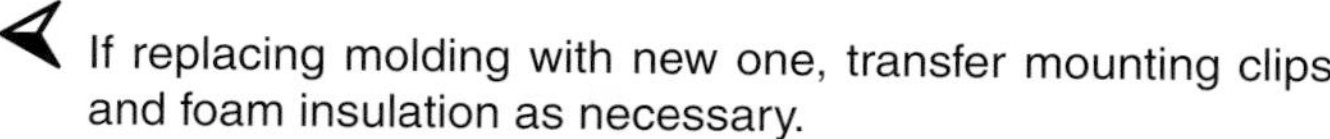

If replacing molding with new one, transfer mounting clips and foam insulation as necessary.

- After installation, recheck pinch protection.

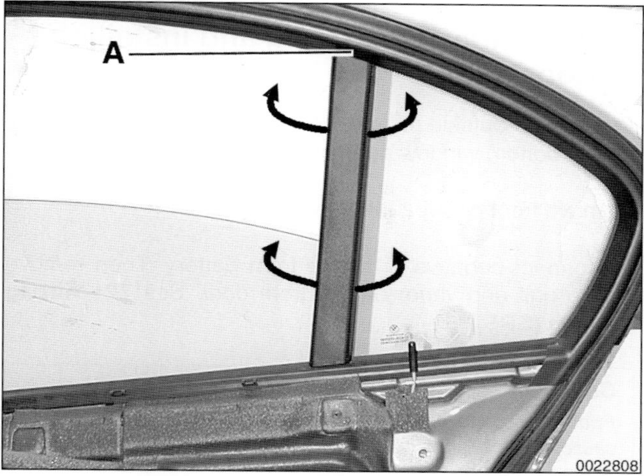

Rear window pinch protection strip, removing

- Remove rear door panel and vapor barrier. See **411 Doors**.

Detach window frame molding strip, peeling it off fixed window partition (**arrows**). Do not tear strip in area **A**.

- Detach electrical connector at top front of door, just below window.

NOTE —
Wire colors for pinch protection strip are black-white.

- After installation, recheck pinch protection.

Front window, adjusting (4-door)

Whenever the front window or window regulator is removed, check window adjustment. The glass should contact the top of the window squarely and should seat against the window seal uniformly.

NOTE —
Poor or non-uniform contact of the window with the seal may result in wind noises and water leaks.

- Remove front door panel. See **411 Doors**.
- Disconnect negative (–) cable from battery. Then remove airbag unit and vapor barrier from door. See **721 Airbag System (SRS)**.

CAUTION —
Prior to disconnecting the battery, read the battery disconnection cautions given at the front of this manual on page viii.

- Partially detach rear of vapor barrier / sound insulation from door and fold forward. Hold in place using adhesive tape.

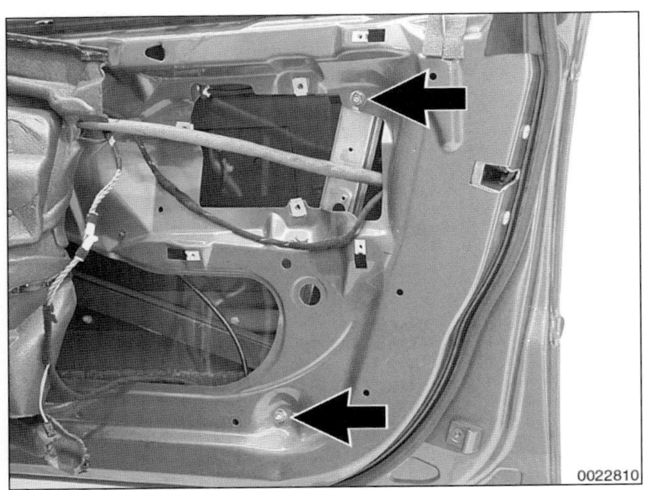

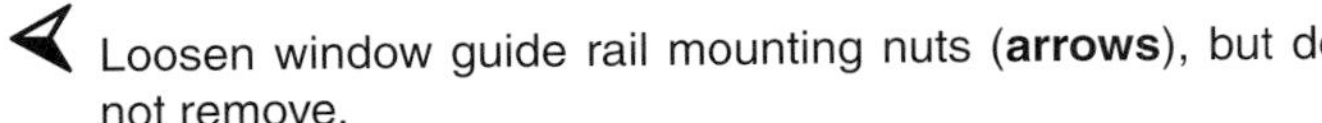
Loosen window guide rail mounting nuts (**arrows**), but do not remove.

- Reconnect battery. Open window fully.
- Tighten guide rail nuts.

Tightening torque
- Window regulator guide rail to door . . . . . 9 Nm (80 in-lb)

Front window, removing and installing (4-door)

- Working on outside of door, use plastic prying tool to gently pry off bottom window opening sealing strip.
- Remove front door panel. See **411 Doors**.
- Disconnect negative (–) cable from battery. Then remove airbag unit and vapor barrier from door. See **721 Airbag System (SRS)**.

> ***CAUTION —***
> *Prior to disconnecting the battery, read the battery disconnection cautions given at the front of this manual on page viii.*

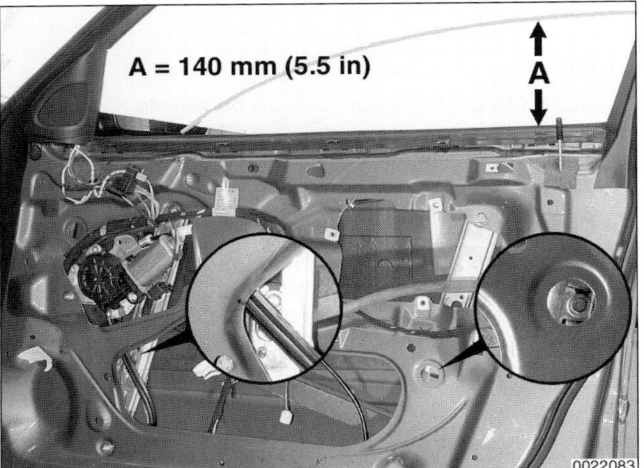

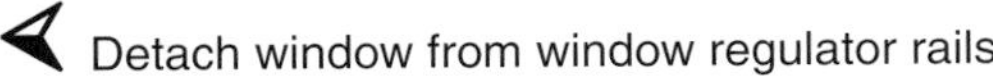
Detach window from window regulator rails:

- Reattach battery. Move window to approx. 140 mm (5.5 in) from bottom.
- Remove window retaining screws (**insets**) at window regulator rails.

> ***WARNING —***
> *Once the window is positioned correctly, disconnect harness connector from power window motor to prevent accidental operation of the window.*

Window glass

Detach plastic window retainers from glass:

- Push expander nut (**1**) out of plastic retainer.
- Squeeze retainer tabs (**2**) and remove from glass.

NOTE —
Replace the plastic window retainers every time the glass is removed from the door.

< Turn window glass carefully inside door cavity and lift out.

– Installation is reverse of removal.
  - Replace plastic window retainers once glass is inside door.
  - Use new mounting bolts when reinstalling side-impact airbag to door.
  - Adjust window. See **Front window, adjusting (4-door)** in this repair group.

Tightening torques
- Side-impact airbag to door . . . . .8.5 Nm (75 in-lb)
- Window to regulator guide . . . . 8 Nm (71 in-lb)

Rear window, removing and installing (4-door)

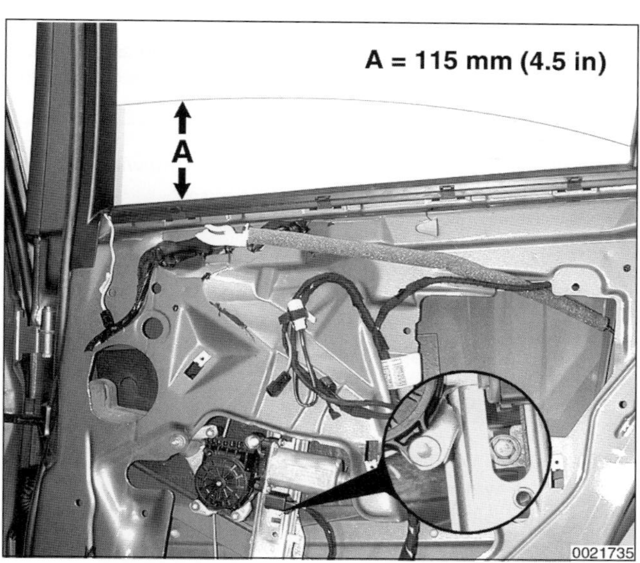

– Remove rear door panel and vapor barrier. See **411 Doors**.

– Model with rear side impact airbag: Disconnect negative (–) cable from battery. Then remove airbag unit from door. See **721 Airbag System (SRS)**.

< Detach window from window regulator rail:
  - If necessary, reattach battery. Move window to approx. 115 mm (4.5 in) from bottom.
  - Remove window retaining screw (**inset**) at window regulator rail.

WARNING —
Once the window is positioned correctly, disconnect harness connector from power window motor to prevent accidental operation of the window.

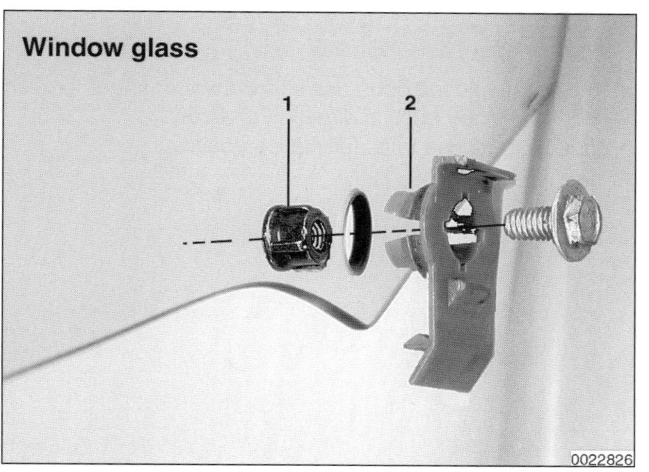

< Detach plastic window retainer from glass:
  - Push expander nut (**1**) out of plastic retainer.
  - Squeeze retainer tabs (**2**) and remove from glass.

NOTE —
Replace the plastic window retainers every time the glass is removed from the door.

– Pull window glass straight up to lift out of door.

– Installation is reverse of removal.
  - Replace plastic window retainer once glass is inside door.
  - If applicable, use new mounting bolts when reinstalling side-impact airbag to door.
  - Rear window does not need adjustment.

Tightening torques
- Side-impact airbag to door . . . . .8.5 Nm (75 in-lb)
- Window to regulator guide . . . . 8 Nm (71 in-lb)

WINDOW SERVICE, 2-DOOR

2-door models are equipped with the window drop down feature:

- When the door latch is activated (door is opened), the window glass moves down slightly to clear the top door seal.
- When the door is closed, the window lifts slightly and jams up tightly against the top door seal.

NOTE —
See **Window motor standardization (Convertibles)** *in this repair group.*

Front window, adjusting (2-door)

The drop-down feature of 2-door cars with frameless windows makes window adjustment critical.

CAUTION —
There is risk of window glass breakage if correct adjustment procedures are not used. If in doubt, leave this procedure to a trained BMW technician.

The following adjustments can be made to the window:

- Longitudinal
- Pretension (or window rake)
- Parallelism (or window tilt)
- Vertical adjustment (or retraction depth)
- Glass protrusion (when open)
- Distance between side window and door window

Emergency operation

Adjusting the window drop-down feature insures low wind noise and water leakage past windows. With the door closed, the window must jam a predetermined amount up into the seal. When the door is opened, the window must lower immediately to clear the seal.

 With door open, close window.

- To simulate closed door, use screwdriver or finger to push door lock rotary latch in direction of **arrow**.
- Window must rise to its full closed position.

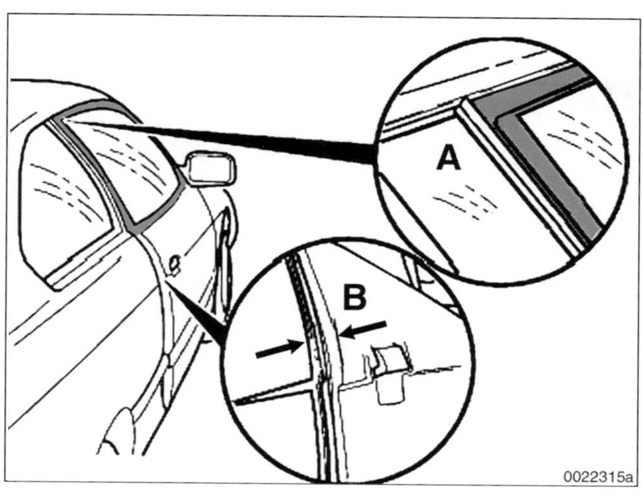

Close door as far as possible without forcing.

- Coupe: Top edge of glass must rest on door seal (**A**).
- Convertible: Gap between door and B-pillar (**B**) must be 25 mm (1 in).

NOTE —
Window must seal with water drain at mirror triangle in A-pillar.

– Use door handle to open rotary latch:

- Window should lower a small amount.

– Close door:

- Window should raise a small amount.

– Reopen door:

- Window should lower a small amount and clear rubber seal.

– If window gets stuck in rubber seal:

- Lower glass.
- Adjust retraction depth. See **Vertical adjustments** n this repair group.

Longitudinal adjustment

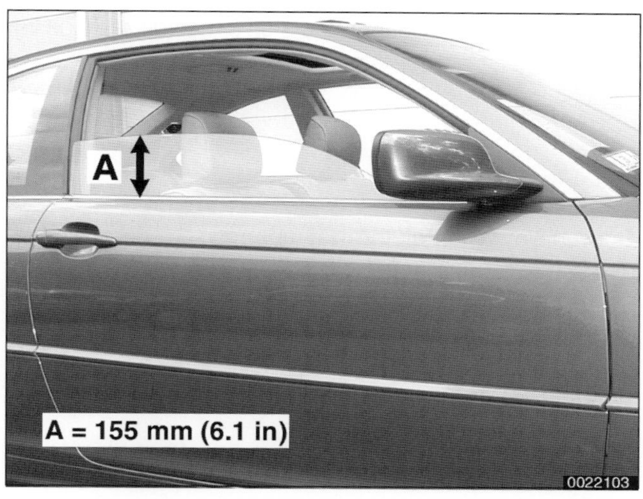

Position window approx. 155 mm (6.1 in) above dead bottom.

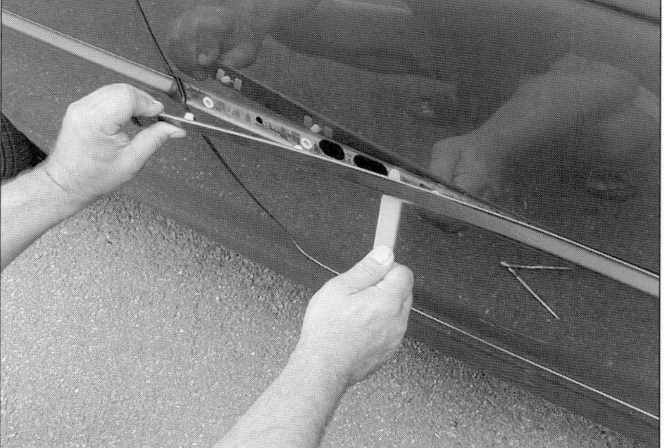

Working carefully with a plastic prying tool, detach outside trim strip from door.

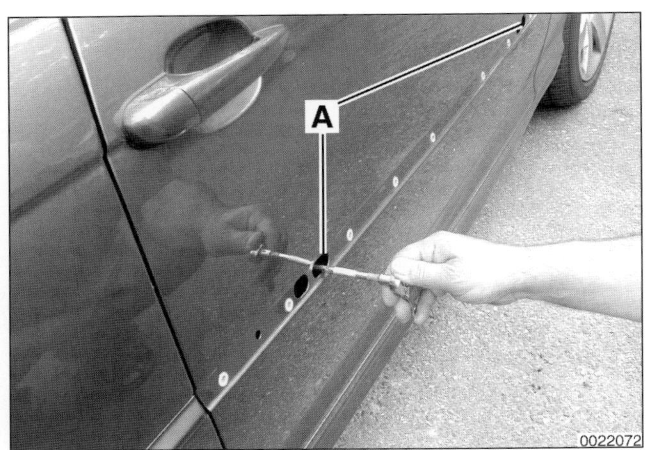

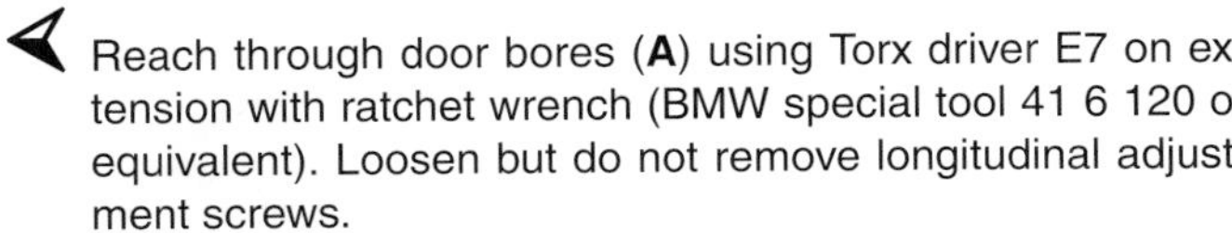

Reach through door bores (**A**) using Torx driver E7 on extension with ratchet wrench (BMW special tool 41 6 120 or equivalent). Loosen but do not remove longitudinal adjustment screws.

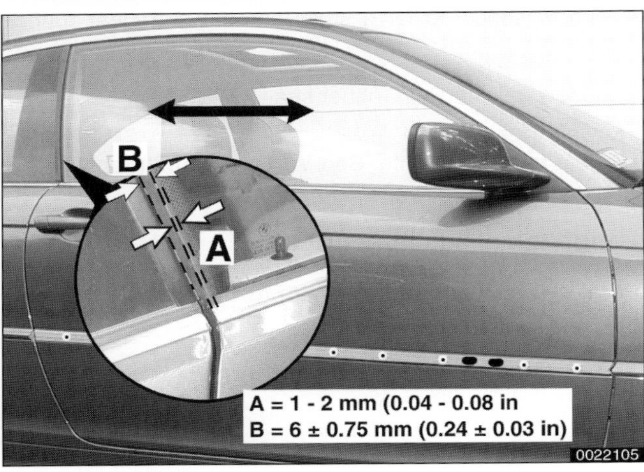

Raise glass to top. Move glass fore or aft to attain correct adjustment.

- Coupe: When fully closed, rear edge of window overlaps door opening seal by dimension **A**.
- If necessary, replace side window sealing trim.

Window longitudinal adjustment

- Dimension **A** . . . . 1 - 2 mm (0.04 - 0.08 in)
- Door window rear edge to side window trim (Coupe) . . 6 ± 0.75 mm (0.24 ± 0.03 in)

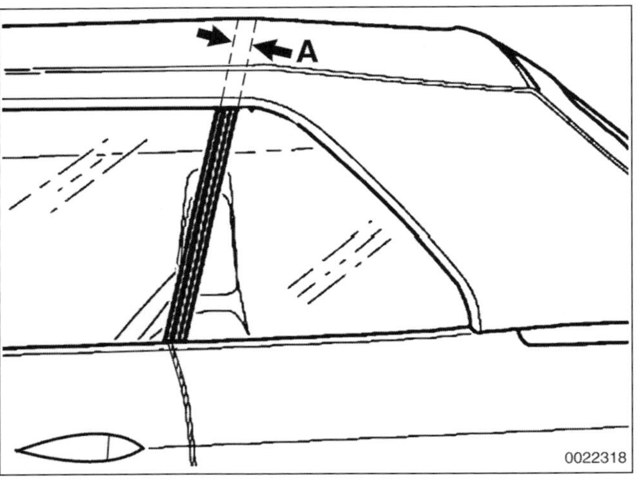

Convertible: When all the way up, measure door window gap to rear window trim.

- Gap **A** is measured from edge of door window to rear of rear window trim.

Window longitudinal adjustment

- Door window rear edge to rear window trim (Convertible) . . . . 25 mm (1 in)

– Tighten longitudinal adjustment screws.

Tightening torque

- Window to guide . . . . 8 Nm (71 in-lb)

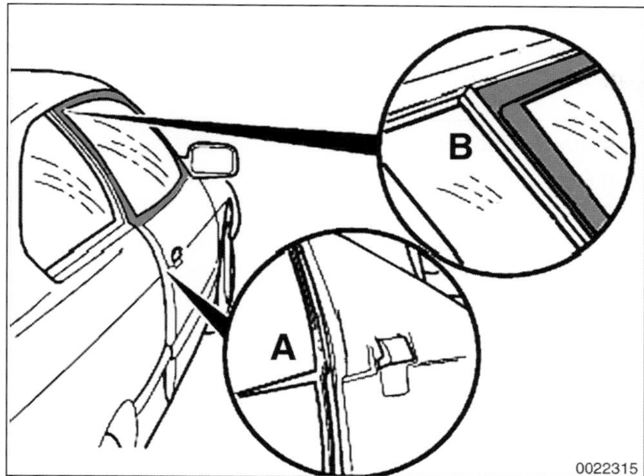

Pretension

Window pretension can also be thought of as the inward rake of the window.

– Remove outer door trim strip as described earlier.

◄ Latch door to first catch of door lock (**A**). Check that top of window rests on rubber door seal (**B**).

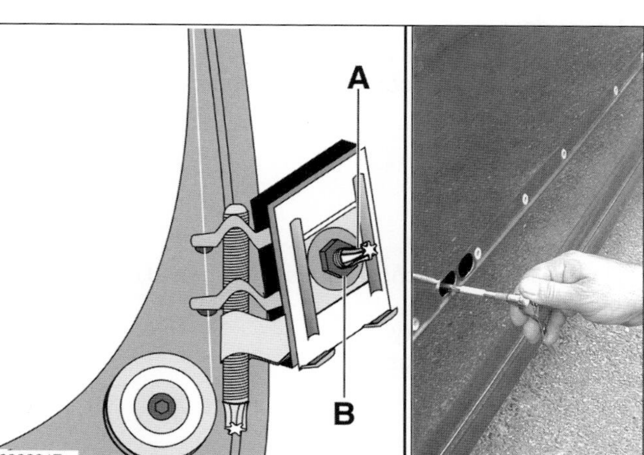

◄ Reach through rear bore in door with BMW special tool 41 6 120 or equivalent.

- Loosen window adjustment Torx screw (**A**) 180° counter-clockwise.
- Turn slider adjustment nut (**B**) until it is hard to move.
- Continue loosening window adjustment Torx screw and tightening slider adjustment nut (see previous step) until correct window rake is reached.
- Tighten window adjustment screw.

Tightening torque
- Window to guide . . . . 8 Nm (71 in-lb)

Vertical adjustments

Adjusting the depth that the window retracts into the door seal insures that wind noise and water leakage past window is kept to a minimum.

◄ **Parallelism**. Top edge of door window must be parallel to contour of water drain in roof.

NOTE —
Window parallelism is also referred to as window tilt.

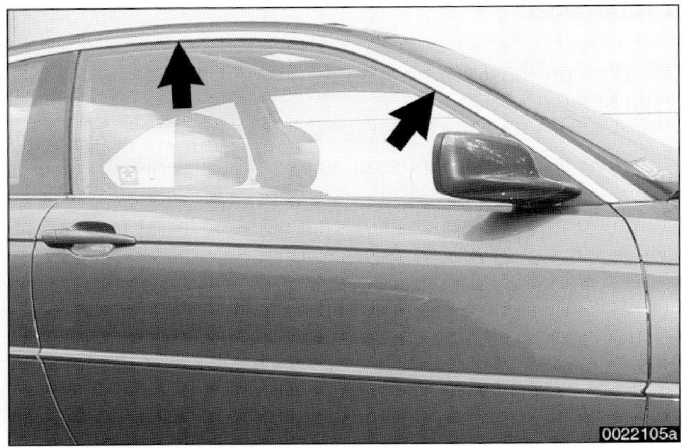

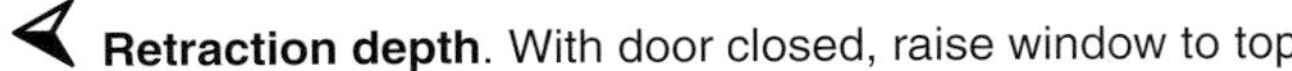

Retraction depth. With door closed, raise window to top.

- Use BMW special tool 51 3 080 or equivalent device to measure depth of window in rubber seal.

Window retraction

- At A-pillar or roof line (**arrows**) . .3 - 4 mm (0.12 - 0.16 in)

– **Window protrusion**. When all the way down, measure door window glass protrusion above top edge of door.

Window protrusion

- Door window above top of door . . . . max. 2 mm (0.08 in)

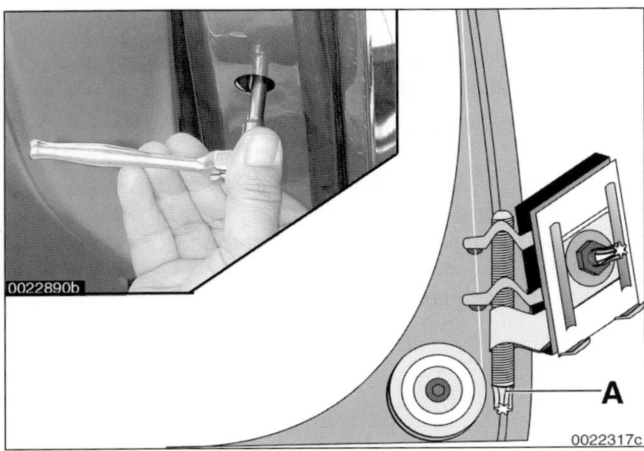

To adjust:

- Lower door glass.
- Pry out rubber plugs at base of door.
- Starting at rear of door, reach through bore in door to turn Torx screw (**A**).

NOTE —
Torx screw size is T20.

- Repeat at front bore.
- Raise window and check for parallelism and correct depth of retraction.
- Repeat as necessary.
- Reinsert rubber plugs.

Front window, removing and installing (2-door)

– Remove interior door panel. See **411 Doors**.

– Disconnect negative (–) cable from battery. Then remove airbag unit and vapor barrier from door. See **721 Airbag System (SRS)**.

> ***CAUTION —***
> *Prior to disconnecting the battery, read the battery disconnection cautions given at the front of this manual on page viii.*

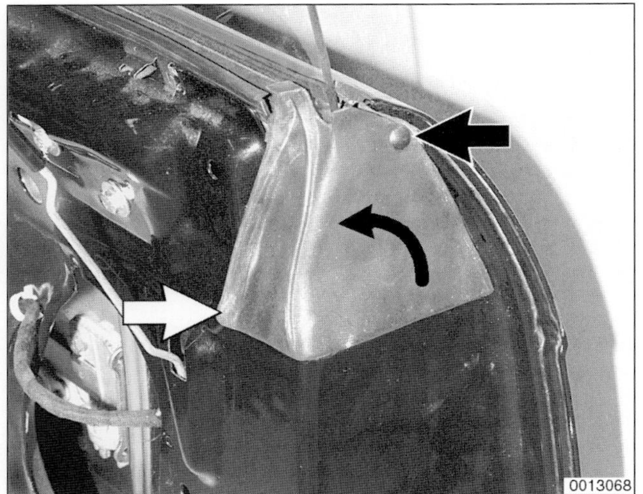

Detach door corner rubber seal mounting clips (**arrows**). Remove seal by pulling up in direction of **curved arrow**.

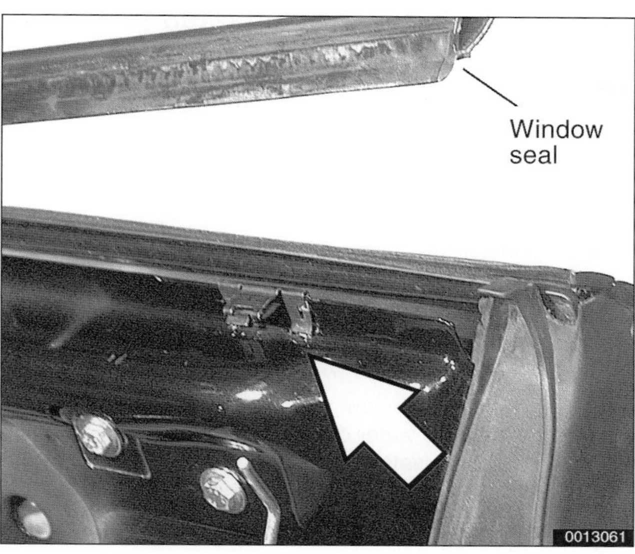

Lift off window inner lip seal.

- If necessary, replace any defective retaining clip (**arrow**).

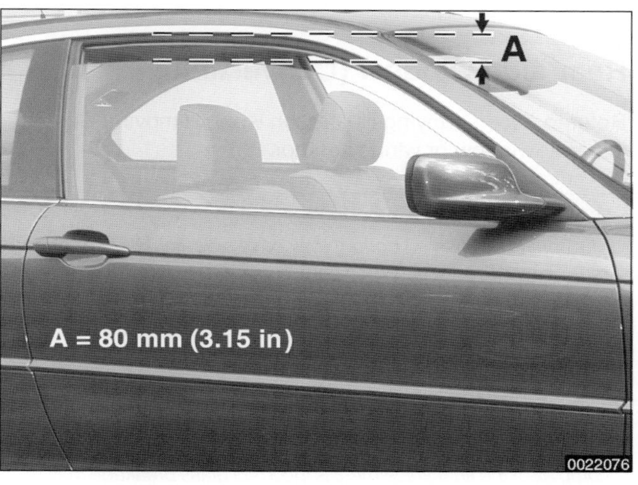

Reconnect battery. Raise door window to approximately 80 mm (3.15 in) below roof line.

> ***WARNING —***
> *Once the window is in place, disconnect harness connector from power window motor to prevent accidental operation of the window.*

– Remove window mounting screws from window regulator rails.

NOTE —

- *Window mounting screws have left-hand thread.*
- *Window rear mounting hardware will stay with glass.*

– Tilt rear edge of window glass up and out of door.

– If glass is being replaced, transfer window rear mounting hardware (mounting shim, threaded sleeve and clamping retainer) from lower rear corner of glass to new window.

– Installation is reverse of removal.

- Install window rear mounting screw with adjusting sleeve through guide rail and threaded sleeve in glass.

NOTE —

- *Window mounting screws have left-hand thread.*

- Use new mounting bolts when reinstalling side-impact air-bag to door.
- Adjust window as described earlier.

Tightening torque

- Side-impact airbag to door . . . . .8.5 Nm (75 in-lb)
- Window to guide . . . . 8 Nm (71 in-lb)

Coupe rear vent window assembly

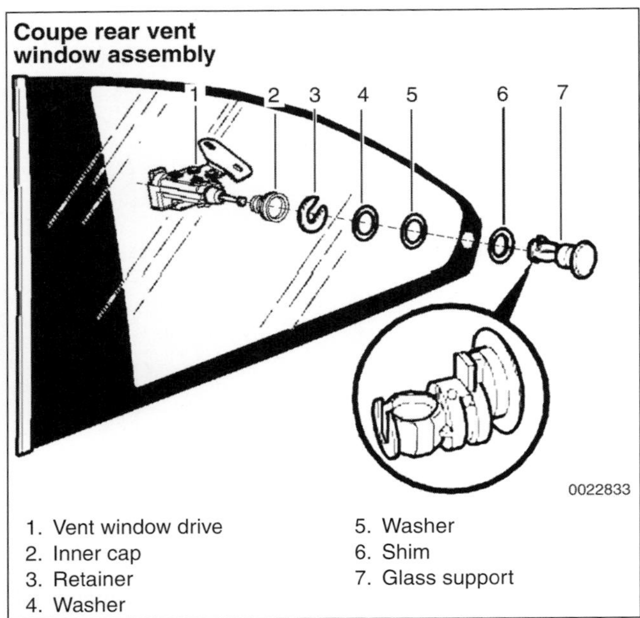

1. Vent window drive
2. Inner cap
3. Retainer
4. Washer
5. Washer
6. Shim
7. Glass support

Rear vent window or vent latch (Coupe)

Refer to accompanying illustration when removing Coupe rear vent window or vent latch mechanism.

- When installing, make sure U-shaped opening in glass support points to rear of car.
- To access rear vent hinges, remove B pillar (door pillar) trim.
- When reinstalling make sure window seals completely. Note gap clearances below.

Vent window clearances

- Front trim strip to rear edge of front window . . . . up to 6 mm (0.24 in)
- Rear of window to water drain . . . up to 1.8 mm (0.07 in)
- Top of window to water drain . . . . 1 mm (0.04 in)

Tightening torques

- Vent window to body (M6 nut). . . . . .6.2 Nm (55 in-lb)

Convertible rear side window mechanism

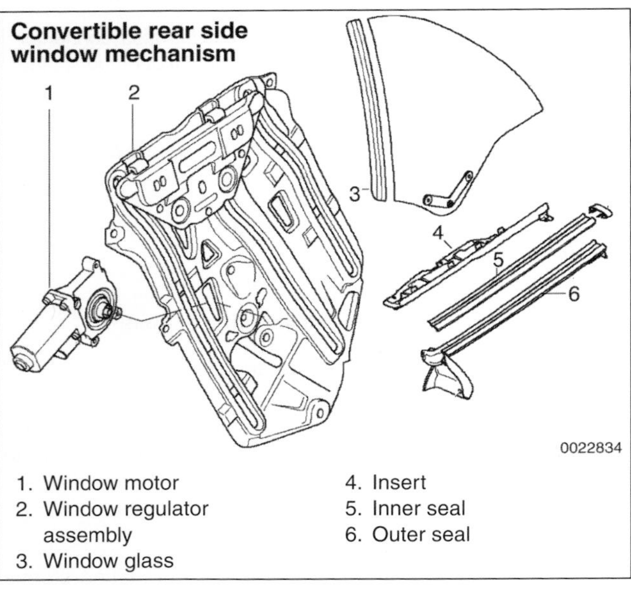

1. Window motor
2. Window regulator assembly
3. Window glass
4. Insert
5. Inner seal
6. Outer seal

Rear side window (Convertible)

Refer to accompanying illustration when removing Convertible rear window or window motor.

> ***WARNING —***
> *M3 Convertible, as an option, may have side-impact airbags for rear seat passengers. When servicing the rear side window on a vehicle with rear side-impact airbags, see* **721 Airbag System (SRS)** *for warnings and cautions and procedures relating to the airbag system.*

> ***CAUTION —***
> *Convertible rear window removal, installation and adjustment is complex. If the final adjustment is incorrect glass breakage may result. This job is best left to be done by a trained technician at a qualified BMW repair facility.*

Rear side window, adjusting (Convertible)

The Convertible rear side window shares the window drop-down feature with the front window: It retracts slightly when the top is raised or lowered, then rises to seal against the folding top once the top is locked in place.

The procedure for setting Convertible rear side window adjustment, while similar in principle to front window adjustment, also depends on correct adjustment of the folding top and of the front window glass.

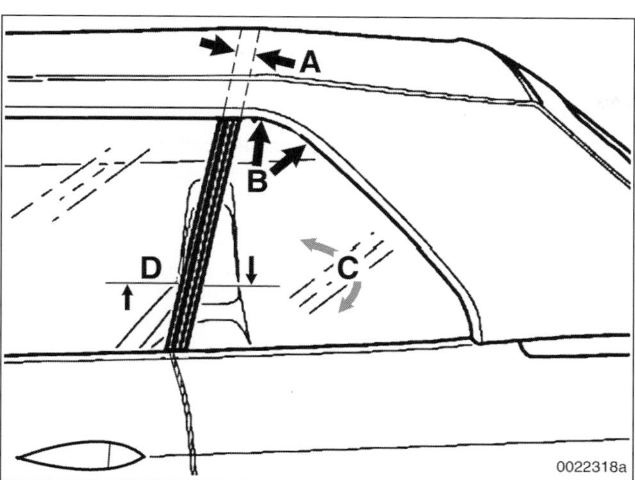

Refer to the accompanying illustration when adjusting Convertible side window.

- **A** Distance to front door window (longitudinal adjustment): Set by loosening Torx bolt through bore in outer shell of car, after removing exterior side trim strip.
- **B** Retraction depth (submersion) into top rubber seal: Remove rear interior side trim panel to access adjustment screws.
- **C** Window centering: Remove rear interior side trim panel to access adjustment screws.
- **D** Side window depth in relation to door window: Remove rear interior side trim panel to access adjustment screws.

Convertible rear side window adjustments

- **A** . . . . .23 - 25 mm (0.9 - 1.0 in)
- **B** Window must jam into convertible top seal when top is closed. With top open, glass must rest firmly against front window seal.
- **C** With convertible top open, window must be centered in channel.
- **D**. . . . . up to 1 mm (0.04 in) toward inside of car

WINDOW REGULATOR SERVICE

Window regulator motor

NOTE —

Because window operation is electronically controlled, the window motor does not have mechanical end positions. For this reason it can be removed and installed with the window in any position and does not need initialization.

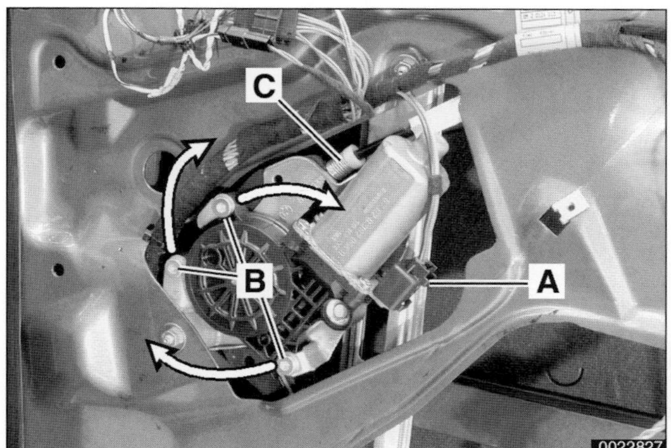

To remove motor:

- Remove inner door panel and vapor barrier.
- Detach window motor electrical harness connector (**A**).
- Remove motor mounting bolts (**B**).
- Twist motor slightly (**arrows**) to clear window regulator mounting tabs.

– When reinstalling:

- Make sure window has not travelled fully downward.
- Manipulate spring-loaded window control cable (**C**) to engage motor teeth to regulator gears.

Window regulator and motor, removing and installing (4-door)

Sedan and Sport Wagon doors are similar. There are two window rails in each front window regulator, only one in the rear. Otherwise the front and rear regulators are similar.

Remove the window regulator and motor as one unit, then separate the two on the workbench.

– Remove door panel. See **411 Doors**.

— Disconnect battery negative cable and remove side impact air bag, if applicable. See **721 Airbag System (SRS)**.

> ***CAUTION —***
> *Prior to disconnecting the battery, read the battery disconnection cautions given at the front of this manual on page viii.*

— Remove vapor barrier.

— Detach window from window regulator as described earlier. Do not remove window from door. Push window up and use wedge to hold in position.

◄ Detach window regulator from door:

- Disconnect electrical harness connector (**A**) to power window motor.
- Remove regulator mounting nuts (**arrows**).

— Remove window regulator through lower door cavity opening, checking for wiring harnesses that might become snagged during removal.

— Installation is reverse of removal.

- Be sure to route wiring harnesses to keep them away from moving window mechanism. Use new wire ties as necessary.
- Adjust front window. See **Front window, adjusting (4-door)**.

Tightening torques

- Window motor to regulator . . . . 5 Nm (4 ft-lb)
- Window regulator to door . . . . 9 Nm (7 ft-lb)
- Window to guide . . . . 8 Nm (71 in-lb)

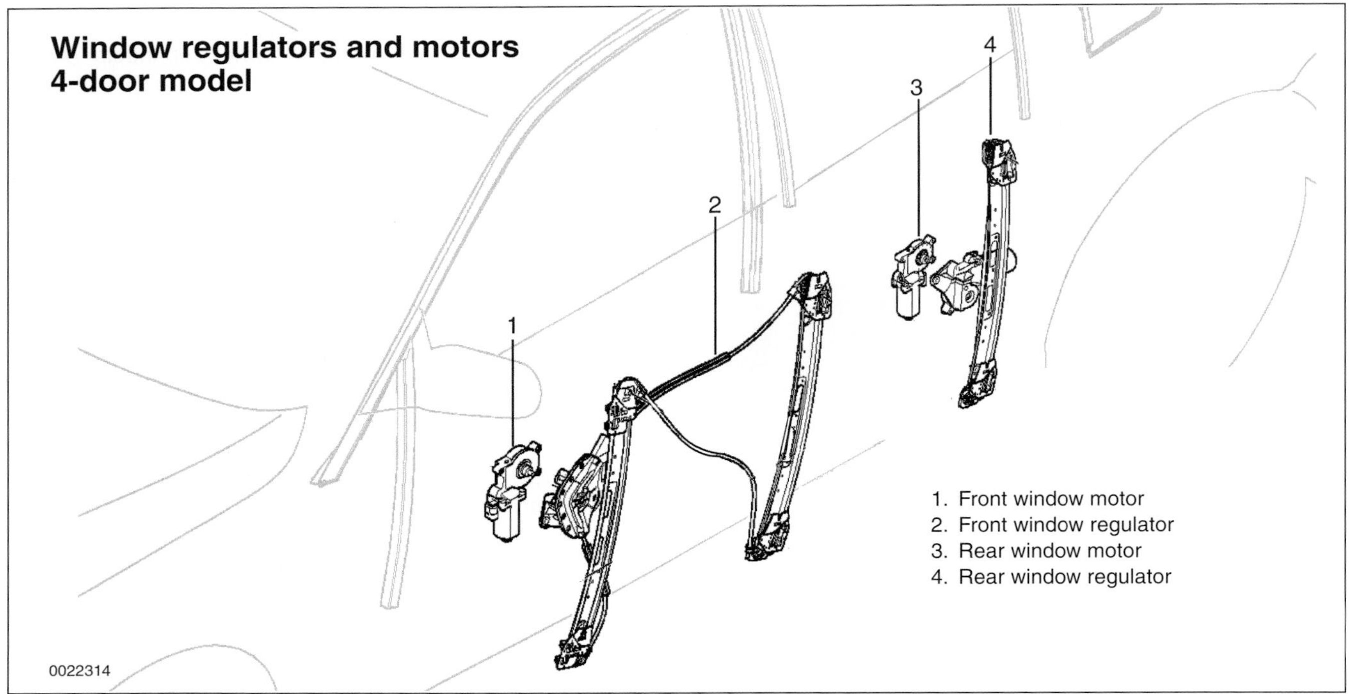

Window motor standardization (Convertibles)

M3 Convertibles manufactured from 03 / 2003 and Convertibles from 09 / 2003 feature anti-pinch protection for the front windows. Pinch protection function is integrated in the individual power window motors. Following repair work on power windows, window motors need to be standardized to activate pinch protection.

– With convertible top in closed position, or hardtop in place, open front windows fully.

– Disconnect and reconnect fuse 57 at the fuse panel. See **610 Electrical Component Locations**.

– Close window by pulling up and holding window switch to second detent.

– When fully closed, keep switch in second detent position for at least 3 seconds.

– Repeat for opposite window.

Window regulator and motor, removing and installing, (2-door)

– Remove door panel. See **411 Doors**.

– Disconnect negative (–) cable from battery. Then remove airbag unit and vapor barrier from door. See **721 Airbag System (SRS)**.

> ***CAUTION —***
> *Prior to disconnecting the battery, read the battery disconnection cautions given at the front of this manual on page viii.*

– Remove door glass. See **Front window, removing and installing (2-door)** in this repair group.

– With battery reconnected, lower window regulator completely.

> ***WARNING —***
> *Once the window regulator is positioned correctly, disconnect harness connector from power window motor to prevent accidental operation of the mechanism.*

2-door front window regulator

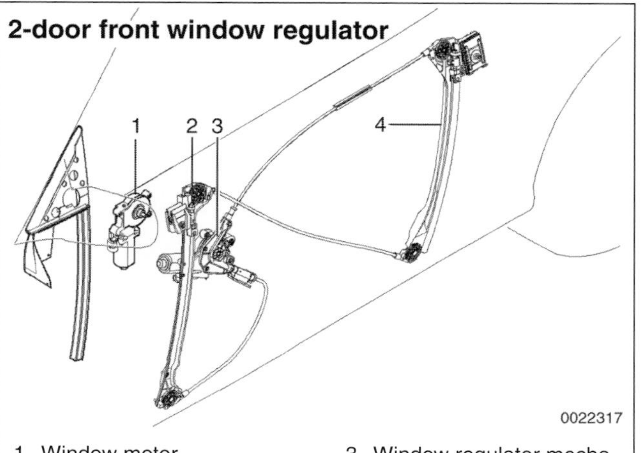

1. Window motor
2. Front window rail
3. Window regulator mechanism
4. Rear window rail

< Detach window regulator from door:

- Disconnect electrical harness connector to power window motor.
- Remove regulator mounting nuts.

– Remove window regulator through lower door cavity opening, checking for wiring harnesses that might become snagged during regulator removal.

– Installation is reverse of removal, noting the following:
  - Inspect rubber insulators. Replace if brittle.
  - After inserting window regulator into door cavity, install and tighten down mounting nuts on rear window rail.
  - Install front window rail mounting nuts but do not tighten.
  - Install glass. See **Front window, removing and installing (2-door)**.
  - Tighten upper nut of front rail.
  - Lower window glass fully.
  - Tighten front rail lower nuts.
  - Adjust window. See **Front window, adjusting (2-door)**.

Tightening torques
- Window motor to regulator . . . . 5 Nm (4 ft-lb)
- Window regulator to door . . . . 9 Nm (7 ft-lb)
- Window to guide . . . . 8 Nm (71 in-lb)

513 Interior Trim

GENERAL

This repair group covers interior trim removal and installation procedures.

Refer to the following repair groups for additional information:

- **250 Gearshift Linkage** for shifter bezel
- **411 Doors** for interior door panels
- **612 Switches**
- **620 Instruments**
- **640 Heating and Air-conditioning** for IHKA control panel
- **650 Radio**
- **721 Airbag System (SRS)**

Special tools

Use plastic prying tools or wrap screwdriver tip with tape to avoid marring interior trim.

Special tools

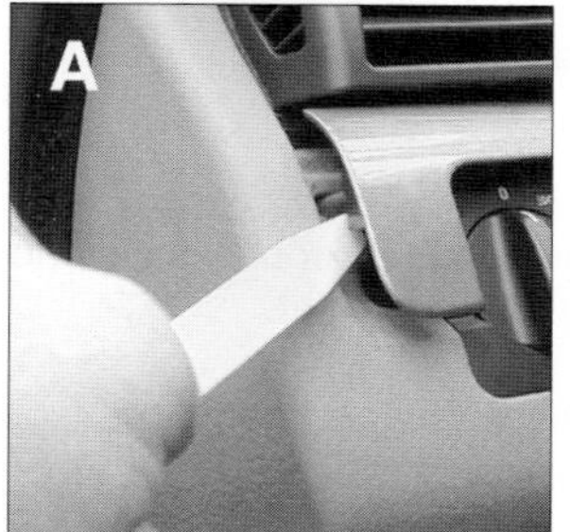

A BMW 00 9 321 . . . . Plastic prying tool

Interior trim repairs

Interior trim and finish panels are clipped or screwed into place. Many of the trim retaining clips are designed to be used only once. When removing trim that is held in place with clips, it is a good idea to have spares on hand before beginning the job.

NOTE —
The BMW E46 is equipped with SRS airbags mounted in the steering wheel, the passenger side dashboard, the front doors, the A-pillars and, as an option in 4-door models, in the rear doors. See **Warnings and cautions** *in this repair group and in* **721 Airbag System (SRS)**.

Warnings and cautions

WARNING —

- *Observe special precautions when servicing the BMW Supplemental Restraint System (SRS). See* **721 Airbag System (SRS)**.
- *Serious injury may result if service is attempted by persons unfamiliar with the BMW SRS and its approved procedures. BMW specifies that all inspection and service should be performed by an authorized BMW dealer.*
- *Before performing any work involving airbags, disconnect the negative (–) battery cable.*
- *Airbags contain a back-up power supply within the SRS control module. Allow a 10 second discharge period after disconnecting the battery cable.*

CAUTION —

- *When working on electrical switches or lights, always disconnect the negative (–) cable from the battery and insulate the cable end to prevent accidental reconnection.*
- *Prior to disconnecting the battery, read the battery disconnection cautions given at the front of this manual on page viii.*
- *To avoid marring the trim when working on interior components, work with plastic prying tools or wrap the tips of screwdrivers and pliers with tape before prying out switches or electrical accessories.*

CENTER CONSOLE

The console between the two front seats starts behind the shifter housing. It houses the parking brake handle, optional telephone and oddments storage tray. The rear portion of the console houses the ashtray and covers the emergency brake cable ends.

Center console, removing and installing

◄ Press rolling cover of rear ashtray down. Depress cover fully to pop ashtray out of console. Remove ashtray.

– Remove retaining screws and bracket.

– Remove ashtray cover and housing. Disconnect electrical harness connector for ashtray courtesy light.

– Remove screws at base of ashtray compartment in console.

0022347

< Unclip parking brake lever trim boot. Pull boot and handle forward off brake lever.

- Gently pry up gearshift lever boot and bezel. Automatic transmission vehicle: Unplug connector for gear indicator light from bezel while removing.

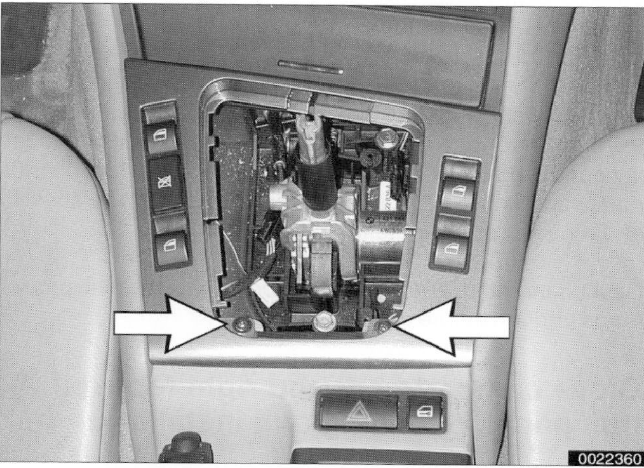
0022360

< Remove center console retaining screws (**arrows**) in gear-shift lever housing opening.

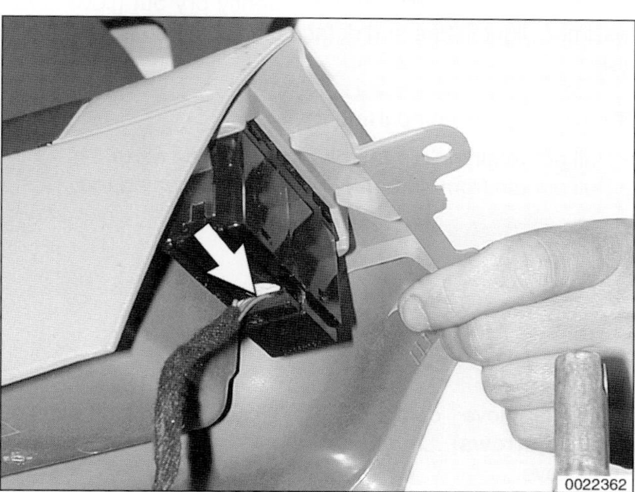
0022362

< Slide center console back and lift up front of console. Disconnect electrical harness connector (**arrow**) from hazard light and central locking switch.

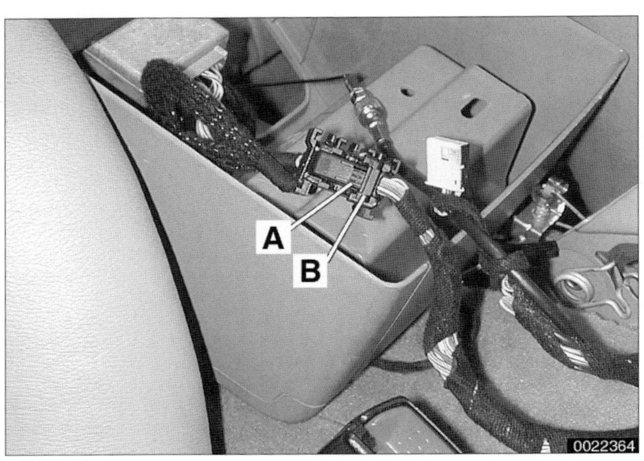

If applicable disconnect wiring for factory installed cellular telephone. To release phone connector, press catch (**A**) and slide lock (**B**) forward. Disconnect antenna connection.

- Vehicle with center armrest: Tilt armrest upright. Lift parking brake lever upwards. Slide center console out between armrest and brake lever.

- Installation is reverse of removal. Make sure to securely fasten all electrical harness connectors during reassembly.

DASHBOARD

The E46 dashboard assembly includes the instrument cluster, passenger side airbag, glove compartment, fuse and relay panel, radio, IHKA control panel or on-board monitor (if equipped with GPS), front ashtray, shifter assembly covers, and window control switches.

Dashboard removal is a complex operation. Read the procedures through before starting work.

Glove compartment and right footwell trim panel, removing and installing

- Open glove compartment door. Gently pry out glove compartment light fixture and detach electrical harness connector.

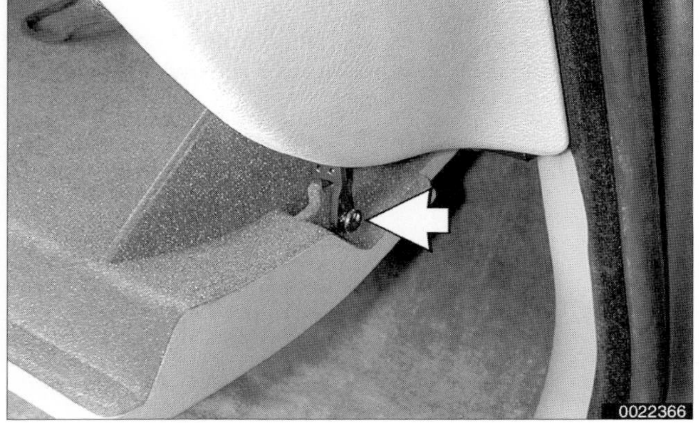

To detach glove compartment:

- Pull out retaining pin (**arrow**) for right side strap.
- Pull out pin from bottom of left side dampening rod.

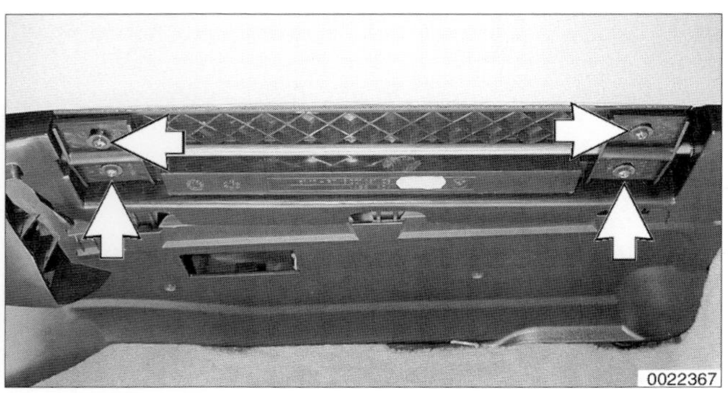

Remove glove compartment hinge mounting bracket screws (**arrows**). Lift glove compartment over support rod to remove.

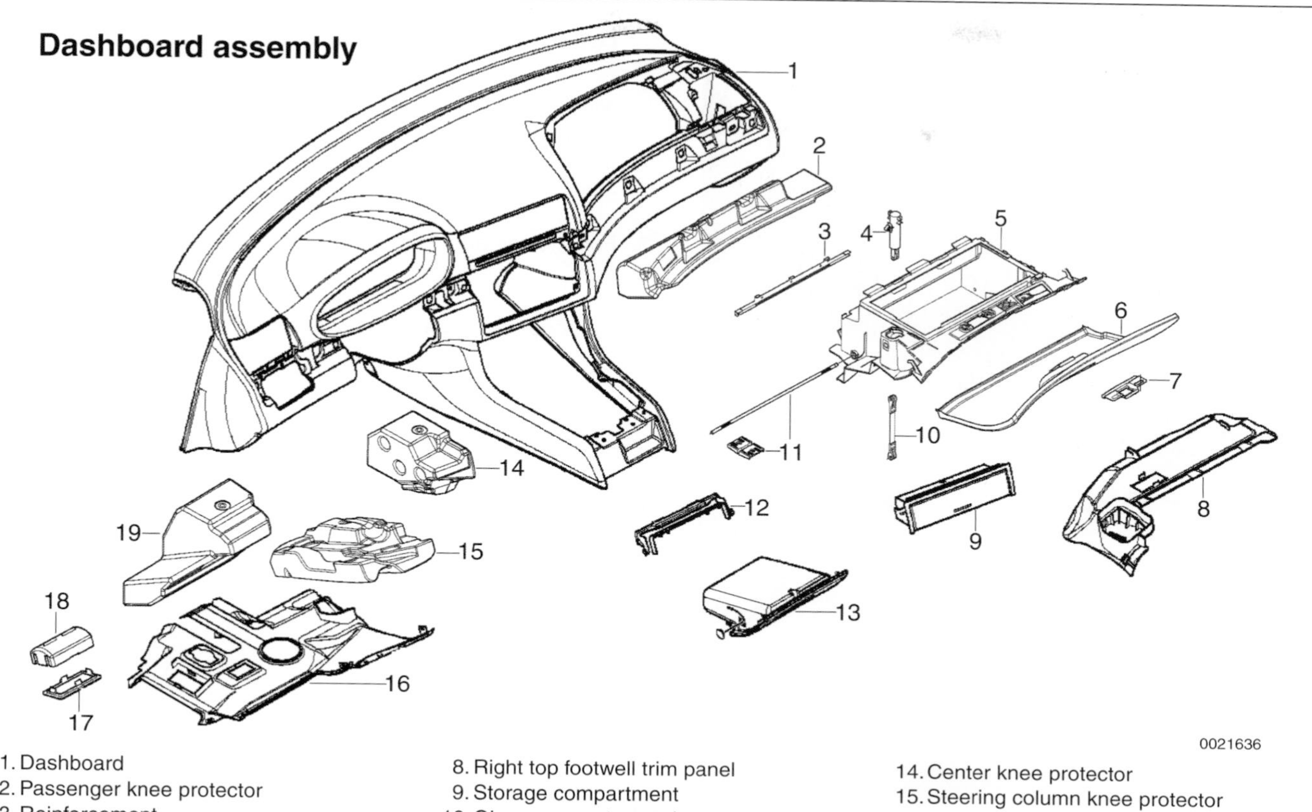

1. Dashboard
2. Passenger knee protector
3. Reinforcement
4. Damper piston
5. Glove compartment
6. Glove compartment door
7. Latch
8. Right top footwell trim panel
9. Storage compartment
10. Glove compartment door strap
11. Glove compartment hinge and support rod
12. Steering column cover
13. Left glove compartment (optional)
14. Center knee protector
15. Steering column knee protector
16. Left footwell (pedal cluster) trim panel
17. Footwell light cover
18. Footwell light socket
19. Left knee protector

Remove glove compartment housing:

- Remove glove compartment housing mounting screws (**arrows**).
- If necessary, release mounting pin (**A**) at right side of housing.
- Pull housing down.

NOTE —

Detach electrical harness from cable guides while removing housing.

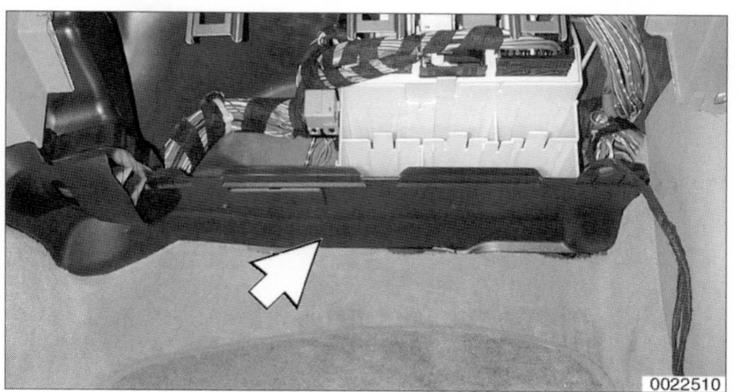

Remove right footwell trim panel (**arrow**) by pulling backward to detach from mounting points.

NOTE —

Detach electrical harness connector(s) from panel while removing.

Steering column trim, removing and installing

NOTE —

In the illustrations for this procedure, the steering wheel is shown removed for photographic purposes. Steering column trim can be removed with the steering wheel installed.

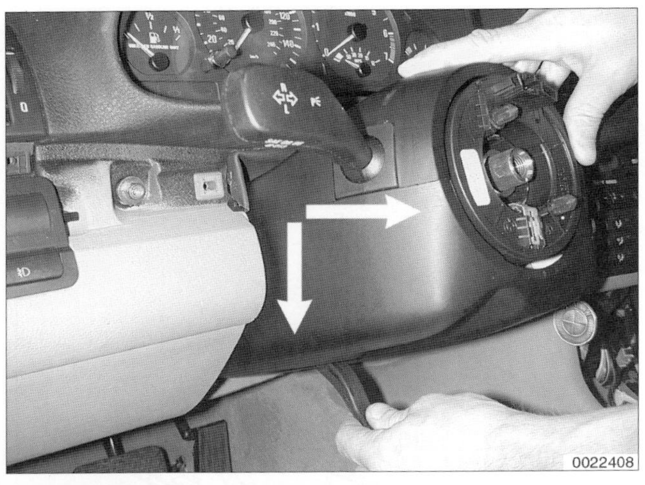

- Fully lower and extend (**arrows**) adjustable steering column.

- Remove upper steering column trim cover retaining screw.

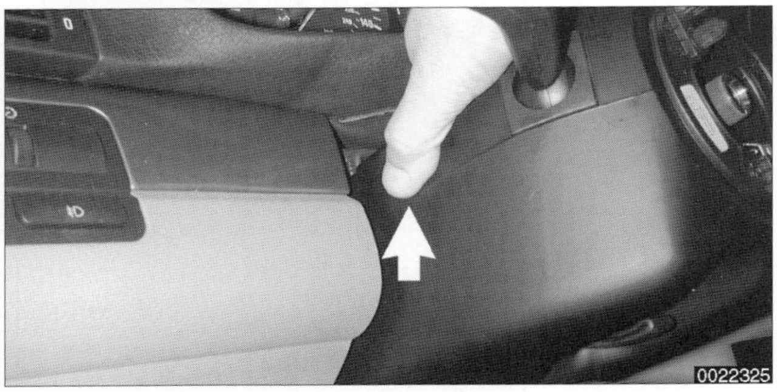

- Push in sides of upper trim cover (**arrow**) to release from lower trim. Pull back and up on upper trim.

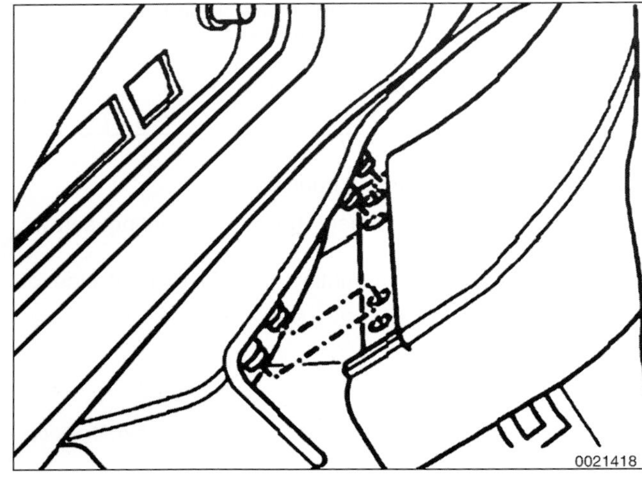

- Pry gently to detach flexible cover from upper trim. Lift off trim.

- Remove left footwell (pedal cluster) trim panel. See **Left footwell (pedal cluster) trim panel, removing and installing** in this repair group.

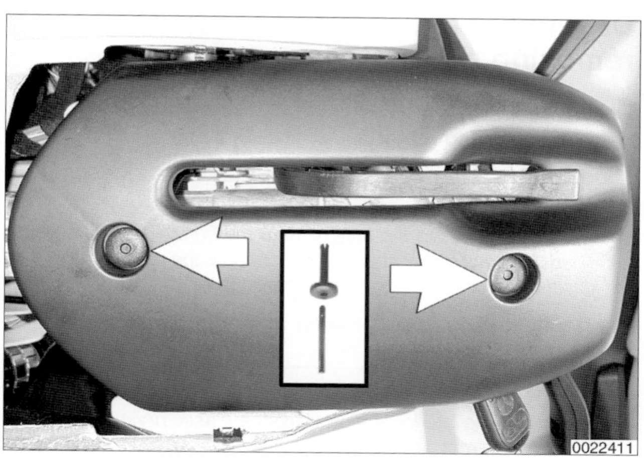

To remove steering column lower trim, drive pins into expansion rivets (**arrows**) to release. Pull down on trim.

- Installation is reverse of removal. Replace any broken or missing fasteners.

Left footwell (pedal cluster) trim panel, removing and installing

- Move steering column to maximum extended position.

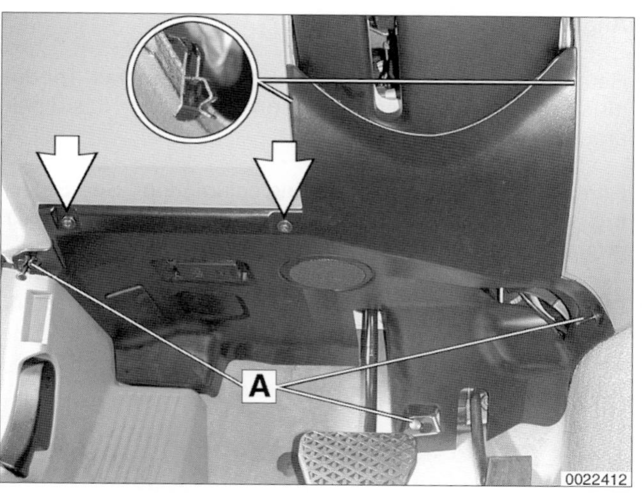

Working at trim panel, remove screws (**arrows**) and expansion rivets (**A**).

- Rotate clips (**inset**) 90° to remove.

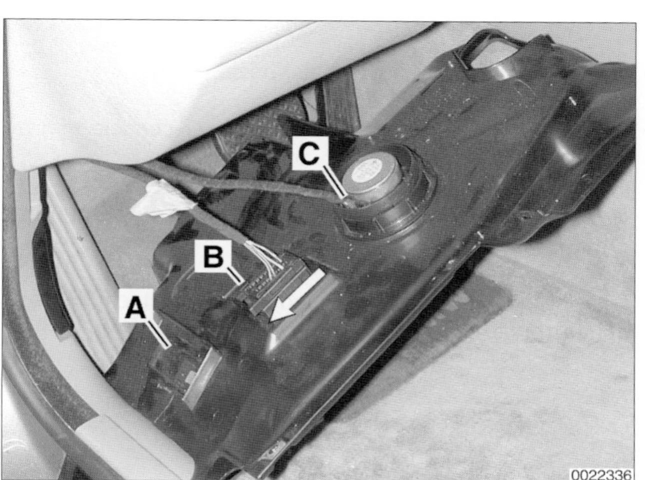

Disconnect electrical harness connectors at left footwell trim panel and remove panel:

- Unplug connector at footwell interior light (**A**), if equipped.
- Slide lock at OBD II connector (**B**) in direction of **arrow**.
- Unplug connector at chime (**C**).

Dashboard and shifter console assembly, removing and installing

– Disconnect negative (–) cable from battery and cover terminal with insulating material.

> **CAUTION —**
> *Prior to disconnecting the battery, read the battery disconnection cautions given at the front of this manual on page viii.*

 Pry gently to remove left, center and right dashboard trim.

> **CAUTION —**
> *To avoid marring interior trim, work with a plastic prying tool.*

NOTE —
- *Left side shown. Center and right trim are similar.*
- *To remove center trim, remove right trim first.*

– Remove steering wheel. See **320 Steering and Wheel and Alignment**.

– Remove left footwell trim panel. See **Left footwell (pedal cluster) trim panel, removing and installing** in this repair group.

– Remove upper and lower steering column trim. See **Steering column trim, removing and installing** in this repair group.

– Detach steering column stalk switch electrical connectors and remove stalk switch. See **612 Switches**.

 Remove shifter knob by pulling straight up.

NOTE —
Apply approx. 90 lb. of force to pull off knob. Do not twist while pulling.

– Gently pry up and remove shifter bezel.

– Unclip bottom of shifter boot from center console trim by pushing forward. Pull boot up around shifter.

– Remove center console. See **Center console, removing and installing** in this repair group.

– Lift off window switch carrier and detach electrical harness connectors to switches.

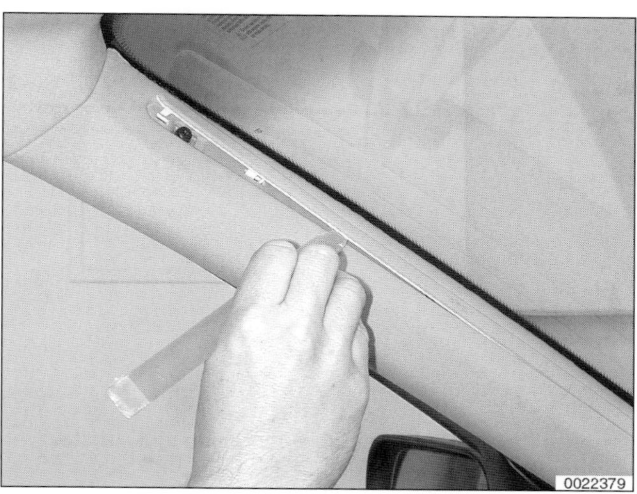

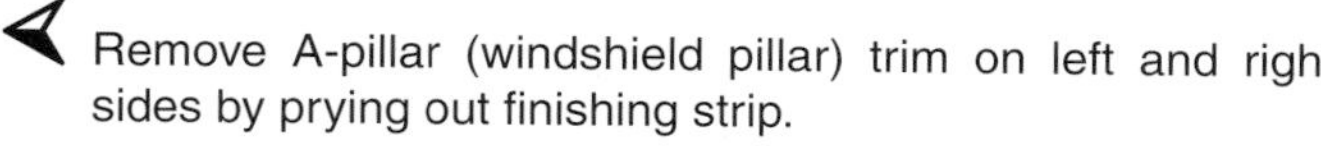

Remove A-pillar (windshield pillar) trim on left and right sides by prying out finishing strip.

> ***CAUTION —***
> *The Head Protection Airbag is behind the A-pillar trim. Do not use sharp instruments to remove trim or finisher strip*

– Remove screws underneath finishing strip.

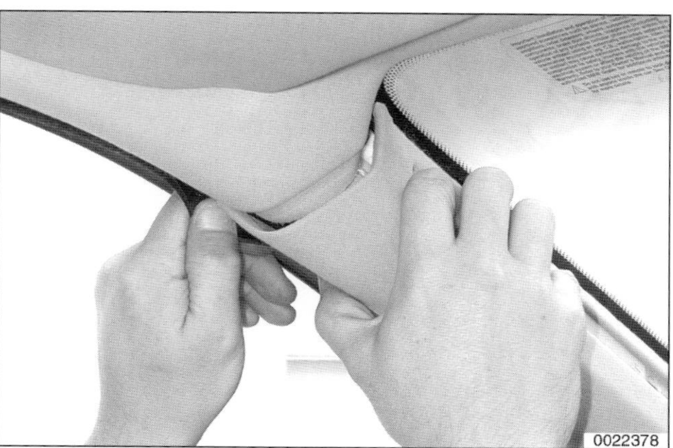

Carefully pull away A-pillar trim.

– Remove headlight switch. See **612 Switches**.

– Remove instrument cluster. See **620 Instruments**.

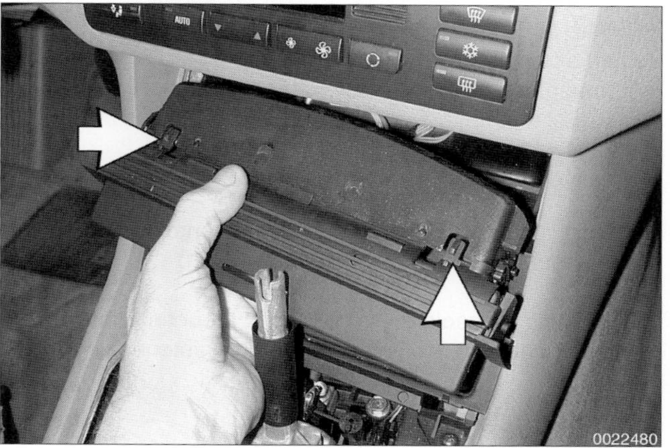

Remove storage compartment below IHKA control panel:

- Open compartment door.
- Push upward on tabs (**arrows**), then pull out.

– Remove IHKA control panel and module. See **640 Heating and Air-conditioning**.

– Reach through IHKA control panel opening and disconnect solar sensor harness connector, if equipped.

– Remove radio. See **650 Radio**.

– Remove glove compartment and right footwell trim. See **Glove compartment and right footwell trim panel, removing and installing** in this repair group.

> ***NOTE —***
> *Detach electrical harness connector(s) from footwell panel while removing.*

– Remove front passenger airbag. See **721 Airbag System (SRS)**.

– Remove dashboard vents. See **640 Heating and Air-conditioning.**

0022392

◀ Remove dashboard mounting screw or expansion rivet (**arrow**) in lower right dashboard.

– Similarly, remove left side dashboard mounting screw or expansion rivet.

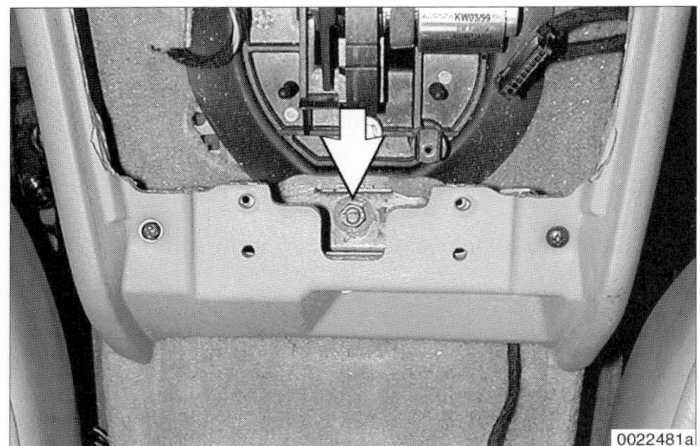
0022481a

◀ Remove dashboard assembly mounting nut (**arrow**) at shifter console.

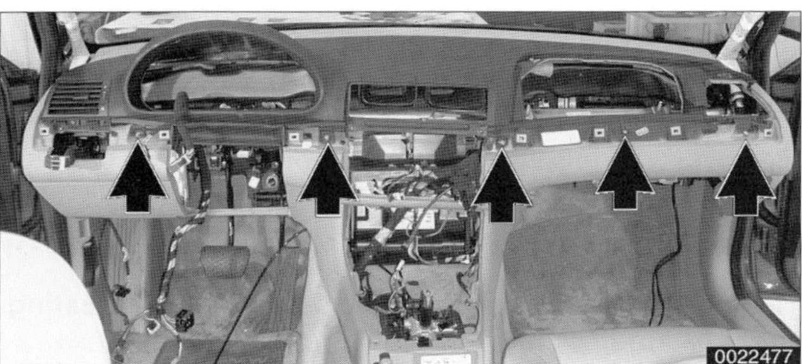
0022477

◀ Remove mounting nuts and screw (**arrows**) at dashboard face.

– To remove dashboard:

- Pull up parking brake fully.
- Push seats fully back.
- Lift dashboard out carefully, checking to make sure that harness connectors, components, hoses and wiring do not get snagged.
- Remove through passenger door.

– When installing, fit dashboard guide pin into locator slot at base of windshield in center.

– Install center console with dashboard mounting nuts loose. Align and center parts before tightening fasteners.

515 Central Locking and Anti-theft

TABLE

515

GENERAL

This section covers repair information for door, trunk lid and tailgate locks and central locking. Also covered are electronic immobilization (EWS) and anti-theft alarm (DWA).

E46 cars are equipped with sophisticated and self-diagnostic electrical systems. When experiencing malfunctions relating to central locking or anti-theft systems, begin diagnosis using a BMW scan tool (DISplus, GT1, MoDiC) or equivalent. An advanced diagnostic scan tool can usually pinpoint electrical faults quickly and safely. Consult an authorized BMW dealer.

Special tools

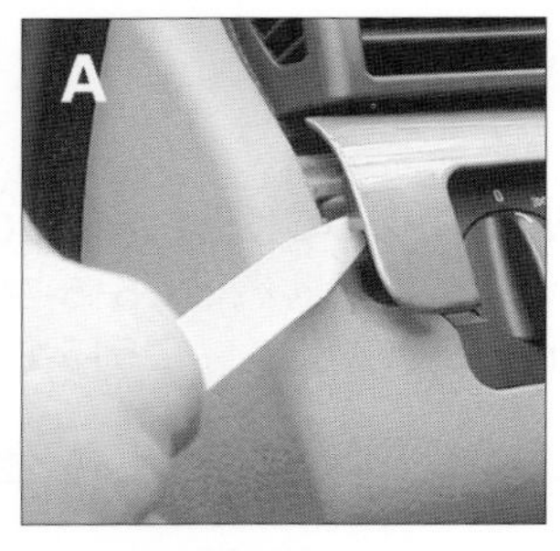

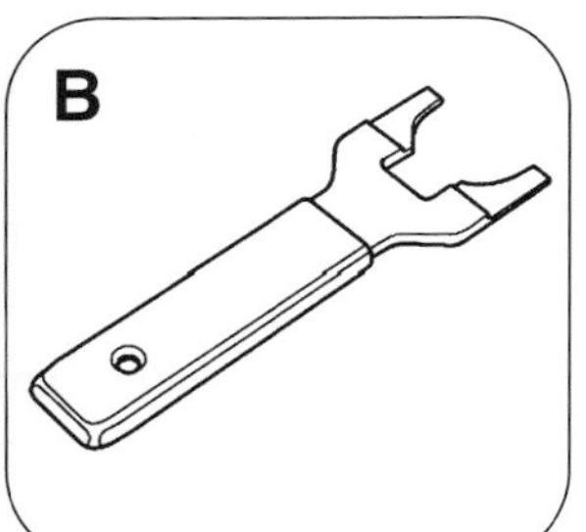

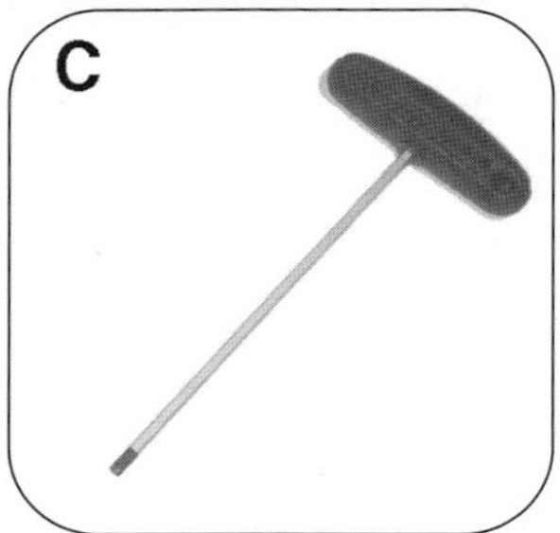

A BMW 00 9 321 . . . . .Plastic prying tool
B BMW 61 3 300 . . . . Ring antenna removal tool
C 4 mm Allen wrench . . . . Front door lock adjustment tool

For additional information see:

- **411 Doors** for door panel removal
- **412 Trunk Lid, Tailgate**
- **600 Electrical System–General**
- **610 Electrical Component Locations**
- **Electrical Wiring Diagrams**.

Special tools

A few special tools may be necessary for repairs in this section.

NOTE —
The BMW E46 is equipped with SRS airbags mounted in the front doors and, as an option in 4-door models, in the rear doors. See **Warnings and cautions** *in this repair group.*

Warnings and cautions

WARNING —

- *Observe special precautions when servicing the BMW Supplemental Restraint System (SRS). See* **721 Airbag System (SRS)**.
- *Serious injury may result if service is attempted by persons unfamiliar with the BMW SRS and its approved procedures. BMW specifies that all inspection and service should be performed by an authorized BMW dealer.*
- *Before performing any work involving airbags, disconnect the negative (–) battery cable.*
- *The airbags system contains a back-up power supply within the SRS control module. Allow a 60 second discharge period after disconnecting the battery cable.*
- *If the airbag warning light on the dashboard illuminates after completion of door lock repairs, the airbags will not deploy in case of an accident. Be sure to have the SRS system diagnosed and repaired immediately.*

CAUTION —

- *When working on electrical components, always disconnect the negative (–) cable from the battery and insulate the cable end to prevent accidental reconnection.*
- *Prior to disconnecting the battery, read the battery disconnection cautions given at the front of this manual on page viii.*
- *To avoid marring the trim when working on interior components, work with plastic prying tools or wrap the tips of screwdrivers and pliers with tape before prying out switches or electrical accessories.*

CENTRAL LOCKING

NOTE —
There is a door lock key cylinder on the driver's door only.

Central locking in E46 vehicles controls the door locks, trunk or tailgate lock and fuel filler flap lock. The Central Body Electronics (ZKE V) control module, known as the General Module (GM V), controls central locking.

Door lock actuators are sealed, self contained units with no replaceable parts. The actuators use Hall effect sensors in place of pin contacts and microswitches to provide door OPEN / CLOSED status signal. Each door lock-button only affects the actuator it controls. There is no effect on the central lock control of other doors.

Door lock actuators can be set to automatically lock when a road speed signal of 2.5 mph is detected by GM V via K-bus. The factory default coding for this feature is OFF, but can be coded ON for individual users with the Key Memory function. See **Car Memory / Key Memory** in this repair group.

The driver door lock cylinder is the only location outside of the vehicle where a key mechanically controls all of the central locking system functions. The outside locks (driver door and trunk) incorporate an overrunning lock cylinder that breaks away and freewheels if an attempt is made to destroy either with a screwdriver or dent puller.

Each rear doors is equipped with a child lock-out lever which prevent the door from being opened from the inside regardless of lock-button position.

The GM V and electronic immobilization (EWS 3.3) interface via the K-bus to monitor double lock status and to initiate double lock override. This feature allows the doors to be opened from the inside if a key accepted by EWS is switched on in the ignition when the doors are double locked. For information about double lock, see **Single lock and double lock function** in this repair group.

Continuous locking / unlocking initiates a timed arrest of the locking system. The GM V counts each time the locks are actuated. After approximately 12 cycles, lock operation is arrested to allow the lock actuators to cool down. Timed arrest is deactivated one actuator cycle for every 8 seconds until the counter is reset to 0. Timed arrest is overridden if a crash signal is received from the multiple restraint system (MRS).

0022918

Central locking switch

The central locking switch is housed in a combined housing with the hazard flasher switch. The switch locks all vehicle locks except for the fuel filler flap.

The switch provides a momentary ground input signal to the GM V. This input single locks each door and the trunk. The fuel filler flap remains unlocked for refueling purposes. If a

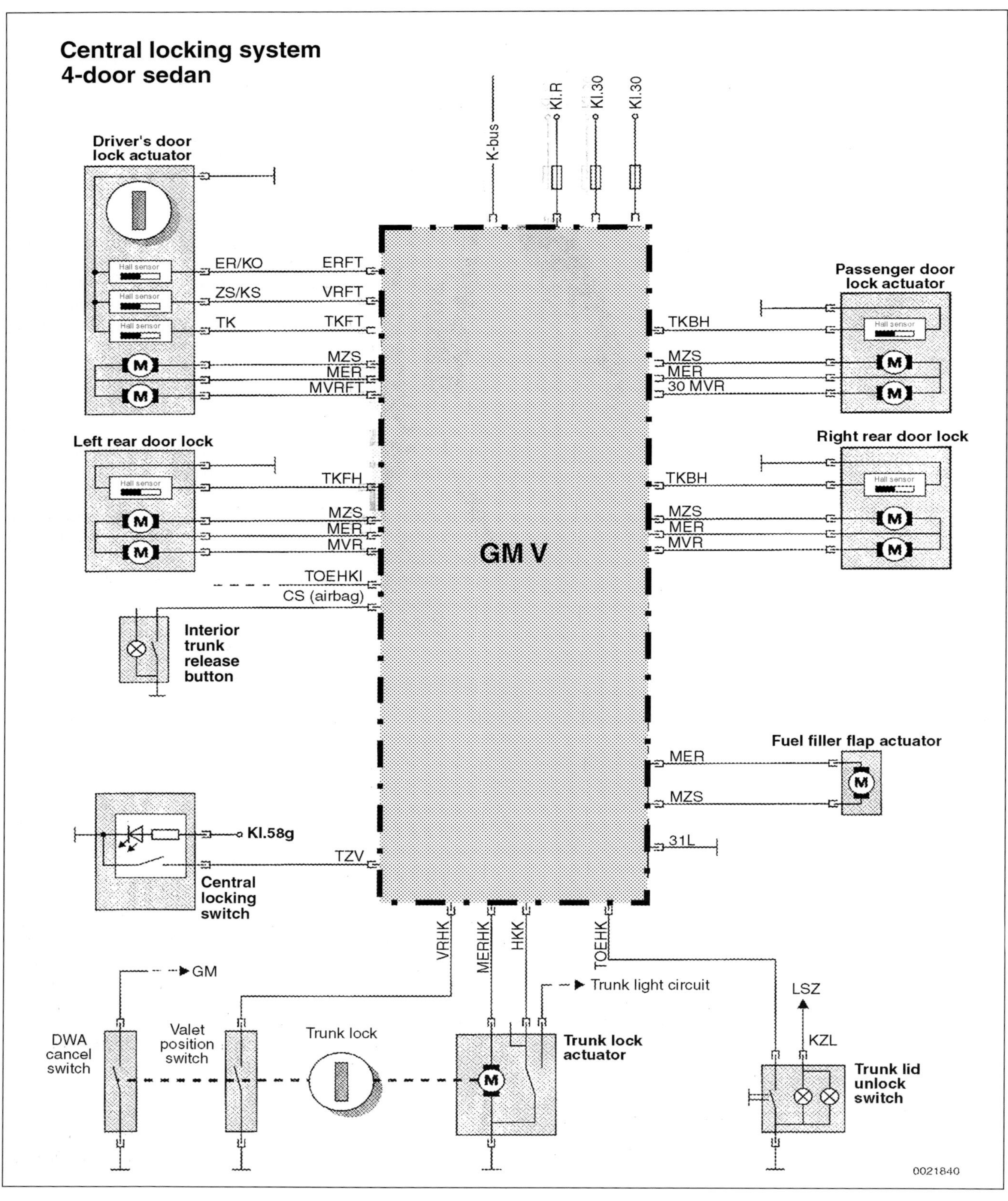

Central locking system
4-door sedan
K-bus
Kl.R
Kl.30
Kl.30
Driver's door lock actuator
Hall sensor
Hall sensor
Hall sensor
ER/KO
ERFT
ZS/KS
VRFT
TK
TKFT
MZS
MER
MVRFT
Passenger door lock actuator
TKBH
MZS
MER
30 MVR
Left rear door lock
TKFH
MZS
MER
MVR
Right rear door lock
TKBH
MZS
MER
MVR
GM V
TOEHKI
CS (airbag)
Interior trunk release button
Fuel filler flap actuator
MER
MZS
31L
Kl.58g
TZV
Central locking switch
VRHK
MERHK
HKK
TOEHK
GM
Trunk light circuit
LSZ
KZL
DWA cancel switch
Valet position switch
Trunk lock
Trunk lock actuator
Trunk lid unlock switch
0021840

door is manually unlocked and opened while centrally locked, the remaining doors stay locked. The opened door can be relocked when closed by manually locking or pushing the central locking switch twice. This resynchronizes all the locks.

Single lock and double lock function

Each door lock actuator incorporates two motors:

Single lock motor controls the mechanical lock mechanism when the central lock switch is pressed to single lock the vehicle. The lock mechanism is fully locked at this point but can still be opened from the interior by pulling the interior door handle twice or by pressing the central lock switch again. When single lock function is activated, the fuel filler flap actuator is not locked.

Double lock motor, also known as central arrest, is activated only when the vehicle is locked from the outside at the driver door lock with a key or when the GM V receives a lock request from the keyless entry (FZV) system. In this case the double lock motor is activated simultaneously with the single lock motor. The double lock motor mechanically offsets an internal rod in the lock actuator, preventing it from unlocking the vehicle from the interior. With double lock activated, the doors cannot be unlocked by any means except by an unlock request at the driver door or via the FZV key.

Trunk lock

The trunk lock can be operated with the key but does not lock or unlock the entire vehicle. When unlocked, the trunk can be opened by pressing the trunk release switch pad located above the license plate or from the remote trunk button in the left kick panel.

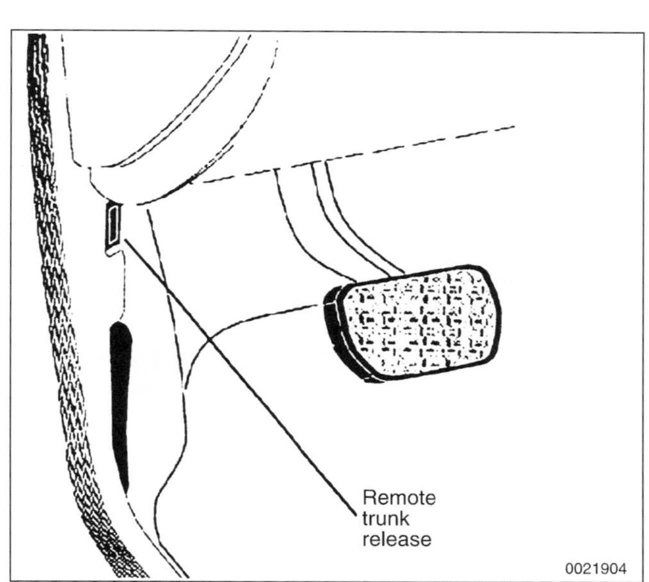

The trunk can also be opened from inside the vehicle by pressing the remote trunk lid release button in driver footwell area. The button provides the GM V with a ground signal when pressed.

The vehicle must be unlocked or single locked from the central lock switch for the remote unlock to work. The remote trunk release is locked out when the trunk is locked in the valet setting or when the GM V detects a vehicle speed over 4 mph via the K-bus.

Pressing the trunk release button on an FZV key opens the trunk.

The trunk lid OPEN / CLOSED and trunk lock key position signals come from the trunk lid switch contact in the trunk lock motor. When closed, the trunk contact provides a ground signal to the GM V signifying a CLOSED trunk. This contact also serves as the trunk light switch when the trunk is OPEN.

The lock actuator motor only operates in one direction to release the latch mechanism. The latch mechanism can also be manually unlocked with the key.

Located on the trunk lock are two additional microswitches for key position status signalling to the GM V.

- **Valet position switch:** With the key lock in the valet position, this switch provides a ground signal to the GM V. The GM V locks out the interior trunk release button preventing the trunk from being opened.
- **DWA cancel switch:** When the trunk is opened with the key, this switch provides a ground signal to the GM preventing the DWA alarm system from activating, if armed.

Keyless entry (FZV)

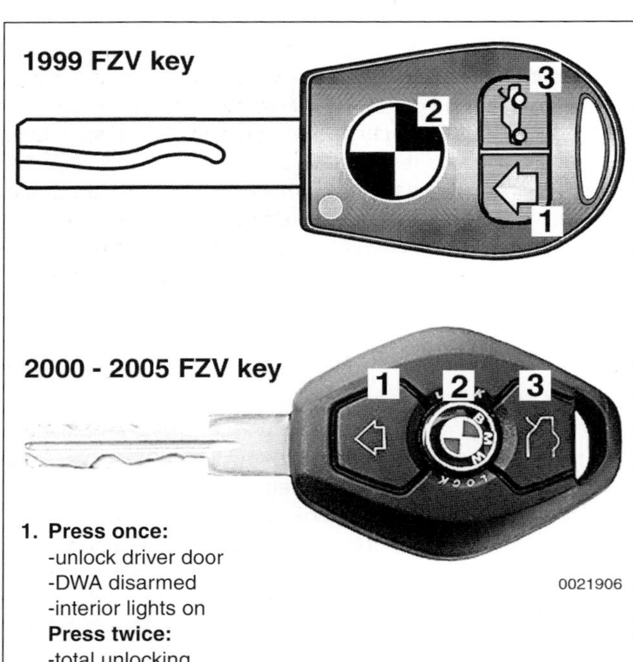

1. **Press once:**
   -unlock driver door
   -DWA disarmed
   -interior lights on
   Press twice:
   -total unlocking
   Hold:
   -convenience opening
2. **Press once:**
   -lock
   -DWA armed
   -interior lights ON when vehicle is locked
   Press twice within 10 seconds:
   -deactivate interior and tilt monitoring
3. **Press momentarily:**
   -trunk lid opens
   Press and hold:
   -panic mode (alarm if equipped)

The E46 keyless entry system (FZV) uses a tiny radio transmitter in the vehicle key to lock and unlock the doors and the trunk by remote control. There are a number of other features incorporated in FZV:

- Locking / unlocking of fuel filler lid
- Selective unlocking of driver door (key in lock cylinder)
- Arming / disarming of DWA alarm system (if equipped)
- Remote unlocking of trunk only
- Comfort opening of windows, sunroof, and convertible top.
- Interior lighting activation (search mode)
- Panic mode alarm activation (if equipped)
- Automatic correction for up to 1000 erroneous activation signals.
- Low transmitter battery fault code storage in the GM V
- 3 volt lithium battery (commercially available CR 2016) used as power supply for key transmitters
- EEPROM storage of key data. Data no longer lost when key battery is replaced; key reinitialization not required.
- Key LED signals operator when transmitting, key initialization status and key self-test
- Keys delivered with four different colored labels. This is helpful to differentiate FZV keys during initialization, preventing possibility of misassigning key ID which would change coded Key Memory functions.

A single unlock request from the driver door with the FZV key unlocks the driver door only. A second unlock request unlocks the remaining doors and trunk. This feature can be modified for individual users with the Key Memory capabilities to activate all lock actuators simultaneously. See **Car Memory / Key Memory** in this repair group.

Starting with 2000 models, the FZV key battery is recharged while the key is in the ignition switch. There is no need to replace the key battery.

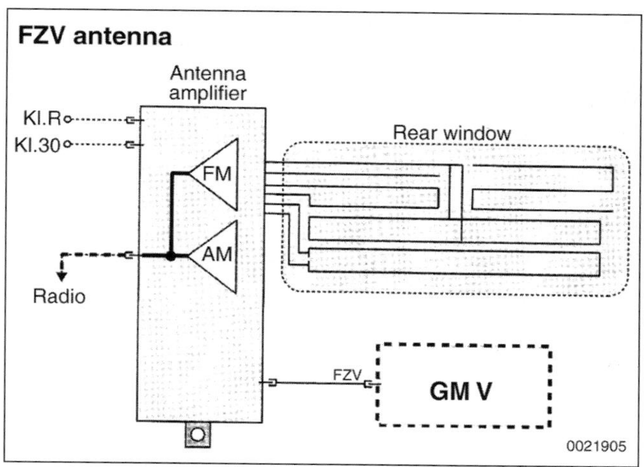

The FZV receiver is part of the antenna amplifier and is installed in the left C-pillar. The receiver produces a digital signal based on the transmitter command and sends it to the GM V for processing. The GM V then carries out all keyless entry, window / sunroof convenience closing features and DWA arming / disarming functions. The frequency of the FZV key radio signal to the antenna amplifier is 315 MHz. The system is also used to convey the key identification number being used to lock / unlock the vehicle. This is required by the Key Memory feature.

Car Memory / Key Memory

A number of safety, security and comfort features and functions can be customized. The identity of the vehicle user is provided by a signal from the keyless entry system (FZV).

Car Memory and Key Memory are actually two separate functions, although they are marketed as a combined feature.

Car Memory

The owner is provided with a list of systems that can be customized. Prior to vehicle delivery, the BMW scan tool (DISplus, GT1 or MoDiC) is used to code the driver preferences into the appropriate control modules. Thereafter these choices cannot be changed without recoding with a BMW scan tool.

The functions that can be set using Car Memory include:

- Alarm system (DWA) features such as arming / disarming with keyless entry (FZV), activation of tilt sensor or interior sensor
- Interior light activation when central locking is used
- Convenience opening of windows and sunroof
- Interior and external lighting preferences
- Heating and A/C preferences (IHKA)
- Seat and mirror position preferences (triggered by Key Memory)
- Instrument cluster display units (km or miles)

Key Memory

Whenever an FZV key is used to lock or unlock the car, the user is identified by the GM V. A maximum of four keys can be programmed with the Key Memory feature. The use of the personalized key then triggers Car Memory functions such as heating and A/C (IHKA) settings or seat, steering column and outside rear view mirror positions.

Most Key Memory programming requires the use of BMW scan tool. However, features such as IHKA blower speed and temperature store automatically without the use of scan tools.

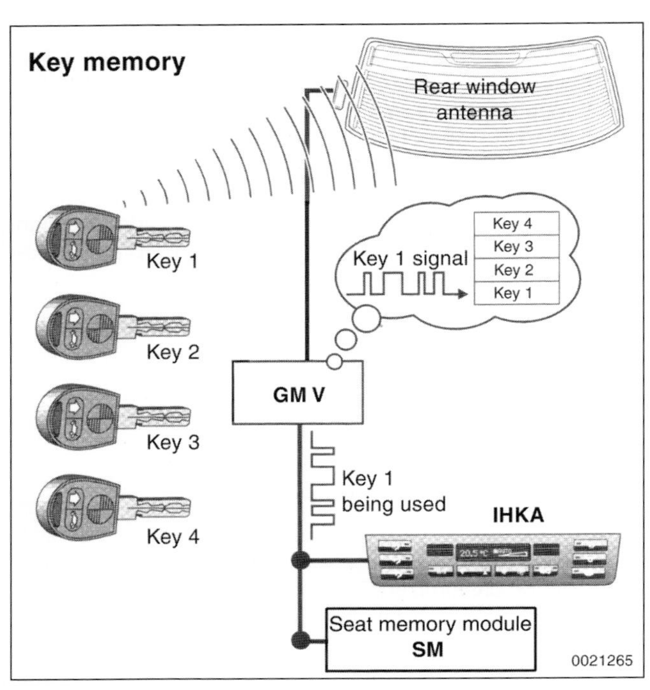

Available Key Memory functions vary based on vehicle equipment. The functions that can be set include:

- Automatic locking after start off
- Selective locking
- Heating / A/C blower speed, heated or cooled air distribution, automatic blower setting.

NOTE —
Key Memory is only activated when using keyless entry. If the driver door is unlocked manually, no electronic input is received at the GM V and Car Memory / Key Memory features are not activated.

FZV key initialization

Initialization of FZV keys is required to establish lock / unlock signal synchronization with the GM V. The initialization procedure provides the GM V with a key identification number and a rolling (changing) code for each key. If initialization is not performed, the GM V does not respond to the key signals.

Initialize up to 4 FZV keys at the same time, with the vehicle unlocked.

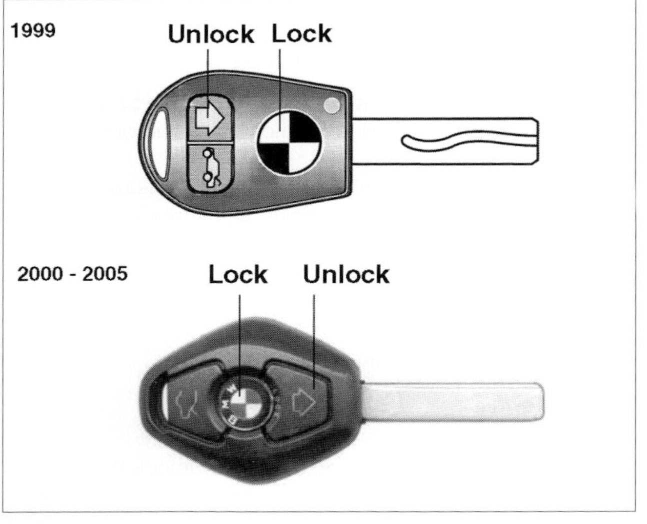

1. Close all doors and have all keys available.
2. Using key no. 1, turn ignition switch on. Within 5 seconds switch ignition OFF and remove key from ignition.
3. Within 30 seconds of turning switch OFF, press and hold **unlock** button.
4. While continuing to hold **unlock** button, quickly press and release **lock** button three times within 10 seconds.
5. Release **unlock** button.
6. If initialization was successful, all locks will be activated and released in rapid succession. If the LED continues to flash or if the locking system fails to respond, repeat the procedure.

To initialize additional remote control keys (make sure that no more than 30 seconds elapse between next initialization procedure) repeat steps 3 through 5. The ignition does not need to be cycled on/off for additional key initialization.

The initialization sequence defines the numbering of the keys in the key memory program. The first key to be initialized receives number one and should be labeled accordingly.

The key memory function responds to the key number. If keys are not initialized in the correct order, Key Memory functions are not assigned correctly.

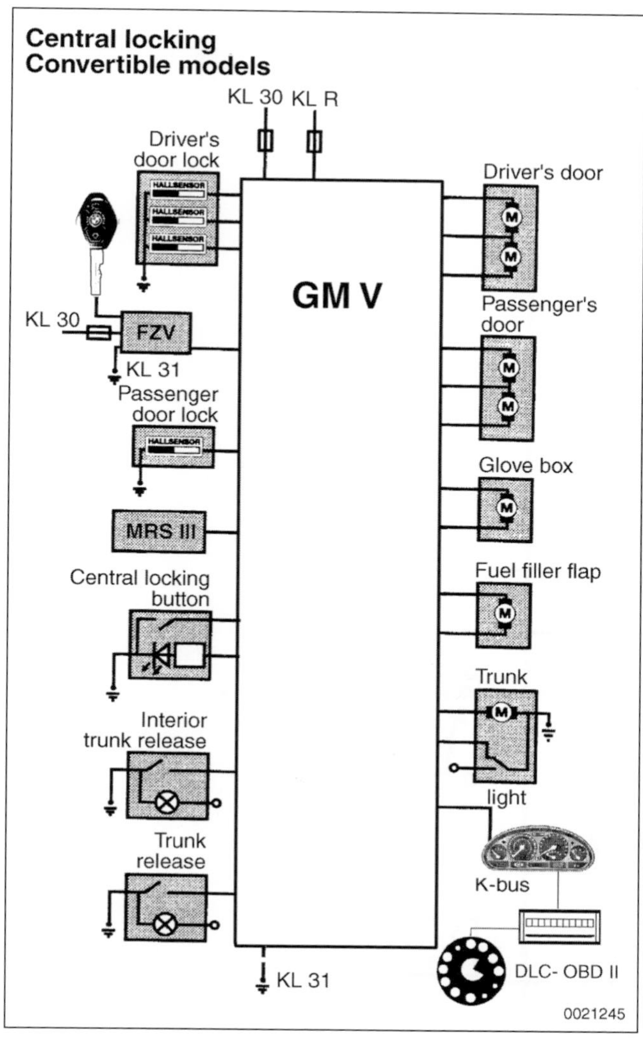

Convertible central locking

In Convertible models, the glove compartment lock is integrated into central locking functions. An additional lock actuator is positioned above the glove compartment lock, locking it whenever central locking is activated.

A microswitch on the glove compartment lock cylinder signals the GM V to lock the trunk electrically. This is the equivalent of valet key position. The trunk can only be opened with either the FZV key or the wallet key.

Also, the trunk is locked whenever the top storage compartment is unlocked while the top is raised or lowered. The top storage cover motor Hall sensor signals the GM V whenever the cover is unlocked.

The Convertible Top Module (CVM II) receives a signal from the GM V over the K-bus to lock out convertible top operation whenever the trunk is OPEN.

The FZV antenna for the Convertible is incorporated into the rear view mirror.

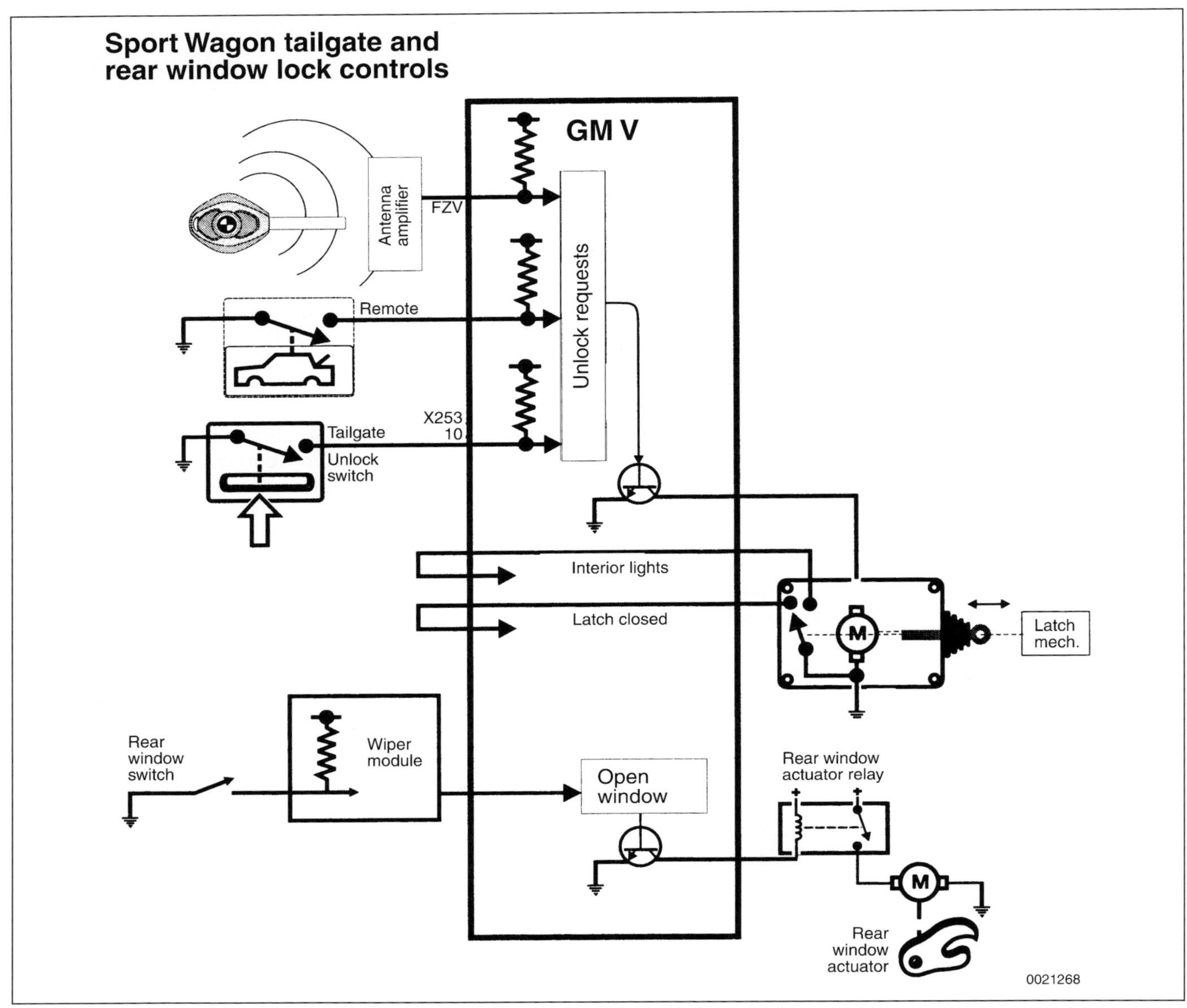

Tailgate and rear window locking

The Sport Wagon tailgate can be opened from:

- FZV key
- Interior tailgate release button at driver kick panel
- Unlock microswitch above rear license plate

Any of these input requests to the GM V activates the tailgate latch motor. The GM V also switches on the interior lights with a tailgate unlock request.

The rear window is opened with the release switch on the rear wiper arm cover. Pressing the switch signals the GM V to activate the rear window release relay.

DOOR HANDLES AND LOCKS

Any time a door lock is removed and reinstalled, be sure to check and reset:

- Unlocking of rotary latch
- Outside door handle overtravel

Perform these adjustments and measurements by closing the door lock rotary latch with a screwdriver, then attempting to open it with the outside door handle. Both adjustment procedures are described below, under **Rotary latch adjustments**.

Rotary latch adjustments

> ***CAUTION —***
> - *After door lock repairs, do not close the door before resetting rotary latch adjustment. The door may lock and be unopenable from outside.*
> - *Carry out rotary latch checks and adjustments with the door open. If the door is closed with the incorrect latch setting, it may not be possible to open the door without destroying the inner door panel.*

Rotary latch unlocking, resetting

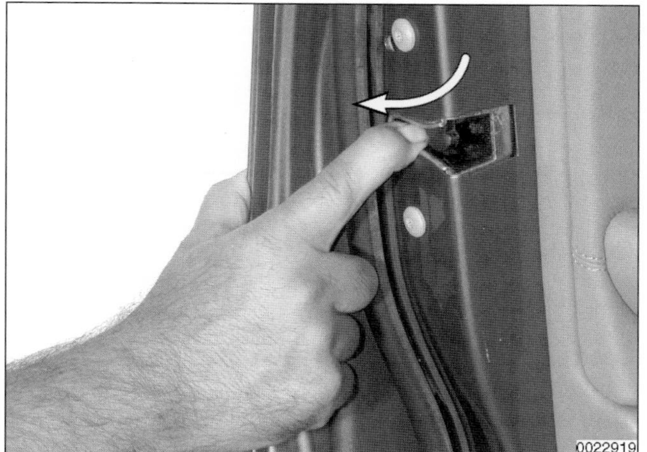

◄ With door open, use screwdriver or finger to push door lock rotary latch in direction of **arrow**.

– Lock doors with key or lock button.

– Unlock car.

– Open rotary latch using outside handle.

– If latch unlocks, adjustment is correct.

◄ If latch fails to unlock:

- Remove latch adjuster access hole cover.
- Use 4 mm Allen wrench to loosen adjustment screw, then retighten.
- Carry out check again.

NOTE —
The right side latch adjusting screw is threaded left-handed.

Tightening torque
- Door lock adjustment screw . . . . 3 + 2 Nm (27 + 18 in-lb)

Door lock and handle assembly

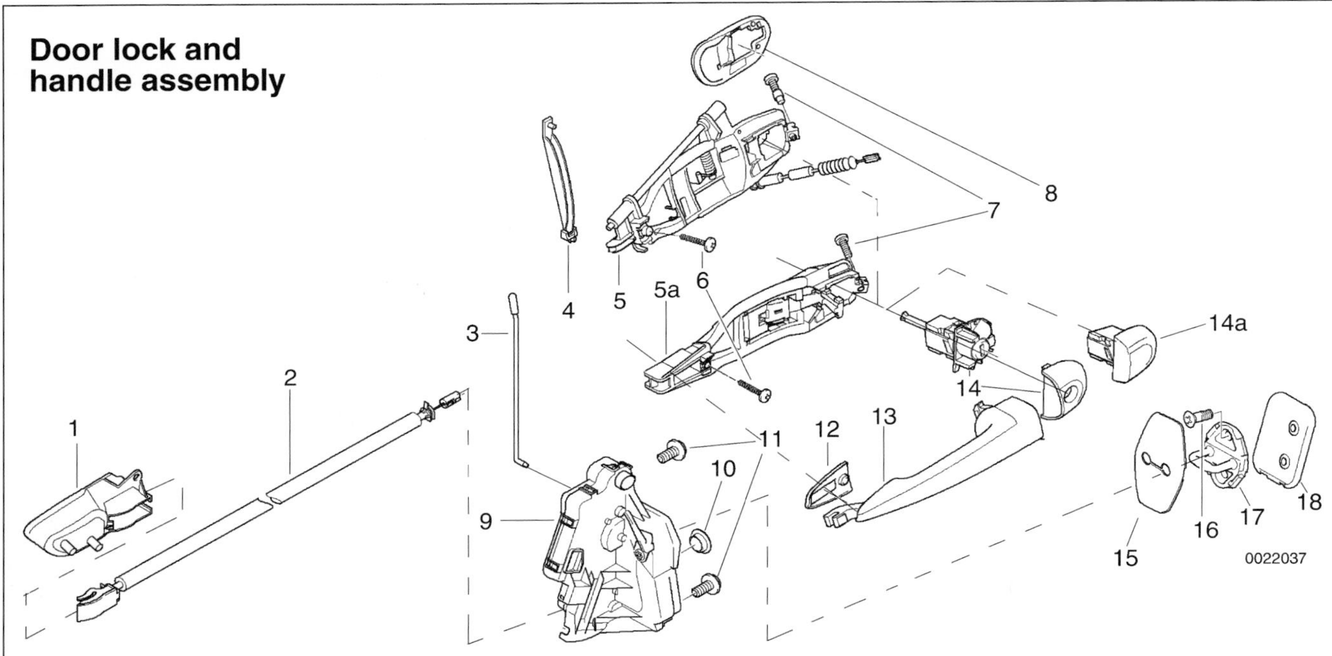

1. Inside door lock release
2. Inside door release Bowden cable
3. Lock button and rod
4. Models from 09 / 2000: Bowden cable bracket
5. Models from 09 / 2000: Door handle inner mechanism

5a. Models to 09 / 2000: Door handle inner mechanism

6. Inner handle mounting bolt
7. Key cylinder mounting bolt (Torx)
8. Gasket
9. Door lock with rotary latch
10. Plug
11. Bolt M6 (always replace) -tighten to 9 Nm (80 in-lb)
12. Gasket
13. Outer door handle
14. Driver door: Door lock cylinder and cover

14a. Rear or right door: Outer handle rear anchor

15. Door striker cover
16. Torx bolt M8 -tighten to 24 Nm (18 ft-lb)
17. Door lock striker
18. Lock plate

Outside handle overtravel, resetting

– With door open, close rotary latch using screwdriver.

– Open rotary latch using outside door handle.

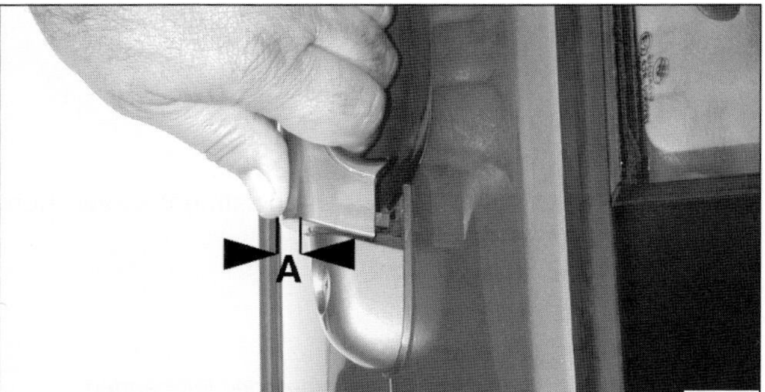

Measure additional distance (**A**) handle can travel once rotary latch releases.

- If correct measurement **A** is obtained, rotary latch adjustment is correct.
- If correct measurement **A** is not obtained, readjust rotary latch through access hole, as described above, and check handle overtravel again.
- If measurement **A** is still not obtained, replace door lock.

Outside door handle overtravel

- Measurement **A** . . . . min. 2 mm (0.08 in)

Door lock, removing and installing

The front and rear door locks for E46 4-door models are similar. Early production cars, up to 09 / 2000, use a lock actuator with an external lever which couples with the outside door handle mechanism. Cars produced from 09 / 2000 use a Bowden cable to attach the outside door handle to the lock release mechanism.

> ***WARNING —***
> *E46 cars are fitted with side-impact airbags in the front doors. Optionally, the rear doors in 4-door models may also be fitted with airbags. When servicing the door lock on a car with door-mounted airbags, always disconnect the negative (–) battery terminal. See* **721 Airbag System (SRS)** *for cautions and procedures relating to the airbag system.*

– Disconnect negative (–) cable from battery.

> ***CAUTION —***
> *Prior to disconnecting the battery, read the battery disconnection cautions given at the front of this manual on page viii.*

– Remove front door trim panel, door airbag, and vapor barrier. See **411 Doors**.

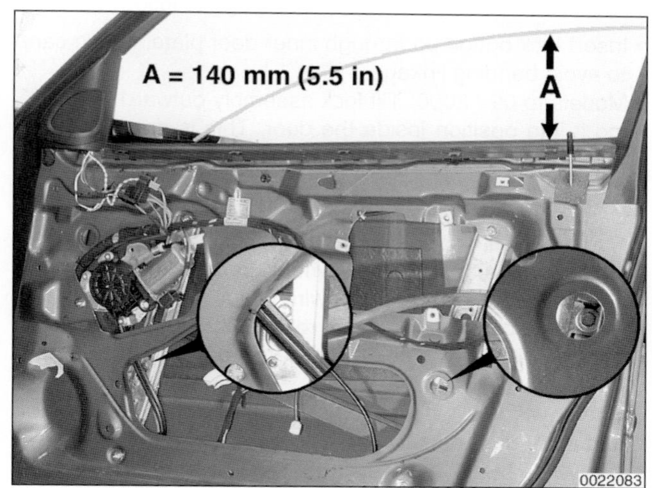

◄ Detach window from window regulator rails:

- Reattach battery. Move window to approx. 140 mm (5.5 in) from bottom. Turn ignition OFF and remove key.
- Remove window retaining screws (**insets**) at window regulator rails.

NOTE —
Be prepared to retrieve the captured nut corresponding to the retaining screw on the back side of the window rail. It may fall to the bottom of the door cavity.

- Be sure to separate plastic lug at base of window from rail.
- Reconnect window motor and turn ignition ON
- Raise window to top. Turn ignition OFF and remove key

> ***CAUTION —***
> *Guide the window up manually in order to avoid binding.*

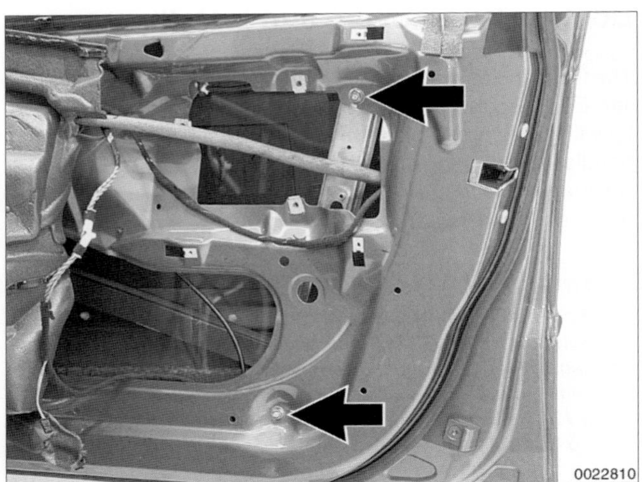

0022810

 Remove window regulator rear rail:

- Remove top and bottom rail mounting fasteners (**arrows**).
- Slide rail down, allowing it to hang to side out of the way.

— Driver door: Remove door lock cylinder. See **Driver door lock cylinder, removing and installing** in this repair group.

— Models from 09 / 2000: Carefully pry outside door handle Bowden cable off lock assembly.

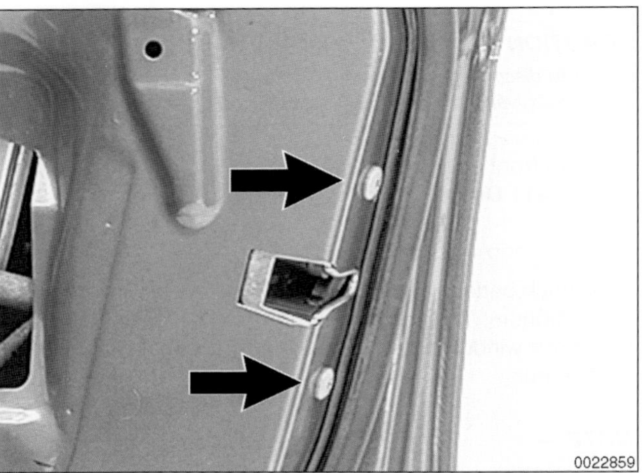

0022859

Remove lock mounting bolts (**arrows**) from rear edge of door. Support lock to prevent it from falling into bottom of door cavity.

— Disconnect harness connector from lock assembly.

— Remove lock assembly, complete with lock-button linkage.

— Installation is reverse of removal, noting the following:

- Insert lock button up through inner door plate, taking care to avoid bending linkage.
- Models to 09 / 2000: Tilt lock assembly outward while lifting it into position inside the door. This is done to make sure lock lever is inserted between outside door handle pawl and outer door skin.
- Use new door lock mounting bolts.
- Use new self-locking mounting bolts when reinstalling side-impact airbag to door (where applicable).
- Secure wire harnesses with wire ties, as applicable.
- Be sure to check unlocking of rotary latch and outside door handle overtravel. See **Rotary latch adjustments** in this repair group.
- Check window function before reinstalling vapor barrier and inner door panel.

Tightening torques

- Airbag to door (replace screws) . . . . . . .8.5 Nm (75 in-lb)
- Door lock to door
  M6 bolt (always replace) . . . . 9 Nm (80 in-lb)
- Window guide to door . . . . 9 Nm (80 in-lb)
- Window to guide . . . . 8 Nm (71 in-lb)

Driver door lock cylinder, removing and installing

Only the driver door is equipped with a lock cylinder. The procedure for removing the door handle rear anchor on the other three doors is similar to that for removing the driver door lock cylinder.

◄ Open door and remove plastic plug (Sedan or Sport Wagon, shown in illustration) or rubber covering (Coupe or Convertible) at lock cylinder mounting bolt access hole in upper rear door edge.

NOTE —
Sedan or Sport Wagon: Remove inner plug by prying with screwdriver, then peel off outer (oval) plastic trim.

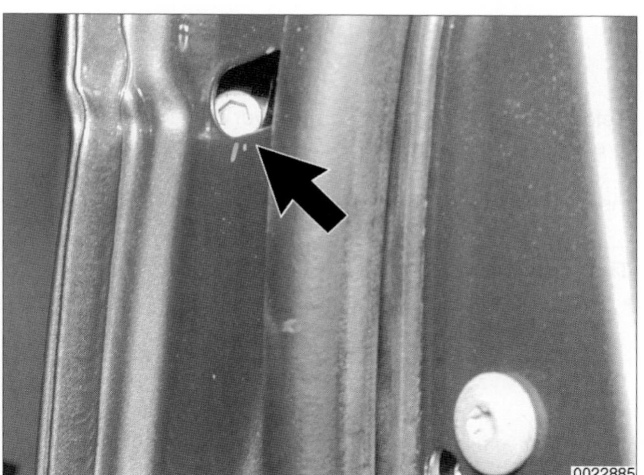

◄ Remove lock cylinder mounting screw (**arrow**).

– Pull out lock cylinder.

NOTE —
Use key in cylinder to help pull cylinder out.

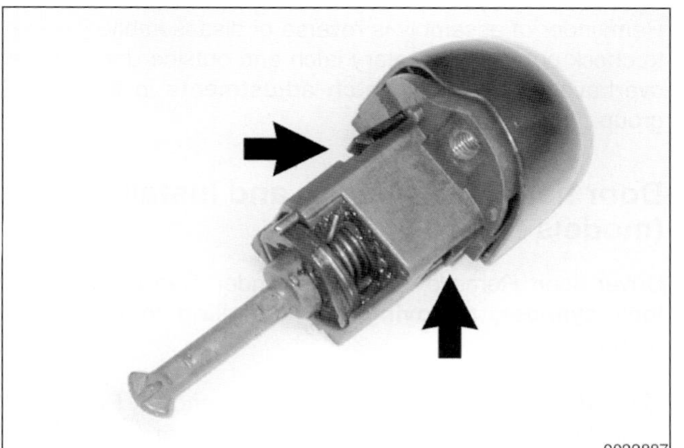

◄ Use a small screw driver to pry cylinder cover locking tabs (**arrows**). Slide cover off cylinder gently to avoid breaking tabs.

– Installation is reverse of removal.

- Sedan or Sport Wagon: Replace cylinder mounting bolt access hole trim cover if necessary.

Door handle, removing and installing (models to 09 / 2000)

– Driver door: Remove door lock cylinder. See **Driver door lock cylinder, removing and installing** in this repair group.

– Other doors: Remove door handle rear anchor. Procedure is similar to removing driver door lock cylinder.

< Pull handle out as far as it will go, then backward approx. 2 mm (0.08 in).

– Push handle in slightly (approx. 4 mm / 0.16 in).

– Remove door handle from door by angling out of door cavity.

NOTE —
Make sure the lock release pawl at the rear of the handle and the mounting guide at the front of the handle are intact.

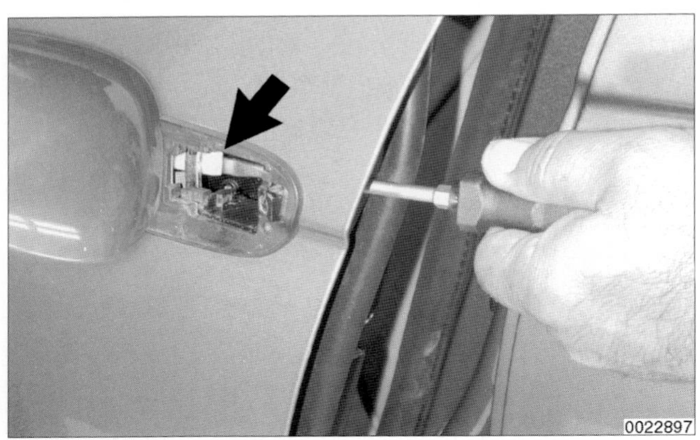

< Before reinstalling, insert screwdriver through access hole in edge of door to push lock release lever (**arrow**) outward.

– Insert outside handle and press forward until click is heard.

Tightening torque
- Outside handle to lock (left-hand thread) . . . . .2.0 Nm (18 in-lb)

NOTE —
Take care that the door handle base gasket is not deformed when the handle is installed.

– Remainder of assembly is reverse of disassembly. Be sure to check unlocking of rotary latch and outside door handle overtravel. See **Rotary latch adjustments** in this repair group.

Door handle, removing and installing (models from 09 / 2000)

– Driver door: Remove door lock cylinder. See **Driver door lock cylinder, removing and installing** in this repair group.

– Other doors: Remove door handle rear anchor. Procedure is similar to removing driver door lock cylinder.

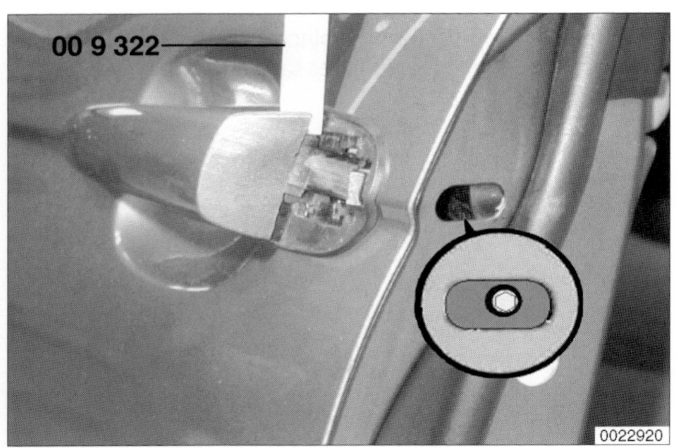

< Pull outside door handle out and wedge BMW special tool 00 9 322 under handle.

– Working in lock cylinder mounting bolt access hole, tighten down screw (*counterclockwise* direction). Lock is now in installation position. Remove special tool 00 9 322.

– Pull outside door handle outward and unhook from front guide.

NOTE —
Make sure the lock release bore at the rear of the handle and the mounting guide at the front of the handle are intact.

– Before reinstalling handle, make sure lock mechanism is in installation position as described earlier:

- Distance between inner door handle lever and outer door skin must not exceed measurement **A**.
- If measurement exceeds specification, pull lever outward with fingers until measurement is correct.

Installation distance: inner door handle lever to door
- Measurement **A** . . . . less than 8 mm (0.32 in)

– Insert handle and snap into place.

Tightening torque
- Outside handle to lock (left-hand thread) . . . . 2.0 Nm (18 in-lb)

NOTE —
Take care that the door handle base gasket is not deformed when the handle is installed.

– Remainder of assembly is reverse of disassembly. Be sure to check unlocking of rotary latch and outside door handle overtravel. See **Rotary latch adjustments** in this repair group.

Door handle inner mechanism, removing and installing (models to 09 / 2000)

WARNING —
E46 cars are fitted with side-impact airbags in the front doors. Optionally, the rear doors in 4-door models may also be fitted with airbags. When servicing the door lock on a car with door-mounted airbags, always disconnect the negative (–) battery terminal. See **721 Airbag System (SRS)** *for cautions and procedures relating to the airbag system.*

– Disconnect negative (–) cable from battery.

CAUTION —
Prior to disconnecting the battery, read the battery disconnection cautions given at the front of this manual on page viii.

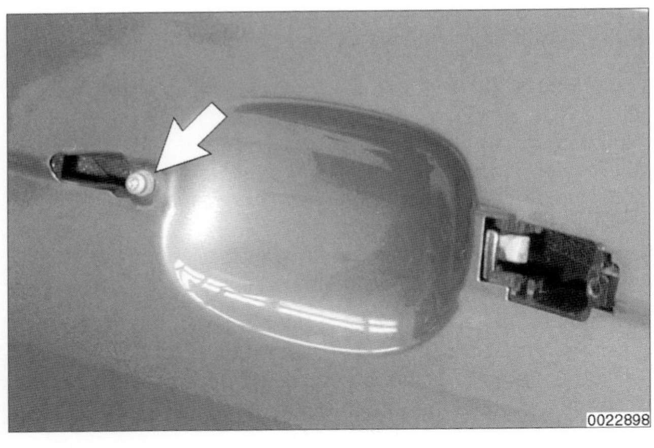

- Remove front door trim panel, door airbag, and vapor barrier. See **411 Doors**.
- Remove door lock and outside door handle. See **Door lock, removing and installing** and **Door handle, removing and installing (models to 09 / 2000)** in this repair group.
- Remove outside handle base seals.
- Loosen inner handle mounting bolt (**arrow**).
- Working inside door opening, slide inner handle toward front and remove.
- Installation is reverse of removal.

NOTE —
Inspect mounting bolt and replace if necessary.

Door handle inner mechanism, removing and installing (models from 09 / 2000)

> ***WARNING —***
> *E46 cars are fitted with side-impact airbags in the front doors. Optionally, the rear doors in 4-door models may also be fitted with airbags. When servicing the door lock on a car with door-mounted airbags, always disconnect the negative (–) battery terminal. See* **721 Airbag System (SRS)** *for cautions and procedures relating to the airbag system.*

- Disconnect negative (–) cable from battery.

> ***CAUTION —***
> *Prior to disconnecting the battery, read the battery disconnection cautions given at the front of this manual on page viii.*

- Remove front door trim panel, door airbag, and vapor barrier. See **411 Doors**.
- Remove door lock and outside door handle. See **Door lock, removing and installing** and **Door handle, removing and installing (models from 09 / 2000)** in this repair group.
- Remove outside handle base seals.
- Lever out Bowden cable from door handle with screwdriver.
- Sedan or Sport Wagon: Slide Bowden cable out of guide.

NOTE —
Place foam insulation on bowden cable in original position during reinstallation.

– Coupe or Convertible: Remove inner door guide (plastic) to gain access to Bowden cable.

NOTE —
Take care to not damage inner door guide during removal and installation.

– Loosen handle mounting bolt.

– Working inside door opening, slide inner handle toward front and remove.

– Installation is reverse of removal.

NOTE —
- *Inspect handle mounting bolt and replace if necessary.*
- *Fit Bowden cable end in lock actuator correctly.*

Door striker, replacing

– Remove striker plastic cover.

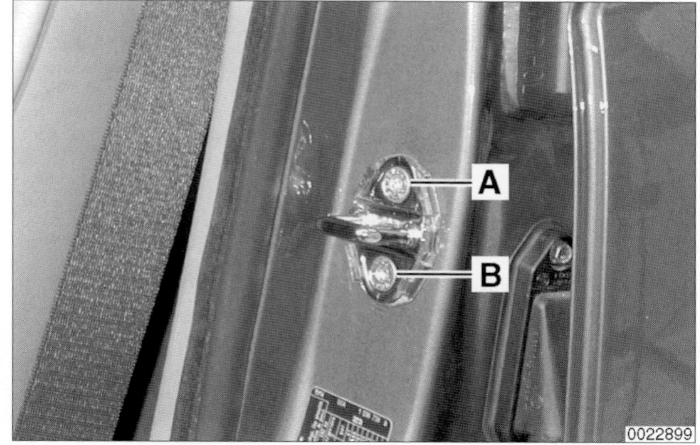

◄ Remove striker top mounting bolt (**A**).

- Screw M8 stud into top bolt hole to keep striker backing plate from falling down into door pillar cavity.
- Remove lower bolt (**B**).

– Remove and reinstall striker and gasket while holding on to stud. Install striker mounting bolts finger-tight.

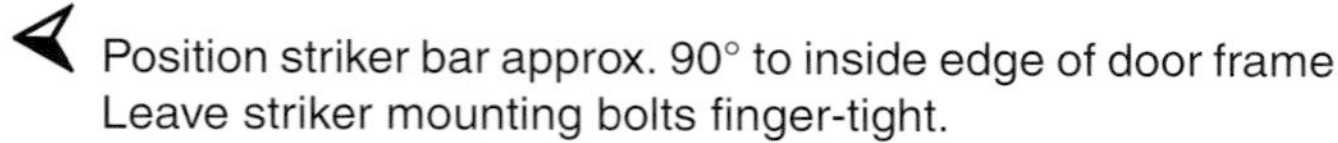

◄ Position striker bar approx. 90° to inside edge of door frame. Leave striker mounting bolts finger-tight.

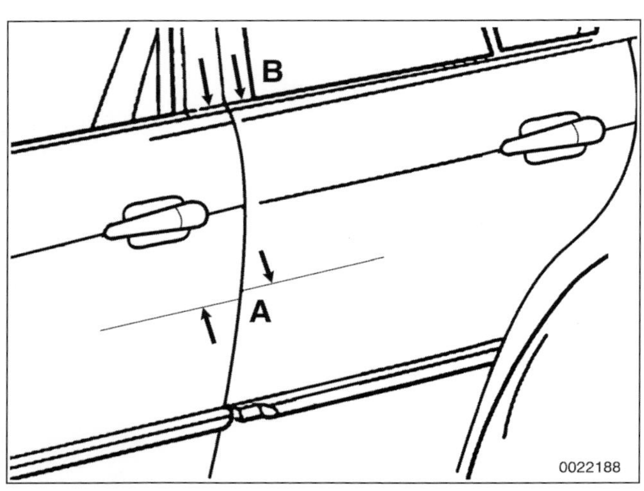

Set position of striker:

- When closed, rear edge of front door must be even with front edge of rear door (Sedan or Sport Wagon) or with rear quarter panel (Coupe or Convertible). Maximum deviation allowed measured at **A**.
- When closed, shoulder of front door must be flush to shoulder of rear door (Sedan or Sport Wagon) or with top of rear quarter panel (Coupe or Convertible). No deviation is allowed at measurement **B**.
- When door is closed, striker must not contact lock housing.
- With door closed, there must be no in or out movement of door.

Door striker position

- Deviation from parallelism of closed door (**A**) . . . . max. 1 mm (0.04 in)
- Deviation from flush at door shoulder (**B**) 0

– Torque striker bolts. Recheck door alignment. Reinstall striker plastic cover.

Tightening torque

- Striker plate to door pillar . . . . 24 Nm (18 ft-lb)

LUGGAGE COMPARTMENT LOCKS

Trunk locking mechanism

The trunk lock cylinder does not actuate central locking control.

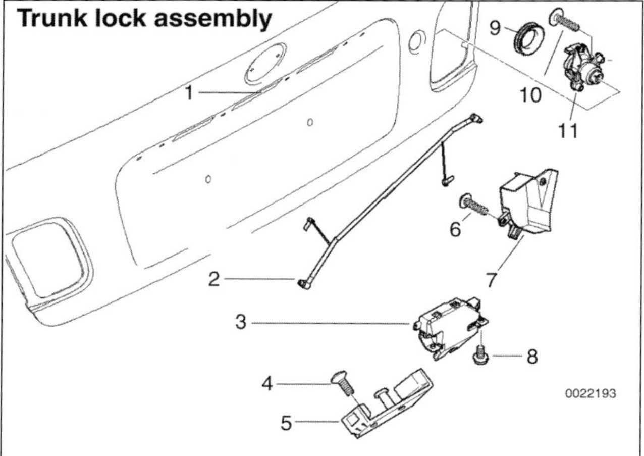

1. Trunk release microswitch
2. Connecting rod
3. Lock with microswitch
4. Torx screw M6
5. Striker plate
6. Trim screw
7. Lock cover
8. Torx bolt M6
9. Lock cylinder gasket
10. Self-threading screw
11. Lock cylinder

The trunk can be unlocked by using:

- Central locking button
- Left door key
- FZV (keyless entry) system
- Trunk lock cylinder in the right side of trunk lid
- Trunk release in driver footwell
- Microswitch in center of license plate light strip

– Remove trunk lock microswitch:

- Remove licence plate light strip.
- Separate electrical harness connector from strip.
- Separate microswitch from strip.

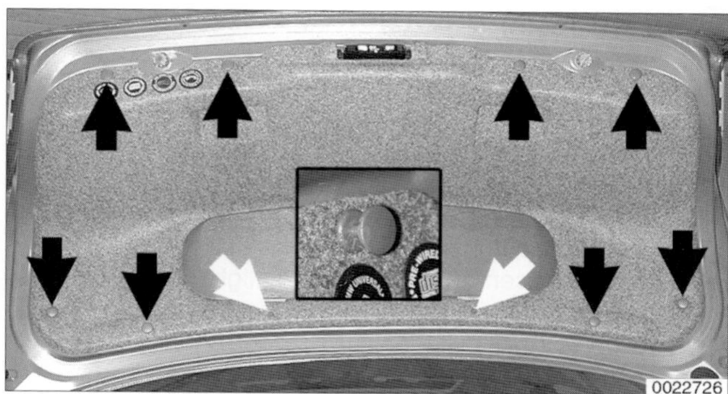

Access trunk lock cylinder or lock:

- Raise trunk lid.
- Open tool kit and remove screws attaching tool kit to trunk lid (**white arrows**). Unclip retaining strap at trunk lid and remove tool kit.
- Remove insulating liner expansion rivets (**black arrows**). and remove trunk liner. Expansion rivets are released by prying upper portion (**inset**).
- Lift off trim panel.

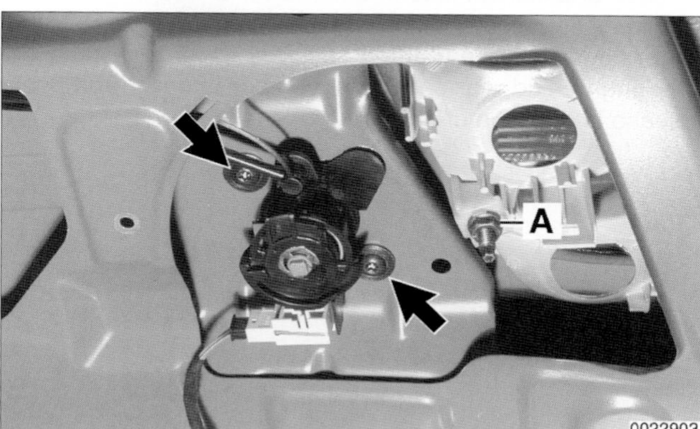

Remove trunk lock cylinder:

- Remove right taillight socket from trunk lid. See **630 Lights**.
- Remove right tail lens mounting nut (**A**) and detach tail lens from trunk lid.
- Remove lock cylinder cover mounting screws (**arrows**). Slide cover to right to remove.

NOTE —

- *Convertible: Remove third brake light to access trunk lock mechanism.*
- *Use new self-tapping screws to reinstall trunk lock cylinder.*

Remove trunk lock striker: Pry out rear trunk edge trim caps (**arrows**) to access striker mounting screws.

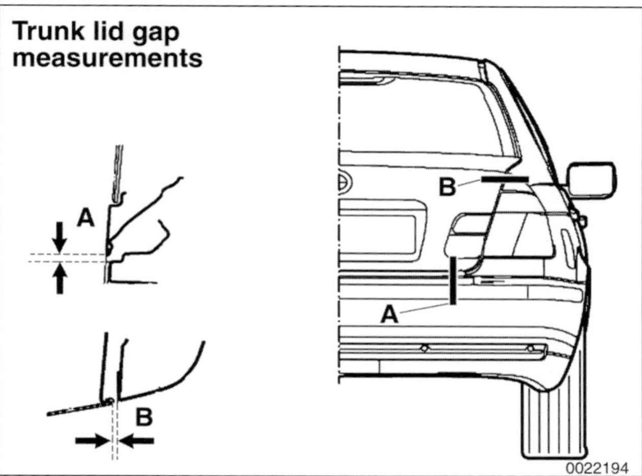

When reinstalling, or to adjust trunk lid alignment, adjust position of trunk lock striker with mounting bolts finger tight.

- Set gap measurements as listed below.
- Check trunk lid lock operation with lid open.
- Also see **412 Trunk Lid, Tailgate.**

Trunk position gap adjustment	
• Trunk lid to rear panel (**A**)	5 ± 1.5 mm (0.2 ± 0.06 in)
• Trunk lid to rear fender (**B**)	4.25 ± 0.75 mm (0.17 ± 0.03 in)

NOTE —

Do not lubricate lock or lock striker with grease.

Tailgate lock, emergency release

The Sport Wagon tailgate can be unlocked using:

- Central locking switch
- Left door key
- FZV (keyless entry) system
- Tailgate release button in left front kick panel
- Microswitch in center of license plate light strip.

There is no key lock cylinder in the tailgate.

In case of electrical failure, there is an emergency tailgate lock release located inside the rear cargo area, along the lower edge of the rear apron behind a small access cover. Working behind rear seat, remove access cover and push release in direction of **arrow** to open tailgate.

Release

0021495

Tailgate and rear window locking mechanism

Remove tailgate lock microswitch:

- Remove license plate light strip.
- Separate electrical harness connector from strip.
- Separate microswitch from strip.

Tailgate lock assembly

0022245

1. Torx bolt M6
2. Rear window lock
3. Rear window lock cover
4. Nut M6
5. Rear window striker mounting bracket and wiper pivot
6. Rear window lock striker
7. Tailgate lock
8. Torx bolt M8
9. Tailgate lock striker
10. Lock plate
11. Tailgate release microswitch
12. Tailgate grip
13. Tailgate grip gasket
14. Tailgate

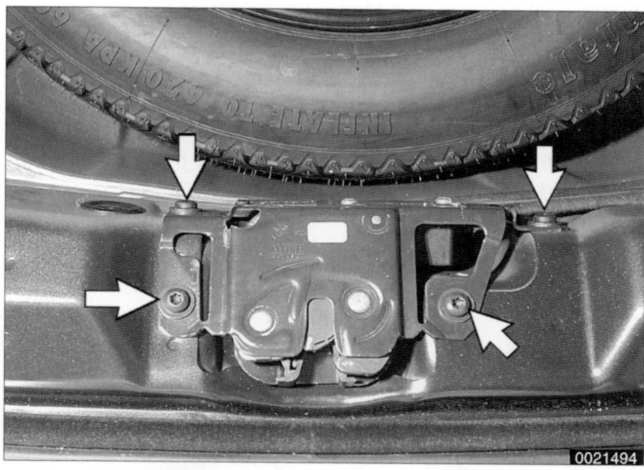

 Remove tailgate lock:

- Open tailgate and remove cargo compartment rear trim.
- Mark position of lock on rear panel.
- Remove lock mounting bolts (**arrows**).
- Detach lock mechanism electrical harness connector.
- Separate electric lock actuator and emergency release lever from tailgate lock mechanism.

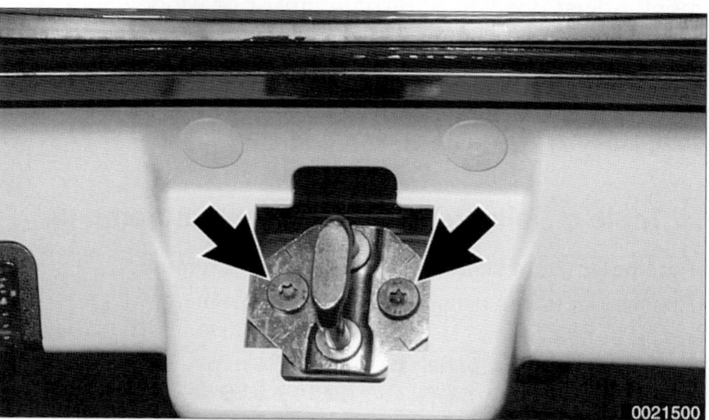

 Remove tailgate lock striker:

- Open tailgate and pry out lock striker trim from bottom of tailgate.
- Remove one of two striker mounting screw (**arrows**).
- Thread in M8 stud to keep striker lock plate from falling inside tailgate.
- Remove second screw and striker.
- Reinstall striker bolts finger tight. Adjust striker position before tightening bolts.

– Adjust striker position:

- Close tailgate slowly, allowing striker to center itself on lock.
- Striker must not touch lock housing.
- Tighten striker mounting bolts, then check tailgate to body gaps. See **Table a**.

NOTE —
Do not lubricate lock or lock striker with grease.

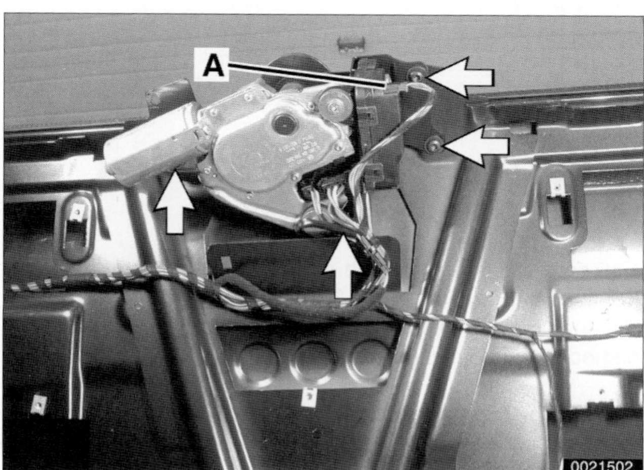

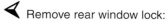

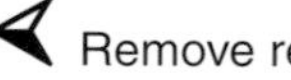 Remove rear window lock:

- Open tailgate. Remove tailgate trim panel.
- Detach window lock and rear wiper electrical harness connector (**A**).
- Remove lock mounting screws (**arrows**).
- Slide lock out from under rear window wiper motor.
- Reinstall lock mounting bolts finger tight. Adjust lock position before tightening bolts.

– Adjust lock position:

- Close window slowly, allowing lock to center itself on striker.
- Tighten lock mounting bolts, then check rear window to body gaps. See **Table a**.
- Tighten lock mounting bolts.

Tightening torque

- Rear window lock and wiper motor to tailgate . . . . 10 Nm (7 ft-lb)

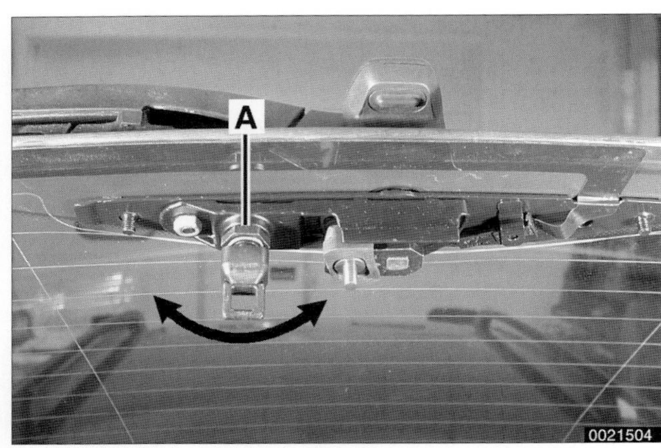

 Adjust rear window lock striker height by loosening lock nut **A**, then turning striker in or out.

- Retighten lock nut.
- Recheck rear window to body gaps. See **Table a**.
- Check and adjust position of rear wiper shaft relative to wiper drive disk and wiper motor end stop. See **611 Wipers and Washers**.

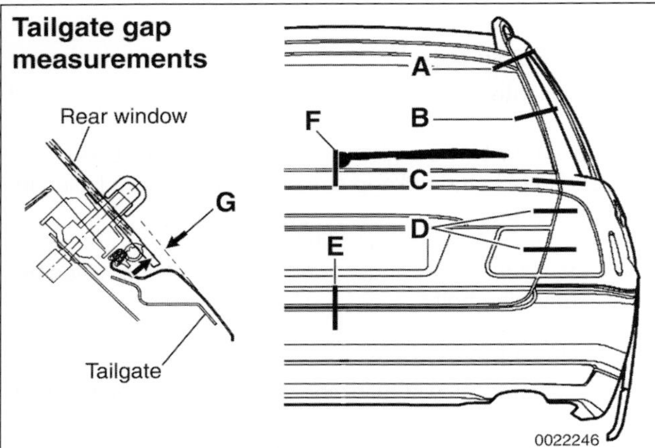

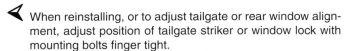

When reinstalling, or to adjust tailgate or rear window alignment, adjust position of tailgate striker or window lock with mounting bolts finger tight.

- Twist tailgate rubber buffers to set gap measurements. See **Table a**.
- Also see **412 Trunk Lid, Tailgate.**

Table a. Tailgate to body gap measurements

Parameter (from sketch)	Gap measurement
Rear spoiler to side panel (**A**)	3.75 ± 1.3 mm (0.15 ± 0.05 in)
Rear window to side panel (**B**)	3.5 ± 1.4 mm (0.14 ± 0.06 in)
Tailgate to side panel (**C**)	3.6 mm ± 0.75 mm (0.14 ± 0.03 in)
Tailgate to side panel (height)	Flush to 2 mm (0.08 in) lower
Tailgate light to corner light (**D**)	4.25 ± 0.75 mm (0.17 ± 0.03 in)
Tailgate to rear bumper (**E**)	5 ± 1 mm (0.2 ± 0.04 in)
Rear window to tailgate (**F**)	4 ± 1 mm (0.16 ± 0.04 in)
Rear window to tailgate (**G**)	5.4 ± 1 mm (0.21 ± 0.04 in)

ELECTRONIC IMMOBILIZATION (EWS)

E46 cars are equipped with passive theft-prevention. Electronic immobilization (EWS 3.3) makes it impossible to start the engine using any means other than the special keys furnished with the vehicle.

The ignition key is embedded with a computer chip and permanently coded. The key communicates with the vehicle using a transponder in the key and a ring antenna surrounding the steering lock cylinder.

A primary code is programmed into the key and into the vehicle itself. A secondary code is changed every time the vehicle is started. If the key code and EWS control module code do not match, the engine management control module and the starter are disabled. EWS ignition keys cannot be duplicated.

The system is designed to have up to ten keys. Only an authorized BMW dealer can provide replacement keys.

NOTE —

- *EWS is sometimes also referred to as Driveaway Protection.*
- *If a vehicle key is lost or stolen, the electronic authorization for that key can be cancelled using the BMW scan tool DISplus, GT1 or MoDiC.*
- *Force applied to a key can damage the electronic circuitry. A damaged key will not start the engine. In that case, purchase a new key and have it initialized by an authorized BMW dealer. See* **FZV key initialization** *in this repair group.*
- *Starting with 2000 models, the battery in the FZV ignition key is recharged while the key is in the ignition switch. There is no need to replace the key battery.*

EWS control module, replacing

– Turn off ignition and remove key.

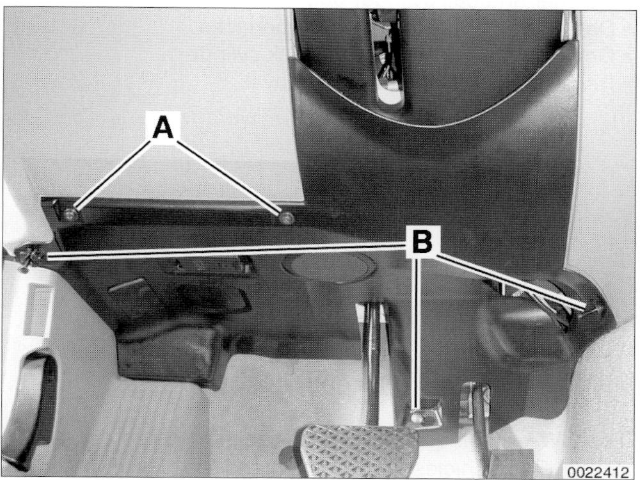

 Remove left footwell (pedal cluster) trim panel.

- Remove screws (**A**).
- Remove fasteners (**B**).
- Lower panel.

Disconnect electrical harness connectors at footwell panel and remove panel:

- Unplug connector at footwell interior light (**A**), if equipped.
- Slide lock at OBD II connector (**B**) in direction of **arrow**.
- Unplug connector at speaker if equipped (**C**).

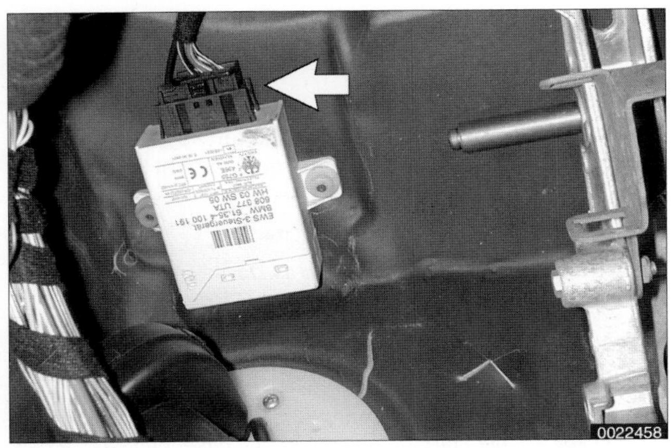

Remove EWS control module harness connector (**arrow**).

– Remove module mounting screws. Remove module.

NOTE —
The EWS module is identified with EWS markings.

– Installation is reverse of removal.

– Recode and program EWS control module using BMW scan tool (DISplus, GT1 or MoDiC) or equivalent.

Ring antenna

To remove EWS ring antenna prior to removing ignition lock cylinder, remove upper and lower steering column trim. Use BMW special tool 61 3 300 to lever ring antenna off lock cylinder. Alternatively, remove lock cylinder first.

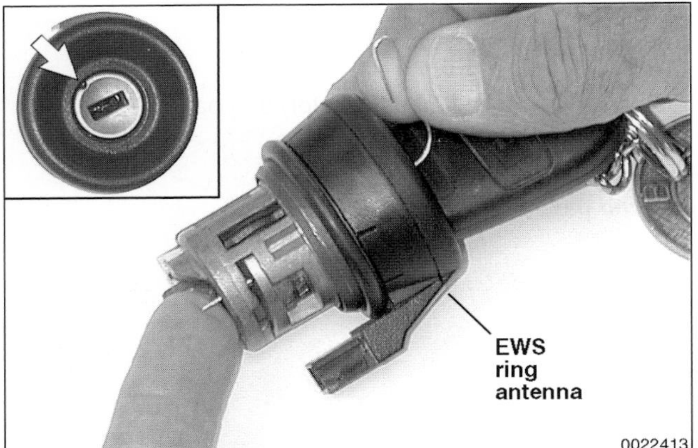

With ignition key in ON position (60° from LOCKED):

- Insert a thin piece of stiff wire into opening (**arrow**) in lock cylinder and pull cylinder out.
- Detach ring antenna harness connector.
- Gently work ring antenna off lock cylinder.
- Reinstallation is reverse of removal.

ANTI-THEFT ALARM (DWA)

The DWA anti-theft system is a dealer installed accessory option. E46 vehicles are prewired and the General Module (GM V) is preprogrammed to accept DWA hardware. Once the DWA system components are installed, the GM V must be coded (using the BMW diagnostic scan tool) to recognize the installed components and carry out DWA functions.

The GM V utilizes existing components and / or circuits as parts of the DWA system:

- Door lock hall effect sensor contacts
- Trunk lid or tailgate switch contacts
- Trunk lock key position switch
- Hood switch
- DWA status LED

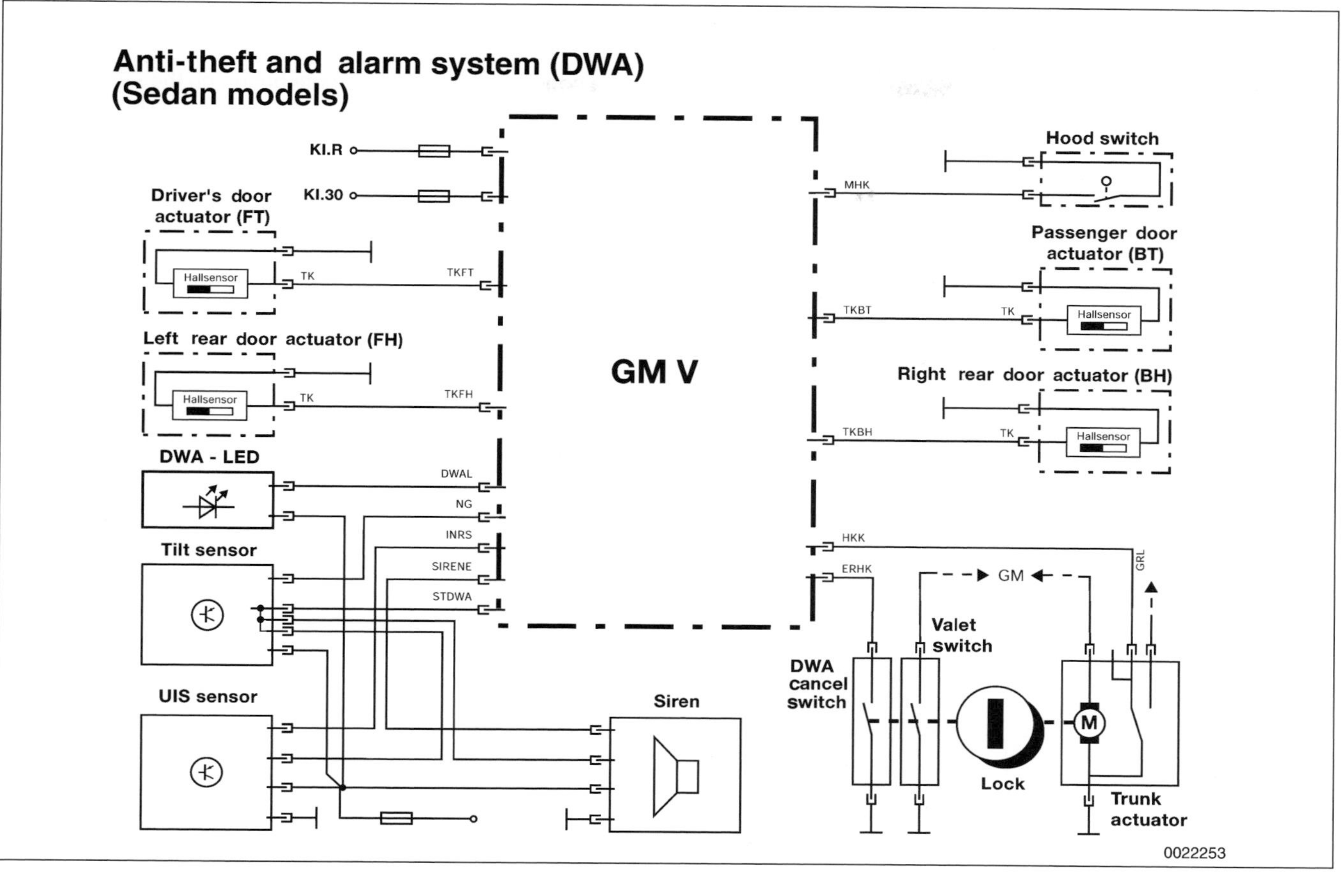

The DWA accessory kit includes the following:

- Tilt sensor in right trunk area
- UIS (interior monitoring sensor) in center of headliner
- Siren in cowl area next to IHKA housing

DWA alarm arming / disarming

The DWA alarm is armed every time the vehicle is locked from the outside with the door lock cylinder or FZV key. When armed, the LED in the rear view mirror flashes as an acknowledgment, along with flashing exterior lights and a momentary chirp from the siren.

The GM V monitors all required input signals for CLOSED status (door closed, trunk closed, etc.) The inputs must be in CLOSED status for a minimum of 3 seconds for the GM V to include them as a monitored component. After 3 seconds any input signal not in CLOSED status is excluded, preventing false alarm activation.

If the DWA is armed a second time within 10 seconds, the tilt sensor and interior protection sensor are also excluded as alarm activation components. This function is useful for preventing false alarm activation if the vehicle is transported on a train or flat bed truck.

While armed, the trunk can be opened without the alarm being triggered as follows:

- If opened with the trunk remote button on the FZV key, the GM V prevents the alarm from activating. (This feature is customizable under the Car Memory function.)
- If opened with the key at the trunk lock cylinder, the trunk key position switch signals the GM V and in the same manner prevents the alarm from activating.
- In either case, when the trunk is returned to the CLOSED position, it no longer activates the alarm.

Alarm operation

When the alarm is triggered, the siren sounds for 30 seconds and the headlight low beams and hazard lights flash for 5 minutes. The GM V signals the Light Center Switch (LSZ) via the K-bus to flash the lights. Following an alarm trigger, the system resets and triggers again in case of additional tampering to the vehicle.

Door contacts

The door lock Hall effect sensors provide door OPEN / CLOSED status:

- When door latch is CLOSED, current flow through sensor is <5 mA.
- When door is OPEN, current flow through sensor is >12 mA.

With DWA armed, the GM V activates the siren if it receives a door OPEN signal.

Trunk lid switch contact

The trunk switch contact is located in the trunk lock assembly. When closed, the trunk contact provides a ground signal to the GM V, signifying CLOSED trunk.

With the DWA armed, the GM V activates the siren if it receives a trunk OPEN signal.

Trunk lock key position switches

There are two switches mounted in one block (**arrow**) on the trunk lock cylinder:

- **Valet position switch.** With the key lock in the valet position, this switch provides a ground signal to the GM V. The GM V locks out the interior trunk release button, preventing the trunk from being opened.
- **DWA deactivation switch.** When the trunk is opened mechanically with the key, this switch provides a ground signal to the GM V, preventing DWA from activating if armed.

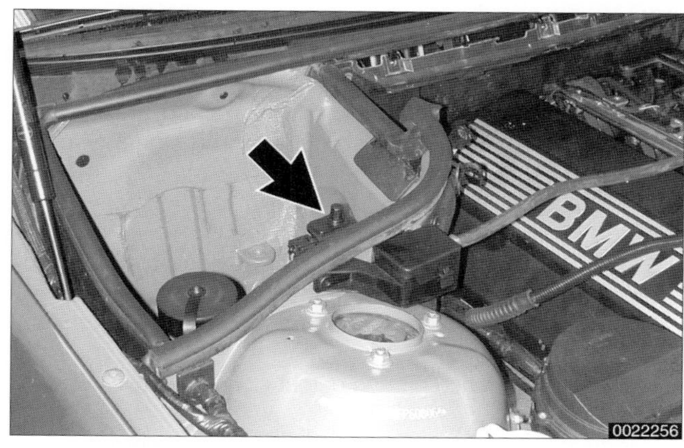

Hood contact switch

Located in the right side engine compartment, the hood contact switch (**arrow**) provides a ground signal to the GM V signifying an open hood. The plunger of this switch can be pulled up past a detent causing the switch contact to close. This feature can be used to simulate a CLOSED hood with the hood open when diagnosing the DWA system.

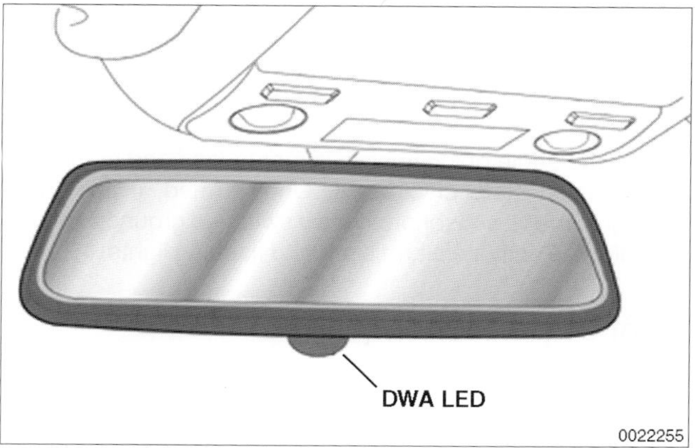

DWA LED

The DWA indicator LED is located in the rear view mirror. All E46 vehicles are equipped with the LED. It is not part of the retailer installed accessory DWA system.

The LED is provided with constant battery voltage (KL 30). The GM V provides a switched ground signal providing the various blinking signals used to convey DWA status to the vehicle operator. DWA LED status is summarized in **Table b**.

Table b. DWA LED status

DWA status	DWA LED condition
Disarmed	OFF
Armed	Continual slow flash
Armed with one or more monitored inputs not in CLOSED position (trunk not closed, etc.)	Rapid flash for 10 seconds, then continual slow flash
Alarm activated	Rapid flash for 5 minutes, then continual slow flash
Rearmed in less than 10 seconds	ON for 1 second
Disarmed after activated alarm	Rapid flash for 10 seconds, then OFF

Tilt sensor

Located in the right trunk area above the battery, the solid state tilt sensor monitors the vehicle parked angle when DWA is armed. The sensor requires three signal wires to perform its function:

- **KL 30.** Constant battery voltage
- **STDWA signal.** Switched ground (provided by GM V) indicates DWA armed / disarmed status. Tilt sensor relays STDWA signal to alarm siren and interior protection sensor.
- **NG signal.** Switched ground output signal to GM V, used for two purposes:
  -Momentary acknowledgment that tilt sensor received STDWA and is currently monitoring vehicle angle.
  -If tilt sensor detects change in vehicle angle when DWA is armed, NG signal is switched ON to inform GM V to activate alarm siren.

When the tilt sensor receives the STDWA signal from the GM V, the angle of the vehicle is memorized and monitored by the solid state electronics. Once armed, if the angle changes, the tilt sensor provides a switched ground signal to the GM V to activate alarm siren and flashing lights.

Interior protection (UIS)

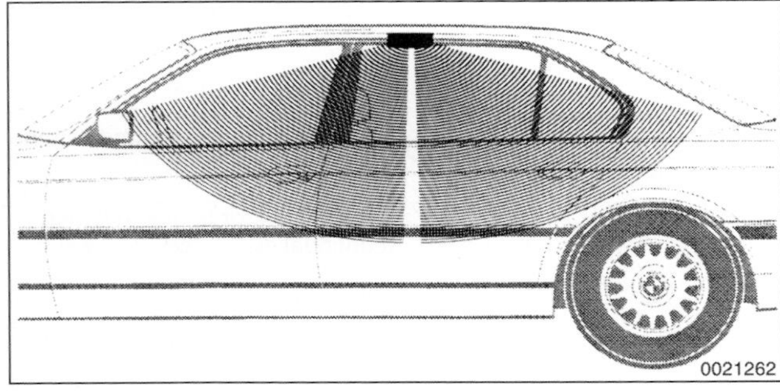

The combined ultrasonic transmitter and receiver in UIS monitors the vehicle interior for motion.

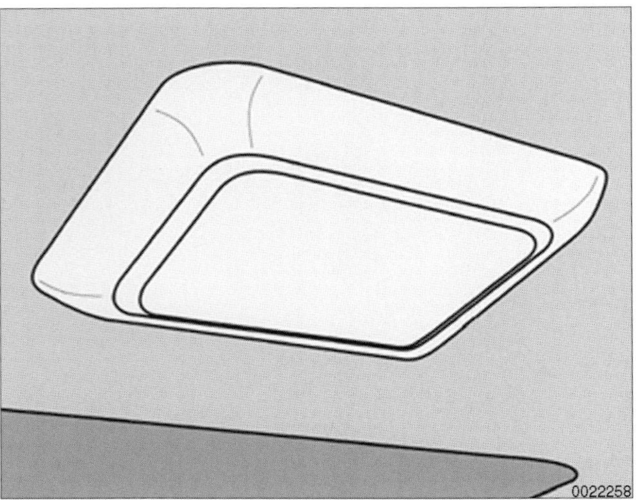

The UIS is mounted in the center of the headliner panel even with the door pillar (B-pillar). Due to the design of the vehicles interior, the sensor is unidirectional and must be installed in the proper direction to ensure proper operation of the system (trim cover ensures directional installation).

Every time the DWA system is armed (STDWA signal), the sensor adapts to stationary interior objects. The sensor emits ultrasonic waves in a programmed timed cycle. It receives echoes of the emitted signals. The UIS amplifies the received sound wave signals and compares them with the transmitted waves. The UIS also checks the incoming echoes for background hiss (wind noise through a partially open window) and adapts for this.

If the echoes are consistently similar, no movement is detected. If the echoes are altered or inconsistent, the UIS changes to a constant cycle and the echo is compared again. If the inconsistency is still present the UIS sends the activate siren signal (INRS) to the GM V.

As with the tilt sensor, the UIS is also switched OFF when the vehicle is locked two times within ten seconds. This allows the sensor to be switched OFF for transportation purposes.

Convertible interior protection (SDR)

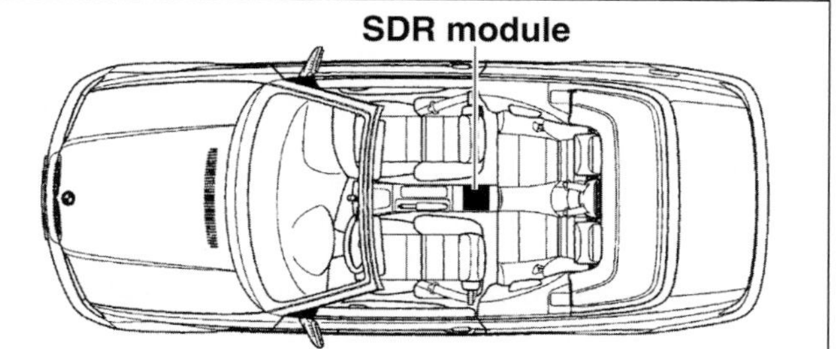

In Convertible models, the interior motion detector for the alarm system is a short distance radar (SDR) detector located on the center tunnel, under the center console next to the parking brake handle. The central position allows the most effective monitoring of the vehicle interior.

The SDR detector consists of two printed circuit boards, one being the transmitter / receiver and the other the processing electronics. The module housing is highly conductive material for high frequency transmission.

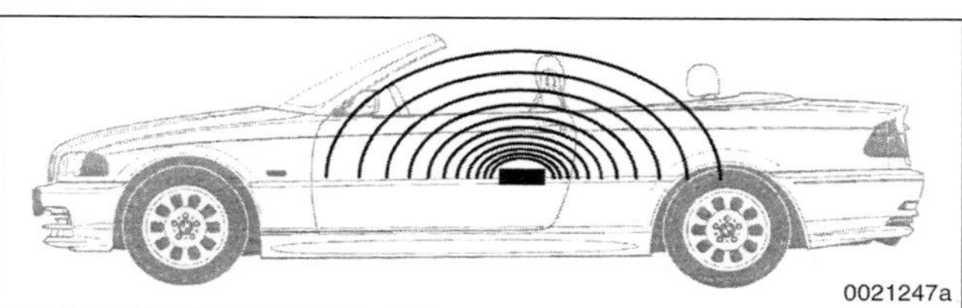

The SDR sensor transmits an electromagnetic field in a hemispherical pattern within the vehicle interior. The monitoring radius is preset in the module. The receiving antenna monitors reflected signals from the interior. The module evaluates these signals as a base line for vehicle security. Any objects that come into this monitoring radius are detected and evaluated by the SDR module.

The module operates in pulse mode. The radar unit transmits a signal, then pauses for the reflected signals to be received by the module.

The detection range of the radar is adjusted by rapid switching when the system is armed. This allows the sensor to adjust its range to either the windshield with the top lowered or to the soft top when it is raised.

The module signals the GM V to trigger the alarm if a new object is detected within its sensing hemisphere. However, false alarms may be triggered by objects falling into the interior when the system is armed with the top lowered. Also, large metal objects, such as the seat backrests, shield the microwave pulse and create a sensor "shadow" effect in the interior.

As with the tilt sensor and the UIS, the SDR sensor can be switched OFF by activating the central locking system twice within 10 seconds.

Alarm siren

The DWA siren is installed in the right rear engine compartment. This location provides a secure position with loud acoustic output.

The siren contains electronic circuitry and a rechargeable battery that is used to power the siren if the vehicle battery is

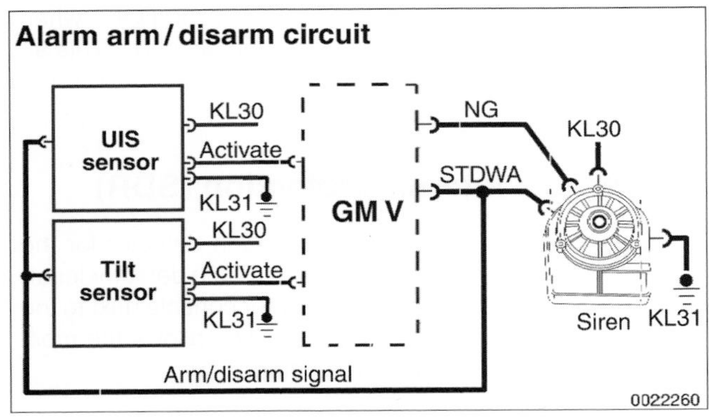

disconnected. The siren battery is recharged from the vehicle battery when DWA is not in the armed state.

The siren has four wires connecting it to the alarm system:

- **KL 30** (power)
- **KL 31** (ground)
- **STDWA signal** (arm / disarm signal from GM V)
- **NG signal** (activate siren output signal to the GM V)

The arm / disarm output signal from the GM V (STDWA) is provided to the tilt sensor, UIS sensor and the siren simultaneously. The arm / disarm signal is a switched ground that signals the components of DWA armed / disarmed status.

The activate the siren, the NG signal is high whether DWA is armed or disarmed. If a monitored input activates the alarm, the high signal to the siren is switched to a 50% duty cycle at the GM V. The control circuitry in the siren activates the siren. If the DWA is armed and the battery is disconnected, the siren circuitry recognizes the normally high NG signal as suddenly going low. In this case the siren is also activated.

Panic mode operation

When the trunk button on an FZV key is pressed and held, the GM V activates the siren for the panic mode. The panic mode is functional with either an armed or disarmed DWA system.

Emergency disarming

Emergency disarming occurs automatically if a key is used to turn the ignition switch ON and EWS accepts it. EWS signals the GM V to unlock the doors and to deactivate the DWA.

520 Seats

GENERAL

This repair group covers removal and installation of the front and rear seats.

Seat design and upholstery

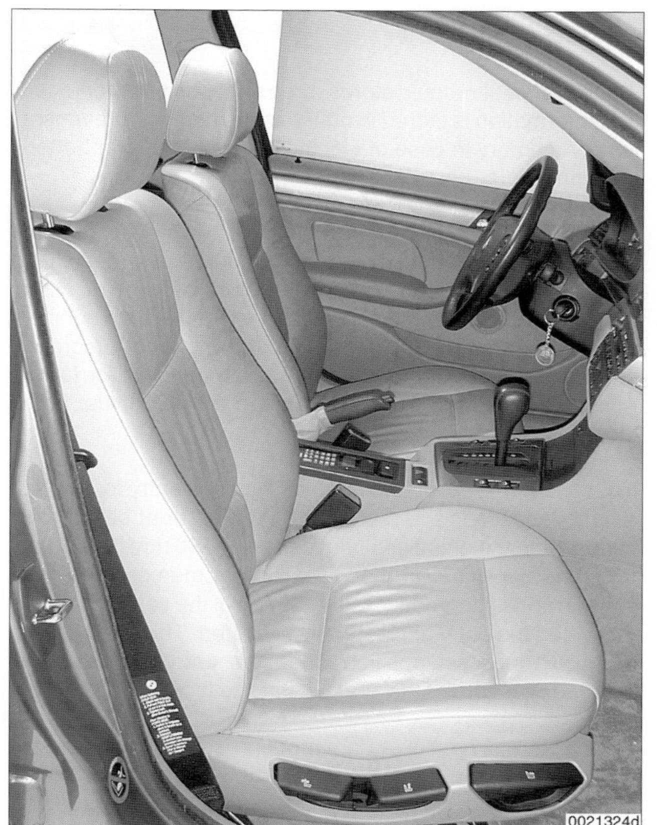

0021324d

E46 front seats come in either manual or powered version. They offer firm support and comfort. Their internal construction is engineered to work together with the vehicle suspension to absorb vibration. The internal ventilation system of the seats adds to the built-in comfort of these seats.

The Convertible front Seat Integrated Seatbelt (SGS) system incorporates the seat belt in the seat backrest.

Vinyl is the most common upholstery, and leather is an available option. The leather appears not only on the seats but on the door panels and other areas as well.

Front seatback nets are standard.

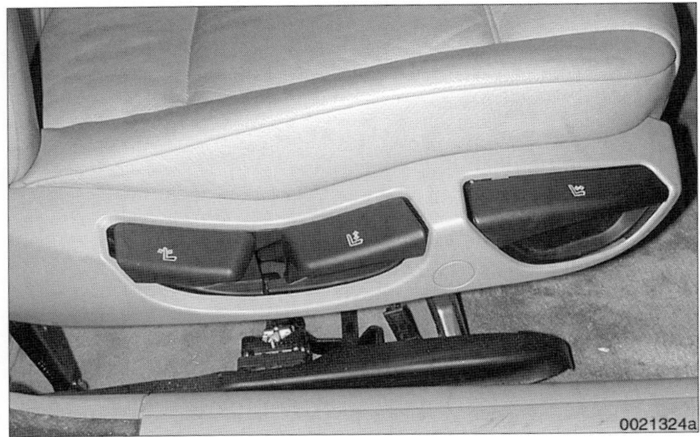

Seat adjustments

Regardless of level of trim, E46 seats offer the following minimum adjustments, with manual (**photo**) or power controls (**below**):

- Fore-aft position
- Backrest angle
- Cushion height
- Head restraints

M3 sport seats include an additional pneumatic power lumbar support.

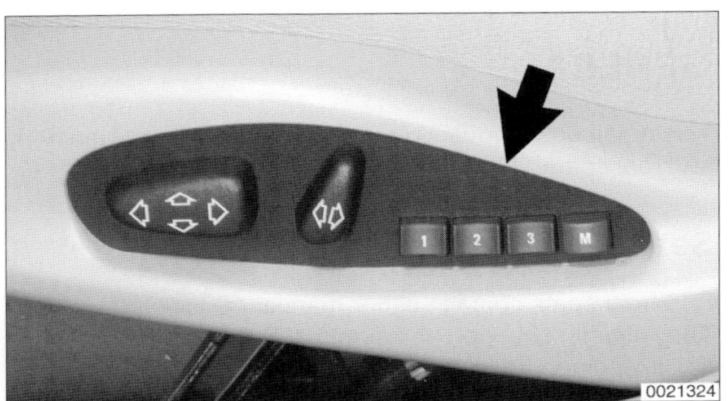

Seat memory system

In cars with seat memory, the driver's front seat incorporates two control modules: One in the seat adjusting switch (**arrow**) and the second under the seat cushion. The two modules process the following:

- Seat adjustments
- Comfort entry aid switch (2-door models)
- Seat backrest lock microswitch (2-door models)
- Seat belt fastened
- K-bus communication with the General Module (GM V) and instrument cluster

The driver seat module stores three seat positions for recall. The information is stored in non-volatile memory, preventing loss of memory in case of electrical power failure or battery disconnection.

The seat adjusting switch block in the driver seat communicates with the seat cushion control module over dedicated lines. The output stages for seat motor movement are in the seat cushion control module. Seat positions are recognized through the use of Hall sensors in the motors. All components of the seat memory system are monitored for faults. Access fault codes using BMW scan tool (DISplus, GT1, MoDiC) or equivalent.

In Coupe and Convertible models, the easy entry feature facilitates access to the rear seats. When a front backrest is folded over, the entire seat moves forward 90 mm (3.54 in) to facilitate rear entry. In models with seat memory, the seat control module memorizes the position of the seat and headrest when the entry aid feature is activated. The seat returns to its previous set position when the entry aid button is pressed rearward or the seat backrest is locked.

The passenger seat on 4-door models uses a simplified control system within the switch block and does not include a memory module. No on-board diagnostics are incorporated into the passenger seat on these models.

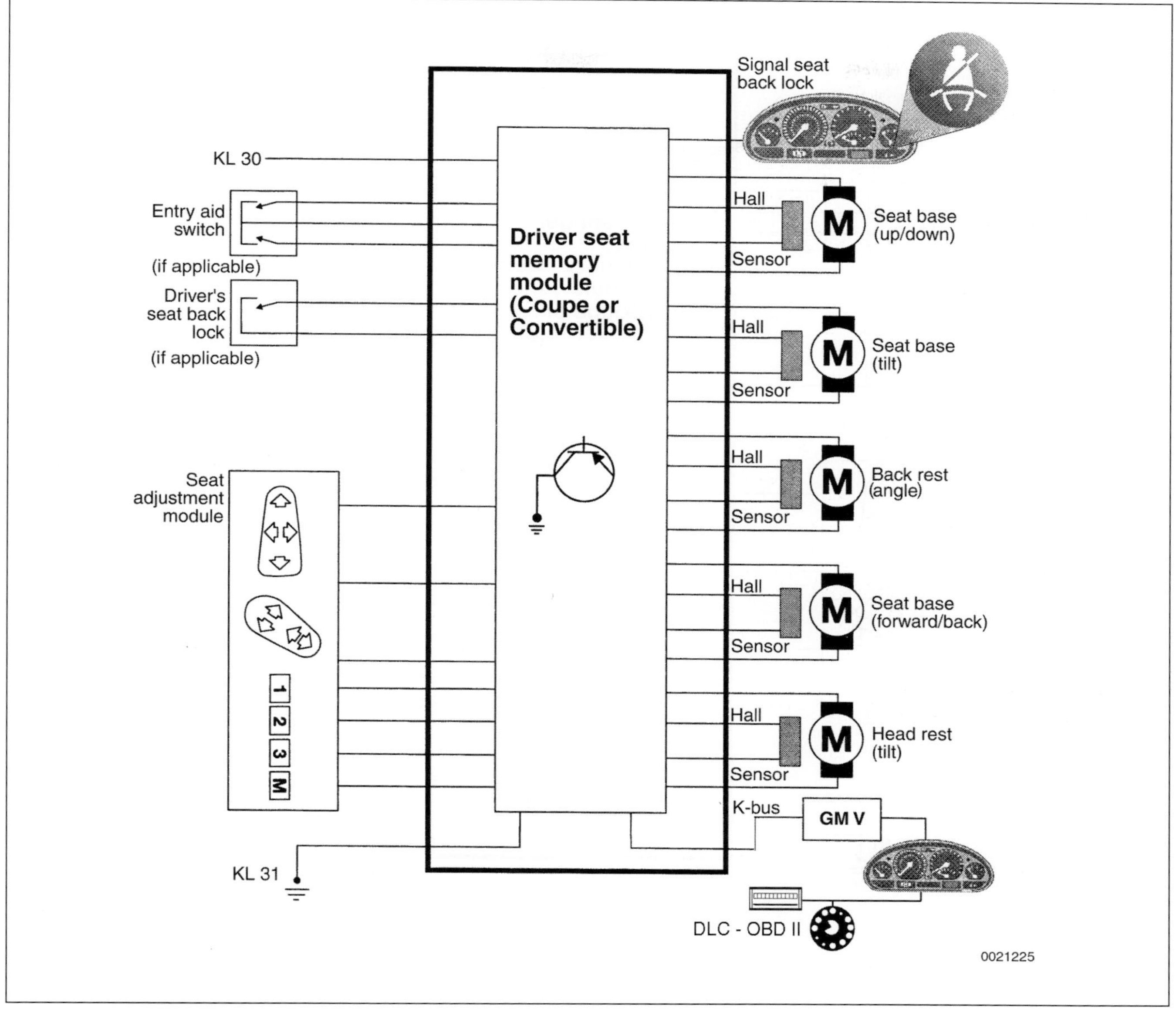
Signal seat back lock
KL 30
Entry aid switch
(if applicable)
Driver's seat back lock
(if applicable)
Driver seat memory module (Coupe or Convertible)
Hall
Sensor
Seat base (up/down)
Seat base (tilt)
Back rest (angle)
Seat base (forward/back)
Head rest (tilt)
Seat adjustment module
1
2
3
M
K-bus
GM V
KL 31
DLC - OBD II
0021225

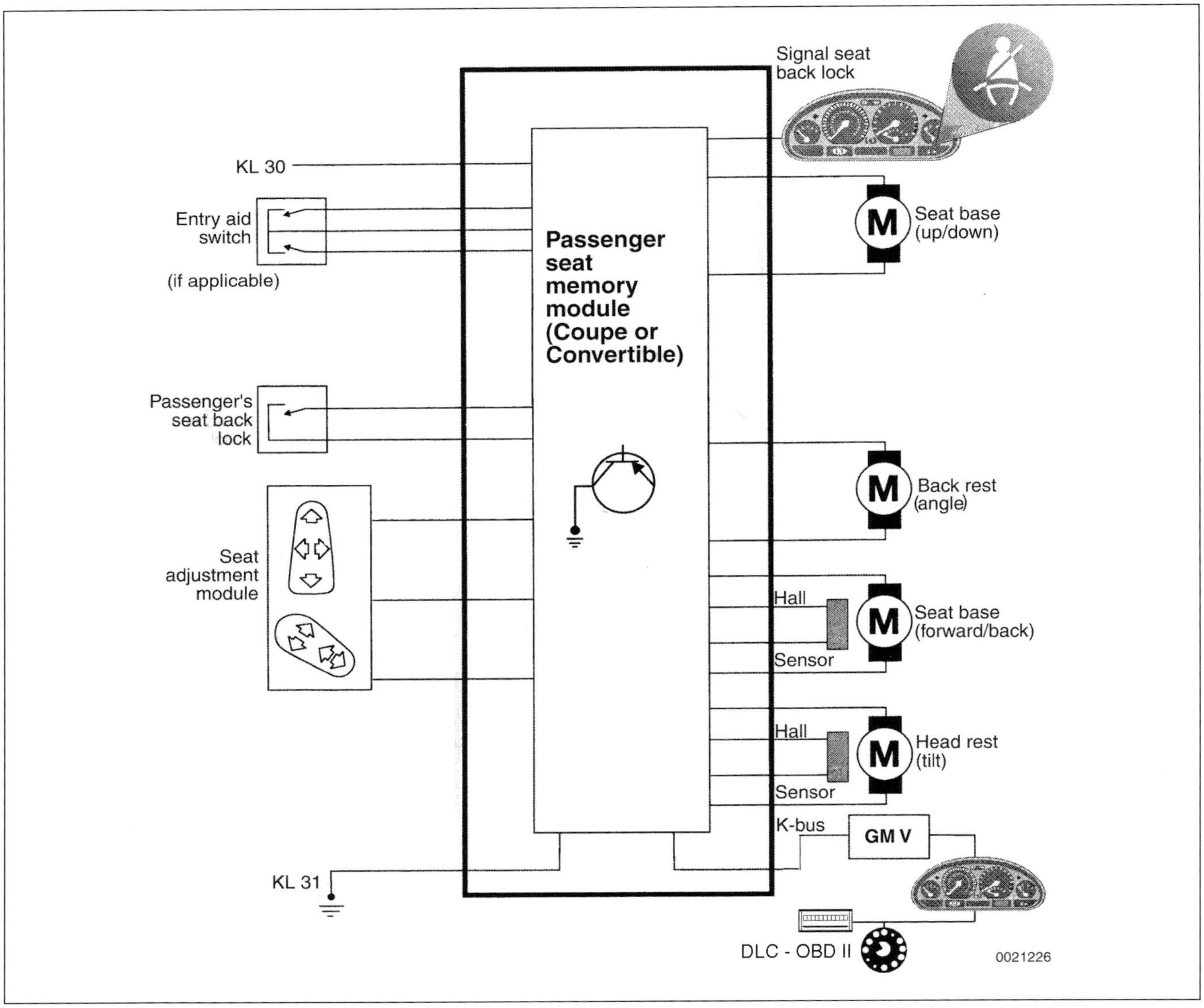

Signal seat back lock

KL 30

Entry aid switch

(if applicable)

Passenger seat memory module (Coupe or Convertible)

Seat base (up/down)

Passenger's seat back lock

Back rest (angle)

Seat adjustment module

Hall

Sensor

Seat base (forward/back)

Hall

Sensor

Head rest (tilt)

K-bus

GM V

KL 31

DLC - OBD II

0021226

Rear seat configuration

Split rear folding seats are optional in the Sedan and standard in the Sport Wagon and Coupe. They are split ⅓ right to ⅔ left with a folding center armrest in the left portion. The armrest, when folded down, is equipped with a storage compartment and cupholders.

FRONT SEATS

Seat removal and installation is similar for all versions. Seat disassembly differs in detail among the many models of seats.

Seat repair and component replacement is possible once the seat has been removed from the vehicle.

Front seat, removing and installing

WARNING —

- *The front seats are equipped with pyrotechnic seat belt tensioners. These tensioners are powerful devices controlled by the SRS system and should be handled with extreme care. Incorrect handling can trigger the tensioner and cause injury. See warnings and cautions in* **721 Airbag System (SRS)**.
- *BMW recommends that all repair or replacement work on pyrotechnic devices must be carried out by a qualified BMW technician.*
- *The airbags system contains a back-up power supply within the SRS control module. Allow a 60 second discharge period after disconnecting the battery cable.*
- *Pyrotechnic devices cannot be repaired. Always replace them.*
- *Never treat pyrotechnic components with cleaning agents or grease.*
- *Do not expose pyrotechnic components to temperatures above 75°C (167°F).*
- *Pyrotechnic components can only be tested electrically when installed, using BMW scan tool (DISplus, GT1, MoDiC) or equivalent.*
- *Do not fire a pyrotechnic gas generator prior to disposal. It must be fired by a special disposal company or shipped back to BMW in the packaging of the new components.*
- *During body straightening and welding with an electric arc welder, always disconnect the battery and the connection to the pyrotechnic gas generators.*

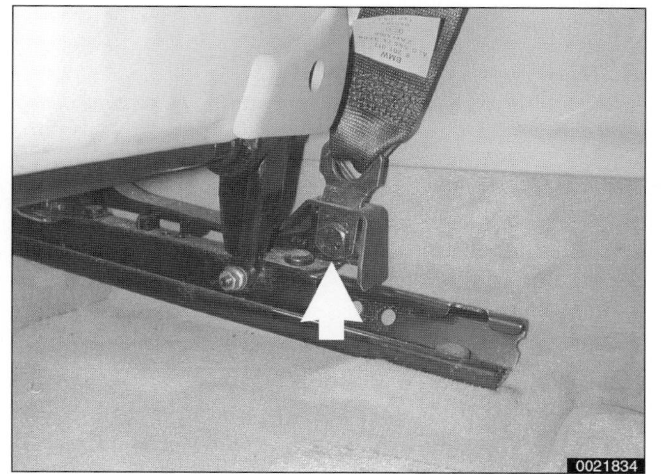

 4-door model: raise seat and move to its forward position. Working at base of seat near door, remove seat belt mounting bolt (**arrow**).

– Remove headrest (not Convertible).

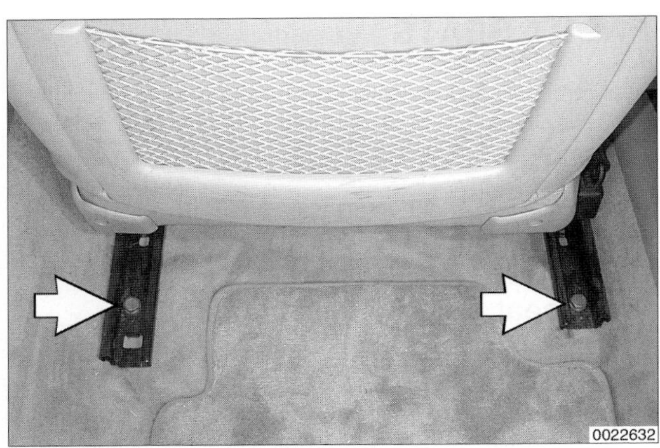

◀ Remove two mounting bolts (**arrows**) at rear of seat rails.

– Move seat to its rearmost position, keeping it raised.

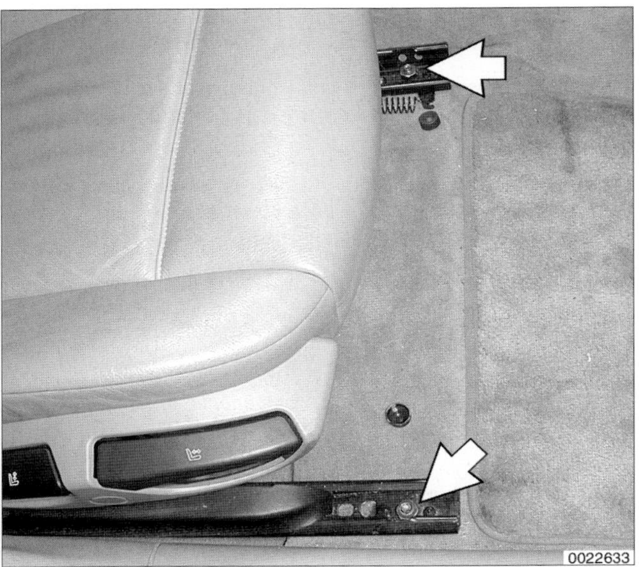

◀ Remove plastic caps over front seat mounting nuts, then remove mounting nuts (**arrows**).

– Disconnect negative (–) cable from battery.

> ***CAUTION —***
> *Prior to disconnecting the battery, read the battery disconnection cautions given at the front of this manual on page viii.*

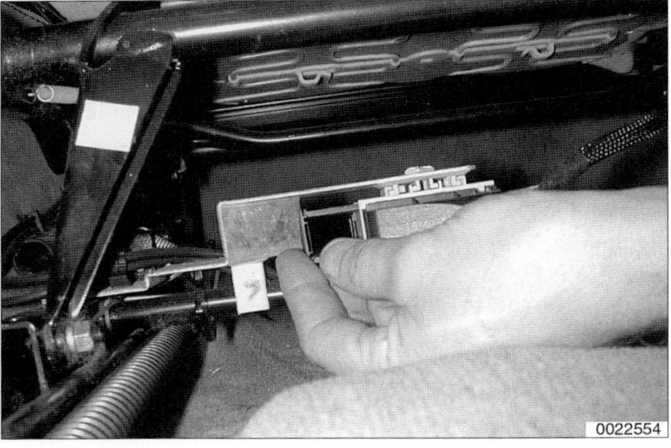

◀ Tilt seat back to access electrical harness connectors. Slide lock to release and disconnect. Cut or untwist wire ties as necessary.

– Remove seat from car. Headrests may be removed to provide additional clearance.

NOTE —
Use a blanket to protect door sill from scuffing by seat rail during seat removal.

– Installation is reverse of removal. Use wire ties or equivalent means to keep seat harness wiring from fraying.

Tightening torque
- Front seat to floor . . . . 45 Nm (33 ft-lb)
- Seat belt end to seat. . . . . 48 Nm (35 ft-lb)

REAR SEATS

Rear seat cushion and backrest, removing and installing (fixed seat back models)

– Pull front of rear seat cushion up to release clips. While holding front of cushion up, pull forward to remove.

◄ Remove rear seat backrest:

- Pull top outer corners of backrest forward (**A**) to detach from top retainers.
- Pull entire backrest up (**B**) to detach from bottom hooks.
- Slide backrest out sideways to clear seat belts.

NOTE —

If the car is equipped with heated rear seats, detach electrical harness connector(s) as you remove the seat components.

– When reinstalling, be sure to pull seat belts and buckles up through appropriate slots in seat cushion.

Rear seat cushion and backrest, removing and installing (fold-down seat back models)

– Pull front of rear seat cushion up and out of clips. While holding front of cushion up, pull forward to remove.

– Tilt backrests forward.

NOTE —

Remove rear headrests, if equipped, by pulling straight up.

◄ Remove backrest side section by pulling out (**A**) and up (**B**).

– Working between two sections of backrest, remove backrest center mount screws.

– Remove outer backrest mounting screws.

– Raise backrests in middle slightly and separate left and right backrest guide. Lift backrest(s) out through rear door(s).

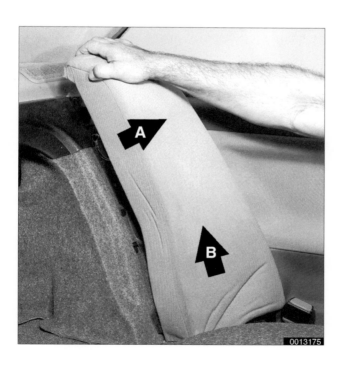

540 Sunroof

GENERAL

This repair group covers the slide-tilt sunroof assembly.

Component locations, initialization, sunroof panel replacement, and sunroof height adjustment are covered. Replacement of the cable assembly or frame require that the headliner be removed. Removal and repair of the sunroof assembly and other components inside the roof cavity is beyond the scope of this manual.

Sunroof electronic controls, initializing

Initialize the sunroof in the following situations:

- Malfunctions such as lack of one-touch function, lack of comfort opening / closing or lack of pinch protection
- If sunroof motor has been removed and reinstalled
- If power supply to sunroof has been interrupted
- If repairs have been performed on slide-tilt mechanism

Normalization

During normalization the mechanical end positions of the sunroof are detected and stored by the General Module (GM V).

0021832

Press and hold sunroof switch in “lift” direction.

- After reaching end position, keep switch pressed for approximately 20 seconds longer.
- The sunroof motor will briefly jerk upwards, signalling normalization is complete.

Characteristic curve

The characteristic resistance curve of the E46 sunroof is learned using coding software. This resets the pinch-protection feature. See your BMW dealer service department.

540

Sunroof panel, emergency closing

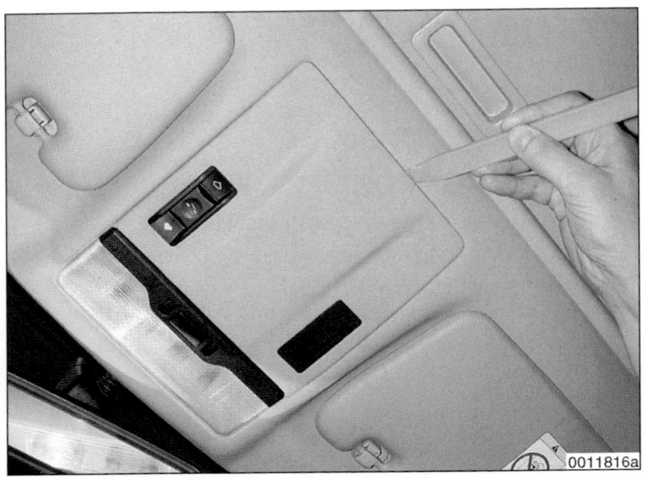
0011816a

◀ Remove access panel from below sunroof motor by gently prying at the rearmost edge with a plastic tool.

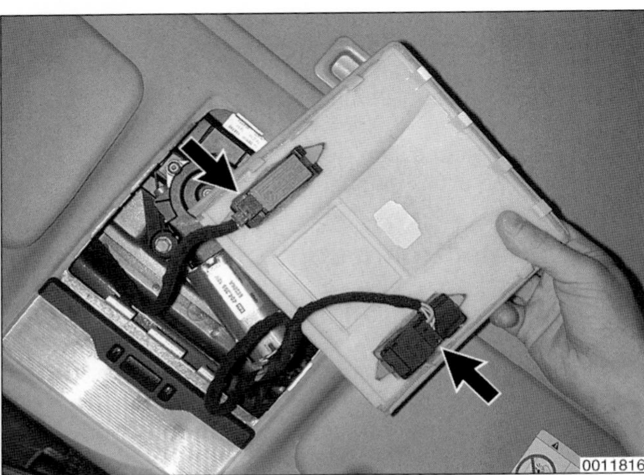
0011816

◀ Disconnect the electrical connections (**arrows**) and lay switch panel aside.

0011817

◀ Insert Allen key into drive in sunroof motor and turn to manually close sunroof.

NOTE —

The Allen key for manually (emergency) closing the sunroof is in the tool kit in the trunk lid (Sedan, Coupe, Convertible) or under the cargo area floor panel (Sport Wagon).

Sunroof panel, adjusting

NOTE —

If water is entering car through headliner, be sure to check drains in front corners of sunroof carrier

The sunroof is controlled by a set of cables that move the sunroof panel along guide rails when the motor is operated. The sunroof can be adjusted without removing it from the car.

The sunroof panel should be adjusted under the following circumstances:

- Sunroof misaligned with roof
- Sunroof does not close squarely
- Wind noise at high speeds (sunroof closed)
- Sunroof has been removed

Correct sunroof alignment:

- Fully close sunroof.
- Use credit card to test for even gap. Card should insert through gap with equal resistance all around sunroof perimeter.

– To adjust sunroof height, shut sunroof fully.

0021996

Slide sunroof liner back into roof cavity until approx. 90 mm (3.5 in) is exposed.

Sunroof panel is retained by three Torx screws (**arrows**) on each side. Adjust sunroof height:

- Loosen Torx screws until sunroof can just be moved.
- Push sunroof panel forward.
- Push sunroof panel up or down until correct height is achieved.
- Tighten screws. Recheck height.
- Check sunroof function.

Sunroof height adjustment specifications

- Rear .... flush to1 mm (0.04 in) higher than roof top
- Front ....flush to 1 mm (0.04 in) lower than roof top

Tightening torque

- Sunroof panel to roof (Torx) ....4.5 Nm (40 in-lb)

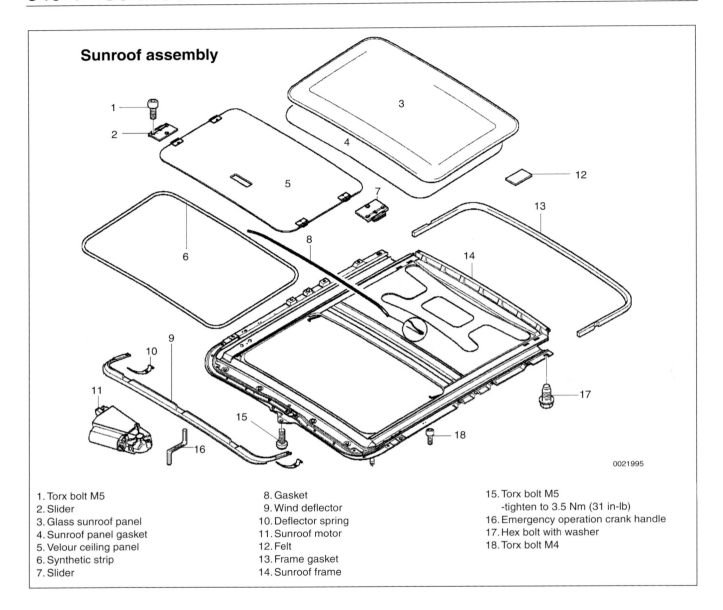

Sunroof assembly

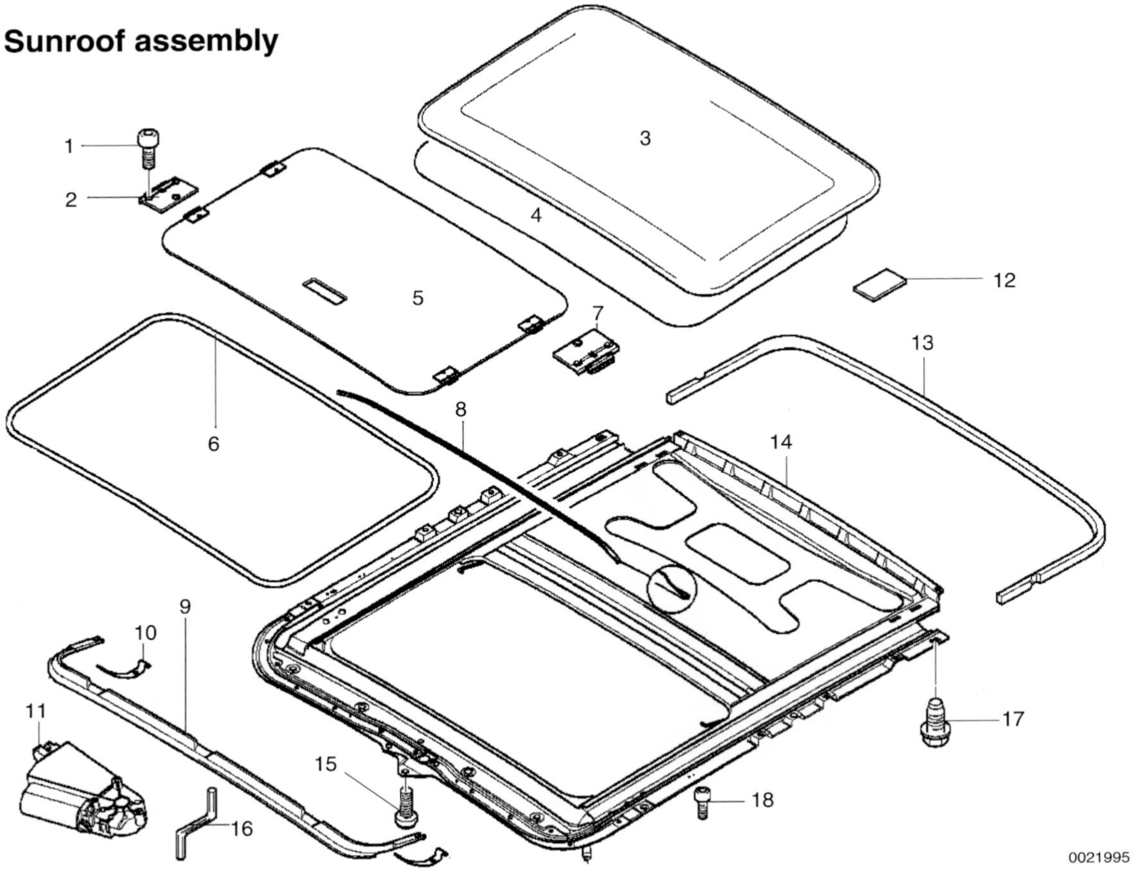

0021995

1. Torx bolt M5
2. Slider
3. Glass sunroof panel
4. Sunroof panel gasket
5. Velour ceiling panel
6. Synthetic strip
7. Slider
8. Gasket
9. Wind deflector
10. Deflector spring
11. Sunroof motor
12. Felt
13. Frame gasket
14. Sunroof frame
15. Torx bolt M5
    -tighten to 3.5 Nm (31 in-lb)
16. Emergency operation crank handle
17. Hex bolt with washer
18. Torx bolt M4

SUNROOF COMPONENTS

Sunroof assembly removal and installation involves headliner removal, and is not covered in this manual. After sunroof repairs be sure to follow initialization and adjustment procedures given earlier.

Sunroof panel, removing and installing

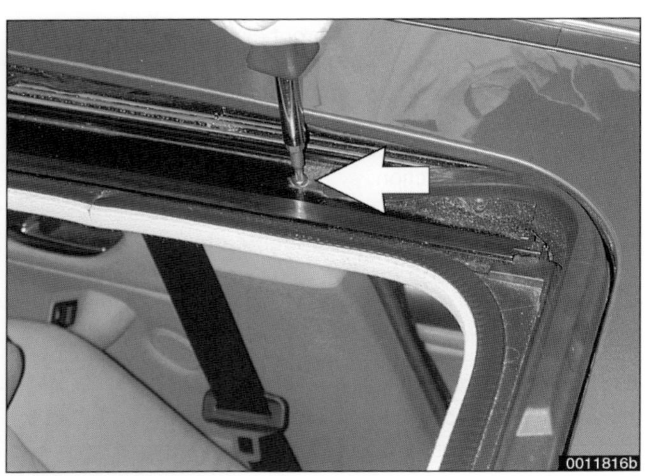

Open sunroof and remove wind blocker by removing Torx screw (**arrow**) on each side.

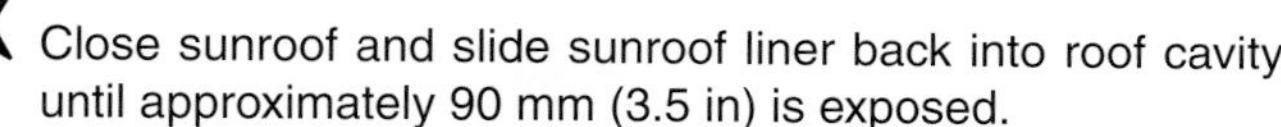

◀ Close sunroof and slide sunroof liner back into roof cavity until approximately 90 mm (3.5 in) is exposed.

◀ Remove three Torx screws (**arrows**) on each side, and lift panel out.

– Installation is reverse of removal. Adjust sunroof height and gap. See **Sunroof panel, adjusting** in this repair group.

Tightening torque

- Wind blocker to roof (Torx) . . . . 1 Nm (9 in-lb)
- Sunroof panel to roof (Torx) . . . . .4.5 Nm (40 in-lb)

Sunroof panel gasket, replacing

– Remove sunroof panel. See **Sunroof panel, removing and installing** in this repair group.

- Pull old seal from panel.
- Coat new seal and channel in sunroof panel with soapy water.
- Starting at back center of panel, install new seal, taking care to not pull seal too tightly around four corners of panel.

– Remainder of installation is reverse of removal. Adjust sunroof height and gap. See **Sunroof panel, adjusting** in this repair group.

Tightening torque

- Wind blocker to roof (Torx) . . . . 1 Nm (9 in-lb)
- Sunroof panel to roof (Torx) . . . . .4.5 Nm (40 in-lb)

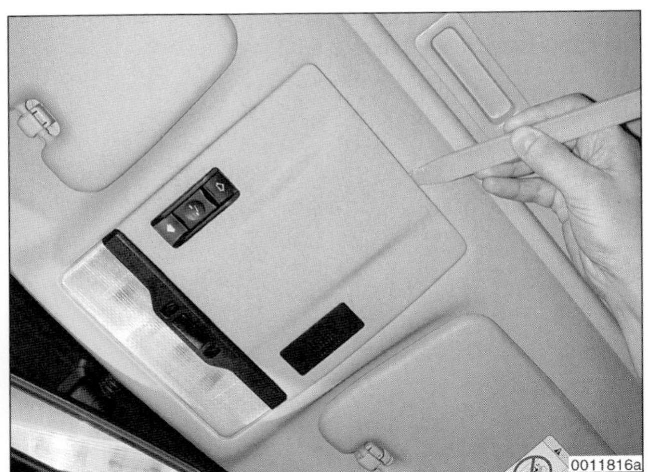

Sunroof motor, replacing

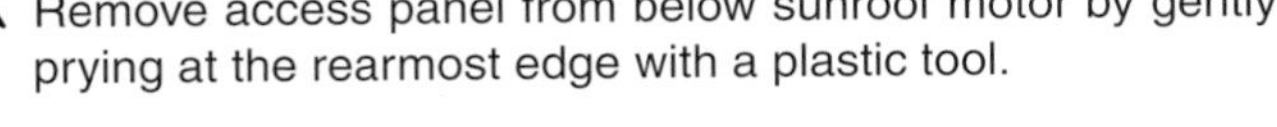

◀ Remove access panel from below sunroof motor by gently prying at the rearmost edge with a plastic tool.

◀ Remove sunroof motor mounting screws (**arrows**).

– Installation is reverse of removal. To reinitialize motor, see **Sunroof electronic controls, initializing** in this repair group.

Tightening torque

- Sunroof motor to sunroof carrier. . . . . . .2.8 Nm (25 in-lb)

541 Convertible Top

GENERAL

This repair group covers the automatic electro-hydraulic convertible top. Information on the Rollover Protection System is also included here.

NOTE —

- *The convertible top control module (CVM II) is located behind the left rear side trim panel. For the location of other convertible top electric components see* **610 Electrical Component Locations**.
- *The glass rear window in the Convertible is not replaceable separately.*

541

Convertible battery

BMW has designed a special Convertible battery tray with link rods (**arrows**) which serve to dampen body flexing and vibration.

> ***CAUTION —***
> *The E46 Convertible requires a special battery which is designed for constant vibration. A battery not designed for this will fail much earlier.*

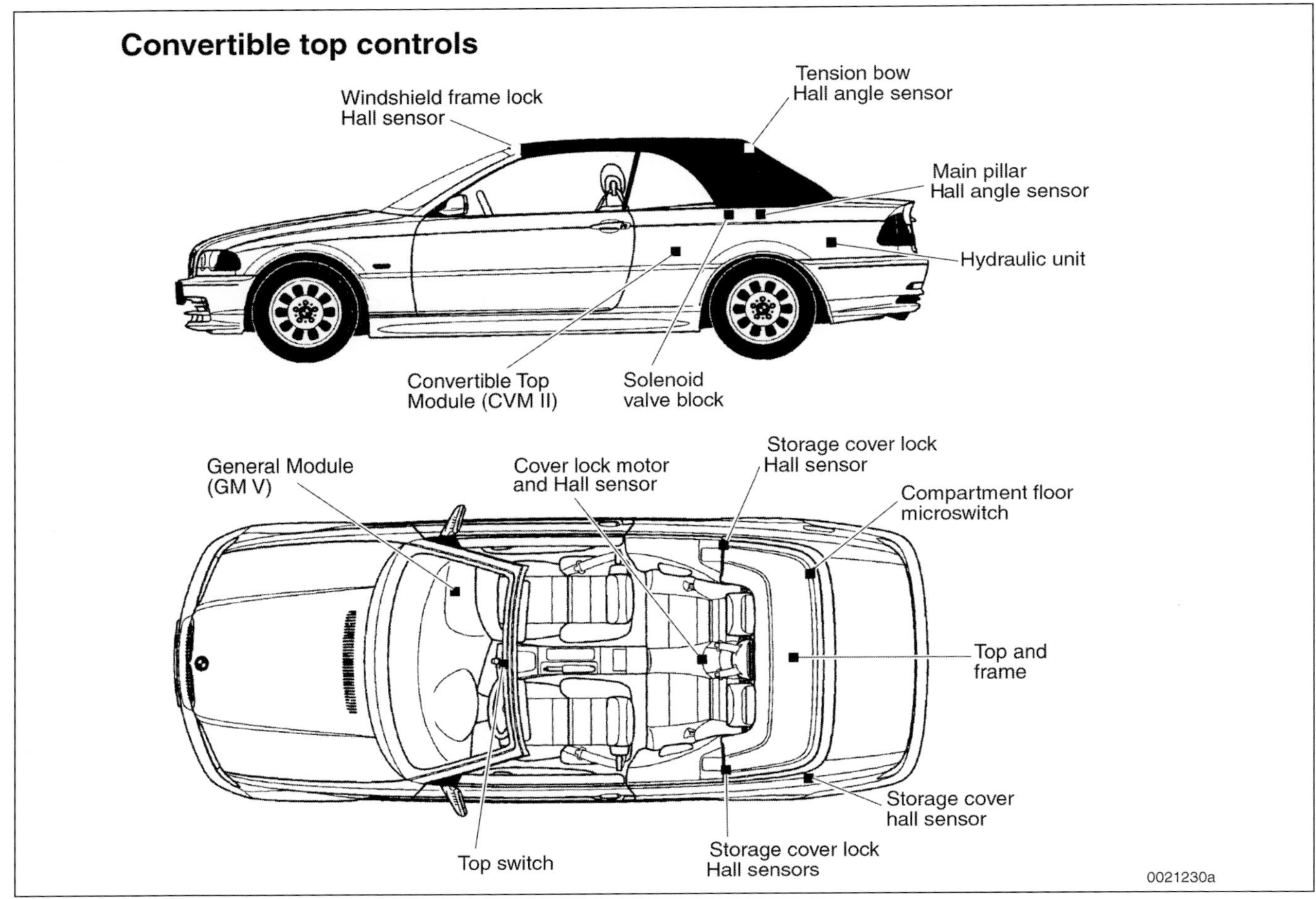

Convertible top operation

The E46 Convertible automatic top system opens and closes the top using hydraulic cylinders and electric motors.

The convertible top system features:

- Convertible Top Module (CVM II) with fault memory storage
- Electro-hydraulic operation
- Convenience opening using FZV (keyless entry) key or door lock cylinder
- Convenience closing using door lock cylinder
- Glass rear window
- Top monitoring during operation using Hall sensors and angle Hall sensors

Emergency operation

- Manually unlock top storage cover:
  - Remove center arm rest.
  - Lift seat upholstery below ski bag.
  - Press button on motor assembly to release motor from gear linkage.
  - Use hand crank (stored on assembly cover) to turn linkage assembly through access hole in motor assembly cover.
  - Unlock top cover and open.
- Switch off ignition. Hydraulic pressure is released in steps after approximately 10 seconds until all pressure is drained from cylinders.
- Manually raise or lower top. Use handcrank to lock or unlock top at windshield top frame.

Hydraulic fluid level, checking or filling

NOTE —
Make sure top is lowered into storage compartment and storage cover is closed.

- Working in trunk, remove trunk trim liner and soundproofing. If necessary, partially remove hydraulic unit to gain view of fill plug and fluid reference mark. DO NOT detach hydraulic lines.

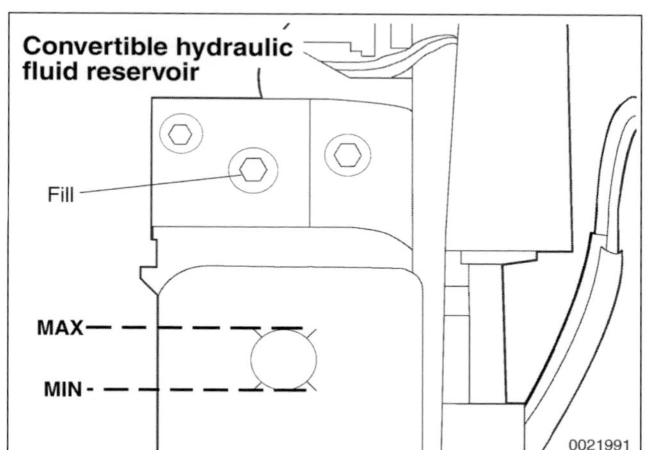

To check:
- Level must be between **MAX** and **MIN** marks.
- Reference mark is circle in translucent reservoir.

- To fill:
  - Detach hydraulic unit and pull out without disconnecting fluid lines.
  - Lay unit on its side and fill through fill plug.
  - Turn unit upright and recheck level.
  - Install new fill plug seal.
- To drain:
  - Detach hydraulic unit and pull out without disconnecting fluid lines.
  - Lay unit on its side and allow to drain through fill plug.
  - Turn unit upright and recheck level.
  - Install new fill plug seal.

Convertible top fluid
- Hydraulic fluid . . . . Aral Vitamol

Tightening torques
- Filler plug to hydraulic unit . . . . . . 10 + 1 Nm (7 + 1 ft-lb)
- Hydraulic unit to body . . . . 10 Nm (7 ft-lb)

NOTE —
The convertible top hydraulic fluid is supplied in the spare parts kit. To restock fluid, check with an authorized BMW dealer parts department.

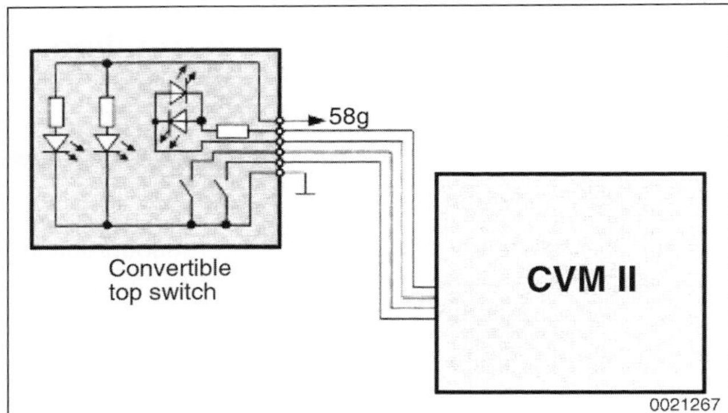

Convertible top switch

The convertible top switch assembly (**arrow**) is in the center console below the IHKA control panel. Two push buttons, one for each direction of travel, provide ground input signals to the Convertible Top Module (CVM II).

Two LEDs are positioned in the center of the switch assembly. The top LED flashes whenever the top is being operated and not locked to the windshield or stored completely in the storage compartment. The lower LED illuminates if the top switch is pushed (open top signal) and the storage compartment floor is in the folded up position. See **Top storage compartment floor** later in this group.

The top ceases moving once the switch is released. The hydraulics hold the top in position and remain under pressure for approximately 20 minutes if the ignition key is left in the ON position.

Convertible Top Module (CVM II)

The CVM II is installed in the left rear of the car behind the side trim (next to the seat). It contains the processing, controlling and monitoring electronics for top operation.

The CVM II communicates with the General Module (GM V) over the K-bus for operation of top storage cover and windows.

The CVM II is fully self-diagnostic and is capable of storing monitored faults. Fault code access and diagnosis is carried out over the K-bus with BMW diagnostic scan tools DIS or MoDiC.

Fault memory storage

Convertible Top Module (CVM II) fault memory is stored in NVRAM. Up to 16 fault codes can be stored in order of occurrence. A distinction is made between permanent and sporadic faults.

If a fault occurs during top operation, all top movement ceases and a fault code is stored in memory. Then the emergency closing procedure must be followed.

Depending on the location and type of the fault, it may be possible to raise or lower the top fully by pressing the switch in the opposite direction.

If the top switch is held ON more than 20 seconds after the top is completely raised or lowered, a fault code is set.
CVM II assumes a fault to ground in the switch or electrical harness. The ignition switch must then be cycled OFF - ON to clear the fault before the top functions again. The fault remains in memory until cleared with BMW scan tool (DISplus, GT1, MoDiC) or equivalent.

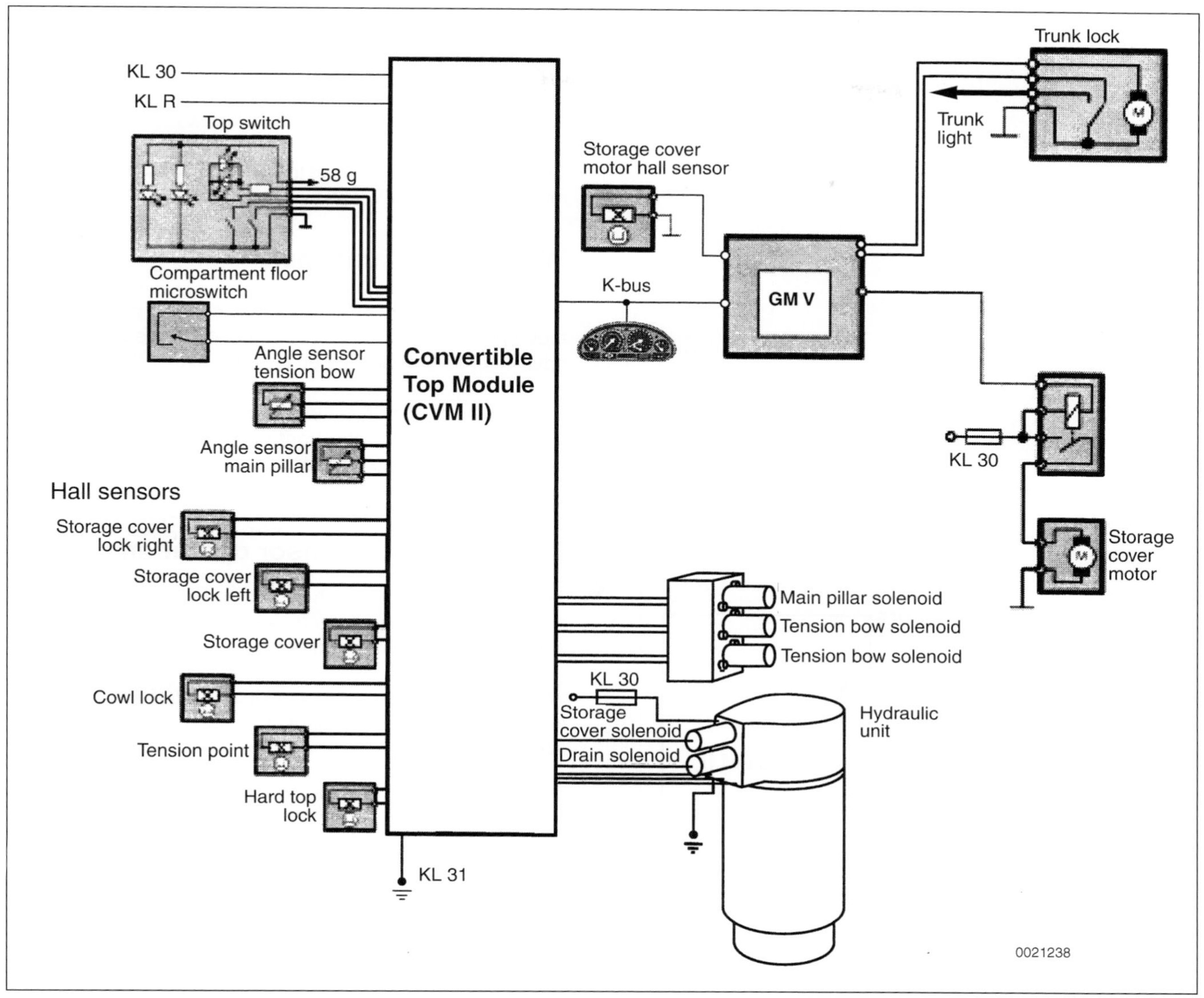

All sequenced movements of the convertible top have time-out limits preset in CVM II. If a time-out occurs before the end position is reached, movement is switched off to prevent damage to any of the top components.

NOTE—

The temperature sensor in the convertible top system signals CVM II to cease operation if hydraulic fluid temperature exceeds 95°C (203°F). However, any functions that have been started are completed before the system is switched off. If temperature exceeds 105°C (221°F) the system is immediately switched off. Close top using the emergency closing procedure. Automatic operation can be resumed when fluid temperature drops below 95°C.

Comfort operation

Comfort closing of the top is possible by using the key in the driver door lock cylinder. Holding the key in the locking position raises the top and closes the windows.

Comfort opening is possible from either the driver door or remotely using the FZV key.

Windshield frame lock

The windshield frame lock assembly consists of the top lock motor positioned in the center of the top frame and two lock drive mechanisms positioned on either side of the top frame.

The lock motor and drive mechanism unlock the top from the windshield and raise the front of the top past the tension point. Flexible drive shafts are used to activate the lock assemblies and drive the tension link rods.

Convertible top sensor operation

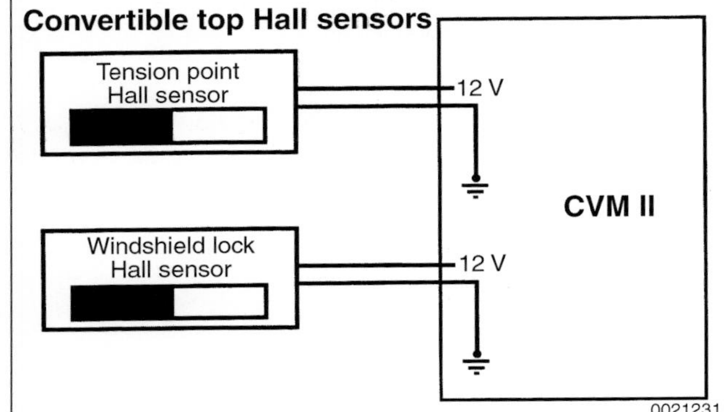

Three Hall sensors which detect the position of the top frame are located on the left lock drive assembly. All three sensors receive power and ground from CVM II.

Windshield lock sensor provides LOW signal when top frame is unlocked from windshield. LED in convertible top switch flashes.

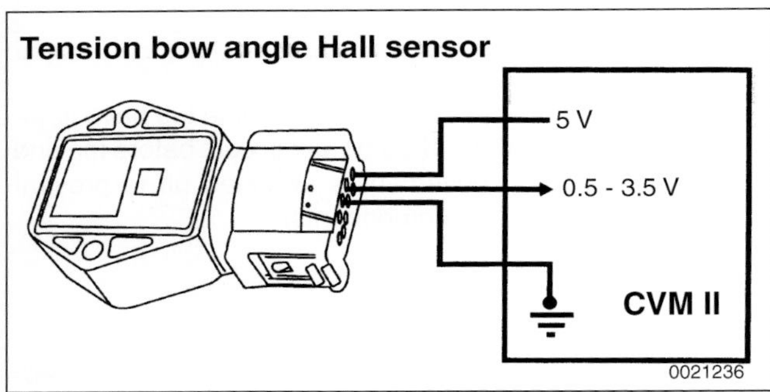

Tension point position sensor provides HIGH signal when top frame is raised past tension point. The angle sensor provides a linear voltage signal input to CVM II (approx. 0.5 - 3.5 volts) as tension bow moves from a vertical to a horizontal position.

Main pillar Hall angle sensor is similar in function and output to tension point position sensor. It is mounted on left side top linkage by left main pillar hydraulic cylinder. The CVM II uses input signal from main pillar angle sensor for top frame positioning.

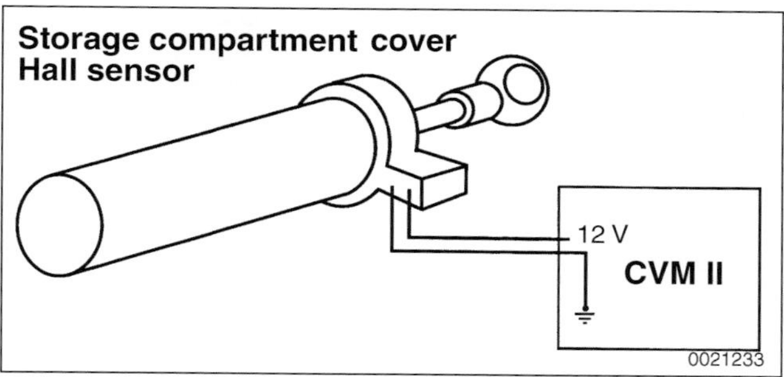

Top storage compartment cover

Top storage compartment cover position is detected and signalled to CVM II by a Hall sensor on left side storage cover hydraulic cylinder in trunk. The sensor provides a HIGH signal when storage cover is fully open.

The CVM II uses this input as a switching signal:

- Activate tension bow solenoid during top lowering.
- Activate main pillar solenoid during top raising.

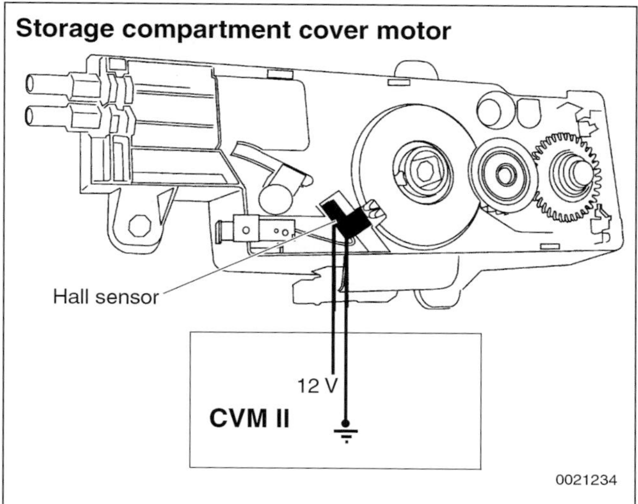

Top storage compartment cover lock motor

The convertible top storage compartment cover lock motor is on driveshaft tunnel under rear seat. It consists of a motor with Hall sensor, gear assembly and two bowden cables connected to cover locks on two sides of cover. The sensor detects locked / unlocked position of cover.

During convertible top operation (raising or lowering) CVM II signals General Module (GM V) over K-bus to unlock storage compartment. The lock motor runs 180° to unlock cover latches. The motor always turns in same direction to lock or unlock.

Once motor has turned 180°, the Hall sensor signals GM V to switch off motor. At the same time, GM V signals CVM II to continue top operation.

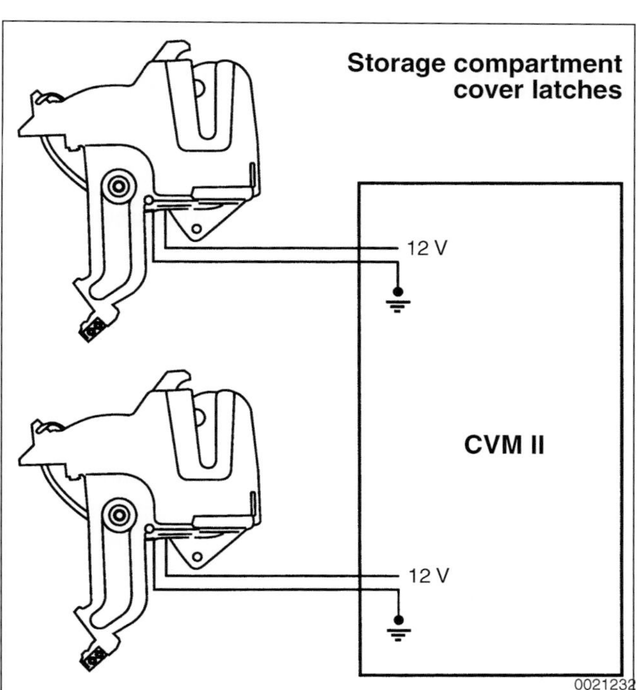

There are two storage compartment cover lock Hall sensors, one mounted on each storage cover latch. The switches receive power and ground from CVM II. Each switch input provides a HIGH signal when cover is unlocked and raised far enough by cover hydraulic cylinders to clear latches.

When cover is completely lowered by hydraulic cylinders, the Hall sensors send a signal to CVM II which signals GM V to relock storage cover.

Top storage compartment floor

The variable convertible top storage compartment is in the trunk. This feature allows the luggage storage area to be enlarged by approximately 40 liters (1.5 cu. ft.) when soft top is raised or removed for hard top installation.

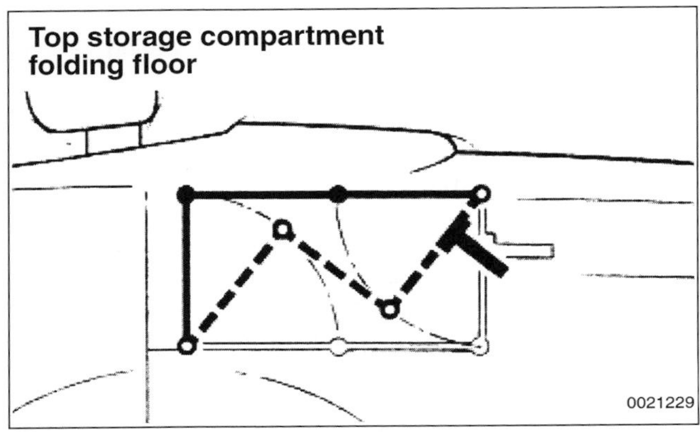

The plastic variable compartment floor is hinged at four point so that it can articulate and be rotated up into top storage space.

A lever on right side of variable floor actuates and locks floor into position.

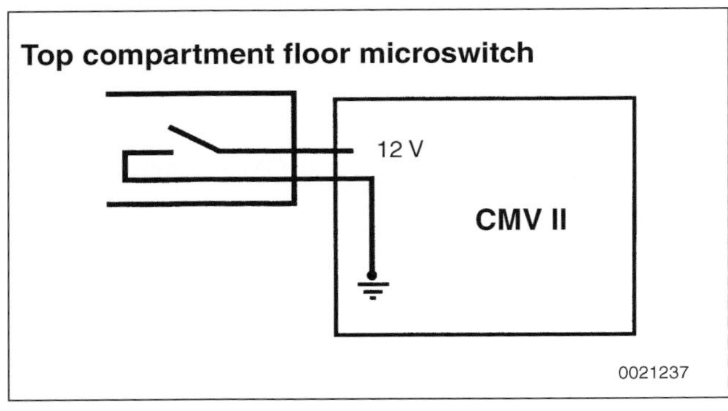

A dampening piston on right side maintains position of variable floor. The lower dampening piston hinge switches a microswitch on right side of variable floor when floor is in folded (raised) position. This signal to CVM II locks out operation of top.

CONVERTIBLE TOP COMPONENTS

Mechanical top components

The metal folding frame of the top is bolted to the sides of the car behind the door pillars (B-pillars).

The three layer soft top consists of:

- Fabric outer layer
- Middle fleece liner
- Inner liner

Refer to the accompanying illustration for mechanical component locations.

Convertible top mechanical components

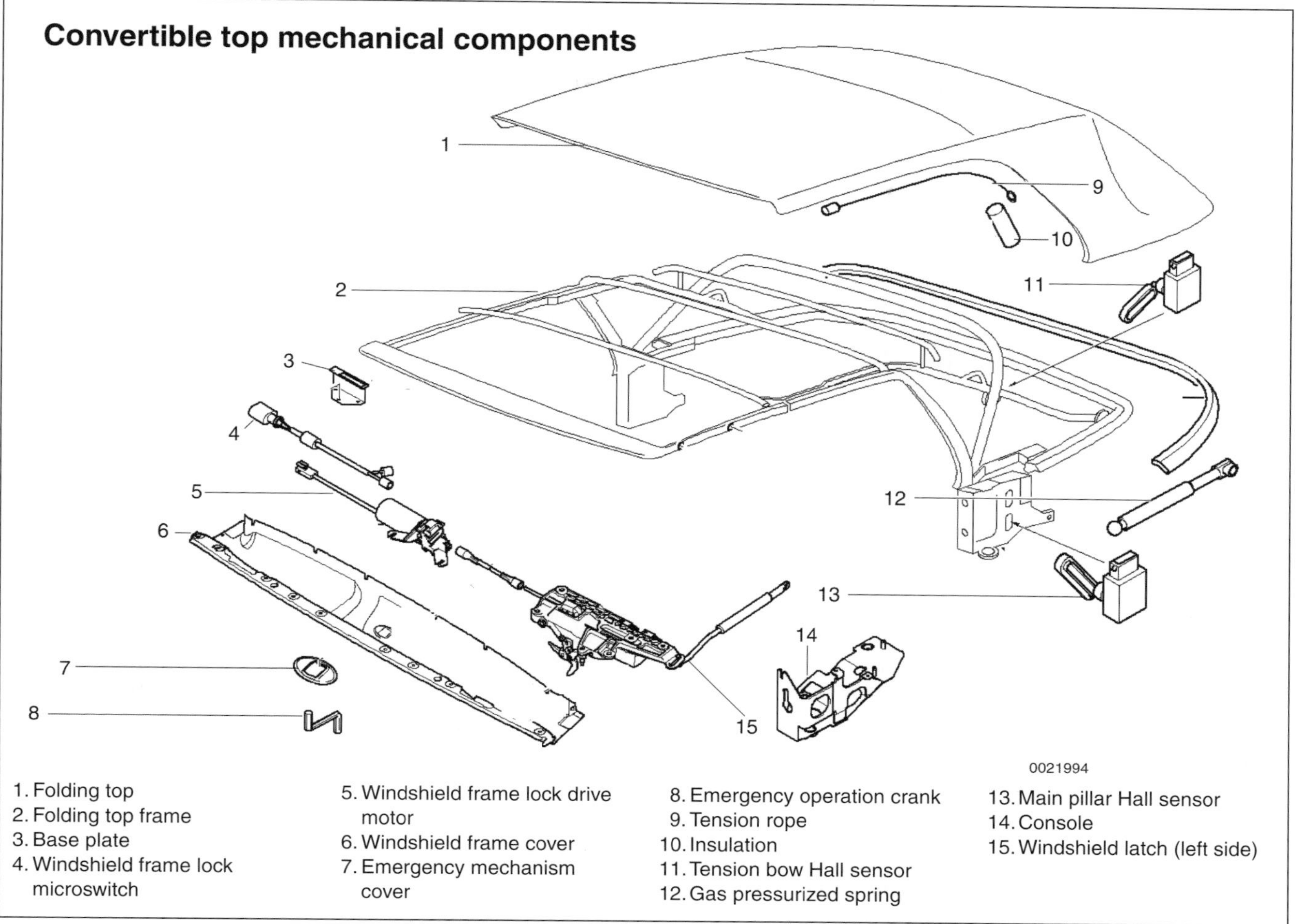

1. Folding top
2. Folding top frame
3. Base plate
4. Windshield frame lock microswitch
5. Windshield frame lock drive motor
6. Windshield frame cover
7. Emergency mechanism cover
8. Emergency operation crank
9. Tension rope
10. Insulation
11. Tension bow Hall sensor
12. Gas pressurized spring
13. Main pillar Hall sensor
14. Console
15. Windshield latch (left side)

Hydraulic system repairs

CAUTION —
- *When working on hydraulic system, system must be at zero pressure.*
- *Disconnect supply and return lines a with convertible top stowed and in untensioned state.*
- *Once hydraulic system has been opened, a function test must be carried out after work has been completed.*
- *Once hydraulic lines have been disconnected from hydraulic components, top must not be moved. Fluid will leak from separated coupling.*
- *Avoid scratching hydraulic piston rods. Even paint mist and welding spots are harmful.*
- *When working around hydraulic cylinders, cover with a protective cloth.*

Working in the trunk at the convertible top hydraulic unit, disconnect the supply and return lines and connect them to each other (short circuit). The system is thus closed and the couplings are protected against damage. The hydraulic sys-

Convertible top hydraulic components

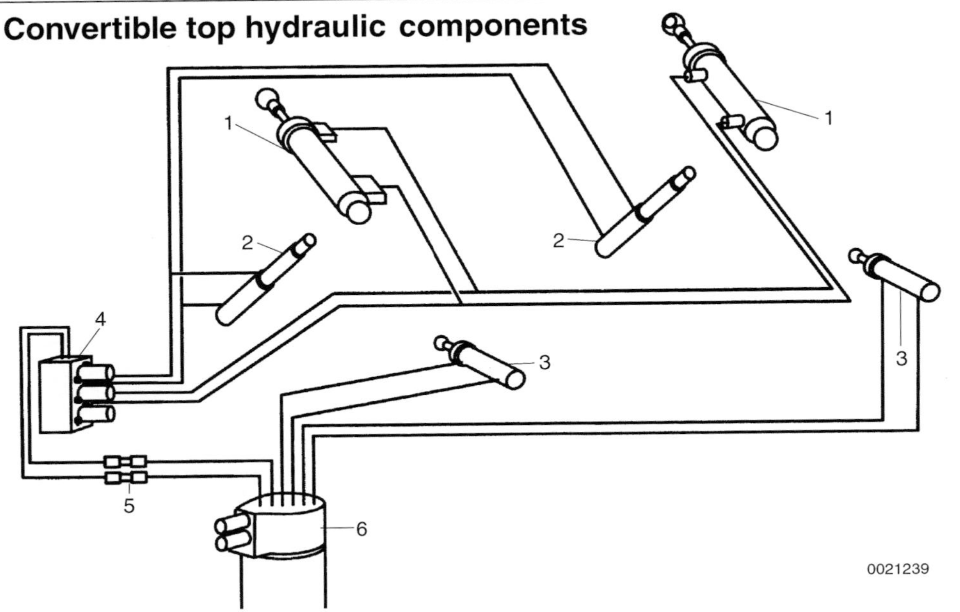

1. **Tension bow** (rear of top) hydraulic cylinders:
   - Operate on top frame linkage to raise and lower bow
   - Located on two sides of tension bow, at sides of rear window
   - Angle Hall sensor on left tension bow linkage detects bow position
   - Hydraulic lines for right tension bow cylinder routed under top fabric along tension bow
2. **Main pillar** hydraulic cylinders:
   - Actuate soft top frame
   - Located on two sides of top frame linkage
   - Angle hall sensor detects position of main top linkage
   - Hydraulic lines for right main pillar cylinder routed under top fabric along tension bow
3. **Top storage compartment cover** hydraulic cylinders:
   - Open and close storage compartment cover
   - Located in trunk
   - Left cylinder equipped with Hall sensor to detect fully opened position of cover
4. Solenoid valve block on left side of top frame:
   - **Solenoid V1** controls operation of main pillar hydraulic cylinder
   - **Solenoid V2** controls tension bow cylinders for raising top
   - **Solenoid V3** controls tension bow cylinders for lowering top
5. Quick disconnect in trunk
6. Hydraulic pump unit:
   - In left side of trunk behind trim
   - Mounted on rubber bushings and covered by sound insulation
   - Unit consists of:
     Hydraulic motor and pump
     Storage cover solenoid valve
     Drain solenoid valve
     Hydraulic fluid reservoir
     Hydraulic fluid temperature sensor
   - Operates at pressures of up to 200 bar (2900 psi)

tem cannot build up high pressure and convertible top can be moved manually.

Hydraulic system compontents and electronics are shown in the accompanying illustrations.

Terms and definitions used in diagnosing and repairing the convertible top hydraulic system are listed in **Table a**. Basic repair procedures for hydraulic system repair are listed in **Table b**.

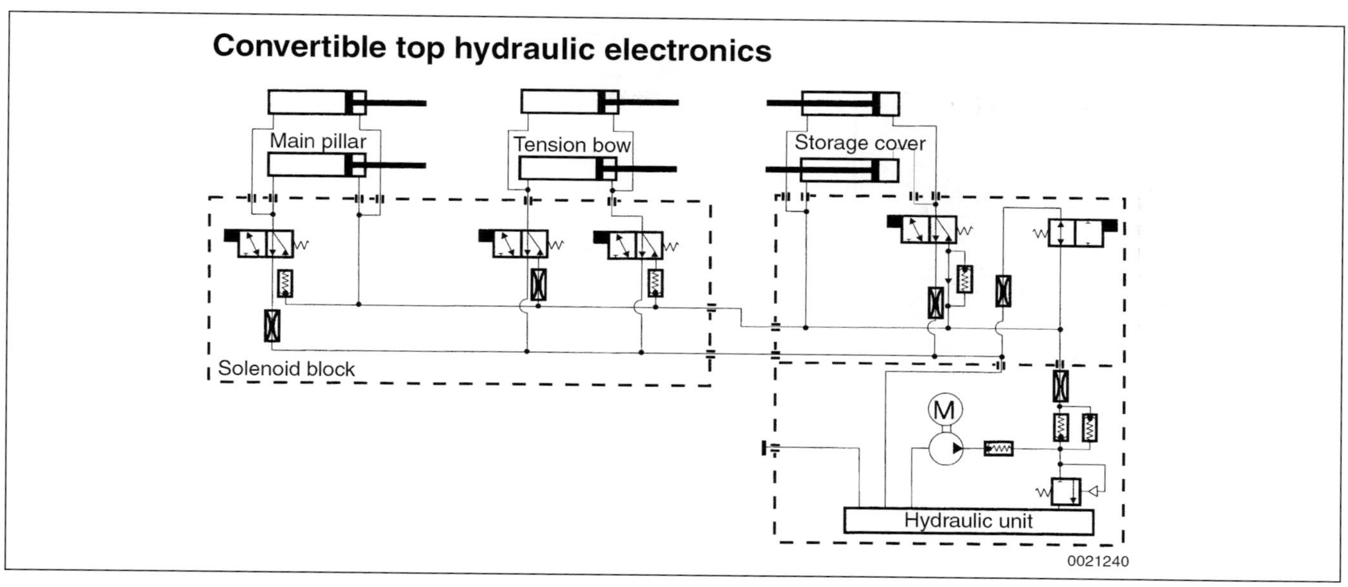

Table a. Definition of hydraulic system terms

Term	Action	Notes
Hydraulic system at zero pressure	Turn ignition to 0 position. Wait 15 seconds.	Hydraulic system has no or very low pressure.
Untensioned state		
Mechanical (emergency) actuation	Open or close top by hand.	See **Emergency operation** in this repair group.
Closed system	All hydraulic lines connected.	Even short-circuiting of lines is possible.
Function test	Open and close top several times (min. 3 times). Check hydraulic unit fluid level and top up if necessary.	Refer to Operating Instructions.
Short circuit	Unfasten quick release coupling. Connect supply and return lines to each other.	Hydraulic system cannot build up pressure. Convertible top can be moved.

Table b. Convertible top hydraulic system repair procedures

Operation	Procedures
Mechanical (manual) operation of top	a. Ignition must be turned off b. Hydraulic lines must be disconnected. (Reconnect when finished) c. After repeated actuation, system fluid is pumped into supply tank of hydraulic unit. If hydraulic components are replaced, there will be too much fluid in system.
Fluid level check	a. Stow convertible top and close storage compartment lid. b. Follow directions in **Hydraulic fluid level, checking or filling** in this group.
Fluid topping up or draining	

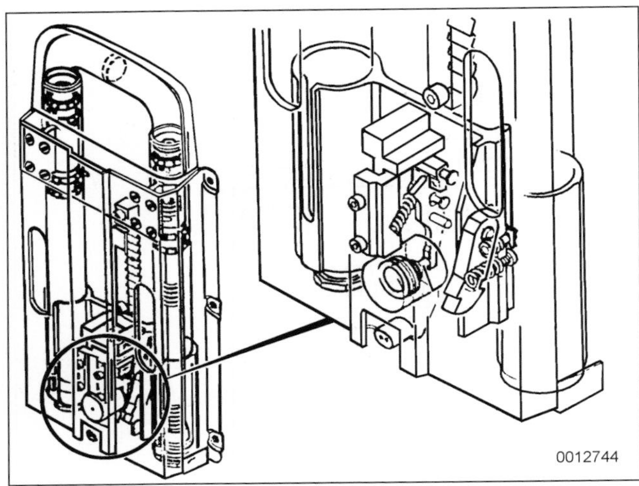

ROLLOVER PROTECTION SYSTEM

Two spring-loaded rollbar cassettes are mounted behind the rear seat. The cassettes are bolted into the reinforced carrier behind the seat backs. When retracted they are covered by the rear headrest which incorporates a flap at the back that opens when the rollbars deploy.

A rollover sensor, mounted in the rear behind the left rear seat back on the rollbar cassette, contains the electronics for rollover detection and deployment final stage for triggering the rollover bar solenoids. Two capacitors are installed for rollbar deployment in case of a power failure during a crash.

The rollover sensor performs a self-check every time the ignition is switched on. The sensor is connected to the diagnostic link (DLC) for troubleshooting purposes.

If faults are detected, the warning lamp in the instrument cluster lights up. In case of a crash, the system attempts to trigger the rollover cassettes to deploy even if a fault code is stored in fault memory.

NOTE —
Diagnosis of convertible top and Rollover Protection System are beyond scope of this book. Your authorized BMW dealer has proper diagnostic equipment and tools to carry out these tasks.

After deployment, the detent pawl in a rollover protection cassette can be retracted by pulling the reset lever forward so that rollbar can be pushed down and locked into the solenoids.

WARNING —
Ensure that area above and adjacent to rollover bars remains clear and unobstructed at all times.

CAUTION —
- *It is not possible to close convertible top with rollover bars extended.*
- *If a hardtop is mounted, be sure to install the protective rollover bar covers provided with hardtop to prevent damaging rear window in case of deployment.*

600 Electrical System–General

TABLES

Special tools

A 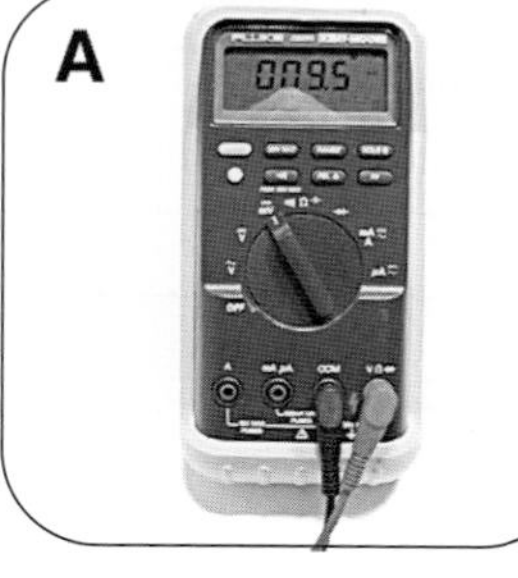

B 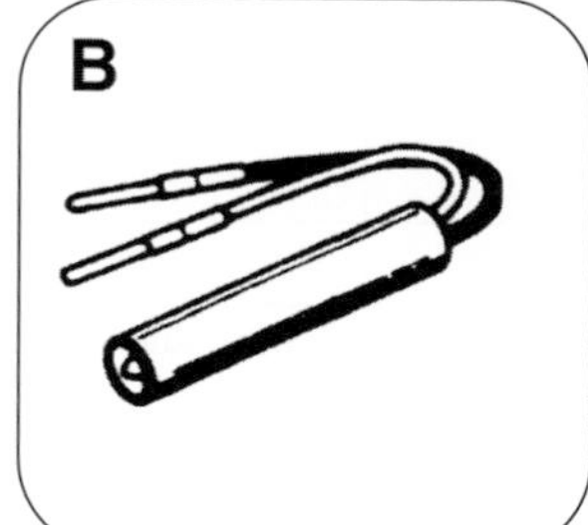

C 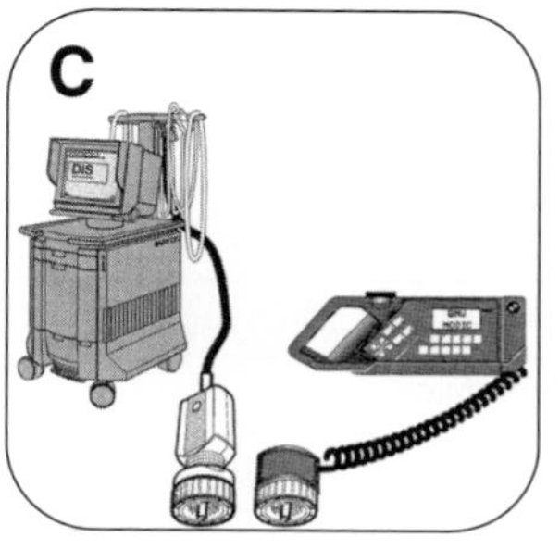

D 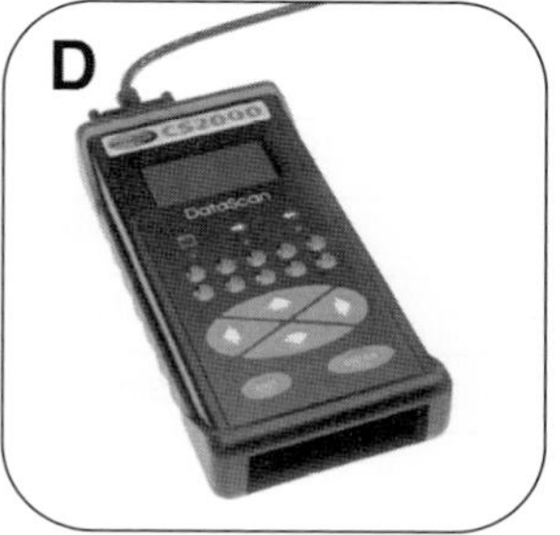

A . . . . automotive digital multimeter
B Baum 1115. . . . . .LED tester with thin spade probes (Source: Baum Tools Unlimited)
C BMW DISplus, GT1, MoDiC. . . . . .scan tools
D . . . . aftermarket scan tool

GENERAL

This repair group presents a brief description of the principal parts of the electrical system. Also covered here are basic electrical system troubleshooting tips.

For additional information on electrical systems and components, refer to the following repair groups:

- **121 Battery, Starter, Alternator**
- **400 Body–General**
- **512 Door Windows**
- **515 Central Locking and Anti-theft**
- **610 Electrical Component Locations**
- **Electrical Wiring Diagrams**

Electrical test equipment

 Always use a digital meter for automotive diagnostic work.

An LED test light is a safe, inexpensive tool that can be used to perform many simple electrical tests that would otherwise require a digital multimeter.

Many systems in E46 cars are designed with self-diagnostic capabilities. The quickest way to diagnose many problems is to use a scan tool to access diagnostic trouble codes (DTCs). See **On-Board Diagnostics** at rear of manual.

BMW acronyms

Acronyms used in wiring diagrams and in this manual are summarized in **Table a**.

Table a. Common BMW acronyms

Acronym	Component or system
A/C	air-conditioning
ABS	antilock brakes
ADB, ADB-X	automatic differential lock
AGS	adaptive transmission control
AIC	rain sensor
ASC	traction control
AUC	automatic air recirculation
BST	Battery Safety Terminal
CAN	Controller Area Network (bus)
CBC	cornering brake control
DBC	dynamic brake control
DK	throttle valve
DLC	diagnostic link connector (20 pin)
DME	digital motor electronics
DMTL	diagnosis module-tank leakage (DME MS 43.0)
DSC	dynamic stability control
DTC	diagnostic trouble code
DWA	antitheft alarm
ECM	engine control module
ECT	engine coolant temperature (sensor)
EDK	electronic throttle (DME MS 43.0)
EDR	electronic throttle system (S54 engine)
EEPROM	flash programmable read-only memory
EGS	electronic transmission control
EPROM	erasable / programmable read-only memory
EWS	electronic immobilizer
FZV	keyless entry
GM	General Module
HPS	head protection airbag
IAT	intake air temperature (sensor)
IHKA	automatic heating and air-conditioning system
ITS	head protection airbag
KL15	battery positive, ignition switch on RUN, power
KL30	battery positive (B+), power
KL31	battery / chassis ground
KL50	ignition start position, power
LDP	fuel tank leak diagnosis pump (DME MS 42.0)
LED	light emitting diode
LEV	low emission vehicle
LSZ	light switch module
MAF	mass air flow sensor
MBC	maximum braking control
MDK	motor driven throttle (DME MS 42.1)
MIL	malfunction indicator light
MRS	multiple restraint system
NLEV	national low emissions vehicle program
NTC	negative temperature coefficient resistor
OBC	on-board computer (board computer)
OBD II	second generation on-board diagnostics
ORVR	on-board refueling vapor recovery
PDC	park distance control (optional)
PWG	accelerator pedal position sensor
RDC	tire pressure control
RPS	rollover protection system
RXD	receive data line
SBE	front passenger seat occupancy sensor
SGS	seat integrated belt system
SHD	sunroof module
SII	service interval indicator
SM	seat memory module
SMG	sequential manual gearbox
SRS	supplemental restraint system
TCM	transmission control module
TDC	top dead center
TLEV	transitional low emissions vehicle
TXD	transmit data line
UIS	ultrasonic interior protection
ULEV	ultra low emissions vehicle
ZKE	Central Body Electronics

Electrical system safety precautions

WARNING —

- *Airbags, front seat belt tensioners and the Battery Safety Terminal (BST) are pyrotechnic (explosive charge) devices. Making repairs without the proper knowledge and special test equipment may cause serious personal injury. See* **721 Airbag System (SRS)**.
- *The ignition system of the car operates at lethal voltages. People with pacemakers or weak hearts should not expose themselves to the ignition system electric currents. Take extra precautions when working on the ignition system or when servicing the engine while it is running or the key is ON. See* **120 Ignition System** *for additional ignition system warnings and cautions.*
- *Keep hands, clothing and other objects clear of the electric radiator cooling fan when working on a warm engine. The fan may start at any time, even when the ignition is switched OFF.*

CAUTION —

- *Turn engine OFF and disconnect the negative (–) cable from the battery before removing any electrical components. Disconnecting the battery may erase fault code(s) stored in control module memory. Check for fault codes using special BMW diagnostic equipment.*
- *Prior to disconnecting the battery, read the battery disconnection cautions given at the front of this manual on page viii.*
- *Connect and disconnect ignition system wires, multiple connectors and ignition test equipment leads only while the ignition is OFF.*
- *Do not disconnect the battery with the engine running.*
- *Do not quick-charge the battery (for boost starting) for longer than one minute, and do not exceed 16.5 volts at the battery with the boosting cables attached. Wait at least one minute before boosting the battery a second time.*
- *Many solid-state control modules are static sensitive. Static discharge permanently damages them. Always handle the modules using proper static prevention equipment and techniques.*
- *Always switch a digital multimeter to the appropriate function and range before making test connections.*
- *To avoid damaging harness connectors or relay panel sockets, use jumper wires with flat-blade connectors that are the same size as the connectors or relay terminals.*
- *Do not try to start the engine of a car which has been heated above 176°F (80°C) (for example, in a paint drying booth). Allow it to cool to normal temperature.*
- *Disconnect the battery before doing any electric welding on the car.*

CAUTION —
- *Do not wash the engine while it is running, or any time the ignition is ON.*
- *Choose test equipment carefully. Use a digital multimeter with at least 10 MΩ input impedance, or an LED test light. An analog (swing-needle) meter or a test light with a normal incandescent bulb may draw enough current to damage sensitive electronic components.*
- *Do not use an ohmmeter to measure resistance on solid state components such as control modules or time delay relays.*
- *Always disconnect the battery before making resistance (ohm) measurements on a circuit.*

E46 ELECTRICAL SYSTEM

E46 cars are electrically complex. Many vehicle systems and subsystems are interconnected or integrated. In addition, the requirements of second generation On-Board Diagnostics (OBD II) are such that there are now many more circuits and wires in the vehicle than ever before. The components must exchange large volumes of data with one another in order to perform their various functions.

This use of dedicated data lines for each link in the system has reached the limits of its capabilities. The solution has been found in the use of specialized, vehicle compatible serial bus systems. The E46 bus system is summarized in **Table b**.

Table b. E46 busses

Bus	Circuits covered
K-bus	Driver information systems (instrument cluster, Check Control, on-board computer) Central Body Electronics (ZKE V) General Module (GM V) Seat memory (SM) Sunroof (SHD) Rain sensor (AIC) Telephone and sound system Headlight module (LSZ) Electronic immobilizer (EWS III) and anti-theft (DWA) Keyless entry (FZV) Park distance control (PDC)
M-bus	Heating and air conditioning (IHKA) components
CAN-bus	Engine management system (DME) Transmission control (AGS) Antilock brakes (ABS) Traction control (ASC) Dynamic stability control (DSC)
D-bus	Data link connector (DLC) OBD II connector Multiple restraint system (MRS II)

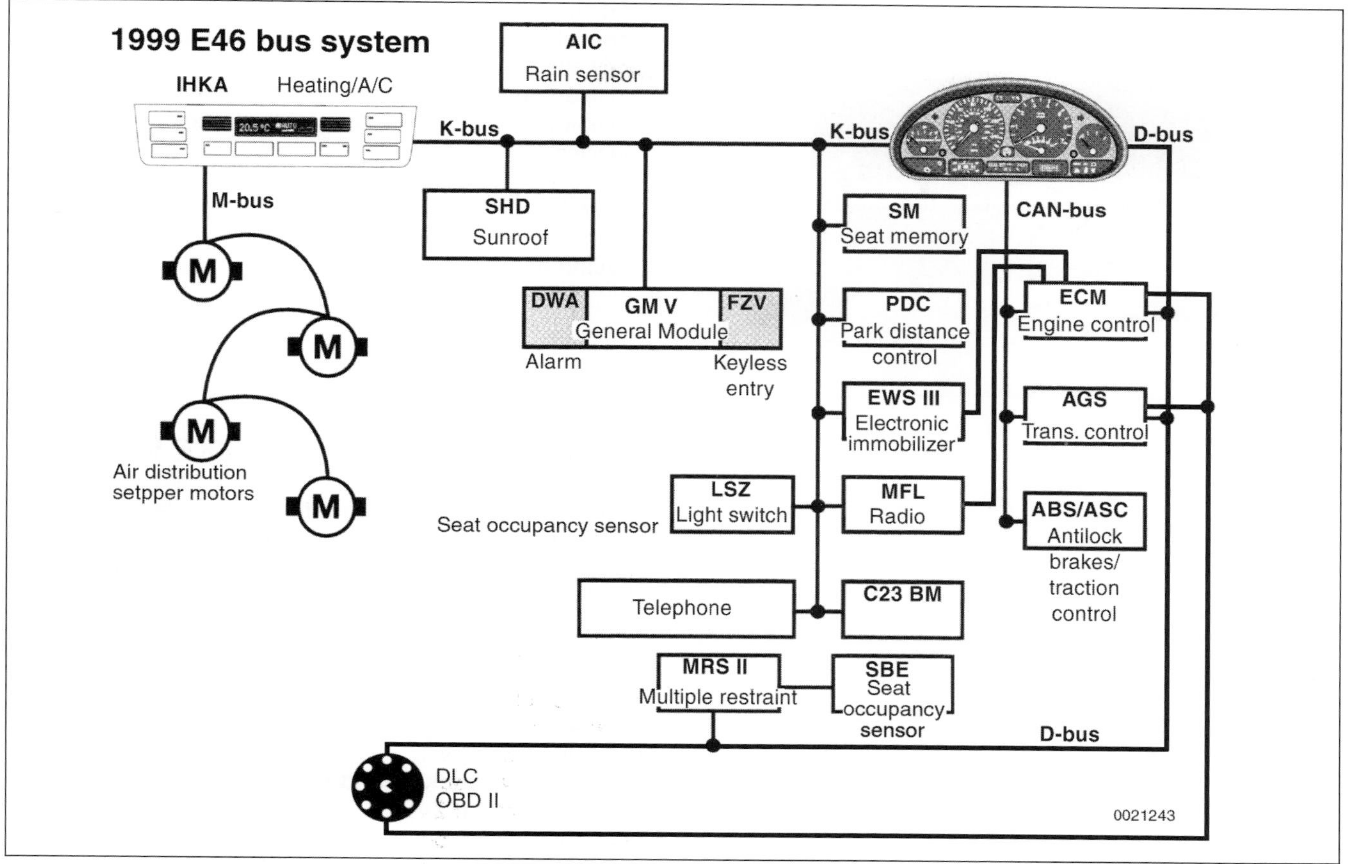

Voltage and polarity

The vehicle electrical system is a 12 volt direct current (dc) negative-ground system. A voltage regulator controls system voltage at approximately 12 volts. All circuits are grounded by direct or indirect connection to the negative (–) terminal of the battery. A number of ground connections throughout the car connect the wiring harness to chassis grounds. These circuits are completed by the battery cable or ground strap between the body and the battery negative (–) terminal.

Wiring, fuses and relays

Electrical components connect using one of the following:

- Heavy cables with lug-type connectors (battery and starter)
- Electrical harnesses with keyed, push-on connectors that lock into place
- Busses with modular connectors

0021264

With the exception of the starter and the charging system, most electrical power is routed from the ignition switch or the battery through the main relay panel in back of the glove compartment or the main fuse box (**arrow**) above the glove compartment. Fuses are color coded to indicate current capacities.

The relays and control modules are mounted in various places throughout the vehicle. See **610 Electrical Component Locations**.

Central Body Electronics (ZKE V)

E46 vehicles are equipped with an integrated complex of electronic modules connected mostly via K-bus. This system, called ZKE V, is primarily controlled by the General Module (GM V).

ZKE V directly controls the following functions:

- Windshield wiper / washer system. See **611 Wipers and Washers**.
- Central locking with power trunk or tailgate release. See **515 Central Locking and Anti-theft**.
- Keyless entry (FZV).
- Power window control. See **512 Door Windows**.
- Car Memory / Key Memory. See **515 Central Locking and Anti-theft**.
- Interior lighting. See **630 Lights**.
- Alarm system (DWA). See **515 Central Locking and Anti-theft**.
- Electronic consumer sleep mode. See **600 Electrical System–General**.

Other functions not directly controlled by ZKE V but interconnected:

- Rain sensor (AIC). See **611 Wiper and Washers**.
- Sunroof operation. See **540 Sunroof**.
- Seat memory. See **520 Seats**.
- Outside rear-view mirror control and heating.
- Windshield washer jet heating.

Redundant vehicle data storage

Vehicle data includes model series and type identification, national variant, options and equipment, engine and transmission serial numbers, total vehicle mileage and service interval information. This information is stored in two different control modules and can be accessed by BMW scan tool (DISplus, GT1, MoDiC) or equivalent.

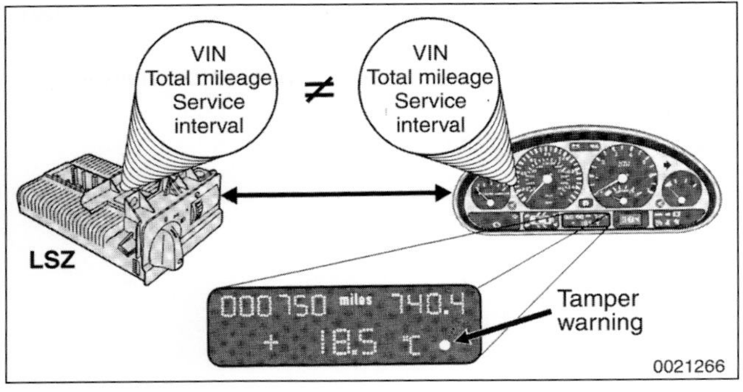

0021266

1999 - 2001: The light control module (LSZ) serves as the redundant vehicle data storage module in parallel with the instrument cluster.

2002 - 2005: The electronic immobilizer (EWS) module and the instrument cluster are the redundant data storage sites.

If one of the two redundant storage modules is replaced, data is transferred from the remaining module to the replacement unit.

Car Memory / Key Memory

A number of features and functions can be customized to the driver(s) preference. Car memory electronics identify the vehicle user by a signal from the FZV key.

Car Memory and Key Memory are actually two separate functions, although they are marketed as a combined feature. See **515 Central Locking and Anti-Theft** for further details.

Electrical consumer sleep mode

Central body electronics (ZKE V) is designed to bring vehicle electrical consumers into "sleep mode" after 16 minutes of inactivity.

In order to test sleep mode:

- Switch ignition OFF.
- Close all doors, trunk or tailgate and hood.
- Lock vehicle using central locking.
- Wait 16 minutes.

If one of a number of inputs into the General Module (GM V) is activated before the vehicle is in sleep mode, the 16 minute cycle starts again. Once the vehicle is in sleep mode, the GM V "wakes up" if it receives a change of signal from one of the following:

- K-bus
- Door jamb sensors
- Trunk lid lock cylinder microswitch
- Interior trunk lid release push-button microswitch
- Central locking button
- Engine hood latch microswitch
- Trunk key position switch
- Interior light switch
- Internal motion sensor
- Tilt sensor
- Driver door lock sensors

NOTE —
If an interior light is accidentally left on, the GM V overrides the signal from it after 16 minutes and implements sleep mode.

WIRING DIAGRAMS

Electrical schematics for selected models in **Electrical Wiring Diagrams** at the rear of this manual make it possible to diagnose and troubleshoot electrical malfunctions.

Wiring schematics and electrical information are also available at the BMW subscription site:

http://www.bmwtechinfo.com

Wiring codes and abbreviations

A lot of information is included in each wiring diagram if you know how to read it. Wire colors in the diagrams are abbreviated. See **Table c**. Combined color codes indicate a multicolored wire. For example the code BL/RT indicates a blue wire with a red stripe.

Sometimes the color of an installed wire may be different than the one on the wiring diagram. Don't be concerned. Just be sure to confirm that the wire connects to the proper terminals.

Table c. Wire color codes

German code	English code	Color
SW	BLK	Black
BL	BLU	Blue
BR	BRN	Brown
GN	GRN	Green
GR	GRY	Grey
	ORG	Orange
RT	RED	Red
VI	VIO	Violet
WS	WHT	White
GE	YEL	Yellow

Circuit designations

BMW identifies many electrical circuits with unique designations which follow the German DIN standard. See **Table d**. For example, if a relay terminal is labeled '30', it tells you that positive (+) voltage is supplied to that terminal at all times directly from the battery.

Table d. Terminal and circuit numbers

Number	Circuit description
1	Low voltage switched terminal of coil
4	High voltage center terminal of coil
+X	Originates at ignition switch. Supplies power when the ignition switch is in the PARK, RUN, or START position
15	Originates at ignition switch. Supplies power when ignition switch is in RUN or START position
30	Battery positive (+) voltage. Supplies power whenever battery is connected. (Not dependent on ignition switch position, unfused)
31	Ground, battery negative (–) terminal
50	Supplies power from battery to starter solenoid when ignition switch is in START position only
+54	Originates at ignition switch. Supplies power when ignition switch is in RUN position only
85	Ground side (–) of relay coil
86	Power-in side (+) of relay coil
87	Relay actuated contact
D	Alternator warning light and field energizing circuit

Component designations

In the wiring diagrams, BMW electrical components are identified using a letter followed by a number. For example, A6000 is the DME control module. The letter A identifies the component as an electronic control module. **Table d** lists the letter code for common components.

Table e. BMW component codes

Letter	Function	Example
A	Electronic control module	A6000 (DME engine control module)
B	Sensor, transducer	B6254 (oil level sensor)
E	Light, electric heater	E46 (left taillight)
F	Fuse	F3 (fuse 3 in fuse panel)
G	Power supply	G6524 (alternator), G1 (battery)
H	Warning light, signal indicator	H7 (left front turn signal bulb)
I	Misc. electrical component	I010644 (interference suppression filter)
K	Relay	K6300 (DME relay)
M	Electric motor, actuator	M2 (electric fuel pump)
N	Navigation, sound system, heating system	N8 (antenna amplifier)
R	Sensor	R10 (pedal position sensor)
S	Switch	S805 (clutch pedal switch)
T	Ignition coil	T6151 (cylinder 1 ignition coil)
U	Radio / interference suppression	U4 (telephone transceiver)
X	Connector; splice connector; ground	X165 (right front engine compartment ground)
Y	Electromechanical component	Y6101 (cylinder 1 fuel injector)

ELECTRICAL TROUBLESHOOTING

Four things are required for current to flow in any electrical circuit: a voltage source, wires or connections to transport the voltage, a load or device that uses the electricity, and a connection to ground.

Most problems can be found using a digital multimeter (volt / ohm / amp meter) to check the following:

- Voltage supply
- Breaks in the wiring (infinite resistance / no continuity)
- A path to ground that completes the circuit

Electric current is logical in its flow, always moving from the voltage source toward ground. Electrical faults can usually be located through a process of elimination. When troubleshooting a complex circuit, separate the circuit into smaller parts. General tests outlined below may be helpful in finding electrical problems. The information is most helpful when used with wiring diagrams.

Be sure to analyze the problem. Use wiring diagrams to determine the most likely cause. Get an understanding of how the circuit works by following the circuit from ground back to the power source.

When making test connections at connectors and components, use care to avoid spreading or damaging the connectors or terminals. Some tests may require jumper wires to bypass components or connections in the wiring harness. When connecting jumper wires, use blade connectors at the wire ends that match the size of the terminal being tested. The small internal contacts are easily spread apart, and this can cause intermittent or faulty connections that can lead to more problems.

Voltage and voltage drops

Wires, connectors, and switches that carry current are designed with very low resistance so that current flows with a minimum loss of voltage. A voltage drop is caused by higher than normal resistance in a circuit. This additional resistance decreases or stops the flow of current. A voltage drop can be noticed by problems ranging from dim headlights to sluggish wipers. Some common sources of voltage drops are corroded or dirty switches, dirty or corroded connections or contacts, and loose or corroded ground wires and ground connections.

A voltage drop test is a good test to make if current is flowing through the circuit, but the circuit is not operating correctly. A voltage drop test helps to pinpoint a corroded ground strap or a faulty switch. Normally, there should be less than 1 volt drop across most wires or closed switches. Voltage drop across a connector or short cable should not exceed 0.5 volts.

A voltage drop test is generally more accurate than a simple resistance check because the resistances involved are often too small to measure with most ohmmeters. For example, a resistance as small as 0.02 Ω would results in a 3 volt drop in a typical 150 amp starter circuit. (150 amps x 0.02 Ω = 3 volts).

Keep in mind that voltage with the key ON and voltage with the engine running are not the same. With the ignition on and the engine OFF (battery voltage), voltage should be approximately 12.6 volts. With the engine running (charging voltage), voltage should be approximately 14.0 volts. Measure voltage at the battery with the ignition ON and then with the engine running to get exact measurements.

Voltage, measuring

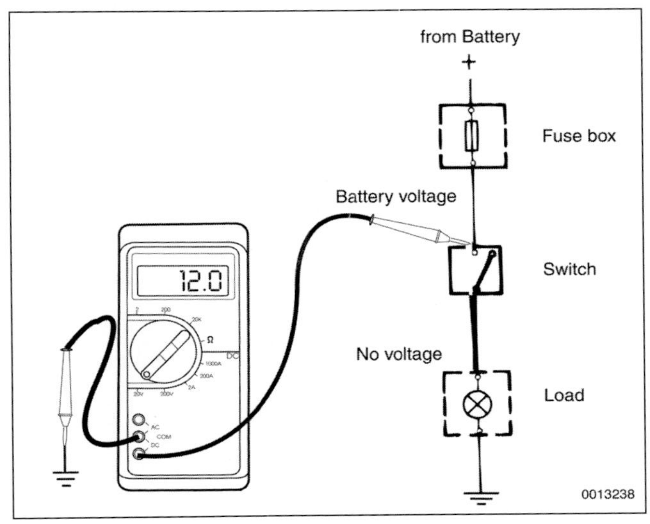

- Connect digital multimeter negative lead to a reliable ground point on car.

NOTE —
The negative (–) battery terminal is always a good ground point.

- Connect digital multimeter positive lead to point in circuit you wish to measure.
  - If a reading is obtained, current is flowing through circuit.
  - If voltage reading deviates more than 1 volt from voltage at the battery, check for a corroded connector or loose ground wire.

Voltage drop, testing

Voltage drop can only be checked when there is a load on the circuit, such as when operating the starter motor or turning on the headlights. Use a digital multimeter to ensure accurate readings.

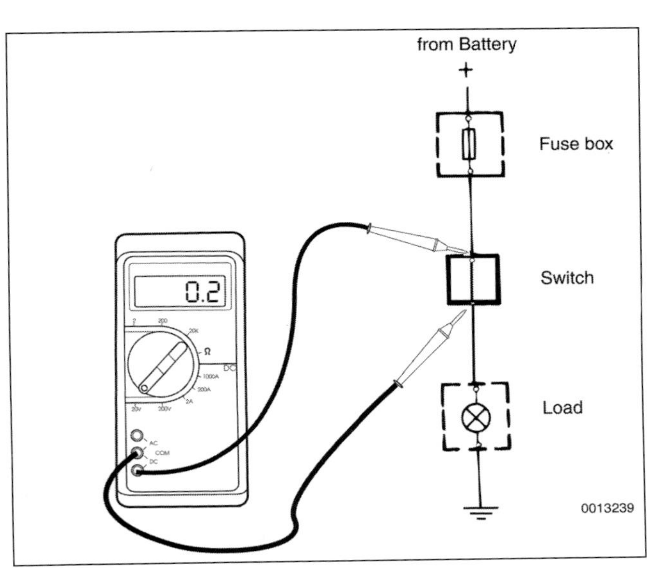

- Connect digital multimeter positive lead to positive (+) battery terminal or a positive power supply close to battery source.
- Connect digital multimeter negative lead to other end of cable or switch being tested.

With power on and circuit working, meter shows voltage drop (difference between two points). This value should not exceed 1 volt.

The maximum voltage drop in an automotive circuit, as recommended by the Society of Automotive Engineers (SAE), is as follows:

- 0 volts for small wire connections
- 0.1 volts for high current connections
- 0.2 volts for high current cables
- 0.3 volts for switch or solenoid contacts

On longer wires or cables, the drop may be slightly higher. In any case, a voltage drop of more than 1.0 volt usually indicates a problem.

Continuity, checking

Continuity tests can be used to check a circuit or switch. Because most automotive circuits are designed to have little or no resistance, a circuit or part of a circuit can be easily checked for faults using an ohmmeter. An open circuit or a circuit with high resistance does not allow current to flow. A circuit with little or no resistance allows current to flow easily.

When checking continuity, turn ignition OFF. On circuits that are powered at all times, disconnect battery. Using the appropriate wiring diagram, a circuit can be easily tested for faulty connections, wires, switches, relays and engine sensors by checking for continuity.

For example, to test brake light switch for continuity:

- With brake pedal in rest position (switch open) there is no continuity (infinite Ω).
- With pedal depressed (switch closed) there is continuity (0Ω).

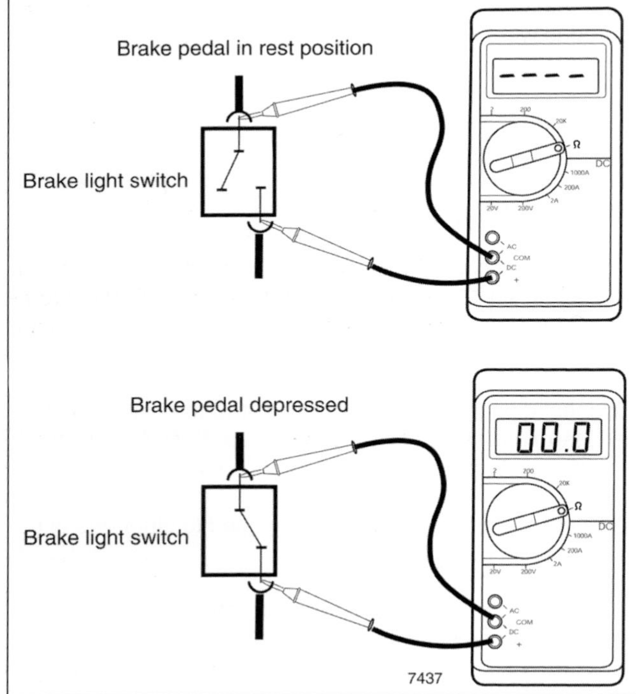

Short circuits

Short circuits are exactly what the name implies. The circuit takes a shorter path than it was designed to take. The most common short that causes problems is a short to ground where the insulation on a positive (+) wire wears away and the metal wire is exposed. When the wire rubs against a metal part of the car or other ground source, the circuit is shorted to ground. If the exposed wire is live (positive battery voltage), a fuse blows and the circuit may possibly be damaged.

Short circuits are often difficult to locate and may vary in nature. Short circuits can be found using a logical approach based on current path.

> ***CAUTION —***
> - *On circuits protected with high rating fuses (25 amp and greater), wires or circuit components may be damaged before the fuse blows. Always check for damage before replacing fuses of this rating.*
> - *When replacing blown fuses, use only fuses having the correct rating. Always confirm the correct fuse rating printed on the fuse / relay panel cover.*

Short circuit, testing with ohmmeter

– Remove blown fuse from circuit and disconnect cables from battery. Disconnect harness connector from circuit load or consumer.

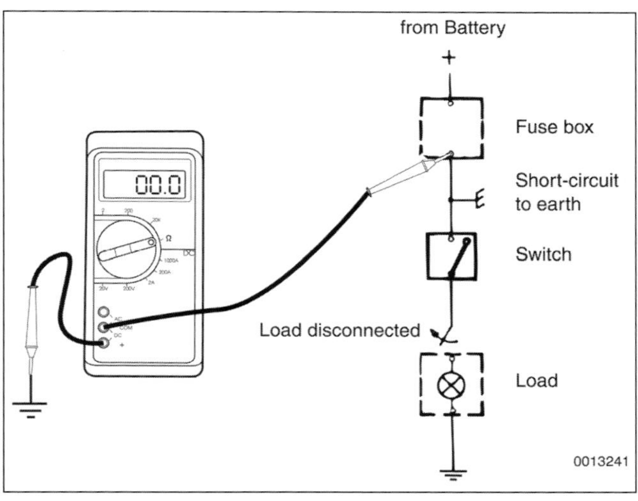

< Using an ohmmeter, connect one test lead to load side of fuse terminal (terminal leading to circuit) and other test lead to ground.

– If there is continuity to ground, there is a short to ground.

– If there is no continuity, work from wire harness nearest to fuse / relay panel and move or wiggle wires while observing meter. Continue to move down harness until meter displays a reading. This is the location of short to ground.

– Visually inspect wire harness at this point for any faults. If no faults are visible, carefully slice open harness cover or wire insulation for further inspection. Repair any faults found.

Short circuit, testing with voltmeter

– Remove blown fuse from circuit. Disconnect harness connector from circuit load or consumer.

NOTE —
Most fuses power more than one consumer. Be sure all consumers are disconnected when checking for a short circuit.

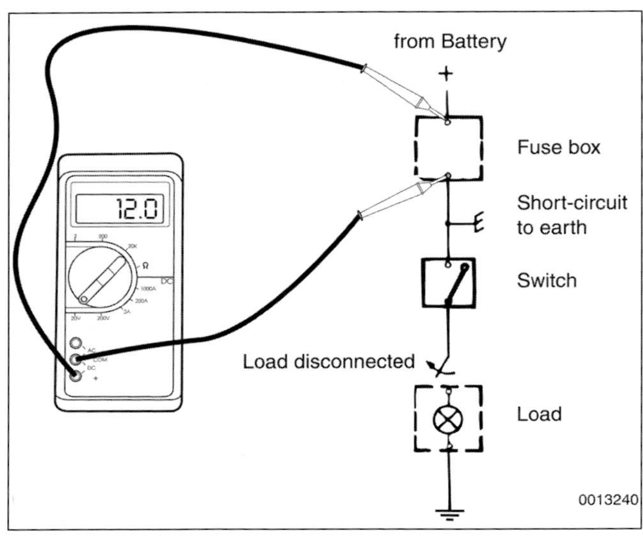

◄ Using a digital multimeter, connect test leads across fuse terminals. Make sure power is present in circuit. If necessary turn key on.

– If voltage is present at voltmeter, there is a short to ground.

– If voltage is not present, work from wire harness nearest to fuse / relay panel and move or wiggle wires while observing meter. Continue to move down harness until meter displays a reading. This is the location of short to ground.

– Visually inspect wire harness at this point for any faults. If no faults are visible, carefully slice open harness cover or wire insulation for further inspection. Repair any faults found.

610 Electrical Component Locations

TABLES

GENERAL

This repair group covers fuse, relay and control module location information. Ground points and other component locations are also covered, primarily via photos or illustrations.

For additional E46 electrical system information, see:

- **600 Electrical System–General**.
- **Electrical Wiring Diagrams**.

Fuses, relays and control modules

The complex nature of E46 electrical systems requires a very large number of fuses and electrical components. Locating this array of equipment is always an important first step in any kind of electrical diagnosis.

Investigating and correcting ground problems often clears mysterious and difficult to trace electrical problem. This repair group covers the major ground locations on the vehicle.

Keep in mind that electrical equipment and accessories installed vary depending on model and model year. Always confirm that the proper electrical component has been identified by using the electrical wiring diagrams at the back of this manual.

Electrical system safety precautions

Please read the following warnings and cautions before doing any work on your electrical system.

WARNING —
The battery safety terminal, pyrotechnic seat belt tensioners, and airbags utilize explosive devices and must be handled with extreme care. Refer to the warnings and cautions in **121 Battery, Alternator, Starter; 720 Seat Belts; and 721 Airbag System (SRS)**.

CAUTION —
- *Prior to disconnecting the battery, read the battery disconnection cautions given at the front of this manual on page viii.*
- *Relay and fuse positions are subject to change and may vary from car to car. If questions arise, an authorized BMW dealer is the best source for the most accurate and up-to-date information.*
- *A good way to verify a relay position is to compare the wiring colors at the relay socket to the colors indicated on the wiring diagrams located at the rear of this manual.*
- *Always switch the ignition off and remove the negative (–) battery cable before removing any electrical components. Connect and disconnect ignition system wires, multiple connectors, and ignition test equipment leads only while the ignition is switched off.*
- *Only use a digital multimeter for electrical tests.*

FUSE POSITIONS

There are three locations for fuses in E46 cars:

- Main harness fuse in trunk
- Fuse panel above glove compartment
- E-box in engine compartment left side

NOTE —
- *In BMW repair information, fuses are numbered F1 through F108. There are two fuses with the same designation: F5 in the main fuse panel is rated 5A and protects the horn circuit. F5 in the E-box fuse carrier is rated 30A and protects the unloader relay circuit in 1999 - 2000 models, and fuel injector relay in 2001 models.*
- *In a few cases, a fuse may have two different amperage ratings depending on equipment in the vehicle. In such cases the second rating is put in parenthesis in the fuse rating tables.*

Main harness fuse

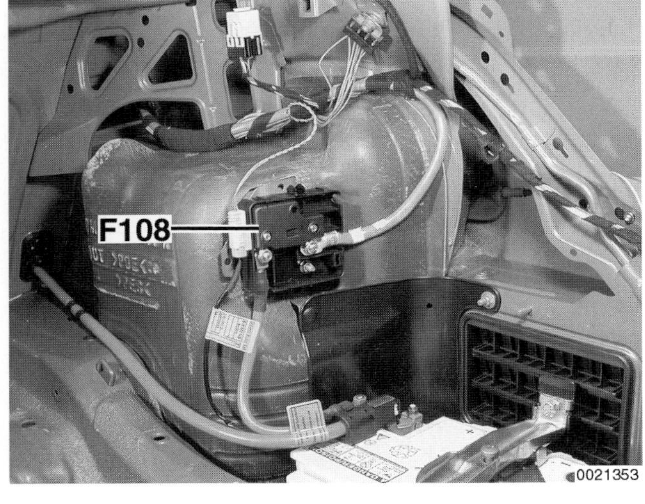

Fig. 1 Main harness fuse in trunk:

- Working ahead of battery in trunk, remove trim liner clips.
- Peel back liner to access F108 (200 amp) fuse (**arrow**) in main power distribution circuit.

Electronics box (E-box) fuse carrier

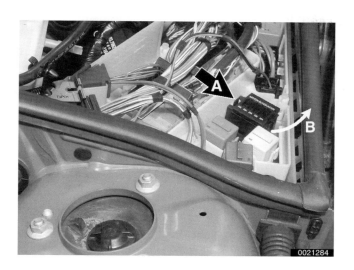

Fig. 2 Engine electronics fuse pack in E-box:

- Working in left rear of engine compartment, remove E-box plastic cover.
- Push on hold-down lock clip (**A**) to release fuse pack carrier.
- Pull up on fuse pack lock clip (**B**) to release fuse pack.

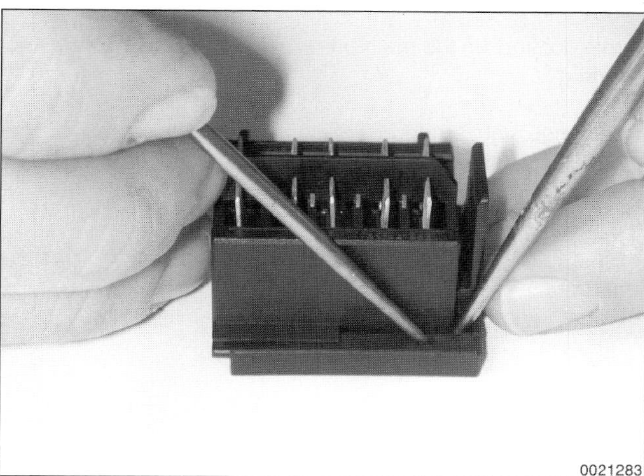

To remove an individual defective fuse inside fuse pack carrier, slide cover off by prying gently while you use pin tool to squeeze lock tabs.

> ***CAUTION —***
> *Once cover is off, fuses can fall out easily. Be sure to keep them in order while replacing defective fuse.*

Table a. E-box fuse pack

Fuse	Rating	Protected circuits
1	30A	Not used (1999 - 2000 models) DME main relay (2001 models) Ignition coils (2001-2005 models)
2	30A	DME control module (ECM) Evaporative emissions valve Fuel injectors Idle speed control valve Resonance valve, intake manifold Secondary air injection pump Suction jet pump valve, LDP system Vanos solenoids
3	20A	A/C compressor clutch relay Camshaft position sensors Crankshaft position sensor DME main relay Fuel pump relay Leakage diagnosis pump (fuel tank) Mass air flow sensor Secondary air injection pump relay Thermostat
4	30A	Changeover valve, running losses (3/2 valve) Oxygen sensors
5	30A	Fuel injector relay (2001-2005 models) Unloader relay to ignition coils (1999 - 2000 models)

Main fuse panel

 **Fig. 3 Fuse panel above glove compartment:**

- Open glove compartment door.
- Working inside compartment, twist each plastic lock tab (**arrows**) at top of compartment 90°.
- Pull down on fuse panel to swing it down.

NOTE —

- *When the fuse box is up in locked position, the plastic tabs should point toward each other. When unlocked, they point to the back of the car.*
- *A small built in flashlight (**A**) is in the glove compartment next to the fuse box.*
- *A red plastic fuse puller (**B**) is in the center of the fuse box.*
- *The sheet of paper with the fuse assignments, below the fuses, can be slid out for reference.*
- *Vertical fuses are active. Horizontal fuses are spares.*

Fuse locations in the main panel are detailed in **Table c** and **Table d**.

Additional high amperage fuses are found on top of the glove compartment fuse panel beneath an access panel.

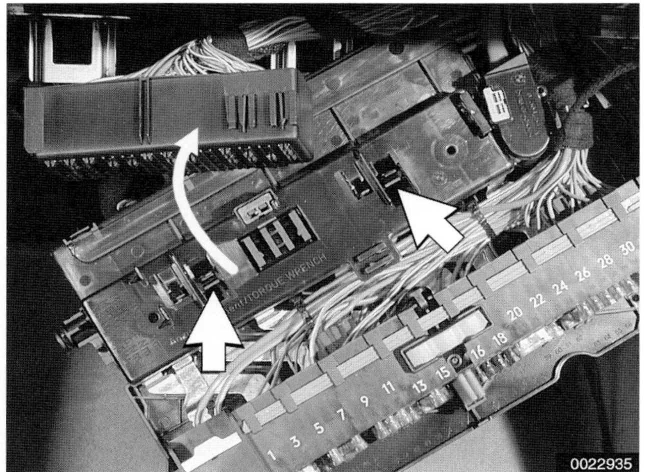

 Lower glove compartment fuse panel fully.

- Slide harness connector block off top of panel (**curved arrow**).
- Detach access panel by squeezing retaining clips (**arrows**).

Fig. 4 High amperage fuses above main fuse panel:

- Fuses F101 through F107 are mounted in this location.

Table b. High amperage fuse positions

Fuse	Rating	Protected circuits
101	50A	Engine cooling fan (1999 models)
102	80A	B+ terminal DME mail relay Engine control module Fuse 5 E-box fuse pack Transmission control module (TCM)
103	80A	not used
104	100A	Preheater relay
105	50A	Ignition switch DLC
106	50A	Light switching center control module
107	50A	Light switching center control module Trailer module
108	200A	Main harness fuse (in trunk, see **Fig. 1**)

Table c. 1999 fuse positions

Fuse	Rating	Protected circuit
1	not used	
2		
3		
4		
5	5A	Horn (see also fuse 55)
6	5A	Make-up mirror light
7	5A	Navigation (see also fuse 41) On-board monitor (see also fuse 41) Radio (see also fuse 41) Telephone (see also fuse 39)
8	not used	
9	5A	Brake light Light module (see also fuse 32) On-board computer Speed control
10	5A	Instrument cluster (see also fuses 34, 43)
11	5A	Airbag Side-impact airbag
12	7.5A	Roller sun blind
13	not used	
14	5A	Electronic immobilizer (EWS) (see also fuse 67) Starter interlock
15	5A	Rain sensor
16	not used	
17		
18		
19		
20		
21		
22		
23		
24	5A	Electrochromic rear view mirror (see also fuse 67) Parking distance control
25	5A	Heated outside mirror, passenger Heated spray nozzles
26	5A	Garage door opener Overheat JP
27	10A	Back-up lights
28	5A	Heater-A/C (see also fuses 62, 63) Heater-A/C blower (see also fuse 37)
29	5A	Engine control (see also fuse 30)

Table c. 1999 fuse positions

Fuse	Rating	Protected circuit
30	7.5A	Engine control (see also fuse 29) OBD II system
31	5A	Outside mirror Tire pressure control (see also fuse 69)
32	5A	Light module (see also fuse 9)
33	5A	ABS/ASC (see also fuses 53, 56) ABS/DSC (see also fuses 40, 53, 56, 61)
34	5A	Instrument cluster (see also fuses 10, 43)
35	not used	
36	50A	Secondary air pump
37	50A	Blower motor
38	10A (15A)	Front fog lights
39	5A	Telephone (see also fuse 7)
40	5A	ABS/DSC (see also fuses 33, 53, 56, 61) Shift gate illumination
41	30A	Navigation (see also fuse 7) On-board monitor (see also fuse 7) Radio (see also fuse 7)
42	not used	
43	5A	Clock Instrument cluster (see also fuses 10, 34) OBD II system
44	20A	Trailer module
45	not used	
46	30A	Sunroof
47	15A (20A)	Cigarette lighter / power outlet
48	30A	Window, front (see also fuse 49)
49	5A	Anti-theft (see also fuse 67) Central locking system (see also fuse 60) Interior light (see also fuse 52) Power window, front (see also fuse 48) Windshield washer system (see also fuses 52, 59)
50	25A	Seat heating
51	30A	Headlight cleaning system
52	30A	Central locking system, trunk Glove box light Interior light (see also fuse 49) Passenger compartment/trunk lighting Windshield washer system (see also fuses 49, 59)
53	30A	ABS/ASC (see also fuses 33, 56) ABS/DSC (see also fuses 33, 40, 56, 61)

Table c. 1999 fuse positions

Fuse	Rating	Protected circuit
54	15A	Fuel pump
55	15A	Horn (see also fuse 5)
56	30A	ABS/ASC (see also fuses 33, 53) ABS/DSC (see also fuses 33, 40, 53, 61)
57	5A	Outside mirror
58	not used	
59	30A	Windshield washer system (see also fuses 49, 52)
60	25A	Central locking (see also fuse 49)
61	30A	ABS/DSC (see also fuses 33, 40, 53, 56)
62	7.5A	A/C (see also fuses 28, 63)
63	7.5A	A/C (see also fuses 28, 62)
64	20A	Auxiliary heater (diesel)
65	30A	Driver seat adjustment
66	not used	
67	5A	Anti-theft (see also fuse 49) Electrochromic rear view mirror (see also fuse 24) Electronic immobilizer (EWS) (see also fuse 14)
68	30A	Heated rear window
69	5A	Tire pressure control (see also fuse 31)
70	30A	Passenger seat adjustment
71	30A (10A Coupe)	Hinged window (Coupe) Window, rear

Table d. 2000-2005 fuse positions

Fuse	Rating	Protected circuit
1	not used	
2	not used	
3	not used	
4	not used	
5	5A	Horn (see also fuse 55)
6	5A	Make-up mirror light Power top (Convertible, see also fuses 12, 35, 42, 46)
7	5A	Heated rear window (see also fuse 68) Navigation system (see also fuse 41) On-board monitor (see also fuse 41) Radio (see also fuse 41) Telephone (see also fuse 39)
8	5A	Sequential transmission (M3, see also fuse 22)
9	5A	Brake light Light module (see also fuse 32) On-board computer Speed control
10	5A	Instrument cluster (see also fuses 34, 43)
11	5A	Airbag Side-impact airbag

Table d. 2000-2005 fuse positions

Fuse	Rating	Protected circuit
12	7.5A	ABS/ASC (see also fuses 33, 42, 53, 56) ABS/DSC (see also fuses 33, 40, 42, 53, 56, 61) ABS/DSC all-wheel drive (see also fuses 33, 35, 40, 42, 53) Manual top (Convertible, see also fuses 42, 46) Power top (Convertible, see also fuses 6, 35, 42, 46) Seat heating (see also fuse 42) Roller sun blind (see also fuse 42) Tire pressure control (see also fuses 31, 42, 69)
13	7.5A	Roll-over protection system (Convertible)
14	5A	Electronic immobilizer (EWS) (see also fuse 67) Starter interlock Gearshift lock
15	5A	Rain sensor Rear wiper (Sport Wagon, see also fuse 45)
16	not used	
17	not used	
18	not used	
19	not used	
20	not used	
21	not used	
22	not used	
23	5A	Heater (see also fuses 28, 62)
24	5A	Electrochromic rear view mirror (see also fuse 67) Park distance control
25	5A	Heated outside mirror, passenger Heated spray nozzles
26	5A	Cigarette lighter Garage door opener
27	10A	Back-up light
28	5A	Air conditioner (see also fuses 62, 63) Blower (see also fuse 50) Heater (see also fuses 23, 62) Heated rear window, Convertible
29	5A	Engine control (see also fuses 27, 30) Engine control (M3, see also fuses 22, 30)
30	7.5A	Engine control (see also fuses 27, 29) Engine control (M3, see also fuses 22, 29) OBD II system (see also fuse 43)
31	5A	Outside mirror (see also fuse 57) Tire pressure control (see also fuses 12, 42, 69)
32	5A	Light module (see also fuse 9)
33	5A	ABS/ASC (see also fuses 12, 42, 53, 56) ABS/DSC (see also fuses 12, 40, 42, 53, 56, 61) ABS/DSC all-wheel drive (see also fuses 12, 35, 40, 42, 53)
34	5A	Instrument cluster (see also fuses 10, 43) Fuel pump control module, MS 45.1
35	50A	Power top (Convertible, see also fuses 6, 12, 42, 46) ABS/DSC all-wheel drive (see also fuses 12, 33, 40, 42, 53)
36	50A	Secondary air pump
37	50A	Engine cooling fan
38	10A (15A)	Front foglights
39	5A	Telephone (see also fuse 7)

Table d. 2000-2005 fuse positions

Fuse	Rating	Protected circuit
40	5A	ABS/DSC (see also fuses 12, 33, 42, 53, 56, 61) ABS/DSC all-wheel drive (see also fuses 12, 33, 35, 42, 53) Shift gate illumination
41	30A	Navigation system (see also fuse 7) On-board monitor (see also fuse 7) Radio/amplifier/CD changer(see also fuse 7)
42	30A	ABS/ASC (see also fuses 12, 33, 53, 56) ABS/DSC (see also fuses 12, 33, 40, 53, 56, 61) ABS/DSC all-wheel drive (see also fuses 12, 33, 35, 40, 53) Manual top (Convertible, see also fuses 12, 46) Power top (Convertible, see also fuses 6, 12, 35, 46) Seat heating (see also fuse 12) Roller sun blind (see also fuse 12) Tire pressure control (see also fuses 12, 31, 69)
43	5A	Instrument cluster (see also fuses 10, 34) OBD II system (see also fuse 30)
44	20A	Trailer module
45	20A	Rear wiper (Sport Wagon, see also fuse 15)
46	30A (20A convert-ible)	Power top (Convertible, see also fuses 6, 12, 35, 42) Manual top (Convertible, see also fuses 12, 42) Sunroof
47	15A	Cigarette lighter / power outlet
48	30A	Power window, front (see also fuse 49)
49	5A	Anti-theft (see also fuse 67) Central locking system (see also fuses 52, 60, Sport Wagon, see fuse 58) Interior light (see also fuse 52) Windshield washer system (see also fuses 52, 59) Window, front (see also fuse 48)
50	40A	Heater-A/C blower (see also fuse 28)
51	30A	Headlight washer system
52	30A	Central locking system (see also fuses 49, 60, Sport Wagon see fuse 58) Glove compartment light Hand lamp Interior lights (see also fuse 49) Passenger compartment/trunk lighting Windshield washer system (see also fuses 49, 59)
53	30A	ABS/ASC (see also fuses 12, 33, 42, 56) ABS/DSC (see also fuses 12, 33, 40, 42, 56, 61) ABS/DSC all-wheel drive (see also fuses 12, 33, 35, 40, 42)

Table d. 2000-2005 fuse positions

Fuse	Rating	Protected circuit
54	15A	Fuel pump
55	15A	Horn (see also fuse 5)
56	30A	ABS/ASC (see also fuses 12, 33, 42, 53) ABS/DSC (see also fuses 12, 33, 40, 42, 53, 61)
57	5A	Outside mirror (see also fuse 31)
58	7.5	Central locking (Sport Wagon, see also fuses 49, 52, 60)
59	30A	Windshield washer system (see also fuses 49, 52)
60	25A	Central locking (see also fuses 49, 52, Sport Wagon, see fuse 58)
61	30A	ABS/DSC (see also fuses 12, 33, 40, 42, 53, 56, 61)
62	7.5A	Heater-A/C (see also fuses 28, 63) Heater (see also fuses 23, 28)
63	7.5A	Heater-A/C (see also fuses 28, 62)
64	not used	
65	30A	Driver seat adjustment
66	5A	Ignition switch, M3
67	5A	Anti-theft (DWA) (see also fuse 49) Electrochromic rear view mirror (see also fuse 24) Electronic immobilizer (EWS) (see also fuse 14)
68	30A	Heated rear window (see also fuse 7)
69	5A	Tire pressure control (see also fuses 12, 31, 42)
70	30A	Passenger seat adjustment
71	30A (10A Coupe)	Hinged window (Coupe) Window, rear

GROUND LOCATIONS

Grounds are widely distributed throughout the vehicle body. Several are found under the interior carpets. Lugs and connectors attached to ground are susceptible to damage and corrosion. Clean or renew them as necessary.

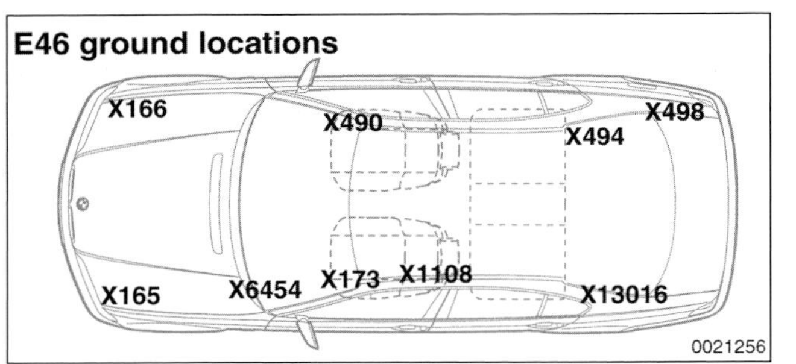

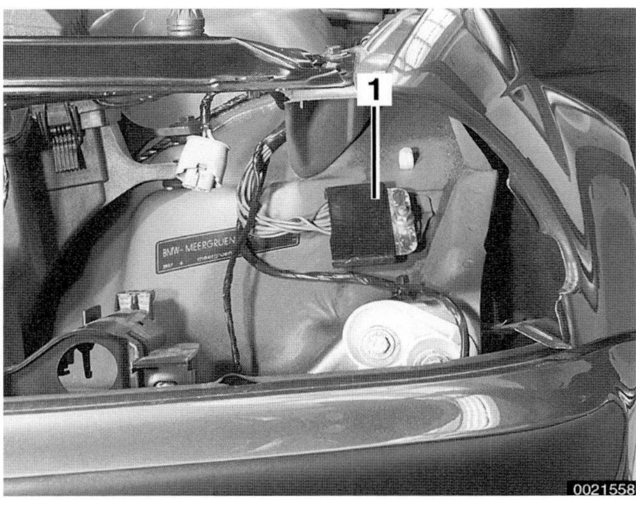

Fig. 5 Left front engine compartment, behind left headlight

1. Ground X165

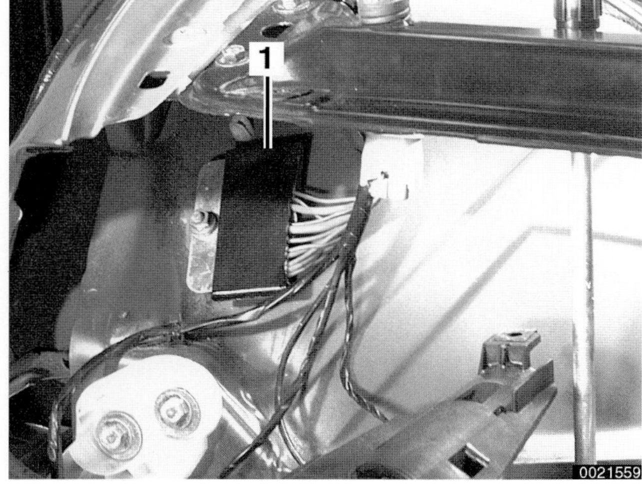

Fig. 6 Right front engine compartment, behind right headlight

1. Ground X166

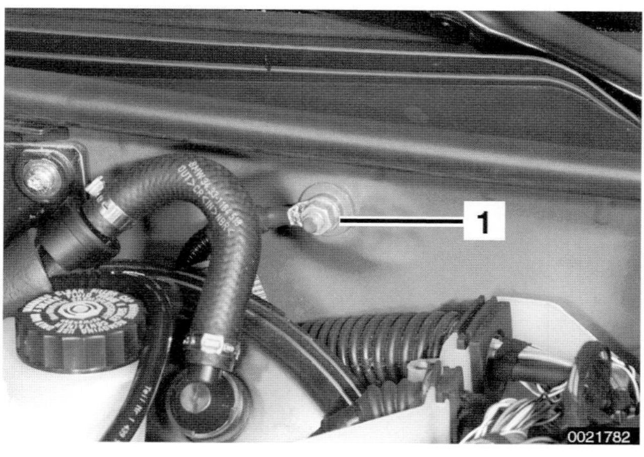

Fig. 7 On bulkhead behind E-box

1.	Ground X6454

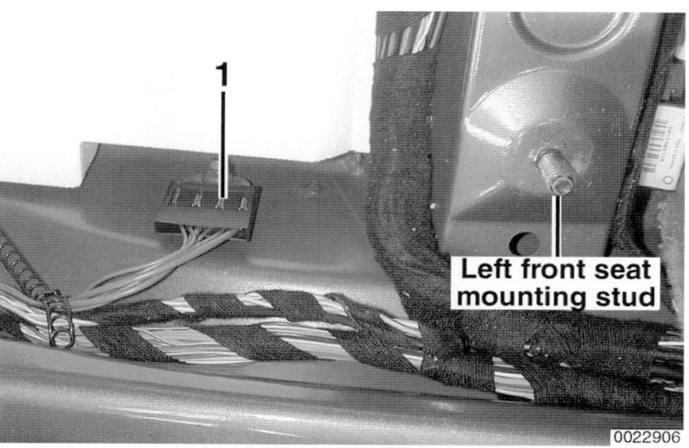

Fig. 8 Under left front carpet on door sill

1.	Ground connector X173

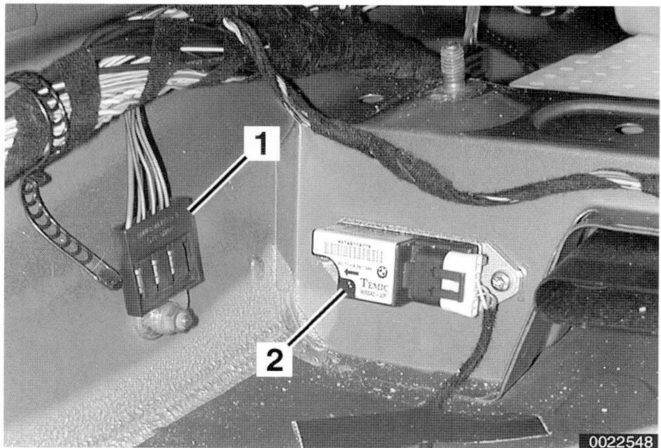

Fig. 9 On door sill, under driver seat carpet

1.	Ground connector X1108
2.	Side impact airbag crash sensor

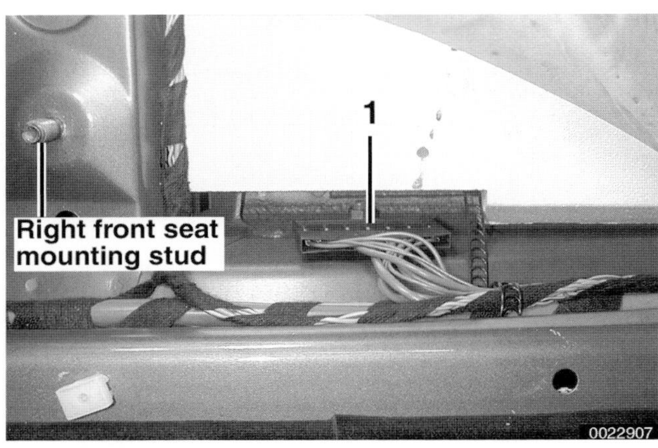

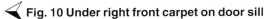

Fig. 10 Under right front carpet on door sill

1. Ground connector X490

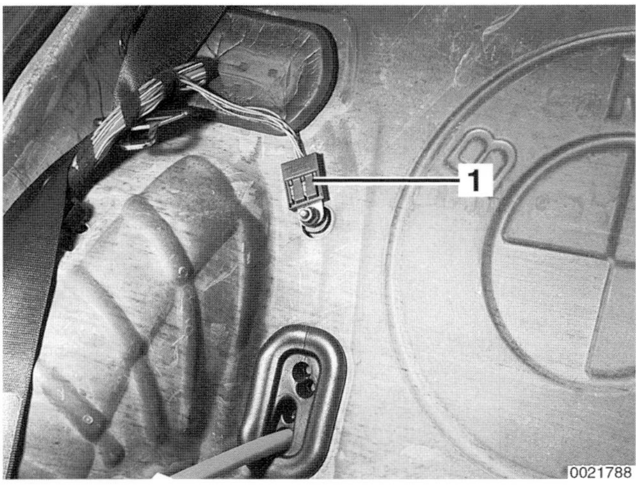

Fig. 11 Behind right rear seat backrest

1. Ground X494

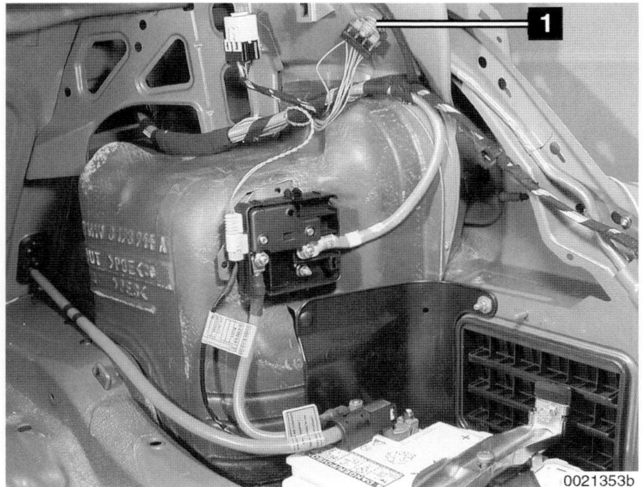

Fig. 12 Right side trunk, behind trim

1. Ground X498

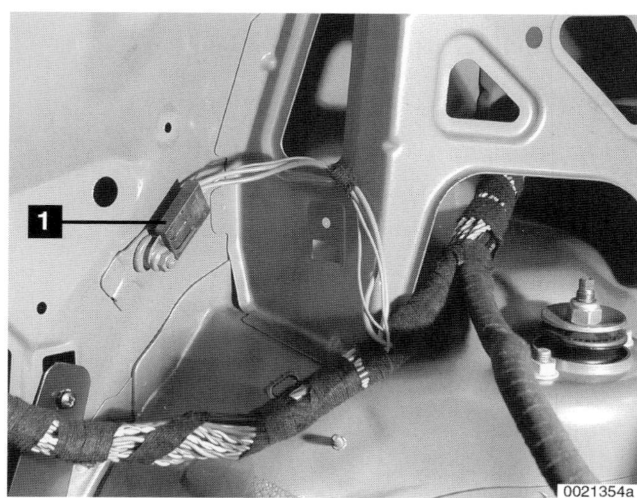

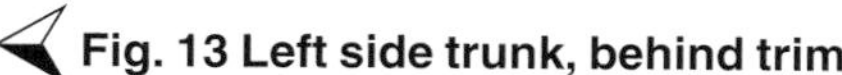
Fig. 13 Left side trunk, behind trim

1. Ground X13016

COMPONENT LOCATIONS

On the following pages are photos and illustrations showing the location of major electrical components in E46 vehicles.

NOTE —

- *Every component is not installed in every car.*
- *Due to changes in production, component locations may vary from what is illustrated. Consult your BMW dealer for the latest information.*
- *The automatic transmission range switch is also sometimes referred to as the gear-position switch.*
- *The EWS 3.3 system is also known as the driveaway protection system or the electronic immobilization system.*
- *All-Season Traction (AST) is a marketing term that refers to ABS/ASC.*

Main relay panel

– To access main relay panel, located under right side of dashboard, remove glove compartment as described in **513 Interior Trim**.

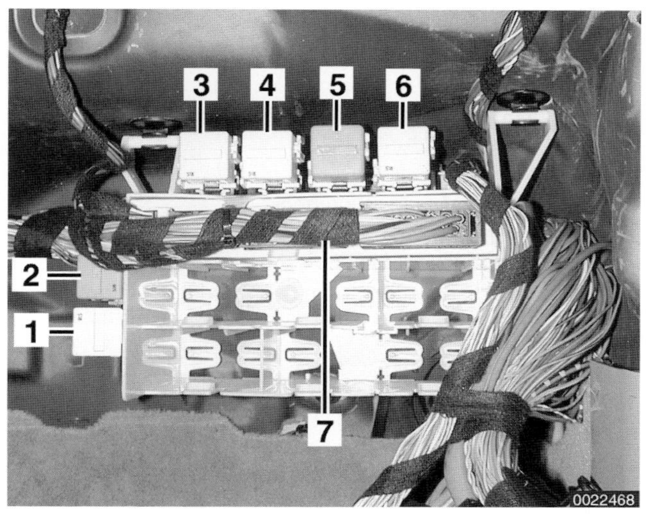

Fig. 14 Behind glove compartment (no headlight cleaning system)

1. A/C relay
2. Secondary air pump relay
3. Fuel pump relay
4. A/C relay
5. Foglight relay
6. Horn relay
7. General module (GM V)

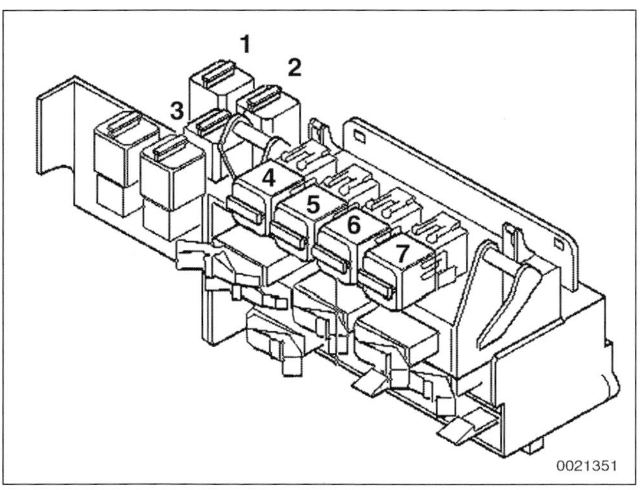

Fig. 15 Behind glove compartment (with headlight cleaning system)

1. Headlight cleaning relay
2. Secondary air pump relay
3. A/C relay
4. Fuel pump relay
5. A/C relay
6. Foglight relay
7. Horn relay

Electronics box (E-box)

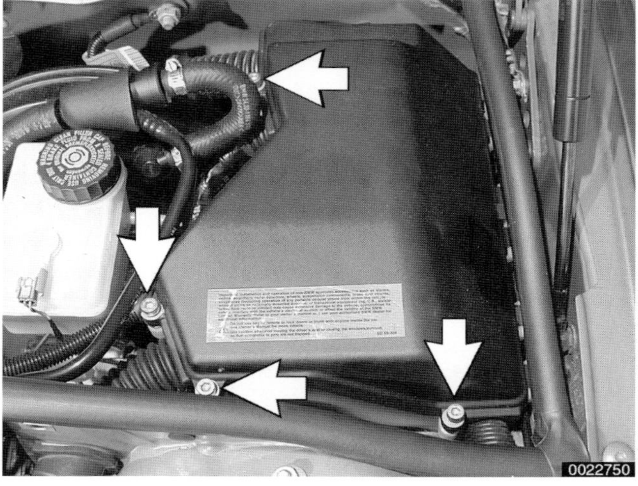

To access E-box components:

- Working in left rear of engine compartment, remove M6 Allen head bolts (**arrows**).
- Lift off E-box cover.

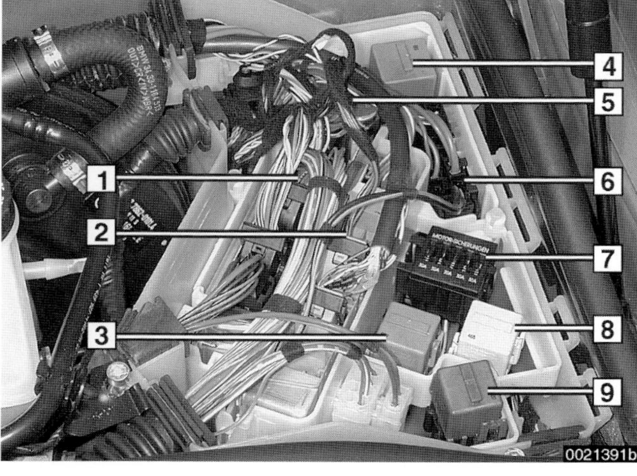

Fig. 16 E-box

1. Engine control module (ECM)
2. Automatic transmission control module (TCM)
3. DME main relay
4. Windshield washer double relay
5. E-box temperature sensor
6. B+ connector
7. Engine electronics fuse pack
8. 1999 - 2000 models: Unloader relay
   2001 models: fuel injector relay
9. Back-up light relay (automatic transmission only)

Component location table

Table e is a cross-referenced listing of electrical components in E46 vehicles. Where available, photos of components in this repair group are referred to in the fourth column.

NOTE —
- *Every attempt has been made in this repair manual to standardize component names. Nevertheless, in some cases, the same component may appear with different names.*
- *No E46 vehicle is equipped with all components illustrated. Where necessary, year and model applications are given in the component location table and the illustrations.*

Table e. E46 component locations

Component	Year, model	Location	Refer to
12 volt auxiliary power socket		see Power socket, 12-volt	
3/2-way valve	1999 - 2000	Under car ahead of fuel filter, under protective cover	
3/2-way valve (changeover)	(Y6167)	Left hand side of engine compartment, towards rear of intake manifold	
A/C blower final stage (resistor pack)		Right side of IHKA housing below glove compartment	Fig. 40
A/C blower relay		Main relay panel behind glove compartment	Fig. 14, Fig. 15
A/C blower		Behind engine compartment rear bulkhead	
A/C compressor		Right front lower engine compartment	
A/C compressor clutch relay (K19)		Main relay panel behind glove compartment	Fig. 14, Fig. 15
A/C compressor solenoid clutch (Y2)		Lower right hand side of engine	
A/C control module (A11)		Center of dashboard	
A/C evaporator temperature sensor		Left side of IHKA housing below instrument cluster	Fig. 39
A/C pressure sensor (B8)		Behind right headlight on top of receiver/drier	Fig. 32
ABS wheel speed sensor connector, front (right/left)		In wheel housing (right/left)	Fig. 62
ABS wheel speed sensor connector, rear (right/left)		Ahead of rear wheel housing (right/left)	
ABS wheel speed sensor, front (right/left)		In front wheel bearing housing (right/left)	Fig. 60
ABS wheel speed sensor, rear (right/left) (B3)		In rear wheel bearing housing (right/left)	Fig. 61
ABS/ASC control module/hydraulic unit (A52)	1999	Left rear engine compartment, below brake master cylinder	
ABS/ASC/DSC warning lights		In instrument cluster	
ABS/DSC charge pressure sensor	rear wheel drive with DSC	Base of master cylinder, left side	Fig. 18
ABS/DSC charge pressure sensor	2001+ rear wheel drive	In ABS/DSC hydraulic unit, right rear engine compartment	
ABS/DSC control module/hydraulic unit (A65)	1999 - 2000; 2001+ all wheel drive	Right rear of engine compartment	Fig. 19
ABS/DSC control module/hydraulic unit	2001+ rear wheel drive	Left rear of engine compartment	
ABS/DSC lateral acceleration sensor	rear wheel drive	Behind driver kickpanel	

Table e. E46 component locations

Component	Year, model	Location	Refer to
ABS/DSC lateral acceleration sensor	2001+ all wheel drive	Combined with rotational rate (yaw) sensor under driver side carpet	
ABS/DSC precharge pump		Left rear engine compartment, below brake master cylinder	Fig. 18
ABS/DSC rotational rate (yaw) sensor		Under driver side carpet	
ABS/DSC steering angle sensor (R33)		Base of upper steering column	Fig. 35
ABS/DSC switch		see ASC/DSC switch	
Accelerator pedal sensor (PWG)		At throttle housing	
Accelerator pedal sensor (PWG)	2001 - 2005	Above accelerator pedal	
Accelerator pedal sensor (R10)		Under accelerator pedal	
Adaptive headlight control module (A214)			
AGS (adaptive transmission control)		see Automatic transmission control module	
Air distribution motors		In IHKA housing under dashboard (see **640 Heating and Air Conditioning)**	
Air flow sensor		see Mass air flow sensor	
Air quality sensor (AUC) (for automatic recirculation system)	2000 - 2005	Right side of radiator	Fig. 17, Fig. 29
Airbag connector, passenger side		Right side dashboard support	Fig. 41
Airbag connector, steering wheel		Under steering wheel airbag	Fig. 34
Airbag control module (MRS module)		Under parking brake lever console, under carpet	Fig. 9
Airbag crash sensor, side-impact airbag (left/right)		Front seat crossmember under carpet (left/right)	
Airbag warning light		In instrument cluster	
Airbag, driver side		Steering wheel center pad	
Airbag, head protection (HPS), electrical connector (left/right)		At bottom of windshield pillar (A pillar) behind dashboard (left/right)	Fig. 42
Airbag, passenger side		Right side dashboard	Fig. 41
Airbag, side-impact (left/right front/rear)		Inside door (left/right, front/rear)	
Alarm control module (DWA)		Above main fuse box behind glove box	
Alarm indicator LED (DWA)		Attached to rear view mirror	
Alarm siren (DWA)		Right side rear of engine compartment near wipers	
Alarm siren battery (DWA)		Inside alarm siren	
All season traction (AST)		see ABS/ASC entries	
Alternator (generator)		Left front of cylinder block	
Amplifier, radio		Left side trunk or cargo compartment behind trim panel	Fig. 54, Fig. 57
Antenna amplifier, diversity	Convertible	On convertible top storage cover	
Antenna amplifier, diversity	Wagon	Behind left side cargo area storage cover	Fig. 57
Antenna amplifier, main	Convertible	Below mast antenna in trunk	
Antenna amplifier, main	Sedan, Coupe	Behind left rear roof pillar (C-pillar) trim panel	Fig. 44
Antenna amplifier, main	Wagon	Below rear spoiler	
Antenna diversity switching module	Convertible	Below mast antenna in trunk	
Antenna, AM	Wagon	In rear spoiler	
Antenna, diversity	Convertible	In convertible top storage cover	
Antenna, diversity	Wagon	Left rear side window	
Antenna, FZV (keyless entry)	Convertible	Interior rear view mirror	
Antenna, FZV (keyless entry)	Sedan, Coupe	Rear window, lower antenna grid	

Table e. E46 component locations

Component	Year, model	Location	Refer to
Antenna, FZV (keyless entry)	Wagon	Center rear window, combined with FM2 antenna	
Antenna, main	Convertible	Mast on left rear fender	
Antenna, main (FM1 and FM2)	Wagon	Rear window center and right	
Antenna, telephone	Convertible	Wound around mast antenna	
Antenna, telephone	Coupe, Sedan, Wagon	In roof above rear window	
Anti-slip (traction)		see ABS/ASC entries	
Anti-slip (traction) control switch		see ASC/DSC switch	
Anti-theft		see Alarm entries	
ASC		see ABS/ASC entries	
ASC+T		see ABS/ASC entries	
ASC/DSC switch		Bottom of center console, left of shifter	
AST		see ABS/ASC entries	
Automatic climate control (IHKA)		see A/C entries	
Automatic transmission control module (TCM) (A7000)		Left rear engine compartment in E-box	Fig. 16
Automatic transmission range switch (gear position/neutral safety switch)	GM trans.	Left side of transmission, inside transmission case	
Automatic transmission range switch (gear position/neutral safety switch)	ZF trans.	Left side of transmission	Fig. 64
Automatic transmission range switch harness connector	ZF trans.	Left side of transmission	Fig. 64
B+ jumper connector		Next to right front strut tower, right rear engine compartment	Fig. 17, Fig. 19
B+ supply, E-box (A2076)		Left side of E-box	Fig. 16
Back-up light switch (automatic transmission)		see Automatic transmission range switch	
Back-up light switch (manual transmission)		Top left side of transmission housing (Getrag) Right front or transmission housing (ZF) see **230 Manual Transmission**	
Back-up light relay (automatic transmission) (K6325)		Left rear engine compartment, in E-box	Fig. 16
Battery		Right side trunk or cargo compartment, under tray	
Battery safety terminal (BST)		On positive battery terminal	
Blower		see A/C blower	
Body electronics control module		see General module (GM V)	
Brake fluid level sensor		Top of brake fluid reservoir, left rear engine compartment	Fig. 17, Fig. 18
Brake fluid pressure sensor		see ABS/DSC charge pressure sensor	
Brake light switch (S29)		At pedal cluster	Fig. 37
Brake pad sensor, left front		Left front brake pad	
Brake pad sensor, right rear		Right rear brake pad	
Brake pad wear sensor connector, left front		In left front wheel housing	Fig. 62
Brake pad wear sensor connector, right rear		Ahead of right rear wheel housing	
Can bus terminal resistor (R8554)		Left side engine compartment in E-box	Fig. 66
Camshaft actuator (VANOS)		see VANOS	
Camshaft position sensor, exhaust (B6224)		Right front of cylinder head	Fig. 29

Table e. E46 component locations

Component	Year, model	Location	Refer to
Camshaft position sensor, intake (B6214)		Left front of cylinder head	Fig. 28
Carbon canister valve	1999 - 2000	Right side of spare tire well under floor pan	
CD changer		Left side of trunk	
Center brake light	Sedan, Coupe	Rear of headliner	
Central locking switch		see Hazard warning/central locking switch	
Changeover valve, intake manifold		see Resonance valve, intake manifold	
Changeover valve, running losses		see 3/2-way valve	
Charge pressure sensor		see ABS/DSC charge pressure sensor	
Child protection window control		see Window lock-out switch, rear	
Chime module, park distance control (PDC)		In left footwell top trim	
Clock		In on-board computer display of instrument cluster	
Clutch pedal position switch (S32)		On pedal cluster	
Clutch switch module (S805)		On clutch pedal	
Combination (stalk) switch		see Turn-signal/headlight dimmer switch (stalk switch) see also Wiper/washer switch (stalk switch)	
Connectors		See X connectors	
Convertible top control module (CVM II)	Convertible	Left rear quarter panel behind trim panel	Fig. 67
Convertible top hydraulic motor	Convertible	In left side of trunk behind trim cover	Fig. 67
Convertible top main pillar Hall sensor	Convertible	Behind rear seat in C pillar position	Fig. 67
Convertible top solenoid valves	Convertible	Left and right rear main pillar, behind quarter panel windows	Fig. 67
Convertible top storage compartment floor microswitch	Convertible	Right side storage compartment hinge in trunk	Fig. 67
Convertible top storage cover Hall sensor	Convertible	Left rear of convertible top cover	Fig. 67
Convertible top storage cover lock Hall sensor	Convertible	Center of cover, between rear seat backrests	Fig. 67
Convertible top storage cover lock motor Hall sensor	Convertible	Center of cover, between rear seat backrests	Fig. 67
Convertible top storage cover motor	Convertible	Center of cover, between rear seat backrests	Fig. 67
Convertible top switch	Convertible	Bottom of center console, ahead of shifter	Fig. 67
Convertible top tension bow Hall sensor	Convertible	Top rear of convertible top	Fig. 67
Convertible top visor latch Hall sensor	Convertible	Top of windshield	Fig. 67
Coolant level sensor		At bottom of coolant expansion tank	
Coolant temperature sensor, radiator outlet		In lower radiator hose, right front of engine	Fig. 31
Coolant temperature sensor		see Engine coolant temperature (ECT) sensor	
Coolant thermostat (B6279)		Front of cylinder head	
Cooling fan		see Engine cooling fan entries	
Crankshaft position sensor (B6203)		Left rear of engine block, under starter motor	Fig. 22
Cruise control cut-off switch		At pedal cluster	Fig. 37
Cruise controls (steering wheel)		Steering wheel right side keypad	
Data link connector (20-pin DLC)	1999 - 2000	Right rear engine compartment (see also OBD II connector)	Fig. 17
Diagnosis module tank leakage (DMTL)	2001 - 2005	see Fuel tank leakage diagnosis pump (LDP or DMTL)	
Digital motor electronics control module		see Engine control module (ECM)	
Directional switch (stalk switch)		see Turn signal/headlight dimmer switch (stalk switch)	
DLC		see Data link connector see also OBD II connector	

Table e. E46 component locations

Component	Year, model	Location	Refer to
DME control module		see Engine control module (ECM)	
DME main relay		Left rear engine compartment in E-box	Fig. 16
DMTL	2001 - 2005	see Fuel tank leakage diagnosis pump (LDP or DMTL)	
Door lock		In door	
Door lock Hall sensor		In door lock mechanism	
Door lock microswitch		In door lock mechanism	
Drive-away protection		see EWS	
DSC		see ABS/DSC entries	
DSC switch		see ASC/DSC switch	
DWA		see Alarm entries	
Dynamic stability control		see ABS/DSC entries	
E-box		Left rear engine compartment, under plastic cover	Fig. 16
E-box cooling fan (M6506)		Bottom rear of E-box or left side of left footwell.	
E-box temperature sensor		Rear of E-box	Fig. 16
ECT sensor		see Engine coolant temperature (ECT) sensor	
EDK throttle motor (Y6390)		At throttle body	
EDR throttle motor (Y5392)		Left side of engine under intake	
Electric coolant thermostat		see Coolant thermostat	
Electronic immobilizer		see EWS entries	
Electronics box		see E-box entries	
Engine compartment light switch		see Engine hood contact switch	
Engine control module (ECM)		Left rear engine compartment in E-box	Fig. 16
Engine coolant temperature (ECT) sensor (B6236) (B6232)		Under rear of intake manifold at rear of cylinder block	Fig. 21
Engine coolant outlet temperature (ECT) sensor (I01023)		Right side of engine near radiator	
Engine cooling fan (electric) (M9)		Models with automatic transmission: In front of radiator Models with standard transmission: In back of radiator	Fig. 17
Engine cooling fan final stage (resistor)		In engine cooling fan housing	
Engine electronics fuse pack		see Fuses, engine electronics	
Engine hood contact switch		Right rear engine compartment	Fig. 19
Engine hood switch (SMG) (A137)(A138)		Engine compartment in left and right lock carrier	
Evaporative control valve (Y6120)		Left front of engine mounted on intake manifold	
Evaporator temperature sensor		see A/C evaporator temperature sensor	
EWS control module (A836)		Left side of passenger compartment bulkhead, above pedal cluster	Fig. 38
EWS ring antenna		Around ignition switch	Fig. 36
EWS transmitter module		In ignition key	
Exhaust camshaft position sensor		Right front of engine, top	Fig. 29
Exhaust camshaft VANOS solenoid		Right front of engine, top	Fig. 29
Exhaust flap soleniod (Y198)		Left side of luggage compartment, behind trim panel	
Exhaust temperature sensor (MS S54) (B5351)		In exhaust ahead of catalyst	
Fog light relay (K47)		Main relay panel behind glove compartment	Fig. 14, Fig. 15
Footwell light, left		In left footwell top trim (pedal cluster trim)	
Footwell light, right		In right footwell top trim	

Table e. E46 component locations

Component	Year, model	Location	Refer to
Fresh air distribution motor		see Air distribution motors	
Fuel filler door lock motor		In right side of trunk or cargo compartment, behind trim	
Fuel injector relay (K6327)	2001 - 2005	Left rear engine compartment in E-box	Fig. 16
Fuel injectors electrical harness		Top of engine, under plastic cover	
Fuel level sensor, left		Top of fuel tank, under left rear seat cushion	Fig. 52
Fuel level sensor, right		Top of fuel tank, under right rear seat cushion, combined with fuel pump	Fig. 52
Fuel pump		Top of fuel tank, under right rear seat cushion, combined with right fuel level sensor. See **160 Fuel Tank and Fuel Pump** for more information.	Fig. 52
Fuel pump control module (A13663) MS45.1		Right side of trunk behind trim panel, 6-pin black connector and 2-pin balck connector for relay	
Fuel pump relay (K96) MS 42.0, MS 43.0 MS S54		Behind glove compartment, main relay panel In trunk, right side behind trim panel in trunk (9-pin black connector)	Fig. 14, Fig. 15
Fuel tank leakage diagnosis pump (LDP or DMTL) (I01065)		Under right rear of vehicle, right side of trunk, under protective cover. Or, right rear wheel well (MS 45).	Fig. 65
Fuel tank vent valve		see Evaporative control valve	
Fuse for main harness F108 (200 amp)		Right wheel housing in trunk	Fig. 1
Fuse panel, main		Above glove compartment	Fig. 14, Fig. 15
Fuses, additional high amperage		Above main fuse panel	Fig. 4
Fuses, engine electronics		Left rear engine compartment in E-box	Fig. 2
FZV antenna		see Antenna, FZV (keyless entry)	
Gas generator, airbag		see Airbag entries	
Gear position indicator light (E82)		Under shifter bezel	Fig. 47
Gear position/neutral safety switch		see Automatic transmission range switch	
General module (GM V)		Main relay panel behind glove compartment	Fig. 14
Generator		see Alternator (generator)	
Glove compartment lock motor		Above glove compartment lock	
GM V		see General module (GM V)	
GPS receiver module		In trunk, mounted behind left rear well	
Ground jumper connection		Right rear engine compartment	Fig. 19
Grounds:			
X1108		Under driver seat carpet on door sill	Fig. 9
X13016		Left side trunk	Fig. 13, Fig. 54
X165		Left front, engine compartment	Fig. 5
X166		Right front, engine compartment	Fig. 6
X173		Under left front carpet on door sill	Fig. 8
X217		Under right side dashboard	
X218		Under right side tunnel carpet	
X490		Under right front seat carpet on door sill	Fig. 10
X494		Behind rear seat backrest	Fig. 11
X498		Right side trunk	Fig. 12, Fig. 53
X6454		On bulkhead, left rear engine compartment	Fig. 7
Hardtop locater mounts (E99, E100)		Left and right sides of convertible top cowl	

Table e. E46 component locations

Component	Year, model	Location	Refer to
Hazard warning/central locking switch (S18)		On center console, behind shifter	
Head protection airbag (HPS)		see Airbag listings	
Headlight dimmer relay		In light control center (LSZ)	
Headlight flasher		see Turn-signal/headlight dimmer switch (stalk switch)	
Headlight vertical aim actuator (left/right) (models with xenon headlights)(M80, M81)		In headlight assembly (left/right)	
Headlight vertical aim load sensor, front (B42)		Front subframe, right side	Fig. 59
Headlight vertical aim load sensor, rear (B64)		Rear subframe, right side	
Headlight washer pump		Front of washer tank, right front engine compartment	
Heater blower		see A/C blower entries	
Heater core temperature sensor		Behind center console below radio	Fig. 45
Heater recirculation distribution motor		see Air distribution motors	
Heater regulator air distribution motor		see Air distribution motors	
Heater valve assembly		Mounted on inner side of left strut tower	Fig. 27
Heating-A/C		see A/C entries	
High beam switch		see Turn signal/headlight dimmer switch (stalk switch)	
Hood switch		see Engine hood security switch	
Horn button		On steering wheel pad	
Horn relay		Main relay panel behind glove compartment	Fig. 14, Fig. 15
Horn (left/right)		Next to front bumper impact absorber (left/right)	
Hot-film mass air flow sensor		see Mass air flow sensor	
Idle speed control valve (Y6130)		Left hand side of engine, under intake manifold	Fig. 23
Ignition coils		Top of cylinder head, under plastic cover	Fig. 25
Ignition relay		see Unloader relay	
Ignition switch		Right side steering column	
IHKA		see A/C entries	
Individual control intake system valve		see Resonance valve, intake manifold	
Inflator assembly, airbag		see Airbag entries	
Instrument cluster control unit (A2)		In instrument cluster	
Intake air temperature (IAT) sensor (B6205)		Center top of engine, between intake manifold and cylinder head	Fig. 25
Intake manifold resonance valve		see Resonance valve, intake manifold	
Interior protection control module (SDR)	Convertible	On center tunnel below console	
Interior protection control module (UIS)	Sedan, Coupe, Wagon	In headliner	
Interior temperature intake fan		In A/C control module in center console	
Interference suppression filter (I01064)		Under roof spoiler (Touring)	
Keyless entry antenna		see Antenna, FZV (keyless entry)	
Kickdown switch, automatic transmission		see Accelerator pedal sensor (PWG)	
Knock sensors (B6240, B6241, B6242, B6243)		Under intake manifold, on engine block	Fig. 24
Lateral acceleration sensor		see ABS/DSC lateral acceleration sensor entries	

Table e. E46 component locations

Component	Year, model	Location	Refer to
LDP		see Fuel tank leakage diagnosis pump (LDP or DMTL)	
Leakage diagnosis pump (LDP)		see Fuel tank leakage diagnosis pump (LDP or DMTL)	
Light control module		In light switch center (LSZ)	
Light control module, adaptive (A214)			
Light switch assembly		In light switch center (LSZ)	
Light switch center (LSZ)		In dashboard, left of steering wheel	
Load-reduction relay		see Unloader relay	
Lumbar support air compressor		Under each seat equipped with support system	
Lumbar support control switch		Below seat base trim	
Lumbar support switch		Four-way toggle switch at base of seat, near seat control switches	
Main fuse panel		see Fuse panel, main	
Main relay panel		see Relay panel, main	
Main harness fuse		see Fuse for main harness F108 (200 amp)	
Mass air flow sensor (B6207)		Left side engine compartment, behind air box	Fig. 17
Mixing actuators		see Air distribution motors	
MRS module		see Airbag control module	
Multi-function clock		In dash cluster below speedometer and tachometer	
Multiple restraint system (MRS) module		see Airbag control module	
Navigation computer		Left side of trunk	
Neutral safety switch		see Automatic transmission range switch	
OBD II connector (16-pin DLC)		In left footwell top trim, under left side of instrument cluster (see also Data link connector)	
Oil level sensor (MS S54) (B6254)		Bottom of oil pan	
Oil pressure switch (B6231)		Left front of engine at oil filter housing	Fig. 26
Oil temperature sensor (B6238)		Left front of engine at oil filter housing	Fig. 26
On-board computer		In instrument cluster	
On-board monitor		In center of dashboard	
Outside air temperature sensor		Under left side of front bumper	
Outside mirror control switch		On left front door arm rest	
Oxygen sensor connector, post-catalyst		Top of engine, between intake manifold and cylinder head cover	Fig. 25
Oxygen sensor connector, precatalyst		Top of engine, between exhaust manifold and cylinder head cover	Fig. 25
Oxygen sensor, post-catalyst		Bottom of exhaust manifold (access from below)	Fig. 58
Oxygen sensor, precatalyst		Top of exhaust manifold	Fig. 25
Oxygen sensor 1 (heated), precatalyst (B62101)		In exhaust pipe, ahead of catalyst	
Oxygen sensor 2 (heated), precatalyst (B62201)		In exhaust pipe, ahead of catalyst	
Oxygen sensor 1 (heated), post-catalyst (B62101) (B62102)		In exhaust pipe, behind catalyst	
Oxygen sensor 2 (heated), post-catalyst (B62201) (B62202)		In exhaust pipe, behind catalyst	
Park angle/tilt sensor		In right side trunk behind trim	
Park distance control (PDC) module		In right side trunk above battery	
Park distance control sensors		Rear bumper trim strip	Fig. 68
Park distance control warning speaker		Right rear speaker, rear parcel shelf	
Parking brake warning switch		Under center console, rear of parking brake handle	Fig. 49

Table e. E46 component locations

Component	Year, model	Location	Refer to
Pedal position sensor		see Accelerator pedal sensor (PWG)	
Pinch protection, window		see Window anti-trap strip	
Power socket, 12-volt	Wagon	Cargo compartment behind left rear seat	Fig. 57
Power window motors		see Window motors	
Power window switches		see Window switches	
Pressure sensitive finger guard		see Window anti-trap strip	
Radiator fan		see Engine cooling fan (electric)	
Radio antenna		see Antenna entries	
Radio controls (steering wheel)		On steering wheel left keypad	
Radio speaker: front tweeter (left/right)		Front door window frame (left/right)	Fig. 33
Radio/cassette/CD player		Center of dashboard	
Rain sensor (B57)		Top center of interior windshield surface, directly ahead of rear view mirror	
Rain sensor control module (AIC)		Attached to rain sensor at top of windshield	
Rear power window lock-out switch		see Window lock-out switch, rear	
Rear window defogger relay	Convertible	Right rear quarter panel behind trim panel	
Rear window defogger relay	Sedan, Coupe	Right trunk wall, behind trim liner	Fig. 53
Rear window defogger relay	Sport Wagon	Right rear cargo area behind trim panel	
Rear window washer pump	Sport Wagon	Behind panel in right rear cargo area	Fig. 56
Relay panel, main		Behind glove compartment	
Resonance valve, intake manifold		Left of intake manifold	Fig. 17
Reversing light switch		see Automatic transmission range switch or Back-up light switch	
Ride level sensor		see Headlight vertical aim sensor entries	
Ring antenna (EWS)		see EWS ring antenna	
Rollover cassette	Convertible	Rear seat headrest	
Rollover sensor	Convertible	Rear seat headrest	
Rotational rate (yaw) sensor		see ABS/DSC rotational rate (yaw) sensor	
Seat backrest motor		Bottom of seat backrest	Fig. 51
Seat control switch module		At base of seat, on side of seat cushion	Fig. 50
Seat cushion tilt motor		Bottom of seat cushion	Fig. 50
Seat forward-back motor		Bottom of seat cushion	Fig. 50
Seat headrest motor		Top of front seat backrest	Fig. 51
Seat heater		In front seat cushion and backrest	
Seat heater switch		Center console, below IHKA control panel	
Seat heater temperature sensor		Front of front seat cushion	
Seat height motor		Back of seat cushion	Fig. 50
Seat load sensor	2000 - 2005	Under passenger seat cushion	
Seat memory module (SM)		Front of seat cushion	Fig. 50
Seat belt lock Hall sensor		In seat belt lock	
Seat belt tensioner, pyrotechnic (left/right)		Base of seat belt lock (left/right)	
Secondary air injection pump (M65) (M63)		Right side engine compartment, above exhaust manifold	Fig. 17, Fig. 30
Secondary air injection pump relay (K6305) (K6304)		Main relay panel behind glove compartment (K6305). Interior passenger side behind right footwell trim (K6304)	Fig. 14, Fig. 15
Secondary air injection pump valve (Y6163)		Rear of engine under intake pipe	Fig. 30

Table e. E46 component locations

Component	Year, model	Location	Refer to
Secondary air mass air flow meter (B6206)		Right side of engine compartment, above exhaust manifold	
Shift interlock cable		Under shifter bezel	Fig. 46
Shiftlock solenoid		Under shifter bezel	
Selector lever shift lock (SMG) (SMGII) (Y19)		Center conslol near selctor lever	
Side-impact airbag		see Airbag entries	
Slip control		see ABS/ASC or ABS/DSC entries	
SMG control module (A70010)		Left side of engine compartment, in E-box	
SMG program switch (S8503)		Center console near shift lever	
SMG II control module (A5300)		Left side of engine, in E-box	
SMG gear change switch left (I01066)		Left side of steering wheel	
SMG gear change switch right (I01181)		Right side of steering wheel	
SMG gear shift sensor (B6572)		Top of transmission	
SMG selector angle sensor (B6573)		Top of transmission	
SMG hydraulic pump (Y69750)		Left side of transmission	
SMG hydraulic pump relay (K6318)		In E-box	
SMG II hydraulic pump relay (K5360)		In E-box	
SMG II hydraulic unit (Y5330)		Left side of engine compartment, under intake pipe	
SMG hydraulic pressure sensor (B6571)		Right side of transmission	
SMG gear solenoid valve 1 (Y6561)		Right side of transmission	
SMG gear solenoid valve 2 (Y6562)		Right side of transmission	
SMG brakes soleniod valve (Y6563)		Right side of transmission	
SMG clutch soleniod valve (Y6564)		Right side of transmission	
SMG clutch position sensor (B6574)		Left side of transmission	
SMG II clutch position sensor (B5141)		Left side of transmission	
SMG rpm sensor (Y8616)		Right side of transmission	
SMG selector lever ASG (A134)		Center console near gear shift	
SMG II transmission speed sensor (Y8516)		Left side of transmission	
SMG II gear position angle sensor (R5140)		Base of gear shift lever	
SMG II longitudinal acceleration sensor (B49)		Under carpet of passenger's seat	
Socket, 12 volt		see Power socket, 12-volt	
Solar sensor	2000 - 2005	Right defroster outlet at base of windshield	
Sound system amplifier		see Amplifier, radio	
Speed sensor		see ABS wheel speed sensor entries	
Spiral spring		see Volute spring	
Starter		Left rear of engine, under intake manifold	
Starter immobilization switch (manual transmission)		On clutch pedal	
Starter terminals 30, 50		Left rear of engine, under intake manifold	Fig. 22
Steering angle sensor		see ABS/DSC steering angle sensor	
Stepper motors		see Air distribution motors	
Steptronic switch	2000 - 2005	Under shifter bezel	
Stop light switch		see Brake light switch	

Table e. E46 component locations

Component	Year, model	Location	Refer to
Sunroof motor		In headliner	Fig. 43
Sunroof/sunshade switch		In center console ahead of shifter	
Supplemental restraint system (SRS)		see Airbag entries	
Tailgate lock (central locking)	Wagon	In tailgate lock	
Tailgate emergency release actuator	Wagon	Rear deck sill, under trim panel, integrated with lock mechanism	
Tailgate unlock switch, exterior	Wagon	Above license plate	
Tailgate unlock switch, interior	Wagon	Left kick panel	
Telephone connector		Under center console	Fig. 48
Telephone antenna		see Antenna entries	
Telephone controls (steering wheel)		Steering wheel left keypad	
Telephone speaker		In left footwell top trim	
Telephone transceiver	Sedan, Coupe	In trunk below parcel shelf	
Thermostat, characteristic map cooling		see Coolant thermostat	
Throttle housing (MDK/EDK)		Under intake manifold	Fig. 23
Throttle actuator (Y6390)		Left front of engine, in front of throttle housing	
Throttle position sensor		see Accelerator pedal sensor (PWG)	
Throttle position sensor (MS S54) (R6252)		Top left side of cylinder head	
Tilt sensor		see Park angle/tilt sensor	
Tire pressure control system (RDC) control unit (A417)		Behind glove compartment	
Toroidal coil		see EWS ring antenna	
Traction control		see ABS/ASC or ABS/DSC entries	
Trailer module		Right side trunk	
Transmission control module		see Automatic transmission module	
Transmission range switch		see Automatic transmission range switch	
Transmission temperature sensor (SMG) (B5238)		Left side of transmission	
Transverse acceleration sensor		see ABS/DSC lateral acceleration sensor entries	
Trunk lid microswitch	Sedan, Coupe, Convertible	In trunk lid lock	
Trunk light switch	Sedan, Coupe, Convertible	In trunk lid lock	
Trunk lock (central locking)	Sedan, Coupe, Convertible	In trunk lid lock	
Turn-signal/headlight dimmer switch (stalk switch)		Left side of steering column	
Ultrasonic sensor (motion detector) (UIS)	Coupe, Sedan, Wagon	In headliner	
Unloader relay		Left rear engine compartment in E-box,	Fig. 16
Valet position switch		On trunk lock cylinder	
VANOS solenoid, exhaust side (Y6276)		Right front of cylinder head	Fig. 29
VANOS solenoid, intake side (Y6275)		Left front of cylinder head	Fig. 17
Variable camshaft control		see VANOS	
Volute spring (I01066)		In center of steering wheel under driver airbag	

Table e. E46 component locations

Component	Year, model	Location	Refer to
Washer fluid level sensor		Bottom of windshield washer tank	
Wheel speed sensor		see ABS wheel speed sensor entries	
Window anti-trap strip	Sedan, Wagon Convertible	Top of window frame in door Integrated into wondow lift motor (2003-2005)	
Window lock-out switch, rear	Sedan, Wagon	Left side shifter bezel	
Window motors		Inside doors	
Window switches		On shifter bezel	
Windshield washer nozzle heaters		In nozzles at rear of engine hood	
Windshield washer pump		At rear of washer tank, right front engine compartment	
Windshield washer relay		Left rear engine compartment in E-box	Fig. 16
Wiper motor		Rear of engine compartment, behind bulkhead	Fig. 20
Wiper/washer switch (stalk)		Right side steering column	
X connectors			
X01120		Component connector (3-pin, black), on rear window (wagon)	
X01185	(SMG)	Component connector (2-pin, bordeaux), in steering wheel	
X01186	(SMG)	Plug connector (3-pin, black), in steering wheel	
X1019		Connector Nighttime illumination, under carpet on RH side of transmission range switch	
X1179		Connector, LH A-pillar bottom	
X1215		Connector Brake light, RH side of steering column	
X10439	(MS 45)	Intermediate connector (2-pin, black), behind rear seat backrest right	
X10148		Connector I-bus signal, behind glove box	
X10170	(SMG)	Component connector (10-pin, green), behind steering wheel	
X10171	(SMG)	Component connector (2-pin, bordeaux), behind steering wheel	
X10189		Connector Consumer cut-off signal, behind glove box	
X10289		Plug connector (1-pin, black), under roof spoiler	
X11197	(to 06/00)	Component connector (20-pin, black), rear of engine compartment right	
X13033		Connector Terminal 30, behind glove box	
X19527	(all)	Plug connector (16-pin, black), in cover of left footwell	
X257		Plug connector (22-pin, black), behind glove box	
X273		Plug connector (22-pin, black), LH B-pillar bottom	
X274		Plug connector (22-pin, black), RH B-pillar bottom	
X5051	(SMG)	Connector Sensor ground, cable duct, bulkhead on right of steering column	
X5141	(SMG)	Component connector (6-pin, black), vehicle underbody left	
X51507	(MS S54)	Plug connector (7-pin, black), under front LH bumper	
X6011		Plug connector (8-pin, black), rear LH side of engine compartment	
X6021		Plug connector (4-pin, black), rear LH side of engine compartment in E-box	
X6053		Plug connector (8-pin, natural), rear LH side of engine compartment in E-box	
X6054		Plug connector (2-pin, natural), rear LH side of engine compartment in E-box	
X60531	(MS 45)	Intermediate connector (8-pin, natural), in E-box	
X60541	(MS 45)	Intermediate connector (2-pin, black), in E-box	

Table e. E46 component locations

Component	Year, model	Location	Refer to
X64101		Plug connector (2-pin, black), rear LH side of engine compartment in E-box	
X64102		Plug connector (2-pin, black), rear LH side of engine compartment	
X6458		Connector Ground, rear LH side of engine compartment in E-box	
X6459		Connector Ground, rear LH side of engine compartment in E-box	
X6460	(MS S54)	Connector Ground, in connector branch, electronics box	
X6462	(MS S54)	Connector Ground, in connector well on front left suspension strut dome	
X6475	(MS S54)	Connector Ground, in connector well on front left suspension strut dome	
X60531	(MS 45)	Intermediate connector (8-pin, natural), in E-box	
X60541	(MS 45)	Intermediate connector (2-pin, black), in E-box	
X6830		Connector Terminal 15, rear LH side of engine compartment in E-box	
X6831	(MS 42)	Connector Terminal 30, LH side of engine under intake manifold	
X6831	(MS 43)	Connector Terminal 15, in E-box	
X6831	(MS S54)	Connector Terminal 15, in connector branch, electronics box	
X6831	(MS 45)	Connector Terminal 15, wiring harness grommet, electronics box	
X6960		Connector Terminal 87, rear LH side of engine compartment in E-box	
X6961	(MS 42)	Connector Voltage supply, rear LH side of engine compartment in E-box	
X6961	(MS 43)	Connector Terminal 87,	
X6961	(MS 45)	Connector Terminal 87, in connector branch, electronics box	
X6962		Connector Terminal 87, rear LH side of engine compartment in E-box	
X6963	(MS 42)	Connector Voltage supply, engine electronics via main relay	
X6963	(MS 43)	Connector Voltage supply Fuel injection valves	
X6963	(MS S54)	Connector Voltage supply, in connector branch, electronics box	
X6964	(MS 42)	Connector, wiring harness grommet, electronics box	
X6964	(MS 43)	Connector Terminal 87, in E-box	
X6964	(MS 45)	Connector Terminal 87, wiring harness grommet, electronics box	
X6965		Connector, wiring harness grommet, electronics box	
X6966	(MS S54)	Connector Terminal 87, in connector well on front left suspension strut dome	
X710		Component connector (3-pin, black), on lift gate	
X8516	(SMG)	Component connector (3-pin, black), on LH side of transmission rear	
X908		Connector Nighttime illumination, RH side of steering column	
Yaw sensor		see ABS/DSC rotational rate (yaw) sensor	
ZKE V control module		see General Module (GM V)	

Engine compartment electrical components

Fig. 17 Engine compartment (1999 323i)

1. Data link connector (DLC) (1999 - mid-2000 models)
2. Hood contact switch
3. B+ jumper connector
4. DSC control module/hydraulic unit
5. Secondary air pump
6. Interior microfilter housing
7. Resonance valve, intake manifold (changeover valve)
8. Mass air flow sensor
9. Brake fluid level sensor
10. Ground lug X6454
11. Electronics box (E-box)
12. Air quality sensor (AUC) (for automatic recirculation control)
13. Intake camshaft VANOS solenoid
14. Engine cooling fan (electric)

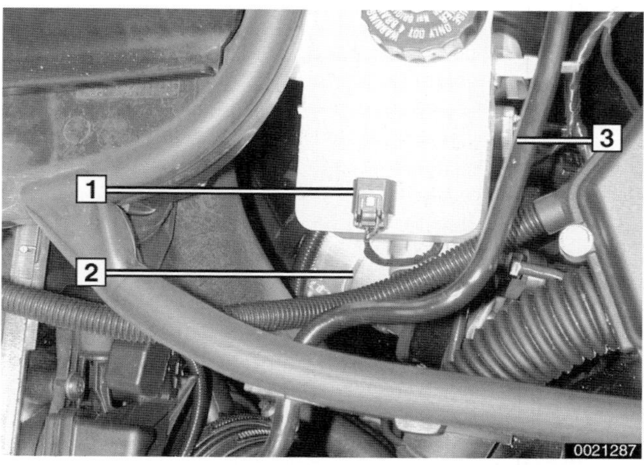

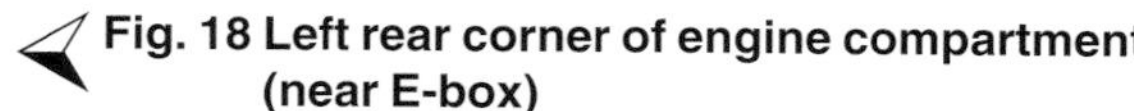
Fig. 18 Left rear corner of engine compartment (near E-box)

1. Brake fluid level sensor
2. DSC precharge pump (Teves DSC MK 20/60)
3. Brake fluid pressure sensor

Fig. 19 Right rear corner of engine compartment (Teves DSC MK 20/60)

1. DSC hydraulic unit
2. Ground jumper connection
3. Hood contact switch
4. B+ jumper connection
5. DSC control module

Fig. 20 Rear of engine compartment, behind bulkhead

1. Wiper assembly electrical harness connector

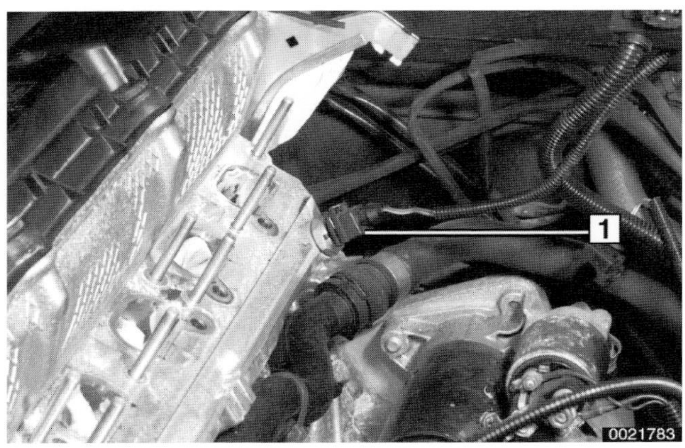

Fig. 21 Under rear of intake manifold

1. Engine coolant temperature (ECT) sensor

Fig. 22 Left rear of engine block, under intake manifold

1. Starter motor terminal 50
2. Starter motor terminal 30
3. Crankshaft position sensor
4. Bore hole for crankshaft locking tool

Fig. 23 Under intake manifold

1. Idle speed control valve
2. Throttle housing (MDK/EDK)

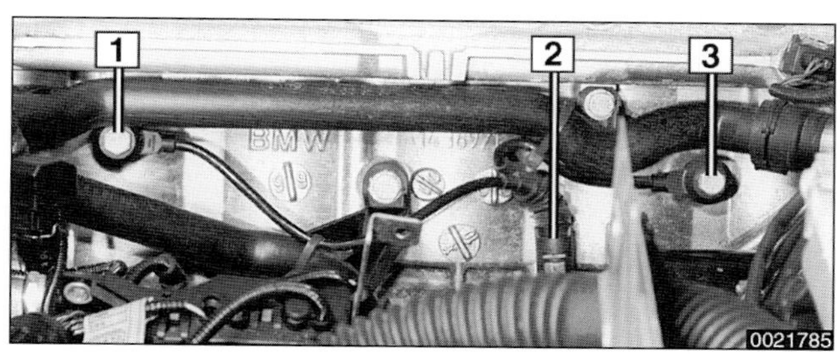

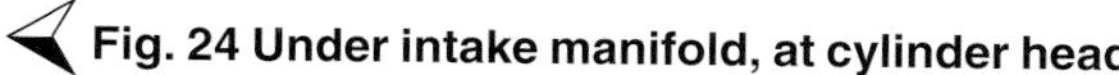

Fig. 24 Under intake manifold, at cylinder head

1. Knock sensor cylinder 1 - 3
2. Knock sensor harness connector
3. Knock sensor cylinder 4 - 6

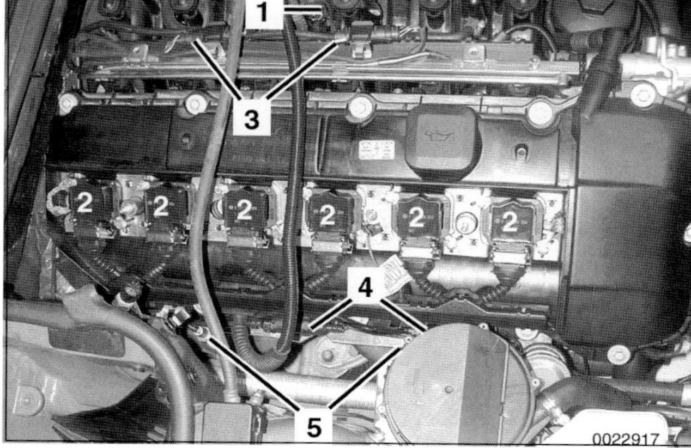

Fig. 25 Center top of engine, under covers

1. Intake air temperature (IAT) sensor
2. Ignition coils
3. Post-catalyst oxygen sensor connectors
4. Precatalyst oxygen sensor connectors
5. Precatalyst oxygen sensors

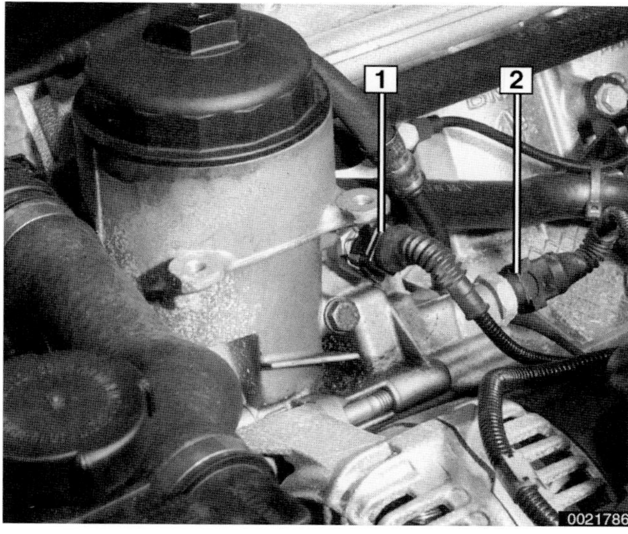

Fig. 26 Left front of engine, at oil filter housing

1. Oil/coolant temperature sensor
2. Oil pressure switch

Fig. 27 Left side of engine compartment

1. Heater control valve

Fig. 28 Cylinder head, left front

1. Intake camshaft position sensor

Fig. 29 Right front of engine, top

1. Exhaust camshaft position sensor
2. Exhaust camshaft VANOS solenoid
3. Air quality sensor (AUC) (for automatic recirculation control)

Fig. 30 Right front of engine

1. Secondary air injection pump
2. Secondary air injection pump valve

Fig. 31 Right front of engine, low

1. Exhaust camshaft position sensor
2. Coolant outlet temperature sensor

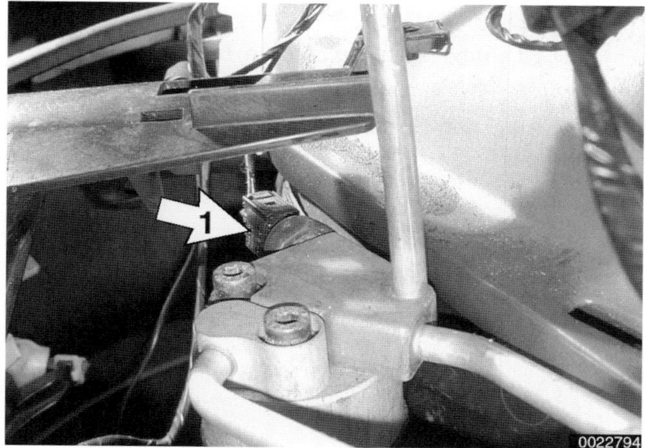

Fig. 32 Top of A/C receiver/drier, right front engine compartment

1. A/C pressure sensor

Car interior electrical components

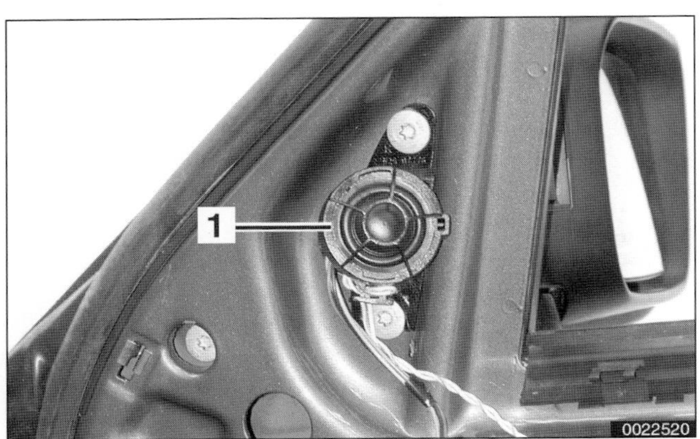

Fig. 33 Front door window frame

1.	Door mounted tweeter

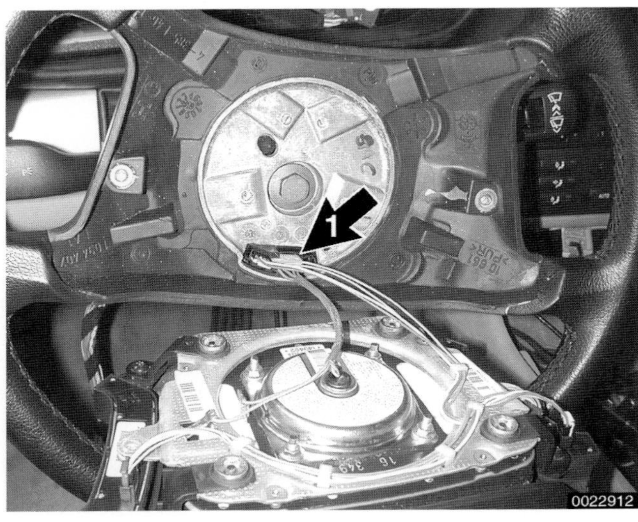

Fig. 34 Underneath horn pad at steering wheel

1.	Airbag connector

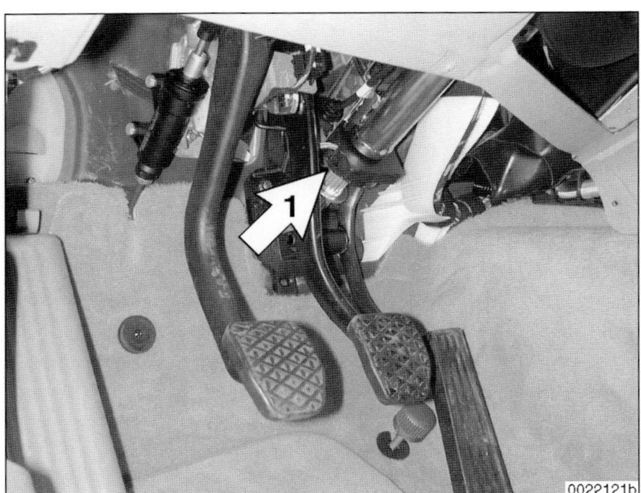

Fig. 35 Left side of steering column, below dashboard

1.	Steering angle sensor

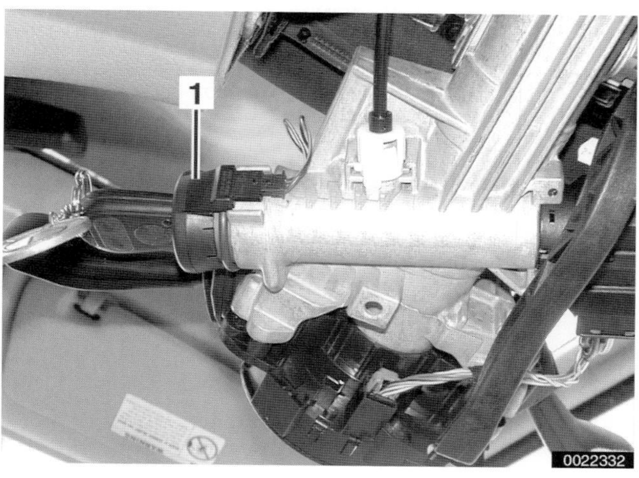

Fig. 36 At ignition switch

1. EWS (electronic immobilizer) ring antenna

Fig. 37 At pedal cluster

1. Cruise control cut-off switch (if equipped)
2. Brake light switch

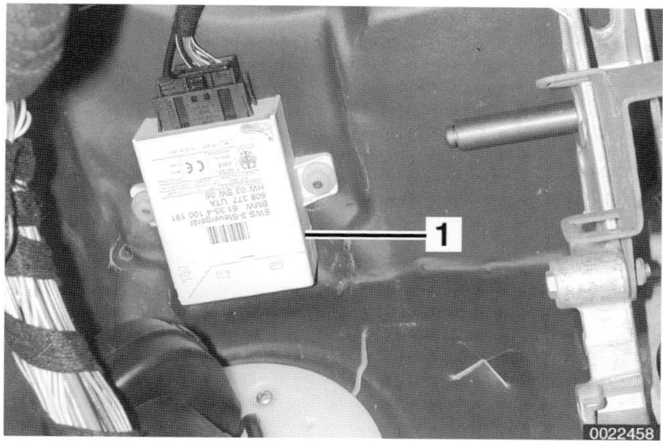

Fig. 38 Above pedal cluster

1. EWS control module

Fig. 39 Left side IHKA housing, below instrument cluster

1.	A/C evaporator temperature sensor

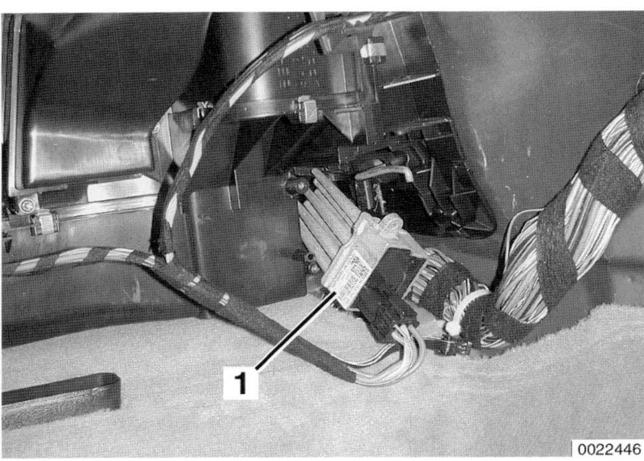

Fig. 40 Right side IHKA housing, below glove compartment

1.	Blower motor resistor pack

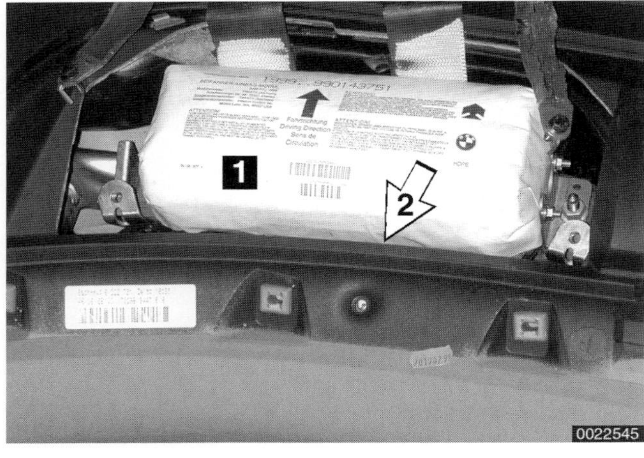

Fig. 41 Right side dashboard

1.	Passenger airbag
2.	Passenger airbag connector

Fig. 42 In windshield pillar (A-pillar)

1. Head protection airbag (HPS) electrical connector

Fig. 43 In headliner

1. Sunroof motor

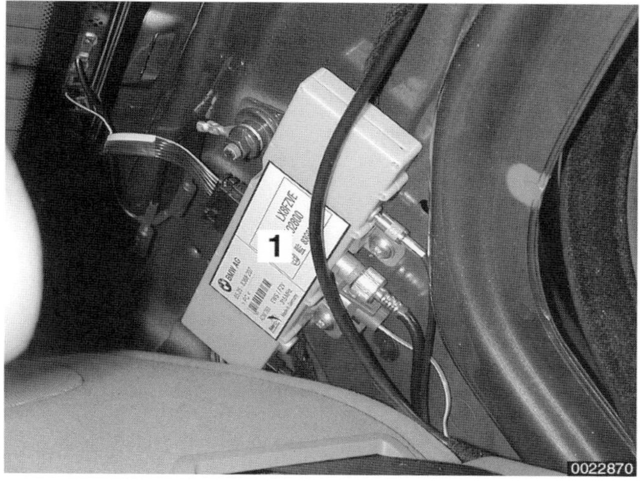

Fig. 44 In left rear roof pillar (C pillar)

1. Antenna amplifier

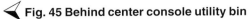

Fig. 45 Behind center console utility bin

1.	Heater core temperature sensor

Fig. 46 Under shifter bezel

1.	Shiftlock solenoid

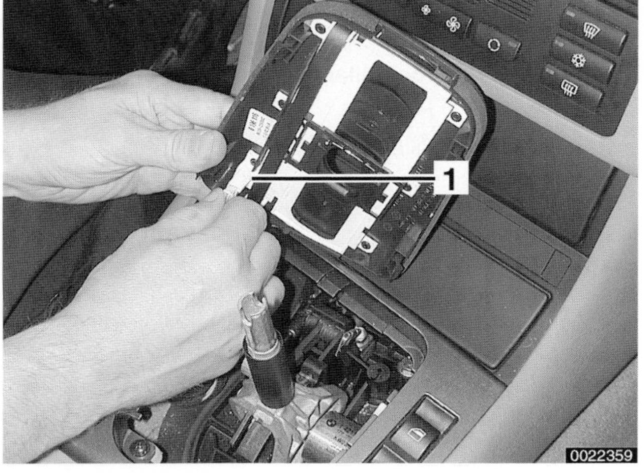

Fig. 47 At shifter bezel

1.	Gear position indicator light

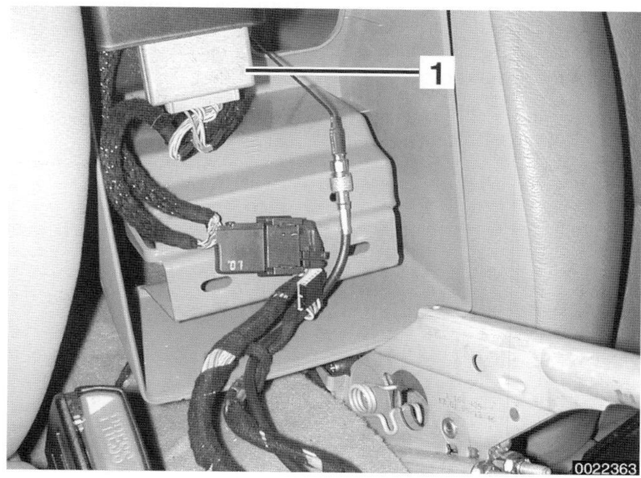

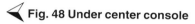

Fig. 48 Under center console

1.	Telephone connector

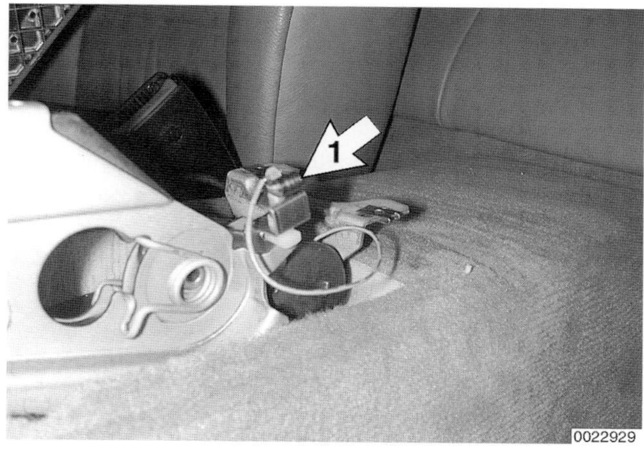

Fig. 49 Under center console, rear of parking brake handle

1.	Parking brake warning switch

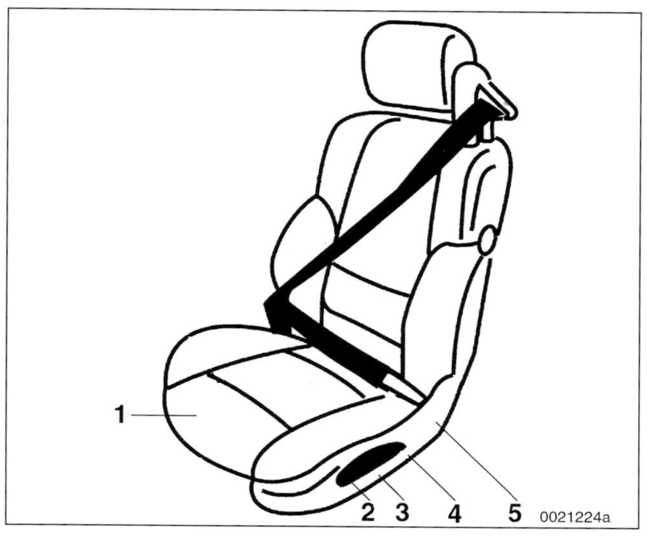

Fig. 50 Driver seat (Convertible seat front view)

1.	Seat memory module
2.	Seat control switch module
3.	Seat tilt motor
4.	Seat forward-back motor
5.	Seat height motor

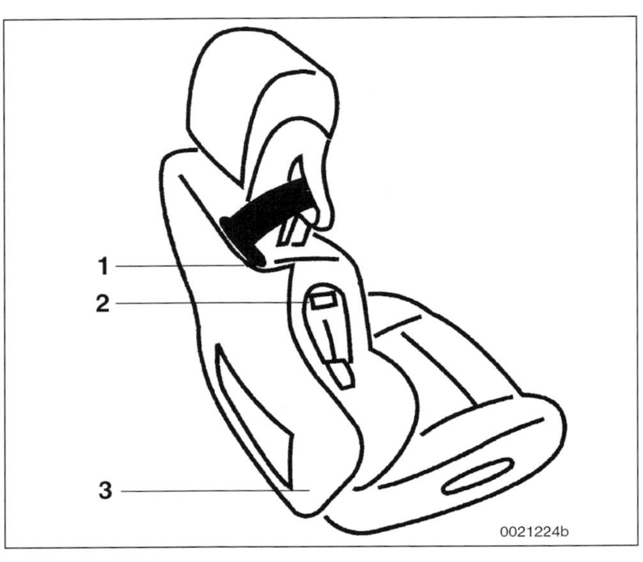

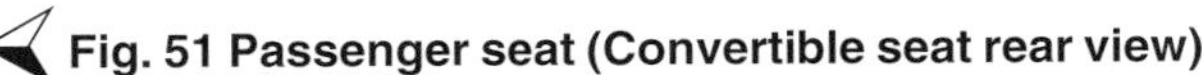

Fig. 51 Passenger seat (Convertible seat rear view)

1. Headrest motor
2. Comfort entry switch
3. Backrest motor

Fig. 52 Below rear seat cushion, under access covers (top of fuel tank)

1. Right side:
   Electric fuel pump and fuel level sender connector
2. Left side:
   Fuel level sender connector

Electrical components in luggage/cargo compartment

Fig. 53 Right side trunk

1. Rear window defogger relay
2. F108 (200 amp fuse) in main harness
3. Battery safety terminal (BST) (explosive charge)
4. Ground X498

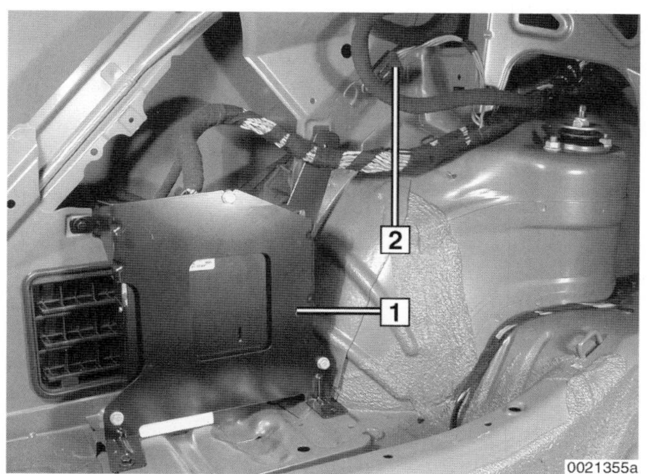

Fig. 54 Left side trunk

1. Sound system amplifier 2. Ground X13016

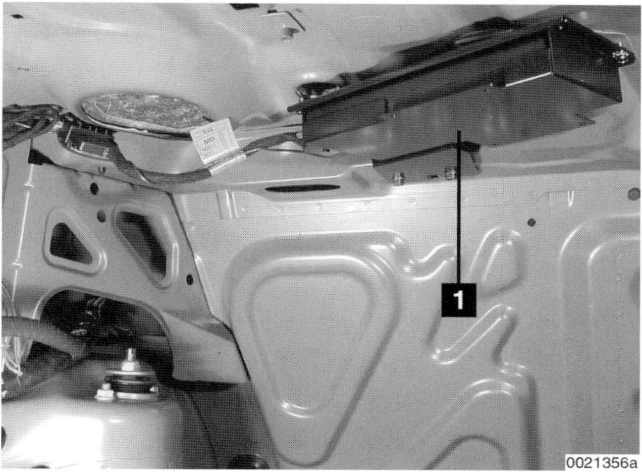

Fig. 55 Trunk, below parcel shelf

1. Telephone transceiver

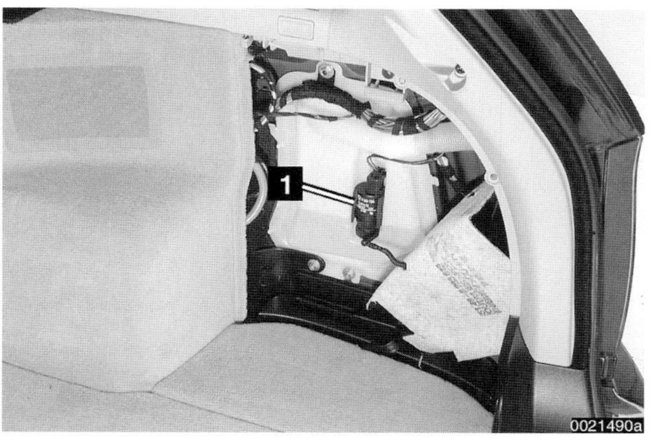

Fig. 56 Right cargo area, behind trim panel (Wagon)

1. Rear window washer pump

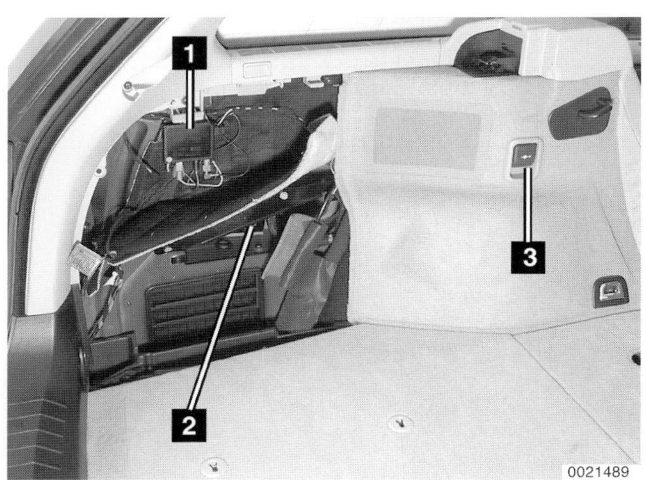

Fig. 57 Left cargo area (Sport Wagon)

1. Antenna diversity amplifier
2. Sound system components
3. Power socket, 12 volt

Electrical components underneath car

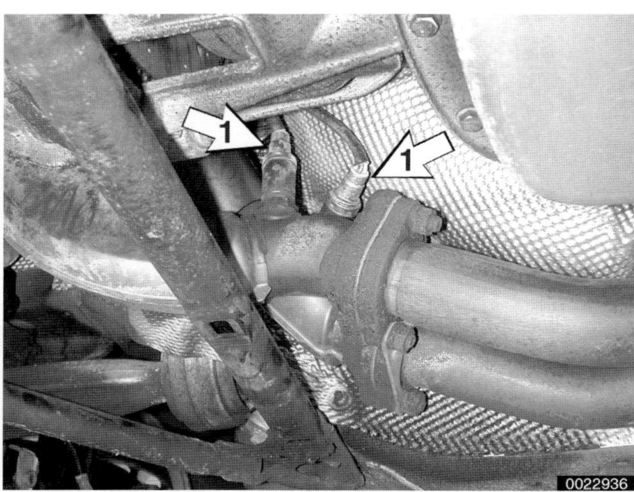

Fig. 58 Underneath right side of engine, at lower end of front exhaust pipes

1. Post-catalyst oxygen sensors

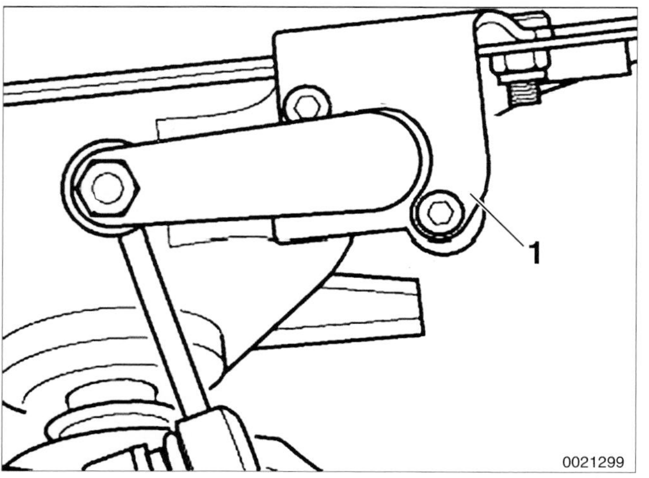

Fig. 59 At front subframe, right side

1. Front ride level sensor

Fig. 60 Right front steering arm (rear wheel drive model shown)

1.	ABS wheel speed sensor, front

NOTE —
Left front wheel speed sensor is similar.

Fig. 61 Right rear wheel bearing housing (1999 rear wheel drive model shown)

ABS wheel speed sensor, rear

NOTE —
Left rear wheel speed sensor is similar.

Fig. 62 In left front wheel housing

1.	ABS wheel speed sensor connector (2-pin grey)
2.	Brake pad wear sensor connector (2-pin black)

NOTE —
- *Right rear wheel speed sensor connector is similar.*
- *The right front and left rear brake pads lack the wear sensor.*

Fig. 63 Rear of automatic transmission (GM)

1. Transmission control (AGS) connector

Fig. 64 Left side of automatic transmission (ZF)

1. Transmission range switch/back-up light switch harness connector
2. Transmission range switch/back-up light switch
3. Transmission control (AGS) harness connector

Fig. 65 Underneath trunk

1. LDP/DMTL fuel tank diagnosis pump

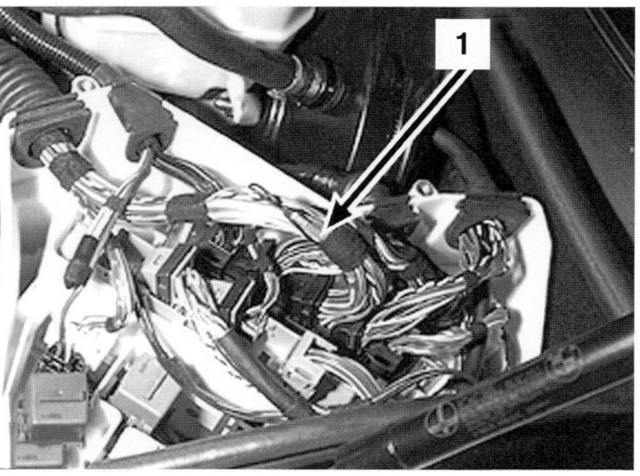

Fig. 66 In E-box box

1. Resistor, CAN terminal (R8554), DME MS 45.1

Convertible top electrical components

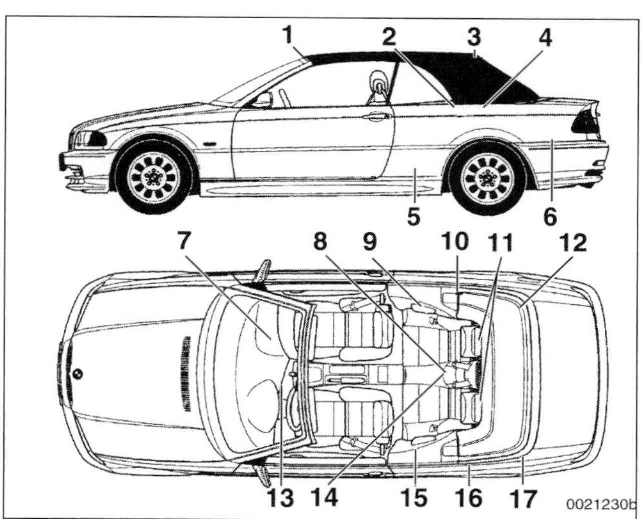

Fig. 67 Convertible

1.	Visor latch hall sensors
2.	Solenoid valves
3.	Tension bow hall sensor
4.	Main pillar hall sensor
5.	Convertible top module (CVM II)
6.	Hydraulic motor
7.	General module (GM V)
8.	Top storage cover lock motor
9.	Rear window defogger relays
10.	Storage cover lock hall sensor
11.	Roll-over cassettes and sensors
12.	Storage compartment floor microswitch
13.	Convertible top switch
14.	Cover lock motor hall sensor
15.	Convertible top module (CVM II)
16.	Storage cover and hard top lock hall sensor
17.	Storage cover hall sensor

Exterior electrical components

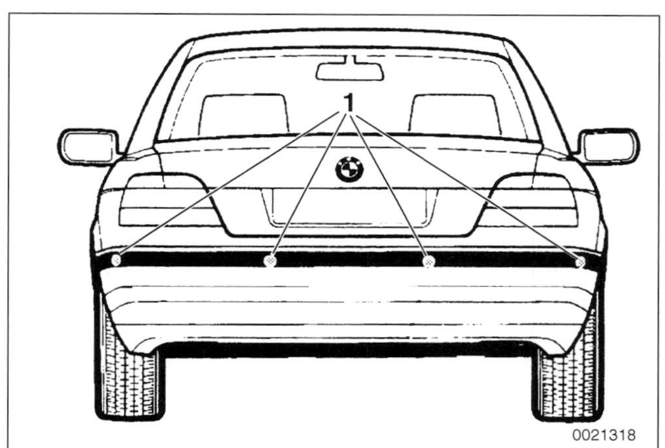

Fig. 68 Rear bumper

1.	Park distance control (PDC) ultrasonic sensors

611 Wipers and Washers

TABLE

Special tools

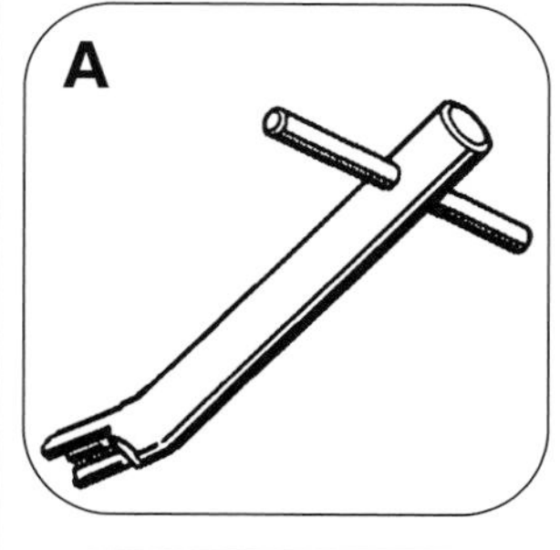

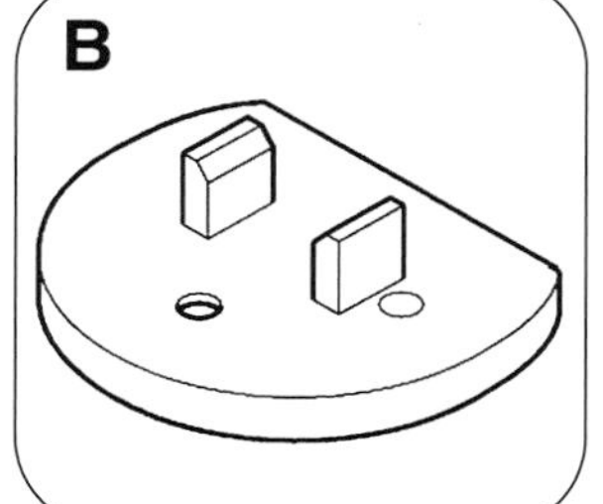

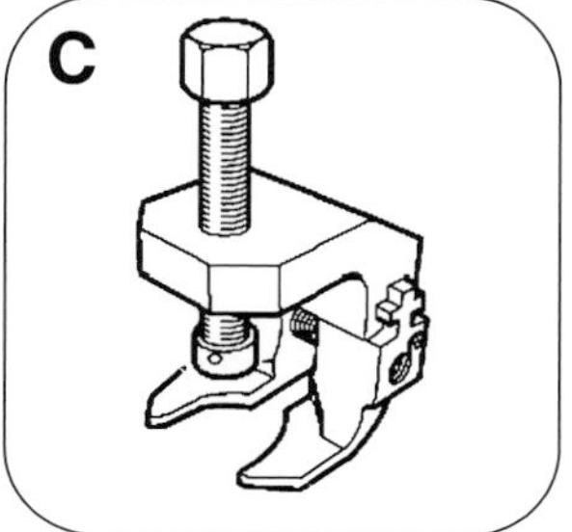

A BMW 00 9 100 . . . . Headlight washer nozzle aligning tool
B BMW 61 1 330 . . . . Rear wiper drive aligning tool
C BMW 61 6 060 . . . . Wiper arm removal tool

GENERAL

This repair group covers repair information for windshield, headlight and rear window (Sport Wagon) wiper and washer systems.

Replacement of the wiper / washer stalk switch assembly is covered in **612 Switches**. Electrical wiring diagrams and relays for the wiper / washer system are covered in **Electrical Wiring Diagrams**.

Special tools

Although most wiper system repairs can be carried out with normal shop tools, a few special tools may be necessary as well.

611

Wiper and washer system

The wiper and washer functions in E46 vehicles are controlled by the ZKE V General Module (GM V). Driver input to the system is via the multi-function stalk switch to the right of the steering column.

Operational faults in the wiper / washer system sets diagnostic trouble codes (DTCs) which can be accessed through BMW scan tool (DISplus, GT1, MoDiC) or equivalent.

The components of the wiper / washer system are described below. Some functions or components are optional, as indicated.

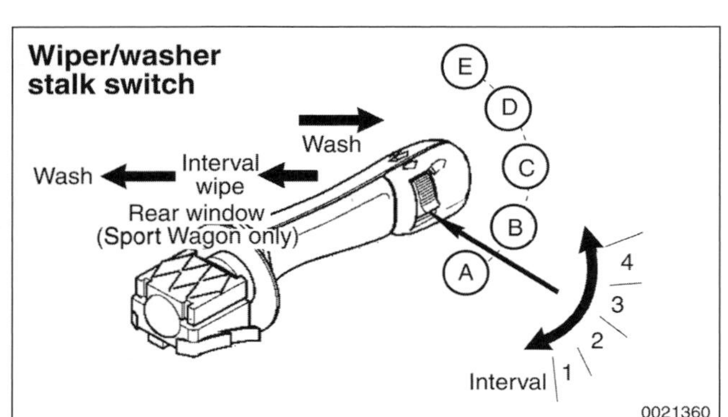

Wiper / washer stalk switch at the steering column has five settings for the windshield:

- **A**: Single wipe (hold stalk switch down)
- **B**: Off
- **C**: Interval (thumb wheel on stalk switch)
- **D**: Slow (automatically switches to interval when car is stopped.)
- **E**: Fast (automatically switches to slow speed when car is stopped.)

In "interval" setting, wiping intervals are dependent on road speed. See **Table a**.

Table a. Wiper interval (seconds)

Thumb wheel position	Vehicle speed (mph)					
	<4	5 - 22	23 - 45	46 - 60	61 - 87	>87
1	26	19	17	15	15	13
2	17	12	11	10	9	7
3	10	6	6	5	4	3
4	5	3	3	2	2	2

The windshield washer system is activated by pulling the stalk switch toward the driver.

In Sport Wagon models with rear wiper / washer, pushing the stalk switch one detent away from the driver activates the interval rear wiper. Pushing the stalk further forward activates the rear window washer.

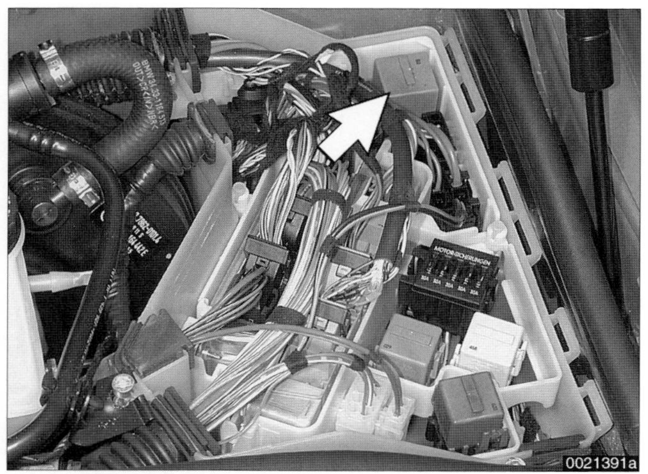

Windshield wiper double relay is in E-box, left rear of engine compartment (**arrow**) under plastic cover.

Rain sensor (optional). The infrared rain sensor and module switch on the windshield wipers automatically when water drops are detected on the windshield. See **Rain sensor system** in this repair group for additional details.

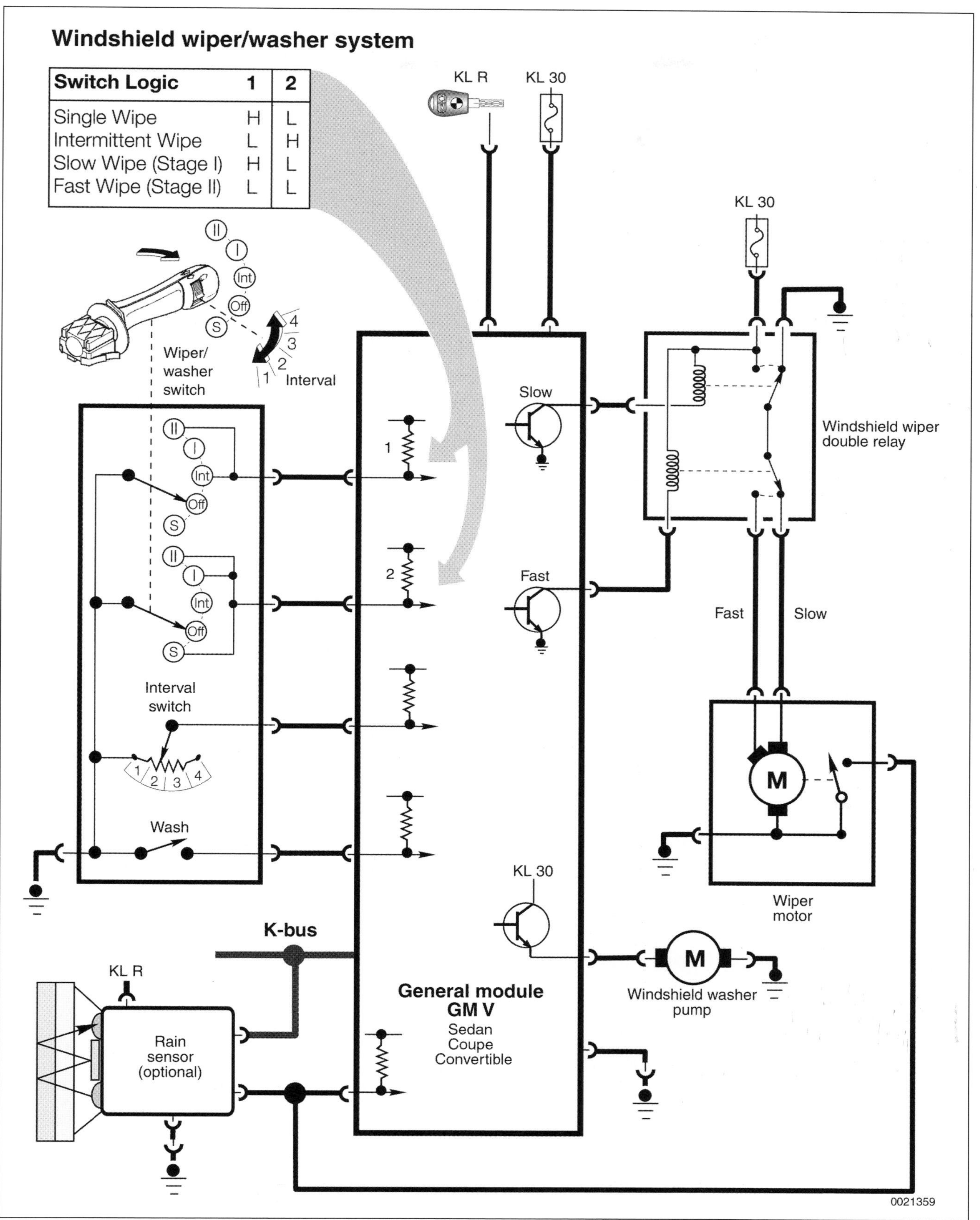
Windshield wiper/washer system
Switch Logic 1 2
Single Wipe H L
Intermittent Wipe L H
Slow Wipe (Stage I) H L
Fast Wipe (Stage II) L L
KL R
KL 30
KL 30
II
I
Int
Off
S
4
3
2
1
Interval
Wiper/
washer
switch
Slow
1
Windshield wiper
double relay
2
Fast
Fast
Slow
Interval
switch
1 2 3 4
Wash
M
Wiper
motor
KL 30
K-bus
KL R
M
Windshield washer
pump
General module
GM V
Sedan
Coupe
Convertible
Rain
sensor
(optional)
0021359

Windshield / headlight washer fluid reservoir is in right front of engine compartment.

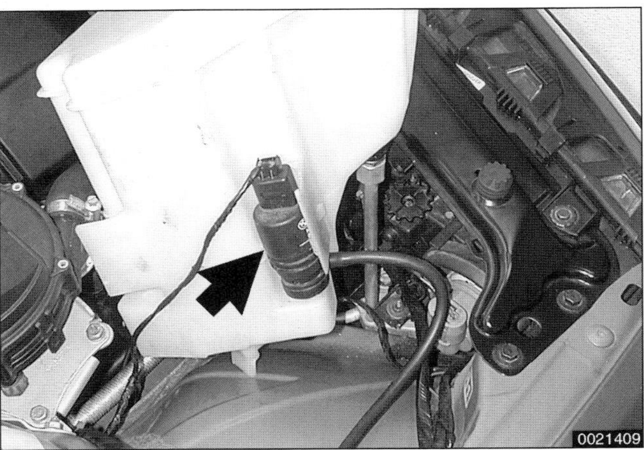

Windshield washer pump (**arrow**) is in rear portion of front washer reservoir.

Headlight washer pump (optional) is in front portion of front washer reservoir.

Windshield washer nozzles are located underneath engine hood. With ignition ON, washer nozzles are automatically heated. The positive temperature coefficient (PTC) nozzle heaters increase resistance as they heat up and automatically cut back on current consumption.

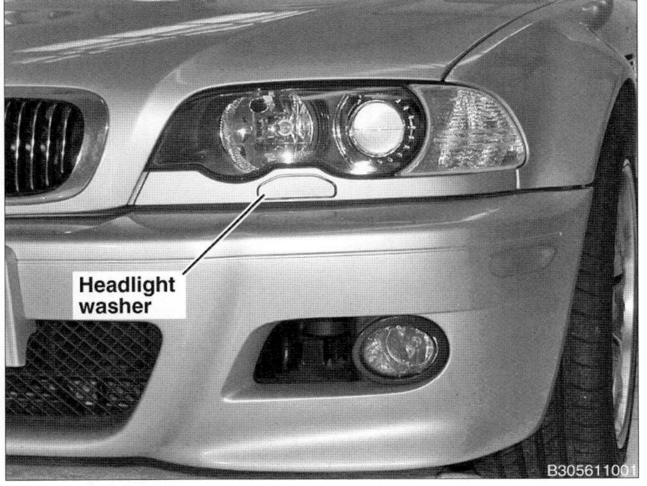

Headlight washer nozzles (standard in M3, M3 Convertible, optional in other models) are in the headlight trim. Headlight washer pump uses fluid from front washer reservoir. If headlights are on, they are cleaned every fifth time windshield washers are activated.

Rear window wiper assembly (Sport Wagon) is mounted to tailgate and linked to rear wiper shaft via a mechanical coupling.

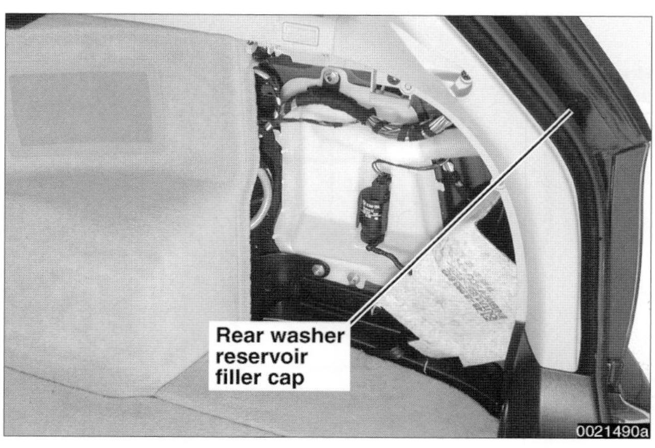

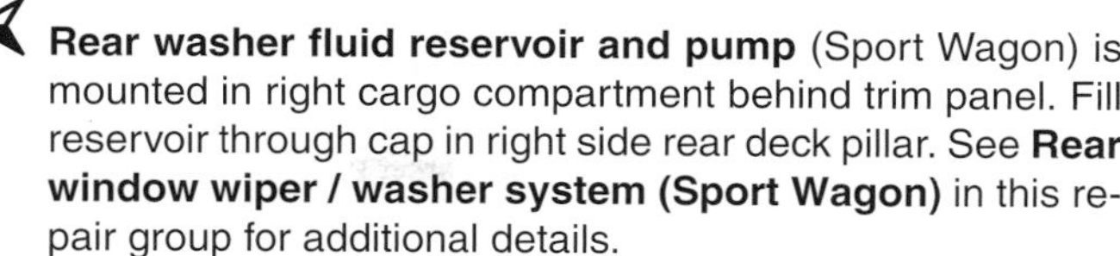

Rear washer fluid reservoir and pump (Sport Wagon) is mounted in right cargo compartment behind trim panel. Fill reservoir through cap in right side rear deck pillar. See **Rear window wiper / washer system (Sport Wagon)** in this repair group for additional details.

Rain sensor system

The optional rain sensor system uses an infrared sensor, located at the top of the windshield in front of the rear view mirror, to detect the presence of water drops (or dirt) on the windshield. The signal from the sensor is communicated to the GM V, which activates the interval wipe cycle if the wiper stalk switch knurled knob (interval control) is in one of the four interval settings.

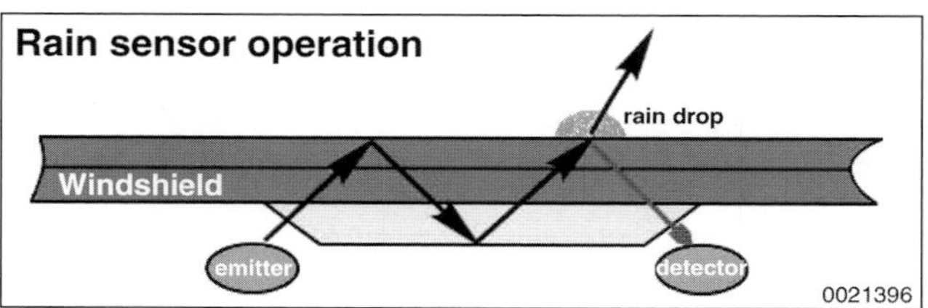

The rain sensor functions by aiming a beam of infrared light through the windshield at a set angle. The beam is reflected back and forth within the windshield until it is detected by the detector component of the rain sensor. Rain drops (or other impurities) on the outside of the windshield cause some of the infrared to be dissipated outside the windshield. As a result the detector "sees" less infrared intensity. This is interpreted as a need for the wiper to be turned on.

System components:

- An optical prism body attached to the top of the windshield
- Infrared emitter and detector diodes
- Optics heater (to prevent condensation from forming on diodes and prism)
- Control module (connected to GM V via K-bus)

The rain sensor is on-line as soon as it receives KL R (ignition on) operating power.

- When windshield wiper stalk switch is placed in intermittent position, GM V signals rain sensor control module via K-bus of request for intermittent wiping and also communicates position of knurled wheel (sensitivity).
- Rain sensor sends a command via K-bus to activate wiper motor.
- If more than 12 seconds pass before GM V receives rain sensor signal, it concludes rain sensor has a defect and operates intermittent wipe function as a non-rain-sensor system. Wiper intermittent cycling is based solely on knurled wheel setting.

The rain sensor continuously monitors the windshield for rain accumulation and signals the GM V to activate the wip-

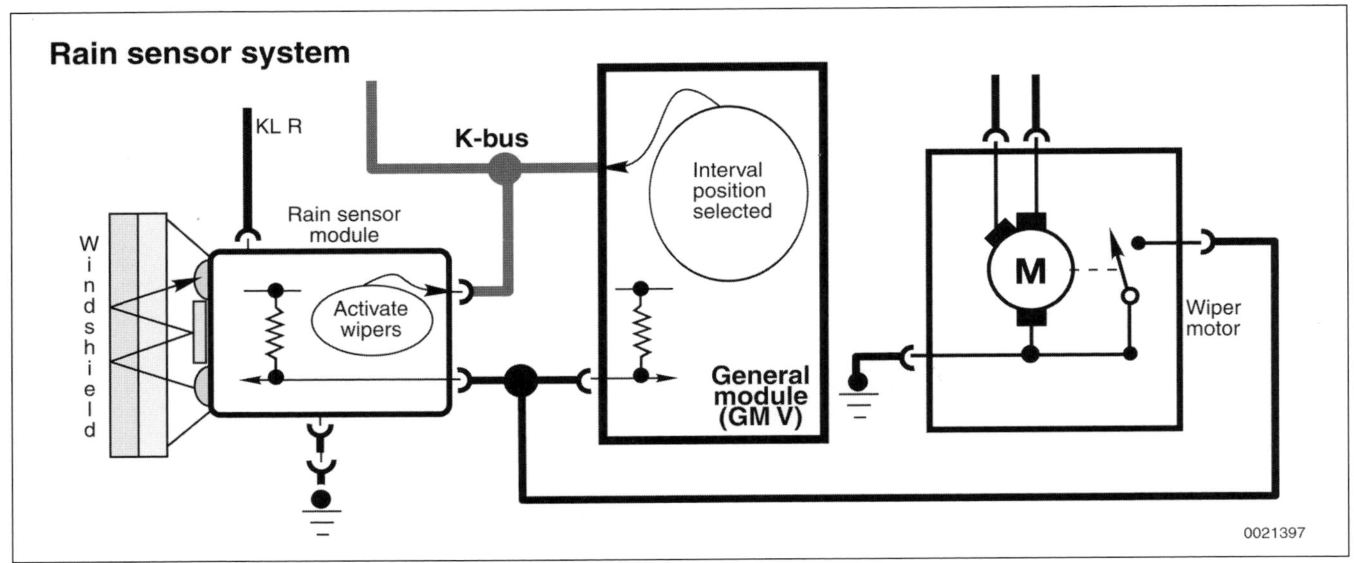

ers based on the knurled wheel position and how fast rain accumulates on the windshield.

The knurled wheel position signal (1 - 4) via the K-bus informs the rain sensor of the selected level of sensitivity:

- Position 1 (least sensitive) delays the wiper activation signal.
- Position 4 (most sensitive) sends the wiper activation signal to the GM V sooner.

Depending on the intensity of the rain the wipers can be operated continuously as if set in the normal wiper stalk switch position regardless of the knurled wheel setting. For this reason, the vehicle speed signal on the K-bus is not utilized on rain sensor equipped wiper systems.

If the ignition switch is turned OFF with the wiper switch in the intermittent position, the rain sensor only becomes active after the ignition is switched ON and one of the following occurs:

- The stalk switch is moved from the intermittent position and then back.
- The knurled wheel setting is adjusted.
- The wash function is activated.

The reasoning behind this switching strategy is to have the driver make a conscious decision to activate the system.

The rain sensor control module adapts to the optics system environment as follows:

- Windshield aging: As vehicle ages, windshield pitting in the rain sensor monitoring area may cause a loss of light in optics system. Control module adapts for loss of light based on intensity of detected infrared light with a cleared windshield. Therefore, rain sensor function is not adversely affected due to windshield aging.
- Dirty windows: Rain sensor adaptation reacts less sensitively to a dirty windshield (dirt, road salt, wax residue) af-

ter a completed wipe cycle. A dirty windshield has a film on it that diminishes ability of infrared to refract into water droplets that are present. This causes a delay in the rain sensor detection capabilities which lengthens time intervals on an intermittent wipe.

CAUTION —

On rain sensor equipped models, make sure the wiper blades are in perfect condition. Only use window cleaner to clean the windshield.

NOTE —

A dirty windshield can cause the rain sensor control module to set a fault due to approaching limits of its adaptation abilities.

Rear window wiper / washer system (Sport Wagon)

The rear wiper motor assembly in Sport Wagon models is mounted in the tailgate through a sound-insulating rubber bushing.

The rear wiper / washer is controlled by the wiper / washer steering column stalk switch via ZKE V system. System functions are:

- Normal interval wipe
- Programmed interval wipe
- Continuous wipe
- Washing

Normal operation is a timed interval of approx. 7 seconds. This is triggered by pressing stalk switch forward to first detent. Full sweep and park position of the wiper arm are recognized by two Hall sensors on motor assembly. If wiper is switched OFF, wiper arm returns to PARK position.

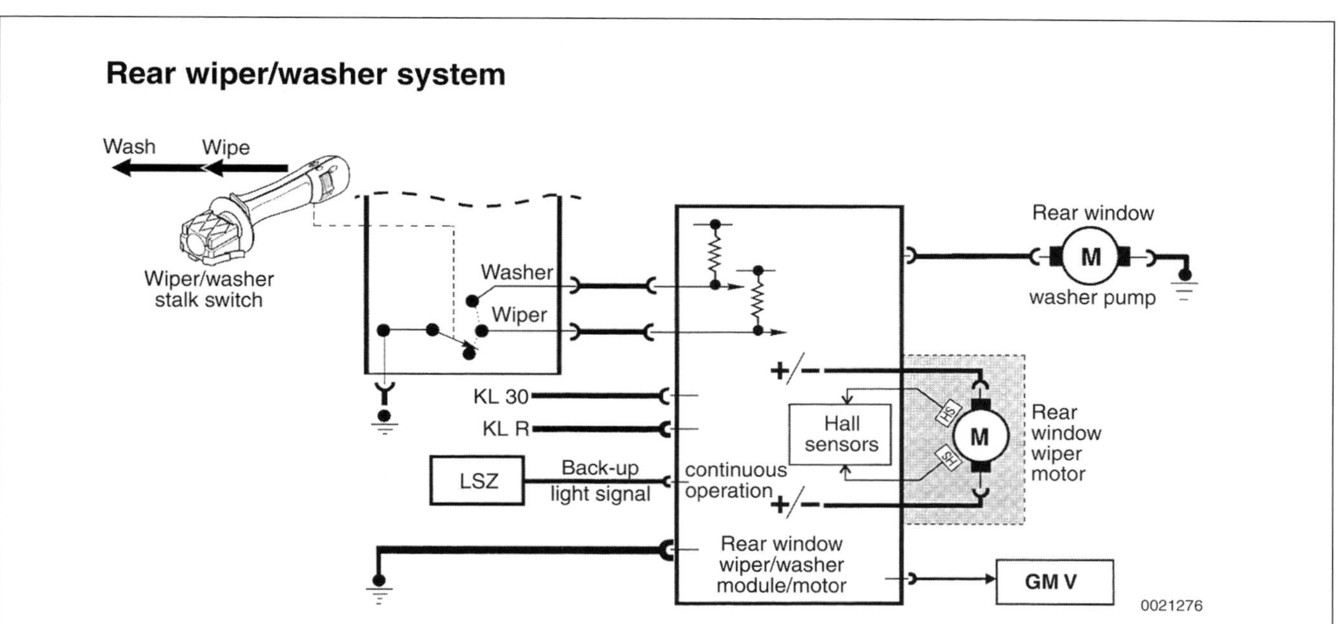

Programmed interval wipe:

- Quickly switch rear wiper ON and OFF.
- Wait the needed interval time.
- Switch rear wiper ON again.

The OFF time is the programmed interval, up to approx. 30 seconds.

Continuous wiping is activated any time rear wiper is ON and transmission is in reverse. Signal is provided by back-up light switch via LSZ (light control module).

Rear window washing is activated when the stalk switch is pushed forward past the first detent:

- Wash cycle 1. Washer pump ON for 1.5 seconds. Wiper ON 1 second later.
- Wash cycle 2. Washer pump ON for 0.5 second after 0.8 second delay. Wiper continues.
- Wash cycle 3. Washer pump ON for 0.5 second after 0.8 second delay. Wiper ON for two wipe-dry cycles.

NOTE —
After washing, the rear wiper remains in interval (normal) wiping mode until switched OFF.

WIPER BLADES

CAUTION —
Never turn on the wiper blades while the hood is open. Damage to the wiper system and hood may occur. To ensure safety during wiper system repair procedures, remove the windshield wiper fuse. See **610 Electrical Component Locations.**

Wiper blade cleaning problems

Streaking is usually caused when wiper blades are coated with road film or car wash wax. Clean blades using soapy water. If cleaning does not cure problem, replace blades. BMW recommends replacing wiper blades twice a year, before and after cold season.

Water drops that remain behind after wiping are usually caused by oil, road film, or diesel exhaust residue on windshield. Use an alcohol or ammonia solution or a non-abrasive cleaner (such as Bon-Ami®) to clean the windshield.

Chatter may be caused by dirty or worn blades, or by wiper arms that are out of alignment. Clean blades and windshield as described above. Adjust wiper arm so that there is even pressure along the blade, and so that blade at rest is perpendicular to windshield. If problems persist, replace blades and wiper arms.

NOTE —
BMW has a special gauge (BMW special tool 00 9 210) available to align the angle of the wiper arm to the windshield glass.

The wiper blades can be renewed in one of two ways:

- Complete blade replacement
- Rubber insert replacement

Insert replacement is the most economical method, although over time the wiper blade itself becomes worn. The rule of thumb is to replace just the inserts every second time.

Wiper blades, replacing

– Pivot wiper arm off windshield.

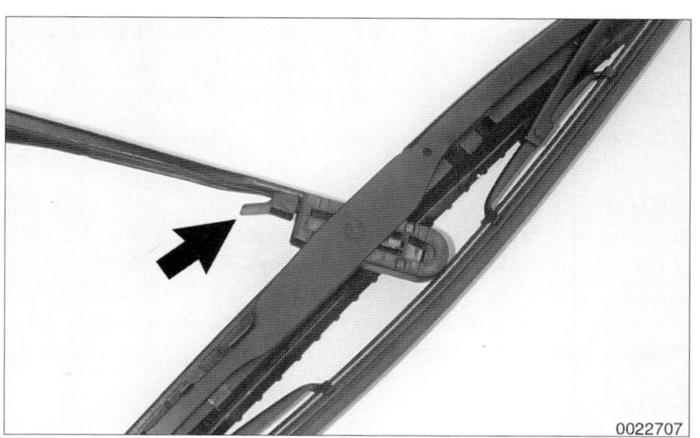

◀ Position wiper blade approximately perpendicular to wiper arm. Remove wiper blade from wiper arm by depressing retaining tab (**arrow**). Slide blade off.

– Installation is reverse of removal. Install wiper blade to wiper arm until retaining tab can be heard to click into position.

NOTE —
Some wiper blade versions have two retaining tabs.

Wiper blade insert, replacing

– Remove wiper blade. See **Wiper blades, replacing** in this repair group.

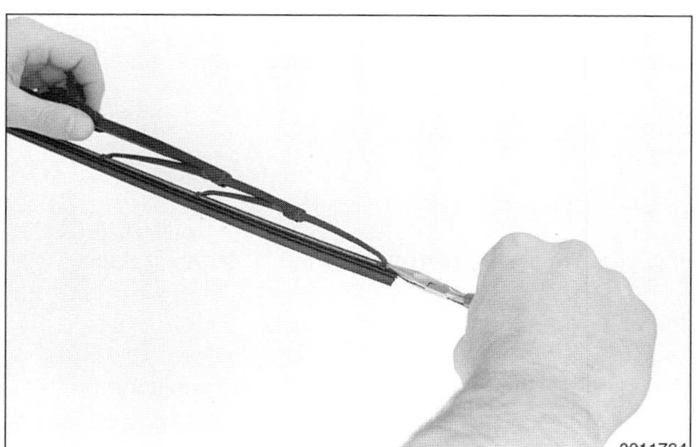

◀ Unhook wiper blade insert from wiper arm guide. If necessary, guide gently using needle nose pliers.

– Pull old insert from wiper arm guides, noting installation position.

– Remove metal support strips from old insert and install into slots in new insert, noting installation direction of cutouts in support strips.

– Slide new insert through wiper blade guides. Lock insert in place at end guides.

NOTE —
The notched cutouts in the retaining strips should engage the molded notches in the insert.

Wiper arm, removing and installing

> ***CAUTION—***
> - *Make sure wipers are parked (stalk switch in OFF position) and the ignition is also OFF.*
> - *Use fender cover to protect windshield.*

NOTE—
Wiper arm removal and installation on the Sport Wagon rear window is similar to the operation on the front wiper arms.

- With engine hood in closed position, remove wiper blade.
- Open hood. Gently pry off cap covering wiper arm retaining nut.

NOTE—
If necessary, raise engine hood to service position to access the front wiper arm fastener. See **410 Fenders, Engine Hood**.

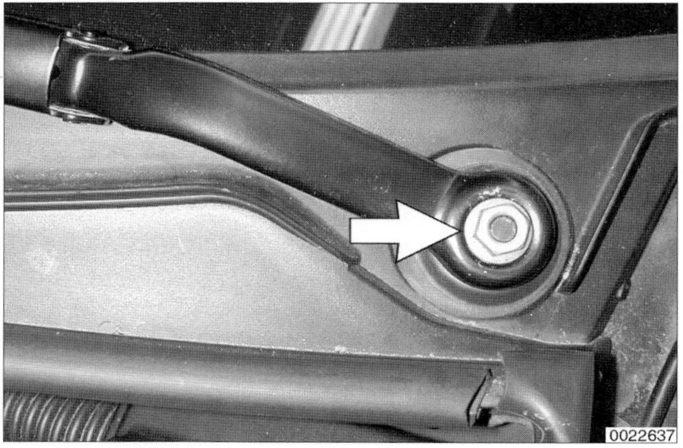

 Remove wiper arm retaining nut (**arrow**). Detach arm from shaft.

NOTE—
Use BMW special tool 61 6 060 or equivalent puller to remove arm.

If wiper arm sleeve (**arrow**) at shaft is loose, replace.

- Install arm and thread nut on loosely.
- Attach wiper blade and check for correct positioning:
  - Front wiper arm tip points right (passenger side).
  - Rear wiper arm tip points left (driver side).
  - Set wiper arm park position, then torque arm.

Wiper arm park position
- Front wiper blade tip distance from windshield gasket
  Right blade . . . . 24 mm (1 in)
  Left blade . . . . 44 mm (1.7 in)
- Rear wiper blade tip distance
  from rear window gasket. . . . . 12 mm (½ in)

Tightening torques
- Front wiper arm to wiper shaft . . . . 30 Nm (22 ft-lb)
- Rear wiper arm to wiper shaft. . . . . 10 Nm (7 ft-lb)

WIPER ASSEMBLIES

Windshield wiper assembly, removing and installing

> *CAUTION —*
> - *Make sure wipers are parked (stalk switch in OFF position) and the ignition is also OFF.*
> - *Use fender cover to protect windshield.*
> - *To avoid damaging the wiper arms and pivots, do not manually slide or force the wiper arms across the windshield.*

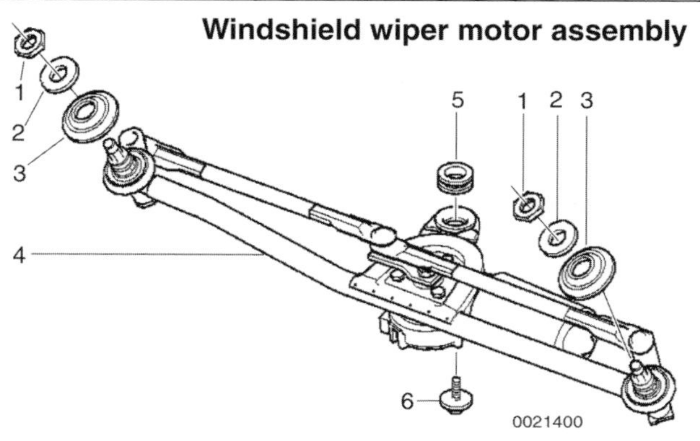

1. Wiper assembly mounting nut -tighten to 10 Nm (7 ft-lb)
2. Washer
3. Rubber damper
4. Motor and rod assembly
5. Rubber damper
6. Center mounting bolt -tighten to 10 Nm (7 ft-lb)

Remove windshield wiper assembly (linkage and motor) as a single unit, then repair or replace wiper motor and other linkage parts.

NOTE —
- *BMW does not provide the windshield wiper motor as a separate component.*
- *If necessary, raise engine hood to service position to access the front wiper assembly. See* **410 Fenders, Engine Hood**.

– Remove wiper arms. See **Wiper arm, removing and installing** in this repair group.

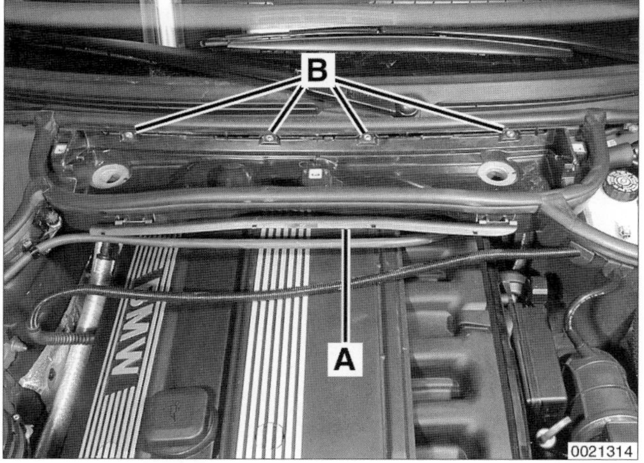

 Remove interior ventilation microfilter housing.

- Remove upper cover and microfilter.
- Open wiring harness loom (**A**) and remove wires.
- Unfasten screws (**B**) and remove lower microfilter housing.

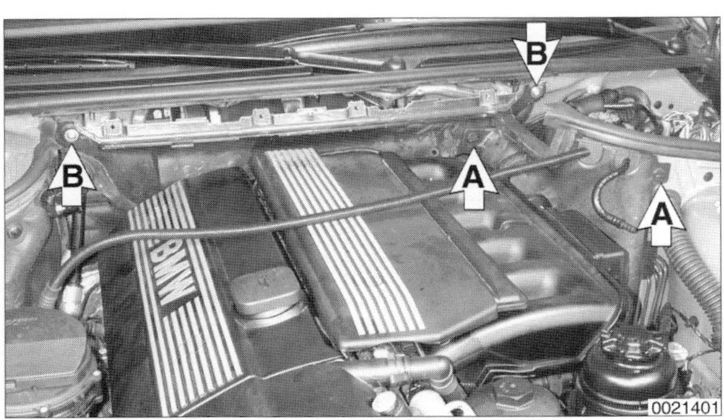

Remove heater bulkhead cover.

- Remove engine compartment side trim panel. Turn locking knobs (**A**) and slide trim panel from mounting lip.
- Remove heater bulkhead cover mounting screws (**B**) and lift cover up and out from bulkhead.

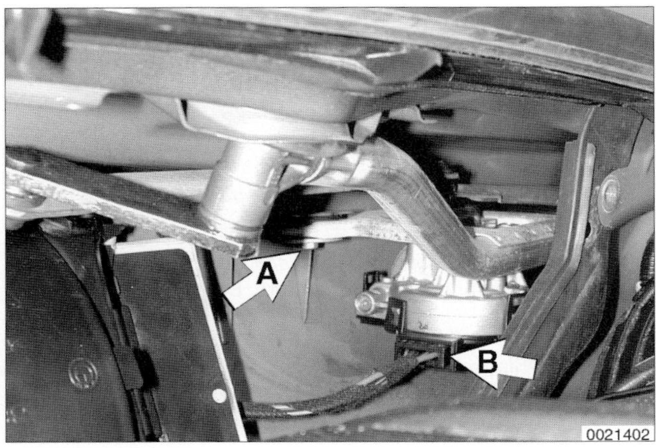

Detach wiper assembly inside cowl cavity:

- Remove assembly center mounting bolt (**A**).
- Disconnect electrical harness connector (**B**).

Remove right link rod (**arrow**) from wiper transmission arm.

– Release retaining clips and remove windshield base trim tray.

Remove large nuts (**arrow**) at base of wiper arm shafts in cowl panel. Remove wiper assembly.

NOTE —
Cover inside edges of cowl panel sheet metal with thick tape to prevent damage during wiper assembly removal.

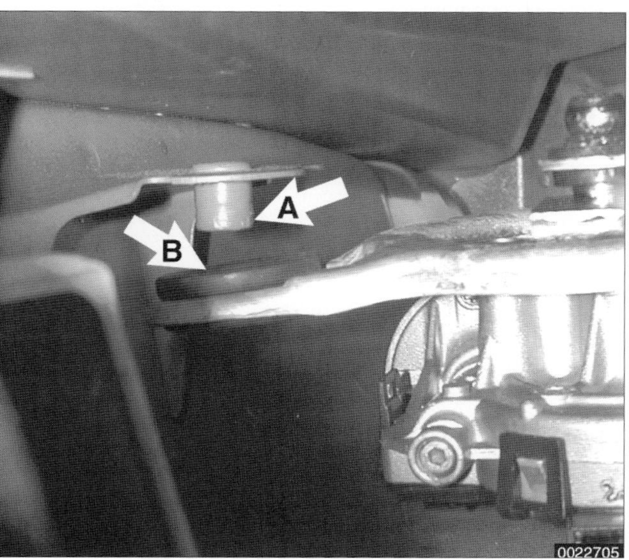

Installation is reverse of removal, noting the following:

- Fit center mounting rubber damper over pin (**A**) into wiper motor mounting arm (**B**).
- Install mounting fasteners finger-tight first.
- Once installed, run wiper motor to PARK position. Switch OFF.
- Install wiper arms but not blades.
- Close hood and fit wiper blades.
- Recheck wiper blade and arm position. See **Wiper arm, removing and installing**.
- Check electrical harness fittings and sealing grommets for correct reinstallation. Replace wire ties cut off during removal.

Tightening torques

- Center wiper assembly mount to cowl . . . 10 Nm (7 ft-lb)
- Wiper arm to wiper shaft. . . . . 30 Nm (22 ft-lb)
- Wiper shaft nut at cowl . . . . 10 Nm (7 ft-lb)

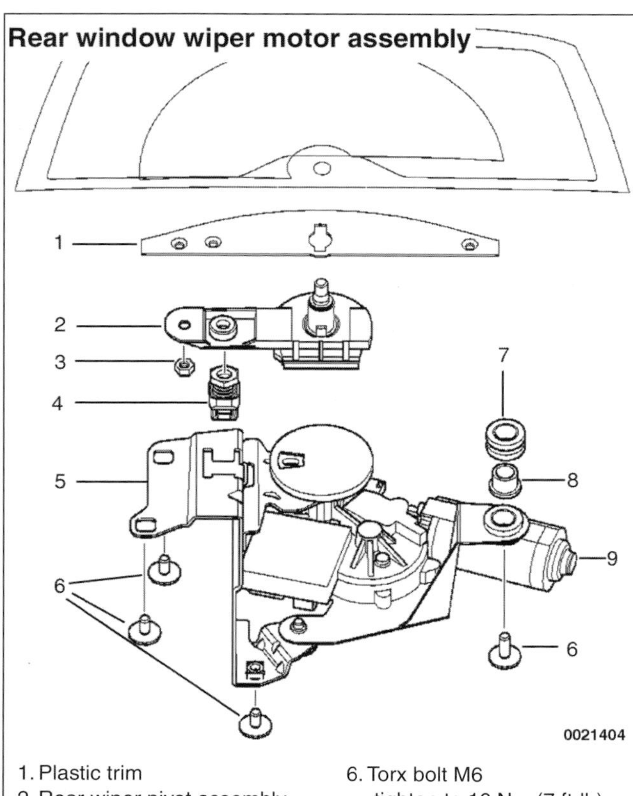

1. Plastic trim
2. Rear wiper pivot assembly
3. Nut M6
   -tighten to 10 Nm (7 ft-lb)
4. Mechanical coupling
5. Wiper motor assembly
6. Torx bolt M6
   -tighten to 10 Nm (7 ft-lb)
7. Damper ring
8. Mounting sleeve
9. Rear wiper motor assembly

Rear window wiper motor, removing and installing (Sport Wagon)

– Open tailgate and remove interior trim panel.

– Detach electrical harness connector(s) and remove wiper motor mounting screws. Remove motor assembly.

– To install:

- Remove rear window lock assembly from rear deck.
- Install wiper motor assembly and thread mounting bolts finger tight.
- Place BMW special tool 61 1 330 on rear window wiper drive and close rear window.
- With rear wiper vertical, allow rear wiper shaft mechanical coupling to snap into special tool bore.
- Tighten down wiper motor assembly.
- Remove special tool.
- Remainder of assembly is reverse of removal.

Tightening torque
- Wiper motor to rear deck (Torx) . . . . 10 Nm (7 ft-lb)

Rear window wiper shaft, removing and installing (Sport Wagon)

– Remove rear wiper arm.

– Lift tailgate window and remove wiper shaft housing plastic trim covers.

– Remove housing mounting nuts. Remove housing.

– Slacken rear window lift nut.

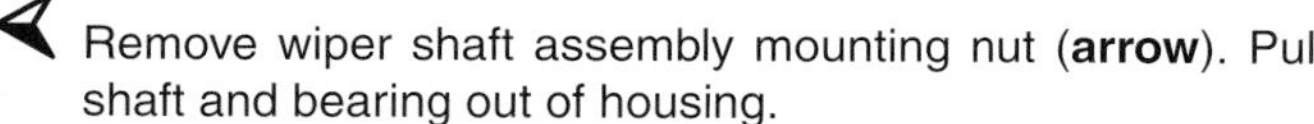

– Remove wiper shaft assembly mounting nut (**arrow**). Pull shaft and bearing out of housing.

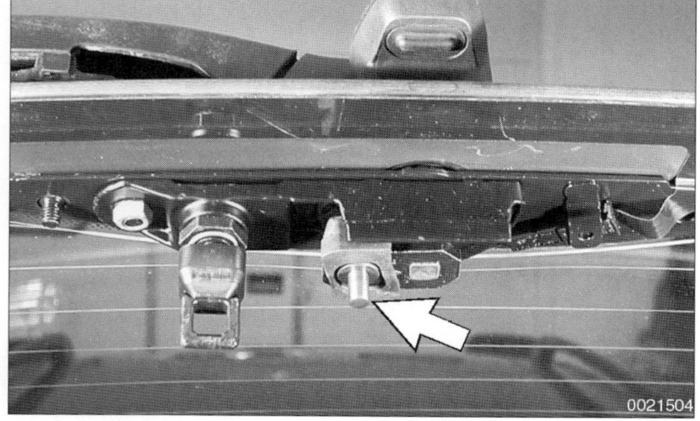

– Installation is reverse of removal. Adjust wiper arm and blade. See **Wiper arm, removing and installing** in this repair group.

Tightening torques
- Rear window button to rear window . . . . . 10 Nm (7 ft-lb)
- Wiper arm to wiper shaft. . . . . 10 Nm (7 ft-lb)
- Wiper shaft housing to rear window . . . . . 10 Nm (7 ft-lb)

WASHER SYSTEMS

Windshield washer system includes:

- Washer fluid reservoir in right front of engine compartment
- Washer fluid pump
- Heated spray nozzles in engine hood

Headlight washer system (where equipped) includes:

- Front washer fluid reservoir (shared with windshield washer system)
- Separate high intensity washer pump
- Headlight spray nozzles in headlight trim

Rear window washer system (Sport Wagon) includes:

- Washer reservoir and pump in right side cargo compartment behind trim panel
- Spray nozzle at top of tailgate window frame

Windshield spray nozzle, removing and installing

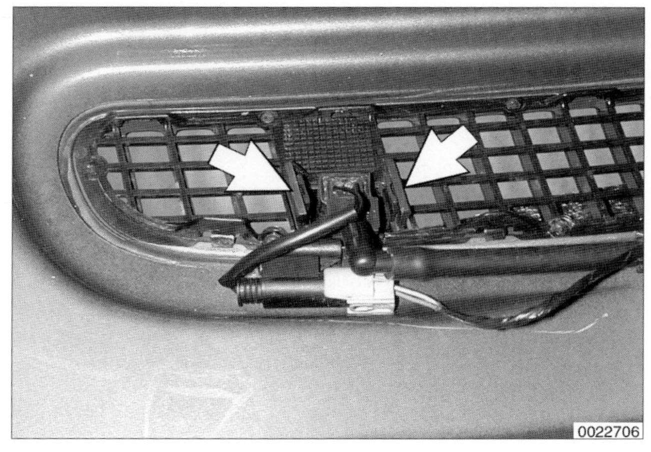

◄ Working under open engine hood, gently squeeze retaining clips (**arrows**) on nozzle sides to free nozzle from plastic intake grille.

– Carefully disconnect hose from nozzle. Disconnect harness connector for nozzle heater.

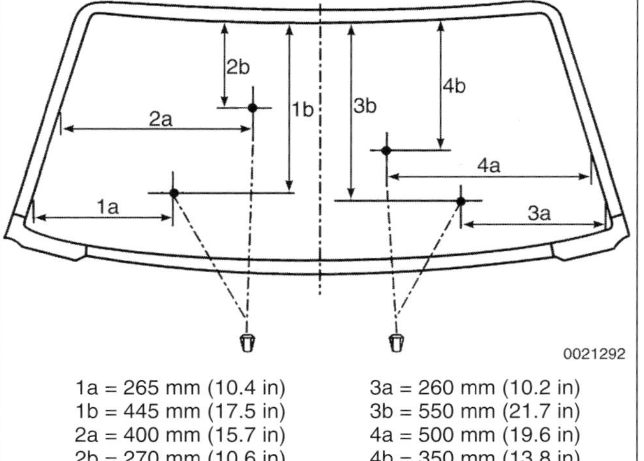

1a = 265 mm (10.4 in)
1b = 445 mm (17.5 in)
2a = 400 mm (15.7 in)
2b = 270 mm (10.6 in)
3a = 260 mm (10.2 in)
3b = 550 mm (21.7 in)
4a = 500 mm (19.6 in)
4b = 350 mm (13.8 in)

◄ Installation is reverse of removal. Check and adjust nozzles before driving. Use measurements in diagram as guide.

NOTE —

Aim windshield spray nozzles by using a sewing needle or a similar diameter stiff piece of wire.

Headlight washer spray nozzle, removing and installing

NOTE —
Headlight washer nozzles are marked L or R on the underside. Do not mix them up.

– Gently pry out spray nozzle and pull out to stop. Tug on nozzle to detach from washer fluid duct.

NOTE —
Be prepared for dripping washer fluid.

– Transfer trim to new nozzle before installing.

– Snap new nozzle on fluid duct by pushing into opening. Check to make sure nozzle is fully snapped into place.

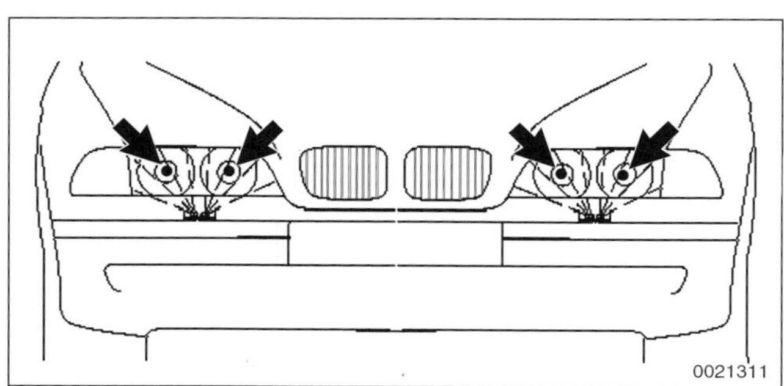

Using BMW special tool 00 9 100 or equivalent, adjust headlight washers so that spray jets strike approximately in center of each beam (**arrows**).

NOTE —
To turn on headlight washer jets, turn on ignition, lights and windshield washer system. To repeat spray procedure, turn off ignition, then back on again. Otherwise the headlight washers are disabled for 3 minutes.

Front washer reservoir and pumps, replacing

– Open hood and siphon washer fluid from reservoir.

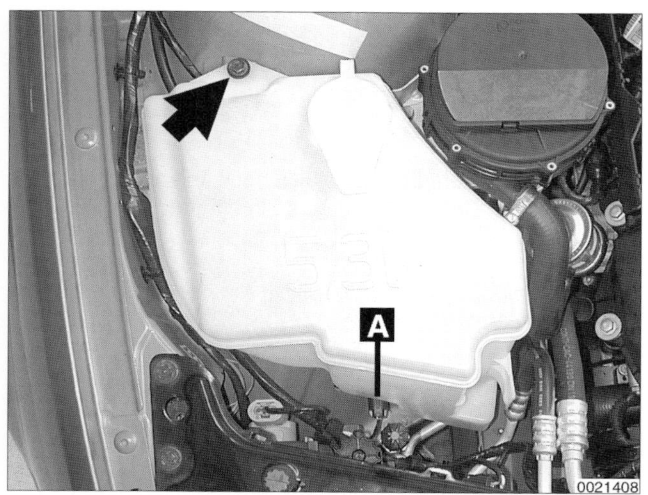

Detach washer fluid level sensor harness connector (**A**) in front bottom of fluid reservoir. Remove reservoir retaining screw (**arrow**).

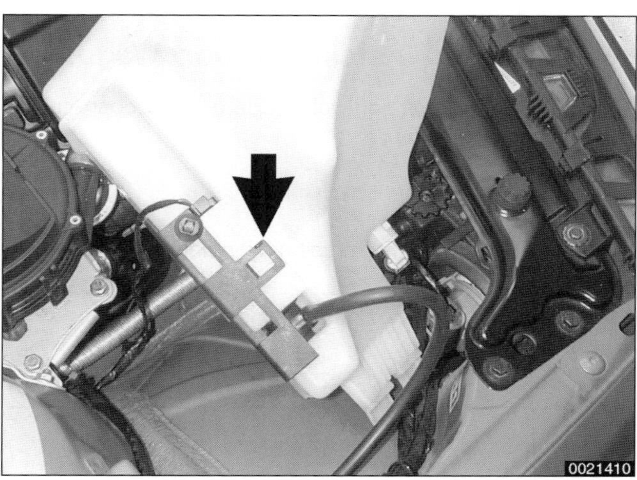

- Lift reservoir. Pry gently at retaining clip (**arrow**) on heat shield to disengage from reservoir.

– Cut off wire tie to release washer pump harness from heat shield. Lay heat shield aside.

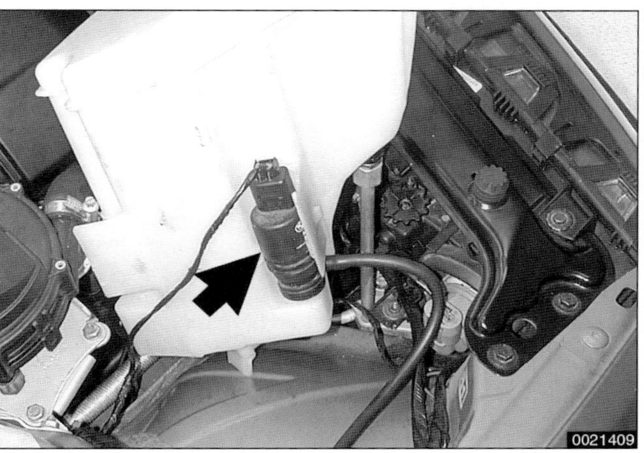

- Remove windshield washer pump (**arrow**) and headlight washer pump (if equipped):
  - Detach pump electrical connector.
  - Twist pump clockwise and pull out of reservoir.

– Installation is reverse of removal, noting the following:
  - Twist washer fluid level sensor clockwise to remove from base of reservoir.
  - Transfer reservoir cover and strainer to new container.
  - Coat fluid pump sealing ring with anti-friction agent.
  - On installation check that fluid hoses are not kinked.
  - Make sure reservoir heat shield is correctly engaged. Replace wire tie.
  - Refill reservoir.

Front washer fluid level sensor, replacing

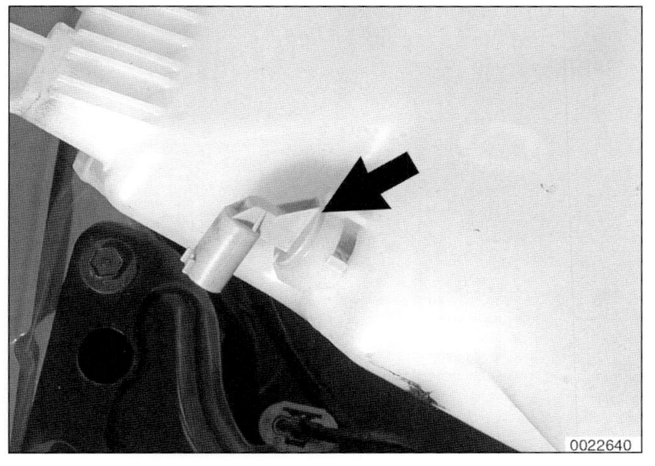

- Remove front washer fluid reservoir. See **Front washer reservoir and pumps, replacing** in this repair group.

– Twist washer fluid level sensor (**arrow**) clockwise to remove from base of reservoir.

– Installation is reverse of removal.

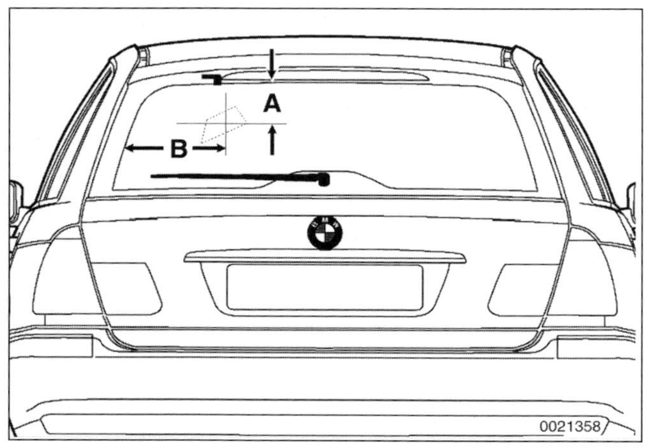

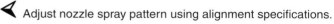

Rear window spray nozzle, removing and installing (Sport Wagon)

– Use plastic prying tool to lever nozzle out of rubber strip at top of tailgate window.

– Push new nozzle into rubber strip.

◄ Adjust nozzle spray pattern using alignment specifications.

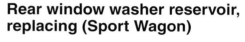

Rear window spray nozzle alignment specifications

- **A** . . . . 100 mm (3.9 in)
- **B** . . . . 320 mm (12.6 in)

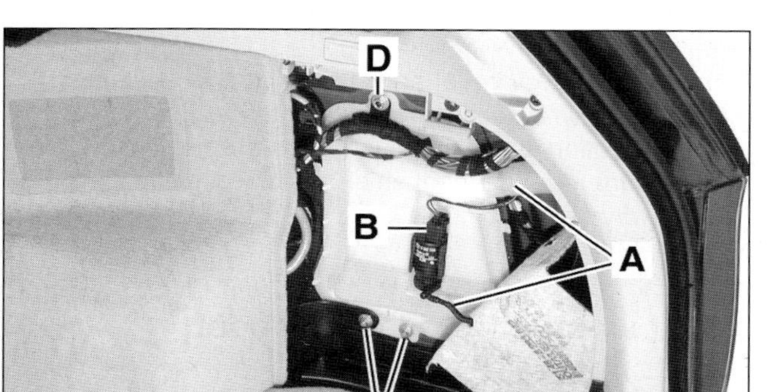

Rear window washer reservoir, replacing (Sport Wagon)

– Working in right rear cargo area, remove side trim panel, then remove sound insulation.

– Siphon out washer fluid reservoir.

◄ Remove reservoir:

- Detach filling and pressure hoses (**A**).
- Remove washer pump electrical harness connector (**B**).
- Loosen mounting nuts at bottom of reservoir (**C**) slightly.
- Remove top mounting nut (**D**) and remove reservoir.

– Remove pump:

- Detach electrical harness connector (**B**).
- Pry pump gently outward and up to remove from reservoir.

– When installing:

- Coat pump sealing ring with anti-friction agent.
- Make sure hoses are not kinked.
- Refill reservoir.

612 Switches

GENERAL

This section covers replacement of electrical switches at the steering wheel, steering column, dashboard, pedal cluster, center console and other locations.

For related information, see also the following repair groups:

- **119 Lubrication System** for oil pressure switch testing
- **520 Seats** for power seat controls
- **540 Sunroof** for sunroof switch
- **541 Convertible Top** for convertible top switch
- **630 Lights** for headlight switch

Special tools

Some special tools are necessary for the repairs detailed in this section.

Special tools

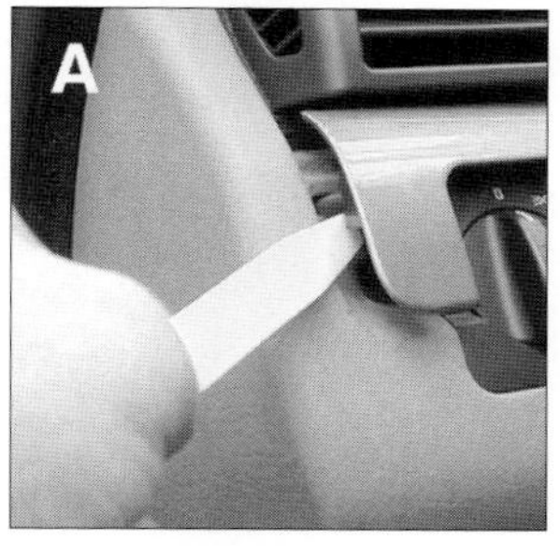

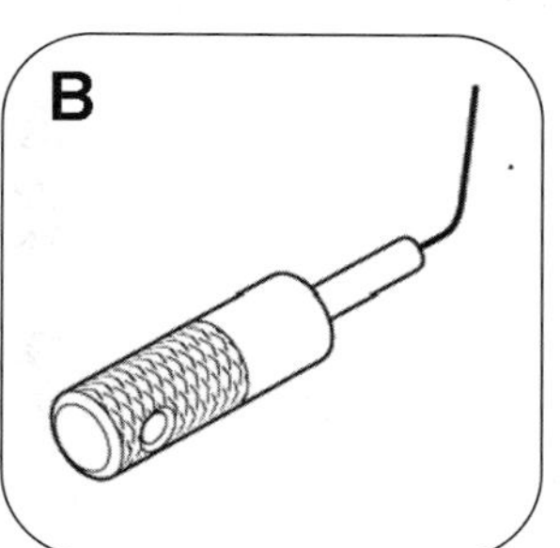

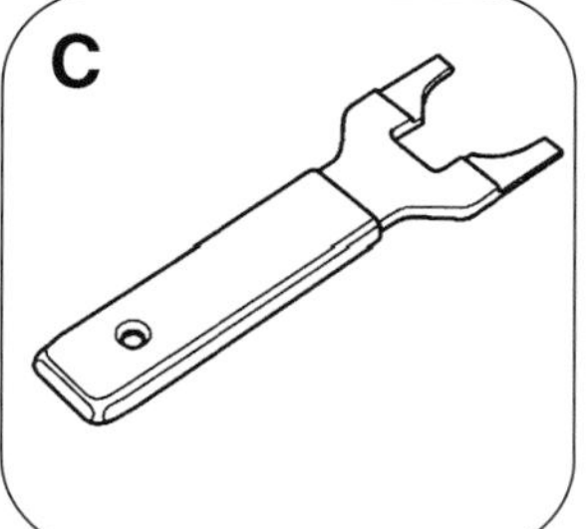

A BMW 00 9 321 . . . . .Plastic prying tool
B BMW 32 3 110. . . . . Ignition cylinder removal tool
C BMW 61 3 300. . . . . Ring antenna removal tool

CAUTION —
- *When working on electrical switches or lights, disconnect the negative (–) cable from the battery and insulate the cable end to prevent accidental reconnection.*
- *Prior to disconnecting the battery, read the battery disconnection cautions given at the front of this manual on page viii.*
- *To avoid marring trim when working on interior components, work with plastic prying tool or wrap the tip of screwdriver or pliers with tape before prying out electrical component.*

612

STEERING WHEEL SWITCHES

E46 vehicles are equipped with either the multi-function (MFL) steering wheel or the sports steering wheel. Incorporated into each steering wheel are an SRS airbag, horn contacts, selected cellular phone and radio controls and cruise control buttons.

To replace the steering wheel switches, remove the airbag first. See **721 Airbag System (SRS)**.

> ***WARNING —***
> *Improper handling of the airbag could cause serious injury. Store the airbag with the horn pad facing up. If stored facing down, accidental deployment could propel it violently into the air, causing injury.*

> ***CAUTION —***
> *Special test equipment is required to retrieve SRS fault codes, diagnose system faults, and turn OFF the SRS warning light. The SRS warning light remains ON until any problem has been corrected and the fault memory has been cleared.*

Multi-function (MFL) steering wheel switches, accessing

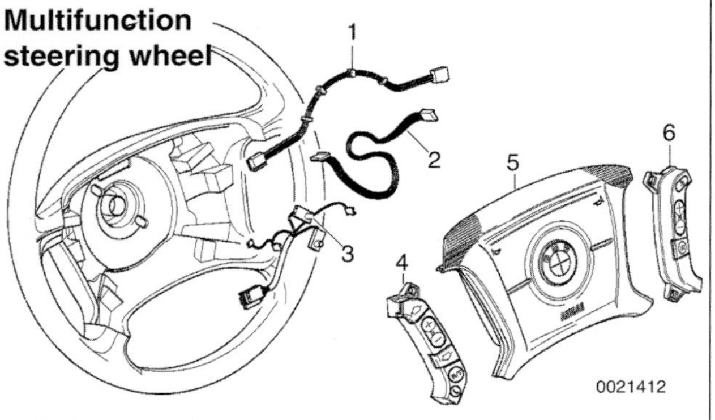

Multifunction steering wheel

1. Cruise control / radio / telephone electrical harness
2. Horn button electrical harness
3. Airbag electrical harness
4. Radio / telephone control switch set
5. Airbag
6. Cruise control switch set

- Remove airbag. See **721 Airbag System (SRS)**.
- Detach electrical harness connectors.
- Remove small screws on back side of airbag pad to release left or right switch set.

NOTE —
BMW does not provide the horn contact switch as a separate part.

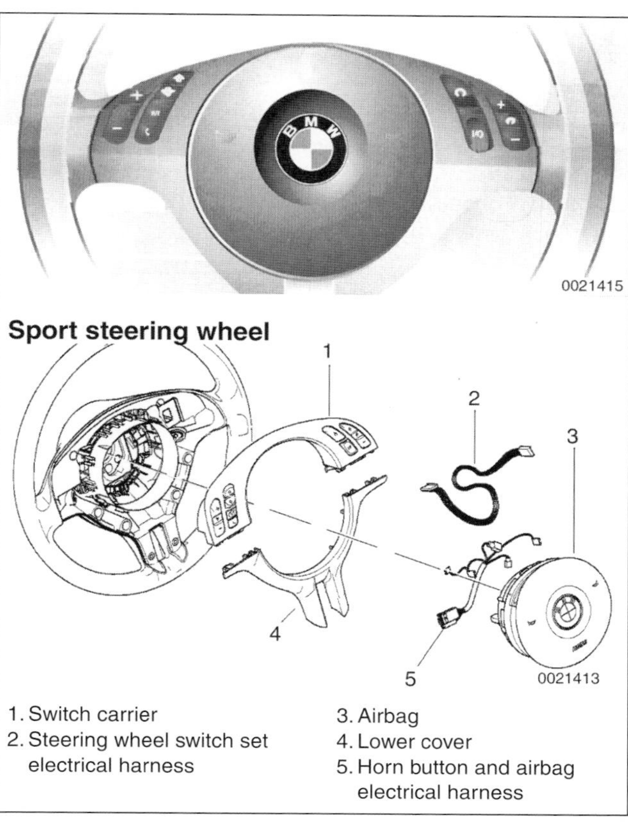

1. Switch carrier
2. Steering wheel switch set electrical harness
3. Airbag
4. Lower cover
5. Horn button and airbag electrical harness

Sport steering wheel switches, accessing

◀ Remove airbag. See **721 Airbag System (SRS)**.

> *NOTE—*
> *There is a special procedure for detaching the airbag from the sport steering wheel. See* **721 Airbag System (SRS)**.

- Remove screws mounting switch carrier to steering wheel.
- Pull switch carrier and trim down to detach from steering wheel. Remove electrical harness connector.
- Separate bottom trim piece from switch carrier.

> *NOTE—*
> *BMW does not provide the horn contact switch as a separate part.*

STEERING COLUMN SWITCHES

To remove any of the steering column switches, it is necessary to first remove the upper and lower column trim pieces. See **513 Interior Trim**.

> *CAUTION—*
> *To prevent marring interior trim, work with plastic prying tools or wrap the tips of screwdrivers and pliers with tape before prying out switches or electrical accessories.*

Ignition lock cylinder, removing and installing

To remove EWS ring antenna prior to removing ignition lock cylinder, remove upper and lower steering column trim. Use BMW special tool 61 3 300 to lever ring antenna off lock cylinder. Alternatively, remove lock cylinder first.

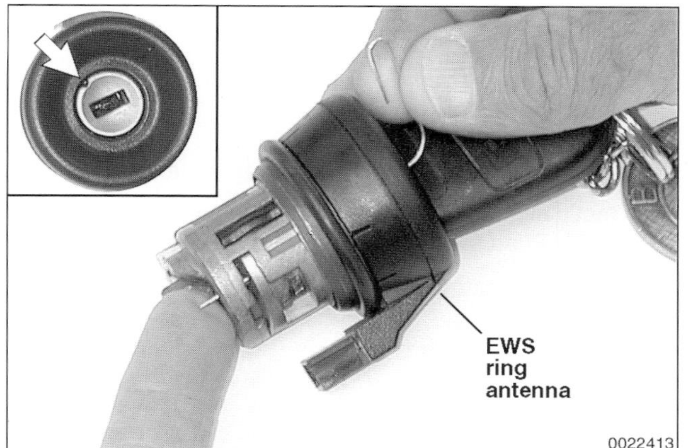

◀ With ignition key in ON position (60° from LOCKED):

- Insert a thin piece of stiff wire into opening (**arrow**) in lock cylinder and pull cylinder out.
- Detach ring antenna harness connector.
- Gently work ring antenna off lock cylinder.
- Reinstallation is reverse of removal.

Ignition switch, removing and installing

NOTE —
Photos for this procedure are from an E39 (5 Series) Sedan. E46 steering column and ignition switch assembly are similar.

– Disconnect negative (–) cable from battery and cover terminal with insulating material.

> ***CAUTION —***
> *Prior to disconnecting the battery, read the battery disconnection cautions given at the front of this manual on page viii.*

– Remove steering column trim. See **513 Interior Trim**.

Pry out electrical connector lock (**arrow**) at ignition switch and detach connector.

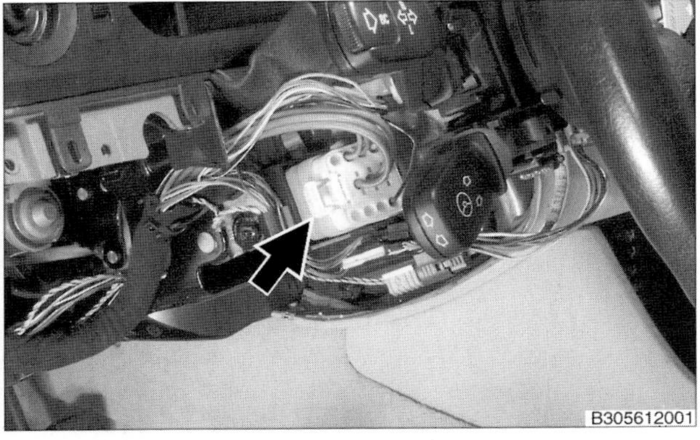

If applicable, remove fasteners (**arrows**) from wiring harness support and remove support.

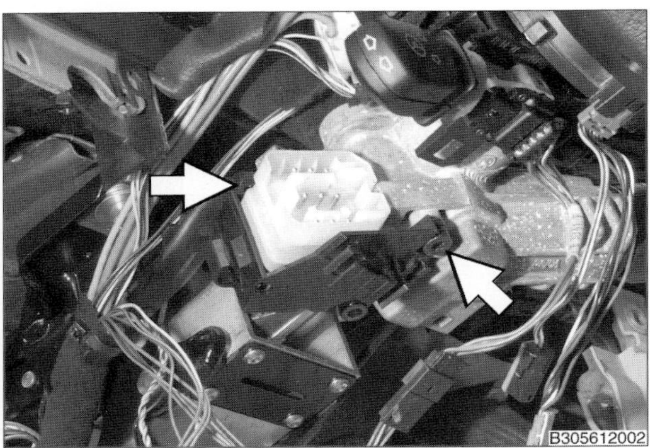

Remove protective paint covering ignition switch fasteners (**arrows**) and remove fasteners.

– Installation is reverse of removal, noting the following:

- Correctly align switch drive to ignition lock drive.
- Secure ignition fasteners with paint after installation.

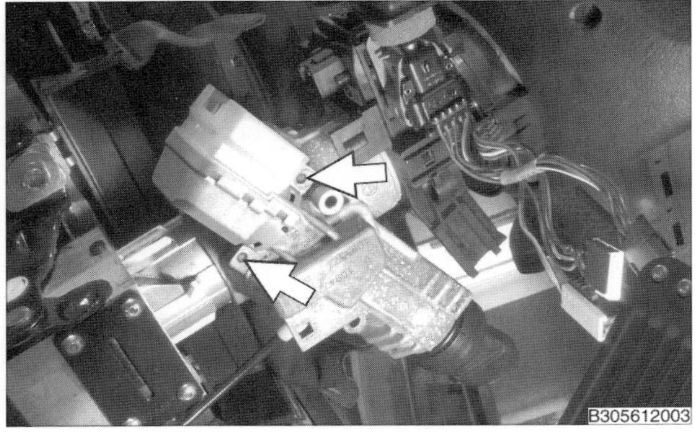

Steering column stalk switch assembly, removing and installing

To replace either the directional / headlight dimmer stalk switch or the wiper / washer stalk switch, first remove the entire stalk switch assembly from the steering column.

> ***CAUTION—***
> *To prevent marring interior trim, work with plastic prying tools or wrap the tips of screwdrivers and pliers with tape before prying out switches or electrical accessories.*

– Disconnect negative (–) cable from battery and cover terminal with insulating material.

> ***CAUTION—***
> *Prior to disconnecting the battery, read the battery disconnection cautions given at the front of this manual on page viii.*

– Remove airbag unit from steering wheel. See **721 Airbag System (SRS)**. Store airbag unit in a safe place with pad facing up.

> ***WARNING—***
> *Any work involving the SRS system should only be performed by an authorized BMW dealer. Making repairs without the proper knowledge and special test equipment may cause serious personal injury. See* **721 Airbag System (SRS).**

– With front wheels pointed straight ahead, remove steering wheel. See **320 Steering and Wheel Alignment**.

– Remove steering column trim. See **513 Interior Trim**.

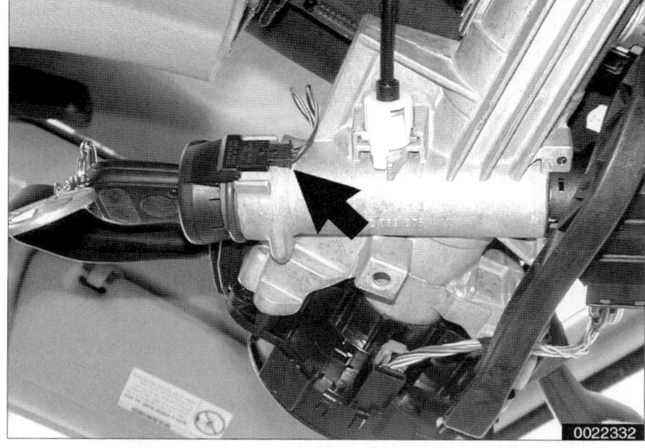

◀ Detach EWS ring antenna electrical harness connector (**arrow**).

◀ Detach wiper / washer switch electrical harness connector (**arrow**).

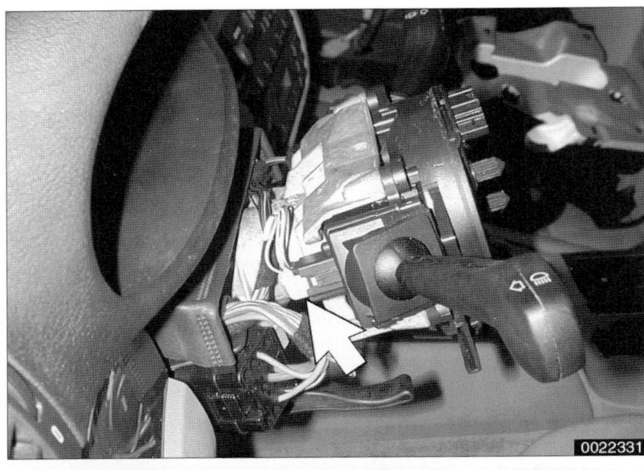

◀ Detach turn signal / headlight dimmer switch electrical harness connector (**arrow**).

◀ Detach driver airbag electrical harness connector (**arrow**).

◀ Remove stalk switch housing retaining screws (**arrows**). Slide switch housing off steering column.

– Installation is reverse of removal, noting the following:
  - Place turn signal indicator in center position before installing.
  - Ensure that self cancelling cams on turn signal switch are not damaged during installation.

Tightening torque
- Steering wheel to steering column spindle shaft . . . . 63 Nm (46 ft-lb)

Turn signal / headlight dimmer switch or wiper switch, removing and installing

– Remove stalk switch. See **Steering column stalk switch assembly, removing and installing** in this repair group. Place assembly face-down on work bench.

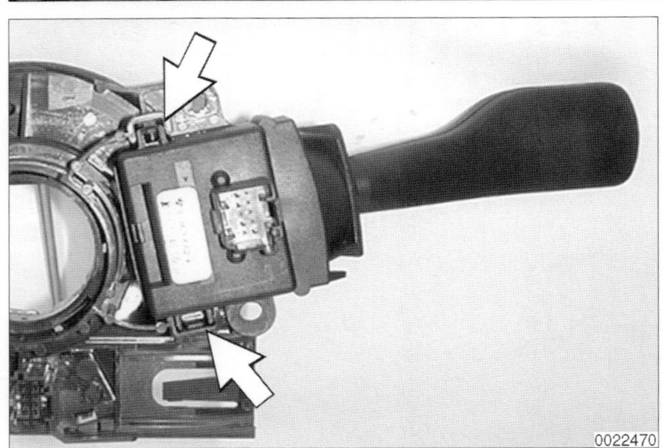

◀ Squeeze locking tabs (**arrows**) on sides of switch and slide out of housing.

– Push in new switch until it snaps into housing.

PEDAL CLUSTER SWITCHES

Brake light switch, replacing

– Remove left footwell trim (above pedals). See **513 Interior Trim**.

Working at pedal cluster:

- Detach electrical harness connector (**arrow**) from brake light switch.
- Slide switch out of holder (toward rear of car).

NOTE —

The brake light switch is held in place via a serrated mounting. Remove switch mounting from pedal cluster bracket.

– Push brake pedal down, install new switch, then allow brake pedal to spring back slowly, automatically adjusting switch position.

Clutch switch, replacing

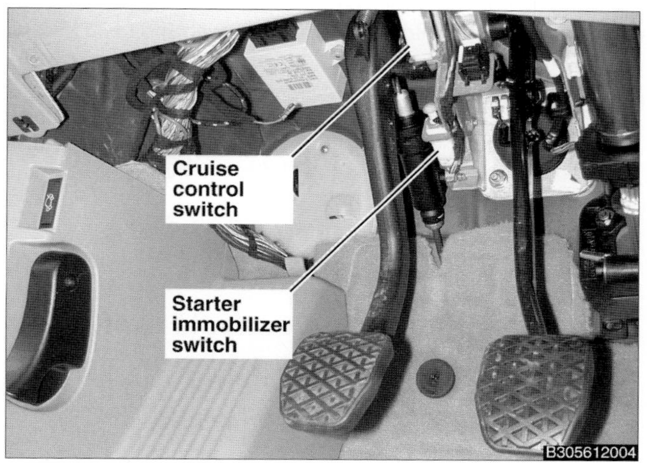

Early production E46 cars are equipped with 2 clutch pedal switches.

- Upper switch is used for cruise control interrupt.
- Lower switch is starter immobilizer.

Later production E46 cars are equipped with a single clutch switch module, attached to the clutch master cylinder. This switch performs both cruise control and starter immobilizer functions.

– To access either version, remove left footwell trim (above pedals). See **513 Interior Trim**.

Version 1

– Remove upper (cruise control) switch:

- Push clutch pedal to floor and lock in position using a pedal prop.
- Detach electrical harness connector from switch.
- Squeeze together retaining clips at front of switch. Slide switch out of holder (toward rear of car).
- Install new switch, then allow clutch pedal to spring back slowly, automatically adjusting switch position.

– Remove lower (starter immobilizer) switch:

- Detach switch electrical connector.
- Squeeze together retaining clips at rear of switch. Slide switch out of holder (toward front of car).
- Install new switch and reattach electrical connector.

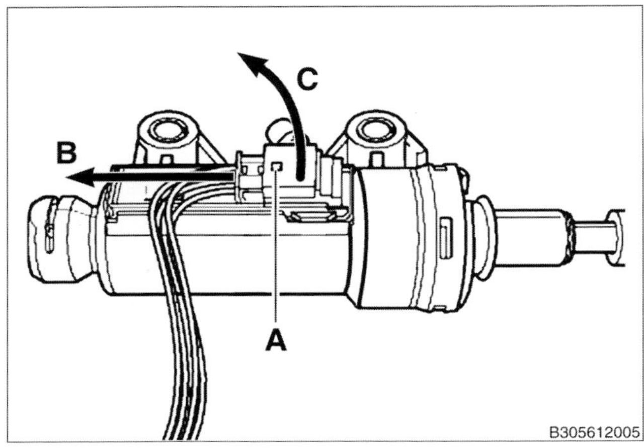

Version 2

Working at clutch master cylinder:

- Press switch module locking button (**A**) to detach electrical connector.
- Pull connector off module (**B**).
- Use screwdriver to lever off module (**C**).

– Installation is reverse of removal. Make sure switch module snaps firmly into place.

OTHER INTERIOR SWITCHES

The ASC or DSC switch is ahead of the shifter console at the bottom of the center dashboard. When equipped, seat heater switches are in the same location.

The right front and right rear window switches are ganged into one unit on the right side of the shifter. The left front and left rear window switches are ganged with the child safety rear window lockout switch (Sedan and Sport Wagon) on the left side of the shifter.

The central locking switch and hazard warning switch are ganged into one unit behind the shifter mechanism.

The left and right electric outside rear view mirrors are controlled by one switch on the driver door armrest.

Lower dashboard and console switches, replacing

– Remove shifter knob by pulling straight up.

NOTE —
Apply approx. 90 lb. of force to pull off knob. Do not twist while pulling.

– Shifter bezel: Lift up by prying gently.

– Shifter boot: Unclip bottom of boot from center console trim by pushing forward. Pull boot up around shifter, but do not remove.

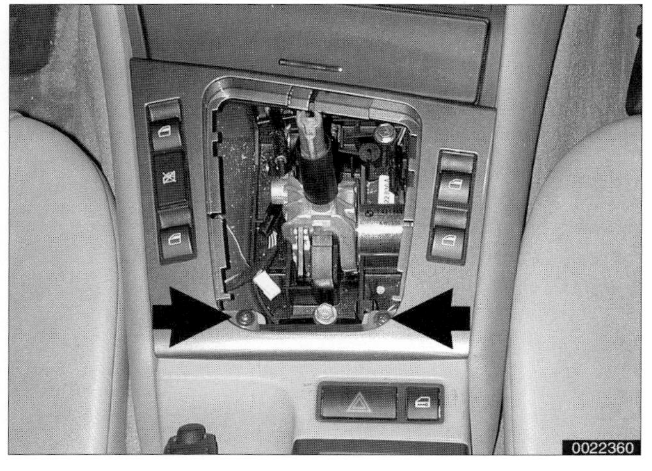

Remove retaining screws (**arrows**) under transmission selector boot / trim.

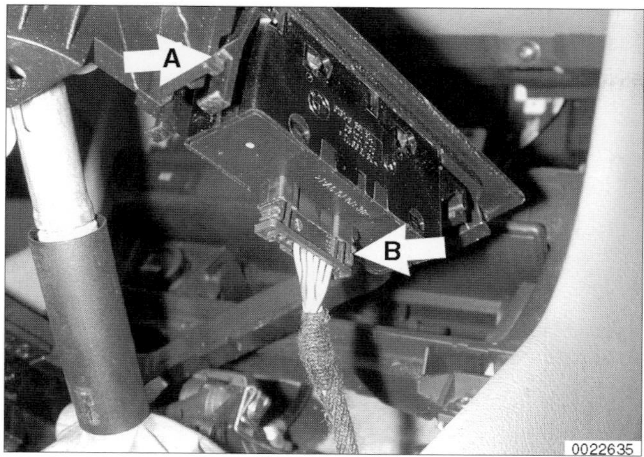

Power window switch, replacing

◀ Unclip switch retainer (**A**) and pull out switches from under console trim.

- Detach electrical harness connector (**B**) from switch assembly.

– Installation is reverse of removal.

ASC, DSC or seat heater switch, replacing

◀ Remove storage compartment below IHKA control panel:

- Open compartment door.
- Push upward in center of compartment, then pull out.

– Remove retaining screws from storage compartment / ash tray housing.

– Slide housing out and disconnect electrical harness connectors. Remove housing from lower dashboard.

– With housing removed, slide switch out of housing by gently pushing from behind.

– Installation is reverse of removal.

Central locking / hazard warning switch, replacing

◀ Working at rear of center console, press rolling cover of rear ashtray down. Depress cover fully to pop ashtray out of console.

– Remove retaining screws and storage tray housing. Disconnect electrical harness connector for storage tray courtesy light.

– Remove screws at base of storage tray compartment in console.

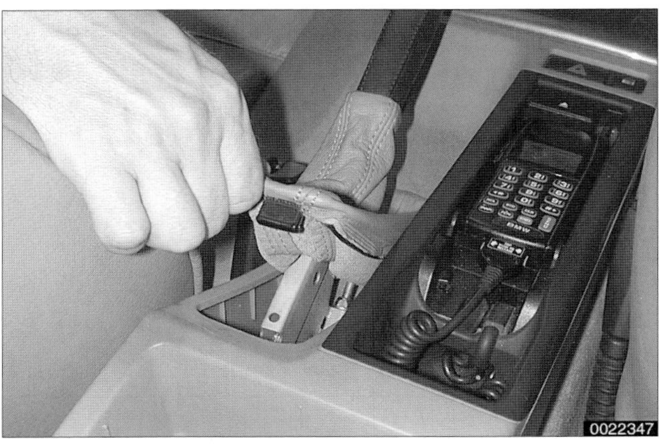
0022347

Unclip parking brake lever trim boot and pull boot and handle forward off lever.

- Slide center console backward and lift up.

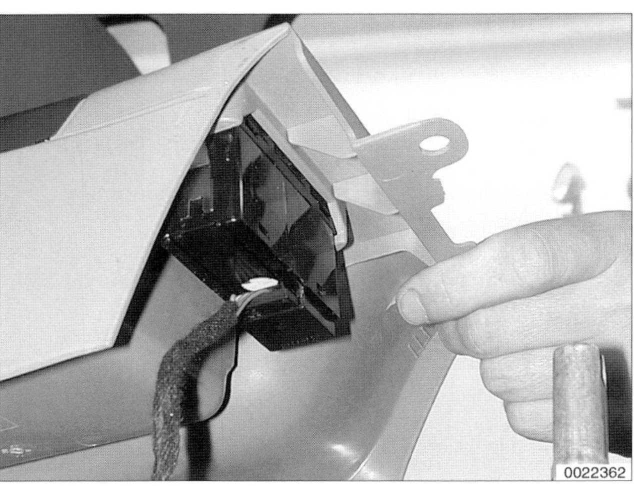
0022362

Disconnect electrical harness protector from hazard warning / central locking switch.

- Depress retaining tabs on each side of switch and push out of console.
- Installation is reverse of removal.

Outside mirror switch, replacing

0022846

Carefully pry outside mirror switch from door arm rest.

- Disconnect harness connector from switch.
- Installation is reverse of removal.

620 Instruments

GENERAL

This repair group covers removal and installation of the instrument cluster. Instrument cluster self-test procedures are also included.

Special tools

Special tools

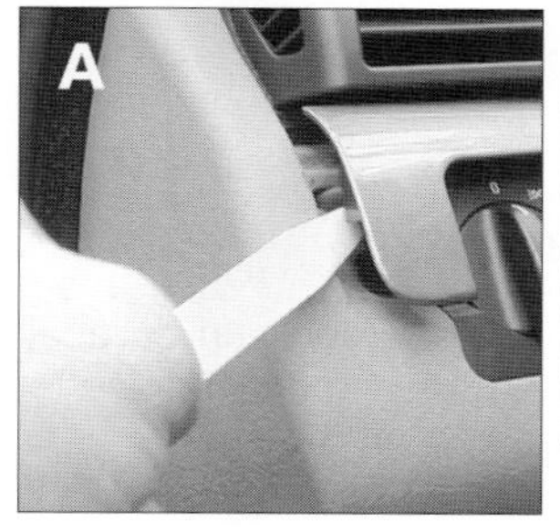

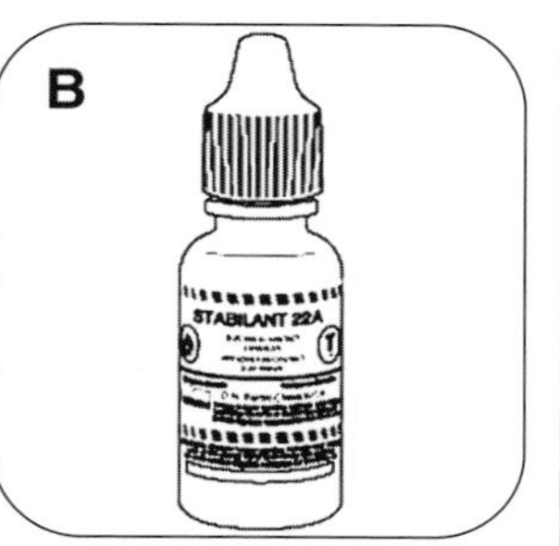

A BMW 00 9 321 . . . . .Plastic prying tool
B Würth Stabilant® 22A. . . . . Electrical contact enhancer

Individual instrument cluster components are not available. Since the instrument cluster is only available as a complete unit, BMW recommends no special tools.

The use of an electrical contact enhancer helps prevent oxidation and intermittent circuit malfunctions at electrical harness connectors.

CAUTION—

- *When servicing the instrument cluster, disconnect the negative (–) cable from the battery and insulate the cable end to prevent accidental reconnection.*
- *Prior to disconnecting the battery, read the battery disconnection cautions given at the front of this manual on page viii.*
- *To avoid marring trim when working on interior components, work with plastic prying tool or wrap the tip of screwdriver or pliers with tape before prying out electrical component.*

INSTRUMENT CLUSTER

The dashboard mounted instrument cluster is the driver control and information center. It is connected to most of the systems and sensors in the car through the use of "bus" networks:

- **K-bus** connects to Central Body Electronics (ZKE V) functions, heating / A/C (IHKA), rain sensor, exterior and interior lights, Multiple Restraint System (MRS), and electronic immobilizer (EWS III).
- **CAN-bus** connects to engine management (DME), transmission control (AGS) and traction / stability control (ASC / DSC).
- **D-bus** connects to 20-pin diagnostic link connector (DLC) and / or 16-pin OBD II diagnostic connector.

620

If the vehicle is equipped with On-Board Computer, pushing the button at the end of the directional stalk switch brings up information of interest to the driver:

- Time
- Outside temperature
- Average fuel consumption
- Cruising range
- Average vehicle speed

These functions are more fully explained in the Owner's Manual.

The cluster also stores important vehicle memory functions such as total mileage and service interval data. Instrument cluster replacement must be followed by special procedures, using BMW scan tools (DISplus, GT1, MoDiC) or equivalent, to synchronize vehicle memory and mileage with the new cluster unit.

NOTE —
Specific vehicle information is stored redundantly in the instrument cluster and the light control module. This information includes:

- *Vehicle identification number (VIN)*
- *Total vehicle mileage*
- *Service interval data*

Instrument cluster layout

The instrument cluster uses stepper motor driven analog gauges for display of engine and road speed, engine temperature, fuel level and economy.

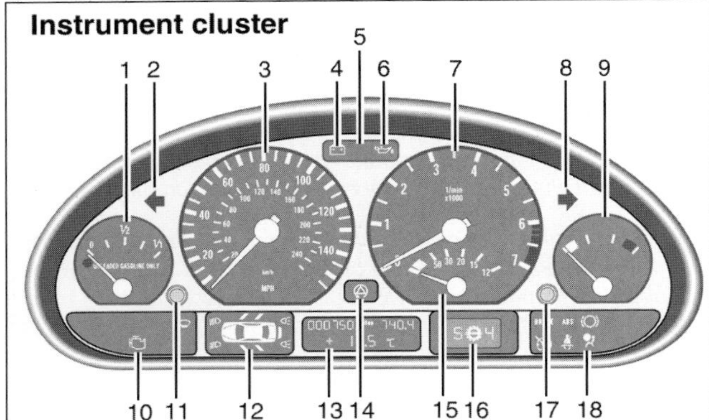

1. Fuel Gauge
2. Left directional
3. Tachometer
4. Alternator warning light
5. High beam warning
6. Oil warning
7. Speedometer
8. Right directional
9. Temperature gauge
10. Warning lights (Check Engine, etc.)
11. Left reset button (odometer / service interval)
12. Check Control LCD
13. Odometer / On-Board Computer LCD
14. ASC / DSC warning
15. Fuel economy gauge
16. Transmission range / program LCD (includes transmission fault indicator)
17. Right reset button (clock)
18. Warning lights (brakes, etc.)

In addition, three LCD blocks display:

- Check Control pictographs
- Service interval and mileage (On-Board Computer)
- Automatic transmission range / program and failure display

Warning indicators and lights are arranged to the right and left of the LCD blocks. The ASC / DSC light, charge indicator, high beam and oil pressure warning lights are located between the speedometer and tachometer.

The instrument cluster is a sealed unit and contains no serviceable components.

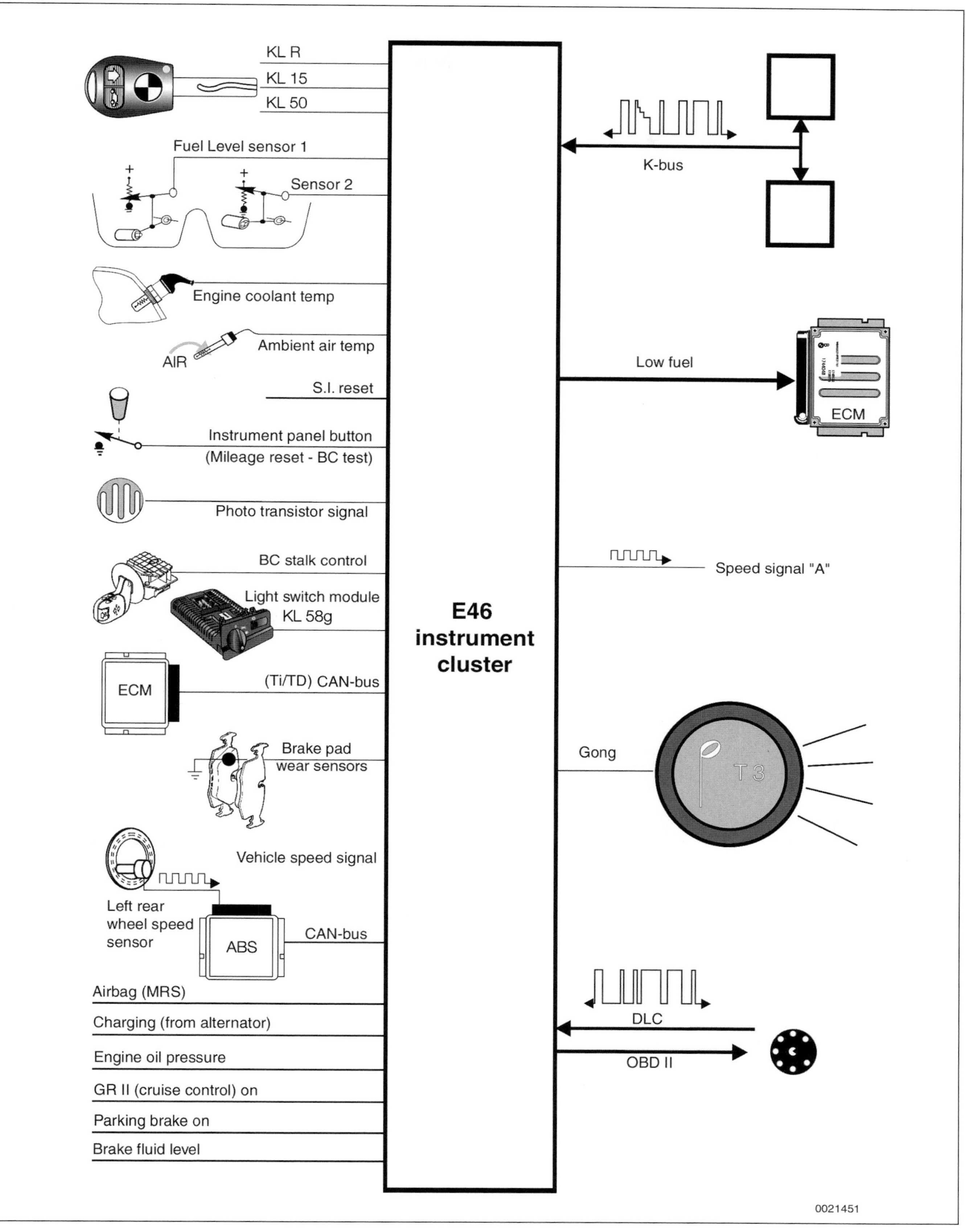
KL R
KL 15
KL 50
Fuel Level sensor 1
Sensor 2
Engine coolant temp
AIR
Ambient air temp
S.I. reset
Instrument panel button
(Mileage reset - BC test)
Photo transistor signal
BC stalk control
Light switch module
KL 58g
ECM
(Ti/TD) CAN-bus
Brake pad
wear sensors
Vehicle speed signal
Left rear
wheel speed
sensor
ABS
CAN-bus
Airbag (MRS)
Charging (from alternator)
Engine oil pressure
GR II (cruise control) on
Parking brake on
Brake fluid level
E46
instrument
cluster
K-bus
Low fuel
ECM
Speed signal "A"
Gong
T 3
DLC
OBD II
0021451

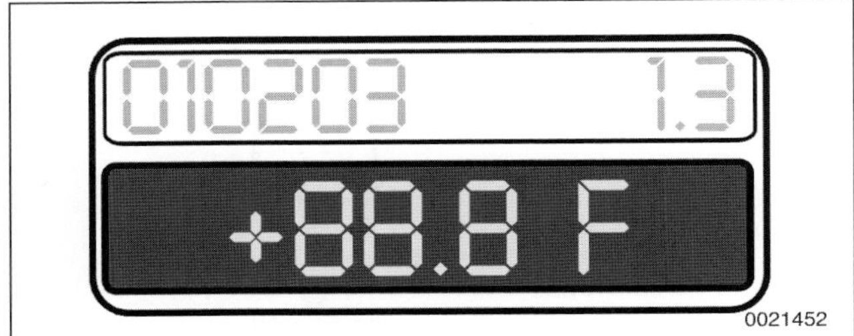

Instrument cluster, self-testing

In addition to the storing diagnostic trouble codes (DTCs) and communicating through the diagnostic link, the instrument cluster is programmed with a series of test menus that can be accessed to check various functions and values. The odometer / On-Board Computer LCD block is used to display the test menus and results. There are a total of 21 test menus.

Table a lists instrument cluster test menus and submenus.

To scroll through numbered test menus:

- Make sure ignition switch is OFF.
- Press and hold left cluster button.
- Turn ignition switch to "radio". Test 1 main menu will be displayed.
- Do nothing and display will automatically scroll through Test 1 submenus.
- Tap or press instrument cluster left button. This signals cluster to display submenus or continue on to next main test menu.

Table a. Instrument cluster test functions

Menu	Sub-menu	Sample output	Meaning
Test 1: Vehicle specific data (see Note below)	1.0	12345	Vehicle identification number (VIN)
	1.1	4812	Body number
	6_1.2	834762	Part number of cluster
	1.3	010203	Coding / diagnosis / bus index
	1.4	3499	Manufacturing date (calendar week / year)
	1.5	04_600	Hardware / software version of cluster (hardware = 04, software = 6.00)
	3_1.6	415_06	Injection status, number of cylinders, engine factor
	1.7		
Test 2: Cluster system test activates gauge drivers, indicators and LEDs to confirm function (see Note below)			
Test 3: SI data	3.0	1500	Liters
	3.1	0	Periodic inspection days (not applicable for US)
Test 4: Fuel consumption data (current)	4.0	0267	26.7 liters / 1000km
	4.1	0073	7.3 liters / hour
Test 5: Fuel consumed / distance traveled	5.0	0195	9.5 liters / 100 km
	5.1	226	Distance left to go (226 km)
Test 6: Fuel level sensor input in liters	6.0	237415	Fuel level averaged • Left side fuel sensor input = 23.7 liters • Right side fuel sensor input = 41.5 liters
	6.1	0652	Total tank level averaged = 65.2 liters
	1_6.2	0667	Indicated value and tank phase • 1 = Both sensors OK • 2 = One sensor faulty • 3 = Implausible input

Table a. Instrument cluster test functions

Menu	Sub-menu	Sample output	Meaning
Test 7: Temperature and speed	7.0	032	Coolant temperature input = 32°C
	7.1	245	Outside temperature input = 24.5°C
	7.2	5283	Engine speed = 5,283 rpm
	7.3	058	Vehicle speed = 58 kph
Test 8: Input values in HEX code	8.0 - 8.3	XXX	HEX code, instrument cluster inputs
Test 9: Battery voltage	9.0	125	12.5 volts
Test 10: Country coding	10.0	02	US (= 02)
Test 11: Cluster code	11.0	000003	Cluster code
Test 12: Not used			
Test 13: Gong test	13.0	"Gong"	Activate gong by pressing button (gong response is delayed).
Test 14: Fault memory (not for diagnosis)			
Tests 15 - 18: Not used			
Test 19: Lock / unlock (see Note below)		L-ON	Display changes from L-ON to L-OFF every second. To unlock test functions, press cluster button immediately when it changes to L-OFF. Tests are automatically locked when exiting test functions.
	19.0	L-OFF	
Test 20: Average fuel consumption correction factor (see Note below)	20.0	XXX9	Press button when correct 1s position is attained.
	20.1	XX5X	Press button when correct 10s position is attained.
	20.2	12XX	Press button when correct 100s position is attained.
Test 21: Software reset	21.0	reset	Reset software

NOTE —

- *Tests 1 and 2 are always unlocked.*
- *Tests 3 - 21 are only accessible after unlocking the test function.*
- *Test 19 is the unlock function for accessing the displays.*
- *If adjustment is necessary, enter into Test 20 using the cluster button. The correction factor number is changed by using the submenus for the 1s, 10s and 100s of the factor number. The digits automatically scroll through 0 - 9 within each group (1s, 10s, 100s).*

0022387

Instrument cluster, removing and installing

◄ Remove instrument cluster retaining screws (**arrows**).

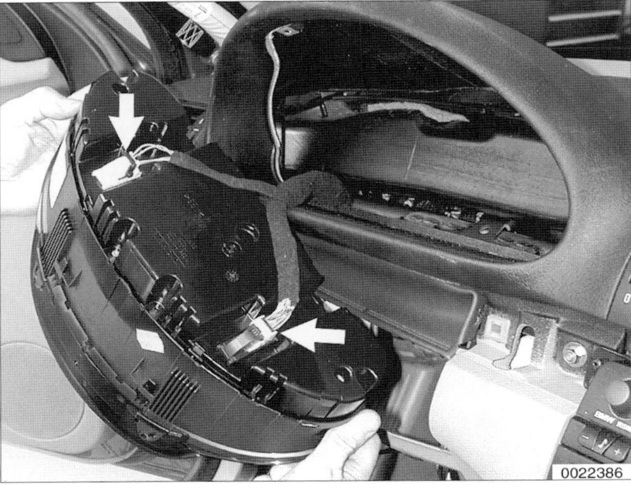
0022386

◄ Place a towel over steering column. Carefully tilt top of cluster out of dashboard. Unlock and disconnect harness connectors (**arrows**) from back of cluster.

NOTE —
Steering wheel does not need to be removed to remove instrument cluster.

0021449

◄ If it is necessary to replace cluster, detach trim by unlocking plastic clips (**arrows**) and pushing through slots.

– Installation is reverse of removal, noting the following:

- Instrument cluster harness connector locking levers must be in up position before installing connector.
- Recode new or replacement cluster using BMW scan tools (DISplus, GT1, MoDiC) or equivalent.

630 Lights

TABLES

GENERAL

This repair group covers interior and exterior lighting, including repairs to the light switch assembly.

Special tools

Some special tools may be necessary to install or adjust lights and light fixtures.

Special Tools

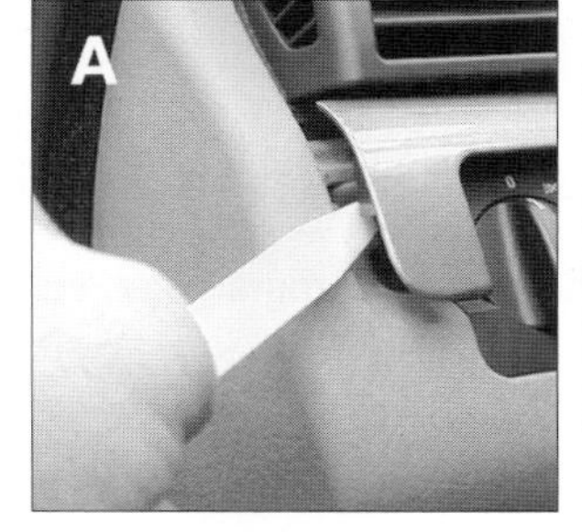

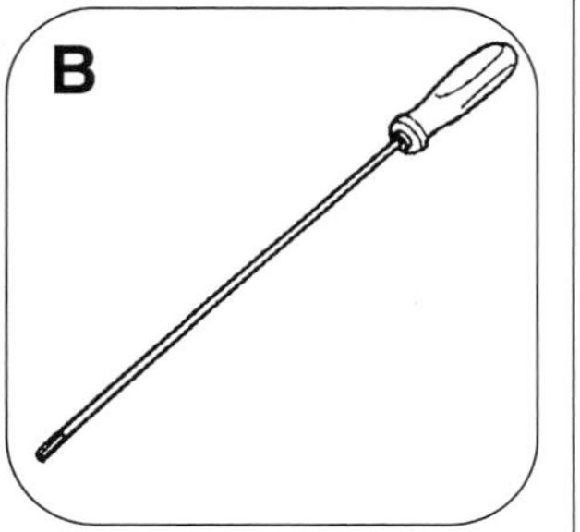

Special tools

- **A** BMW 00 9 321 . . . . . Plastic trim prying tool
- **B** 4 mm / 6 mm Allen . . . . . Foglight / headlight adjusting tool

630

Bulb applications

For convenience, the bulb applications for E46 cars are listed in **Table a**.

Table a. E46 bulb applications

Location	Type & rating
Headlights	
High beam	H7 12V 55W
Low beam (halogen)	H7 12 V 55W
Low beam (xenon)	D2-S
Foglights	
Front	HB4
Rear (Euro only)	12V 21W
Turn signal and taillight	
Back-up	12V 21W
Brake	12V 21W
Brake / taillight	12V 21/4W
License plate	12V 5W
Side turn signal	W5W
Third brake light	LED
Turn signal (front or rear)	12V 21W
Interior lights	
Footwell	Softlite 5W
Glove compartment	Softlite 5W
Passenger compartment, front or rear	Softlite 5W
Reading, front or rear	6W
Trunk or cargo compartment	Softlite 10W
Visor vanity	Softlite 10W

Light switch center (LSZ)

The light switch center (LSZ), mounted in the left side of the dashboard, has the following functions:

- Headlight / taillight / running light control switch
- Foglight switch
- Instrument dimmer control
- Light control module

In addition to normal light control, the LSZ provides the following functions:

- Hot and cold monitoring of the exterior bulbs
- Emergency lighting function
- Short circuit protection
- 1999 - 2001: Redundant storage of mileage and service interval data
- Automatic headlight adjustment (LWR) programmed control (if equipped)

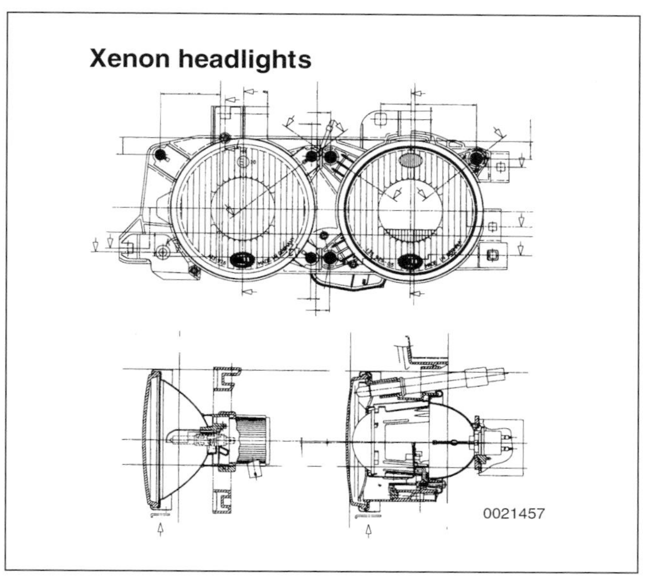

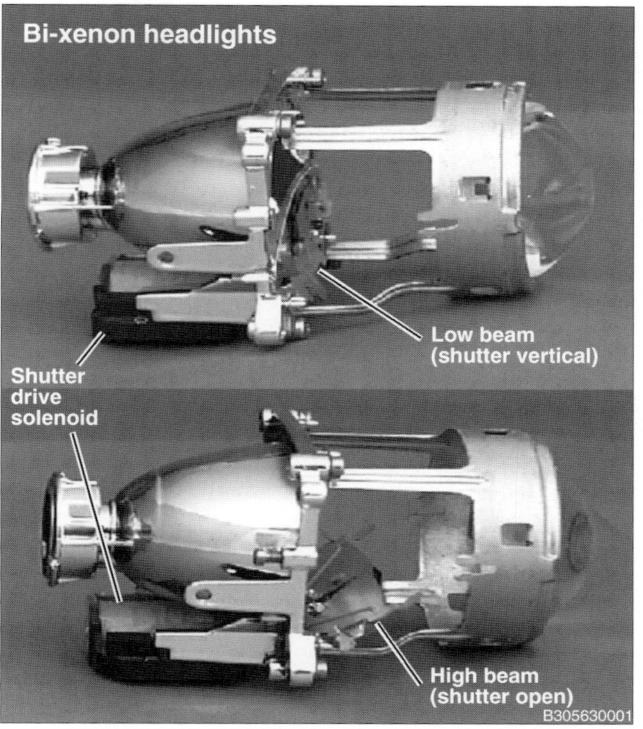

Headlight versions

E46 cars are equipped with halogen headlights as standard equipment. Halogen bulb replacement is performed from the back (engine) side of the headlight assembly. The front face of each headlight assembly is a removable plastic cover.

Optional xenon low-beam headlights illuminate the road ahead and to the sides in greater detail than conventional headlights. Sometimes referred to as High Intensity Discharge (HID) lights, xenon lights use less energy and last longer than other headlight bulbs.

Cars equipped with xenon headlights also feature automatic headlight adjustment control (LWR) for varying passenger and cargo loads.

Components of the headlight system can be purchased from BMW. Use illustrations on the following pages to identify components.

Adaptive headlights

In adaptive bi-xenon headlights, an option available starting in 2002, there is an electrically activated shutter which directs the low beam cone of light in the same direction as the high beams.

Rain / light sensor (RLS)

If the vehicle is equipped with the optional automatic headlight control, the driving lights are turned on and off automatically by the rain / light sensor (RLS), depending on ambient light conditions.

The rain sensor system is augmented by two additional optical sensors, both housed in the rear view mirror at the top of the windshield:

- **Surrounding-light sensor** detects light intensity in a wide angle above the vehicle.
- **Frontal-light sensor** detects light intensity in a narrow cone in front of the vehicle.

A microprocessor uses this data to determine when and whether to turn the lights ON or OFF in the following circumstances:

- Dawn or dusk
- Night
- Driving through a tunnel
- Precipitation such as rain or snow

RLS sensitivity is adjustable by means of the Car Memory feature. See **515 Central Locking and Anti-theft**.

For additional details on rain sensor system, see **611 Wiper and Washers**.

Bulb monitoring

The light control module monitors the following bulbs in both hot and cold states:

- High / low beams
- Brake lights
- Turn signal lights
- Taillights
- Parking lights
- Side marker lights
- License plate lights

Bulb monitoring
Check Control
Monitor
Monitor
Cold bulb
Hot bulb
0021456

Hot and cold monitoring of light bulbs allows the LSZ to detect defective bulbs. Hot monitoring checks the continuity of circuits while the lights are switched on. Cold monitoring consists of a brief pulse of current which is too short for the lights to illuminate. If the module detects a defective bulb, a signal is sent to the instrument cluster and Check Control is illuminated with the appropriate warning.

Home lighting

This convenience feature provides lighting for occupants to leave the vehicle and enter their house. The feature is switched on by activating the headlight flasher switch after the lights and ignition are switched OFF. The lights are switched OFF after the coded time delay or by switching the ignition ON.

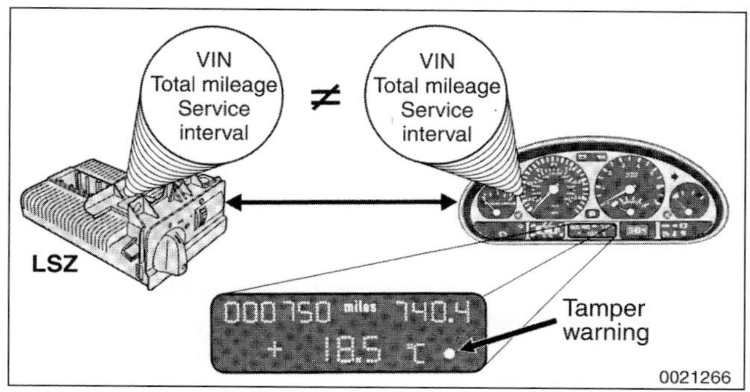

Redundant vehicle data storage

Vehicle data includes model series and type identification, national variant, options and equipment, engine and transmission serial numbers, total vehicle mileage and service interval information. This information is stored in two different control modules and can be accessed by BMW scan tool (DISplus, GT1, MoDiC) or equivalent.

1999 - 2001: The light control module (LSZ) serves as the redundant vehicle data storage module in parallel with the instrument cluster.

2002 - 2005: The electronic immobilizer (EWS) module and the instrument cluster are the redundant data storage sites.

If one of the two redundant storage modules is replaced, data is transferred from the remaining module to the replacement unit when it is recoded.

Emergency (fail safe) lighting

The light control module provides emergency lighting in case of an electronic module failure. Back up hardware allows the following lighting circuits to function:

- Low beam headlights
- Taillights
- Brake lights

The headlights and taillights come on as soon as the ignition is switched ON. The brake lights operate when the brake pedal is pressed.

Warnings and cautions

WARNING —

- *Internal pressure of HID glass bulb may exceed 100 bar (in operation). Bulb temperature may exceed 700 degrees Celsius. Always wear safety glasses and gloves when removing and installing an HID bulb.*

- *Never look directly at an operating HID bulb. The UV emissions of an HID bulb are approximately 2.5 times that of a comparable halogen bulb.*

- *When working on electrical systems, remove the fuse protecting the circuit under repair. See* **610 Electrical Component Locations**.

> **CAUTION —**
> - *The physical and mechanical properties of HID bulb and control module are very sensitive. Use an antistatic mat and work with caution.*
> - *Do not operate the HID control module unless a bulb is connected.*
> - *Before servicing headlight system, switch off all electrical consumers. Switch ignition off and remove ignition key.*
> - *To ensure bulb longevity, do not handle bulb glass with bare fingers. Dirt and skin oils cause a bulb to fail prematurely. If necessary, wipe bulb using a clean cloth dampened with rubbing alcohol.*
> - *Use only original equipment replacement bulbs. Non-original equipment bulbs may cause false failure readings on the Check Control display.*
> - *To avoid marring car paint or trim, work with plastic prying tools or wrap the tips of tools with tape.*

LIGHT SWITCH

Light switch assembly (LSZ), removing and installing

0021440

◄ Pry gently at left dashboard trim to remove.

> **CAUTION —**
> *To avoid marring interior trim, work with a plastic prying tool.*

0021439

◄ Remove light switch mounting screws (**arrows**).

– Lift switch slightly and withdraw from dashboard.

NOTE —
- *If the vehicle is equipped with a left side glove compartment, remove the compartment for improved access to the back of the headlight switch and its electrical harness.*
- *Remove the left side footwell trim (above the pedals) for better access to the headlight switch electrical harness. See* **513 Interior Trim**.

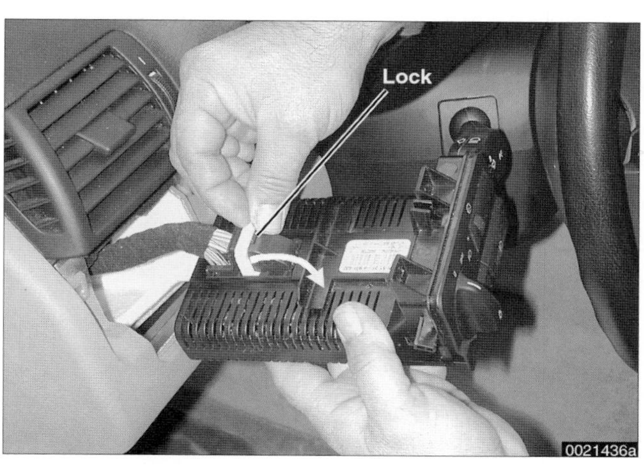

0021436a

To release harness connector latch:

- Swing latch backward (**arrow**).
- Pull electrical harness connector off switch assembly.

– Installation is reverse of removal.

Light control module, separating

– Remove light switch assembly. See **Light switch assembly (LSZ), removing and installing** in this repair group.

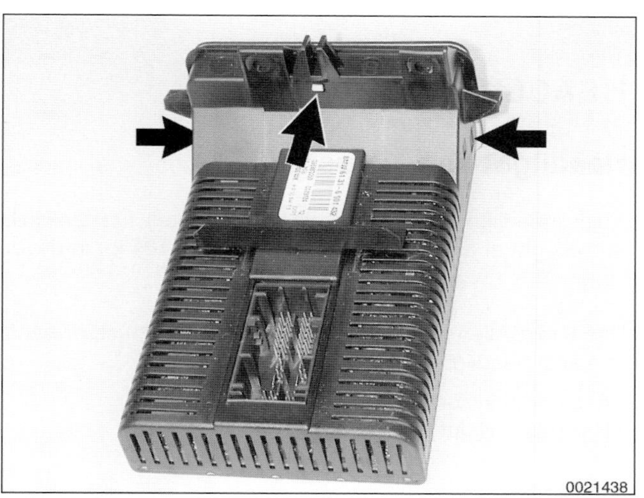
0021438

Press in on LSZ tabs (**arrows**) to separate switch component from control module.

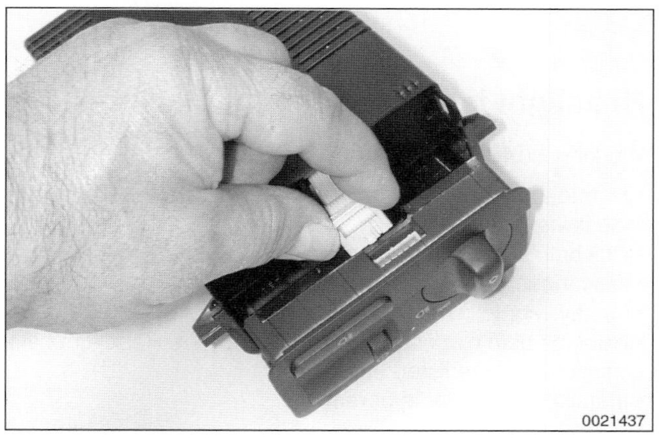
0021437

Gently wiggle harness connector to remove from switch.

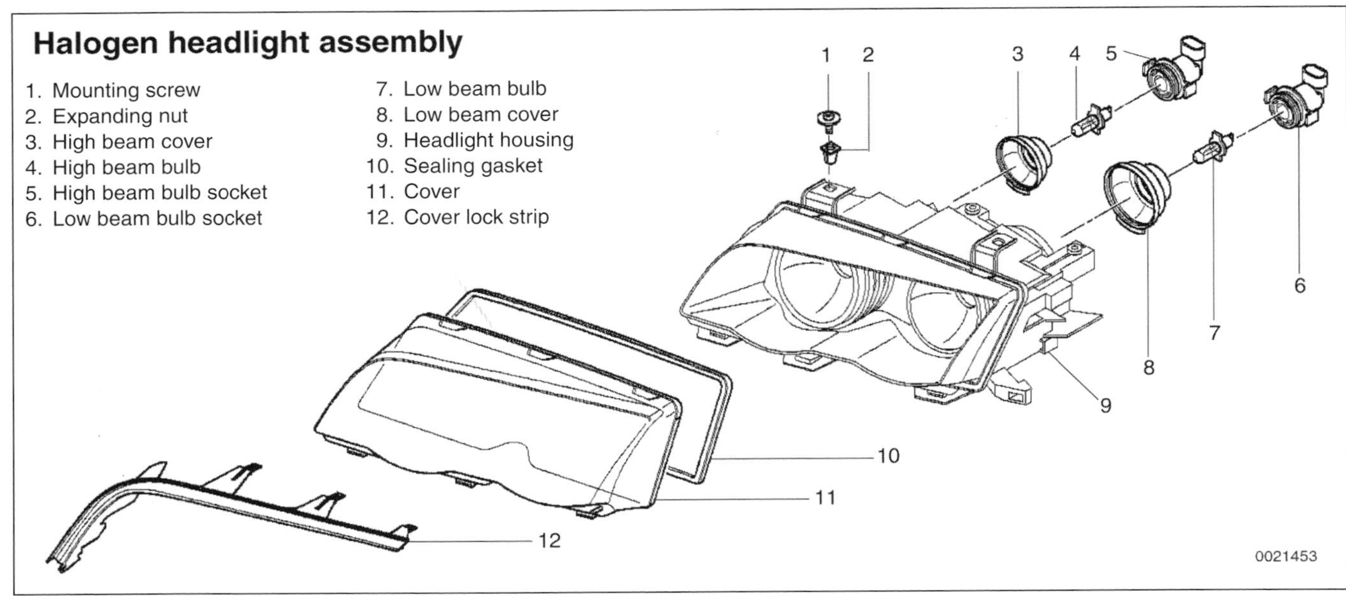

HEADLIGHTS

Headlight aim, adjusting

Adjust headlight aim with correct tire pressures, fuel tank full, and weight of one person (approx. 75 Kg / 165 lb) in driver seat.

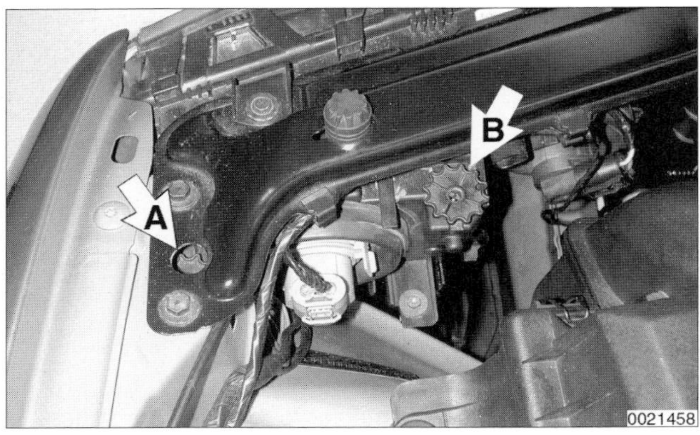

Use 6 mm Allen wrench, phillips head screwdriver, or hand to adjust headlight by turning adjusting knobs.

- **A** is primarily for lateral adjustment.
- **B** is primarily for vertical adjustment.

NOTE —

When adjusting headlights with automatic adjuster system (LWR), wait at least 30 seconds for LWR to cycle and adjust to its calculated position.

Headlight bulb (halogen), replacing

Working in back of headlight assembly:

- Rotate headlight bulb retaining ring (**arrows**) counterclockwise.
- Pull bulb socket and bulb out of headlight assembly.
- Disconnect harness connector from socket.
- Gently wiggle bulb and pull straight out of socket.
- Replace bulb by pushing firmly into socket. Headlight bulb applications are listed below.
- Installation is reverse of removal.

NOTE —

To remove left side high beam bulb, remove air filter housing cover. See **020 Maintenance**.

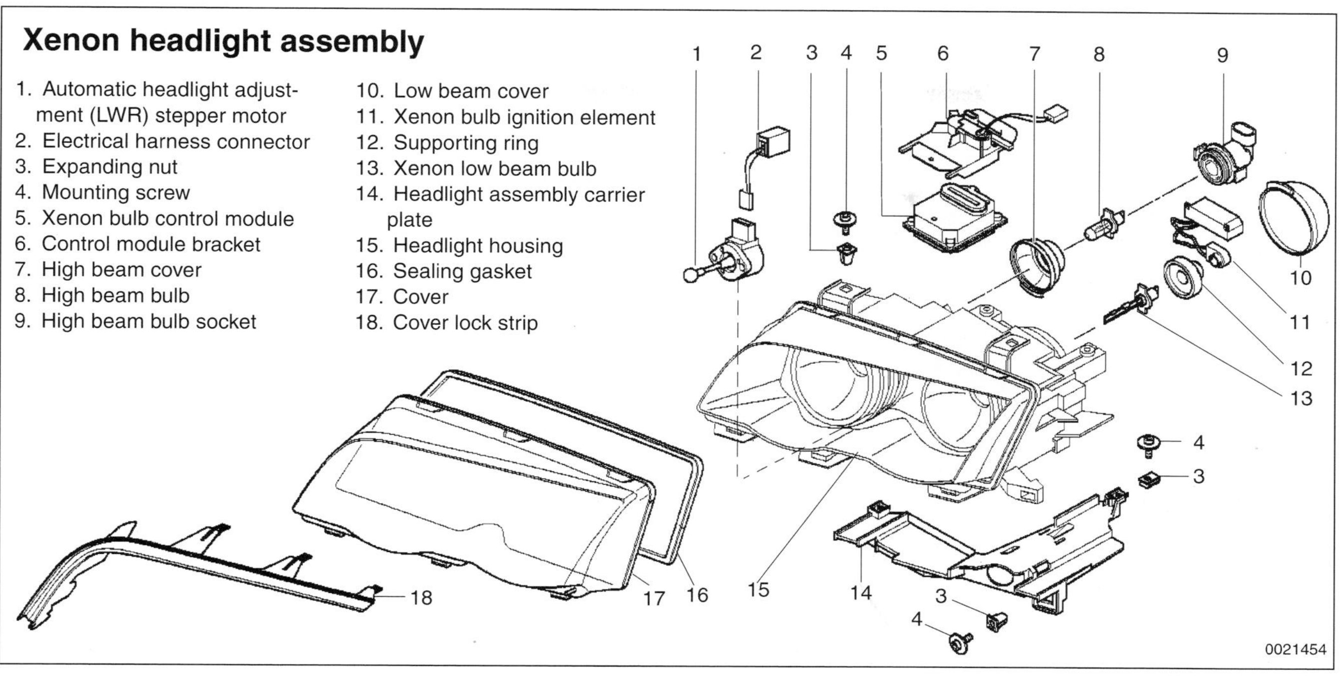

Xenon headlight assembly

1. Automatic headlight adjustment (LWR) stepper motor
2. Electrical harness connector
3. Expanding nut
4. Mounting screw
5. Xenon bulb control module
6. Control module bracket
7. High beam cover
8. High beam bulb
9. High beam bulb socket
10. Low beam cover
11. Xenon bulb ignition element
12. Supporting ring
13. Xenon low beam bulb
14. Headlight assembly carrier plate
15. Headlight housing
16. Sealing gasket
17. Cover
18. Cover lock strip

Headlight bulb (xenon), replacing

– Working in back of headlight assembly:

- Remove low beam cover.
- Twist xenon ignition element counterclockwise and remove.
- Rotate headlight bulb retaining ring counterclockwise. Pull bulb out of headlight assembly.
- Installation is reverse of removal. Headlight bulb applications are listed below.

Headlight bulb application

- Low beam (halogen) H7 12V 55W
- Low bean (xenon) D2-S
- High beam H7 12V 55W

Headlight assembly, removing and installing

– Disconnect harness connectors from headlight assembly.

– If necessary, remove headlight washer spray nozzles. See **611 Wiper and Washers**.

– Remove front turn signal assembly. See **Front turn signal assembly, removing and installing** in this repair group.

< Using plastic prying tool, pry at corners (**arrows**) to detach and remove lower headlight trim.

Remove headlight mounting screws (**arrows**). Lift headlight assembly forward and out of car.

During reassembly:

- Install top mounting screws hand tight.
- Pull headlight assembly toward front of car.
- Close engine hood and check to make sure that gap between hood and headlight assembly (**A**) is correct. See specification below.
- Open hood and tighten down mounting screws.
- Remainder of assembly is reverse of removal.

Headlight to hood gap

- Dimension **A** . . . . 5.0 ± 1.0 mm (0.2 ± 0.04 in.)

– Adjust headlight aim. See **Headlight aim, adjusting** in this repair group.

Headlight lens, removing and installing

– If necessary, remove headlight washer spray nozzles. See **611 Wiper and Washers**.

– Remove front turn signal assembly. See **Front turn signal assembly, removing and installing** in this repair group.

Using plastic prying tool, pry at corners (**arrows**) to detach and remove lower headlight trim.

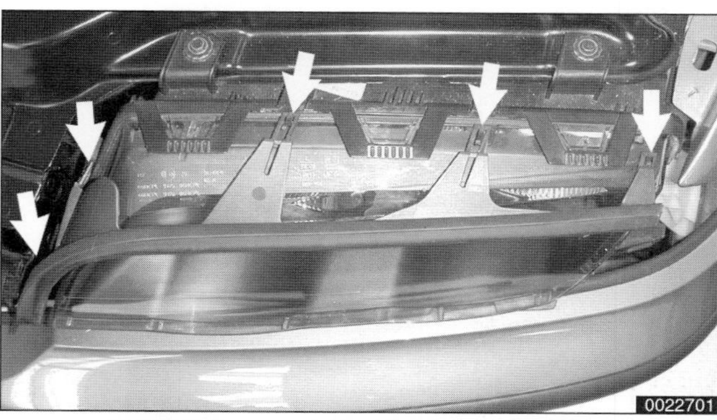
0022701

◀ Unclip headlight lens sealing gasket (**arrows**) and remove.

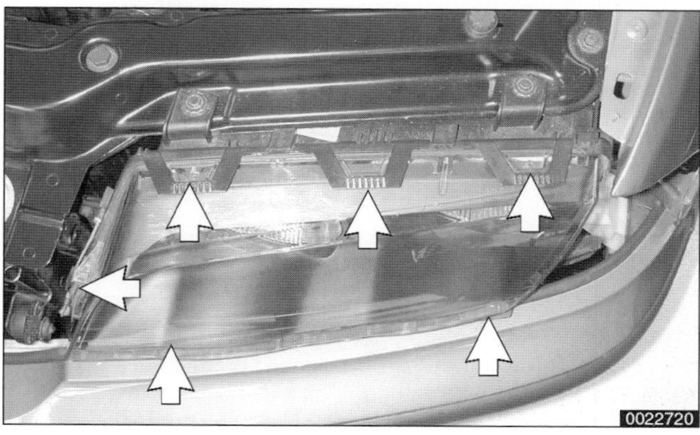
0022720

◀ Release front lens retaining clips (**arrows**).

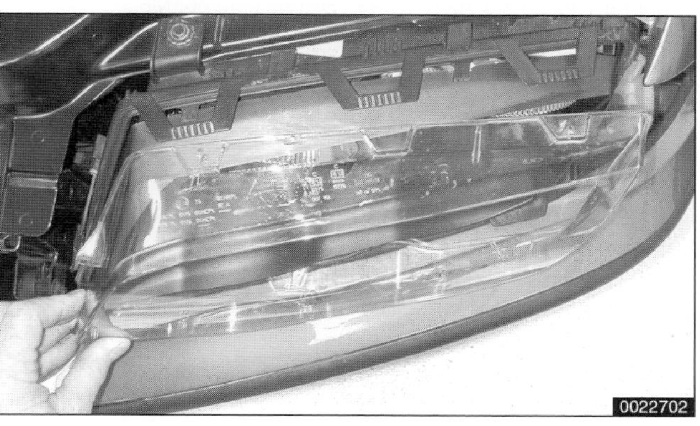
0022702

◀ Pull lens forward to remove.

- Installation is reverse of removal. Replace gasket between lens and body of light if necessary.

Automatic headlight adjustment (LWR)

Vehicles equipped with the optional xenon headlights feature automatic headlight adjustment (LWR). This system automatically adjusts the vertical positioning of the headlights to maintain optimum headlight beam angle for maximum driving visibility and to prevent undue glare for oncoming motorists. The system compensates for vehicle load angle changes.

LWR monitors vehicle load via two hall effect sensors mounted to the front and rear suspension members. When an adjustment to the angle of the headlight beams is necessary, LWR simultaneously activates two stepper motors (one in each headlight assembly). The stepper motors drive a threaded rod that moves the lower edge of the headlight

Headlight vertical aim system components

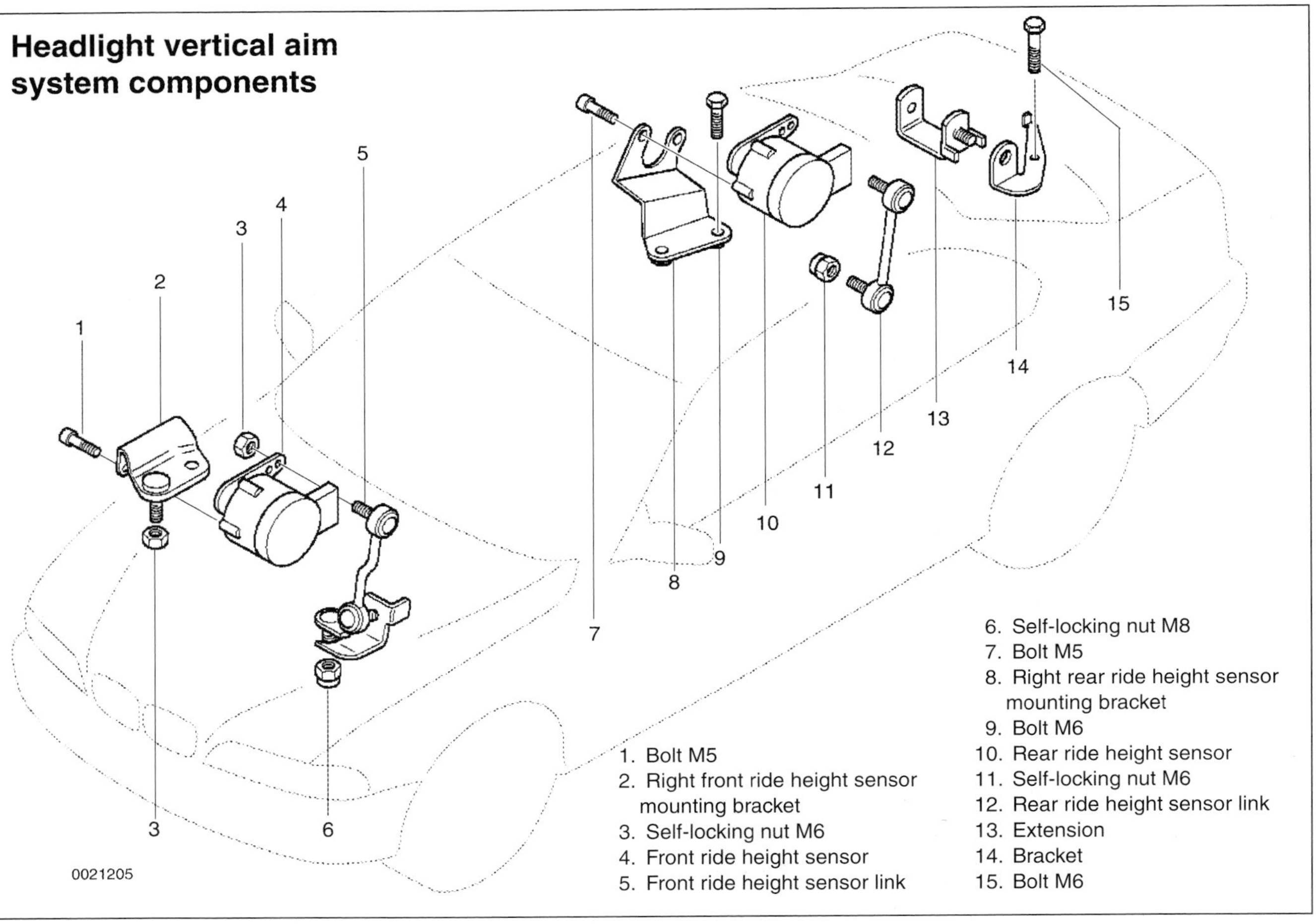

1. Bolt M5
2. Right front ride height sensor mounting bracket
3. Self-locking nut M6
4. Front ride height sensor
5. Front ride height sensor link
6. Self-locking nut M8
7. Bolt M5
8. Right rear ride height sensor mounting bracket
9. Bolt M6
10. Rear ride height sensor
11. Self-locking nut M6
12. Rear ride height sensor link
13. Extension
14. Bracket
15. Bolt M6

0021205

carrier plates. The pivoting movement adjusts the vertical position of the headlight beams.

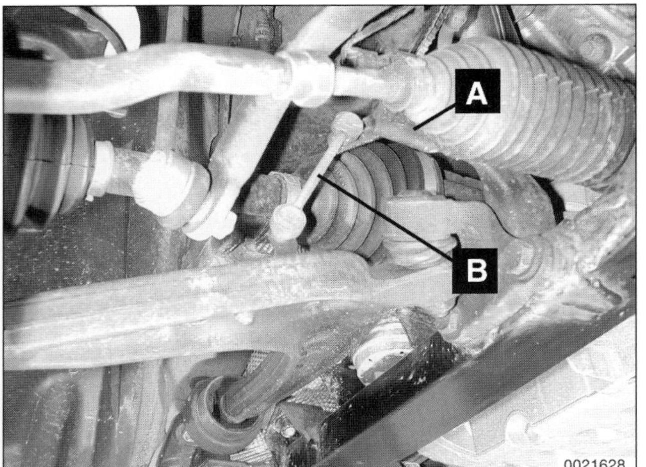

At each axle of the vehicle, the LWR sensor (**A**) is mounted to a fixed point on the suspension subframe. A lever (**B**) is connected to the moving suspension member. The sensor output voltage changes as the suspension moves up and down.

Diagnose LWR problems using BMW scan tool (DISplus, GT1, MoDiC) or equivalent.

NOTE —

LWR is not available with standard halogen headlights.

FRONT FOGLIGHTS

Foglight aim, adjusting

Sedan, Sport Wagon: Use 4 mm Allen wrench to turn plastic adjuster (**arrow**) on outer edge of foglight.

Coupe, Convertible: Use adjuster (**arrow**) on inside upper edge of foglight.

2001 models:

- Using plastic pry tool, pry off foglight cover at slot (**arrow**).
- Adjust using 6 mm Allen on outside upper corner of foglight.

Foglight assembly, removing and installing

– **Sedan, Sport Wagon**:

- Use plastic prying tool to lever out foglight assembly.
- Detach electrical harness connector.

– **Coupe, Convertible**:

- Gently remove lower bumper trim.
- Working at foglight, detach grille and loosen mounting screws.
- Remove foglight assembly with grille attached.
- Detach electrical harness connector.

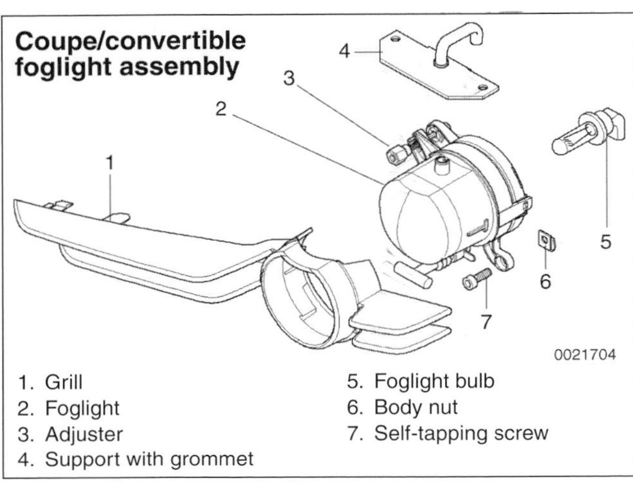

1. Grill
2. Foglight
3. Adjuster
4. Support with grommet
5. Foglight bulb
6. Body nut
7. Self-tapping screw

◄ Unclip grill from foglight.

– Installation is reverse of removal, noting the following:

- Sedan, Sport Wagon: Foglight must be snapped firmly into bumper retainers.
- Coupe, Convertible: Keep ventilation grommets unkinked and firmly seated.
- Adjust foglight. See **Foglight aim, adjusting** in this repair group.

Foglight bulb, replacing

– Remove foglight assembly. See **Foglight assembly, removing and installing** in this repair group.

- Twist and remove bulb from rear of foglight assembly.

> ***CAUTION —***
> *Do not touch bulbs with your bare hands. If necessary wipe bulb using a clean cloth dampened with rubbing alcohol.*

- Installation is reverse of removal. Check electrical connector for corrosion. Spray with contact cleaner, if necessary.

Foglight application	
• Front foglight bulb	HB4

TURN SIGNALS, TAILLIGHTS

Front turn signal assembly, removing and installing

This procedure includes turn signal bulb replacement.

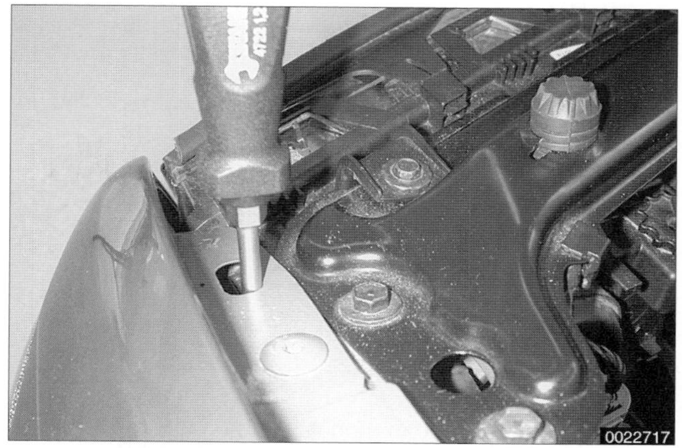

With engine hood open, use screwdriver to press turn signal assembly retaining clip down to disengage from retaining tab on headlight assembly frame.

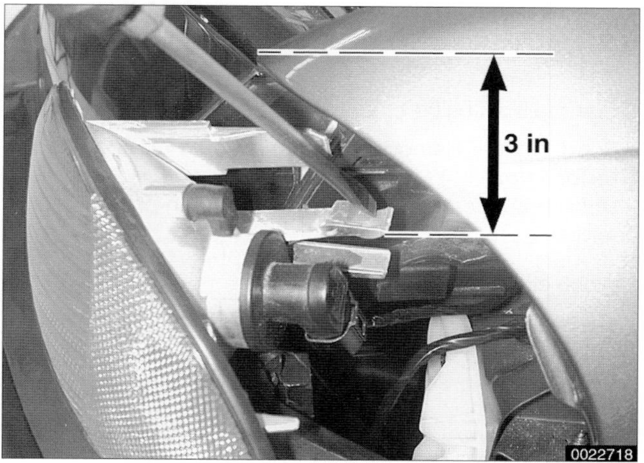

Screwdriver must reach into fender hole a minimum of 3 inches to reach retaining tab.

- Push turn signal forward. Light slides straight out.
- Detach electrical harness connector.
- Twist and remove bulb from rear of turn signal assembly.

> ***CAUTION —***
> *Do not touch bulb with your bare hands. If necessary wipe bulb using a clean cloth dampened with rubbing alcohol.*

NOTE —
Before reinstalling, make sure rubber seal on wrap-around trim (underneath headlights) is firmly glued to trim. Reglue if necessary.

Front turn signal
- Turn signal bulb 12V 21W

Side turn signal assembly

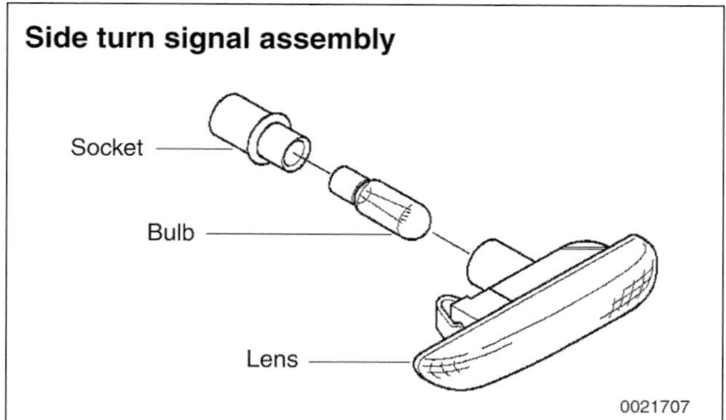

The yellow marker lights on the sides of the front fenders are turn signals. Use plastic prying tool to gently lever assembly out of fender.

Side turn signal
- Side light bulb 12V 5W

Taillight assembly

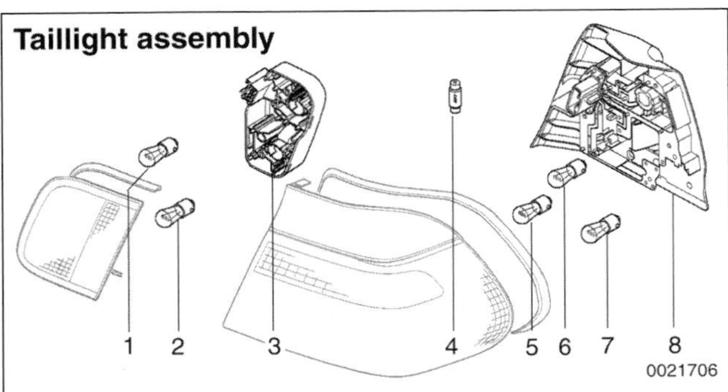

1. Backup light bulb 12V 21W
2. Rear foglight bulb (Euro only) 12V 21W
3. Trunk lid / tailgate bulb carrier
4. Trunk light bulb 12V 10W
5. Taillight / brake light bulb 12V 21/4W
6. Turn signal bulb 12V 21W
7. Brake light bulb 12V 21W

Taillight assembly, removing and installing

In E46 cars, taillight functions are split. The corner bulb carrier on each side contains:

- Taillight bulb
- Turn signal bulb
- Brake light bulb
- Trunk light bulb

The bulb carrier on each corner of trunk lid or tailgate contains:

- Back-up light bulb
- Rear foglight (European models only)

– To access taillight bulbs carriers, open trunk lid or tailgate.

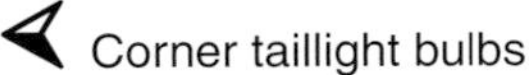

Corner taillight bulbs:

- Sport Wagon: Remove cargo area side trim. See **513 Interior Trim**.
- Unlatch bulb carrier retainer (**arrow**), then pull carrier off taillight assembly.

– Detach electrical harness connector.

– Replace bulbs as necessary.

> **CAUTION —**
> *Do not touch bulb with your bare hands. If necessary wipe bulb using a clean cloth dampened with rubbing alcohol.*

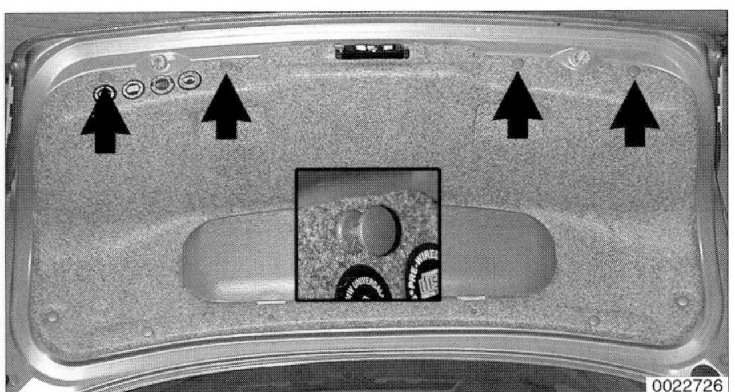

Trunk lid taillight bulbs: Partially remove trunk lid trim panel by removing plastic expansion rivets (**arrows**). Pry out expansion rivet pin (**inset**), then pull off trunk lid.

– Tailgate taillight bulbs: Remove tailgate inside trim panel.

Unlatch bulb carrier retainer (**arrow**), then pull carrier off.

- Detach electrical harness connector.
- Replace bulb(s) as necessary.

> ***CAUTION —***
> *Do not touch bulb with your bare hands. If necessary wipe bulb using a clean cloth dampened with rubbing alcohol.*

- Installation of either bulb carrier is reverse of removal.

Taillight applications

- Backup light bulb. 12V 21W
- Brake light bulb 12V 21W
- Brake light / taillight bulb 12V 21/4W
- Rear foglight (European only). 12V 21W
- Turn signal bulb. . . . . 12 V 21W

Center brake light

The center brake light in all models is an LED unit. There are no replaceable bulbs.

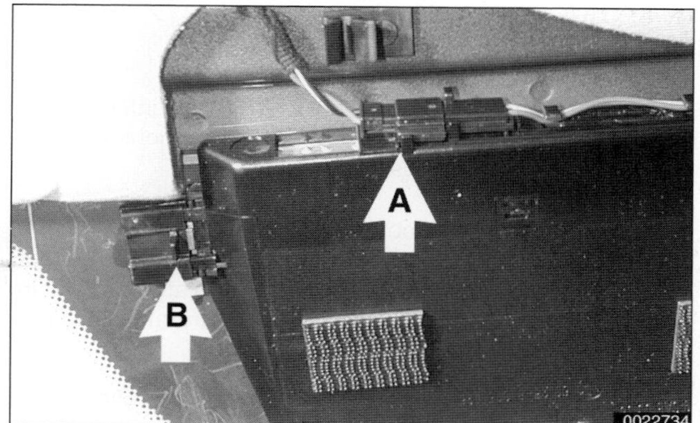

Sedan, Coupe: Working from rear seat in passenger compartment, gently pull off trim cover over third brake light (at top of rear glass).

- Detach electrical harness connector (**A**).
- Remove retaining clips (**B**) on either side and remove assembly.

– **Convertible**: Remove inner trunk lid trim adjacent to license plate light assembly.

- Detach electrical harness connector
- Push center brake light out.

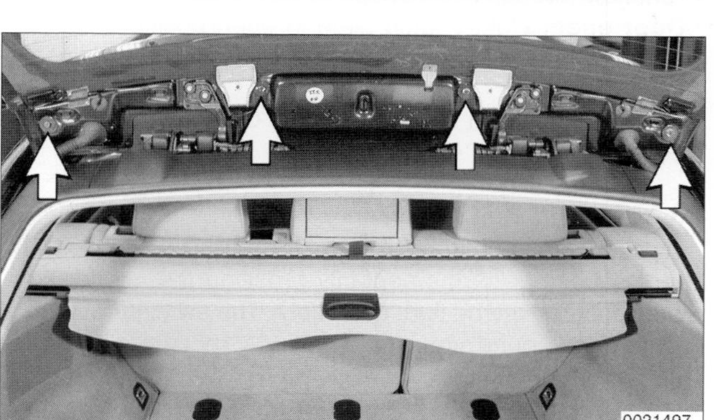

Sport Wagon: Open rear window.

- Carefully detach rear window hinge cover.
- Remove rear spoiler mounting bolts (**arrows**).
- Detach electrical harness connector and rear washer hose from spoiler.
- Remove mounting screws and remove third brake light assembly from spoiler.
- When installing, be sure electrical harness and rear window washer hose are not damaged or kinked.

NOTE —
Replace sealing plastic and grommets as necessary during reassembly.

Tightening torque

- Rear spoiler to rear glass . . . . 6 Nm (4 ft-lb)

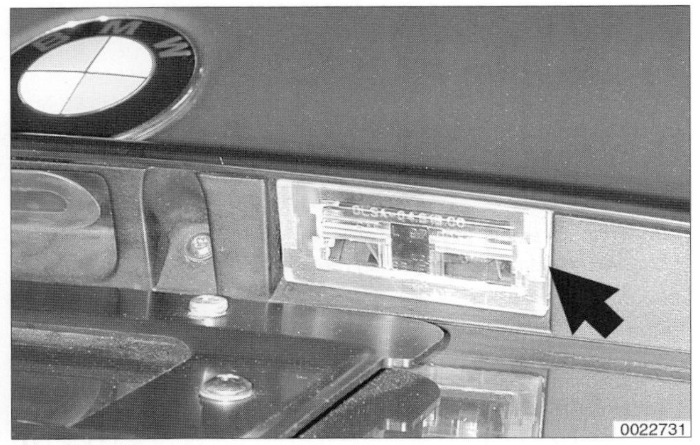

License plate light, removing and installing

Using a plastic prying tool or flat tipped screwdriver, pry gently on right side of license plate light assembly (**arrow**). Lift off lens.

> ***CAUTION —***
> *To avoid marring trim, wrap the screwdriver tip with tape.*

– Remove bulb.

NOTE —
Inspect bulb contact springs for damage and corrosion. Replace socket assembly if necessary.

License plate light application

• License plate bulb 12V 5W

– Installation is reverse of removal.

INTERIOR LIGHTS

The ZKE V General Module (GM V) controls the interior lighting automatically using input from several monitors. The lighting can also be manually controlled.

Each door lock actuator contains a Hall effect sensor for the purpose of monitoring door open / closed status. The sensor is located directly behind the rotary latch plate encased in the lock actuator and is activated by the rotary latch plate position.

- **Door closed:** Rotary latch plate in latched position. Current flow through Hall sensor <5 mA.
- **Door open:** Rotary latch plate in open position. Current flow through Hall sensor >12 mA.

A change in current flow informs the GM V when a door is opened or closed.

The overhead front seat interior / map light unit contains a single main interior light. The light is controlled by the GM V automatically or by momentarily pressing the interior light switch located on the light assembly. The switch provides a momentary ground signal that the GM V recognizes as a request to either turn the light ON or OFF.

If the switch is held for more than 3 seconds, the GM V interprets the continuous ground signal as a request to turn the interior light circuit OFF (workshop mode). Workshop mode is stored in memory: Even if the GM V is removed from the power supply and reconnected, the lights do not come back ON unless the switch is pressed again.

There are two reading / map lights in the front interior light assembly. Each is mechanically controlled by depressing the corresponding switch. The power supply for the map lights is supplied by the GM V.

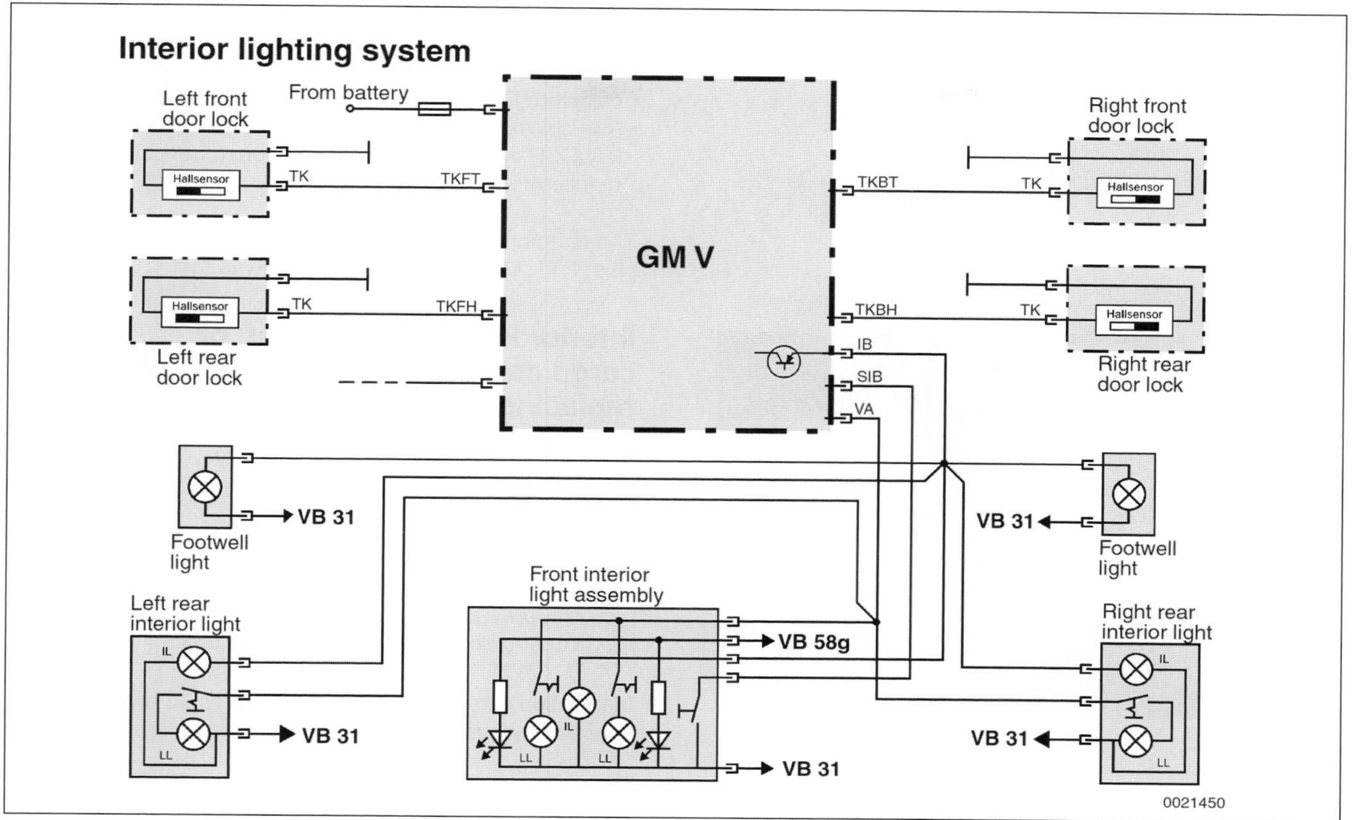

There is a courtesy light in each front footwell. These lights are only operated when the GM V provides power to the interior lighting circuit.

Interior light automatic controls

The GM V provides 12 volts to the interior lighting circuit when the status of one of the following input signals changes:

- Door contact Hall sensor active (door open)
- "Unlock" request received from driver door key lock Hall sensor (ignition switch OFF)
- "Unlock" request from FZV keyless entry system received via K-bus (ignition switch OFF)
- Vehicle exterior lights on for minimum of 2 minutes when ignition switch is OFF
- Crash signal from MRS control module
- Lock button of FZV key pressed with vehicle already locked (interior search function)
- Ignition switch is turned to "radio" position with driver door closed
- Vehicle is locked (single or double) with door contacts closed

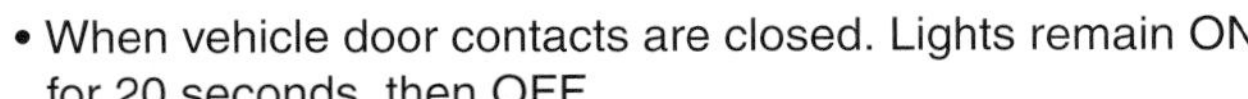

- When vehicle door contacts are closed. Lights remain ON for 20 seconds, then OFF
- After interior search function is activated, lights automatically turn OFF after 8 seconds
- After 16 minutes with door contact active (open door) and key OFF, lights are switched off (consumer cutoff or sleep function)

The component activation function of BMW scan tool (DISplus, GT1, MoDiC) also has the ability to switch the lights.

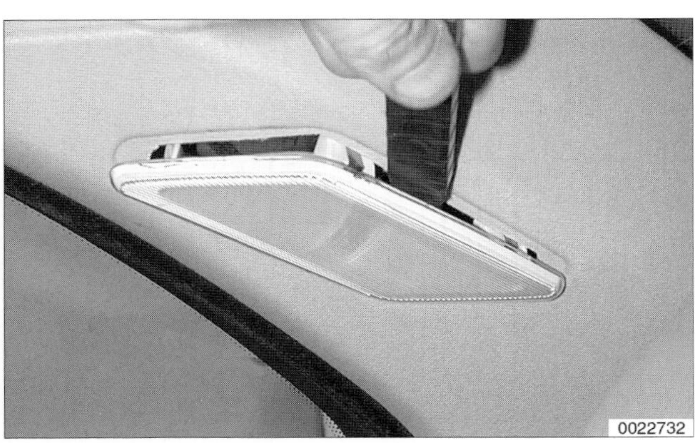

Interior light, footwell light, or cargo compartment light (Sport Wagon), replacing bulb

 Pry interior light fixture gently to remove.

- Detach electrical harness connector.
- Remove bulb and replace.

> ***CAUTION —***
> *Do not touch bulb with your bare hands. If necessary wipe bulb using a clean cloth dampened with rubbing alcohol.*

– Installation is reverse of removal. Bulb types and specifications for various interior lamps are listed below.

Interior light applications

- Footwell light bulb . . . . Softlite 5W
- Glove compartment light bulb . . . . Softlite 5W
- Passenger compartment bulb, front or rear . . Softlite 5W
- Reading bulb, front or rear 6W
- Tailgate courtesy light bulb . . . . Softlite 10W
- Visor vanity light bulb . . . . Softlite 10W

Trunk light bulb, replacing

The trunk light is integrated with the taillight assembly.

 Pry trunk light cover (**arrow**) gently to remove from taillight corner bulb carrier.

- Remove bulb and replace.
- Installation is reverse of removal.

Trunk light application

- Trunk light bulb . . . . Softlite, 10W

640 Heating and Air-conditioning

TABLES

Special tools

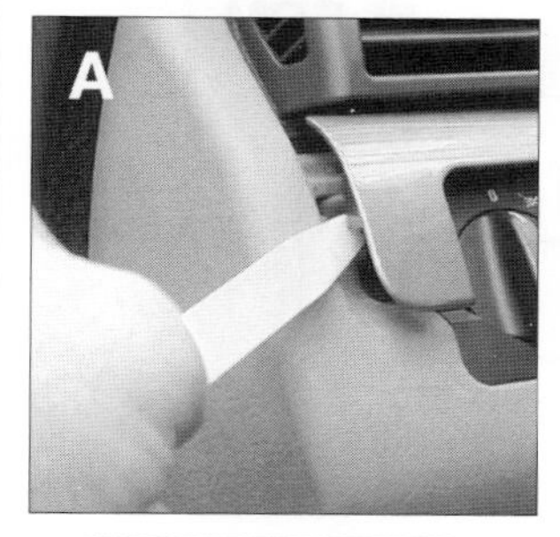

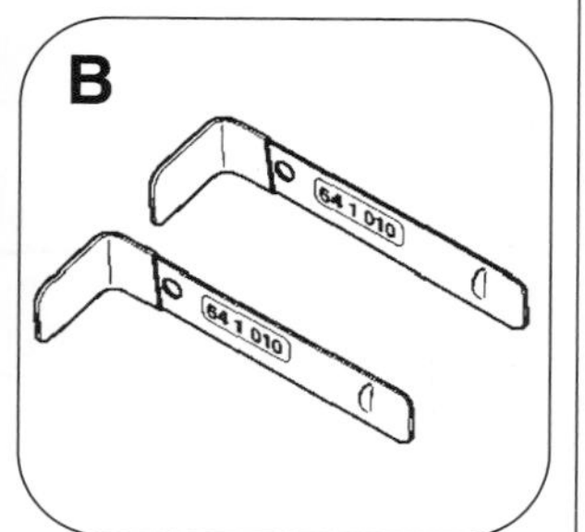

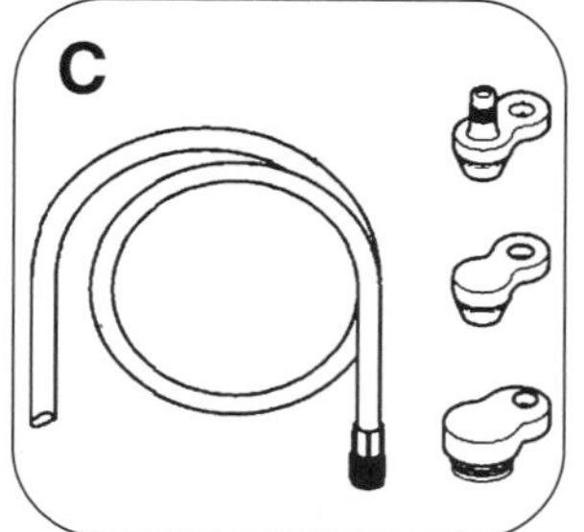

A BMW 00 9 321. . . . . Plastic tool for prying off interior trim
B BMW 64 1 010. . . . . .IHKA control panel removal tools
C BMW 64 5 100. . . . . A/C line plug kit

GENERAL

The repair information in this repair group applies to the heating and air-conditioning system. Many of the procedures require that the A/C refrigerant charge be evacuated. See **A/C system warnings and cautions** later in this repair group.

For information on the engine cooling system, see **170 Radiator and Cooling System**.

Special tools

Some special tools are necessary for heating and A/C repair procedures.

A variety of A/C system evacuation and recharge equipment is available. Follow the equipment manufacturer's recommendations and instructions.

NOTE —
A/C system recharging procedures are beyond the scope of this manual.

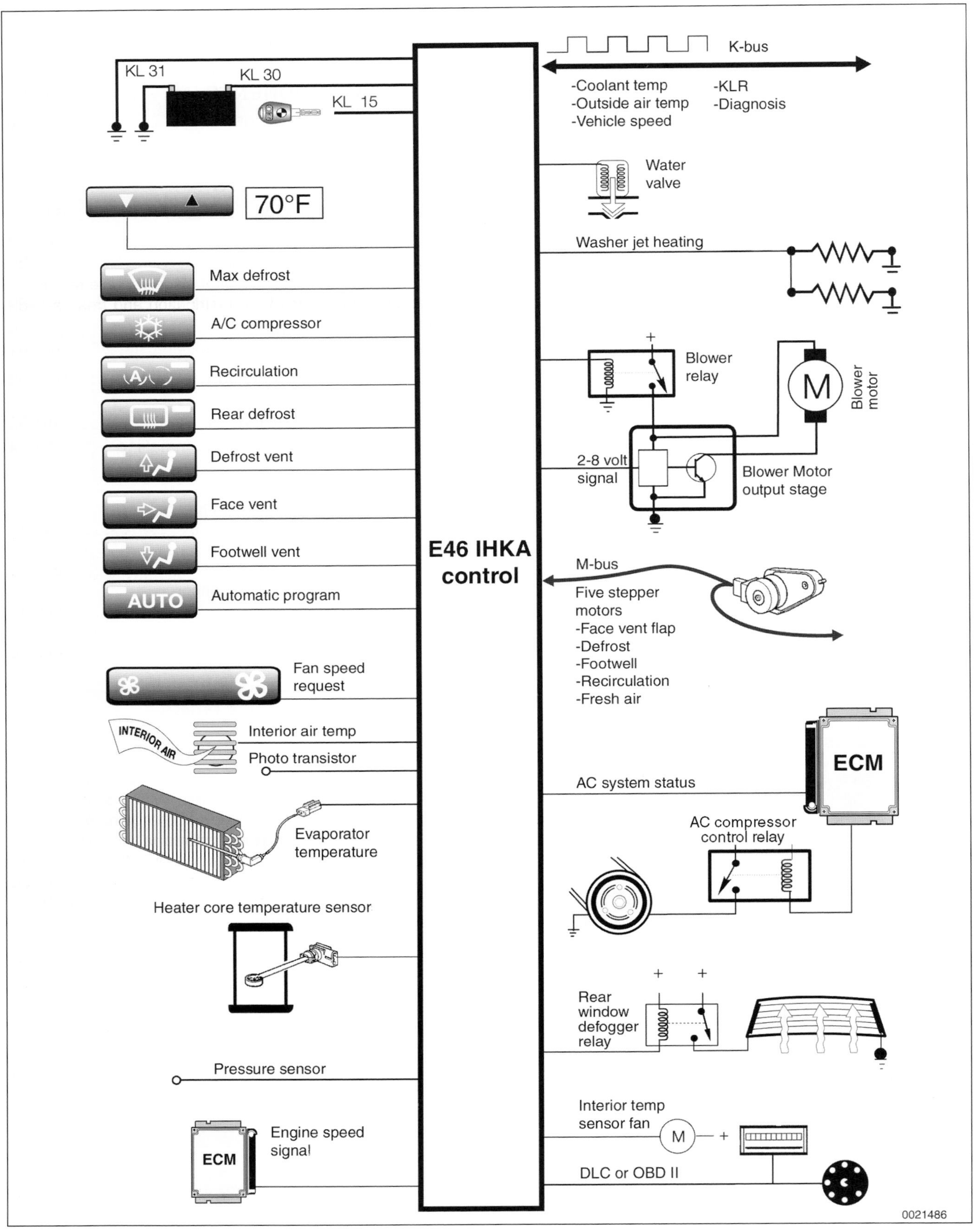
K-bus
KL 31
KL 30
KL 15
-Coolant temp
-Outside air temp
-Vehicle speed
-KLR
-Diagnosis
Water valve
70°F
Washer jet heating
Max defrost
A/C compressor
Recirculation
Rear defrost
Defrost vent
Face vent
Footwell vent
AUTO
Automatic program
Blower relay
Blower motor
M
2-8 volt signal
Blower Motor output stage
E46 IHKA control
M-bus
Five stepper motors
-Face vent flap
-Defrost
-Footwell
-Recirculation
-Fresh air
Fan speed request
INTERIOR AIR
Interior air temp
Photo transistor
ECM
AC system status
Evaporator temperature
AC compressor control relay
Heater core temperature sensor
Rear window defogger relay
Pressure sensor
Interior temp sensor fan
ECM
Engine speed signal
DLC or OBD II
0021486

Integrated heating and cooling system (IHKA)

The E46 integrated automatic climate control system (IHKA) offers powerful cooling and heating, effective ventilation, and smooth operation in A/C mode.

The E46 IHKA design includes the following:

- Single heater core for temperature regulation
- Maximum heating and cooling for defroster functions
- Rear window defogger operation integrated into the heating / cooling system
- Blower controlled through a final stage variable resistor
- Road speed dependent air distribution and fresh air volume
- Self-calibrating air distribution stepper motors controlled via M-bus
- Fresh air microfilter system
- Electronically regulated A/C compressor
- Heater control personalization via Car Memory / Key Memory

Control panel and module

Heating and air conditioning functions are programmed via the center console mounted control panel. The control panel has large, easy to use soft-touch controls and an LED display.

IHKA control panel

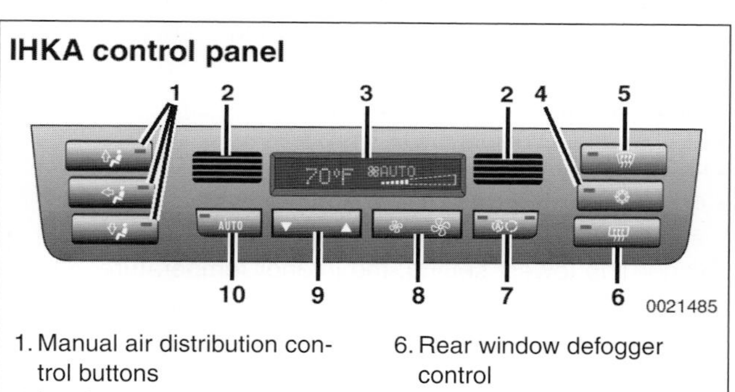

1. Manual air distribution control buttons
2. Interior temperature sensor fan intake / outlet
3. LCD matrix
4. A/C control ("snowflake")
5. Windshield defrost control
6. Rear window defogger control
7. Recirculation control
8. Blower control
9. Temperature control
10. Automatic air distribution

The IHKA control module, integral with the front panel, includes an EEPROM chip for storage of diagnostic trouble codes (DTCs). Inputs to the module include:

- Heater core temperature sensor
- A/C evaporator temperature sensor
- Other programmed functions from Car Memory (such as rear window defrost timing).

Starting with 2002 models, the IHKA control panel was slightly redesigned:

- Interior temperature sensor was no longer fitted with a fan.
- Blower and temperature rocker switches were replaced with individual push buttons.

The module can go into "sleep mode" to reduce power consumption when the ignition is switched OFF but still retain control panel settings and DTC information. If the control module is replaced, program and recode new unit using BMW scan tool (DISplus, GT1, MoDiC) or equivalent.

Heat regulation

The E46 uses a single water valve and heater core to provide passenger compartment heat. The water valve is electrically pulsed to control the flow of coolant through the heater core.

Temperature regulation is based on the following inputs:

- Temperature control switch setting
- Interior temperature sensor signal
- Ambient temperature signal
- Heater core temperature sensor signal
- Evaporator temperature signal
- Solar sensor input (if applicable)

A rocker switch is used to select the desired cabin temperature, shown in the display matrix of the control panel. The range for temperature display is from 15° to 32°C (60° to 90°F).

Blower control

The blower rocker switch on the IHKA control panel is the master switch for the entire system. Selecting slower fan speeds eventually results in the following:

- Blower motor OFF
- All air distribution valves closed
- LED and LCD displays OFF
- Rear window defroster OFF
- A/C compressor OFF

Even in the lowest setting, the interior temperature sensor continues to operate and the IHKA control panel continues to signal the heater valve for heat.

Regulated A/C compressor

The operation of the A/C compressor is modulated, eliminating noticeable on / off cycling. In order to reduce fuel consumption and improve vehicle performance, the system default is with the compressor OFF.

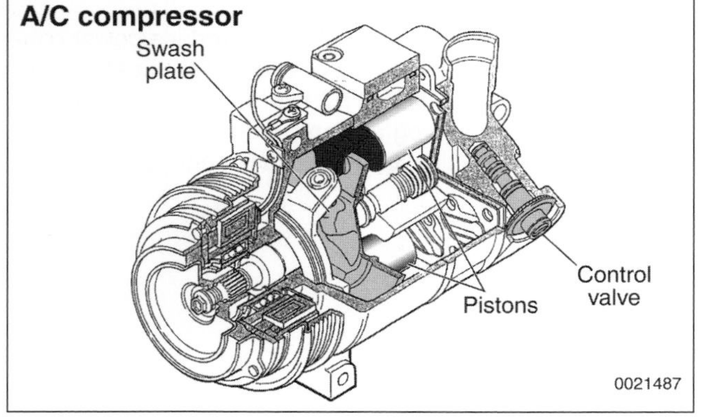

The A/C system uses a variable displacement compressor. The swash plate of the compressor is hinged so that is can vary piston travel based on output requirements of the system.

A/C compressor function is controlled by the Engine Control Module (ECM) based on inputs from the IHKA control panel. Pressing the “snowflake” button requests A/C activation. As long as the evaporator temperature is above 2°C (36°F), the IHKA signals the ECM to activate the compressor.

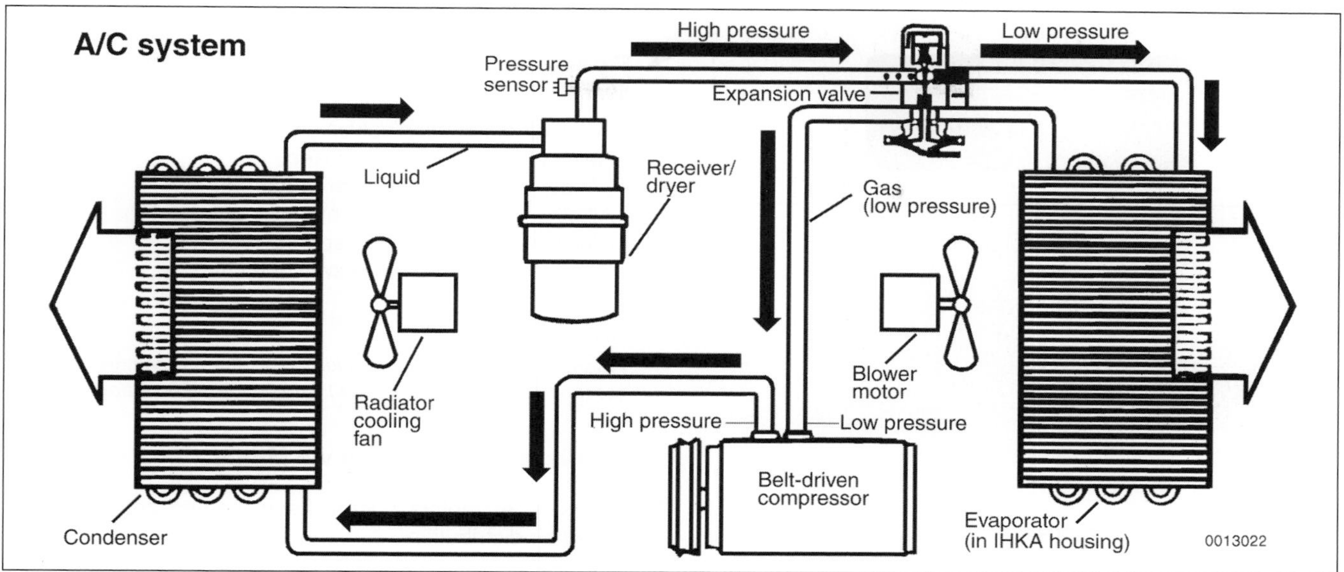

The IHKA control module sends the following signals to the ECM over the K-bus and CAN-bus via the instrument cluster:

- Request for A/C activation
- Load torque for switching the compressor
- Requested cooling fan speed

The IHKA determines the load torque for compressor activation and required engine cooling fan speed from the pressure sensor mounted on the receiver-dryer. The pressure sensor provides a linear voltage input signal (0 - 5 volts) to the IHKA control module. The module processes this signal and determines the load torque of the system (0 - 30 Nm). The higher the pressure in the system, the higher the voltage input signal to the IHKA module. The output signal to the ECM enables the ECM to modify the idle speed, timing and fuel injection amount based on the load that is imposed when the compressor is activated.

Regulated engine cooling fan operation

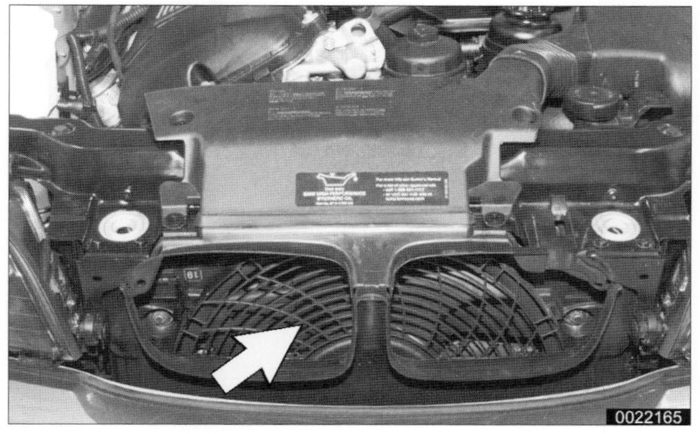

The electric engine cooling fan (**arrow**) operates at variable speeds (15 stages) based on cooling system load. The ECM activates the fan through a pulse modulated final stage control. See **170 Radiator and Cooling System** for further details.

NOTE —

- *Automatic transmission models: The engine cooling fan is located in front of the radiator. A belt-driven fan and fan clutch assembly are installed at the rear of the radiator.*
- *Standard transmission models: The electric engine cooling fan is installed at the rear of the radiator.*

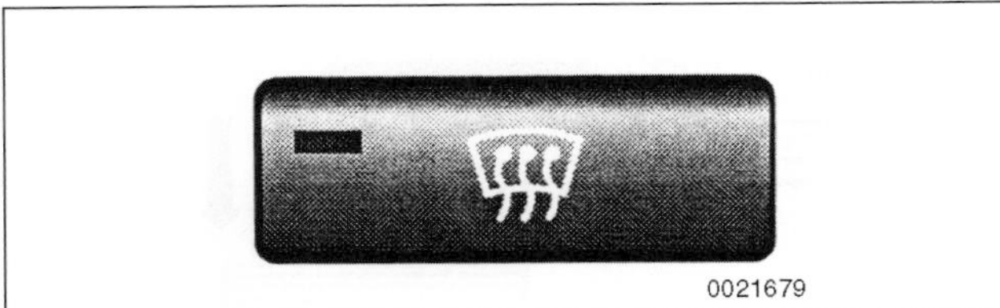
0021679

Maximum defrosting

Pressing the defrost button turns on maximum defrost functions:

- Fresh air distribution valves are opened.
- Recirculation valves are closed.
- Windshield defrost vents are opened.
- All other air distribution vents are closed.
- Blower runs at maximum speed.
- Rear window defroster is switched ON.

NOTE —
When windshield defrosting is turned on, the A/C compressor does not run automatically, although it can be turned on manually.

Air distribution control via M-bus

Five stepper motors control fresh, heated and air conditioned air distribution.

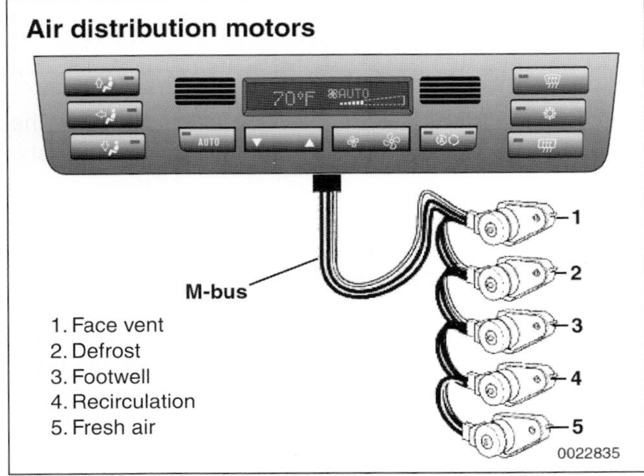

0022835

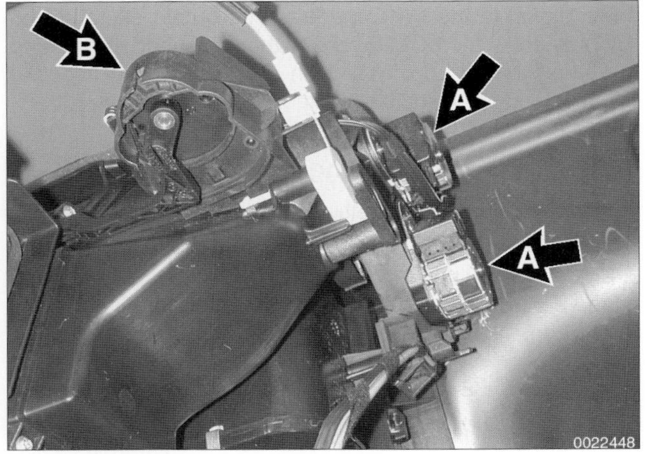

0022448

Two different types of air distribution motors are used in the system. Fast acting motors (**A**) are used for the fresh air / recirculation flaps. (Right side shown.)

– Slower acting motors (**B**) are used for the other operations.

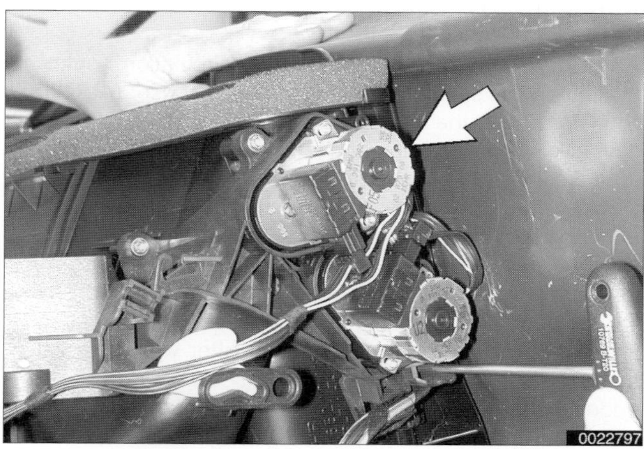

The center dashboard air outlet distribution motor (**arrow**) allows ventilation air temperature to be controlled by the driver or passenger.

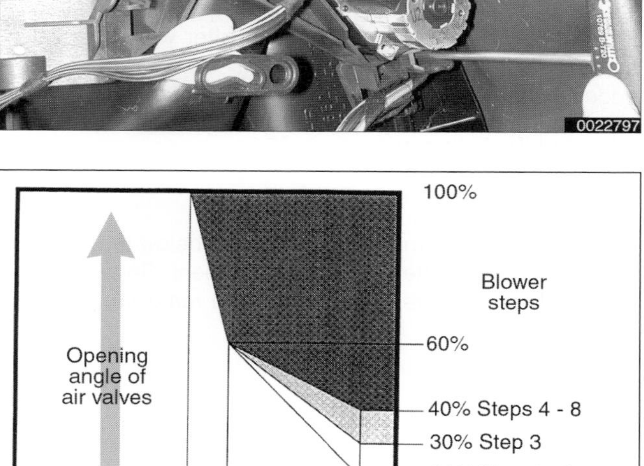

When fresh air is selected, the fresh air inlet distribution flaps are positioned according to road speed and blower motor speed. The motors close the air inlet flaps incrementally according to road speed but the motion is dampened to avoid closing and opening continually due to slight speed changes.

IHKA personalization

Car Memory / Key Memory allows various functions and features of IHKA control to be tailored to the driver's wishes. IHKA functions that can be programmed using BMW scan tool (DISplus, GT1, MoDiC) or equivalent include:

- Automatic activation of recirculation when vehicle is started
- Blower speed adjustment (8-speed blower)
- Automatic opening of ventilation flaps with warm coolant
- Automatic closing of footwell flaps with A/C activation
- Automatic closing of defroster flaps with A/C activation
- Adjustments to set temperature
- Automatic activation of compressor control when ignition is switched ON
- Auto program for blower control when ignition is switched ON

NOTE —

See **515 Central Locking and Anti-theft** *for an explanation of Car Memory / Key Memory.*

0021289a

Automatic air recirculation

As of model year 2000, automatic recirculation control is available. This system uses an air quality sensor (AUC) (**arrow**), located at the top right corner of the radiator, to detect high levels of air pollution and automatically switch the IHKA to recirculation of interior air. The recirculation button on the IHKA control panel can be toggled to allow automatic, manual or no recirculation.

Once recirculation is turned on, it runs until it is turned off using the button. Once the ignition is turned off, the recirculation setting is saved for 15 minutes, after which the IHKA system reverts to fresh air mode. This feature can be overridden using the Car Memory feature, so that recirculating interior air is automatically selected on engine start-up.

0021792

Ventilation microfilter system

The E46 ventilation microfilter is housed below the fresh air inlet at the rear of the engine compartment. Service by releasing three-quick release screws and removing a plastic cover.

Service

The heating system is part of the engine cooling system and is sealed. The only required service is periodic coolant flushing. **See 170 Radiator and Cooling System**.

Servicing the A/C system requires the use of specialized equipment. Follow the equipment manufacturer's instructions.

Rear window defogger

0021680

The electric rear window defogger switch is integrated in the IHKA control panel. Pressing the rear window defogger button activates the rear window heating element for about 17 minutes, although this can be changed through Car Memory. Pressing the button again activates a cycle of 40 seconds on / 80 seconds off for 5 minutes.

The defogger element in the rear glass is integrated with the radio antenna.

The rear window defogger relay (**arrow**) is on the right side of the trunk or cargo compartment (Sport Wagon) behind the trim.

Convertible heated rear window

In the E46 Convertible, both the soft top and the hard top are equipped with rear window defogger. Power is supplied by two relays located on the right side rear quarter panel behind the interior trim cover.

Rear defogger operation is controlled by the IHKA control module.

On hardtop:

- Rear relay is energized.
- Power to hard top window is supplied through connector strip on hard top lock.

On convertible top:

- Rear relay is energized. It powers front relay.
- If convertible top control module (CVM) signals that convertible top is locked to windshield frame, front relay powers rear window heater grid.
- If convertible top is lowered, a signal from CVM to front relay prevents heated top operation.
- Front relay also signals sound system to switch stereo sound ON when top is up, stereo sound OFF when top is down.

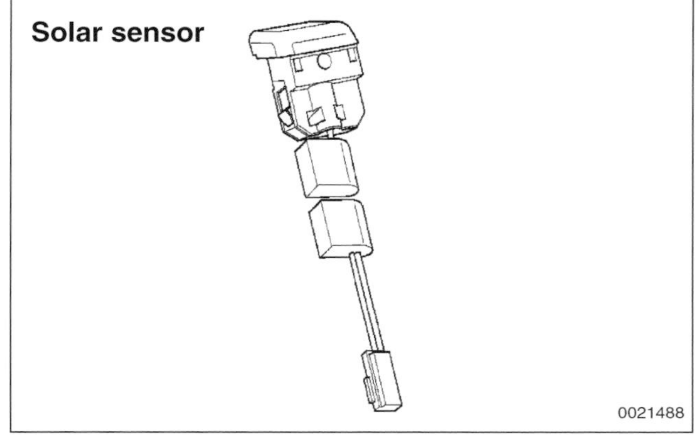

Solar sensor

The solar sensor relays data about the amount and intensity of solar heating to the IHKA control module. Climate control settings are changed to compensate for this additional influence.

The solar sensor consists of a photoresistor installed in the right defroster outlet and a short harness.

The solar sensor receives power (5 volts) and ground from the IHKA control module. Voltage drop across the photoresistor increases as solar radiation increases. The control module calculates voltage drop across the photoresistor and determines the degree of solar heating based on the change in voltage. In response to the solar sensor signal, the IHKA module regulates interior climate settings using the following:

- **Blower.** The blower activation curve is changed.
- **Ventilation.** The opening angles of air distribution flaps are changed.

The control module processes the photoresistor input every 10 seconds and also checks it for plausibility based on mapped values. Values outside the limit indicate a malfunction and the solar sensor signal is ignored by the module. Troubleshoot solar sensor using BMW scan tool (DISplus, GT1, MoDiC) or equivalent.

To access the solar sensor, remove the trim in front of the main dashboard panel, ahead of the dashboard vents.

Troubleshooting

Trouble with the heating and A/C system can be broken down into one or more of the following categories.

Mechanical problems

- Control panel malfunction
- Blower motor malfunction
- Noisy or seized compressor
- Noisy compressor clutch
- Malfunctioning belt

Diagnosis of noisy engine compartment components is covered in **100 Engine–General**. A/C belt replacement is covered in **020 Maintenance**.

Cooling system problems

- Coolant problems
- Cooling fan problems

Cooling system pressure testing and other diagnosis is covered in **170 Radiator and Cooling System**.

Refrigerant leak

Use diagnostic equipment to pinpoint refrigerant leaks. Replace leaky components or seals.

NOTE —
Diagnosis of A/C system components is beyond the scope of this manual. Follow the equipment manufacturer's instructions.

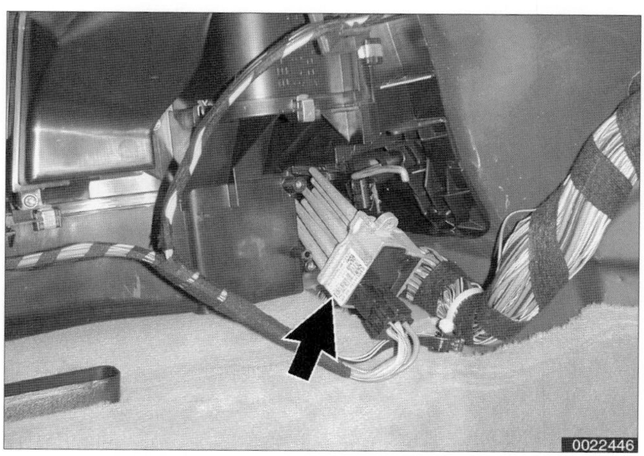

Odors

Mildew in the IHKA housing and in the evaporator fins can cause strong odors.

< Working under right side of dash, remove blower resistor pack (**arrow**). See **Blower resistor pack, replacing** in this repair group.

– Poke a spray wand through IHKA housing opening and spray commercially available cleaning agent on evaporator. Move wand back and forth to cover evaporator fins with liquid.

– Allow 5 minutes for liquid to drip through evaporator drain.

– Start car and run heater and A/C at maximum power for 5 minutes to dry out evaporator.

IHKA function problems

IHKA inputs and outputs are self-diagnosed. If a fault is detected, a diagnostic trouble code (DTC) is initially entered in IHKA control module RAM and then in EEPROM when the ignition is switched OFF, up to a maximum of six DTCs. The IHKA module is connected to the diagnostic link connector (DLC or OBD II) via the K-bus and instrument cluster. Access DTCs using BMW scan tool (DISplus, GT1, MoDiC) or equivalent.

CAUTION —
When troubleshooting problems with the E46 IHKA, be sure to review Car Memory / Key Memory settings prior to condemning a component as faulty.

Substitute value operation

If an input potentiometer, sensor or circuit fails or the signal from it is *not plausible*, the IHKA control module ignores the faulty signal and substitutes a programmed substitute value. See **Table a**.

Table a. Substitute programmed values for IHKA component inputs

Input	Working range	Substitute value
Heat exchanger sensor	5° to 124°C (41° to 255°F)	55°C (131°F)
Evaporator sensor	-10° to 30°C (14° to 86°F)	0°C (32°F)
Interior temperature sensor	10° to 40°C (50° to 104°F)	20°C (68°F)
Exterior temperature		0°C (32°F)
Coolant temperature		100°C (212°F)
Specified temperature	16° to 32°C (61° to 90°F)	22°C (72°F)

NOTE —
The substitute value for the evaporator temperature sensor is below the A/C compressor cycling temperature (2°C / 34°F). If the evaporator temperature sensor signal is not plausible, *the substitute value switches the A/C OFF.*

Table b lists resistance values and fault limits for IHKA temperature sensors.

Table b. Temperature sensor resistance values at 25°C (77°F)

Sensor	Resistance	Fault limit
Heater core	9 kΩ ± 2%	Temp > 125°C (257°F)
Evaporator	9 kΩ ± 2%	Temp > 120°C (248°F)
Interior	10 kΩ ± 2%	Temp ≤-46°C (-51°F)

Table c lists A/C evaporator temperature-dependent resistance values.

Table c. A/C evaporator temperature sensor resistance values

Temperature °C (°F)	Resistance range kΩ
-5 (23)	11.7 - 11.9
0 (32)	8.8 - 9.2
5 (41)	6.8 - 7.2
10 (50)	5.3 - 5.6
15 (59)	4.2 - 4.5
20 (68)	3.3 - 3.6
25 (77)	2.6 - 2.9
30 (86)	2.1 - 2.3
35 (95)	1.7 - 1.9

Table d lists A/C expansion valve pressure values.

Table d. Expansion valve pressure values

Inlet pressure	14 bar (203 psi)
Outlet pressure	1.8 bar (26 psi)
Leak test with detector pressure	1 - 2 bar (14.5 - 29 psi)

A/C system warnings and cautions

WARNING —

- *Wear hand and eye protection (gloves and goggles) when working around the A/C system. If refrigerant does come in contact with your skin or eyes:*
  -Do not rub skin or eyes.
  -Immediately flush skin or eyes with cool water for 15 minutes.
  -Rush to a doctor or hospital.
  -Do not attempt to treat yourself.
- *Work in a well ventilated area. Switch on exhaust ventilation system when working on the refrigerant system.*
- *Do not expose any component of the A/C system to high temperatures (above 80°C / 176°F) or open flames. Excessive heat causes a pressure increase which could burst the system.*
- *Keep refrigerant away from open flames. Poisonous gas is produced if it burns. Do not smoke near refrigerant gases for the same reason.*
- *The A/C system is filled with refrigerant gas which is under pressure. Pressurized refrigerant in the presence of oxygen may form a combustible mixture. Do not introduce compressed air into any refrigerant container (full or empty).*
- *Electric welding near refrigerant hoses causes R-134a to decompose. Discharge system before welding.*

CAUTION —

- *Any person who services a motor vehicle air-conditioner must, by law, be properly trained and certified, and use approved refrigerant recycling equipment. Technicians must complete an EPA-approved recycling course to be certified.*
- *It is recommended that all A/C service be left to an authorized BMW dealer or other qualified A/C service facility.*
- *State and local governments may have additional requirements regarding air conditioning servicing. Always comply with state and local laws.*
- *Do not top off a partially charged refrigerant system. Discharge system, evacuate and then recharge system.*
- *Do not use R-12 refrigerant, refrigerant oils or system components in R-134a system. Component damage and system contamination results.*
- *The mixture of refrigerant oil (PAG oil) and refrigerant R-134a attacks some metals and alloys (for example, copper) and breaks down certain hose materials. Use only hoses and lines that are identified with a green mark (stripe) or the lettering "R-134a".*
- *Immediately plug open connections on A/C components and lines to prevent dirt and moisture contamination.*
- *Do not steam clean A/C condensers or evaporators. Use only cold water or compressed air.*

VENTS AND DUCTS

The IHKA air distribution system includes 5 air distribution motors (stepper motors), right and left footwell ducts, dashboard mounted defroster vents, and three sets of face level vents.

Removal of at least one of the stepper motors (right footwell vent) involves removal of the passenger side airbag in the dashboard.

> ***WARNING —***
> *Airbags are inflated by an explosive device. Handled improperly or without adequate safeguards, the system can be very dangerous. Special precautions must be observed prior to any work at or near the airbags. See* **721 Airbag System (SRS)**.

> ***CAUTION —***
> *When working on interior trim removal, work with plastic prying tools or wrap the tips of screwdrivers and pliers with tape.*

Air distribution motors

The five air distribution motors are installed under the dashboard. They are made accessible by removing either the glove compartment and right footwell trim panel or the left footwell (pedal cluster) trim panel as described below.

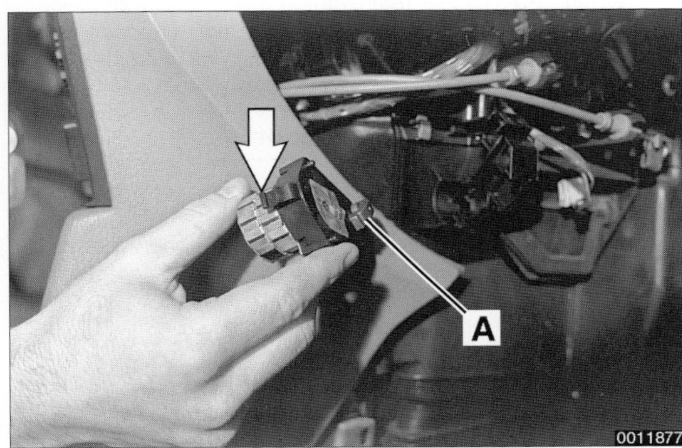

Each motor can be removed after its electrical wiring harness connector has been removed.

- Squeeze plastic clip (**arrow**) to release motor.
- Tilt motor out of housing.

– During installation, be sure to align air distribution flap and motor drive (**A**).

Right side air distribution motors, accessing

Four of the air distribution motors are under the right side of the dashboard:

- Right side fresh air / recirculation
- Defroster
- Ventilation flaps
- Right footwell vent

– Disconnect negative (–) battery cable.

> ***CAUTION —***
> *Prior to disconnecting the battery, read the battery disconnection cautions given at the front of this manual.*

– Remove glove compartment and right footwell trim panel for access. See **513 Interior Trim**.

> **CAUTION —**
> *Disassemble interior trim carefully to avoid damage.*

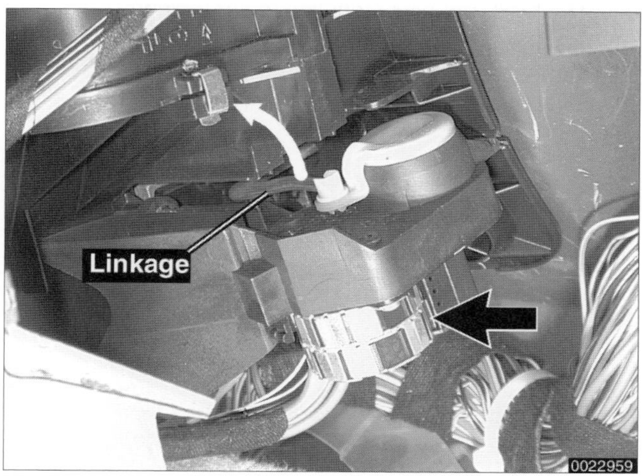

◀ Right side fresh air / recirculation motor (**arrow**):

- For access, remove right footwell duct as described below.
- Unhook linkage, then remove motor.

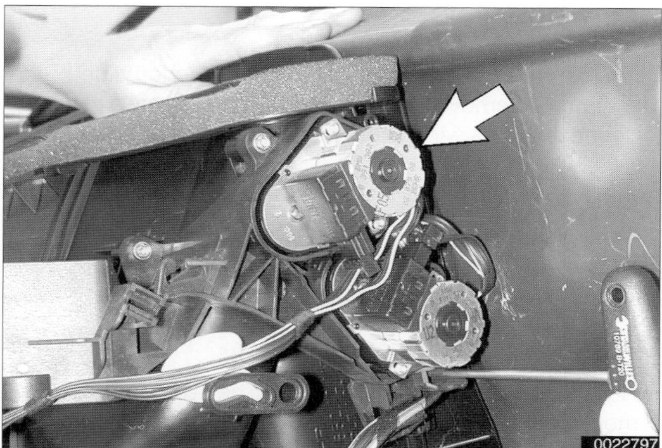

◀ Defroster air distribution motor (**arrow**)

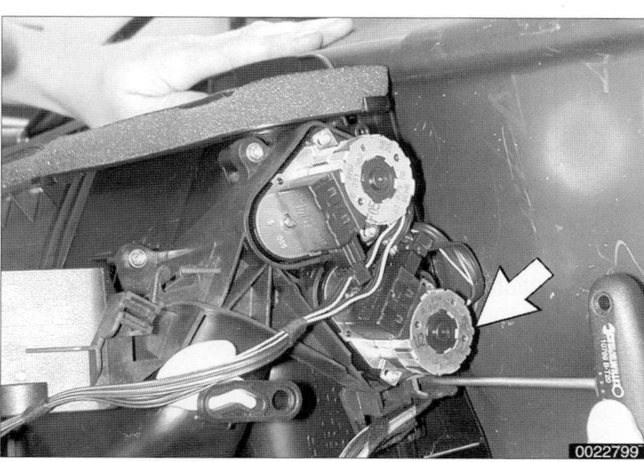

◀ Ventilation distribution motor (**arrow**)

- For access, remove defroster air distribution motor.

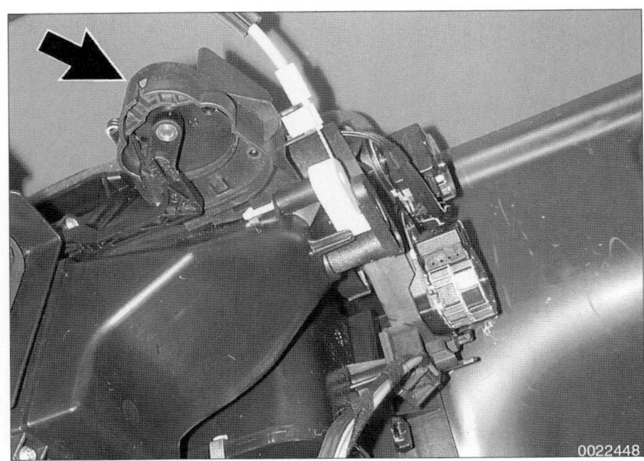

Right footwell vent air distribution motor (**arrow**):

- For access, remove passenger side airbag. See **721 Airbag System (SRS)**.
- Unhook linkage, then remove motor.

Left side air distribution motor, accessing

The fresh air distribution motor is under the left side of the dashboard. Remove the left footwell (pedal cluster) trim panel for access.

> ***CAUTION—***
> *Disassemble interior trim carefully to avoid damage.*

– Move steering column to maximum extended position.

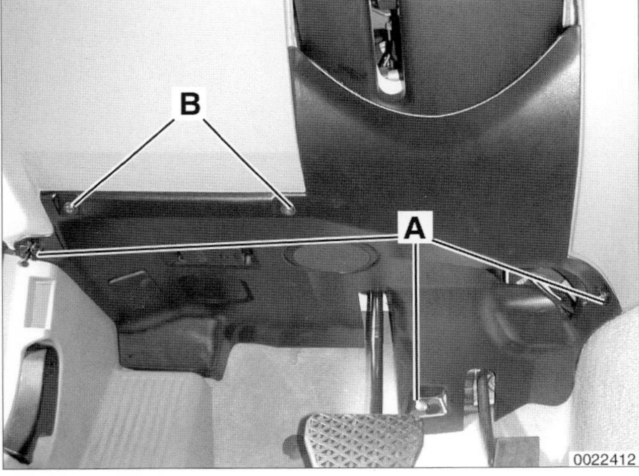

Working at trim panel, remove fasteners.

- Note locking clips (**A**) which must be rotated 90° to remove.
- Remove mounting screws (**B**).
- Unhook retaining clip from steering column lower trim.
- Detach electrical harness connectors from footwell light and speaker (if equipped).
- Release OBD II socket from panel and pull out.

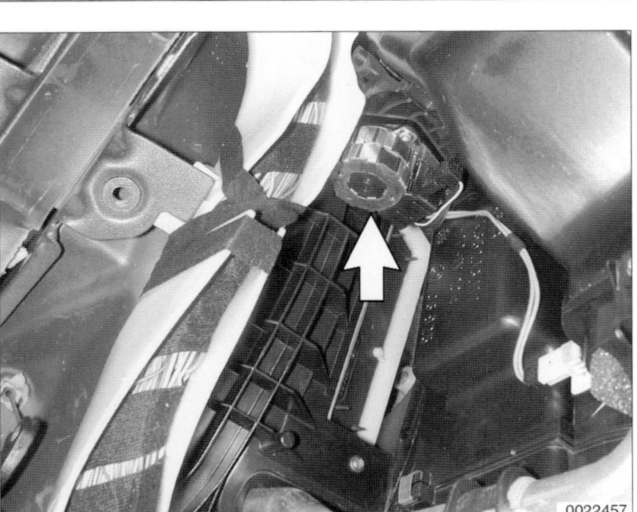

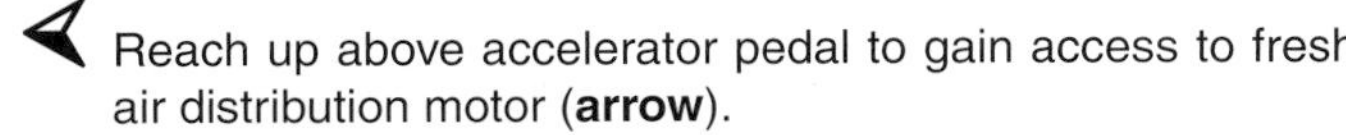
Reach up above accelerator pedal to gain access to fresh air distribution motor (**arrow**).

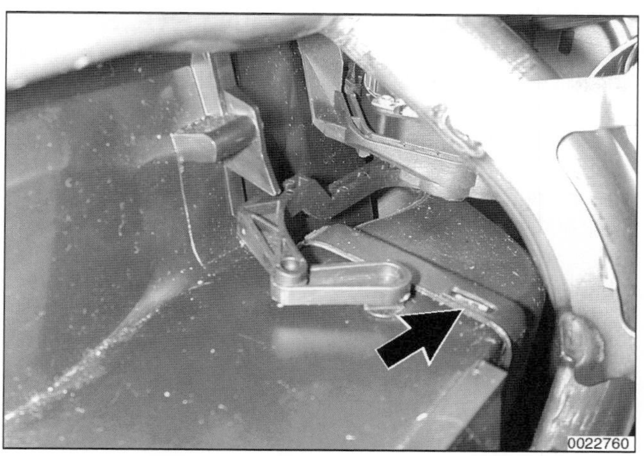
0022760

Right footwell duct, removing and installing

- Remove glove compartment. See **513 Interior Trim**.
- Remove IHKA control panel or GPS On-Board Monitor. See **IHKA control panel, removing and installing** or **On-Board (GPS) Monitor, removing and installing** in this repair group.
- ◄ Reach through control panel opening to detach air duct locking clip (**arrow**) from heater / evaporator housing.
- Separate bottom of air duct from rear compartment duct.
- Pull forward and down to remove.
- Installation is reverse of removal.

Dashboard vent, removing and installing

0021440

◄ Pry gently at dashboard trim to remove.

> ***CAUTION —***
> *To avoid marring interior trim, work with a plastic prying tool.*

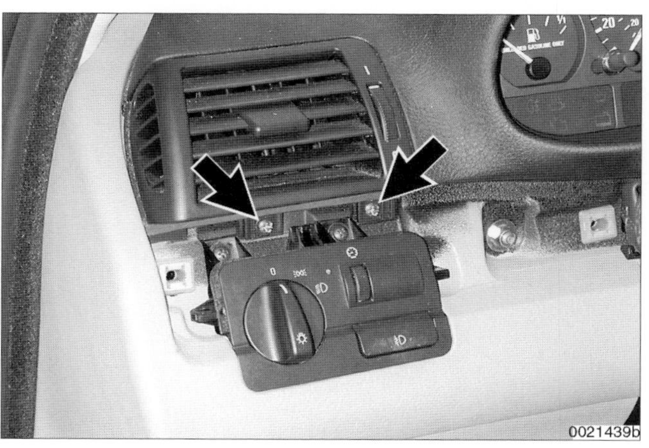
0021439b

- ◄ Remove air vent mounting screws (**arrows**).
- Lift vent slightly and withdraw from dashboard.
- Installation is reverse of removal.
- Removal of right or center dashboard vent is similar.
- To fully remove the center dashboard vent, use pliers to detach control cable housing and remove from control lever.
- Remove trim on right side prior to removing center trim.

HEATING AND A/C CONTROLS

The IHKA control module is integrated with the control panel in the center console below the radio. There is a built-in interior temperature sensor and fan.

The interior temperature sensor fan was discontinued on 2002 and later models.

Models with GPS navigation are equipped with a center console-mounted On-Board Monitor. This combines sound system control, GPS and heating / A/C control functions.

IHKA control panel, removing and installing

If BMW special tools 64 1 010 are available, slide them between IHKA control panel front bezel and dashboard, then pull panel out. Otherwise, use the following procedure.

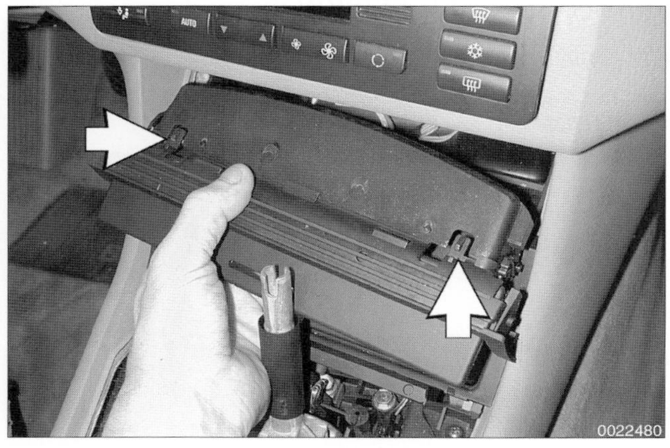

◀ Remove utility compartment below IHKA control panel:

- Open compartment door.
- Push upward in center of compartment to release locking tabs (**arrows**).
- Pull out compartment.

– Shifter bezel: Lift up by prying gently.

– Shifter boot: Unclip bottom of boot from shifter trim (window switch carrier) by pushing forward. Pull boot up around shifter, but do not remove.

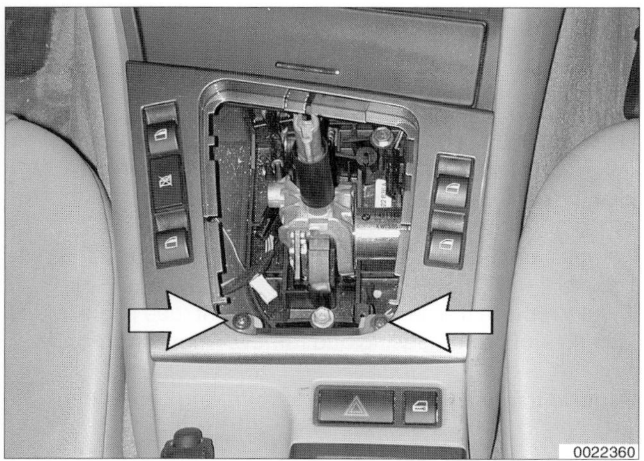

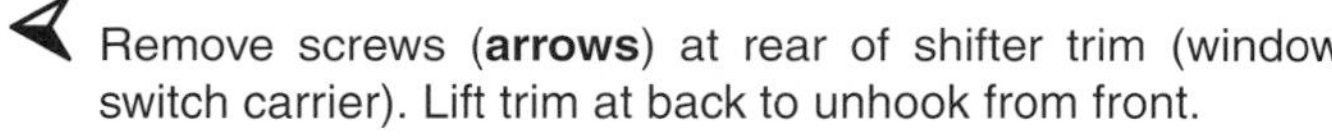

◀ Remove screws (**arrows**) at rear of shifter trim (window switch carrier). Lift trim at back to unhook from front.

◄ Remove screws (**arrows**) at front and rear of ashtray carrier. Lift up ashtray carrier.

- Reach up through opening and push IHKA control module and panel out.
- Detach electrical harness connectors.
- Disassemble panel from module using an anti-static mat as a working surface.

> ***CAUTION —***
> *Do not touch circuit boards with bare fingers.*

- Installation is reverse of removal.
- Recode and program new IHKA control module using BMW scan tool (DISplus, GT1 or MoDiC) or equivalent.

On-Board (GPS) Monitor, removing and installing

- Remove dashboard center vent. See **Dashboard vent, removing and installing** in this repair group.
- Pull off menu button on face of monitor. Reach through apertures with screwdriver to twist catches. This releases monitor from console.
- Pull out monitor and detach electrical harness connectors in back.
- Installation is reverse of removal.
- Recode and program new On-Board Monitor using BMW scan tool (DISplus, GT1 or MoDiC) or equivalent.

Heater core temperature sensor, removing and installing

- Remove IHKA control panel or On-Board Monitor. See **IHKA control panel, removing and installing** or **On-Board (GPS) Monitor, removing and installing** in this repair group.

◄ Reach through dashboard opening and detach heater core temperature sensor electrical harness connector (**arrow**).

- Pull sensor out of IHKA housing.
- Installation is reverse of removal.

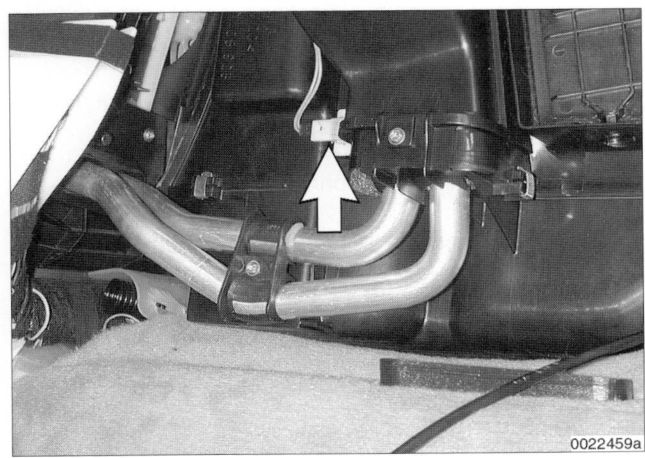
0022459a

Evaporator temperature sensor

To gain access to evaporator temperature sensor (**arrow**):

- Remove left footwell trim panel (above pedals). See **513 Interior Trim**.
- Sensor is installed in left side of IHKA housing above coolant pipes.

BLOWER COMPONENTS

Blower, removing and installing

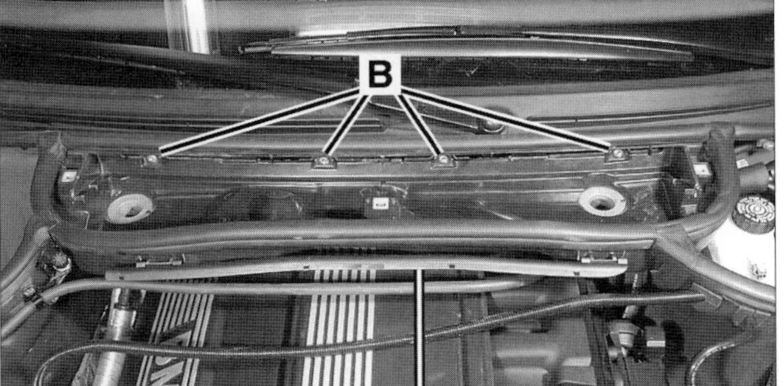

0021314

Remove housing for interior ventilation microfilter.

- Remove upper cover and microfilter.
- Open wiring harness loom (**A**) and remove wires.
- Unfasten screws (**B**) and remove lower housing.

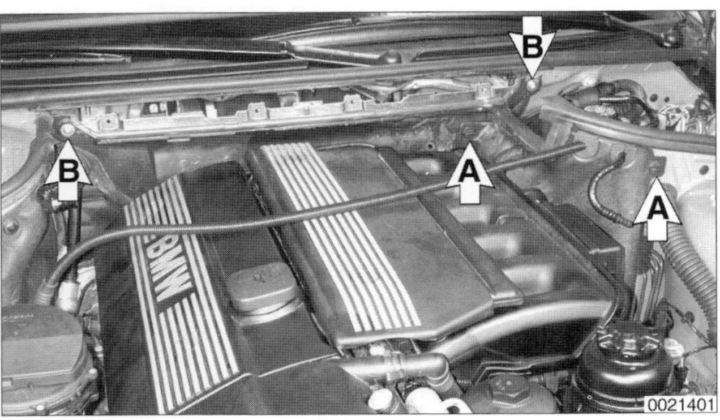

0021401

Remove heater bulkhead cover:

- Remove engine compartment side trim panel. Turn locking clips (**A**) and slide trim panel up.
- Remove heater bulkhead cover mounting screws (**B**) and lift cover off bulkhead.

◄ Remove intake manifold cover:

- Remove plastic trim covers (**arrows**).
- Remove cover hold down bolts and lift off cover.

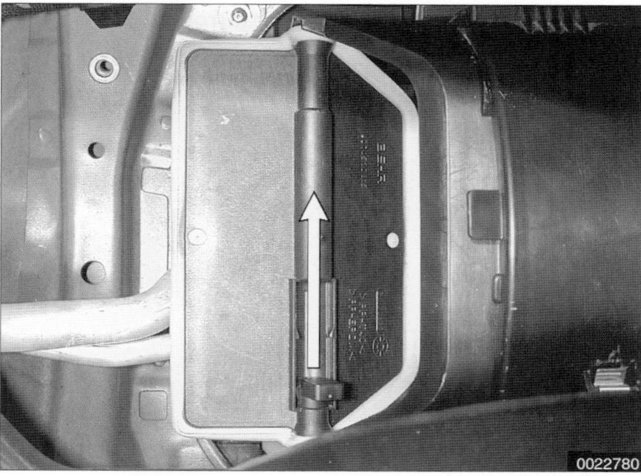

◄ Working inside right side of cowl, pull up on lever (**arrow**) and detach right air intake flap from blower housing.

◄ Pry off blower cover retaining clips (**A**). Remove screw (**B**) and lift off outer blower housing cover.

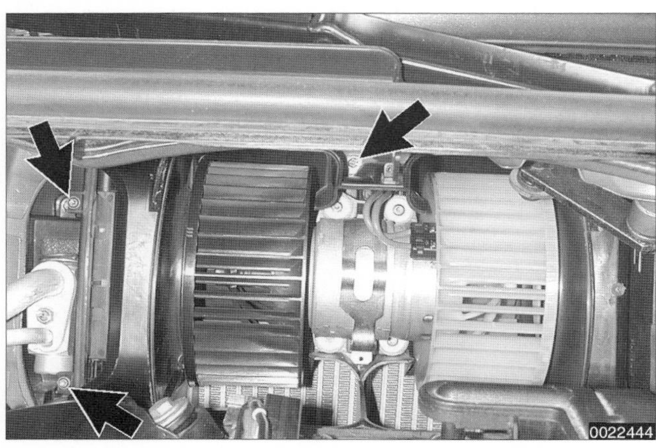

◀ Remove blower cover retaining screws (**arrows**). Lift off cover.

◀ Detach electrical harness connector (**arrow**).

◀ Pry off blower motor retaining strap.

– Pull blower motor forward to remove.

– Installation is reverse of removal:

- Align slot in blower motor with mounting tab in blower motor housing.

Blower resistor pack, replacing

NOTE —

The blower motor resistor pack is also referred to as the final stage unit.

– Remove right footwell air duct. See **Right footwell duct, removing and installing** in this repair group.

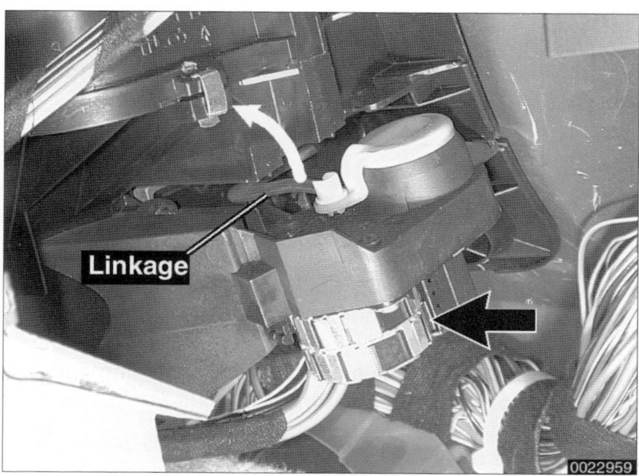

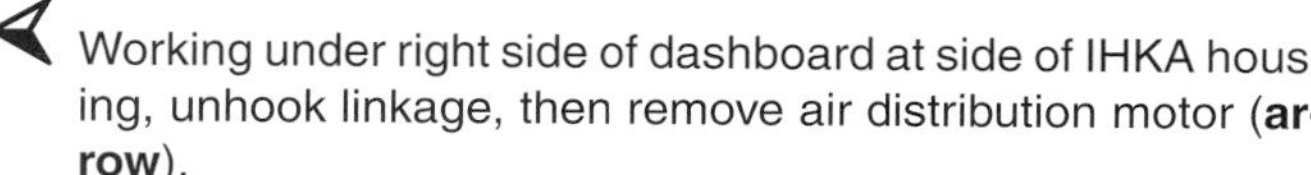

Working under right side of dashboard at side of IHKA housing, unhook linkage, then remove air distribution motor (**arrow**).

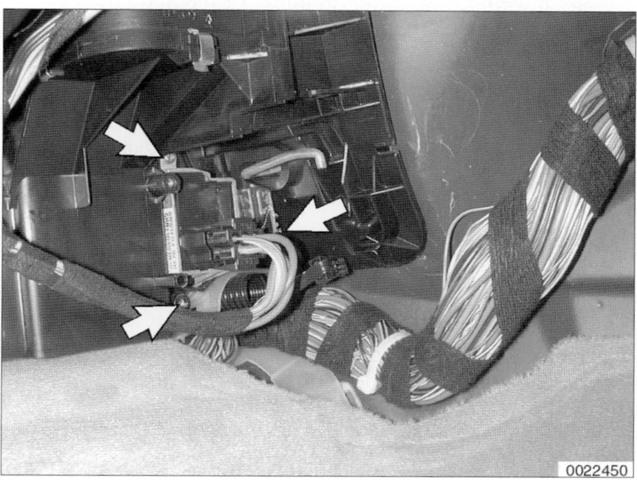

To remove blower resistor pack from IHKA housing:

- Remove mounting screws (**arrows**).
- Detach electrical harness connector.
- Press retaining clip away from switch to release switch.

– Installation is reverse of removal.

- Make sure electrical harness is routed as before.
- Align guides and clips correctly.

HEATER COMPONENTS

The heater valve is located in the left side of the engine compartment, attached to the left strut tower. The solenoid operated valve controls coolant flow through the heater core.

The IHKA housing, located underneath the center of the dashboard, houses the heater core, the A/C evaporator, the heating and A/C blower and associated sensors and air distribution motors.

> ***CAUTION —***
> *Removal of either the heater core or the IHKA housing involves dashboard removal. Before starting work, disconnect the battery negative (–) cable in the trunk. Be sure to read the battery disconnection cautions at the beginning of this manual and the airbag warnings in* **721 Airbag System (SRS)**.

Heater valve, replacing

- Drain engine coolant. See **170 Radiator and Cooling System**.

> ***WARNING —***
> *Allow the cooling system to cool before opening or draining the cooling system.*

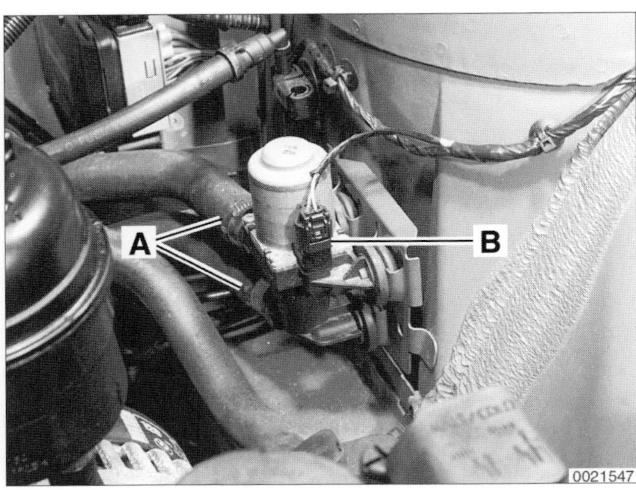

- Disconnect hoses (**A**) and electrical harness connector (**B**) at heater valve on left inner fender.
- Carefully pull heater valve out of rubber mounting and pull up and out of engine compartment.
- Installation is reverse of removal.
  - Inspect hoses and rubber mounts. Replace as necessary.
  - Use new hose clamps.

Tightening torque
- Coolant hose clamp
  32 - 48 mm (2¼ - 4 in.) . . . . .2.5 Nm (22 in-lb)

Heater core, replacing

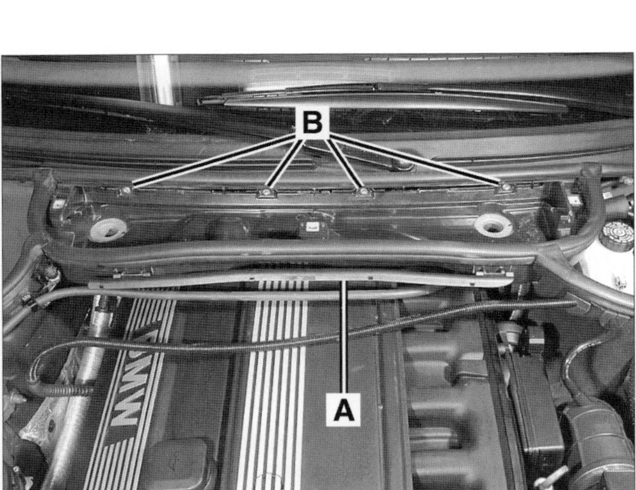

- Remove housing for interior ventilation microfilter.
  - Remove upper cover and microfilter.
  - Open wiring harness loom (**A**) and remove wires.
  - Unfasten screws (**B**) and remove lower housing.
- Drain engine coolant. See **170 Radiator and Cooling System**.

> ***WARNING —***
> *Allow the cooling system to cool before opening or draining the cooling system.*

- Remove center console and dashboard. See **513 Interior Trim**.

- Working at rear engine compartment bulkhead, loosen hose clamps (**arrows**) and detach heater hoses.
- Blow out excess coolant from heater core using compressed air at coolant lines.
- Release right air duct from IHKA housing.

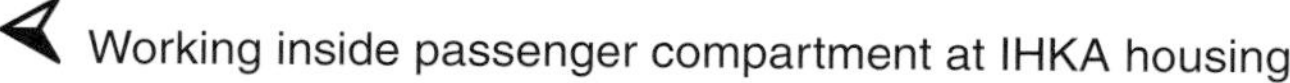

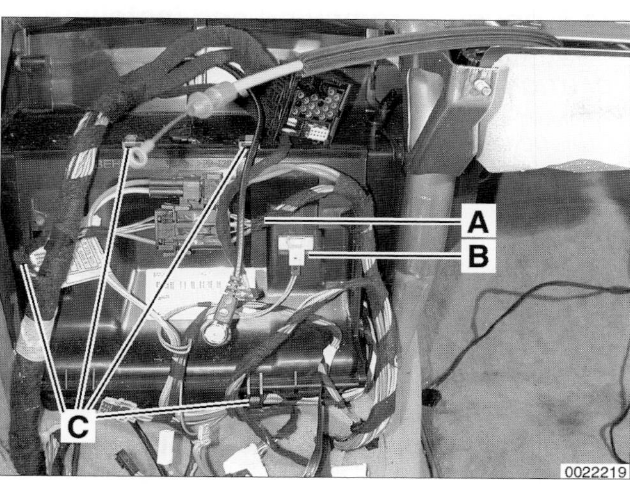

◀ Working inside passenger compartment at IHKA housing:

- Detach wiring harness (**A**) from housing.
- Remove heater core temperature sensor (**B**) by pulling straight out.
- Remove retaining clips (**C**) from housing cover.
- Lift off front of cover, then unhook tabs from housing at rear.

◀ Remove coolant pipe retaining clamps mounting screws (**arrows**).

◀ To remove heater core from IHKA housing:

- Remove coolant pipe retainers (**arrows**) to detach pipes.
- Tilt heater core to remove from housing.

– Installation is reverse of removal.

- Fit lugs in back of housing cover in heater housing slots.
- Use new sealing O-rings and coat with anti-seize agent.
- Fill and bleed cooling system. See **170 Radiator and Cooling System**.

> ***CAUTION —***
> *Replace coolant flange O-rings and tighten fasteners to specified torques.*

Tightening torque

- Coolant hose clamp
  32 - 48 mm (2¼ - 4 in.) . . . . 2.5 Nm (22 in-lb)

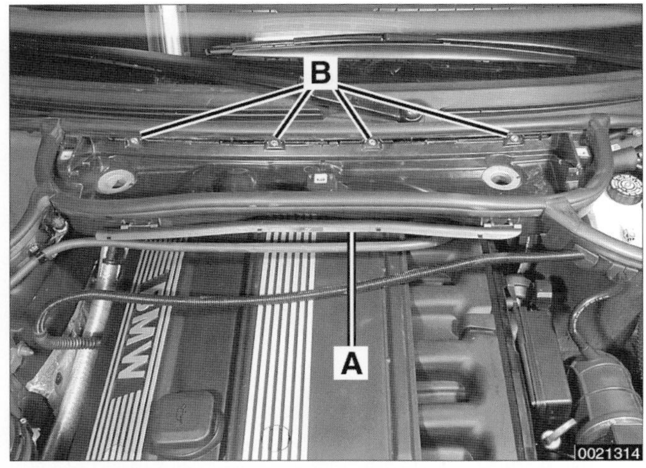

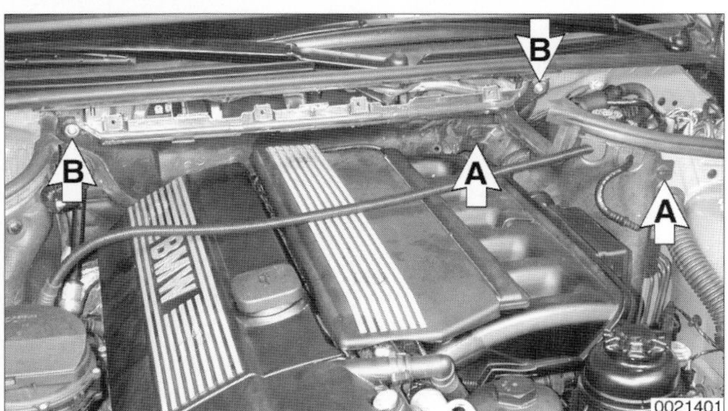

IHKA housing, removing and installing

> ***CAUTION —***
> - *Removing the IHKA housing requires evacuating the A/C system. DO NOT attempt this procedure without proper tools and training.*
> - *Any person who services a motor vehicle air conditioner must, by law, be properly trained and certified, and use approved refrigerant recycling equipment. Technicians must complete an EPA-approved recycling course to be certified*

◄ Remove housing for interior ventilation microfilter.

- Remove upper cover and microfilter.
- Open wiring harness loom (**A**) and remove wires.
- Unfasten screws (**B**) and remove lower housing.

◄ Remove heater bulkhead cover:

- Remove engine compartment side trim panel. Turn locking clips (**A**) and slide trim panel up.
- Remove heater bulkhead cover mounting screws (**B**) and lift cover off bulkhead.

– Drain engine coolant. See **170 Radiator and Cooling System**.

> ***WARNING —***
> *Allow the cooling system to cool before opening or draining the cooling system.*

◄ Working at rear engine compartment bulkhead, loosen hose clamps (**arrows**) and detach heater hoses.

– Blow out excess coolant from heater core using compressed air at coolant lines.

– Following manufacturer's instructions, connect approved refrigerant recovery / recycling / recharging unit to A/C system and discharge system.

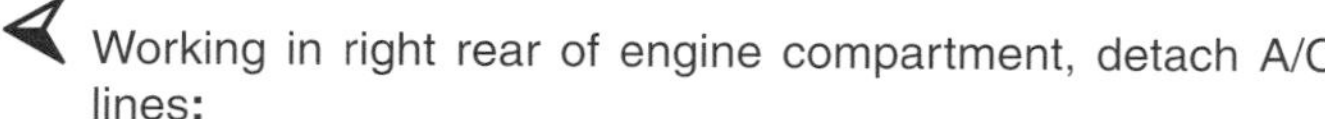

Working in right rear of engine compartment, detach A/C lines:

- Remove A/C recharging port bracket mounting nut (**A**).
- Remove allen bolts (**B**) at bulkhead.
- Using BMW special tool 64 5 102 or equivalent, detach and plug A/C lines.

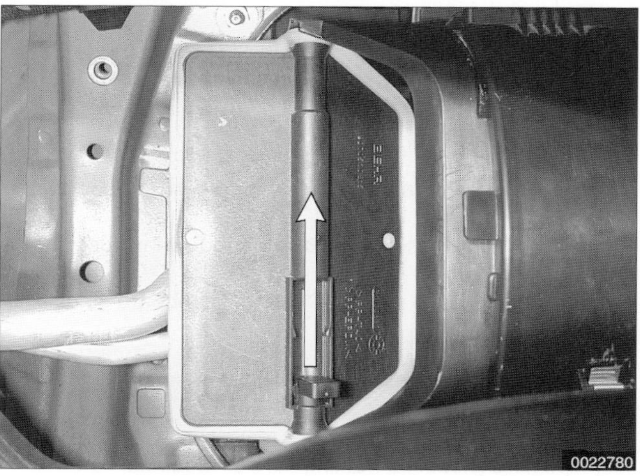

Working inside right side of cowl, pull up on lever (**arrow**) and detach right air intake flap from blower housing.

– Working in right front of IHKA housing, detach double pipe (A/C line) from expansion valve.

- Lay double pipe aside.
- Plug up open A/C ports.

Remove IHKA housing mounting nuts (**arrows**) at bulkhead.

– Remove center console and dashboard. See **513 Interior Trim**.

– Working inside passenger compartment below steering column, drill out steering column shear bolt. See **320 Steering and Wheel Alignment**.

- Remove steering column mounting bolts.
- Lower column.

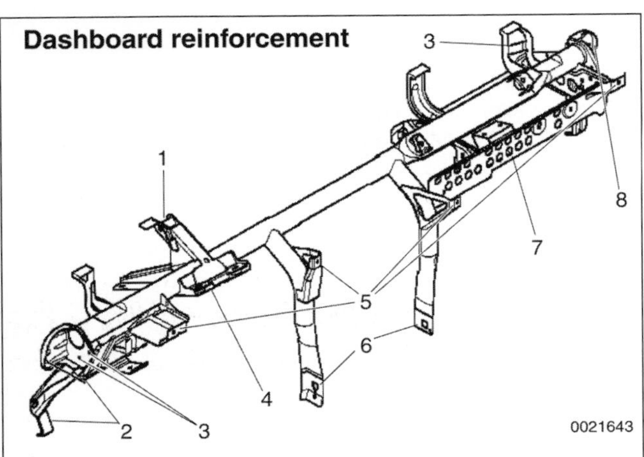

Under dash attachments:

1. Bulkhead	5. Dashboard mounts
2. Left A-pillar	6. Center tunnel
3. Head protection airbag	7. Relay panel
4. Steering column	8. Right A-pillar

Remove dashboard reinforcement fasteners:

- Detach bulkhead brace (**1**).
- Detach left and right A-pillar braces (**2** and **8**).
- Detach head protection airbag (**3**).
- Remove center tunnel mounting bolts (**6**).

– Detach heater housing electrical harness connectors.

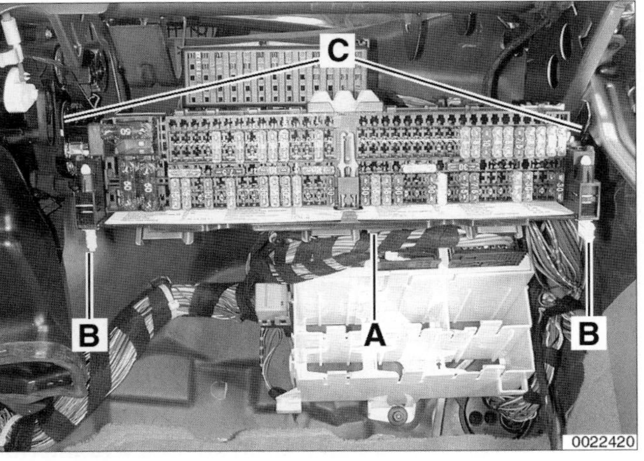

Working at right side of dash:

- Cut wire tie (**A**) at dashboard reinforcement support for relay panel.
- Turn fuse panel lock tabs (**B**) 90° and swing fuse panel down.
- Detach fuse panel pivots (**C**) from dashboard reinforcement.

– Lift off dashboard reinforcement, making sure all electrical harnesses and hoses are free.

– Remove IHKA housing, making sure all electrical harnesses and hoses are free.

– Installation is reverse of removal. Note the following:

- Make sure A/C condensate drain is routed correctly.
- Replace wire ties, sealing O-rings and hose clamps.
- Use new shear bolt at steering column mounting. Tighten bolt until head shears off.
- Evacuate and recharge A/C system using specialized equipment.
- Fill and bleed cooling system. See **170 Radiator and Cooling System**.

> ***CAUTION —***
> *Replace heater and A/C flange O-rings and tighten fasteners to specified torques.*

Tightening torques

- Coolant hose clamp
  32 - 48 mm (2¼ - 4 in.) . . . . .2.5 Nm (22 in-lb)
- Steering column to
  dashboard reinforcement . . . . 22 Nm (16 ft-lb)

AIR CONDITIONING COMPONENTS

This section covers removal and installation of air conditioning refrigerant components. A/C testing and diagnosis, refrigerant discharge, evacuation and recharge are not covered here.

The A/C condenser, compressor, receiver dryer, pressure sensor, refrigerant lines and expansion valve are either installed in the engine compartment or accessible from the engine compartment.

The A/C evaporator is located in the IHKA housing. Removal of the IHKA housing involves dashboard removal. Before starting work, disconnect the battery negative (–) cable in the trunk. Be sure to read the battery disconnection cautions at the beginning of this manual and the airbag warnings in **721 Airbag System (SRS)**.

A/C compressor, replacing

– Following manufacturer's instructions, connect an approved refrigerant recovery / recycling / recharging unit to A/C system and discharge system.

> ***WARNING —***
> *Do not discharge / charge the A/C system without proper equipment and training. Damage to the vehicle and personal injury may result.*

– Remove splash shield from under engine.

– Mark A/C drive belt with direction of rotation.

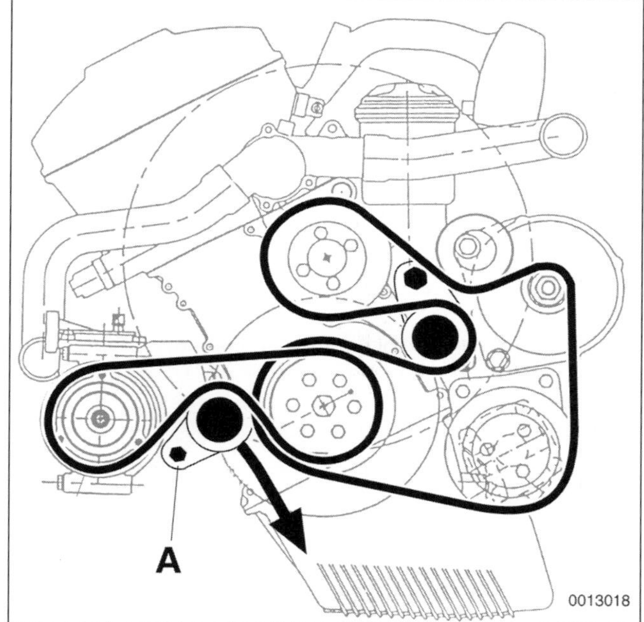

< Release tension on A/C belt:

- Use long-handled wrench to turn tensioner pulley release lug (**A**) clockwise (against spring tension).
- Remove drive belt.
- For additional information on belt removal, see **020 Maintenance**.

– Detach and set aside front washer fluid reservoir. See **611 Wipers and Washers**.

– Disconnect electrical harness connector from compressor.

< Remove A/C pressure hose and suction hose flange bolts (**arrows**) from compressor. Plug hoses immediately.

– All-wheel-drive model: Unbolt and lower front stabilizer bar. See **310 Front Suspension**.

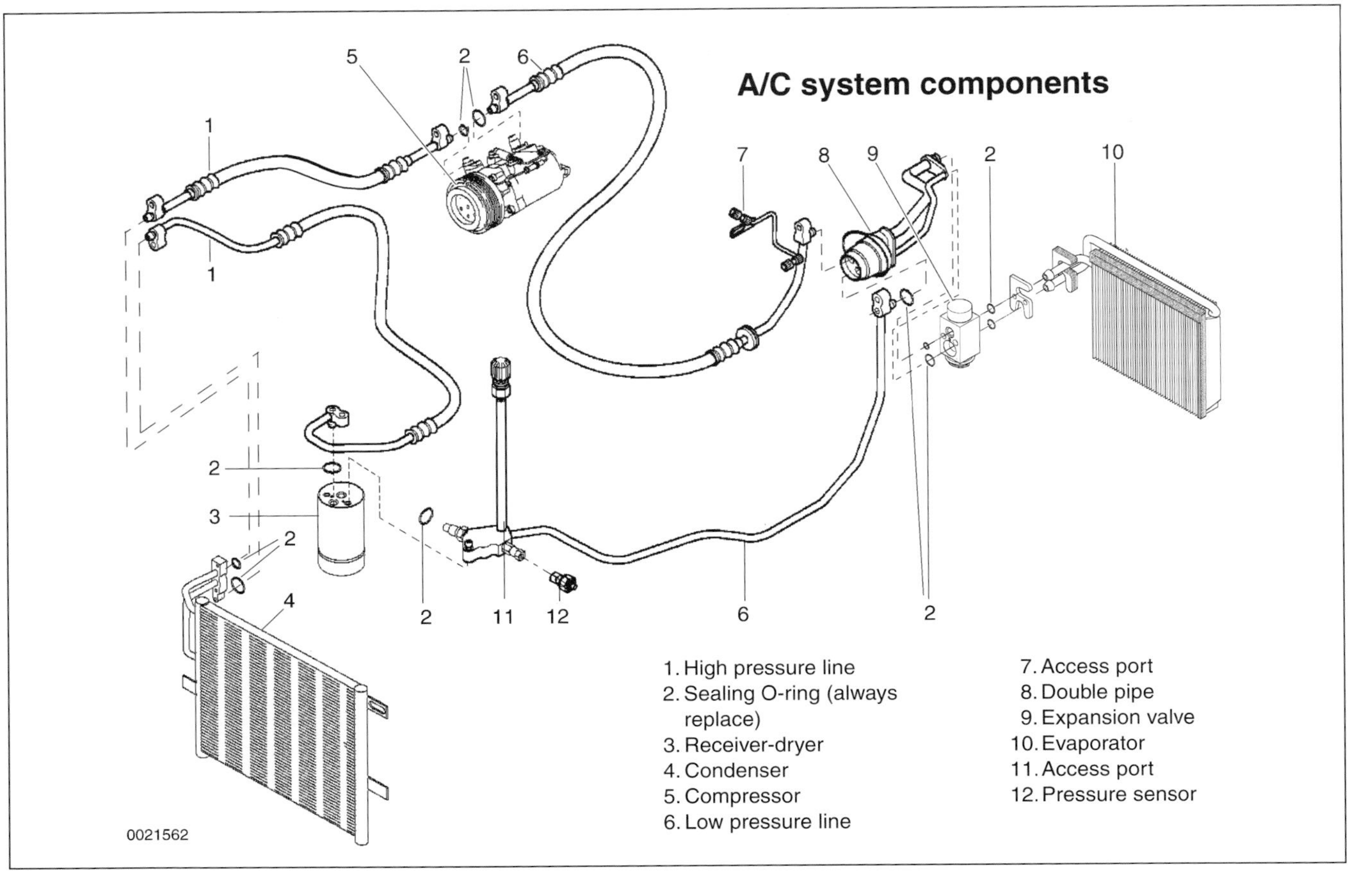

A/C system components

1. High pressure line
2. Sealing O-ring (always replace)
3. Receiver-dryer
4. Condenser
5. Compressor
6. Low pressure line
7. Access port
8. Double pipe
9. Expansion valve
10. Evaporator
11. Access port
12. Pressure sensor

0021562

◀ Support compressor while removing compressor mounting bolts (**arrows**). Remove compressor.

– Installation is reverse of removal.

> ***CAUTION —***
> - *Always replace O-rings when reconnecting refrigerant lines.*
> - *When installing a new compressor always replace receiver-dryer unit.*

Tightening torque
- A/C line to A/C compressor . . . . 20 Nm (15 ft-lb)

– Recharge system following equipment manufacturer's instructions. See **Table e** for A/C system fluid specifications.

Table e. A/C system fluid specifications

Fluid	Quantity
R-134a refrigerant	740 ± 25 g (2 lb ± 1 oz.)
Refrigerant oil	PAG oil

A/C condenser, replacing

The A/C condenser is located in front of the radiator.

– Following manufacturer's instructions, connect an approved refrigerant recovery / recycling / recharging unit to A/C system and discharge system.

> ***WARNING —***
> *Do not discharge / charge the A/C system without proper equipment and training. Damage to the vehicle and personal injury may result.*

Remove complete air filter housing:

- Detach vacuum line at intake boot (**A**).
- Disconnect electrical harness connector on mass air flow sensor (**B**).
- Release mass air flow sensor clips (**C**).
- Remove filter housing mounting screws (**D**).
- Detach air duct connections (**E**) and lift complete air filter housing out of engine compartment, pulling it forward away from mass air flow sensor.

– Remove intake hood, cooling fan and shroud, and radiator. See **170 Radiator and Cooling System**.

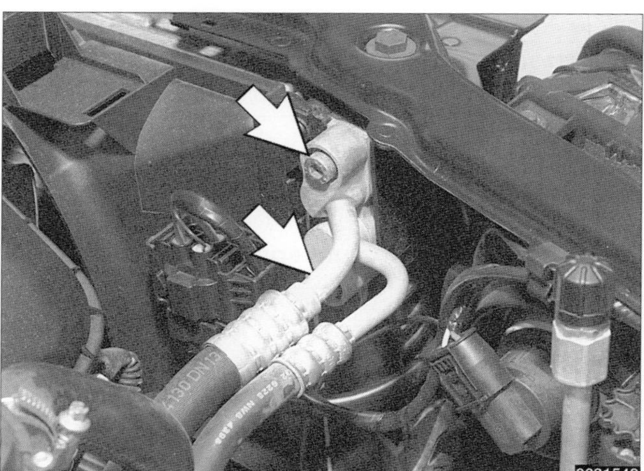

Remove Allen bolts (**arrows**) and detach A/C lines from upper right corner of condenser. Plug lines immediately.

– Remove fastener (expansion rivet) from top left corner of condenser.

– Remove Torx screw from top right corner of condenser, just below refrigerant line flange.

– Lift up condenser to disengage from plastic bracket and remove from above.

– Installation is reverse of removal.

> ***CAUTION —***
> - *Always replace O-rings when reconnecting refrigerant lines.*
> - *When installing a new condenser always replace receiver-dryer unit.*

– Recharge system following equipment manufacturer's instructions.

A/C system fluid specifications

Fluid	Quantity
R-134a refrigerant	740 ± 25 g (2 lb ± 1 oz.)
Refrigerant oil	PAG oil

A/C receiver-dryer, replacing

Replace the receiver-dryer if:

- There is dirt in the A/C system.
- The compressor seized or was replaced for any reason.
- The condenser or evaporator were replaced.
- The A/C system leaks and there is no more refrigerant.
- The A/C system was open for 24 hours or more.

The receiver-dryer is mounted in the front right corner of the engine compartment behind and below the headlight assembly.

– Following manufacturer's instructions, connect an approved refrigerant recovery / recycling / recharging unit to A/C system and discharge system.

– Remove right headlight assembly. See **630 Lights**.

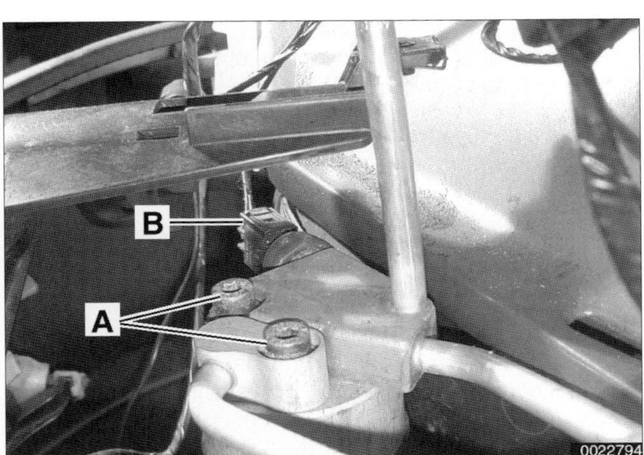

< Remove refrigerant pressure line mounting bolts (**A**) from receiver-dryer.

- Plug lines immediately.
- Disconnect high pressure switch harness connector (**B**).

– Working underneath right front of car, remove splash shield retaining screws. Remove splash shield.

– Loosen receiver-dryer mounting strap bolts and slide receiver-dryer down and out.

– Installation is reverse of removal.

> ***CAUTION —***
> *Always replace O-rings when reconnecting refrigerant lines.*

– Recharge system following equipment manufacturer's instructions.

A/C system fluid specifications

Fluid	Quantity
R-134a refrigerant	740 ± 25 g (2 lb ± 1 oz.)
Refrigerant oil	PAG oil

A/C expansion valve, removing and installing

– Following manufacturer's instructions, connect an approved refrigerant recovery / recycling / recharging unit to A/C system and discharge system.

> ***WARNING —***
> *Do not discharge / charge the A/C system without proper equipment and training. Damage to the vehicle and personal injury may result.*

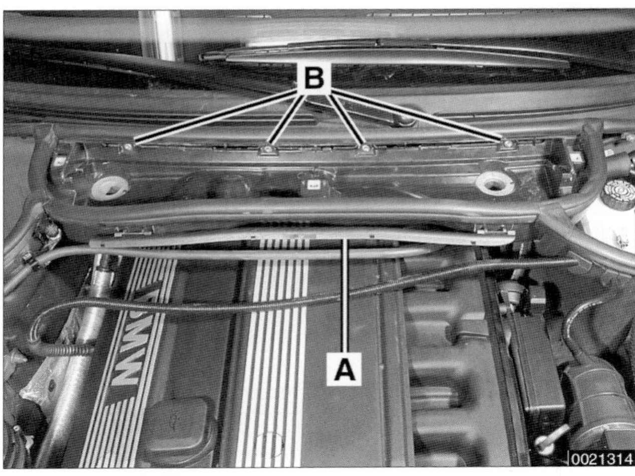

Remove housing for interior ventilation microfilter.

- Remove upper cover and microfilter.
- Open wiring harness loom (**A**) and remove wires.
- Unfasten screws (**B**) and remove lower housing.

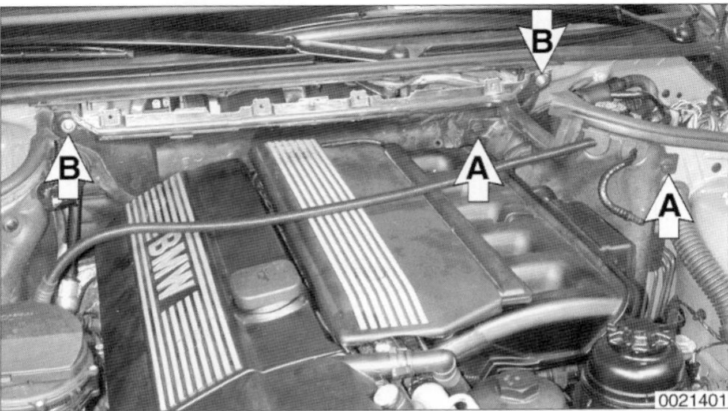

To remove heater bulkhead cover:

- Remove engine compartment side trim panel. Turn locking clips (**A**) and slide trim panel up.
- Remove heater bulkhead cover mounting screws (**B**) and lift cover off bulkhead.

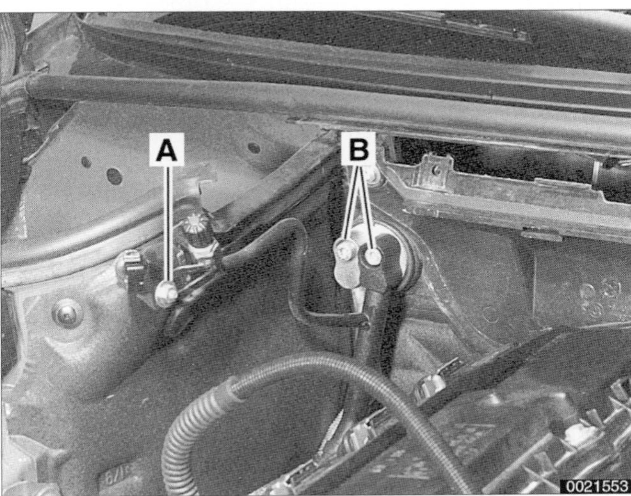

Working in right rear of engine compartment, detach A/C lines:

- Remove A/C recharging port bracket mounting nut (**A**).
- Remove allen bolts (**B**) at bulkhead. Release and plug open A/C lines.

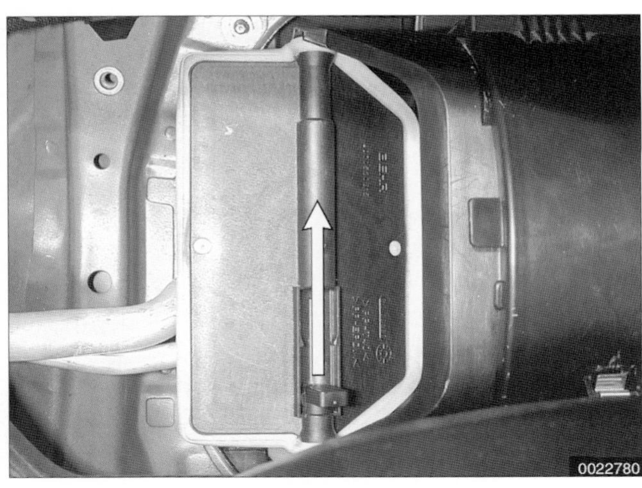

Working inside right side of cowl, pull up on lever (**arrow**) and detach right air intake flap from blower housing.

– Working in right front of IHKA housing, detach double pipe (A/C line) from expansion valve.
  - Lay double pipe aside.
  - Plug up open A/C ports.

– Remove expansion valve mounting bolts and remove valve.

– Installation is reverse of removal.

> ***CAUTION —***
> *Always replace O-rings when reconnecting refrigerant lines.*

– Recharge system following equipment manufacturer's instructions.

A/C system fluid specifications

Fluid	Quantity
R-134a refrigerant	740 ± 25 g (2 lb ± 1 oz.)
Refrigerant oil	PAG oil

A/C evaporator, removing and installing

> ***CAUTION —***
> *Evaporator removal involves removal of the complete dashboard. Before starting work, disconnect the battery negative (–) cable in the trunk. Be sure to read the battery disconnection cautions on page viii and the airbag warnings in* **721 Airbag System (SRS)**.

– Following manufacturer's instructions, connect an approved refrigerant recovery / recycling / recharging unit to A/C system and discharge system.

– Drain engine coolant. See **170 Radiator and Cooling System**.

– Remove complete IHKA housing. See **IHKA housing, removing and installing** in this repair group.

– Remove heater core. See **Heater core, replacing** in this repair group.

– Working on left side of IHKA housing:
  - Detach evaporator temperature sensor electrical harness connector and pull out sensor.
  - Detach wiring harness from housing.
  - Detach linkage from fresh air distribution motor.

– Working on right side of IHKA housing:
  - Unclip and remove fresh air / recirculation motor.
  - Remove evaporator cover mounting screw and remove cover.

– Detach and remove microswitch at side of IHKA housing.

- Working in front of IHKA housing:
  - Remove blower housing mounting screws. Lift out blower housing.
  - Remove double coolant pipe.

- Pry off evaporator housing retaining clips and remove cover. Pull evaporator and expansion valve out of bottom of housing.

- If installing new evaporator, switch over expansion valve. Use new sealing O-rings.

> ***CAUTION —***
> *Do not bend cooling fins on evaporator. If necessary, straighten with fin comb.*

- Installation is reverse of removal.
  - Make sure electrical harnesses are routed as before.
  - Recharge system following equipment manufacturer's instructions.

A/C system fluid specifications

Fluid	Quantity
R-134a refrigerant	740 ± 25 g (2 lb ± 1 oz.)
Refrigerant oil	PAG oil

650 Radio

GENERAL

This section covers the BMW factory-installed sound system, including radio, amplifier and speaker removal. Radio antenna information is also included.

On-Board (GPS) Monitor removal is covered in **640 Heating and Air-conditioning**.

Special tools

Special tools

A BMW 00 9 321 . . . . Plastic prying tool

Use BMW special tool 00 9 321 or equivalent plastic prying tool to pry out plastic interior parts without damage or marring.

Radio tag

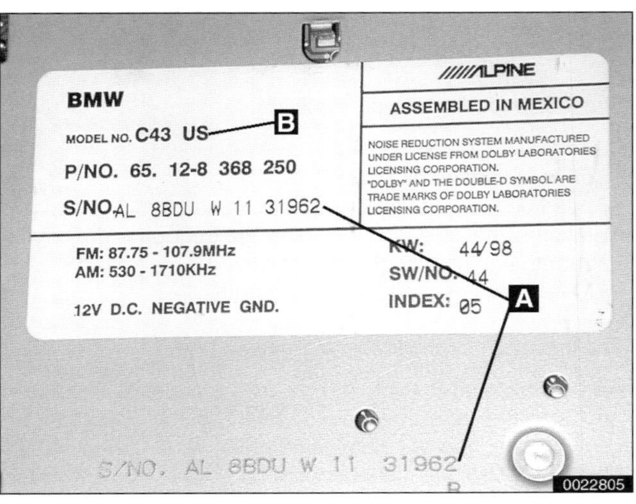

A tag on the bottom of the radio contains the serial number (**A**) and model number (**B**).

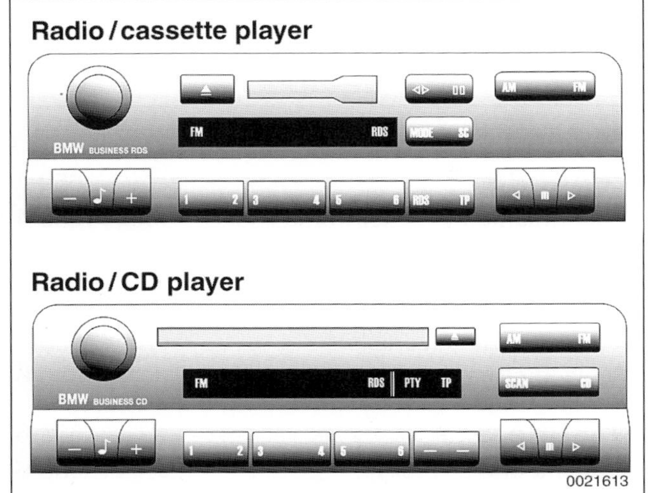

Sound system

The standard E46 radio features a cassette player. The optional radio has a single in-dash CD player. Both radios are prewired for the optional CD changer that mounts in the trunk. Another option, the On-Board Monitor, integrates GPS navigation with radio and IHKA controls. Basic radio controls are also incorporated in the steering wheel.

Sound system components are interconnected via K-bus. Theft proofing of the radio by code is no longer required as the radio does not function without the K-bus connection and a valid signal from the instrument cluster.

Other features of the sound system include:

- Autostoring of stations
- Vehicle speed dependent volume
- Telephone muting

Diversity antenna, described later in this group, is optional on some models and standard on the Convertible and Sport Wagon.

RDS

Radio Data System (RDS) is a transmit and receive system operated in the FM band. It is a data service offered by radio stations in which the information is transmitted inaudibly with the audio programs. The name of the station is displayed in the radio when the RDS system is active. Program identification, program service name and RDS quality are also displayed.

Troubleshooting

Although electronic radio and sound system troubleshooting is beyond the scope of this manual, there are number of self-tests that are possible with the standard BMW radio installed in E46 cars.

Radio test functions are activated by pressing the M button within 8 seconds of switching the radio on. Hold it pressed in for 8 seconds to start the tests.

The test functions include:

- Radio serial number
- Software version display
- Speed dependent volume control adjustment
- Station signal strength, including FM frequency set, signal strength and quality of signal received
- AM frequency set and signal strength

The test also checks antenna functions:

- Antenna signal strength (F number) indicates the quality of the signal received by the antenna. The scale ranges from 0 to 15, with the optimum value being 15. If the value falls below 10, radio stations can not be listened to in stereo.

RADIO AND AUDIO ACCESSORIES

Radio, removing and installing

> ***CAUTION —***
> - *Before beginning work on the radio or sound system, verify that the radio is an original equipment BMW radio and that the wiring harness is not modified.*
> - *Refer servicing of aftermarket sound equipment to an authorized agent of the equipment manufacturer.*

– Prying gently, remove right dashboard trim, then center dashboard trim. See **513 Interior Trim**.

> ***CAUTION —***
> *To avoid marring interior trim, work with a plastic prying tool.*

◄ Remove radio mounting screws (**arrows**).

– Pull radio out of instrument panel opening. Detach electrical harness connector and antenna lead.

– Installation is reverse of removal.

Amplifier

The sound system amplifier is installed behind the left rear trim in the trunk or cargo compartment.

– Sedan or Coupe: Remove left side trunk trim clips and peel back trim.

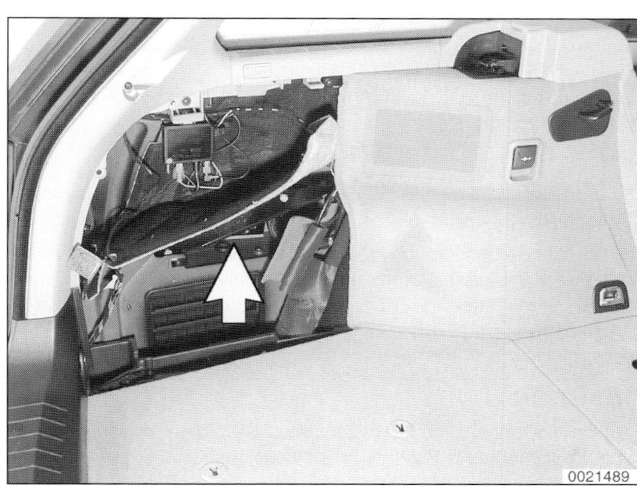

◄ Sport Wagon: Remove left cargo compartment trim cover. Sound system amplifier (**arrow**) is behind sound insulation.

– Convertible:

- Disconnect battery negative terminal.
- Remove lower section of rear seat left side trim.
- If necessary, remove convertible top module. See **541 Convertible Top**.
- Amplifier is attached to side wall.

CD changer

The optional CD changer is located in the left side of the trunk or cargo compartment, behind the trim panel. An access door allows loading of up to 6 CDs.

SPEAKERS

Each model in the E46 model line-up features a slightly different speaker setup. Speaker and other component locations also vary depending on the type of sound system installed. Some of the common speaker installations are covered in this section.

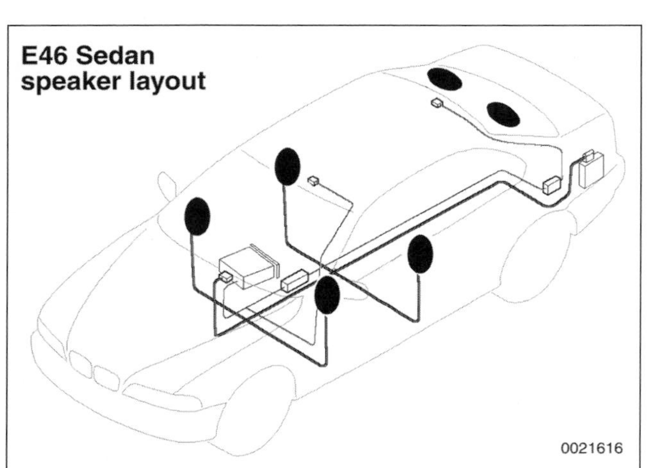

Sedan and **Sport Wagon**: The standard installation is six speakers, one in each door and two in the rear. The rear speakers in the Sedan are in the parcel shelf. The rear speakers in the Sport Wagon are mounted on the left and right wheel housings behind trim covers.

Coupe: A tweeter and a mid-range speaker are installed in each front door panel. Another speaker pair is in the left and right rear side trim panels.

Convertible: The standard speaker set-up consists of four speakers mounted in the rear side trim panels, two on each side. One speaker on each side is a 130 mm wide band and the other is a tweeter.

The Harman / Kardon system incorporates an additional subwoofer installed in the trunk. The amplification for this subwoofer comes from the main sound system amplifier.

In the Convertible, the subwoofer is installed in the ski bag cover. It is hinged so that it can be swung aside when the ski bag is used. A magnet on the subwoofer cover holds it in-place against the rear bulkhead while the ski bag is used. The subwoofer functions in either position.

Also in the Convertible, the sound system receives a signal from the rear window defroster relay when the top is lowered. This switches off the stereophonic function.

Door mounted speaker, removing

> ***WARNING —***
> *E46 cars are equipped with front door airbags. Rear door airbags are optional. Before performing any work involving airbags, disconnect the negative (–) battery cable. See* **721 Airbag System (SRS)**.

> ***CAUTION —***
> *Prior to disconnecting the battery, read the battery disconnection cautions given at the front of this manual.*

– Remove interior door panel. See **411 Doors**.

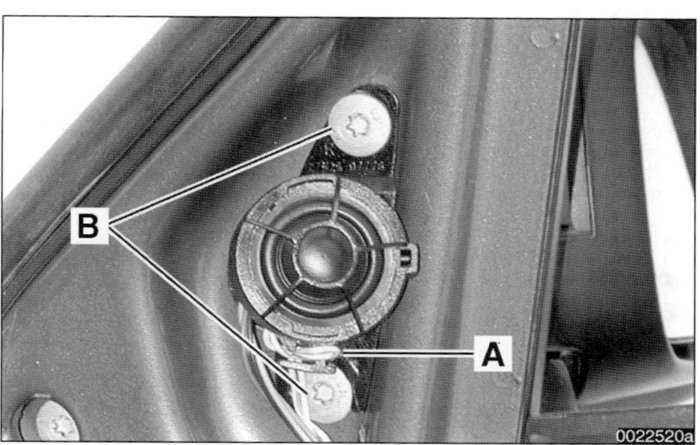

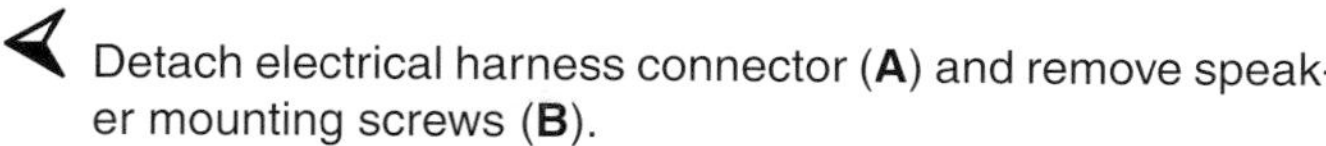

Detach electrical harness connector (**A**) and remove speaker mounting screws (**B**).

- Remove speaker.

Rear speaker, removing and installing (Sedan or Coupe)

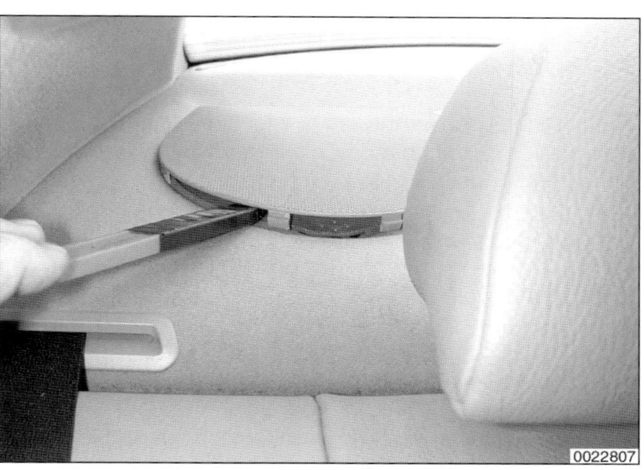

Working at rear parcel shelf, pry speaker cover by inner edge and remove.

> ***CAUTION —***
> *To avoid marring interior trim, work with a plastic prying tool.*

- Remove mounting screws, lift up speaker and detach electrical harness connector.
- When reinstalling, make sure speaker and harness are seated as before.

Rear side panel speaker, removing (Convertible)

- Disconnect battery negative terminal.

> ***CAUTION —***
> *Prior to disconnecting the battery, read the battery disconnection cautions given at the front of this manual on page viii.*

- Remove lower section of rear seat side trim.
- If necessary, remove convertible top module. See **541 Convertible Top** (left side only).
- Speaker is attached to side wall.

Subwoofer, removing

– Coupe:
  - Working in trunk under parcel shelf, remove subwoofer mounting screws.
  - Unhook and pull subwoofer down. Remove electrical harness connector.

– Convertible:
  - Working in trunk, unhook and swing out subwoofer.
  - Squeeze plastic harness cover and remove.
  - Detach electrical harness connector.
  - Using plastic pry tool, gently pry subwoofer at bottom left and pull out.

ANTENNA

Antenna and diversity

The antenna used for the radio, telephone and FZV remote entry system is integrated with the rear window defogger in Sedan and Coupe.

Convertible and Sport Wagon feature a diversity antenna system to provide the strongest possible radio station signal to the sound system.

In this system there are two (or more) antennas. Both the main and the auxiliary antenna(s) receive radio signals and both signals are amplified in separate amplifiers. The signals are then transmitted to the diversity switching module, which locks onto the strongest signal and sends it to the radio receiver.

Sport Wagon antenna system

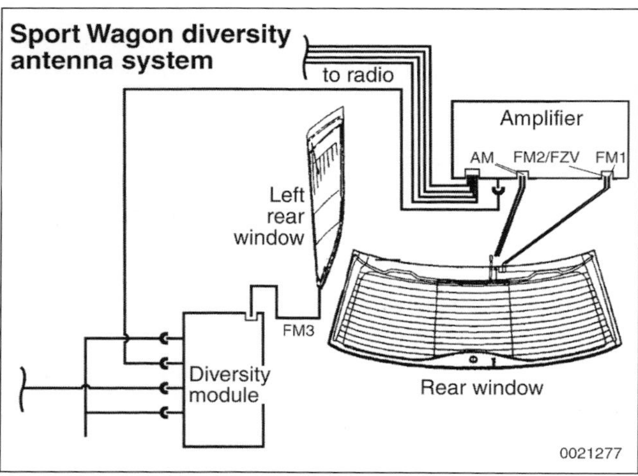

The diversity antenna system on the E46 Sport Wagon consists of the following;

- FM1 antenna in rear window (right half)
- FM2 antenna in rear window (center)
- FM3 antenna in left rear side window
- AM antenna in rear spoiler
- FZV (keyless entry) antenna combined with FM2 antenna

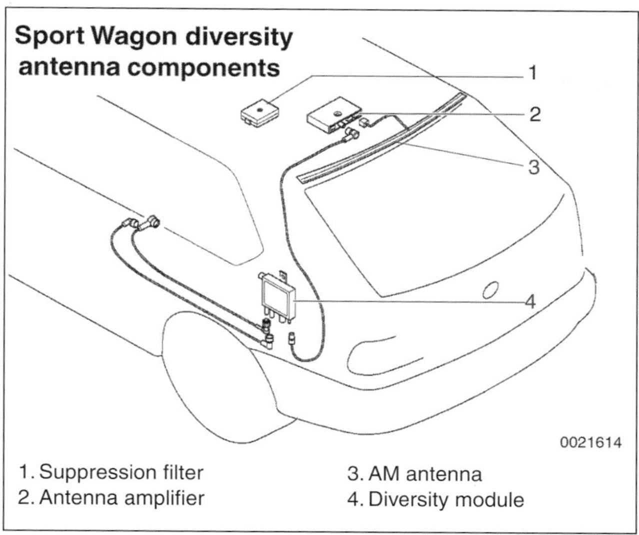

1. Suppression filter
2. Antenna amplifier
3. AM antenna
4. Diversity module

The FM1 / FM2 antenna amplifier is located beneath the rear spoiler. The signal from this amplifier is transmitted to the diversity module in the cargo compartment behind the left trim panel.

The FM3 antenna has a separate amplifier integrated into the diversity module. The module selects the clearest signal from the three antennas and transmits that to the sound system.

The AM antenna is glued to the bottom of the rear spoiler.

Convertible antenna system

The diversity antenna system on the E46 Convertible consists of the following:

- Main antenna mast on left rear fender
- Auxiliary antenna in convertible top storage cover
- Main antenna amplifier, mounted directly below the antenna mast
- Auxiliary antenna amplifier, mounted on convertible top storage cover and powered through antenna lead
- Diversity switching module, mounted below antenna mast in trunk

Additional rear window defogger and antenna information is in **640 Heating and Air-conditioning**.

NOTE —
The telephone antenna is wound around the main antenna mast.

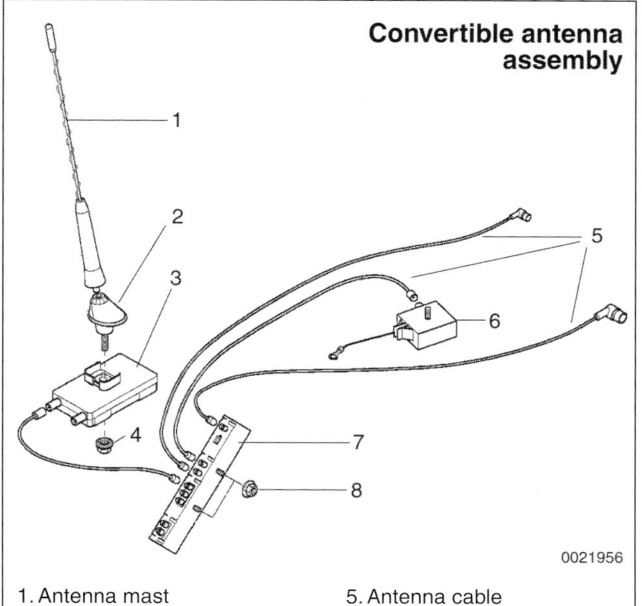

1. Antenna mast
2. Antenna head
3. Antenna base
4. Nut M5
5. Antenna cable
6. Antenna FM amplifier
7. Antenna diversity amplifier
8. Nut M6

Antenna, removing (Convertible)

Unscrew and remove antenna mast.

- Detach and remove wheel housing trim liner in left side of trunk.
- Through elongated hole of antenna retaining bracket, unscrew M5 nut.
  - This releases antenna head from base.
  - Place antenna base down on bracket.
  - Remove antenna head from above fender.
- To remove base, slide toward rear of car, then detach cable connections.
- When installing, make sure the offset of antenna head points toward back of car.

Antenna amplifier, accessing

- Convertible main antenna amplifier:
  - Detach and remove wheel housing trim liner in left side of trunk.
  - Antenna amplifier is mounted below antenna bracket.
- Convertible auxiliary antenna amplifier:
  - Open convertible top compartment lid.
  - Auxiliary amplifier is attached to left rear corner of lid.

0022870

◄ Sedan or Coupe antenna amplifier: Remove left rear roof pillar (C-pillar) trim panel.

- Sedan or Coupe antenna trap circuit (suppressor): Remove right rear roof pillar (C-pillar) trim panel.

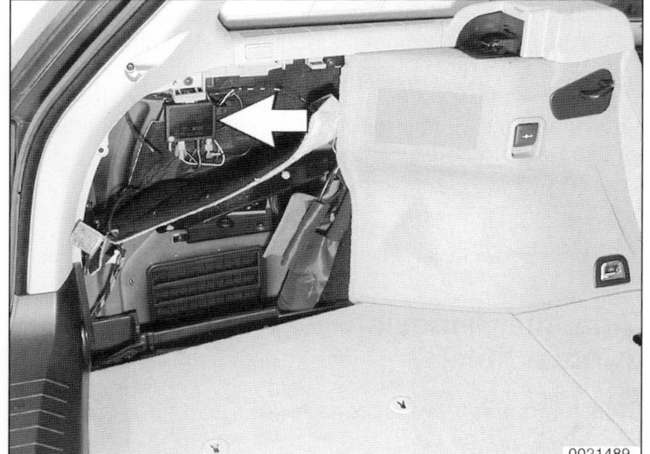
0021489

◄ Sport Wagon FM3 antenna / diversity module (**arrow**): Remove left cargo compartment trim cover.

- Sport Wagon FM1 / FM2 antenna amplifier:
  - Remove rear spoiler. See **412 Trunk Lid, Tailgate**.
  - Amplifier is in center of rear window underneath spoiler.

720 Seat Belts

GENERAL

This section covers repairs to the seat belts.

E46 models are equipped with 3-point shoulder belts at four seating positions.

- **Sport Wagon**: Additional 3-point shoulder belt in center of rear seat
- **Sedan** and **Coupe**: Either lap belt or a 3-point shoulder belt in center of rear seat
- **Convertible**: Seat-integrated seat belt system (SGS) in front

The front seat belt locks are equipped with pyrotechnic (explosive charge) automatic tensioners. These tensioners are designed to automatically retract and tension the seat belt by 55 mm (approximately 2 inches) in case of an accident.

Pyrotechnic tensioners are controlled by the Multiple Restraint System (MRS) control module. MRS electronics integrate seat belt operation and airbag deployment. Additional MRS information is in **721 Airbag System (SRS)**.

720

Child safety seat installation anchors

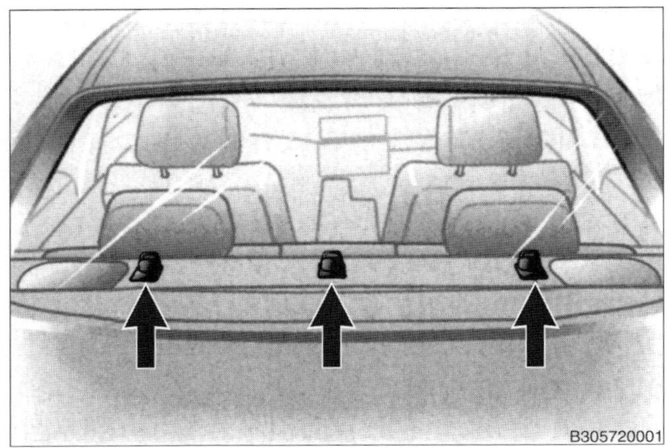

Sedan or **Coupe**: Upper child seat tether anchors (**arrows**) at rear parcel shelf.

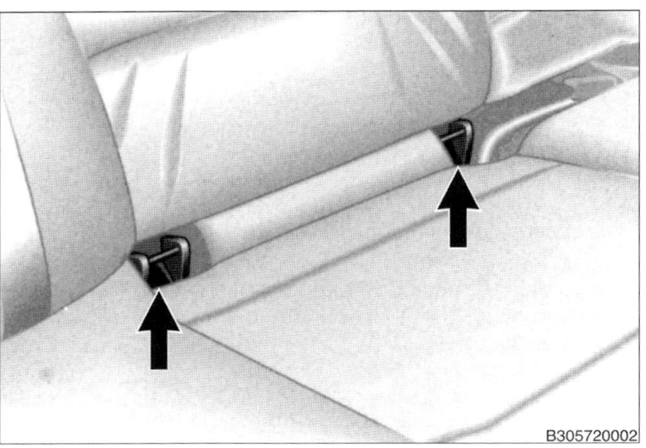

Sedan or **Coupe**: LATCH child-restraint anchors (**arrows**) at base of rear backrest, near seat belt mounting points.

NOTE —
LATCH is the acronym for Lower Anchors and Tethers for CHildren.

Convertible: Two tether points behind rear seat headrests.

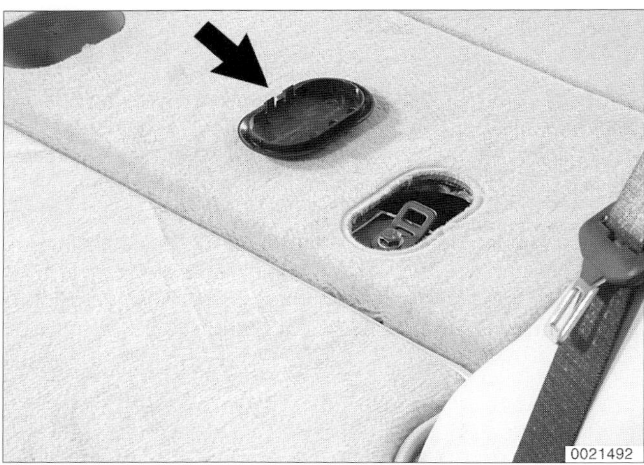

Sport Wagon: Three tether points behind rear seat, under plastic covers (**arrow**), in cargo compartment floor.

NOTE —
For information on proper installation of child safety seats, child safety seat recalls, or for location of child safety seat inspection station in your area, visit the National Highway Traffic Safety Administration (NHTSA) website at **www.nhtsa.dot.gov**.

Troubleshooting

The seat belt reel should lock when driving quickly through curves, during severe braking or in case of a collision. The automatic reel does not require any servicing and should never be opened.

In case of an accident, follow the seat belt troubleshooting procedures in **Table a**.

Table a. Seat belt troubleshooting

Problem	Probable cause	Repairs
Damage to seat belt.	Accident in which bumper impact absorbers were permanently deformed.	Replace complete automatic seat belt. Also check and replace, if necessary: -Seat belt mounting on car body. -Seat belt mounting on seat runner.
Belt creased, unraveled, pinched, cut or melted. Belt buckle or belt lock plastic casing worn, damaged or missing.	Seat belts aged or worn.	Replace complete automatic seat belt.
Seat belt buckle is *not* ejected with spring pressure when red button on seat belt lock is pressed.	Seat belt lock mechanism worn or damaged.	Replace seat belt lock.
Seat belt automatic reel does not lock when pulled out suddenly.	Automatic reel defective.	Replace reel assembly.
Seat belt automatic reel jams when pulled out.	Automatic reel loose.	Tighten reel mounting bolt.
	Return spring broken inside reel.	Replace reel assembly.
Seat belt does not retract automatically. (See note below.)	Automatic reel loose.	Tighten reel mounting bolt.
	Return spring broken inside reel.	Replace reel assembly.
Belt squeaks when fastened or unfastened.	Excessive friction in belt guides.	Replace reel assembly.
	Automatic reel loose.	Tighten reel mounting bolt.
	Return spring broken inside reel.	Replace reel assembly.
Seat belt pyrotechnic tensioner triggered.	Accident	Replace complete automatic seat belt. Also check retaining bracket of belt tensioner for twist.
Convertible only:		
Front seat back requires excessive force to lock or unlock.	Accident damage to seat via seat belt .	Replace front seat.
Seat back lock warning light on when seat back is locked; or warning light ON when seat back is shaken.	Seat back lock microswitch defective.	Replace microswitch.
	Microswitch electrical harness connectors loose or defective.	Repair electrical leads.
	Seat back lock damaged.	If fault persists, replace front seat.
Contact surface of inertia reel warped.	Accident damage.	Replace front seat.
Seat back warped or deformed.		
Head restraint carrier not parallel.		
Seat movement sticky or sluggish at some point in its range; unusual noises.	Accident damage (side).	
Front seat shows evidence of contact with body structural part (e.g., door).	Accident damage (side).	
Front seat shows evidence of contact with external objects.	Accident damage (rollover).	

NOTE —
The rear bench seat belt strap may not retract fully due to increased friction between strap and seat cover. A small remaining loop in belt strap when fully retracted is acceptable.

Seat belt warnings

See also **Airbag system warnings** in **721 Airbag System (SRS)**.

WARNING —

- *If the airbag warning light is ON, the seat belt tensioners will not be triggered in case of an accident. Be sure to have the airbag system inspected and repaired immediately.*
- *Pyrotechnic seat belt tensioners are powerful devices. Handle with extreme care. Incorrect handling can trigger the tensioner and cause injury.*
- *BMW recommends that all repair or replacement work on pyrotechnic devices be carried out by a qualified BMW technician.*
- *Be sure to disconnect the battery and wait 1 minute before attempting to work on pyrotechnic devices.*
- *Pyrotechnic devices cannot be repaired. Always replace them.*
- *Never treat pyrotechnic components with cleaning agents or grease.*
- *Do not expose pyrotechnic components to temperatures above 75°C (167°F).*
- *Pyrotechnic components can only be tested electrically when installed, using BMW scan tool (DISplus, GT1, MoDiC) or equivalent.*
- *Do not fire a pyrotechnic gas generator prior to disposal. It must be fired by a special disposal company or shipped back to BMW in the packaging of the new components.*
- *During body straightening and welding with an electric arc welder, disconnect the battery and the connection to the pyrotechnic gas generators.*
- *Do not install a rear facing child safety seat in the front passenger seat position.*
- *In vehicles equipped with rear side-impact airbags, be sure that child safety seats are installed correctly.*
- *If seat belts are subjected to occupant loading in a collision, replace them as a set (including all hardware) for maximum safety.*
- *Do not modify or repair seat belts or seat belt mounting points.*
- *Do not bleach or dye seat belt webbing. Webbing that is severely faded or redyed does not meet the strength requirements of a collision. Clean belts with a luke-warm soap solution only.*
- *Periodically inspect seat belts for webbing defects such as cuts or pulled threads.*
- *Immediately after replacing a damaged or worn seat belt, destroy the old belt to prevent it from being used again.*

FRONT SEAT BELT ASSEMBLY

Front seat belt tensioner, removing and installing

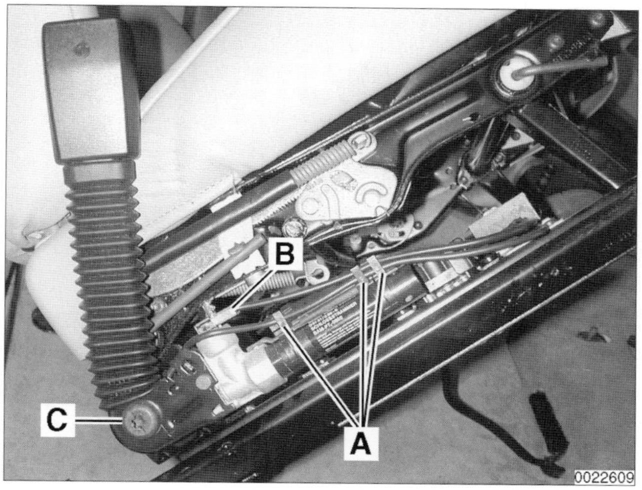

– Detach battery negative (–) cable.

> ***CAUTION —***
> *Prior to disconnecting the battery, read the battery disconnection cautions given at the front of this manual.*

– Remove front seat. See **520 Seats**.

◄ Remove pyrotechnic belt tensioner:

- Detach tensioner harness connector from seat rail by cutting wire tie (**A**).
- Detach harness connection (**B**).
- Remove tensioner mounting bolt (**C**).

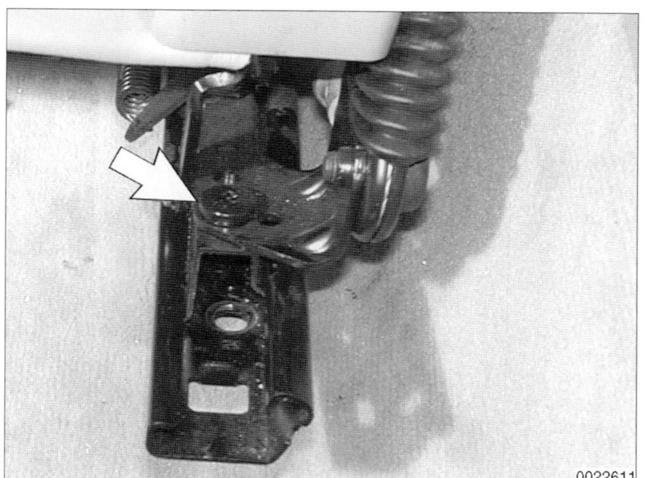

◄ Check tensioner mounting bracket (**arrow**) for damage or bending. Replace if necessary.

> ***CAUTION —***
> *A bent tensioner mounting bracket may make it impossible to adjust seat height.*

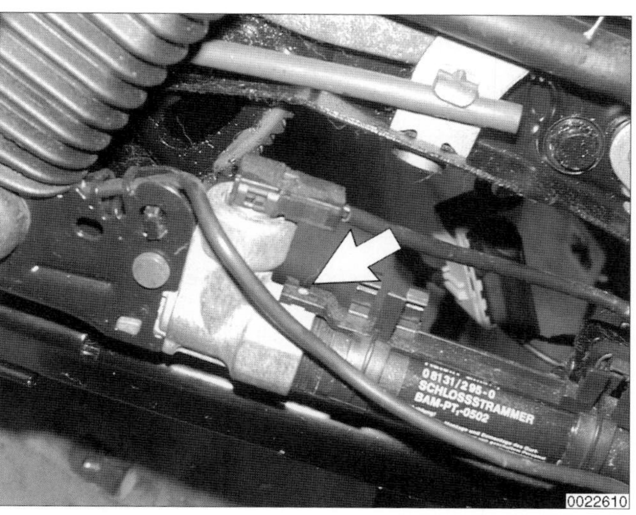

◄ When reinstalling:

- Replace wire ties to relieve tension on pyrotechnic belt tensioner electrical connector.
- Make sure tensioner connector mounting bracket (**arrow**) is installed correctly.

Tightening torques

- Front seat to floor (M10 fastener) . . . . . . 45 Nm (33 ft-lb)
- Seat belt to seat . . . . 48 Nm (35 ft-lb)
- Tensioner mounting bracket to seat rail . 24 Nm (18 ft-lb)
- Tensioner to mounting bracket . . . . 48 Nm (35 ft-lb)

Front seat belt assembly (Sedan, Coupe, Sport Wagon)

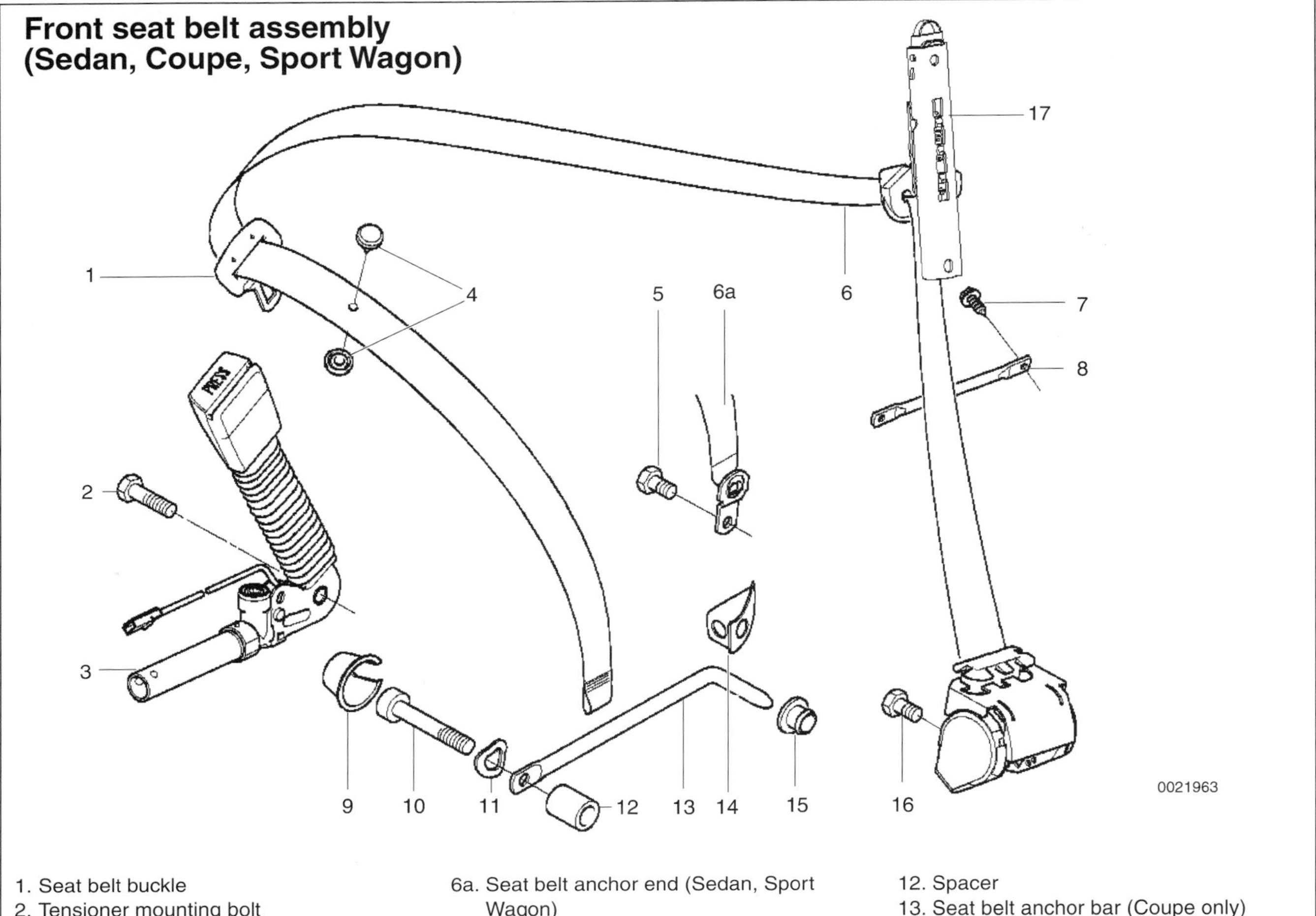

1. Seat belt buckle
2. Tensioner mounting bolt
   -tighten to 48 Nm (35 ft-lb)
3. Seat belt lock with pyrotechnic tensioner
4. Seat belt stop button
5. Seat belt anchor bolt
   -tighten to 48 Nm (35 ft-lb)
6. Seat belt reel assembly

6a. Seat belt anchor end (Sedan, Sport Wagon)

7. Bolt M8
8. B-pillar cross-brace
9. Plastic cap
10. Bolt M10
    -tighten to 31 Nm (23 ft-lb)
11. Spring washer
12. Spacer
13. Seat belt anchor bar (Coupe only)
14. Cap
15. Grommet
16. Seat belt reel mounting bolt M10
    -tighten to 31 Nm (23 ft-lb)
17. Seat belt height adjuster

Front seat belt reel, removing and installing (Sedan, Coupe, Sport Wagon)

– Detach battery negative (–) cable.

> ***CAUTION —***
> *Prior to disconnecting the battery, read the battery disconnection cautions given at the front of this manual.*

– Remove front seat as described in **520 Seats**.

– Coupe: Working just inside door sill:

- Pry off plastic protective cap over end of seat belt anchor bar.
- Remove anchor bar bolt and slip off end of seat belt from bar.

NOTE —
Replace anchor bar if it is bent.

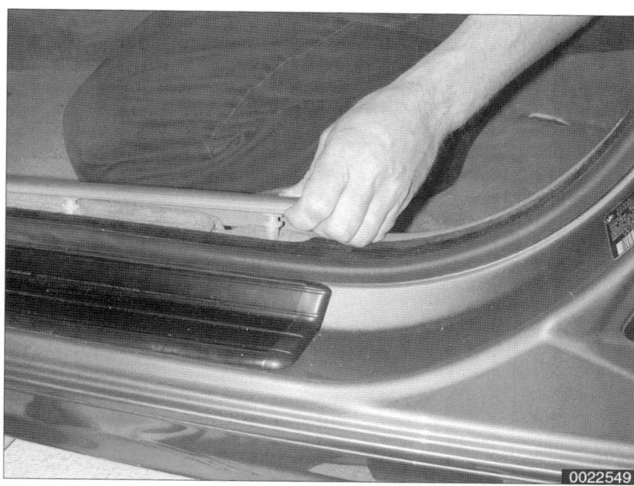
0022549

Prying gently upward, remove plastic door sill protector strip.

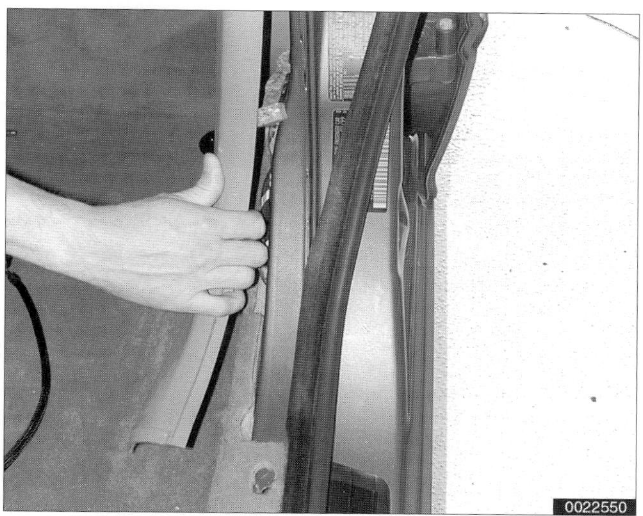
0022550

Sedan, Sport Wagon: Remove lower door pillar (B-pillar) plastic trim.

- Pry gently along bottom of trim to disengage clips from pillar.
- Slide trim down and out.

– Coupe: Remove rear side panel. See **411 Doors**.

NOTE —
Partially peel rubber door seal(s) away from B-pillar.

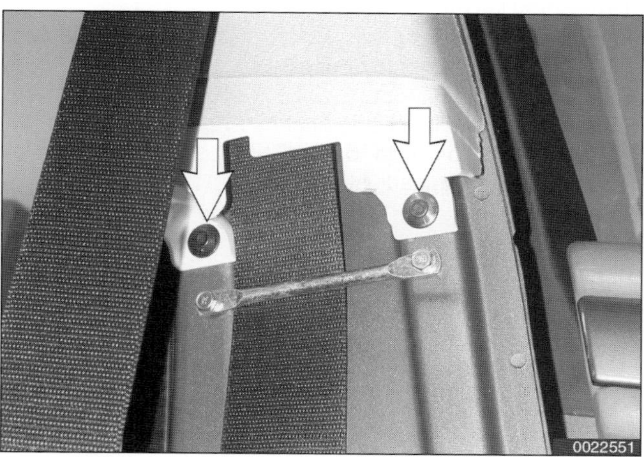
0022551

Remove upper B-pillar plastic trim expansion rivets (**arrows**).

Pull B-pillar upper trim down to remove.

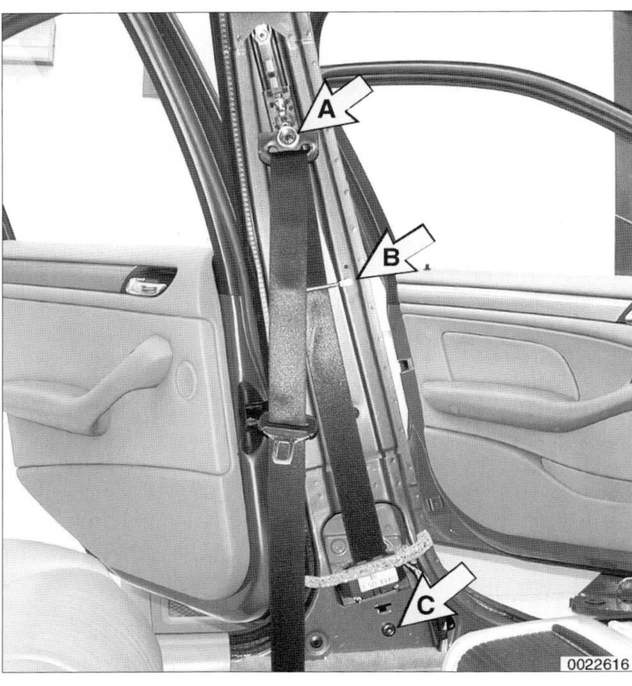

Remove automatic reel from B-pillar:

- Remove upper seat belt anchor bolt (**A**).
- Remove cross-brace mounting bolts (**B**).
- Remove sound insulation at base of B-pillar. Then remove automatic seat belt reel mounting bolt (**C**).
- Lift out reel.

– If it is necessary to remove sliding seat belt height adjuster, unscrew mounting bolts from B-pillar.

– Installation is reverse of removal. Install automatic reel housing to B-pillar by sliding tab into locating slot.

Tightening torques

- Front seat to floor (M10) . . . . 45 Nm (33 ft-lb)
- Seat belt anchor bar to door sill . . . . 31 Nm (23 ft-lb)
- Seat belt to seat . . . . 48 Nm (35 ft-lb)
- Seat belt to B-pillar sliding anchor . . . . . 31 Nm (23 ft-lb)
- Seat belt reel to B-pillar bottom . . . . 31 Nm (23 ft-lb)
- Sliding seat height adjuster to B-pillar. . . . . 24 Nm (18 ft-lb)

Seat-integrated seat belt system (SGS) (Convertible)

Convertible front seats are designed with integrated seat belts which channel the forces acting on a front seat occupant during a collision to the reinforced floor.

The fixed anchor point and the seat belt lock / tensioner are mounted on the seat frame. The upper seat belt guide is attached to the headrest. In this way the belt is optimally positioned regardless of headrest position.

The inertia reel is attached to the inside of the seat backrest. The mechanism is connected to the backrest hinge through a lever and a cable drive (coupler mechanism). As the angle of the backrest is adjusted, the cable drive will change the angle of the inertia lock. In this way the reel is in the proper position for locking at any seat back angle.

The seat belt lock and tensioner on the SGS system is a pyrotechnic device similar to that on other E46 models. When working on SGS belts, be sure to read **Seat belt warnings** in this repair group.

NOTE —

- *SGS seat belt removal can only be carried out with the seat out of the car. See* **520 Seats**.
- *Once the seat has been removed, partially disassemble the backrest to access the seat belt mechanism. See accompanying illustration for assembly details and torque values.*

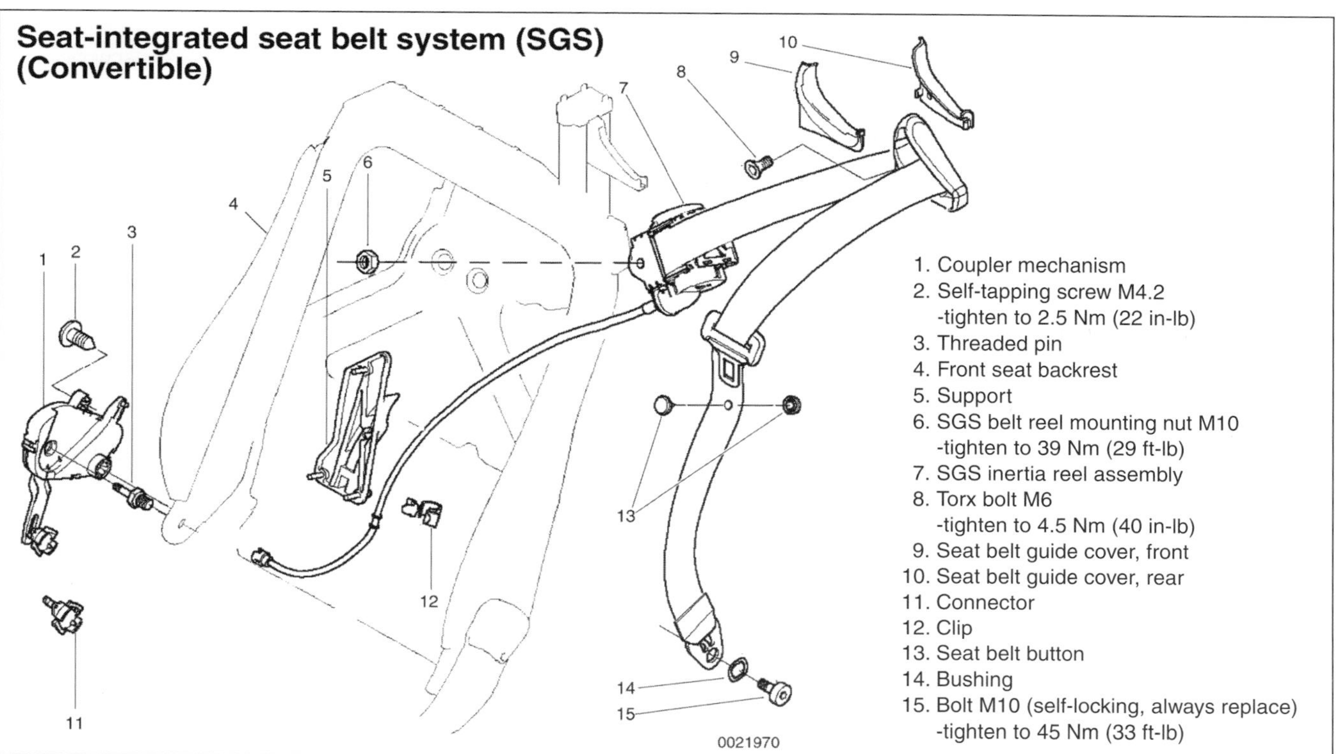

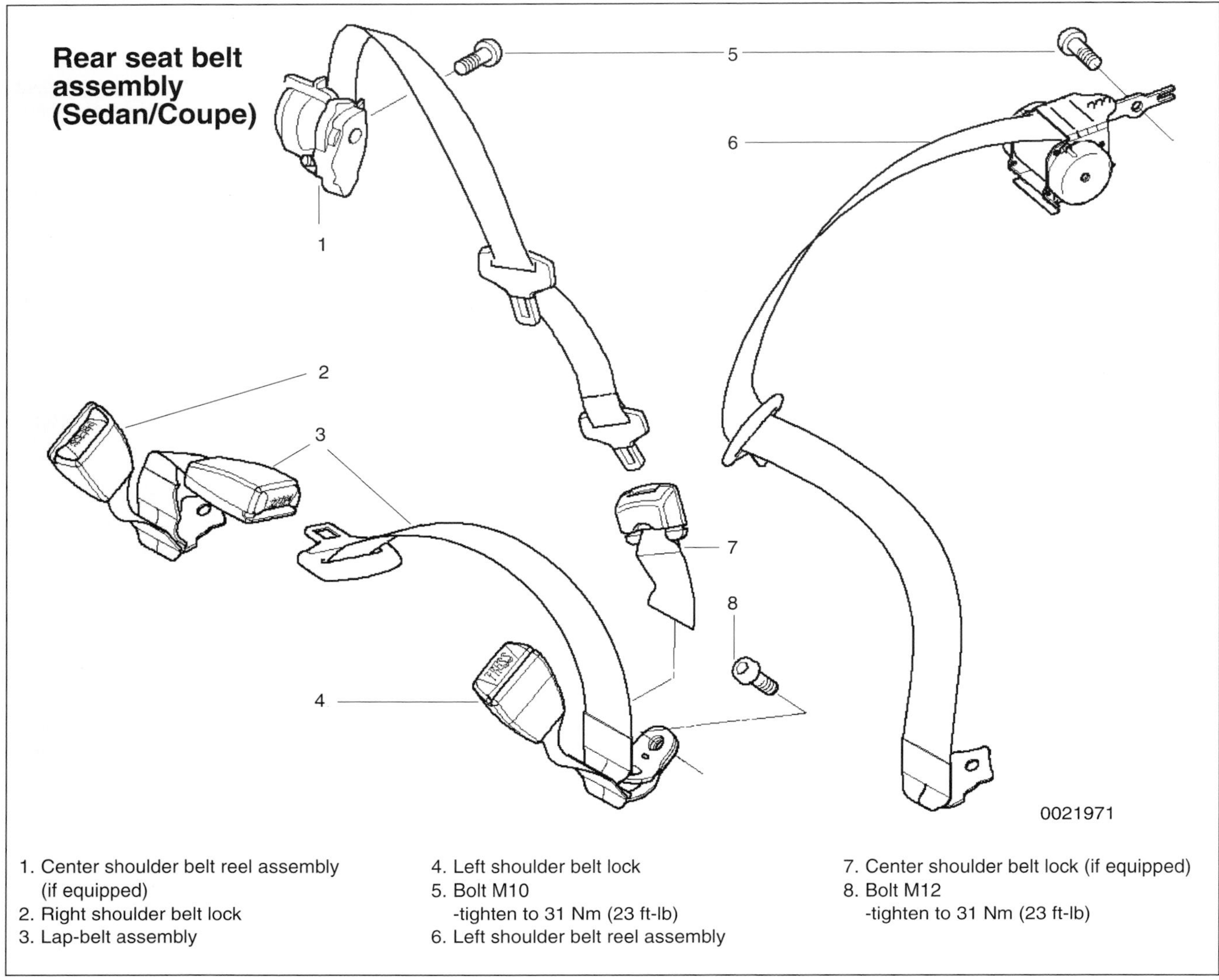

1. Center shoulder belt reel assembly (if equipped)
2. Right shoulder belt lock
3. Lap-belt assembly
4. Left shoulder belt lock
5. Bolt M10
   -tighten to 31 Nm (23 ft-lb)
6. Left shoulder belt reel assembly
7. Center shoulder belt lock (if equipped)
8. Bolt M12
   -tighten to 31 Nm (23 ft-lb)

REAR SEAT BELT ASSEMBLY

Rear seat belts (Sedan, Coupe)

– Remove rear parcel shelf to access shoulder belt assembly mounting bolts.

– Remove rear seat cushion to access rear seat belt lock mounting bolts. See **520 Seats**.

– The accompanying illustration provides information on rear seat belt component locations and fastener torques.

– When installing seat belt lock straps:
  - Install right lock strap (which is shorter) underneath middle lock strap.
  - Install left lock strap underneath middle lap belt strap.
  - Metal strap ends must rest against stop on floor underneath seat.

Rear seat belts (Sport Wagon)

– Center shoulder belt:
  - Remove shoulder belt guide trim at top of seat backrest. Feed belt out through slot in trim.
  - Working in cargo compartment, partially remove backrest cover to access shoulder belt reel.
  - Remove shoulder belt reel mounting bolt inside backrest.

NOTE —

Remove Bowden cable from backrest brackets and unhook from backrest release latch. Center seat belt reel can be then be removed.

– Outboard shoulder belt:
  - Remove roof-pillar (C-pillar) trim.
  - Remove center shoulder belt.

– Lift up rear seat cushion(s) to access rear seat belt lock mounting bolt(s).

The accompanying illustration provides information on rear seat belt component locations and fastener torques.

– When installing seat belt lock straps:
  - Install right belt lock strap (which is shorter) underneath center belt lock strap.
  - Install left belt lock strap underneath center lap belt strap.
  - Metal strap ends must rest against stop on floor underneath seat.

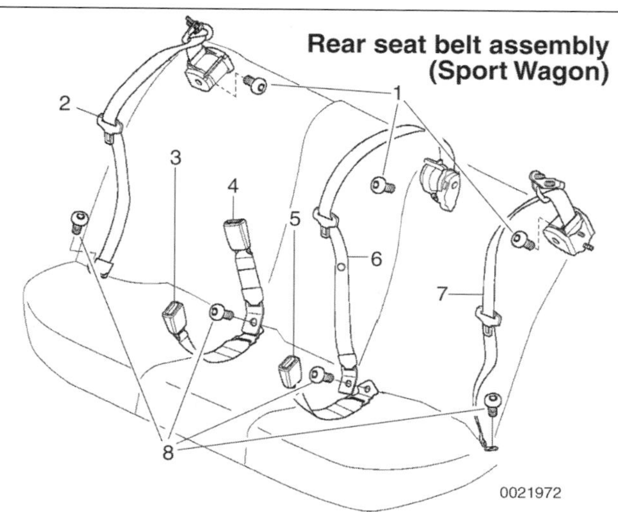

1. Bolt M10
   -tighten to 31 Nm (23 ft-lb)
2. Right shoulder belt reel assembly.
3. Center belt lock
4. Right belt lock
5. Left belt lock
6. Center shoulder belt reel assembly
7. Left shoulder belt reel assembly
8. Bolt M12
   -tighten to 31 Nm (23 ft-lb)

Rear seat belts (Convertible)

– Access shoulder belt or seat belt lock mounting bolts:
  - Remove center armrest.
  - Push shoulder belts toward sides and feed out of top guides.
  - Lift seat cushion up and forward to remove.
  - Remove lower backrest securing screws located below backrest. Lift backrest straight up and unhook from tabs in back.
  - Remove rear head restraints by pulling straight up.
  - Remove cover of rollover protection bars for right and left side.
  - Open convertible top compartment cover.

– Shoulder belt reels are bolted to convertible top storage compartment.

The accompanying illustration provides information on rear seat belt component locations and fastener torques.

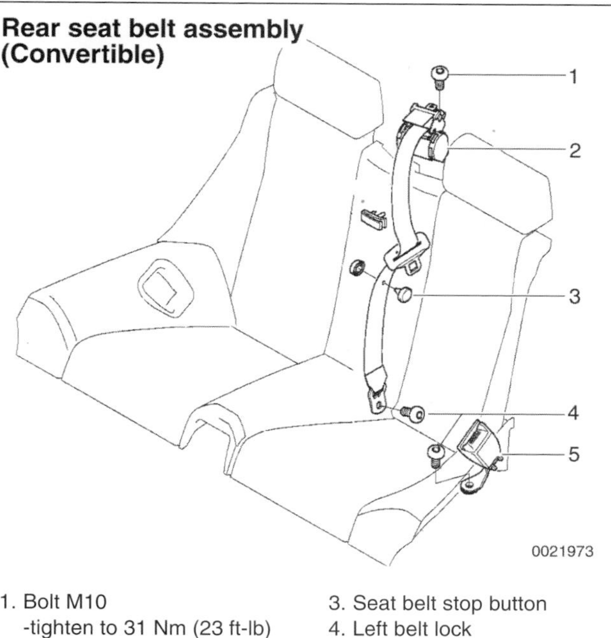

1. Bolt M10
   -tighten to 31 Nm (23 ft-lb)
2. Left shoulder belt reel assembly.
3. Seat belt stop button
4. Left belt lock
5. Bolt M12
   -tighten to 31 Nm (23 ft-lb)

721 Airbag System (SRS)

GENERAL

This repair group covers airbag components. Airbag system repair and fault diagnosis is not covered here. Diagnostics, component testing, and airbag system repair should be carried out by trained BMW service technicians.

NOTE —
- *Airbags are also known as the Supplemental Restraint System (SRS). In the E46 cars the occupant safety system is called the Multiple Restraint System (MRS).*
- *Special test equipment is required to retrieve airbag fault codes, diagnose system faults, and reset / turn off the airbag warning light. The warning light remains ON until any problem has been corrected and the fault memory has been cleared.*

Individual airbag system components can only be tested electronically when installed in the car using BMW scan tool (DISplus, GT1, MoDiC) or equivalent.

Special tools

Most airbag system repairs can be performed with normal shop tools. Use BMW special tool 00 9 321 or equivalent plastic prying tool to pry out plastic interior parts without damage or marring.

Special tools

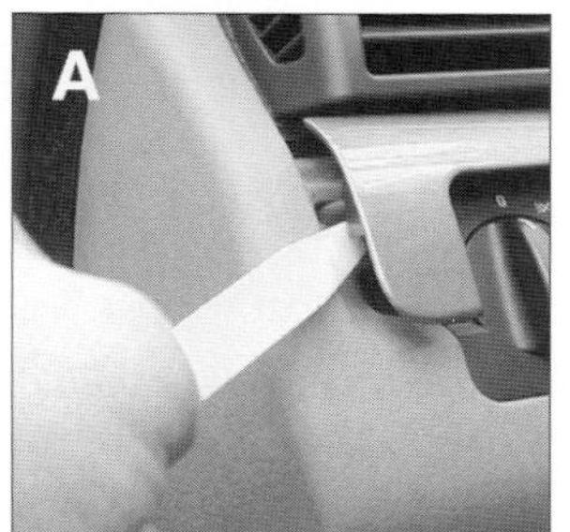

A BMW 00 9 321 . . . . .Plastic prying tool

E46 airbags

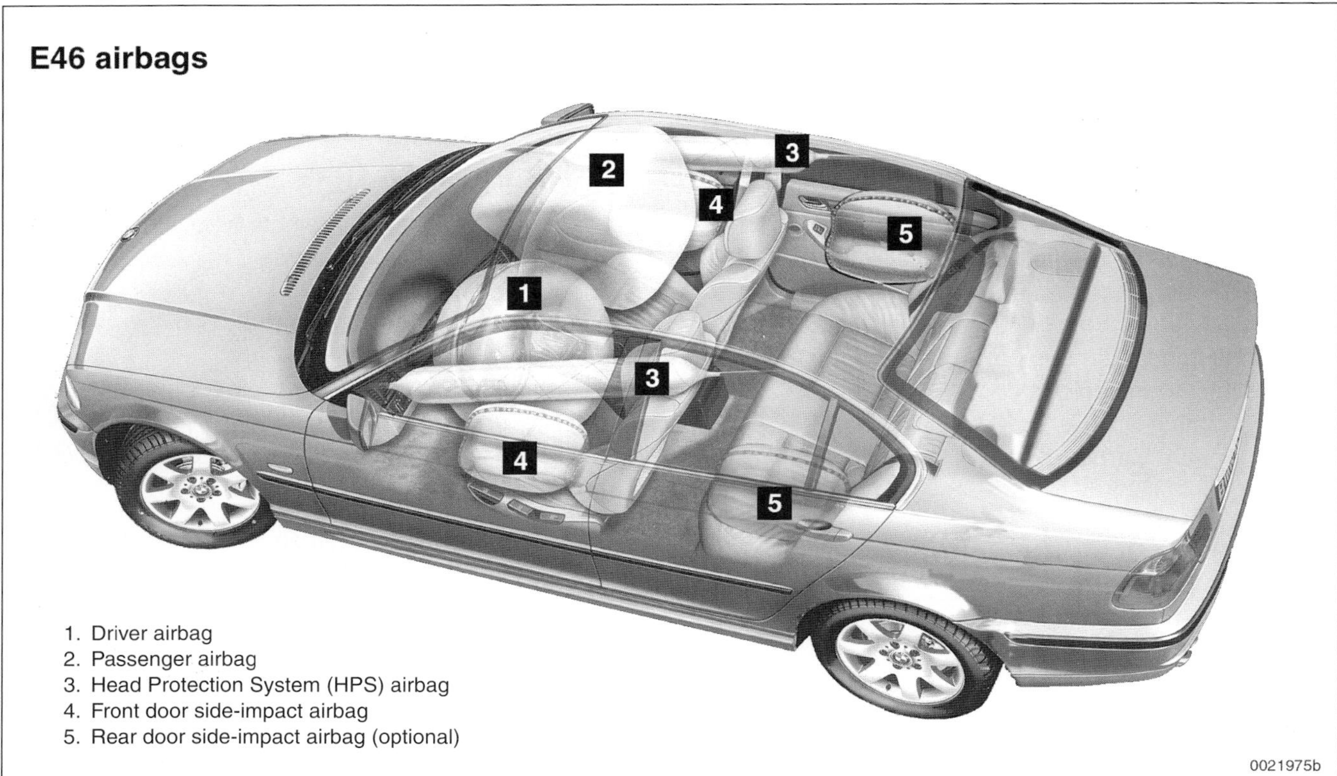

1. Driver airbag
2. Passenger airbag
3. Head Protection System (HPS) airbag
4. Front door side-impact airbag
5. Rear door side-impact airbag (optional)

0021975b

Multiple Restraint System (MRS)

The E46 airbag system consists of the following:

- Driver airbag in the center of the steering wheel hub
- Passenger airbag in the right side of the dashboard
- Front side-impact airbags, one in each front door
- Head Protection System (HPS) airbags, one in each front roof pillar (A-pillar)

As an option, Sedan or Sport Wagon may be equipped with:

- Rear side-impact airbags, one in each rear door

Airbags, seat belt pyrotechnic tensioners and Battery safety Terminal (BST) are integrated into the Multiple Restraint System (MRS).

Two generations of MRS technology were employed in E46 cars:

- **MRS II** from model introduction to 08 / 1999
- **MRS III** 09 / 1999 and later

The primary difference between the two systems is the use of 2-stage airbags in MRS III.

The MRS control module is located on the center tunnel, underneath the rug below the parking brake handle. If the module is replaced, recode and program new unit using BMW scan tool (DISplus, GT1, MoDiC) or equivalent.

2-stage airbag

Beginning with the 2000 model year (09/1999 production), 2-stage airbags were used in the front. This ensures that the force of airbag inflation is not greater than necessary to provide protection. The airbags are designed to provide "soft" deployment if the acceleration sensor detects a low-speed impact, with a "hard" deployment only in higher speed impacts.

Head protection airbags (HPS)

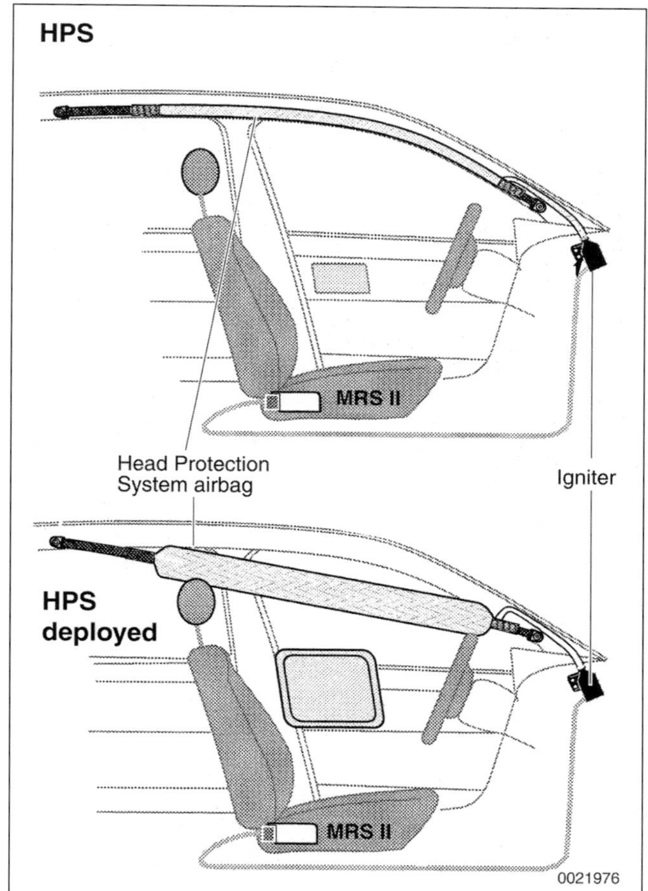

This protective system covers a large area between the front roof pillar (A-pillar) and the rear section of the roof. A hollow flexible tube about 5 feet long and 1.5 inches in diameter is anchored inside the A-pillar and front roof rail and concealed by interior trim.

Upon severe side impact, a gas generator unit fills the head protection system (HPS) tube with inert gas. The expanding tube pops out of the trim to form a straight tube 5.1 inches in diameter and stretched in a straight line from the lower windshield pillar to above the rear door. The inflated tube is located to prevent the front occupant's head from contacting the A-pillar, the B-pillar, or side window. The tube's sloping position allows protection for both short and tall people. The inflated tube is stiff enough to retain much of its effectiveness even if the window is broken. The HPS tube remains inflated for approximately 7 to 8 seconds to extend protection time in case the vehicle encounters additional side impacts during the crash.

BMW literature uses the acronyms HPS and ITS interchangeably for the Head Protection System.

Rear side-impact airbags

Similar to the standard-equipment front side-impact airbags, the rear airbags are built into the doors of 4-door models. These were offered as a special order option on certain models only. They can be deactivated to protect infants or small children riding in the rear seat.

To activate or deactivate, use BMW scan tool (DISplus, GT1, MoDiC) or equivalent.

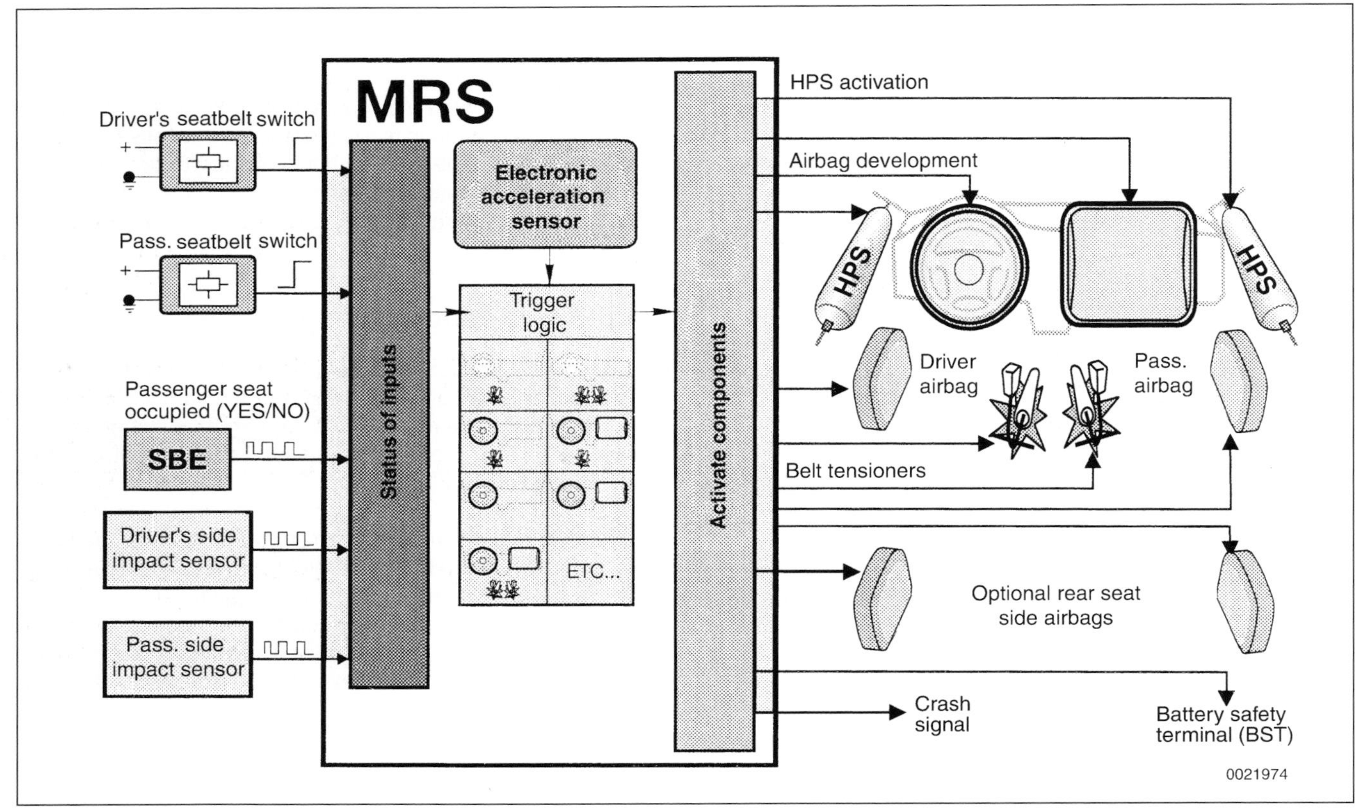

MRS deployment logic

Primary sensing and triggering functions for the front-impact airbags and seat belt tensioners are combined into a single MRS control module located above the center tunnel, under the rug, beneath the parking brake handle.

Side-impact and head protection airbags are controlled by separate sensors, one for each side of the vehicle.

MRS deployment logic provides two thresholds for the activation of the safety system, depending upon the severity of impact and whether or not occupants have fastened their seat belts:

- Belts fastened, low impact speed: Lower deployment threshold. Only seat belt pyrotechnic tensioners are deployed.
- Belts fastened, high impact speed: Higher deployment threshold. Tensioners and front-impact airbags are deployed.
- Belts not fastened, low or high impact speed: Airbags are deployed.
- Passenger seat not occupied: Neither belt tensioner nor airbag is deployed on that side.

B305721001

Airbag warning light

The MRS control module detects and stores system status.

The airbag warning light in the instrument cluster displays the status of the airbag system when the ignition key is in "accessory" or ON positions.

- System normal: Warning light ON briefly, then OFF.
- System malfunction: Warning light fails to come ON.
- System malfunction: Warning light ON briefly, then OFF and ON again.

The airbag warning light also comes ON if seat belt pyrotechnic tensioners are triggered.

Airbag system warnings

See also **Seat belt warnings** in **720 Seat Belts**.

WARNING —

- *If the airbag warning light is ON, the airbags will not be triggered in case of an accident. Be sure to have the system inspected and repaired immediately.*
- *The airbag is an explosive device. Handled improperly or without adequate safeguards, the airbag system can be very dangerous. Observe special precautions prior to any work at or near the airbags.*
- *The airbag is a vehicle safety system. Serious injury may result if system service is attempted by persons unfamiliar with the BMW airbag system and its approved service procedures. BMW advises that all inspection and service be performed by an authorized BMW dealer.*
- *Disconnect the battery and cover the negative (–) battery terminal with an insulator before starting diagnostic, troubleshooting or service work associated with the airbags, and before doing any welding on the car.*
- *After disconnecting the battery, wait 1 minute before beginning work on airbag components.*
- *Airbag system components can only be tested electrically when installed, using BMW scan tool (DISplus, GT1, MoDiC) or equivalent.*
- *If an airbag has been activated due to an accident, BMW specifies that airbag components be replaced. For more information on post-collision airbag service, see an authorized BMW dealer.*
- *Do not fire an airbag unit prior to disposal. It must be fired by a special disposal company or shipped back to BMW in the packaging of the new components.*
- *When removing a fired airbag unit, avoid contact with the skin; wear gloves. In case of skin contact, wash with water.*

> ***WARNING —***
> - *Do not allow airbag system components to come in contact with cleaning solutions or grease. Do not subject airbag components to temperatures above 167°F (75°C). When reconnecting the battery, no person should be inside the vehicle.*
> - *Place an airbag unit that has been removed from its packaging with the padded side facing upward. Do not leave an airbag unit unattended.*
> - *If the airbag unit or airbag control module has been dropped from a height of ½ meter (1½ ft.) or more, do not instal.*

AIRBAG ELECTRONICS

Airbag harnesses and connectors

If an airbag system electrical harness shows visible signs of wear or damage, replace or repair.

— To repair airbag harness:
- Disconnect negative (–) cable from battery and cover negative terminal with insulating material.
- Disconnect harness connector at airbag module or on intermediate plug.
- Cut through one cable, then the other, and repair.

> ***CAUTION —***
> - *Do not under any circumstances cut through both wires of an airbag harness at the same time.*
> - *Perform only one repair on an airbag harness wire. If more than one spot is damaged, replace the entire section of harness.*

MRS control module, replacing

— Disconnect negative (–) cable from battery and cover negative terminal with insulating material.

> ***CAUTION —***
> *Prior to disconnecting the battery, read the battery disconnection cautions given at the front of this manual.*

— Remove center utility tray between front seats. See **513 Interior Trim**.

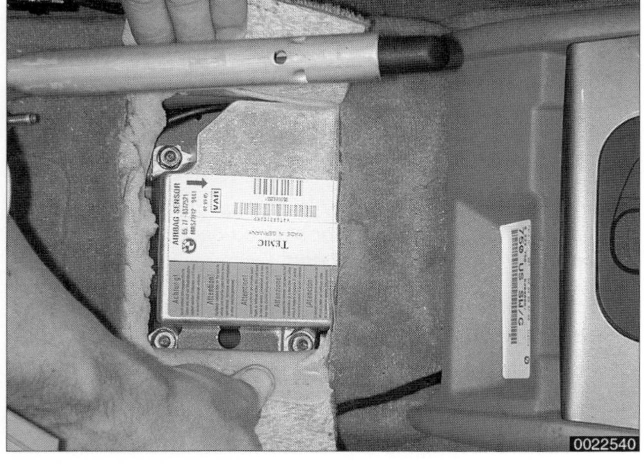

◀ Cut open carpet on top of center tunnel to access MRS II module.

— Remove module mounting nuts and lift up control module. Detach electrical harness connector.

— Installation is reverse of removal. Be sure to reconnect MRS module ground cable.

— Recode and program new module using BMW scan tool (DISplus, GT1, MoDiC) or equivalent.

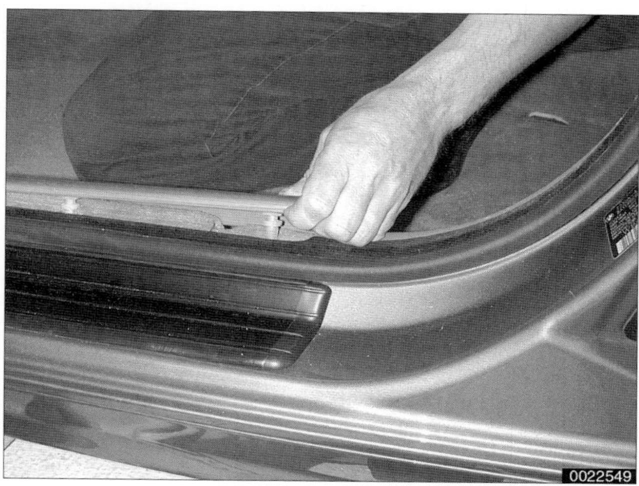

Side-impact crash sensor, removing and installing

– Make sure ignition key is OFF.

– Remove front seat. See **520 Seats**.

◄ Remove plastic door sill trim. Lift to release clips at one end, then slide off. Fold up carpet towards rear seat floor. If necessary, remove floor level heater duct.

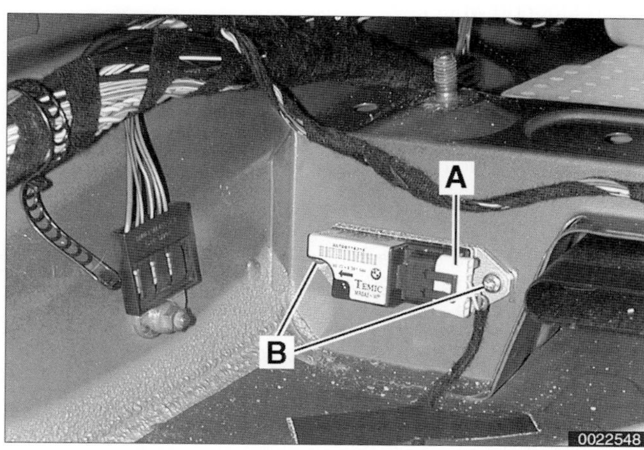

◄ Detach electrical connector from crash sensor (**A**). Remove sensor retaining screws (**B**) and remove sensor.

– Installation is reverse of removal. Make sure arrow on sensor points to door sill.

AIRBAGS

Driver airbag, removing and installing

– Disconnect negative (–) cable from battery and cover terminal with insulating material.

> ***WARNING —***
> *After disconnecting the battery, wait 1 minute before beginning work on airbag components.*

> ***CAUTION —***
> *Prior to disconnecting the battery, read the battery disconnection cautions given at the front of this manual.*

◄ Multifunction (MFL) steering wheel:

- Working behind steering wheel, completely loosen Torx screws (T30) while holding airbag in place.
- Support airbag unit to prevent it from falling out.

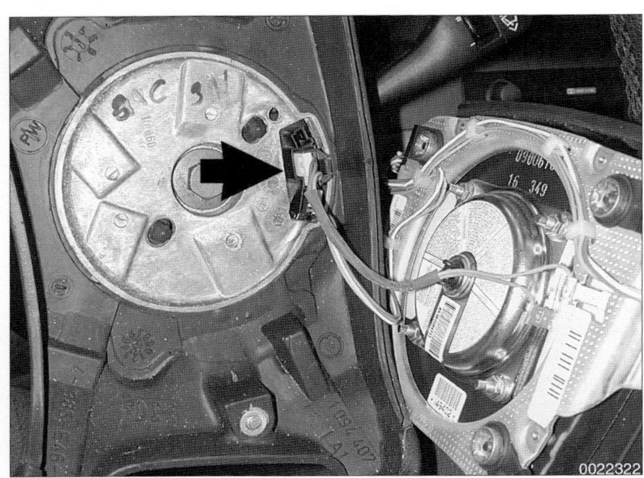

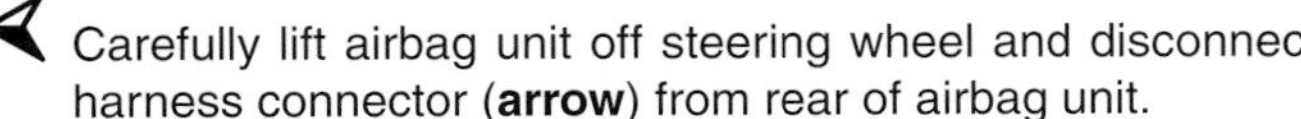

Carefully lift airbag unit off steering wheel and disconnect harness connector (**arrow**) from rear of airbag unit.

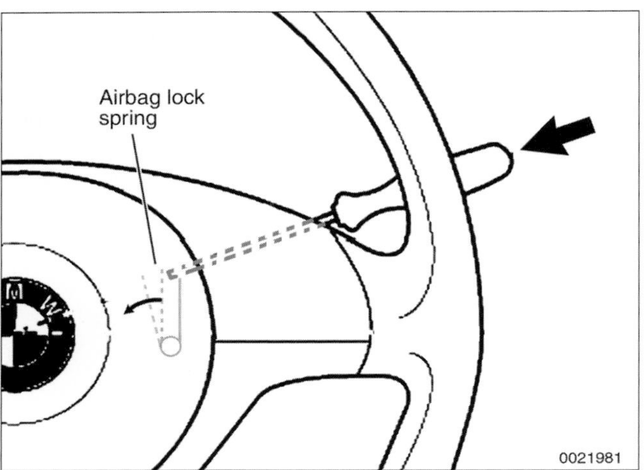

Sport steering wheel:

- Insert screwdriver through opening in rear of steering wheel and push against spring tension to release airbag unit lock.
- Repeat procedure on other side of steering wheel.
- Lift off airbag unit and detach electrical connectors.

> ***WARNING —***
> - *Store the removed airbag unit with the horn pad facing up. If stored facing down, accidental deployment could propel it violently into the air, causing injury.*
> - *Once an airbag is removed, do not drive the car.*
> - *Do not connect the battery with the airbag disconnected. A fault code will be stored, setting off the airbag warning light. Special tools are needed to reset the fault memory.*

— Installation is reverse of removal.

- MFL steering wheel: Torque airbag using specification listed below.
- Sport steering wheel: Press airbag unit mounting pins into spring locks in steering wheel until they snap in firmly.

> ***CAUTION —***
> *Do not pinch airbag harness in center of steering wheel when installing airbag.*

Tightening torque

- Airbag to steering wheel (MFL). . . . . 8 Nm (71 in-lb)

Once the airbag unit is installed and all other service procedures have been completed, start the engine and check that the airbag warning light goes OFF. If the warning light stays ON, the airbag system will not function as designed. Have the system diagnosed and repaired by an authorized BMW dealer.

Passenger airbag, removing and installing

– Disconnect negative (–) cable from battery and cover negative terminal with insulating material.

> ***WARNING —***
> *After disconnecting the battery, wait 1 minute before beginning work on airbag components.*

> ***CAUTION —***
> *Prior to disconnecting the battery, read the battery disconnection cautions given at the front of this manual.*

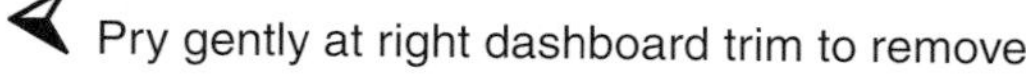

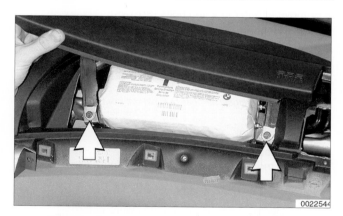

◄ Pry gently at right dashboard trim to remove.

> ***CAUTION —***
> *To avoid marring interior trim, work with a plastic prying tool.*

– Remove right dashboard fresh air outlet mounting screws and pull outlet out of dash.

0022542

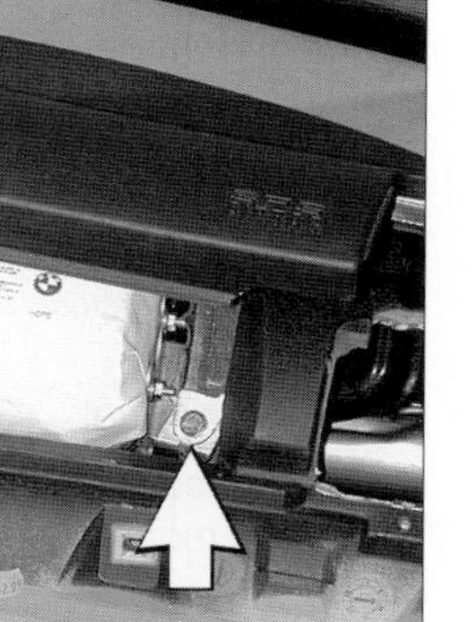

0022544

◄ Lift cover from top of passenger side airbag on dashboard.

- Remove cover strap retaining bolts (**arrows**) to detach cover completely from dashboard.

> ***CAUTION —***
> *The plastic retainer at the right end of the cover may snap during removal. Be sure to have extra retainers on hand for reassembly*

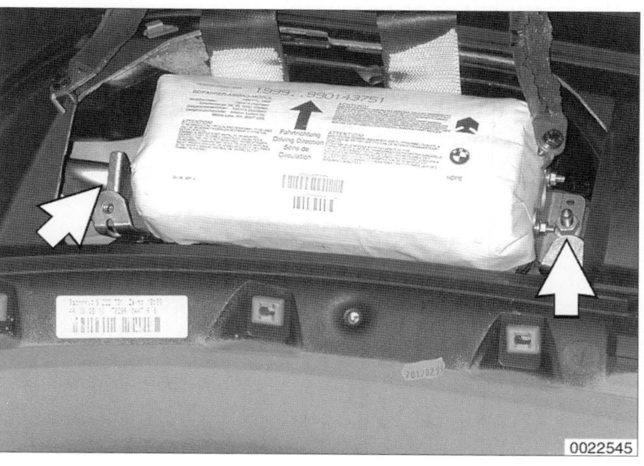

0022545

◄ Remove airbag mounting fasteners (**arrows**).

– Lift airbag and disconnect electrical harness connector. Remove airbag.

> ***WARNING —***
> *Store the removed airbag unit with the soft pad facing up. If stored facing down, accidental deployment could propel it violently into the air, causing injury.*

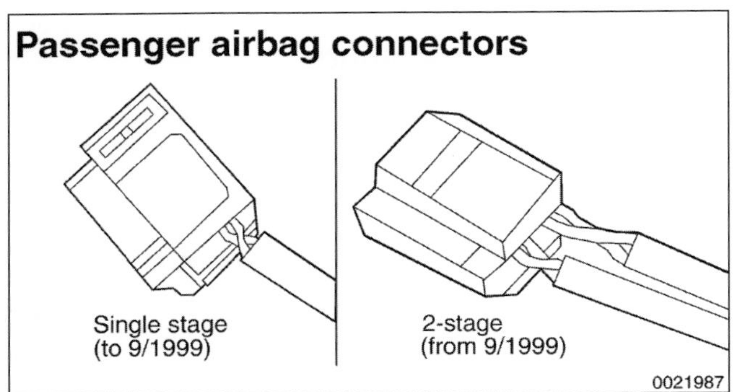

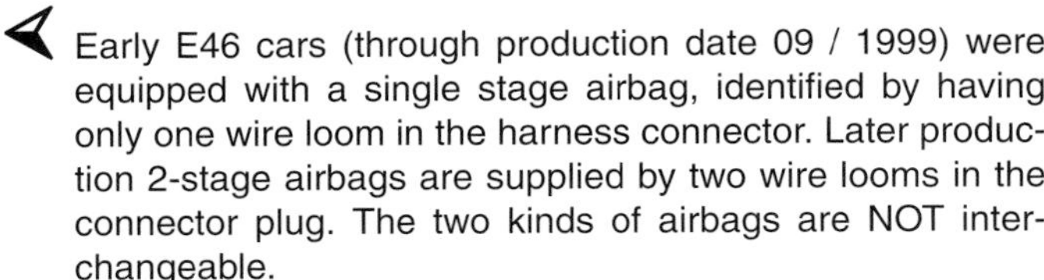

Early E46 cars (through production date 09 / 1999) were equipped with a single stage airbag, identified by having only one wire loom in the harness connector. Later production 2-stage airbags are supplied by two wire looms in the connector plug. The two kinds of airbags are NOT interchangeable.

– Installation is reverse of removal. Make sure wiring harness is not pinched when installing airbag unit in dashboard.

Tightening torques
- Airbag cover strap to dashboard (M6) . . . . 9 Nm (7 ft-lb)
- Passenger air bag to dashboard (M8) . . 22 Nm (16 ft-lb)

Door mounted side-impact airbag, removing and installing

– Disconnect negative (–) cable from battery and cover negative terminal with insulating material.

> ***CAUTION —***
> *Prior to disconnecting the battery, read the battery disconnection cautions given at the front of this manual.*

– Remove inside door panel. See **411 Doors**.

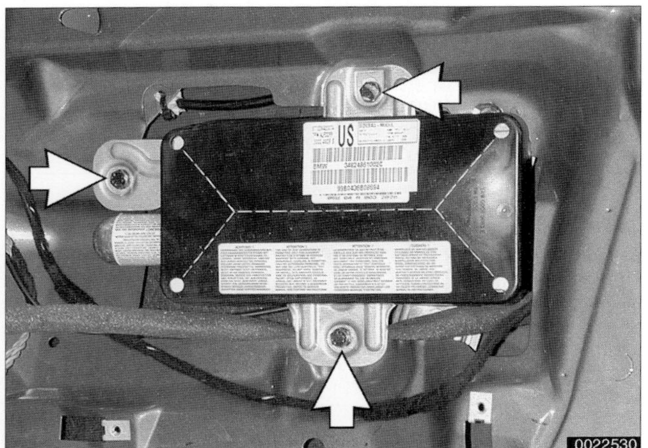

Front door airbag:
- Remove airbag mounting bolts (**arrows**).
- Turn over airbag unit and cut off electrical harness wire tie.
- Detach harness connector.

> ***CAUTION —***
> *When removing and installing the airbag unit, pay attention to the routing of the electrical harness to avoid kinks or breaks in the wire.*

– Rear door airbag:
- Detach electrical harness connector.
- Remove mounting bolts and remove airbag from door.

– Installation is reverse of removal.
- Route electrical harnesses as they were before.
- Use new wire ties as necessary.
- Use new self-locking mounting bolts.

Tightening torque
- Side-impact airbag to door . . . . 9 Nm (7 ft-lb)

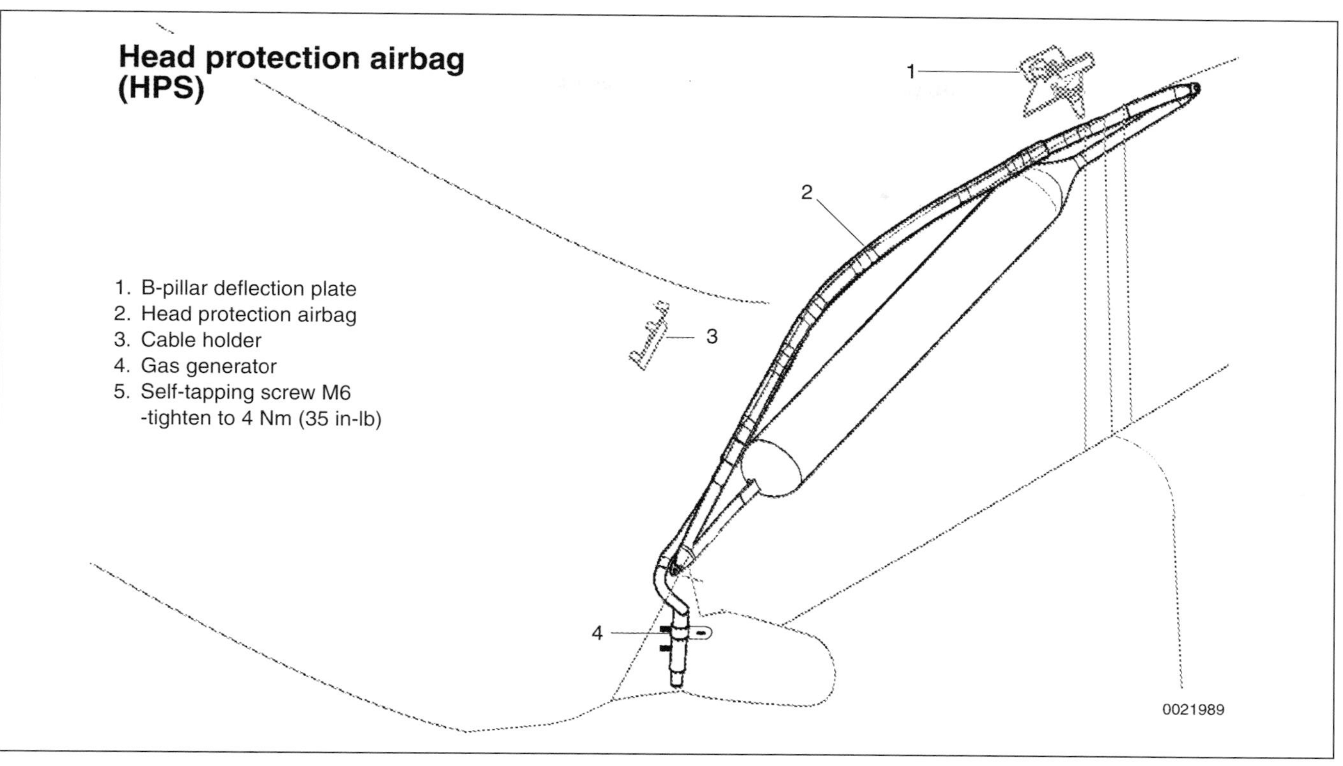

Head protection airbag (HPS) components

Replacement of a head protection airbag (HPS) is an extensive operation. Replacement includes removal of the following components:

- Complete dashboard
- Complete headliner
- Windshield pillar (A-pillar) trim
- Door pillar (B-pillar) trim

– Before starting work on HPS airbag, disconnect negative (-) battery cable and cover terminal with insulating material.

> ***CAUTION —***
>
> *Prior to disconnecting the battery, read the battery disconnection cautions given at the front of this manual.*

Tightening torque

- HPS airbag to body. . . . . 11 Nm (8 ft-lb)
- HPS airbag mounting bracket to A or B-pillar. .2.5 Nm (22 in-lb)
- HPS gas generator to dashboard reinforcement M6 self-tapping screw. . . . . 4 Nm (35 in-lb)

ELE Electrical Wiring Diagrams

ELECTRICAL COMPONENT LOCATIONS (relay and fuse positions, ground locations)see **Repair Group 610**

GENERAL

This section presents electrical wiring schematics for E46 models.

NOTE —
*A supplemental wiring diagram section, which includes late model engine management and other late model system schematics, can be found on page **ELE-317**.*

Special tools

Electrical repairs require the use of appropriate tools.

Special Tools

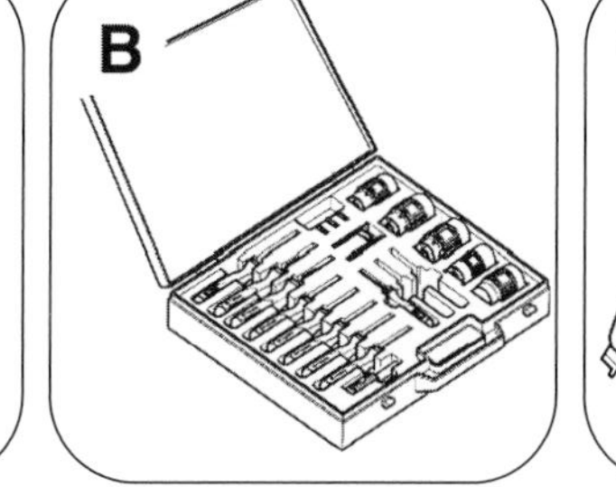
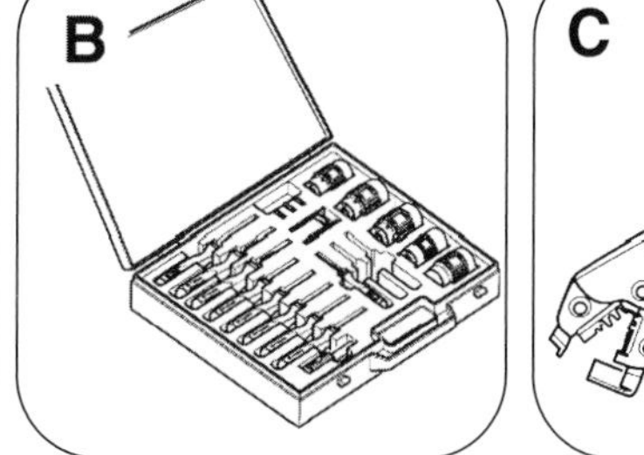

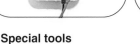

Special tools

A Fluke 87 ... Automotive digital multimeter
B BMW 61 1 150 ... Wiring harness end repair tools
C BMW 61 9 041 ... Wire end crimp tool

How to find a circuit or electrical component

- Look up the component or circuit in **Wiring Diagram Index**.
- Go to the main schematics page indicated for the component.
- Find the BMW electrical component code for connectors, fuses or other components that are connected to the circuit you are researching.
- Look up (by code or name) the components in **Wiring Diagram Index**.
- Go back to the schematics page indicated by the table to continue following the circuit.

NOTE —
Component locations can be found in **610 Electrical Component Locations**.

Schematic conventions

The schematics divide the vehicle electrical system into individual circuits. Interacting electrical components are shown on one schematic.

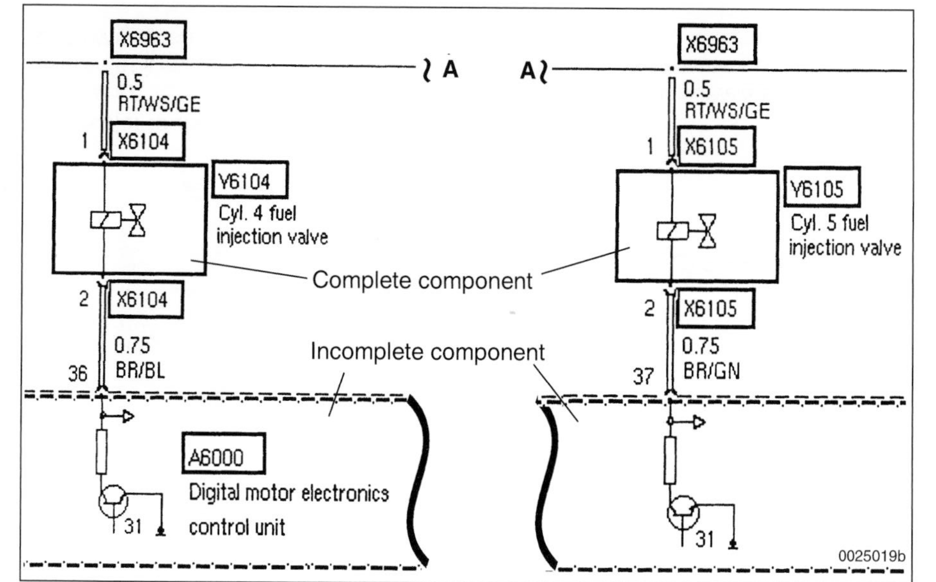

If a schematic spans several pages, this fact is clearly indicated at the top of each page.

- If a component, such as a control module, continues across several pages, a vertical tilde (≀) indicates the break.
- If a circuit continues across several pages, a vertical tilde and matching letters (**A**, **B**, **C**, etc.) indicate the break and the matching wires.
- A component (or connector) which is completely represented in the schematic is shown as a solid box.
- A component (or connector) which has other connectors in addition to the ones shown in the schematic is shown with a dashed line.
- Alternate current paths for different models are indicated by large brackets ().

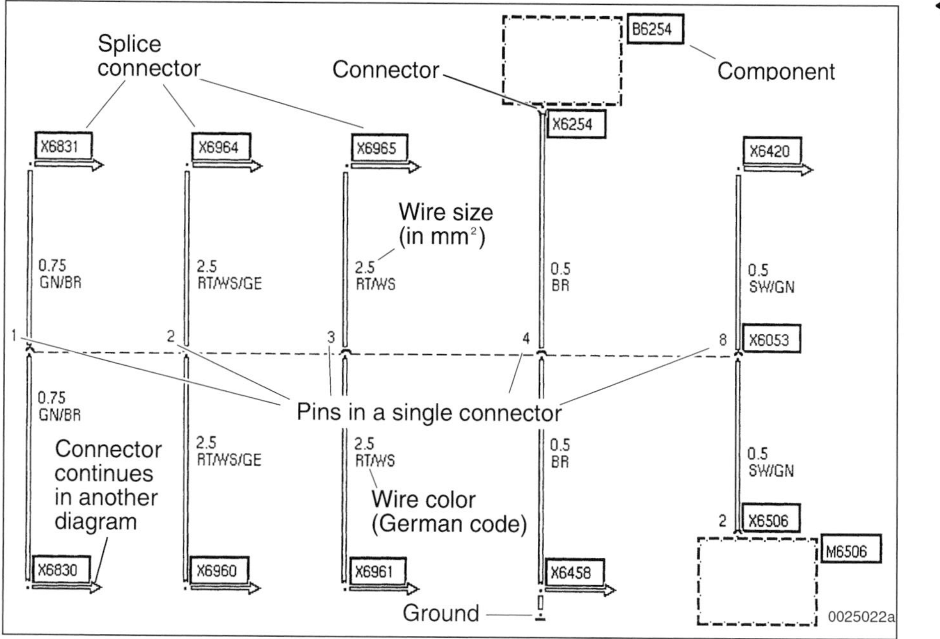

Electrical components are represented in such a way that their general layout and function are self-explanatory. They are usually arranged in the diagrams so that the current path can be followed from positive at the top to negative at the bottom.

Switches and relays are always shown in rest position (generally OFF).

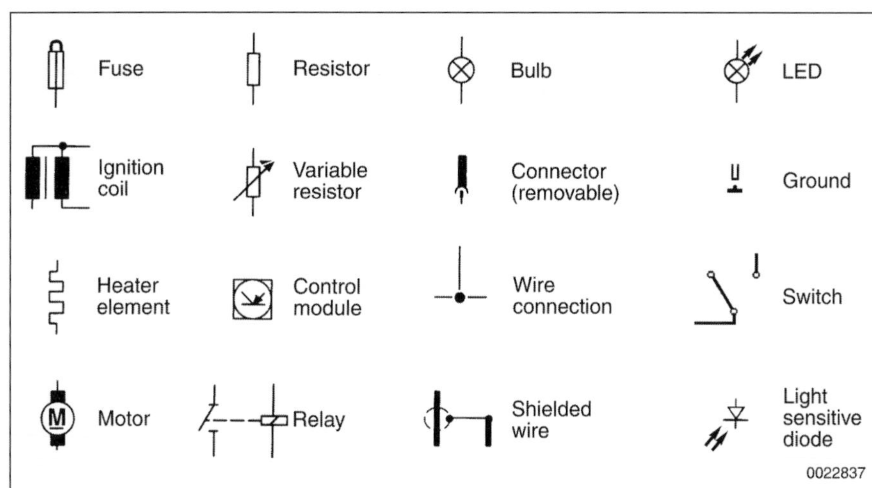

Symbols

The schematics utilize simplified electrical symbols.

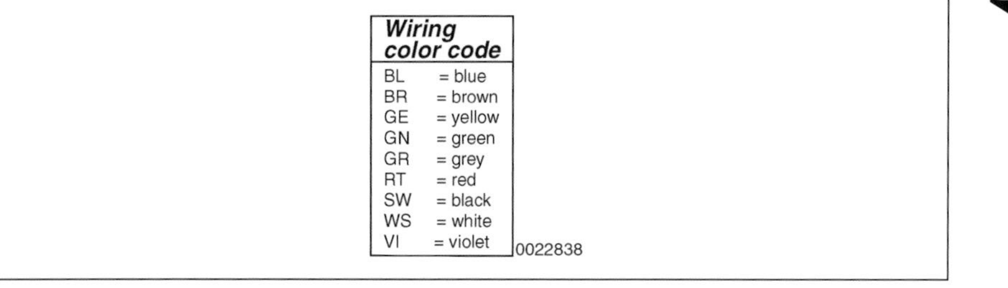

Wiring color code

BL	= blue
BR	= brown
GE	= yellow
GN	= green
GR	= grey
RT	= red
SW	= black
WS	= white
VI	= violet

0022838

Wire insulation colors in this section are given with color abbreviations.

Wire sizes follow the DIN (European) convention.

NOTE —

For example, an 0.5 wire is ½ mm^2 in cross-section area. This corresponds to approx. SAE 16 gauge wire.

Porsche identifies many electrical circuits with unique designations which follow the DIN standard. Also, BMW designates electrical components, junctions and grounds with a unique alphanumeric designation, most of which also ollow the DIN standard. See **600 Electrical System–General**

ELECTRICAL COMPONENT INDEX

ELECTRICAL COMPONENT INDEX *(CONT.)*

ELECTRICAL COMPONENT INDEX *(CONT.)*

ELECTRICAL COMPONENT INDEX *(CONT.)*

ELECTRICAL COMPONENT INDEX *(CONT.)*

ELECTRICAL COMPONENT INDEX *(CONT.)*

ELECTRICAL COMPONENT INDEX *(CONT.)*

ELECTRICAL COMPONENT INDEX *(CONT.)*

ELECTRICAL COMPONENT INDEX *(CONT.)*

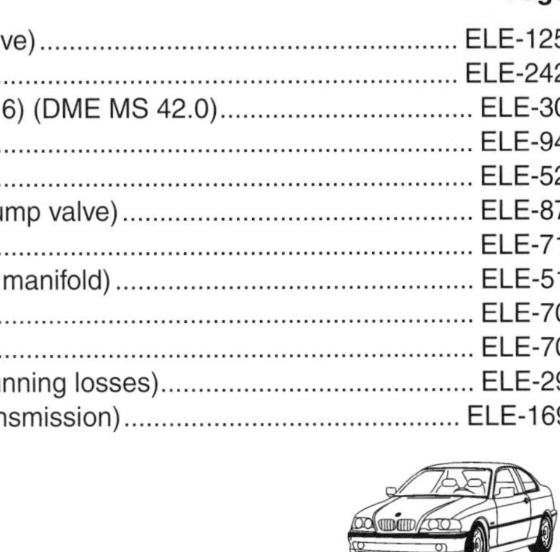

Fuse carrier, engine electronics (A8680)

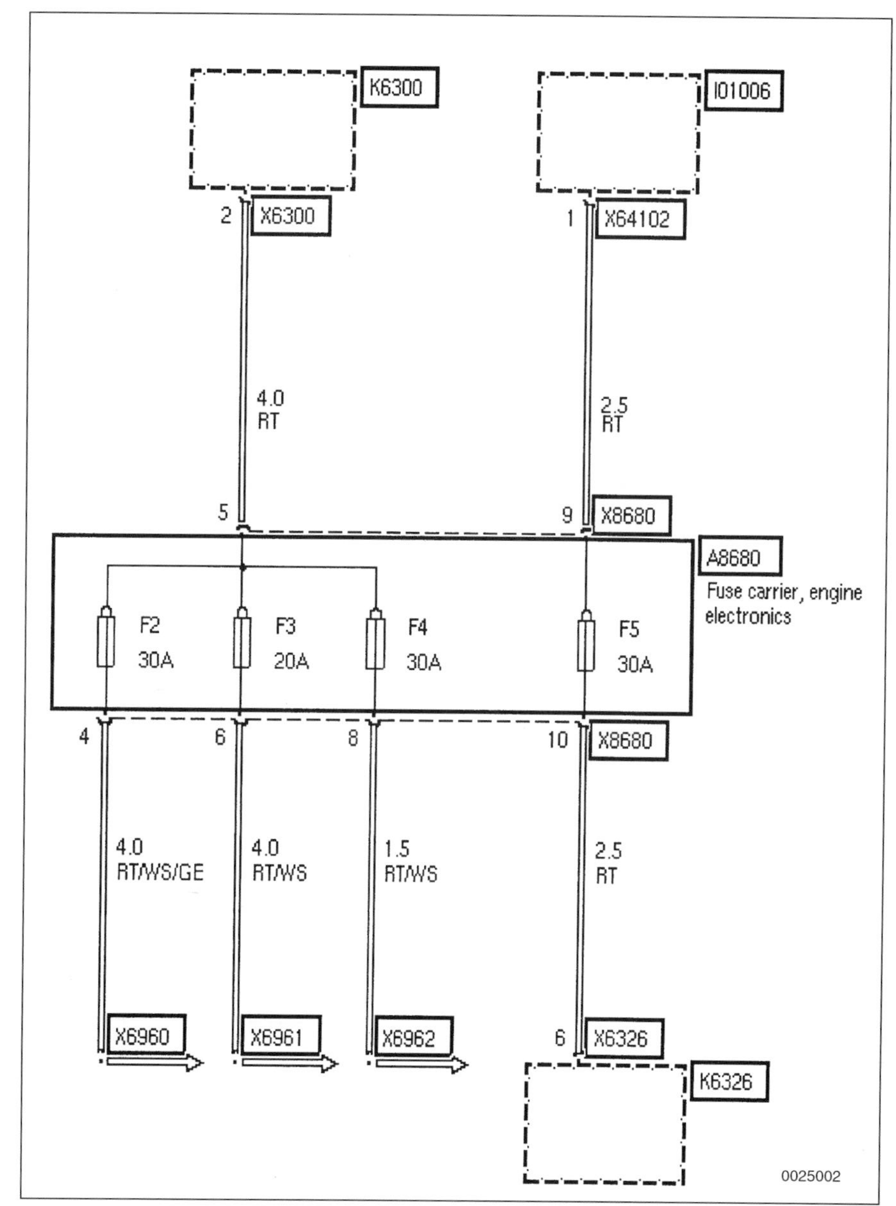

Splice connector (X6961)

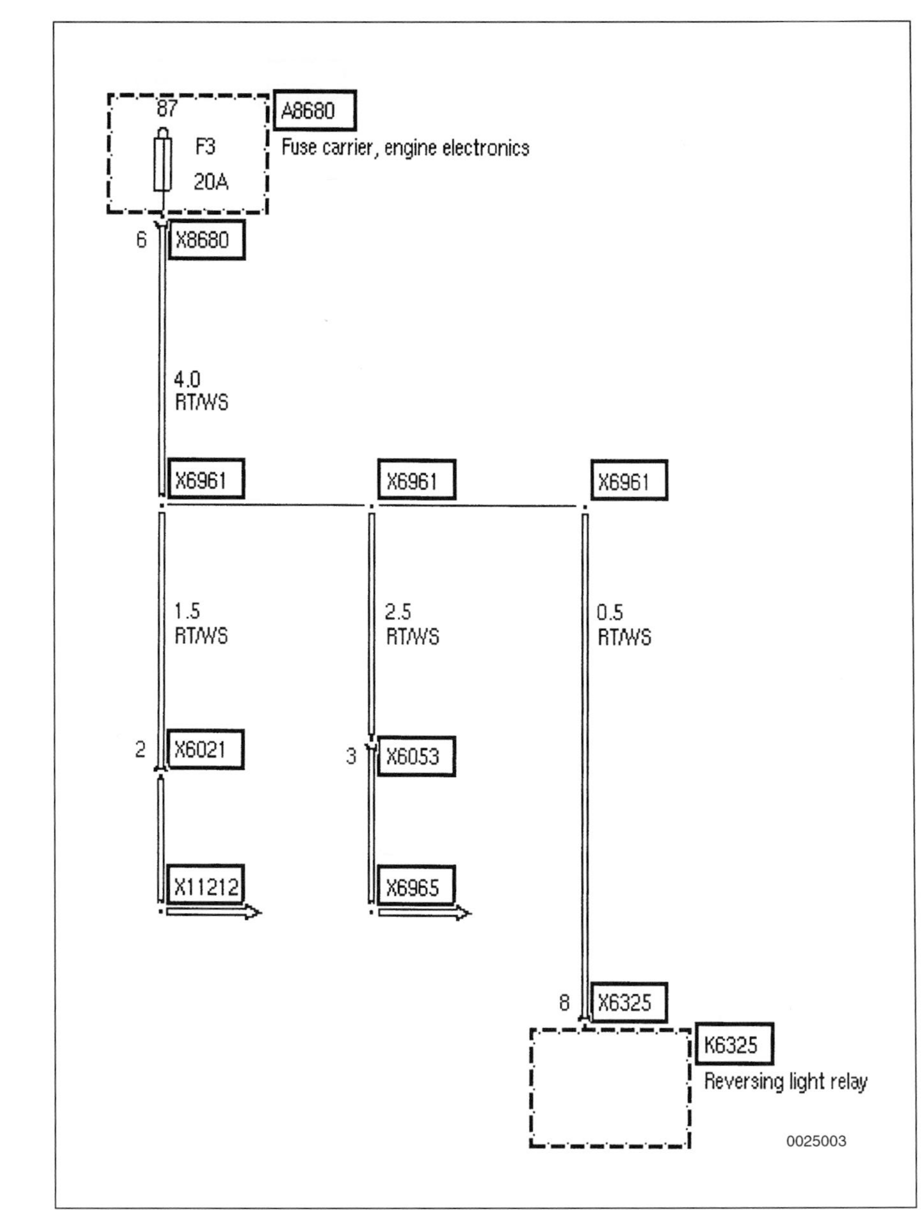

Engine harness connector (X6021)

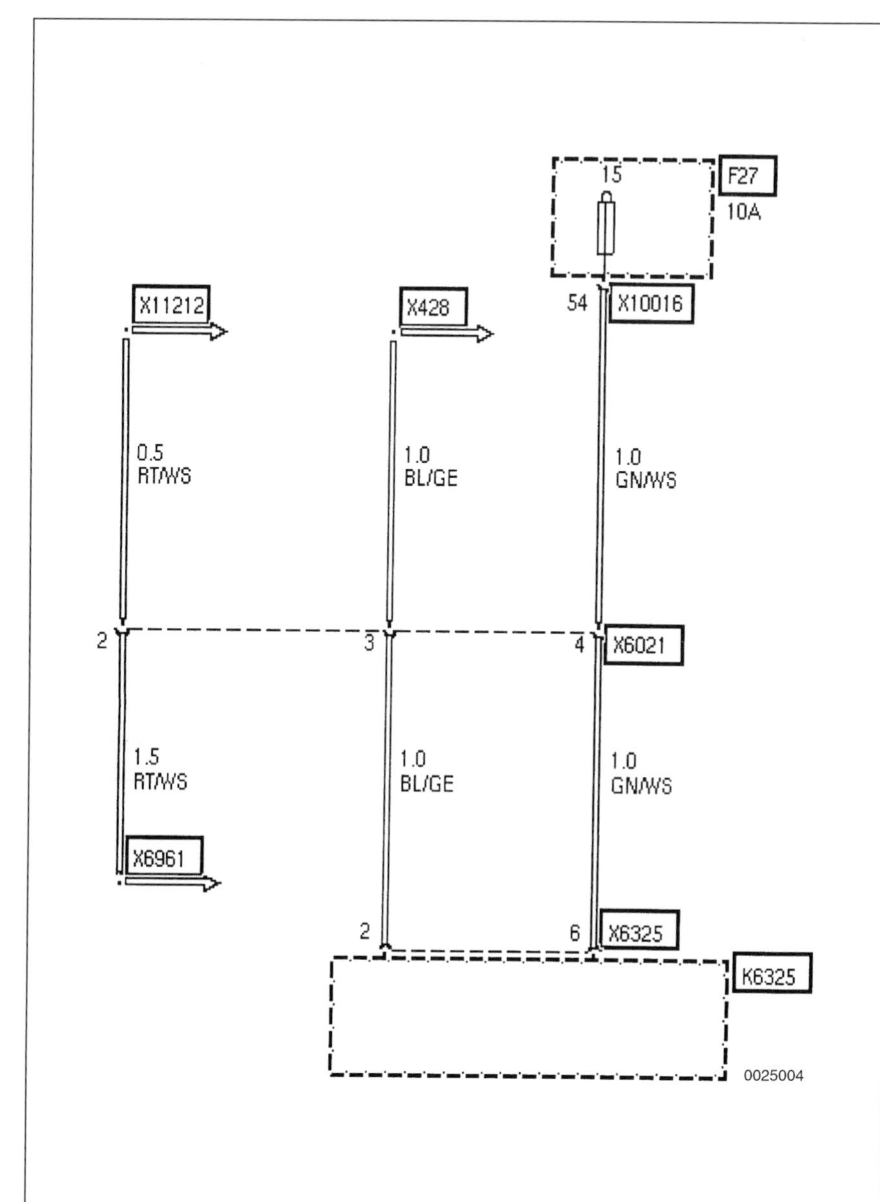

Splice connector (X11212)

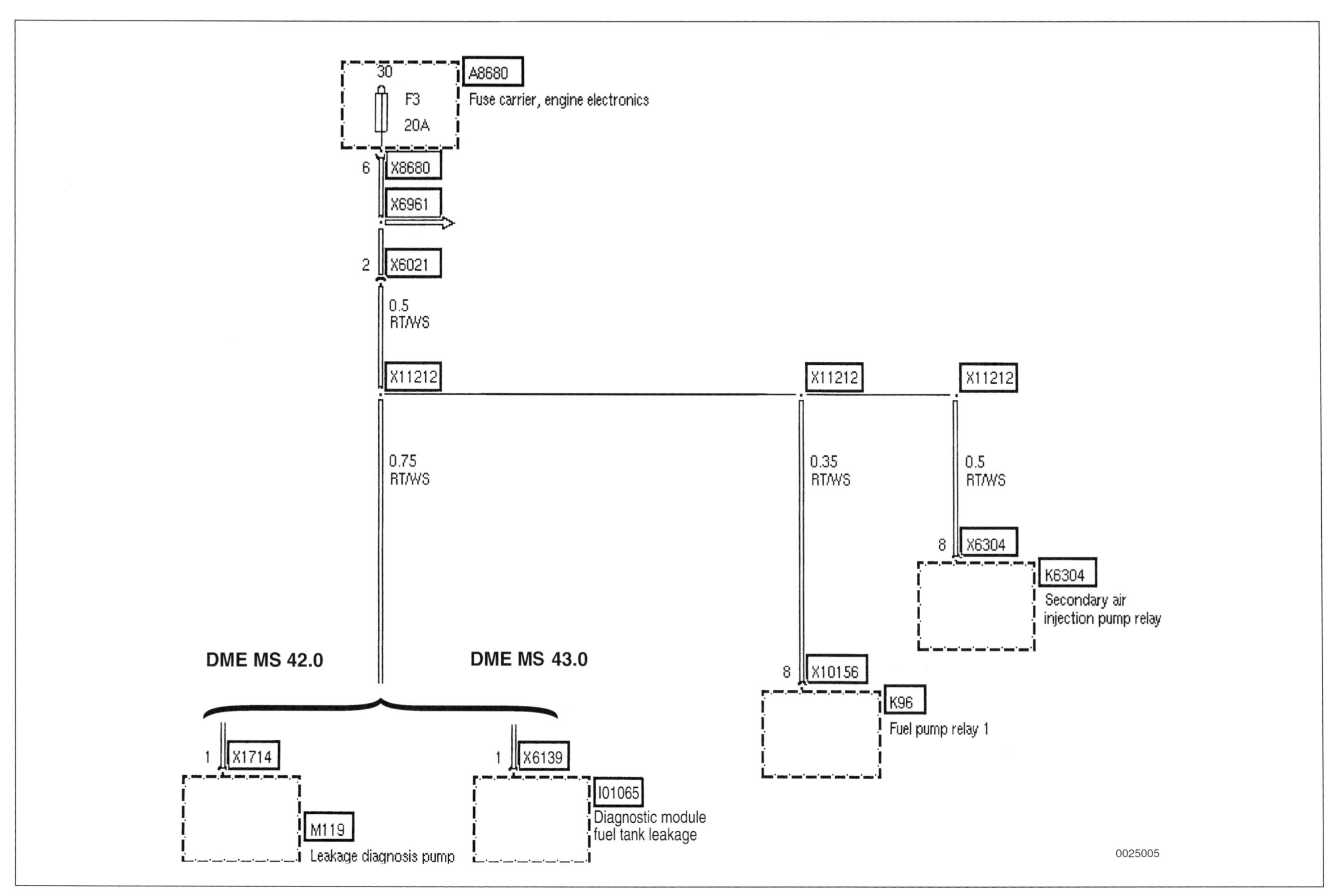

Fuel pump/fuel level sensor assembly (M2)

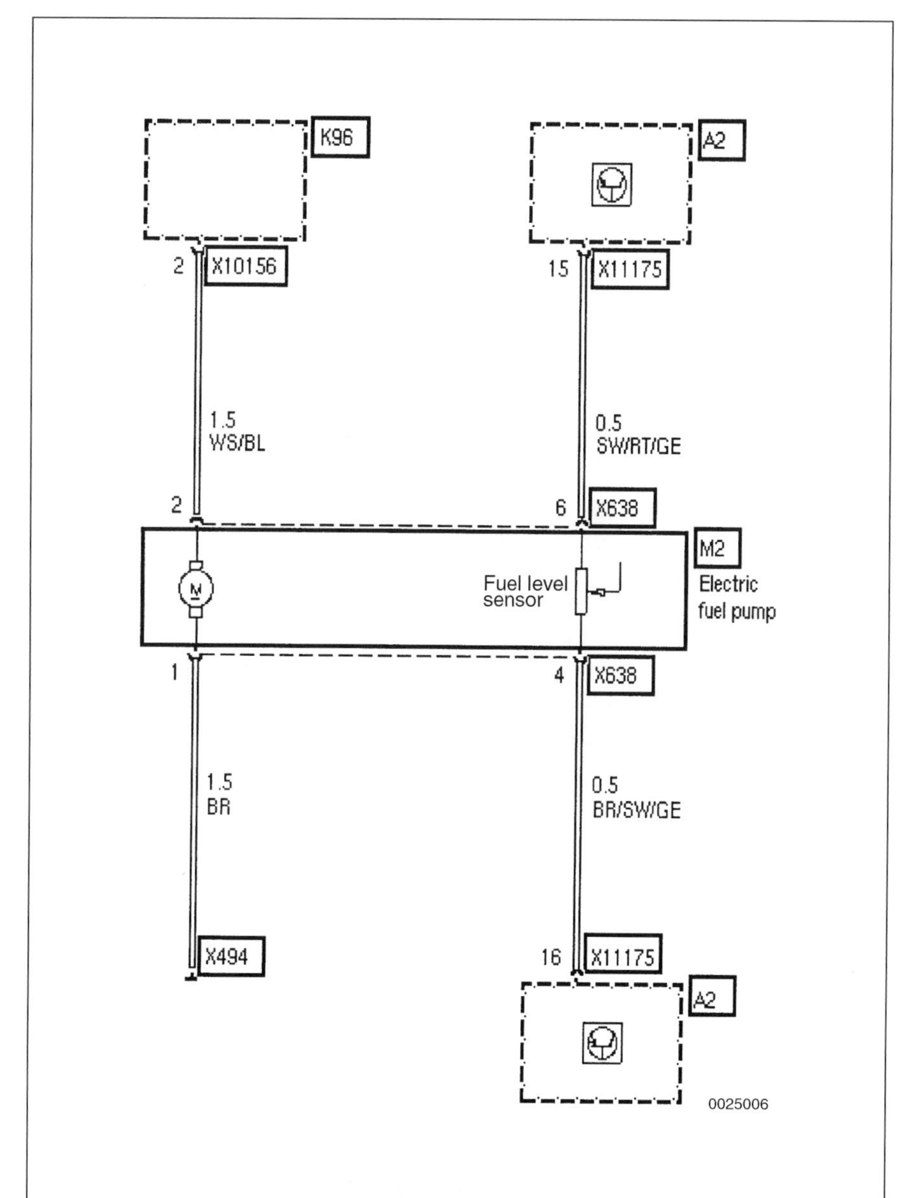

Ground (X494)

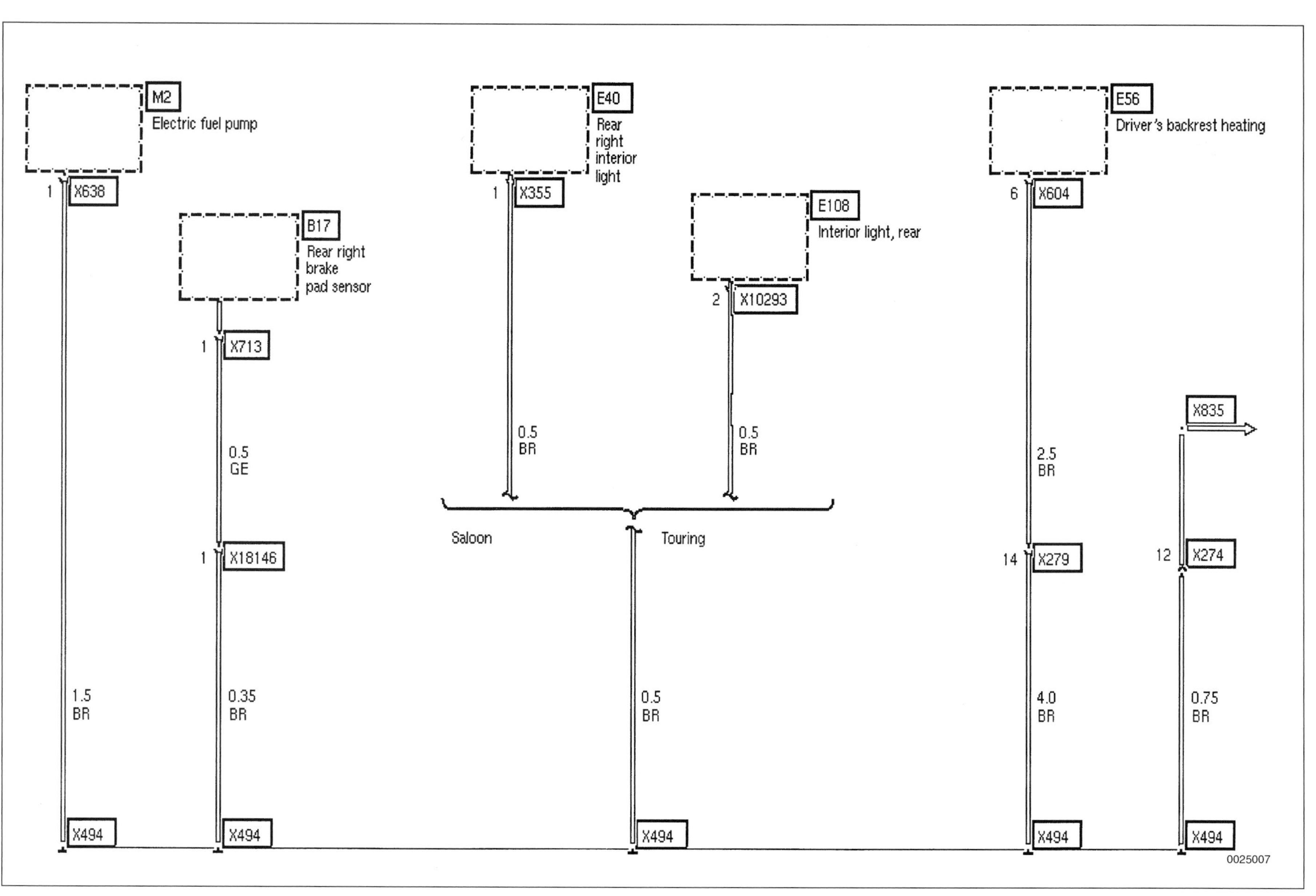
M2
Electric fuel pump
1
X638
1.5
BR
X494
B17
Rear right
brake
pad sensor
1
X713
0.5
GE
1
X18146
0.35
BR
X494
E40
Rear
right
interior
light
1
X355
0.5
BR
E108
Interior light, rear
2
X10293
0.5
BR
Saloon
Touring
0.5
BR
X494
E56
Driver's backrest heating
6
X604
2.5
BR
14
X279
4.0
BR
X494
X835
12
X274
0.75
BR
X494
0025007

DME control unit (A6000), module 1

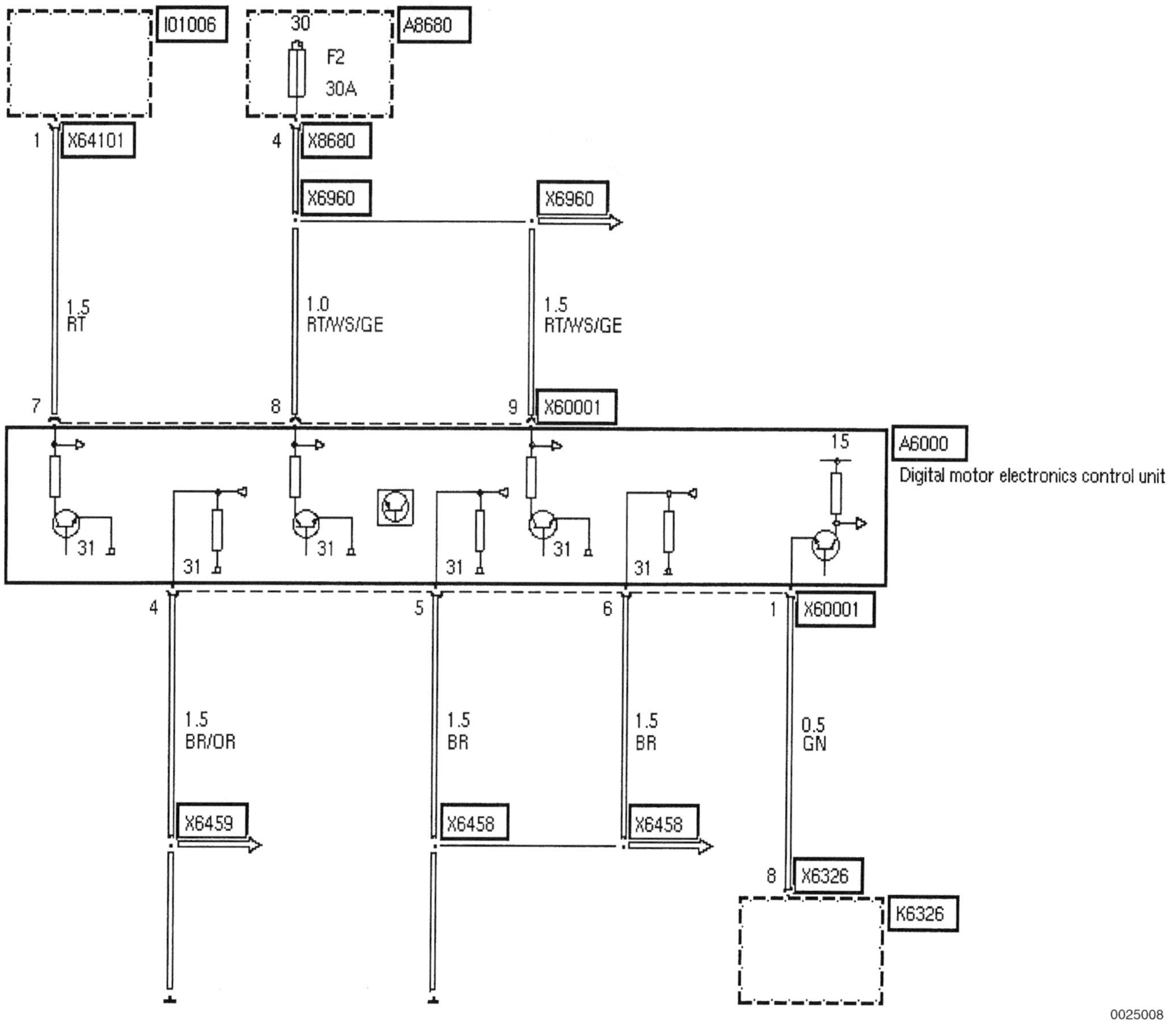

I01006
A8680
30
F2
30A
1 X64101
4 X8680
X6960
X6960
1.5
RT
1.0
RT/WS/GE
1.5
RT/WS/GE
7
8
9 X60001
A6000
Digital motor electronics control unit
15
31
31
31
31
31
31
31
4
5
6
1 X60001
1.5
BR/OR
1.5
BR
1.5
BR
0.5
GN
X6459
X6458
X6458
8 X6326
K6326
0025008

DME control unit (A6000), module 2
1 of 2

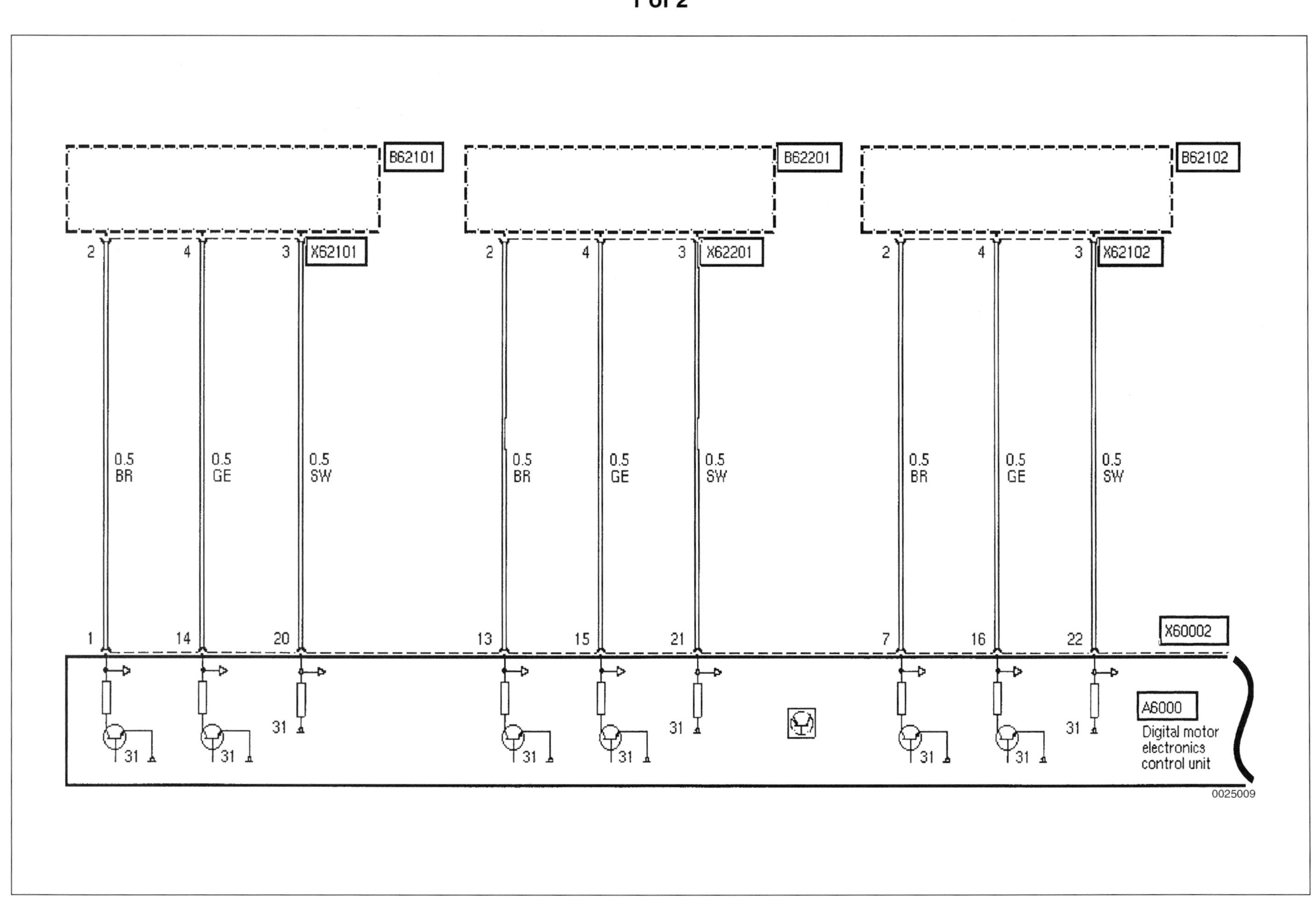

DME control unit (A6000), module 2

2 of 2

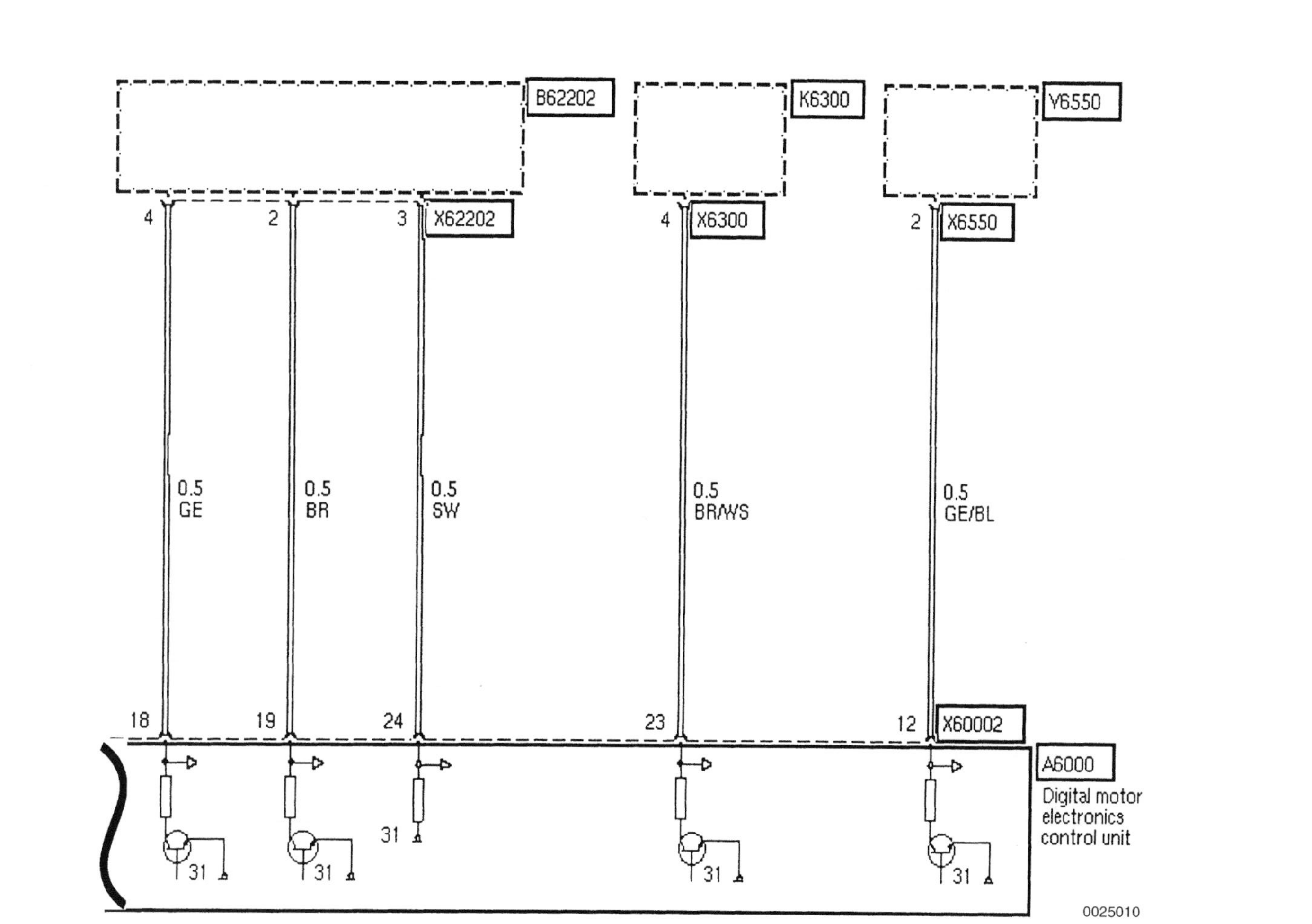

DME control unit (A6000), module 3
1 of 3

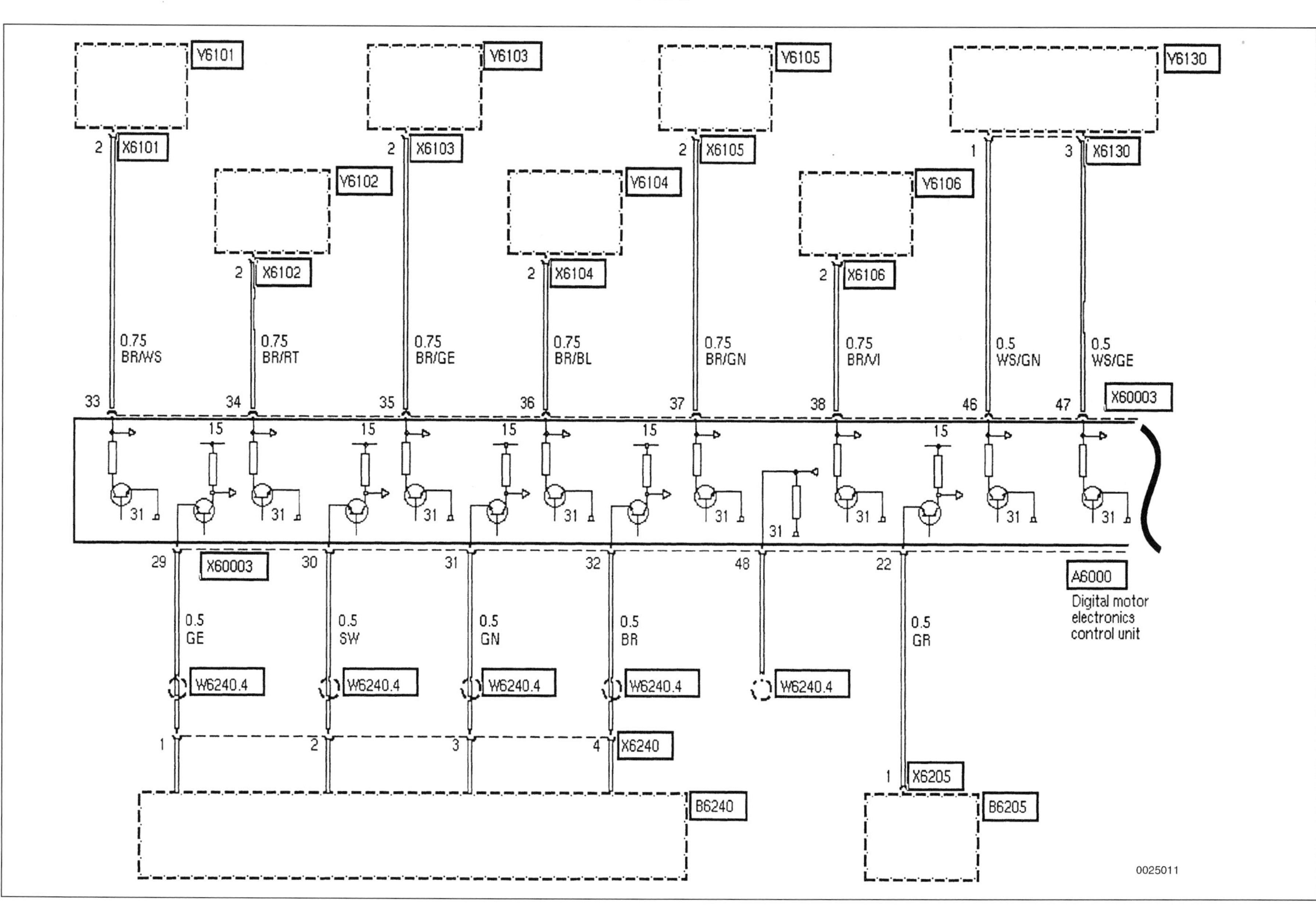

DME control unit (A6000), module 3
2 of 3

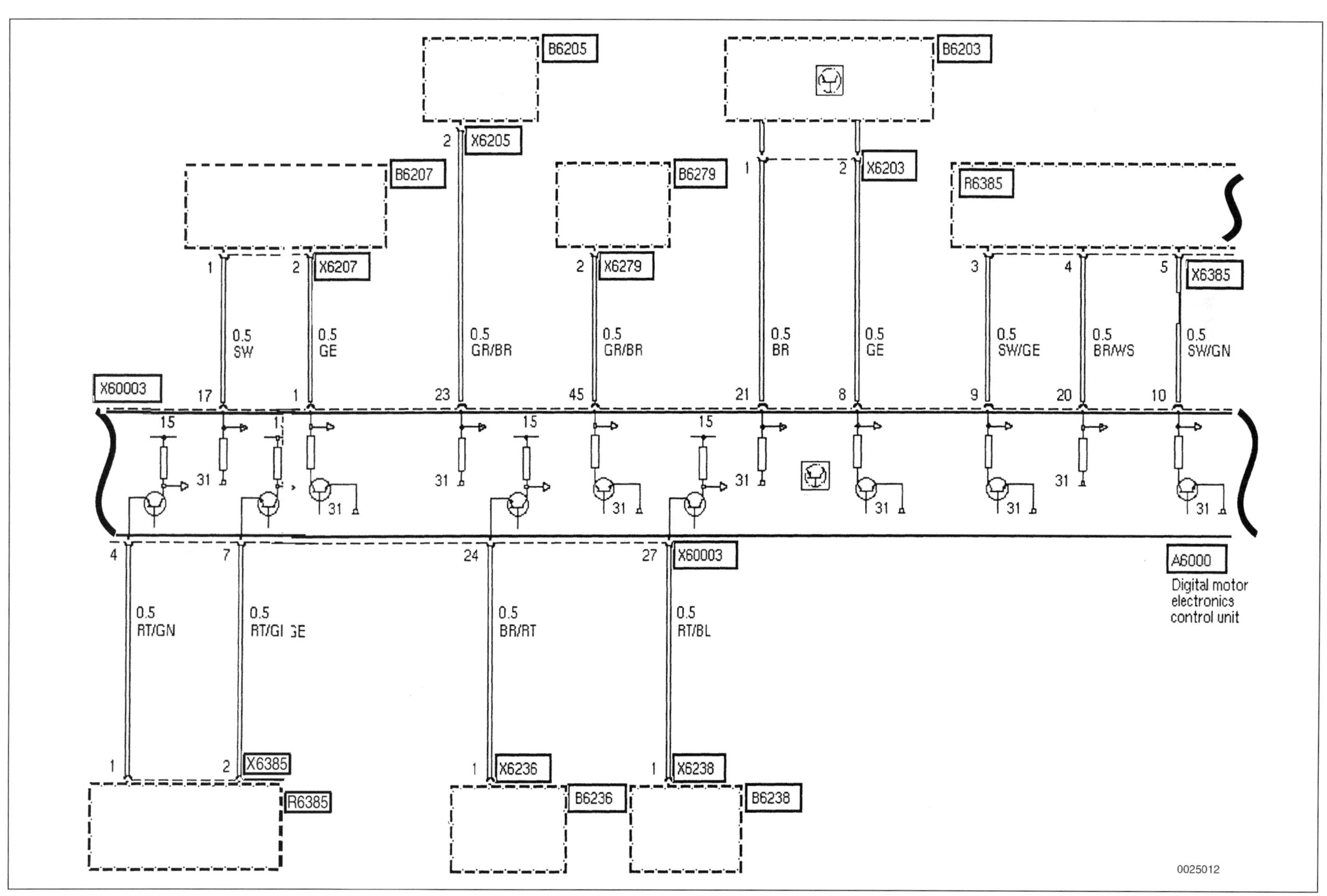

DME control unit (A6000), module 3

3 of 3

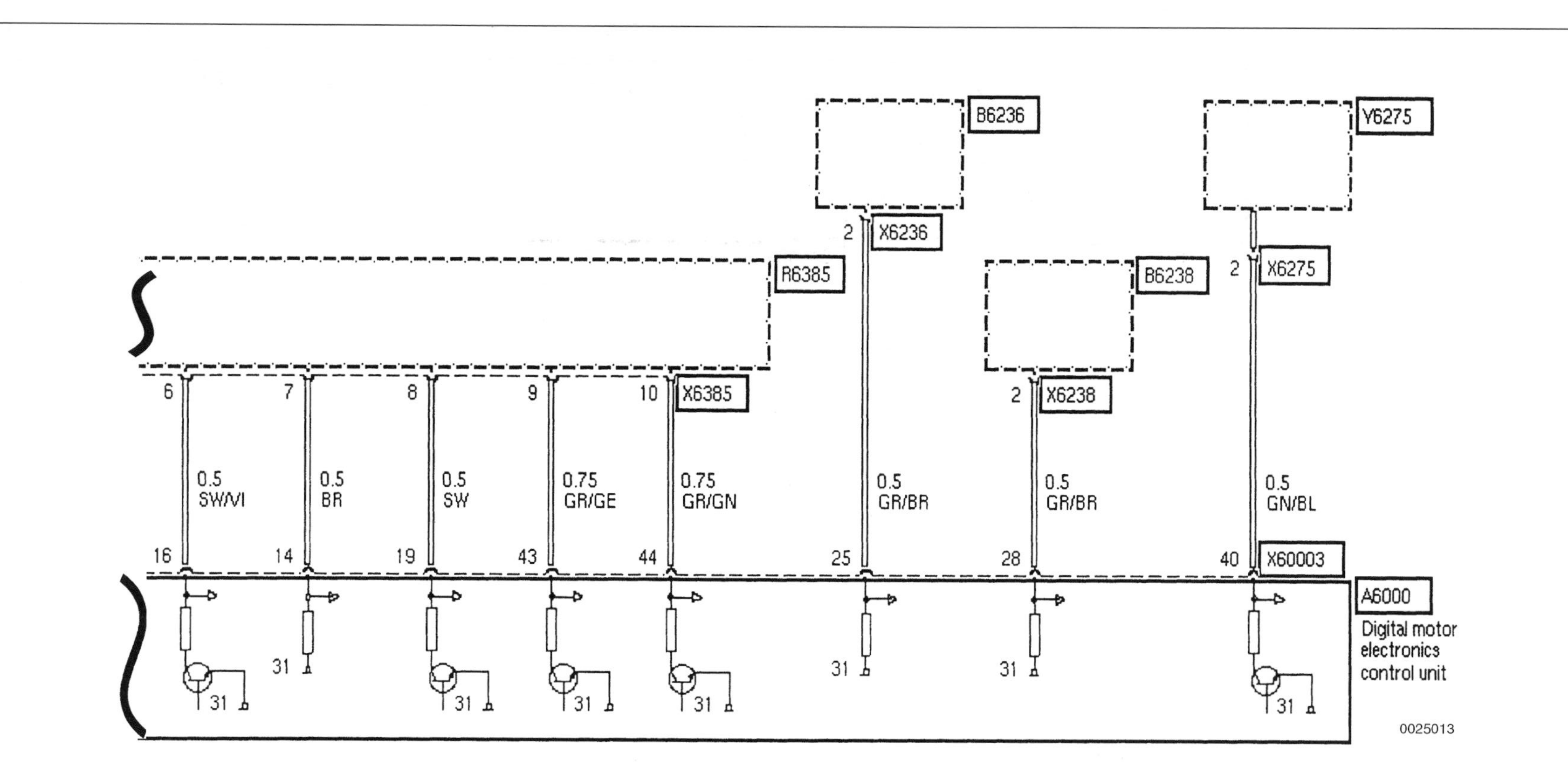

DME control unit (A6000), module 4
1 of 3

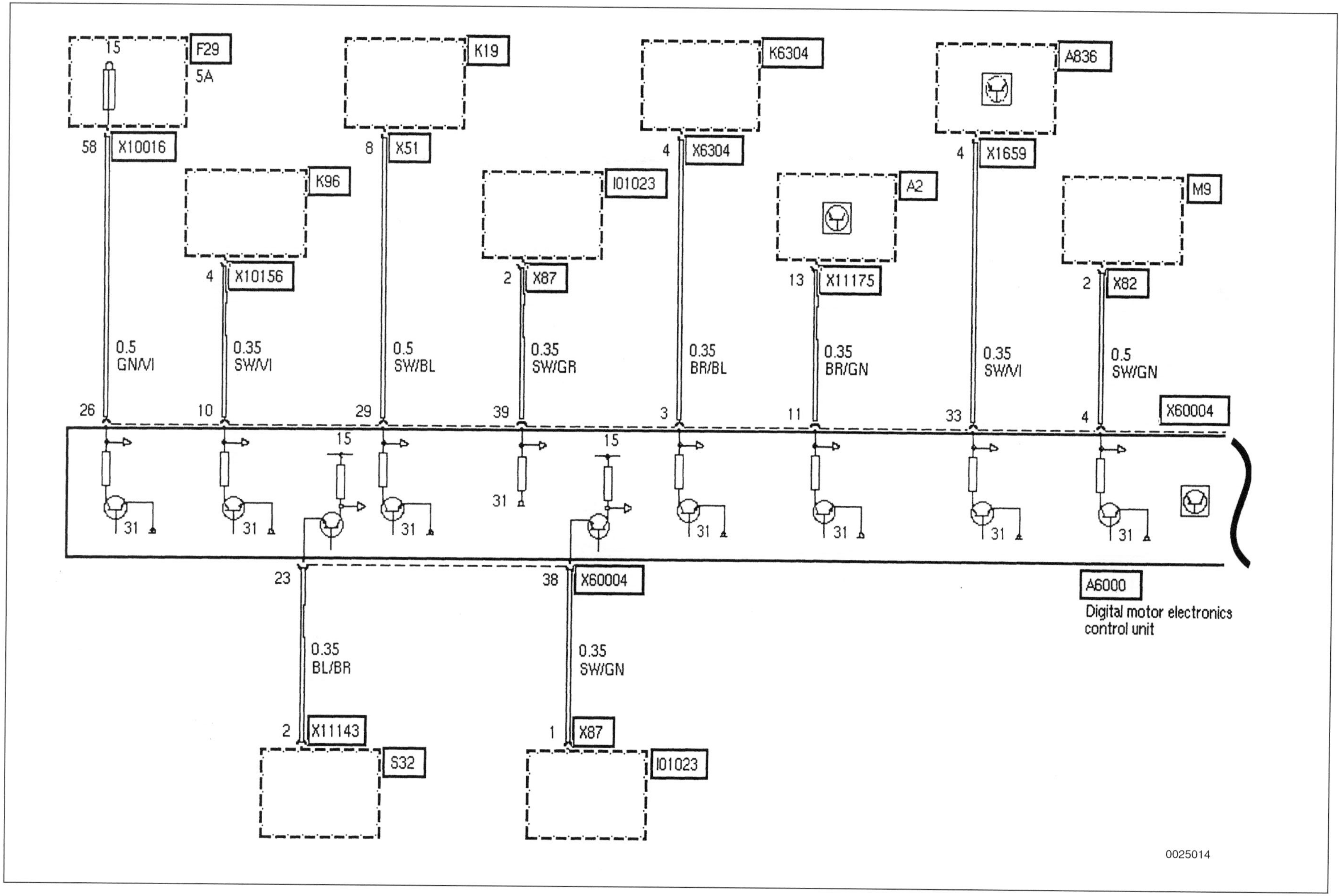

F29
5A
15
58 X10016
0.5
GN/VI
26

K96
4 X10156
0.35
SW/VI
10

K19
8 X51
0.5
SW/BL
29

I01023
2 X87
0.35
SW/GR
39

K6304
4 X6304
0.35
BR/BL
3

A2
13 X11175
0.35
BR/GN
11

A836
4 X1659
0.35
SW/VI
33

M9
2 X82
0.5
SW/GN
4

X60004

15
15
31

23
0.35
BL/BR
2 X11143
S32

38 X60004
0.35
SW/GN
1 X87
I01023

A6000
Digital motor electronics control unit

0025014

DME control unit (A6000), module 4
2 of 3

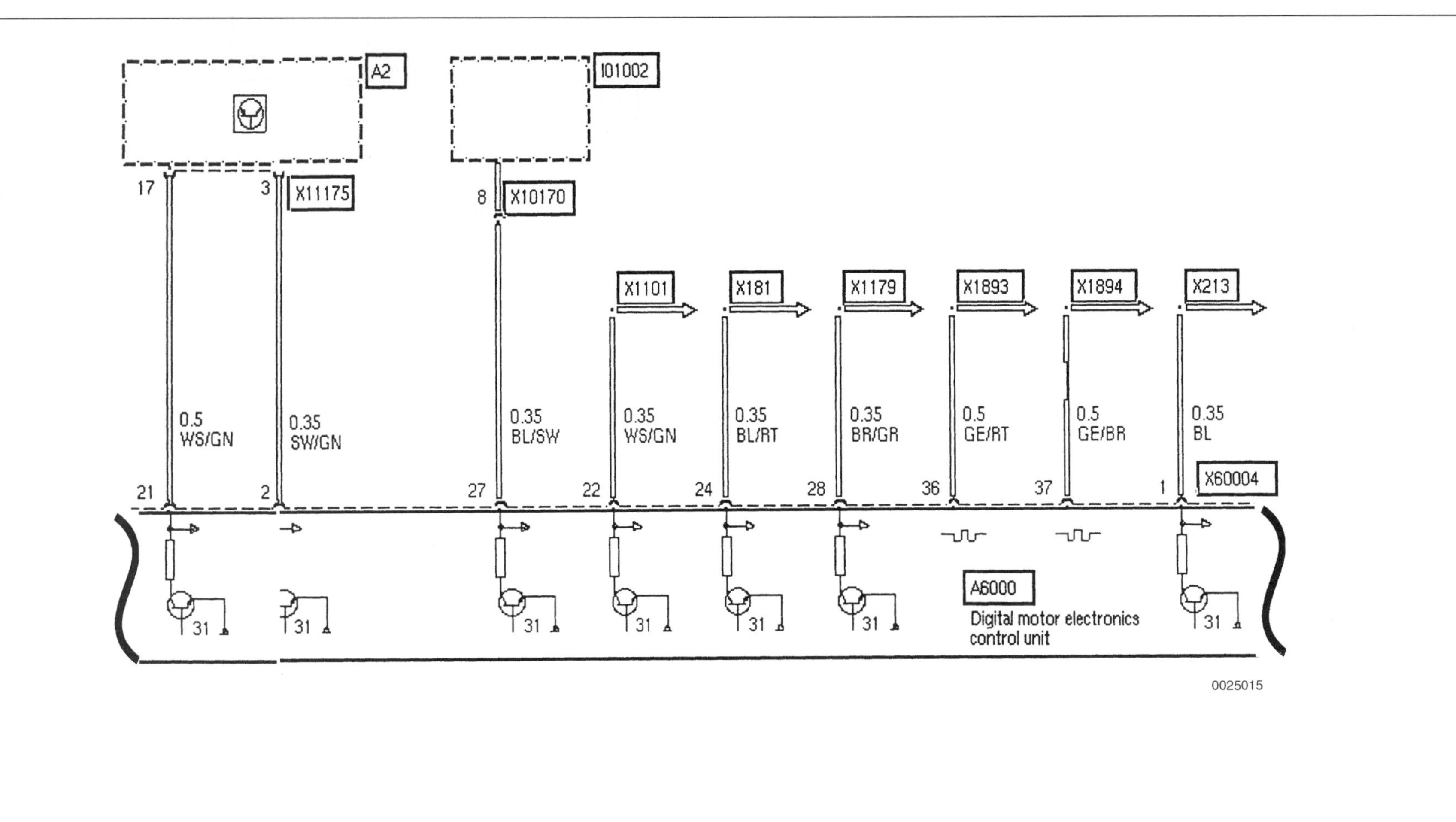

DME control unit (A6000), module 4

3 of 3

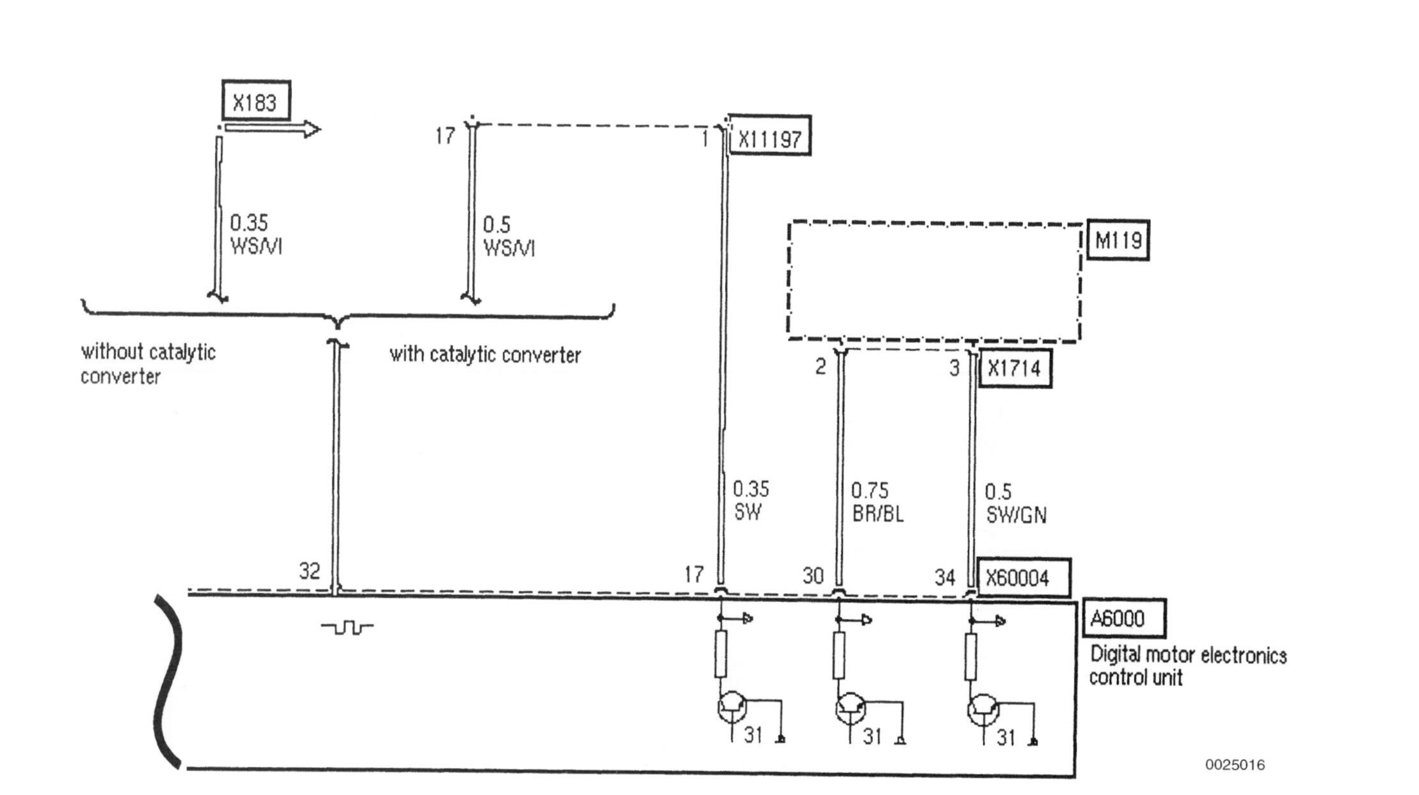

DME control unit (A6000), module 5

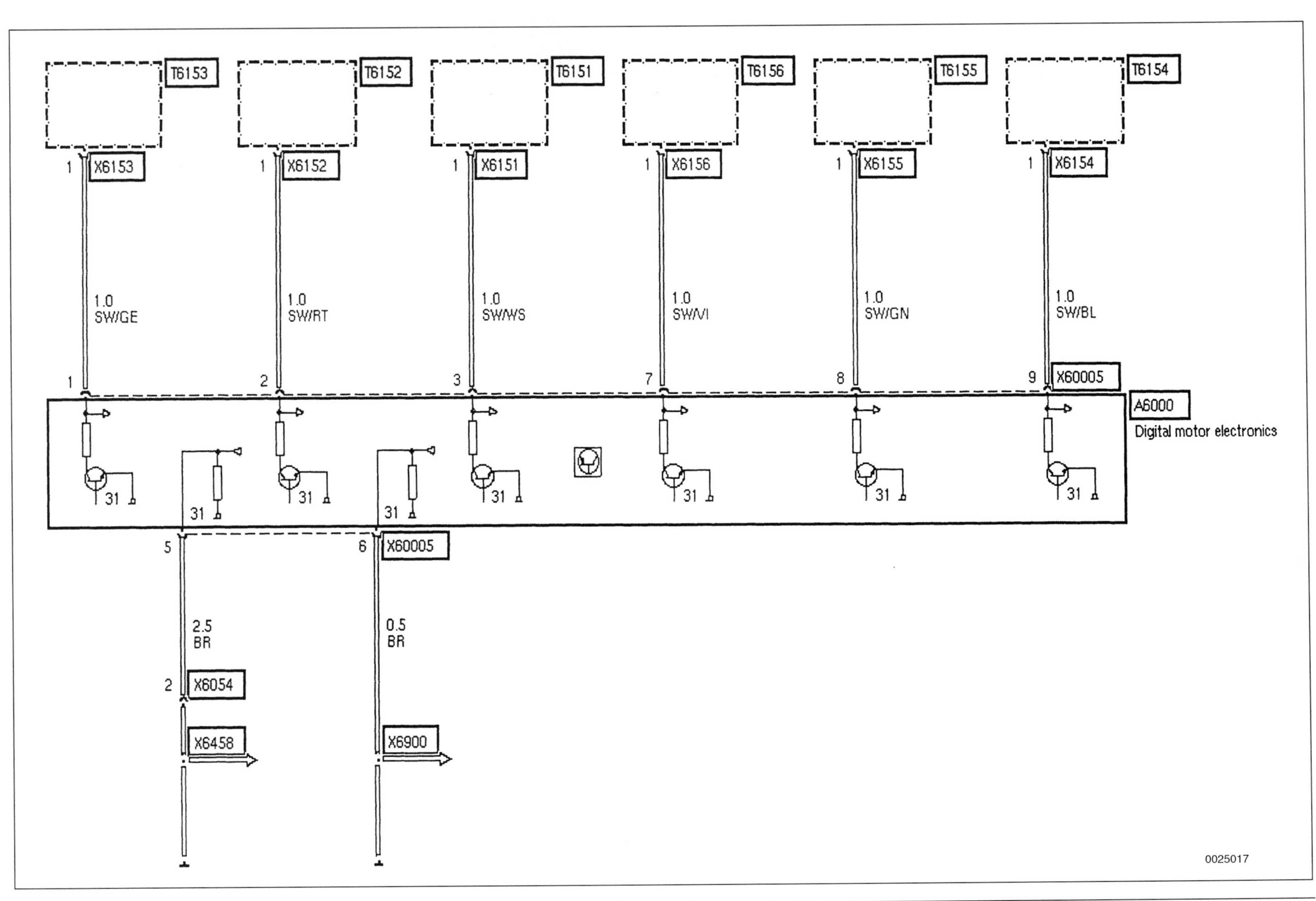

Fuel changeover valve (3/2-way valve) (Y6550)

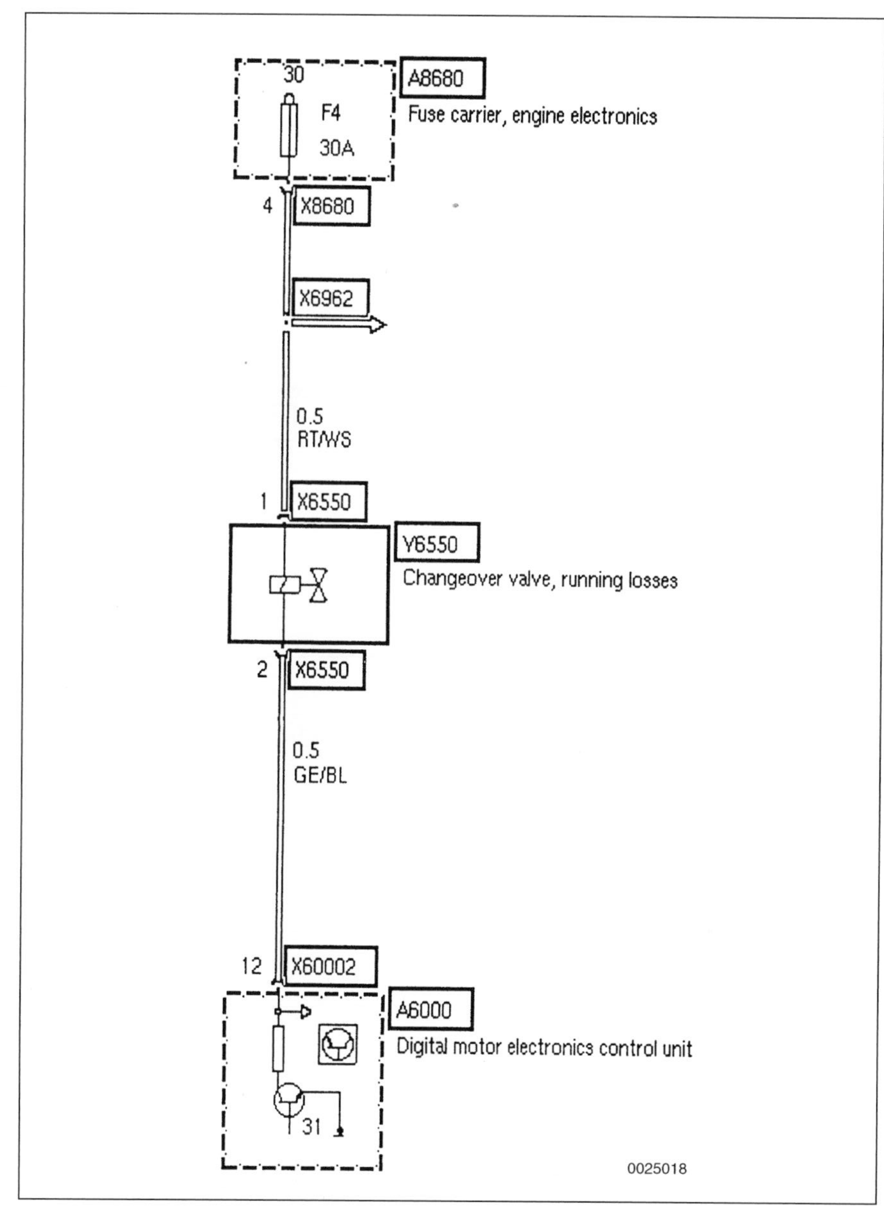

Fuel injectors (Y6101 - Y6106) (DME MS 42.0)
1 of 2

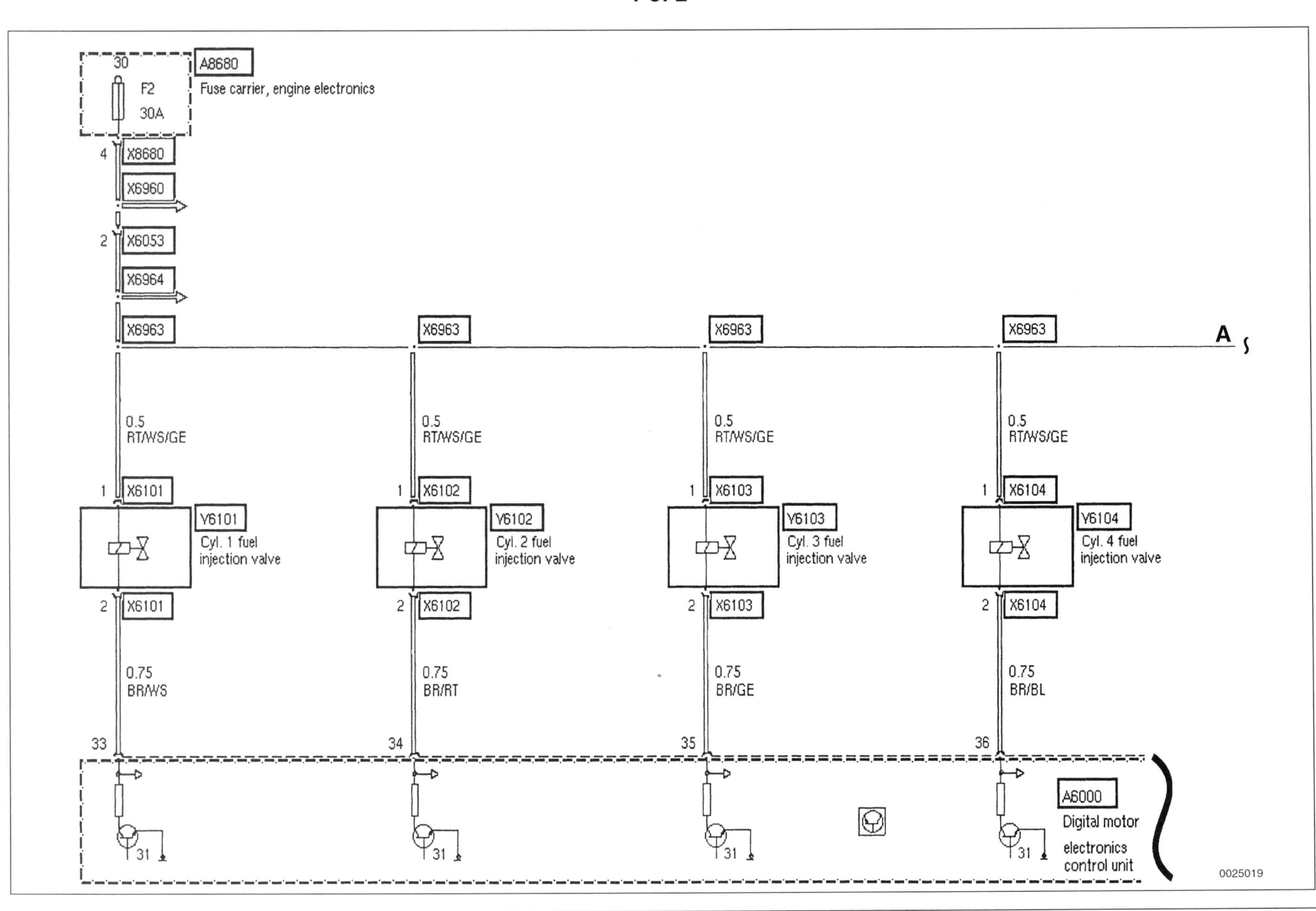

Fuel injectors (Y6101 - Y6106) (DME MS 42.0)

2 of 2

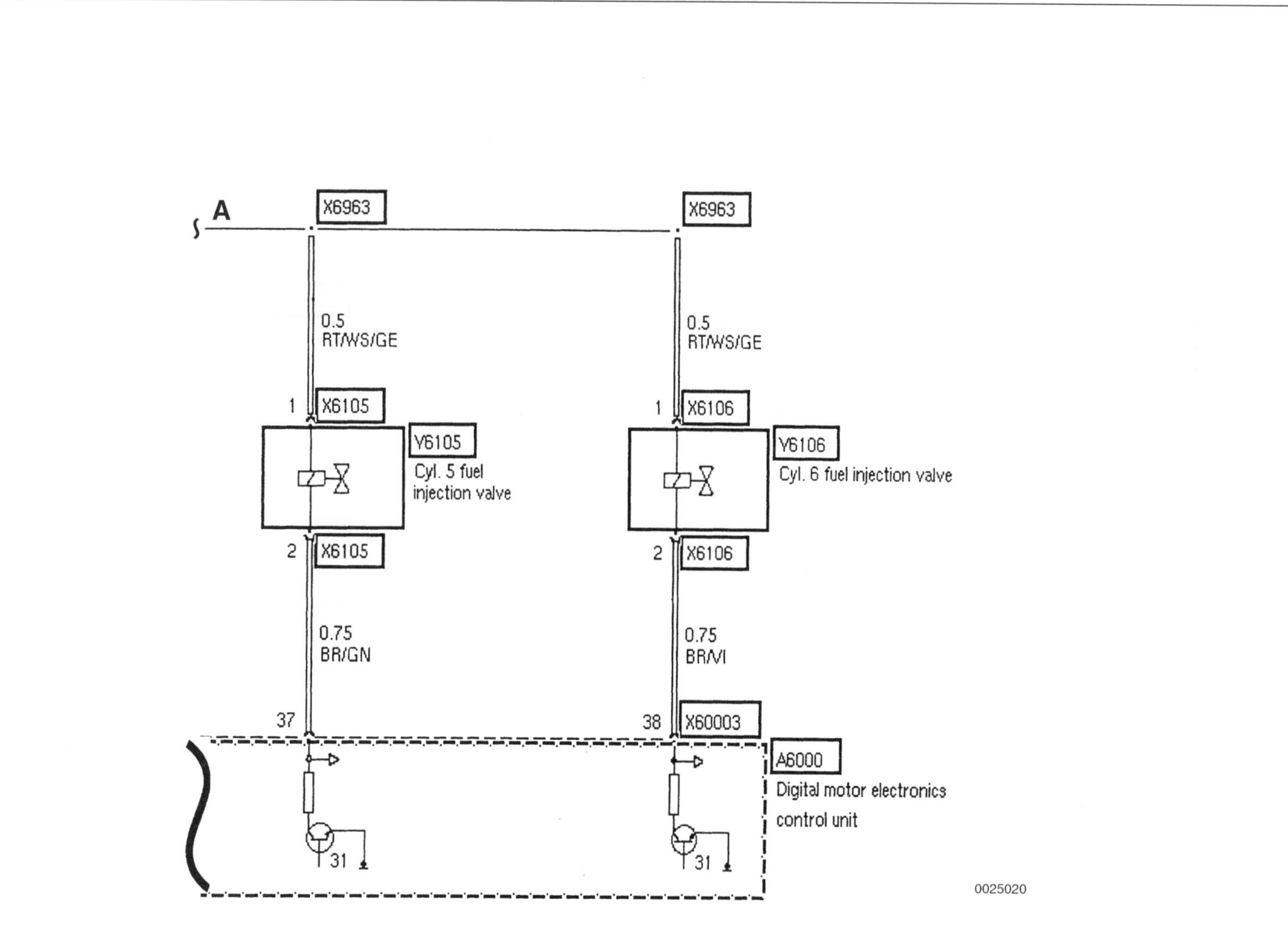

Splice connector (X6960)

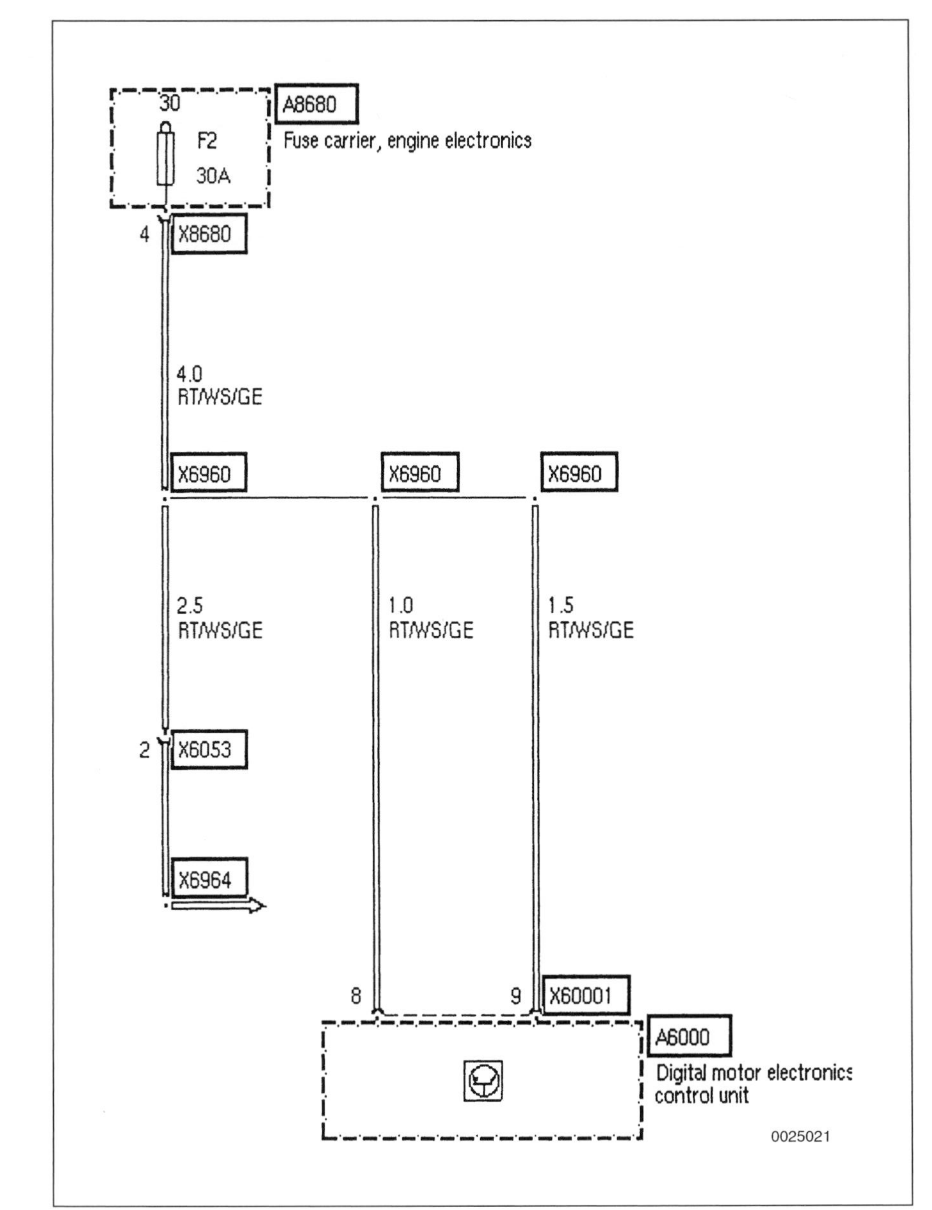

Engine harness connector (X6053)

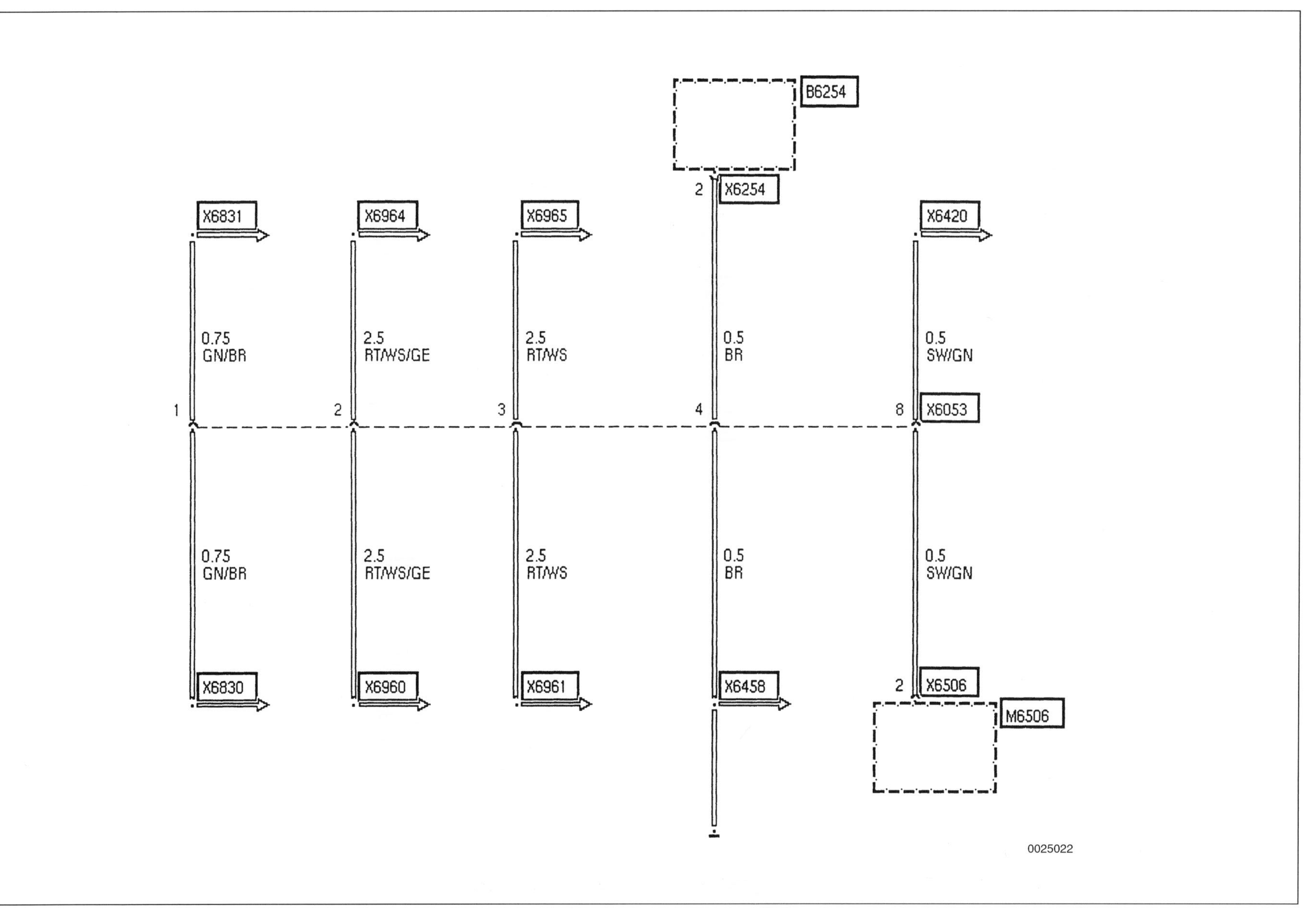

Engine harness splice connector (X6964)
1 of 2

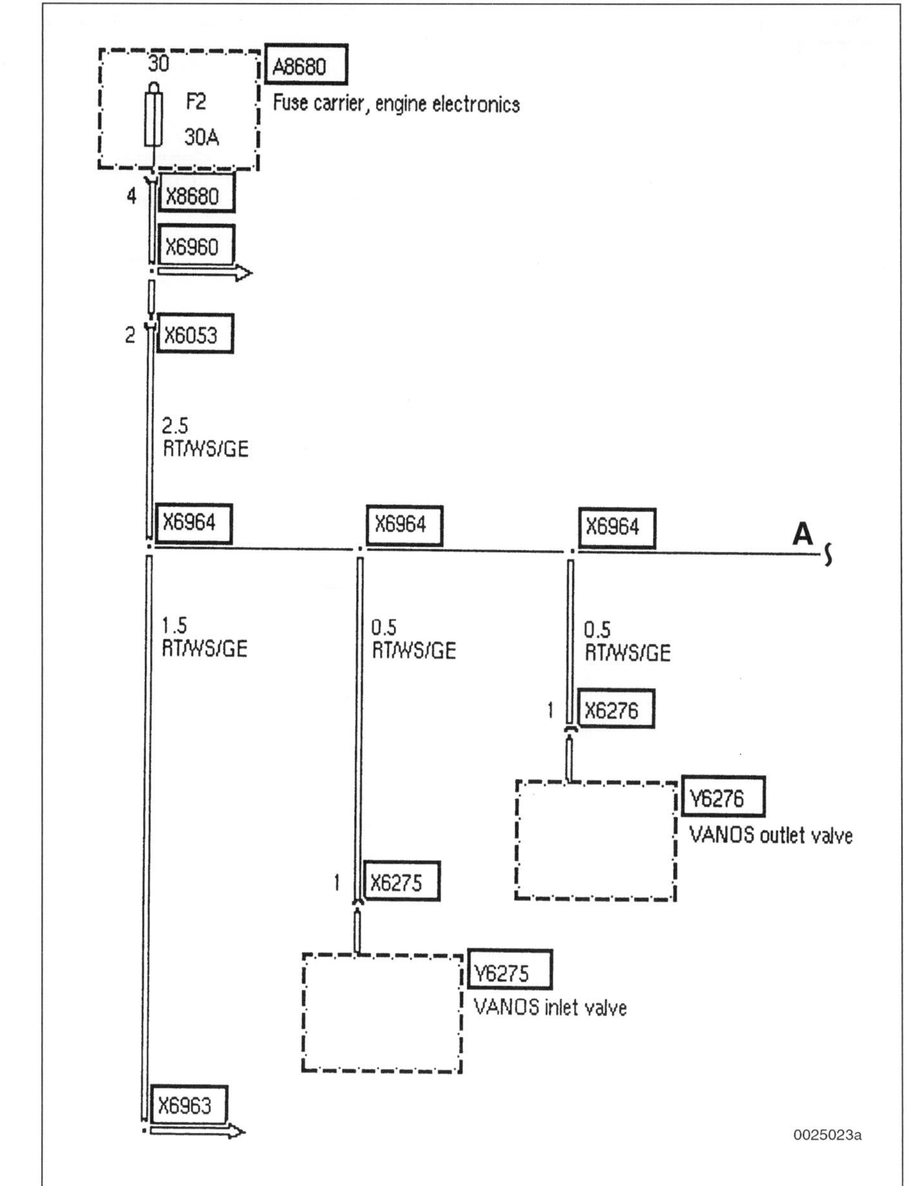

Engine harness splice connector (X6964)
2 of 2

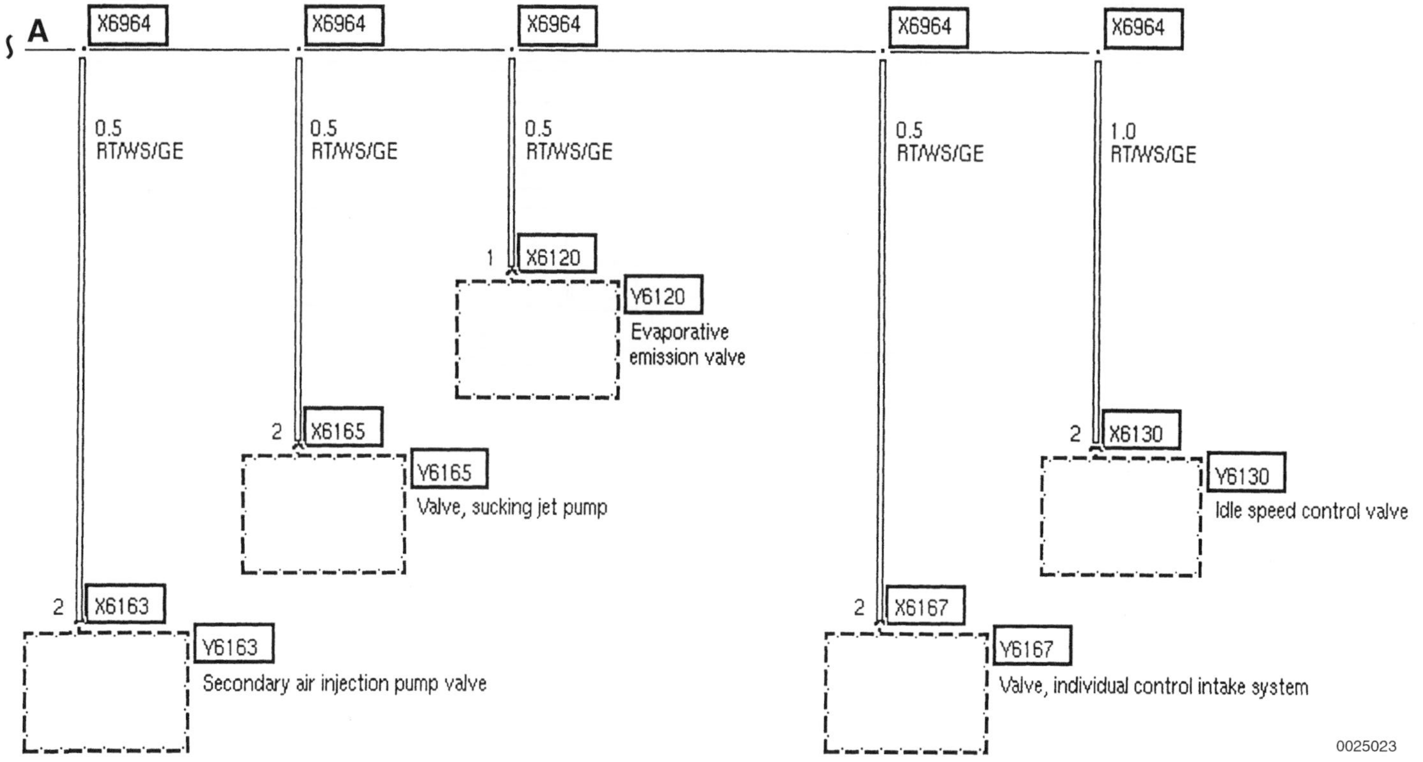

A
X6964
0.5
RT/WS/GE
2 X6163
Y6163
Secondary air injection pump valve
X6964
0.5
RT/WS/GE
2 X6165
Y6165
Valve, sucking jet pump
X6964
0.5
RT/WS/GE
1 X6120
Y6120
Evaporative emission valve
X6964
0.5
RT/WS/GE
2 X6167
Y6167
Valve, individual control intake system
X6964
1.0
RT/WS/GE
2 X6130
Y6130
Idle speed control valve
0025023

Multifunction steering wheel

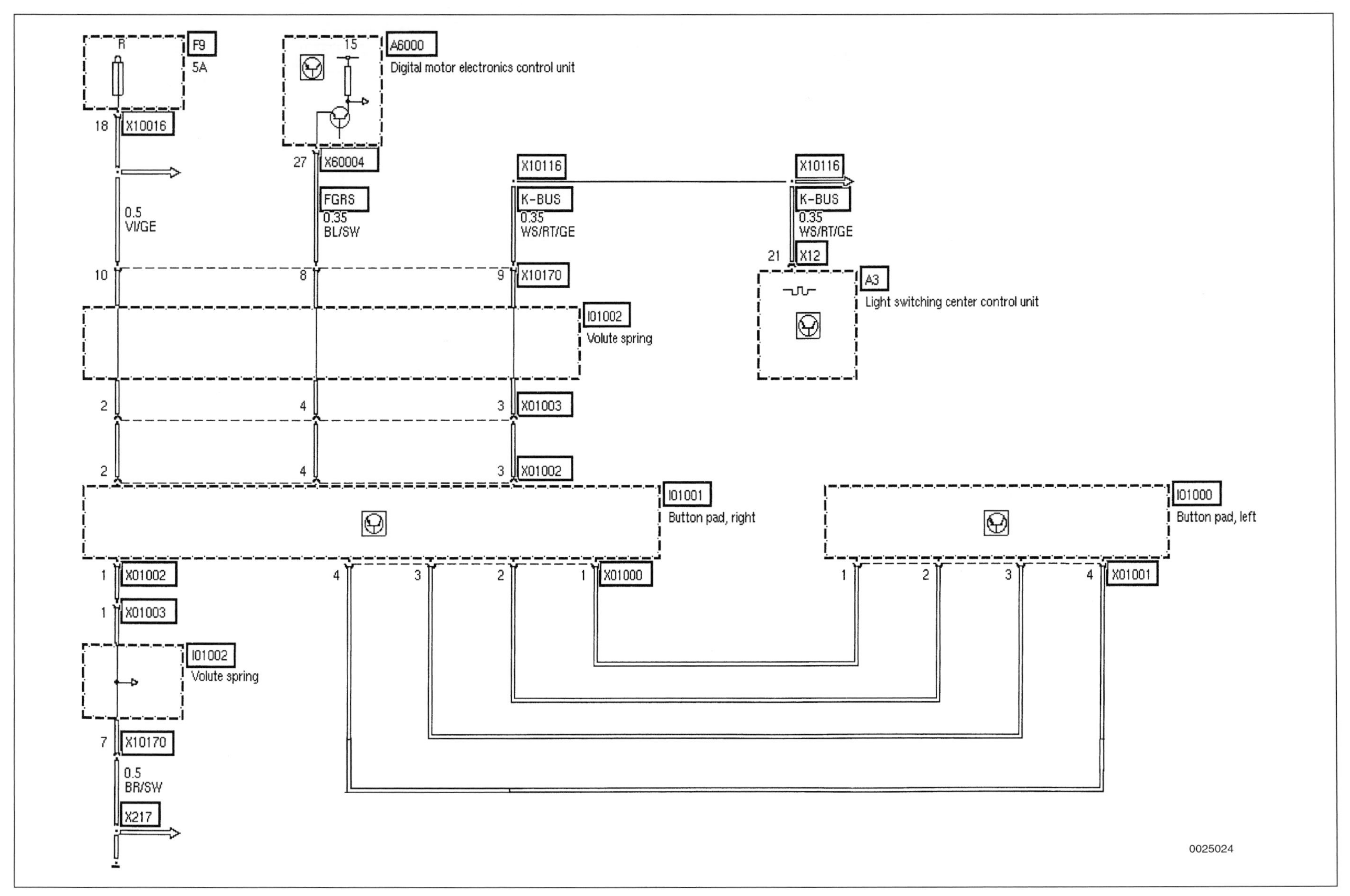

Fuse 9 (F9)

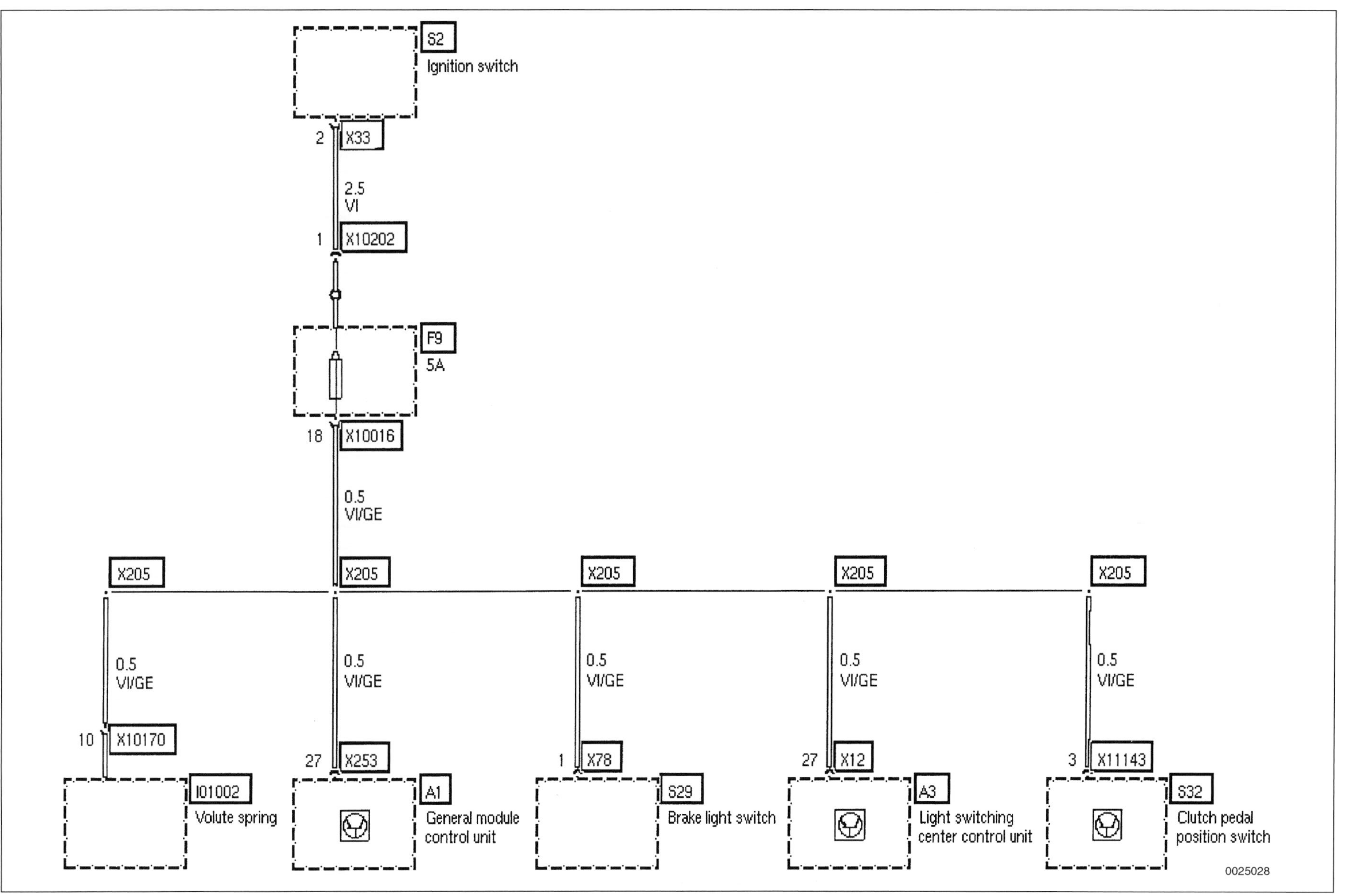

S2
Ignition switch
2
X33
2.5
VI
1
X10202
F9
5A
18
X10016
0.5
VI/GE
X205
X205
X205
X205
X205
0.5
VI/GE
0.5
VI/GE
0.5
VI/GE
0.5
VI/GE
0.5
VI/GE
10
X10170
I01002
Volute spring
27
X253
A1
General module
control unit
1
X78
S29
Brake light switch
27
X12
A3
Light switching
center control unit
3
X11143
S32
Clutch pedal
position switch
0025028

K-bus splice connector (X10116)
1 of 3

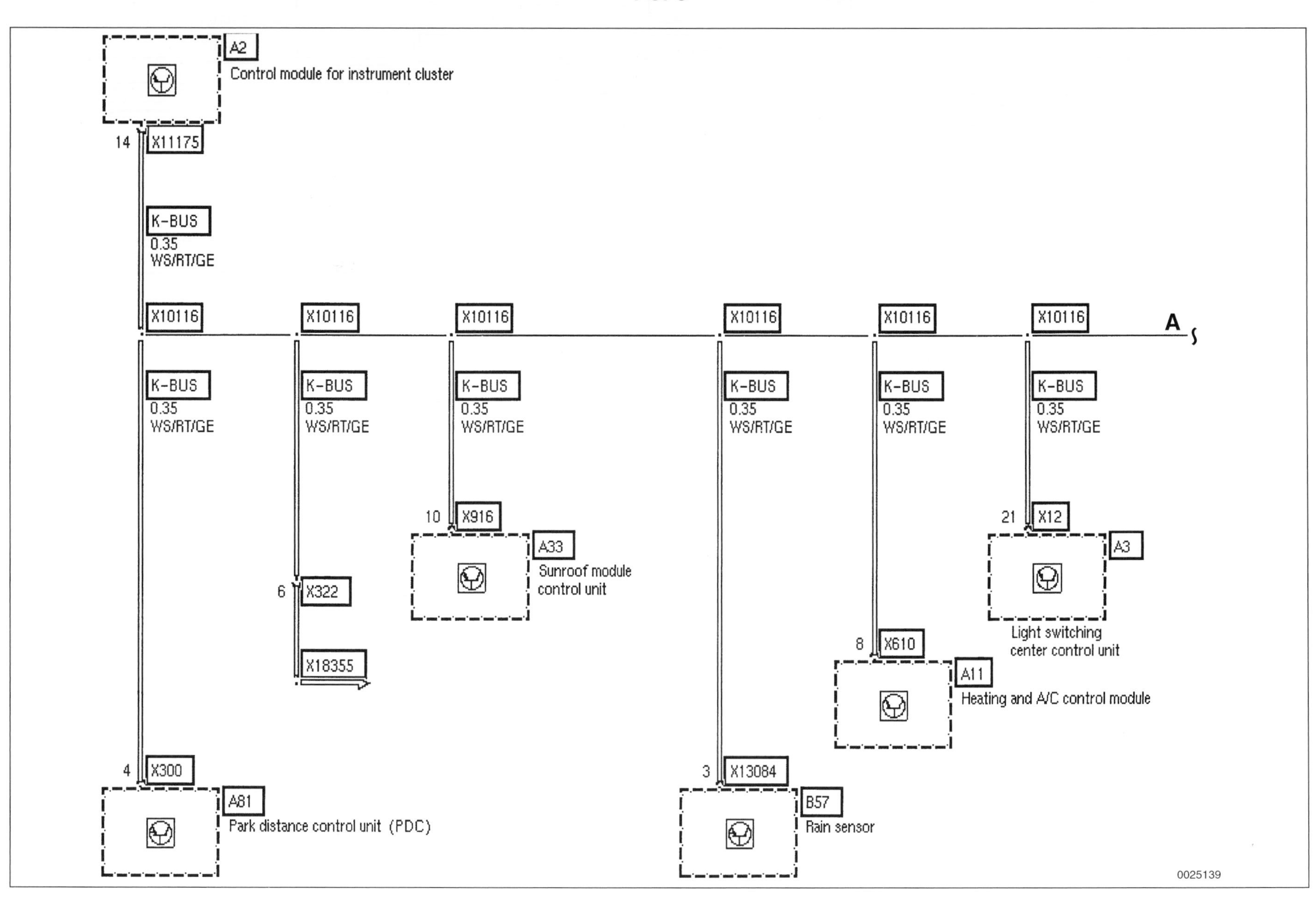

K-bus splice connector (X10116)
2 of 3

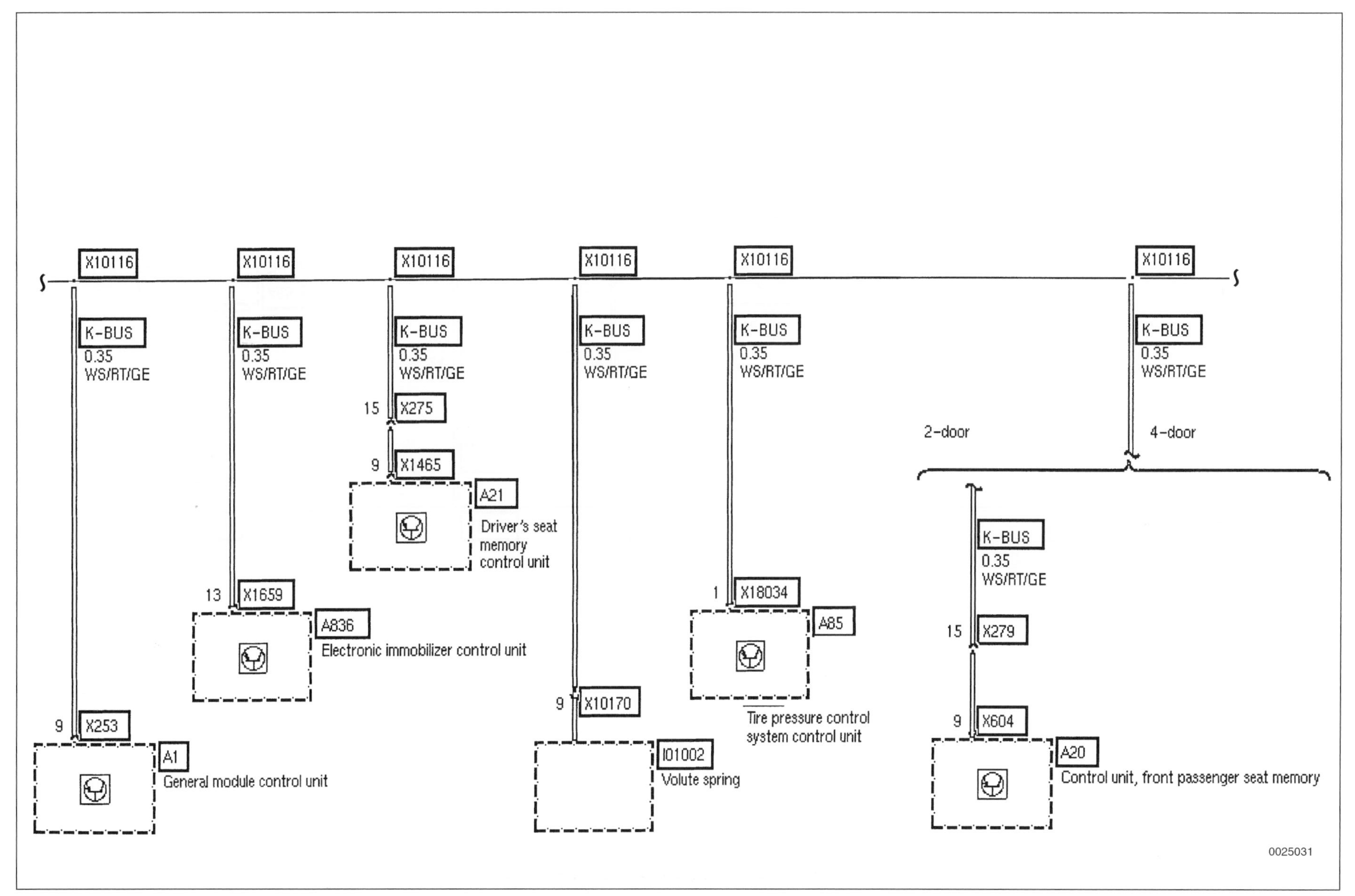

K-bus splice connector (X10116)
3 of 3

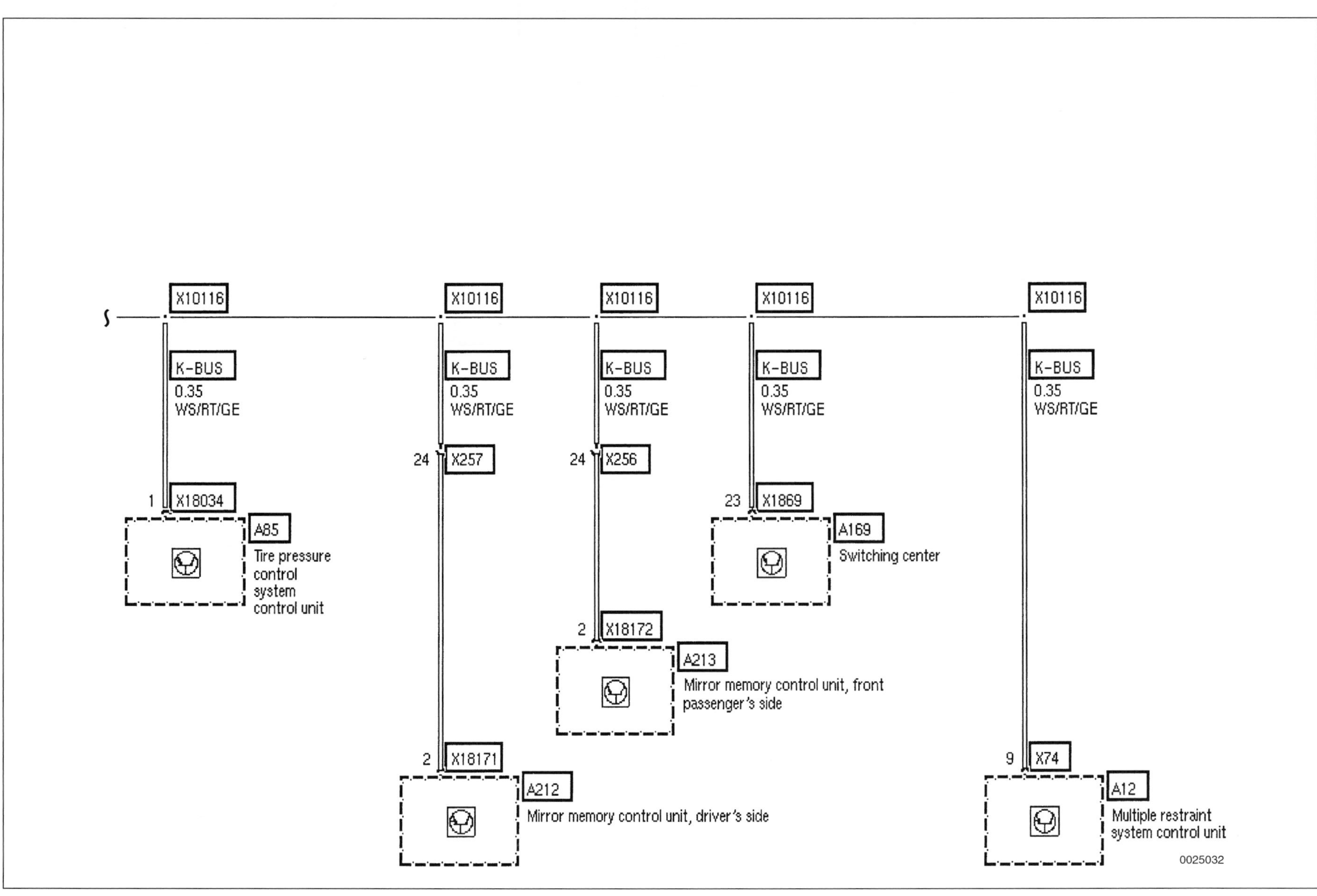

Volute spring (I01002)

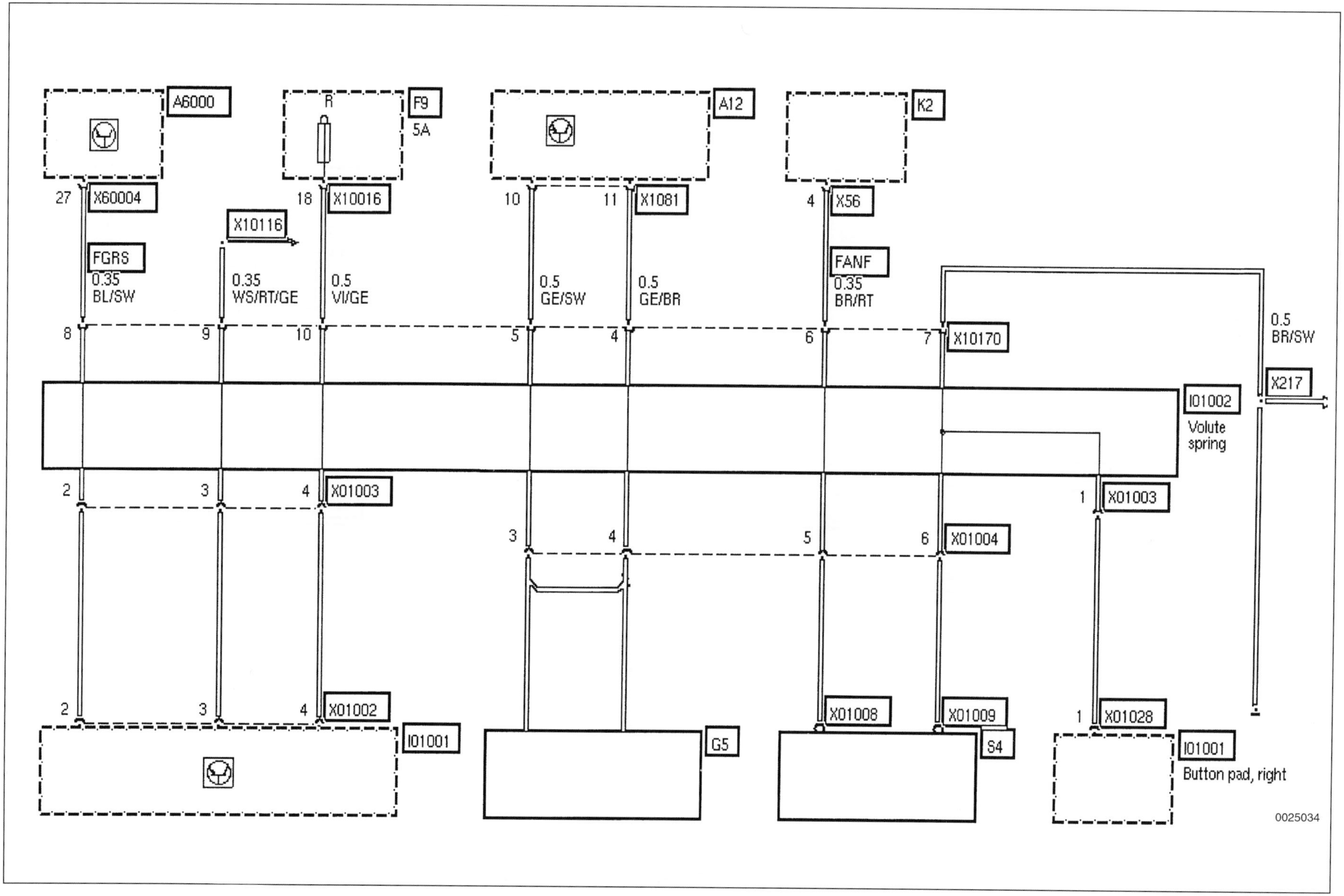

Splice connector (X217)
1 of 2

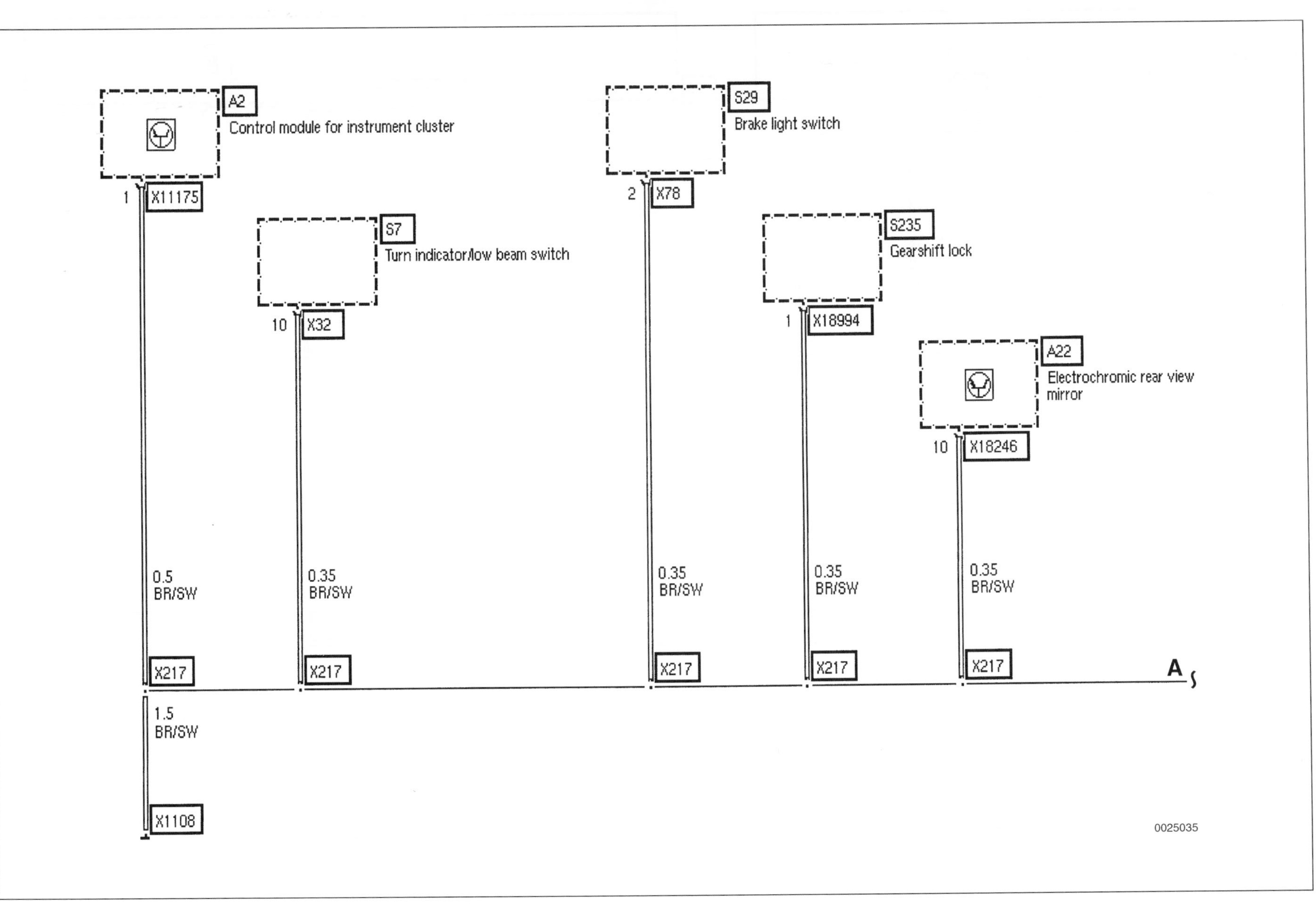

Splice connector (X217)
2 of 2

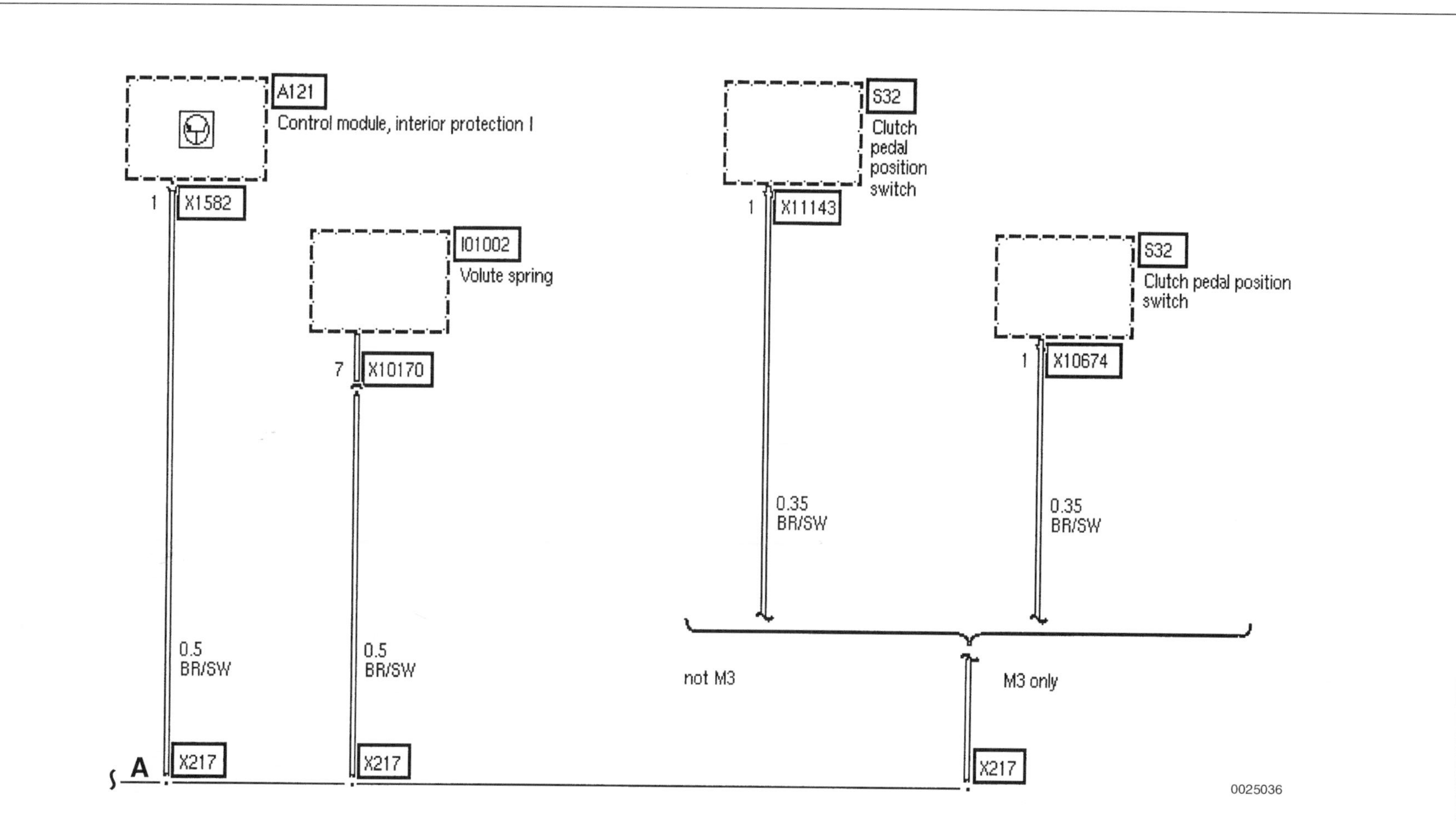

Brake light switch (S29)

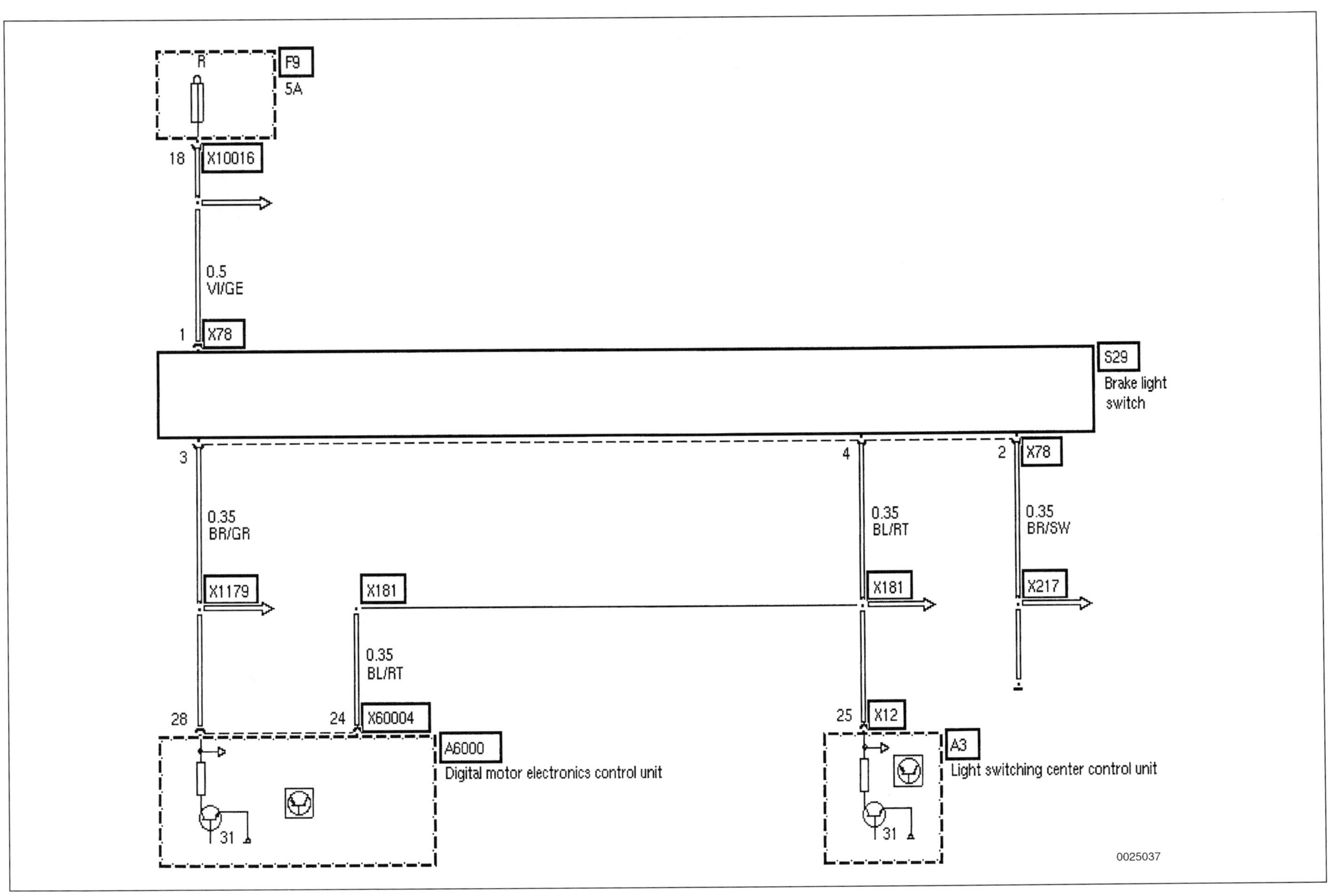

Brake light test signal splice connector (X1179)

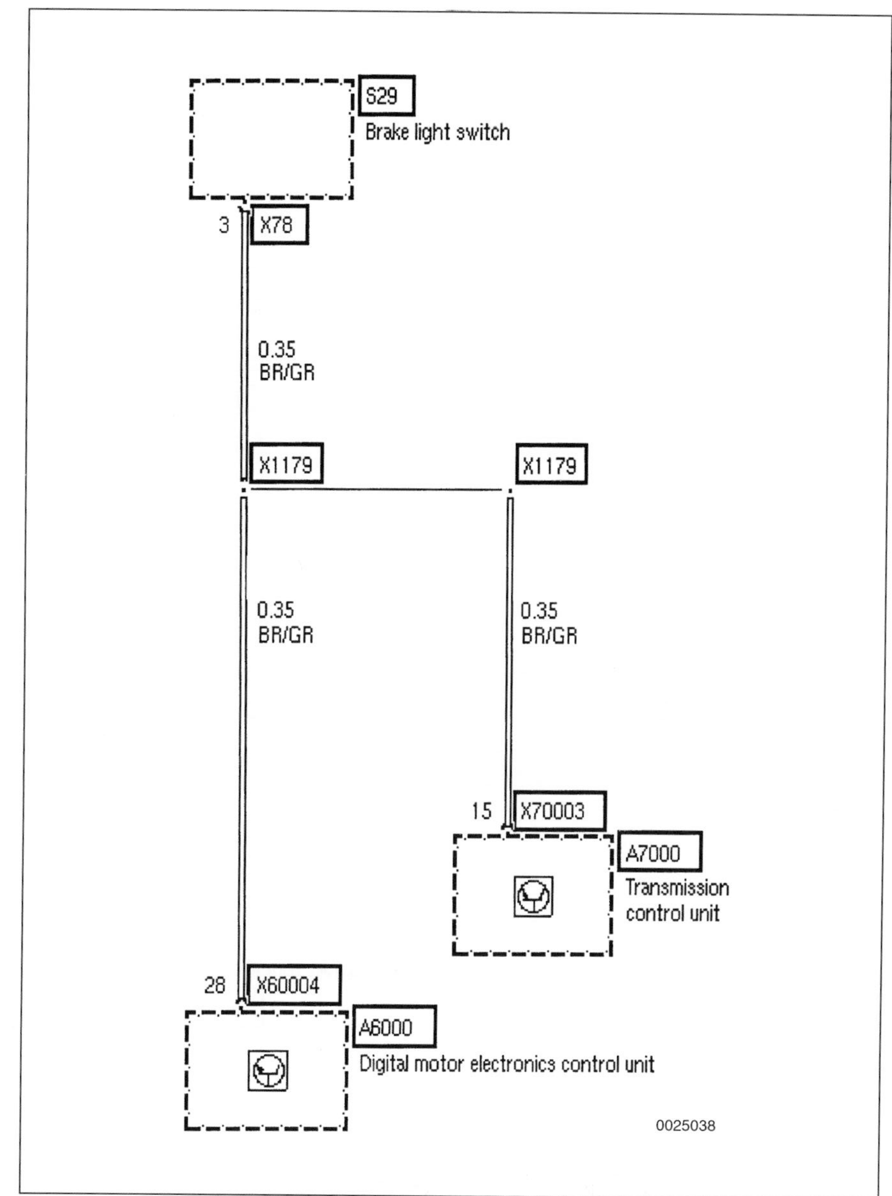

Brake light splice connector (X181)

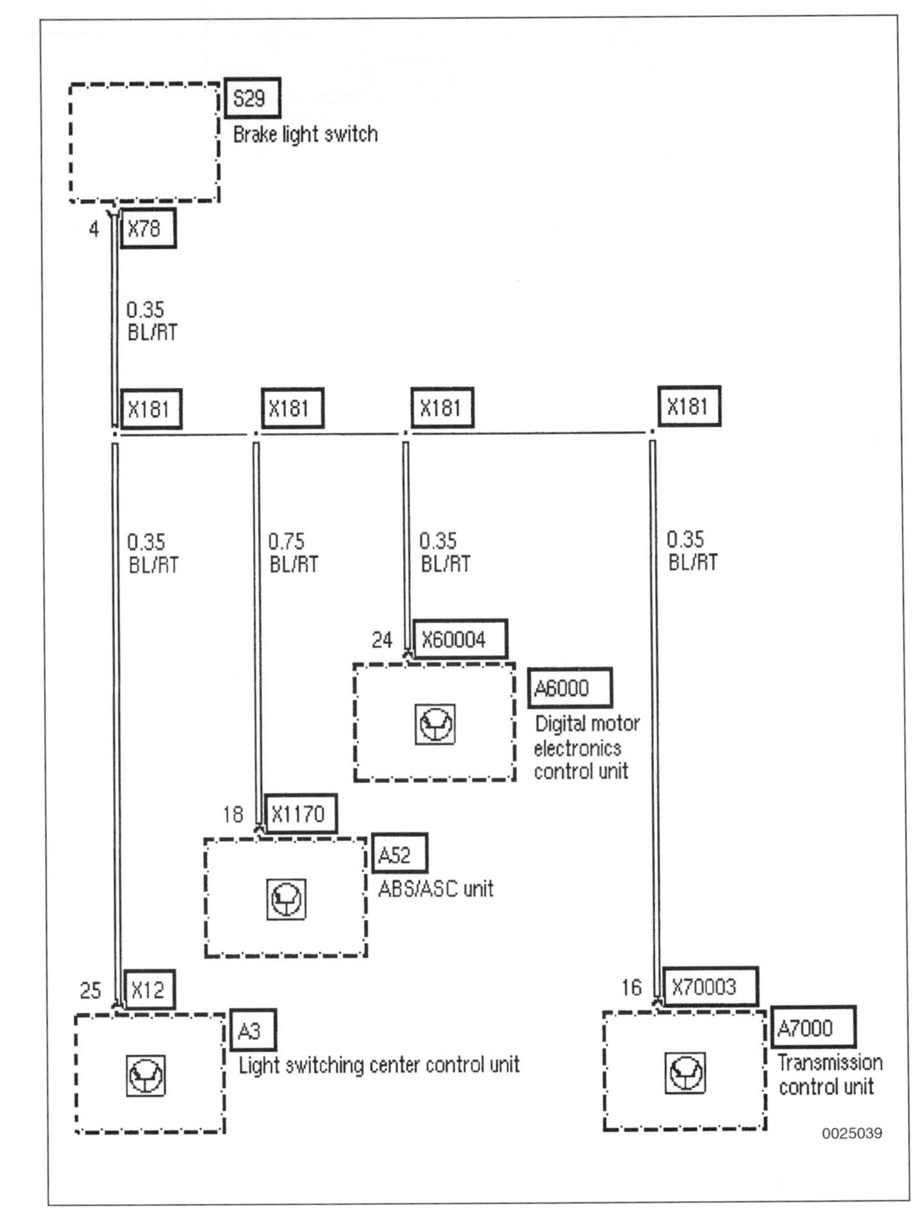

Knock sensors (B6240)

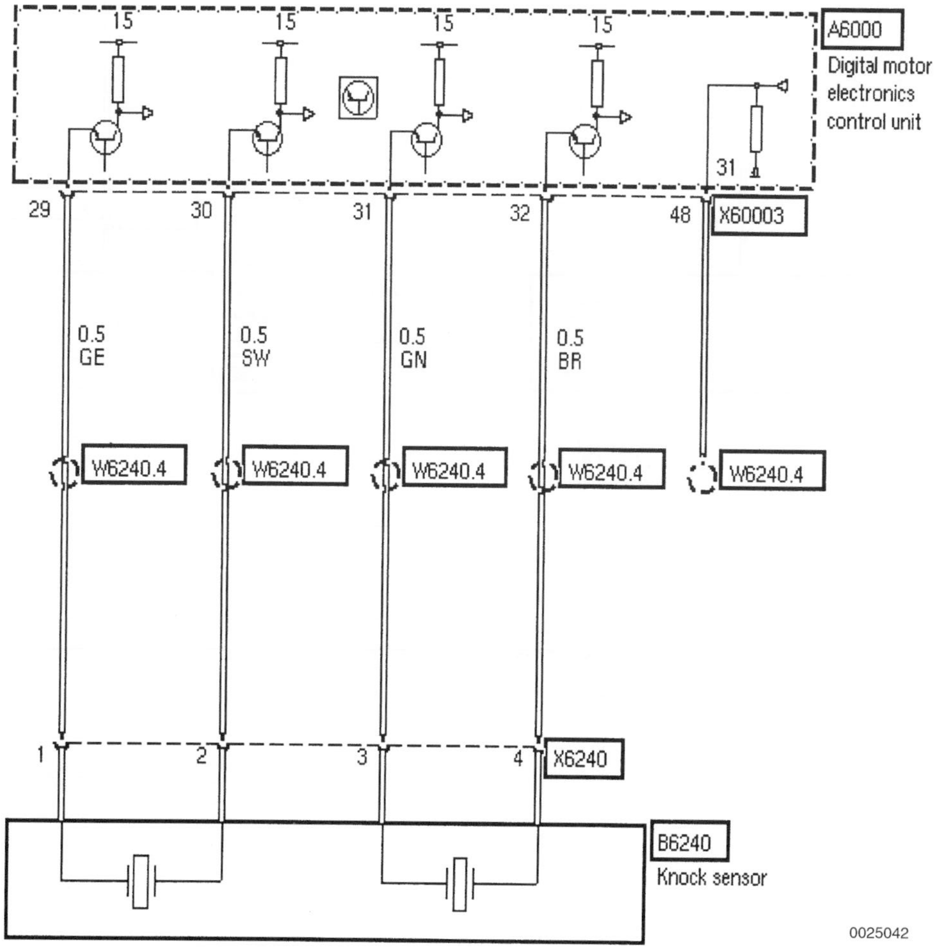

A6000
Digital motor electronics control unit

15 15 15 15 31

29 30 31 32 48 X60003

0.5 GE
0.5 SW
0.5 GN
0.5 BR

W6240.4 W6240.4 W6240.4 W6240.4 W6240.4

1 2 3 4 X6240

B6240
Knock sensor

0025042

Oxygen sensors, precatalyst (B62101, B62201)

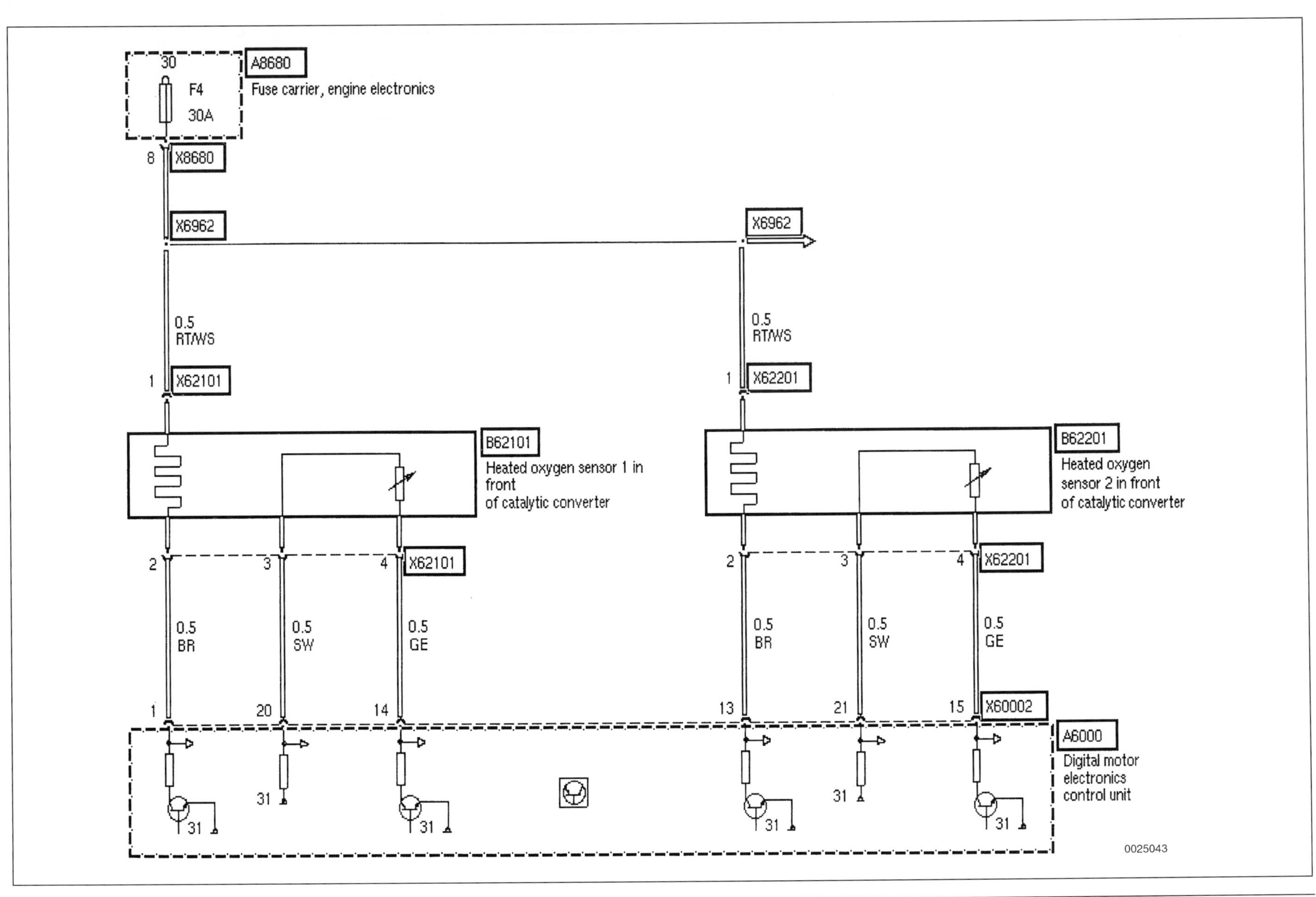

Oxygen sensors, post-catalyst (B62102, B62202)

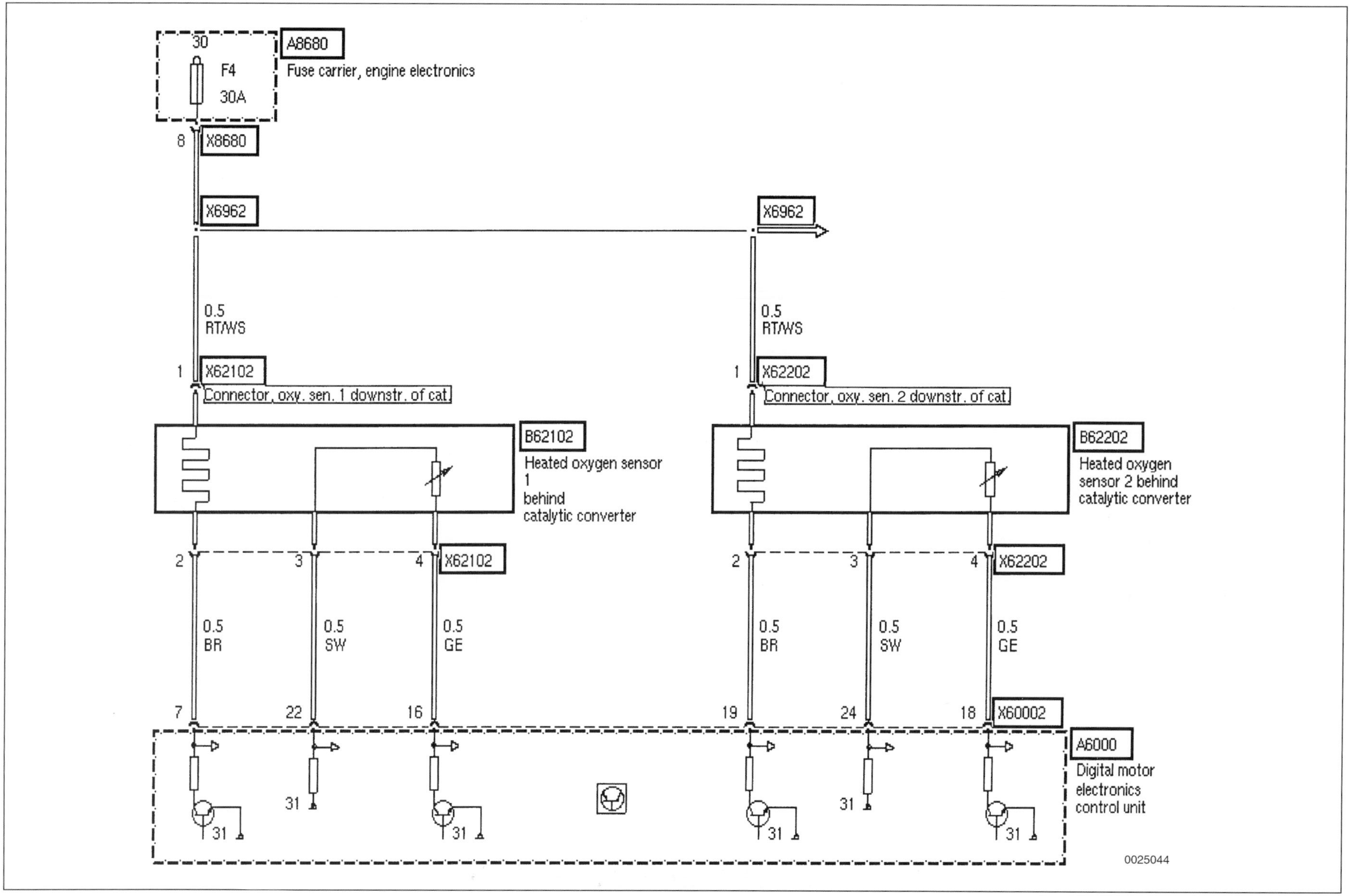

A8680
Fuse carrier, engine electronics
30
F4
30A
8 X8680
X6962
X6962
0.5
RT/WS
1 X62102
Connector, oxy. sen. 1 downstr. of cat.
0.5
RT/WS
1 X62202
Connector, oxy. sen. 2 downstr. of cat.
B62102
Heated oxygen sensor
1
behind
catalytic converter
B62202
Heated oxygen
sensor 2 behind
catalytic converter
2 3 4 X62102
0.5 BR
0.5 SW
0.5 GE
2 3 4 X62202
0.5 BR
0.5 SW
0.5 GE
7 22 16
19 24 18 X60002
31
31
31
31
31
31
A6000
Digital motor
electronics
control unit
0025044

Throttle valve (MDK) (DME MS 42.0) (R6385)

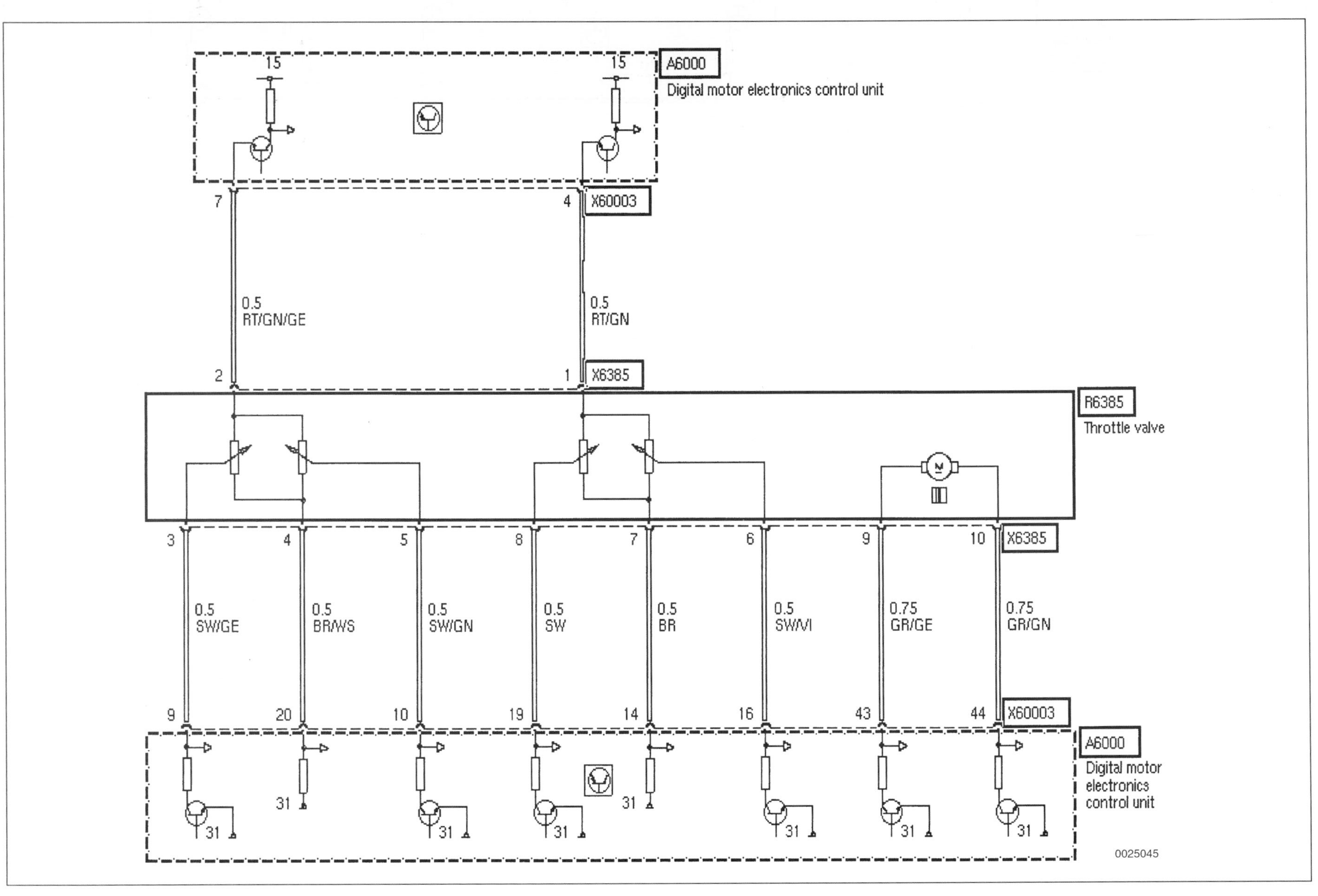

Changeover valve, intake manifold (Y6167)

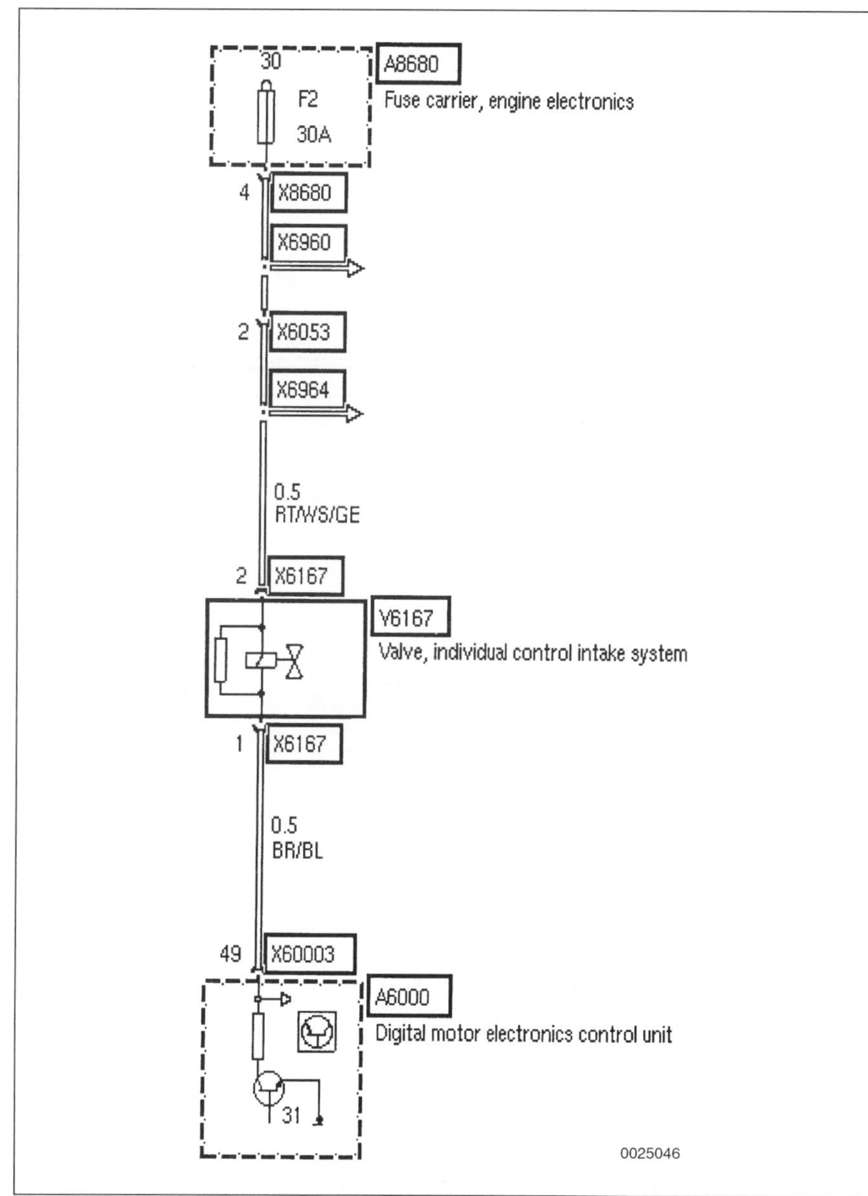

Idle speed control valve (Y6130)

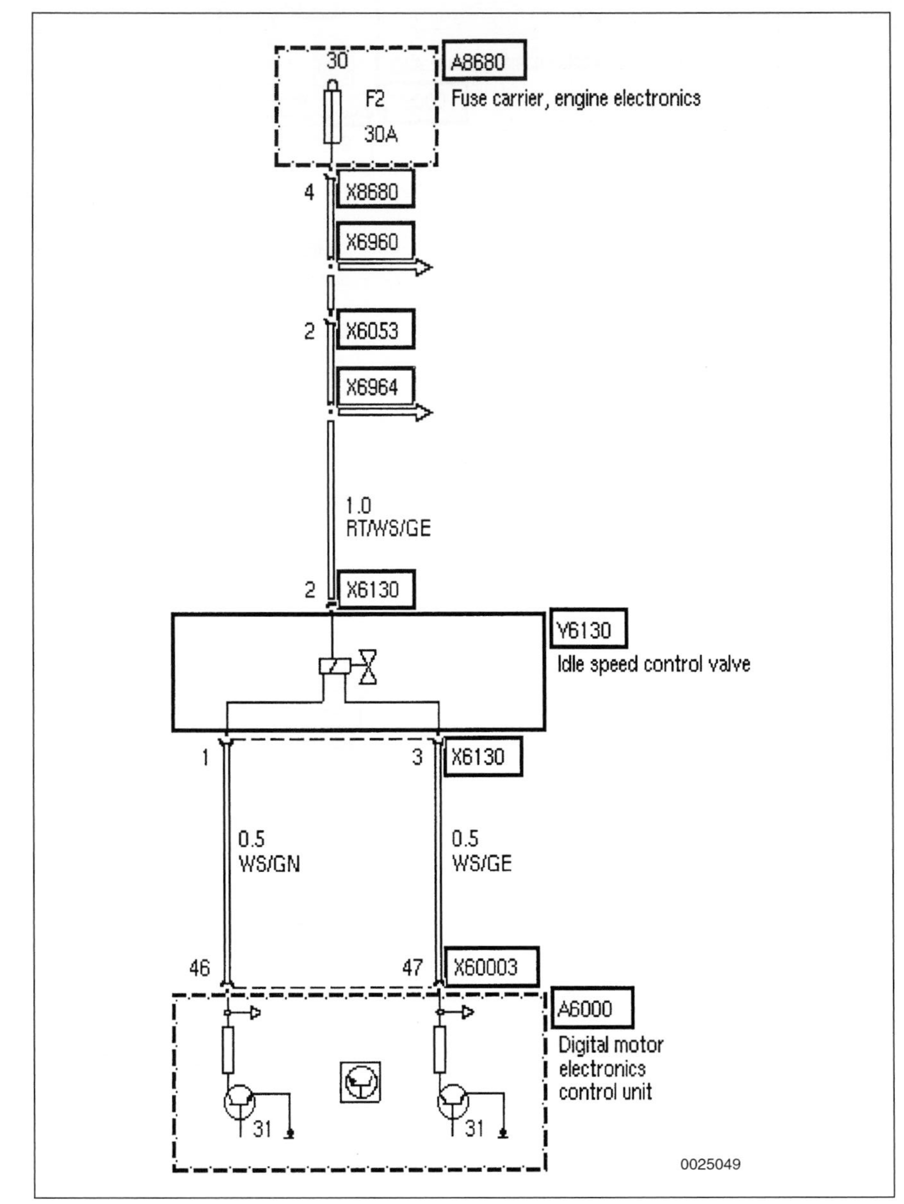

Mass air flow sensor (B6207)

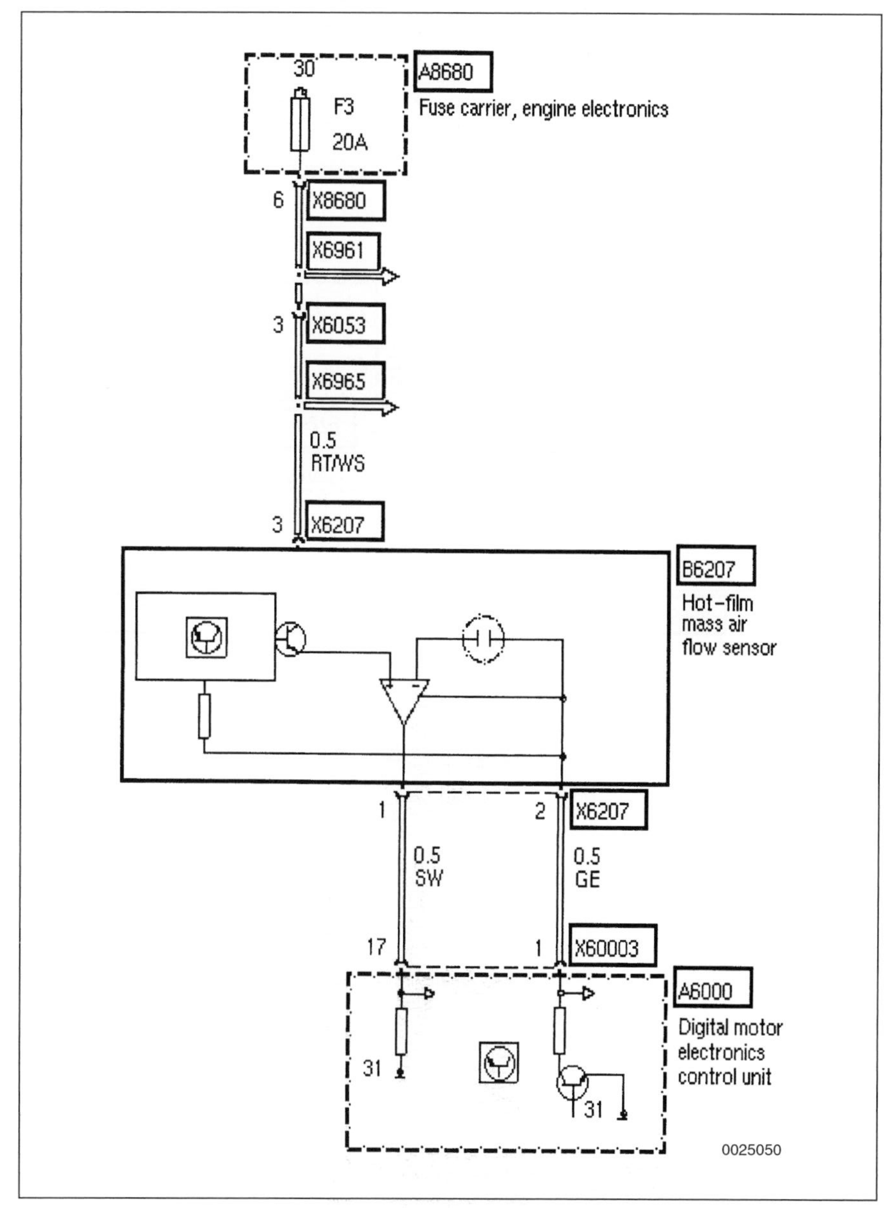

Splice connector (X6965)

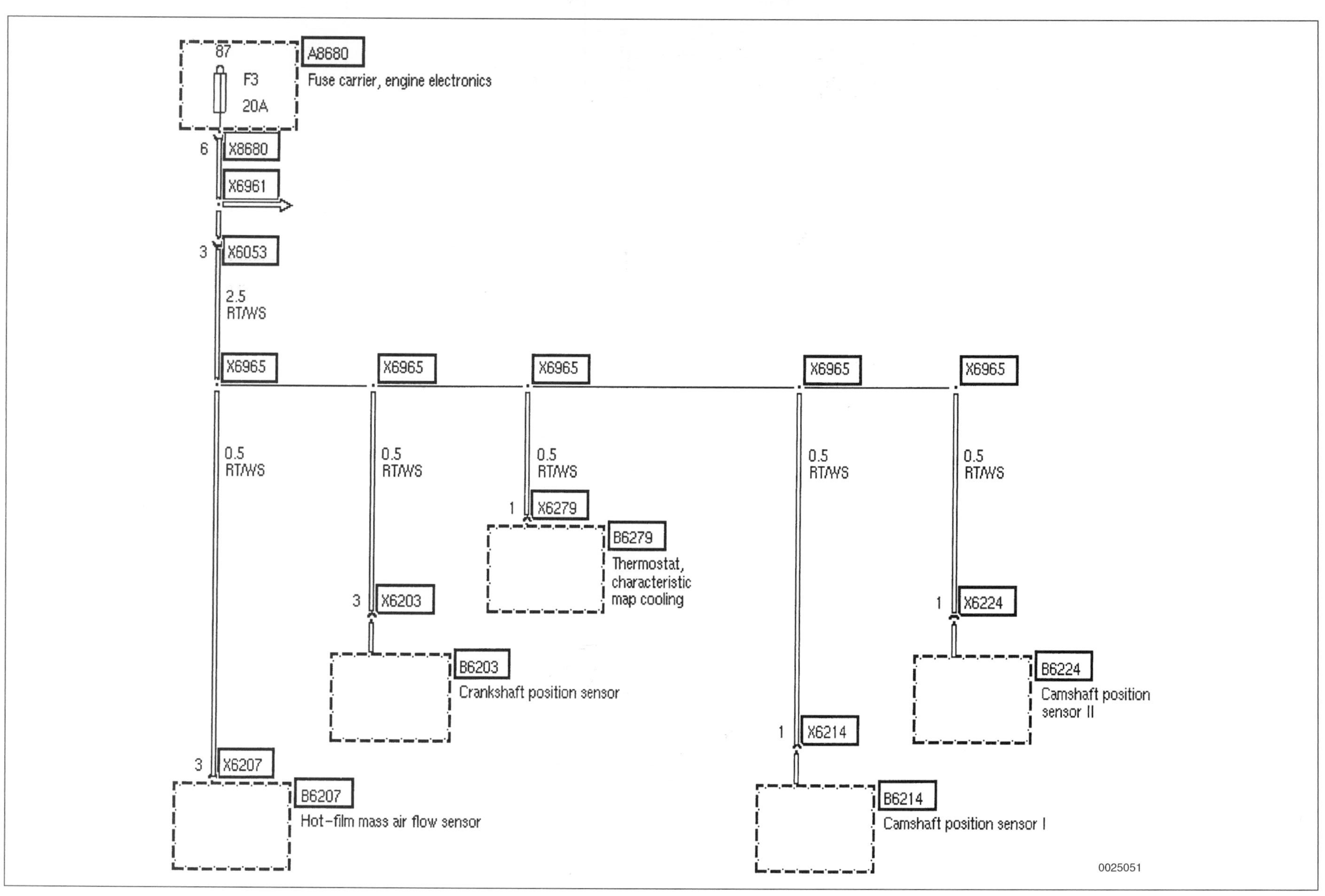

Intake air temperature (IAT) sensor (B6205)

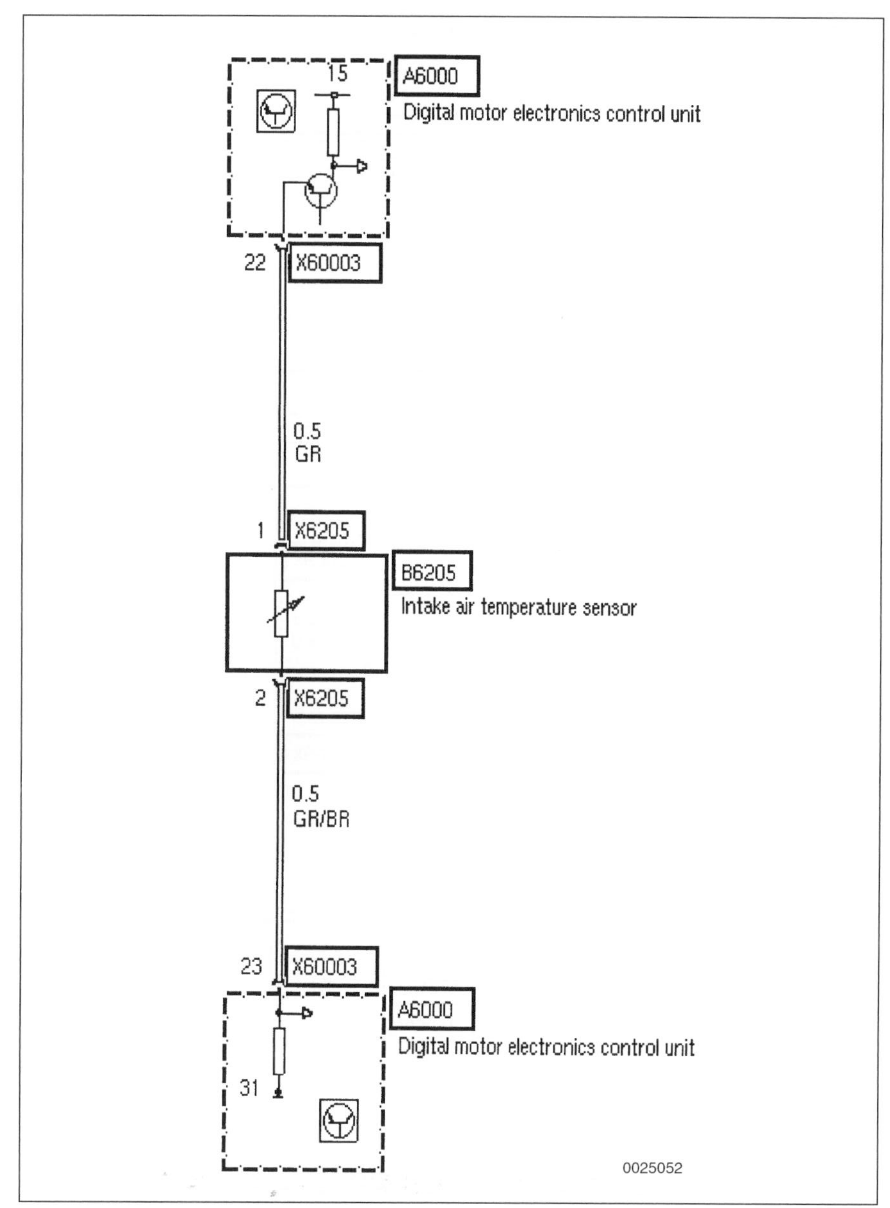

Crankshaft position sensor (B6203)

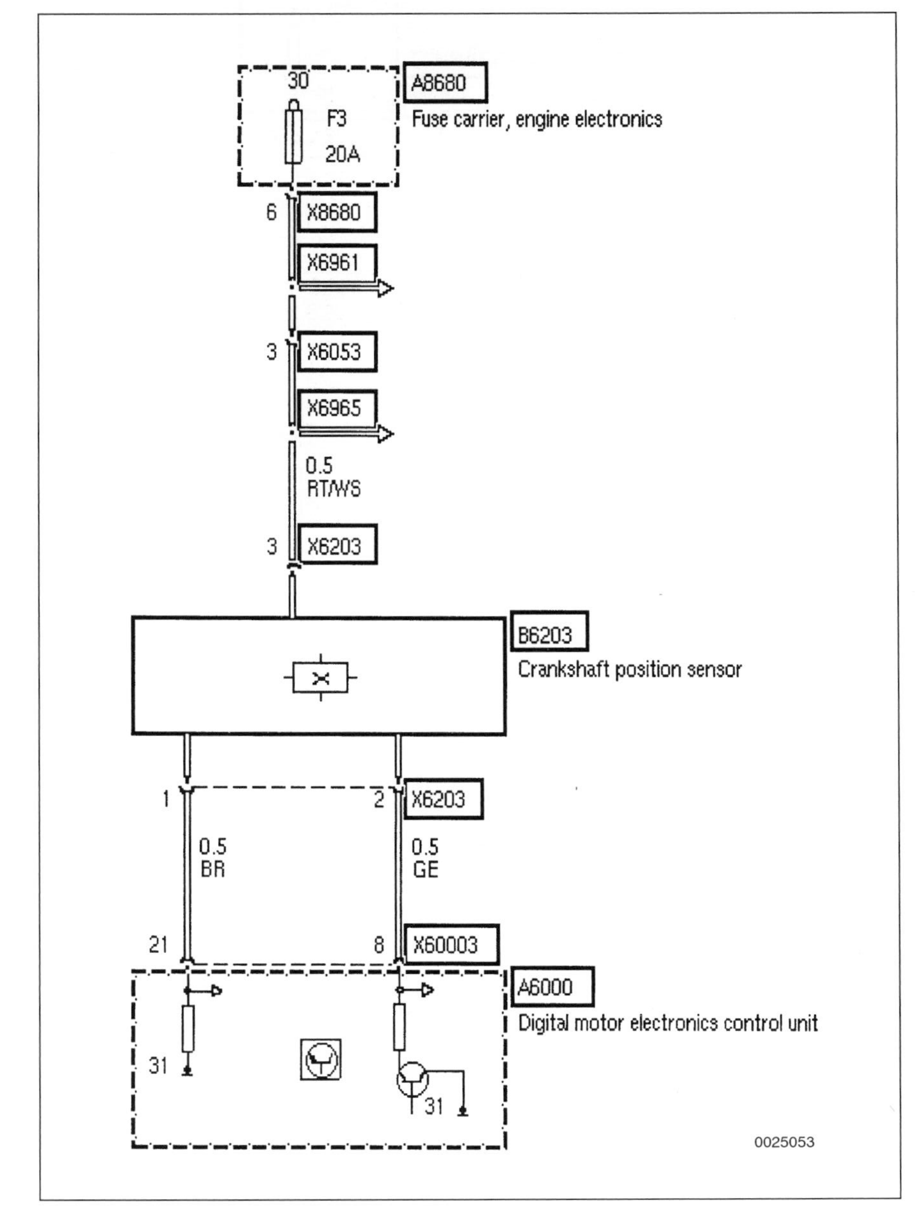

Thermostat (B6279)

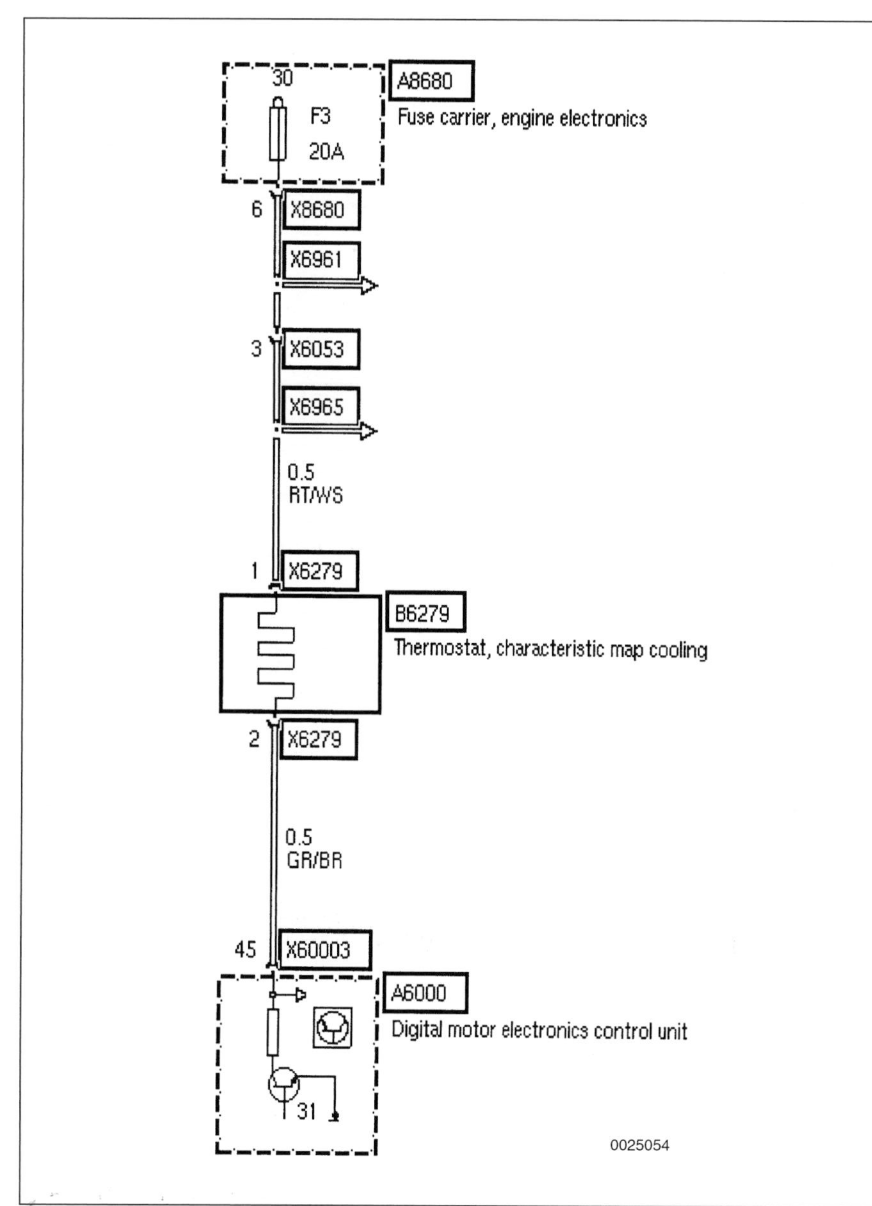

30
F3
20A
A8680
Fuse carrier, engine electronics
6
X8680
X6961
3
X6053
X6965
0.5
RT/WS
1
X6279
B6279
Thermostat, characteristic map cooling
2
X6279
0.5
GR/BR
45
X60003
A6000
Digital motor electronics control unit
31
0025054

Engine coolant temperature (ECT) sensor (B6236)

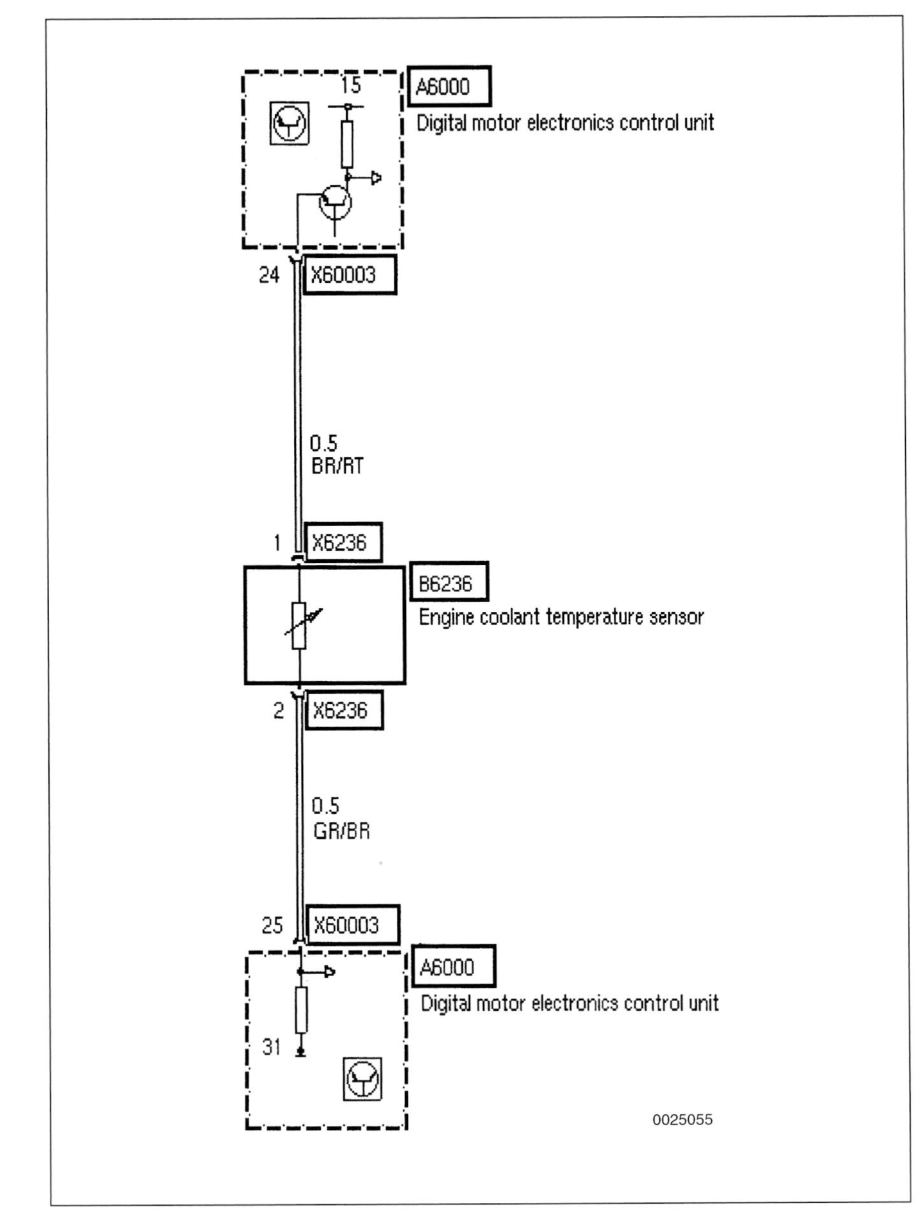

Engine cooling fan (M9)

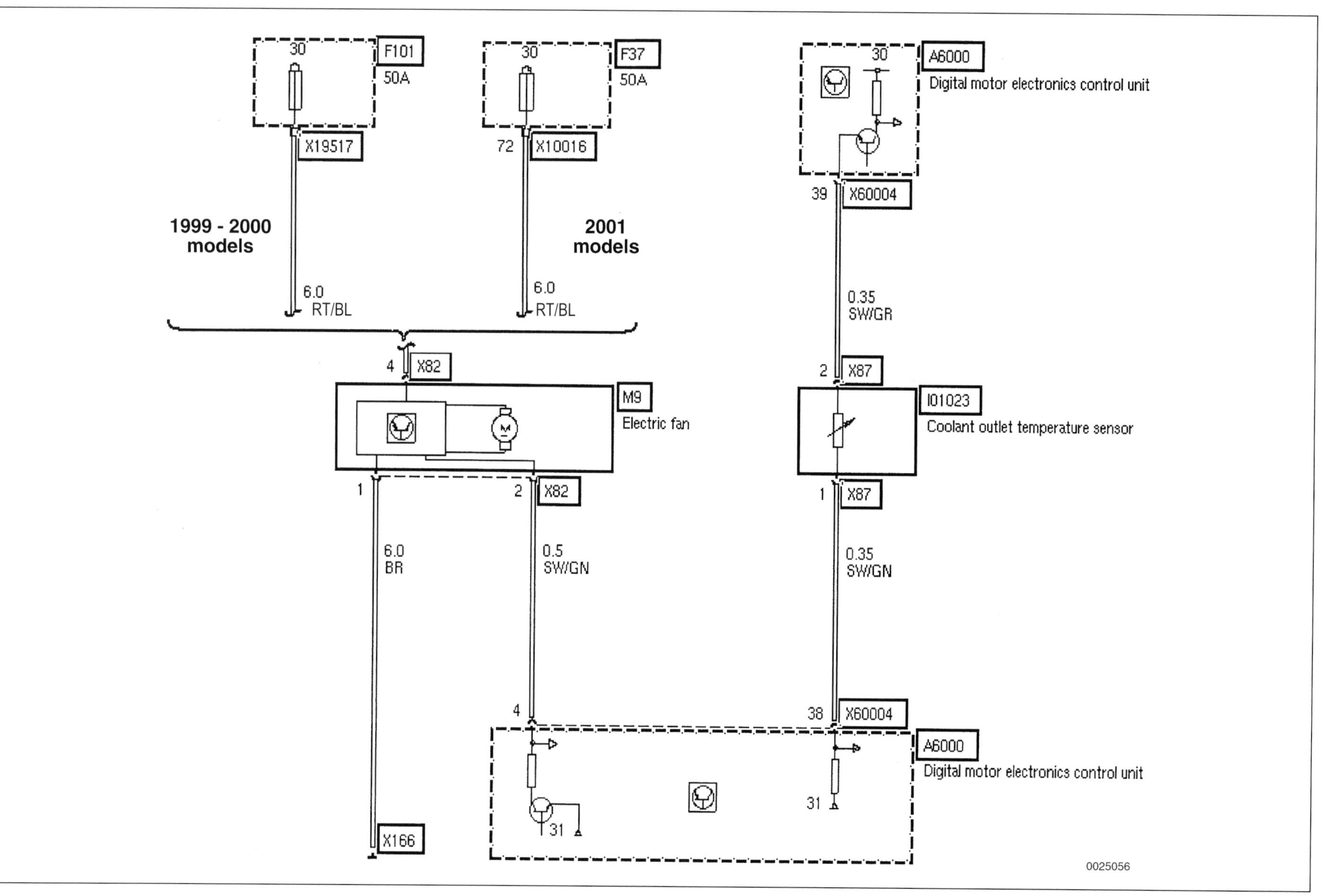

Ground (X166)
1 of 2

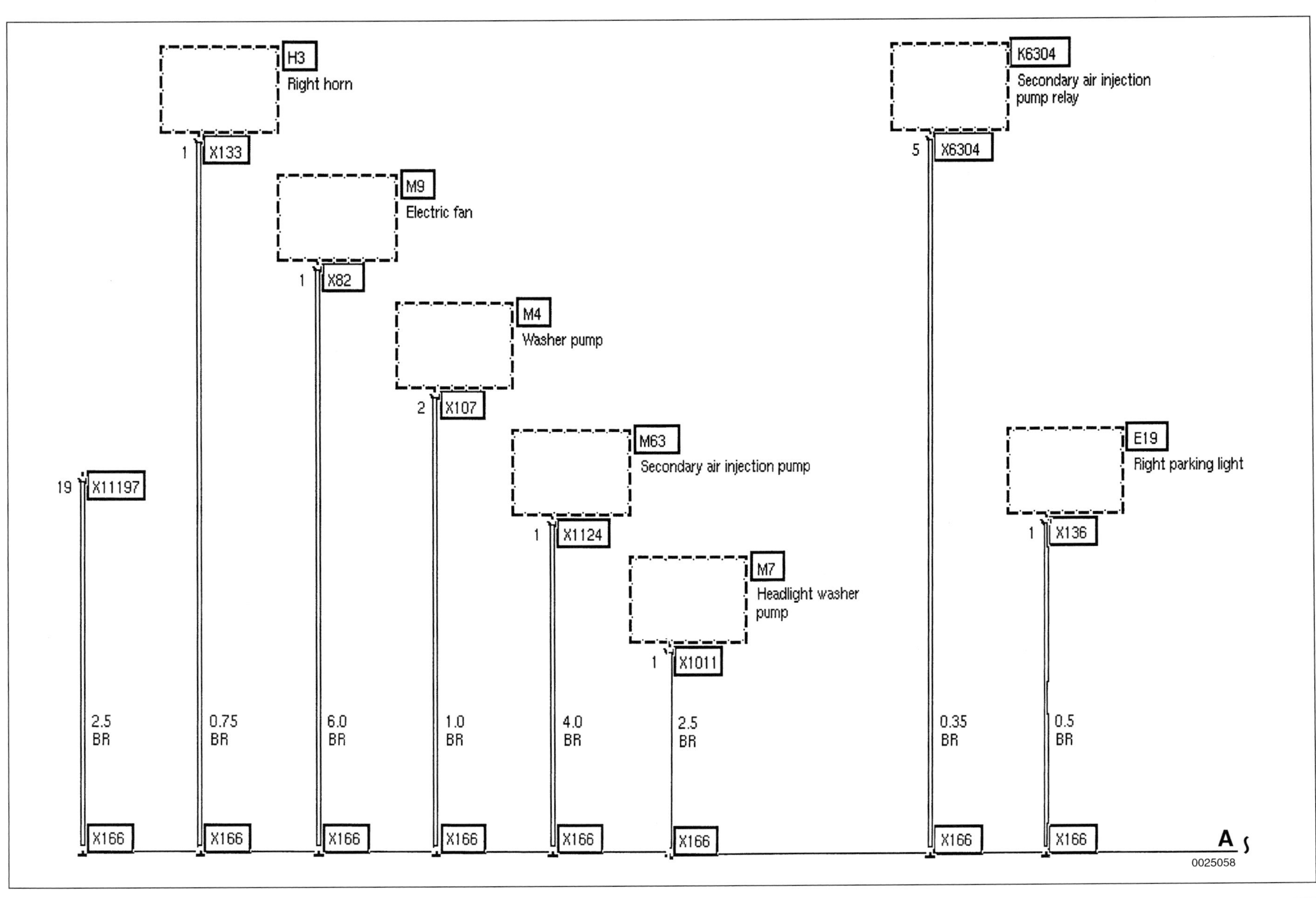

Ground (X166)
2 of 2

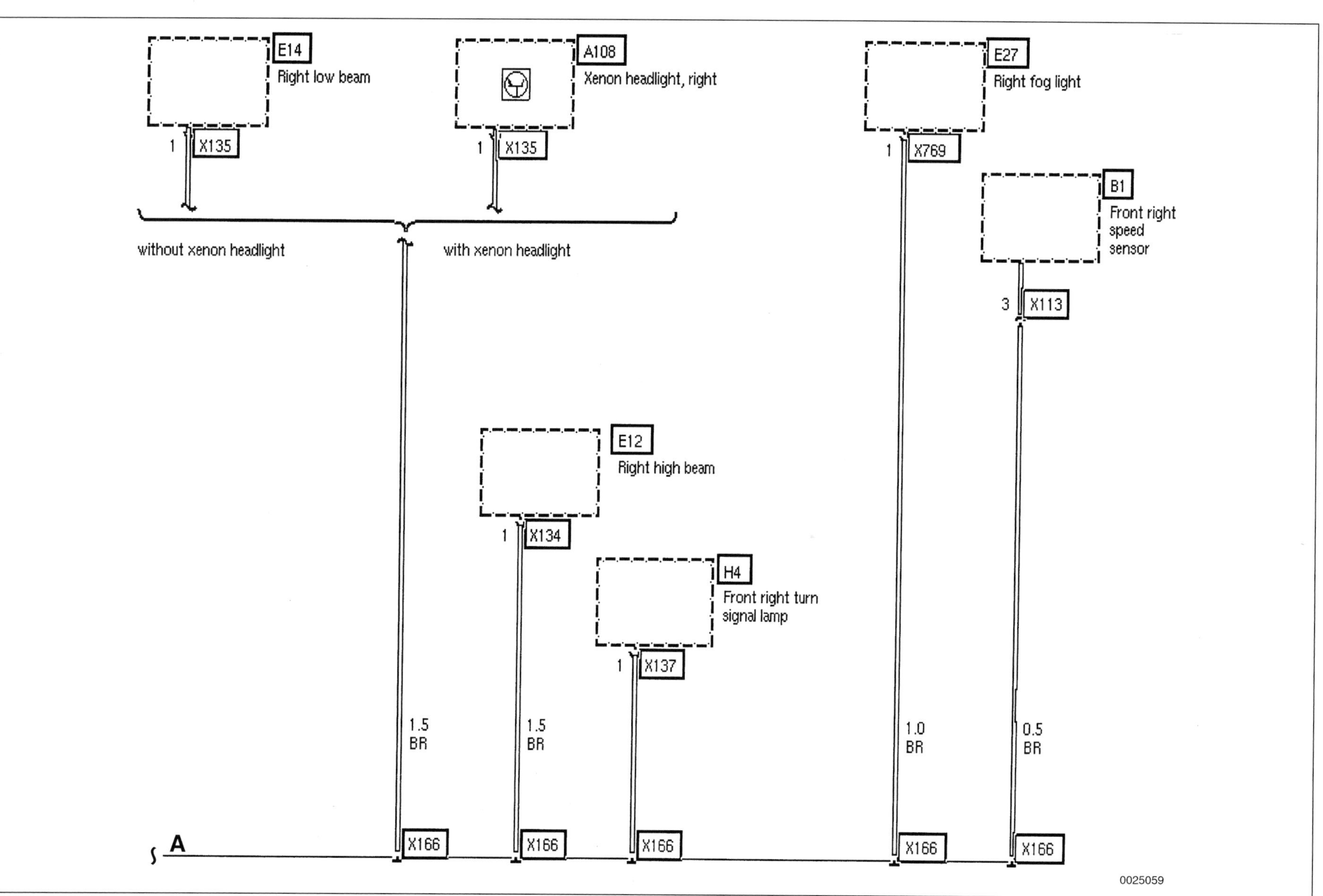

Oil temperature sensor (B6238)

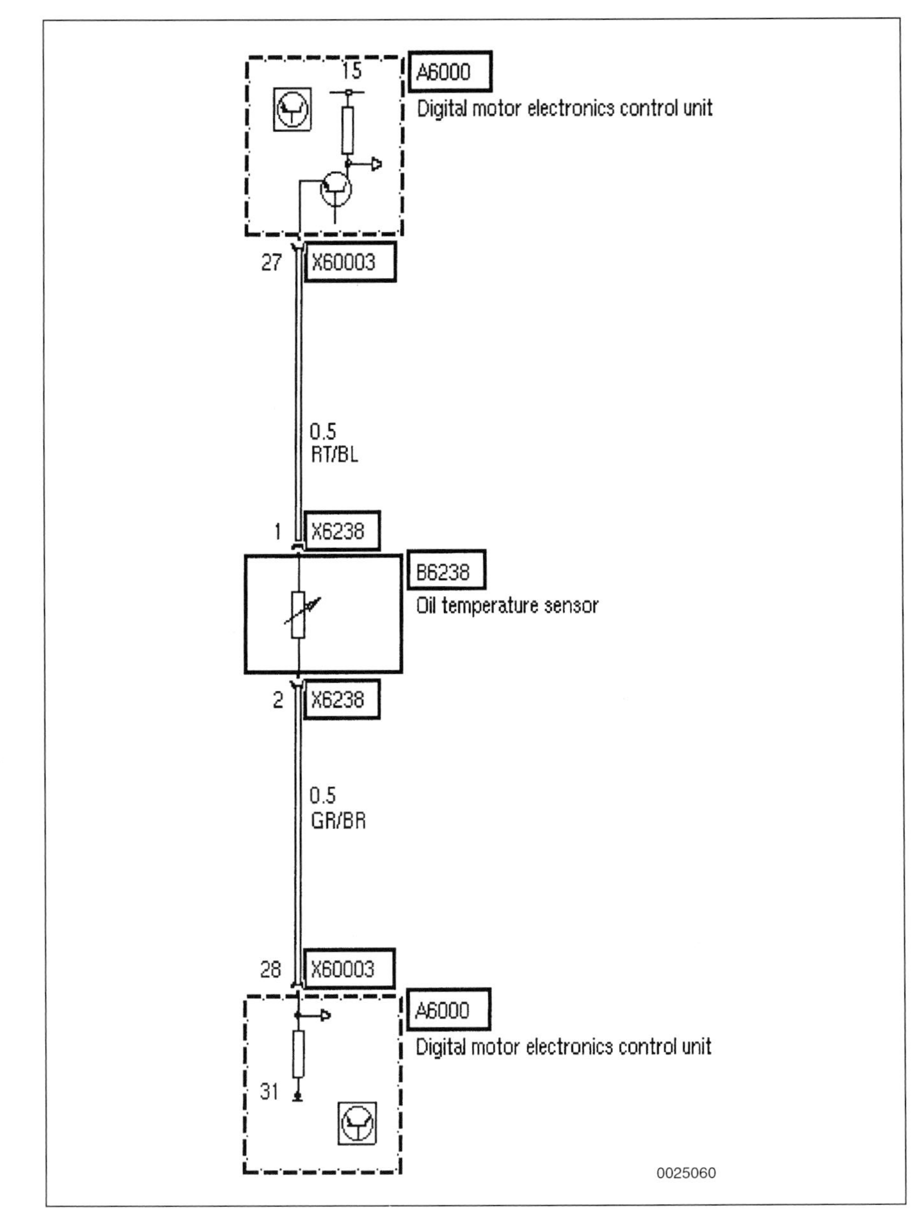

Fuse 37 (F37)

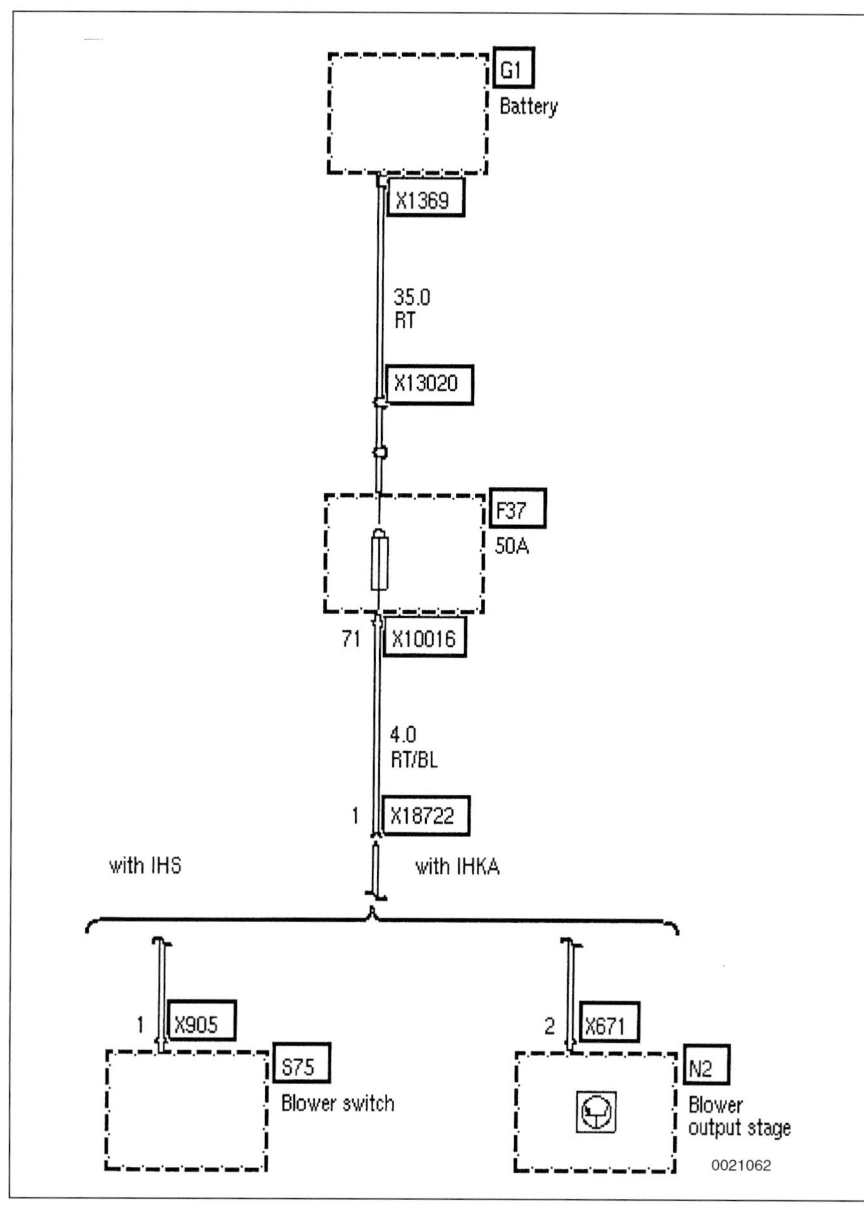
G1
Battery
X1369
35.0
RT
X13020
F37
50A
71
X10016
4.0
RT/BL
1
X18722
with IHS
with IHKA
1
X905
S75
Blower switch
2
X671
N2
Blower
output stage
0021062

This page left intentionally blank

Transmission control unit (A7000), module 1

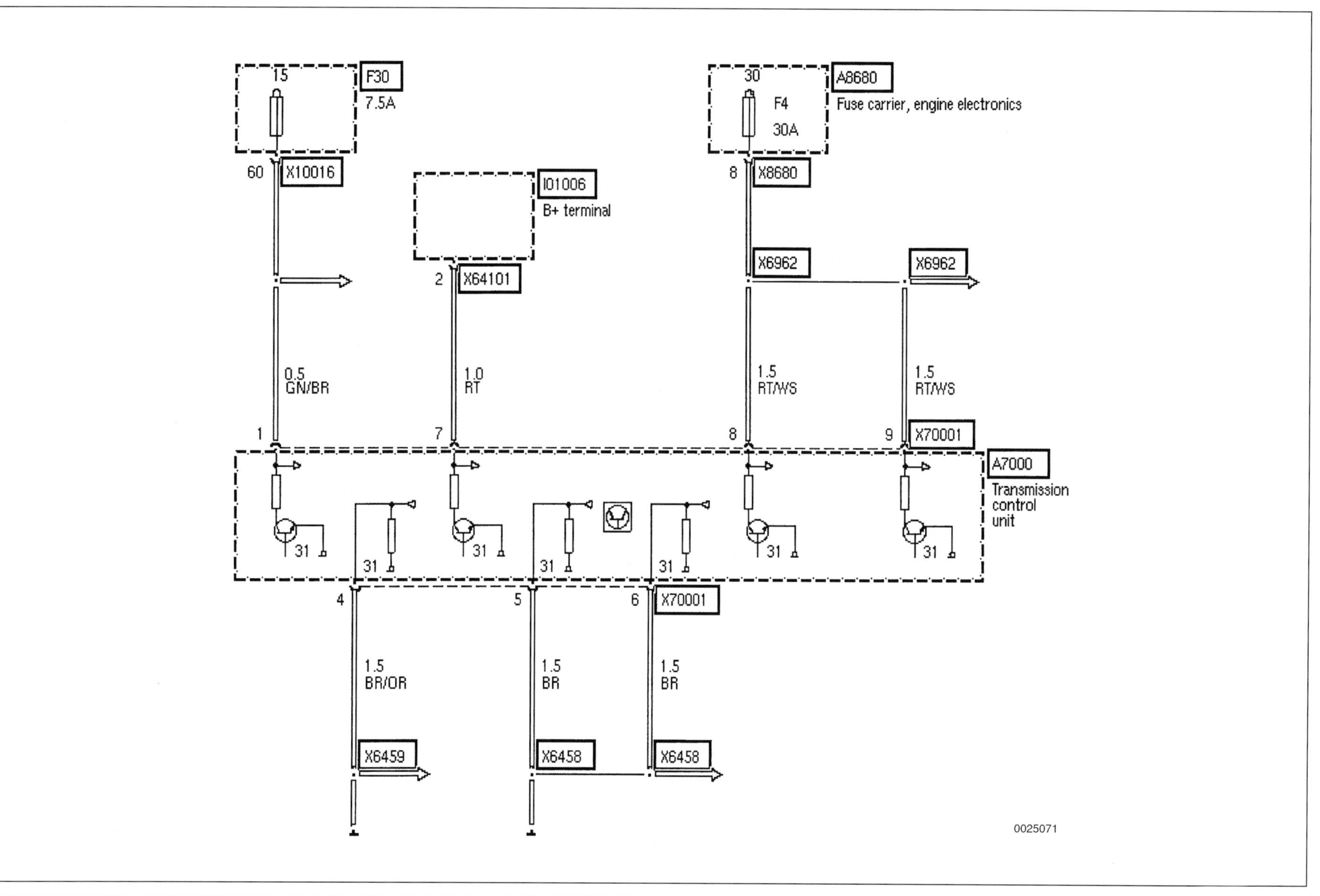

Instrument cluster control unit (A2)
1 of 3

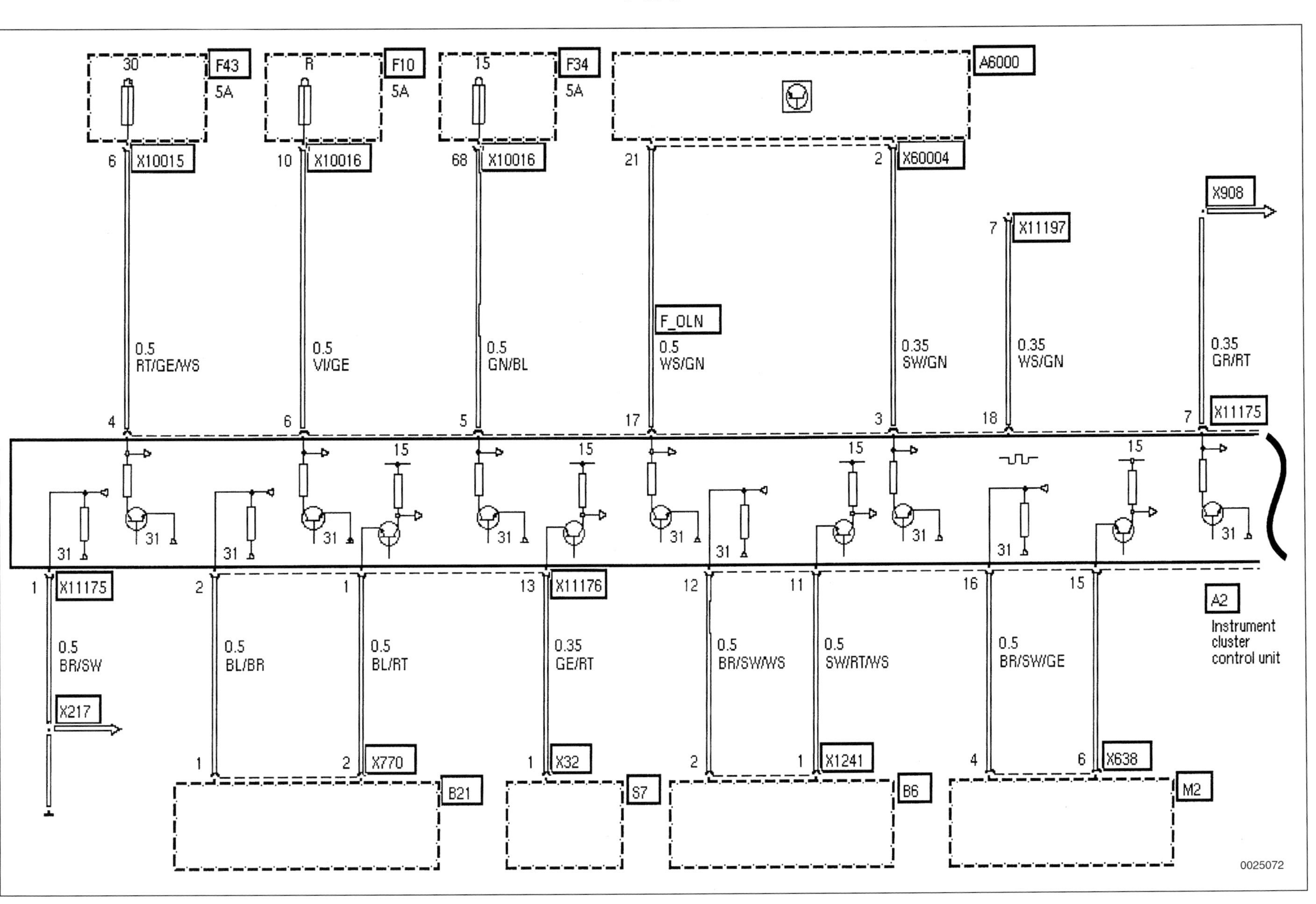

Instrument cluster control unit (A2)
2 of 3

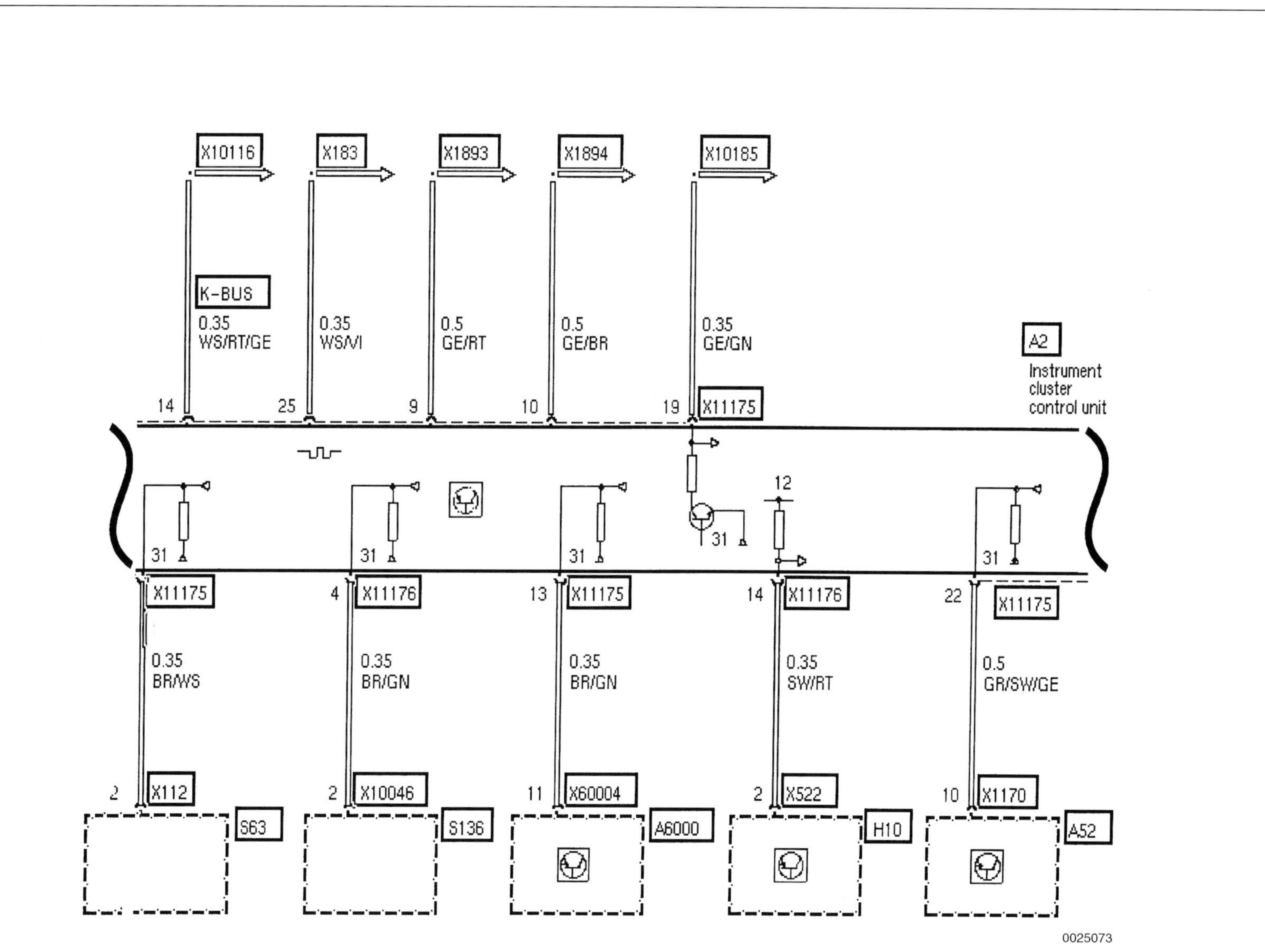

Instrument cluster control unit (A2)
3 of 3

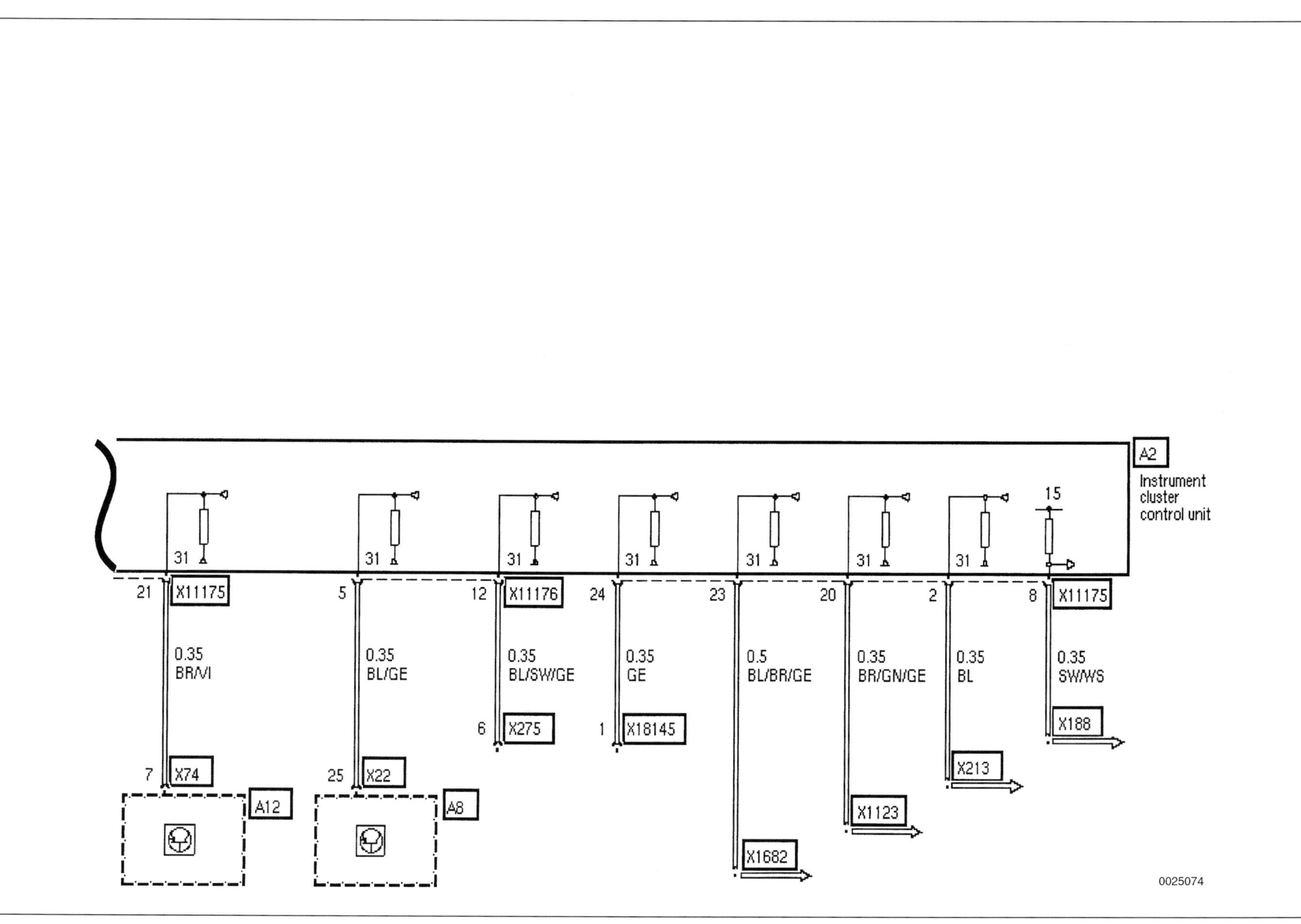

Camshaft position sensors (B6214, B6224)

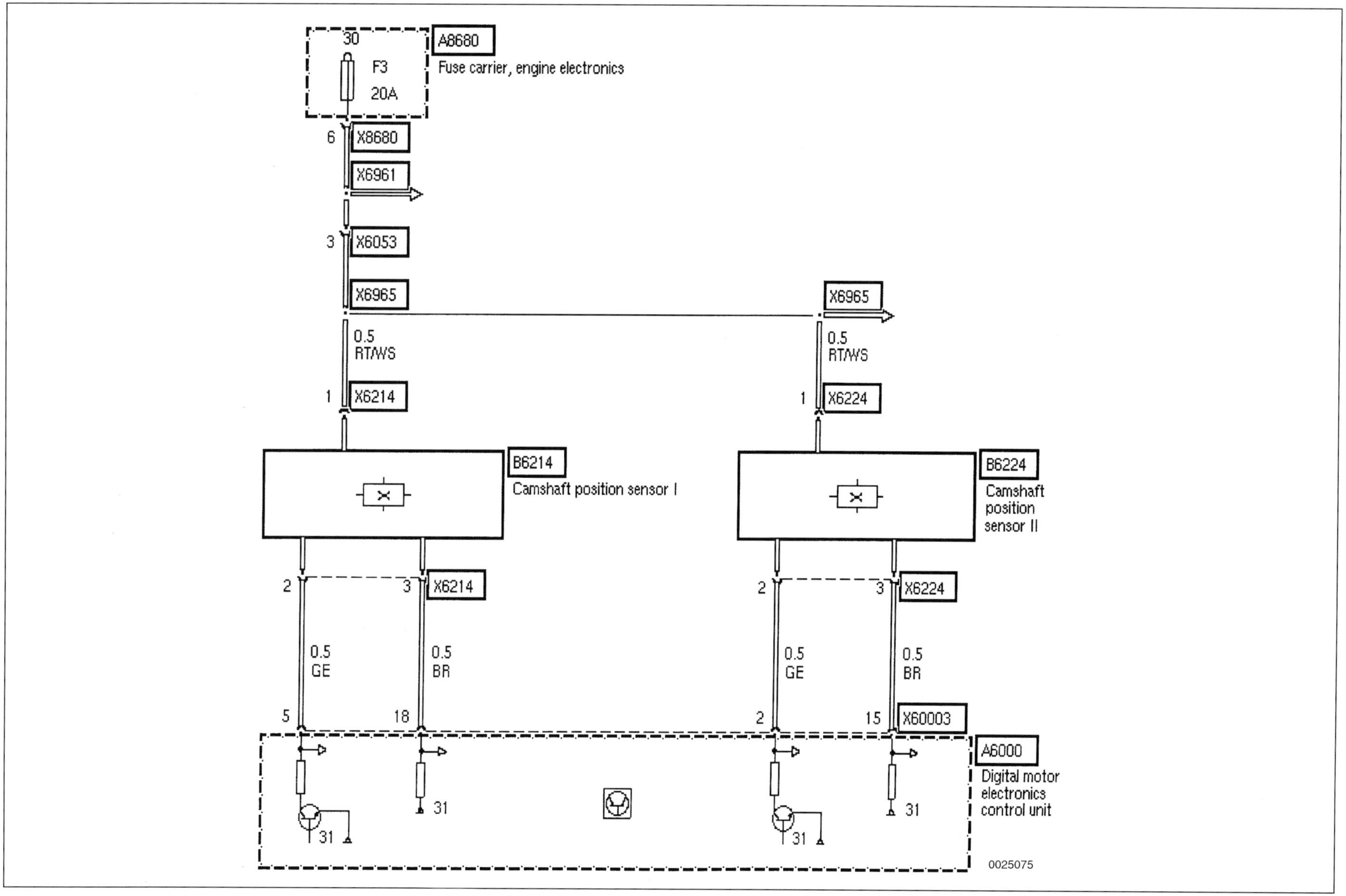

VANOS solenoid valves (Y6275, Y6276)

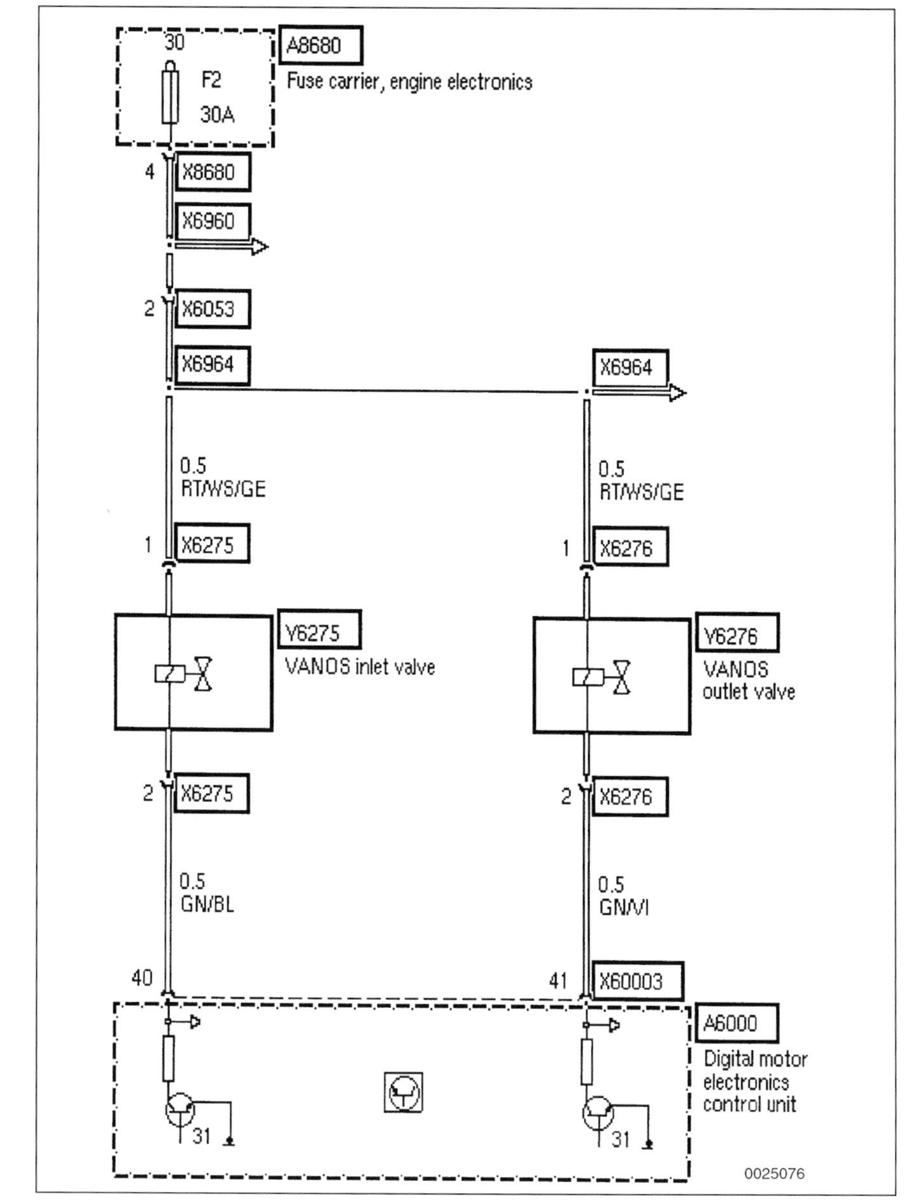

Suction jet pump (Y6165)

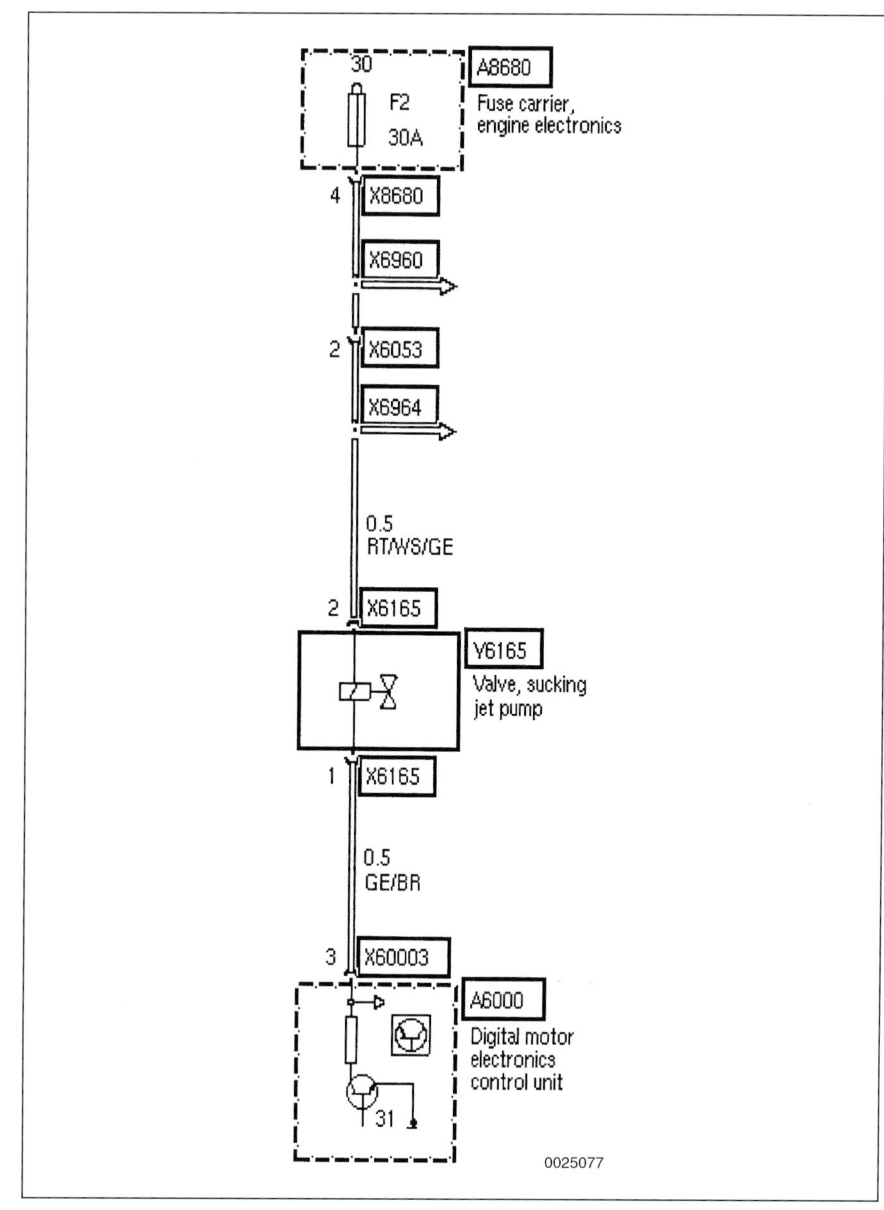

Diagnostic Link Connector (20-pin DLC) (X11197)

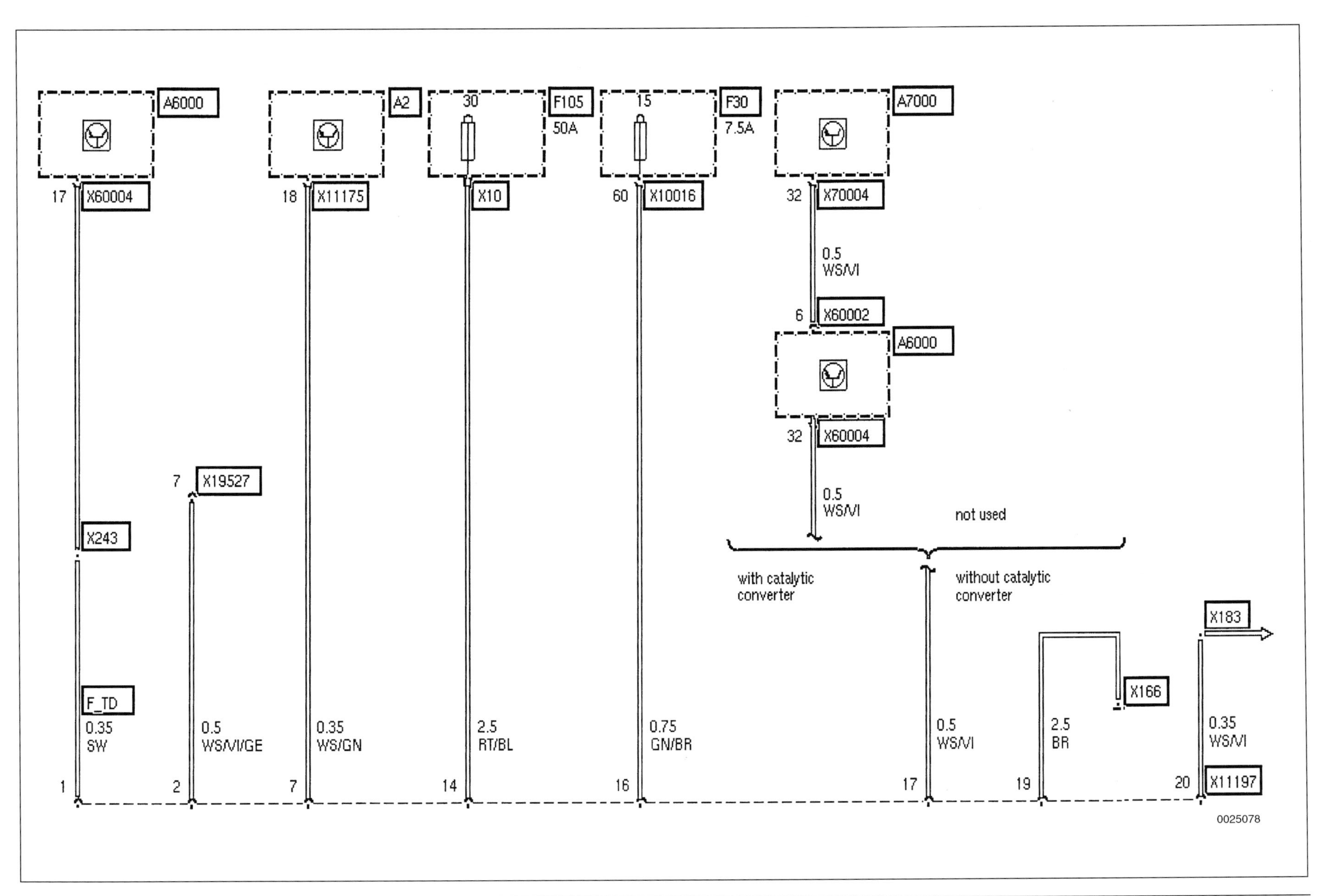

Fuse 105 (F105)

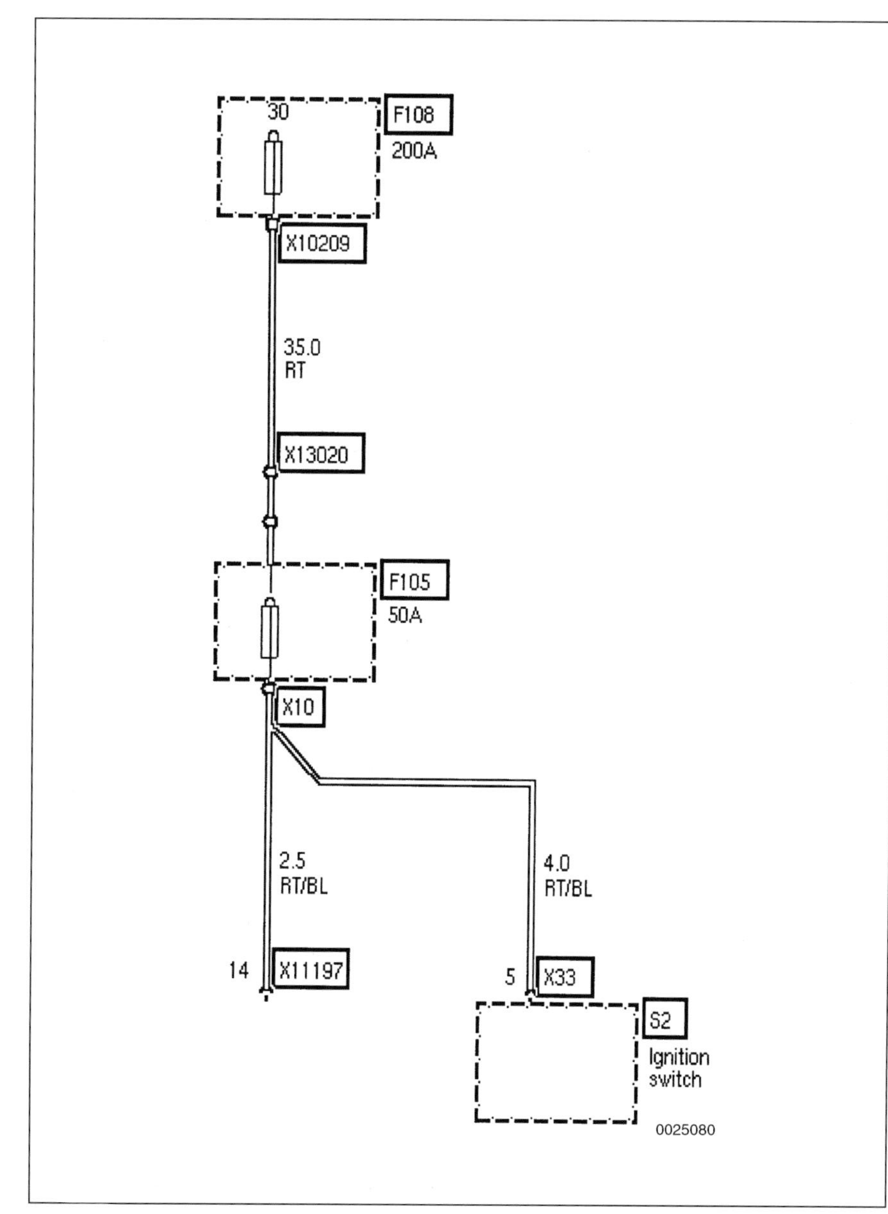

Fuse 30 (F30)

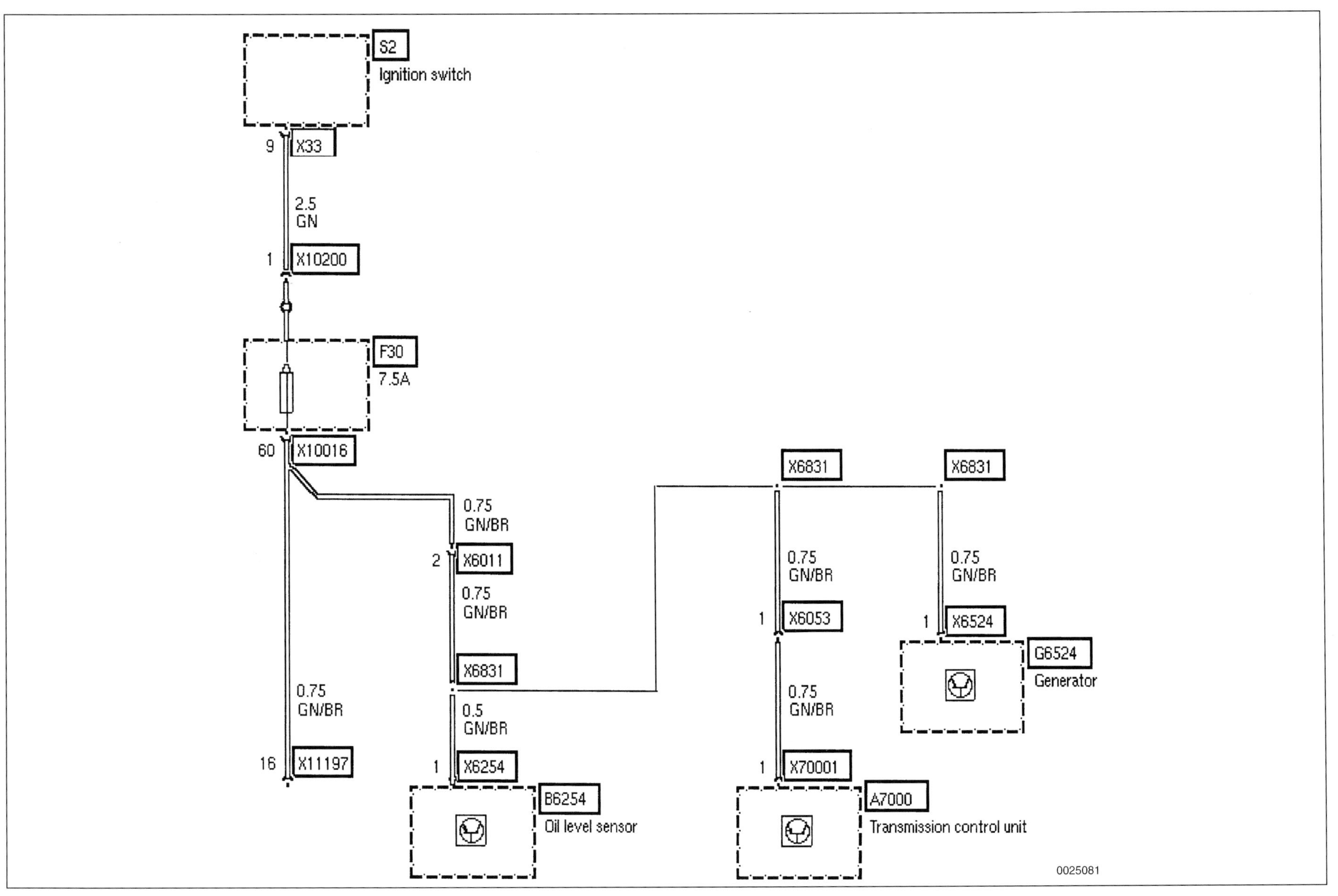
S2
Ignition switch
9
X33
2.5
GN
1
X10200
F30
7.5A
60
X10016
0.75
GN/BR
2
X6011
0.75
GN/BR
X6831
0.5
GN/BR
1
X6254
B6254
Oil level sensor
0.75
GN/BR
16
X11197
X6831
0.75
GN/BR
1
X6053
0.75
GN/BR
1
X70001
A7000
Transmission control unit
X6831
0.75
GN/BR
1
X6524
G6524
Generator
0025081

Splice connector (X243)

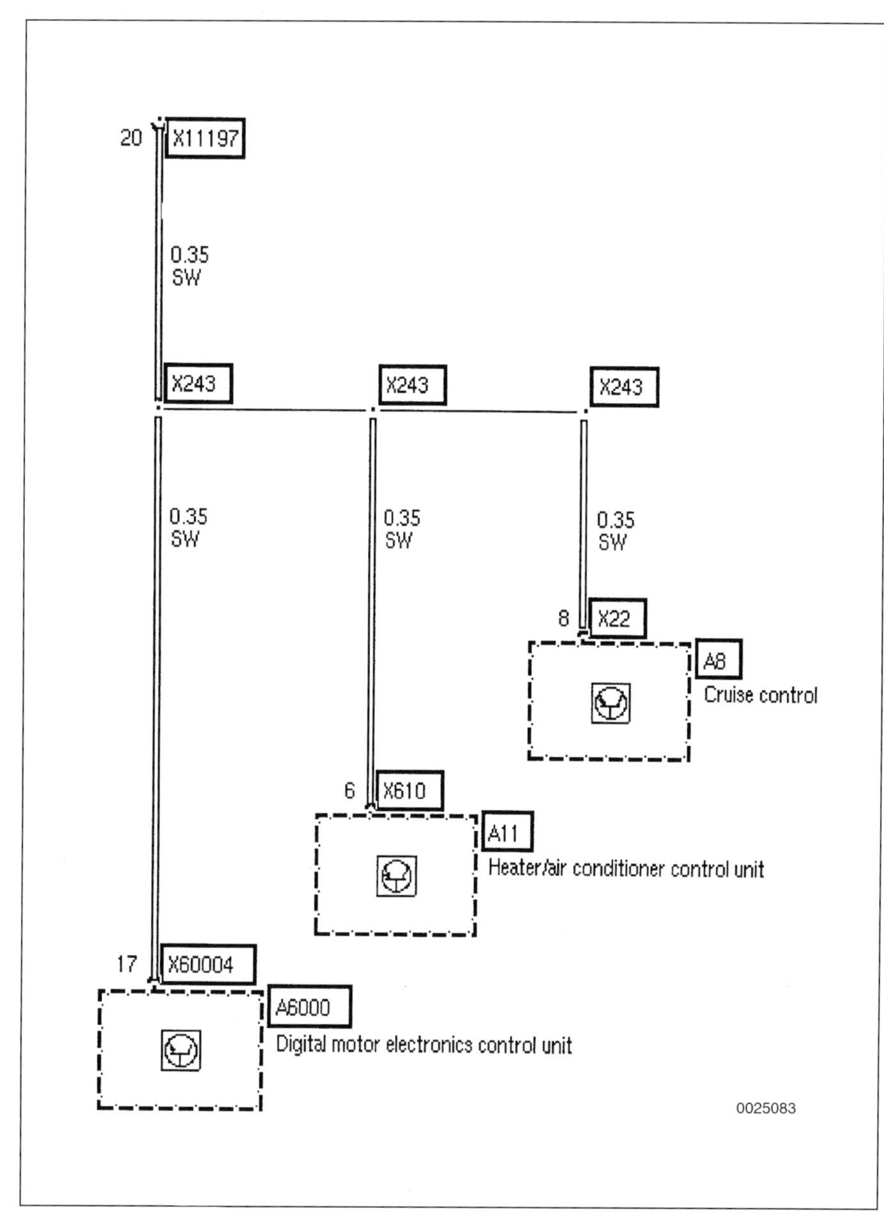

OBD II socket (16-pin DLC) (I01019)

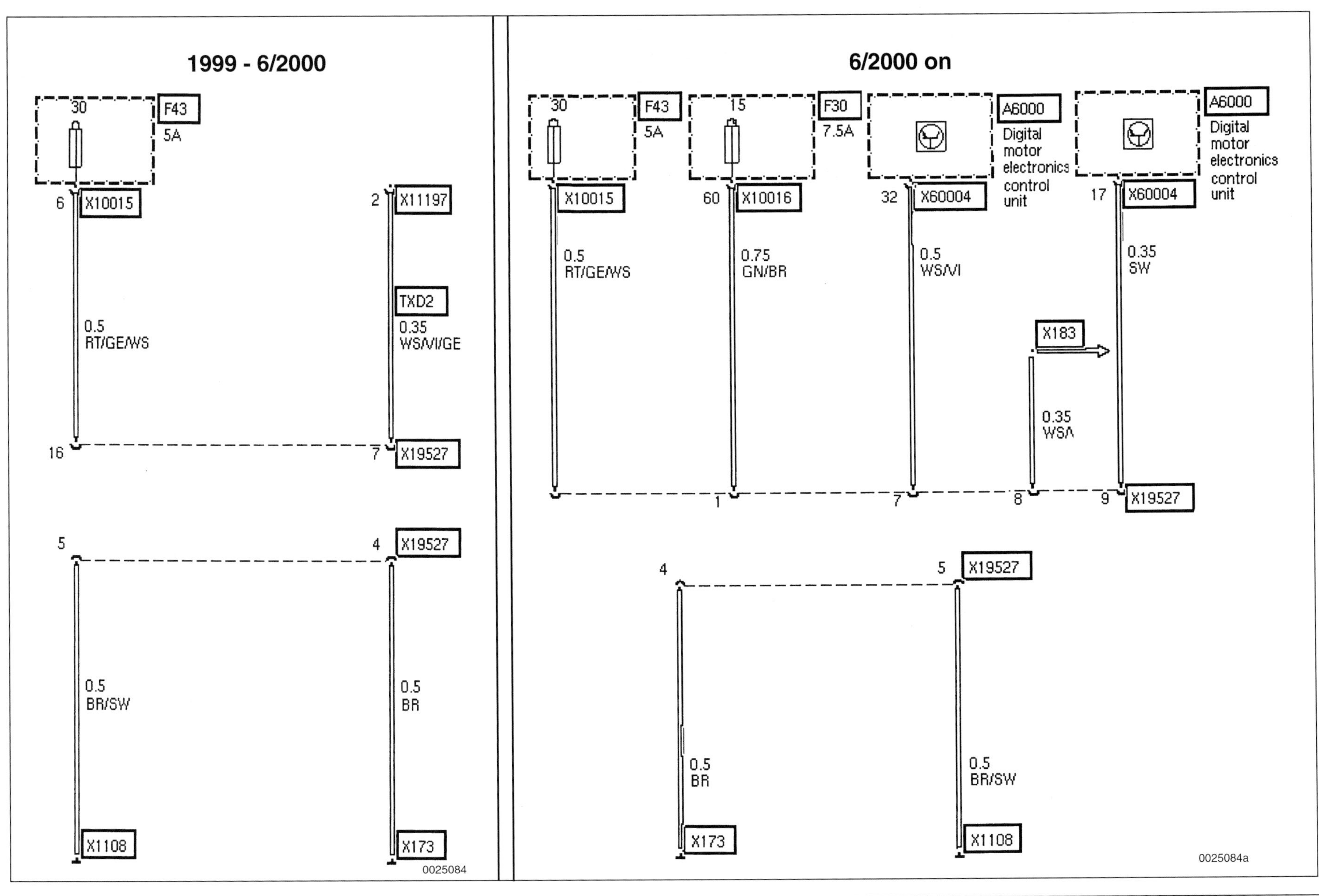

Splice connector (X183)

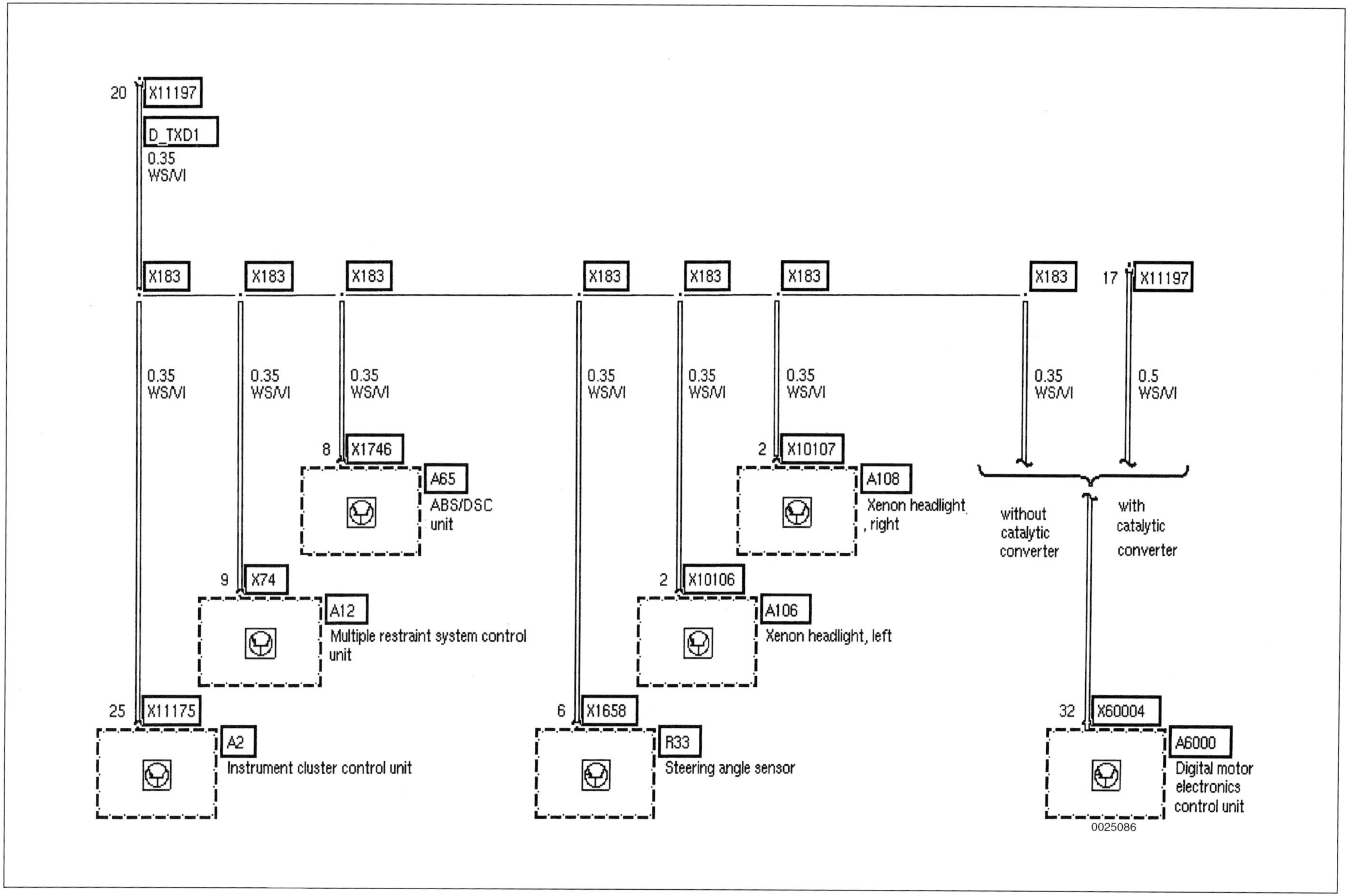

Vehicle speed signal

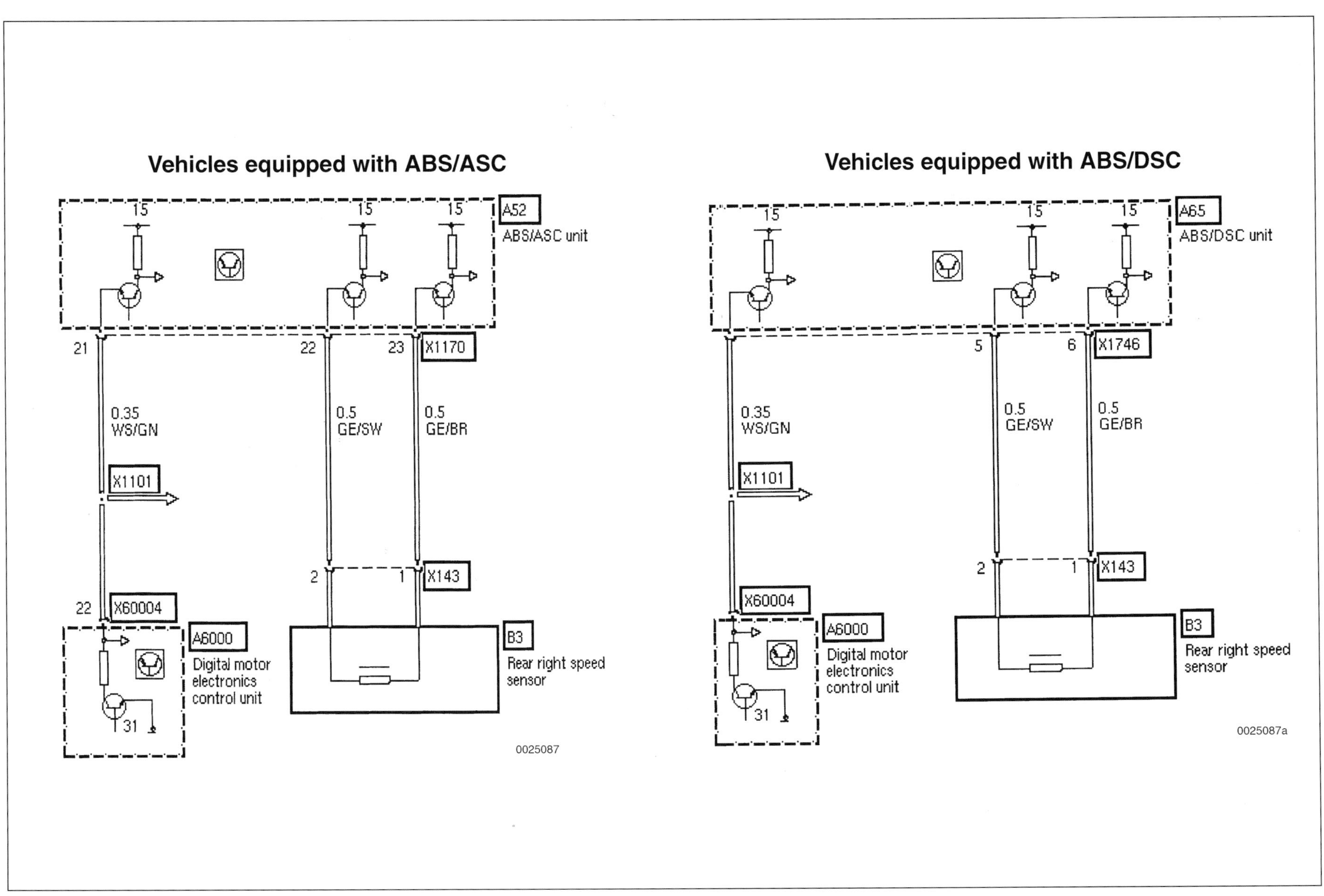

ABS/ASC control unit (A52)
1 of 2

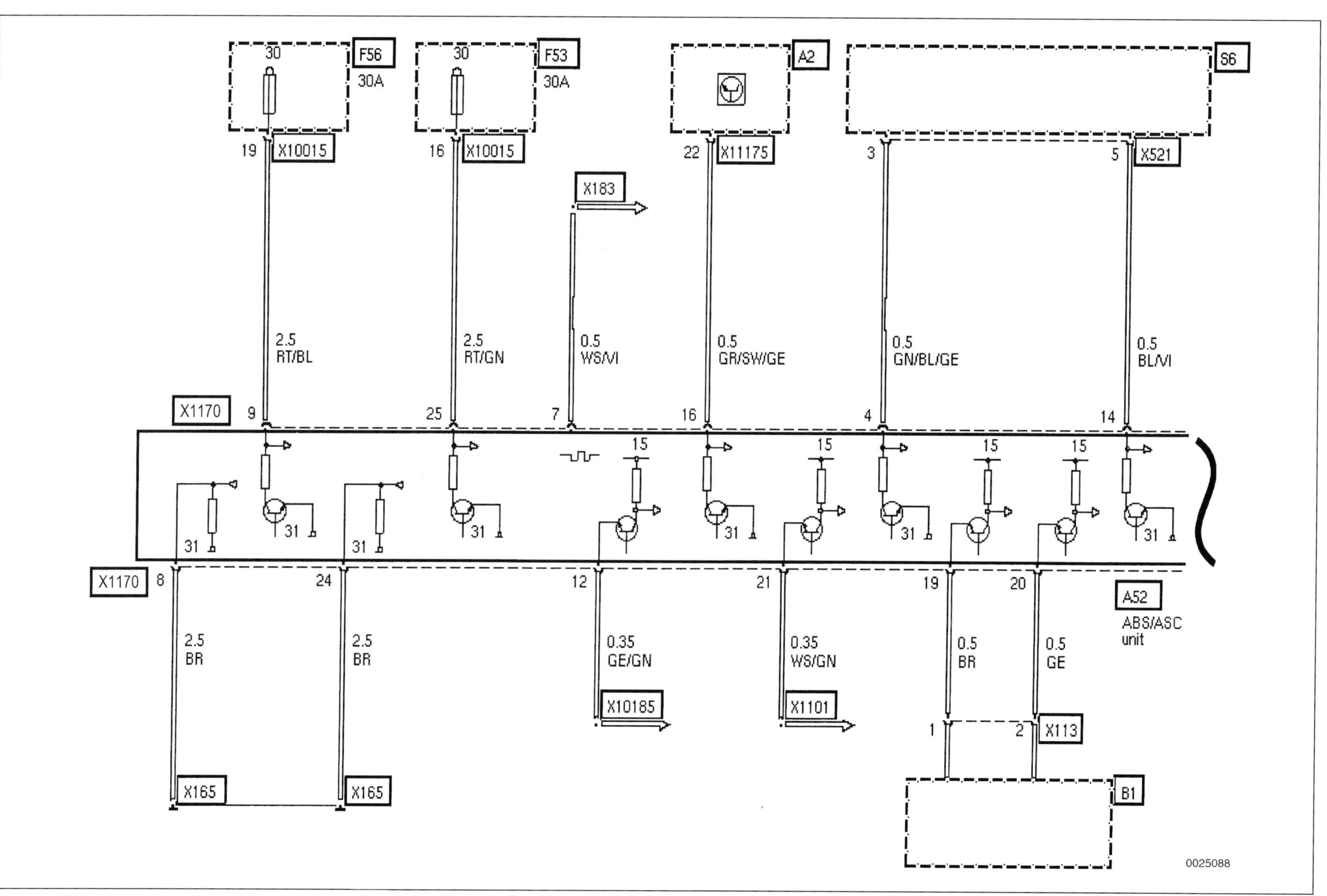

ABS/ASC control unit (A52)
2 of 2

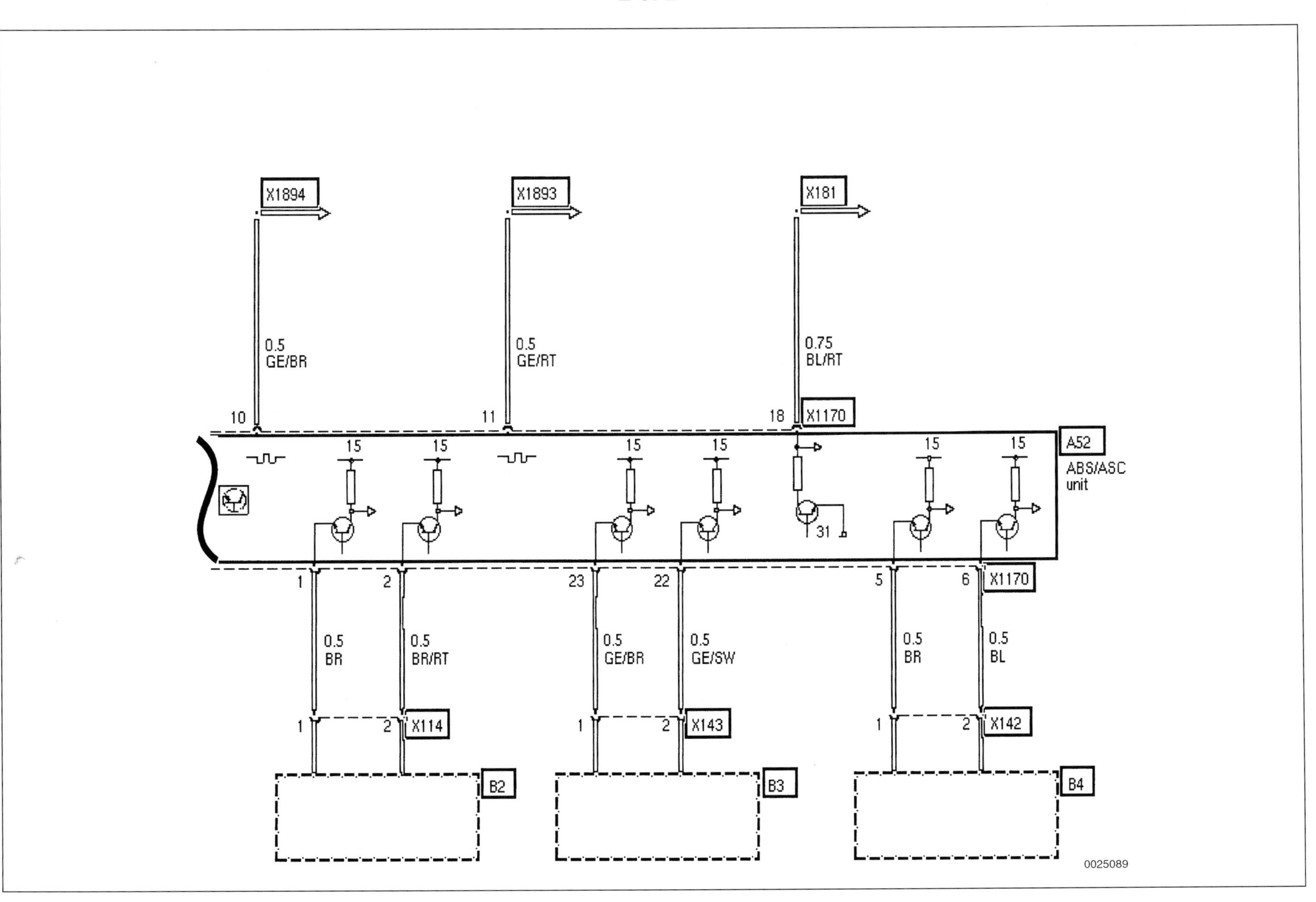

Splice connector (X1101)

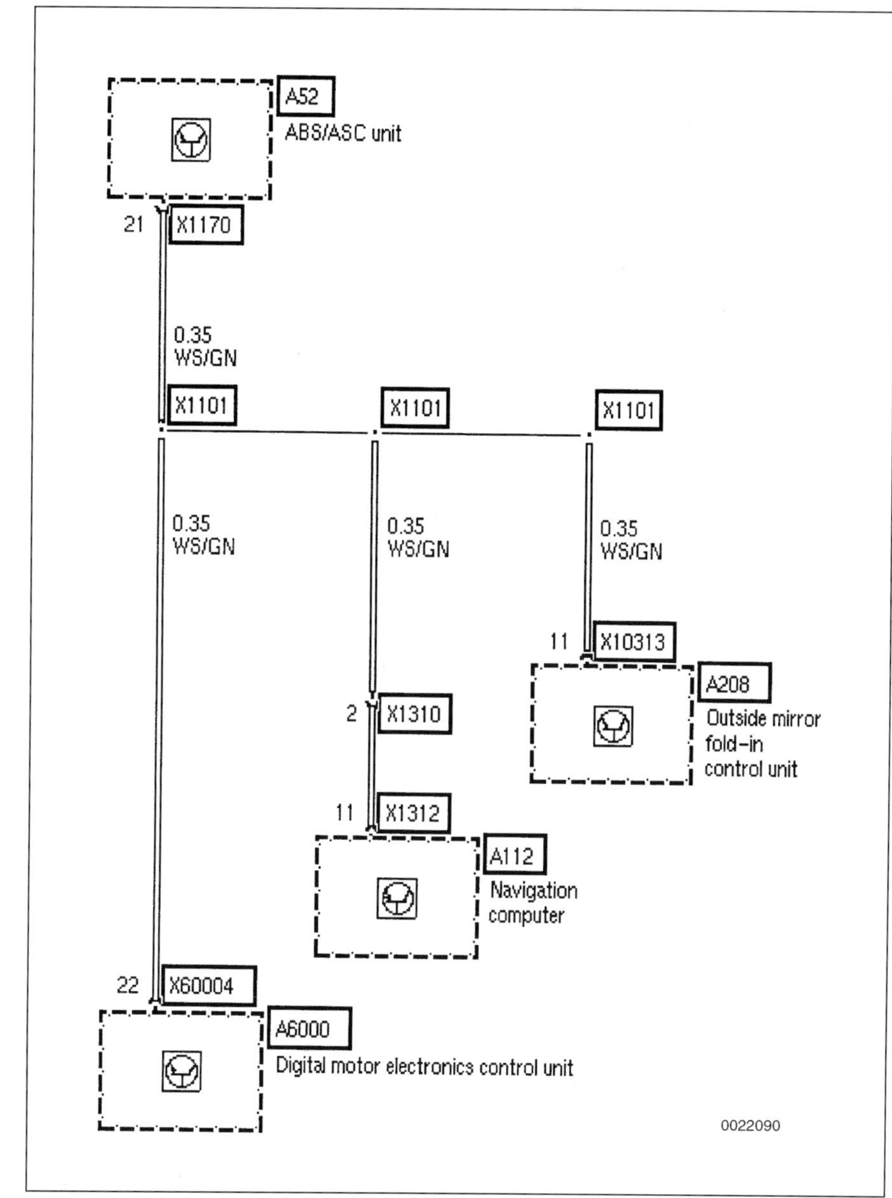
A52
ABS/ASC unit
21
X1170
0.35
WS/GN
X1101
X1101
X1101
0.35
WS/GN
0.35
WS/GN
0.35
WS/GN
11
X10313
A208
Outside mirror
fold-in
control unit
2
X1310
11
X1312
A112
Navigation
computer
22
X60004
A6000
Digital motor electronics control unit
0022090

Electronic immobilizer (EWS 3.3) control unit (A836)
1 of 2

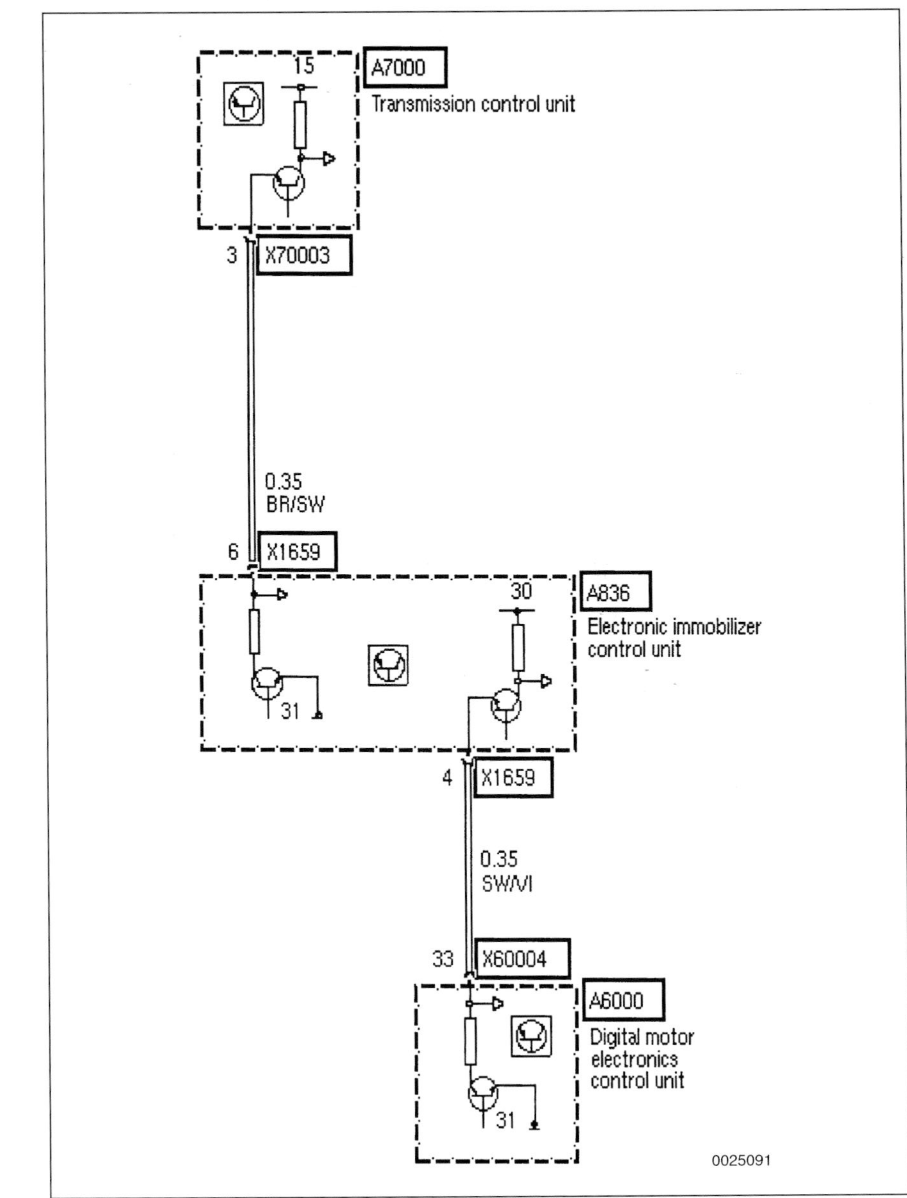

Electronic immobilizer (EWS 3.3) control unit (A836)
2 of 2

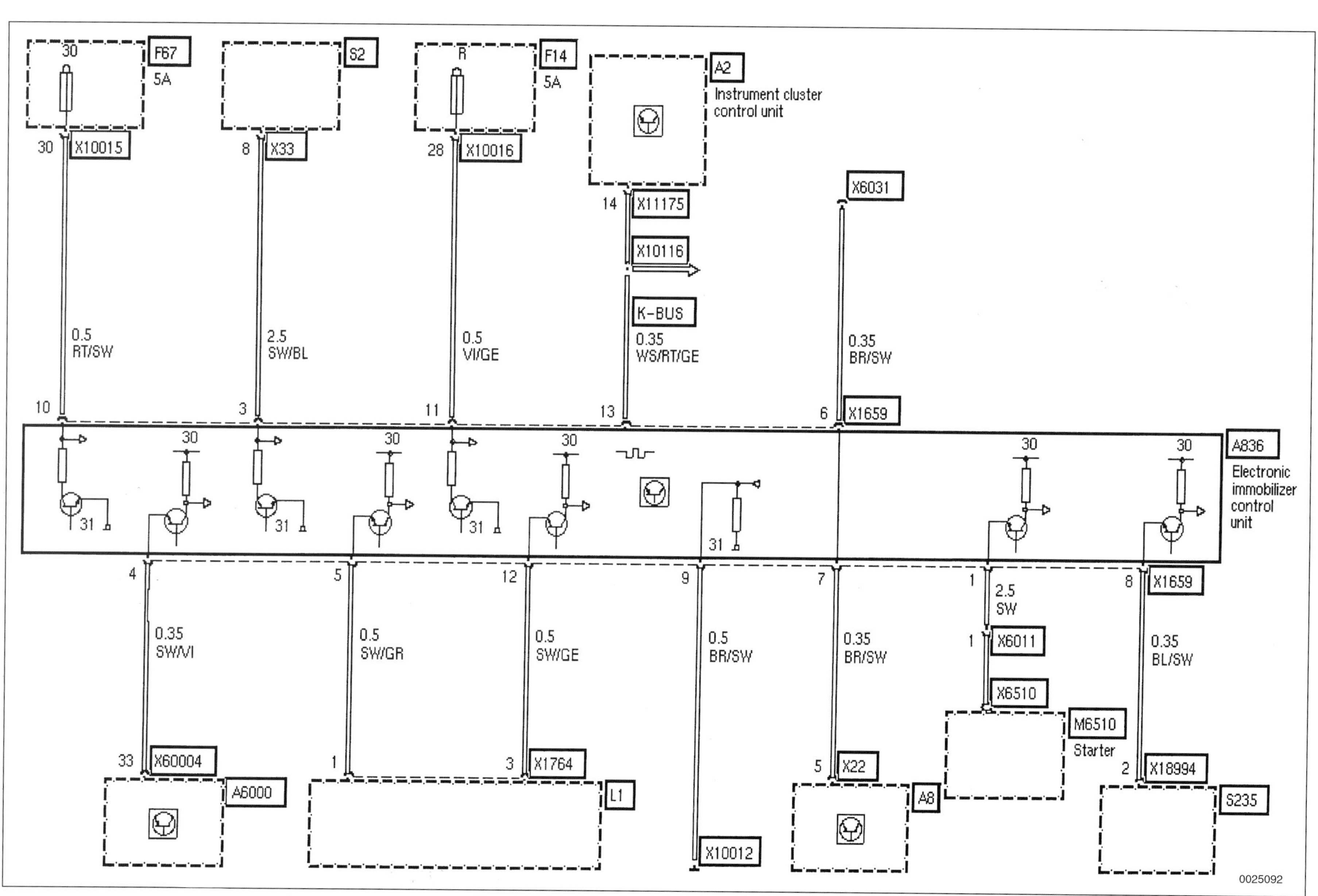

CAN-bus splice connectors (X1893, X1894)

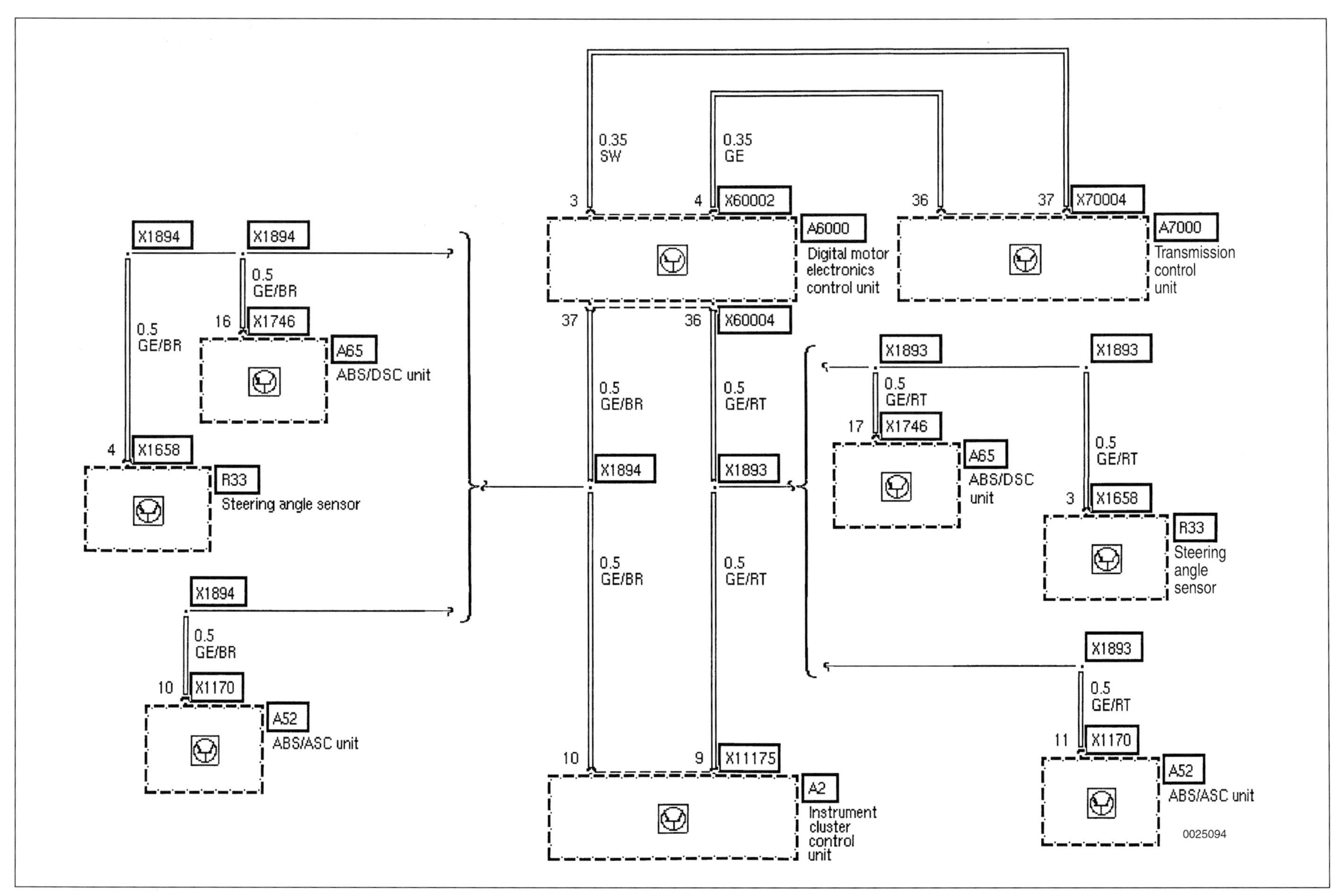

Secondary air injection pump (M63)

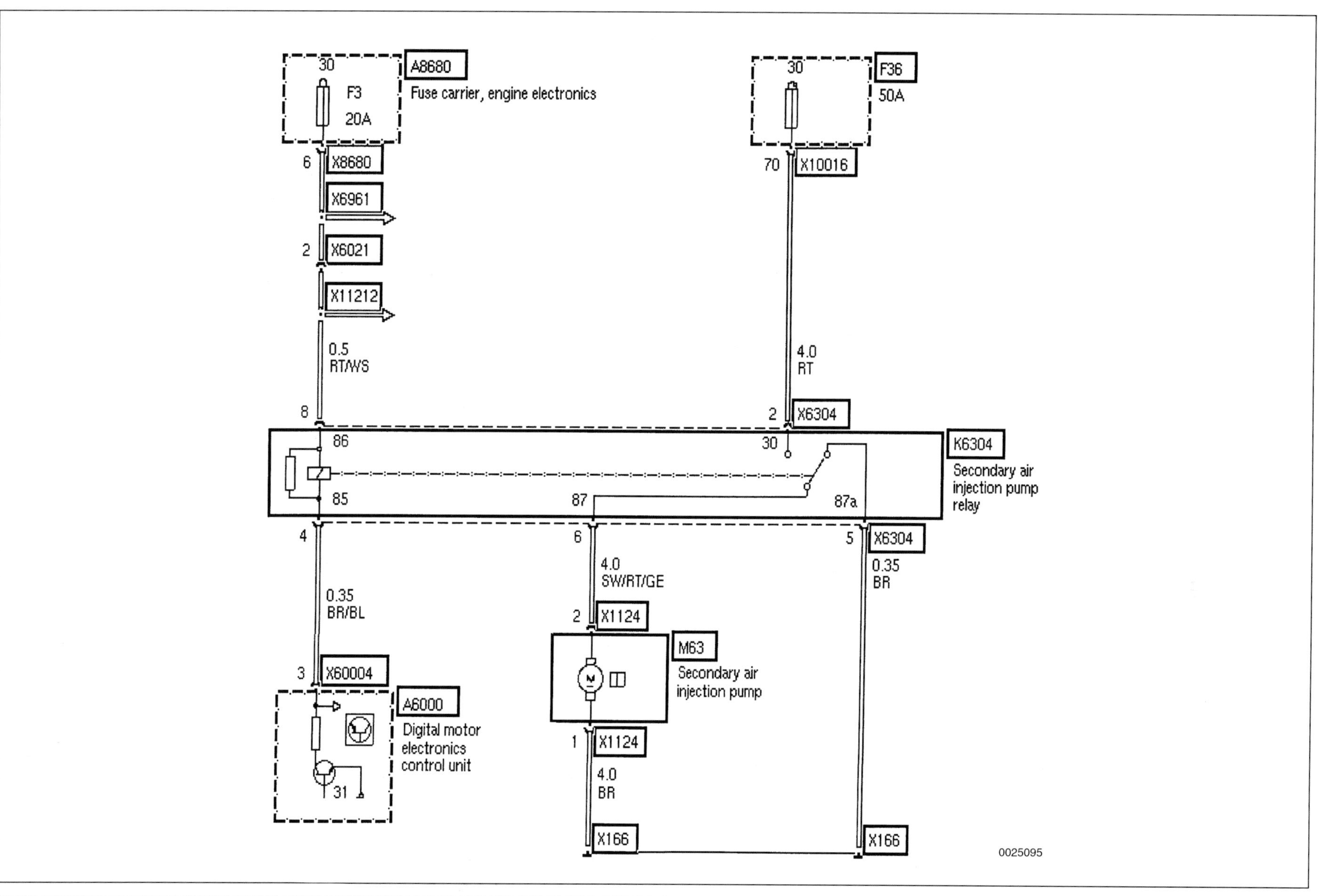

Fuse 36 (F36)

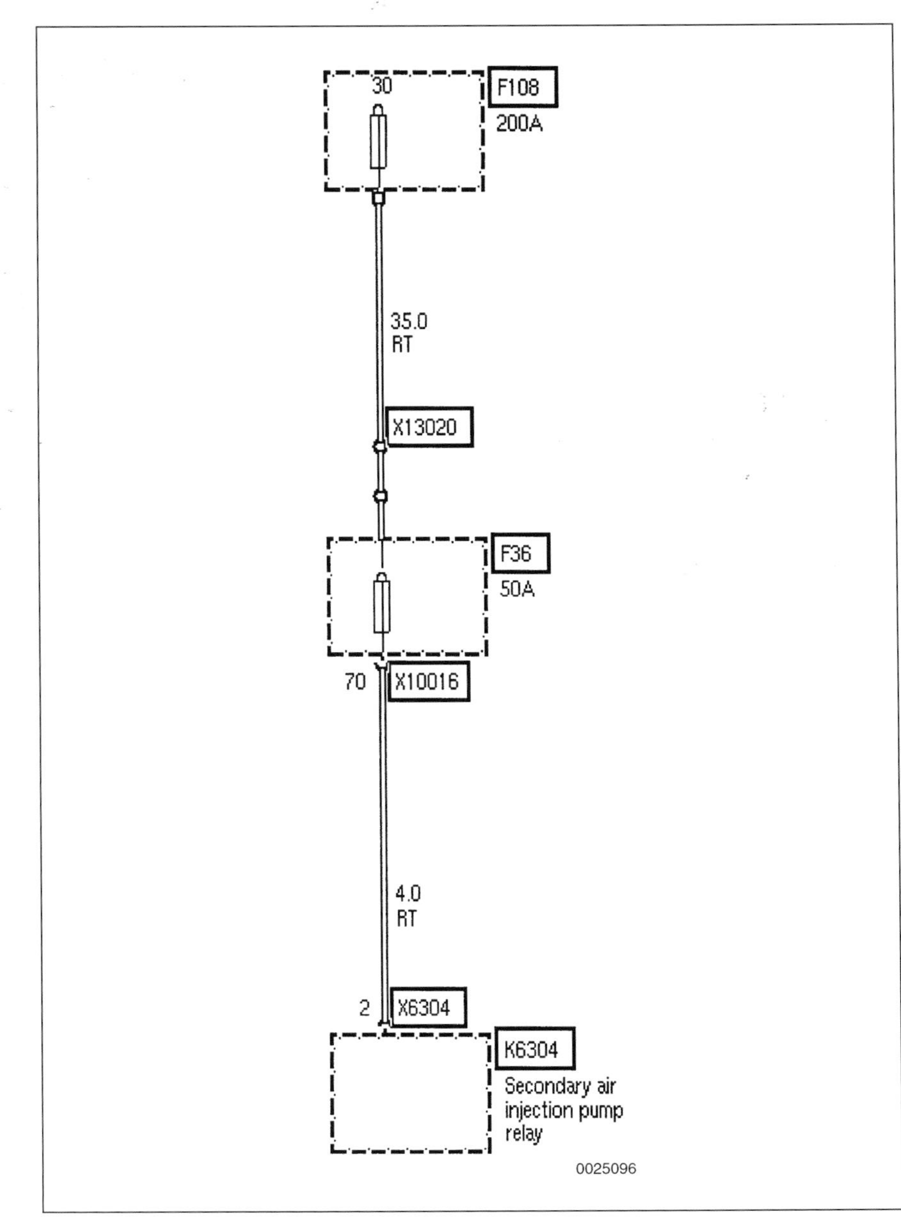
30
F108
200A
35.0
RT
X13020
F36
50A
70
X10016
4.0
RT
2
X6304
K6304
Secondary air
injection pump
relay
0025096

Secondary air injection pump valve (Y6163)

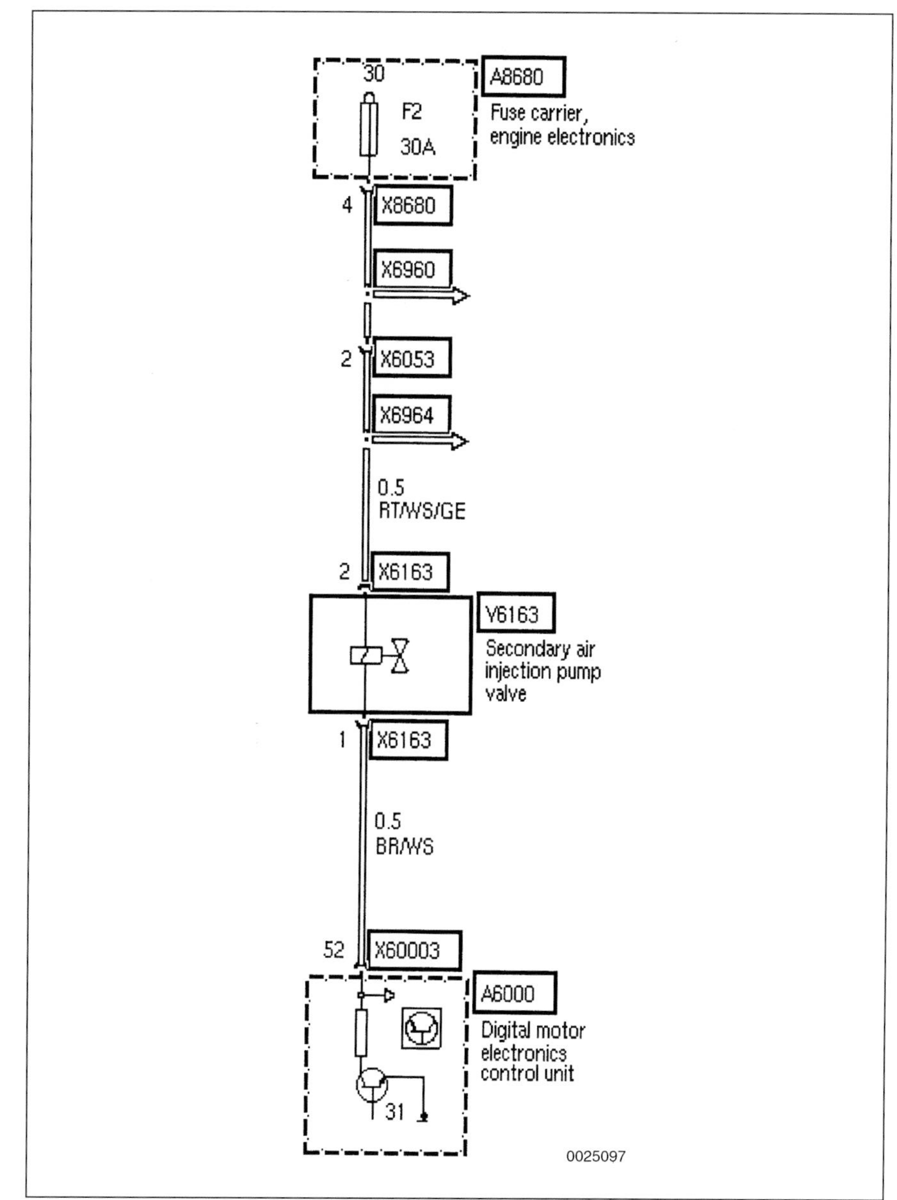

DME main relay (K6300)

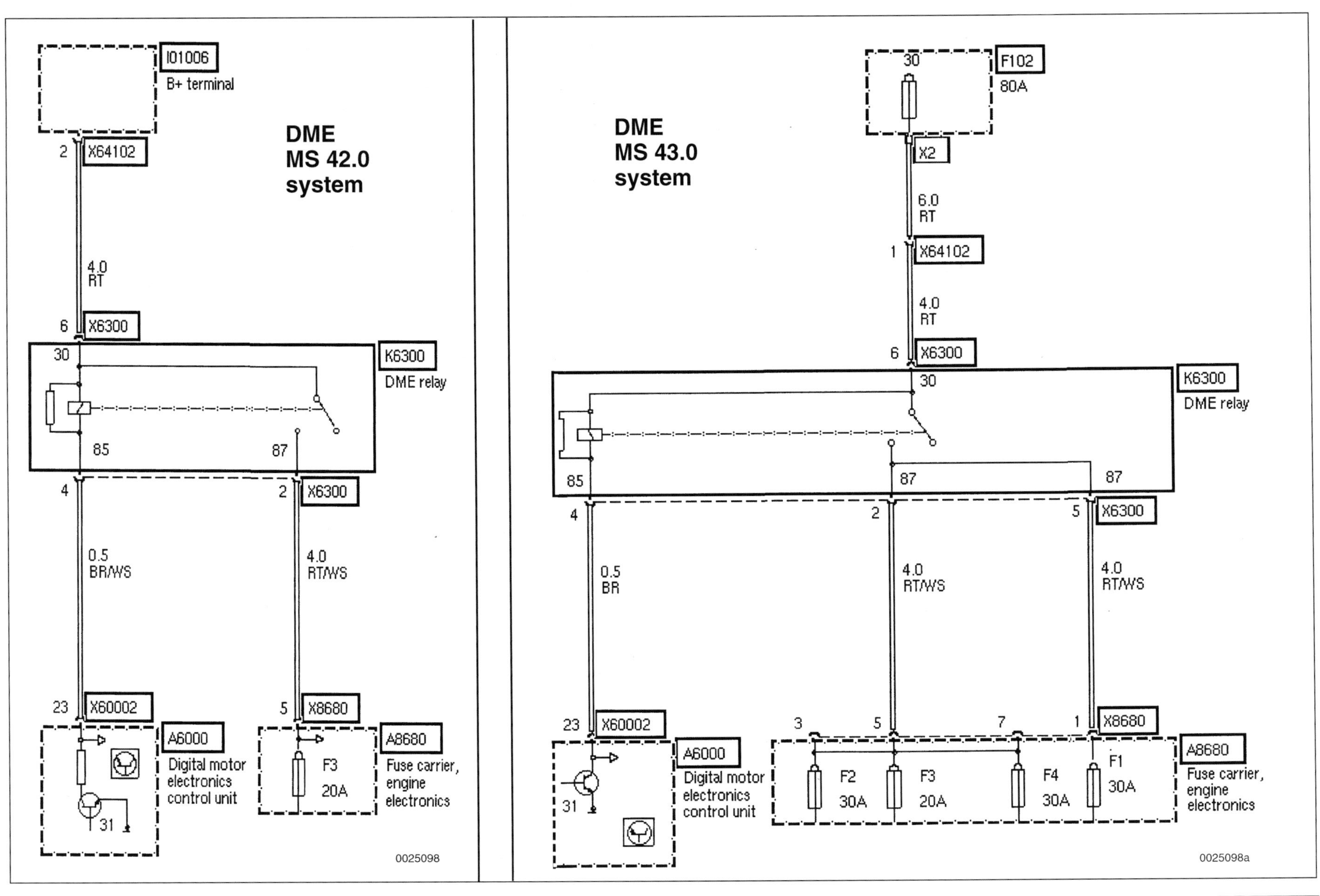

B+ terminal, E-box (I01006)

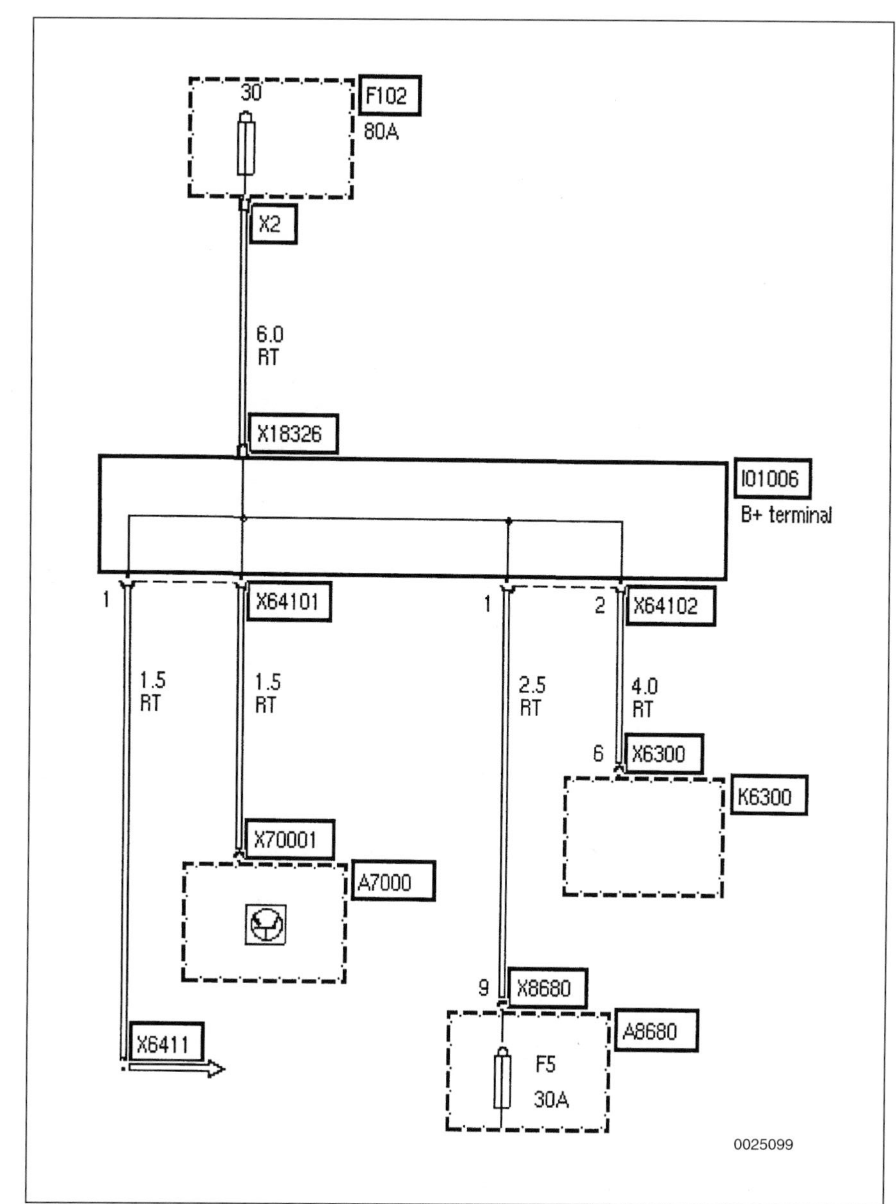

DME control unit power and ground supply (DME MS 42.0)

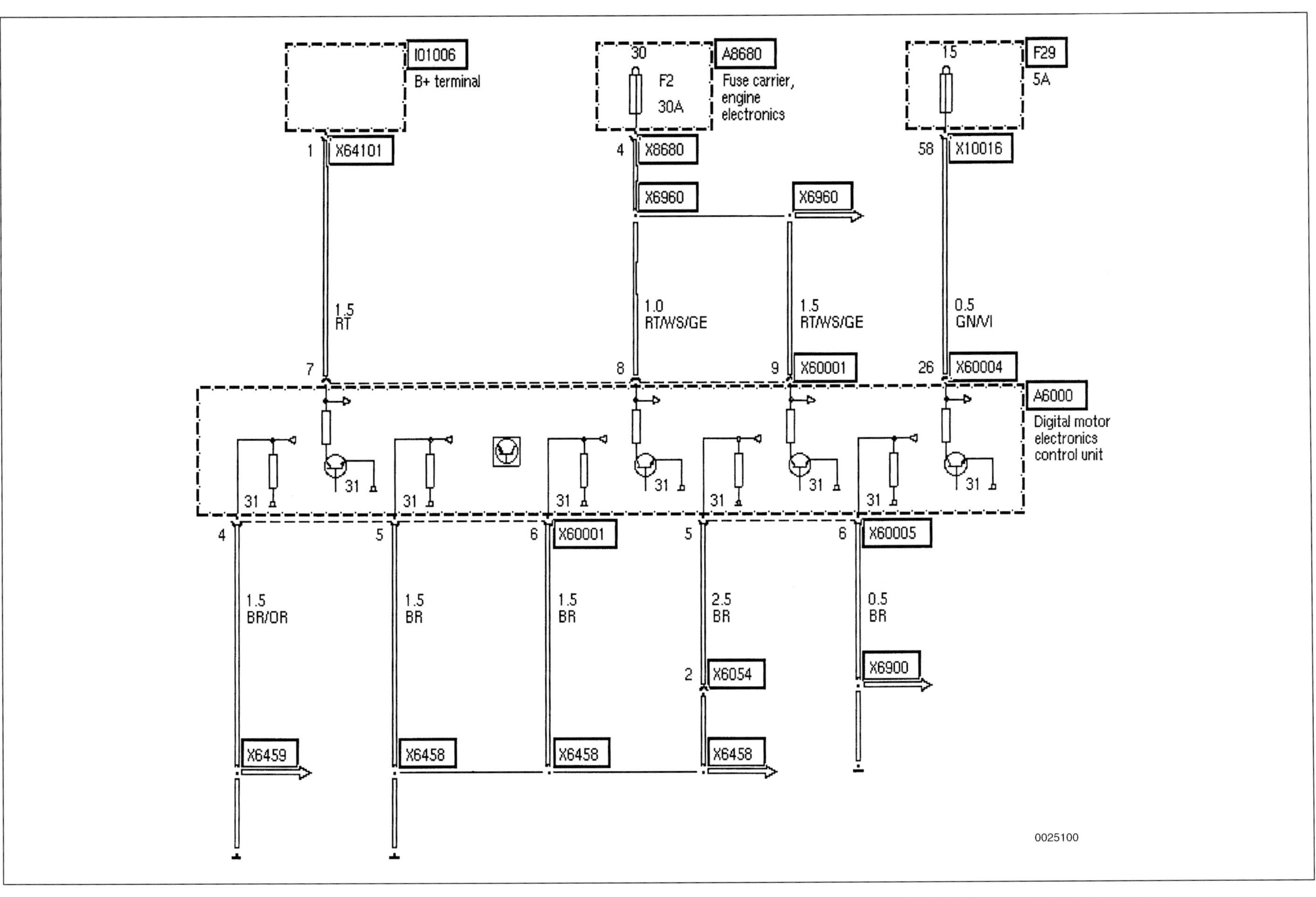

Fuse 29 (F29)

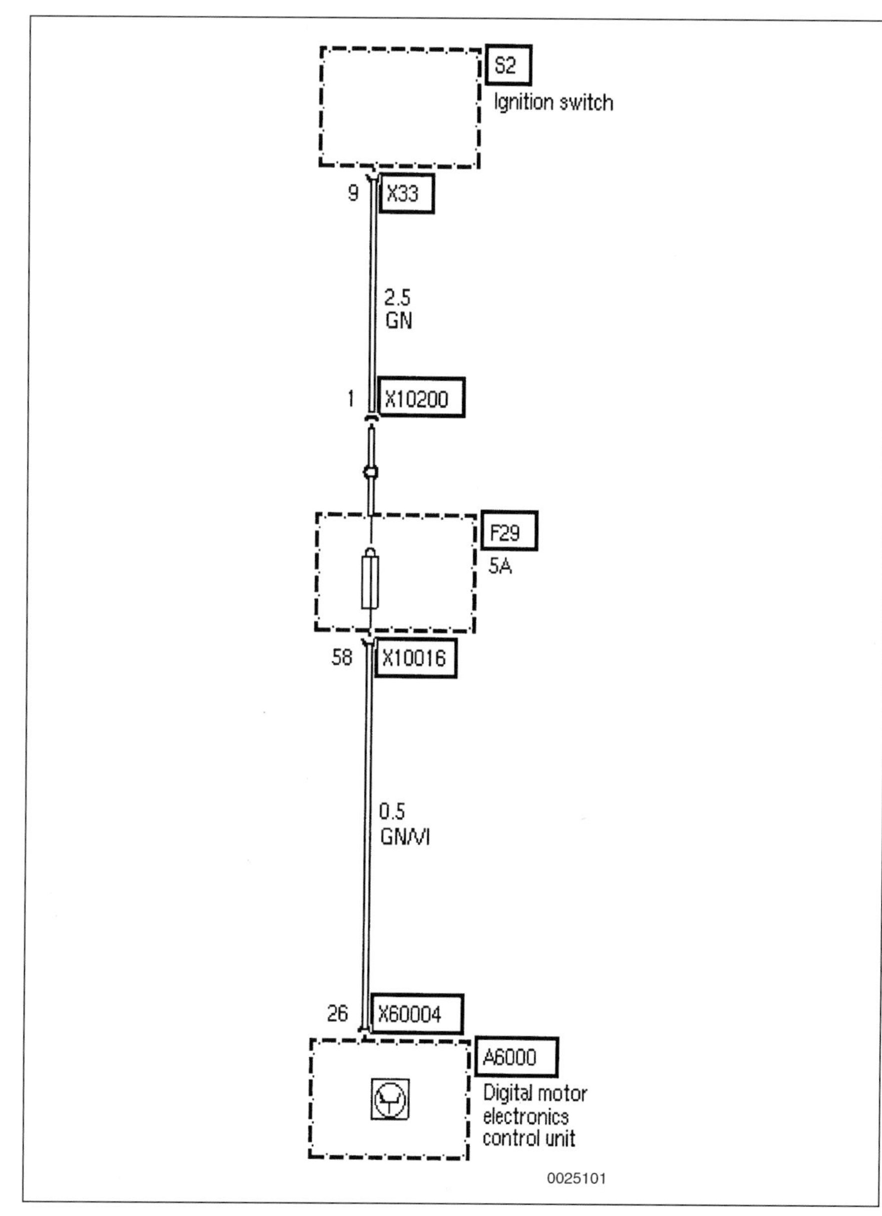
S2
Ignition switch
9
X33
2.5
GN
1
X10200
F29
5A
58
X10016
0.5
GN/VI
26
X60004
A6000
Digital motor
electronics
control unit
0025101

Splice connector (X6458)

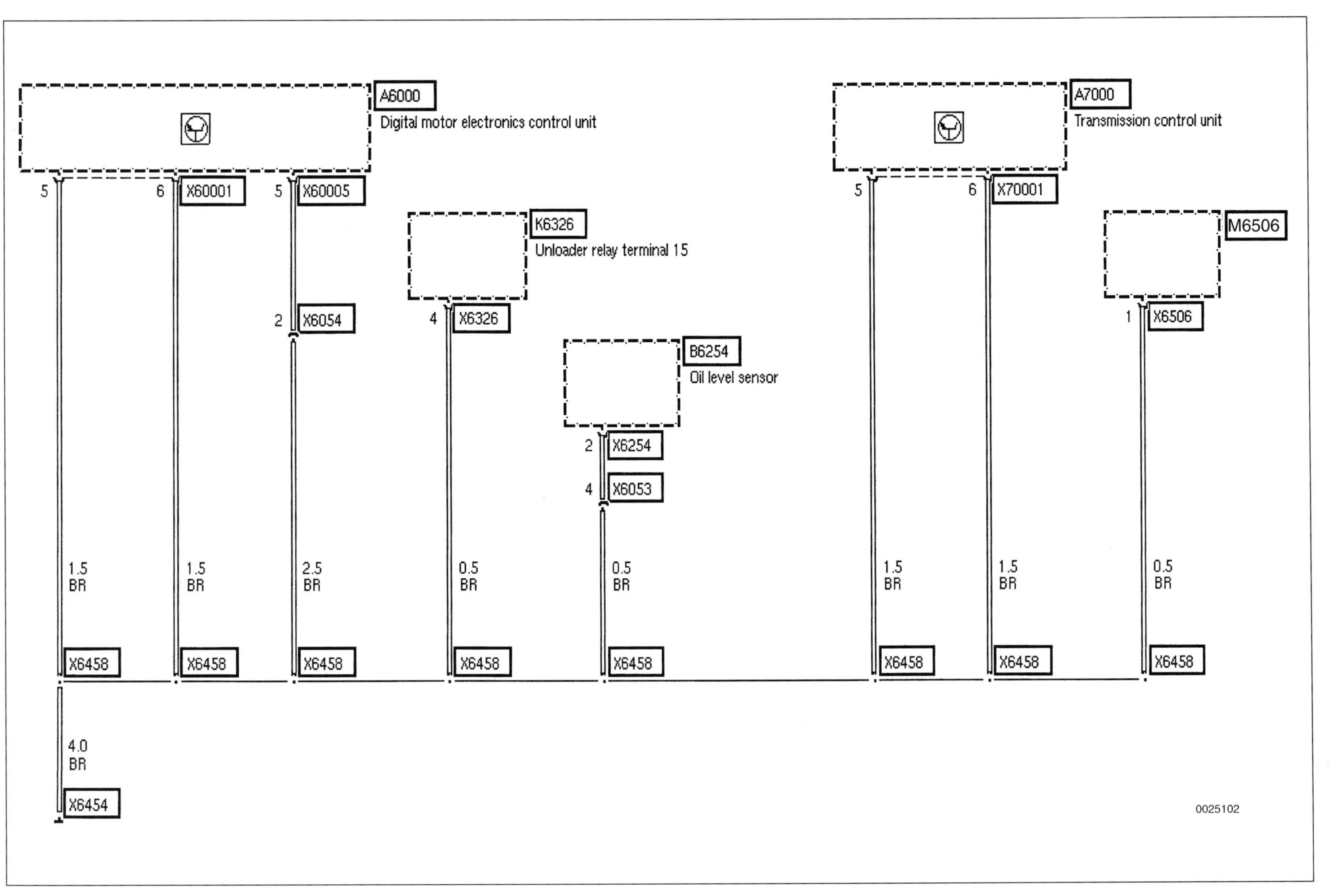

Ignition coils ground (X6456)

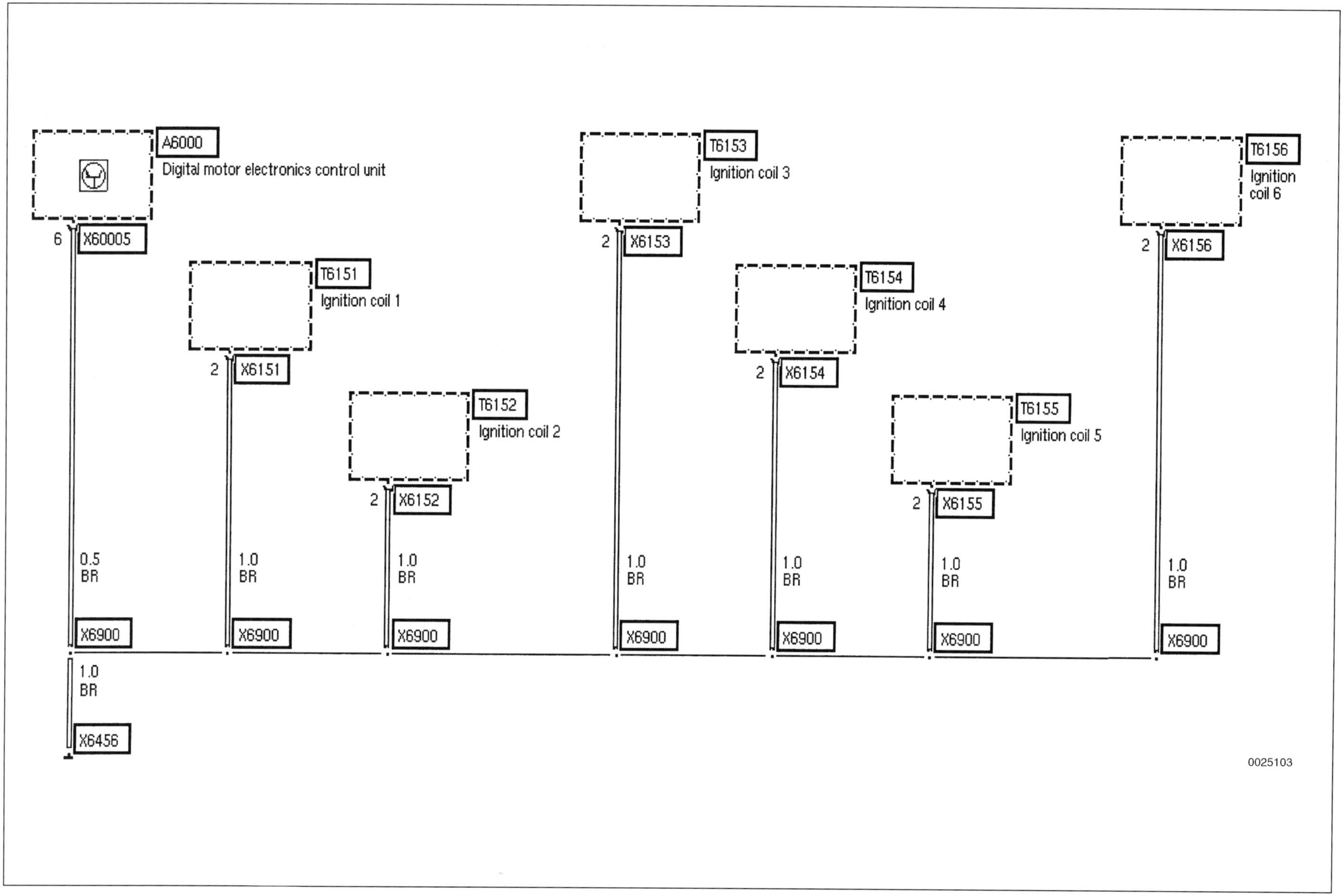

Fuel tank vent valve (Y6120)

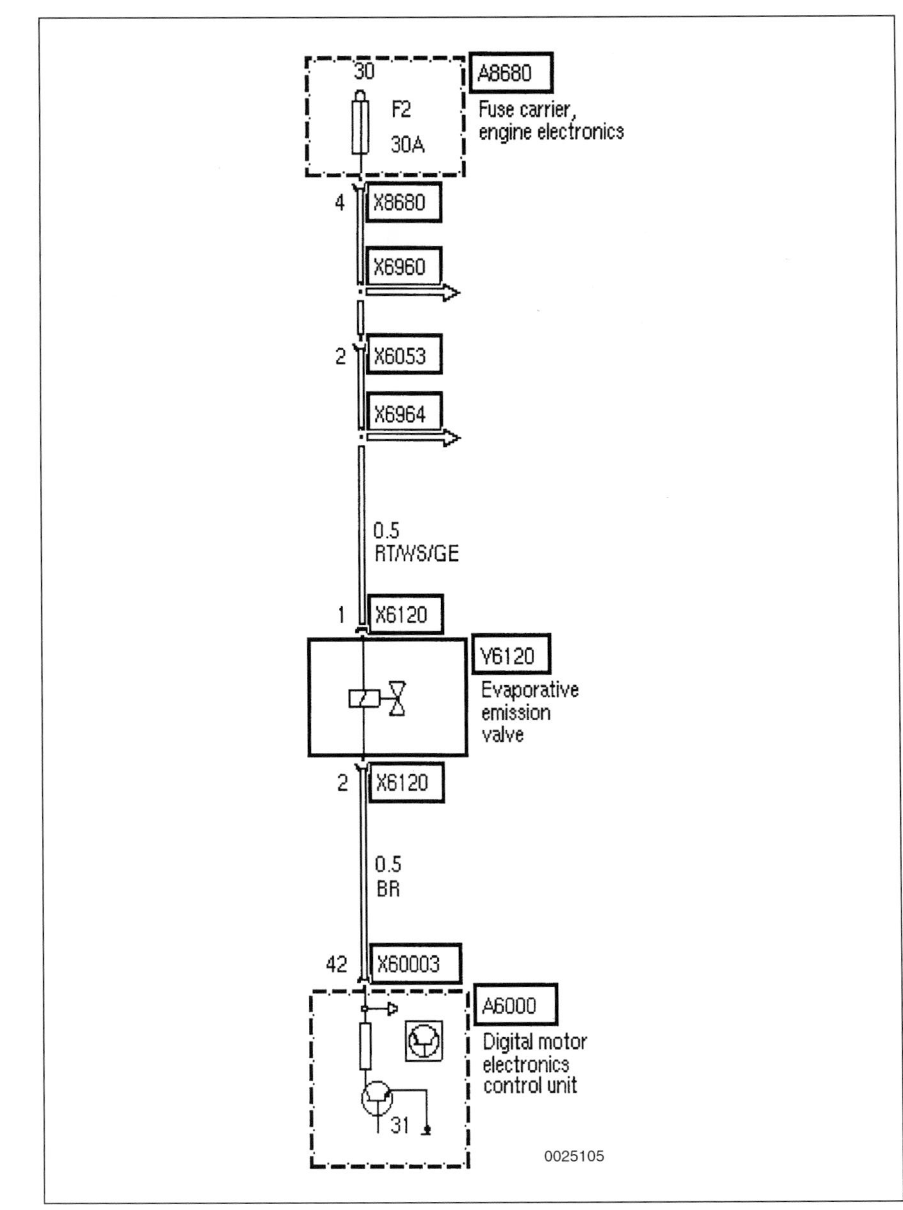

Fuel tank leakage diagnosis pump (M119, I01065)

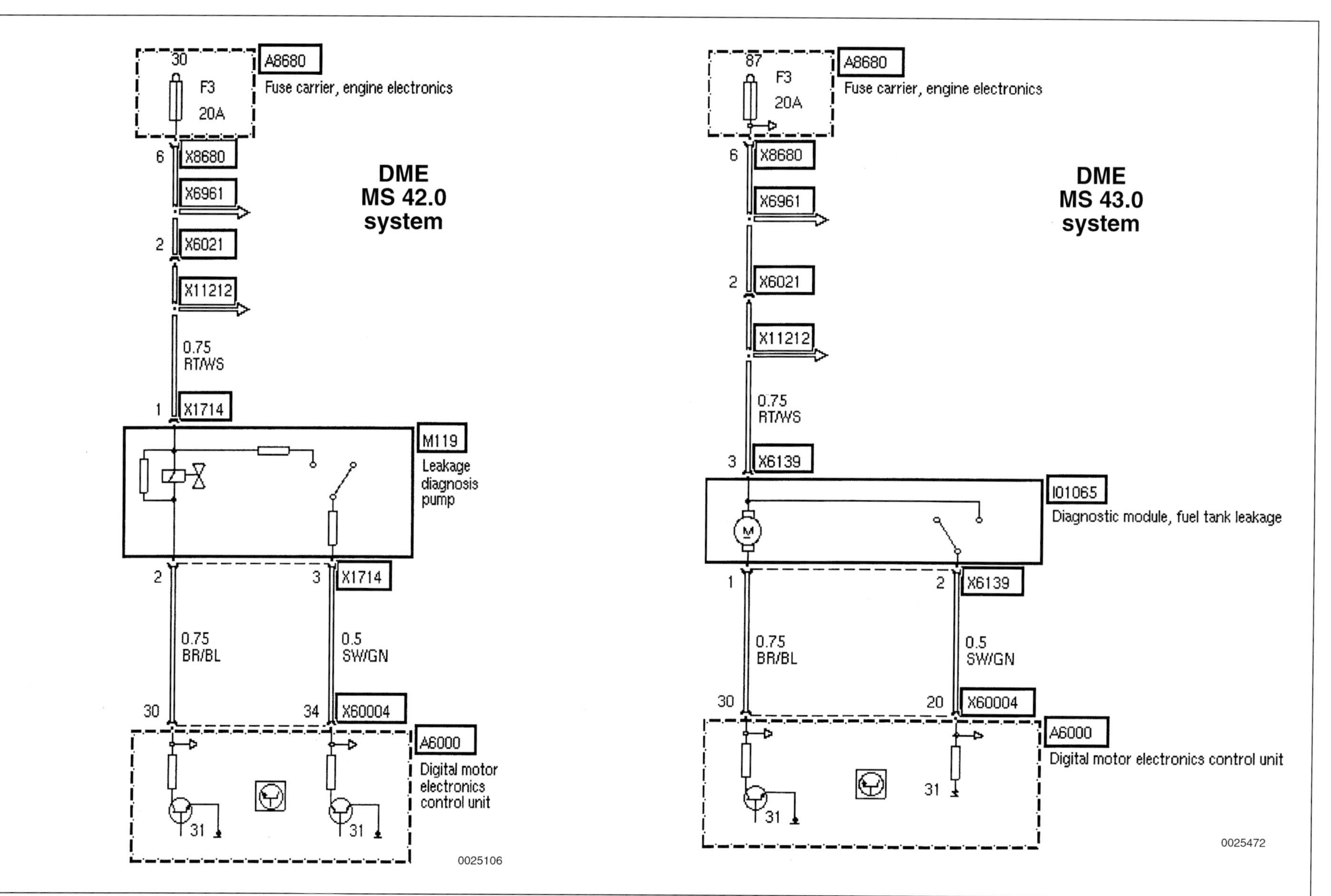

Ignition coil 1 (DME MS 42.0) (T6151)

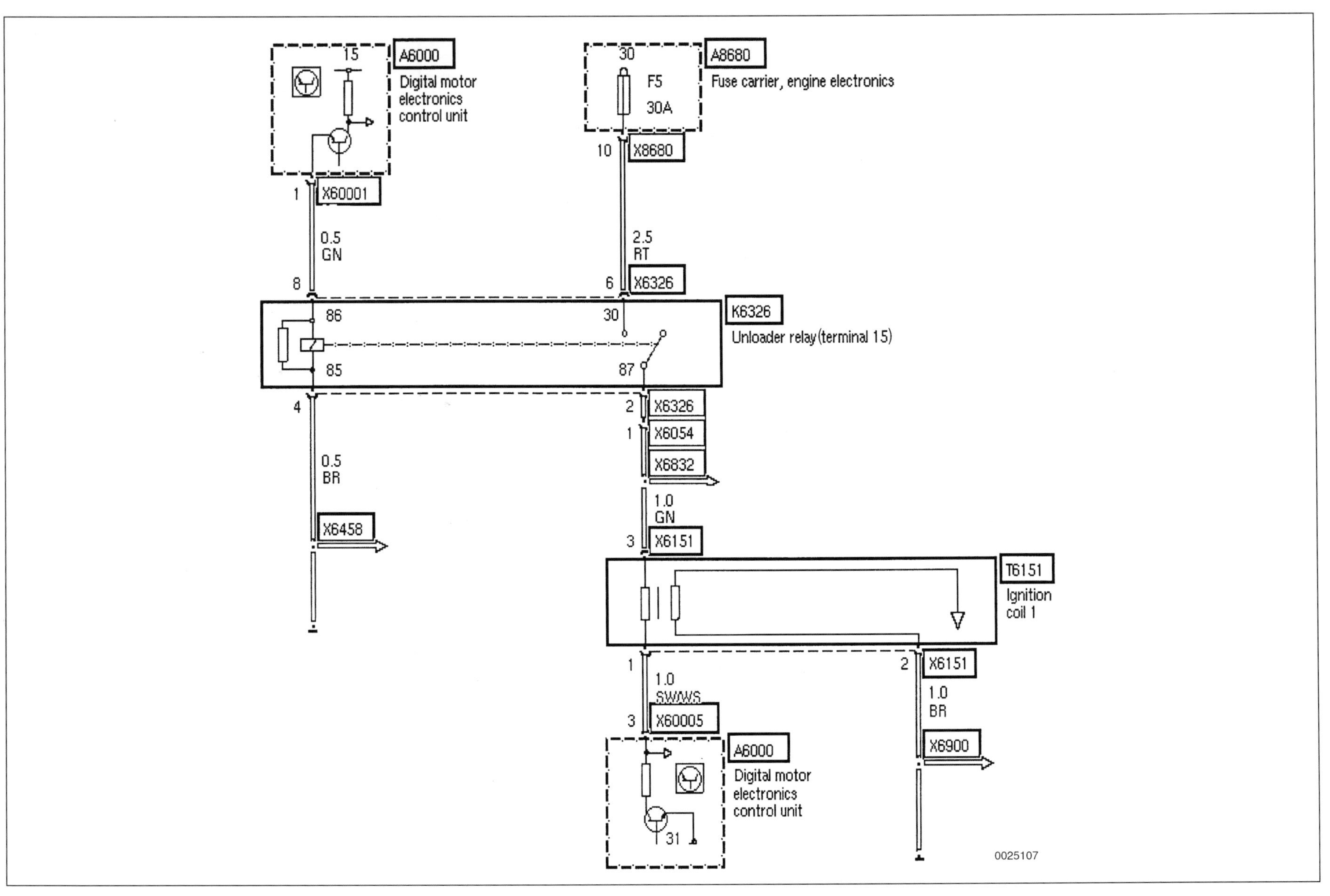

Splice connector (X6832)

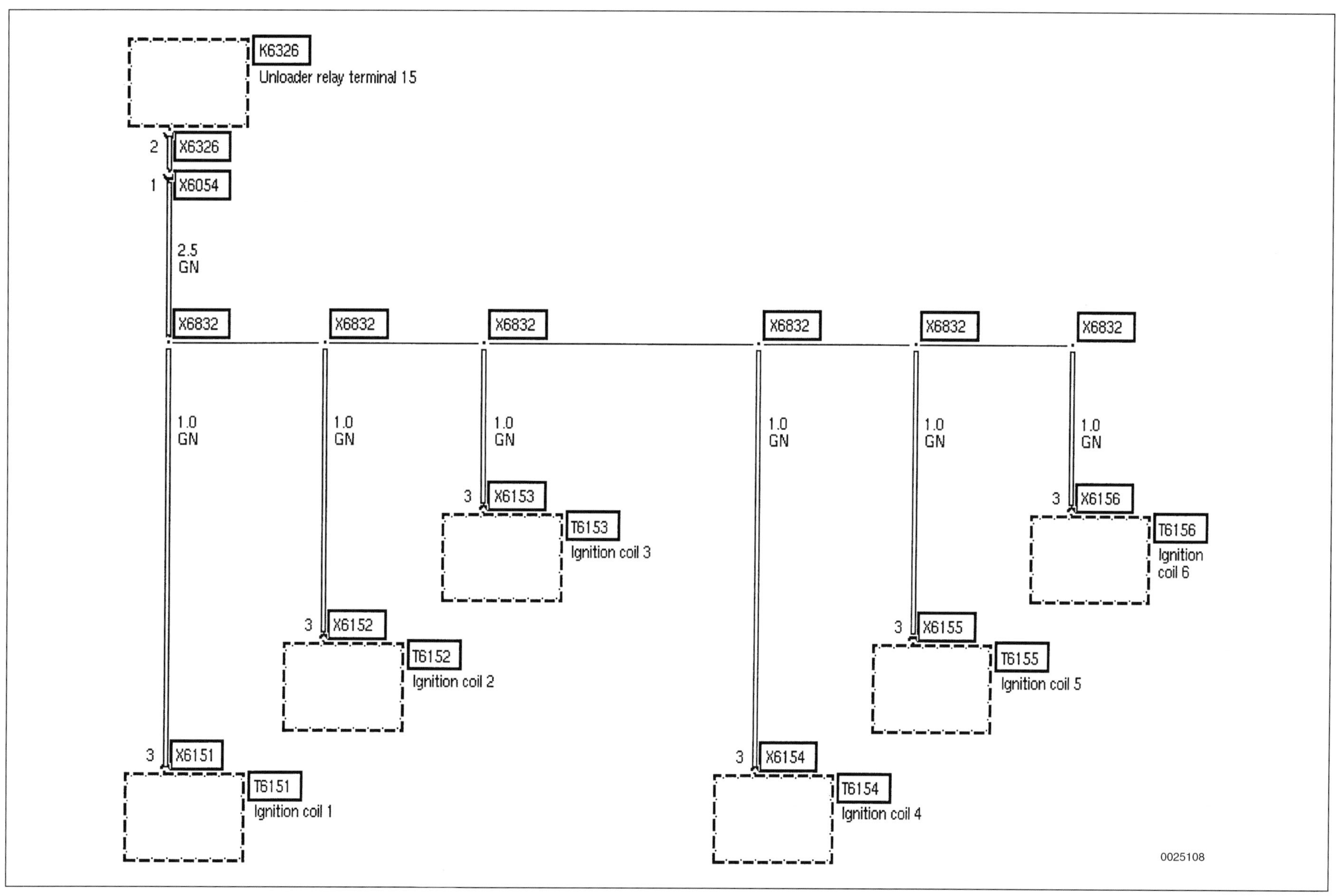

Ignition coil 2 (DME MS 42.0) (T6152)

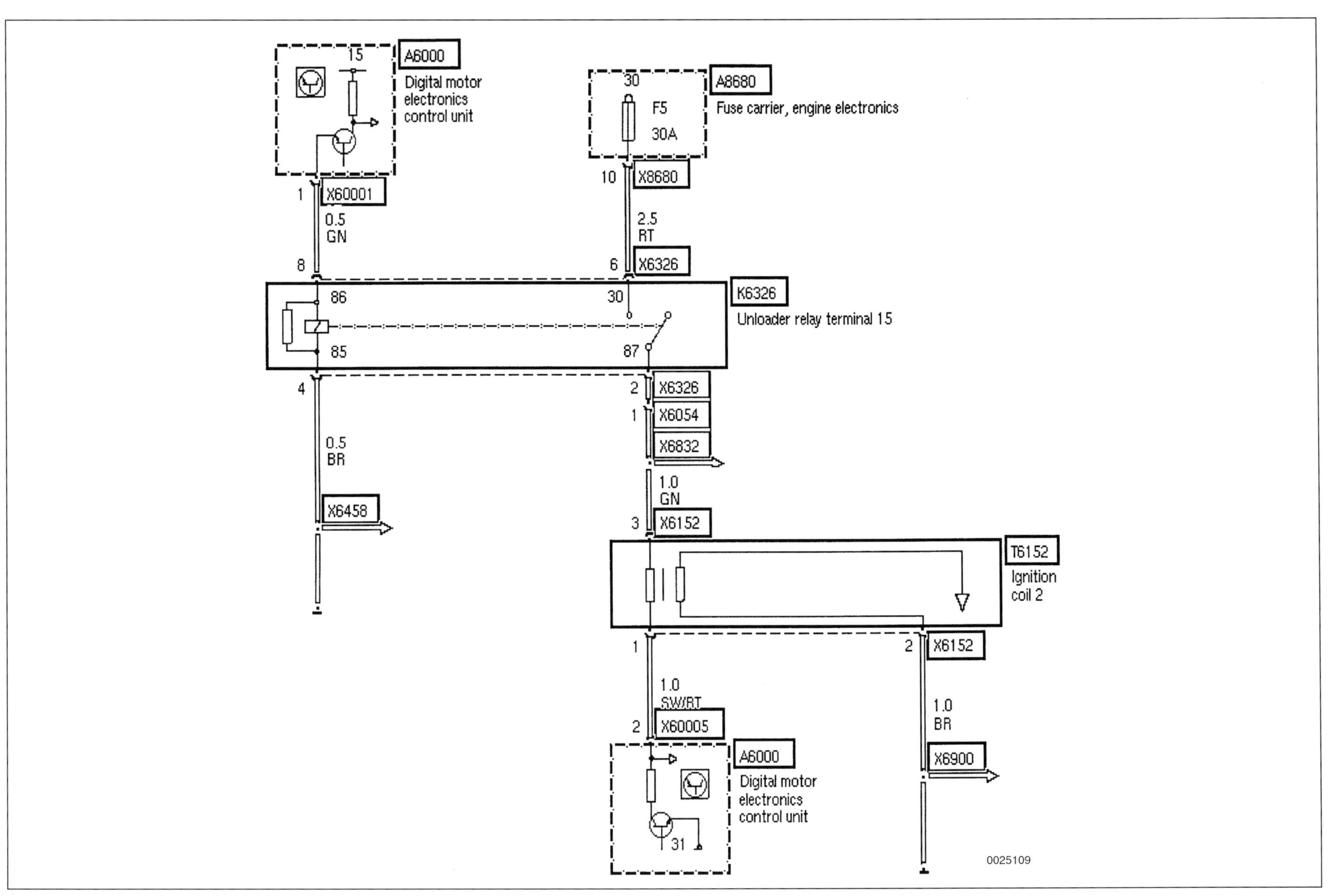

Ignition coil 3 (DME MS 42.0) (T6153)

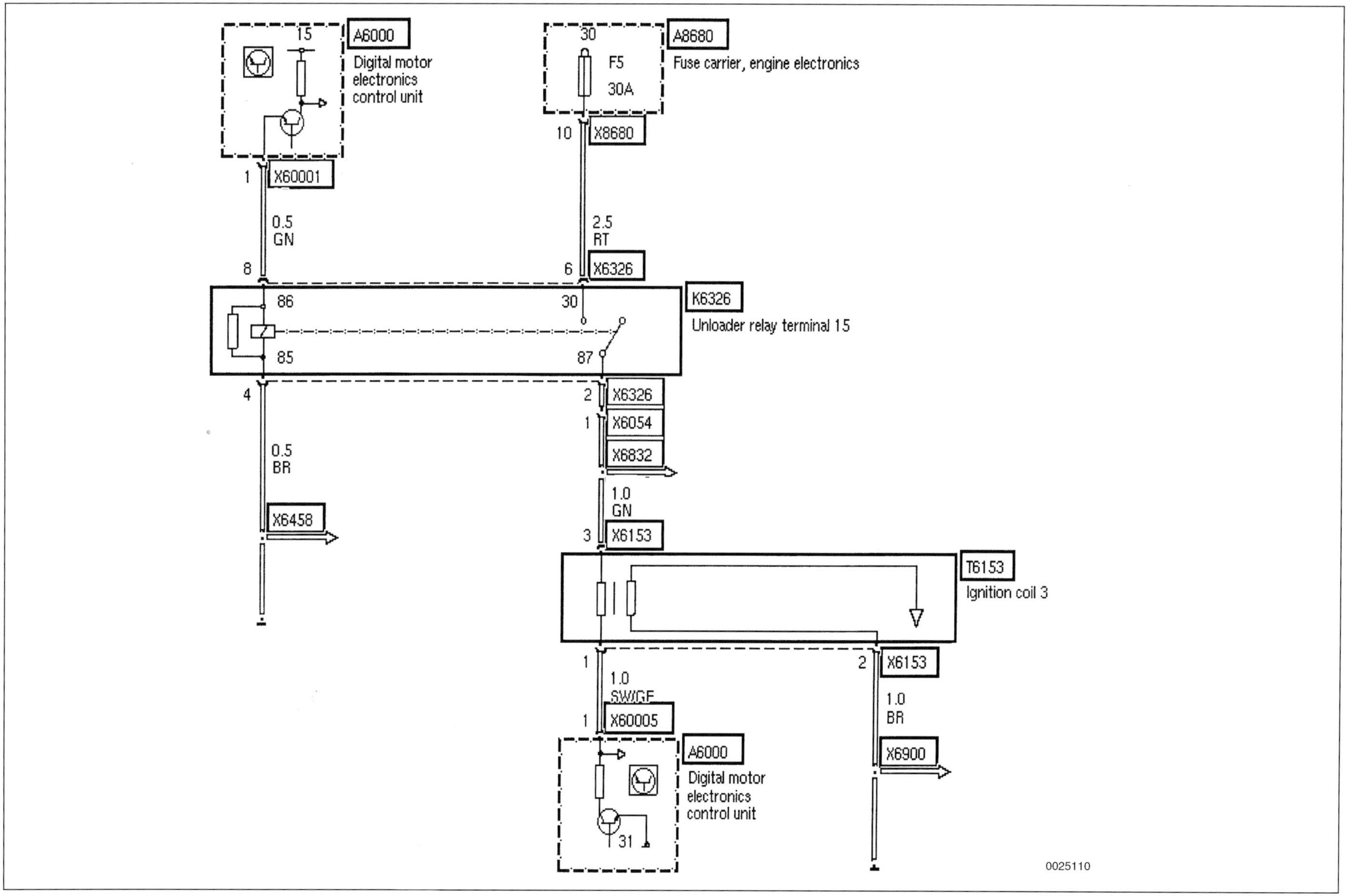

15
A6000
Digital motor electronics control unit
1 X60001
0.5 GN
8

30
F5
30A
A8680
Fuse carrier, engine electronics
10 X8680
2.5 RT
6 X6326

86
30
K6326
Unloader relay terminal 15
85
87

4
0.5 BR
X6458

2 X6326
1 X6054
X6832
1.0 GN
3 X6153

T6153
Ignition coil 3

1
1.0 SW/GE
1 X60005
A6000
Digital motor electronics control unit
31

2 X6153
1.0 BR
X6900

0025110

Ignition coil 4 (DME MS 42.0) (T6154)

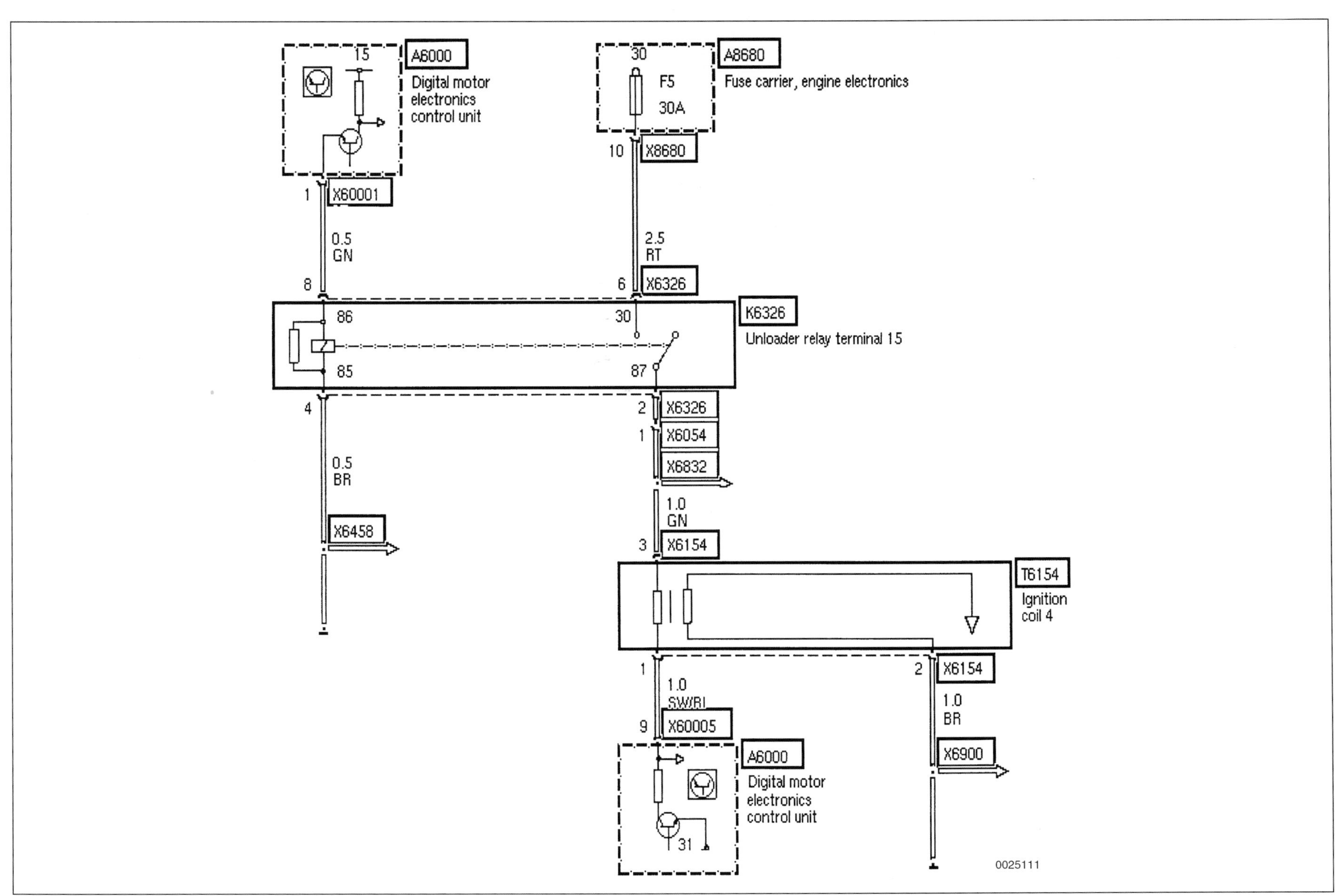

Ignition coil 5 (DME MS 42.0) (T6155)

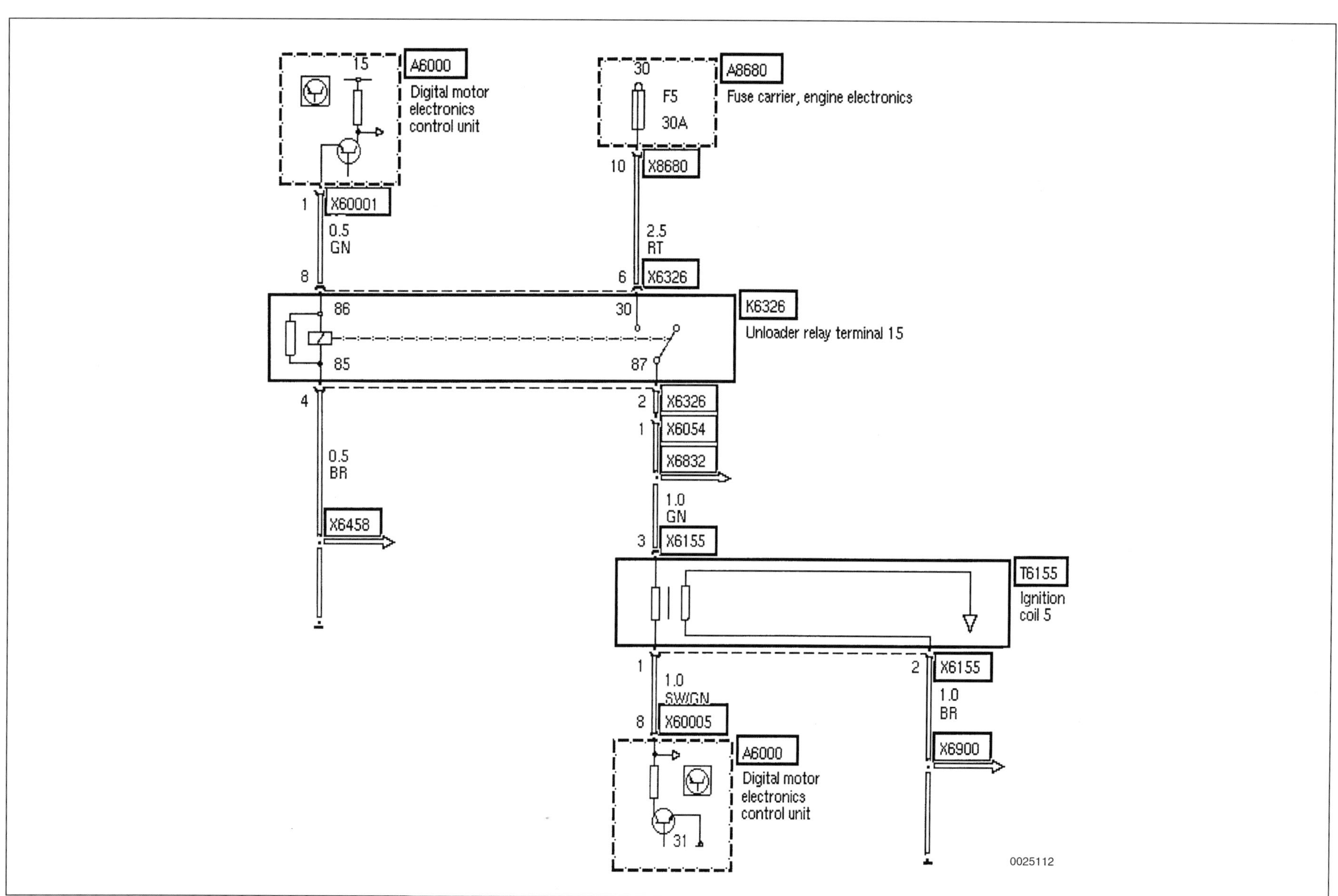

Ignition coil 6 (DME MS 42.0) (T6156)

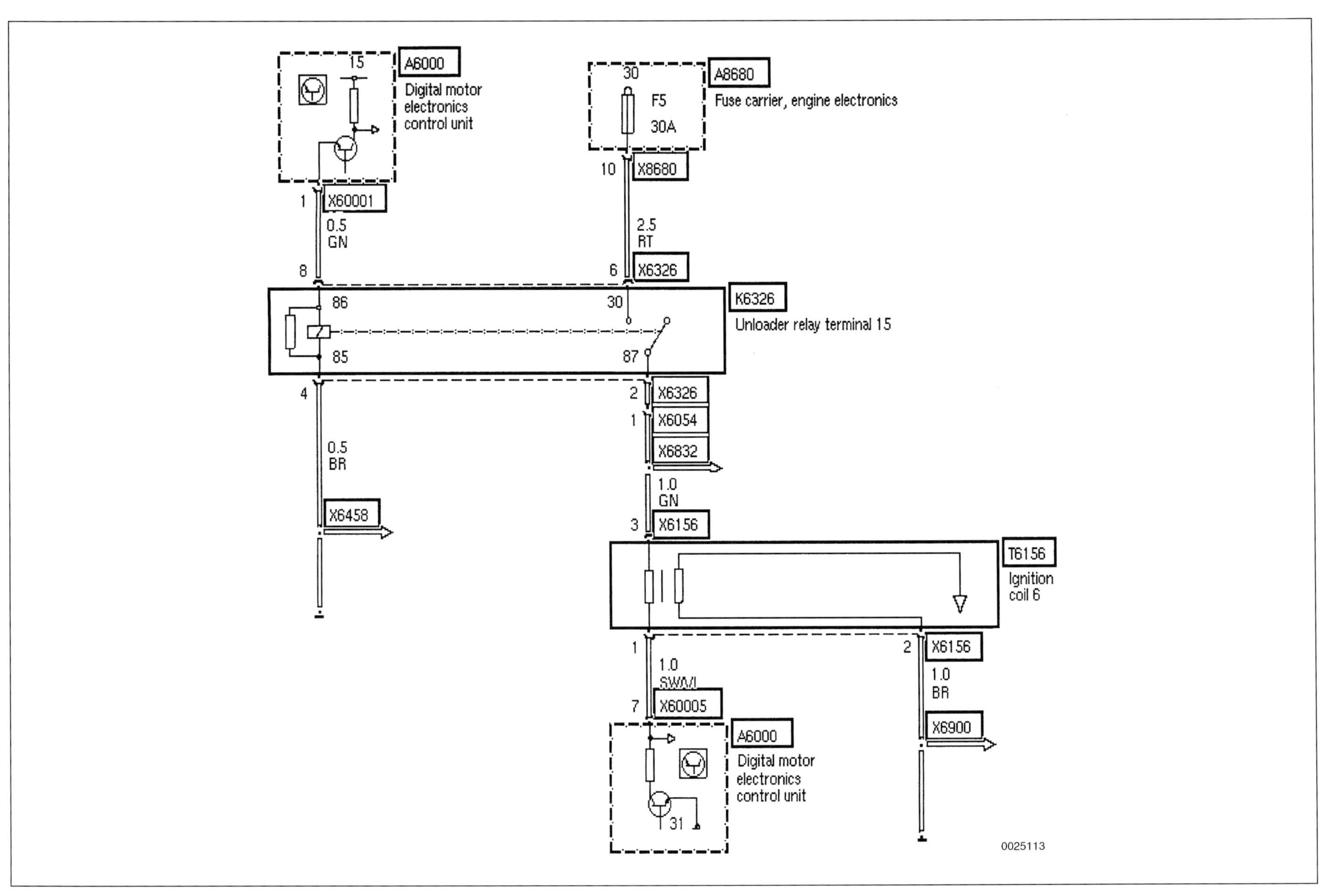

E-box cooling fan (M6506)

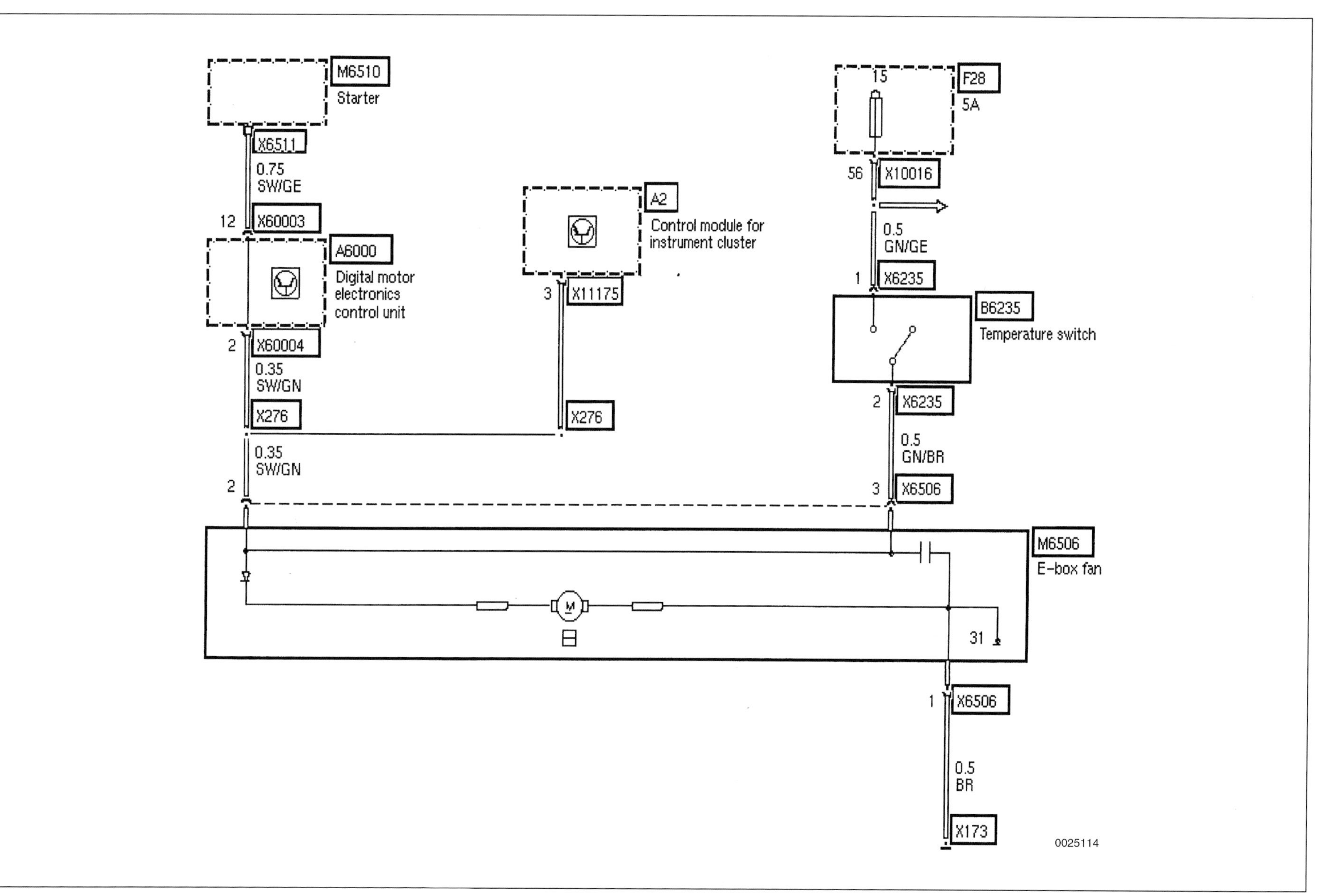

Fuse 28 (F28)

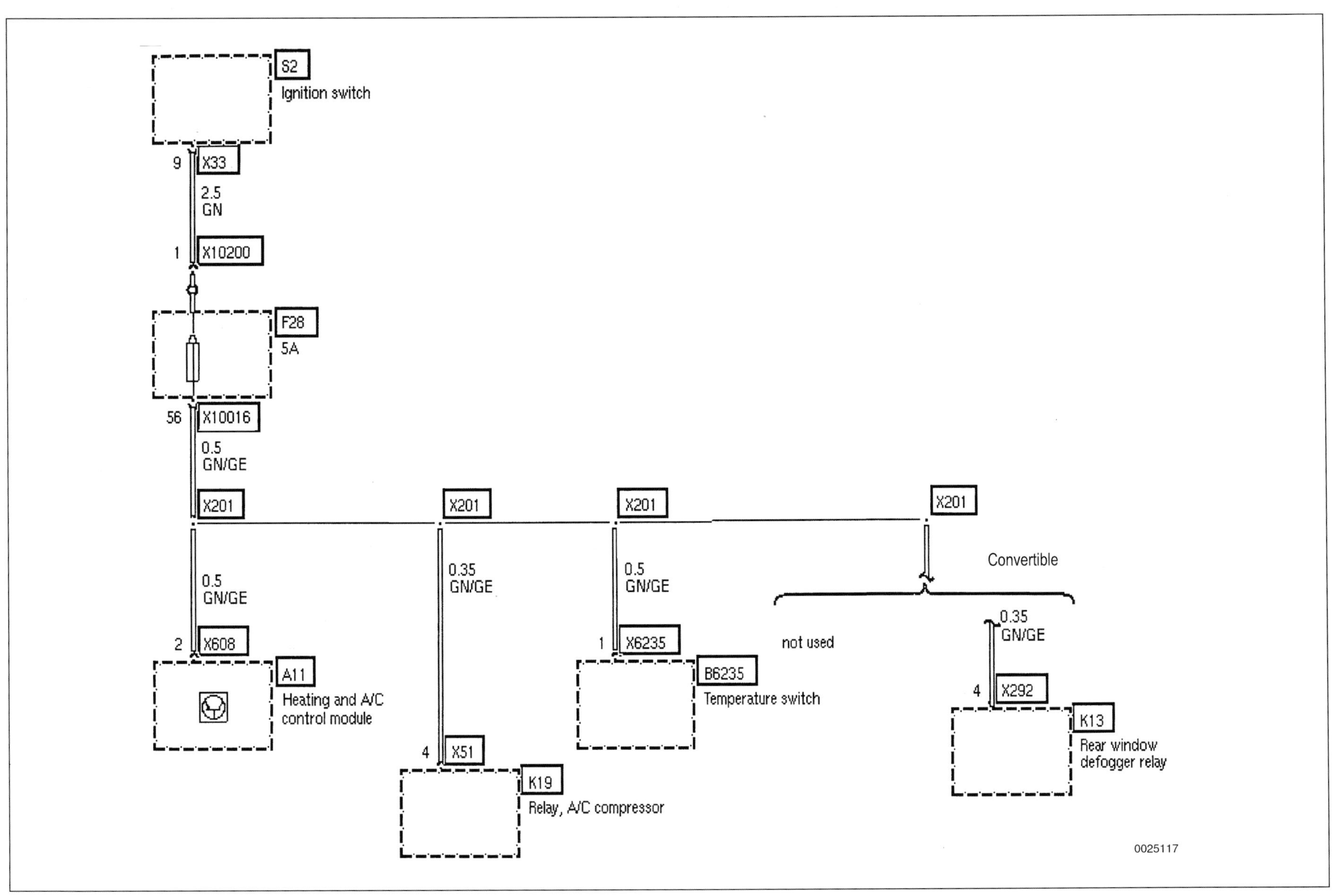
S2
Ignition switch
9
X33
2.5
GN
1
X10200
F28
5A
56
X10016
0.5
GN/GE
X201
X201
X201
X201
0.5
GN/GE
0.35
GN/GE
0.5
GN/GE
Convertible
not used
0.35
GN/GE
2
X608
A11
Heating and A/C
control module
4
X51
K19
Relay, A/C compressor
1
X6235
B6235
Temperature switch
4
X292
K13
Rear window
defogger relay
0025117

Ground (X173)
1 of 2

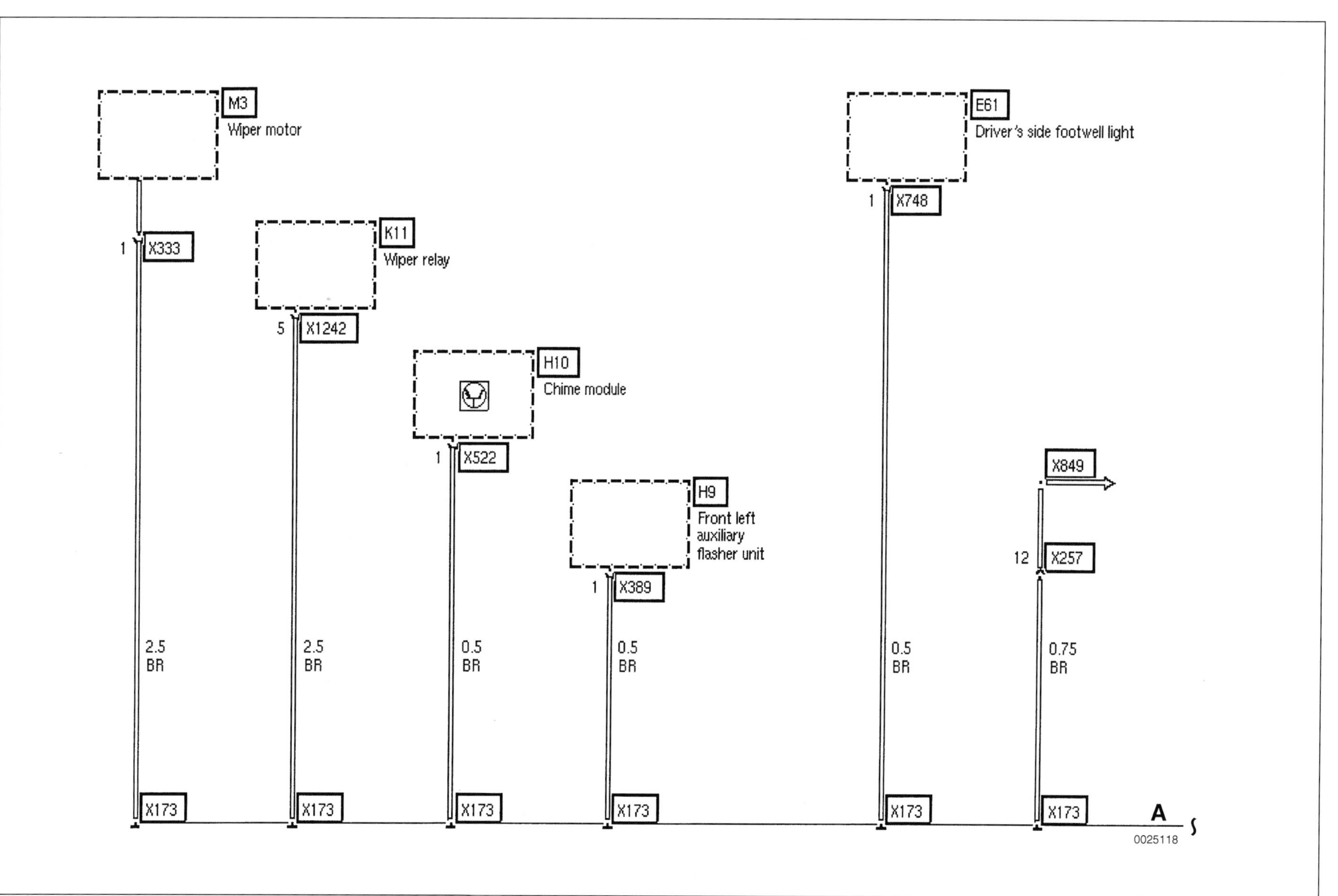

Ground (X173)
2 of 2

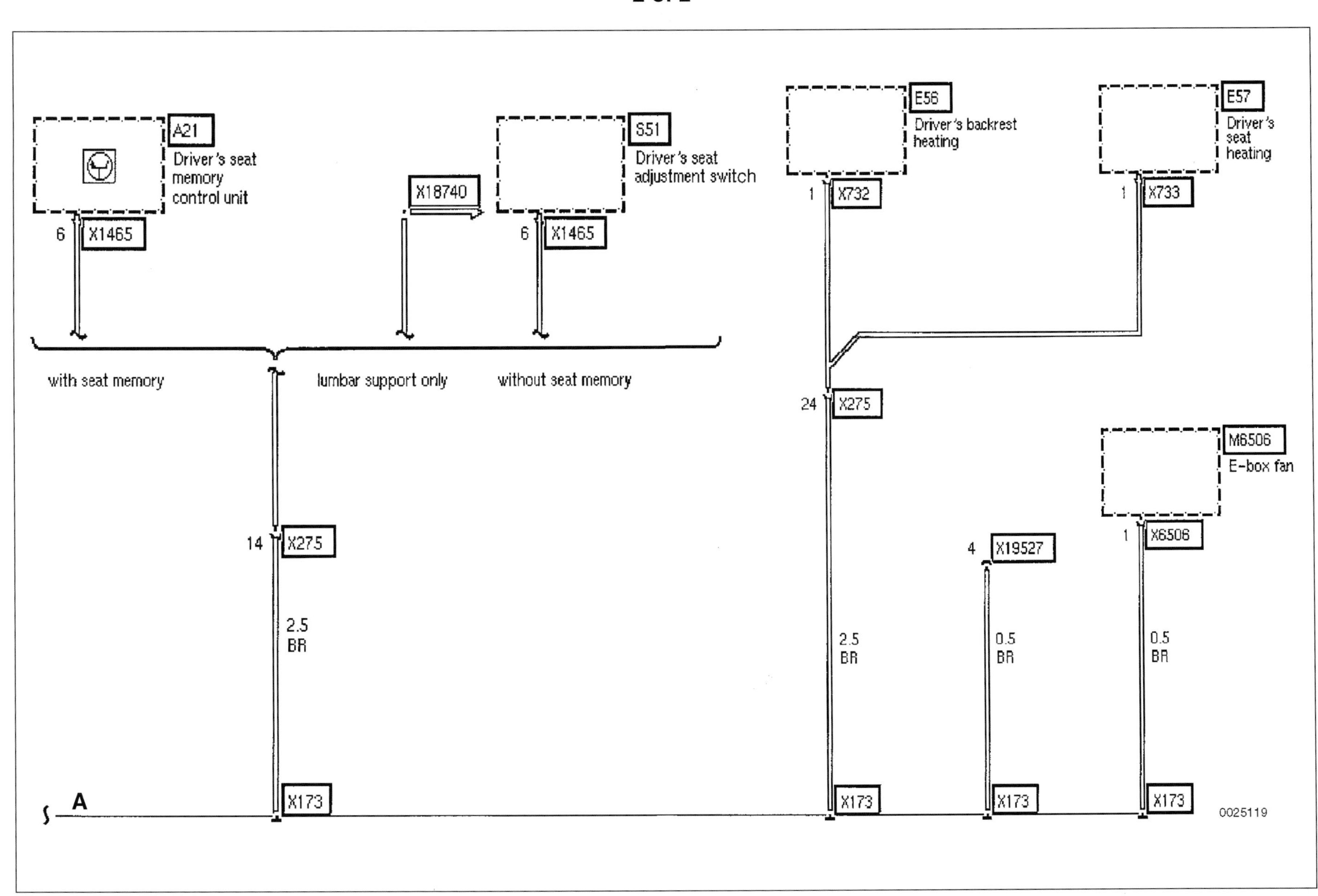

Starter (M6510)

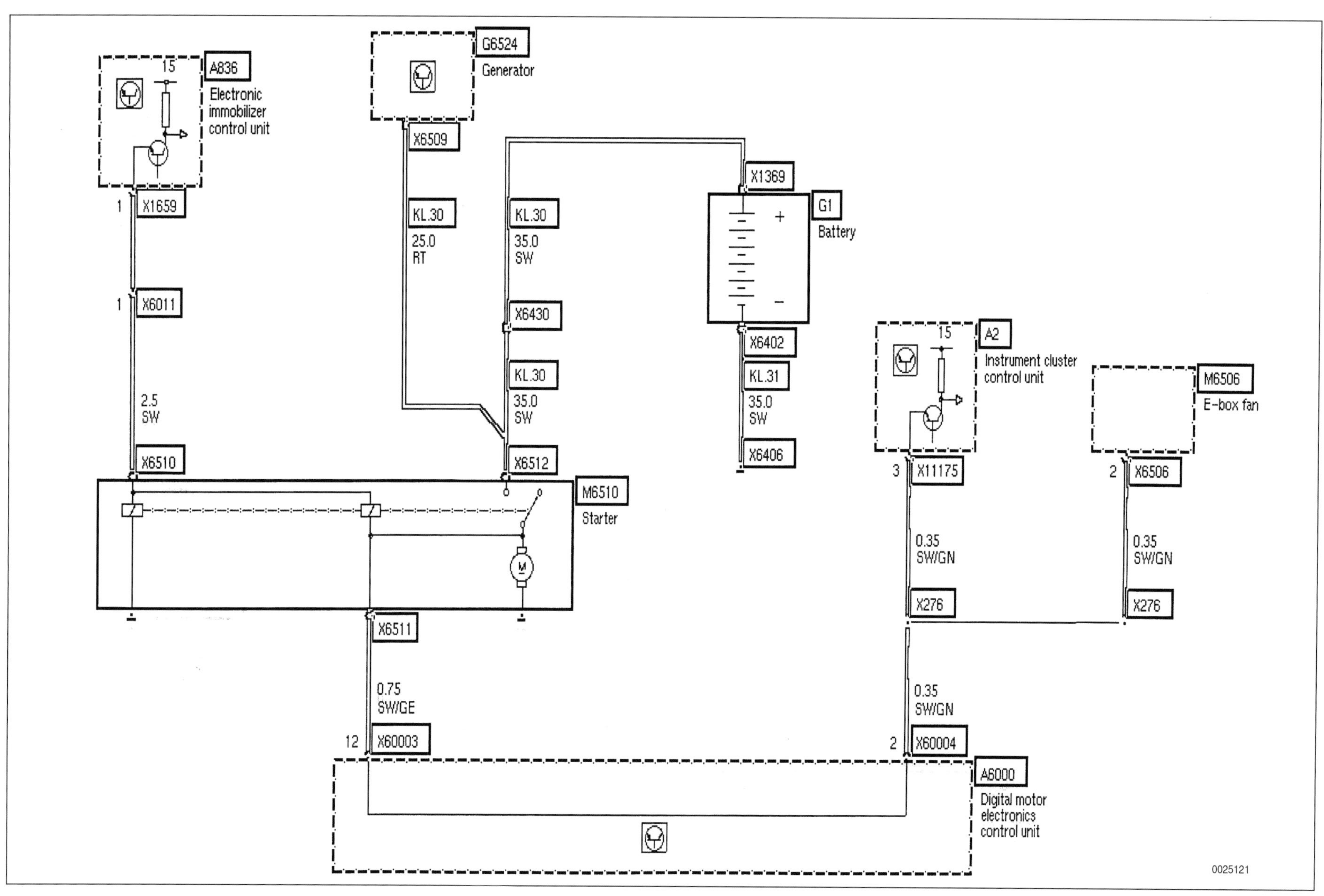

Engine harness connector (X6011)

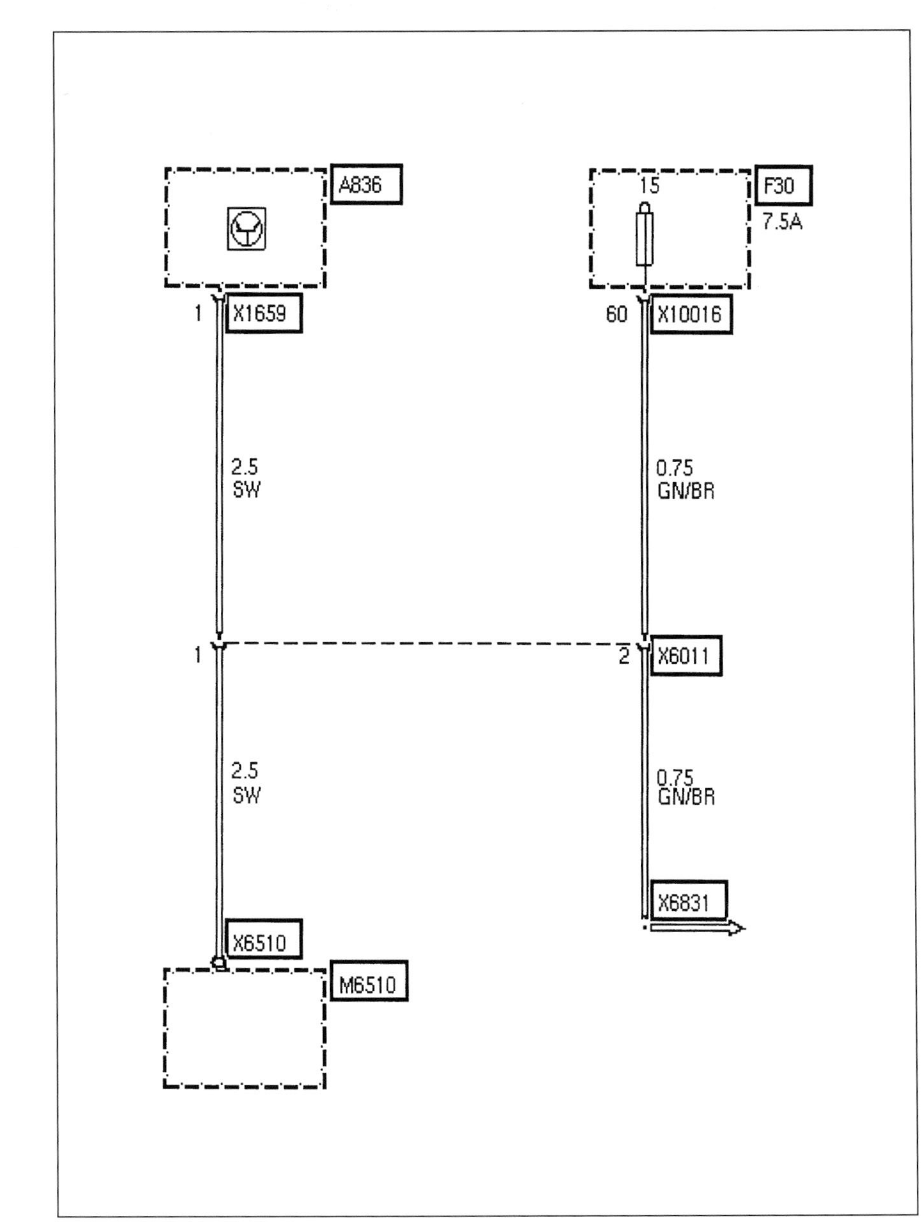

Battery (G1)
1 of 3

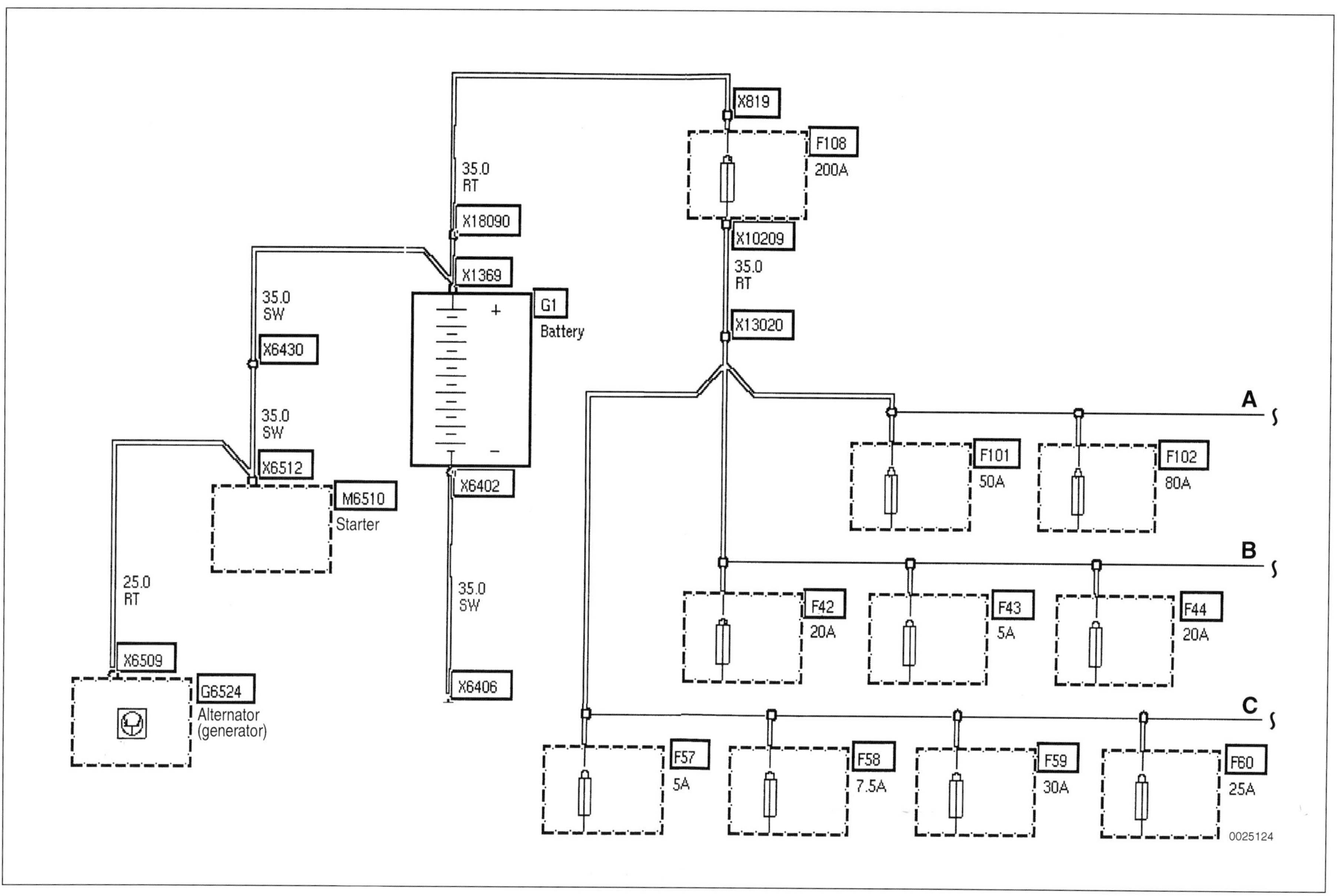

Battery (G1)
2 of 3

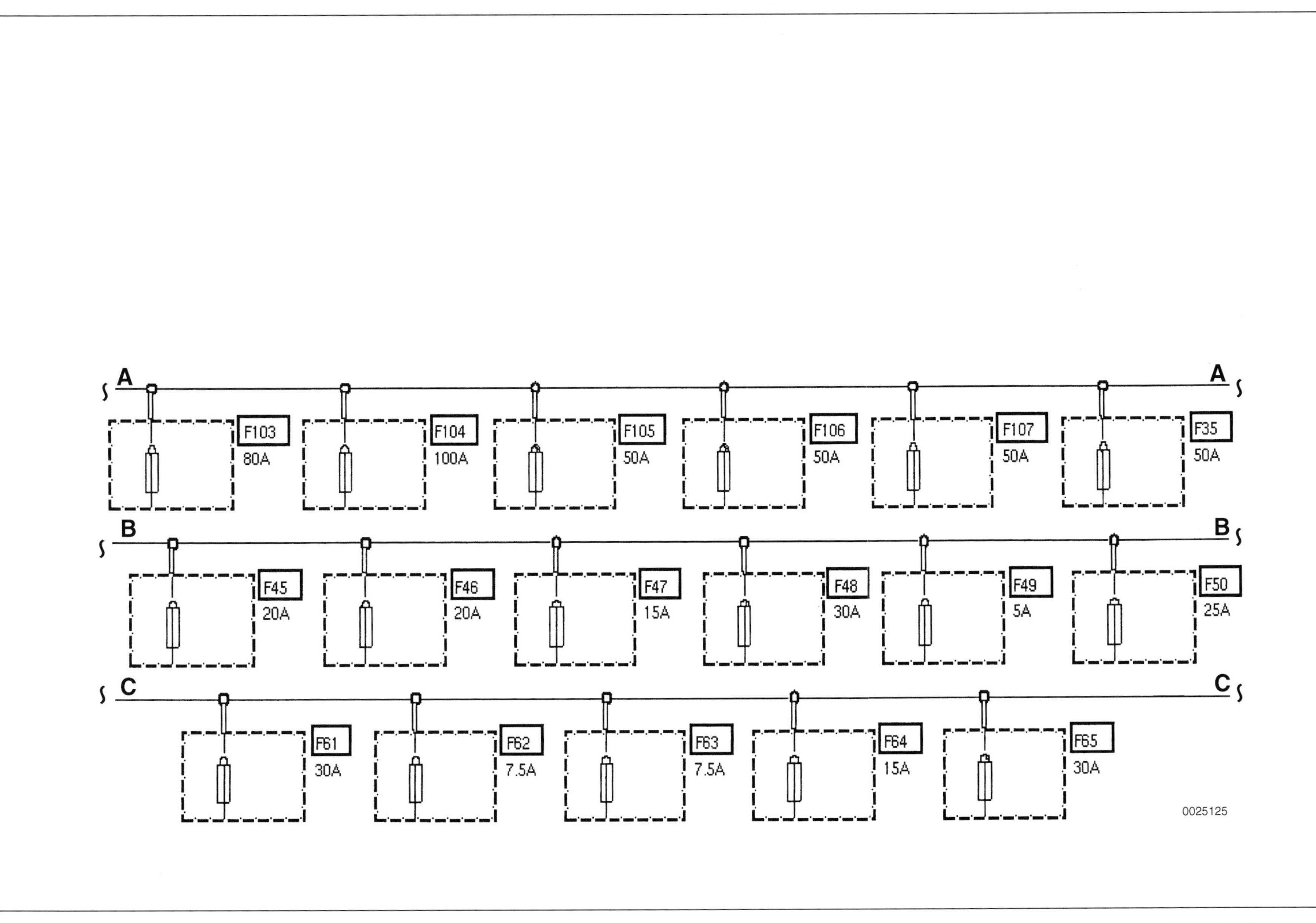

Battery (G1)
3 of 3

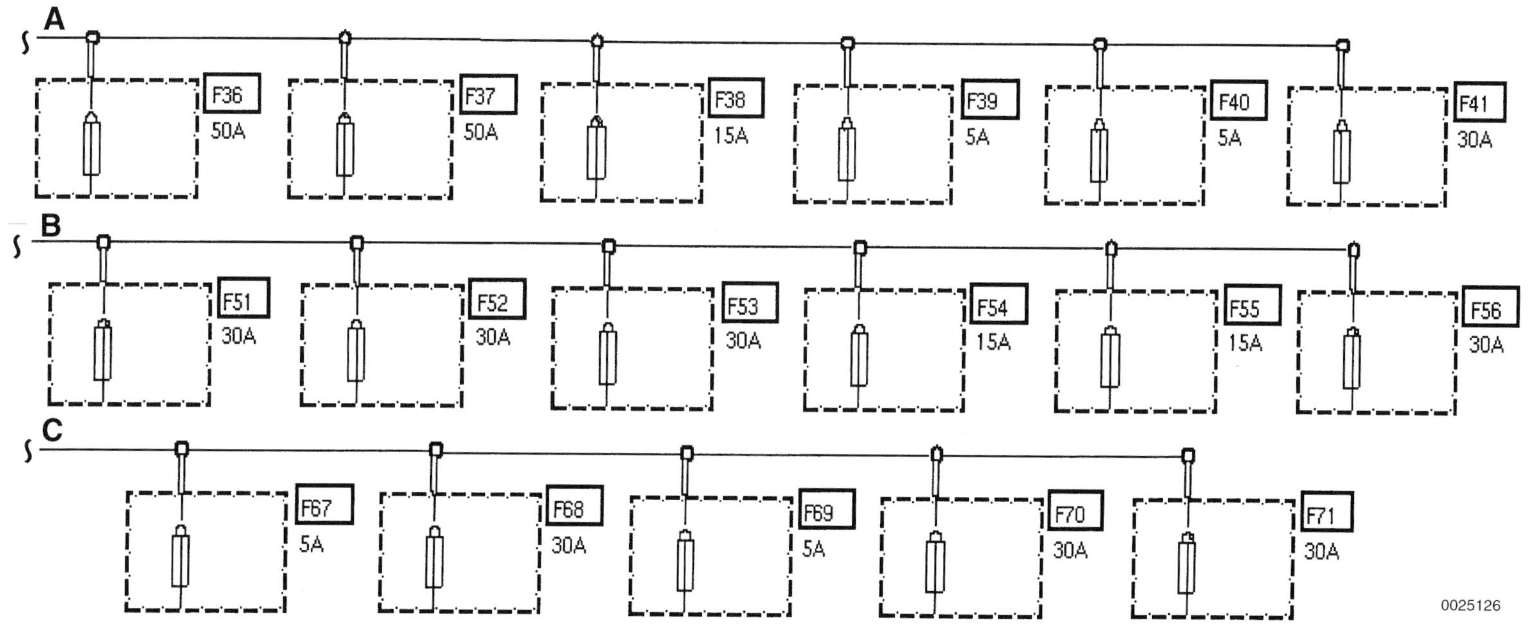

Alternator (generator) (G6524)

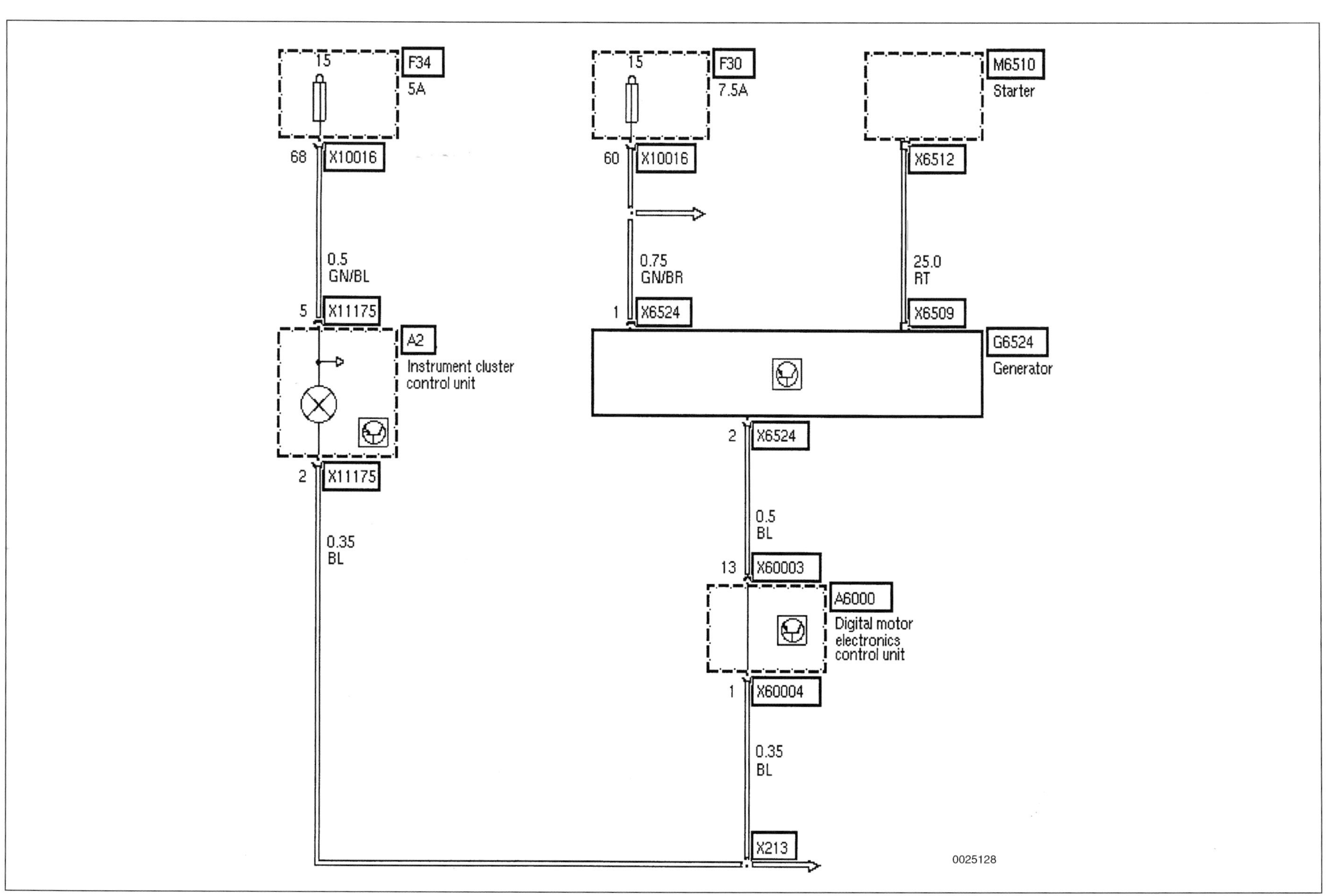

Fuse 34 (F34)

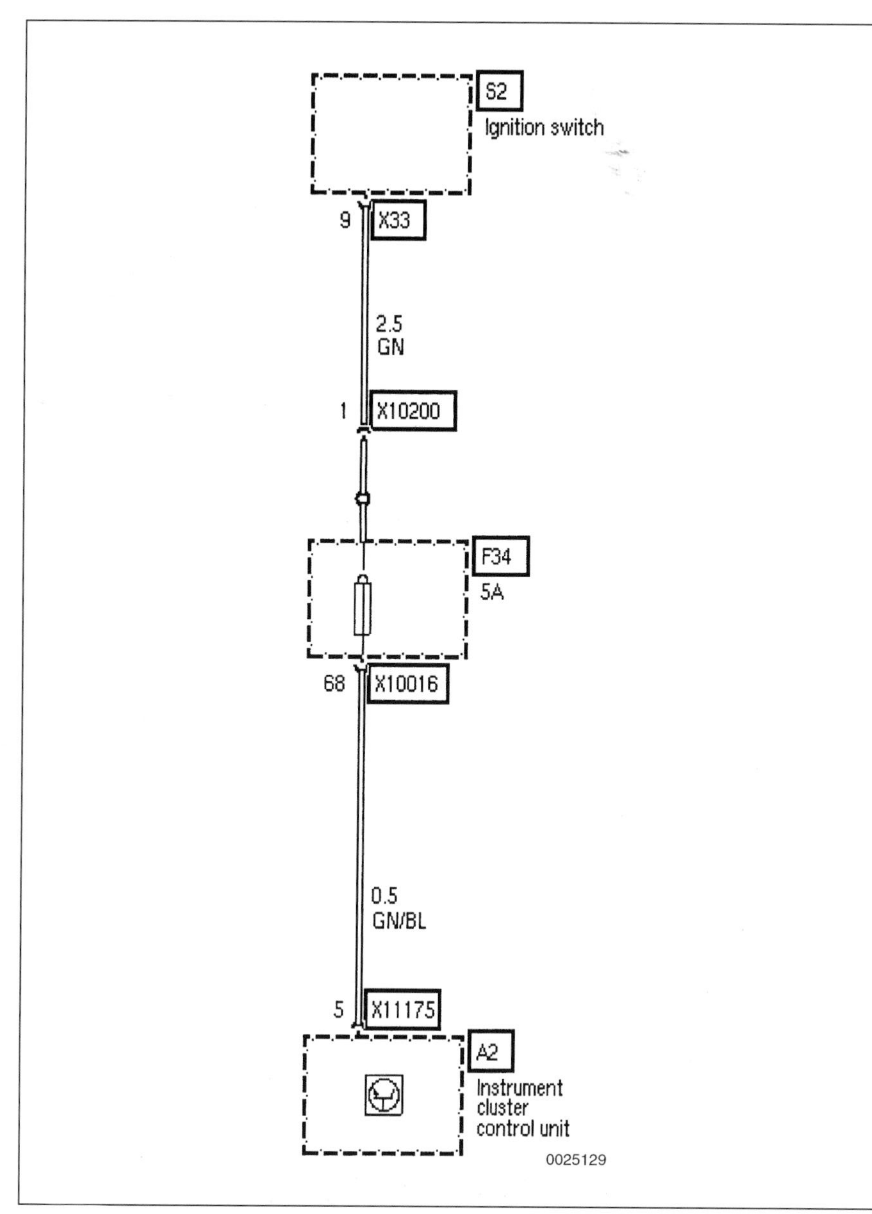

S2
Ignition switch
9
X33
2.5
GN
1
X10200
F34
5A
68
X10016
0.5
GN/BL
5
X11175
A2
Instrument
cluster
control unit
0025129

Fuel pump relay (K96)

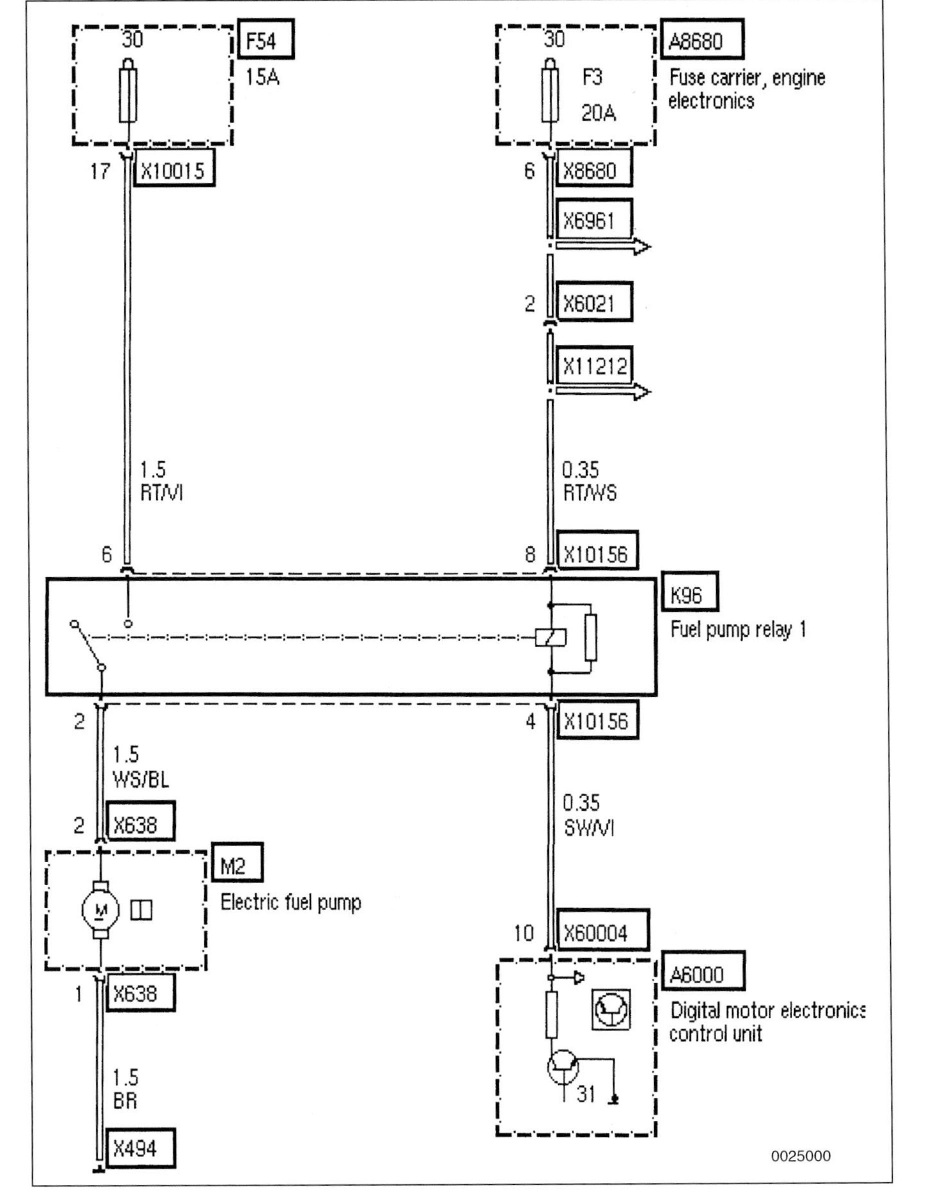

Splice connector (X213)

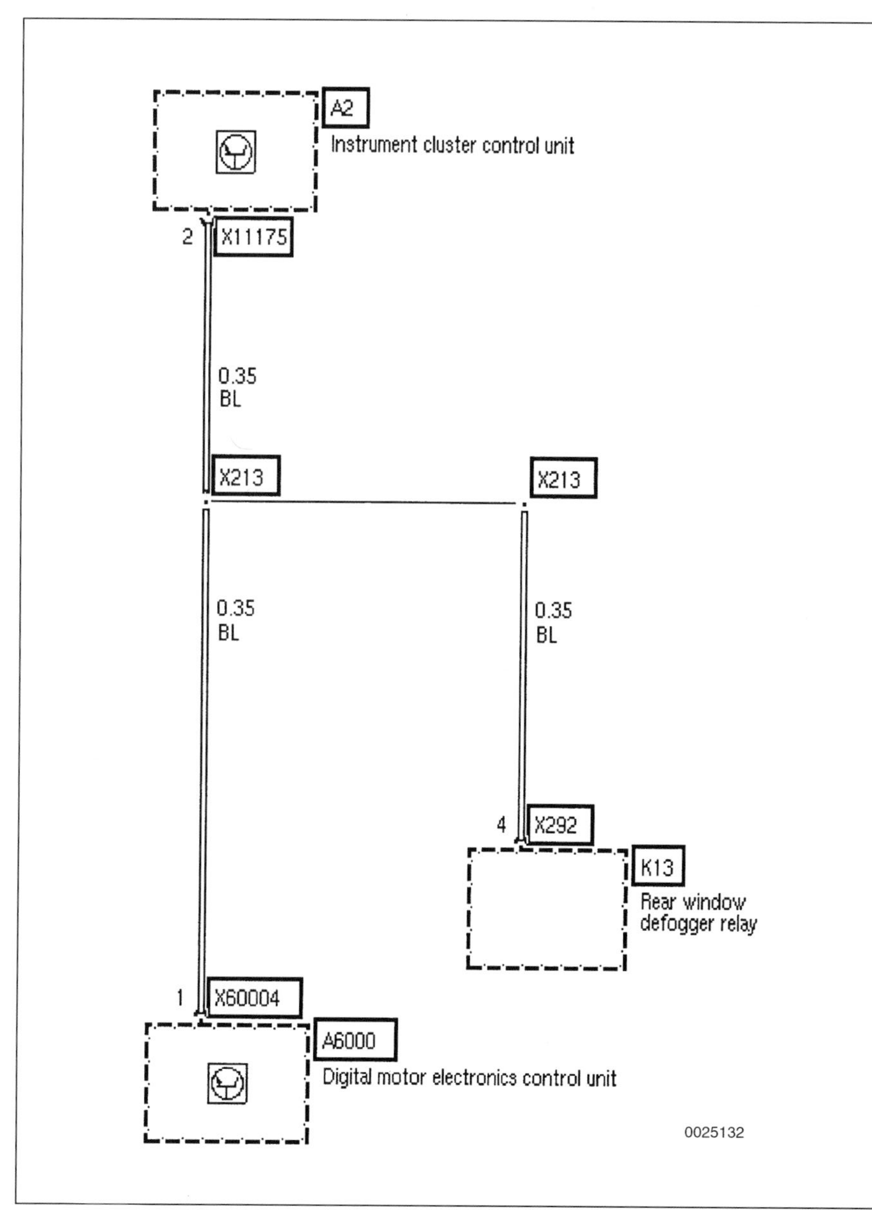

Charging socket (I01012)

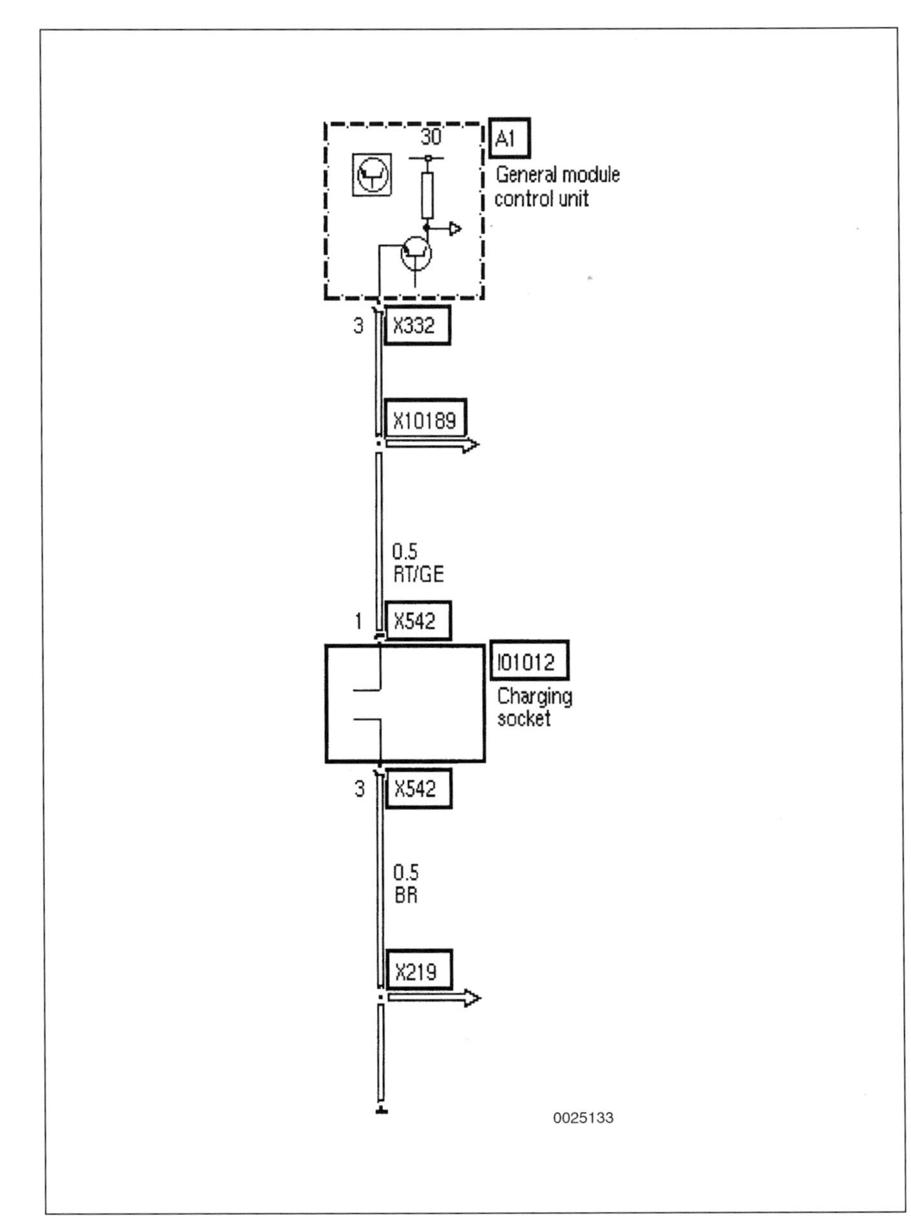

Splice connector (X10189)

1 of 2

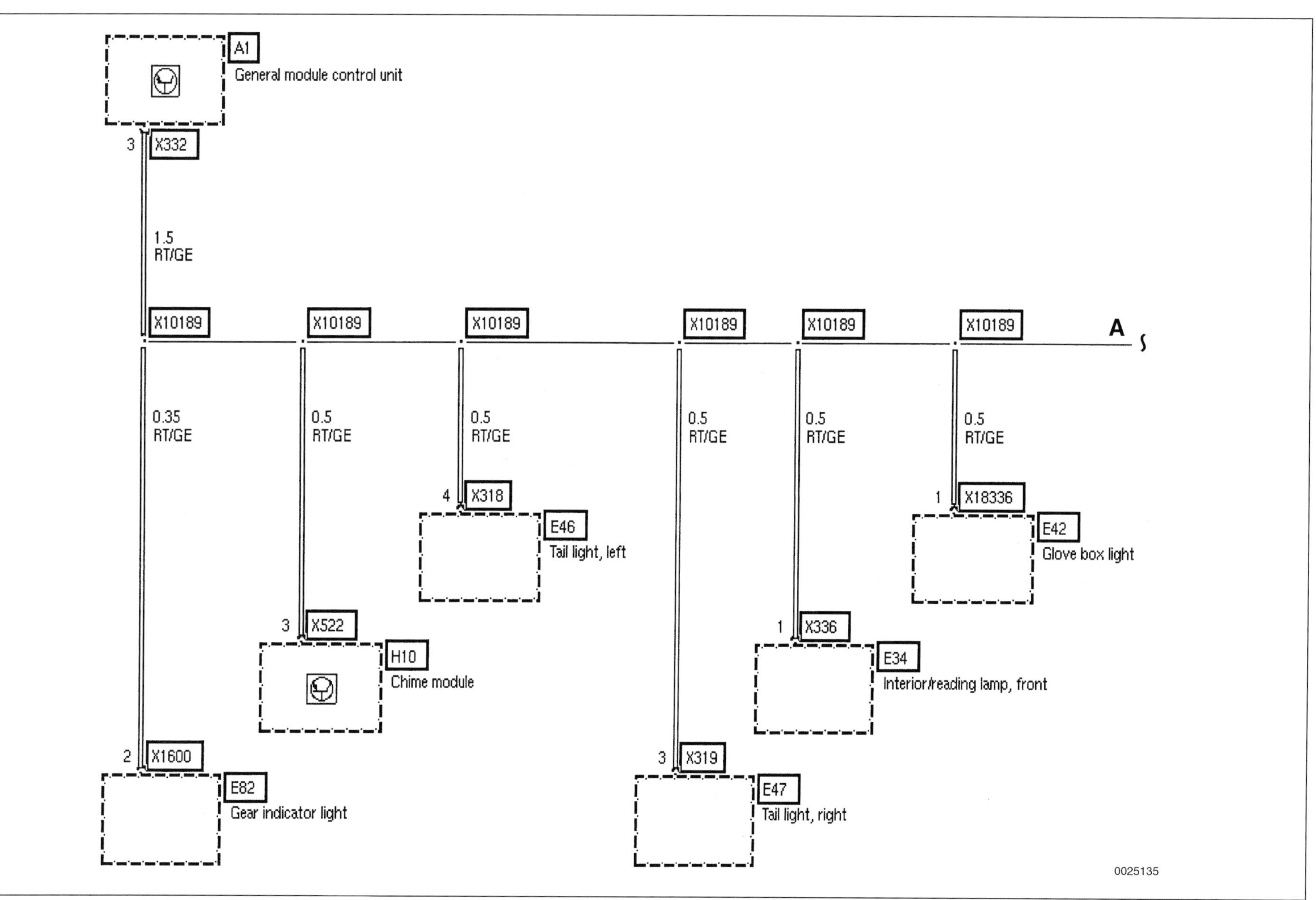

Splice connector (X10189)
2 of 2

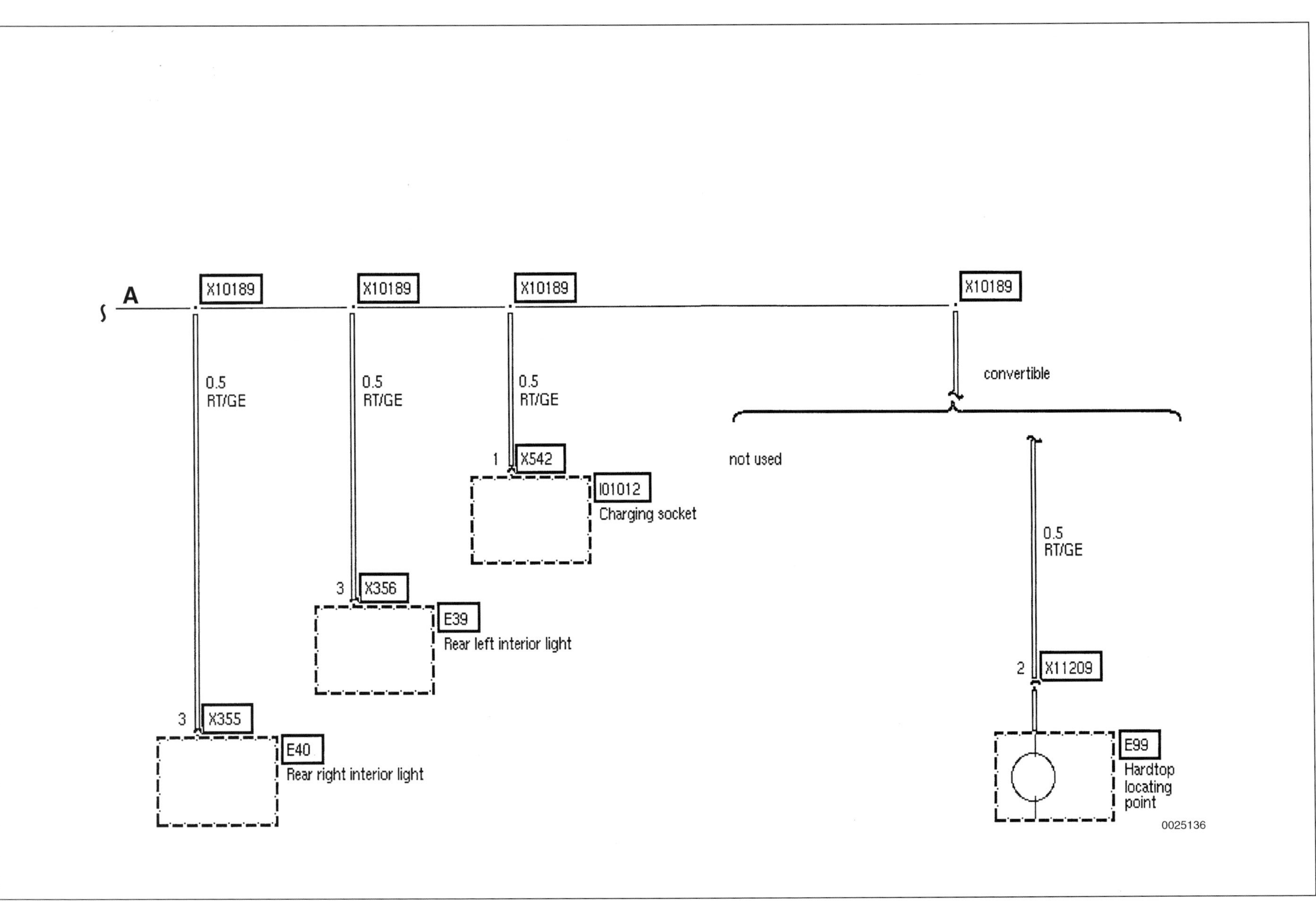

Splice connector (X219)
1 of 2

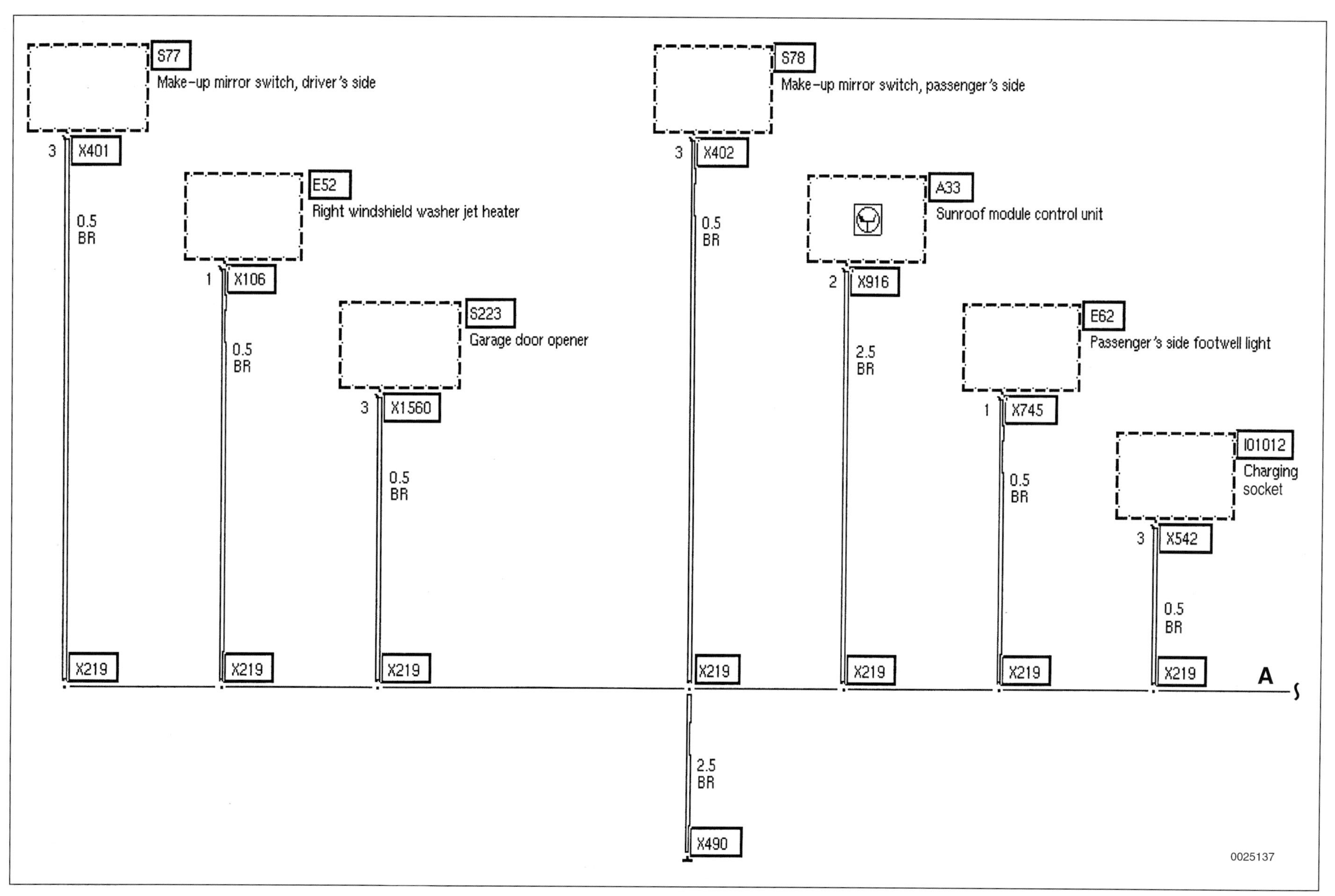

Splice connector (X219)
2 of 2

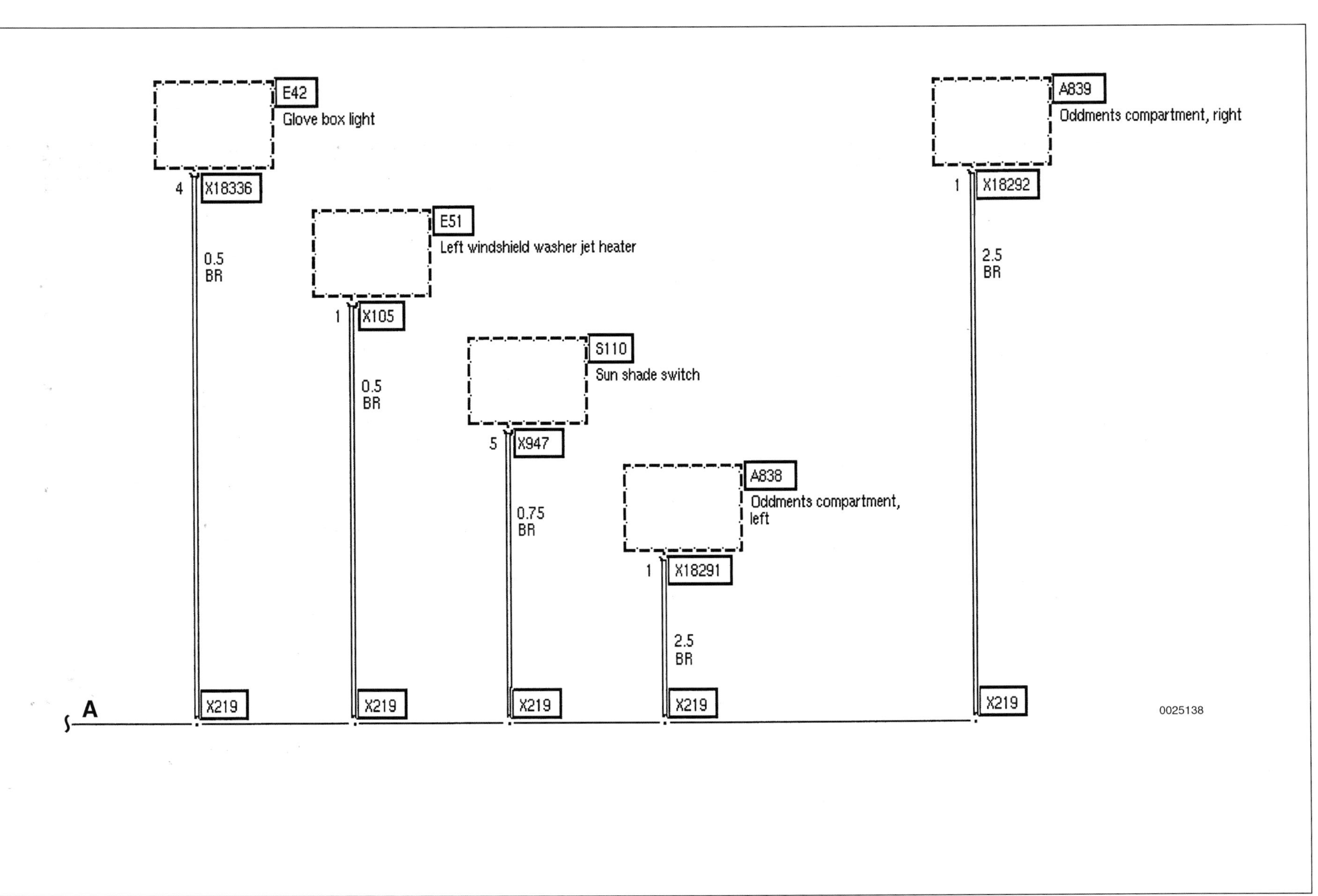

Park distance control (PDC) unit (A81)

1 of 2

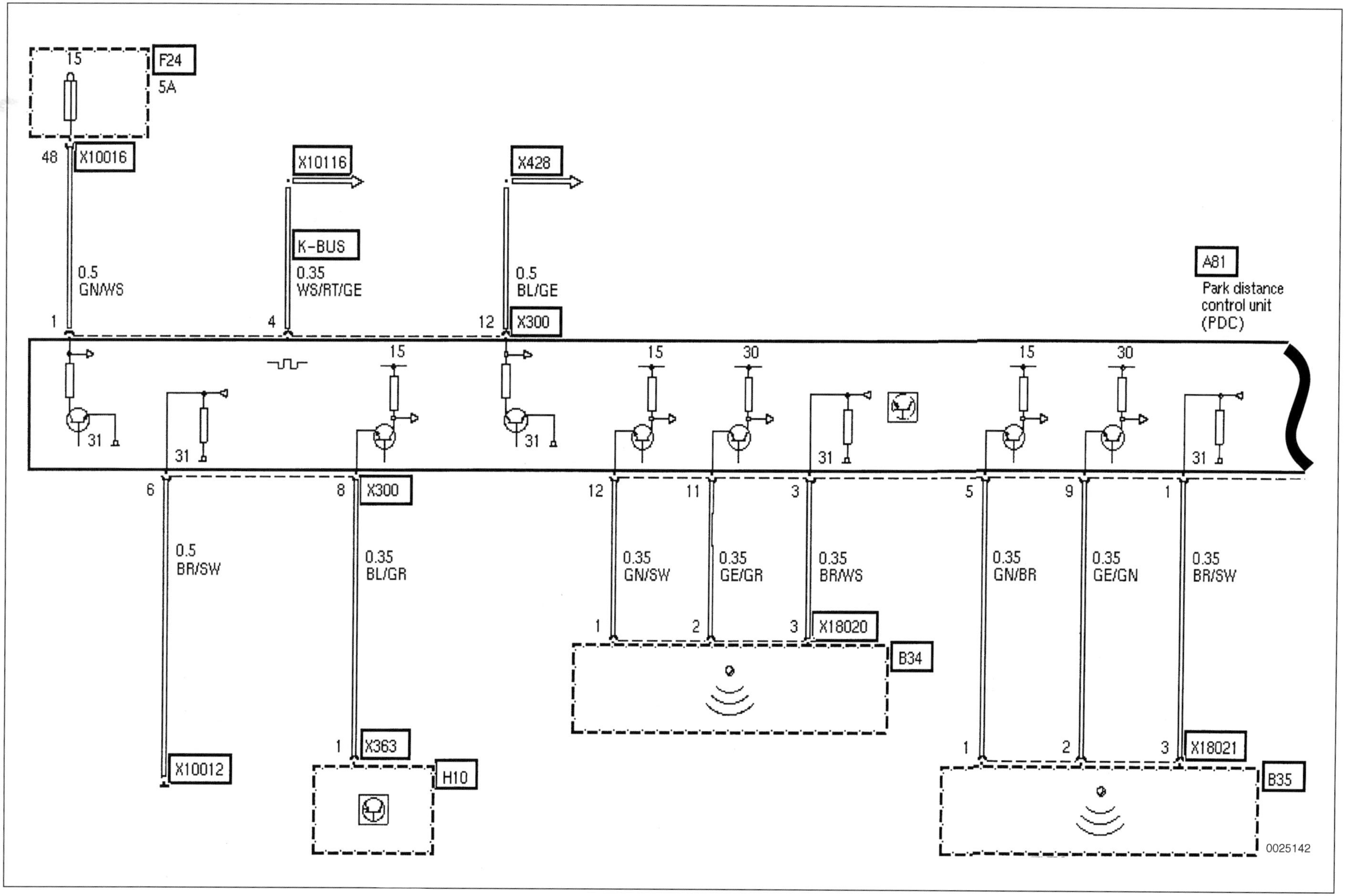

Park distance control (PDC) unit (A81)
2 of 2

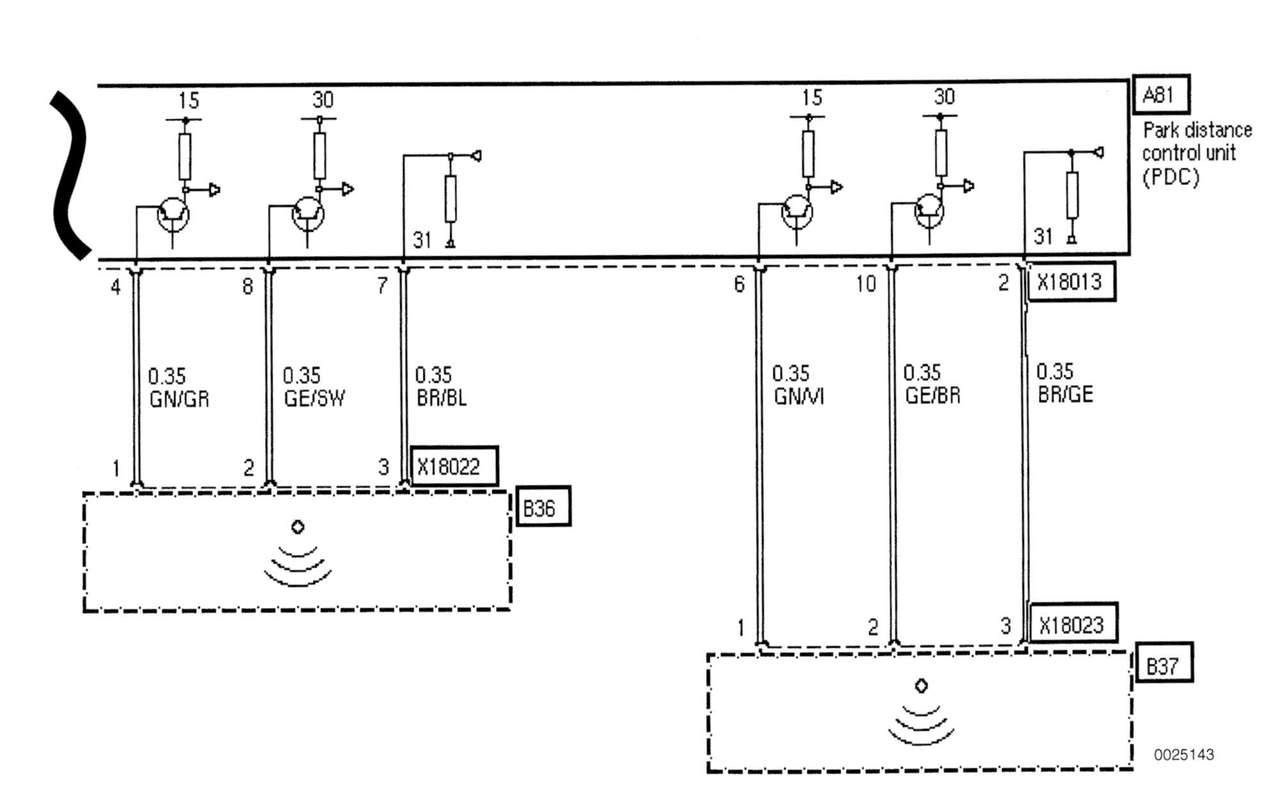

Connector (X322)

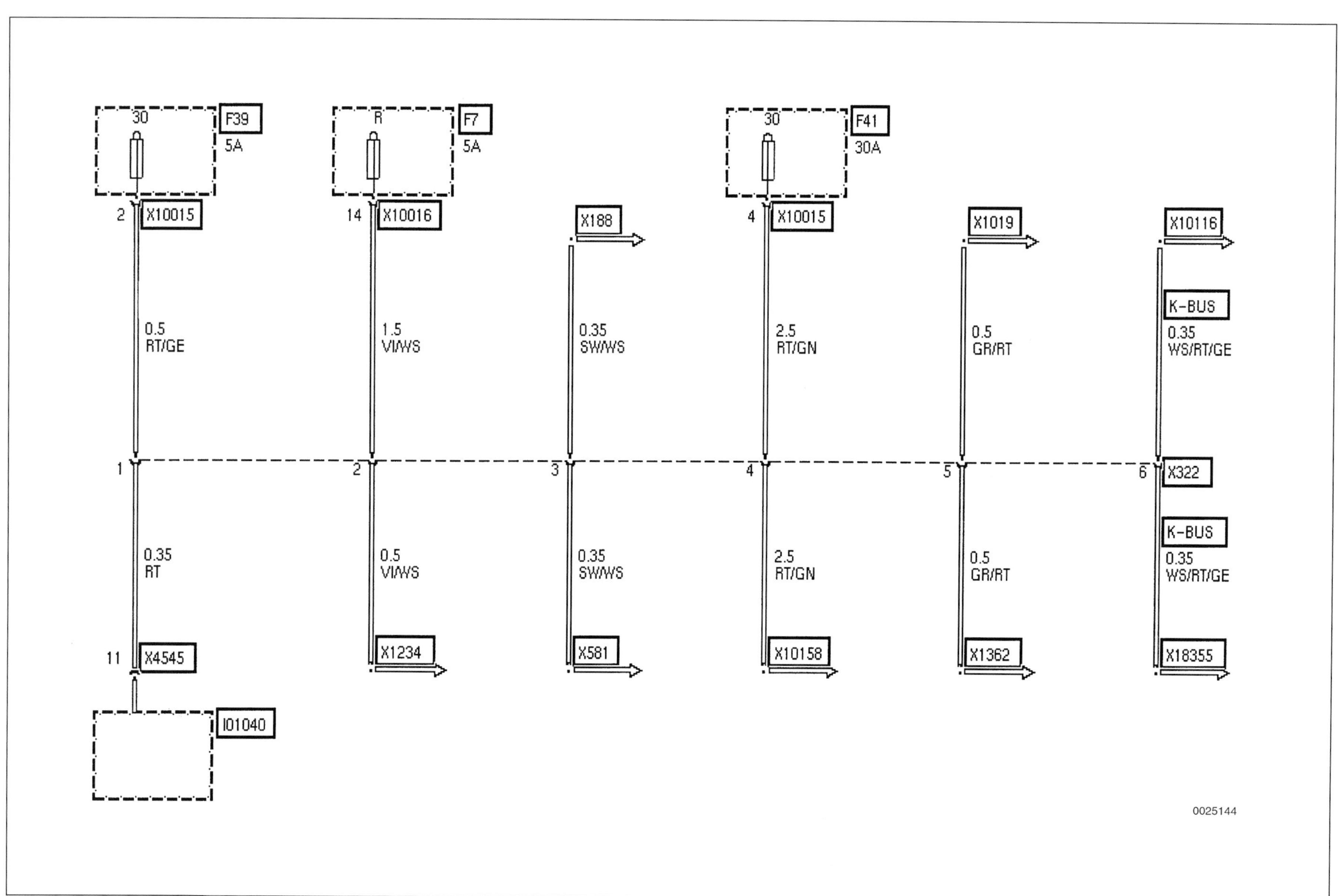

Splice connector (X18355)

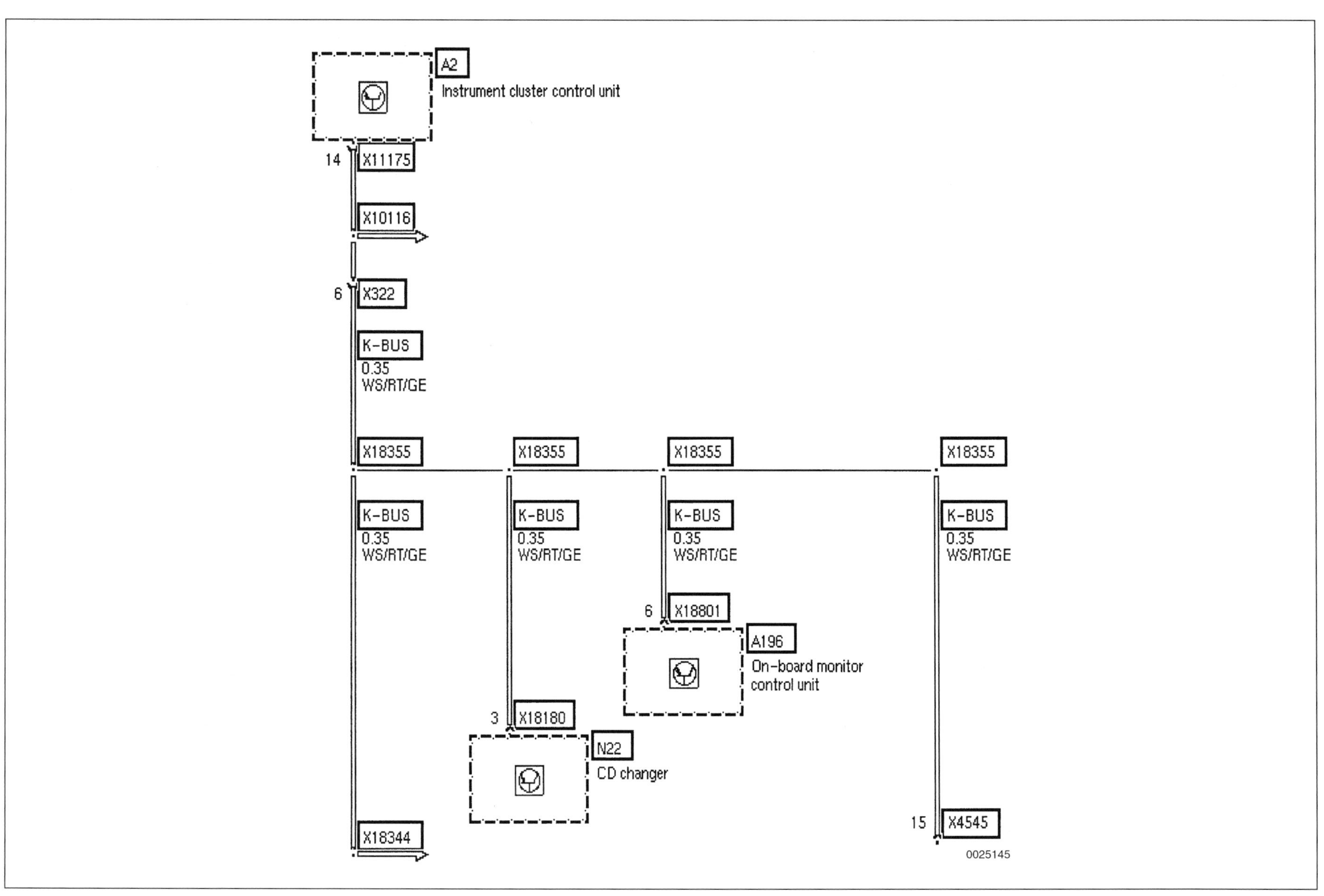

A/C and heating control module (A11)
1 of 2

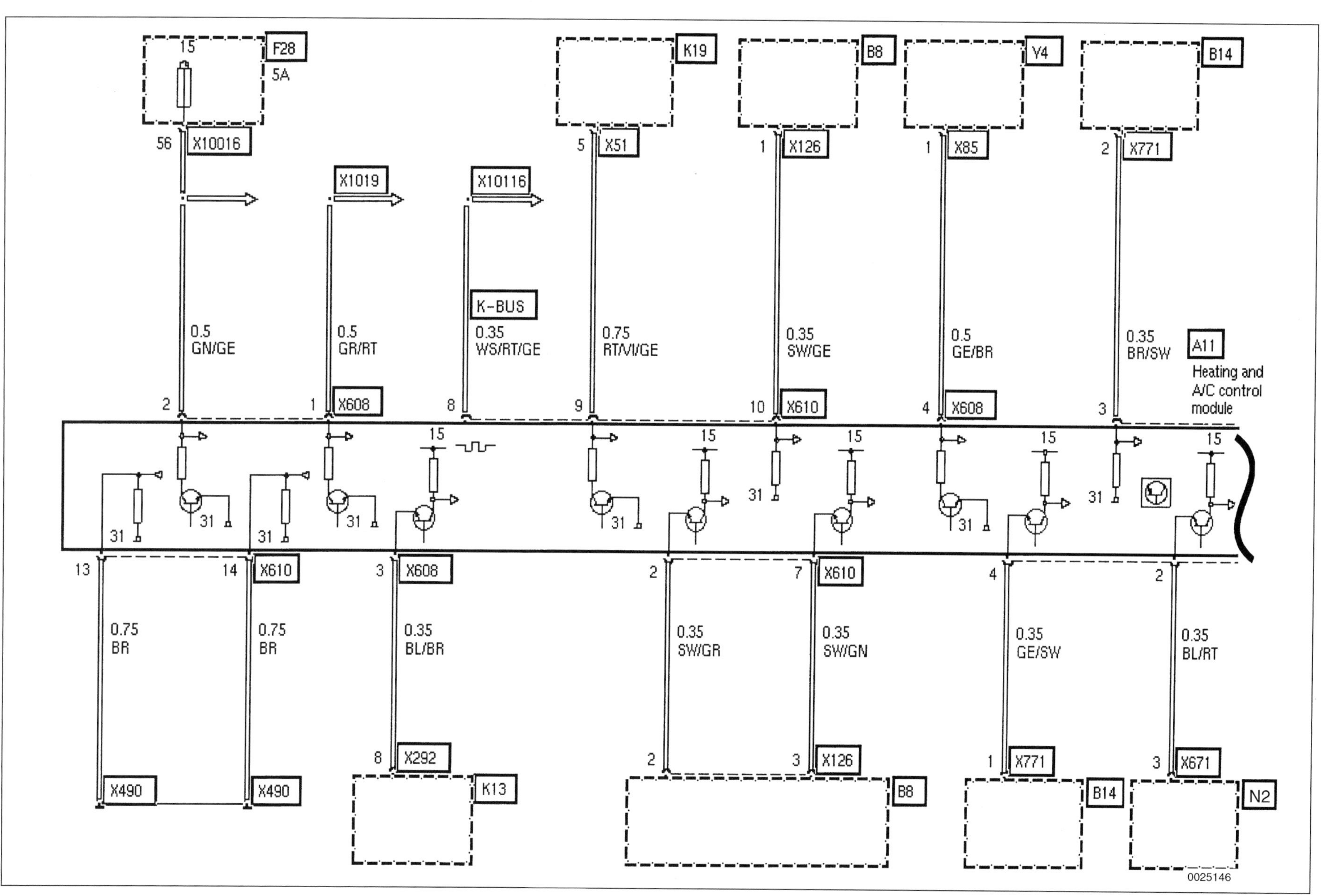

A/C and heating control module (A11)
2 of 2

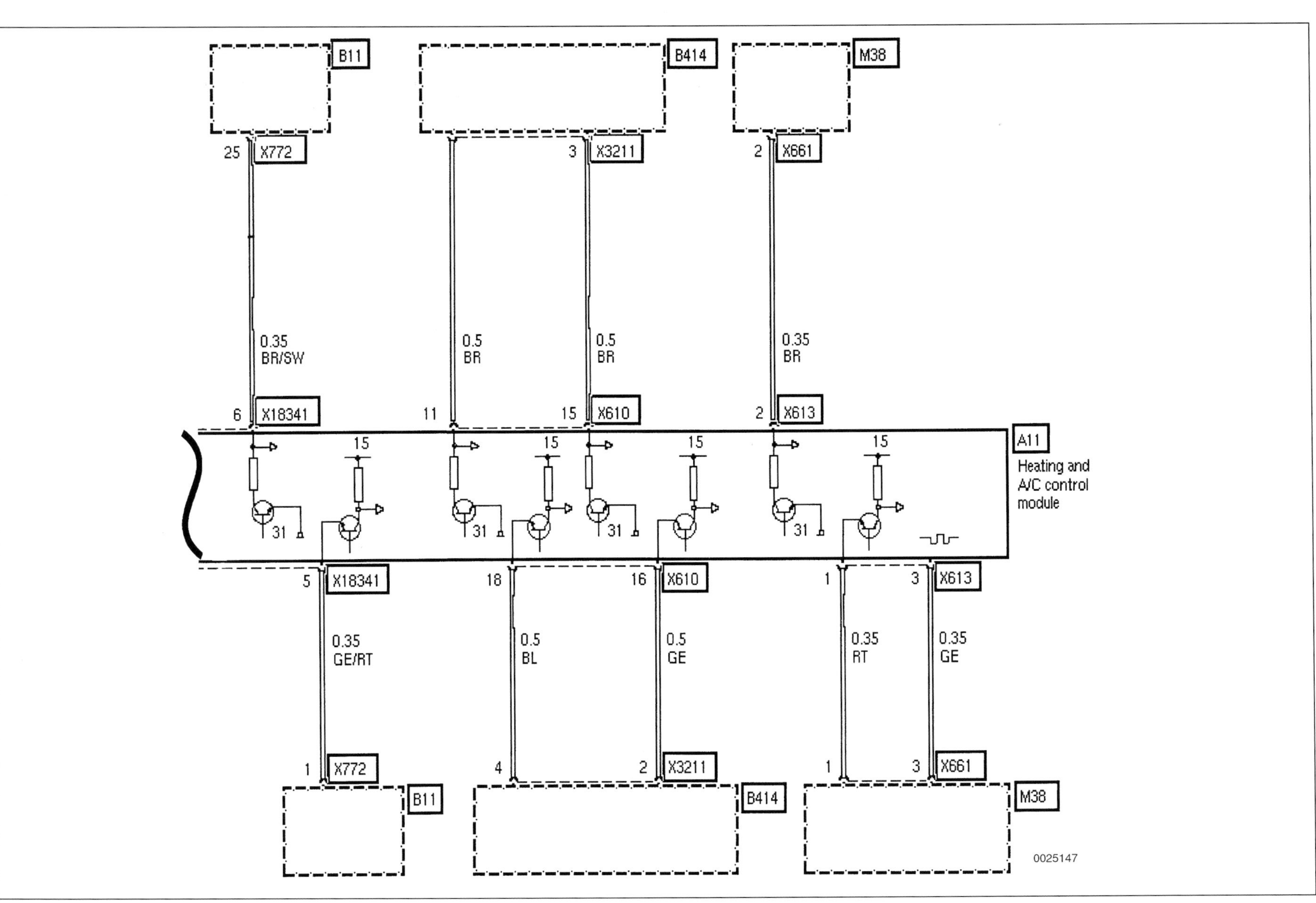

Light switching center control unit (A3)

1 of 6

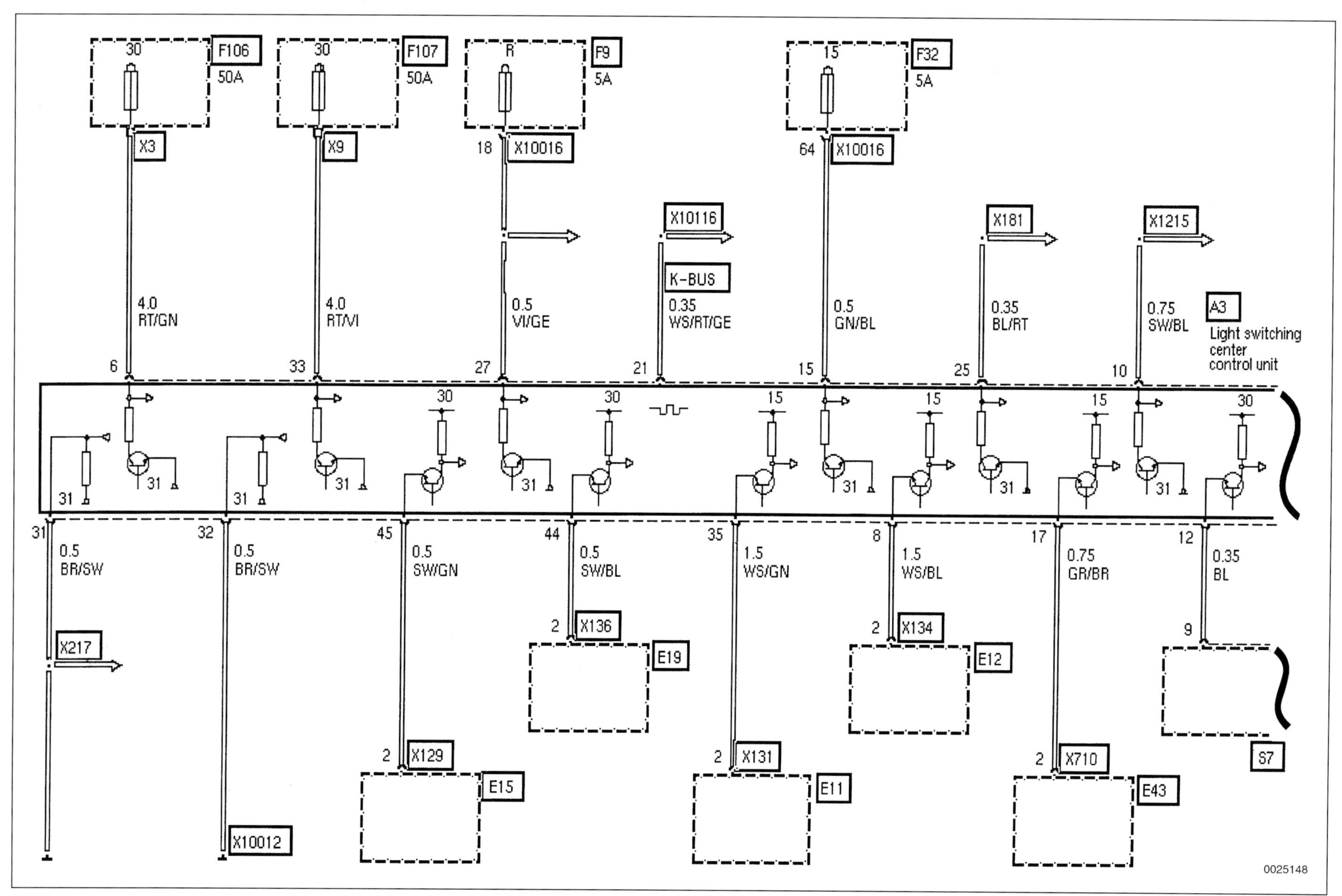

Light switching center control unit (A3)

2 of 6

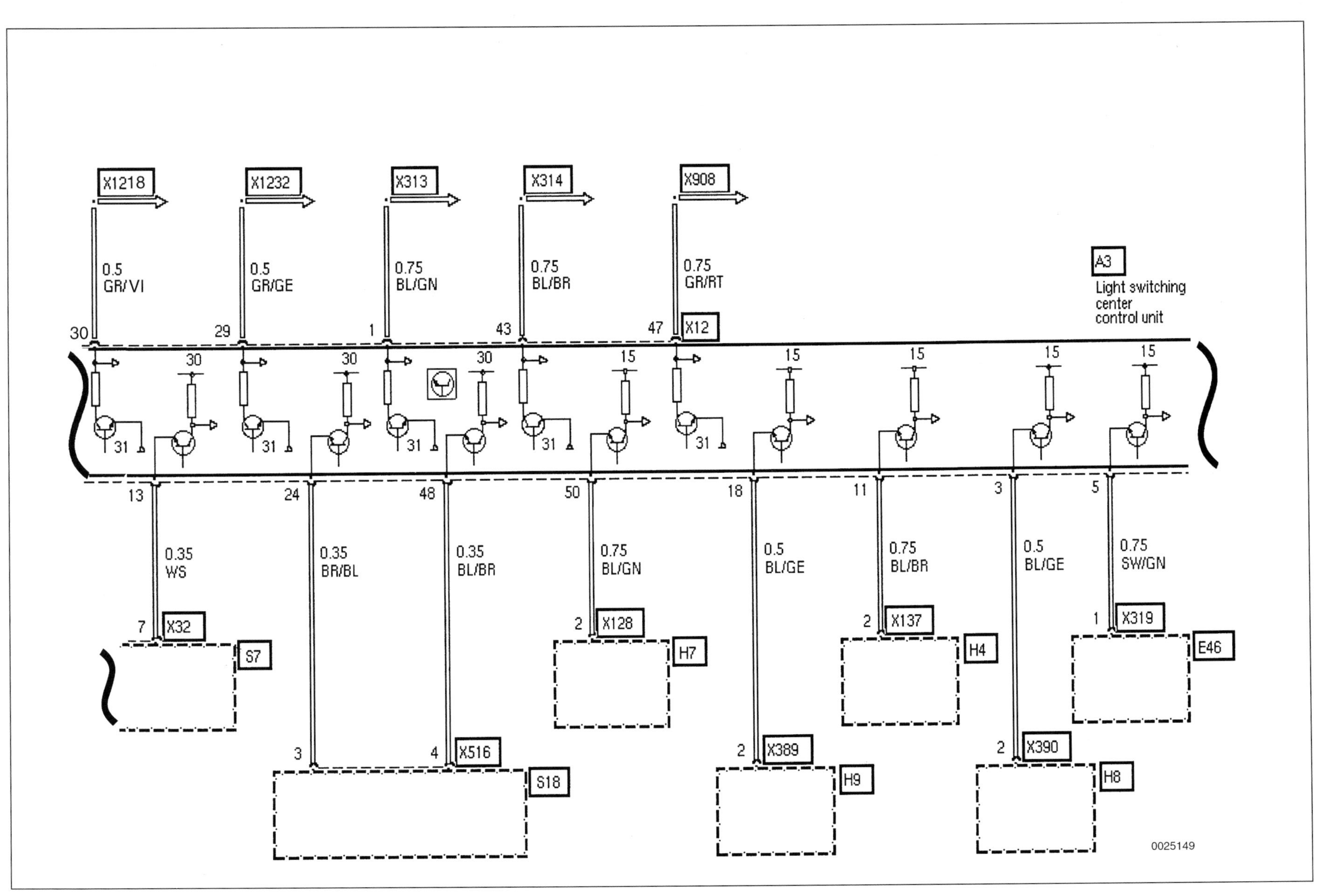

NO POSTAGE
NECESSARY
IF MAILED
IN THE
UNITED STATES

BUSINESS REPLY MAIL

FIRST-CLASS MAIL PERMIT NO. 29544 BOSTON MA

POSTAGE WILL BE PAID BY ADDRESSEE

BENTLEY PUBLISHERS™ | Automotive Reference™

Bentley Publishers
1734 Massachusetts Avenue
Cambridge, MA 02138-9940
USA

1734 Massachusetts Ave.
Cambridge, MA 02138 USA
Tel: 800-423-4595 • Fax: 617-876-9235
Automotive Reference®

Please fill out this postage prepaid card so that we may keep you informed of any new products.

Name ______________ Address ______________

City ________ State ____ Zip _____ Country ______ Phone ______

E-mail address ______________

What make, model and year car(s) do you own? ______________

Where did you buy your Bentley book?

- ❑ Bookstore ❑ Catalog/mail order
- ❑ BentleyPublishers.com ❑ Other

  Please specify name ______________

How did you find out about this book?

- ❑ Previously owned Bentley books

  Please specify title(s) ______________
- ❑ BentleyPublishers.com
- ❑ Recommended by a friend
- ❑ Magazine advertisement or ❑ Review

  Which magazine? ______________

What magazines do you read?

- ❑ *Road & Track* ❑ *VW Trends* ❑ *european car*
- ❑ *Car and Driver* ❑ Other ______________

Would you like to be on our mailing list for upcoming products in these categories?

- ❑ BMW ❑ Volkswagen and Audi
- ❑ Corvette ❑ Performance / engineering
- ❑ Honda, Mazda, and other Asian models
- ❑ Porsche ❑ All new titles

What automotive subjects are you interested in?

- ❑ Auto history
- ❑ European cars
- ❑ Tuning/high-performance driving
- ❑ How-to service and repair
- ❑ Favorite racing series ______________
- ❑ Other ______________

Comments on this book? ______________

____

What other books would you like to see us publish? ______________

❑ Please send me your free catalog of Bentley Publishers automotive products.

B305-03

Light switching center control unit (A3)
3 of 6

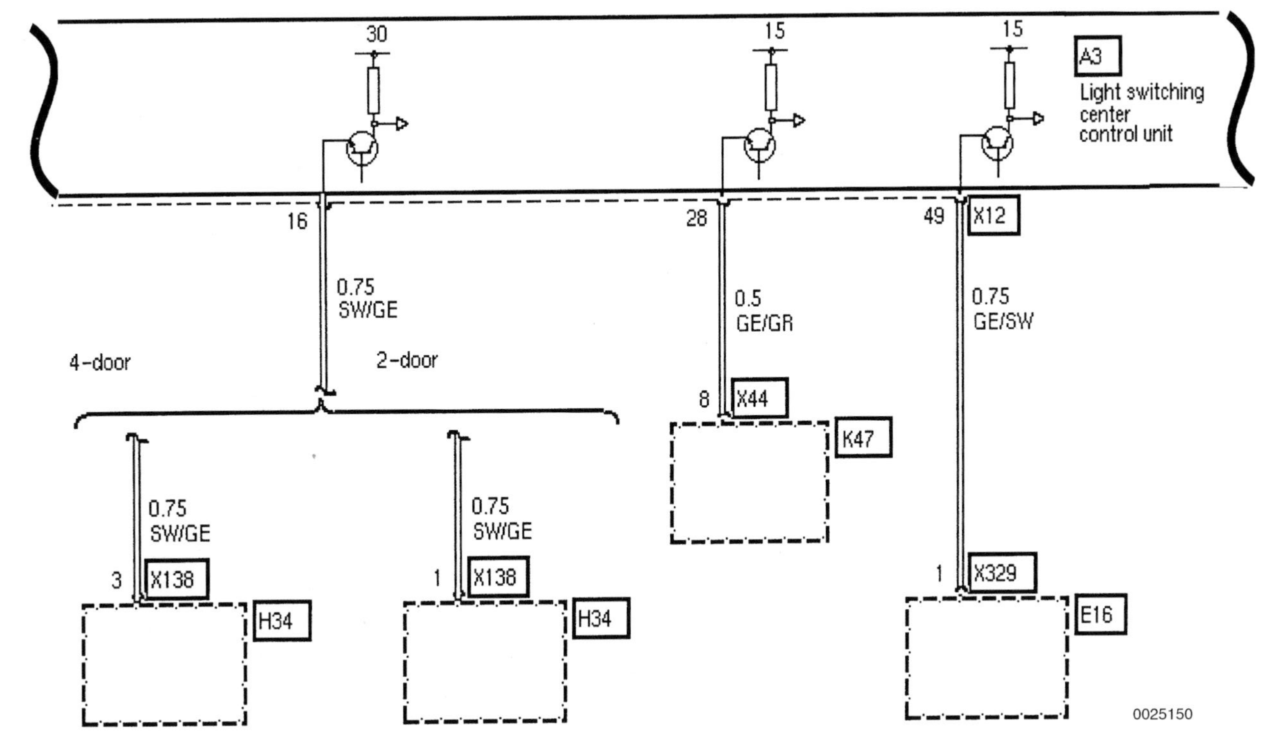

Light switching center control unit (A3)
4 of 6

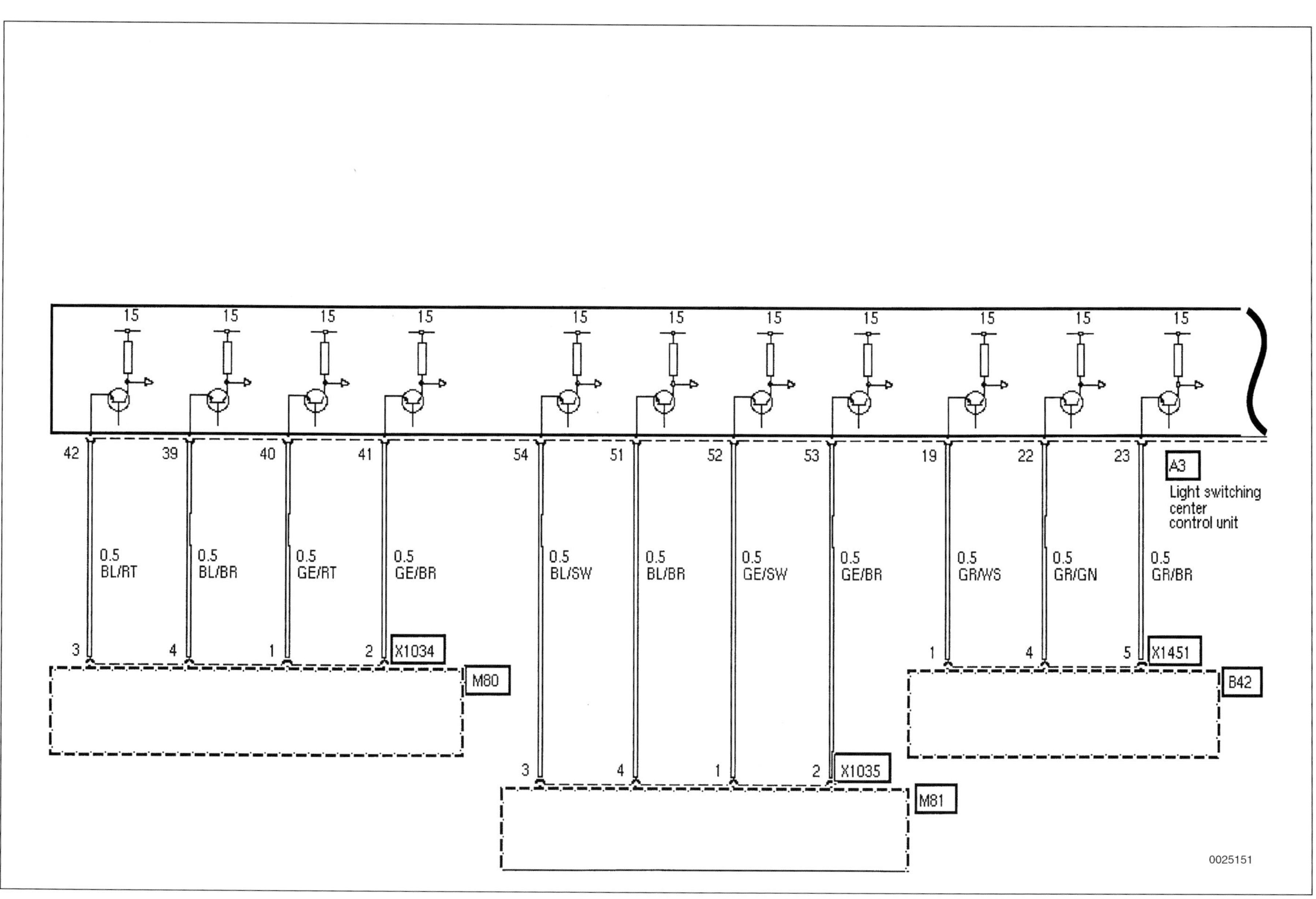

Light switching center control unit (A3)
5 of 6

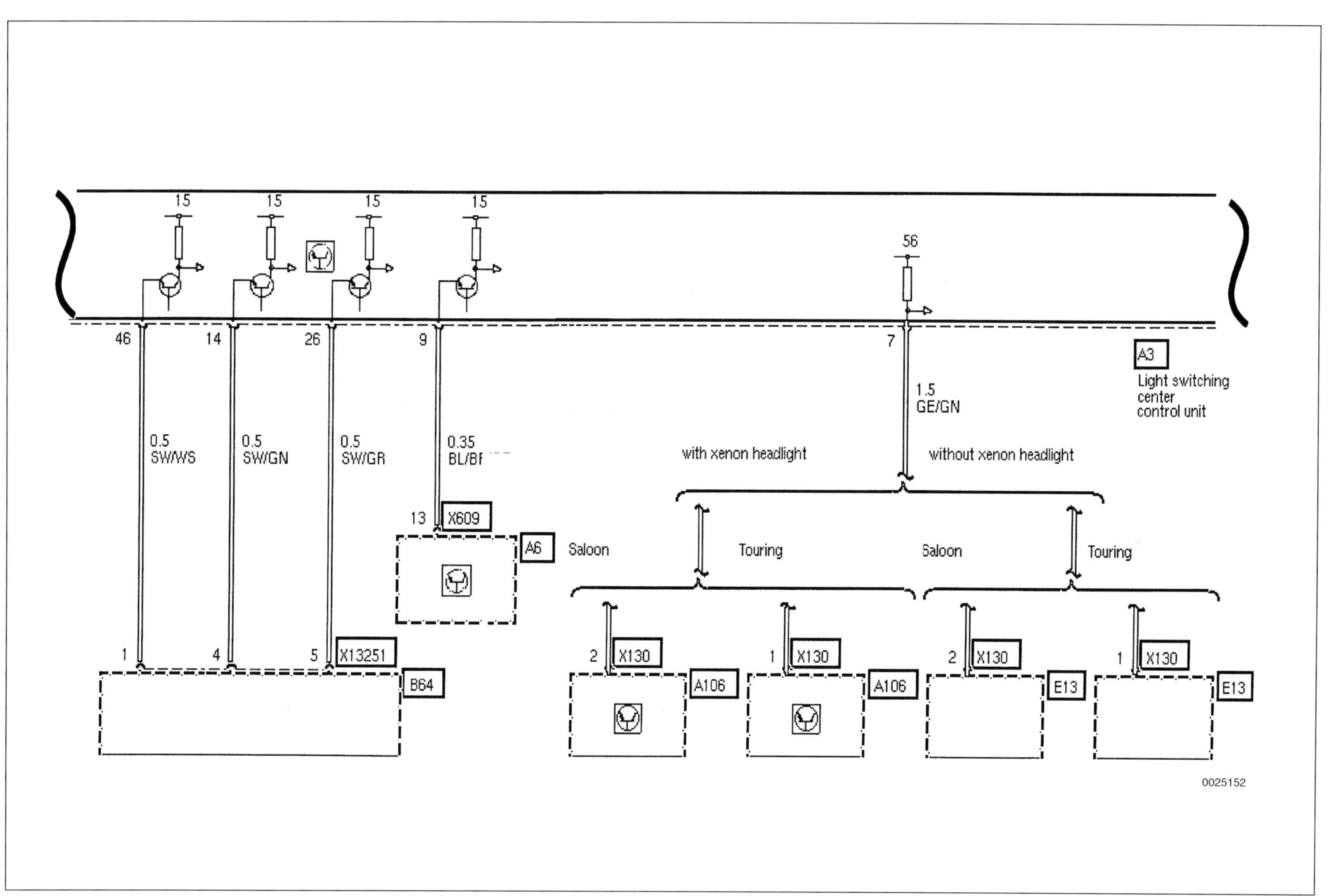

Light switching center control unit (A3)

6 of 6

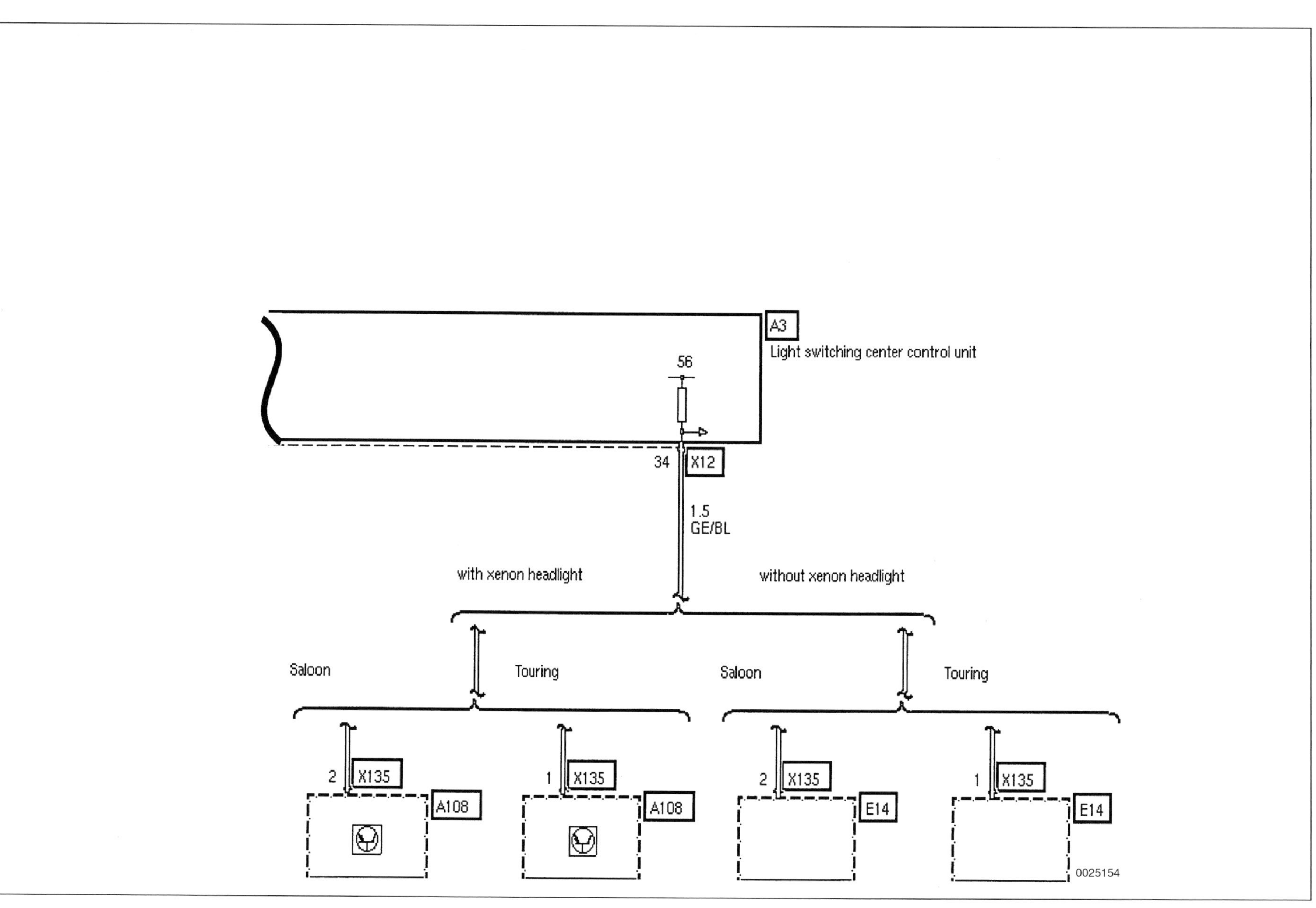

General module (GM V) (A1)
1 of 6

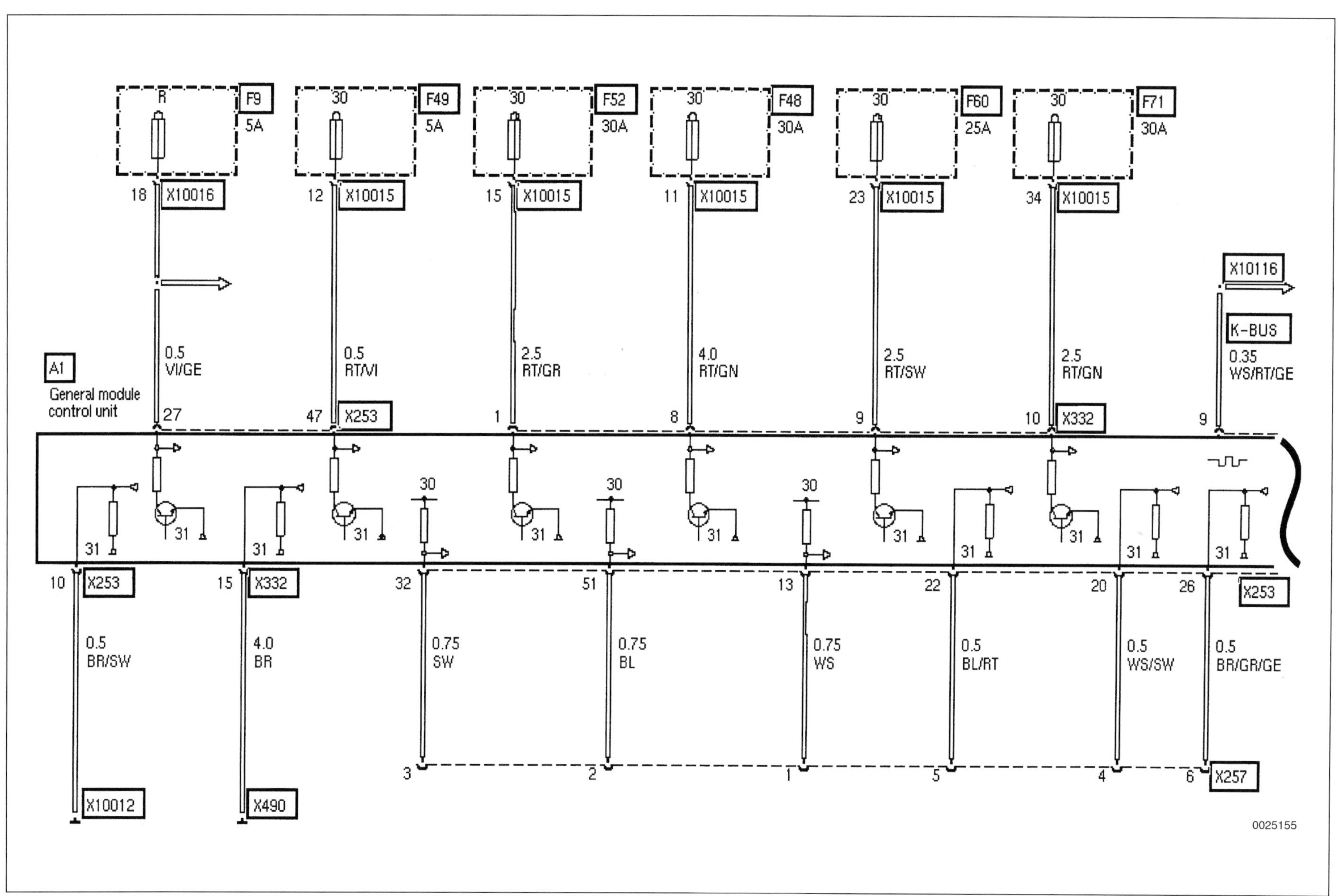

General module (GM V) (A1)
2 of 6

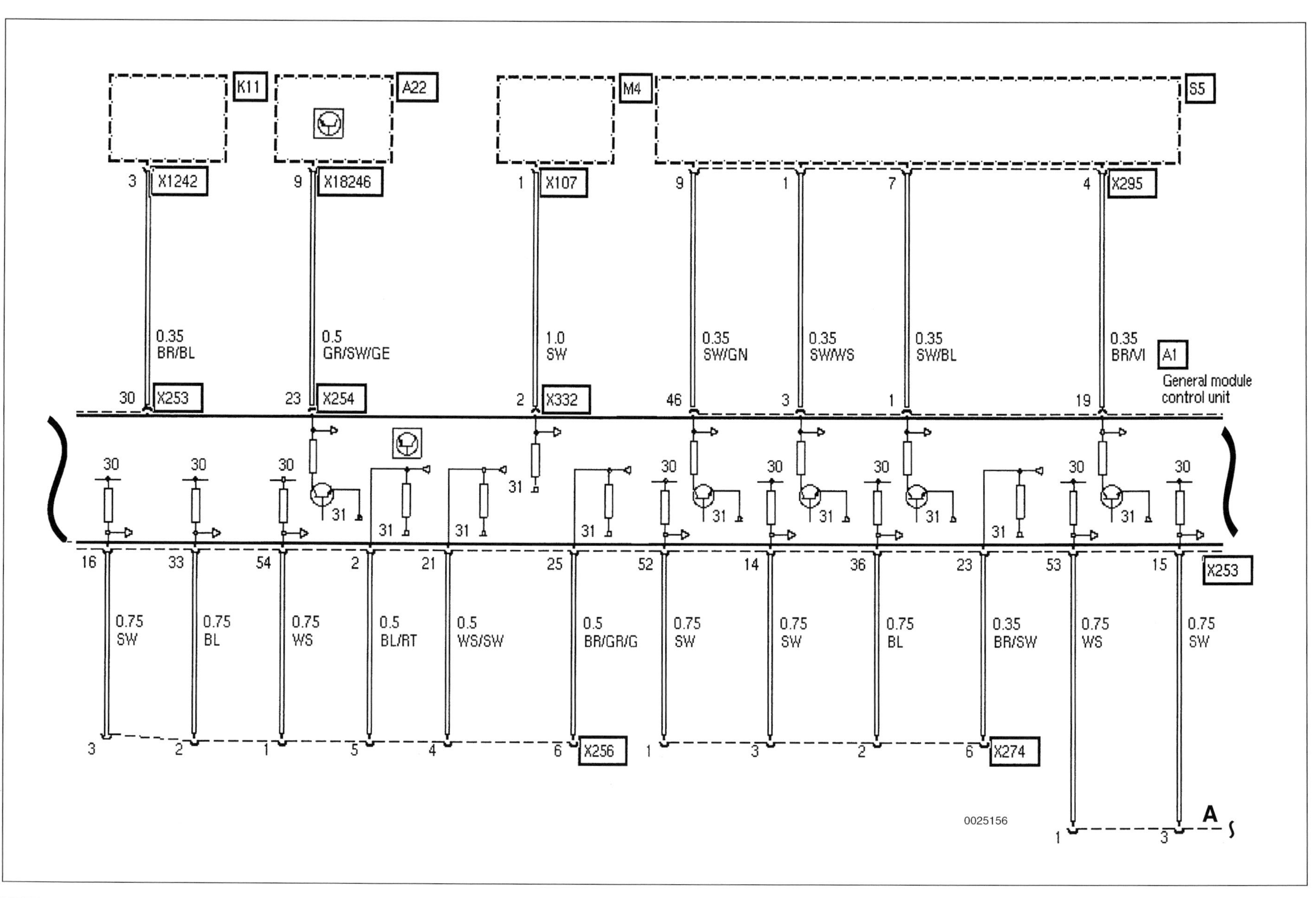

General module (GM V) (A1)
3 of 6

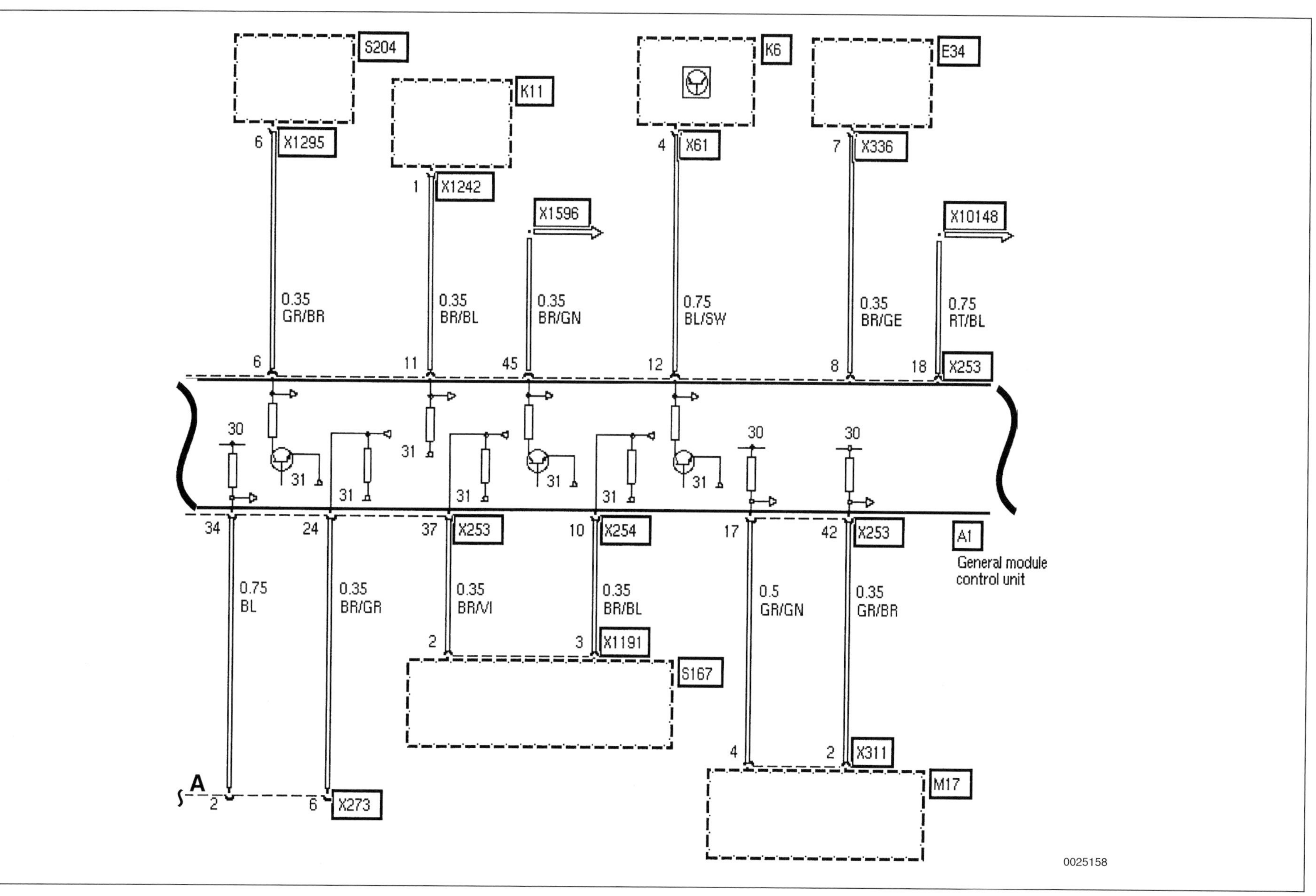

General module (GM V) (A1)
4 of 6

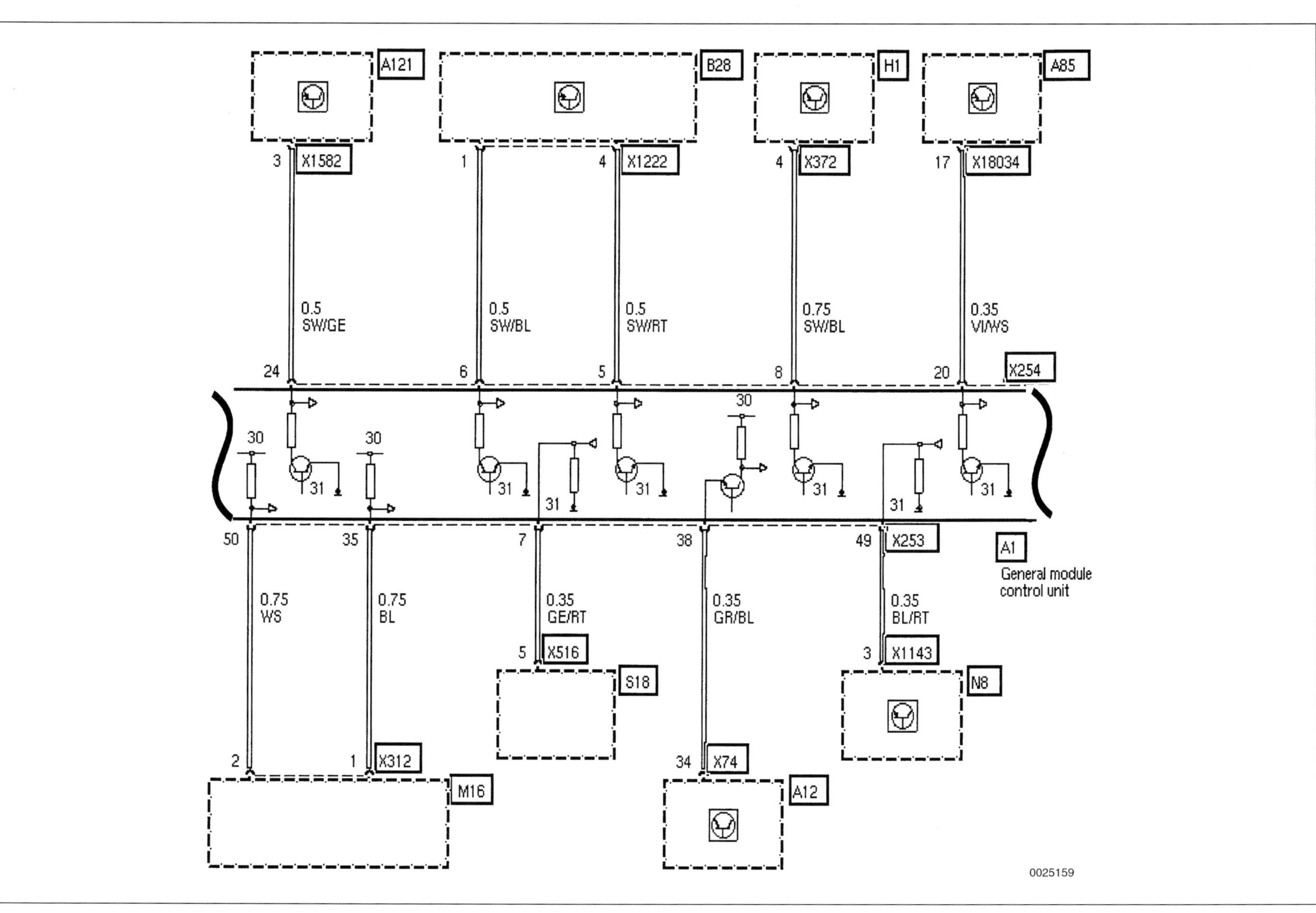

General module (GM V) (A1)
5 of 6

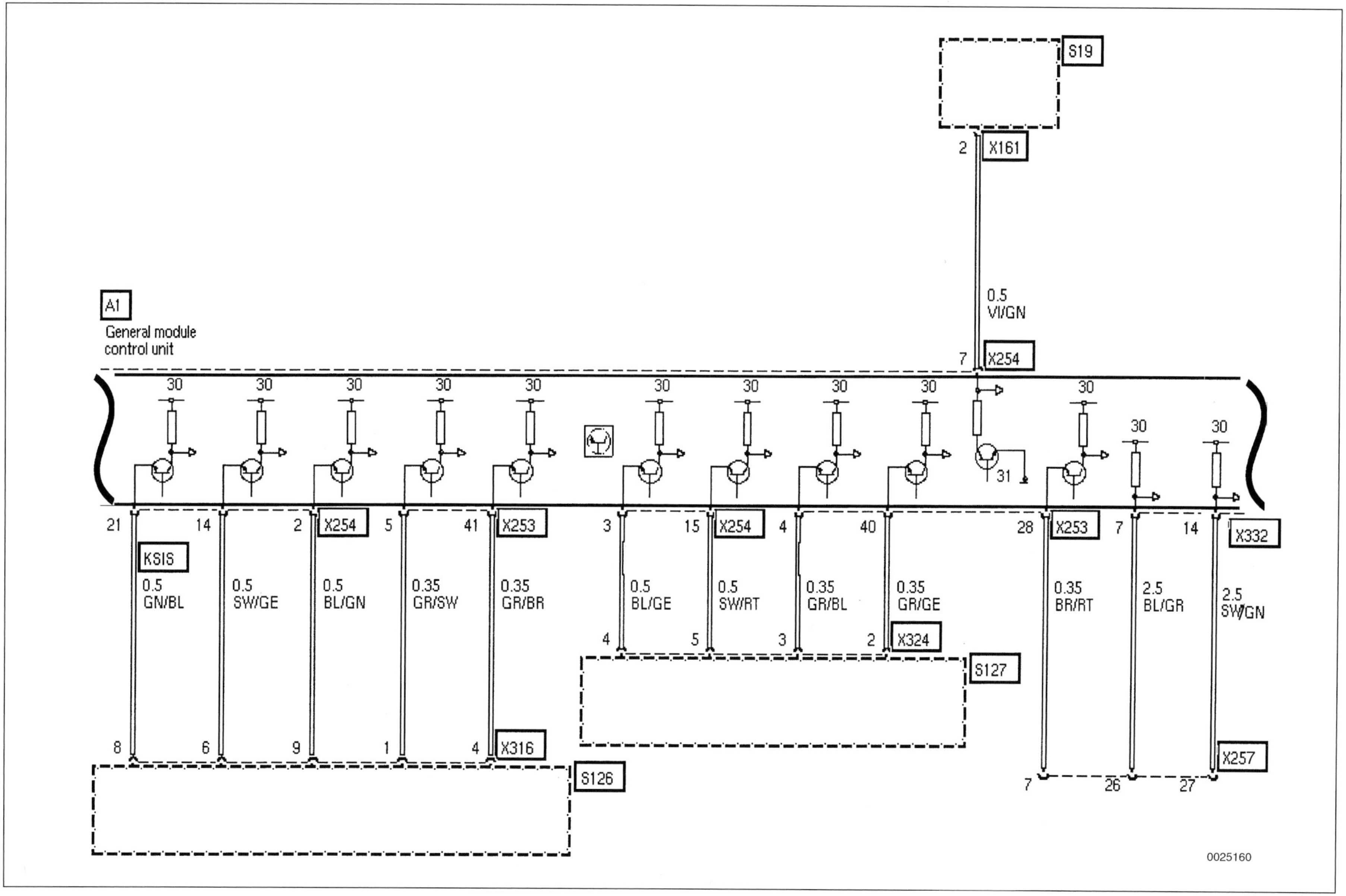

General module (A1)
6 of 6

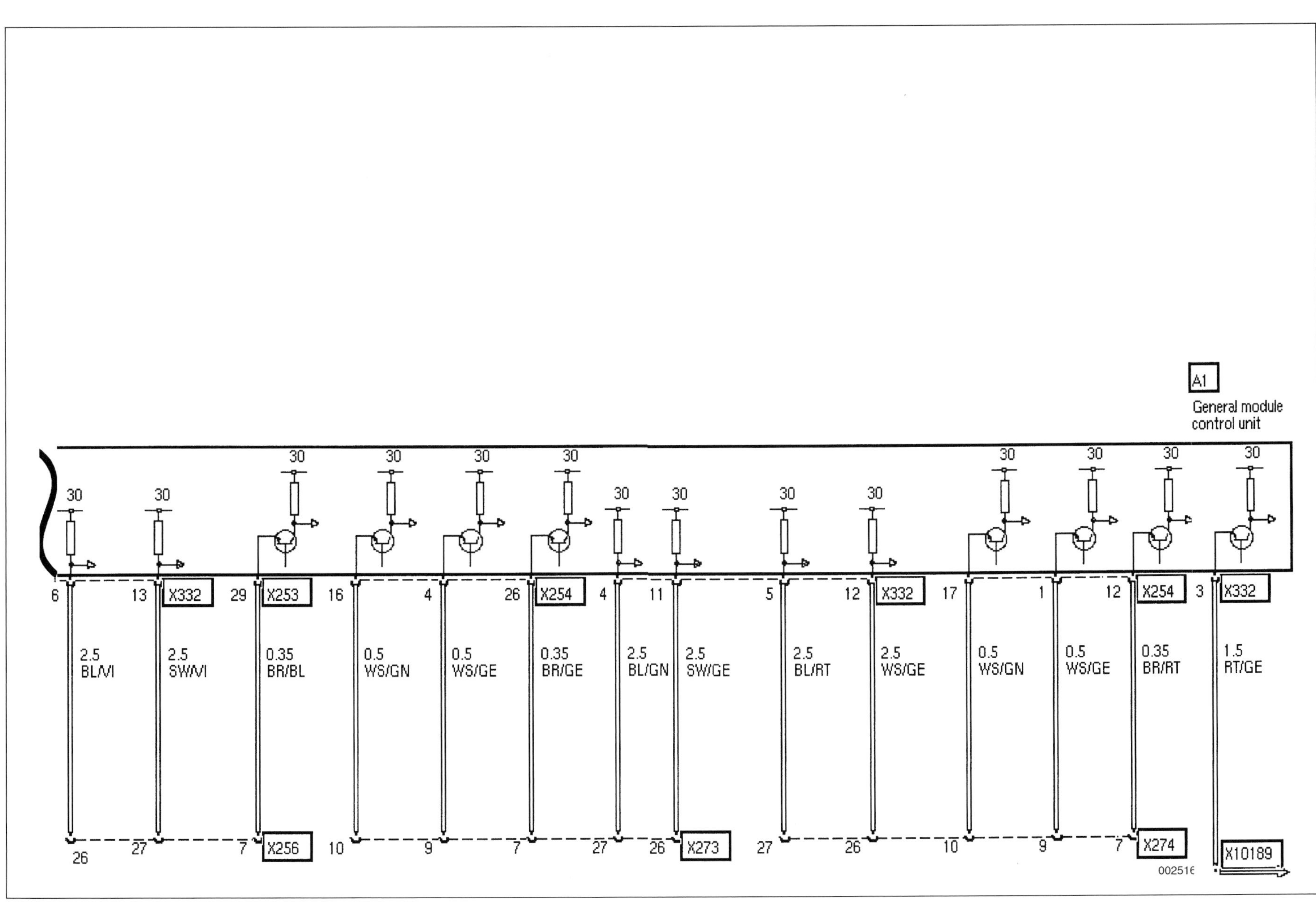

Connector (X275)
1 of 2

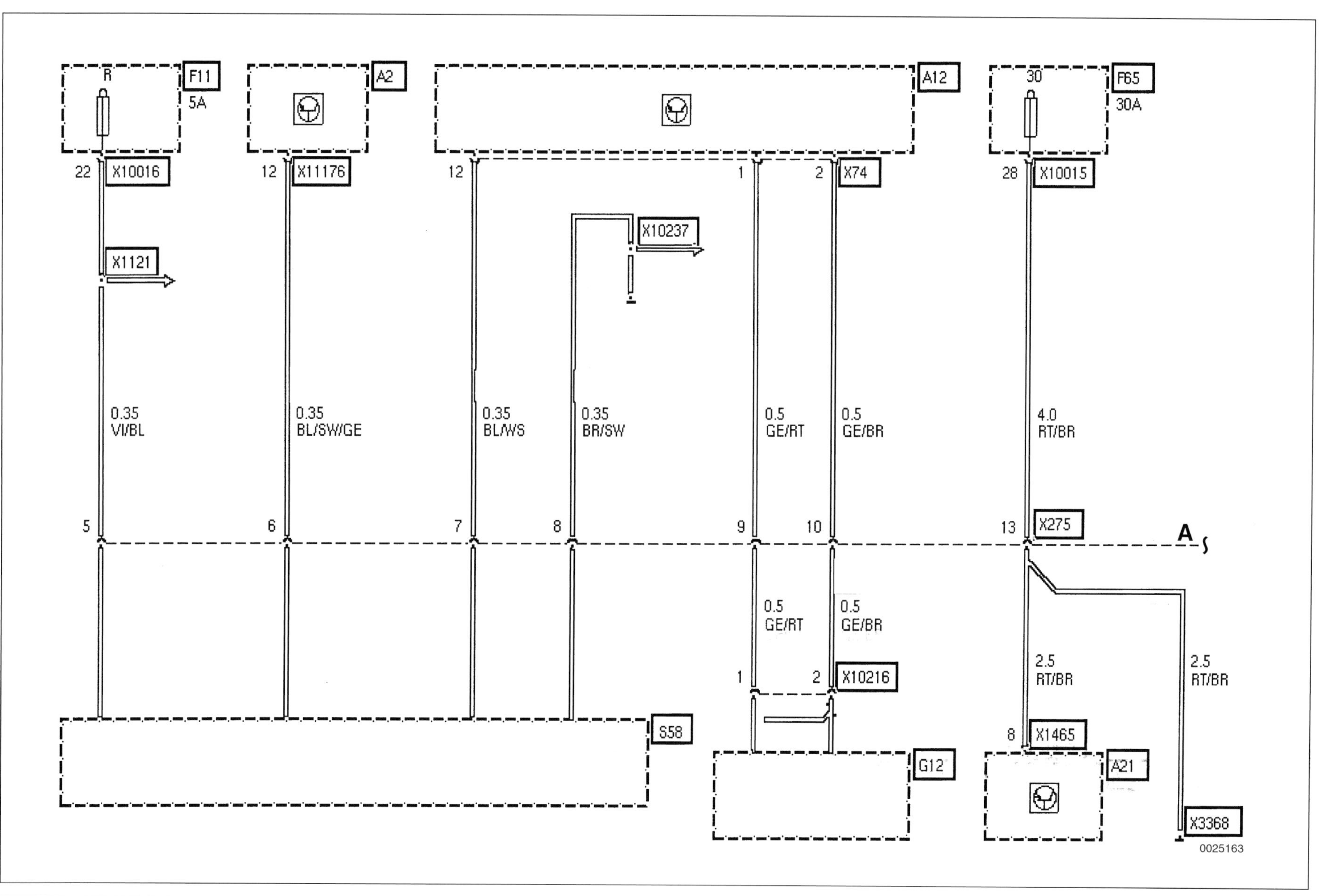

Connector (X275)
2 of 2

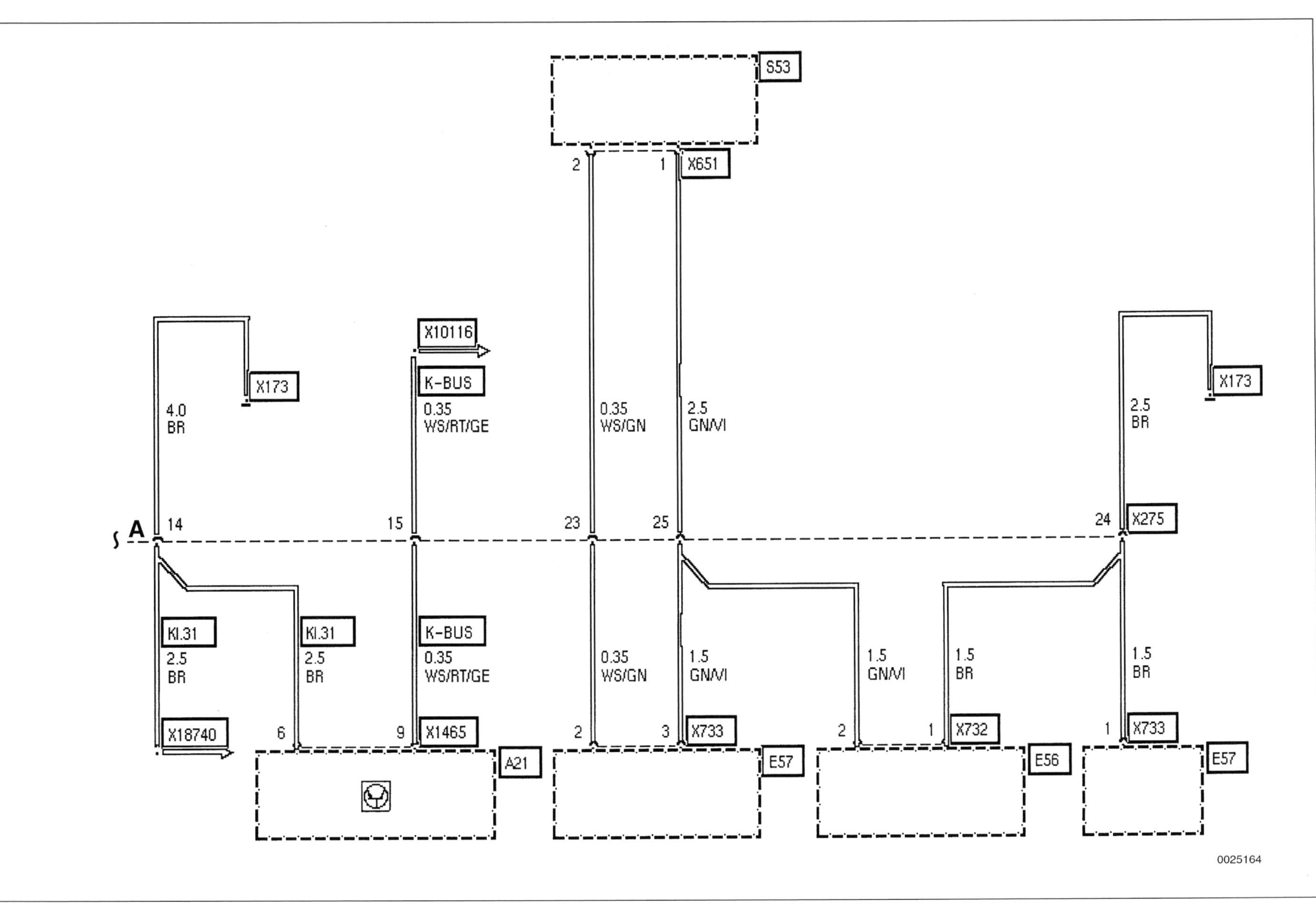

Seat memory control unit, driver side (A21)
1 of 2

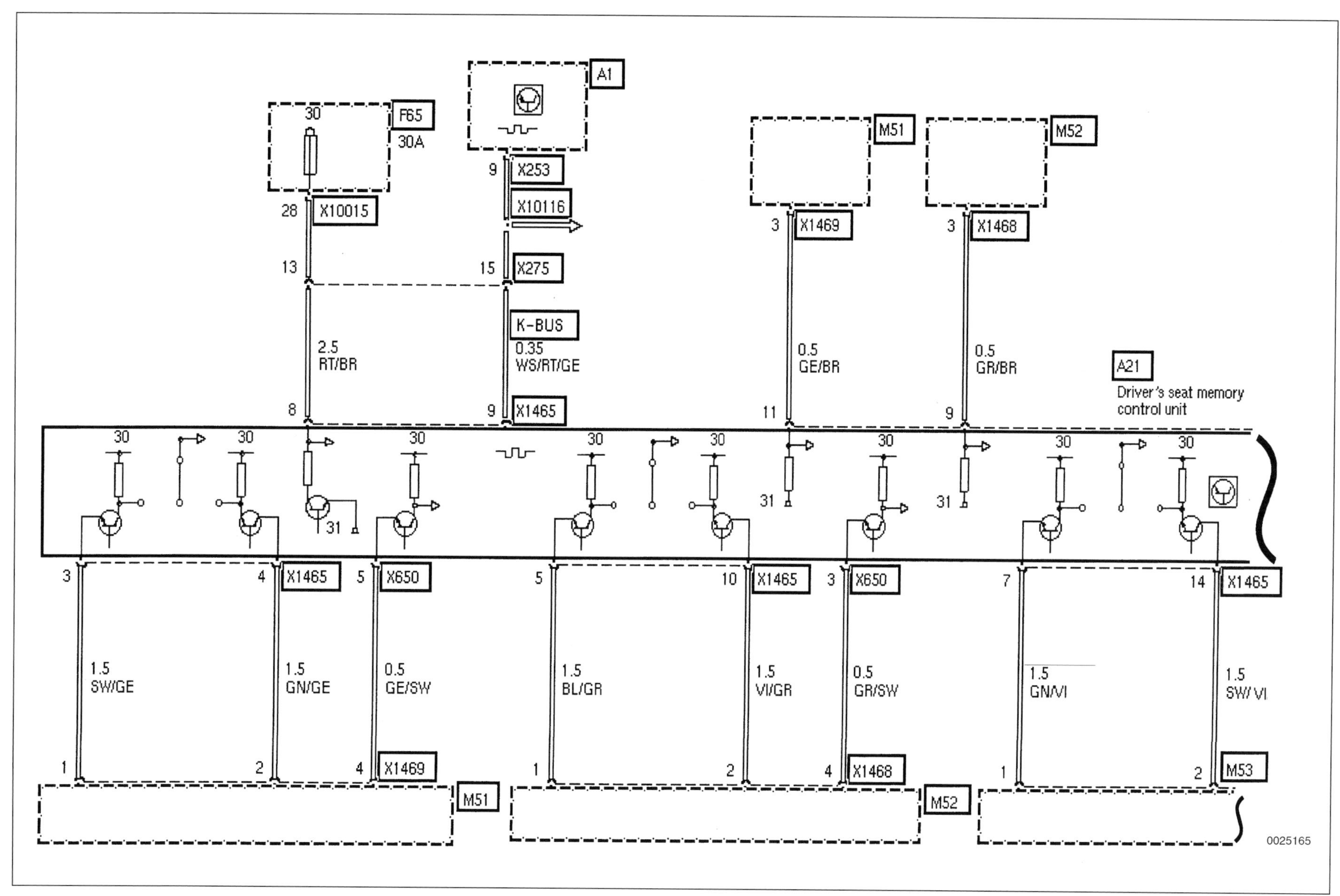

Seat memory control unit, driver side (A21)
2 of 2

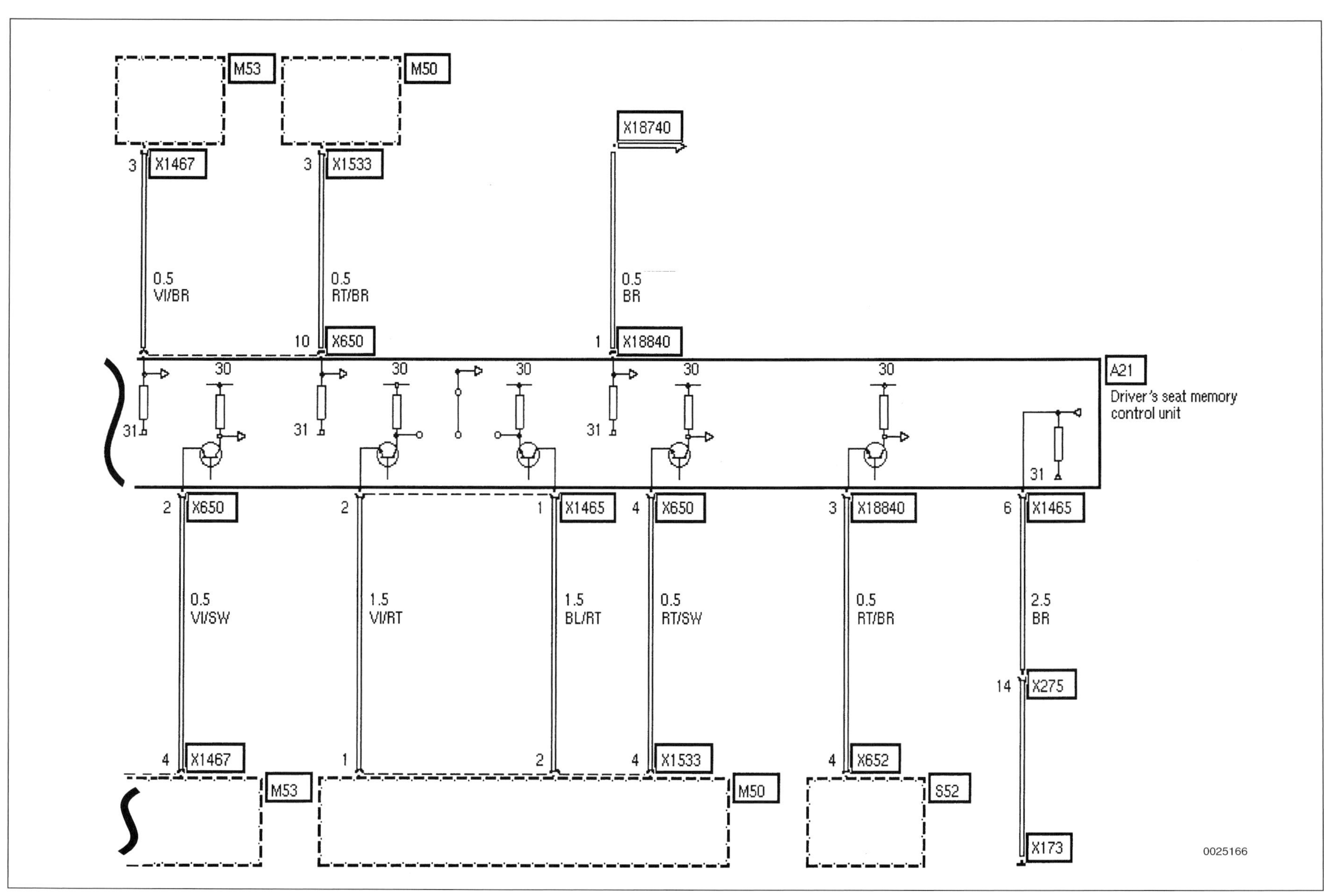

Tire pressure control system (RDC) control unit (A85)

1 of 2

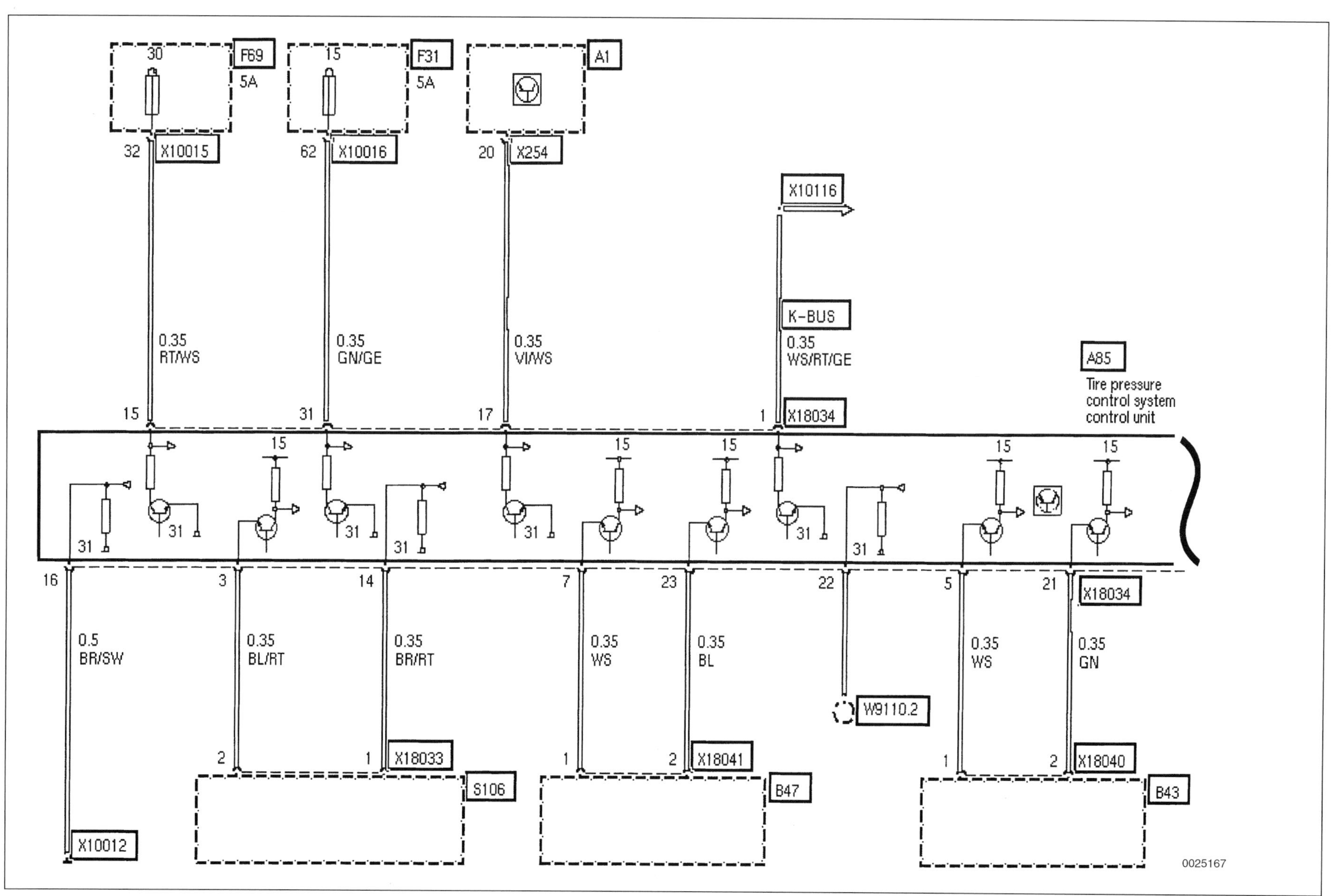

Tire pressure control system (RDC) control unit (A85)
2 of 2

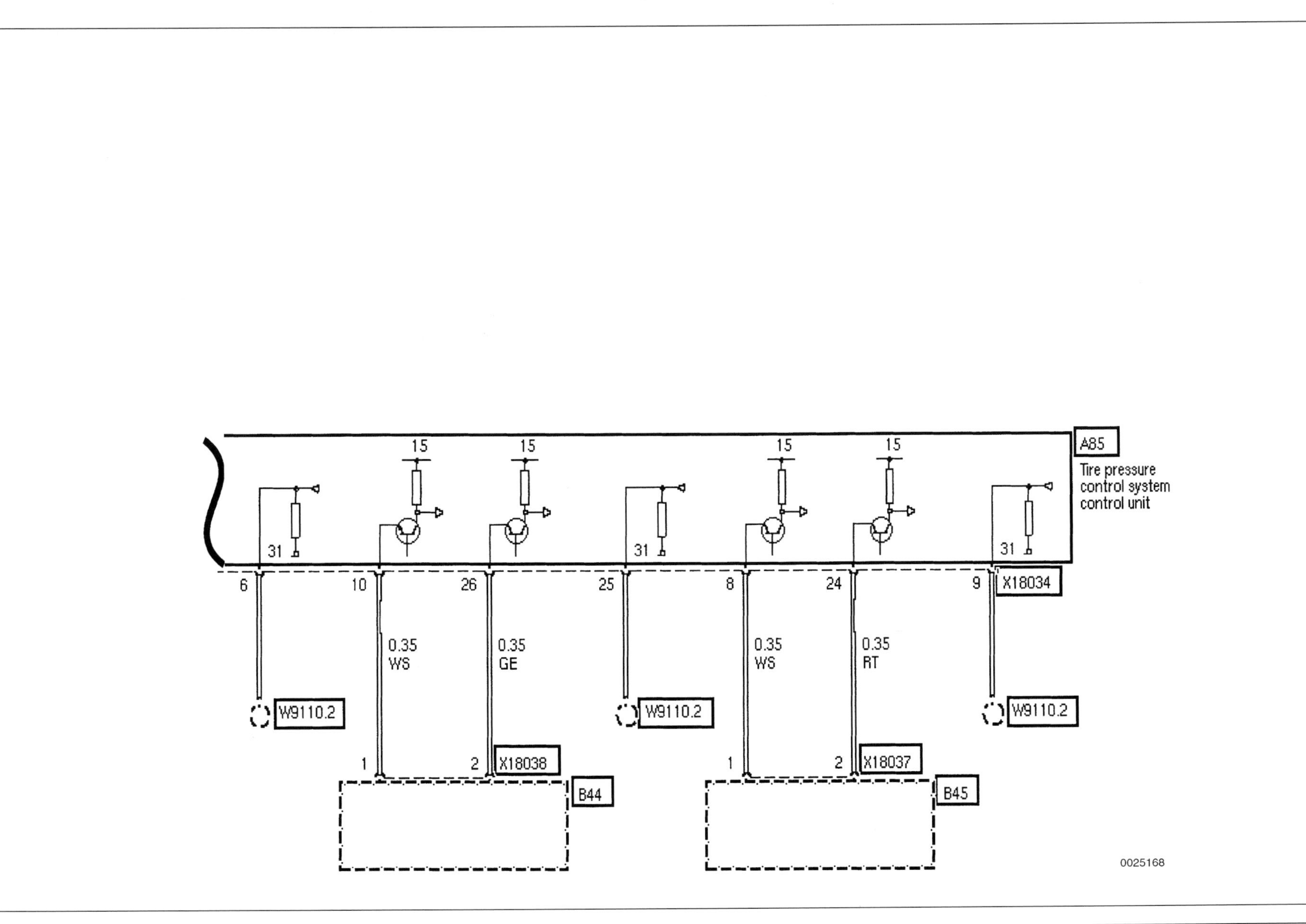

Connector (X279)
1 of 2

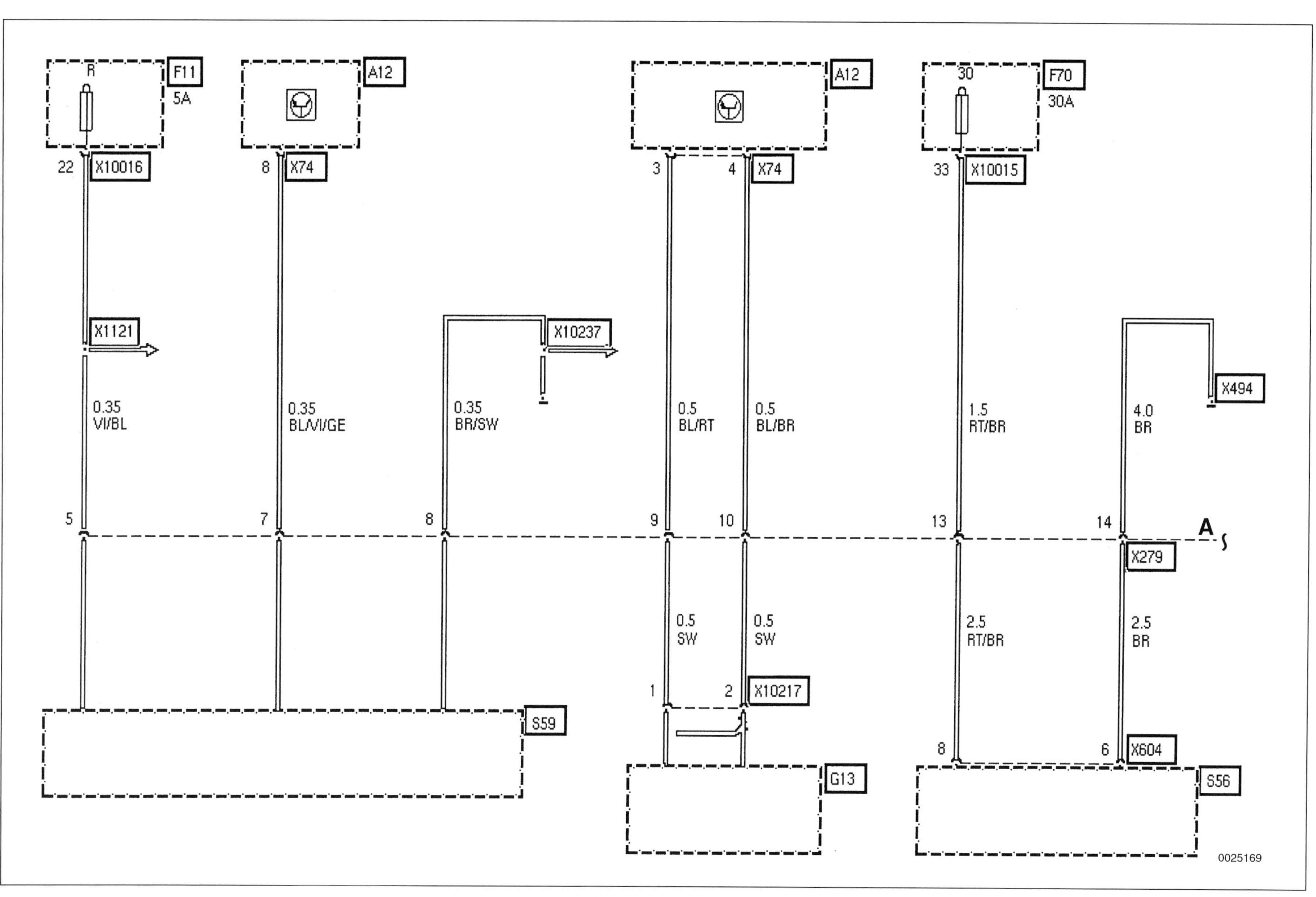

Connector (X279)
2 of 2

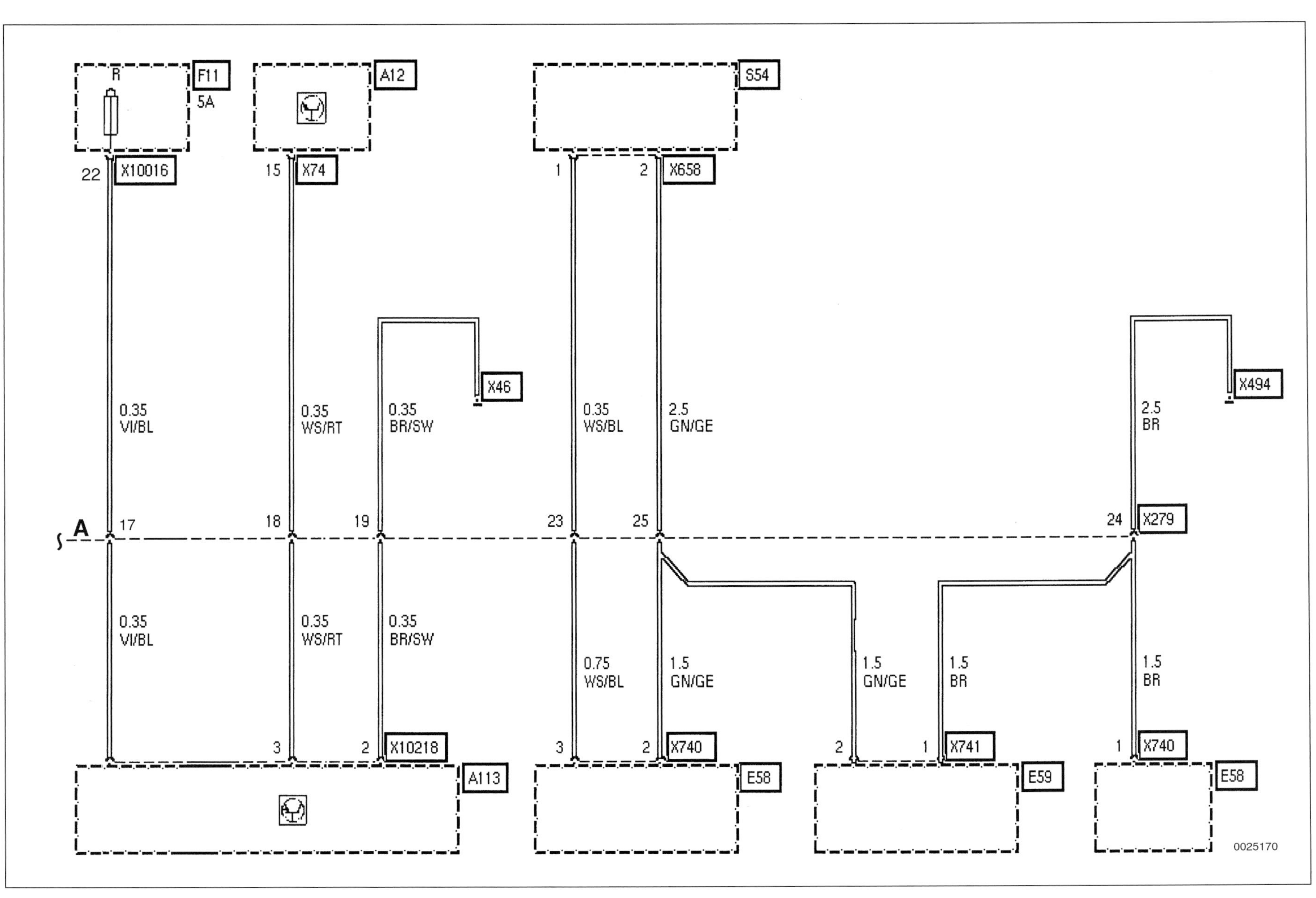

Fuse 67 (F67)

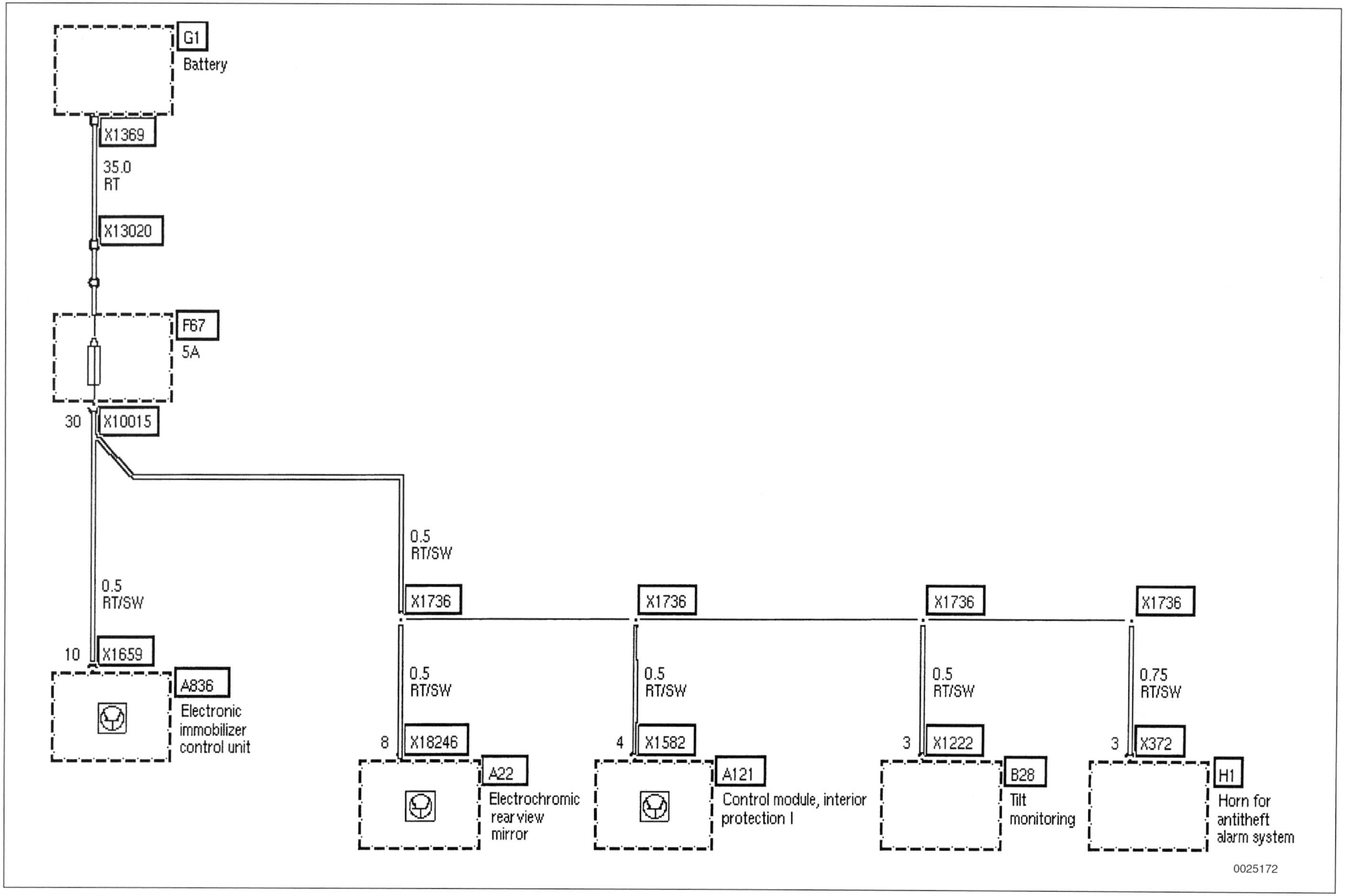

G1
Battery
X1369
35.0
RT
X13020
F67
5A
30
X10015
0.5
RT/SW
10
X1659
A836
Electronic immobilizer control unit
0.5
RT/SW
X1736
0.5
RT/SW
8
X18246
A22
Electrochromic rear view mirror
X1736
0.5
RT/SW
4
X1582
A121
Control module, interior protection I
X1736
0.5
RT/SW
3
X1222
B28
Tilt monitoring
X1736
0.75
RT/SW
3
X372
H1
Horn for antitheft alarm system
0025172

Fuse 14 (F14)

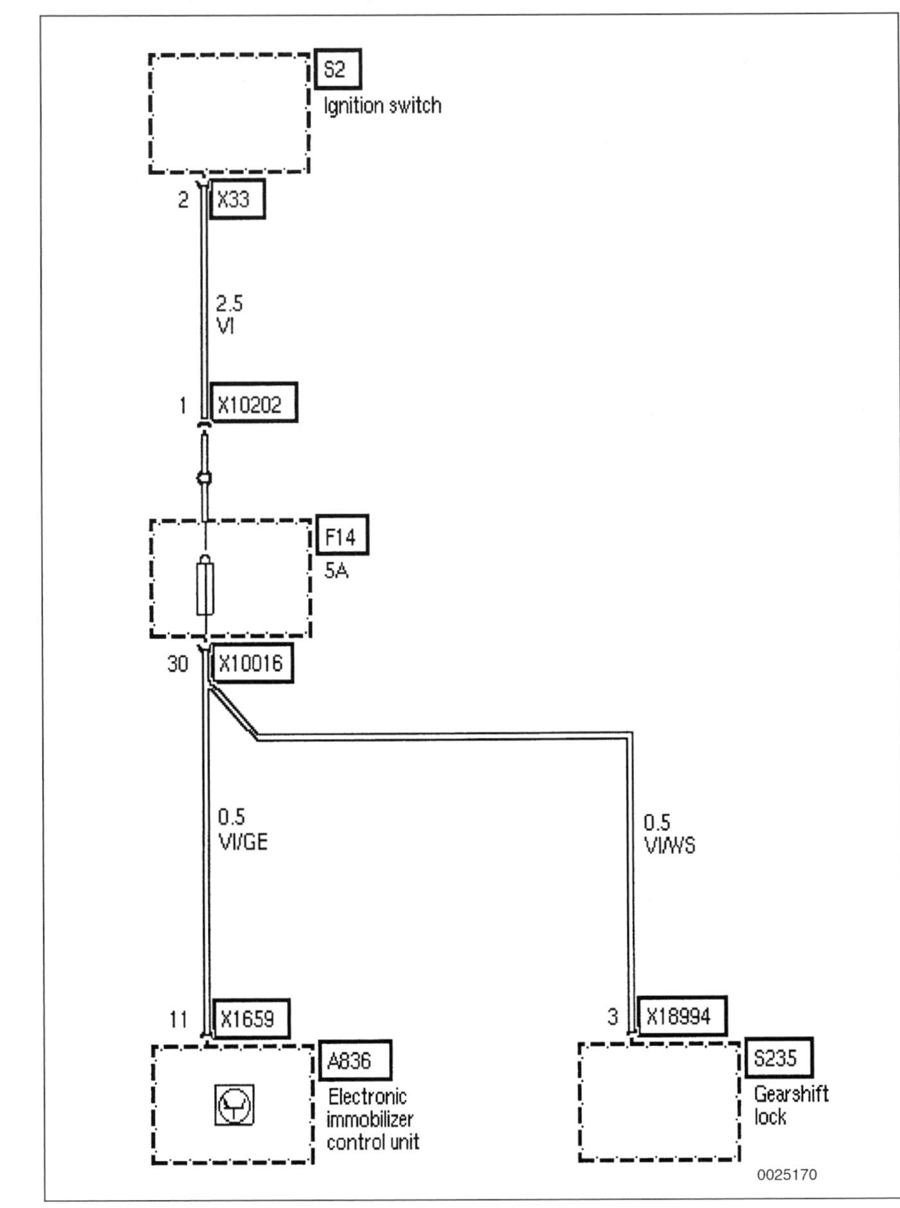
S2
Ignition switch
2
X33
2.5
VI
1
X10202
F14
5A
30
X10016
0.5
VI/GE
0.5
VI/WS
11
X1659
A836
Electronic
immobilizer
control unit
3
X18994
S235
Gearshift
lock
0025170

Ground (X10012)
1 of 2

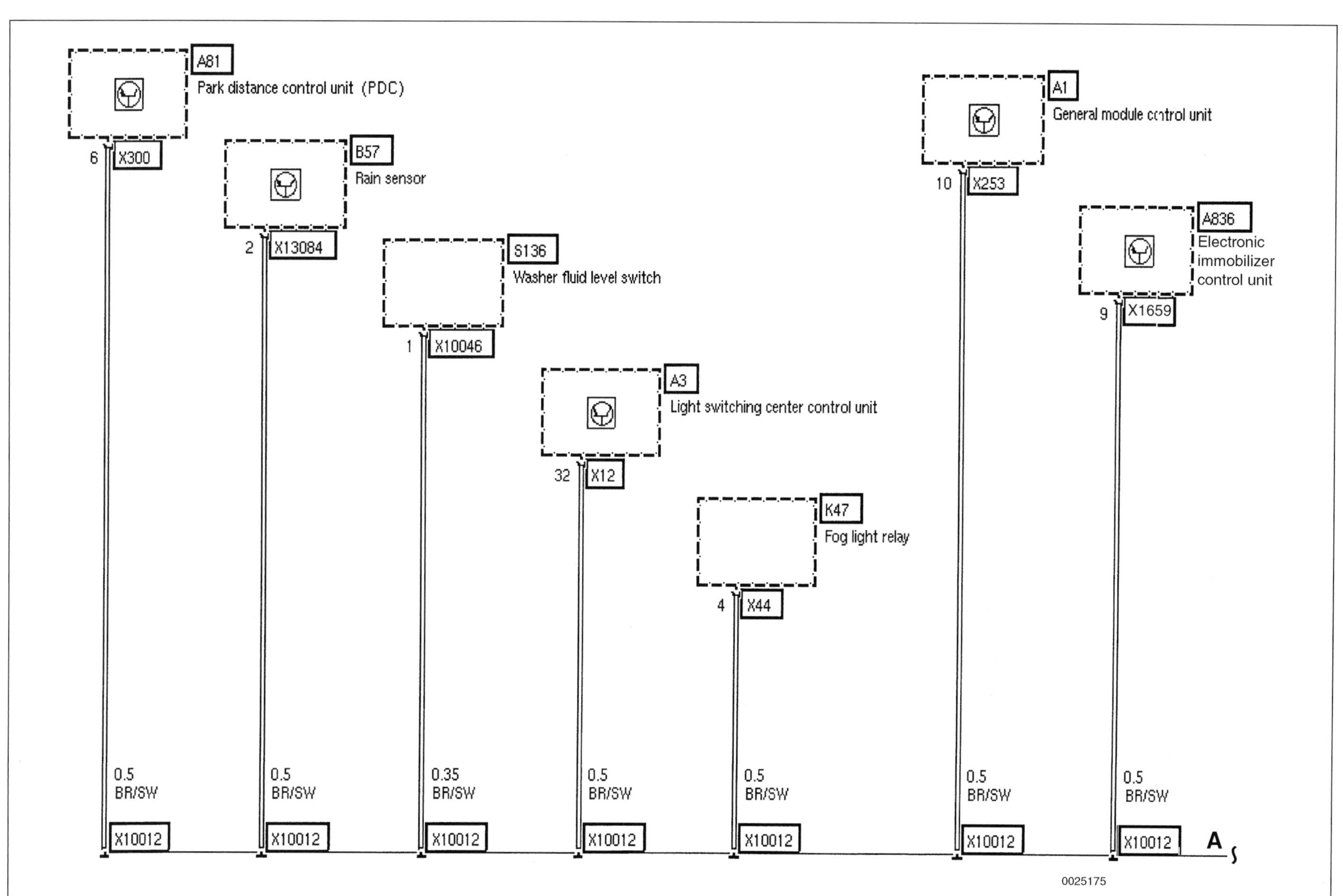

Ground (X10012)
2 of 2

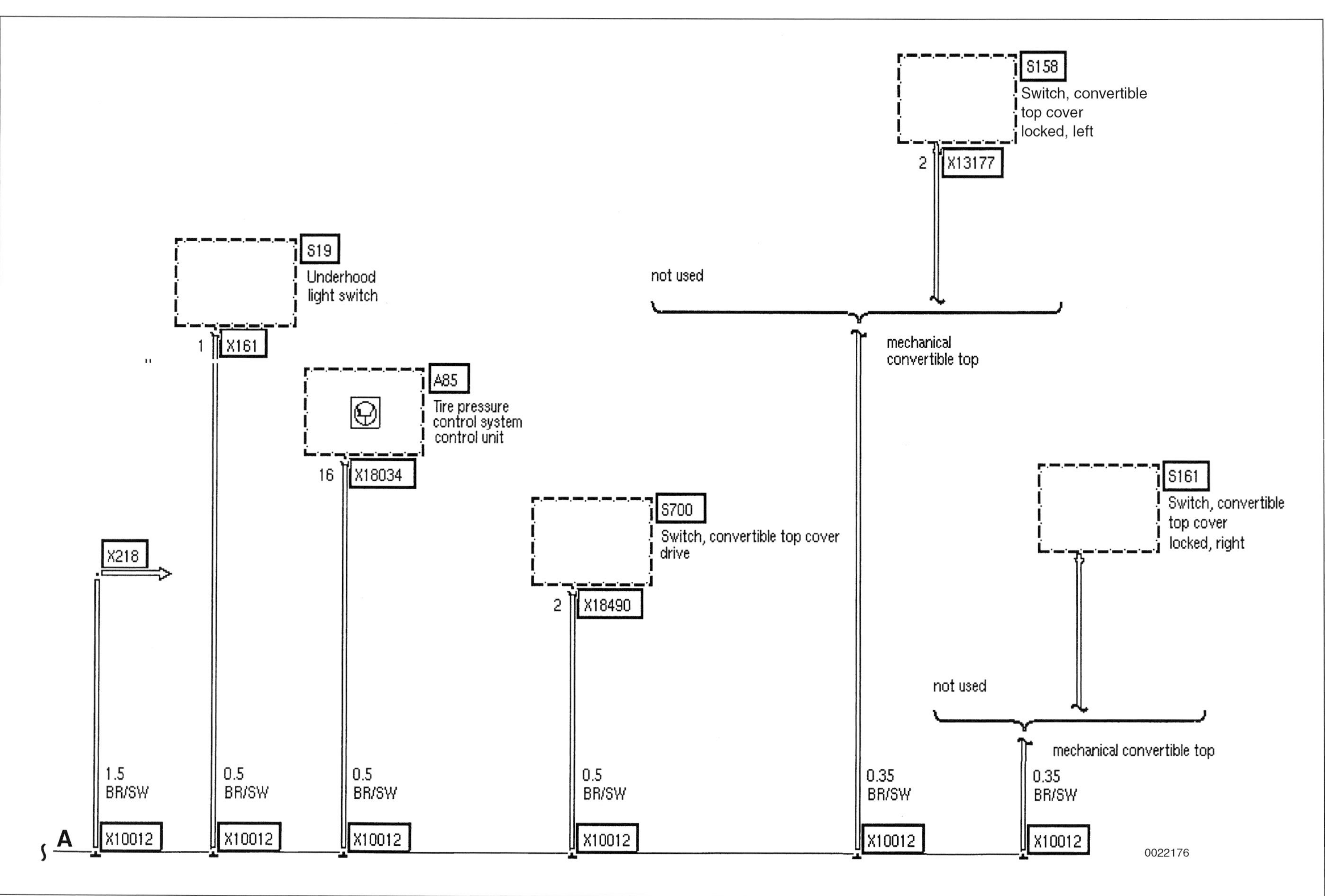

EWS ring antenna (L1)

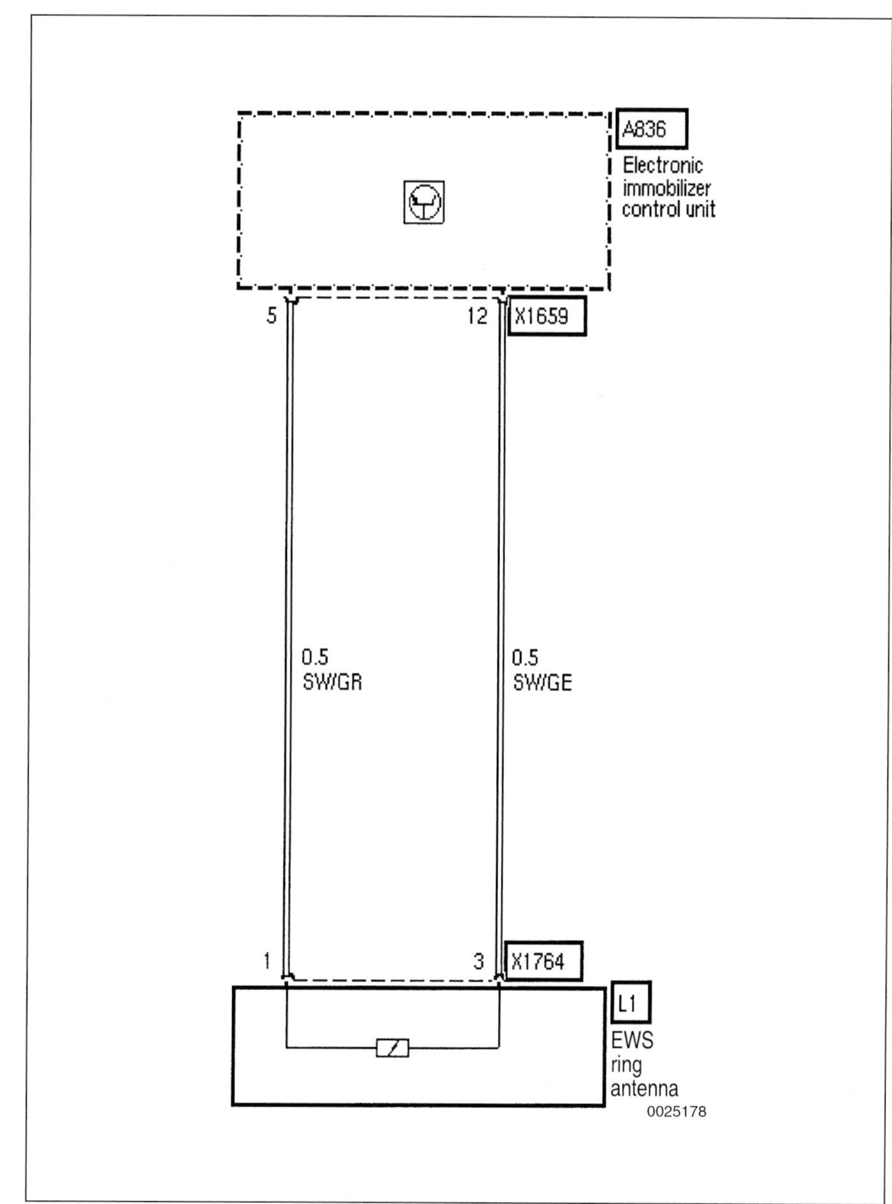

Ignition switch (S2)

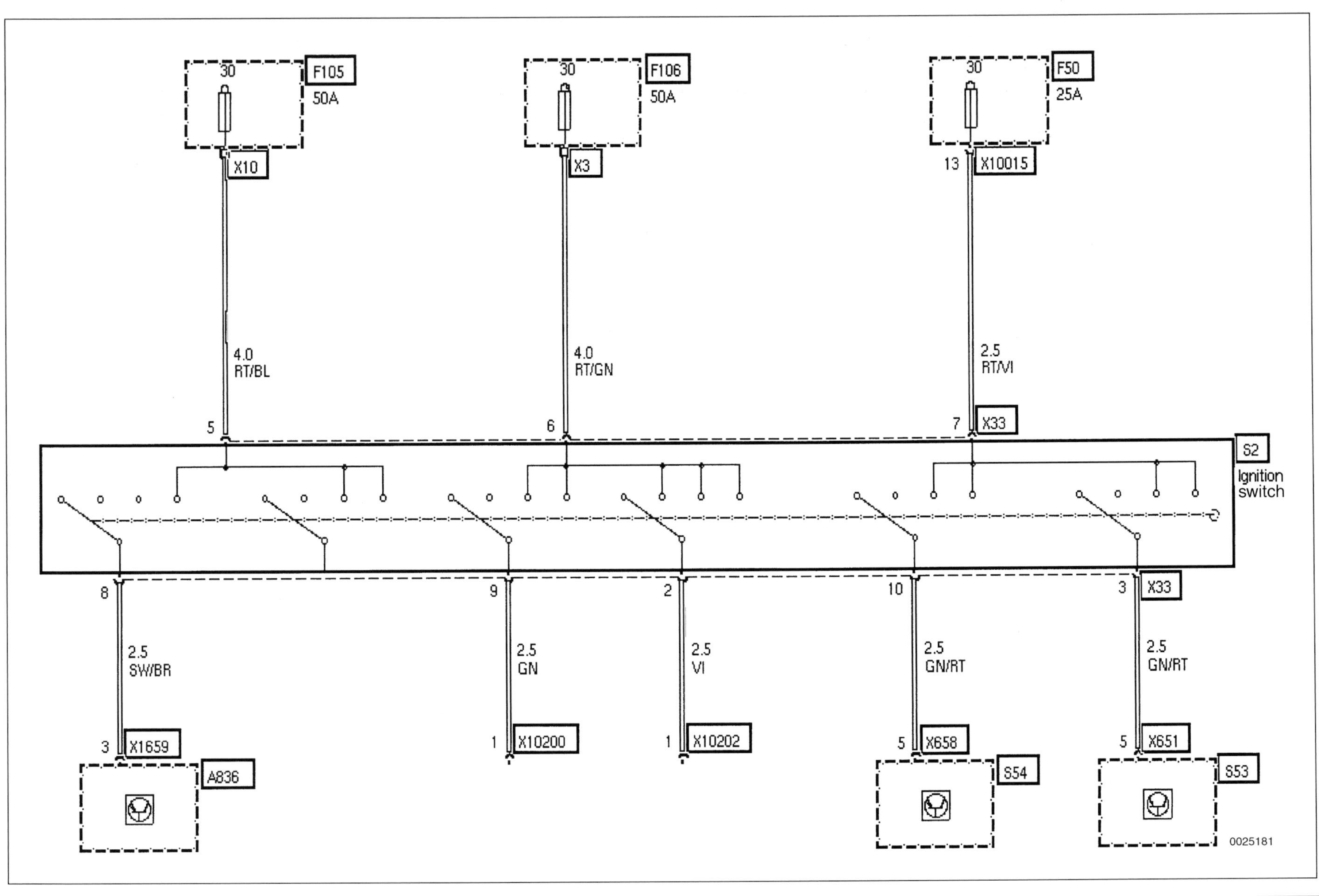

Starter immobilization switch (manual transmission) (S235)

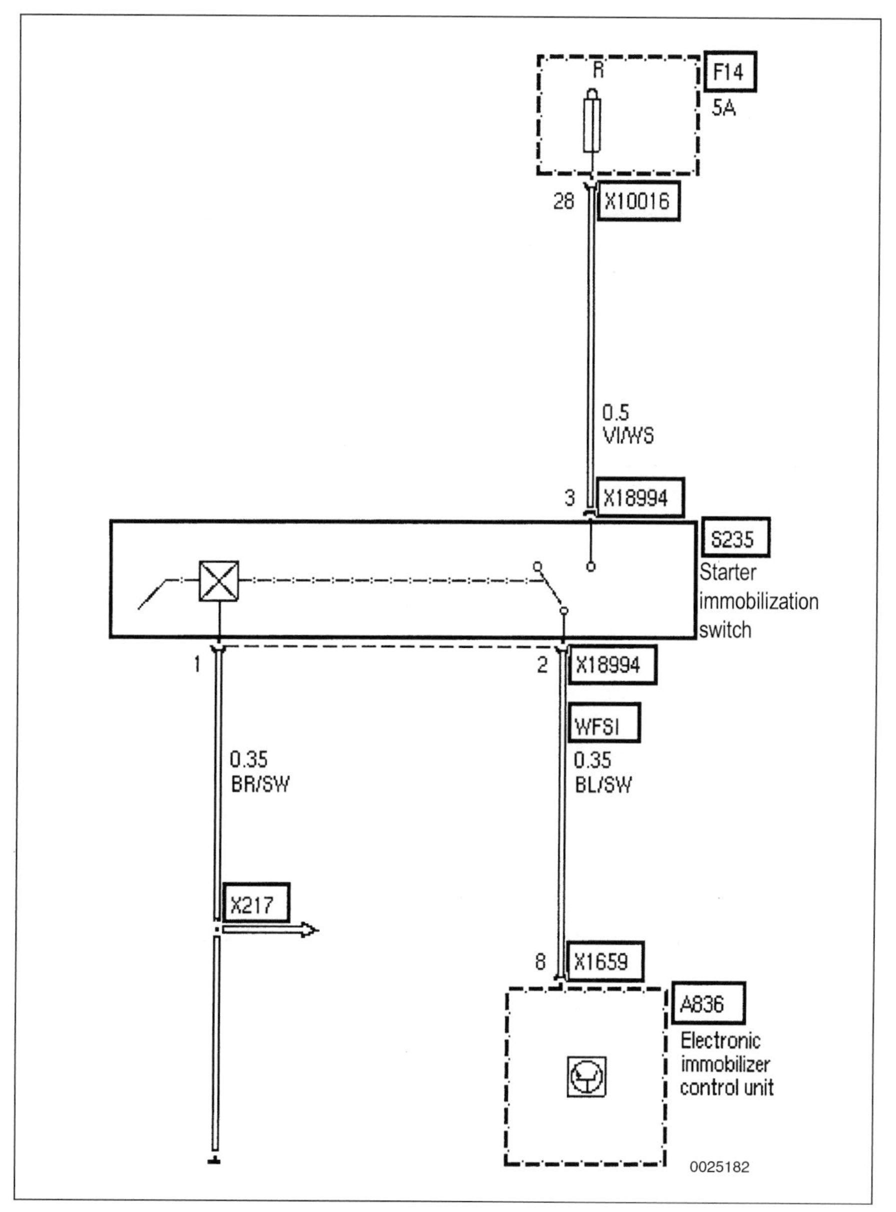

Fuse 54 (F54)

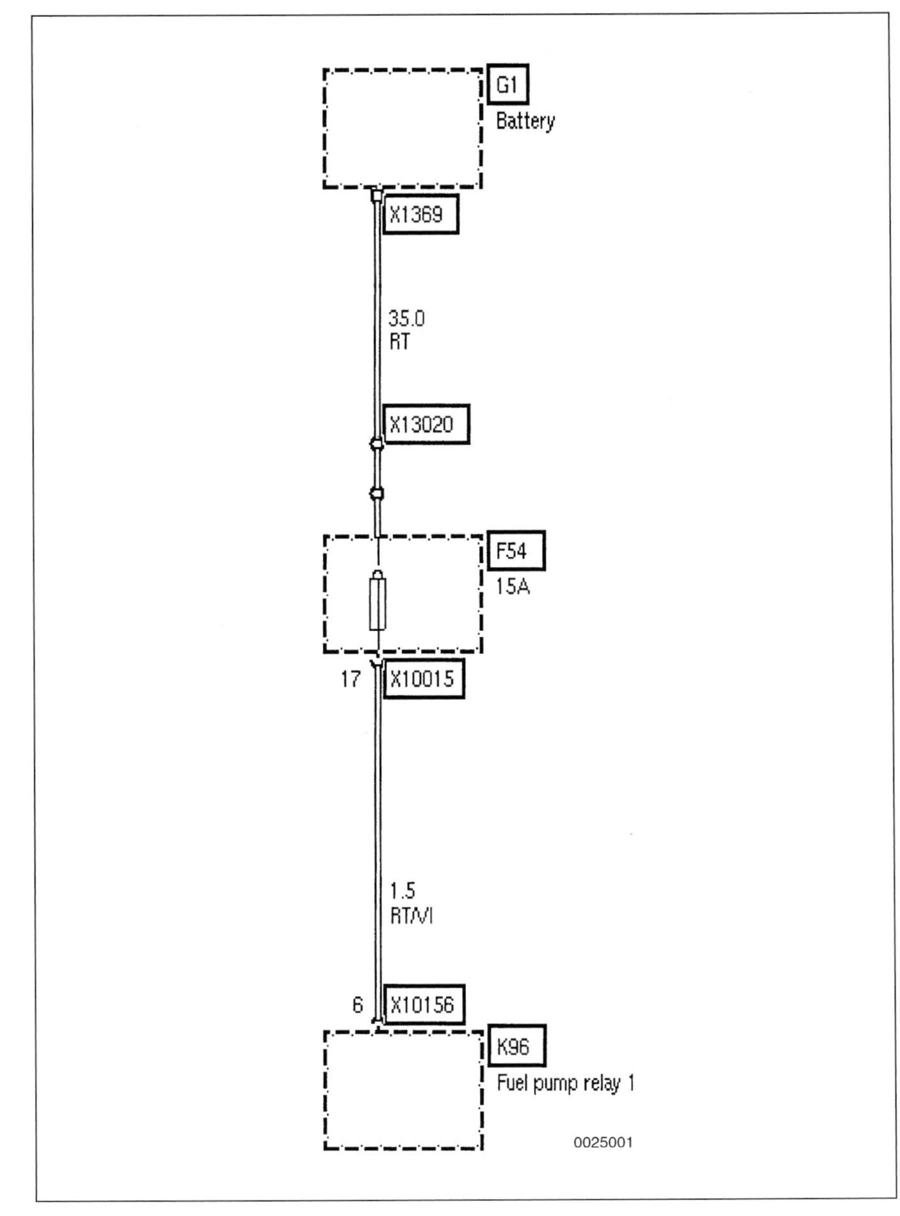
G1
Battery
X1369
35.0
RT
X13020
F54
15A
17
X10015
1.5
RT/VI
6
X10156
K96
Fuel pump relay 1
0025001

DME/AGS interface

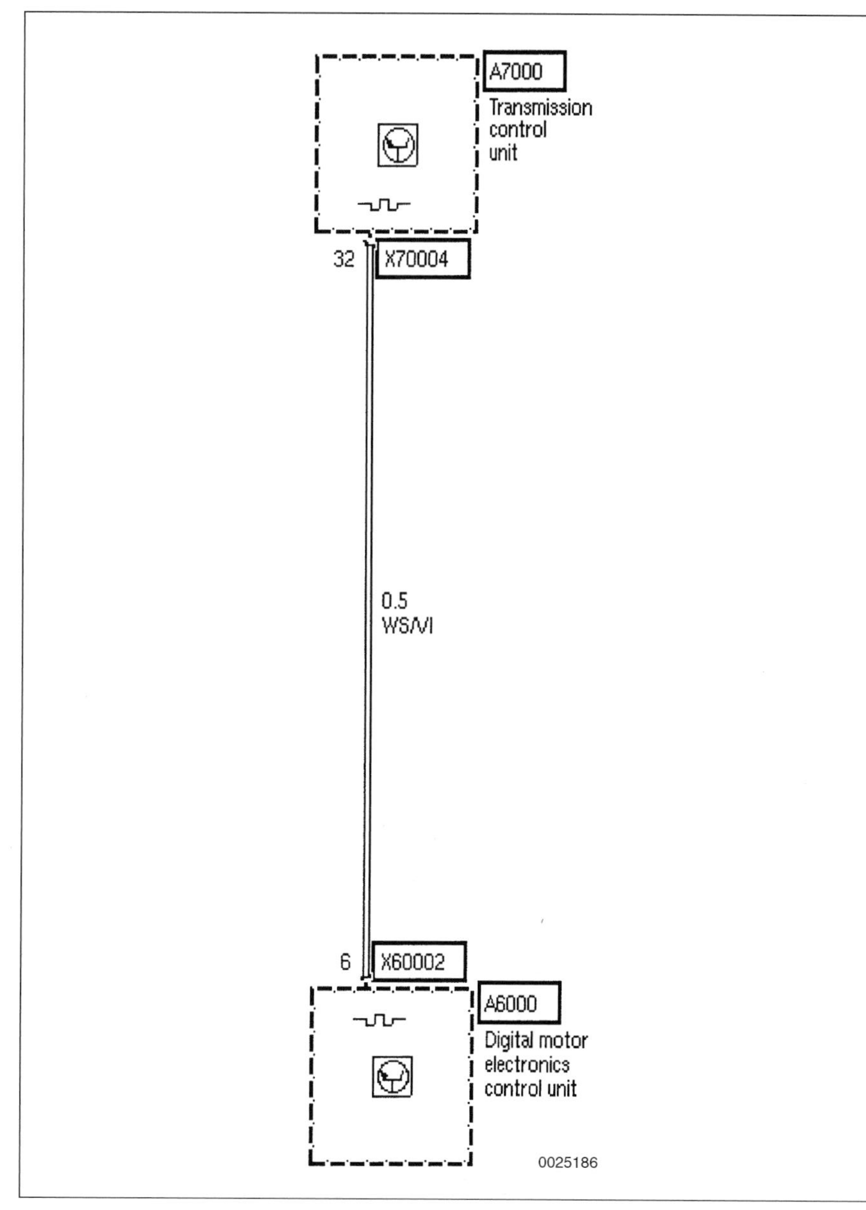

Shift lock (Y19)

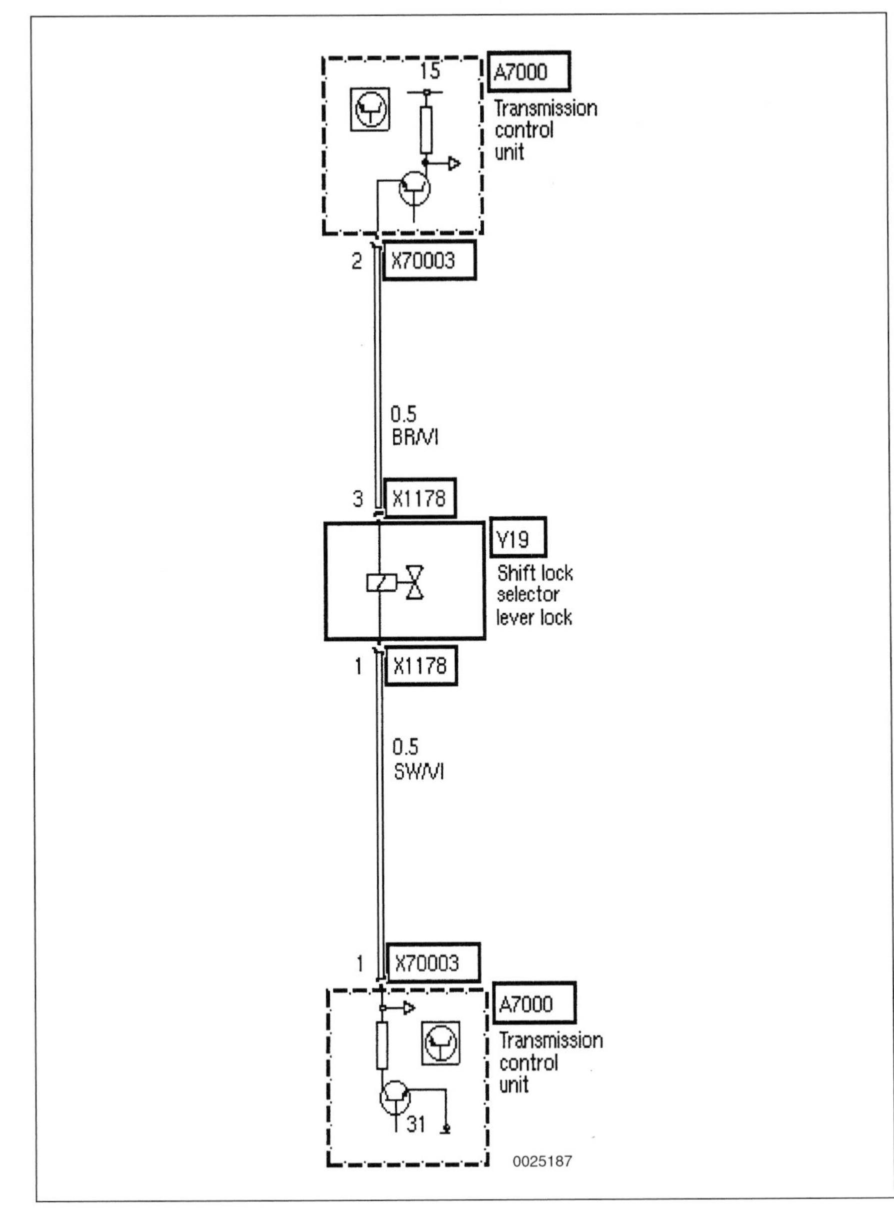

Transmission range position switch (S8532)

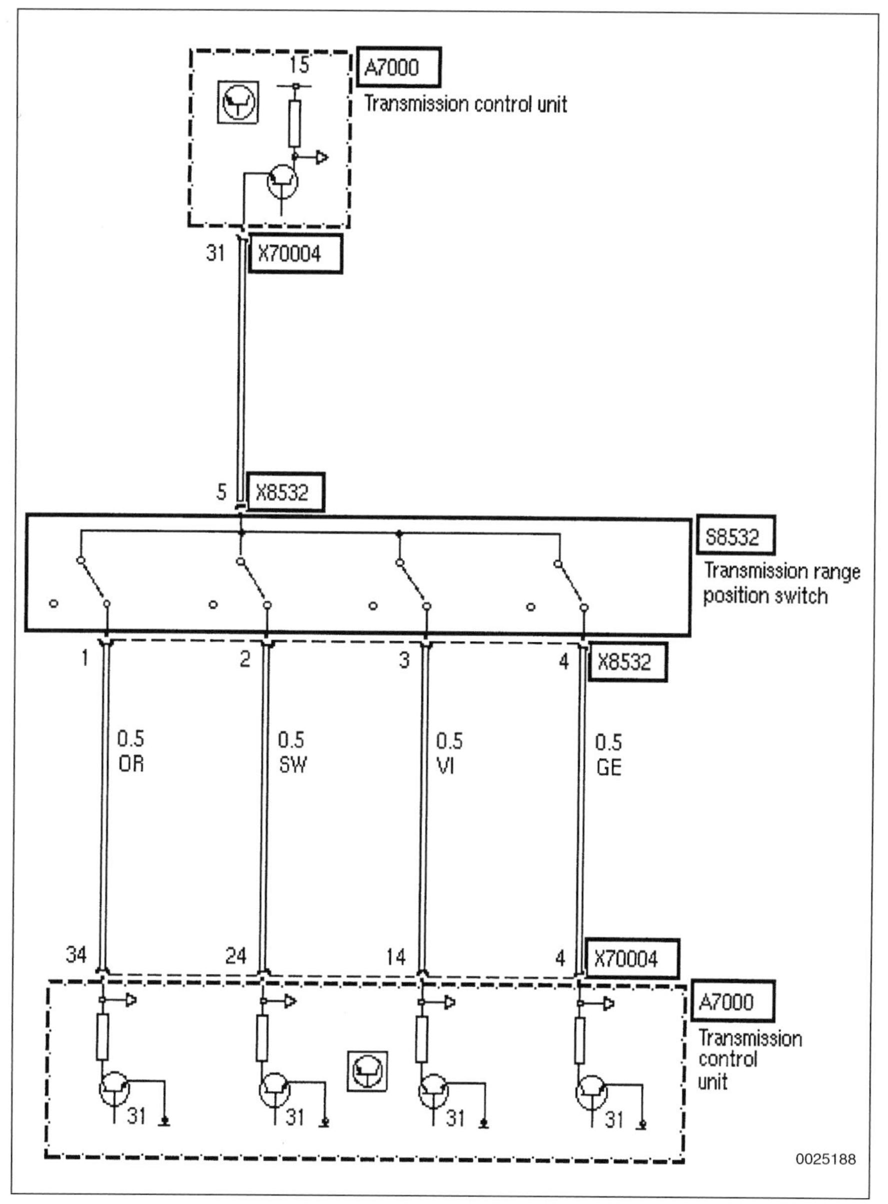

Steptronic switch (S224)

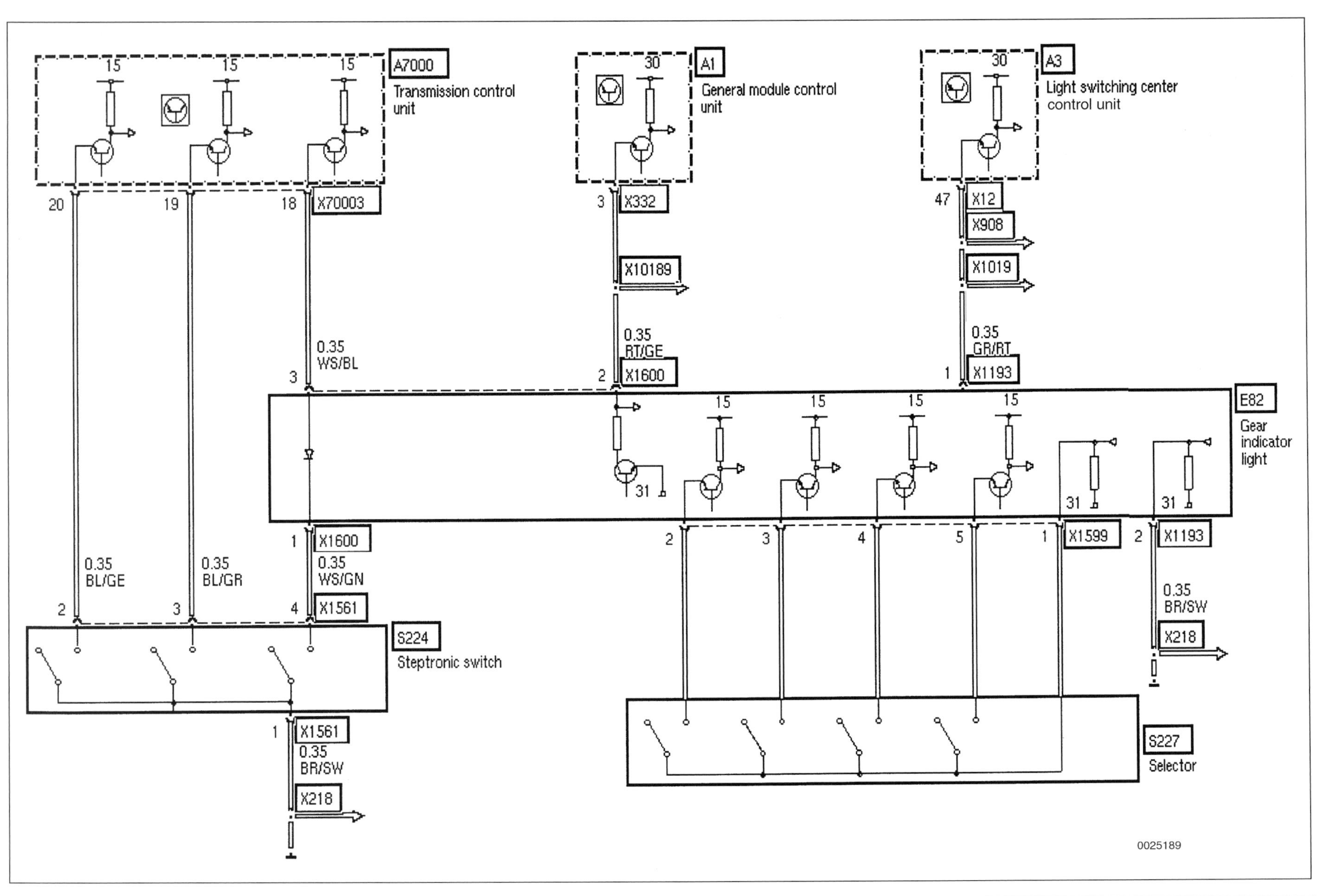

Splice connector (X218)

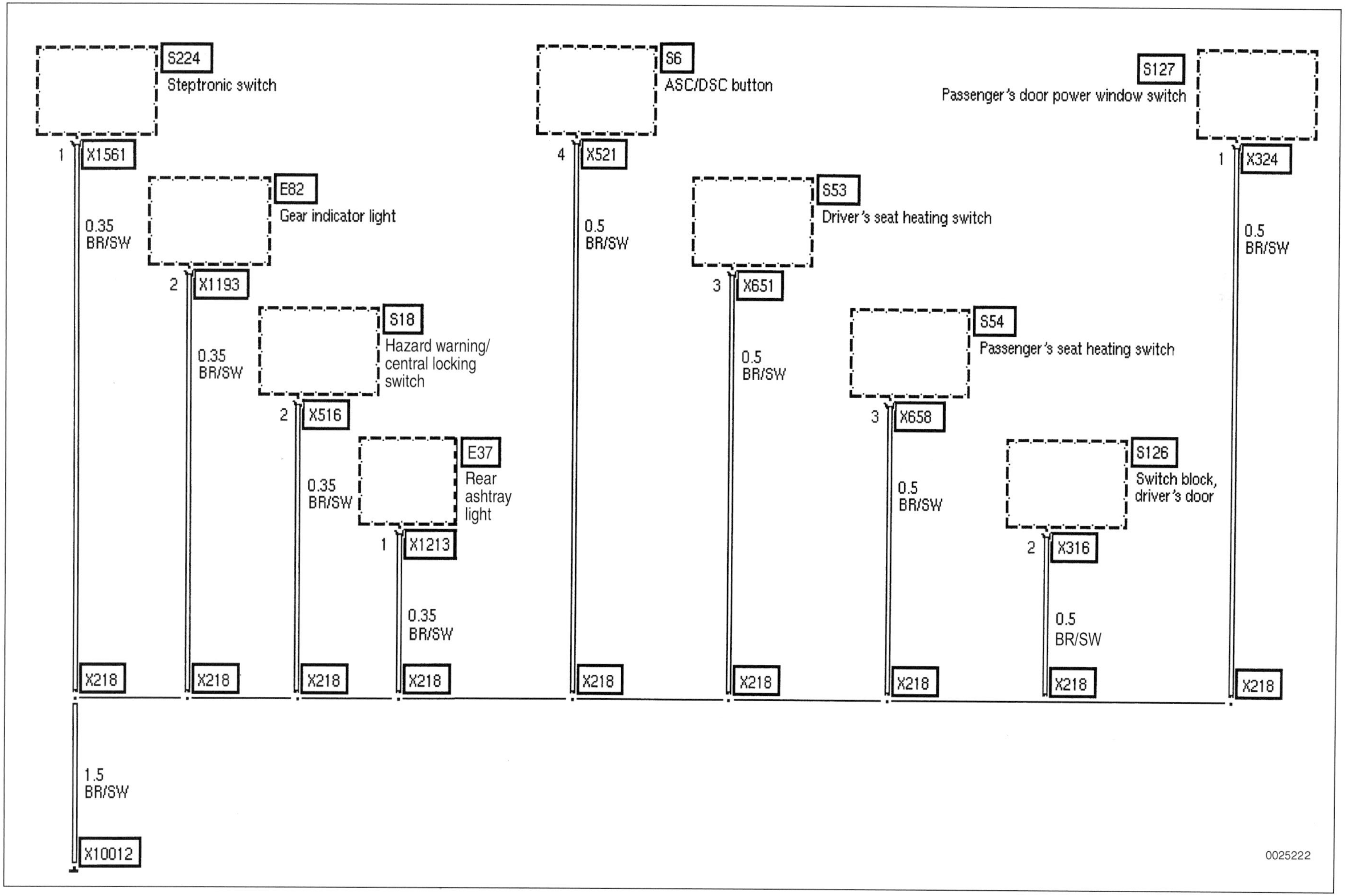

Instrument lighting splice connector (X1019)
1 of 2

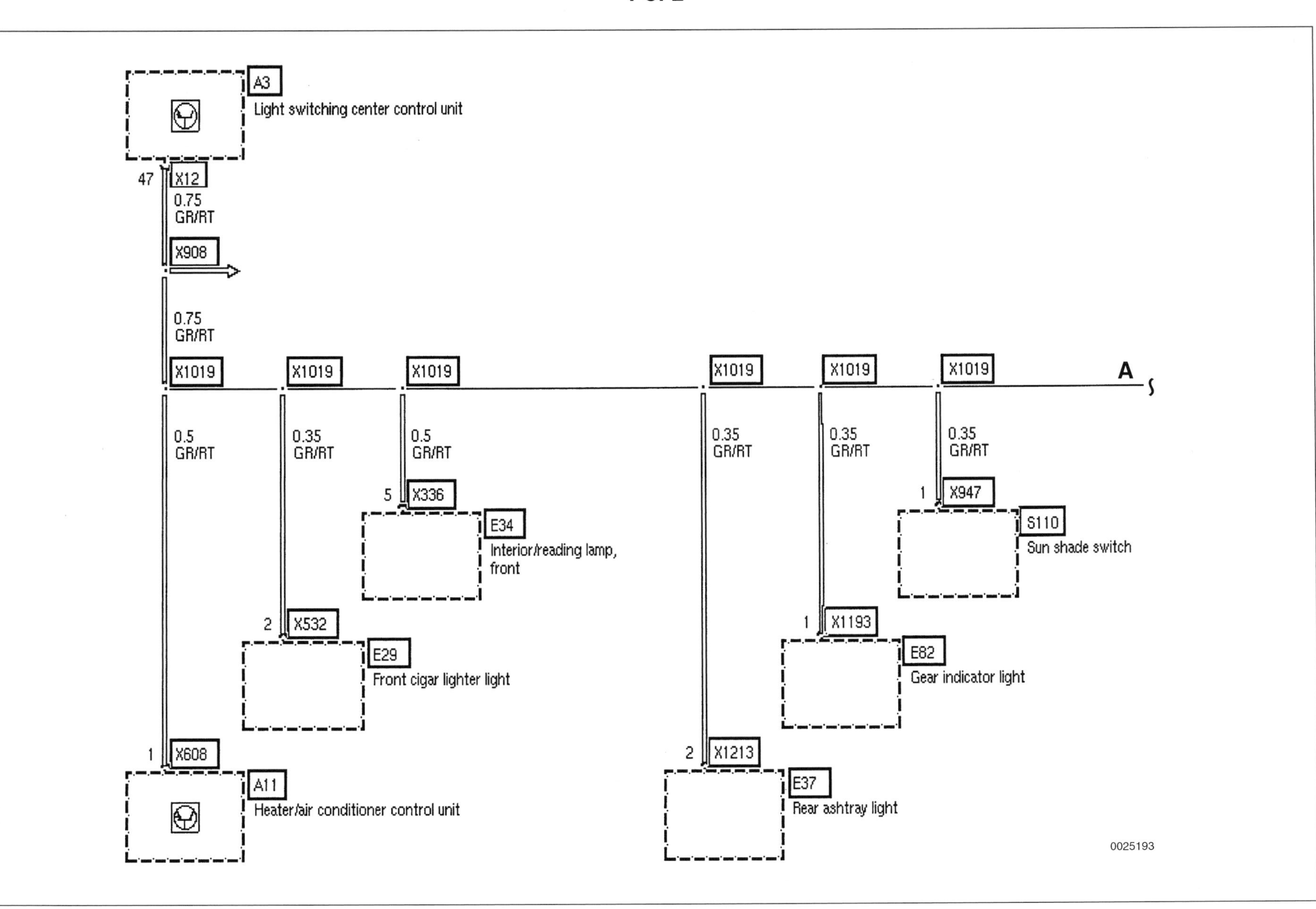

Instrument lighting splice connector (X1019)

2 of 2

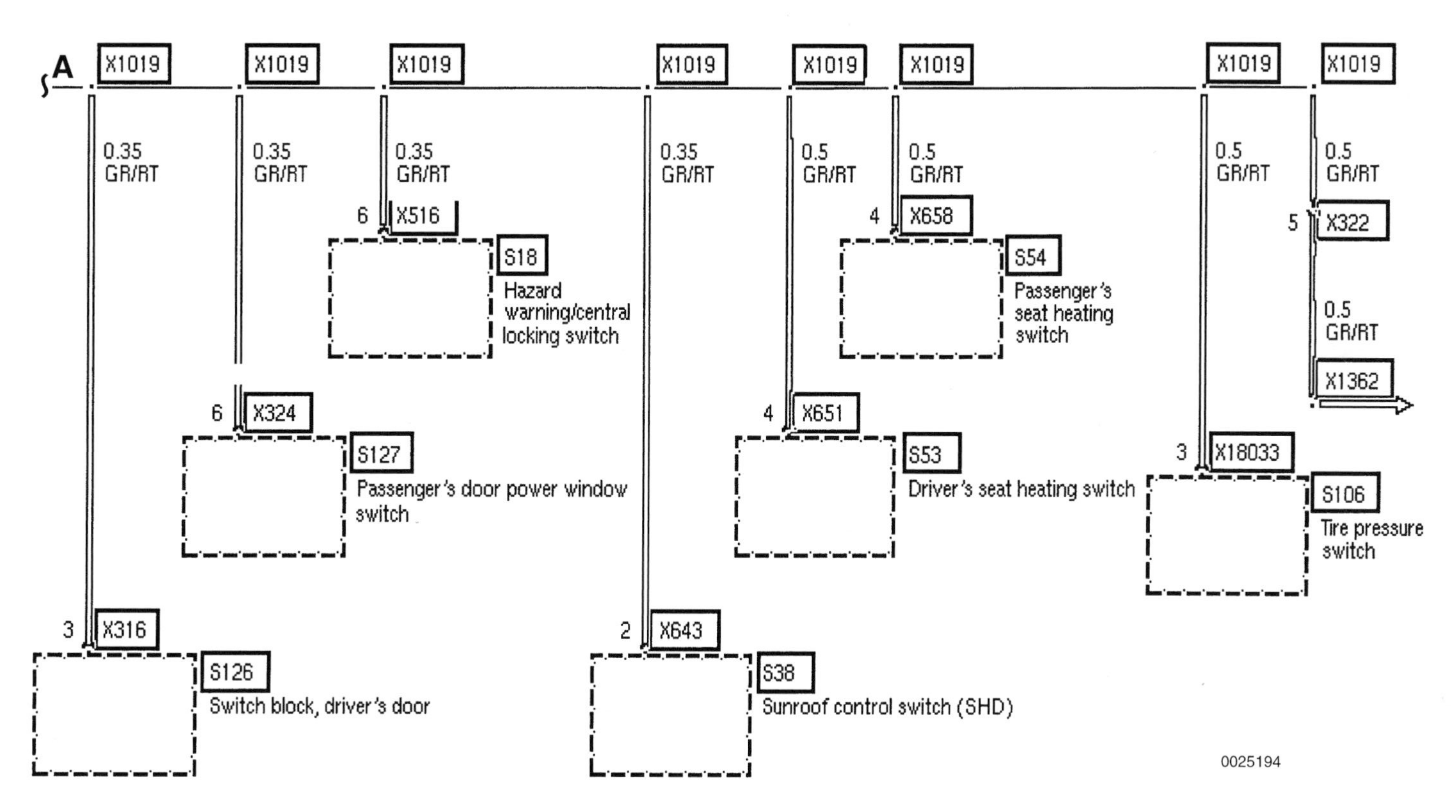

Back-up lights relay (K6325)

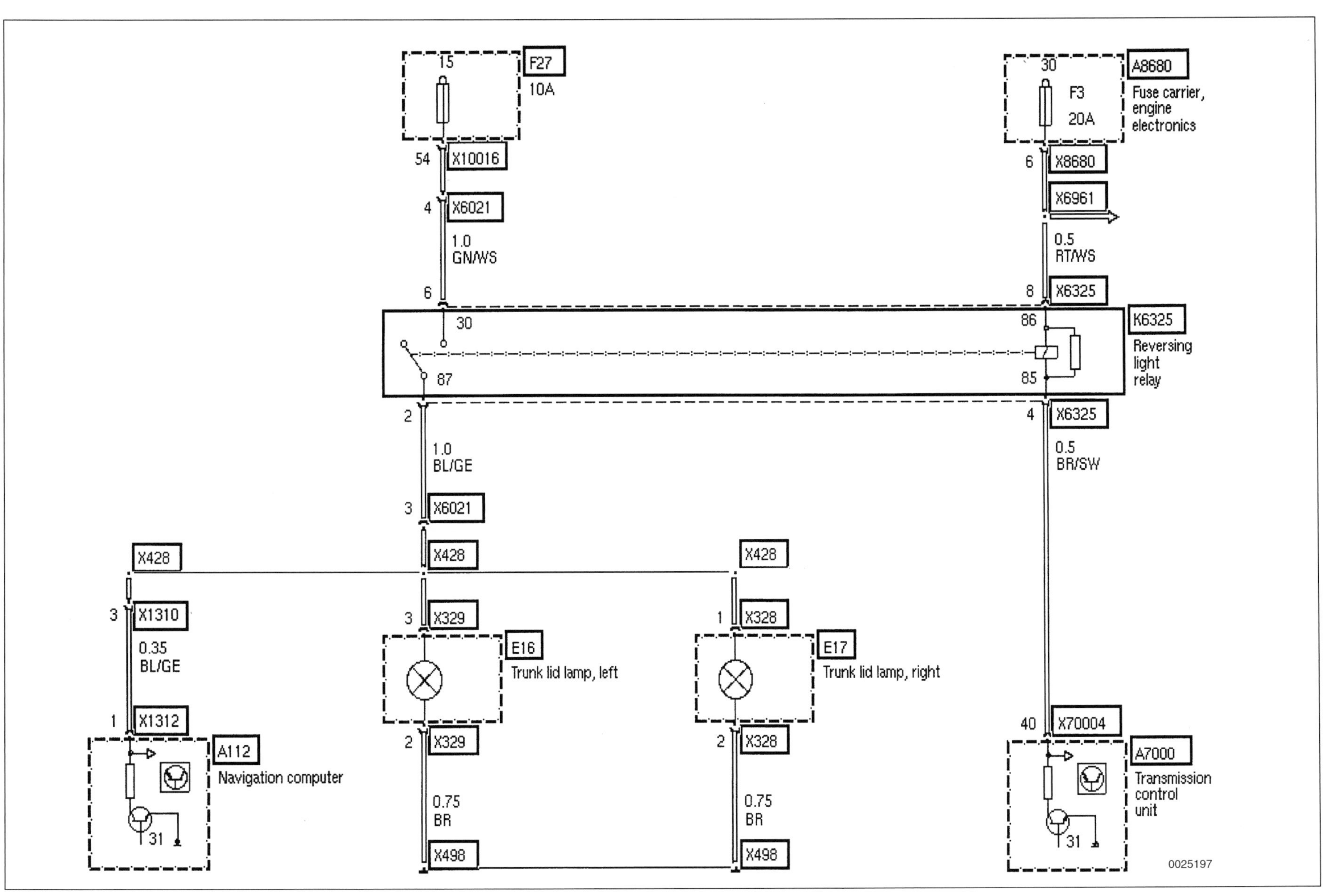

Fuse 27 (F27)

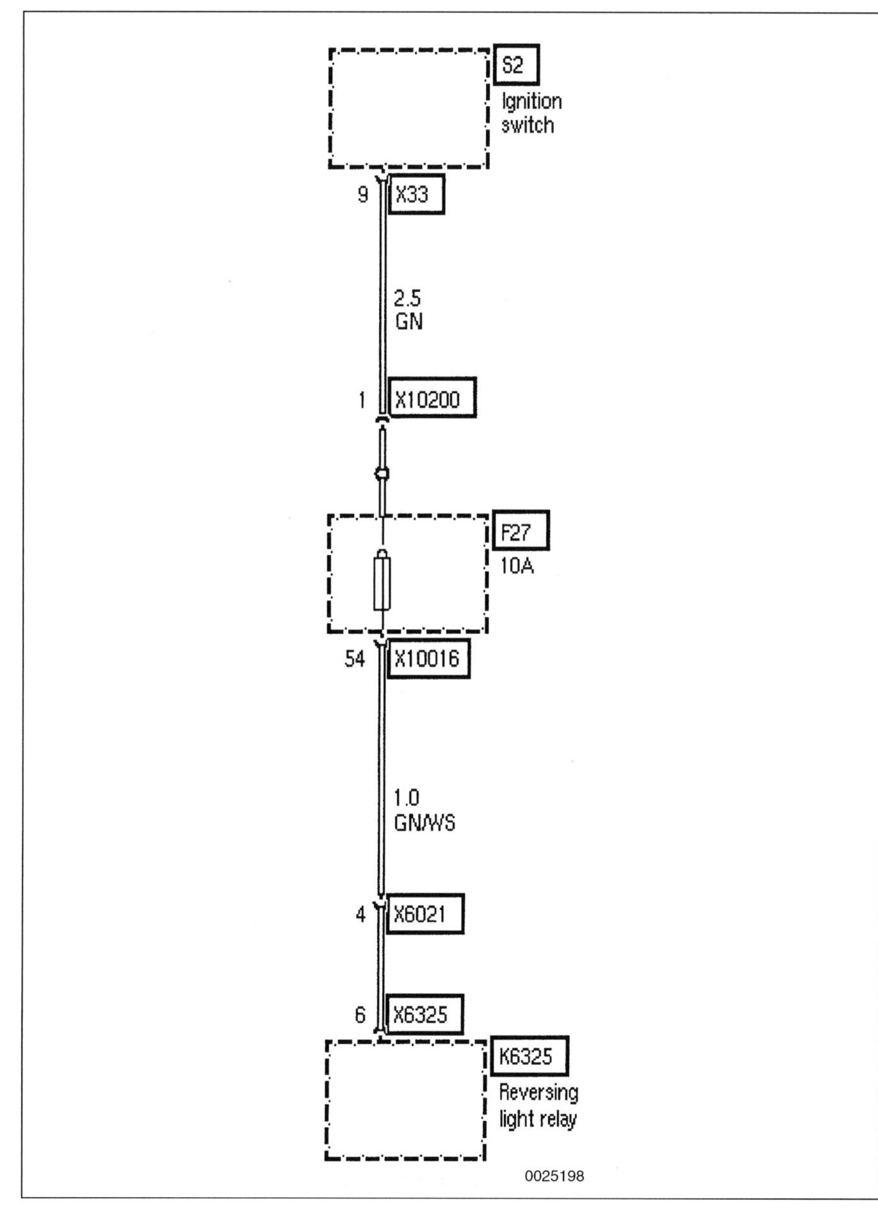
S2
Ignition switch
9
X33
2.5
GN
1
X10200
F27
10A
54
X10016
1.0
GN/WS
4
X6021
6
X6325
K6325
Reversing light relay
0025198

Connector (X428)

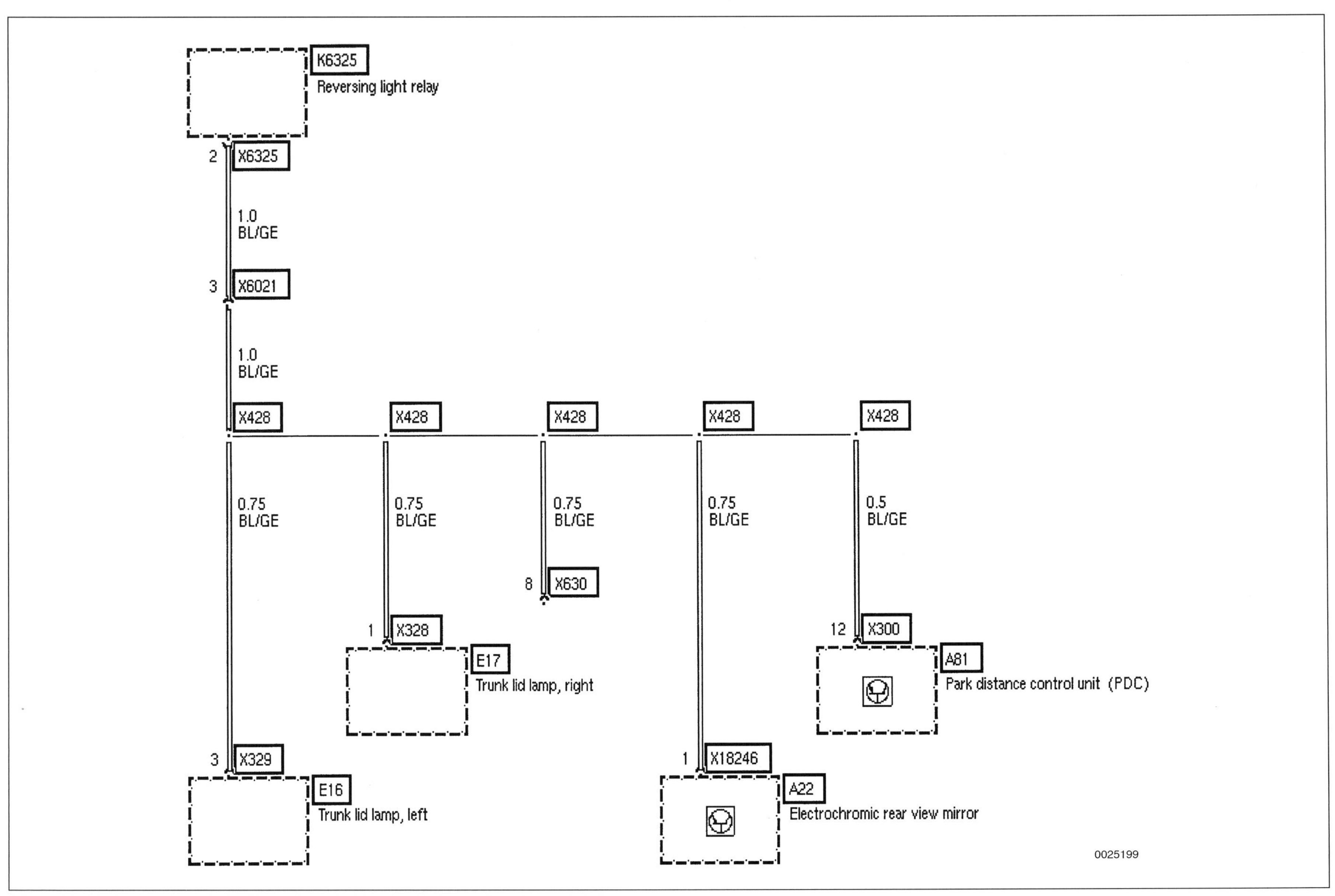

Trunk lid lights, left (E16)

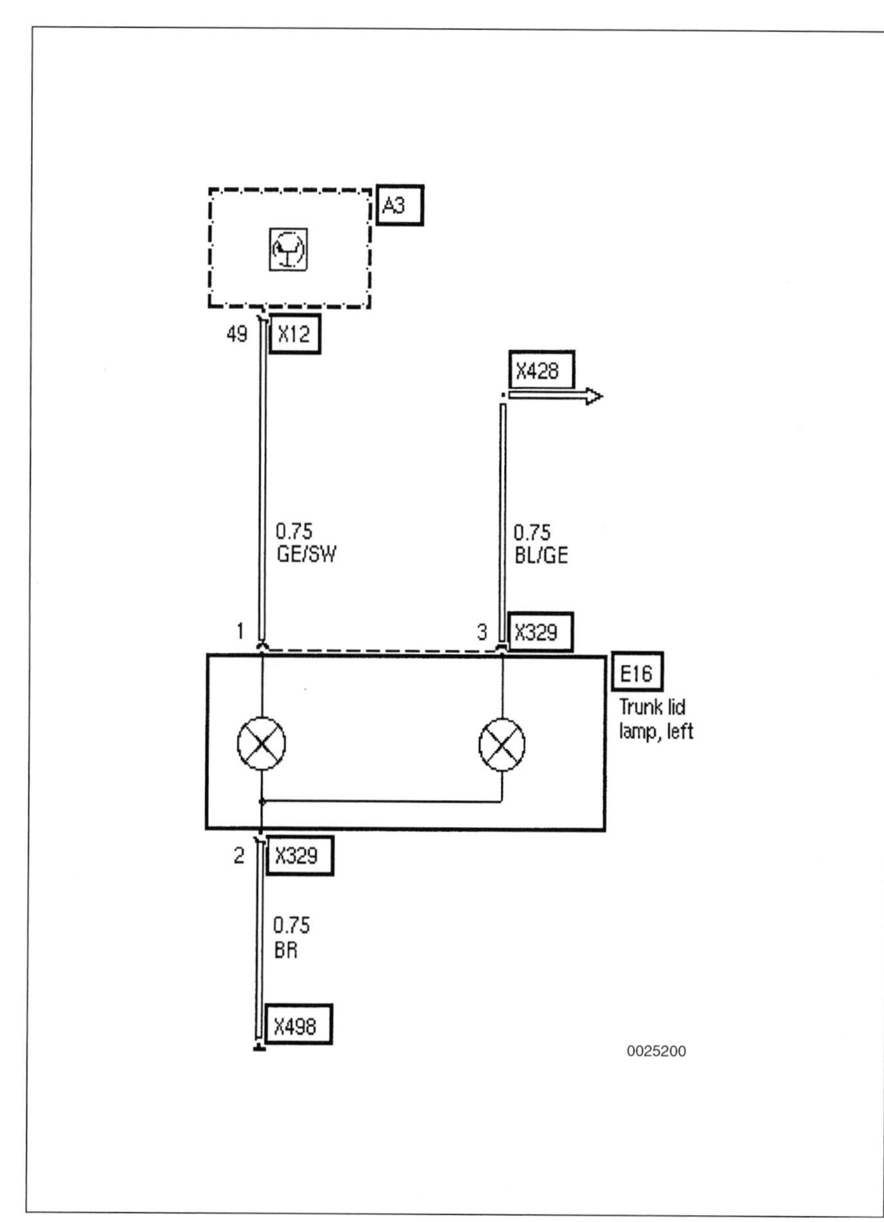

Ground (X498)
1 of 2

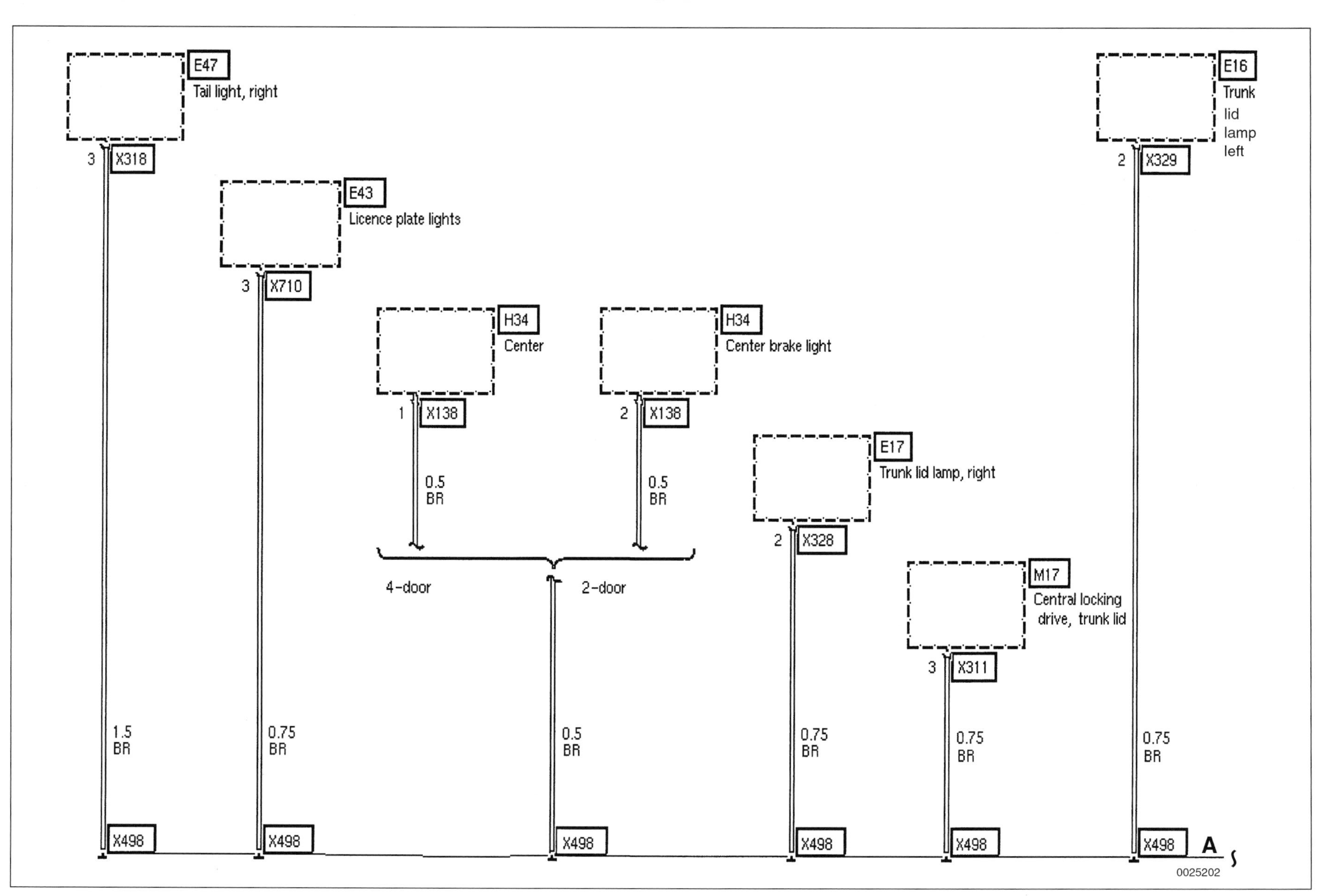

Ground (X498)
2 of 2

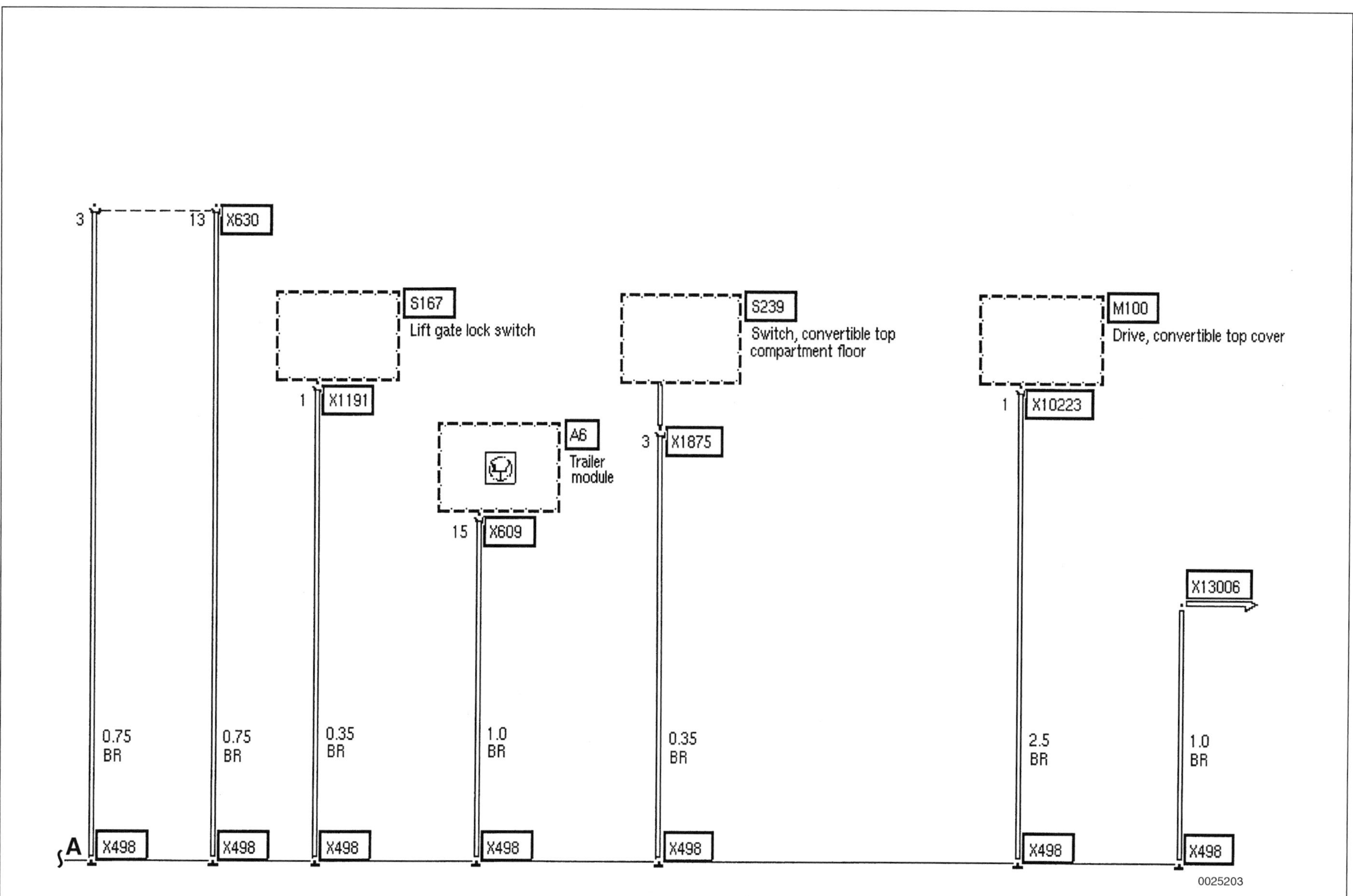

Trunk lid lights, right (E17)

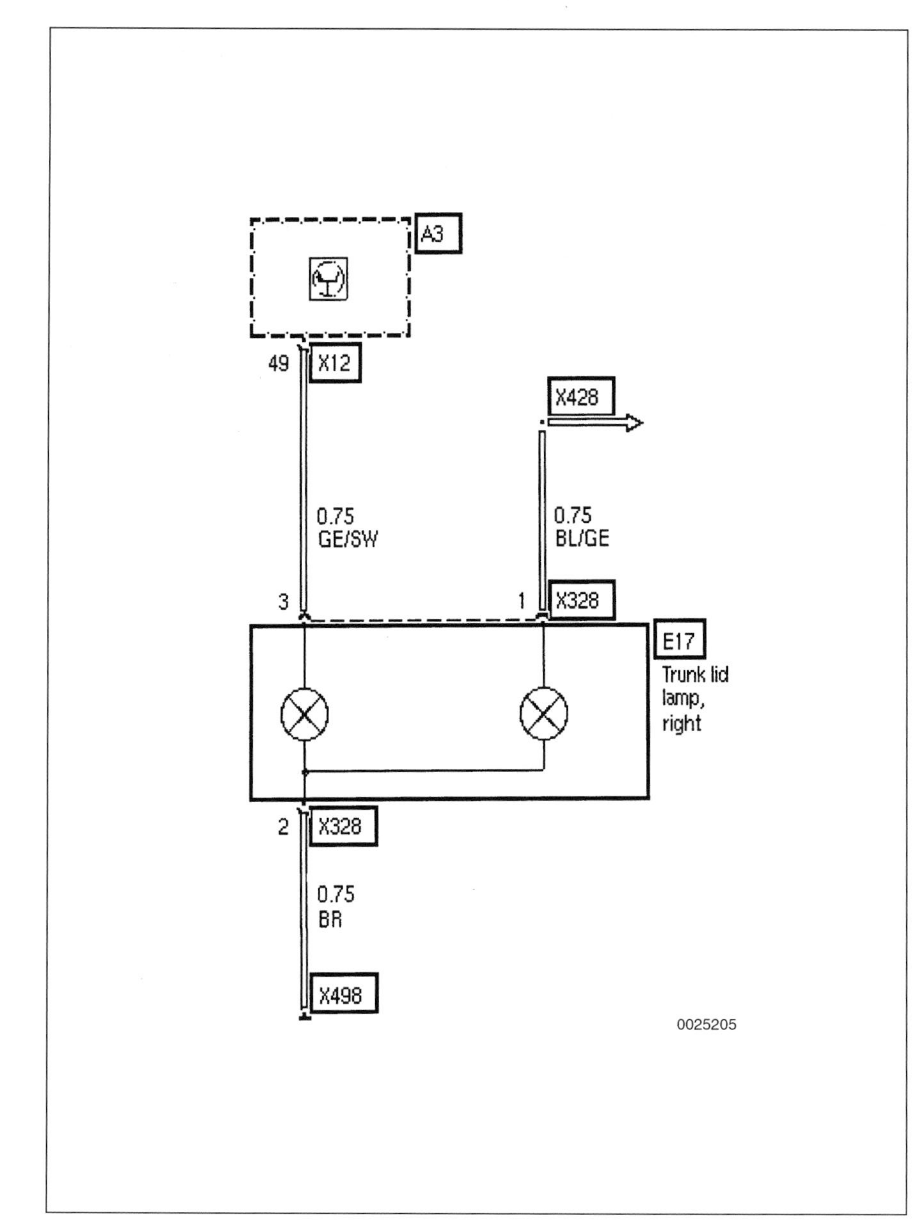

Transmission control unit (A7000)

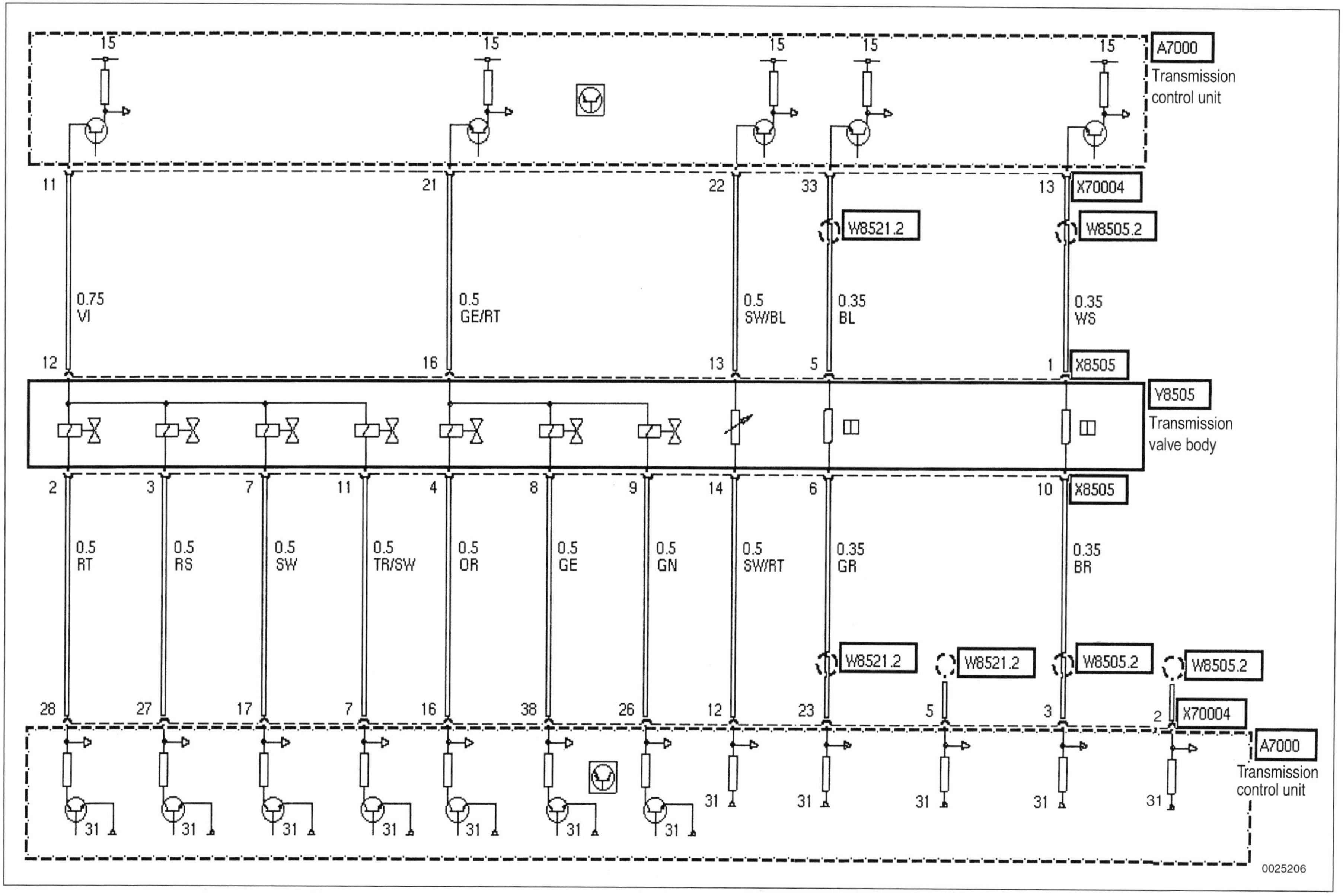

A7000 Transmission control unit

15 15 15 15 15

11 21 22 33 13

X70004

W8521.2 W8505.2

0.75 VI | 0.5 GE/RT | 0.5 SW/BL | 0.35 BL | 0.35 WS

12 16 13 5 1

X8505

V8505 Transmission valve body

2 3 7 11 4 8 9 14 6 10

X8505

0.5 RT | 0.5 RS | 0.5 SW | 0.5 TR/SW | 0.5 OR | 0.5 GE | 0.5 GN | 0.5 SW/RT | 0.35 GR | 0.35 BR

W8521.2 W8521.2 W8505.2 W8505.2

28 27 17 7 16 38 26 12 23 5 3 2

X70004

A7000 Transmission control unit

31 31 31 31 31 31 31 31 31 31 31 31

0025206

Kickdown switch (S8507)

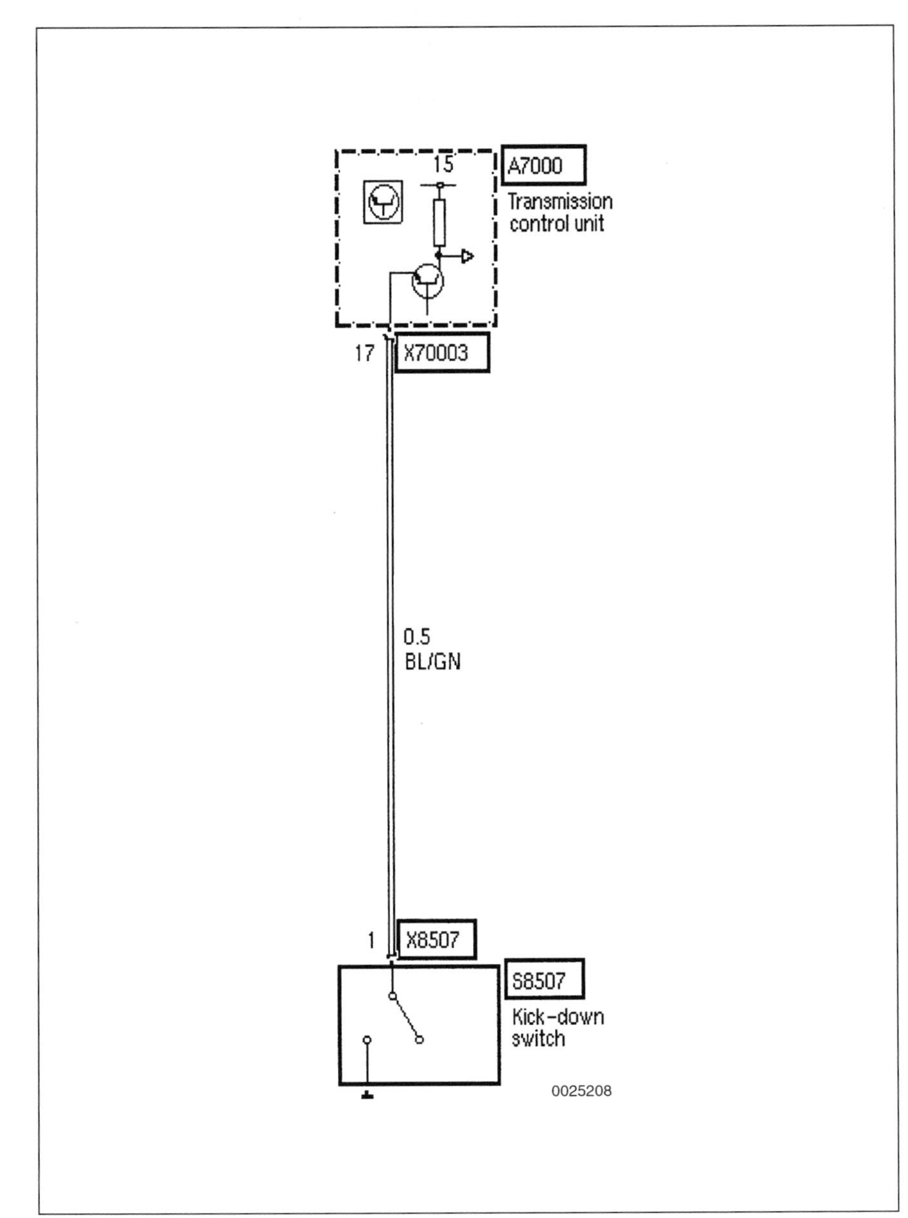

Fuse 56 (F56)

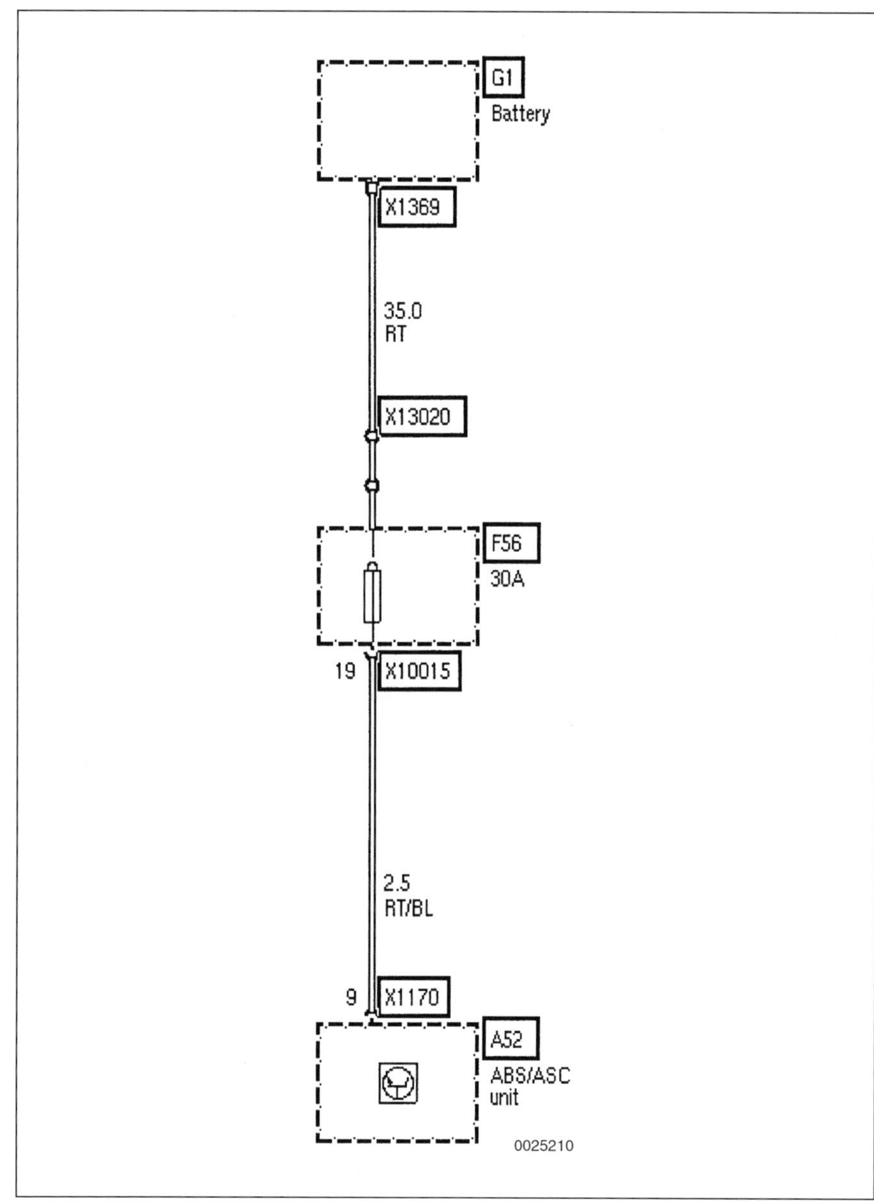

G1
Battery
X1369
35.0
RT
X13020
F56
30A
19
X10015
2.5
RT/BL
9
X1170
A52
ABS/ASC
unit
0025210

Fuse 53 (F53)

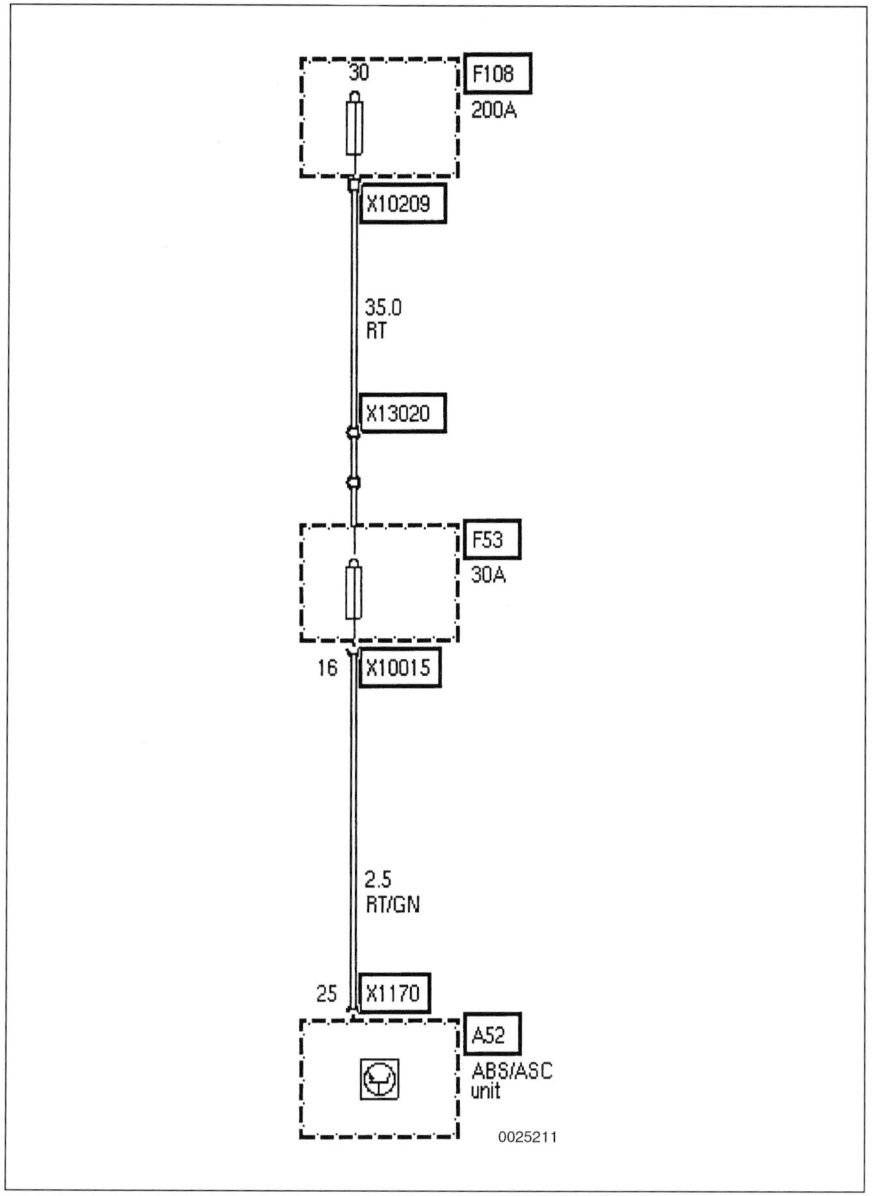

30
F108
200A
X10209
35.0
RT
X13020
F53
30A
16
X10015
2.5
RT/GN
25
X1170
A52
ABS/ASC
unit
0025211

Fuse 33 (F33)

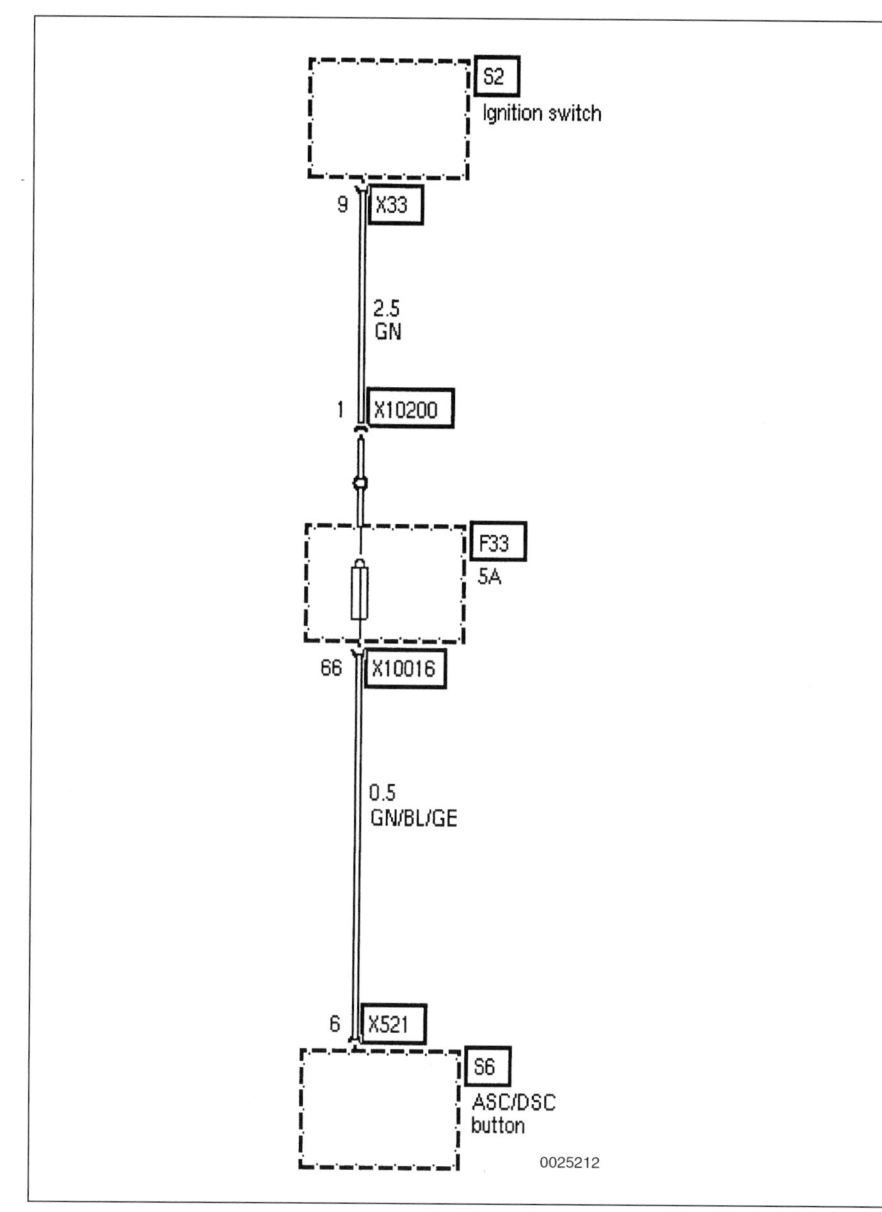

S2
Ignition switch
9
X33
2.5
GN
1
X10200
F33
5A
66
X10016
0.5
GN/BL/GE
6
X521
S6
ASC/DSC
button
0025212

Ground (X165)

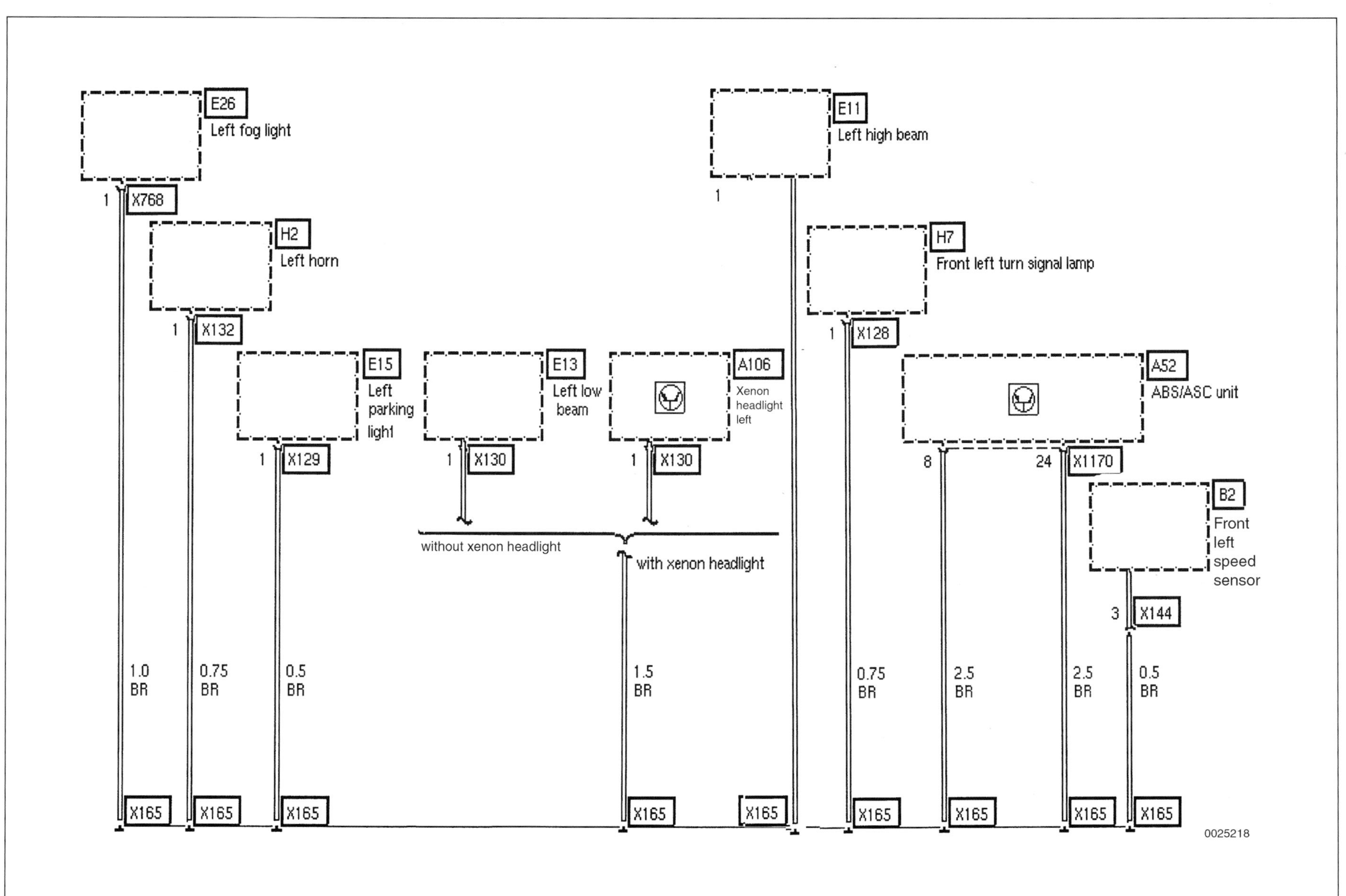
E26
Left fog light
1
X768
1.0
BR
X165
H2
Left horn
1
X132
0.75
BR
X165
E15
Left
parking
light
1
X129
0.5
BR
X165
E13
Left low
beam
1
X130
A106
Xenon
headlight
left
1
X130
without xenon headlight
with xenon headlight
1.5
BR
X165
E11
Left high beam
1
X165
H7
Front left turn signal lamp
1
X128
0.75
BR
X165
A52
ABS/ASC unit
8
2.5
BR
X165
24
X1170
2.5
BR
X165
B2
Front
left
speed
sensor
3
X144
0.5
BR
X165
0025218

ABS/ASC warning light

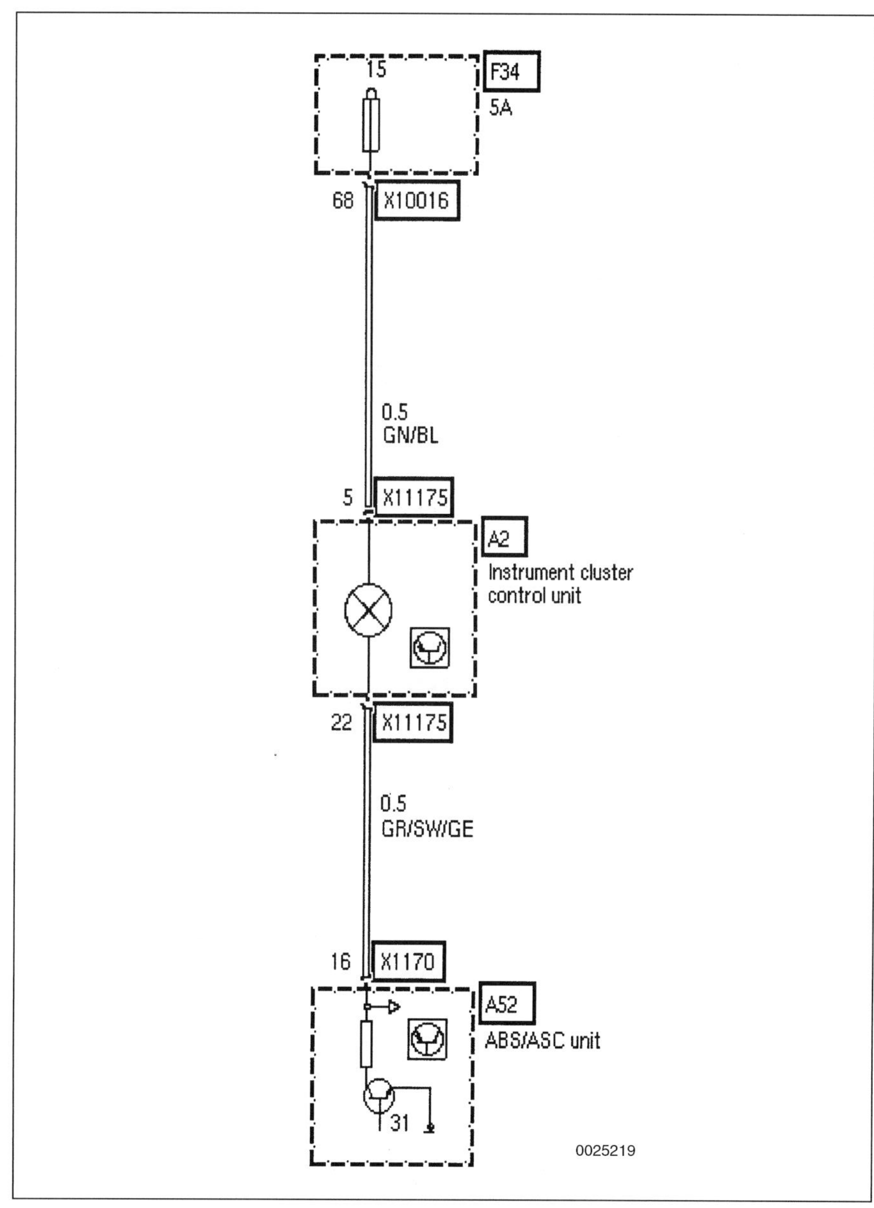

ASC/DSC button (S6)

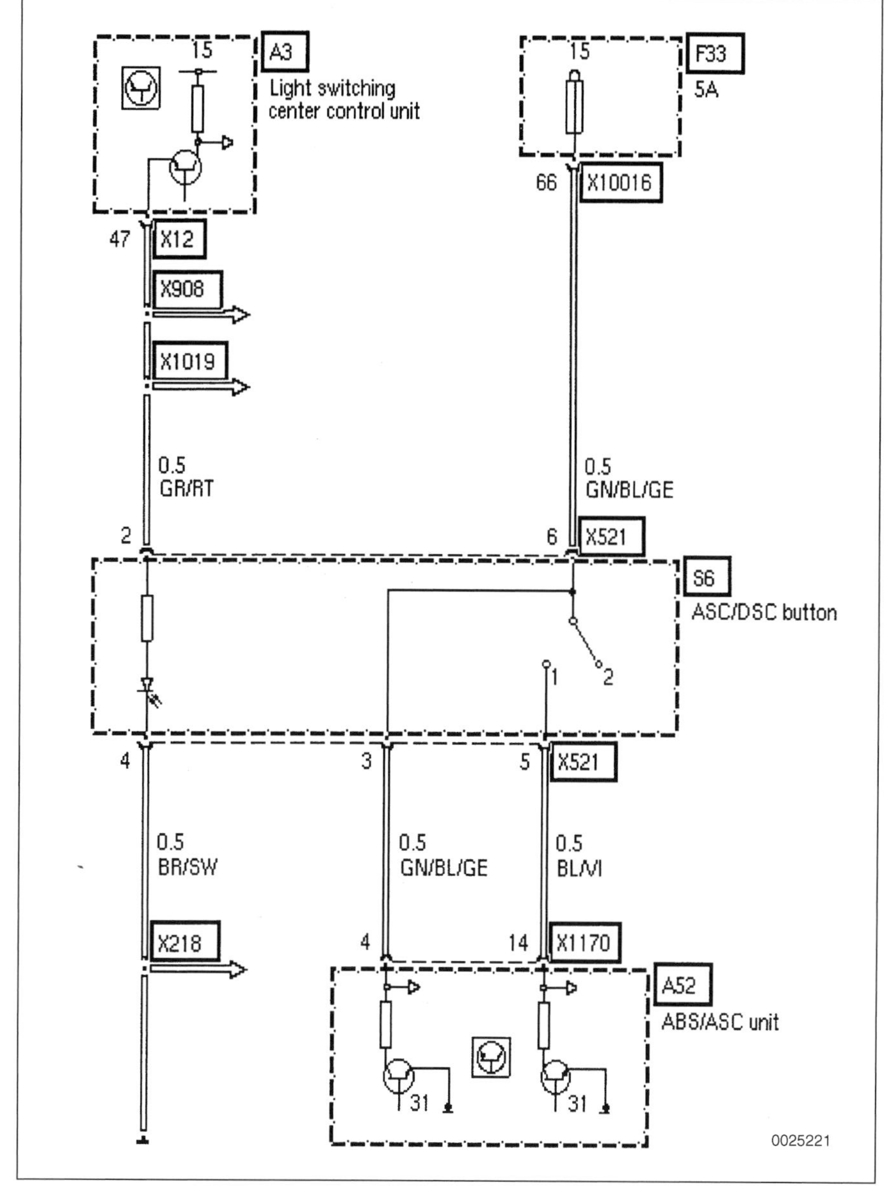

Mirror, electrochromic rear view (A22)

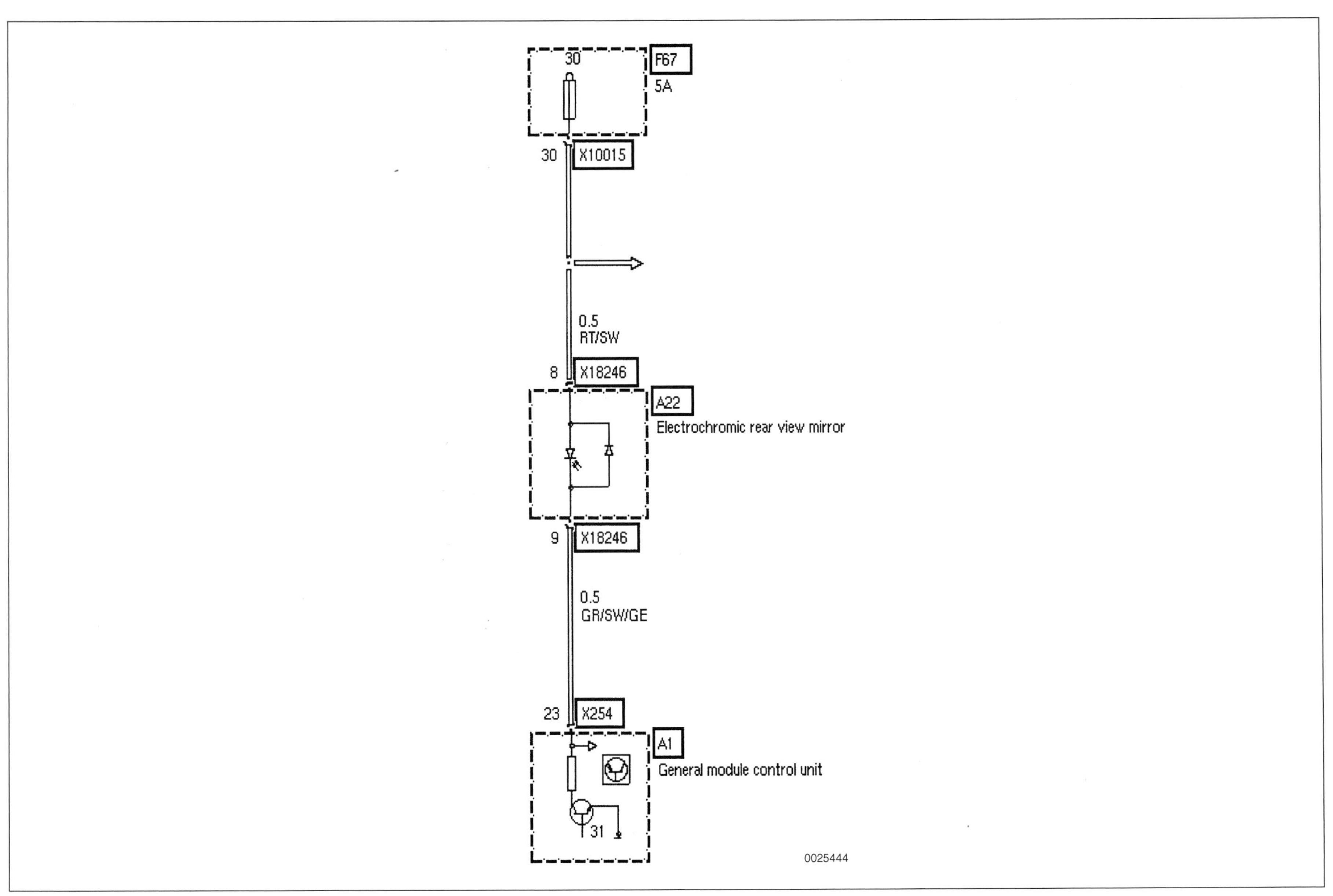

This page left intentionally blank

This page left intentionally blank

ABS/ASC wheel speed sensors, rear (B3, B4)

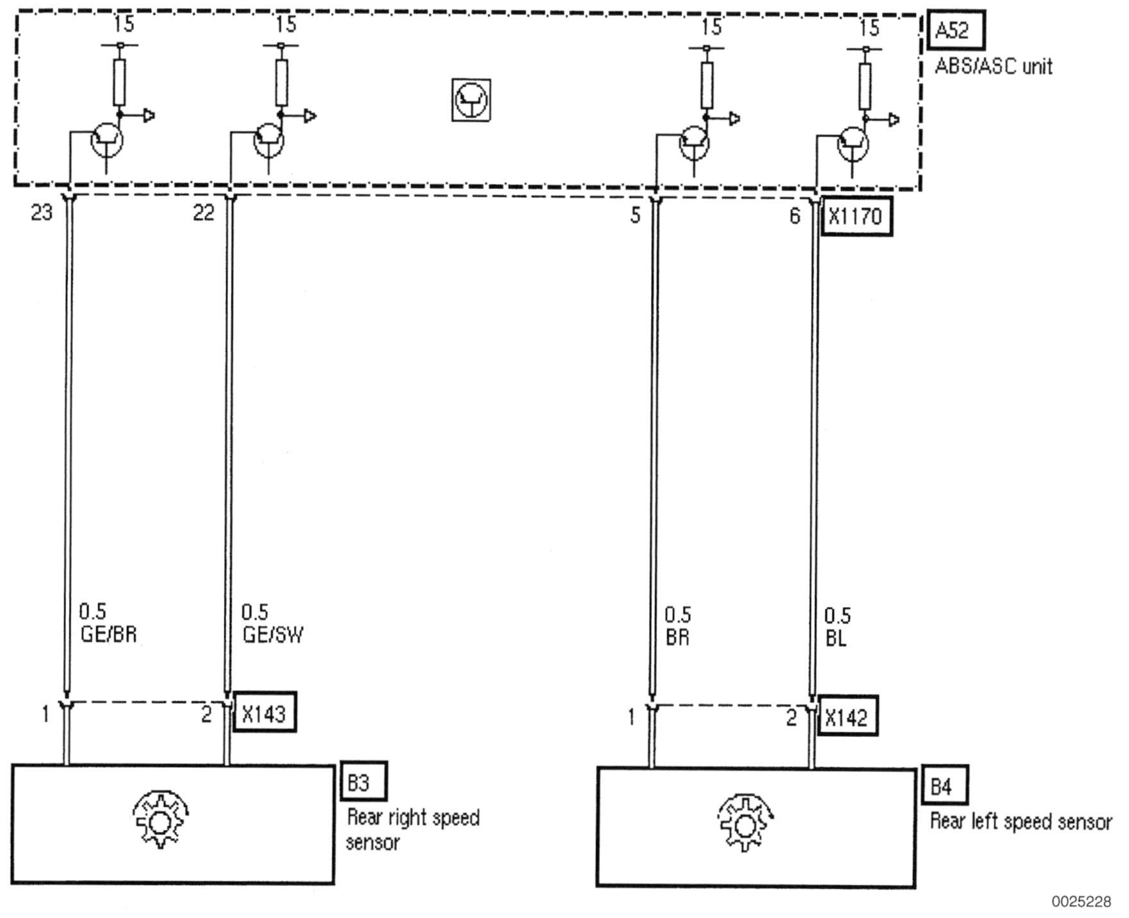

15
15
15
15
A52
ABS/ASC unit
23
22
5
6
X1170
0.5
GE/BR
0.5
GE/SW
0.5
BR
0.5
BL
1
2
X143
1
2
X142
B3
Rear right speed sensor
B4
Rear left speed sensor
0025228

ABS/ASC wheel speed sensors, front (B1, B2)

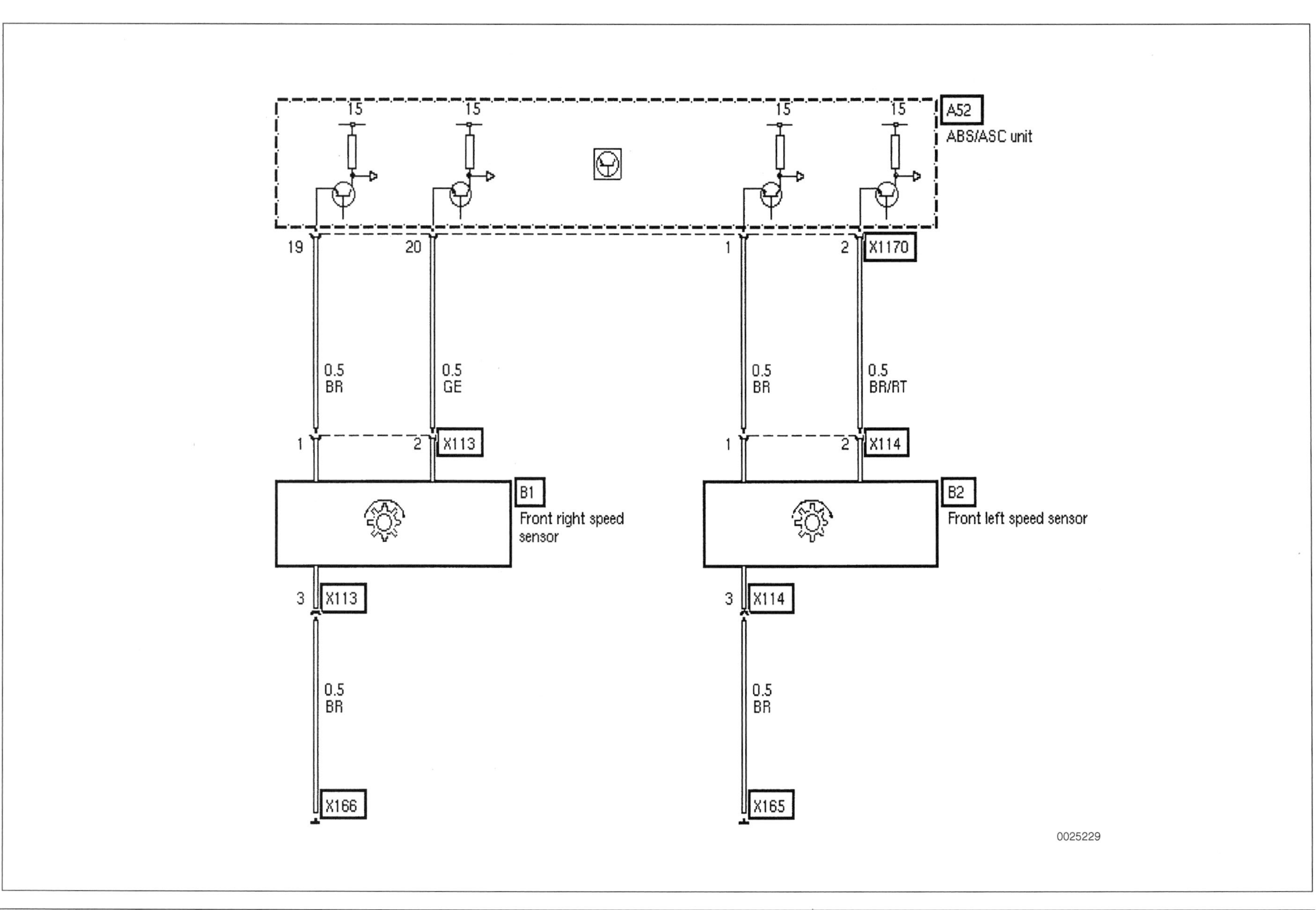

Connector (X10185)

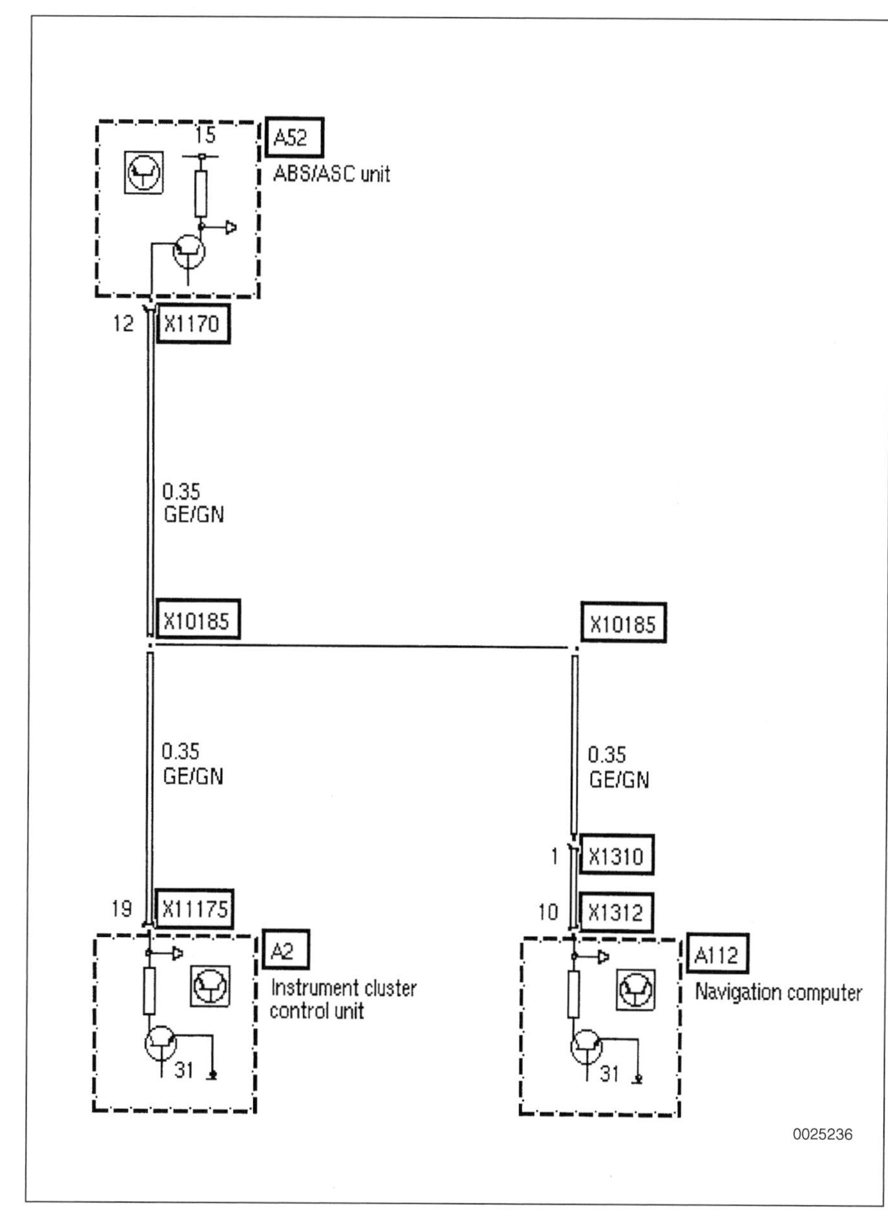

Connector (X1310)

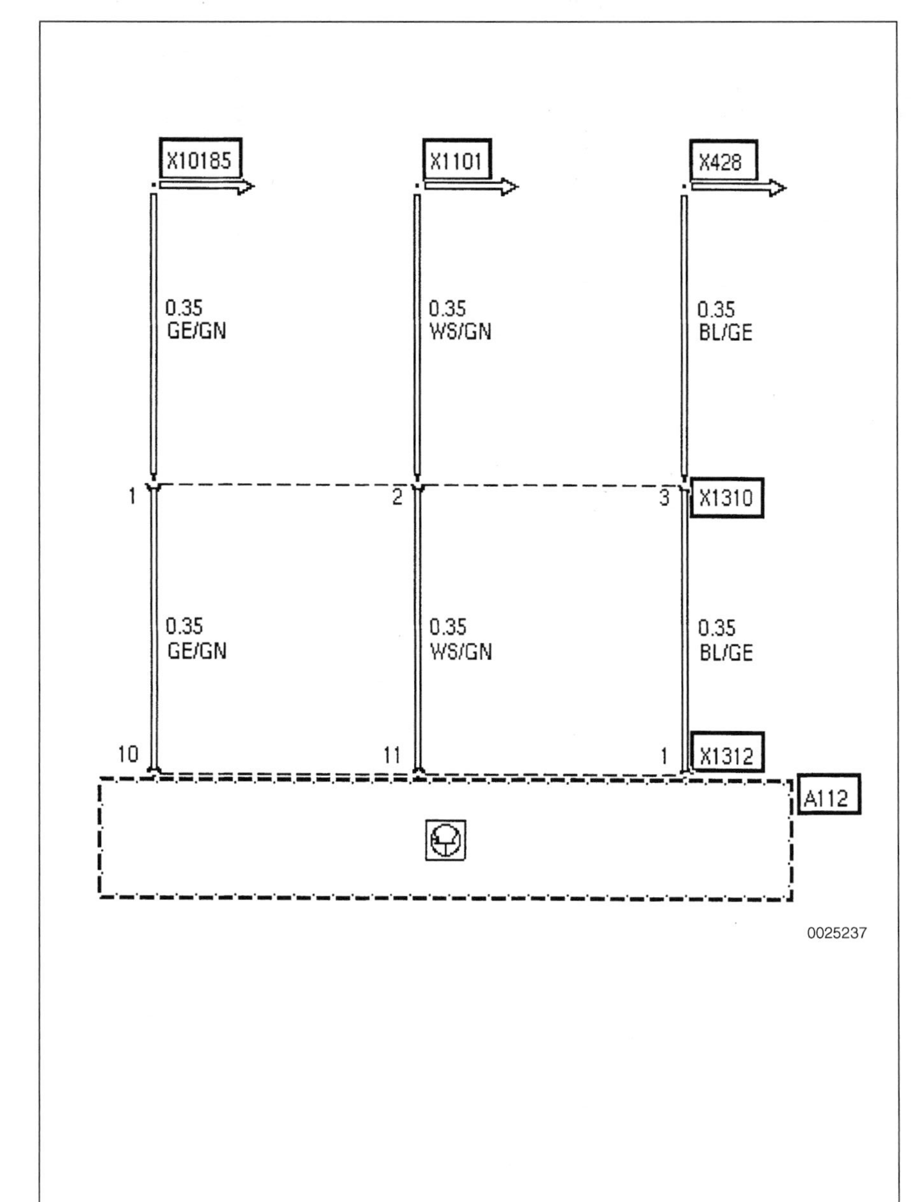

Navigation computer (A112)
1 of 2

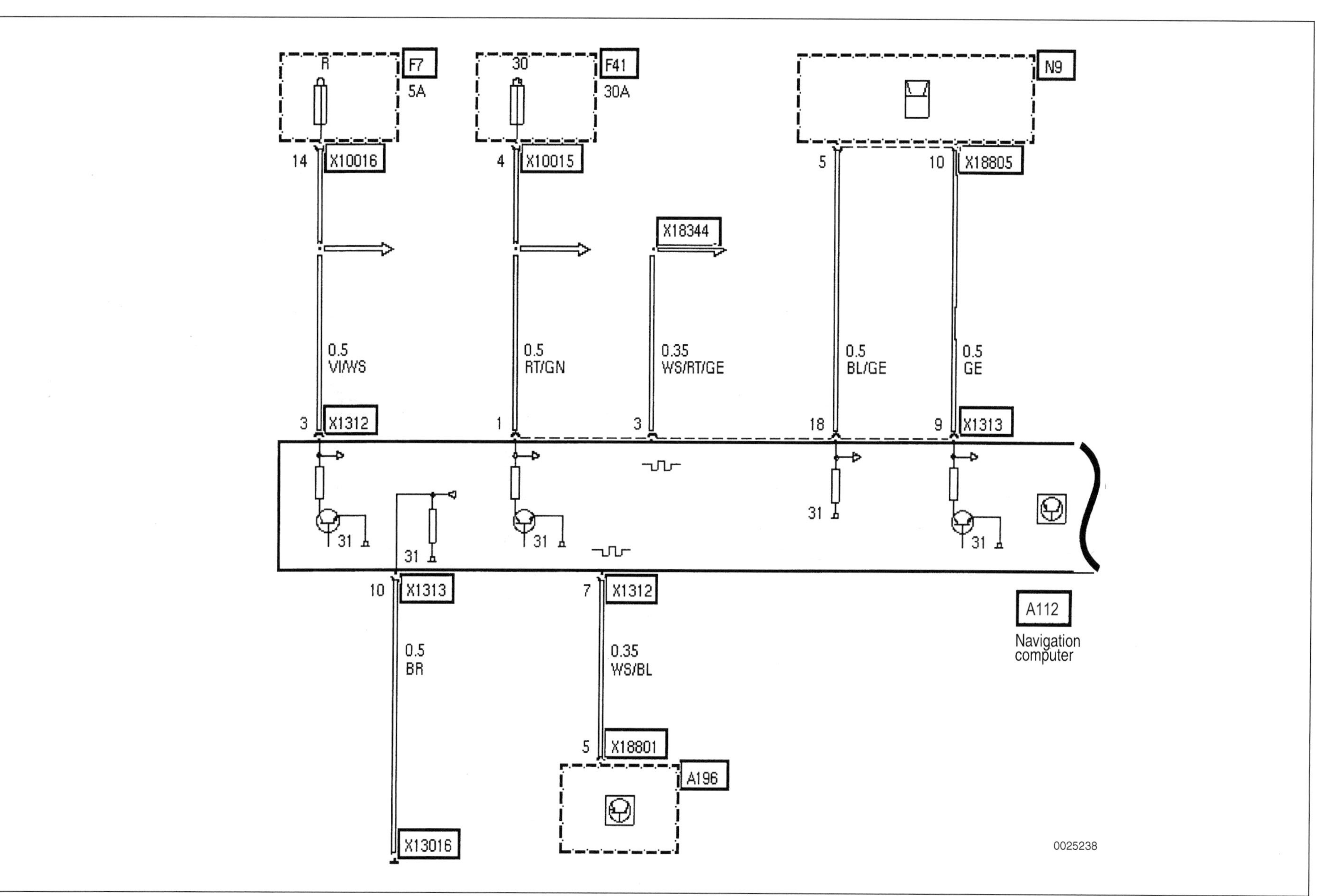

Navigation computer (A112)
2 of 2

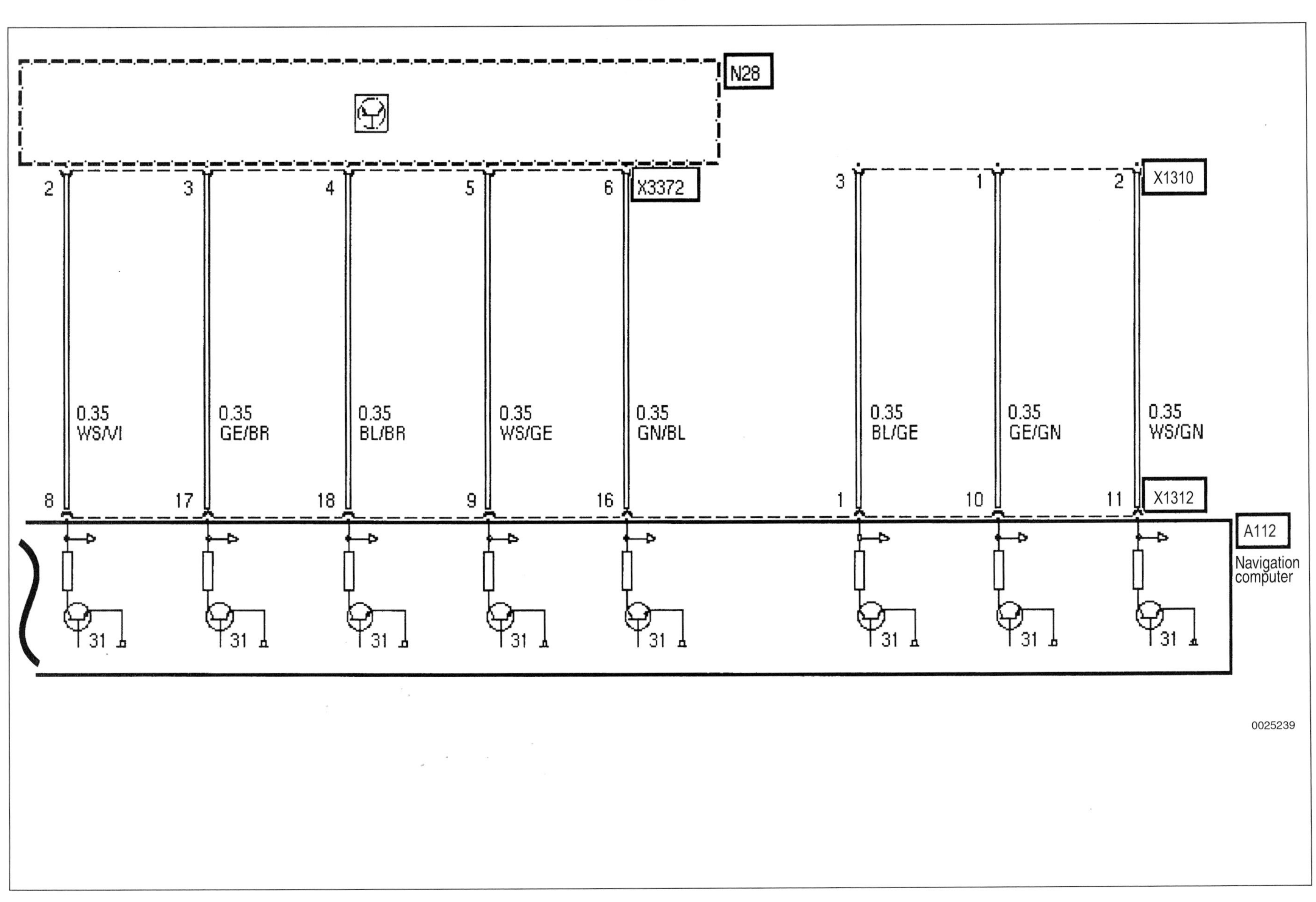

Fuse 69 (F69)

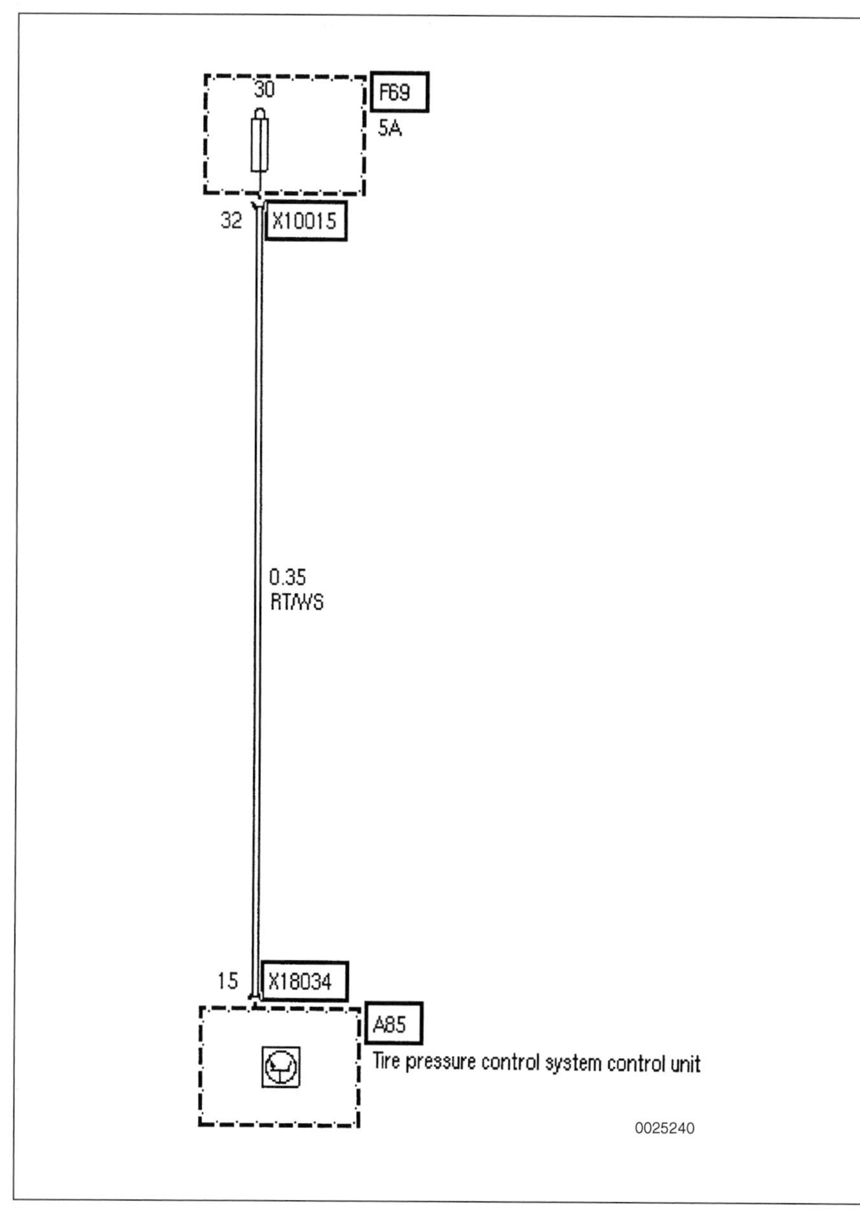

30
F69
5A
32
X10015
0.35
RT/WS
15
X18034
A85
Tire pressure control system control unit
0025240

Fuse 31 (F31)

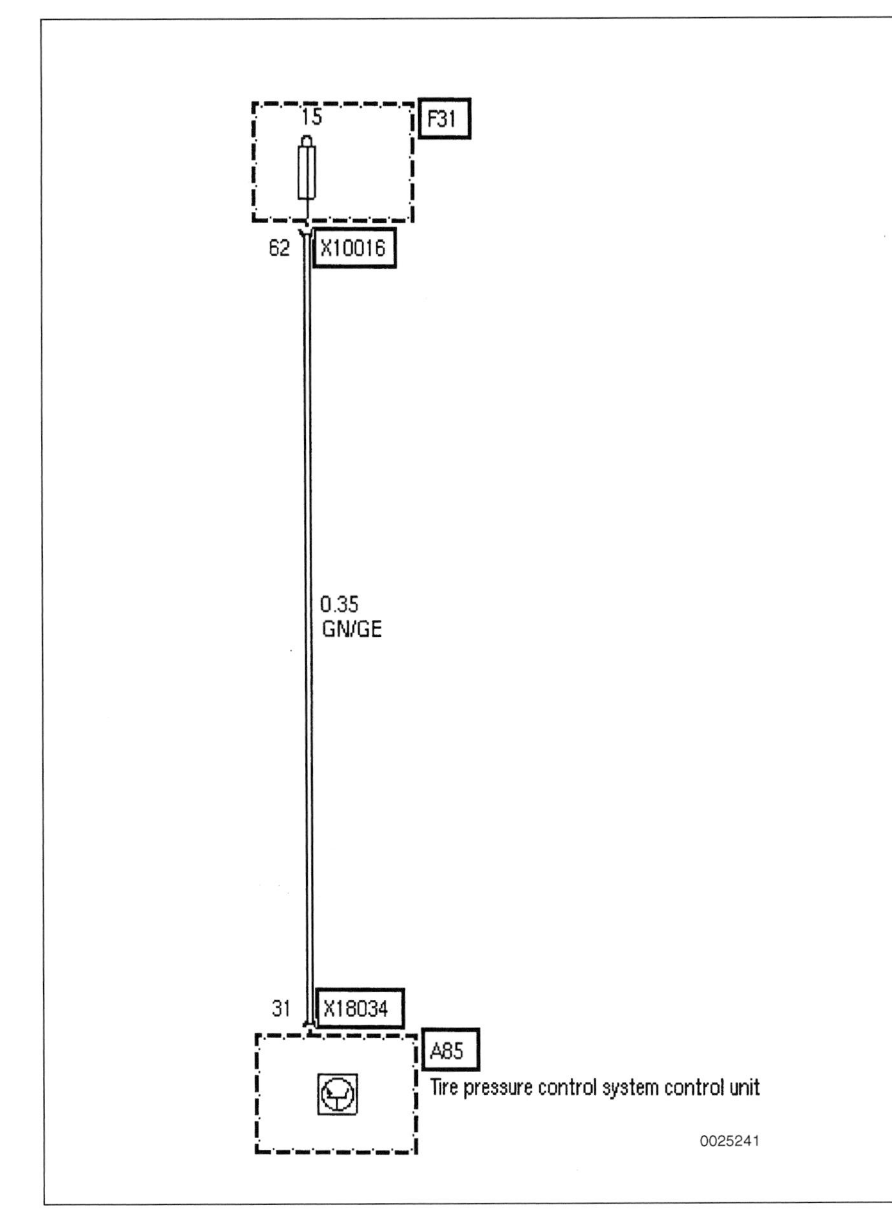
15
F31
62
X10016
0.35
GN/GE
31
X18034
A85
Tire pressure control system control unit
0025241

Tire pressure control (RDC) switch (S106)

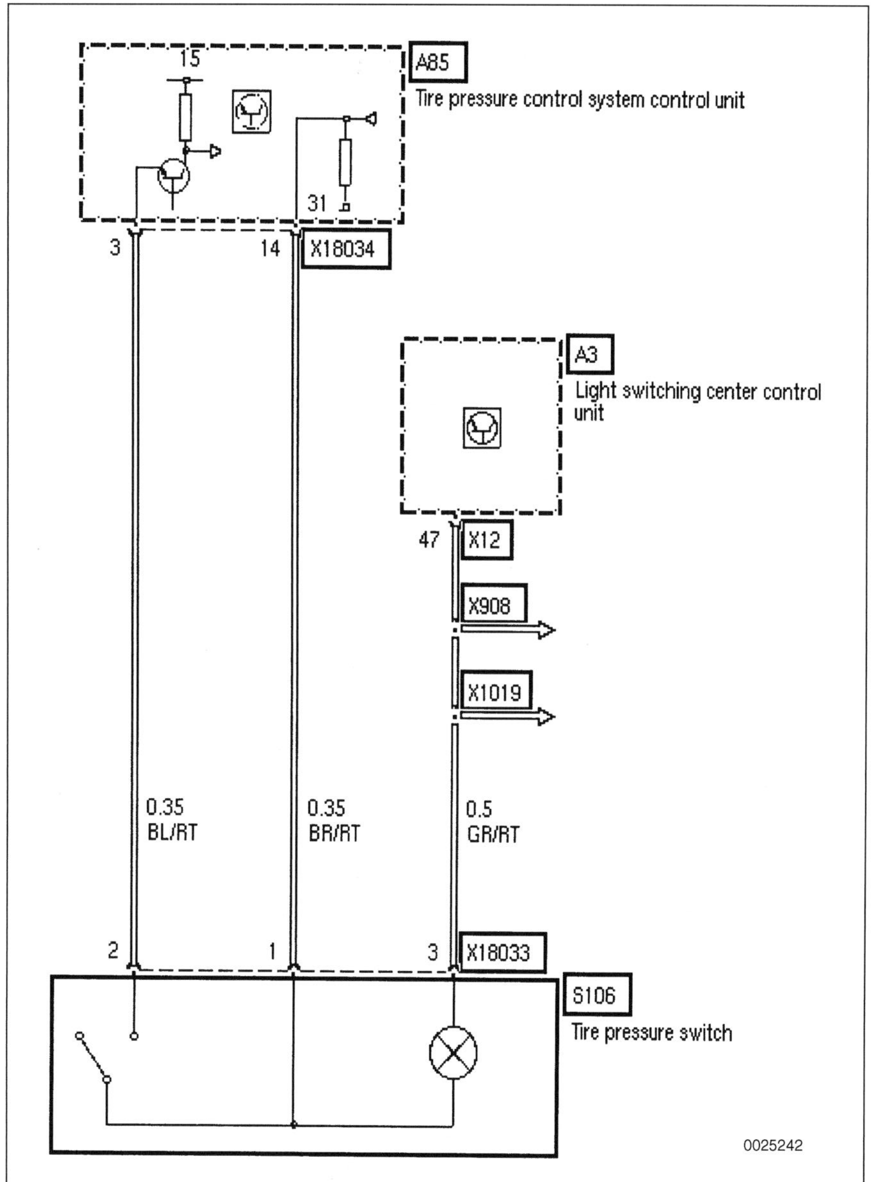

Tire pressure control (RDC) sensors (B43, B44, B45, B47)

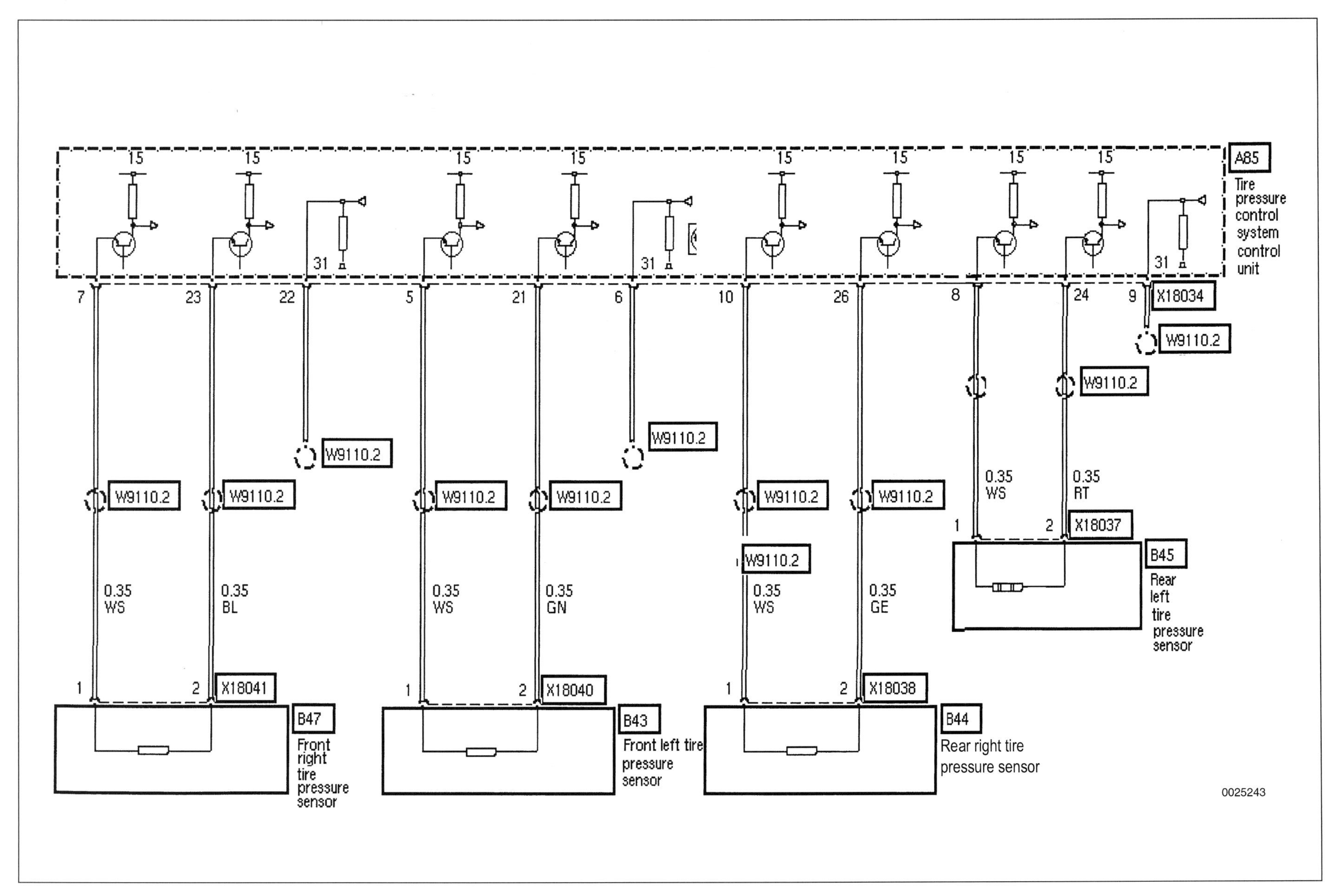

Fuse 106 (F106)

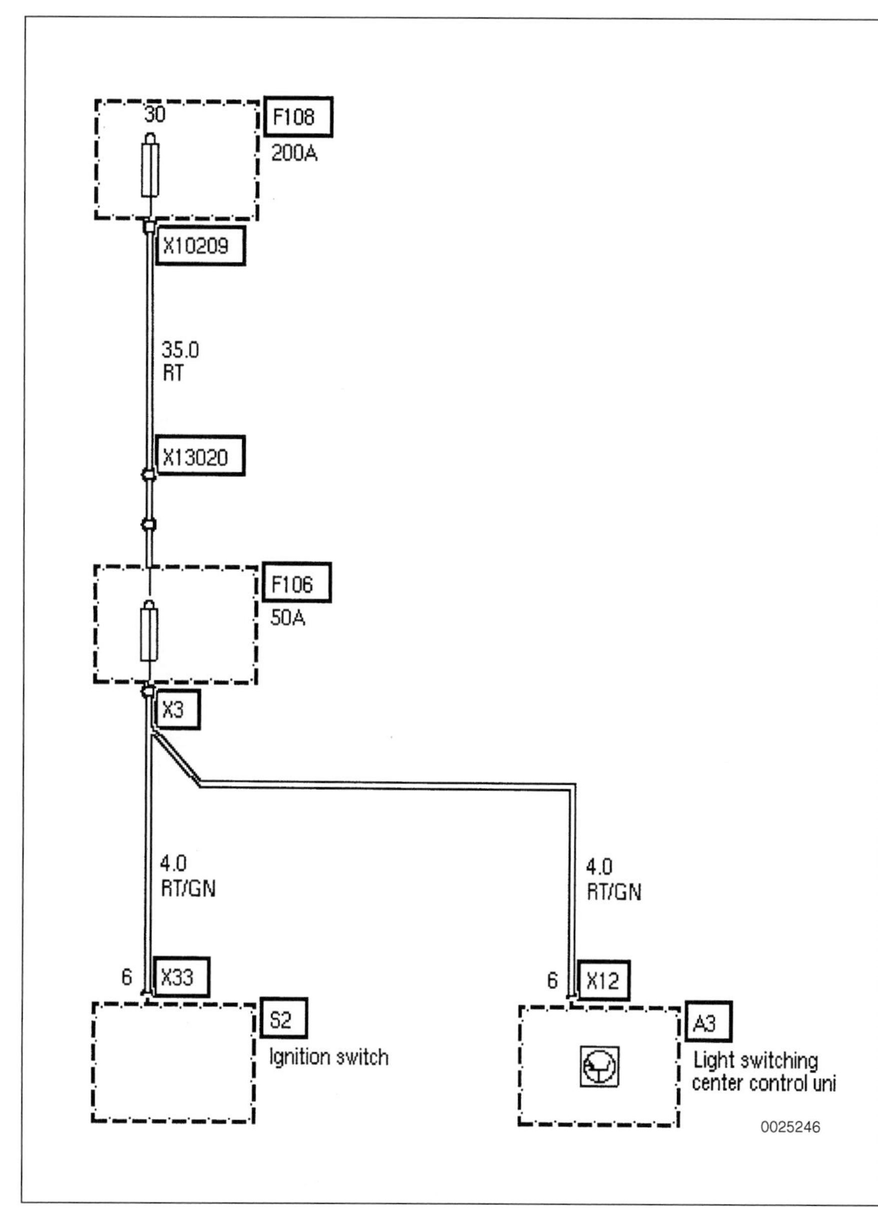

Fuse 107 (F107)

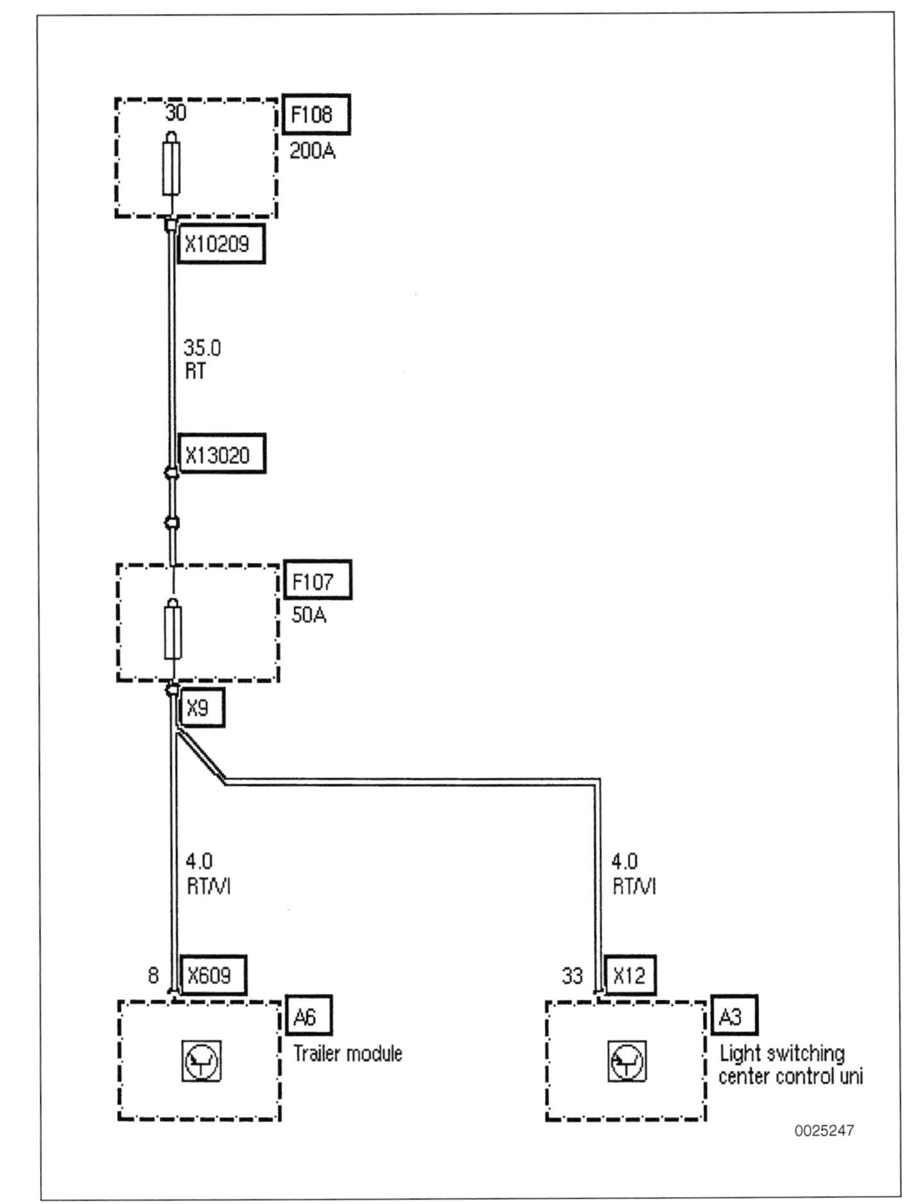

This page left intentionally blank

Fuse 32 (F32)

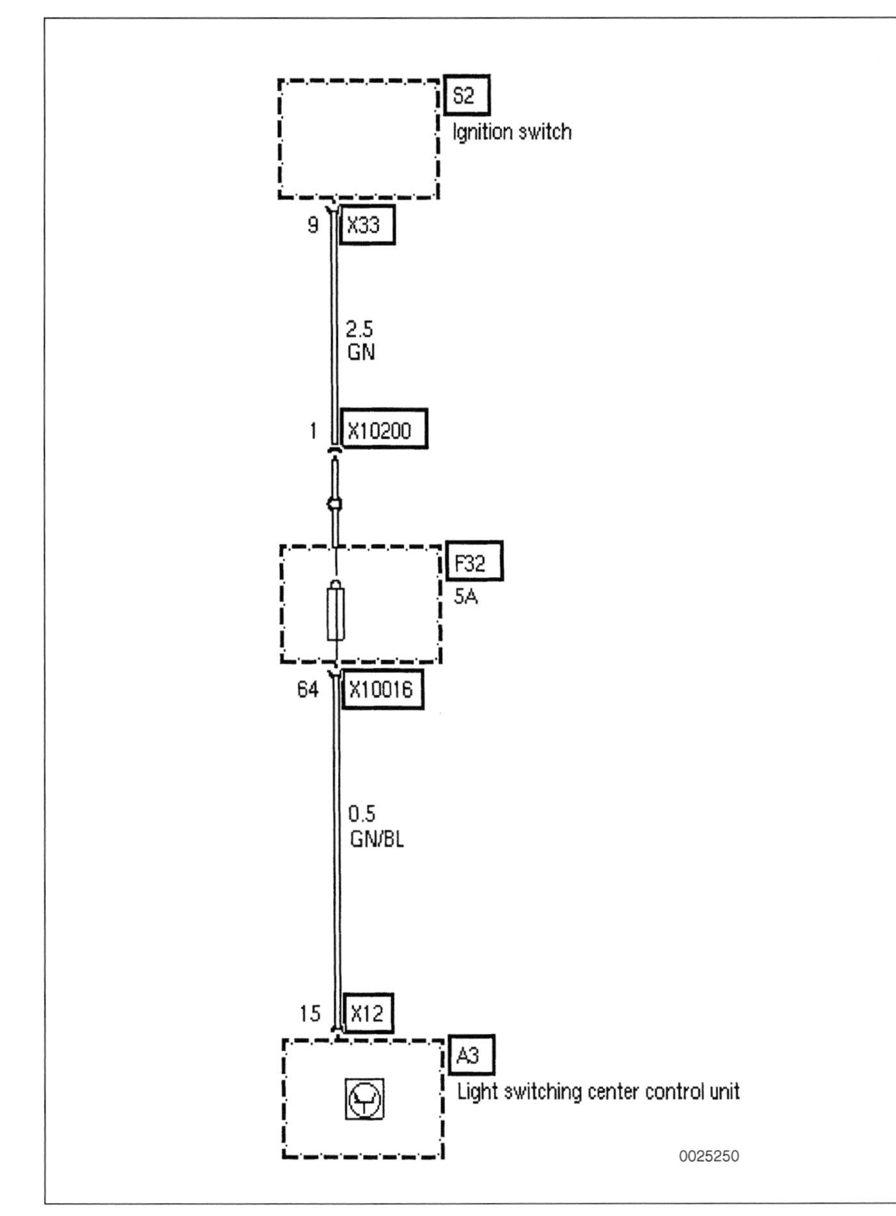
S2
Ignition switch
9
X33
2.5
GN
1
X10200
F32
5A
64
X10016
0.5
GN/BL
15
X12
A3
Light switching center control unit
0025250

Parking lights, rear

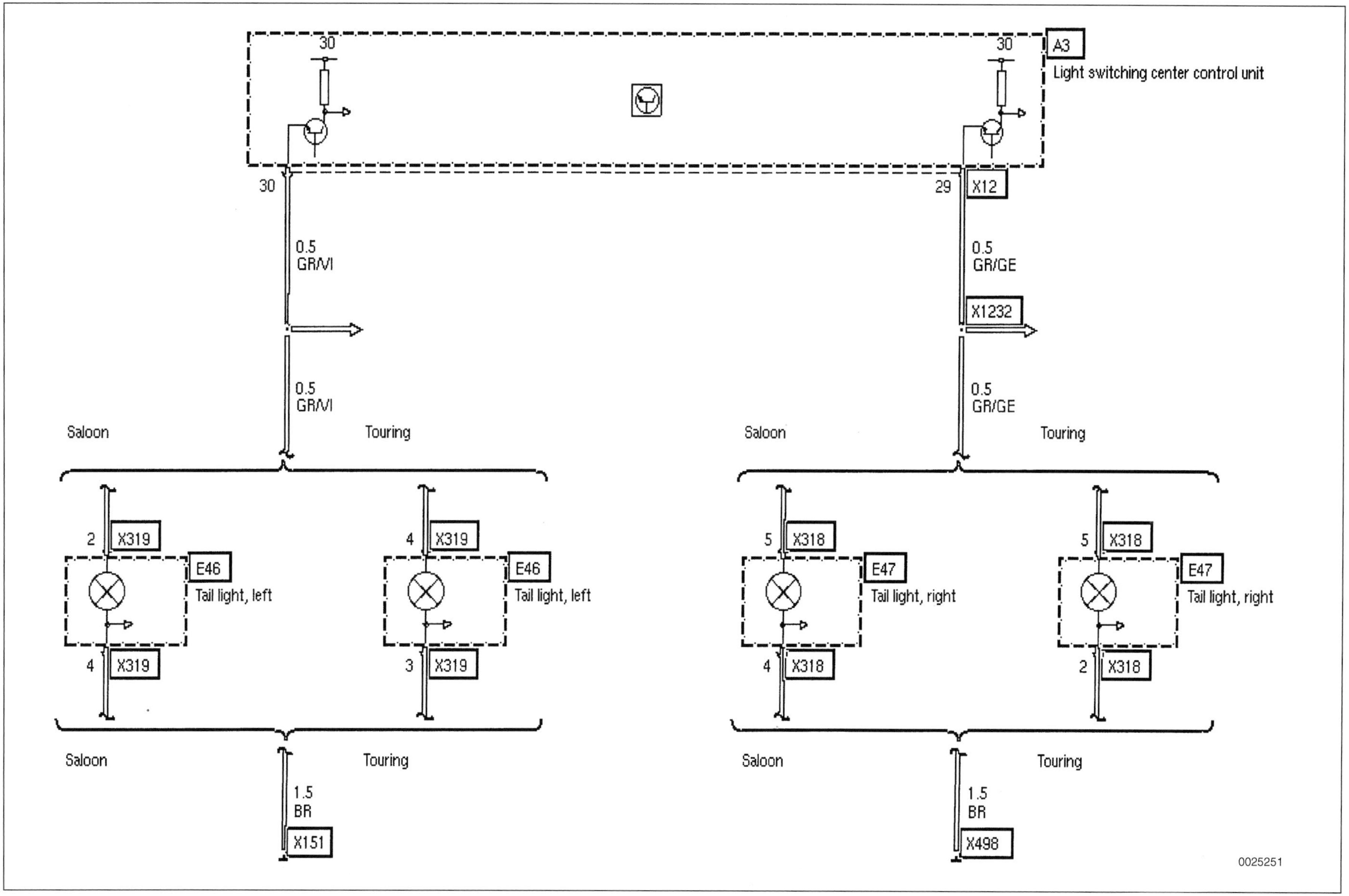

Splice connector (X1218)

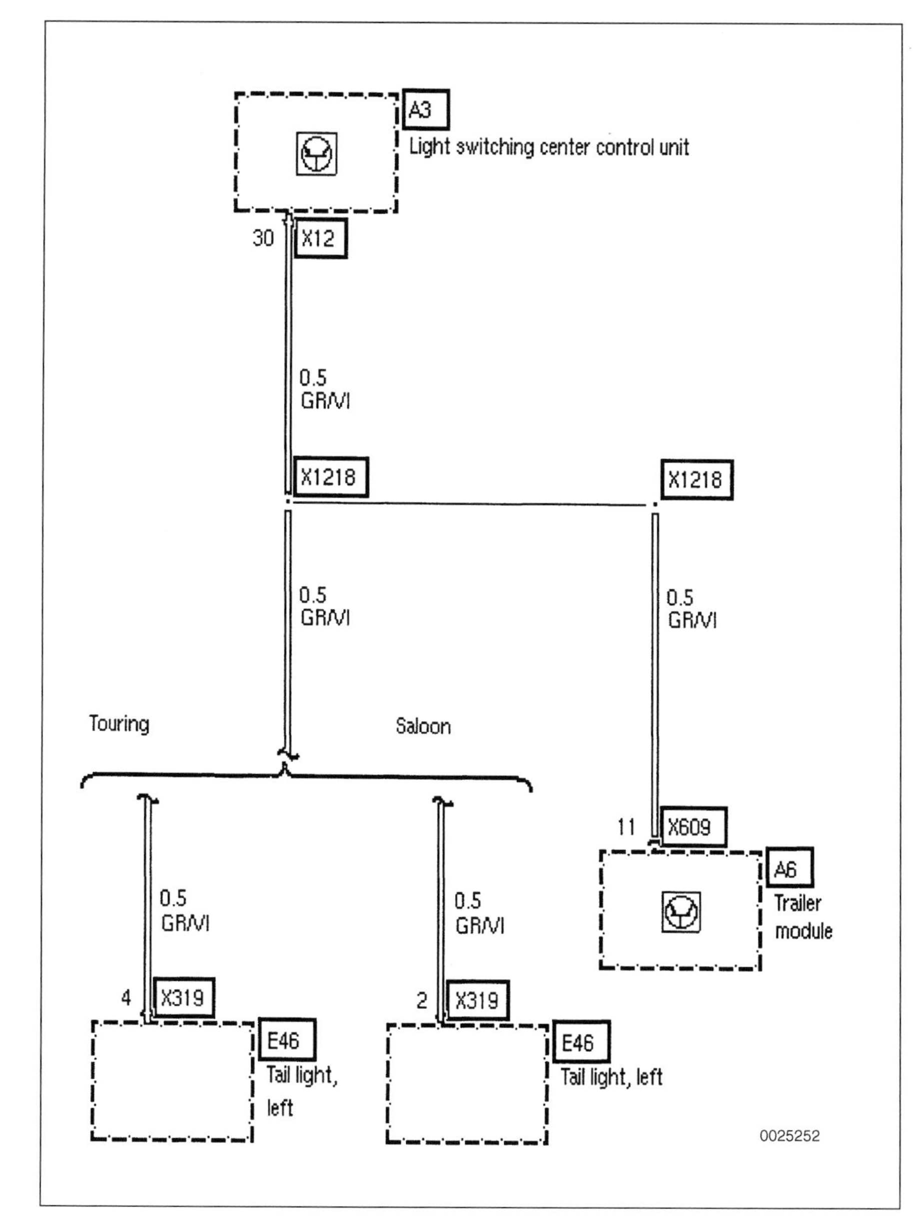

Taillight, left (E46)

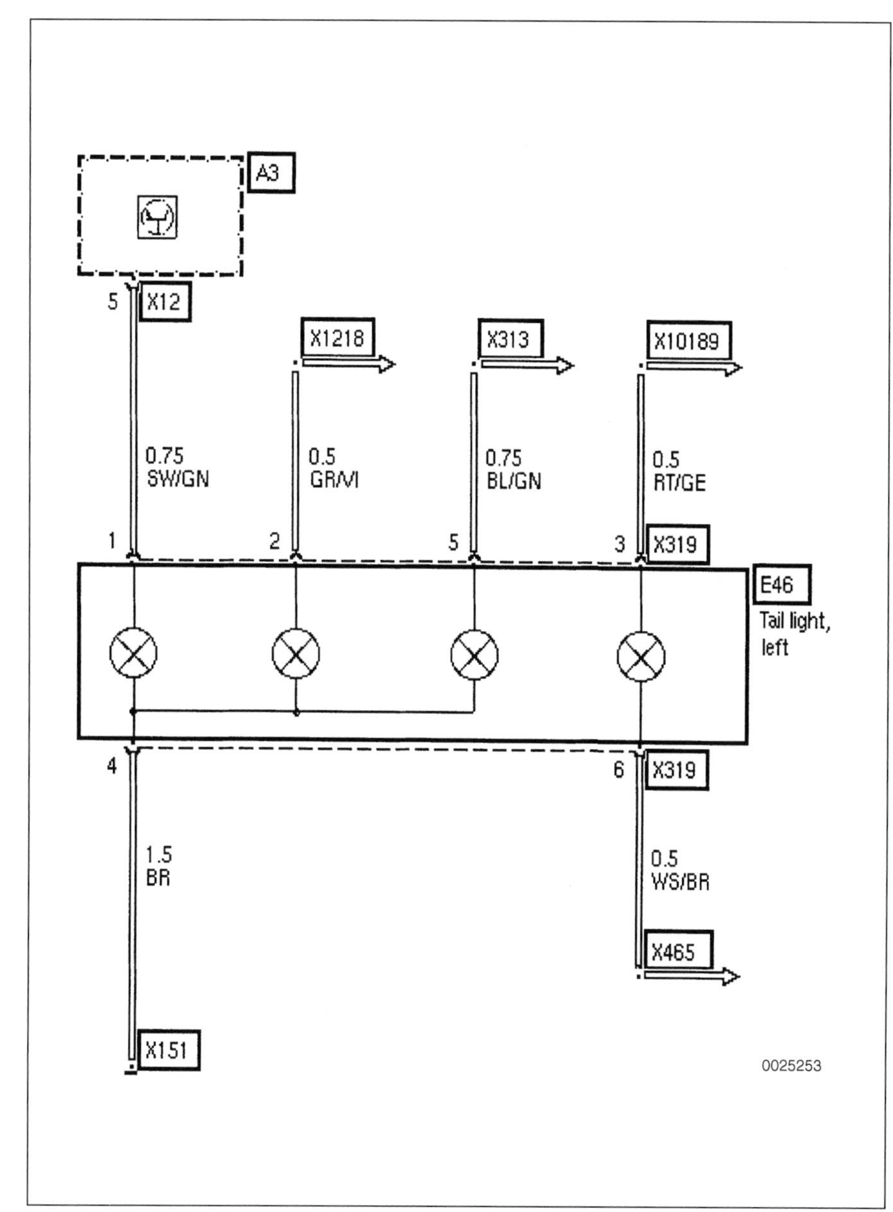

Ground (X151)
1 of 2

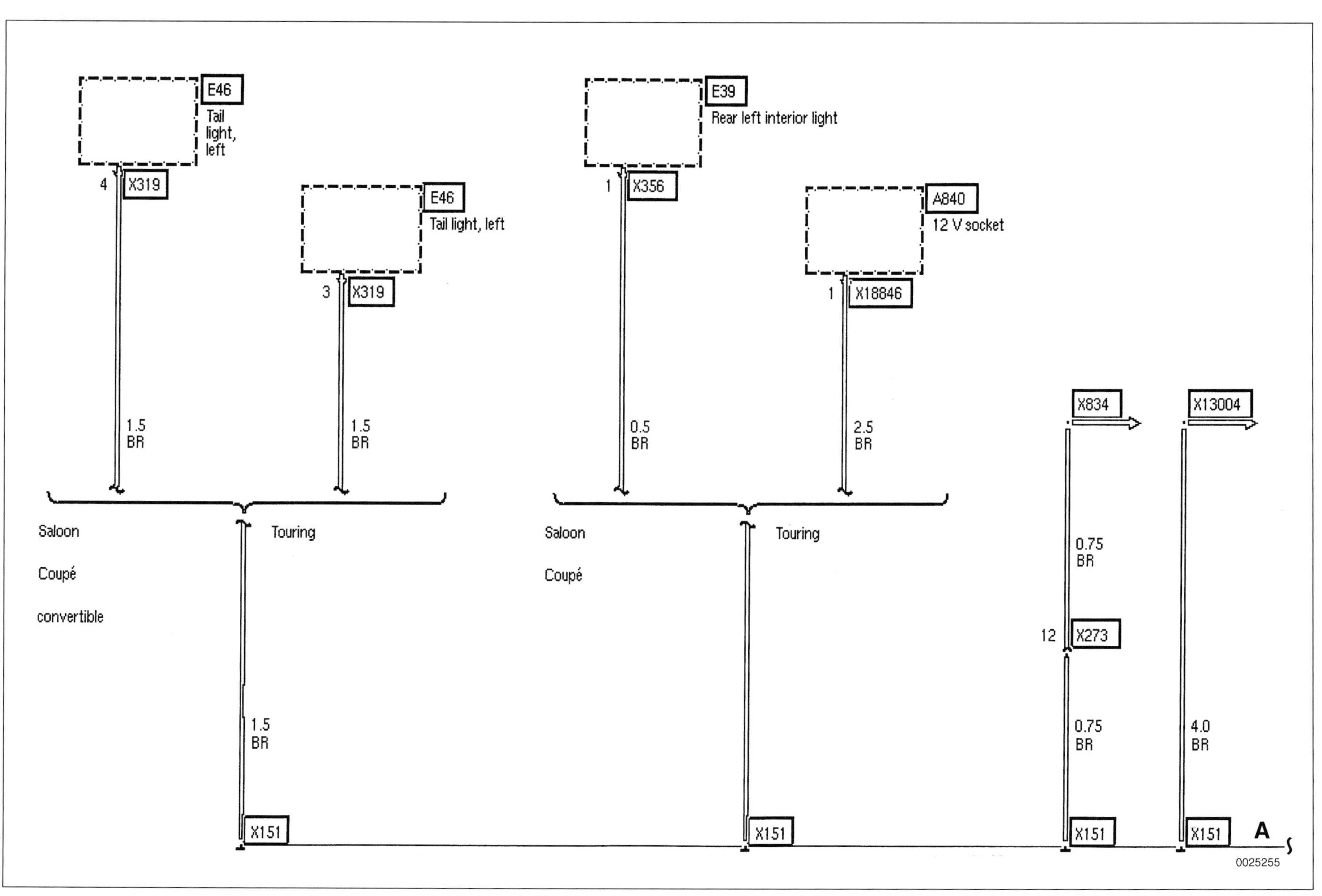

Ground (X151)
2 of 2

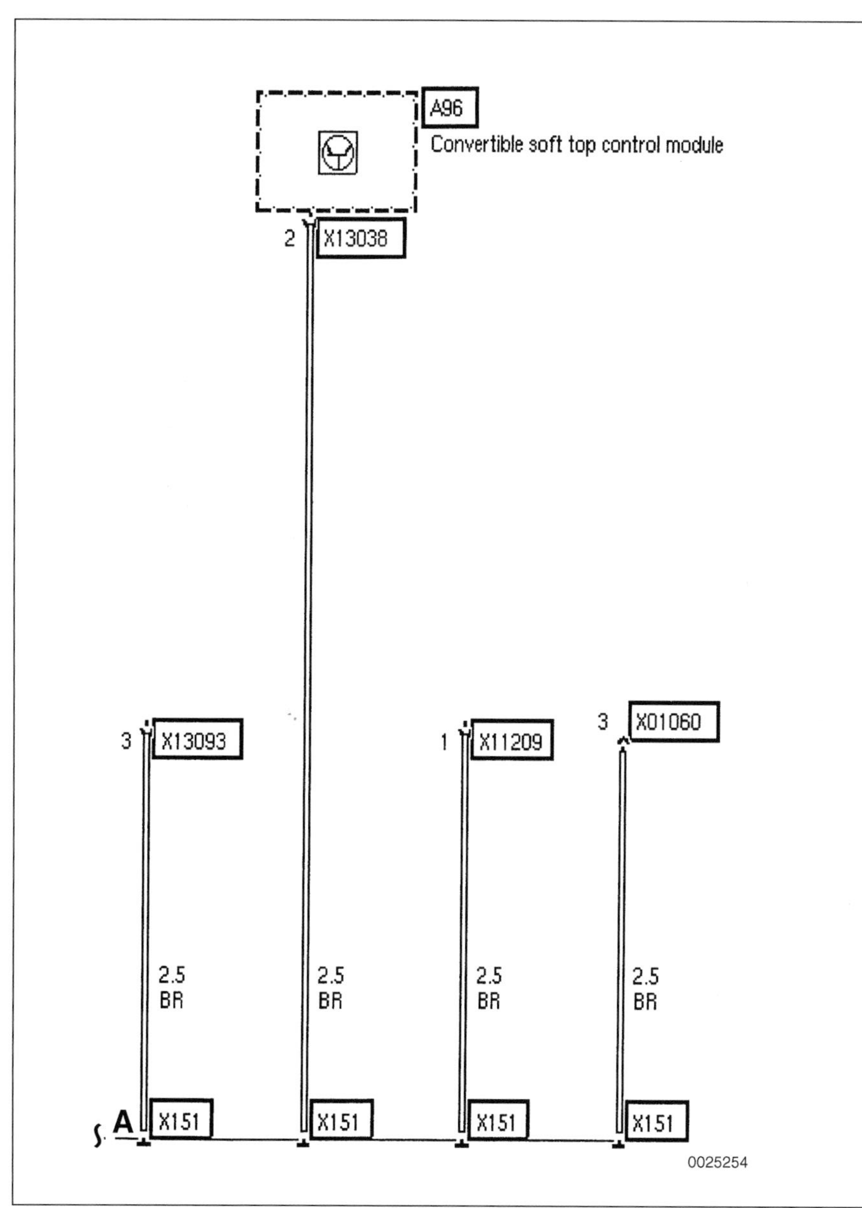

Splice connector (X1232)

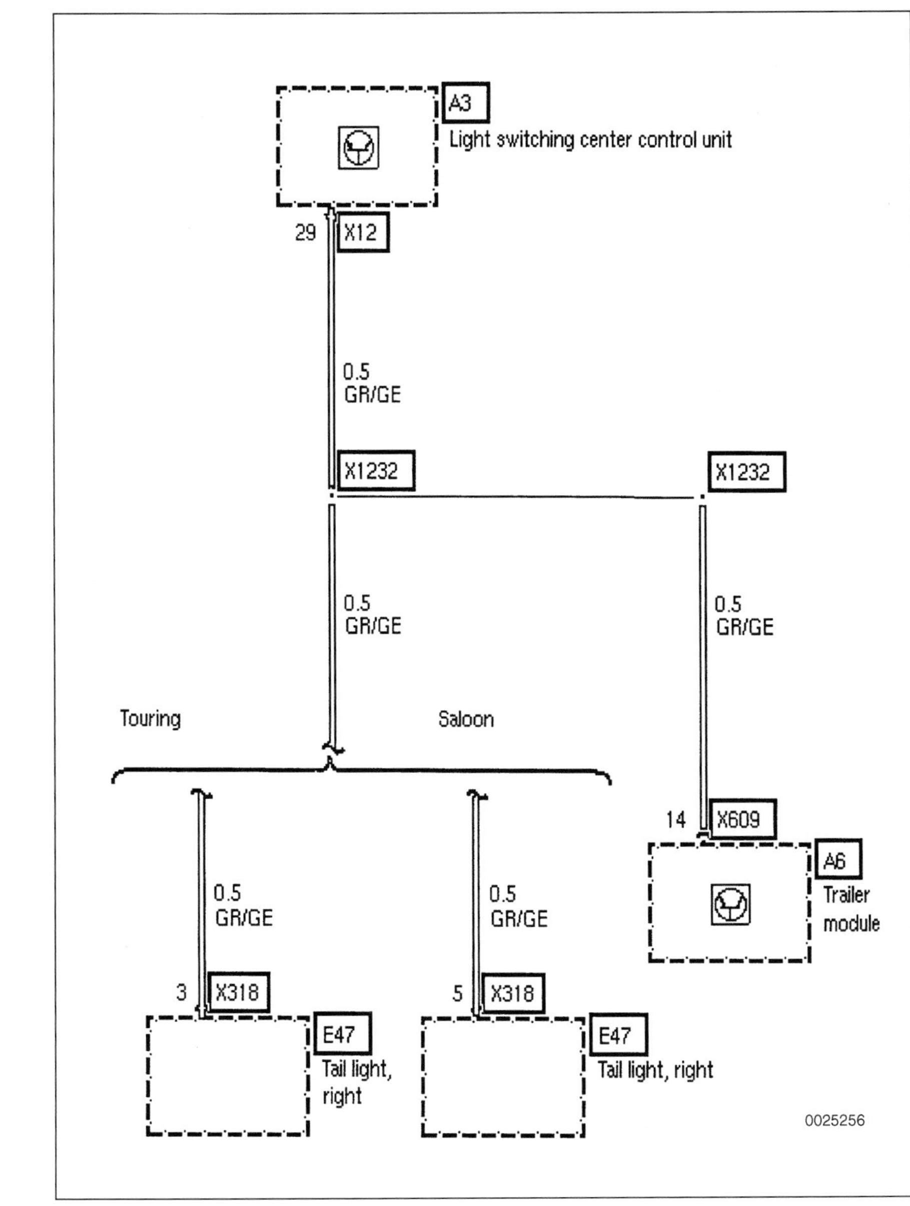

Taillight, right (E47)

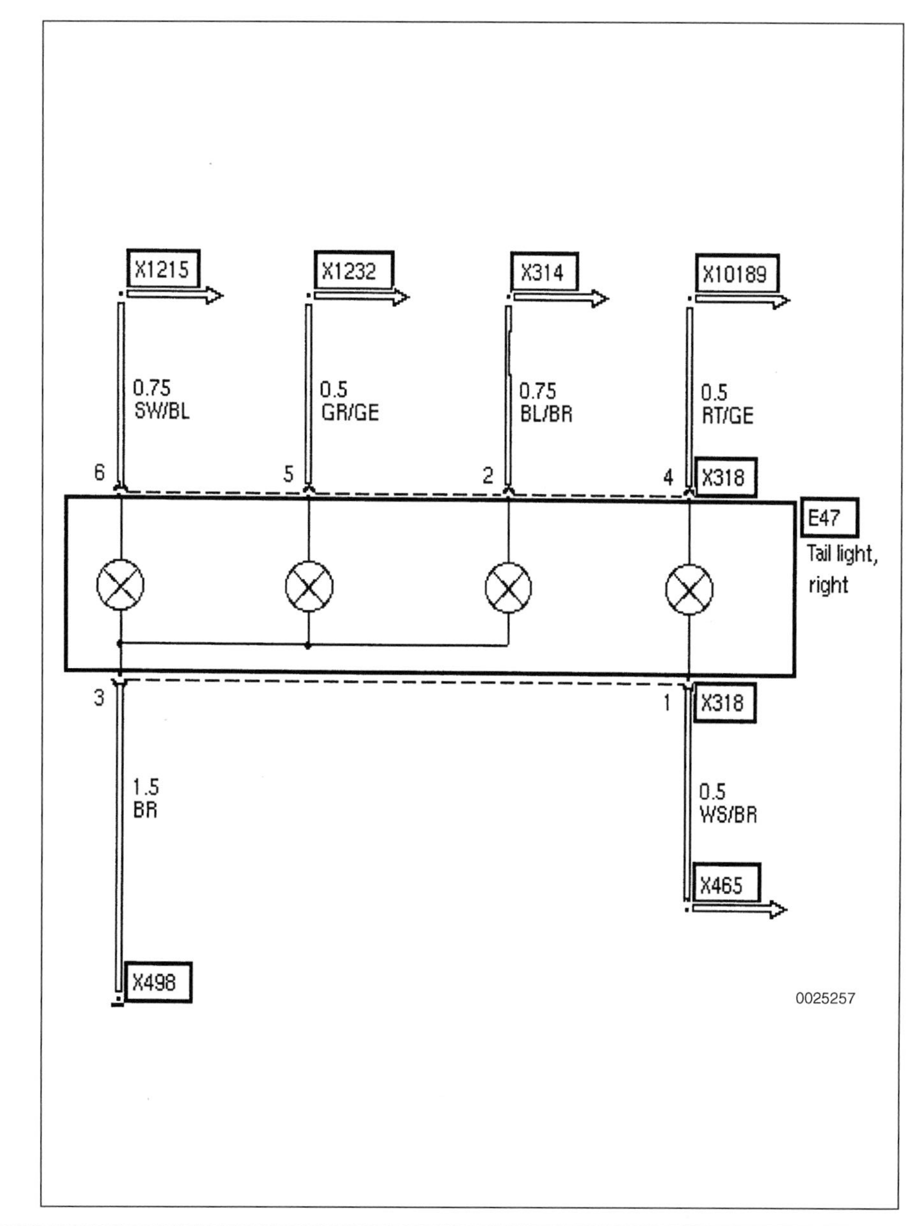

License plate light (E43)

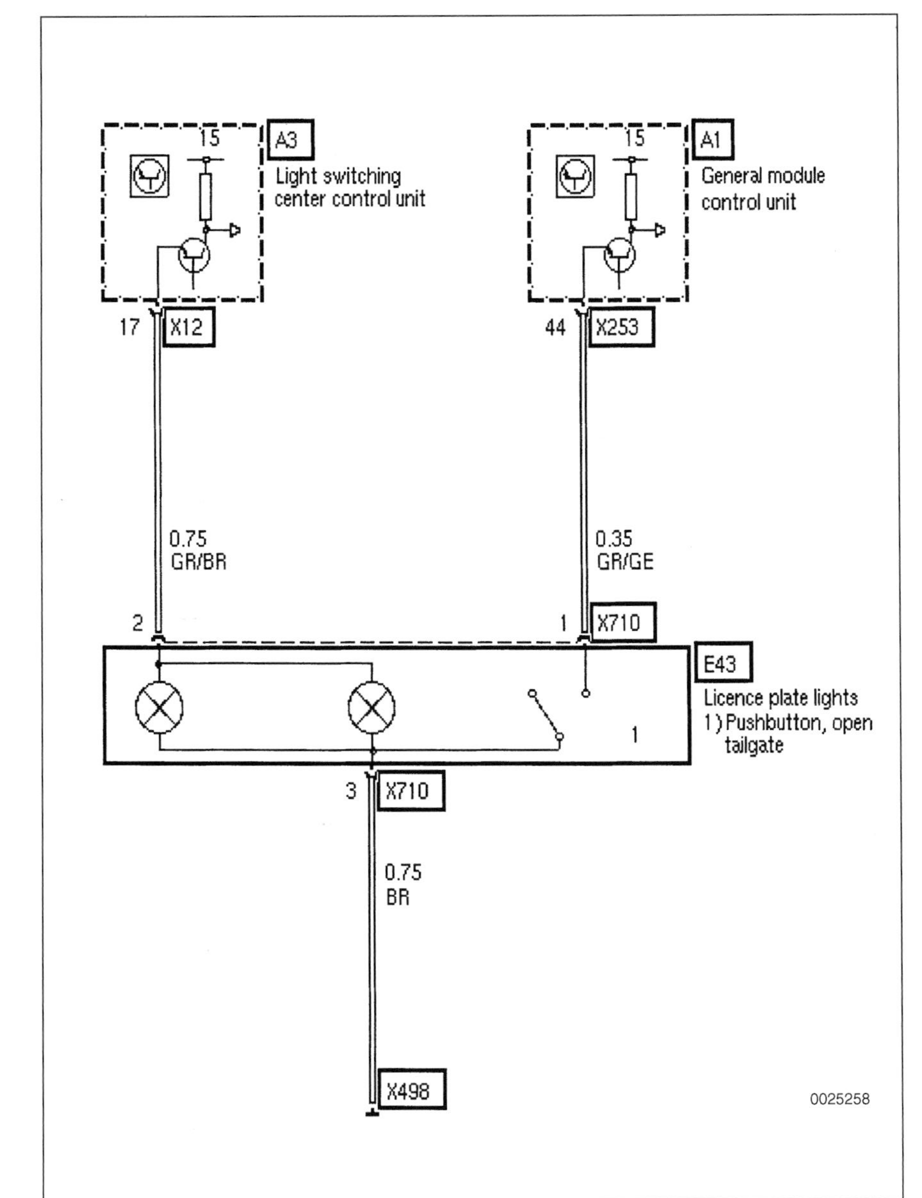

Exterior lights, left side (H7, H9)

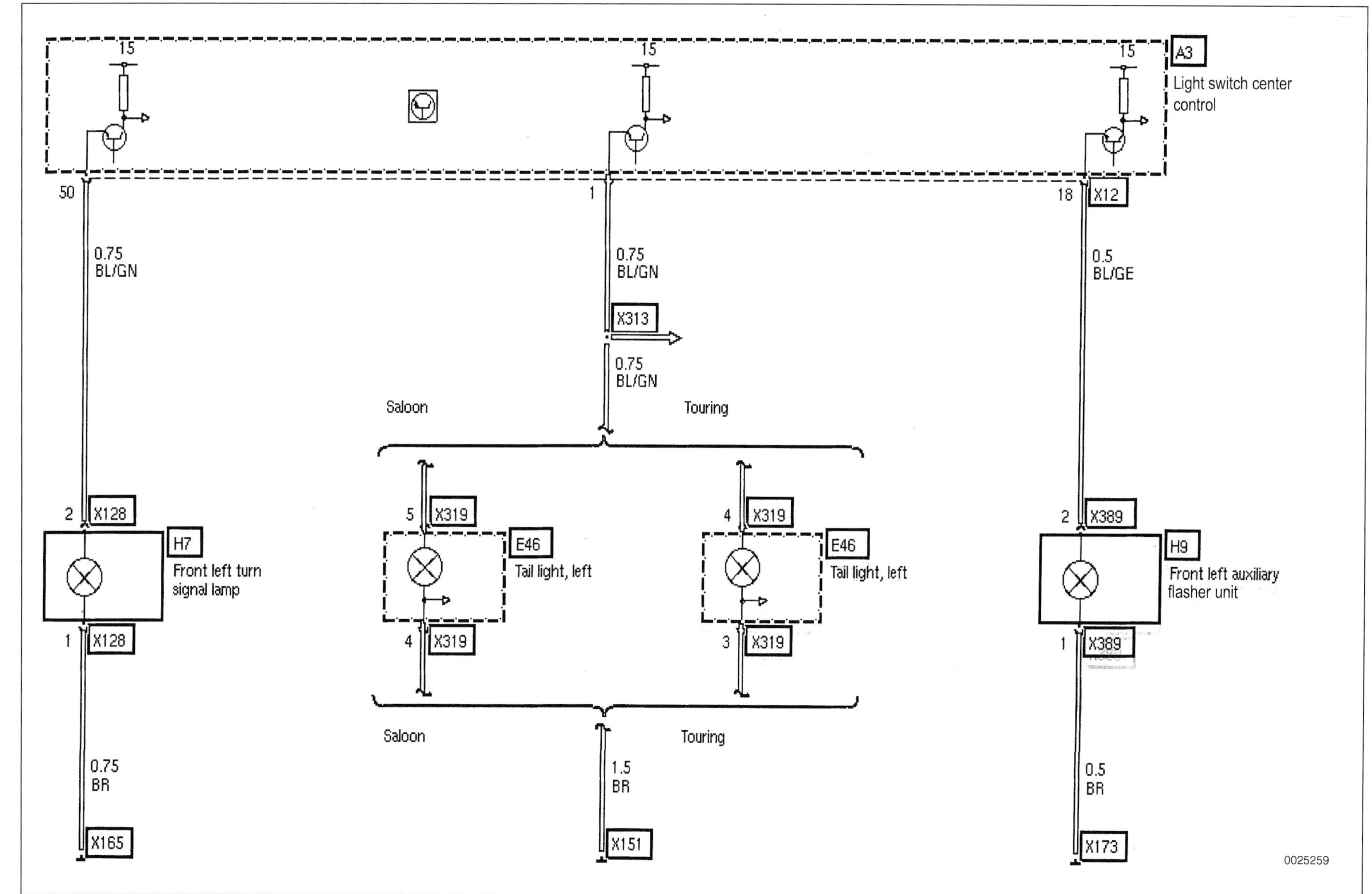

Splice connector (X313)

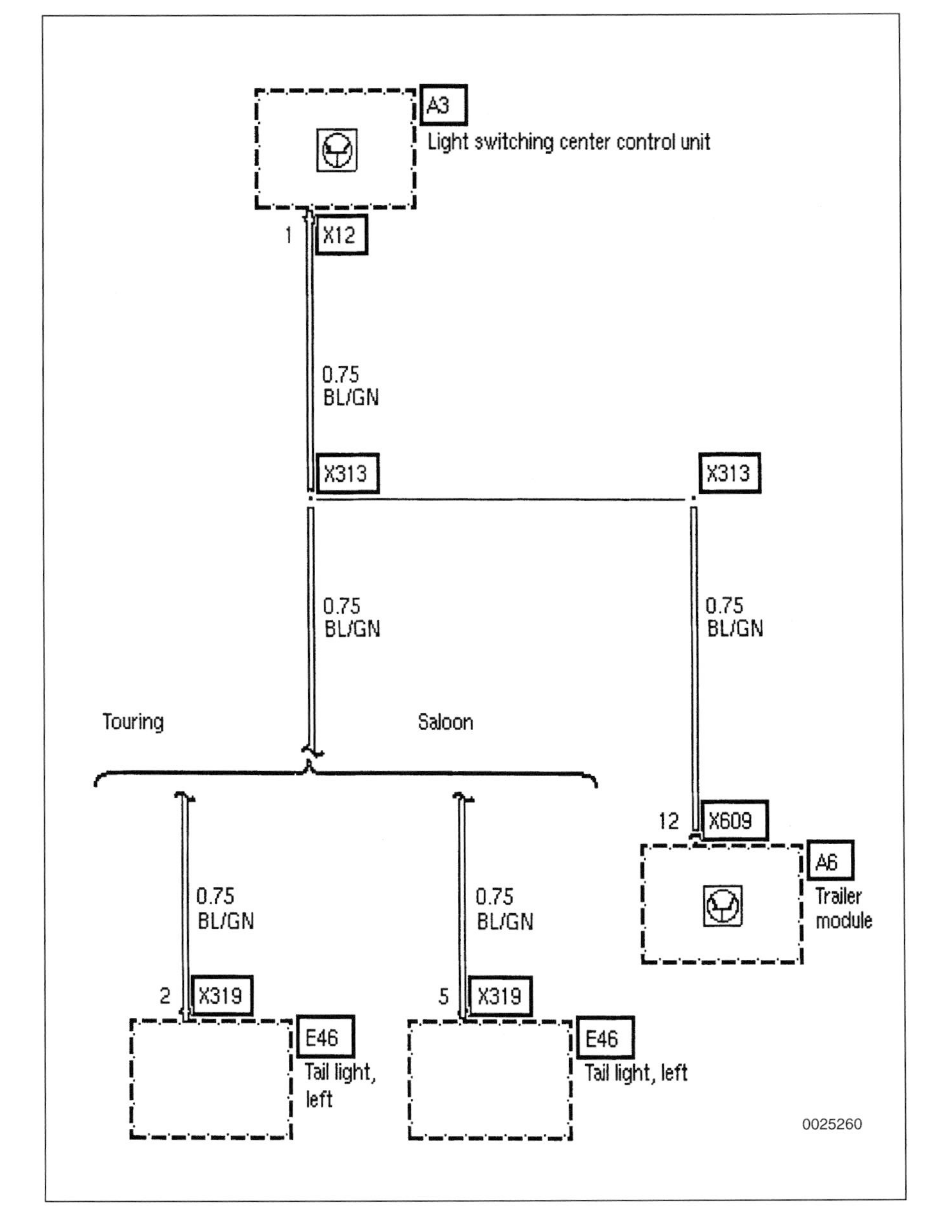

Exterior lights, right side (H4, H8)

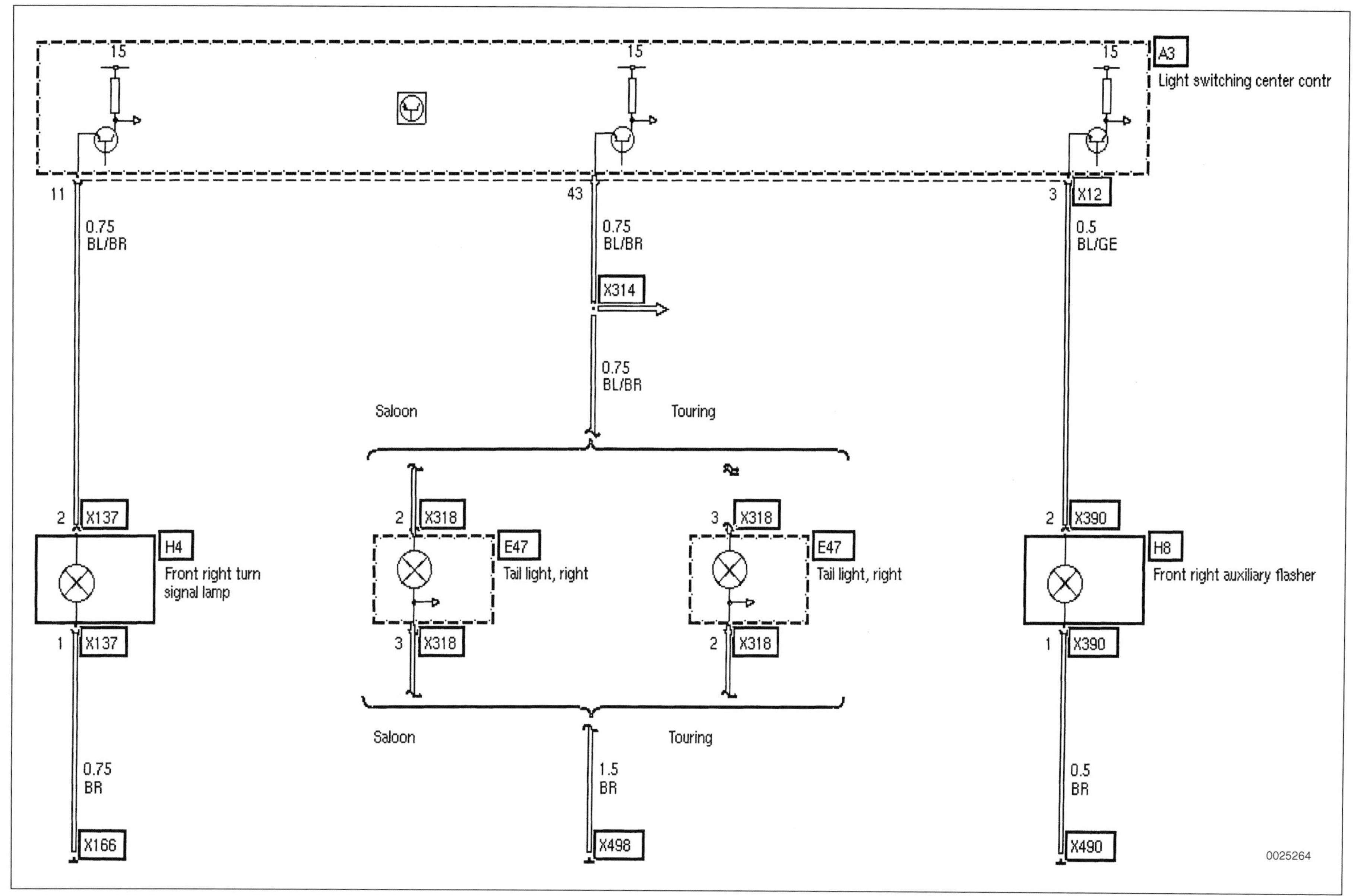

Splice connector (X314)

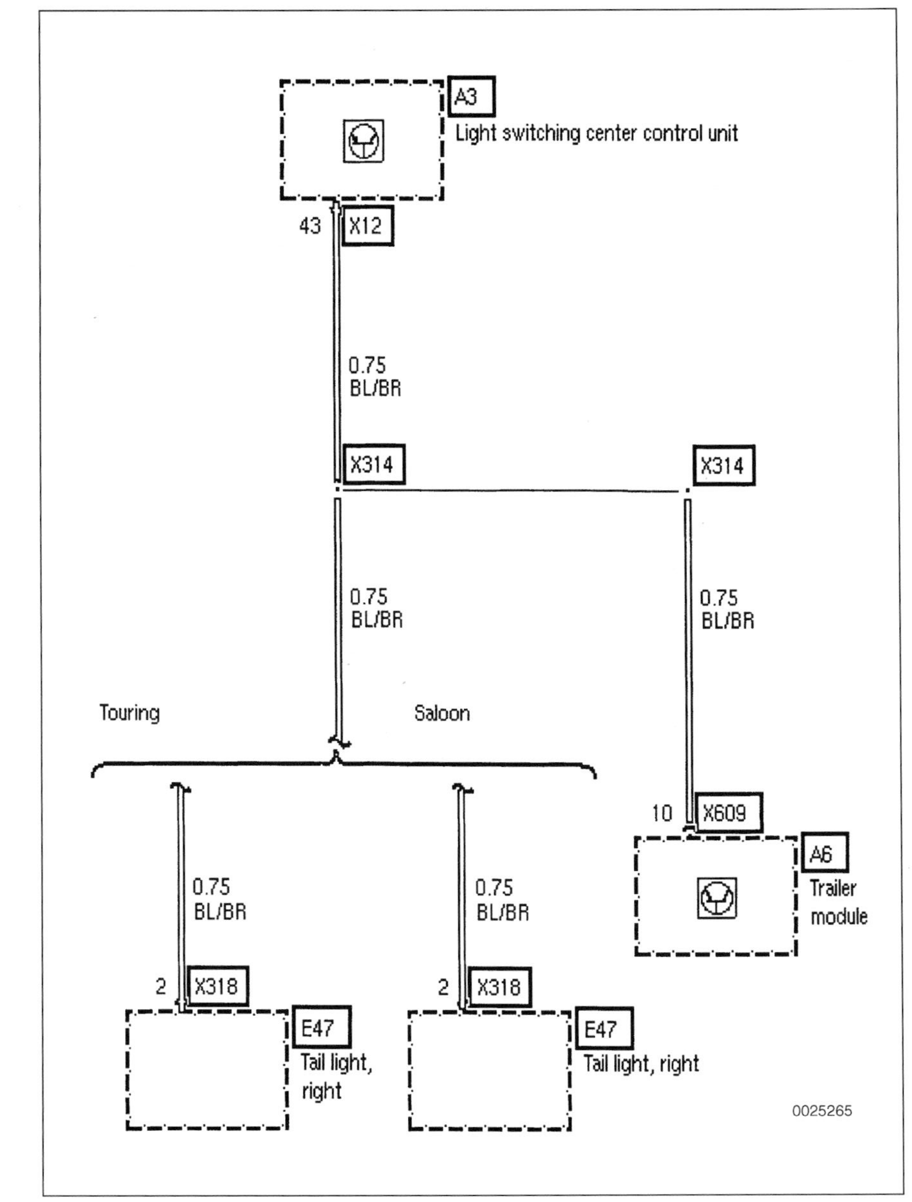

Ground (X490)
1 of 2

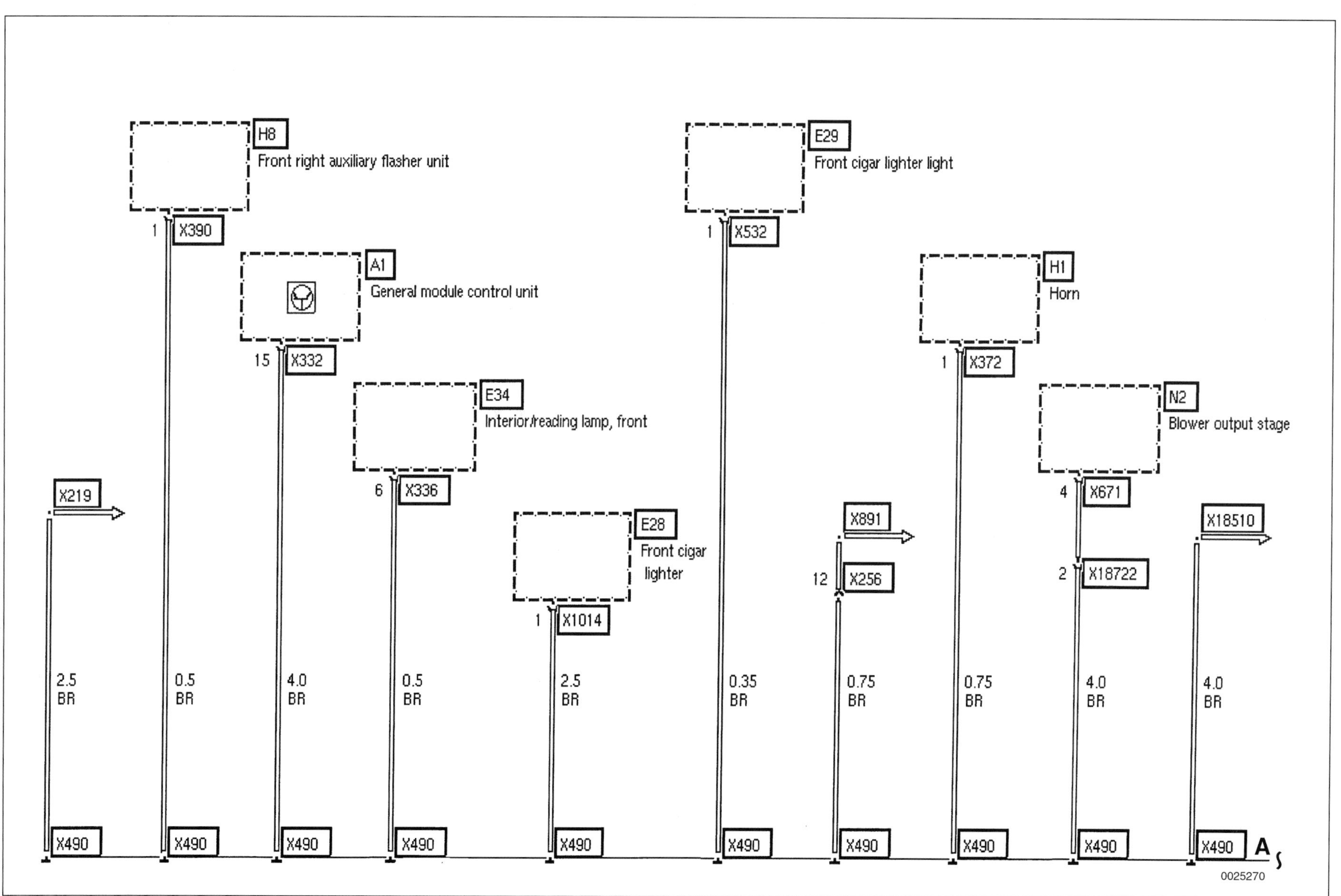

Ground (X490)
2 of 2

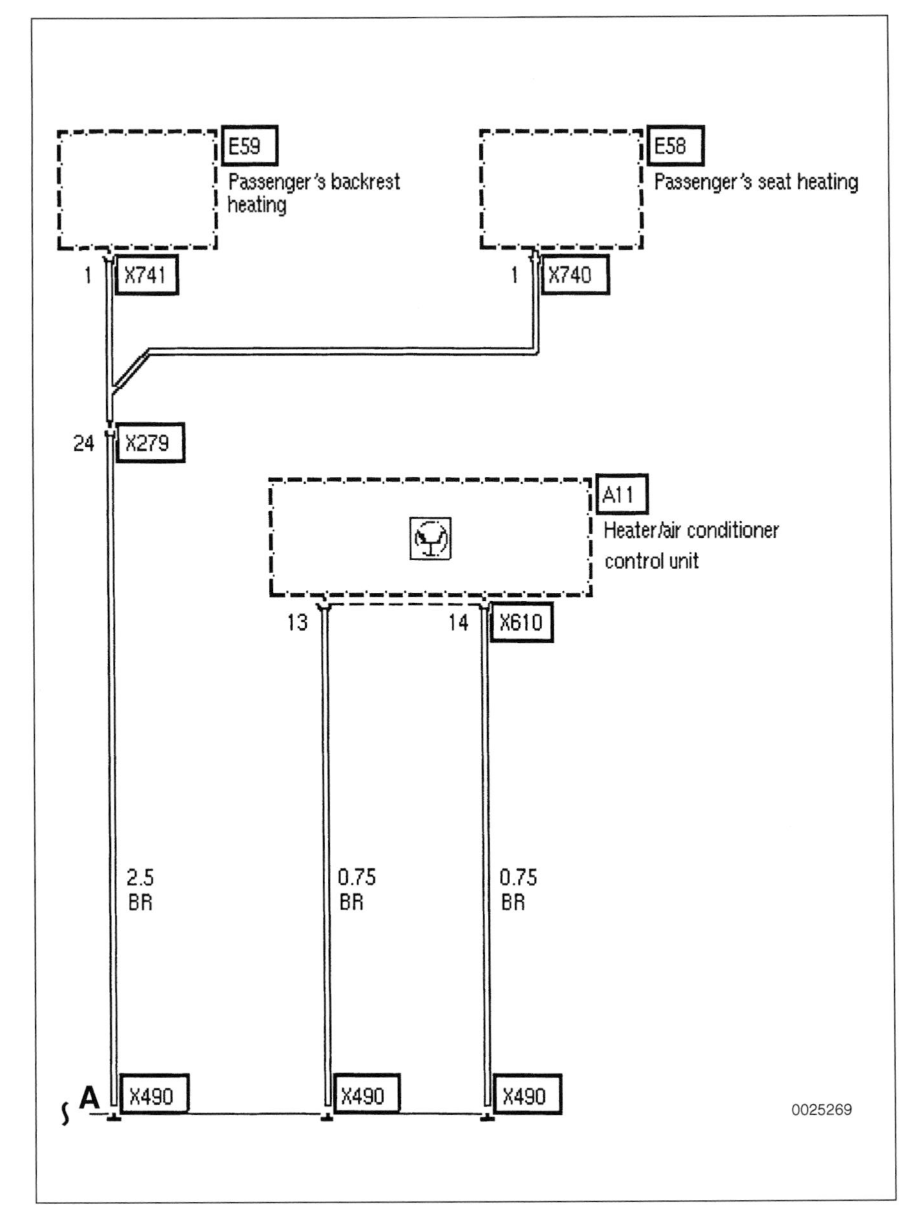

Headlight, low beams (E13, E14)

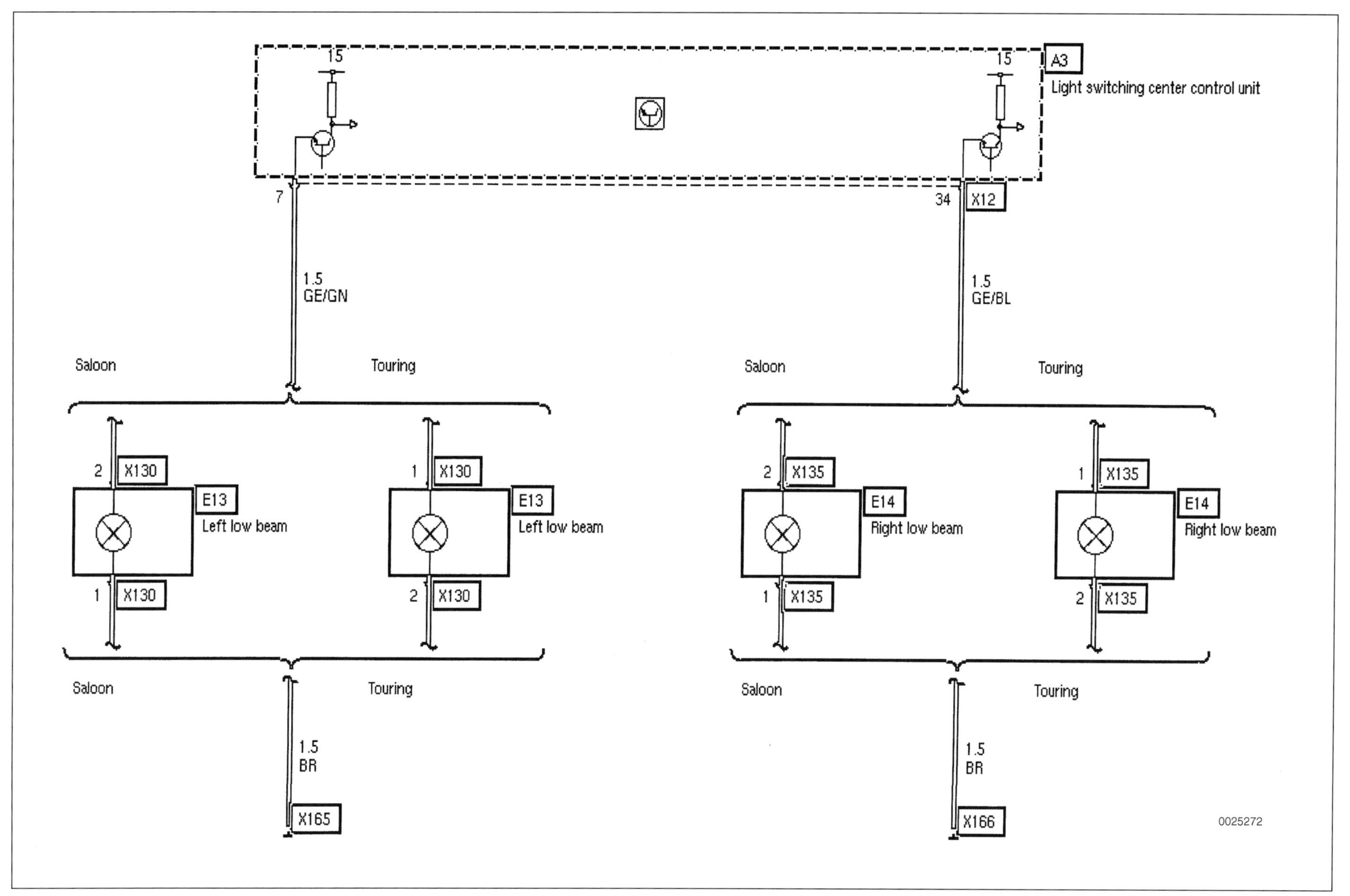

Turn signal/low beam switch (S7)

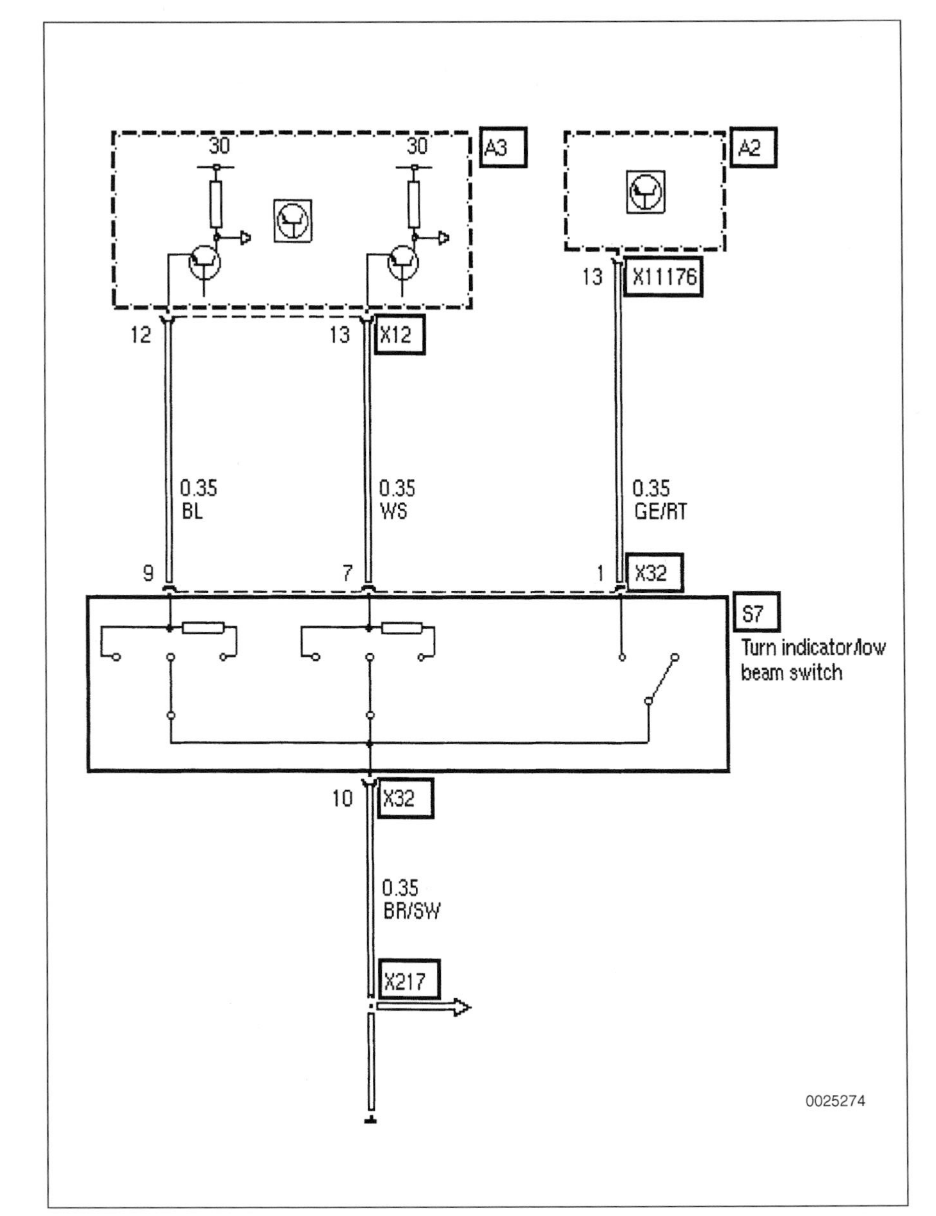

Headlight, high beams (E11, E12)

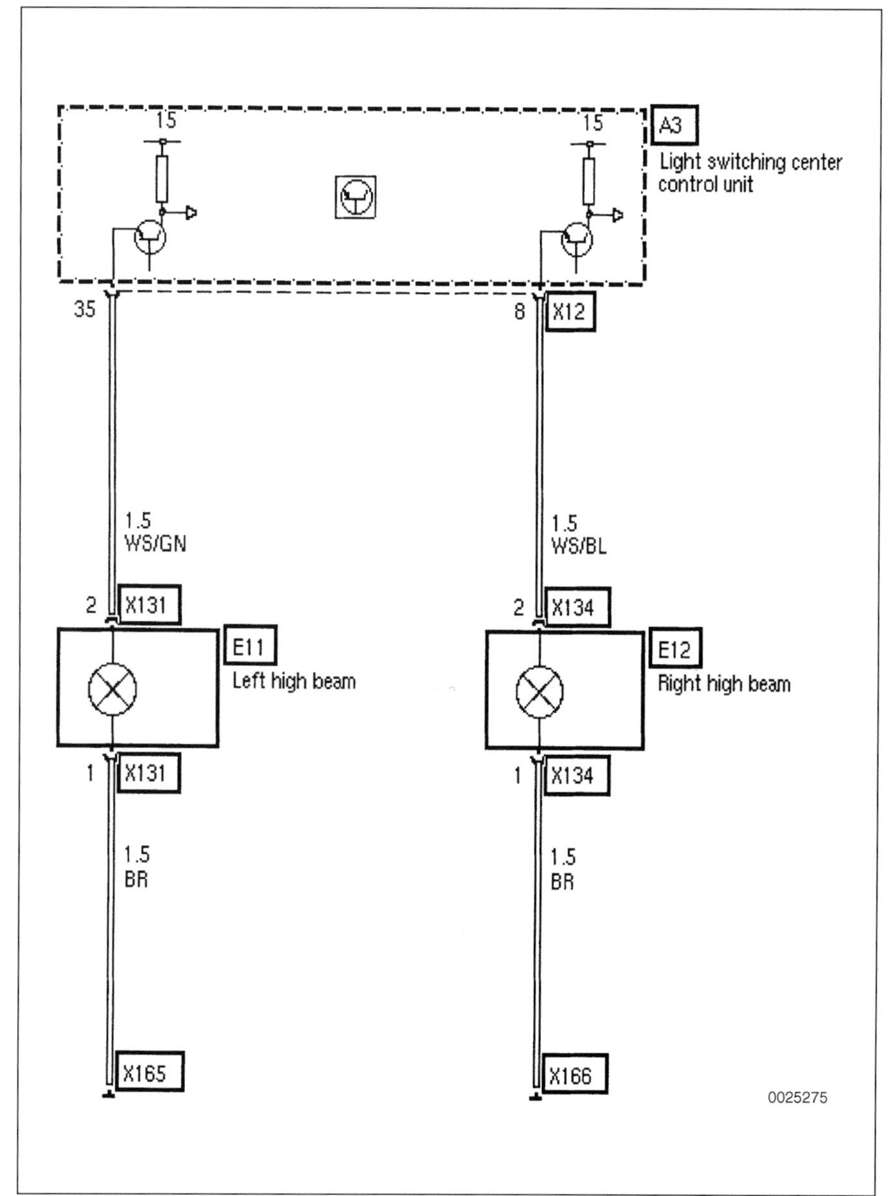

This page left intentionally blank

Brake lights

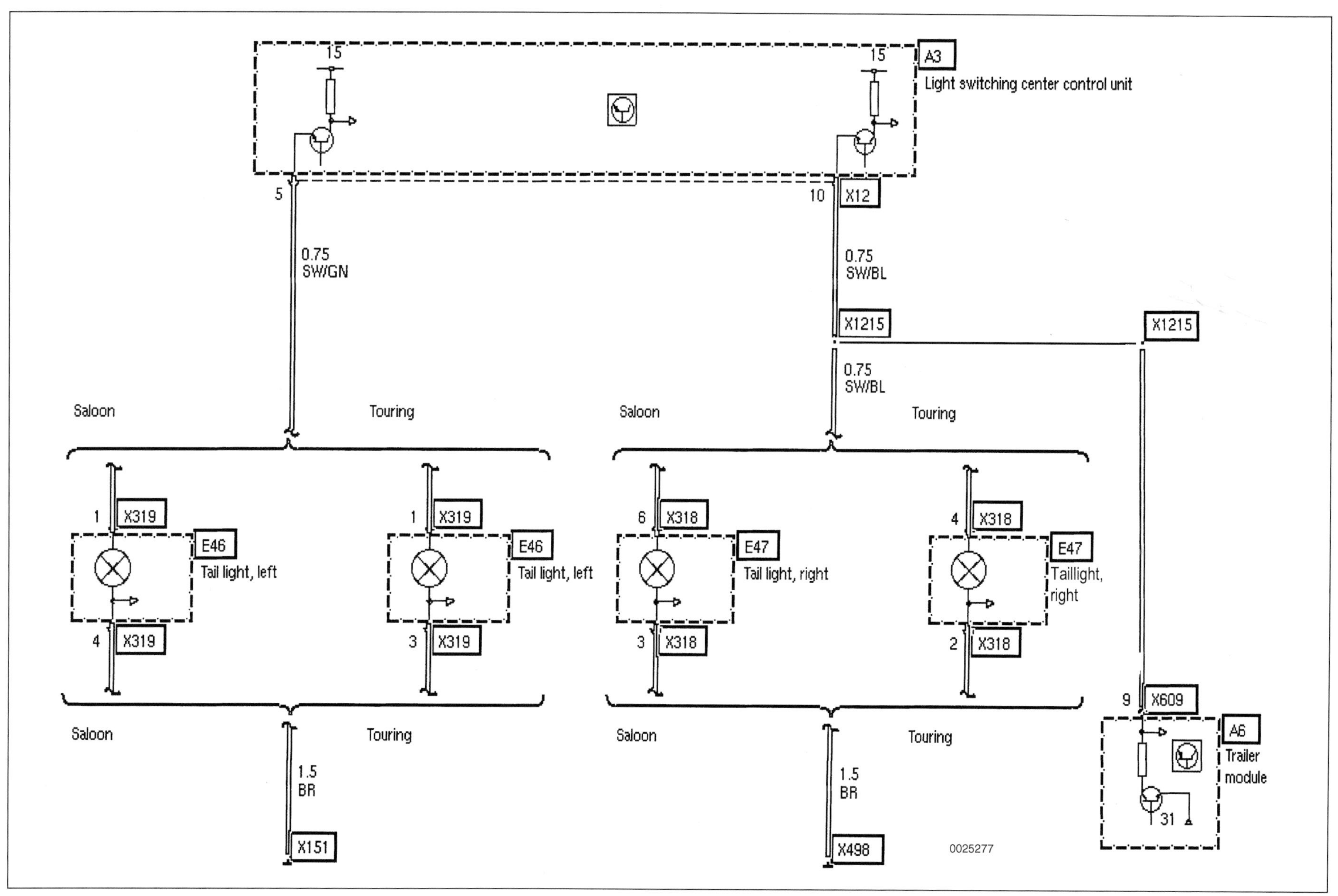

Splice connector (X1215)

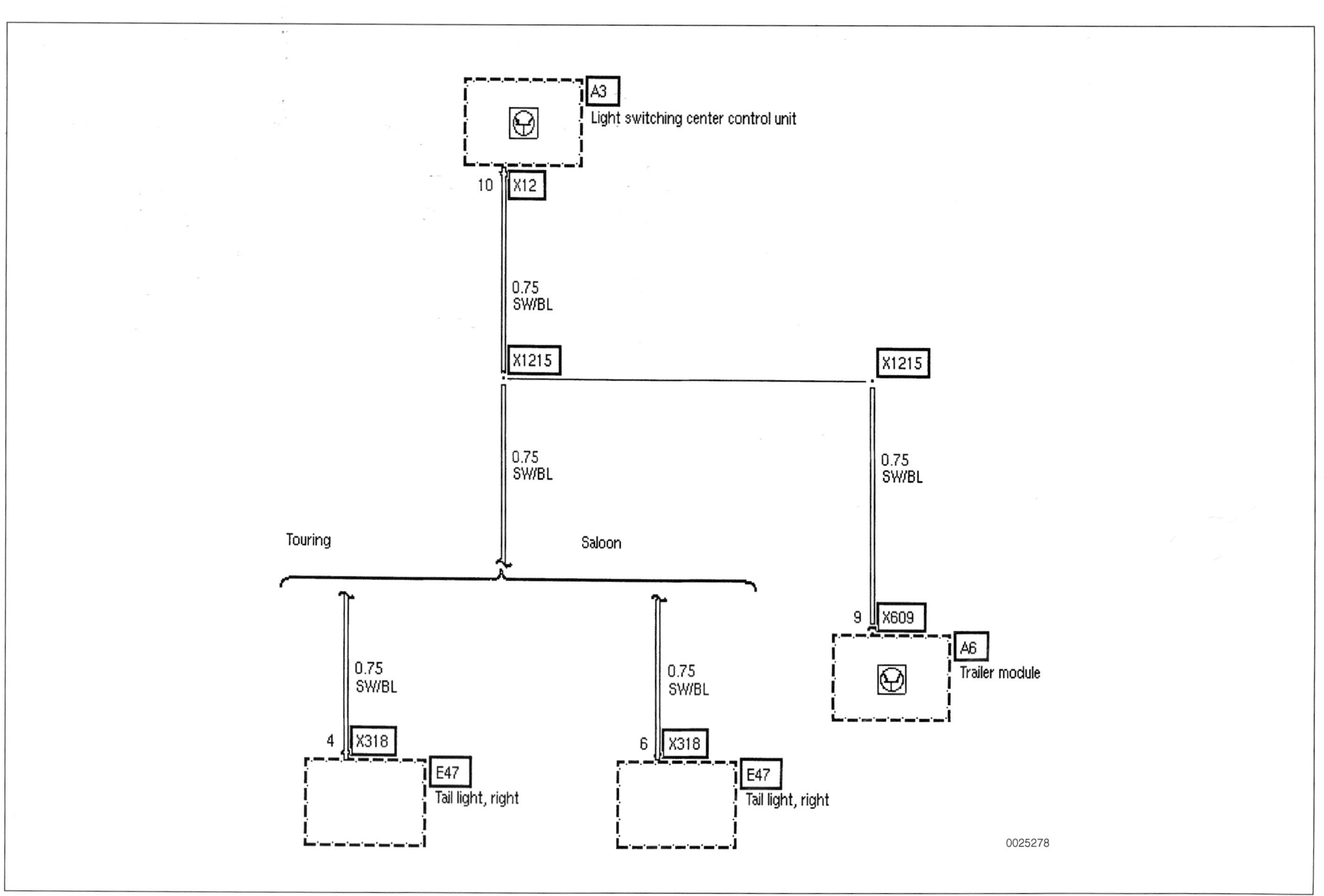

Center brake light (H34)

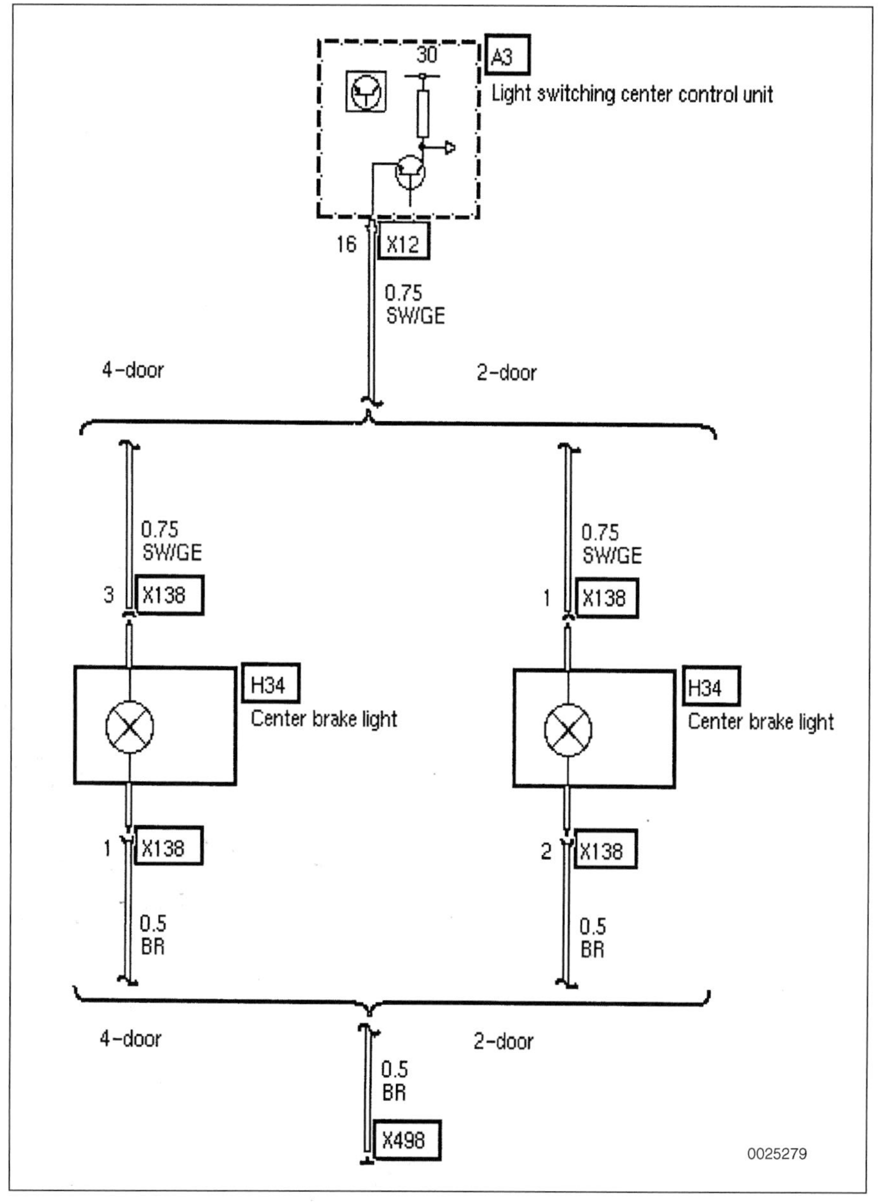

Hazard warning/central locking switch (S18)

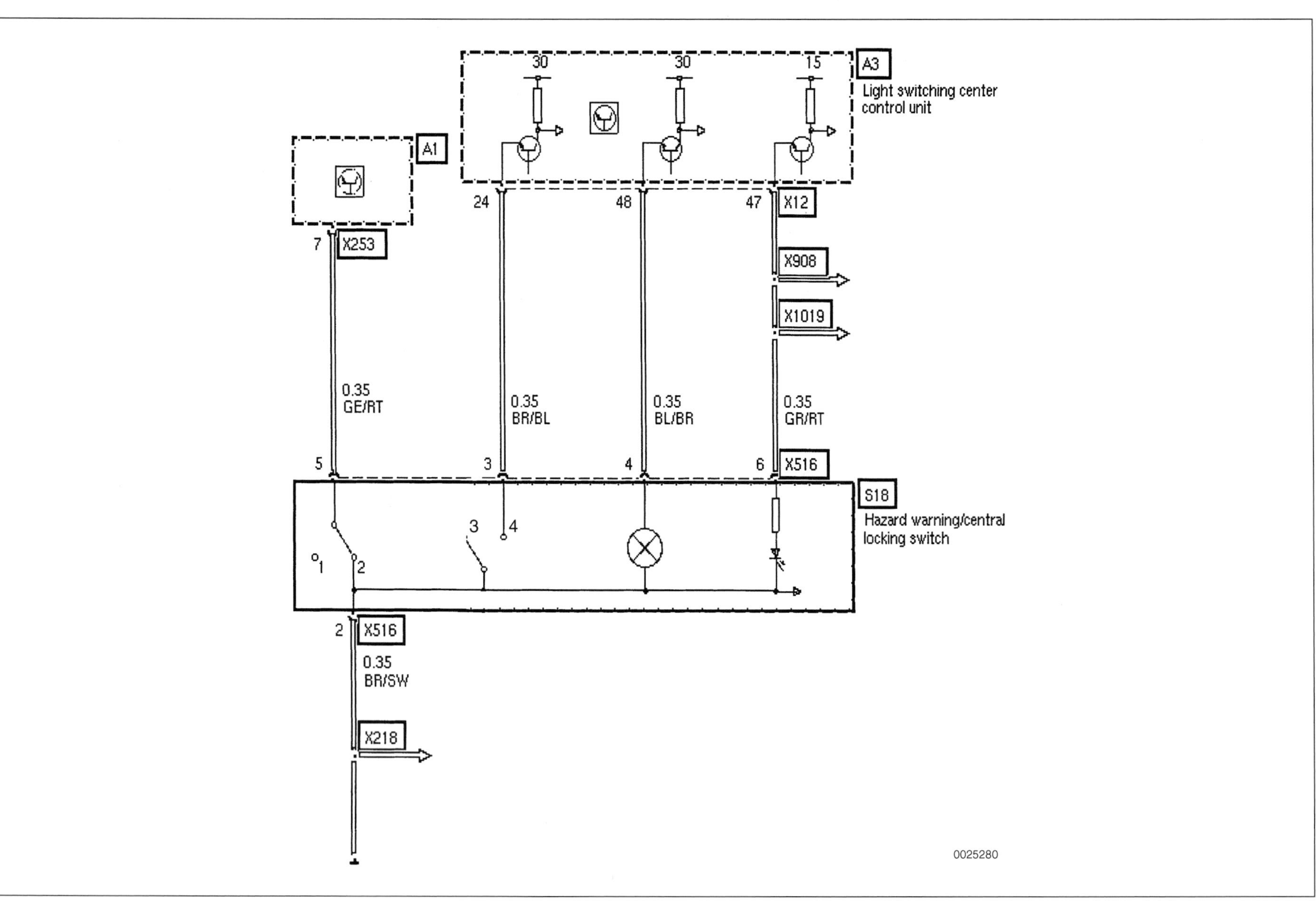

Foglights (E26, E27)

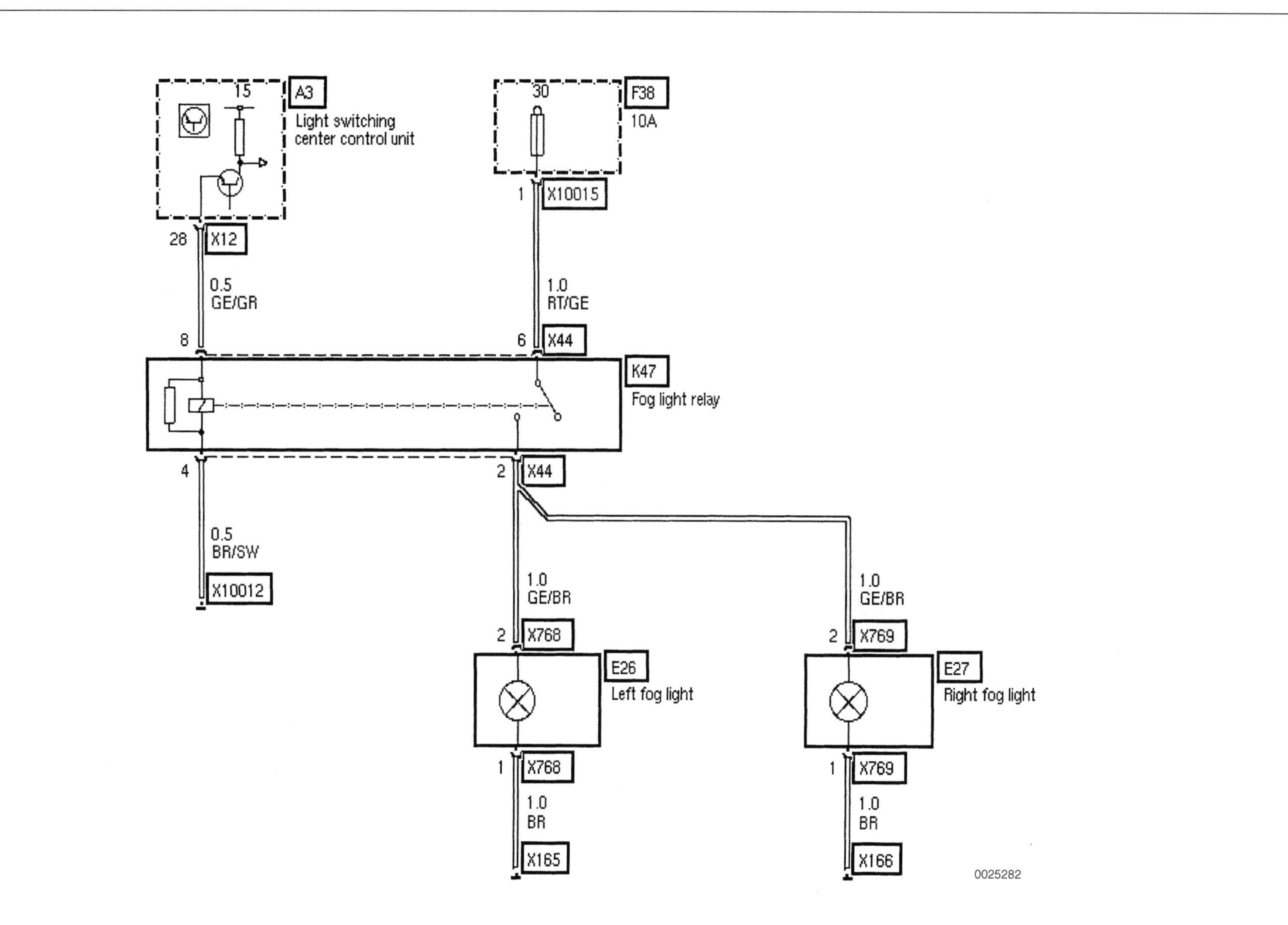

Fuse 38 (F38)

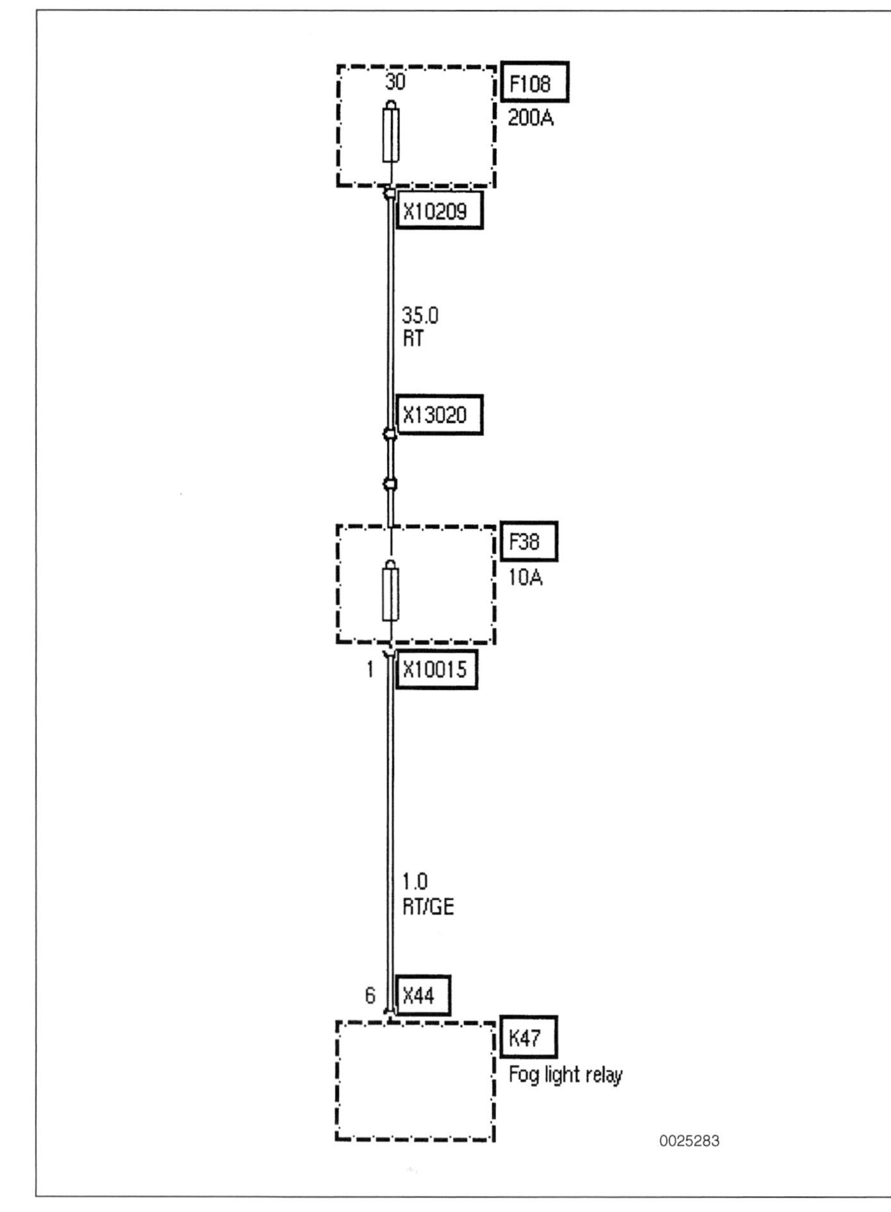
30
F108
200A
X10209
35.0
RT
X13020
F38
10A
1
X10015
1.0
RT/GE
6
X44
K47
Fog light relay
0025283

Foglight, left rear

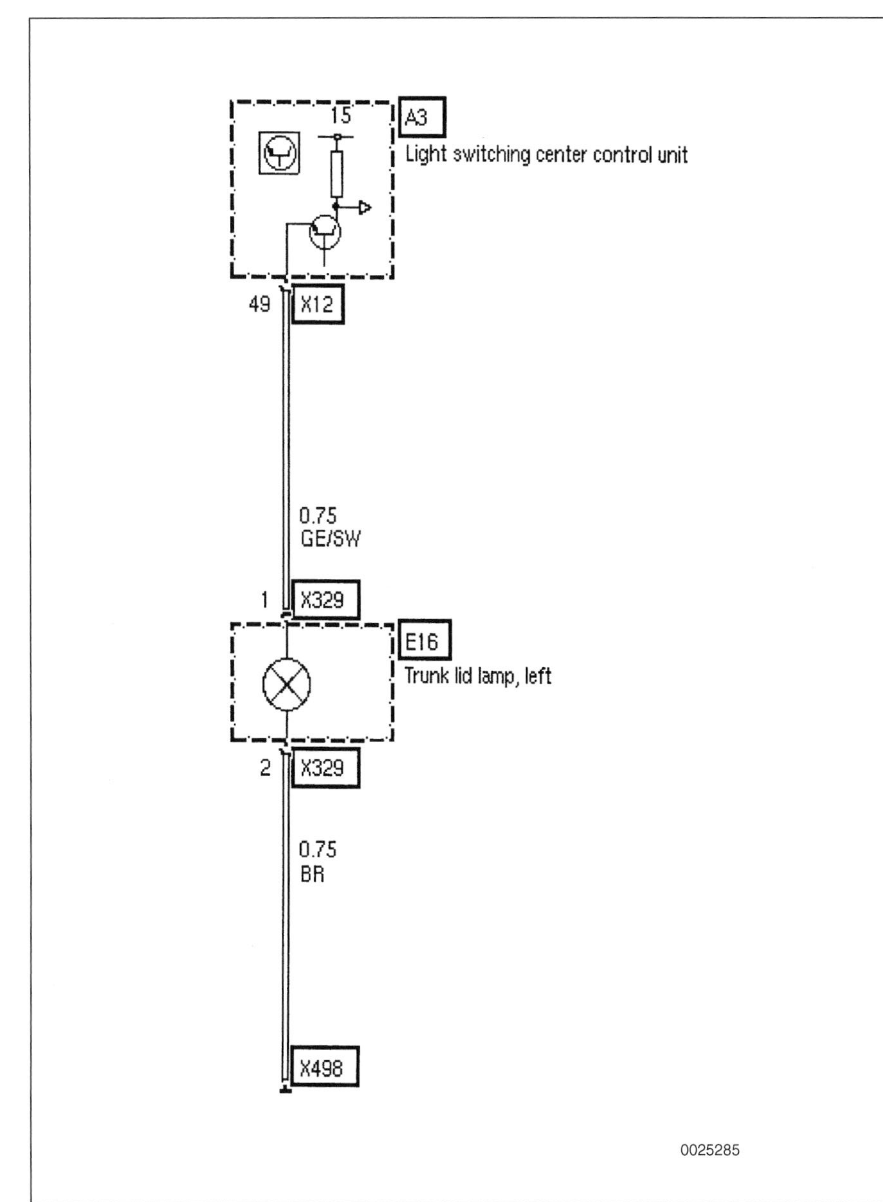

Back-up lights switch

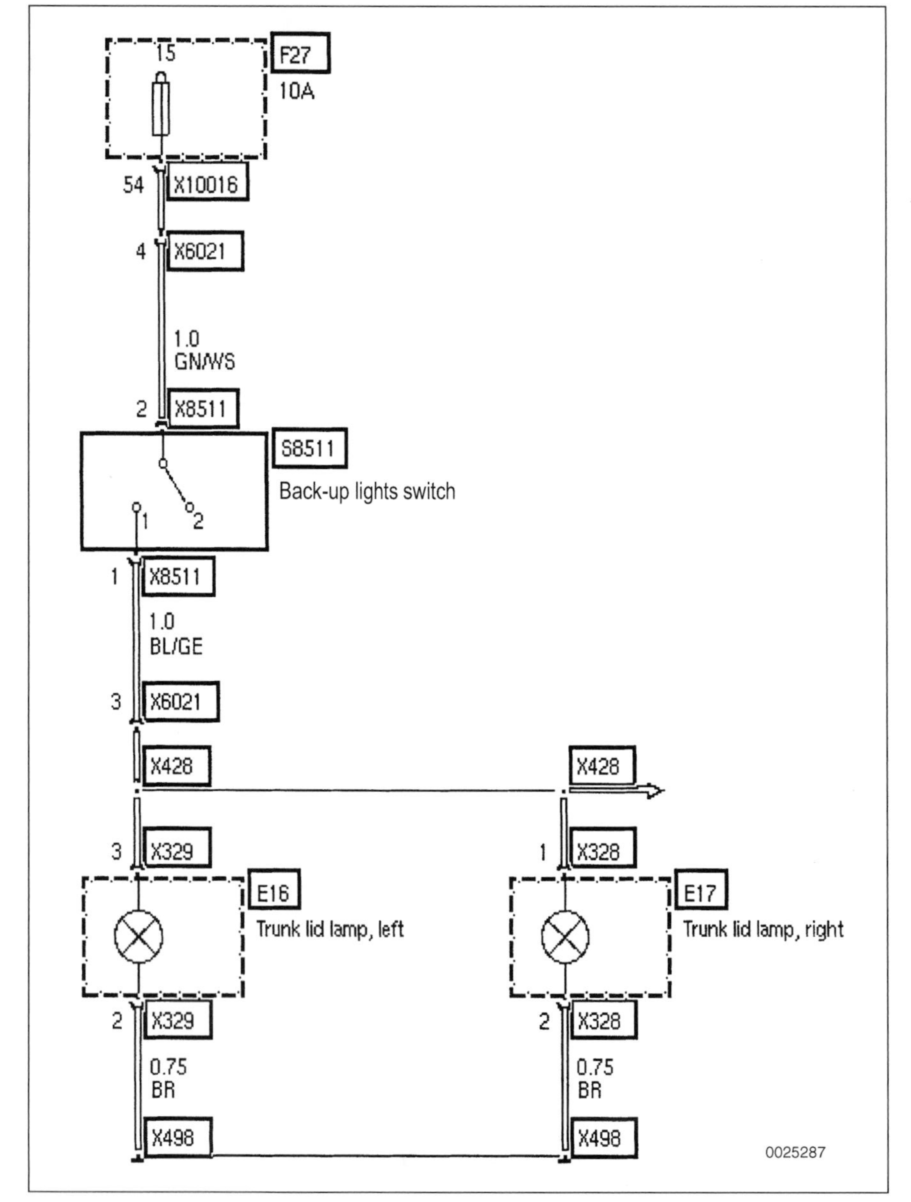

Oddments compartments (A838, A839)

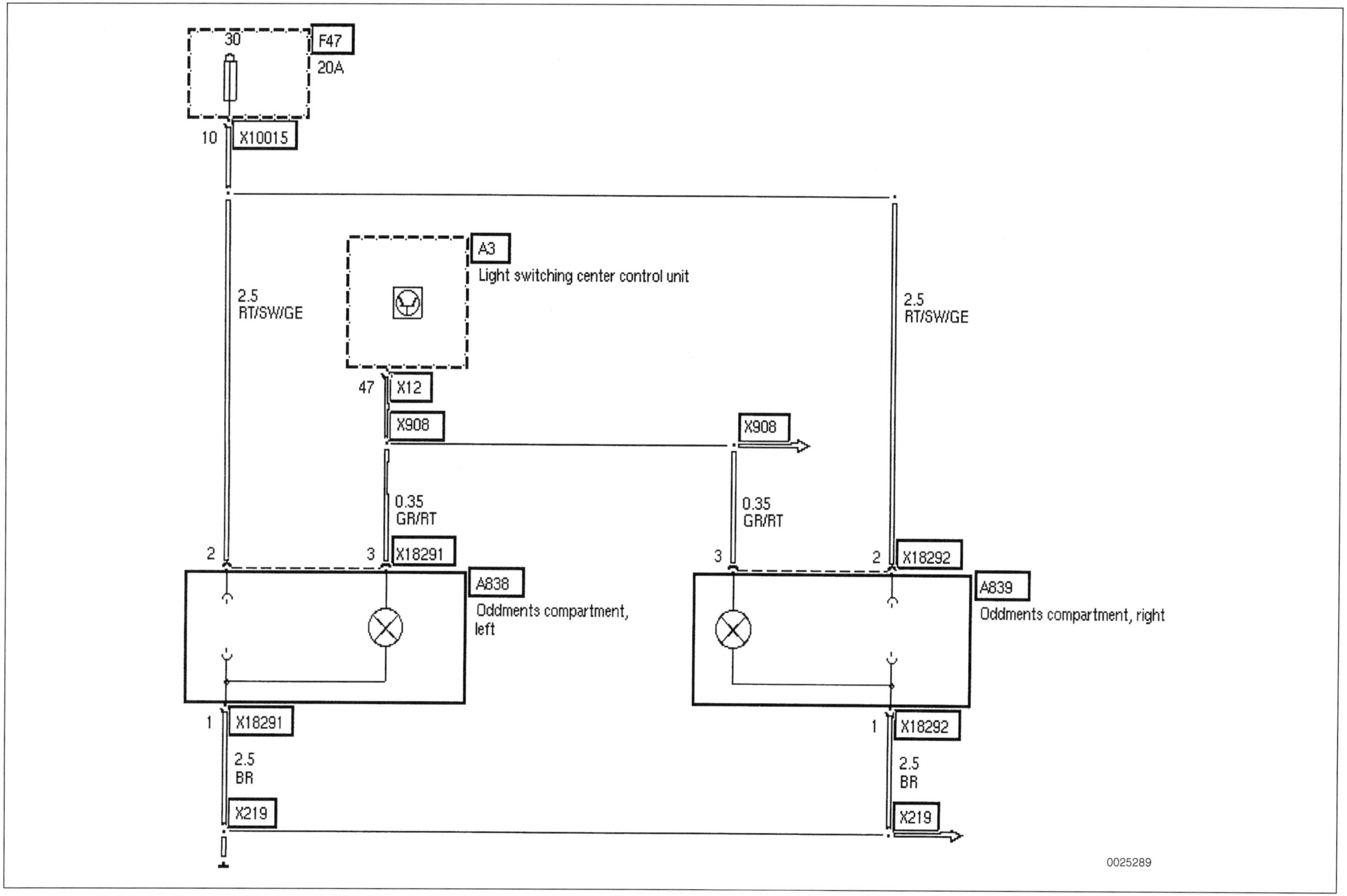

30
F47
20A
10
X10015
2.5
RT/SW/GE
A3
Light switching center control unit
2.5
RT/SW/GE
47
X12
X908
X908
0.35
GR/RT
0.35
GR/RT
2
3
X18291
3
2
X18292
A838
Oddments compartment,
left
A839
Oddments compartment, right
1
X18291
1
X18292
2.5
BR
2.5
BR
X219
X219
0025289

Interior/reading light, front (E34)

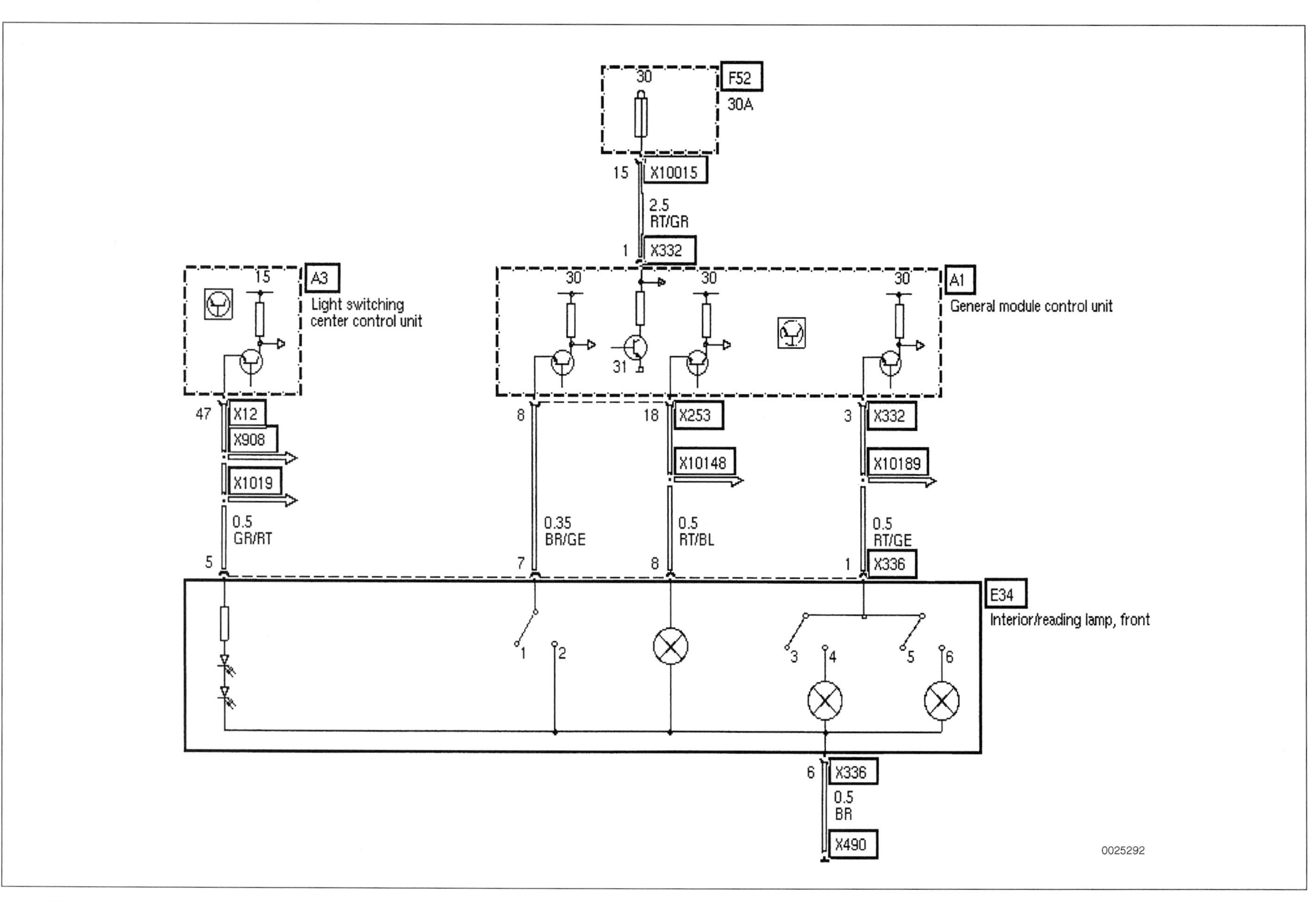

Fuse 52 (F52)

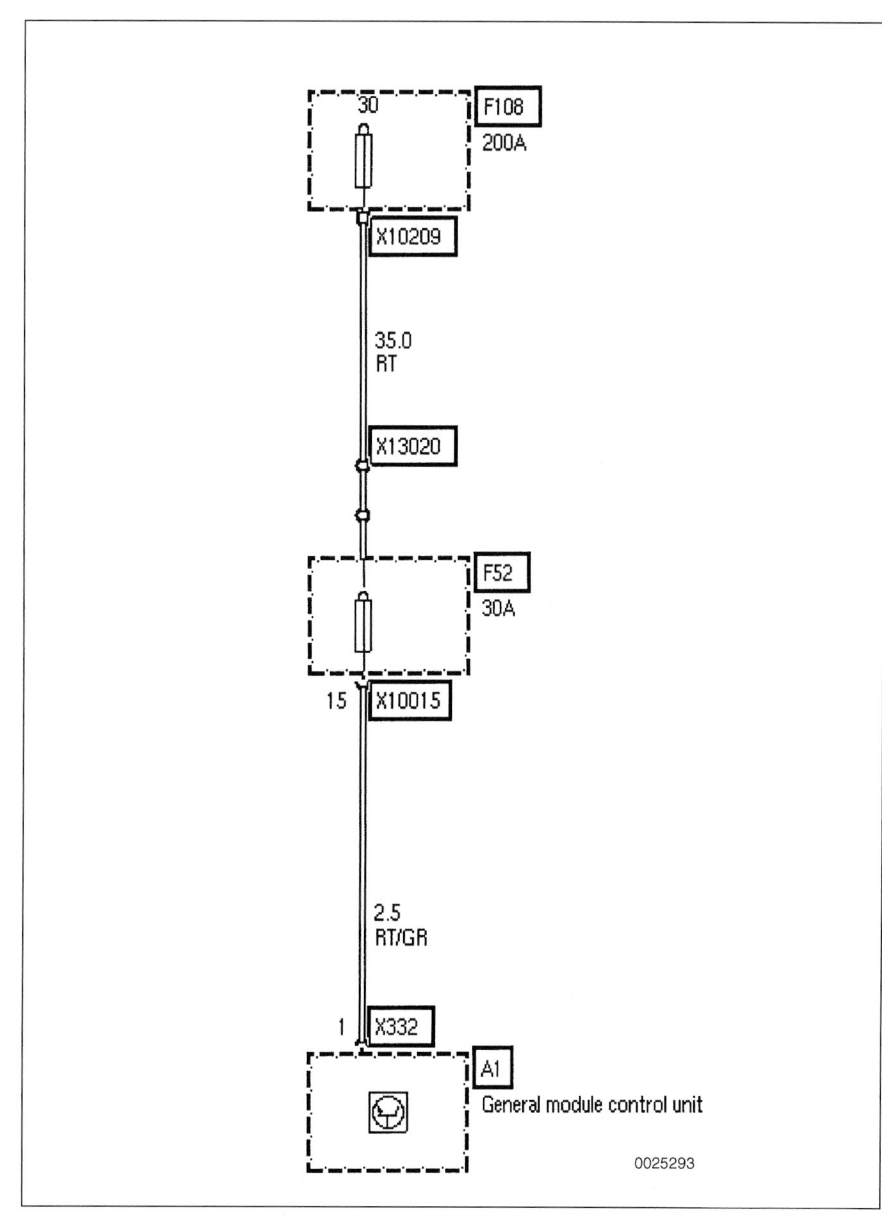
30
F108
200A
X10209
35.0
RT
X13020
F52
30A
15
X10015
2.5
RT/GR
1
X332
A1
General module control unit
0025293

Splice connector (X10148)

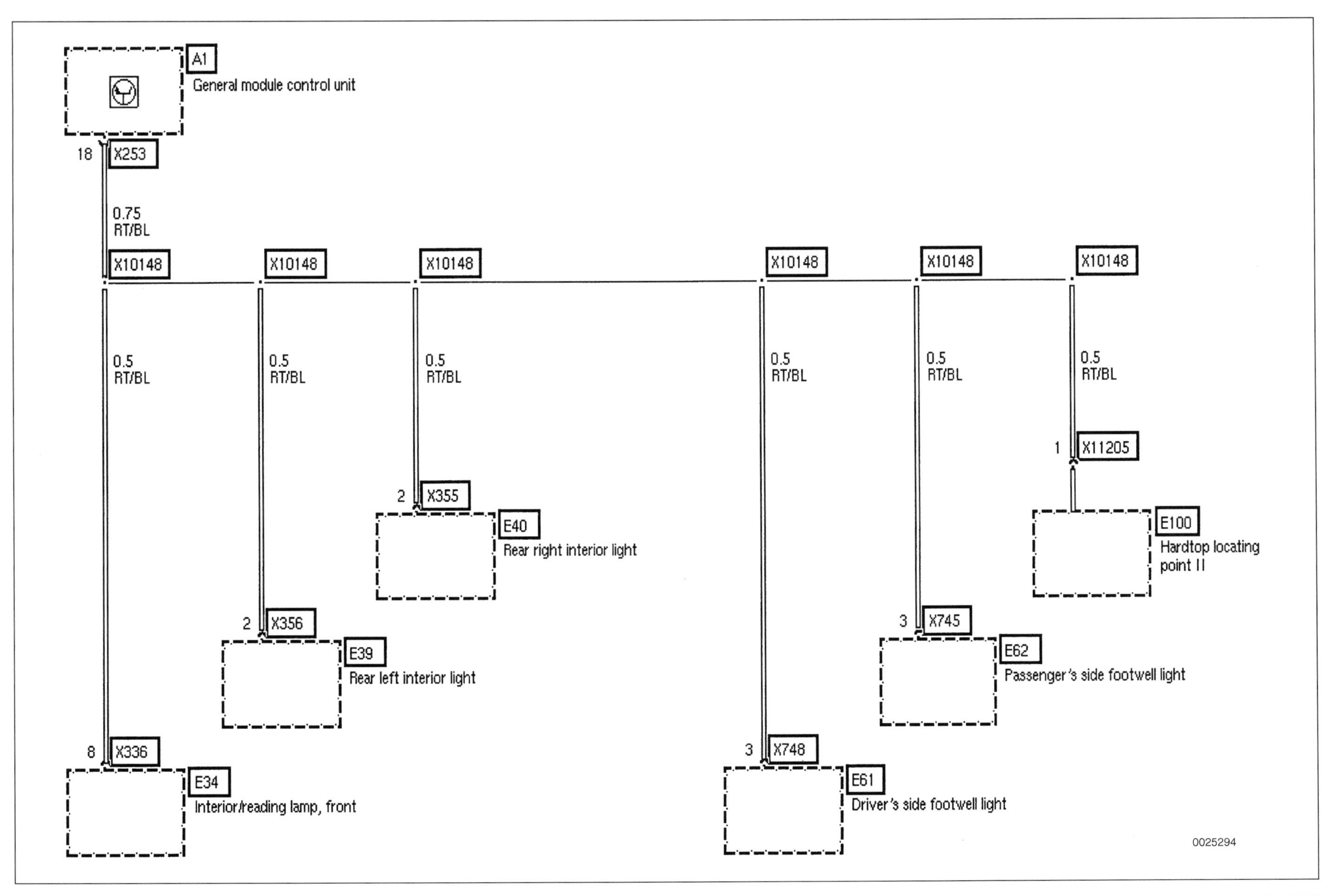

Interior light, left rear (E39)

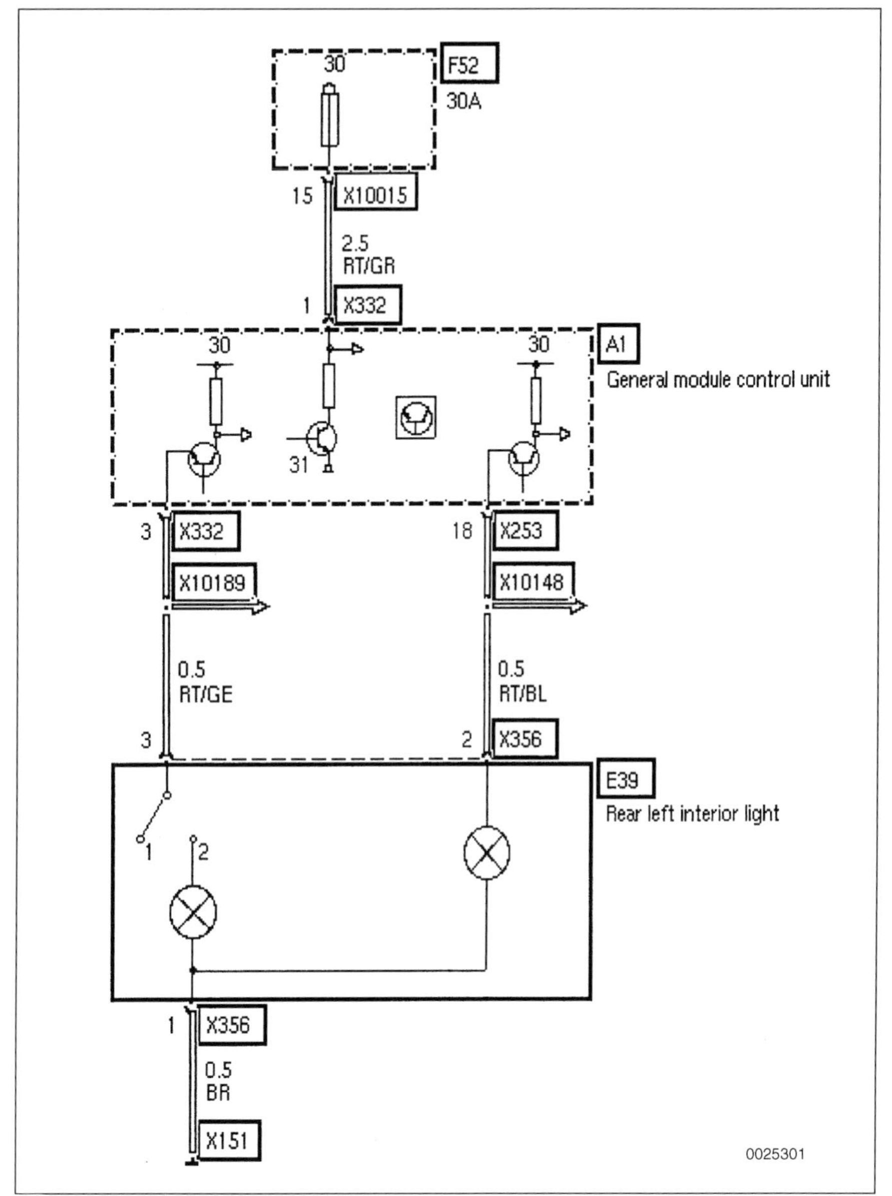

This page left intentionally blank

Interior light, right rear (E40)

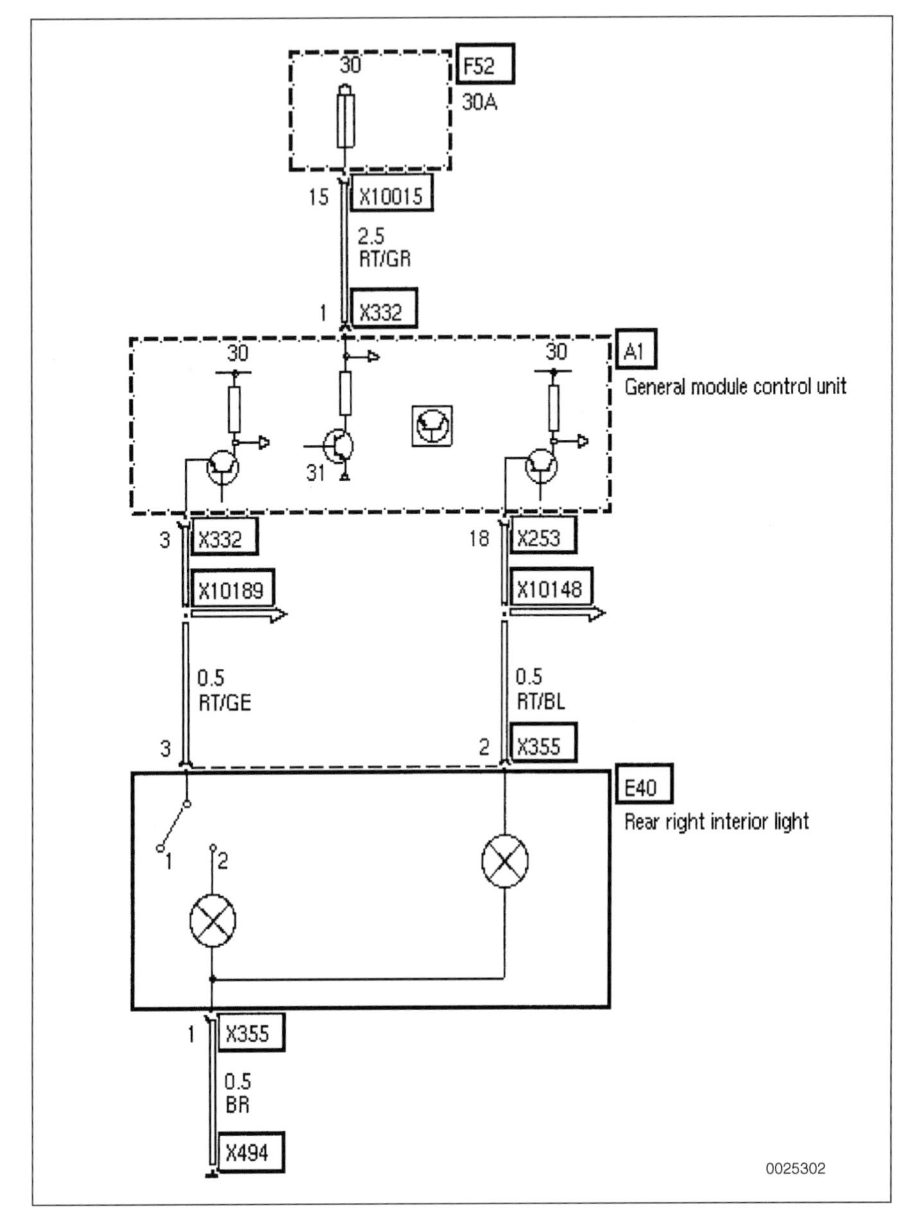

Glove compartment light (E42)

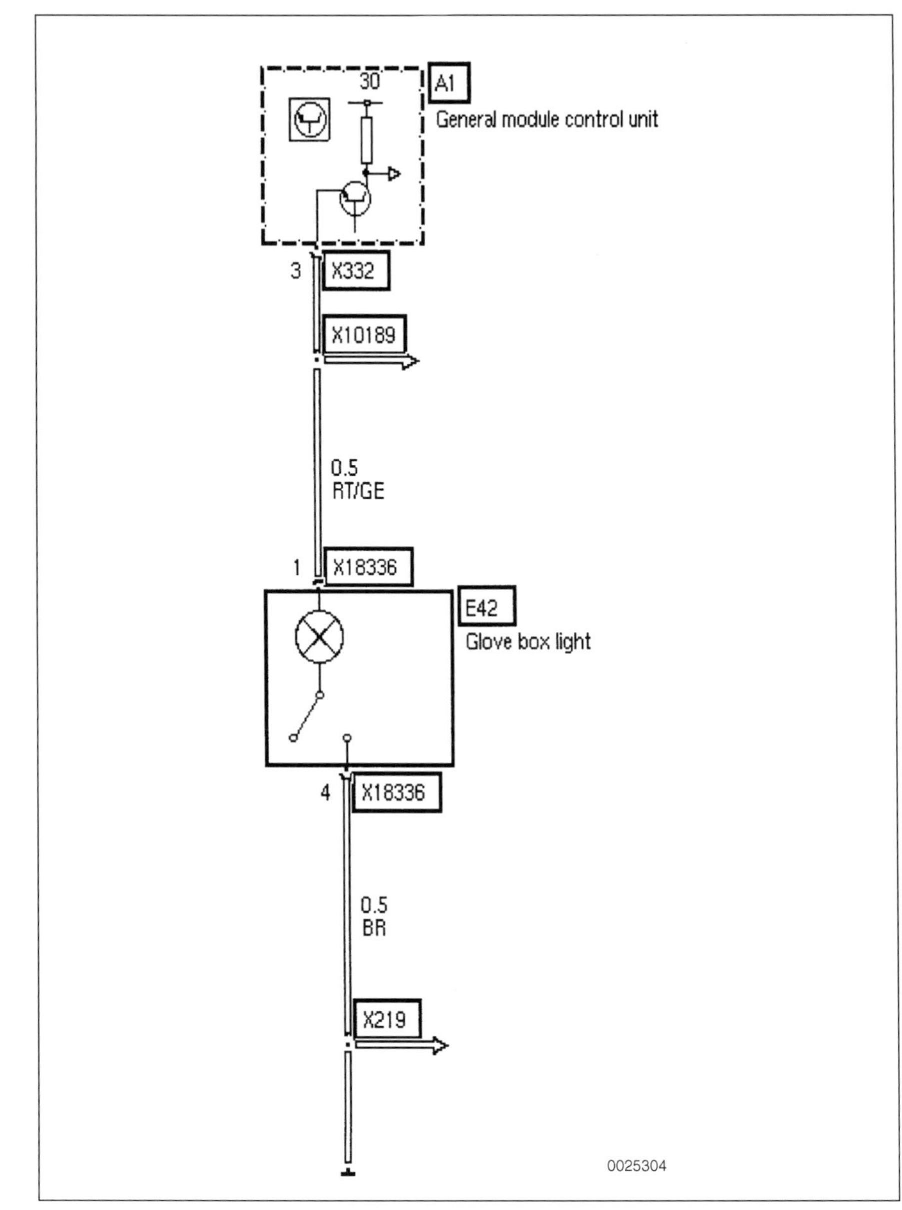

Footwell lights (E61, E62)

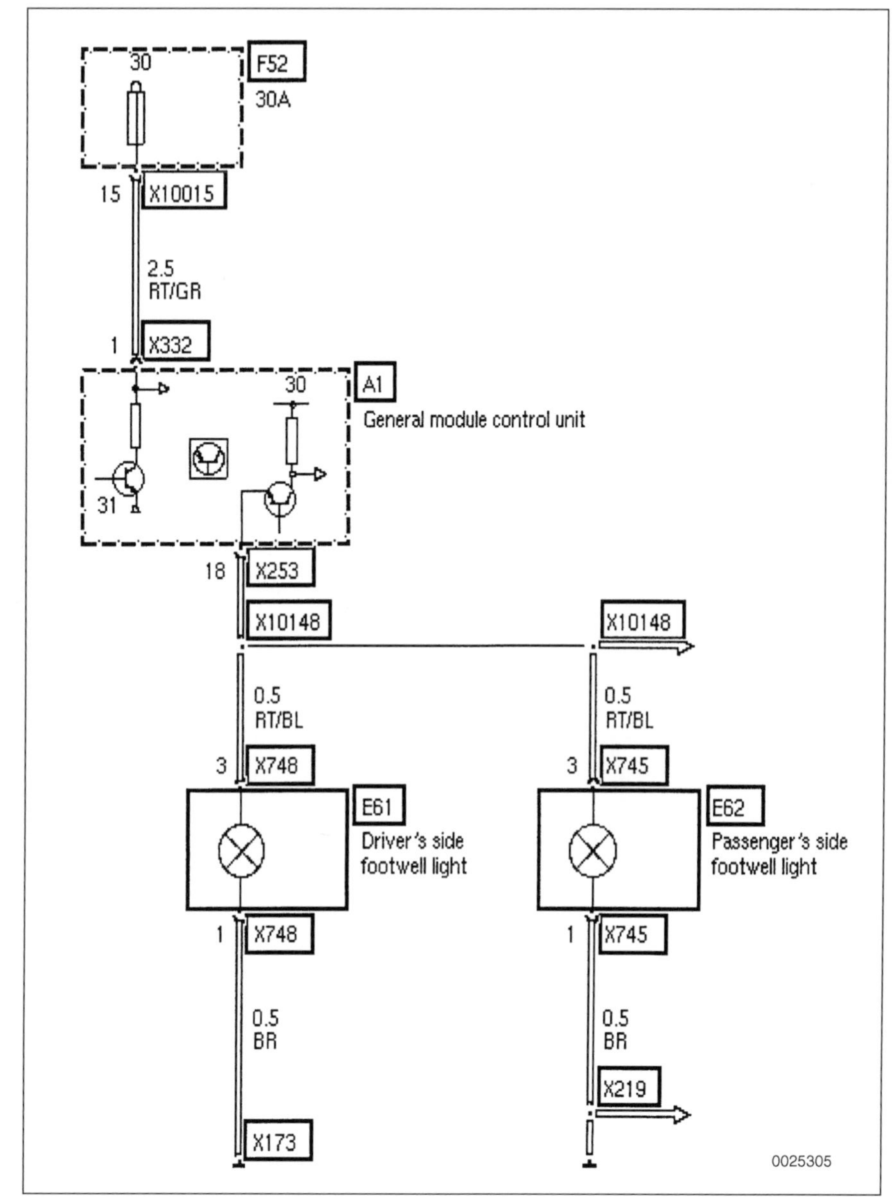

Trunk lights (E47)

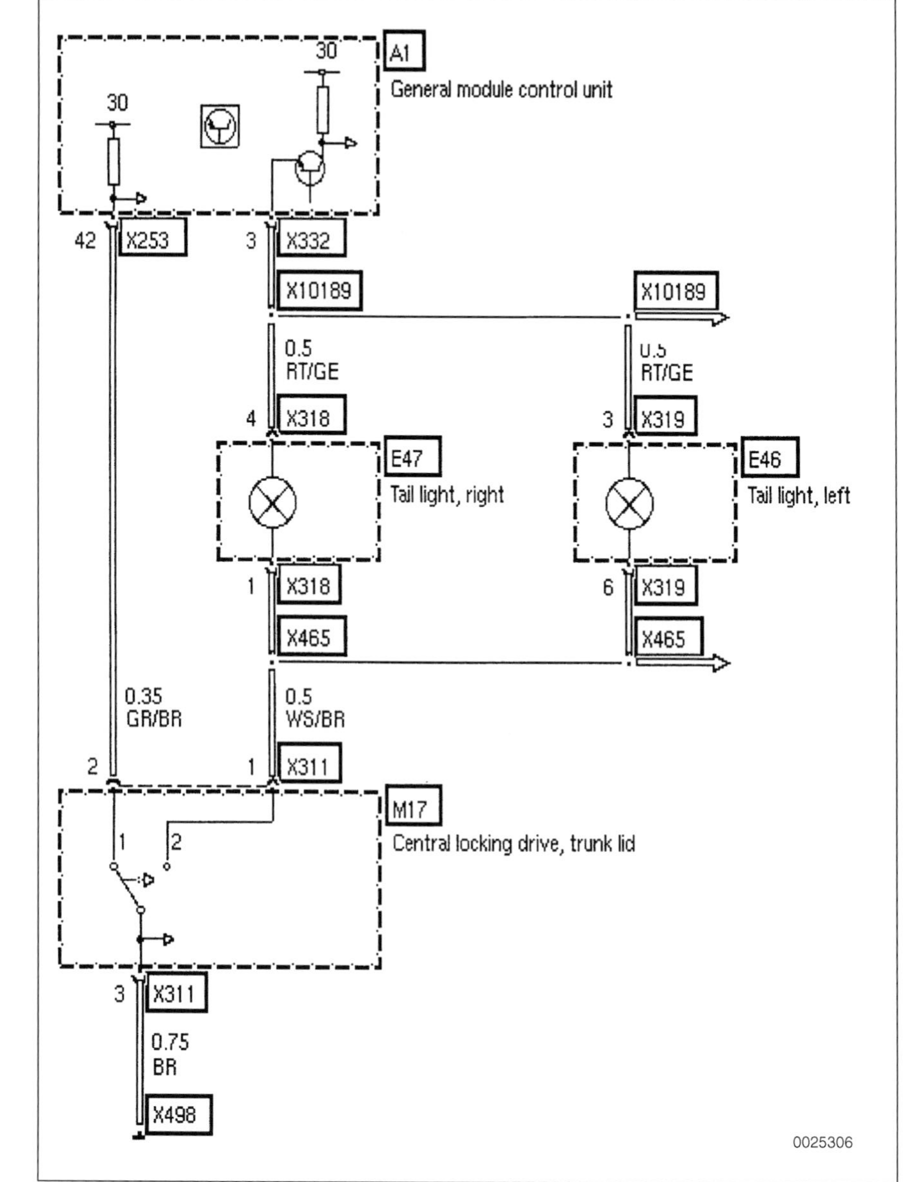

Splice connector (X465)

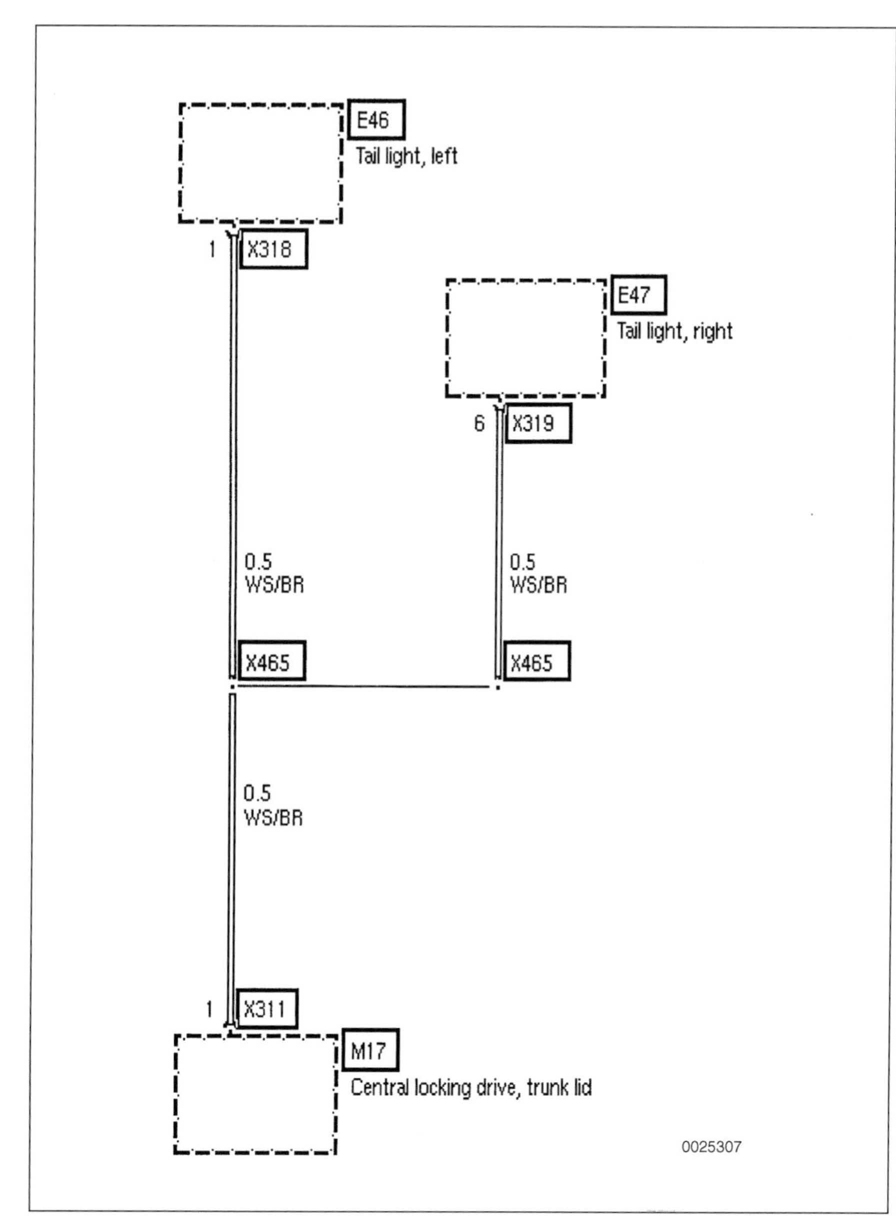

Makeup mirror lights (E35, E36)

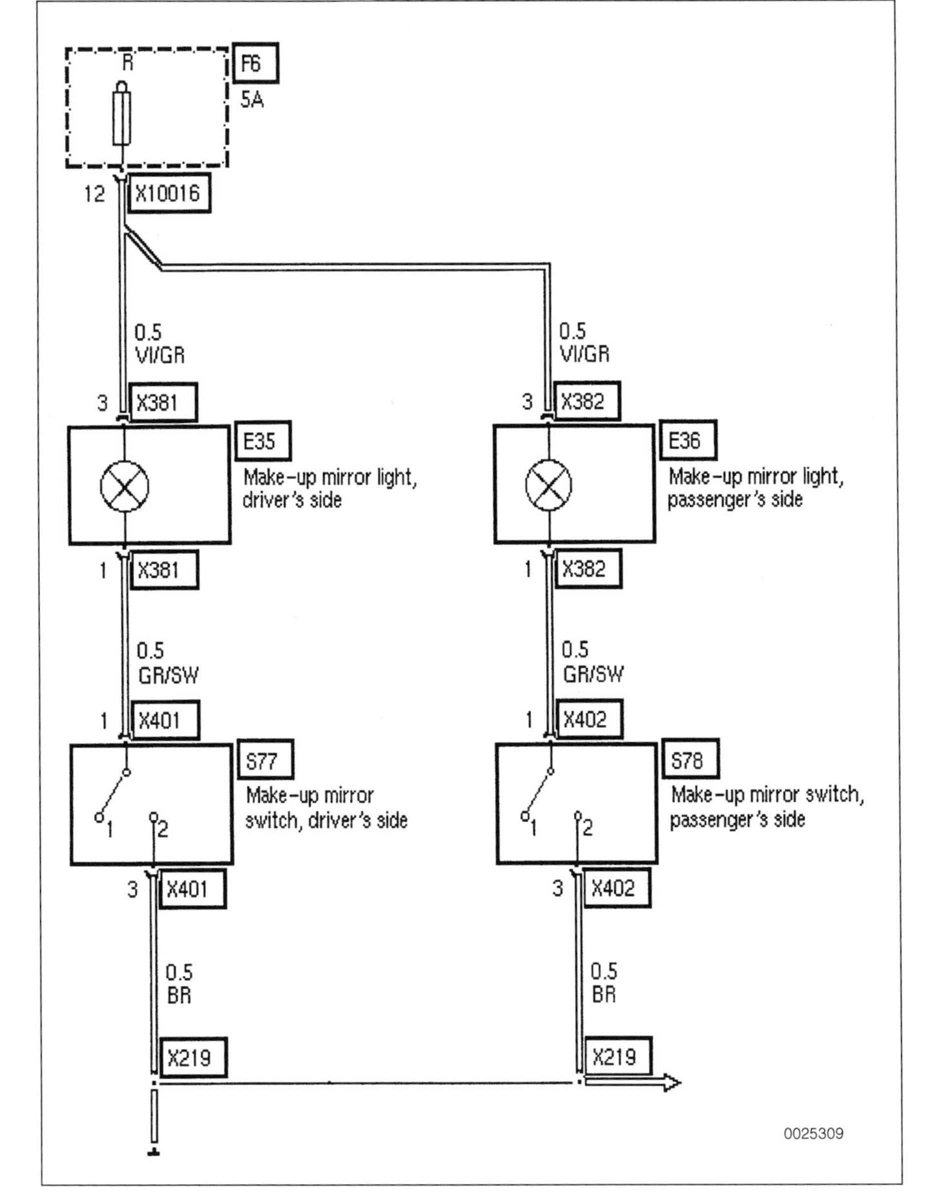

Fuse 6 (F6)

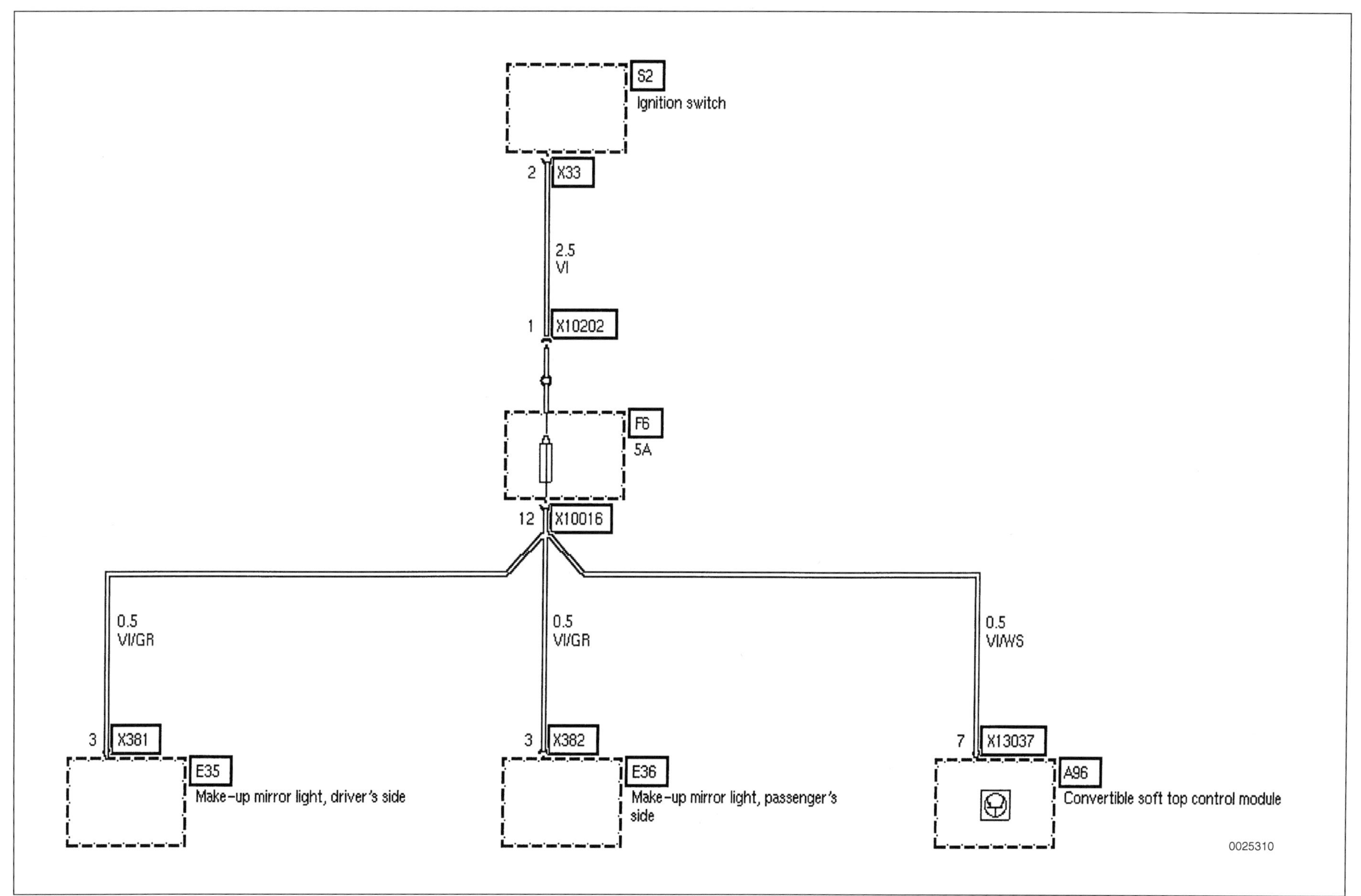
S2
Ignition switch
2
X33
2.5
VI
1
X10202
F6
5A
12
X10016
0.5
VI/GR
0.5
VI/GR
0.5
VI/WS
3
X381
E35
Make-up mirror light, driver's side
3
X382
E36
Make-up mirror light, passenger's side
7
X13037
A96
Convertible soft top control module
0025310

Cigar lighter, front (E28)

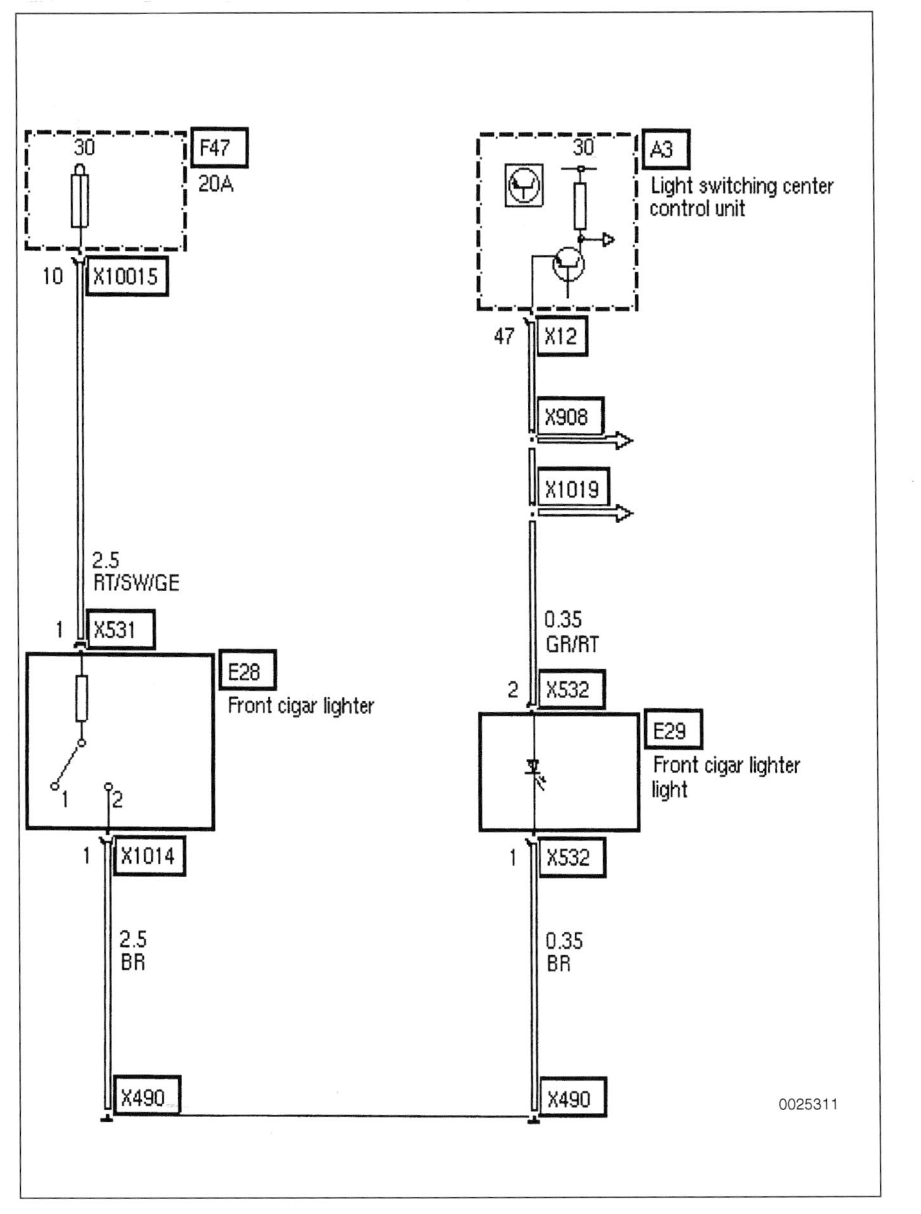

Ashtray light, rear (E37)

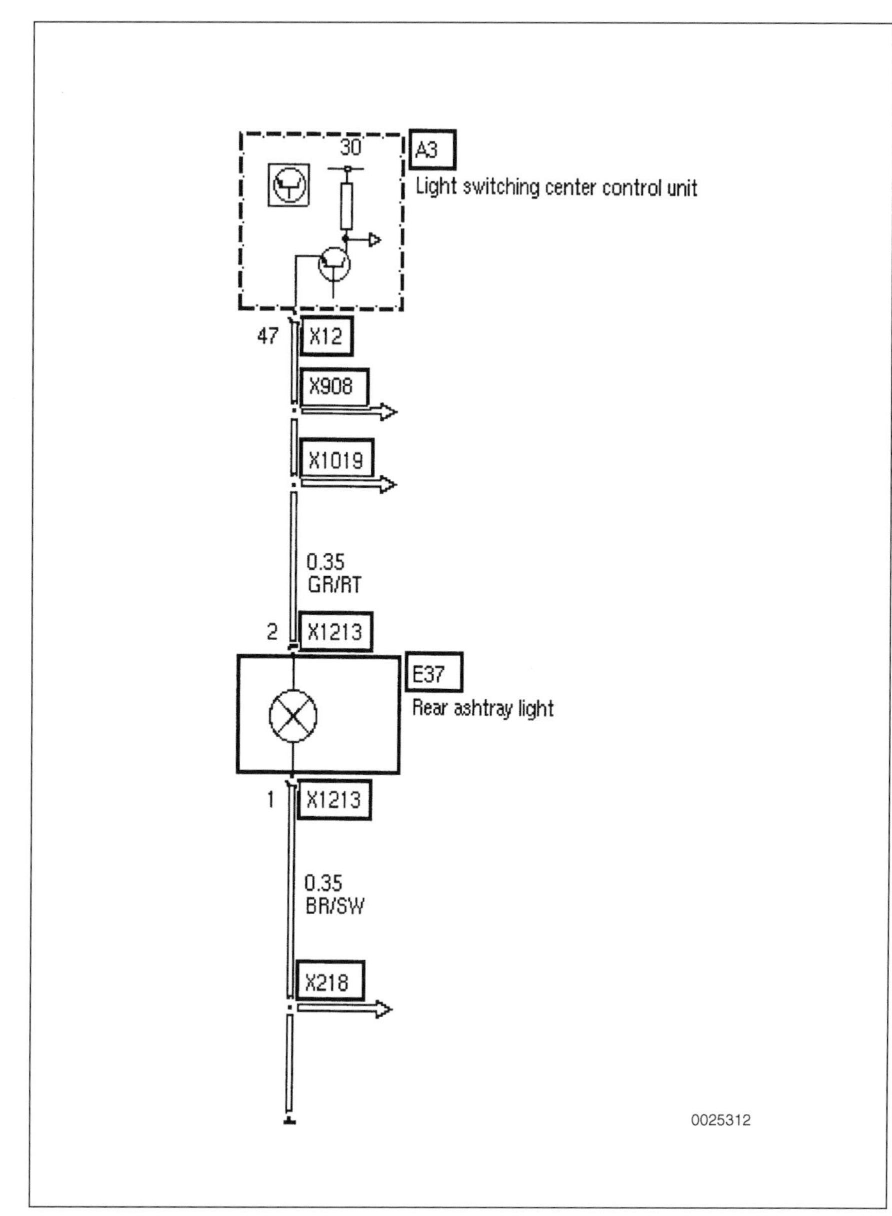

Door lock, driver door (S47)

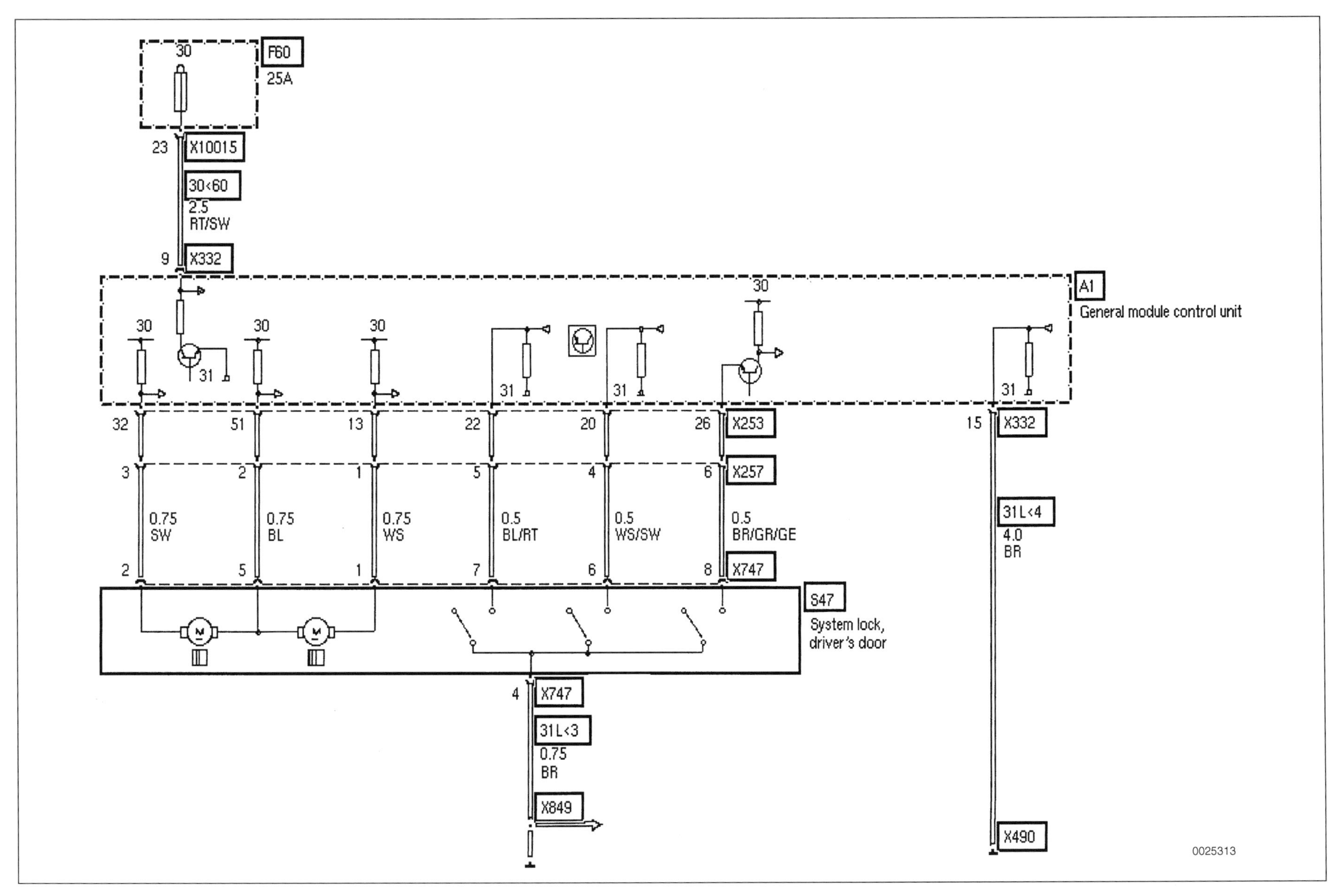

Fuse 60 (F60)

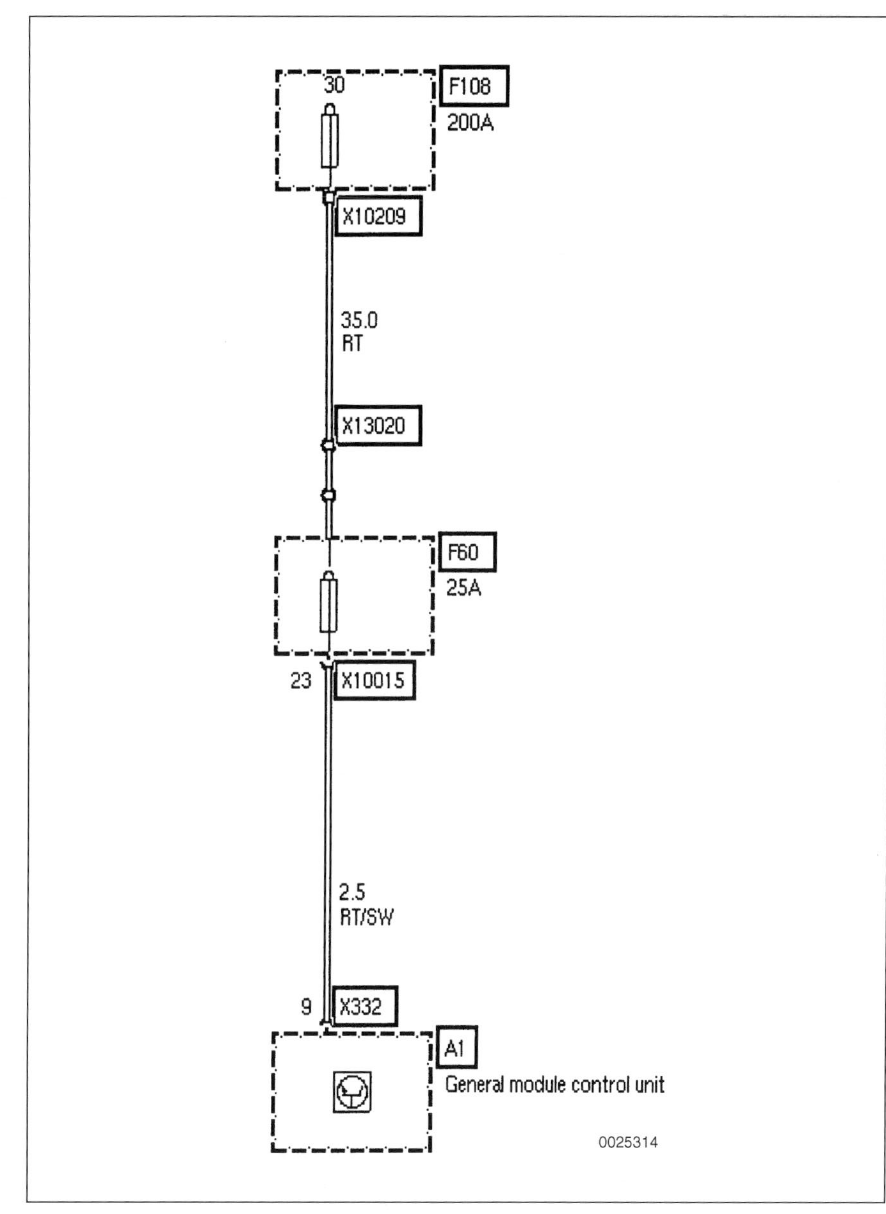

30
F108
200A
X10209
35.0
RT
X13020
F60
25A
23
X10015
2.5
RT/SW
9
X332
A1
General module control unit
0025314

Door connector, driver door (X257)
1 of 2

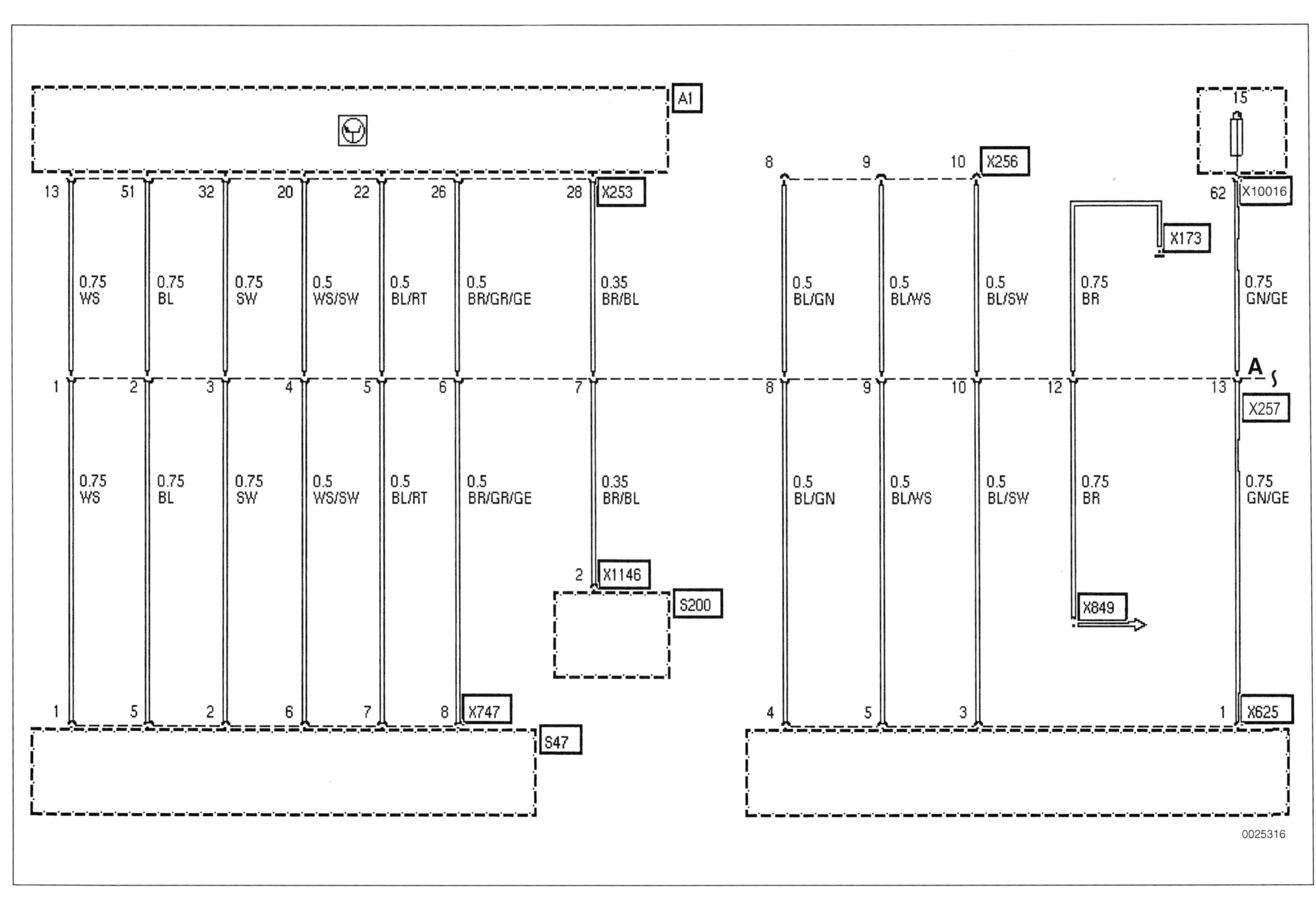

Door connector, driver door (X257)
2 of 2

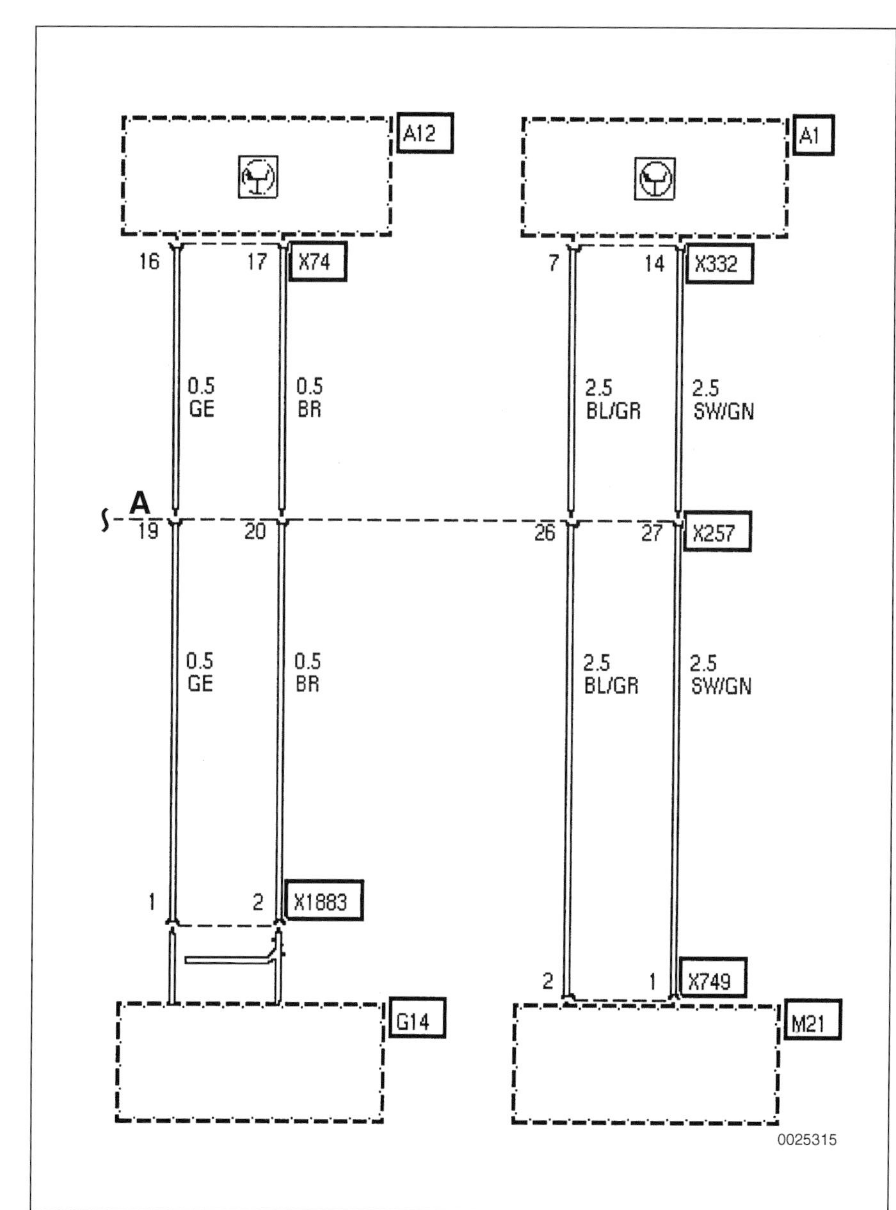

Splice connector (X849)

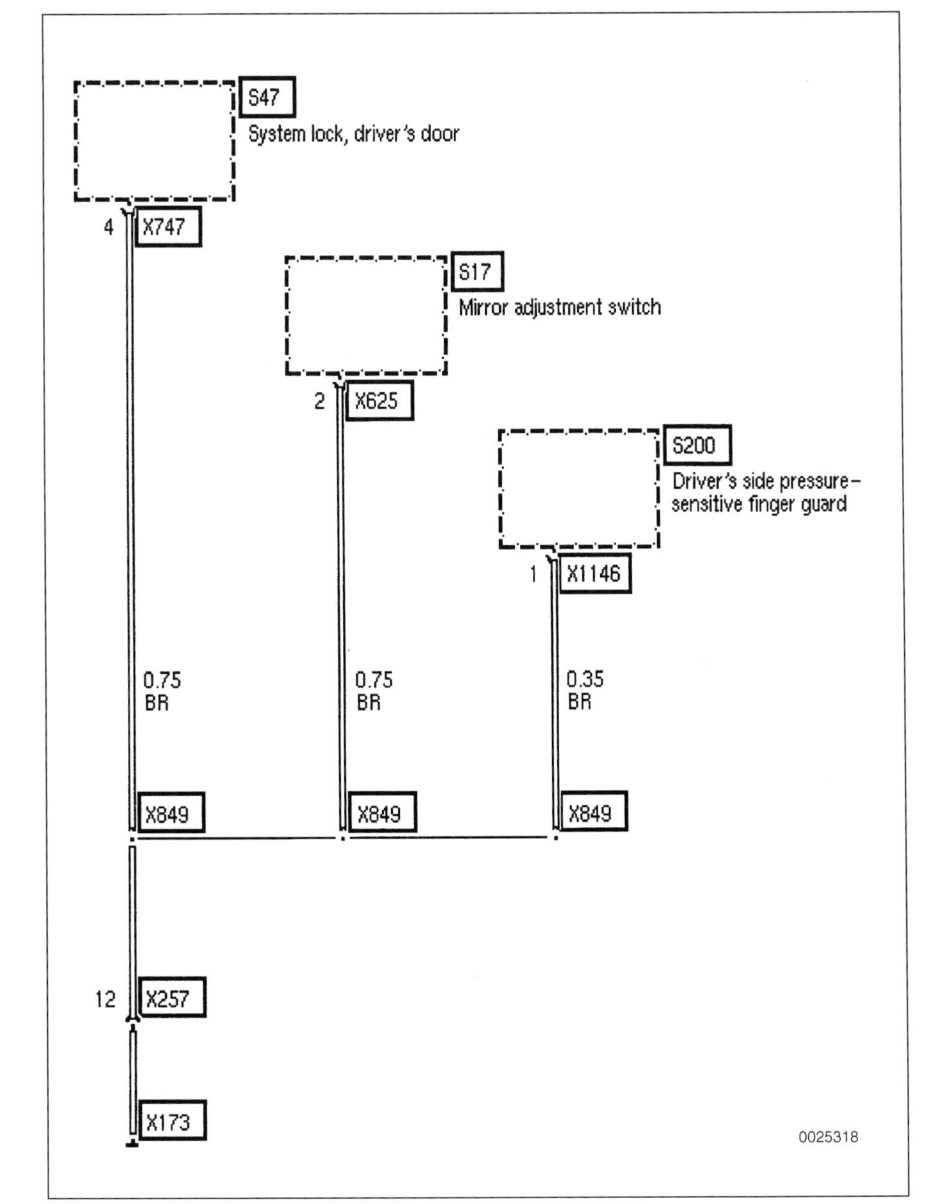

Door lock, passenger door (S49)

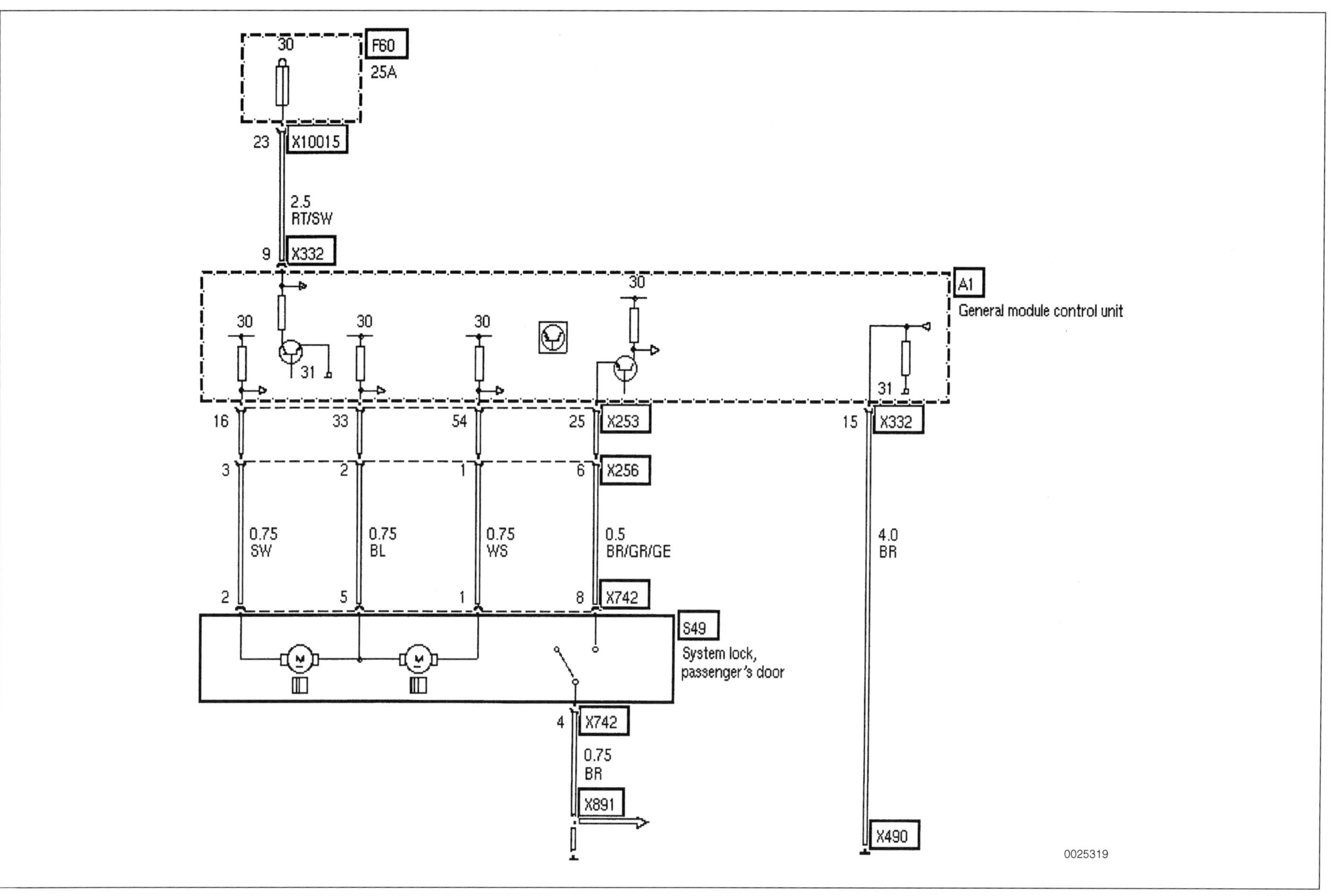

Splice connector (X891)

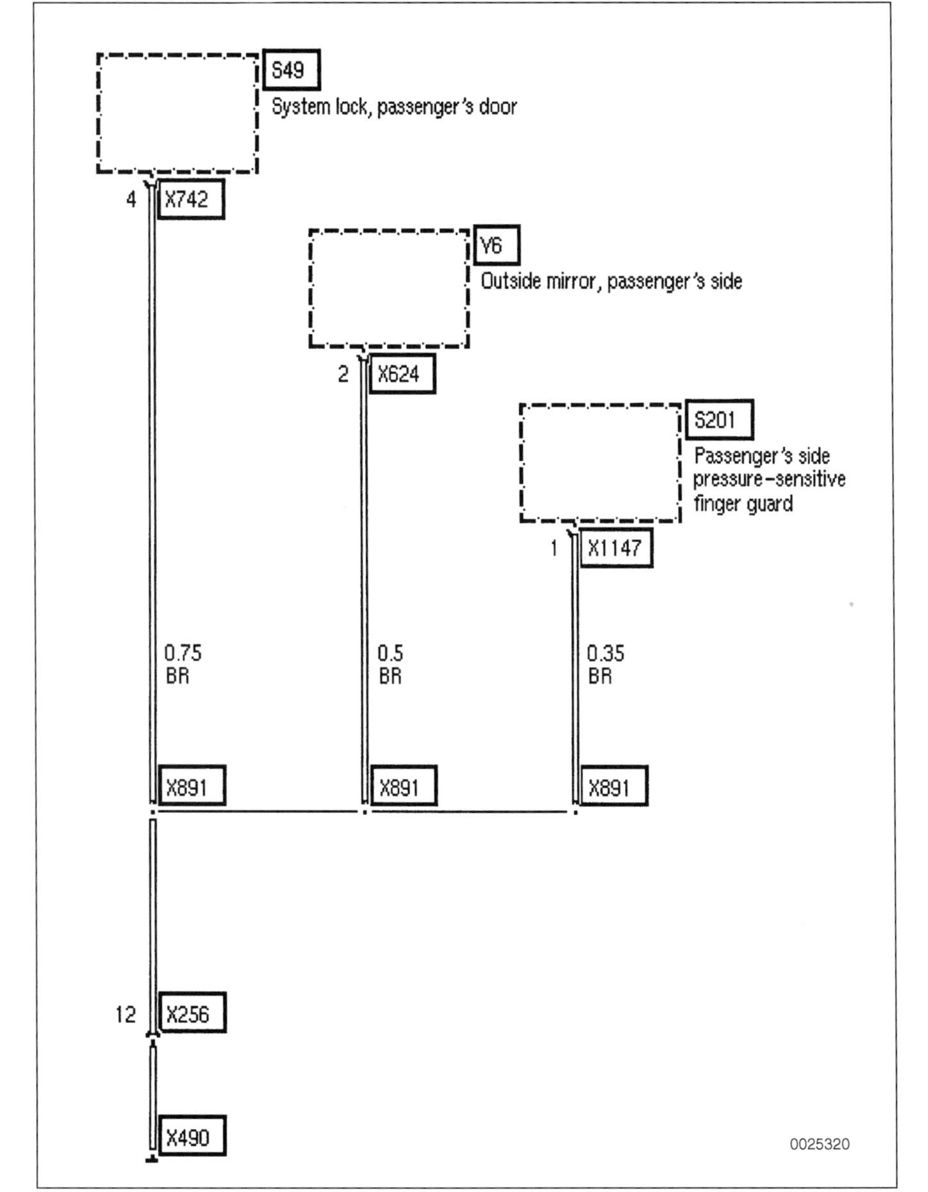

Door locks, rear (M14, M15)

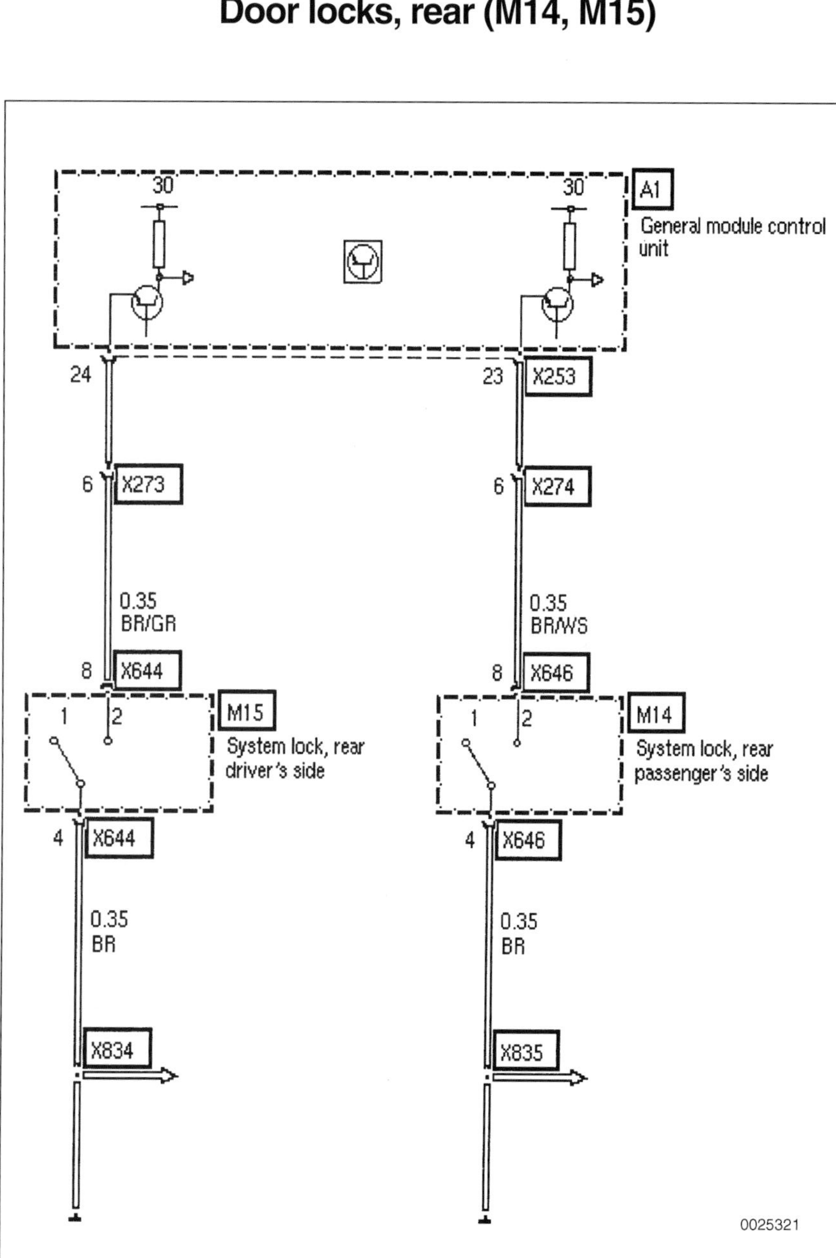

Door connector, left rear (X273)
1 of 2

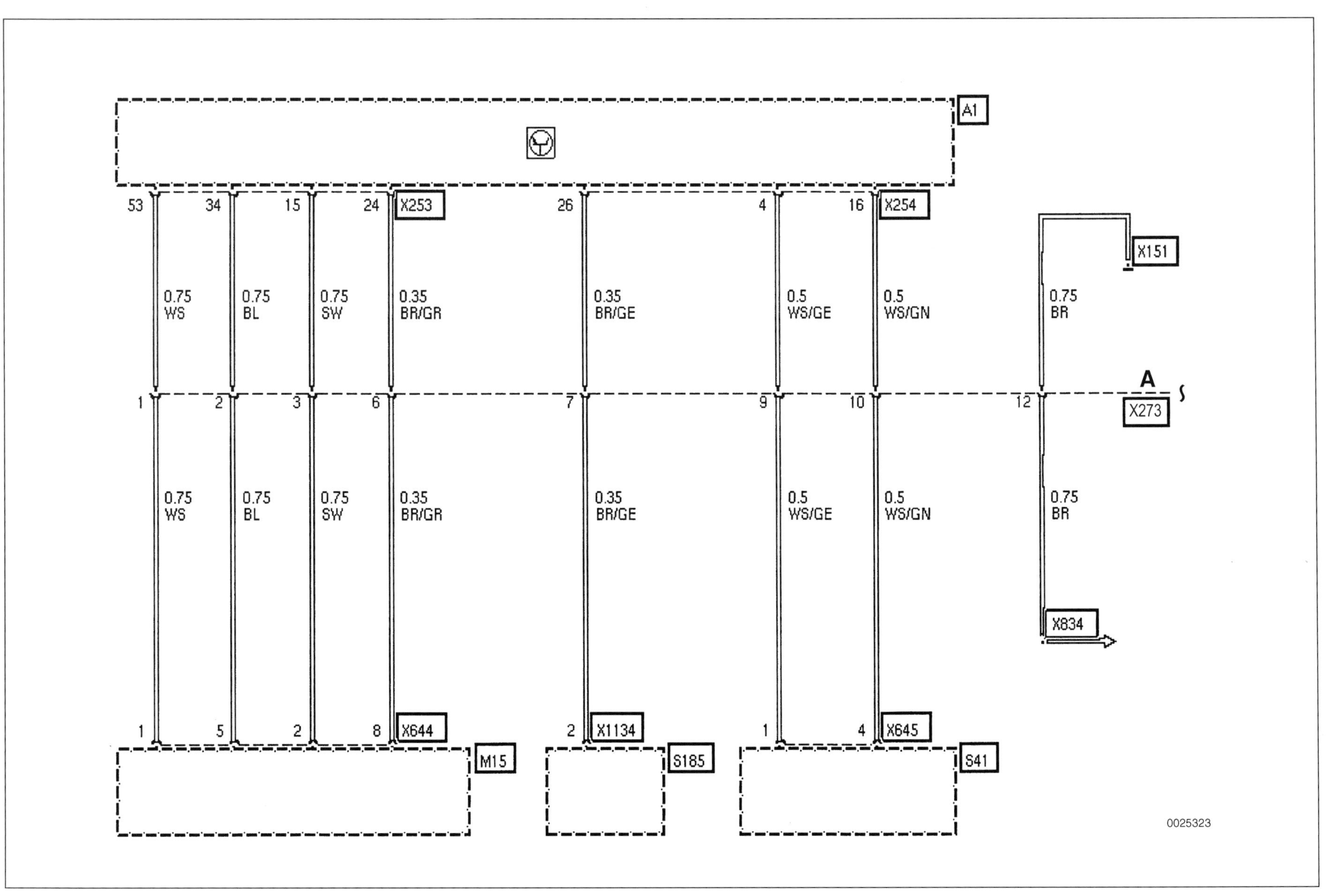

Door connector, left rear (X273)
2 of 2

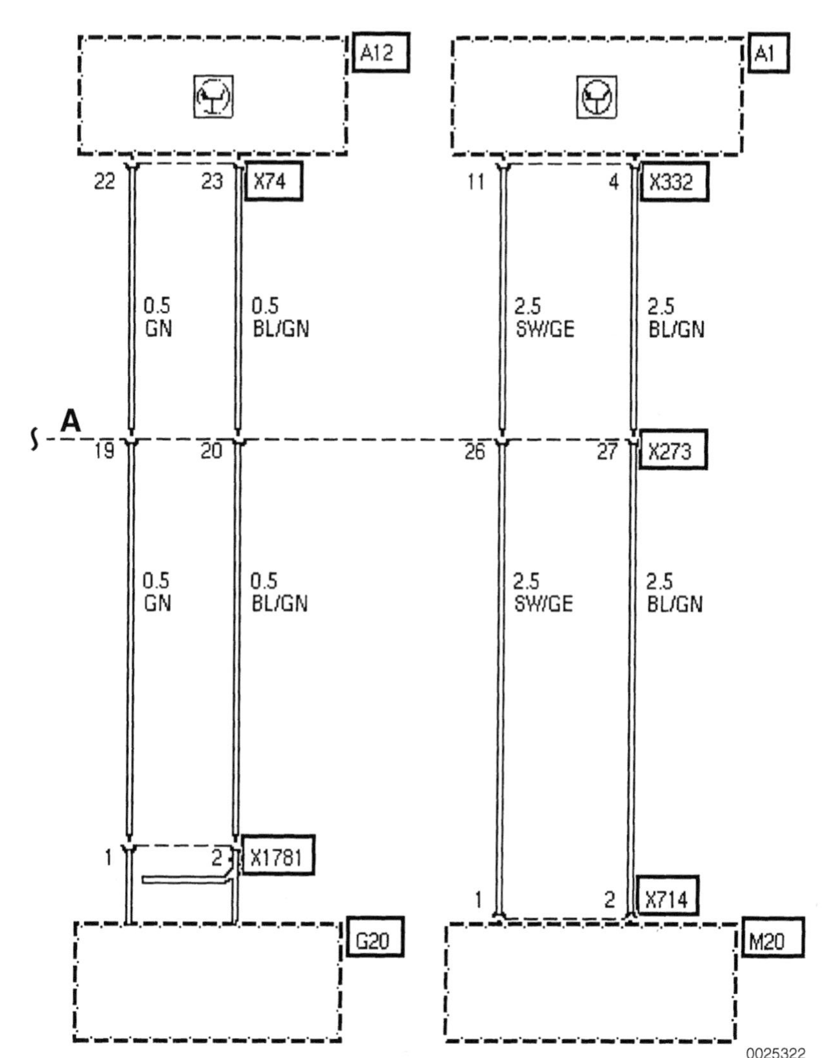

Door connector, right rear (X274)
1 of 2

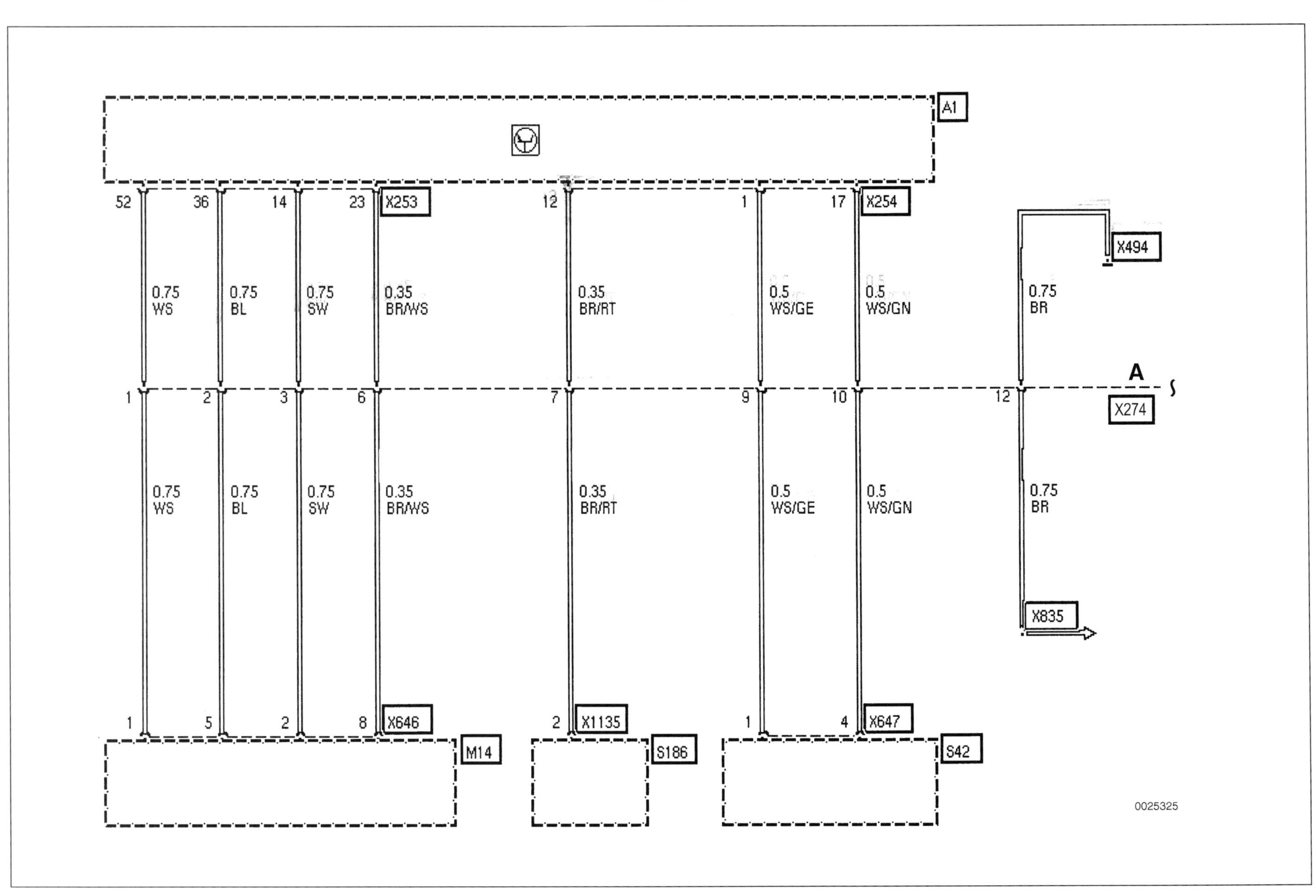

Door connector, right rear (X274)
2 of 2

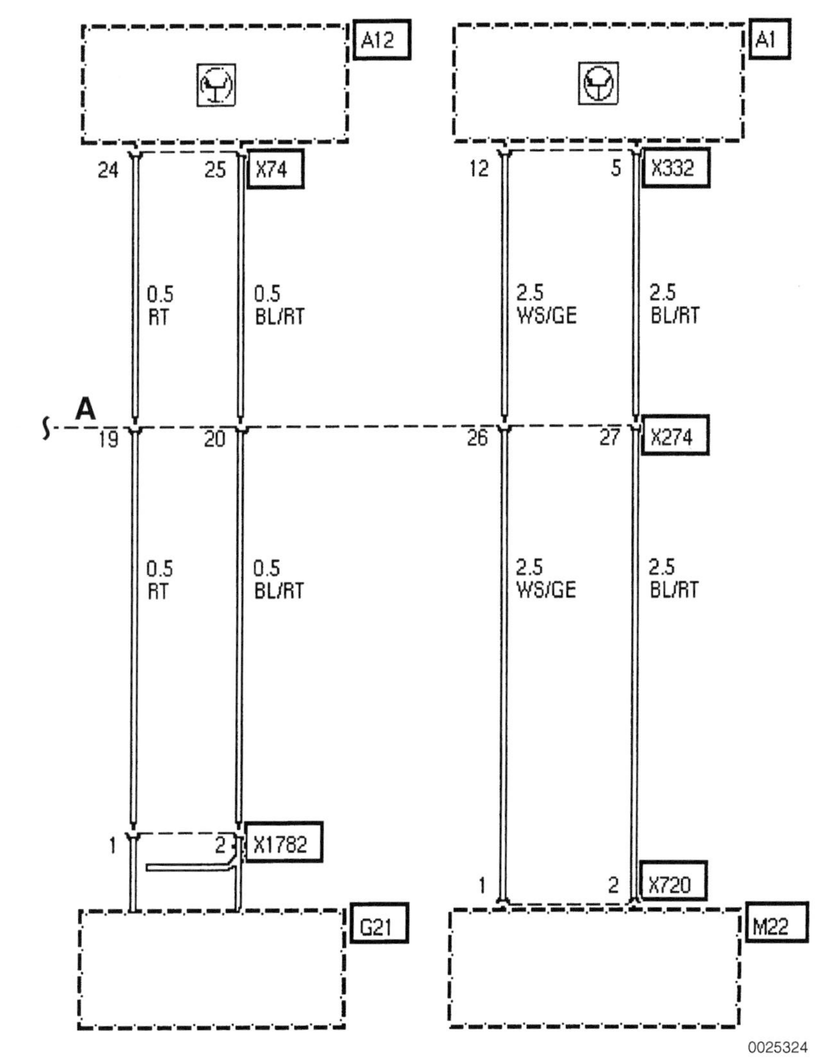

Splice connector (X834)

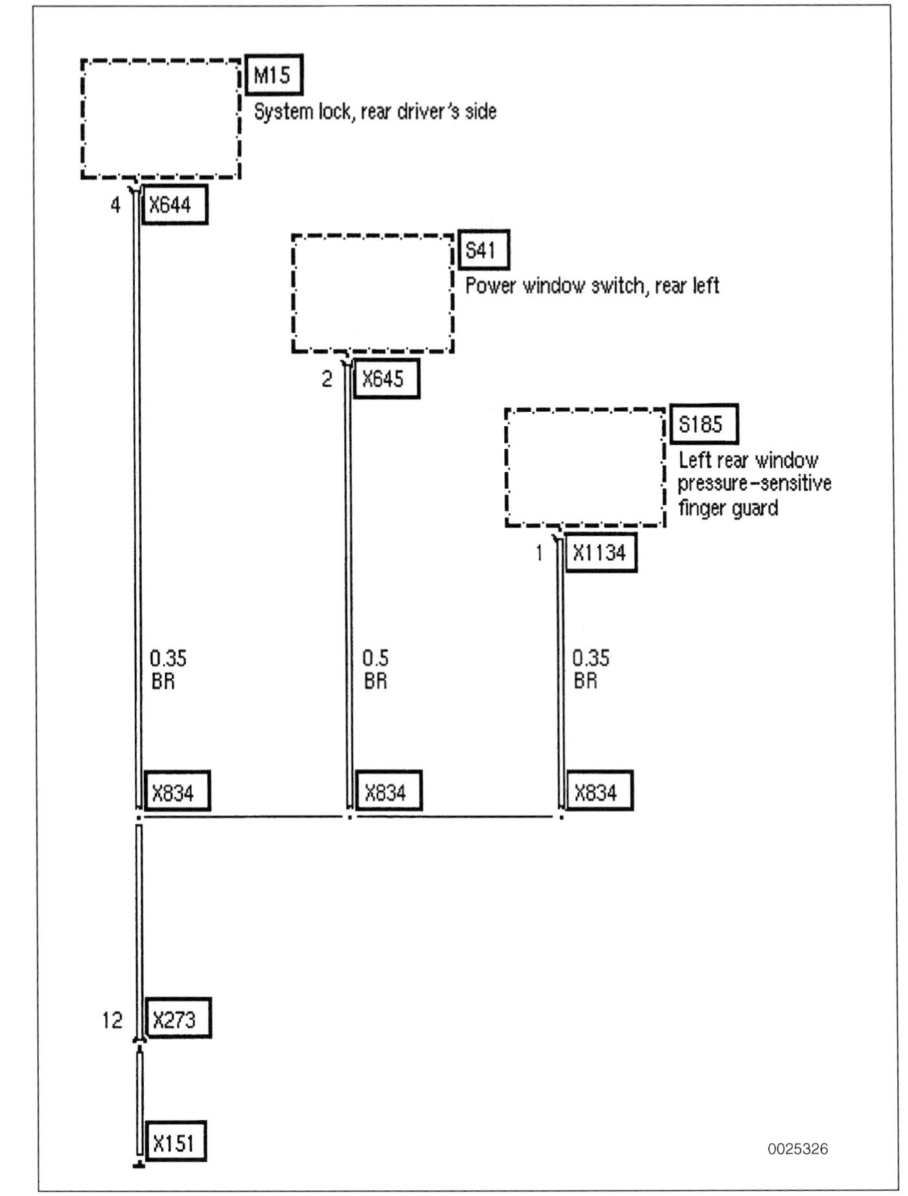

Splice connector (X835)

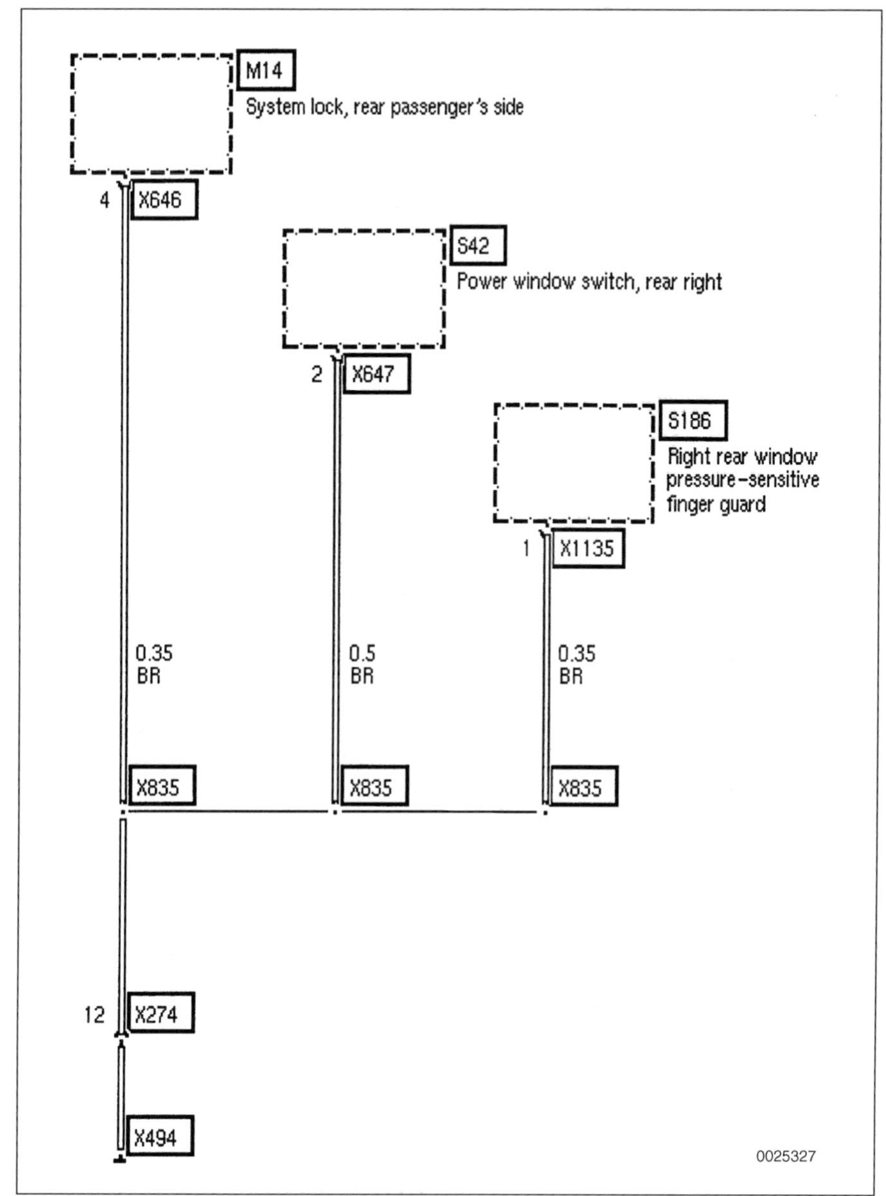

Trunk lid/tailgate lock (M17, S167)

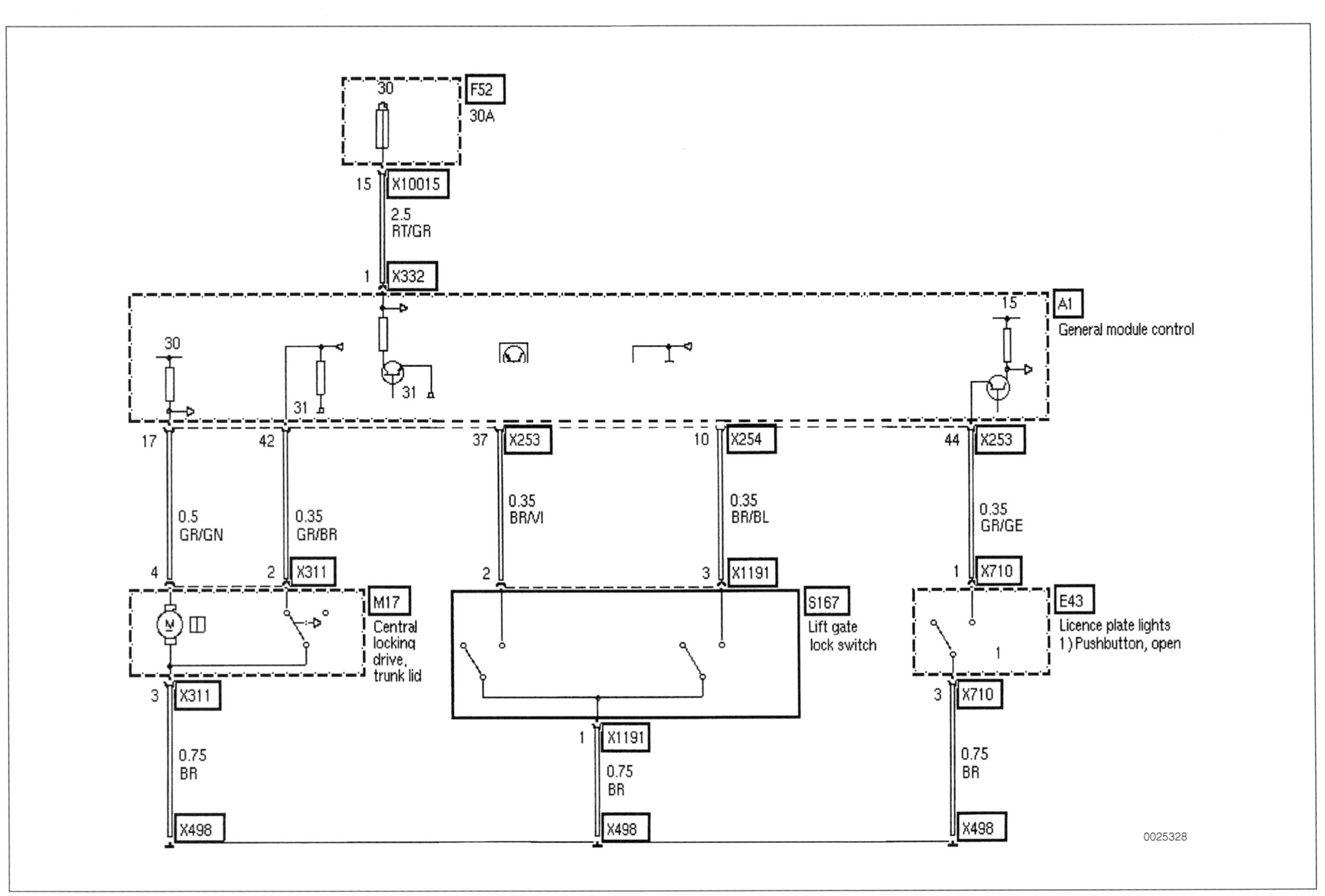

Headlight vertical aim actuators (M80, M81)

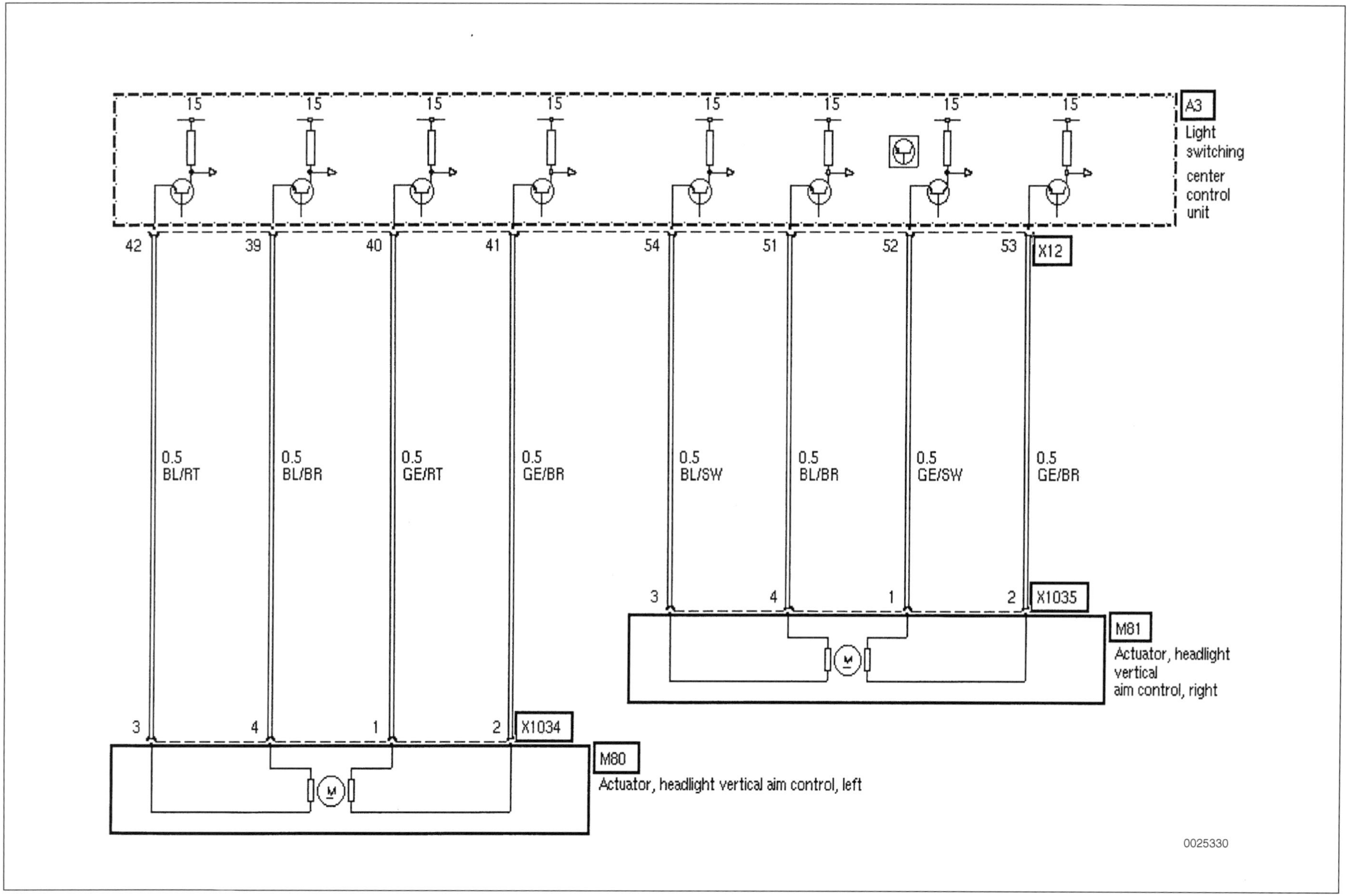

Headlight vertical aim load sensors (B42, B64)

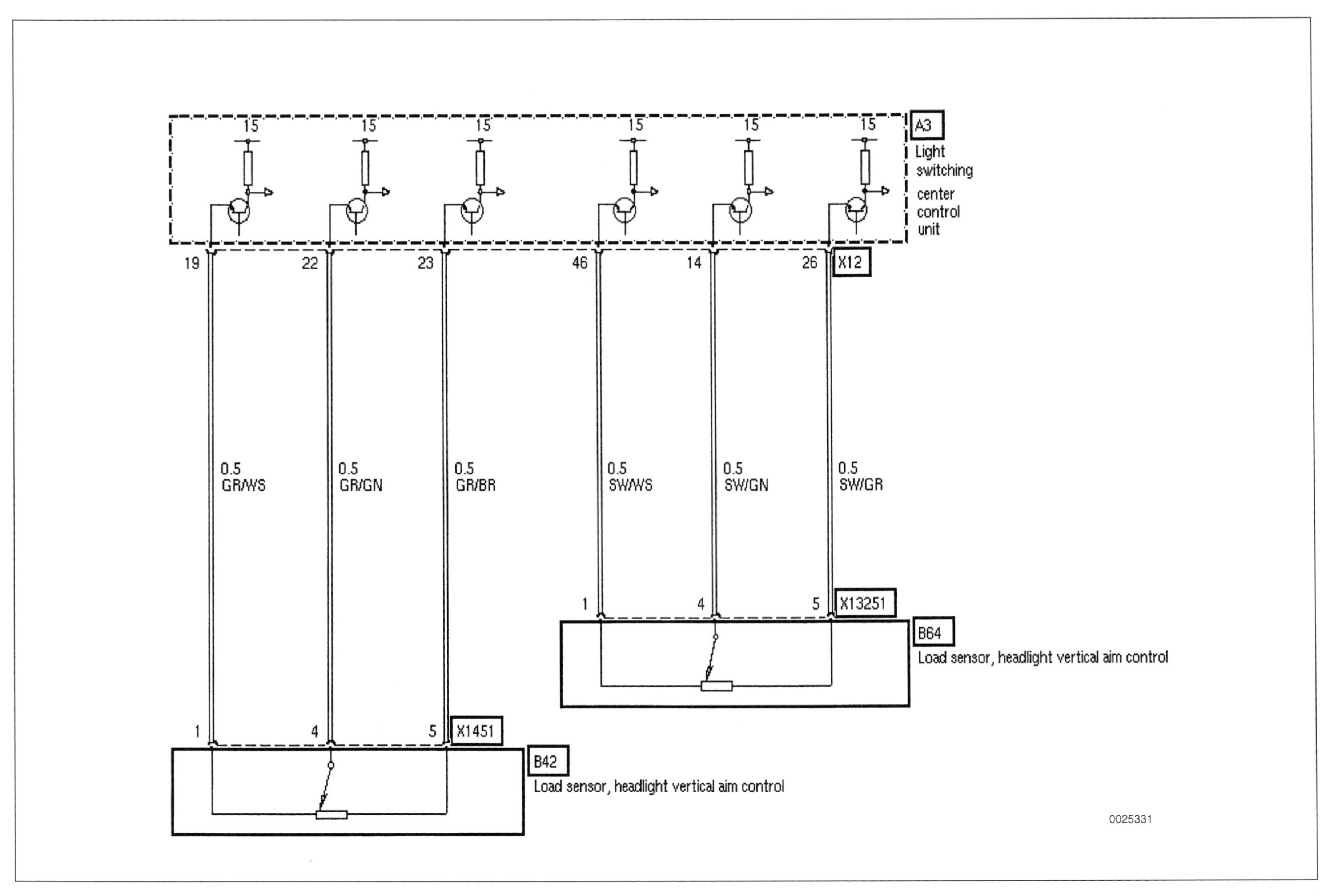

Fuel level sensors (B6, M2)

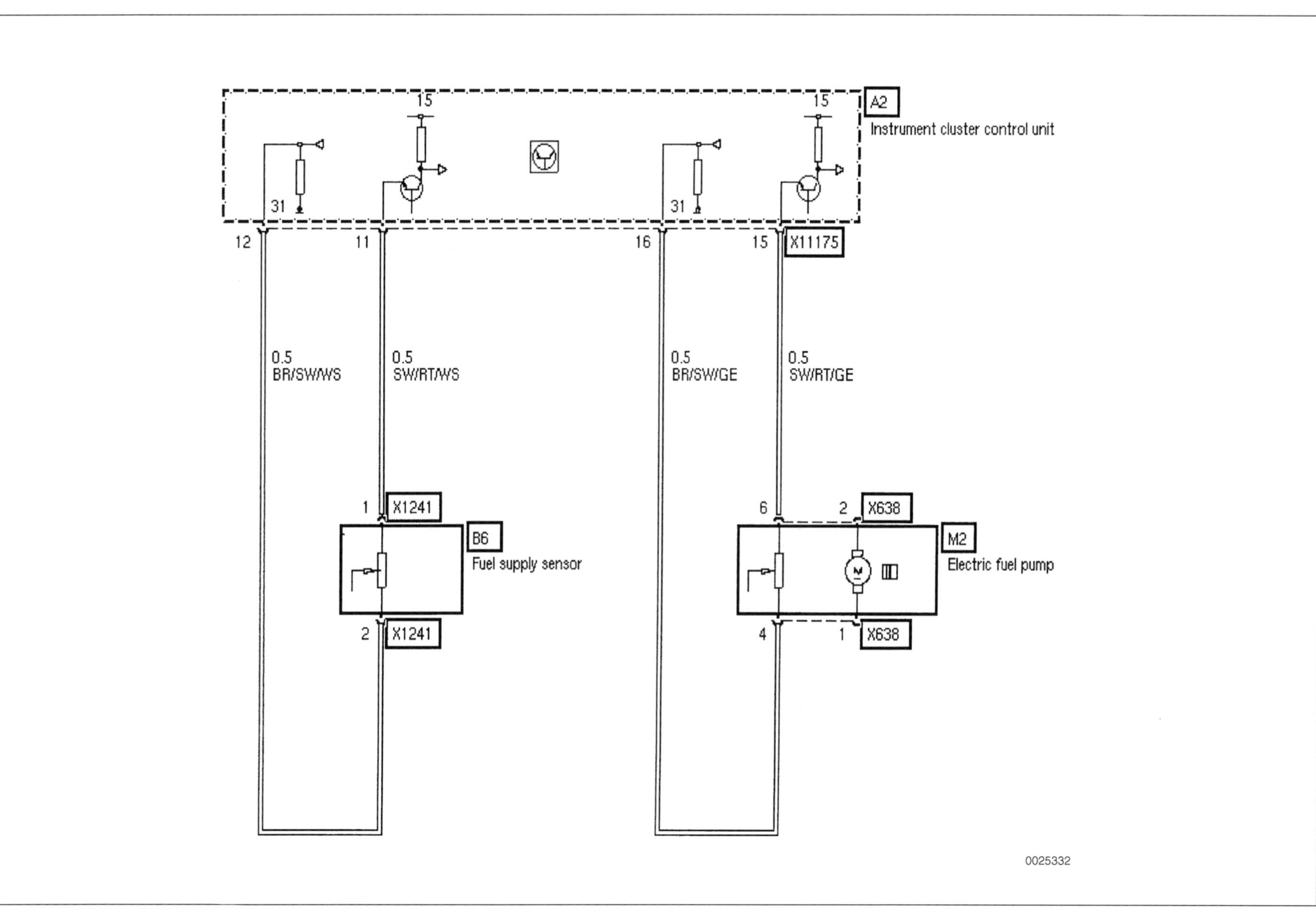

This page left intentionally blank

Outside temperature sensor (B21)

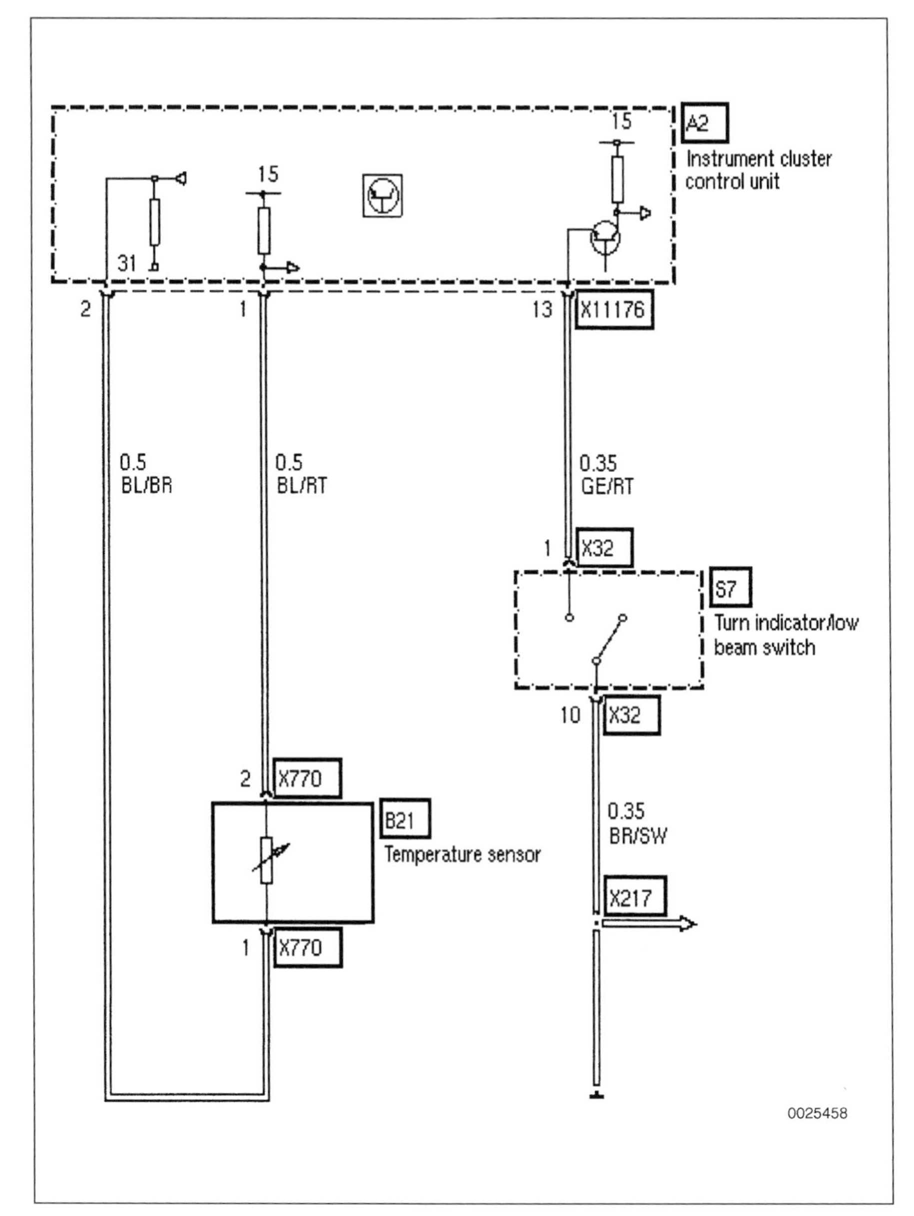

Engine coolant level switch (S63)

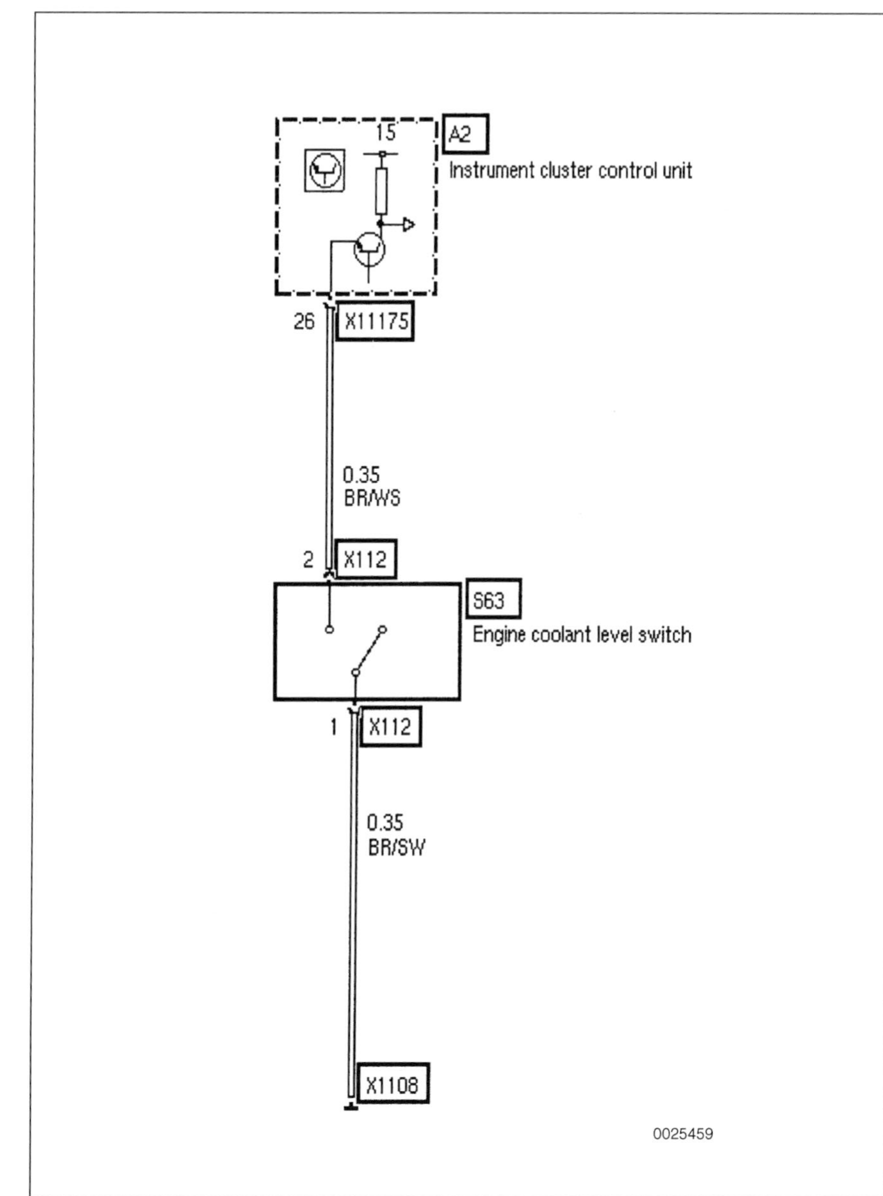

Ground (X1108)

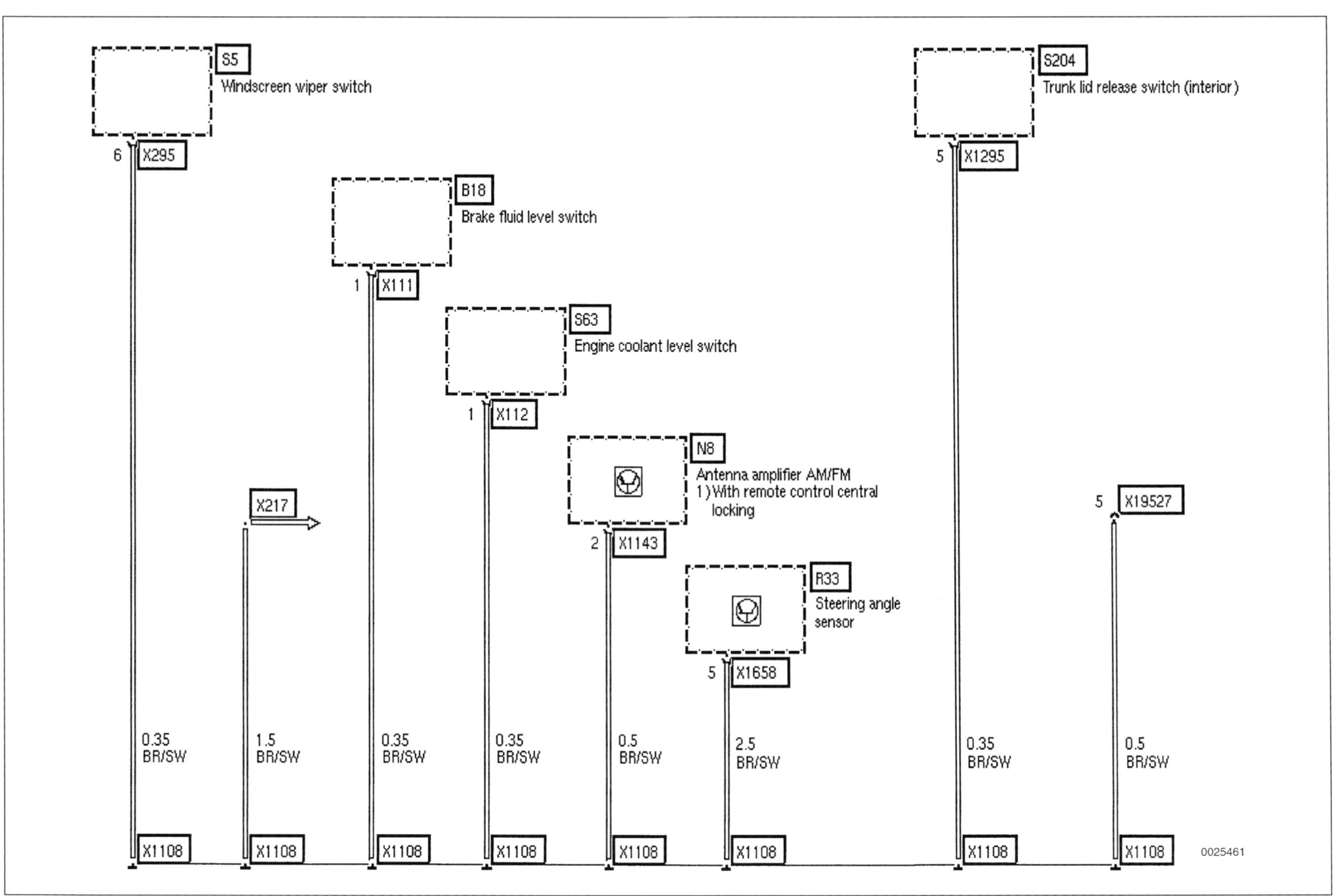

Oil pressure switch (B6231)

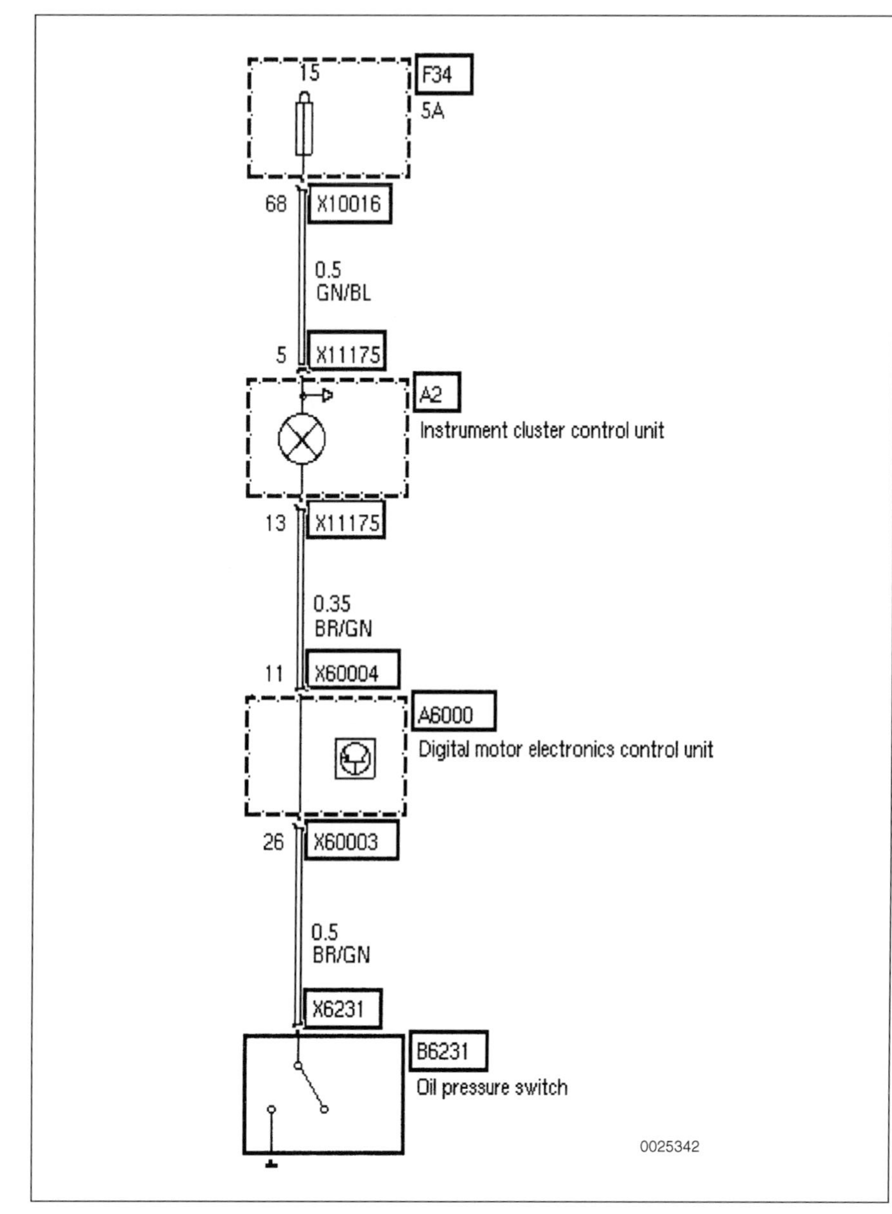

Oil level sensor (B6254)

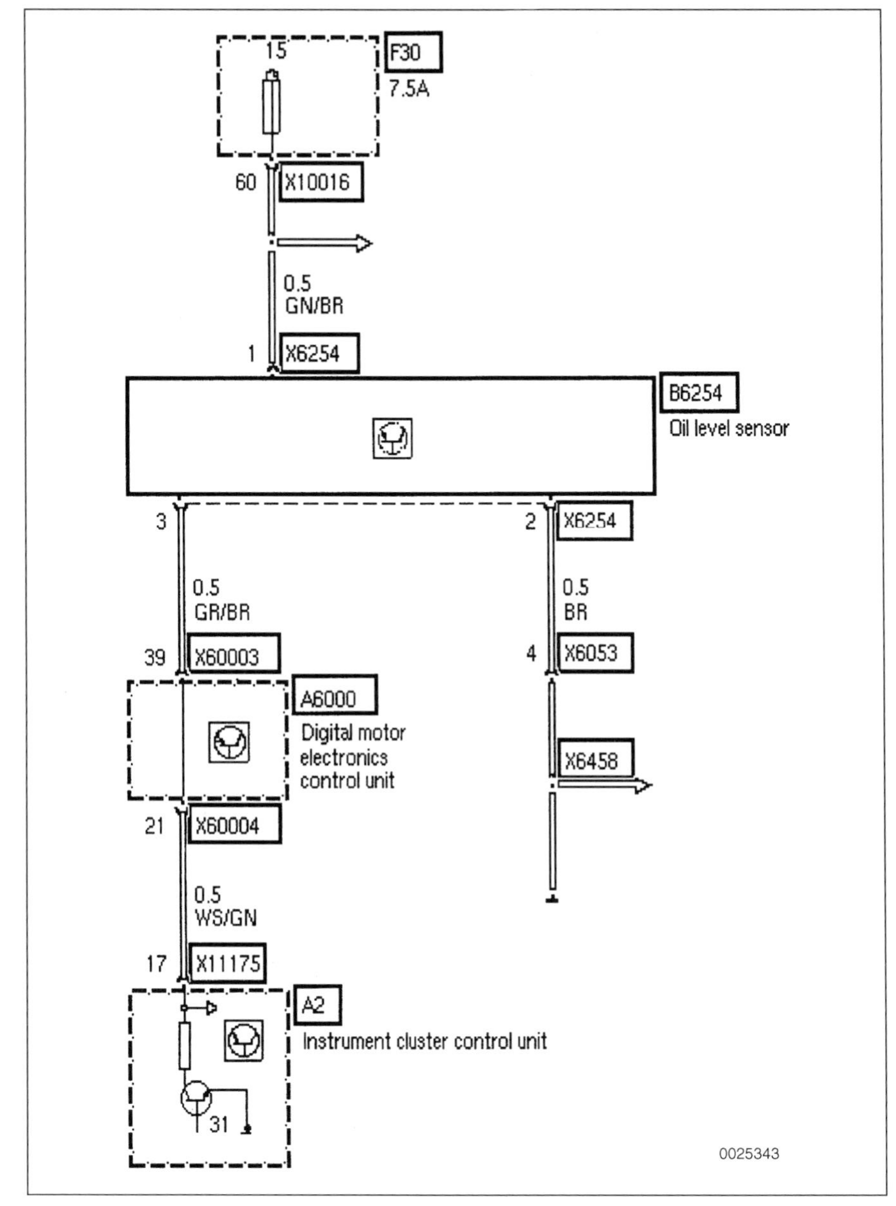

Seatbelt contact, driver side (S58)

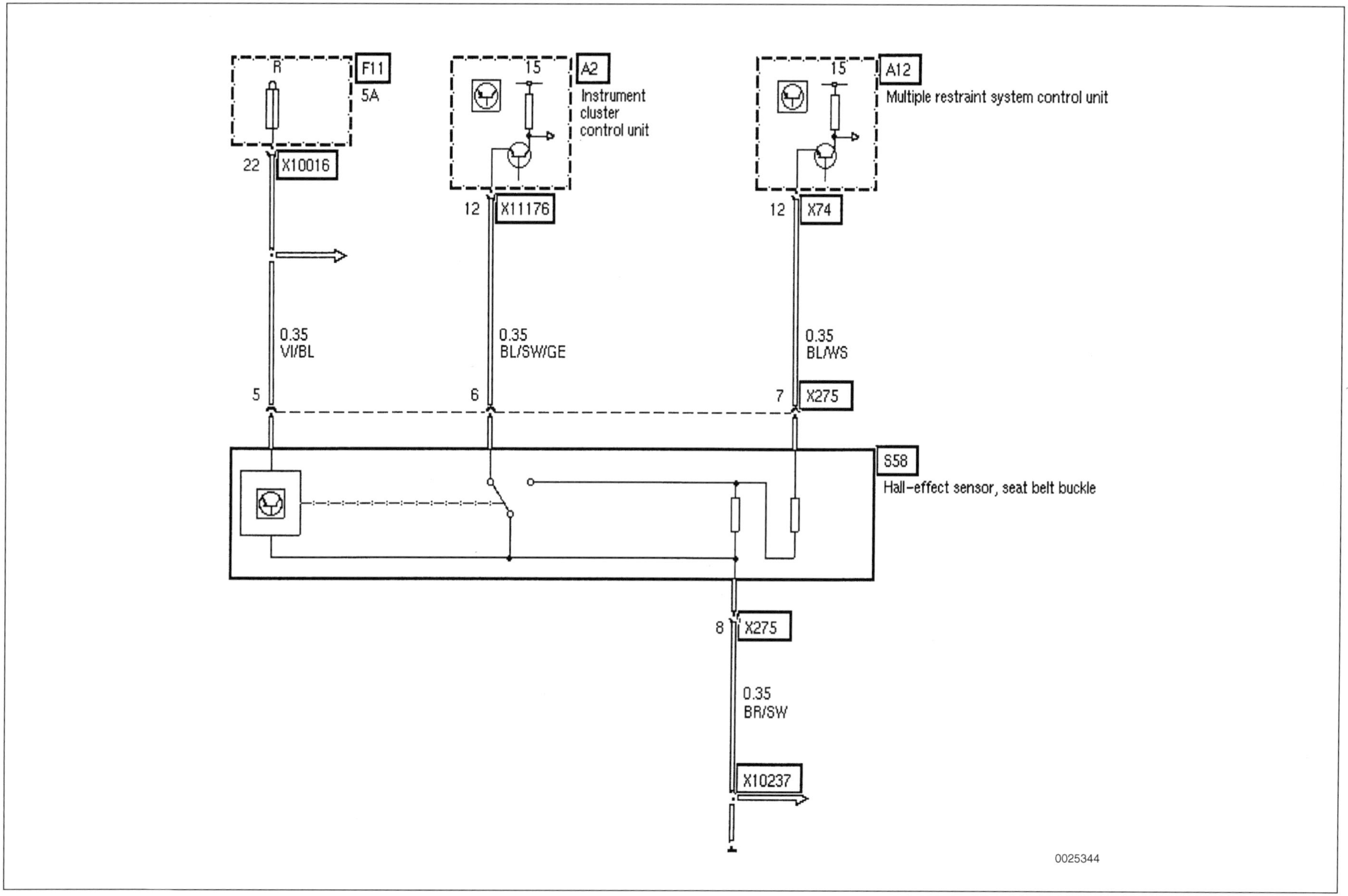

Fuse 11 (F11)

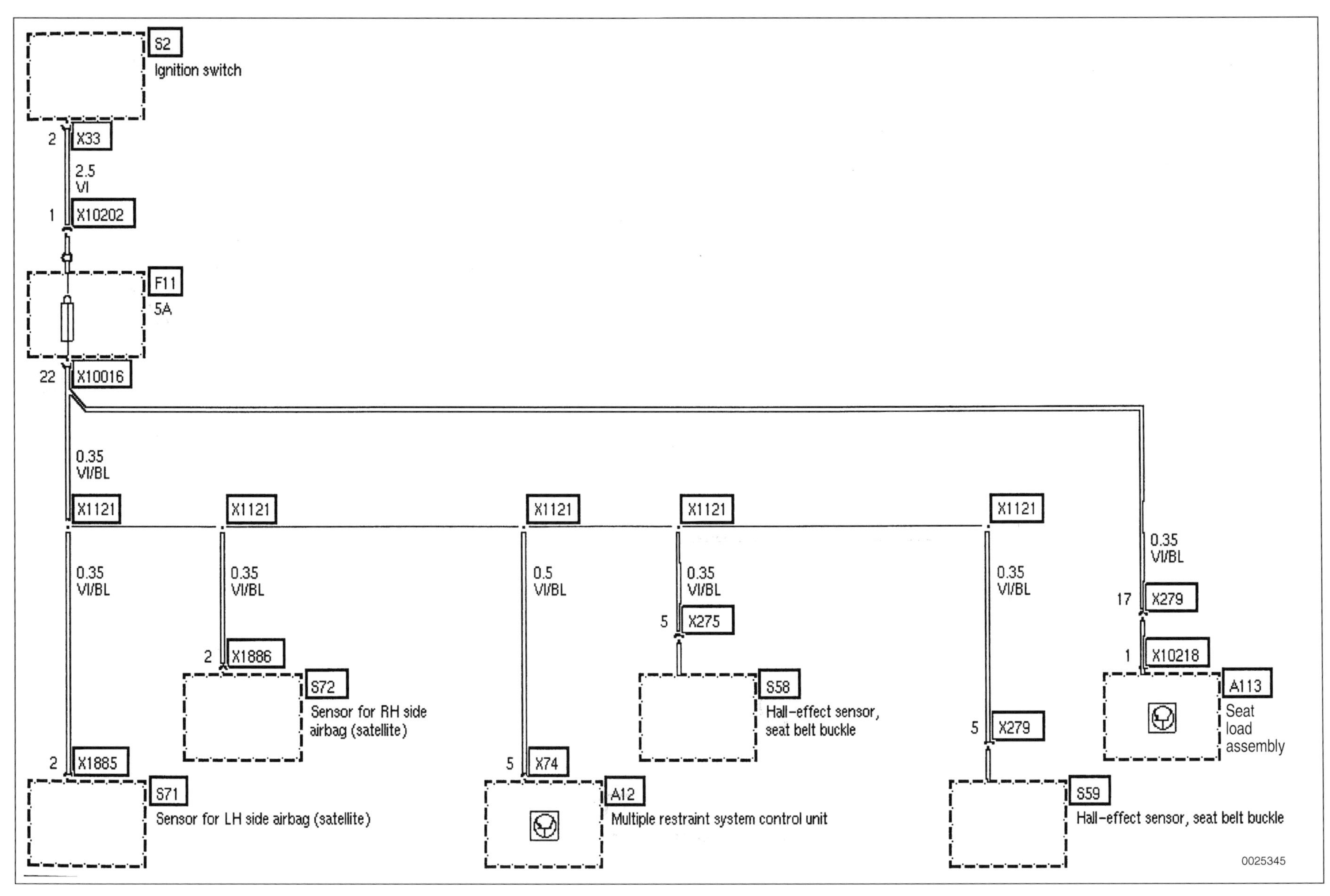
S2
Ignition switch
2
X33
2.5
VI
1
X10202
F11
5A
22
X10016
0.35
VI/BL
X1121
X1121
X1121
X1121
X1121
0.35
VI/BL
0.35
VI/BL
0.5
VI/BL
0.35
VI/BL
0.35
VI/BL
0.35
VI/BL
17
X279
1
X10218
A113
Seat
load
assembly
5
X275
S58
Hall-effect sensor,
seat belt buckle
2
X1886
S72
Sensor for RH side
airbag (satellite)
2
X1885
S71
Sensor for LH side airbag (satellite)
5
X74
A12
Multiple restraint system control unit
5
X279
S59
Hall-effect sensor, seat belt buckle
0025345

Multiple restraint system (MRS) control unit (A12)

1 of 3

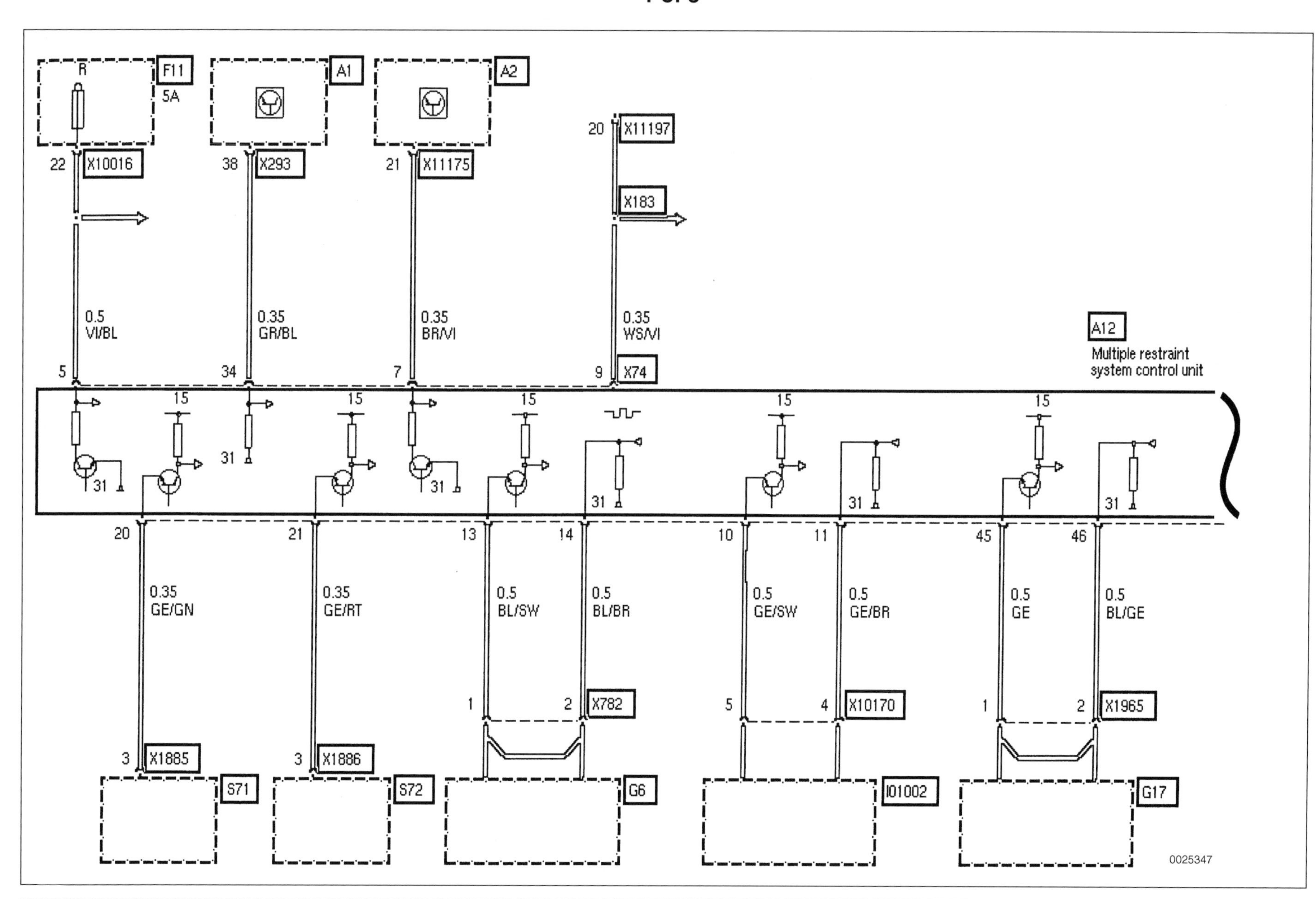

Multiple restraint system (MRS) control unit (A12)

2 of 3

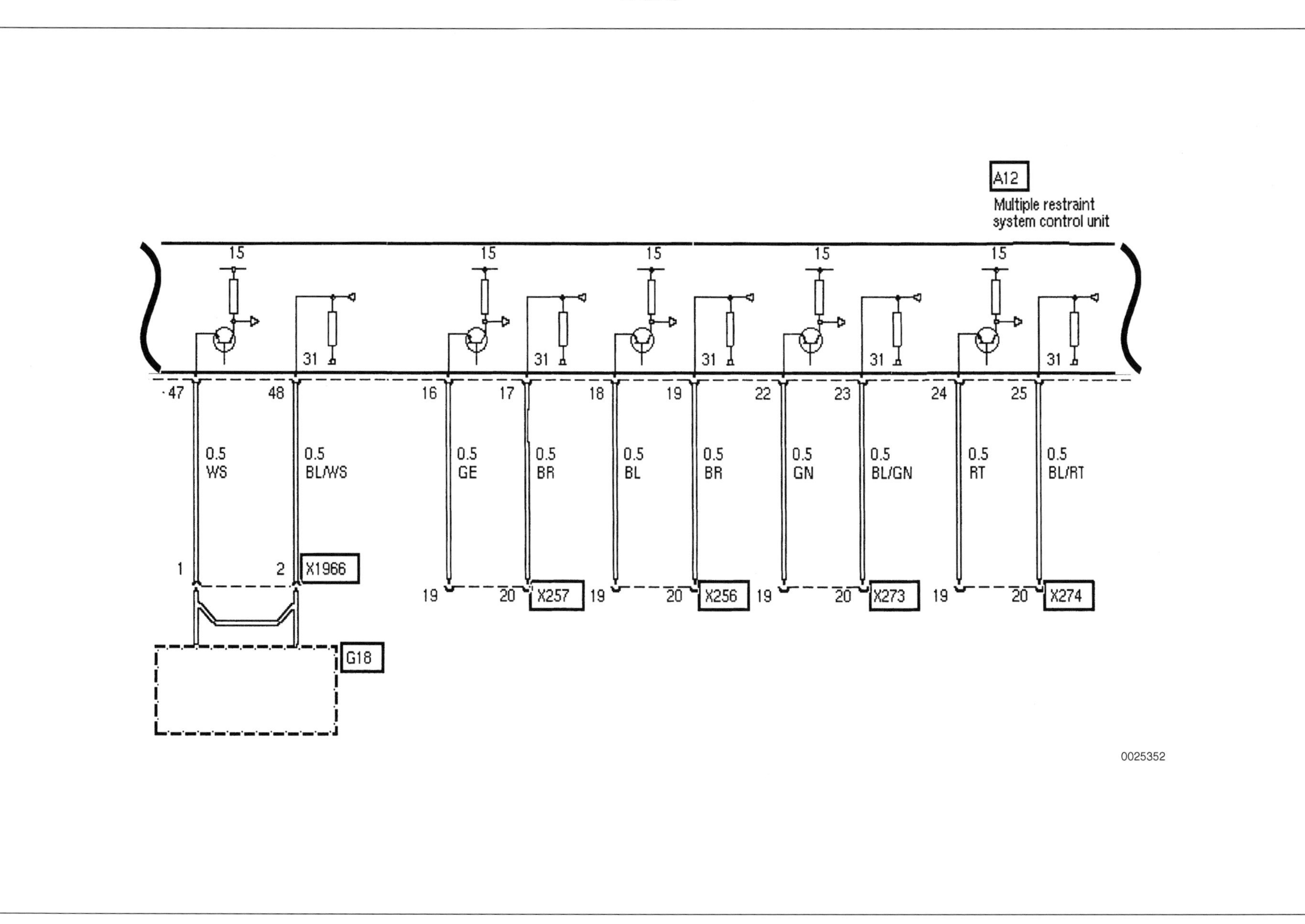

Multiple restraint system (MRS) control unit (A12)

3 of 3

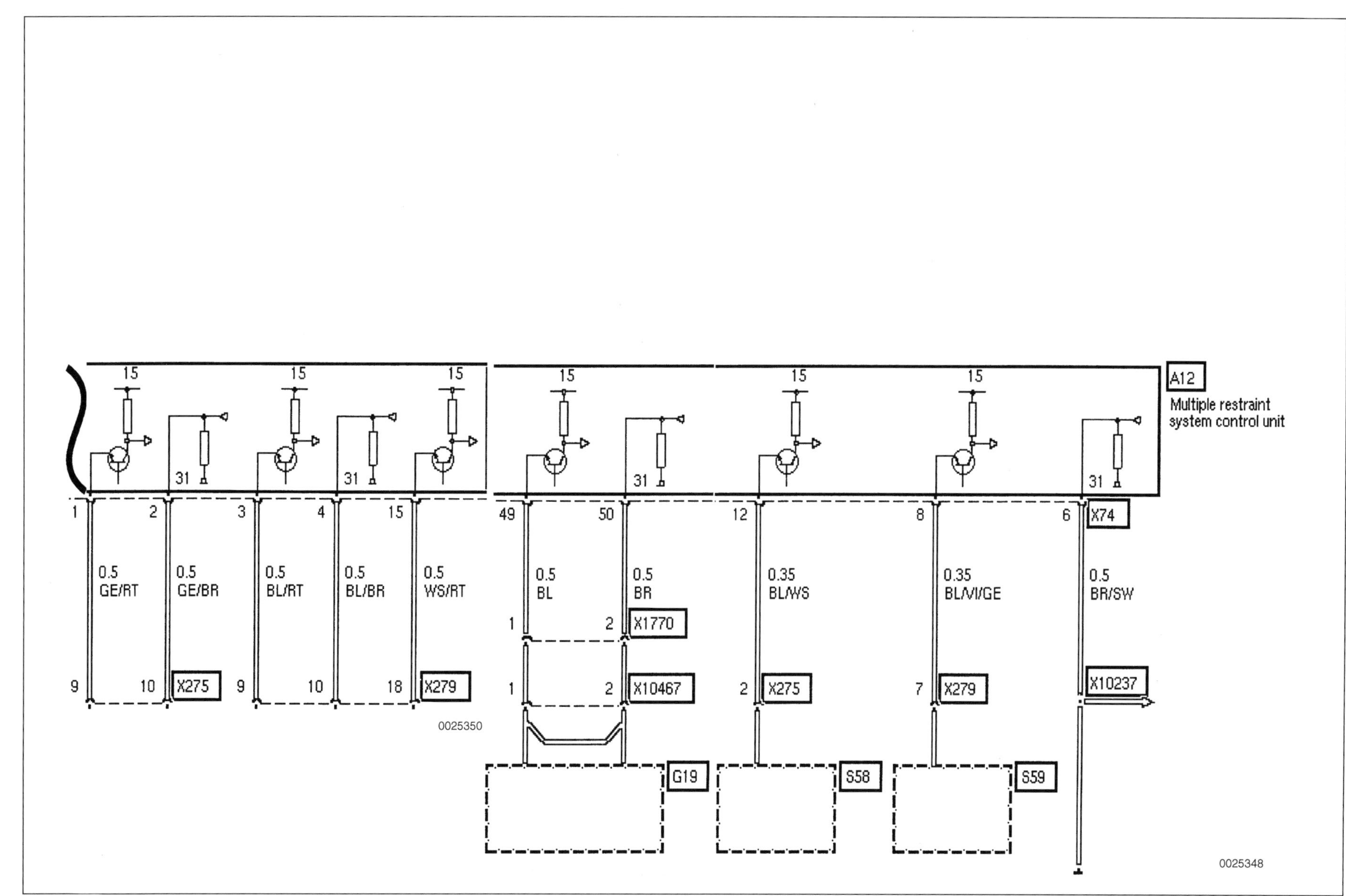

Brake warning light

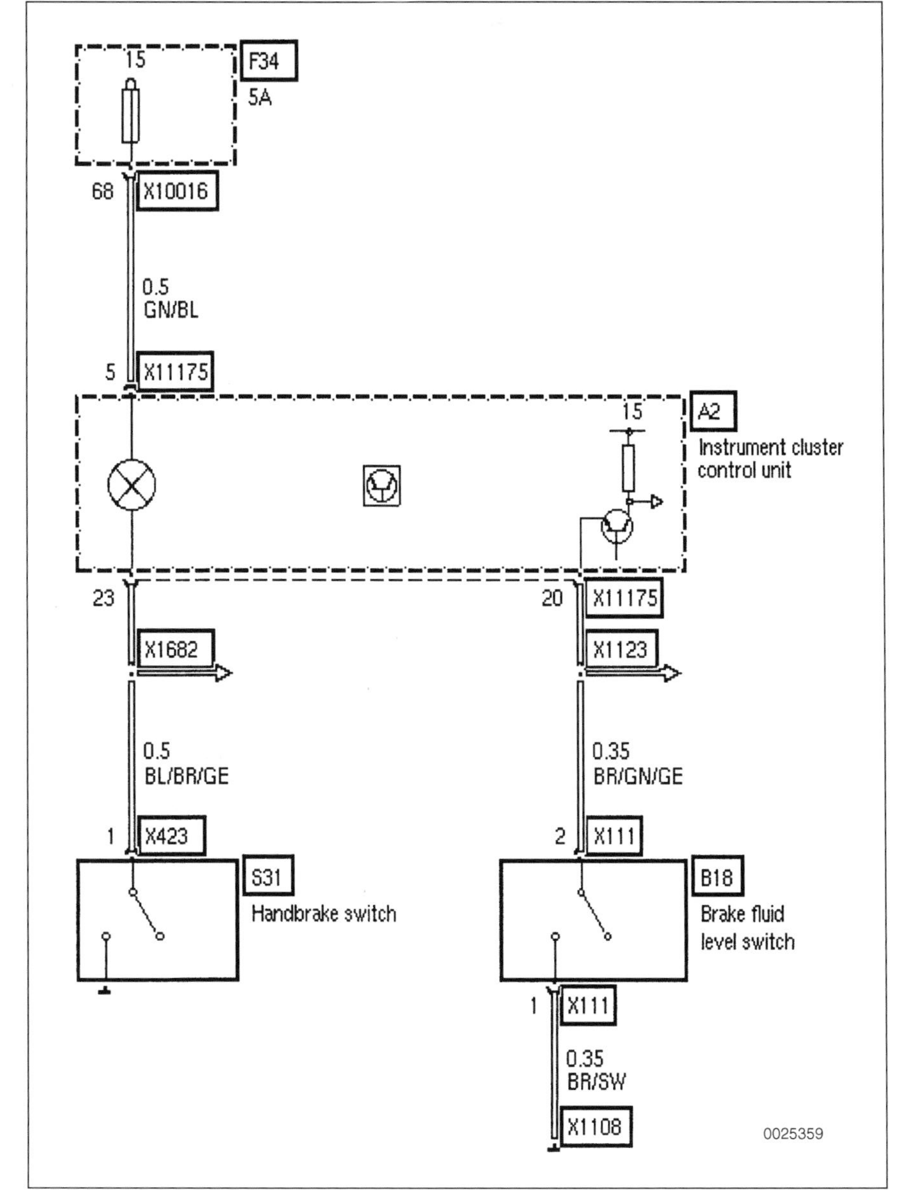

Seat belt contact, passenger side (S59)

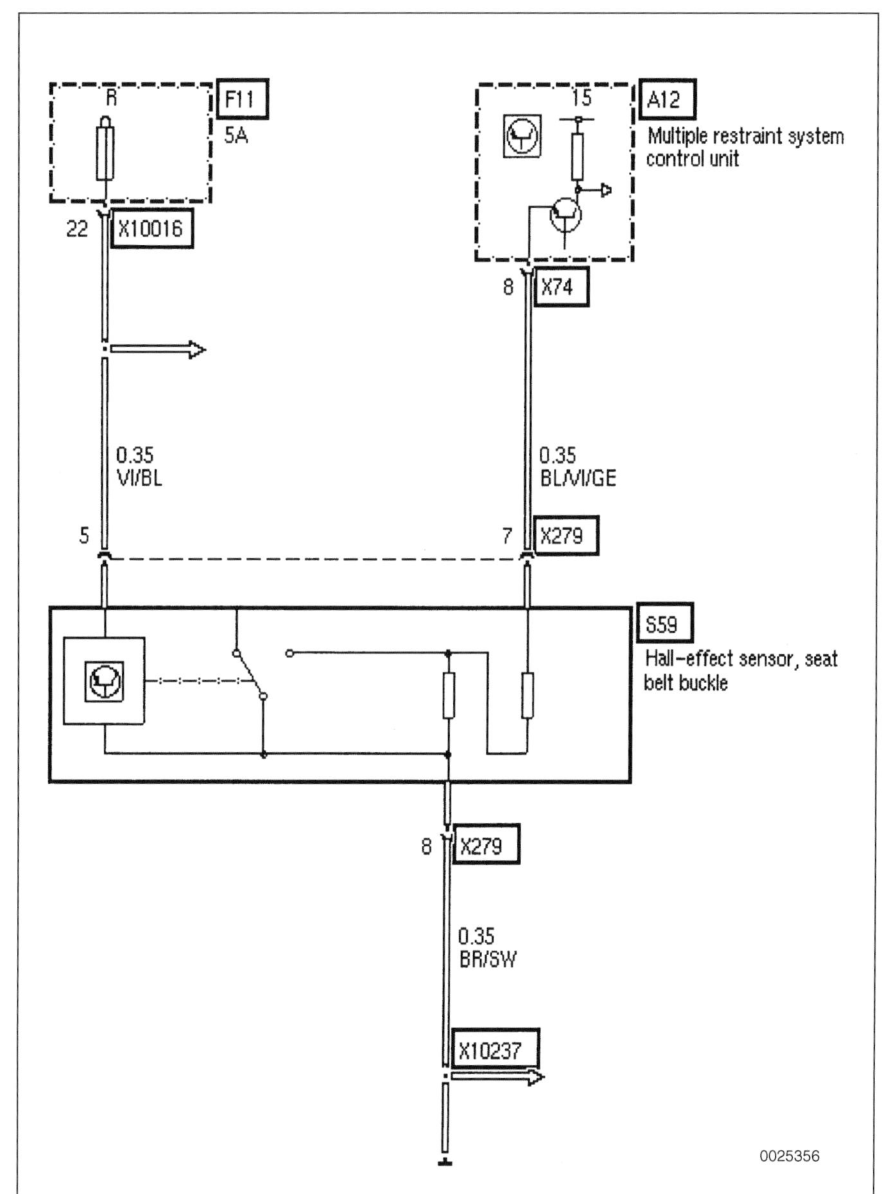

Splice connector (X1682)

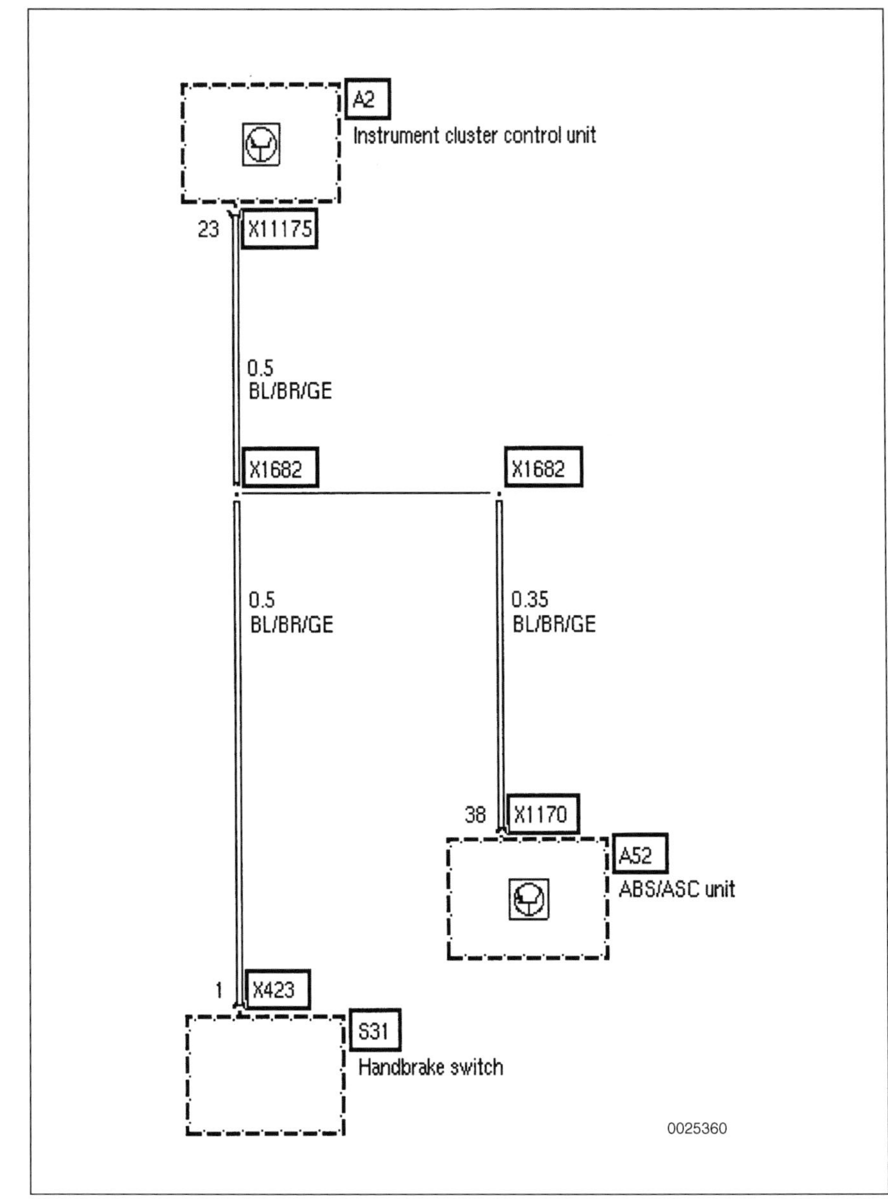

Splice connector (X1123)

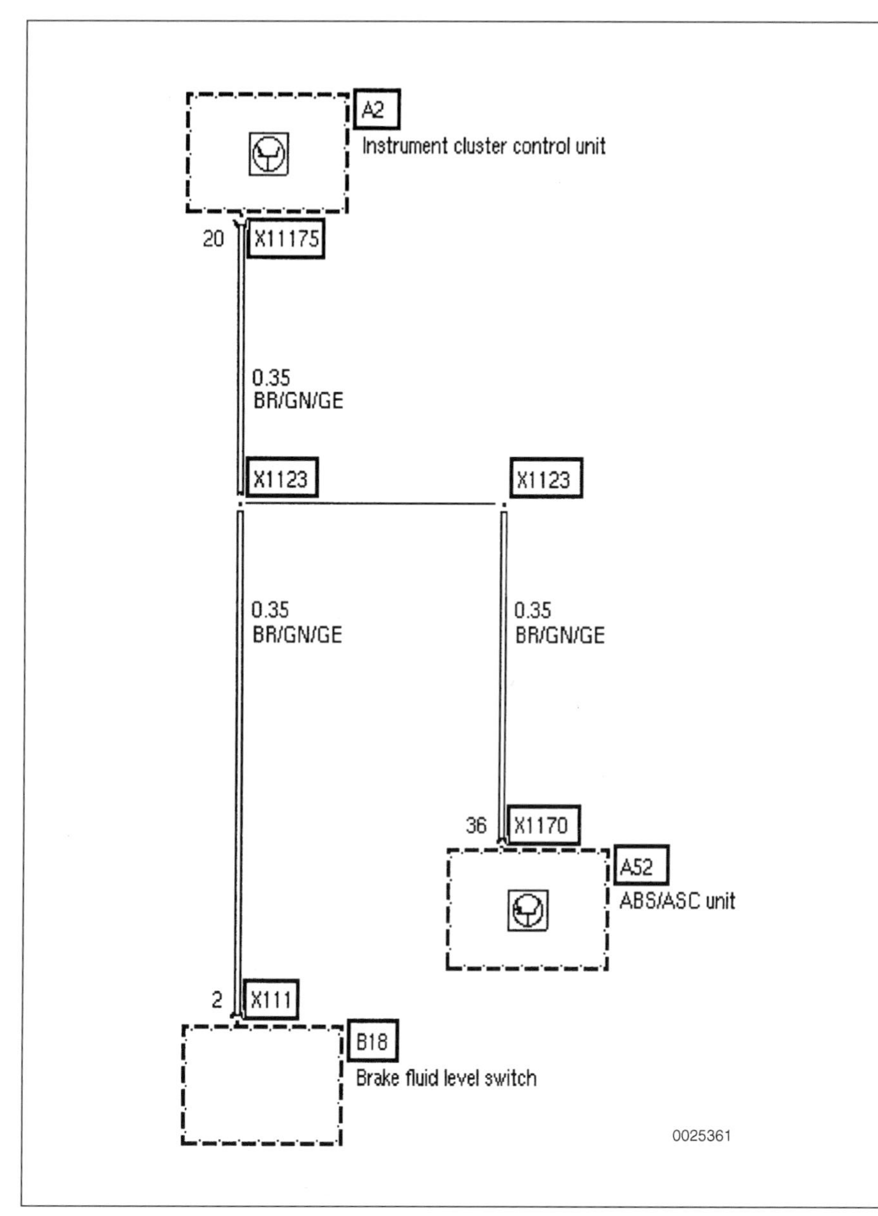

Brake pad wear sensors (B16, B17)

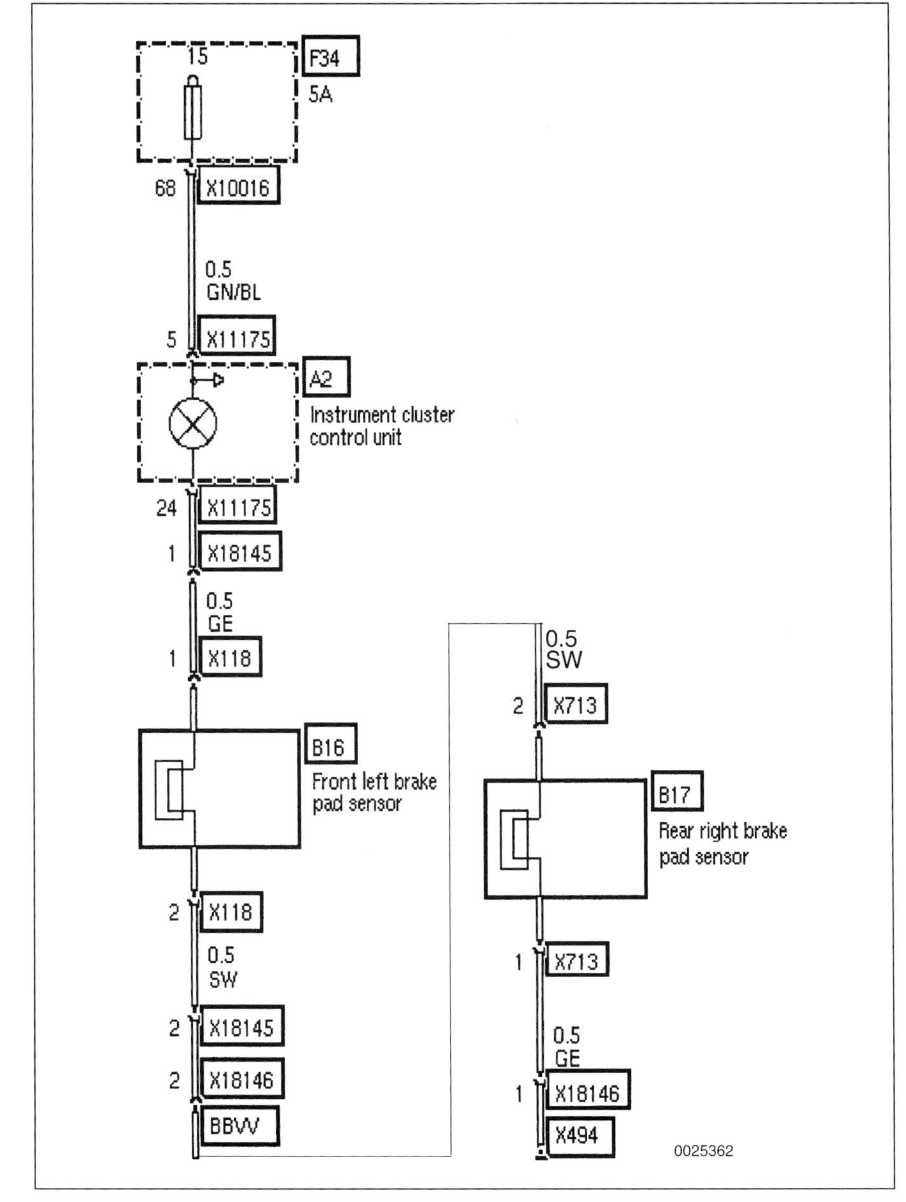

DSC indicator light

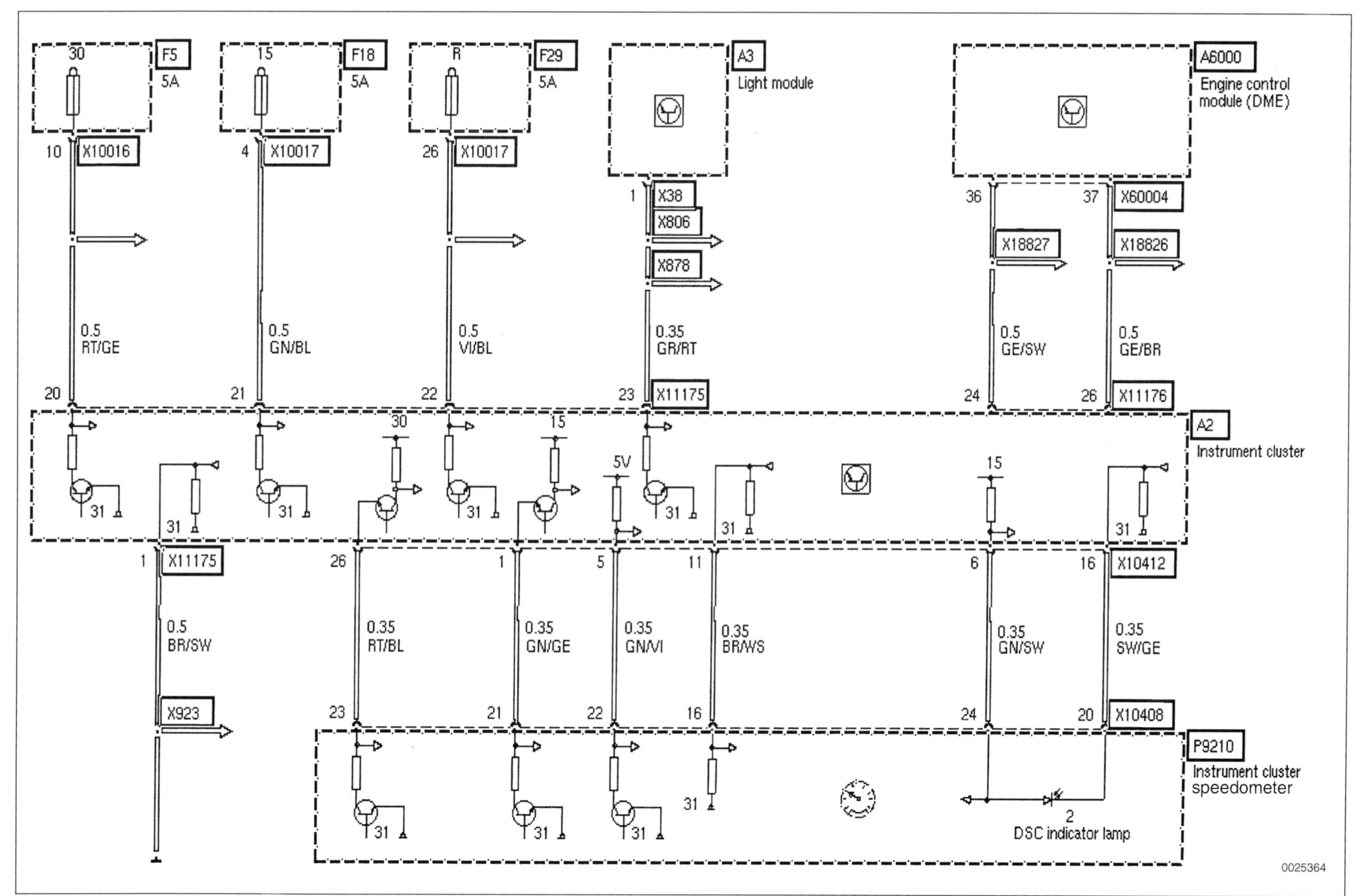

Fuse 5 (F5)

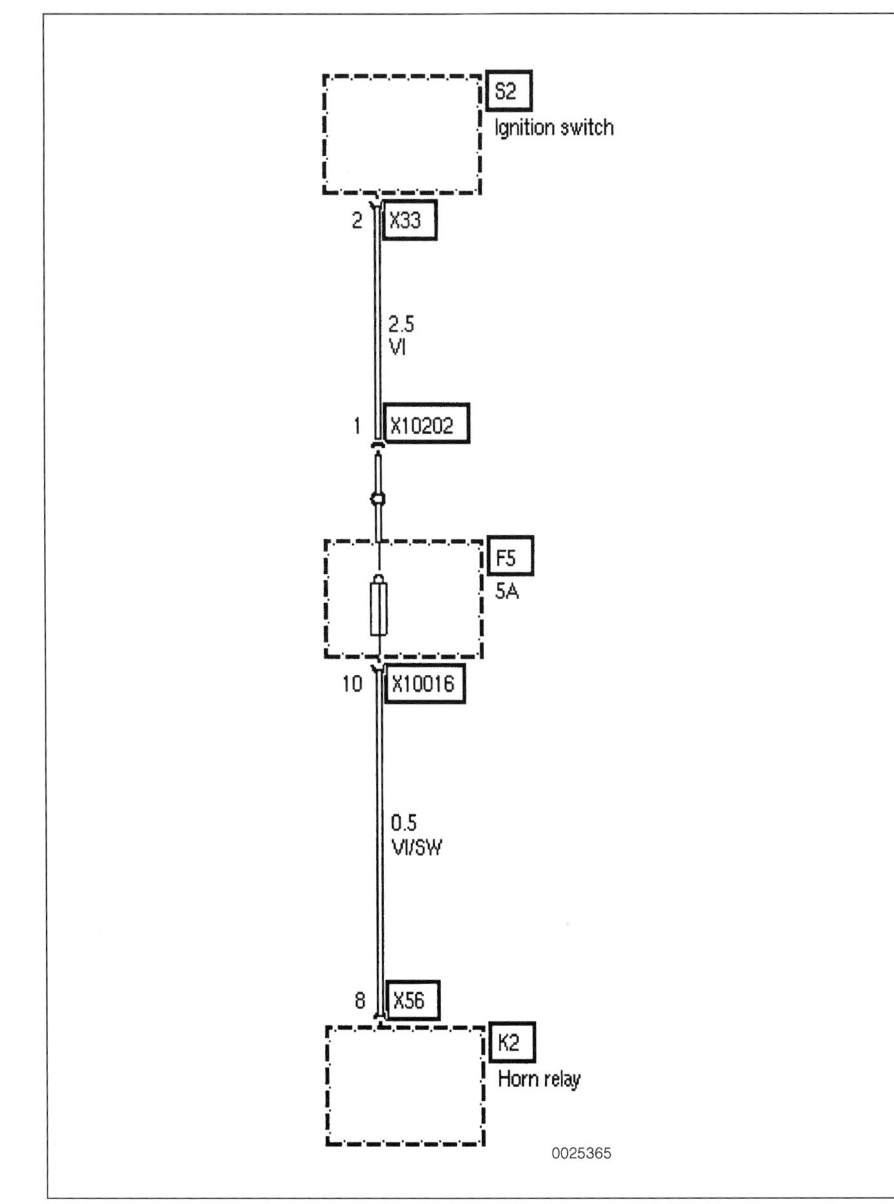
S2
Ignition switch
2
X33
2.5
VI
1
X10202
F5
5A
10
X10016
0.5
VI/SW
8
X56
K2
Horn relay
0025365

Washer fluid level switch (S136)

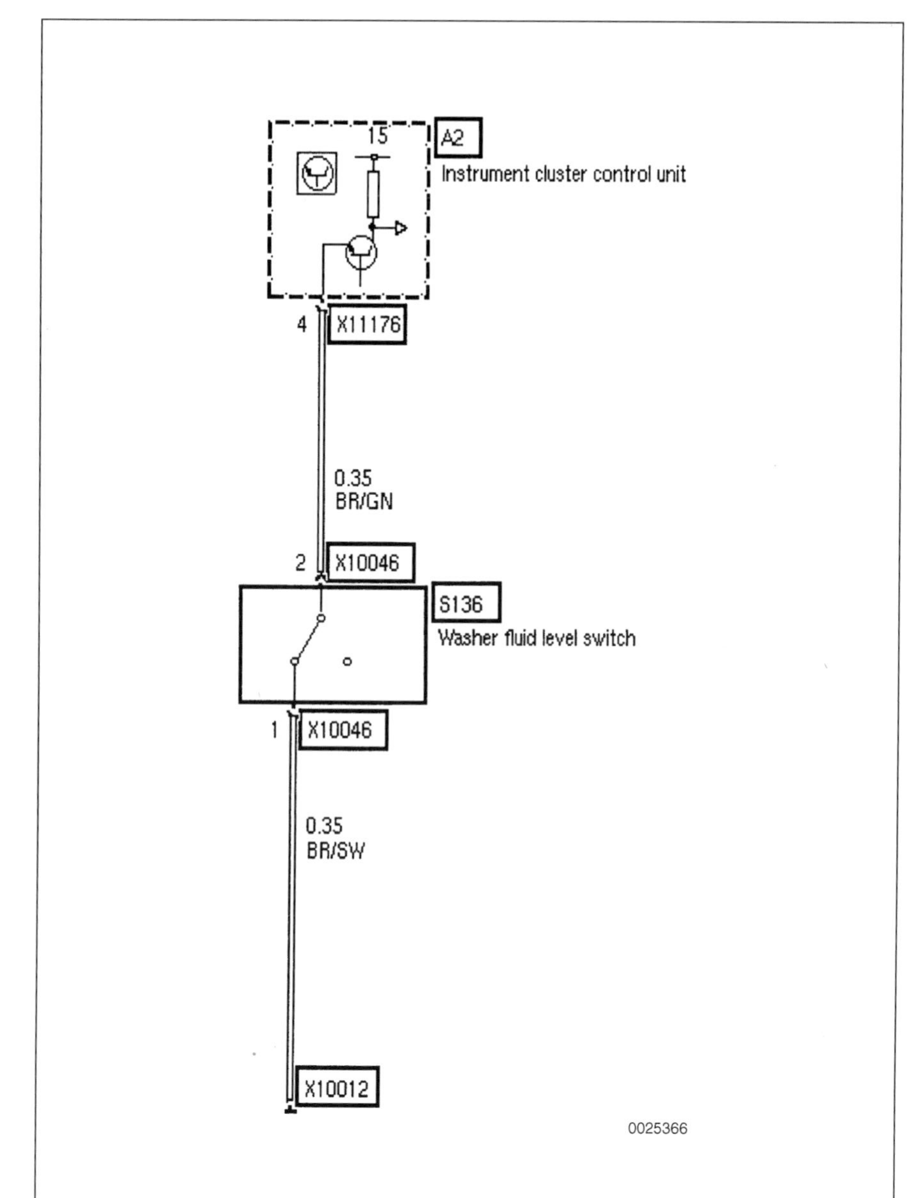

Airbag indicator light

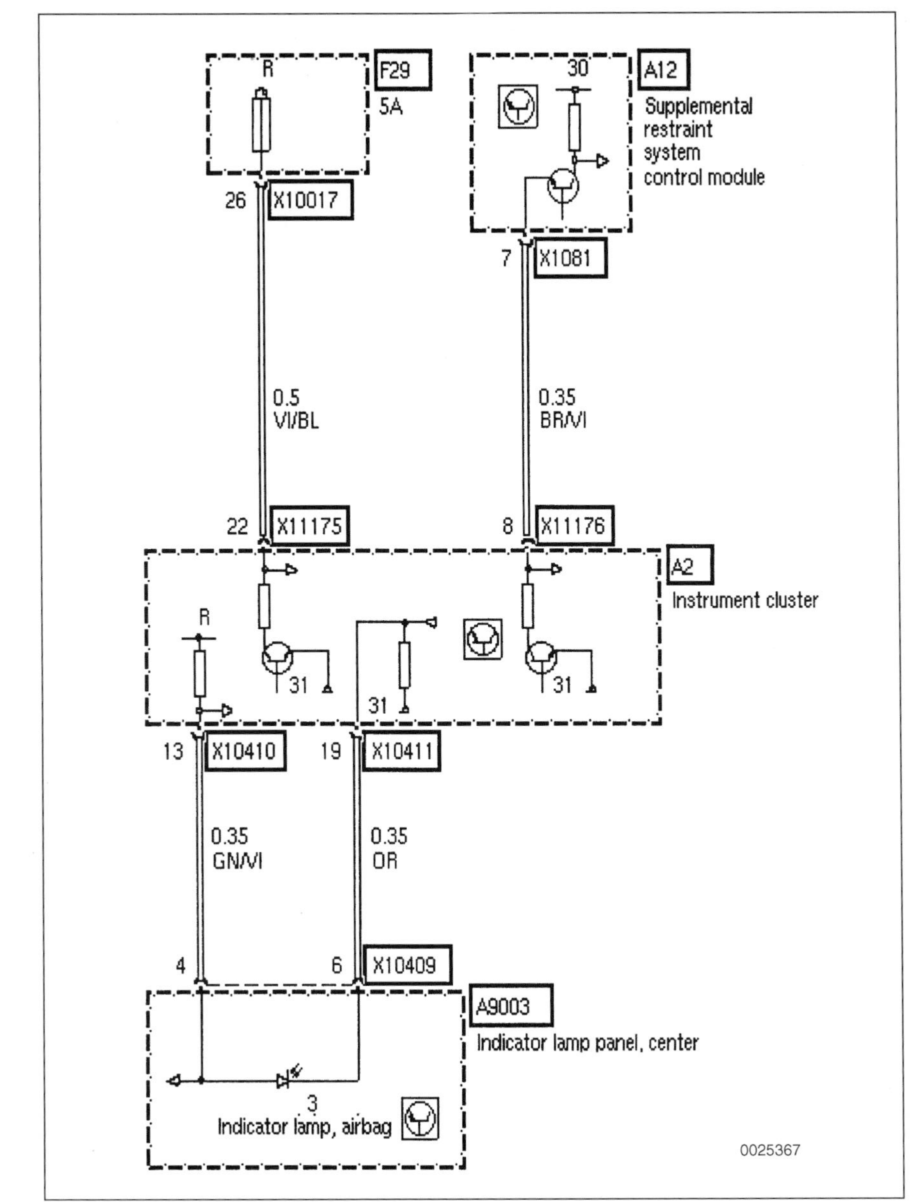

Chime module (park distance control) (H10)

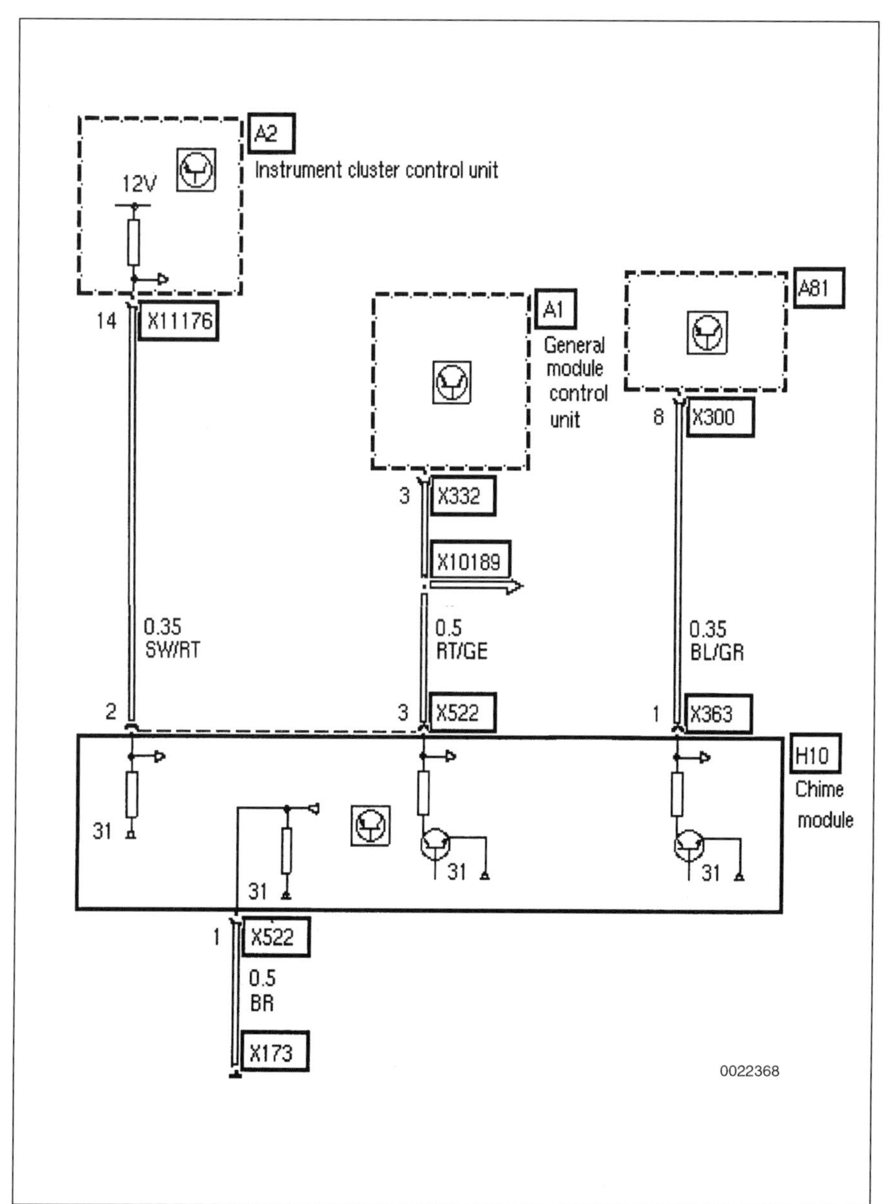

Splice connector (X581)

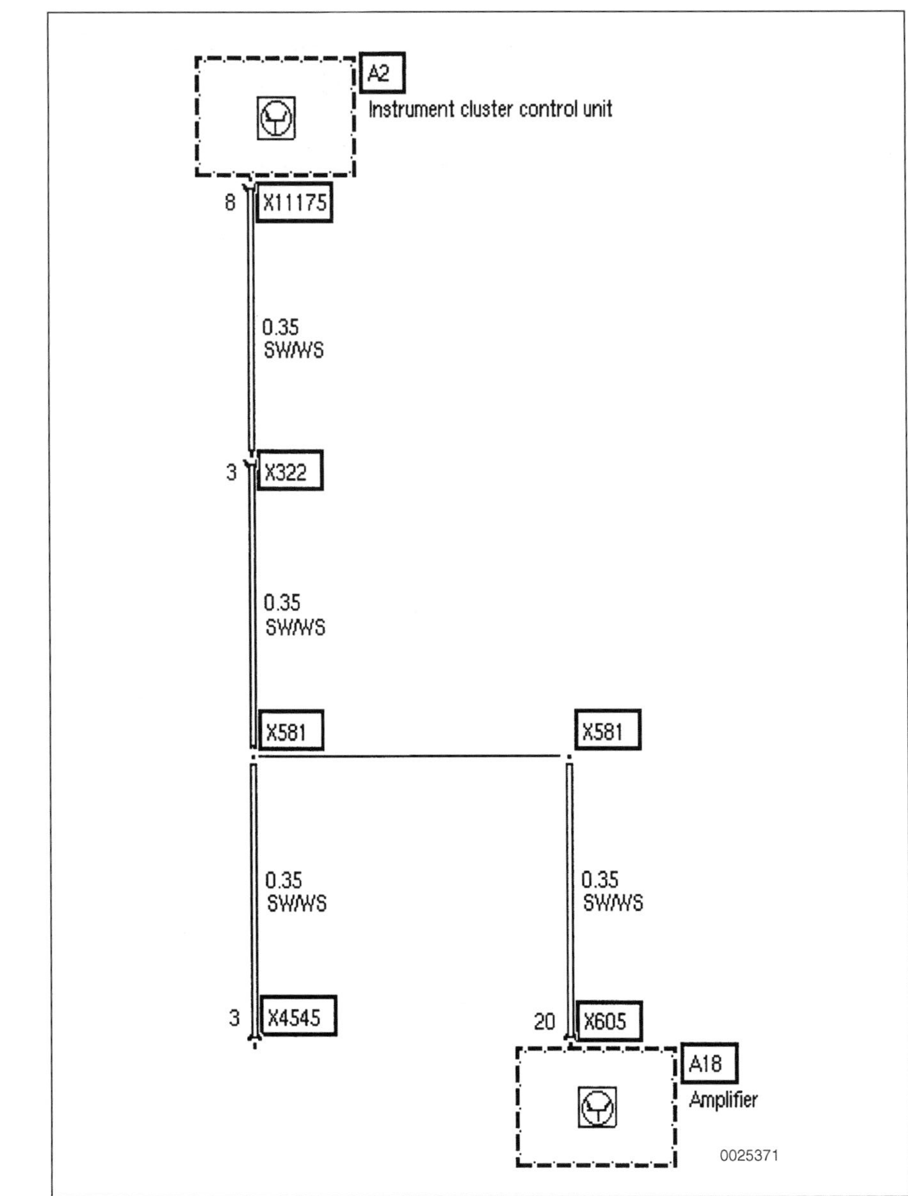

Fuse 41 (F41)

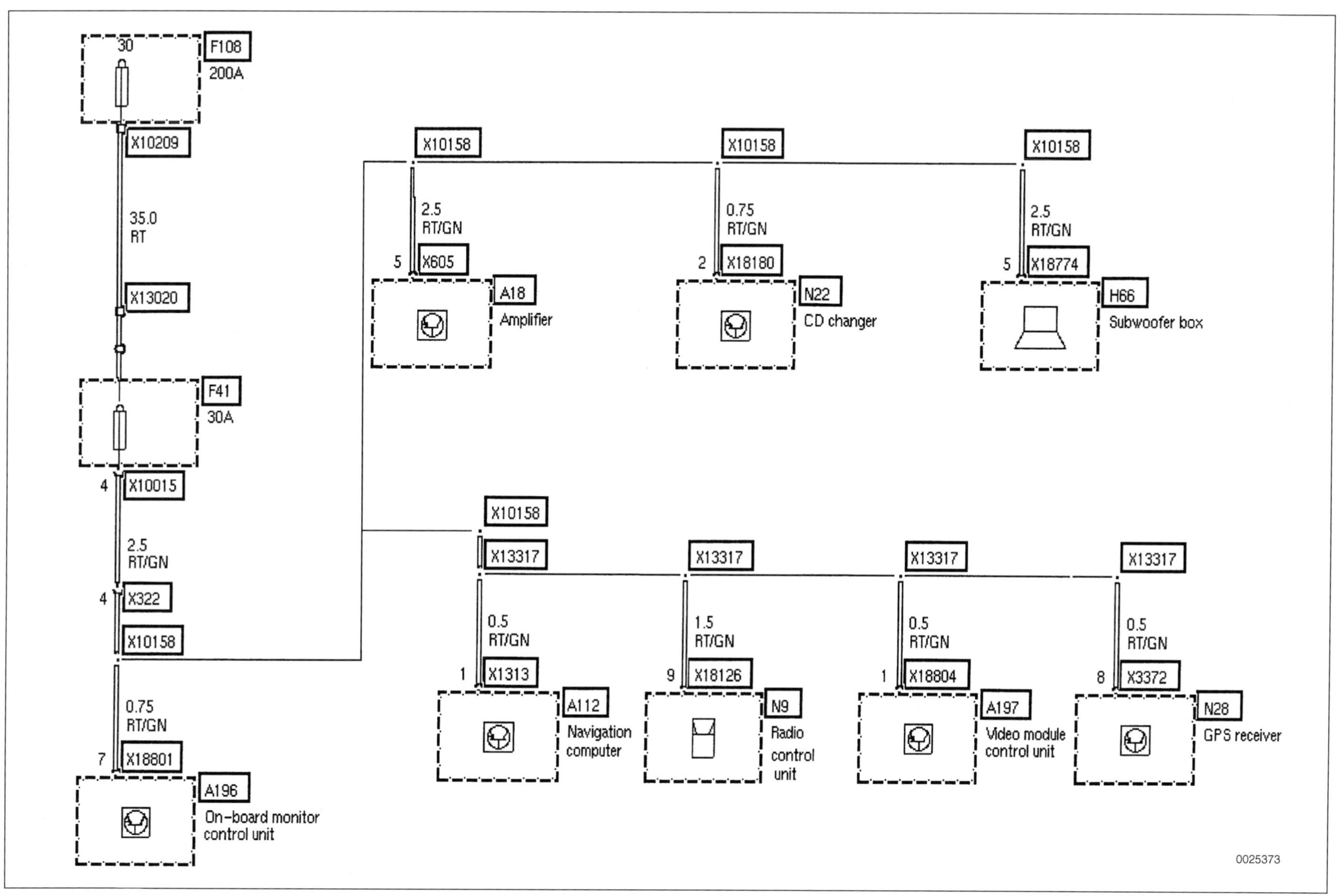

30
F108
200A
X10209
35.0
RT
X13020
F41
30A
4
X10015
2.5
RT/GN
4
X322
X10158
0.75
RT/GN
7
X18801
A196
On-board monitor
control unit
X10158
2.5
RT/GN
5
X605
A18
Amplifier
X10158
0.75
RT/GN
2
X18180
N22
CD changer
X10158
2.5
RT/GN
5
X18774
H66
Subwoofer box
X10158
X13317
0.5
RT/GN
1
X1313
A112
Navigation
computer
X13317
1.5
RT/GN
9
X18126
N9
Radio
control
unit
X13317
0.5
RT/GN
1
X18804
A197
Video module
control unit
X13317
0.5
RT/GN
8
X3372
N28
GPS receiver
0025373

Splice connector (X18344)

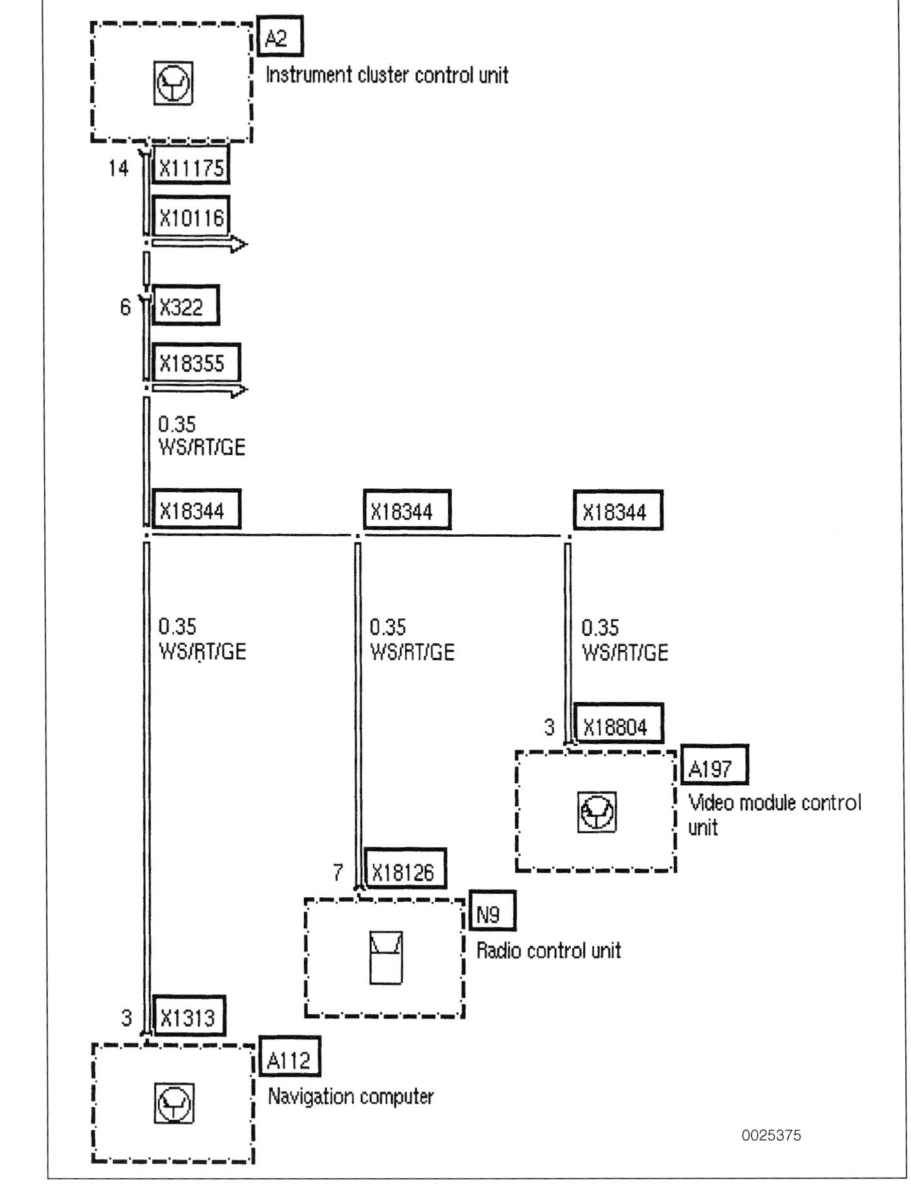

Radio control unit (N9)
1 of 3

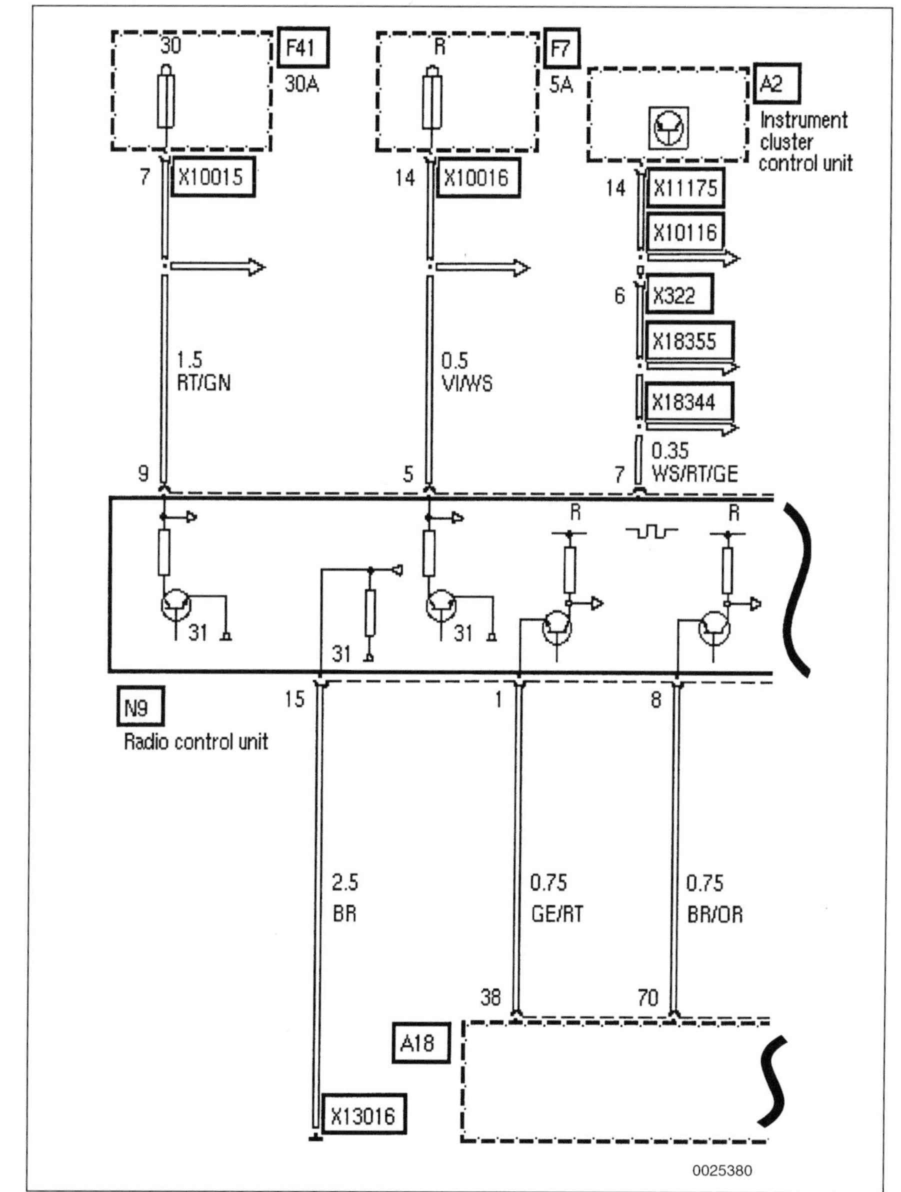

Radio control unit (N9)
2 of 3

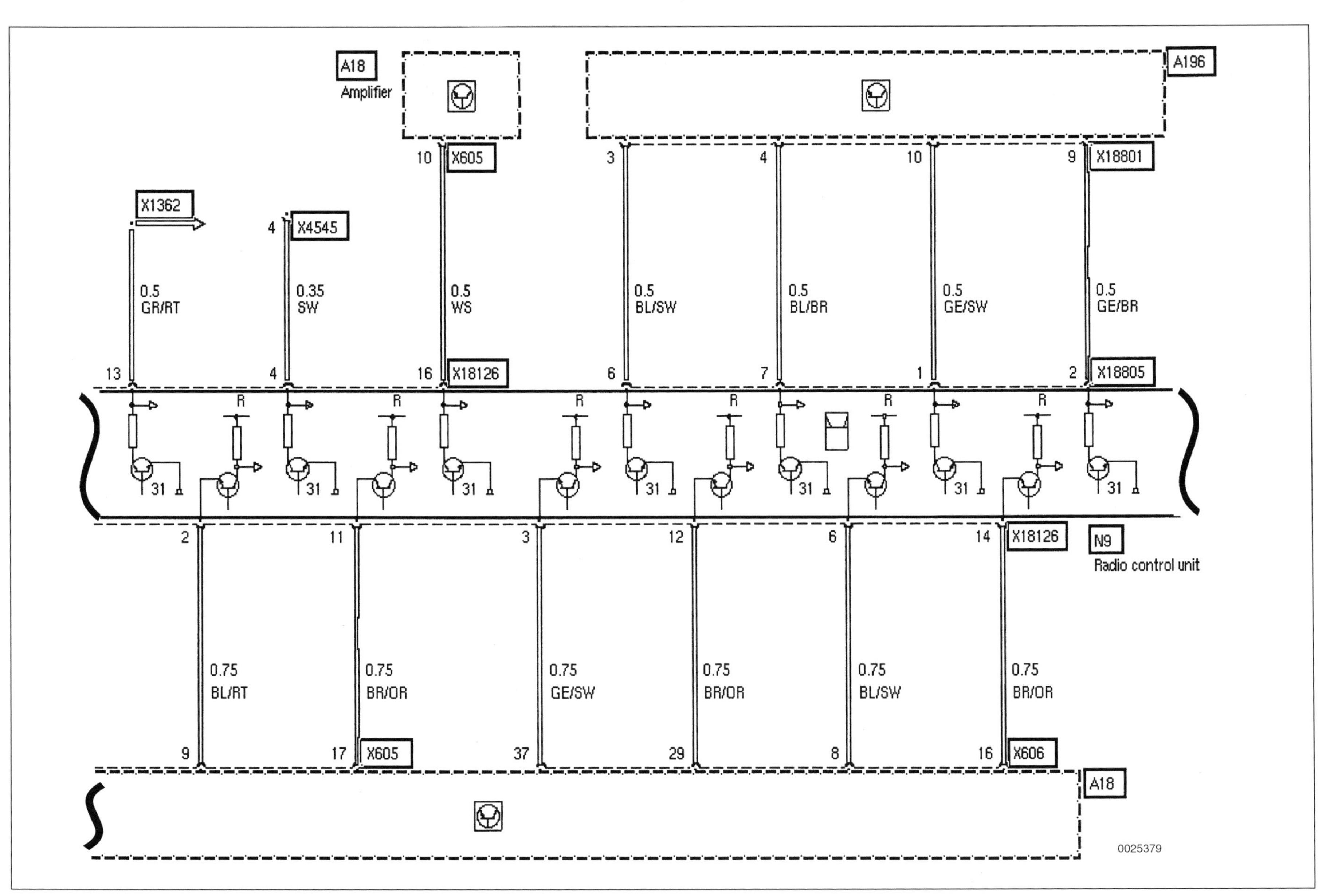

Radio control unit (N9)

3 of 3

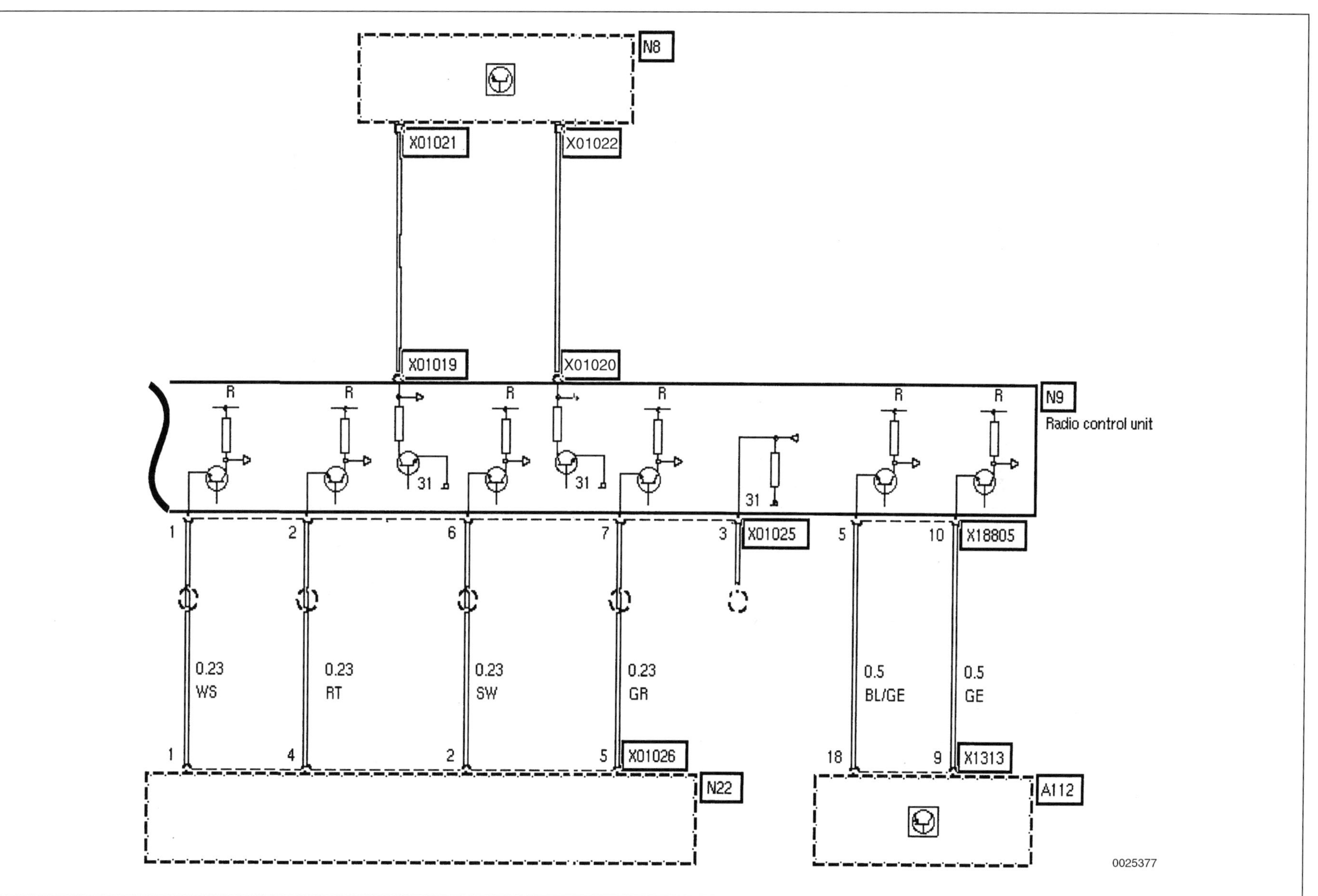

Ground (X13016)

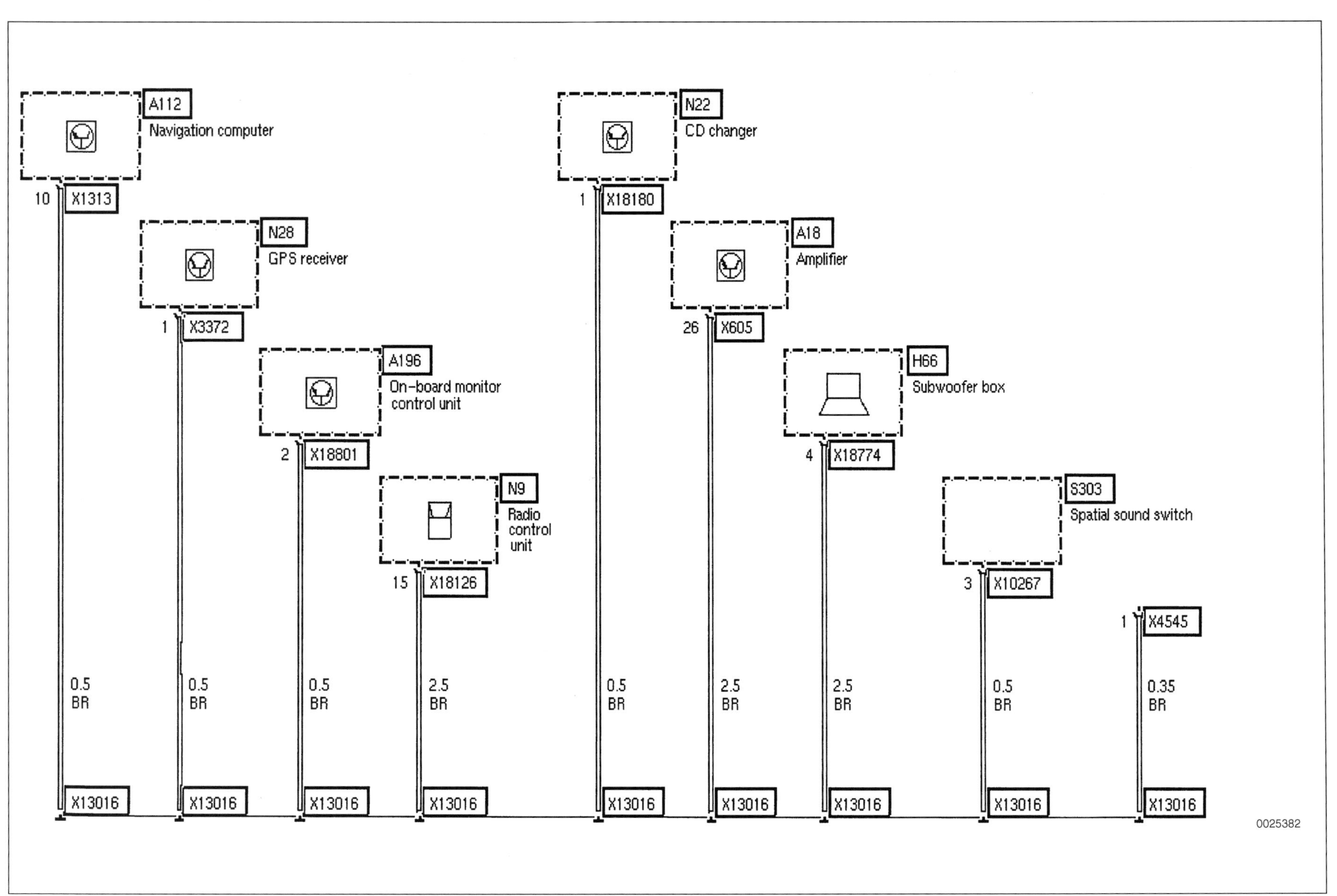

CD changer (N22)

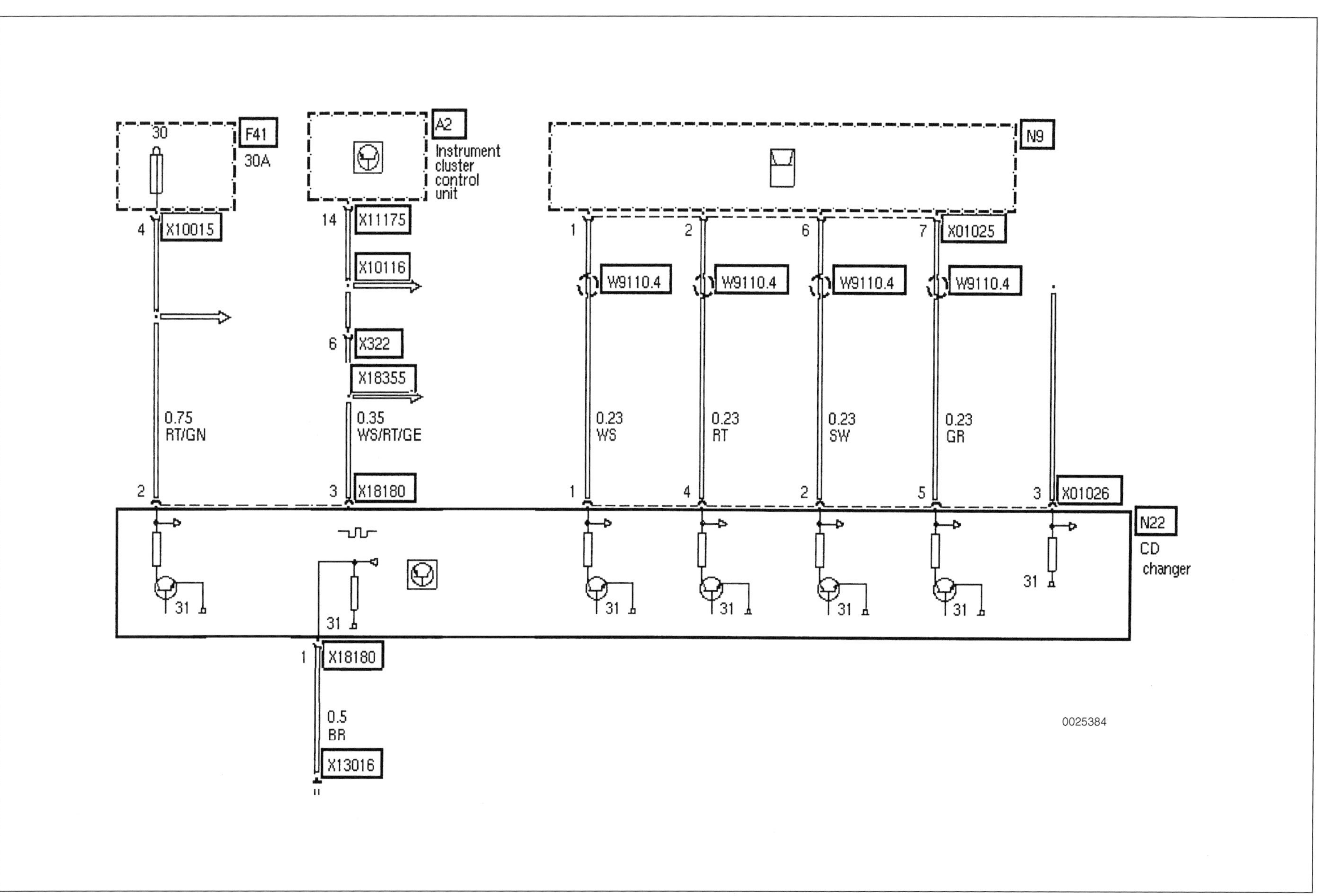

On-board monitor control unit (A196)

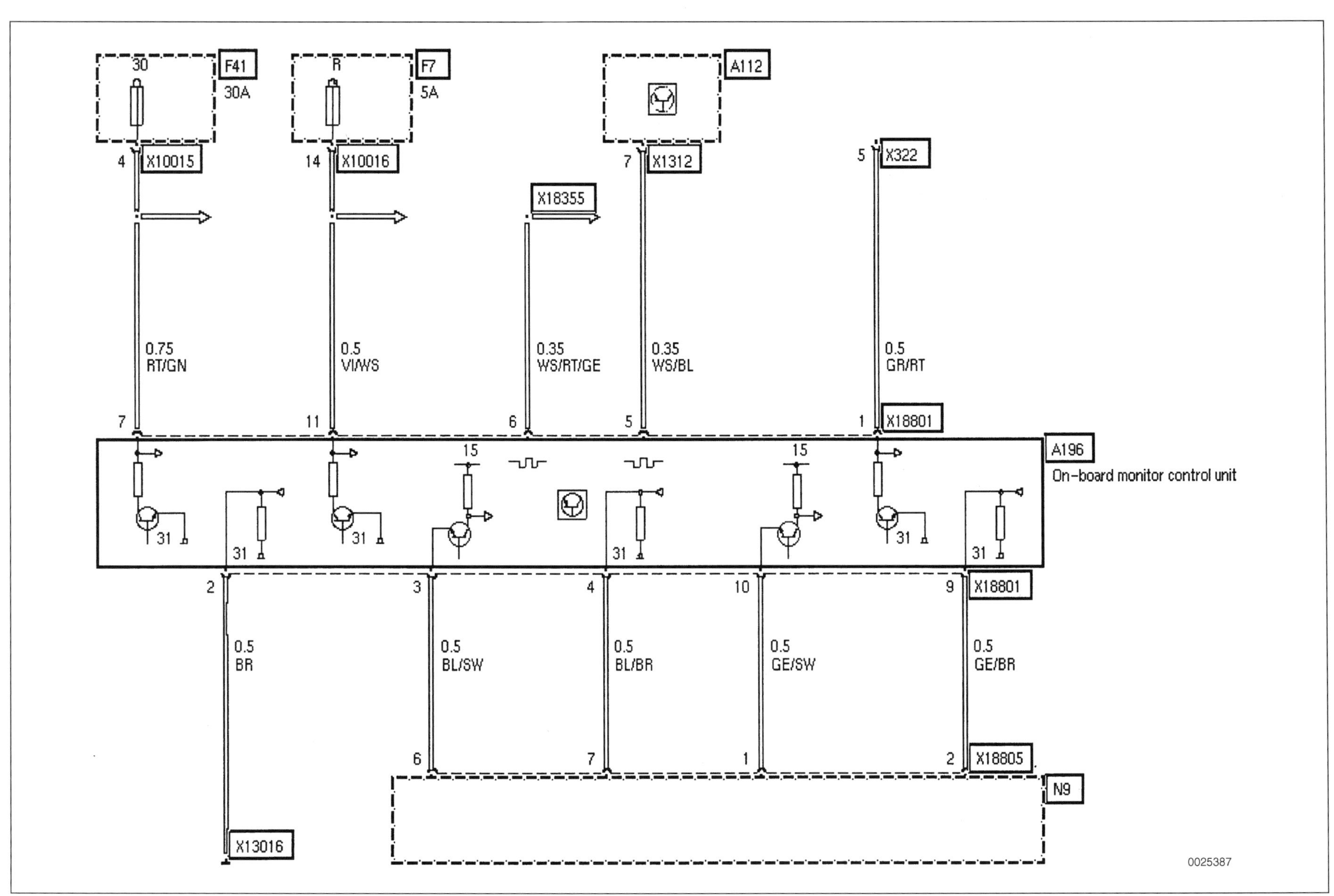

Telephone transceiver (U400)
1 of 2

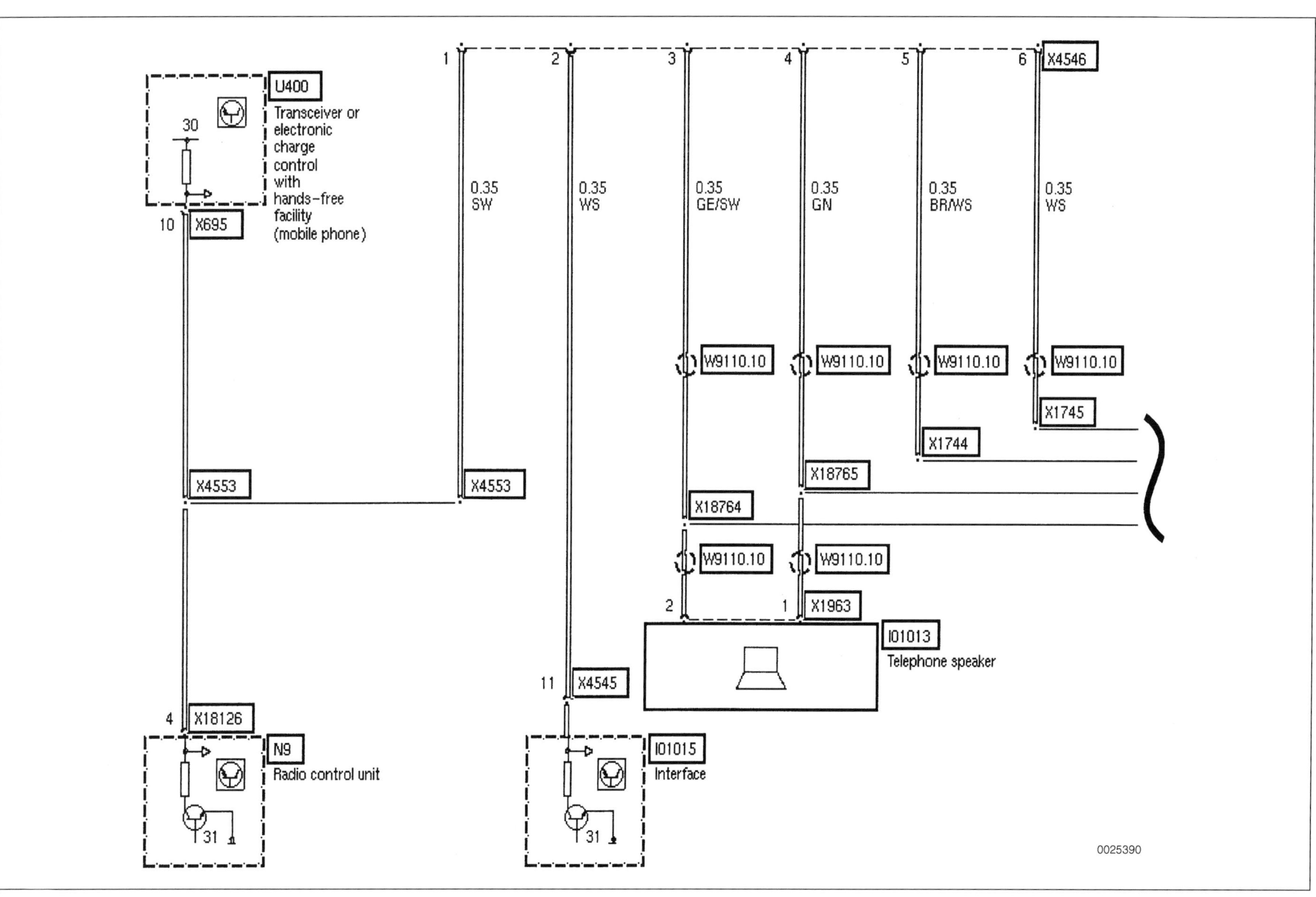

Telephone transceiver (U400)
2 of 2

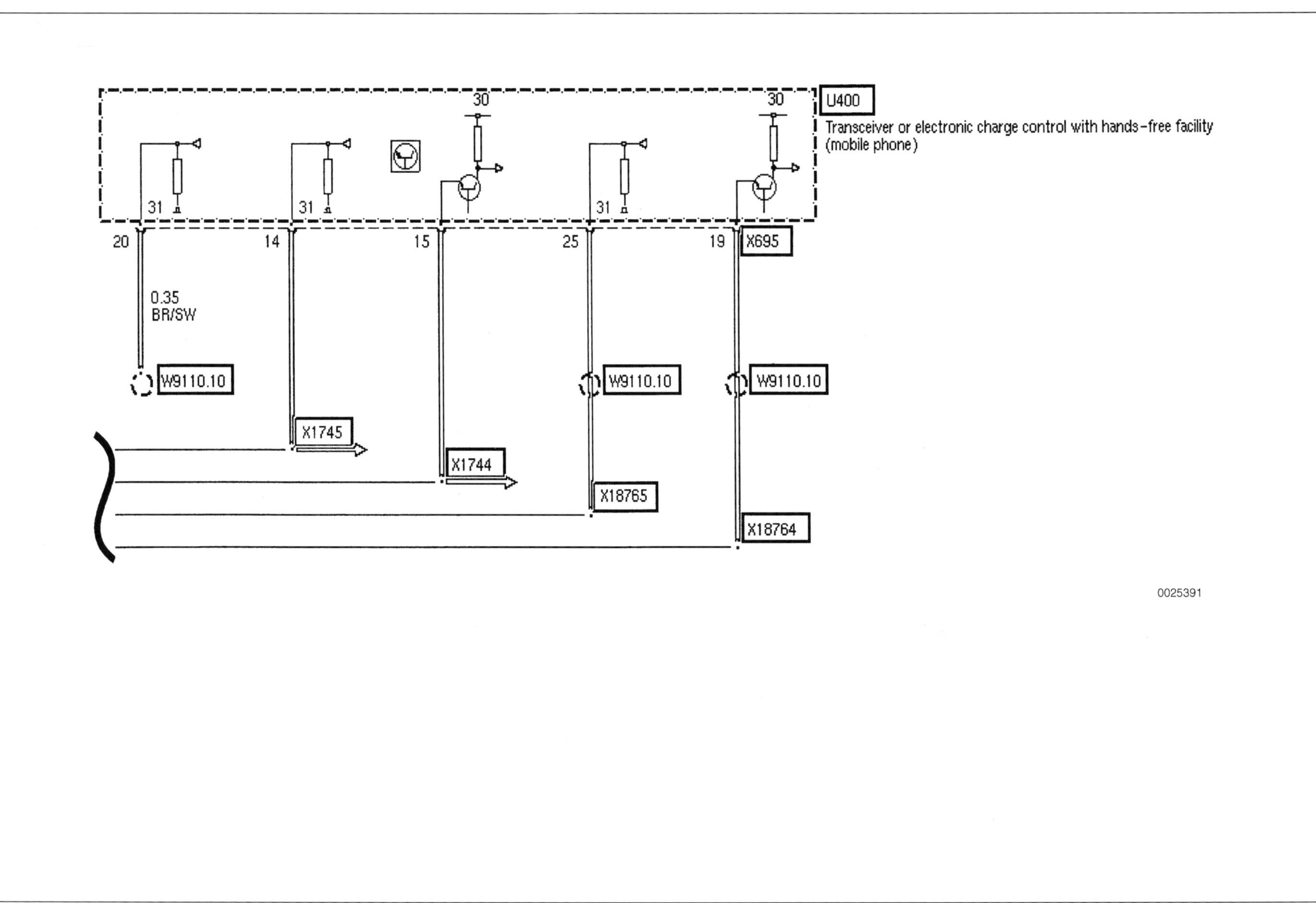

Telephone splice connectors (X1744, X1745)

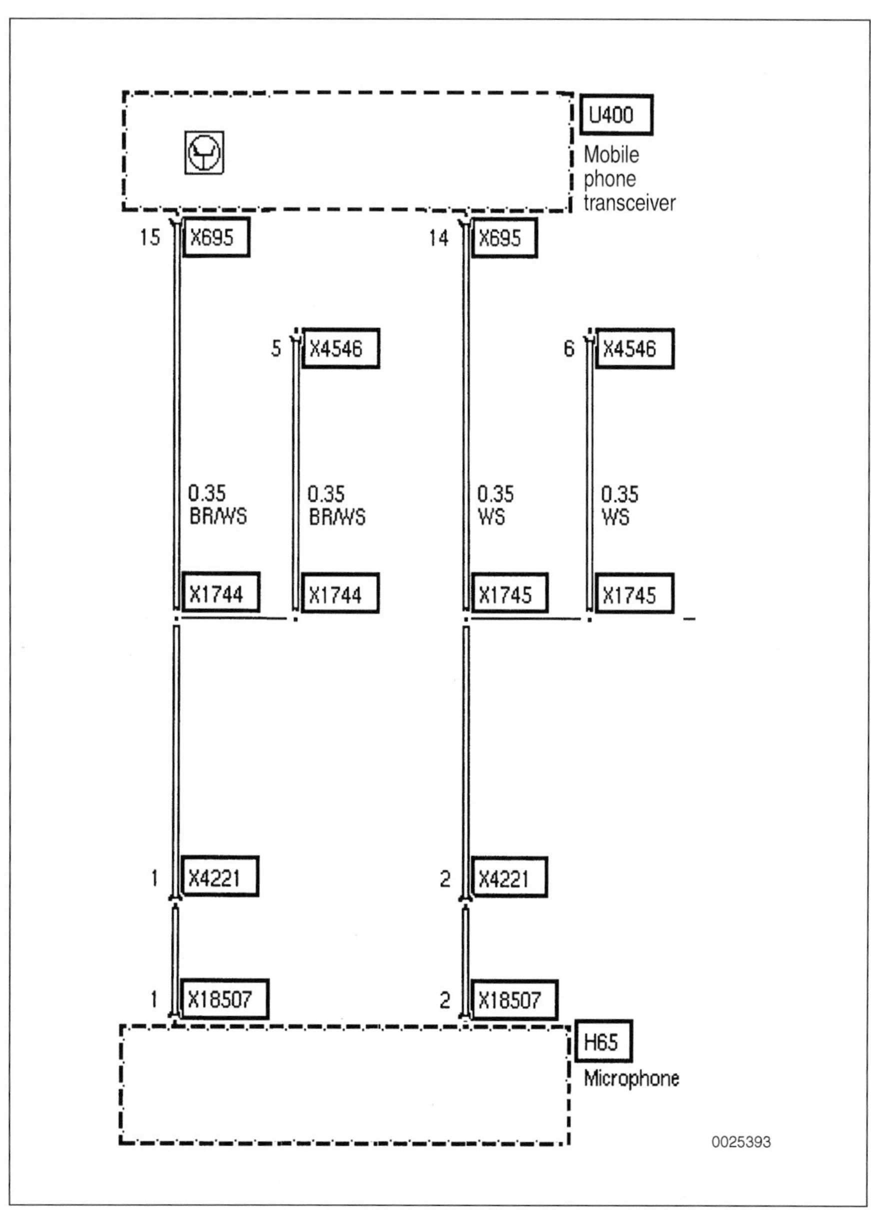

Telephone, mobile (I01014)
1 of 2

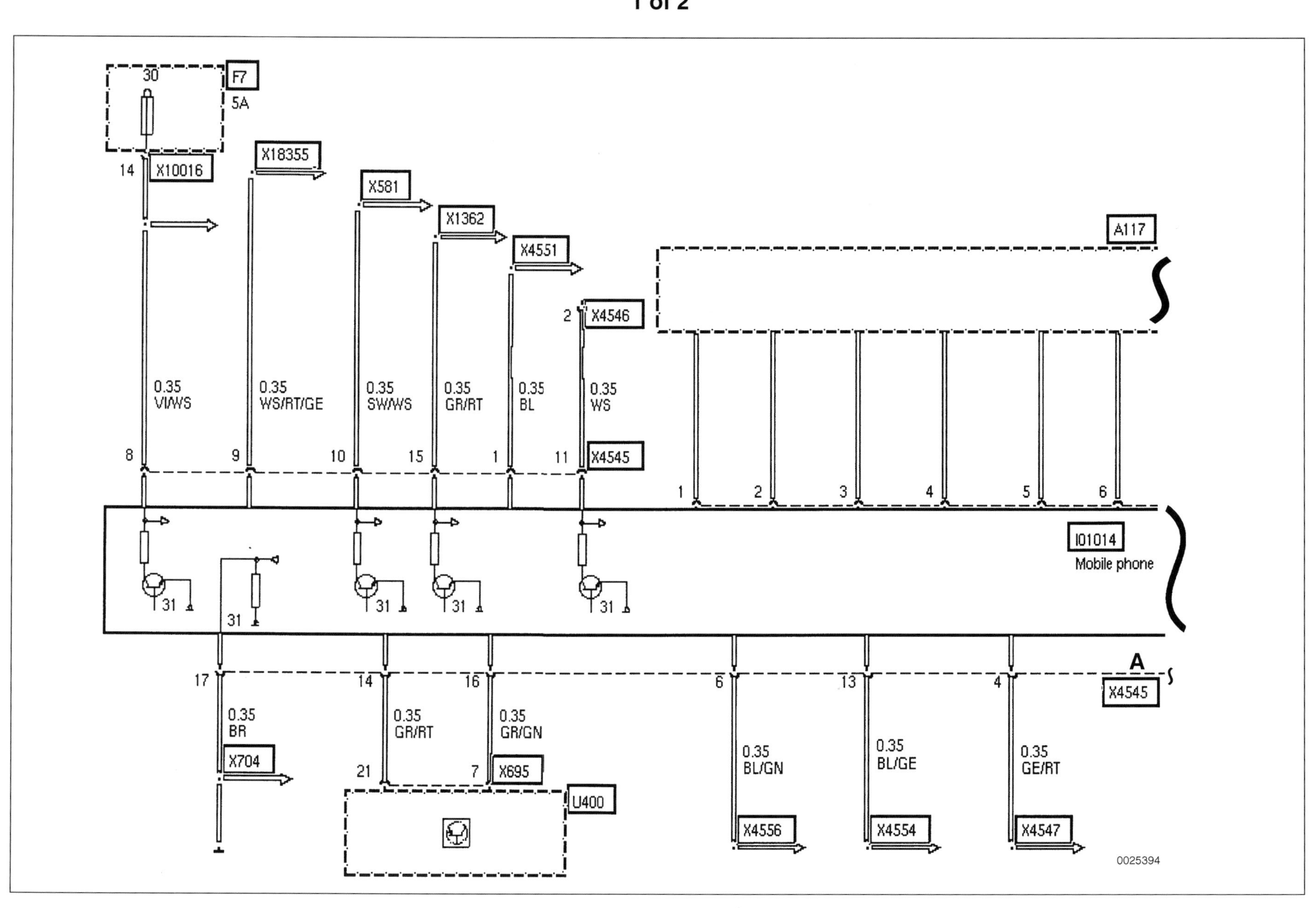

Telephone, mobile (I01014)
2 of 2

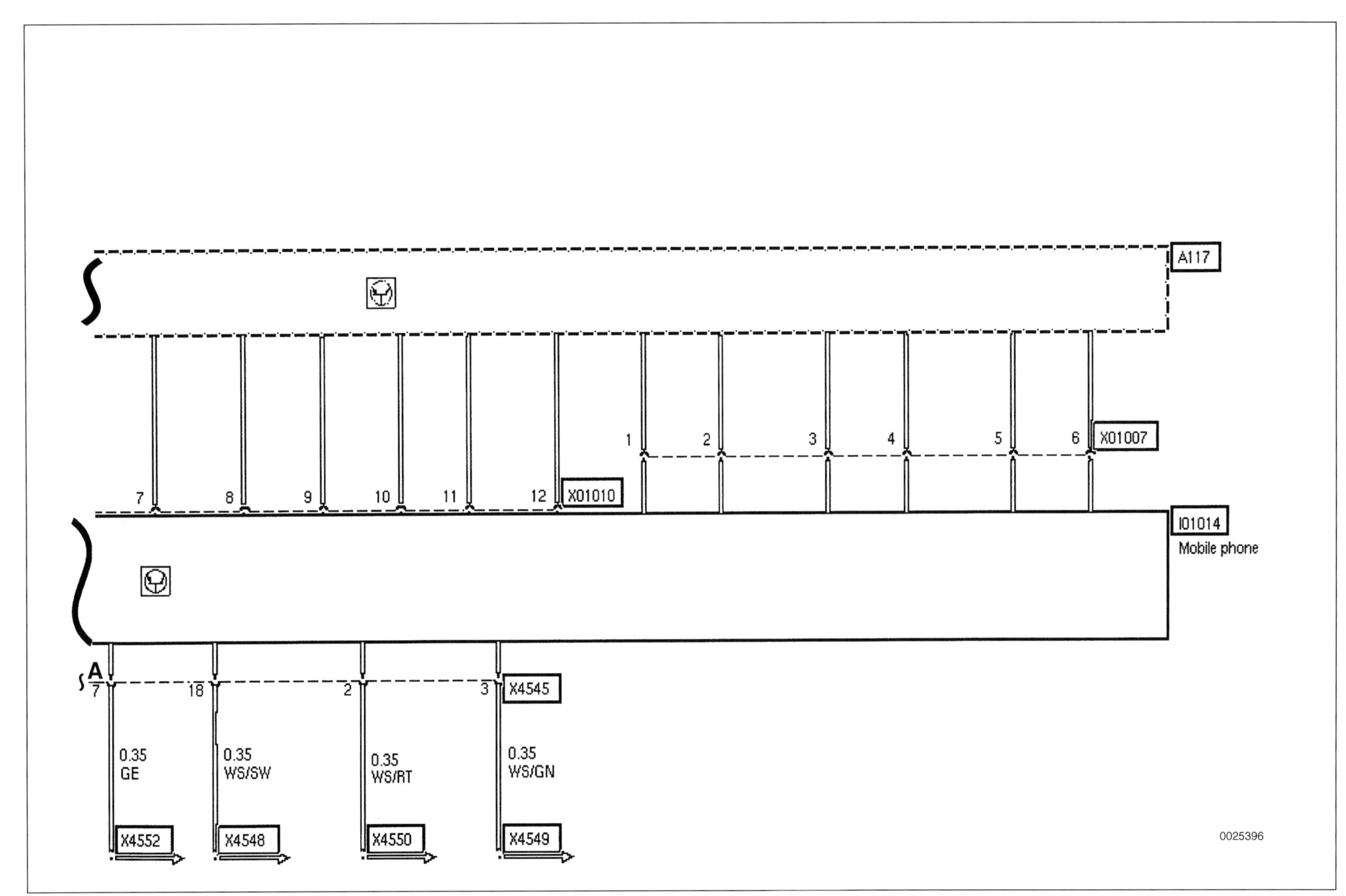

Speakers, front (bass and tweeter) (H41, H44, H50, H59)

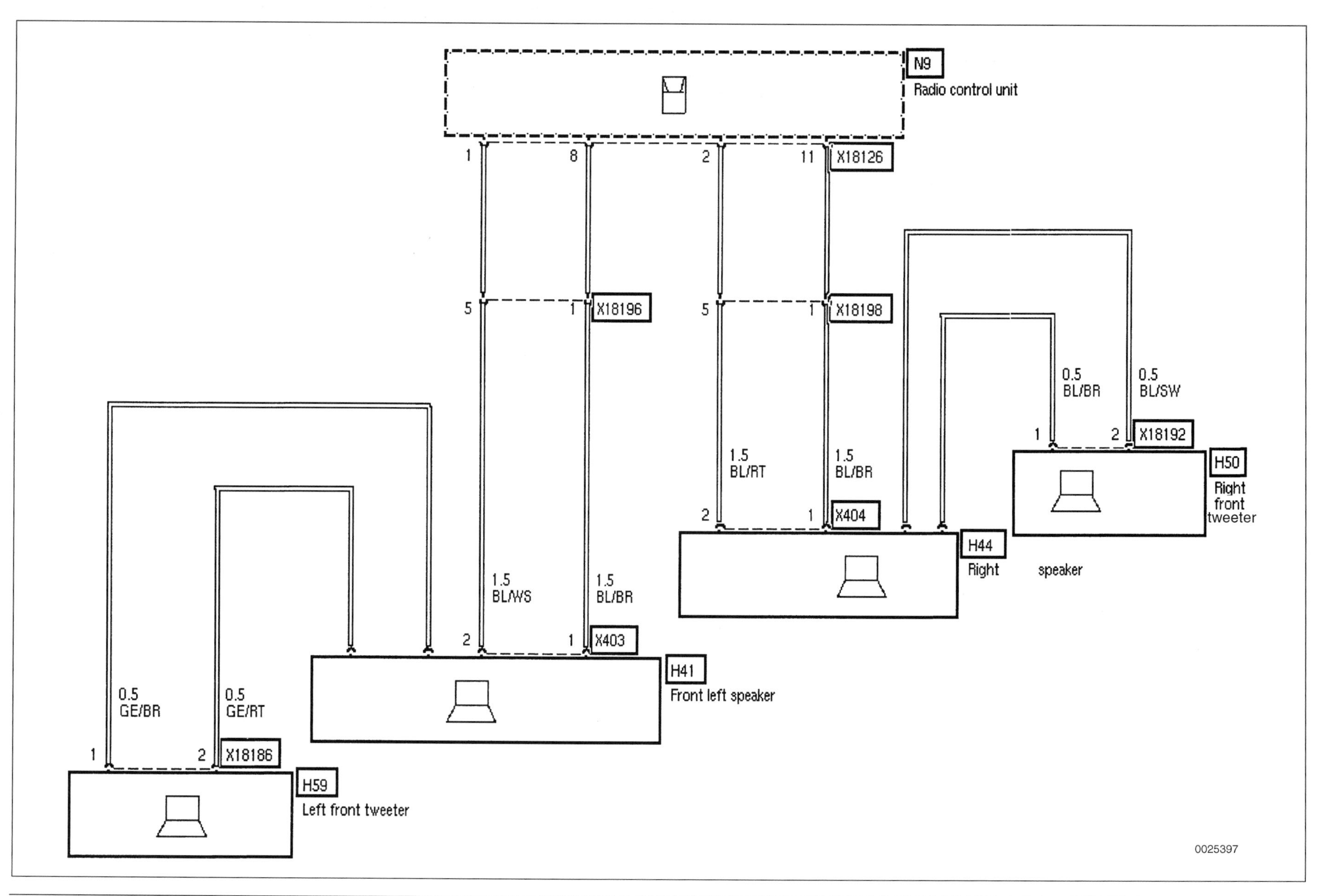

Connector (X18196)

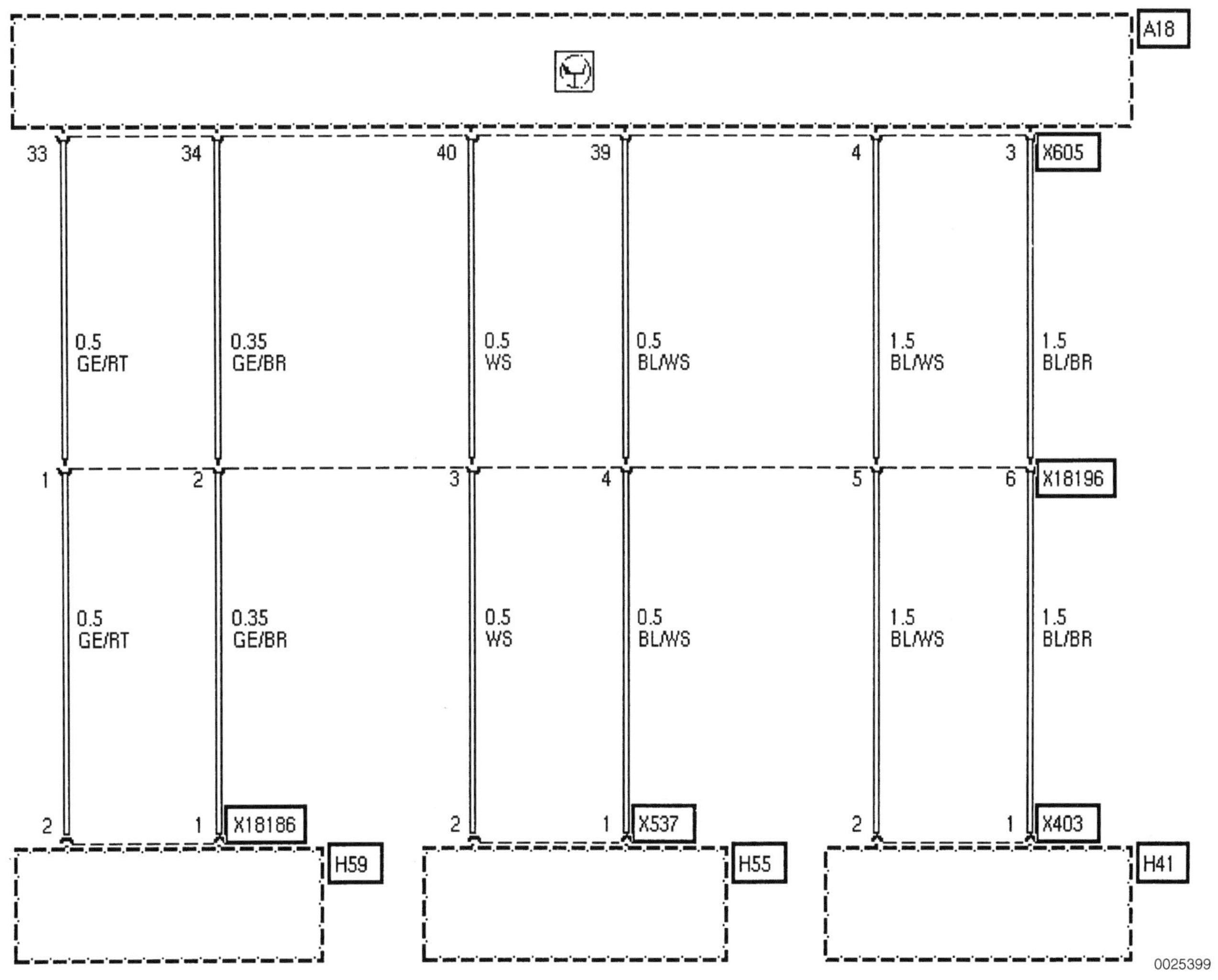

Connector (X18198)

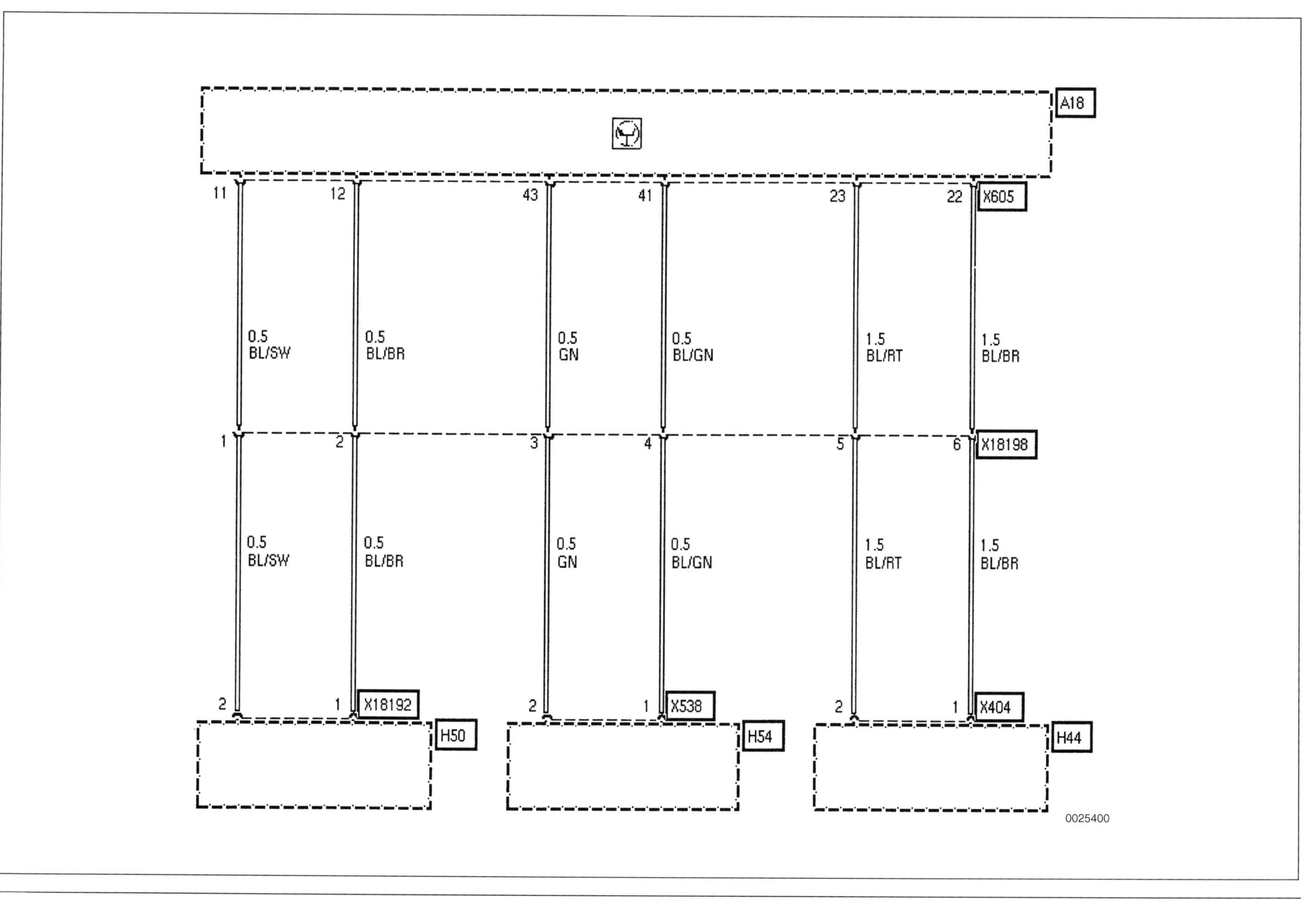

Speakers, rear (H45, H46)

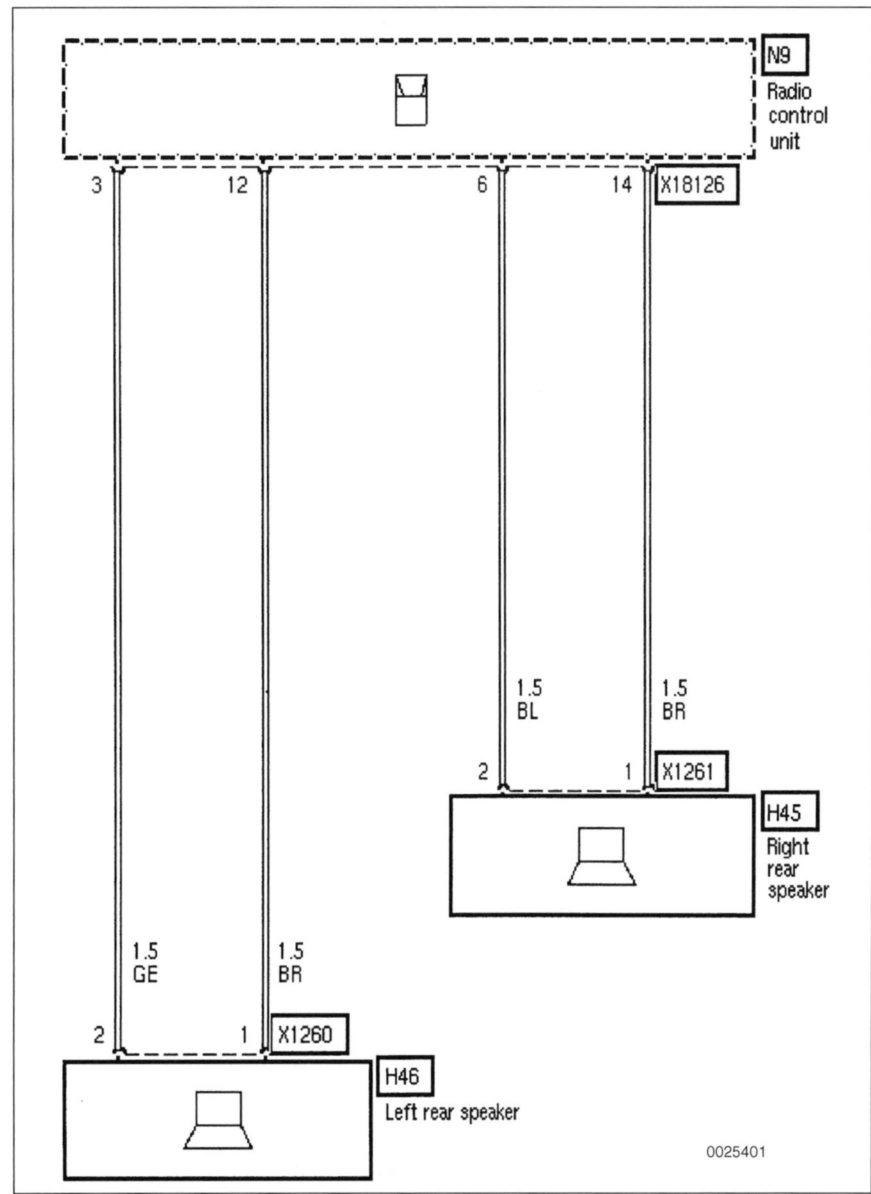

Antenna amplifier (N8)

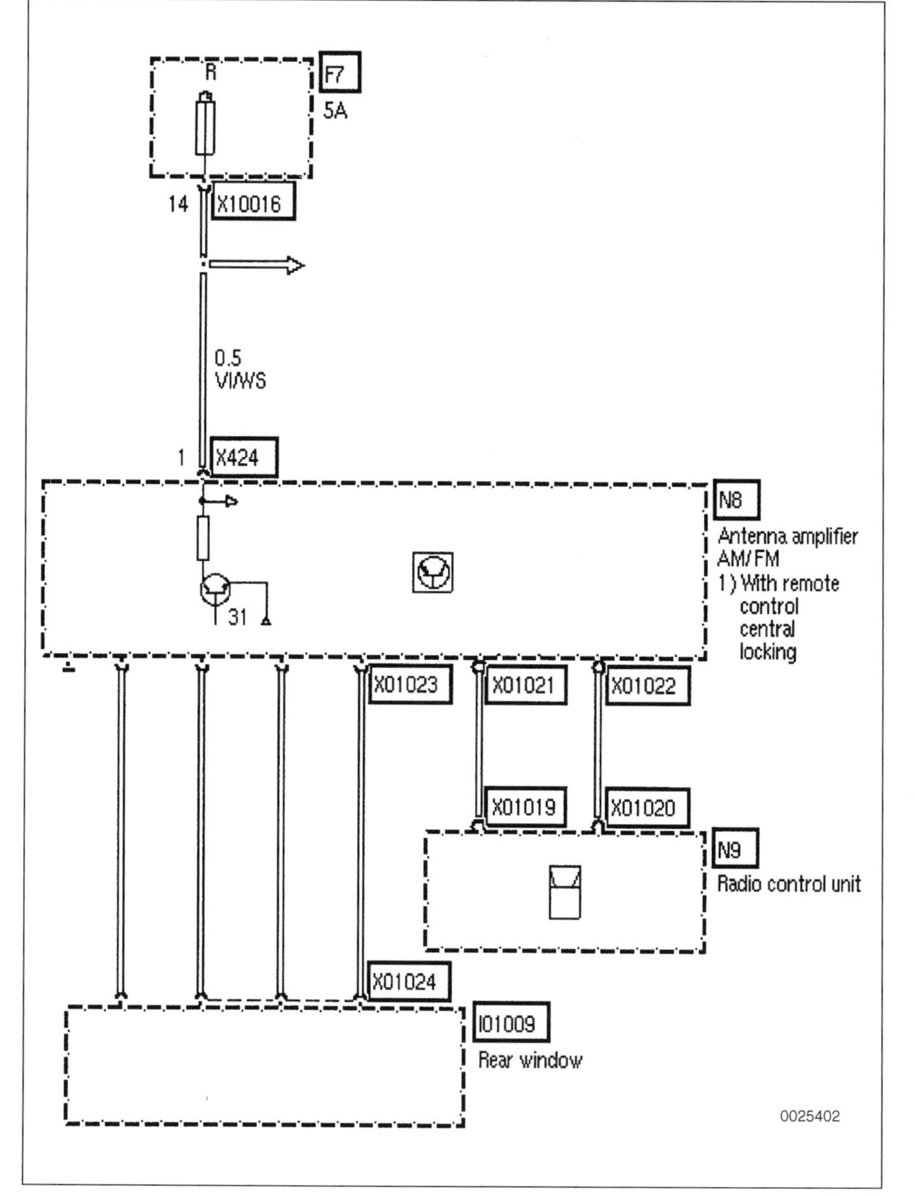

Defogger, rear window (K13)

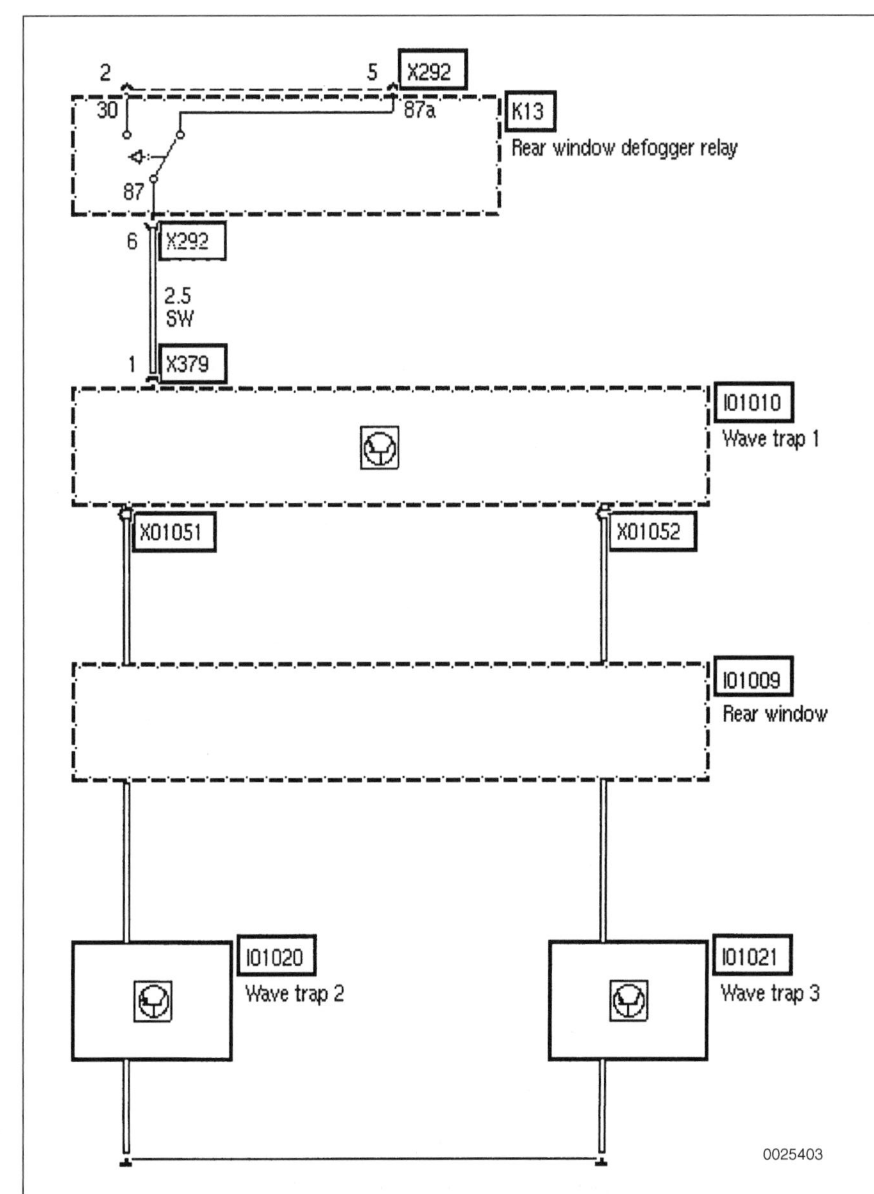

GPS receiver (N28)

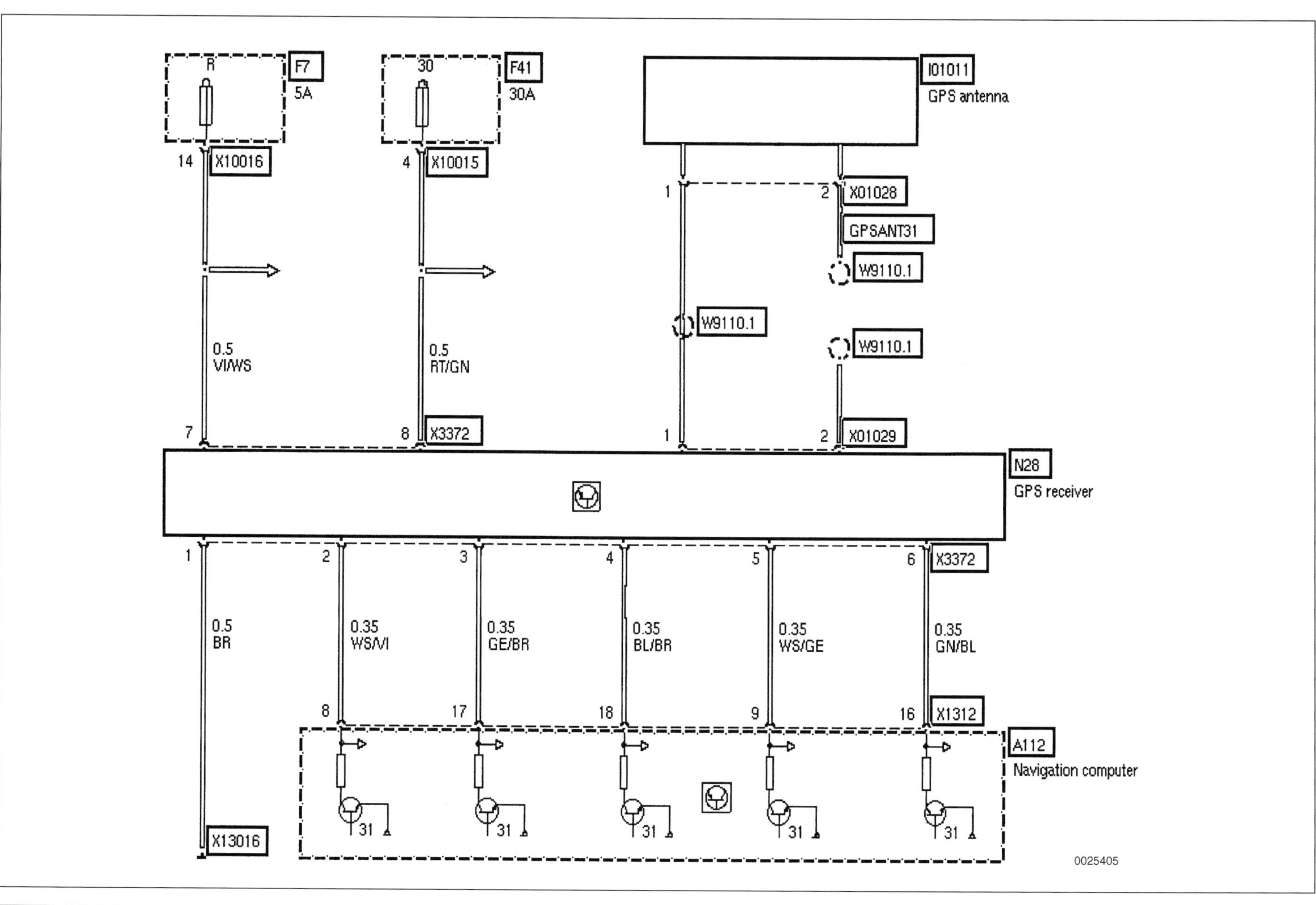

ABS/DSC control unit (A65)

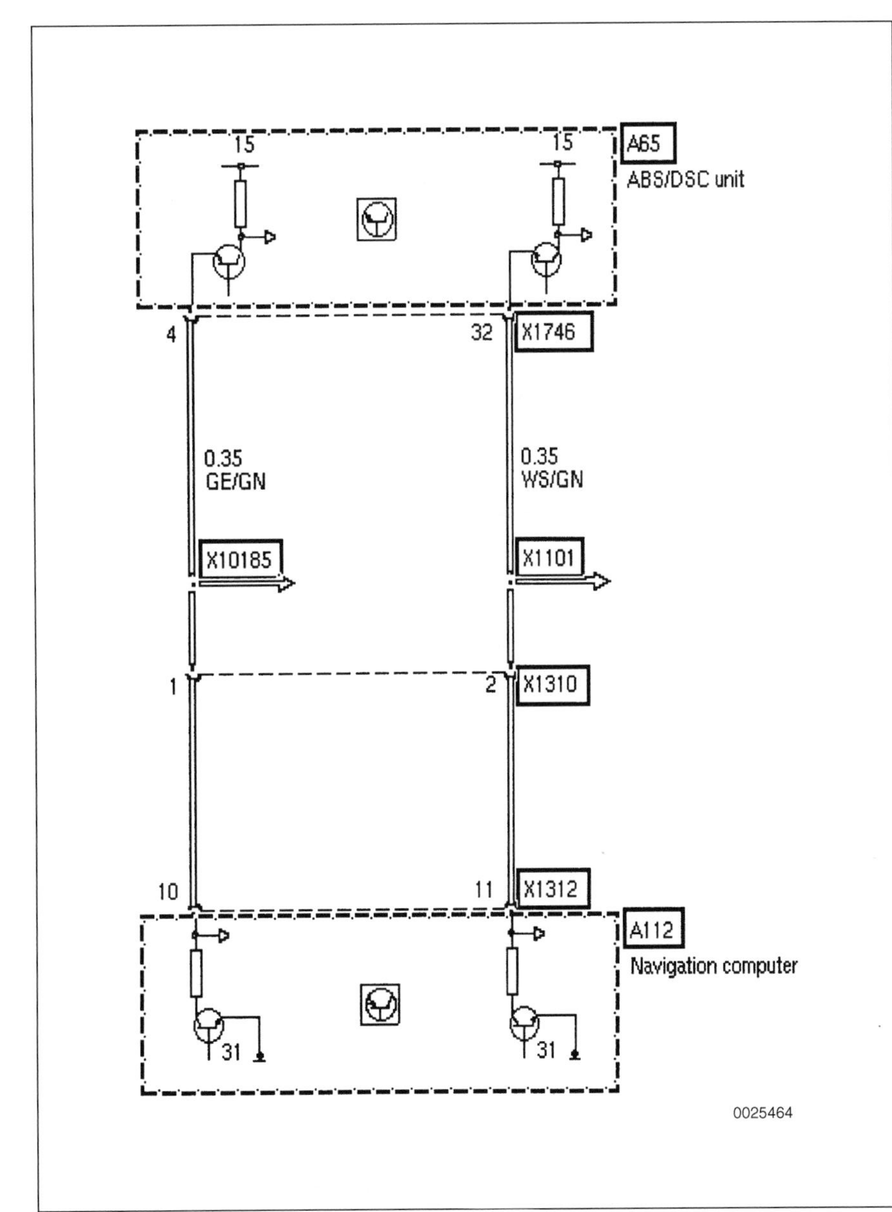

Splice connector (X10237)

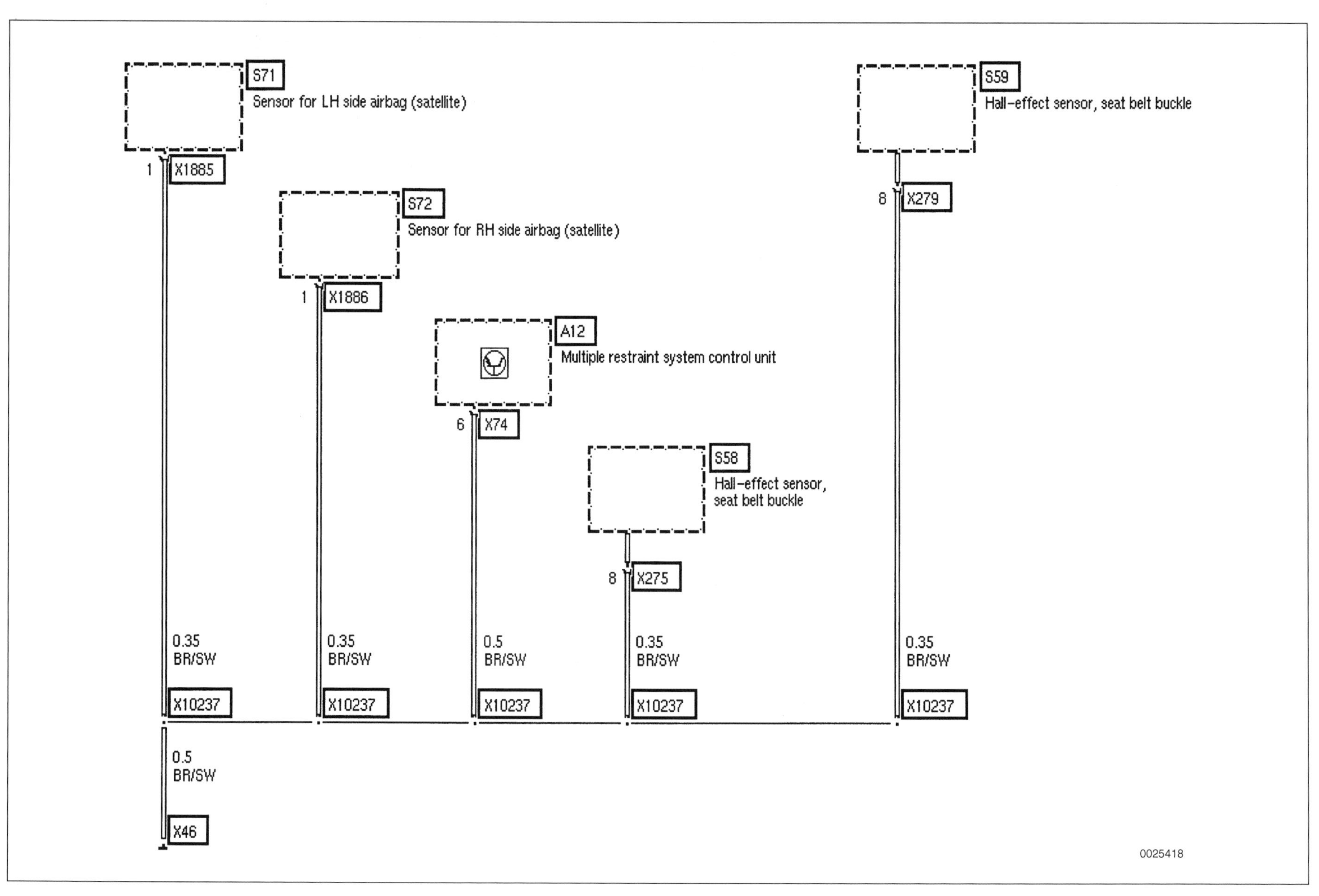

Airbag crash sensors, side-impact (S71, S72)

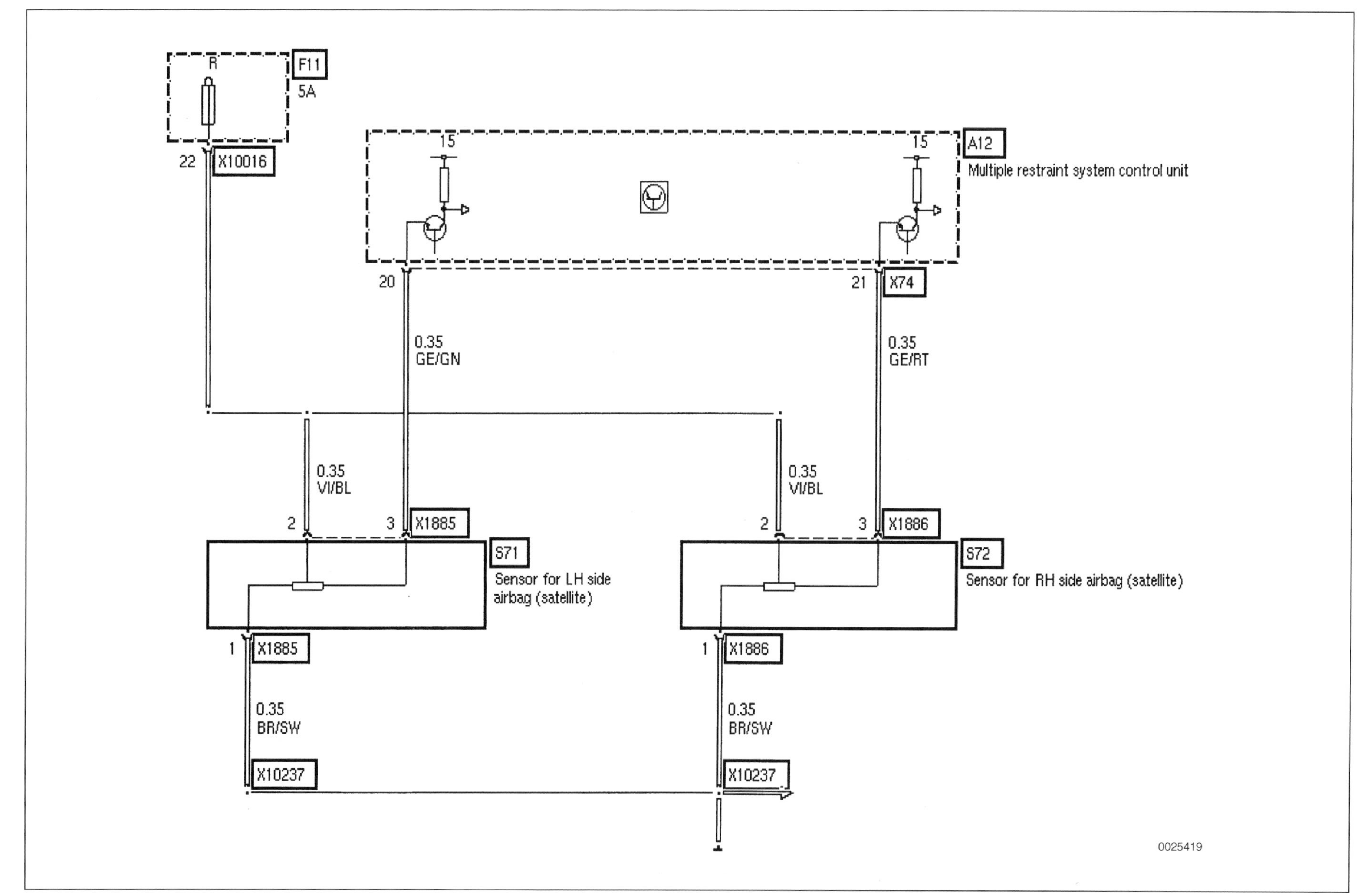

Airbags, front (G5, G6)

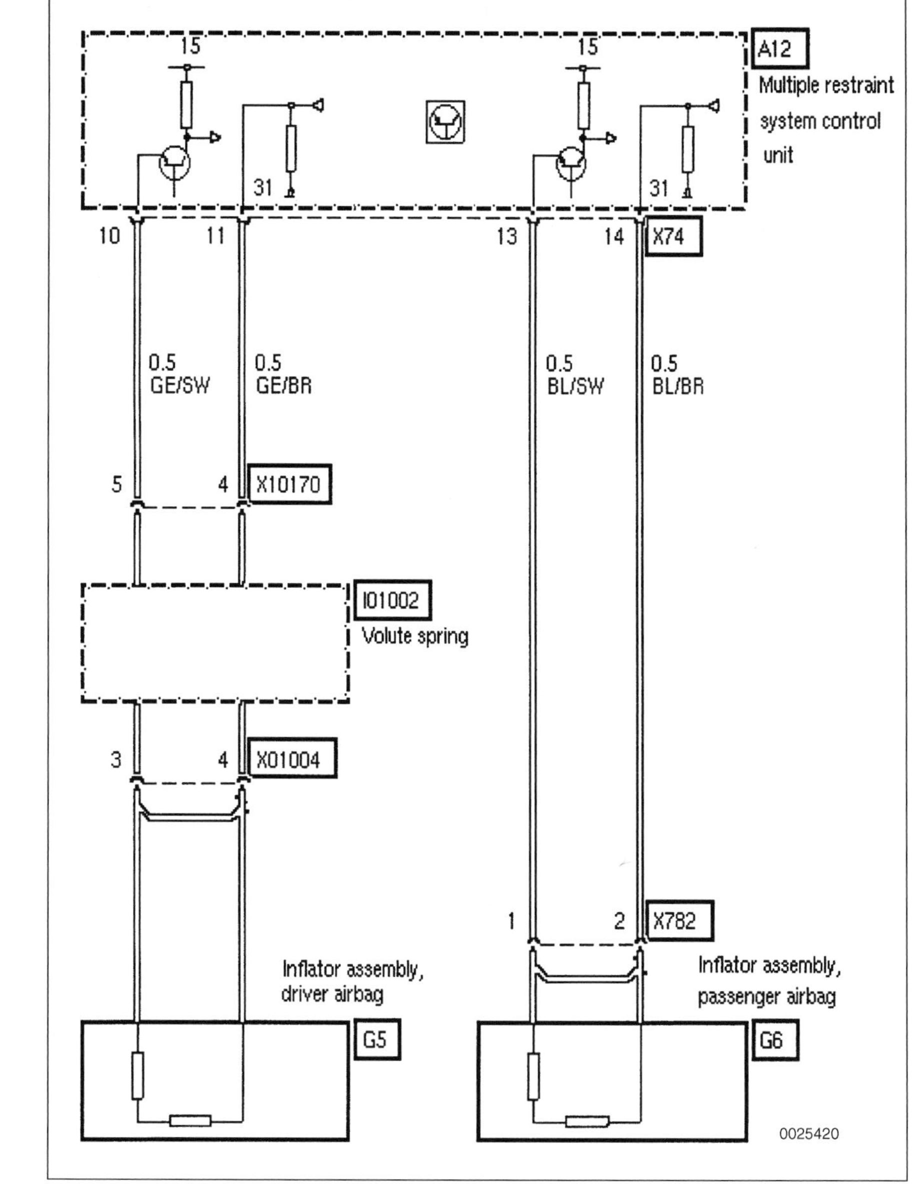

Airbags, head protection system (HPS) (G17, G18)

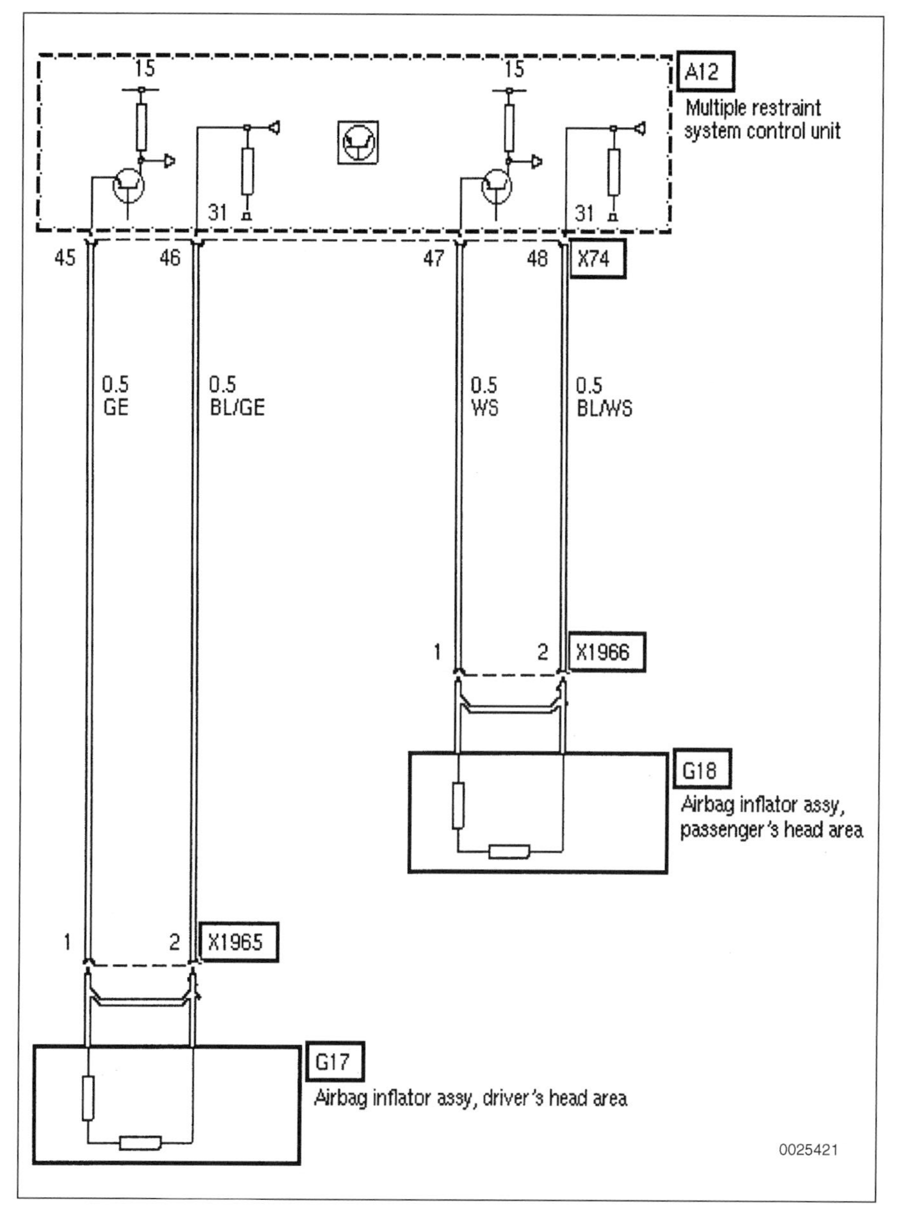

Airbags, side-impact, front (G14, G15)

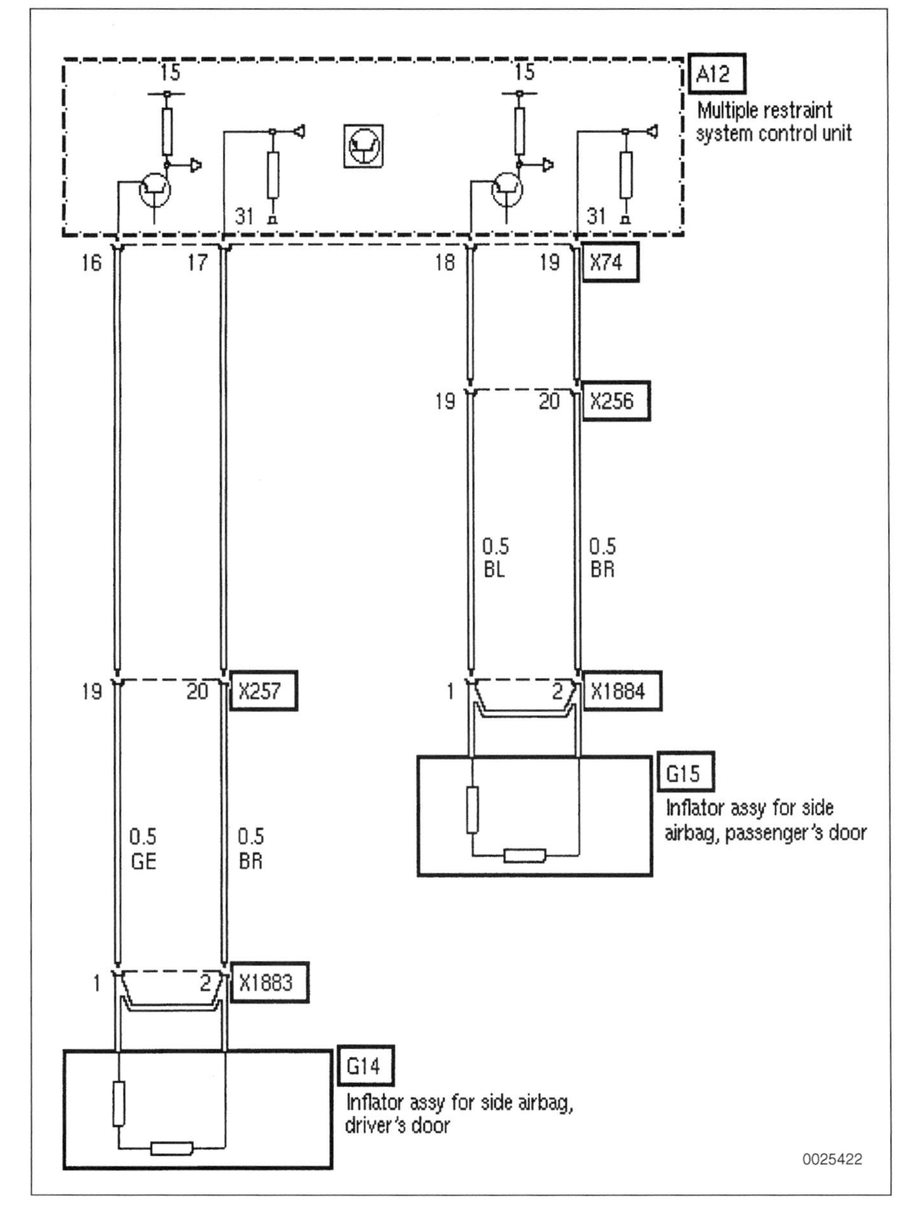

Airbags, side-impact, rear (G20, G21)

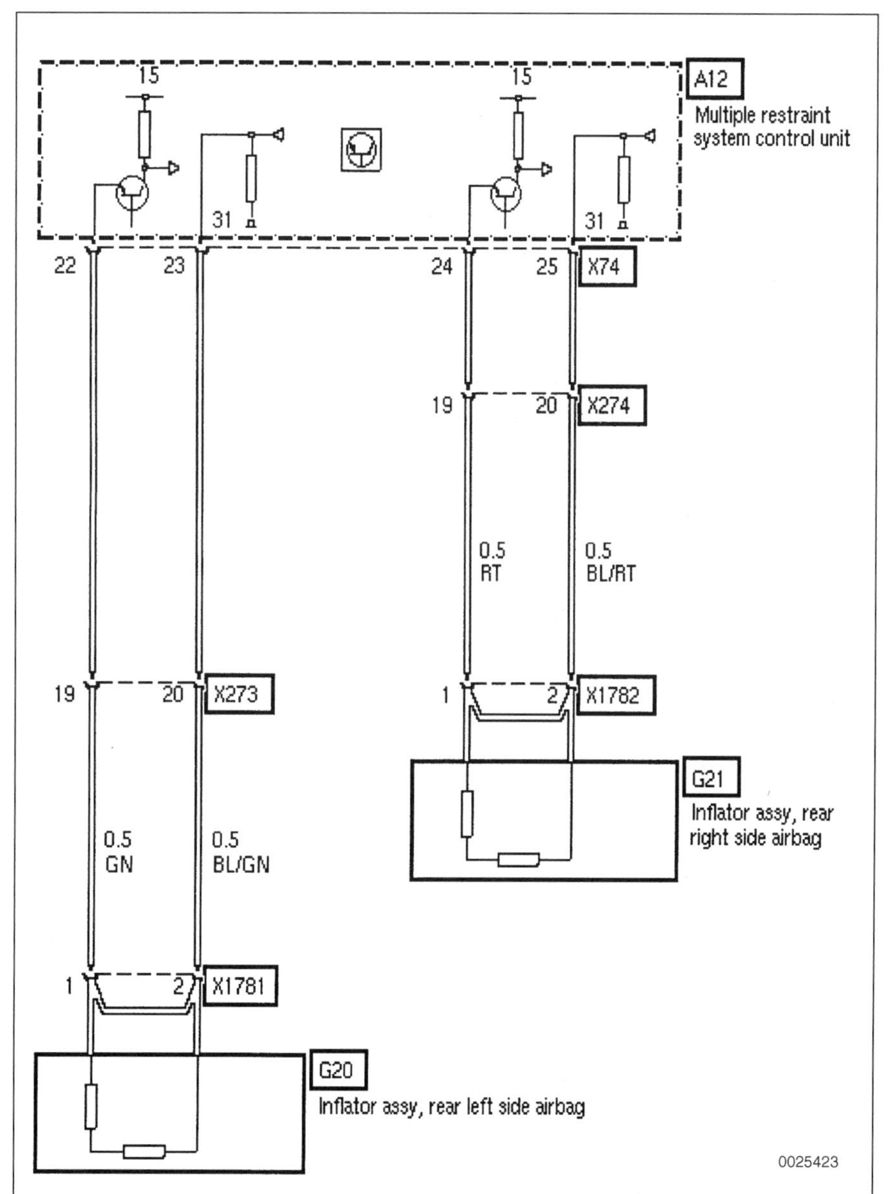

Seat belt tensioners, pyrotechnic (G12, G13)

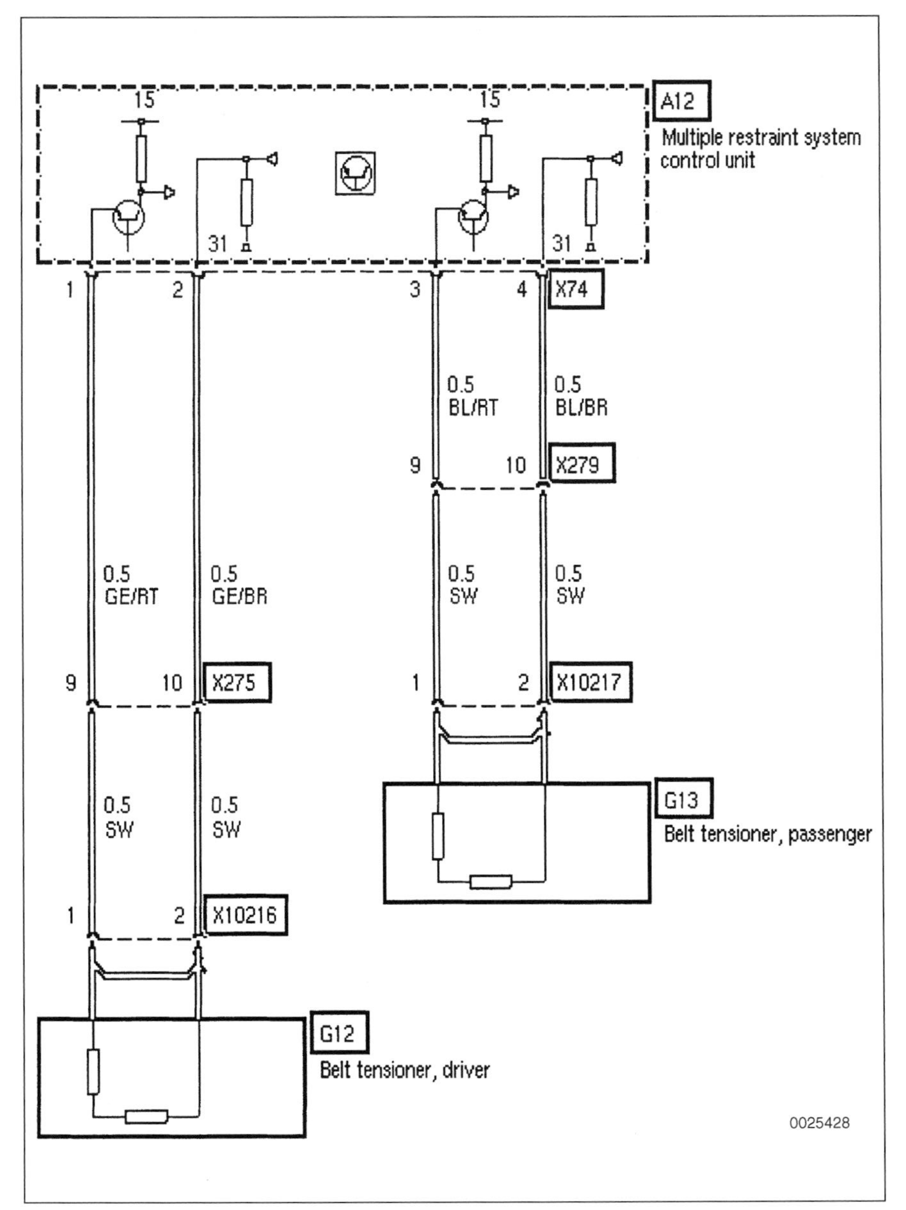

Seat load sensor (A113)

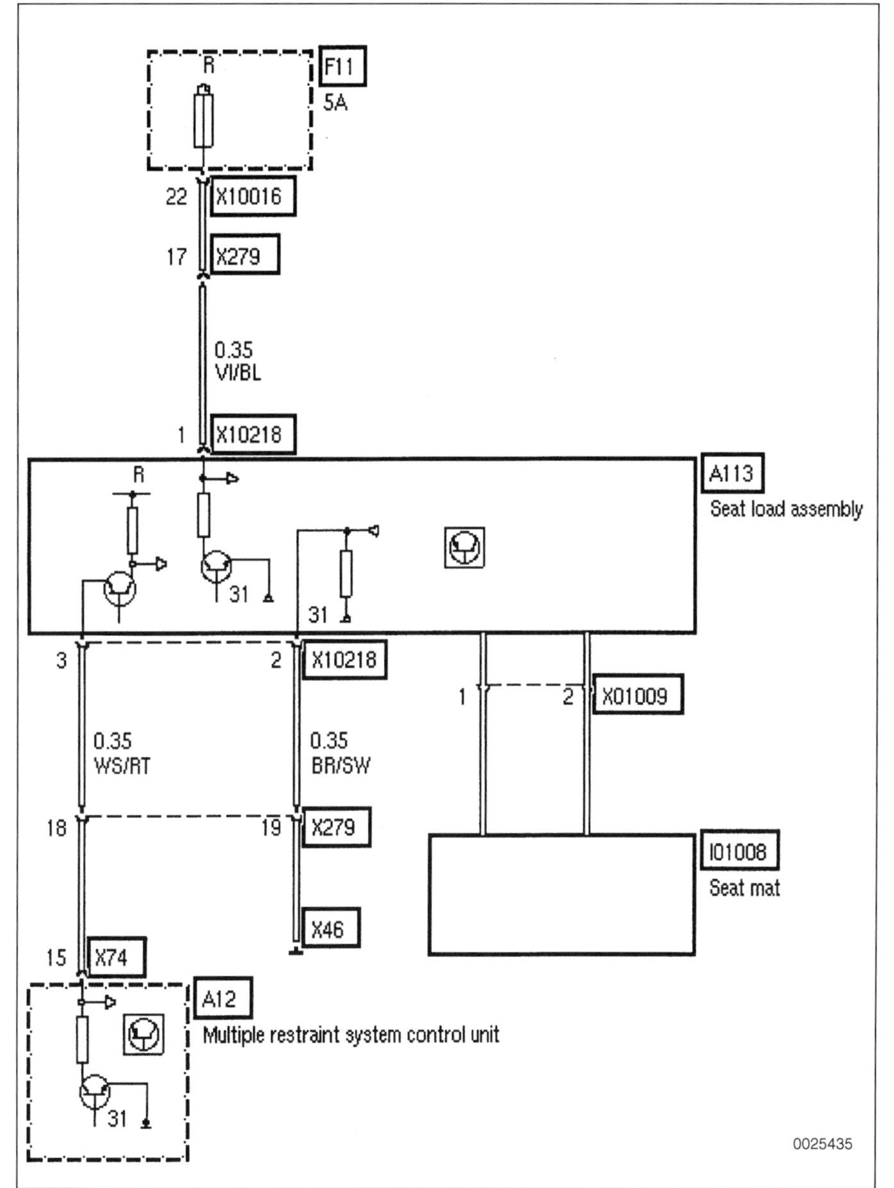

Ground (X46)

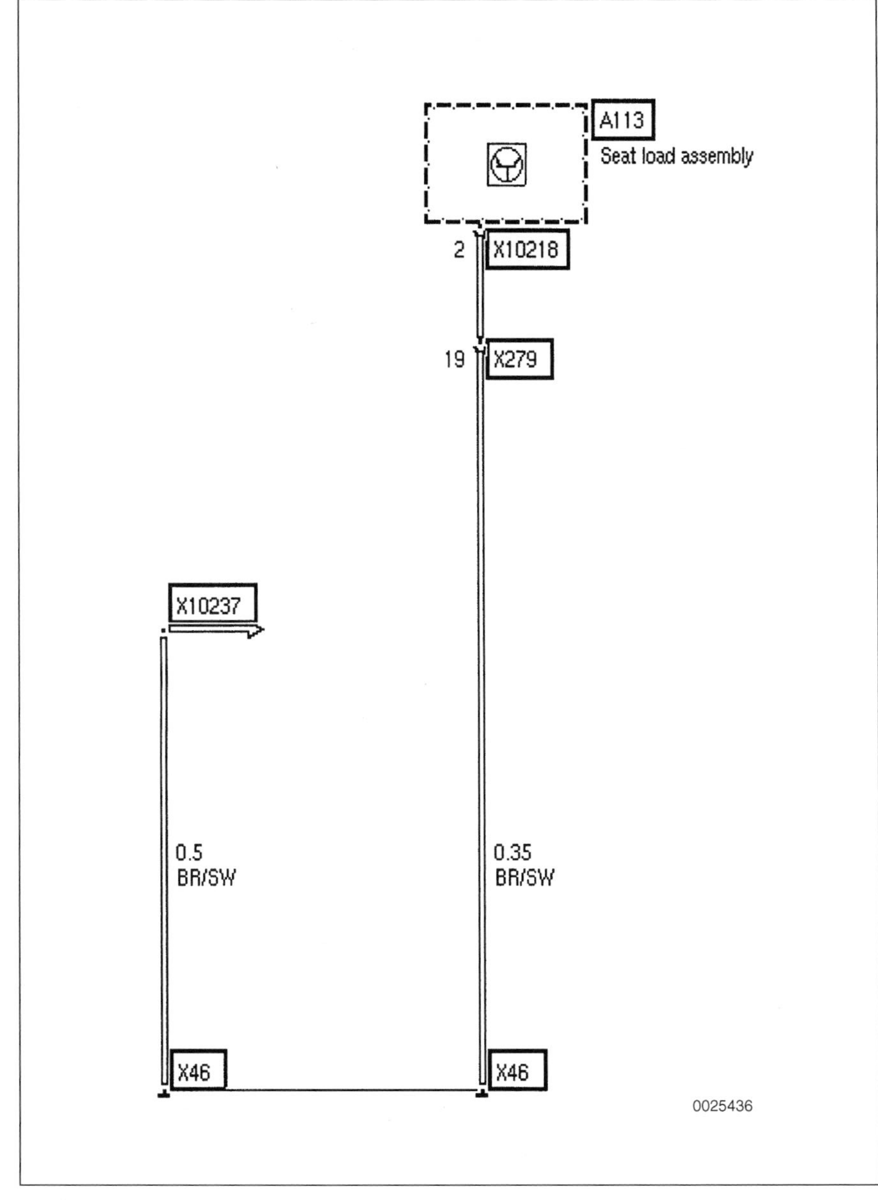
A113
Seat load assembly
2
X10218
19
X279
X10237
0.5
BR/SW
0.35
BR/SW
X46
X46
0025436

Battery safety terminal (G19)

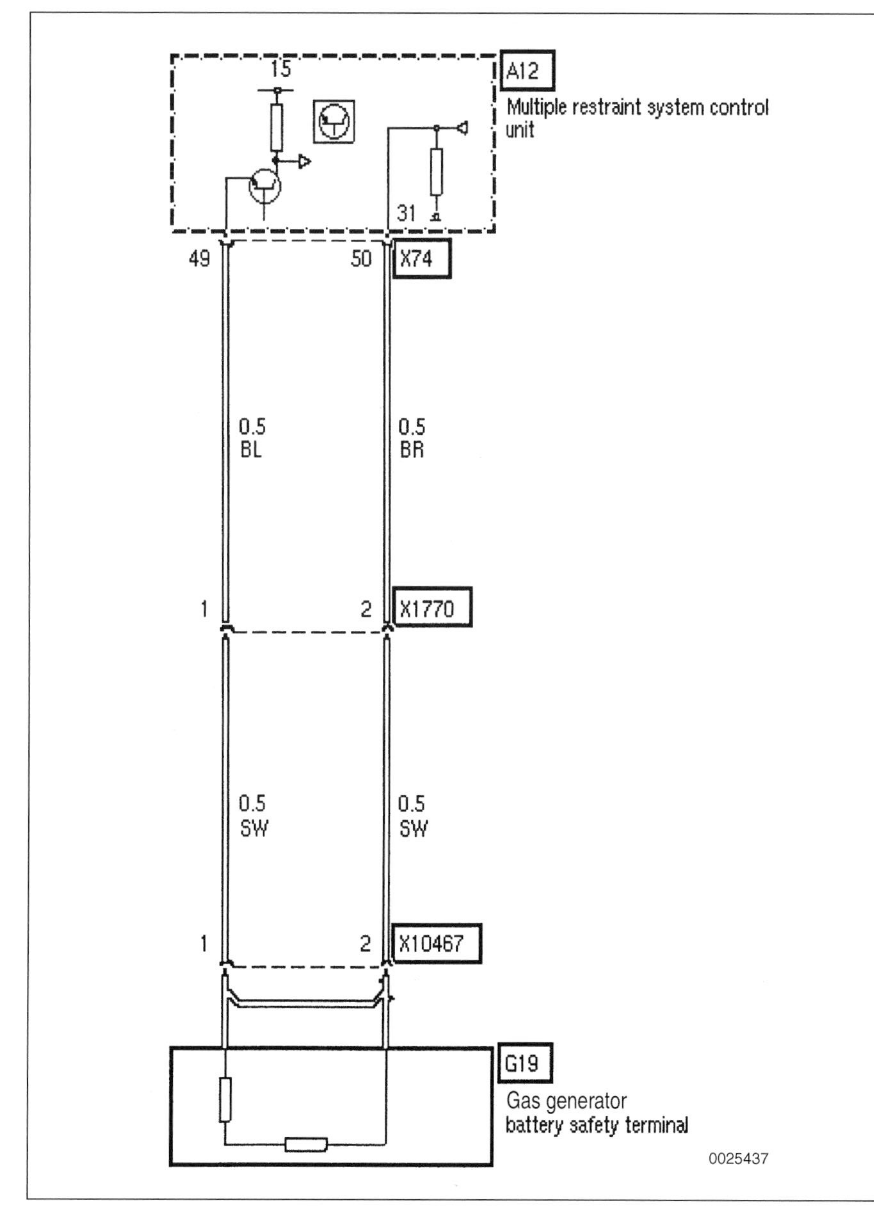

Engine hood contact switch (S19)

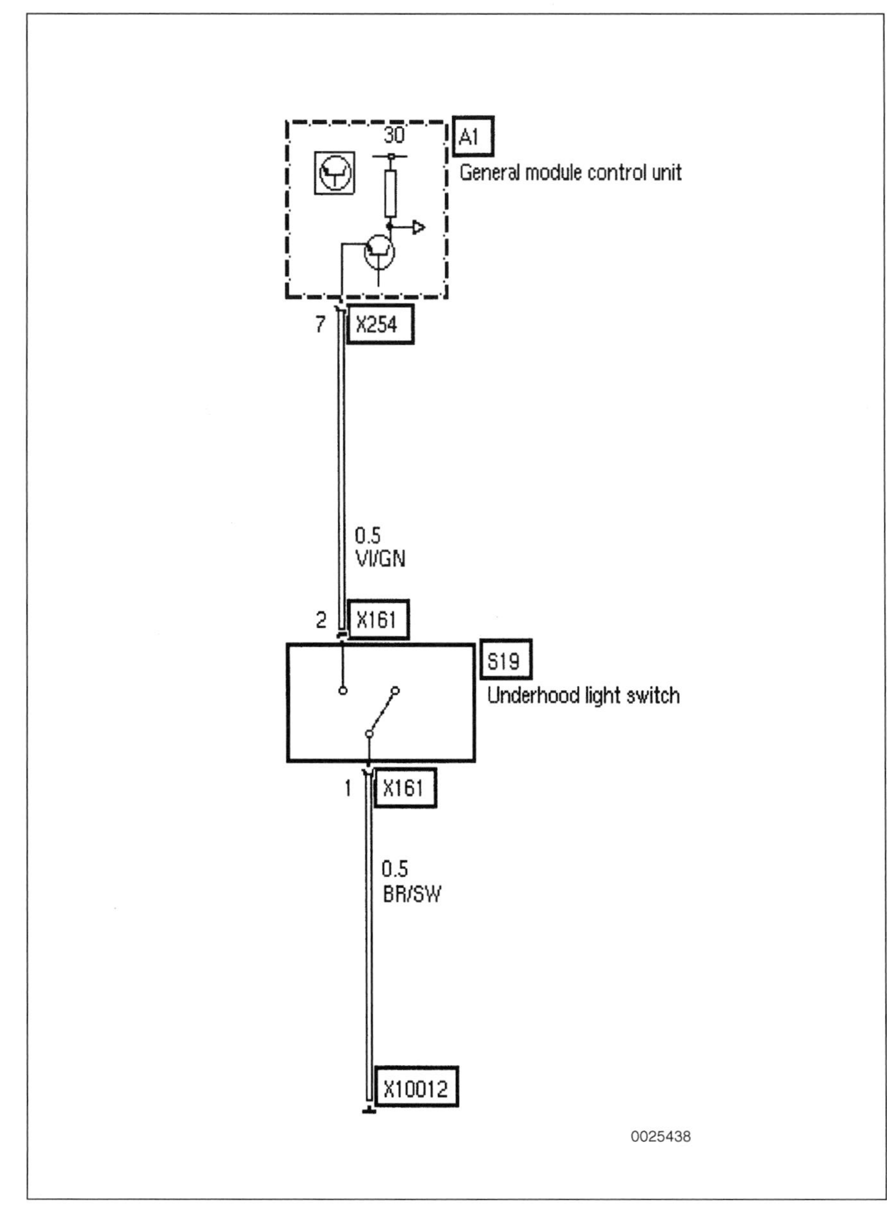

Anti-theft alarm system (DWA)
1 of 2

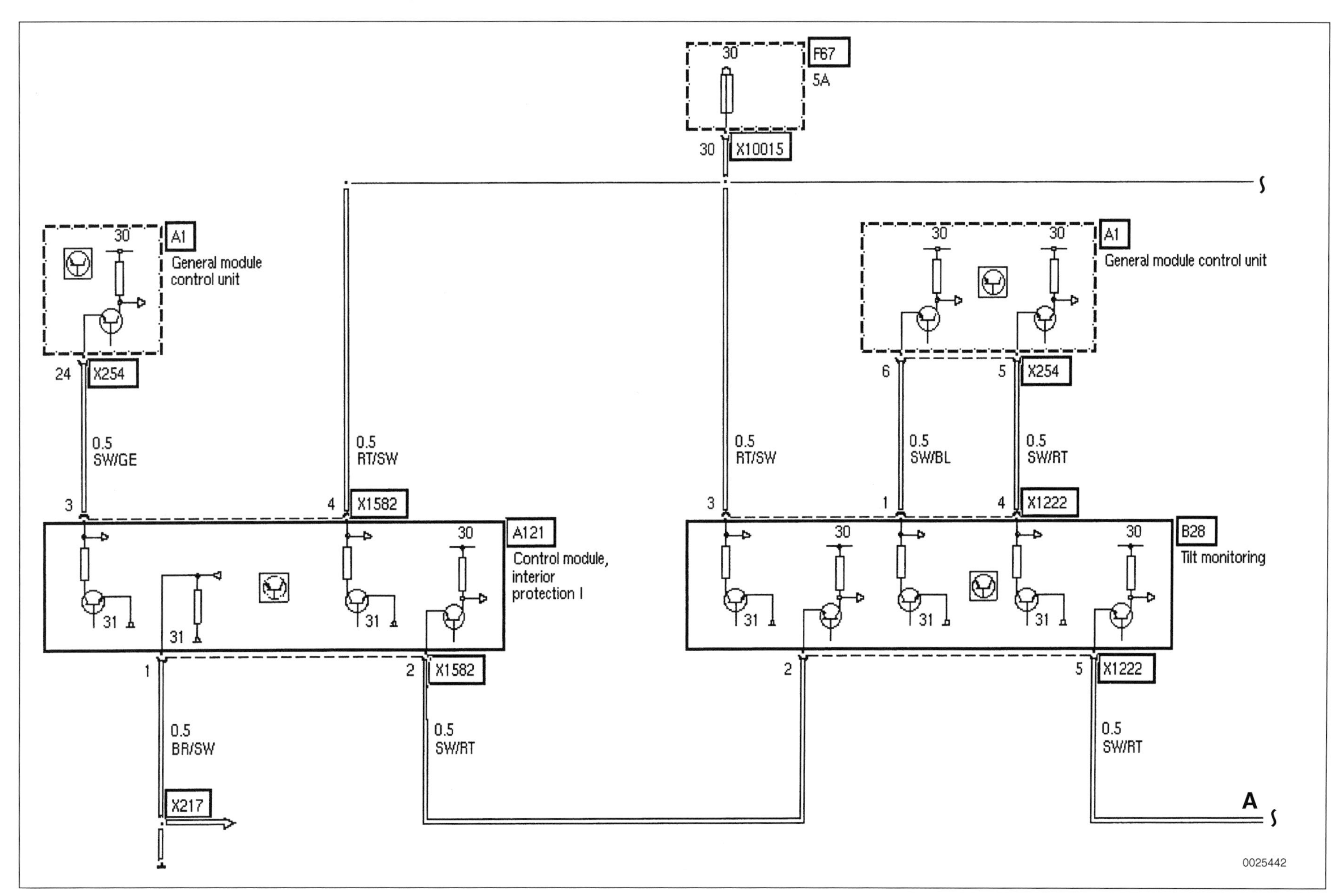

Anti-theft alarm system (DWA)
2 of 2

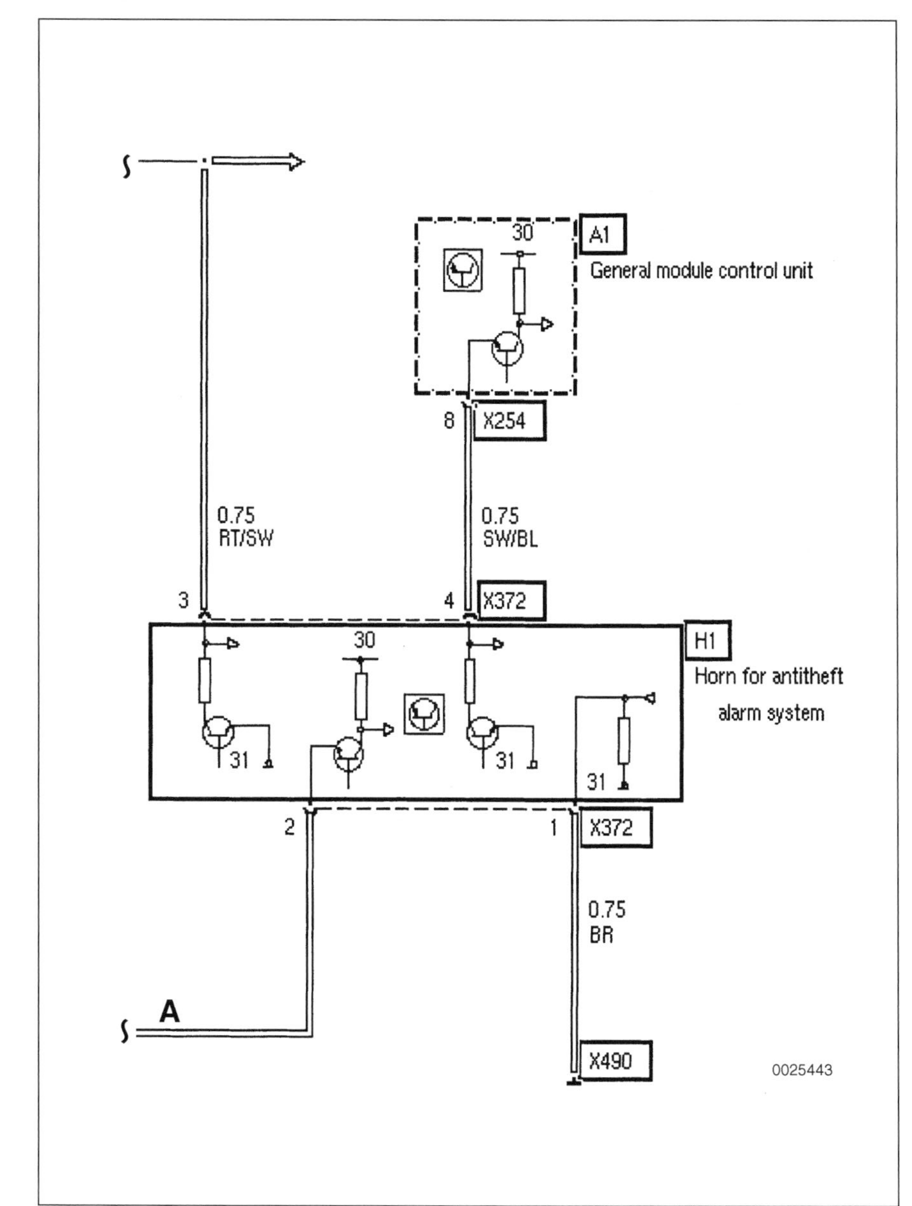

Window switch, left front (S126)

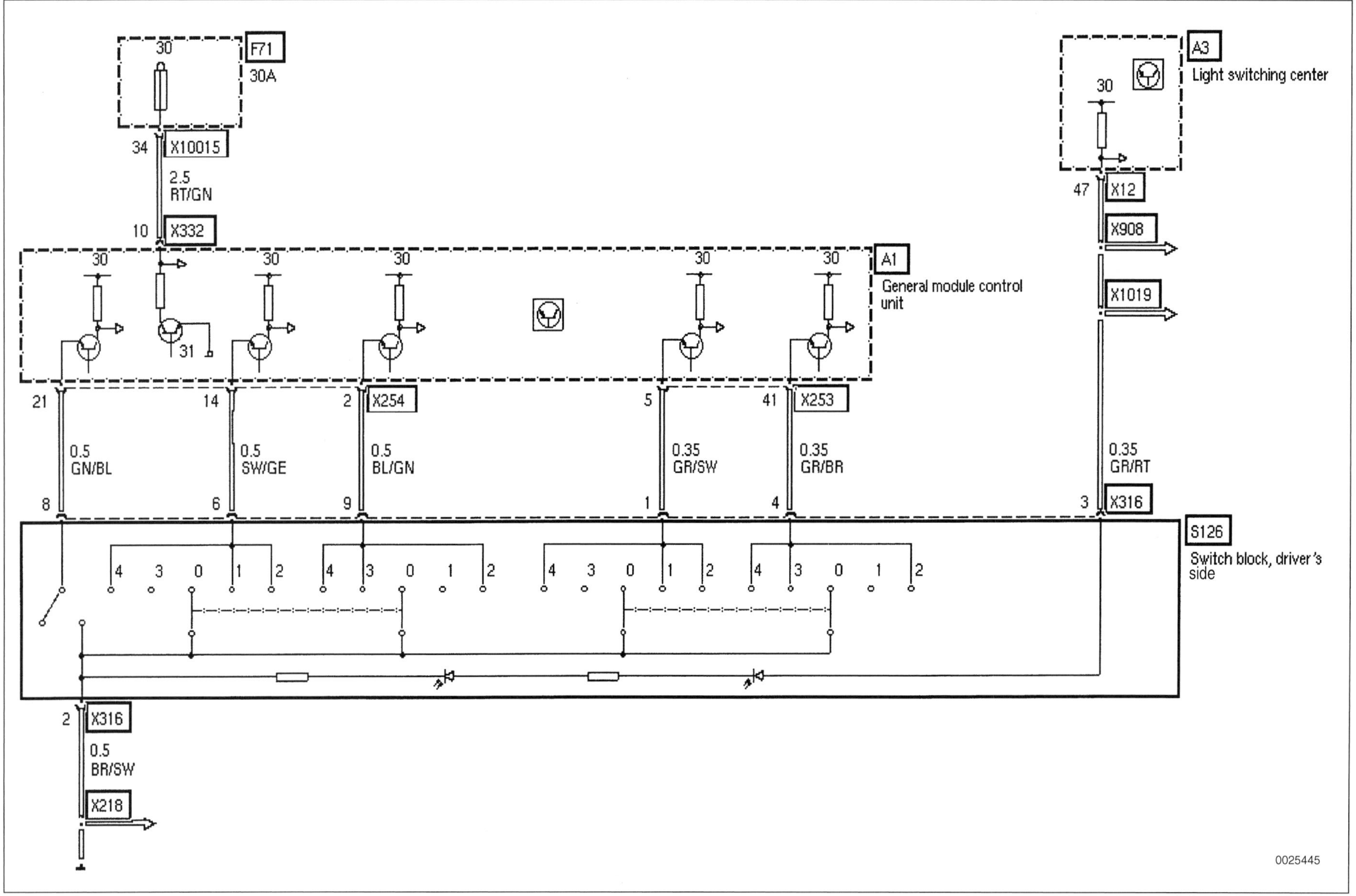

Window switch, right front (S127)

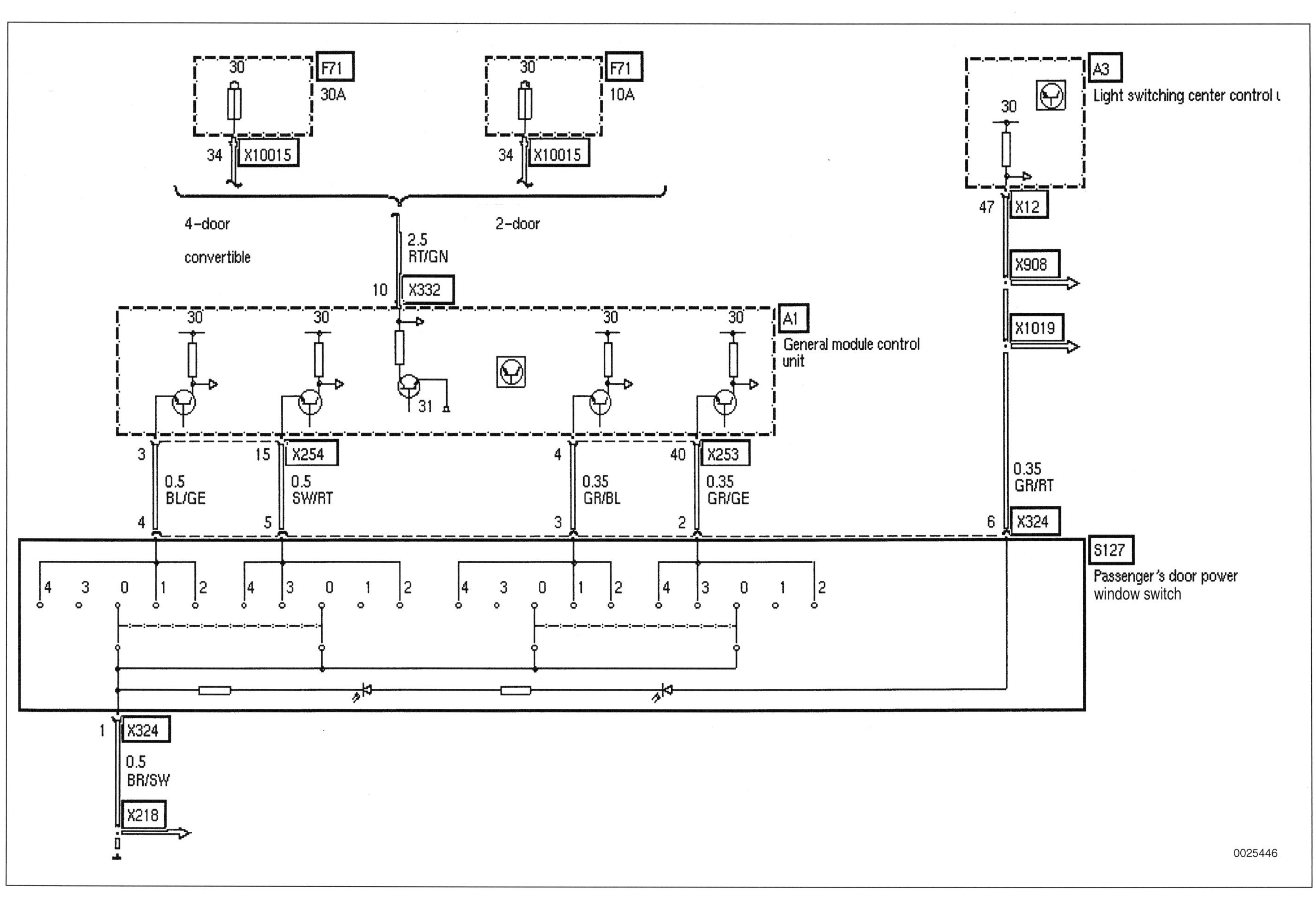

Fuse 71 (F71)

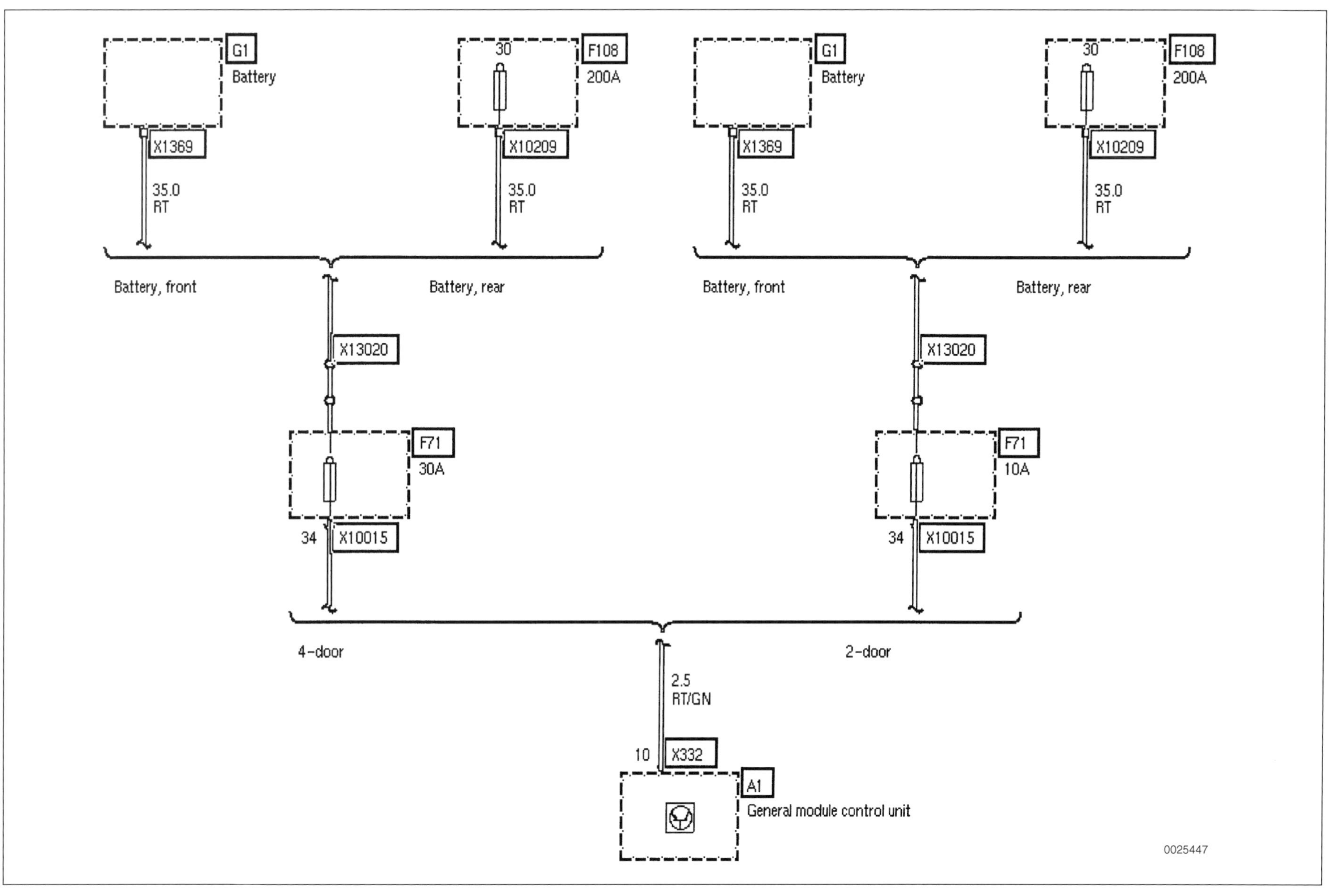
G1
Battery
X1369
35.0
RT
30
F108
200A
X10209
35.0
RT
Battery, front
Battery, rear
X13020
F71
30A
34
X10015
G1
Battery
X1369
35.0
RT
30
F108
200A
X10209
35.0
RT
Battery, front
Battery, rear
X13020
F71
10A
34
X10015
4-door
2-door
2.5
RT/GN
10
X332
A1
General module control unit
0025447

Window switch, left rear (S41)

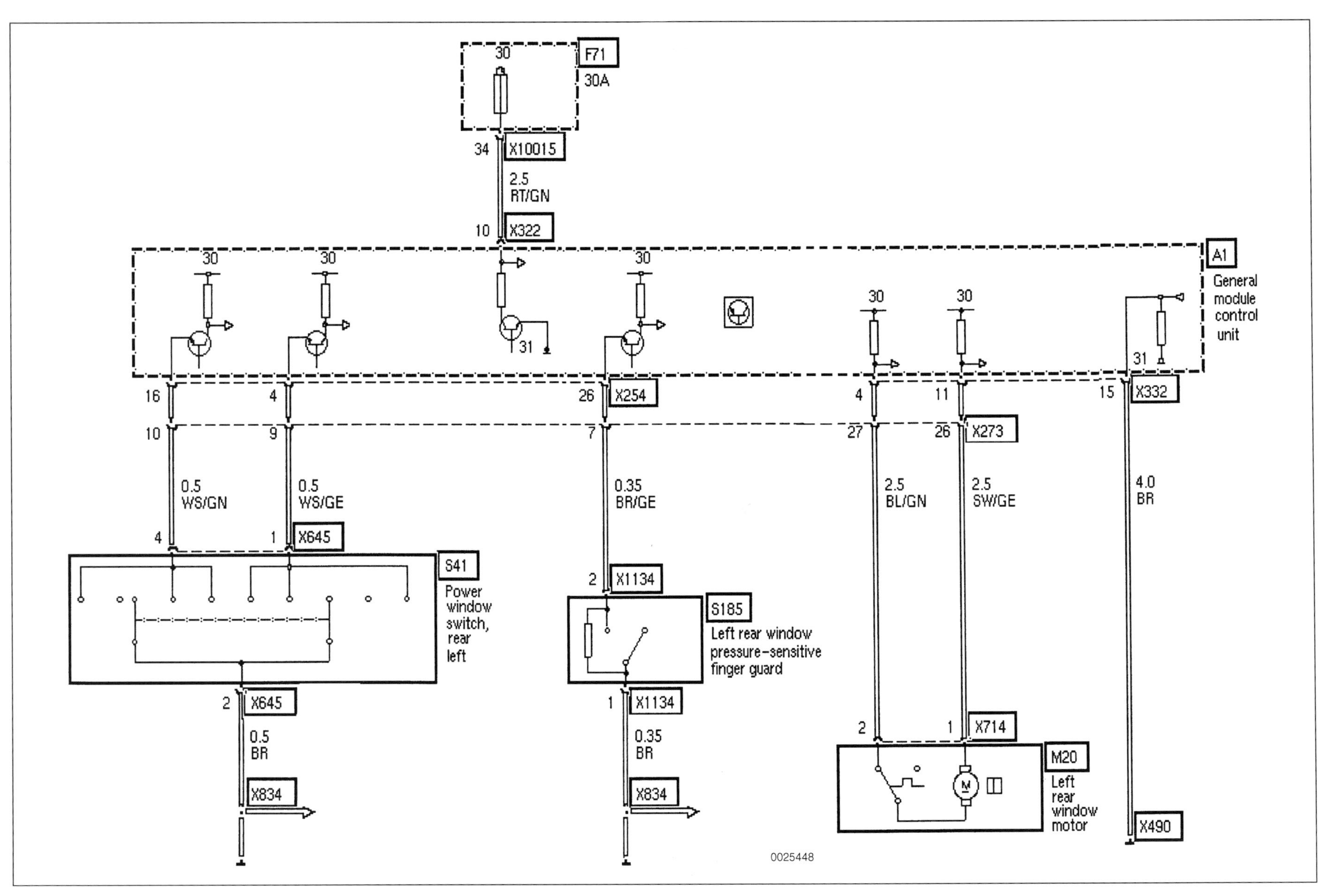

Window switch, right rear (S42)

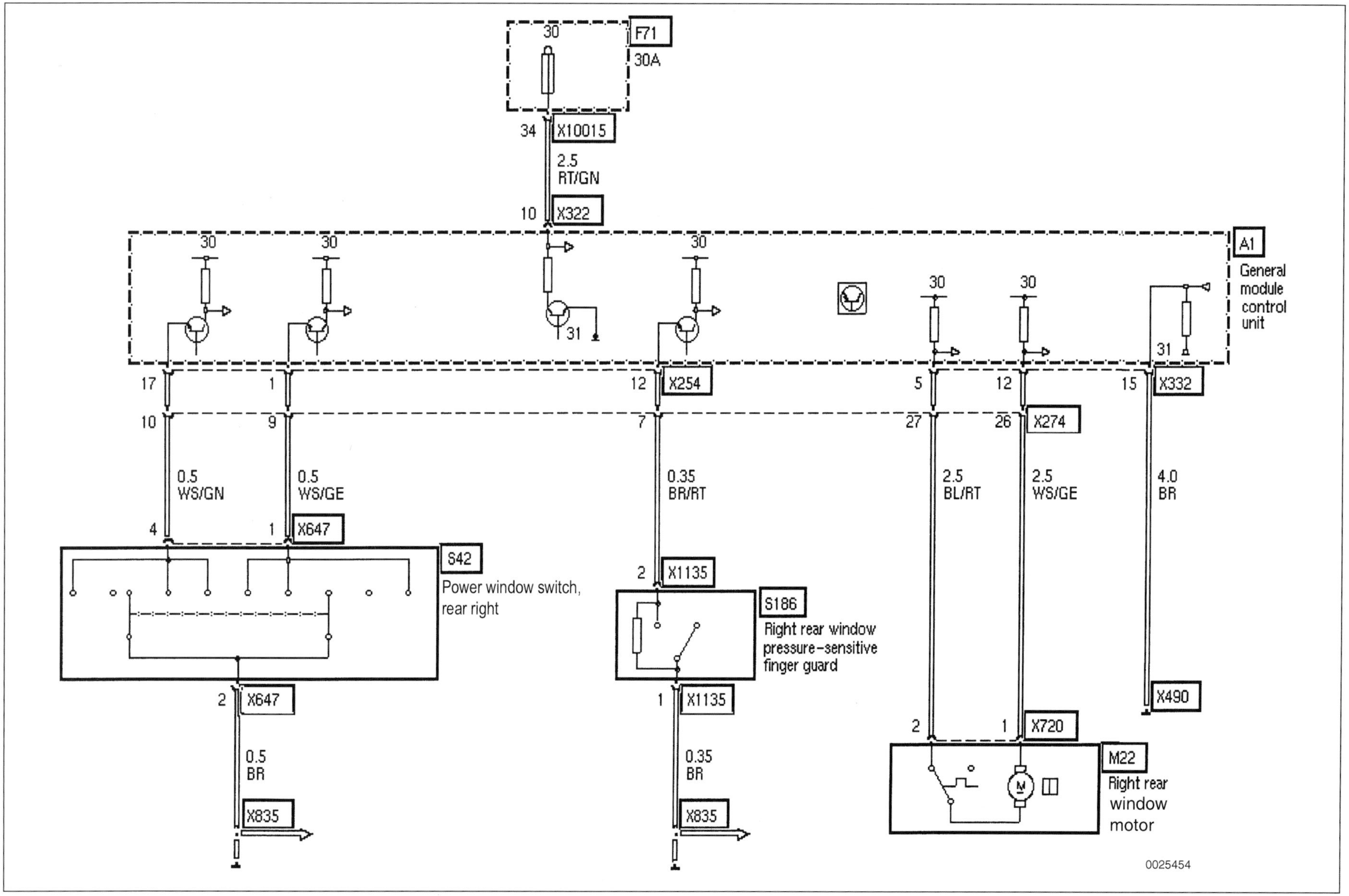

A/C compressor clutch relay (K19)

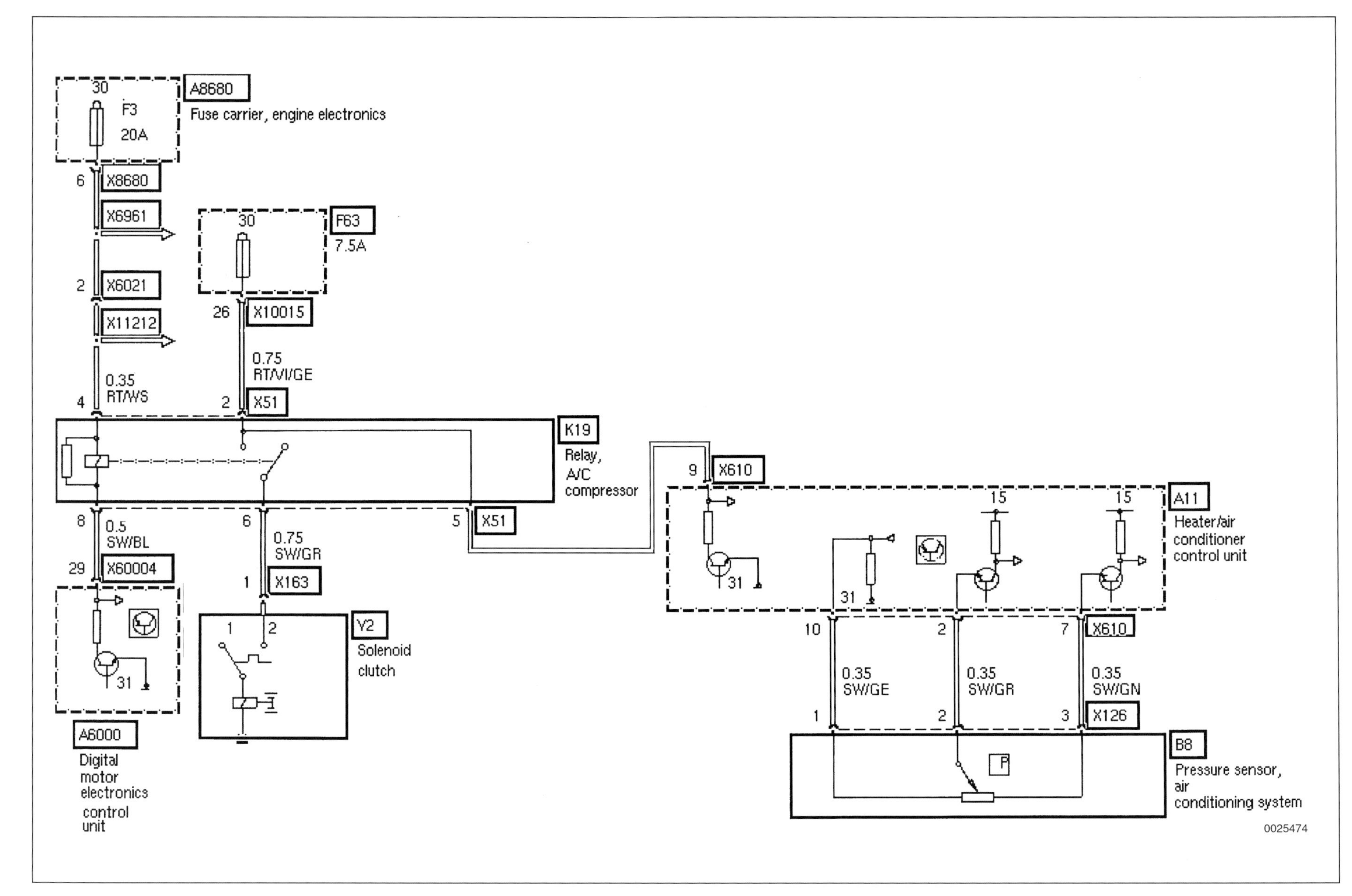

Supplemental Electrical Wiring Diagrams

ELECTRICAL COMPONENT LOCATIONS (relay and fuse positions, ground locations)see **Repair Group 610**

NOTE —
The main wiring diagram section, which includes most of the E46 system schematics, can be found on page ***ELE-1***

ELECTRICAL COMPONENT INDEX

ELECTRICAL COMPONENT INDEX *(CONT.)*

ELECTRICAL COMPONENT INDEX *(CONT.)*

MS 43.0 Engine Management
Exhaust flap, 330i models

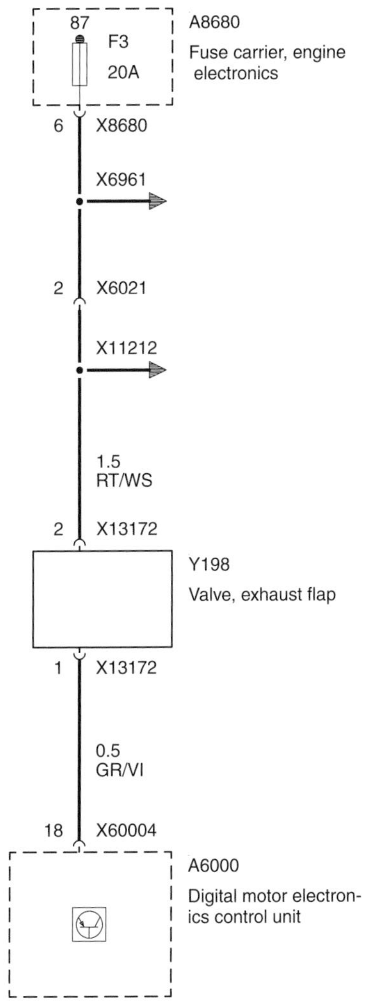

MS 43.0 Engine Management
Fuel pump

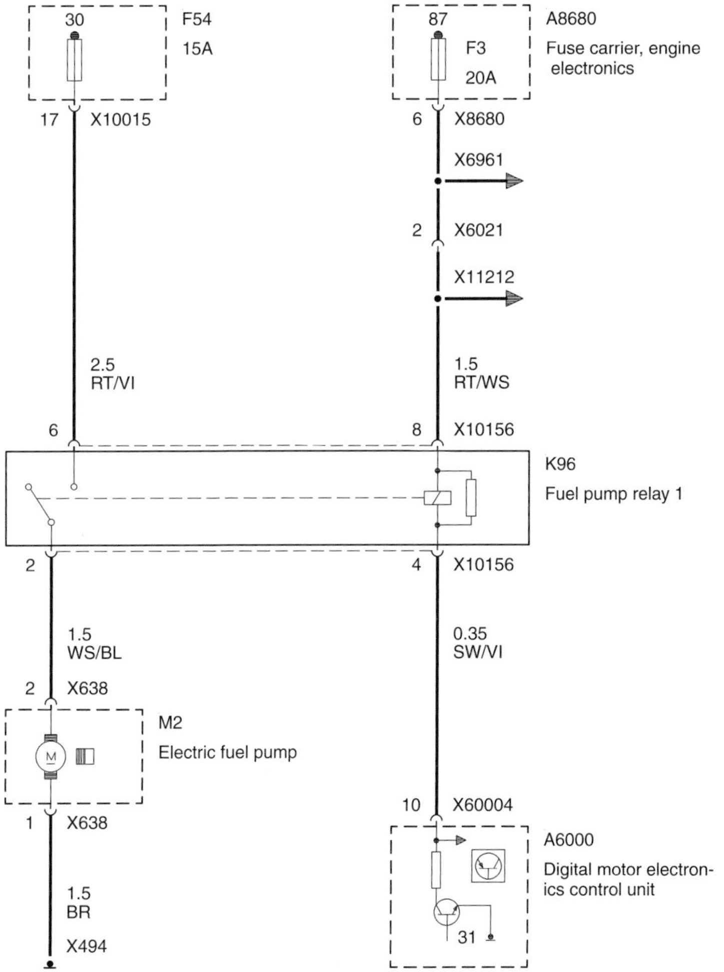

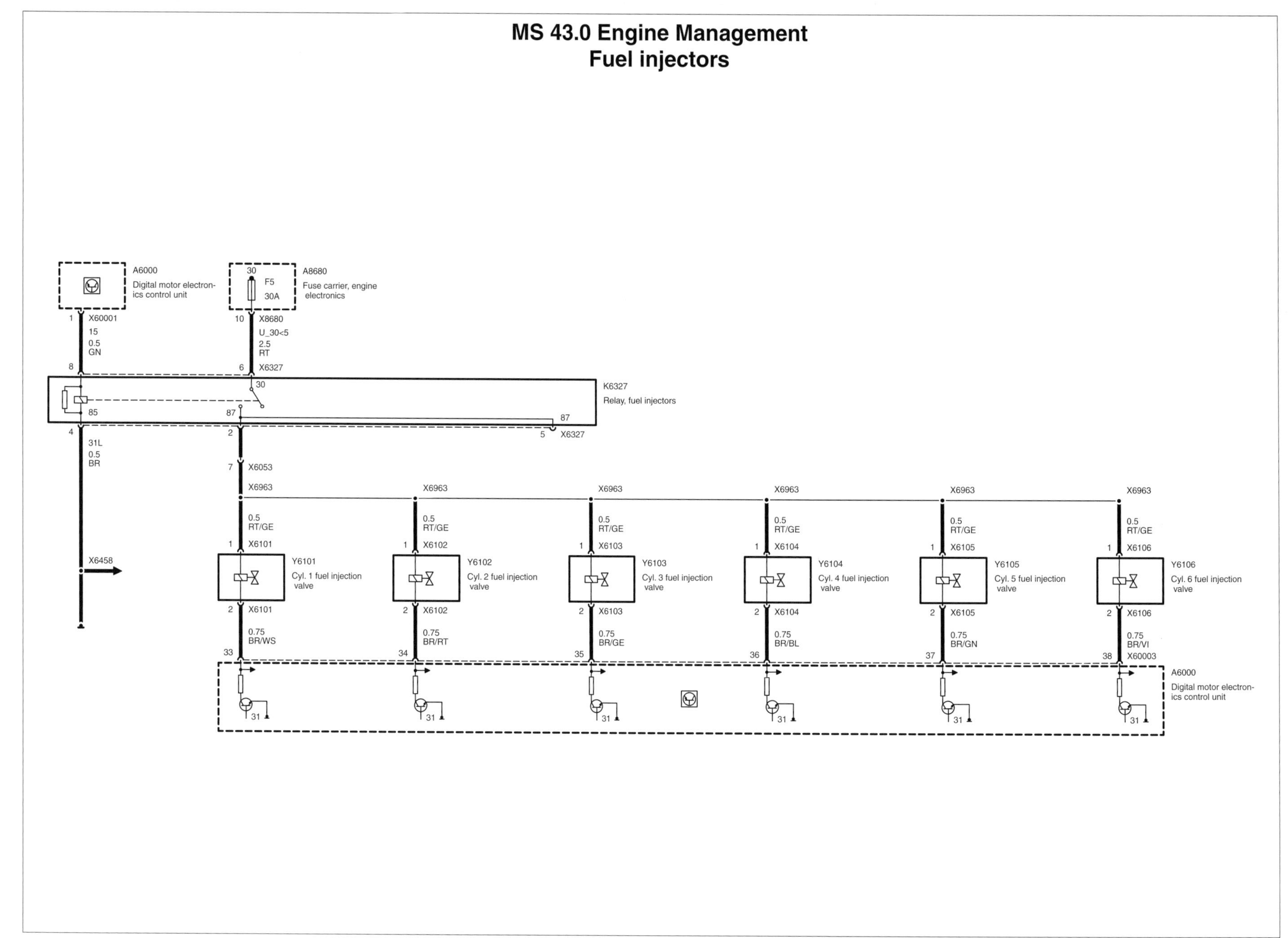
MS 43.0 Engine Management
Fuel injectors
A6000
Digital motor electronics control unit
A8680
Fuse carrier, engine electronics
30
F5
30A
1
X60001
15
0.5
GN
10
X8680
U_30<5
2.5
RT
8
6
X6327
30
K6327
Relay, fuel injectors
85
87
87
4
2
5
X6327
31L
0.5
BR
7
X6053
X6963
X6458
0.5
RT/GE
X6101
Y6101
Cyl. 1 fuel injection valve
X6102
Y6102
Cyl. 2 fuel injection valve
X6103
Y6103
Cyl. 3 fuel injection valve
X6104
Y6104
Cyl. 4 fuel injection valve
X6105
Y6105
Cyl. 5 fuel injection valve
X6106
Y6106
Cyl. 6 fuel injection valve
0.75
BR/WS
BR/RT
BR/GE
BR/BL
BR/GN
BR/VI
X60003
33
34
35
36
37
38
31

MS 43.0 Engine Management
Pedal position sensor

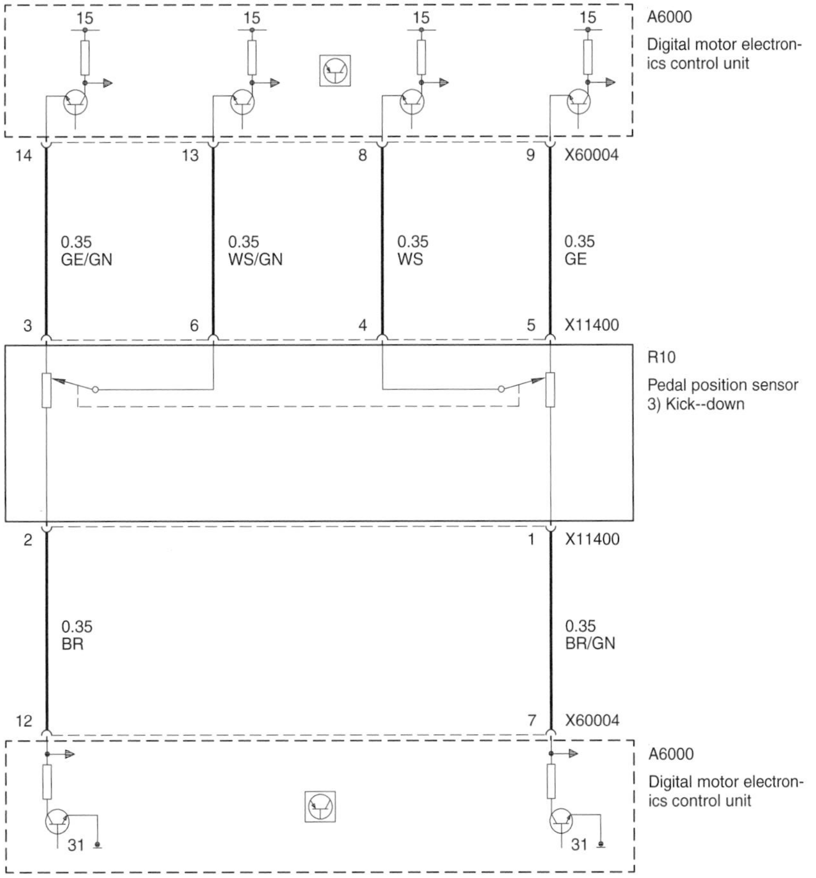

A6000
Digital motor electronics control unit

15 15 15 15

14 13 8 9 X60004

0.35 GE/GN
0.35 WS/GN
0.35 WS
0.35 GE

3 6 4 5 X11400

R10
Pedal position sensor
3) Kick--down

2 1 X11400

0.35 BR
0.35 BR/GN

12 7 X60004

A6000
Digital motor electronics control unit

31 31

MS 43.0 Engine Management
Knock sensors

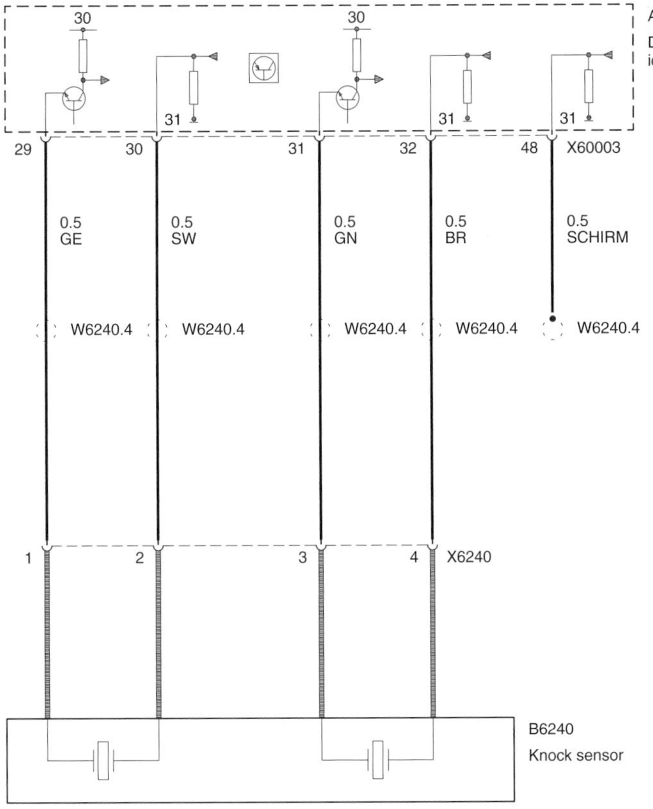

A6000
Digital motor electronics control unit

30 30 31 31 31

29 30 31 32 48 X60003

0.5 GE
0.5 SW
0.5 GN
0.5 BR
0.5 SCHIRM

W6240.4 W6240.4 W6240.4 W6240.4 W6240.4

1 2 3 4 X6240

B6240
Knock sensor

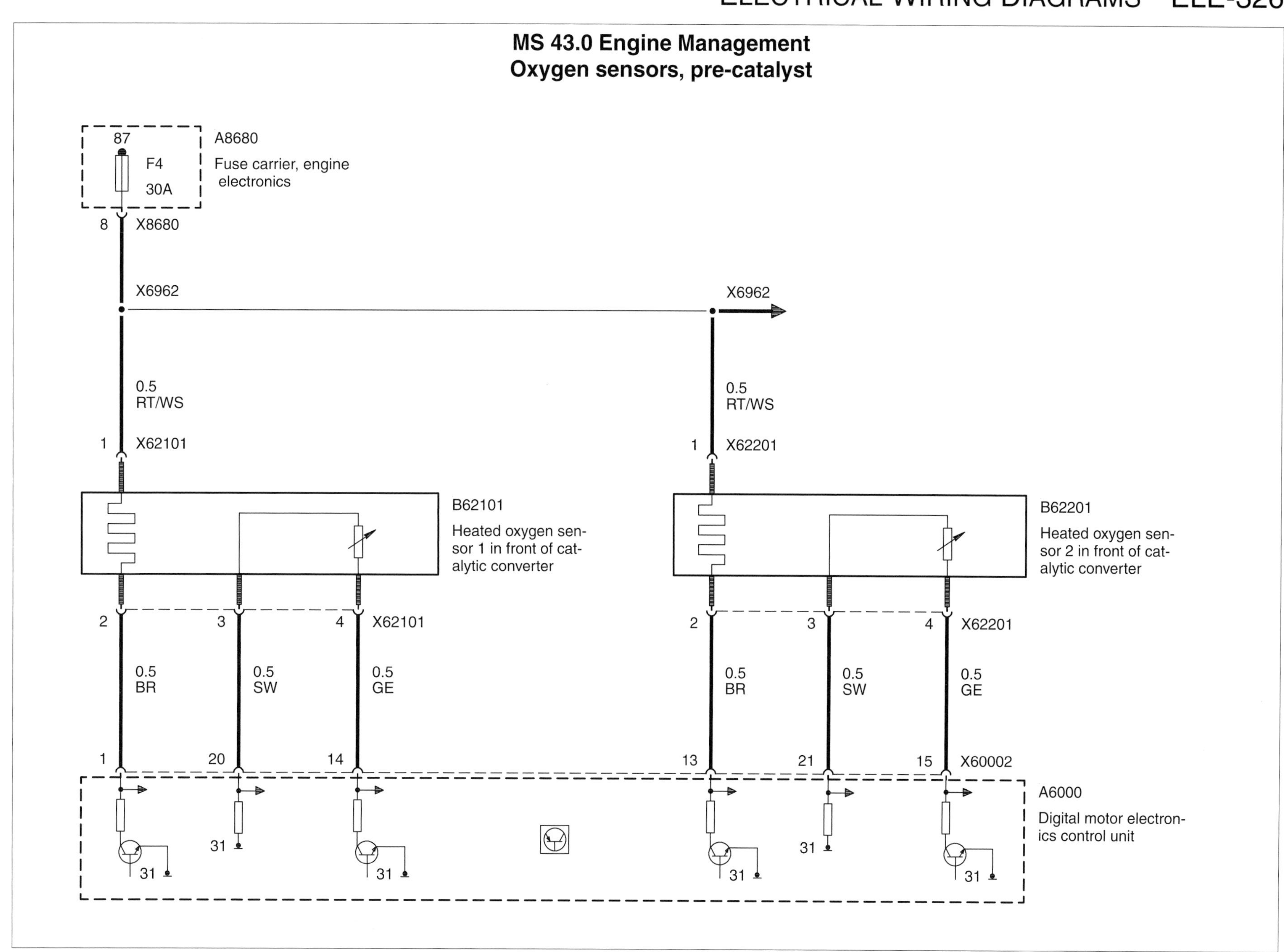
MS 43.0 Engine Management
Oxygen sensors, pre-catalyst
87
F4
30A
A8680
Fuse carrier, engine electronics
8
X8680
X6962
X6962
0.5
RT/WS
1
X62101
0.5
RT/WS
1
X62201
B62101
Heated oxygen sensor 1 in front of catalytic converter
B62201
Heated oxygen sensor 2 in front of catalytic converter
2
3
4
X62101
2
3
4
X62201
0.5
BR
0.5
SW
0.5
GE
0.5
BR
0.5
SW
0.5
GE
1
20
14
13
21
15
X60002
A6000
Digital motor electronics control unit
31
31
31
31
31
31

MS 43.0 Engine Management
Oxygen sensors, post-catalyst

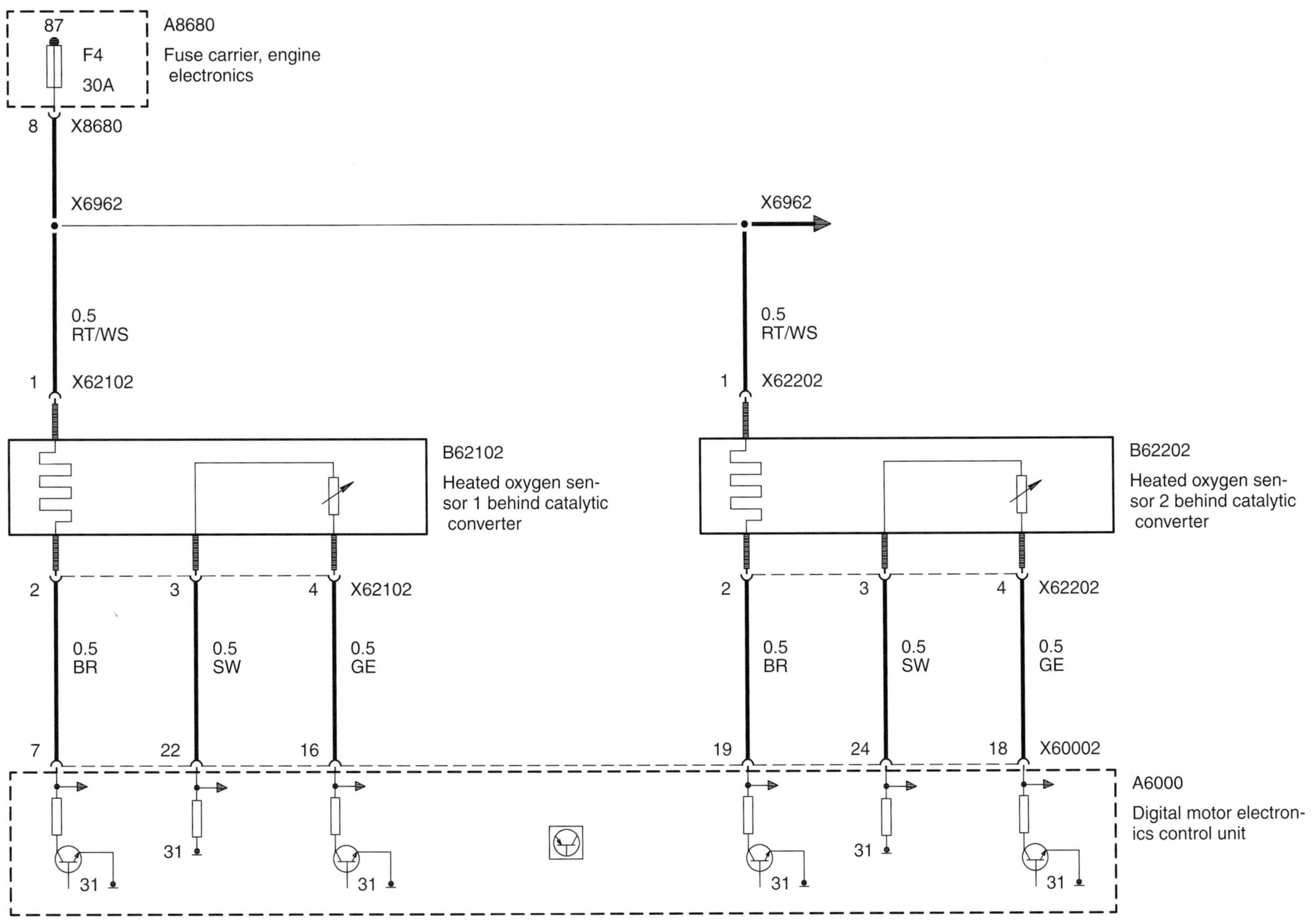

MS 43.0 Engine Management
Motor driven throttle

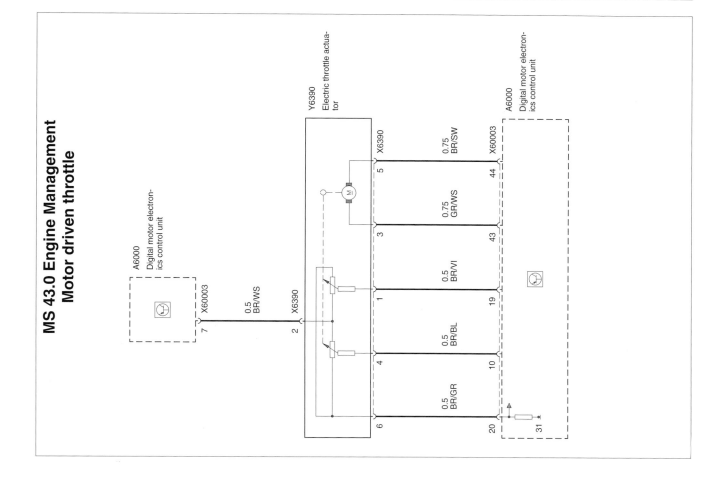

A6000
Digital motor electronics control unit
7 X60003
0.5
BR/WS
2 X6390
Y6390
Electric throttle actuator
6 4 1 3 5 X6390
0.5 BR/GR
0.5 BR/BL
0.5 BR/VI
0.75 GR/WS
0.75 BR/SW
20 10 19 43 44 X60003
31
A6000
Digital motor electronics control unit

MS 43.0 Engine Management
DISA changeover valve

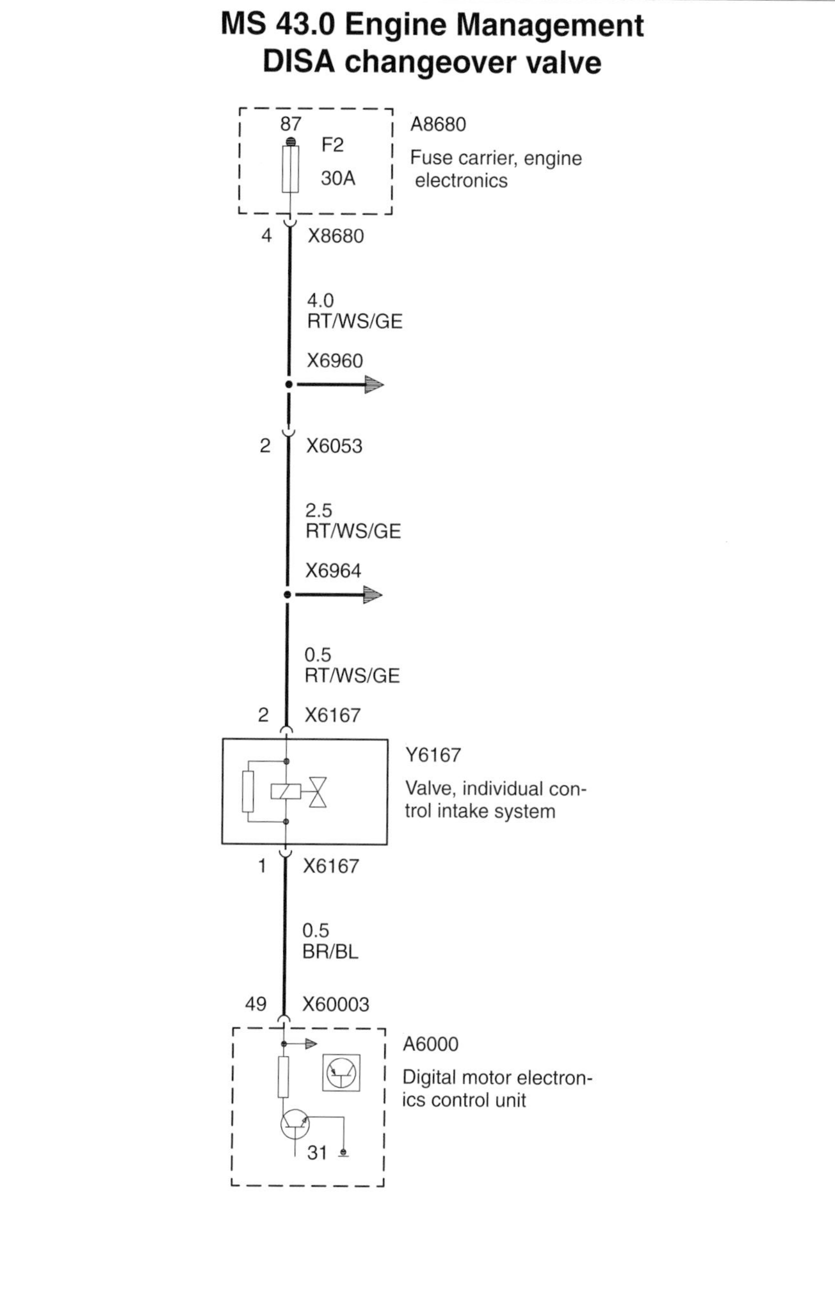

MS 43.0 Engine Management
Idle speed control valve

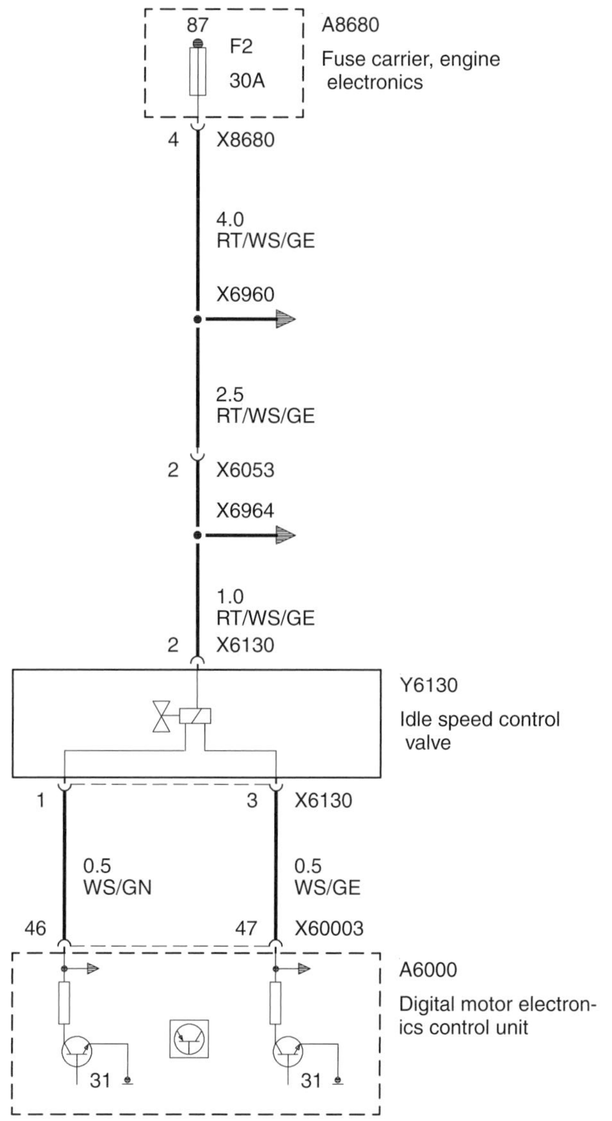

MS 43.0 Engine Management
Mass Air Flow Sensor

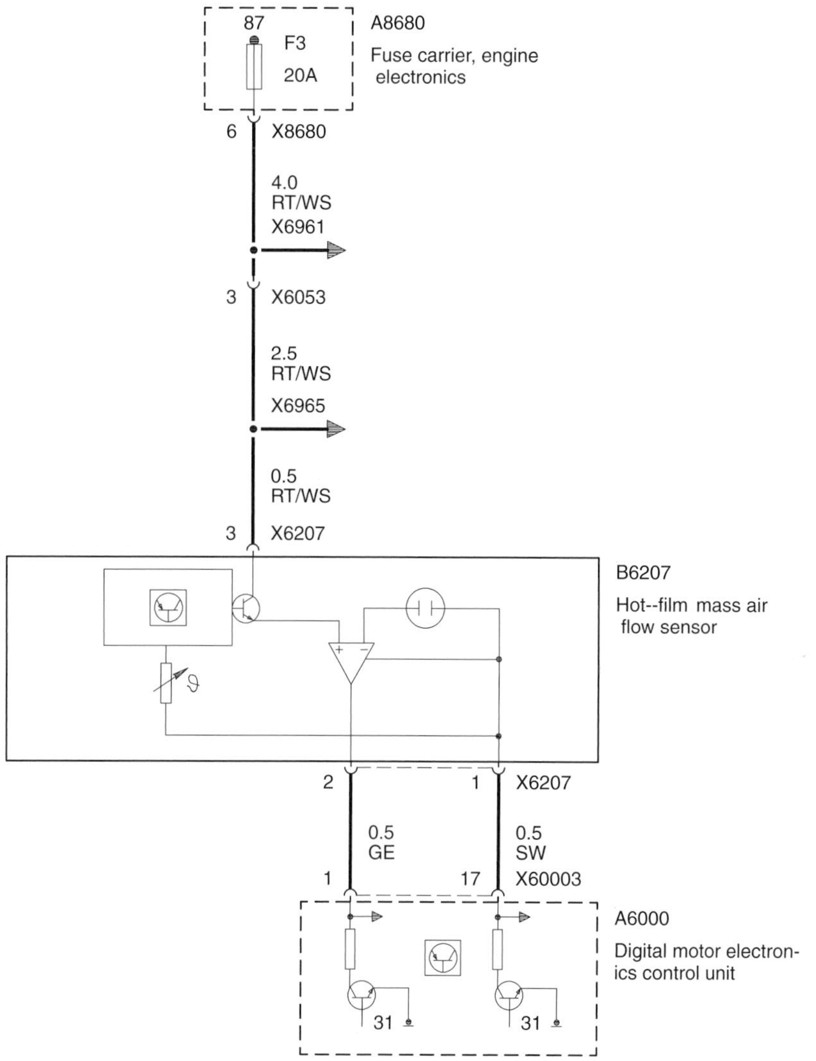

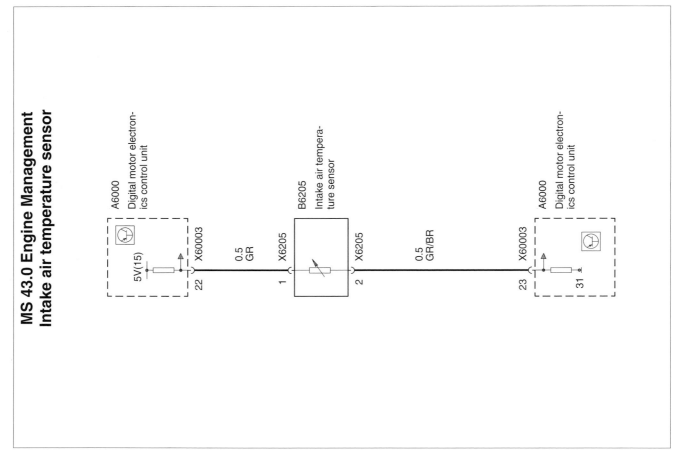

MS 43.0 Engine Management
Intake air temperature sensor

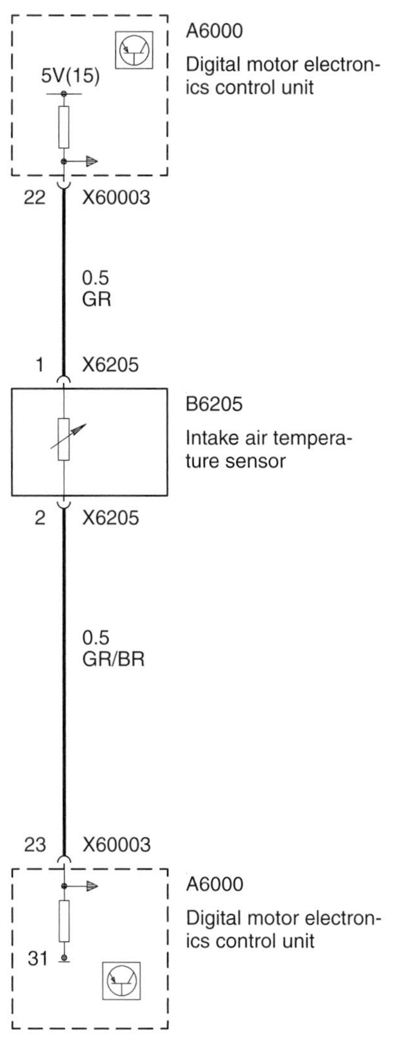

MS 43.0 Engine Management
Crankshaft position sensor

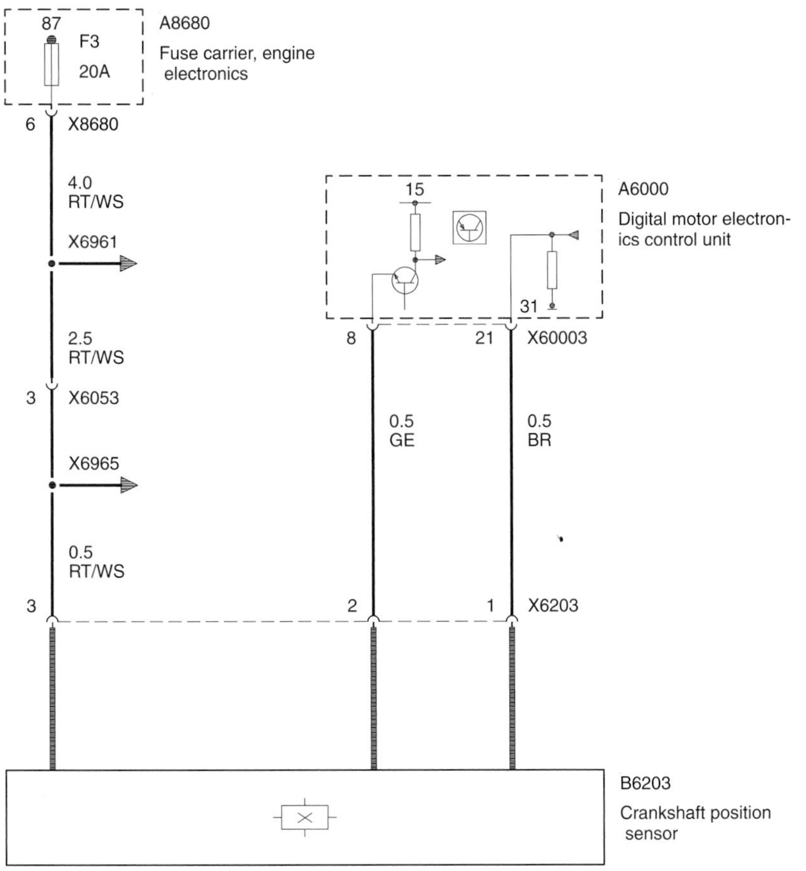

MS 43.0 Engine Management
Thermostat (electrically-heated)

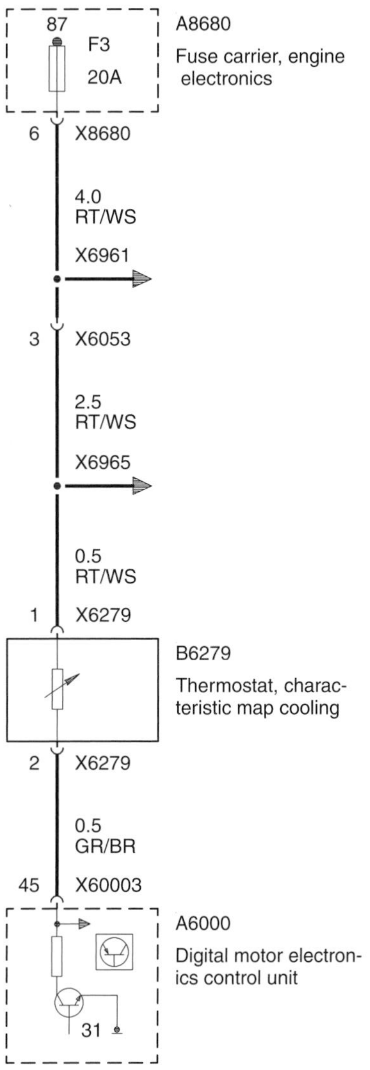

A8680
Fuse carrier, engine electronics
87
F3
20A
6 X8680
4.0
RT/WS
X6961
3 X6053
2.5
RT/WS
X6965
0.5
RT/WS
1 X6279
B6279
Thermostat, characteristic map cooling
2 X6279
0.5
GR/BR
45 X60003
A6000
Digital motor electronics control unit
31

MS 43.0 Engine Management
Engine coolant temperature sensor

A6000
Digital motor electronics control unit
15
24 X60003
0.5
BR/RT
1 X6236
B6236
Engine coolant temperature sensor
2 X6236
0.5
GR/BR
25 X60003
A6000
Digital motor electronics control unit
31

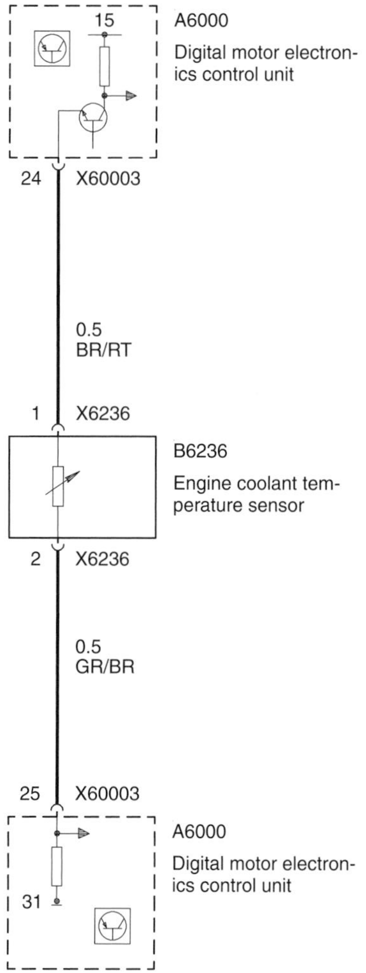

MS 43.0 Engine Management
Engine oil temperature sensor

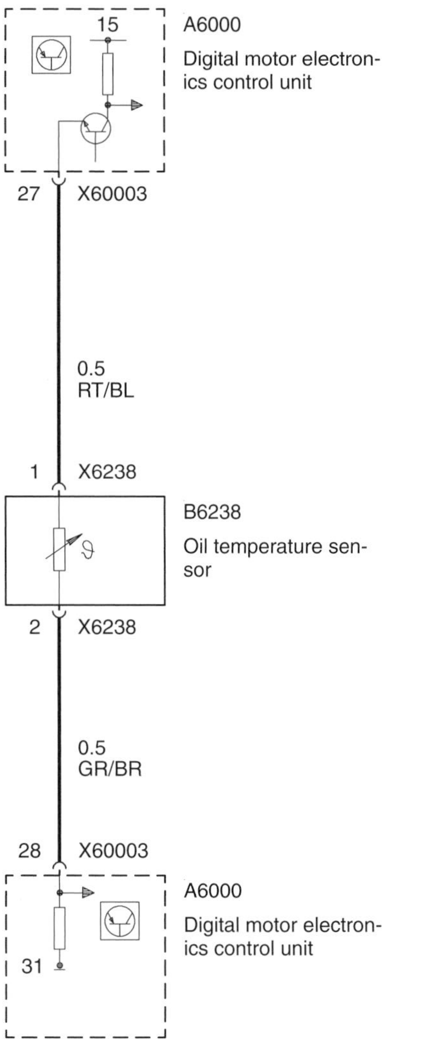

15
A6000
Digital motor electronics control unit
27 X60003
0.5
RT/BL
1 X6238
B6238
Oil temperature sensor
2 X6238
0.5
GR/BR
28 X60003
A6000
Digital motor electronics control unit
31

MS 43.0 Engine Management
VANOS control valves

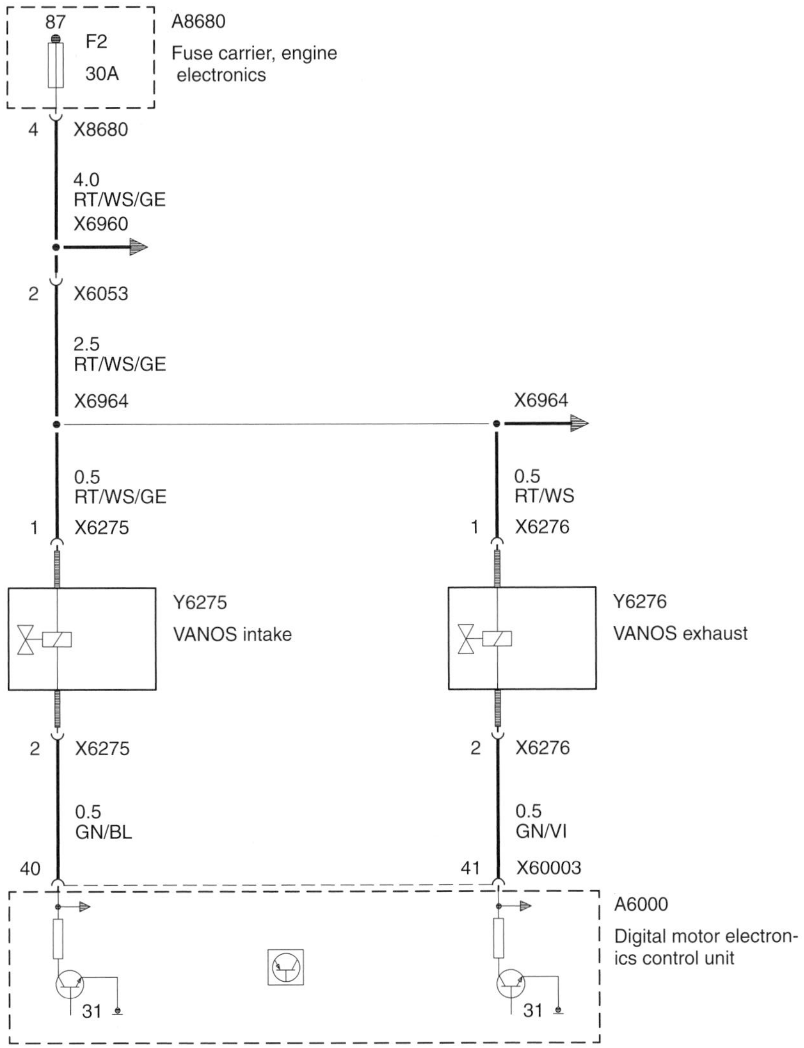

87
F2
30A
A8680
Fuse carrier, engine electronics
4 X8680
4.0
RT/WS/GE
X6960
2 X6053
2.5
RT/WS/GE
X6964
X6964
0.5
RT/WS/GE
1 X6275
0.5
RT/WS
1 X6276
Y6275
VANOS intake
Y6276
VANOS exhaust
2 X6275
2 X6276
0.5
GN/BL
0.5
GN/VI
40
41 X60003
A6000
Digital motor electronics control unit
31
31

MS 43.0 Engine Management
Camshaft position sensors

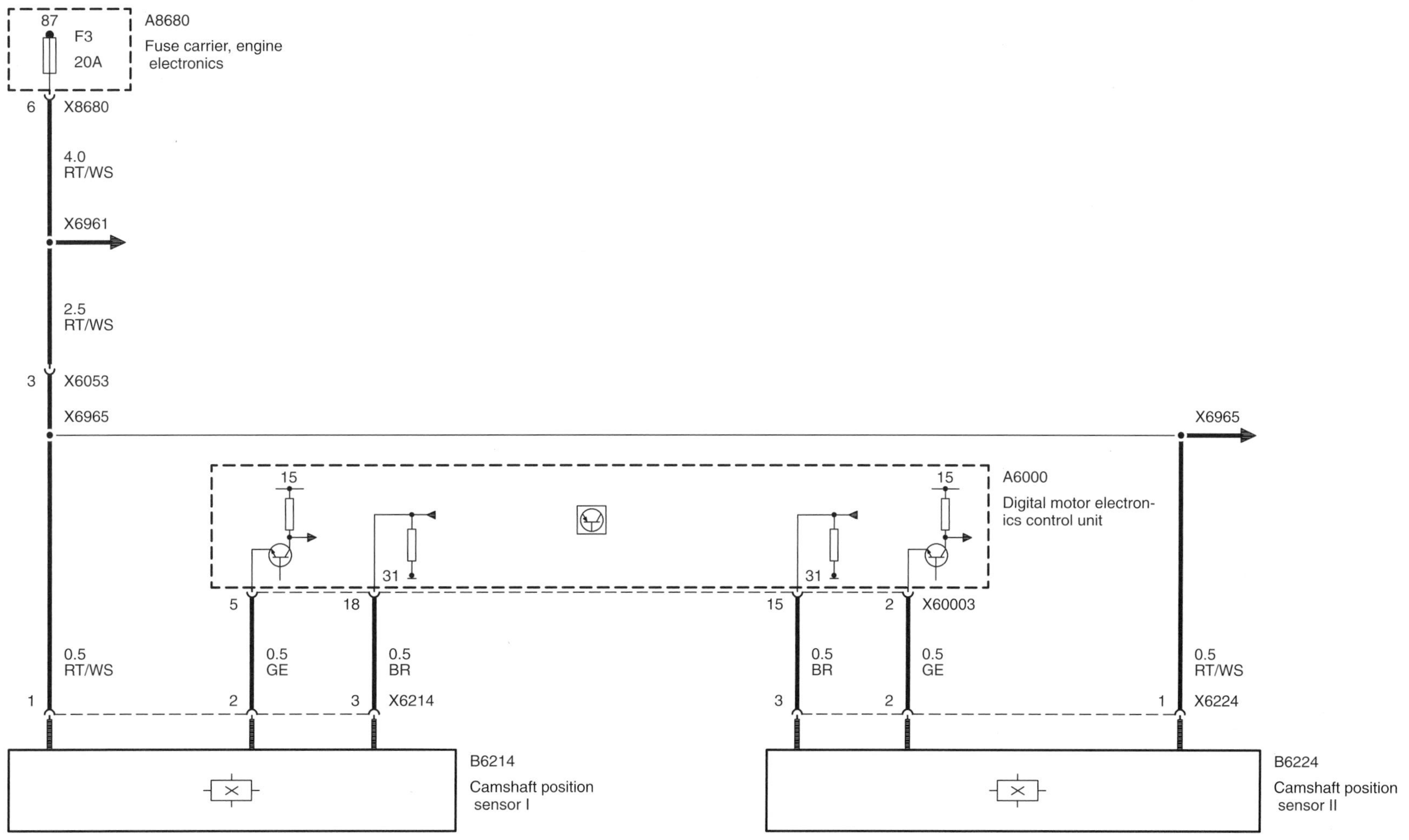

87
F3
20A
A8680
Fuse carrier, engine electronics
6 X8680
4.0 RT/WS
X6961
2.5 RT/WS
3 X6053
X6965
X6965
15
15
A6000
Digital motor electronics control unit
31
31
5
18
15
2 X60003
0.5 RT/WS
0.5 GE
0.5 BR
0.5 BR
0.5 GE
0.5 RT/WS
1
2
3 X6214
3
2
1 X6224
B6214
Camshaft position sensor I
B6224
Camshaft position sensor II

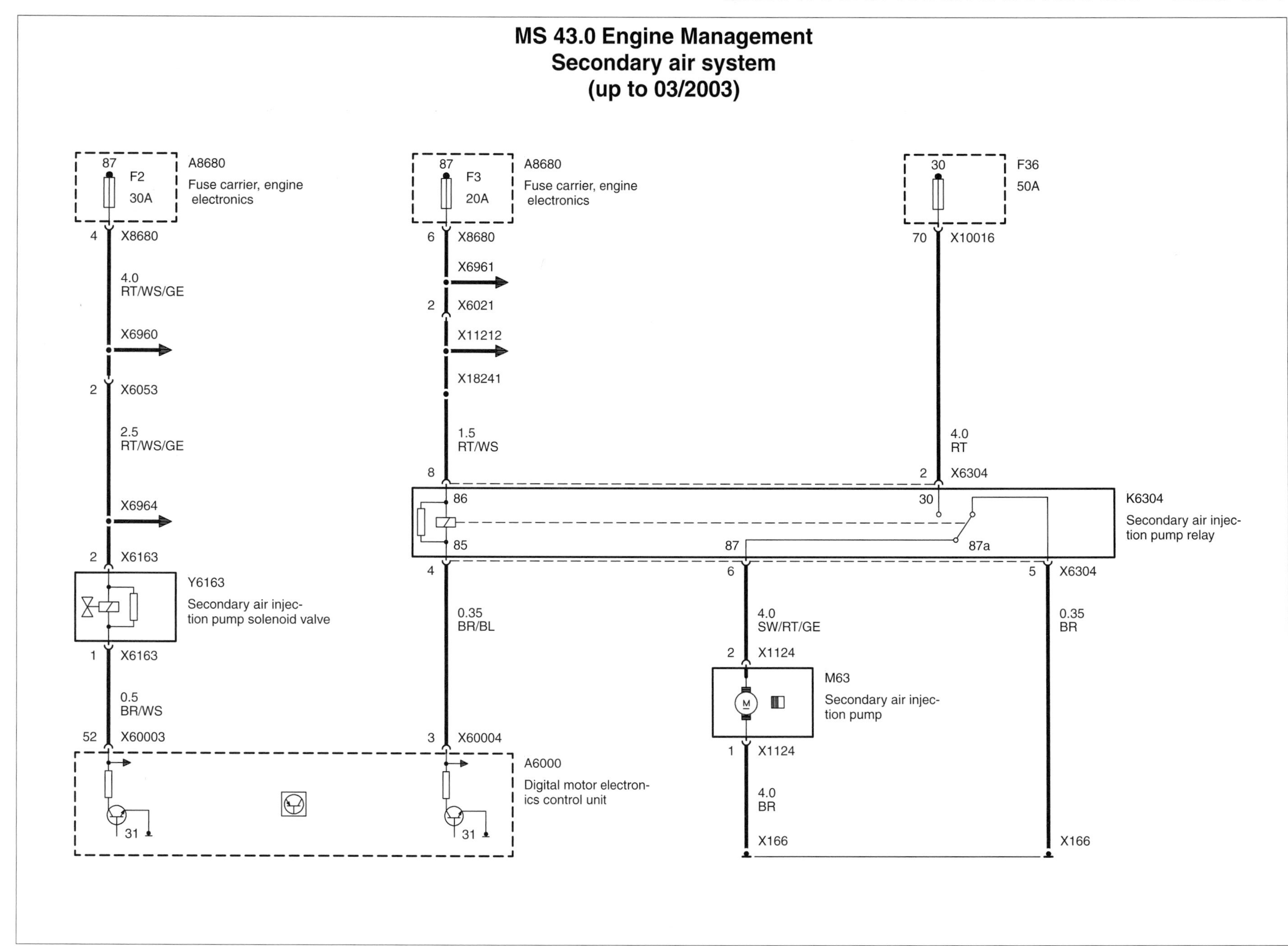
MS 43.0 Engine Management
Secondary air system
(up to 03/2003)
87
F2
30A
A8680
Fuse carrier, engine electronics
4
X8680
4.0
RT/WS/GE
X6960
2
X6053
2.5
RT/WS/GE
X6964
2
X6163
Y6163
Secondary air injection pump solenoid valve
1
X6163
0.5
BR/WS
52
X60003
31
87
F3
20A
A8680
Fuse carrier, engine electronics
6
X8680
X6961
2
X6021
X11212
X18241
1.5
RT/WS
8
86
85
4
0.35
BR/BL
3
X60004
31
A6000
Digital motor electronics control unit
30
F36
50A
70
X10016
4.0
RT
2
X6304
30
87
87a
K6304
Secondary air injection pump relay
6
4.0
SW/RT/GE
2
X1124
M
M63
Secondary air injection pump
1
X1124
4.0
BR
X166
5
X6304
0.35
BR
X166

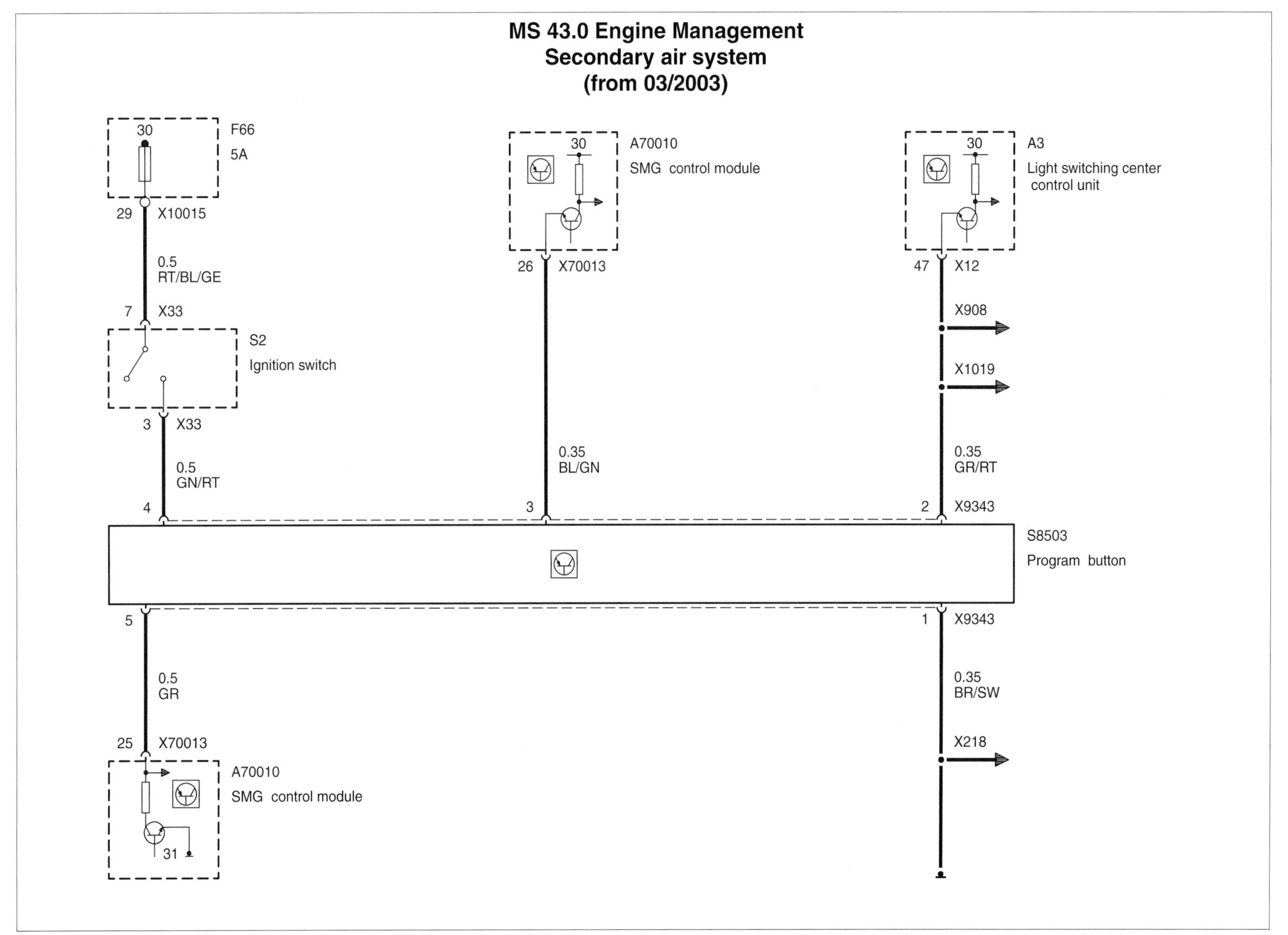
MS 43.0 Engine Management
Secondary air system
(from 03/2003)
30
F66
5A
29
X10015
0.5
RT/BL/GE
7
X33
S2
Ignition switch
3
X33
0.5
GN/RT
4
30
A70010
SMG control module
26
X70013
0.35
BL/GN
3
30
A3
Light switching center
control unit
47
X12
X908
X1019
0.35
GR/RT
2
X9343
S8503
Program button
5
0.5
GR
25
X70013
A70010
SMG control module
31
1
X9343
0.35
BR/SW
X218

MS 43.0 Engine Management
DME main relay

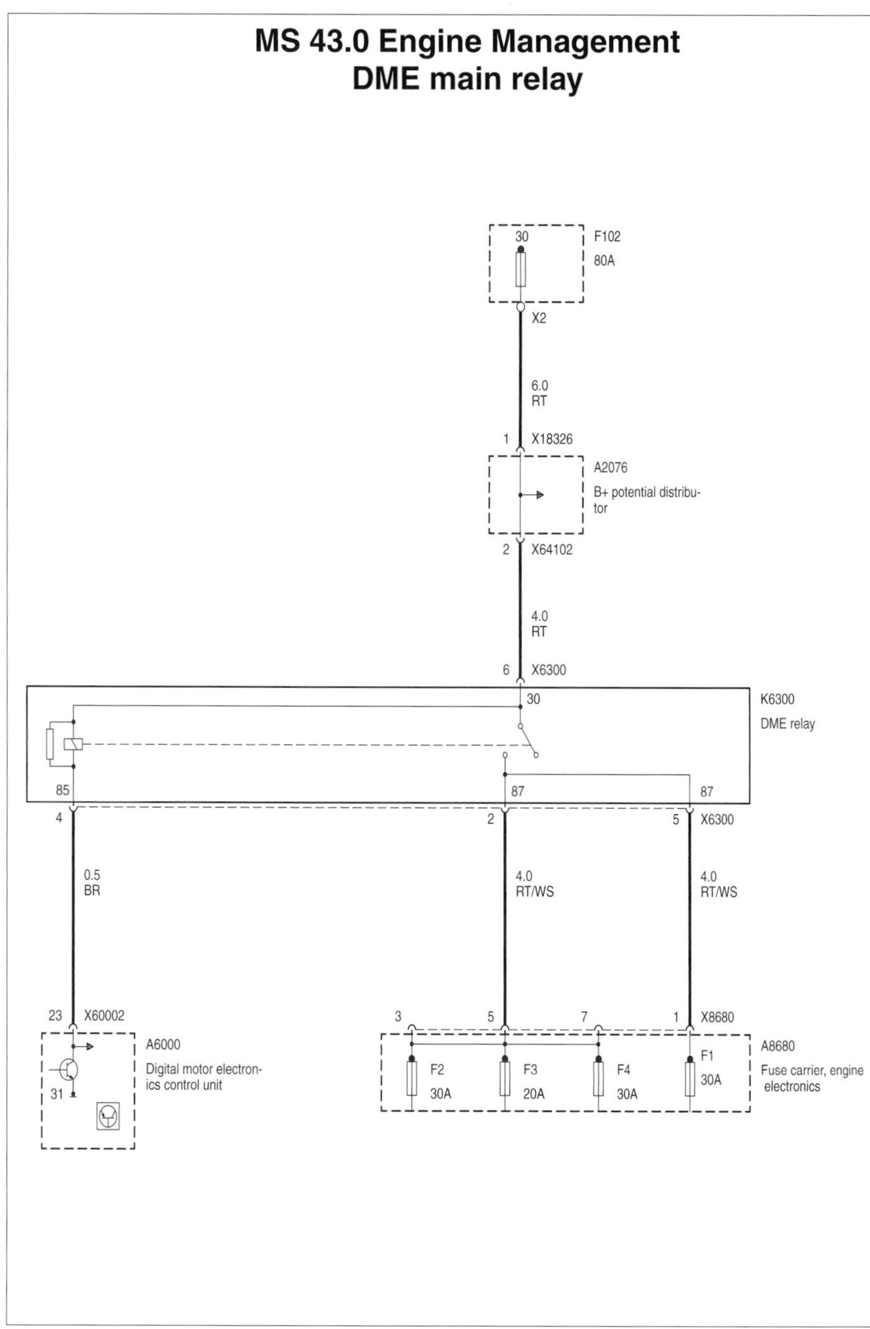

MS 43.0 Engine Management
Fuel tank ventilation valve

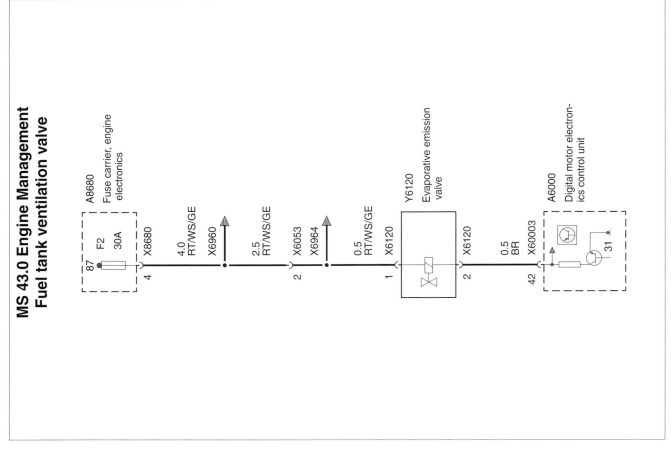

87
F2
30A
A8680
Fuse carrier, engine electronics
4 X8680
4.0
RT/WS/GE
X6960
2.5
RT/WS/GE
2 X6053
X6964
0.5
RT/WS/GE
1 X6120
Y6120
Evaporative emission valve
2 X6120
0.5
BR
42 X60003
A6000
Digital motor electronics control unit
31

MS 43.0 Engine Management
Fuel tank leakage diagnosis module
(up to 09/2002)

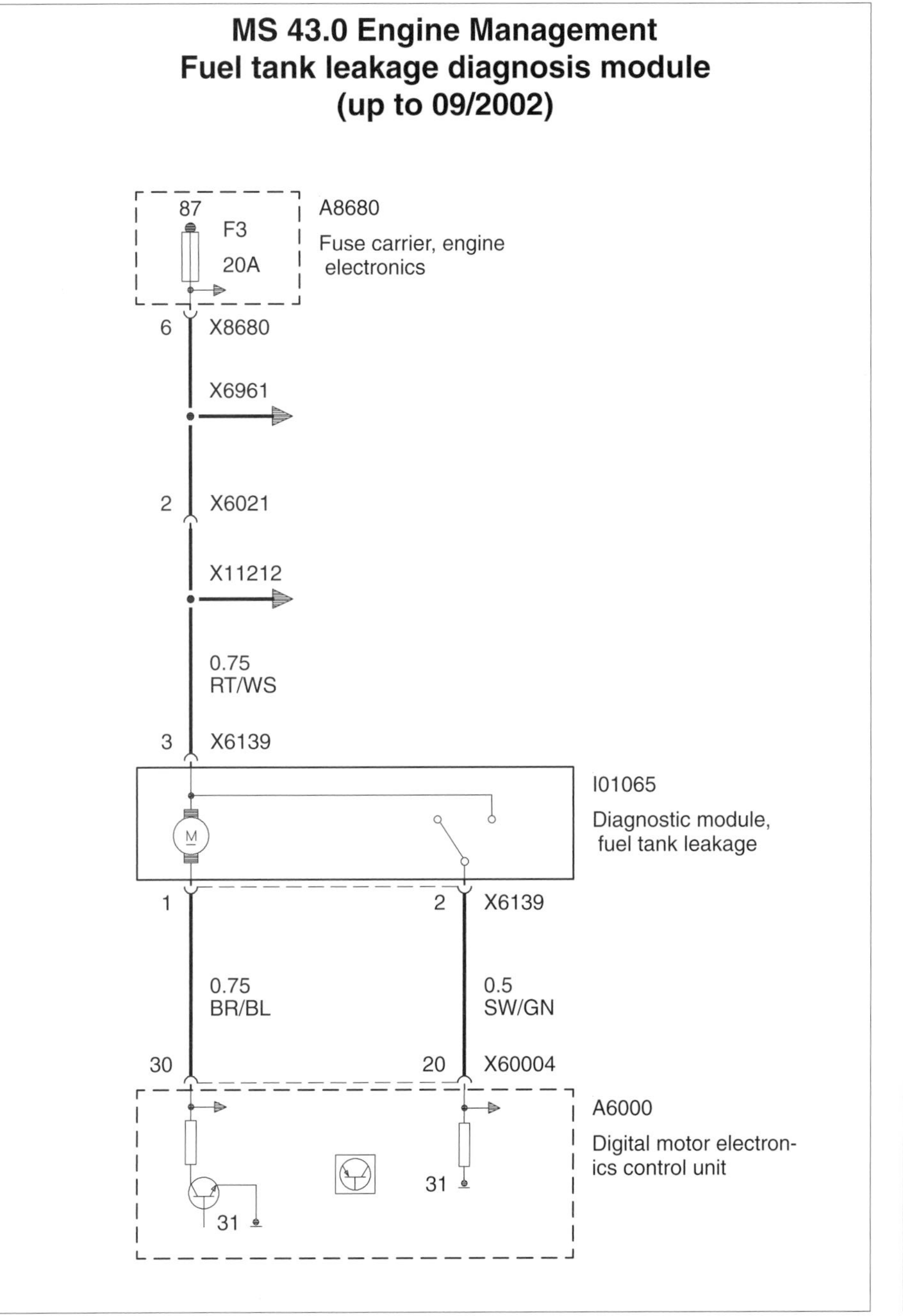

MS 43.0 Engine Management
Fuel tank leakage diagnosis module
(from 09/2002)

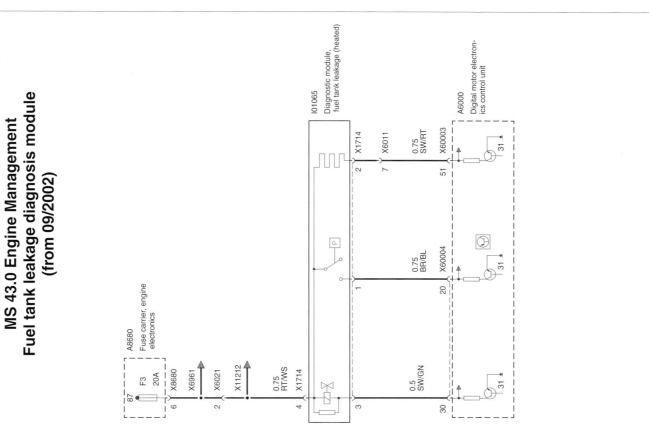

87
F3
20A
A8680
Fuse carrier, engine electronics
6 X8680
X6961
2 X6021
X11212
0.75
RT/WS
4 X1714
P
I01065
Diagnostic module, fuel tank leakage (heated)
3
1
2 X1714
7 X6011
0.5
SW/GN
0.75
BR/BL
0.75
SW/RT
30
20 X60004
51 X60003
A6000
Digital motor electronics control unit
31
31
31

MS 43.0 Engine Management
Power supply, DME control module

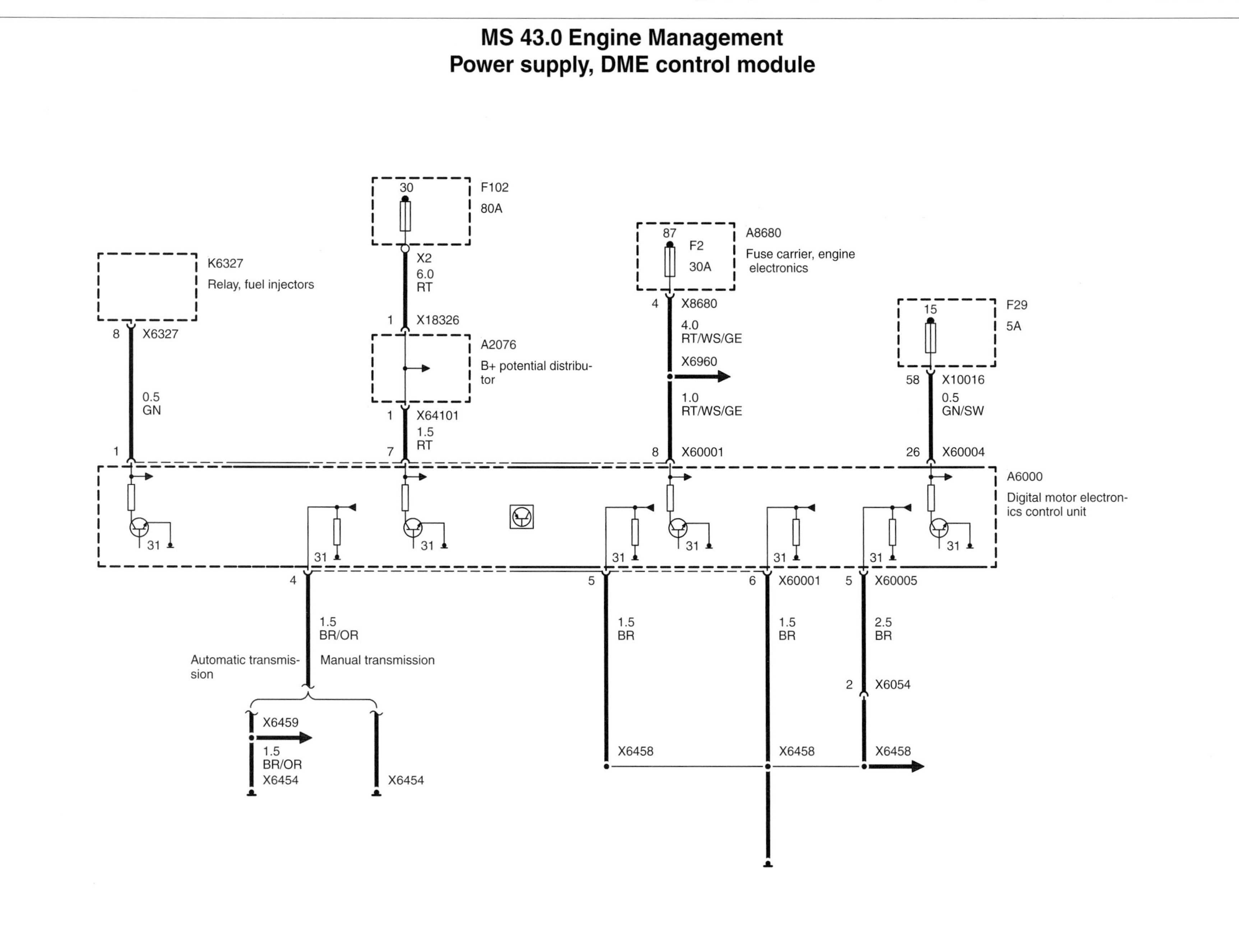

MS 43.0 Engine Management
Ignition coils
(page 1 of 2)

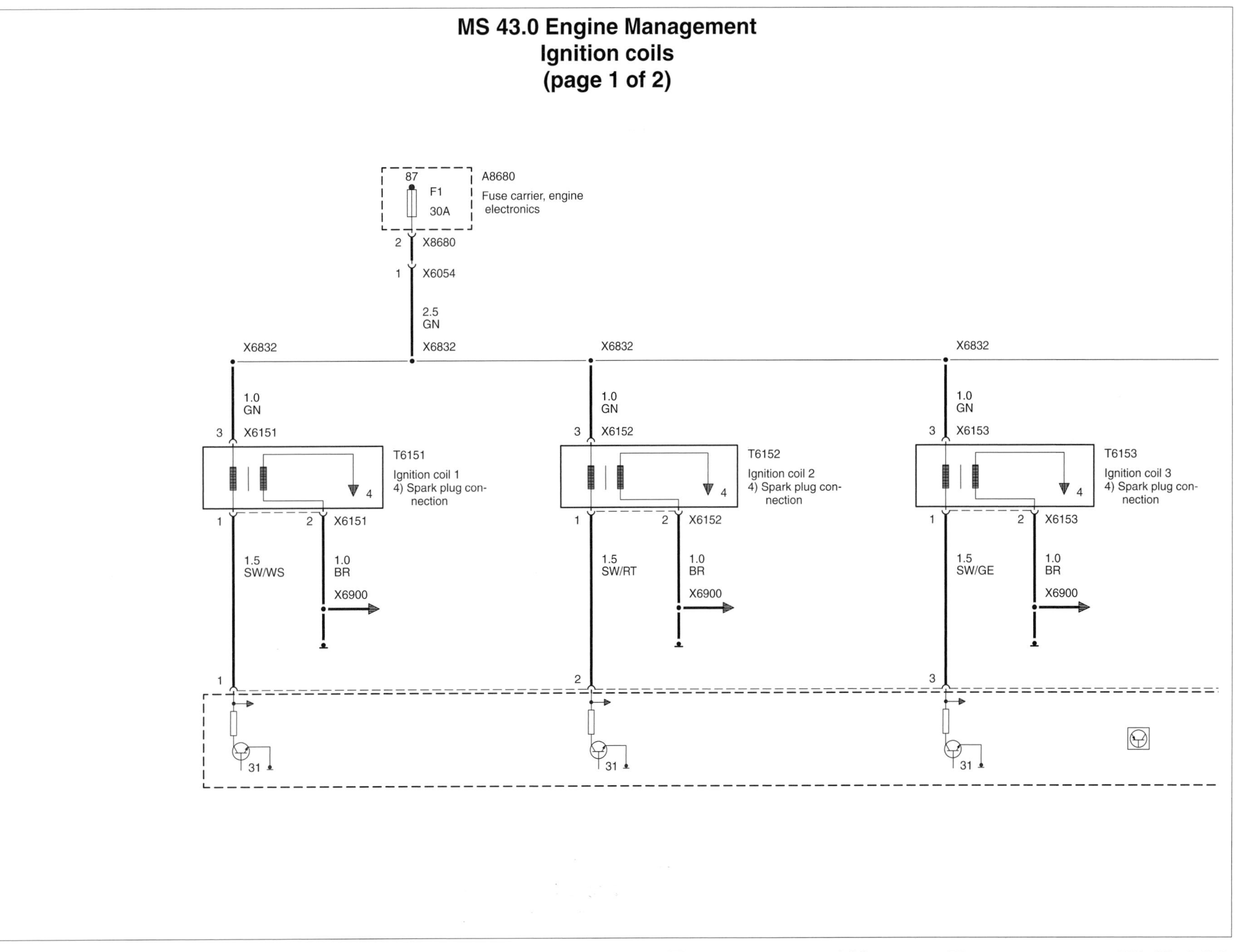

MS 43.0 Engine Management
Ignition coils
(page 2 of 2)

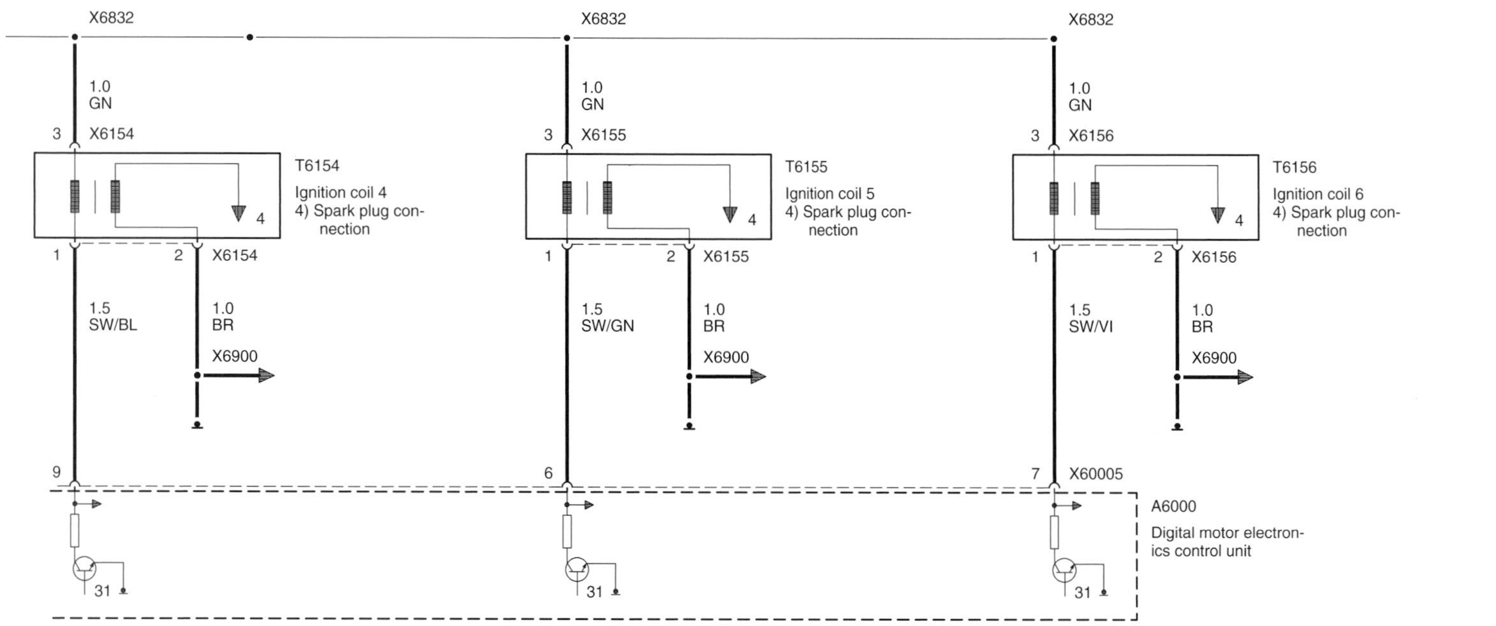

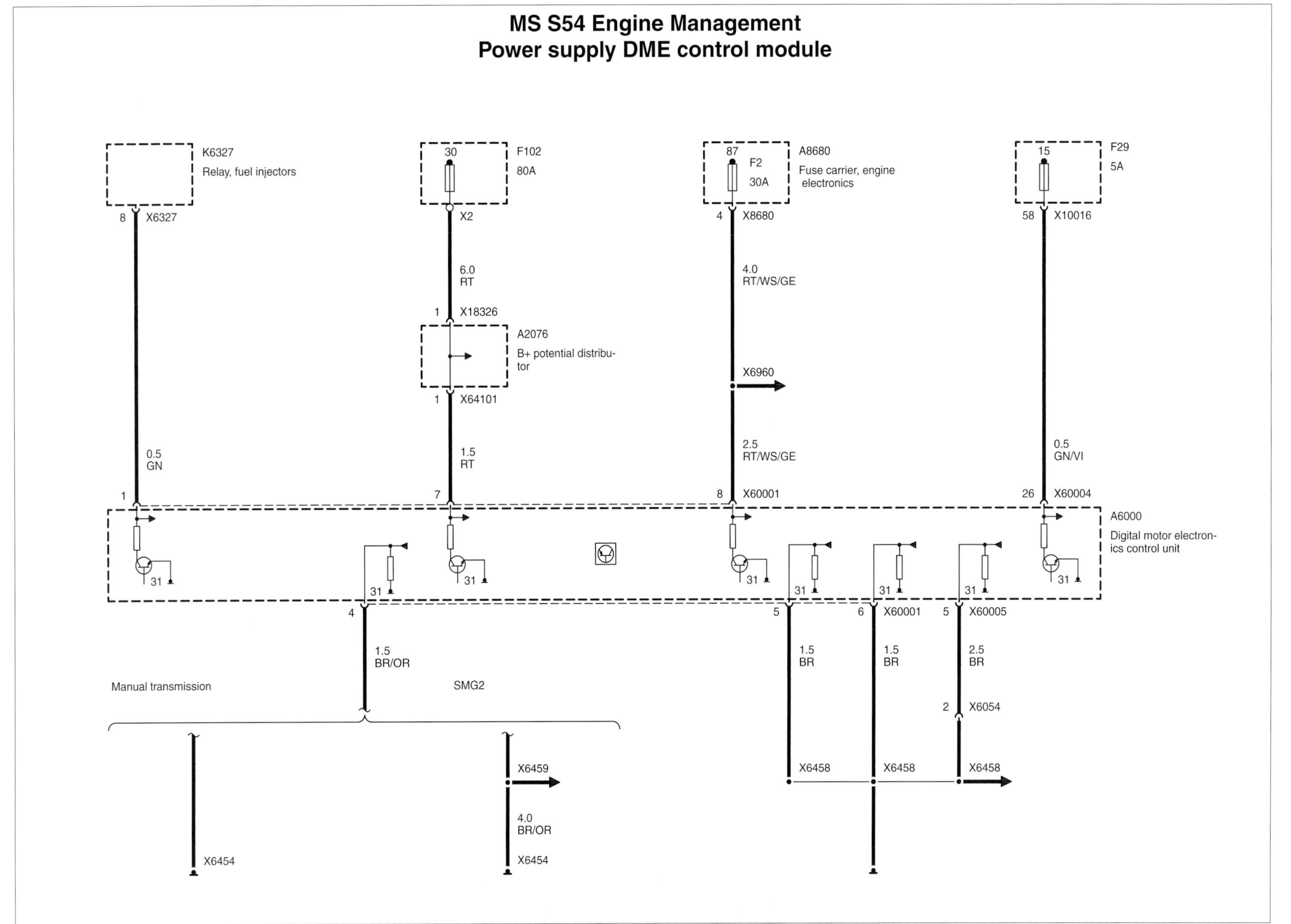
MS S54 Engine Management
Power supply DME control module
K6327
Relay, fuel injectors
8
X6327
0.5
GN
1
30
F102
80A
X2
6.0
RT
1
X18326
A2076
B+ potential distribu-
tor
1
X64101
1.5
RT
7
87
F2
30A
A8680
Fuse carrier, engine
electronics
4
X8680
4.0
RT/WS/GE
X6960
2.5
RT/WS/GE
8
X60001
15
F29
5A
58
X10016
0.5
GN/VI
26
X60004
A6000
Digital motor electron-
ics control unit
31
4
1.5
BR/OR
Manual transmission
SMG2
X6454
X6459
4.0
BR/OR
X6454
5
1.5
BR
X6458
6
X60001
1.5
BR
X6458
5
X60005
2.5
BR
2
X6054
X6458

MS S54 Engine Management
CAN bus connectors

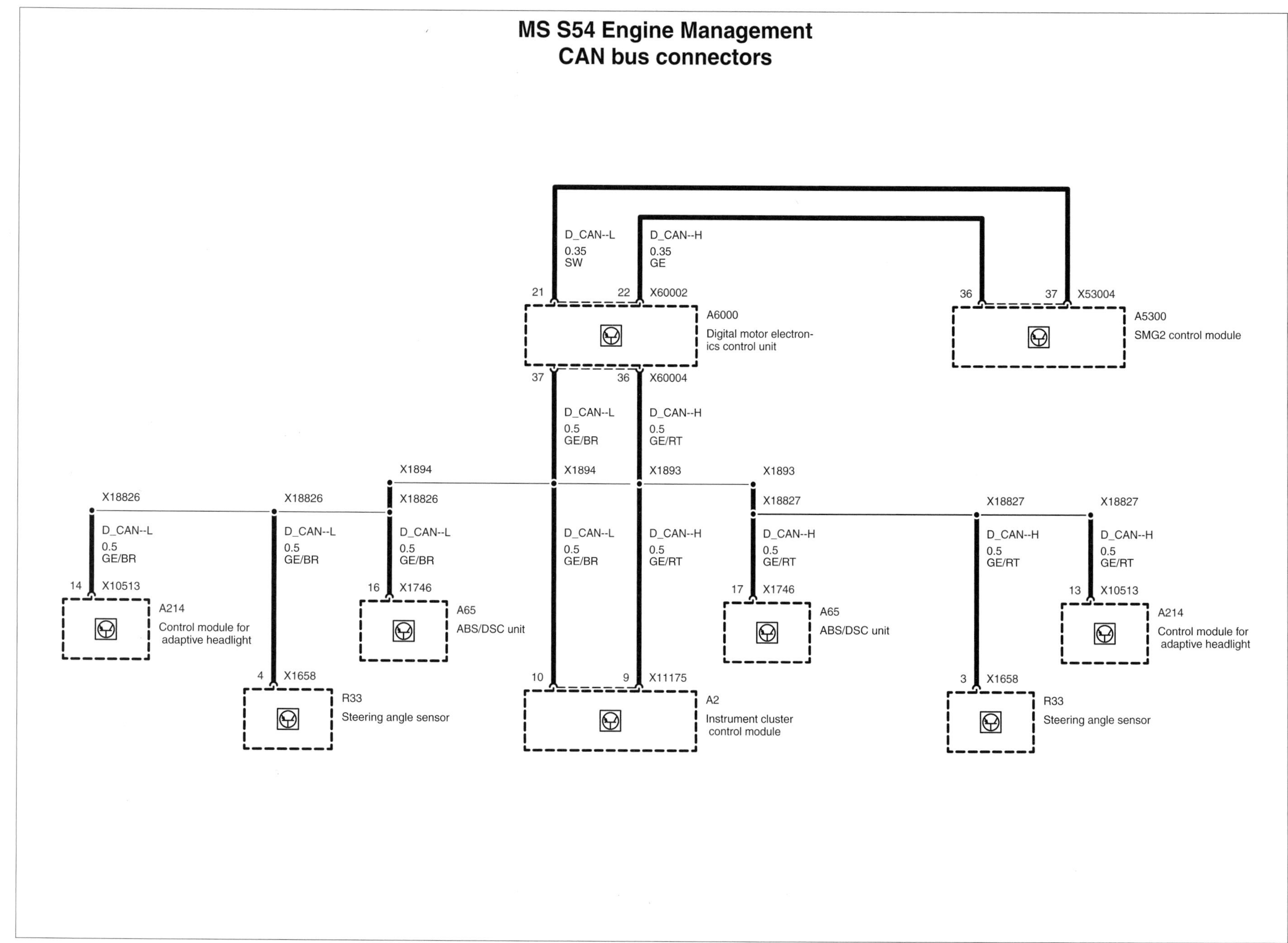

MS S54 Engine Management
A/C compressor control

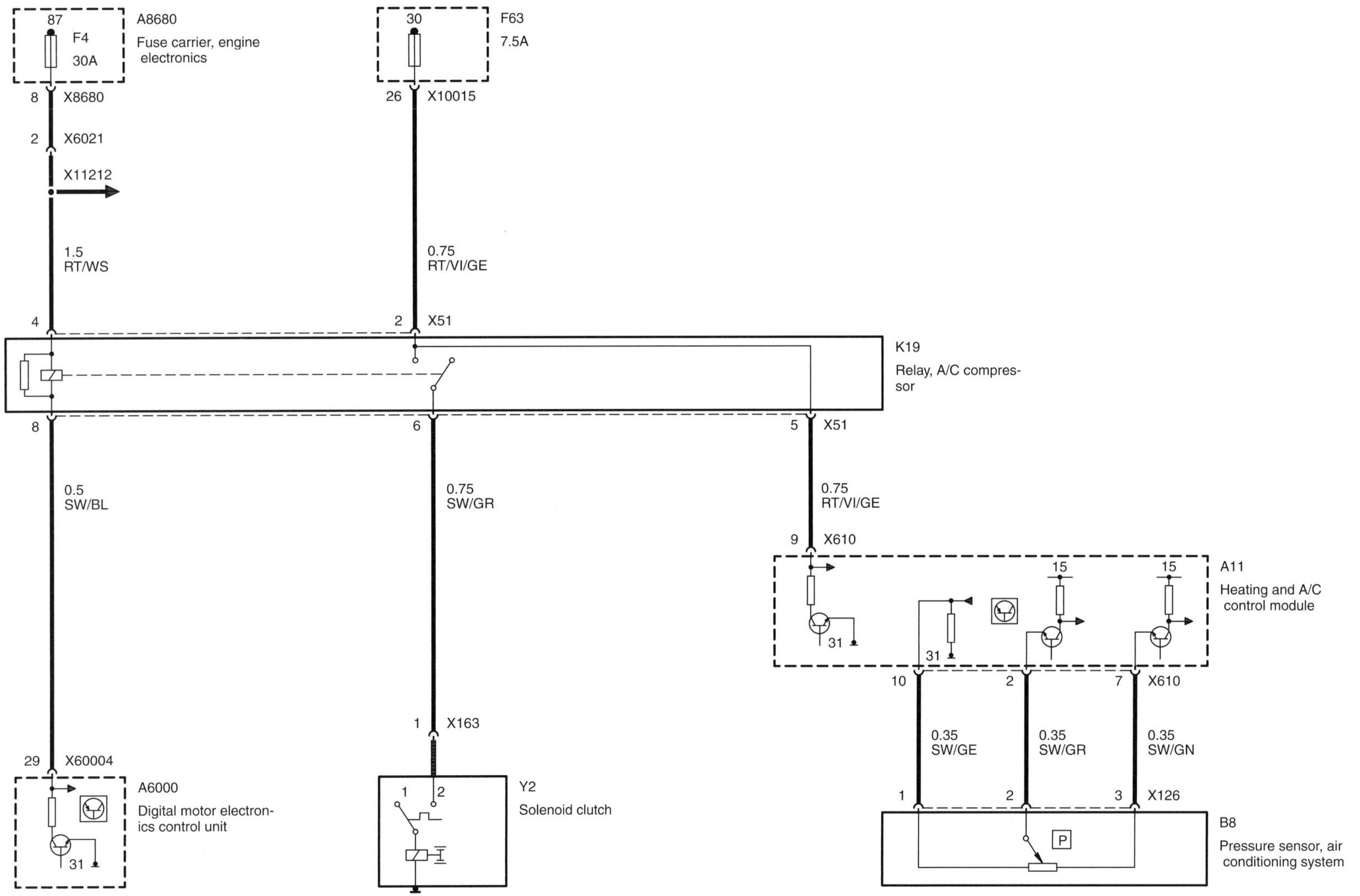

MS S54 Engine Management
Clutch pedal switch
(up to 03/2001)

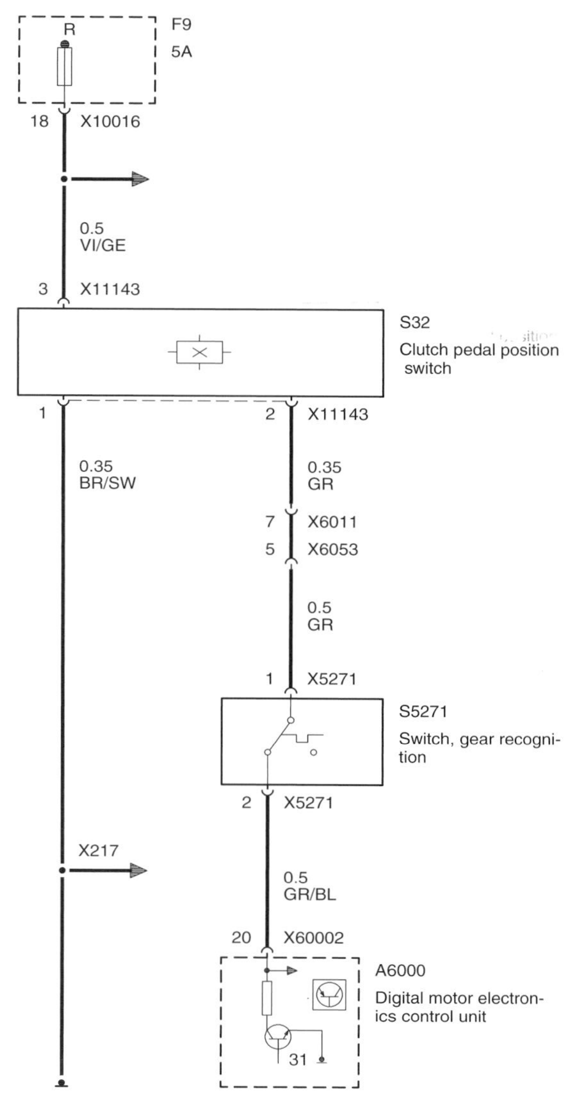

F9
5A
R
18 X10016
0.5
VI/GE
3 X11143
S32
Clutch pedal position switch
1
0.35
BR/SW
2 X11143
0.35
GR
7 X6011
5 X6053
0.5
GR
1 X5271
S5271
Switch, gear recognition
2 X5271
X217
0.5
GR/BL
20 X60002
A6000
Digital motor electronics control unit
31

MS S54 Engine Management
Clutch switch, gear recognition switch
(from 03/2001)

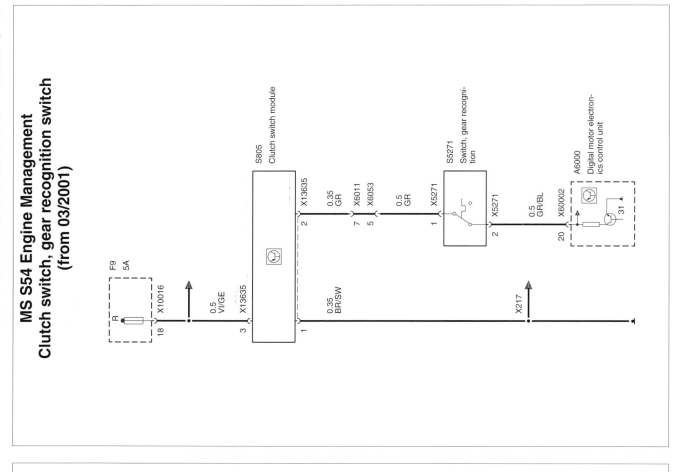

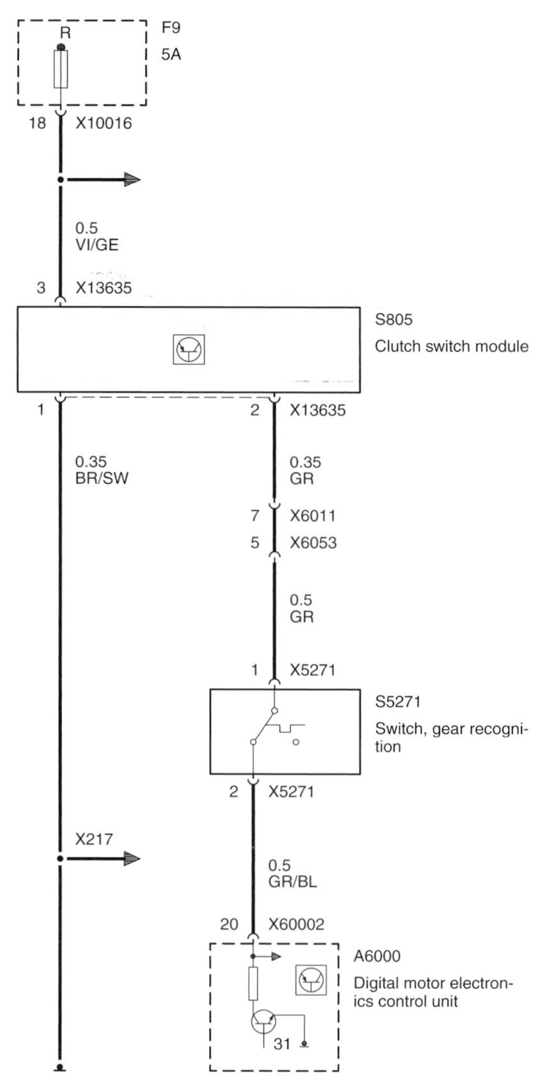

F9
5A
R
18 X10016
0.5
VI/GE
3 X13635
S805
Clutch switch module
1
0.35
BR/SW
2 X13635
0.35
GR
7 X6011
5 X6053
0.5
GR
1 X5271
S5271
Switch, gear recognition
2 X5271
X217
0.5
GR/BL
20 X60002
A6000
Digital motor electronics control unit
31

MS S54 Engine Management
Camshaft position sensor

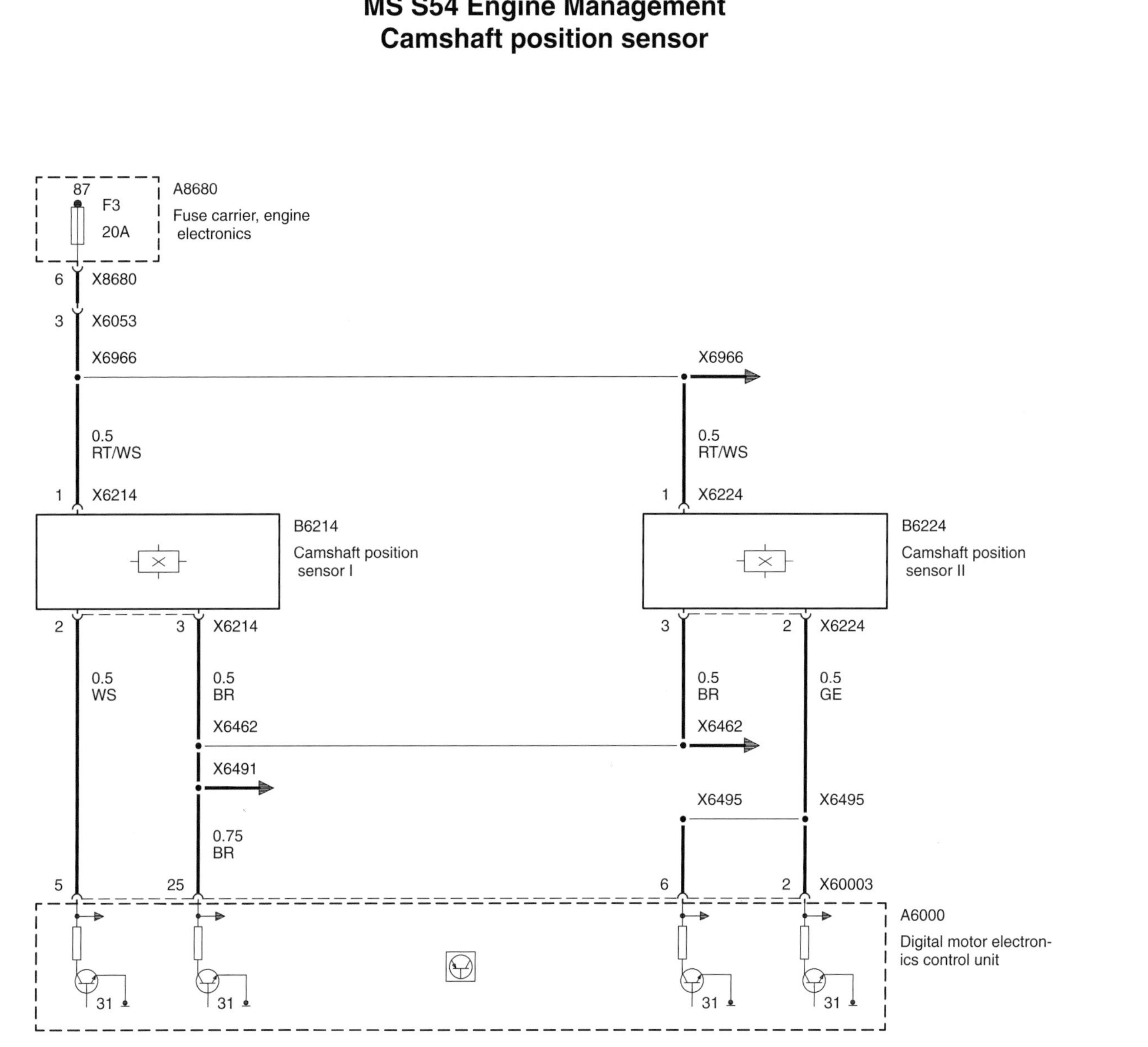

MS S54 Engine Management
Knock sensors

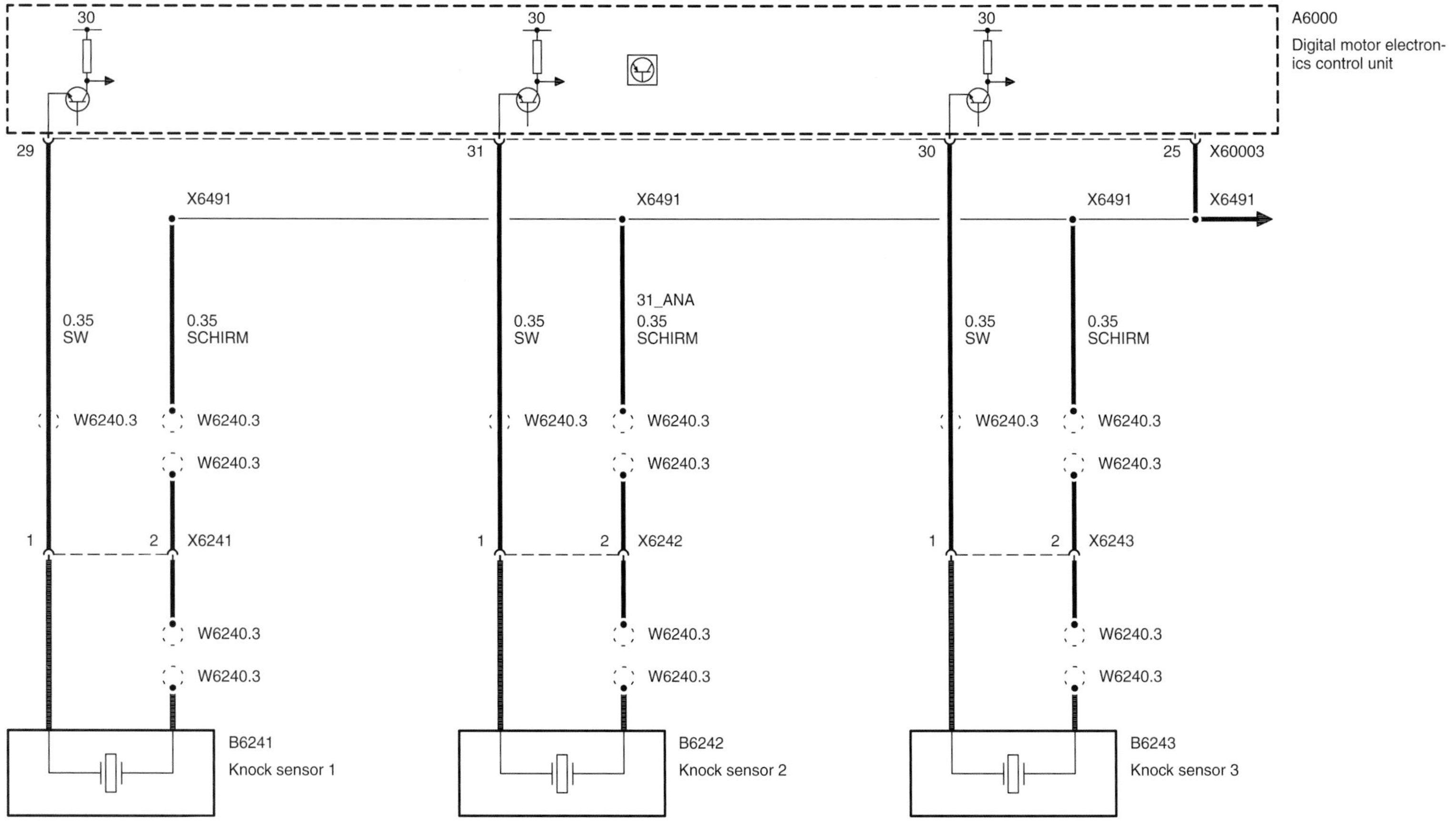

A6000
Digital motor electronics control unit

30
30
30
29
31
30
25
X60003
X6491
X6491
X6491
X6491

0.35
SW
0.35
SCHIRM
0.35
SW
31_ANA
0.35
SCHIRM
0.35
SW
0.35
SCHIRM

W6240.3
W6240.3
W6240.3
W6240.3
W6240.3
W6240.3
W6240.3
W6240.3
W6240.3

1
2
X6241
1
2
X6242
1
2
X6243

W6240.3
W6240.3
W6240.3
W6240.3
W6240.3
W6240.3

B6241
Knock sensor 1
B6242
Knock sensor 2
B6243
Knock sensor 3

MS S54 Engine Management
Mass air flow sensor

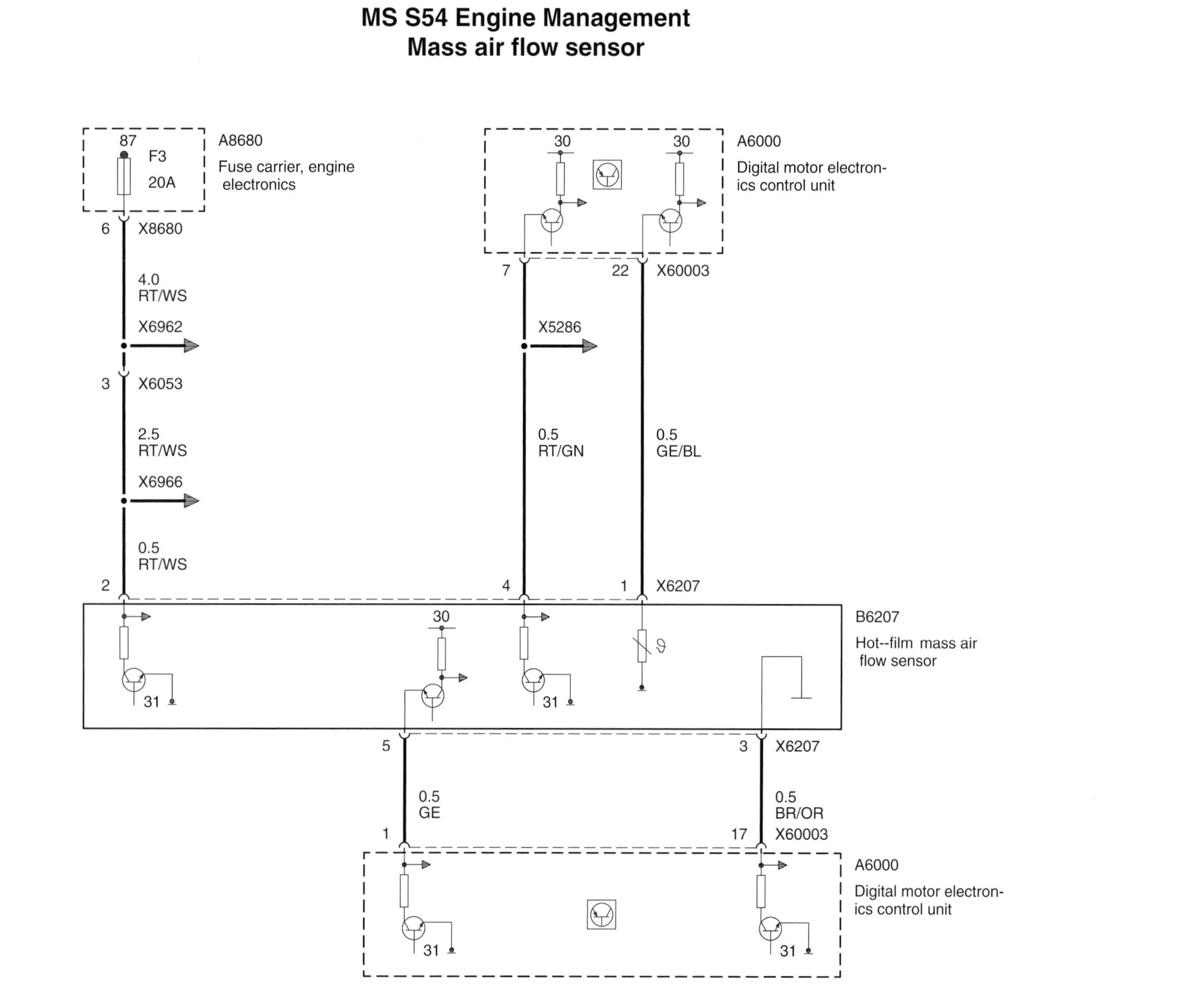

MS S54 Engine Management
Engine coolant temperature sensor

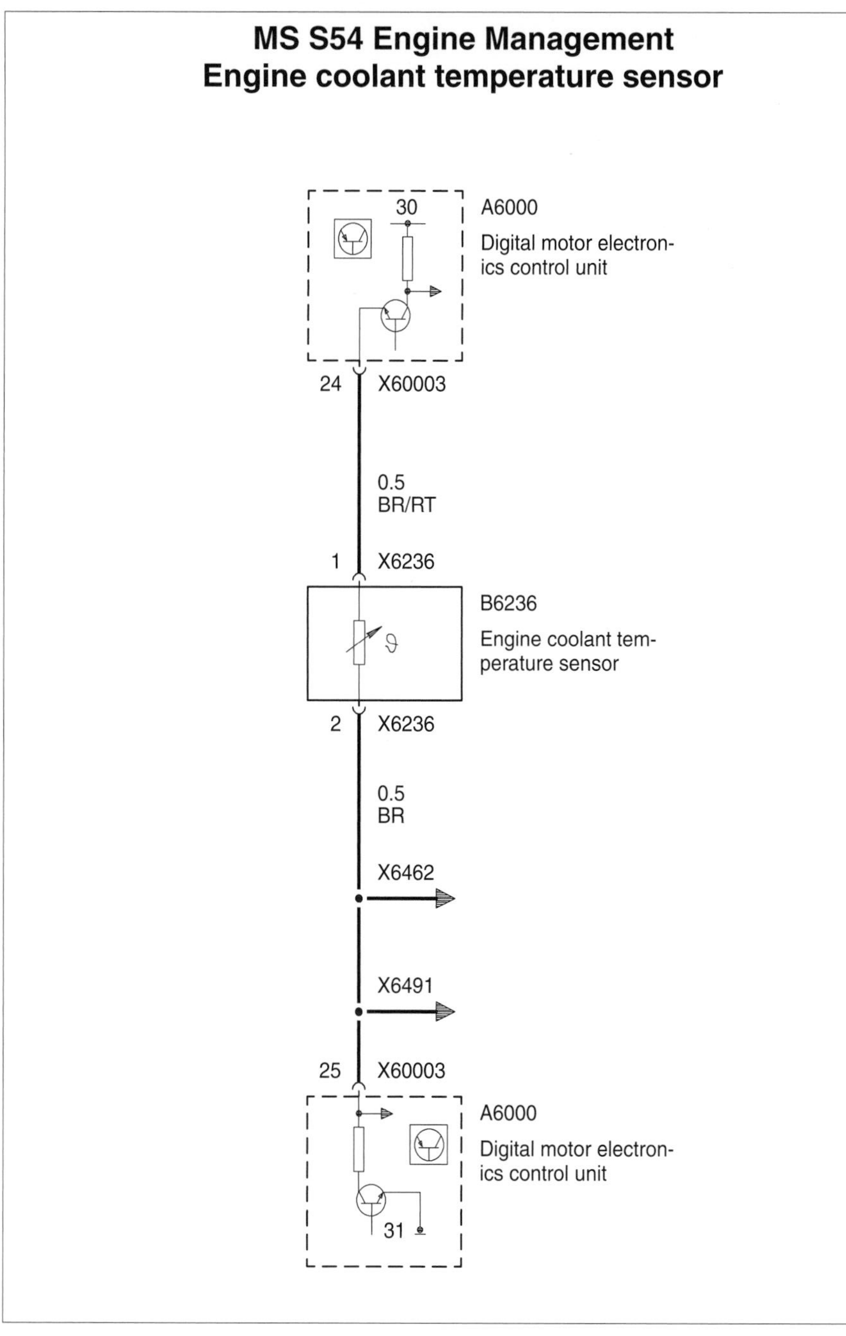

MS S54 Engine Management
Exhaust temperature sensor

30
A6000
Digital motor electronics control unit
10
X60002
0.5
BL/SW
2
X5351
B5351
Exhaust temperature sensor
1
X5351
X6460
0.5
BR
5
X60002
A6000
Digital motor electronics control unit
31

MS S54 Engine Management
Motor driven throttle (EDR)

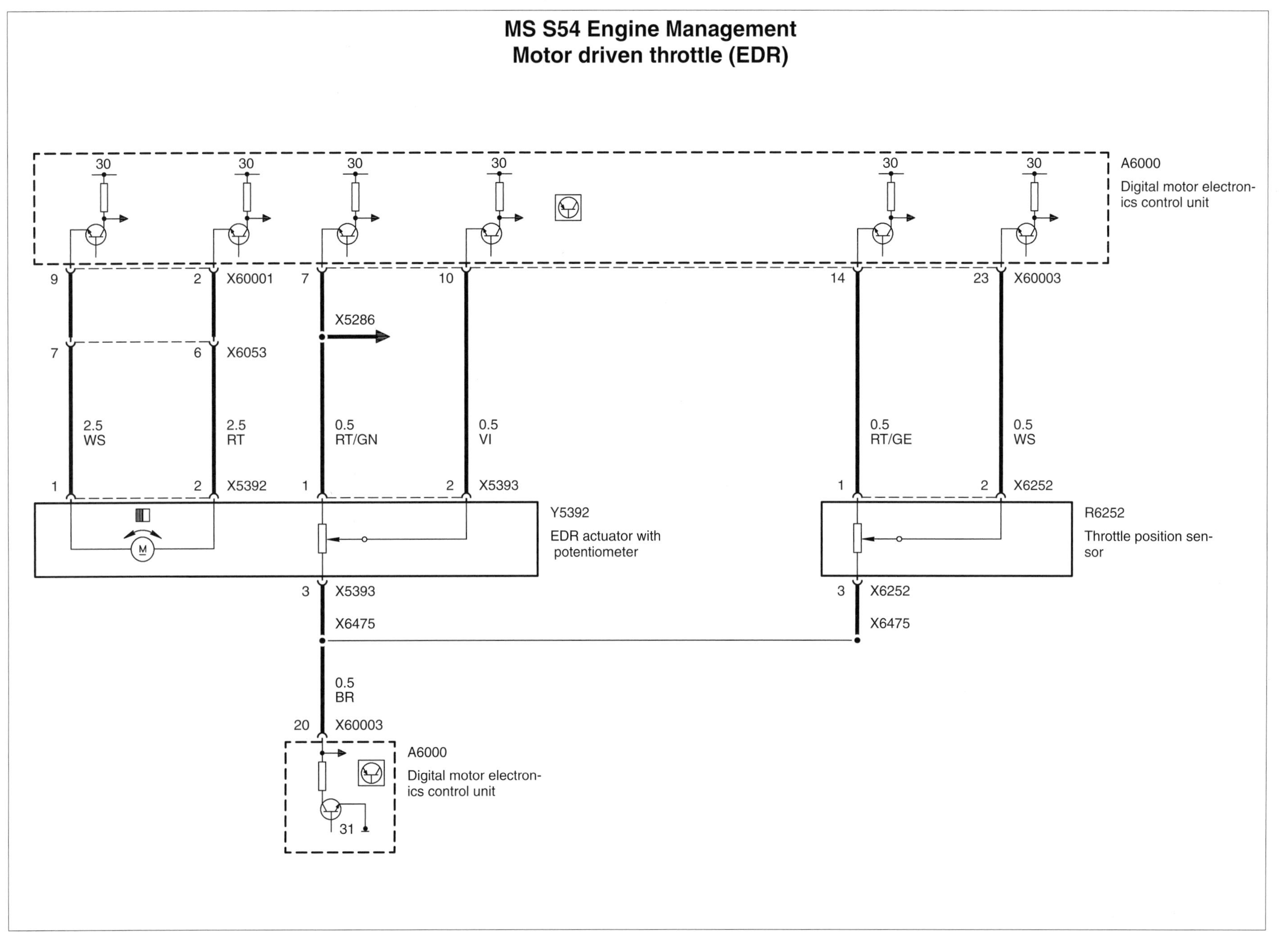

MS S54 Engine Management
Oxygen sensors, pre-catalyst

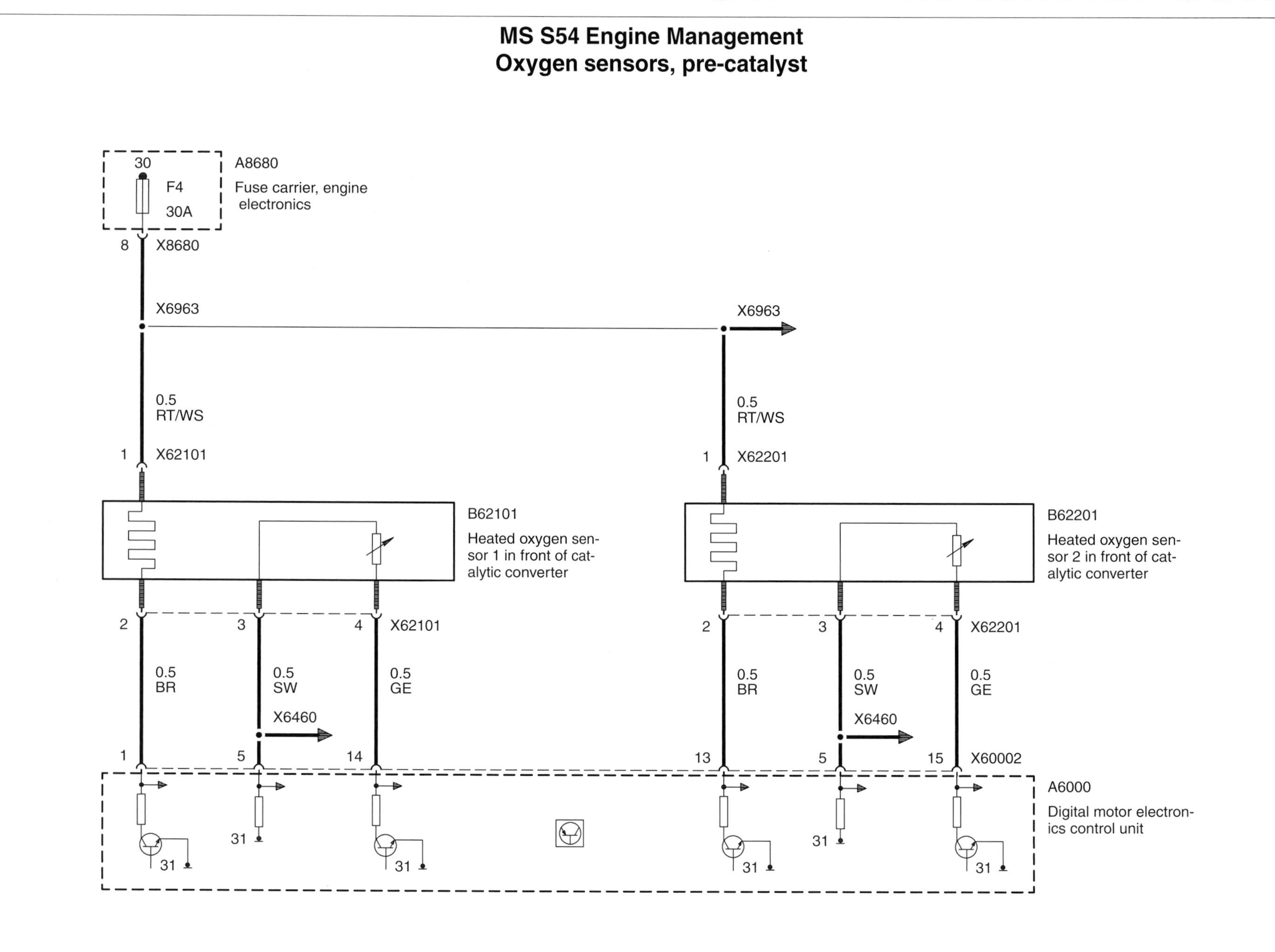

MS S54 Engine Management
Oxygen sensors, post-catalyst

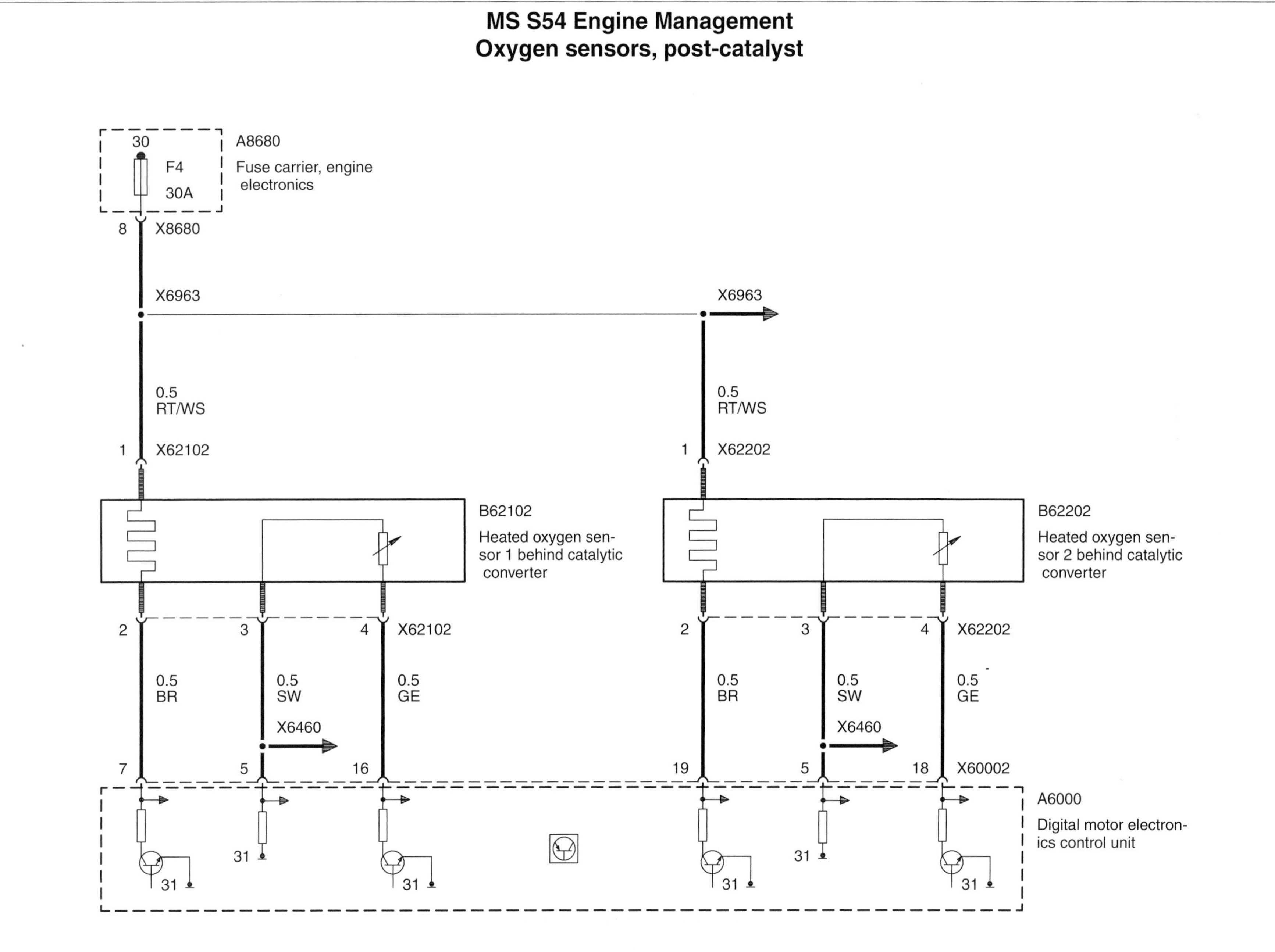

MS S54 Engine Management
Pedal position sensor

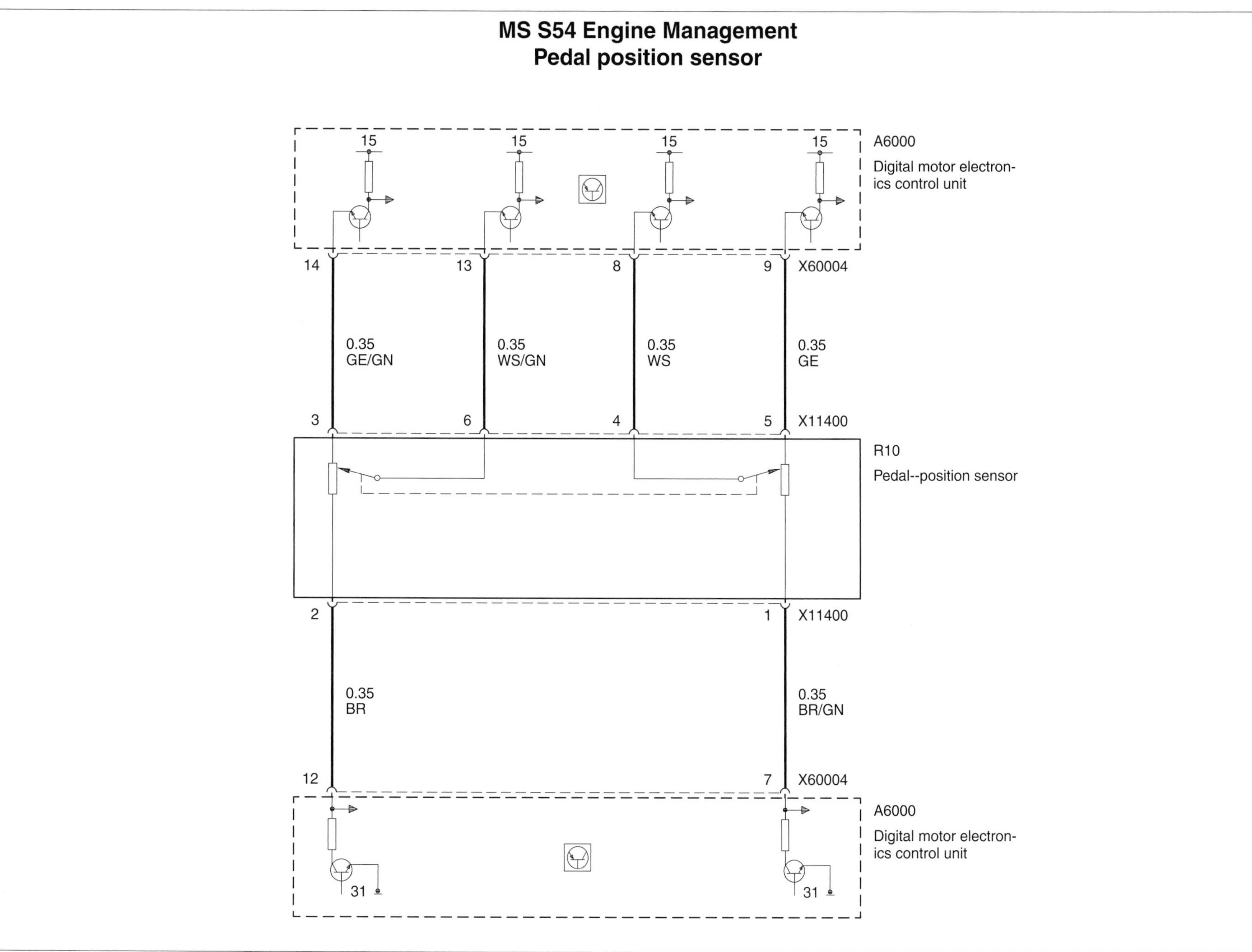

MS S54 Engine Management
Crankshaft position sensor

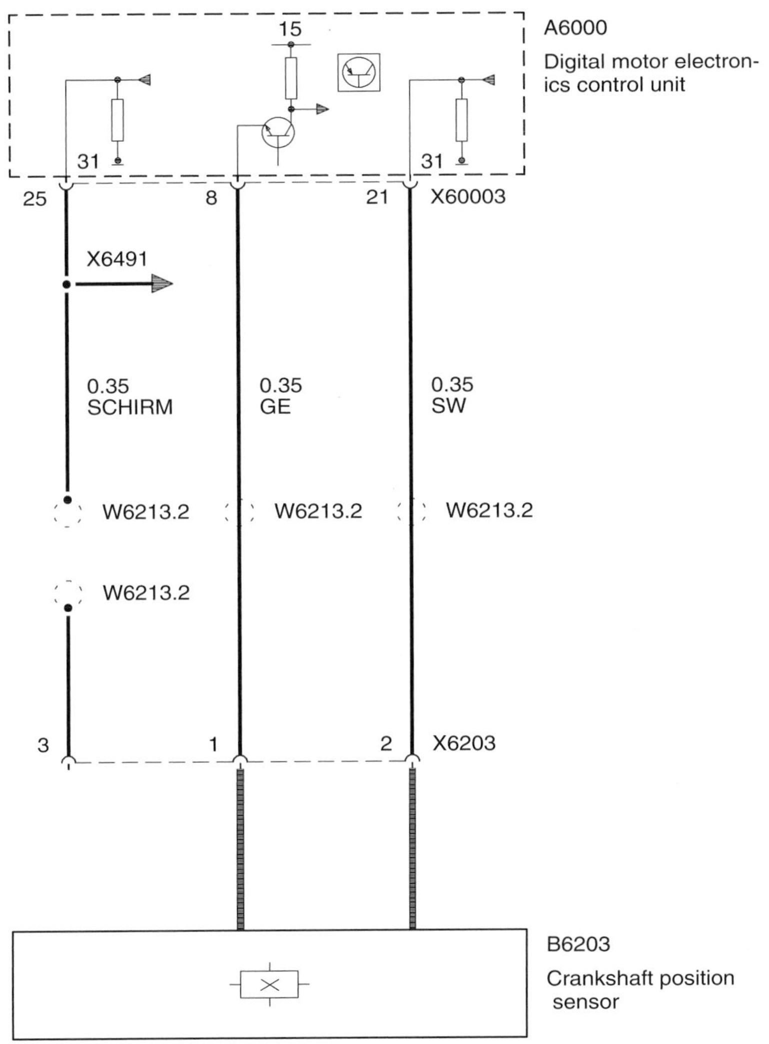

MS S54 Engine Management
Oil-level sensor

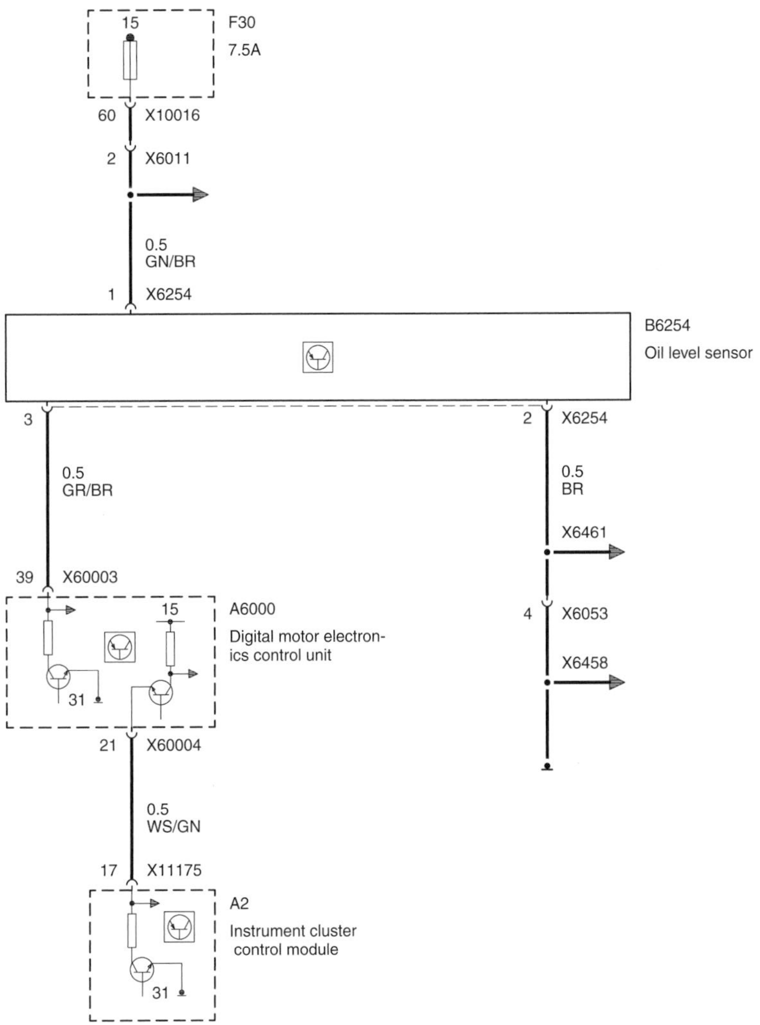

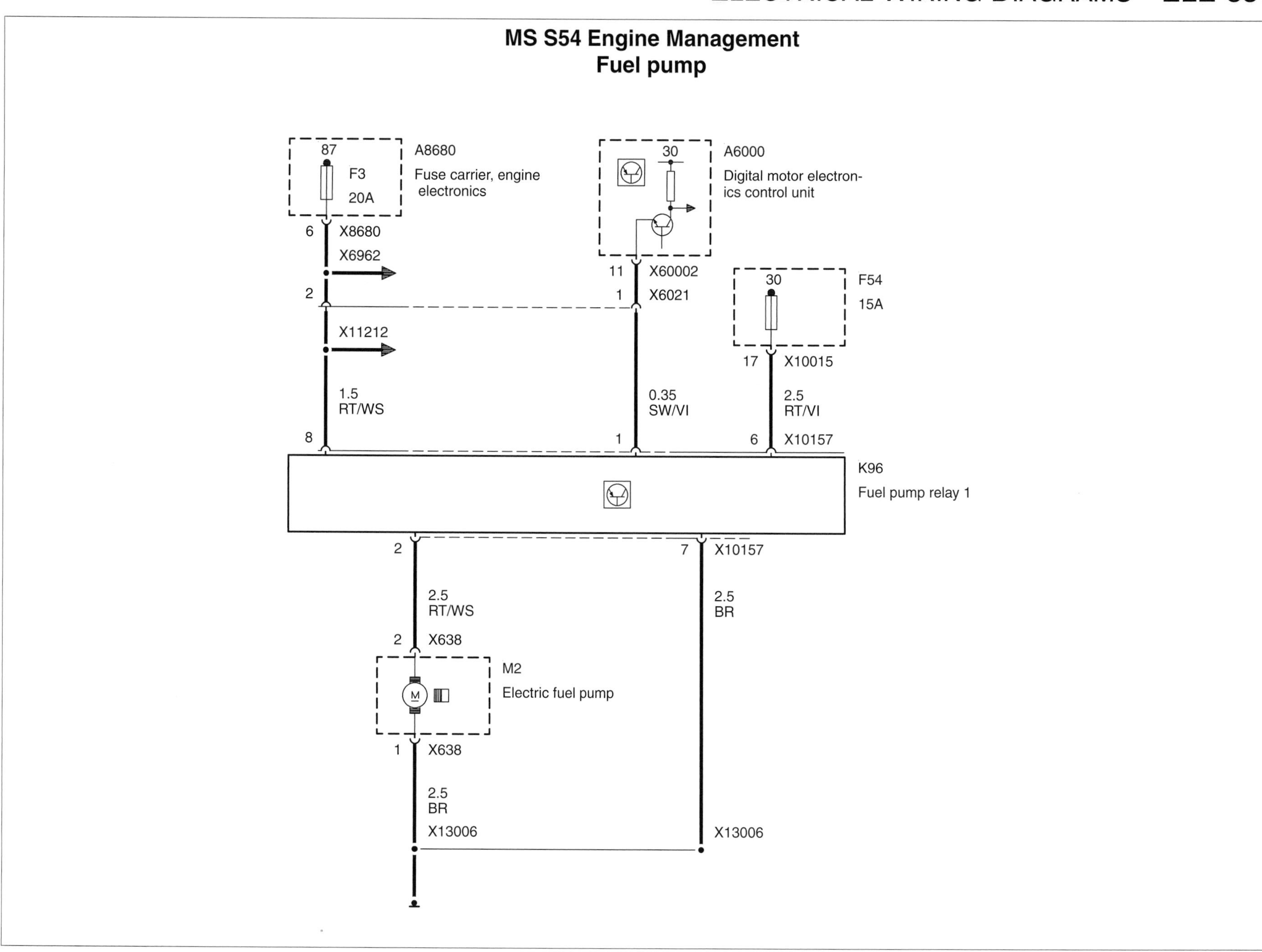
MS S54 Engine Management
Fuel pump
87
F3
20A
A8680
Fuse carrier, engine electronics
6
X8680
X6962
2
X11212
1.5
RT/WS
8
30
A6000
Digital motor electronics control unit
11
X60002
1
X6021
0.35
SW/VI
1
30
F54
15A
17
X10015
2.5
RT/VI
6
X10157
K96
Fuel pump relay 1
2
7
X10157
2.5
RT/WS
2
X638
M2
Electric fuel pump
M
1
X638
2.5
BR
X13006
2.5
BR
X13006

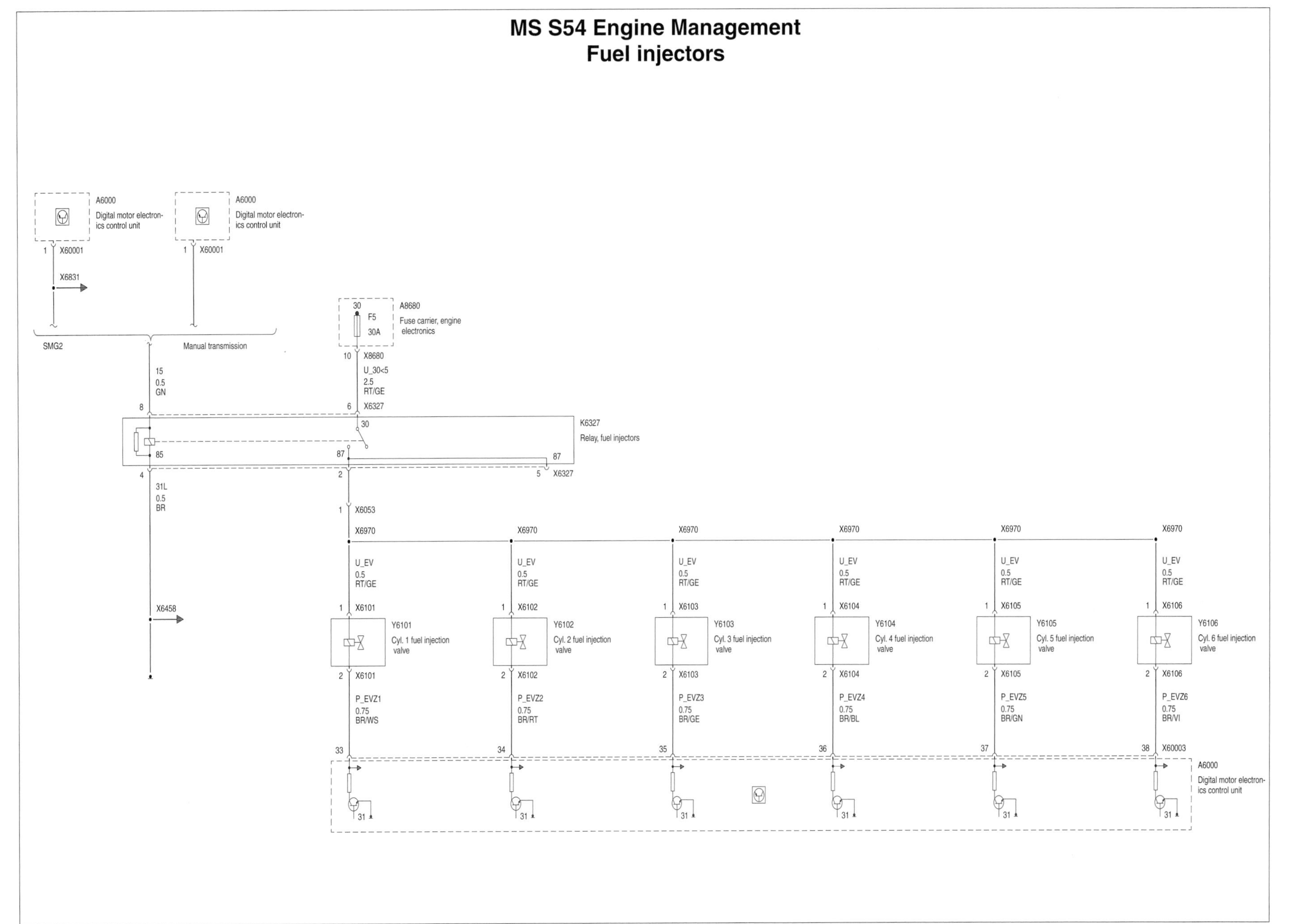
MS S54 Engine Management
Fuel injectors
A6000
Digital motor electronics control unit
1 X60001
X6831
SMG2
A6000
Digital motor electronics control unit
1 X60001
Manual transmission
15
0.5
GN
8
30
F5
30A
A8680
Fuse carrier, engine electronics
10 X8680
U_30<5
2.5
RT/GE
6 X6327
30
K6327
Relay, fuel injectors
85
87
87
4
2
5 X6327
31L
0.5
BR
X6458
1 X6053
X6970
U_EV
0.5
RT/GE
1 X6101
Y6101
Cyl. 1 fuel injection valve
2 X6101
P_EVZ1
0.75
BR/WS
33
X6970
U_EV
0.5
RT/GE
1 X6102
Y6102
Cyl. 2 fuel injection valve
2 X6102
P_EVZ2
0.75
BR/RT
34
X6970
U_EV
0.5
RT/GE
1 X6103
Y6103
Cyl. 3 fuel injection valve
2 X6103
P_EVZ3
0.75
BR/GE
35
X6970
U_EV
0.5
RT/GE
1 X6104
Y6104
Cyl. 4 fuel injection valve
2 X6104
P_EVZ4
0.75
BR/BL
36
X6970
U_EV
0.5
RT/GE
1 X6105
Y6105
Cyl. 5 fuel injection valve
2 X6105
P_EVZ5
0.75
BR/GN
37
X6970
U_EV
0.5
RT/GE
1 X6106
Y6106
Cyl. 6 fuel injection valve
2 X6106
P_EVZ6
0.75
BR/VI
38 X60003
A6000
Digital motor electronics control unit
31
31
31
31
31
31

MS S54 Engine Management
Fuel tank ventilation valve

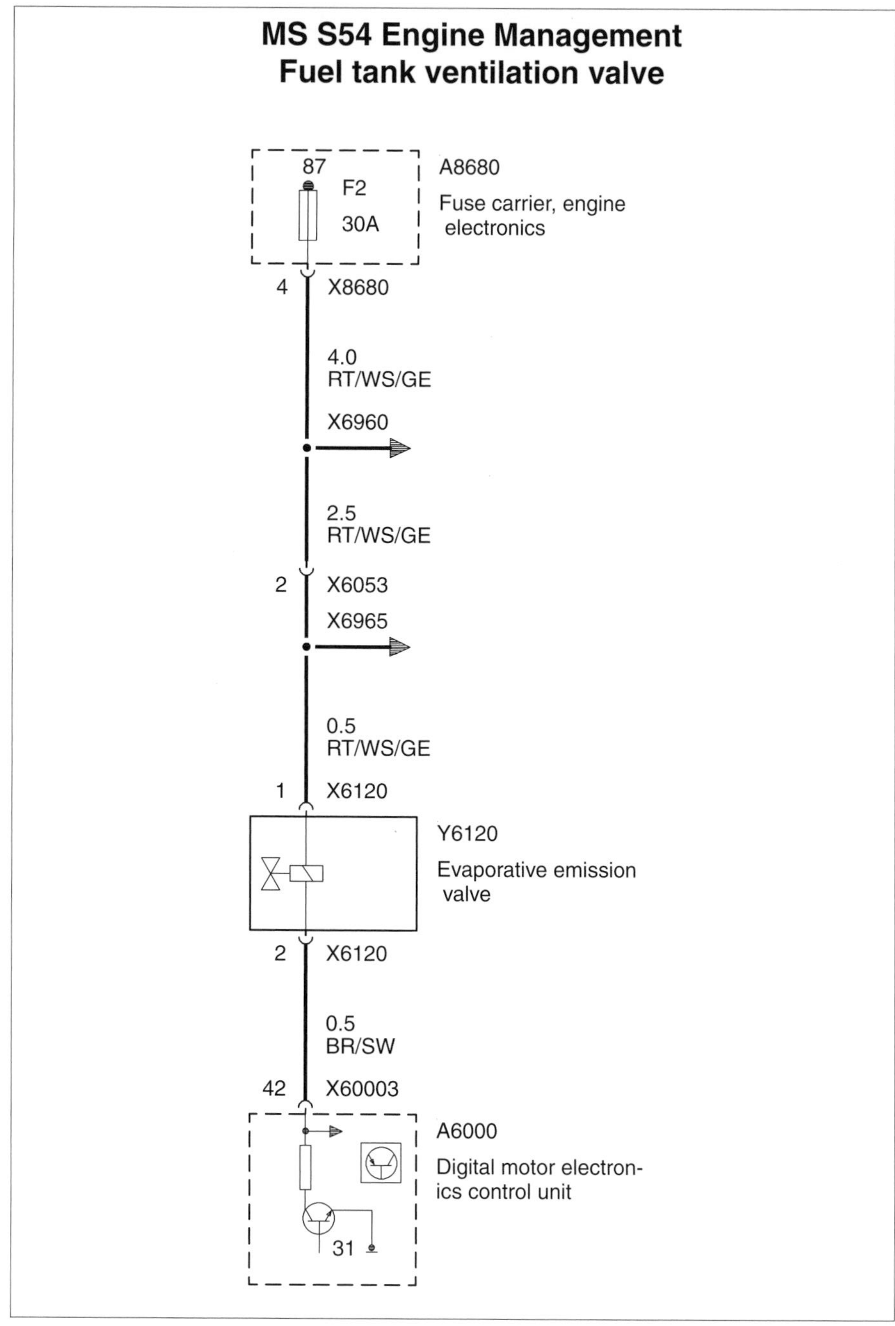

MS S54 Engine Management
Idle speed control valve

87
F2
30A
A8680
Fuse carrier, engine electronics
4
X8680
4.0
RT/WS/GE
X6960
2.5
RT/WS/GE
2
X6053
X6965
1.0
RT/WS/GE
2
X6130
Y6130
Idle speed control valve
1
3
X6130
0.5
WS/GN
0.5
WS/GE
46
47
X60003
A6000
Digital motor electronics control unit
31
31

MS S54 Engine Management
VANOS control valves

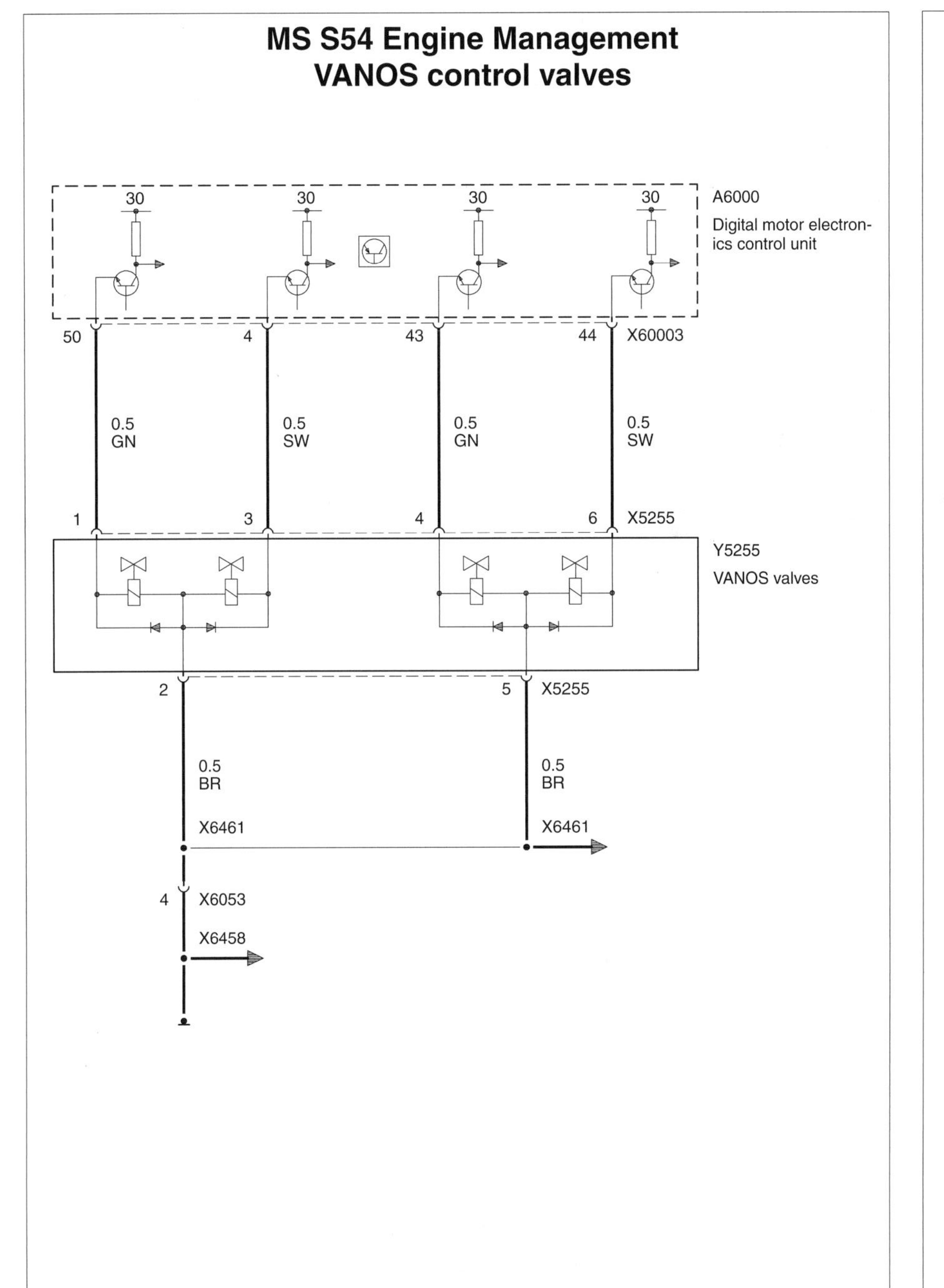

This page intentionally left blank

MS S54 Engine Management
Ignition coils

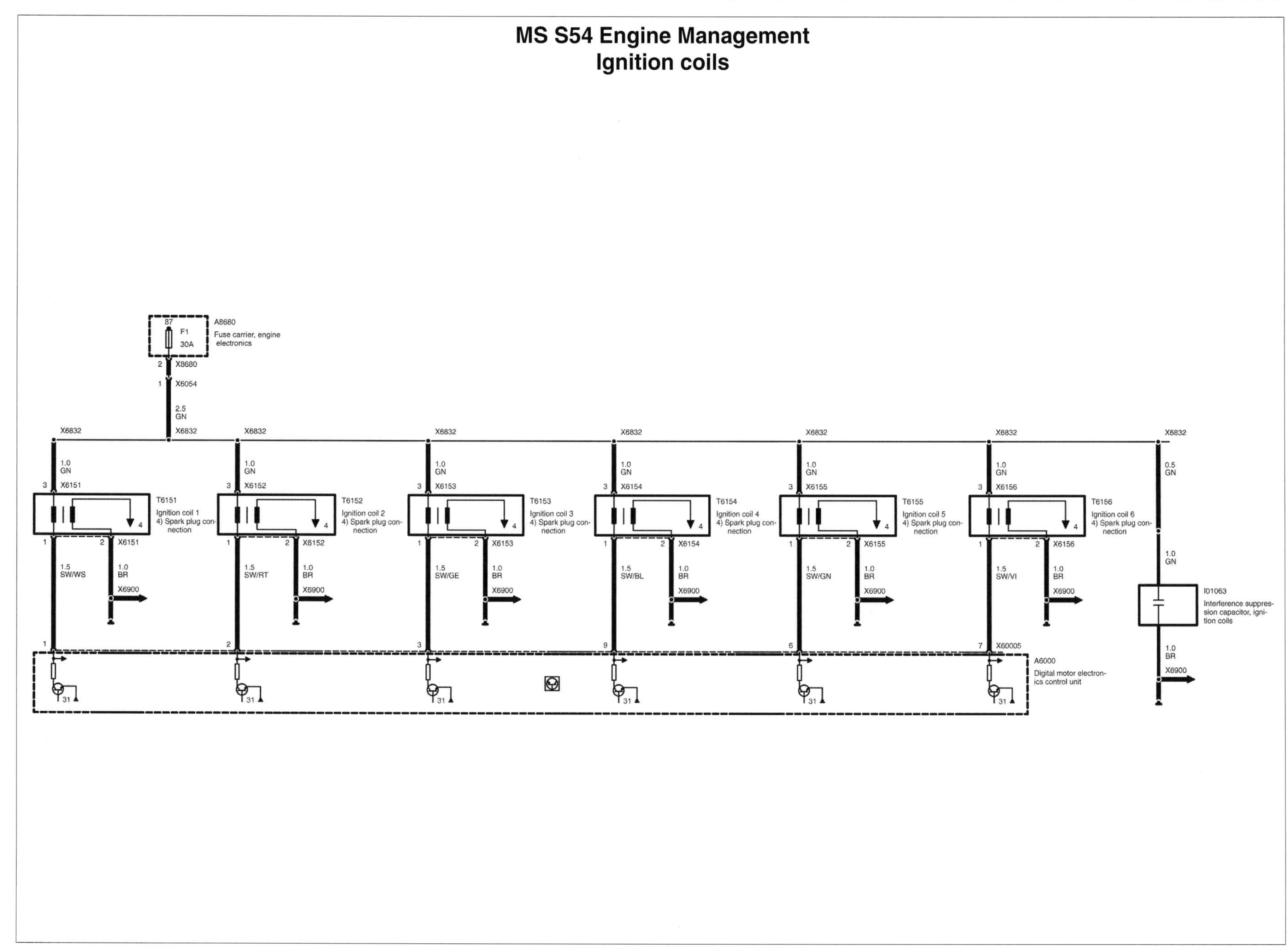

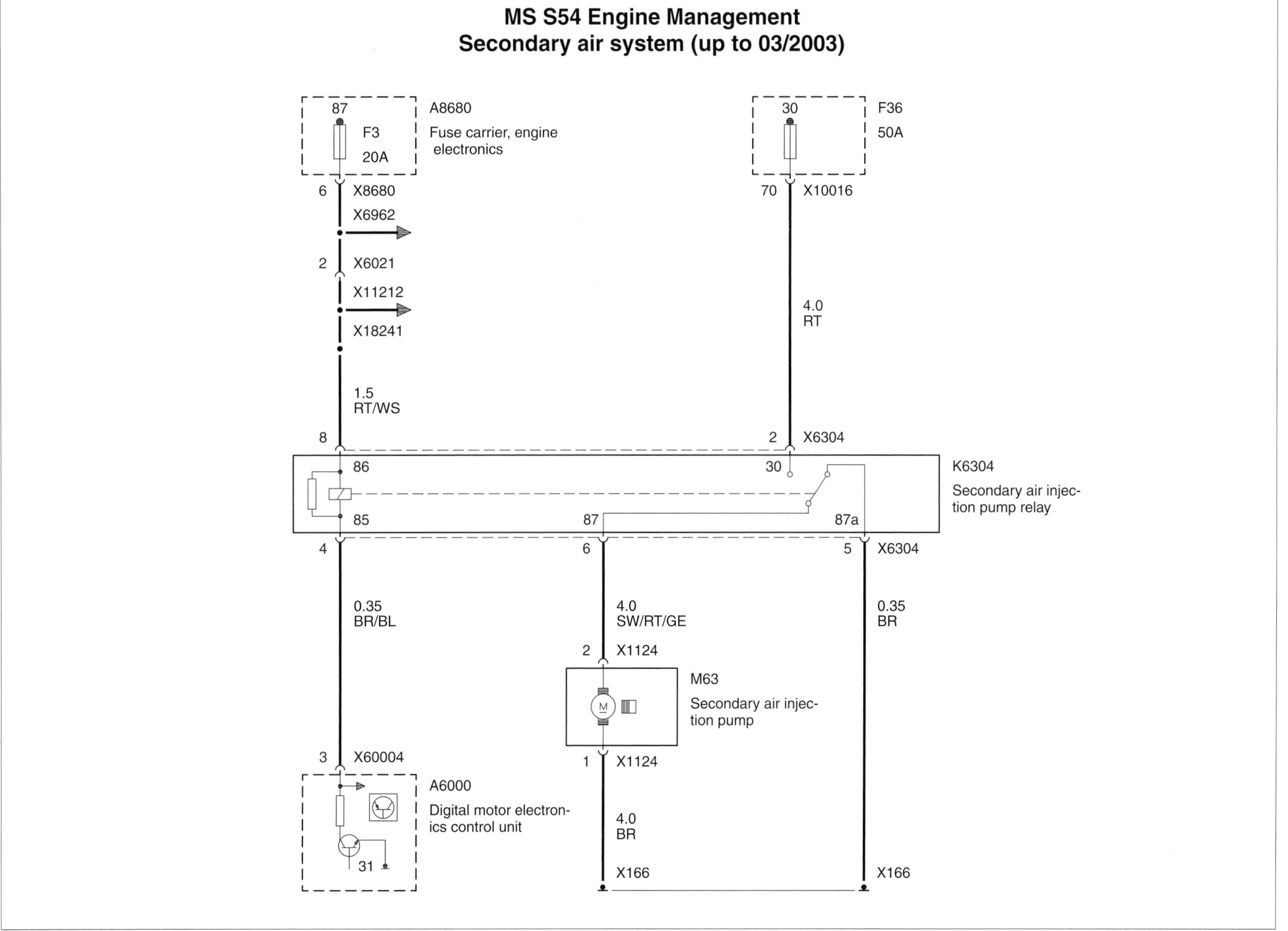
MS S54 Engine Management
Secondary air system (up to 03/2003)
87
F3
20A
A8680
Fuse carrier, engine electronics
30
F36
50A
6
X8680
X6962
2
X6021
X11212
X18241
70
X10016
4.0
RT
1.5
RT/WS
8
2
X6304
86
30
K6304
Secondary air injection pump relay
85
87
87a
4
6
5
X6304
0.35
BR/BL
4.0
SW/RT/GE
0.35
BR
2
X1124
M63
Secondary air injection pump
3
X60004
1
X1124
A6000
Digital motor electronics control unit
4.0
BR
31
X166
X166

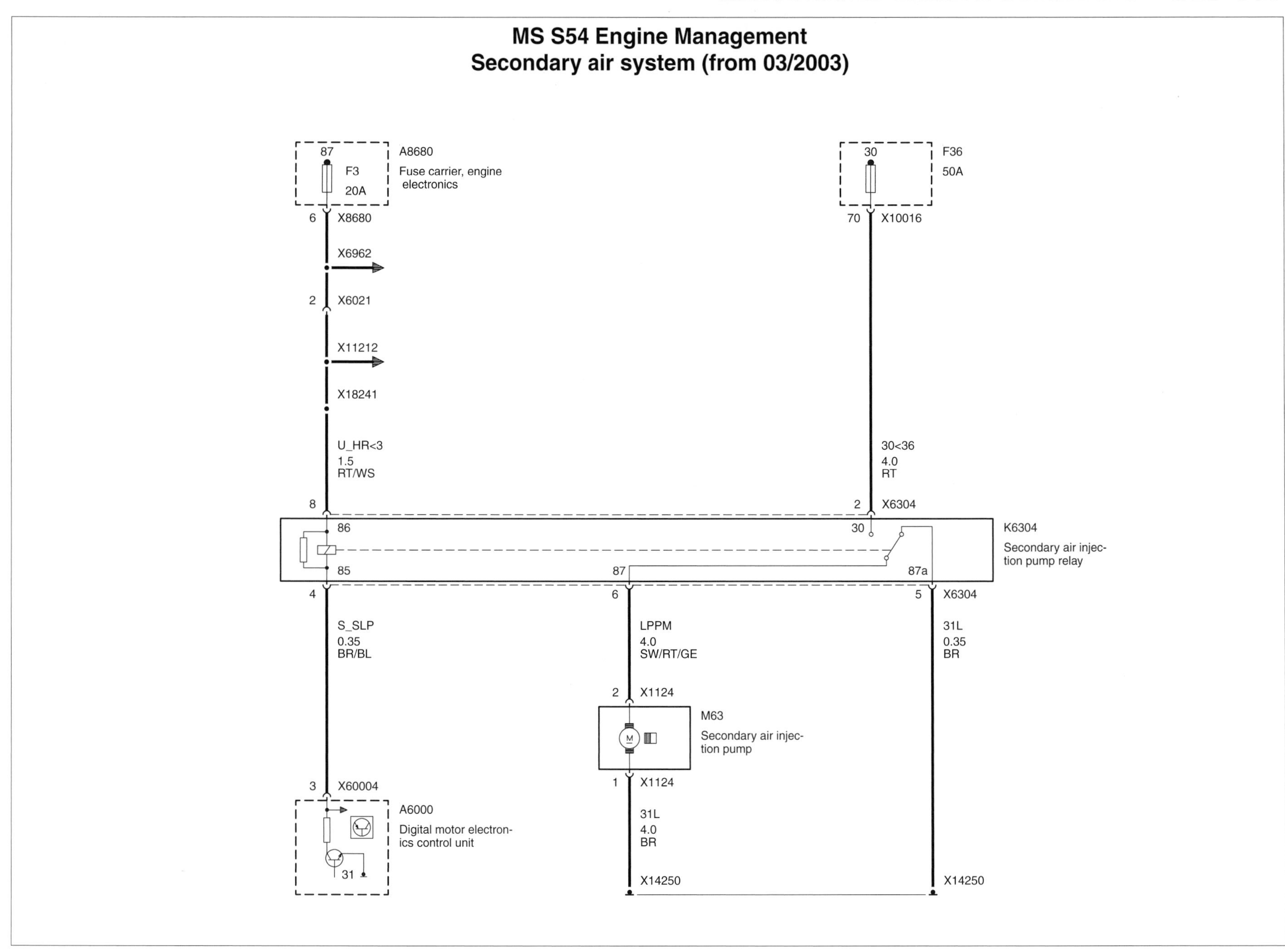
MS S54 Engine Management
Secondary air system (from 03/2003)
87
F3
20A
A8680
Fuse carrier, engine electronics
6
X8680
X6962
2
X6021
X11212
X18241
U_HR<3
1.5
RT/WS
8
30
F36
50A
70
X10016
30<36
4.0
RT
2
X6304
86
85
30
87
87a
K6304
Secondary air injection pump relay
4
6
5
X6304
S_SLP
0.35
BR/BL
LPPM
4.0
SW/RT/GE
31L
0.35
BR
2
X1124
M63
Secondary air injection pump
1
X1124
31L
4.0
BR
X14250
X14250
3
X60004
A6000
Digital motor electronics control unit
31

MS 45.1 Engine Management
Oxygen sensors, pre-catalyst

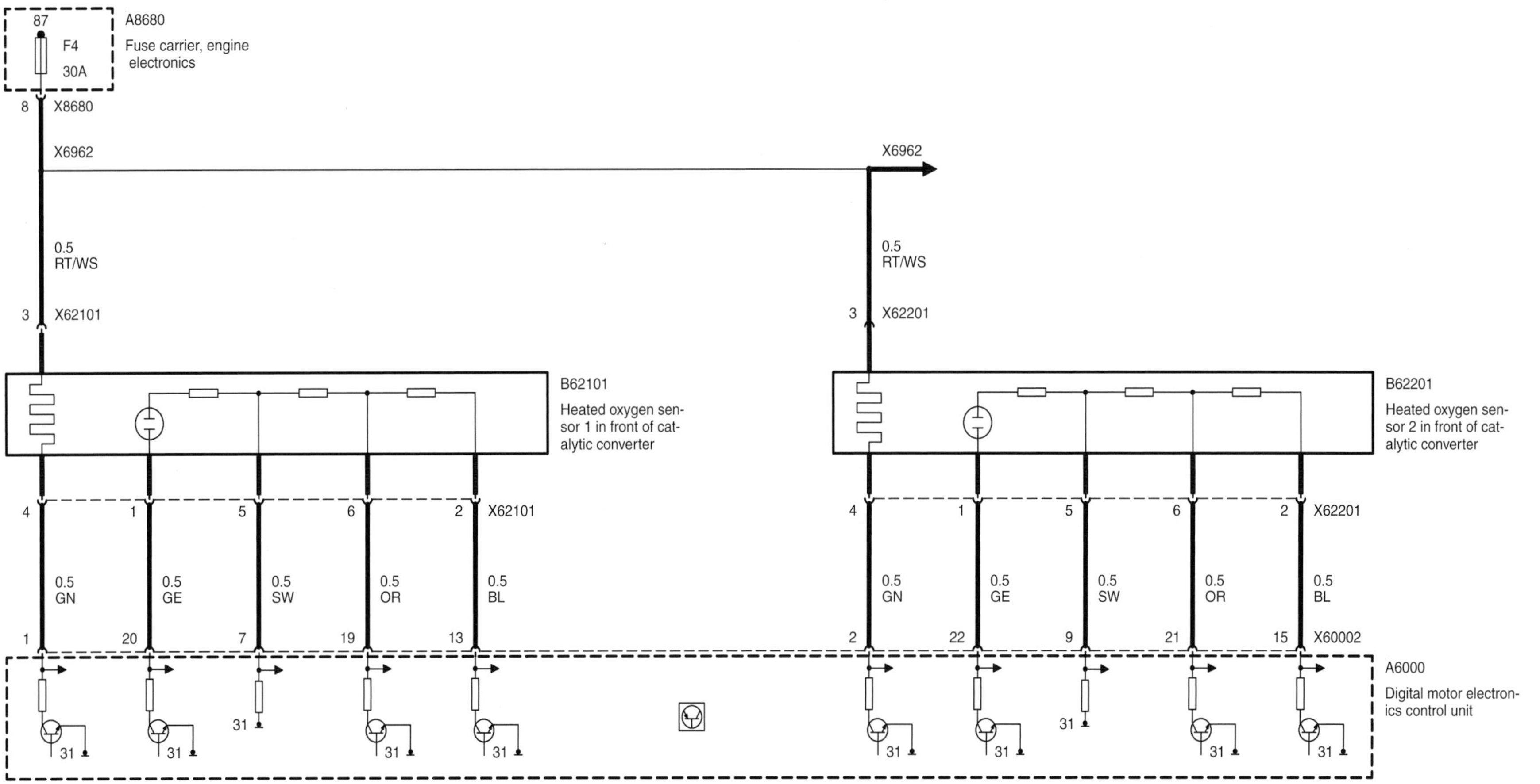

87
F4
30A
A8680
Fuse carrier, engine electronics
8 X8680
X6962
0.5 RT/WS
3 X62101
B62101
Heated oxygen sensor 1 in front of catalytic converter
4 1 5 6 2 X62101
0.5 GN
0.5 GE
0.5 SW
0.5 OR
0.5 BL
1 20 7 19 13

X6962
0.5 RT/WS
3 X62201
B62201
Heated oxygen sensor 2 in front of catalytic converter
4 1 5 6 2 X62201
0.5 GN
0.5 GE
0.5 SW
0.5 OR
0.5 BL
2 22 9 21 15 X60002

A6000
Digital motor electronics control unit
31 31 31 31 31 31 31 31 31 31

MS 45.1 Engine Management
Oxygen sensors, post-catalyst

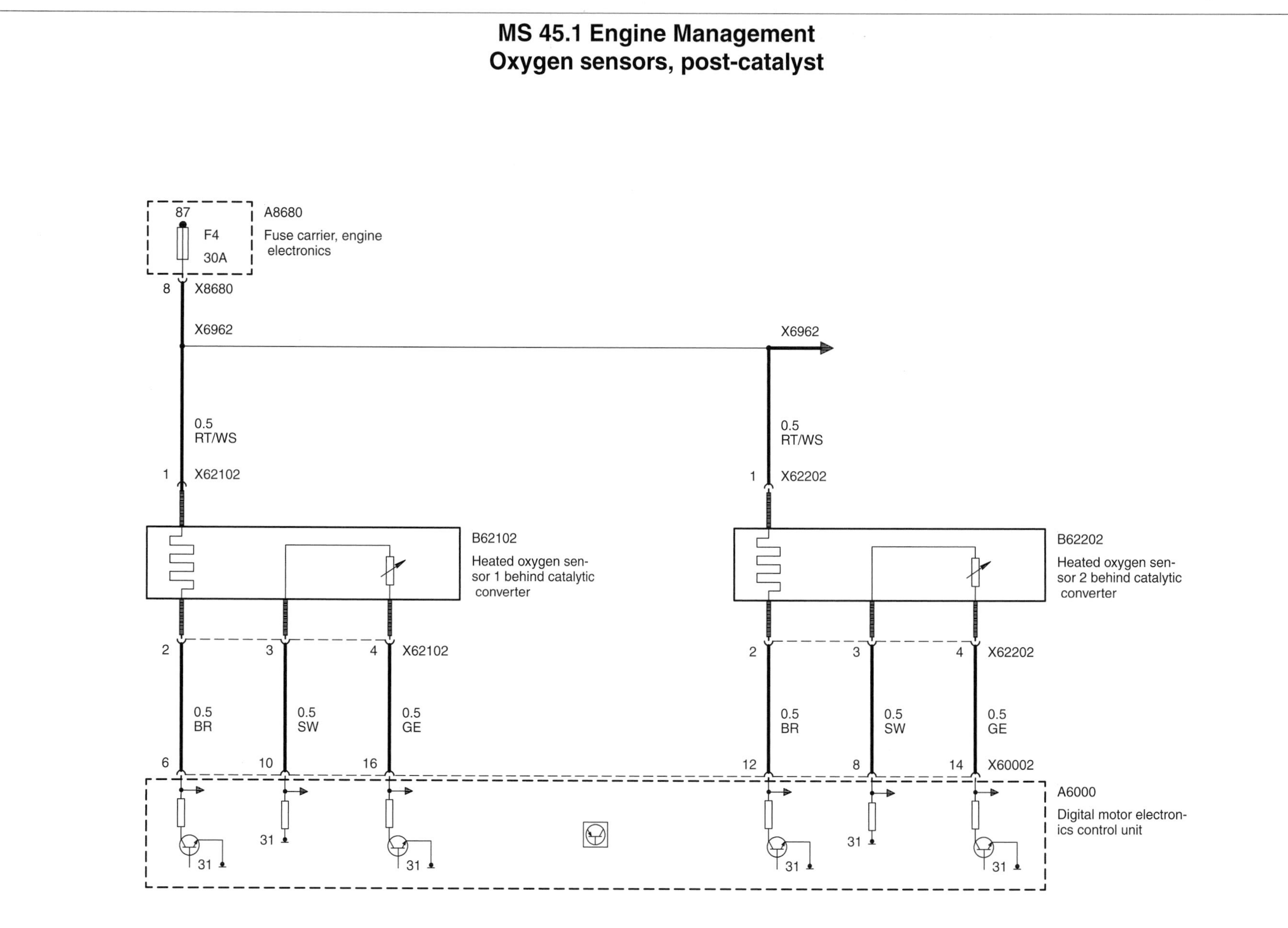

MS 45.1 Engine Management
Fuel injectors
(page 1 of 2)

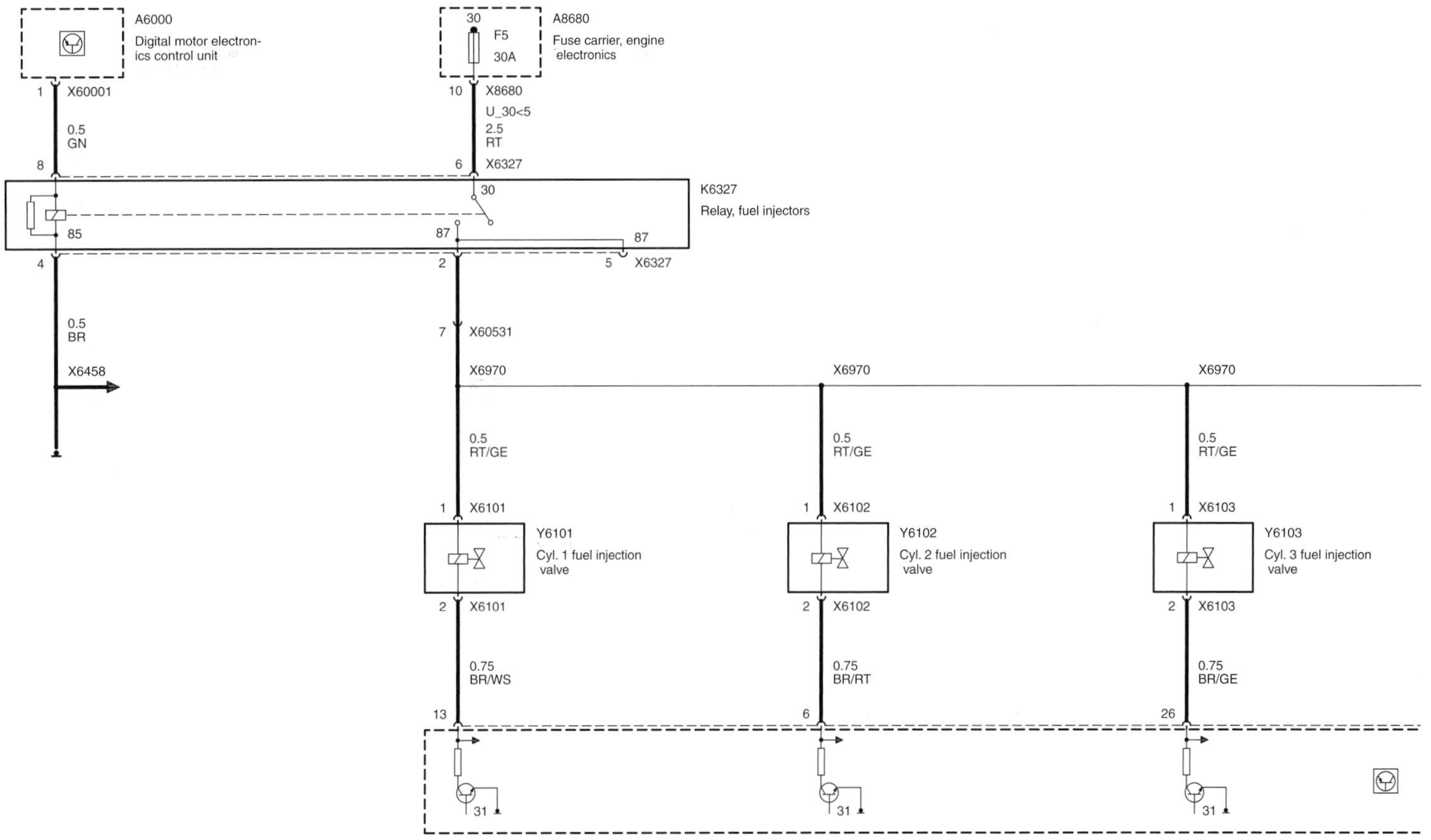

35

MS 45.1 Engine Management
Fuel injectors
(page 2 of 2)

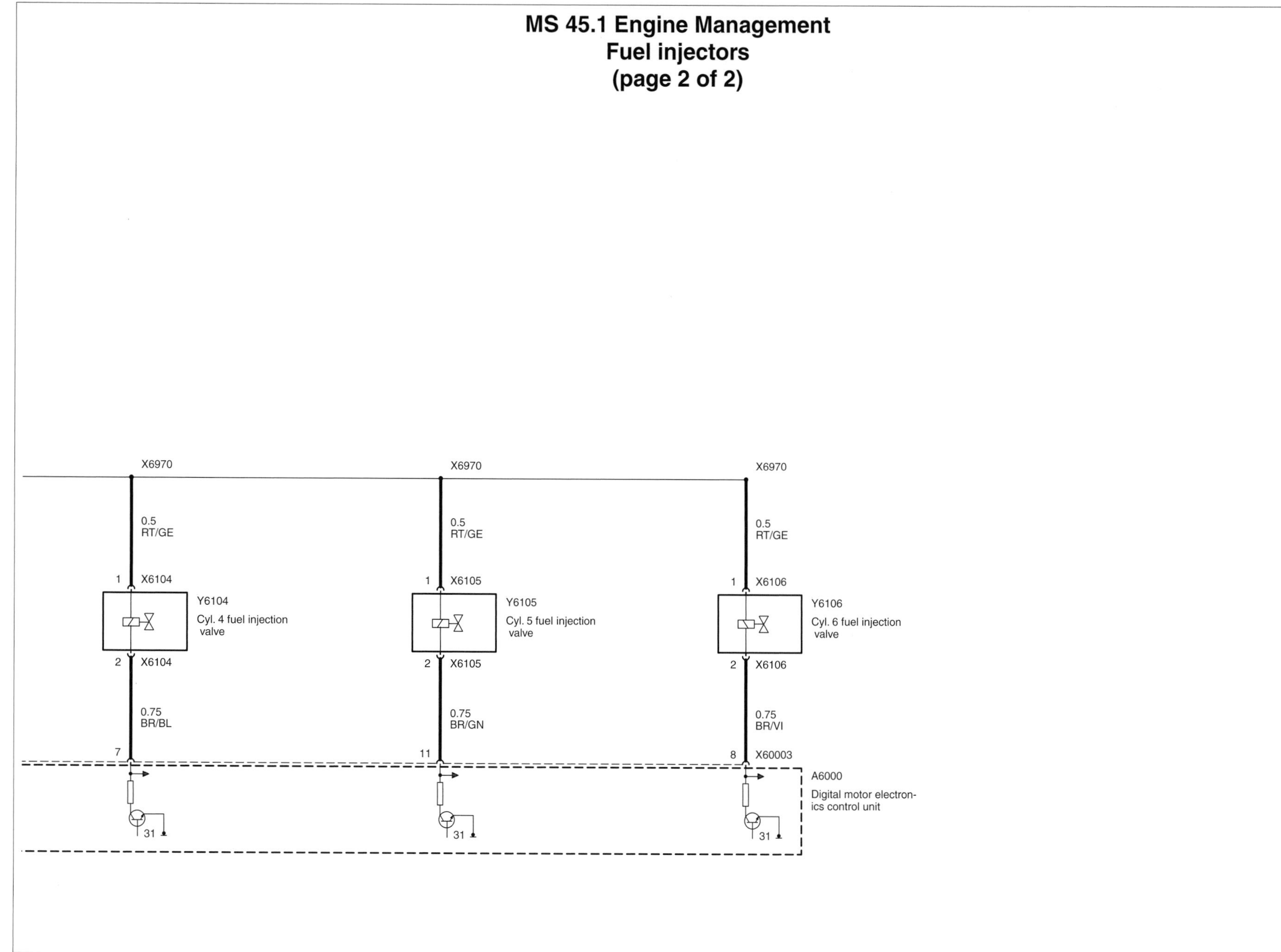

MS 45.1 Engine Management
Fuel pump

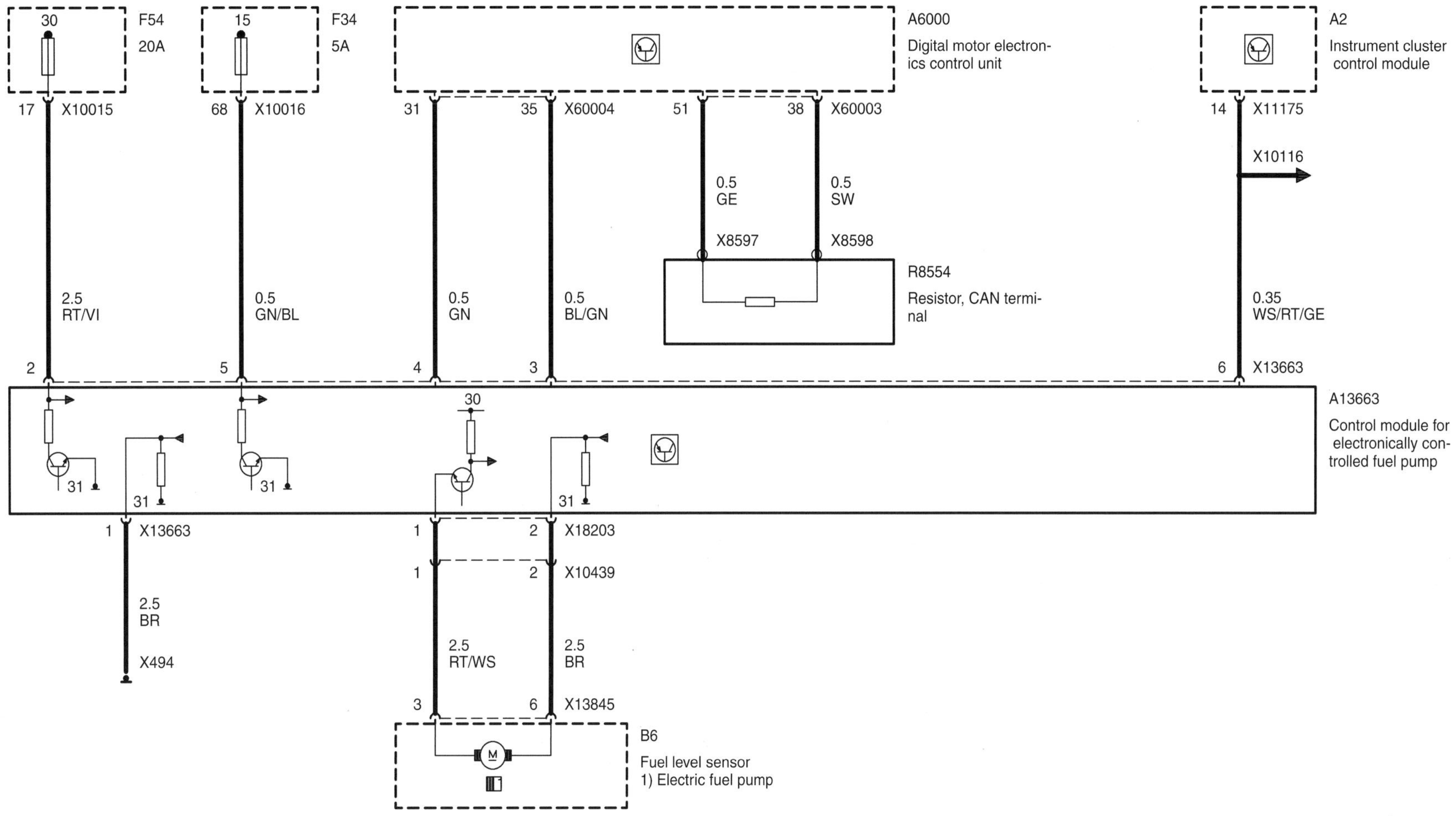

MS 45.1 Engine Management
Pedal position sensor

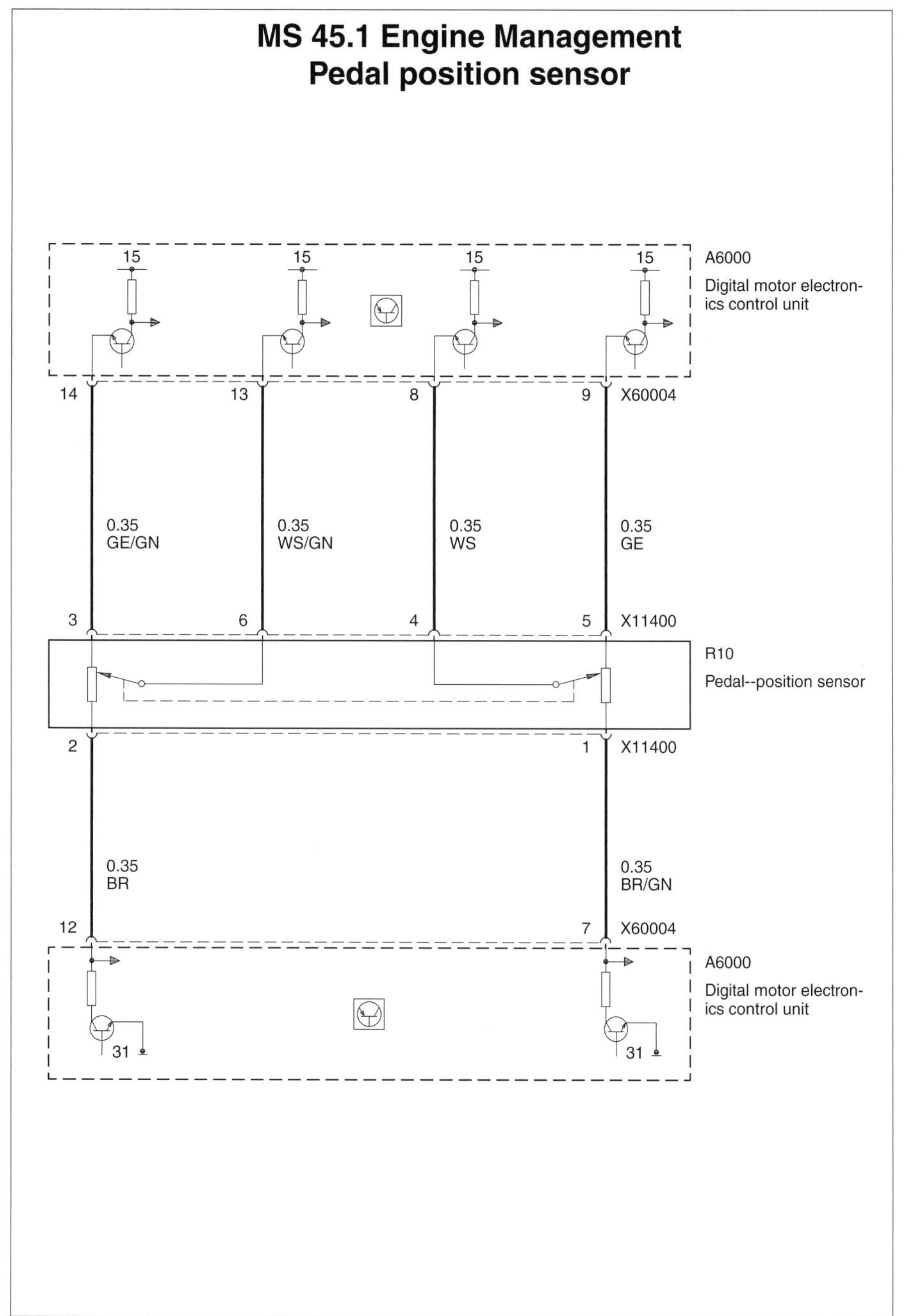

MS 45.1 Engine Management
Knock sensors

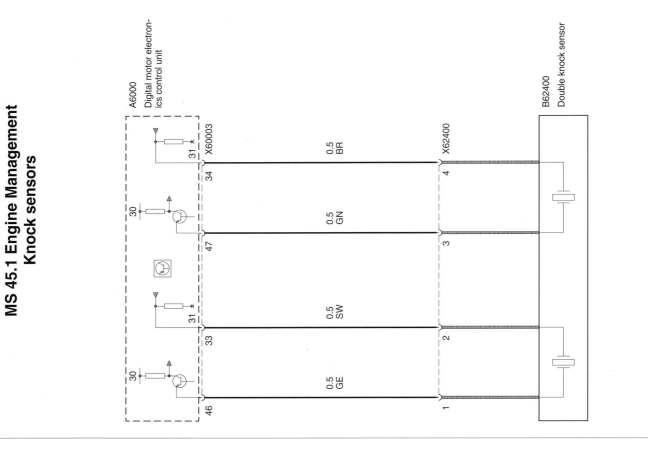

30
30
A6000
Digital motor electronics control unit
31
31
46
33
47
34
X60003
0.5
GE
0.5
SW
0.5
GN
0.5
BR
1
2
3
4
X62400
B62400
Double knock sensor

MS 45.1 Engine Management
Motor driven throttle (EDK)

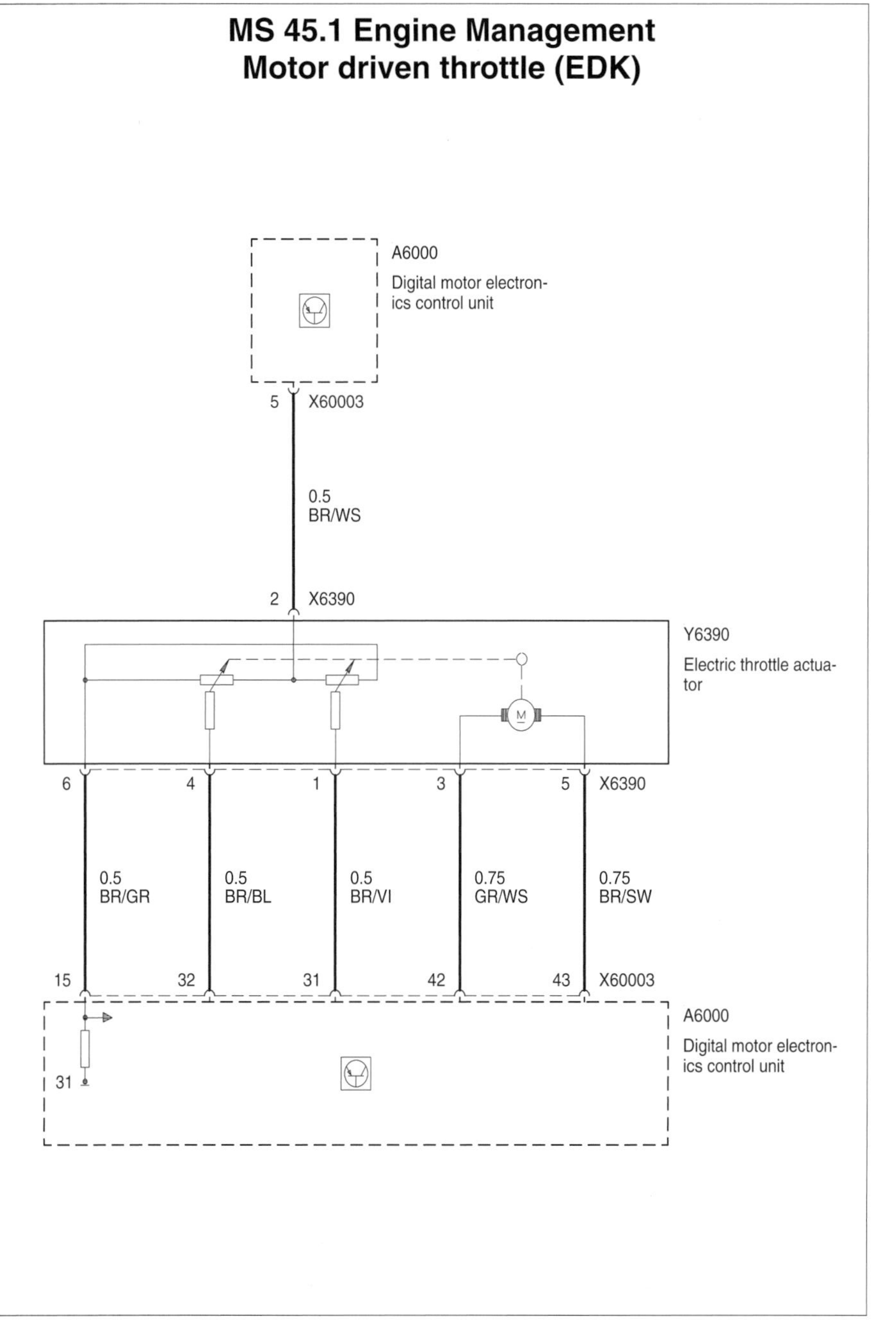

MS 45.1 Engine Management
DISA changeover valve

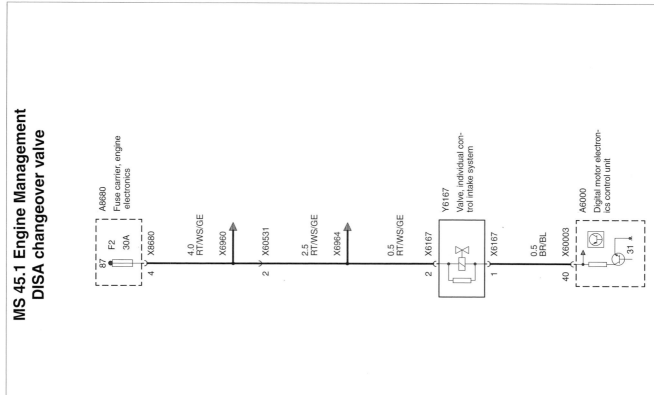

87
F2
30A
A8680
Fuse carrier, engine electronics
4
X8680
4.0
RT/WS/GE
X6960
2
X60531
2.5
RT/WS/GE
X6964
0.5
RT/WS/GE
2
X6167
Y6167
Valve, individual control intake system
1
X6167
0.5
BR/BL
40
X60003
A6000
Digital motor electronics control unit
31

MS 45.1Engine Management
Idle speed control valve

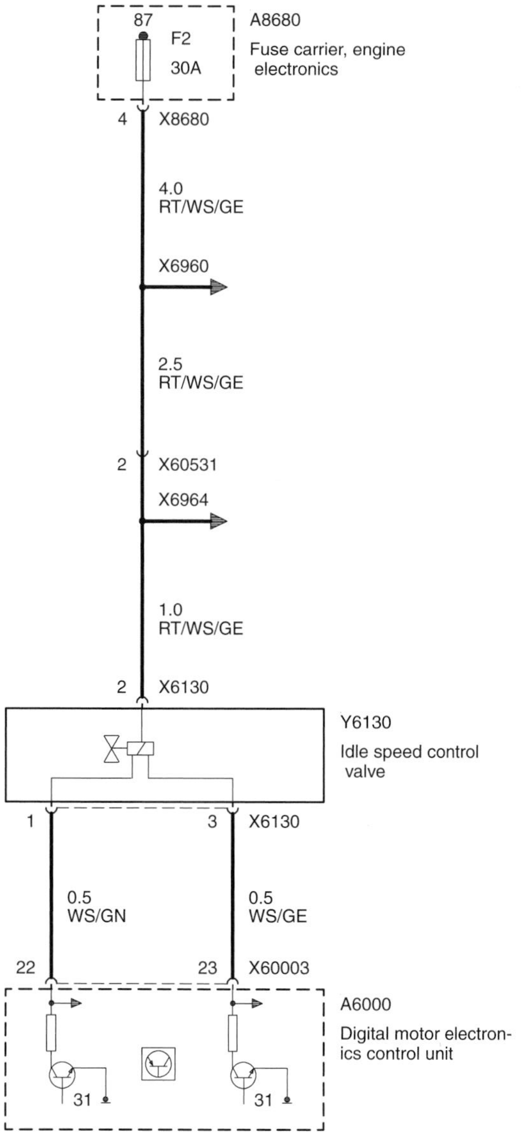

MS 45.1 Engine Management
Mass Air Flow sensor

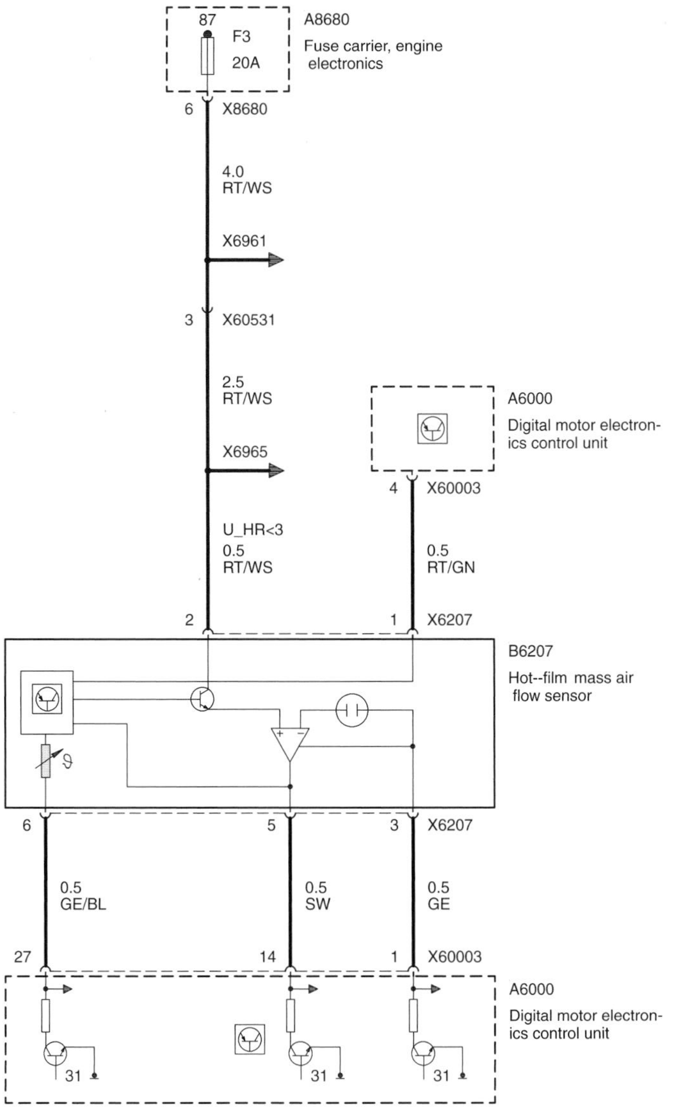

MS 45.1 Engine Management
Crankshaft position sensor

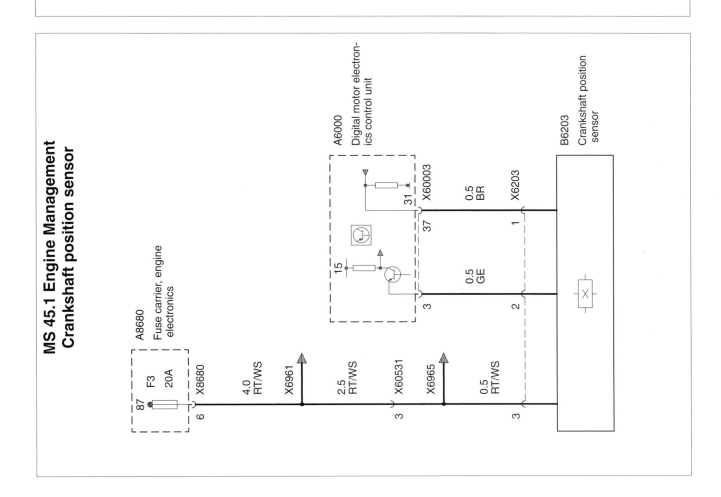

87
F3
20A
A8680
Fuse carrier, engine electronics
6
X8680
4.0
RT/WS
X6961
2.5
RT/WS
3
X60531
X6965
0.5
RT/WS
3
15
A6000
Digital motor electronics control unit
31
3
37
X60003
0.5
GE
0.5
BR
2
1
X6203
B6203
Crankshaft position sensor

MS 45.1 Engine Management
Thermostat (electrically heated)

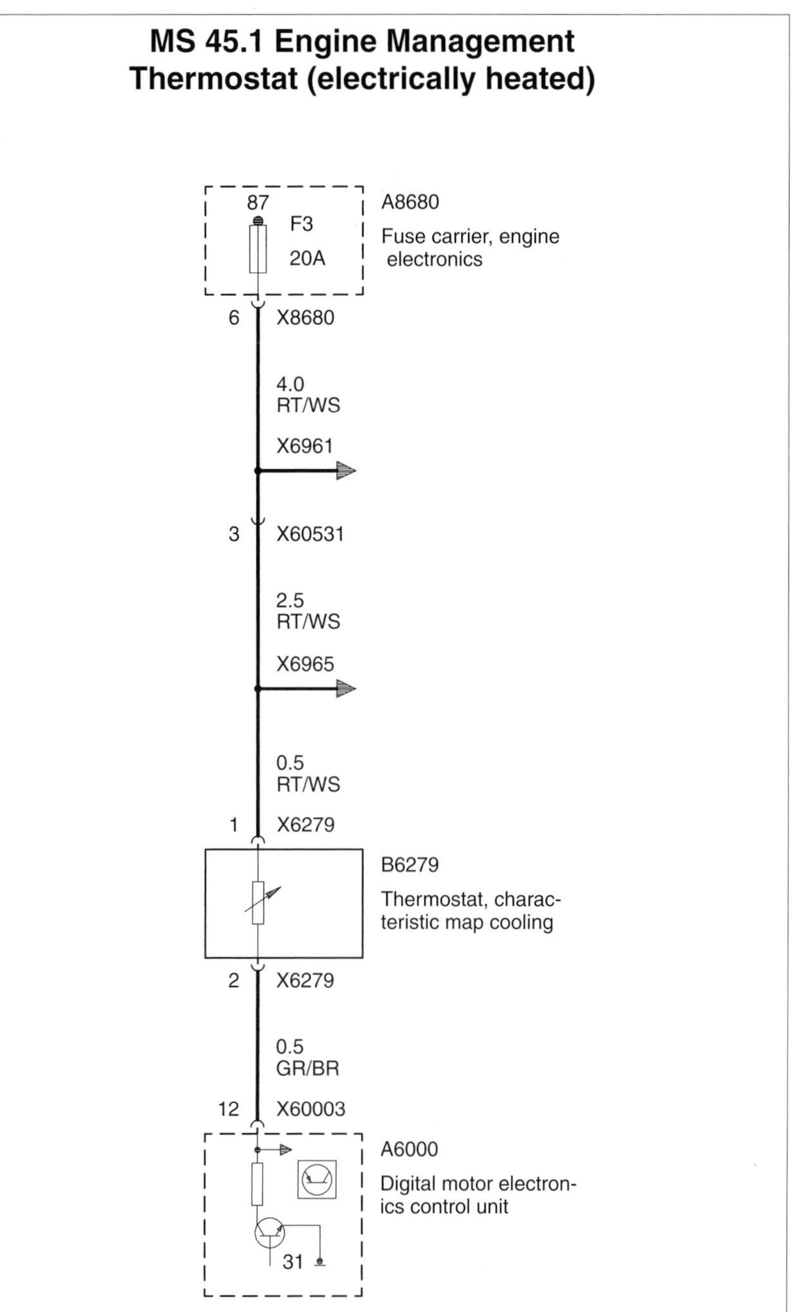

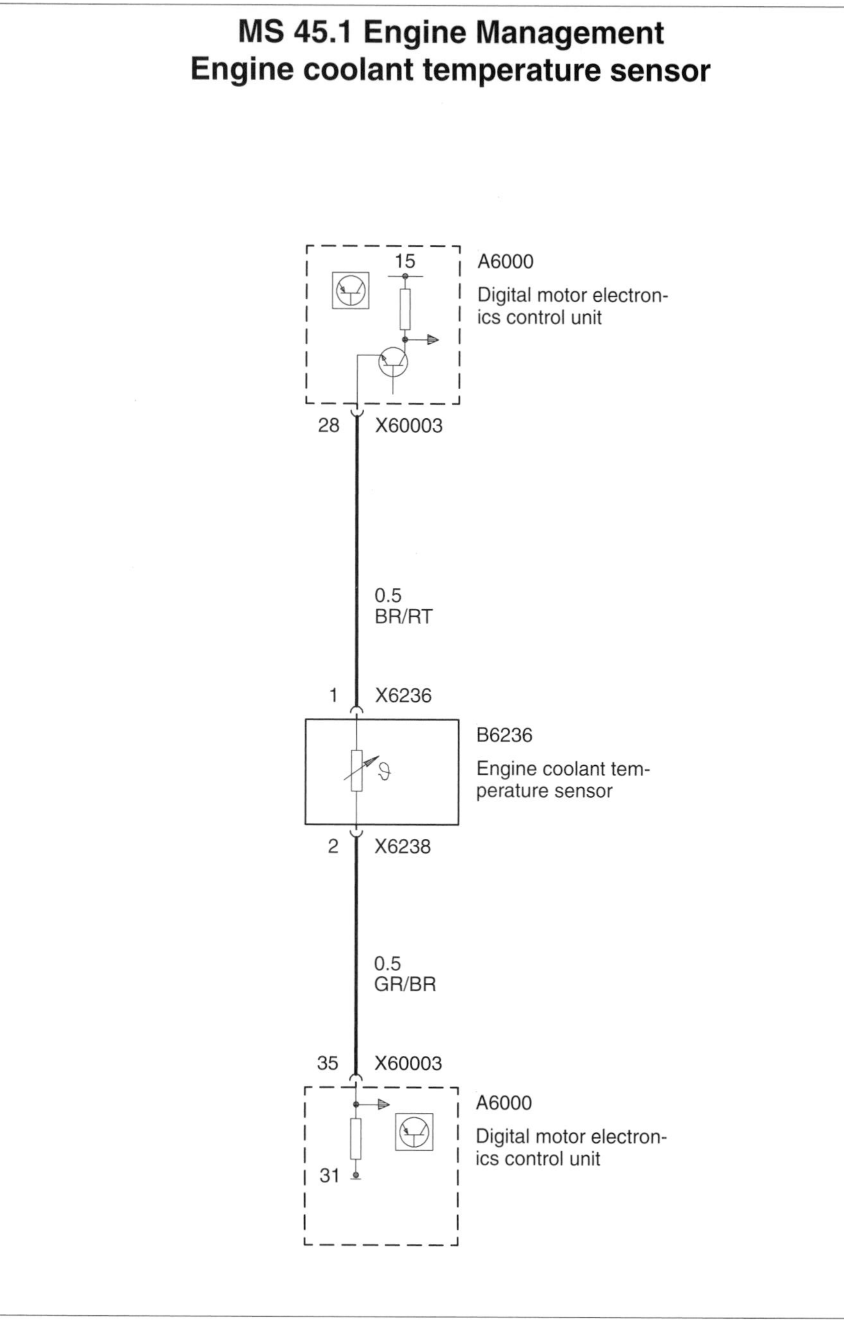

MS 45.1 Engine Management
Engine oil temperature sensor

15
A6000
Digital motor electronics control unit
44 X60003
0.5
RT/BL
1 X6238
B6238
Oil temperature sensor
2 X6238
0.5
GR/BR
45 X60003
A6000
Digital motor electronics control unit
31

MS 45.1 Engine Management
Engine oil level sensor

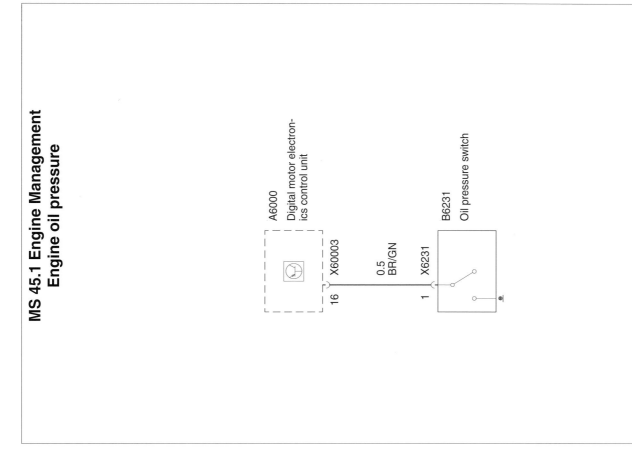

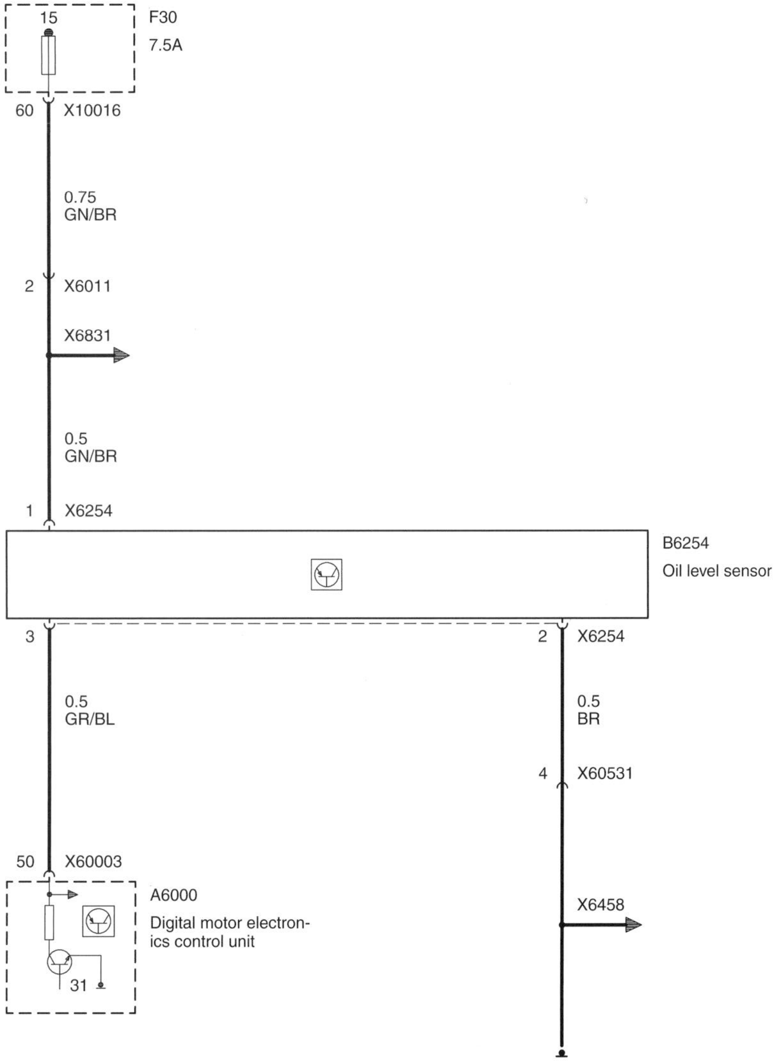

MS 45.1 Engine Management
Engine oil pressure

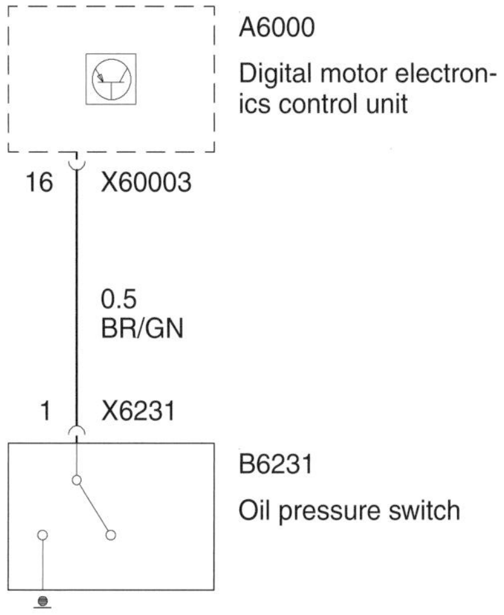

MS 45.1 Engine Management
Camshaft position sensors

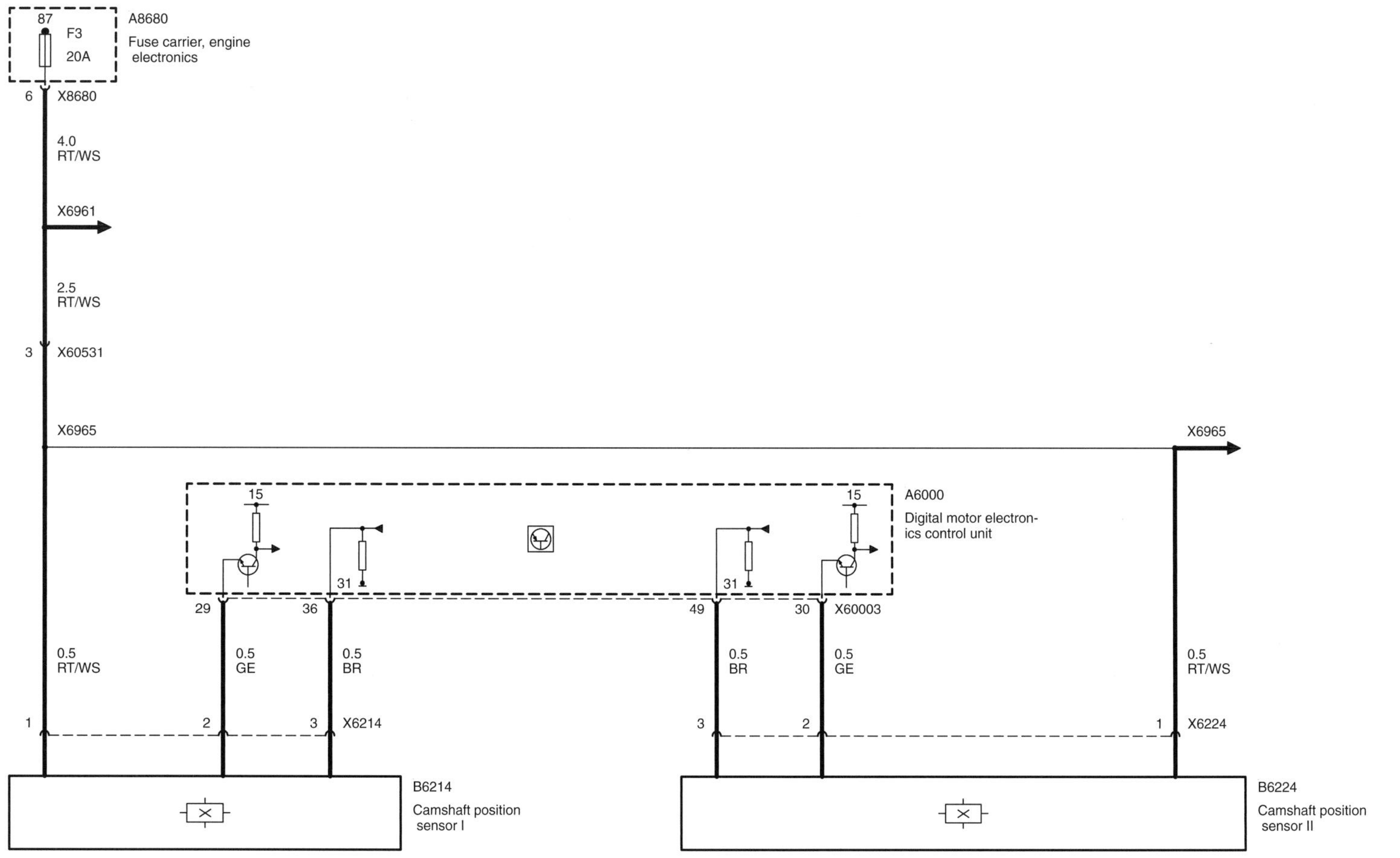

87
F3
20A
A8680
Fuse carrier, engine electronics
6 X8680
4.0 RT/WS
X6961
2.5 RT/WS
3 X60531
X6965
X6965
15
15
A6000
Digital motor electronics control unit
31
31
29
36
49
30 X60003
0.5 RT/WS
0.5 GE
0.5 BR
0.5 BR
0.5 GE
0.5 RT/WS
1
2
3 X6214
3
2
1 X6224
B6214
Camshaft position sensor I
B6224
Camshaft position sensor II

MS 45.1 Engine Management
Fuel supply, local CAN bus

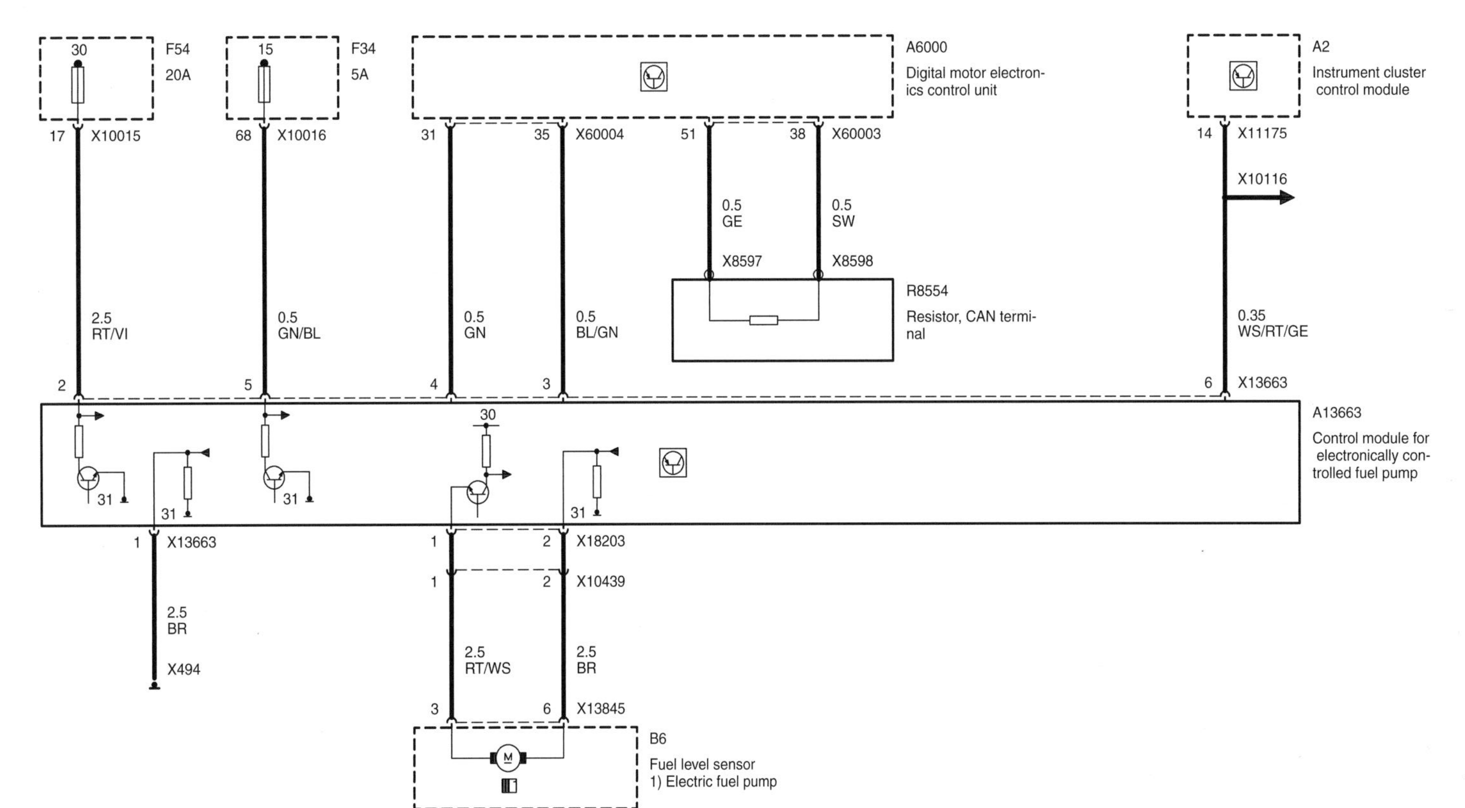

MS 45.1 Engine Management
Secondary air system
(up to 03/2003)

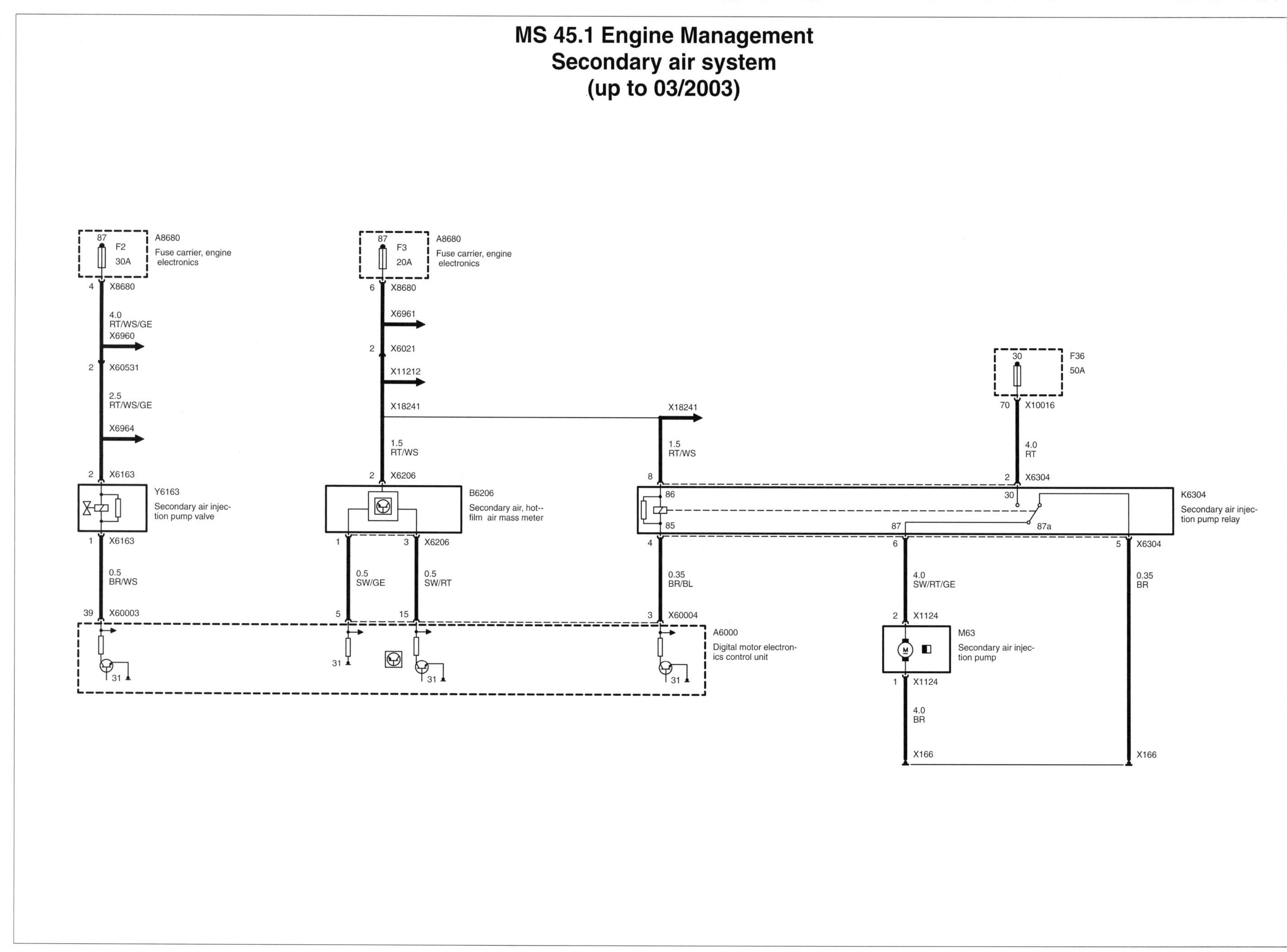

MS 45.1 Engine Management
Secondary air system (from 03/2003)
(page 1 of 2)

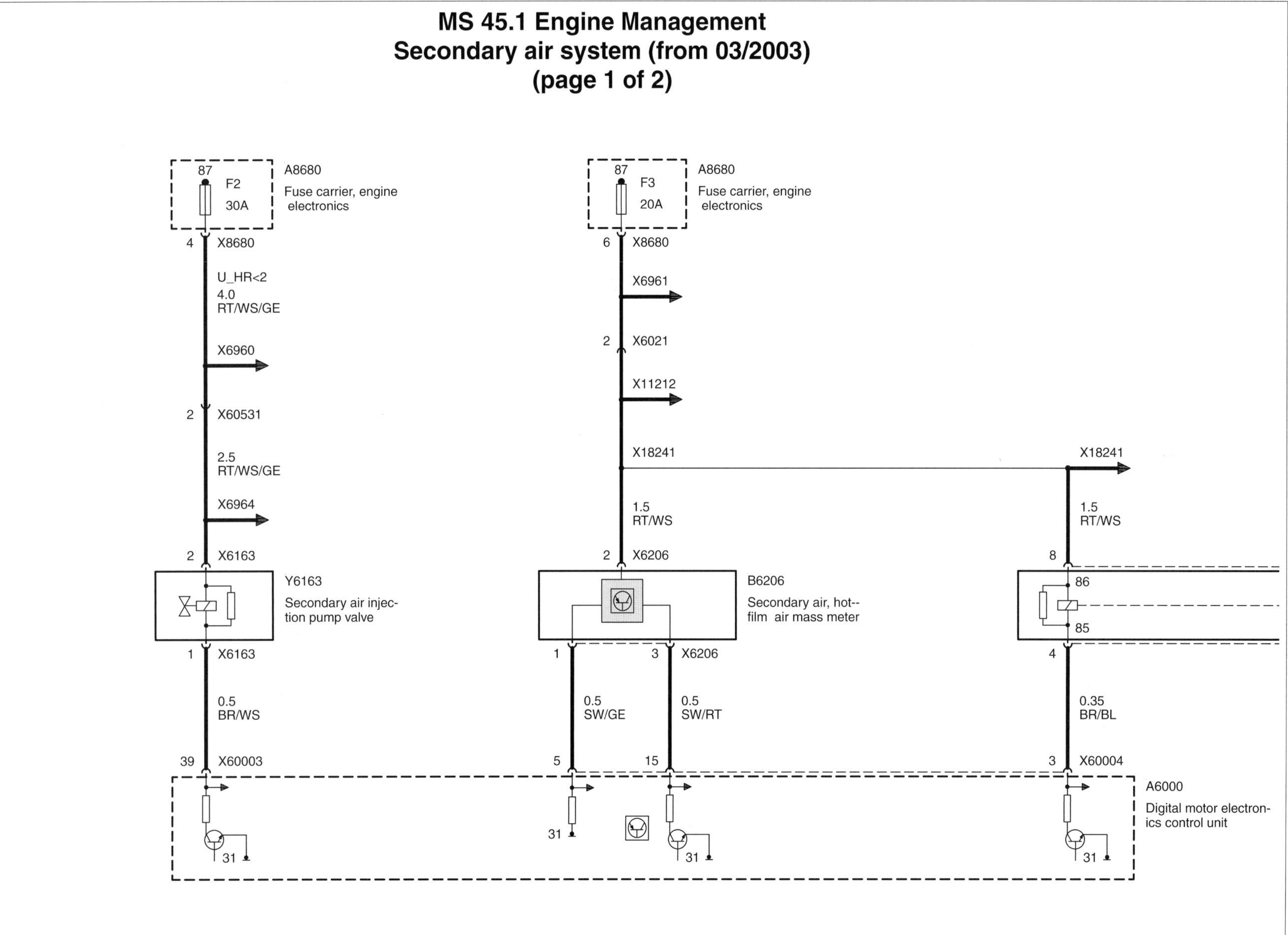

MS 45.1 Engine Management
Secondary air system (from 03/2003)
(page 2 of 2)

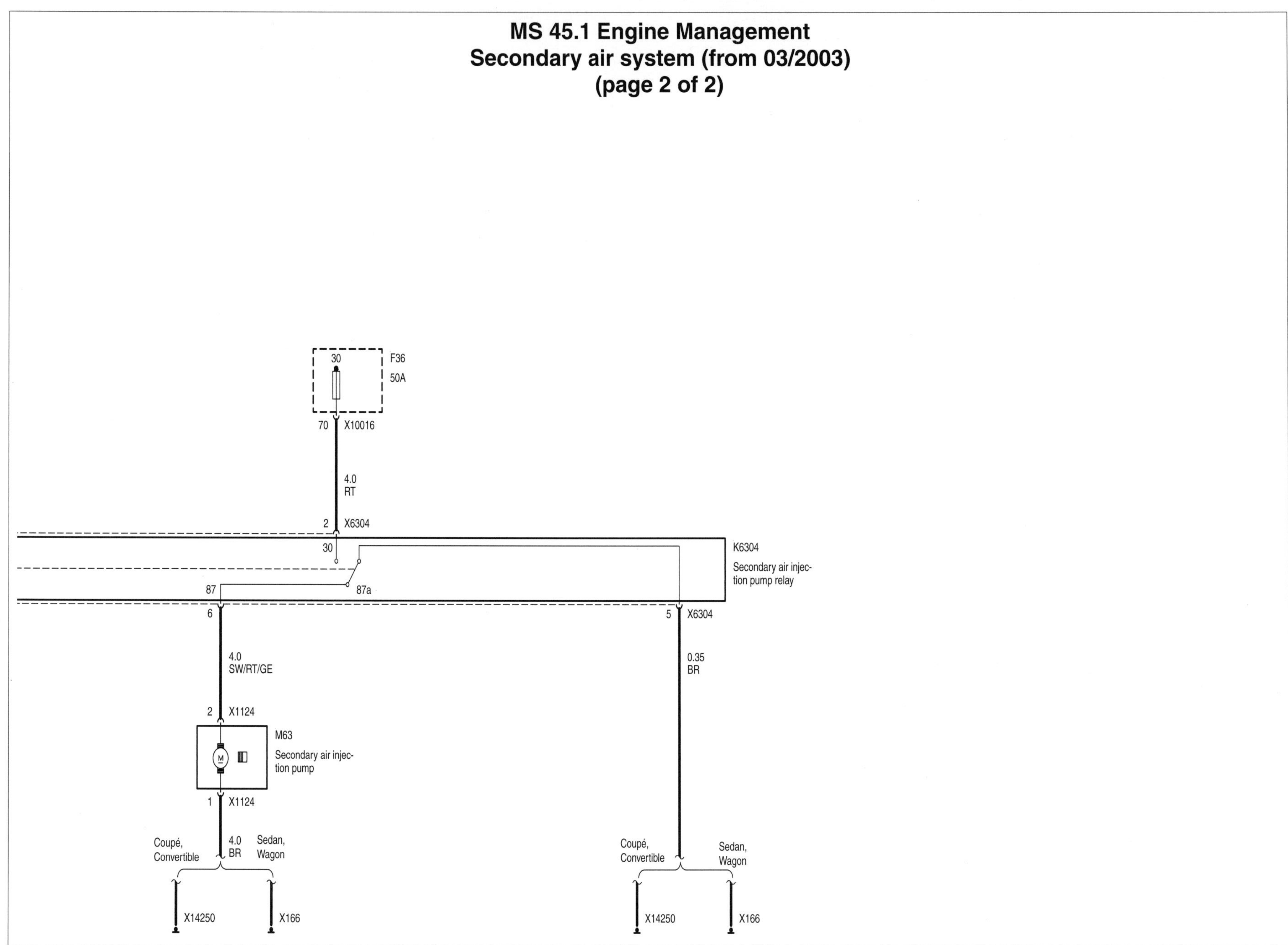

MS 45.1 Engine Management
DME main relay

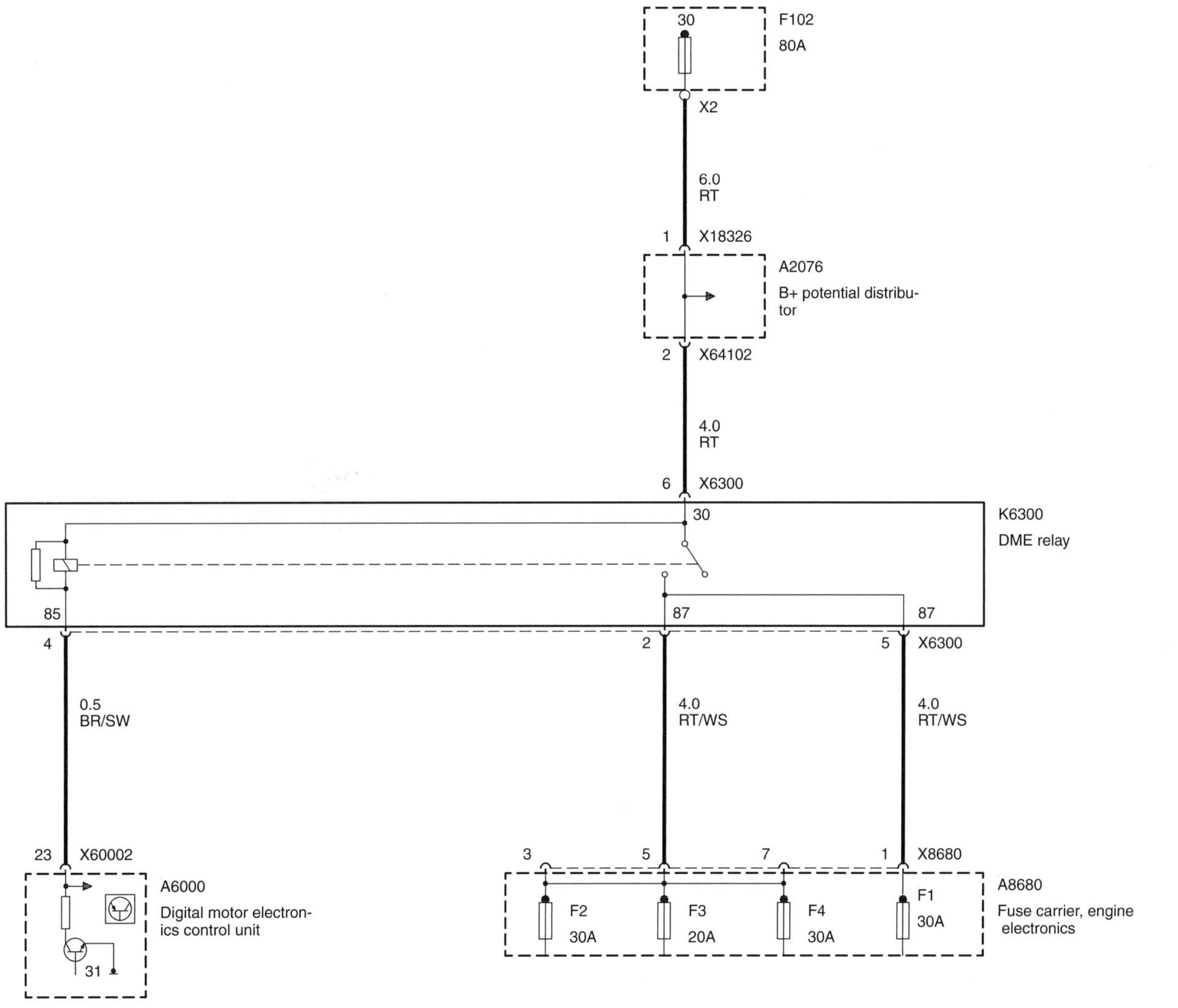

MS 45.1 Engine Management
Power supply, DME control module

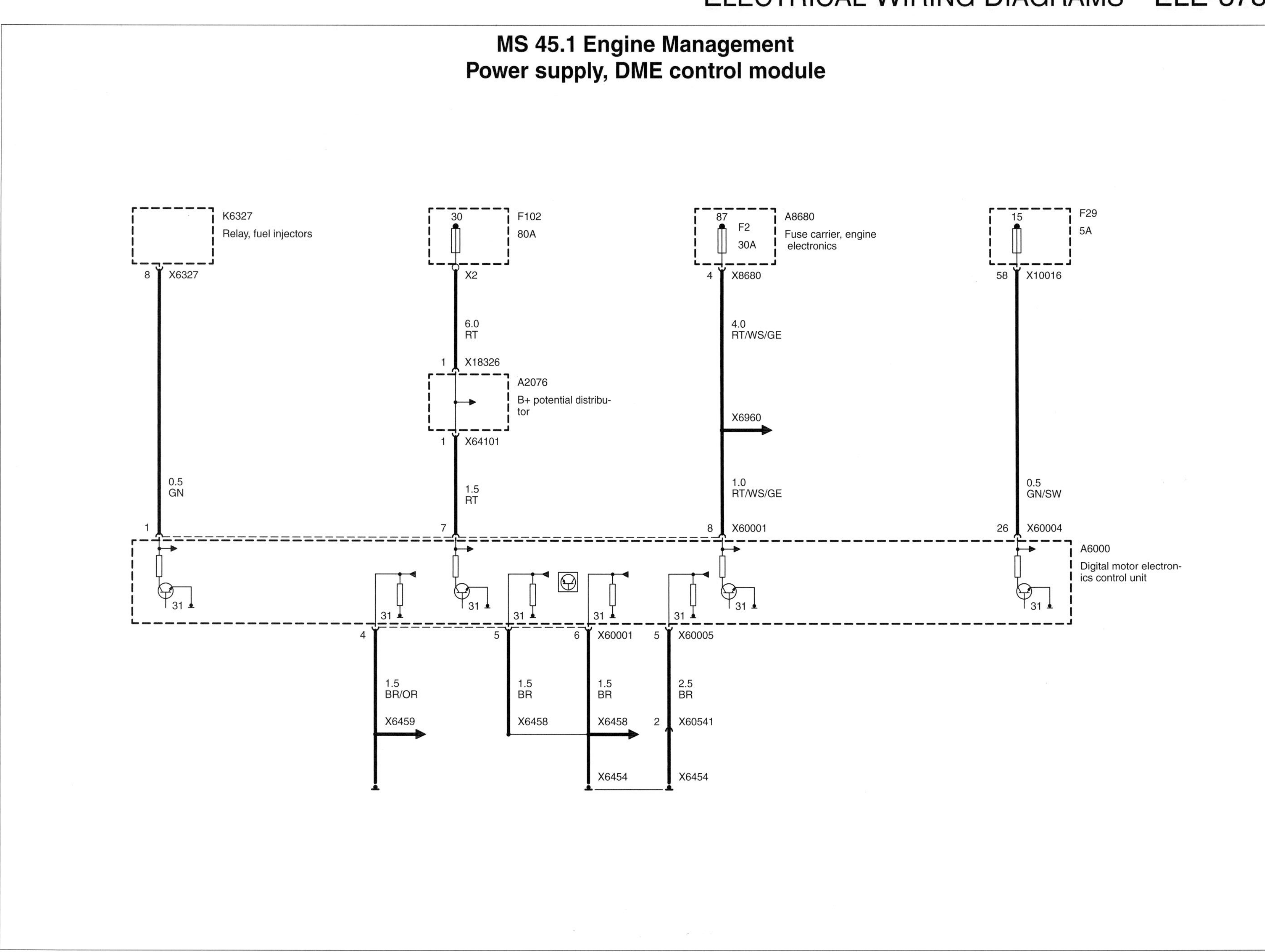

MS 45.1 Engine Management
Fuel tank ventilation valve

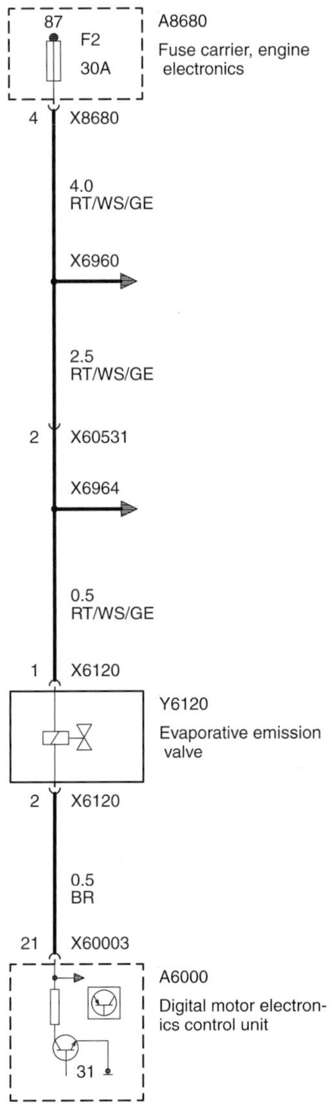

MS 45.1 Engine Management
Fuel tank leakage diagnosis module

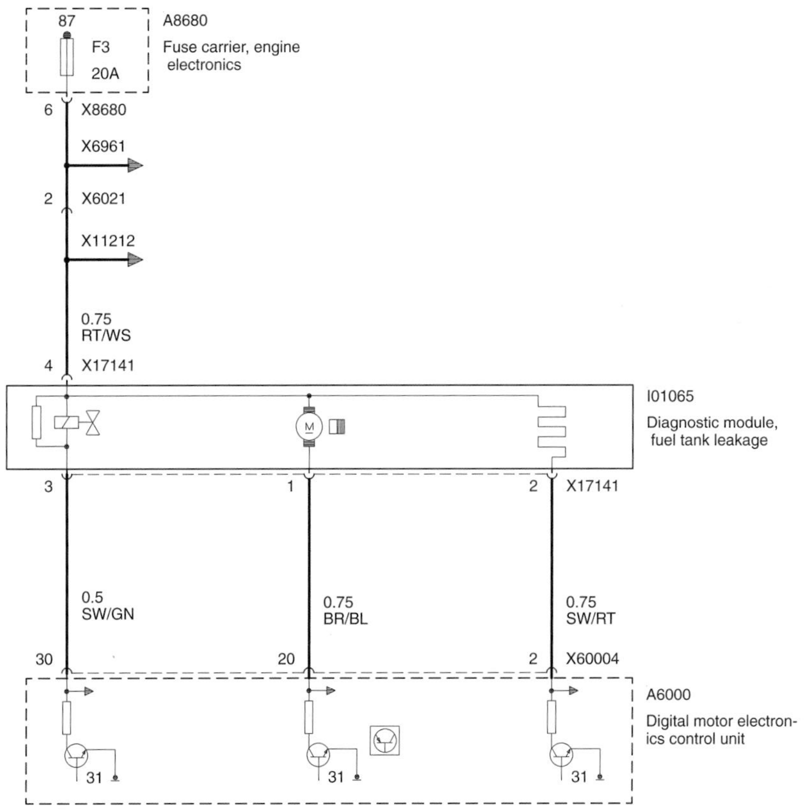

MS 45.1 Engine Management
Ignition coils
(page 1 of 2)

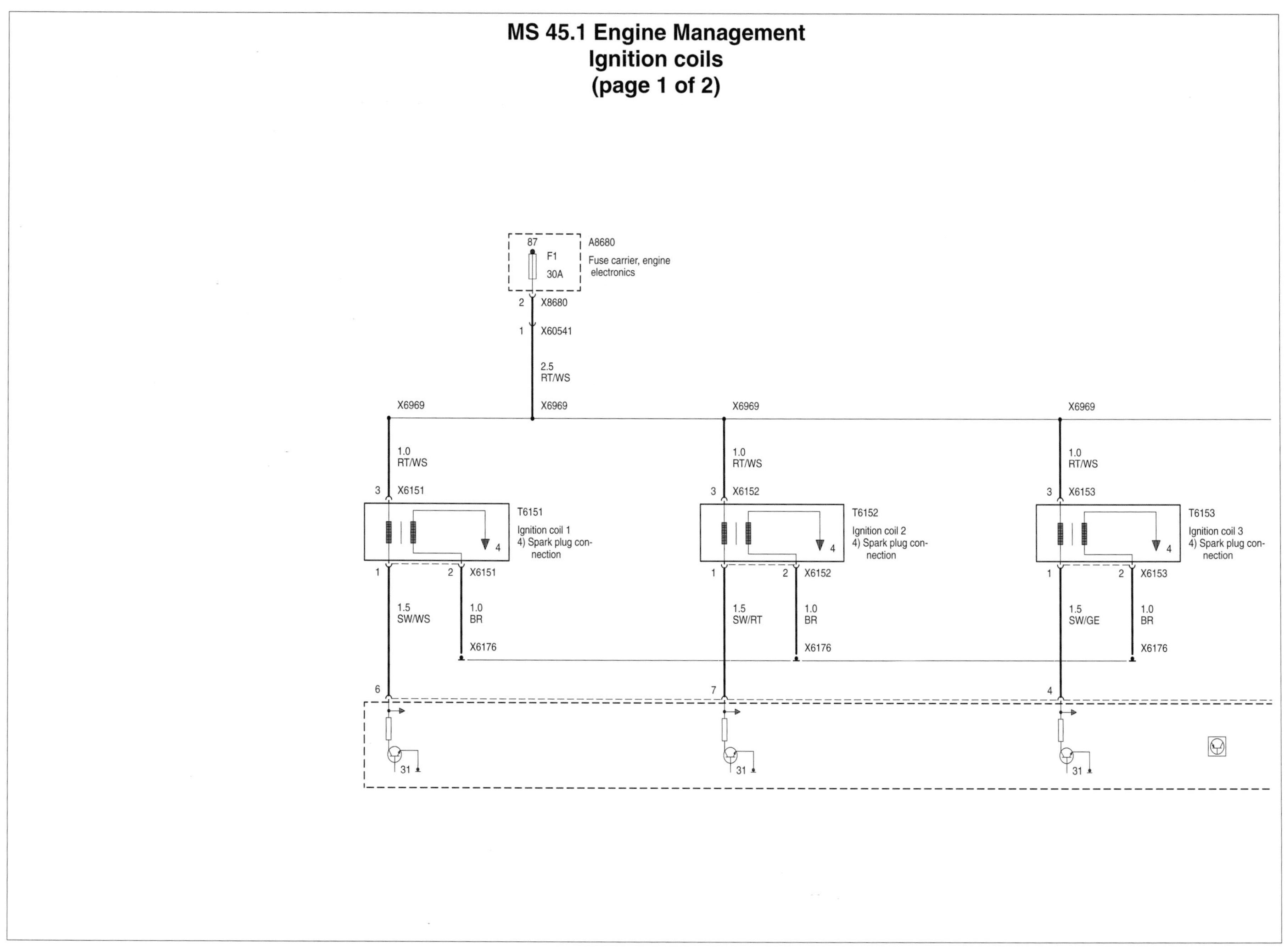

MS 45.1 Engine Management
Ignition coils
(page 2 of 2)

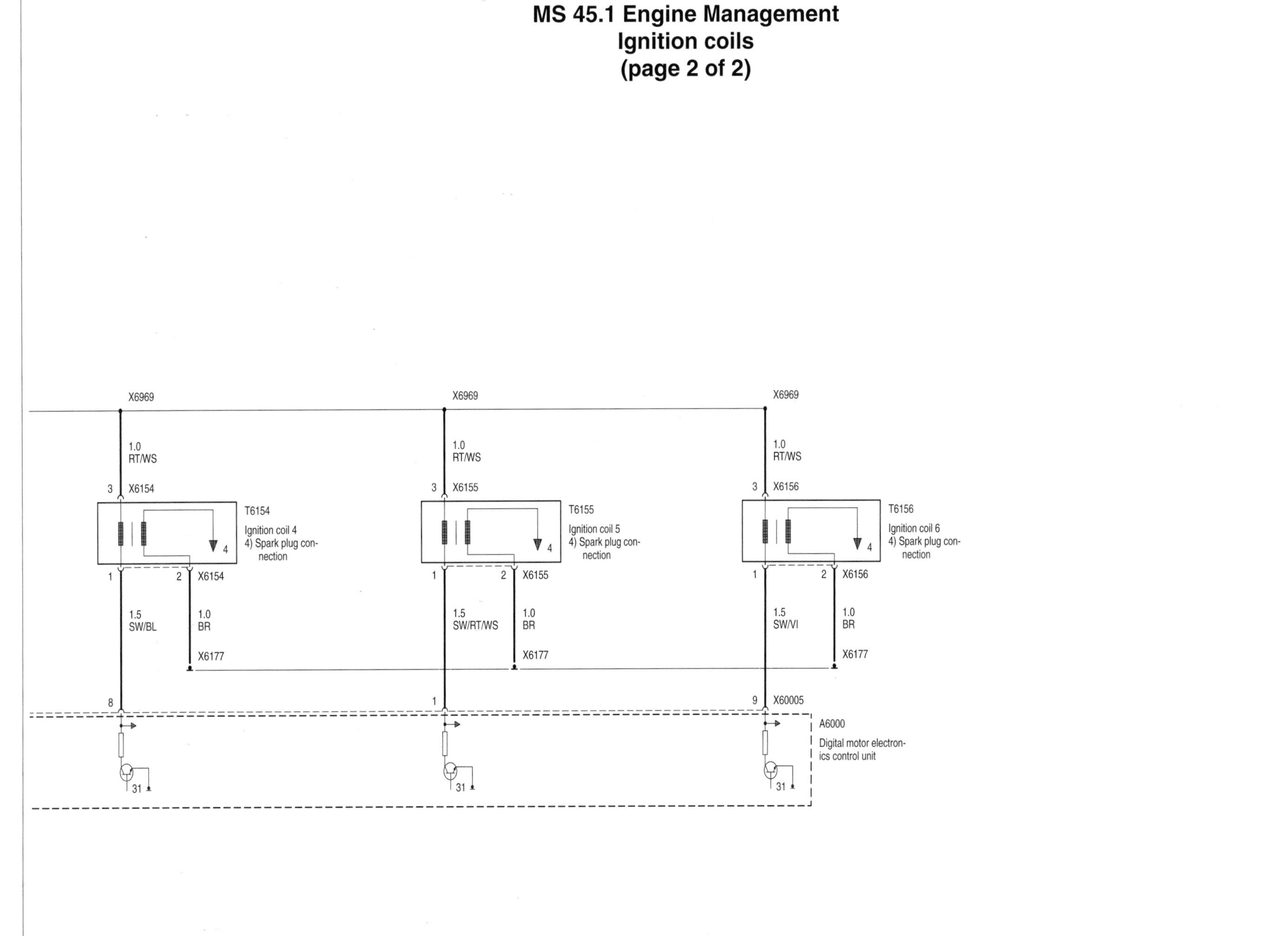

MS 45.1 Engine Management
E-box fan

87
F3
20A
A8680
Fuse carrier, engine electronics
6 X8680
X6961
2 X6021
X11212
A6000
Digital motor electronics control unit
19 X60004
0.5
RT/WS
0.5
BR/OR
2
1 X6506
M6506
E--box fan

This page intentionally left blank

SMG Transmission (325i / 330i models)
SMG interfaces

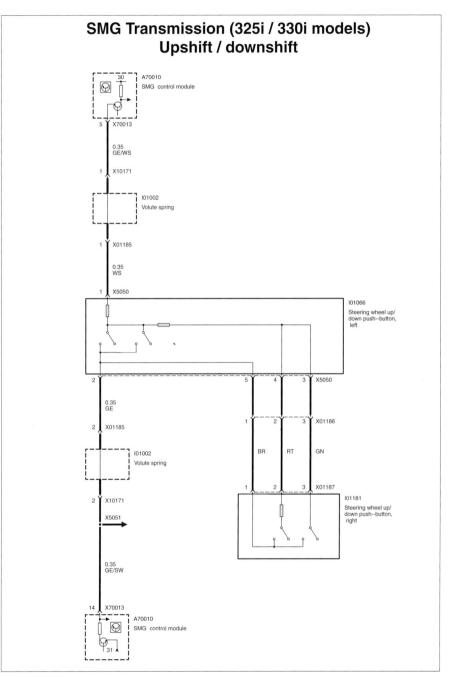

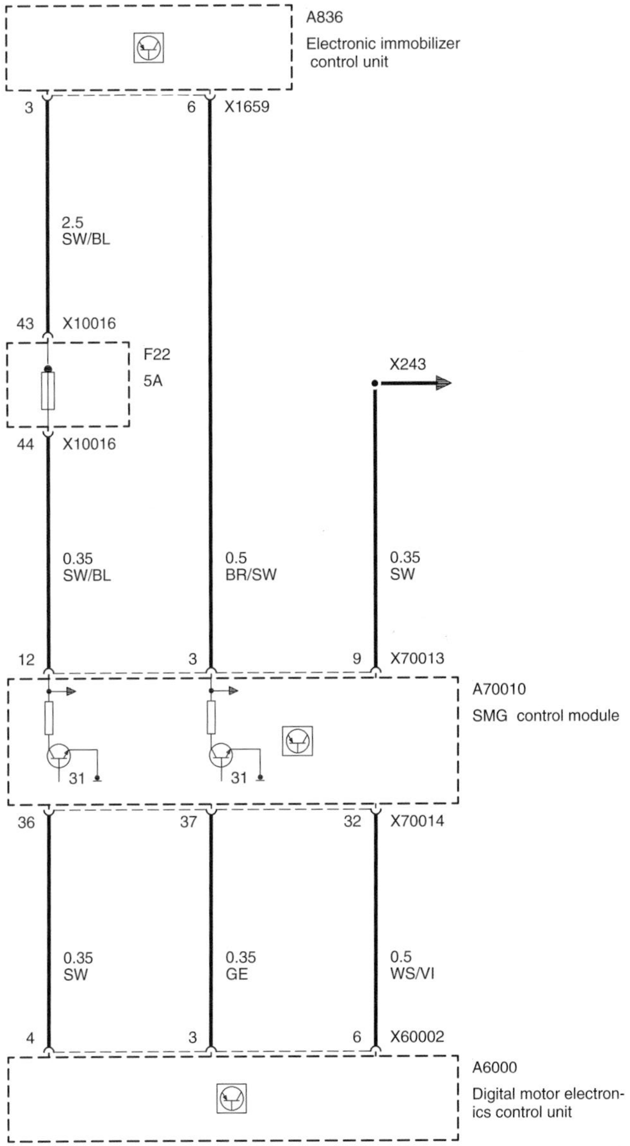

SMG Transmission (325i / 330i models)
Upshift / downshift

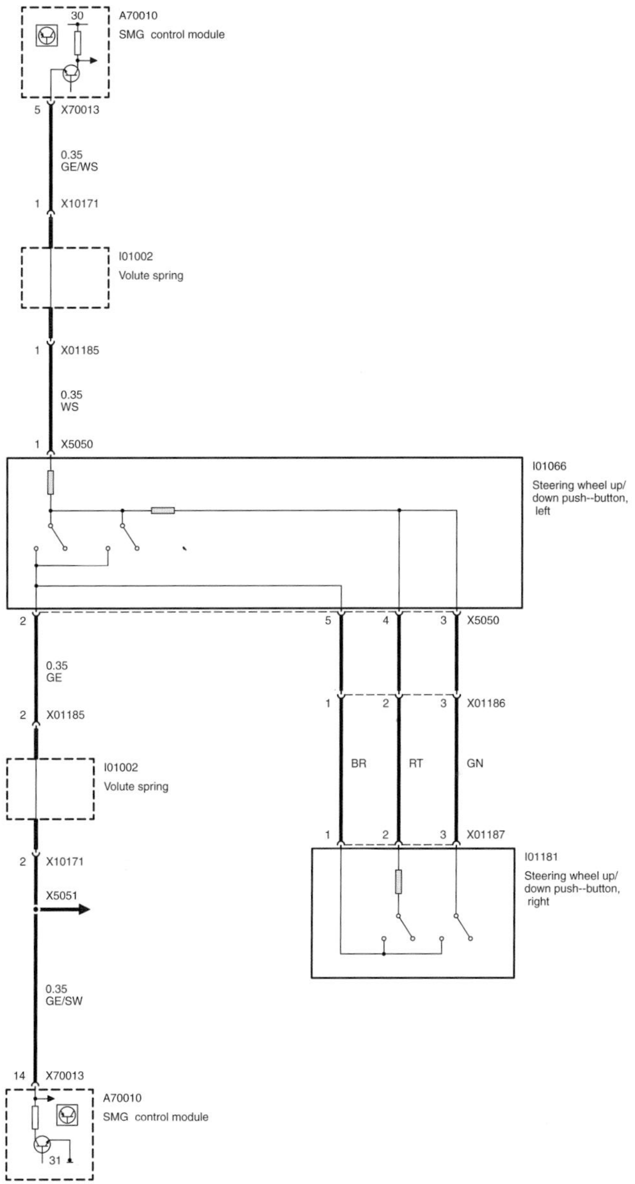

SMG Transmission (325i / 330i models)
Sport program switch

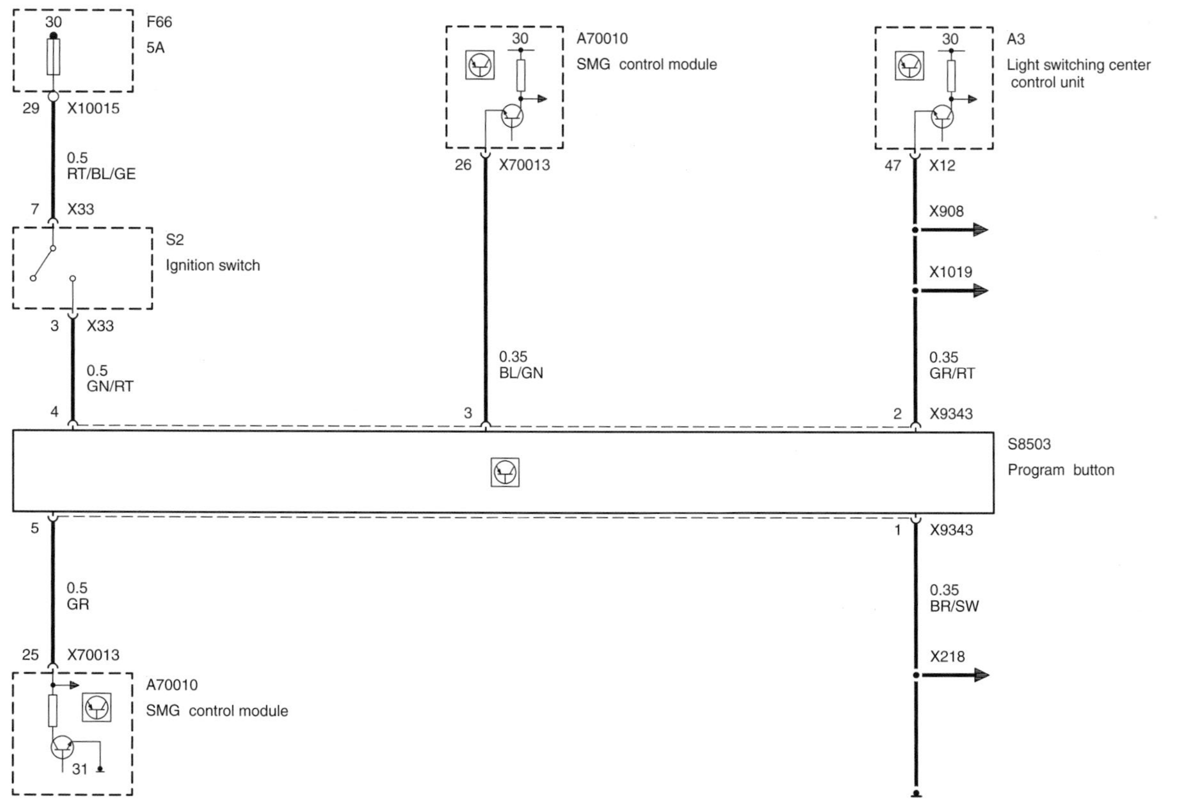

SMG Transmission (325i / 330i models)
Gearshift / selector angle position

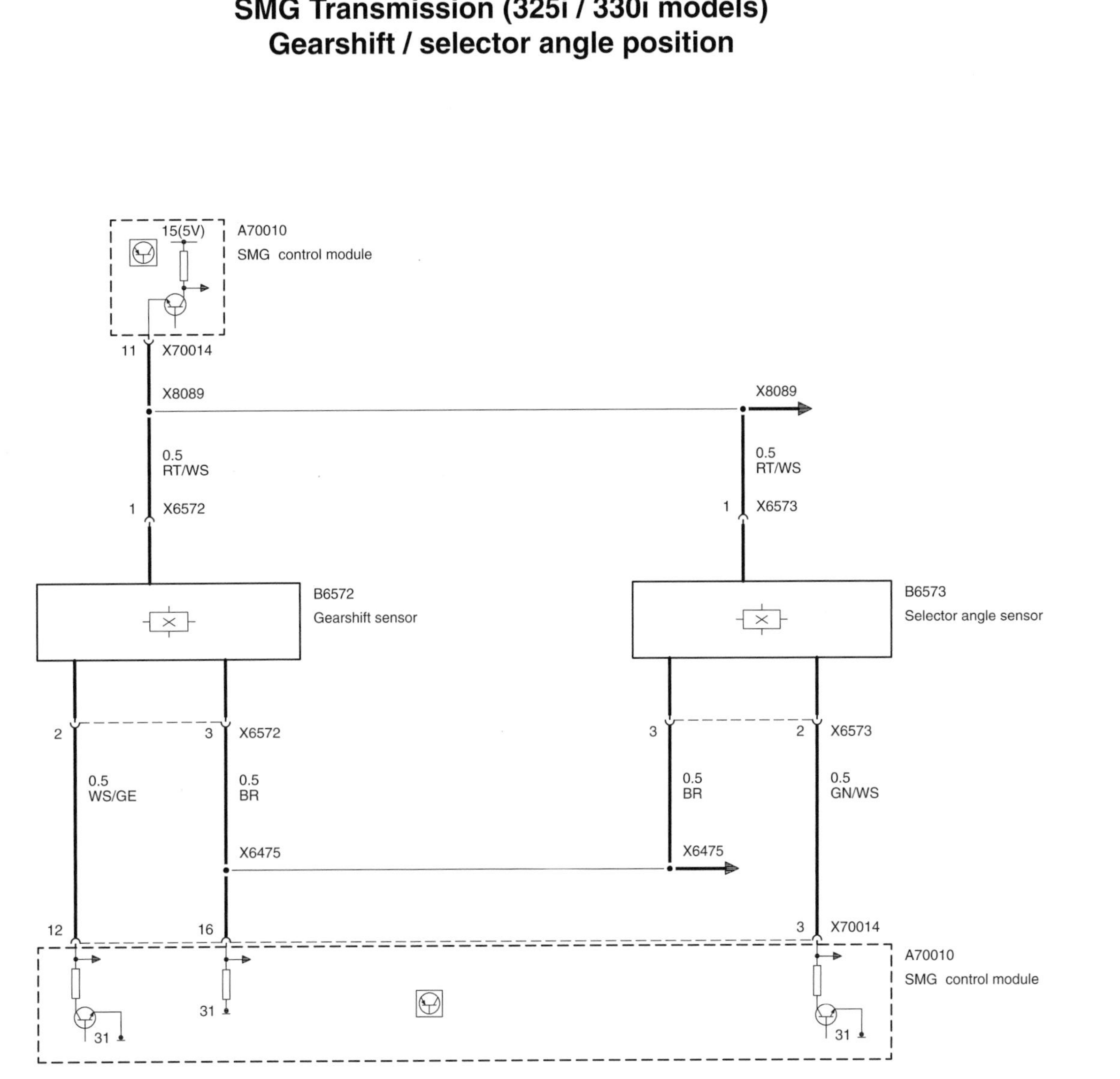

SMG Transmission (325i / 330i models)
SMG hydraulic system
(page 1 of 2)

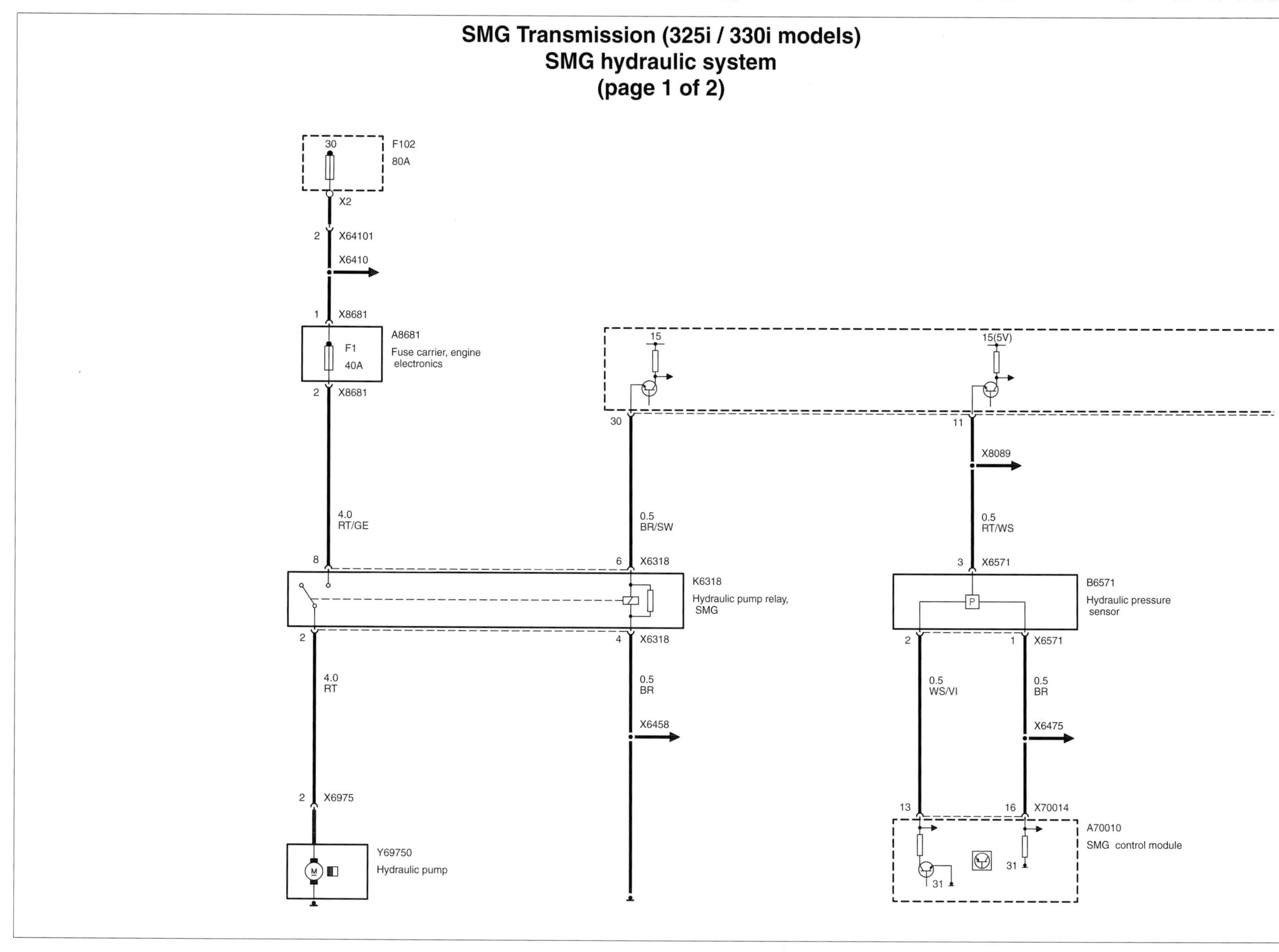

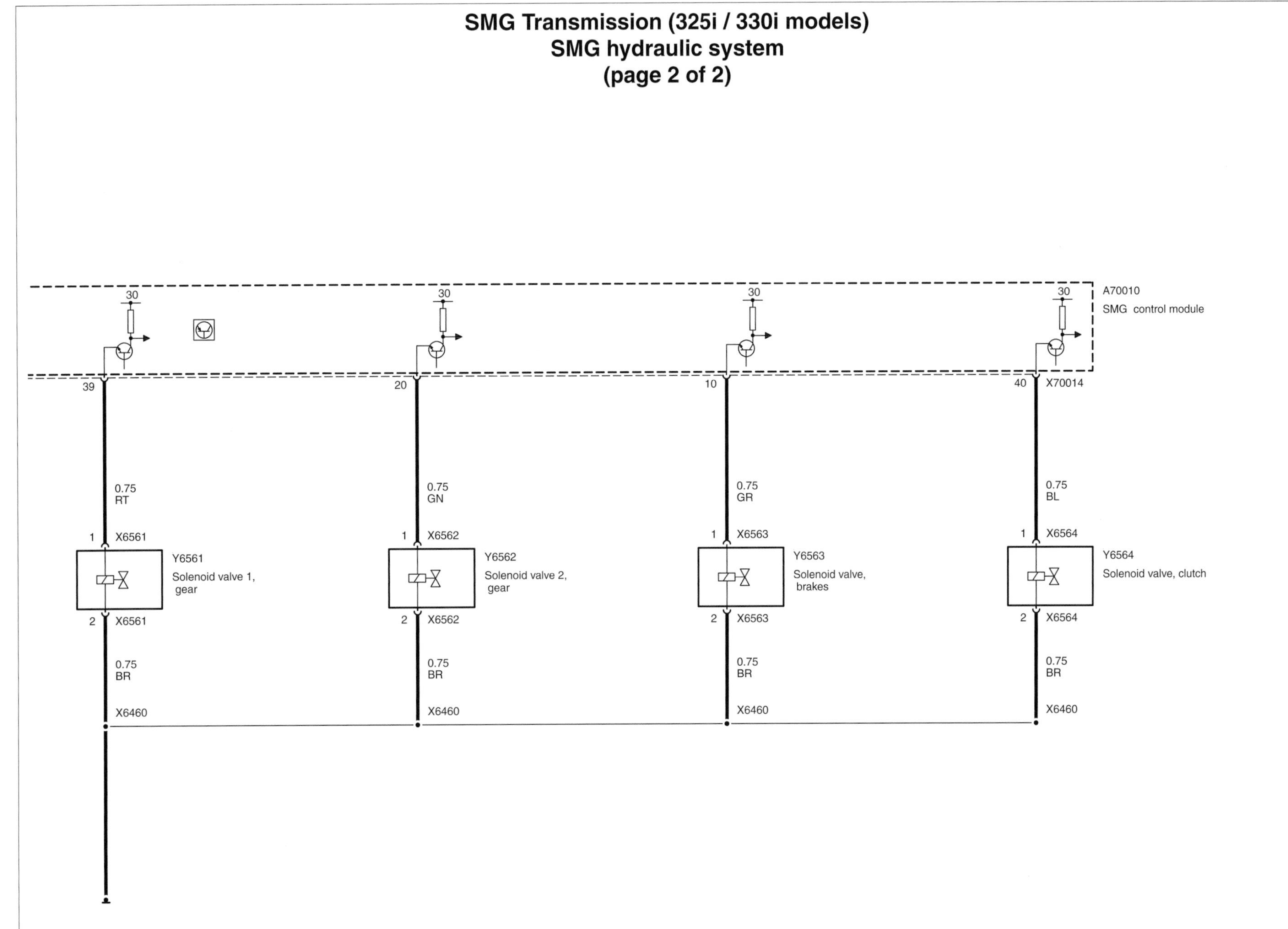
SMG Transmission (325i / 330i models)
SMG hydraulic system
(page 2 of 2)
A70010
SMG control module
30
30
30
30
39
20
10
40
X70014
0.75
RT
0.75
GN
0.75
GR
0.75
BL
1
X6561
1
X6562
1
X6563
1
X6564
Y6561
Solenoid valve 1,
gear
Y6562
Solenoid valve 2,
gear
Y6563
Solenoid valve,
brakes
Y6564
Solenoid valve, clutch
2
X6561
2
X6562
2
X6563
2
X6564
0.75
BR
0.75
BR
0.75
BR
0.75
BR
X6460
X6460
X6460
X6460

SMG Transmission (325i / 330i models)
Clutch position

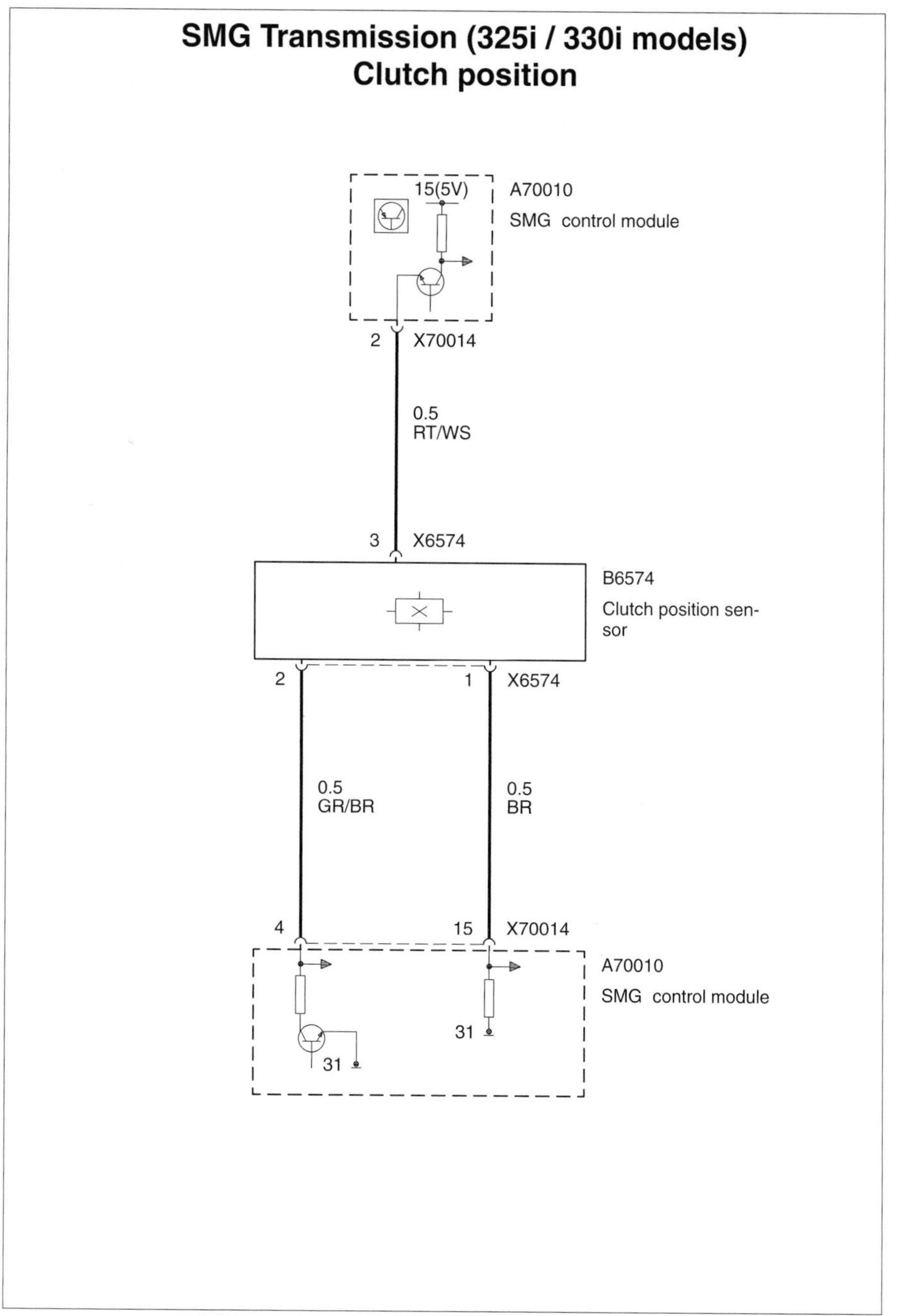

SMG Transmission (325i / 330i models)
Speed, transmission main shaft

Y8616
Rpm sensor, transmission main shaft
1
2
X8616
0.5
GE
0.5
SW
W8516
W8516
W8516
23
24
X70014
A70010
SMG control module
31
31
X6461
0.5
BR
X6458

SMG Transmission (325i / 330i models)
Power supply
(up to 09/2002)

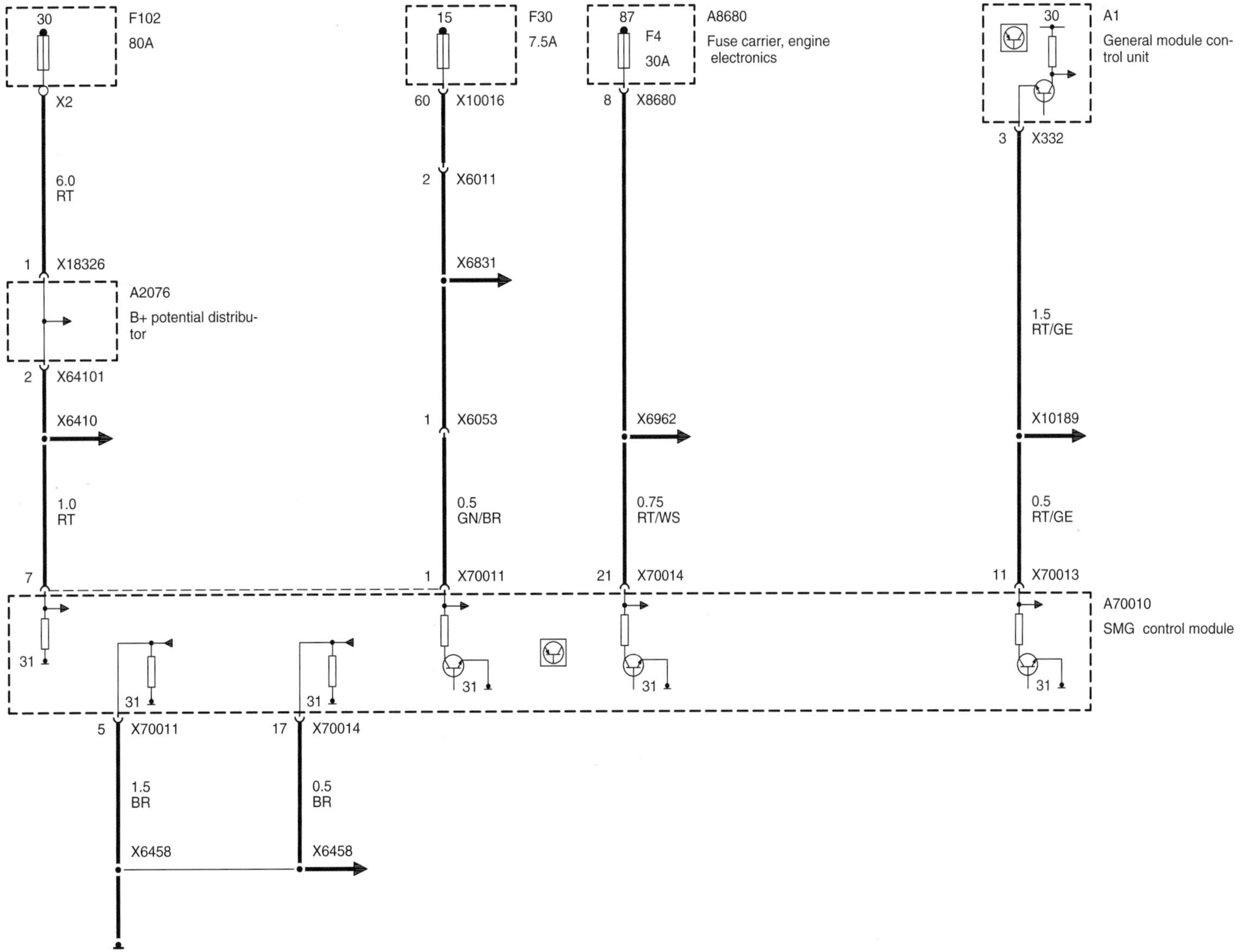

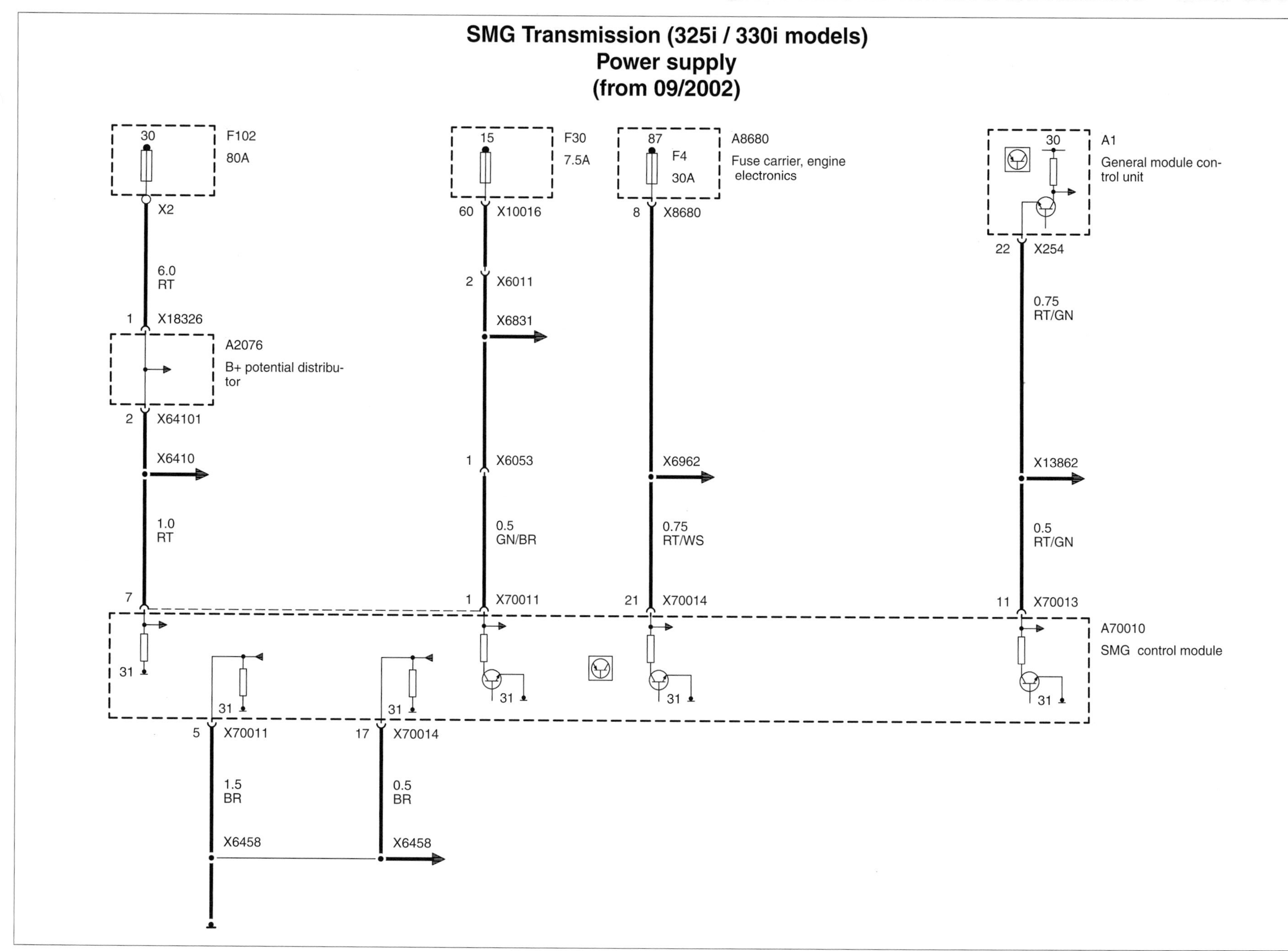
SMG Transmission (325i / 330i models)
Power supply
(from 09/2002)
30
F102
80A
X2
6.0
RT
1
X18326
A2076
B+ potential distributor
2
X64101
X6410
1.0
RT
7
31
15
F30
7.5A
60
X10016
2
X6011
X6831
1
X6053
0.5
GN/BR
1
X70011
87
F4
30A
A8680
Fuse carrier, engine electronics
8
X8680
X6962
0.75
RT/WS
21
X70014
30
A1
General module control unit
22
X254
0.75
RT/GN
X13862
0.5
RT/GN
11
X70013
A70010
SMG control module
31
5
X70011
1.5
BR
X6458
17
X70014
0.5
BR
X6458

SMG Transmission (325i / 330i models)
Selector lever
(up to 09/2002)

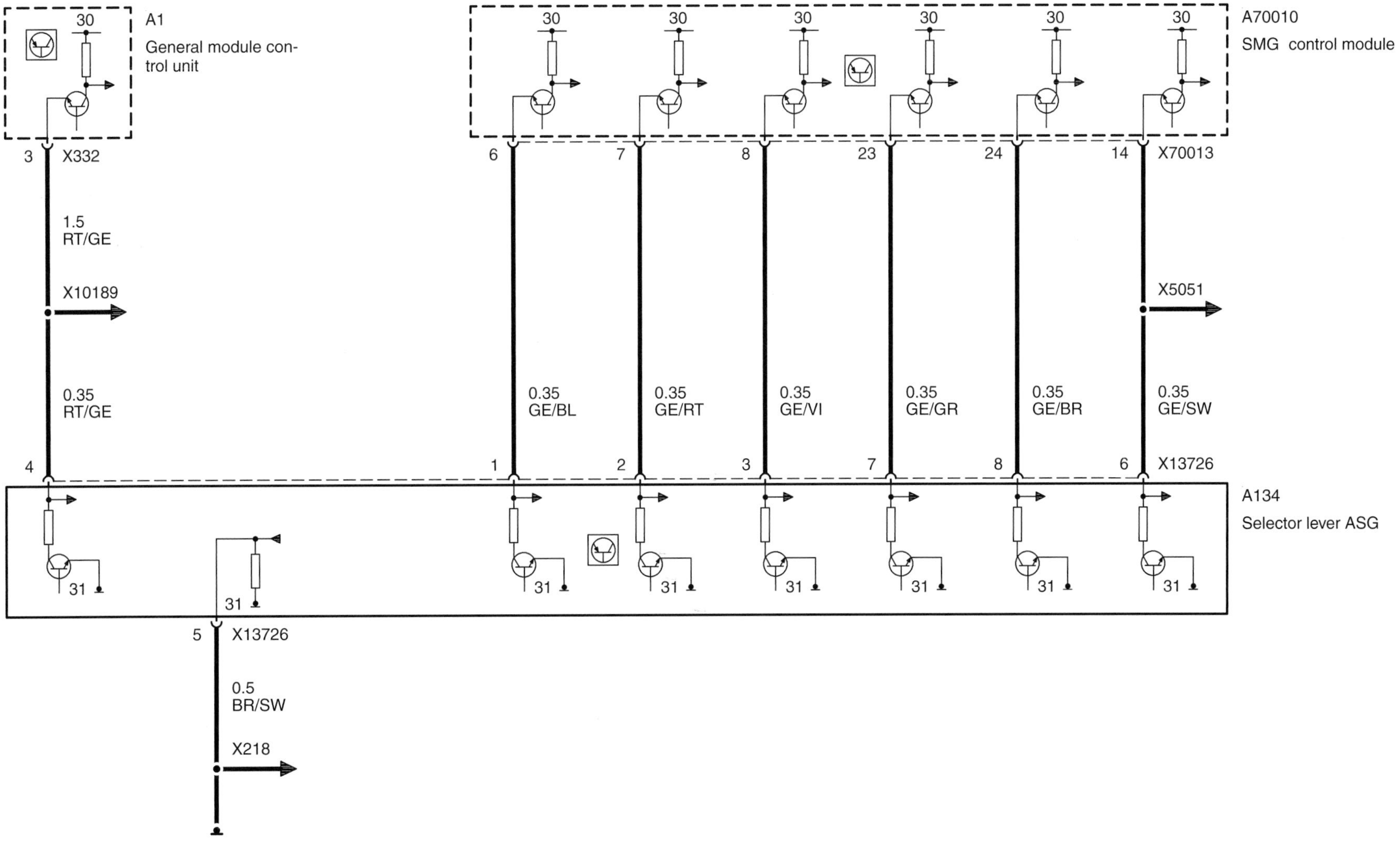

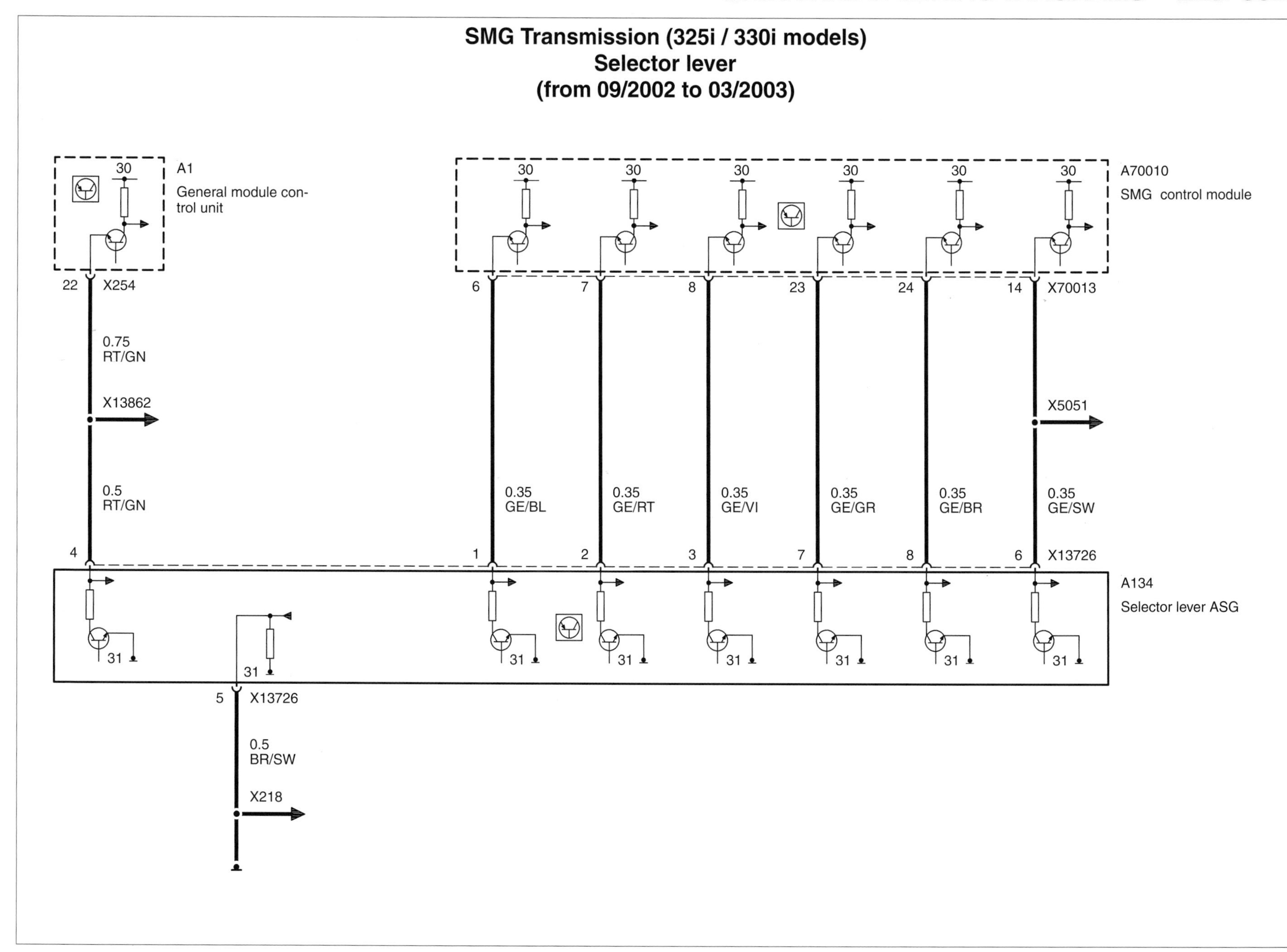
SMG Transmission (325i / 330i models)
Selector lever
(from 09/2002 to 03/2003)
A1
General module control unit
30
22
X254
0.75
RT/GN
X13862
0.5
RT/GN
4
A70010
SMG control module
30
6
7
8
23
24
14
X70013
X5051
0.35
GE/BL
0.35
GE/RT
0.35
GE/VI
0.35
GE/GR
0.35
GE/BR
0.35
GE/SW
1
2
3
7
8
6
X13726
A134
Selector lever ASG
31
5
X13726
0.5
BR/SW
X218

SMG Transmission (325i / 330i models)
Selector lever
(from 03/2003)

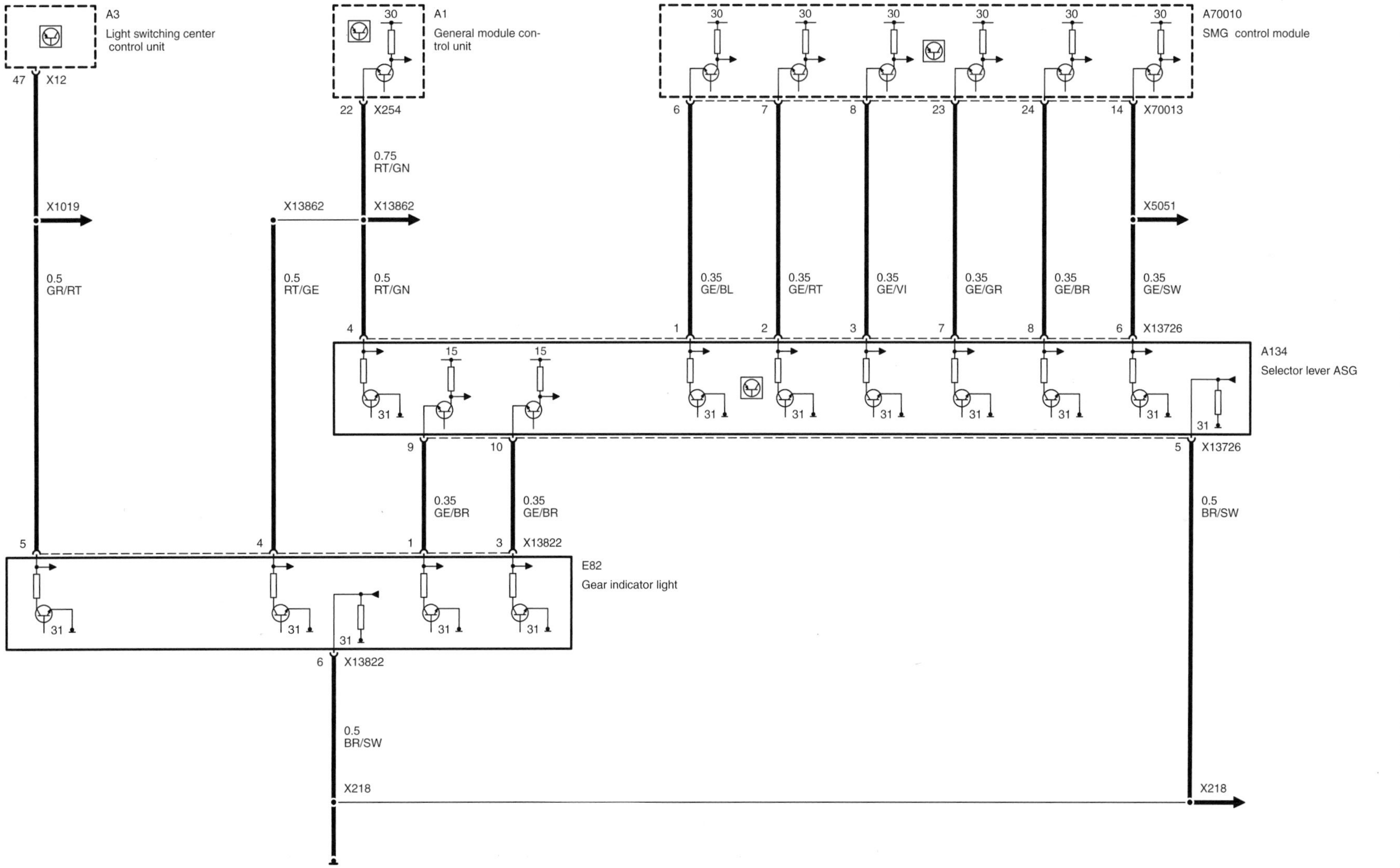

A3
Light switching center control unit
47 X12
X1019
0.5 GR/RT

A1
General module control unit
30
22 X254
0.75 RT/GN
X13862
X13862
0.5 RT/GN
0.5 RT/GE

A70010
SMG control module
30 30 30 30 30 30
6 7 8 23 24 14 X70013
X5051
0.35 GE/BL
0.35 GE/RT
0.35 GE/VI
0.35 GE/GR
0.35 GE/BR
0.35 GE/SW
4 1 2 3 7 8 6 X13726

A134
Selector lever ASG
15 15
31 31 31 31 31 31 31 31
9 10 5 X13726
0.35 GE/BR
0.35 GE/BR
0.5 BR/SW

5 4 1 3 X13822
E82
Gear indicator light
31 31 31 31 31
6 X13822
0.5 BR/SW
X218
X218

SMG Transmission (325i / 330i models)
Brake light switch

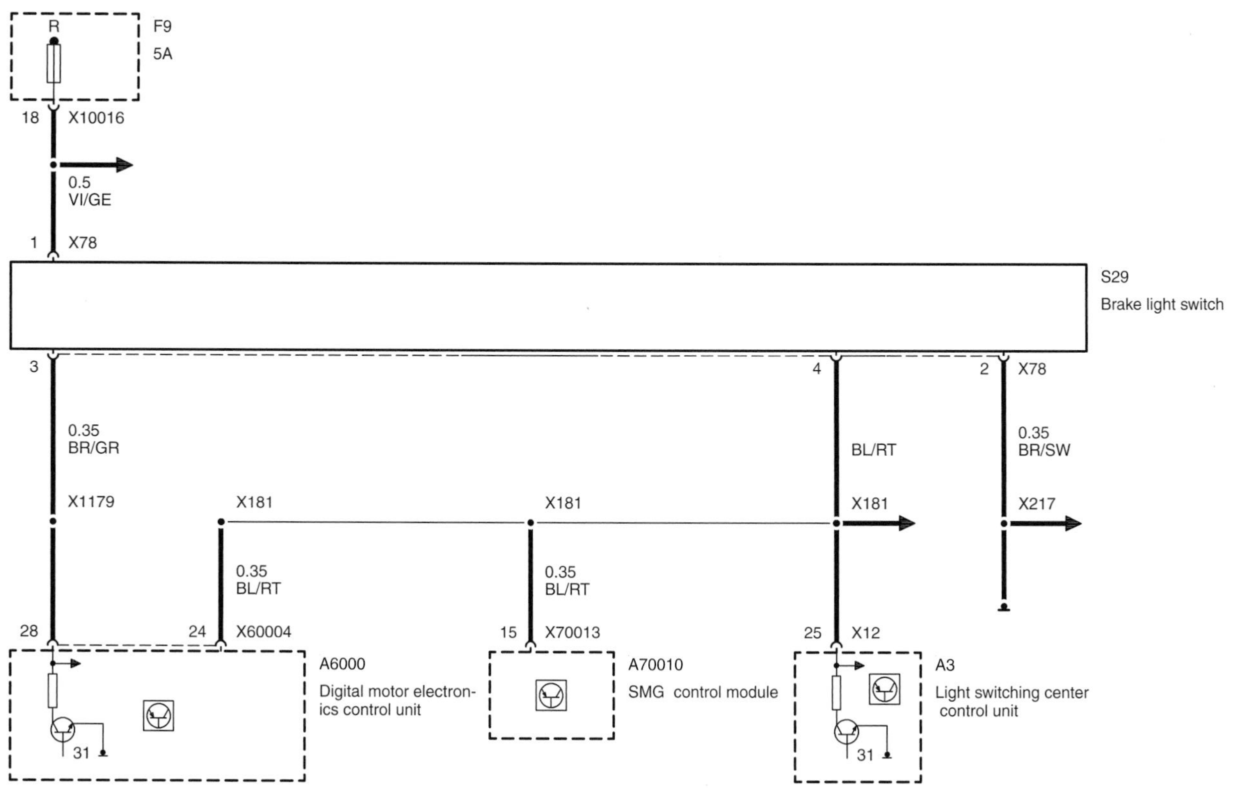

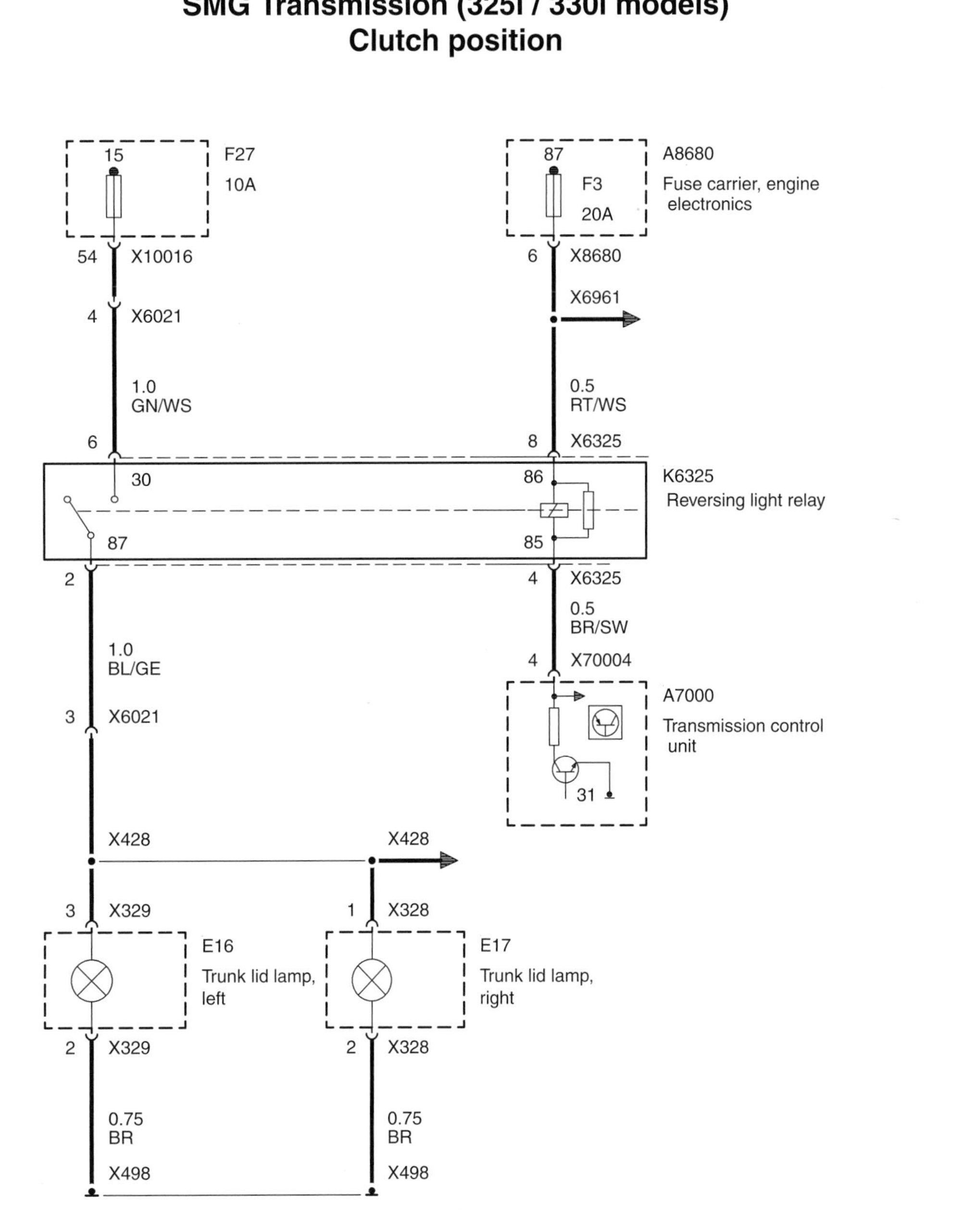
SMG Transmission (325i / 330i models)
Clutch position
15
F27
10A
54
X10016
4
X6021
1.0
GN/WS
6
87
F3
20A
A8680
Fuse carrier, engine electronics
6
X8680
X6961
0.5
RT/WS
8
X6325
30
86
K6325
Reversing light relay
87
85
2
4
X6325
0.5
BR/SW
4
X70004
A7000
Transmission control unit
31
1.0
BL/GE
3
X6021
X428
X428
3
X329
1
X328
E16
Trunk lid lamp, left
E17
Trunk lid lamp, right
2
X329
2
X328
0.75
BR
0.75
BR
X498
X498

SMG Transmission (325i / 330i models)
Shift lock selector lever lock

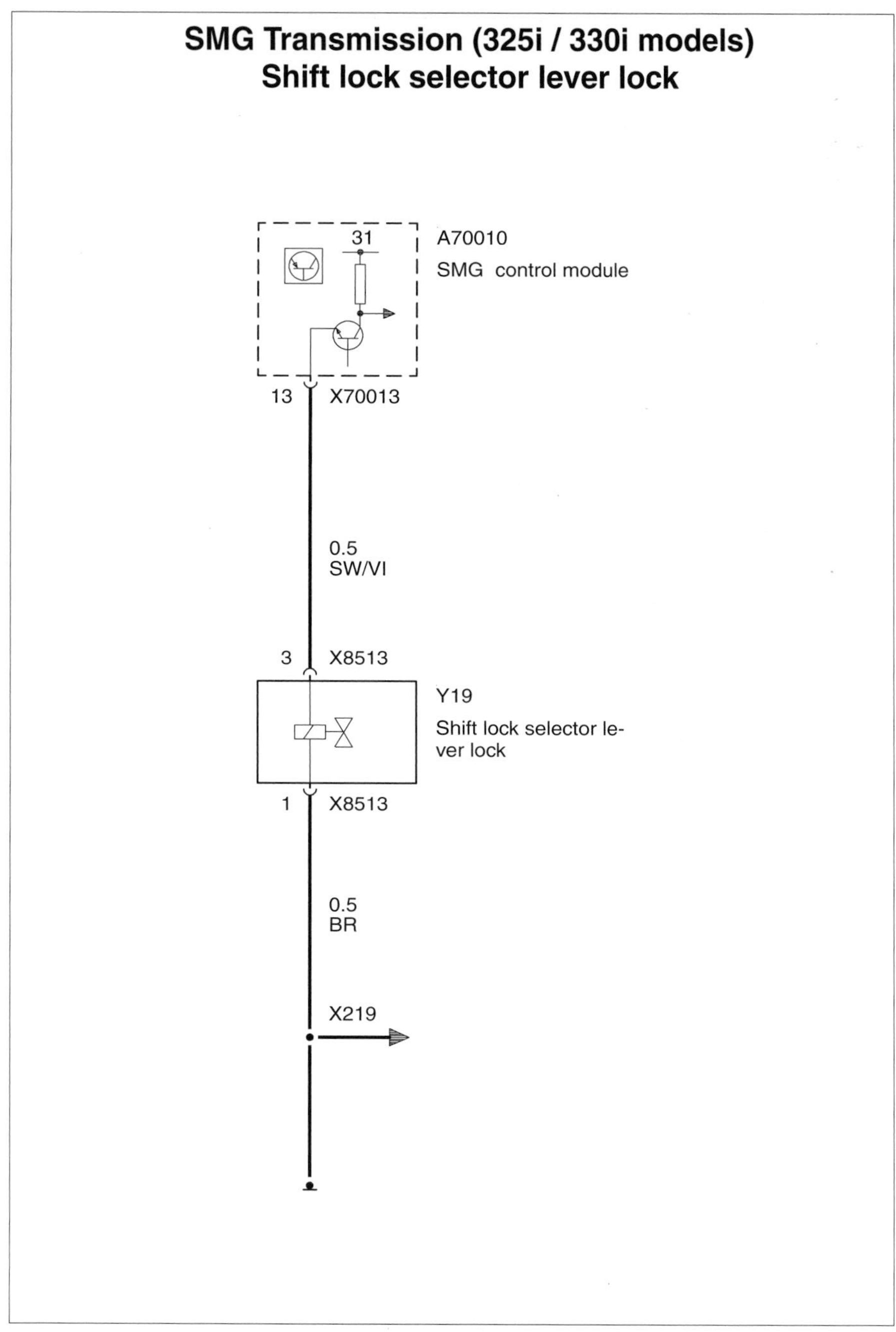

SMG II Transmission (M3)
Transmission gear oil temperature sensor

30
A5300
SMG2 control module
13
X53004
0.5
BR/SW
1
X5238
B5238
Transmission fluid
temperature sensor
2
X5238
X06462
0.5
BR
31
X53004
A5300
SMG2 control module
31

SMG II Transmission (M3)
Upshift/downshift

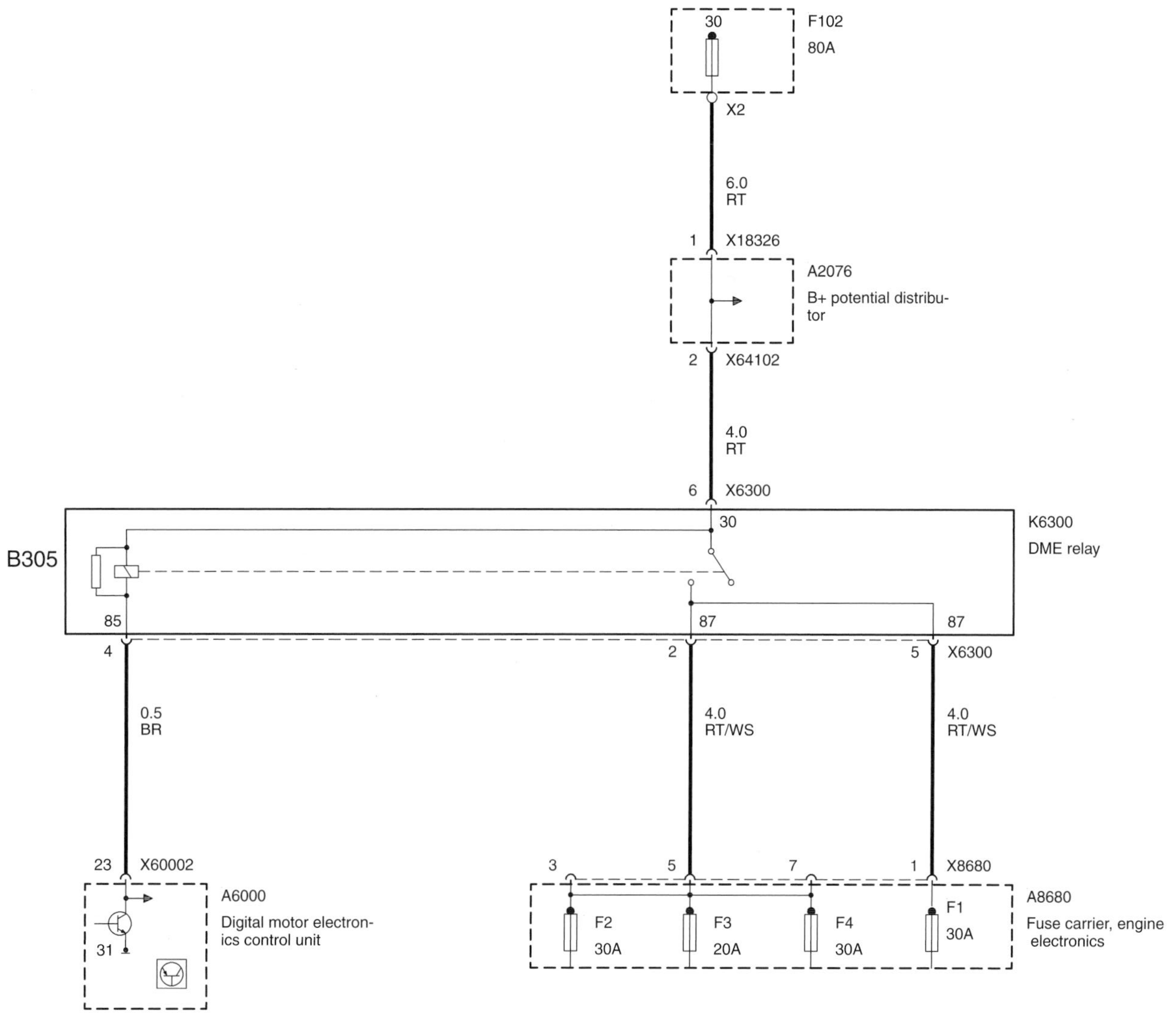

F102
80A
30
X2
6.0
RT
1
X18326
A2076
B+ potential distributor
2
X64102
4.0
RT
6
X6300
30
K6300
DME relay
B305
85
87
87
4
2
5
X6300
0.5
BR
4.0
RT/WS
4.0
RT/WS
23
X60002
A6000
Digital motor electronics control unit
31
3
5
7
1
X8680
A8680
Fuse carrier, engine electronics
F2
30A
F3
20A
F4
30A
F1
30A

SMG II Transmission (M3)
Hood contacts
(up to 03/2003)

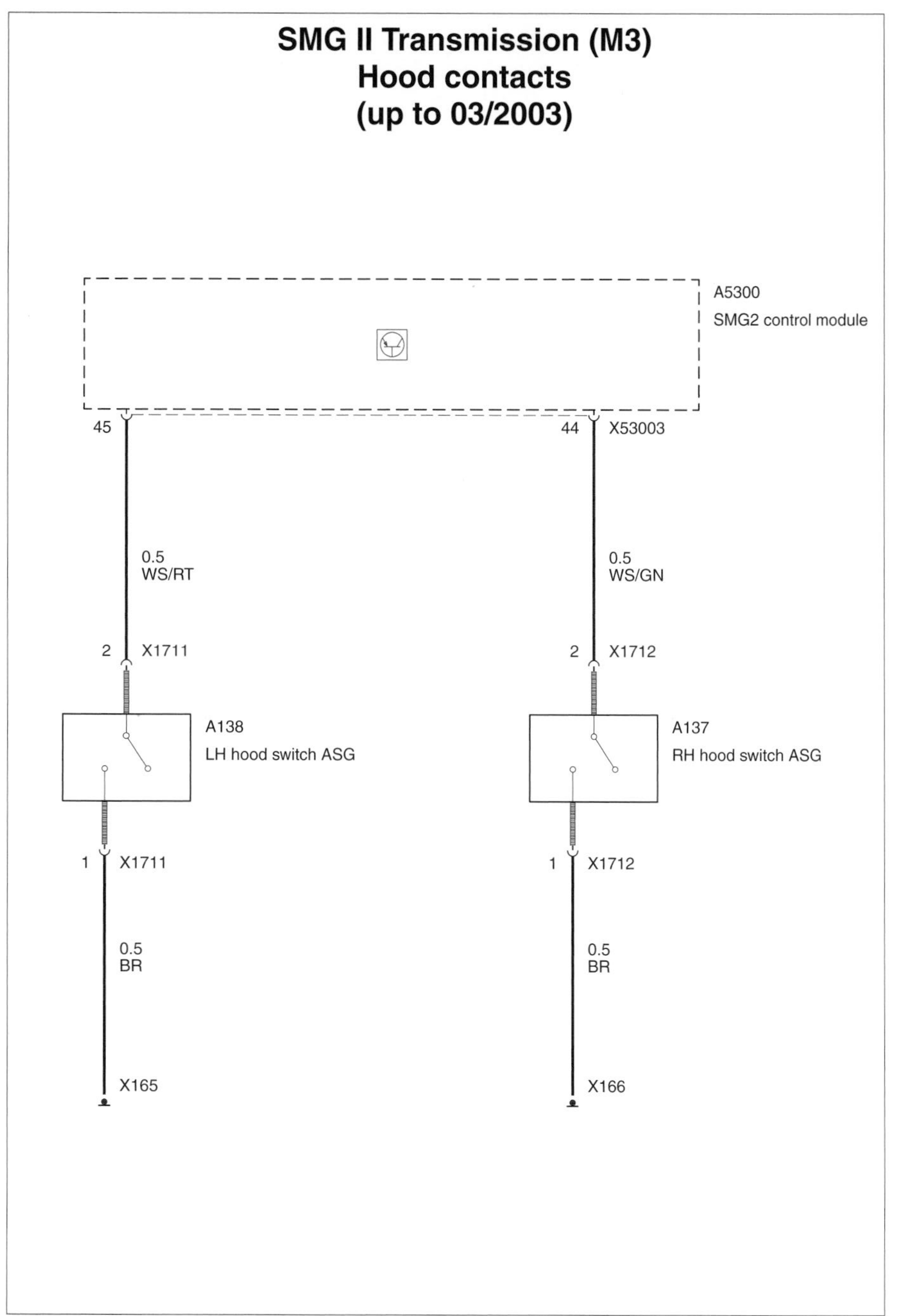

SMG II Transmission (M3)
Hood contacts
(from 03/2003)

A5300
SMG2 control module
45
44
X53003
0.5
WS/RT
0.5
WS/GN
2
X1711
2
X1712
A138
LH hood switch ASG
A137
RH hood switch ASG
1
X1711
1
X1712
0.5
BR
0.5
BR
X14249
X14250

SMG II Transmission (M3)
Selector position angle sensor

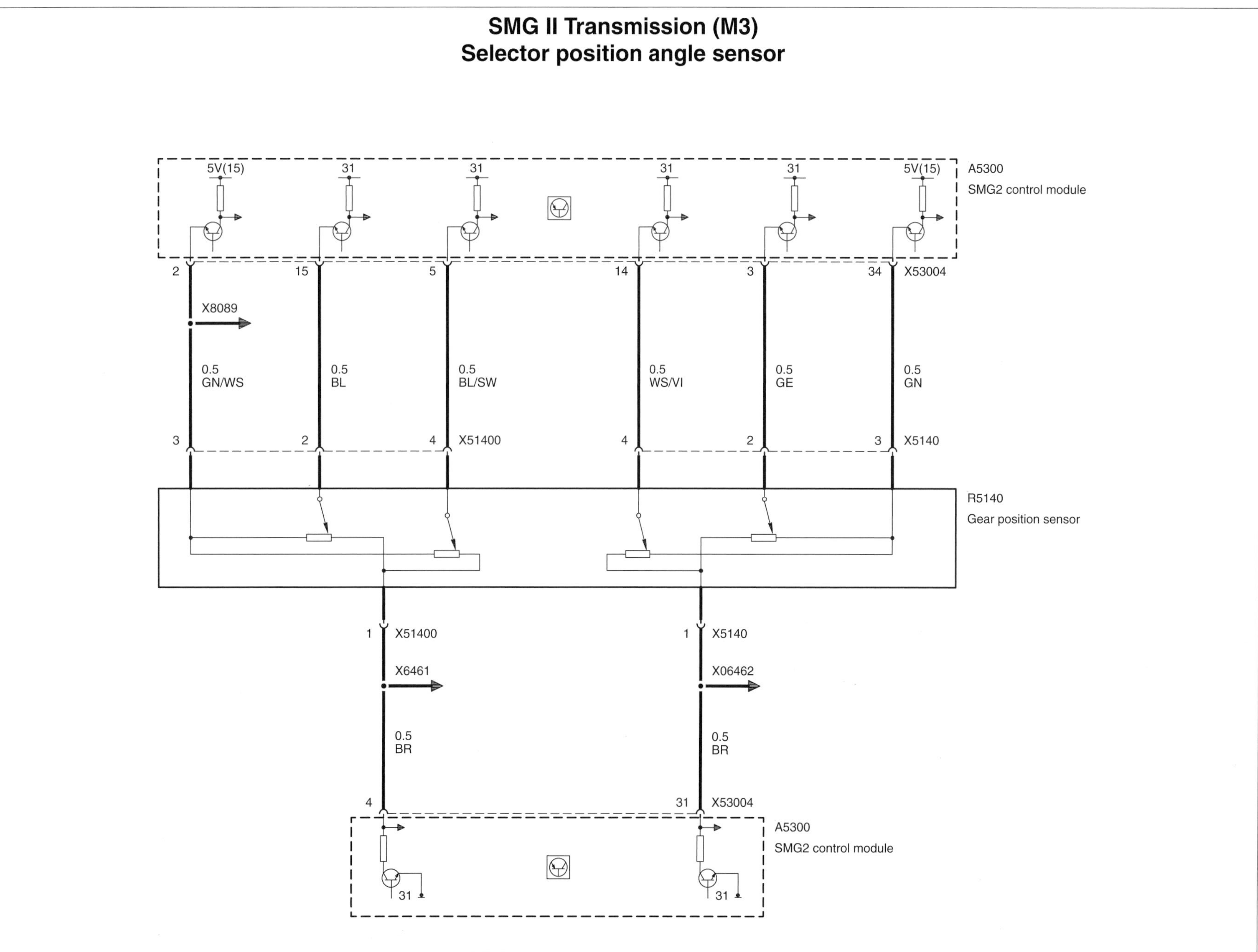

SMG II Transmission (M3)
Transmission speed sensor
(up to 09/2001)

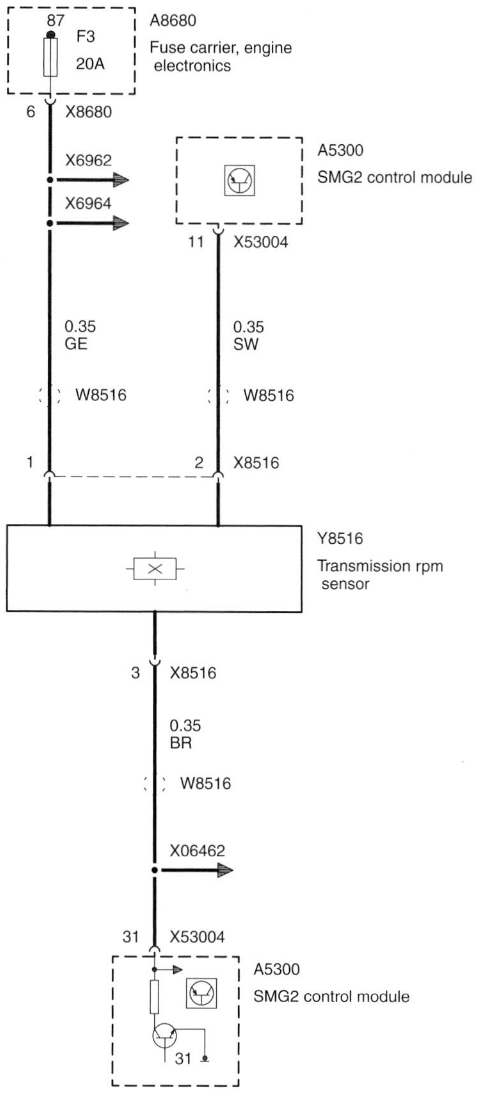

SMG II Transmission (M3)
Transmission speed sensor
(from 09/2001)

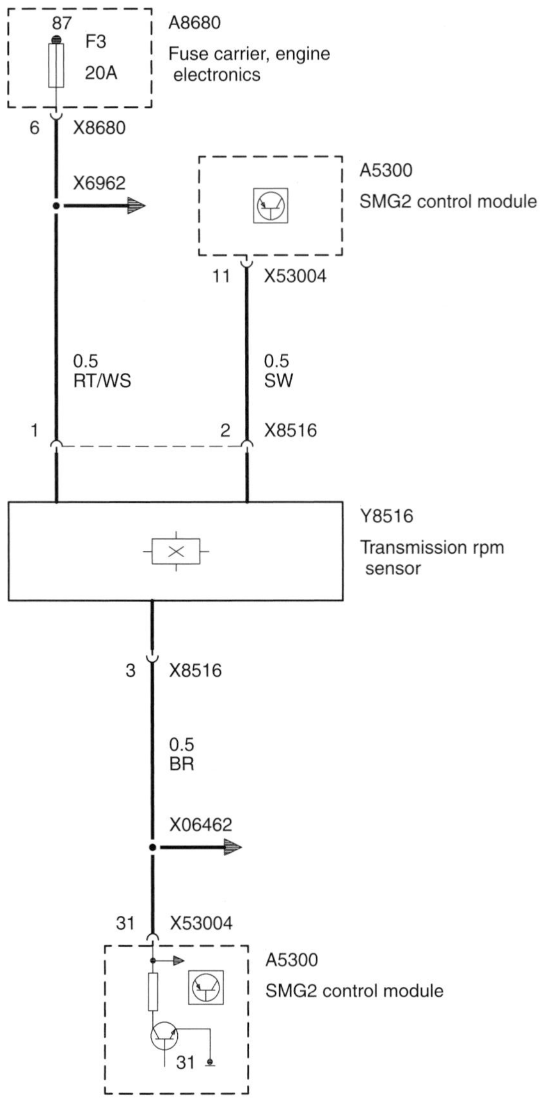

SMG II Transmission (M3)
Selector lever

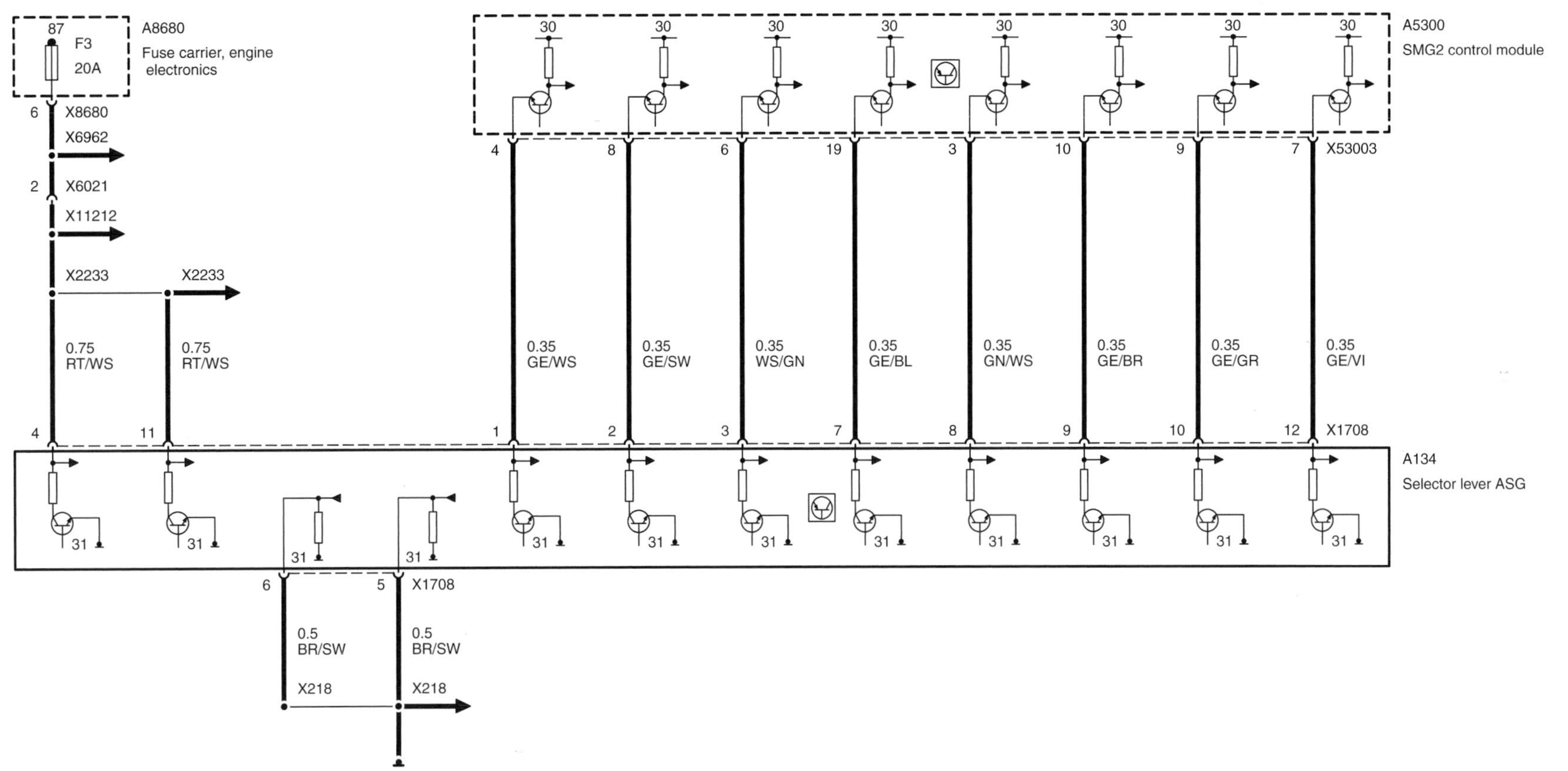

SMG II Transmission (M3)
Clutch position sensor

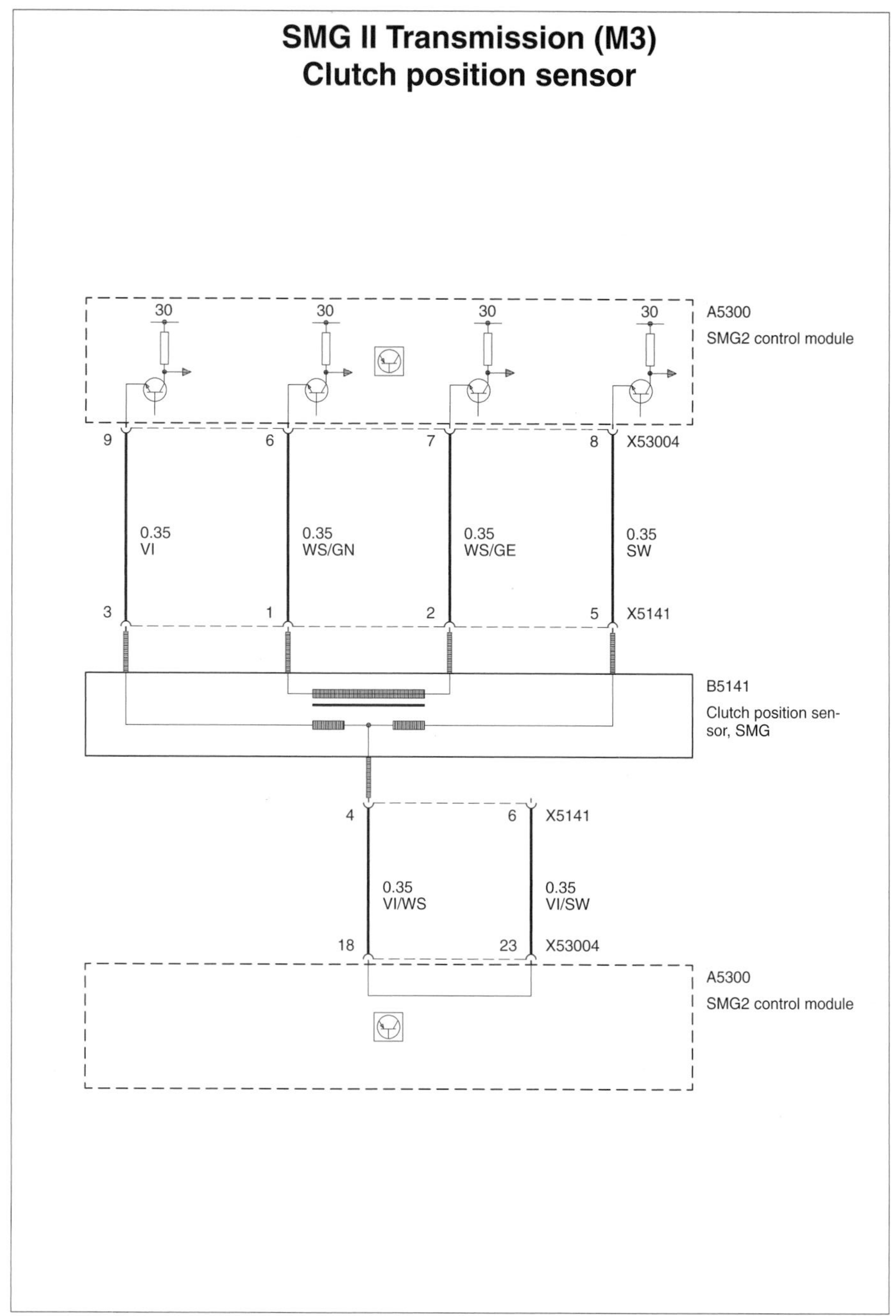

SMG II Transmission (M3)
Longitudinal acceleration sensor

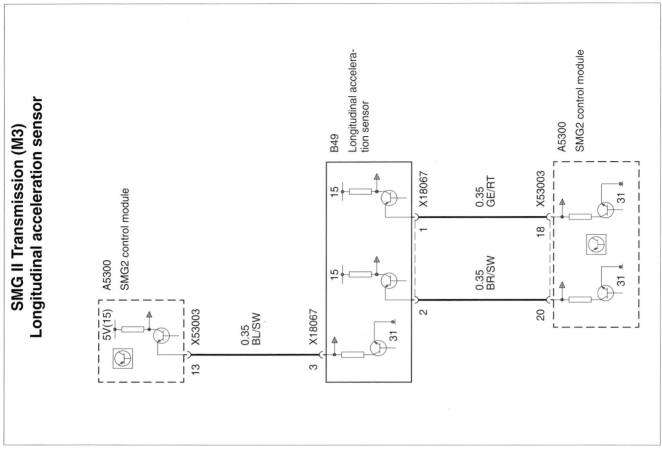

5V(15)
A5300
SMG2 control module
13 X53003
0.35
BL/SW
3 X18067
15
15
B49
Longitudinal accelera-
tion sensor
31
2
1
X18067
0.35
BR/SW
0.35
GE/RT
20
18
X53003
A5300
SMG2 control module
31
31

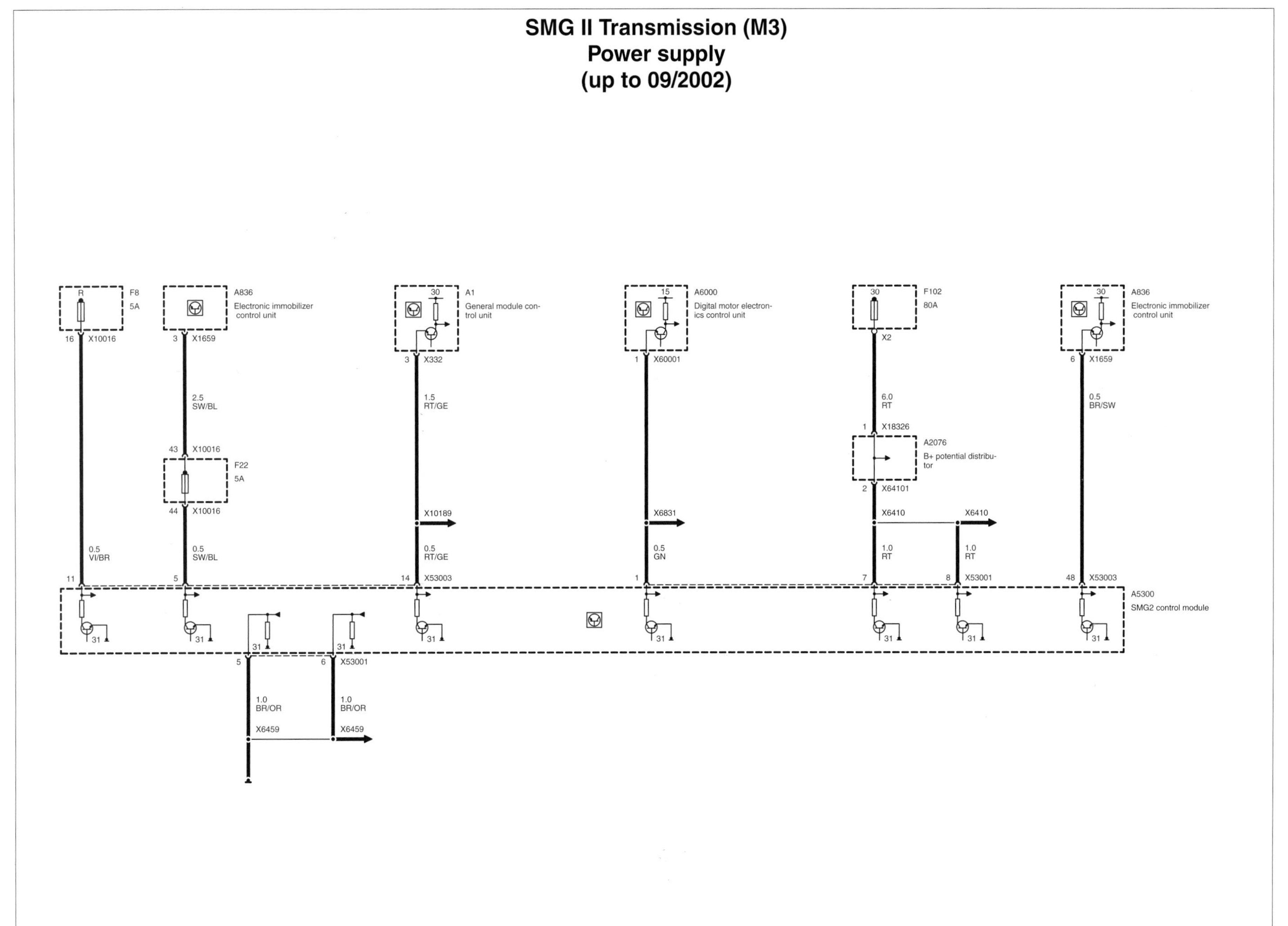
SMG II Transmission (M3)
Power supply
(up to 09/2002)
F8
5A
R
16 X10016
0.5
VI/BR
11
A836
Electronic immobilizer
control unit
3 X1659
2.5
SW/BL
43 X10016
F22
5A
44 X10016
0.5
SW/BL
5
A1
General module con-
trol unit
30
3 X332
1.5
RT/GE
X10189
0.5
RT/GE
14 X53003
A6000
Digital motor electron-
ics control unit
15
1 X60001
X6831
0.5
GN
1
F102
80A
30
X2
6.0
RT
1 X18326
A2076
B+ potential distribu-
tor
2 X64101
X6410
1.0
RT
7
X6410
1.0
RT
8 X53001
A836
Electronic immobilizer
control unit
30
6 X1659
0.5
BR/SW
48 X53003
A5300
SMG2 control module
31
5
6 X53001
1.0
BR/OR
X6459
1.0
BR/OR
X6459

SMG II Transmission (M3)
Power supply
(from 09/2002)

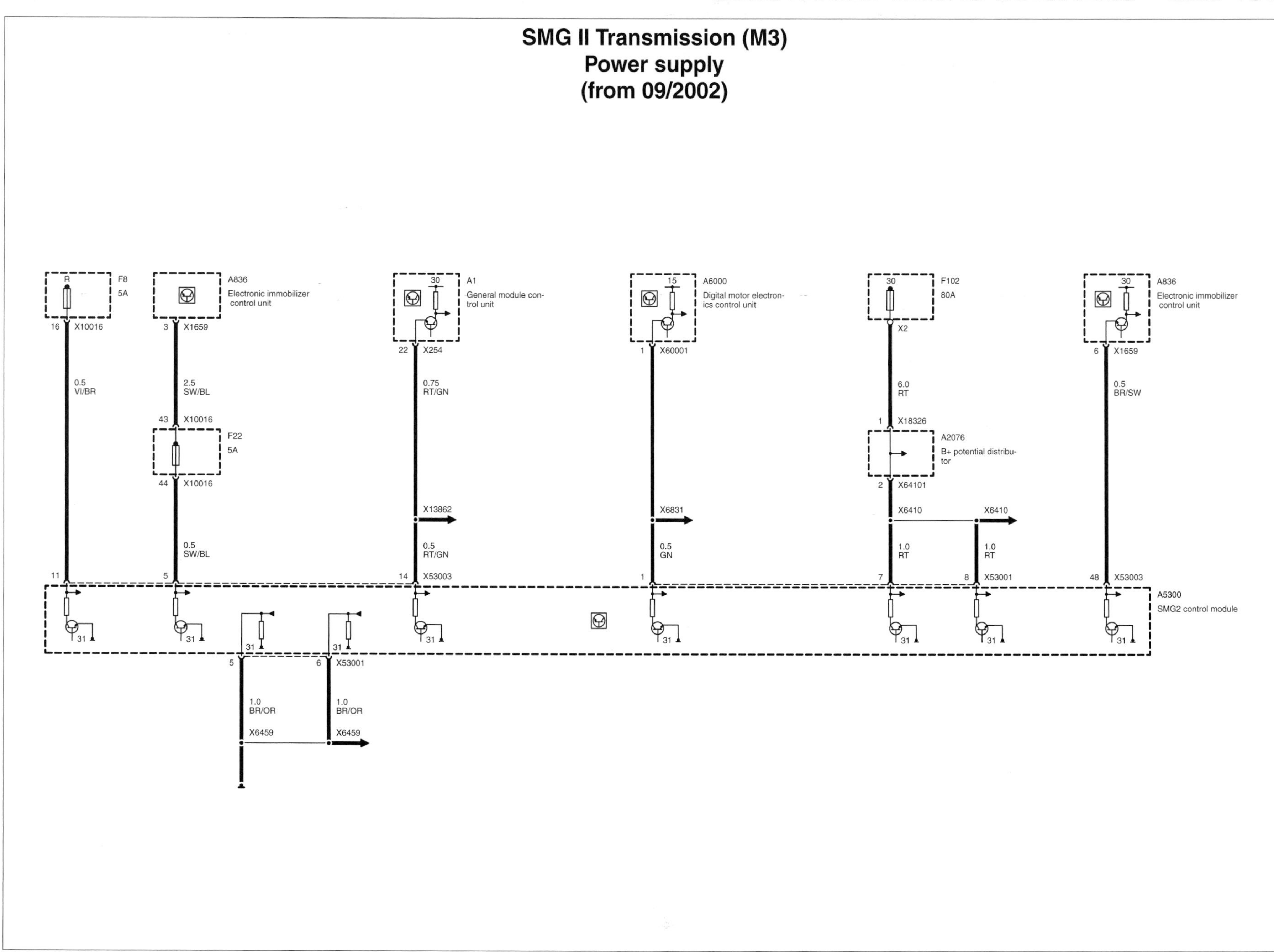

SMG II Transmission (M3)
Hydraulic unit

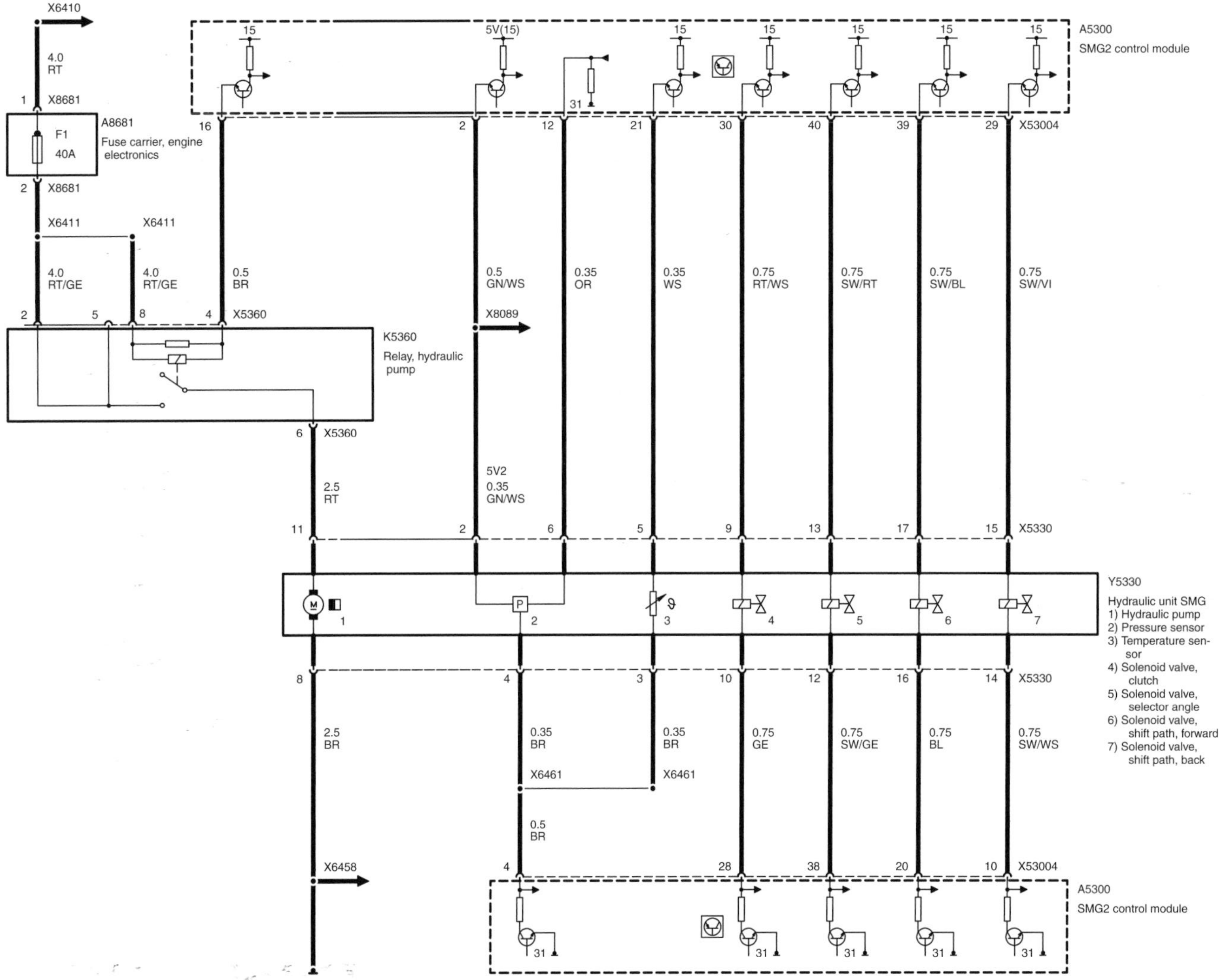

SMG II Transmission (M3)
Selector lever shift lock

87
F3
20A
A8680
Fuse carrier, engine electronics
6 X8680
X6962
2 X6021
X11212
X2233
0.75
RT/WS
3 X8513
Y19
Shift lock selector lever lock
1 X8513
0.5
SW/VI
26 X53003
A5300
SMG2 control module
31

This page intentionally left blank

Multifunction steering wheel

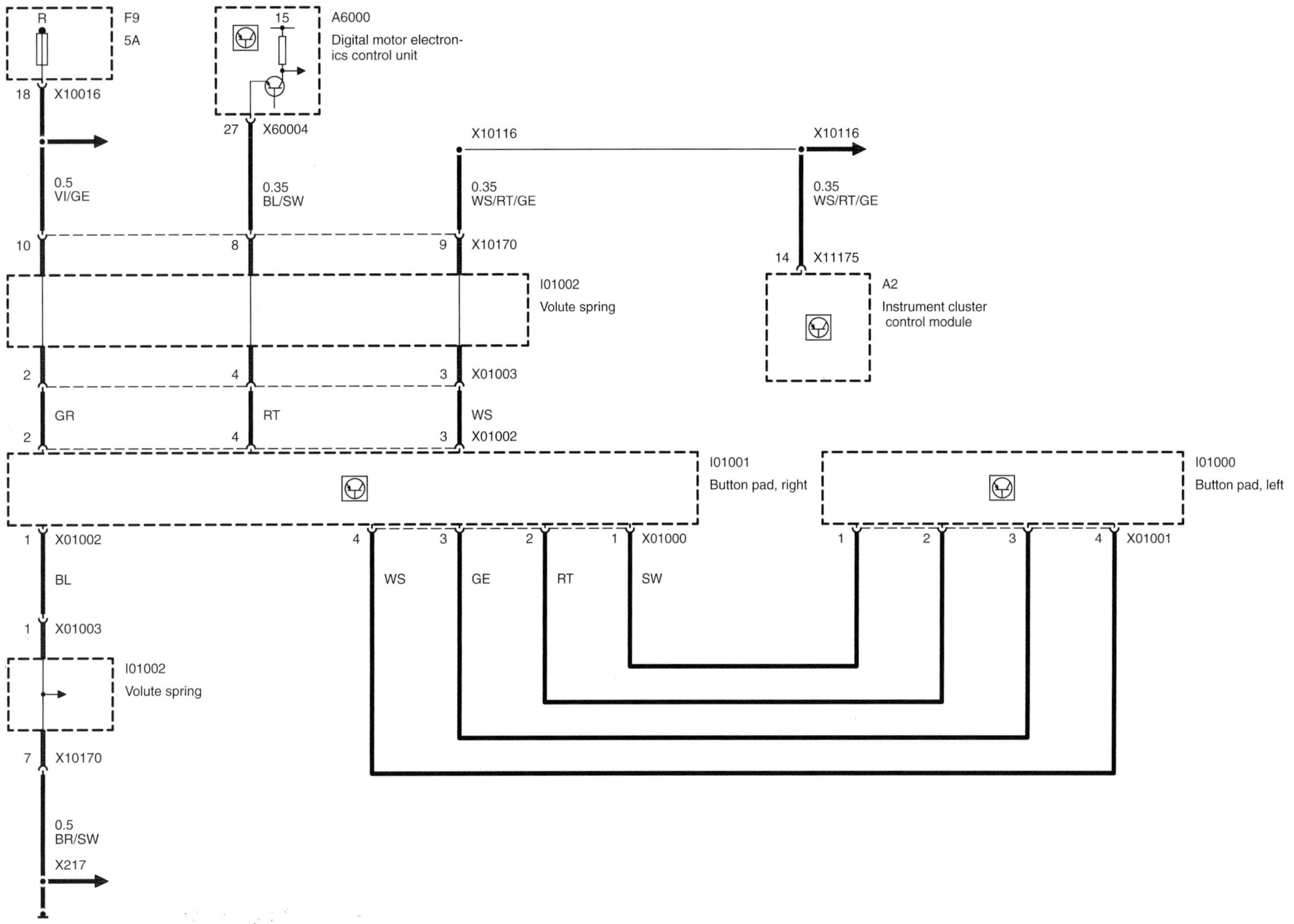

Brake light switch

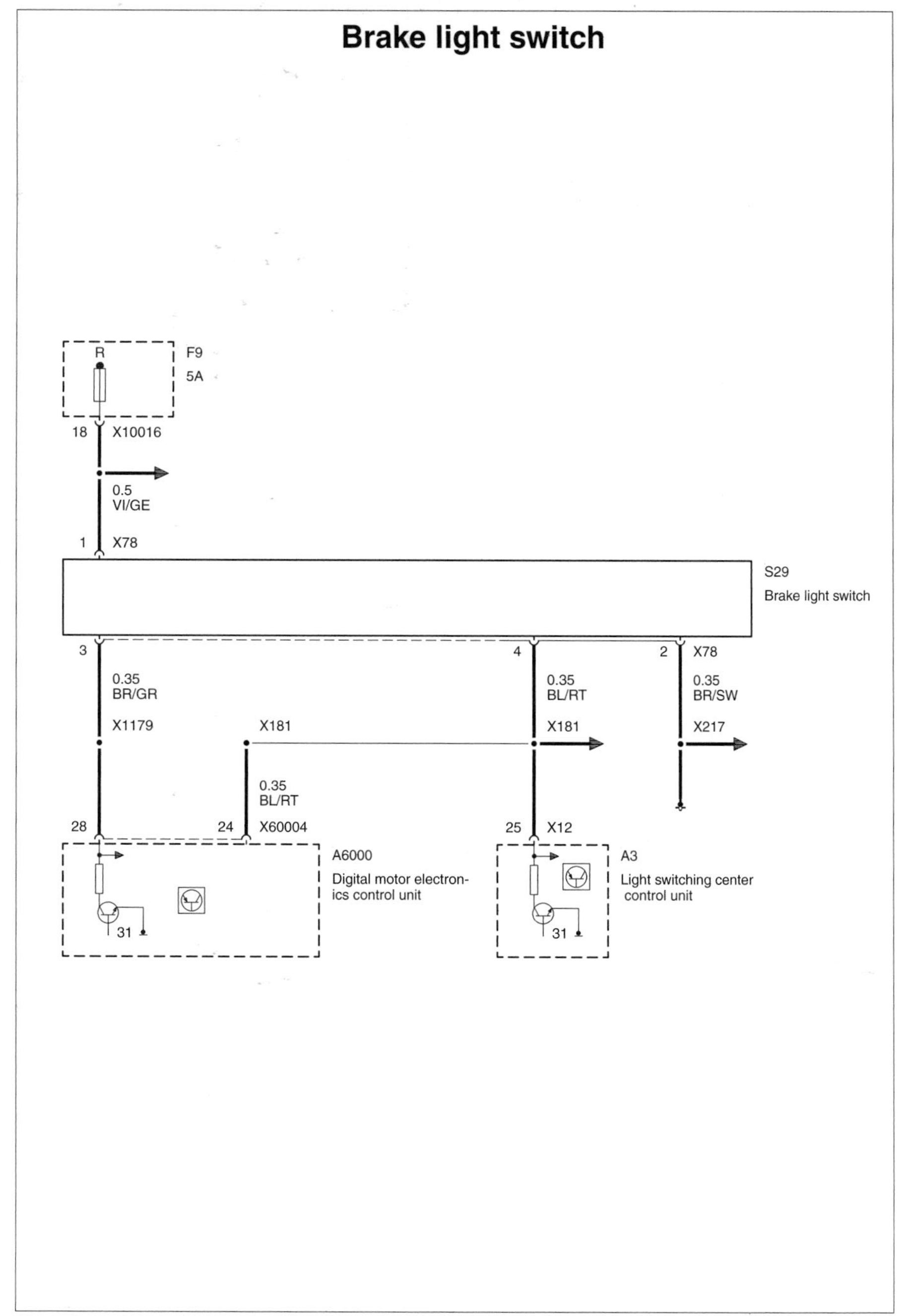

Clutch switch (up to 03/2001)

15
A6000
Digital motor electron-
ics control unit
R
F9
5A
18
X10016
23
X60004
0.35
BL/BR
0.5
VI/GE
2
3
X11143
S32
Clutch pedal position
switch
1
X11143
0.35
BR/SW
X217

Clutch switch (from 03/2001)

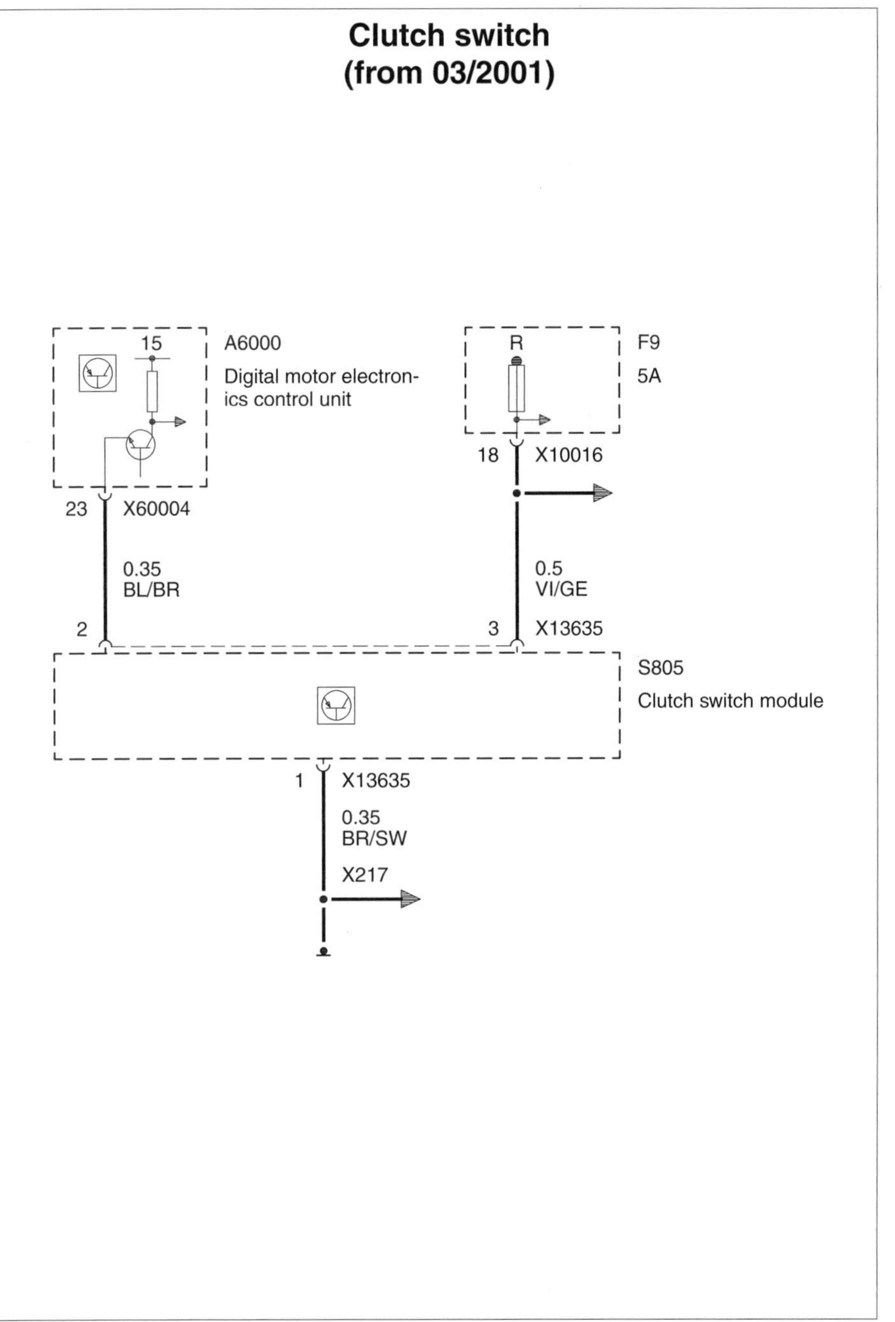

A/C compressor control

87
F3
20A
A8680
Fuse carrier, engine electronics
6 X8680
X6961
30
F63
7.5A
2 X6021
26 X10015
X11212
1.5
RT/WS
0.75
RT/VI/GE
4
2 X51
K19
Relay, A/C compressor
8
6
5 X51
0.5
SW/BL
0.75
SW/GR
0.75
RT/VI/GE
9 X610
A11
Heating and A/C control module
15
15
31
31
10
2
7 X610
1 X163
0.35
SW/GE
0.35
SW/GR
0.35
SW/GN
1
2
Y2
Solenoid clutch
1
2
3 X126
B8
Pressure sensor, air conditioning system
P
29 X60004
A6000
Digital motor electronics control unit
31

Engine cooling system (from 09/1999)

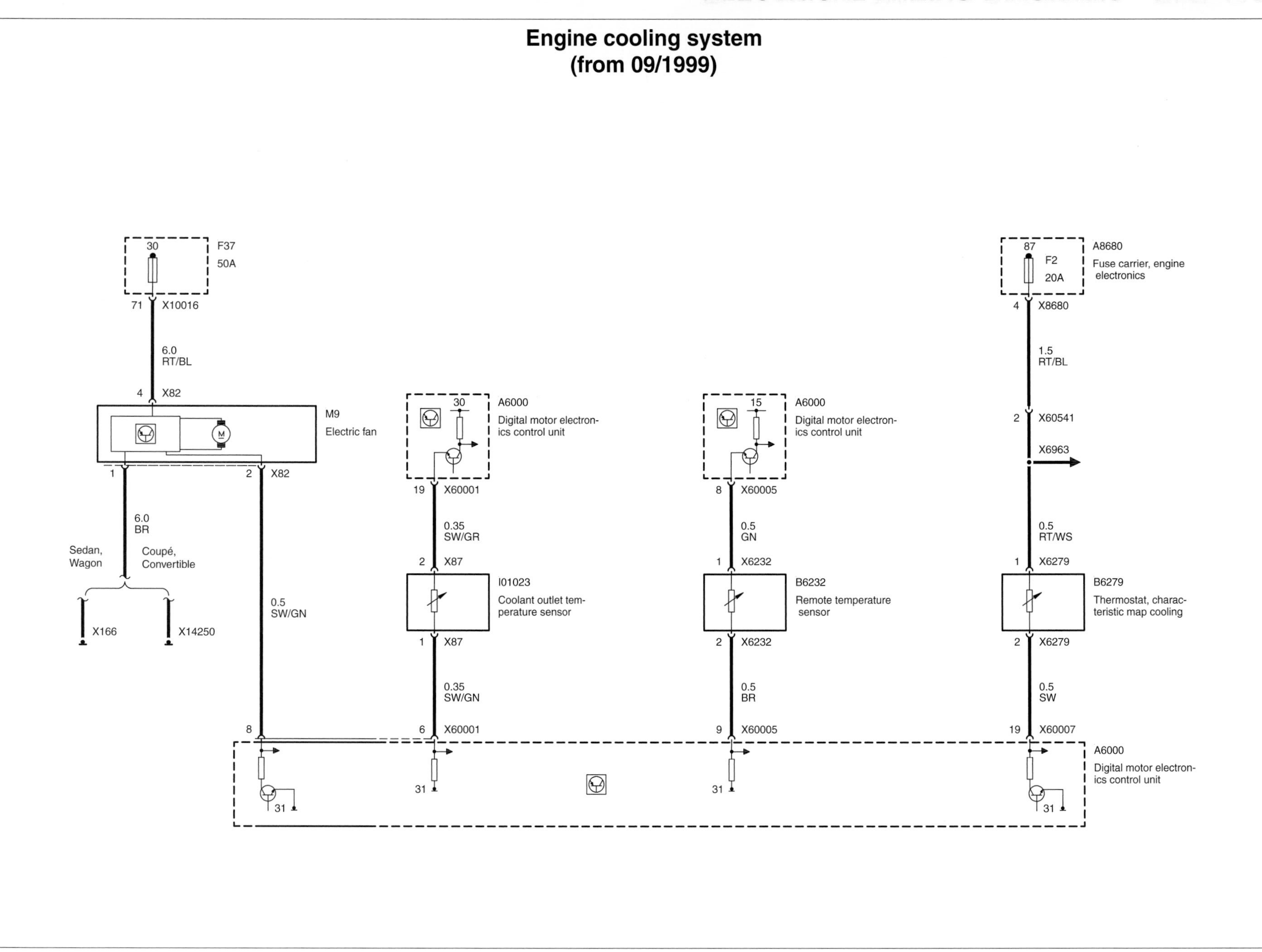

Engine cooling fan (up to 03/2003)

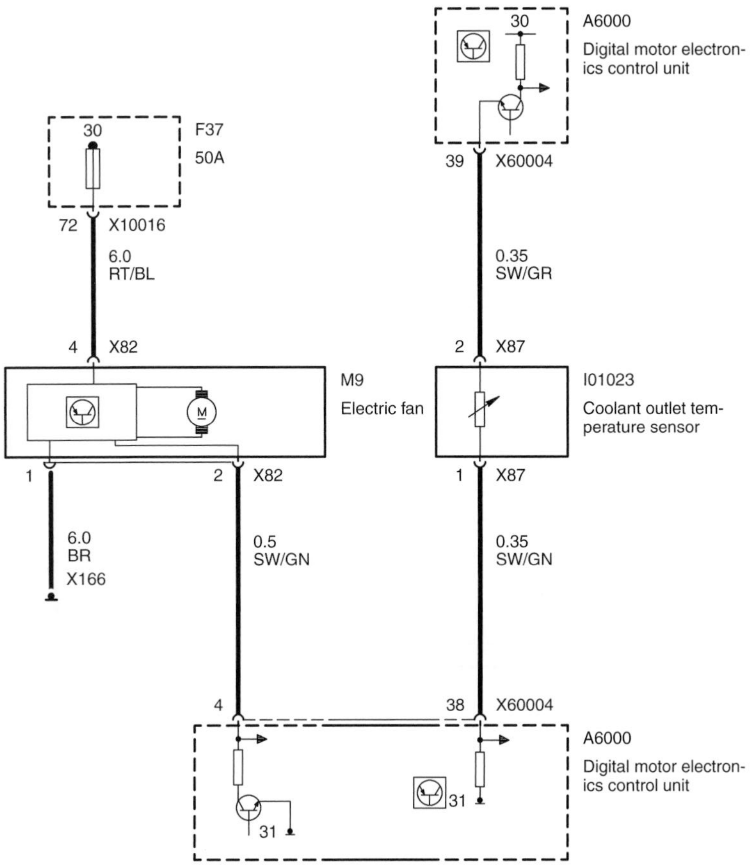

Engine cooling fan sedan and wagon (from 03/2003)

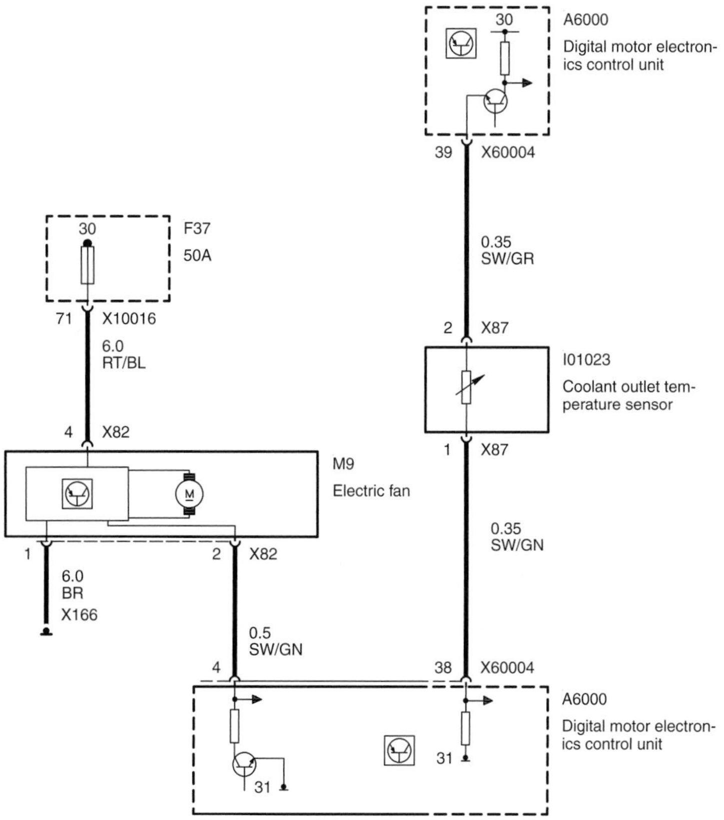

Engine cooling fan coupe and convertible (from 03/2003)

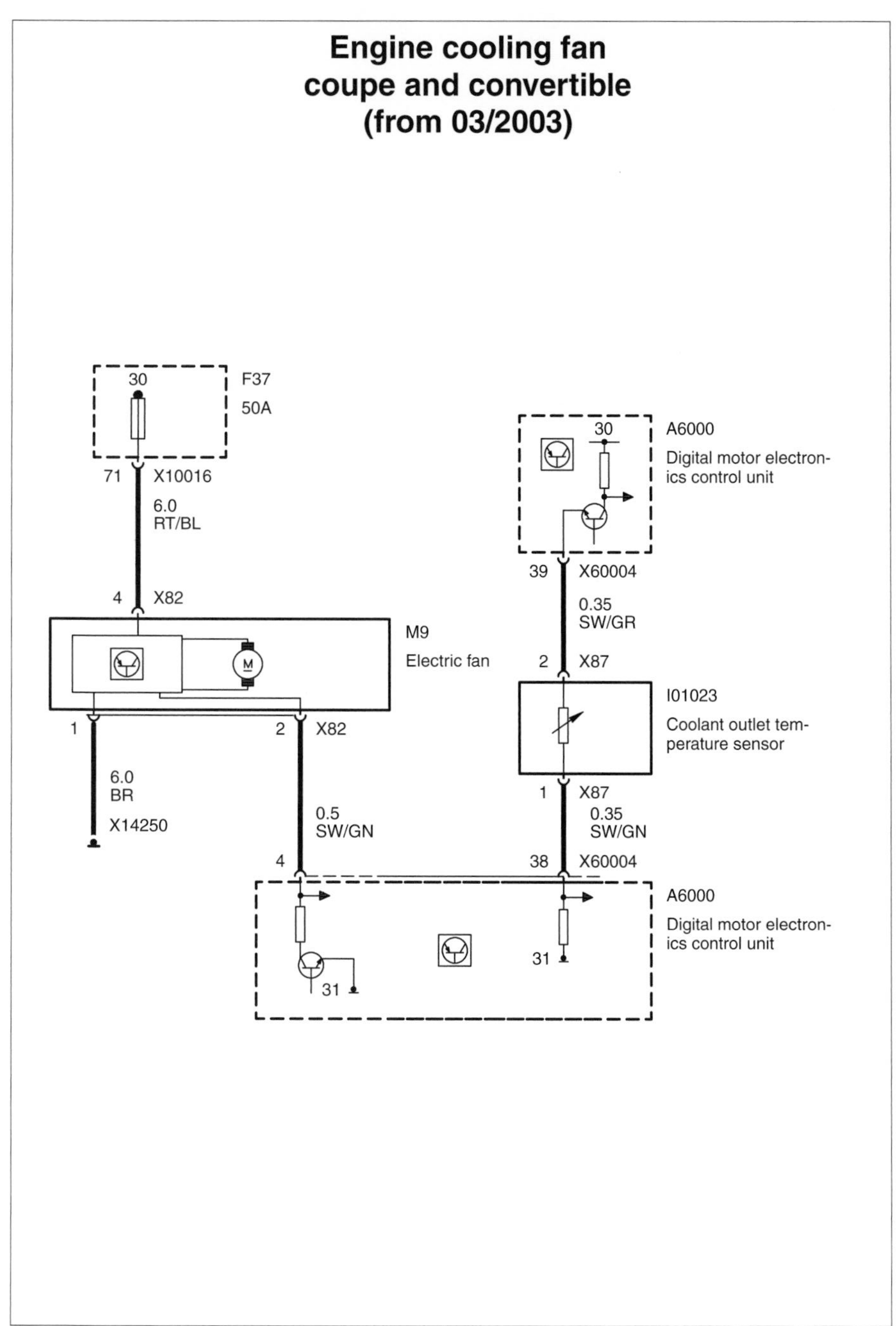

OBD II socket

A7000
32
X70004
0.5
WS/VI
3
X60001
A6000
32
X60004
F43
5A
30
6
X10015
F30
7.5A
60
15
X10016
X183
X243
0.5
RT/GE/WS
0.75
GN/BR
0.5
WS/VI
0.35
WS/VI
0.35
SW
16
1
7
8
9
X19527
4
5
X19527
0.5
BR
X173
0.5
BR/SW
X1108

Road speed signal ASC Mark 20 (up to 09/2001)

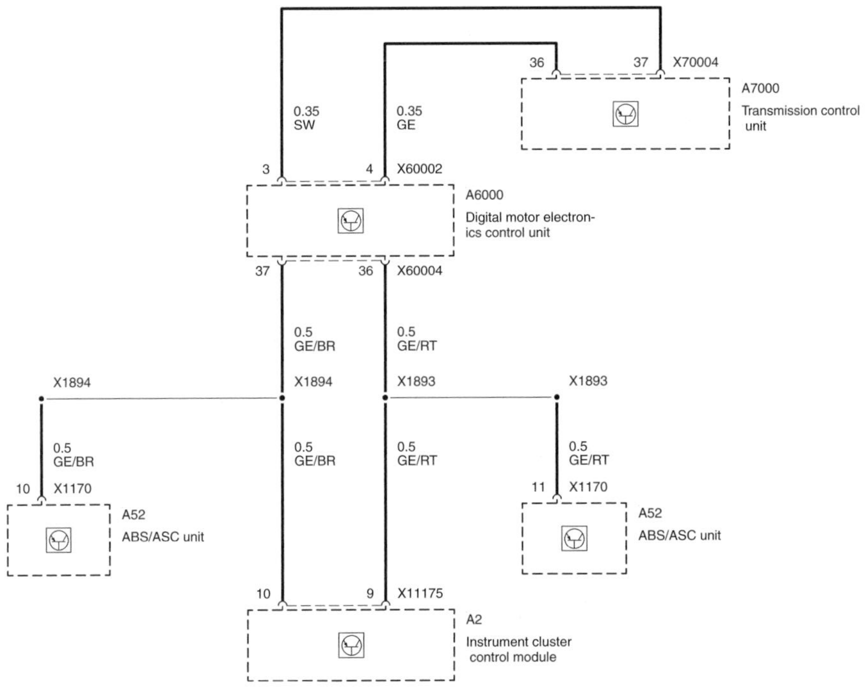

Road speed signal DSC Mark 20

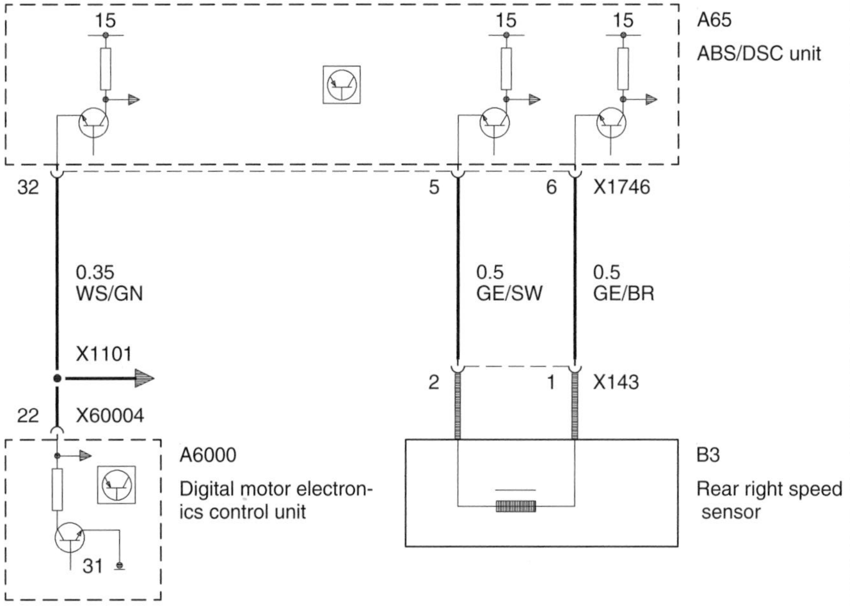

Road speed signal
DSC Mark 60

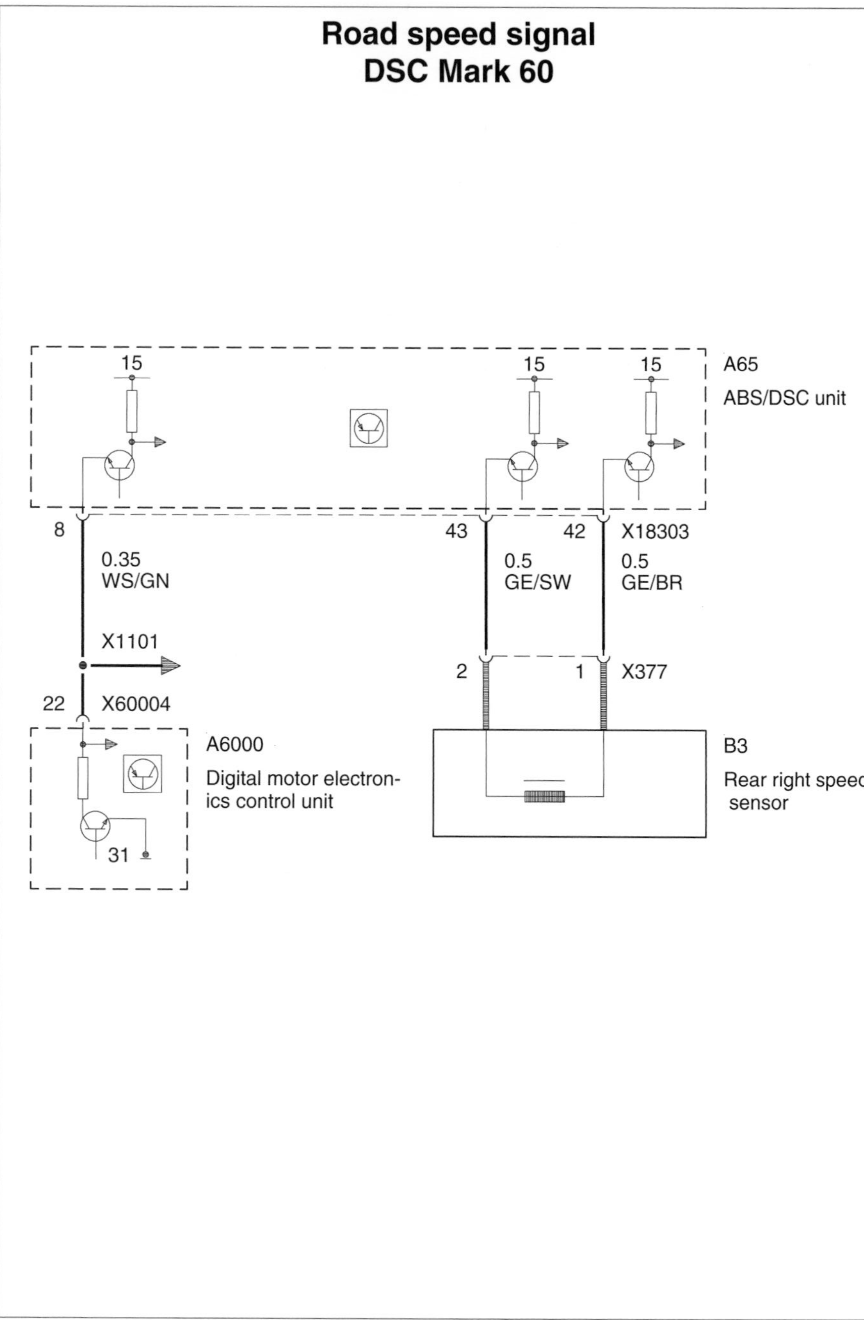

Processed wheel speed
Right rear sensor

15
A52
ABS/ASC unit
8
X18303
0.35
WS/GN
X1101
0.35
WS/GN
22
X60004
A6000
Digital motor electron-
ics control unit
31

Interface signals

15
A7000
Transmission control unit
3 X70003
0.35
BR/SW
6 X1659
30
A836
Electronic immobilizer control unit
31
4 X1659
0.35
SW/VI
33 X60004
A6000
Digital motor electronics control unit
31

This page intentionally left blank

CAN bus connector (from 09/2001)

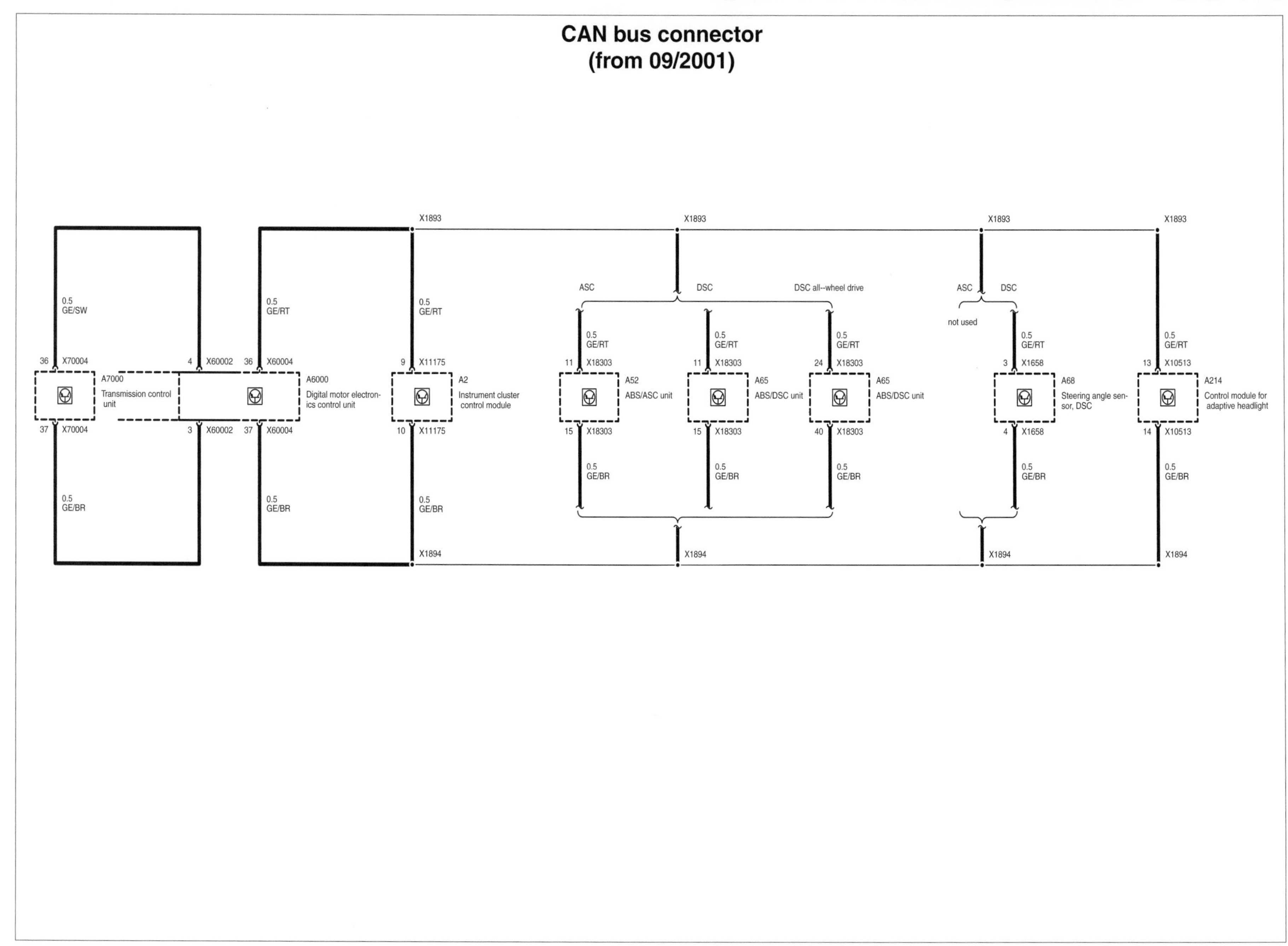

CAN bus connector ASC Mark 20 (up to 09/2001)

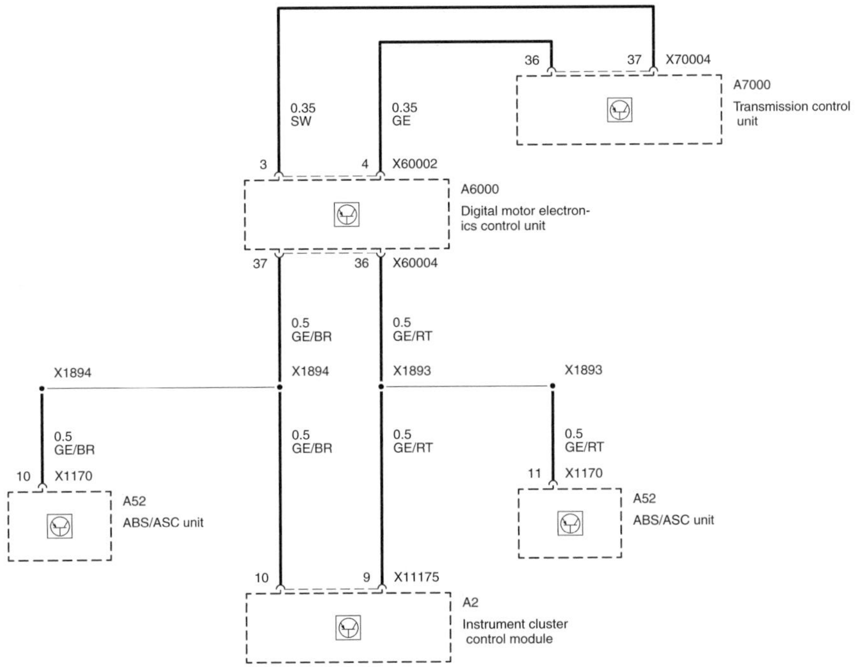

A7000 Transmission control unit
36 37 X70004

0.35 SW
0.35 GE

3 4 X60002

A6000 Digital motor electronics control unit

37 36 X60004

0.5 GE/BR
0.5 GE/RT

X1894
X1894
X1893
X1893

0.5 GE/BR
0.5 GE/BR
0.5 GE/RT
0.5 GE/RT

10 X1170
A52 ABS/ASC unit

11 X1170
A52 ABS/ASC unit

10 9 X11175
A2 Instrument cluster control module

CAN bus connector DSC Mark 20

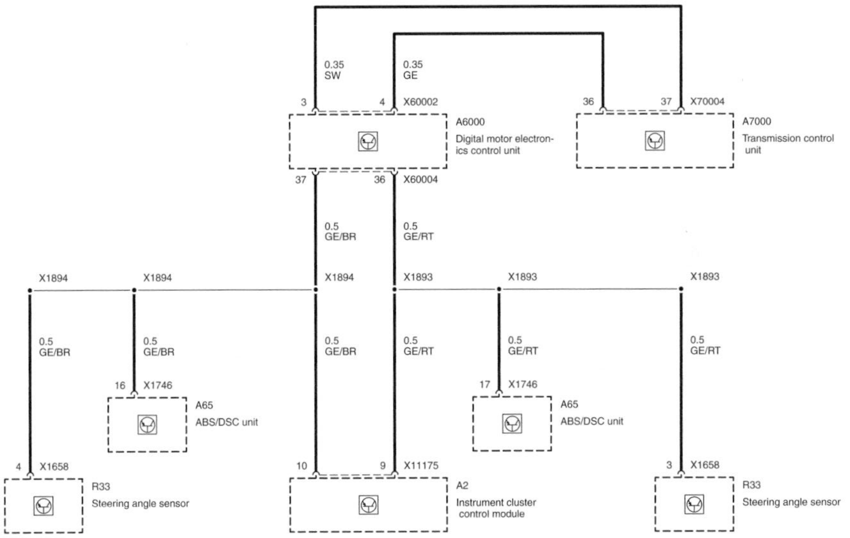

0.35 SW
0.35 GE

3 4 X60002
A6000 Digital motor electronics control unit

36 37 X70004
A7000 Transmission control unit

37 36 X60004

0.5 GE/BR
0.5 GE/RT

X1894
X1894
X1894
X1893
X1893
X1893

0.5 GE/BR
0.5 GE/BR
0.5 GE/BR
0.5 GE/RT
0.5 GE/RT
0.5 GE/RT

16 X1746
A65 ABS/DSC unit

17 X1746
A65 ABS/DSC unit

4 X1658
R33 Steering angle sensor

10 9 X11175
A2 Instrument cluster control module

3 X1658
R33 Steering angle sensor

CAN bus connector DSC III 5.7

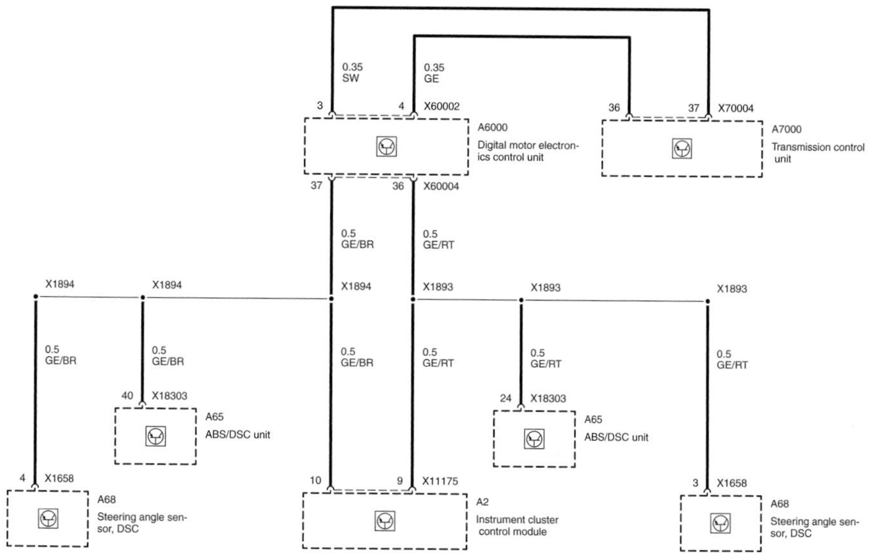

CAN bus connector DSC Mark 60

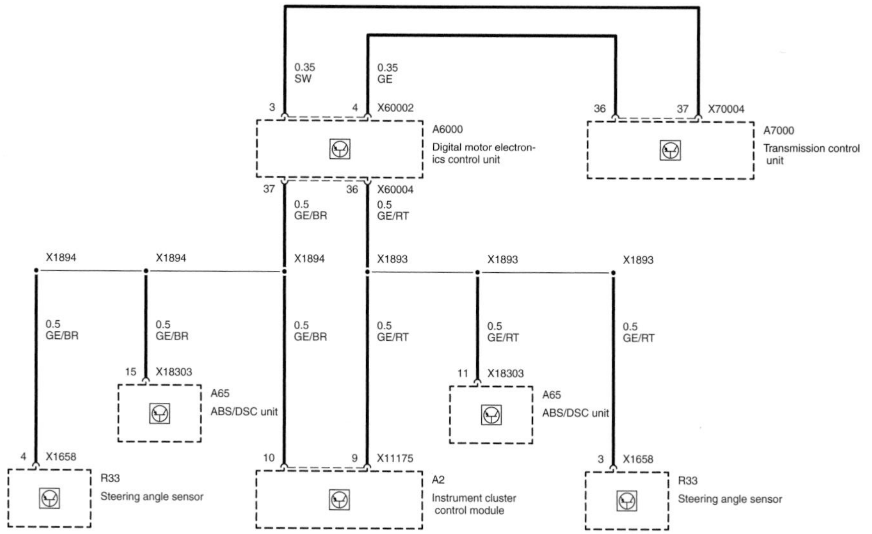

Charging system MS 42

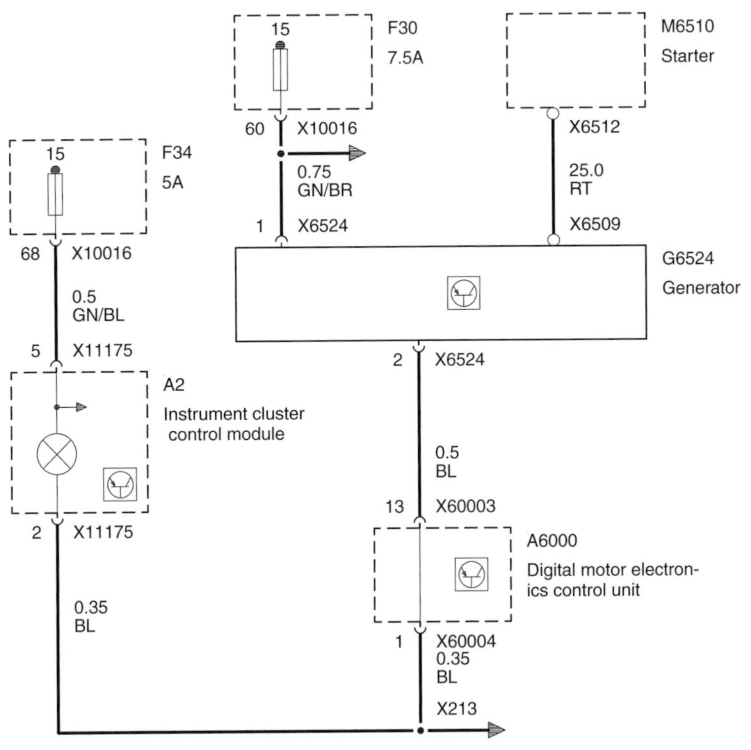

F34
5A
15
68 X10016
0.5
GN/BL
5 X11175
A2
Instrument cluster control module
2 X11175
0.35
BL

F30
7.5A
15
60 X10016
0.75
GN/BR
1 X6524

M6510
Starter
X6512
25.0
RT
X6509

G6524
Generator
2 X6524
0.5
BL
13 X60003
A6000
Digital motor electronics control unit
1 X60004
0.35
BL
X213

Charging system MS 43

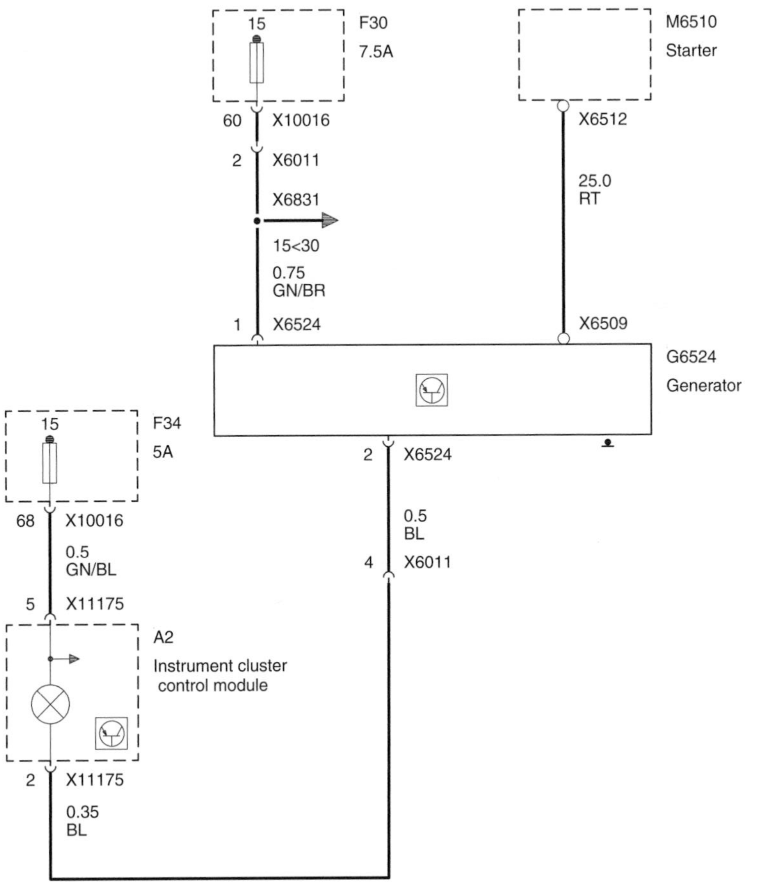

F30
7.5A
15
60 X10016
2 X6011
X6831
15<30
0.75
GN/BR
1 X6524

M6510
Starter
X6512
25.0
RT
X6509

G6524
Generator
2 X6524
0.5
BL
4 X6011

F34
5A
15
68 X10016
0.5
GN/BL
5 X11175
A2
Instrument cluster control module
2 X11175
0.35
BL

Charging system MS 45.1

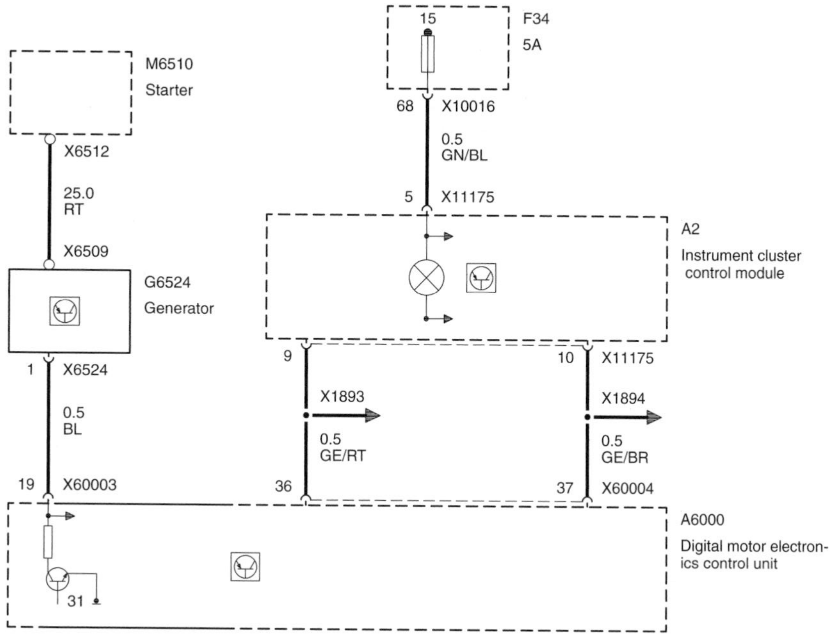

Charging system MS S54 (up to 03/2004)

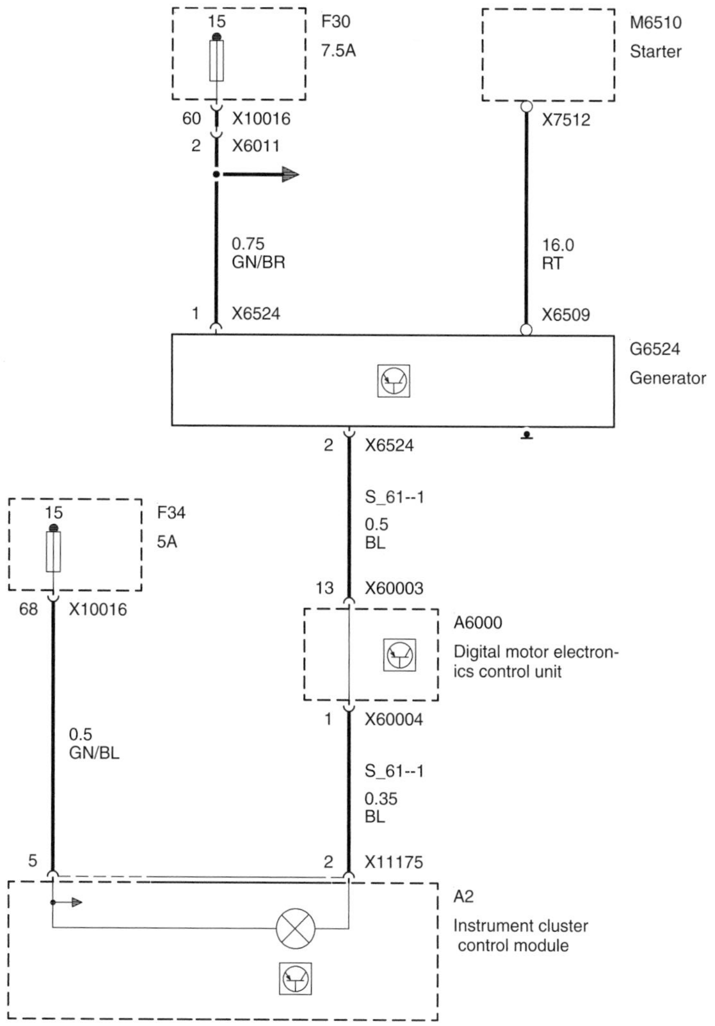

Charging system MS S54 (from 03/2004)

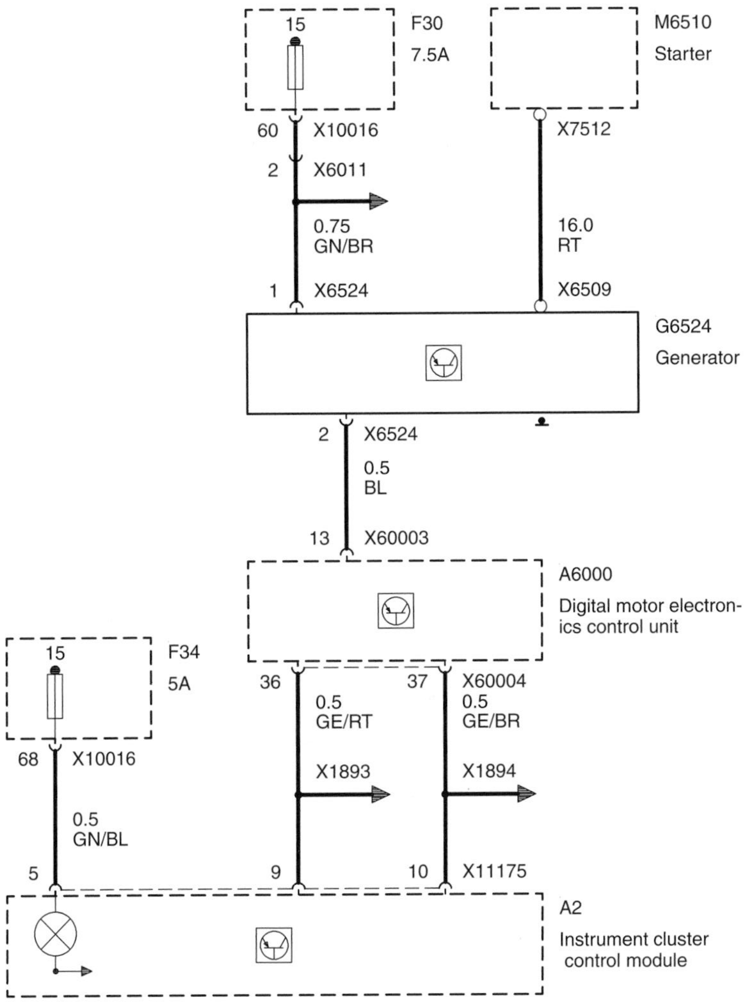

Power window, convertible Driver's side (from 09/2003)

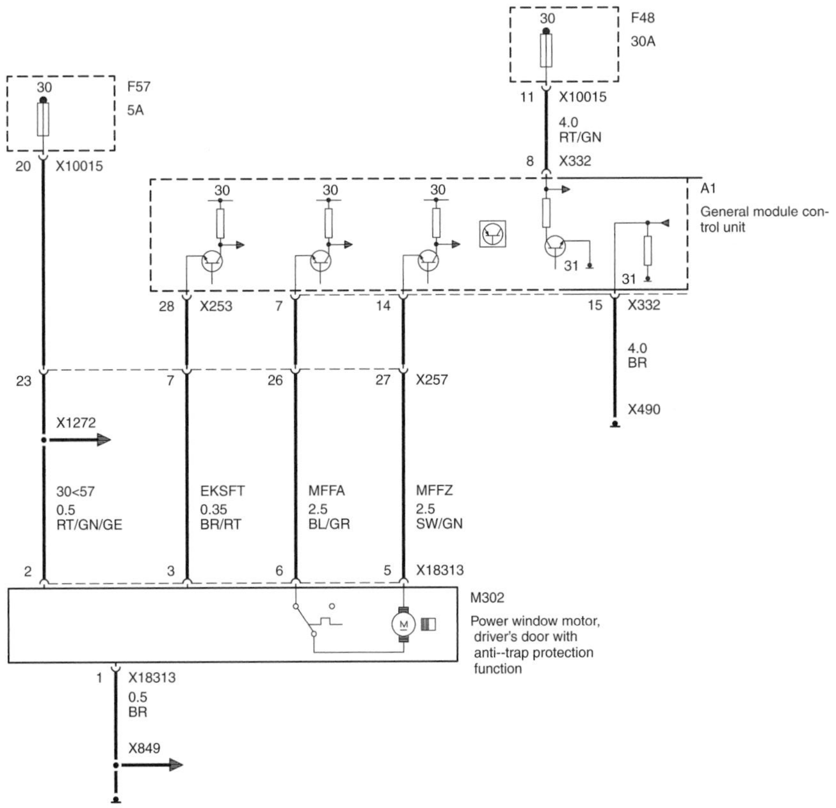

Power window, convertible Passenger's side (from 09/2003)

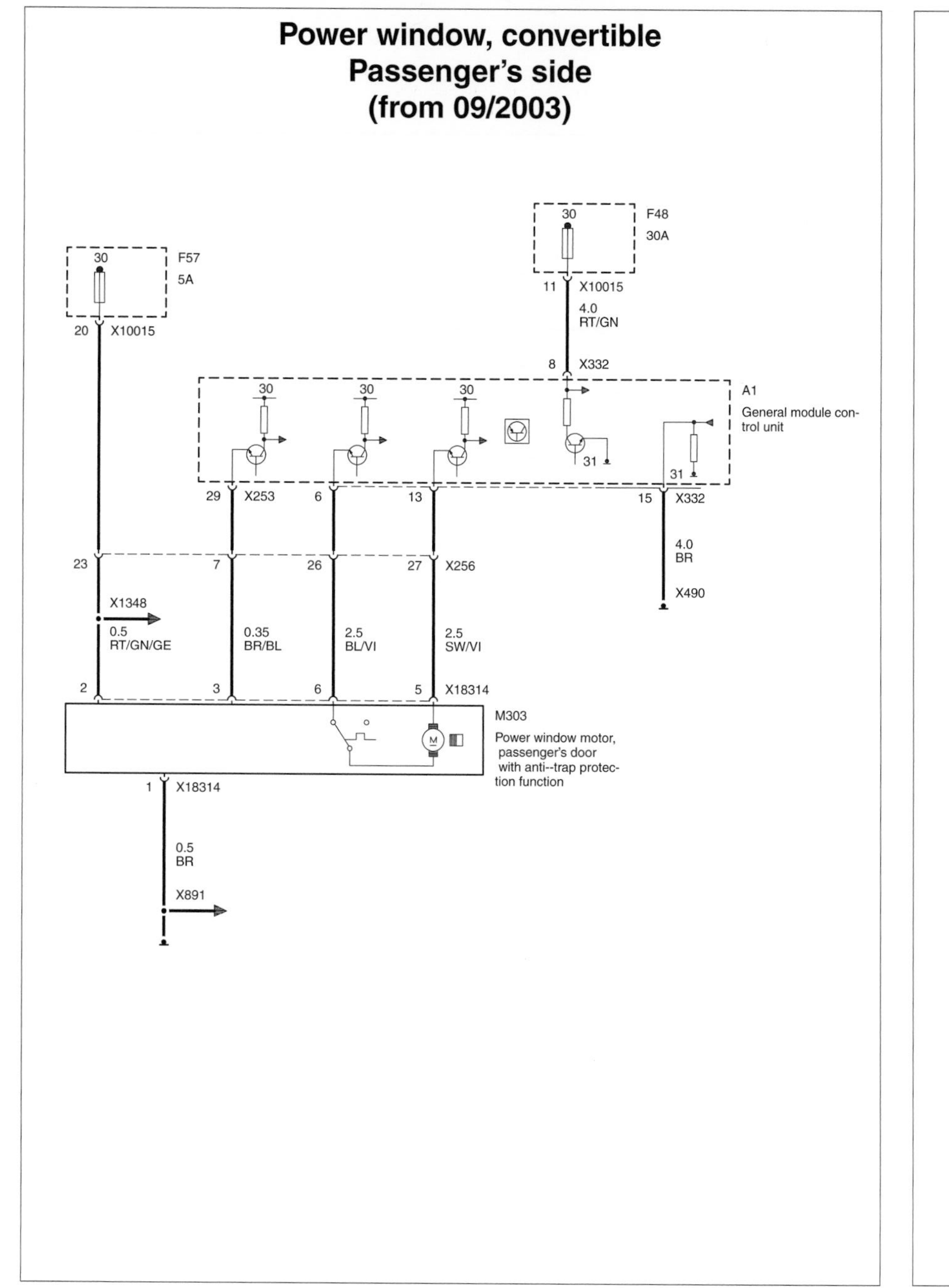

This page intentionally left blank

General module
Coupe (from 09/2003)
(page 1 of 4)

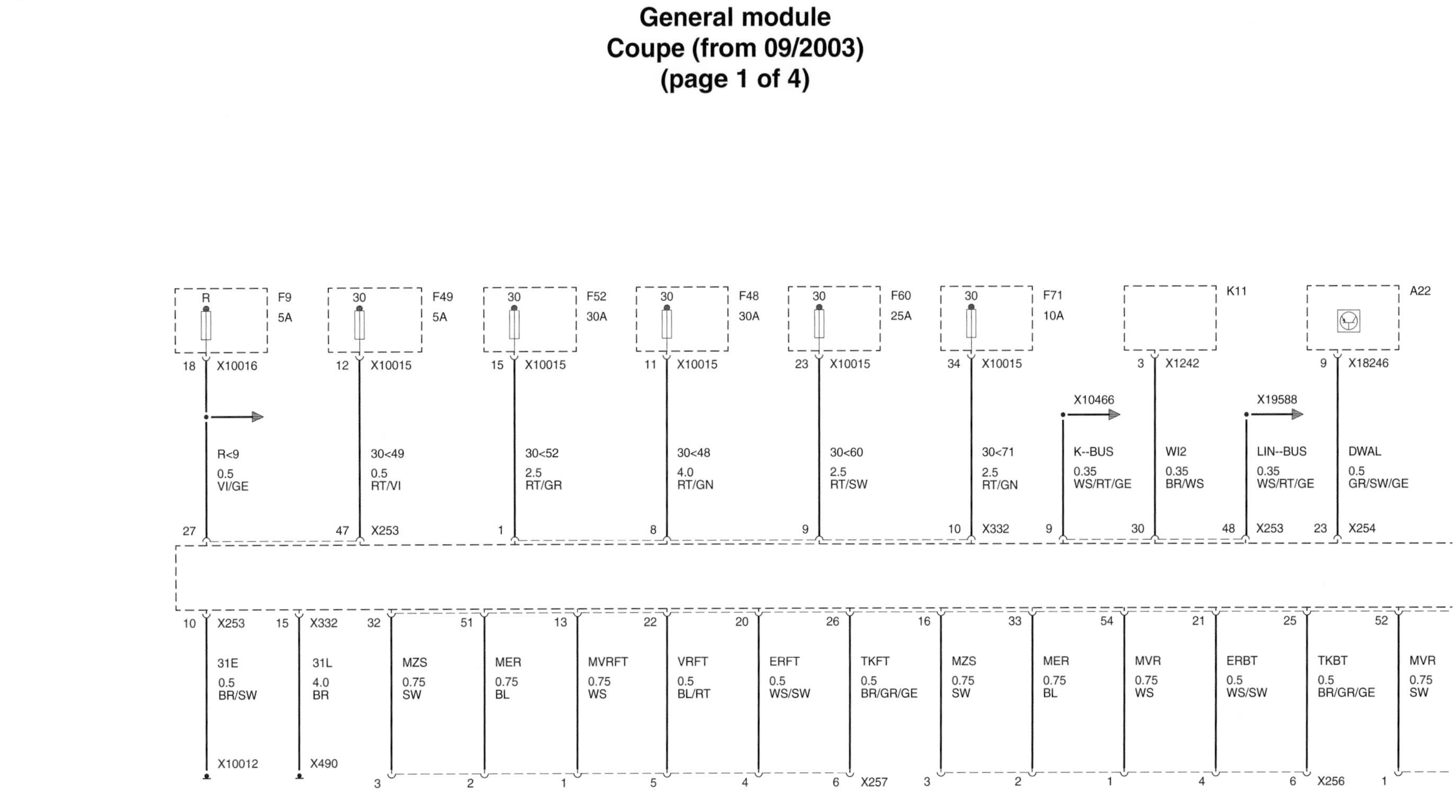

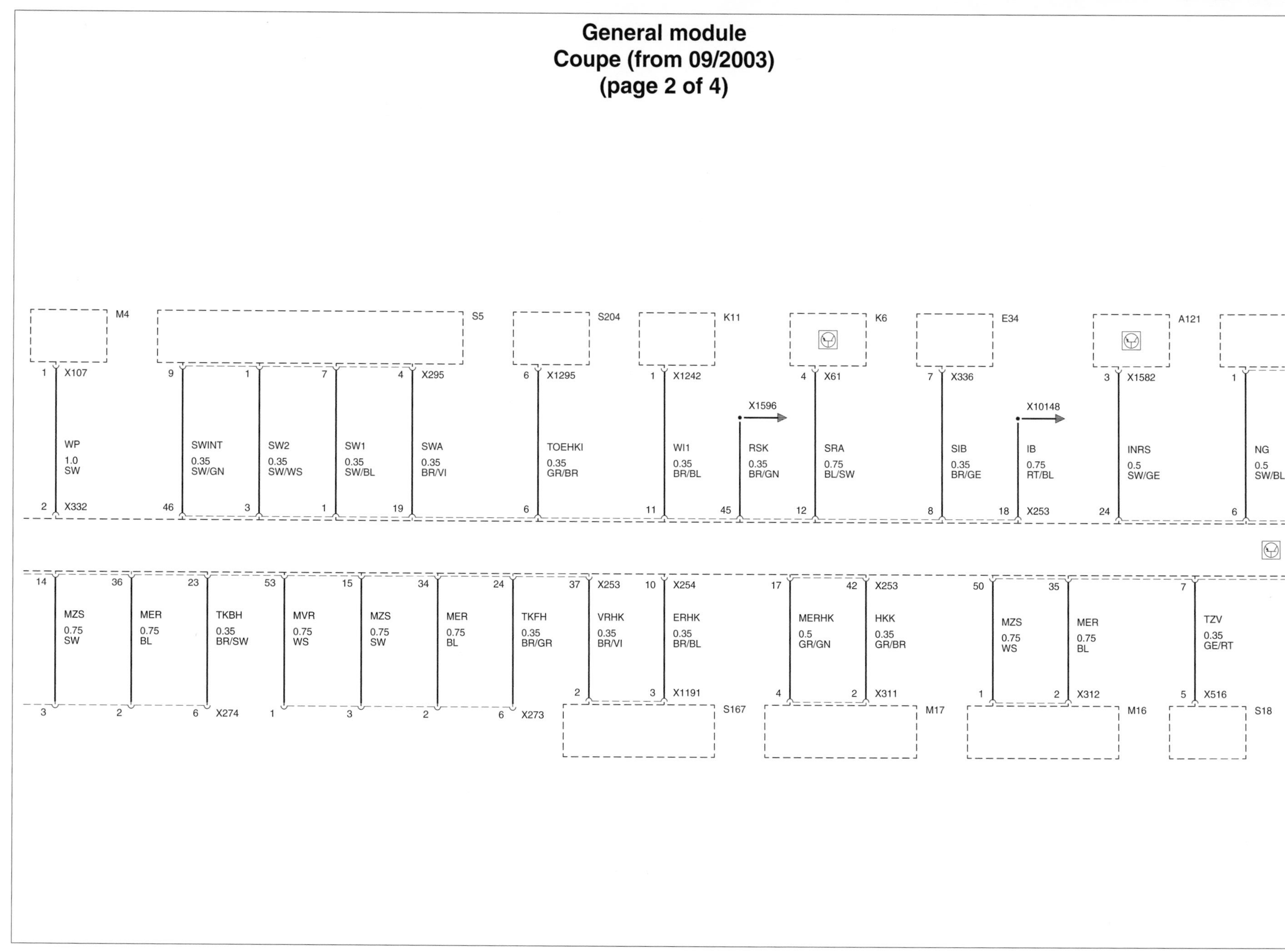
General module
Coupe (from 09/2003)
(page 2 of 4)
M4
S5
S204
K11
K6
E34
A121
X107
X295
X1295
X1242
X61
X336
X1582
X1596
X10148
WP 1.0 SW
SWINT 0.35 SW/GN
SW2 0.35 SW/WS
SW1 0.35 SW/BL
SWA 0.35 BR/VI
TOEHKI 0.35 GR/BR
WI1 0.35 BR/BL
RSK 0.35 BR/GN
SRA 0.75 BL/SW
SIB 0.35 BR/GE
IB 0.75 RT/BL
INRS 0.5 SW/GE
NG 0.5 SW/BL
X332
X253
MZS 0.75 SW
MER 0.75 BL
TKBH 0.35 BR/SW
MVR 0.75 WS
MZS 0.75 SW
MER 0.75 BL
TKFH 0.35 BR/GR
VRHK 0.35 BR/VI
ERHK 0.35 BR/BL
MERHK 0.5 GR/GN
HKK 0.35 GR/BR
MZS 0.75 WS
MER 0.75 BL
TZV 0.35 GE/RT
X253
X254
X253
X274
X273
X1191
X311
X312
X516
S167
M17
M16
S18

General module
Coupe (from 09/2003)
(page 3 of 4)

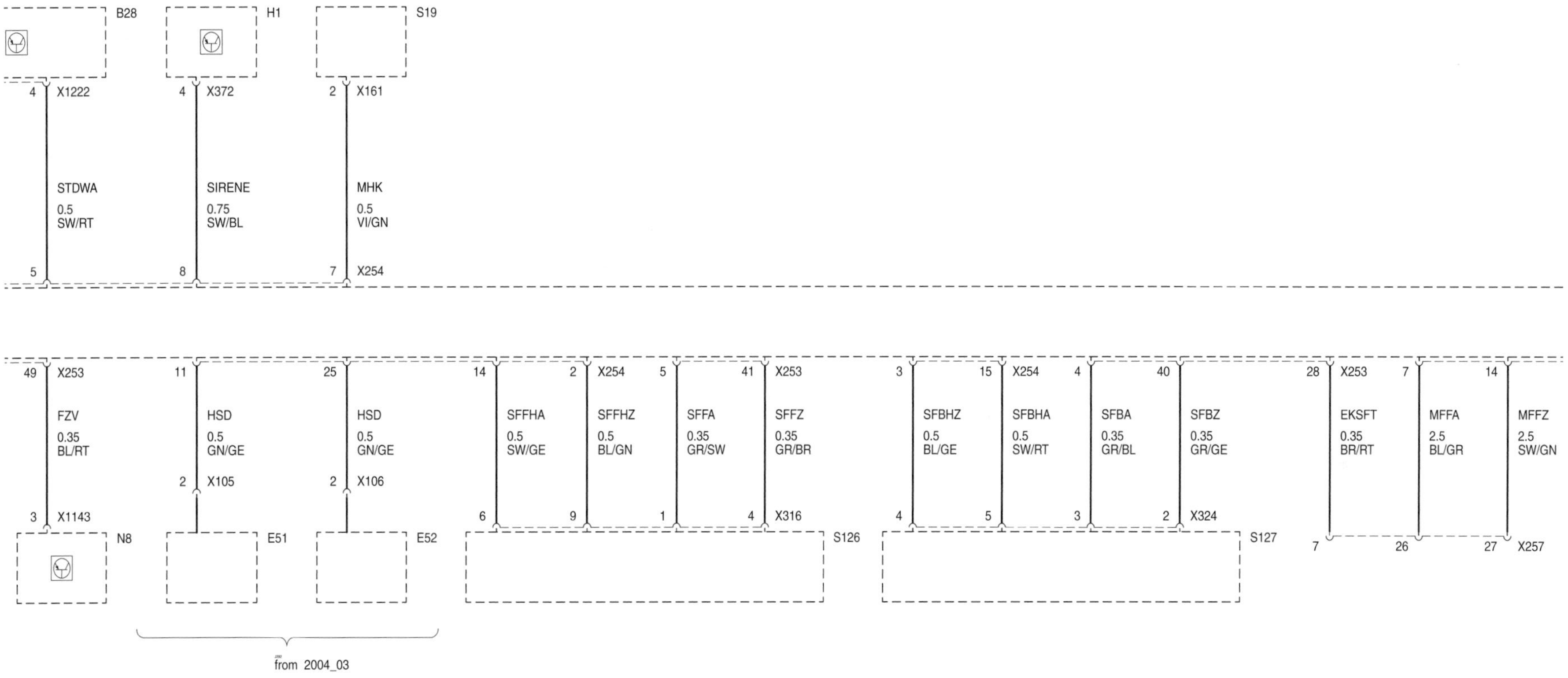

B28
4 X1222
STDWA
0.5
SW/RT
5

H1
4 X372
SIRENE
0.75
SW/BL
8

S19
2 X161
MHK
0.5
VI/GN
7 X254

49 X253
FZV
0.35
BL/RT
3 X1143
N8

11
HSD
0.5
GN/GE
2 X105
E51

25
HSD
0.5
GN/GE
2 X106
E52

from 2004_03

14
SFFHA
0.5
SW/GE
6

2 X254
SFFHZ
0.5
BL/GN
9

5
SFFA
0.35
GR/SW
1

41 X253
SFFZ
0.35
GR/BR
4 X316
S126

3
SFBHZ
0.5
BL/GE
4

15 X254
SFBHA
0.5
SW/RT
5

4
SFBA
0.35
GR/BL
3

40
SFBZ
0.35
GR/GE
2 X324
S127

28 X253
EKSFT
0.35
BR/RT
7

7
MFFA
2.5
BL/GR
26

14
MFFZ
2.5
SW/GN
27 X257

General module
Coupe (from 09/2003)
(page 4 of 4)

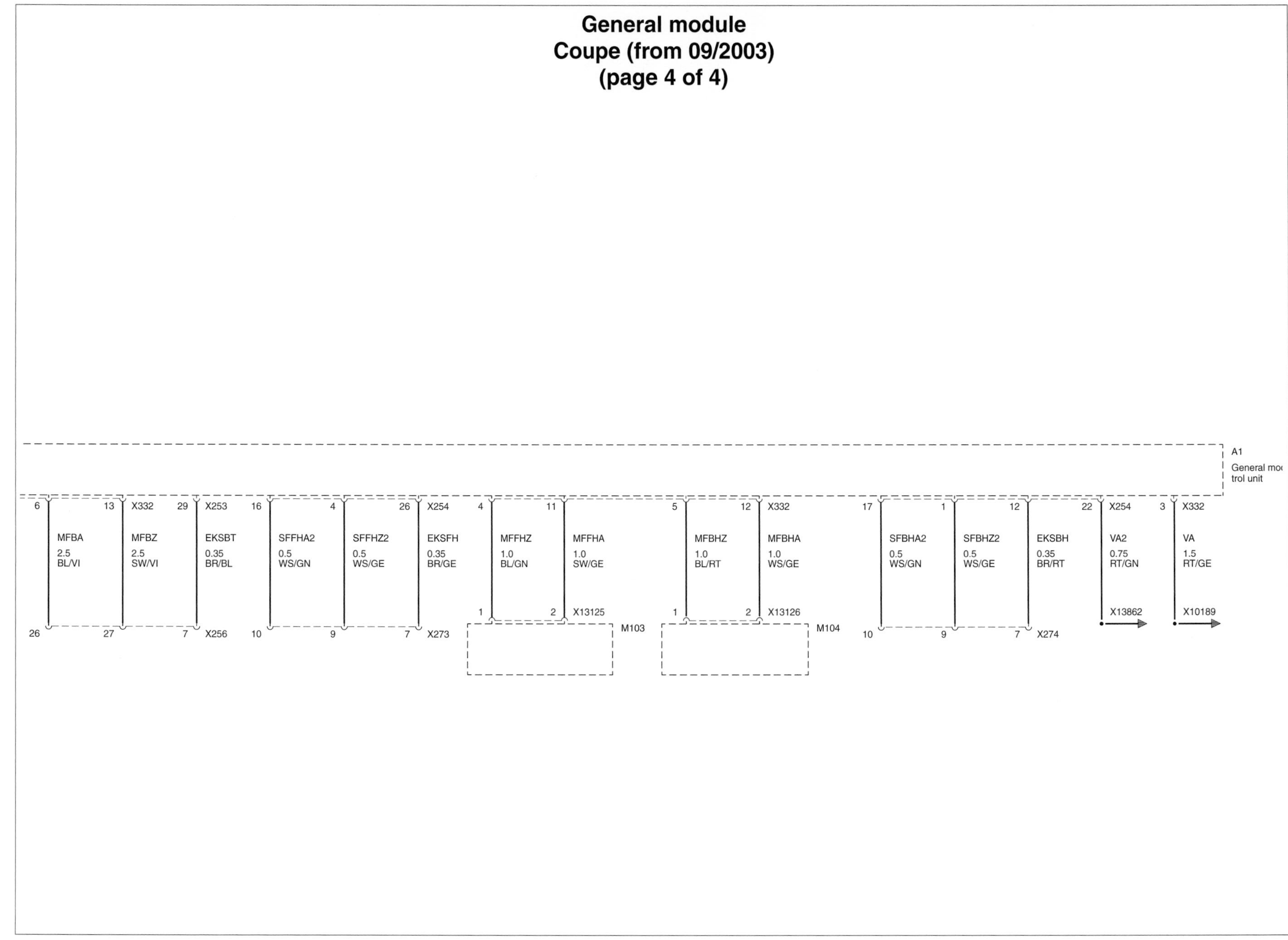

Lights
Power supply, LSZ

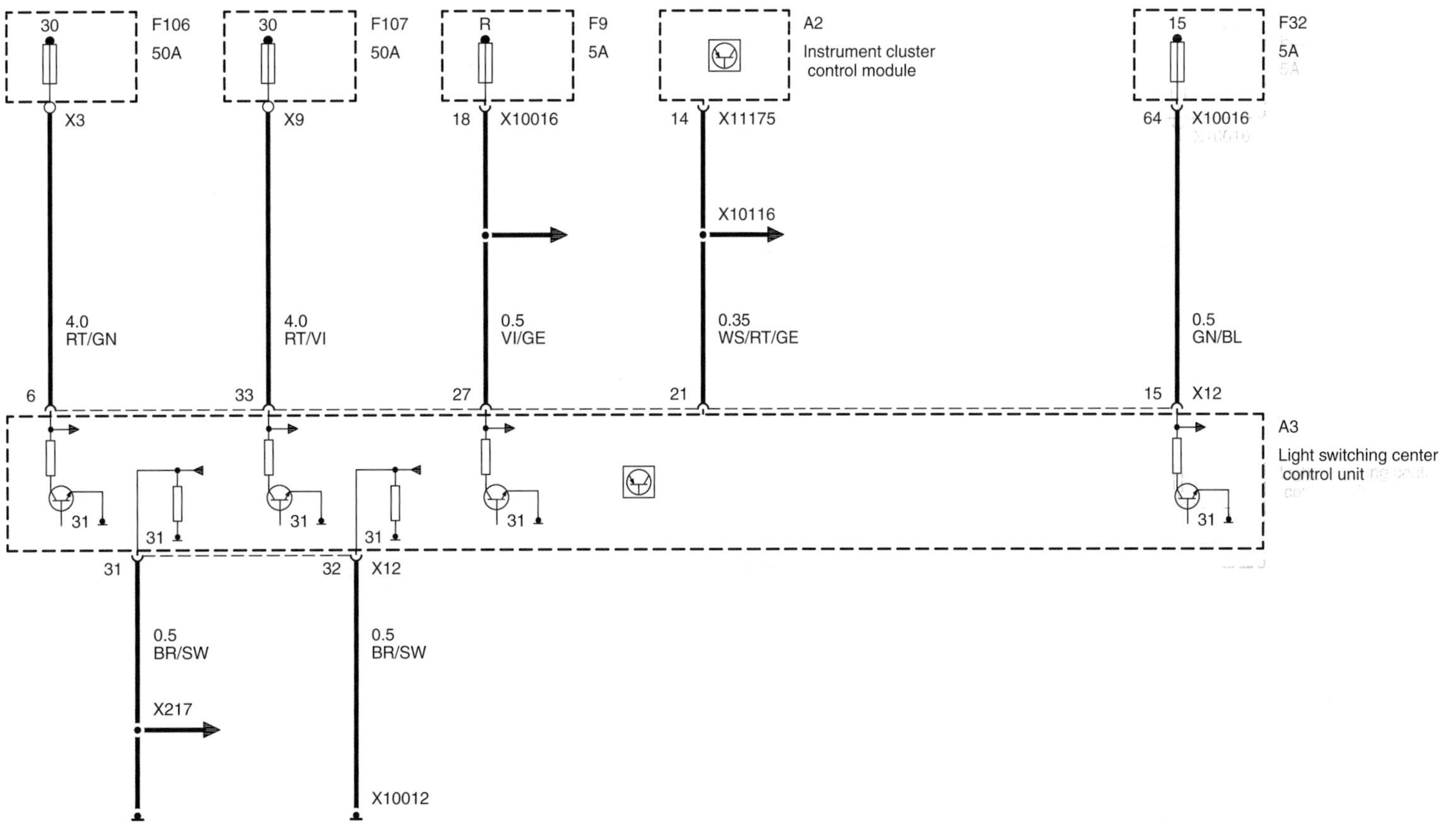

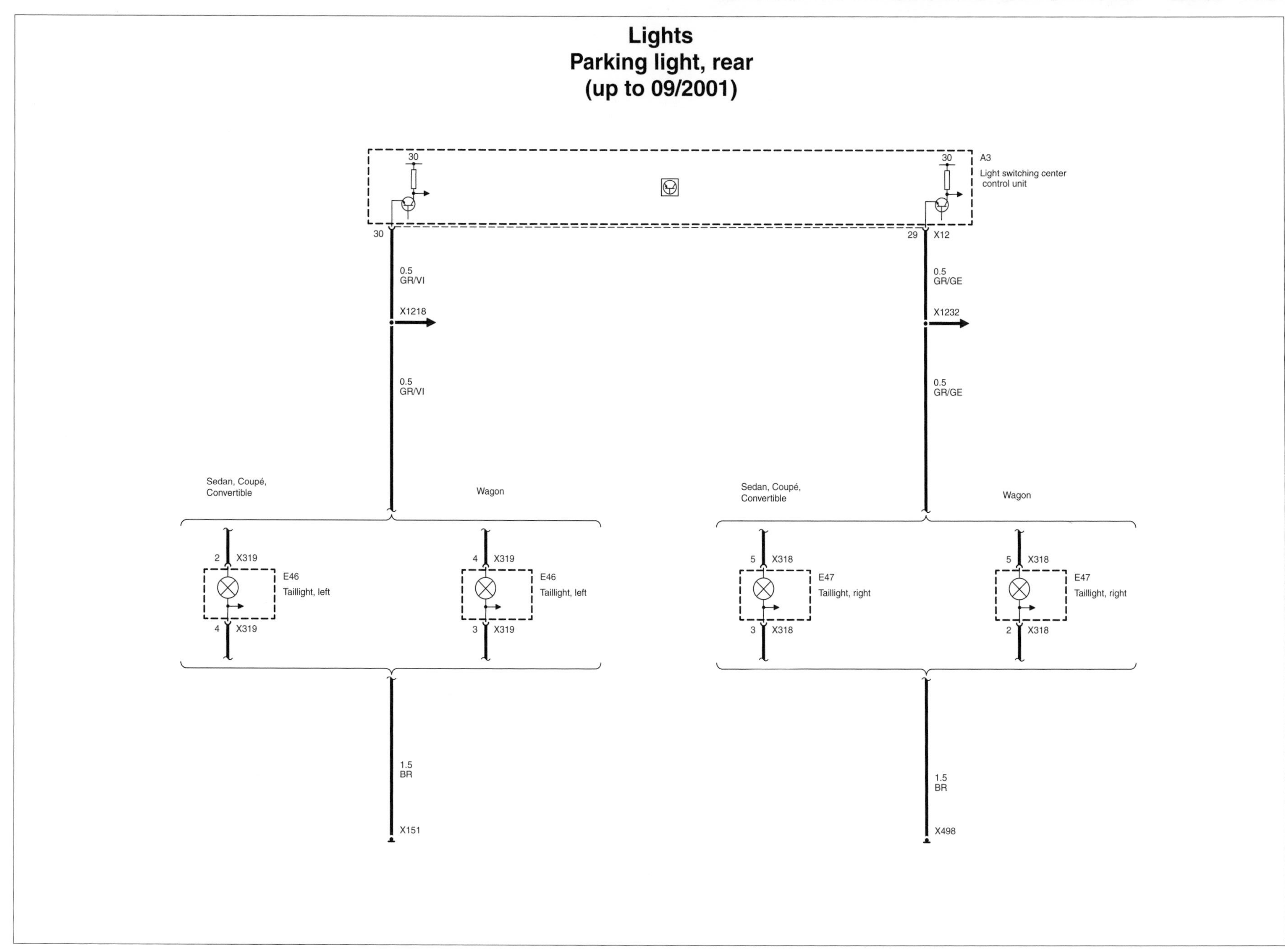
Lights
Parking light, rear
(up to 09/2001)
30
30
A3
Light switching center control unit
30
29
X12
0.5
GR/VI
X1218
0.5
GR/VI
0.5
GR/GE
X1232
0.5
GR/GE
Sedan, Coupé, Convertible
Wagon
Sedan, Coupé, Convertible
Wagon
2
X319
E46
Taillight, left
4
X319
4
X319
E46
Taillight, left
3
X319
5
X318
E47
Taillight, right
3
X318
5
X318
E47
Taillight, right
2
X318
1.5
BR
X151
1.5
BR
X498

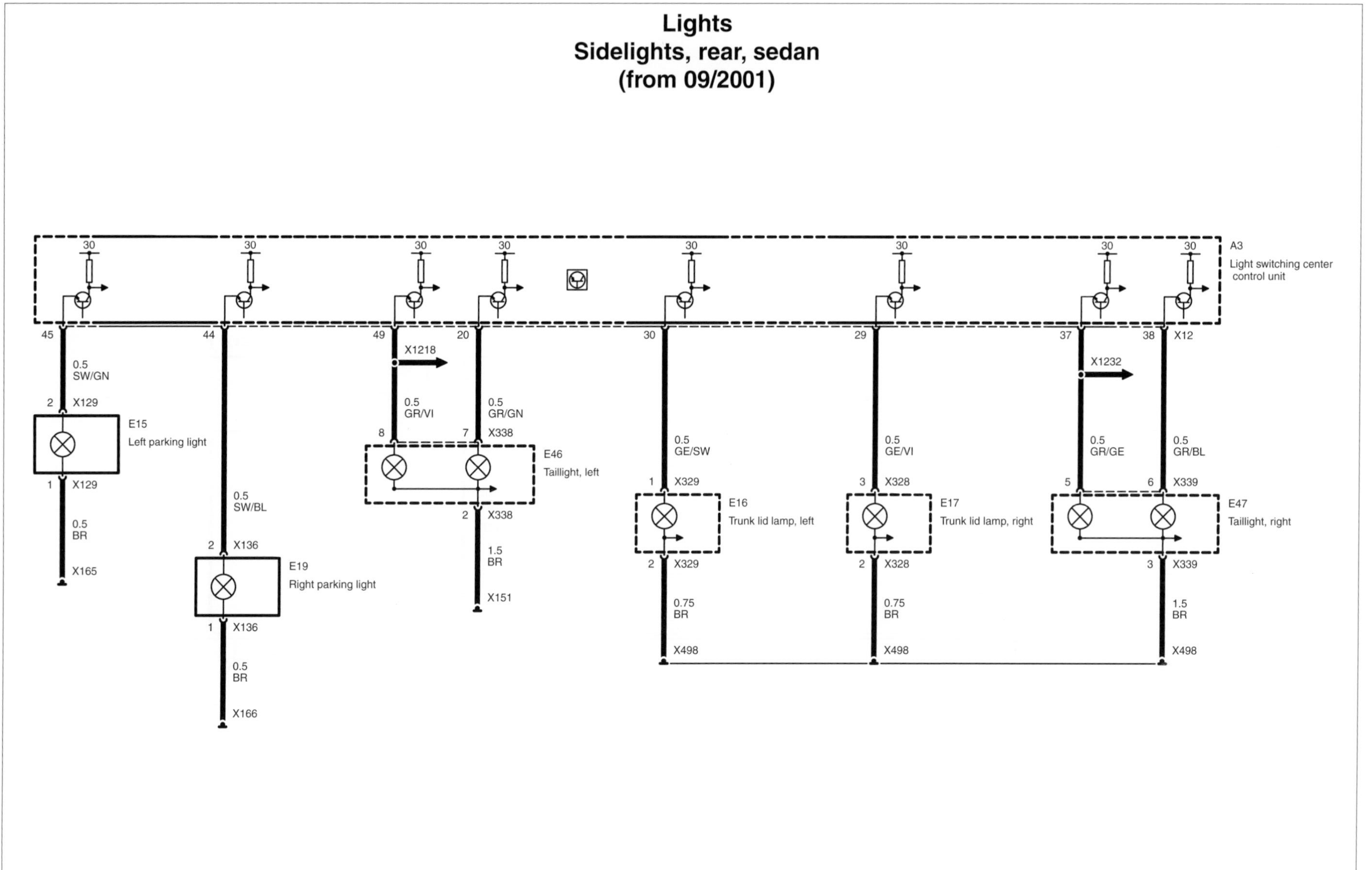

Lights
Sidelights, rear, sedan
(from 09/2001)
A3
Light switching center control unit
30
45
44
49
20
30
29
37
38
X12
0.5
SW/GN
X129
E15
Left parking light
0.5
BR
X165
0.5
SW/BL
X136
E19
Right parking light
X166
X1218
0.5
GR/VI
0.5
GR/GN
X338
E46
Taillight, left
1.5
BR
X151
0.5
GE/SW
X329
E16
Trunk lid lamp, left
0.75
BR
X498
0.5
GE/VI
X328
E17
Trunk lid lamp, right
X1232
0.5
GR/GE
0.5
GR/BL
X339
E47
Taillight, right

Lights
Sidelights, rear, coupe / convertible
(09/2001 to 03/2003)

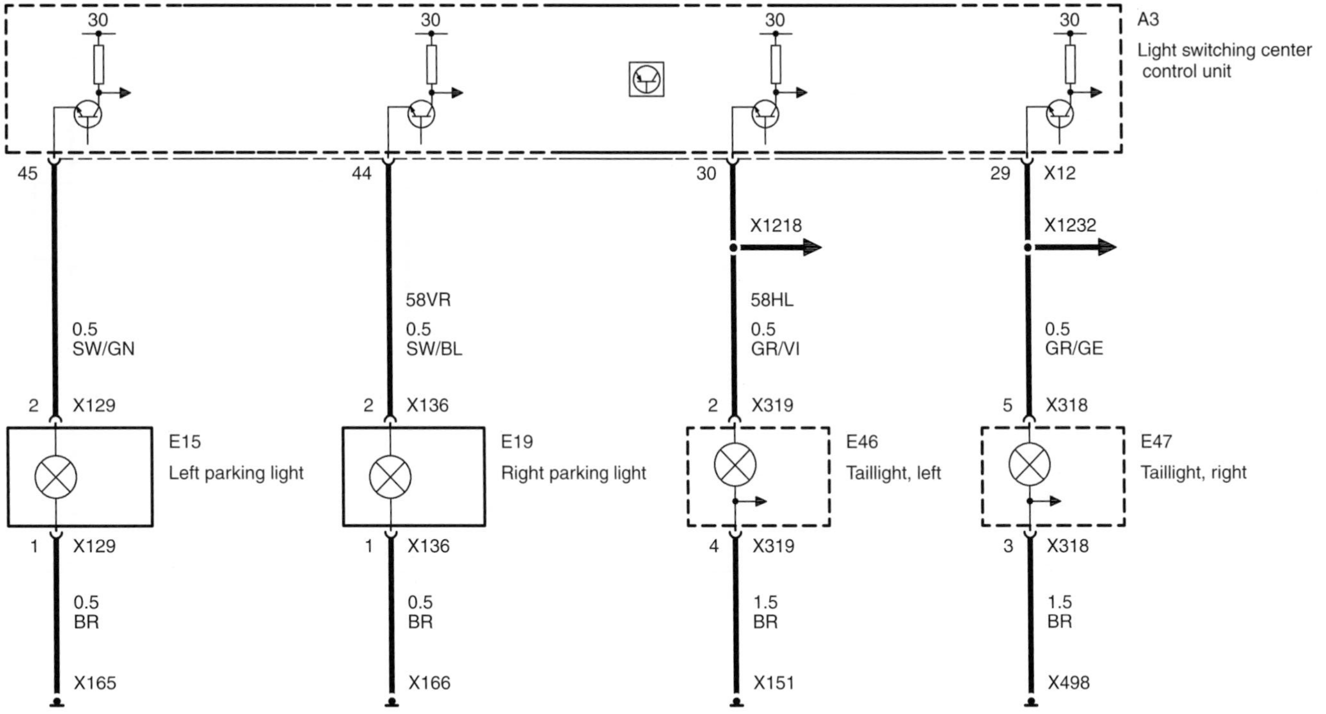

30
30
30
30
A3
Light switching center control unit

45
44
30
29 X12
X1218
X1232

0.5
SW/GN

58VR
0.5
SW/BL

58HL
0.5
GR/VI

0.5
GR/GE

2 X129
2 X136
2 X319
5 X318

E15
Left parking light

E19
Right parking light

E46
Taillight, left

E47
Taillight, right

1 X129
1 X136
4 X319
3 X318

0.5
BR

0.5
BR

1.5
BR

1.5
BR

X165
X166
X151
X498

Lights
Sidelights, rear, coupe / convertible
(from 03/2003)

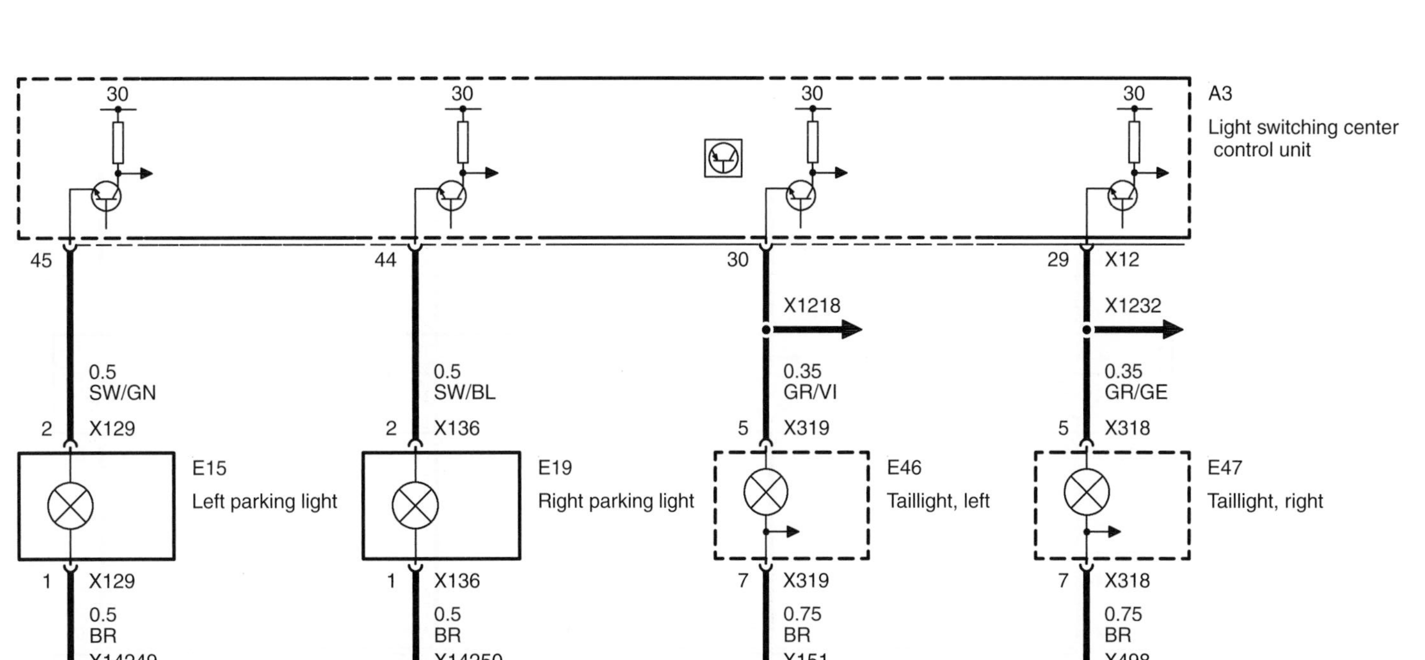

Lights
Sidelights, rear, wagon
(from 09/2001)

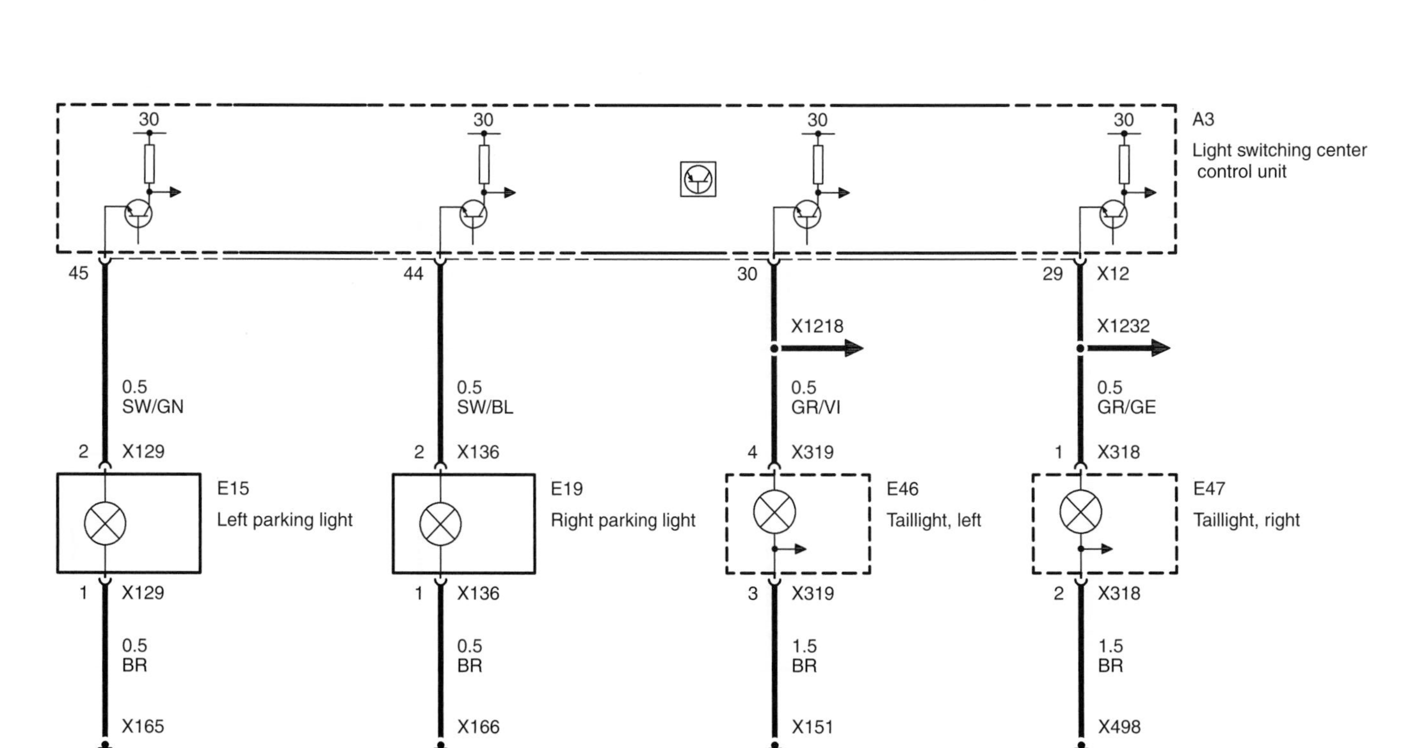

Lights
License plate light

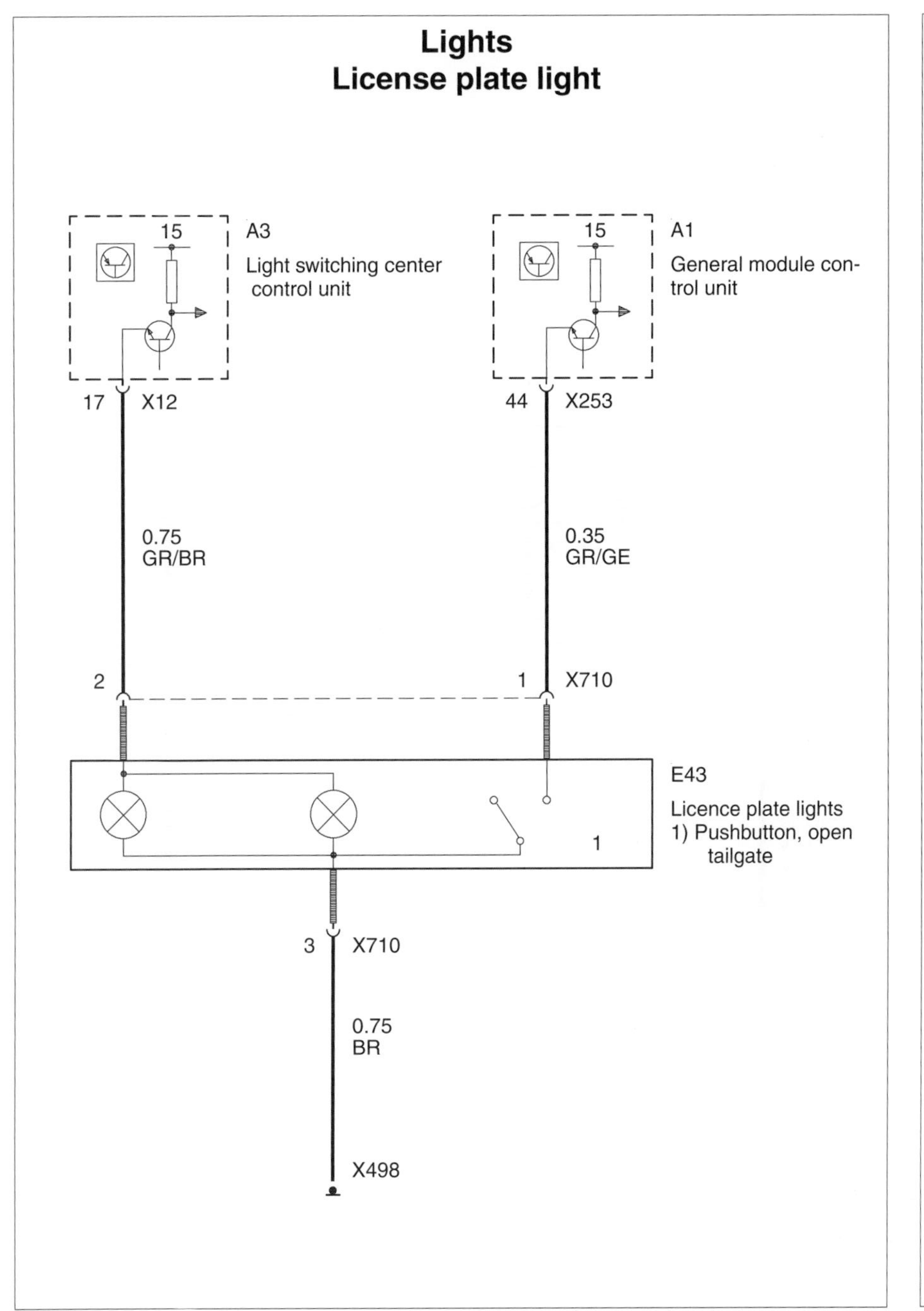

This page intentionally left blank

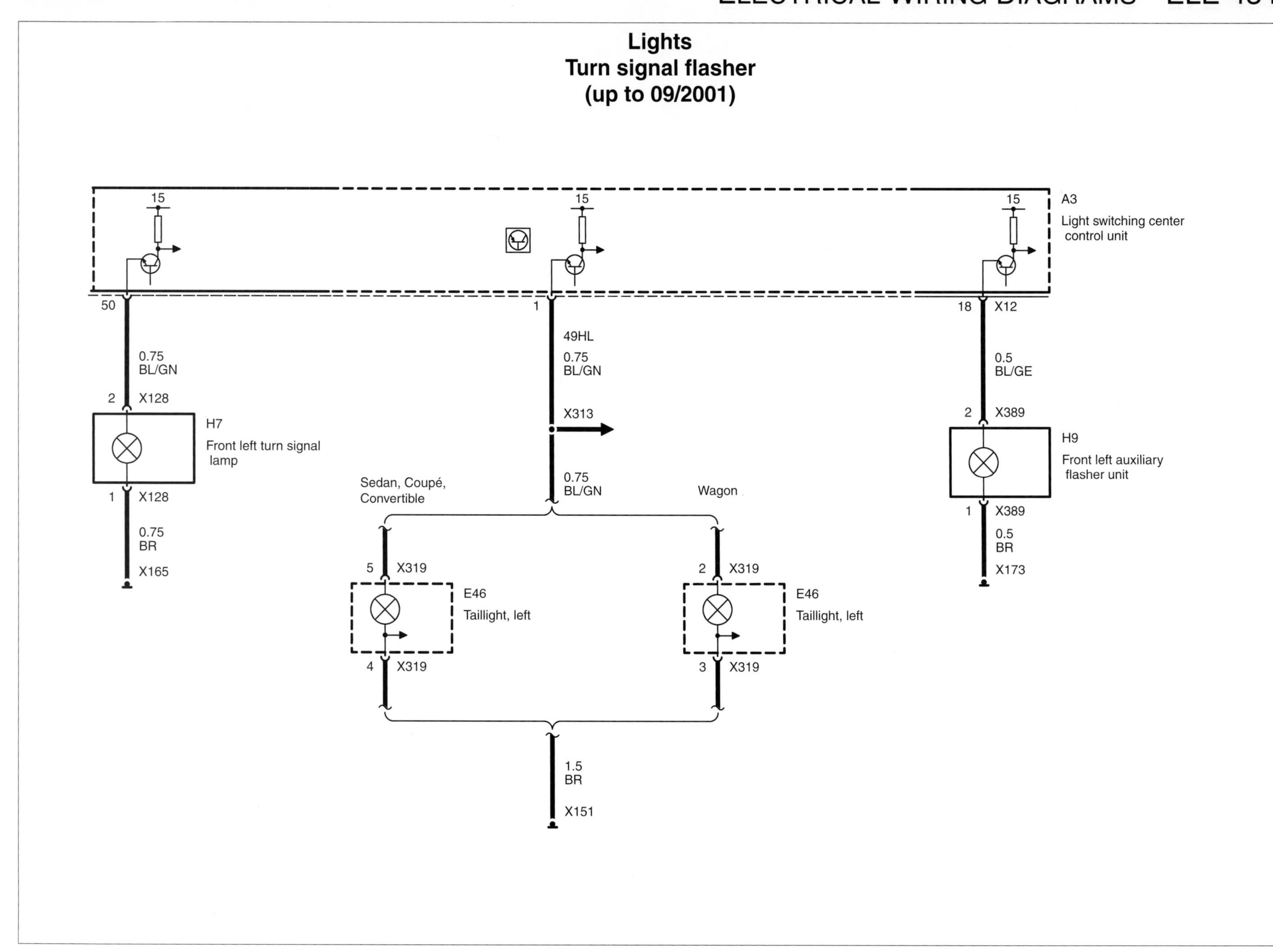
Lights
Turn signal flasher
(up to 09/2001)
15
15
15
A3
Light switching center control unit
50
1
18
X12
0.75
BL/GN
49HL
0.75
BL/GN
0.5
BL/GE
2
X128
X313
2
X389
H7
Front left turn signal lamp
H9
Front left auxiliary flasher unit
1
X128
0.75
BL/GN
Sedan, Coupé, Convertible
Wagon
1
X389
0.75
BR
X165
0.5
BR
X173
5
X319
2
X319
E46
Taillight, left
E46
Taillight, left
4
X319
3
X319
1.5
BR
X151

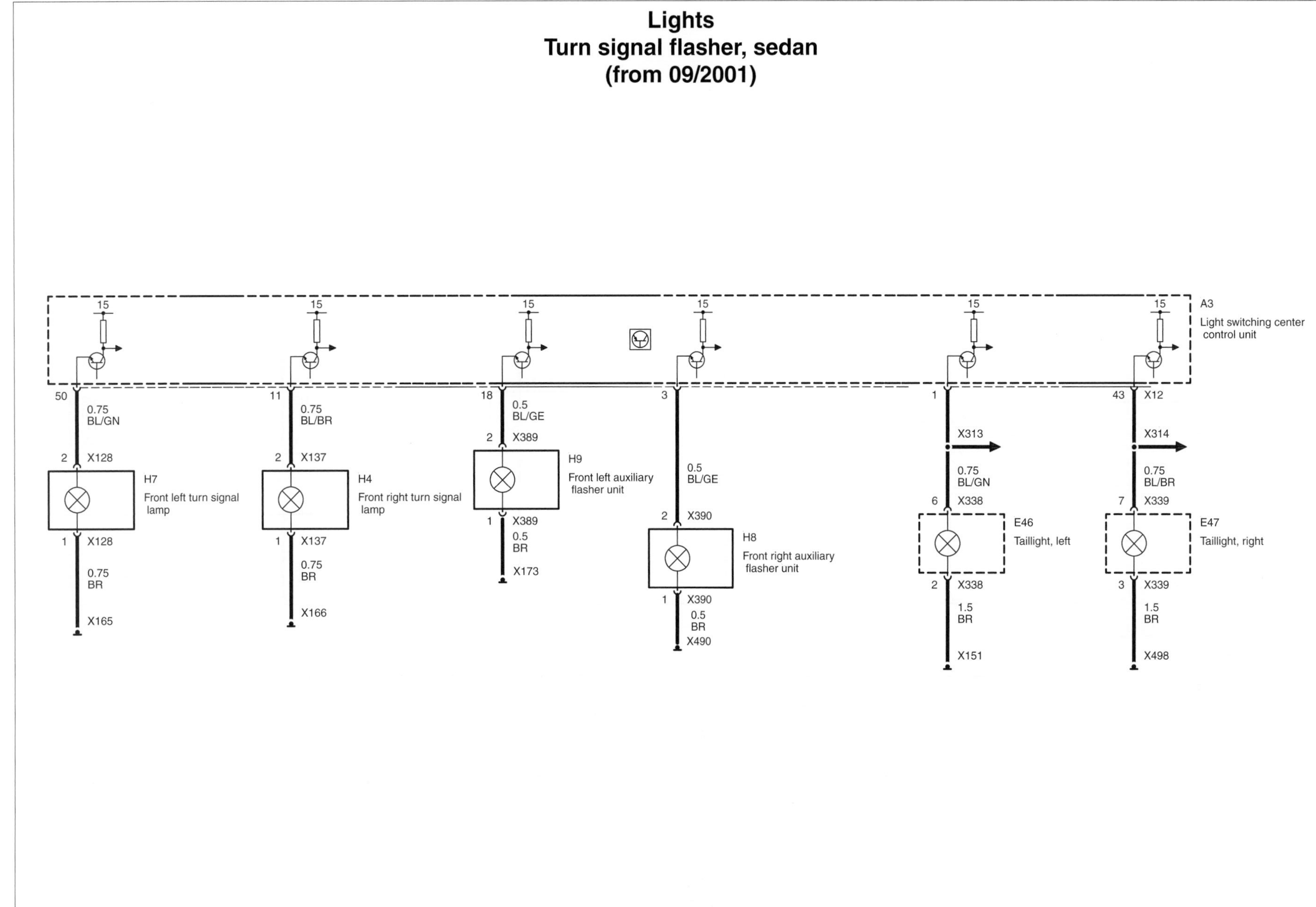

Lights
Turn signal flasher, sedan
(from 09/2001)
A3
Light switching center control unit
15
50
0.75
BL/GN
2
X128
H7
Front left turn signal lamp
1
X128
0.75
BR
X165
11
0.75
BL/BR
X137
H4
Front right turn signal lamp
X137
0.75
BR
X166
18
0.5
BL/GE
X389
H9
Front left auxiliary flasher unit
X389
0.5
BR
X173
3
0.5
BL/GE
X390
H8
Front right auxiliary flasher unit
X390
0.5
BR
X490
X313
0.75
BL/GN
6
X338
E46
Taillight, left
X338
1.5
BR
X151
43
X12
X314
0.75
BL/BR
7
X339
E47
Taillight, right
3
X339
1.5
BR
X498

Lights
Turn signal flasher, coupe / convertible
(from 09/2001 to 03/2003)

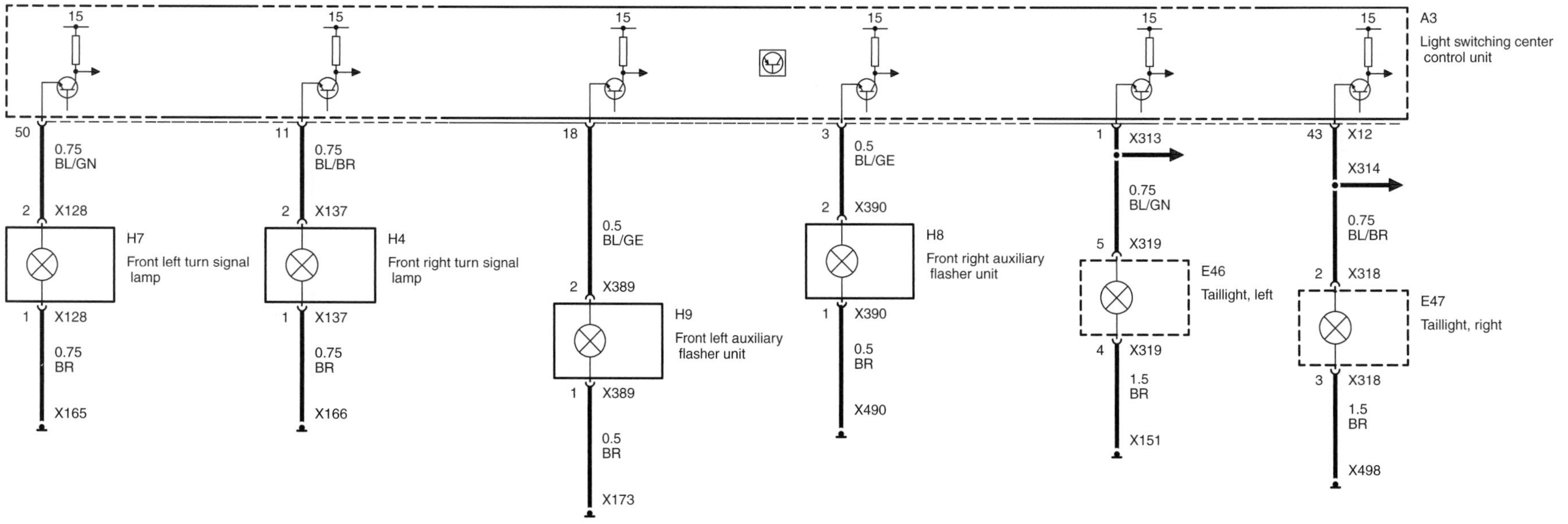

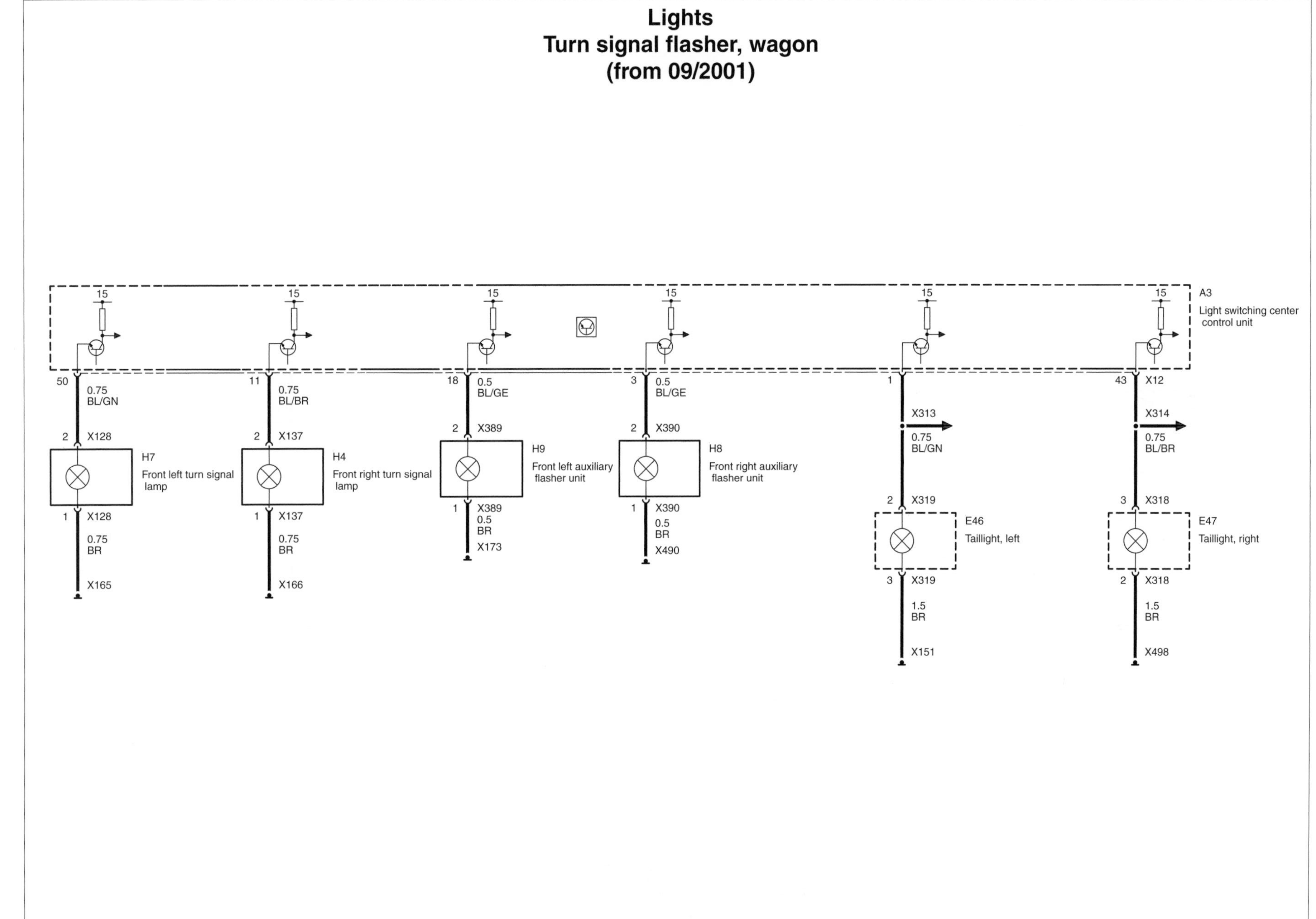
Lights
Turn signal flasher, wagon
(from 09/2001)
15
A3
Light switching center control unit
50
0.75
BL/GN
2
X128
H7
Front left turn signal lamp
1
X128
0.75
BR
X165
11
0.75
BL/BR
2
X137
H4
Front right turn signal lamp
1
X137
0.75
BR
X166
18
0.5
BL/GE
2
X389
H9
Front left auxiliary flasher unit
1
X389
0.5
BR
X173
3
0.5
BL/GE
2
X390
H8
Front right auxiliary flasher unit
1
X390
0.5
BR
X490
1
X313
0.75
BL/GN
2
X319
E46
Taillight, left
3
X319
1.5
BR
X151
43
X12
X314
0.75
BL/BR
3
X318
E47
Taillight, right
2
X318
1.5
BR
X498

Lights
Turn signal flasher, coupe / convertible, w/out MS S54 (from 03/2003)

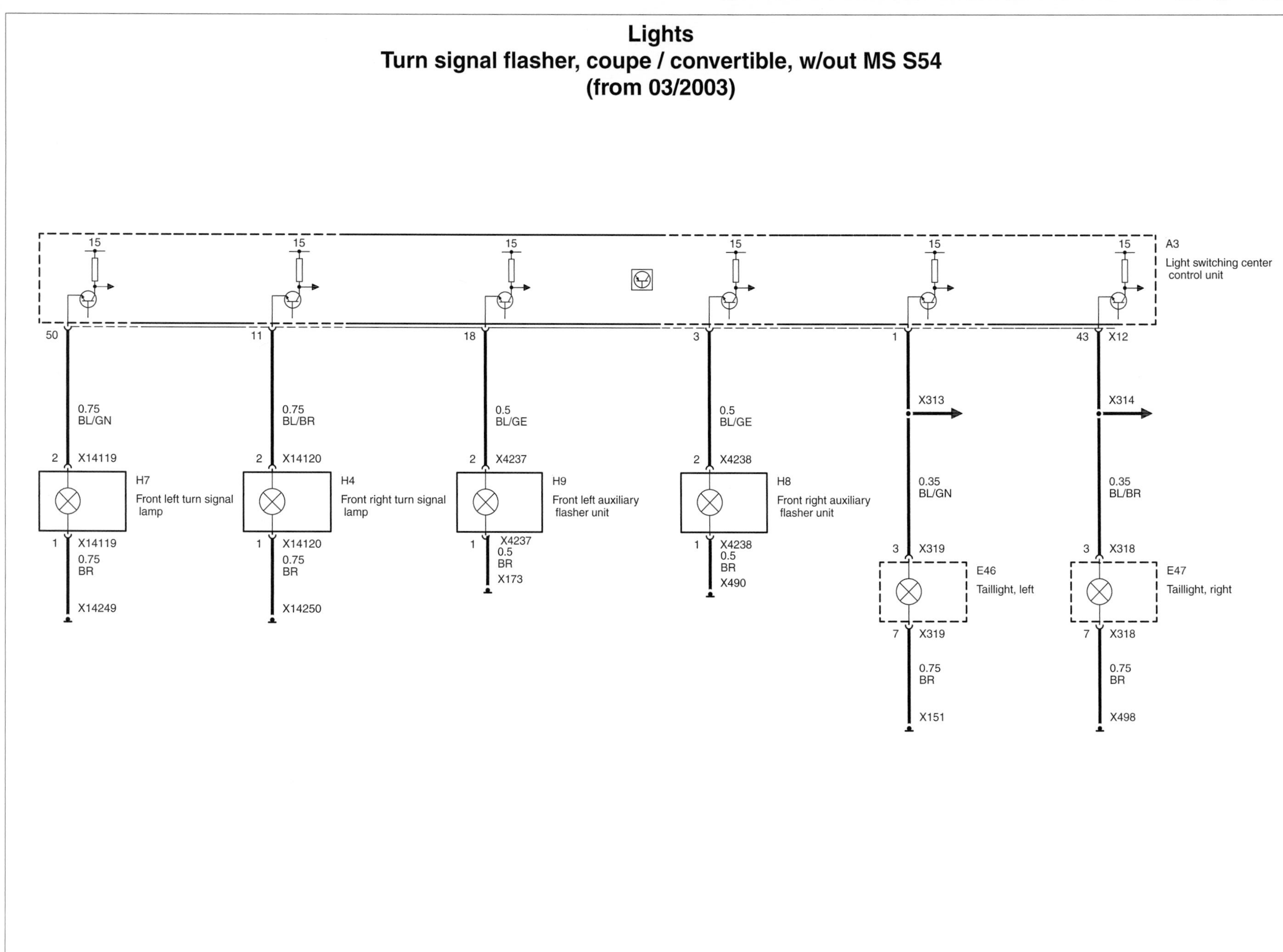

Lights
Turn signal flasher, coupe / convertible, w/ MS S54 (from 03/2003)

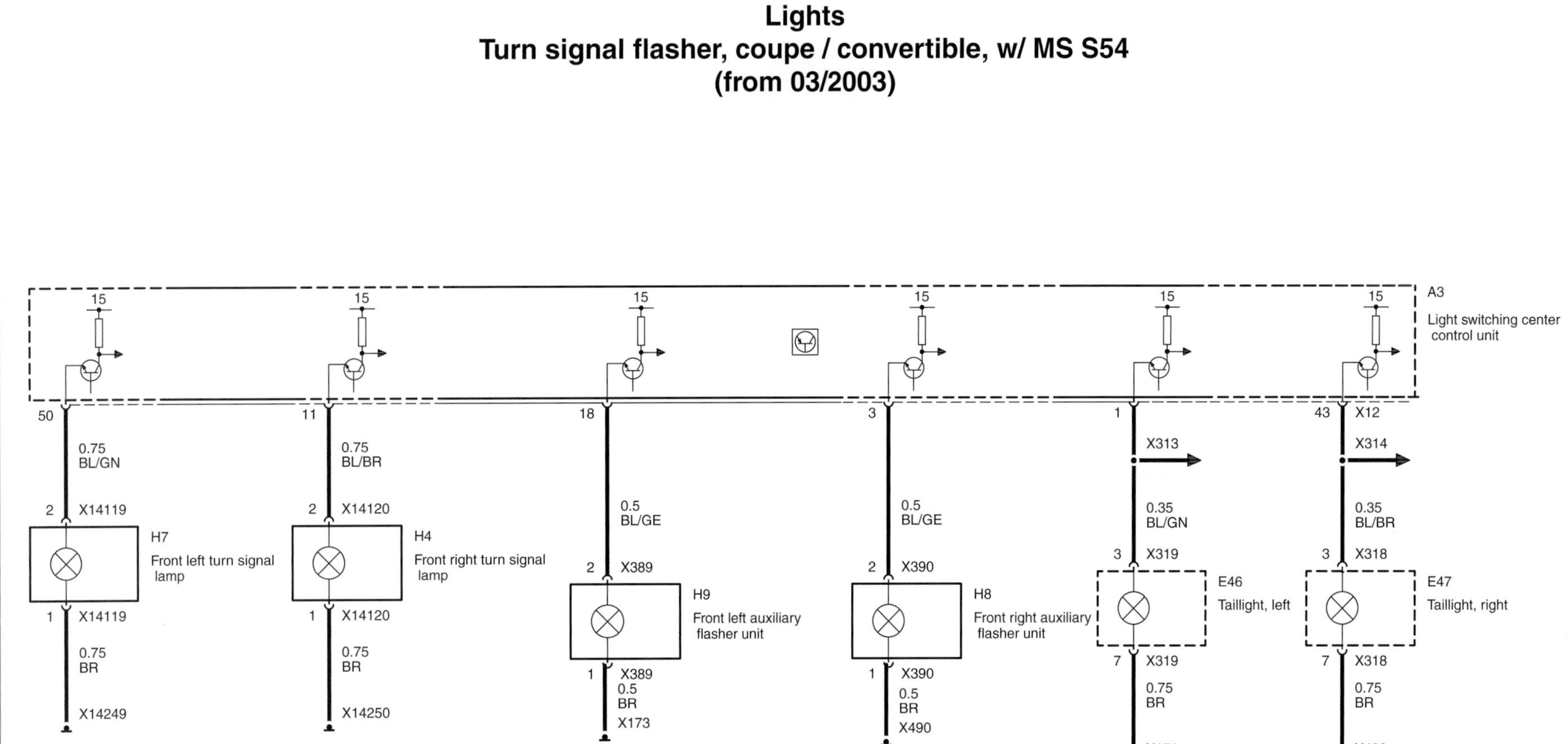

Lights
Low beams w/out Xenon
(up to 09/2001)

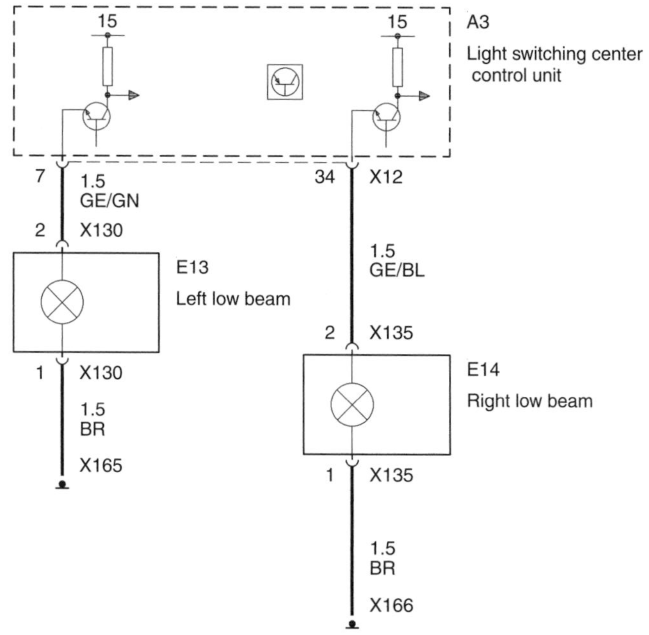

Lights
Low beams w/out Xenon
(09/2001 to 03/2003)

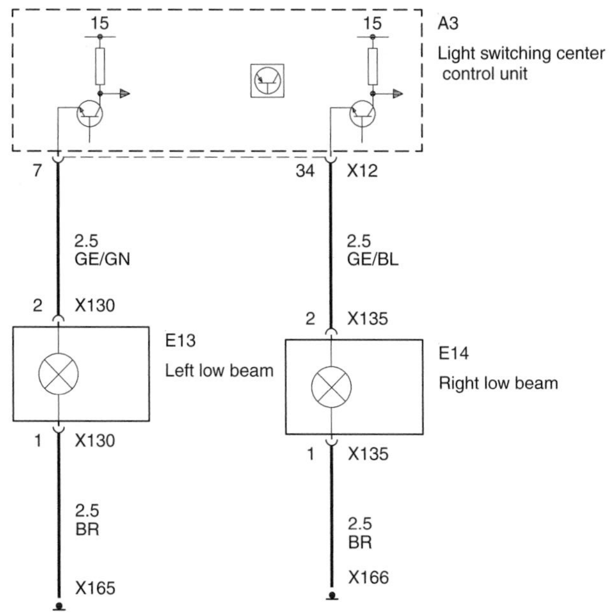

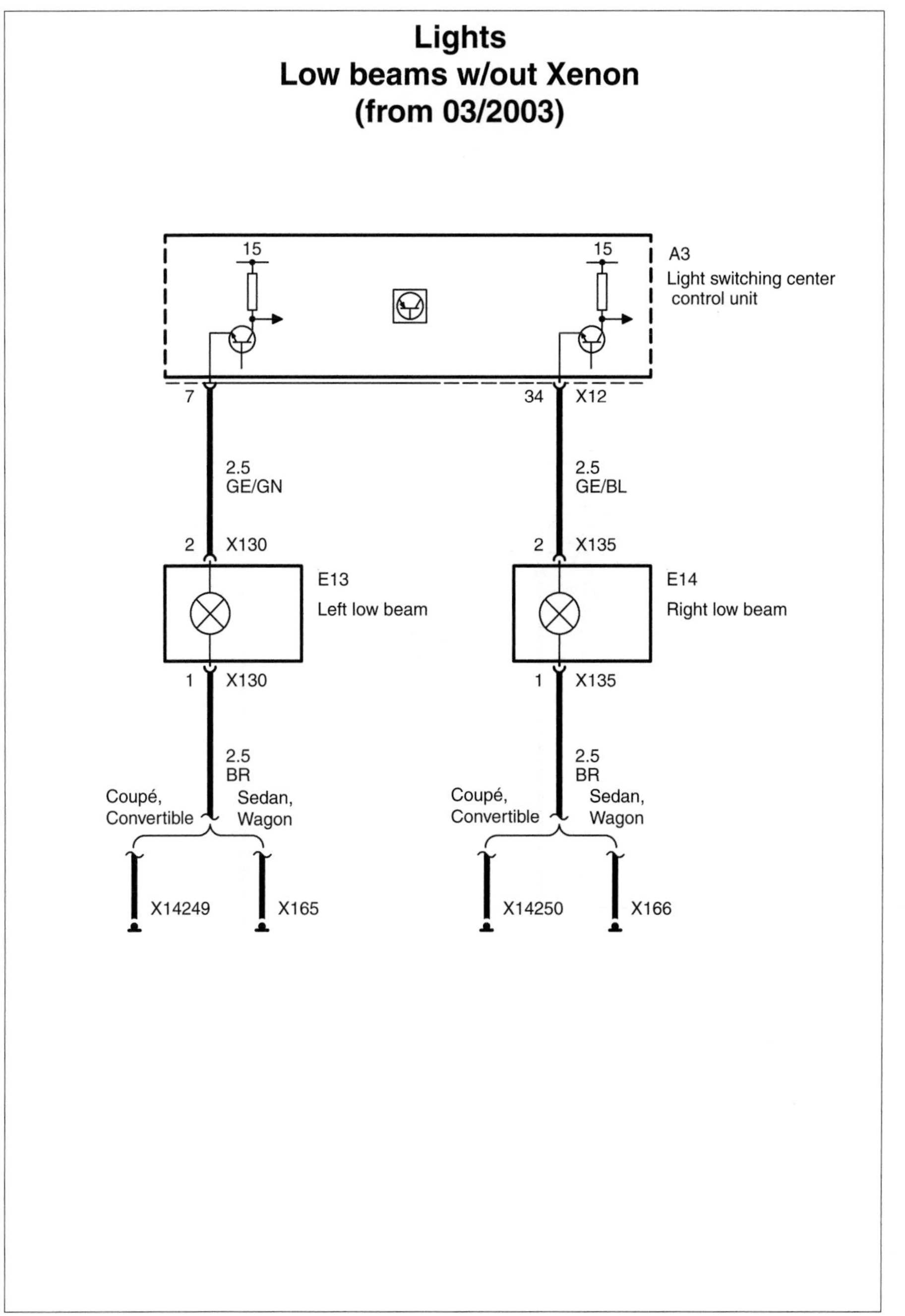

This page intentionally left blank

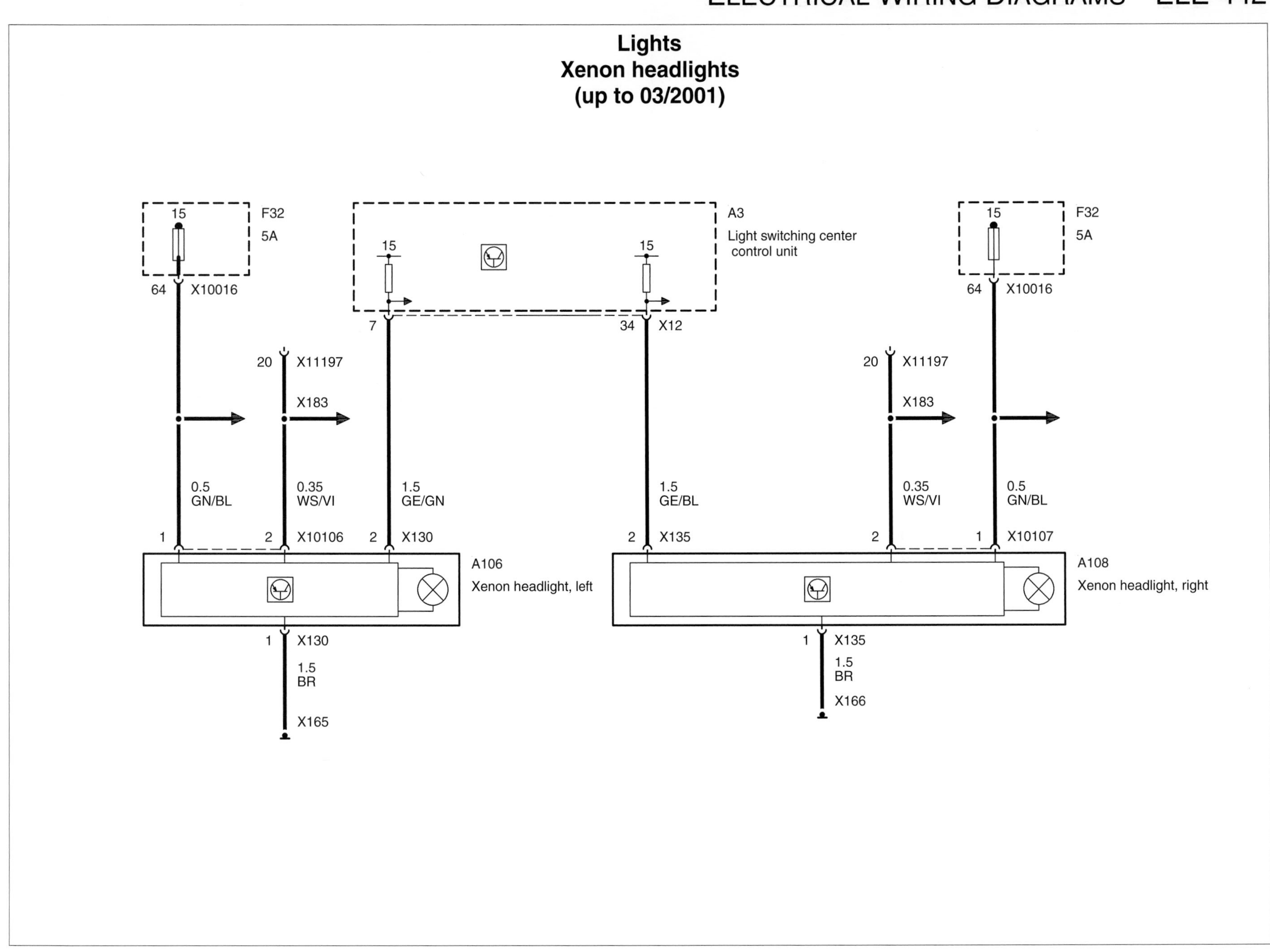
Lights
Xenon headlights
(up to 03/2001)
15
F32
5A
64
X10016
A3
Light switching center control unit
15
15
7
34
X12
20
X11197
X183
0.5
GN/BL
0.35
WS/VI
1.5
GE/GN
1.5
GE/BL
1
2
X10106
2
X130
2
X135
1
X10107
A106
Xenon headlight, left
A108
Xenon headlight, right
1
X130
1.5
BR
X165
1
X135
1.5
BR
X166

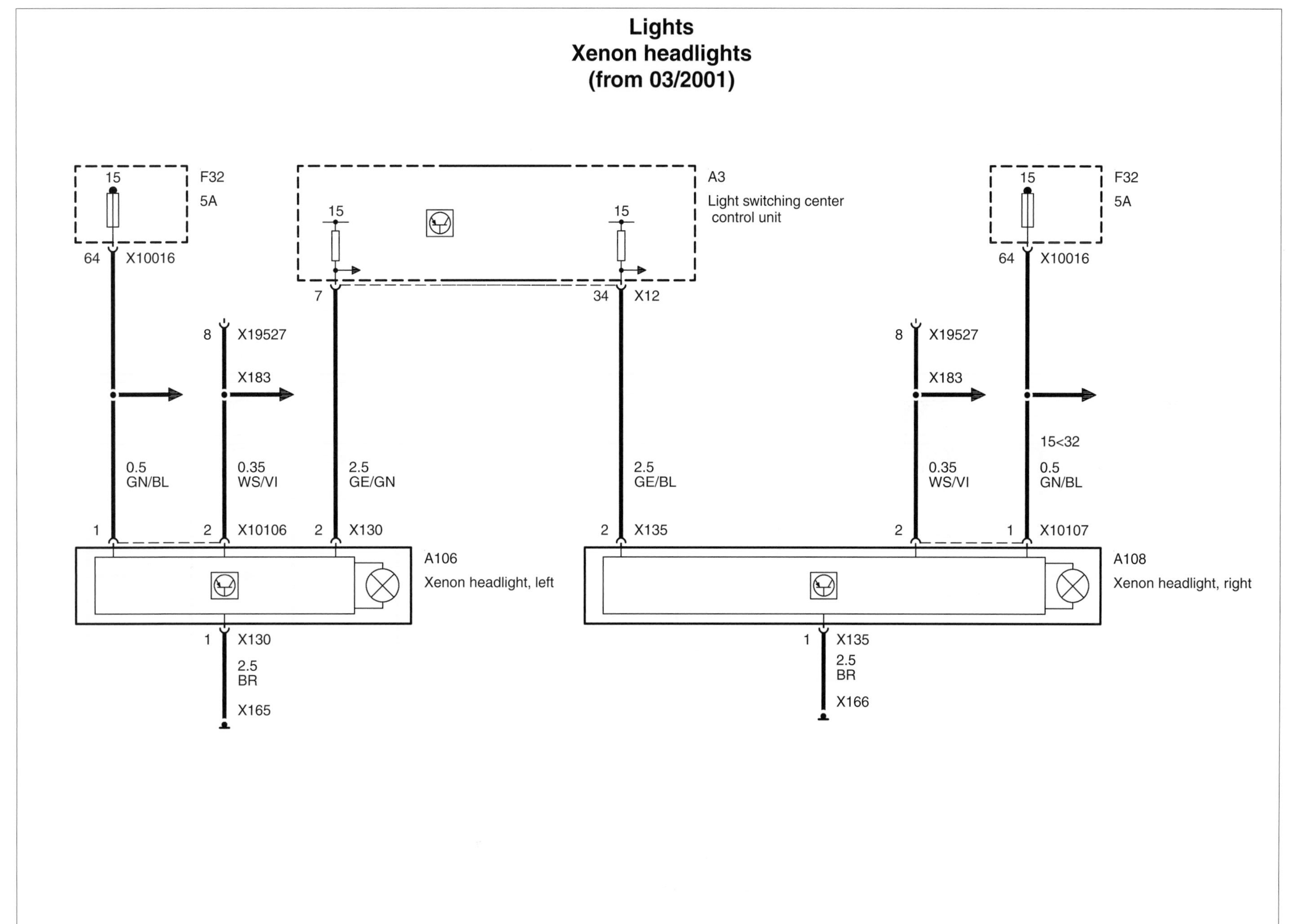
Lights
Xenon headlights
(from 03/2001)
15
F32
5A
64
X10016
15
15
A3
Light switching center
control unit
7
34
X12
8
X19527
X183
0.5
GN/BL
0.35
WS/VI
2.5
GE/GN
2.5
GE/BL
15<32
1
2
X10106
2
X130
2
X135
1
X10107
A106
Xenon headlight, left
A108
Xenon headlight, right
1
X130
2.5
BR
X165
1
X135
X166

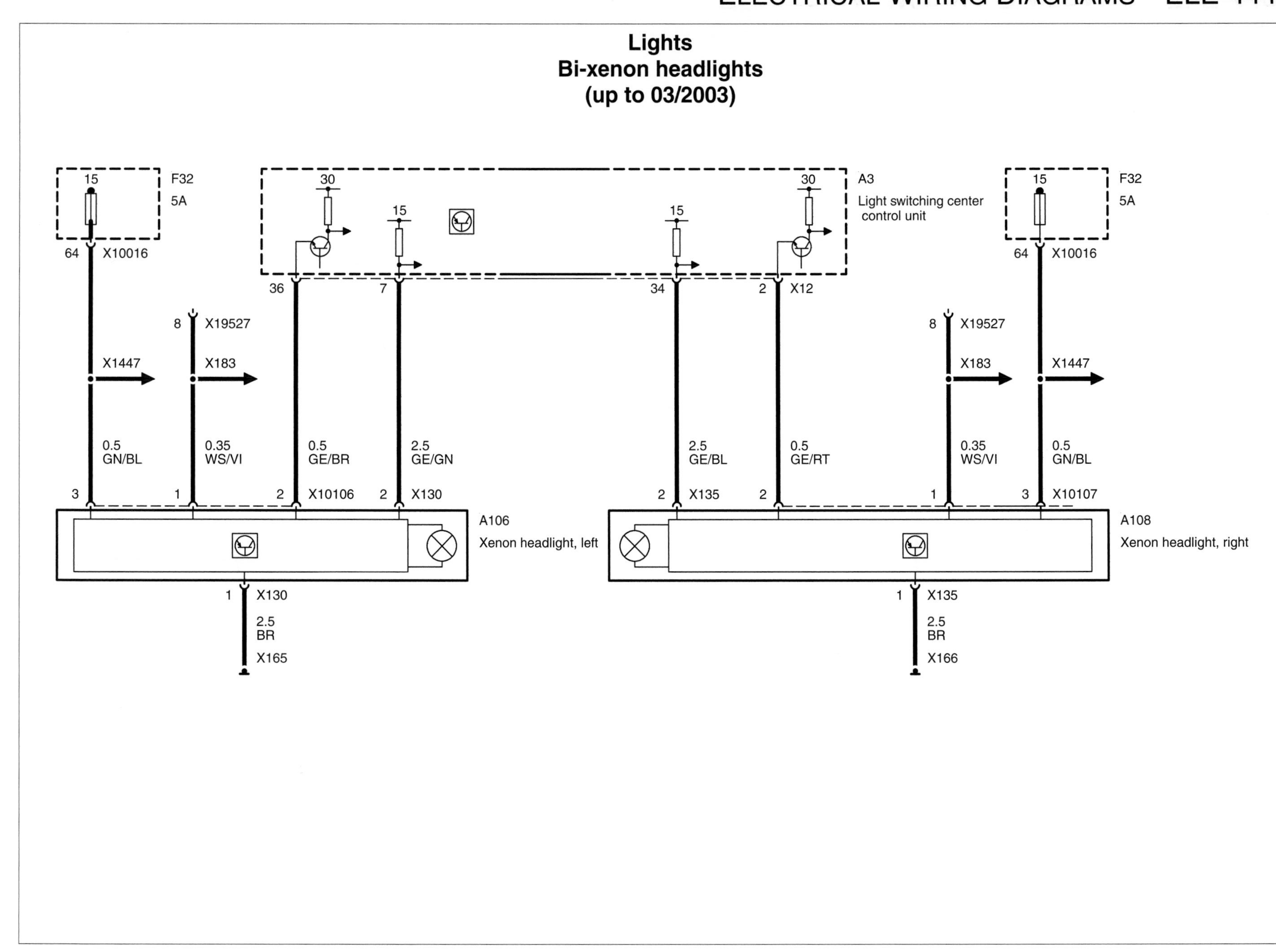
Lights
Bi-xenon headlights
(up to 03/2003)
F32
5A
15
64
X10016
X1447
0.5
GN/BL
3
8
X19527
X183
0.35
WS/VI
1
A3
Light switching center control unit
30
15
36
0.5
GE/BR
2
X10106
7
2.5
GE/GN
X130
34
2.5
GE/BL
X135
X12
0.5
GE/RT
X10107
A106
Xenon headlight, left
A108
Xenon headlight, right
X130
2.5
BR
X165
X135
2.5
BR
X166

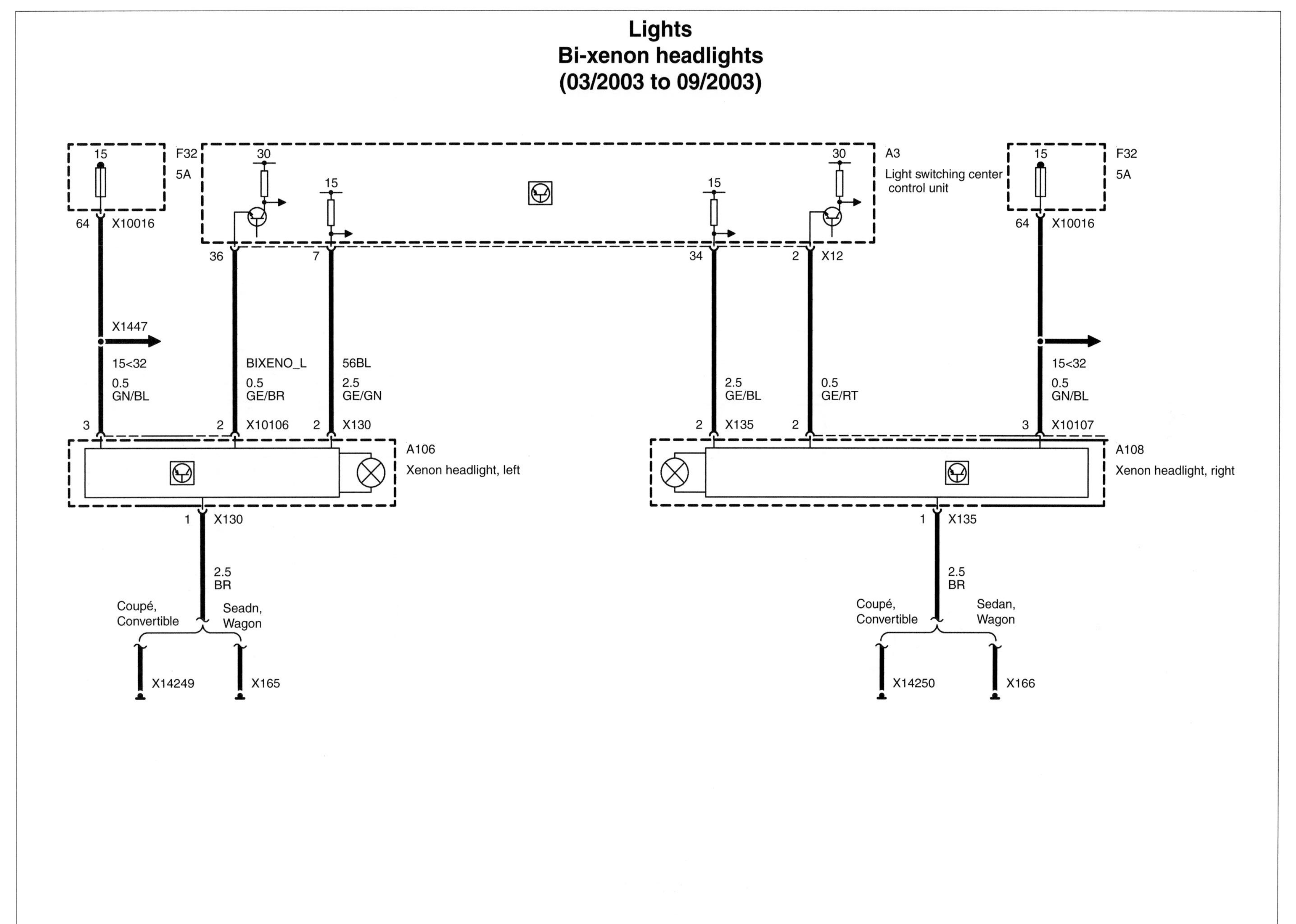

Lights
Bi-xenon headlights
(03/2003 to 09/2003)
15
F32
5A
64
X10016
30
15
A3
Light switching center control unit
36
7
34
2
X12
X1447
15<32
0.5
GN/BL
BIXENO_L
0.5
GE/BR
56BL
2.5
GE/GN
2.5
GE/BL
0.5
GE/RT
3
2
X10106
X130
X135
X10107
A106
Xenon headlight, left
A108
Xenon headlight, right
1
2.5
BR
Coupé,
Convertible
Seadn,
Wagon
Sedan,
Wagon
X14249
X165
X14250
X166

Lights
Bi-xenon headlights
(from 09/2003)

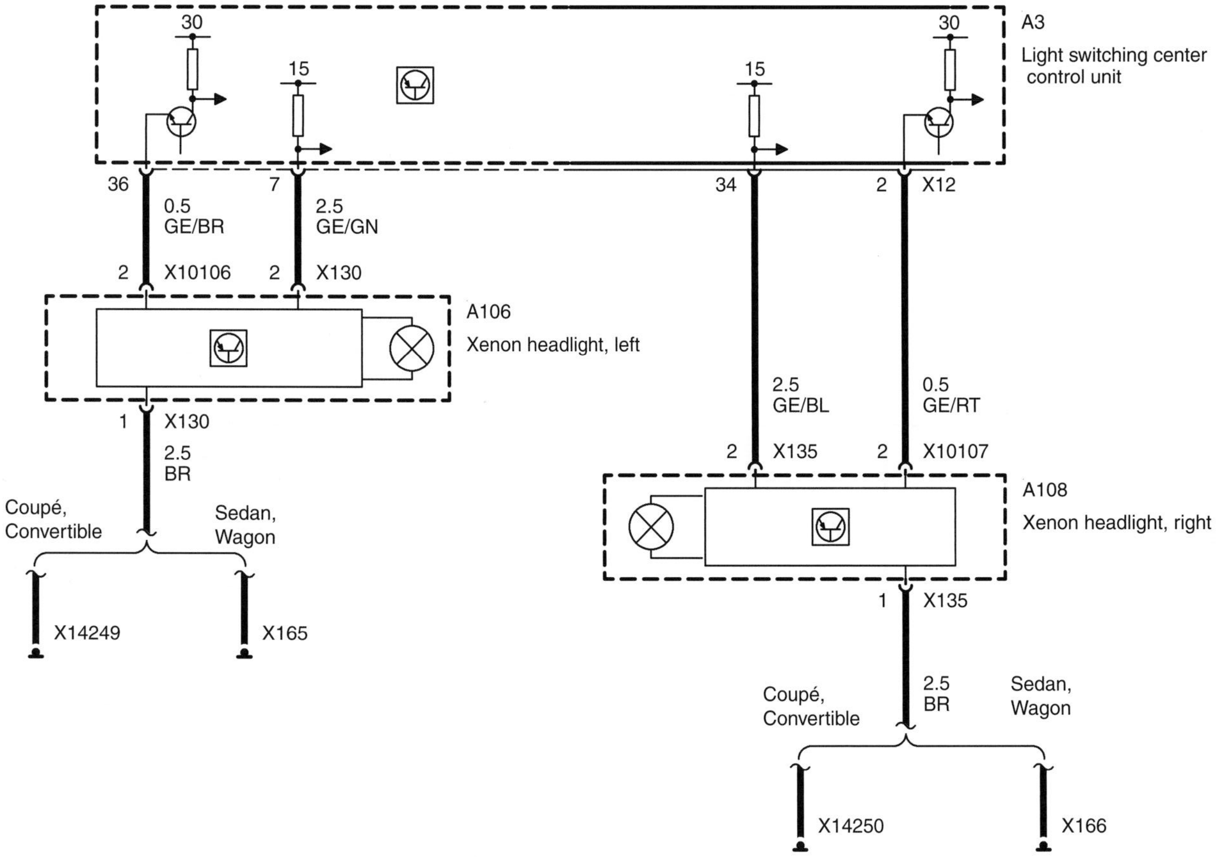

Lights
Turn signal indicator / headlight stalk

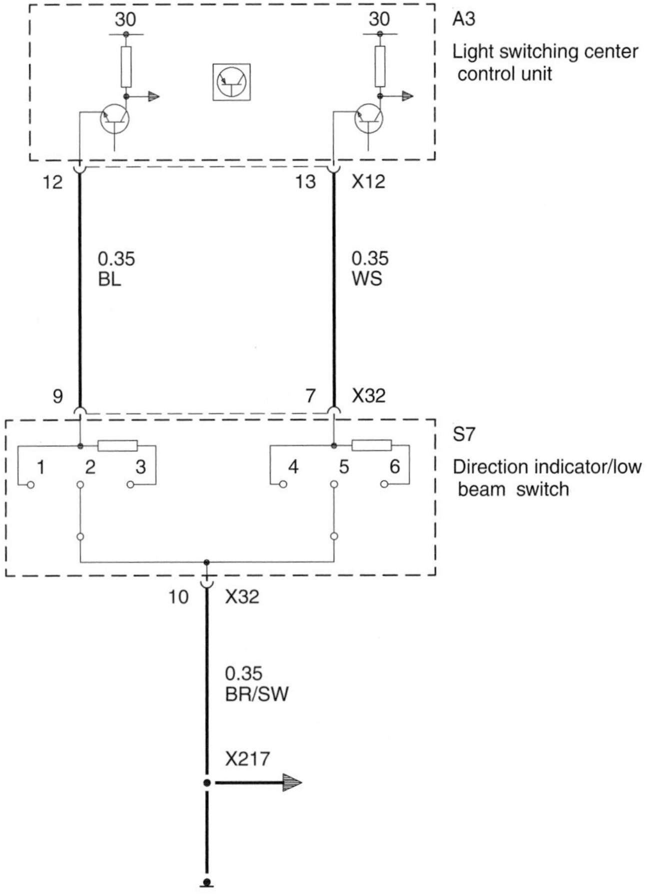

30
30
A3
Light switching center control unit
12
13
X12
0.35
BL
0.35
WS
9
7
X32
S7
Direction indicator/low beam switch
1
2
3
4
5
6
10
X32
0.35
BR/SW
X217

Lights
High beams w/o Xenon
(up to 03/2003)

15
15
A3
Light switching center control unit
35
8
X12
1.5
WS/GN
1.5
WS/BL
2
X131
2
X134
E11
Left high beam
E12
Right high beam
1
X131
1
X134
1.5
BR
1.5
BR
X165
X166

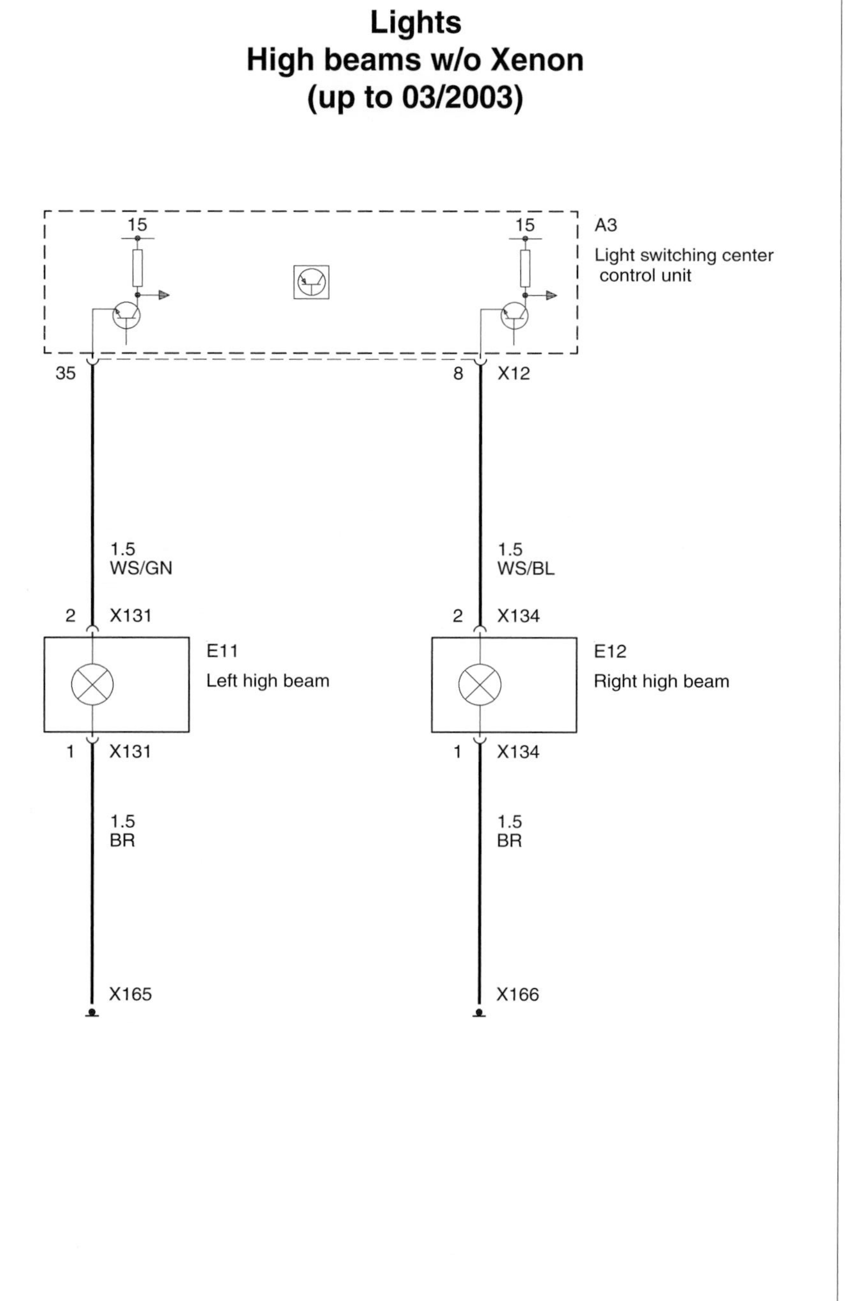

Lights
High beams w/o Xenon (from 03/2003)

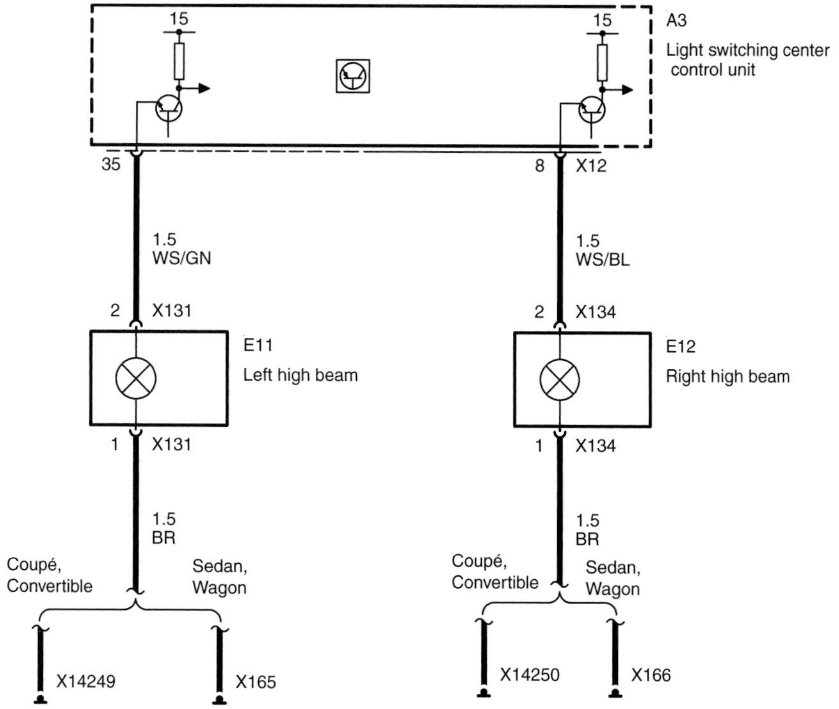

Lights
Manual headlight vertical aim control w/out xenon

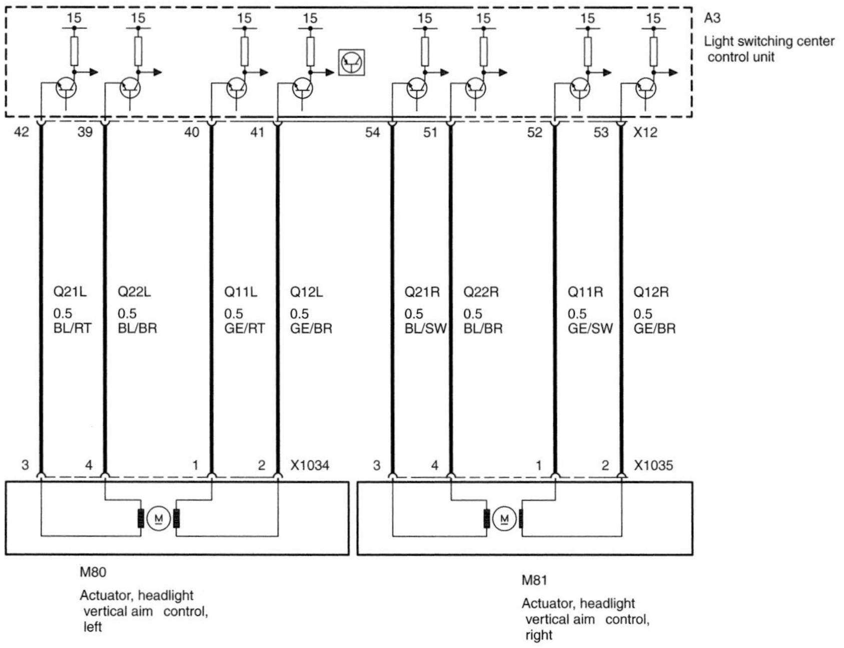

Lights
Automatic headlight vertical aim control w/xenon

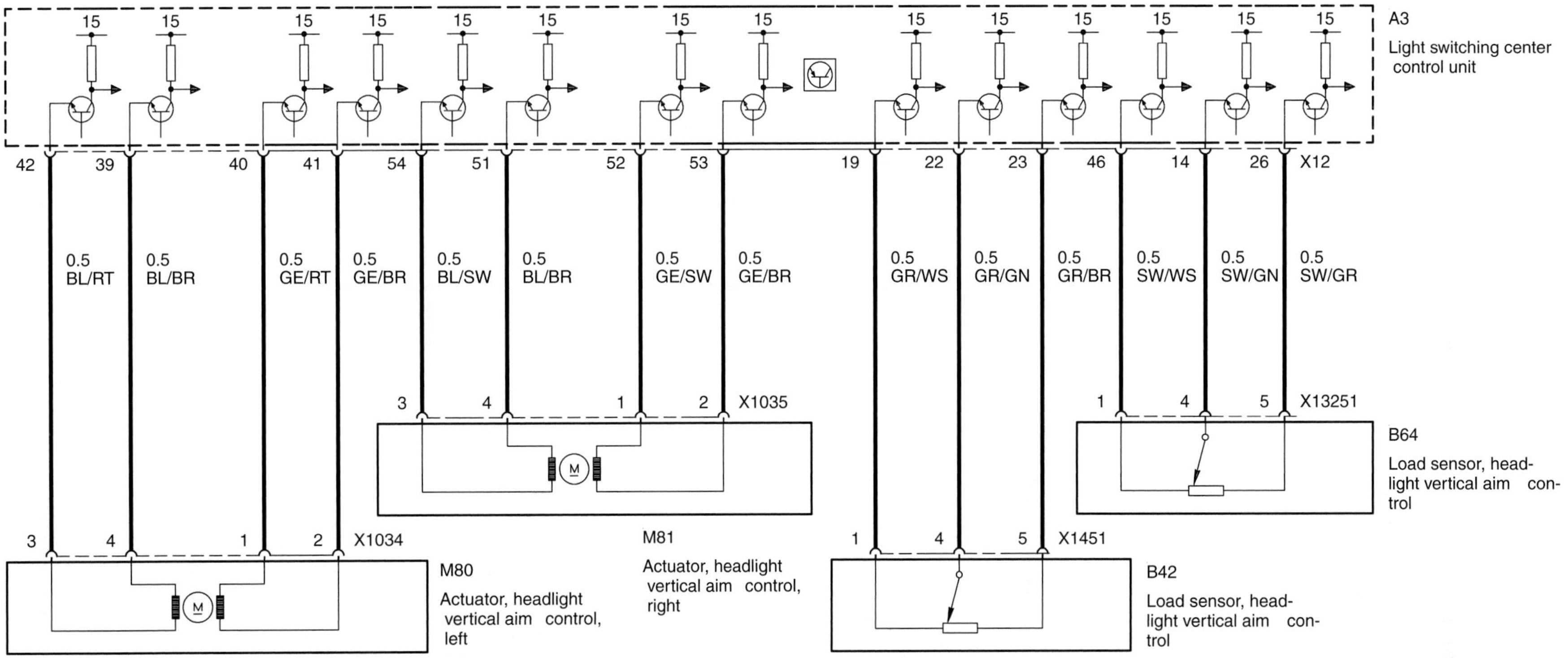

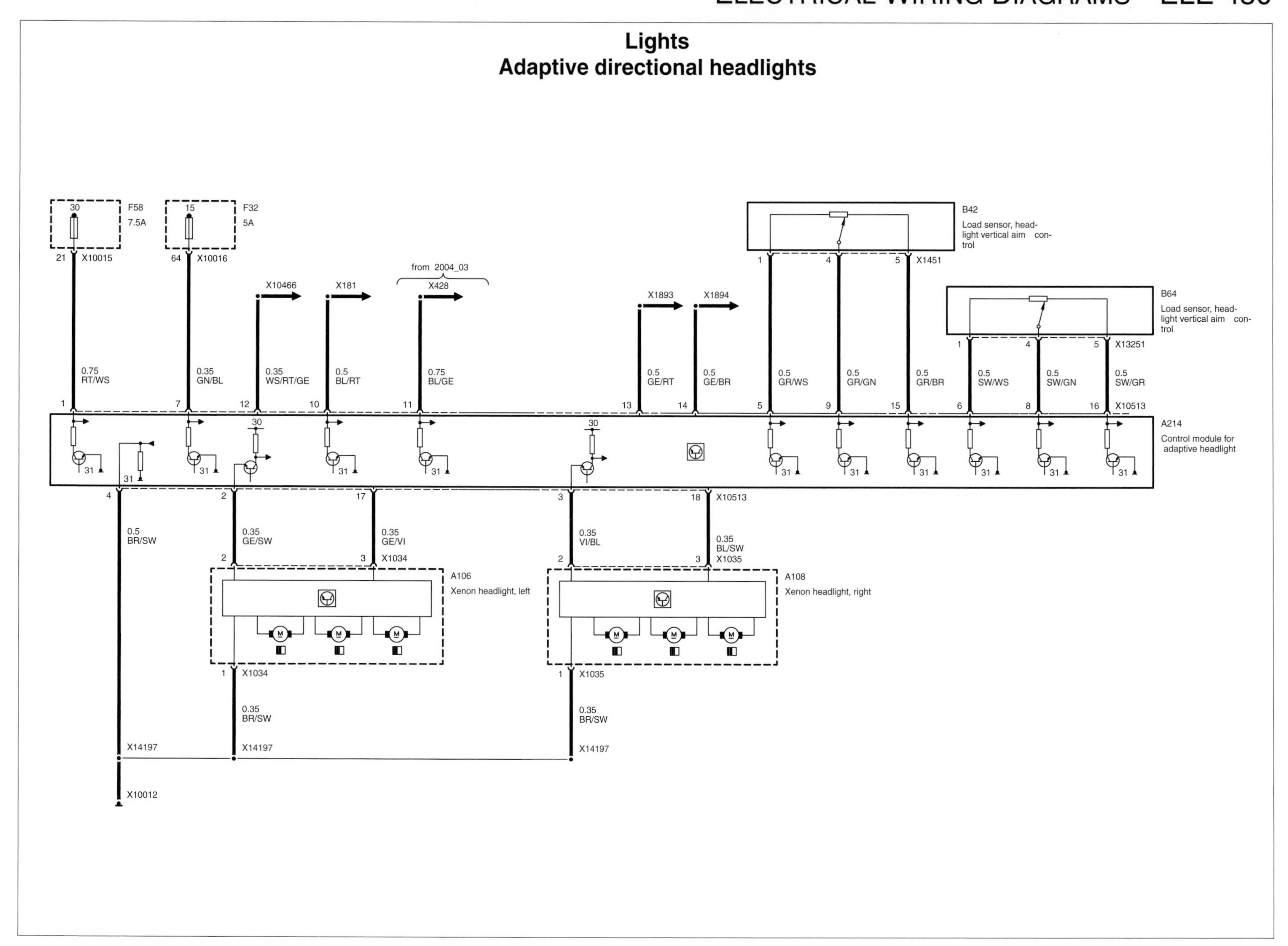

Lights
Adaptive directional headlights
F58
7.5A
30
21
X10015
F32
5A
15
64
X10016
0.75
RT/WS
0.35
GN/BL
X10466
0.35
WS/RT/GE
X181
0.5
BL/RT
from 2004_03
X428
0.75
BL/GE
X1893
0.5
GE/RT
X1894
0.5
GE/BR
B42
Load sensor, head-light vertical aim control
X1451
0.5
GR/WS
0.5
GR/GN
0.5
GR/BR
B64
Load sensor, head-light vertical aim control
X13251
0.5
SW/WS
0.5
SW/GN
0.5
SW/GR
X10513
A214
Control module for adaptive headlight
31
30
0.5
BR/SW
0.35
GE/SW
0.35
GE/VI
X1034
A106
Xenon headlight, left
0.35
VI/BL
0.35
BL/SW
X1035
A108
Xenon headlight, right
X1034
0.35
BR/SW
X1035
0.35
BR/SW
X14197
X10012

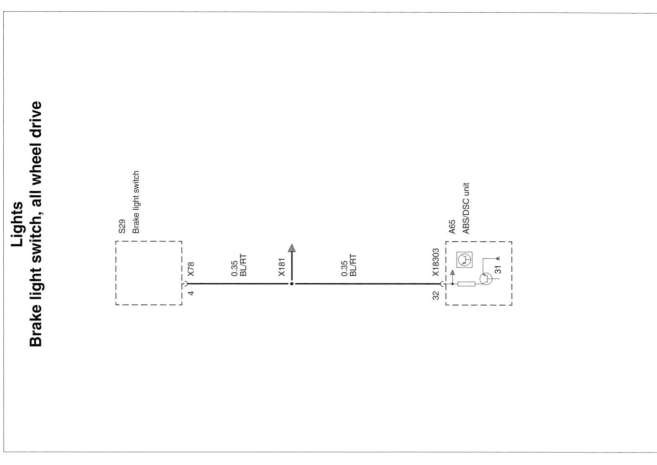

Lights
Rain sensor

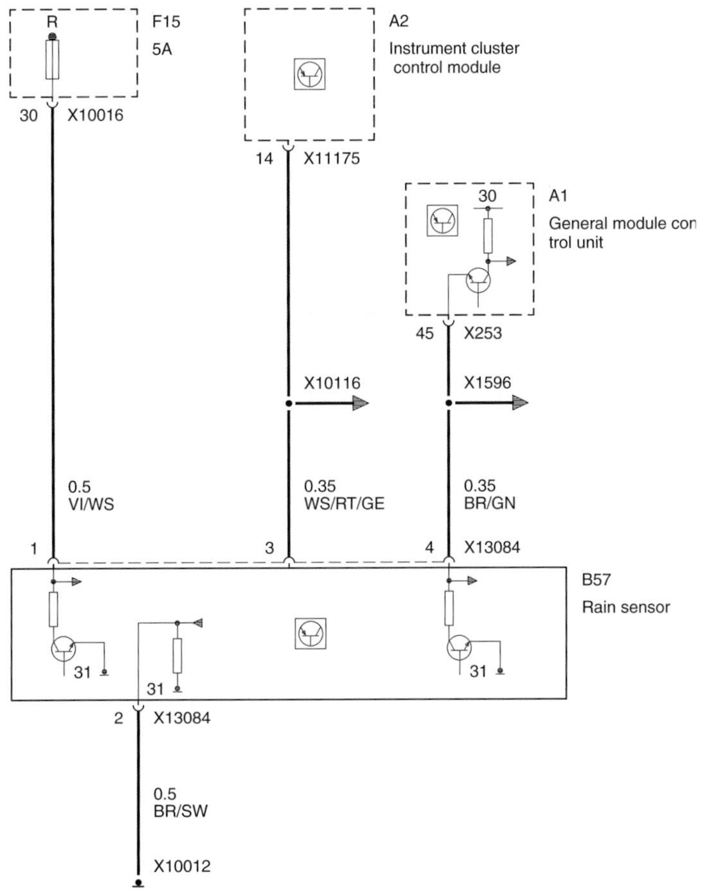

Lights
Brake light switch, all wheel drive

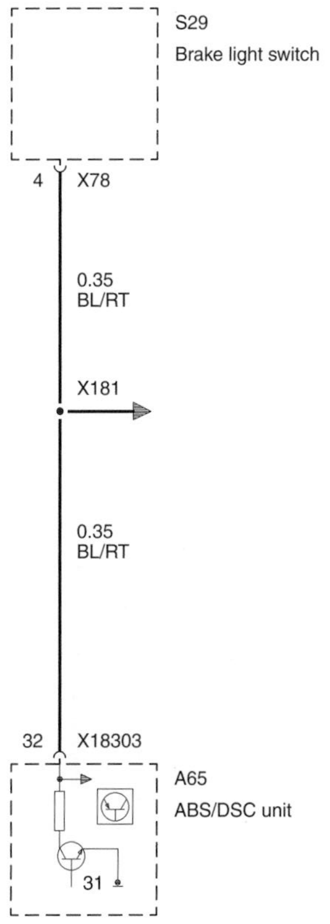

Lights
Brake light switch, MS S54

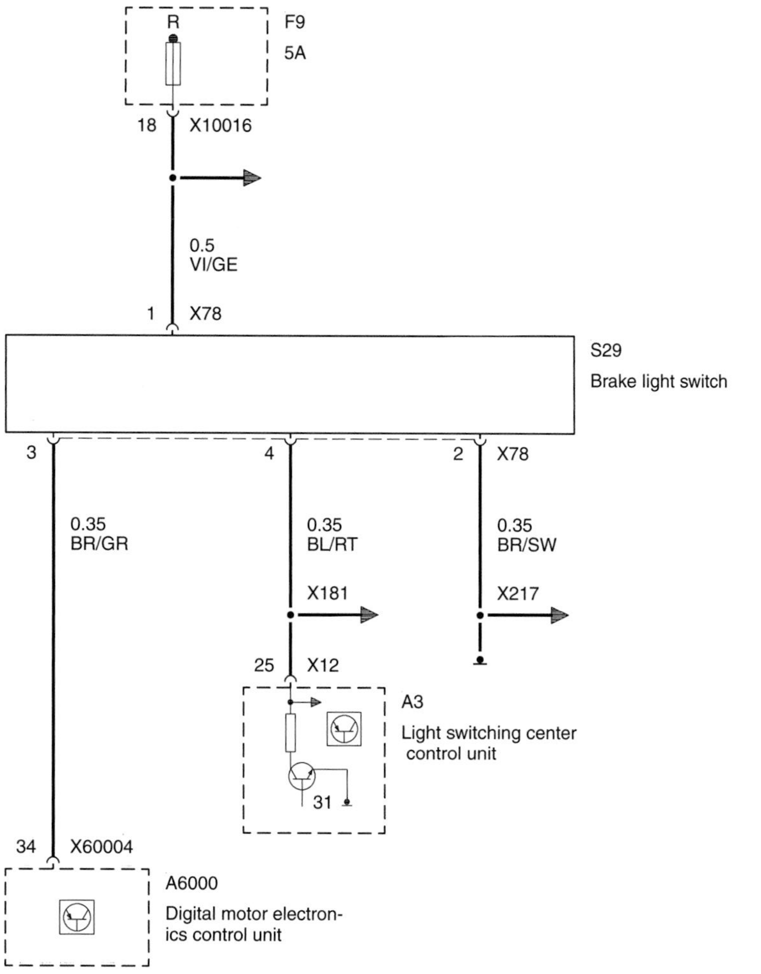

Lights
Brake light switch, MS 43

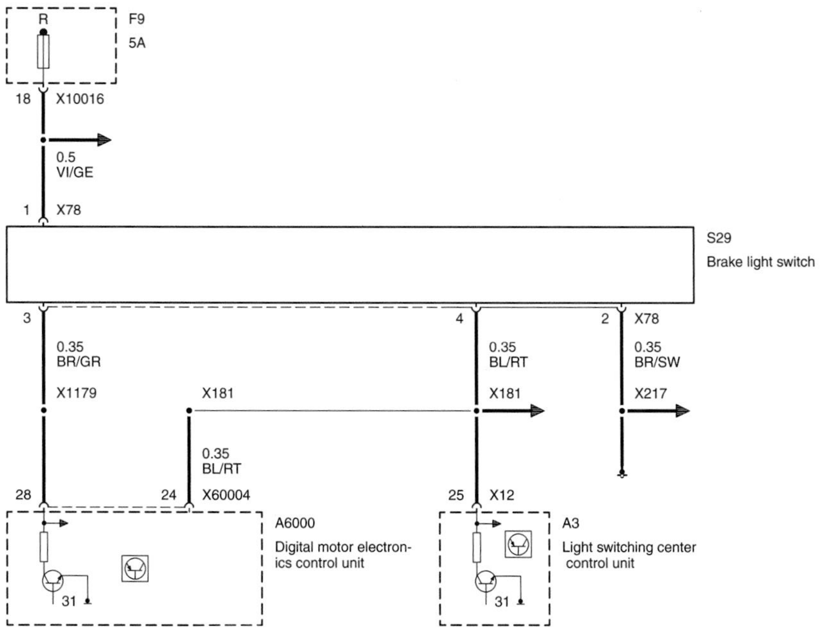

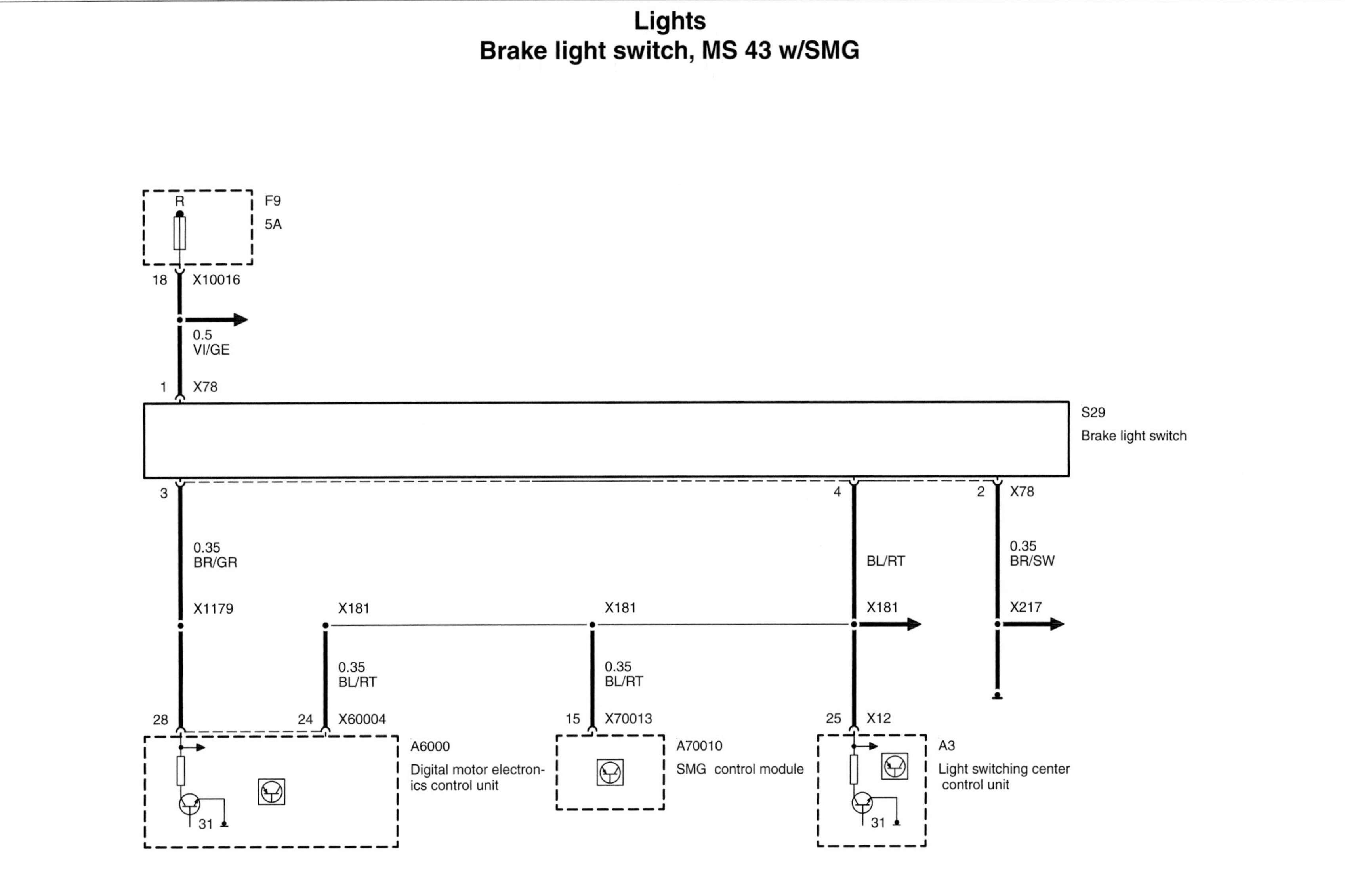
Lights
Brake light switch, MS 43 w/SMG
R
F9
5A
18
X10016
0.5
VI/GE
1
X78
S29
Brake light switch
3
4
2
X78
0.35
BR/GR
BL/RT
0.35
BR/SW
X1179
X181
X181
X181
X217
0.35
BL/RT
0.35
BL/RT
28
24
X60004
15
X70013
25
X12
A6000
Digital motor electron-
ics control unit
A70010
SMG control module
A3
Light switching center
control unit
31
31

Lights
Brake light switch, all wheel drive w/tire pressure warning

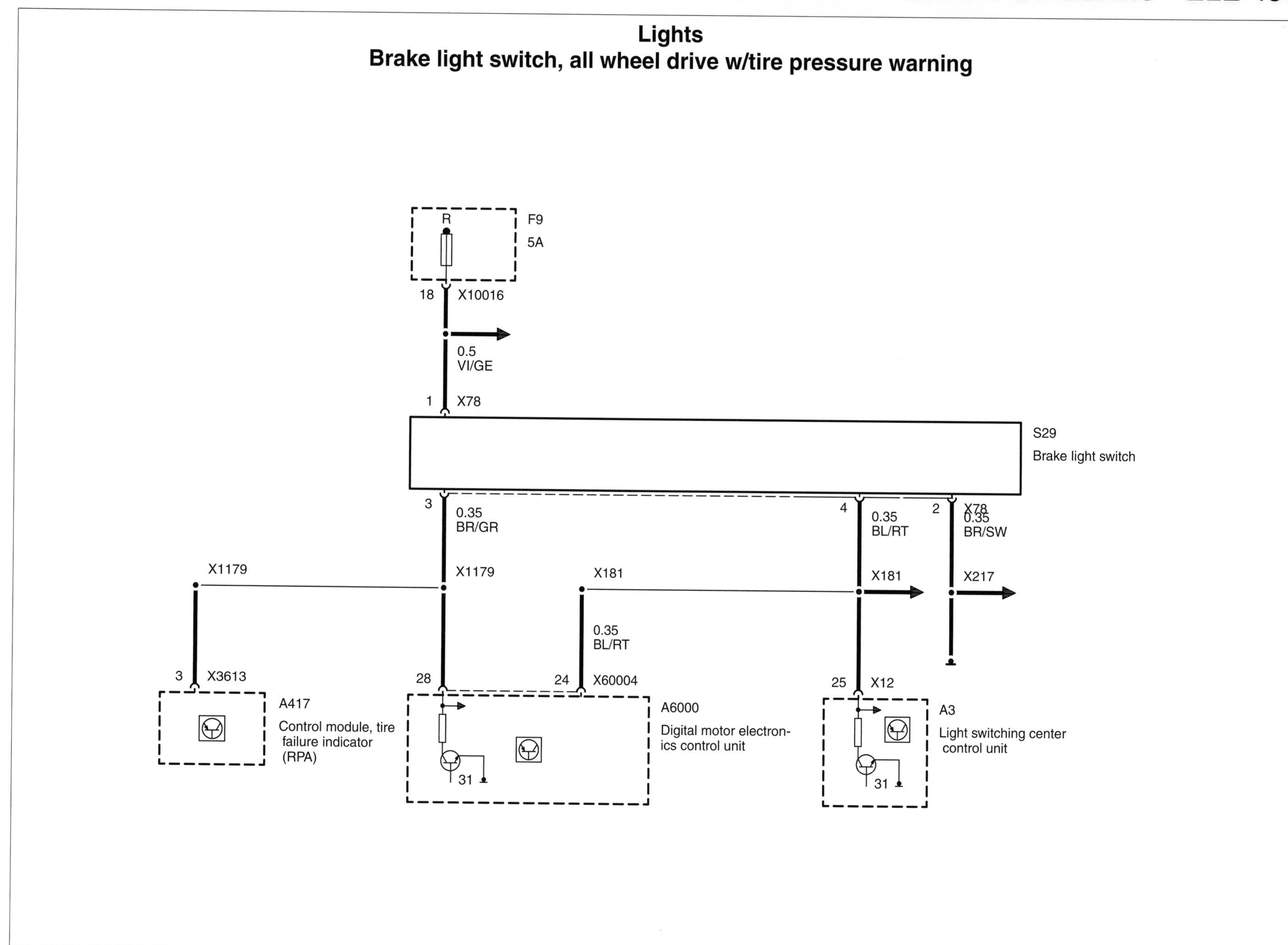

Lights
Brake lights
(up to 09/2001)

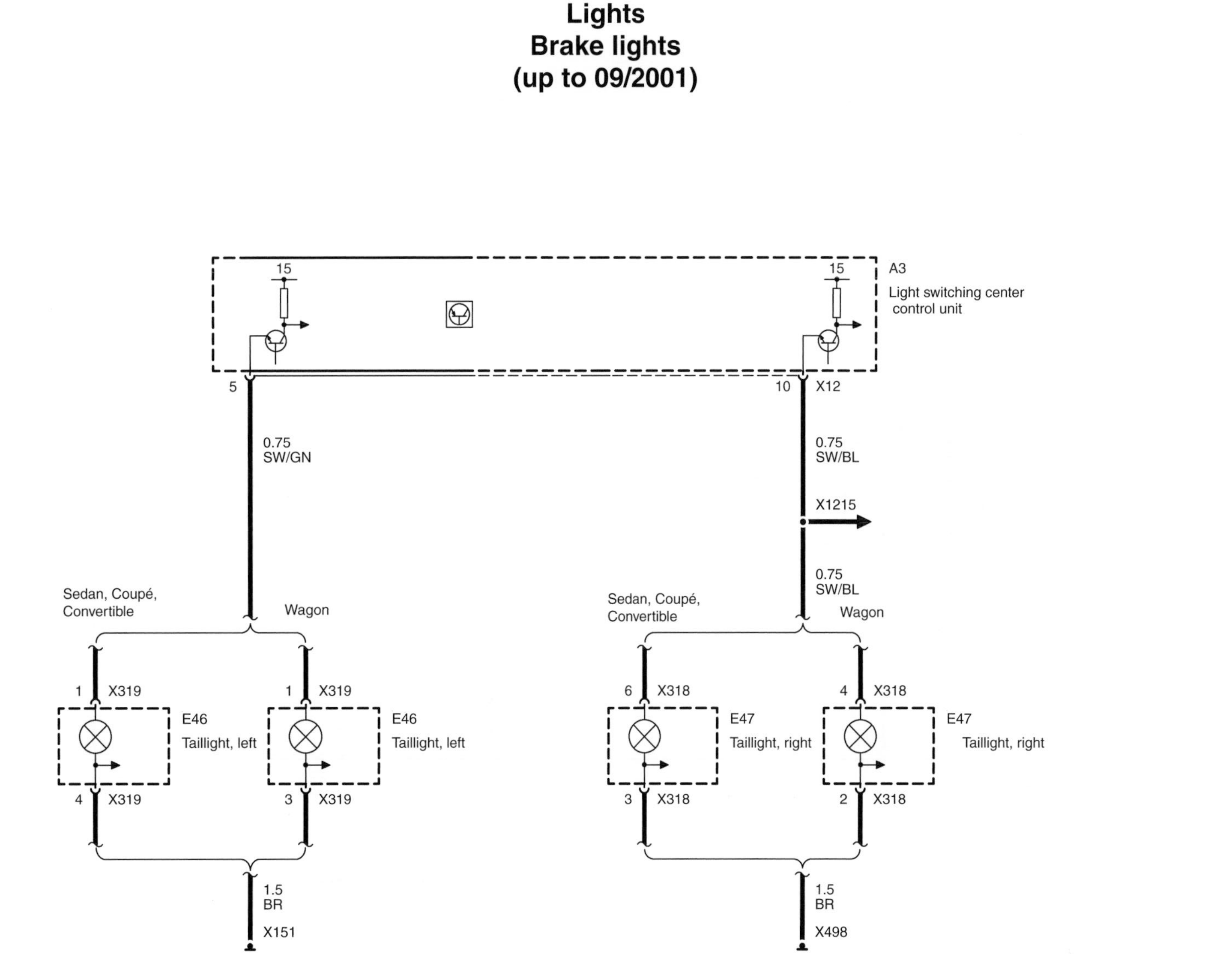

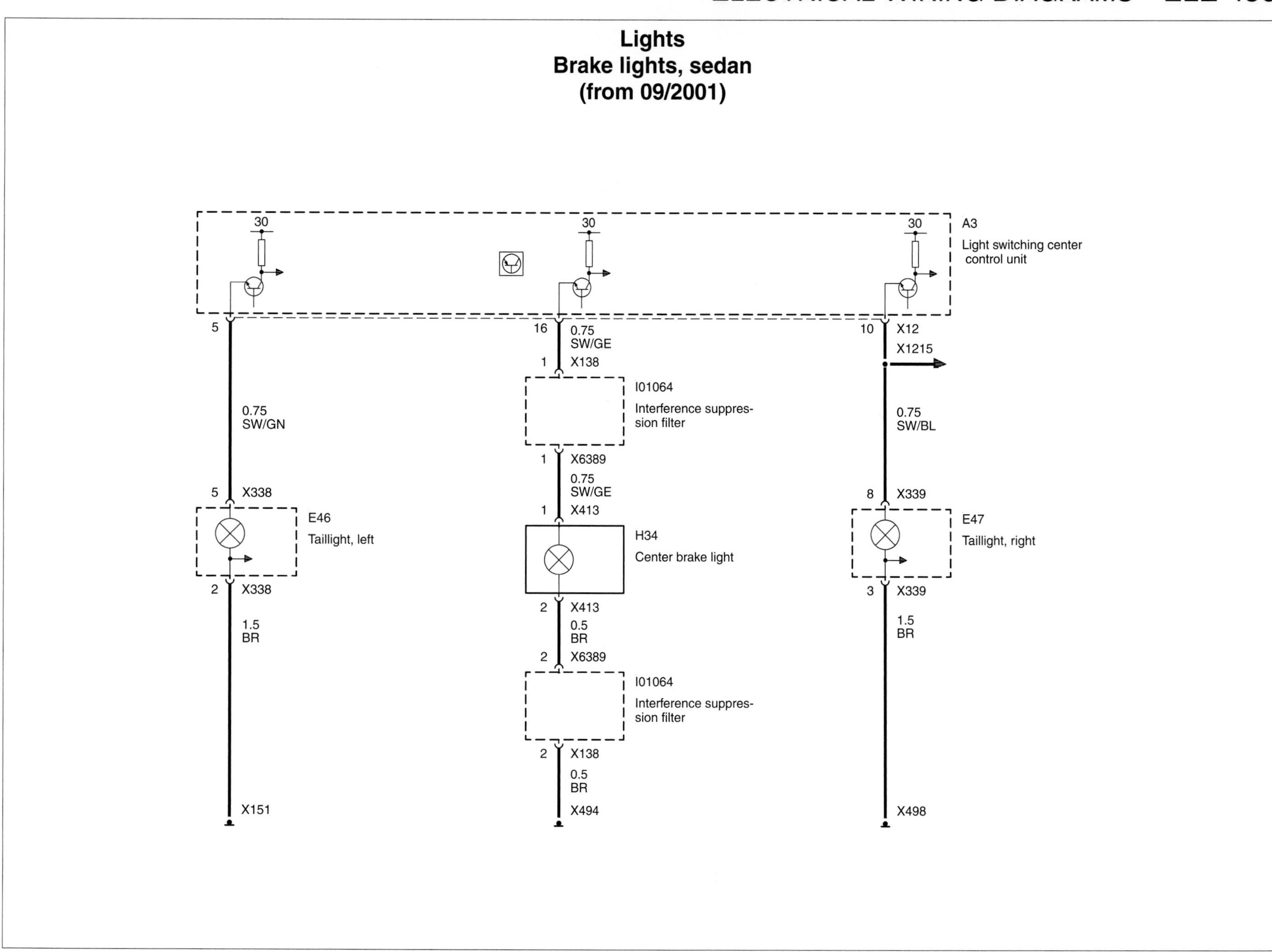
Lights
Brake lights, sedan
(from 09/2001)
30
30
30
A3
Light switching center control unit
5
16
0.75
SW/GE
1
X138
10
X12
X1215
I01064
Interference suppres-sion filter
0.75
SW/GN
0.75
SW/BL
1
X6389
0.75
SW/GE
5
X338
1
X413
8
X339
E46
Taillight, left
H34
Center brake light
E47
Taillight, right
2
X338
2
X413
3
X339
1.5
BR
0.5
BR
1.5
BR
2
X6389
I01064
Interference suppres-sion filter
2
X138
0.5
BR
X151
X494
X498

Lights
Brake lights, coupe / convertible (from 09/2001 to 03/2003)

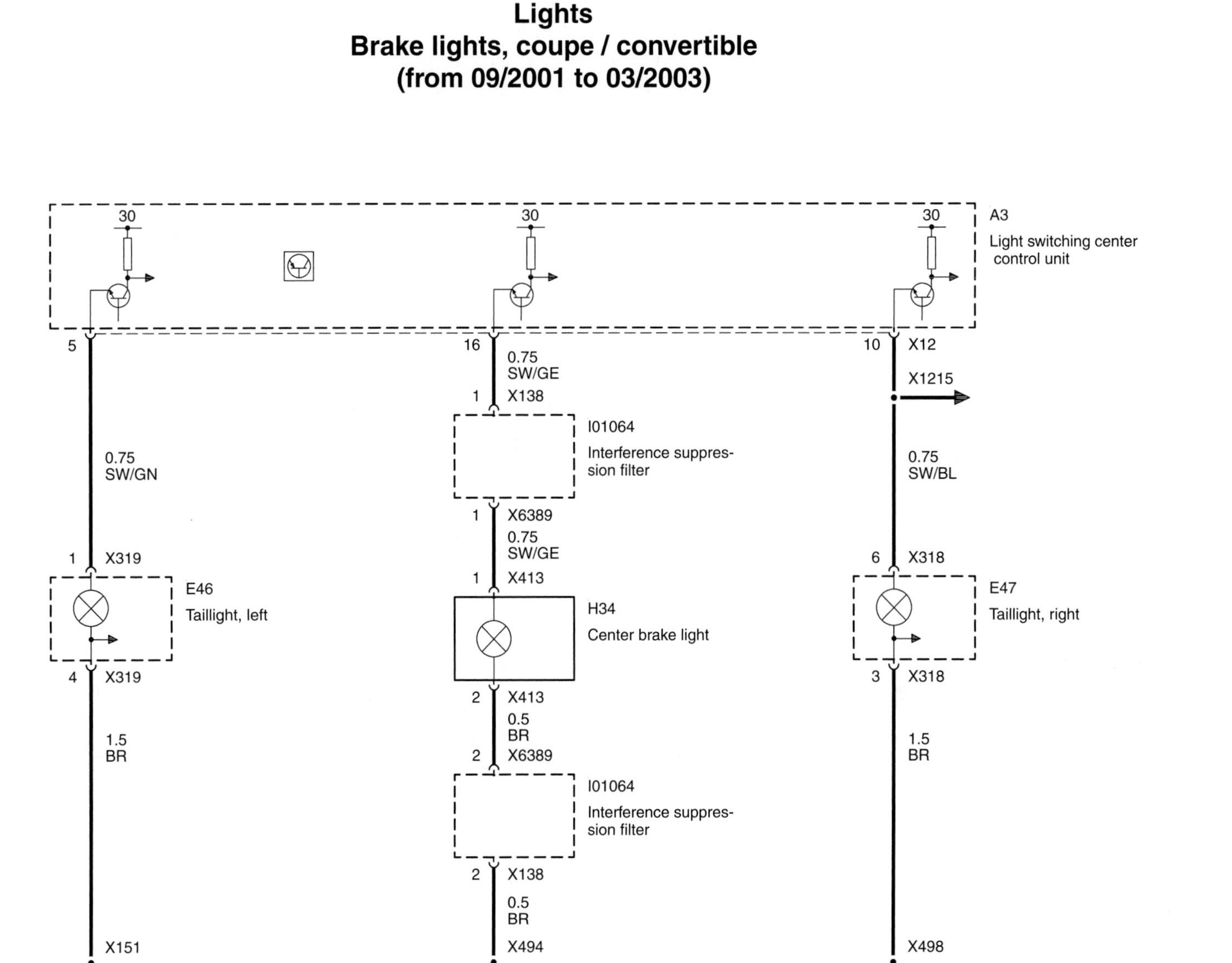

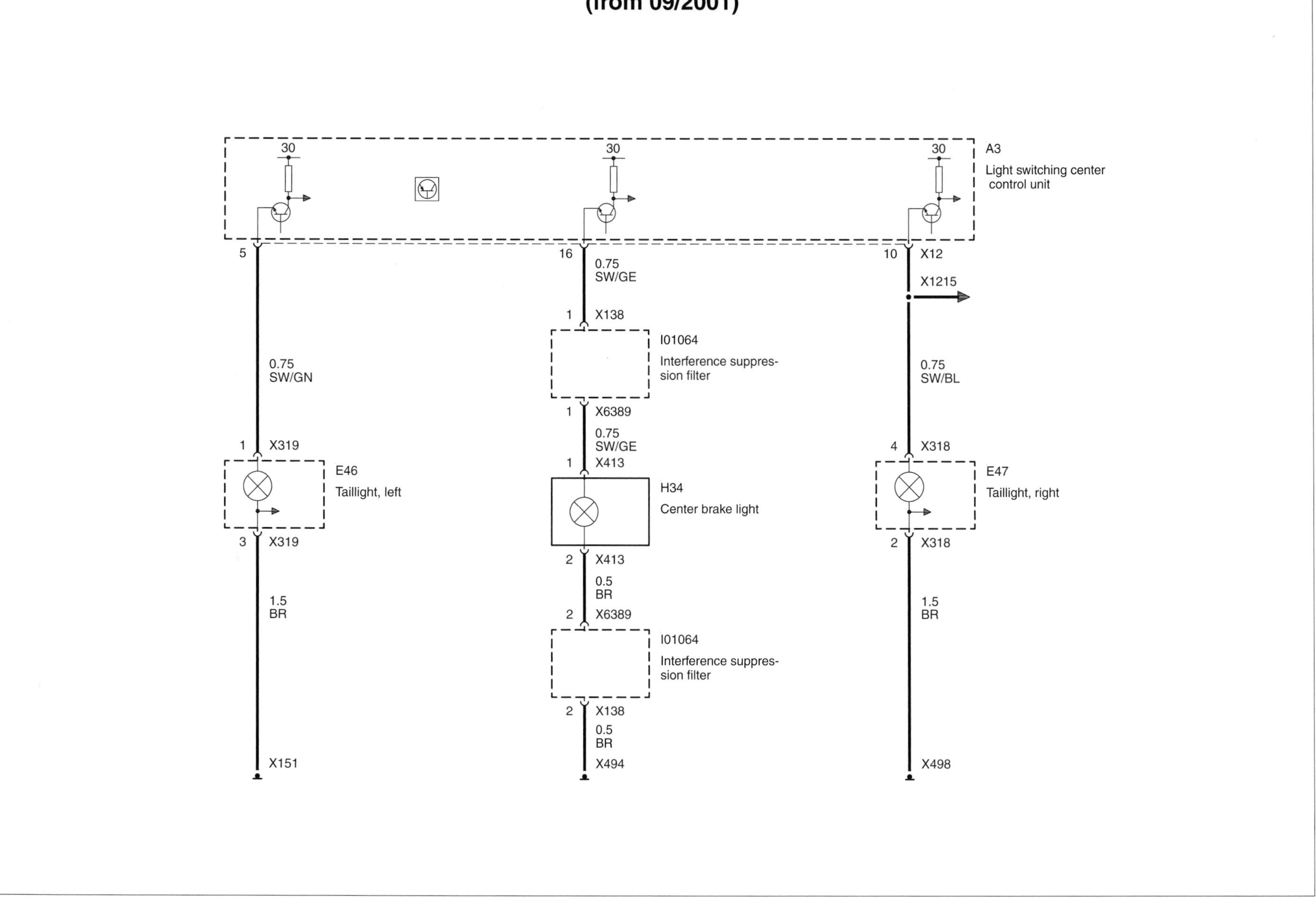
Lights
Brake lights, wagon
(from 09/2001)
30
30
30
A3
Light switching center control unit
5
16
10
X12
0.75
SW/GE
X1215
1
X138
I01064
Interference suppression filter
0.75
SW/GN
0.75
SW/BL
1
X6389
0.75
SW/GE
1
X413
1
X319
4
X318
E46
Taillight, left
H34
Center brake light
E47
Taillight, right
3
X319
2
X413
2
X318
0.5
BR
1.5
BR
2
X6389
1.5
BR
I01064
Interference suppression filter
2
X138
0.5
BR
X151
X494
X498

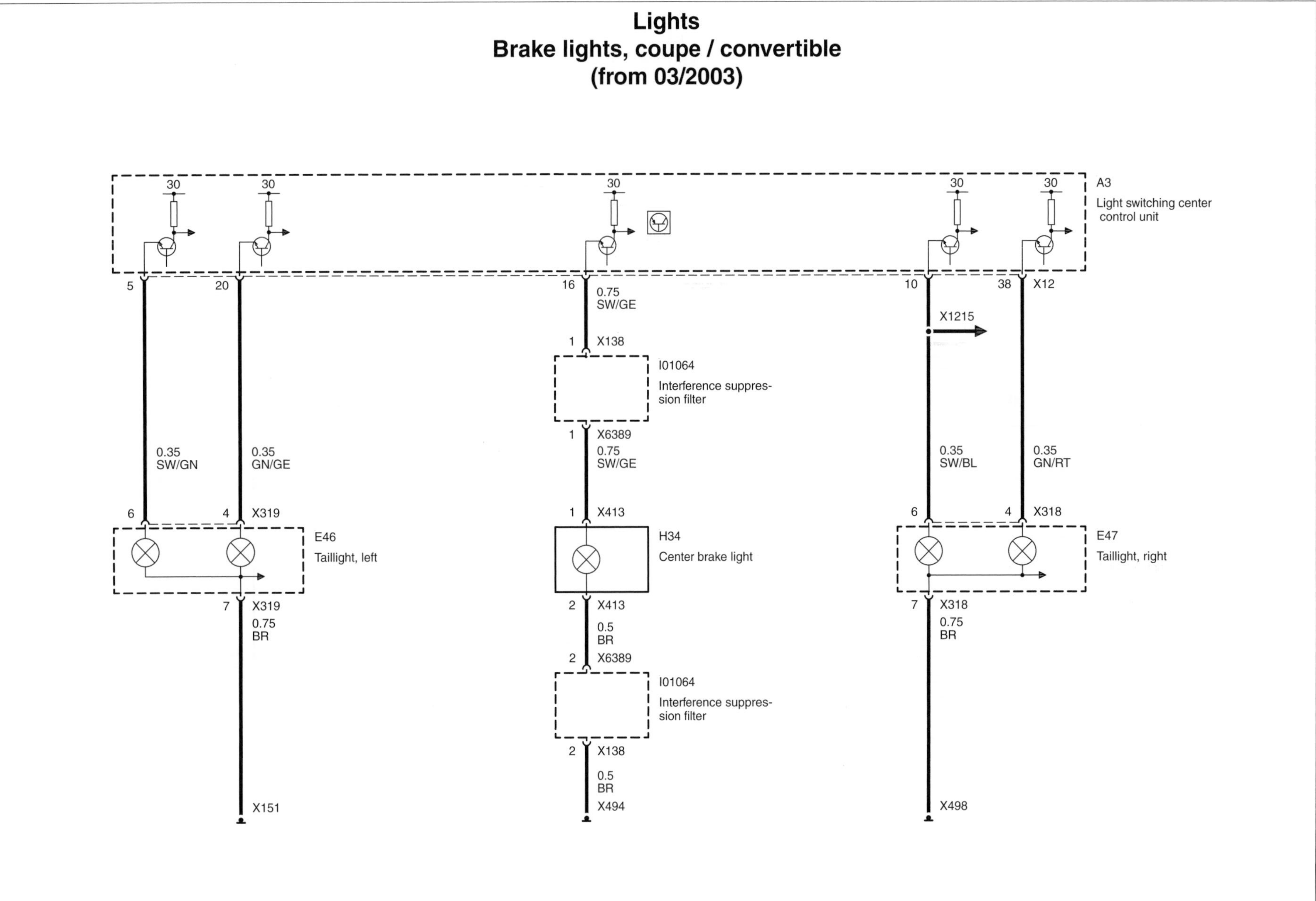

Lights
Brake lights, coupe / convertible
(from 03/2003)
30
A3
Light switching center control unit
5
20
16
10
38
X12
0.75
SW/GE
X1215
1
X138
I01064
Interference suppres-sion filter
X6389
0.35
SW/GN
0.35
GN/GE
0.35
SW/BL
0.35
GN/RT
6
4
X319
X413
X318
E46
Taillight, left
H34
Center brake light
E47
Taillight, right
7
0.75
BR
2
0.5
BR
X151
X494
X498

Lights
Hazard warning switch

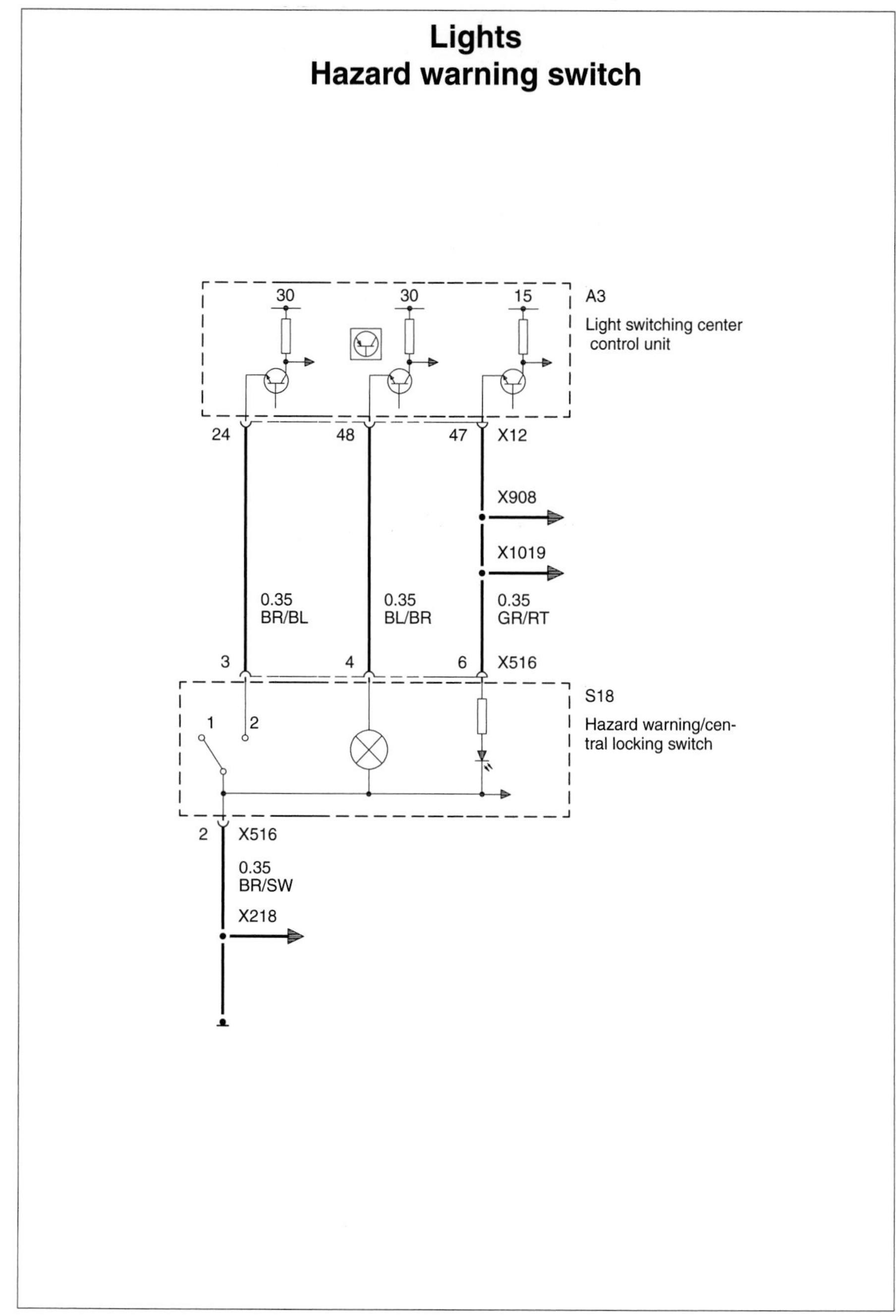

Lights
Fog lights w/out DME MS S54 (up to 03/2001)

F38
10A
30
1 X10015
A3
Light switching center control unit
15
28 X12
0.5
GE/GR
1.0
RT/GE
8
6 X44
K47
Fog light relay
4
2 X44
0.5
BR/SW
X10012
1.0
GE/BR
2 X768
E26
Left fog light
1 X768
1.0
BR
X165
1.0
GE/BR
2 X769
E27
Right fog light
1 X769
1.0
BR
X166

Lights
Fog lights w/ DME MS S54
(up to 03/2001)

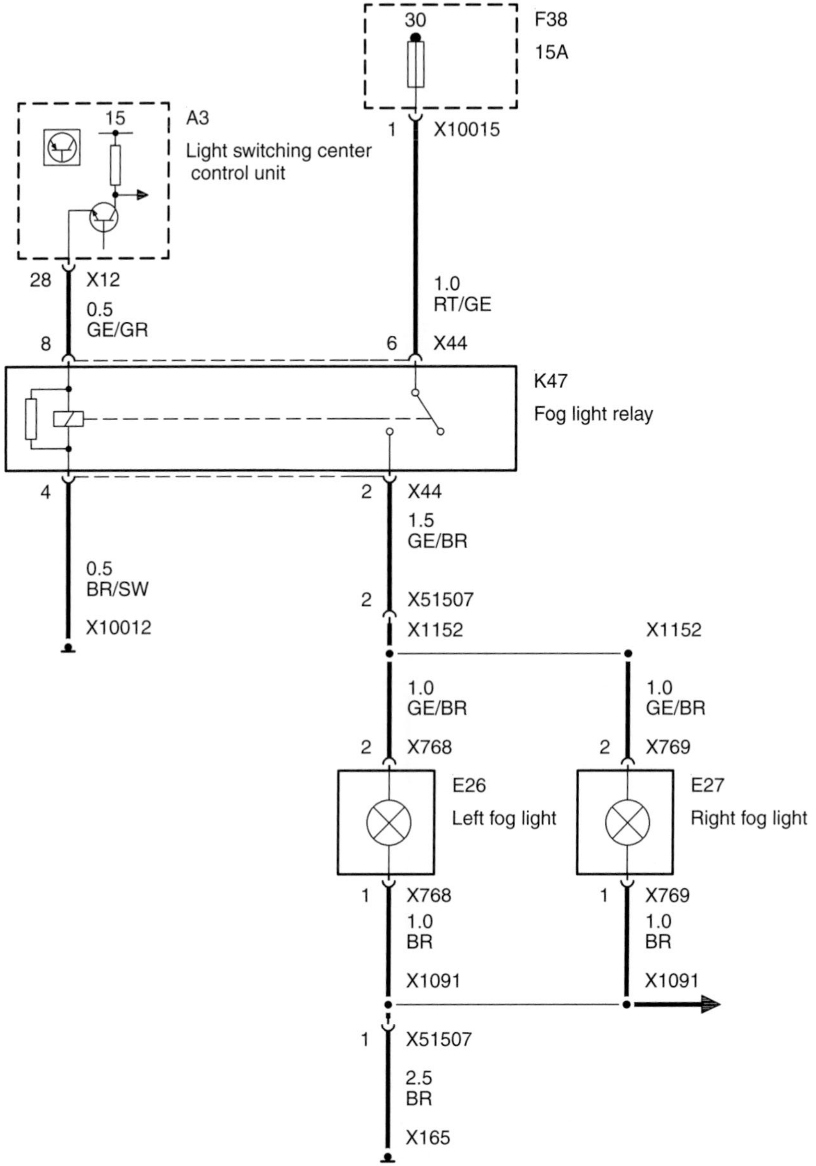

F38
15A
30
1 X10015
A3
Light switching center control unit
15
28 X12
0.5
GE/GR
1.0
RT/GE
8
6 X44
K47
Fog light relay
4
2 X44
1.5
GE/BR
0.5
BR/SW
X10012
2 X51507
X1152
X1152
1.0
GE/BR
2 X768
1.0
GE/BR
2 X769
E26
Left fog light
E27
Right fog light
1 X768
1.0
BR
1 X769
1.0
BR
X1091
X1091
1 X51507
2.5
BR
X165

Lights
Fog lights w/out DME MS S54
(from 03/2001 to 09/2001)

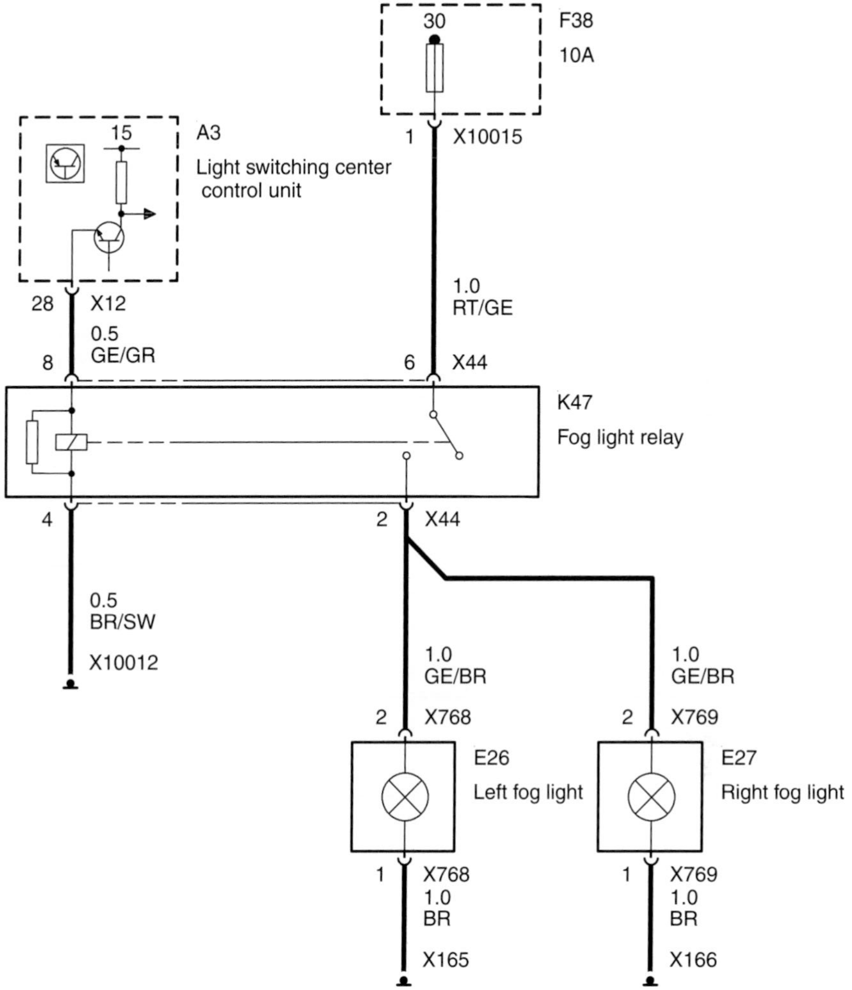

F38
10A
30
1 X10015
A3
Light switching center control unit
15
28 X12
0.5
GE/GR
1.0
RT/GE
8
6 X44
K47
Fog light relay
4
2 X44
0.5
BR/SW
X10012
1.0
GE/BR
2 X768
1.0
GE/BR
2 X769
E26
Left fog light
E27
Right fog light
1 X768
1.0
BR
X165
1 X769
1.0
BR
X166

Lights
Fog lights w/ DME MS S54
(from 03/2001 to 09/2001)

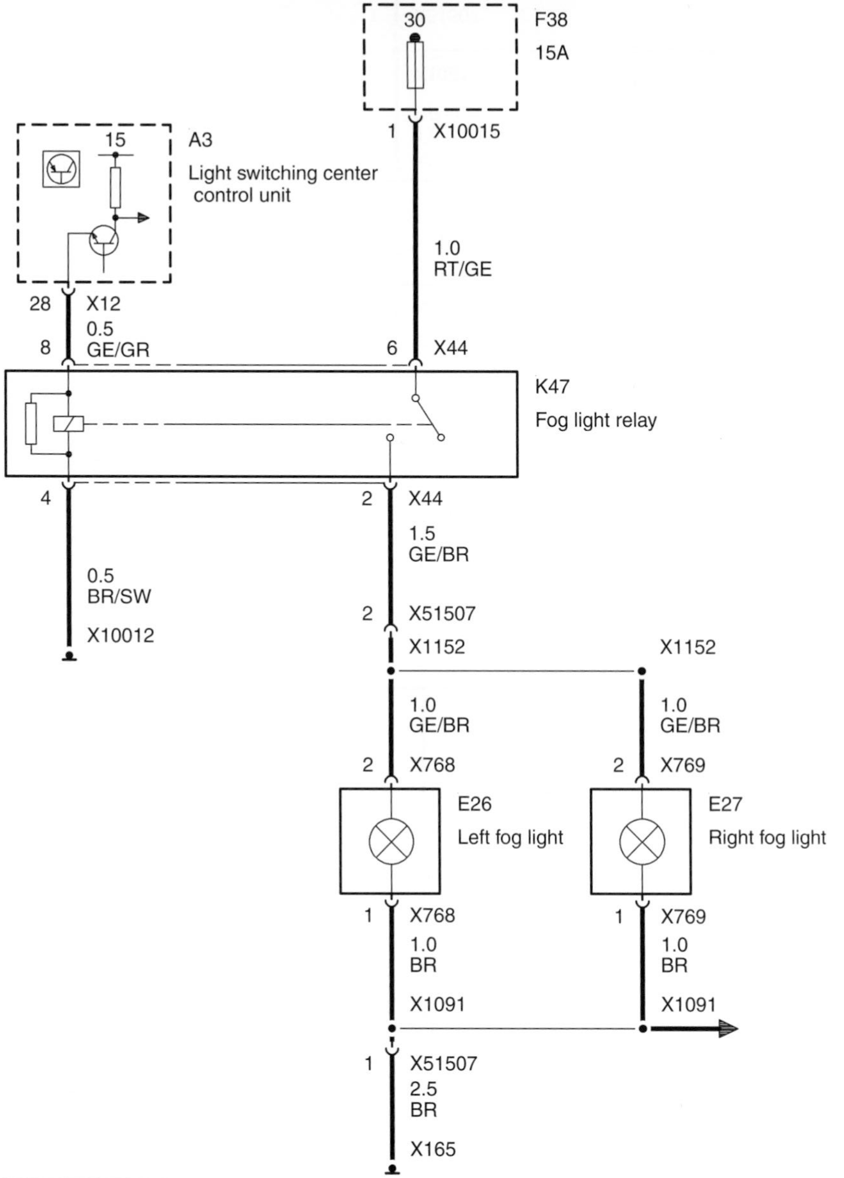

F38
15A
30
1 X10015
1.0
RT/GE
6 X44
A3
Light switching center control unit
15
28 X12
0.5
8 GE/GR
K47
Fog light relay
4
0.5
BR/SW
X10012
2 X44
1.5
GE/BR
2 X51507
X1152
X1152
1.0
GE/BR
2 X768
E26
Left fog light
1 X768
1.0
BR
X1091
1.0
GE/BR
2 X769
E27
Right fog light
1 X769
1.0
BR
X1091
1 X51507
2.5
BR
X165

Lights
Front and rear fog lights, sedan
(from 09/2001)

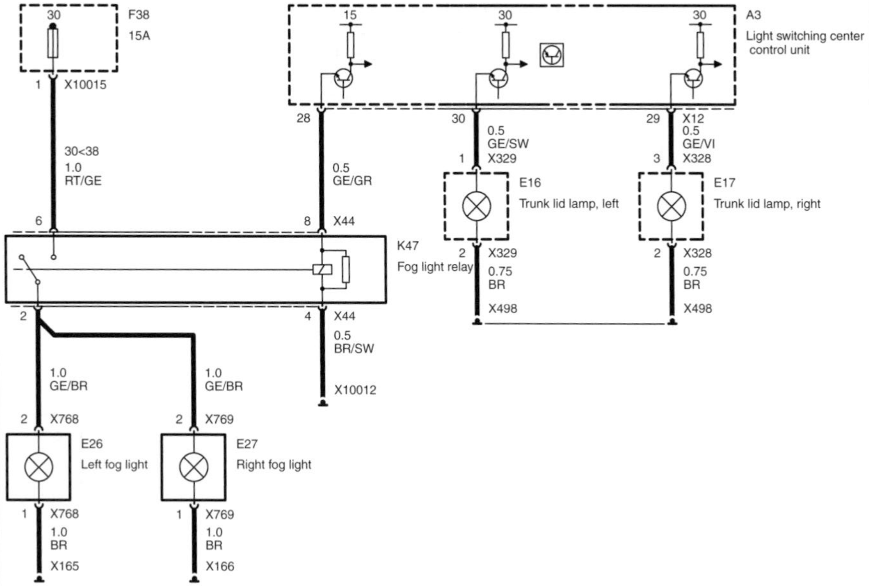

F38
15A
30
1 X10015
30<38
1.0
RT/GE
6
A3
Light switching center control unit
15
30
30
28
0.5
GE/GR
8 X44
K47
Fog light relay
2
4 X44
0.5
BR/SW
X10012
30
0.5
GE/SW
1 X329
E16
Trunk lid lamp, left
2 X329
0.75
BR
X498
29 X12
0.5
GE/VI
3 X328
E17
Trunk lid lamp, right
2 X328
0.75
BR
X498
1.0
GE/BR
2 X768
E26
Left fog light
1 X768
1.0
BR
X165
1.0
GE/BR
2 X769
E27
Right fog light
1 X769
1.0
BR
X166

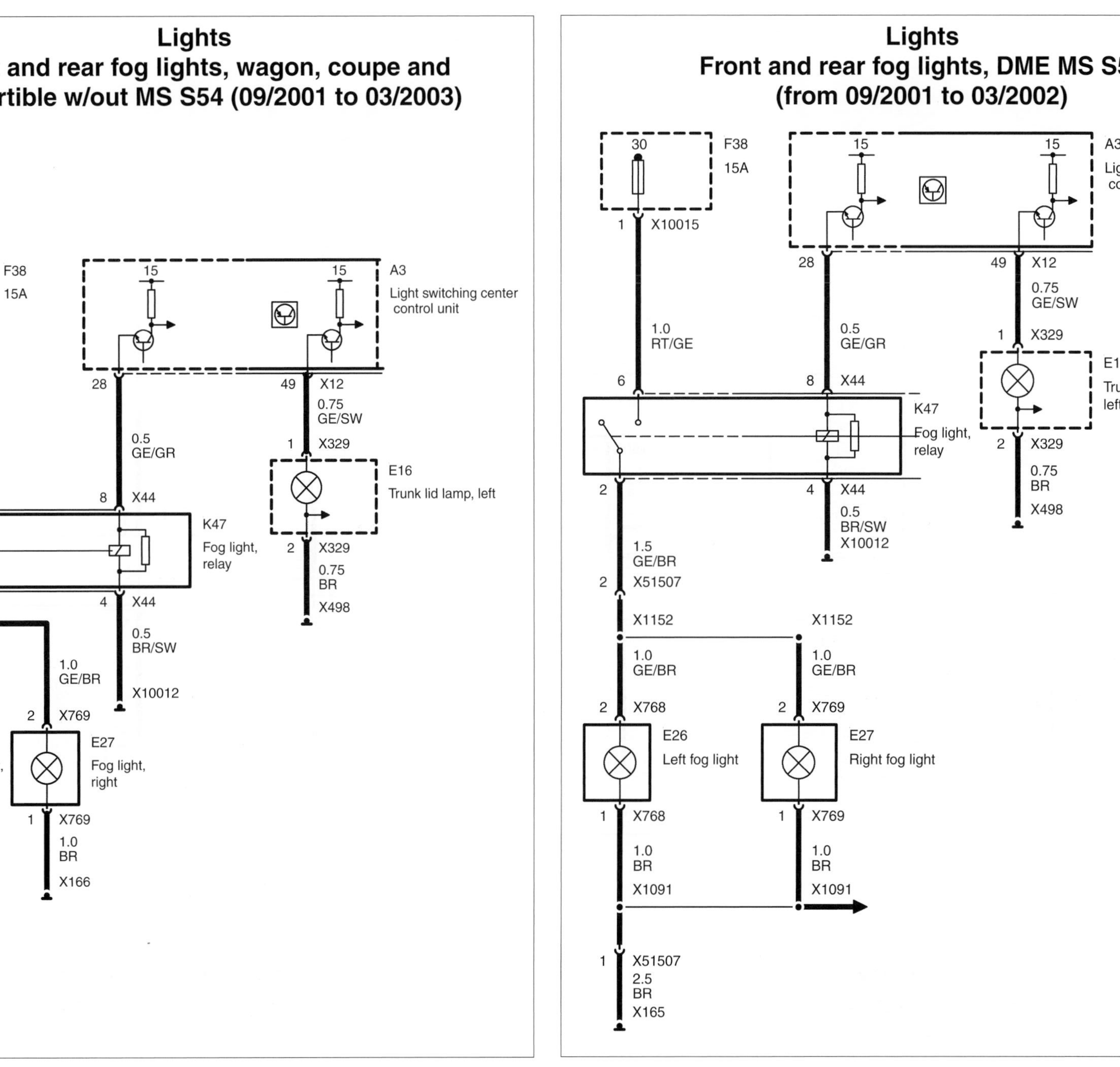

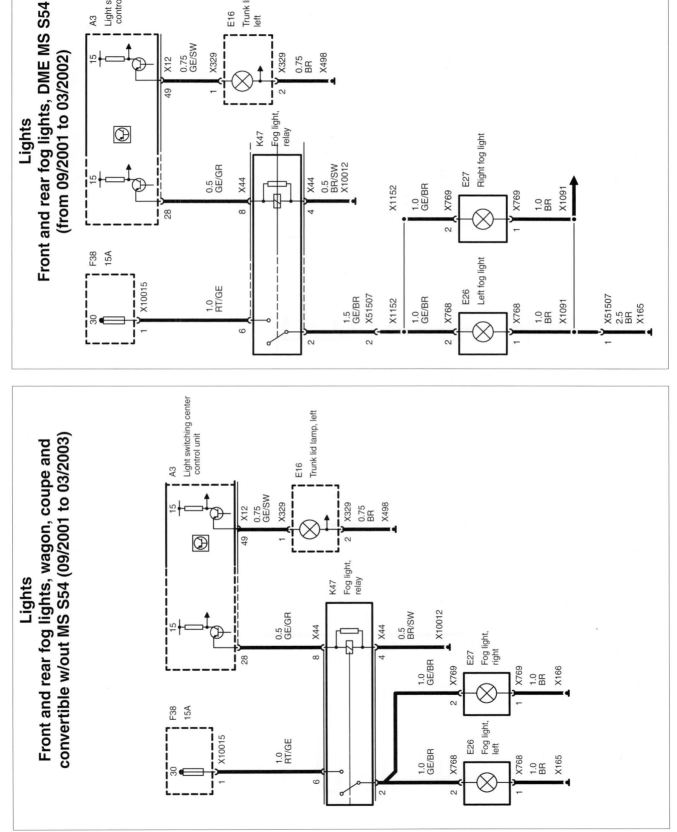

Lights
Front and rear fog lights, wagon, coupe and convertible w/out MS S54 (09/2001 to 03/2003)
30
F38
15A
1
X10015
1.0
RT/GE
15
15
A3
Light switching center control unit
28
49
X12
0.75
GE/SW
0.5
GE/GR
1
X329
E16
Trunk lid lamp, left
2
X329
0.75
BR
X498
6
8
X44
K47
Fog light, relay
2
4
X44
0.5
BR/SW
X10012
1.0
GE/BR
1.0
GE/BR
2
X768
2
X769
E26
Fog light, left
E27
Fog light, right
1
X768
1.0
BR
X165
1
X769
1.0
BR
X166
Lights
Front and rear fog lights, DME MS S54 (from 09/2001 to 03/2002)
30
F38
15A
1
X10015
15
15
A3
Light switching center control unit
28
49
X12
0.75
GE/SW
1
X329
E16
Trunk lid lamp, left
2
X329
0.75
BR
X498
1.0
RT/GE
0.5
GE/GR
6
8
X44
K47
Fog light, relay
2
4
X44
0.5
BR/SW
X10012
1.5
GE/BR
2
X51507
X1152
X1152
1.0
GE/BR
1.0
GE/BR
2
X768
2
X769
E26
Left fog light
E27
Right fog light
1
X768
1
X769
1.0
BR
X1091
1.0
BR
X1091
1
X51507
2.5
BR
X165

Lights
Front and rear fog lights, wagon (from 03/2003)

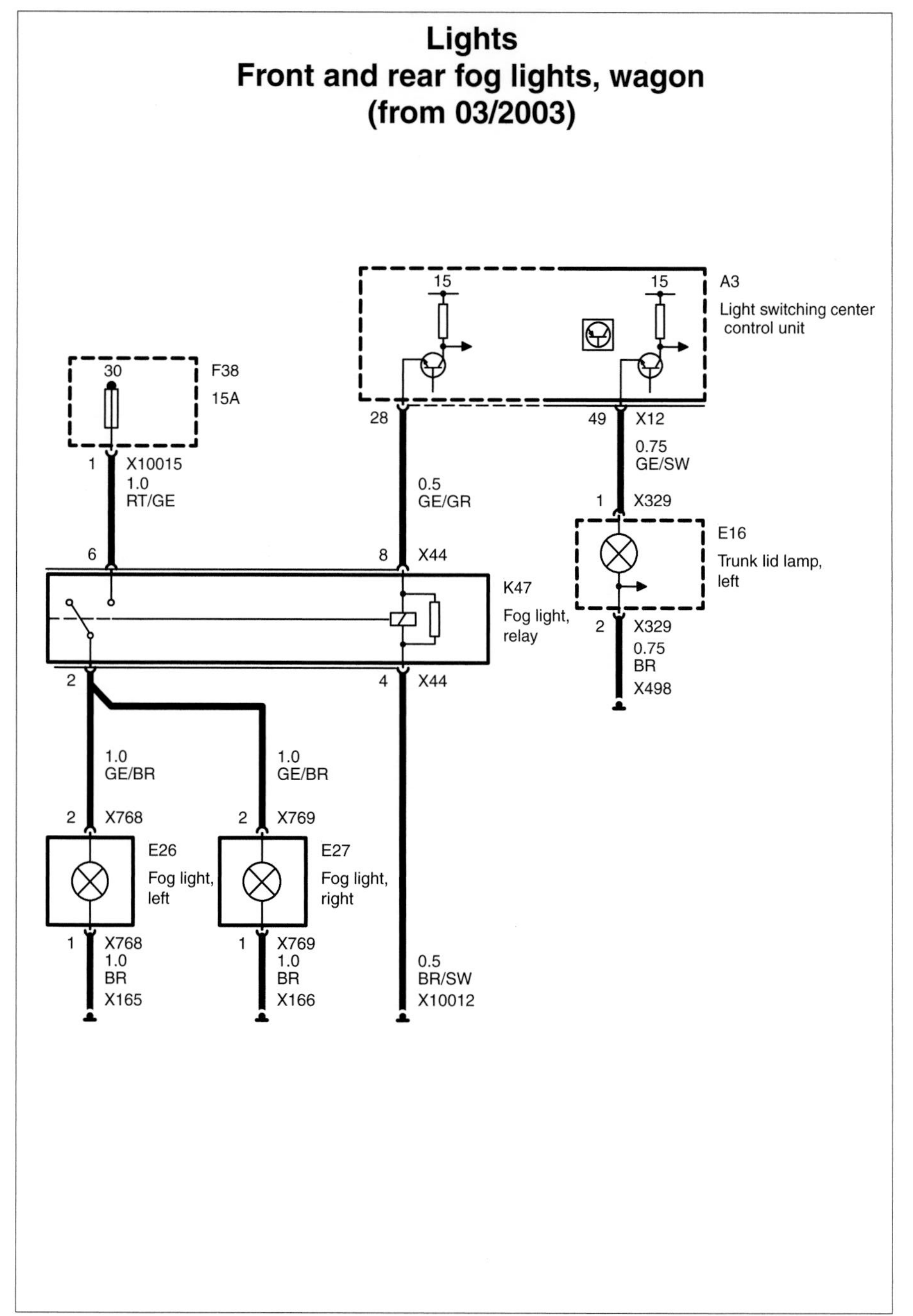

Lights
Front and rear fog lights, coupe / convertible w/out DME MS S54 (from 03/2003)

F38
15A
30
1
X10015
1.0
RT/GE
A3
Light switching center control unit
15
15
28
49
X12
0.75
GE/SW
1
X329
E16
Trunk lid lamp, left
2
X329
0.75
BR
X498
0.5
GE/GR
6
8
X44
K47
Fog light relay
2
4
X44
1.0
GE/BR
1.0
GE/BR
2
X768
2
X769
E26
Fog light, left
E27
Fog light, right
1
X768
1.0
BR
X14249
1
X769
1.0
BR
X14250
0.5
BR/SW
X10012

Lights
Front and rear fog lights, coupe / convertible w/DME MS S54 (from 03/2003)

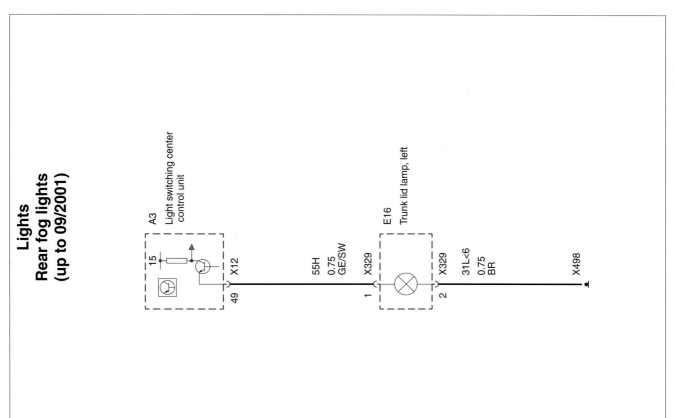

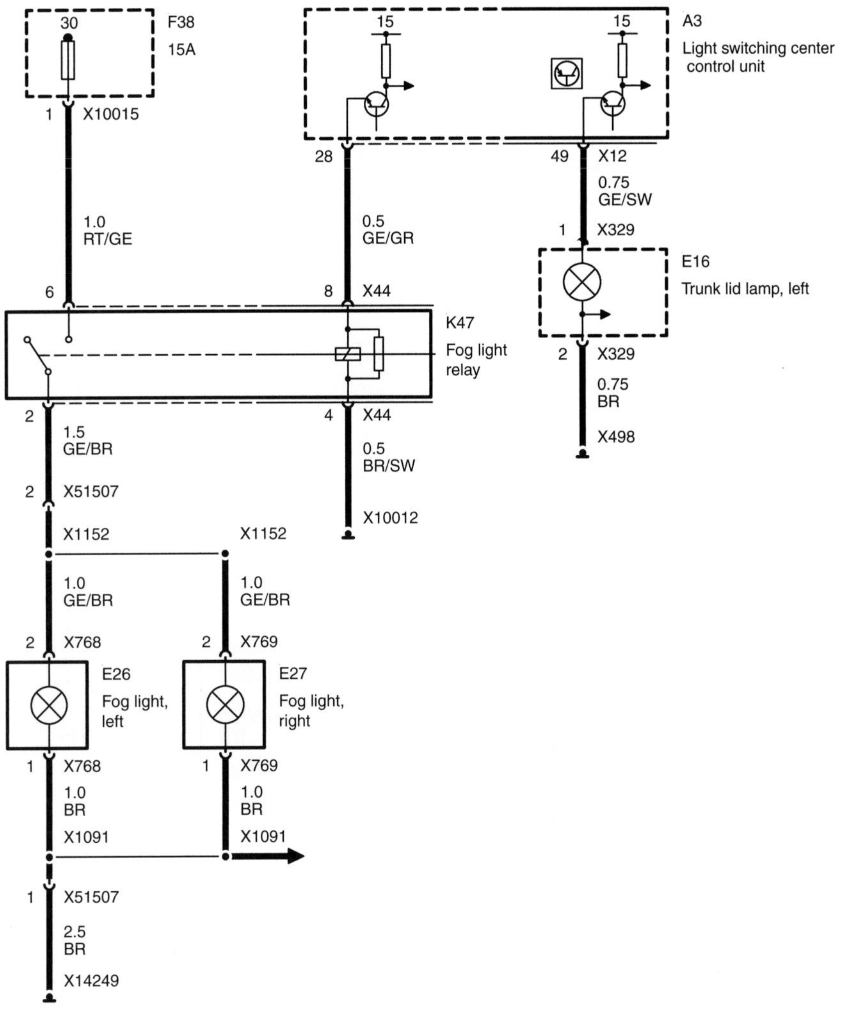

Lights
Rear fog lights (up to 09/2001)

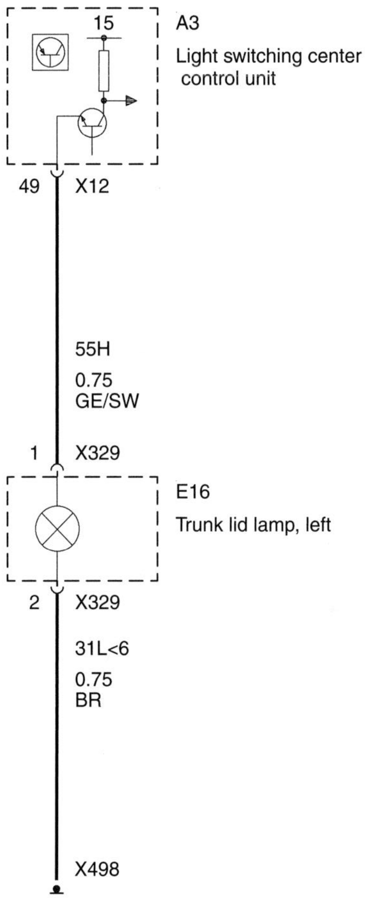

Lights
Backup lights, w/auto transmission

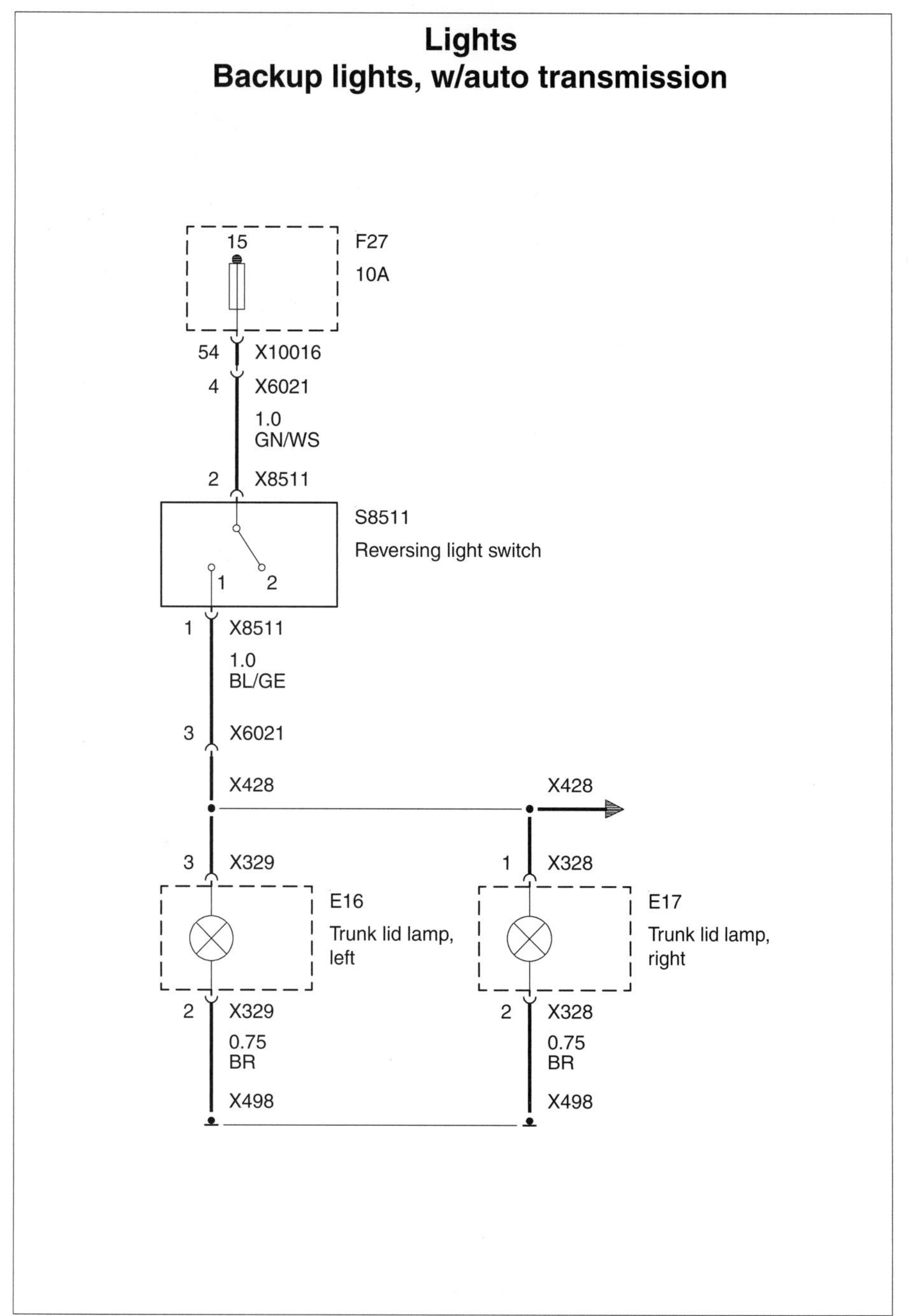

Lights
Backup lights, MS 43, MS 45 w/auto transmission

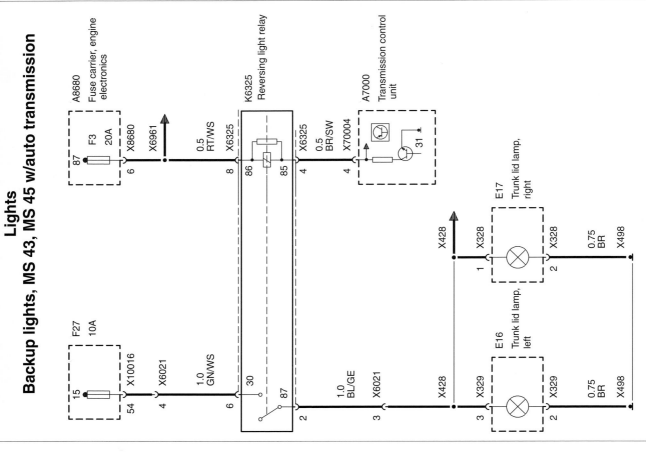

15
F27
10A
54
X10016
4
X6021
1.0
GN/WS
6
87
A8680
F3
Fuse carrier, engine
electronics
20A
6
X8680
X6961
0.5
RT/WS
8
X6325
30
86
K6325
Reversing light relay
87
85
2
4
X6325
0.5
BR/SW
4
X70004
1.0
BL/GE
A7000
Transmission control
unit
3
X6021
31
X428
X428
3
X329
1
X328
E16
Trunk lid lamp,
left
E17
Trunk lid lamp,
right
2
X329
2
X328
0.75
BR
0.75
BR
X498
X498

Lights
Interior lighting, convertible

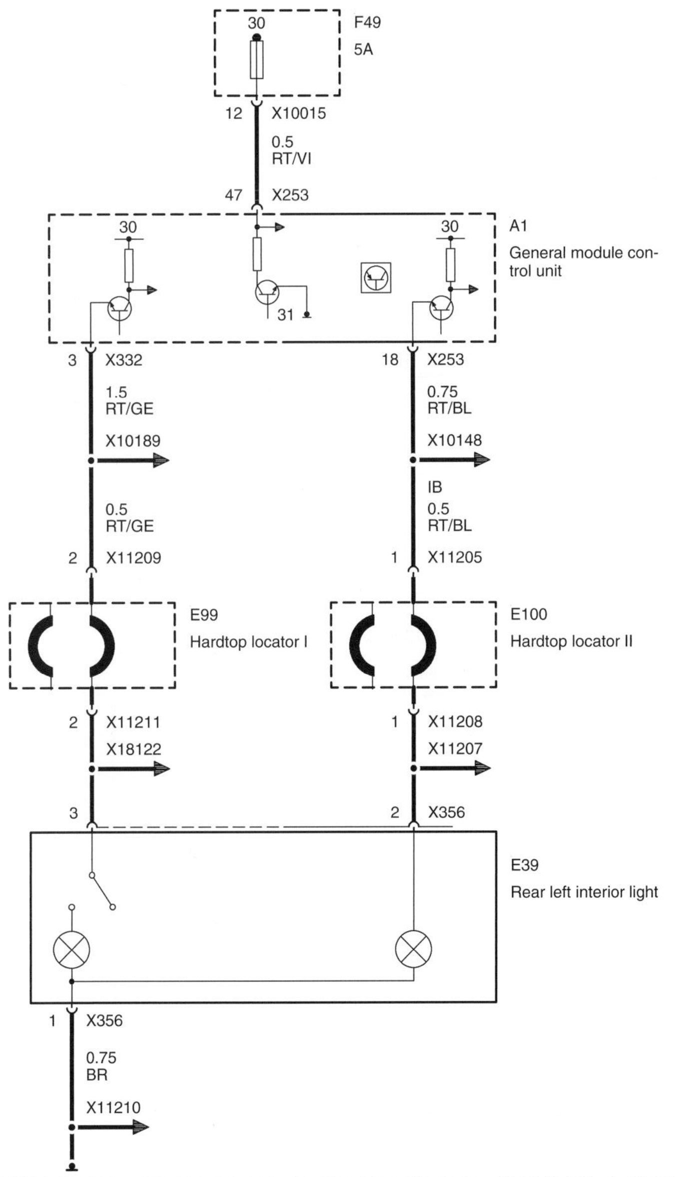

F49
5A
30
12 X10015
0.5
RT/VI
47 X253
A1
General module control unit
30
30
31
3 X332
1.5
RT/GE
X10189
0.5
RT/GE
2 X11209
E99
Hardtop locator I
2 X11211
X18122
3
18 X253
0.75
RT/BL
X10148
IB
0.5
RT/BL
1 X11205
E100
Hardtop locator II
1 X11208
X11207
2 X356
E39
Rear left interior light
1 X356
0.75
BR
X11210

Lights
Oddments tray package

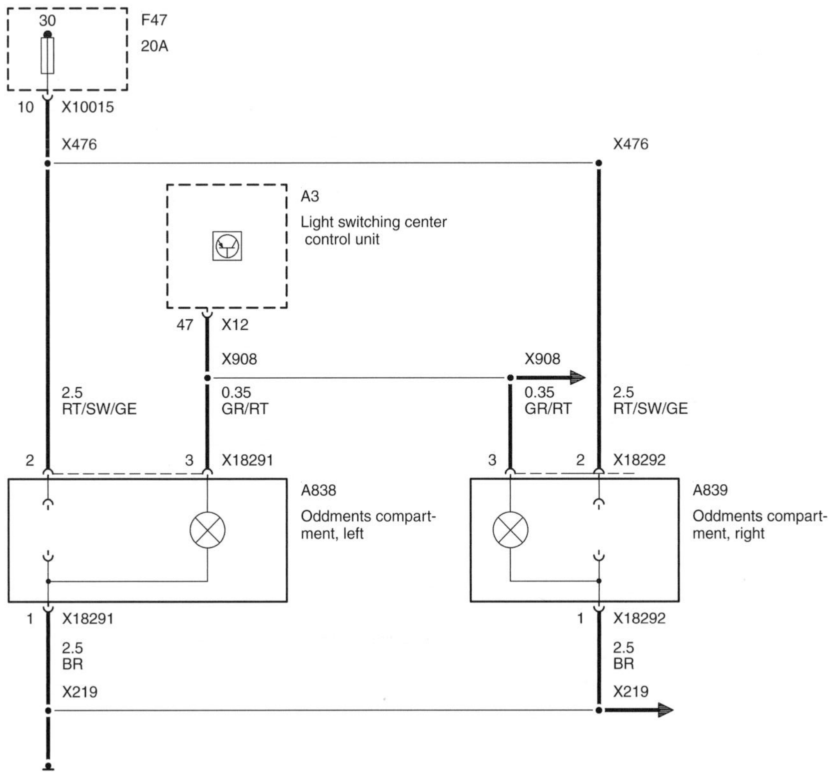

F47
20A
30
10 X10015
X476
X476
A3
Light switching center control unit
47 X12
X908
X908
2.5
RT/SW/GE
0.35
GR/RT
0.35
GR/RT
2.5
RT/SW/GE
2
3 X18291
3
2 X18292
A838
Oddments compartment, left
A839
Oddments compartment, right
1 X18291
2.5
BR
X219
1 X18292
2.5
BR
X219

Lights
Interior lighting, front

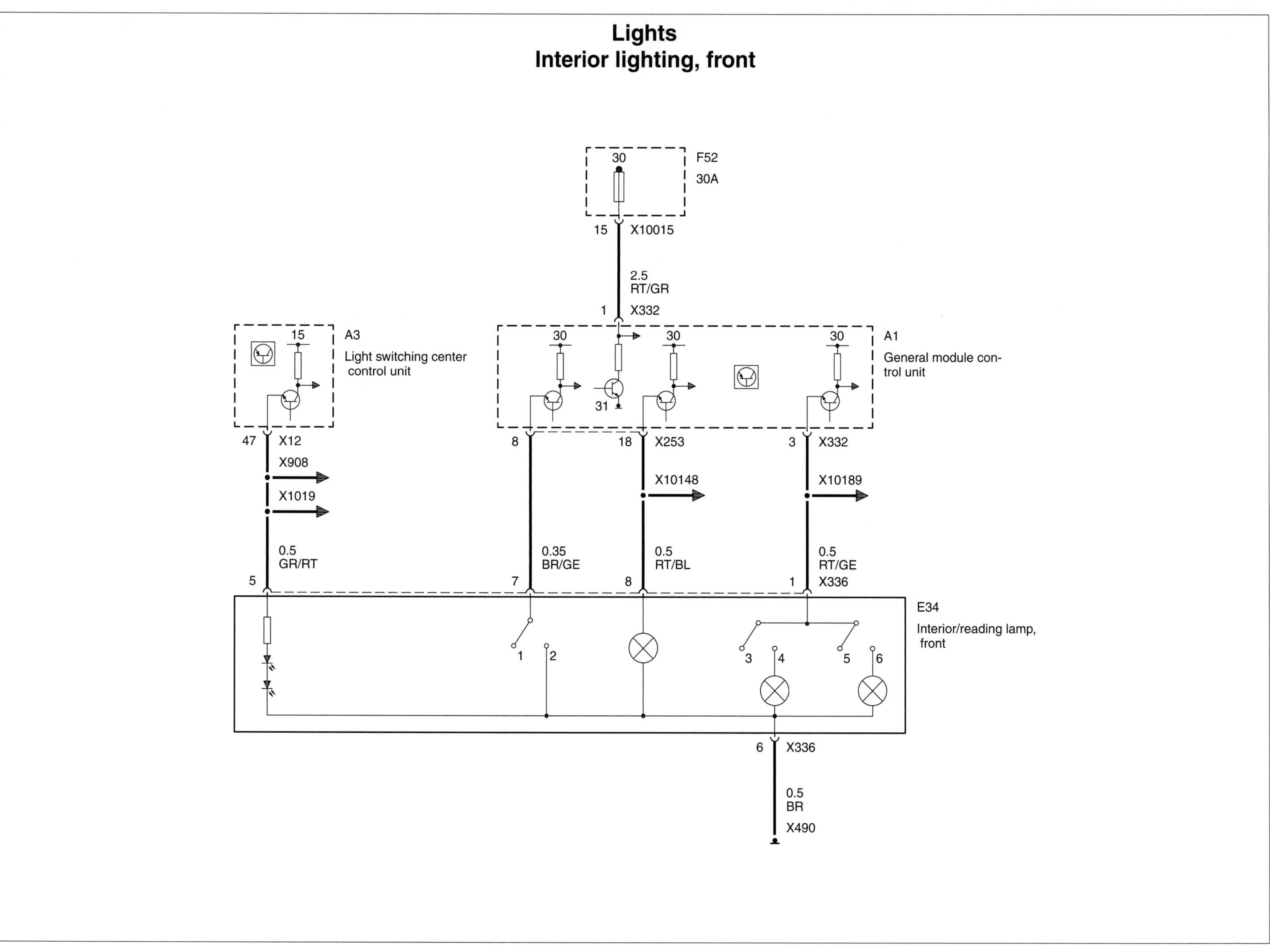

Lights
Interior lighting, rear, sedan / coupe

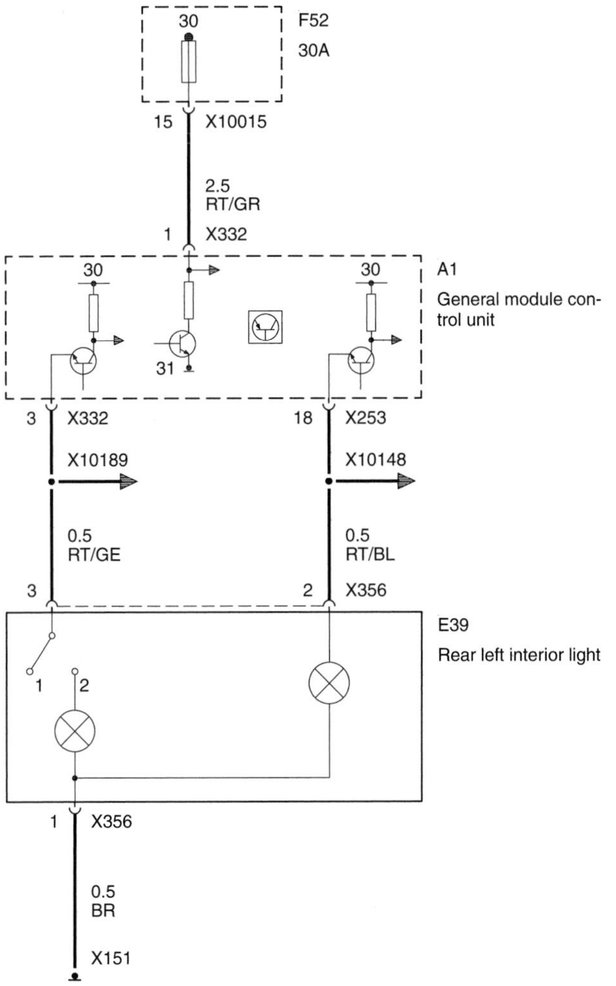

F52
30A
30
15 X10015
2.5
RT/GR
1 X332
A1
General module control unit
30
31
30
3 X332
18 X253
X10189
X10148
0.5
RT/GE
0.5
RT/BL
3
2 X356
E39
Rear left interior light
1 2
1 X356
0.5
BR
X151

Lights
Interior lighting, rear, wagon (up to 06/2000)

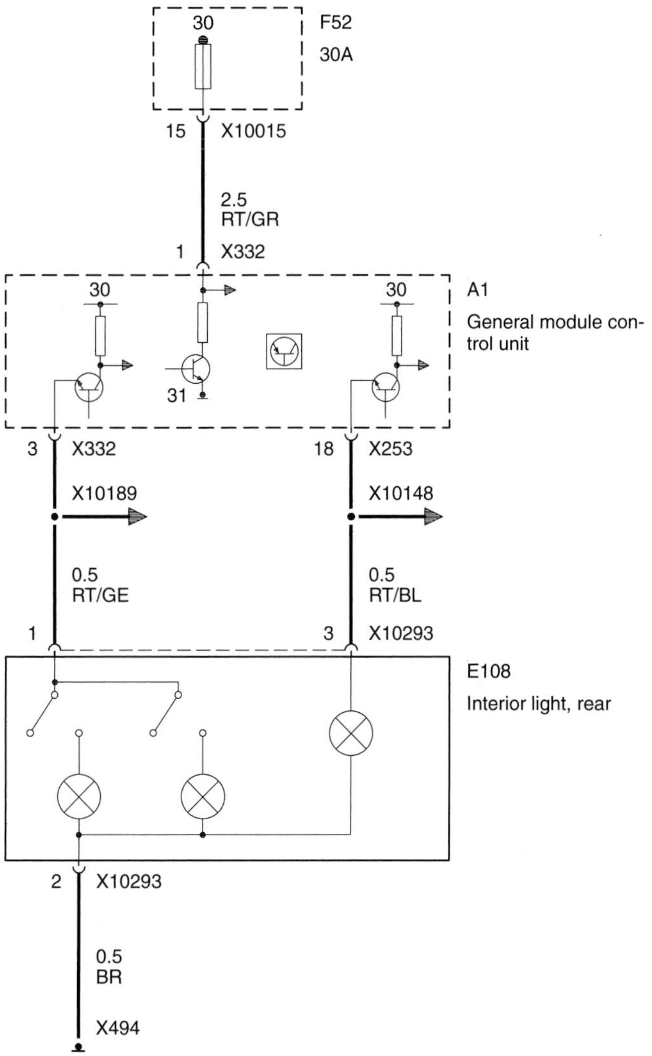

F52
30A
30
15 X10015
2.5
RT/GR
1 X332
A1
General module control unit
30
31
30
3 X332
18 X253
X10189
X10148
0.5
RT/GE
0.5
RT/BL
1
3 X10293
E108
Interior light, rear
2 X10293
0.5
BR
X494

Lights
Interior lighting, rear, wagon (from 06/2000)

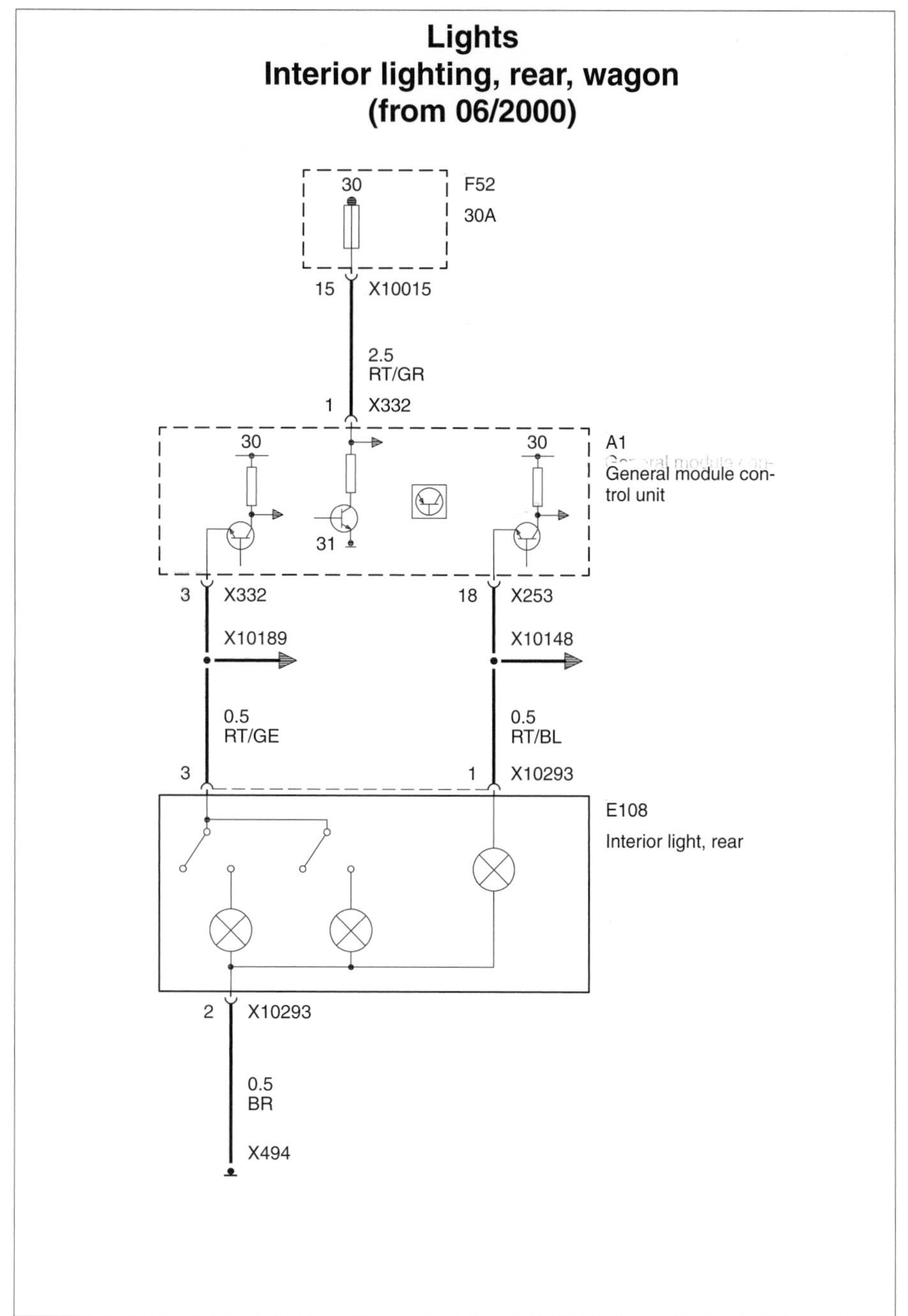

Lights
Interior lighting, rear, wagon

30
F52
30A
15
X10015
2.5
RT/GR
1
X332
30
30
A1
General module control unit
31
3
X332
18
X253
X10189
X10148
0.5
RT/GE
0.5
RT/BL
1
3
X10293
E108
Interior light, rear
2
X10293
0.5
BR
X494

Lights
Glove box light

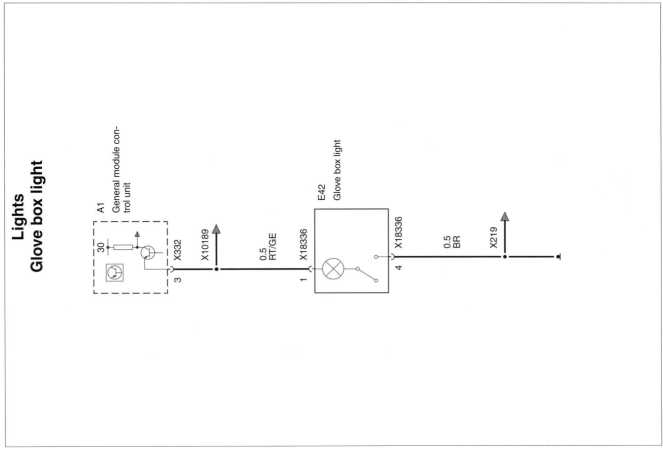

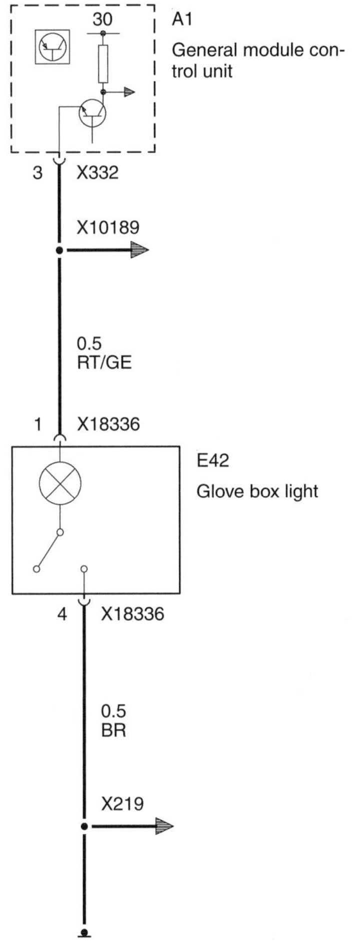

Lights
Footwell lights

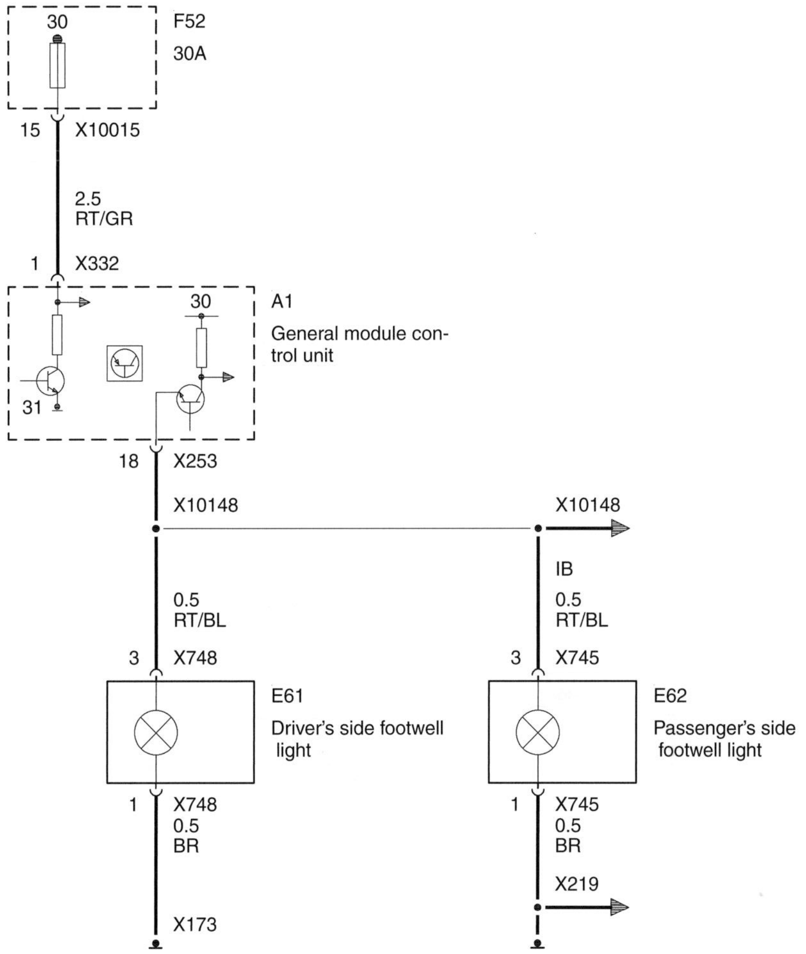

Lights
Luggage compartment lighting, coupe / convertible (up to 03/2003)

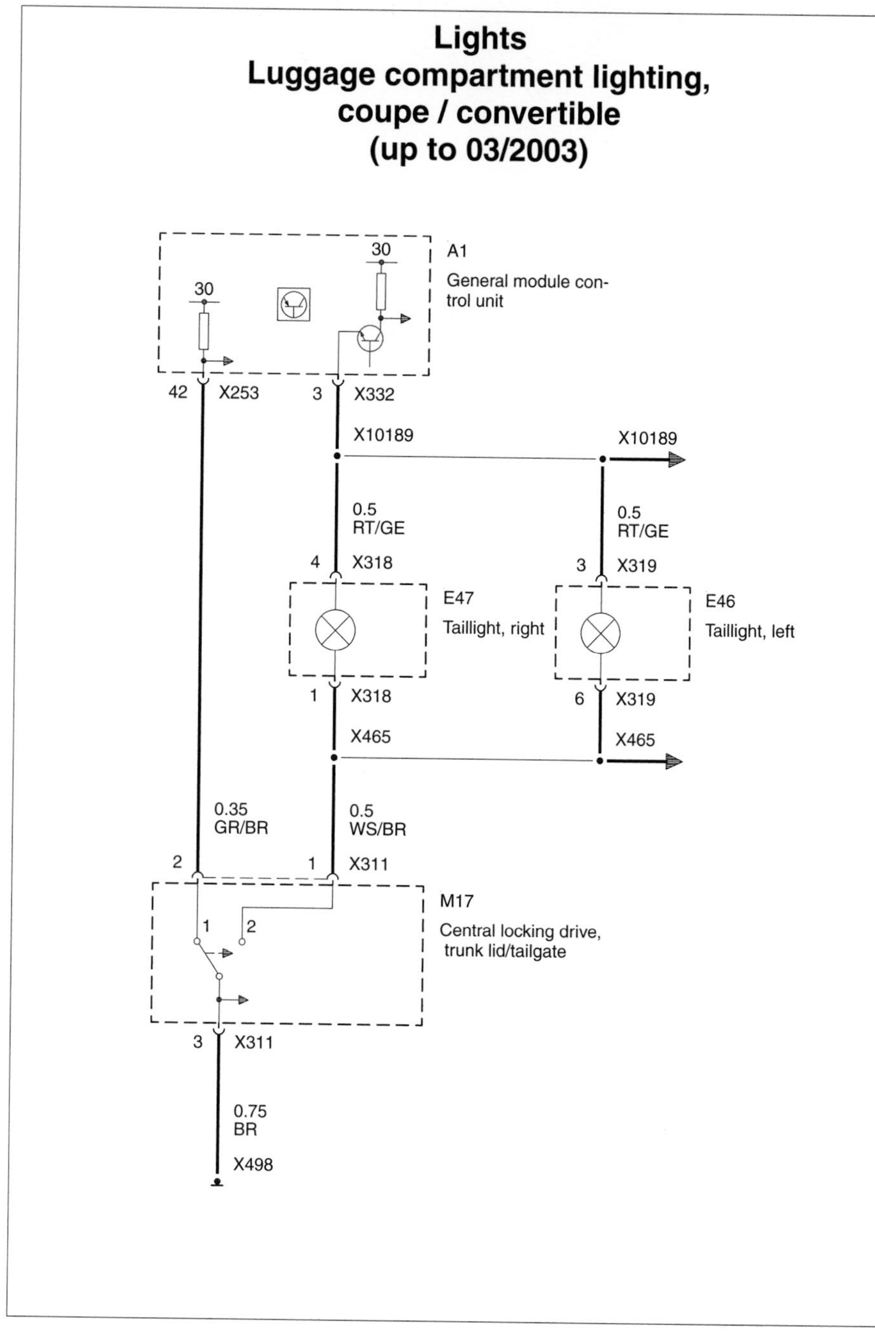

Lights
Luggage compartment lighting, sedan (from 09/2001)

Lights
Luggage compartment lighting, wagon

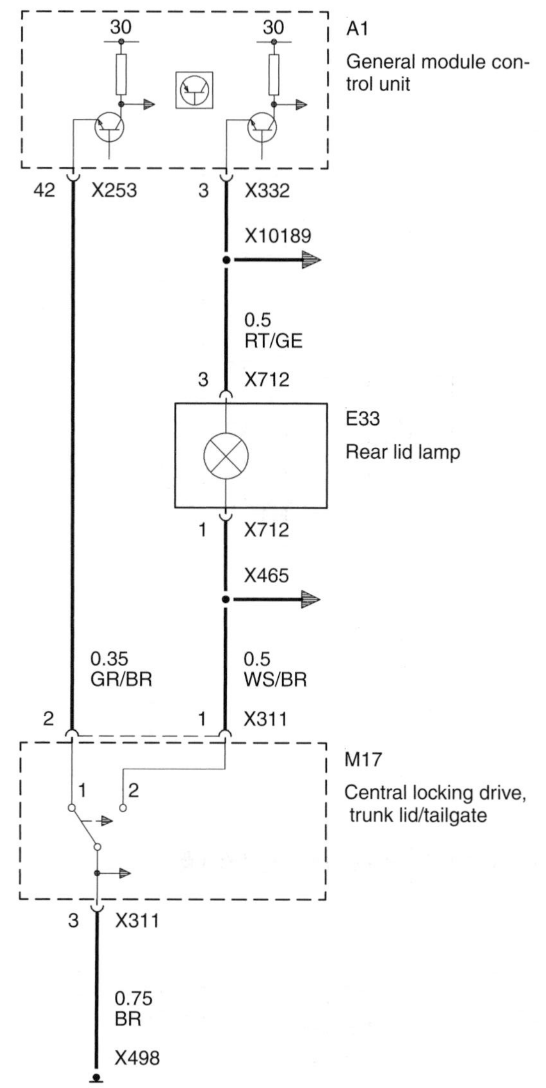

A1
General module control unit

30 30
42 X253
3 X332
X10189
0.5 RT/GE
3 X712

E33
Rear lid lamp

1 X712
X465
0.35 GR/BR
0.5 WS/BR
2 1 X311

M17
Central locking drive, trunk lid/tailgate

1 2
3 X311
0.75 BR
X498

Lights
Luggage compartment lighting, sedan (up to 09/2001)

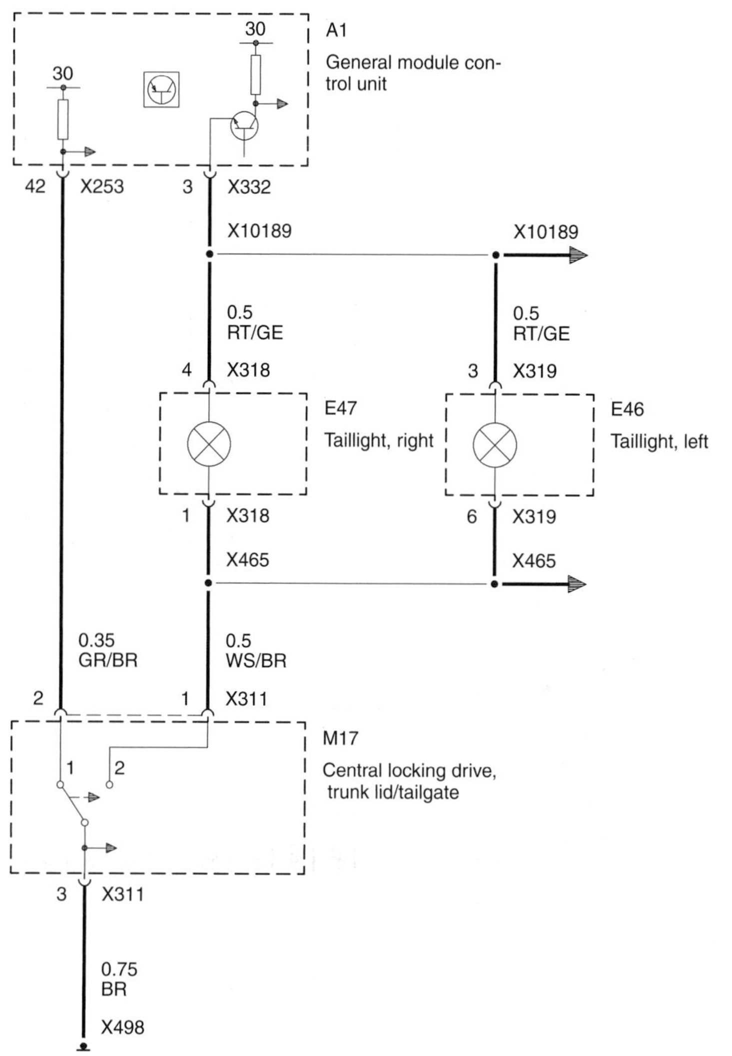

A1
General module control unit

30 30
42 X253
3 X332
X10189
X10189
0.5 RT/GE
0.5 RT/GE
4 X318
3 X319

E47
Taillight, right

E46
Taillight, left

1 X318
6 X319
X465
X465
0.35 GR/BR
0.5 WS/BR
2 1 X311

M17
Central locking drive, trunk lid/tailgate

1 2
3 X311
0.75 BR
X498

Lights
Luggage compartment lighting, coupe / convertible (from 03/2003)

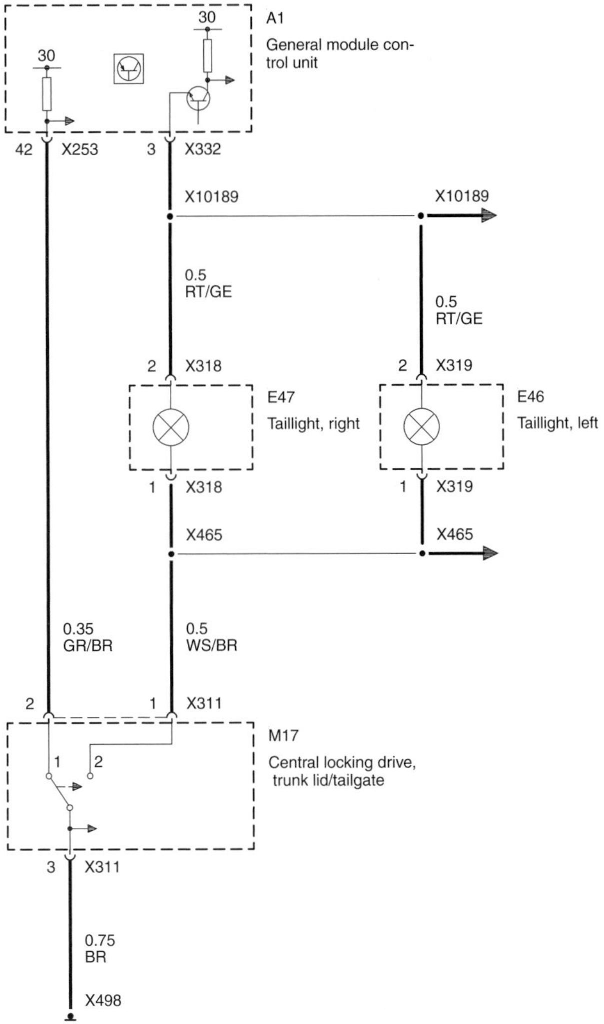

A1
General module control unit
30
30
42 X253
3 X332
X10189
X10189
0.5
RT/GE
0.5
RT/GE
2 X318
E47
Taillight, right
1 X318
2 X319
E46
Taillight, left
1 X319
X465
X465
0.35
GR/BR
0.5
WS/BR
2
1 X311
M17
Central locking drive, trunk lid/tailgate
1
2
3 X311
0.75
BR
X498

Lights
Vanity mirror light

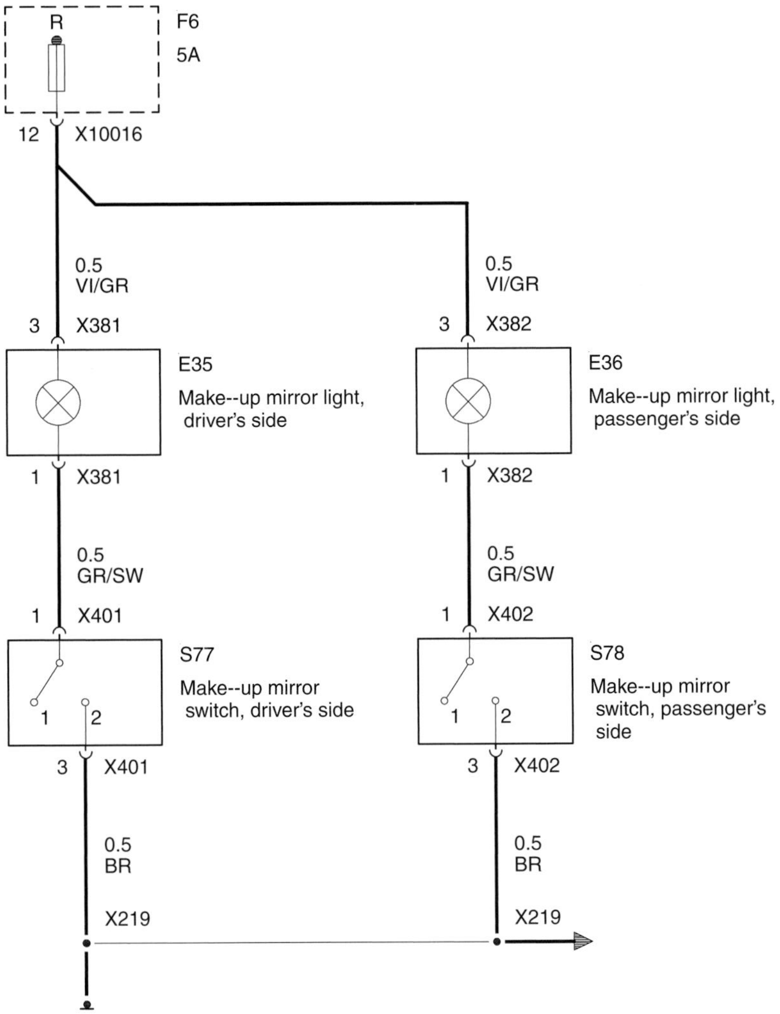

R
F6
5A
12 X10016
0.5
VI/GR
3 X381
E35
Make--up mirror light, driver's side
1 X381
0.5
GR/SW
1 X401
S77
Make--up mirror switch, driver's side
1
2
3 X401
0.5
BR
X219
0.5
VI/GR
3 X382
E36
Make--up mirror light, passenger's side
1 X382
0.5
GR/SW
1 X402
S78
Make--up mirror switch, passenger's side
1
2
3 X402
0.5
BR
X219

Lights
Front cigar lighter, sedan / coupe / convertible

30
F47
20A
10
X10015
30<47
2.5
RT/SW/GE
1
X531
E28
Front cigar lighter
1
2
1
X1014
2.5
BR
X490
30
A3
Light switching center control unit
47
X12
X908
X1019
0.35
GR/RT
2
X532
E29
Front cigar lighter light
1
X532
0.35
BR
X490

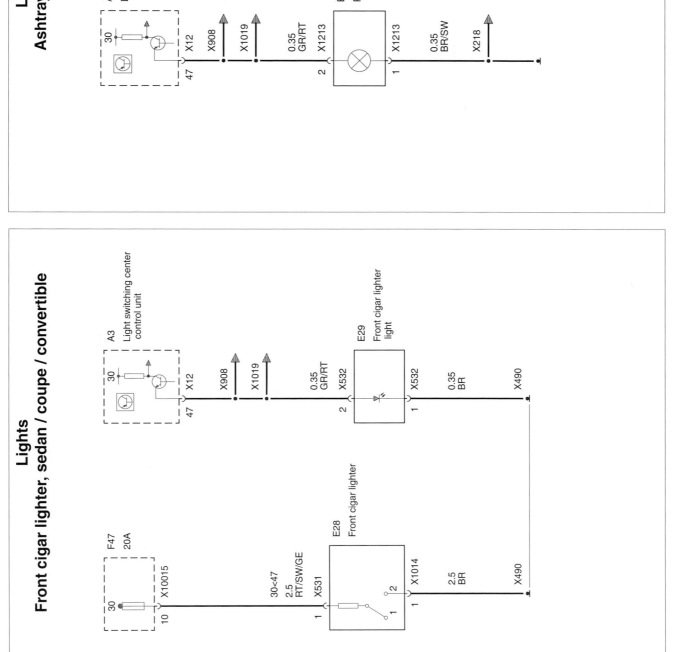

Lights
Ashtray light, rear

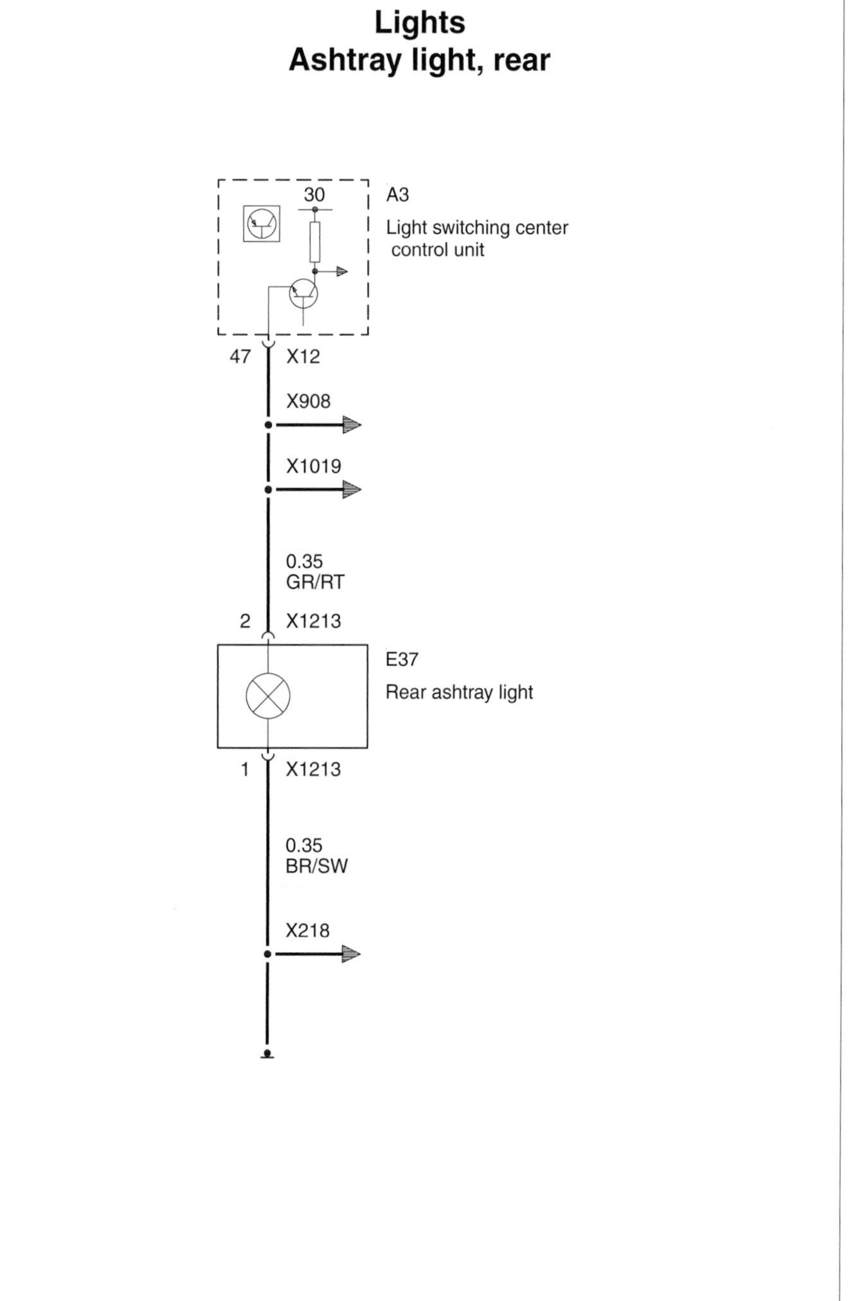

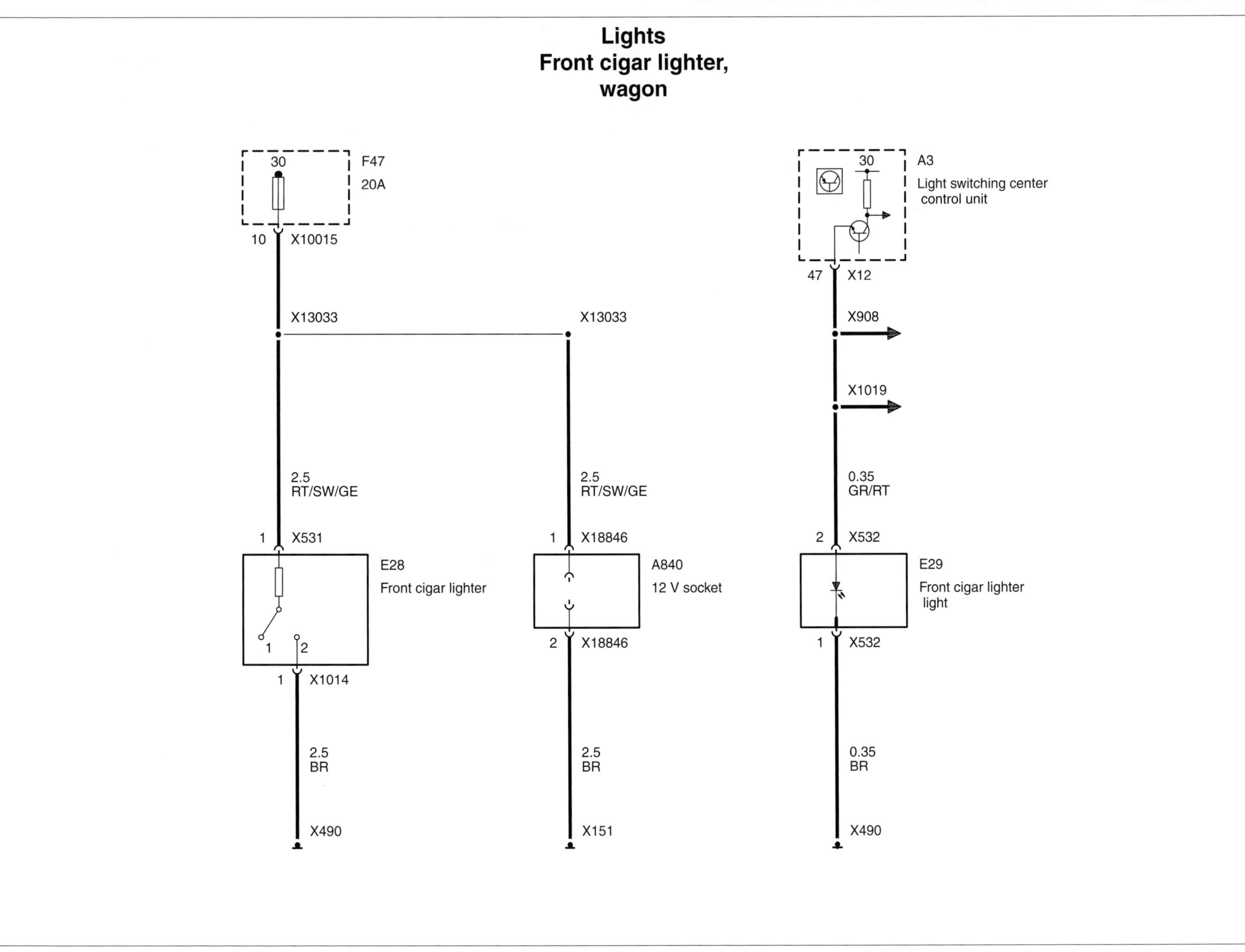
Lights
Front cigar lighter,
wagon
30
F47
20A
10
X10015
X13033
X13033
2.5
RT/SW/GE
2.5
RT/SW/GE
1
X531
E28
Front cigar lighter
1
2
1
X1014
2.5
BR
X490
1
X18846
A840
12 V socket
2
X18846
2.5
BR
X151
30
A3
Light switching center
control unit
47
X12
X908
X1019
0.35
GR/RT
2
X532
E29
Front cigar lighter
light
1
X532
0.35
BR
X490

Lights
Rear left interior light, convertible

F49
5A
30
12 X10015
0.5 RT/VI
47 X253

A1
General module control unit
30
30
31
3 X332
1.5 RT/GE
X10189
0.5 RT/GE
2 X11209
18 X253
0.75 RT/BL
X10148
IB
0.5 RT/BL
1 X11205

E99
Hardtop locator I
E100
Hardtop locator II

2 X11211
X18122
1 X11208
X11207
3
2 X356

E39
Rear left interior light

1 X356
0.75 BR
X11210

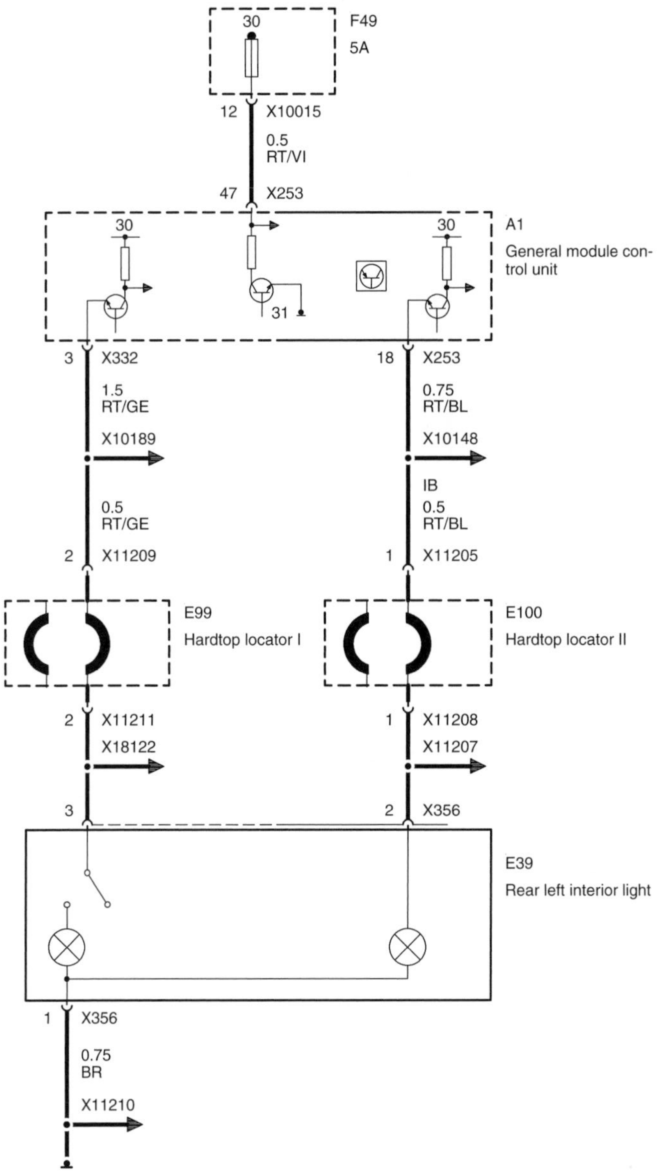

Lights
Rear right interior light, convertible

F49
5A
30
12 X10015
0.5 RT/VI
47 X253

A1
General module control unit
30
30
31
3 X332
1.5 RT/GE
X10189
0.5 RT/GE
2 X11209
18 X253
0.75 RT/BL
X10148
0.5 RT/BL
1 X11205

E99
Hardtop locator I
E100
Hardtop locator II

2 X11211
X18122
1 X11208
X11207
3
2 X355

E40
Rear right interior light

1 X355
0.75 BR
X11210

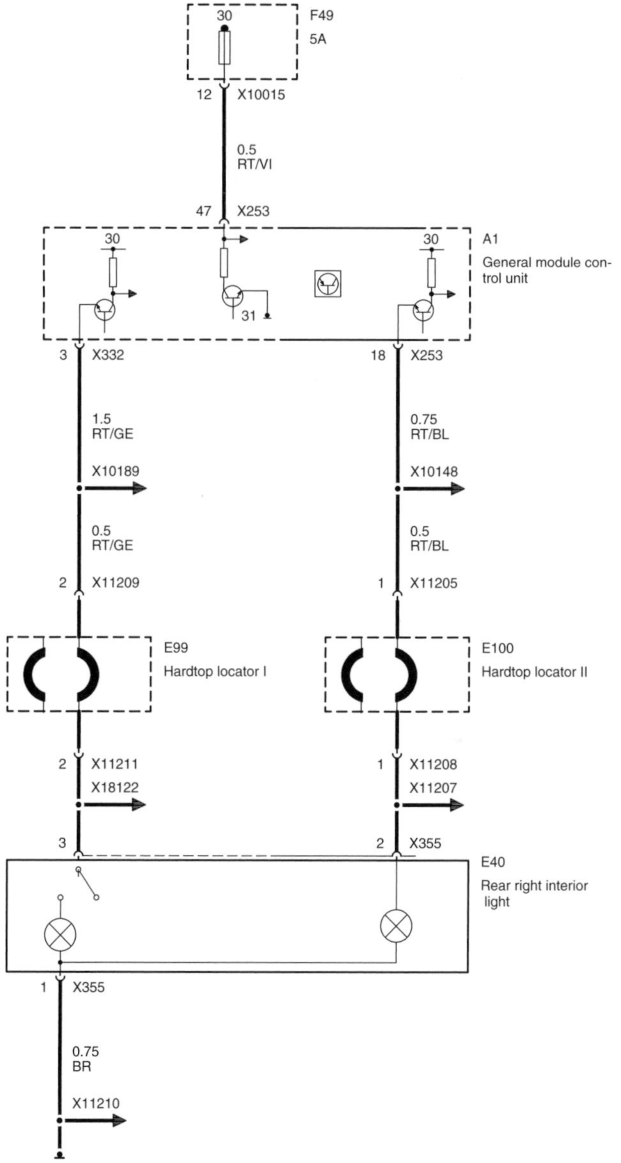

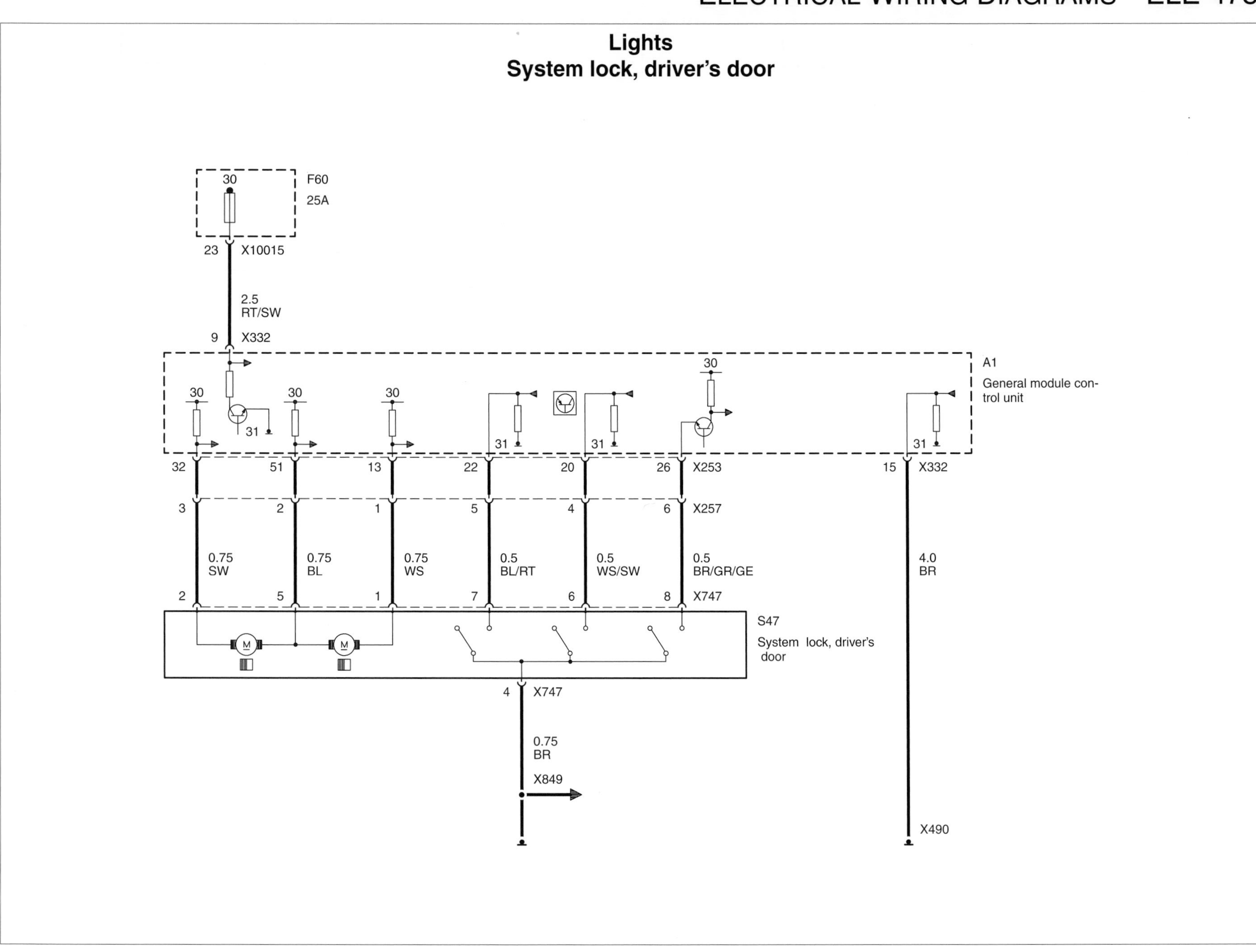
Lights
System lock, driver's door
30
F60
25A
23
X10015
2.5
RT/SW
9
X332
A1
General module control unit
30
30
30
30
31
31
31
31
32
51
13
22
20
26
X253
15
X332
3
2
1
5
4
6
X257
0.75
SW
0.75
BL
0.75
WS
0.5
BL/RT
0.5
WS/SW
0.5
BR/GR/GE
4.0
BR
2
5
1
7
6
8
X747
S47
System lock, driver's door
4
X747
0.75
BR
X849
X490

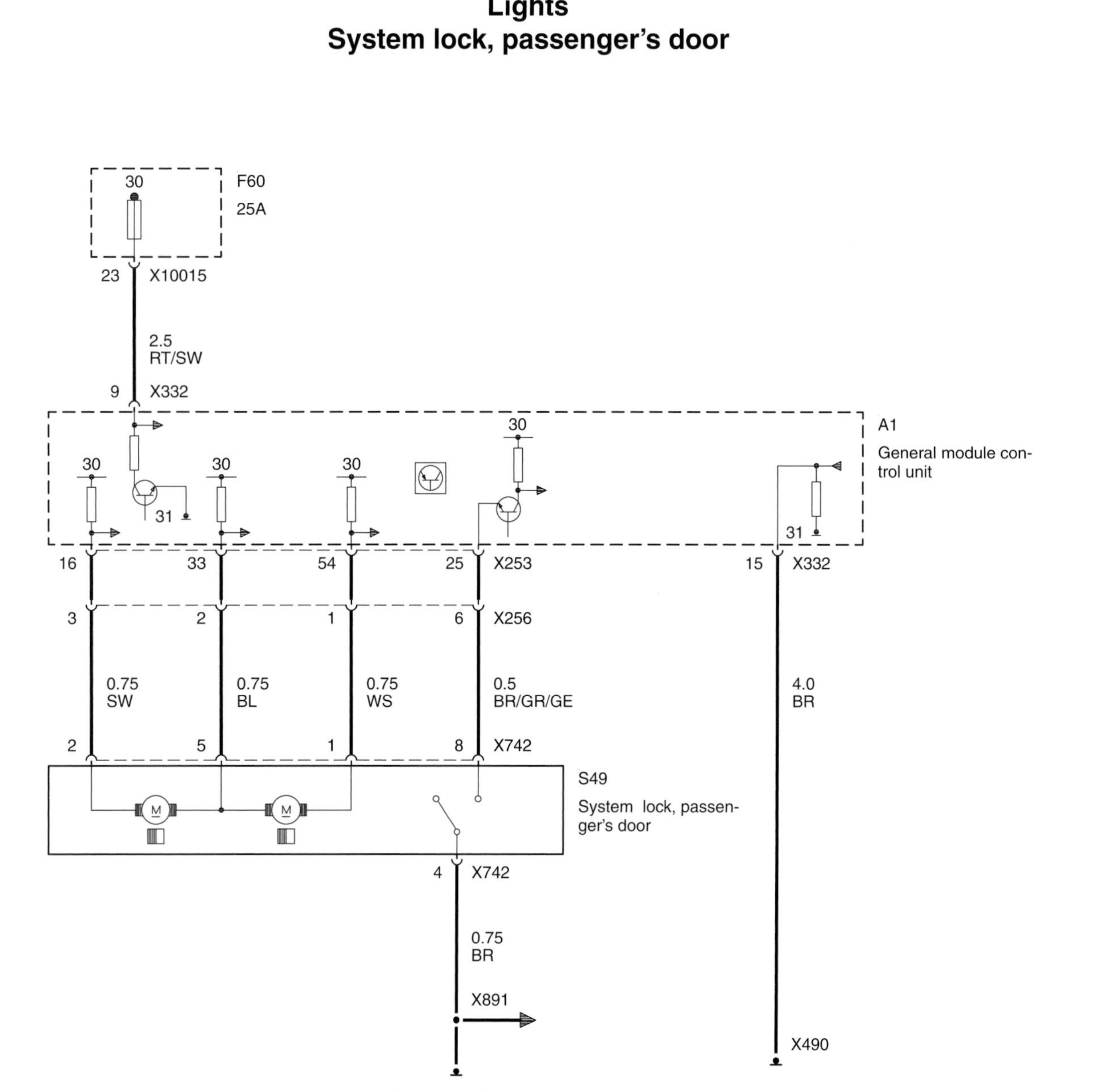
Lights
System lock, passenger's door
30
F60
25A
23
X10015
2.5
RT/SW
9
X332
A1
General module control unit
30
30
30
30
31
31
16
33
54
25
X253
15
X332
3
2
1
6
X256
0.75
SW
0.75
BL
0.75
WS
0.5
BR/GR/GE
4.0
BR
2
5
1
8
X742
S49
System lock, passenger's door
4
X742
0.75
BR
X891
X490

Lights
Rear door contacts

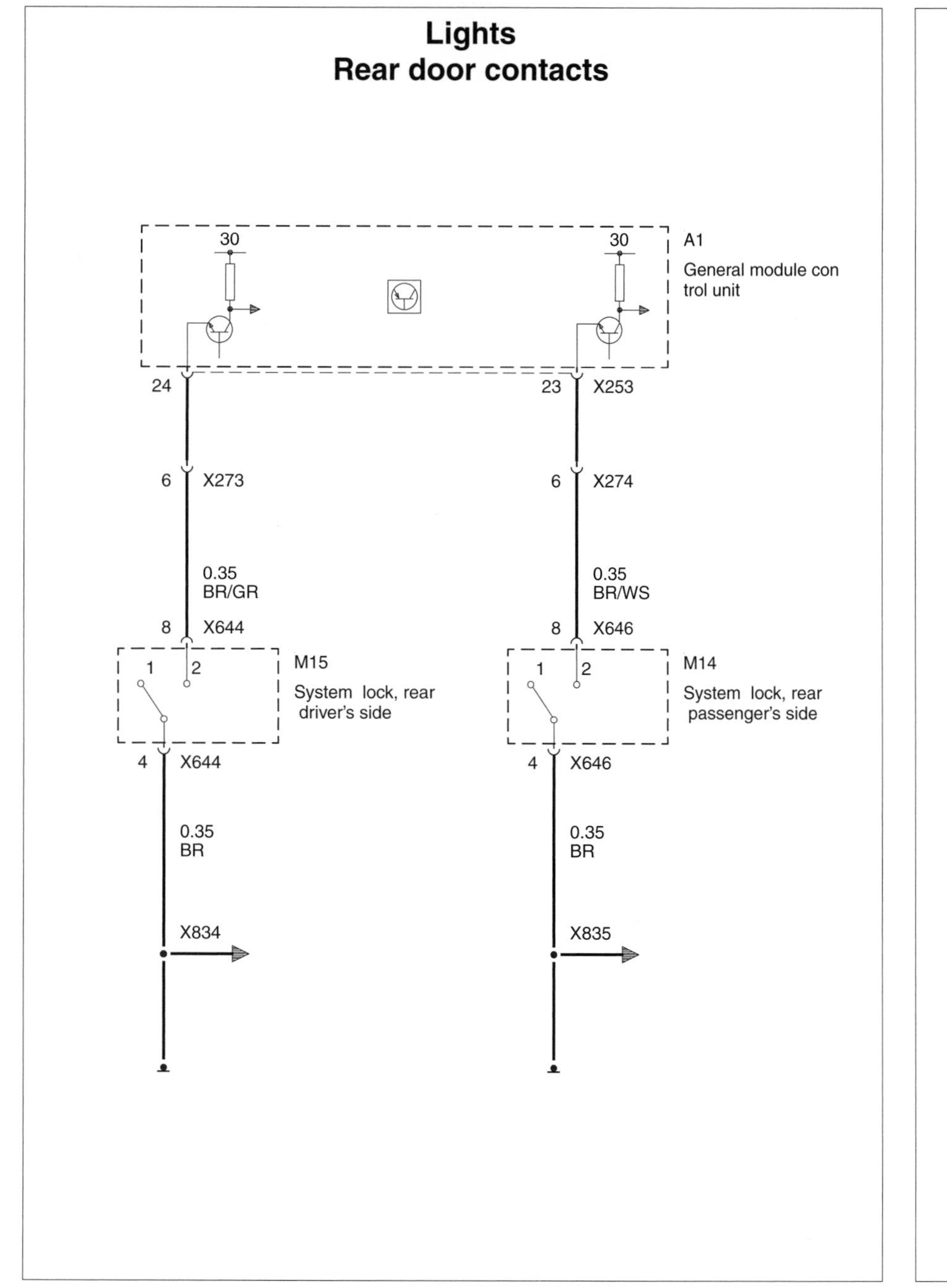

This page intentionally left blank

Lights
Trunk lid unlocking, sedan / coupe

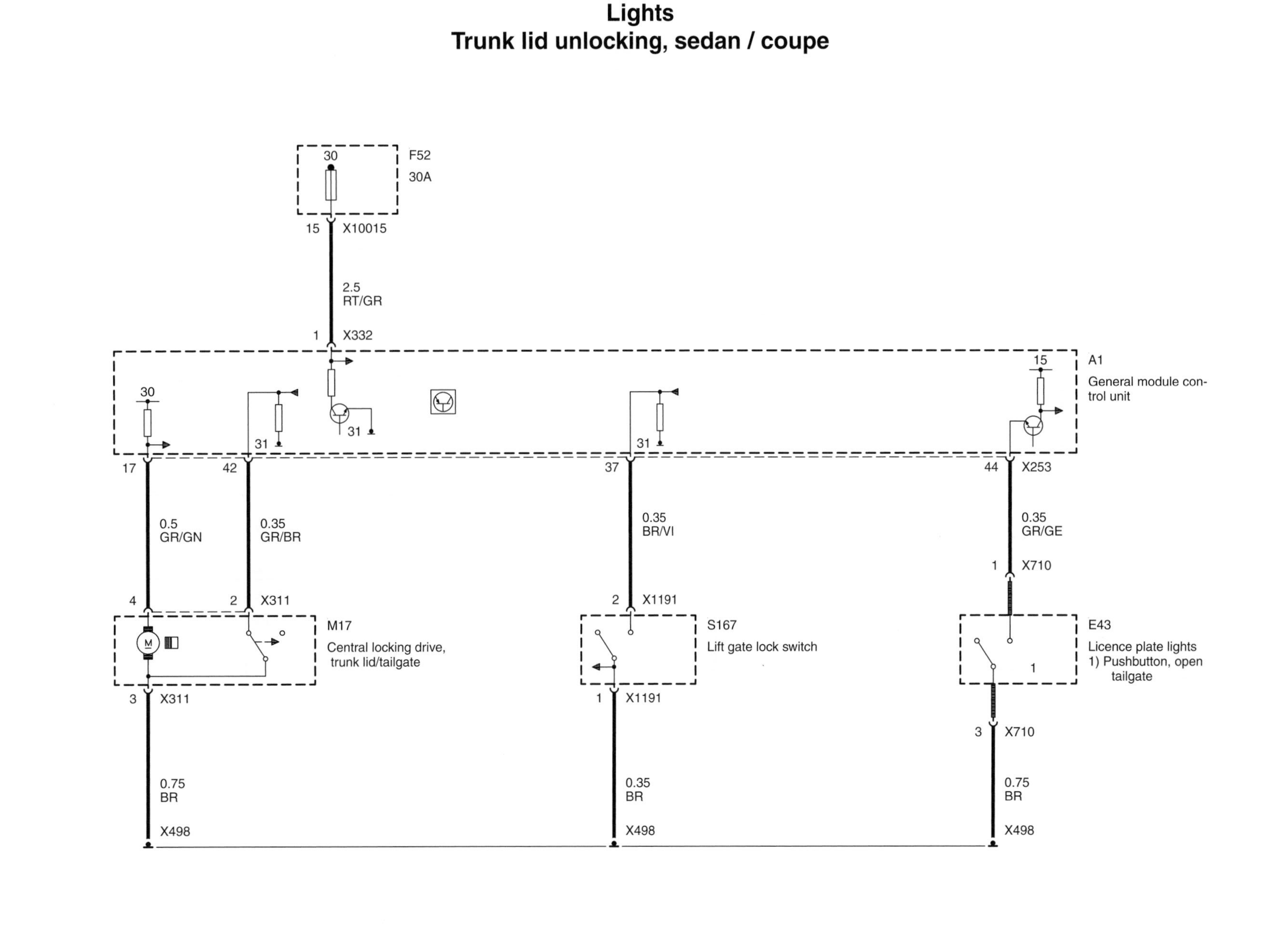

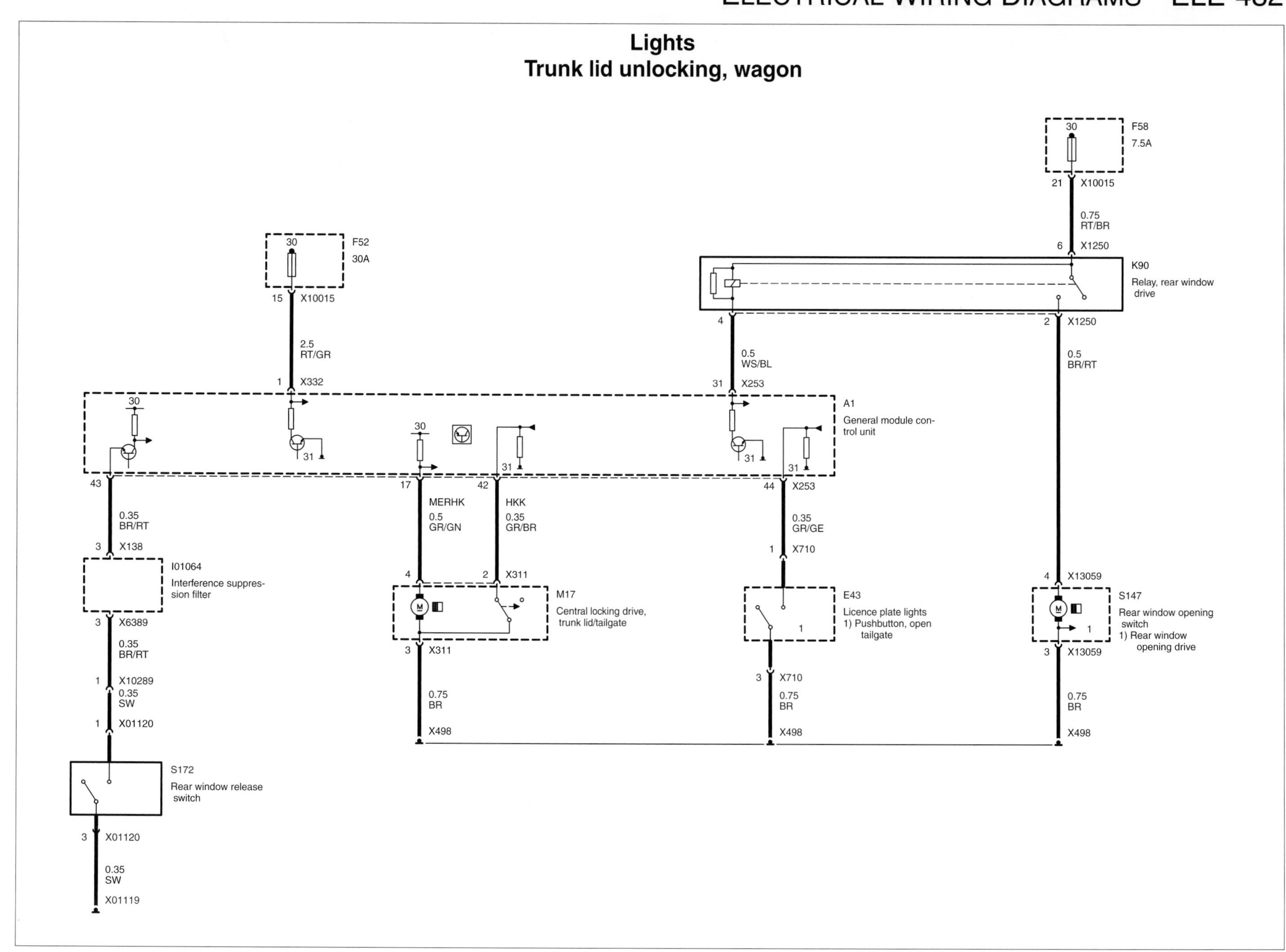

Lights
Trunk lid unlocking, wagon
F58
7.5A
30
21 X10015
0.75 RT/BR
6 X1250
K90
Relay, rear window drive
4
2 X1250
0.5 BR/RT
0.5 WS/BL
31 X253
A1
General module control unit
F52
30A
30
15 X10015
2.5 RT/GR
1 X332
30
31
43
17
42
44 X253
MERHK
0.5 GR/GN
HKK
0.35 GR/BR
0.35 GR/GE
1 X710
4
2 X311
M17
Central locking drive, trunk lid/tailgate
3 X311
0.75 BR
X498
E43
Licence plate lights
1) Pushbutton, open tailgate
3 X710
4 X13059
S147
Rear window opening switch
1) Rear window opening drive
3 X13059
0.35 BR/RT
3 X138
I01064
Interference suppression filter
3 X6389
1 X10289
0.35 SW
1 X01120
S172
Rear window release switch
3 X01120
X01119

Lights
Trunk lid unlocking, convertible

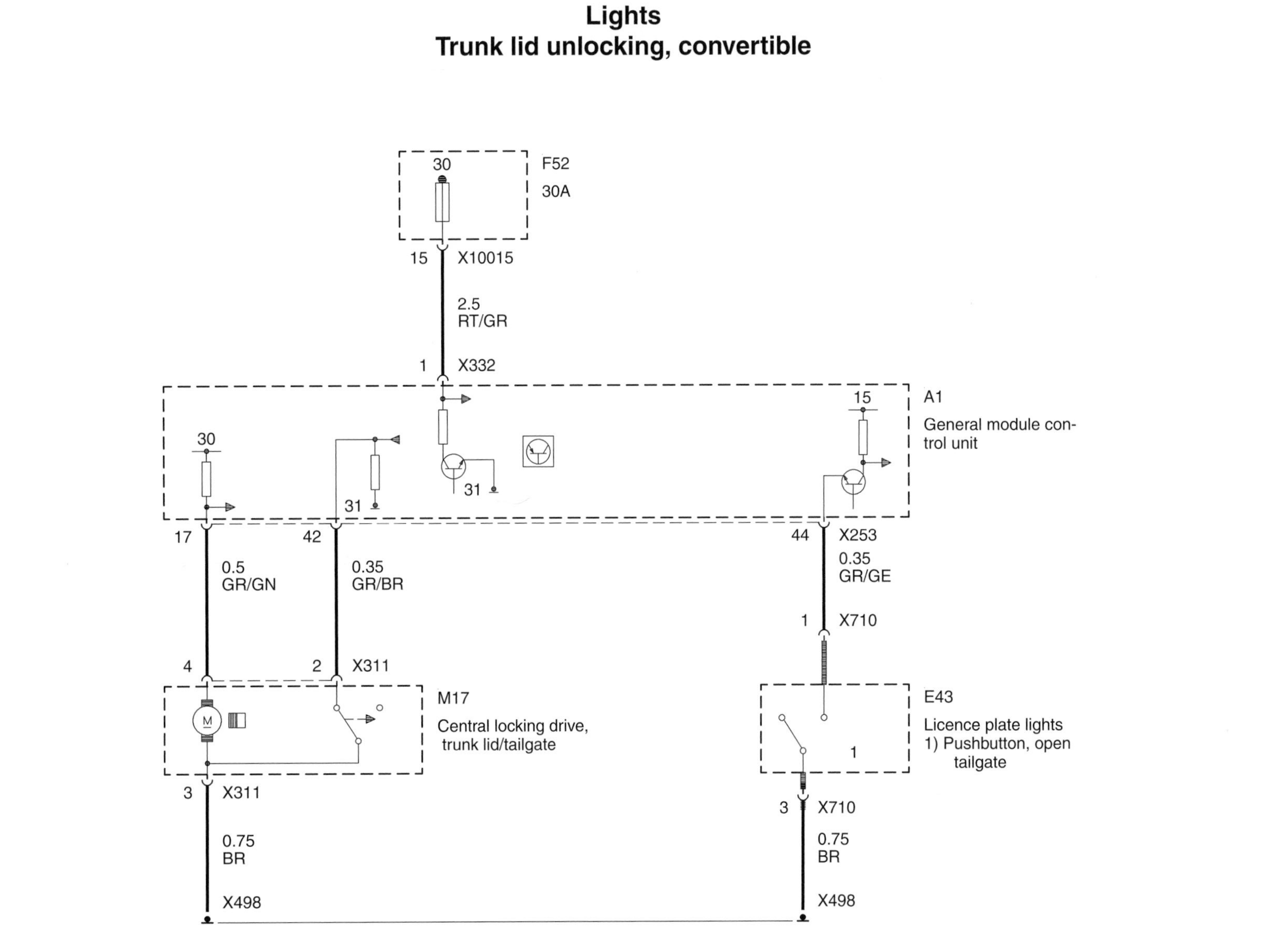

OBD On-Board Diagnostics

GENERAL

This chapter outlines the fundamentals and equipment requirements of the SAE (Society of Automotive Engineers and CARB (California Air Resource Board) On-Board Diagnostics II standard as it applies to BMW vehicles. Also covered here is a comprehensive listing of BMW and OBD II diagnostic trouble codes (DTCs).

ON-BOARD DIAGNOSTICS (OBD II)

OBD II standards have been applied to all passenger vehicles sold in the United States from model year 1996.

OBD capabilities are incorporated into engine software to monitor virtually every component that can affect vehicle emissions. Each emission-influencing component is checked by a diagnostic routine to verify that it is functioning properly. If a problem or malfunction is detected, the OBD II system illuminates the malfunction indicator light (MIL) on the instrument panel.

The OBD II system also stores important information about the detected malfunction in the engine control module (ECM) so that a repair technician can find the problem and repair it accurately.

NOTE —
- *Specialized OBD II scan tool equipment is needed to access the fault memory and OBD II data.*
- *The OBD II fault memory (including the MIL) can only be reset using a special scan tool. Removing the connector from the engine control module (ECM) or disconnecting the battery will not erase the fault memory.*

Malfunction Indicator Light (MIL)

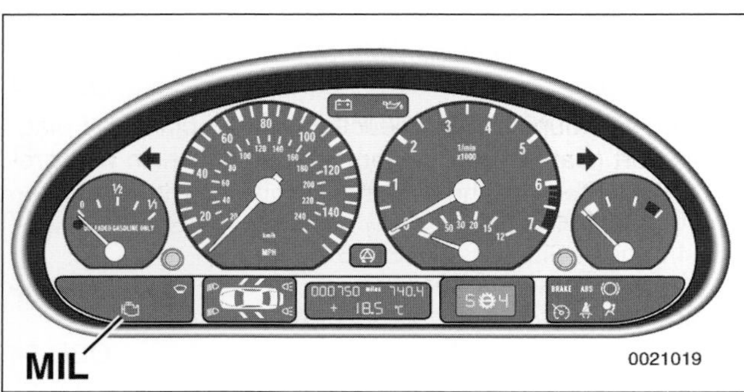

The OBD II system is designed to illuminate the Malfunction Indicator Light (MIL) when emission levels exceed 1.5 times the Federal standards.

NOTE —
On model year 1999 and 2000 cars, the MIL is labeled Check Engine. On later models, the MIL is labeled Service Engine Soon.

Conditions that illuminate the MIL:

- Engine management system fault detected for two consecutive OBD II drive cycles (see **Drive cycle**).
- Catalyst damaging fault.
- Malfunction in component(s) monitoring emissions.
- Manufacturer-defined specifications exceeded.
- Implausible sensor input signal.
- Misfire.
- Leak detected in fuel tank evaporative system.
- No purge flow detected from purge valve / evaporative system.
- Failure of DME to enter closed-loop operation within specified time.
- Engine management system enters “limp home” mode.

Additional information on MIL:

- A fault code is stored within the engine control module (ECM) upon the first occurrence of a fault being identified.
- Two **complete** consecutive drive cycles with the fault present illuminate the MIL. The exception to the two-fault requirement is a catalyst-damaging fault which turns the light on immediately.
- If the second drive cycle is not completed and the fault not checked, the engine control module (ECM) counts the third drive cycle as the next consecutive drive cycle. The MIL is illuminated if the fault is still present.
- Once the MIL is illuminated, it remains illuminated unless the system is tested and found to be without faults through three complete consecutive drive cycles.
- In all cases except catalyst-damaging fault(s), the fault code is cleared from memory automatically if fault is not detected through **40** consecutive drive cycles.
- In case of a catalyst-damaging fault, the fault code is cleared from memory automatically if the fault is not detected through **80** consecutive drive cycles.

Scan tool and scan tool display

Owing to the advanced nature of OBD II adaptive strategies, all diagnostics need to start with a scan tool. The aftermarket scan tools can be connected to either the 16-pin OBD II Data Link Connector (DLC) or the BMW 20-pin DLC in the engine compartment. Data from the OBD II DLC may be limited, depending on scan tool and vehicle.

OBD II standards mandate that the 16-pin DLC must be located within three (3) feet of the driver and must not require any tools to be exposed. The communication protocol used by BMW is ISO 9141.

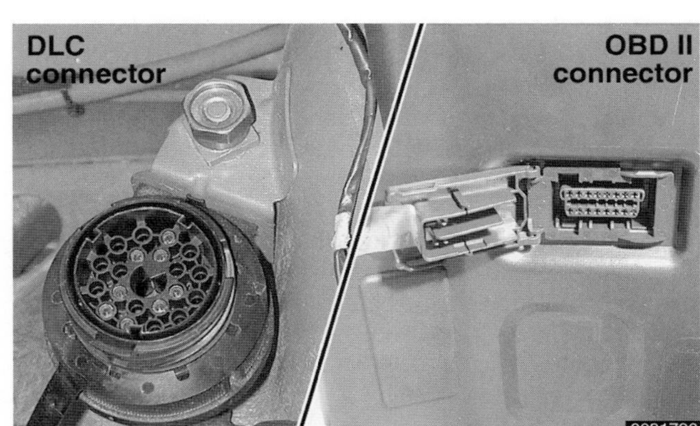

Starting with June 2000 production, the 20-pin BMW diagnostic port (**Data Link Connector** or **DLC**) which was previously located in the engine compartment has been deleted. All diagnostic, coding and programming functions are incorporated into the **OBD II** diagnostic port, located under left side of dashboard.

NOTE —

- *On cars built up 06-2000: when accessing emissions related DTCs through the 16-pin OBD II DLC, the BMW 20-pin DLC cap must be installed.*
- *Professional diagnostic scan tools available at the time of this printing include the BMW factory tools (*DISplus *and* MoDiC*) and a small number of aftermarket BMW-specific tools. The* CS2000' *from Baum Tools Unlimited, the* Retriever *from Assenmacher Specialty Tools, and the* MT2500 *from Snap-On Tools are examples of quality OBD scan tools.*
- *In addition to the professional line of scan tools, inexpensive 'generic' OBD II scan tool software programs and handheld units are readily available. These tools do have limited capabilities, but they are nonetheless powerful diagnostic tools. These tools read live data streams and freeze frame data as well as a host of other valuable diagnostic data.*
- *For the do-it-yourself owner, simple aftermarket DTC readers are also available. These inexpensive BMW-only tools are capable of checking for DTCs as well as turning off the illuminated MIL and resetting the service indicator lights.*

Diagnostic monitors

Diagnostic monitors are software routines which run tests and checks on specific systems, components, or functions.

A complete drive cycle (see **Drive cycle** in this repair group) is required for the tests to be valid. The diagnostic monitor signals the engine control module (ECM) of the loss or impairment of the signal or component and determines if a signal or sensor is faulty based on 3 conditions:

- Signal or component shorted to ground
- Signal or component shorted to B+
- Signal or component missing (open circuit)

The OBD II system must monitor *all* emission control systems that are on-board. Not all vehicles have a full complement of emission control systems. For example, a vehicle may not be equipped with secondary air injection, so naturally no secondary air readiness/function code would be present.

OBD II requires monitoring of the following:

- **Oxygen sensor monitoring**
- **Catalyst monitoring**
- **Misfire monitoring**
- **Evaporative system monitoring**
- **Secondary air monitoring**
- **Fuel system monitoring**

Monitoring these emissions related functions is done using DME input sensors and output accouters based on preprogrammed data sets. If the ECM cannot determine the environment or engine operating conditions due to missing or faulty signals it will set a fault code and, depending on conditions, illuminate the MIL.

Oxygen sensor monitoring: When drive conditions allow, response rate and switching time of each oxygen sensor is monitored. In addition, the heater function is also monitored. The OBD II "diagnostic executive" knows the difference between upstream and downstream oxygen sensors and reads each one individually.

All oxygen sensors are monitored separately. In order for the oxygen sensor to be effectively monitored, the system must be in closed loop operation.

Catalyst monitoring: This strategy monitors the two heated oxygen sensors per bank of cylinders. It compares the oxygen content going into the catalytic converter to the oxygen leaving the converter.

The diagnostic executive knows that most of the oxygen should be used up during the oxidation phase and if it sees higher than programmed values, a fault will be set and the MIL will illuminate.

Misfire detection: This strategy monitors crankshaft speed fluctuations and determines if a misfire occurs by variations in speed between each crankshaft sensor trigger point. This strategy is so finely tuned that it can even determine the severity of the misfire.

The diagnostic executive must determine if misfire is occurring, as well as other pertinent misfire information.

- Specific cylinder(s)
- Severity of the misfire event
- Emissions relevant or catalyst damaging

Misfire detection is an on-going monitoring process that is only disabled under certain limited conditions.

Secondary air injection monitoring: Secondary air injection is used to reduce HC and CO emissions during engine warm up. Immediately following a cold engine start (-10 to 40°C), fresh air/oxygen is pumped directly into the exhaust manifold. By injecting oxygen into the exhaust manifold, catalyst warm-up time is reduced.

System components:

- Electric air injection motor/pump
- Electric motor/pump relay
- Non-return valve
- Vacuum/vent valve
- Stainless steel air injection pipes
- Vacuum reservoir

The secondary air system is monitored via the use of the pre-catalyst oxygen sensors. Once the air pump is active and air is injected into the system, the signal at the oxygen sensor will reflect a lean condition. If the oxygen sensor signal does not change, a fault will be set and identify the faulty bank(s). If after completing the next cold start a fault is again present, the MIL will be illuminated.

Fuel system monitoring: This monitors receives high priority. It looks at the fuel delivery needed (long/short term fuel trim) for proper engine operation based on programmed data. If too much or not enough fuel is delivered over a predetermined time, a DTC is set and the MIL is turned on.

NOTE —

Fuel trim refers to adjustments to base fuel schedule. Long-term fuel trim refers to gradual adjustments to the fuel calibration adjustment as compared to short term fuel trim. Long term fuel trim adjustments compensate for gradual changes that occur over time.

Fuel system monitoring monitors the calculated injection time (ti) in relation to engine speed, load, and the pre-catalytic converter oxygen sensor(s) signals as a result of residual oxygen in the exhaust stream.

The diagnostic executive uses the precatalyst oxygen sensor signal as a correction factor for adjusting and optimizing the mixture pilot control under all engine operating conditions.

Evaporative system monitoring: This monitor checks the sealed integrity of the fuel storage system and related fuel lines.

This monitor has the ability to detect very small leaks anywhere in the system. A pressure test is be performed on the EVAP system on a continuous basis as the drive cycle allows. A leak detection pump (LDP) is used to pressurize and check system integrity.

Drive cycle

The OBD II drive cycle is a specific driving routine used by the EPA to test vehicle emissions. The purpose of the drive cycle is to run all of the emission-related on-board diagnostics over a broad range of driving conditions.

A drive cycle is considered complete when all of the diagnostic monitors have run their tests without interruption. For a drive cycle to be initiated, the vehicle must be started cold and brought up to an oil temperature of 160°F, at least 40°F above its original starting temperature.

Once a drive cycle is completed, the system status or inspection/maintenance (I/M) readiness codes are set to "Yes." When all codes are set to "Yes" the system is described as having established "readiness".

System status codes will be set to "No" in the following cases:

- Battery or ECM is disconnected.
- DTCs have been erased after completion of repairs but drive cycle has not be completed.

A scan tool can be used to determine I/M readiness.

Readiness codes

I/M readiness codes

1	2	3	4	5	6	7	8
1	0	1	1	0	0	0	0

1. Catalyst efficiency
2. Catalyst heating (not yet = 0)
3. EVAP monitoring
4. Secondary air injection
5. A/C Refrigerant (R12 only)
6. Oxygen sensor
7. Oxygen sensor heater
8. EGR (Not yet = 0)

The inspection/maintenance (I/M) readiness codes are mandated as part of OBD II. The readiness code will be stored after complete diagnostic monitoring of all components and systems has been carried out. The readiness code function was put into place to prevent manipulating an I/M emission test procedure by clearing faults codes or disconnecting the ECM or battery.

The readiness code can be displayed using an aftermarket scan tool. The code is binary: either "0" or "1". When all zeros are displayed, the system has established its readiness.

Diagnostic trouble codes (DTCs)

The SAE mandates a 5-digit diagnostic trouble code (DTC) standard. Emission related DTCs start with the letter "P" for power train and are commonly referred to as "P-codes". When the malfunction indicator light (MIL) is illuminated it indicates that a DTC has been stored:

- DTCs are stored as soon as they occur, whether or not the MIL illuminates.
- DTCs store and display a time stamp.
- DTCs record the current fault status.

DTC digit interpretation

- **1st digit:**
  - P .... powertrain
  - B .... body
  - C .... chassis
- **2nd digit:**
  - 0 .... SAE
  - 1 .... BMW
- **3rd digit:**
  - 0 .... total system
  - 1 .... air/fuel induction
  - 2 .... fuel injection
  - 3 .... ignition system or misfire
  - 4 .... auxiliary emission control
  - 5 .... vehicle speed & idle control
  - 6 .... ECM inputs/outputs
  - 7 .... transmission
- **4th - 5th digits** .... individual circuits or components

DTC example: P 0 3 0 6

- **P:** A powertrain problem
- **0**: SAE sanctioned or 'generic'
- **3:** Related to an ignition system/misfire
- **06** Misfire has been detected at cylinder #6.

Freeze frame data: DTCs provide a "freeze frame" or snapshot of a vehicle performance or emissions fault at the moment that the fault first occurs. This information is accessible through generic scan tools.

The freeze frame should contain, but isn't limited to, following data:

- Engine load (calculated)
- Engine RPM
- Short- and long-term fuel trim
- Vehicle speed
- Coolant temperature
- Intake manifold pressure
- Open/closed loop operation
- Fuel pressure (if available)
- DTC

BMW FAULT CODE TABLES (DTCS)

BMW fault codes (FC) expand on the SAE sanctioned DTCs and are accessible primarily through BMW (or BMW specific) diagnostic scan tools. Below is a comprehensive listing of SAE P-codes, the corresponding BMW FCs and an explanation of their meanings

Table a. M52 TU engine: Siemens DME MS42.1 from 06/01/1998 to 05/31/1999		
PCode	**BMW-FC**	**PCode text**
P0101	8	Mass or Volume Air Flow Circuit Range/Performance
P0111	14	Intake Air Temperature Sensor 1 Circuit Range/Performance
P0116	10	Engine Coolant Temperature Circuit Range/Performance
P0120	112	Throttle/Pedal Position Sensor/Switch 'A' Circuit
P0120	113	Throttle/Pedal Position Sensor/Switch 'A' Circuit
P0120	118	Throttle/Pedal Position Sensor/Switch 'A' Circuit
P0120	173	Throttle/Pedal Position Sensor/Switch 'A' Circuit
P0120	174	Throttle/Pedal Position Sensor/Switch 'A' Circuit
P0125	222	Insufficient Coolant Temperature for Closed Loop Fuel Control
P0128	168	Coolant Thermostat (Coolant Temperature Below Thermostat Regulating Temperature)
P0130	150	O2 Sensor Circuit (Bank 1 Sensor 1)
P0130	151	O2 Sensor Circuit (Bank 1 Sensor 1)
P0130	152	O2 Sensor Circuit (Bank 1 Sensor 1)
P0133	229	O2 Sensor Circuit Slow Response (Bank 1 Sensor 1)
P0134	186	O2 Sensor Circuit No Activity Detected (Bank 1 Sensor 1)
P0135	25	O2 Sensor Heater Circuit (Bank 1 Sensor 1)
P0136	156	O2 Sensor Circuit (Bank 1 Sensor 2)
P0136	157	O2 Sensor Circuit (Bank 1 Sensor 2)
P0136	215	O2 Sensor Circuit (Bank 1 Sensor 2)
P0139	220	O2 Sensor Circuit Slow Response (Bank 1 Sensor 2)
P0141	61	O2 Sensor Heater Circuit (Bank 1 Sensor 2)
P0150	153	O2 Sensor Circuit (Bank 2 Sensor 1)
P0150	154	O2 Sensor Circuit (Bank 2 Sensor 1)
P0150	155	O2 Sensor Circuit (Bank 2 Sensor 1)
P0153	230	O2 Sensor Circuit Slow Response (Bank 2 Sensor 1)
P0154	187	O2 Sensor Circuit No Activity Detected (Bank 2 Sensor 1)
P0155	55	O2 Sensor Heater Circuit (Bank 2 Sensor 1)
P0156	159	O2 Sensor Circuit (Bank 2 Sensor 2)
P0156	160	O2 Sensor Circuit (Bank 2 Sensor 2)
P0156	216	O2 Sensor Circuit (Bank 2 Sensor 2)
P0159	221	O2 Sensor Circuit Slow Response (Bank 2 Sensor 2)
P0161	79	O2 Sensor Heater Circuit (Bank 2 Sensor 2)
P0170	202	Fuel Trim (Bank 1)
P0173	203	Fuel Trim (Bank 2)
P0201	6	Injector Circuit/Open - Cylinder 1
P0202	5	Injector Circuit/Open - Cylinder 2
P0203	22	Injector Circuit/Open - Cylinder 3
P0204	24	Injector Circuit/Open - Cylinder 4

Table a. M52 TU engine: Siemens DME MS42.1 from 06/01/1998 to 05/31/1999		
PCode	**BMW-FC**	**PCode text**
P0205	33	Injector Circuit/Open - Cylinder 5
P0206	23	Injector Circuit/Open - Cylinder 6
P0301	238	Cylinder 1 Misfire Detected
P0302	239	Cylinder 2 Misfire Detected
P0303	240	Cylinder 3 Misfire Detected
P0304	241	Cylinder 4 Misfire Detected
P0305	242	Cylinder 5 Misfire Detected
P0306	243	Cylinder 6 Misfire Detected
P0325	57	Knock Sensor 1 Circuit (Bank 1 or Single Sensor)
P0330	59	Knock Sensor 2 Circuit (Bank 2)
P0335	83	Crankshaft Position Sensor 'A' Circuit
P0340	65	Camshaft Position Sensor 'A' Circuit (Bank 1 or Single Sensor)
P0412	62	Secondary Air Injection System Switching Valve A Circuit
P0420	233	Catalyst System Efficiency Below Threshold (Bank 1)
P0430	234	Catalyst System Efficiency Below Threshold (Bank 2)
P0440	250	Evaporative Emission System
P0442	145	Evaporative Emission System Leak Detected (small leak)
P0443	68	Evaporative Emission System Purge Control Valve Circuit
P0500	214	Vehicle Speed Sensor 'A'
P0505	204	Idle Air Control System
P0600	217	Serial Communication Link
P0601	100	Internal Control Module Memory Check Sum Error
P0601	170	Internal Control Module Memory Check Sum Error
P0601	171	Internal Control Module Memory Check Sum Error
P1132	188	O2 Sensor Heater Control Circuit (Bank 1 Sensor 1)
P1133	189	O2 Sensor Heater Control Circuit (Bank 2 Sensor 1)
P1140	149	Mass or Volume Air Flow Circuit Range/Performance Problem
P1145	50	Solenoid Valve Running Losses Control Circuit Electrical
P1161	122	Fuel Trim Adaptation Additive High (Bank 2) (M52: Engine Oil Temperature Sensor Circuit)
P1180	223	O2 Sensor Signal Circuit Slow Switching from Rich to Lean (Bank 1 Sensor 2)
P1181	224	O2 Sensor Signal Circuit Slow Switching from Rich to Lean (Bank 2 Sensor 2)
P1186	190	O2 Sensor Heater Control Circuit (Bank 1 Sensor 2)
P1187	191	O2 Sensor Heater Control Circuit (Bank 2 Sensor 2)
P1188	227	Fuel Control (Bank 1 Sensor 1)
P1189	228	Fuel Control (Bank 2 Sensor 1)
P1190	235	Pre Catalyst Fuel Trim System (Bank 1)
P1191	236	Pre Catalyst Fuel Trim System (Bank 2)
P1192	225	Post Catalyst Fuel Trim System (Bank 1)
P1193	226	Post Catalyst Fuel Trim System (Bank 2)

Table a. M52 TU engine: Siemens DME MS42.1 from 06/01/1998 to 05/31/1999		
PCode	**BMW-FC**	**PCode text**
P1397	18	Camshaft Position Sensor 'B' Circuit (Bank 1)
P1421	246	Secondary Air System (Bank 2)
P1423	245	Secondary Air System (Bank 1)
P1432	247	Secondary Air Injection System Incorrect Flow Detected
P1453	35	Secondary Air Injection Pump Relay Control Circuit Electrical
P1470	126	Leakage Diagnostic Pump Control Circuit Electrical
P1475	140	Leakage Diagnostic Pump Reed Switch Did not Close
P1476	143	Leakage Diagnostic Pump Clamped Tube (M52 MY99/00: Leakage Diagnostic Pump Reed Switch Circuit)
P1478	146	Evaporative Emission System Leak Detected (very small leak)
P1509	53	Idle-Speed Control Valve Opening Solenoid Control Circuit Signal Electrical
P1519	103	Oil-Condition Sensor Temperature Measurement (M62/M52/S52: 'A' Camshaft Position Actuator Bank 1)
P1520	104	Oil-Condition Sensor Level Measurement (M52: 'B' Camshaft Position Actuator Bank 1)
P1522	105	Oil-Condition Sensor Permeability Measurement (M62: 'A' Camshaft Position Actuator Bank 2; M52: 'A' Camshaft Position Actuator Tight or Jammed)
P1523	106	'A' Camshaft Position Actuator Signal Low (Bank 1) (M52: 'B' Camshaft Position Actuator Tight or Jammed)
P1525	21	'A' Camshaft Position Actuator Control Open Circuit (Bank 1)
P1529	19	'B' Camshaft Position Actuator Control Circuit Signal Low (Bank 1)
P1542	110	Pedal Position Sensor Electrical
P1542	111	Pedal Position Sensor Electrical
P1542	117	Pedal Position Sensor Electrical
P1542	120	Pedal Position Sensor Electrical
P1542	172	Pedal Position Sensor Electrical
P1542	175	Pedal Position Sensor Electrical
P1542	176	Pedal Position Sensor Electrical
P1550	27	Idle-Speed Control Valve Closing Coil Electrical
P1580	109	Throttle Valve Mechanically Stuck (M73: Throttle Valve 1 Spring Test)
P1580	114	Throttle Valve Mechanically Stuck (M73: Throttle Valve 1 Spring Test)
P1580	119	Throttle Valve Mechanically Stuck (M73: Throttle Valve 1 Spring Test)
P1593	124	DISA (Differentiated Intake Manifold) Control Circuit Electrical
P1622	123	Map Cooling Thermostat Control Circuit Electrical
P1623	115	Pedal Position Sensor Potentiometer Supply
P1623	116	Pedal Position Sensor Potentiometer Supply

Table b. M52 TU engine: Siemens DME MS42.1 from 06/01/1999 to 10/31/2000		
PCode	**BMW-FC**	**PCode text**
P0101	8	Mass or Volume Air Flow Circuit Range/Performance
P0111	14	Intake Air Temperature Sensor 1 Circuit Range/Performance
P0116	10	Engine Coolant Temperature Circuit Range/Performance

Table b. M52 TU engine: Siemens DME MS42.1 from 06/01/1999 to 10/31/2000		
PCode	**BMW-FC**	**PCode text**
P0120	112	Throttle/Pedal Position Sensor/Switch 'A' Circuit
P0120	113	Throttle/Pedal Position Sensor/Switch 'A' Circuit
P0120	118	Throttle/Pedal Position Sensor/Switch 'A' Circuit
P0120	173	Throttle/Pedal Position Sensor/Switch 'A' Circuit
P0120	174	Throttle/Pedal Position Sensor/Switch 'A' Circuit
P0125	222	Insufficient Coolant Temperature for Closed Loop Fuel Control
P0128	168	Coolant Thermostat (Coolant Temperature Below Thermostat Regulating Temperature)
P0130	150	O2 Sensor Circuit (Bank 1 Sensor 1)
P0130	151	O2 Sensor Circuit (Bank 1 Sensor 1)
P0130	152	O2 Sensor Circuit (Bank 1 Sensor 1)
P0133	229	O2 Sensor Circuit Slow Response (Bank 1 Sensor 1)
P0134	186	O2 Sensor Circuit No Activity Detected (Bank 1 Sensor 1)
P0135	25	O2 Sensor Heater Circuit (Bank 1 Sensor 1)
P0136	156	O2 Sensor Circuit (Bank 1 Sensor 2)
P0136	157	O2 Sensor Circuit (Bank 1 Sensor 2)
P0136	215	O2 Sensor Circuit (Bank 1 Sensor 2)
P0141	61	O2 Sensor Heater Circuit (Bank 1 Sensor 2)
P0150	153	O2 Sensor Circuit (Bank 2 Sensor 1)
P0150	154	O2 Sensor Circuit (Bank 2 Sensor 1)
P0150	155	O2 Sensor Circuit (Bank 2 Sensor 1)
P0153	230	O2 Sensor Circuit Slow Response (Bank 2 Sensor 1)
P0154	187	O2 Sensor Circuit No Activity Detected (Bank 2 Sensor 1)
P0155	55	O2 Sensor Heater Circuit (Bank 2 Sensor 1)
P0156	159	O2 Sensor Circuit (Bank 2 Sensor 2)
P0156	160	O2 Sensor Circuit (Bank 2 Sensor 2)
P0156	216	O2 Sensor Circuit (Bank 2 Sensor 2)
P0161	79	O2 Sensor Heater Circuit (Bank 2 Sensor 2)
P0170	202	Fuel Trim (Bank 1)
P0173	203	Fuel Trim (Bank 2)
P0201	6	Injector Circuit/Open - Cylinder 1
P0202	5	Injector Circuit/Open - Cylinder 2
P0203	22	Injector Circuit/Open - Cylinder 3
P0204	24	Injector Circuit/Open - Cylinder 4
P0205	33	Injector Circuit/Open - Cylinder 5
P0206	23	Injector Circuit/Open - Cylinder 6
P0301	238	Cylinder 1 Misfire Detected
P0302	239	Cylinder 2 Misfire Detected
P0303	240	Cylinder 3 Misfire Detected
P0304	241	Cylinder 4 Misfire Detected

Table b. M52 TU engine: Siemens DME MS42.1 from 06/01/1999 to 10/31/2000		
PCode	**BMW-FC**	**PCode text**
P0305	242	Cylinder 5 Misfire Detected
P0306	243	Cylinder 6 Misfire Detected
P0325	57	Knock Sensor 1 Circuit (Bank 1 or Single Sensor)
P0330	59	Knock Sensor 2 Circuit (Bank 2)
P0335	83	Crankshaft Position Sensor 'A' Circuit
P0340	65	Camshaft Position Sensor 'A' Circuit (Bank 1 or Single Sensor)
P0412	62	Secondary Air Injection System Switching Valve A Circuit
P0420	233	Catalyst System Efficiency Below Threshold (Bank 1)
P0430	234	Catalyst System Efficiency Below Threshold (Bank 2)
P0440	250	Evaporative Emission System
P0442	145	Evaporative Emission System Leak Detected (small leak)
P0443	68	Evaporative Emission System Purge Control Valve Circuit
P0500	214	Vehicle Speed Sensor 'A'
P0505	204	Idle Air Control System
P0600	217	Serial Communication Link
P0601	100	Internal Control Module Memory Check Sum Error
P0601	170 I	Internal Control Module Memory Check Sum Error
P0601	171	Internal Control Module Memory Check Sum Error
P1132	188	O2 Sensor Heater Control Circuit (Bank 1 Sensor 1)
P1133	189	O2 Sensor Heater Control Circuit (Bank 2 Sensor 1)
P1140	149	Mass or Volume Air Flow Circuit Range/Performance Problem
P1145	50	Solenoid Valve Running Losses Control Circuit Electrical
P1161	122	Fuel Trim Adaptation Additive High (Bank 2) (M52: Engine Oil Temperature Sensor Circuit)
P1180	223	O2 Sensor Signal Circuit Slow Switching from Rich to Lean (Bank 1 Sensor 2)
P1181	224	O2 Sensor Signal Circuit Slow Switching from Rich to Lean (Bank 2 Sensor 2)
P1184	220	HO2S Sensor Voltage Excursion Electrical (Bank 1 Sensor 1)
P1185	221	HO2S Sensor Voltage Excursion Electrical (Bank 2 Sensor 1)
P1186	190	O2 Sensor Heater Control Circuit (Bank 1 Sensor 2)
P1187	191	O2 Sensor Heater Control Circuit (Bank 2 Sensor 2)
P1188	227	Fuel Control (Bank 1 Sensor 1)
P1189	228	Fuel Control (Bank 2 Sensor 1)
P1190	235	Pre Catalyst Fuel Trim System (Bank 1)
P1191	236	Pre Catalyst Fuel Trim System (Bank 2)
P1192	225	Post Catalyst Fuel Trim System (Bank 1)
P1193	226	Post Catalyst Fuel Trim System (Bank 2)
P1397	18	Camshaft Position Sensor 'B' Circuit (Bank 1)
P1421	246	Secondary Air System (Bank 2)
P1423	245	Secondary Air System (Bank 1)
P1432	247	Secondary Air Injection System Incorrect Flow Detected

Table b. M52 TU engine: Siemens DME MS42.1 from 06/01/1999 to 10/31/2000		
PCode	**BMW-FC**	**PCode text**
P1453	35	Secondary Air Injection Pump Relay Control Circuit Electrical
P1470	126	Leakage Diagnostic Pump Control Circuit Electrical
P1475	140	Leakage Diagnostic Pump Reed Switch Did not Close
P1476	143	Leakage Diagnostic Pump Clamped Tube (M52 MY99/00: Leakage Diagnostic Pump Reed Switch Circuit)
P1478	146	Evaporative Emission System Leak Detected (very small leak)
P1509	53	Idle-Speed Control Valve Opening Solenoid Control Circuit Signal Electrical
P1519	103	Oil-Condition Sensor Temperature Measurement (M62/M52/S52: 'A' Camshaft Position Actuator Bank 1)
P1520	104	Oil-Condition Sensor Level Measurement (M52: 'B' Camshaft Position Actuator Bank 1)
P1522	105	Oil-Condition Sensor Permeability Measurement (M62: 'A' Camshaft Position Actuator Bank 2; M52: 'A' Camshaft Position Actuator Tight or Jammed)
P1523	106	'A' Camshaft Position Actuator Signal Low (Bank 1) (M52: 'B' Camshaft Position Actuator Tight or Jammed)
P1525	21	'A' Camshaft Position Actuator Control Open Circuit (Bank 1)
P1529	19	'B' Camshaft Position Actuator Control Circuit Signal Low (Bank 1)
P1542	110	Pedal Position Sensor Electrical
P1542	111	Pedal Position Sensor Electrical
P1542	117	Pedal Position Sensor Electrical
P1542	120	Pedal Position Sensor Electrical
P1542	172	Pedal Position Sensor Electrical
P1542	175	Pedal Position Sensor Electrical
P1542	176	Pedal Position Sensor Electrical
P1550	27	Idle-Speed Control Valve Closing Coil Electrical
P1580	109	Throttle Valve Mechanically Stuck (M73: Throttle Valve 1 Spring Test)
P1580	114	Throttle Valve Mechanically Stuck (M73: Throttle Valve 1 Spring Test)
P1580	119	Throttle Valve Mechanically Stuck (M73: Throttle Valve 1 Spring Test)
P1593	124	DISA (Differentiated Intake Manifold) Control Circuit Electrical
P1622	123	Map Cooling Thermostat Control Circuit Electrical
P1623	115	Pedal Position Sensor Potentiometer Supply
P1623	116	Pedal Position Sensor Potentiometer Supply

Table c. M54 engine: Siemens DME MS43.0 from 04/01/2000 to 08/31/2001		
PCode	**BMW-FC**	**PCode text**
P0011	103	'A' Camshaft Position Timing Over-Advanced or System Performance (Bank 1)
P0012	105	'A' Camshaft Position Timing Over-Retarded (Bank 1)
P0014	104	'B' Camshaft Position Timing Over-Advanced or System Performance (Bank 1)
P0015	106	'B' Camshaft Position Timing Over-Retarded (Bank 1)
P0101	149	Mass or Volume Air Flow Circuit Range/Performance
P0102	8	Mass or Volume Air Flow Circuit Low Input
P0103	8	Mass or Volume Air Flow Circuit High Input

Table c. M54 engine: Siemens DME MS43.0 from 04/01/2000 to 08/31/2001		
PCode	**BMW-FC**	**PCode text**
P0107	197	Manifold Absolute Pressure/Barometric Pressure Circuit Low Input
P0108	197	Manifold Absolute Pressure/Barometric Pressure Circuit High Input
P0112	14	Intake Air Temperature Sensor 1 Circuit Low
P0113	14	Intake Air Temperature Sensor 1 Circuit High
P0117	10	Engine Coolant Temperature Circuit Low
P0118	10	Engine Coolant Temperature Circuit High
P0121	118	Throttle/Pedal Position Sensor/Switch 'A' Circuit Range/Performance
P0122	112	Throttle/Pedal Position Sensor/Switch 'A' Circuit Low
P0123	112	Throttle/Pedal Position Sensor/Switch 'A' Circuit High
P0125	222	Insufficient Coolant Temperature for Closed Loop Fuel Control
P0128	168	Coolant Thermostat (Coolant Temperature Below Thermostat Regulating Temperature)
P0131	150	O2 Sensor Circuit Low Voltage (Bank 1 Sensor 1)
P0132	150	O2 Sensor Circuit High Voltage (Bank 1 Sensor 1)
P0133	229	O2 Sensor Circuit Slow Response (Bank 1 Sensor 1)
P0133	231	O2 Sensor Circuit Slow Response (Bank 1 Sensor 1)
P0134	150	O2 Sensor Circuit No Activity Detected (Bank 1 Sensor 1)
P0135	188	O2 Sensor Heater Circuit (Bank 1 Sensor 1)
P0137	152	O2 Sensor Circuit Low Voltage (Bank 1 Sensor 2)
P0138	152	O2 Sensor Circuit High Voltage (Bank 1 Sensor 2)
P0139	215	O2 Sensor Circuit Slow Response (Bank 1 Sensor 2)
P0139	248	O2 Sensor Circuit Slow Response (Bank 1 Sensor 2)
P0140	152	O2 Sensor Circuit No Activity Detected (Bank 1 Sensor 2)
P0141	190	O2 Sensor Heater Circuit (Bank 1 Sensor 2)
P0151	151	O2 Sensor Circuit Low Voltage (Bank 2 Sensor 1)
P0152	151	O2 Sensor Circuit High Voltage (Bank 2 Sensor 1)
P0153	230	O2 Sensor Circuit Slow Response (Bank 2 Sensor 1)
P0153	232	O2 Sensor Circuit Slow Response (Bank 2 Sensor 1)
P0154	151	O2 Sensor Circuit No Activity Detected (Bank 2 Sensor 1)
P0155	189	O2 Sensor Heater Circuit (Bank 2 Sensor 1)
P0157	153	O2 Sensor Circuit Low Voltage (Bank 2 Sensor 2)
P0158	153	O2 Sensor Circuit High Voltage (Bank 2 Sensor 2)
P0159	216	O2 Sensor Circuit Slow Response (Bank 2 Sensor 2)
P0159	249	O2 Sensor Circuit Slow Response (Bank 2 Sensor 2)
P0160	153	O2 Sensor Circuit No Activity Detected (Bank 2 Sensor 2)
P0161	191	O2 Sensor Heater Circuit (Bank 2 Sensor 2)
P0171	202	System Too Lean (Bank 1)
P0171	227	System Too Lean (Bank 1)
P0172	202	System Too Rich (Bank 1)
P0172	227	System Too Rich (Bank 1)

Table c. M54 engine: Siemens DME MS43.0 from 04/01/2000 to 08/31/2001		
PCode	**BMW-FC**	**PCode text**
P0174	203	System Too Lean (Bank 2)
P0174	228	System Too Lean (Bank 2)
P0175	203	System Too Rich (Bank 2)
P0175	228	System Too Rich (Bank 2)
P0197	122	Engine Oil Temperature Sensor Low
P0198	122	Engine Oil Temperature Sensor High
P0201	6	Injector Circuit/Open - Cylinder 1
P0202	5 I	Injector Circuit/Open - Cylinder 2
P0203	22	Injector Circuit/Open - Cylinder 3
P0204	24	Injector Circuit/Open - Cylinder 4
P0205	33	Injector Circuit/Open - Cylinder 5
P0206	23	Injector Circuit/Open - Cylinder 6
P0221	119	Throttle/Pedal Position Sensor/Switch 'B' Circuit Range/Performance
P0222	113	Throttle/Pedal Position Sensor/Switch 'B' Circuit Low
P0223	113	Throttle/Pedal Position Sensor/Switch 'B' Circuit High
P0261	6	Cylinder 1 Injector Circuit Low
P0262	6	Cylinder 1 Injector Circuit High
P0264	5	Cylinder 2 Injector Circuit Low
P0265	5	Cylinder 2 Injector Circuit High
P0267	22	Cylinder 3 Injector Circuit Low
P0268	22	Cylinder 3 Injector Circuit High
P0270	24	Cylinder 4 Injector Circuit Low
P0271	24	Cylinder 4 Injector Circuit High
P0273	33	Cylinder 5 Injector Circuit Low
P0274	33	Cylinder 5 Injector Circuit High
P0276	23	Cylinder 6 Injector Circuit Low
P0277	23	Cylinder 6 Injector Circuit High
P0301	238	Cylinder 1 Misfire Detected
P0302	239	Cylinder 2 Misfire Detected
P0303	240	Cylinder 3 Misfire Detected
P0304	241	Cylinder 4 Misfire Detected
P0305	242	Cylinder 5 Misfire Detected
P0306	243	Cylinder 6 Misfire Detected
P0313	238	Misfire Detected with Low Fuel
P0313	239	Misfire Detected with Low Fuel
P0313	240	Misfire Detected with Low Fuel
P0313	241	Misfire Detected with Low Fuel
P0313	242	Misfire Detected with Low Fuel
P0313	243	Misfire Detected with Low Fuel

Table c. M54 engine: Siemens DME MS43.0 from 04/01/2000 to 08/31/2001		
PCode	**BMW-FC**	**PCode text**
P0327	57	Knock Sensor 1 Circuit Low (Bank 1 or Single Sensor)
P0332	59	Knock Sensor 2 Circuit Low (Bank 2)
P0335	83	Crankshaft Position Sensor 'A' Circuit
P0339	83	Crankshaft Position Sensor 'A' Circuit Intermittent
P0340	65	Camshaft Position Sensor 'A' Circuit (Bank 1 or Single Sensor)
P0344	65	Camshaft Position Sensor 'A' Circuit Intermittent (Bank 1 or Single Sensor)
P0365	18	Camshaft Position Sensor 'B' Circuit (Bank 1)
P0369	18	Camshaft Position Sensor 'B' Circuit Intermittent (Bank 1)
P0413	62	Secondary Air Injection System Switching Valve A Circuit Open
P0414	62	Secondary Air Injection System Switching Valve A Circuit Shorted
P0420	233	Catalyst System Efficiency Below Threshold (Bank 1)
P0430	234	Catalyst System Efficiency Below Threshold (Bank 2)
P0441	250	Evaporative Emission System Incorrect Purge Flow
P0443	68	Evaporative Emission System Purge Control Valve Circuit
P0444	68	Evaporative Emission System Purge Control Valve Circuit Open
P0445	68	Evaporative Emission System Purge Control Valve Circuit Shorted
P0455	143	Evaporative Emission System Leak Detected (large leak)
P0456	143	Evaporative Emission System Leak Detected (very small leak)
P0491	245	Secondary Air Injection System Insufficient Flow (Bank 1)
P0500	214	Vehicle Speed Sensor 'A'
P0505	204	Idle Air Control System
P0600	217	Serial Communication Link
P0604	100	Internal Control Module Random Access Memory (RAM) Error
P1111	11	Engine Coolant Temperature Sensor Radiator Outlet Low Input
P1112	11	Engine Coolant Temperature Sensor Radiator Outlet High Input
P1120	114	Pedal Position Sensor Circuit
P1121	117	Pedal Position Sensor 1 Range/Performance Problem
P1122	110	Pedal Position Sensor 1 Low Input
P1123	110	Pedal Position Sensor 1 High Input
P1134	25	O2 Sensor Heater Circuit Signal Intermittent (Bank 1 Sensor 1)
P1135	25	O2 Sensor Heater Circuit Low Voltage (Bank 1 Sensor 1)
P1136	25	O2 Sensor Heater Circuit High Voltage (Bank 1 Sensor 1)
P1137	79	O2 Sensor Heater Circuit Signal Intermittent (Bank 1 Sensor 2)
P1138	79	O2 Sensor Heater Circuit Low Voltage (Bank 1 Sensor 2)
P1139	79	O2 Sensor Heater Circuit High Voltage (Bank 1 Sensor 2)
P1151	55	O2 Sensor Heater Circuit Signal Intermittent (Bank 2 Sensor 1)
P1152	55	O2 Sensor Heater Circuit Low Voltage (Bank 2 Sensor 1)
P1153	55	O2 Sensor Heater Circuit High Voltage (Bank 2 Sensor 1)
P1155	61	O2 Sensor Heater Circuit Signal Intermittent (Bank 2 Sensor 2)

Table c. M54 engine: Siemens DME MS43.0 from 04/01/2000 to 08/31/2001		
PCode	**BMW-FC**	**PCode text**
P1156	61	O2 Sensor Heater Circuit Low Voltage (Bank 2 Sensor 2)
P1157	61	O2 Sensor Heater Circuit High Voltage (Bank 2 Sensor 2)
P1190	235	Pre Catalyst Fuel Trim System (Bank 1)
P1191	236	Pre Catalyst Fuel Trim System (Bank 2)
P1192	225	Post Catalyst Fuel Trim System (Bank 1)
P1193	226	Post Catalyst Fuel Trim System (Bank 2)
P1222	111	Pedal Position Sensor 2 Low Input
P1223	111	Pedal Position Sensor 2 High Input
P1342	238	Misfire During Start Cylinder 1
P1343	238	Misfire Cylinder 1 with Fuel Cut-Off
P1344	239	Misfire During Start Cylinder 2
P1345	239	Misfire Cylinder 2 with Fuel Cut-Off
P1346	240	Misfire During Start Cylinder 3
P1347	240	Misfire Cylinder 3 with Fuel Cut-Off
P1348	241	Misfire During Start Cylinder 4
P1349	241	Misfire Cylinder 4 with Fuel Cut-Off
P1350	242	Misfire during Start Cylinder 5
P1351	242	Misfire Cylinder 5 with Fuel Cut-Off
P1352	243	Misfire during Start Cylinder 6
P1500	211	Idle-Speed Control Valve Stuck Open
P1501	211	Idle-Speed Control Valve Stuck Closed
P1502	27	Idle-Speed Control Valve Closing Solenoid Control Circuit Signal High
P1503	27	Idle-Speed Control Valve Closing Solenoid Control Circuit Signal Low
P1504	27	Idle-Speed Control Valve Closing Solenoid Control Open Circuit
P1506	53	Idle-Speed Control Valve Opening Solenoid Control Circuit Signal High
P1507	53	Idle-Speed Control Valve Opening Solenoid Control Circuit Signal Low
P1508	53	Idle-Speed Control Valve Opening Solenoid Control Open Circuit
P1353	243	Misfire Cylinder 6 with Fuel Cut-Off
P1413	35	Secondary Air Injection Pump Relay Control Circuit Signal Low
P1414	35	Secondary Air Injection Pump Relay Control Circuit Signal High
P1444	142	Diagnostic Module Tank Leakage (DM-TL) Pump Control Open Circuit
P1445	140	Diagnostic Module Tank Leakage (DM-TL) Pump Control Circuit Signal Low
P1446	140	Diagnostic Module Tank Leakage (DM-TL) Pump Control Circuit Signal High
P1447	142	Diagnostic Module Tank Leakage (DM-TL) Pump Current Too High during Switching Solenoid Test
P1448	142	Diagnostic Module Tank Leakage (DM-TL) Pump Current Too Low
P1449	142	Diagnostic Module Tank Leakage (DM-TL) Pump Current Too High
P1451	126	Diagnostic Module Tank Leakage (DM-TL) Switching Solenoid Control Circuit Signal Low
P1452	126	Diagnostic Module Tank Leakage (DM-TL) Switching Solenoid Control Circuit Signal High
P1512	124	DISA (Differentiated Intake Manifold) Control Circuit Signal Low

Table c. M54 engine: Siemens DME MS43.0 from 04/01/2000 to 08/31/2001		
PCode	**BMW-FC**	**PCode text**
P1513	124	DISA (Differentiated Intake Manifold) Control Circuit Signal High
P1523	21	'A' Camshaft Position Actuator Signal Low (Bank 1) (M52: 'B' Camshaft Position Actuator Tight or Jammed)
P1524	21	'A' Camshaft Position Actuator Control Circuit Signal High (Bank 1)
P1525	21	'A' Camshaft Position Actuator Control Open Circuit (Bank 1)
P1529	19	'B' Camshaft Position Actuator Control Circuit Signal Low (Bank 1)
P1530	19	'B' Camshaft Position Actuator Control Circuit Signal High (Bank 1) (S54 to 09/00: Throttle Valve Position Control, Control Deviation)
P1531	19	'B' Camshaft Position Actuator Control Open Circuit (Bank 1)
P1602	48	Control Module Self-Test, Control Module Defective
P1602	58	Control Module Self-Test, Control Module Defective
P1602	63	Control Module Self-Test, Control Module Defective
P1602	66	Control Module Self-Test, Control Module Defective
P1602	67	Control Module Self-Test, Control Module Defective
P1602	70	Control Module Self-Test, Control Module Defective
P1602	71	Control Module Self-Test, Control Module Defective
P1602	72	Control Module Self-Test, Control Module Defective
P1603	49	Control Module Self-Test, Torque Monitoring
P1604	50	Control Module Self-Test, Speed Monitoring
P1604	51	Control Module Self-Test, Speed Monitoring
P1619	123	Map Cooling Thermostat Control Circuit Signal Low
P1620	123	Map Cooling Thermostat Control Circuit Signal High
P1624	146	Pedal Position Sensor Potentiometer Supply Channel 1 Electrical (M52: Coolant Thermostat (Coolant Temperature Below Thermostat Regulating Temperature))
P1625	147	Pedal Position Sensor Potentiometer Supply Channel 2 Electrical
P1632	115	Throttle Valve Adaptation Conditions Not Met
P1633	115	Throttle Valve Adaptation Limp-Home Position Unknown
P1634	115	Throttle Valve Adaptation Spring Test Failed
P1634	135	Throttle Valve Adaptation Spring Test Failed
P1634	136	Throttle Valve Adaptation Spring Test Failed
P1635	115	Throttle Valve Adaptation Lower Mechanical Stop not Adapted
P1636	109	Throttle Valve Control Circuit
P1637	162	Throttle Valve Position Control, Control Deviation
P1638	160	Throttle Valve Position Control Throttle Stuck Temporarily
P1639	161	Throttle Valve Position Control Throttle Stuck Permanently

Table d. M54 engine: Siemens DME MS43.0 from 09/01/2001 to 08/31/2002		
PCode	**BMW-FC**	**PCode text**
P0011	103	'A' Camshaft Position Timing Over-Advanced or System Performance (Bank 1)
P0012	105	'A' Camshaft Position Timing Over-Retarded (Bank 1)

Table d. M54 engine: Siemens DME MS43.0 from 09/01/2001 to 08/31/2002		
PCode	**BMW-FC**	**PCode text**
P0014	104	'B' Camshaft Position Timing Over-Advanced or System Performance (Bank 1)
P0015	106	'B' Camshaft Position Timing Over-Retarded (Bank 1)
P0030	25	HO2S Heater Control Circuit (Bank 1 Sensor 1)
P0031	25	HO2S Heater Control Circuit Low (Bank 1 Sensor 1)
P0032	25	HO2S Heater Control Circuit High (Bank 1 Sensor 1)
P0036	79	HO2S Heater Control Circuit (Bank 1 Sensor 2)
P0037	79	HO2S Heater Control Circuit Low (Bank 1 Sensor 2)
P0038	79	HO2S Heater Control Circuit High (Bank 1 Sensor 2)
P0050	55	HO2S Heater Control Circuit (Bank 2 Sensor 1)
P0051	55	HO2S Heater Control Circuit Low (Bank 2 Sensor 1)
P0052	55	HO2S Heater Control Circuit High (Bank 2 Sensor 1)
P0056	61	HO2S Heater Control Circuit (Bank 2 Sensor 2)
P0057	61	HO2S Heater Control Circuit Low (Bank 2 Sensor 2)
P0058	61	HO2S Heater Control Circuit High (Bank 2 Sensor 2)
P0101	149	Mass or Volume Air Flow Circuit Range/Performance
P0102	8	Mass or Volume Air Flow Circuit Low Input
P0103	8	Mass or Volume Air Flow Circuit High Input
P0107	197	Manifold Absolute Pressure/Barometric Pressure Circuit Low Input
P0108	197	Manifold Absolute Pressure/Barometric Pressure Circuit High Input
P0112	14	Intake Air Temperature Sensor 1 Circuit Low
P0113	14	Intake Air Temperature Sensor 1 Circuit High
P0117	10	Engine Coolant Temperature Circuit Low
P0118	10	Engine Coolant Temperature Circuit High
P0121	118	Throttle/Pedal Position Sensor/Switch 'A' Circuit Range/Performance
P0122	112	Throttle/Pedal Position Sensor/Switch 'A' Circuit Low
P0123	112	Throttle/Pedal Position Sensor/Switch 'A' Circuit High
P0125	222	Insufficient Coolant Temperature for Closed Loop Fuel Control
P0128	168	Coolant Thermostat (Coolant Temperature Below Thermostat Regulating Temperature)
P0131	150	O2 Sensor Circuit Low Voltage (Bank 1 Sensor 1)
P0132	150	O2 Sensor Circuit High Voltage (Bank 1 Sensor 1)
P0133	229	O2 Sensor Circuit Slow Response (Bank 1 Sensor 1)
P0134	150	O2 Sensor Circuit No Activity Detected (Bank 1 Sensor 1)
P0135	188	O2 Sensor Heater Circuit (Bank 1 Sensor 1)
P0137	152	O2 Sensor Circuit Low Voltage (Bank 1 Sensor 2)
P0138	152	O2 Sensor Circuit High Voltage (Bank 1 Sensor 2)
P0140	152	O2 Sensor Circuit No Activity Detected (Bank 1 Sensor 2)
P0141	190	O2 Sensor Heater Circuit (Bank 1 Sensor 2)
P0151	151	O2 Sensor Circuit Low Voltage (Bank 2 Sensor 1)
P0152	151	O2 Sensor Circuit High Voltage (Bank 2 Sensor 1)

Table d. M54 engine: Siemens DME MS43.0 from 09/01/2001 to 08/31/2002		
PCode	**BMW-FC**	**PCode text**
P0153	230	O2 Sensor Circuit Slow Response (Bank 2 Sensor 1)
P0154	151	O2 Sensor Circuit No Activity Detected (Bank 2 Sensor 1)
P0155	189	O2 Sensor Heater Circuit (Bank 2 Sensor 1)
P0157	153	O2 Sensor Circuit Low Voltage (Bank 2 Sensor 2)
P0158	153	O2 Sensor Circuit High Voltage (Bank 2 Sensor 2)
P0160	153	O2 Sensor Circuit No Activity Detected (Bank 2 Sensor 2)
P0161	191	O2 Sensor Heater Circuit (Bank 2 Sensor 2)
P0171	227	System Too Lean (Bank 1)
P0172	227	System Too Rich (Bank 1)
P0174	228	System Too Lean (Bank 2)
P0175	228	System Too Rich (Bank 2)
P0197	122	Engine Oil Temperature Sensor Low
P0198	122	Engine Oil Temperature Sensor High
P0201	6	Injector Circuit/Open - Cylinder 1
P0202	5	Injector Circuit/Open - Cylinder 2
P0203	22	Injector Circuit/Open - Cylinder 3
P0204	24	Injector Circuit/Open - Cylinder 4
P0205	33	Injector Circuit/Open - Cylinder 5
P0206	23	Injector Circuit/Open - Cylinder 6
P0221	119	Throttle/Pedal Position Sensor/Switch 'B' Circuit Range/Performance
P0222	113	Throttle/Pedal Position Sensor/Switch 'B' Circuit Low
P0223	113	Throttle/Pedal Position Sensor/Switch 'B' Circuit High
P0261	6	Cylinder 1 Injector Circuit Low
P0262	6	Cylinder 1 Injector Circuit High
P0264	5	Cylinder 2 Injector Circuit Low
P0265	5	Cylinder 2 Injector Circuit High
P0267	22	Cylinder 3 Injector Circuit Low
P0268	22	Cylinder 3 Injector Circuit High
P0270	24	Cylinder 4 Injector Circuit Low
P0271	24	Cylinder 4 Injector Circuit High
P0273	33	Cylinder 5 Injector Circuit Low
P0274	33	Cylinder 5 Injector Circuit High
P0276	23	Cylinder 6 Injector Circuit Low
P0277	23	Cylinder 6 Injector Circuit High
P0301	238	Cylinder 1 Misfire Detected
P0302	239	Cylinder 2 Misfire Detected
P0303	240	Cylinder 3 Misfire Detected
P0304	241	Cylinder 4 Misfire Detected
P0305	242	Cylinder 5 Misfire Detected

Table d. M54 engine: Siemens DME MS43.0 from 09/01/2001 to 08/31/2002		
PCode	**BMW-FC**	**PCode text**
P0306	243	Cylinder 6 Misfire Detected
P0313	238	Misfire Detected with Low Fuel
P0313	239	Misfire Detected with Low Fuel
P0313	240	Misfire Detected with Low Fuel
P0313	241	Misfire Detected with Low Fuel
P0313	242	Misfire Detected with Low Fuel
P0313	243	Misfire Detected with Low Fuel
P0327	57	Knock Sensor 1 Circuit Low (Bank 1 or Single Sensor)
P0332	59	Knock Sensor 2 Circuit Low (Bank 2)
P0335	83	Crankshaft Position Sensor 'A' Circuit
P0339	83	Crankshaft Position Sensor 'A' Circuit Intermittent
P0340	65	Camshaft Position Sensor 'A' Circuit (Bank 1 or Single Sensor)
P0344	65	Camshaft Position Sensor 'A' Circuit Intermittent (Bank 1 or Single Sensor)
P0365	18	Camshaft Position Sensor 'B' Circuit (Bank 1)
P0369	18	Camshaft Position Sensor 'B' Circuit Intermittent (Bank 1)
P0413	62	Secondary Air Injection System Switching Valve A Circuit Open
P0414	62	Secondary Air Injection System Switching Valve A Circuit Shorted
P0420	233	Catalyst System Efficiency Below Threshold (Bank 1)
P0430	234	Catalyst System Efficiency Below Threshold (Bank 2)
P0441	250	Evaporative Emission System Incorrect Purge Flow
P0443	68	Evaporative Emission System Purge Control Valve Circuit
P0444	68	Evaporative Emission System Purge Control Valve Circuit Open
P0445	68	Evaporative Emission System Purge Control Valve Circuit Shorted
P0455	143	Evaporative Emission System Leak Detected (large leak)
P0456	143	Evaporative Emission System Leak Detected (very small leak)
P0491	245	Secondary Air Injection System Insufficient Flow (Bank 1)
P0492	246	Secondary Air Injection System Insufficient Flow (Bank 2)
P0500	214	Vehicle Speed Sensor 'A'
P0505	204	Idle Air Control System
P0600	217	Serial Communication Link
P0604	100	Internal Control Module Random Access Memory (RAM) Error
P1083	202	Fuel Control Limit Mixture Too Lean (Bank 1 Sensor 1)
P1084	202	Fuel Control Limit Mixture Too Rich (Bank 1 Sensor 1)
P1085	203	Fuel Control Limit Mixture Too Lean (Bank 2 Sensor 1)
P1086	203	Fuel Control Limit Mixture Too Rich (Bank 2 Sensor 1)
P1087	229	O2 Sensor Circuit Slow Response in Lean Control Range (Bank 1 Sensor 1)
P1088	229	O2 Sensor Circuit Slow Response in Rich Control Range (Bank 1 Sensor 1)
P1089	230	O2 Sensor Circuit Slow Response in Lean Control Range (Bank 1 Sensor 2)
P1090	235	Pre Catalyst Fuel Trim System Too Lean (Bank 1)

Table d. M54 engine: Siemens DME MS43.0 from 09/01/2001 to 08/31/2002		
PCode	**BMW-FC**	**PCode text**
P1091	236	Pre Catalyst Fuel Trim System Too Lean (Bank 2)
P1092	235	Pre Catalyst Fuel Trim System Too Rich (Bank 1)
P1093	236	Pre Catalyst Fuel Trim System Too Rich (Bank 2)
P1094	230	O2 Sensor Circuit Slow Response in Rich Control Range (Bank 2 Sensor 1)
P1111	11	Engine Coolant Temperature Sensor Radiator Outlet Low Input
P1112	11	Engine Coolant Temperature Sensor Radiator Outlet High Input
P1120	114	Pedal Position Sensor Circuit
P1121	117	Pedal Position Sensor 1 Range/Performance Problem
P1122	110	Pedal Position Sensor 1 Low Input
P1123	110	Pedal Position Sensor 1 High Input
P1143	215	O2 Sensor Activity Check Signal Too High (Bank 1 Sensor 2)
P1144	215	O2 Sensor Activity Check Signal Too Low (Bank 1 Sensor 2)
P1149	216	O2 Sensor Activity Check Signal Too High (Bank 2 Sensor 2)
P1150	216	O2 Sensor Activity Check Signal Too Low (Bank 2 Sensor 2)
P1171	196	Ambient Pressure Sensor Variant Recognition Value in Boot Range Implausible
P1172	196	Ambient Pressure Sensor Variant Recognition Error Value Stored in Boot Range
P1173	196	Ambient Pressure Sensor Variant Recognition Learning Failed
P1222	111	Pedal Position Sensor 2 Low Input
P1223	111	Pedal Position Sensor 2 High Input
P1314	202	Fuel Mixture Deviation Detected with Low Fuel
P1314	203	Fuel Mixture Deviation Detected with Low Fuel
P1314	227	Fuel Mixture Deviation Detected with Low Fuel
P1314	228	Fuel Mixture Deviation Detected with Low Fuel
P1342	238	Misfire During Start Cylinder 1
P1343	238	Misfire Cylinder 1 with Fuel Cut-Off
P1344	239	Misfire During Start Cylinder 2
P1345	239	Misfire Cylinder 2 with Fuel Cut-Off
P1346	240	Misfire During Start Cylinder 3
P1347	240	Misfire Cylinder 3 with Fuel Cut-Off
P1348	241	Misfire During Start Cylinder 4
P1349	241	Misfire Cylinder 4 with Fuel Cut-Off
P1350	242	Misfire during Start Cylinder 5
P1351	242	Misfire Cylinder 5 with Fuel Cut-Off
P1352	243	Misfire during Start Cylinder 6
P1353	243	Misfire Cylinder 6 with Fuel Cut-Off
P1413	35	Secondary Air Injection Pump Relay Control Circuit Signal Low
P1414	35	Secondary Air Injection Pump Relay Control Circuit Signal High
P1445	140	Diagnostic Module Tank Leakage (DM-TL) Pump Control Circuit Signal Low
P1446	140	Diagnostic Module Tank Leakage (DM-TL) Pump Control Circuit Signal High

Table d. M54 engine: Siemens DME MS43.0 from 09/01/2001 to 08/31/2002		
PCode	**BMW-FC**	**PCode text**
P1447	142	Diagnostic Module Tank Leakage (DM-TL) Pump Current Too High during Switching Solenoid Test
P1448	142	Diagnostic Module Tank Leakage (DM-TL) Pump Current Too Low
P1449	142	Diagnostic Module Tank Leakage (DM-TL) Pump Current Too High
P1451	126	Diagnostic Module Tank Leakage (DM-TL) Switching Solenoid Control Circuit Signal Low
P1452	126	Diagnostic Module Tank Leakage (DM-TL) Switching Solenoid Control Circuit Signal High
P1500	211	Idle-Speed Control Valve Stuck Open
P1501	211	Idle-Speed Control Valve Stuck Closed
P1502	27	Idle-Speed Control Valve Closing Solenoid Control Circuit Signal High
P1503	27	Idle-Speed Control Valve Closing Solenoid Control Circuit Signal Low
P1504	27	Idle-Speed Control Valve Closing Solenoid Control Open Circuit
P1506	53	Idle-Speed Control Valve Opening Solenoid Control Circuit Signal High
P1507	53	Idle-Speed Control Valve Opening Solenoid Control Circuit Signal Low
P1508	53	Idle-Speed Control Valve Opening Solenoid Control Open Circuit
P1512	124	DISA (Differentiated Intake Manifold) Control Circuit Signal Low
P1513	124	DISA (Differentiated Intake Manifold) Control Circuit Signal High
P1523	21	'A' Camshaft Position Actuator Signal Low (Bank 1) (M52: 'B' Camshaft Position Actuator Tight or Jammed)
P1524	21	'A' Camshaft Position Actuator Control Circuit Signal High (Bank 1)
P1525	21	'A' Camshaft Position Actuator Control Open Circuit (Bank 1)
P1529	19	'B' Camshaft Position Actuator Control Circuit Signal Low (Bank 1)
P1530	19	'B' Camshaft Position Actuator Control Circuit Signal High (Bank 1) (S54 to 09/00: Throttle Valve Position Control, Control Deviation)
P1531	19	'B' Camshaft Position Actuator Control Open Circuit (Bank 1)
P1602	48	Control Module Self-Test, Control Module Defective
P1602	58	Control Module Self-Test, Control Module Defective
P1602	63	Control Module Self-Test, Control Module Defective
P1602	66	Control Module Self-Test, Control Module Defective
P1602	67	Control Module Self-Test, Control Module Defective
P1602	70	Control Module Self-Test, Control Module Defective
P1602	71	Control Module Self-Test, Control Module Defective
P1602	72	Control Module Self-Test, Control Module Defective
P1603	49	Control Module Self-Test, Torque Monitoring
P1604	50	Control Module Self-Test, Speed Monitoring
P1619	123	Map Cooling Thermostat Control Circuit Signal Low
P1620	123	Map Cooling Thermostat Control Circuit Signal High
P1624	146	Pedal Position Sensor Potentiometer Supply Channel 1 Electrical (M52: Coolant Thermostat (Coolant Temperature Below Thermostat Regulating Temperature))
P1625	147	Pedal Position Sensor Potentiometer Supply Channel 2 Electrical
P1632	115	Throttle Valve Adaptation Conditions Not Met
P1633	115	Throttle Valve Adaptation Limp-Home Position Unknown

Table d. M54 engine: Siemens DME MS43.0 from 09/01/2001 to 08/31/2002		
PCode	**BMW-FC**	**PCode text**
P1634	115	Throttle Valve Adaptation Spring Test Failed
P1635	115	Throttle Valve Adaptation Lower Mechanical Stop not Adapted
P1636	109	Throttle Valve Control Circuit
P1637	162	Throttle Valve Position Control, Control Deviation
P1638	160	Throttle Valve Position Control Throttle Stuck Temporarily
P1639	161	Throttle Valve Position Control Throttle Stuck Permanently
P1675	135	Throttle Valve Actuator Start Test Re-Adaptation Required
P1694	136	Throttle Valve Actuator Start Test Spring Test and Limp-Home Position Failed
P2096	225	Post Catalyst Fuel Trim System Too Lean (Bank 1)
P2098	226	Post Catalyst Fuel Trim System Too Lean (Bank 2)

Table e. M54 engine: Siemens DME MS43.0 from 09/01/2002 to 02/28/2003		
PCode	**BMW-FC**	**PCode text**
P0011	103	'A' Camshaft Position Timing Over-Advanced or System Performance (Bank 1)
P0012	105	'A' Camshaft Position Timing Over-Retarded (Bank 1)
P0014	104	'B' Camshaft Position Timing Over-Advanced or System Performance (Bank 1)
P0015	106	'B' Camshaft Position Timing Over-Retarded (Bank 1)
P0030	25	HO2S Heater Control Circuit (Bank 1 Sensor 1)
P0031	25	HO2S Heater Control Circuit Low (Bank 1 Sensor 1)
P0032	25	HO2S Heater Control Circuit High (Bank 1 Sensor 1)
P0036	79	HO2S Heater Control Circuit (Bank 1 Sensor 2)
P0037	79	HO2S Heater Control Circuit Low (Bank 1 Sensor 2)
P0038	79	HO2S Heater Control Circuit High (Bank 1 Sensor 2)
P0050	55	HO2S Heater Control Circuit (Bank 2 Sensor 1)
P0051	55	HO2S Heater Control Circuit Low (Bank 2 Sensor 1)
P0052	55	HO2S Heater Control Circuit High (Bank 2 Sensor 1)
P0056	61	HO2S Heater Control Circuit (Bank 2 Sensor 2)
P0057	61	HO2S Heater Control Circuit Low (Bank 2 Sensor 2)
P0058	61	HO2S Heater Control Circuit High (Bank 2 Sensor 2)
P0101	149	Mass or Volume Air Flow Circuit Range/Performance
P0102	8	Mass or Volume Air Flow Circuit Low Input
P0103	8	Mass or Volume Air Flow Circuit High Input
P0107	197	Manifold Absolute Pressure/Barometric Pressure Circuit Low Input
P0108	197	Manifold Absolute Pressure/Barometric Pressure Circuit High Input
P0112	14	Intake Air Temperature Sensor 1 Circuit Low
P0113	14	Intake Air Temperature Sensor 1 Circuit High
P0117	10	Engine Coolant Temperature Circuit Low
P0118	10	Engine Coolant Temperature Circuit High

Table e. M54 engine: Siemens DME MS43.0 from 09/01/2002 to 02/28/2003		
P0121	118	Throttle/Pedal Position Sensor/Switch 'A' Circuit Range/Performance
P0122	112	Throttle/Pedal Position Sensor/Switch 'A' Circuit Low
P0123	112	Throttle/Pedal Position Sensor/Switch 'A' Circuit High
P0125	222	Insufficient Coolant Temperature for Closed Loop Fuel Control
P0128	168	Coolant Thermostat (Coolant Temperature Below Thermostat Regulating Temperature)
P0131	150	O2 Sensor Circuit Low Voltage (Bank 1 Sensor 1)
P0132	150	O2 Sensor Circuit High Voltage (Bank 1 Sensor 1)
P0133	229	O2 Sensor Circuit Slow Response (Bank 1 Sensor 1)
P0134	150	O2 Sensor Circuit No Activity Detected (Bank 1 Sensor 1)
P0135	188	O2 Sensor Heater Circuit (Bank 1 Sensor 1)
P0137	152	O2 Sensor Circuit Low Voltage (Bank 1 Sensor 2)
P0138	152	O2 Sensor Circuit High Voltage (Bank 1 Sensor 2)
P0140	152	O2 Sensor Circuit No Activity Detected (Bank 1 Sensor 2)
P0141	190	O2 Sensor Heater Circuit (Bank 1 Sensor 2)
P0151	151	O2 Sensor Circuit Low Voltage (Bank 2 Sensor 1)
P0152	151	O2 Sensor Circuit High Voltage (Bank 2 Sensor 1)
P0153	230	O2 Sensor Circuit Slow Response (Bank 2 Sensor 1)
P0154	151	O2 Sensor Circuit No Activity Detected (Bank 2 Sensor 1)
P0155	189	O2 Sensor Heater Circuit (Bank 2 Sensor 1)
P0157	153	O2 Sensor Circuit Low Voltage (Bank 2 Sensor 2)
P0158	153	O2 Sensor Circuit High Voltage (Bank 2 Sensor 2)
P0160	153	O2 Sensor Circuit No Activity Detected (Bank 2 Sensor 2)
P0161	191	O2 Sensor Heater Circuit (Bank 2 Sensor 2)
P0171	227	System Too Lean (Bank 1)
P0172	227	System Too Rich (Bank 1)
P0174	228	System Too Lean (Bank 2)
P0175	228	System Too Rich (Bank 2)
P0197	122	Engine Oil Temperature Sensor Low
P0198	122	Engine Oil Temperature Sensor High
P0201	6	Injector Circuit/Open - Cylinder 1
P0202	5	Injector Circuit/Open - Cylinder 2
P0203	22	Injector Circuit/Open - Cylinder 3
P0204	24	Injector Circuit/Open - Cylinder 4
P0205	33	Injector Circuit/Open - Cylinder 5
P0206	23	Injector Circuit/Open - Cylinder 6
P0221	119	Throttle/Pedal Position Sensor/Switch 'B' Circuit Range/Performance
P0222	113	Throttle/Pedal Position Sensor/Switch 'B' Circuit Low
P0223	113	Throttle/Pedal Position Sensor/Switch 'B' Circuit High
P0261	6	Cylinder 1 Injector Circuit Low
P0262	6	Cylinder 1 Injector Circuit High

Table e. M54 engine: Siemens DME MS43.0 from 09/01/2002 to 02/28/2003		
P0264	5	Cylinder 2 Injector Circuit Low
P0265	5	Cylinder 2 Injector Circuit High
P0267	22	Cylinder 3 Injector Circuit Low
P0268	22	Cylinder 3 Injector Circuit High
P0270	24	Cylinder 4 Injector Circuit Low
P0271	24	Cylinder 4 Injector Circuit High
P0273	33	Cylinder 5 Injector Circuit Low
P0274	33	Cylinder 5 Injector Circuit High
P0276	23	Cylinder 6 Injector Circuit Low
P0277	23	Cylinder 6 Injector Circuit High
P0301	238	Cylinder 1 Misfire Detected
P0302	239	Cylinder 2 Misfire Detected
P0303	240	Cylinder 3 Misfire Detected
P0304	241	Cylinder 4 Misfire Detected
P0305	242	Cylinder 5 Misfire Detected
P0306	243	Cylinder 6 Misfire Detected
P0313	238	Misfire Detected with Low Fuel
P0313	239	Misfire Detected with Low Fuel
P0313	240	Misfire Detected with Low Fuel
P0313	241	Misfire Detected with Low Fuel
P0313	242	Misfire Detected with Low Fuel
P0313	243	Misfire Detected with Low Fuel
P0327	57	Knock Sensor 1 Circuit Low (Bank 1 or Single Sensor)
P0332	59	Knock Sensor 2 Circuit Low (Bank 2)
P0335	83	Crankshaft Position Sensor 'A' Circuit
P0339	83	Crankshaft Position Sensor 'A' Circuit Intermittent
P0340	65	Camshaft Position Sensor 'A' Circuit (Bank 1 or Single Sensor)
P0344	65	Camshaft Position Sensor 'A' Circuit Intermittent (Bank 1 or Single Sensor)
P0365	18	Camshaft Position Sensor 'B' Circuit (Bank 1)
P0369	18	Camshaft Position Sensor 'B' Circuit Intermittent (Bank 1)
P0413	62	Secondary Air Injection System Switching Valve A Circuit Open
P0414	62	Secondary Air Injection System Switching Valve A Circuit Shorted
P0420	233	Catalyst System Efficiency Below Threshold (Bank 1)
P0430	234	Catalyst System Efficiency Below Threshold (Bank 2)
P0441	250	Evaporative Emission System Incorrect Purge Flow
P0443	68	Evaporative Emission System Purge Control Valve Circuit
P0444	68	Evaporative Emission System Purge Control Valve Circuit Open
P0445	68	Evaporative Emission System Purge Control Valve Circuit Shorted
P0455	143	Evaporative Emission System Leak Detected (large leak)
P0456	143	Evaporative Emission System Leak Detected (very small leak)

Table e. M54 engine: Siemens DME MS43.0 from 09/01/2002 to 02/28/2003		
P0491	245	Secondary Air Injection System Insufficient Flow (Bank 1)
P0492	246	Secondary Air Injection System Insufficient Flow (Bank 2)
P0500	214	Vehicle Speed Sensor 'A'
P0505	204	Idle Air Control System
P0600	217	Serial Communication Link
P0604	100	Internal Control Module Random Access Memory (RAM) Error
P1083	202	Fuel Control Limit Mixture Too Lean (Bank 1 Sensor 1)
P1084	202	Fuel Control Limit Mixture Too Rich (Bank 1 Sensor 1)
P1085	203	Fuel Control Limit Mixture Too Lean (Bank 2 Sensor 1)
P1086	203	Fuel Control Limit Mixture Too Rich (Bank 2 Sensor 1)
P1087	229	O2 Sensor Circuit Slow Response in Lean Control Range (Bank 1 Sensor 1)
P1088	229	O2 Sensor Circuit Slow Response in Rich Control Range (Bank 1 Sensor 1)
P1089	230	O2 Sensor Circuit Slow Response in Lean Control Range (Bank 1 Sensor 2)
P1090	235	Pre Catalyst Fuel Trim System Too Lean (Bank 1)
P1091	236	Pre Catalyst Fuel Trim System Too Lean (Bank 2)
P1092	235	Pre Catalyst Fuel Trim System Too Rich (Bank 1)
P1093	236	Pre Catalyst Fuel Trim System Too Rich (Bank 2)
P1094	230	O2 Sensor Circuit Slow Response in Rich Control Range (Bank 2 Sensor 1)
P1111	11	Engine Coolant Temperature Sensor Radiator Outlet Low Input
P1112	11	Engine Coolant Temperature Sensor Radiator Outlet High Input
P1120	114	Pedal Position Sensor Circuit
P1121	117	Pedal Position Sensor 1 Range/Performance Problem
P1122	110	Pedal Position Sensor 1 Low Input
P1123	110	Pedal Position Sensor 1 High Input
P1143	215	O2 Sensor Activity Check Signal Too High (Bank 1 Sensor 2)
P1144	215	O2 Sensor Activity Check Signal Too Low (Bank 1 Sensor 2)
P1149	216	O2 Sensor Activity Check Signal Too High (Bank 2 Sensor 2)
P1150	216	O2 Sensor Activity Check Signal Too Low (Bank 2 Sensor 2)
P1171	196	Ambient Pressure Sensor Variant Recognition Value in Boot Range Implausible
P1172	196	Ambient Pressure Sensor Variant Recognition Error Value Stored in Boot Range
P1173	196	Ambient Pressure Sensor Variant Recognition Learning Failed
P1222	111	Pedal Position Sensor 2 Low Input
P1223	111	Pedal Position Sensor 2 High Input
P1314	202	Fuel Mixture Deviation Detected with Low Fuel
P1314	203	Fuel Mixture Deviation Detected with Low Fuel
P1314	227	Fuel Mixture Deviation Detected with Low Fuel
P1314	228	Fuel Mixture Deviation Detected with Low Fuel
P1342	238	Misfire During Start Cylinder 1
P1343	238	Misfire Cylinder 1 with Fuel Cut-Off
P1344	239	Misfire During Start Cylinder 2

Table e. M54 engine: Siemens DME MS43.0 from 09/01/2002 to 02/28/2003		
P1345	239	Misfire Cylinder 2 with Fuel Cut-Off
P1346	240	Misfire During Start Cylinder 3
P1347	240	Misfire Cylinder 3 with Fuel Cut-Off
P1348	241	Misfire During Start Cylinder 4
P1349	241	Misfire Cylinder 4 with Fuel Cut-Off
P1350	242	Misfire during Start Cylinder 5
P1351	242	Misfire Cylinder 5 with Fuel Cut-Off
P1352	243	Misfire during Start Cylinder 6
P1353	243	Misfire Cylinder 6 with Fuel Cut-Off
P1413	35	Secondary Air Injection Pump Relay Control Circuit Signal Low
P1414	35	Secondary Air Injection Pump Relay Control Circuit Signal High
P1445	140	Diagnostic Module Tank Leakage (DM-TL) Pump Control Circuit Signal Low
P1446	140	Diagnostic Module Tank Leakage (DM-TL) Pump Control Circuit Signal High
P1447	142	Diagnostic Module Tank Leakage (DM-TL) Pump Current Too High during Switching Solenoid Test
P1448	142	Diagnostic Module Tank Leakage (DM-TL) Pump Current Too Low
P1449	142	Diagnostic Module Tank Leakage (DM-TL) Pump Current Too High
P1451	126	Diagnostic Module Tank Leakage (DM-TL) Switching Solenoid Control Circuit Signal Low
P1452	126	Diagnostic Module Tank Leakage (DM-TL) Switching Solenoid Control Circuit Signal High
P1500	211	Idle-Speed Control Valve Stuck Open
P1501	211	Idle-Speed Control Valve Stuck Closed
P1502	27	Idle-Speed Control Valve Closing Solenoid Control Circuit Signal High
P1503	27	Idle-Speed Control Valve Closing Solenoid Control Circuit Signal Low
P1504	27	Idle-Speed Control Valve Closing Solenoid Control Open Circuit
P1506	53	Idle-Speed Control Valve Opening Solenoid Control Circuit Signal High
P1507	53	Idle-Speed Control Valve Opening Solenoid Control Circuit Signal Low
P1508	53	Idle-Speed Control Valve Opening Solenoid Control Open Circuit
P1512	124	DISA (Differentiated Intake Manifold) Control Circuit Signal Low
P1513	124	DISA (Differentiated Intake Manifold) Control Circuit Signal High
P1523	21	'A' Camshaft Position Actuator Signal Low (Bank 1) (M52: 'B' Camshaft Position Actuator Tight or Jammed)
P1524	21	'A' Camshaft Position Actuator Control Circuit Signal High (Bank 1)
P1525	21	'A' Camshaft Position Actuator Control Open Circuit (Bank 1)
P1529	19	'B' Camshaft Position Actuator Control Circuit Signal Low (Bank 1)
P1530	19	'B' Camshaft Position Actuator Control Circuit Signal High (Bank 1) (S54 to 09/00: Throttle Valve Position Control, Control Deviation)
P1531	19	'B' Camshaft Position Actuator Control Open Circuit (Bank 1)
P1602	48	Control Module Self-Test, Control Module Defective
P1602	58	Control Module Self-Test, Control Module Defective
P1602	63	Control Module Self-Test, Control Module Defective
P1602	66	Control Module Self-Test, Control Module Defective
P1602	67	Control Module Self-Test, Control Module Defective

Table e. M54 engine: Siemens DME MS43.0 from 09/01/2002 to 02/28/2003		
P1602	70	Control Module Self-Test, Control Module Defective
P1602	71	Control Module Self-Test, Control Module Defective
P1602	72	Control Module Self-Test, Control Module Defective
P1603	49	Control Module Self-Test, Torque Monitoring
P1604	50	Control Module Self-Test, Speed Monitoring
P1619	123	Map Cooling Thermostat Control Circuit Signal Low
P1620	123	Map Cooling Thermostat Control Circuit Signal High
P1624	146	Pedal Position Sensor Potentiometer Supply Channel 1 Electrical (M52: Coolant Thermostat (Coolant Temperature Below Thermostat Regulating Temperature))
P1625	147	Pedal Position Sensor Potentiometer Supply Channel 2 Electrical
P1632	115	Throttle Valve Adaptation Conditions Not Met
P1633	115	Throttle Valve Adaptation Limp-Home Position Unknown
P1634	115	Throttle Valve Adaptation Spring Test Failed
P1635	115	Throttle Valve Adaptation Lower Mechanical Stop not Adapted
P1636	109	Throttle Valve Control Circuit
P1637	162	Throttle Valve Position Control, Control Deviation
P1638	160	Throttle Valve Position Control Throttle Stuck Temporarily
P1639	161	Throttle Valve Position Control Throttle Stuck Permanently
P1675	135	Throttle Valve Actuator Start Test Re-Adaptation Required
P1694	136	Throttle Valve Actuator Start Test Spring Test and Limp-Home Position Failed
P2096	225	Post Catalyst Fuel Trim System Too Lean (Bank 1)
P2098	226	Post Catalyst Fuel Trim System Too Lean (Bank 2)

Table f. M54 engine: Siemens DME MS43.0 from 03/01/2003		
PCode	**BMW-FC**	**PCode text**
P0011	103	'A' Camshaft Position Timing Over-Advanced or System Performance (Bank 1)
P0012	105	'A' Camshaft Position Timing Over-Retarded (Bank 1)
P0014	104	'B' Camshaft Position Timing Over-Advanced or System Performance (Bank 1)
P0015	106	'B' Camshaft Position Timing Over-Retarded (Bank 1)
P0030	25	HO2S Heater Control Circuit (Bank 1 Sensor 1)
P0031	25	HO2S Heater Control Circuit Low (Bank 1 Sensor 1)
P0032	25	HO2S Heater Control Circuit High (Bank 1 Sensor 1)
P0036	79	HO2S Heater Control Circuit (Bank 1 Sensor 2)
P0037	79	HO2S Heater Control Circuit Low (Bank 1 Sensor 2)
P0038	79	HO2S Heater Control Circuit High (Bank 1 Sensor 2)
P0050	55	HO2S Heater Control Circuit (Bank 2 Sensor 1)
P0051	55	HO2S Heater Control Circuit Low (Bank 2 Sensor 1)
P0052	55	HO2S Heater Control Circuit High (Bank 2 Sensor 1)
P0056	61	HO2S Heater Control Circuit (Bank 2 Sensor 2)

Table f. M54 engine: Siemens DME MS43.0 from 03/01/2003		
PCode	**BMW-FC**	**PCode text**
P0057	61	HO2S Heater Control Circuit Low (Bank 2 Sensor 2)
P0058	61	HO2S Heater Control Circuit High (Bank 2 Sensor 2)
P0101	149	Mass or Volume Air Flow Circuit Range/Performance
P0102	8	Mass or Volume Air Flow Circuit Low Input
P0103	8	Mass or Volume Air Flow Circuit High Input
P0112	14	Intake Air Temperature Sensor 1 Circuit Low
P0113	14	Intake Air Temperature Sensor 1 Circuit High
P0117	10	Engine Coolant Temperature Circuit Low
P0118	10	Engine Coolant Temperature Circuit High
P0121	118	Throttle/Pedal Position Sensor/Switch 'A' Circuit Range/Performance
P0122	112	Throttle/Pedal Position Sensor/Switch 'A' Circuit Low
P0123	112	Throttle/Pedal Position Sensor/Switch 'A' Circuit High
P0125	222	Insufficient Coolant Temperature for Closed Loop Fuel Control
P0128	168	Coolant Thermostat (Coolant Temperature Below Thermostat Regulating Temperature)
P0131	150	O2 Sensor Circuit Low Voltage (Bank 1 Sensor 1)
P0132	150	O2 Sensor Circuit High Voltage (Bank 1 Sensor 1)
P0133	229	O2 Sensor Circuit Slow Response (Bank 1 Sensor 1)
P0134	150	O2 Sensor Circuit No Activity Detected (Bank 1 Sensor 1)
P0135	188	O2 Sensor Heater Circuit (Bank 1 Sensor 1)
P0137	152	O2 Sensor Circuit Low Voltage (Bank 1 Sensor 2)
P0138	152	O2 Sensor Circuit High Voltage (Bank 1 Sensor 2)
P0140	152	O2 Sensor Circuit No Activity Detected (Bank 1 Sensor 2)
P0141	190	O2 Sensor Heater Circuit (Bank 1 Sensor 2)
P0151	151	O2 Sensor Circuit Low Voltage (Bank 2 Sensor 1)
P0152	151	O2 Sensor Circuit High Voltage (Bank 2 Sensor 1)
P0153	230	O2 Sensor Circuit Slow Response (Bank 2 Sensor 1)
P0154	151	O2 Sensor Circuit No Activity Detected (Bank 2 Sensor 1)
P0155	189	O2 Sensor Heater Circuit (Bank 2 Sensor 1)
P0157	153	O2 Sensor Circuit Low Voltage (Bank 2 Sensor 2)
P0158	153	O2 Sensor Circuit High Voltage (Bank 2 Sensor 2)
P0160	153	O2 Sensor Circuit No Activity Detected (Bank 2 Sensor 2)
P0161	191	O2 Sensor Heater Circuit (Bank 2 Sensor 2)
P0171	227	System Too Lean (Bank 1)
P0172	227	System Too Rich (Bank 1)
P0174	228	System Too Lean (Bank 2)
P0175	228	System Too Rich (Bank 2)
P0197	122	Engine Oil Temperature Sensor Low
P0198	122	Engine Oil Temperature Sensor High
P0201	6	Injector Circuit/Open - Cylinder 1

Table f. M54 engine: Siemens DME MS43.0 from 03/01/2003		
PCode	BMW-FC	PCode text
P0202	5	Injector Circuit/Open - Cylinder 2
P0203	22	Injector Circuit/Open - Cylinder 3
P0204	24	Injector Circuit/Open - Cylinder 4
P0205	33	Injector Circuit/Open - Cylinder 5
P0206	23	Injector Circuit/Open - Cylinder 6
P0221	119	Throttle/Pedal Position Sensor/Switch 'B' Circuit Range/Performance
P0222	113	Throttle/Pedal Position Sensor/Switch 'B' Circuit Low
P0223	113	Throttle/Pedal Position Sensor/Switch 'B' Circuit High
P0261	6	Cylinder 1 Injector Circuit Low
P0262	6	Cylinder 1 Injector Circuit High
P0264	5	Cylinder 2 Injector Circuit Low
P0265	5	Cylinder 2 Injector Circuit High
P0267	22	Cylinder 3 Injector Circuit Low
P0268	22	Cylinder 3 Injector Circuit High
P0270	24	Cylinder 4 Injector Circuit Low
P0271	24	Cylinder 4 Injector Circuit High
P0273	33	Cylinder 5 Injector Circuit Low
P0274	33	Cylinder 5 Injector Circuit High
P0276	23	Cylinder 6 Injector Circuit Low
P0277	23	Cylinder 6 Injector Circuit High
P0301	238	Cylinder 1 Misfire Detected
P0302	239	Cylinder 2 Misfire Detected
P0303	240	Cylinder 3 Misfire Detected
P0304	241	Cylinder 4 Misfire Detected
P0305	242	Cylinder 5 Misfire Detected
P0306	243	Cylinder 6 Misfire Detected
P0313	238	Misfire Detected with Low Fuel
P0313	239	Misfire Detected with Low Fuel
P0313	240	Misfire Detected with Low Fuel
P0313	241	Misfire Detected with Low Fuel
P0313	242	Misfire Detected with Low Fuel
P0313	243	Misfire Detected with Low Fuel
P0327	57	Knock Sensor 1 Circuit Low (Bank 1 or Single Sensor)
P0332	59	Knock Sensor 2 Circuit Low (Bank 2)
P0335	83	Crankshaft Position Sensor 'A' Circuit
P0339	83	Crankshaft Position Sensor 'A' Circuit Intermittent
P0340	65	Camshaft Position Sensor 'A' Circuit (Bank 1 or Single Sensor)
P0344	65	Camshaft Position Sensor 'A' Circuit Intermittent (Bank 1 or Single Sensor)
P0365	18	Camshaft Position Sensor 'B' Circuit (Bank 1)

Table f. M54 engine: Siemens DME MS43.0 from 03/01/2003		
PCode	BMW-FC	PCode text
P0369	18	Camshaft Position Sensor 'B' Circuit Intermittent (Bank 1)
P0413	62	Secondary Air Injection System Switching Valve A Circuit Open
P0414	62	Secondary Air Injection System Switching Valve A Circuit Shorted
P0420	233	Catalyst System Efficiency Below Threshold (Bank 1)
P0430	234	Catalyst System Efficiency Below Threshold (Bank 2)
P0441	250	Evaporative Emission System Incorrect Purge Flow
P0443	68	Evaporative Emission System Purge Control Valve Circuit
P0444	68	Evaporative Emission System Purge Control Valve Circuit Open
P0445	68	Evaporative Emission System Purge Control Valve Circuit Shorted
P0455	143	Evaporative Emission System Leak Detected (large leak)
P0456	143	Evaporative Emission System Leak Detected (very small leak)
P0491	245	Secondary Air Injection System Insufficient Flow (Bank 1)
P0492	246	Secondary Air Injection System Insufficient Flow (Bank 2)
P0500	214	Vehicle Speed Sensor 'A'
P0505	204	Idle Air Control System
P0600	217	Serial Communication Link
P0604	100	Internal Control Module Random Access Memory (RAM) Error
P1083	202	Fuel Control Limit Mixture Too Lean (Bank 1 Sensor 1)
P1084	202	Fuel Control Limit Mixture Too Rich (Bank 1 Sensor 1)
P1085	203	Fuel Control Limit Mixture Too Lean (Bank 2 Sensor 1)
P1086	203	Fuel Control Limit Mixture Too Rich (Bank 2 Sensor 1)
P1087	229	O2 Sensor Circuit Slow Response in Lean Control Range (Bank 1 Sensor 1)
P1088	229	O2 Sensor Circuit Slow Response in Rich Control Range (Bank 1 Sensor 1)
P1089	230	O2 Sensor Circuit Slow Response in Lean Control Range (Bank 1 Sensor 2)
P1090	235	Pre Catalyst Fuel Trim System Too Lean (Bank 1)
P1091	236	Pre Catalyst Fuel Trim System Too Lean (Bank 2)
P1092	235	Pre Catalyst Fuel Trim System Too Rich (Bank 1)
P1093	236	Pre Catalyst Fuel Trim System Too Rich (Bank 2)
P1094	230	O2 Sensor Circuit Slow Response in Rich Control Range (Bank 2 Sensor 1)
P1111	11	Engine Coolant Temperature Sensor Radiator Outlet Low Input
P1112	11	Engine Coolant Temperature Sensor Radiator Outlet High Input
P1120	114	Pedal Position Sensor Circuit
P1121	117	Pedal Position Sensor 1 Range/Performance Problem
P1122	110	Pedal Position Sensor 1 Low Input
P1123	110	Pedal Position Sensor 1 High Input
P1171	196	Ambient Pressure Sensor Variant Recognition Value in Boot Range Implausible
P1172	196	Ambient Pressure Sensor Variant Recognition Error Value Stored in Boot Range
P1173	196	Ambient Pressure Sensor Variant Recognition Learning Failed
P1222	111	Pedal Position Sensor 2 Low Input

Table f. M54 engine: Siemens DME MS43.0 from 03/01/2003		
PCode	**BMW-FC**	**PCode text**
P1223	111	Pedal Position Sensor 2 High Input
P1314	202	Fuel Mixture Deviation Detected with Low Fuel
P1314	203	Fuel Mixture Deviation Detected with Low Fuel
P1314	227	Fuel Mixture Deviation Detected with Low Fuel
P1314	228	Fuel Mixture Deviation Detected with Low Fuel
P1342	238	Misfire During Start Cylinder 1
P1343	238	Misfire Cylinder 1 with Fuel Cut-Off
P1344	239	Misfire During Start Cylinder 2
P1345	239	Misfire Cylinder 2 with Fuel Cut-Off
P1346	240	Misfire During Start Cylinder 3
P1347	240	Misfire Cylinder 3 with Fuel Cut-Off
P1348	241	Misfire During Start Cylinder 4
P1349	241	Misfire Cylinder 4 with Fuel Cut-Off
P1350	242	Misfire during Start Cylinder 5
P1351	242	Misfire Cylinder 5 with Fuel Cut-Off
P1352	243	Misfire during Start Cylinder 6
P1353	243	Misfire Cylinder 6 with Fuel Cut-Off
P1413	35	Secondary Air Injection Pump Relay Control Circuit Signal Low
P1414	35	Secondary Air Injection Pump Relay Control Circuit Signal High
P1445	140	Diagnostic Module Tank Leakage (DM-TL) Pump Control Circuit Signal Low
P1446	140	Diagnostic Module Tank Leakage (DM-TL) Pump Control Circuit Signal High
P1447	142	Diagnostic Module Tank Leakage (DM-TL) Pump Current Too High during Switching Solenoid Test
P1448	142	Diagnostic Module Tank Leakage (DM-TL) Pump Current Too Low
P1449	142	Diagnostic Module Tank Leakage (DM-TL) Pump Current Too High
P1451	126	Diagnostic Module Tank Leakage (DM-TL) Switching Solenoid Control Circuit Signal Low
P1452	126	Diagnostic Module Tank Leakage (DM-TL) Switching Solenoid Control Circuit Signal High
P1500	211	Idle-Speed Control Valve Stuck Open
P1501	211	Idle-Speed Control Valve Stuck Closed
P1502	27	Idle-Speed Control Valve Closing Solenoid Control Circuit Signal High
P1503	27	Idle-Speed Control Valve Closing Solenoid Control Circuit Signal Low
P1504	27	Idle-Speed Control Valve Closing Solenoid Control Open Circuit
P1506	53	Idle-Speed Control Valve Opening Solenoid Control Circuit Signal High
P1507	53	Idle-Speed Control Valve Opening Solenoid Control Open Circuit Low
P1508	53	Idle-Speed Control Valve Opening Solenoid Control Open Circuit
P1512	124	DISA (Differentiated Intake Manifold) Control Circuit Signal Low
P1513	124	DISA (Differentiated Intake Manifold) Control Circuit Signal High
P1525	21	'A' Camshaft Position Actuator Control Open Circuit (Bank 1)
P1531	19	'B' Camshaft Position Actuator Control Open Circuit (Bank 1)
P1602	48	Control Module Self-Test, Control Module Defective

Table f. M54 engine: Siemens DME MS43.0 from 03/01/2003		
PCode	**BMW-FC**	**PCode text**
P1602	58	Control Module Self-Test, Control Module Defective
P1602	63	Control Module Self-Test, Control Module Defective
P1602	66	Control Module Self-Test, Control Module Defective
P1602	67	Control Module Self-Test, Control Module Defective
P1602	70	Control Module Self-Test, Control Module Defective
P1602	71	Control Module Self-Test, Control Module Defective
P1602	72	Control Module Self-Test, Control Module Defective
P1603	49	Control Module Self-Test, Torque Monitoring
P1604	50	Control Module Self-Test, Speed Monitoring
P1619	123	Map Cooling Thermostat Control Circuit Signal Low
P1620	123	Map Cooling Thermostat Control Circuit Signal High
P1624	146	Pedal Position Sensor Potentiometer Supply Channel 1 Electrical (M52: Coolant Thermostat (Coolant Temperature Below Thermostat Regulating Temperature))
P1625	147	Pedal Position Sensor Potentiometer Supply Channel 2 Electrical
P1632	115	Throttle Valve Adaptation Conditions Not Met
P1633	115	Throttle Valve Adaptation Limp-Home Position Unknown
P1634	115	Throttle Valve Adaptation Spring Test Failed
P1635	115	Throttle Valve Adaptation Lower Mechanical Stop not Adapted
P1636	109	Throttle Valve Control Circuit
P1637	162	Throttle Valve Position Control, Control Deviation
P1638	160	Throttle Valve Position Control Throttle Stuck Temporarily
P1639	161	Throttle Valve Position Control Throttle Stuck Permanently
P1675	135	Throttle Valve Actuator Start Test Re-Adaptation Required
P1694	136	Throttle Valve Actuator Start Test Spring Test and Limp-Home Position Failed
P2088	21	'A' Camshaft Position Actuator Control Circuit Low (Bank 1)
P2089	21	'A' Camshaft Position Actuator Control Circuit High (Bank 1)
P2090	19	'B' Camshaft Position Actuator Control Circuit Low (Bank 1)
P2091	19	'B' Camshaft Position Actuator Control Circuit High (Bank 1)
P2096	225	Post Catalyst Fuel Trim System Too Lean (Bank 1)
P2098	226	Post Catalyst Fuel Trim System Too Lean (Bank 2)
P2228	197	Barometric Pressure Circuit Low
P2229	197	Barometric Pressure Circuit High
P2270	215	O2 Sensor Signal Stuck Lean (Bank 1 Sensor 2)
P2271	215	O2 Sensor Signal Stuck Rich (Bank 1 Sensor 2)
P2272	216	O2 Sensor Signal Stuck Lean (Bank 2 Sensor 2)
P2273	216	O2 Sensor Signal Stuck Rich (Bank 2 Sensor 2)

Table g. M54bin engine: Siemens DME MS45.1 from 09/01/2002		
PCode	**BMW-FC**	**PCode text**
P0012	10426	'A' Camshaft Position Timing Over-Retarded (Bank 1)
P0015	10428	'B' Camshaft Position Timing Over-Retarded (Bank 1)
P0030	10013	HO2S Heater Control Circuit (Bank 1 Sensor 1)
P0031	10013	HO2S Heater Control Circuit Low (Bank 1 Sensor 1)
P0032	10013	HO2S Heater Control Circuit High (Bank 1 Sensor 1)
P0036	10006	HO2S Heater Control Circuit (Bank 1 Sensor 2)
P0037	10006	HO2S Heater Control Circuit Low (Bank 1 Sensor 2)
P0038	10006	HO2S Heater Control Circuit High (Bank 1 Sensor 2)
P0040	10602	O2 Sensor Signals Swapped Bank 1 Sensor 1 / Bank 2 Sensor 1
P0041	10603	O2 Sensor Signals Swapped Bank 1 Sensor 2 / Bank 2 Sensor 2
P0050	10005	HO2S Heater Control Circuit (Bank 2 Sensor 1)
P0051	10005	HO2S Heater Control Circuit Low (Bank 2 Sensor 1)
P0052	10005	HO2S Heater Control Circuit High (Bank 2 Sensor 1)
P0056	10007	HO2S Heater Control Circuit (Bank 2 Sensor 2)
P0057	10007	HO2S Heater Control Circuit Low (Bank 2 Sensor 2)
P0058	10007	HO2S Heater Control Circuit High (Bank 2 Sensor 2)
P0101	10461	Mass or Volume Air Flow Circuit Range/Performance
P0102	10115	Mass or Volume Air Flow Circuit Low Input
P0103	10115	Mass or Volume Air Flow Circuit High Input
P0112	10124	Intake Air Temperature Sensor 1 Circuit Low
P0113	10124	Intake Air Temperature Sensor 1 Circuit High
P0117	10123	Engine Coolant Temperature Circuit Low
P0118	10123	Engine Coolant Temperature Circuit High
P0121	10036	Throttle/Pedal Position Sensor/Switch 'A' Circuit Range /Performance
P0121	10118	Throttle/Pedal Position Sensor/Switch 'A' Circuit Range /Performance
P0122	10118	Throttle/Pedal Position Sensor/Switch 'A' Circuit Low
P0123	10118	Throttle/Pedal Position Sensor/Switch 'A' Circuit High
P0125	10206	Insufficient Coolant Temperature for Closed Loop Fuel Control
P0128	10139	Coolant Thermostat (Coolant Temperature Below Thermostat Regulating Temperature)
P0131	10662	O2 Sensor Circuit Low Voltage (Bank 1 Sensor 1)
P0132	10010	O2 Sensor Circuit High Voltage (Bank 1 Sensor 1)
P0133	10015	O2 Sensor Circuit Slow Response (Bank 1 Sensor 1)
P0134	10663	O2 Sensor Circuit No Activity Detected (Bank 1 Sensor 1)
P0135	10394	O2 Sensor Heater Circuit (Bank 1 Sensor 1)
P0137	10654	O2 Sensor Circuit Low Voltage (Bank 1 Sensor 2)
P0138	10012	O2 Sensor Circuit High Voltage (Bank 1 Sensor 2)
P0140	10655	O2 Sensor Circuit No Activity Detected (Bank 1 Sensor 2)
P0141	10396	O2 Sensor Heater Circuit (Bank 1 Sensor 2)
P0151	10658	O2 Sensor Circuit Low Voltage (Bank 2 Sensor 1)

Table g. M54bin engine: Siemens DME MS45.1 from 09/01/2002		
PCode	**BMW-FC**	**PCode text**
P0152	10018	O2 Sensor Circuit High Voltage (Bank 2 Sensor 1)
P0153	10021	O2 Sensor Circuit Slow Response (Bank 2 Sensor 1)
P0154	10659	O2 Sensor Circuit No Activity Detected (Bank 2 Sensor 1)
P0155	10395	O2 Sensor Heater Circuit (Bank 2 Sensor 1)
P0157	10656	O2 Sensor Circuit Low Voltage (Bank 2 Sensor 2)
P0158	10020	O2 Sensor Circuit High Voltage (Bank 2 Sensor 2)
P0160	10657	O2 Sensor Circuit No Activity Detected (Bank 2 Sensor 2)
P0161	10397	O2 Sensor Heater Circuit (Bank 2 Sensor 2)
P0171	10370	System Too Lean (Bank 1)
P0172	10370	System Too Rich (Bank 1)
P0174	10371	System Too Lean (Bank 2)
P0175	10371	System Too Rich (Bank 2)
P0197	10258	Engine Oil Temperature Sensor Low
P0198	10258	Engine Oil Temperature Sensor High
P0201	10150	Injector Circuit/Open - Cylinder 1
P0202	10154	Injector Circuit/Open - Cylinder 2
P0203	10152	Injector Circuit/Open - Cylinder 3
P0204	10155	Injector Circuit/Open - Cylinder 4
P0205	10151	Injector Circuit/Open - Cylinder 5
P0206	10153	Injector Circuit/Open - Cylinder 6
P0221	10037	Throttle/Pedal Position Sensor/Switch 'B' Circuit Range/Performance
P0221	10119	Throttle/Pedal Position Sensor/Switch 'B' Circuit Range/Performance
P0222	10119	Throttle/Pedal Position Sensor/Switch 'B' Circuit Low
P0223	10119	Throttle/Pedal Position Sensor/Switch 'B' Circuit High
P0261	10150	Cylinder 1 Injector Circuit Low
P0262	10150	Cylinder 1 Injector Circuit High
P0264	10154	Cylinder 2 Injector Circuit Low
P0265	10154	Cylinder 2 Injector Circuit High
P0267	10152	Cylinder 3 Injector Circuit Low
P0268	10152	Cylinder 3 Injector Circuit High
P0270	10155	Cylinder 4 Injector Circuit Low
P0271	10155	Cylinder 4 Injector Circuit High
P0273	10151	Cylinder 5 Injector Circuit Low
P0274	10151	Cylinder 5 Injector Circuit High
P0276	10153	Cylinder 6 Injector Circuit Low
P0277	10153	Cylinder 6 Injector Circuit High
P0300	10062	Random/Multiple Cylinder Misfire Detected
P0301	10050	Cylinder 1 Misfire Detected
P0302	10054	Cylinder 2 Misfire Detected

Table g. M54bin engine: Siemens DME MS45.1 from 09/01/2002		
PCode	**BMW-FC**	**PCode text**
P0303	10052	Cylinder 3 Misfire Detected
P0304	10055	Cylinder 4 Misfire Detected
P0305	10051	Cylinder 5 Misfire Detected
P0306	10053	Cylinder 6 Misfire Detected
P0313	10386	Misfire Detected with Low Fuel
P0316	10062	Engine Misfire Detected on Startup (First 1000 Revolutions)
P0328	10210	Knock Sensor 1 Circuit High (Bank 1 or Single Sensor)
P0335	10389	Crankshaft Position Sensor 'A' Circuit
P0340	10390	Camshaft Position Sensor 'A' Circuit (Bank 1 or Single Sensor)
P0363	10062	Misfire Detected - Fueling Disabled
P0365	10391	Camshaft Position Sensor 'B' Circuit (Bank 1)
P0370	10008	Timing Reference High Resolution Signal 'A'
P0420	10040	Catalyst System Efficiency Below Threshold (Bank 1)
P0430	10045	Catalyst System Efficiency Below Threshold (Bank 2)
P0440	10093	Evaporative Emission System
P0442	10188	Evaporative Emission System Leak Detected (small leak)
P0443	10098	Evaporative Emission System Purge Control Valve Circuit
P0444	10098	Evaporative Emission System Purge Control Valve Circuit Open
P0445	10098	Evaporative Emission System Purge Control Valve Circuit Shorted
P0455	10188	Evaporative Emission System Leak Detected (large leak)
P0491	10080	Secondary Air Injection System Insufficient Flow (Bank 1)
P0492	10080	Secondary Air Injection System Insufficient Flow (Bank 2)
P0500	10120	Vehicle Speed Sensor 'A'
P0505	10241	Idle Air Control System
P0604	10105	Internal Control Module Random Access Memory (RAM) Error
P0700	10650	Transmission Control System (MIL Request)
P1087	10015	O2 Sensor Circuit Slow Response in Lean Control Range (Bank 1 Sensor 1)
P1088	10015	O2 Sensor Circuit Slow Response in Rich Control Range (Bank 1 Sensor 1)
P1089	10021	O2 Sensor Circuit Slow Response in Lean Control Range (Bank 1 Sensor 2)
P1094	10021	O2 Sensor Circuit Slow Response in Rich Control Range (Bank 2 Sensor 1)
P1111	10125	Engine Coolant Temperature Sensor Radiator Outlet Low Input
P1112	10125	Engine Coolant Temperature Sensor Radiator Outlet High Input
P1120	10247	Pedal Position Sensor Circuit
P1121	10248	Pedal Position Sensor 1 Range/Performance Problem
P1122	10231	Pedal Position Sensor 1 Low Input
P1123	10231	Pedal Position Sensor 1 High Input
P1222	10232	Pedal Position Sensor 2 Low Input
P1223	10232	Pedal Position Sensor 2 High Input
P1247	10461	Barometric Pressure Plausibility

Table g. M54bin engine: Siemens DME MS45.1 from 09/01/2002		
PCode	**BMW-FC**	**PCode text**
P1315	10086	Camshaft Position Sensor 'A' Circuit Signal Duration after Initialization (Bank 1)
P1316	10086	Camshaft Position Sensor 'A' Signal Duration during Initialization (Bank 1)
P1318	10087	Camshaft Position Sensor 'B' Circuit Signal Duration after Initialization (Bank 1)
P1319	10087	Camshaft Position Sensor 'B' Signal Duration during Initialization (Bank 1)
P1326	10422	'A' Camshaft Position Timing Reference Position out of Range (Bank 1)
P1328	10211	Knock Sensor 2 Circuit High Input (Bank 1)
P1331	10424	'B' Camshaft Position Timing Reference Position out of Range (Bank 1)
P1338	10088	Camshaft Position Sensor 'A' Faulty Phase Position (Bank 1)
P1339	10092	Camshaft Position Sensor 'B' Faulty Phase Position (Bank 1)
P1342	10050	Misfire During Start Cylinder 1
P1343	10050	Misfire Cylinder 1 with Fuel Cut-Off
P1344	10054	Misfire During Start Cylinder 2
P1345	10054	Misfire Cylinder 2 with Fuel Cut-Off
P1346	10052	Misfire During Start Cylinder 3
P1347	10052	Misfire Cylinder 3 with Fuel Cut-Off
P1348	10055	Misfire During Start Cylinder 4
P1349	10055	Misfire Cylinder 4 with Fuel Cut-Off
P1350	10051	Misfire during Start Cylinder 5
P1351	10051	Misfire Cylinder 5 with Fuel Cut-Off
P1352	10053	Misfire during Start Cylinder 6
P1353	10053	Misfire Cylinder 6 with Fuel Cut-Off
P1413	10084	Secondary Air Injection Pump Relay Control Circuit Signal Low
P1414	10084	Secondary Air Injection Pump Relay Control Circuit Signal High
P1415	10080	Mass or Volume Air Flow Too Low
P1429	10201	Diagnostic Module Tank Leakage (DM-TL) Heater
P1430	10201	Diagnostic Module Tank Leakage (DM-TL) Heater Low
P1431	10201	Diagnostic Module Tank Leakage (DM-TL) Heater High
P1434	10189	Diagnostic Module Tank Leakage (DM-TL)
P1444	10186	Diagnostic Module Tank Leakage (DM-TL) Pump Control Open Circuit
P1445	10186	Diagnostic Module Tank Leakage (DM-TL) Pump Control Circuit Signal Low
P1446	10186	Diagnostic Module Tank Leakage (DM-TL) Pump Control Circuit Signal High
P1447	10189	Diagnostic Module Tank Leakage (DM-TL) Pump Current Too High during Switching Solenoid Test
P1448	10189	Diagnostic Module Tank Leakage (DM-TL) Pump Current Too Low
P1449	10189	Diagnostic Module Tank Leakage (DM-TL) Pump Current Too High
P1450	10002	Diagnostic Module Tank Leakage (DM-TL) Switching Solenoid Control Open Circuit
P1451	10002	Diagnostic Module Tank Leakage (DM-TL) Switching Solenoid Control Circuit Signal Low
P1452	10002	Diagnostic Module Tank Leakage (DM-TL) Switching Solenoid Control Circuit Signal High
P1453	10084	Secondary Air Injection Pump Relay Control Circuit Electrical
P1502	10198	Idle-Speed Control Valve Closing Solenoid Control Circuit Signal High

Table g. M54bin engine: Siemens DME MS45.1 from 09/01/2002		
PCode	BMW-FC	PCode text
P1503	10198	Idle-Speed Control Valve Closing Solenoid Control Circuit Signal Low
P1504	10198	Idle-Speed Control Valve Closing Solenoid Control Open Circuit
P1506	10199	Idle-Speed Control Valve Opening Solenoid Control Circuit Signal High
P1507	10199	Idle-Speed Control Valve Opening Solenoid Control Circuit Signal Low
P1508	10199	Idle-Speed Control Valve Opening Solenoid Control Open Circuit
P1510	10461	Idle-Speed Control Valve Stuck
P1511	10270	DISA (Differentiated Intake Manifold) Control Circuit Electrical
P1512	10270	DISA (Differentiated Intake Manifold) Control Circuit Signal Low
P1513	10270	DISA (Differentiated Intake Manifold) Control Circuit Signal High
P1525	10165	'A' Camshaft Position Actuator Control Open Circuit (Bank 1)
P1531	10173	'B' Camshaft Position Actuator Control Open Circuit (Bank 1)
P16A9	10404	Control Module Self-Test, Speed Monitoring Reset
P1611	10220	Serial Communication Link Transmission Control Module
P1618	10103	Control Module Self-Test, AD-Converter Monitoring
P1619	10140	Map Cooling Thermostat Control Circuit Signal Low
P1620	10140	Map Cooling Thermostat Control Circuit Signal High
P1622	10140	Map Cooling Thermostat Control Circuit Electrical
P1624	10048	Pedal Position Sensor Potentiometer Supply Channel 1 Electrical (M52: Coolant Thermostat (Coolant Temperature Below Thermostat Regulating Temperature))
P1625	10049	Pedal Position Sensor Potentiometer Supply Channel 2 Electrical
P1632	10134	Throttle Valve Adaptation Conditions Not Met
P1633	10134	Throttle Valve Adaptation Limp-Home Position Unknown
P1634	10134	Throttle Valve Adaptation Spring Test Failed
P1634	10145	Throttle Valve Adaptation Spring Test Failed
P1635	10134	Throttle Valve Adaptation Lower Mechanical Stop not Adapted
P1635	10419	Throttle Valve Adaptation Lower Mechanical Stop not Adapted
P1636	10132	Throttle Valve Control Circuit
P1637	10066	Throttle Valve Position Control, Control Deviation
P1638	10064	Throttle Valve Position Control Throttle Stuck Temporarily
P1639	10065	Throttle Valve Position Control Throttle Stuck Permanently
P1675	10149	Throttle Valve Actuator Start Test Re-Adaptation Required
P1694	10145	Throttle Valve Actuator Start Test Spring Test and Limp-Home Position Failed
P16A0	10288	Internal Control Module Memory Checksum Error in Boot Software
P16A1	10288	Internal Control Module Memory Checksum Error in Application Software
P16A2	10288	Internal Control Module Memory Checksum Error in Data
P16A3	10345	Internal Control Module Non-Volatile Memory (NVMY) Error
P16A4	10346	Timeout Control Module Knock Sensor SPI-Bus
P16A5	10347	Timeout Control Module Multiple Output Stage SPI-Bus
P16A6	10401	Control Module Self-Test, Cruise Control Monitoring

Table g. M54bin engine: Siemens DME MS45.1 from 09/01/2002		
PCode	**BMW-FC**	**PCode text**
P16A7	10402	Control Module Self-Test, Hot Film Air Mass Meter Monitoring
P16A8	10402	Control Module Self-Test, Throttle Position Monitoring
P16B0	10405	Control Module Self-Test, Pedal Position Sensor Monitoring
P16B1	10410	Control Module Self-Test, Idle Air Control System Integrated Component Plausibility
P16B2	10410	Control Module Self-Test, Idle Air Control System PD-Component Plausibility
P16B3	10411	Control Module Self-Test, MSR (Engine-Drag-Torque Control) Monitoring
P16B4	10411	Control Module Self-Test, DCC (Distance Cruise Control) Monitoring
P16B5	10411	Control Module Self-Test, AMT (Automatic Manual Transmission) Monitoring
P16B6	10411	Control Module Self-Test, ETC Monitoring
P16B7	10412	Control Module Self-Test, Clutch Torque Monitoring Maximum Value Plausibility
P16B8	10412	Control Module Self-Test, Clutch Torque Monitoring Minimum Value Plausibility
P16B9	10412	Control Module Self-Test, Torque Loss Monitoring
P16C0	10412	Control Module Self-Test, Driving Dynamics Control Switch Monitoring
P16C1	10413	Control Module Self-Test, Torque Monitoring Current Indicated Value Plausibility
P16C2	10417	Control Module Self-Test, Speed Limitation Monitoring
P16C3	10418	Control Module Self-Test, Speed Limitation Reset
P2088	10165	'A' Camshaft Position Actuator Control Circuit Low (Bank 1)
P2089	10165	'A' Camshaft Position Actuator Control Circuit High (Bank 1)
P2090	10173	'B' Camshaft Position Actuator Control Circuit Low (Bank 1)
P2091	10173	'B' Camshaft Position Actuator Control Circuit High (Bank 1)
P2096	10472	Post Catalyst Fuel Trim System Too Lean (Bank 1)
P2097	10472	Post Catalyst Fuel Trim System Too Rich (Bank 1)
P2098	10473	Post Catalyst Fuel Trim System Too Lean (Bank 2)
P2099	10473	Post Catalyst Fuel Trim System Too Rich (Bank 2)
P2228	10164	Barometric Pressure Circuit Low
P2229	10164	Barometric Pressure Circuit High
P2270	10480	O2 Sensor Signal Stuck Lean (Bank 1 Sensor 2)
P2271	10480	O2 Sensor Signal Stuck Rich (Bank 1 Sensor 2)
P2272	10481	O2 Sensor Signal Stuck Lean (Bank 2 Sensor 2)
P2273	10481	O2 Sensor Signal Stuck Rich (Bank 2 Sensor 2)
P3010	10486	O2 Sensor Low Input after Cold Start (Bank 1 Sensor 2)
P3011	10487	O2 Sensor Low Input after Cold Start (Bank 2 Sensor 2)
P3040	10480	O2 Sensor Lean and Rich Voltage Thresholds not Reached (Bank 1 Sensor 2)
P3041	10481	O2 Sensor Lean and Rich Voltage Thresholds not Reached (Bank 2 Sensor 2)
P3198	10205	Engine Coolant Temperature Gradient Too High
P3199	10207	Engine Coolant Temperature Signal Stuck
P3238	10289	Control Module Monitoring TPU Chip Defective

Table h. M56 engine: Siemens DME MS45.1 from 09/01/02		
PCode	**BMW-FC**	**PCode text**
P0012	10426	'A' Camshaft Position Timing Over-Retarded (Bank 1)
P0015	10428	'B' Camshaft Position Timing Over-Retarded (Bank 1)
P0030	10660	HO2S Heater Control Circuit (Bank 1 Sensor 1)
P0031	10660	HO2S Heater Control Circuit Low (Bank 1 Sensor 1)
P0032	10660	HO2S Heater Control Circuit High (Bank 1 Sensor 1)
P0036	10006	HO2S Heater Control Circuit (Bank 1 Sensor 2)
P0037	10006	HO2S Heater Control Circuit Low (Bank 1 Sensor 2)
P0038	10006	HO2S Heater Control Circuit High (Bank 1 Sensor 2)
P0040	10602	O2 Sensor Signals Swapped Bank 1 Sensor 1 / Bank 2 Sensor 1
P0041	10603	O2 Sensor Signals Swapped Bank 1 Sensor 2 / Bank 2 Sensor 2
P0050	10661	HO2S Heater Control Circuit (Bank 2 Sensor 1)
P0051	10661	HO2S Heater Control Circuit Low (Bank 2 Sensor 1)
P0052	10661	HO2S Heater Control Circuit High (Bank 2 Sensor 1)
P0056	10007	HO2S Heater Control Circuit (Bank 2 Sensor 2)
P0057	10007	HO2S Heater Control Circuit Low (Bank 2 Sensor 2)
P0058	10007	HO2S Heater Control Circuit High (Bank 2 Sensor 2)
P0101	10461	Mass or Volume Air Flow Circuit Range/Performance
P0102	10115	Mass or Volume Air Flow Circuit Low Input
P0103	10115	Mass or Volume Air Flow Circuit High Input
P0112	10124	Intake Air Temperature Sensor 1 Circuit Low
P0113	10124	Intake Air Temperature Sensor 1 Circuit High
P0117	10123	Engine Coolant Temperature Circuit Low
P0118	10123	Engine Coolant Temperature Circuit High
P0121	10036	Throttle/Pedal Position Sensor/Switch 'A' Circuit Range/Performance
P0121	10118	Throttle/Pedal Position Sensor/Switch 'A' Circuit Range/Performance
P0122	10118	Throttle/Pedal Position Sensor/Switch 'A' Circuit Low
P0123	10118	Throttle/Pedal Position Sensor/Switch 'A' Circuit High
P0125	10206	Insufficient Coolant Temperature for Closed Loop Fuel Control
P0128	10139	Coolant Thermostat (Coolant Temperature Below Thermostat Regulating Temperature)
P0131	10470	O2 Sensor Circuit Low Voltage (Bank 1 Sensor 1)
P0132	10470	O2 Sensor Circuit High Voltage (Bank 1 Sensor 1)
P0133	10594	O2 Sensor Circuit Slow Response (Bank 1 Sensor 1)
P0135	10394	O2 Sensor Heater Circuit (Bank 1 Sensor 1)
P0135	10435	O2 Sensor Heater Circuit (Bank 1 Sensor 1)
P0137	10654	O2 Sensor Circuit Low Voltage (Bank 1 Sensor 2)
P0138	10012	O2 Sensor Circuit High Voltage (Bank 1 Sensor 2)
P0140	10655	O2 Sensor Circuit No Activity Detected (Bank 1 Sensor 2)
P0141	10396	O2 Sensor Heater Circuit (Bank 1 Sensor 2)
P0151	10471	O2 Sensor Circuit Low Voltage (Bank 2 Sensor 1)

Table h. M56 engine: Siemens DME MS45.1 from 09/01/02		
PCode	**BMW-FC**	**PCode text**
P0152	10471	O2 Sensor Circuit High Voltage (Bank 2 Sensor 1)
P0153	10595	O2 Sensor Circuit Slow Response (Bank 2 Sensor 1)
P0155	10395	O2 Sensor Heater Circuit (Bank 2 Sensor 1)
P0155	10436	O2 Sensor Heater Circuit (Bank 2 Sensor 1)
P0157	10656	O2 Sensor Circuit Low Voltage (Bank 2 Sensor 2)
P0158	10020	O2 Sensor Circuit High Voltage (Bank 2 Sensor 2)
P0160	10657	O2 Sensor Circuit No Activity Detected (Bank 2 Sensor 2)
P0161	10397	O2 Sensor Heater Circuit (Bank 2 Sensor 2)
P0171	10370	System Too Lean (Bank 1)
P0172	10370	System Too Rich (Bank 1)
P0174	10371	System Too Lean (Bank 2)
P0175	10371	System Too Rich (Bank 2)
P0197	10258	Engine Oil Temperature Sensor Low
P0198	10258	Engine Oil Temperature Sensor High
P0201	10150	Injector Circuit/Open - Cylinder 1
P0202	10154	Injector Circuit/Open - Cylinder 2
P0203	10152	Injector Circuit/Open - Cylinder 3
P0204	10155	Injector Circuit/Open - Cylinder 4
P0205	10151	Injector Circuit/Open - Cylinder 5
P0206	10153	Injector Circuit/Open - Cylinder 6
P0221	10037	Throttle/Pedal Position Sensor/Switch 'B' Circuit Range/Performance
P0221	10119	Throttle/Pedal Position Sensor/Switch 'B' Circuit Range/Performance
P0222	10119	Throttle/Pedal Position Sensor/Switch 'B' Circuit Low
P0223	10119	Throttle/Pedal Position Sensor/Switch 'B' Circuit High
P0261	10150	Cylinder 1 Injector Circuit Low
P0262	10150	Cylinder 1 Injector Circuit High
P0264	10154	Cylinder 2 Injector Circuit Low
P0265	10154	Cylinder 2 Injector Circuit High
P0267	10152	Cylinder 3 Injector Circuit Low
P0268	10152	Cylinder 3 Injector Circuit High
P0270	10155	Cylinder 4 Injector Circuit Low
P0271	10155	Cylinder 4 Injector Circuit High
P0273	10151	Cylinder 5 Injector Circuit Low
P0274	10151	Cylinder 5 Injector Circuit High
P0276	10153	Cylinder 6 Injector Circuit Low
P0277	10153	Cylinder 6 Injector Circuit High
P0300	10062	Random/Multiple Cylinder Misfire Detected
P0301	10050	Cylinder 1 Misfire Detected
P0302	10054	Cylinder 2 Misfire Detected

Table h. M56 engine: Siemens DME MS45.1 from 09/01/02		
PCode	**BMW-FC**	**PCode text**
P0303	10052	Cylinder 3 Misfire Detected
P0304	10055	Cylinder 4 Misfire Detected
P0305	10051	Cylinder 5 Misfire Detected
P0306	10053	Cylinder 6 Misfire Detected
P0313	10386	Misfire Detected with Low Fuel
P0316	10062	Engine Misfire Detected on Startup (First 1000 Revolutions)
P0328	10210	Knock Sensor 1 Circuit High (Bank 1 or Single Sensor)
P0335	10389	Crankshaft Position Sensor 'A' Circuit
P0363	10062	Misfire Detected - Fueling Disabled
P0370	10008	Timing Reference High Resolution Signal 'A'
P0411	10081	Secondary Air Injection System Incorrect Flow Detected
P0412	10085	Secondary Air Injection System Switching Valve A Circuit
P0413	10085	Secondary Air Injection System Switching Valve A Circuit Open
P0414	10085	Secondary Air Injection System Switching Valve A Circuit Shorted
P0420	10040	Catalyst System Efficiency Below Threshold (Bank 1)
P0430	10045	Catalyst System Efficiency Below Threshold (Bank 2)
P0440	10093	Evaporative Emission System
P0442	10188	Evaporative Emission System Leak Detected (small leak)
P0443	10098	Evaporative Emission System Purge Control Valve Circuit
P0444	10098	Evaporative Emission System Purge Control Valve Circuit Open
P0445	10098	Evaporative Emission System Purge Control Valve Circuit Shorted
P0455	10188	Evaporative Emission System Leak Detected (large leak)
P0500	10120	Vehicle Speed Sensor 'A'
P0505	10241	Idle Air Control System
P0604	10105	Internal Control Module Random Access Memory (RAM) Error
P0700	10650	Transmission Control System (MIL Request)
P1111	10125	Engine Coolant Temperature Sensor Radiator Outlet Low Input
P1112	10125	Engine Coolant Temperature Sensor Radiator Outlet High Input
P1120	10247	Pedal Position Sensor Circuit
P1121	10248	Pedal Position Sensor 1 Range/Performance Problem
P1122	10231	Pedal Position Sensor 1 Low Input
P1123	10231	Pedal Position Sensor 1 High Input
P1222	10232	Pedal Position Sensor 2 Low Input
P1223	10232	Pedal Position Sensor 2 High Input
P1247	10461	Barometric Pressure Plausibility
P1315	10086	Camshaft Position Sensor 'A' Circuit Signal Duration after Initialization (Bank 1)
P1316	10086	Camshaft Position Sensor 'A' Signal Duration during Initialization (Bank 1)
P1318	10087	Camshaft Position Sensor 'B' Circuit Signal Duration after Initialization (Bank 1)
P1319	10087	Camshaft Position Sensor 'B' Signal Duration during Initialization (Bank 1)

Table h. M56 engine: Siemens DME MS45.1 from 09/01/02		
PCode	**BMW-FC**	**PCode text**
P1326	10422	'A' Camshaft Position Timing Reference Position out of Range (Bank 1)
P1328	10211	Knock Sensor 2 Circuit High Input (Bank 1)
P1331	10424	'B' Camshaft Position Timing Reference Position out of Range (Bank 1)
P1338	10088	Camshaft Position Sensor 'A' Faulty Phase Position (Bank 1)
P1339	10092	Camshaft Position Sensor 'B' Faulty Phase Position (Bank 1)
P1342	10050	Misfire During Start Cylinder 1
P1343	10050	Misfire Cylinder 1 with Fuel Cut-Off
P1344	10054	Misfire During Start Cylinder 2
P1345	10054	Misfire Cylinder 2 with Fuel Cut-Off
P1346	10052	Misfire During Start Cylinder 3
P1347	10052	Misfire Cylinder 3 with Fuel Cut-Off
P1348	10055	Misfire During Start Cylinder 4
P1349	10055	Misfire Cylinder 4 with Fuel Cut-Off
P1350	10051	Misfire during Start Cylinder 5
P1351	10051	Misfire Cylinder 5 with Fuel Cut-Off
P1352	10053	Misfire during Start Cylinder 6
P1353	10053	Misfire Cylinder 6 with Fuel Cut-Off
P1411	10081	Secondary Air Pump No Activity Detected
P1412	10081	Secondary Air Pump/Secondary Air Valve Large Leak
P1413	10084	Secondary Air Injection Pump Relay Control Circuit Signal Low
P1414	10084	Secondary Air Injection Pump Relay Control Circuit Signal High
P1416	10082	Secondary Air Injection Valve Stuck Off
P1418	10081	Secondary Air Injection Valve/Secondary Air Hose Clamped
P1419	10096	Secondary Air Mass Flow Sensor Circuit
P1429	10201	Diagnostic Module Tank Leakage (DM-TL) Heater
P1430	10201	Diagnostic Module Tank Leakage (DM-TL) Heater Low
P1431	10201	Diagnostic Module Tank Leakage (DM-TL) Heater High
P1434	10189	Diagnostic Module Tank Leakage (DM-TL)
P1444	10186	Diagnostic Module Tank Leakage (DM-TL) Pump Control Open Circuit
P1445	10186	Diagnostic Module Tank Leakage (DM-TL) Pump Control Circuit Signal Low
P1446	10186	Diagnostic Module Tank Leakage (DM-TL) Pump Control Circuit Signal High
P1447	10189	Diagnostic Module Tank Leakage (DM-TL) Pump Current Too High during Switching Solenoid Test
P1448	10189	Diagnostic Module Tank Leakage (DM-TL) Pump Current Too Low
P1449	10189	Diagnostic Module Tank Leakage (DM-TL) Pump Current Too High
P1450	10002	Diagnostic Module Tank Leakage (DM-TL) Switching Solenoid Control Open Circuit
P1451	10002	Diagnostic Module Tank Leakage (DM-TL) Switching Solenoid Control Circuit Signal Low
P1452	10002	Diagnostic Module Tank Leakage (DM-TL) Switching Solenoid Control Circuit Signal High
P1453	10084	Secondary Air Injection Pump Relay Control Circuit Electrical
P1502	10198	Idle-Speed Control Valve Closing Solenoid Control Circuit Signal High

Table h. M56 engine: Siemens DME MS45.1 from 09/01/02		
PCode	**BMW-FC**	**PCode text**
P1503	10198	Idle-Speed Control Valve Closing Solenoid Control Circuit Signal Low
P1504	10198	Idle-Speed Control Valve Closing Solenoid Control Open Circuit
P1506	10199	Idle-Speed Control Valve Opening Solenoid Control Circuit Signal High
P1507	10199	Idle-Speed Control Valve Opening Solenoid Control Circuit Signal Low
P1508	10199	Idle-Speed Control Valve Opening Solenoid Control Open Circuit
P1510	10461	Idle-Speed Control Valve Stuck
P1511	10270	DISA (Differentiated Intake Manifold) Control Circuit Electrical
P1512	10270	DISA (Differentiated Intake Manifold) Control Circuit Signal Low
P1513	10270	DISA (Differentiated Intake Manifold) Control Circuit Signal High
P1525	10165	'A' Camshaft Position Actuator Control Open Circuit (Bank 1)
P1531	10173	'B' Camshaft Position Actuator Control Open Circuit (Bank 1)
P16A9	10404	Control Module Self-Test, Speed Monitoring Reset
P1611	10220	Serial Communication Link Transmission Control Module
P1618	10103	Control Module Self-Test, AD-Converter Monitoring
P1619	10140	Map Cooling Thermostat Control Circuit Signal Low
P1620	10140	Map Cooling Thermostat Control Circuit Signal High
P1622	10140	Map Cooling Thermostat Control Circuit Electrical
P1624	10048	Pedal Position Sensor Potentiometer Supply Channel 1 Electrical (M52: Coolant Thermostat (Coolant Temperature Below Thermostat Regulating Temperature))
P1625	10049	Pedal Position Sensor Potentiometer Supply Channel 2 Electrical
P1632	10134	Throttle Valve Adaptation Conditions Not Met
P1633	10134	Throttle Valve Adaptation Limp-Home Position Unknown
P1634	10134	Throttle Valve Adaptation Spring Test Failed
P1634	10145	Throttle Valve Adaptation Spring Test Failed
P1635	10134	Throttle Valve Adaptation Lower Mechanical Stop not Adapted
P1635	10419	Throttle Valve Adaptation Lower Mechanical Stop not Adapted
P1636	10132	Throttle Valve Control Circuit
P1637	10066	Throttle Valve Position Control, Control Deviation
P1638	10064	Throttle Valve Position Control Throttle Stuck Temporarily
P1639	10065	Throttle Valve Position Control Throttle Stuck Permanently
P1675	10149	Throttle Valve Actuator Start Test Re-Adaptation Required
P1694	10145	Throttle Valve Actuator Start Test Spring Test and Limp-Home Position Failed
P16A0	10288	Internal Control Module Memory Checksum Error in Boot Software
P16A1	10288	Internal Control Module Memory Checksum Error in Application Software
P16A2	10288	Internal Control Module Memory Checksum Error in Data
P16A3	10345	Internal Control Module Non-Volatile Memory (NVMY) Error
P16A4	10346	Timeout Control Module Knock Sensor SPI-Bus
P16A5	10347	Timeout Control Module Multiple Output Stage SPI-Bus
P16A6	10401	Control Module Self-Test, Cruise Control Monitoring

Table h. M56 engine: Siemens DME MS45.1 from 09/01/02		
PCode	BMW-FC	PCode text
P16A7	10402	Control Module Self-Test, Hot Film Air Mass Meter Monitoring
P16A8	10402	Control Module Self-Test, Throttle Position Monitoring
P16B0	10405	Control Module Self-Test, Pedal Position Sensor Monitoring
P16B1	10410	Control Module Self-Test, Idle Air Control System Integrated Component Plausibility
P16B2	10410	Control Module Self-Test, Idle Air Control System PD-Component Plausibility
P16B3	10411	Control Module Self-Test, MSR (Engine-Drag-Torque Control) Monitoring
P16B4	10411	Control Module Self-Test, DCC (Distance Cruise Control) Monitoring
P16B5	10411	Control Module Self-Test, AMT (Automatic Manual Transmission) Monitoring
P16B6	10411	Control Module Self-Test, ETC Monitoring
P16B7	10412	Control Module Self-Test, Clutch Torque Monitoring Maximum Value Plausibility
P16B8	10412	Control Module Self-Test, Clutch Torque Monitoring Minimum Value Plausibility
P16B9	10412	Control Module Self-Test, Torque Loss Monitoring
P16C0	10412	Control Module Self-Test, Driving Dynamics Control Switch Monitoring
P16C1	10413	Control Module Self-Test, Torque Monitoring Current Indicated Value Plausibility
P16C2	10417	Control Module Self-Test, Speed Limitation Monitoring
P16C3	10418	Control Module Self-Test, Speed Limitation Reset
P2088	10165	'A' Camshaft Position Actuator Control Circuit Low (Bank 1)
P2089	10165	'A' Camshaft Position Actuator Control Circuit High (Bank 1)
P2090	10173	'B' Camshaft Position Actuator Control Circuit Low (Bank 1)
P2091	10173	'B' Camshaft Position Actuator Control Circuit High (Bank 1)
P2096	10482	Post Catalyst Fuel Trim System Too Lean (Bank 1)
P2097	10482	Post Catalyst Fuel Trim System Too Rich (Bank 1)
P2098	10483	Post Catalyst Fuel Trim System Too Lean (Bank 2)
P2099	10483	Post Catalyst Fuel Trim System Too Rich (Bank 2)
P2195	10630	O2 Sensor Signal Stuck Lean (Bank 1 Sensor 1)
P2196	10632	O2 Sensor Signal Stuck Rich (Bank 1 Sensor 1)
P2197	10631	O2 Sensor Signal Stuck Lean (Bank 2 Sensor 1)
P2198	10633	O2 Sensor Signal Stuck Rich (Bank 2 Sensor 1)
P2228	10164	Barometric Pressure Circuit Low
P2229	10164	Barometric Pressure Circuit High
P2231	10592	O2 Sensor Signal Circuit Shorted to Heater Circuit (Bank 1 Sensor 1)
P2234	10593	O2 Sensor Signal Circuit Shorted to Heater Circuit (Bank 2 Sensor 1)
P2237	10611	O2 Sensor Positive Current Control Circuit/Open (Bank 1 Sensor 1)
P2240	10612	O2 Sensor Positive Current Control Circuit/Open (Bank 2 Sensor 1)
P2243	10611	O2 Sensor Reference Voltage Circuit/Open (Bank 1 Sensor 1)
P2247	10612	O2 Sensor Reference Voltage Circuit/Open (Bank 2 Sensor 1)
P2251	10611	O2 Sensor Negative Current Control Circuit/Open (Bank 1 Sensor 1)
P2254	10612	O2 Sensor Negative Current Control Circuit/Open (Bank 2 Sensor 1)
P2270	10437	O2 Sensor Signal Stuck Lean (Bank 1 Sensor 2)

Table h. M56 engine: Siemens DME MS45.1 from 09/01/02		
PCode	**BMW-FC**	**PCode text**
P2271	10437	O2 Sensor Signal Stuck Rich (Bank 1 Sensor 2)
P2272	10438	O2 Sensor Signal Stuck Lean (Bank 2 Sensor 2)
P2273	10438	O2 Sensor Signal Stuck Rich (Bank 2 Sensor 2)
P2297	10433	O2 Sensor Out of Range During Deceleration (Bank 1 Sensor 1)
P2298	10434	O2 Sensor Out of Range During Deceleration (Bank 2 Sensor 1)
P2414	10598	O2 Sensor Exhaust Sample Error (Bank 1 Sensor 1)
P2415	10599	O2 Sensor Exhaust Sample Error (Bank 2 Sensor 1)
P2626	10611	O2 Sensor Pumping Current Trim Circuit/Open (Bank 1 Sensor 1)
P2629	10612	O2 Sensor Pumping Current Trim Circuit/Open (Bank 2 Sensor 1)
P3010	10486	O2 Sensor Low Input after Cold Start (Bank 1 Sensor 2)
P3011	10487	O2 Sensor Low Input after Cold Start (Bank 2 Sensor 2)
P3014	10470	O2 Sensor WRAF-IC Supply Voltage Too Low (Bank 1 Sensor 1)
P3015	10471	O2 Sensor IC Supply Voltage Too Low (Bank 2 Sensor 1)
P3022	10495	O2 Sensor Disturbed SPI Communication to WRAF-IC (Bank 1 Sensor 1)
P3023	10496	O2 Sensor Disturbed SPI Communication to WRAF-IC (Bank 2 Sensor 1)
P3024	10495	O2 Sensor Initialization Error WRAF-IC (Bank 1 Sensor 1)
P3025	10496	O2 Sensor Initialization Error WRAF-IC (Bank 2 Sensor 1)
P3026	10435	O2 Sensor Operating Temperature not Reached (Bank 1 Sensor 1)
P3027	10436	O2 Sensor Operating Temperature not Reached (Bank 2 Sensor 1)
P3034	10433	O2 Sensor Characteristic Curve Gradient Too Low (Bank 1 Sensor 1)
P3035	10434	O2 Sensor Characteristic Curve Gradient Too Low (Bank 2 Sensor 1)
P3198	10205	Engine Coolant Temperature Gradient Too High
P3199	10207	Engine Coolant Temperature Signal Stuck
P3238	10289	Control Module Monitoring TPU Chip Defective

Table i. S54 engine: Siemens DME MS S54 from 05/01/2000 to 08/31/2000		
PCode	**BMW-FC**	**PCode text**
P0011	184	'A' Camshaft Position Timing Over-Advanced or System Performance (Bank 1)
P0013	185	'B' Camshaft Position Actuator Circuit (Bank 1)
P0100	41	Mass or Volume Air Flow Circuit
P0111	77	Intake Air Temperature Sensor 1 Circuit Range/Performance
P0115	105	Engine Coolant Temperature Circuit
P0116	78	Engine Coolant Temperature Circuit Range/Performance
P0120	120	Throttle/Pedal Position Sensor/Switch 'A' Circuit
P0120	121	Throttle/Pedal Position Sensor/Switch 'A' Circuit
P0130	13	O2 Sensor Circuit (Bank 1 Sensor 1)
P0133	214	O2 Sensor Circuit Slow Response (Bank 1 Sensor 1)
P0133	216	O2 Sensor Circuit Slow Response (Bank 1 Sensor 1)

Table i. S54 engine: Siemens DME MS S54 from 05/01/2000 to 08/31/2000		
PCode	**BMW-FC**	**PCode text**
P0134	218	O2 Sensor Circuit No Activity Detected (Bank 1 Sensor 1)
P0135	37	O2 Sensor Heater Circuit (Bank 1 Sensor 1)
P0136	87	O2 Sensor Circuit (Bank 1 Sensor 2)
P0139	92	O2 Sensor Circuit Slow Response (Bank 1 Sensor 2)
P0141	39	O2 Sensor Heater Circuit (Bank 1 Sensor 2)
P0150	12	O2 Sensor Circuit (Bank 2 Sensor 1)
P0153	215	O2 Sensor Circuit Slow Response (Bank 2 Sensor 1)
P0153	217	O2 Sensor Circuit Slow Response (Bank 2 Sensor 1)
P0154	219	O2 Sensor Circuit No Activity Detected (Bank 2 Sensor 1)
P0155	38	O2 Sensor Heater Circuit (Bank 2 Sensor 1)
P0156	88	O2 Sensor Circuit (Bank 2 Sensor 2)
P0159	93	O2 Sensor Circuit Slow Response (Bank 2 Sensor 2)
P0161	40	O2 Sensor Heater Circuit (Bank 2 Sensor 2)
P0170	144	Fuel Trim (Bank 1)
P0173	145	Fuel Trim (Bank 2)
P0201	3	Injector Circuit/Open - Cylinder 1
P0202	5	Injector Circuit/Open - Cylinder 2
P0203	4	Injector Circuit/Open - Cylinder 3
P0204	33	Injector Circuit/Open - Cylinder 4
P0205	31	Injector Circuit/Open - Cylinder 5
P0206	32	Injector Circuit/Open - Cylinder 6
P0300	204	Random/Multiple Cylinder Misfire Detected
P0300	213	Random/Multiple Cylinder Misfire Detected
P0301	196	Cylinder 1 Misfire Detected
P0301	205	Cylinder 1 Misfire Detected
P0302	197	Cylinder 2 Misfire Detected
P0302	206	Cylinder 2 Misfire Detected
P0303	198	Cylinder 3 Misfire Detected
P0303	207	Cylinder 3 Misfire Detected
P0304	199	Cylinder 4 Misfire Detected
P0304	208	Cylinder 4 Misfire Detected
P0305	200	Cylinder 5 Misfire Detected
P0305	209	Cylinder 5 Misfire Detected
P0306	201	Cylinder 6 Misfire Detected
P0306	210	Cylinder 6 Misfire Detected
P0335	16	Crankshaft Position Sensor 'A' Circuit
P0340	7	Camshaft Position Sensor 'A' Circuit (Bank 1 or Single Sensor)
P0385	10	Crankshaft Position Sensor 'B' Circuit
P0411	170	Secondary Air Injection System Incorrect Flow Detected

Table i. S54 engine: Siemens DME MS S54 from 05/01/2000 to 08/31/2000		
PCode	**BMW-FC**	**PCode text**
P0412	63	Secondary Air Injection System Switching Valve A Circuit
P0418	19	Secondary Air Injection System Control 'A' Circuit
P0420	178	Catalyst System Efficiency Below Threshold (Bank 1)
P0430	179	Catalyst System Efficiency Below Threshold (Bank 2)
P0440	232	Evaporative Emission System
P0442	180	Evaporative Emission System Leak Detected (small leak)
P0443	36	Evaporative Emission System Purge Control Valve Circuit
P0500	135	Vehicle Speed Sensor 'A'
P0505	128	Idle Air Control System
P0601	150	Internal Control Module Memory Check Sum Error
P0601	157	Internal Control Module Memory Check Sum Error
P0605	30	Internal Control Module Read Only Memory (ROM) Error
P0605	122	Internal Control Module Read Only Memory (ROM) Error
P0605	158	Internal Control Module Read Only Memory (ROM) Error
P0605	163	Internal Control Module Read Only Memory (ROM) Error
P0605	231	Internal Control Module Read Only Memory (ROM) Error
P1115	105	Ambient Air Temperature Sensor Error Value Received (M52LEV, S54 to 09/00: Coolant Temperature Sensor Plausibility)
P1140	73	Mass or Volume Air Flow Circuit Range/Performance Problem
P1188	174	Fuel Control (Bank 1 Sensor 1)
P1189	175	Fuel Control (Bank 2 Sensor 1)
P1317	15	'B' Camshaft Position Actuator Plausibility
P1472	27	Diagnostic Module Tank Leakage (DM-TL) Switching Solenoid Control Circuit Electrical
P1473	127	Diagnostic Module Tank Leakage (DM-TL) Pump Current Plausibility
P1509	29	Idle-Speed Control Valve Opening Solenoid Control Circuit Signal Electrical
P1550	2	Idle-Speed Control Valve Closing Coil Electrical
P1552	67	'A' Camshaft Position Actuator Control Open Circuit (Bank 1)
P1556	72	Air Conditioning Compressor Signal Low (S54 to 09/00: 'A' Camshaft Position Actuator Control Open Circuit (Bank 1)
P1560	22	'B' Camshaft Position Actuator Control Open Circuit (Bank 1)
P1565	21	Multifunction Steering Wheel (MFL) Interface, Bit Error or Buttons '+' and '-' Pressed Simultaneously (S54 to 09/00: 'B' Camshaft Position Actuator Control Open Circuit (Bank 1)
P1585	149	Misfire Detected with Low Fuel
P1640	155	Internal Control Module RAM/ROM Error
P1640	156	Internal Control Module RAM/ROM Error

Table j. S54 engine: Siemens DME MS S54 from 09/01/2000 to 02/28/2001		
PCode	**BMW-FC**	**PCode text**
P0011	184	'A' Camshaft Position Timing Over-Advanced or System Performance (Bank 1)
P0012	184	'A' Camshaft Position Timing Over-Retarded (Bank 1)

Table j. S54 engine: Siemens DME MS S54 from 09/01/2000 to 02/28/2001		
PCode	**BMW-FC**	**PCode text**
P0014	185	'B' Camshaft Position Timing Over-Advanced or System Performance (Bank 1)
P0015	185	'B' Camshaft Position Timing Over-Retarded (Bank 1)
P0101	73	Mass or Volume Air Flow Circuit Range/Performance
P0102	41	Mass or Volume Air Flow Circuit Low Input
P0103	41	Mass or Volume Air Flow Circuit High Input
P0111	77	Intake Air Temperature Sensor 1 Circuit Range/Performance
P0112	77	Intake Air Temperature Sensor 1 Circuit Low
P0113	77	Intake Air Temperature Sensor 1 Circuit High
P0115	105	Engine Coolant Temperature Circuit
P0117	78	Engine Coolant Temperature Circuit Low
P0118	78	Engine Coolant Temperature Circuit High
P0121	118	Throttle/Pedal Position Sensor/Switch 'A' Circuit Range/Performance
P0121	120	Throttle/Pedal Position Sensor/Switch 'A' Circuit Range/Performance
P0121	121	Throttle/Pedal Position Sensor/Switch 'A' Circuit Range/Performance
P0122	118	Throttle/Pedal Position Sensor/Switch 'A' Circuit High
P0123	118	Throttle/Pedal Position Sensor/Switch 'A' Circuit Low
P0128	105	Coolant Thermostat (Coolant Temperature Below Thermostat Regulating Temperature)
P0131	13	O2 Sensor Circuit Low Voltage (Bank 1 Sensor 1)
P0132	13	O2 Sensor Circuit High Voltage (Bank 1 Sensor 1)
P0133	214	O2 Sensor Circuit Slow Response (Bank 1 Sensor 1)
P0134	13	O2 Sensor Circuit No Activity Detected (Bank 1 Sensor 1)
P0134	218	O2 Sensor Circuit No Activity Detected (Bank 1 Sensor 1)
P0135	37	O2 Sensor Heater Circuit (Bank 1 Sensor 1)
P0137	87	O2 Sensor Circuit Low Voltage (Bank 1 Sensor 2)
P0138	87	O2 Sensor Circuit High Voltage (Bank 1 Sensor 2)
P0139	92	O2 Sensor Circuit Slow Response (Bank 1 Sensor 2)
P0140	87	O2 Sensor Circuit No Activity Detected (Bank 1 Sensor 2)
P0141	39	O2 Sensor Heater Circuit (Bank 1 Sensor 2)
P0151	12	O2 Sensor Circuit Low Voltage (Bank 2 Sensor 1)
P0152	12	O2 Sensor Circuit High Voltage (Bank 2 Sensor 1)
P0153	215	O2 Sensor Circuit Slow Response (Bank 2 Sensor 1)
P0154	12	O2 Sensor Circuit No Activity Detected (Bank 2 Sensor 1)
P0154	219	O2 Sensor Circuit No Activity Detected (Bank 2 Sensor 1)
P0155	38	O2 Sensor Heater Circuit (Bank 2 Sensor 1)
P0157	88	O2 Sensor Circuit Low Voltage (Bank 2 Sensor 2)
P0158	88	O2 Sensor Circuit High Voltage (Bank 2 Sensor 2)
P0159	93	O2 Sensor Circuit Slow Response (Bank 2 Sensor 2)
P0160	88	O2 Sensor Circuit No Activity Detected (Bank 2 Sensor 2)
P0161	40	O2 Sensor Heater Circuit (Bank 2 Sensor 2)

Table j. S54 engine: Siemens DME MS S54 from 09/01/2000 to 02/28/2001		
PCode	**BMW-FC**	**PCode text**
P0171	144	System Too Lean (Bank 1)
P0171	174	System Too Lean (Bank 1)
P0172	144	System Too Rich (Bank 1)
P0172	174	System Too Rich (Bank 1)
P0174	145	System Too Lean (Bank 2)
P0174	175	System Too Lean (Bank 2)
P0175	145	System Too Rich (Bank 2)
P0175	175	System Too Rich (Bank 2)
P0201	3	Injector Circuit/Open - Cylinder 1
P0202	5	Injector Circuit/Open - Cylinder 2
P0203	4	Injector Circuit/Open - Cylinder 3
P0204	33	Injector Circuit/Open - Cylinder 4
P0205	31	Injector Circuit/Open - Cylinder 5
P0206	32	Injector Circuit/Open - Cylinder 6
P0221	119	Throttle/Pedal Position Sensor/Switch 'B' Circuit Range/Performance
P0222	119	Throttle/Pedal Position Sensor/Switch 'B' Circuit Low
P0223	119	Throttle/Pedal Position Sensor/Switch 'B' Circuit High
P0261	3	Cylinder 1 Injector Circuit Low
P0262	3	Cylinder 1 Injector Circuit High
P0264	5	Cylinder 2 Injector Circuit Low
P0265	5	Cylinder 2 Injector Circuit High
P0267	4	Cylinder 3 Injector Circuit Low
P0268	4	Cylinder 3 Injector Circuit High
P0270	33	Cylinder 4 Injector Circuit Low
P0271	33	Cylinder 4 Injector Circuit High
P0273	31	Cylinder 5 Injector Circuit Low
P0274	31	Cylinder 5 Injector Circuit High
P0276	32	Cylinder 6 Injector Circuit Low
P0277	32	Cylinder 6 Injector Circuit High
P0300	213	Random/Multiple Cylinder Misfire Detected
P0301	205	Cylinder 1 Misfire Detected
P0302	206	Cylinder 2 Misfire Detected
P0303	207	Cylinder 3 Misfire Detected
P0304	208	Cylinder 4 Misfire Detected
P0305	209	Cylinder 5 Misfire Detected
P0306	210	Cylinder 6 Misfire Detected
P0335	16	Crankshaft Position Sensor 'A' Circuit
P0340	7	Camshaft Position Sensor 'A' Circuit (Bank 1 or Single Sensor)
P0365	10	Camshaft Position Sensor 'B' Circuit (Bank 1)

Table j. S54 engine: Siemens DME MS S54 from 09/01/2000 to 02/28/2001		
PCode	BMW-FC	PCode text
P0369	162	Camshaft Position Sensor 'B' Circuit Intermittent (Bank 1)
P0394	15	Camshaft Position Sensor 'B' Circuit Intermittent (Bank 2)
P0411	170	Secondary Air Injection System Incorrect Flow Detected
P0413	63	Secondary Air Injection System Switching Valve A Circuit Open
P0414	63	Secondary Air Injection System Switching Valve A Circuit Shorted
P0418	19	Secondary Air Injection System Control 'A' Circuit
P0420	178	Catalyst System Efficiency Below Threshold (Bank 1)
P0430	179	Catalyst System Efficiency Below Threshold (Bank 2)
P0440	232	Evaporative Emission System
P0442	180	Evaporative Emission System Leak Detected (small leak)
P0443	36	Evaporative Emission System Purge Control Valve Circuit
P0444	36	Evaporative Emission System Purge Control Valve Circuit Open
P0445	36	Evaporative Emission System Purge Control Valve Circuit Shorted
P0491	170	Secondary Air Injection System Insufficient Flow (Bank 1)
P0492	170	Secondary Air Injection System Insufficient Flow (Bank 2)
P0500	135	Vehicle Speed Sensor 'A'
P0506	128	Idle Air Control System RPM Lower Than Expected
P0507	128	Idle Air Control System RPM Higher Than Expected
P0601	150	Internal Control Module Memory Check Sum Error
P0601	157	Internal Control Module Memory Check Sum Error
P0604	157	Internal Control Module Random Access Memory (RAM) Error
P0605	150	Internal Control Module Read Only Memory (ROM) Error
P0605	157	Internal Control Module Read Only Memory (ROM) Error
P0606	30	ECM/PCM Processor
P0606	107	ECM/PCM Processor
P0606	158	ECM/PCM Processor
P0606	163	ECM/PCM Processor
P1121	111	Pedal Position Sensor 1 Range/Performance Problem
P1122	60	Pedal Position Sensor 1 Low Input
P1123	60	Pedal Position Sensor 1 High Input
P1134	37	O2 Sensor Heater Circuit Signal Intermittent (Bank 1 Sensor 1)
P1135	37	O2 Sensor Heater Circuit Low Voltage (Bank 1 Sensor 1)
P1136	37	O2 Sensor Heater Circuit High Voltage (Bank 1 Sensor 1)
P1137	39	O2 Sensor Heater Circuit Signal Intermittent (Bank 1 Sensor 2)
P1138	39	O2 Sensor Heater Circuit Low Voltage (Bank 1 Sensor 2)
P1139	39	O2 Sensor Heater Circuit High Voltage (Bank 1 Sensor 2)
P1151	38	O2 Sensor Heater Circuit Signal Intermittent (Bank 2 Sensor 1)
P1152	38	O2 Sensor Heater Circuit Low Voltage (Bank 2 Sensor 1)
P1153	38	O2 Sensor Heater Circuit High Voltage (Bank 2 Sensor 1)

Table j. S54 engine: Siemens DME MS S54 from 09/01/2000 to 02/28/2001		
PCode	BMW-FC	PCode text
P1155	40	O2 Sensor Heater Circuit Signal Intermittent (Bank 2 Sensor 2)
P1156	40	O2 Sensor Heater Circuit Low Voltage (Bank 2 Sensor 2)
P1157	40	O2 Sensor Heater Circuit High Voltage (Bank 2 Sensor 2)
P1178	216	O2 Sensor Signal Circuit Slow Switching from Rich to Lean (Bank 1 Sensor 1)
P1179	217	O2 Sensor Signal Circuit Slow Switching from Rich to Lean (Bank 2 Sensor 1)
P1221	112	Pedal Position Sensor 2 Range/Performance Problem
P1222	61	Pedal Position Sensor 2 Low Input
P1223	61	Pedal Position Sensor 2 High Input
P1340	213	Multiple Cylinder Misfire During Start
P1341	204	Multiple Cylinder Misfire with Fuel Cut-Off
P1342	205	Misfire During Start Cylinder 1
P1343	196	Misfire Cylinder 1 with Fuel Cut-Off
P1344	206	Misfire During Start Cylinder 2
P1345	197	Misfire Cylinder 2 with Fuel Cut-Off
P1346	207	Misfire During Start Cylinder 3
P1347	198	Misfire Cylinder 3 with Fuel Cut-Off
P1348	208	Misfire During Start Cylinder 4
P1349	199	Misfire Cylinder 4 with Fuel Cut-Off
P1350	209	Misfire during Start Cylinder 5
P1351	200	Misfire Cylinder 5 with Fuel Cut-Off
P1352	210	Misfire during Start Cylinder 6
P1353	201	Misfire Cylinder 6 with Fuel Cut-Off
P1447	127	Diagnostic Module Tank Leakage (DM-TL) Pump Current Too High during Switching Solenoid Test
P1448	127	Diagnostic Module Tank Leakage (DM-TL) Pump Current Too Low
P1449	127	Diagnostic Module Tank Leakage (DM-TL) Pump Current Too High
P1450	27	Diagnostic Module Tank Leakage (DM-TL) Switching Solenoid Control Open Circuit
P1451	27	Diagnostic Module Tank Leakage (DM-TL) Switching Solenoid Control Circuit Signal Low
P1452	27	Diagnostic Module Tank Leakage (DM-TL) Switching Solenoid Control Circuit Signal High
P1504	2	Idle-Speed Control Valve Closing Solenoid Control Open Circuit
P1507	29	Idle-Speed Control Valve Opening Solenoid Control Circuit Signal Low
P1508	29	Idle-Speed Control Valve Opening Solenoid Control Open Circuit
P1509	29	Idle-Speed Control Valve Opening Solenoid Control Circuit Signal Electrical
P1525	67	'A' Camshaft Position Actuator Control Open Circuit (Bank 1)
P1525	72	'A' Camshaft Position Actuator Control Open Circuit (Bank 1)
P1531	21	'B' Camshaft Position Actuator Control Open Circuit (Bank 1)
P1531	22	'B' Camshaft Position Actuator Control Open Circuit (Bank 1)
P1550	2	Idle-Speed Control Valve Closing Coil Electrical
P1585	149	Misfire Detected with Low Fuel
P1602	122	Control Module Self-Test, Control Module Defective

Table j. S54 engine: Siemens DME MS S54 from 09/01/2000 to 02/28/2001		
PCode	**BMW-FC**	**PCode text**
P1602	231	Control Module Self-Test, Control Module Defective
P1634	107	Throttle Valve Adaptation Spring Test Failed
P1636	45	Throttle Valve Control Circuit
P1637	107	Throttle Valve Position Control, Control Deviation
P1637	230	Throttle Valve Position Control, Control Deviation
P1639	107	Throttle Valve Position Control Throttle Stuck Permanently
P1640	155	Internal Control Module RAM/ROM Error
P1640	156	Internal Control Module RAM/ROM Error
P1663	156	EWS (Electronic Immobilizer) Rolling Code Faulty Storage in EEPROM

Table k. S54 engine: Siemens DME MS S54 from 03/01/2001 to 08/31/2001		
PCode	**BMW-FC**	**PCode text**
P0011	184	'A' Camshaft Position Timing Over-Advanced or System Performance (Bank 1)
P0012	184	'A' Camshaft Position Timing Over-Retarded (Bank 1)
P0014	185	'B' Camshaft Position Timing Over-Advanced or System Performance (Bank 1)
P0015	185	'B' Camshaft Position Timing Over-Retarded (Bank 1)
P0101	73	Mass or Volume Air Flow Circuit Range/Performance
P0102	41	Mass or Volume Air Flow Circuit Low Input
P0103	41	Mass or Volume Air Flow Circuit High Input
P0111	77	Intake Air Temperature Sensor 1 Circuit Range/Performance
P0112	77	Intake Air Temperature Sensor 1 Circuit Low
P0113	77	Intake Air Temperature Sensor 1 Circuit High
P0116	105	Engine Coolant Temperature Circuit Range/Performance
P0117	78	Engine Coolant Temperature Circuit Low
P0118	78	Engine Coolant Temperature Circuit High
P0121	118	Throttle/Pedal Position Sensor/Switch 'A' Circuit Range/Performance
P0121	120	Throttle/Pedal Position Sensor/Switch 'A' Circuit Range/Performance
P0121	121	Throttle/Pedal Position Sensor/Switch 'A' Circuit Range/Performance
P0122	118	Throttle/Pedal Position Sensor/Switch 'A' Circuit Low
P0123	118	Throttle/Pedal Position Sensor/Switch 'A' Circuit High
P0128	105	Coolant Thermostat (Coolant Temperature Below Thermostat Regulating Temperature)
P0131	13	O2 Sensor Circuit Low Voltage (Bank 1 Sensor 1)
P0132	13	O2 Sensor Circuit High Voltage (Bank 1 Sensor 1)
P0133	214	O2 Sensor Circuit Slow Response (Bank 1 Sensor 1)
P0134	13	O2 Sensor Circuit No Activity Detected (Bank 1 Sensor 1)
P0134	218	O2 Sensor Circuit No Activity Detected (Bank 1 Sensor 1)
P0135	37	O2 Sensor Heater Circuit (Bank 1 Sensor 1)
P0137	87	O2 Sensor Circuit Low Voltage (Bank 1 Sensor 2)

Table k. S54 engine: Siemens DME MS S54 from 03/01/2001 to 08/31/2001		
PCode	**BMW-FC**	**PCode text**
P0138	87	O2 Sensor Circuit High Voltage (Bank 1 Sensor 2)
P0139	92	O2 Sensor Circuit Slow Response (Bank 1 Sensor 2)
P0140	87	O2 Sensor Circuit No Activity Detected (Bank 1 Sensor 2)
P0141	39	O2 Sensor Heater Circuit (Bank 1 Sensor 2)
P0151	12	O2 Sensor Circuit Low Voltage (Bank 2 Sensor 1)
P0152	12	O2 Sensor Circuit High Voltage (Bank 2 Sensor 1)
P0153	215	O2 Sensor Circuit Slow Response (Bank 2 Sensor 1)
P0154	12	O2 Sensor Circuit No Activity Detected (Bank 2 Sensor 1)
P0154	219	O2 Sensor Circuit No Activity Detected (Bank 2 Sensor 1)
P0155	38	O2 Sensor Heater Circuit (Bank 2 Sensor 1)
P0157	88	O2 Sensor Circuit Low Voltage (Bank 2 Sensor 2)
P0158	88	O2 Sensor Circuit High Voltage (Bank 2 Sensor 2)
P0159	93	O2 Sensor Circuit Slow Response (Bank 2 Sensor 2)
P0160	88	O2 Sensor Circuit No Activity Detected (Bank 2 Sensor 2)
P0161	40	O2 Sensor Heater Circuit (Bank 2 Sensor 2)
P0171	144	System Too Lean (Bank 1)
P0171	174	System Too Lean (Bank 1)
P0172	144	System Too Rich (Bank 1)
P0172	174	System Too Rich (Bank 1)
P0174	145	System Too Lean (Bank 2)
P0174	175	System Too Lean (Bank 2)
P0175	145	System Too Rich (Bank 2)
P0175	175	System Too Rich (Bank 2)
P0201	3	Injector Circuit/Open - Cylinder 1
P0202	5	Injector Circuit/Open - Cylinder 2
P0203	4	Injector Circuit/Open - Cylinder 3
P0204	33	Injector Circuit/Open - Cylinder 4
P0205	31	Injector Circuit/Open - Cylinder 5
P0206	32	Injector Circuit/Open - Cylinder 6
P0221	119	Throttle/Pedal Position Sensor/Switch 'B' Circuit Range/Performance
P0222	119	Throttle/Pedal Position Sensor/Switch 'B' Circuit Low
P0223	119	Throttle/Pedal Position Sensor/Switch 'B' Circuit High
P0261	3	Cylinder 1 Injector Circuit Low
P0262	3	Cylinder 1 Injector Circuit High
P0264	5	Cylinder 2 Injector Circuit Low
P0265	5	Cylinder 2 Injector Circuit High
P0267	4	Cylinder 3 Injector Circuit Low
P0268	4	Cylinder 3 Injector Circuit High
P0270	33	Cylinder 4 Injector Circuit Low

Table k. S54 engine: Siemens DME MS S54 from 03/01/2001 to 08/31/2001		
PCode	**BMW-FC**	**PCode text**
P0271	33	Cylinder 4 Injector Circuit High
P0273	31	Cylinder 5 Injector Circuit Low
P0274	31	Cylinder 5 Injector Circuit High
P0276	32	Cylinder 6 Injector Circuit Low
P0277	32	Cylinder 6 Injector Circuit High
P0300	213	Random/Multiple Cylinder Misfire Detected
P0301	205	Cylinder 1 Misfire Detected
P0302	206	Cylinder 2 Misfire Detected
P0303	207	Cylinder 3 Misfire Detected
P0304	208	Cylinder 4 Misfire Detected
P0305	209	Cylinder 5 Misfire Detected
P0306	210	Cylinder 6 Misfire Detected
P0335	16	Crankshaft Position Sensor 'A' Circuit
P0340	7	Camshaft Position Sensor 'A' Circuit (Bank 1 or Single Sensor)
P0365	10	Camshaft Position Sensor 'B' Circuit (Bank 1)
P0369	162	Camshaft Position Sensor 'B' Circuit Intermittent (Bank 1)
P0394	15	Camshaft Position Sensor 'B' Circuit Intermittent (Bank 2)
P0411	170	Secondary Air Injection System Incorrect Flow Detected
P0413	63	Secondary Air Injection System Switching Valve A Circuit Open
P0414	63	Secondary Air Injection System Switching Valve A Circuit Shorted
P0418	19	Secondary Air Injection System Control 'A' Circuit
P0420	178	Catalyst System Efficiency Below Threshold (Bank 1)
P0430	179	Catalyst System Efficiency Below Threshold (Bank 2)
P0440	232	Evaporative Emission System
P0442	180	Evaporative Emission System Leak Detected (small leak)
P0443	36	Evaporative Emission System Purge Control Valve Circuit
P0444	36	Evaporative Emission System Purge Control Valve Circuit Open
P0445	36	Evaporative Emission System Purge Control Valve Circuit Shorted
P0491	170	Secondary Air Injection System Insufficient Flow (Bank 1)
P0492	170	Secondary Air Injection System Insufficient Flow (Bank 2)
P0500	135	Vehicle Speed Sensor 'A'
P0506	128	Idle Air Control System RPM Lower Than Expected
P0507	128	Idle Air Control System RPM Higher Than Expected
P0601	150	Internal Control Module Memory Check Sum Error
P0601	157	Internal Control Module Memory Check Sum Error
P0604	157	Internal Control Module Random Access Memory (RAM) Error
P0605	150 I	Internal Control Module Read Only Memory (ROM) Error
P0605	157	Internal Control Module Read Only Memory (ROM) Error
P0606	30	ECM/PCM Processor

Table k. S54 engine: Siemens DME MS S54 from 03/01/2001 to 08/31/2001		
PCode	**BMW-FC**	**PCode text**
P0606	107	ECM/PCM Processor
P0606	158	ECM/PCM Processor
P0606	163	ECM/PCM Processor
P1121	111	Pedal Position Sensor 1 Range/Performance Problem
P1122	60	Pedal Position Sensor 1 Low Input
P1123	60	Pedal Position Sensor 1 High Input
P1134	37	O2 Sensor Heater Circuit Signal Intermittent (Bank 1 Sensor 1)
P1135	37	O2 Sensor Heater Circuit Low Voltage (Bank 1 Sensor 1)
P1136	37	O2 Sensor Heater Circuit High Voltage (Bank 1 Sensor 1)
P1137	39	O2 Sensor Heater Circuit Signal Intermittent (Bank 1 Sensor 2)
P1138	39	O2 Sensor Heater Circuit Low Voltage (Bank 1 Sensor 2)
P1139	39	O2 Sensor Heater Circuit High Voltage (Bank 1 Sensor 2)
P1151	38	O2 Sensor Heater Circuit Signal Intermittent (Bank 2 Sensor 1)
P1152	38	O2 Sensor Heater Circuit Low Voltage (Bank 2 Sensor 1)
P1153	38	O2 Sensor Heater Circuit High Voltage (Bank 2 Sensor 1)
P1155	40	O2 Sensor Heater Circuit Signal Intermittent (Bank 2 Sensor 2)
P1156	40	O2 Sensor Heater Circuit Low Voltage (Bank 2 Sensor 2)
P1157	40	O2 Sensor Heater Circuit High Voltage (Bank 2 Sensor 2)
P1178	216	O2 Sensor Signal Circuit Slow Switching from Rich to Lean (Bank 1 Sensor 1)
P1179	217	O2 Sensor Signal Circuit Slow Switching from Rich to Lean (Bank 2 Sensor 1)
P1221	112	Pedal Position Sensor 2 Range/Performance Problem
P1222	61	Pedal Position Sensor 2 Low Input
P1223	61	Pedal Position Sensor 2 High Input
P1340	213	Multiple Cylinder Misfire During Start
P1341	204	Multiple Cylinder Misfire with Fuel Cut-Off
P1342	205	Misfire During Start Cylinder 1
P1503	2 I	Idle-Speed Control Valve Closing Solenoid Control Circuit Signal Low
P1343	196	Misfire Cylinder 1 with Fuel Cut-Off
P1344	206	Misfire During Start Cylinder 2
P1345	197	Misfire Cylinder 2 with Fuel Cut-Off
P1346	207	Misfire During Start Cylinder 3
P1347	198	Misfire Cylinder 3 with Fuel Cut-Off
P1348	208	Misfire During Start Cylinder 4
P1349	199	Misfire Cylinder 4 with Fuel Cut-Off
P1350	209	Misfire during Start Cylinder 5
P1351	200	Misfire Cylinder 5 with Fuel Cut-Off
P1352	210	Misfire during Start Cylinder 6
P1353	201	Misfire Cylinder 6 with Fuel Cut-Off
P1447	127	Diagnostic Module Tank Leakage (DM-TL) Pump Current Too High during Switching Solenoid Test

Table k. S54 engine: Siemens DME MS S54 from 03/01/2001 to 08/31/2001		
PCode	**BMW-FC**	**PCode text**
P1448	127	Diagnostic Module Tank Leakage (DM-TL) Pump Current Too Low
P1449	127	Diagnostic Module Tank Leakage (DM-TL) Pump Current Too High
P1450	27	Diagnostic Module Tank Leakage (DM-TL) Switching Solenoid Control Open Circuit
P1451	27	Diagnostic Module Tank Leakage (DM-TL) Switching Solenoid Control Circuit Signal Low
P1452	27	Diagnostic Module Tank Leakage (DM-TL) Switching Solenoid Control Circuit Signal High
P1504	2	Idle-Speed Control Valve Closing Solenoid Control Open Circuit
P1507	29	Idle-Speed Control Valve Opening Solenoid Control Circuit Signal Low
P1508	29	Idle-Speed Control Valve Opening Solenoid Control Open Circuit
P1509	29	Idle-Speed Control Valve Opening Solenoid Control Circuit Signal Electrical
P1525	67	'A' Camshaft Position Actuator Control Open Circuit (Bank 1)
1525	72	'A' Camshaft Position Actuator Control Open Circuit (Bank 1)
P1531	22	'B' Camshaft Position Actuator Control Open Circuit (Bank 1)
P1550	2	Idle-Speed Control Valve Closing Coil Electrical
P1585	149	Misfire Detected with Low Fuel
P1602	122	Control Module Self-Test, Control Module Defective
P1602	231	Control Module Self-Test, Control Module Defective
P1634	107	Throttle Valve Adaptation Spring Test Failed
P1636	45	Throttle Valve Control Circuit
P1637	107	Throttle Valve Position Control, Control Deviation
P1637	230	Throttle Valve Position Control, Control Deviation
P1639	107	Throttle Valve Position Control Throttle Stuck Permanently
P1640	155	Internal Control Module RAM/ROM Error
P1640	156	Internal Control Module RAM/ROM Error
P1663	156	EWS (Electronic Immobilizer) Rolling Code Faulty Storage in EEPROM

Table l. S54 engine: Siemens DME MS S54 from 09/01/2001 to 08/31/2002		
PCode	**BMW-FC**	**PCode text**
P0011	184	'A' Camshaft Position Timing Over-Advanced or System Performance (Bank 1)
P0012	184	'A' Camshaft Position Timing Over-Retarded (Bank 1)
P0014	185	'B' Camshaft Position Timing Over-Advanced or System Performance (Bank 1)
P0015	185	'B' Camshaft Position Timing Over-Retarded (Bank 1)
P0030	37	HO2S Heater Control Circuit (Bank 1 Sensor 1)
P0031	37	HO2S Heater Control Circuit Low (Bank 1 Sensor 1)
P0032	37	HO2S Heater Control Circuit High (Bank 1 Sensor 1)
P0036	39	HO2S Heater Control Circuit (Bank 1 Sensor 2)
P0037	39	HO2S Heater Control Circuit Low (Bank 1 Sensor 2)
P0038	39	HO2S Heater Control Circuit High (Bank 1 Sensor 2)
P0050	38	HO2S Heater Control Circuit (Bank 2 Sensor 1)

Table I. S54 engine: Siemens DME MS S54 from 09/01/2001 to 08/31/2002		
PCode	**BMW-FC**	**PCode text**
P0051	38	HO2S Heater Control Circuit Low (Bank 2 Sensor 1)
P0052	38	HO2S Heater Control Circuit High (Bank 2 Sensor 1)
P0056	40	HO2S Heater Control Circuit (Bank 2 Sensor 2)
P0057	40	HO2S Heater Control Circuit Low (Bank 2 Sensor 2)
P0058	40	HO2S Heater Control Circuit High (Bank 2 Sensor 2)
P0101	73	Mass or Volume Air Flow Circuit Range/Performance
P0102	41	Mass or Volume Air Flow Circuit Low Input
P0103	41	Mass or Volume Air Flow Circuit High Input
P0111	77	Intake Air Temperature Sensor 1 Circuit Range/Performance
P0112	77	Intake Air Temperature Sensor 1 Circuit Low
P0113	77	Intake Air Temperature Sensor 1 Circuit High
P0116	105	Engine Coolant Temperature Circuit Range/Performance
P0117	78	Engine Coolant Temperature Circuit Low
P0118	78	Engine Coolant Temperature Circuit High
P0121	118	Throttle/Pedal Position Sensor/Switch 'A' Circuit Range/Performance
P0121	120	Throttle/Pedal Position Sensor/Switch 'A' Circuit Range/Performance
P0121	121	Throttle/Pedal Position Sensor/Switch 'A' Circuit Range/Performance
P0122	118	Throttle/Pedal Position Sensor/Switch 'A' Circuit Low
P0123	118	Throttle/Pedal Position Sensor/Switch 'A' Circuit High
P0128	105	Coolant Thermostat (Coolant Temperature Below Thermostat Regulating Temperature)
P0131	13	O2 Sensor Circuit Low Voltage (Bank 1 Sensor 1)
P0132	13	O2 Sensor Circuit High Voltage (Bank 1 Sensor 1)
P0133	214	O2 Sensor Circuit Slow Response (Bank 1 Sensor 1)
P0134	13	O2 Sensor Circuit No Activity Detected (Bank 1 Sensor 1)
P0134	218	O2 Sensor Circuit No Activity Detected (Bank 1 Sensor 1)
P0135	37	O2 Sensor Heater Circuit (Bank 1 Sensor 1)
P0137	87	O2 Sensor Circuit Low Voltage (Bank 1 Sensor 2)
P0138	87	O2 Sensor Circuit High Voltage (Bank 1 Sensor 2)
P0139	92	O2 Sensor Circuit Slow Response (Bank 1 Sensor 2)
P0140	87	O2 Sensor Circuit No Activity Detected (Bank 1 Sensor 2)
P0141	39	O2 Sensor Heater Circuit (Bank 1 Sensor 2)
P0151	12	O2 Sensor Circuit Low Voltage (Bank 2 Sensor 1)
P0152	12	O2 Sensor Circuit High Voltage (Bank 2 Sensor 1)
P0153	215	O2 Sensor Circuit Slow Response (Bank 2 Sensor 1)
P0154	12	O2 Sensor Circuit No Activity Detected (Bank 2 Sensor 1)
P0154	219	O2 Sensor Circuit No Activity Detected (Bank 2 Sensor 1)
P0155	38	O2 Sensor Heater Circuit (Bank 2 Sensor 1)
P0157	88	O2 Sensor Circuit Low Voltage (Bank 2 Sensor 2)
P0158	88	O2 Sensor Circuit High Voltage (Bank 2 Sensor 2)

Table I. S54 engine: Siemens DME MS S54 from 09/01/2001 to 08/31/2002		
PCode	**BMW-FC**	**PCode text**
P0159	93	O2 Sensor Circuit Slow Response (Bank 2 Sensor 2)
P0160	88	O2 Sensor Circuit No Activity Detected (Bank 2 Sensor 2)
P0161	40	O2 Sensor Heater Circuit (Bank 2 Sensor 2)
P0171	144	System Too Lean (Bank 1)
P0171	174	System Too Lean (Bank 1)
P0172	144	System Too Rich (Bank 1)
P0172	174	System Too Rich (Bank 1)
P0174	145	System Too Lean (Bank 2)
P0174	175	System Too Lean (Bank 2)
P0175	145	System Too Rich (Bank 2)
P0175	175	System Too Rich (Bank 2)
P0201	3	Injector Circuit/Open - Cylinder 1
P0202	5	Injector Circuit/Open - Cylinder 2
P0203	4	Injector Circuit/Open - Cylinder 3
P0204	33	Injector Circuit/Open - Cylinder 4
P0205	31	Injector Circuit/Open - Cylinder 5
P0206	32	Injector Circuit/Open - Cylinder 6
P0221	119	Throttle/Pedal Position Sensor/Switch 'B' Circuit Range/Performance
P0222	119	Throttle/Pedal Position Sensor/Switch 'B' Circuit Low
P0223	119	Throttle/Pedal Position Sensor/Switch 'B' Circuit High
P0261	3	Cylinder 1 Injector Circuit Low
P0262	3	Cylinder 1 Injector Circuit High
P0264	5	Cylinder 2 Injector Circuit Low
P0265	5	Cylinder 2 Injector Circuit High
P0267	4	Cylinder 3 Injector Circuit Low
P0268	4	Cylinder 3 Injector Circuit High
P0270	33	Cylinder 4 Injector Circuit Low
P0271	33	Cylinder 4 Injector Circuit High
P0273	31	Cylinder 5 Injector Circuit Low
P0274	31	Cylinder 5 Injector Circuit High
P0276	32	Cylinder 6 Injector Circuit Low
P0277	32	Cylinder 6 Injector Circuit High
P0300	213	Random/Multiple Cylinder Misfire Detected
P0301	205	Cylinder 1 Misfire Detected
P0302	206	Cylinder 2 Misfire Detected
P0303	207	Cylinder 3 Misfire Detected
P0304	208	Cylinder 4 Misfire Detected
P0305	209	Cylinder 5 Misfire Detected
P0306	210	Cylinder 6 Misfire Detected

Table I. S54 engine: Siemens DME MS S54 from 09/01/2001 to 08/31/2002		
PCode	**BMW-FC**	**PCode text**
P0335	16	Crankshaft Position Sensor 'A' Circuit
P0340	7	Camshaft Position Sensor 'A' Circuit (Bank 1 or Single Sensor)
P0365	10	Camshaft Position Sensor 'B' Circuit (Bank 1)
P0369	162	Camshaft Position Sensor 'B' Circuit Intermittent (Bank 1)
P0394	15	Camshaft Position Sensor 'B' Circuit Intermittent (Bank 2)
P0411	170	Secondary Air Injection System Incorrect Flow Detected
P0413	63	Secondary Air Injection System Switching Valve A Circuit Open
P0414	63	Secondary Air Injection System Switching Valve A Circuit Shorted
P0418	19	Secondary Air Injection System Control 'A' Circuit
P0420	178	Catalyst System Efficiency Below Threshold (Bank 1)
P0430	179	Catalyst System Efficiency Below Threshold (Bank 2)
P0441	232	Evaporative Emission System Incorrect Purge Flow
P0442	180	Evaporative Emission System Leak Detected (small leak)
P0443	36	Evaporative Emission System Purge Control Valve Circuit
P0444	36	Evaporative Emission System Purge Control Valve Circuit Open
P0445	36	Evaporative Emission System Purge Control Valve Circuit Shorted
P0491	170	Secondary Air Injection System Insufficient Flow (Bank 1)
P0492	170	Secondary Air Injection System Insufficient Flow (Bank 2)
P0500	135	Vehicle Speed Sensor 'A'
P0506	128 I	Idle Air Control System RPM Lower Than Expected
P0507	128	Idle Air Control System RPM Higher Than Expected
P0601	150	Internal Control Module Memory Check Sum Error
P0601	157	Internal Control Module Memory Check Sum Error
P0604	150	Internal Control Module Random Access Memory (RAM) Error
P0604	157	Internal Control Module Random Access Memory (RAM) Error
P0605	150	Internal Control Module Read Only Memory (ROM) Error
P0605	157	Internal Control Module Read Only Memory (ROM) Error
P1502	2	Idle-Speed Control Valve Closing Solenoid Control Circuit Signal High
P1503	2	Idle-Speed Control Valve Closing Solenoid Control Circuit Signal Low
P0606	30	ECM/PCM Processor
P0606	107	ECM/PCM Processor
P0606	158	ECM/PCM Processor
P0606	163	ECM/PCM Processor
P1121	111	Pedal Position Sensor 1 Range/Performance Problem
P1122	60	Pedal Position Sensor 1 Low Input
P1123	60	Pedal Position Sensor 1 High Input
P1178	216	O2 Sensor Signal Circuit Slow Switching from Rich to Lean (Bank 1 Sensor 1)
P1179	217	O2 Sensor Signal Circuit Slow Switching from Rich to Lean (Bank 2 Sensor 1)
P1221	112	Pedal Position Sensor 2 Range/Performance Problem

Table I. S54 engine: Siemens DME MS S54 from 09/01/2001 to 08/31/2002		
PCode	**BMW-FC**	**PCode text**
P1222	61	Pedal Position Sensor 2 Low Input
P1223	61	Pedal Position Sensor 2 High Input
P1340	213	Multiple Cylinder Misfire During Start
P1341	204	Multiple Cylinder Misfire with Fuel Cut-Off
P1342	205	Misfire During Start Cylinder 1
P1343	196	Misfire Cylinder 1 with Fuel Cut-Off
P1344	206	Misfire During Start Cylinder 2
P1345	197	Misfire Cylinder 2 with Fuel Cut-Off
P1346	207	Misfire During Start Cylinder 3
P1347	198	Misfire Cylinder 3 with Fuel Cut-Off
P1348	208	Misfire During Start Cylinder 4
P1349	199	Misfire Cylinder 4 with Fuel Cut-Off
P1350	209	Misfire during Start Cylinder 5
P1351	200	Misfire Cylinder 5 with Fuel Cut-Off
P1352	210	Misfire during Start Cylinder 6
P1353	201	Misfire Cylinder 6 with Fuel Cut-Off
P1434	176	Diagnostic Module Tank Leakage (DM-TL)
P1447	127	Diagnostic Module Tank Leakage (DM-TL) Pump Current Too High during Switching Solenoid Test
P1448	127	Diagnostic Module Tank Leakage (DM-TL) Pump Current Too Low
P1449	127	Diagnostic Module Tank Leakage (DM-TL) Pump Current Too High
P1450	27	Diagnostic Module Tank Leakage (DM-TL) Switching Solenoid Control Open Circuit
P1451	27	Diagnostic Module Tank Leakage (DM-TL) Switching Solenoid Control Circuit Signal Low
P1452	27	Diagnostic Module Tank Leakage (DM-TL) Switching Solenoid Control Circuit Signal High
P1504	2	Idle-Speed Control Valve Closing Solenoid Control Open Circuit
P1506	29	Idle-Speed Control Valve Opening Solenoid Control Circuit Signal High
P1507	29	Idle-Speed Control Valve Opening Solenoid Control Circuit Signal Low
P1508	29	Idle-Speed Control Valve Opening Solenoid Control Open Circuit
P1525	67	'A' Camshaft Position Actuator Control Open Circuit (Bank 1)
P1525	72	'A' Camshaft Position Actuator Control Open Circuit (Bank 1)
P1531	21	'B' Camshaft Position Actuator Control Open Circuit (Bank 1)
P1531	22	'B' Camshaft Position Actuator Control Open Circuit (Bank 1)
P1585	149	Misfire Detected with Low Fuel
P1602	122	Control Module Self-Test, Control Module Defective
P1602	231	Control Module Self-Test, Control Module Defective
P1634	107	Throttle Valve Adaptation Spring Test Failed
P1636	45	Throttle Valve Control Circuit
P1637	107	Throttle Valve Position Control, Control Deviation
P1637	230	Throttle Valve Position Control, Control Deviation
P1639	107	Throttle Valve Position Control Throttle Stuck Permanently

Table l. S54 engine: Siemens DME MS S54 from 09/01/2001 to 08/31/2002		
PCode	**BMW-FC**	**PCode text**
P1640	155	Internal Control Module RAM/ROM Error
P1640	156	Internal Control Module RAM/ROM Error
P1663	155	EWS (Electronic Immobilizer) Rolling Code Faulty Storage in EEPROM
P1663	156	EWS (Electronic Immobilizer) Rolling Code Faulty Storage in EEPROM

Table m. S54 engine: Siemens DME MS S54 from 09/01/2002		
PCode	**BMW-FC**	**PCode text**
P0011	184	'A' Camshaft Position Timing Over-Advanced or System Performance (Bank 1)
P0012	184	'A' Camshaft Position Timing Over-Retarded (Bank 1)
P0014	185	'B' Camshaft Position Timing Over-Advanced or System Performance (Bank 1)
P0015	185	'B' Camshaft Position Timing Over-Retarded (Bank 1)
P0017	162	Crankshaft Position - Camshaft Position Correlation (Bank 1 Sensor B)
P0030	37	HO2S Heater Control Circuit (Bank 1 Sensor 1)
P0031	37	HO2S Heater Control Circuit Low (Bank 1 Sensor 1)
P0032	37	HO2S Heater Control Circuit High (Bank 1 Sensor 1)
P0036	39	HO2S Heater Control Circuit (Bank 1 Sensor 2)
P0037	39	HO2S Heater Control Circuit Low (Bank 1 Sensor 2)
P0038	39	HO2S Heater Control Circuit High (Bank 1 Sensor 2)
P0050	38	HO2S Heater Control Circuit (Bank 2 Sensor 1)
P0051	38	HO2S Heater Control Circuit Low (Bank 2 Sensor 1)
P0052	38	HO2S Heater Control Circuit High (Bank 2 Sensor 1)
P0056	40	HO2S Heater Control Circuit (Bank 2 Sensor 2)
P0057	40	HO2S Heater Control Circuit Low (Bank 2 Sensor 2)
P0058	40	HO2S Heater Control Circuit High (Bank 2 Sensor 2)
P0101	73	Mass or Volume Air Flow Circuit Range/Performance
P0102	41	Mass or Volume Air Flow Circuit Low Input
P0103	41	Mass or Volume Air Flow Circuit High Input
P0111	77	Intake Air Temperature Sensor 1 Circuit Range/Performance
P0112	77	Intake Air Temperature Sensor 1 Circuit Low
P0113	77	Intake Air Temperature Sensor 1 Circuit High
P0116	105	Engine Coolant Temperature Circuit Range/Performance
P0117	78	Engine Coolant Temperature Circuit Low
P0118	78	Engine Coolant Temperature Circuit High
P0121	118	Throttle/Pedal Position Sensor/Switch 'A' Circuit Range/Performance
P0121	120	Throttle/Pedal Position Sensor/Switch 'A' Circuit Range/Performance
P0121	121	Throttle/Pedal Position Sensor/Switch 'A' Circuit Range/Performance
P0122	118	Throttle/Pedal Position Sensor/Switch 'A' Circuit Low
P0123	118	Throttle/Pedal Position Sensor/Switch 'A' Circuit High
P0125	105	Insufficient Coolant Temperature for Closed Loop Fuel Control

Table m. S54 engine: Siemens DME MS S54 from 09/01/2002		
PCode	**BMW-FC**	**PCode text**
P0128	105	Coolant Thermostat (Coolant Temperature Below Thermostat Regulating Temperature)
P0131	13	O2 Sensor Circuit Low Voltage (Bank 1 Sensor 1)
P0132	13	O2 Sensor Circuit High Voltage (Bank 1 Sensor 1)
P0133	214	O2 Sensor Circuit Slow Response (Bank 1 Sensor 1)
P0134	13	O2 Sensor Circuit No Activity Detected (Bank 1 Sensor 1)
P0135	37	O2 Sensor Heater Circuit (Bank 1 Sensor 1)
P0137	87	O2 Sensor Circuit Low Voltage (Bank 1 Sensor 2)
P0138	87	O2 Sensor Circuit High Voltage (Bank 1 Sensor 2)
P0139	92	O2 Sensor Circuit Slow Response (Bank 1 Sensor 2)
P0140	87	O2 Sensor Circuit No Activity Detected (Bank 1 Sensor 2)
P0141	39	O2 Sensor Heater Circuit (Bank 1 Sensor 2)
P0151	12	O2 Sensor Circuit Low Voltage (Bank 2 Sensor 1)
P0152	12	O2 Sensor Circuit High Voltage (Bank 2 Sensor 1)
P0153	215	O2 Sensor Circuit Slow Response (Bank 2 Sensor 1)
P0154	12	O2 Sensor Circuit No Activity Detected (Bank 2 Sensor 1)
P0155	38	O2 Sensor Heater Circuit (Bank 2 Sensor 1)
P0157	88	O2 Sensor Circuit Low Voltage (Bank 2 Sensor 2)
P0158	88	O2 Sensor Circuit High Voltage (Bank 2 Sensor 2)
P0159	93	O2 Sensor Circuit Slow Response (Bank 2 Sensor 2)
P0160	88	O2 Sensor Circuit No Activity Detected (Bank 2 Sensor 2)
P0161	40	O2 Sensor Heater Circuit (Bank 2 Sensor 2)
P0171	144	System Too Lean (Bank 1)
P0171	174	System Too Lean (Bank 1)
P0172	144	System Too Rich (Bank 1)
P0172	174	System Too Rich (Bank 1)
P0174	145	System Too Lean (Bank 2)
P0174	175	System Too Lean (Bank 2)
P0175	145	System Too Rich (Bank 2)
P0175	175	System Too Rich (Bank 2)
P0200	183	Injector Circuit/Open
P0201	3	Injector Circuit/Open - Cylinder 1
P0202	5	Injector Circuit/Open - Cylinder 2
P0203	4	Injector Circuit/Open - Cylinder 3
P0204	33	Injector Circuit/Open - Cylinder 4
P0205	31	Injector Circuit/Open - Cylinder 5
P0206	32	Injector Circuit/Open - Cylinder 6
P0216	182	Injector/Injection Timing Control Circuit
P0221	119	Throttle/Pedal Position Sensor/Switch 'B' Circuit Range/Performance
P0222	119	Throttle/Pedal Position Sensor/Switch 'B' Circuit Low

Table m. S54 engine: Siemens DME MS S54 from 09/01/2002		
PCode	**BMW-FC**	**PCode text**
P0223	119	Throttle/Pedal Position Sensor/Switch 'B' Circuit High
P0261	3	Cylinder 1 Injector Circuit Low
P0262	3	Cylinder 1 Injector Circuit High
P0264	5	Cylinder 2 Injector Circuit Low
P0265	5	Cylinder 2 Injector Circuit High
P0267	4	Cylinder 3 Injector Circuit Low
P0268	4	Cylinder 3 Injector Circuit High
P0270	33	Cylinder 4 Injector Circuit Low
P0271	33	Cylinder 4 Injector Circuit High
P0273	31	Cylinder 5 Injector Circuit Low
P0274	31	Cylinder 5 Injector Circuit High
P0276	32	Cylinder 6 Injector Circuit Low
P0277	32	Cylinder 6 Injector Circuit High
P0300	213	Random/Multiple Cylinder Misfire Detected
P0301	205	Cylinder 1 Misfire Detected
P0302	206	Cylinder 2 Misfire Detected
P0303	207	Cylinder 3 Misfire Detected
P0304	208	Cylinder 4 Misfire Detected
P0305	209	Cylinder 5 Misfire Detected
P0306	210	Cylinder 6 Misfire Detected
P0313	149	Misfire Detected with Low Fuel
P0316	213	Engine Misfire Detected on Startup (First 1000 Revolutions)
P0335	16	Crankshaft Position Sensor 'A' Circuit
P0340	7	Camshaft Position Sensor 'A' Circuit (Bank 1 or Single Sensor)
P0363	204	Misfire Detected - Fueling Disabled
P0365	10	Camshaft Position Sensor 'B' Circuit (Bank 1)
P0394	15	Camshaft Position Sensor 'B' Circuit Intermittent (Bank 2)
P0411	170	Secondary Air Injection System Incorrect Flow Detected
P0413	63	Secondary Air Injection System Switching Valve A Circuit Open
P0414	63	Secondary Air Injection System Switching Valve A Circuit Shorted
P0418	19	Secondary Air Injection System Control 'A' Circuit
P0420	178	Catalyst System Efficiency Below Threshold (Bank 1)
P0430	179	Catalyst System Efficiency Below Threshold (Bank 2)
P0441	232	Evaporative Emission System Incorrect Purge Flow
P0442	180	Evaporative Emission System Leak Detected (small leak)
P0443	36	Evaporative Emission System Purge Control Valve Circuit
P0444	36	Evaporative Emission System Purge Control Valve Circuit Open
P0445	36	Evaporative Emission System Purge Control Valve Circuit Shorted
P0491	170	Secondary Air Injection System Insufficient Flow (Bank 1)

Table m. S54 engine: Siemens DME MS S54 from 09/01/2002		
PCode	BMW-FC	PCode text
P0492	170	Secondary Air Injection System Insufficient Flow (Bank 2)
P0500	135	Vehicle Speed Sensor 'A'
P0505	136	Idle Air Control System
P0506	128	Idle Air Control System RPM Lower Than Expected
P0507	128	Idle Air Control System RPM Higher Than Expected
P0601	150	Internal Control Module Memory Check Sum Error
P0601	157	Internal Control Module Memory Check Sum Error
P0604	150	Internal Control Module Random Access Memory (RAM) Error
P0604	157	Internal Control Module Random Access Memory (RAM) Error
P0605	150	Internal Control Module Read Only Memory (ROM) Error
P0605	157	Internal Control Module Read Only Memory (ROM) Error
P0606	30	ECM/PCM Processor
P0606	107	ECM/PCM Processor
P0606	158	ECM/PCM Processor
P0606	163	ECM/PCM Processor
P1121	111	Pedal Position Sensor 1 Range/Performance Problem
P1122	60	Pedal Position Sensor 1 Low Input
P1123	60	Pedal Position Sensor 1 High Input
P1178	216	O2 Sensor Signal Circuit Slow Switching from Rich to Lean (Bank 1 Sensor 1)
P1179	217	O2 Sensor Signal Circuit Slow Switching from Rich to Lean (Bank 2 Sensor 1)
P1185	219	HO2S Sensor Voltage Excursion Electrical (Bank 2 Sensor 1)
P1221	112	Pedal Position Sensor 2 Range/Performance Problem
P1222	61	Pedal Position Sensor 2 Low Input
P1223	61	Pedal Position Sensor 2 High Input
P1342	205	Misfire During Start Cylinder 1
P1343	196	Misfire Cylinder 1 with Fuel Cut-Off
P1344	206	Misfire During Start Cylinder 2
P1345	197	Misfire Cylinder 2 with Fuel Cut-Off
P1346	207	Misfire During Start Cylinder 3
P1347	198	Misfire Cylinder 3 with Fuel Cut-Off
P1348	208	Misfire During Start Cylinder 4
P1349	199	Misfire Cylinder 4 with Fuel Cut-Off
P1350	209	Misfire during Start Cylinder 5
P1351	200	Misfire Cylinder 5 with Fuel Cut-Off
P1352	210	Misfire during Start Cylinder 6
P1353	201	Misfire Cylinder 6 with Fuel Cut-Off
P1434	176	Diagnostic Module Tank Leakage (DM-TL)
P1446	127	Diagnostic Module Tank Leakage (DM-TL) Pump Control Circuit Signal High
P1447	127	Diagnostic Module Tank Leakage (DM-TL) Pump Current Too High during Switching Solenoid Test

Table m. S54 engine: Siemens DME MS S54 from 09/01/2002

PCode	BMW-FC	PCode text
P1448	127	Diagnostic Module Tank Leakage (DM-TL) Pump Current Too Low
P1449	127	Diagnostic Module Tank Leakage (DM-TL) Pump Current Too High
P1450	27	Diagnostic Module Tank Leakage (DM-TL) Switching Solenoid Control Open Circuit
P1451	27	Diagnostic Module Tank Leakage (DM-TL) Switching Solenoid Control Circuit Signal Low
P1452	27	Diagnostic Module Tank Leakage (DM-TL) Switching Solenoid Control Circuit Signal High
P1500	136	Idle-Speed Control Valve Stuck Open
P1501	136	Idle-Speed Control Valve Stuck Closed
P1502	2	Idle-Speed Control Valve Closing Solenoid Control Circuit Signal High
P1503	2	Idle-Speed Control Valve Closing Solenoid Control Circuit Signal Low
P1504	2	Idle-Speed Control Valve Closing Solenoid Control Open Circuit
P1506	29	Idle-Speed Control Valve Opening Solenoid Control Circuit Signal High
P1507	29	Idle-Speed Control Valve Opening Solenoid Control Circuit Signal Low
P1508	29	Idle-Speed Control Valve Opening Solenoid Control Open Circuit
P1525	67	'A' Camshaft Position Actuator Control Open Circuit (Bank 1)
P1525	72	'A' Camshaft Position Actuator Control Open Circuit (Bank 1)
P1531	21	'B' Camshaft Position Actuator Control Open Circuit (Bank 1)
P1531	22	'B' Camshaft Position Actuator Control Open Circuit (Bank 1)
P1602	122	Control Module Self-Test, Control Module Defective
P1603	195	Control Module Self-Test, Torque Monitoring
P1634	107	Throttle Valve Adaptation Spring Test Failed
P1636	45	Throttle Valve Control Circuit
P1637	107	Throttle Valve Position Control, Control Deviation
P1637	230	Throttle Valve Position Control, Control Deviation
P1639	107	Throttle Valve Position Control Throttle Stuck Permanently
P1640	155	Internal Control Module RAM/ROM Error
P1640	156	Internal Control Module RAM/ROM Error
P1663	155	EWS (Electronic Immobilizer) Rolling Code Faulty Storage in EEPROM
P1663	156	EWS (Electronic Immobilizer) Rolling Code Faulty Storage in EEPROM

WARNING

Your common sense, good judgement and general alertness are crucial to safe and successful service work. Before attempting any work on your BMW, be sure to read **001 General Warnings and Cautions** *and the copyright page at the front of the manual. Review these warnings and cautions each time you prepare to work on your car. Please also read any warnings and cautions that accompany the procedures in the manual.*

WARNING

Your common sense, good judgement and general alertness are crucial to safe and successful service work. Before attempting any work on your BMW, be sure to read **001 General Warnings and Cautions** *and the copyright page at the front of the manual. Review these warnings and cautions each time you prepare to work on your car. Please also read any warnings and cautions that accompany the procedures in the manual.*

D

E

4 INDEX

WARNING

Your common sense, good judgement and general alertness are crucial to safe and successful service work. Before attempting any work on your BMW, be sure to read **001 General Warnings and Cautions** *and the copyright page at the front of the manual. Review these warnings and cautions each time you prepare to work on your car. Please also read any warnings and cautions that accompany the procedures in the manual.*

6 INDEX

> ***WARNING***
>
> *Your common sense, good judgement and general alertness are crucial to safe and successful service work. Before attempting any work on your BMW, be sure to read* **001 General Warnings and Cautions** *and the copyright page at the front of the manual. Review these warnings and cautions each time you prepare to work on your car. Please also read any warnings and cautions that accompany the procedures in the manual.*

R

S

WARNING

Your common sense, good judgement and general alertness are crucial to safe and successful service work. Before attempting any work on your BMW, be sure to read **001 General Warnings and Cautions** *and the copyright page at the front of the manual. Review these warnings and cautions each time you prepare to work on your car. Please also read any warnings and cautions that accompany the procedures in the manual.*

Selected Books and Repair Information From Bentley Publishers

Driving

Alex Zanardi - My Sweetest Victory
Alex Zanardi with Gianluca Gasparini
ISBN 978-0-8376-1249-2

The Unfair Advantage
Mark Donohue ISBN 978-0-8376-0069-7

Going Faster! Mastering the Art of Race Driving
The Skip Barber Racing School
ISBN 978-0-8376-0226-4

A French Kiss With Death: Steve McQueen and the Making of *Le Mans*
Michael Keyser ISBN 978-0-8376-0234-9

Sports Car and Competition Driving
Paul Frère with foreword *by Phil Hill*
ISBN 978-0-8376-0202-8

Engineering / Reference

Supercharged! Design, Testing, and Installation of Supercharger Systems
Corky Bell ISBN 978-0-8376-0168-7

Maximum Boost: Designing, Testing, and Installing Turbocharger Systems
Corky Bell ISBN 978-0-8376-0160-1

Bosch Fuel Injection and Engine Management
Charles O. Probst, SAE
ISBN 978-0-8376-0300-1

Race Car Aerodynamics
Joseph Katz ISBN 978-0-8376-0142-7

Road & Track Illustrated Automotive Dictionary
John Dinkel ISBN 978-0-8376-0143-4

Scientific Design of Exhaust and Intake Systems
Philip H. Smith ISBN 978-0-8376-0309-4

Alfa Romeo

Alfa Romeo All-Alloy Twin Cam Companion 1954–1994
Pat Braden ISBN 978-0-8376-0275-2

Alfa Romeo Owner's Bible™
Pat Braden ISBN 978-0-8376-0707-8

Audi

Audi TT: 2000–2006, 1.8L turbo, 3.2L, including roadster and quattro
Bentley Publishers ISBN 978-0-8376-1500-4

Audi A6 Service Manual: 1998–2004, including A6, allroad quattro, S6, RS6
Bentley Publishers
ISBN 978-0-8376-1499-1

BMW

BMW Z3 Service Manual: 1996–2002, including Z3 Roadster, Z3 Coupe, M Roadster, M Coupe
Bentley Publishers ISBN 978-0-8376-1250-8

BMW 3 Series (E46) Service Manual: 1999–2005, M3, 323i, 325i, 325xi, 328i, 330i, 330xi, Sedan, Coupe, Convertible, Wagon
Bentley Publishers
ISBN 978-0-8376-1277-5

BMW 3 Series (E36) Service Manual: 1992–1998, 318i/is/iC, 323is/iC, 325i/is/iC, 328i/is/iC, M3
Bentley Publishers ISBN 978-0-8376-0326-1

BMW 5 Series Service Manual: 1997–2002 525i, 528i, 530i, 540i, Sedan, Sport Wagon
Bentley Publishers ISBN 978-0-8376-0317-9

BMW 6 Series Enthusiast's Companion™
Jeremy Walton ISBN 978-0-8376-0193-9

BMW 7 Series Service Manual: 1988–1994, 735i, 735iL, 740i, 740iL, 750iL
Bentley Publishers ISBN 978-0-8376-0328-5

Bosch

Bosch Automotive Handbook 6th Edition
Robert Bosch, GmbH ISBN 978-0-8376-1243-0

Bosch Handbook for Automotive Electrics and Electronics
Robert Bosch, GmbH ISBN 978-0-8376-1050-4

Bosch Handbook for Diesel-Engine Management
Robert Bosch, GmbH ISBN 978-0-8376-1353-6

Bosch Handbook for Gasoline-Engine Management
Robert Bosch, GmbH ISBN 978-0-8376-1390-1

Chevrolet

Corvette Illustrated Encyclopedia
Tom Benford ISBN 978-0-8376-0928-7

Corvette Fuel Injection & Electronic Engine Management 1982–2001:
Charles O. Probst, SAE ISBN 978-0-8376-0861-7

Zora Arkus-Duntov: The Legend Behind Corvette
Jerry Burton ISBN 978-0-8376-0858-7

Chevrolet by the Numbers 1965–1969: The Essential Chevrolet Parts Reference
Alan Colvin ISBN 978-0-8376-0956-0

Ford

Ford Fuel Injection and Electronic Engine Control: 1988–1993
Charles O. Probst, SAE ISBN 978-0-8376-0301-8

The Official Ford Mustang 5.0 Technical Reference & Performance Handbook: 1979–1993
Al Kirschenbaum ISBN 978-0-8376-0210-3

Jeep

Jeep CJ Rebuilder's Manual: 1972-1986
Moses Ludel ISBN 978-0-8376-0151-9

Jeep Owner's Bible™ - Third Edition
Moses Ludel ISBN 978- 0-8376-1117-4

Mercedes-Benz

Mercedes-Benz Technical Companion™
staff of The Star and members of the Mercedes-Benz Club of America ISBN 978-0-8376-1033-7

Mercedes-Benz E-Class (W124) Owner's Bible™: 1986–1995
Bentley Publishers ISBN 978-0-8376-0230-1

MINI Cooper

MINI Cooper Service Manual: 2002-2004
Bentley Publishers ISBN 978-0-8376-1068-9

Porsche

Porsche: Excellence Was Expected
Karl Ludvigsen ISBN 978-0-8376-0235-6

Porsche 911 Enthusiast's Companion™
Adrian Streather ISBN 978-0-8376-0293-6

Porsche 911 Carrera Service Manual: 1984–1989
Bentley Publishers ISBN 978-0-8376-0291-2

Porsche 911 SC Service Manual: 1978–1983
Bentley Publishers ISBN 978-0-8376-0290-5

Porsche Boxster, Boxster S Service Manual: 1997–2004
Bentley Publishers ISBN 978-0-8376-1333-8

Volkswagen

Battle for the Beetle
Karl Ludvigsen ISBN 978-0-8376-0071-0

Jetta, Golf, GTI Service Manual: 1999–2005 1.8L turbo, 1.9L TDI diesel, PD diesel, 2.0L gasoline, 2.8L VR6
Bentley Publishers ISBN 978-0-8376-1251-5

New Beetle Service Manual: 1998–2002 1.8L turbo, 1.9L TDI diesel, 2.0L gasoline
Bentley Publishers ISBN 978-0-8376-0376-6

New Beetle 1998–2006, New Beetle Convertible 2003-2006 Official Factory Repair Manual on CD-ROM
Volkswagen of America ISBN 978-0-8376-1497-7

Passat Service Manual: 1998–2005, 1.8L turbo, 2.8L V6, 4.0L W8, including wagon and 4MOTION
Bentley Publishers ISBN 978-0-8376-1483-0

Passat, Passat Wagon 1998–2005 Official Factory Repair Manual on DVD-ROM
Volkswagen of America ISBN 978-0-8376-1267-6

Golf, GTI, Jetta 1993–1999, Cabrio 1995–2002 Official Factory Repair Manual on CD-ROM
Volkswagen of America ISBN 978-0-8376-1263-8

Jetta, Golf, GTI: 1993–1999, Cabrio: 1995-2002 Service Manual
Bentley Publishers ISBN 978-0-8376-0366-7

BentleyPublishers™ .com

Automotive Reference

Bentley Publishers has published service manuals and automobile books since 1950. Please write to us at 1734 Massachusetts Ave., Cambridge, MA 02138, visit our web site, or call 1-800-423-4595 for a free copy of our catalog.